S0-BVP-409

*The O*NET Dictionary of Occupational Titles™ 1998-1999 Edition*

Based on information obtained from the U.S. Department of Labor and other sources.

Please see the last few pages for ordering information as well as a sampling of JIST products, including the following:

- *The Occupational Outlook Handbook*
- *The Young Person's Occupational Outlook Handbook*
- *The Enhanced Occupational Outlook Handbook*
- *The Enhanced Guide for Occupational Exploration*
- *The Complete Guide for Occupational Exploration*
- *The Dictionary of Occupational Titles (the now "classic" 1991 edition)*
- *Franchise Opportunities Handbook*
- *Luddens' Adult Guide to Colleges and Universities*
- *America's Fastest Growing Jobs*
- *America's Top Jobs for People Without a Four-Year Degree*
- *America's Top Jobs for College Graduates*
- *America's Top 300 Jobs*
- *America's Top Resumes for America's Top Jobs*
- *Gallery of Best Resumes*

Software:

- *JIST's Multimedia Occupational Outlook Handbook CD-ROM*
- *Young Person's Electronic Occupational Outlook Handbook*
- *JIST's Electronic Enhanced Dictionary of Occupational Titles*
- *JIST's Career Explorer™ CD-ROM*
- *Mike Farr's Get a Job Workshop on CD-ROM*

The O*NET Dictionary of Occupational Titles™
1998-1999 Edition

Developed under the direction of J. Michael Farr and LaVerne Ludden, with database work by Paul Mangin.

JIST Works, Inc.
720 North Park Avenue
Indianapolis, IN 46202
ISBN 1-56370-509-5 Hardcover
ISBN 1-56370-510-9 Softcover

Please see the last pages of this book for a listing of other JIST products and an order form. Visit our Web site at www. JIST.com for free chapters of books, ordering information, and other fun materials.

IMPORTANT NOTICE ON THE LIMITATIONS OF USE OF THIS BOOK

*The O*NET Dictionary of Occupational Titles* ™ was designed to update and replace the *Dictionary of Occupational Titles*. The DOT was last published by the U.S. Department of Labor in 1991 and included the disclaimer that follows, with minor alterations. This disclaimer also applies to *The O*NET Dictionary of Occupational Titles*™.

Occupational information contained in this book reflects jobs as they have been found to occur, but they may not coincide in every respect with the content of jobs as performed in particular establishments or at certain localities. Users of this information demanding specific job requirements should supplement this data with local information detailing jobs within their community.

In using this book, it should be noted that the U.S. Employment Service, the U.S. Department of Labor, or JIST Works, Inc., has no responsibility for establishing wage levels for workers in the United States or settling jurisdictional matters in relation to different occupations. In preparing vocational definitions, no data were collected concerning these and related matters. Therefore, the occupational information in this book cannot be regarded as determining standards for any aspect of the employer-employee relationship. Data contained in this publication should not be considered a judicial or legislative standard for wages, hours, or other contractual or bargaining elements.

The use of any information, no matter how carefully collected, researched, screened, or presented does have its limitations. The information provided in the O*NET database—and this book—has been carefully collected and thoughtfully presented. Even so, errors and inaccuracies can be introduced and, for this reason, we can accept no responsibility for any errors in fact nor in any decisions made or actions taken as a result of the information provided. As in all things, we humbly suggest that you accept your own judgment regarding important decisions.

ABOUT THIS BOOK

Please don't be intimidated by the formal look of this book. We have worked hard to make it an easy-to-use, valuable resource for a variety of nontechnical purposes.

We believe this new reference will be of great help to job seekers, students, businesses, educators, career counselors, and many others. It presents, in a practical format, a major new standard for organizing and describing occupations.

The information database used to create this book was developed by the U.S. Department of Labor (DOL) and first released in 1998. Called the O*NET (for the Occupational Information Network), it represents a large departure from the past system. Many governmental, business, educational, and other organizations rely on the standardized occupational classification system developed by the DOL. The O*NET system is the standard that others now will use in collecting data on wages, job growth, and related facts.

The O*NET is clearly an important new information source. As an electronic database, however, its details are not readily available. As a result, the DOL released the O*NET database to developers, such as JIST, to adapt the data into software and print formats that will reach a wide audience.

This book is the first to provide the O*NET material in printed form, and we hope it serves as a beneficial tool for you. In a very real sense, this book is the result of cooperation between a governmental and a private organization. In this case, we think your taxes are being spent wisely.

CREDITS

Although several people have their names on the cover, this book represents many years of work by hundreds of dedicated individuals. The O*NET database that serves as the basis for this book was created by researchers and developers under the direction of the U.S. Department of Labor. They, in turn, were assisted by thousands of employers who provided details on the nature of work in thousands of job samplings used in the database's development.

There is more: while the O*NET database was first released in 1998, it is based on the substantial work done on an earlier database used to develop the *Dictionary of Occupational Titles* (DOT). That DOT database was first used in the 1939 DOT edition and has been continuously updated. The DOT formed the basis for much of the occupational information used by employers, job seekers, career counselors, educational and training institutions, researchers, policy makers, and others.

Because of their large numbers, most who worked on the occupational material used in this book are not credited. Even so, we appreciate their efforts and present this book in their honor and in the honor of the good people at the U.S. Department of Labor who made it possible.

TABLE OF CONTENTS

O*NET Occupations Within Groupings of Related Jobs

Section 1—Executives, Managers, and Administrators

General Managers

Specialty Managers

Executives

Services Managers

Section 2—Professional and Support Specialists—Financial Specialists Engineers, Scientists, Mathematicians, Social Scientists, Social Services Workers, Religious Workers, and Legal Workers

Financial Specialists

Purchasers and Buyers

Human Resources Workers

Inspectors and Compliance Officers

Management Support Workers

Engineers

Architects and Surveyors

Engineering Technologists and Technicians

Physical Scientists

Life Scientists

Life and Physical Sciences Technologists and Technicians

Computer Scientists

Mathematical Scientists and Technicians

Social Scientists

Social Services Workers

Religious Workers

Lawyers and Judges

Legal Assistants

Section 3—Professional and Support Specialties—Educators, Librarians, Counselors, Health Care Workers, Artists, Writers, Performers, and Other Professional Workers

College and University Faculty

Preschool, Kindergarten, Elementary, Secondary, and Special Education Teachers and Instructors

Librarians, Curators, and Counselors

Diagnosing and Treating Practitioners

Medical Therapists

Health Care Providers

Medical Technologists and Technicians

Artistic, Creative, and Entertainment Providers

Other Professional, Paraprofessional, and Technical Workers

Section 4—Sales Workers

Sales Supervisors and Managers

Sales Agents

Technical, Wholesale, and Retail Sales Workers

Mail Clerks, Carriers, and Messengers

Material Recording, Scheduling, and Distributing Workers

Section 6—Service Workers

Service Supervisors and Managers

Private Household Workers

Protective Service Workers

Food Service Workers

Medical Assistants and Aides

Cleaning and Building Service Workers

Personal Service Workers

Section 7—Agricultural, Forestry, and Fishing Workers

Agriculture, Forestry, and Fishing Supervisors

Timber Cutting and Related Logging Workers

Plant and Animal Workers

Farm Workers

Other Agricultural Workers

Section 8—Mechanics, Installers, Repairers, Construction Trades, Extractive Trades, Metal and Plastics Working, Woodworking, Apparel, Precision Printing, and Food Processing Workers

Blue Collar Worker Supervisors

Inspectors, Testers, and Graders

Industrial Equipment Mechanics

Motor Vehicle Mechanics

Communications Equipment Mechanics

Line Installers and Electronic Equipment Repairers

Other Mechanics, Installers, and Repairers

Carpenters, Drywall Workers, and Lathers

Electricians

Masons, Concrete Workers, Tile Setters, and Reinforcing Metal Workers

Painters and Paperhangers

Plumbing Workers

Flooring Installers

Highway and Rail Workers

Other Construction Workers

Extractive Trades Workers

Metalworking and Plastics Working Occupations

Woodworking Occupations

Apparel Occupations

Precision Printing Occupations

Food Processing Occupations

Other Precision Occupations

Section 9—Machine Setters, Operators, and Tenders, Production Workers, Hand Workers, Plant and System Workers, Transportation Workers, and Helpers

Machine Cutting, Turning, Drilling, Grinding, and Polishing Setters, Operators, and Tenders

Punching, Pressing, Extruding, Rolling, and Forming Machine Setters and Operators

Metal Fabricating Machine Setters, Operators, and Related Workers

Molding, Casting, Plating, and Heating Machine Setters and Operators

Other Metal and Plastic Machine Setters and Operators

Woodworking Machine Setters and Operators

Printing, Binding, and Related Machine Setters and Operators

Textile and Related Machine Setters, Operators, and Related Workers

Other Machine Setters, Operators, and Tenders

Precision Production Occupations

Hand Workers, Including Assemblers and Fabricators

Plant and Systems Occupations

Motor Vehicle Operators

Rail Transportation Workers

Water Transportation and Related Workers

Air Transportation Workers

Other Transportation-Related Workers

Material Moving Equipment Operators

Helpers—Mechanics and Repairers

Helpers—Construction

Helpers—Feeders and Offbearers

Helpers—Material Movers

Helpers—Production, Washing, and Packing

Military

INTRODUCTION

This introduction provides information to help you understand and begin using *The O*NET Dictionary of Occupational Titles*™. We have tried to keep this short and nontechnical. If you are interested in technical information, several appendices in the back provide additional details.

WHAT IS THE O*NET?

The O*NET is not a book—it is a new computerized database of information on occupations. Developed by the U.S. Department of Labor, the O*NET name is a short form of "The Occupational Information Network," the database's formal name.

The O*NET database was first released in early 1998. It was developed to replace an older occupational database that was the basis of the 1991 edition of the *Dictionary of Occupational Titles* (DOT). In its current form, the O*NET database provides information on 1,172 occupations. In the years to come, new occupations will be added, and the information on all occupations will be updated regularly.

At the time of this writing, this is the first and only book presenting the new O*NET information in printed form. The U.S. Department of Labor has decided that its role is to create and maintain the O*NET database in electronic form and has no plans to release it in print.

As mentioned, the most recent edition of the DOT was released in book form by the U.S. Department of Labor in 1991. That DOT provided information on 12,741 occupational titles, far more occupations than in the O*NET database. Many of those 12,741 occupations were similar and were combined into more general descriptions. Others were highly specialized or employed few people and their descriptions were not included in the new O*NET. The result is a list of occupations that is smaller and more useful -- the O*NET.

The new O*NET and the old DOT systems have similarities because the new O*NET system is built on the solid foundation provided by the older DOT system. If you are familiar with the Dictionary of Occupational Titles, you will probably feel quite comfortable with the O*NET descriptions in this book. Because this book bridges the new O*NET with the DOT, we have referred to both systems in the title -- *The O*NET Dictionary of Occupational Titles*™.

THE O*NET DATA ELEMENTS

Remember that the O*NET is not a book -- it is a database with many details about each occupation. In addition to a narrative description, each O*NET occupation includes material on 445 data element descriptors. If you were to print the complete information for one occupation, you would have a very long, boring, and confusing description.

Consider this: If you were asked to describe your best friend, you would most likely omit many details. For example, you probably would not mention blood type, cholesterol level, mom's name, or what your friend had for lunch. Instead, you would select points that you felt better described this person. Those other details could be very important to someone at some time, but not in this situation.

In a similar way, if you were to look at all the information available for each occupation in the O*NET database, you would quickly understand why printing them in book form would not make sense. For example, following is the summary information on just one of the 445 O*NET data elements available for each occupation.

O*NET Data Dictionary

Element: **Rate Control**

Description: **The ability to time the adjustments of a movement or equipment control in anticipation of changes in the speed and/or direction of a continuously moving object or scene**

Content Model Key: **I.A.2.b.4**

I. Worker Characteristics
A. Abilities
2. Psychomotor Abilities
b. Control Movement Abilities
4. Rate Control

Variable	Variable Description	File Name	Field Values	Scale, Ques Codes
A28LV00M	Rate Control-Level	Means_AB	1-7, 0(NR)	LV, A

Left Label	Value	Right Value
Requires precisely timed control adjustments to random changes of a high-speed object moving in several directions.	**7.00**	
	6.50	**Operating aircraft controls used to land a jet on an aircraft carrier in rough weather**
	4.80	**Shooting a duck in flight.**
	3.60	**Keeping up with a car you are following when the speed of that car changes.**
	2.40	**Riding a bicycle alongside a jogger.**
Requires timed control adjustments to a slow-moving, almost predictable object moving in a single direction	**1.00**	

Variable	Variable Description	File Name	Field Values	Scale, Ques Codes
A28IM00M	Rate Control-Importance	Means_AB	1-5	IM, A

Rate Control is a very important element for a job such as aircraft pilot, an occupation that requires a high level of skill in this factor, but would be of little meaning to most office workers, for example. So including Rate Control information on each occupation would not be helpful -- and including details on the 445 data elements for each occupation would create many pages of little interest to most people.

There is also the practical matter that a book attempting to do this would be thousands of pages long and require many volumes. Who would buy or read it? For this reason, we have used a variety of techniques to reduce the information provided for each occupation—and increase the usefulness of each description for most users. Appendix D provides brief descriptions for the many O*NET data elements included in this book. We say more about how we selected the ones we included later in this introduction.

IF YOU WANT MORE DETAILS ABOUT THE O*NET OCCUPATIONS

You may want more detailed information about occupations than we can provide in this book. For example, you just may want to know the Rate Control measures for one or more specific occupations -- or have some other specialized need that can't be met by this book. If so, we suggest that you gain access to the O*NET database in its electronic form.

Keep in mind that the U.S. Department of Labor, which creates the data, does not plan to release the O*NET in printed form -- this book is the only printed version of which we are aware. Unfortunately, access to the electronic form of the O*NET database is limited. At the time we write this, the O*NET database was being released only to software developers and not to the public.

In the months to come, we anticipate that the O*NET data will be included in various software programs released by commercial and governmental sources -- although it may take awhile. JIST, the publisher of this book, plans to include the O*NET data in revisions of its current occupational information software. Call JIST and get on our mailing list if interested. Information on contacting us is in the back of this book. The government may also put the O*NET database on the Internet but, until it does, access to it will remain limited.

SAMPLE O*NET DESCRIPTION

Our challenge in developing this book was to create a printed description of each O*NET occupation that would be useful to most people and that would be practical in book form. We've stayed up late many nights considering how to do this. Because we know that a picture is worth a thousand words, we have provided here a sample O*NET description that we developed for this book. We've added callouts to point out the various elements of the description and will explain each element following the description itself.

While short, this description is packed with useful information that we think will be quite helpful for most readers. Most content is easy enough to understand, although some details will interest only those who require it.

Sample O*NET Description

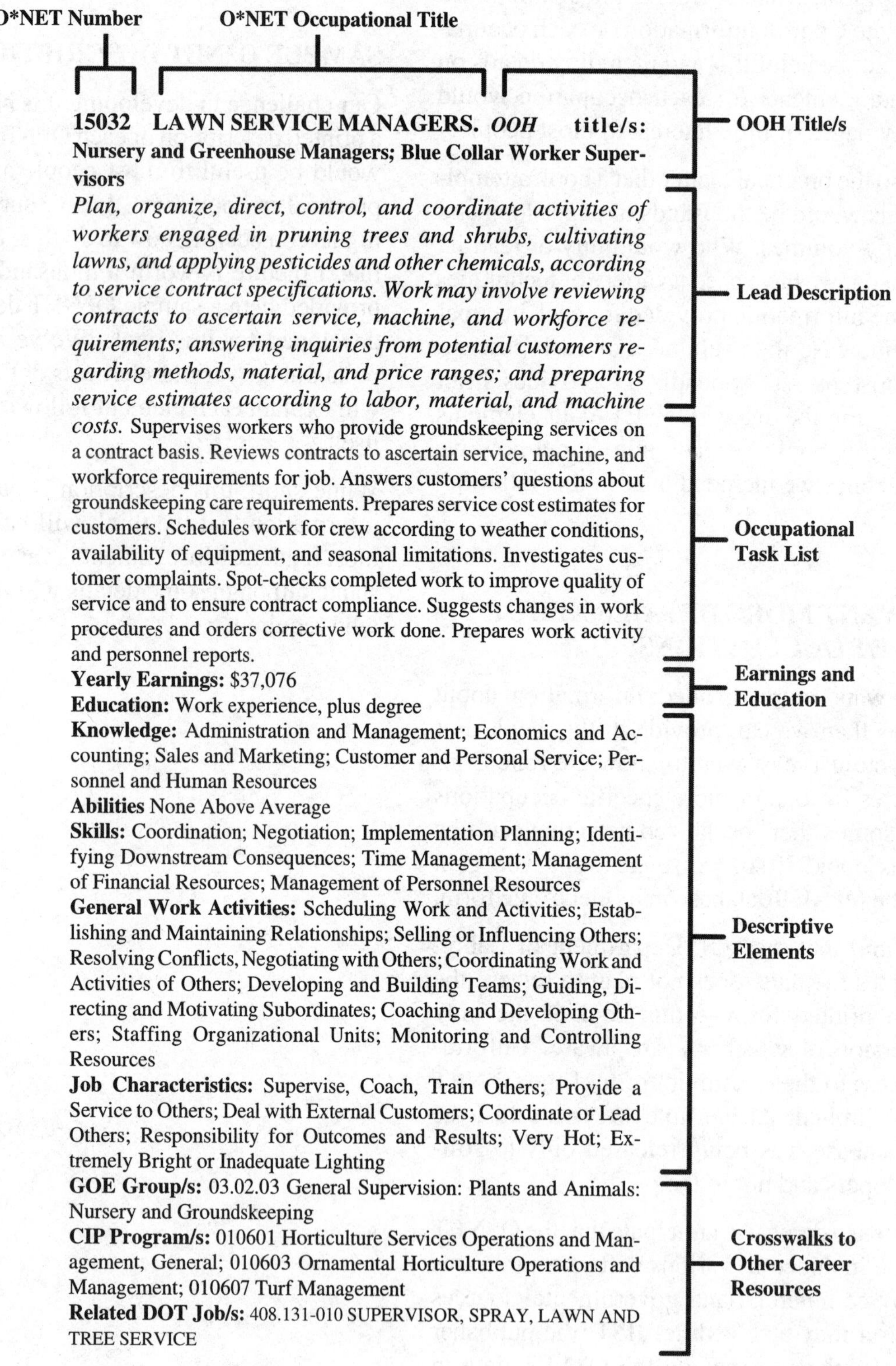

15032 LAWN SERVICE MANAGERS. ***OOH*** **title/s: Nursery and Greenhouse Managers; Blue Collar Worker Supervisors**

Plan, organize, direct, control, and coordinate activities of workers engaged in pruning trees and shrubs, cultivating lawns, and applying pesticides and other chemicals, according to service contract specifications. Work may involve reviewing contracts to ascertain service, machine, and workforce requirements; answering inquiries from potential customers regarding methods, material, and price ranges; and preparing service estimates according to labor, material, and machine costs. Supervises workers who provide groundskeeping services on a contract basis. Reviews contracts to ascertain service, machine, and workforce requirements for job. Answers customers' questions about groundskeeping care requirements. Prepares service cost estimates for customers. Schedules work for crew according to weather conditions, availability of equipment, and seasonal limitations. Investigates customer complaints. Spot-checks completed work to improve quality of service and to ensure contract compliance. Suggests changes in work procedures and orders corrective work done. Prepares work activity and personnel reports.

Yearly Earnings: $37,076

Education: Work experience, plus degree

Knowledge: Administration and Management; Economics and Accounting; Sales and Marketing; Customer and Personal Service; Personnel and Human Resources

Abilities None Above Average

Skills: Coordination; Negotiation; Implementation Planning; Identifying Downstream Consequences; Time Management; Management of Financial Resources; Management of Personnel Resources

General Work Activities: Scheduling Work and Activities; Establishing and Maintaining Relationships; Selling or Influencing Others; Resolving Conflicts, Negotiating with Others; Coordinating Work and Activities of Others; Developing and Building Teams; Guiding, Directing and Motivating Subordinates; Coaching and Developing Others; Staffing Organizational Units; Monitoring and Controlling Resources

Job Characteristics: Supervise, Coach, Train Others; Provide a Service to Others; Deal with External Customers; Coordinate or Lead Others; Responsibility for Outcomes and Results; Very Hot; Extremely Bright or Inadequate Lighting

GOE Group/s: 03.02.03 General Supervision: Plants and Animals: Nursery and Groundskeeping

CIP Program/s: 010601 Horticulture Services Operations and Management, General; 010603 Ornamental Horticulture Operations and Management; 010607 Turf Management

Related DOT Job/s: 408.131-010 SUPERVISOR, SPRAY, LAWN AND TREE SERVICE

THE PARTS OF THE O*NET DESCRIPTIONS PROVIDED IN THIS BOOK

Brief descriptions follow for each element included in an O*NET occupational description. Please note that we have used the words occupation and job interchangeably in this introduction and this book. While there may be technical differences, they are the same for our purposes.

- **O*NET Number—**Each O*NET occupation is assigned a unique number. These are not random numbers, because they relate to the O*NET occupational groups and subgroups. You can see how this system works by looking at the list of O*NET occupations following the table of contents. Occupations in this book are presented in numerical order, using their assigned O*NET number.
- **O*NET Occupational Title**—This is the title typically used for the listed occupation.
- **OOH Title/s**—When possible, we cross-reference the most closely related job title or titles in the *Occupational Outlook Handbook* (OOH). The OOH is a standard, widely used reference book updated every two years by the U.S. Department of Labor. Because it provides such helpful information, we highly recommend you read the OOH descriptions related to O*NET jobs that interest you. While the O*NET database does not provide related OOH job titles, we felt it important to create this connection and hope you find it useful.
- **O*Net Occupational Description**—This gives you a brief but useable description for each O*NET job. The description is divided as follows. The first part, the "Lead Description," is printed in italics and provides a one- or two-sentence description of the job. This is sometimes followed by (also in italics) statements such as "Include wholesale or retail trade merchandising managers" or "Exclude procurement managers" that provide related titles that are or are not described in other O*NET occupations. This is then followed, in regular type, by an "Occupational Task List" that describes occupational "tasks" specific to the job being described. Presented in sentence form, this list provides a useful review of what a person working in that job would typically do.
- **Yearly Earnings**—This represents the mean annual earnings received by those in this occupation. The O*NET database does not provide this information yet, so we obtained earnings information from U.S. Census Bureau data and cross-referenced it to the O*NET jobs

  In reviewing earnings, note that the earnings figures can be misleading for a variety of reasons. For example, new or recent entrants to the occupation will often earn substantially less than the amount listed, because they often have much less experience than the average person working in that occupation. Pay rates also often vary considerably in different regions of the country; smaller employers often pay less; workers with more training or experience tend to earn more; and there are many other factors to consider. In other cases, the earnings data we obtained from the U.S. Census disagrees with other sources of information. For example, the census lists physicians as having considerably lower earnings than data from other government sources. So consider the earnings information as a guideline that may not apply to your situation. You can often obtain local earnings information from your state employment service or other sources -- ask your librarian for help. You also can ask people who work in those occupations what someone would earn at differing levels of experience.
- **Education**—While this section of the O*NET description is titled "Education" for simplicity, it includes information on the education, training, and work experience typically required for entry into that job. Please note, however, that some (or many) who work in the job may have higher or lower levels than indicated in the O*NET descriptions. Depending on the job, it is quite possible that some new entrants become employed in these jobs although they do not meet these criteria. Certification or licensing may also be required for some jobs but accurate information on these requirements was not available yet from the O*NET database. You will need to determine such requirements from other sources, such as the *Occupational Outlook Handbook*. The definitions of educational levels used in the book are found in another section of this introduction.

- **Knowledge**—This section of the O*NET description refers to areas of knowledge required to successfully perform in the occupation described. The knowledge may have been obtained from a variety of formal or informal sources, including high school or college courses or majors, training programs, self-employment, military, paid or volunteer work experience, or other life experience. If you are considering additional education or training, this section gives you some idea of the courses or programs that would be helpful for each job.
- **Abilities**—This section contains "enduring attributes" that influence the job performance of workers. These attributes are regarded as traits because they don't change over long periods of time. Abilities affect how quickly a person can learn new skills and the level of skill that can be achieved. Sometimes people refer to this as aptitude or even talent. Usually an ability increases your interest in learning and practicing a skill. For example, you may find that math is easy for you. So when you are taught a concept like calculating the mean and standard deviation -- to help control product quality, for example -- you are able to quickly learn how to use this in your job. We have included those abilities in a job description that have numerical ratings that are above average for that job. Appendix D contains a list of abilities found in the O*NET along with a definition of each.
- **Skills**—This section lists a variety of skills needed to perform at above average levels in each job. Depending on the occupation, some of these skills are quite complex, while others are relatively basic. All of us possess thousands of skills, although we take most of them for granted. For example, have you ever considered the complexity of physical skills needed to drive a car? This task is so complex that the most sophisticated machines cannot do it nearly as well as most sixteen year olds. Yet we take doing this -- and many other things -- for granted. While all of the many skills we possess to do a given job are not listed in the O*NET database, it does include many skills that are important across a range of jobs. To avoid overwhelming you with details, only those skills with higher numerical ratings in the database are listed for each job. Appendix D provides brief definitions of all the skills included in the O*NET database and used in the descriptions.
- **General Work Activities**—This section of the O*NET description lists the general types of work activities needed to perform the job described. As with the Skills section, some jobs list very complex activities as well as more basic ones. When a job involves supervision of others, this is often mentioned and can give you a good idea of the level of responsibility typically required. We list only those activities with an above average or higher numerical rating in the O*NET database (actually, those that were one standard deviation over the mean). Appendix D provides a complete list of these activities.
- **Job Characteristics**—This section includes several types of information we think you will find helpful. Measures are available for occupational requirements such as Interacting with Others, Mental Processes, Role Relationships, Communication Methods, Responsibility for Others, and many more. If present in the job, the nature of interaction with and level of responsibility for others are listed. Hazardous or unpleasant working conditions are listed when present, with entries such as cramped work space, awkward positions, electrical shock, loud noise, unpleasant/angry people, frustrating circumstances (one of our favorites), and many others. In addition, this section lists special clothing requirements, when present, such as uniforms or protective/safety clothing. When these factors were given higher numerical ratings, we included them in the occupational description.
- **GOE Group/s**—The Guide for Occupational Exploration (GOE) is a system for organizing jobs based on interests. We provided related GOE group numbers and names so you can cross-reference this important system. Developed by the U.S. Department of Labor, the GOE is designed as a more intuitive system to help counselors, students, job seekers, career changers, and others identify occupations for further exploration. It organizes all jobs into just 12 major groupings and

then into more specific subgroups of related jobs. This is a very helpful way to find a variety of jobs that you might otherwise overlook.

For example, suppose that you are interested in the "creative expression of feelings or ideas" -- that's the Artistic Interest area. That area is further divided into eight more specific groupings of related jobs such as Literary Arts, Visual Arts, Performing Arts -- Drama, and others. If you were interested in the Literary Arts group, that is again divided into three even more specific groupings, including Editing, Creative Writing, and Critiquing -- and a variety of jobs are then listed within these groupings.

It sounds complex, but it's not. The GOE can quickly open you up to a world of possibilities that you might overlook using more traditional occupational groupings. The major books that present the GOE system are the *Enhanced Guide for Occupational Exploration* and the *Complete Guide for Occupational Exploration*. Both should be available at larger libraries and both are published by JIST. Appendix B provides a complete listing of the GOE groupings along with cross-references to other major reference systems.

- **CIP Program/s**—The Classification of Instructional Programs (CIP) is a system of categorizing training and educational programs and courses. The CIP is widely used by a variety of occupational, education, and training reference systems. For each occupation, we include information on the related CIP numeric code and title. This will give you some information on the type of training and education typically required for entry into the occupation described. The U.S. Department of Education has a reference guide describing all of the CIP programs.

- **Related DOT Job/s**—As mentioned earlier in this introduction, the *Dictionary of Occupational Titles* (DOT) is a standard reference book that describes over 12,741 jobs. This part of the O*NET description lists the DOT job number and title for all related DOT jobs. There are several uses of this information. The first is that the DOT system is referred to in a variety of interest tests (such as the Self-Directed Search) and other career information systems. While the new O*NET is intended to eventually replace the DOT, many current systems will use the DOT structure for years to come. Even if you don't need to cross-reference the DOT, the information is quite useful, since it provides specialized job titles that are not in the O*NET database. In some cases, the DOT job titles will give you ideas for jobs that would be more interesting to you than the more general O*NET job. You can look up these descriptions in the DOT for additional information.

*Note: Some information often overlaps in each O*NET description. For example, the Work Activities statements will often be similar to those in the Occupational Task Statement. The Skills statements also may be similar to content provided elsewhere. The reason is in how the information was developed. The occupational task descriptions were written specifically for each job, based on information collected from employer surveys and other sources. Information for Knowledge, Abilities, Skills, General Work Activities, and Job Characteristics were created quite differently. For these, a list of characteristics was developed that would apply to many or all jobs. Each occupation was given a numerical rating for each characteristic, with higher numbers referring to higher levels of competence. Listing the measures for all these characteristics would be impractical, so we include only those that have above average numerical ratings for each occupation. (Our definition of above average is one standard deviation above the mean.) This results in much shorter lists but ones that are more useful for most people. For some jobs, there are no characteristics with above average numerical measures. For example, the sample description for Lawn Service Managers shows such an occurrence in the Abilities section, where it states "None above average." This doesn't mean that these characteristics are unimportant but rather none has met our technical definition for above average. Another technical issue is that you may notice that some information for a job description seems contradictory or outright inaccurate.*

*For example, the O*NET description for Actuaries indicates that one of this job's characteristics is to "Deal with Physically Aggressive People." While the O*NET database does include a higher numerical* *rating that results in this characteristic being included in the description, we just don't think that Actuaries have to do this very often. This example might be an error in the O*NET database that will be corrected in a future release, but we have decided to include the information as provided by the U.S. Department of Labor. All of this is another way for us to emphasize that you need to be careful in how you interpret any information, and that even carefully collected data can include errors or lead you to inaccurate conclusions. Data does have its limitations and, as in all things, you will need to use good common sense in interpreting the contents of this book and any other reference.*

TIPS FOR USING THE *O*NET DICTIONARY OF OCCUPATIONAL TITLES*™

In the years to come, the O*NET will become the major and most authoritative source of occupational information for employers, job seekers, students, career changers, and many others. Most occupational information sources will rely on or cross-reference to the O*NET as the standard for detailed, reliable information on occupations. As the first and perhaps only print version of the O*NET, *The O*NET Dictionary of Occupational Titles*™ is intended for use by a variety of audiences. While it will be used for a variety of purposes, we expect its primary uses to be the following:

- ***information for businesses and employers***
- ***exploring career alternatives***
- ***information for job seekers***
- ***considering various education or training options***
- ***researching technical and legal issues***

Following are brief comments on how *The O*NET Dictionary of Occupational Titles*™ could assist individuals in meeting these needs. Additional resource materials on career planning, job search and other topics are presented in the bibliography.

Tips for Employer and Human Resource Development Use

The O*NET descriptions in this book provide a variety of valuable information for use in business and other situations. Some of these uses include the following.

- **Write job descriptions:** Each O*NET description has been carefully constructed to accurately reflect the tasks, skills, abilities, and other attributes required in that job. This information provides an excellent source of objective information to use in writing job descriptions. As an example, look back at the sample job description for Lawn Service Manager presented earlier in the introduction.

  From that, you would find the key skills needed in the position, the level of responsibility for others involved, education and training required, and a variety of special knowledge needed to succeed in that job -- most of the content needed to write a solid job description. Of course, employers would need to customize their descriptions, but the O*NET descriptions provide an excellent starting point.

- **Structure employment interviews and hiring decisions:** Employers can use the O*NET descriptions to identify key skills and experiences to look for when screening applicants during an employment interview. This can be done informally or, if desired, a more formal list of required competencies could be developed and then used by interviewers to more objectively rate each applicant on each measure. Of course, employer-specific requirements should be added as needed to the basic requirements for job performance provided by the O*NET descriptions.

- **Set pay levels:** We have already noted the limitations for using any pay information, and those same cautions apply when used by an employer. The salary information does, however, provide some guidance on the pay level for an experienced worker. Entry-level workers will often be paid less (sometimes much less), and local conditions often determine the "going rate" to attract the employee skills needed. There are no hard guidelines, so use your judgment.

- **Identify training requirements:** Employers can use O*NET descriptions to identify training needed for current or new employees to gain proficiency in various jobs. An employer may identify skills or other weaknesses in a potential employee that can be corrected through brief training and, therefore, increase the applicant pool for certain positions. The O*NET information also would be helpful for existing employees seeking upward mobility to a more challenging or different job with the same employer, by helping them identify areas of skills, training, knowledge, or other factors that they need to develop for success in a new position.

Tips for Exploring Career Alternatives

Virtually all workers in North America work in one of the occupations described in this book. While the descriptions are quite brief, they provide substantial information that can be used as a preliminary source for identifying one or more career options to explore more thoroughly.

If you are using this book to explore career options, the best way to begin is by identifying clusters of jobs that interest you most. We suggest you do this by looking at the listing of O*NET jobs following the table of contents. The occupations there are arranged into groups of similar jobs, with the group titles presented in bold type. Once you locate a group of jobs that seems interesting to you, identify specific job titles within the same or similar groups for further exploration. In this way, you will often identify jobs that you may otherwise not consider. Read the O*NET descriptions for those jobs that most interest you and, for those you want to know more about, use one of the resources that follow.

- **Read the *Occupational Outlook Handbook*:** Each O*NET description includes a reference to one or more job titles found in a separate book titled the *Occupational Outlook Handbook.* We like the OOH and recommend it highly. Its descriptions are longer and provide details that would be useful to anyone considering the occupation. The OOH is available in most libraries and through many bookstores. The OOH descriptions are also provided in a book titled *America's Top 300 Jobs*. One or the other of these books should be available in most libraries or bookstores.

- **Read the *Dictionary of Occupational Titles* (DOT) and the *Guide for Occupational Exploration* (GOE):** The DOT and GOE are widely used reference books whose organizational systems are cross-referenced by many other books, interest inventories, and other materials. The O*NET descriptions include related DOT and GOE numbers and job titles or interest groups, allowing you to cross-reference these important systems. The DOT was published by the U.S. Department of Labor and provides brief descriptions for over 12,000 job titles. The last edition of the DOT was released in 1991, and there are no plans to update it in its current form.

  Two current editions of the GOE exist -- the *Complete Guide for Occupational Exploration* and the *Enhanced Guide for Occupational Exploration.* Both organize jobs into groupings based on interests and provide useful information on these groupings and the jobs within the groups. The CGOE cross-references all jobs in the DOT to the GOE interest groups, and the EGOE includes DOT descriptions for 2,800 of the largest jobs. Use the DOT and GOE cross-references included in this book's O*NET descriptions to find information on related jobs in these and other information sources.

- **Get additional information from the library or the Internet:** Ask the librarian to direct you to books, periodicals, and other sources of information on an occupation that interests you. Professional journals are often available for a wide variety of occupations and industries. You can also often obtain substantial information from professional associations and other sources on the Internet. JIST's Internet site provides links to other career-related sites. Visit www.JIST.com

- **Talk to people who work in the jobs that interest you:** The best source of information is often overlooked -- the people who work in jobs that interest you. They are often willing to answer your questions and to give you sources of additional information.

Tips for Job Seekers

The O*NET job descriptions in this book can help a job seeker in two important ways:

- **Identify new job targets:** Many job seekers miss employment opportunities by overlooking jobs they can do but with which they are not familiar. For this reason, you should carefully review all the O*NET job titles, with particular emphasis on those in clusters you are already considering. A listing of O*NET jobs within clusters follows the table of contents in this book. Review it if you are looking for a job. As you identify possible new job targets, look up their O*NET descriptions to determine if you might qualify. If so, you should consider pursuing these jobs. In the interview, point out the qualities that you do have and state that you can quickly learn any needed skills.

- **To prepare for interviews:** The O*NET descriptions provide very useful information for you in preparing for an interview. For example, once you have set up an interview for a position, carefully review the O*NET description for that job. Doing so will help you identify skills and experience you should emphasize in your interview. We also encourage you to carefully review the O*NET descriptions of jobs you have held in the past. Doing so will identify skills and other characteristics that you can present in your interview for a new position.

  Even past jobs that seem unrelated to your current interests often provide skills and experience that you can use to convince an employer that you can do the position you seek. Careful preparation such as this can make the difference between your getting a job offer or not. We have often found that better-prepared job seekers will get a job over those with superior credentials. The difference is in how well they present themselves in the interview. Those who read and understand the skills they have to do the job they seek -- and communicate this to an employer -- will have a distinct advantage over those who do not.

Tips for Considering Education or Training Options

People with more training or education tend to earn more than those with less. While most training and education will benefit you in some way, too many people do not spend enough time investigating such an important decision. Before you spend substantial time and money on courses or training programs, spend some time investigating what you hope to gain.

Each O*NET description provides several sources of education and training information. The Education section of each job description is the most obvious one, but additional information is found in the Knowledge and CIP Program/s sections of each O*NET description. Following are additional details on how each of these sections can be used to better understand the training or education needed for a given job.

The Education Section: This includes information on the training or education level typically required for entry into the listed occupation. There are 11 levels of education used in the O*NET descriptions. They are as follows:

- *Short-term O-J-T (On the Job Training)*—It is possible to work in these occupations and achieve an average level of performance within a few days or weeks through on-the-job training.
- *Moderate-term O-J-T*—Occupations that require this type of training can be performed adequately after a 1- to 12-month period of combined on-the-job and informal training. Typically, untrained workers observe experienced workers perform tasks and are gradually moved into progressively more difficult assignments.
- *Long-term O-J-T*—This type of training requires more than 12 months of on-the-job training or combined work experience and formal classroom instruction. This includes occupations that use formal apprenticeships for training workers that may take up to four years. It also includes intensive occupation-specific, employer-sponsored training like police academies. Furthermore, it includes occupations that require natural talent that must be developed over many years.

- *Work experience in a related occupation*—This type of job requires a worker to have experience in a related occupation such as police detectives, who are selected based on their experience as police patrol officers.
- *Postsecondary vocational training*—This requirement can vary from training that involves a few months but is usually less than one year. In a few instances there may be as many as four years of training.
- *Associate's degree*—This degree usually requires two years of full-time academic work beyond high school.
- *Bachelor's degree*—This is a degree that requires approximately four-to-five years of full-time academic work beyond high school.
- *Work experience, plus degree*—Jobs in this category are often management-related and require some experience in a related non-managerial position.
- *Master's degree*—Completion of a master's degree usually requires one-to-two years of full-time study beyond the bachelor's degree.
- *Doctoral degree*—This degree normally requires two or more years of full-time academic work beyond the bachelor's degree.
- *First professional degree*—This type of degree normally requires a minimum of at least two years of education beyond the bachelor's degree and frequently requires three years.

The Knowledge section: The Knowledge section of each O*NET description includes specific areas of knowledge that would be helpful or necessary in performing the job. Some of these listings include course names, training programs, areas of study, or college majors related to performance in the occupation. Other sections of each description, such as the Skills and Generalized Work Activities sections, can provide clues on the training or education that would be helpful for the listed job.

The CIP code section: Each occupational description includes a CIP code and title. This refers to the Classification of Instructional Programs, a widely used system to organize training and education programs. The CIP code and title tell you the type of training or educational programs typically available that help prepare for that occupation. Program names used in various schools and training programs may differ from those listed in the CIP, but the CIP information will give you some idea of the types of programs available.

While the O*NET descriptions in this book provide some information on the level of training, education, or experience needed for various occupations, you obviously need more detail. As with occupational data, a wide variety of training and education information is available. Bookstores and libraries have many books on the topic; much is available on the Internet; and local schools and training programs provide orientation and admission information. All these resources should be used before making an important decision on education or training.

Tips for Corporate and Institutional Educators and Human Resource Development People

O*NET descriptions provide an excellent source of information on the skills and knowledge needed to succeed in a given job. If you are responsible for developing or teaching a course or curriculum for a school or training program, the descriptions provide exact points that need to be learned. An outcome-oriented program could then be developed to teach specific, measurable knowledge or competencies. Remember that the O*NET database provides specific measures for many elements included in this book, and these measures can be obtained from accessing the database itself.

In a similar way, a business could use the descriptions in this book to help define the on-the-job or more formal training program needed to prepare employees for specific positions. For example, in reviewing the O*NET description for Lawn Service Managers, you would notice the emphasis this position requires in working with people -- it includes such statements as "Customer and personal service," "Establishing and maintaining relationships," and "Coaching and developing others." A training program for this position, then, could not just deal with grass and weeds -- other skills are essential for success.

Tips for Researching Technical and Legal Issues -- "Caveat Datum"*

The O*NET database -- and the O*NET descriptions in this book -- provide substantial technical information on jobs and their many characteristics and requirements. This information is provided by the U.S. government and great care has been taken to make it both accurate and reliable. Even so, the information does have limitations. For example, the O*NET job title "Sales Managers" will have enormous differences in requirements from one employer to another -- in such points as level of responsibility, stress, travel requirements, computer literacy requirements, product knowledge, physical lifting of samples, and many other factors. These differences can simply not be included in one description database and many job-to-job differences will exist. That is why the U.S. Department of Labor has never approved or encouraged the use of its occupational information to support formal litigation or as the final, authoritative basis for legal or other formal matters.

In a similar way, we urge anyone using this book to understand that the validity of the underlying information has limitations. For example, an occupation that lists "Bachelor's degree" as a typical training requirement for entry often has some or even many people successfully working in these jobs with less education -- or much more.

One source of occupational information can simply not cover all variations of a given job -- too many differences exist in the requirements for the same job title among different employers. That is why we recommend that you use your own judgment in understanding the information in this book. While it has been carefully collected and reviewed, it has limitations and should not be used as the final authoritative source for legal or technical issues.

* You have probably heard of "caveat emptor," which is Latin for "let the buyer beware." We think "caveat datum," which loosely translated means "beware of the data," is particularly appropriate as our advice for regarding the O*NET data as the basis for settling legal issues.

YOUR SUGGESTIONS ARE WELCOME

While it was impractical to include details on all 445 data elements for each occupation found in the O*NET database, the O*NET descriptions in this book include substantial details in a useful format. In addition to the narrative description and occupational task elements, we included higher-than-average requirements for 218 data elements for each occupation -- plus the crosswalk information for the GOE, CIP, and DOT. While some compromises were involved in constructing helpful descriptions, we think the information will be valuable for many uses. We hope you agree.

Because we intend to revise this book as updated O*NET data becomes available, please let us know what you would like us to include in future editions. Please send your comments and suggestions to

Editor, *The O*NET Dictionary of Occupational Titles™*

JIST Works, Inc.
720 North Park Avenue
Indianapolis, IN 46202
(or e-mail to JISTworks@aol.com)

Thanks!

Section 1
Executives, Managers, and Administrators

General Managers

13002A TREASURERS, CONTROLLERS, AND CHIEF FINANCIAL OFFICERS. OOH Title/s: Financial Managers; General Managers and Top Executives

Plan, direct, and coordinate the financial activities of an organization at the highest level of management. Include financial reserve officers. Directs financial planning, procurement, and investment of funds for organization. Directs preparation of budgets. Prepares reports or directs preparation of reports summarizing organization's current and forecasted financial position, business activity, and reports required by regulatory agencies. Prepares financial reports or directs preparation of reports. Recommends to management major economic objectives and policies. Delegates authority for receipt, disbursement, banking, protection, and custody of funds, securities, and financial instruments. Analyzes past, present, and expected operations. Plans and implements new operating procedures to improve efficiency and reduce costs. Ensures that institution reserves meet legal requirements. Coordinates activities of assigned program and interprets policies and practices. Arranges audits of company accounts. Advises management on investments and loans for short- and long-range financial plans. Manages accounting department. Evaluates need for procurement of funds and investment of surplus. Determines methods and procedures for carrying out assigned program. Develops policies and procedures for account collections and extension of credit to customers.

Yearly Earnings: $37,180

Education: Work experience, plus degree

Knowledge: Administration and Management; Economics and Accounting; Sales and Marketing; Personnel and Human Resources; Mathematics; Psychology; English Language; History and Archeology; Philosophy and Theology; Law, Government, and Jurisprudence; Communications and Media

Abilities: Oral Comprehension; Written Comprehension; Oral Expression; Written Expression; Fluency of Ideas; Originality; Problem Sensitivity; Deductive Reasoning; Inductive Reasoning; Information Ordering; Category Flexibility; Mathematical Reasoning; Number Facility; Memorization; Speed of Closure; Perceptual Speed; Selective Attention; Near Vision; Speech Recognition; Speech Clarity

Skills: Reading Comprehension; Writing; Speaking; Mathematics; Critical Thinking; Active Learning; Learning Strategies; Monitoring; Coordination; Persuasion; Negotiation; Problem Identification; Information Gathering; Information Organization; Synthesis/Reorganization; Idea Generation; Idea Evaluation; Implementation Planning; Solution Appraisal; Operations Analysis; Visioning; Systems Perception; Identifying Downstream Consequences; Identification of Key Causes; Judgment and Decision Making; Systems Evaluation; Time Management; Management of Financial Resources; Management of Material Resources; Management of Personnel Resources

General Work Activities: Getting Information Needed to Do the Job; Monitoring Processes, Material, or Surroundings; Identifying Objects, Actions, and Events; Estimating Needed Characteristics; Judging Qualities of Things, Services, People; Processing Information; Evaluating Information against Standards; Analyzing Data or Information; Making Decisions and Solving Problems; Thinking Creatively; Updating and Using Job-Relevant Knowledge; Developing Objectives and Strategies; Scheduling Work and Activities; Organizing, Planning, and Prioritizing; Operating Vehicles or Equipment; Implementing Ideas, Programs, etc.; Documenting/Recording Information; Interpreting Meaning of Information to Others; Communicating with Other Workers; Communicating with Persons Outside Organization; Establishing and Maintaining Relationships; Selling or Influencing Others; Resolving Conflicts, Negotiating with Others; Coordinating Work and Activities of Others; Developing and Building Teams; Guiding, Directing and Motivating Subordinates; Coaching and Developing Others; Provide Consultation and Advice to Others; Performing Administrative Activities; Staffing Organizational Units; Monitoring and Controlling Resources

Job Characteristics: Take a Position Opposed to Others; Coordinate or Lead Others; Responsibility for Outcomes and Results; Sitting; Consequence of Error; Frustrating Circumstances; Importance of Being Exact or Accurate; Importance of Being Sure All is Done; Importance of Being Aware of New Events

GOE Group/s: 11.05.02 Business Administration: Administrative Specialization; 11.06.02 Finance: Records Systems Analysis; 11.06.03 Finance: Risk and Profit Analysis; 11.06.05 Finance: Budget and Financial Control

CIP Program/s: 520801 Finance, General; 520807 Investments and Securities

Related DOT Job/s: 160.167-058 CONTROLLER; 161.117-018 TREASURER; 186.117-070 TREASURER, FINANCIAL INSTITUTION; 186.117-078 VICE PRESIDENT, FINANCIAL INSTITUTION; 186.167-054 RESERVE OFFICER

13002B FINANCIAL MANAGERS, BRANCH OR DEPARTMENT. OOH Title/s: Financial Managers

Direct and coordinate financial activities of workers in a branch, office, or department of an establishment, such as branch bank, brokerage firm, risk and insurance department, or credit department. Directs and coordinates activities of workers engaged in conducting credit investigations and collecting delinquent accounts of customers. Plans, directs, and coordinates risk and insurance programs of establishment to control risks and losses. Manages branch or office of financial institution. Directs and coordinates activities to implement institution policies, procedures, and practices concerning granting or extending lines of credit and loans. Prepares financial and regulatory reports required by law, regulations, and board of directors. Analyzes and classifies risks as to frequency and financial impact of risk on company. Selects appropriate technique to minimize loss, such as avoidance and loss prevention and reduction. Prepares operational and risk reports for management analysis. Directs floor operations of brokerage firm engaged in buying and selling securities at exchange. Establishes procedures for custody and control of assets, records, loan collateral, and securities to ensure safekeeping. Evaluates effectiveness of current collection policies and procedures. Directs insurance negotiations, selects insurance brokers and carriers, and places insurance. Evaluates data pertaining to costs to plan budget. Reviews collection reports to ascertain status of collections and balances outstanding. Monitors order flow and transactions that brokerage firm executes on floor of exchange. Reviews reports of securities transactions and price lists to analyze market conditions. Establishes credit limitations on customer account. Examines, evaluates, and processes loan applications. Submits delinquent accounts to attorney or outside agency for collection.

Yearly Earnings: $37,180

Education: Work experience, plus degree

Knowledge: Administration and Management; Economics and Accounting; Sales and Marketing; Personnel and Human Resources; Mathematics; Psychology; English Language; History and Archeology; Law, Government, and Jurisprudence

Abilities: Oral Comprehension; Written Comprehension; Oral Expression; Written Expression; Fluency of Ideas; Originality; Problem Sensitivity; Deductive Reasoning; Inductive Reasoning; Information Ordering; Category Flexibility; Mathematical Reasoning; Number Facility; Memorization; Speed of Closure; Selective Attention; Time Sharing; Near Vision; Far Vision; Speech Recognition; Speech Clarity

Skills: Reading Comprehension; Active Listening; Writing; Speaking; Mathematics; Critical Thinking; Active Learning; Learning Strategies; Monitoring; Social Perceptiveness; Coordination; Persuasion; Negotiation; Service Orientation; Problem Identification; Information Gathering; Information Organization; Synthesis/Reorganization; Idea Generation; Idea Evaluation; Implementation Planning; Solution Appraisal; Operations Analysis; Visioning; Systems Perception; Identifying Downstream Consequences; Identification of Key Causes; Judgment and Decision Making; Systems Evaluation; Time Management; Management of Financial Resources; Management of Material Resources; Management of Personnel Resources
General Work Activities: Getting Information Needed to Do the Job; Monitoring Processes, Material, or Surroundings; Identifying Objects, Actions, and Events; Estimating Needed Characteristics; Judging Qualities of Things, Services, People; Processing Information; Evaluating Information against Standards; Analyzing Data or Information; Making Decisions and Solving Problems; Thinking Creatively; Updating and Using Job-Relevant Knowledge; Developing Objectives and Strategies; Scheduling Work and Activities; Organizing, Planning, and Prioritizing; Operating Vehicles or Equipment; Documenting/Recording Information; Interpreting Meaning of Information to Others; Communicating with Other Workers; Communicating with Persons Outside Organization; Establishing and Maintaining Relationships; Selling or Influencing Others; Resolving Conflicts, Negotiating with Others; Performing for or Working with Public; Coordinating Work and Activities of Others; Developing and Building Teams; Teaching Others; Guiding, Directing and Motivating Subordinates; Coaching and Developing Others; Provide Consultation and Advice to Others; Performing Administrative Activities; Staffing Organizational Units; Monitoring and Controlling Resources
Job Characteristics: Objective or Subjective Information; Supervise, Coach, Train Others; Persuade Someone to a Course of Action; Take a Position Opposed to Others; Coordinate or Lead Others; Responsibility for Outcomes and Results; Frequency in Conflict Situations; Deal with Unpleasant or Angry People; Sitting; Consequence of Error; Frustrating Circumstances; Degree of Automation; Importance of Being Aware of New Events
GOE Group/s: 11.05.04 Business Administration: Sales and Purchasing Management; 11.06.03 Finance: Risk and Profit Analysis; 11.11.04 Business Management: Services
CIP Program/s: 520801 Finance, General; 520807 Investments and Securities
Related DOT Job/s: 169.167-086 MANAGER, CREDIT AND COLLECTION; 186.117-066 RISK AND INSURANCE MANAGER; 186.117-074 TRUST OFFICER; 186.117-082 FOREIGN-EXCHANGE DEALER; 186.117-086 MANAGER, EXCHANGE FLOOR; 186.137-014 OPERATIONS OFFICER; 186.167-070 ASSISTANT BRANCH MANAGER, FINANCIAL INSTITUTION; 186.167-082 FACTOR; 186.167-086 MANAGER, FINANCIAL INSTITUTION

13005A HUMAN RESOURCES MANAGERS. OOH

Title/s: Personnel, Training, and Labor Relations Specialists and Managers

Plan, direct, and coordinate human resource management activities of an organization to maximize the strategic use of human resources,and maintain functions such as employee compensation, recruitment, personnel policies, and regulatory compliance. Formulates policies and procedures for recruitment, testing, placement, classification, orientation, benefits, and labor and industrial relations. Plans, directs, supervises, and coordinates work activities of subordinates and staff relating to employment, compensation, labor relations, and employee relations. Directs preparation and distribution of written and verbal information to inform employees of benefits, compensation, and personnel policies. Evaluates and modifies benefits policies to establish competitive programs and to ensure compliance with legal requirements. Analyzes compensation policies, government regulations, and prevailing wage rates to develop competitive compensation plan. Develops methods to improve employment policies, processes, and practices, and recommends changes to management. Prepares personnel forecast to project employment needs. Prepares budget for personnel operations. Prepares and delivers presentations and reports to corporate officers or other management regarding human resource management policies and practices and recommendations for change. Negotiates bargaining agreements and resolves labor disputes. Meets with shop stewards and supervisors to resolve grievances. Conducts exit interviews to identify reasons for employee termination and writes separation notices. Plans and conducts new employee orientation to foster positive attitude toward organizational objectives. Writes directives advising department managers of organization policy in personnel matters such as equal employment opportunity, sexual harassment, and discrimination. Studies legislation, arbitration decisions, and collective bargaining contracts to assess industry trends. Maintains records and compiles statistical reports concerning personnel-related data such as hires, transfers, performance appraisals, and absenteeism rates. Analyzes statistical data and reports to identify and determine causes of personnel problems and develop recommendations for improvement of organization's personnel policies and practices. Represents organization at personnel-related hearings and investigations. Contracts with vendors to provide employee services, such as canteen, transportation, or relocation service. Investigates industrial accidents and prepares reports for insurance carrier.
Yearly Earnings: $35,256
Education: Work experience, plus degree
Knowledge: Administration and Management; Economics and Accounting; Personnel and Human Resources; Mathematics; Psychology; Education and Training; English Language; Law, Government, and Jurisprudence
Abilities: Oral Comprehension; Written Comprehension; Oral Expression; Written Expression; Fluency of Ideas; Originality; Problem Sensitivity; Deductive Reasoning; Inductive Reasoning; Information Ordering; Category Flexibility; Mathematical Reasoning; Number Facility; Memorization; Speed of Closure; Flexibility of Closure; Perceptual Speed; Selective Attention; Time Sharing; Gross Body Equilibrium; Far Vision
Skills: Active Listening; Writing; Speaking; Critical Thinking; Active Learning; Learning Strategies; Monitoring; Social Perceptiveness; Coordination; Persuasion; Negotiation; Instructing; Problem Identification; Information Gathering; Synthesis/Reorganization; Idea Generation; Idea Evaluation; Implementation Planning; Solution Appraisal; Programming; Visioning; Systems Perception; Identifying Downstream Consequences; Identification of Key Causes; Judgment and Decision Making; Systems Evaluation; Time Management; Management of Financial Resources; Management of Material Resources; Management of Personnel Resources
General Work Activities: Getting Information Needed to Do the Job; Monitoring Processes, Material, or Surroundings; Estimating Needed Characteristics; Judging Qualities of Things, Services, People; Processing Information; Evaluating Information against Standards; Analyzing Data or Information; Making Decisions and Solving Problems; Thinking Creatively; Updating and Using Job-Relevant Knowledge; Developing Objectives and Strategies; Scheduling Work and Activities; Organizing, Planning, and Prioritizing; Operating Vehicles or Equipment; Implementing Ideas, Programs, etc.; Documenting/Recording Information; Interpreting Meaning of Information to Others; Communicating with Other Workers; Communicating with Persons Outside Organization; Establishing and Maintaining Relationships; Selling or Influencing Others; Resolving Conflicts, Negotiating with

Others; Coordinating Work and Activities of Others; Developing and Building Teams; Teaching Others; Guiding, Directing and Motivating Subordinates; Coaching and Developing Others; Provide Consultation and Advice to Others; Performing Administrative Activities; Staffing Organizational Units; Monitoring and Controlling Resources
Job Characteristics: Objective or Subjective Information; Job-Required Social Interaction; Supervise, Coach, Train Others; Persuade Someone to a Course of Action; Take a Position Opposed to Others; Coordinate or Lead Others; Responsibility for Outcomes and Results; Sitting; Consequence of Error; Frustrating Circumstances; Importance of Being Sure All is Done
GOE Group/s: 11.05.02 Business Administration: Administrative Specialization; 11.05.03 Business Administration: Management Services: Government
CIP Program/s: 521001 Human Resources Management; 521002 Labor/Personnel Relations and Studies
Related DOT Job/s: 166.117-010 DIRECTOR, INDUSTRIAL RELATIONS; 166.117-018 MANAGER, PERSONNEL; 166.167-018 MANAGER, BENEFITS; 166.167-022 MANAGER, COMPENSATION; 166.167-030 MANAGER, EMPLOYMENT; 188.117-086 DIRECTOR, MERIT SYSTEM

13005B TRAINING AND DEVELOPMENT MANAGERS. OOH Title/s: Personnel, Training, and Labor Relations Specialists and Managers; Police, Detectives, and Special Agents

Plan, direct, and coordinate the training activities of an organization. Analyzes training needs to develop new training programs or to modify and improve existing programs. Plans and develops training procedures utilizing knowledge of relative effectiveness of individual training, classroom training, demonstrations, on-the-job training, meetings, conferences, and workshops. Formulates training policies and schedules, utilizing knowledge of identified training needs. Evaluates effectiveness of training programs and instructor performance. Develops and organizes training manuals, multimedia visual aids, and other educational materials. Coordinates established courses with technical and professional courses provided by community schools, and designates training procedures. Develops testing and evaluation procedures. Confers with management and supervisory personnel to identify training needs based on projected production processes, changes, and other factors. Reviews and evaluates training and apprenticeship programs for compliance with government standards. Prepares training budget for department or organization. Trains instructors and supervisors in effective training techniques. Interprets and clarifies regulatory policies governing apprenticeship training programs, and provides information and assistance to trainees and labor and management representatives.
Yearly Earnings: $35,256
Education: Work experience, plus degree
Knowledge: Administration and Management; Personnel and Human Resources; Psychology; Education and Training; Law, Government, and Jurisprudence
Abilities: Oral Comprehension; Written Comprehension; Oral Expression; Written Expression; Fluency of Ideas; Originality; Problem Sensitivity; Deductive Reasoning; Inductive Reasoning; Category Flexibility; Mathematical Reasoning; Number Facility; Memorization; Speed of Closure; Flexibility of Closure; Perceptual Speed; Selective Attention; Time Sharing; Far Vision
Skills: Speaking; Critical Thinking; Learning Strategies; Instructing; Problem Identification; Information Gathering; Idea Generation; Idea Evaluation; Implementation Planning; Operations Analysis; Visioning; Identifying Downstream Consequences; Identification of Key Causes; Systems Evaluation; Time Management; Management of Financial Resources; Management of Personnel Resources
General Work Activities: Getting Information Needed to Do the Job; Monitoring Processes, Material, or Surroundings; Identifying Objects, Actions, and Events; Estimating Needed Characteristics; Judging Qualities of Things, Services, People; Processing Information; Evaluating Information against Standards; Analyzing Data or Information; Making Decisions and Solving Problems; Thinking Creatively; Developing Objectives and Strategies; Scheduling Work and Activities; Organizing, Planning, and Prioritizing; Implementing Ideas, Programs, etc.; Documenting/Recording Information; Interpreting Meaning of Information to Others; Communicating with Other Workers; Establishing and Maintaining Relationships; Resolving Conflicts, Negotiating with Others; Coordinating Work and Activities of Others; Developing and Building Teams; Teaching Others; Guiding, Directing and Motivating Subordinates; Coaching and Developing Others; Provide Consultation and Advice to Others; Performing Administrative Activities; Staffing Organizational Units; Monitoring and Controlling Resources
Job Characteristics: Objective or Subjective Information; Job-Required Social Interaction; Supervise, Coach, Train Others; Provide a Service to Others; Take a Position Opposed to Others; Coordinate or Lead Others; Responsibility for Outcomes and Results
GOE Group/s: 11.07.03 Services Administration: Education Services
CIP Program/s: 440401 Public Administration; 521001 Human Resources Management
Related DOT Job/s: 166.167-026 MANAGER, EDUCATION AND TRAINING; 188.117-010 APPRENTICESHIP CONSULTANT; 375.167-054 POLICE ACADEMY PROGRAM COORDINATOR

13005C LABOR RELATIONS MANAGERS. OOH Title/s: Personnel, Training, and Labor Relations Specialists and Managers

Plan, direct, and coordinate the labor relations program of an organization. Analyze and interpret collective bargaining agreements and advise management and union officials in development, application, and interpretation of labor relations policies and practices. Represents management in labor contract negotiations to reconcile opposing claims and recommend concessions, or proposes adoption of new procedures. Analyzes collective bargaining agreements to interpret intent, spirit, and terms of contract. Compiles information on disagreement and determines points of issue, according to knowledge of labor, business, and government responsibilities under law. Advises management and union officials on development, application, and interpretation of company labor relations policies and practices. Arranges and schedules meetings between parties in labor dispute to investigate and resolve grievances. Monitors implementation of policies concerning wages, hours, and working conditions to ensure compliance to labor contract terms. Supervises work activities of employees involved in labor relations functions of organization. Completes statistical reports on cases, findings, and resolved issues.
Yearly Earnings: $35,256
Education: Work experience, plus degree
Knowledge: Administration and Management; Personnel and Human Resources; Mathematics; English Language; Law, Government, and Jurisprudence
Abilities: Oral Comprehension; Written Comprehension; Oral Expression; Written Expression; Fluency of Ideas; Originality; Problem Sensitivity; Inductive Reasoning; Information Ordering; Memorization; Speech Clarity
Skills: Active Listening; Persuasion; Negotiation; Programming; Visioning; Identifying Downstream Consequences; Time Management; Management of Personnel Resources
General Work Activities: Getting Information Needed to Do the Job; Monitoring Processes, Material, or Surroundings; Identifying Objects,

Actions, and Events; Judging Qualities of Things, Services, People; Processing Information; Evaluating Information against Standards; Analyzing Data or Information; Making Decisions and Solving Problems; Thinking Creatively; Updating and Using Job-Relevant Knowledge; Developing Objectives and Strategies; Scheduling Work and Activities; Organizing, Planning, and Prioritizing; Interpreting Meaning of Information to Others; Communicating with Other Workers; Establishing and Maintaining Relationships; Selling or Influencing Others; Resolving Conflicts, Negotiating with Others; Coordinating Work and Activities of Others; Developing and Building Teams; Guiding, Directing and Motivating Subordinates; Coaching and Developing Others; Provide Consultation and Advice to Others; Performing Administrative Activities; Staffing Organizational Units; Monitoring and Controlling Resources

Job Characteristics: Objective or Subjective Information; Job-Required Social Interaction; Supervise, Coach, Train Others; Persuade Someone to a Course of Action; Take a Position Opposed to Others; Coordinate or Lead Others; Responsibility for Outcomes and Results; Frequency in Conflict Situations; Deal with Unpleasant or Angry People; Sitting; Consequence of Error; Frustrating Circumstances; Importance of Being Sure All is Done

GOE Group/s: 11.04.03 Law: Conciliation; 11.05.02 Business Administration: Administrative Specialization

CIP Program/s: 521001 Human Resources Management; 521002 Labor/Personnel Relations and Studies

Related DOT Job/s: 166.167-034 MANAGER, LABOR RELATIONS; 188.217-010 COMMISSIONER OF CONCILIATION

13005E EMPLOYEE ASSISTANCE SPECIALISTS. OOH Title/s: Public Relations Specialists

Coordinate activities of employers to set up and operate programs to help employees overcome behavioral or medical problems, such as substance abuse, that affect job performance. Develops or leads group to develop employee assistance programs, policies, and procedures. Plans and conducts training sessions for company officials to develop skills to identify and assist with resolving employee behavioral problems. Consults with employer to establish referral network for group or individual counseling of troubled employees. Consults with staff of employee assistance program to monitor progress of program. Consults with employer representatives to develop education and prevention program. Analyzes character and type of business establishments, and compiles list of prospective employers to implement assistance programs. Contacts prospective employers to explain program advantages and fees, and negotiates participation agreement with interested employers. Writes announcements and advertisements for newspapers and other publications to promote employee assistance program within business community.

Yearly Earnings: $31,772

Education: Bachelor's degree

Knowledge: Administration and Management; Sales and Marketing; Customer and Personal Service; Personnel and Human Resources; Psychology; Sociology and Anthropology; Therapy and Counseling; Education and Training

Abilities: Oral Comprehension; Written Comprehension; Oral Expression; Written Expression; Originality; Problem Sensitivity; Deductive Reasoning; Inductive Reasoning; Information Ordering; Near Vision; Speech Clarity

Skills: Reading Comprehension; Active Listening; Speaking; Critical Thinking; Active Learning; Learning Strategies; Monitoring; Social Perceptiveness; Coordination; Persuasion; Negotiation; Instructing; Service Orientation; Problem Identification; Information Gathering; Idea Generation; Idea Evaluation; Implementation Planning; Systems Evaluation; Management of Personnel Resources

General Work Activities: Getting Information Needed to Do the Job; Monitoring Processes, Material, or Surroundings; Judging Qualities of Things, Services, People; Processing Information; Making Decisions and Solving Problems; Thinking Creatively; Developing Objectives and Strategies; Scheduling Work and Activities; Organizing, Planning, and Prioritizing; Communicating with Other Workers; Communicating with Persons Outside Organization; Establishing and Maintaining Relationships; Assisting and Caring for Others; Selling or Influencing Others; Resolving Conflicts, Negotiating with Others; Coordinating Work and Activities of Others; Developing and Building Teams; Teaching Others; Guiding, Directing and Motivating Subordinates; Coaching and Developing Others; Provide Consultation and Advice to Others; Performing Administrative Activities

Job Characteristics: Objective or Subjective Information; Job-Required Social Interaction; Supervise, Coach, Train Others; Persuade Someone to a Course of Action; Provide a Service to Others; Coordinate or Lead Others; Sitting; Frustrating Circumstances

GOE Group/s: 11.05.02 Business Administration: Administrative Specialization

CIP Program/s: 511501 Alcohol/Drug Abuse Counseling

Related DOT Job/s: 166.167-050 PROGRAM SPECIALIST, EMPLOYEE-HEALTH MAINTENANCE

13008 PURCHASING MANAGERS. OOH Title/s: Purchasers and Buyers

Plan, direct, and coordinate the activities of buyers, purchasing officers, and related workers involved in purchasing materials, products, or services. Include wholesale or retail trade merchandising managers. Directs and coordinates activities of personnel engaged in buying, selling, and distributing materials, equipment, machinery, and supplies. Develops and implements office, operations, and systems instructions, policies, and procedures. Conducts inventory and directs buyers in purchase of products, materials, and supplies. Determines merchandise costs and formulates and coordinates merchandising policies and activities to ensure profit. Represents company in formulating policies and negotiating contracts with suppliers and unions. Prepares, reviews, and processes requisitions and purchase orders for supplies and equipment. Analyzes market and delivery systems to determine present and future material availability. Prepares report regarding market conditions and merchandise costs. Consults with department personnel to develop and plan sales promotion programs. Studies work flow, sequence of operations, and office arrangement to determine need for new or improved office machines.

Yearly Earnings: $39,780

Education: Work experience, plus degree

Knowledge: Administration and Management; Economics and Accounting; Sales and Marketing; Personnel and Human Resources; Production and Processing; Mathematics; Sociology and Anthropology

Abilities: Fluency of Ideas; Originality; Category Flexibility; Mathematical Reasoning; Number Facility; Speech Clarity

Skills: Active Listening; Writing; Speaking; Social Perceptiveness; Coordination; Persuasion; Negotiation; Problem Identification; Information Gathering; Information Organization; Idea Generation; Idea Evaluation; Implementation Planning; Systems Perception; Identifying Downstream Consequences; Identification of Key Causes; Judgment and Decision Making; Systems Evaluation; Time Management; Management of Financial Resources; Management of Material Resources; Management of Personnel Resources

General Work Activities: Getting Information Needed to Do the Job; Estimating Needed Characteristics; Judging Qualities of Things, Services, People; Evaluating Information against Standards; Analyzing Data or Information; Making Decisions and Solving Problems; Developing Objectives and Strategies; Scheduling Work and Activities;

Organizing, Planning, and Prioritizing; Implementing Ideas, Programs, etc.; Documenting/Recording Information; Interpreting Meaning of Information to Others; Communicating with Other Workers; Communicating with Persons Outside Organization; Establishing and Maintaining Relationships; Selling or Influencing Others; Resolving Conflicts, Negotiating with Others; Coordinating Work and Activities of Others; Developing and Building Teams; Guiding, Directing and Motivating Subordinates; Provide Consultation and Advice to Others; Performing Administrative Activities; Monitoring and Controlling Resources
Job Characteristics: Objective or Subjective Information; Job-Required Social Interaction; Supervise, Coach, Train Others; Persuade Someone to a Course of Action; Take a Position Opposed to Others; Deal with External Customers; Coordinate or Lead Others; Responsibility for Outcomes and Results; Frequency in Conflict Situations; Sitting
GOE Group/s: 11.05.02 Business Administration: Administrative Specialization; 11.05.04 Business Administration: Sales and Purchasing Management
CIP Program/s: 080705 General Retailing Operations; 520201 Business Administration and Management, General; 520202 Purchasing, Procurement and Contracts Management
Related DOT Job/s: 162.167-014 BUYER, TOBACCO, HEAD; 162.167-022 MANAGER, PROCUREMENT SERVICES; 184.117-078 SUPERINTENDENT, COMMISSARY; 185.167-034 MANAGER, MERCHANDISE

13011A ADVERTISING AND PROMOTIONS MANAGERS. OOH Title/s: Marketing, Advertising, and Public Relations Managers

Plan and direct advertising policies and programs or produce collateral materials, such as posters, contests, coupons, or give-aways, to create extra interest in the purchase of a product or service for a department, an entire organization, or on an account basis. Directs activities of workers engaged in developing and producing advertisements. Plans and executes advertising policies of organization. Plans and prepares advertising and promotional material. Confers with department heads and/or staff to discuss topics such as contracts, selection of advertising media, or product to be advertised. Formulates plans to extend business with established accounts and transacts business as agent for advertising accounts. Coordinates activities of departments, such as sales, graphic arts, media, finance, and research. Confers with clients to provide marketing or technical advice. Monitors and analyzes sales promotion results to determine cost effectiveness of promotion campaign. Inspects layouts and advertising copy and edits scripts, audio and video tapes, and other promotional material for adherence to specifications. Supervises and trains service representatives. Reads trade journals and professional literature to stay informed on trends, innovations, and changes that affect media planning. Consults publications to learn about conventions and social functions, and organizes prospect files for promotional purposes. Represents company at trade association meetings to promote products. Directs product research and development. Contacts organizations to explain services and facilities offered or to secure props, audio-visual materials, and sound effects. Adjusts broadcasting schedules due to program cancellation. Directs conversion of products from USA to foreign standards. Inspects premises of assigned stores for adequate security and compliance with safety codes and ordinances.
Yearly Earnings: $43,784
Education: Work experience, plus degree
Knowledge: Administration and Management; Economics and Accounting; Sales and Marketing; Customer and Personal Service; Personnel and Human Resources; Mathematics; Psychology; Sociology and Anthropology; Geography; Education and Training; English Language; Foreign Language; Fine Arts; History and Archeology; Philosophy and Theology; Public Safety and Security; Law, Government, and Jurisprudence; Telecommunications; Communications and Media
Abilities: Oral Comprehension; Written Comprehension; Oral Expression; Written Expression; Fluency of Ideas; Originality; Problem Sensitivity; Deductive Reasoning; Inductive Reasoning; Category Flexibility; Mathematical Reasoning; Number Facility; Memorization; Speed of Closure; Visualization; Selective Attention; Time Sharing; Near Vision; Far Vision; Visual Color Discrimination; Speech Recognition; Speech Clarity
Skills: Reading Comprehension; Active Listening; Writing; Speaking; Critical Thinking; Active Learning; Learning Strategies; Monitoring; Social Perceptiveness; Coordination; Persuasion; Negotiation; Instructing; Service Orientation; Problem Identification; Information Gathering; Information Organization; Synthesis/Reorganization; Idea Generation; Idea Evaluation; Implementation Planning; Solution Appraisal; Operations Analysis; Product Inspection; Visioning; Systems Perception; Identifying Downstream Consequences; Identification of Key Causes; Judgment and Decision Making; Systems Evaluation; Time Management; Management of Financial Resources; Management of Material Resources; Management of Personnel Resources
General Work Activities: Getting Information Needed to Do the Job; Monitoring Processes, Material, or Surroundings; Estimating Needed Characteristics; Judging Qualities of Things, Services, People; Processing Information; Evaluating Information against Standards; Analyzing Data or Information; Making Decisions and Solving Problems; Thinking Creatively; Updating and Using Job-Relevant Knowledge; Developing Objectives and Strategies; Scheduling Work and Activities; Organizing, Planning, and Prioritizing; Operating Vehicles or Equipment; Implementing Ideas, Programs, etc.; Documenting/Recording Information; Interpreting Meaning of Information to Others; Communicating with Other Workers; Communicating with Persons Outside Organization; Establishing and Maintaining Relationships; Selling or Influencing Others; Resolving Conflicts, Negotiating with Others; Performing for or Working with Public; Coordinating Work and Activities of Others; Developing and Building Teams; Teaching Others; Guiding, Directing and Motivating Subordinates; Coaching and Developing Others; Provide Consultation and Advice to Others; Performing Administrative Activities; Staffing Organizational Units; Monitoring and Controlling Resources
Job Characteristics: Objective or Subjective Information; Job-Required Social Interaction; Supervise, Coach, Train Others; Persuade Someone to a Course of Action; Provide a Service to Others; Take a Position Opposed to Others; Deal with External Customers; Coordinate or Lead Others; Responsibility for Outcomes and Results; Frequency in Conflict Situations; Sitting; Consequence of Error; Frustrating Circumstances; Importance of Being Sure All is Done; Importance of Being Aware of New Events
GOE Group/s: 11.09.01 Promotion: Sales
CIP Program/s: 080901 Hospitality and Recreation Marketing Operations, General; 080902 Hotel/Motel Services Marketing Operations; 090201 Advertising; 090701 Radio and Television Broadcasting; 500602 Film-Video Making/Cinematography and Production; 520902 Hotel/Motel and Restaurant Management; 521401 Business Marketing and Marketing Management
Related DOT Job/s: 159.167-022 EXECUTIVE PRODUCER, PROMOS; 163.117-018 MANAGER, PROMOTION; 164.117-010 MANAGER, ADVERTISING; 164.117-014 MANAGER, ADVERTISING AGENCY; 164.117-018 MEDIA DIRECTOR; 164.167-010 ACCOUNT EXECUTIVE

13011B SALES MANAGERS. OOH Title/s: Marketing, Advertising, and Public Relations Managers; Retail Sales Worker Supervisors and Managers

Direct the actual distribution or movement of a product or service to customers. Coordinate sales distribution by estab-

lishing sales territories, quotas, and goals, and establish training programs for sales representatives. Analyze sales statistics gathered by staff to determine sales potential and inventory requirements, and monitor the preferences of customers. Directs and coordinates activities involving sales of manufactured goods, service outlets, technical services, operating retail chain, and advertising services for publication. Plans and directs staffing, training, and performance evaluations to develop and control sales and service programs. Directs, coordinates, and reviews activities in sales and service accounting and recordkeeping, and receiving and shipping operations. Analyzes marketing potential of new and existing store locations, sales statistics, and expenditures to formulate policy. Confers or consults with department heads to plan advertising services, secure information on appliances and equipment, and customer-required specifications. Reviews operational records and reports to project sales and determine profitability. Advises dealers and distributors on policies and operating procedures to ensure functional effectiveness of business. Directs foreign sales and service outlets of organization. Visits franchised dealers to stimulate interest in establishment or expansion of leasing programs. Directs clerical staff to maintain export correspondence, bid requests, and credit collections, and current information on tariffs, licenses, and restrictions. Confers with potential customers regarding equipment needs and advises customers on types of equipment to purchase. Resolves customer complaints regarding sales and service. Represents company at trade association meetings to promote products. Directs product research and development. Inspects premises of assigned stores for adequate security exits and compliance with safety codes and ordinances. Direct conversion of products from USA to foreign standards.

Yearly Earnings: $43,784

Education: Work experience, plus degree

Knowledge: Administration and Management; Clerical; Economics and Accounting; Sales and Marketing; Customer and Personal Service; Personnel and Human Resources; Mathematics; Psychology; Sociology and Anthropology; Geography; Education and Training; English Language; Foreign Language; History and Archeology; Philosophy and Theology; Public Safety and Security; Law, Government, and Jurisprudence; Communications and Media; Transportation

Abilities: Oral Comprehension; Written Comprehension; Oral Expression; Written Expression; Fluency of Ideas; Originality; Problem Sensitivity; Deductive Reasoning; Inductive Reasoning; Category Flexibility; Mathematical Reasoning; Number Facility; Memorization; Selective Attention; Time Sharing; Near Vision; Far Vision; Speech Recognition; Speech Clarity

Skills: Active Listening; Speaking; Critical Thinking; Active Learning; Learning Strategies; Monitoring; Social Perceptiveness; Coordination; Persuasion; Negotiation; Instructing; Service Orientation; Problem Identification; Information Gathering; Synthesis/Reorganization; Idea Generation; Idea Evaluation; Implementation Planning; Solution Appraisal; Operations Analysis; Visioning; Systems Perception; Identifying Downstream Consequences; Identification of Key Causes; Judgment and Decision Making; Systems Evaluation; Time Management; Management of Financial Resources; Management of Material Resources; Management of Personnel Resources

General Work Activities: Getting Information Needed to Do the Job; Monitoring Processes, Material, or Surroundings; Identifying Objects, Actions, and Events; Inspecting Equipment, Structures, or Material; Estimating Needed Characteristics; Judging Qualities of Things, Services, People; Processing Information; Evaluating Information against Standards; Analyzing Data or Information; Making Decisions and Solving Problems; Thinking Creatively; Updating and Using Job-Relevant Knowledge; Developing Objectives and Strategies; Scheduling Work and Activities; Organizing, Planning, and Prioritizing; Operating Vehicles or Equipment; Implementing Ideas, Programs, etc.; Documenting/Recording Information; Interpreting Meaning of Information to Others; Communicating with Other Workers; Communicating with Persons Outside Organization; Establishing and Maintaining Relationships; Selling or Influencing Others; Resolving Conflicts, Negotiating with Others; Performing for or Working with Public; Coordinating Work and Activities of Others; Developing and Building Teams; Teaching Others; Guiding, Directing and Motivating Subordinates; Coaching and Developing Others; Provide Consultation and Advice to Others; Performing Administrative Activities; Staffing Organizational Units; Monitoring and Controlling Resources

Job Characteristics: Objective or Subjective Information; Job-Required Social Interaction; Supervise, Coach, Train Others; Persuade Someone to a Course of Action; Provide a Service to Others; Take a Position Opposed to Others; Deal with External Customers; Coordinate or Lead Others; Responsibility for Outcomes and Results; Frequency in Conflict Situations; Deal with Unpleasant or Angry People; Sitting; Consequence of Error; Frustrating Circumstances; Importance of Being Sure All is Done; Importance of Being Aware of New Events

GOE Group/s: 05.02.03 Managerial Work: Mechanical: Processing and Manufacturing; 11.05.04 Business Administration: Sales and Purchasing Management; 11.09.01 Promotion: Sales; 11.11.05 Business Management: Wholesale-Retail

CIP Program/s: 080705 General Retailing Operations; 081208 Vehicle Marketing Operations; 090201 Advertising; 521401 Business Marketing and Marketing Management; 521403 International Business Marketing

Related DOT Job/s: 163.117-014 MANAGER, EXPORT; 163.167-010 MANAGER, ADVERTISING; 163.167-018 MANAGER, SALES; 163.167-022 MANAGER, UTILITY SALES AND SERVICE; 163.267-010 FIELD REPRESENTATIVE; 185.117-014 AREA SUPERVISOR, RETAIL CHAIN STORE; 185.167-042 MANAGER, PROFESSIONAL EQUIPMENT SALES-AND-SERVICE; 187.167-162 MANAGER, VEHICLE LEASING AND RENTAL; 189.117-018 MANAGER, CUSTOMER TECHNICAL SERVICES

13011C MARKETING MANAGERS. OOH Title/s: Marketing, Advertising, and Public Relations Managers

Determine the demand for products and services offered by a firm and its competitors and identify potential customers. Develop pricing strategies with the goal of maximizing the firm's profits or share of the market while ensuring the firm's customers are satisfied. Oversee product development or monitor trends that indicate the need for new products and services. Plans and administers marketing and distribution of broadcasting television programs and negotiates agreements for ancillary properties. Develops marketing strategy, based on knowledge of establishment policy, nature of market, and cost and mark-up factors. Coordinates and publicizes product marketing activities. Directs activities of world trade department in chamber of commerce to assist business concerns in developing and utilizing foreign markets. Conducts economic and commercial surveys in foreign countries to locate markets for products and services. Analyzes foreign business developments and fashion and trade journals regarding fashion trends and opportunities for selling and buying products. Promotes new fashions and coordinates promotional activities, such as fashion shows, to induce consumer acceptance. Reviews inventory of television programs and films produced and distribution rights to determine potential markets for broadcasting station. Consults with buying personnel to gain advice regarding type of fashions store will purchase and feature for season. Advises exporters and importers on documentation procedures and certifies commercial documents that are required by foreign countries. Confers with legal staff to resolve problems, such as copyrights and royalty sharing with outside producers and distributors. Advises business and other groups on local, national, and international legislation affecting world trade. Negotiates with media agents to secure agreements for transla-

tion of materials into other media. Entertains foreign governmental officials and business representatives to promote trade relations. Prepare report of marketing activities for state and federal agencies. Contracts with models, musicians, caterers, and other personnel to manage staging of fashion shows. Selects garments and accessories to be shown at fashion shows. Arranges for reproduction of visual materials and edits materials according to specific market or customer requirements. Promotes travel to other countries. Compiles catalog of audio-visual offerings and sets prices and rental fees. Provides information on current fashion, style trends, and use of accessories.
Yearly Earnings: $43,784
Education: Work experience, plus degree
Knowledge: Administration and Management; Economics and Accounting; Sales and Marketing; Customer and Personal Service; Personnel and Human Resources; Mathematics; Psychology; Sociology and Anthropology; Geography; Education and Training; English Language; Foreign Language; Fine Arts; History and Archeology; Philosophy and Theology; Law, Government, and Jurisprudence; Communications and Media; Transportation
Abilities: Oral Comprehension; Written Comprehension; Oral Expression; Written Expression; Fluency of Ideas; Originality; Problem Sensitivity; Deductive Reasoning; Inductive Reasoning; Information Ordering; Category Flexibility; Mathematical Reasoning; Number Facility; Memorization; Visualization; Selective Attention; Time Sharing; Near Vision; Visual Color Discrimination; Auditory Attention; Speech Recognition; Speech Clarity
Skills: Reading Comprehension; Active Listening; Writing; Speaking; Critical Thinking; Active Learning; Learning Strategies; Monitoring; Social Perceptiveness; Coordination; Persuasion; Negotiation; Service Orientation; Problem Identification; Information Gathering; Information Organization; Synthesis/Reorganization; Idea Generation; Idea Evaluation; Implementation Planning; Solution Appraisal; Operations Analysis; Visioning; Systems Perception; Identifying Downstream Consequences; Identification of Key Causes; Judgment and Decision Making; Systems Evaluation; Time Management; Management of Financial Resources; Management of Material Resources; Management of Personnel Resources
General Work Activities: Getting Information Needed to Do the Job; Monitoring Processes, Material, or Surroundings; Estimating Needed Characteristics; Judging Qualities of Things, Services, People; Processing Information; Evaluating Information against Standards; Analyzing Data or Information; Making Decisions and Solving Problems; Thinking Creatively; Updating and Using Job-Relevant Knowledge; Developing Objectives and Strategies; Scheduling Work and Activities; Organizing, Planning, and Prioritizing; Operating Vehicles or Equipment; Implementing Ideas, Programs, etc.; Documenting/Recording Information; Interpreting Meaning of Information to Others; Communicating with Other Workers; Communicating with Persons Outside Organization; Establishing and Maintaining Relationships; Selling or Influencing Others; Resolving Conflicts, Negotiating with Others; Performing for or Working with Public; Coordinating Work and Activities of Others; Developing and Building Teams; Teaching Others; Guiding, Directing and Motivating Subordinates; Coaching and Developing Others; Provide Consultation and Advice to Others; Performing Administrative Activities; Staffing Organizational Units; Monitoring and Controlling Resources
Job Characteristics: Objective or Subjective Information; Job-Required Social Interaction; Supervise, Coach, Train Others; Persuade Someone to a Course of Action; Provide a Service to Others; Take a Position Opposed to Others; Deal with External Customers; Coordinate or Lead Others; Responsibility for Outcomes and Results; Frequency in Conflict Situations; Sitting; Consequence of Error; Frustrating Circumstances; Importance of Being Aware of New Events
GOE Group/s: 11.05.02 Business Administration: Administrative Specialization; 11.05.04 Business Administration: Sales and Purchasing Management; 11.09.01 Promotion: Sales
CIP Program/s: 080101 Apparel and Accessories Marketing Operations, General; 080102 Fashion Merchandising; 080204 Business Services Marketing Operations; 200301 Clothing, Apparel and Textile Workers and Managers, General; 200306 Fashion and Fabric Consultant; 521401 Business Marketing and Marketing Management; 521403 International Business Marketing
Related DOT Job/s: 162.117-034 ; 163.117-022 DIRECTOR, MEDIA MARKETING; 164.117-022 ; 185.157-010 FASHION COORDINATOR; 185.157-014 SUPERVISOR OF SALES; 187.167-170 MANAGER, WORLD TRADE AND MARITIME DIVISION

13011D FUNDRAISING DIRECTORS. OOH Title/s: Marketing, Advertising, and Public Relations Managers

Plan and direct activities to solicit and maintain funds for special projects and nonprofit organizations,such as charities, universities, museums, and other organizations dependent upon voluntary financial contributions. Plan and directs solicitation of funds for broadcasting stations and institutions such as zoos and museums. Establishes fundraising goals. Assigns responsibilities for personal solicitation efforts. Plans and coordinates benefit events. Develops schedule for disbursing solicited funds. Develops public relations materials to enhance institution image and promote fundraising program. Organizes direct mail campaign to reach potential contributors. Researches public and private grant agencies and foundations to identify sources of funding. Supervises and coordinates activities of workers engaged in maintaining records of contributors and grants and preparing letters of appreciation. Purchases mailing list of potential donors or negotiates agreements with other organizations for exchange of mailing lists. Specializes in solicitation of funding from government, foundation, or corporation sources. Serves as liaison between broadcast departmental staff and funding establishment personnel to provide project information and to solve problems.
Yearly Earnings: $43,784
Education: Work experience, plus degree
Knowledge: Administration and Management; Economics and Accounting; Sales and Marketing; Psychology; Sociology and Anthropology; Geography; English Language; Foreign Language; Fine Arts; Philosophy and Theology; Law, Government, and Jurisprudence; Telecommunications; Communications and Media
Abilities: Oral Comprehension; Written Comprehension; Oral Expression; Written Expression; Fluency of Ideas; Originality; Inductive Reasoning; Mathematical Reasoning; Number Facility; Memorization; Time Sharing; Far Vision; Speech Recognition; Speech Clarity
Skills: Active Listening; Speaking; Monitoring; Social Perceptiveness; Coordination; Persuasion; Negotiation; Service Orientation; Information Gathering; Information Organization; Synthesis/Reorganization; Idea Generation; Idea Evaluation; Implementation Planning; Solution Appraisal; Visioning; Systems Perception; Identifying Downstream Consequences; Identification of Key Causes; Judgment and Decision Making; Systems Evaluation; Time Management; Management of Financial Resources; Management of Material Resources; Management of Personnel Resources
General Work Activities: Judging Qualities of Things, Services, People; Evaluating Information against Standards; Making Decisions and Solving Problems; Thinking Creatively; Developing Objectives and Strategies; Scheduling Work and Activities; Organizing, Planning, and Prioritizing; Operating Vehicles or Equipment; Implementing Ideas, Programs, etc.; Interpreting Meaning of Information to Others; Communicating with Other Workers; Communicating with Persons Outside Organization; Establishing and Maintaining Relationships; Selling or Influencing Others; Resolving Conflicts, Negotiating with

Others; Performing for or Working with Public; Coordinating Work and Activities of Others; Developing and Building Teams; Guiding, Directing and Motivating Subordinates; Coaching and Developing Others; Provide Consultation and Advice to Others; Performing Administrative Activities; Staffing Organizational Units; Monitoring and Controlling Resources
Job Characteristics: Objective or Subjective Information; Job-Required Social Interaction; Supervise, Coach, Train Others; Persuade Someone to a Course of Action; Deal with External Customers; Coordinate or Lead Others; Responsibility for Outcomes and Results; Sitting; Frustrating Circumstances
GOE Group/s: 11.05.04 Business Administration: Sales and Purchasing Management; 11.09.02 Promotion: Fund and Membership Solicitation
CIP Program/s: 090501 Public Relations and Organizational Communications; 500701 Art, General; 500704 Arts Management; 510799 Health and Medical Administrative Services, Other; 520201 Business Administration and Management, General; 521401 Business Marketing and Marketing Management
Related DOT Job/s: 163.117-026 DIRECTOR, UNDERWRITER SOLICITATION; 165.117-010 DIRECTOR, FUNDRAISING; 165.117-014 DIRECTOR, FUNDS DEVELOPMENT

13014A PROPERTY OFFICERS AND CONTRACT ADMINISTRATORS. OOH Title/s: Administrative Services Managers
Coordinate property procurement and disposition activities of a business, agency, or other organization. Administer contracts for purchase or sale of equipment, materials, products, or services. Directs activities concerned with unclaimed property, and contracts for purchase of equipment, materials, products, or services. Authorizes obtaining and purchase of materials, supplies and equipment, and equipment maintenance. Prepares plans for selling and maintaining materials and property. Prepares, reviews, and negotiates bids and estimates with firms, bidders, and customers. Recommends disposal of materials and property. Examines performance requirements, property-related data, delivery schedules, and estimates of costs of material, equipment, and production. Advises company departments concerning contractual rights and obligations. Inspects inventory and transfers or fills material and equipment requests. Examines and evaluates materials and property to ensure conformance to company standards. Coordinates work of sales department.
Yearly Earnings: $39,936
Education: Work experience, plus degree
Knowledge: Administration and Management; Economics and Accounting; Sales and Marketing; Law, Government, and Jurisprudence; Transportation
Abilities: Written Comprehension; Oral Expression; Written Expression; Problem Sensitivity; Deductive Reasoning; Inductive Reasoning; Category Flexibility; Mathematical Reasoning; Number Facility; Perceptual Speed; Gross Body Equilibrium; Near Vision; Speech Recognition
Skills: Reading Comprehension; Writing; Speaking; Coordination; Negotiation; Implementation Planning; Judgment and Decision Making; Time Management; Management of Financial Resources; Management of Material Resources; Management of Personnel Resources
General Work Activities: Monitoring Processes, Material, or Surroundings; Estimating Needed Characteristics; Judging Qualities of Things, Services, People; Processing Information; Analyzing Data or Information; Making Decisions and Solving Problems; Developing Objectives and Strategies; Scheduling Work and Activities; Organizing, Planning, and Prioritizing; Operating Vehicles or Equipment; Implementing Ideas, Programs, etc.; Communicating with Other Workers; Communicating with Persons Outside Organization; Establishing and Maintaining Relationships; Selling or Influencing Others; Resolving Conflicts, Negotiating with Others; Coordinating Work and Activities of Others; Developing and Building Teams; Guiding, Directing and Motivating Subordinates; Coaching and Developing Others; Provide Consultation and Advice to Others; Performing Administrative Activities; Staffing Organizational Units; Monitoring and Controlling Resources
Job Characteristics: Persuade Someone to a Course of Action; Take a Position Opposed to Others; Coordinate or Lead Others; Responsibility for Outcomes and Results; Sitting
GOE Group/s: 11.05.04 Business Administration: Sales and Purchasing Management; 11.12.01 Contracts and Claims: Claims and Settlement; 11.12.02 Contracts and Claims: Rental and Leasing; 11.12.04 Contracts and Claims: Procurement Negotiations
CIP Program/s: 440401 Public Administration; 520201 Business Administration and Management, General; 520202 Purchasing, Procurement and Contracts Management; 520203 Logistics and Materials Management
Related DOT Job/s: 162.117-014 CONTRACT ADMINISTRATOR; 163.167-026 PROPERTY-DISPOSAL OFFICER; 188.117-122 PROPERTY-UTILIZATION OFFICER; 188.167-106 UNCLAIMED PROPERTY OFFICER

13014B ADMINISTRATIVE SERVICES MANAGERS. OOH Title/s: Administrative Services Managers; Retail Sales Worker Supervisors and Managers; Health Services Managers
Plan, direct, and coordinate supportive services of an organization, such as recordkeeping, mail distribution, telephone reception, and other office support services. May oversee facilities planning and maintenance and custodial operations. Include facilities managers. Exclude procurement managers. Coordinates activities of clerical and administrative personnel in establishment or organization. Analyzes and organizes office operations, procedures, and production to improve efficiency. Recommends cost-saving methods, such as supply changes and disposal of records to improve efficiency of department. Prepares and reviews reports and schedules to ensure accuracy and efficiency. Formulates budgetary reports. Hires and terminates clerical and administrative personnel. Conducts classes to teach procedures to staff.
Yearly Earnings: $39,936
Education: Work experience, plus degree
Knowledge: Administration and Management; Clerical; Economics and Accounting; Personnel and Human Resources; Mathematics; Psychology; Education and Training; English Language
Abilities: Oral Comprehension; Oral Expression; Written Expression; Fluency of Ideas; Originality; Mathematical Reasoning; Number Facility; Memorization; Time Sharing; Wrist-Finger Speed; Near Vision; Speech Recognition; Speech Clarity
Skills: Reading Comprehension; Writing; Speaking; Learning Strategies; Monitoring; Social Perceptiveness; Coordination; Persuasion; Instructing; Idea Generation; Idea Evaluation; Visioning; Identification of Key Causes; Judgment and Decision Making; Systems Evaluation; Time Management; Management of Financial Resources; Management of Material Resources; Management of Personnel Resources
General Work Activities: Analyzing Data or Information; Thinking Creatively; Developing Objectives and Strategies; Scheduling Work and Activities; Organizing, Planning, and Prioritizing; Operating Vehicles or Equipment; Implementing Ideas, Programs, etc.; Documenting/Recording Information; Interpreting Meaning of Information to Others; Communicating with Other Workers; Establishing and Maintaining Relationships; Resolving Conflicts, Negotiating with Others; Coordinating Work and Activities of Others; Developing and Building Teams; Teaching Others; Guiding, Directing and Motivating Subordi-

nates; Coaching and Developing Others; Provide Consultation and Advice to Others; Performing Administrative Activities; Staffing Organizational Units; Monitoring and Controlling Resources
Job Characteristics: Objective or Subjective Information; Job-Required Social Interaction; Supervise, Coach, Train Others; Persuade Someone to a Course of Action; Take a Position Opposed to Others; Coordinate or Lead Others; Responsibility for Outcomes and Results; Frequency in Conflict Situations; Deal with Physical, Aggressive People; Sitting; Frustrating Circumstances; Degree of Automation
GOE Group/s: 07.01.02 Administrative Detail: Administration; 11.07.02 Services Administration: Health and Safety Services
CIP Program/s: 510701 Health System/Health Services Administration; 520201 Business Administration and Management, General; 520204 Office Supervision and Management
Related DOT Job/s: 169.167-034 MANAGER, OFFICE; 187.117-062 RADIOLOGY ADMINISTRATOR; 188.117-130 COURT ADMINISTRATOR; 189.167-014 DIRECTOR, SERVICE

13017A ENGINEERING MANAGERS. OOH Title/s: Engineering, Science, and Data Processing Managers

Plan, direct, and coordinate activities in such fields as architecture, engineering, and related research and development. These persons spend the greatest portion of their time in managerial work, for which a background consistent with that described for engineers is required. Exclude natural science managers; mathematical managers; computer operations, information systems, computer programming, and data processing managers; as well as managers of computer-related occupations. Establishes procedures and directs testing, operation, maintenance, and repair of transmitter equipment. Evaluates contract proposals, directs negotiation of research contracts, and prepares bids and contracts. Plans and directs installation, maintenance, testing, and repair of facilities and equipment. Directs, reviews, and approves product design and changes, and directs testing. Plans, coordinates, and directs engineering project, organizes and assigns staff, and directs integration of technical activities with products. Plans and directs oilfield development, gas and oil production, and geothermal drilling. Analyzes technology, resource needs, and market demand, and confers with management, production, and marketing staff to plan and assess feasibility of project. Plans, directs, and coordinates survey work with activities of other staff, certifies survey work, and writes land legal descriptions. Administers highway planning, construction, and maintenance, and reviews and recommends or approves contracts and cost estimates. Directs engineering of water control, treatment, and distribution projects. Confers with and prepares reports for officials, and speaks to public to solicit support.
Yearly Earnings: $39,936
Education: Work experience, plus degree
Knowledge: Administration and Management; Economics and Accounting; Sales and Marketing; Personnel and Human Resources; Engineering and Technology; Design; Building and Construction; Mechanical; Mathematics; Physics; Chemistry; Psychology; Geography; English Language; History and Archeology; Public Safety and Security; Law, Government, and Jurisprudence; Telecommunications; Communications and Media
Abilities: Oral Comprehension; Written Comprehension; Oral Expression; Written Expression; Fluency of Ideas; Originality; Problem Sensitivity; Deductive Reasoning; Inductive Reasoning; Information Ordering; Category Flexibility; Mathematical Reasoning; Number Facility; Memorization; Speed of Closure; Spatial Orientation; Visualization; Selective Attention; Time Sharing; Gross Body Equilibrium; Near Vision; Far Vision; Visual Color Discrimination; Peripheral Vision; Speech Recognition; Speech Clarity
Skills: Reading Comprehension; Active Listening; Writing; Speaking; Mathematics; Science; Critical Thinking; Active Learning; Monitoring; Social Perceptiveness; Coordination; Persuasion; Negotiation; Problem Identification; Information Gathering; Information Organization; Synthesis/Reorganization; Idea Generation; Idea Evaluation; Implementation Planning; Solution Appraisal; Operations Analysis; Technology Design; Equipment Selection; Installation; Programming; Testing; Product Inspection; Equipment Maintenance; Troubleshooting; Repairing; Visioning; Systems Perception; Identifying Downstream Consequences; Identification of Key Causes; Judgment and Decision Making; Systems Evaluation; Time Management; Management of Financial Resources; Management of Material Resources; Management of Personnel Resources
General Work Activities: Getting Information Needed to Do the Job; Monitoring Processes, Material, or Surroundings; Identifying Objects, Actions, and Events; Inspecting Equipment, Structures, or Material; Estimating Needed Characteristics; Judging Qualities of Things, Services, People; Processing Information; Evaluating Information against Standards; Analyzing Data or Information; Making Decisions and Solving Problems; Thinking Creatively; Updating and Using Job-Relevant Knowledge; Developing Objectives and Strategies; Scheduling Work and Activities; Organizing, Planning, and Prioritizing; Operating Vehicles or Equipment; Drafting and Specifying Technical Devices, etc.; Implementing Ideas, Programs, etc.; Repairing and Maintaining Mechanical Equipment; Repairing and Maintaining Electrical Equipment; Documenting/Recording Information; Interpreting Meaning of Information to Others; Communicating with Other Workers; Communicating with Persons Outside Organization; Establishing and Maintaining Relationships; Selling or Influencing Others; Resolving Conflicts, Negotiating with Others; Coordinating Work and Activities of Others; Developing and Building Teams; Teaching Others; Guiding, Directing and Motivating Subordinates; Coaching and Developing Others; Provide Consultation and Advice to Others; Performing Administrative Activities; Staffing Organizational Units; Monitoring and Controlling Resources
Job Characteristics: Objective or Subjective Information; Supervise, Coach, Train Others; Take a Position Opposed to Others; Coordinate or Lead Others; Responsibility for Outcomes and Results; Frequency in Conflict Situations; High Places; Consequence of Error; Frustrating Circumstances; Importance of Being Exact or Accurate
GOE Group/s: 05.01.03 Engineering: Systems Design; 05.01.08 Engineering: General Engineering; 05.02.01 Managerial Work: Mechanical: Systems; 05.02.06 Managerial Work: Mechanical: Services; 11.05.03 Business Administration: Management Services: Government; 11.12.04 Contracts and Claims: Procurement Negotiations
CIP Program/s: 140801 Civil Engineering, General; 140805 Water Resources Engineering; 143001 Engineering/Industrial Management; 151102 Surveying
Related DOT Job/s: 003.167-034 ENGINEER-IN-CHARGE, TRANSMITTER; 003.167-070 ENGINEERING MANAGER, ELECTRONICS; 005.167-010 CHIEF ENGINEER, WATERWORKS; 005.167-022 HIGHWAY-ADMINISTRATIVE ENGINEER; 007.167-014 PLANT ENGINEER; 010.161-014 CHIEF PETROLEUM ENGINEER; 010.167-018 SUPERINTENDENT, OIL-WELL SERVICES; 018.167-022 MANAGER, LAND SURVEYING; 019.167-014 PROJECT ENGINEER; 162.117-030 RESEARCH-CONTRACTS SUPERVISOR

13017B NATURAL SCIENCES MANAGERS. OOH Title/s: Engineering, Science, and Data Processing Managers

Plan, direct, and coordinate activities in such fields as life sciences, physical sciences, mathematics, statistics, and related research and development. These persons spend the greatest portion of their time in managerial work, for which a background consistent with that described for mathematicians or

natural scientists is required. Exclude engineering managers; computer operations, information systems, computer programming, and data processing managers; as well as managers of computer-related occupations. Schedules, directs, and assigns duties to engineers, technicians, researchers, and other staff. Plans and directs research, development, and production activities of chemical plant. Coordinates successive phases of problem analysis, solution proposals, and testing. Prepares and administers budget, approves and reviews expenditures, and prepares financial reports. Reviews project activities, and prepares and reviews research, testing, and operational reports. Confers with scientists, engineers, regulators, and others to plan and review projects and to provide technical assistance. Advises and assists in obtaining patents or other legal requirements. Provides technical assistance to agencies conducting environmental studies.
Yearly Earnings: $39,936
Education: Work experience, plus degree
Knowledge: Administration and Management; Economics and Accounting; Personnel and Human Resources; Production and Processing; Engineering and Technology; Mathematics; Physics; Chemistry; Biology; Psychology; Geography; Education and Training; English Language; Foreign Language; History and Archeology; Law, Government, and Jurisprudence
Abilities: Oral Comprehension; Written Comprehension; Oral Expression; Written Expression; Fluency of Ideas; Originality; Problem Sensitivity; Deductive Reasoning; Inductive Reasoning; Information Ordering; Category Flexibility; Mathematical Reasoning; Number Facility; Memorization; Speed of Closure; Perceptual Speed; Visualization; Selective Attention; Time Sharing; Near Vision; Far Vision; Speech Recognition; Speech Clarity
Skills: Reading Comprehension; Active Listening; Writing; Speaking; Mathematics; Science; Critical Thinking; Active Learning; Learning Strategies; Monitoring; Social Perceptiveness; Coordination; Persuasion; Negotiation; Instructing; Problem Identification; Information Gathering; Information Organization; Synthesis/Reorganization; Idea Generation; Idea Evaluation; Implementation Planning; Solution Appraisal; Operations Analysis; Technology Design; Equipment Selection; Testing; Product Inspection; Troubleshooting; Visioning; Systems Perception; Identifying Downstream Consequences; Identification of Key Causes; Judgment and Decision Making; Systems Evaluation; Time Management; Management of Financial Resources; Management of Material Resources; Management of Personnel Resources
General Work Activities: Getting Information Needed to Do the Job; Monitoring Processes, Material, or Surroundings; Identifying Objects, Actions, and Events; Estimating Needed Characteristics; Judging Qualities of Things, Services, People; Processing Information; Evaluating Information against Standards; Analyzing Data or Information; Making Decisions and Solving Problems; Thinking Creatively; Updating and Using Job-Relevant Knowledge; Developing Objectives and Strategies; Scheduling Work and Activities; Organizing, Planning, and Prioritizing; Operating Vehicles or Equipment; Drafting and Specifying Technical Devices, etc.; Implementing Ideas, Programs, etc.; Documenting/Recording Information; Interpreting Meaning of Information to Others; Communicating with Other Workers; Communicating with Persons Outside Organization; Establishing and Maintaining Relationships; Selling or Influencing Others; Resolving Conflicts, Negotiating with Others; Coordinating Work and Activities of Others; Developing and Building Teams; Teaching Others; Guiding, Directing and Motivating Subordinates; Coaching and Developing Others; Provide Consultation and Advice to Others; Performing Administrative Activities; Staffing Organizational Units; Monitoring and Controlling Resources
Job Characteristics: Supervise, Coach, Train Others; Take a Position Opposed to Others; Coordinate or Lead Others; Responsibility for Outcomes and Results; Frequency in Conflict Situations
GOE Group/s: 02.01.02 Physical Sciences: Technology; 05.01.08 Engineering: General Engineering
CIP Program/s: 030101 Natural Resources Conservation, General; 030102 Environmental Science/Studies
Related DOT Job/s: 008.167-010 TECHNICAL DIRECTOR, CHEMICAL PLANT; 022.161-010 CHEMICAL LABORATORY CHIEF; 029.167-014 PROJECT MANAGER, ENVIRONMENTAL RESEARCH

13017C COMPUTER AND INFORMATION SYSTEMS MANAGERS. OOH Title/s: Engineering, Science, and Data Processing Managers

Plan, direct, and coordinate activities in such fields as electronic data processing, information systems, systems analysis, and computer programming. These persons spend the greatest portion of their time in managerial work, for which a background consistent with that described for computer professionals—such as computer systems analysts, computer scientists, database administrators, computer programmers, and computer support specialists—would be required. Evaluates data processing project proposals and assesses project feasibility. Directs department, prepares and reviews operational reports, adjusts schedule to meet priorities, and prepares progress reports. Establishes work standards, directs training, participates in staffing and promotion decisions, and disciplines workers. Consults with users, management, vendors, and technicians to determine computing needs and system requirements. Analyzes workflow; assigns, schedules, and reviews work; and directs and coordinates with other departments. Meets with department heads, managers, supervisors, vendors, and others to solicit cooperation and resolve problems. Approves, prepares, monitors, and adjusts operational budget. Develops and interprets organizational goals, policies, and procedures, and reviews project plans.
Yearly Earnings: $39,936
Education: Work experience, plus degree
Knowledge: Administration and Management; Clerical; Economics and Accounting; Sales and Marketing; Customer and Personal Service; Personnel and Human Resources; Computers and Electronics; Mathematics; Psychology; Education and Training; English Language; Communications and Media
Abilities: Oral Comprehension; Written Comprehension; Oral Expression; Written Expression; Fluency of Ideas; Originality; Problem Sensitivity; Deductive Reasoning; Inductive Reasoning; Information Ordering; Category Flexibility; Mathematical Reasoning; Number Facility; Memorization; Speed of Closure; Selective Attention; Time Sharing; Near Vision; Speech Recognition; Speech Clarity
Skills: Reading Comprehension; Active Listening; Writing; Speaking; Mathematics; Active Learning; Learning Strategies; Monitoring; Social Perceptiveness; Coordination; Persuasion; Negotiation; Instructing; Service Orientation; Problem Identification; Information Gathering; Information Organization; Synthesis/Reorganization; Idea Generation; Idea Evaluation; Implementation Planning; Solution Appraisal; Operations Analysis; Technology Design; Programming; Visioning; Systems Perception; Identifying Downstream Consequences; Identification of Key Causes; Judgment and Decision Making; Systems Evaluation; Time Management; Management of Financial Resources; Management of Material Resources; Management of Personnel Resources
General Work Activities: Getting Information Needed to Do the Job; Monitoring Processes, Material, or Surroundings; Identifying Objects, Actions, and Events; Estimating Needed Characteristics; Judging Qualities of Things, Services, People; Processing Information; Evaluating Information against Standards; Analyzing Data or Information; Making Decisions and Solving Problems; Thinking Creatively; Updating and Using Job-Relevant Knowledge; Developing Objectives and

Strategies; Scheduling Work and Activities; Organizing, Planning, and Prioritizing; Operating Vehicles or Equipment; Implementing Ideas, Programs, etc.; Documenting/Recording Information; Interpreting Meaning of Information to Others; Communicating with Other Workers; Communicating with Persons Outside Organization; Establishing and Maintaining Relationships; Selling or Influencing Others; Resolving Conflicts, Negotiating with Others; Coordinating Work and Activities of Others; Developing and Building Teams; Teaching Others; Guiding, Directing and Motivating Subordinates; Coaching and Developing Others; Provide Consultation and Advice to Others; Performing Administrative Activities; Staffing Organizational Units; Monitoring and Controlling Resources
Job Characteristics: Objective or Subjective Information; Job-Required Social Interaction; Supervise, Coach, Train Others; Take a Position Opposed to Others; Coordinate or Lead Others; Responsibility for Outcomes and Results; Frequency in Conflict Situations; Sitting; Frustrating Circumstances; Degree of Automation
GOE Group/s: 11.01.01 Mathematics and Statistics: Data Processing Design
CIP Program/s: 521201 Management Information Systems and Business Data Processing
Related DOT Job/s: 169.167-030 MANAGER, DATA PROCESSING; 169.167-082 MANAGER, COMPUTER OPERATIONS

Specialty Managers

15002 POSTMASTERS AND MAIL SUPERINTENDENTS. OOH Title/s: Blue Collar Worker Supervisors; General Managers and Top Executives
Direct and coordinate operational, administrative, management, and supportive services of a U.S. post office; or coordinate activities of workers engaged in postal and related work in assigned post office. Organizes and supervises directly, or through subordinates, such activities as processing incoming and outgoing mail to ensure efficient service to patrons. Directs and coordinates operational, management, and supportive services of associate post offices within district area known as sectional center. Directs and coordinates operations of several sectional centers within district. Prepares and submits detailed and summary reports of post office activities to designated supervisors. Confers with suppliers to obtain bids for proposed purchases, requisitions supplies, and disburses funds as specified by law. Selects, trains, and evaluates performance of employees and prepares work schedules. Negotiates labor disputes. Selects, trains, and terminates postmasters and managers of associate postal units. Resolves customer complaints and informs public of postal laws and regulations.
Yearly Earnings: $32,136
Education: Work experience in a related occupation
Knowledge: Administration and Management; Clerical; Economics and Accounting; Customer and Personal Service; Personnel and Human Resources; Psychology; Geography; Education and Training; Law, Government, and Jurisprudence; Transportation
Abilities: None above average
Skills: Reading Comprehension; Active Listening; Writing; Speaking; Critical Thinking; Active Learning; Learning Strategies; Monitoring; Social Perceptiveness; Coordination; Persuasion; Negotiation; Instructing; Problem Identification; Information Organization; Synthesis/Reorganization; Idea Generation; Idea Evaluation; Implementation Planning; Solution Appraisal; Visioning; Systems Perception; Identifying Downstream Consequences; Identification of Key Causes; Judgment and Decision Making; Systems Evaluation; Time Management; Management of Financial Resources; Management of Material Resources; Management of Personnel Resources
General Work Activities: Estimating Needed Characteristics; Judging Qualities of Things, Services, People; Processing Information; Making Decisions and Solving Problems; Updating and Using Job-Relevant Knowledge; Developing Objectives and Strategies; Scheduling Work and Activities; Organizing, Planning, and Prioritizing; Implementing Ideas, Programs, etc.; Documenting/Recording Information; Communicating with Other Workers; Establishing and Maintaining Relationships; Resolving Conflicts, Negotiating with Others; Performing for or Working with Public; Coordinating Work and Activities of Others; Developing and Building Teams; Guiding, Directing and Motivating Subordinates; Coaching and Developing Others; Performing Administrative Activities; Staffing Organizational Units; Monitoring and Controlling Resources
Job Characteristics: Supervise, Coach, Train Others; Deal with External Customers; Coordinate or Lead Others; Responsibility for Outcomes and Results; Deal with Unpleasant or Angry People; Special Uniform; Importance of Being Exact or Accurate
GOE Group/s: 11.05.03 Business Administration: Management Services: Government
CIP Program/s: 440401 Public Administration; 520201 Business Administration and Management, General
Related DOT Job/s: 188.167-066 POSTMASTER; 188.167-086 SECTIONAL CENTER MANAGER, POSTAL SERVICE

15005A COLLEGE AND UNIVERSITY ADMINISTRATORS. OOH Title/s: Education Administrators; General Managers and Top Executives
Plan, direct, and coordinate research and instructional programs at postsecondary institutions, including universities, colleges, and junior and community colleges. Exclude college presidents. Establishes operational policies and procedures and develops academic objectives. Directs work activities of personnel engaged in administration of academic institutions, departments, and alumni organizations. Meets with academic and administrative personnel to disseminate information, identify problems, monitor progress reports, and ensure adherence to goals and objectives. Evaluates personnel and physical plant operations, student programs, and statistical and research data to implement procedures or modifications to administrative policies. Advises staff and students on problems relating to policies, program administration, and financial and personal matters, and recommends solutions. Estimates and allocates department funding based on financial success of previous courses and other pertinent factors. Completes and submits operating budget for approval, controls expenditures, and maintains financial reports and records. Consults with staff, students, alumni, and subject experts to determine needs/feasibility, and to formulate admission policies and educational programs. Represents college/university as liaison officer with accrediting agencies and to exchange information between academic institutions and in community. Determines course schedules and correlates room assignments to ensure optimum use of buildings and equipment. Confers with other academic staff to explain admission requirements and transfer credit policies, and compares course equivalencies to university/college curriculum. Negotiates with foundation and industry representatives to secure loans for university and identify costs and materials for building construction. Recruits, employs, trains, and terminates department personnel. Reviews student misconduct reports requiring disciplinary action and counsels students to ensure conformance to university policies. Coordinates alumni functions and encourages alumni endorsement of recruiting and fundraising activities. Plans and promotes athletic policies, sports events, ticket sales, and student participation in social, cultural, and recreational activities. Assists faculty and staff to conduct orientation programs, teach classes, issue student transcripts, and prepare commencement lists. Audits financial status of student organization and facility accounts, and certifies in-

come reports from event ticket sales. Advises student organizations, sponsors faculty activities, and arranges for caterers, entertainers, and decorators at scheduled events. Selects and counsels candidates for financial aid, and coordinates issuing and collecting of student aid payments.

Yearly Earnings: $39,208

Education: Work experience, plus degree

Knowledge: Administration and Management; Economics and Accounting; Sales and Marketing; Customer and Personal Service; Personnel and Human Resources; Mathematics; Psychology; Sociology and Anthropology; Therapy and Counseling; Education and Training; English Language; Foreign Language; History and Archeology; Philosophy and Theology; Public Safety and Security; Law, Government, and Jurisprudence; Communications and Media

Abilities: Oral Comprehension; Written Comprehension; Oral Expression; Written Expression; Fluency of Ideas; Originality; Problem Sensitivity; Deductive Reasoning; Inductive Reasoning; Category Flexibility; Mathematical Reasoning; Number Facility; Memorization; Speed of Closure; Selective Attention; Near Vision; Far Vision; Speech Recognition; Speech Clarity

Skills: Reading Comprehension; Active Listening; Writing; Speaking; Mathematics; Critical Thinking; Active Learning; Learning Strategies; Monitoring; Social Perceptiveness; Coordination; Persuasion; Negotiation; Instructing; Service Orientation; Problem Identification; Information Gathering; Information Organization; Synthesis/Reorganization; Idea Generation; Idea Evaluation; Implementation Planning; Solution Appraisal; Operations Analysis; Product Inspection; Visioning; Systems Perception; Identifying Downstream Consequences; Identification of Key Causes; Judgment and Decision Making; Systems Evaluation; Time Management; Management of Financial Resources; Management of Material Resources; Management of Personnel Resources

General Work Activities: Getting Information Needed to Do the Job; Monitoring Processes, Material, or Surroundings; Estimating Needed Characteristics; Judging Qualities of Things, Services, People; Processing Information; Evaluating Information against Standards; Analyzing Data or Information; Making Decisions and Solving Problems; Thinking Creatively; Updating and Using Job-Relevant Knowledge; Developing Objectives and Strategies; Scheduling Work and Activities; Organizing, Planning, and Prioritizing; Operating Vehicles or Equipment; Implementing Ideas, Programs, etc.; Documenting/Recording Information; Interpreting Meaning of Information to Others; Communicating with Other Workers; Communicating with Persons Outside Organization; Establishing and Maintaining Relationships; Selling or Influencing Others; Resolving Conflicts, Negotiating with Others; Performing for or Working with Public; Coordinating Work and Activities of Others; Developing and Building Teams; Teaching Others; Guiding, Directing and Motivating Subordinates; Coaching and Developing Others; Provide Consultation and Advice to Others; Performing Administrative Activities; Staffing Organizational Units; Monitoring and Controlling Resources

Job Characteristics: Objective or Subjective Information; Job-Required Social Interaction; Supervise, Coach, Train Others; Persuade Someone to a Course of Action; Take a Position Opposed to Others; Coordinate or Lead Others; Responsibility for Outcomes and Results; Frequency in Conflict Situations; Deal with Unpleasant or Angry People; Deal with Physical, Aggressive People; Sitting; Frustrating Circumstances; Importance of Being Sure All is Done

GOE Group/s: 10.01.02 Social Services: Counseling and Social Work; 11.05.02 Business Administration: Administrative Specialization; 11.07.03 Services Administration: Education Services; 11.09.02 Promotion: Fund and Membership Solicitation

CIP Program/s: 130101 Education, General; 130401 Education Administration and Supervision, General; 130403 Adult and Continuing Education Administration; 130406 Higher Education Administration; 130407 Community and Junior College Administration; 130603 Educational Statistics and Research Methods; 131102 College/Postsecondary Student Counseling and Personnel Services

Related DOT Job/s: 090.117-010 ACADEMIC DEAN; 090.117-014 ALUMNI SECRETARY; 090.117-018 DEAN OF STUDENTS; 090.117-022 DIRECTOR, ATHLETIC; 090.117-026 DIRECTOR, EXTENSION WORK; 090.117-030 FINANCIAL-AIDS OFFICER; 090.167-010 DEPARTMENT HEAD, COLLEGE OR UNIVERSITY; 090.167-014 DIRECTOR OF ADMISSIONS; 090.167-018 DIRECTOR OF INSTITUTIONAL RESEARCH; 090.167-022 DIRECTOR OF STUDENT AFFAIRS; 090.167-026 DIRECTOR, SUMMER SESSIONS; 090.167-030 REGISTRAR, COLLEGE OR UNIVERSITY; 186.117-010 BUSINESS MANAGER, COLLEGE OR UNIVERSITY

15005B EDUCATIONAL PROGRAM DIRECTORS.

OOH Title/s: Education Administrators; Health Services Managers

Plan, develop, and administer programs to provide educational opportunities for students. Establishes program philosophy, plans, policies, and academic codes of ethics to maintain educational standards for student screening, placement, and training. Plans, directs, and monitors instructional methods and content for educational, vocational, or student activity programs. Reviews and approves new programs or recommends modifications to existing programs. Evaluates programs to determine effectiveness, efficiency, and utilization, and to ensure activities comply with federal, state, and local regulations. Prepares and submits budget requests, or grant proposals to solicit program funding. Determines scope of educational program offerings, and prepares drafts of course schedules and descriptions to estimate staffing and facility requirements. Coordinates outreach activities with businesses, communities, and other institutions or organizations to identify educational needs and establish and coordinate programs. Collects and analyzes survey data, regulatory information, and demographic and employment trends to forecast enrollment patterns and curriculum changes. Directs and coordinates activities of teachers or administrators at daycare centers, schools, public agencies, and institutions. Determines allocations of funds for staff, supplies, materials, and equipment, and authorizes purchases. Organizes and directs committees of specialists, volunteers, and staff to provide technical and advisory assistance for programs. Plans and coordinates consumer research and educational services to assist organizations in product development and marketing. Recruits, hires, trains, and evaluates primary and supplemental staff, and recommends personnel actions for programs and services. Contacts and addresses commercial, community, or political groups to promote educational programs and services or to lobby for legislative changes. Writes articles, manuals, and other publications and assists in the distribution of promotional literature. Confers with parents and staff to discuss educational activities, policies, and student behavioral or learning problems. Counsels and provides guidance to students regarding personal, academic, or behavioral problems. Reviews and interprets government codes and develops programs to ensure facility safety, security, and maintenance. Completes, maintains, or assigns preparation of attendance, activity, planning, or personnel reports and records for officials and agencies. Teaches classes or courses to students.

Yearly Earnings: $39,208

Education: Work experience, plus degree

Knowledge: Administration and Management; Clerical; Economics and Accounting; Sales and Marketing; Customer and Personal Service; Personnel and Human Resources; Food Production; Mathematics; Psychology; Sociology and Anthropology; Therapy and Counseling; Education and Training; English Language; History and Archeology; Philosophy and Theology; Public Safety and Security; Law, Govern-

ment, and Jurisprudence; Telecommunications; Communications and Media
Abilities: Oral Comprehension; Written Comprehension; Oral Expression; Written Expression; Fluency of Ideas; Originality; Problem Sensitivity; Deductive Reasoning; Inductive Reasoning; Information Ordering; Category Flexibility; Mathematical Reasoning; Number Facility; Memorization; Speed of Closure; Selective Attention; Time Sharing; Near Vision; Far Vision; Speech Recognition; Speech Clarity
Skills: Reading Comprehension; Active Listening; Writing; Speaking; Critical Thinking; Active Learning; Learning Strategies; Monitoring; Social Perceptiveness; Coordination; Persuasion; Negotiation; Instructing; Service Orientation; Problem Identification; Information Gathering; Information Organization; Synthesis/Reorganization; Idea Generation; Idea Evaluation; Implementation Planning; Solution Appraisal; Operations Analysis; Visioning; Systems Perception; Identifying Downstream Consequences; Identification of Key Causes; Judgment and Decision Making; Systems Evaluation; Time Management; Management of Financial Resources; Management of Material Resources; Management of Personnel Resources
General Work Activities: Getting Information Needed to Do the Job; Monitoring Processes, Material, or Surroundings; Estimating Needed Characteristics; Judging Qualities of Things, Services, People; Processing Information; Evaluating Information against Standards; Analyzing Data or Information; Making Decisions and Solving Problems; Thinking Creatively; Developing Objectives and Strategies; Scheduling Work and Activities; Organizing, Planning, and Prioritizing; Operating Vehicles or Equipment; Implementing Ideas, Programs, etc.; Documenting/Recording Information; Interpreting Meaning of Information to Others; Communicating with Other Workers; Communicating with Persons Outside Organization; Establishing and Maintaining Relationships; Selling or Influencing Others; Resolving Conflicts, Negotiating with Others; Performing for or Working with Public; Coordinating Work and Activities of Others; Developing and Building Teams; Teaching Others; Guiding, Directing and Motivating Subordinates; Coaching and Developing Others; Provide Consultation and Advice to Others; Performing Administrative Activities; Staffing Organizational Units; Monitoring and Controlling Resources
Job Characteristics: Objective or Subjective Information; Job-Required Social Interaction; Supervise, Coach, Train Others; Persuade Someone to a Course of Action; Take a Position Opposed to Others; Coordinate or Lead Others; Responsible for Others' Health and Safety; Responsibility for Outcomes and Results; Frequency in Conflict Situations; Deal with Unpleasant or Angry People; Frustrating Circumstances
GOE Group/s: 07.01.02 Administrative Detail: Administration; 10.01.02 Social Services: Counseling and Social Work; 10.02.01 Nursing, Therapy, and Specialized Teaching Services: Nursing; 11.02.03 Educational and Library Services: Teaching, Home Economics, Agriculture; 11.07.01 Services Administration: Social Services; 11.07.02 Services Administration: Health and Safety Services; 11.07.03 Services Administration: Education Services
CIP Program/s: 020102 Agricultural Extension; 130101 Education, General; 130301 Curriculum and Instruction; 130401 Education Administration and Supervision, General; 130402 Administration of Special Education; 130403 Adult and Continuing Education Administration; 130404 Educational Supervision; 130405 Elementary, Middle and Secondary Education Administration; 130406 Higher Education Administration; 130407 Community and Junior College Administration; 130501 Educational/Instructional Media Design; 130601 Educational Evaluation and Research; 130604 Educational Assessment, Testing and Measurement; 131001 Special Education, General; 131003 Education of the Deaf and Hearing Impaired; 131005 Education of the Emotionally Handicapped; 131006 Education of the Mentally Handicapped; 131007 Education of the Multiple Handicapped; 131008 Education of the Physically Handicapped; 131011 Education of the Specific Learning Disabled; 131012 Education of the Speech Impaired; 131101 Counselor Education Counseling and Guidance Services; 131102 College/Postsecondary Student Counseling and Personnel Services; 131204 Pre-Elementary/Early Childhood/Kindergarten Teacher Education; 131301 Agricultural Teacher Education (Vocational); 131308 Home Economics Teacher Education (Vocational); 190901 Clothing/Apparel and Textile Studies; 200201 Child Care and Guidance Workers and Managers, General; 200203 Child Care Services Manager; 200501 Home Furnishings and Equipment Installers and Consultants, General; 511602 Nursing Administration (Post-R.N.); 511608 Nursing Science (Post-R.N.); 512899 Dental Residency Programs, Other
Related DOT Job/s: 072.117-010 DIRECTOR, DENTAL SERVICES; 075.117-010 CONSULTANT, EDUCATIONAL, STATE BOARD OF NURSING; 075.117-018 DIRECTOR, EDUCATIONAL, COMMUNITY-HEALTH NURSING; 090.167-034 DIRECTOR, FIELD SERVICES; 091.107-010 ASSISTANT PRINCIPAL; 092.167-010 DIRECTOR, DAY CARE CENTER; 094.117-010 DIRECTOR, COMMISSION FOR THE BLIND; 094.167-014 DIRECTOR, SPECIAL EDUCATION; 096.161-010 HOME-SERVICE DIRECTOR; 096.167-010 DISTRICT EXTENSION SERVICE AGENT; 096.167-014 SPECIALIST-IN-CHARGE, EXTENSION SERVICE; 097.167-010 DIRECTOR, VOCATIONAL TRAINING; 099.117-010 DIRECTOR, EDUCATIONAL PROGRAM; 099.117-014 EDUCATION SUPERVISOR, CORRECTIONAL INSTITUTION; 099.117-018 PRINCIPAL; 099.117-030 DIRECTOR, EDUCATION; 099.167-034 DIRECTOR OF PUPIL PERSONNEL PROGRAM; 169.267-022 SECRETARY, BOARD-OF-EDUCATION

15008A NURSING DIRECTORS. OOH Title/s: Health Services Managers; Education Administrators

Plan, direct, and coordinate facilities or programs providing nursing care. Include directors of schools of nursing. Plans curricula and schedules health education instruction training and counseling for nursing school, in-service, and community programs. Plans, directs, and administers nursing services or educational programs in health care facilities. Establishes and revises policies and procedures, such as selection, performance, and compensation standards, organizational objectives, and medical and maintenance procedures. Prepares budget and administers health care programs and services within budgetary limitations. Recruits, interviews, selects, and assigns nursing and health services staff, faculty, and students. Conducts studies and site visits to assess program needs and evaluate the cost-effectiveness and efficiency of existing services. Prepares, maintains, and updates nursing policy and procedure manuals. Establishes records of management systems for health services, patients, staff, and nursing students. Consults with legal counsel, community groups, medical staff, and administrators regarding the application of nursing principles to industrial and social welfare problems. Directs collection, analysis, and interpretation of health service and utilization statistics. Acts as liaison between health care institution or facility and community to promote cooperative relationships and plan integrated programming.
Yearly Earnings: $37,076
Education: Work experience, plus degree
Knowledge: Administration and Management; Clerical; Economics and Accounting; Sales and Marketing; Customer and Personal Service; Personnel and Human Resources; Mathematics; Biology; Psychology; Sociology and Anthropology; Medicine and Dentistry; Therapy and Counseling; Education and Training
Abilities: Oral Comprehension; Written Comprehension; Oral Expression; Written Expression; Originality; Speech Clarity
Skills: Reading Comprehension; Active Listening; Writing; Speaking; Mathematics; Critical Thinking; Active Learning; Learning Strategies; Monitoring; Social Perceptiveness; Coordination; Persuasion; Negotiation; Instructing; Problem Identification; Information Gathering;

Idea Generation; Idea Evaluation; Implementation Planning; Solution Appraisal; Visioning; Systems Perception; Identifying Downstream Consequences; Identification of Key Causes; Judgment and Decision Making; Systems Evaluation; Time Management; Management of Financial Resources; Management of Material Resources; Management of Personnel Resources
General Work Activities: Getting Information Needed to Do the Job; Evaluating Information against Standards; Analyzing Data or Information; Making Decisions and Solving Problems; Thinking Creatively; Updating and Using Job-Relevant Knowledge; Developing Objectives and Strategies; Scheduling Work and Activities; Organizing, Planning, and Prioritizing; Documenting/Recording Information; Communicating with Other Workers; Communicating with Persons Outside Organization; Establishing and Maintaining Relationships; Assisting and Caring for Others; Resolving Conflicts, Negotiating with Others; Performing for or Working with Public; Coordinating Work and Activities of Others; Developing and Building Teams; Teaching Others; Guiding, Directing and Motivating Subordinates; Coaching and Developing Others; Provide Consultation and Advice to Others; Performing Administrative Activities; Staffing Organizational Units; Monitoring and Controlling Resources
Job Characteristics: Objective or Subjective Information; Job-Required Social Interaction; Supervise, Coach, Train Others; Deal with External Customers; Coordinate or Lead Others; Responsible for Others' Health and Safety; Responsibility for Outcomes and Results; Diseases/Infections; Sitting; Consequence of Error; Importance of Being Sure All is Done
GOE Group/s: 11.07.02 Services Administration: Health and Safety Services
CIP Program/s: 510299 Communication Disorders Sciences and Services, Other; 511602 Nursing Administration (Post-R.N.); 520201 Business Administration and Management, General
Related DOT Job/s: 075.117-014 DIRECTOR, COMMUNITY-HEALTH NURSING; 075.117-022 DIRECTOR, NURSING SERVICE; 075.117-026 DIRECTOR, OCCUPATIONAL HEALTH NURSING; 075.117-030 DIRECTOR, SCHOOL OF NURSING

15008B MEDICAL AND HEALTH SERVICES MANAGERS. OOH Title/s: Health Services Managers

Plan, direct, and coordinate medicine and health services in hospitals, clinics, managed care organizations, public health agencies, or similar organizations. Include hospital administrators, long-term care administrators, and other health care facility administrators. Administers fiscal operations, such as planning budgets, authorizing expenditures, and coordinating financial reporting. Directs and coordinates activities of medical, nursing, technical, clerical, service, and maintenance personnel of health care facility or mobile unit. Develops or expands medical programs or health services for research, rehabilitation, and community health promotion. Develops organizational policies and procedures, and establishes evaluative or operational criteria for facility or medical unit. Implements and administers programs and services for health care or medical facility. Establishes work schedules and assignments for staff, according to workload, space, and equipment availability. Prepares activity reports to inform management of the status and implementation plans of programs, services, and quality initiatives. Recruits, hires, and evaluates the performance of medical staff and auxiliary personnel. Reviews and analyzes facility activities and data to aid planning and cash- and risk-management and to improve service utilization. Consults with medical, business, and community groups to discuss service problems, coordinate activities and plans, and promote health programs. Develops instructional materials and conducts in-service and community-based educational programs. Inspects facilities for emergency readiness and compliance of access, safety, and sanitation regulations, and recommends building or equipment modifications. Develops and maintains computerized records management system to store or process personnel or activity data.
Yearly Earnings: $37,076
Education: Work experience, plus degree
Knowledge: Administration and Management; Clerical; Economics and Accounting; Sales and Marketing; Customer and Personal Service; Personnel and Human Resources; Mathematics; Psychology; Medicine and Dentistry; Therapy and Counseling; Education and Training; Public Safety and Security; Communications and Media
Abilities: Written Comprehension; Oral Expression; Written Expression; Fluency of Ideas; Originality; Information Ordering; Mathematical Reasoning; Time Sharing; Speech Recognition; Speech Clarity
Skills: Reading Comprehension; Active Listening; Writing; Speaking; Learning Strategies; Monitoring; Social Perceptiveness; Coordination; Instructing; Problem Identification; Idea Generation; Idea Evaluation; Implementation Planning; Solution Appraisal; Operations Analysis; Visioning; Systems Perception; Identifying Downstream Consequences; Identification of Key Causes; Judgment and Decision Making; Systems Evaluation; Time Management; Management of Financial Resources; Management of Material Resources; Management of Personnel Resources
General Work Activities: Getting Information Needed to Do the Job; Monitoring Processes, Material, or Surroundings; Inspecting Equipment, Structures, or Material; Estimating Needed Characteristics; Processing Information; Evaluating Information against Standards; Analyzing Data or Information; Making Decisions and Solving Problems; Thinking Creatively; Updating and Using Job-Relevant Knowledge; Developing Objectives and Strategies; Scheduling Work and Activities; Organizing, Planning, and Prioritizing; Operating Vehicles or Equipment; Implementing Ideas, Programs, etc.; Communicating with Other Workers; Establishing and Maintaining Relationships; Assisting and Caring for Others; Performing for or Working with Public; Coordinating Work and Activities of Others; Developing and Building Teams; Teaching Others; Guiding, Directing and Motivating Subordinates; Coaching and Developing Others; Provide Consultation and Advice to Others; Performing Administrative Activities; Staffing Organizational Units; Monitoring and Controlling Resources
Job Characteristics: Objective or Subjective Information; Supervise, Coach, Train Others; Deal with External Customers; Coordinate or Lead Others; Responsibility for Outcomes and Results; Frequency in Conflict Situations; Sitting; Importance of Being Aware of New Events
GOE Group/s: 11.07.02 Services Administration: Health and Safety Services
CIP Program/s: 510299 Communication Disorders Sciences and Services, Other; 510701 Health System/Health Services Administration; 510702 Hospital/Health Facilities Administration; 510706 Medical Records Administration; 511602 Nursing Administration (Post-R.N.); 512916 Emergency Medicine Residency; 520201 Business Administration and Management, General
Related DOT Job/s: 076.117-010 COORDINATOR OF REHABILITATION SERVICES; 079.117-010 EMERGENCY MEDICAL SERVICES COORDINATOR; 079.167-014 MEDICAL-RECORD ADMINISTRATOR; 169.167-090; 187.117-010 ADMINISTRATOR, HEALTH CARE FACILITY; 187.117-058 DIRECTOR, OUTPATIENT SERVICES

15011A LAND LEASING AND DEVELOPMENT MANAGERS. OOH Title/s: Property and Real Estate Managers

Plan, direct, and coordinate the acquisition or disposition of land, rights-of-way, or property rights for development, mineral, oil, or gas rights, or other special use through options, purchase, or lease agreements. Makes final decisions regarding sales, leases, and purchases of real property based on evaluation of costs, available resources, and organizational interests. Negotiates terms and conditions of agreements with property owners, public officials, and community representatives, and signs contracts to finalize transactions. Directs and coordinates collection and auditing of funds from sales, purchases, and leases. Directs staff activities, such as preparing appraisal reports and feasibility studies, identifying availability and quality of land, and ascertaining ownership. Administers and interprets general policies made by company officials and ensures conformance to established standards. Studies financial transactions of competing companies or brokers to determine expenditure necessary to obtain leases and other contracts. Prepares statistical abstracts to reveal trends in tax rates and proportion of workforce having specified skills in a given community. Evaluates and promotes industrial-development potential of company properties. Plans and directs field staff activities such as mineral sampling, surveying, and water testing to determine optimal land usage. Coordinates research activities with public utilities, universities, and other groups. Authorizes or requests authorization for maintenance of noncontrolled company properties such as dwellings, hotels, or commissaries. Determines roads, bridges, and utility systems that must be maintained during construction. Settles claims for property or crop damage.

Yearly Earnings: $22,620

Education: Bachelor's degree

Knowledge: Administration and Management; Economics and Accounting; Sales and Marketing; Mathematics; Geography; English Language; Law, Government, and Jurisprudence

Abilities: Mathematical Reasoning; Number Facility; Speech Clarity

Skills: Reading Comprehension; Active Listening; Writing; Speaking; Critical Thinking; Active Learning; Social Perceptiveness; Coordination; Persuasion; Negotiation; Service Orientation; Problem Identification; Information Gathering; Information Organization; Synthesis/Reorganization; Idea Generation; Idea Evaluation; Implementation Planning; Solution Appraisal; Programming; Systems Perception; Identifying Downstream Consequences; Identification of Key Causes; Judgment and Decision Making; Systems Evaluation; Time Management; Management of Financial Resources; Management of Material Resources; Management of Personnel Resources

General Work Activities: Getting Information Needed to Do the Job; Monitoring Processes, Material, or Surroundings; Estimating Needed Characteristics; Judging Qualities of Things, Services, People; Processing Information; Evaluating Information against Standards; Analyzing Data or Information; Making Decisions and Solving Problems; Thinking Creatively; Developing Objectives and Strategies; Scheduling Work and Activities; Organizing, Planning, and Prioritizing; Implementing Ideas, Programs, etc.; Documenting/Recording Information; Interpreting Meaning of Information to Others; Communicating with Other Workers; Communicating with Persons Outside Organization; Establishing and Maintaining Relationships; Selling or Influencing Others; Resolving Conflicts, Negotiating with Others; Performing for or Working with Public; Coordinating Work and Activities of Others; Developing and Building Teams; Guiding, Directing and Motivating Subordinates; Coaching and Developing Others; Provide Consultation and Advice to Others; Performing Administrative Activities; Staffing Organizational Units; Monitoring and Controlling Resources

Job Characteristics: Objective or Subjective Information; Job-Required Social Interaction; Supervise, Coach, Train Others; Persuade Someone to a Course of Action; Take a Position Opposed to Others; Deal with External Customers; Coordinate or Lead Others; Responsibility for Outcomes and Results; Frequency in Conflict Situations; Deal with Unpleasant or Angry People; Deal with Physical, Aggressive People

GOE Group/s: 11.05.01 Business Administration: Management Services: Non-Government; 11.12.02 Contracts and Claims: Rental and Leasing

CIP Program/s: 521501 Real Estate

Related DOT Job/s: 186.117-042 MANAGER, LAND DEVELOPMENT; 186.117-046 MANAGER, LEASING; 186.117-058 REAL-ESTATE AGENT; 191.117-050 RIGHT-OF-WAY SUPERVISOR

15011B PROPERTY, REAL ESTATE, AND COMMUNITY ASSOCIATION MANAGERS. OOH

Title/s: Property and Real Estate Managers

Plan, direct, and coordinate selling, buying, leasing, or governance activities of commercial, industrial, or residential real estate properties. Include managers of homeowner and condominium associations, rented or leased housing units, buildings, or land (including rights-of-way). Exclude workers whose duties are not primarily managerial. Workers who are engaged primarily in direct buying, selling, or renting of real estate are reported as sales workers. Manages and oversees operations, maintenance, and administrative functions for commercial, industrial, or residential properties. Directs collection of monthly assessments, rental fees and deposits, and payment of insurance premiums, mortgage, taxes, and incurred operating expenses. Meets with clients to negotiate management and service contracts, determine priorities, and discuss financial and operational status of property. Plans, schedules, and coordinates general maintenance, major repairs, and remodeling or construction projects for commercial or residential property. Investigates complaints, disturbances, and violations, and resolves problems following management rules and regulations. Recruits, hires, and trains managerial, clerical, and maintenance staff, or contracts with vendors for security, maintenance, extermination, or groundskeeping personnel. Directs and coordinates the activities of staff and contract personnel and evaluates performance. Maintains records of sales, rental or usage activity, special permits issued, maintenance and operating costs, or property availability. Purchases building and maintenance supplies, equipment, or furniture. Develops and administers annual operating budget. Negotiates for sale, lease, or development of property, and completes or reviews appropriate documents and forms. Inspects facilities and equipment, and inventories building contents to document damage and determine repair needs. Assembles and analyzes construction and vendor service contract bids. Confers with legal authority to ensure transactions and terminations of contracts and agreements are in accordance with court orders, laws, and regulations. Maintains contact with insurance carrier, fire and police departments, and other agencies to ensure protection and compliance with codes and regulations. Prepares reports summarizing financial and operational status of property or facility. Meets with prospective leasers to show property, explain terms of occupancy, and provide information about local area.

Yearly Earnings: $22,620

Education: Bachelor's degree

Knowledge: Administration and Management; Economics and Accounting; Sales and Marketing; Personnel and Human Resources; Building and Construction; Law, Government, and Jurisprudence

Abilities: Written Expression; Mathematical Reasoning; Number Facility; Speech Recognition

Skills: Reading Comprehension; Active Listening; Writing; Speaking; Social Perceptiveness; Coordination; Persuasion; Negotiation; Service Orientation; Problem Identification; Information Gathering; Idea Generation; Idea Evaluation; Implementation Planning; Solution Appraisal; Visioning; Systems Perception; Identifying Downstream Consequences; Identification of Key Causes; Judgment and Decision Making; Systems Evaluation; Time Management; Management of

Financial Resources; Management of Material Resources; Management of Personnel Resources
General Work Activities: Getting Information Needed to Do the Job; Estimating Needed Characteristics; Judging Qualities of Things, Services, People; Processing Information; Making Decisions and Solving Problems; Developing Objectives and Strategies; Scheduling Work and Activities; Organizing, Planning, and Prioritizing; Documenting/Recording Information; Communicating with Other Workers; Communicating with Persons Outside Organization; Selling or Influencing Others; Resolving Conflicts, Negotiating with Others; Coordinating Work and Activities of Others; Developing and Building Teams; Guiding, Directing and Motivating Subordinates; Provide Consultation and Advice to Others; Performing Administrative Activities; Staffing Organizational Units; Monitoring and Controlling Resources
Job Characteristics: Objective or Subjective Information; Job-Required Social Interaction; Supervise, Coach, Train Others; Persuade Someone to a Course of Action; Provide a Service to Others; Take a Position Opposed to Others; Deal with External Customers; Coordinate or Lead Others; Responsibility for Outcomes and Results; Frequency in Conflict Situations; Deal with Unpleasant or Angry People; Deal with Physical, Aggressive People
GOE Group/s: 05.02.02 Managerial Work: Mechanical: Maintenance and Construction; 11.05.03 Business Administration: Management Services: Government; 11.11.01 Business Management: Lodging; 11.11.04 Business Management: Services; 11.11.05 Business Management: Wholesale-Retail; 11.12.02 Contracts and Claims: Rental and Leasing
CIP Program/s: 521501 Real Estate
Related DOT Job/s: 186.117-062 RENTAL MANAGER, PUBLIC EVENTS FACILITIES; 186.167-018 MANAGER, APARTMENT HOUSE; 186.167-030 MANAGER, HOUSING PROJECT; 186.167-042 MANAGER, MARKET; 186.167-046 MANAGER, PROPERTY; 186.167-062 CONDOMINIUM MANAGER; 186.167-066 MANAGER, REAL-ESTATE FIRM; 187.167-190 SUPERINTENDENT, BUILDING

15011C PROPERTY RECORDS MANAGERS. OOH Title/s: Property and Real Estate Managers

Direct and coordinate activities in an organization relating to searching, examining, and recording information for property-related documents to determine status of property titles or property rights. Directs and coordinates researching and recordkeeping activities concerning ownership, contractual terms and conditions, and expiration dates of land documents. Prepares work schedules, and assigns projects to prioritize activities for title search staff. Monitors status of pending research assignments, and confers with staff to resolve production and quality problems. Confers with employees and other managers to establish and modify policies and procedures. Conducts performance appraisals and makes recommendations for personnel actions such as promotions, remedial training, transfers, and terminations. Authorizes royalty payments, bonuses, and other compensation as specified by terms and conditions of legal documents. Oversees the signing of real estate closing documents to verify transfer of title and proper disbursement of documents and escrow funds. Develops and conducts training programs for new hires, and provides continuing in-service training for current employees. Oversees preparation of timesheets, and reviews payroll information. Recruits, interviews, and hires title department personnel. Performs difficult and involved title searches. Reviews accuracy and completeness of legal documents, such as title reports, deeds, affidavits, and other data, to ensure the legality of business transactions. Discusses search delays and title defects, such as outstanding liens or judgments, with legal counsel. Prepares reports to summarize terms and conditions of existing contracts, leases, and agreements, and to provide information for renegotiations. Completes purchase orders for equipment and supplies.
Yearly Earnings: $22,620
Education: Bachelor's degree
Knowledge: Administration and Management; Economics and Accounting; Personnel and Human Resources; Education and Training; English Language; Law, Government, and Jurisprudence
Abilities: Written Comprehension; Written Expression; Speech Clarity
Skills: Reading Comprehension; Active Listening; Writing; Speaking; Active Learning; Learning Strategies; Social Perceptiveness; Coordination; Persuasion; Negotiation; Instructing; Information Gathering; Information Organization; Idea Generation; Idea Evaluation; Implementation Planning; Solution Appraisal; Systems Perception; Identifying Downstream Consequences; Identification of Key Causes; Judgment and Decision Making; Systems Evaluation; Time Management; Management of Financial Resources; Management of Material Resources; Management of Personnel Resources
General Work Activities: Getting Information Needed to Do the Job; Estimating Needed Characteristics; Judging Qualities of Things, Services, People; Processing Information; Evaluating Information against Standards; Analyzing Data or Information; Scheduling Work and Activities; Organizing, Planning, and Prioritizing; Implementing Ideas, Programs, etc.; Communicating with Other Workers; Establishing and Maintaining Relationships; Resolving Conflicts, Negotiating with Others; Coordinating Work and Activities of Others; Developing and Building Teams; Teaching Others; Guiding, Directing and Motivating Subordinates; Coaching and Developing Others; Provide Consultation and Advice to Others; Performing Administrative Activities; Staffing Organizational Units; Monitoring and Controlling Resources
Job Characteristics: Objective or Subjective Information; Job-Required Social Interaction; Supervise, Coach, Train Others; Persuade Someone to a Course of Action; Take a Position Opposed to Others; Coordinate or Lead Others; Responsibility for Outcomes and Results; Frequency in Conflict Situations; Sitting; Frustrating Circumstances
GOE Group/s: 11.05.02 Business Administration: Administrative Specialization; 11.11.04 Business Management: Services
CIP Program/s: 220103 Paralegal/Legal Assistant; 521501 Real Estate
Related DOT Job/s: 186.167-038 MANAGER, LAND LEASES-AND-RENTALS; 186.167-090 MANAGER, TITLE SEARCH

15014 INDUSTRIAL PRODUCTION MANAGERS. OOH Title/s: Industrial Production Managers; Education Administrators; Health Services Managers

Plan, organize, direct, control, and coordinate the work activities and resources necessary for manufacturing products in accordance with cost, quality, and quantity specifications. Directs and coordinates production, processing, distribution, and marketing activities of industrial organization. Reviews processing schedules and production orders to determine staffing requirements, work procedures, and duty assignments. Reviews plans and confers with research and support staff to develop new products and processes or the quality of existing products. Initiates and coordinates inventory and cost control programs. Analyzes production, quality control, maintenance, and other operational reports to detect production problems. Reviews operations and confers with technical or administrative staff to resolve production or processing problems. Negotiates material prices with suppliers. Develops budgets and approves expenditures for supplies, materials, and human resources. Coordinates and recommends procedures for facility and equipment maintenance or modification. Examines samples of raw products or directs testing during processing to ensure finished products conform to prescribed quality standards. Prepares and maintains production reports and personnel records. Hires, trains, evaluates, and discharges staff. Resolves personnel griev-

ances. Plans and develops sales or promotional programs for products in new and existing markets.
Yearly Earnings: $39,936
Education: Bachelor's degree
Knowledge: Administration and Management; Economics and Accounting; Sales and Marketing; Customer and Personal Service; Personnel and Human Resources; Production and Processing; Food Production; Chemistry; Psychology; Sociology and Anthropology; Education and Training; Law, Government, and Jurisprudence; Communications and Media; Transportation
Abilities: Oral Comprehension; Written Comprehension; Oral Expression; Written Expression; Fluency of Ideas; Originality; Problem Sensitivity; Deductive Reasoning; Inductive Reasoning; Information Ordering; Category Flexibility; Mathematical Reasoning; Number Facility; Memorization; Speed of Closure; Flexibility of Closure; Perceptual Speed; Near Vision; Visual Color Discrimination; Speech Recognition; Speech Clarity
Skills: Speaking; Critical Thinking; Active Learning; Monitoring; Social Perceptiveness; Coordination; Persuasion; Negotiation; Problem Identification; Information Gathering; Synthesis/Reorganization; Idea Generation; Idea Evaluation; Implementation Planning; Solution Appraisal; Operations Analysis; Equipment Selection; Installation; Product Inspection; Equipment Maintenance; Troubleshooting; Visioning; Systems Perception; Identifying Downstream Consequences; Identification of Key Causes; Judgment and Decision Making; Systems Evaluation; Time Management; Management of Financial Resources; Management of Material Resources; Management of Personnel Resources
General Work Activities: Getting Information Needed to Do the Job; Monitoring Processes, Material, or Surroundings; Identifying Objects, Actions, and Events; Inspecting Equipment, Structures, or Material; Estimating Needed Characteristics; Judging Qualities of Things, Services, People; Processing Information; Evaluating Information against Standards; Analyzing Data or Information; Making Decisions and Solving Problems; Thinking Creatively; Updating and Using Job-Relevant Knowledge; Developing Objectives and Strategies; Scheduling Work and Activities; Organizing, Planning, and Prioritizing; Operating Vehicles or Equipment; Implementing Ideas, Programs, etc.; Documenting/Recording Information; Interpreting Meaning of Information to Others; Communicating with Other Workers; Establishing and Maintaining Relationships; Selling or Influencing Others; Resolving Conflicts, Negotiating with Others; Coordinating Work and Activities of Others; Developing and Building Teams; Teaching Others; Guiding, Directing and Motivating Subordinates; Coaching and Developing Others; Provide Consultation and Advice to Others; Performing Administrative Activities; Staffing Organizational Units; Monitoring and Controlling Resources
Job Characteristics: Objective or Subjective Information; Job-Required Social Interaction; Supervise, Coach, Train Others; Persuade Someone to a Course of Action; Take a Position Opposed to Others; Coordinate or Lead Others; Responsible for Others' Health and Safety; Responsibility for Outcomes and Results; Frequency in Conflict Situations; Deal with Unpleasant or Angry People; Frustrating Circumstances; Importance of Being Aware of New Events
GOE Group/s: 03.01.01 Managerial Work: Plants and Animals: Farming; 05.02.03 Managerial Work: Mechanical: Processing and Manufacturing; 11.05.02 Business Administration: Administrative Specialization; 11.07.01 Services Administration: Social Services
CIP Program/s: 010401 Agricultural and Food Products Processing Operations and Management; 020301 Food Sciences and Technology; 130101 Education, General; 130401 Education Administration and Supervision, General; 130403 Adult and Continuing Education Administration; 142801 Textile Sciences and Engineering; 430102 Corrections/Correctional Administration; 520201 Business Administration and Management, General; 520205 Operations Management and Supervision
Related DOT Job/s: 180.167-054 SUPERINTENDENT; 182.167-022 SUPERINTENDENT, CONCRETE-MIXING PLANT; 183.117-010 MANAGER, BRANCH; 183.117-014 PRODUCTION SUPERINTENDENT; 183.161-014 WINE MAKER; 183.167-010 BREWING DIRECTOR; 183.167-014 GENERAL SUPERINTENDENT, MILLING; 183.167-018 GENERAL SUPERVISOR; 183.167-022 GENERAL SUPERVISOR; 183.167-026 MANAGER, FOOD PROCESSING PLANT; 183.167-034 SUPERINTENDENT, CAR CONSTRUCTION; 187.167-090 MANAGER, DENTAL LABORATORY; 188.167-094 SUPERINTENDENT, INDUSTRIES, CORRECTIONAL FACILITY

15017A LANDSCAPING MANAGERS. OOH Title/s: Construction Managers

Plan and direct landscaping functions and sequences of work to landscape grounds of private residences, public areas, or commercial and industrial properties, according to landscape design and clients' specifications. Confers with prospective client and studies landscape designs, drawings, and bills of materials to ascertain scope of landscaping work required. Formulates and submits estimate and contract for client or bid to industrial concern or governmental agency. Calculates labor, equipment, material, and overhead costs to determine minimum estimate or bid which will provide for margin of profit. Plans landscaping functions and sequences of work at various sites to obtain optimum utilization of workforce and equipment. Inspects work at sites for compliance with terms and specifications of contract. Inspects grounds or area to determine equipment requirements for grading, tilling, or replacing top soil, and labor requirements. Directs and coordinates activities of workers engaged in performing landscaping functions in contractual agreement. Purchases and ensures that materials are on-site as needed.
Yearly Earnings: $39,936
Education: Bachelor's degree
Knowledge: Administration and Management; Economics and Accounting; Sales and Marketing; Customer and Personal Service; Personnel and Human Resources; Design; Chemistry; Biology
Abilities: Fluency of Ideas; Originality; Information Ordering; Visualization
Skills: Mathematics; Coordination; Negotiation; Implementation Planning; Operations Analysis; Equipment Selection; Product Inspection; Visioning; Systems Perception; Identifying Downstream Consequences; Identification of Key Causes; Systems Evaluation; Time Management; Management of Financial Resources; Management of Material Resources; Management of Personnel Resources
General Work Activities: Scheduling Work and Activities; Establishing and Maintaining Relationships; Selling or Influencing Others; Coordinating Work and Activities of Others; Developing and Building Teams; Guiding, Directing and Motivating Subordinates; Monitoring and Controlling Resources
Job Characteristics: Supervise, Coach, Train Others; Persuade Someone to a Course of Action; Deal with External Customers; Coordinate or Lead Others; Responsibility for Outcomes and Results
GOE Group/s: 03.01.03 Managerial Work: Plants and Animals: Specialty Cropping
CIP Program/s: 010601 Horticulture Services Operations and Management, General; 010605 Landscaping Operations and Management
Related DOT Job/s: 182.167-014 LANDSCAPE CONTRACTOR

15017B CONSTRUCTION MANAGERS. OOH Title/s: Construction Managers

Plan, direct, coordinate, and budget, usually through subordinate supervisory personnel, activities concerned with the construction and maintenance of structures, facilities, and systems.

Participate in the conceptual development of a construction project and oversee its organization, scheduling, and implementation. Include specialized construction fields such as carpentry or plumbing. Include general superintendents, project managers, and constructors who manage, coordinate, and supervise the construction process. Plans, organizes, and directs activities concerned with construction and maintenance of structures, facilities, and systems. Confers with supervisory personnel to discuss such matters as work procedures, complaints, and construction problems. Inspects and reviews construction work, repair projects, and reports to ensure work conforms to specifications. Studies job specifications to plan and approve construction of project. Directs and supervises workers on construction site to ensure project meets specifications. Contracts workers to perform construction work in accordance with specifications. Requisitions supplies and materials to complete construction project. Interprets and explains plans and contract terms to administrative staff, workers, and clients. Formulates reports concerning such areas as work progress, costs, and scheduling. Dispatches workers to construction sites to work on specified projects. Investigates reports of damage at construction sites to ensure proper procedures are being carried out.

Yearly Earnings: $39,936

Education: Bachelor's degree

Knowledge: Administration and Management; Personnel and Human Resources; Design; Building and Construction; Public Safety and Security; Law, Government, and Jurisprudence

Abilities: Speech Recognition

Skills: Active Listening; Writing; Speaking; Mathematics; Critical Thinking; Active Learning; Monitoring; Coordination; Persuasion; Negotiation; Problem Identification; Idea Generation; Idea Evaluation; Implementation Planning; Solution Appraisal; Operations Analysis; Equipment Selection; Product Inspection; Visioning; Identifying Downstream Consequences; Identification of Key Causes; Judgment and Decision Making; Systems Evaluation; Time Management; Management of Financial Resources; Management of Material Resources; Management of Personnel Resources

General Work Activities: Getting Information Needed to Do the Job; Monitoring Processes, Material, or Surroundings; Identifying Objects, Actions, and Events; Inspecting Equipment, Structures, or Material; Estimating Needed Characteristics; Judging Qualities of Things, Services, People; Processing Information; Making Decisions and Solving Problems; Updating and Using Job-Relevant Knowledge; Developing Objectives and Strategies; Scheduling Work and Activities; Organizing, Planning, and Prioritizing; Drafting and Specifying Technical Devices, etc.; Implementing Ideas, Programs, etc.; Establishing and Maintaining Relationships; Coordinating Work and Activities of Others; Developing and Building Teams; Guiding, Directing and Motivating Subordinates; Staffing Organizational Units; Monitoring and Controlling Resources

Job Characteristics: Supervise, Coach, Train Others; Take a Position Opposed to Others; Coordinate or Lead Others; Responsibility for Outcomes and Results; Frequency in Conflict Situations; Sounds, Noise Levels are Distracting, etc.; Very Hot; High Places; Climbing Ladders, Scaffolds, Poles, etc.; Consequence of Error; Importance of Being Exact or Accurate; Importance of Being Sure All is Done

GOE Group/s: 05.02.02 Managerial Work: Mechanical: Maintenance and Construction; 11.12.04 Contracts and Claims: Procurement Negotiations

CIP Program/s: 000000 NO CIP ASSIGNED

Related DOT Job/s: 182.167-010 CONTRACTOR; 182.167-018 RAILROAD-CONSTRUCTION DIRECTOR; 182.167-026 SUPERINTENDENT, CONSTRUCTION; 182.167-030 SUPERINTENDENT, MAINTENANCE OF WAY; 182.167-034 SUPERVISOR, BRIDGES AND BUILDINGS

15021A MINING SUPERINTENDENTS AND SUPERVISORS. OOH Title/s: General Managers and Top Executives; Blue Collar Worker Supervisors

Plan, direct, and coordinate mining operations to extract mineral ore or aggregate from underground or surface mines, quarries, or pits. Confers with engineering, supervisory, and maintenance personnel to plan and coordinate mine development and operations. Directs opening or closing of mine sections, pits, or other work areas, and installation or removal of equipment. Studies land contours and rock formations to specify locations for mine shafts, pillars, and timbers and to determine equipment needs. Directs and coordinates enforcement of mining laws and safety regulations and reports violations. Studies maps and blueprints to determine prospective locations for mine haulage ways, access roads, rail tracks, and conveyor systems. Reviews, consolidates, and oversees updating of mine records, such as geological and survey reports, air quality, safety reports, and production logs. Inspects mine to detect production, equipment, safety, and personnel problems, and recommends steps to improve conditions and increase production. Calculates mining and quarrying operational costs and potential income, and determines activities to maximize income. Negotiates with workers, supervisors, union personnel, and other parties to resolve grievances or settle complaints.

Yearly Earnings: $39,936

Education: Work experience, plus degree

Knowledge: Administration and Management; Economics and Accounting; Personnel and Human Resources; Production and Processing; Design; Building and Construction; Geography; Public Safety and Security

Abilities: Oral Comprehension; Mathematical Reasoning; Spatial Orientation

Skills: Active Listening; Science; Active Learning; Monitoring; Coordination; Persuasion; Negotiation; Idea Evaluation; Implementation Planning; Management of Financial Resources; Management of Material Resources; Management of Personnel Resources

General Work Activities: Monitoring Processes, Material, or Surroundings; Inspecting Equipment, Structures, or Material; Estimating Needed Characteristics; Processing Information; Evaluating Information against Standards; Analyzing Data or Information; Making Decisions and Solving Problems; Developing Objectives and Strategies; Scheduling Work and Activities; Organizing, Planning, and Prioritizing; Drafting and Specifying Technical Devices, etc.; Implementing Ideas, Programs, etc.; Communicating with Other Workers; Communicating with Persons Outside Organization; Establishing and Maintaining Relationships; Resolving Conflicts, Negotiating with Others; Coordinating Work and Activities of Others; Developing and Building Teams; Guiding, Directing and Motivating Subordinates; Coaching and Developing Others; Provide Consultation and Advice to Others; Performing Administrative Activities; Staffing Organizational Units; Monitoring and Controlling Resources

Job Characteristics: Supervise, Coach, Train Others; Take a Position Opposed to Others; Coordinate or Lead Others; Responsible for Others' Health and Safety; Responsibility for Outcomes and Results; Extremely Bright or Inadequate Lighting; Cramped Work Space, Awkward Positions; Hazardous Conditions; Climbing Ladders, Scaffolds, Poles, etc.; Common Protective or Safety Attire; Specialized Protective or Safety Attire; Consequence of Error; Importance of Being Exact or Accurate; Importance of Being Sure All is Done

GOE Group/s: 05.02.05 Managerial Work: Mechanical: Mining, Logging, and Petroleum Production

CIP Program/s: 000000 NO CIP ASSIGNED

Related DOT Job/s: 181.117-014 MINE SUPERINTENDENT; 181.167-018 SUPERVISOR, MINE

15021C OIL AND GAS DRILLING AND PRODUCTION SUPERINTENDENTS. OOH Title/s: General Managers and Top Executives; Blue Collar Worker Supervisors

Plan, direct, and coordinate activities required to erect, install, and maintain equipment for exploratory or production drilling of oil and gas. May direct technical processes and analyses to resolve drilling problems and to monitor and control operating costs and production efficiency. Plans and directs erection of drilling rigs and installation and maintenance of equipment, such as pumping units and compressor stations. Determines procedures to resolve drilling problems, service well equipment, clean wells, and dismantle and store derricks and drill equipment. Directs technical processes related to drilling, such as treatment of oil and gas, sediment analysis, well logging, and formation testing. Analyzes production reports and formulates drilling and production procedures to control well production in accordance with proration regulations. Directs petroleum exploration parties engaged in drilling for samples of subsurface stratigraphy and in seismic prospecting.

Yearly Earnings: $39,936

Education: Work experience, plus degree

Knowledge: Administration and Management; Production and Processing; Engineering and Technology; Building and Construction; Physics

Abilities: Fluency of Ideas; Deductive Reasoning; Inductive Reasoning; Information Ordering; Category Flexibility; Memorization; Speed of Closure; Flexibility of Closure; Perceptual Speed; Spatial Orientation; Visualization; Selective Attention; Time Sharing; Response Orientation; Gross Body Equilibrium; Far Vision; Peripheral Vision

Skills: Science; Critical Thinking; Coordination; Negotiation; Instructing; Problem Identification; Implementation Planning; Equipment Selection; Installation; Operation Monitoring; Operation and Control; Identifying Downstream Consequences; Identification of Key Causes; Time Management; Management of Material Resources; Management of Personnel Resources

General Work Activities: Getting Information Needed to Do the Job; Monitoring Processes, Material, or Surroundings; Identifying Objects, Actions, and Events; Inspecting Equipment, Structures, or Material; Estimating Needed Characteristics; Judging Qualities of Things, Services, People; Processing Information; Analyzing Data or Information; Making Decisions and Solving Problems; Updating and Using Job-Relevant Knowledge; Developing Objectives and Strategies; Scheduling Work and Activities; Organizing, Planning, and Prioritizing; Controlling Machines and Processes; Drafting and Specifying Technical Devices, etc.; Documenting/Recording Information; Communicating with Other Workers; Resolving Conflicts, Negotiating with Others; Coordinating Work and Activities of Others; Developing and Building Teams; Guiding, Directing and Motivating Subordinates; Coaching and Developing Others; Provide Consultation and Advice to Others; Performing Administrative Activities; Staffing Organizational Units; Monitoring and Controlling Resources

Job Characteristics: Job-Required Social Interaction; Supervise, Coach, Train Others; Coordinate or Lead Others; Responsible for Others' Health and Safety; Responsibility for Outcomes and Results; Sounds, Noise Levels are Distracting, etc.; Contaminants; Whole Body Vibration; High Places; Hazardous Conditions; Hazardous Equipment; Climbing Ladders, Scaffolds, Poles, etc.; Common Protective or Safety Attire; Specialized Protective or Safety Attire; Consequence of Error; Importance of Being Sure All is Done

GOE Group/s: 05.02.01 Managerial Work: Mechanical: Systems

CIP Program/s: 000000 NO CIP ASSIGNED

Related DOT Job/s: 181.167-014 SUPERINTENDENT, DRILLING AND PRODUCTION

15023A TRANSPORTATION MANAGERS. OOH Title/s: Communication, Transportation, and Utilities Operations Managers

Plan, direct, and coordinate the transportation operations within an organization, or the activities of organizations that provide transportation services. Directs and coordinates, through subordinates, activities of operations department to obtain use of equipment, facilities, and human resources. Confers and cooperates with management and other in formulating and implementing administrative, operational, and customer relations policies and procedures. Analyzes expenditures and other financial reports to develop plans, policies, and budgets for increasing profits and improving services. Enforces compliance of operations personnel with administrative policies, procedures, safety rules, and government regulations. Reviews transportation schedules, worker assignments, and routes to ensure compliance with standards for personnel selection, safety, and union contract terms. Conducts investigations in cooperation with government agencies to determine causes of transportation accidents and to improve safety procedures. Oversees activities relating to dispatching, routing, and tracking transportation vehicles, such as aircraft and railroad cars. Prepares management recommendations, such as need for increasing fares, tariffs, or expansion or changes to existing schedules. Recommends or authorizes capital expenditures for acquisition of new equipment or property to increase efficiency and services of operations department. Oversees process of investigation and response to customer or shipper complaints relating to operations department. Oversees workers assigning tariff classifications and preparing billing according to mode of transportation and destination of shipment. Acts as organization representative before commissions or regulatory bodies during hearings, such as to increase rates and change routes and schedules. Inspects or oversees repairs and maintenance to equipment, vehicles, and facilities to enforce standards for safety, efficiency, cleanliness, and appearance. Oversees procurement process, including research and testing of equipment, vendor contacts, and approval of requisitions. Negotiates and authorizes contracts with equipment and materials suppliers. Participates in union contract negotiations and settlement of grievances.

Yearly Earnings: $39,936

Education: Work experience, plus degree

Knowledge: Administration and Management; Economics and Accounting; Sales and Marketing; Personnel and Human Resources; Mathematics; Geography; Public Safety and Security; Law, Government, and Jurisprudence; Transportation

Abilities: Oral Comprehension; Written Comprehension; Oral Expression; Fluency of Ideas; Originality; Problem Sensitivity; Deductive Reasoning; Mathematical Reasoning; Time Sharing; Speech Clarity

Skills: Reading Comprehension; Monitoring; Coordination; Persuasion; Negotiation; Idea Generation; Idea Evaluation; Implementation Planning; Solution Appraisal; Operations Analysis; Equipment Selection; Visioning; Systems Perception; Identifying Downstream Consequences; Identification of Key Causes; Judgment and Decision Making; Systems Evaluation; Time Management; Management of Financial Resources; Management of Material Resources; Management of Personnel Resources

General Work Activities: Getting Information Needed to Do the Job; Monitoring Processes, Material, or Surroundings; Identifying Objects, Actions, and Events; Inspecting Equipment, Structures, or Material; Estimating Needed Characteristics; Judging Qualities of Things, Services, People; Processing Information; Evaluating Information against Standards; Making Decisions and Solving Problems; Thinking Creatively; Developing Objectives and Strategies; Scheduling Work and Activities; Organizing, Planning, and Prioritizing; Communicating with Other Workers; Communicating with Persons Outside Organization; Selling or Influencing Others; Resolving Conflicts, Negotiating with Others; Coordinating Work and Activities of Others; Developing and Building Teams; Guiding, Directing and Motivating Subordinates; Performing Administrative Activities; Staffing Organizational Units; Monitoring and Controlling Resources

Job Characteristics: Job-Required Social Interaction; Supervise, Coach, Train Others; Persuade Someone to a Course of Action; Take a Position Opposed to Others; Coordinate or Lead Others; Responsible for Others' Health and Safety; Responsibility for Outcomes and Results; Frequency in Conflict Situations; Consequence of Error; Frustrating Circumstances; Importance of Being Sure All is Done; Importance of Being Aware of New Events

GOE Group/s: 05.02.02 Managerial Work: Mechanical: Maintenance and Construction; 05.02.04 Managerial Work: Mechanical: Communications; 05.02.07 Managerial Work: Mechanical: Materials Handling; 07.01.02 Administrative Detail: Administration; 07.05.01 Records Processing: Coordinating and Scheduling; 11.05.01 Business Administration: Management Services: Non-Government; 11.05.02 Business Administration: Administrative Specialization; 11.05.03 Business Administration: Management Services: Government; 11.10.05 Regulations Enforcement: Company Policy; 11.11.03 Business Management: Transportation; 11.12.02 Contracts and Claims: Rental and Leasing

CIP Program/s: 010301 Agricultural Production Workers and Managers, General; 010304 Crop Production Operations and Management; 010501 Agricultural Supplies Retailing and Wholesaling; 080709 General Distribution Operations; 430201 Fire Protection and Safety Technologists and Technicians; 490104 Aviation Management; 520201 Business Administration and Management, General; 520203 Logistics and Materials Management

Related DOT Job/s: 180.167-062 MANAGER, AERIAL PLANTING AND CULTIVATION; 184.117-014 DIRECTOR, TRANSPORTATION; 184.117-018 DISTRICT SUPERVISOR; 184.117-026 MANAGER, AIRPORT; 184.117-034 MANAGER, AUTOMOTIVE SERVICES; 184.117-038 MANAGER, FLIGHT OPERATIONS; 184.117-042 MANAGER, HARBOR DEPARTMENT; 184.117-050 MANAGER, OPERATIONS; 184.117-054 MANAGER, REGIONAL; 184.117-058 MANAGER, SCHEDULE PLANNING; 184.117-066 MANAGER, TRAFFIC; 184.117-086 MANAGER, CAR INSPECTION AND REPAIR; 184.117-090 REGIONAL SUPERINTENDENT, RAILROAD CAR INSPECTION AND REPAIR; 184.167-010 BOAT DISPATCHER; 184.167-042 GENERAL AGENT, OPERATIONS; 184.167-054 MANAGER, BUS TRANSPORTATION; 184.167-058 MANAGER, CARGO-AND-RAMP-SERVICES; 184.167-066 MANAGER, FLIGHT CONTROL; 184.167-070 MANAGER, FLIGHT-RESERVATIONS; 184.167-082 MANAGER, STATION; 184.167-090 MANAGER, TRAFFIC; 184.167-094 MANAGER, TRAFFIC; 184.167-098 MANAGER, TRAFFIC I; 184.167-102 MANAGER, TRAFFIC I; 184.167-106 MANAGER, TRAFFIC II; 184.167-110 MANAGER, TRUCK TERMINAL; 184.167-122 PORT-TRAFFIC MANAGER; 184.167-130 STATION MANAGER; 184.167-158 SUPERINTENDENT, DIVISION; 184.167-170 SUPERINTENDENT, MAINTENANCE; 184.167-174 SUPERINTENDENT, MAINTENANCE; 184.167-178 SUPERINTENDENT, MAINTENANCE OF EQUIPMENT; 184.167-182 SUPERINTENDENT, MARINE; 184.167-186 SUPERINTENDENT, MARINE OIL TERMINAL; 184.167-206 SUPERINTENDENT, STATIONS; 184.167-214 SUPERINTENDENT, TERMINAL; 184.167-226 SUPERINTENDENT, TRANSPORTATION; 184.167-242 SUPERVISOR, TERMINAL OPERATIONS; 184.167-254 TERMINAL SUPERINTENDENT; 184.167-266 TRANSPORTATION-MAINTENANCE SUPERVISOR; 184.167-274 WHARFINGER, CHIEF; 184.167-282 DIVISION ROAD SUPERVISOR; 184.167-286 GENERAL CAR SUPERVISOR, YARD; 184.167-290 SUPERVISOR, COMMUNICATIONS-AND-SIGNALS; 184.167-294 SUPERVISOR, TRAIN OPERATIONS; 184.267-010 FREIGHT-TRAFFIC CONSULTANT; 186.117-030 GENERAL CLAIMS AGENT; 196.167-010 CHIEF PILOT; 909.127-010 SAFETY COORDINATOR

15023B COMMUNICATIONS MANAGERS. OOH

Title/s: Communication, Transportation, and Utilities Operations Managers

Plan, direct, and coordinate the communication operations within an organization, or the activities of organizations that provide communication services, such as radio and TV broadcasting or telecommunications. Supervises personnel directly or through subordinates, and coordinates worker or departmental activities. Directs investigation of rates, services, activities, or station operations to ensure compliance with government regulations. Prepares or directs preparation of plans, proposals, reports, or other documents. Develops operating procedures and policies and interprets for personnel. Analyzes reports, data, studies, or governmental rulings to determine status, appropriate response, or effect on operations or profitability. Confers with officials, administrators, management, or others to discuss programs, services, production, or procedures. Directs, coordinates, and inspects equipment installations to ensure compliance with regulations, standards, and deadlines. Plans work activities and prepares schedules. Directs testing and inspection of equipment for operational performance. Makes recommendations or advises personnel regarding procedures, acquisitions, complaints, or business activities. Negotiates settlements, contractual agreements, or services with company representatives or owners. Reviews and authorizes or approves recommendations, contracts, plans, or requisitions for equipment and supplies. Prepares budget for department, station, or program, and monitors expenses. Determines workforce requirement, hires and discharges workers, and assigns work. Conducts studies to determine effectiveness and adequacy of equipment, work load, or estimated equipment and maintenance costs. Reviews accounts and records and verifies accuracy of cash balances.

Yearly Earnings: $39,936

Education: Work experience, plus degree

Knowledge: Administration and Management; Economics and Accounting; Personnel and Human Resources; Computers and Electronics; Engineering and Technology; Mathematics; Psychology; English Language; Telecommunications; Communications and Media

Abilities: Oral Comprehension; Written Comprehension; Oral Expression; Written Expression; Fluency of Ideas; Originality; Problem Sensitivity; Deductive Reasoning; Inductive Reasoning; Information Ordering; Category Flexibility; Mathematical Reasoning; Number Facility; Memorization; Speed of Closure; Flexibility of Closure; Perceptual Speed; Speech Clarity

Skills: Active Listening; Writing; Speaking; Monitoring; Social Perceptiveness; Coordination; Persuasion; Negotiation; Instructing; Information Gathering; Idea Generation; Idea Evaluation; Implementation Planning; Solution Appraisal; Operations Analysis; Product Inspection; Visioning; Systems Perception; Identifying Downstream Consequences; Identification of Key Causes; Judgment and Decision Making; Systems Evaluation; Time Management; Management of Financial Resources; Management of Material Resources; Management of Personnel Resources

General Work Activities: Getting Information Needed to Do the Job; Monitoring Processes, Material, or Surroundings; Inspecting Equipment, Structures, or Material; Estimating Needed Characteristics; Processing Information; Analyzing Data or Information; Making Decisions and Solving Problems; Updating and Using Job-Relevant Knowledge; Developing Objectives and Strategies; Scheduling Work and Activities; Organizing, Planning, and Prioritizing; Implementing Ideas, Programs, etc.; Communicating with Other Workers; Communicating with Persons Outside Organization; Establishing and Maintaining Relationships; Selling or Influencing Others; Resolving Conflicts, Negotiating with Others; Coordinating Work and Activities of Others; Guiding, Directing and Motivating Subordinates; Perform-

ing Administrative Activities; Staffing Organizational Units; Monitoring and Controlling Resources
Job Characteristics: Objective or Subjective Information; Job-Required Social Interaction; Supervise, Coach, Train Others; Persuade Someone to a Course of Action; Take a Position Opposed to Others; Coordinate or Lead Others; Responsibility for Outcomes and Results; Frequency in Conflict Situations; Deal with Unpleasant or Angry People; Sitting; Frustrating Circumstances; Importance of Being Aware of New Events
GOE Group/s: 05.02.01 Managerial Work: Mechanical: Systems; 05.02.04 Managerial Work: Mechanical: Communications; 05.05.05 Craft Technology: Electrical-Electronic Systems Installation and Repair; 07.01.02 Administrative Detail: Administration; 11.05.02 Business Administration: Administrative Specialization; 11.10.05 Regulations Enforcement: Company Policy; 11.12.01 Contracts and Claims: Claims and Settlement
CIP Program/s: 520201 Business Administration and Management, General; 520203 Logistics and Materials Management
Related DOT Job/s: 168.167-070 REGULATORY ADMINISTRATOR; 169.167-070 DIRECTOR, EDUCATIONAL PROGRAMMING; 184.117-062 MANAGER, STATION; 184.117-070 OPERATIONS MANAGER; 184.117-074 REVENUE-SETTLEMENTS ADMINISTRATOR; 184.117-082 SUPERINTENDENT, COMMUNICATIONS; 184.161-010 CABLE SUPERVISOR; 184.167-018 DIRECTOR, OPERATIONS; 184.167-062 MANAGER, COMMUNICATIONS STATION; 184.167-086 MANAGER, TELEGRAPH OFFICE; 184.167-134 STATIONS-RELATIONS-CONTACT REPRESENTATIVE; 184.167-230 SUPERVISOR OF COMMUNICATIONS; 184.167-258 TESTING-AND-REGULATING CHIEF; 193.167-018 SUPERINTENDENT, RADIO COMMUNICATIONS; 194.162-010 PROGRAM DIRECTOR, CABLE TELEVISION

15023C UTILITIES MANAGERS. OOH Title/s: Communication, Transportation, and Utilities Operations Managers

Plan, direct, and coordinate the activities or operations of organizations that provide utility services, such as electricity, natural gas, sanitation, and water. Schedules and coordinates activities such as processing and distribution of services, patrolling and inspection of facilities, and maintenance activities. Formulates, implements, and interprets policies and procedures. Develops plans to meet expanded needs, such as increasing capacity or facilities or modifying equipment. Plans methods and sequence of operations to obtain optimum utilization of facilities and land or to facilitate system modifications. Authorizes repair, movement, installation, or construction of equipment, supplies, or facilities. Hires, discharges, supervises, and coordinates activities of workers directly or through subordinates. Confers with management, personnel, customers, and other to solve technical or administrative problems, discuss matters, and coordinate activities. Analyzes data, trends, reports, consumption, or test results to determine adequacy of facilities, system performance, or development areas. Develops test procedures, directs and schedules testing activities, and analyzes results. Investigates and evaluates new developments in materials, tools, or equipment. Forecasts consumption of utilities to meet demands or to determine construction, equipment, or maintenance requirements. Inspects project, operations, or site to determine progress, need for repair, or compliance with specifications and regulations. Prepares budget estimates based on anticipated material, equipment, and personnel needs. Determines action to be taken in event of emergencies, such as machine, equipment, or power failure. Prepares reports, directives, records, work orders, specifications for work methods, and other documents.
Yearly Earnings: $39,936
Education: Work experience, plus degree
Knowledge: Administration and Management; Economics and Accounting; Sales and Marketing; Personnel and Human Resources; Engineering and Technology; Design; Building and Construction; Mathematics; Physics; Psychology
Abilities: Problem Sensitivity; Deductive Reasoning; Inductive Reasoning; Mathematical Reasoning; Number Facility; Time Sharing
Skills: Active Listening; Writing; Speaking; Mathematics; Critical Thinking; Active Learning; Monitoring; Social Perceptiveness; Coordination; Negotiation; Problem Identification; Information Gathering; Information Organization; Synthesis/Reorganization; Idea Generation; Idea Evaluation; Implementation Planning; Solution Appraisal; Operations Analysis; Equipment Selection; Visioning; Systems Perception; Identifying Downstream Consequences; Identification of Key Causes; Judgment and Decision Making; Systems Evaluation; Time Management; Management of Financial Resources; Management of Material Resources; Management of Personnel Resources
General Work Activities: Identifying Objects, Actions, and Events; Inspecting Equipment, Structures, or Material; Estimating Needed Characteristics; Processing Information; Evaluating Information against Standards; Analyzing Data or Information; Making Decisions and Solving Problems; Updating and Using Job-Relevant Knowledge; Developing Objectives and Strategies; Scheduling Work and Activities; Organizing, Planning, and Prioritizing; Implementing Ideas, Programs, etc.; Communicating with Other Workers; Establishing and Maintaining Relationships; Resolving Conflicts, Negotiating with Others; Coordinating Work and Activities of Others; Developing and Building Teams; Guiding, Directing and Motivating Subordinates; Coaching and Developing Others; Performing Administrative Activities; Staffing Organizational Units; Monitoring and Controlling Resources
Job Characteristics: Objective or Subjective Information; Job-Required Social Interaction; Supervise, Coach, Train Others; Persuade Someone to a Course of Action; Take a Position Opposed to Others; Coordinate or Lead Others; Responsible for Others' Health and Safety; Responsibility for Outcomes and Results; Frequency in Conflict Situations; Sitting; Frustrating Circumstances; Importance of Being Sure All is Done; Importance of Being Aware of New Events
GOE Group/s: 05.01.03 Engineering: Systems Design; 05.02.01 Managerial Work: Mechanical: Systems; 05.02.02 Managerial Work: Mechanical: Maintenance and Construction; 05.02.06 Managerial Work: Mechanical: Services; 11.05.03 Business Administration: Management Services: Government; 11.09.03 Promotion: Public Relations
CIP Program/s: 010101 Agricultural Business and Management, General; 010299 Agricultural Mechanization, Other; 030101 Natural Resources Conservation, General; 440401 Public Administration; 520201 Business Administration and Management, General; 520203 Logistics and Materials Management
Related DOT Job/s: 184.117-030 MANAGER, AREA DEVELOPMENT; 184.117-046 MANAGER, IRRIGATION DISTRICT; 184.161-014 SUPERINTENDENT, WATER-AND-SEWER SYSTEMS; 184.167-078 MANAGER, SOLID-WASTE-DISPOSAL; 184.167-126 SERVICE SUPERVISOR III; 184.167-138 SUPERINTENDENT OF GENERATION; 184.167-150 SUPERINTENDENT, DISTRIBUTION I; 184.167-154 SUPERINTENDENT, DISTRIBUTION II; 184.167-162 SUPERINTENDENT, ELECTRIC POWER; 184.167-166 SUPERINTENDENT, GENERATING PLANT; 184.167-198 SUPERINTENDENT, PIPELINES; 184.167-202 SUPERINTENDENT, POWER; 184.167-210 SUPERINTENDENT, SYSTEM OPERATION; 184.167-218 SUPERINTENDENT, TESTS; 184.167-222 SUPERINTENDENT, TRANSMISSION; 184.167-238 SUPERVISOR, SEWER SYSTEM; 184.167-246 SUPERVISOR, WATERWORKS; 184.167-270 WATER CONTROL SUPERVISOR; 914.167-010 DISPATCHER, CHIEF II

15023D STORAGE AND DISTRIBUTION MANAGERS. OOH Title/s: Communication, Transportation, and Utilities Operations Managers

Plan, direct, and coordinate the storage and distribution operations within an organization, or the activities of organizations that are engaged in storing and distributing materials and products. Establishes standard and emergency operating procedures for receiving, handling, storing, shipping, or salvaging products or materials. Confers with department heads to coordinate warehouse activities, such as production, sales, records control, and purchasing. Plans, develops, and implements warehouse safety and security programs and activities. Reviews invoices, work orders, consumption reports, and demand forecasts to estimate peak delivery periods and issue work assignments. Supervises the activities of workers engaged in receiving, storing, testing, and shipping products or materials. Inspects physical condition of warehouse and equipment and prepares work orders for testing, maintenance, or repair. Negotiates contracts, settlements, and freight-handling agreements to resolve problems between foreign and domestic shippers. Develops and implements plans for facility modification or expansion, such as equipment purchase or changes in space allocation or structural design. Examines invoices and shipping manifests for conformity to tariff and customs regulations, and contacts customs officials to effect release of shipments. Interviews, selects, and trains warehouse and supervisory personnel. Schedules air or surface pickup, delivery, or distribution of products or materials. Prepares or directs preparation of correspondence, reports, and operations, maintenance, and safety manuals. Interacts with customers or shippers to solicit new business, answer questions about services offered or required, and investigate complaints. Examines products or materials to estimate quantities or weight and type of container required for storage or transport.

Yearly Earnings: $39,936

Education: Work experience, plus degree

Knowledge: Administration and Management; Economics and Accounting; Sales and Marketing; Personnel and Human Resources; Production and Processing; Design; Mathematics; Psychology; Education and Training; Public Safety and Security; Law, Government, and Jurisprudence; Communications and Media; Transportation

Abilities: Written Comprehension; Problem Sensitivity; Deductive Reasoning; Inductive Reasoning; Mathematical Reasoning; Number Facility; Speed of Closure; Visualization; Selective Attention; Time Sharing

Skills: Learning Strategies; Coordination; Negotiation; Instructing; Problem Identification; Implementation Planning; Operations Analysis; Product Inspection; Visioning; Systems Perception; Identifying Downstream Consequences; Systems Evaluation; Time Management; Management of Material Resources; Management of Personnel Resources

General Work Activities: Monitoring Processes, Material, or Surroundings; Inspecting Equipment, Structures, or Material; Estimating Needed Characteristics; Scheduling Work and Activities; Organizing, Planning, and Prioritizing; Communicating with Other Workers; Establishing and Maintaining Relationships; Selling or Influencing Others; Resolving Conflicts, Negotiating with Others; Coordinating Work and Activities of Others; Developing and Building Teams; Teaching Others; Guiding, Directing and Motivating Subordinates; Coaching and Developing Others; Performing Administrative Activities; Staffing Organizational Units; Monitoring and Controlling Resources

Job Characteristics: Objective or Subjective Information; Job-Required Social Interaction; Supervise, Coach, Train Others; Persuade Someone to a Course of Action; Take a Position Opposed to Others; Deal with External Customers; Coordinate or Lead Others; Responsible for Others' Health and Safety; Responsibility for Outcomes and Results; Frequency in Conflict Situations; Deal with Physical, Aggressive People; Frustrating Circumstances

GOE Group/s: 05.02.01 Managerial Work: Mechanical: Systems; 05.02.07 Managerial Work: Mechanical: Materials Handling; 11.05.02 Business Administration: Administrative Specialization; 11.11.03 Business Management: Transportation

CIP Program/s: 080709 General Distribution Operations; 520201 Business Administration and Management, General; 521101 International Business; 521403 International Business Marketing

Related DOT Job/s: 181.117-010 MANAGER, BULK PLANT; 184.117-022 IMPORT-EXPORT AGENT; 184.167-038 DISPATCHER, CHIEF I; 184.167-114 MANAGER, WAREHOUSE; 184.167-118 OPERATIONS MANAGER; 184.167-146 SUPERINTENDENT, COMPRESSOR STATIONS; 184.167-190 SUPERINTENDENT, MEASUREMENT; 189.167-038 SUPERINTENDENT, AMMUNITION STORAGE

15026A LODGING MANAGERS. OOH Title/s: Hotel Managers and Assistants

Plan, direct, and coordinate activities of an organization or department that provides lodging and other accommodations. Exclude food-service managers in lodging establishments. Coordinates front-office activities of hotel or motel and resolves problems. Manages and maintains temporary or permanent lodging facilities. Answers inquiries pertaining to hotel policies and services and resolves occupants' complaints. Confers and cooperates with other department heads to ensure coordination of hotel activities. Interviews and hires applicants. Assigns duties and shifts to workers and observes performances to ensure operating procedures. Purchases supplies and arranges for outside services, such as fuel delivery, laundry, maintenance and repair, and trash collection. Receives and processes advance registration payments, sends out letters of confirmation, and returns checks when registration cannot be accepted. Shows and rents or assigns accommodations. Arranges for medical aid for park patrons. Collects rent and records data pertaining to rent funds and expenditures. Patrols facilities and grounds and investigates disturbances. Greets and registers guests. Arranges telephone answering service, delivers mail and packages, and answers questions regarding locations for eating and entertainment. Makes minor electrical, plumbing, and structural repairs. Rents equipment, such as rowboats, water skis, and fishing tackle, and coordinates intramural activities of patrons of park. Mows and waters lawns, and cultivates flower beds and shrubbery. Cleans accommodations after guests' departure. Cleans public areas, such as entrances, halls, and laundry rooms, and fires boilers. Sells light lunches, candy, tobacco, and other sundry items.

Yearly Earnings: $21,580

Education: Work experience in a related occupation

Knowledge: Administration and Management; Clerical; Economics and Accounting; Sales and Marketing; Customer and Personal Service; Personnel and Human Resources; Food Production; Building and Construction; Psychology; Sociology and Anthropology; Geography; Medicine and Dentistry; Foreign Language; History and Archeology; Philosophy and Theology; Public Safety and Security; Law, Government, and Jurisprudence; Telecommunications

Abilities: Problem Sensitivity; Category Flexibility; Mathematical Reasoning; Number Facility; Memorization; Flexibility of Closure; Perceptual Speed; Spatial Orientation; Time Sharing; Response Orientation; Dynamic Strength; Stamina; Gross Body Equilibrium; Near Vision; Far Vision; Night Vision; Peripheral Vision; Glare Sensitivity; Hearing Sensitivity; Sound Localization; Speech Recognition; Speech Clarity

Skills: Social Perceptiveness; Coordination; Negotiation; Service Orientation; Implementation Planning; Equipment Maintenance; Repairing; Time Management; Management of Financial Resources;

Management of Material Resources; Management of Personnel Resources
General Work Activities: Developing Objectives and Strategies; Scheduling Work and Activities; Organizing, Planning, and Prioritizing; Performing General Physical Activities; Operating Vehicles or Equipment; Repairing and Maintaining Mechanical Equipment; Repairing and Maintaining Electrical Equipment; Communicating with Other Workers; Communicating with Persons Outside Organization; Establishing and Maintaining Relationships; Assisting and Caring for Others; Selling or Influencing Others; Resolving Conflicts, Negotiating with Others; Performing for or Working with Public; Coordinating Work and Activities of Others; Developing and Building Teams; Guiding, Directing and Motivating Subordinates; Coaching and Developing Others; Provide Consultation and Advice to Others; Performing Administrative Activities; Staffing Organizational Units; Monitoring and Controlling Resources
Job Characteristics: Job-Required Social Interaction; Supervise, Coach, Train Others; Provide a Service to Others; Take a Position Opposed to Others; Deal with External Customers; Responsible for Others' Health and Safety; Responsibility for Outcomes and Results; Frequency in Conflict Situations; Deal with Unpleasant or Angry People; Walking or Running
GOE Group/s: 11.11.01 Business Management: Lodging
CIP Program/s: 120504 Food and Beverage/Restaurant Operations Manager; 520702 Franchise Operation; 520901 Hospitality/Administration Management; 520902 Hotel/Motel and Restaurant Management
Related DOT Job/s: 187.117-038 MANAGER, HOTEL OR MOTEL; 187.137-018 MANAGER, FRONT OFFICE; 320.137-014 MANAGER, LODGING FACILITIES

15026B FOOD-SERVICE MANAGERS. OOH Title/s: Restaurant and Food Service Managers

Plan, direct, and coordinate activities of an organization or department that serves food and beverages. Monitors compliance with health and fire regulations regarding food preparation and serving and building maintenance in lodging and dining facility. Plans menus and food utilization based on anticipated number of guests, nutritional value, palatability, popularity, and costs. Organizes and directs worker-training programs, resolves personnel problems, hires new staff, and evaluates employee performance in dining and lodging facilities. Coordinates assignments of cooking personnel to ensure economical use of food and timely preparation. Estimates food, liquor, wine, and other beverage consumption to anticipate amount to be purchased or requisitioned. Monitors food preparation and methods, size of portions, and garnishing and presentation of food to ensure food is prepared and presented in accepted manner. Monitors budget and payroll records, and reviews financial transactions to ensure expenditures are authorized and budgeted. Investigates and resolves complaints regarding food quality and service or accommodations. Reviews menus and analyzes recipes to determine labor and overhead costs, and assigns prices to menu items. Establishes and enforces nutrition standards for dining establishment based on accepted industry standards. Keeps records required by government agencies regarding sanitation and food subsidies, where indicated. Tests cooked food by tasting and smelling to ensure palatability and flavor conformity. Coordinates activities of residential camp workers, including assignment of living quarters. Assists underage workers to obtain work permits and health and birth certificates, and arranges for medical care for sick or injured workers. Creates specialty dishes and develops recipes to be used in dining facility.
Yearly Earnings: $21,580
Education: Work experience in a related occupation
Knowledge: Administration and Management; Clerical; Economics and Accounting; Sales and Marketing; Customer and Personal Service; Personnel and Human Resources; Production and Processing; Food Production; Psychology; Medicine and Dentistry; Therapy and Counseling; Education and Training; Public Safety and Security; Law, Government, and Jurisprudence
Abilities: Oral Expression; Fluency of Ideas; Originality; Problem Sensitivity; Deductive Reasoning; Category Flexibility; Mathematical Reasoning; Number Facility; Memorization; Time Sharing; Gross Body Equilibrium; Far Vision; Visual Color Discrimination; Night Vision; Peripheral Vision; Auditory Attention; Speech Recognition; Speech Clarity
Skills: Speaking; Learning Strategies; Monitoring; Social Perceptiveness; Coordination; Negotiation; Instructing; Service Orientation; Problem Identification; Idea Generation; Implementation Planning; Systems Perception; Systems Evaluation; Time Management; Management of Financial Resources; Management of Material Resources; Management of Personnel Resources
General Work Activities: Estimating Needed Characteristics; Thinking Creatively; Developing Objectives and Strategies; Scheduling Work and Activities; Communicating with Other Workers; Establishing and Maintaining Relationships; Assisting and Caring for Others; Resolving Conflicts, Negotiating with Others; Coordinating Work and Activities of Others; Developing and Building Teams; Guiding, Directing and Motivating Subordinates; Coaching and Developing Others; Performing Administrative Activities; Staffing Organizational Units; Monitoring and Controlling Resources
Job Characteristics: Objective or Subjective Information; Job-Required Social Interaction; Supervise, Coach, Train Others; Take a Position Opposed to Others; Deal with External Customers; Coordinate or Lead Others; Responsible for Others' Health and Safety; Responsibility for Outcomes and Results; Frequency in Conflict Situations; Deal with Unpleasant or Angry People; Walking or Running
GOE Group/s: 05.10.04 Crafts: Structural-Mechanical-Electrical-Electronic; 11.05.02 Business Administration: Administrative Specialization; 11.11.01 Business Management: Lodging; 11.11.04 Business Management: Services
CIP Program/s: 080901 Hospitality and Recreation Marketing Operations, General; 080906 Food Sales Operations; 120503 Culinary Arts/Chef Training; 120504 Food and Beverage/Restaurant Operations Manager; 120507 Waiter/Waitress and Dining Room Manager; 190501 Foods and Nutrition Studies, General; 190505 Food Systems Administration; 200401 Institutional Food Workers and Administrators, General; 200405 Food Caterer; 200409 Institutional Food Services Administrator; 520702 Franchise Operation; 520901 Hospitality/Administration Management; 520902 Hotel/Motel and Restaurant Management
Related DOT Job/s: 185.137-010 MANAGER, FAST FOOD SERVICES; 187.161-010 EXECUTIVE CHEF; 187.167-026 DIRECTOR, FOOD SERVICES; 187.167-050 MANAGER, AGRICULTURAL-LABOR CAMP; 187.167-066 MANAGER, CAMP; 187.167-106 MANAGER, FOOD SERVICE; 187.167-126 MANAGER, LIQUOR ESTABLISHMENT; 187.167-206 DIETARY MANAGER; 187.167-210 DIRECTOR, FOOD AND BEVERAGE; 319.137-014 MANAGER, FLIGHT KITCHEN; 319.137-018 MANAGER, INDUSTRIAL CAFETERIA; 320.137-010 MANAGER, BOARDING HOUSE

15031 NURSERY AND GREENHOUSE MANAGERS. OOH Title/s: Farm Operators and Managers

Plan, organize, direct, control, and coordinate activities of workers engaged in propagating, cultivating, and harvesting horticultural specialties, such as trees, shrubs, flowers, mushrooms, and other plants. Work may involve training new employees in gardening techniques, inspecting facilities for signs

of disrepair, and delegating repair duties to staff. Manages nursery to grow horticultural plants for sale to trade or retail customers, for display or exhibition, or for research. Hires workers and directs supervisors and workers planting seeds, controlling plant growth and disease, and potting or cutting plants for marketing. Determines type and quantity of horticultural plants to be grown, such as trees, shrubs, flowers, ornamental plants, or vegetables, based on budget, projected sales volume, or executive directive. Grows horticultural plants under controlled conditions hydroponically. Considers such factors as whether plants need hothouse/greenhouse or natural weather growing conditions. Selects and purchases seed, plant nutrients, and disease-control chemicals. Tours work areas to observe work being done, to inspect crops, and to evaluate plant and soil conditions. Confers with horticultural personnel in planning facility renovations or additions. Coordinates clerical, recordkeeping, inventory, requisition, and marketing activities. Sells gardening accessories, such as sprays, garden implements, and plant nutrients. Negotiates contracts for lease of lands or trucks or for purchase of trees. Represents establishment and provides horticultural information to public through radio, television, or newspaper media. Designs floral exhibits and prepares scale drawings of exhibits.
Yearly Earnings: $19,604
Education: Work experience in a related occupation
Knowledge: Administration and Management; Clerical; Economics and Accounting; Sales and Marketing; Customer and Personal Service; Personnel and Human Resources; Production and Processing; Food Production; Design; Chemistry; Biology; Education and Training; Communications and Media
Abilities: Originality; Category Flexibility; Number Facility
Skills: Active Listening; Speaking; Monitoring; Coordination; Negotiation; Instructing; Idea Generation; Implementation Planning; Solution Appraisal; Operations Analysis; Systems Perception; Judgment and Decision Making; Systems Evaluation; Time Management; Management of Financial Resources; Management of Material Resources; Management of Personnel Resources
General Work Activities: Thinking Creatively; Developing Objectives and Strategies; Scheduling Work and Activities; Communicating with Persons Outside Organization; Establishing and Maintaining Relationships; Selling or Influencing Others; Resolving Conflicts, Negotiating with Others; Performing for or Working with Public; Coordinating Work and Activities of Others; Developing and Building Teams; Guiding, Directing and Motivating Subordinates; Coaching and Developing Others; Provide Consultation and Advice to Others; Performing Administrative Activities; Staffing Organizational Units; Monitoring and Controlling Resources
Job Characteristics: Supervise, Coach, Train Others; Persuade Someone to a Course of Action; Coordinate or Lead Others; Responsibility for Outcomes and Results; Deal with Unpleasant or Angry People; Very Hot; Kneeling, Crouching, or Crawling
GOE Group/s: 03.01.03 Managerial Work: Plants and Animals: Specialty Cropping
CIP Program/s: 010101 Agricultural Business and Management, General; 010102 Agricultural Business/Agribusiness Operations; 010104 Farm and Ranch Management; 010601 Horticulture Services Operations and Management, General; 010604 Greenhouse Operations and Management; 010606 Nursery Operations and Management; 020401 Plant Sciences, General; 020403 Horticulture Science
Related DOT Job/s: 180.117-010 MANAGER, CHRISTMAS-TREE FARM; 180.161-014 SUPERINTENDENT, HORTICULTURE; 180.167-042 MANAGER, NURSERY

15032 LAWN SERVICE MANAGERS. OOH Title/s: Nursery and Greenhouse Managers; Blue Collar Worker Supervisors
Plan, organize, direct, control, and coordinate activities of workers engaged in pruning trees and shrubs, cultivating lawns, and applying pesticides and other chemicals, according to service contract specifications. Work may involve reviewing contracts to ascertain service, machine, and workforce requirements; answering inquiries from potential customers regarding methods, material, and price ranges; and preparing service estimates according to labor, material, and machine costs. Supervises workers who provide groundskeeping services on a contract basis. Reviews contracts to ascertain service, machine, and workforce requirements for job. Answers customers' questions about groundskeeping care requirements. Prepares service cost estimates for customers. Schedules work for crew according to weather conditions, availability of equipment, and seasonal limitations. Investigates customer complaints. Spot-checks completed work to improve quality of service and to ensure contract compliance. Suggests changes in work procedures and orders corrective work done. Prepares work activity and personnel reports.
Yearly Earnings: $37,076
Education: Work experience, plus degree
Knowledge: Administration and Management; Economics and Accounting; Sales and Marketing; Customer and Personal Service; Personnel and Human Resources
Abilities: None above average
Skills: Coordination; Negotiation; Implementation Planning; Identifying Downstream Consequences; Time Management; Management of Financial Resources; Management of Personnel Resources
General Work Activities: Scheduling Work and Activities; Establishing and Maintaining Relationships; Selling or Influencing Others; Resolving Conflicts, Negotiating with Others; Coordinating Work and Activities of Others; Developing and Building Teams; Guiding, Directing and Motivating Subordinates; Coaching and Developing Others; Staffing Organizational Units; Monitoring and Controlling Resources
Job Characteristics: Supervise, Coach, Train Others; Provide a Service to Others; Deal with External Customers; Coordinate or Lead Others; Responsibility for Outcomes and Results; Very Hot; Extremely Bright or Inadequate Lighting
GOE Group/s: 03.02.03 General Supervision: Plants and Animals: Nursery and Groundskeeping
CIP Program/s: 010601 Horticulture Services Operations and Management, General; 010603 Ornamental Horticulture Operations and Management; 010607 Turf Management
Related DOT Job/s: 408.131-010 SUPERVISOR, SPRAY, LAWN AND TREE SERVICE

Executives

19005A GOVERNMENT SERVICE EXECUTIVES. OOH Title/s: General Managers and Top Executives; Health Services Managers
Determine and formulate policies and provide overall direction of federal, state, local, or international government activities. Plan, direct, and coordinate operational activities at the highest level of management with the help of subordinate managers. Directs organization charged with administering and monitoring regulated activities to interpret and clarify laws and to ensure compliance with laws. Administers, interprets, and explains policies, rules, regulations, and laws to organizations and individuals under authority of commission or applicable legislation. Develops, plans, organizes, and

administers policies and procedures for organization to ensure that administrative and operational objectives are met. Directs and coordinates activities of workers in public organization to ensure continuing operations, maximize returns on investments, and increase productivity. Prepares budget and directs and monitors expenditures of department funds. Directs and conducts studies and research, and prepares reports and other publications relating to operational trends and program objectives and accomplishments. Consults with staff and others in government, business, and private organizations to discuss issues, coordinate activities, and resolve problems. Negotiates contracts and agreements with federal and state agencies and other organizations, and prepares budget for funding and implementation of programs. Evaluates findings of investigations, surveys, and studies to formulate policies and techniques and recommend improvements for personnel actions, programs, or business services. Implements corrective action plan to solve problems. Directs, coordinates, and conducts activities between United States government and foreign entities to provide information to promote international interest and harmony. Reviews and analyzes legislation, laws, and public policy, and recommends changes to promote and support interests of general population, as well as special groups. Prepares, reviews, and submits reports concerning activities, expenses, budget, government statutes and rulings, and other items affecting business or program services. Develops, directs, and coordinates testing, hiring, training, and evaluation of staff personnel. Conducts or directs investigations or hearings to resolve complaints and violations of laws. Establishes and maintains comprehensive and current recordkeeping system of activities and operational procedures in business office. Plans, promotes, organizes, and coordinates public community service program and maintains cooperative working relationships among public and agency participants. Delivers speeches, writes articles, and presents information for organization at meetings or conventions to promote services, exchange ideas, and accomplish objectives. Participates in activities to promote business and expand services, and provides technical assistance in conducting of conferences, seminars, and workshops. Testifies in court, before control or review board, or at legislature.

Yearly Earnings: $37,024

Education: Work experience, plus degree

Knowledge: Administration and Management; Clerical; Economics and Accounting; Sales and Marketing; Customer and Personal Service; Personnel and Human Resources; Mathematics; Psychology; Sociology and Anthropology; Geography; Education and Training; English Language; Foreign Language; History and Archeology; Philosophy and Theology; Public Safety and Security; Law, Government, and Jurisprudence; Communications and Media

Abilities: Oral Comprehension; Written Comprehension; Oral Expression; Written Expression; Fluency of Ideas; Originality; Problem Sensitivity; Deductive Reasoning; Inductive Reasoning; Information Ordering; Category Flexibility; Mathematical Reasoning; Number Facility; Memorization; Speed of Closure; Flexibility of Closure; Time Sharing; Near Vision; Speech Recognition; Speech Clarity

Skills: Reading Comprehension; Active Listening; Writing; Speaking; Mathematics; Critical Thinking; Active Learning; Learning Strategies; Monitoring; Social Perceptiveness; Coordination; Persuasion; Negotiation; Instructing; Service Orientation; Problem Identification; Information Gathering; Information Organization; Synthesis/Reorganization; Idea Generation; Idea Evaluation; Implementation Planning; Solution Appraisal; Operations Analysis; Visioning; Systems Perception; Identifying Downstream Consequences; Identification of Key Causes; Judgment and Decision Making; Systems Evaluation; Time Management; Management of Financial Resources; Management of Material Resources; Management of Personnel Resources

General Work Activities: Getting Information Needed to Do the Job; Monitoring Processes, Material, or Surroundings; Identifying Objects, Actions, and Events; Estimating Needed Characteristics; Judging Qualities of Things, Services, People; Processing Information; Evaluating Information against Standards; Analyzing Data or Information; Making Decisions and Solving Problems; Thinking Creatively; Updating and Using Job-Relevant Knowledge; Developing Objectives and Strategies; Scheduling Work and Activities; Organizing, Planning, and Prioritizing; Operating Vehicles or Equipment; Implementing Ideas, Programs, etc.; Documenting/Recording Information; Interpreting Meaning of Information to Others; Communicating with Other Workers; Communicating with Persons Outside Organization; Establishing and Maintaining Relationships; Selling or Influencing Others; Resolving Conflicts, Negotiating with Others; Performing for or Working with Public; Coordinating Work and Activities of Others; Developing and Building Teams; Teaching Others; Guiding, Directing and Motivating Subordinates; Coaching and Developing Others; Provide Consultation and Advice to Others; Performing Administrative Activities; Staffing Organizational Units; Monitoring and Controlling Resources

Job Characteristics: Objective or Subjective Information; Job-Required Social Interaction; Supervise, Coach, Train Others; Persuade Someone to a Course of Action; Take a Position Opposed to Others; Deal with External Customers; Coordinate or Lead Others; Responsibility for Outcomes and Results; Frequency in Conflict Situations; Deal with Unpleasant or Angry People; Sitting; Frustrating Circumstances

GOE Group/s: 03.01.02 Managerial Work: Plants and Animals: Specialty Breeding; 04.01.01 Safety and Law Enforcement: Managing; 04.01.02 Safety and Law Enforcement: Investigating; 05.02.01 Managerial Work: Mechanical: Systems; 05.02.02 Managerial Work: Mechanical: Maintenance and Construction; 11.01.02 Mathematics and Statistics: Data Analysis; 11.05.03 Business Administration: Management Services: Government; 11.07.01 Services Administration: Social Services; 11.07.02 Services Administration: Health and Safety Services; 11.07.03 Services Administration: Education Services; 11.07.04 Services Administration: Recreation Services; 11.09.03 Promotion: Public Relations; 11.10.01 Regulations Enforcement: Finance; 11.10.02 Regulations Enforcement: Individual Rights; 11.10.03 Regulations Enforcement: Health and Safety; 11.10.04 Regulations Enforcement: Immigration and Customs

CIP Program/s: 020401 Plant Sciences, General; 020409 Range Science and Management; 030101 Natural Resources Conservation, General; 030102 Environmental Science/Studies; 030203 Natural Resources Law Enforcement and Protective Services; 030601 Wildlife and Wildlands Management; 080705 General Retailing Operations; 310301 Parks, Recreation and Leisure Facilities Management; 420601 Counseling Psychology; 430102 Corrections/Correctional Administration; 430103 Criminal Justice/Law Enforcement Administration; 430107 Law Enforcement/Police Science; 430202 Fire Services Administration; 440201 Community Organization, Resources and Services; 440401 Public Administration; 450601 Economics, General; 450604 Development Economics and International Development; 450605 International Economics; 450901 International Relations and Affairs; 500701 Art, General; 500704 Arts Management; 510301 Community Health Liaison; 511501 Alcohol/Drug Abuse Counseling; 512202 Environmental Health; 520201 Business Administration and Management, General; 520901 Hospitality/Administration Management

Related DOT Job/s: 050.117-010 DIRECTOR, EMPLOYMENT RESEARCH AND PLANNING; 079.167-010 COMMUNITY-SERVICES-AND-HEALTH-EDUCATION OFFICER; 137.137-010 DIRECTOR, TRANSLATION; 168.167-090 MANAGER, REGULATED PROGRAM; 169.117-010 EXECUTIVE SECRETARY, STATE BOARD OF NURSING; 185.167-062 SUPERVISOR, LIQUOR STORES AND AGENCIES; 186.117-022 DEPUTY INSURANCE COMMISSIONER; 187.117-018 DIRECTOR,

INSTITUTION; 187.117-054 SUPERINTENDENT, RECREATION; 188.117-014 BUSINESS-ENTERPRISE OFFICER; 188.117-018 CHIEF, FISHERY DIVISION; 188.117-022 CIVIL PREPAREDNESS OFFICER; 188.117-026 COMMISSIONER, CONSERVATION OF RESOURCES; 188.117-030 COMMISSIONER, PUBLIC WORKS; 188.117-034 DIRECTOR, AERONAUTICS COMMISSION; 188.117-038 DIRECTOR, AGRICULTURAL SERVICES; 188.117-042 DIRECTOR, ARTS-AND-HUMANITIES COUNCIL; 188.117-046 DIRECTOR, COMPLIANCE; 188.117-050 DIRECTOR, CONSUMER AFFAIRS; 188.117-054 DIRECTOR, CORRECTIONAL AGENCY; 188.117-058 DIRECTOR, COUNCIL ON AGING; 188.117-062 DIRECTOR, FIELD REPRESENTATIVES; 188.117-066 DIRECTOR, LABOR STANDARDS; 188.117-070 DIRECTOR, LAW ENFORCEMENT; 188.117-074 DIRECTOR, LICENSING AND REGISTRATION; 188.117-078 DIRECTOR, EMPLOYMENT SERVICES; 188.117-082 DIRECTOR, MEDICAL FACILITIES SECTION; 188.117-090 DIRECTOR, REVENUE; 188.117-094 DIRECTOR, UNEMPLOYMENT INSURANCE; 188.117-098 DISTRICT CUSTOMS DIRECTOR; 188.117-102 ECONOMIC DEVELOPMENT COORDINATOR; 188.117-106 FOREIGN-SERVICE OFFICER; 188.117-110 HOUSING-MANAGEMENT OFFICER; 188.117-114 MANAGER, CITY; 188.117-118 POLICE COMMISSIONER I; 188.117-126 WELFARE DIRECTOR; 188.117-134 DIRECTOR, REGULATORY AGENCY; 188.137-010 SUPERVISOR; 188.167-014 ASSESSOR-COLLECTOR, IRRIGATION TAX; 188.167-018 CHIEF WARDEN; 188.167-022 DIRECTOR OF VITAL STATISTICS; 188.167-026 DIRECTOR, CLASSIFICATION AND TREATMENT; 188.167-030 DIRECTOR, FINANCIAL RESPONSIBILITY DIVISION; 188.167-034 DIRECTOR, SAFETY COUNCIL; 188.167-042 DIRECTOR, STATE-ASSESSED PROPERTIES; 188.167-046 DISTRICT CUSTOMS DIRECTOR, DEPUTY; 188.167-050 ELECTION ASSISTANT; 188.167-054 FEDERAL AID COORDINATOR; 188.167-058 MANAGER, OFFICE; 188.167-062 PARK SUPERINTENDENT; 188.167-070 RELOCATION COMMISSIONER; 188.167-078 ROADS SUPERVISOR; 188.167-082 SECRETARY OF STATE; 188.167-098 SUPERINTENDENT, SANITATION; 188.167-102 TRAFFIC-SAFETY ADMINISTRATOR; 195.167-042 ALCOHOL-AND-DRUG-ABUSE-ASSISTANCE PROGRAM ADMINISTRATOR; 199.167-022 ENVIRONMENTAL ANALYST; 373.117-010 FIRE CHIEF; 375.117-010 POLICE CHIEF; 375.167-026 HARBOR MASTER; 379.137-018 WILDLIFE AGENT, REGIONAL

19005B PRIVATE SECTOR EXECUTIVES. OOH

Title/s: General Managers and Top Executives; Financial Managers; Retail Sales Worker Supervisors and Managers

Determine and formulate policies and business strategies, and provide overall direction of private sector organizations. Plan, direct, and coordinate operational activities at the highest level of management, with the help of subordinate managers. Directs, plans, and implements policies and objectives of organization or business in accordance with charter and board of directors. Directs activities of organization to plan procedures, establish responsibilities, and coordinate functions among departments and sites. Confers with board members, organization officials, and staff members to establish policies and formulate plans. Analyzes operations to evaluate performance of company and staff and to determine areas of cost reduction and program improvement. Reviews financial statements and sales and activity reports to ensure that organization's objectives are achieved. Directs and coordinates organization's financial and budget activities to fund operations, maximize investments, and increase efficiency. Assigns or delegates responsibilities to subordinates. Directs and coordinates activities of business or department concerned with production, pricing, sales, and/or distribution of products. Directs and coordinates activities of business involved with buying and selling investment products and financial services. Directs nonmerchandising departments of business, such as advertising, purchasing, credit, and accounting. Establishes internal control procedures. Prepares reports and budgets. Presides over or serves on board of directors, management committees, or other governing boards. Negotiates or approves contracts with suppliers and distributors, and with maintenance, janitorial, and security providers. Promotes objectives of institution or business before associations, public, government agencies, or community groups. Screens, selects, hires, transfers, and discharges employees. Administers program for selection of sites, construction of buildings, and provision of equipment and supplies. Directs in-service training of staff.

Yearly Earnings: $39,936

Education: Work experience, plus degree

Knowledge: Administration and Management; Economics and Accounting; Sales and Marketing; Customer and Personal Service; Personnel and Human Resources; Production and Processing; Food Production; Engineering and Technology; Building and Construction; Mathematics; Psychology; Sociology and Anthropology; Geography; Therapy and Counseling; Education and Training; English Language; Foreign Language; History and Archeology; Philosophy and Theology; Public Safety and Security; Law, Government, and Jurisprudence; Communications and Media; Transportation

Abilities: Oral Comprehension; Written Comprehension; Oral Expression; Written Expression; Fluency of Ideas; Originality; Problem Sensitivity; Deductive Reasoning; Inductive Reasoning; Information Ordering; Category Flexibility; Mathematical Reasoning; Number Facility; Memorization; Speed of Closure; Perceptual Speed; Selective Attention; Time Sharing; Near Vision; Auditory Attention; Speech Recognition; Speech Clarity

Skills: Reading Comprehension; Active Listening; Writing; Speaking; Mathematics; Critical Thinking; Active Learning; Learning Strategies; Monitoring; Social Perceptiveness; Coordination; Persuasion; Negotiation; Service Orientation; Problem Identification; Information Gathering; Information Organization; Synthesis/Reorganization; Idea Generation; Idea Evaluation; Implementation Planning; Solution Appraisal; Operations Analysis; Visioning; Systems Perception; Identifying Downstream Consequences; Identification of Key Causes; Judgment and Decision Making; Systems Evaluation; Time Management; Management of Financial Resources; Management of Material Resources; Management of Personnel Resources

General Work Activities: Getting Information Needed to Do the Job; Monitoring Processes, Material, or Surroundings; Identifying Objects, Actions, and Events; Estimating Needed Characteristics; Judging Qualities of Things, Services, People; Processing Information; Evaluating Information against Standards; Analyzing Data or Information; Making Decisions and Solving Problems; Thinking Creatively; Updating and Using Job-Relevant Knowledge; Developing Objectives and Strategies; Scheduling Work and Activities; Organizing, Planning, and Prioritizing; Operating Vehicles or Equipment; Implementing Ideas, Programs, etc.; Documenting/Recording Information; Interpreting Meaning of Information to Others; Communicating with Other Workers; Communicating with Persons Outside Organization; Establishing and Maintaining Relationships; Selling or Influencing Others; Resolving Conflicts, Negotiating with Others; Performing for or Working with Public; Coordinating Work and Activities of Others; Developing and Building Teams; Teaching Others; Guiding, Directing and Motivating Subordinates; Coaching and Developing Others; Provide Consultation and Advice to Others; Performing Administrative Activities; Staffing Organizational Units; Monitoring and Controlling Resources

Job Characteristics: Objective or Subjective Information; Job-Required Social Interaction; Supervise, Coach, Train Others; Persuade Someone to a Course of Action; Take a Position Opposed to Others; Coordinate or Lead Others; Responsibility for Outcomes and Results; Frequency in Conflict Situations; Deal with Unpleasant or Angry People; Sitting; Consequence of Error; Frustrating Circumstances; Degree of Automation; Importance of Being Sure All is Done

GOE Group/s: 11.05.01 Business Administration: Management Services: Non-Government; 11.05.02 Business Administration: Administrative Specialization; 11.05.04 Business Administration: Sales and Purchasing Management; 11.07.03 Services Administration: Education Services
CIP Program/s: 080705 General Retailing Operations; 130101 Education, General; 130401 Education Administration and Supervision, General; 130405 Elementary, Middle and Secondary Education Administration; 130406 Higher Education Administration; 130407 Community and Junior College Administration; 520201 Business Administration and Management, General; 520701 Enterprise Management and Operation, General; 520801 Finance, General; 520807 Investments and Securities
Related DOT Job/s: 090.117-034 PRESIDENT, EDUCATIONAL INSTITUTION; 099.117-022 SUPERINTENDENT, SCHOOLS; 137.137-010 ; 185.117-010 MANAGER, DEPARTMENT STORE; 186.117-034 MANAGER, BROKERAGE OFFICE; 186.117-054 PRESIDENT, FINANCIAL INSTITUTION; 187.167-074 MANAGER, CEMETERY; 189.117-022 MANAGER, INDUSTRIAL ORGANIZATION; 189.117-026 PRESIDENT; 189.117-034 VICE PRESIDENT; 189.117-038 USER REPRESENTATIVE, INTERNATIONAL ACCOUNTING; 189.117-046 MANAGER, BAKERY; 189.167-022 MANAGER, DEPARTMENT; 189.167-030 PROGRAM MANAGER

Services Managers

19999A AMUSEMENT AND RECREATION ESTABLISHMENT MANAGERS. OOH Title/s: Hotel Managers and Assistants; Recreation Workers

Plan, direct, and coordinate the activities of organizations that provide amusement or recreational facilities or services to the public. Plans, organizes, and coordinates programs of recreational activities, entertainment, or instructional classes. Formulates and establishes operational policies, such as hours of operation, fee amounts, and accounting procedures. Determines work activities necessary to operate facility, and assigns duties to staff accordingly. Prepares, compiles, and maintains budgets, schedules of activities or personnel, and inventory or accounting records. Hires, promotes, and discharges workers. Enforces laws, safety regulations, and establishment rules concerning personnel or patron behavior. Purchases or orders supplies and equipment. Confers with patrons or employees to resolve grievances or work problems. Trains staff or instructs patrons in recreational activities, such as swimming, skating, dancing, riding animals, or shooting firearms. Inspects facilities for cleanliness, maintenance needs, or compliance with health and safety regulations. Plans and initiates promotional projects and writes materials to publicize and advertise recreational facilities and activities. Advises patrons of available facilities and activities and registers them for rental of facility or equipment, or for particular activity. Collects fees and issues receipts to patrons for use of facilities or participation in activities. Sells recreational supplies and equipment or lessons to patrons.
Yearly Earnings: $37,076
Education: Work experience, plus degree
Knowledge: Administration and Management; Economics and Accounting; Sales and Marketing; Customer and Personal Service; Personnel and Human Resources; Education and Training; Public Safety and Security; Law, Government, and Jurisprudence
Abilities: Fluency of Ideas; Originality; Number Facility; Perceptual Speed; Gross Body Equilibrium; Far Vision
Skills: Social Perceptiveness; Negotiation; Instructing; Problem Identification; Idea Generation; Equipment Selection; Time Management; Management of Financial Resources; Management of Material Resources; Management of Personnel Resources
General Work Activities: Estimating Needed Characteristics; Developing Objectives and Strategies; Scheduling Work and Activities; Organizing, Planning, and Prioritizing; Communicating with Other Workers; Communicating with Persons Outside Organization; Establishing and Maintaining Relationships; Selling or Influencing Others; Resolving Conflicts, Negotiating with Others; Performing for or Working with Public; Coordinating Work and Activities of Others; Developing and Building Teams; Teaching Others; Guiding, Directing and Motivating Subordinates; Coaching and Developing Others; Performing Administrative Activities; Staffing Organizational Units; Monitoring and Controlling Resources
Job Characteristics: Objective or Subjective Information; Job-Required Social Interaction; Supervise, Coach, Train Others; Persuade Someone to a Course of Action; Deal with External Customers; Coordinate or Lead Others; Responsibility for Outcomes and Results
GOE Group/s: 01.05.01 Performing Arts:Dance: Instructing and Choreography; 11.07.04 Services Administration: Recreation Services; 11.11.02 Business Management: Recreation and Amusement; 11.11.04 Business Management: Services
CIP Program/s: 080705 General Retailing Operations; 080901 Hospitality and Recreation Marketing Operations, General; 080903 Recreation Products/Services Marketing Operations; 310301 Parks, Recreation and Leisure Facilities Management; 500201 Crafts, Folk Art and Artisanry; 520201 Business Administration and Management, General; 520901 Hospitality/Administration Management
Related DOT Job/s: 153.137-010 MANAGER, POOL; 187.117-034 GENERAL MANAGER, ROAD PRODUCTION; 187.117-042 MANAGER, RECREATION ESTABLISHMENT; 187.161-014 MANAGER, HANDICRAFT-OR-HOBBY SHOP; 187.167-054 MANAGER, AQUATIC FACILITY; 187.167-086 MANAGER, DANCE STUDIO; 187.167-094 MANAGER, DUDE RANCH; 187.167-102 MANAGER, FISH-AND-GAME CLUB; 187.167-114 MANAGER, GOLF CLUB; 187.167-118 MANAGER, GUN CLUB; 187.167-122 MANAGER, HOTEL RECREATIONAL FACILITIES; 187.167-146 MANAGER, SKATING RINK; 187.167-154 MANAGER, THEATER; 187.167-166 MANAGER, WINTER SPORTS; 187.167-202 DIRECTOR, CRAFT CENTER; 187.167-222 MANAGER, BOWLING ALLEY; 187.167-230 MANAGER, RECREATION FACILITY; 195.167-018 DIRECTOR, CAMP; 329.161-010 MANAGER, CAMP; 349.224-010 ANIMAL-RIDE MANAGER; 359.137-010 SUPERVISOR, HOSPITALITY HOUSE; 969.137-014 SUPERVISOR, SHOW OPERATIONS

19999B SOCIAL AND COMMUNITY SERVICE MANAGERS. OOH Title/s: Social Workers; General Managers and Top Executives

Plan, organize, and coordinate the activities of a social service program or community outreach organization. Oversee the program or organization's budget and policies regarding participant involvement, program requirements, and benefits. Work may involve directing social workers, counselors, or probation officers. Confers and consults with individuals, groups, and committees to determine needs and to plan, implement, and extend organization's programs and services. Determines organizational policies and defines scope of services offered and administration of procedures. Establishes and maintains relationships with other agencies and organizations in community to meet and not duplicate community needs and services. Assigns duties to staff or volunteers. Plans, directs, and prepares fundraising activities and public relations materials. Researches and analyzes member or community needs as basis for community development. Participates in program activities to serve clients of agency. Prepares, distributes, and maintains records and reports, such as budgets, personnel records, or training manuals. Coordinates volunteer service programs, such as Red Cross, hospital volunteers, or vocational training for disabled individuals. Speaks to community

groups to explain and interpret agency purpose, programs, and policies. Advises volunteers and volunteer leaders to ensure quality of programs and effective use of resources. Instructs and trains agency staff or volunteers in skills required to provide services. Interviews, recruits, or hires volunteers and staff. Observes workers to evaluate performance and ensure that work meets established standards.
Yearly Earnings: $37,076
Education: Work experience, plus degree
Knowledge: Administration and Management; Economics and Accounting; Customer and Personal Service; Personnel and Human Resources; Sociology and Anthropology; Education and Training; English Language; Communications and Media
Abilities: Written Comprehension; Written Expression; Fluency of Ideas; Originality; Category Flexibility; Mathematical Reasoning; Perceptual Speed; Selective Attention; Speech Clarity
Skills: Speaking; Learning Strategies; Social Perceptiveness; Coordination; Persuasion; Negotiation; Instructing; Service Orientation; Problem Identification; Idea Generation; Implementation Planning; Visioning; Identification of Key Causes; Time Management; Management of Financial Resources; Management of Material Resources; Management of Personnel Resources
General Work Activities: Getting Information Needed to Do the Job; Monitoring Processes, Material, or Surroundings; Identifying Objects, Actions, and Events; Estimating Needed Characteristics; Judging Qualities of Things, Services, People; Processing Information; Evaluating Information against Standards; Analyzing Data or Information; Making Decisions and Solving Problems; Thinking Creatively; Developing Objectives and Strategies; Scheduling Work and Activities; Organizing, Planning, and Prioritizing; Operating Vehicles or Equipment; Implementing Ideas, Programs, etc.; Documenting/Recording Information; Interpreting Meaning of Information to Others; Communicating with Other Workers; Communicating with Persons Outside Organization; Establishing and Maintaining Relationships; Assisting and Caring for Others; Selling or Influencing Others; Resolving Conflicts, Negotiating with Others; Performing for or Working with Public; Coordinating Work and Activities of Others; Developing and Building Teams; Teaching Others; Guiding, Directing and Motivating Subordinates; Coaching and Developing Others; Provide Consultation and Advice to Others; Performing Administrative Activities; Staffing Organizational Units; Monitoring and Controlling Resources
Job Characteristics: Objective or Subjective Information; Job-Required Social Interaction; Supervise, Coach, Train Others; Persuade Someone to a Course of Action; Take a Position Opposed to Others; Deal with External Customers; Coordinate or Lead Others; Responsibility for Outcomes and Results; Sitting; Frustrating Circumstances
GOE Group/s: 11.07.01 Services Administration: Social Services; 11.07.02 Services Administration: Health and Safety Services
CIP Program/s: 440201 Community Organization, Resources and Services; 440401 Public Administration; 440701 Social Work; 510701 Health System/Health Services Administration; 510702 Hospital/Health Facilities Administration; 511602 Nursing Administration (Post-R.N.); 520201 Business Administration and Management, General
Related DOT Job/s: 187.117-022 DISTRICT ADVISER; 187.117-026 EXECUTIVE DIRECTOR, SHELTERED WORKSHOP; 187.117-046 PROGRAM DIRECTOR, GROUP WORK; 187.117-066 EXECUTIVE DIRECTOR, RED CROSS; 187.167-022 COORDINATOR, VOLUNTEER SERVICES; 187.167-038 DIRECTOR, VOLUNTEER SERVICES; 187.167-214 DIRECTOR, SERVICE; 187.167-234 DIRECTOR, COMMUNITY ORGANIZATION; 195.117-010 ADMINISTRATOR, SOCIAL WELFARE; 195.167-022 DIRECTOR, FIELD; 195.167-038 REHABILITATION CENTER MANAGER

19999C ASSOCIATION MANAGERS AND ADMINISTRATORS. OOH Title/s: General Managers and Top Executives

Direct and coordinate activities of professional, trade, or business associations to achieve goals, objectives, and standards of association. Coordinates committees or board of directors of association to evaluate services, recommend new programs, or promote association. Plans, directs, or participates in preparation and presentation of educational material to membership or public using various media. Plans, develops, and implements new programs and ideas based on evaluation of current programs. Directs and coordinates association functions, such as conventions, exhibits, and local or regional workshops or meetings. Directs surveys and compilation of membership data, such as average income, benefits, standards, or common problems. Advises chapters, members, or businesses of association regarding financial, organizational, growth, or membership problems. Analyzes factors affecting association, members, or member organizations, such as legislation and taxation or economic conditions and trends. Prepares monthly or annual budget reports and oversees finances of association. Represents association at public, social, or business receptions, or in negotiations with representatives of government, business, or labor organizations. Visits members or chapters of association to ensure association standards are being met and to promote goodwill.
Yearly Earnings: $37,076
Education: Work experience, plus degree
Knowledge: Administration and Management; Economics and Accounting; Mathematics; Education and Training
Abilities: Oral Comprehension; Written Comprehension; Oral Expression; Written Expression; Originality; Deductive Reasoning; Inductive Reasoning; Information Ordering; Category Flexibility; Mathematical Reasoning; Number Facility; Memorization; Near Vision; Speech Recognition; Speech Clarity
Skills: Writing; Speaking; Mathematics; Critical Thinking; Learning Strategies; Monitoring; Social Perceptiveness; Coordination; Persuasion; Negotiation; Instructing; Problem Identification; Information Gathering; Idea Generation; Idea Evaluation; Implementation Planning; Solution Appraisal; Programming; Visioning; Systems Perception; Identifying Downstream Consequences; Identification of Key Causes; Judgment and Decision Making; Systems Evaluation; Management of Financial Resources; Management of Personnel Resources
General Work Activities: Getting Information Needed to Do the Job; Monitoring Processes, Material, or Surroundings; Estimating Needed Characteristics; Judging Qualities of Things, Services, People; Processing Information; Evaluating Information against Standards; Analyzing Data or Information; Making Decisions and Solving Problems; Thinking Creatively; Updating and Using Job-Relevant Knowledge; Developing Objectives and Strategies; Scheduling Work and Activities; Organizing, Planning, and Prioritizing; Interpreting Meaning of Information to Others; Communicating with Other Workers; Communicating with Persons Outside Organization; Establishing and Maintaining Relationships; Selling or Influencing Others; Resolving Conflicts, Negotiating with Others; Performing for or Working with Public; Coordinating Work and Activities of Others; Developing and Building Teams; Teaching Others; Guiding, Directing and Motivating Subordinates; Coaching and Developing Others; Provide Consultation and Advice to Others; Performing Administrative Activities; Staffing Organizational Units; Monitoring and Controlling Resources
Job Characteristics: Objective or Subjective Information; Job-Required Social Interaction; Supervise, Coach, Train Others; Persuade Someone to a Course of Action; Take a Position Opposed to Others; Deal with External Customers; Coordinate or Lead Others; Responsibility for Outcomes and Results; Sitting; Frustrating Circumstances

GOE Group/s: 11.05.01 Business Administration: Management Services: Non-Government; 11.05.02 Business Administration: Administrative Specialization
CIP Program/s: 511602 Nursing Administration (Post-R.N.); 520201 Business Administration and Management, General
Related DOT Job/s: 075.117-034 EXECUTIVE DIRECTOR, NURSES' ASSOCIATION; 187.117-030 EXECUTIVE VICE PRESIDENT, CHAMBER OF COMMERCE; 187.167-018 BUSINESS REPRESENTATIVE, LABOR UNION; 187.167-042 DIVISION MANAGER, CHAMBER OF COMMERCE; 189.117-010 ASSOCIATION EXECUTIVE; 189.167-026 MEMBERSHIP DIRECTOR

19999D SERVICE ESTABLISHMENT MANAGERS. OOH Title/s: General Managers and Top Executives

Manage service establishment or direct and coordinate service activities within an establishment. Plan, direct, and coordinate service operations within an organization, or the activities of organizations that provide services. Directs worker activities in service establishments, such as travel agencies, health clubs, or beauty salons, or in customer service departments. Plans and adjusts work schedule and assigns duties to meet customer demands. Coordinates sales promotion activities and sells services to clients. Communicates with customer to ascertain needs, advise on services, adjust complaints, or negotiate contracts. Keeps records of work hours, labor costs, expenditures, receipts, and materials used, to analyze and prepare operation reports or budget. Observes worker performance and reviews employees' work to ensure accuracy or quality of work. Interviews and hires personnel. Orients and trains new personnel in job duties, safety and health rules, company policies, and performance requirements. Confers with employees to give performance feedback, assist with providing services, and solve problems. Transfers or discharges employees, according to work performance. Requisitions or purchases equipment or supplies to enable establishment to provide services.
Yearly Earnings: $37,076
Education: Work experience, plus degree
Knowledge: Administration and Management; Economics and Accounting; Sales and Marketing; Customer and Personal Service; Personnel and Human Resources; Education and Training
Abilities: Number Facility; Perceptual Speed; Time Sharing; Far Vision; Sound Localization
Skills: Speaking; Social Perceptiveness; Persuasion; Negotiation; Instructing; Service Orientation; Idea Generation; Implementation Planning; Systems Perception; Identification of Key Causes; Time Management; Management of Financial Resources; Management of Material Resources; Management of Personnel Resources
General Work Activities: Judging Qualities of Things, Services, People; Scheduling Work and Activities; Organizing, Planning, and Prioritizing; Communicating with Other Workers; Communicating with Persons Outside Organization; Establishing and Maintaining Relationships; Selling or Influencing Others; Resolving Conflicts, Negotiating with Others; Performing for or Working with Public; Coordinating Work and Activities of Others; Developing and Building Teams; Teaching Others; Guiding, Directing and Motivating Subordinates; Coaching and Developing Others; Performing Administrative Activities; Staffing Organizational Units; Monitoring and Controlling Resources
Job Characteristics: Objective or Subjective Information; Job-Required Social Interaction; Supervise, Coach, Train Others; Persuade Someone to a Course of Action; Provide a Service to Others; Deal with External Customers; Coordinate or Lead Others; Responsibility for Outcomes and Results; Frequency in Conflict Situations; Deal with Unpleasant or Angry People; Sitting; Frustrating Circumstances
GOE Group/s: 05.02.07 Managerial Work: Mechanical: Materials Handling; 05.10.02 Crafts: Mechanical; 11.11.04 Business Management: Services; 11.11.05 Business Management: Wholesale-Retail
CIP Program/s: 010201 Agricultural Mechanization, General; 081105 Travel Services Marketing Operations; 200301 Clothing, Apparel and Textile Workers and Managers, General; 200309 Drycleaner and Launderer (Commercial); 520903 Travel-Tourism Management
Related DOT Job/s: 183.167-030 SERVICE SUPERVISOR, LEASED MACHINERY AND EQUIPMENT; 187.167-058 MANAGER, BARBER OR BEAUTY SHOP; 187.167-082 MANAGER, CUSTOMER SERVICES; 187.167-158 MANAGER, TRAVEL AGENCY; 187.167-194 SUPERINTENDENT, LAUNDRY; 187.167-226 MANAGER, MARINA DRY DOCK; 339.137-010 MANAGER, HEALTH CLUB; 389.134-010 SUPERVISOR, EXTERMINATION

19999E GAMBLING ESTABLISHMENT MANAGERS. OOH Title/s: General Managers and Top Executives

Plan, direct, and coordinate the activities of organizations or establishments, such as casinos, cardrooms, and racetracks, that provide gambling or games-of-chance activities to the public. Review operational expenses, budget estimates, betting accounts, and collection reports for accuracy. Observes and supervises operation to ensure that employees render prompt and courteous service to patrons. Establishes policies on types of gambling offered, odds, extension of credit, and serving food and beverages. Directs workers compiling summary sheets for each race or event to show amount wagered and amount to be paid to winners. Prepares work schedules, assigns work stations, and keeps attendance records. Resolves customer complaints regarding service. Interviews and hires workers. Trains new workers and evaluates their performance. Explains and interprets house rules, such as game rules and betting limits, to patrons. Records, issues receipts for, and pays off bets.
Yearly Earnings: $37,076
Education: Work experience, plus degree
Knowledge: Administration and Management; Economics and Accounting; Customer and Personal Service; Personnel and Human Resources; Mathematics
Abilities: Mathematical Reasoning; Number Facility; Time Sharing
Skills: Speaking; Critical Thinking; Monitoring; Social Perceptiveness; Negotiation; Instructing; Service Orientation; Idea Generation; Identifying Downstream Consequences; Identification of Key Causes; Time Management; Management of Financial Resources; Management of Material Resources; Management of Personnel Resources
General Work Activities: Processing Information; Developing Objectives and Strategies; Scheduling Work and Activities; Organizing, Planning, and Prioritizing; Communicating with Other Workers; Establishing and Maintaining Relationships; Selling or Influencing Others; Resolving Conflicts, Negotiating with Others; Performing for or Working with Public; Coordinating Work and Activities of Others; Developing and Building Teams; Guiding, Directing and Motivating Subordinates; Coaching and Developing Others; Performing Administrative Activities; Staffing Organizational Units; Monitoring and Controlling Resources
Job Characteristics: Objective or Subjective Information; Job-Required Social Interaction; Supervise, Coach, Train Others; Deal with External Customers; Coordinate or Lead Others; Responsibility for Outcomes and Results
GOE Group/s: 07.03.01 Financial Detail: Paying and Receiving; 11.06.03 Finance: Risk and Profit Analysis; 11.11.02 Business Management: Recreation and Amusement
CIP Program/s: 520201 Business Administration and Management, General; 520901 Hospitality/Administration Management

Related DOT Job/s: 187.167-014 BOOKMAKER; 187.167-070 MANAGER, CASINO; 187.167-134 MANAGER, MUTUEL DEPARTMENT; 343.137-010 MANAGER, CARDROOM; 343.137-014 SUPERVISOR, CARDROOM

19999F SECURITY MANAGERS. OOH Title/s: Private Detectives and Investigators; General Managers and Top Executives

Plan, direct, and coordinate implementation of security procedures, systems, and personnel to protect private or public property and personnel from theft, fire, and personal injury. Inspects premises to determine security needs, test alarm systems and safety equipment, or detect safety hazards. Analyzes security needs; plans and directs implementation of security measures, such as security or safety systems; and estimates costs of operation. Develops and establishes security procedures for establishment or for protection of individual, group, or property. Confers with management to determine need for programs and to formulate and coordinate security programs with establishment activities. Directs activities of personnel in developing, revising, or updating company security measures, to comply with federal regulations. Confers with client regarding security needs, evaluation of services, or problems with security systems. Assigns workers to shifts, posts, or patrol, according to protection requirements or size and nature of establishment. Interviews and hires security workers. Observes workers' performance of duties to evaluate efficiency and to detect and correct inefficient or improper work practices. Trains workers in security operations, such as first aid, fire safety, and detecting and apprehending intruders or shoplifters. Conducts background investigations of job applicants or employees to obtain information such as personal histories, character references, or wage garnishments. Monitors or supervises monitoring of alarm system controls and investigation of alarm signals. Conducts or directs surveillance of premises or suspects. Interprets company policies and procedures for workers. Studies federal security regulations, and consults with federal representatives for interpretation or application of particular regulations to company operations. Responds to calls from subordinates to direct activities during fires, storms, riots, and other emergencies. Prepares reports concerning investigations, security needs and recommendations, or security manual of procedures. Investigates crimes committed against client or establishment, such as fraud, robbery, arson, or patent infringement. Confers and cooperates with police, fire, and civil defense authorities to coordinate activities during emergency. Contacts business establishments to promote sales of security services.
Yearly Earnings: $37,076
Education: Work experience, plus degree
Knowledge: Administration and Management; Sales and Marketing; Customer and Personal Service; Personnel and Human Resources; Education and Training; Public Safety and Security; Law, Government, and Jurisprudence
Abilities: Written Comprehension; Fluency of Ideas; Deductive Reasoning; Inductive Reasoning; Speed of Closure; Flexibility of Closure; Perceptual Speed; Spatial Orientation; Selective Attention; Time Sharing; Response Orientation; Rate Control; Reaction Time; Gross Body Equilibrium; Near Vision; Far Vision; Night Vision; Peripheral Vision; Hearing Sensitivity; Auditory Attention; Sound Localization
Skills: Critical Thinking; Active Learning; Learning Strategies; Coordination; Persuasion; Negotiation; Instructing; Problem Identification; Information Gathering; Idea Generation; Idea Evaluation; Implementation Planning; Solution Appraisal; Operations Analysis; Equipment Selection; Visioning; Identifying Downstream Consequences; Identification of Key Causes; Systems Evaluation; Time Management; Management of Financial Resources; Management of Material Resources; Management of Personnel Resources
General Work Activities: Getting Information Needed to Do the Job; Monitoring Processes, Material, or Surroundings; Estimating Needed Characteristics; Judging Qualities of Things, Services, People; Processing Information; Analyzing Data or Information; Making Decisions and Solving Problems; Thinking Creatively; Developing Objectives and Strategies; Scheduling Work and Activities; Organizing, Planning, and Prioritizing; Interpreting Meaning of Information to Others; Communicating with Other Workers; Communicating with Persons Outside Organization; Establishing and Maintaining Relationships; Assisting and Caring for Others; Selling or Influencing Others; Resolving Conflicts, Negotiating with Others; Performing for or Working with Public; Coordinating Work and Activities of Others; Developing and Building Teams; Teaching Others; Guiding, Directing and Motivating Subordinates; Coaching and Developing Others; Provide Consultation and Advice to Others; Performing Administrative Activities; Staffing Organizational Units; Monitoring and Controlling Resources
Job Characteristics: Job-Required Social Interaction; Supervise, Coach, Train Others; Persuade Someone to a Course of Action; Provide a Service to Others; Deal with External Customers; Coordinate or Lead Others; Responsible for Others' Health and Safety; Responsibility for Outcomes and Results; Frequency in Conflict Situations; Deal with Unpleasant or Angry People; Deal with Physical, Aggressive People; Special Uniform; Specialized Protective or Safety Attire; Consequence of Error; Frustrating Circumstances; Importance of Being Sure All is Done; Importance of Being Aware of New Events
GOE Group/s: 11.05.02 Business Administration: Administrative Specialization
CIP Program/s: 430109 Security and Loss Prevention Services
Related DOT Job/s: 189.167-034 SECURITY OFFICER; 189.167-050 SUPERINTENDENT, PLANT PROTECTION; 189.167-054 SECURITY CONSULTANT; 372.167-014 GUARD, CHIEF; 372.167-022 MANAGER, ARMORED TRANSPORT SERVICE; 376.137-010 MANAGER, INTERNAL SECURITY; 379.137-022 SUPERVISOR, PROTECTIVE-SIGNAL OPERATIONS

19999G ALL OTHER MANAGERS AND ADMINISTRATORS. OOH Title/s: Engineering, Science, and Data Processing Managers; Retail Sales Worker Supervisors and Managers

All other managers and administrators not classified separately above.
Yearly Earnings: $37,076
Education: Work experience, plus degree
GOE Group/s: 11.05.02 Business Administration: Administrative Specialization
CIP Program/s: 080705 General Retailing Operations; 520201 Business Administration and Management, General
Related DOT Job/s: 181.167-010 MANAGER, FIELD PARTY, GEOPHYSICAL PROSPECTING; 189.117-014 DIRECTOR, RESEARCH AND DEVELOPMENT; 189.117-030 PROJECT DIRECTOR; 189.117-042 DIRECTOR, QUALITY ASSURANCE; 189.167-018 MANAGEMENT TRAINEE; 199.267-034 RESEARCH ASSISTANT II

Section 2
Professional and Support Specialists—Financial Specialists, Engineers, Scientists, Mathematicians, Social Scientists, Social Services Workers, Religious Workers, and Legal Workers

Financial Specialists

21102 UNDERWRITERS. OOH Title/s: Underwriters

Review individual applications for insurance to evaluate degree of risk involved and determine acceptance of applications. Examines documents to determine degree of risk from such factors as applicant financial standing and value and condition of property. Evaluates possibility of losses due to catastrophe or excessive insurance. Declines excessive risks. Authorizes reinsurance of policy when risk is high. Decreases value of policy when risk is substandard, and specifies applicable endorsements or applies rating to ensure safe, profitable distribution of risks, using reference materials. Reviews company records to determine amount of insurance in force on single risk or group of closely related risks. Writes to field representatives, medical personnel, and others to obtain further information, quote rates, or explain company underwriting policies.

Yearly Earnings: $30,992
Education: Bachelor's degree
Knowledge: Clerical; Economics and Accounting; Mathematics
Abilities: Written Comprehension; Mathematical Reasoning
Skills: Mathematics; Critical Thinking; Information Gathering; Judgment and Decision Making; Systems Evaluation
General Work Activities: Getting Information Needed to Do the Job; Monitoring Processes, Material, or Surroundings; Judging Qualities of Things, Services, People; Processing Information; Evaluating Information against Standards; Making Decisions and Solving Problems
Job Characteristics: Sitting
GOE Group/s: 11.06.03 Finance: Risk and Profit Analysis
CIP Program/s: 520801 Finance, General; 520805 Insurance and Risk Management
Related DOT Job/s: 169.267-046 UNDERWRITER

21105 CREDIT ANALYSTS. OOH Title/s: Loan Officers and Counselors

Analyze current credit data and financial statements of individuals or firms to determine the degree of risk involved in extending credit or lending money. Prepare reports with this credit information for use in decision making. Analyzes credit data and financial statements to determine degree of risk involved in extending credit or lending money. Generates financial ratios, using computer program, to evaluate customer's financial status. Analyzes financial data, such as income growth, quality of management, and market share, to determine profitability of loan. Compares liquidity, profitability, and credit history with similar establishments of same industry and geographic location. Evaluates customer records and recommends payment plan based on earnings, savings data, payment history, and purchase activity. Completes loan application, including credit analysis and summary of loan request, and submits to loan committee for approval. Confers with credit association and other business representatives to exchange credit information. Reviews individual or commercial customer files to identify and select delinquent accounts for collection. Consults with customers to resolve complaints and verify financial and credit transactions, and adjusts accounts as needed.

Yearly Earnings: $33,020
Education: Bachelor's degree
Knowledge: Economics and Accounting; Personnel and Human Resources; Computers and Electronics; Mathematics; Geography; History and Archeology; Philosophy and Theology; Law, Government, and Jurisprudence
Abilities: Deductive Reasoning; Mathematical Reasoning; Number Facility; Near Vision; Speech Recognition
Skills: Active Listening; Speaking; Mathematics; Critical Thinking; Active Learning; Monitoring; Negotiation; Service Orientation; Problem Identification; Information Gathering; Information Organization; Idea Evaluation; Solution Appraisal; Programming; Systems Perception; Identifying Downstream Consequences; Identification of Key Causes; Judgment and Decision Making; Systems Evaluation; Management of Financial Resources
General Work Activities: Evaluating Information against Standards; Operating Vehicles or Equipment; Performing Administrative Activities
Job Characteristics: Persuade Someone to a Course of Action; Take a Position Opposed to Others; Frequency in Conflict Situations; Deal with Unpleasant or Angry People; Sitting; Frustrating Circumstances
GOE Group/s: 07.01.04 Administrative Detail: Financial Work; 11.06.03 Finance: Risk and Profit Analysis
CIP Program/s: 520801 Finance, General; 520803 Banking and Financial Support Services
Related DOT Job/s: 160.267-022 CREDIT ANALYST; 186.267-022 LOAN REVIEW ANALYST; 241.267-022 CREDIT ANALYST

21108 LOAN OFFICERS AND COUNSELORS. OOH Title/s: Loan Officers and Counselors

Evaluate, authorize, or recommend approval of commercial, real estate, or credit loans. Advise borrowers on financial status and methods of payments. Include mortgage loan officers or agents, collection analysts, and loan servicing officers. Analyzes applicant financial status, credit, and property evaluation to determine feasibility of granting loan. Approves loan within specified limits. Refers loan to loan committee for approval. Evaluates acceptability of loan to corporations that buy real estate loans on secondary mortgage markets. Interviews applicant and requests specified information for loan application. Contacts applicant or creditors to resolve questions regarding application information. Ensures loan agreements are complete and accurate according to policy. Computes payment schedule. Submits application to credit analyst for verification and recommendation. Petitions court to transfer title and deeds of collateral to bank. Confers with underwriters to aid in resolving mortgage application problems. Analyzes potential loan markets to develop prospects for loans. Arranges for maintenance and liquidation of delinquent property. Contacts customers to arrange payment of delinquent loan balances. Supervises loan personnel.

Yearly Earnings: $33,020
Education: Bachelor's degree
Knowledge: Clerical; Economics and Accounting; Sales and Marketing; Customer and Personal Service; Personnel and Human Resources; Mathematics; Law, Government, and Jurisprudence; Communications and Media
Abilities: Oral Comprehension; Written Comprehension; Oral Expression; Written Expression; Problem Sensitivity; Deductive Reasoning; Inductive Reasoning; Information Ordering; Category Flexibility; Mathematical Reasoning; Number Facility; Memorization; Near Vision; Speech Recognition; Speech Clarity
Skills: Active Listening; Speaking; Information Gathering; Judgment and Decision Making; Management of Personnel Resources
General Work Activities: Getting Information Needed to Do the Job; Monitoring Processes, Material, or Surroundings; Judging Qualities of Things, Services, People; Processing Information; Evaluating Information against Standards; Analyzing Data or Information; Making Decisions and Solving Problems; Scheduling Work and Activities; Operating Vehicles or Equipment; Documenting/Recording Information; Interpreting Meaning of Information to Others; Communicating with Other Workers; Communicating with Persons Outside Organization; Establishing and Maintaining Relationships; Selling or Influencing Others; Resolving Conflicts, Negotiating with Others; Performing

for or Working with Public; Coordinating Work and Activities of Others; Developing and Building Teams; Guiding, Directing and Motivating Subordinates; Coaching and Developing Others; Provide Consultation and Advice to Others; Performing Administrative Activities; Staffing Organizational Units; Monitoring and Controlling Resources
Job Characteristics: Supervise, Coach, Train Others; Provide a Service to Others; Deal with External Customers; Responsibility for Outcomes and Results; Frequency in Conflict Situations; Deal with Unpleasant or Angry People; Sitting
GOE Group/s: 11.05.02 Business Administration: Administrative Specialization; 11.06.03 Finance: Risk and Profit Analysis
CIP Program/s: 080401 Financial Services Marketing Operations; 520801 Finance, General; 520803 Banking and Financial Support Services; 520806 International Finance
Related DOT Job/s: 186.167-078 COMMERCIAL LOAN COLLECTION OFFICER; 186.267-018 LOAN OFFICER; 186.267-026 UNDERWRITER, MORTGAGE LOAN

21111 TAX PREPARERS. OOH Title/s: Bookkeeping, Accounting, and Auditing Clerks

Prepare tax returns for individuals or small businesses, but do not have the background or responsibilities of an accredited accountant or certified public accountant. May work for established tax return firm. Reviews financial records, such as income statements and documentation of expenditures, to determine forms needed to prepare return. Computes taxes owed, using adding machine, and completes entries on forms, following tax form instructions and tax tables. Consults tax law handbook or bulletins to determine procedure for preparation of atypical returns. Interviews client to obtain additional information on taxable income and deductible expenses and allowances. Verifies totals on forms prepared by others to detect errors in arithmetic or procedure, as needed. Calculates form preparation fee according to complexity of return and amount of time required to prepare forms.
Yearly Earnings: $19,500
Education: Moderate-term O-J-T
Knowledge: Clerical; Economics and Accounting; Mathematics; Law, Government, and Jurisprudence
Abilities: Deductive Reasoning; Mathematical Reasoning; Number Facility
Skills: Active Listening; Mathematics
General Work Activities: Processing Information; Evaluating Information against Standards; Performing Administrative Activities
Job Characteristics: Provide a Service to Others; Sitting; Importance of Being Exact or Accurate; Importance of Being Sure All is Done
GOE Group/s: 07.02.02 Mathematical Detail: Accounting
CIP Program/s: 520302 Accounting Technician; 521601 Taxation
Related DOT Job/s: 219.362-070 TAX PREPARER

21114A ACCOUNTANTS. OOH Title/s: Accountants and Auditors

Analyze financial information and prepare financial reports to determine or maintain record of assets, liabilities, profit and loss, tax liability, or other financial activities within an organization. Exclude auditors. Analyzes operations, trends, costs, revenues, financial commitments, and obligations incurred, to project future revenues and expenses, using computer. Develops, maintains, and analyzes budgets, and prepares periodic reports comparing budgeted costs to actual costs. Analyzes records of financial transactions to determine accuracy and completeness of entries, using computer. Prepares balance sheet, profit and loss statement, amortization and depreciation schedules, and other financial reports, using calculator or computer. Reports finances of establishment to management, and advises management about resource utilization, tax strategies, and assumptions underlying budget forecasts. Develops, implements, modifies, and documents budgeting, cost, general, property, and tax accounting systems. Predicts revenues and expenditures, and submits reports to management. Computes taxes owed; ensures compliance with tax payment, reporting, and other tax requirements; and represents establishment before taxing authority. Surveys establishment operations to ascertain accounting needs. Establishes table of accounts, and assigns entries to proper accounts. Audits contracts and prepares reports to substantiate transactions prior to settlement. Prepares forms and manuals for workers performing accounting and bookkeeping tasks. Appraises, evaluates, and inventories real property and equipment, and records description, value, location, and other information. Adapts accounting and recordkeeping functions to current technology of computerized accounting systems. Directs activities of workers performing accounting and bookkeeping tasks.
Yearly Earnings: $31,928
Education: Bachelor's degree
Knowledge: Administration and Management; Clerical; Economics and Accounting; Personnel and Human Resources; Computers and Electronics; Mathematics; Sociology and Anthropology; Education and Training; English Language; Philosophy and Theology; Law, Government, and Jurisprudence
Abilities: Written Comprehension; Written Expression; Fluency of Ideas; Originality; Deductive Reasoning; Mathematical Reasoning; Number Facility; Memorization; Speed of Closure; Flexibility of Closure; Perceptual Speed; Finger Dexterity; Near Vision
Skills: Reading Comprehension; Active Listening; Writing; Speaking; Mathematics; Critical Thinking; Active Learning; Learning Strategies; Monitoring; Persuasion; Negotiation; Instructing; Problem Identification; Information Gathering; Information Organization; Synthesis/Reorganization; Idea Generation; Idea Evaluation; Implementation Planning; Solution Appraisal; Operations Analysis; Equipment Selection; Product Inspection; Visioning; Systems Perception; Identifying Downstream Consequences; Identification of Key Causes; Judgment and Decision Making; Systems Evaluation; Time Management; Management of Financial Resources; Management of Material Resources; Management of Personnel Resources
General Work Activities: Getting Information Needed to Do the Job; Monitoring Processes, Material, or Surroundings; Estimating Needed Characteristics; Judging Qualities of Things, Services, People; Processing Information; Evaluating Information against Standards; Analyzing Data or Information; Making Decisions and Solving Problems; Thinking Creatively; Updating and Using Job-Relevant Knowledge; Developing Objectives and Strategies; Scheduling Work and Activities; Organizing, Planning, and Prioritizing; Operating Vehicles or Equipment; Implementing Ideas, Programs, etc.; Documenting/Recording Information; Interpreting Meaning of Information to Others; Communicating with Other Workers; Communicating with Persons Outside Organization; Coordinating Work and Activities of Others; Guiding, Directing and Motivating Subordinates; Provide Consultation and Advice to Others; Performing Administrative Activities; Monitoring and Controlling Resources
Job Characteristics: Provide a Service to Others; Sitting; Importance of Being Exact or Accurate
GOE Group/s: 11.06.01 Finance: Accounting and Auditing
CIP Program/s: 520301 Accounting
Related DOT Job/s: 160.162-010 ACCOUNTANT, TAX; 160.162-018 ACCOUNTANT; 160.162-022 ACCOUNTANT, BUDGET; 160.162-026 ACCOUNTANT, COST; 160.167-022 ACCOUNTANT, PROPERTY; 160.167-026 ACCOUNTANT, SYSTEMS; 160.167-042 BURSAR

21114B AUDITORS. OOH Title/s: Accountants and Auditors

Examine and analyze accounting records to determine financial status of establishment and prepare financial reports concerning operating procedures. Reviews data about material assets, net worth, liabilities, capital stock, surplus, income, and expenditures. Analyzes annual reports, financial statements, and other records, using accepted accounting and statistical procedures, to determine financial condition. Evaluates reports from commission regarding solvency and profitability of company. Inspects account books and system for efficiency, effectiveness, and use of accepted accounting procedures to record transactions. Inspects cash on hand, notes receivable and payable, negotiable securities, and canceled checks. Reports to management about asset utilization and audit results, and recommends changes in operations and financial activities. Reviews taxpayer accounts, and conducts audits on-site, by correspondence, or by summoning taxpayer to office. Analyzes data for deficient controls, duplicated effort, extravagance, fraud, or noncompliance with laws, regulations, and management policies. Audits records to determine unemployment insurance premiums, liabilities, and compliance with tax laws. Examines payroll and personnel records to determine worker's compensation coverage. Examines records, tax returns, and related documents pertaining to settlement of decedent's estate. Verifies journal and ledger entries by examining inventory. Studies costs and revenue requirements, and designs new rate structure. Confers with company officials about financial and regulatory matters. Evaluates taxpayer finances to determine tax liability, notifies taxpayer of liability, and advises taxpayer of appeal rights. Examines records and interviews workers to ensure recording of transactions and compliance with laws and regulations. Supervises auditing of establishments, and determines scope of investigation required. Prepares and presents testimony to regulatory commission hearings. Directs activities of personnel engaged in filing, recording, compiling, and transmitting financial records.
Yearly Earnings: $31,928
Education: Bachelor's degree
Knowledge: Administration and Management; Clerical; Economics and Accounting; Computers and Electronics; Mathematics; English Language; Philosophy and Theology; Law, Government, and Jurisprudence
Abilities: Written Comprehension; Oral Expression; Written Expression; Problem Sensitivity; Deductive Reasoning; Inductive Reasoning; Mathematical Reasoning; Number Facility; Memorization; Speed of Closure; Flexibility of Closure; Perceptual Speed; Selective Attention; Near Vision
Skills: Reading Comprehension; Active Listening; Writing; Speaking; Mathematics; Critical Thinking; Active Learning; Monitoring; Problem Identification; Information Gathering; Information Organization; Synthesis/Reorganization; Idea Generation; Idea Evaluation; Implementation Planning; Solution Appraisal; Visioning; Systems Perception; Identifying Downstream Consequences; Identification of Key Causes; Judgment and Decision Making; Systems Evaluation; Time Management; Management of Financial Resources; Management of Personnel Resources
General Work Activities: Getting Information Needed to Do the Job; Monitoring Processes, Material, or Surroundings; Estimating Needed Characteristics; Judging Qualities of Things, Services, People; Processing Information; Evaluating Information against Standards; Analyzing Data or Information; Making Decisions and Solving Problems; Updating and Using Job-Relevant Knowledge; Developing Objectives and Strategies; Scheduling Work and Activities; Organizing, Planning, and Prioritizing; Operating Vehicles or Equipment; Documenting/Recording Information; Interpreting Meaning of Information to Others; Communicating with Other Workers; Communicating with Persons Outside Organization; Coordinating Work and Activities of Others; Guiding, Directing and Motivating Subordinates; Provide Consultation and Advice to Others; Performing Administrative Activities; Monitoring and Controlling Resources
Job Characteristics: Supervise, Coach, Train Others; Provide a Service to Others; Deal with External Customers; Coordinate or Lead Others; Responsibility for Outcomes and Results; Frequency in Conflict Situations; Deal with Unpleasant or Angry People; Sitting; Consequence of Error; Importance of Being Exact or Accurate
GOE Group/s: 11.06.01 Finance: Accounting and Auditing; 11.06.03 Finance: Risk and Profit Analysis
CIP Program/s: 520301 Accounting; 520801 Finance, General
Related DOT Job/s: 160.167-030 AUDITOR, COUNTY OR CITY; 160.167-034 AUDITOR, INTERNAL; 160.167-038 AUDITOR, TAX; 160.167-054 AUDITOR; 160.267-014 DIRECTOR, UTILITY ACCOUNTS

21114C DATA PROCESSING AUDITORS. OOH Title/s: Accountants and Auditors

Plan and conduct audits of data processing systems and applications to safeguard assets, ensure accuracy of data, and promote operational efficiency. Gathers data by interviewing workers, examining records, and using computer. Analyzes data to evaluate effectiveness of controls, accuracy of reports, and efficiency and security of operations. Establishes objectives and plan for audit, following general audit plan and previous audit reports. Writes audit report and recommendations, using computer. Devises, writes, and tests computer program to obtain information needed for audit. Devises controls for new or modified computer application, for error detection, and to prevent inaccuracy and data loss.
Yearly Earnings: $31,928
Education: Bachelor's degree
Knowledge: Administration and Management; Clerical; Economics and Accounting; Computers and Electronics; Mathematics; Philosophy and Theology; Telecommunications
Abilities: Written Comprehension; Problem Sensitivity; Information Ordering; Category Flexibility; Speed of Closure; Flexibility of Closure; Perceptual Speed; Wrist-Finger Speed
Skills: Reading Comprehension; Active Listening; Writing; Speaking; Critical Thinking; Active Learning; Learning Strategies; Monitoring; Problem Identification; Information Gathering; Information Organization; Synthesis/Reorganization; Idea Generation; Idea Evaluation; Implementation Planning; Solution Appraisal; Operations Analysis; Technology Design; Equipment Selection; Programming; Testing; Product Inspection; Visioning; Systems Perception; Identifying Downstream Consequences; Identification of Key Causes; Judgment and Decision Making; Systems Evaluation
General Work Activities: Getting Information Needed to Do the Job; Monitoring Processes, Material, or Surroundings; Identifying Objects, Actions, and Events; Judging Qualities of Things, Services, People; Processing Information; Evaluating Information against Standards; Analyzing Data or Information; Making Decisions and Solving Problems; Thinking Creatively; Updating and Using Job-Relevant Knowledge; Developing Objectives and Strategies; Organizing, Planning, and Prioritizing; Operating Vehicles or Equipment; Documenting/Recording Information; Interpreting Meaning of Information to Others; Communicating with Other Workers; Provide Consultation and Advice to Others; Performing Administrative Activities; Monitoring and Controlling Resources
Job Characteristics: Provide a Service to Others; Sitting
GOE Group/s: 11.06.01 Finance: Accounting and Auditing
CIP Program/s: 110201 Computer Programming; 520301 Accounting; 521201 Management Information Systems and Business Data Processing; 521202 Business Computer Programming/Programmer; 521203 Business Systems Analysis and Design

Related DOT Job/s: 160.162-030 AUDITOR, DATA PROCESSING

21117 BUDGET ANALYSTS. OOH Title/s: Budget Analysts

Examine budget estimates for completeness, accuracy, and conformance with procedures and regulations. Examine requests for budget revisions, recommend approval or denial, and draft correspondence. Analyze monthly department budgeting and accounting reports for the purpose of maintaining expenditure controls. Provide technical assistance to officials in the preparation of budgets. Analyzes accounting records to determine financial resources required to implement program, and submits recommendations for budget allocations. Reviews operating budgets periodically to analyze trends affecting budget needs. Analyzes costs in relation to services performed during previous fiscal years to prepare comparative analyses of operating programs. Recommends approval or disapproval of requests for funds. Advises staff on cost analysis and fiscal allocations. Correlates appropriations for specific programs with appropriations for divisional programs, and includes items for emergency funds. Directs preparation of regular and special budget reports to interpret budget directives and to establish policies for carrying out directives. Consults with unit heads to ensure adjustments are made in accordance with program changes to facilitate long-term planning. Directs compilation of data based on statistical studies and analyses of past and current years to prepare budgets. Testifies regarding proposed budgets before examining and fund-granting authorities to clarify reports and gain support for estimated budget needs. Administers personnel functions of budget department, such as training, work scheduling, promotions, transfers, and performance ratings.
Yearly Earnings: $33,020
Education: Bachelor's degree
Knowledge: Administration and Management; Economics and Accounting; Personnel and Human Resources; Computers and Electronics; Mathematics; Education and Training
Abilities: Written Comprehension; Deductive Reasoning; Mathematical Reasoning; Number Facility
Skills: Reading Comprehension; Active Listening; Writing; Speaking; Mathematics; Critical Thinking; Active Learning; Learning Strategies; Monitoring; Coordination; Persuasion; Negotiation; Instructing; Problem Identification; Information Gathering; Information Organization; Synthesis/Reorganization; Idea Generation; Idea Evaluation; Implementation Planning; Solution Appraisal; Visioning; Systems Perception; Identifying Downstream Consequences; Identification of Key Causes; Judgment and Decision Making; Systems Evaluation; Time Management; Management of Financial Resources; Management of Material Resources; Management of Personnel Resources
General Work Activities: Getting Information Needed to Do the Job; Monitoring Processes, Material, or Surroundings; Estimating Needed Characteristics; Judging Qualities of Things, Services, People; Processing Information; Evaluating Information against Standards; Analyzing Data or Information; Making Decisions and Solving Problems; Updating and Using Job-Relevant Knowledge; Developing Objectives and Strategies; Organizing, Planning, and Prioritizing; Documenting/Recording Information; Interpreting Meaning of Information to Others; Communicating with Other Workers; Establishing and Maintaining Relationships; Developing and Building Teams; Teaching Others; Guiding, Directing and Motivating Subordinates; Coaching and Developing Others; Provide Consultation and Advice to Others; Performing Administrative Activities; Staffing Organizational Units; Monitoring and Controlling Resources
Job Characteristics: Consequence of Error; Importance of Being Exact or Accurate; Importance of Being Sure All is Done
GOE Group/s: 11.06.05 Finance: Budget and Financial Control
CIP Program/s: 440401 Public Administration; 520201 Business Administration and Management, General; 520206 Non-Profit and Public Management; 520301 Accounting; 520801 Finance, General; 520808 Public Finance
Related DOT Job/s: 161.117-010 BUDGET OFFICER; 161.267-030 BUDGET ANALYST

21199B FINANCIAL COUNSELORS. OOH Title/s: Indirectly related to Financial Managers

Provide financial counseling to individuals regarding debt management or special financial aid for students. Interviews client with debt problems to determine available monthly income after living expenses to meet credit obligations. Counsels client on financial problems, such as excessive spending and borrowing of funds. Establishes payment priorities to plan payoff method and estimate time for debt liquidation. Explains to individuals and groups financial assistance available to college and university students, such as loans, grants, and scholarships. Calculates amount of debt and funds available. Interviews students to obtain information and compares data on students' applications with eligibility requirements to determine eligibility for assistance program. Determines amount of aid to be granted, considering such factors as funds available, extent of demand, and needs of students. Contacts creditors to arrange for payment adjustments so that payments are feasible for client and agreeable to creditors. Opens account for client and disburses funds from account to creditors as agent for client. Prepares required records and reports. Authorizes release of funds to students. Assists in selection of candidates for specific financial awards or aid.
Yearly Earnings: $37,180
Education: Work experience, plus degree
Knowledge: Economics and Accounting; Customer and Personal Service; Mathematics; Therapy and Counseling
Abilities: Mathematical Reasoning; Number Facility
Skills: Active Listening; Speaking; Service Orientation; Judgment and Decision Making; Management of Financial Resources
General Work Activities: Developing Objectives and Strategies; Communicating with Persons Outside Organization; Establishing and Maintaining Relationships; Assisting and Caring for Others; Selling or Influencing Others; Resolving Conflicts, Negotiating with Others; Performing for or Working with Public; Teaching Others; Coaching and Developing Others; Provide Consultation and Advice to Others; Performing Administrative Activities; Monitoring and Controlling Resources
Job Characteristics: Objective or Subjective Information; Job-Required Social Interaction; Persuade Someone to a Course of Action; Provide a Service to Others; Take a Position Opposed to Others; Deal with External Customers; Frequency in Conflict Situations; Deal with Physical, Aggressive People; Sitting
GOE Group/s: 07.01.01 Administrative Detail: Interviewing
CIP Program/s: 520801 Finance, General; 520804 Financial Planning
Related DOT Job/s: 160.207-010 CREDIT COUNSELOR; 169.267-018 FINANCIAL-AID COUNSELOR

21199D ALL OTHER FINANCIAL SPECIALISTS. OOH Title/s: Indirectly related to Financial Managers

All other financial specialists not classified separately above.
Yearly Earnings: $37,180
Education: Work experience, plus degree
GOE Group/s: 11.06.03 Finance: Risk and Profit Analysis
CIP Program/s: 520801 Finance, General; 520803 Banking and Financial Support Services
Related DOT Job/s: 169.267-042 LETTER-OF-CREDIT DOCUMENT EXAMINER

Purchasers and Buyers

21302 WHOLESALE AND RETAIL BUYERS, EXCEPT FARM PRODUCTS. OOH Title/s: Purchasers and Buyers

Buy merchandise or commodities (other than farm products) for resale to consumers at the wholesale or retail level, including both durable and nondurable goods. Analyze past buying trends, sales records, price, and quality of merchandise to determine value and yield. Select, order, and authorize payment for merchandise according to contractual agreements. May conduct meetings with sales personnel and introduce new products. Include assistant buyers. Selects and orders merchandise from suppliers, or purchases merchandise from other merchants. Obtains and analyzes information about customer needs and preferences. Consults with store or merchandise managers about budget and goods to be purchased. Confers with assistant buyers and sales clerks to determine likes and dislikes of customers. Analyzes sales records to determine what goods are in demand. Examines and selects merchandise at local and remote sites. Inspects, grades, or approves merchandise or products to determine value or yield. Conducts staff meetings with sales personnel to introduce new merchandise. Authorizes payment of invoices or return of merchandise. Sets or recommends mark-up rates and selling prices. Arranges for transportation of purchases. Determines markdowns on slow-selling merchandise. Trains sales personnel and/or assistant buyers. Provides clerks with information, such as price, mark-ups or mark-downs, manufacturer number, season code, and style number, to print on price tags. Approves advertising materials.

Yearly Earnings: $26,624

Education: Bachelor's degree

Knowledge: Administration and Management; Economics and Accounting; Sales and Marketing; Customer and Personal Service; Personnel and Human Resources; Mathematics; Psychology; Sociology and Anthropology; Geography; Education and Training; Foreign Language; Philosophy and Theology; Communications and Media; Transportation

Abilities: Oral Comprehension; Oral Expression; Fluency of Ideas; Originality; Deductive Reasoning; Inductive Reasoning; Category Flexibility; Mathematical Reasoning; Number Facility; Memorization; Speed of Closure; Near Vision; Visual Color Discrimination; Auditory Attention; Speech Recognition

Skills: Active Listening; Speaking; Active Learning; Monitoring; Social Perceptiveness; Persuasion; Negotiation; Instructing; Service Orientation; Information Gathering; Idea Evaluation; Implementation Planning; Solution Appraisal; Operations Analysis; Product Inspection; Systems Perception; Identification of Key Causes; Management of Financial Resources; Management of Material Resources; Management of Personnel Resources

General Work Activities: Estimating Needed Characteristics; Making Decisions and Solving Problems; Developing Objectives and Strategies; Organizing, Planning, and Prioritizing; Communicating with Other Workers; Communicating with Persons Outside Organization; Establishing and Maintaining Relationships; Selling or Influencing Others; Resolving Conflicts, Negotiating with Others; Coordinating Work and Activities of Others; Developing and Building Teams; Teaching Others; Guiding, Directing and Motivating Subordinates; Coaching and Developing Others; Performing Administrative Activities; Staffing Organizational Units; Monitoring and Controlling Resources

Job Characteristics: Objective or Subjective Information; Job-Required Social Interaction; Supervise, Coach, Train Others; Persuade Someone to a Course of Action; Take a Position Opposed to Others; Responsibility for Outcomes and Results; Frequency in Conflict Situations; Deal with Unpleasant or Angry People; Consequence of Error; Frustrating Circumstances; Importance of Being Aware of New Events

GOE Group/s: 08.01.03 Sales Technology: Purchasing and Sales

CIP Program/s: 010501 Agricultural Supplies Retailing and Wholesaling; 080704 General Buying Operations; 080705 General Retailing Operations; 200301 Clothing, Apparel and Textile Workers and Managers, General; 200306 Fashion and Fabric Consultant; 200501 Home Furnishings and Equipment Installers and Consultants, General; 521403 International Business Marketing

Related DOT Job/s: 162.157-018 BUYER; 162.157-022 BUYER, ASSISTANT

21305A PURCHASING AGENTS AND BUYERS, FARM PRODUCTS. OOH Title/s: Purchasers and Buyers

Arrange or contract for the purchase of farm products for further processing or resale. Negotiates contracts with farmers for production or purchase of agricultural products such as milk, grains, and Christmas trees. Arranges sales, loans, or financing for supplies, such as equipment, seed, feed, fertilizer, and chemicals. Reviews orders and determines product types and quantities required to meet demand. Plans and arranges for transportation for crops, milk, or other products to dairy or processing facility. Inspects and tests crops or other farm products to determine quality and to detect evidence of disease or insect damage. Estimates production possibilities by surveying property and studying factors such as history of crop rotation, soil fertility, and irrigation facilities. Maintains records of business transactions. Advises farm groups and growers on land preparation and livestock care to maximize quantity and quality of production. Coordinates and directs activities of workers engaged in cutting, transporting, storing, or milling products, and in maintaining records. Writes articles for publication.

Yearly Earnings: $31,564

Education: Bachelor's degree

Knowledge: Administration and Management; Clerical; Economics and Accounting; Sales and Marketing; Production and Processing; Food Production; Mathematics; Biology; English Language; Communications and Media; Transportation

Abilities: Written Expression; Category Flexibility; Mathematical Reasoning; Number Facility; Memorization; Gross Body Equilibrium; Speech Clarity

Skills: Writing; Speaking; Mathematics; Coordination; Persuasion; Negotiation; Management of Financial Resources; Management of Material Resources

General Work Activities: Inspecting Equipment, Structures, or Material; Estimating Needed Characteristics; Judging Qualities of Things, Services, People; Making Decisions and Solving Problems; Developing Objectives and Strategies; Organizing, Planning, and Prioritizing; Communicating with Persons Outside Organization; Establishing and Maintaining Relationships; Selling or Influencing Others; Resolving Conflicts, Negotiating with Others; Coordinating Work and Activities of Others; Guiding, Directing and Motivating Subordinates; Provide Consultation and Advice to Others; Monitoring and Controlling Resources

Job Characteristics: Persuade Someone to a Course of Action; Take a Position Opposed to Others; Deal with External Customers; Coordinate or Lead Others; Frequency in Conflict Situations; Walking or Running

GOE Group/s: 03.01.01 Managerial Work: Plants and Animals: Farming; 08.01.03 Sales Technology: Purchasing and Sales; 11.05.04 Business Administration: Sales and Purchasing Management

CIP Program/s: 010301 Agricultural Production Workers and Managers, General; 010302 Agricultural Animal Husbandry and Production Management; 010501 Agricultural Supplies Retailing and

Wholesaling; 030401 Forest Harvesting and Production Technologists and Technicians; 080704 General Buying Operations; 080706 General Selling Skills and Sales Operations; 521403 International Business Marketing
Related DOT Job/s: 162.117-010 CHRISTMAS-TREE CONTRACTOR; 162.117-022 FIELD CONTRACTOR; 162.117-026 FIELD-CONTACT TECHNICIAN; 162.167-010 BUYER, GRAIN; 162.167-018 CLEAN-RICE BROKER

21308A PURCHASING AGENTS AND CONTRACT SPECIALISTS. OOH Title/s: Purchasers and Buyers

Coordinate activities involved with procuring goods and services from suppliers. May negotiate with suppliers to draw up procurement contracts and administer, terminate, or renegotiate contracts. Exclude purchasing agents and buyers of farm products. Negotiates or renegotiates and administers contracts with suppliers, vendors, and other representatives. Locates and arranges for purchase of goods and services necessary for efficient operation of organization. Formulates policies and procedures for bid proposals and procurement of goods and services. Analyzes price proposals, financial reports, and other data and information to determine reasonable prices. Prepares purchase orders, or bid proposals and reviews requisitions for goods and services. Directs and coordinates workers' activities involving bid proposals and procurement of goods and services. Evaluates and monitors contract performance to determine need for changes and to ensure compliance with contractual obligations. Arbitrates claims and resolves complaints generated during performance of contract. Maintains and reviews computerized or manual records of items purchased, costs, delivery, product performance, and inventories. Confers with personnel, users, and vendors to discuss defective or unacceptable goods or services, and determines corrective action.
Yearly Earnings: $31,304
Education: Bachelor's degree
Knowledge: Administration and Management; Clerical; Economics and Accounting; Sales and Marketing; Computers and Electronics; Law, Government, and Jurisprudence; Transportation
Abilities: Oral Expression; Mathematical Reasoning
Skills: Reading Comprehension; Active Listening; Writing; Speaking; Mathematics; Critical Thinking; Active Learning; Monitoring; Coordination; Persuasion; Negotiation; Problem Identification; Information Gathering; Synthesis/Reorganization; Idea Generation; Implementation Planning; Identifying Downstream Consequences; Identification of Key Causes; Judgment and Decision Making; Systems Evaluation; Management of Financial Resources; Management of Material Resources
General Work Activities: Monitoring Processes, Material, or Surroundings; Identifying Objects, Actions, and Events; Estimating Needed Characteristics; Judging Qualities of Things, Services, People; Processing Information; Analyzing Data or Information; Making Decisions and Solving Problems; Developing Objectives and Strategies; Organizing, Planning, and Prioritizing; Documenting/Recording Information; Establishing and Maintaining Relationships; Selling or Influencing Others; Resolving Conflicts, Negotiating with Others; Guiding, Directing and Motivating Subordinates; Provide Consultation and Advice to Others; Performing Administrative Activities; Monitoring and Controlling Resources
Job Characteristics: Persuade Someone to a Course of Action; Take a Position Opposed to Others; Frequency in Conflict Situations; Deal with Unpleasant or Angry People; Sitting
GOE Group/s: 08.01.03 Sales Technology: Purchasing and Sales; 11.05.02 Business Administration: Administrative Specialization; 11.05.04 Business Administration: Sales and Purchasing Management; 11.12.04 Contracts and Claims: Procurement Negotiations
CIP Program/s: 010501 Agricultural Supplies Retailing and Wholesaling; 080704 General Buying Operations; 200401 Institutional Food Workers and Administrators, General; 200409 Institutional Food Services Administrator; 520201 Business Administration and Management, General; 520202 Purchasing, Procurement and Contracts Management
Related DOT Job/s: 162.117-018 CONTRACT SPECIALIST; 162.157-030 OUTSIDE PROPERTY AGENT; 162.157-038 PURCHASING AGENT; 163.117-010 MANAGER, CONTRACTS

21308B PROCUREMENT ENGINEERS. OOH Title/s: Purchasers and Buyers

Coordinate the development and use of engineering specifications and requirements to facilitate the procurement of parts, tools, equipment, or other products or materials. Develops and establishes specifications and performance test requirements for equipment to be purchased. Coordinates engineering, tool design, purchasing, and other activities to facilitate production and procurement of tooling. Coordinates procurement and production activities to expedite movement of tools between departments or vendors. Analyzes technical data, designs, preliminary specifications, and availability of parts and equipment. Evaluates tooling orders to determine whether tooling should be manufactured in-house or purchased from outside vendors. Calculates and records tool requirements, and maintains records of procurement, status, and disposition information. Prepares requisitions for tooling purchases, and processes requests for tool repairs. Investigates equipment makers and potential suppliers, and recommends those most desirable. Advises personnel, suppliers, and customers of nature and function of parts and equipment. Arranges conferences between suppliers, engineers, purchasers, inspectors, and other personnel to facilitate procurement process.
Yearly Earnings: $31,304
Education: Bachelor's degree
Knowledge: Administration and Management; Clerical; Economics and Accounting; Sales and Marketing; Production and Processing; Engineering and Technology; Design; Mathematics; Physics
Abilities: Oral Comprehension; Written Comprehension; Written Expression; Mathematical Reasoning; Number Facility; Time Sharing
Skills: Reading Comprehension; Active Listening; Writing; Mathematics; Science; Critical Thinking; Active Learning; Learning Strategies; Monitoring; Coordination; Persuasion; Negotiation; Problem Identification; Information Gathering; Synthesis/Reorganization; Idea Evaluation; Implementation Planning; Solution Appraisal; Operations Analysis; Technology Design; Equipment Selection; Visioning; Identifying Downstream Consequences; Identification of Key Causes; Judgment and Decision Making; Systems Evaluation; Time Management; Management of Financial Resources; Management of Material Resources
General Work Activities: Getting Information Needed to Do the Job; Monitoring Processes, Material, or Surroundings; Estimating Needed Characteristics; Judging Qualities of Things, Services, People; Evaluating Information against Standards; Analyzing Data or Information; Making Decisions and Solving Problems; Updating and Using Job-Relevant Knowledge; Developing Objectives and Strategies; Scheduling Work and Activities; Organizing, Planning, and Prioritizing; Drafting and Specifying Technical Devices, etc.; Documenting/Recording Information; Communicating with Other Workers; Communicating with Persons Outside Organization; Establishing and Maintaining Relationships; Coordinating Work and Activities of Others; Provide Consultation and Advice to Others; Performing Administrative Activities
Job Characteristics: Sitting; Consequence of Error; Importance of Being Sure All is Done

GOE Group/s: 05.02.03 Managerial Work: Mechanical: Processing and Manufacturing; 05.03.03 Engineering Technology: Expediting and Coordinating
CIP Program/s: 140201 Aerospace, Aeronautical and Astronautical Engineering; 520201 Business Administration and Management, General; 520202 Purchasing, Procurement and Contracts Management
Related DOT Job/s: 162.157-034 PROCUREMENT ENGINEER; 169.167-054 TOOLING COORDINATOR, PRODUCTION ENGINEERING

21308C PRICE ANALYSTS. OOH Title/s: Purchasers and Buyers
Compile and analyze statistical data to determine feasibility of buying products and to establish price objectives for contract transactions. Compiles and analyzes statistical data to establish price objectives and to determine purchasing feasibility. Evaluates findings and makes recommendations regarding feasibility of manufacturing or purchasing needed products. Compiles information from periodicals, catalogs, and other sources to keep informed on price trends and manufacturing processes. Determines manufacturing costs within company divisions to obtain data for cost analysis studies. Confers with vendors and analyzes vendors' operations to determine factors that affect prices. Prepares reports, charts, and graphs to track statistical data, price information, and cost analysis findings.
Yearly Earnings: $31,304
Education: Bachelor's degree
Knowledge: Economics and Accounting; Mathematics
Abilities: Written Comprehension; Written Expression; Deductive Reasoning; Mathematical Reasoning; Number Facility
Skills: Reading Comprehension; Writing; Speaking; Mathematics; Critical Thinking; Active Learning; Persuasion; Problem Identification; Information Gathering; Information Organization; Synthesis/Reorganization; Idea Generation; Idea Evaluation; Solution Appraisal; Operations Analysis; Programming; Visioning; Systems Perception; Identifying Downstream Consequences; Identification of Key Causes; Judgment and Decision Making; Systems Evaluation; Management of Financial Resources
General Work Activities: Estimating Needed Characteristics; Judging Qualities of Things, Services, People; Evaluating Information against Standards; Analyzing Data or Information; Making Decisions and Solving Problems; Updating and Using Job-Relevant Knowledge; Developing Objectives and Strategies; Documenting/Recording Information; Interpreting Meaning of Information to Others; Provide Consultation and Advice to Others; Monitoring and Controlling Resources
Job Characteristics: Sitting; Consequence of Error; Importance of Being Exact or Accurate
GOE Group/s: 11.06.03 Finance: Risk and Profit Analysis
CIP Program/s: 520201 Business Administration and Management, General; 520202 Purchasing, Procurement and Contracts Management
Related DOT Job/s: 162.167-030 PURCHASE-PRICE ANALYST

Human Resources Workers

21502 CLAIMS TAKERS, UNEMPLOYMENT BENEFITS. OOH Title/s: Insurance Claims Clerks
Interview unemployed workers and compile data to determine eligibility for unemployment benefits. Interviews claimants returning at specified intervals to certify claimants for continuing benefits. Reviews data on job applications or claim forms to ensure completeness. Assists applicants completing application forms for job referrals or unemployment compensation claims. Answers questions concerning registration for jobs or application for unemployment benefits. Assists applicants in filling out forms, using knowledge of information required or native language of applicant. Schedules unemployment insurance claimants for adjudication interview when question of eligibility arises. Refers applicants to job opening or interview with other staff, in accordance with administrative guidelines or office procedure.
Yearly Earnings: $23,764
Education: Moderate-term O-J-T
Knowledge: Clerical; Customer and Personal Service; Personnel and Human Resources; Therapy and Counseling; Foreign Language
Abilities: None above average
Skills: Speaking; Service Orientation
General Work Activities: Performing for or Working with Public
Job Characteristics: Job-Required Social Interaction; Deal with External Customers; Frequency in Conflict Situations; Deal with Unpleasant or Angry People; Deal with Physical, Aggressive People; Sitting
GOE Group/s: 07.04.01 Oral Communications: Interviewing
CIP Program/s: 440401 Public Administration; 521001 Human Resources Management
Related DOT Job/s: 169.367-010 EMPLOYMENT-AND-CLAIMS AIDE

21505 SPECIAL AGENTS, INSURANCE. OOH Title/s: Public Relations Specialists
Recruit independent insurance sales agents in field and maintain contact between them and home office. Advise agents on matters pertaining to conduct of business, such as cancellations, overdue accounts, technical problems, claims procedures, new business contacts, and new products. May gather information for underwriter. Recruits independent sales agents in field. Maintains contact between agent and home office. Advises agent on matters pertaining to conduct of business, such as cancellations, overdue accounts, and new business prospects. Gathers information for underwriters. Selects and hires sales agents based on selection criteria of company. Drafts contract between agent and company.
Yearly Earnings: $31,200
Education: Long-term O-J-T
Knowledge: Administration and Management; Economics and Accounting; Sales and Marketing; Personnel and Human Resources; Psychology; Geography
Abilities: Written Expression
Skills: Reading Comprehension; Active Listening; Writing; Speaking; Social Perceptiveness; Persuasion; Negotiation; Visioning; Management of Personnel Resources
General Work Activities: Making Decisions and Solving Problems; Communicating with Other Workers; Establishing and Maintaining Relationships; Developing and Building Teams; Coaching and Developing Others; Provide Consultation and Advice to Others; Staffing Organizational Units
Job Characteristics: Supervise, Coach, Train Others; Persuade Someone to a Course of Action; Take a Position Opposed to Others; Coordinate or Lead Others; Sitting
GOE Group/s: 11.05.02 Business Administration: Administrative Specialization
CIP Program/s: 081001 Insurance Marketing Operations; 520801 Finance, General; 520805 Insurance and Risk Management
Related DOT Job/s: 166.167-046 SPECIAL AGENT

21508 EMPLOYMENT INTERVIEWERS, PRIVATE OR PUBLIC EMPLOYMENT SERVICE. OOH Title/s: Employment Interviewers
Interview job applicants in employment office and refer them to prospective employers for consideration. Search application files, notify selected applicants of job openings, and refer qualified applicants to prospective employers. Contact employers to verify referral results. Record and evaluate various pertinent

data. Interviews job applicants to select people meeting employer qualifications. Refers selected applicants to person placing job order, according to policy of organization. Reviews employment applications and evaluates work history, education and training, job skills, compensation needs, and other qualifications of applicants. Records additional knowledge, skills, abilities, interests, test results, and other data pertinent to selection and referral of applicants. Reviews job orders and matches applicants with job requirements, utilizing manual or computerized file search. Informs applicants of job duties and responsibilities, compensation and benefits, work schedules, working conditions, promotional opportunities, and other related information. Keeps records of applicants not selected for employment. Searches for and recruits applicants for open positions. Conducts or arranges for skills, intelligence, or psychological testing of applicants. Performs reference and background checks on applicants. Evaluates selection and testing techniques by conducting research or follow-up activities and conferring with management and supervisory personnel. Contacts employers to solicit orders for job vacancies, and records information on forms to describe duties, hiring requirements, and related data. Refers applicants to vocational counseling services.
Yearly Earnings: $31,772
Education: Bachelor's degree
Knowledge: Administration and Management; Clerical; Sales and Marketing; Customer and Personal Service; Personnel and Human Resources; Psychology; Sociology and Anthropology; Therapy and Counseling
Abilities: Oral Comprehension
Skills: Active Listening; Speaking; Social Perceptiveness; Service Orientation; Idea Generation; Management of Personnel Resources
General Work Activities: Judging Qualities of Things, Services, People; Documenting/Recording Information; Establishing and Maintaining Relationships; Assisting and Caring for Others; Performing for or Working with Public; Staffing Organizational Units
Job Characteristics: Objective or Subjective Information; Deal with External Customers; Sitting; Importance of Being Sure All is Done
GOE Group/s: 11.03.04 Social Research: Occupational
CIP Program/s: 521001 Human Resources Management
Related DOT Job/s: 166.267-010 EMPLOYMENT INTERVIEWER

21511A JOB AND OCCUPATIONAL ANALYSTS. OOH Title/s: Personnel, Training, and Labor Relations Specialists and Managers

Collect, analyze, and classify occupational data to develop job or occupational descriptions or profiles to facilitate personnel management decision making and to develop career information. Analyzes organizational, occupational, and industrial data to facilitate organizational functions and provide technical information to business, industry, and government. Researches job and worker requirements, structural and functional relationships among jobs and occupations, and occupational trends. Observes and interviews employees to collect job, organizational, and occupational information. Prepares reports, such as job descriptions, organization and flow charts, and career path reports, to summarize job analysis information. Consults with business, industry, government, and union officials to arrange for, plan, and design occupational studies and surveys. Prepares research results for publication in form of journals, books, manuals, and film. Determines need for and develops job analysis instruments and materials. Evaluates and improves methods and techniques for selecting, promoting, evaluating, and training workers. Plans and develops curricula and materials for training programs and conducts training.
Yearly Earnings: $31,772
Education: Bachelor's degree
Knowledge: Administration and Management; Clerical; Personnel and Human Resources; Food Production; Computers and Electronics; Mathematics; Psychology; Education and Training; English Language; History and Archeology; Philosophy and Theology; Communications and Media
Abilities: Oral Comprehension; Oral Expression; Written Expression; Originality; Deductive Reasoning; Number Facility; Time Sharing; Near Vision; Night Vision; Auditory Attention; Speech Clarity
Skills: Reading Comprehension; Active Listening; Writing; Speaking; Critical Thinking; Active Learning; Learning Strategies; Monitoring; Social Perceptiveness; Coordination; Persuasion; Negotiation; Instructing; Service Orientation; Information Gathering; Information Organization; Synthesis/Reorganization; Idea Generation; Idea Evaluation; Implementation Planning; Solution Appraisal; Operations Analysis; Programming; Visioning; Systems Perception; Identifying Downstream Consequences; Identification of Key Causes; Systems Evaluation; Management of Personnel Resources
General Work Activities: Getting Information Needed to Do the Job; Monitoring Processes, Material, or Surroundings; Analyzing Data or Information; Organizing, Planning, and Prioritizing; Communicating with Other Workers; Communicating with Persons Outside Organization; Teaching Others; Provide Consultation and Advice to Others
Job Characteristics: Supervise, Coach, Train Others; Sitting
GOE Group/s: 11.03.04 Social Research: Occupational
CIP Program/s: 521001 Human Resources Management
Related DOT Job/s: 166.067-010 OCCUPATIONAL ANALYST; 166.267-018 JOB ANALYST

21511B EMPLOYER RELATIONS AND PLACEMENT SPECIALISTS. OOH Title/s: Personnel, Training, and Labor Relations Specialists and Managers

Develop relationships with employers to facilitate placement of job applicants or students in employment opportunities. Establishes and maintains relationships with employers to determine personnel needs, promote use of service, and monitor progress of placed individuals. Confers with employers to resolve problems relating to employment service effectiveness, employer compliance, and employer recruitment activities. Arranges job interviews for applicants. Receives and records information from employers regarding employment opportunities. Directs and coordinates job placement programs and job analysis services. Conducts surveys of local labor market, and assists employers in revising organizational policies such as job standards and compensation. Promotes, develops, and terminates on-the-job and auxiliary training programs and assists in writing contracts. Instructs applicants in resume writing, job search, and interviewing skills, and conducts in-service training for personnel of placement service. Interviews applicants to determine interests, qualifications, and employment eligibility, and assists in developing employment and curriculum plans. Collects, organizes, and analyzes occupational, educational, and economic information for placement services and to maintain occupational library. Develops placement office procedures, establishes work loads, assigns tasks, and reviews activity reports.
Yearly Earnings: $31,772
Education: Bachelor's degree
Knowledge: Administration and Management; Clerical; Sales and Marketing; Customer and Personal Service; Personnel and Human Resources; Computers and Electronics; Psychology; Sociology and Anthropology; Geography; Therapy and Counseling; Education and Training
Abilities: Oral Expression; Written Expression; Fluency of Ideas; Originality; Deductive Reasoning; Near Vision; Speech Recognition; Speech Clarity
Skills: Active Listening; Writing; Speaking; Critical Thinking; Active Learning; Learning Strategies; Monitoring; Social Perceptiveness; Co-

ordination; Persuasion; Negotiation; Instructing; Service Orientation; Problem Identification; Information Gathering; Information Organization; Synthesis/Reorganization; Idea Generation; Idea Evaluation; Implementation Planning; Solution Appraisal; Operations Analysis; Programming; Visioning; Systems Perception; Identifying Downstream Consequences; Identification of Key Causes; Judgment and Decision Making; Systems Evaluation; Time Management; Management of Financial Resources; Management of Personnel Resources
General Work Activities: Judging Qualities of Things, Services, People; Scheduling Work and Activities; Organizing, Planning, and Prioritizing; Communicating with Other Workers; Communicating with Persons Outside Organization; Establishing and Maintaining Relationships; Assisting and Caring for Others; Selling or Influencing Others; Resolving Conflicts, Negotiating with Others; Coordinating Work and Activities of Others; Developing and Building Teams; Teaching Others; Guiding, Directing and Motivating Subordinates; Coaching and Developing Others; Performing Administrative Activities; Staffing Organizational Units
Job Characteristics: Objective or Subjective Information; Job-Required Social Interaction; Supervise, Coach, Train Others; Persuade Someone to a Course of Action; Coordinate or Lead Others; Responsibility for Outcomes and Results; Frequency in Conflict Situations; Sitting
GOE Group/s: 10.01.02 Social Services: Counseling and Social Work; 11.03.04 Social Research: Occupational; 11.09.03 Promotion: Public Relations
CIP Program/s: 521001 Human Resources Management
Related DOT Job/s: 166.167-014 DIRECTOR OF PLACEMENT; 166.257-010 EMPLOYER RELATIONS REPRESENTATIVE; 166.267-034 JOB DEVELOPMENT SPECIALIST; 187.167-034 DIRECTOR, NURSES' REGISTRY

21511C EMPLOYEE RELATIONS SPECIALISTS.

OOH Title/s: Personnel, Training, and Labor Relations Specialists and Managers

Perform a variety of duties to promote employee welfare, such as resolving human relations problems and promoting employee health and well-being. Interviews workers and discusses with personnel human relations, and work-related problems that adversely affect morale, health, and productivity. Evaluates and resolves human relations, labor relations, and work-related problems, and meets with management to determine appropriate action. Explains and provides advice to workers about company and governmental rules, regulations, and procedures, and need for compliance. Counsels employees regarding work, family, or personal problems. Explains company compensation and benefit programs, such as medical, insurance, retirement, and savings plans, and enrolls workers in specified programs. Arranges for employee library, lunchroom, recreational facilities, and activities. Develops, schedules, and conducts technical, management, and interpersonal skills training to improve employee performance. Prepares newsletter and other reports to communicate information about employee concerns and comments and organizational actions taken. Attends conferences and meetings, as employee-management liaison, to facilitate communication between parties. Prepares reports and enters and updates medical, insurance, retirement, and other personnel forms and records, using computer. Audits benefit accounts and examines records to ensure compliance with standards and regulations. Arranges for employee physical examinations, first aid, and other medical attention. Inspects facilities to determine if lighting, sanitation, and security are adequate and to ensure compliance to standards. Supervises clerical or administrative personnel.
Yearly Earnings: $31,772
Education: Bachelor's degree
Knowledge: Administration and Management; Clerical; Economics and Accounting; Customer and Personal Service; Personnel and Human Resources; Computers and Electronics; Psychology; Sociology and Anthropology; Therapy and Counseling; Education and Training; Law, Government, and Jurisprudence; Communications and Media
Abilities: Oral Expression; Fluency of Ideas; Originality; Near Vision; Auditory Attention; Speech Clarity
Skills: Reading Comprehension; Active Listening; Writing; Speaking; Critical Thinking; Active Learning; Learning Strategies; Monitoring; Social Perceptiveness; Coordination; Persuasion; Negotiation; Instructing; Service Orientation; Problem Identification; Information Organization; Idea Generation; Idea Evaluation; Implementation Planning; Solution Appraisal; Operations Analysis; Programming; Visioning; Systems Perception; Identifying Downstream Consequences; Identification of Key Causes; Systems Evaluation; Time Management; Management of Financial Resources; Management of Material Resources; Management of Personnel Resources
General Work Activities: Getting Information Needed to Do the Job; Judging Qualities of Things, Services, People; Processing Information; Scheduling Work and Activities; Organizing, Planning, and Prioritizing; Operating Vehicles or Equipment; Interpreting Meaning of Information to Others; Communicating with Other Workers; Establishing and Maintaining Relationships; Assisting and Caring for Others; Resolving Conflicts, Negotiating with Others; Developing and Building Teams; Teaching Others; Guiding, Directing and Motivating Subordinates; Coaching and Developing Others; Provide Consultation and Advice to Others; Performing Administrative Activities
Job Characteristics: Objective or Subjective Information; Job-Required Social Interaction; Supervise, Coach, Train Others; Persuade Someone to a Course of Action; Take a Position Opposed to Others; Coordinate or Lead Others; Responsibility for Outcomes and Results; Frequency in Conflict Situations; Deal with Unpleasant or Angry People; Sitting; Frustrating Circumstances
GOE Group/s: 07.01.01 Administrative Detail: Interviewing; 11.02.02 Educational and Library Services: Teaching, Vocational and Industrial; 11.03.04 Social Research: Occupational; 11.05.02 Business Administration: Administrative Specialization; 11.10.03 Regulations Enforcement: Health and Safety
CIP Program/s: 521001 Human Resources Management; 521002 Labor/Personnel Relations and Studies; 521003 Organizational Behavior Studies
Related DOT Job/s: 166.117-014 MANAGER, EMPLOYEE WELFARE; 166.167-042 SENIOR ENLISTED ADVISOR; 166.267-030 RETIREMENT OFFICER; 166.267-042 EMPLOYEE RELATIONS SPECIALIST; 166.267-046 HUMAN RESOURCE ADVISOR

21511D EMPLOYEE TRAINING SPECIALISTS. OOH Title/s: Personnel, Training, and Labor Relations Specialists and Managers; Education Administrators; Public Relations Specialists

Coordinate and conduct employee training programs to train new and existing employees how to perform required work, improve work methods, or comply with policies, procedures, or regulations. Develops and conducts orientation and training for employees or customers of industrial or commercial establishment. Confers with managers, instructors, or customer representatives of industrial or commercial establishment to determine training needs. Evaluates training materials, such as outlines, text, and handouts, prepared by instructors. Assigns instructors to conduct training and assists them in obtaining required training materials. Schedules classes based on availability of classrooms, equipment, and instructors. Coordinates recruitment and placement of participants in skill training. Organizes and develops training procedure manuals and guides. Attends meetings and seminars to obtain information useful to train staff and to inform management of training programs and goals. Maintains records and writes reports to monitor and evaluate training activities and program effectiveness. Supervises instructors, monitors and evaluates instructor performance, and refers instructors to classes for skill development. Monitors training costs to ensure budget is not exceeded, and prepares budget report to justify expenditures. Refers trainees with social problems to appropriate service agency. Screens, hires, and assigns workers to positions based on qualifications.

Yearly Earnings: $31,772

Education: Bachelor's degree

Knowledge: Administration and Management; Clerical; Economics and Accounting; Sales and Marketing; Customer and Personal Service; Personnel and Human Resources; Psychology; Sociology and Anthropology; Therapy and Counseling; Education and Training; Foreign Language; Communications and Media

Abilities: Oral Expression; Written Expression; Fluency of Ideas; Originality; Mathematical Reasoning; Selective Attention; Wrist-Finger Speed; Near Vision; Far Vision; Night Vision; Speech Recognition; Speech Clarity

Skills: Active Listening; Writing; Speaking; Active Learning; Learning Strategies; Monitoring; Social Perceptiveness; Coordination; Persuasion; Negotiation; Instructing; Service Orientation; Problem Identification; Information Gathering; Information Organization; Idea Generation; Idea Evaluation; Implementation Planning; Solution Appraisal; Operations Analysis; Programming; Visioning; Systems Perception; Identifying Downstream Consequences; Identification of Key Causes; Judgment and Decision Making; Systems Evaluation; Time Management; Management of Financial Resources; Management of Material Resources; Management of Personnel Resources

General Work Activities: Thinking Creatively; Developing Objectives and Strategies; Scheduling Work and Activities; Communicating with Other Workers; Communicating with Persons Outside Organization; Establishing and Maintaining Relationships; Resolving Conflicts, Negotiating with Others; Coordinating Work and Activities of Others; Developing and Building Teams; Teaching Others; Guiding, Directing and Motivating Subordinates; Coaching and Developing Others; Provide Consultation and Advice to Others; Staffing Organizational Units; Monitoring and Controlling Resources

Job Characteristics: Objective or Subjective Information; Job-Required Social Interaction; Supervise, Coach, Train Others; Take a Position Opposed to Others; Coordinate or Lead Others; Responsibility for Outcomes and Results; Frustrating Circumstances

GOE Group/s: 07.01.02 Administrative Detail: Administration; 10.02.01 Nursing, Therapy, and Specialized Teaching Services: Nursing; 11.07.03 Services Administration: Education Services; 11.11.03 Business Management: Transportation

CIP Program/s: 130401 Education Administration and Supervision, General; 130403 Adult and Continuing Education Administration; 440401 Public Administration; 521001 Human Resources Management

Related DOT Job/s: 079.127-010 INSERVICE COORDINATOR, AUXILIARY PERSONNEL; 166.167-038 PORT PURSER; 166.167-054 TECHNICAL TRAINING COORDINATOR; 169.167-062 COORDINATOR, SKILL-TRAINING PROGRAM; 239.137-010 COMMERCIAL-INSTRUCTOR SUPERVISOR

21511E PERSONNEL RECRUITERS. OOH Title/s: Personnel, Training, and Labor Relations Specialists and Managers; Clerical Supervisors and Managers

Seek out, interview, and screen applicants to fill existing and future job openings and promote career opportunities within organization. Interviews applicants to obtain work history, training, education, job skills, and other background information. Provides potential applicants with information regarding facilities, operations, benefits, and job or career opportunities in organization. Conducts reference and background checks on applicants. Contacts college representatives to arrange for and schedule on-campus interviews with students. Reviews and evaluates applicant qualifications or eligibility for specified licensing, according to established guidelines and designated licensing codes. Notifies applicants by mail or telephone to inform them of employment possibilities, consideration, and selection. Hires or refers applicants to other hiring personnel in organization. Arranges for interviews and travel and lodging for selected applicants at company expense. Evaluates recruitment and selection criteria to ensure conformance to professional, statistical, and testing standards, and recommends revision as needed. Assists and advises establishment management in organizing, preparing, and implementing recruiting and retention programs. Speaks to civic, social, and other groups to provide information concerning job possibilities and career opportunities. Prepares and maintains employment records and authorizes paperwork assigning applicant to positions. Corrects and scores portions of examinations used to screen and select applicants. Projects yearly recruitment expenditures for budgetary consideration and control.

Yearly Earnings: $31,772

Education: Bachelor's degree

Knowledge: Administration and Management; Clerical; Sales and Marketing; Personnel and Human Resources; Computers and Electronics; Psychology; Philosophy and Theology; Law, Government, and Jurisprudence

Abilities: Originality; Mathematical Reasoning; Number Facility; Time Sharing; Auditory Attention; Speech Recognition; Speech Clarity

Skills: Active Listening; Writing; Speaking; Learning Strategies; Monitoring; Social Perceptiveness; Persuasion; Negotiation; Instructing; Service Orientation; Information Organization; Idea Generation; Idea Evaluation; Implementation Planning; Visioning; Identifying Downstream Consequences; Judgment and Decision Making; Systems Evaluation; Management of Financial Resources; Management of Personnel Resources

General Work Activities: Judging Qualities of Things, Services, People; Communicating with Persons Outside Organization; Staffing Organizational Units; Monitoring and Controlling Resources

Job Characteristics: Objective or Subjective Information; Job-Required Social Interaction; Persuade Someone to a Course of Action; Sitting

GOE Group/s: 11.03.04 Social Research: Occupational

CIP Program/s: 130101 Education, General; 130401 Education Administration and Supervision, General; 130405 Elementary, Middle and Secondary Education Administration; 130601 Educational Evaluation and Research; 130603 Educational Statistics and Research Methods; 130604 Educational Assessment, Testing and Measurement; 521001 Human Resources Management

Related DOT Job/s: 099.167-010 CERTIFICATION AND SELECTION SPECIALIST; 166.267-026 RECRUITER; 166.267-038 PERSONNEL RECRUITER; 205.367-050 SUPERVISOR, CONTINGENTS

21511F LABOR RELATIONS SPECIALISTS. OOH Title/s: Personnel, Training, and Labor Relations Specialists and Managers

Mediate, arbitrate, and conciliate disputes over negotiations of labor agreements or labor relations disputes. Conducts arbitration hearings concerning disputes over negotiations of labor contracts and agreements between labor and management. Mediates and assists disagreeing parties to compromise or otherwise negotiate on agreement regarding dispute. Renders decision to settle dispute, protect public interests, prevent employee wage loss, and minimize business interruptions, and issues report concerning settlement. Interrogates parties and

clarifies problems to focus discussion on crucial points of disagreement. Investigates labor disputes upon request of bona fide party, following labor laws, industry practices, and labor relations social policies. Analyzes information to evaluate contentions of parties regarding disputed contract provisions. Promotes use of fact-finding, mediation, conciliation, and advisory services to prevent or resolve labor disputes and maintain labor relations. Prepares and issues reports regarding results of arbitration, decisions reached, or outcomes of negotiations. Conducts representation elections and oversees balloting procedures according to written consent agreement of concerned parties in labor dispute.
Yearly Earnings: $31,772
Education: Bachelor's degree
Knowledge: Administration and Management; Customer and Personal Service; Personnel and Human Resources; Psychology; Law, Government, and Jurisprudence
Abilities: Oral Comprehension; Written Comprehension; Oral Expression; Written Expression; Fluency of Ideas; Originality; Problem Sensitivity; Deductive Reasoning; Inductive Reasoning; Speed of Closure; Selective Attention; Near Vision; Auditory Attention; Speech Recognition; Speech Clarity
Skills: Active Listening; Writing; Speaking; Critical Thinking; Active Learning; Learning Strategies; Monitoring; Social Perceptiveness; Coordination; Persuasion; Negotiation; Service Orientation; Problem Identification; Information Gathering; Information Organization; Synthesis/Reorganization; Idea Generation; Idea Evaluation; Implementation Planning; Solution Appraisal; Visioning; Systems Perception; Identifying Downstream Consequences; Identification of Key Causes; Judgment and Decision Making; Systems Evaluation; Management of Financial Resources; Management of Personnel Resources
General Work Activities: Getting Information Needed to Do the Job; Processing Information; Analyzing Data or Information; Making Decisions and Solving Problems; Thinking Creatively; Updating and Using Job-Relevant Knowledge; Developing Objectives and Strategies; Organizing, Planning, and Prioritizing; Communicating with Other Workers; Communicating with Persons Outside Organization; Establishing and Maintaining Relationships; Selling or Influencing Others; Resolving Conflicts, Negotiating with Others; Developing and Building Teams; Provide Consultation and Advice to Others
Job Characteristics: Objective or Subjective Information; Job-Required Social Interaction; Persuade Someone to a Course of Action; Take a Position Opposed to Others; Coordinate or Lead Others; Frequency in Conflict Situations; Deal with Unpleasant or Angry People; Deal with Physical, Aggressive People; Sitting; Frustrating Circumstances
GOE Group/s: 11.04.03 Law: Conciliation
CIP Program/s: 521001 Human Resources Management; 521002 Labor/Personnel Relations and Studies
Related DOT Job/s: 169.107-010 ARBITRATOR; 169.207-010 CONCILIATOR

Inspectors and Compliance Officers

21902 COST ESTIMATORS. OOH Title/s: Cost Estimators
Prepare cost estimates for product manufacturing, construction projects, or services, to aid management in bidding on or determining price of product or service. May specialize according to particular service performed or type of product manufactured. Analyzes blueprints, specifications, proposals, and other documentation, to prepare time, cost, and labor estimates. Prepares estimates for selecting vendors or subcontractors and determining cost effectiveness. Reviews data to determine material and labor requirements, and prepares itemized list. Prepares estimates used for management purposes, such as planning, organizing, and scheduling work. Prepares time, cost, and labor estimates for products, projects, or services, applying specialized methodologies, techniques, or processes. Computes cost factors used for preparing estimates for management and determining cost effectiveness. Conducts special studies to develop and establish standard hour and related cost data or to effect cost reduction. Consults with clients, vendors, or other individuals to discuss and formulate estimates and resolve issues.
Yearly Earnings: $25,636
Education: Work experience in a related occupation
Knowledge: Administration and Management; Economics and Accounting; Production and Processing; Building and Construction; Mathematics
Abilities: Mathematical Reasoning; Number Facility
Skills: Reading Comprehension; Writing; Mathematics; Active Learning; Negotiation; Information Gathering; Information Organization; Synthesis/Reorganization; Idea Generation; Idea Evaluation; Implementation Planning; Solution Appraisal; Visioning; Systems Perception; Identifying Downstream Consequences; Judgment and Decision Making; Systems Evaluation; Management of Financial Resources; Management of Material Resources
General Work Activities: Estimating Needed Characteristics; Evaluating Information against Standards; Developing Objectives and Strategies; Documenting/Recording Information; Communicating with Other Workers; Communicating with Persons Outside Organization; Provide Consultation and Advice to Others
Job Characteristics: Sitting; Consequence of Error; Importance of Being Exact or Accurate; Importance of Being Sure All is Done
GOE Group/s: 05.03.02 Engineering Technology: Drafting
CIP Program/s: 520201 Business Administration and Management, General; 520202 Purchasing, Procurement and Contracts Management
Related DOT Job/s: 169.267-038 ESTIMATOR

21905 MANAGEMENT ANALYSTS. OOH Title/s: Management Analysts and Consultants
Review, analyze, and suggest improvements to business and organizational systems to assist management in operating more efficiently and effectively. Conduct organizational studies and evaluations, design systems and procedures, conduct work simplification and measurement studies, and prepare operations and procedures manuals. Exclude computer systems analysts. Reviews forms and reports, and confers with management and users about format, distribution, and purpose to identify problems and improvements. Develops and implements records management program for filing, protection, and retrieval of records, and assures compliance with program. Reviews records retention schedules and recordkeeping requirements to plan transfer of active records to inactive or archival storage or destruction. Reports findings and prepares recommendations for new systems, procedures, or organizational changes. Interviews personnel and conducts on-site observation to ascertain unit functions, work performed, and methods, equipment, and personnel used. Prepares manuals and trains workers in use of new forms, reports, procedures, or equipment, according to organizational policy. Designs, evaluates, recommends, and approves changes of forms and reports. Implements new systems, trains personnel in use, and reviews operations to ensure that systems are applied and functioning as designed. Recommends purchase of storage equipment, and designs area layout to locate equipment in space available. Directs records management personnel and supporting technical, micrographics, and printing workers.
Yearly Earnings: $41,028
Education: Master's degree

Knowledge: Administration and Management; Clerical; Economics and Accounting; Personnel and Human Resources; Production and Processing; Mathematics; Psychology; Education and Training; English Language; Law, Government, and Jurisprudence
Abilities: Oral Comprehension; Written Expression; Fluency of Ideas; Originality; Problem Sensitivity; Category Flexibility; Speed of Closure; Visualization; Speech Clarity
Skills: Reading Comprehension; Active Listening; Writing; Speaking; Critical Thinking; Active Learning; Learning Strategies; Monitoring; Social Perceptiveness; Coordination; Persuasion; Negotiation; Instructing; Problem Identification; Information Gathering; Information Organization; Synthesis/Reorganization; Idea Generation; Idea Evaluation; Implementation Planning; Solution Appraisal; Operations Analysis; Equipment Selection; Visioning; Systems Perception; Identifying Downstream Consequences; Identification of Key Causes; Judgment and Decision Making; Systems Evaluation; Time Management; Management of Material Resources; Management of Personnel Resources
General Work Activities: Getting Information Needed to Do the Job; Monitoring Processes, Material, or Surroundings; Identifying Objects, Actions, and Events; Estimating Needed Characteristics; Judging Qualities of Things, Services, People; Processing Information; Evaluating Information against Standards; Analyzing Data or Information; Making Decisions and Solving Problems; Thinking Creatively; Developing Objectives and Strategies; Scheduling Work and Activities; Organizing, Planning, and Prioritizing; Operating Vehicles or Equipment; Drafting and Specifying Technical Devices, etc.; Implementing Ideas, Programs, etc.; Documenting/Recording Information; Interpreting Meaning of Information to Others; Communicating with Other Workers; Communicating with Persons Outside Organization; Establishing and Maintaining Relationships; Resolving Conflicts, Negotiating with Others; Coordinating Work and Activities of Others; Developing and Building Teams; Teaching Others; Guiding, Directing and Motivating Subordinates; Coaching and Developing Others; Provide Consultation and Advice to Others; Performing Administrative Activities; Staffing Organizational Units; Monitoring and Controlling Resources
Job Characteristics: Objective or Subjective Information; Job-Required Social Interaction; Supervise, Coach, Train Others; Persuade Someone to a Course of Action; Take a Position Opposed to Others; Coordinate or Lead Others; Responsibility for Outcomes and Results; Frustrating Circumstances
GOE Group/s: 05.01.06 Engineering: Work Planning and Utilization; 11.01.01 Mathematics and Statistics: Data Processing Design; 11.06.02 Finance: Records Systems Analysis
CIP Program/s: 520201 Business Administration and Management, General
Related DOT Job/s: 161.117-014 DIRECTOR, RECORDS MANAGEMENT; 161.167-010 MANAGEMENT ANALYST; 161.167-014 MANAGER, FORMS ANALYSIS; 161.167-018 MANAGER, RECORDS ANALYSIS; 161.167-022 MANAGER, REPORTS ANALYSIS; 161.267-010 CLERICAL-METHODS ANALYST; 161.267-018 FORMS ANALYST; 161.267-022 RECORDS-MANAGEMENT ANALYST; 161.267-026 REPORTS ANALYST

21908A CONSTRUCTION AND BUILDING INSPECTORS. OOH Title/s: Construction and Building Inspectors; Inspectors and Compliance Officers, Except Construction

Inspect structures using engineering skills to determine structural soundness and compliance with specifications, building codes, and other regulations. Inspections may be general in nature or limited to a specific area, such as electrical systems or plumbing. Inspects bridges, dams, highways, building, wiring, plumbing, electrical circuits, sewer, heating system, and foundation for conformance to specifications and codes. Reviews and interprets plans, blueprints, specifications, and construction methods to ensure compliance to legal requirements. Measures dimensions and verifies level, alignment, and elevation of structures and fixtures to ensure compliance to building plans and codes. Approves and signs plans that meet required specifications. Records and notifies owners, violators, and authorities of violations of construction specifications and building codes. Issues violation notices, stop-work orders, and permits for construction and occupancy. Confers with owners, violators, and authorities to explain regulations and recommend alterations in construction or specifications. Reviews complaints, obtains evidence, and testifies in court that construction does not conform to code. Maintains daily logs, inventory, and inspection and construction records, and prepares reports. Evaluates premises for cleanliness, including garbage disposal and lack of vermin infestation. Computes estimates of work completed and approves payment for contractors.
Yearly Earnings: $34,372
Education: Work experience in a related occupation
Knowledge: Economics and Accounting; Design; Building and Construction; Mathematics; Physics; Public Safety and Security; Law, Government, and Jurisprudence
Abilities: Written Comprehension; Written Expression; Problem Sensitivity; Inductive Reasoning; Flexibility of Closure; Spatial Orientation; Stamina; Gross Body Equilibrium; Near Vision; Far Vision; Visual Color Discrimination; Speech Clarity
Skills: Active Listening; Writing; Speaking; Mathematics; Critical Thinking; Active Learning; Persuasion; Negotiation; Problem Identification; Operations Analysis; Testing; Product Inspection; Troubleshooting; Visioning; Systems Perception; Identifying Downstream Consequences; Identification of Key Causes; Judgment and Decision Making; Systems Evaluation; Management of Financial Resources
General Work Activities: Inspecting Equipment, Structures, or Material; Processing Information
Job Characteristics: Take a Position Opposed to Others; Responsible for Others' Health and Safety; Frequency in Conflict Situations; Deal with Unpleasant or Angry People; Extremely Bright or Inadequate Lighting; Cramped Work Space, Awkward Positions; Radiation; High Places; Climbing Ladders, Scaffolds, Poles, etc.; Walking or Running; Kneeling, Crouching, or Crawling; Keeping or Regaining Balance; Bending or Twisting the Body; Frustrating Circumstances; Importance of Being Sure All is Done
GOE Group/s: 05.03.06 Engineering Technology: Industrial and Safety; 05.07.02 Quality Control: Mechincal
CIP Program/s: 150101 Architectural Engineering Technologists and Technicians; 150303 Electrical, Electronic and Communications Engineering Technologists and Technicians; 151001 Construction/Building Technologists and Technicians; 430201 Fire Protection and Safety Technologists and Technicians; 460301 Electrical and Power Transmission Installer, General; 460302 Electrician; 460403 Construction/Building Inspector; 460501 Plumber and Pipefitter; 470201 Heating, Air Conditioning and Refrigeration Mechanics and Repairers
Related DOT Job/s: 168.167-030 INSPECTOR, BUILDING; 168.167-034 INSPECTOR, ELECTRICAL; 168.167-046 INSPECTOR, HEATING AND REFRIGERATION; 168.167-050 INSPECTOR, PLUMBING; 168.267-102 PLAN CHECKER; 168.367-018 CODE INSPECTOR; 182.267-010 CONSTRUCTION INSPECTOR

21908B ELEVATOR INSPECTORS. OOH Title/s: Construction and Building Inspectors

Inspect elevators and other lifting and conveying devices to verify conformance to laws and ordinances regulating design, installation, and safe operation. Inspects electrical and mechanical

features of elevators and other lifting devices to validate conformance to safety regulations and procedures. Conducts tests of elevator's speed, brakes, and safety devices. Recommends corrections for unsafe conditions of elevators and lifting devices. Investigates and determines cause of accidents involving lifting devices. Consults with engineers, installers, and owners regarding corrections of unsafe conditions. Records and formulates reports of inspections and investigations of unsafe conditions or accidents. Computes maximum loads for elevators and other lifting or conveying devices. Seals operating device of unsafe elevators and other lifting devices.
Yearly Earnings: $34,372
Education: Work experience in a related occupation
Knowledge: Design; Building and Construction; Public Safety and Security; Law, Government, and Jurisprudence
Abilities: Selective Attention; Stamina; Gross Body Equilibrium; Visual Color Discrimination; Sound Localization
Skills: Science; Persuasion; Testing; Troubleshooting
General Work Activities: Repairing and Maintaining Mechanical Equipment; Repairing and Maintaining Electrical Equipment
Job Characteristics: Take a Position Opposed to Others; Responsible for Others' Health and Safety; Cramped Work Space, Awkward Positions; High Places; Standing; Climbing Ladders, Scaffolds, Poles, etc.; Kneeling, Crouching, or Crawling; Keeping or Regaining Balance; Consequence of Error; Frustrating Circumstances; Importance of Being Exact or Accurate; Importance of Being Sure All is Done
GOE Group/s: 05.03.06 Engineering Technology: Industrial and Safety
CIP Program/s: 460403 Construction/Building Inspector
Related DOT Job/s: 168.167-038 INSPECTOR, ELEVATORS

21911A HEALTH OFFICERS AND INSPECTORS.

OOH Title/s: Inspectors and Compliance Officers, Except Construction

Plan, develop, and enforce health programs to maintain health and sanitation standards, regulations, and procedures designed to protect the public. May investigate cases of communicable diseases and implement programs to prevent further spread of the disease. Inspects facilities, equipment, accommodations, operating procedures, and staff competence to ensure health and sanitation regulation compliance. Investigates complaints concerning violations of public health laws or substandard products or services. Interviews individuals to obtain information and evidence regarding communicable diseases or violations of health and sanitation regulations. Collects samples and performs laboratory analyses to detect disease or to determine purity and cleanliness of tested item. Examines credentials, licenses, or permits to ensure compliance with licensing requirements. Recommends corrective action or changes in facilities, standards, or administrative methods in response to complaints, license applications, undesirable conditions, or violations of law. Imposes quarantines because of contagious diseases, or orders closing of establishments not conforming to health standards. Confers with school and state authorities and community groups to develop health standards and programs. Reviews records and reports concerning laboratory results, staffing, personal references, floor plans, fire inspections, and sanitation. Collaborates with other personnel in investigations and in establishment of public health programs or testing procedures. Informs individuals of specific regulations affecting establishments. Cites or arrests violators, and testifies in court. Prepares reports and documents of investigation data, activities, findings, and recommendations for corrective measures. Destroys or prohibits sale of unsafe food, drugs, or consumer products. Promotes public and environmental health programs. Organizes and conducts training programs in environmental and health practices. Reviews legislative developments to determine changes in legal requirements and probable effects on production processes.
Yearly Earnings: $34,372
Education: Work experience in a related occupation
Knowledge: Food Production; Chemistry; Biology; Medicine and Dentistry; Education and Training; Public Safety and Security; Law, Government, and Jurisprudence; Communications and Media
Abilities: Written Expression; Problem Sensitivity; Inductive Reasoning; Memorization; Perceptual Speed; Spatial Orientation
Skills: Reading Comprehension; Active Listening; Speaking; Science; Monitoring; Persuasion; Negotiation; Information Gathering; Implementation Planning; Programming; Identifying Downstream Consequences; Identification of Key Causes
General Work Activities: Getting Information Needed to Do the Job; Monitoring Processes, Material, or Surroundings; Inspecting Equipment, Structures, or Material; Judging Qualities of Things, Services, People; Processing Information; Evaluating Information against Standards; Analyzing Data or Information; Making Decisions and Solving Problems; Updating and Using Job-Relevant Knowledge; Developing Objectives and Strategies; Organizing, Planning, and Prioritizing; Drafting and Specifying Technical Devices, etc.; Implementing Ideas, Programs, etc.; Documenting/Recording Information; Interpreting Meaning of Information to Others; Communicating with Other Workers; Communicating with Persons Outside Organization; Selling or Influencing Others; Performing for or Working with Public; Teaching Others; Provide Consultation and Advice to Others
Job Characteristics: Persuade Someone to a Course of Action; Take a Position Opposed to Others; Deal with External Customers; Responsible for Others' Health and Safety; Frequency in Conflict Situations; Deal with Unpleasant or Angry People; Extremely Bright or Inadequate Lighting; Diseases/Infections; High Places; Frustrating Circumstances; Importance of Being Exact or Accurate; Importance of Being Sure All is Done
GOE Group/s: 05.02.03 Managerial Work: Mechanical: Processing and Manufacturing; 11.10.03 Regulations Enforcement: Health and Safety; 11.10.05 Regulations Enforcement: Company Policy
CIP Program/s: 020301 Food Sciences and Technology; 120301 Funeral Services and Mortuary Science; 141401 Environmental/Environmental Health Engineering; 150506 Water Quality and Wastewater Treatment Technologists and Technicians; 150507 Environmental and Pollution Control Technologists and Technicians; 150701 Occupational Safety and Health Technologists and Technicians; 200401 Institutional Food Workers and Administrators, General; 200409 Institutional Food Services Administrator; 480701 Woodworkers, General; 480702 Furniture Designer and Maker; 510301 Community Health Liaison; 510702 Hospital/Health Facilities Administration; 512001 Pharmacy (B. Pharm., Pharm.D.); 512002 Pharmacy Administration and Pharmaceutics; 512201 Public Health, General
Related DOT Job/s: 079.117-018 SANITARIAN; 168.167-018 HEALTH OFFICER, FIELD; 168.167-042 INSPECTOR, HEALTH CARE FACILITIES; 168.167-066 QUALITY-CONTROL COORDINATOR; 168.267-030 DINING-SERVICE INSPECTOR; 168.267-042 FOOD AND DRUG INSPECTOR; 168.267-046 INSPECTOR, FURNITURE AND BEDDING; 168.267-078 MORTICIAN INVESTIGATOR; 187.117-050 PUBLIC HEALTH SERVICE OFFICER

21911B ENVIRONMENTAL COMPLIANCE INSPECTORS.

OOH Title/s: Inspectors and Compliance Officers, Except Construction

Inspect and investigate sources of pollution to protect the public and environment and ensure conformance with federal, state, and local regulations and ordinances. Inspects solid waste disposal and treatment facilities, wastewater treatment facilities, or other water courses or sites for conformance with regulations. Inspects establishments to ensure that handling, storage, and disposal of fertilizers, pesticides, and other hazardous chemicals conform with regulations. Investigates complaints and suspected violations concerning illegal dumping, pollution, pesticides, product quality, or labeling laws. Conducts field tests and collects samples for laboratory analysis. Interviews individuals to determine nature of suspected violations and to obtain evidence of violation. Examines permits, licenses, applications, and records to ensure compliance with licensing requirements. Makes recommendations for corrective action, or issues citations for violations. Conducts research on hazardous waste management projects to determine magnitude of disposal problem, treatment, and disposal alternatives and costs. Reviews and evaluates applications for registration of products containing dangerous materials or pollution-control discharge permits. Advises individuals and groups concerning pollution-control regulations, and inspection and investigation findings, and encourages voluntary action to correct problems. Studies laws and statutes to determine nature of code violation and type of action to be taken. Evaluates label information for accuracy and conformance to regulatory requirements. Prepares, organizes, and maintains records to document activities, recommend action, provide reference materials, and prepare technical and evidentiary reports. Assists in the development of spill-prevention programs and hazardous waste rules and regulations, and recommends corrective action in event of hazardous spill.

Yearly Earnings: $34,372

Education: Work experience in a related occupation

Knowledge: Production and Processing; Food Production; Mathematics; Physics; Chemistry; Biology; Public Safety and Security; Law, Government, and Jurisprudence; Communications and Media

Abilities: Written Comprehension; Oral Expression; Written Expression; Fluency of Ideas; Problem Sensitivity; Deductive Reasoning; Inductive Reasoning; Information Ordering; Category Flexibility; Memorization; Speed of Closure; Flexibility of Closure; Perceptual Speed

Skills: Reading Comprehension; Active Listening; Writing; Speaking; Science; Critical Thinking; Monitoring; Persuasion; Negotiation; Problem Identification; Information Gathering; Information Organization; Implementation Planning; Programming; Testing; Visioning; Identifying Downstream Consequences; Identification of Key Causes; Judgment and Decision Making; Systems Evaluation; Management of Material Resources

General Work Activities: Monitoring Processes, Material, or Surroundings; Identifying Objects, Actions, and Events; Inspecting Equipment, Structures, or Material; Judging Qualities of Things, Services, People; Processing Information; Evaluating Information against Standards; Analyzing Data or Information; Making Decisions and Solving Problems; Updating and Using Job-Relevant Knowledge; Developing Objectives and Strategies; Drafting and Specifying Technical Devices, etc.; Documenting/Recording Information; Interpreting Meaning of Information to Others; Communicating with Other Workers; Communicating with Persons Outside Organization; Assisting and Caring for Others; Selling or Influencing Others; Provide Consultation and Advice to Others

Job Characteristics: Persuade Someone to a Course of Action; Take a Position Opposed to Others; Deal with External Customers; Responsible for Others' Health and Safety; Frequency in Conflict Situations; Deal with Unpleasant or Angry People; Contaminants; Diseases/Infections; Hazardous Conditions; Climbing Ladders, Scaffolds, Poles, etc.; Walking or Running

GOE Group/s: 05.03.06 Engineering Technology: Industrial and Safety; 11.10.03 Regulations Enforcement: Health and Safety

CIP Program/s: 010401 Agricultural and Food Products Processing Operations and Management; 010501 Agricultural Supplies Retailing and Wholesaling; 020301 Food Sciences and Technology; 020401 Plant Sciences, General; 020408 Plant Protection (Pest Management); 150506 Water Quality and Wastewater Treatment Technologists and Technicians; 150507 Environmental and Pollution Control Technologists and Technicians

Related DOT Job/s: 168.267-054 INSPECTOR, INDUSTRIAL WASTE; 168.267-082 AGRICULTURAL-CHEMICALS INSPECTOR; 168.267-086 HAZARDOUS-WASTE MANAGEMENT SPECIALIST; 168.267-090 INSPECTOR, WATER-POLLUTION CONTROL; 168.267-098 PESTICIDE-CONTROL INSPECTOR; 168.267-106 REGISTRATION SPECIALIST, AGRICULTURAL CHEMICALS; 168.267-110 SANITATION INSPECTOR

21911C IMMIGRATION AND CUSTOMS INSPECTORS. OOH Title/s: Inspectors and Compliance Officers, Except Construction

Investigate and inspect persons, common carriers, goods, and merchandise arriving in or departing from the United States or between states to detect violations of immigration and customs laws and regulations. Inspects cargo, baggage, personal articles, and common carriers entering or leaving U.S. for compliance with revenue laws and U.S. Customs Service regulations. Examines visas and passports and interviews persons to determine eligibility for admission, residence, and travel in U.S. Examines, classifies, weighs, measures, and appraises merchandise to enforce regulations of U.S. Customs Service and to prevent illegal importing and exporting. Determines investigative and seizure techniques to be used, and seizes contraband, undeclared merchandise, vehicles, and air- or seacraft carrying smuggled merchandise. Arrests, detains, paroles, or arranges for deportation of persons in violation of customs or immigration laws. Keeps records and writes reports of activities, findings, transactions, violations, discrepancies, and decisions. Reviews private and public records and documents to establish, assemble, and verify facts and secure legal evidence. Determines duty and taxes to be paid, investigates applications for duty refunds or petitions for remission or mitigation of penalties. Interprets and explains laws and regulations to others. Issues or denies permits. Institutes civil and criminal prosecutions, and assists other governmental agencies with regulation violation issues. Collects samples of merchandise for examination, appraising, or testing, and requests laboratory analyses. Testifies in administrative and judicial proceedings.

Yearly Earnings: $34,372

Education: Work experience in a related occupation

Knowledge: Sociology and Anthropology; Geography; Foreign Language; Public Safety and Security; Law, Government, and Jurisprudence; Communications and Media; Transportation

Abilities: Problem Sensitivity; Memorization; Selective Attention; Time Sharing

Skills: None above average

General Work Activities: Judging Qualities of Things, Services, People; Documenting/Recording Information; Interpreting Meaning of Information to Others; Performing for or Working with Public

Job Characteristics: Job-Required Social Interaction; Take a Position Opposed to Others; Frequency in Conflict Situations; Deal with Unpleasant or Angry People; Deal with Physical, Aggressive People; Walking or Running; Special Uniform; Importance of Being Aware of New Events

GOE Group/s: 04.01.02 Safety and Law Enforcement: Investigating; 05.09.03 Material Control: Verifying, Recording, and Marking; 11.10.04 Regulations Enforcement: Immigration and Customs

CIP Program/s: 430107 Law Enforcement/Police Science; 430109 Security and Loss Prevention Services; 521403 International Business Marketing

Related DOT Job/s: 168.167-022 IMMIGRATION INSPECTOR; 168.267-018 CUSTOMS IMPORT SPECIALIST; 168.267-022 CUSTOMS INSPECTOR; 168.387-010 OPENER-VERIFIER-PACKER, CUSTOMS; 188.167-090 SPECIAL AGENT, CUSTOMS

21911D LICENSING EXAMINERS AND INSPECTORS. OOH Title/s: Inspectors and Compliance Officers, Except Construction

Examine, evaluate, and investigate eligibility for, conformity with, or liability under licenses or permits. Evaluates information to determine license, permit, or passport eligibility or liability incurred. Determines eligibility or liability and approves or disallows application or license. Administers oral, written, road, or flight test to determine applicant's eligibility for licensing. Scores tests and rates ability of applicant through observation of equipment operation and control. Reviews applications, records, and documents to determine relevant eligibility information. Visits establishments to determine that valid licenses and permits are displayed and that licensing standards are being upheld. Issues licenses to individuals meeting standards. Confers with officials and technical or professional specialists, and interviews individuals to obtain information or clarify facts. Prepares reports of activities, evaluations, recommendations, and decisions. Prepares correspondence to inform concerned parties of decisions made and to appeal rights. Warns violators of infractions or penalties. Provides information, and answers questions of individuals or groups concerning licensing, permit, or passport regulations.

Yearly Earnings: $34,372

Education: Work experience in a related occupation

Knowledge: Law, Government, and Jurisprudence; Transportation

Abilities: None above average

Skills: Active Listening; Speaking; Monitoring

General Work Activities: Judging Qualities of Things, Services, People; Processing Information; Interpreting Meaning of Information to Others; Communicating with Persons Outside Organization; Performing for or Working with Public

Job Characteristics: Take a Position Opposed to Others; Deal with External Customers; Frequency in Conflict Situations; Deal with Unpleasant or Angry People; Sitting

GOE Group/s: 05.04.01 Air and Water Vehicle Operation: Air; 07.01.05 Administrative Detail: Certifying; 07.01.07 Administrative Detail: Test Administration; 11.10.03 Regulations Enforcement: Health and Safety

CIP Program/s: 131304 Driver and Safety Teacher Education; 430107 Law Enforcement/Police Science; 440401 Public Administration; 490102 Aircraft Pilot and Navigator (Professional)

Related DOT Job/s: 168.167-074 REVIEWING OFFICER, DRIVER'S LICENSE; 168.267-034 DRIVER'S LICENSE EXAMINER; 168.267-066 LICENSE INSPECTOR; 169.267-014 EXAMINER; 169.267-030 PASSPORT-APPLICATION EXAMINER; 196.163-010 FLIGHT-OPERATIONS INSPECTOR

21911E INDUSTRIAL AND OCCUPATIONAL SAFETY AND HEALTH INSPECTORS. OOH Title/s: Inspectors and Compliance Officers, Except Construction

Inspect and evaluate places of employment and properties to ensure compliance with safety and health laws. Inspects worksites, machinery, equipment, or insured properties for hazards, violations, and conformance with governmental standards. Analyzes unsafe conditions and assigns rating according to established factors. Observes work activities and practices to determine compliance with safety precautions and safety equipment used. Measures and evaluates voluntary compliance and effectiveness of safety program, using established goals. Tests noise levels and measures air quality, using precision instruments. Confers with management to ensure compliance with regulations and demonstrate use of safety equipment and first aid procedures. Recommends changes in policies and procedures to prevent accidents and illness. Photographs work environments or property areas to record risk or violations and to provide documentation. Investigates accidents to ascertain causes and analyzes history of accidents and claims to develop accident-prevention programs. Plans and directs safety and health activities and training in work environment to evaluate and control hazards. Orders suspension of activity posing threat to workers or other individuals. Maintains records and prepares reports of findings, violations, and recommendations for corrective action. Develops and conducts training to promote health and safety, safe operation of equipment, and compliance with precautions. Assists management with preparation of safety and health budget. Testifies in legal proceedings.

Yearly Earnings: $34,372

Education: Work experience in a related occupation

Knowledge: Administration and Management; Clerical; Production and Processing; Education and Training; English Language; Public Safety and Security; Law, Government, and Jurisprudence; Communications and Media

Abilities: Written Comprehension; Oral Expression; Written Expression; Problem Sensitivity; Deductive Reasoning; Inductive Reasoning; Category Flexibility; Memorization; Speed of Closure; Flexibility of Closure; Perceptual Speed; Hearing Sensitivity; Speech Clarity

Skills: Reading Comprehension; Active Listening; Writing; Speaking; Critical Thinking; Monitoring; Coordination; Persuasion; Negotiation; Instructing; Problem Identification; Information Gathering; Information Organization; Implementation Planning; Product Inspection; Identifying Downstream Consequences; Judgment and Decision Making; Systems Evaluation

General Work Activities: Getting Information Needed to Do the Job; Monitoring Processes, Material, or Surroundings; Identifying Objects, Actions, and Events; Inspecting Equipment, Structures, or Material; Judging Qualities of Things, Services, People; Processing Information; Making Decisions and Solving Problems; Drafting and Specifying Technical Devices, etc.; Implementing Ideas, Programs, etc.; Documenting/Recording Information; Interpreting Meaning of Information to Others; Communicating with Other Workers; Communicating with Persons Outside Organization; Teaching Others; Coaching and Developing Others; Provide Consultation and Advice to Others

Job Characteristics: Persuade Someone to a Course of Action; Take a Position Opposed to Others; Deal with External Customers; Responsible for Others' Health and Safety; Frequency in Conflict Situations; Deal with Unpleasant or Angry People; Sounds, Noise Levels are Distracting, etc.; Very Hot; Extremely Bright or Inadequate Lighting; Radiation; High Places; Hazardous Conditions; Climbing Ladders, Scaffolds, Poles, etc.; Walking or Running; Common Protective or Safety Attire; Specialized Protective or Safety Attire; Consequence of Error; Importance of Being Sure All is Done

GOE Group/s: 03.01.04 Managerial Work: Plants and Animals: Forestry and Logging; 11.10.03 Regulations Enforcement: Health and Safety

CIP Program/s: 030405 Logging/Timber Harvesting; 150701 Occupational Safety and Health Technologists and Technicians; 430201 Fire Protection and Safety Technologists and Technicians; 512206 Occupational Health and Industrial Hygiene

Related DOT Job/s: 168.161-014 INDUSTRIAL-SAFETY-AND-HEALTH TECHNICIAN; 168.167-062 OCCUPATIONAL-SAFETY-AND-HEALTH INSPECTOR; 168.167-078 SAFETY INSPECTOR; 168.167-086 SAFETY MANAGER; 168.264-014 SAFETY INSPECTOR; 168.267-070 LOGGING-OPERATIONS INSPECTOR; 168.267-074 MINE INSPECTOR

21911F EQUAL OPPORTUNITY REPRESENTATIVES AND OFFICERS. OOH Title/s: Inspectors and Compliance Officers, Except Construction

Monitor and evaluate compliance with equal opportunity laws, guidelines, and policies to ensure that employment practices and contracting arrangements give equal opportunity without

regard to race, religion, color, national origin, sex, age, or disability. Interprets civil rights laws and equal opportunity governmental regulations for individuals and employers. Investigates employment practices and alleged violations of law to document and correct discriminatory factors. Studies equal opportunity complaints to clarify issues. Prepares report of findings and recommendations for corrective action. Consults with community representatives to develop technical assistance agreements in accordance with governmental regulations. Conducts surveys and evaluates findings to determine existence of systematic discrimination. Reviews contracts to determine company actions required to meet governmental equal opportunity provisions. Confers with management or other personnel to resolve or settle equal opportunity issues and disputes. Acts as representative between minority placement agencies and employers. Develops guidelines for nondiscriminatory employment practices for use by employers.
Yearly Earnings: $34,372
Education: Work experience in a related occupation
Knowledge: Personnel and Human Resources; Sociology and Anthropology; English Language; Law, Government, and Jurisprudence
Abilities: Oral Comprehension; Written Comprehension; Oral Expression; Written Expression; Problem Sensitivity; Deductive Reasoning; Inductive Reasoning; Information Ordering; Category Flexibility; Gross Body Equilibrium; Speech Clarity
Skills: Active Listening; Writing; Speaking; Monitoring; Social Perceptiveness; Persuasion; Negotiation; Information Gathering; Implementation Planning; Visioning; Identification of Key Causes
General Work Activities: Getting Information Needed to Do the Job; Identifying Objects, Actions, and Events; Judging Qualities of Things, Services, People; Processing Information; Evaluating Information against Standards; Analyzing Data or Information; Making Decisions and Solving Problems; Updating and Using Job-Relevant Knowledge; Developing Objectives and Strategies; Organizing, Planning, and Prioritizing; Implementing Ideas, Programs, etc.; Documenting/Recording Information; Interpreting Meaning of Information to Others; Communicating with Other Workers; Communicating with Persons Outside Organization; Resolving Conflicts, Negotiating with Others; Provide Consultation and Advice to Others
Job Characteristics: Objective or Subjective Information; Persuade Someone to a Course of Action; Take a Position Opposed to Others; Deal with External Customers; Frequency in Conflict Situations; Deal with Unpleasant or Angry People; Sitting; Frustrating Circumstances
GOE Group/s: 11.10.02 Regulations Enforcement: Individual Rights
CIP Program/s: 440201 Community Organization, Resources and Services; 440401 Public Administration; 521001 Human Resources Management
Related DOT Job/s: 168.167-014 EQUAL-OPPORTUNITY REPRESENTATIVE; 168.267-114 EQUAL OPPORTUNITY OFFICER

21911H GOVERNMENT PROPERTY INSPECTORS AND INVESTIGATORS. OOH Title/s: Inspectors and Compliance Officers, Except Construction

Investigate regulated activities to ensure compliance with federal, state, or municipal laws. Investigate or inspect government property to ensure compliance with contract agreements and government regulations. Investigates regulated activities to detect violation of law relating to such activities as revenue collection, employment practices, or fraudulent benefit claims. Inspects manufactured or processed products to ensure compliance with contract specifications and legal requirements. Locates and interviews plaintiffs, witnesses, or representatives of business or government to gather facts relevant to inspection or alleged violation. Inspects government-owned equipment and materials in hands of private contractors to prevent waste, damage, theft, and other irregularities. Examines records, reports, and documents to establish facts and detect discrepancies. Investigates character of applicant for special license or permit and misuses of license or permit. Submits samples of product to government laboratory for testing, as indicated by departmental procedures. Prepares correspondence, reports of inspections or investigations, and recommendations for administrative or legal authorities. Testifies in court or at administrative proceedings concerning findings of investigation.
Yearly Earnings: $34,372
Education: Work experience in a related occupation
Knowledge: Personnel and Human Resources; English Language; Public Safety and Security; Law, Government, and Jurisprudence; Communications and Media
Abilities: Written Comprehension; Oral Expression; Written Expression; Problem Sensitivity; Inductive Reasoning; Memorization; Flexibility of Closure; Perceptual Speed
Skills: Reading Comprehension; Writing; Speaking; Critical Thinking; Persuasion; Negotiation; Problem Identification; Information Gathering; Visioning; Identifying Downstream Consequences; Judgment and Decision Making
General Work Activities: Getting Information Needed to Do the Job; Monitoring Processes, Material, or Surroundings; Identifying Objects, Actions, and Events; Inspecting Equipment, Structures, or Material; Judging Qualities of Things, Services, People; Processing Information; Organizing, Planning, and Prioritizing; Documenting/Recording Information; Interpreting Meaning of Information to Others; Communicating with Other Workers; Communicating with Persons Outside Organization
Job Characteristics: Take a Position Opposed to Others; Deal with External Customers; Responsible for Others' Health and Safety; Frequency in Conflict Situations; Deal with Unpleasant or Angry People; Walking or Running; Frustrating Circumstances
GOE Group/s: 05.03.06 Engineering Technology: Industrial and Safety; 11.10.01 Regulations Enforcement: Finance
CIP Program/s: 150702 Quality Control Technologists and Technicians; 430107 Law Enforcement/Police Science
Related DOT Job/s: 168.267-050 INSPECTOR, GOVERNMENT PROPERTY; 168.267-062 INVESTIGATOR; 168.287-014 INSPECTOR, QUALITY ASSURANCE

21911J FINANCIAL EXAMINERS. OOH Title/s: Inspectors and Compliance Officers, Except Construction

Enforce or ensure compliance with laws and regulations governing financial and securities institutions and financial and real estate transactions. May examine, verify correctness of, or establish authenticity of records. Investigates activities of institutions to enforce laws and regulations and to ensure legality of transactions and operations or financial solvency. Reviews, analyzes, and interprets new, proposed, or revised laws, regulations, policies, and procedures. Establishes guidelines for and directs implementation of procedures and policies to comply with new and revised regulations. Recommends action to ensure compliance with laws and regulations or to protect solvency of institution. Reviews applications for merger, acquisition, establishment of new institution, acceptance in Federal Reserve System, or registration of securities sales. Determines if application action is in public interest and in accordance with regulations, and recommends acceptance or rejection of application. Schedules audits and examines records and reports to determine regulatory compliance. Confers with officials of real estate, securities, or financial institution industries to exchange views and discuss issues or pending cases. Directs workers engaged in designing, writing, and publishing guidelines, manuals, bulletins, and reports. Conducts or arranges for educational classes and training programs.
Yearly Earnings: $34,372

Education: Work experience in a related occupation
Knowledge: Administration and Management; Economics and Accounting; Mathematics; Education and Training; English Language; Law, Government, and Jurisprudence
Abilities: Oral Comprehension; Written Comprehension; Oral Expression; Written Expression; Problem Sensitivity; Deductive Reasoning; Inductive Reasoning; Category Flexibility; Mathematical Reasoning; Number Facility; Memorization; Perceptual Speed; Near Vision
Skills: Reading Comprehension; Active Listening; Writing; Speaking; Mathematics; Monitoring; Persuasion; Negotiation; Problem Identification; Information Gathering; Systems Perception; Judgment and Decision Making; Systems Evaluation; Management of Financial Resources
General Work Activities: Getting Information Needed to Do the Job; Monitoring Processes, Material, or Surroundings; Identifying Objects, Actions, and Events; Estimating Needed Characteristics; Judging Qualities of Things, Services, People; Processing Information; Evaluating Information against Standards; Analyzing Data or Information; Making Decisions and Solving Problems; Updating and Using Job-Relevant Knowledge; Developing Objectives and Strategies; Scheduling Work and Activities; Organizing, Planning, and Prioritizing; Implementing Ideas, Programs, etc.; Documenting/Recording Information; Interpreting Meaning of Information to Others; Communicating with Other Workers; Communicating with Persons Outside Organization; Coordinating Work and Activities of Others; Developing and Building Teams; Teaching Others; Guiding, Directing and Motivating Subordinates; Provide Consultation and Advice to Others; Performing Administrative Activities
Job Characteristics: Supervise, Coach, Train Others; Persuade Someone to a Course of Action; Take a Position Opposed to Others; Coordinate or Lead Others; Responsibility for Outcomes and Results; Frequency in Conflict Situations; Deal with Unpleasant or Angry People; Sitting; Importance of Being Sure All is Done
GOE Group/s: 11.10.01 Regulations Enforcement: Finance
CIP Program/s: 520801 Finance, General
Related DOT Job/s: 160.167-046 CHIEF BANK EXAMINER; 186.117-090 ; 188.167-038 DIRECTOR, SECURITIES AND REAL ESTATE

21911K AVIATION INSPECTORS. OOH Title/s: Inspectors and Compliance Officers, Except Construction

Inspect aircraft, maintenance procedures, air navigational aids, air traffic controls, and communications equipment to ensure conformance with federal safety regulations. Inspects aircraft and components to identify damage or defects and to determine structural and mechanical airworthiness, using hand tools and test instruments. Examines maintenance record and flight log to determine if service and maintenance checks and overhauls were performed at prescribed intervals. Examines access plates and doors for security. Starts aircraft and observes gauges, meters, and other instruments to detect evidence of malfunction. Conducts flight test program to test equipment, instruments, and systems under various conditions, including adverse weather, using both manual and automatic controls. Recommends purchase, repair, or modification of equipment. Schedules and coordinates inflight testing program with ground crews and air traffic control to assure ground tracking, equipment monitoring, and related services. Prepares reports to document flight activities and inspection findings. Approves or disapproves issuance of certificate of airworthiness. Investigates air accidents to determine cause. Analyzes training program and conducts examinations to assure competency of persons operating, installing, and repairing equipment.
Yearly Earnings: $34,372
Education: Work experience in a related occupation
Knowledge: Personnel and Human Resources; Computers and Electronics; Engineering and Technology; Mechanical; Physics; Education and Training; English Language; Public Safety and Security; Law, Government, and Jurisprudence; Telecommunications; Transportation
Abilities: Written Comprehension; Written Expression; Problem Sensitivity; Deductive Reasoning; Inductive Reasoning; Information Ordering; Category Flexibility; Number Facility; Speed of Closure; Flexibility of Closure; Perceptual Speed; Spatial Orientation; Control Precision; Response Orientation; Rate Control; Reaction Time; Gross Body Equilibrium; Far Vision; Peripheral Vision
Skills: Writing; Science; Critical Thinking; Problem Identification; Information Gathering; Equipment Selection; Programming; Testing; Operation Monitoring; Product Inspection; Troubleshooting; Visioning; Systems Perception; Identifying Downstream Consequences; Identification of Key Causes; Judgment and Decision Making; Systems Evaluation
General Work Activities: Getting Information Needed to Do the Job; Monitoring Processes, Material, or Surroundings; Identifying Objects, Actions, and Events; Inspecting Equipment, Structures, or Material; Judging Qualities of Things, Services, People; Processing Information; Analyzing Data or Information; Making Decisions and Solving Problems; Updating and Using Job-Relevant Knowledge; Scheduling Work and Activities; Controlling Machines and Processes; Interacting with Computers; Drafting and Specifying Technical Devices, etc.; Implementing Ideas, Programs, etc.; Documenting/Recording Information; Interpreting Meaning of Information to Others; Communicating with Other Workers; Coordinating Work and Activities of Others; Teaching Others; Provide Consultation and Advice to Others
Job Characteristics: Take a Position Opposed to Others; Responsible for Others' Health and Safety; Frequency in Conflict Situations; Sounds, Noise Levels are Distracting, etc.; Extremely Bright or Inadequate Lighting; Cramped Work Space, Awkward Positions; High Places; Climbing Ladders, Scaffolds, Poles, etc.; Keeping or Regaining Balance; Consequence of Error; Frustrating Circumstances; Importance of Being Exact or Accurate; Importance of Being Sure All is Done
GOE Group/s: 05.03.06 Engineering Technology: Industrial and Safety; 05.04.01 Air and Water Vehicle Operation: Air
CIP Program/s: 150801 Aeronautical and Aerospace Engineering Technologists and Technicians; 470609 Aviation Systems and Avionics Maintenance Technologists and Technicians; 490102 Aircraft Pilot and Navigator (Professional)
Related DOT Job/s: 168.264-010 INSPECTOR, AIR-CARRIER; 196.163-014 SUPERVISING AIRPLANE PILOT

21911L PRESSURE VESSEL INSPECTORS. OOH Title/s: Inspectors and Compliance Officers, Except Construction

Inspect pressure vessel equipment for conformance with safety laws and standards regulating their design, fabrication, installation, repair, and operation. Inspects drawings, designs, and specifications for piping, boilers and other vessels. Evaluates factors, such as materials used, safety devices, regulators, construction quality, riveting, welding, pitting, corrosion, cracking, and safety valve operation. Performs standard tests to verify condition of equipment and calibration of meters and gauges, using test equipment and hand tools. Inspects gas mains to determine that rate of flow, pressure, location, construction, and installation conform to standards. Calculates allowable limits of pressure, strength, and stresses. Recommends or orders actions to correct violations of legal requirements or to eliminate unsafe conditions. Examines permits and inspection records to determine that inspection schedule and remedial actions conform to procedures and regulations. Witnesses acceptance and installation tests. Keeps records and prepares reports of inspections and investigations for administrative or legal authorities. Confers with engineers, manufacturers, contractors, owners, and operators concerning problems in construction,

operation, and repair. Investigates accidents to determine causes and to develop methods of preventing recurrences.
Yearly Earnings: $34,372
Education: Work experience in a related occupation
Knowledge: Engineering and Technology; Design; Building and Construction; Mechanical; Mathematics; Physics; Public Safety and Security; Law, Government, and Jurisprudence
Abilities: None above average
Skills: Operations Analysis; Testing; Operation Monitoring; Product Inspection
General Work Activities: Identifying Objects, Actions, and Events; Inspecting Equipment, Structures, or Material; Processing Information; Controlling Machines and Processes
Job Characteristics: Take a Position Opposed to Others; Frequency in Conflict Situations; Cramped Work Space, Awkward Positions; Consequence of Error
GOE Group/s: 05.03.06 Engineering Technology: Industrial and Safety; 11.10.03 Regulations Enforcement: Health and Safety
CIP Program/s: 470303 Industrial Machinery Maintenance and Repair; 470501 Stationary Energy Sources Installer and Operator
Related DOT Job/s: 168.167-026 INSPECTOR, BOILER; 168.264-018 GAS INSPECTOR

21911M PUBLIC TRANSPORTATION INSPECTORS. OOH Title/s: Inspectors and Compliance Officers, Except Construction
Monitor operation of public transportation systems to ensure good service and compliance with regulations. Investigate accidents, equipment failures, and complaints. Observes employees performing assigned duties to note their deportment, treatment of passengers, and adherence to company regulations and schedules. Observes and records time required to load and unload passengers or freight volume of traffic on vehicle and at stops. Investigates schedule delays, accidents, and complaints. Inspects company vehicles and other property for evidence of abuse, damage, and mechanical malfunction, and directs repair. Determines need for changes in service, such as additional vehicles, route changes, and revised schedules, to improve service and efficiency. Drives automobile along route to detect conditions hazardous to equipment and passengers, and negotiates with local governments to eliminate hazards. Submits written reports to management with recommendations for improving service. Reports disruptions to service. Assists in dispatching equipment when necessary. Recommends promotions and disciplinary actions involving transportation personnel.
Yearly Earnings: $34,372
Education: Work experience in a related occupation
Knowledge: Administration and Management; Customer and Personal Service; Personnel and Human Resources; Geography; Public Safety and Security; Law, Government, and Jurisprudence; Transportation
Abilities: None above average
Skills: Monitoring; Operations Analysis; Systems Evaluation; Management of Personnel Resources
General Work Activities: Inspecting Equipment, Structures, or Material; Scheduling Work and Activities; Interacting with Computers; Staffing Organizational Units
Job Characteristics: Take a Position Opposed to Others; Responsible for Others' Health and Safety; Frequency in Conflict Situations; Importance of Being Sure All is Done
GOE Group/s: 11.10.05 Regulations Enforcement: Company Policy
CIP Program/s: 140801 Civil Engineering, General; 140804 Transportation and Highway Engineering
Related DOT Job/s: 168.167-082 TRANSPORTATION INSPECTOR; 184.163-010 TRAFFIC INSPECTOR

21911N MARINE CARGO INSPECTORS. OOH Title/s: Inspectors and Compliance Officers, Except Construction
Inspect cargoes of seagoing vessels to certify compliance with health and safety regulations in cargo handling and stowage. Inspects loaded cargo in holds and cargo handling devices to determine compliance with regulations and need for maintenance. Reads vessel documents to ascertain cargo capabilities according to design and cargo regulations. Calculates gross and net tonnage, hold capacities, volume of stored fuel and water, cargo weight, and ship stability factors, using mathematical formulas. Determines type of license and safety equipment required, and computes applicable tolls and wharfage fees. Examines blueprints of ship and takes physical measurements to determine capacity and depth of vessel in water, using measuring instruments. Writes certificates of admeasurement, listing details such as design, length, depth, and breadth of vessel, and method of propulsion. Issues certificate of compliance when violations are not detected, or recommends remedial procedures to correct deficiencies. Times roll of ship, using stopwatch. Analyzes data, formulates recommendations, and writes reports of findings. Advises crew in techniques of stowing dangerous and heavy cargo, according to knowledge of hazardous cargo.
Yearly Earnings: $34,372
Education: Work experience in a related occupation
Knowledge: Design; Mathematics; Physics; Public Safety and Security; Law, Government, and Jurisprudence; Transportation
Abilities: Problem Sensitivity; Inductive Reasoning; Mathematical Reasoning; Number Facility; Memorization; Speed of Closure; Flexibility of Closure; Perceptual Speed; Spatial Orientation; Gross Body Equilibrium
Skills: Mathematics; Persuasion
General Work Activities: Inspecting Equipment, Structures, or Material; Documenting/Recording Information; Interpreting Meaning of Information to Others; Performing Administrative Activities
Job Characteristics: Take a Position Opposed to Others; Responsible for Others' Health and Safety; Frequency in Conflict Situations; Extremely Bright or Inadequate Lighting; Climbing Ladders, Scaffolds, Poles, etc.; Walking or Running; Frustrating Circumstances; Importance of Being Sure All is Done
GOE Group/s: 05.03.02 Engineering Technology: Drafting; 11.10.03 Regulations Enforcement: Health and Safety
CIP Program/s: 000000 NO CIP ASSIGNED
Related DOT Job/s: 168.267-094 MARINE-CARGO SURVEYOR; 169.284-010 ADMEASURER

21911P CORONERS. OOH Title/s: Inspectors and Compliance Officers, Except Construction
Direct activities such as autopsies, pathological and toxicological analyses, and inquests relating to the investigation of deaths occurring within a legal jurisdiction to, determine cause of death or to fix responsibility for accidental, violent, or unexplained deaths. Directs activities of physicians and technologists conducting autopsies and pathological and toxicological analyses to determine cause of death. Directs investigations into circumstances of deaths to fix responsibility for accidental, violent, or unexplained deaths. Confers with officials of public health and law enforcement agencies to coordinate interdepartmental activities. Directs activities of workers involved in preparing documents for permanent records. Testifies at inquests, hearings, and court trials. Coordinates activities for disposition of unclaimed corpse and personal effects of deceased. Provides information concerning death circumstances to relatives of deceased.
Yearly Earnings: $34,372
Education: Work experience in a related occupation

Knowledge: Administration and Management; Chemistry; Biology; Medicine and Dentistry; English Language; Foreign Language; Public Safety and Security; Law, Government, and Jurisprudence
Abilities: Oral Expression; Written Expression; Fluency of Ideas; Problem Sensitivity; Deductive Reasoning; Inductive Reasoning; Information Ordering; Category Flexibility; Speed of Closure; Flexibility of Closure; Perceptual Speed; Near Vision; Speech Clarity
Skills: Reading Comprehension; Active Listening; Writing; Speaking; Mathematics; Science; Critical Thinking; Active Learning; Coordination; Problem Identification; Information Gathering; Information Organization; Synthesis/Reorganization; Idea Evaluation; Programming; Time Management; Management of Personnel Resources
General Work Activities: Monitoring Processes, Material, or Surroundings; Identifying Objects, Actions, and Events; Inspecting Equipment, Structures, or Material; Judging Qualities of Things, Services, People; Processing Information; Analyzing Data or Information; Making Decisions and Solving Problems; Implementing Ideas, Programs, etc.; Documenting/Recording Information; Interpreting Meaning of Information to Others; Communicating with Other Workers; Coordinating Work and Activities of Others; Guiding, Directing and Motivating Subordinates; Provide Consultation and Advice to Others
Job Characteristics: Supervise, Coach, Train Others; Coordinate or Lead Others; Responsibility for Outcomes and Results; Frequency in Conflict Situations; Contaminants; Diseases/Infections; Common Protective or Safety Attire; Frustrating Circumstances
GOE Group/s: 02.02.01 Life Sciences: Animal Specialization
CIP Program/s: 512919 Forensic Pathology Residency
Related DOT Job/s: 168.161-010 CORONER

21911R AGRICULTURAL INSPECTORS. OOH Title/s: Inspectors and Compliance Officers, Except Construction

Inspect agricultural commodities, processing equipment, and facilities to enforce compliance with government regulations. Inspects facilities and equipment for adequacy, sanitation, and compliance with regulations. Inspects horticultural products or livestock to detect harmful disease, infestation, or growth rate. Examines, weighs, and measures commodities, such as poultry, eggs, meat, and seafood, to certify wholesomeness, grade, and weight. Inspects livestock to determine effectiveness of medication and feeding programs. Writes reports of findings and recommendations, and advises farmer, grower, or processor of corrective action to be taken. Collects samples of pests or suspected diseased animals or materials and routes to laboratory for identification and analysis. Advises farmers and growers of development programs or new equipment and techniques to aid in quality production, applying agricultural knowledge. Testifies in legal proceedings.
Yearly Earnings: $34,372
Education: Work experience in a related occupation
Knowledge: Production and Processing; Food Production; Biology; Law, Government, and Jurisprudence
Abilities: Oral Expression; Written Expression; Originality; Problem Sensitivity; Deductive Reasoning; Inductive Reasoning; Information Ordering; Category Flexibility; Memorization; Speed of Closure; Flexibility of Closure; Perceptual Speed; Wrist-Finger Speed; Gross Body Equilibrium; Speech Clarity
Skills: Product Inspection
General Work Activities: Monitoring Processes, Material, or Surroundings; Inspecting Equipment, Structures, or Material; Judging Qualities of Things, Services, People; Processing Information; Drafting and Specifying Technical Devices, etc.; Interpreting Meaning of Information to Others; Communicating with Persons Outside Organization; Provide Consultation and Advice to Others
Job Characteristics: Persuade Someone to a Course of Action; Take a Position Opposed to Others; Deal with External Customers; Responsible for Others' Health and Safety; Frequency in Conflict Situations; Deal with Unpleasant or Angry People; Sounds, Noise Levels are Distracting, etc.; Very Hot; Diseases/Infections; Walking or Running; Frustrating Circumstances; Importance of Being Sure All is Done
GOE Group/s: 11.10.03 Regulations Enforcement: Health and Safety
CIP Program/s: 010401 Agricultural and Food Products Processing Operations and Management; 020401 Plant Sciences, General; 020408 Plant Protection (Pest Management)
Related DOT Job/s: 168.287-010 INSPECTOR, AGRICULTURAL COMMODITIES; 411.267-010 FIELD SERVICE TECHNICIAN, POULTRY

21911T RADIATION-PROTECTION SPECIALISTS. OOH Title/s: Inspectors and Compliance Officers, Except Construction

Inspect and test X ray or other radiation-producing equipment and utilization areas, and evaluate operating procedures to detect and control radiation hazards in hospitals, laboratories, medical offices, and other establishments that use equipment that produces radiation harmful to humans. Visits hospitals, medical offices, and other establishments to inspect X ray machines and premises. Tests equipment to determine that kilovolt potential, alignment of components, and other elements of equipment meet standards for safe operation. Operates equipment to determine need for calibration, repair, or replacement of parts. Measures density of lead shielding in walls, using radiometric equipment. Computes cumulative radiation levels and refers to regulations to determine if amount of shielding is sufficient to absorb radiation emissions. Examines license of equipment operator for authenticity. Observes operating practices of equipment operator to determine competence in use of equipment. Reviews plans and specifications for proposed X ray installations for conformance to legal requirements and radiation safety practices. Contacts organizations submitting inadequate specifications to explain changes in shielding or layout needed to conform to regulations. Confers with physicians, dentists, and X ray personnel to explain procedures and legal requirements pertaining to use of equipment. Demonstrates exposure techniques to improve procedures and minimize amount of radiation delivered to patients and operator.
Yearly Earnings: $34,372
Education: Work experience in a related occupation
Knowledge: Mathematics; Physics; Medicine and Dentistry; Education and Training; Public Safety and Security; Law, Government, and Jurisprudence
Abilities: Oral Expression; Problem Sensitivity; Deductive Reasoning; Information Ordering; Mathematical Reasoning; Number Facility; Memorization; Perceptual Speed; Finger Dexterity; Control Precision
Skills: Science; Instructing; Problem Identification; Programming; Testing; Operation Monitoring; Operation and Control; Systems Perception; Management of Material Resources
General Work Activities: Monitoring Processes, Material, or Surroundings; Identifying Objects, Actions, and Events; Inspecting Equipment, Structures, or Material; Judging Qualities of Things, Services, People; Processing Information; Evaluating Information against Standards; Analyzing Data or Information; Controlling Machines and Processes; Drafting and Specifying Technical Devices, etc.; Interpreting Meaning of Information to Others; Communicating with Persons Outside Organization; Teaching Others; Provide Consultation and Advice to Others
Job Characteristics: Persuade Someone to a Course of Action; Take a Position Opposed to Others; Responsible for Others' Health and Safety; Radiation; Common Protective or Safety Attire; Specialized Protective or Safety Attire; Consequence of Error; Importance of Being Exact or Accurate; Importance of Being Sure All is Done
GOE Group/s: 11.10.03 Regulations Enforcement: Health and Safety

CIP Program/s: 510907 Medical Radiologic Technologists and Technicians
Related DOT Job/s: 168.261-010 RADIATION-PROTECTION SPECIALIST

21914 TAX EXAMINERS, COLLECTORS, AND REVENUE AGENTS. OOH Title/s: Tax Examiners, Collectors, and Revenue Agents

Determine tax liability or collect taxes from individuals or business firms, according to prescribed laws and regulations. Examines and analyzes tax assets and liabilities to determine resolution of delinquent tax problems. Investigates legal instruments, other documents, financial transactions, operation methods, and industry practices to assess inclusiveness of accounting records and tax returns. Conducts independent field audits and investigations of federal income tax returns to verify or amend tax liabilities. Examines selected tax returns to determine nature and extent of audits to be performed. Selects appropriate remedy, such as partial-payment agreement, offer of compromise, or seizure and sale of property. Analyzes accounting books and records to determine appropriateness of accounting methods employed and compliance with statutory provisions. Secures taxpayer's agreement to discharge tax assessment, or submits contested determination to other administrative or judicial conferees for appeals hearings. Directs service of legal documents, such as subpoenas, warrants, notices of assessment, and garnishments. Confers with taxpayer or representative to explain issues involved and applicability of pertinent tax laws and regulations. Participates in informal appeals hearings on contested cases from other agents. Serves as member of regional appeals board to reexamine unresolved issues in terms of relevant laws and regulations. Recommends criminal prosecutions and civil penalties.
Yearly Earnings: $36,192
Education: Bachelor's degree
Knowledge: Economics and Accounting; Mathematics; Law, Government, and Jurisprudence
Abilities: Written Comprehension; Deductive Reasoning; Mathematical Reasoning; Number Facility; Speech Recognition
Skills: Reading Comprehension; Active Listening; Writing; Speaking; Mathematics; Critical Thinking; Active Learning; Monitoring; Persuasion; Negotiation; Problem Identification; Information Gathering; Information Organization; Synthesis/Reorganization; Idea Evaluation; Solution Appraisal; Judgment and Decision Making; Systems Evaluation; Management of Financial Resources
General Work Activities: Getting Information Needed to Do the Job; Monitoring Processes, Material, or Surroundings; Judging Qualities of Things, Services, People; Processing Information; Evaluating Information against Standards; Analyzing Data or Information; Making Decisions and Solving Problems; Updating and Using Job-Relevant Knowledge; Operating Vehicles or Equipment; Documenting/Recording Information; Interpreting Meaning of Information to Others; Communicating with Persons Outside Organization; Resolving Conflicts, Negotiating with Others; Provide Consultation and Advice to Others; Performing Administrative Activities
Job Characteristics: Frequency in Conflict Situations; Sitting
GOE Group/s: 11.06.01 Finance: Accounting and Auditing
CIP Program/s: 520301 Accounting
Related DOT Job/s: 160.167-050 REVENUE AGENT; 188.167-074 REVENUE OFFICER

21917 ASSESSORS. OOH Title/s: Real Estate Agents, Brokers, and Appraisers

Appraise real and personal property to determine its fair value. May assess taxes in accordance with prescribed schedules. Appraises real and personal property, such as aircraft, marine craft, buildings, and land, to determine fair value. Inspects property, considering factors such as market value, location, and building or replacement costs, to determine appraisal value. Assesses and computes taxes according to prescribed tax tables and schedules. Writes and submits appraisal and tax reports for public record. Interprets property laws, formulates operational policies, and directs assessment office activities.
Yearly Earnings: $30,888
Education: Work experience in a related occupation
Knowledge: Economics and Accounting; Mathematics; Geography; Law, Government, and Jurisprudence
Abilities: Inductive Reasoning; Mathematical Reasoning; Number Facility; Gross Body Equilibrium
Skills: Information Gathering; Product Inspection; Systems Perception; Identifying Downstream Consequences; Judgment and Decision Making
General Work Activities: Estimating Needed Characteristics; Judging Qualities of Things, Services, People; Evaluating Information against Standards; Interacting with Computers; Interpreting Meaning of Information to Others; Provide Consultation and Advice to Others; Performing Administrative Activities
Job Characteristics: Objective or Subjective Information; Take a Position Opposed to Others; Walking or Running
GOE Group/s: 11.06.03 Finance: Risk and Profit Analysis
CIP Program/s: 521501 Real Estate
Related DOT Job/s: 188.167-010 APPRAISER

21921 CLAIMS EXAMINERS, PROPERTY AND CASUALTY INSURANCE. OOH Title/s: Adjusters, Investigators, and Collectors

Review settled insurance claims to determine that payments and settlements have been made in accordance with company practices and procedures, ensuring that adjusters have followed proper methods. Report overpayments, underpayments, and other irregularities. Confer with legal counsel on claims requiring litigation. Analyzes data used in settling claim to determine its validity in payment of claims. Reports overpayments, underpayments, and other irregularities. Confers with legal counsel on claims requiring litigation.
Yearly Earnings: $23,764
Education: Bachelor's degree
Knowledge: Law, Government, and Jurisprudence
Abilities: Number Facility
Skills: Reading Comprehension; Mathematics; Monitoring; Problem Identification; Information Gathering; Judgment and Decision Making; Systems Evaluation
General Work Activities: Processing Information; Analyzing Data or Information
Job Characteristics: Take a Position Opposed to Others; Frequency in Conflict Situations; Sitting; Importance of Being Sure All is Done
GOE Group/s: 07.02.03 Mathematical Detail: Statistical Reporting and Analysis
CIP Program/s: 520801 Finance, General; 520805 Insurance and Risk Management
Related DOT Job/s: 168.267-014 CLAIM EXAMINER

Management Support Workers

21999A COMPUTER SECURITY SPECIALISTS. OOH Title/s: Computer Scientists and Systems Analysts

Plan, coordinate, and implement security measures for information systems to regulate access to computer data files and prevent unauthorized modification, destruction, or disclosure of

information. Develops plans to safeguard computer files against accidental or unauthorized modification, destruction, or disclosure and to meet emergency data processing needs. Coordinates implementation of computer system plan with establishment personnel and outside vendors. Tests data processing system to ensure functioning of data processing activities and security measures. Modifies computer security files to incorporate new software, correct errors, or change individual access status. Confers with personnel to discuss issues such as computer data access needs, security violations, and programming changes. Monitors use of data files and regulates access to safeguard information in computer files. Writes reports to document computer security and emergency measures policies, procedures, and test results.
Yearly Earnings: $43,940
Education: Bachelor's degree
Knowledge: Administration and Management; Computers and Electronics; Philosophy and Theology; Public Safety and Security
Abilities: Oral Comprehension; Written Comprehension; Fluency of Ideas; Deductive Reasoning; Inductive Reasoning; Information Ordering; Speed of Closure; Flexibility of Closure; Visualization
Skills: Synthesis/Reorganization; Idea Generation; Implementation Planning; Operations Analysis; Technology Design; Installation; Programming; Testing; Management of Material Resources
General Work Activities: Inspecting Equipment, Structures, or Material; Judging Qualities of Things, Services, People; Analyzing Data or Information; Making Decisions and Solving Problems; Thinking Creatively; Updating and Using Job-Relevant Knowledge; Developing Objectives and Strategies; Scheduling Work and Activities; Organizing, Planning, and Prioritizing; Operating Vehicles or Equipment; Drafting and Specifying Technical Devices, etc.; Implementing Ideas, Programs, etc.; Repairing and Maintaining Electrical Equipment; Documenting/Recording Information; Interpreting Meaning of Information to Others; Communicating with Other Workers; Coordinating Work and Activities of Others; Provide Consultation and Advice to Others; Monitoring and Controlling Resources
Job Characteristics: Provide a Service to Others; Coordinate or Lead Others; Importance of Being Sure All is Done
GOE Group/s: 11.01.01 Mathematics and Statistics: Data Processing Design; 11.10.05 Regulations Enforcement: Company Policy
CIP Program/s: 110101 Computer and Information Sciences, General; 110501 Computer Systems Analysis; 521201 Management Information Systems and Business Data Processing; 521203 Business Systems Analysis and Design; 521204 Business Systems Networking and Telecommunications; 521205 Business Computer Facilities Operator
Related DOT Job/s: 033.162-010 COMPUTER SECURITY COORDINATOR; 033.162-014 DATA RECOVERY PLANNER; 033.362-010 COMPUTER SECURITY SPECIALIST

21999B LEGISLATIVE ASSISTANTS. OOH Title/s: Indirectly related to Inspectors and Compliance Officers, Except Construction

Perform research into governmental laws and procedures to resolve problems or complaints of constituents or to assist legislator in preparation of proposed legislation. Conducts research in such areas as laws, procedures, and systems of government and subject matter of proposed legislation. Analyzes voting records, existing and pending legislation, political activity, or constituent problems to determine action to take. Confers with personnel, such as constituents, representatives of federal agencies, and members of press to gather and provide information. Attends committee meetings to obtain information on proposed legislation. Briefs legislator on issues and recommends action to be taken. Prepares correspondence, reports, and preliminary drafts of bills and speeches. Assists in campaign activities.
Yearly Earnings: $31,564
Education: Bachelor's degree
Knowledge: English Language; Law, Government, and Jurisprudence
Abilities: Oral Comprehension; Written Comprehension; Oral Expression; Written Expression; Fluency of Ideas; Originality; Deductive Reasoning; Inductive Reasoning; Speed of Closure; Gross Body Equilibrium; Far Vision
Skills: Reading Comprehension; Active Listening; Writing; Critical Thinking; Active Learning; Coordination; Persuasion; Negotiation; Problem Identification; Information Gathering; Synthesis/Reorganization; Idea Generation; Idea Evaluation; Implementation Planning; Solution Appraisal; Visioning; Systems Perception; Identifying Downstream Consequences; Identification of Key Causes; Judgment and Decision Making; Systems Evaluation
General Work Activities: Getting Information Needed to Do the Job; Monitoring Processes, Material, or Surroundings; Judging Qualities of Things, Services, People; Processing Information; Evaluating Information against Standards; Analyzing Data or Information; Making Decisions and Solving Problems; Thinking Creatively; Developing Objectives and Strategies; Organizing, Planning, and Prioritizing; Documenting/Recording Information; Interpreting Meaning of Information to Others; Communicating with Other Workers; Communicating with Persons Outside Organization; Establishing and Maintaining Relationships; Selling or Influencing Others; Resolving Conflicts, Negotiating with Others; Performing for or Working with Public; Provide Consultation and Advice to Others; Performing Administrative Activities
Job Characteristics: Objective or Subjective Information; Job-Required Social Interaction; Sitting
GOE Group/s: 07.01.06 Administrative Detail: Investigating; 11.05.03 Business Administration: Management Services: Government
CIP Program/s: 220103 Paralegal/Legal Assistant; 440501 Public Policy Analysis
Related DOT Job/s: 169.167-066 LEGISLATIVE ASSISTANT; 169.262-010 CASEWORKER

21999C EXECUTIVE SECRETARIES AND ADMINISTRATIVE ASSISTANTS. OOH Title/s: Secretaries

Aid executive by coordinating office services, such as personnel, budget preparation and control, housekeeping, records control, and special management studies. Coordinates and directs office services, such as records and budget preparation, personnel, and housekeeping, to aid executives. Prepares records and reports, such as recommendations for solutions of administrative problems and annual reports. Files and retrieves corporation documents, records, and reports. Analyzes operating practices and procedures to create new or to revise existing methods. Interprets administrative and operating policies and procedures for employees. Studies management methods to improve workflow, simplify reporting procedures, or implement cost reductions. Plans conferences. Reads and answers correspondence.
Yearly Earnings: $31,564
Education: Bachelor's degree
Knowledge: Administration and Management; Clerical; Economics and Accounting
Abilities: Wrist-Finger Speed; Near Vision
Skills: Coordination; Synthesis/Reorganization; Programming; Time Management; Management of Financial Resources; Management of Material Resources; Management of Personnel Resources
General Work Activities: Scheduling Work and Activities; Operating Vehicles or Equipment; Establishing and Maintaining Relationships; Performing Administrative Activities; Monitoring and Controlling Resources

Job Characteristics: Provide a Service to Others; Coordinate or Lead Others; Sitting
GOE Group/s: 07.01.02 Administrative Detail: Administration; 11.05.02 Business Administration: Administrative Specialization
CIP Program/s: 520201 Business Administration and Management, General; 520204 Office Supervision and Management; 520401 Administrative Assistant/Secretarial Science, General; 520402 Executive Assistant/Secretary
Related DOT Job/s: 169.167-010 ADMINISTRATIVE ASSISTANT; 169.167-014 ADMINISTRATIVE SECRETARY

21999D LAND LEASING AND PERMIT AGENTS.

OOH Title/s: Property and Real Estate Managers

Arrange for property leases or permits for special use, such as mineral prospecting or movie production. Negotiates agreements, such as leases, options, and royalty payments, with property representatives. Draws up agreements according to negotiated terms, applying knowledge of company policies and local, state, and federal laws. Confers with others regarding characteristics of location desired and lease and use of property. Obtains signatures on documents from company and property representatives. Seeks new locations for prospecting or production activities. Consults with authorities and landowners, and researches company policies and local, state, and Federal laws to obtain regulatory information. Searches public records to determine legal ownership of land and mineral rights for property. Writes purchase orders and bank checks as specified by leases, agreements, and contracts. Draws sketches of locations and terrain to be traversed. Posts markers on property to indicate locations.
Yearly Earnings: $31,564
Education: Bachelor's degree
Knowledge: Economics and Accounting; Geography; Law, Government, and Jurisprudence
Abilities: Written Comprehension; Written Expression; Perceptual Speed
Skills: Writing; Negotiation; Management of Material Resources
General Work Activities: Getting Information Needed to Do the Job; Monitoring Processes, Material, or Surroundings; Processing Information; Making Decisions and Solving Problems; Communicating with Persons Outside Organization; Establishing and Maintaining Relationships; Selling or Influencing Others; Resolving Conflicts, Negotiating with Others; Provide Consultation and Advice to Others; Performing Administrative Activities; Monitoring and Controlling Resources
Job Characteristics: Persuade Someone to a Course of Action; Deal with External Customers; Frustrating Circumstances
GOE Group/s: 11.12.02 Contracts and Claims: Rental and Leasing
CIP Program/s: 521501 Real Estate
Related DOT Job/s: 191.117-030 LEASE BUYER; 191.117-042 PERMIT AGENT, GEOPHYSICAL PROSPECTING; 191.117-046 RIGHT-OF-WAY AGENT; 191.167-018 LOCATION MANAGER

21999F MEETING AND CONVENTION PLANNERS.

OOH Title/s: Hotel Managers and Assistants

Coordinate activities of staff and convention personnel to make arrangements for group meetings and conventions. Directs and coordinates activities of staff and convention personnel to make arrangements, prepare facilities, and provide services for events. Consults with customer to determine objectives and requirements for events, such as meetings, conferences, and conventions. Plans and develops programs, budgets, and services, such as lodging, catering, and entertainment, according to customer requirements. Evaluates and selects providers of services, such as meeting facilities, speakers, and transportation, according to customer requirements. Negotiates contracts with such providers as hotels, convention centers, and speakers. Inspects rooms and displays for conformance to customer requirements, and conducts post-meeting evaluations to improve future events. Speaks with attendees and resolves complaints to maintain goodwill. Obtains permits from fire and health departments to erect displays and exhibits and to serve food at events. Reviews bills for accuracy and approves payment. Maintains records of events. Reads trade publications, attends seminars, and consults with other meeting professionals to keep abreast of meeting management standards and trends.
Yearly Earnings: $31,564
Education: Bachelor's degree
Knowledge: Administration and Management; Economics and Accounting; Sales and Marketing; Customer and Personal Service; Sociology and Anthropology; Foreign Language; Public Safety and Security; Law, Government, and Jurisprudence; Telecommunications; Communications and Media
Abilities: Oral Comprehension; Category Flexibility
Skills: Speaking; Monitoring; Social Perceptiveness; Coordination; Persuasion; Negotiation; Service Orientation; Implementation Planning; Time Management; Management of Financial Resources; Management of Material Resources; Management of Personnel Resources
General Work Activities: Scheduling Work and Activities; Organizing, Planning, and Prioritizing; Communicating with Other Workers; Communicating with Persons Outside Organization; Establishing and Maintaining Relationships; Selling or Influencing Others; Resolving Conflicts, Negotiating with Others; Performing for or Working with Public; Coordinating Work and Activities of Others; Developing and Building Teams; Guiding, Directing and Motivating Subordinates; Coaching and Developing Others; Performing Administrative Activities; Monitoring and Controlling Resources
Job Characteristics: Deal with External Customers; Coordinate or Lead Others; Responsibility for Outcomes and Results; Frequency in Conflict Situations; Deal with Unpleasant or Angry People; Sitting; Frustrating Circumstances
GOE Group/s: 11.11.01 Business Management: Lodging
CIP Program/s: 190501 Foods and Nutrition Studies, General; 190505 Food Systems Administration; 200401 Institutional Food Workers and Administrators, General; 200405 Food Caterer; 520902 Hotel/Motel and Restaurant Management; 520903 Travel-Tourism Management
Related DOT Job/s: 169.117-022 ; 187.167-078 MANAGER, CONVENTION

21999G GRANT COORDINATORS. OOH Title/s:

Marketing, Advertising, and Public Relations Specialists; Budget Analysts

Research, develop, and coordinate development of proposals for funding and funding sources to establish or maintain grant-funded programs in public or private organizations. Prepares proposal narrative justifying budgetary expenditures for approval by organization officials. Writes and submits grant proposal application to funding agency or foundation. Directs and coordinates evaluation and monitoring of grant-funded programs. Consults with personnel to determine goals, objectives, and budgetary requirements of organizations, such as nonprofit agencies, institutions, or school systems. Researches availability of grant funds from public and private agencies to determine feasibility of developing programs to supplement budget allocations. Completes reports as specified by grant. Confers with representatives of funding sources to complete details of proposal. Maintains files on grants.
Yearly Earnings: $43,784
Education: Work experience, plus degree
Knowledge: Administration and Management; Economics and Accounting; English Language; Law, Government, and Jurisprudence

Abilities: Oral Comprehension; Written Comprehension; Oral Expression; Written Expression; Fluency of Ideas; Perceptual Speed; Selective Attention
Skills: Writing; Coordination; Persuasion; Negotiation; Information Gathering; Information Organization; Idea Evaluation; Systems Perception; Identifying Downstream Consequences; Management of Financial Resources; Management of Material Resources; Management of Personnel Resources
General Work Activities: Getting Information Needed to Do the Job; Monitoring Processes, Material, or Surroundings; Identifying Objects, Actions, and Events; Estimating Needed Characteristics; Judging Qualities of Things, Services, People; Processing Information; Evaluating Information against Standards; Analyzing Data or Information; Making Decisions and Solving Problems; Thinking Creatively; Developing Objectives and Strategies; Organizing, Planning, and Prioritizing; Documenting/Recording Information; Communicating with Other Workers; Communicating with Persons Outside Organization; Establishing and Maintaining Relationships; Selling or Influencing Others; Resolving Conflicts, Negotiating with Others; Coordinating Work and Activities of Others; Developing and Building Teams; Guiding, Directing and Motivating Subordinates; Provide Consultation and Advice to Others; Performing Administrative Activities; Staffing Organizational Units; Monitoring and Controlling Resources
Job Characteristics: Persuade Someone to a Course of Action; Coordinate or Lead Others; Sitting; Frustrating Circumstances; Importance of Being Sure All is Done
GOE Group/s: 11.05.02 Business Administration: Administrative Specialization
CIP Program/s: 440401 Public Administration
Related DOT Job/s: 169.117-014 GRANT COORDINATOR

21999H CUSTOMS BROKERS. OOH Title/s: Purchasers and Buyers
Prepare and compile documents required by federal government for discharge of foreign cargo at domestic port to serve as intermediary between importers, merchant shipping companies, airlines, railroads, trucking companies, pipeline operators, and the United States Customs Service. Completes entry papers from shipper's invoice, in accordance with federal regulations, for discharge of foreign cargo at domestic port. Submits entry papers to U.S. Customs Service, according to federal regulations. Prepares papers for shipper to appeal duty charges imposed by Customs Service. Quotes duty rates on goods to be imported, based on knowledge of federal tariffs and excise taxes. Arranges for payment of duties as specified by law. Registers foreign ships with U.S. Coast Guard. Provides storage and transportation of imported goods from port to final destination.
Yearly Earnings: $31,564
Education: Bachelor's degree
Knowledge: Economics and Accounting; Geography; Foreign Language; Law, Government, and Jurisprudence; Transportation
Abilities: None above average
Skills: None above average
General Work Activities: Resolving Conflicts, Negotiating with Others; Performing for or Working with Public; Performing Administrative Activities; Monitoring and Controlling Resources
Job Characteristics: Job-Required Social Interaction; Deal with External Customers; Sitting; Importance of Being Sure All is Done
GOE Group/s: 11.04.04 Law: Abstracting, Document Preparation
CIP Program/s: 521101 International Business; 521403 International Business Marketing
Related DOT Job/s: 186.117-018 CUSTOMS BROKER

21999J ALL OTHER MANAGEMENT SUPPORT WORKERS. OOH Title/s: Inspectors and Compliance Officers, Except Construction; Lawyers and Judges; Personnel, Training, and Labor Relations Specialists and Managers; Firefighting Occupations; Postal Clerks and Mail Carriers; Police, Detectives, and Special Agents
All other management support workers not classified separately above.
Yearly Earnings: $31,564
Education: Bachelor's degree
GOE Group/s: 02.04.01 Laboratory Technology: Physical Sciences; 08.01.03 Sales Technology: Purchasing and Sales; 11.04.04 Law: Abstracting, Document Preparation; 11.05.02 Business Administration: Administrative Specialization; 11.11.03 Business Management: Transportation
CIP Program/s: 080706 General Selling Skills and Sales Operations; 100104 Radio and Television Broadcasting Technologists and Technicians; 150611 Metallurgical Technologists and Technicians; 220103 Paralegal/Legal Assistant; 490399 Water Transportation Workers, Other; 520801 Finance, General; 520807 Investments and Securities; 521501 Real Estate
Related DOT Job/s: 100.117-014 LIBRARY CONSULTANT; 110.167-010 BAR EXAMINER; 166.267-014 HOSPITAL-INSURANCE REPRESENTATIVE; 168.267-026 DEALER-COMPLIANCE REPRESENTATIVE; 168.367-010 ATTENDANCE OFFICER; 168.367-014 RATER, TRAVEL ACCOMMODATIONS; 169.167-022 FIRE ASSISTANT; 169.167-026 LABORATORY ASSISTANT, LIAISON INSPECTION; 169.167-078 UTILIZATION COORDINATOR; 184.167-250 TARIFF PUBLISHING AGENT; 187.167-062 MANAGER, BRANCH OPERATION EVALUATION; 189.117-050 ; 189.157-010 BUSINESS-OPPORTUNITY-AND-PROPERTY-INVESTMENT BROKER; 197.167-014 PURSER; 199.167-018 ENERGY-CONTROL OFFICER; 239.167-010 COMMUNICATIONS COORDINATOR; 239.367-018 MAIL-DISTRIBUTION-SCHEME EXAMINER; 310.267-010 ANALYST, FOOD AND BEVERAGE; 375.267-026 POLICE INSPECTOR I; 378.267-014 DISASTER OR DAMAGE CONTROL SPECIALIST

Engineers

22102 AEROSPACE ENGINEERS. OOH Title/s: Aerospace Engineers; Engineering, Science, and Data Processing Managers
Perform a variety of engineering work in designing, constructing, and testing aircraft, missiles, and spacecraft. May conduct basic and applied research to evaluate adaptability of materials and equipment to aircraft design and manufacture. May recommend improvements in testing equipment and techniques. Include aeronautical and astronautical engineers. Develops design criteria for aeronautical or aerospace products or systems, including testing methods, production costs, quality standards, and completion dates. Analyzes project requests and proposals and engineering data to determine feasibility, producibility, cost, and production time of aerospace or aeronautical product. Formulates conceptual design of aeronautical or aerospace products or systems to meet customer requirements. Formulates mathematical models or other methods of computer analysis to develop, evaluate, or modify design according to customer engineering requirements. Plans and conducts experimental, environmental, operational, and stress tests on models and prototypes of aircraft and aerospace systems and equipment. Evaluates product data and design from inspections and reports for conformance to engineering principles, customer requirements, and quality standards. Directs and coordinates activities of engineering or technical personnel

designing, fabricating, modifying, or testing aircraft or aerospace products. Directs research and development programs to improve production methods, parts, and equipment technology and to reduce costs. Reviews performance reports and documentation from customers and field engineers, and inspects malfunctioning or damaged products to determine problem. Plans and coordinates activities concerned with investigating and resolving customers reports of technical problems with aircraft or aerospace vehicles. Writes technical reports and other documentation, such as handbooks and bulletins, for use by engineering staff, management, and customers. Maintains records of performance reports for future reference. Evaluates and approves selection of vendors by study of past performance and new advertisements.

Yearly Earnings: $46,592

Education: Bachelor's degree

Knowledge: Administration and Management; Economics and Accounting; Customer and Personal Service; Personnel and Human Resources; Production and Processing; Computers and Electronics; Engineering and Technology; Design; Building and Construction; Mechanical; Mathematics; Physics; English Language; Telecommunications; Communications and Media

Abilities: Oral Comprehension; Written Comprehension; Oral Expression; Written Expression; Fluency of Ideas; Originality; Deductive Reasoning; Inductive Reasoning; Information Ordering; Mathematical Reasoning; Number Facility; Speed of Closure; Visualization

Skills: Reading Comprehension; Active Listening; Writing; Speaking; Mathematics; Science; Critical Thinking; Active Learning; Learning Strategies; Monitoring; Coordination; Instructing; Problem Identification; Information Gathering; Information Organization; Synthesis/Reorganization; Idea Generation; Idea Evaluation; Implementation Planning; Solution Appraisal; Operations Analysis; Technology Design; Equipment Selection; Installation; Programming; Testing; Operation Monitoring; Operation and Control; Product Inspection; Troubleshooting; Repairing; Visioning; Systems Perception; Identifying Downstream Consequences; Identification of Key Causes; Judgment and Decision Making; Systems Evaluation; Time Management; Management of Financial Resources; Management of Material Resources; Management of Personnel Resources

General Work Activities: Getting Information Needed to Do the Job; Monitoring Processes, Material, or Surroundings; Identifying Objects, Actions, and Events; Inspecting Equipment, Structures, or Material; Estimating Needed Characteristics; Judging Qualities of Things, Services, People; Processing Information; Evaluating Information against Standards; Analyzing Data or Information; Making Decisions and Solving Problems; Thinking Creatively; Updating and Using Job-Relevant Knowledge; Developing Objectives and Strategies; Organizing, Planning, and Prioritizing; Operating Vehicles or Equipment; Drafting and Specifying Technical Devices, etc.; Implementing Ideas, Programs, etc.; Documenting/Recording Information; Interpreting Meaning of Information to Others; Communicating with Other Workers; Communicating with Persons Outside Organization; Resolving Conflicts, Negotiating with Others; Coordinating Work and Activities of Others; Developing and Building Teams; Teaching Others; Guiding, Directing and Motivating Subordinates; Coaching and Developing Others; Provide Consultation and Advice to Others; Performing Administrative Activities; Monitoring and Controlling Resources

Job Characteristics: Responsibility for Outcomes and Results; Consequence of Error; Importance of Being Exact or Accurate; Importance of Being Sure All is Done

GOE Group/s: 05.01.01 Engineering: Research; 05.01.04 Engineering: Testing and Quality Control; 05.01.06 Engineering: Work Planning and Utilization; 05.01.07 Engineering: Design; 05.01.08 Engineering: General Engineering

CIP Program/s: 140201 Aerospace, Aeronautical and Astronautical Engineering

Related DOT Job/s: 002.061-010 AERODYNAMICIST; 002.061-014 AERONAUTICAL ENGINEER; 002.061-018 AERONAUTICAL TEST ENGINEER; 002.061-022 AERONAUTICAL-DESIGN ENGINEER; 002.061-026 AERONAUTICAL-RESEARCH ENGINEER; 002.061-030 STRESS ANALYST; 002.167-010 VALUE ENGINEER; 002.167-014 FIELD-SERVICE ENGINEER; 002.167-018 AERONAUTICAL PROJECT ENGINEER

22105A CERAMIC ENGINEERS. OOH Title/s: Metallurgical, Ceramic, and Materials Engineers

Conduct research, design machinery, and develop processing techniques related to the manufacturing of ceramic products. Conducts research into methods of processing, forming, and firing of clays to develop new ceramic products. Designs machinery, equipment, and apparatus for forming, firing, and handling products. Develops processing techniques and directs technical work concerned with manufacture of ceramic products. Directs testing of physical, chemical, and heat-resisting properties of materials. Analyzes results of tests to determine combinations of materials which will improve quality of products. Coordinates testing activities of finished products for such characteristics as texture, color, durability, glazing, and refractory properties. Directs and coordinates manufacturing of prototype ceramic product. Designs and directs others in fabrication of testing and test-control apparatus and equipment. Directs and coordinates activities concerned with development, procurement, installation, and calibration of test and recording instruments, equipment, and control devices. Prepares or directs preparation of product layout and detailed drawings. Prepares technical reports for use by engineering and management personnel.

Yearly Earnings: $46,592

Education: Bachelor's degree

Knowledge: Administration and Management; Production and Processing; Computers and Electronics; Engineering and Technology; Design; Mathematics; Physics; Chemistry; English Language

Abilities: Written Expression; Originality; Deductive Reasoning; Number Facility; Visualization; Visual Color Discrimination; Speech Clarity

Skills: Reading Comprehension; Active Listening; Writing; Speaking; Mathematics; Science; Critical Thinking; Active Learning; Coordination; Problem Identification; Information Gathering; Information Organization; Synthesis/Reorganization; Idea Generation; Idea Evaluation; Implementation Planning; Solution Appraisal; Operations Analysis; Technology Design; Equipment Selection; Installation; Programming; Testing; Product Inspection; Visioning; Systems Perception; Identifying Downstream Consequences; Identification of Key Causes; Judgment and Decision Making; Systems Evaluation; Time Management; Management of Material Resources; Management of Personnel Resources

General Work Activities: Getting Information Needed to Do the Job; Monitoring Processes, Material, or Surroundings; Identifying Objects, Actions, and Events; Inspecting Equipment, Structures, or Material; Estimating Needed Characteristics; Judging Qualities of Things, Services, People; Evaluating Information against Standards; Analyzing Data or Information; Making Decisions and Solving Problems; Thinking Creatively; Updating and Using Job-Relevant Knowledge; Developing Objectives and Strategies; Scheduling Work and Activities; Organizing, Planning, and Prioritizing; Drafting and Specifying Technical Devices, etc.; Implementing Ideas, Programs, etc.; Documenting/Recording Information; Interpreting Meaning of Information to Others; Communicating with Other Workers; Selling or Influencing Others; Coordinating Work and Activities of Others; Developing and Building Teams; Teaching Others; Guiding, Directing and Motivating Subordinates; Provide Consultation and Advice to Others

Job Characteristics: Objective or Subjective Information; Job-Required Social Interaction; Supervise, Coach, Train Others; Persuade Someone to a Course of Action; Take a Position Opposed to Others; Coordinate or Lead Others; Responsibility for Outcomes and Results; Hazardous Equipment; Consequence of Error; Importance of Being Exact or Accurate
GOE Group/s: 05.01.01 Engineering: Research; 05.01.04 Engineering: Testing and Quality Control; 05.01.07 Engineering: Design
CIP Program/s: 140601 Ceramic Sciences and Engineering
Related DOT Job/s: 006.061-010 CERAMIC DESIGN ENGINEER; 006.061-014 CERAMIC ENGINEER; 006.061-018 CERAMIC RESEARCH ENGINEER; 006.061-022 CERAMICS TEST ENGINEER

22105B METALLURGISTS. OOH Title/s: Metallurgical, Ceramic, and Materials Engineers

Investigate properties of metals and develop methods to produce new alloys, applications, and processes of extracting metals from their ores, and to commercially fabricate products from metals. Conducts microscopic and macroscopic studies of metals and alloys to determine their physical characteristics, properties, and reactions to processing techniques. Tests and investigates alloys to develop new or improved grades or production methods, and to determine compliance with manufacturing standards. Develops and improves processes for melting, hot-working, cold-working, heat-treating, molding, and pouring metals. Originates, controls, and develops processes used in extracting metals from their ores. Studies ore reduction problems to determine most efficient methods of producing metals commercially. Consults with engineers to develop methods of manufacturing alloys at minimum costs. Interprets findings and prepares drawings, charts, and graphs for reference or instructional purposes. Makes experimental sand molds, and tests sand for permeability, strength, and chemical composition. Writes reports referencing findings, conclusions, and recommendations. Directs laboratory personnel in preparing samples, and designates area of samples for microscopic or macroscopic examinations. Controls temperature adjustments, charge mixtures, and other variables on blast and steel-melting furnaces.
Yearly Earnings: $46,592
Education: Bachelor's degree
Knowledge: Administration and Management; Production and Processing; Engineering and Technology; Design; Physics; Chemistry; Geography; English Language
Abilities: Oral Comprehension; Written Comprehension; Written Expression; Originality; Deductive Reasoning; Inductive Reasoning; Category Flexibility; Mathematical Reasoning; Number Facility; Memorization; Near Vision
Skills: Reading Comprehension; Active Listening; Writing; Speaking; Mathematics; Science; Critical Thinking; Active Learning; Instructing; Problem Identification; Information Gathering; Information Organization; Synthesis/Reorganization; Idea Generation; Idea Evaluation; Implementation Planning; Solution Appraisal; Operations Analysis; Technology Design; Testing; Operation Monitoring; Operation and Control; Product Inspection; Visioning; Systems Perception; Identifying Downstream Consequences; Judgment and Decision Making
General Work Activities: Getting Information Needed to Do the Job; Monitoring Processes, Material, or Surroundings; Judging Qualities of Things, Services, People; Evaluating Information against Standards; Analyzing Data or Information; Making Decisions and Solving Problems; Thinking Creatively; Updating and Using Job-Relevant Knowledge; Developing Objectives and Strategies; Operating Vehicles or Equipment; Drafting and Specifying Technical Devices, etc.; Implementing Ideas, Programs, etc.; Documenting/Recording Information; Interpreting Meaning of Information to Others; Communicating with Other Workers; Communicating with Persons Outside Organization; Coordinating Work and Activities of Others; Developing and Building Teams; Guiding, Directing and Motivating Subordinates; Provide Consultation and Advice to Others; Staffing Organizational Units; Monitoring and Controlling Resources
Job Characteristics: None above average
GOE Group/s: 02.01.02 Physical Sciences: Technology; 05.01.01 Engineering: Research; 05.01.04 Engineering: Testing and Quality Control; 05.01.06 Engineering: Work Planning and Utilization
CIP Program/s: 142001 Metallurgical Engineering; 400701 Metallurgy
Related DOT Job/s: 011.061-010 FOUNDRY METALLURGIST; 011.061-014 METALLOGRAPHER; 011.061-018 METALLURGIST, EXTRACTIVE; 011.061-022 METALLURGIST, PHYSICAL

22105C WELDING ENGINEERS. OOH Title/s: Metallurgical, Ceramic, and Materials Engineers

Develop welding techniques, procedures, and applications of welding equipment to problems involving fabrication of metals. Conducts research and development investigations to improve existing or to develop new welding equipment. Conducts research and development investigations to develop new or to modify current welding techniques and procedures. Conducts research and development investigations to develop and test new fabrication processes and procedures. Establishes welding procedures for production and welding personnel, to ensure compliance with specifications, processes, and heating requirements. Evaluates new equipment, techniques, and materials in welding field for possible application to current welding problems or production processes. Prepares technical reports identifying results of research and development and preventive maintenance investigations. Directs and coordinates technical inspections to ensure compliance with established welding procedures and standards. Contacts other agencies, engineering personnel, or clients to exchange ideas, information, or technical advice.
Yearly Earnings: $46,592
Education: Bachelor's degree
Knowledge: Engineering and Technology; Design; Building and Construction; Mathematics; Physics
Abilities: Written Expression; Fluency of Ideas; Originality; Problem Sensitivity; Inductive Reasoning; Flexibility of Closure
Skills: Active Listening; Writing; Speaking; Mathematics; Science; Critical Thinking; Active Learning; Coordination; Problem Identification; Information Gathering; Information Organization; Synthesis/Reorganization; Idea Generation; Idea Evaluation; Implementation Planning; Solution Appraisal; Operations Analysis; Technology Design; Equipment Selection; Testing; Product Inspection; Troubleshooting; Visioning; Systems Perception; Identifying Downstream Consequences; Identification of Key Causes; Judgment and Decision Making; Systems Evaluation; Management of Material Resources
General Work Activities: Getting Information Needed to Do the Job; Identifying Objects, Actions, and Events; Inspecting Equipment, Structures, or Material; Estimating Needed Characteristics; Judging Qualities of Things, Services, People; Processing Information; Evaluating Information against Standards; Analyzing Data or Information; Making Decisions and Solving Problems; Thinking Creatively; Updating and Using Job-Relevant Knowledge; Developing Objectives and Strategies; Scheduling Work and Activities; Organizing, Planning, and Prioritizing; Controlling Machines and Processes; Drafting and Specifying Technical Devices, etc.; Implementing Ideas, Programs, etc.; Repairing and Maintaining Mechanical Equipment; Documenting/Recording Information; Interpreting Meaning of Information to Others; Communicating with Other Workers; Communicating with Persons Outside Organization; Selling or Influencing Others; Developing and Building Teams; Provide Consultation and Advice to Others

Job Characteristics: Supervise, Coach, Train Others; Persuade Someone to a Course of Action; Take a Position Opposed to Others; Coordinate or Lead Others; Responsibility for Outcomes and Results; Sounds, Noise Levels are Distracting, etc.
GOE Group/s: 05.01.08 Engineering: General Engineering
CIP Program/s: 142001 Metallurgical Engineering
Related DOT Job/s: 011.061-026 WELDING ENGINEER

22105D MATERIALS ENGINEERS. OOH Title/s: Metallurgical, Ceramic, and Materials Engineers
*Evaluate materials and develop machinery and processes to manufacture materials for use in products that must meet specialized design and performance specifications. Develop new uses for known materials. Include those working with composite materials or specializing in one type of material, such as graphite, metal and metal alloys, ceramics and glass, plastics and polymers, and naturally occurring materials. Include metallurgists and metallurgical engineers, ceramic engineers, and welding engineers.*Reviews new product plans and makes recommendations for material selection based on design objectives and cost. Plans and implements laboratory operations to develop material and fabrication procedures that maintain cost and performance standards. Evaluates technical and economic factors relating to process or product design objectives. Reviews product failure data and interprets laboratory test results to determine material or process causes. Confers with producers of material during investigation and evaluation of material for product applications.
Yearly Earnings: $46,592
Education: Bachelor's degree
Knowledge: Economics and Accounting; Production and Processing; Engineering and Technology; Design; Mathematics; Physics; Chemistry; English Language
Abilities: Written Comprehension; Written Expression; Fluency of Ideas; Originality; Problem Sensitivity; Deductive Reasoning; Inductive Reasoning; Mathematical Reasoning; Number Facility; Flexibility of Closure; Perceptual Speed; Visualization; Selective Attention
Skills: Reading Comprehension; Active Listening; Writing; Speaking; Mathematics; Science; Critical Thinking; Active Learning; Coordination; Problem Identification; Information Gathering; Information Organization; Synthesis/Reorganization; Idea Generation; Idea Evaluation; Implementation Planning; Solution Appraisal; Operations Analysis; Technology Design; Equipment Selection; Product Inspection; Troubleshooting; Visioning; Systems Perception; Identifying Downstream Consequences; Identification of Key Causes; Judgment and Decision Making; Systems Evaluation
General Work Activities: Getting Information Needed to Do the Job; Monitoring Processes, Material, or Surroundings; Identifying Objects, Actions, and Events; Estimating Needed Characteristics; Judging Qualities of Things, Services, People; Processing Information; Evaluating Information against Standards; Analyzing Data or Information; Making Decisions and Solving Problems; Thinking Creatively; Updating and Using Job-Relevant Knowledge; Developing Objectives and Strategies; Scheduling Work and Activities; Organizing, Planning, and Prioritizing; Drafting and Specifying Technical Devices, etc.; Implementing Ideas, Programs, etc.; Interpreting Meaning of Information to Others; Communicating with Other Workers; Selling or Influencing Others; Developing and Building Teams; Provide Consultation and Advice to Others; Monitoring and Controlling Resources
Job Characteristics: Objective or Subjective Information; Persuade Someone to a Course of Action; Take a Position Opposed to Others; Coordinate or Lead Others; Responsibility for Outcomes and Results; Sitting
GOE Group/s: 05.01.06 Engineering: Work Planning and Utilization
CIP Program/s: 143101 Materials Science
Related DOT Job/s: 019.061-014 MATERIALS ENGINEER

22108 MINING ENGINEERS, INCLUDING MINE SAFETY. OOH Title/s: Mining Engineers
Determine the location and plan the extraction of coal, metallic ores, nonmetallic minerals, and building materials, such as stone and gravel. Work involves conducting preliminary surveys of deposits or undeveloped mines and planning their development; examining deposits or mines to determine whether they can be worked at a profit; making geological and topographical surveys; evolving methods of mining best suited to character, type, and size of deposits; and supervising mining operations. Lays out and directs mine construction operations. Plans and coordinates mining processes and labor utilization. Plans, conducts, or directs others in performing mining experiments to test or prove research findings. Evaluates data to develop new mining products, equipment, or processes. Devises methods to solve environmental problems and reclaim mine sites. Analyzes labor requirements, equipment needs, and operational costs to prepare budget. Plans and supervises construction of access roads, power supplies, and water, communication, ventilation, and drainage systems. Directs and coordinates manufacturing or building of prototype mining product or system. Inspects mining areas for unsafe equipment and working conditions, tests air, and recommends installation or alteration of air-circulation equipment. Prepares technical reports for use by mining, engineering, and management personnel. Prepares or directs preparation of product or system layout and detailed drawings and schematics. Determines conditions under which tests are to be conducted and sequences and phases of test operations. Designs and maintains protective and rescue equipment and safety devices. Instructs mine personnel in safe working practices, first aid, and compliance with mining laws and practices, and promotes safety. Leads rescue activities, investigates accidents, reports causes, and recommends remedial actions. Confers with others to clarify or resolve problems. Designs and directs other personnel in fabrication of testing and test-control apparatus and equipment. Directs and coordinates activities concerned with development, procurement, installation, and calibration of test and recording instruments, equipment, and control devices.
Yearly Earnings: $46,592
Education: Bachelor's degree
Knowledge: Administration and Management; Economics and Accounting; Personnel and Human Resources; Production and Processing; Engineering and Technology; Design; Building and Construction; Mechanical; Mathematics; Physics; Chemistry; Geography; Education and Training; English Language; Public Safety and Security; Law, Government, and Jurisprudence; Transportation
Abilities: Oral Comprehension; Written Comprehension; Oral Expression; Written Expression; Fluency of Ideas; Originality; Problem Sensitivity; Deductive Reasoning; Inductive Reasoning; Information Ordering; Number Facility; Speed of Closure; Flexibility of Closure; Visualization; Gross Body Equilibrium; Far Vision; Night Vision
Skills: Reading Comprehension; Active Listening; Writing; Speaking; Mathematics; Science; Critical Thinking; Active Learning; Learning Strategies; Monitoring; Coordination; Persuasion; Negotiation; Instructing; Problem Identification; Information Gathering; Information Organization; Synthesis/Reorganization; Idea Generation; Idea Evaluation; Implementation Planning; Solution Appraisal; Operations Analysis; Technology Design; Equipment Selection; Installation; Programming; Testing; Product Inspection; Troubleshooting; Visioning; Systems Perception; Identifying Downstream Consequences; Identification of Key Causes; Judgment and Decision Making; Systems Evaluation; Time Management; Management of Financial Resources;

Management of Material Resources; Management of Personnel Resources
General Work Activities: Getting Information Needed to Do the Job; Monitoring Processes, Material, or Surroundings; Identifying Objects, Actions, and Events; Inspecting Equipment, Structures, or Material; Estimating Needed Characteristics; Judging Qualities of Things, Services, People; Processing Information; Evaluating Information against Standards; Analyzing Data or Information; Making Decisions and Solving Problems; Thinking Creatively; Updating and Using Job-Relevant Knowledge; Developing Objectives and Strategies; Scheduling Work and Activities; Organizing, Planning, and Prioritizing; Drafting and Specifying Technical Devices, etc.; Implementing Ideas, Programs, etc.; Repairing and Maintaining Mechanical Equipment; Documenting/Recording Information; Interpreting Meaning of Information to Others; Communicating with Other Workers; Resolving Conflicts, Negotiating with Others; Coordinating Work and Activities of Others; Developing and Building Teams; Guiding, Directing and Motivating Subordinates; Provide Consultation and Advice to Others; Monitoring and Controlling Resources
Job Characteristics: Objective or Subjective Information; Supervise, Coach, Train Others; Persuade Someone to a Course of Action; Take a Position Opposed to Others; Coordinate or Lead Others; Responsible for Others' Health and Safety; Responsibility for Outcomes and Results; Frequency in Conflict Situations; Extremely Bright or Inadequate Lighting; Hazardous Conditions; Specialized Protective or Safety Attire; Consequence of Error; Importance of Being Sure All is Done
GOE Group/s: 05.01.01 Engineering: Research; 05.01.02 Engineering: Environmental Protection; 05.01.04 Engineering: Testing and Quality Control; 05.01.06 Engineering: Work Planning and Utilization; 05.01.07 Engineering: Design
CIP Program/s: 142101 Mining and Mineral Engineering; 142501 Petroleum Engineering
Related DOT Job/s: 010.061-010 DESIGN ENGINEER, MINING-AND-OIL-FIELD EQUIPMENT; 010.061-014 MINING ENGINEER; 010.061-022 RESEARCH ENGINEER, MINING-AND-OIL-WELL EQUIPMENT; 010.061-026 SAFETY ENGINEER, MINES; 010.061-030 TEST ENGINEER, MINING-AND-OIL-FIELD EQUIPMENT

22111 PETROLEUM ENGINEERS. OOH Title/s: Petroleum Engineers; Engineering, Science, and Data Processing Managers

Devise methods to improve oil and gas well production and determine the need for new or modified tool designs. Oversee drilling and offer technical advice to achieve economical and satisfactory progress. Designs or modifies mining and oil field machinery and tools, applying engineering principles. Conducts engineering research experiments to improve or modify mining and oil machinery and operations. Develops plans for oil and gas field drilling, and for product recovery and treatment. Confers with scientific, engineering, and technical personnel to resolve design, research, and testing problems. Evaluates findings to develop, design, or test equipment or processes. Monitors production rates, and plans rework processes to improve production. Analyzes data to recommend placement of wells and supplementary processes to enhance production. Assists engineering and other personnel to solve operating problems. Coordinates activities of workers engaged in research, planning, and development. Inspects oil and gas wells to determine that installations are completed. Assigns work to staff to obtain maximum utilization of personnel. Interprets drilling and testing information for personnel. Tests machinery and equipment to ensure conformance to performance specifications and to ensure safety. Writes technical reports for engineering and management personnel.
Yearly Earnings: $46,592
Education: Bachelor's degree
Knowledge: Administration and Management; Personnel and Human Resources; Production and Processing; Engineering and Technology; Design; Mechanical; Mathematics; Physics; English Language
Abilities: Oral Comprehension; Written Comprehension; Oral Expression; Written Expression; Fluency of Ideas; Originality; Problem Sensitivity; Deductive Reasoning; Inductive Reasoning; Information Ordering; Category Flexibility; Mathematical Reasoning; Number Facility; Memorization; Speed of Closure; Flexibility of Closure; Perceptual Speed; Spatial Orientation; Visualization; Time Sharing; Response Orientation; Rate Control; Gross Body Equilibrium; Peripheral Vision; Depth Perception; Glare Sensitivity; Hearing Sensitivity; Auditory Attention; Sound Localization
Skills: Reading Comprehension; Writing; Speaking; Mathematics; Science; Critical Thinking; Active Learning; Monitoring; Coordination; Instructing; Problem Identification; Information Gathering; Information Organization; Synthesis/Reorganization; Idea Generation; Idea Evaluation; Implementation Planning; Solution Appraisal; Operations Analysis; Technology Design; Equipment Selection; Installation; Programming; Testing; Operation Monitoring; Operation and Control; Product Inspection; Troubleshooting; Systems Perception; Identifying Downstream Consequences; Identification of Key Causes; Judgment and Decision Making; Systems Evaluation; Time Management; Management of Financial Resources; Management of Material Resources; Management of Personnel Resources
General Work Activities: Getting Information Needed to Do the Job; Monitoring Processes, Material, or Surroundings; Identifying Objects, Actions, and Events; Inspecting Equipment, Structures, or Material; Estimating Needed Characteristics; Judging Qualities of Things, Services, People; Evaluating Information against Standards; Analyzing Data or Information; Making Decisions and Solving Problems; Thinking Creatively; Updating and Using Job-Relevant Knowledge; Developing Objectives and Strategies; Scheduling Work and Activities; Organizing, Planning, and Prioritizing; Operating Vehicles or Equipment; Drafting and Specifying Technical Devices, etc.; Implementing Ideas, Programs, etc.; Communicating with Other Workers; Coordinating Work and Activities of Others; Guiding, Directing and Motivating Subordinates; Provide Consultation and Advice to Others
Job Characteristics: Supervise, Coach, Train Others; Take a Position Opposed to Others; Coordinate or Lead Others; Responsibility for Outcomes and Results; Deal with Physical, Aggressive People; Hazardous Conditions; Walking or Running; Consequence of Error; Frustrating Circumstances; Degree of Automation; Importance of Being Exact or Accurate; Importance of Being Sure All is Done; Importance of Being Aware of New Events
GOE Group/s: 05.01.01 Engineering: Research; 05.01.04 Engineering: Testing and Quality Control; 05.01.07 Engineering: Design; 05.01.08 Engineering: General Engineering; 05.02.03 Managerial Work: Mechanical: Processing and Manufacturing
CIP Program/s: 142101 Mining and Mineral Engineering; 142501 Petroleum Engineering
Related DOT Job/s: 010.061-010 ; 010.061-018 PETROLEUM ENGINEER; 010.061-022 ; 010.061-030 ; 010.161-010 CHIEF ENGINEER, RESEARCH; 010.167-010 CHIEF ENGINEER; 010.167-014 DISTRICT SUPERVISOR, MUD-ANALYSIS WELL LOGGING

22114 CHEMICAL ENGINEERS. OOH Title/s: Chemical Engineers

Design chemical plant equipment and devise processes for manufacturing chemicals and products such as gasoline, synthetic rubber, plastics, detergents, cement, paper, and pulp by applying principles and technology of chemistry, physics, and engineering. Devises processes to separate components of liquids or gases, using absorbent such as fuller's earth or carbons. Conducts research to develop new and improved chemical manufacturing proc-

esses. Designs and plans layout, and oversees workers engaged in constructing and improving equipment to implement chemical processes on commercial scale. Designs measurement and control systems for chemical plants based on data collected in laboratory experiments and in pilot plant operations. Develops electrochemical processes to generate electric currents, using controlled chemical reactions, or to produce chemical changes, using electric currents. Determines most effective arrangement of operations, such as mixing, crushing, heat transfer, distillation, and drying. Performs laboratory studies of steps in manufacture of new product, and tests proposed process in small-scale operation (pilot plant). Performs tests throughout stages of production to determine degree of control over variables, including temperature, density, specific gravity, and pressure. Develops safety procedures to be employed by workers operating equipment or working in close proximity to ongoing chemical reactions. Prepares estimate of production costs and production progress reports for management. Directs activities of workers who operate equipment such as absorption and evaporation towers and electromagnets to effect required chemical reaction. Directs workers using absorption method to remove soluble constituent or vapor by dissolving in a liquid.
Yearly Earnings: $46,592
Education: Bachelor's degree
Knowledge: Administration and Management; Economics and Accounting; Production and Processing; Computers and Electronics; Engineering and Technology; Design; Mechanical; Mathematics; Physics; Chemistry; Biology; English Language; Public Safety and Security; Law, Government, and Jurisprudence
Abilities: Oral Comprehension; Written Comprehension; Oral Expression; Written Expression; Fluency of Ideas; Originality; Problem Sensitivity; Deductive Reasoning; Inductive Reasoning; Information Ordering; Category Flexibility; Mathematical Reasoning; Number Facility; Memorization; Speed of Closure; Perceptual Speed; Spatial Orientation; Visualization; Selective Attention; Time Sharing; Control Precision; Response Orientation; Reaction Time; Gross Body Equilibrium; Near Vision; Far Vision; Visual Color Discrimination; Peripheral Vision; Depth Perception; Glare Sensitivity; Hearing Sensitivity; Auditory Attention; Speech Clarity
Skills: Reading Comprehension; Writing; Speaking; Mathematics; Science; Critical Thinking; Active Learning; Learning Strategies; Monitoring; Coordination; Instructing; Problem Identification; Information Gathering; Information Organization; Synthesis/Reorganization; Idea Generation; Idea Evaluation; Implementation Planning; Solution Appraisal; Operations Analysis; Technology Design; Equipment Selection; Installation; Programming; Testing; Operation Monitoring; Product Inspection; Troubleshooting; Visioning; Systems Perception; Identifying Downstream Consequences; Identification of Key Causes; Judgment and Decision Making; Systems Evaluation; Time Management; Management of Financial Resources; Management of Material Resources; Management of Personnel Resources
General Work Activities: Getting Information Needed to Do the Job; Monitoring Processes, Material, or Surroundings; Identifying Objects, Actions, and Events; Inspecting Equipment, Structures, or Material; Estimating Needed Characteristics; Judging Qualities of Things, Services, People; Processing Information; Evaluating Information against Standards; Analyzing Data or Information; Making Decisions and Solving Problems; Thinking Creatively; Updating and Using Job-Relevant Knowledge; Developing Objectives and Strategies; Scheduling Work and Activities; Organizing, Planning, and Prioritizing; Controlling Machines and Processes; Operating Vehicles or Equipment; Drafting and Specifying Technical Devices, etc.; Implementing Ideas, Programs, etc.; Documenting/Recording Information; Interpreting Meaning of Information to Others; Communicating with Other Workers; Selling or Influencing Others; Coordinating Work and Activities of Others; Developing and Building Teams; Guiding, Directing and Motivating Subordinates; Provide Consultation and Advice to Others; Performing Administrative Activities; Monitoring and Controlling Resources
Job Characteristics: Supervise, Coach, Train Others; Responsible for Others' Health and Safety; Responsibility for Outcomes and Results; Contaminants; Hazardous Conditions; Common Protective or Safety Attire; Specialized Protective or Safety Attire; Consequence of Error; Frustrating Circumstances; Degree of Automation; Importance of Being Exact or Accurate; Importance of Being Sure All is Done
GOE Group/s: 05.01.01 Engineering: Research; 05.01.04 Engineering: Testing and Quality Control; 05.01.07 Engineering: Design; 05.01.08 Engineering: General Engineering
CIP Program/s: 140701 Chemical Engineering; 142801 Textile Sciences and Engineering; 143201 Polymer/Plastics Engineering
Related DOT Job/s: 008.061-010 ABSORPTION-AND-ADSORPTION ENGINEER; 008.061-014 CHEMICAL DESIGN ENGINEER, PROCESSES; 008.061-018 CHEMICAL ENGINEER; 008.061-022 CHEMICAL RESEARCH ENGINEER; 008.061-026 CHEMICAL-TEST ENGINEER

22117 NUCLEAR ENGINEERS. OOH Title/s: Nuclear Engineers

Conduct research on nuclear engineering problems. or apply principles and theory of nuclear science to problems concerned with release, control, and utilization of nuclear energy. Determines potential hazard and accident conditions which may exist in fuel handling and storage and recommends preventive measures. Performs experiments to determine acceptable methods of nuclear material usage, nuclear fuel reclamation, and waste disposal. Formulates equations that describe phenomena occurring during fission of nuclear fuels, and develops analytical models for research. Analyzes available data and consults with other scientists to determine parameters of experimentation and suitability of analytical models. Plans and designs nuclear research to discover facts or to test, prove, or modify known nuclear theories. Conducts tests to research nuclear fuel behavior and nuclear machinery and equipment performance. Examines accidents and obtains data to formulate preventive measures. Evaluates research findings to develop new concepts of thermonuclear analysis and new uses of radioactive models. Synthesizes analyses of tests results and prepares technical reports of findings and recommendations. Inspects nuclear fuels, waste, equipment, test-reactor vessel and related systems, and control instrumentation to identify potential problems or hazards. Monitors nuclear operations to identify potential or inherent design, construction, or operational problems to ensure safe operations. Designs and develops nuclear machinery and equipment, such as reactor cores, radiation shielding, and associated instrumentation and control mechanisms. Designs and oversees construction and operation of nuclear fuels reprocessing systems and reclamation systems. Computes cost estimates of construction projects, prepares project proposals, and discusses projects with vendors, contractors, and nuclear facility's review board. Formulates and initiates corrective actions and orders plant shutdown in emergency situations. Maintains reports to summarize work and document plant operations. Writes operational instructions relative to nuclear plant operation and nuclear fuel and waste handling and disposal. Directs operating and maintenance activities of operational nuclear facility.
Yearly Earnings: $46,592
Education: Bachelor's degree
Knowledge: Administration and Management; Economics and Accounting; Computers and Electronics; Engineering and Technology; Design; Building and Construction; Mathematics; Physics; Chemistry; Education and Training; English Language; Public Safety and Security
Abilities: Oral Comprehension; Written Comprehension; Oral Expression; Written Expression; Fluency of Ideas; Originality; Problem Sensitivity; Deductive Reasoning; Inductive Reasoning; Information

Ordering; Mathematical Reasoning; Number Facility; Speed of Closure; Flexibility of Closure; Perceptual Speed; Visualization; Selective Attention; Time Sharing; Control Precision; Response Orientation; Rate Control; Reaction Time; Hearing Sensitivity; Auditory Attention; Speech Recognition; Speech Clarity

Skills: Reading Comprehension; Active Listening; Writing; Speaking; Mathematics; Science; Critical Thinking; Active Learning; Learning Strategies; Monitoring; Coordination; Persuasion; Instructing; Problem Identification; Information Gathering; Information Organization; Synthesis/Reorganization; Idea Generation; Idea Evaluation; Implementation Planning; Solution Appraisal; Operations Analysis; Technology Design; Equipment Selection; Installation; Programming; Testing; Operation Monitoring; Operation and Control; Product Inspection; Equipment Maintenance; Troubleshooting; Repairing; Visioning; Systems Perception; Identifying Downstream Consequences; Identification of Key Causes; Judgment and Decision Making; Systems Evaluation; Time Management; Management of Financial Resources; Management of Material Resources; Management of Personnel Resources

General Work Activities: Getting Information Needed to Do the Job; Monitoring Processes, Material, or Surroundings; Identifying Objects, Actions, and Events; Inspecting Equipment, Structures, or Material; Estimating Needed Characteristics; Judging Qualities of Things, Services, People; Processing Information; Evaluating Information against Standards; Analyzing Data or Information; Making Decisions and Solving Problems; Thinking Creatively; Updating and Using Job-Relevant Knowledge; Developing Objectives and Strategies; Scheduling Work and Activities; Organizing, Planning, and Prioritizing; Operating Vehicles or Equipment; Drafting and Specifying Technical Devices, etc.; Implementing Ideas, Programs, etc.; Documenting/Recording Information; Interpreting Meaning of Information to Others; Communicating with Other Workers; Communicating with Persons Outside Organization; Coordinating Work and Activities of Others; Provide Consultation and Advice to Others; Performing Administrative Activities; Monitoring and Controlling Resources

Job Characteristics: Supervise, Coach, Train Others; Take a Position Opposed to Others; Coordinate or Lead Others; Responsible for Others' Health and Safety; Responsibility for Outcomes and Results; Radiation; High Places; Hazardous Conditions; Climbing Ladders, Scaffolds, Poles, etc.; Specialized Protective or Safety Attire; Consequence of Error; Degree of Automation; Importance of Being Exact or Accurate; Importance of Being Sure All is Done; Importance of Being Aware of New Events; Pace Determined by Speed of Equipment

GOE Group/s: 05.01.01 Engineering: Research; 05.01.02 Engineering: Environmental Protection; 05.01.03 Engineering: Systems Design; 05.01.04 Engineering: Testing and Quality Control; 05.01.07 Engineering: Design

CIP Program/s: 140801 Civil Engineering, General; 140802 Geotechnical Engineering; 142301 Nuclear Engineering

Related DOT Job/s: 005.061-042 WASTE-MANAGEMENT ENGINEER, RADIOACTIVE MATERIALS; 015.061-010 DESIGN ENGINEER, NUCLEAR EQUIPMENT; 015.061-014 NUCLEAR ENGINEER; 015.061-018 RESEARCH ENGINEER, NUCLEAR EQUIPMENT; 015.061-022 TEST ENGINEER, NUCLEAR EQUIPMENT; 015.061-026 NUCLEAR-FUELS RECLAMATION ENGINEER; 015.061-030 NUCLEAR-FUELS RESEARCH ENGINEER; 015.067-010 NUCLEAR-CRITICALITY SAFETY ENGINEER; 015.137-010 RADIATION-PROTECTION ENGINEER; 015.167-010 NUCLEAR-PLANT TECHNICAL ADVISOR; 015.167-014 NUCLEAR-TEST-REACTOR PROGRAM COORDINATOR

22121 CIVIL ENGINEERS, INCLUDING TRAFFIC.

OOH Title/s: Civil Engineers

Perform engineering duties in planning, designing, and overseeing construction and maintenance of structures and facilities such as roads, railroads, airports, bridges, harbors, channels, dams, irrigation projects, pipelines, power plants, water and sewage systems, and waste disposal units. Include traffic engineers who specialize in studying vehicular and pedestrian traffic conditions. Analyzes survey reports, maps, drawings, blueprints, aerial photography, and other topographical or geologic data to plan projects. Plans and designs transportation or hydraulic systems and structures, following construction and government standards, using design software and drawing tools. Estimates quantities and cost of materials, equipment, or labor to determine project feasibility. Directs construction, operations, and maintenance activities at project site. Computes load and grade requirements, water flow rates, and material stress factors to determine design specifications. Directs or participates in surveying to lay out installations and establish reference points, grades, and elevations to guide construction. Inspects project sites to monitor progress and ensure conformance to design specifications and safety or sanitation standards. Conducts studies of traffic patterns or environmental conditions to identify engineering problems and assess the potential impact of projects. Tests soils and materials to determine the adequacy and strength of foundations, concrete, asphalt, or steel. Provides technical advice regarding design, construction, or program modifications and structural repairs to industrial and managerial personnel. Prepares or presents public reports, such as bid proposals, deeds, environmental impact statements, and property and right-of-way descriptions.

Yearly Earnings: $44,148

Education: Bachelor's degree

Knowledge: Administration and Management; Economics and Accounting; Computers and Electronics; Engineering and Technology; Design; Building and Construction; Mathematics; Physics; Geography; English Language; Public Safety and Security; Law, Government, and Jurisprudence; Transportation

Abilities: Oral Comprehension; Written Comprehension; Oral Expression; Written Expression; Fluency of Ideas; Originality; Problem Sensitivity; Deductive Reasoning; Inductive Reasoning; Information Ordering; Mathematical Reasoning; Number Facility; Speed of Closure; Flexibility of Closure; Visualization; Time Sharing

Skills: Reading Comprehension; Active Listening; Writing; Speaking; Mathematics; Science; Critical Thinking; Active Learning; Monitoring; Coordination; Persuasion; Problem Identification; Information Gathering; Synthesis/Reorganization; Idea Generation; Idea Evaluation; Implementation Planning; Solution Appraisal; Operations Analysis; Technology Design; Equipment Selection; Installation; Programming; Testing; Product Inspection; Troubleshooting; Visioning; Systems Perception; Identifying Downstream Consequences; Identification of Key Causes; Judgment and Decision Making; Systems Evaluation; Management of Financial Resources; Management of Material Resources; Management of Personnel Resources

General Work Activities: Getting Information Needed to Do the Job; Identifying Objects, Actions, and Events; Inspecting Equipment, Structures, or Material; Estimating Needed Characteristics; Processing Information; Evaluating Information against Standards; Analyzing Data or Information; Making Decisions and Solving Problems; Updating and Using Job-Relevant Knowledge; Developing Objectives and Strategies; Scheduling Work and Activities; Organizing, Planning, and Prioritizing; Operating Vehicles or Equipment; Drafting and Specifying Technical Devices, etc.; Implementing Ideas, Programs, etc.; Documenting/Recording Information; Interpreting Meaning of Information to Others; Communicating with Other Workers; Communicating with Persons Outside Organization; Coordinating Work and Activities of Others; Provide Consultation and Advice to Others

Job Characteristics: Responsibility for Outcomes and Results; High Places; Climbing Ladders, Scaffolds, Poles, etc.; Consequence of

Error; Frustrating Circumstances; Importance of Being Exact or Accurate; Importance of Being Sure All is Done
GOE Group/s: 05.01.02 Engineering: Environmental Protection; 05.01.03 Engineering: Systems Design; 05.01.06 Engineering: Work Planning and Utilization; 05.01.07 Engineering: Design; 05.01.08 Engineering: General Engineering
CIP Program/s: 010201 Agricultural Mechanization, General; 140401 Architectural Engineering; 140801 Civil Engineering, General; 140802 Geotechnical Engineering; 140803 Structural Engineering; 140804 Transportation and Highway Engineering; 140805 Water Resources Engineering
Related DOT Job/s: 005.061-010 AIRPORT ENGINEER; 005.061-014 CIVIL ENGINEER; 005.061-018 HYDRAULIC ENGINEER; 005.061-022 IRRIGATION ENGINEER; 005.061-026 RAILROAD ENGINEER; 005.061-030 SANITARY ENGINEER; 005.061-034 STRUCTURAL ENGINEER; 005.061-038 TRANSPORTATION ENGINEER; 005.167-014 DRAINAGE-DESIGN COORDINATOR; 005.167-018 FOREST ENGINEER; 005.167-026 PRODUCTION ENGINEER, TRACK; 019.167-018 RESOURCE-RECOVERY ENGINEER

22123 AGRICULTURAL ENGINEERS. OOH Title/s: Engineers

Apply knowledge of engineering technology and biological science to agricultural problems concerned with power and machinery, electrification, structures, soil and water conservation, and processing of agricultural products. Designs and directs manufacture of equipment for land tillage and fertilization, plant and animal disease and insect control, and for harvesting or moving commodities. Designs and supervises erection of crop storage, animal shelter, and residential structures and heating, lighting, cooling, plumbing, and waste disposal systems. Designs and supervises installation of equipment and instruments used to evaluate and process farm products, and to automate agricultural operations. Develops criteria for design, manufacture, or construction of equipment, structures, and facilities. Plans and directs construction of rural electric-power distribution systems, and irrigation, drainage, and flood control systems for soil and water conservation. Designs sensing, measuring, and recording devices and instrumentation used to study plant or animal life. Studies such problems as effect of temperature, humidity, and light on plants and animals and effectiveness of different insecticides. Conducts research to develop agricultural machinery and equipment. Designs agricultural machinery and equipment. Conducts tests on agricultural machinery and equipment. Conducts radio and television educational programs to provide assistance to farmers, local groups, and related farm cooperatives.
Yearly Earnings: $45,032
Education: Bachelor's degree
Knowledge: Administration and Management; Economics and Accounting; Production and Processing; Food Production; Computers and Electronics; Engineering and Technology; Design; Building and Construction; Mechanical; Mathematics; Physics; Chemistry; Biology; Sociology and Anthropology; Geography; Education and Training; English Language; Philosophy and Theology; Law, Government, and Jurisprudence; Communications and Media; Transportation
Abilities: Oral Comprehension; Written Comprehension; Written Expression; Fluency of Ideas; Originality; Problem Sensitivity; Deductive Reasoning; Inductive Reasoning; Information Ordering; Category Flexibility; Mathematical Reasoning; Number Facility; Memorization; Speed of Closure; Flexibility of Closure; Visualization; Selective Attention; Time Sharing; Speech Clarity
Skills: Reading Comprehension; Active Listening; Writing; Speaking; Mathematics; Science; Critical Thinking; Active Learning; Learning Strategies; Monitoring; Coordination; Persuasion; Negotiation; Instructing; Problem Identification; Information Gathering; Information Organization; Synthesis/Reorganization; Idea Generation; Idea Evaluation; Implementation Planning; Solution Appraisal; Operations Analysis; Technology Design; Equipment Selection; Installation; Programming; Testing; Product Inspection; Troubleshooting; Visioning; Systems Perception; Identifying Downstream Consequences; Identification of Key Causes; Judgment and Decision Making; Systems Evaluation; Time Management; Management of Personnel Resources
General Work Activities: Getting Information Needed to Do the Job; Monitoring Processes, Material, or Surroundings; Identifying Objects, Actions, and Events; Inspecting Equipment, Structures, or Material; Estimating Needed Characteristics; Judging Qualities of Things, Services, People; Processing Information; Evaluating Information against Standards; Analyzing Data or Information; Making Decisions and Solving Problems; Thinking Creatively; Updating and Using Job-Relevant Knowledge; Developing Objectives and Strategies; Scheduling Work and Activities; Organizing, Planning, and Prioritizing; Operating Vehicles or Equipment; Drafting and Specifying Technical Devices, etc.; Implementing Ideas, Programs, etc.; Documenting/Recording Information; Interpreting Meaning of Information to Others; Communicating with Other Workers; Communicating with Persons Outside Organization; Coordinating Work and Activities of Others; Developing and Building Teams; Teaching Others; Guiding, Directing and Motivating Subordinates; Coaching and Developing Others; Provide Consultation and Advice to Others
Job Characteristics: Supervise, Coach, Train Others; Persuade Someone to a Course of Action; Take a Position Opposed to Others; Coordinate or Lead Others; Very Hot; Extremely Bright or Inadequate Lighting; Hazardous Conditions
GOE Group/s: 05.01.01 Engineering: Research; 05.01.04 Engineering: Testing and Quality Control; 05.01.07 Engineering: Design; 05.01.08 Engineering: General Engineering
CIP Program/s: 140101 Engineering, General; 140301 Agricultural Engineering
Related DOT Job/s: 013.061-010 AGRICULTURAL ENGINEER; 013.061-014 AGRICULTURAL-RESEARCH ENGINEER; 013.061-018 DESIGN-ENGINEER, AGRICULTURAL EQUIPMENT; 013.061-022 TEST ENGINEER, AGRICULTURAL EQUIPMENT

22126A ELECTRICAL ENGINEERS. OOH Title/s: Electrical and Electronics Engineers

Design, develop, test, or supervise the manufacturing and installation of electrical equipment, components, or systems for commercial, industrial, military, or scientific use. Exclude computer engineers. Designs electrical instruments, equipment, facilities, components, products, and systems for commercial, industrial, and domestic purposes. Plans and implements research methodology and procedures to apply principles of electrical theory to engineering projects. Prepares and studies technical drawings, specifications of electrical systems, and topographical maps to ensure installation and operations conform to standards and customer requirements. Develops applications of controls, instruments, and systems for new commercial, domestic, and industrial uses. Directs operations and coordinates manufacturing, construction, installation, maintenance, and testing activities to ensure compliance with specifications, applicable codes, and customer requirements. Plans layout of electric power-generating plants and distribution lines and stations. Conducts field surveys and studies maps, graphs, diagrams, and other data to identify and correct power system problems. Performs detailed calculations to compute and establish manufacturing, construction, and installation standards and specifications. Confers with engineers, customers, and others to discuss existing or potential engineering projects and products. Inspects completed installations and observes operations for conformance to design and equipment specifications, and operational and safety standards. Evaluates and analyzes data regarding electric power systems and

stations, and recommends changes to improve operating efficiency. Estimates labor, material, and construction costs, and prepares specifications for purchase of materials and equipment. Collects data relating to commercial and residential development, population, and power system interconnection to determine operating efficiency of electrical systems. Compiles data and writes reports regarding existing and potential engineering studies and projects. Operates computer-assisted engineering and design software and equipment to perform engineering tasks. Investigates customer or public complaints, determines nature and extent of problem, and recommends remedial measures.
Yearly Earnings: $47,996
Education: Bachelor's degree
Knowledge: Administration and Management; Economics and Accounting; Production and Processing; Computers and Electronics; Engineering and Technology; Design; Building and Construction; Mechanical; Mathematics; Physics; Public Safety and Security; Telecommunications
Abilities: Oral Comprehension; Written Comprehension; Oral Expression; Written Expression; Fluency of Ideas; Originality; Problem Sensitivity; Deductive Reasoning; Inductive Reasoning; Information Ordering; Category Flexibility; Mathematical Reasoning; Number Facility; Memorization; Speed of Closure; Flexibility of Closure; Spatial Orientation; Visualization; Finger Dexterity; Wrist-Finger Speed
Skills: Reading Comprehension; Active Listening; Writing; Speaking; Mathematics; Science; Critical Thinking; Active Learning; Learning Strategies; Problem Identification; Information Gathering; Information Organization; Synthesis/Reorganization; Idea Generation; Idea Evaluation; Implementation Planning; Solution Appraisal; Operations Analysis; Technology Design; Equipment Selection; Programming; Testing; Operation Monitoring; Troubleshooting; Visioning; Systems Perception; Identifying Downstream Consequences; Identification of Key Causes; Judgment and Decision Making; Systems Evaluation; Management of Financial Resources; Management of Material Resources
General Work Activities: Getting Information Needed to Do the Job; Monitoring Processes, Material, or Surroundings; Identifying Objects, Actions, and Events; Inspecting Equipment, Structures, or Material; Estimating Needed Characteristics; Judging Qualities of Things, Services, People; Processing Information; Evaluating Information against Standards; Analyzing Data or Information; Making Decisions and Solving Problems; Thinking Creatively; Updating and Using Job-Relevant Knowledge; Developing Objectives and Strategies; Organizing, Planning, and Prioritizing; Operating Vehicles or Equipment; Drafting and Specifying Technical Devices, etc.; Implementing Ideas, Programs, etc.; Repairing and Maintaining Electrical Equipment; Documenting/Recording Information; Interpreting Meaning of Information to Others; Communicating with Other Workers; Communicating with Persons Outside Organization; Coordinating Work and Activities of Others; Developing and Building Teams; Guiding, Directing and Motivating Subordinates; Provide Consultation and Advice to Others; Monitoring and Controlling Resources
Job Characteristics: Objective or Subjective Information; Persuade Someone to a Course of Action; Take a Position Opposed to Others; Responsibility for Outcomes and Results; Frustrating Circumstances; Degree of Automation; Importance of Being Exact or Accurate; Importance of Being Sure All is Done
GOE Group/s: 05.01.01 Engineering: Research; 05.01.03 Engineering: Systems Design; 05.01.04 Engineering: Testing and Quality Control; 05.01.07 Engineering: Design; 05.01.08 Engineering: General Engineering
CIP Program/s: 141001 Electrical, Electronics and Communication Engineering; 142801 Textile Sciences and Engineering
Related DOT Job/s: 003.061-010 ELECTRICAL ENGINEER; 003.061-014 ELECTRICAL TEST ENGINEER; 003.061-018 ELECTRICAL-DESIGN ENGINEER; 003.061-022 ELECTRICAL-PROSPECTING ENGINEER; 003.061-026 ELECTRICAL-RESEARCH ENGINEER; 003.061-046 ILLUMINATING ENGINEER; 003.167-014 DISTRIBUTION-FIELD ENGINEER; 003.167-018 ELECTRICAL ENGINEER, POWER SYSTEM; 003.167-022 ELECTROLYSIS-AND-CORROSION-CONTROL ENGINEER; 003.167-026 ENGINEER OF SYSTEM DEVELOPMENT; 003.167-038 INDUCTION-COORDINATION POWER ENGINEER; 003.167-046 POWER-DISTRIBUTION ENGINEER; 003.167-050 POWER-TRANSMISSION ENGINEER; 003.167-054 PROTECTION ENGINEER

22126B ELECTRONICS ENGINEERS, EXCEPT COMPUTER. OOH Title/s: Electrical and Electronics Engineers

Research, design, develop, and test electronic components and systems for commercial, industrial, military, or scientific use, utilizing knowledge of electronic theory and materials properties. Design electronic circuits and components for use in fields such as telecommunications, aerospace guidance and propulsion control, acoustics, or instruments and controls. Exclude computer hardware engineers. Designs electronic components, products, and systems for commercial, industrial, medical, military, and scientific applications. Develops operational, maintenance, and testing procedures for electronic products, components, equipment, and systems. Plans and develops applications and modifications for electronic properties used in components, products, and systems, to improve technical performance. Plans and implements research, methodology, and procedures to apply principles of electronic theory to engineering projects. Directs and coordinates activities concerned with manufacture, construction, installation, maintenance, operation, and modification of electronic equipment, products, and systems. Evaluates operational systems and recommends repair or design modifications based on factors such as environment, service, cost, and system capabilities. Analyzes system requirements, capacity, cost, and customer needs to determine feasibility of project and to develop system plan. Conducts studies to gather information regarding current services, equipment capacities, traffic data, and acquisition and installation costs. Inspects electronic equipment, instruments, products, and systems to ensure conformance to specifications, safety standards, and applicable codes and regulations. Prepares engineering sketches and specifications for construction, relocation, and installation of transmitting and receiving equipment, facilities, products, and systems. Confers with engineers, customers, and others to discuss existing and potential engineering projects or products. Operates computer-assisted engineering and design software and equipment to perform engineering tasks. Provides technical assistance to field and laboratory staff regarding equipment standards and problems, and applications of transmitting and receiving methods. Prepares, reviews, and maintains maintenance schedules and operational reports and charts. Reviews or prepares budget and cost estimates for equipment, construction, and installation projects, and controls expenditures. Determines material and equipment needs, and orders supplies. Investigates causes of personal injury resulting from contact with high-voltage communications equipment.
Yearly Earnings: $47,996
Education: Bachelor's degree
Knowledge: Administration and Management; Economics and Accounting; Customer and Personal Service; Production and Processing; Computers and Electronics; Engineering and Technology; Design; Building and Construction; Mechanical; Mathematics; Physics; English Language; Telecommunications; Communications and Media
Abilities: Oral Comprehension; Written Comprehension; Oral Expression; Written Expression; Fluency of Ideas; Originality; Problem Sensitivity; Deductive Reasoning; Inductive Reasoning; Information Ordering; Category Flexibility; Mathematical Reasoning; Number Fa-

cility; Memorization; Speed of Closure; Flexibility of Closure; Visualization; Time Sharing; Finger Dexterity; Wrist-Finger Speed; Near Vision

Skills: Reading Comprehension; Writing; Mathematics; Science; Critical Thinking; Active Learning; Problem Identification; Information Gathering; Idea Generation; Idea Evaluation; Solution Appraisal; Operations Analysis; Technology Design; Equipment Selection; Programming; Operation Monitoring; Visioning; Systems Perception; Identifying Downstream Consequences; Identification of Key Causes; Judgment and Decision Making; Systems Evaluation; Management of Financial Resources; Management of Material Resources

General Work Activities: Getting Information Needed to Do the Job; Monitoring Processes, Material, or Surroundings; Identifying Objects, Actions, and Events; Inspecting Equipment, Structures, or Material; Estimating Needed Characteristics; Judging Qualities of Things, Services, People; Processing Information; Evaluating Information against Standards; Analyzing Data or Information; Making Decisions and Solving Problems; Thinking Creatively; Updating and Using Job-Relevant Knowledge; Developing Objectives and Strategies; Scheduling Work and Activities; Organizing, Planning, and Prioritizing; Operating Vehicles or Equipment; Drafting and Specifying Technical Devices, etc.; Implementing Ideas, Programs, etc.; Repairing and Maintaining Electrical Equipment; Documenting/Recording Information; Interpreting Meaning of Information to Others; Communicating with Other Workers; Communicating with Persons Outside Organization; Coordinating Work and Activities of Others; Developing and Building Teams; Guiding, Directing and Motivating Subordinates; Provide Consultation and Advice to Others; Monitoring and Controlling Resources

Job Characteristics: Take a Position Opposed to Others; Coordinate or Lead Others; Responsible for Others' Health and Safety; Responsibility for Outcomes and Results; Hazardous Conditions; Consequence of Error; Importance of Being Exact or Accurate; Importance of Being Sure All is Done

GOE Group/s: 05.01.01 Engineering: Research; 05.01.03 Engineering: Systems Design; 05.01.04 Engineering: Testing and Quality Control; 05.01.07 Engineering: Design; 05.01.08 Engineering: General Engineering

CIP Program/s: 140901 Computer Engineering; 141001 Electrical, Electronics and Communication Engineering

Related DOT Job/s: 003.061-030 ELECTRONICS ENGINEER; 003.061-034 ELECTRONICS-DESIGN ENGINEER; 003.061-038 ELECTRONICS-RESEARCH ENGINEER; 003.061-042 ELECTRONICS-TEST ENGINEER; 003.061-050 PLANNING ENGINEER, CENTRAL OFFICE FACILITIES; 003.167-010 CABLE ENGINEER, OUTSIDE PLANT; 003.167-030 ENGINEER-IN-CHARGE, STUDIO OPERATIONS; 003.167-042 OUTSIDE-PLANT ENGINEER; 003.167-058 SUPERVISOR, MICROWAVE; 003.167-066 TRANSMISSION-AND-PROTECTION ENGINEER; 003.187-010 CENTRAL-OFFICE EQUIPMENT ENGINEER; 003.187-014 COMMERCIAL ENGINEER; 003.187-018 CUSTOMER-EQUIPMENT ENGINEER; 031.167-018

22127 COMPUTER ENGINEERS. OOH Title/s: Computer Scientists and Systems Analysts

Analyze data processing requirements to plan EDP system to provide system capabilities required for projected work loads. Plan layout and installation of new system or modification of existing system. May set up and control analog or hybrid computer systems to solve scientific and engineering problems. Analyzes software requirements to determine feasibility of design within time and cost constraints. Analyzes information to determine, recommend, and plan layout for type of computers and peripheral equipment modifications to existing systems. Consults with engineering staff to evaluate interface between hardware and software and operational and performance requirements of overall system. Evaluates factors such as reporting formats required, cost constraints, and need for security restrictions to determine hardware configuration. Formulates and designs software system, using scientific analysis and mathematical models to predict and measure outcome and consequences of design. Confers with data processing and project managers to obtain information on limitations and capabilities for data processing projects. Develops and directs software system testing procedures, programming, and documentation. Coordinates installation of software system. Monitors functioning of equipment to ensure system operates in conformance with specifications. Consults with customer concerning maintenance of software system. Specifies power supply requirements and configuration. Enters data into computer terminal to store, retrieve, and manipulate data for analysis of system capabilities and requirements. Recommends purchase of equipment to control dust, temperature, and humidity in area of system installation. Trains users to use new or modified equipment.

Yearly Earnings: $43,940

Education: Bachelor's degree

Knowledge: Administration and Management; Clerical; Economics and Accounting; Customer and Personal Service; Computers and Electronics; Engineering and Technology; Design; Mathematics; Education and Training; English Language; Telecommunications; Communications and Media

Abilities: Oral Comprehension; Written Comprehension; Oral Expression; Written Expression; Fluency of Ideas; Originality; Problem Sensitivity; Deductive Reasoning; Inductive Reasoning; Information Ordering; Category Flexibility; Mathematical Reasoning; Number Facility; Memorization; Speed of Closure; Visualization; Selective Attention; Near Vision; Speech Recognition; Speech Clarity

Skills: Reading Comprehension; Active Listening; Writing; Speaking; Mathematics; Science; Critical Thinking; Active Learning; Learning Strategies; Monitoring; Coordination; Persuasion; Instructing; Problem Identification; Information Gathering; Information Organization; Synthesis/Reorganization; Idea Generation; Idea Evaluation; Implementation Planning; Solution Appraisal; Operations Analysis; Technology Design; Equipment Selection; Installation; Programming; Testing; Operation Monitoring; Operation and Control; Product Inspection; Troubleshooting; Visioning; Systems Perception; Identifying Downstream Consequences; Identification of Key Causes; Judgment and Decision Making; Systems Evaluation; Management of Financial Resources; Management of Material Resources; Management of Personnel Resources

General Work Activities: Getting Information Needed to Do the Job; Monitoring Processes, Material, or Surroundings; Identifying Objects, Actions, and Events; Inspecting Equipment, Structures, or Material; Estimating Needed Characteristics; Judging Qualities of Things, Services, People; Processing Information; Evaluating Information against Standards; Analyzing Data or Information; Making Decisions and Solving Problems; Thinking Creatively; Updating and Using Job-Relevant Knowledge; Developing Objectives and Strategies; Organizing, Planning, and Prioritizing; Operating Vehicles or Equipment; Drafting and Specifying Technical Devices, etc.; Implementing Ideas, Programs, etc.; Repairing and Maintaining Electrical Equipment; Documenting/Recording Information; Interpreting Meaning of Information to Others; Communicating with Other Workers; Communicating with Persons Outside Organization; Establishing and Maintaining Relationships; Performing for or Working with Public; Coordinating Work and Activities of Others; Developing and Building Teams; Teaching Others; Coaching and Developing Others; Provide Consultation and Advice to Others; Performing Administrative Activities; Monitoring and Controlling Resources

Job Characteristics: Supervise, Coach, Train Others; Provide a Service to Others; Take a Position Opposed to Others; Deal with External

Customers; Sitting; Degree of Automation; Importance of Being Exact or Accurate; Importance of Being Sure All is Done
GOE Group/s: 05.01.03 Engineering: Systems Design; 11.01.01 Mathematics and Statistics: Data Processing Design
CIP Program/s: 110401 Information Sciences and Systems; 140901 Computer Engineering
Related DOT Job/s: 030.062-010 SOFTWARE ENGINEER; 033.167-010 COMPUTER SYSTEMS HARDWARE ANALYST

22128 INDUSTRIAL ENGINEERS, EXCEPT SAFETY. OOH Title/s: Industrial Engineers; Engineering, Science, and Data Processing Managers; Inspectors, Testers, and Graders

Perform engineering duties in planning and overseeing the utilization of production facilities and personnel in department or other subdivision of industrial establishment. Plan equipment layout, work flow, and accident prevention measures to maintain efficient and safe utilization of plant facilities. Plan and oversee work, study, and training programs to promote efficient worker utilization. Develop and oversee quality control, inventory control, and production record systems. Exclude industrial product safety engineers. Analyzes statistical data and product specifications to determine standards and establish quality and reliability objectives of finished product. Develops manufacturing methods, labor utilization standards, and cost analysis systems to promote efficient staff and facility utilization. Drafts and designs layout of equipment, materials, and workspace to illustrate maximum efficiency, using drafting tools and computer. Plans and establishes sequence of operations to fabricate and assemble parts or products and to promote efficient utilization of resources. Reviews production schedules, engineering specifications, orders, and related information to obtain knowledge of manufacturing methods, procedures, and activities. Studies operations sequence, material flow, functional statements, organization charts, and project information to determine worker functions and responsibilities. Formulates sampling procedures and designs and develops forms and instructions for recording, evaluating, and reporting quality and reliability data. Applies statistical methods and performs mathematical calculations to determine manufacturing processes, staff requirements, and production standards. Coordinates quality control objectives and activities to resolve production problems, maximize product reliability, and minimize cost. Communicates with management and user personnel to develop production and design standards. Recommends methods for improving utilization of personnel, material, and utilities. Estimates production cost and effect of product design changes for management review, action, and control. Completes production reports, purchase orders, and material, tool, and equipment lists. Directs workers engaged in product measurement, inspection, and testing activities to ensure quality control and reliability. Records or oversees recording of information to ensure currency of engineering drawings and documentation of production problems. Regulates and alters workflow schedules, according to established manufacturing sequences and lead times, to expedite production operations. Implements methods and procedures for disposition of discrepant material and defective or damaged parts, and assesses cost and responsibility. Evaluates precision and accuracy of production and testing equipment and engineering drawings to formulate corrective action plan. Confers with vendors, staff, and management personnel regarding purchases, procedures, product specifications, manufacturing capabilities, and project status. Schedules deliveries based on production forecasts, material substitutions, storage and handling facilities, and maintenance requirements.
Yearly Earnings: $41,080
Education: Bachelor's degree
Knowledge: Administration and Management; Clerical; Economics and Accounting; Personnel and Human Resources; Production and Processing; Engineering and Technology; Design; Mathematics; Physics; Psychology; Education and Training; Public Safety and Security
Abilities: Oral Comprehension; Written Comprehension; Oral Expression; Written Expression; Fluency of Ideas; Originality; Deductive Reasoning; Inductive Reasoning; Information Ordering; Category Flexibility; Mathematical Reasoning; Number Facility; Visualization; Speech Recognition
Skills: Reading Comprehension; Mathematics; Science; Critical Thinking; Active Learning; Problem Identification; Information Gathering; Idea Generation; Idea Evaluation; Implementation Planning; Operations Analysis; Technology Design; Product Inspection; Visioning; Identifying Downstream Consequences; Judgment and Decision Making; Systems Evaluation; Time Management; Management of Material Resources
General Work Activities: Getting Information Needed to Do the Job; Monitoring Processes, Material, or Surroundings; Identifying Objects, Actions, and Events; Estimating Needed Characteristics; Judging Qualities of Things, Services, People; Processing Information; Evaluating Information against Standards; Analyzing Data or Information; Making Decisions and Solving Problems; Thinking Creatively; Updating and Using Job-Relevant Knowledge; Developing Objectives and Strategies; Scheduling Work and Activities; Organizing, Planning, and Prioritizing; Operating Vehicles or Equipment; Drafting and Specifying Technical Devices, etc.; Implementing Ideas, Programs, etc.; Documenting/Recording Information; Interpreting Meaning of Information to Others; Communicating with Other Workers; Coordinating Work and Activities of Others; Developing and Building Teams; Guiding, Directing and Motivating Subordinates; Provide Consultation and Advice to Others; Monitoring and Controlling Resources
Job Characteristics: Take a Position Opposed to Others; Coordinate or Lead Others; Responsibility for Outcomes and Results; Frequency in Conflict Situations; Importance of Being Aware of New Events
GOE Group/s: 05.01.04 Engineering: Testing and Quality Control; 05.01.06 Engineering: Work Planning and Utilization; 05.02.03 Managerial Work: Mechanical: Processing and Manufacturing; 05.03.02 Engineering Technology: Drafting; 05.03.03 Engineering Technology: Expediting and Coordinating
CIP Program/s: 141701 Industrial/Manufacturing Engineering; 142801 Textile Sciences and Engineering; 143001 Engineering/Industrial Management; 150603 Industrial/Manufacturing Technologists and Technicians
Related DOT Job/s: 011.161-010 SUPERVISOR, METALLURGICAL-AND-QUALITY-CONTROL-TESTING; 012.061-018 STANDARDS ENGINEER; 012.067-010 METROLOGIST; 012.167-010 CONFIGURATION MANAGEMENT ANALYST; 012.167-014 MANAGER, QUALITY CONTROL; 012.167-018 FACTORY LAY-OUT ENGINEER; 012.167-030 INDUSTRIAL ENGINEER; 012.167-038 LIAISON ENGINEER; 012.167-042 MANUFACTURING ENGINEER; 012.167-046 PRODUCTION ENGINEER; 012.167-050 PRODUCTION PLANNER; 012.167-054 QUALITY CONTROL ENGINEER; 012.167-062 SUPERVISOR, VENDOR QUALITY; 012.167-070 TIME-STUDY ENGINEER; 012.167-074 TOOL PLANNER; 012.167-078 DOCUMENTATION ENGINEER; 012.167-082 MATERIAL SCHEDULER; 012.187-014 SHOE-LAY-OUT PLANNER; 019.167-010 LOGISTICS ENGINEER; 822.261-014 EQUIPMENT INSPECTOR

22132A INDUSTRIAL SAFETY AND HEALTH ENGINEERS. OOH Title/s: Engineering, Science, and Data Processing Managers; Engineers

Plan, implement, and coordinate safety programs to prevent or correct unsafe environmental working conditions. Devises and implements safety or industrial health program to prevent, correct, or control unsafe environmental conditions. Examines plans and specifications for new machinery or equipment to determine if all safety requirements have been included. Conducts or coordinates training of workers concerning safety laws and regulations; use of safety equipment, devices, and clothing; and first aid. Inspects facilities, machinery, and safety equipment to identify and correct potential hazards, and to ensure compliance with safety regulations. Conducts or directs testing of air quality, noise, temperature, or radiation to verify compliance with health and safety regulations. Provides technical guidance to organizations regarding how to handle health-related problems, such as water and air pollution. Compiles, analyzes, and interprets statistical data related to exposure factors concerning occupational illnesses and accidents. Installs or directs installation of safety devices on machinery. Investigates causes of industrial accidents or injuries to develop solutions to minimize or prevent recurrence. Conducts plant or area surveys to determine safety levels for exposure to materials and conditions. Checks floors of plant to ensure they are strong enough to support heavy machinery. Designs and builds safety devices for machinery or safety clothing. Prepares reports of findings from investigation of accidents, inspection of facilities, or testing of environment. Maintains liaison with outside organizations, such as fire departments, mutual aid societies, and rescue teams.

Yearly Earnings: $45,032

Education: Bachelor's degree

Knowledge: Administration and Management; Engineering and Technology; Design; Building and Construction; Mathematics; Physics; Chemistry; Biology; Education and Training; Public Safety and Security; Law, Government, and Jurisprudence

Abilities: Oral Comprehension; Written Expression; Fluency of Ideas; Problem Sensitivity; Deductive Reasoning; Inductive Reasoning; Category Flexibility; Mathematical Reasoning; Number Facility; Flexibility of Closure

Skills: Writing; Speaking; Mathematics; Science; Critical Thinking; Active Learning; Learning Strategies; Monitoring; Coordination; Persuasion; Instructing; Problem Identification; Information Organization; Synthesis/Reorganization; Idea Generation; Idea Evaluation; Implementation Planning; Solution Appraisal; Operations Analysis; Technology Design; Equipment Selection; Installation; Programming; Testing; Product Inspection; Visioning; Systems Perception; Identifying Downstream Consequences; Identification of Key Causes; Judgment and Decision Making; Systems Evaluation

General Work Activities: Getting Information Needed to Do the Job; Monitoring Processes, Material, or Surroundings; Identifying Objects, Actions, and Events; Inspecting Equipment, Structures, or Material; Estimating Needed Characteristics; Judging Qualities of Things, Services, People; Processing Information; Evaluating Information against Standards; Analyzing Data or Information; Making Decisions and Solving Problems; Thinking Creatively; Updating and Using Job-Relevant Knowledge; Developing Objectives and Strategies; Scheduling Work and Activities; Organizing, Planning, and Prioritizing; Operating Vehicles or Equipment; Drafting and Specifying Technical Devices, etc.; Implementing Ideas, Programs, etc.; Repairing and Maintaining Mechanical Equipment; Repairing and Maintaining Electrical Equipment; Documenting/Recording Information; Interpreting Meaning of Information to Others; Communicating with Other Workers; Communicating with Persons Outside Organization; Coordinating Work and Activities of Others; Developing and Building Teams; Teaching Others; Coaching and Developing Others; Provide Consultation and Advice to Others

Job Characteristics: Supervise, Coach, Train Others; Responsible for Others' Health and Safety; Specialized Protective or Safety Attire; Consequence of Error; Importance of Being Exact or Accurate

GOE Group/s: 05.01.02 Engineering: Environmental Protection

CIP Program/s: 140101 Engineering, General; 141401 Environmental/Environmental Health Engineering

Related DOT Job/s: 012.061-014 SAFETY ENGINEER; 012.167-034 INDUSTRIAL-HEALTH ENGINEER; 012.167-058 SAFETY MANAGER

22132B FIRE-PREVENTION AND PROTECTION ENGINEERS. OOH Title/s: Engineers

Research causes of fires; determine fire protection methods; and design or recommend materials or equipment, such as structural components or fire-detection equipment, to assist organizations in safeguarding life and property against fire, explosion, and related hazards. Determines fire causes and methods of fire prevention. Studies properties concerning fire prevention factors, such as fire-resistance of construction, contents, water supply and delivery, and exits. Recommends and advises on use of fire-detection equipment, extinguishing devices, or methods to alleviate conditions conducive to fire. Conducts research on fire retardants and fire safety of materials and devices to determine cause and methods of fire prevention. Advises and plans for prevention of destruction by fire, wind, water, or other causes of damage. Evaluates fire departments and laws and regulations affecting fire prevention or fire safety. Organizes and trains personnel to carry out fire-protection programs. Designs fire-detection equipment, alarm systems, fire-extinguishing devices and systems, or structural components protection. Teaches courses on fire prevention and protection.

Yearly Earnings: $45,032

Education: Bachelor's degree

Knowledge: Sales and Marketing; Engineering and Technology; Design; Building and Construction; Physics; Chemistry; Geography; Education and Training; Public Safety and Security; Law, Government, and Jurisprudence; Telecommunications; Communications and Media

Abilities: Deductive Reasoning; Inductive Reasoning; Category Flexibility

Skills: Speaking; Science; Active Learning; Instructing; Information Gathering; Idea Generation; Implementation Planning; Solution Appraisal; Operations Analysis; Technology Design; Equipment Selection; Testing; Product Inspection; Identifying Downstream Consequences; Judgment and Decision Making; Systems Evaluation

General Work Activities: Getting Information Needed to Do the Job; Identifying Objects, Actions, and Events; Inspecting Equipment, Structures, or Material; Estimating Needed Characteristics; Processing Information; Evaluating Information against Standards; Analyzing Data or Information; Making Decisions and Solving Problems; Thinking Creatively; Updating and Using Job-Relevant Knowledge; Developing Objectives and Strategies; Drafting and Specifying Technical Devices, etc.; Implementing Ideas, Programs, etc.; Interpreting Meaning of Information to Others; Communicating with Other Workers; Communicating with Persons Outside Organization; Selling or Influencing Others; Performing for or Working with Public; Developing and Building Teams; Teaching Others; Guiding, Directing and Motivating Subordinates; Coaching and Developing Others; Provide Consultation and Advice to Others

Job Characteristics: Supervise, Coach, Train Others; Climbing Ladders, Scaffolds, Poles, etc.; Specialized Protective or Safety Attire

GOE Group/s: 05.01.01 Engineering: Research; 05.01.02 Engineering: Environmental Protection

CIP Program/s: 140101 Engineering, General

Related DOT Job/s: 012.167-022 FIRE-PREVENTION RESEARCH ENGINEER; 012.167-026 FIRE-PROTECTION ENGINEER

22132C PRODUCT SAFETY ENGINEERS. OOH Title/s: Engineers

Develop and conduct tests to evaluate product safety levels, and recommend measures to reduce or eliminate hazards. Conducts research to evaluate safety levels for products. Evaluates potential

health hazards or damage which could occur from misuse of product, and engineers solutions to improve safety. Investigates causes of accidents, injuries, or illnesses from product usage to develop solutions to minimize or prevent recurrence. Advises and recommends procedures for detection, prevention, and elimination of physical, chemical, or other product hazards. Participates in preparation of product usage and precautionary label instructions. Prepares reports of findings from investigation of accidents.
Yearly Earnings: $45,032
Education: Bachelor's degree
Knowledge: Production and Processing; Engineering and Technology; Physics; Chemistry; Biology; English Language; Public Safety and Security
Abilities: Written Expression; Fluency of Ideas; Problem Sensitivity; Deductive Reasoning; Inductive Reasoning; Category Flexibility
Skills: Writing; Mathematics; Science; Critical Thinking; Active Learning; Monitoring; Problem Identification; Information Gathering; Information Organization; Synthesis/Reorganization; Idea Generation; Idea Evaluation; Implementation Planning; Solution Appraisal; Operations Analysis; Technology Design; Testing; Product Inspection; Troubleshooting; Identifying Downstream Consequences; Identification of Key Causes; Judgment and Decision Making
General Work Activities: Getting Information Needed to Do the Job; Monitoring Processes, Material, or Surroundings; Identifying Objects, Actions, and Events; Inspecting Equipment, Structures, or Material; Judging Qualities of Things, Services, People; Processing Information; Evaluating Information against Standards; Analyzing Data or Information; Making Decisions and Solving Problems; Operating Vehicles or Equipment; Drafting and Specifying Technical Devices, etc.; Implementing Ideas, Programs, etc.; Documenting/Recording Information; Interpreting Meaning of Information to Others; Communicating with Other Workers; Provide Consultation and Advice to Others
Job Characteristics: Take a Position Opposed to Others; Responsible for Others' Health and Safety; Specialized Protective or Safety Attire
GOE Group/s: 05.01.02 Engineering: Environmental Protection
CIP Program/s: 140101 Engineering, General
Related DOT Job/s: 012.061-010 PRODUCT-SAFETY ENGINEER

22135 MECHANICAL ENGINEERS. OOH Title/s: Mechanical Engineers

Perform engineering duties in planning and designing tools, engines, machines, and other mechanically functioning equipment. Oversee installation, operation, maintenance, and repair of such equipment as centralized heat, gas, water, and steam systems. Designs products and systems to meet process requirements, applying knowledge of engineering principles. Oversees installation to ensure machines and equipment are installed and functioning according to specifications. Coordinates building, fabrication, and installation of product design and operation, maintenance, and repair activities to utilize machines and equipment. Specifies system components or directs modification of products to ensure conformance with engineering design and performance specifications. Inspects, evaluates, and arranges field installations, and recommends design modifications to eliminate machine or system malfunctions. Alters or modifies design to obtain specified functional and operational performance. Investigates equipment failures and difficulties, diagnoses faulty operation, and makes recommendations to maintenance crew. Examines gas-powered equipment after installation to ensure proper functioning, and solves problems concerned with equipment. Studies industrial processes to determine where and how application of gas fuel-consuming equipment can be made. Researches and analyzes data, such as customer design proposal, specifications, and manuals, to determine feasibility of design or application. Plans and directs engineering personnel in fabrication of test control apparatus and equipment, and develops procedures for testing products. Confers with establishment personnel and engineers to implement operating procedures and resolve system malfunctions, and to provide technical information. Develops models of alternate processing methods to test feasibility or new applications of system components, and recommends implementation of procedures. Tests ability of machines, such as robot, to perform tasks, using teach pendant and precision measuring instruments and following specifications. Selects or designs robot tools to meet specifications, using robot manuals and either drafting tools or computer and software programs. Assists drafter in developing structural design of product, using drafting tools or computer-assisted design/drafting equipment and software. Conducts experiments to test and analyze existing designs and equipment to obtain data on performance of product, and prepares reports. Determines parts supply, maintenance tasks, safety procedures, and service schedules required to maintain machines and equipment in prescribed condition. Writes operating programs, using existing computer program, or writes own computer programs, applying knowledge of programming language and computer. Participates in meetings, seminars, and training sessions to stay apprised of new developments in field.
Yearly Earnings: $46,540
Education: Bachelor's degree
Knowledge: Production and Processing; Computers and Electronics; Engineering and Technology; Design; Building and Construction; Mechanical; Mathematics; Physics
Abilities: Oral Comprehension; Written Comprehension; Oral Expression; Written Expression; Fluency of Ideas; Originality; Problem Sensitivity; Deductive Reasoning; Inductive Reasoning; Information Ordering; Category Flexibility; Mathematical Reasoning; Number Facility; Memorization; Speed of Closure; Flexibility of Closure; Perceptual Speed; Visualization; Selective Attention; Time Sharing; Near Vision; Visual Color Discrimination; Hearing Sensitivity; Sound Localization; Speech Recognition
Skills: Reading Comprehension; Mathematics; Science; Critical Thinking; Active Learning; Monitoring; Problem Identification; Information Gathering; Information Organization; Synthesis/Reorganization; Idea Generation; Idea Evaluation; Solution Appraisal; Operations Analysis; Technology Design; Equipment Selection; Programming; Testing; Product Inspection; Troubleshooting; Visioning; Systems Perception; Judgment and Decision Making; Management of Material Resources
General Work Activities: Getting Information Needed to Do the Job; Monitoring Processes, Material, or Surroundings; Identifying Objects, Actions, and Events; Inspecting Equipment, Structures, or Material; Estimating Needed Characteristics; Judging Qualities of Things, Services, People; Processing Information; Evaluating Information against Standards; Analyzing Data or Information; Making Decisions and Solving Problems; Thinking Creatively; Updating and Using Job-Relevant Knowledge; Developing Objectives and Strategies; Organizing, Planning, and Prioritizing; Operating Vehicles or Equipment; Drafting and Specifying Technical Devices, etc.; Implementing Ideas, Programs, etc.; Documenting/Recording Information; Interpreting Meaning of Information to Others; Communicating with Other Workers; Provide Consultation and Advice to Others
Job Characteristics: Supervise, Coach, Train Others; Take a Position Opposed to Others; Coordinate or Lead Others; Responsibility for Outcomes and Results; Frequency in Conflict Situations; Hazardous Equipment; Consequence of Error; Frustrating Circumstances; Degree of Automation; Importance of Being Exact or Accurate; Importance of Being Sure All is Done
GOE Group/s: 05.01.01 Engineering: Research; 05.01.04 Engineering: Testing and Quality Control; 05.01.06 Engineering: Work Planning and Utilization; 05.01.07 Engineering: Design; 05.01.08

Engineering: General Engineering; 05.03.07 Engineering Technology: Mechanical

CIP Program/s: 141901 Mechanical Engineering; 142801 Textile Sciences and Engineering; 150505 Solar Technologists and Technicians; 150805 Mechanical Engineering/Mechanical Technologists and Technicians

Related DOT Job/s: 007.061-010 AUTOMOTIVE ENGINEER; 007.061-014 MECHANICAL ENGINEER; 007.061-018 MECHANICAL-DESIGN ENGINEER, FACILITIES; 007.061-022 MECHANICAL-DESIGN ENGINEER, PRODUCTS; 007.061-026 TOOL DESIGNER; 007.061-030 TOOL-DESIGNER APPRENTICE; 007.061-034 UTILIZATION ENGINEER; 007.061-038 APPLICATIONS ENGINEER, MANUFACTURING; 007.061-042 STRESS ANALYST; 007.161-022 MECHANICAL RESEARCH ENGINEER; 007.161-034 TEST ENGINEER, MECHANICAL EQUIPMENT; 007.161-038 SOLAR-ENERGY-SYSTEMS DESIGNER

22138 MARINE ENGINEERS. OOH Title/s: Engineers

Design, develop, and take responsibility for the installation of ship machinery and related equipment, including propulsion machines and power supply systems. Exclude marine architects. Designs and oversees testing, installation, and repair of marine apparatus and equipment. Conducts analytical, environmental, operational, or performance studies to develop design for products, such as marine engines, equipment, and structures. Prepares or directs preparation of product or system layout and detailed drawings and schematics. Evaluates operation of marine equipment during acceptance testing and shakedown cruises. Analyzes data to determine feasibility of product proposal. Directs and coordinates manufacturing or building of prototype marine product or system. Confers with research personnel to clarify or resolve problems and develop or modify design. Investigates and observes tests on machinery and equipment for compliance with standards. Conducts environmental, operational, or performance tests on marine machinery and equipment. Plans, conducts, or directs personnel in performing engineering experiments to test or prove theories and principles. Determines conditions under which tests are to be conducted and sequences and phases of test operations. Maintains and coordinates repair of marine machinery and equipment for installation on vessels. Inspects marine equipment and machinery to draw up work requests and job specifications. Reviews work requests and compares them with previous work completed on ship to ensure costs are economically sound. Prepares technical reports on types of testing conducted, completed repairs, and cost of repairs for engineering, management, or sales personnel. Prepares technical reports for use by engineering, management, or sales personnel. Maintains contact and formulates reports for contractors and clients to ensure completion of work at minimum cost. Coordinates activities with those of regulatory bodies to ensure repairs and alterations are at minimum cost, consistent with safety. Obtains readings on tail shaft and tail shaft bearings, using measuring devices. Procures materials needed to repair marine equipment and machinery.

Yearly Earnings: $45,032

Education: Bachelor's degree

Knowledge: Administration and Management; Economics and Accounting; Engineering and Technology; Design; Building and Construction; Mechanical; Mathematics; Physics; Chemistry; Geography; English Language; Public Safety and Security; Law, Government, and Jurisprudence; Transportation

Abilities: Written Comprehension; Written Expression; Fluency of Ideas; Originality; Problem Sensitivity; Deductive Reasoning; Inductive Reasoning; Information Ordering; Number Facility; Memorization; Speed of Closure; Perceptual Speed; Visualization; Selective Attention; Gross Body Equilibrium

Skills: Reading Comprehension; Active Listening; Writing; Speaking; Mathematics; Science; Critical Thinking; Active Learning; Monitoring; Coordination; Negotiation; Problem Identification; Information Gathering; Information Organization; Synthesis/Reorganization; Idea Generation; Idea Evaluation; Implementation Planning; Solution Appraisal; Operations Analysis; Technology Design; Equipment Selection; Installation; Testing; Operation Monitoring; Product Inspection; Equipment Maintenance; Troubleshooting; Visioning; Systems Perception; Identifying Downstream Consequences; Identification of Key Causes; Judgment and Decision Making; Systems Evaluation; Time Management; Management of Material Resources; Management of Personnel Resources

General Work Activities: Getting Information Needed to Do the Job; Monitoring Processes, Material, or Surroundings; Identifying Objects, Actions, and Events; Inspecting Equipment, Structures, or Material; Estimating Needed Characteristics; Processing Information; Evaluating Information against Standards; Analyzing Data or Information; Making Decisions and Solving Problems; Thinking Creatively; Updating and Using Job-Relevant Knowledge; Developing Objectives and Strategies; Scheduling Work and Activities; Organizing, Planning, and Prioritizing; Operating Vehicles or Equipment; Drafting and Specifying Technical Devices, etc.; Implementing Ideas, Programs, etc.; Repairing and Maintaining Mechanical Equipment; Documenting/Recording Information; Interpreting Meaning of Information to Others; Communicating with Other Workers; Coordinating Work and Activities of Others; Developing and Building Teams; Guiding, Directing and Motivating Subordinates; Provide Consultation and Advice to Others; Monitoring and Controlling Resources

Job Characteristics: Objective or Subjective Information; Supervise, Coach, Train Others; Take a Position Opposed to Others; Coordinate or Lead Others; Responsible for Others' Health and Safety; Responsibility for Outcomes and Results; Frequency in Conflict Situations; Deal with Physical, Aggressive People; Hazardous Conditions; Hazardous Equipment; Consequence of Error; Frustrating Circumstances; Importance of Being Exact or Accurate; Importance of Being Sure All is Done

GOE Group/s: 05.01.01 Engineering: Research; 05.01.03 Engineering: Systems Design; 05.01.04 Engineering: Testing and Quality Control; 05.01.06 Engineering: Work Planning and Utilization; 05.01.07 Engineering: Design; 05.03.06 Engineering Technology: Industrial and Safety

CIP Program/s: 140101 Engineering, General; 142201 Naval Architecture and Marine Engineering

Related DOT Job/s: 014.061-010 DESIGN ENGINEER, MARINE EQUIPMENT; 014.061-014 MARINE ENGINEER; 014.061-018 RESEARCH ENGINEER, MARINE EQUIPMENT; 014.061-022 TEST ENGINEER, MARINE EQUIPMENT; 014.167-010 MARINE SURVEYOR; 014.167-014 PORT ENGINEER

22197 PRODUCTION ENGINEERS. OOH Title/s: Engineers

Develop, advance, and improve products, processes, or materials, and build or supervise the building of prototypes. May operate machinery, equipment, or hand tools to produce their prototypes. Conducts research and analytical studies to develop design or specifications for products. Directs and coordinates manufacturing of building of prototype or system. Confers with research and other engineering personnel to clarify and resolve problems, and prepares design modifications as needed. Prepares or directs preparation of product or system layout and detailed drawings and schematics. Analyzes data to determine feasibility of product proposal. Plans and develops experimental test programs. Analyzes test data and reports to determine if design meets functional and performance specifications. Evaluates engineering test results for possible application to development of systems or other uses.

Yearly Earnings: $45,032

Education: Bachelor's degree
Knowledge: Administration and Management; Production and Processing; Computers and Electronics; Engineering and Technology; Design; Mechanical; Mathematics; Physics; English Language
Abilities: Fluency of Ideas; Originality; Problem Sensitivity; Information Ordering; Mathematical Reasoning; Visualization; Speech Clarity
Skills: Reading Comprehension; Active Listening; Writing; Speaking; Mathematics; Science; Critical Thinking; Active Learning; Learning Strategies; Monitoring; Coordination; Problem Identification; Information Gathering; Information Organization; Synthesis/Reorganization; Idea Generation; Idea Evaluation; Implementation Planning; Solution Appraisal; Operations Analysis; Technology Design; Equipment Selection; Programming; Testing; Operation Monitoring; Operation and Control; Product Inspection; Troubleshooting; Visioning; Systems Perception; Identifying Downstream Consequences; Identification of Key Causes; Judgment and Decision Making; Systems Evaluation; Time Management; Management of Material Resources; Management of Personnel Resources
General Work Activities: Getting Information Needed to Do the Job; Monitoring Processes, Material, or Surroundings; Identifying Objects, Actions, and Events; Inspecting Equipment, Structures, or Material; Estimating Needed Characteristics; Judging Qualities of Things, Services, People; Processing Information; Evaluating Information against Standards; Analyzing Data or Information; Making Decisions and Solving Problems; Thinking Creatively; Updating and Using Job-Relevant Knowledge; Developing Objectives and Strategies; Scheduling Work and Activities; Organizing, Planning, and Prioritizing; Controlling Machines and Processes; Operating Vehicles or Equipment; Drafting and Specifying Technical Devices, etc.; Implementing Ideas, Programs, etc.; Documenting/Recording Information; Interpreting Meaning of Information to Others; Communicating with Other Workers; Selling or Influencing Others; Coordinating Work and Activities of Others; Developing and Building Teams; Guiding, Directing and Motivating Subordinates; Coaching and Developing Others; Provide Consultation and Advice to Others
Job Characteristics: Persuade Someone to a Course of Action; Coordinate or Lead Others; Responsibility for Outcomes and Results; Frequency in Conflict Situations; Frustrating Circumstances; Importance of Being Exact or Accurate; Importance of Being Sure All is Done
GOE Group/s: 02.02.01 Life Sciences: Animal Specialization; 05.01.04 Engineering: Testing and Quality Control; 05.01.07 Engineering: Design; 05.01.08 Engineering: General Engineering; 05.03.09 Engineering Technology: Packaging and Storing
CIP Program/s: 140101 Engineering, General; 140501 Bioengineering and Biomedical Engineering; 141101 Engineering Mechanics; 141201 Engineering Physics; 141301 Engineering Science
Related DOT Job/s: 019.061-010 BIOMEDICAL ENGINEER; 019.061-018 OPTICAL ENGINEER; 019.061-026 RELIABILITY ENGINEER; 019.081-010 MAINTAINABILITY ENGINEER; 019.081-014 PHOTOGRAPHIC ENGINEER; 019.187-010 PACKAGING ENGINEER

22199 ALL OTHER ENGINEERS. OOH Title/s: Engineers

All other engineers not classified separately above.
Yearly Earnings: $45,032
Education: Bachelor's degree
GOE Group/s: 05.01.08 Engineering: General Engineering
CIP Program/s: 140101 Engineering, General; 141101 Engineering Mechanics; 141201 Engineering Physics; 141301 Engineering Science
Related DOT Job/s: 019.061-022 ORDNANCE ENGINEER

Architects and Surveyors

22302 ARCHITECTS, EXCEPT LANDSCAPE AND MARINE. OOH Title/s: Architects

Plan and design structures, such as private residences, office buildings, theaters, factories, and other structural property. Prepares information regarding design, structure specifications, materials, color, equipment, estimated costs, and construction time. Plans layout of project. Integrates engineering element into unified design. Prepares scale drawings. Consults with client to determine functional and spatial requirements of structure. Estimates costs and construction time. Conducts periodic on-site observation of work during construction to monitor compliance with plans. Directs activities of workers engaged in preparing drawings and specification documents. Prepares contract documents for building contractors. Represents client in obtaining bids and awarding construction contracts. Administers construction contracts. Prepares operating and maintenance manuals, studies, and reports.
Yearly Earnings: $36,816
Education: Bachelor's degree
Knowledge: Administration and Management; Economics and Accounting; Sales and Marketing; Customer and Personal Service; Personnel and Human Resources; Engineering and Technology; Design; Building and Construction; Mathematics; Physics; Geography; English Language; Fine Arts; History and Archeology; Public Safety and Security; Law, Government, and Jurisprudence; Communications and Media
Abilities: Oral Comprehension; Written Comprehension; Oral Expression; Written Expression; Fluency of Ideas; Originality; Problem Sensitivity; Deductive Reasoning; Inductive Reasoning; Information Ordering; Category Flexibility; Mathematical Reasoning; Number Facility; Memorization; Speed of Closure; Flexibility of Closure; Spatial Orientation; Visualization; Selective Attention; Time Sharing; Gross Body Equilibrium; Near Vision; Far Vision; Visual Color Discrimination; Night Vision; Speech Recognition
Skills: Reading Comprehension; Active Listening; Writing; Speaking; Mathematics; Monitoring; Coordination; Negotiation; Service Orientation; Problem Identification; Information Gathering; Information Organization; Synthesis/Reorganization; Idea Generation; Idea Evaluation; Implementation Planning; Solution Appraisal; Operations Analysis; Technology Design; Equipment Selection; Product Inspection; Visioning; Systems Perception; Identification of Key Causes; Judgment and Decision Making; Time Management; Management of Financial Resources; Management of Material Resources; Management of Personnel Resources
General Work Activities: Getting Information Needed to Do the Job; Identifying Objects, Actions, and Events; Inspecting Equipment, Structures, or Material; Estimating Needed Characteristics; Judging Qualities of Things, Services, People; Processing Information; Evaluating Information against Standards; Analyzing Data or Information; Making Decisions and Solving Problems; Thinking Creatively; Updating and Using Job-Relevant Knowledge; Developing Objectives and Strategies; Scheduling Work and Activities; Organizing, Planning, and Prioritizing; Operating Vehicles or Equipment; Drafting and Specifying Technical Devices, etc.; Implementing Ideas, Programs, etc.; Documenting/Recording Information; Communicating with Persons Outside Organization; Establishing and Maintaining Relationships; Selling or Influencing Others; Resolving Conflicts, Negotiating with Others; Coordinating Work and Activities of Others; Developing and Building Teams; Guiding, Directing and Motivating Subordinates; Coaching and Developing Others; Provide Consultation and Advice to Others; Performing Administrative Activities; Staffing Organizational Units; Monitoring and Controlling Resources

Job Characteristics: Objective or Subjective Information; Coordinate or Lead Others; Responsibility for Outcomes and Results; Deal with Unpleasant or Angry People; High Places; Climbing Ladders, Scaffolds, Poles, etc.; Consequence of Error; Frustrating Circumstances; Importance of Being Exact or Accurate; Importance of Being Sure All is Done
GOE Group/s: 05.01.07 Engineering: Design; 05.01.08 Engineering: General Engineering
CIP Program/s: 040201 Architecture; 040401 Architectural Environmental Design
Related DOT Job/s: 001.061-010 ARCHITECT; 001.167-010 SCHOOL-PLANT CONSULTANT

22305 MARINE ARCHITECTS. OOH Title/s: Architects

Design and oversee construction and repair of marine craft and floating structures such as ships, barges, tugs, dredges, submarines, torpedoes, floats, and buoys. May confer with marine engineers. Oversees construction and testing of prototype in model basin, and develops sectional and waterline curves of hull to establish center of gravity, ideal hull form, and buoyancy and stability data. Confers with marine engineering personnel to establish arrangement of boiler room equipment and propulsion machinery, heating and ventilating systems, refrigeration equipment, piping, and other functional equipment. Designs complete hull and superstructure according to specifications and test data, in conformity with standards of safety, efficiency, and economy. Designs layout of craft interior, including cargo space, passenger compartments, ladder wells, and elevators. Studies design proposals and specifications to establish basic characteristics of craft, such as size, weight, speed, propulsion, displacement, and draft. Evaluates performance of craft during dock and sea trials to determine design changes and conformance with national and international standards.
Yearly Earnings: $36,816
Education: Bachelor's degree
Knowledge: Administration and Management; Computers and Electronics; Engineering and Technology; Design; Building and Construction; Mechanical; Mathematics; Physics; Geography; English Language; Public Safety and Security; Law, Government, and Jurisprudence; Transportation
Abilities: Oral Comprehension; Written Comprehension; Oral Expression; Written Expression; Fluency of Ideas; Originality; Problem Sensitivity; Deductive Reasoning; Inductive Reasoning; Information Ordering; Mathematical Reasoning; Number Facility; Memorization; Speed of Closure; Perceptual Speed; Spatial Orientation; Visualization; Gross Body Equilibrium; Far Vision; Glare Sensitivity
Skills: Reading Comprehension; Active Listening; Speaking; Mathematics; Science; Critical Thinking; Active Learning; Learning Strategies; Monitoring; Coordination; Problem Identification; Information Gathering; Information Organization; Synthesis/Reorganization; Idea Generation; Idea Evaluation; Implementation Planning; Solution Appraisal; Operations Analysis; Technology Design; Equipment Selection; Testing; Product Inspection; Troubleshooting; Visioning; Systems Perception; Identifying Downstream Consequences; Identification of Key Causes; Judgment and Decision Making; Systems Evaluation; Time Management
General Work Activities: Getting Information Needed to Do the Job; Monitoring Processes, Material, or Surroundings; Identifying Objects, Actions, and Events; Inspecting Equipment, Structures, or Material; Estimating Needed Characteristics; Judging Qualities of Things, Services, People; Processing Information; Evaluating Information against Standards; Analyzing Data or Information; Making Decisions and Solving Problems; Thinking Creatively; Updating and Using Job-Relevant Knowledge; Developing Objectives and Strategies; Scheduling Work and Activities; Organizing, Planning, and Prioritizing; Drafting and Specifying Technical Devices, etc.; Implementing Ideas, Programs, etc.; Documenting/Recording Information; Interpreting Meaning of Information to Others; Communicating with Other Workers; Communicating with Persons Outside Organization; Establishing and Maintaining Relationships; Coordinating Work and Activities of Others; Developing and Building Teams; Guiding, Directing and Motivating Subordinates; Provide Consultation and Advice to Others
Job Characteristics: Objective or Subjective Information; Take a Position Opposed to Others; Responsibility for Outcomes and Results; Extremely Bright or Inadequate Lighting; Keeping or Regaining Balance; Consequence of Error; Importance of Being Exact or Accurate; Importance of Being Sure All is Done
GOE Group/s: 05.01.07 Engineering: Design
CIP Program/s: 140101 Engineering, General; 142201 Naval Architecture and Marine Engineering
Related DOT Job/s: 001.061-014 ARCHITECT, MARINE

22308 LANDSCAPE ARCHITECTS. OOH Title/s: Landscape Architects

Plan and design land areas for such projects as parks and other recreational facilities, airports, highways, hospitals, schools, land subdivisions, and commercial, industrial, and residential sites. Prepares site plans, specifications, and cost estimates for land development, coordinating arrangement of existing and proposed land features and structures. Compiles and analyzes data on conditions, such as location, drainage, and location of structures, for environmental reports and landscaping plans. Inspects landscape work to ensure compliance with specifications, approves quality of materials and work, and advises client and construction personnel. Confers with clients, engineering personnel, and architects on overall program.
Yearly Earnings: $36,816
Education: Bachelor's degree
Knowledge: Administration and Management; Economics and Accounting; Customer and Personal Service; Engineering and Technology; Design; Building and Construction; Mathematics; Physics; Biology; Geography; English Language; Fine Arts; History and Archeology; Public Safety and Security; Law, Government, and Jurisprudence
Abilities: Written Comprehension; Fluency of Ideas; Originality; Information Ordering; Spatial Orientation; Visualization; Far Vision
Skills: Reading Comprehension; Active Listening; Writing; Speaking; Mathematics; Critical Thinking; Active Learning; Learning Strategies; Monitoring; Coordination; Persuasion; Negotiation; Problem Identification; Information Gathering; Information Organization; Synthesis/Reorganization; Idea Generation; Idea Evaluation; Implementation Planning; Solution Appraisal; Operations Analysis; Product Inspection; Visioning; Systems Perception; Identifying Downstream Consequences; Identification of Key Causes; Judgment and Decision Making; Systems Evaluation; Management of Financial Resources; Management of Material Resources
General Work Activities: Getting Information Needed to Do the Job; Estimating Needed Characteristics; Analyzing Data or Information; Making Decisions and Solving Problems; Thinking Creatively; Organizing, Planning, and Prioritizing; Drafting and Specifying Technical Devices, etc.; Implementing Ideas, Programs, etc.; Communicating with Persons Outside Organization; Selling or Influencing Others; Provide Consultation and Advice to Others; Monitoring and Controlling Resources
Job Characteristics: Objective or Subjective Information; Provide a Service to Others; Deal with External Customers; Coordinate or Lead Others; Frequency in Conflict Situations
GOE Group/s: 05.01.07 Engineering: Design
CIP Program/s: 040401 Architectural Environmental Design; 040601 Landscape Architecture

Related DOT Job/s: 001.061-018 LANDSCAPE ARCHITECT

22311A CARTOGRAPHERS AND PHOTOGRAMMETRISTS. OOH Title/s: Surveyors

Collect, analyze, and interpret geographic information provided by geodetic surveys, aerial photographs, and satellite data. Research, study, and prepare maps and other spatial data in digital or graphic form for legal, social, political, educational, and design purposes. Prepares mosaic prints, contour maps, profile sheets, and related cartographic material, applying mastery of photogrammetric techniques and principles. Determines and defines production specifications, such as projection, scale, size, and colors of map product. Analyzes survey data, source maps and photos, computer or automated mapping products, and other records to determine location and names of features. Develops design concept of map product. Identifies, scales, and orients geodetic points, elevations, and other planimetric or topographic features, applying standard math formulas. Studies legal records to establish boundaries of local, national, and international properties. Travels over photographed area to observe, identify, record, and verify all features shown and not shown in photograph. Revises existing maps and charts and corrects maps in various stages of compilation. Determines guidelines for source material to be used, such as maps, automated mapping products, photographic survey data, and place names.

Yearly Earnings: $26,780

Education: Postsecondary vocational training

Knowledge: Design; Geography; Foreign Language; History and Archeology

Abilities: Mathematical Reasoning; Number Facility; Speed of Closure; Flexibility of Closure; Spatial Orientation; Selective Attention; Near Vision; Far Vision; Visual Color Discrimination; Night Vision; Depth Perception; Glare Sensitivity

Skills: Reading Comprehension; Mathematics; Information Gathering; Information Organization; Synthesis/Reorganization; Operations Analysis; Equipment Selection; Programming; Management of Material Resources

General Work Activities: Getting Information Needed to Do the Job; Interacting with Computers; Drafting and Specifying Technical Devices, etc.

Job Characteristics: Importance of Being Exact or Accurate

GOE Group/s: 05.03.02 Engineering Technology: Drafting

CIP Program/s: 151102 Surveying; 450702 Cartography; 480101 Drafting, General; 480103 Civil/Structural Drafting

Related DOT Job/s: 018.131-010 SUPERVISOR, CARTOGRAPHY; 018.261-010 DRAFTER, CARTOGRAPHIC; 018.261-026 PHOTOGRAMMETRIST; 018.262-010 FIELD-MAP EDITOR

22311B SURVEYORS. OOH Title/s: Surveyors

Make exact measurements and determine property boundaries. Provide data relevant to the shape, contour, gravitation, location, elevation, or dimension of land or land features on or near the earth's surface for engineering, mapmaking, mining, land evaluation, construction, and other purposes. Plans ground surveys designed to establish base lines, elevations, and other geodetic measurements. Determines photographic equipment to be used and altitude from which to photograph terrain, and directs aerial surveys of specified geographical area. Drafts or directs others to draft maps of survey data. Prepares survey proposal, or directs one or more phases of survey proposal preparation. Surveys water bodies to determine navigable channels and to secure data for construction of breakwaters, piers, and other marine structures. Analyzes survey objectives and specifications, utilizing knowledge of survey uses. Determines appropriate and economical methods and procedures for establishing survey control. Computes data necessary for driving and connecting underground passages, underground storage, and volume of underground deposits. Coordinates findings with work of engineering and architectural personnel, clients, and others concerned with project. Establishes fixed points for use in making maps, using geodetic and engineering instruments. Prepares charts and tables and makes precise determinations of elevations, and records other characteristics of terrain. Computes geodetic measurements and interprets survey data to determine position, shape, and elevations of geomorphic and topographic features. Conducts research in surveying and mapping methods, using knowledge of techniques of photogrammetric map compilation, electronic data processing, and flight and control planning. Locates and marks sites selected for geophysical prospecting activities, such as locating petroleum or mineral products. Estimates cost of survey. Studies weight, shape, size, and mass of earth, and variations in earth's gravitational field, using astronomic observations and complex computations. Takes instrument readings of sun or stars, and calculates longitude and latitude to determine specific area location. Keeps accurate notes, records, and sketches to describe and certify work performed.

Yearly Earnings: $26,780

Education: Postsecondary vocational training

Knowledge: Administration and Management; Economics and Accounting; Computers and Electronics; Engineering and Technology; Design; Mathematics; Physics; Biology; Sociology and Anthropology; Geography; Education and Training; English Language; Foreign Language; History and Archeology; Philosophy and Theology; Public Safety and Security; Telecommunications; Transportation

Abilities: Written Comprehension; Oral Expression; Written Expression; Fluency of Ideas; Originality; Deductive Reasoning; Inductive Reasoning; Category Flexibility; Mathematical Reasoning; Number Facility; Speed of Closure; Flexibility of Closure; Spatial Orientation; Visualization; Selective Attention; Time Sharing; Stamina; Gross Body Equilibrium; Near Vision; Far Vision; Night Vision; Glare Sensitivity; Speech Recognition; Speech Clarity

Skills: Reading Comprehension; Writing; Mathematics; Science; Critical Thinking; Active Learning; Learning Strategies; Monitoring; Coordination; Persuasion; Negotiation; Instructing; Problem Identification; Information Gathering; Information Organization; Synthesis/Reorganization; Idea Generation; Idea Evaluation; Implementation Planning; Solution Appraisal; Operations Analysis; Equipment Selection; Programming; Visioning; Systems Perception; Identifying Downstream Consequences; Identification of Key Causes; Judgment and Decision Making; Systems Evaluation; Time Management; Management of Financial Resources; Management of Material Resources; Management of Personnel Resources

General Work Activities: Getting Information Needed to Do the Job; Monitoring Processes, Material, or Surroundings; Estimating Needed Characteristics; Evaluating Information against Standards; Analyzing Data or Information; Making Decisions and Solving Problems; Developing Objectives and Strategies; Organizing, Planning, and Prioritizing; Drafting and Specifying Technical Devices, etc.; Provide Consultation and Advice to Others

Job Characteristics: Supervise, Coach, Train Others; Coordinate or Lead Others; Responsibility for Outcomes and Results; Radiation; Walking or Running; Importance of Being Exact or Accurate

GOE Group/s: 02.01.01 Physical Sciences: Theoretical Research; 05.01.06 Engineering: Work Planning and Utilization; 05.03.01 Engineering Technology: Surveying

CIP Program/s: 150805 Mechanical Engineering/Mechanical Technologists and Technicians; 151102 Surveying; 450701 Geography; 450702 Cartography

Related DOT Job/s: 018.161-010 SURVEYOR, MINE; 018.167-018 LAND SURVEYOR; 018.167-026 PHOTOGRAMMETRIC ENGINEER;

018.167-038 SURVEYOR, GEODETIC; 018.167-042 SURVEYOR, GEOPHYSICAL PROSPECTING; 018.167-046 SURVEYOR, MARINE; 024.061-014 GEODESIST; 184.167-026 DIRECTOR, PHOTOGRAMMETRY FLIGHT OPERATIONS

Engineering Technologists and Technicians

22502 CIVIL ENGINEERING TECHNICIANS. OOH

Title/s: Engineering Technicians

Apply theory and principles of civil engineering in planning, designing, and overseeing construction and maintenance of structures and facilities, under the direction of engineering staff or physical scientists. Inspects project site and evaluates contractor work to detect design malfunctions and ensure conformance to design specifications and applicable codes. Analyzes proposed site factors, and designs maps, graphs, tracings, and diagrams to illustrate findings. Plans and conducts field surveys to locate new sites and analyze details of project sites. Drafts detailed dimensional drawings, and designs layouts for projects and to ensure conformance to specifications. Develops plans and estimates costs for installation of systems, utilization of facilities, or construction of structures. Reads and reviews project blueprints and structural specifications to determine dimensions of structure or system and material requirements. Calculates dimensions, square footage, profile and component specifications, and material quantities, using calculator or computer. Reports maintenance problems occurring at project site to supervisor, and negotiates changes to resolve system conflicts. Conducts materials test and analysis, using tools and equipment, and applying engineering knowledge. Confers with supervisor to determine project details, such as plan preparation, acceptance testing, and evaluation of field conditions. Prepares reports and documents project activities and data. Evaluates facility to determine suitability for occupancy and square footage availability. Responds to public suggestions and complaints.

Yearly Earnings: $28,808

Education: Associate degree

Knowledge: Computers and Electronics; Engineering and Technology; Design; Building and Construction; Mathematics; Law, Government, and Jurisprudence

Abilities: Written Expression; Problem Sensitivity; Category Flexibility; Mathematical Reasoning; Number Facility; Visualization; Time Sharing; Depth Perception; Glare Sensitivity

Skills: Active Listening; Writing; Mathematics; Science; Critical Thinking; Active Learning; Negotiation; Problem Identification; Information Gathering; Information Organization; Synthesis/Reorganization; Idea Generation; Idea Evaluation; Implementation Planning; Solution Appraisal; Operations Analysis; Technology Design; Equipment Selection; Testing; Product Inspection; Identifying Downstream Consequences; Identification of Key Causes; Judgment and Decision Making; Systems Evaluation; Management of Material Resources

General Work Activities: Getting Information Needed to Do the Job; Monitoring Processes, Material, or Surroundings; Identifying Objects, Actions, and Events; Inspecting Equipment, Structures, or Material; Estimating Needed Characteristics; Judging Qualities of Things, Services, People; Processing Information; Evaluating Information against Standards; Analyzing Data or Information; Making Decisions and Solving Problems; Thinking Creatively; Updating and Using Job-Relevant Knowledge; Developing Objectives and Strategies; Organizing, Planning, and Prioritizing; Drafting and Specifying Technical Devices, etc.; Implementing Ideas, Programs, etc.; Documenting/Recording Information; Interpreting Meaning of Information to Others; Communicating with Other Workers; Selling or Influencing Others; Resolving Conflicts, Negotiating with Others; Developing and Building Teams; Monitoring and Controlling Resources

Job Characteristics: Persuade Someone to a Course of Action; Take a Position Opposed to Others; Coordinate or Lead Others; Responsibility for Outcomes and Results; High Places; Climbing Ladders, Scaffolds, Poles, etc.; Importance of Being Sure All is Done

GOE Group/s: 05.01.06 Engineering: Work Planning and Utilization; 05.03.02 Engineering Technology: Drafting; 05.03.06 Engineering Technology: Industrial and Safety

CIP Program/s: 040501 Interior Architecture; 150101 Architectural Engineering Technologists and Technicians; 150201 Civil Engineering/Civil Technologists and Technicians; 151001 Construction/Building Techmologists and Technicians

Related DOT Job/s: 005.261-014 CIVIL ENGINEERING TECHNICIAN; 019.261-018 FACILITIES PLANNER; 019.261-026 FIRE-PROTECTION ENGINEERING TECHNICIAN; 199.261-014 PARKING ANALYST

22505A ELECTRONICS ENGINEERING TECHNICIANS. OOH Title/s: Engineering Technicians

Lay out, build, test, troubleshoot, repair, and modify developmental and production electronic components, parts, equipment, and systems, such as computer equipment, missile control instrumentation, electron tubes, test equipment, and machine tool numerical controls, applying principles and theories of electronics, electrical circuitry, engineering mathematics, electronic and electrical testing, and physics. Reads blueprints, wiring diagrams, schematic drawings, and engineering instructions for assembling electronics units, applying knowledge of electronic theory and components. Fabricates parts, such as coils, terminal boards, and chassis, using bench lathes, drills, or other machine tools. Assembles circuitry or electronic components, according to engineering instructions, technical manuals, and knowledge of electronics, using hand tools and power tools. Tests electronics unit, using standard test equipment, to evaluate performance and determine needs for adjustments. Adjusts and replaces defective or improperly functioning circuitry and electronics components, using hand tools and soldering iron. Designs basic circuitry and sketches for design documentation, as directed by engineers, using drafting instruments and computer-aided design equipment. Assists engineers in development of testing techniques, laboratory equipment, and circuitry or installation specifications, by writing reports and recording data.

Yearly Earnings: $31,148

Education: Associate degree

Knowledge: Production and Processing; Computers and Electronics; Engineering and Technology; Design; Building and Construction; Mathematics; Physics

Abilities: None above average

Skills: Mathematics; Science; Critical Thinking; Active Learning; Problem Identification; Information Gathering; Information Organization; Operations Analysis; Technology Design; Equipment Selection; Installation; Testing; Operation Monitoring; Troubleshooting; Repairing

General Work Activities: Inspecting Equipment, Structures, or Material; Updating and Using Job-Relevant Knowledge; Operating Vehicles or Equipment; Drafting and Specifying Technical Devices, etc.; Repairing and Maintaining Electrical Equipment; Documenting/Recording Information

Job Characteristics: Radiation; Degree of Automation

GOE Group/s: 05.01.01 Engineering: Research; 05.05.05 Craft Technology: Electrical-Electronic Systems Installation and Repair

CIP Program/s: 150301 Computer Engineering Technologists and Technicians; 150303 Electrical, Electronic and Communications Engineering Technologists and Technicians; 150402 Computer Mainte-

nance Technologists and Technicians; 150403 Electromechanical Technologists and Technicians; 150405 Robotics Technologists and Technicians; 470101 Electrical and Electronics Equipment Installer and Repairer; 470105 Industrial Electronics Installer and Repairer
Related DOT Job/s: 003.161-014 ELECTRONICS TECHNICIAN; 003.161-018 TECHNICIAN, SEMICONDUCTOR DEVELOPMENT; 725.381-010 TUBE REBUILDER; 726.261-010 ELECTRONICS ASSEMBLER, DEVELOPMENTAL

22505B CALIBRATION AND INSTRUMENTATION TECHNICIANS. OOH Title/s: Engineering Technicians

Develop, test, calibrate, operate, and repair electrical, mechanical, electromechanical, electrohydraulic, or electronic measuring and recording instruments, apparatus, and equipment. Plans sequence of testing and calibration program for instruments and equipment, according to blueprints, schematics, technical manuals, and other specifications. Sets up test equipment and conducts tests on performance and reliability of mechanical, structural, or electromechanical equipment. Modifies performance and operation of component parts and circuitry to specifications, using test equipment and precision instruments. Selects sensing, telemetering, and recording instrumentation and circuitry. Disassembles and reassembles instruments and equipment, using hand tools, and inspects instruments and equipment for defects. Sketches plans for developing jigs, fixtures, instruments, and related nonstandard apparatus. Analyzes and converts test data, using mathematical formulas, and reports results and proposed modifications. Performs preventive and corrective maintenance of test apparatus and peripheral equipment. Confers with engineers, supervisor, and other technical workers to assist with equipment installation, maintenance, and repair techniques.
Yearly Earnings: $31,148
Education: Associate degree
Knowledge: Computers and Electronics; Engineering and Technology; Design; Mechanical; Mathematics
Abilities: Written Comprehension; Deductive Reasoning; Information Ordering; Mathematical Reasoning
Skills: Technology Design; Equipment Selection; Installation; Testing; Product Inspection; Equipment Maintenance; Troubleshooting
General Work Activities: Inspecting Equipment, Structures, or Material; Evaluating Information against Standards; Analyzing Data or Information; Controlling Machines and Processes; Drafting and Specifying Technical Devices, etc.; Repairing and Maintaining Mechanical Equipment; Repairing and Maintaining Electrical Equipment
Job Characteristics: None above average
GOE Group/s: 02.04.01 Laboratory Technology: Physical Sciences; 05.01.01 Engineering: Research; 05.01.08 Engineering: General Engineering
CIP Program/s: 150303 Electrical, Electronic and Communications Engineering Technologists and Technicians; 150403 Electromechanical Technologists and Technicians; 150404 Instrumentation Technologists and Technicians; 150801 Aeronautical and Aerospace Engineering Technologists and Technicians; 470401 Instrument Calibration and Repairer
Related DOT Job/s: 003.261-010 INSTRUMENTATION TECHNICIAN; 019.281-010 CALIBRATION LABORATORY TECHNICIAN; 828.261-018 SENIOR TECHNICIAN, CONTROLS

22505C ELECTRICAL ENGINEERING TECHNICIANS. OOH Title/s: Engineering Technicians

Apply electrical theory and related knowledge to test and modify developmental or operational electrical machinery and electrical control equipment and circuitry in industrial or commercial plants and laboratories. Sets up and operates test equipment to evaluate performance of developmental parts, assemblies, or systems under simulated operating conditions. Modifies electrical prototypes, parts, assemblies, and systems to correct functional deviations. Plans method and sequence of operations for testing and developing experimental electronic and electrical equipment. Assembles electrical and electronic systems and prototypes, according to engineering data and knowledge of electrical principles, using hand tools and measuring instruments. Analyzes and interprets test information. Draws diagrams and writes engineering specifications to clarify design details and functional criteria of experimental electronics units. Collaborates with electrical engineer and other personnel to solve developmental problems. Maintains and repairs testing equipment.
Yearly Earnings: $31,148
Education: Associate degree
Knowledge: Computers and Electronics; Engineering and Technology; Design; Mathematics; Physics
Abilities: Deductive Reasoning; Information Ordering; Mathematical Reasoning; Visualization
Skills: Active Learning; Synthesis/Reorganization; Operations Analysis; Technology Design; Equipment Selection; Installation; Testing; Troubleshooting
General Work Activities: Identifying Objects, Actions, and Events; Inspecting Equipment, Structures, or Material; Evaluating Information against Standards; Analyzing Data or Information; Thinking Creatively; Updating and Using Job-Relevant Knowledge; Operating Vehicles or Equipment; Drafting and Specifying Technical Devices, etc.; Implementing Ideas, Programs, etc.; Repairing and Maintaining Electrical Equipment
Job Characteristics: None above average
GOE Group/s: 05.01.01 Engineering: Research; 05.03.05 Engineering Technology: Electrical-Electronic
CIP Program/s: 150303 Electrical, Electronic and Communications Engineering Technologists and Technicians
Related DOT Job/s: 003.161-010 ELECTRICAL TECHNICIAN; 726.261-014 ELECTRICIAN, RESEARCH

22508 INDUSTRIAL ENGINEERING TECHNICIANS AND TECHNOLOGISTS. OOH Title/s: Engineering Technicians; Inspectors and Compliance Officers, Except Construction

Study and record time, motion, method, and speed involved in performance of production, maintenance, clerical, and other worker operations for such purposes as establishing standard production rates or improving efficiency. Usually work under the direction of engineering staff. Studies time, motion, methods, and speed involved in maintenance, production, and other operations to establish standard production rate and improve efficiency. Observes workers operating equipment or performing tasks to determine time involved and fatigue rate, using timing devices. Prepares charts, graphs, and diagrams to illustrate workflow, routing, floor layouts, material handling, and machine utilization. Recommends revision to methods of operation, material handling, equipment layout, or other changes to increase production or improve standards. Records test data, applying statistical quality control procedures. Observes workers using equipment to verify that equipment is being operated and maintained according to quality assurance standards. Recommends modifications to existing quality or production standards to achieve optimum quality within limits of equipment capability. Evaluates data and writes reports to validate or indicate deviations from existing standards. Aids in planning work assignments in accordance with worker performance, machine capacity, production schedules, and anticipated delays. Prepares graphs or charts of data, or enters data into computer for analysis. Interprets engineering drawings, schematic diagrams, or formulas, and

confers with management or engineering staff to determine quality and reliability standards. Reads worker logs, product processing sheets, and specification sheets to verify that records adhere to quality assurance specifications. Tests and inspects products at various stages of production process for quality control purposes. Compiles and evaluates statistical data to determine and maintain quality and reliability of products. Selects products for tests at specified stages in production process, and tests products for such qualities as dimensions and performance characteristics. Sets up and performs destructive and nondestructive tests on materials, parts, or products to measure performance, life, or material characteristics.
Yearly Earnings: $28,808
Education: Associate degree
Knowledge: Administration and Management; Clerical; Economics and Accounting; Personnel and Human Resources; Production and Processing; Computers and Electronics; Engineering and Technology; Design; Mechanical; Mathematics; Physics; Psychology; Sociology and Anthropology; English Language; Philosophy and Theology; Public Safety and Security; Communications and Media
Abilities: Written Expression; Fluency of Ideas; Originality; Inductive Reasoning; Information Ordering; Category Flexibility; Mathematical Reasoning; Number Facility; Speed of Closure; Perceptual Speed; Visualization; Selective Attention; Time Sharing; Far Vision
Skills: Reading Comprehension; Writing; Speaking; Mathematics; Science; Critical Thinking; Active Learning; Learning Strategies; Monitoring; Persuasion; Problem Identification; Information Gathering; Information Organization; Synthesis/Reorganization; Idea Generation; Idea Evaluation; Implementation Planning; Solution Appraisal; Operations Analysis; Technology Design; Equipment Selection; Programming; Testing; Operation Monitoring; Product Inspection; Visioning; Systems Perception; Identifying Downstream Consequences; Identification of Key Causes; Judgment and Decision Making; Systems Evaluation
General Work Activities: Getting Information Needed to Do the Job; Identifying Objects, Actions, and Events; Estimating Needed Characteristics; Judging Qualities of Things, Services, People; Processing Information; Evaluating Information against Standards; Analyzing Data or Information; Developing Objectives and Strategies; Scheduling Work and Activities; Operating Vehicles or Equipment; Drafting and Specifying Technical Devices, etc.; Documenting/Recording Information; Interpreting Meaning of Information to Others; Communicating with Other Workers
Job Characteristics: Persuade Someone to a Course of Action; Sounds, Noise Levels are Distracting, etc.; Extremely Bright or Inadequate Lighting; Sitting; Importance of Being Exact or Accurate
GOE Group/s: 02.04.01 Laboratory Technology: Physical Sciences; 05.03.06 Engineering Technology: Industrial and Safety
CIP Program/s: 150603 Industrial/Manufacturing Technologists and Technicians; 150702 Quality Control Technologists and Technicians
Related DOT Job/s: 012.261-014 QUALITY CONTROL TECHNICIAN; 012.267-010 INDUSTRIAL ENGINEERING TECHNICIAN; 168.367-022 PERSONNEL QUALITY ASSURANCE AUDITOR

22511 MECHANICAL ENGINEERING TECHNICIANS AND TECHNOLOGISTS. OOH Title/s: Engineering Technicians

Apply theory and principles of mechanical engineering to develop and test machinery and equipment, under direction of engineering staff or physical scientists. Reviews project instructions and blueprints to ascertain test specifications, procedures, and objectives, and tests nature of technical problems, such as redesign. Sets up and conducts tests of complete units and components under operational conditions to investigate proposals for improving equipment performance. Devises, fabricates, and assembles new or modified mechanical components for products, such as industrial machinery or equipment and measuring instruments. Analyzes test results in relation to design or rated specifications and test objectives, and modifies or adjusts equipment to meet specifications. Tests equipment, using test devices attached to generator, voltage regulator, or other electrical parts, such as generators or spark plugs. Sets up prototype and test apparatus and operates test controlling equipment to observe and record prototype test results. Reviews project instructions and specifications to identify, modify, and plan requirements fabrication, assembly, and testing. Discusses changes in design, method of manufacture and assembly, and drafting techniques and procedures with staff, and coordinates corrections. Calculates required capacities for equipment of proposed system to obtain specified performance, and submits data to engineering personnel for approval. Drafts detail drawing or sketch for drafting room completion or to request parts fabrication by machine, sheet, or wood shops. Records test procedures and results, numerical and graphical data, and recommendations for changes in product or test methods. Confers with technicians, submits reports of test results to engineering department, and recommends design or material changes. Evaluates tool drawing designs by measuring drawing dimensions and comparing with original specifications for form and function, using engineering skills. Operates drill press, grinders, engine lathe, or other machines to modify parts tested or to fabricate experimental parts for testing. Reads dials and meters to determine amperage, voltage, electrical out- and input at specific operating temperature to analyze parts performance. Prepares parts sketches and writes work orders and purchase requests to be furnished by outside contractors. Inspects lines and figures for clarity, and returns erroneous drawings to designer for correction. Estimates cost factors, including labor and material for purchased and fabricated parts and costs for assembly, testing, and installing.
Yearly Earnings: $28,808
Education: Associate degree
Knowledge: Administration and Management; Engineering and Technology; Design; Mechanical; Mathematics; Physics
Abilities: Oral Comprehension; Written Comprehension; Oral Expression; Written Expression; Fluency of Ideas; Problem Sensitivity; Deductive Reasoning; Inductive Reasoning; Information Ordering; Mathematical Reasoning; Number Facility; Speed of Closure; Perceptual Speed; Visualization; Time Sharing; Rate Control; Wrist-Finger Speed
Skills: Active Listening; Mathematics; Science; Active Learning; Information Organization; Synthesis/Reorganization; Idea Generation; Idea Evaluation; Implementation Planning; Operations Analysis; Technology Design; Equipment Selection; Testing; Operation Monitoring; Operation and Control; Troubleshooting; Visioning; Systems Perception; Identifying Downstream Consequences; Judgment and Decision Making; Management of Material Resources
General Work Activities: Monitoring Processes, Material, or Surroundings; Identifying Objects, Actions, and Events; Inspecting Equipment, Structures, or Material; Evaluating Information against Standards; Analyzing Data or Information; Thinking Creatively; Updating and Using Job-Relevant Knowledge; Controlling Machines and Processes; Drafting and Specifying Technical Devices, etc.; Implementing Ideas, Programs, etc.; Repairing and Maintaining Mechanical Equipment; Communicating with Other Workers
Job Characteristics: Hazardous Conditions; Hazardous Equipment; Importance of Being Exact or Accurate
GOE Group/s: 05.01.01 Engineering: Research; 05.01.07 Engineering: Design; 05.03.02 Engineering Technology: Drafting; 05.03.07 Engineering Technology: Mechanical
CIP Program/s: 150501 Heating, Air Conditioning and Refrigeration Technologists and Technicians; 150503 Energy Management and Systems Technologists and Technicians; 150803 Automotive Engineering

Technologists and Technicians; 150805 Mechanical Engineering/Mechanical Technologists and Technicians; 480101 Drafting, General; 480105 Mechanical Drafting
Related DOT Job/s: 007.161-026 MECHANICAL-ENGINEERING TECHNICIAN; 007.161-030 OPTOMECHANICAL TECHNICIAN; 007.167-010 DIE-DRAWING CHECKER; 007.181-010 HEAT-TRANSFER TECHNICIAN; 007.267-010 DRAWINGS CHECKER, ENGINEERING; 007.267-014 TOOL DESIGN CHECKER; 017.261-010 AUTO-DESIGN CHECKER

22514A ARCHITECTURAL DRAFTERS. OOH Title/s: Drafters

Prepare detailed drawings of architectural designs and plans for buildings and structures according to specifications provided by architect. Draws rough and detailed scale plans, to scale, for foundations, buildings, and structures, according to specifications. Prepares colored drawings of landscape and interior designs for presentation to client. Lays out and plans interior room arrangements for commercial buildings, and draws charts, forms, and records, using computer-assisted equipment. Develops diagrams for construction, fabrication, and installation of equipment, structures, components, and systems, using field documents and specifications. Lays out schematics and wiring diagrams used to erect, install, and repair establishment cable and electrical systems, using computer equipment. Traces copies of plans and drawings, using transparent paper or cloth, ink, pencil, and standard drafting instruments, for reproduction purposes. Drafts and corrects topographical maps to represent geological stratigraphy, mineral deposits, and pipeline systems, using survey data and aerial photographs. Calculates heat loss and gain of buildings and structures to determine required equipment specifications, following standard procedures. Builds landscape models, using data provided by landscape architect.
Yearly Earnings: $28,756
Education: Postsecondary vocational training
Knowledge: Computers and Electronics; Engineering and Technology; Design; Mathematics; Physics; Fine Arts
Abilities: Fluency of Ideas; Category Flexibility; Mathematical Reasoning; Number Facility; Speed of Closure; Spatial Orientation; Visualization; Arm-Hand Steadiness; Manual Dexterity; Finger Dexterity; Wrist-Finger Speed; Near Vision; Visual Color Discrimination
Skills: Mathematics; Operations Analysis; Programming; Visioning
General Work Activities: Thinking Creatively; Operating Vehicles or Equipment; Drafting and Specifying Technical Devices, etc.
Job Characteristics: Sitting; Using Hands on Objects, Tools, or Controls; Importance of Being Exact or Accurate; Importance of Being Sure All is Done
GOE Group/s: 05.03.02 Engineering Technology: Drafting
CIP Program/s: 150501 Heating, Air Conditioning and Refrigeration Technologists and Technicians; 480101 Drafting, General; 480102 Architectural Drafting; 480103 Civil/Structural Drafting
Related DOT Job/s: 001.261-010 DRAFTER, ARCHITECTURAL; 001.261-014 DRAFTER, LANDSCAPE; 005.281-014 DRAFTER, STRUCTURAL; 014.281-010 DRAFTER, MARINE; 017.261-026 DRAFTER, COMMERCIAL; 017.261-034 DRAFTER, HEATING AND VENTILATING; 017.261-038 DRAFTER, PLUMBING; 017.281-018 DRAFTER, ASSISTANT; 017.281-030 DRAFTER, OIL AND GAS

22514B ELECTRONIC DRAFTERS. OOH Title/s: Drafters

Draw wiring diagrams, circuit board assembly diagrams, schematics, and layout drawings used for manufacture, installation, and repair of electronic equipment. Drafts detail and assembly drawings and designs of electromechanical equipment and related data processing systems. Creates master layout of design components and circuitry and printed circuit boards, according to specifications and utilizing computer-assisted equipment. Plots electrical test points on layout sheet, using pencil, and draws schematics to wire test fixture heads to frame. Consults with engineers to discuss and interpret design concepts and determine requirements of detailed working drawings. Examines electronic schematics and analyzes logic diagrams and design documents to plan layout of printed circuit board components and circuitry. Compares logic element configuration on display screen with engineering schematics, and calculates figures to convert, redesign, and modify element. Reviews blueprints to determine customer requirements, and consults with assembler regarding schematics, wiring procedures, and conductor paths. Copies drawings of printed circuit board fabrication, using print machine or blueprinting procedure. Selects drill size to drill test head, according to test design and specifications, and submits guide layout to designated department. Generates computer tapes of final layout design to produce layered photomasks and photoplotting design onto film. Compiles data, computes quantities, and prepares cost estimates to determine equipment needs, and requisitions materials as required. Examines and verifies master layout for electrical and mechanical accuracy. Keys and programs specified commands and engineering specifications into computer system to change functions and test final layout. Reviews work orders and procedural manuals, and confers with vendors and design staff to resolve problems and modify design. Locates files relating to specified design projection database library, loads program into computer, and records completed job data. Supervises and coordinates work activities of workers engaged in drafting, designing layouts, assembling, and testing printed circuit boards.
Yearly Earnings: $28,756
Education: Postsecondary vocational training
Knowledge: Administration and Management; Computers and Electronics; Engineering and Technology; Design; Mathematics; Telecommunications
Abilities: Oral Comprehension; Written Comprehension; Oral Expression; Fluency of Ideas; Deductive Reasoning; Information Ordering; Category Flexibility; Mathematical Reasoning; Number Facility; Speed of Closure; Flexibility of Closure; Perceptual Speed; Visualization; Arm-Hand Steadiness; Manual Dexterity; Wrist-Finger Speed; Near Vision
Skills: Mathematics; Science; Active Learning; Coordination; Problem Identification; Information Organization; Synthesis/Reorganization; Operations Analysis; Technology Design; Equipment Selection; Installation; Programming; Testing; Troubleshooting; Visioning; Systems Perception; Identification of Key Causes; Systems Evaluation; Management of Financial Resources; Management of Material Resources; Management of Personnel Resources
General Work Activities: Getting Information Needed to Do the Job; Inspecting Equipment, Structures, or Material; Processing Information; Evaluating Information against Standards; Analyzing Data or Information; Making Decisions and Solving Problems; Updating and Using Job-Relevant Knowledge; Scheduling Work and Activities; Operating Vehicles or Equipment; Drafting and Specifying Technical Devices, etc.; Interpreting Meaning of Information to Others; Coordinating Work and Activities of Others; Guiding, Directing and Motivating Subordinates; Provide Consultation and Advice to Others
Job Characteristics: Supervise, Coach, Train Others; Responsibility for Outcomes and Results; Sitting; Using Hands on Objects, Tools, or Controls; Importance of Being Exact or Accurate; Importance of Being Sure All is Done
GOE Group/s: 05.03.02 Engineering Technology: Drafting
CIP Program/s: 150301 Computer Engineering Technologists and Technicians; 150303 Electrical, Electronic and Communications Engineering Technologists and Technicians; 480101 Drafting, General; 480104 Electrical/Electronics Drafting; 520201 Business Administra-

tion and Management, General; 520205 Operations Management and Supervision
Related DOT Job/s: 003.131-010 SUPERVISOR, DRAFTING AND PRINTED CIRCUIT DESIGN; 003.261-018 INTEGRATED CIRCUIT LAYOUT DESIGNER; 003.261-022 PRINTED CIRCUIT DESIGNER; 003.281-014 DRAFTER, ELECTRONIC; 003.362-010 DESIGN TECHNICIAN, COMPUTER-AIDED; 017.261-014 DESIGN DRAFTER, ELECTROMECHANISMS; 726.364-014 TEST FIXTURE DESIGNER

22514C CIVIL DRAFTERS. OOH Title/s: Drafters

Prepare drawings and topographical and relief maps used in civil engineering projects, such as highways, bridges, pipelines, flood control projects, and water and sewerage control systems. Draws maps, diagrams, and profiles, using cross-sections and surveys, to represent elevations, topographical contours, subsurface formations, and structures. Drafts plans and detailed drawings for structures, installations, and construction projects, such as highways, sewage disposal systems, and dikes. Plots boreholes for oil and gas wells, from photographic subsurface survey recordings and other data, using computer-assisted drafting equipment. Finishes and duplicates drawings, according to required mediums and specifications for reproduction, using blueprinting, photographing, or other duplicating methods. Identifies symbols located on topographical surveys to denote geological and geophysical formations or oil field installations. Calculates excavation tonnage and prepares graphs and fill-hauling diagrams used in earth-moving operations. Reviews rough sketches, drawings, specifications, and other engineering data received from civil engineer. Computes and represents characteristics and dimensions of borehole, such as depth, degree, and direction of inclination. Correlates, interprets, and modifies data obtained from topographical surveys, well logs, and geophysical prospecting reports. Accompanies field survey crew to locate grading markers or to collect data required to revise construction drawings.
Yearly Earnings: $28,756
Education: Postsecondary vocational training
Knowledge: Computers and Electronics; Engineering and Technology; Design; Mathematics; Physics; Geography
Abilities: Oral Comprehension; Written Comprehension; Inductive Reasoning; Information Ordering; Mathematical Reasoning; Number Facility; Perceptual Speed; Spatial Orientation; Wrist-Finger Speed; Near Vision
Skills: Mathematics; Operations Analysis; Programming
General Work Activities: Evaluating Information against Standards; Operating Vehicles or Equipment; Drafting and Specifying Technical Devices, etc.
Job Characteristics: Consequence of Error; Importance of Being Exact or Accurate; Importance of Being Sure All is Done
GOE Group/s: 05.03.02 Engineering Technology: Drafting
CIP Program/s: 480101 Drafting, General; 480103 Civil/Structural Drafting
Related DOT Job/s: 005.281-010 DRAFTER, CIVIL; 010.281-010 DRAFTER, DIRECTIONAL SURVEY; 010.281-014 DRAFTER, GEOLOGICAL; 010.281-018 DRAFTER, GEOPHYSICAL

22514D MECHANICAL DRAFTERS. OOH Title/s: Drafters

Prepare detailed working diagrams of machinery and mechanical devices, including dimensions, fastening methods, and other engineering information. Develops detailed design drawings and specifications for mechanical equipment, dies/tools, and controls, according to engineering sketches and design proposals. Lays out and draws schematic, orthographic, or angle views to depict functional relationships of components, assemblies, systems, and machines. Designs scale or full-size blueprints of specialty items, such as furniture and automobile body or chassis components. Draws freehand sketches of designs,and traces finished drawings onto designated paper for reproduction of blueprints. Lays out, draws, and reproduces illustrations for reference manuals and technical publications to describe operation and maintenance of mechanical systems. Shades or colors drawings to clarify and emphasize details and dimensions, and eliminates background, using ink, crayon, airbrush, and overlays. Positions instructions and comments onto drawings, and illustrates and describes installation and maintenance details. Reviews and analyzes specifications, sketches, engineering drawings, ideas, and related design data to determine factors affecting component designs. Computes mathematical formulas to develop and design detailed specifications for components or machinery, using computer-assisted equipment. Modifies and revises designs to correct operating deficiencies or to reduce production problems. Observes set-up and gauges during programmed machine or equipment trial run to verify conformance of signals and systems to specifications. Measures machine set-up and parts during production to ensure compliance with design specifications, using precision measuring instruments. Compiles and analyzes test data to determine effect of machine design on various factors, such as temperature and pressure. Confers with customer representatives to review schematics and to answer questions pertaining to installation of systems. Coordinates and works in conjunction with other workers to design, lay out, or detail components and systems. Directs work activities of detailer, and confers with staff and supervisors to resolve design or other problems.
Yearly Earnings: $28,756
Education: Postsecondary vocational training
Knowledge: Computers and Electronics; Engineering and Technology; Design; Mathematics; Physics; Fine Arts
Abilities: Written Comprehension; Fluency of Ideas; Originality; Deductive Reasoning; Information Ordering; Category Flexibility; Mathematical Reasoning; Number Facility; Spatial Orientation; Visualization; Arm-Hand Steadiness; Manual Dexterity; Finger Dexterity; Near Vision; Visual Color Discrimination
Skills: Mathematics; Science; Critical Thinking; Negotiation; Information Gathering; Information Organization; Synthesis/Reorganization; Idea Generation; Idea Evaluation; Implementation Planning; Solution Appraisal; Operations Analysis; Technology Design; Equipment Selection; Programming; Testing; Operation Monitoring; Product Inspection; Troubleshooting; Visioning; Systems Perception; Identifying Downstream Consequences; Identification of Key Causes; Judgment and Decision Making; Systems Evaluation; Management of Material Resources; Management of Personnel Resources
General Work Activities: Getting Information Needed to Do the Job; Inspecting Equipment, Structures, or Material; Operating Vehicles or Equipment; Drafting and Specifying Technical Devices, etc.; Communicating with Persons Outside Organization; Coordinating Work and Activities of Others; Guiding, Directing and Motivating Subordinates
Job Characteristics: Supervise, Coach, Train Others; Take a Position Opposed to Others; Coordinate or Lead Others; Responsibility for Outcomes and Results; Sitting; Frustrating Circumstances; Importance of Being Exact or Accurate; Importance of Being Sure All is Done
GOE Group/s: 05.03.02 Engineering Technology: Drafting
CIP Program/s: 150403 Electromechanical Technologists and Technicians; 150404 Instrumentation Technologists and Technicians; 150805 Mechanical Engineering/Mechanical Technologists and Technicians; 480101 Drafting, General; 480104 Electrical/Electronics Drafting; 480105 Mechanical Drafting
Related DOT Job/s: 002.261-010 DRAFTER, AERONAUTICAL; 003.261-014 CONTROLS DESIGNER; 007.161-010 DIE DESIGNER; 007.161-014 DIE-DESIGNER APPRENTICE; 007.161-018 ENGINEERING ASSISTANT, MECHANICAL EQUIPMENT; 007.261-014 DRAFTER, CASTINGS; 007.261-018 DRAFTER, PATENT; 007.261-022 DRAFTER,

TOOL DESIGN; 007.281-010 DRAFTER, MECHANICAL; 017.261-018 DETAILER; 017.261-022 DETAILER, FURNITURE; 017.261-030 DRAFTER, DETAIL; 017.261-042 DRAFTER, AUTOMOTIVE DESIGN; 017.281-010 AUTO-DESIGN DETAILER; 017.281-014 DRAFTER APPRENTICE; 017.281-026 DRAFTER, AUTOMOTIVE DESIGN LAYOUT; 017.281-034 TECHNICAL ILLUSTRATOR

22517 ESTIMATORS AND DRAFTERS, UTILITIES. OOH Title/s: Drafters

Develop specifications and instructions for installation of voltage transformers, overhead or underground cables, and related electrical equipment used to conduct electrical energy from transmission lines or high-voltage distribution lines to consumers. Makes other drawings, such as pertaining to wiring connections or cross-sections of underground cables, as required for instructions to installation crew. Drafts sketches to scale. Draws master sketch showing relation of proposed installation to existing facilities. Takes measurements, such as distances to be spanned by wire and cable, which affect installation and arrangement of equipment. Performs land surveying duties, and prepares specifications and diagrams for installation of gas-distribution pipes owned by gas-electric utility. Reviews completed construction drawings and cost estimates for accuracy and conformity to standards and regulations. Studies work order request to determine type of service, such as lighting or power, demanded by installation. Estimates material, equipment, and incidentals needed for installation. Visits site of proposed installation and draws rough sketch of location. Estimates labor and material costs, using price lists and records on previous projects. Inspects completed installation of electrical equipment and related building circuitry to verify conformance to specifications. Consults power distribution engineering staff on difficulties encountered. Directs maintenance of files of blueprints, maps, construction sketches, cost estimates, and related records. Supervises other workers.

Yearly Earnings: $28,756
Education: Postsecondary vocational training
Knowledge: Administration and Management; Economics and Accounting; Personnel and Human Resources; Engineering and Technology; Design; Building and Construction; Mathematics; Physics; Psychology; Sociology and Anthropology; Geography; English Language; Public Safety and Security
Abilities: Fluency of Ideas; Originality; Number Facility; Memorization; Speed of Closure; Spatial Orientation; Visualization
Skills: Active Listening; Mathematics; Monitoring; Coordination; Information Organization; Synthesis/Reorganization; Idea Generation; Idea Evaluation; Implementation Planning; Solution Appraisal; Operations Analysis; Technology Design; Equipment Selection; Product Inspection; Visioning; Identifying Downstream Consequences; Judgment and Decision Making; Systems Evaluation; Time Management; Management of Financial Resources; Management of Material Resources; Management of Personnel Resources
General Work Activities: Getting Information Needed to Do the Job; Inspecting Equipment, Structures, or Material; Estimating Needed Characteristics; Drafting and Specifying Technical Devices, etc.; Documenting/Recording Information; Communicating with Other Workers; Coordinating Work and Activities of Others; Guiding, Directing and Motivating Subordinates
Job Characteristics: Supervise, Coach, Train Others; Take a Position Opposed to Others; Coordinate or Lead Others; Responsibility for Outcomes and Results; Extremely Bright or Inadequate Lighting; Radiation; High Places; Hazardous Conditions; Importance of Being Sure All is Done
GOE Group/s: 05.03.02 Engineering Technology: Drafting
CIP Program/s: 480101 Drafting, General; 480103 Civil/Structural Drafting; 480104 Electrical/Electronics Drafting
Related DOT Job/s: 003.281-010 DRAFTER, ELECTRICAL; 019.161-010 SUPERVISOR, ESTIMATOR AND DRAFTER; 019.261-014 ESTIMATOR AND DRAFTER

22521A SURVEYING TECHNICIANS. OOH Title/s: Surveyors

Adjust and operate surveying instruments, such as the theodolite and electronic distance-measuring equipment, and compile notes, make sketches, and enter data into computers. Obtains land survey data, such as angles, elevations, points, and contours, using electronic distance measuring equipment and other surveying instruments. Compiles notes, sketches, and records of survey data obtained and work performed. Directs work of subordinate members of party, performing surveying duties not requiring licensure.

Yearly Earnings: $26,780
Education: Postsecondary vocational training
Knowledge: Engineering and Technology; Design; Mathematics; Geography
Abilities: Spatial Orientation
Skills: None above average
General Work Activities: Controlling Machines and Processes; Guiding, Directing and Motivating Subordinates
Job Characteristics: Very Hot; Importance of Being Exact or Accurate
GOE Group/s: 05.03.01 Engineering Technology: Surveying
CIP Program/s: 151102 Surveying
Related DOT Job/s: 018.167-010 CHIEF OF PARTY; 018.167-034 SURVEYOR ASSISTANT, INSTRUMENTS

22521B MAPPING TECHNICIANS. OOH Title/s: Surveyors

Calculate mapmaking information from field notes, and draw and verify accuracy of topographical maps. Computes and measures scaled distances between reference points to establish exact relative position of adjoining prints. Traces contours and topographical details to produce map. Calculates latitude, longitude, angles, areas, and other information for mapmaking from survey field notes, using reference tables and computer. Verifies identification of topographical features and accuracy of contour lines by comparison with aerial photographs, old maps, and other reference materials. Forms three-dimensional image of aerial photographs taken from different locations, using mathematical aids and plotting instruments. Lays out and matches aerial photographs in sequence taken, looking for missing areas. Marks errors and makes corrections, such as numbering grid lines or lettering names of rivers or towns. Trims, aligns, and joins prints to form photographic mosaic, maintaining scaled distances between reference points. Analyzes aerial photographs to detect and interpret significant military, industrial, resource, or topographical data. Stores, retrieves, and compares map information, using computers and databanks. Supervises and coordinates activities of workers engaged in drafting maps or in production of blueprints, photostats, and photographs.

Yearly Earnings: $26,780
Education: Postsecondary vocational training
Knowledge: Administration and Management; Computers and Electronics; Design; Mathematics; Geography
Abilities: Mathematical Reasoning; Number Facility; Flexibility of Closure; Spatial Orientation; Wrist-Finger Speed; Near Vision; Far Vision; Visual Color Discrimination
Skills: Mathematics; Synthesis/Reorganization; Technology Design; Management of Personnel Resources
General Work Activities: Evaluating Information against Standards; Operating Vehicles or Equipment; Drafting and Specifying Technical Devices, etc.; Communicating with Other Workers; Coordinating

Work and Activities of Others; Guiding, Directing and Motivating Subordinates
Job Characteristics: Supervise, Coach, Train Others; Responsibility for Outcomes and Results; Importance of Being Exact or Accurate
GOE Group/s: 05.03.01 Engineering Technology: Surveying; 05.03.02 Engineering Technology: Drafting
CIP Program/s: 151102 Surveying; 450702 Cartography; 480101 Drafting, General; 480103 Civil/Structural Drafting
Related DOT Job/s: 018.167-014 GEODETIC COMPUTATOR; 018.167-030 SUPERVISOR, MAPPING; 018.261-018 EDITOR, MAP; 018.261-022 MOSAICIST; 018.281-010 STEREO-PLOTTER OPERATOR; 029.167-010 AERIAL-PHOTOGRAPH INTERPRETER

22599A SOUND ENGINEERING TECHNICIANS.

OOH Title/s: Broadcast Technicians

Operate machines and equipment to record, synchronize, mix, or reproduce music, voices, and previously recorded sound effects. Records speech, music, and other sounds on recording media, using recording equipment. Mixes and edits voices, music, and taped sound effects during stage performances, using sound-mixing board. Synchronizes and equalizes prerecorded dialog, music, and sound effects with visual action of motion picture or television production, using control console. Reproduces and duplicates sound recordings from original recording media, using sound editing and duplication equipment. Regulates volume level and quality of sound during motion picture, phonograph, television, or radio production recording sessions, using control console. Sets up, adjusts, and tests recording equipment to prepare for recording session. Keeps log of recordings. Maintains recording equipment. Supervises workers preparing and producing sound effects for radio, film, and videotape productions.
Yearly Earnings: $31,148
Education: Associate degree
Knowledge: Computers and Electronics; Engineering and Technology; Telecommunications; Communications and Media
Abilities: Flexibility of Closure; Selective Attention; Response Orientation; Hearing Sensitivity; Auditory Attention; Sound Localization
Skills: Equipment Selection; Operation Monitoring; Operation and Control; Equipment Maintenance; Troubleshooting; Management of Personnel Resources
General Work Activities: Thinking Creatively; Repairing and Maintaining Electrical Equipment; Developing and Building Teams; Guiding, Directing and Motivating Subordinates
Job Characteristics: Supervise, Coach, Train Others; Sitting; Using Hands on Objects, Tools, or Controls; Degree of Automation
GOE Group/s: 01.06.02 Craft Arts: Arts and Crafts; 05.10.03 Crafts: Electrical-Electronic; 05.10.05 Crafts: Reproduction
CIP Program/s: 100104 Radio and Television Broadcasting Technologists and Technicians
Related DOT Job/s: 194.262-014 SOUND CONTROLLER; 194.262-018 SOUND MIXER; 194.362-010 RECORDING ENGINEER; 194.362-014 RE-RECORDING MIXER; 194.382-014 TAPE TRANSFERRER; 962.167-010 MANAGER, SOUND EFFECTS; 962.382-010 RECORDIST

22599B METALLURGICAL TECHNICIANS. OOH

Title/s: Engineering Technicians

Examine and test minerals and metal samples to determine their physical and chemical properties. Examines and tests metal samples to determine their physical properties, using microscopes, electromagnetic irradiation machines, and manual measuring instruments. Tests metal parts, using radiographic, penetrant, ultrasonic, and magnetic particle methods, to determine if parts meet nondestructive specifications. Examines metal and mineral samples, using spectrograph, spectrometer, densitometer, and other measuring instruments, and records results. Investigates physical and chemical properties of metals, evaluates ore extraction processes, and analyzes data to select testing methods. Measures physical properties of metal specimens, such as tensile strength, hardness, and ductility, using tension testing machines, and records results. Conducts experiments and evaluates data to develop equipment, techniques, and procedures for welding and heat treating.
Yearly Earnings: $28,808
Education: Associate degree
Knowledge: Engineering and Technology; Physics; Chemistry
Abilities: Deductive Reasoning; Inductive Reasoning; Information Ordering; Number Facility; Finger Dexterity
Skills: Mathematics; Science; Equipment Selection; Programming; Testing
General Work Activities: Monitoring Processes, Material, or Surroundings; Identifying Objects, Actions, and Events; Judging Qualities of Things, Services, People; Processing Information; Updating and Using Job-Relevant Knowledge; Controlling Machines and Processes; Operating Vehicles or Equipment; Interpreting Meaning of Information to Others
Job Characteristics: Radiation; Importance of Being Exact or Accurate
GOE Group/s: 02.04.01 Laboratory Technology: Physical Sciences; 05.01.01 Engineering: Research; 05.07.01 Quality Control: Structural
CIP Program/s: 150611 Metallurgical Technologists and Technicians; 150702 Quality Control Technologists and Technicians
Related DOT Job/s: 011.261-010 METALLURGICAL TECHNICIAN; 011.261-014 WELDING TECHNICIAN; 011.261-018 NONDESTRUCTIVE TESTER; 011.261-022 LABORATORY ASSISTANT, METALLURGICAL; 011.281-014 SPECTROSCOPIST; 011.361-010 TESTER

22599C AEROSPACE ENGINEERING TECHNICIANS. OOH Title/s: Engineering Technicians

Operate, install, calibrate, and maintain integrated computer/communications systems consoles, simulators, and other data acquisition, test, and measurement instrument equipment, to launch, track, position, and evaluate air and space vehicles. May record and interpret test data. May fabricate, assemble, and test aircraft parts and mechanisms in laboratory. Determines data required, plans data acquisition operations, and sets up required data acquisition, test, and measurement equipment. Inspects, diagnoses, maintains, and operates test setup and equipment to detect malfunctions, and adjusts, repairs, or replaces faulty components. Tests aircraft systems under simulated operational conditions, using test instrumentation and equipment, to determine design or fabrication parameters. Sets up, operates, maintains, and monitors computer systems and devices for data acquisition and analysis to detect malfunctions. Constructs and maintains test facilities for aircraft parts and systems, according to specifications, using hand tools, power tools, and test instruments. Discusses test data requirements and results with other personnel, determines data required, and calculates and modifies test parameters or equipment. Records and interprets test data on parts, assemblies, and mechanisms, and confers with engineering personnel regarding test procedures and results. Fabricates and installs parts and systems to be tested in test equipment, using hand tools, power tools, and test instruments. Inputs commands and data into computer systems to modify programs for specific test requirements or for equipment maintenance and calibration.
Yearly Earnings: $28,808
Education: Associate degree
Knowledge: Computers and Electronics; Engineering and Technology; Mechanical; Mathematics; Physics
Abilities: Oral Comprehension; Written Comprehension; Oral Expression; Written Expression; Deductive Reasoning; Inductive Reasoning;

Information Ordering; Mathematical Reasoning; Number Facility; Memorization; Visualization; Wrist-Finger Speed; Near Vision
Skills: Mathematics; Science; Critical Thinking; Information Gathering; Solution Appraisal; Operations Analysis; Technology Design; Equipment Selection; Installation; Programming; Testing; Operation Monitoring; Operation and Control; Product Inspection; Equipment Maintenance; Troubleshooting; Repairing
General Work Activities: Getting Information Needed to Do the Job; Monitoring Processes, Material, or Surroundings; Identifying Objects, Actions, and Events; Inspecting Equipment, Structures, or Material; Estimating Needed Characteristics; Judging Qualities of Things, Services, People; Processing Information; Evaluating Information against Standards; Analyzing Data or Information; Making Decisions and Solving Problems; Thinking Creatively; Updating and Using Job-Relevant Knowledge; Developing Objectives and Strategies; Organizing, Planning, and Prioritizing; Controlling Machines and Processes; Operating Vehicles or Equipment; Drafting and Specifying Technical Devices, etc.; Implementing Ideas, Programs, etc.; Repairing and Maintaining Mechanical Equipment; Repairing and Maintaining Electrical Equipment; Documenting/Recording Information; Interpreting Meaning of Information to Others; Communicating with Other Workers; Provide Consultation and Advice to Others; Monitoring and Controlling Resources
Job Characteristics: Consequence of Error; Importance of Being Exact or Accurate; Importance of Being Sure All is Done
GOE Group/s: 05.01.04 Engineering: Testing and Quality Control; 05.03.05 Engineering Technology: Electrical-Electronic; 05.10.04 Crafts: Structural-Mechanical-Electrical-Electronic
CIP Program/s: 150801 Aeronautical and Aerospace Engineering Technologists and Technicians; 150805 Mechanical Engineering/Mechanical Technologists and Technicians
Related DOT Job/s: 002.261-014 RESEARCH MECHANIC; 002.262-010 FLIGHT-TEST DATA ACQUISITION TECHNICIAN; 710.361-014 TEST EQUIPMENT MECHANIC; 869.261-026 WIND TUNNEL MECHANIC

22599D AGRICULTURAL TECHNICIANS. OOH Title/s: Engineering Technicians

Lay out and complete detailed drawings of agricultural machinery and equipment, and test agricultural equipment and techniques. Lays out agricultural systems and machinery, such as irrigation and electric systems and agricultural harvesting and processing equipment, using drafting tools. Evaluates performance of agricultural equipment and components, using operating specifications, test equipment, and recording instruments. Designs products to perform within specifications, using design principles and knowledge of biology and engineering. Documents test procedures and computes and records test results, using test data log. Maintains knowledge of functions, operations, and maintenance of agricultural industry equipment and materials for proper utilization.
Yearly Earnings: $28,808
Education: Associate degree
Knowledge: Engineering and Technology; Design; Mechanical
Abilities: Written Comprehension; Fluency of Ideas; Originality; Deductive Reasoning; Inductive Reasoning; Information Ordering; Mathematical Reasoning; Number Facility; Memorization; Wrist-Finger Speed; Near Vision
Skills: Mathematics; Science; Operations Analysis; Technology Design; Equipment Selection; Programming; Testing; Operation Monitoring; Operation and Control; Product Inspection; Equipment Maintenance
General Work Activities: Inspecting Equipment, Structures, or Material; Thinking Creatively; Updating and Using Job-Relevant Knowledge; Organizing, Planning, and Prioritizing; Controlling Machines and Processes; Drafting and Specifying Technical Devices, etc.; Implementing Ideas, Programs, etc.
Job Characteristics: Importance of Being Sure All is Done
GOE Group/s: 05.01.07 Engineering: Design; 05.03.07 Engineering Technology: Mechanical
CIP Program/s: 010201 Agricultural Mechanization, General
Related DOT Job/s: 013.161-010 AGRICULTURAL-ENGINEERING TECHNICIAN; 019.261-022 TEST TECHNICIAN

22599E CHEMICAL ENGINEERING TECHNICIANS.

OOH Title/s: Engineering Technicians
Conduct tests, prepare diagrams and flowcharts, and compile and record data to assist chemical engineers in developing, improving, and testing chemical plant processes, products, and equipment. Develops and tests pilot-plant units and prototype processing systems. Sets up test apparatus, tests developmental and production equipment and instruments, and observes and records operating characteristics. Prepares diagrams and flowcharts, and compiles engineering data to develop procedures for chemical processing operations. Fabricates, installs, and modifies equipment to ensure that standards are met. Observes chemical or physical operational processes, and recommends modification or change. Prepares chemical solutions, using formulas, for use in processing materials. Performs preventive and corrective maintenance of chemical processing equipment. Writes technical reports, and submits findings. Confers with and instructs technical personnel and equipment operators so that specified procedures are used.
Yearly Earnings: $28,808
Education: Associate degree
Knowledge: Production and Processing; Engineering and Technology; Mechanical; Chemistry
Abilities: Oral Comprehension; Written Comprehension; Oral Expression; Written Expression; Fluency of Ideas; Originality; Problem Sensitivity; Deductive Reasoning; Inductive Reasoning; Information Ordering; Category Flexibility; Mathematical Reasoning; Number Facility; Memorization; Speed of Closure; Flexibility of Closure; Perceptual Speed; Visualization; Selective Attention; Time Sharing; Near Vision; Hearing Sensitivity; Sound Localization
Skills: Writing; Mathematics; Science; Critical Thinking; Active Learning; Learning Strategies; Instructing; Operations Analysis; Technology Design; Equipment Selection; Installation; Programming; Testing; Operation Monitoring; Operation and Control; Product Inspection; Equipment Maintenance; Troubleshooting; Repairing
General Work Activities: Getting Information Needed to Do the Job; Monitoring Processes, Material, or Surroundings; Identifying Objects, Actions, and Events; Inspecting Equipment, Structures, or Material; Processing Information; Evaluating Information against Standards; Analyzing Data or Information; Making Decisions and Solving Problems; Thinking Creatively; Updating and Using Job-Relevant Knowledge; Developing Objectives and Strategies; Controlling Machines and Processes; Operating Vehicles or Equipment; Drafting and Specifying Technical Devices, etc.; Implementing Ideas, Programs, etc.; Repairing and Maintaining Mechanical Equipment; Repairing and Maintaining Electrical Equipment; Documenting/Recording Information; Interpreting Meaning of Information to Others; Communicating with Other Workers; Teaching Others; Provide Consultation and Advice to Others
Job Characteristics: Supervise, Coach, Train Others; Coordinate or Lead Others; Hazardous Conditions; Specialized Protective or Safety Attire; Importance of Being Exact or Accurate; Importance of Being Sure All is Done
GOE Group/s: 05.01.08 Engineering: General Engineering
CIP Program/s: 150506 Water Quality and Wastewater Treatment Technologists and Technicians; 150607 Plastics Technologists and Technicians; 150903 Petroleum Technologists and Technicians

Related DOT Job/s: 008.261-010 CHEMICAL-ENGINEERING TECHNICIAN

22599F LASER TECHNICIANS. OOH Title/s: Engineering Technicians

Construct, install, and test gas or solid-state laser devices, according to engineering specifications and project instructions. Sets up electronic and optical instruments to test laser device, using electrical or optical inputs. Operates controls of vacuum pump and gas transfer equipment to fill laser body with specified volume and pressure of gases, and tests laser body for pressure leaks, using leak detector. Reviews assembly layout, blueprints, and sketches, and confers with engineering personnel to interpret production details of laser for workers. Analyzes test data and prepares technical reports for engineering personnel to recommend solutions to technical problems. Installs and aligns optical parts, such as mirrors and wave plates, in laser body, using precision instruments. Assembles laser body in chassis, and installs and aligns electronic components, tubing, and wiring to connect controls.
Yearly Earnings: $31,148
Education: Associate degree
Knowledge: Computers and Electronics; Engineering and Technology; Design; Physics
Abilities: Oral Comprehension; Written Comprehension; Oral Expression; Written Expression; Inductive Reasoning; Information Ordering; Number Facility; Visualization; Finger Dexterity; Control Precision; Near Vision
Skills: Mathematics; Science; Operations Analysis; Technology Design; Equipment Selection; Installation; Programming; Testing; Operation Monitoring
General Work Activities: Monitoring Processes, Material, or Surroundings; Identifying Objects, Actions, and Events; Inspecting Equipment, Structures, or Material; Evaluating Information against Standards; Analyzing Data or Information; Making Decisions and Solving Problems; Updating and Using Job-Relevant Knowledge; Controlling Machines and Processes; Drafting and Specifying Technical Devices, etc.; Repairing and Maintaining Electrical Equipment; Documenting/Recording Information; Interpreting Meaning of Information to Others; Communicating with Other Workers; Provide Consultation and Advice to Others
Job Characteristics: Radiation; Specialized Protective or Safety Attire; Importance of Being Exact or Accurate; Importance of Being Sure All is Done
GOE Group/s: 05.03.05 Engineering Technology: Electrical-Electronic
CIP Program/s: 150304 Laser and Optical Technologists and Technicians
Related DOT Job/s: 019.261-034 LASER TECHNICIAN

22599G ALL OTHER ENGINEERING AND RELATED TECHNICIANS AND TECHNOLOGISTS. OOH Title/s: Aircraft Pilots; Drafters; Engineering Technicians

All other engineering and related technicians and technologists not classified separately above.
Yearly Earnings: $28,808
Education: Associate degree
GOE Group/s: 05.03.02 Engineering Technology: Drafting; 05.04.01 Air and Water Vehicle Operation: Air
CIP Program/s: 150805 Mechanical Engineering/Mechanical Technologists and Technicians; 480101 Drafting, General; 490102 Aircraft Pilot and Navigator (Professional)
Related DOT Job/s: 007.261-010 CHIEF DRAFTER; 017.161-010 DRAFTER, CHIEF, DESIGN; 196.263-026 CONTROLLER, REMOTELY-PILOTED VEHICLE; 196.263-042 TEST PILOT

Physical Scientists

24102A PHYSICISTS. OOH Title/s: Physicists and Astronomers

Conduct research into the phases of physical phenomena, develop theories and laws on the basis of observation and experiments, and devise methods to apply laws and theories to industry and other fields. Observes structure and properties of matter and transformation and propagation of energy, using masers, lasers, telescopes, and other equipment. Analyzes results of experiments designed to detect and measure previously unobserved physical phenomena. Conducts instrumental analyses to determine physical properties of materials. Describes and expresses observations and conclusions in mathematical terms. Conducts application analysis to determine commercial, industrial, scientific, medical, military, or other uses for electro-optical devices. Assists in developing standards of permissible concentrations of radioisotopes in liquids and gases. Designs electronic circuitry and optical components with scientific characteristics to fit within specified mechanical limits and perform according to specifications. Assists with development of manufacturing, assembly, and fabrication processes of lasers, masers, infrared, and other light-emitting and light-sensitive devices. Conducts research pertaining to potential environmental impact of proposed atomic energy-related industrial development to determine qualifications for licensing. Directs testing and monitoring of contamination of radioactive equipment and recording of personnel and plant area radiation exposure data. Consults other scientists regarding innovations to ensure equipment or plant design conforms to health physics standards for protection of personnel. Incorporates methods for maintenance and repair of components and designs, and develops test instrumentation and test procedures. Advises authorities in procedures to be followed in radiation incidents or hazards, and assists in civil defense planning. Supervises subordinate personnel, including graduate students, in scientific activities or research. Writes for or serves as consultant for professional journals or other media. Trains technicians to assist in scientific experimentation and research.
Yearly Earnings: $39,000
Education: Doctor's degree
Knowledge: Personnel and Human Resources; Production and Processing; Computers and Electronics; Engineering and Technology; Design; Mathematics; Physics; Chemistry; Education and Training; English Language; Foreign Language; History and Archeology; Communications and Media
Abilities: Oral Comprehension; Written Comprehension; Oral Expression; Written Expression; Fluency of Ideas; Originality; Problem Sensitivity; Deductive Reasoning; Inductive Reasoning; Information Ordering; Category Flexibility; Mathematical Reasoning; Number Facility; Memorization; Speed of Closure; Speech Recognition; Speech Clarity
Skills: Reading Comprehension; Writing; Speaking; Mathematics; Science; Critical Thinking; Active Learning; Learning Strategies; Monitoring; Coordination; Instructing; Problem Identification; Information Gathering; Information Organization; Synthesis/Reorganization; Idea Generation; Idea Evaluation; Implementation Planning; Solution Appraisal; Operations Analysis; Technology Design; Equipment Selection; Programming; Testing; Operation Monitoring; Visioning; Systems Perception; Identifying Downstream Consequences; Identification of Key Causes; Judgment and Decision Making; Systems Evaluation; Time Management; Management of Personnel Resources
General Work Activities: Getting Information Needed to Do the Job; Monitoring Processes, Material, or Surroundings; Identifying Objects, Actions, and Events; Inspecting Equipment, Structures, or Material;

Estimating Needed Characteristics; Judging Qualities of Things, Services, People; Processing Information; Evaluating Information against Standards; Analyzing Data or Information; Making Decisions and Solving Problems; Thinking Creatively; Updating and Using Job-Relevant Knowledge; Developing Objectives and Strategies; Organizing, Planning, and Prioritizing; Operating Vehicles or Equipment; Drafting and Specifying Technical Devices, etc.; Implementing Ideas, Programs, etc.; Repairing and Maintaining Electrical Equipment; Documenting/Recording Information; Interpreting Meaning of Information to Others; Communicating with Other Workers; Communicating with Persons Outside Organization; Coordinating Work and Activities of Others; Developing and Building Teams; Teaching Others; Guiding, Directing and Motivating Subordinates; Coaching and Developing Others; Provide Consultation and Advice to Others
Job Characteristics: Supervise, Coach, Train Others; Take a Position Opposed to Others; Radiation; Sitting; Specialized Protective or Safety Attire; Importance of Being Aware of New Events
GOE Group/s: 02.01.01 Physical Sciences: Theoretical Research; 05.01.02 Engineering: Environmental Protection; 05.01.07 Engineering: Design
CIP Program/s: 400201 Astronomy; 400301 Astrophysics; 400501 Chemistry, General; 400506 Physical and Theoretical Chemistry; 400703 Earth and Planetary Sciences; 400801 Physics, General; 400802 Chemical and Atomic/Molecular Physics; 400804 Elementary Particle Physics; 400805 Plasma and High-Temperature Physics; 400806 Nuclear Physics; 400807 Optics; 400808 Solid State and Low-Temperature Physics; 400809 Acoustics; 400810 Theoretical and Mathematical Physics; 512205 Health Physics/Radiologic Health
Related DOT Job/s: 015.021-010 HEALTH PHYSICIST; 023.061-010 ELECTRO-OPTICAL ENGINEER; 023.061-014 PHYSICIST; 023.067-010 PHYSICIST, THEORETICAL

24102B ASTRONOMERS. OOH Title/s: Physicists and Astronomers

Observe, research, and interpret celestial and astronomical phenomena to increase basic knowledge; and apply such information to practical problems. Studies celestial phenomena from ground or above atmosphere, using various optical devices such as telescopes situated on ground or attached to satellites. Studies history, structure, extent, and evolution of stars, stellar systems, and universe. Calculates orbits and determines sizes, shapes, brightness, and motions of different celestial bodies. Computes positions of sun, moon, planets, stars, nebulae, and galaxies. Determines exact time by celestial observations, and conducts research into relationships between time and space. Analyzes wave lengths of radiation from celestial bodies, as observed in all ranges of spectrum. Develops mathematical tables giving positions of sun, moon, planets, and stars at given times for use by air and sea navigators. Designs optical, mechanical, and electronic instruments for astronomical research.
Yearly Earnings: $39,000
Education: Doctor's degree
Knowledge: Computers and Electronics; Engineering and Technology; Design; Mathematics; Physics; Geography; English Language; History and Archeology
Abilities: Written Comprehension; Written Expression; Fluency of Ideas; Deductive Reasoning; Inductive Reasoning; Category Flexibility; Mathematical Reasoning; Number Facility; Far Vision; Night Vision; Peripheral Vision; Depth Perception; Glare Sensitivity
Skills: Reading Comprehension; Writing; Mathematics; Science; Critical Thinking; Active Learning; Information Gathering; Information Organization; Synthesis/Reorganization; Idea Generation; Idea Evaluation; Operations Analysis; Technology Design; Equipment Selection; Programming; Systems Perception; Identifying Downstream Consequences
General Work Activities: Getting Information Needed to Do the Job; Monitoring Processes, Material, or Surroundings; Identifying Objects, Actions, and Events; Estimating Needed Characteristics; Judging Qualities of Things, Services, People; Processing Information; Evaluating Information against Standards; Analyzing Data or Information; Making Decisions and Solving Problems; Thinking Creatively; Updating and Using Job-Relevant Knowledge; Developing Objectives and Strategies; Organizing, Planning, and Prioritizing; Operating Vehicles or Equipment; Drafting and Specifying Technical Devices, etc.; Implementing Ideas, Programs, etc.; Documenting/Recording Information; Interpreting Meaning of Information to Others; Provide Consultation and Advice to Others
Job Characteristics: High Places; Importance of Being Aware of New Events
GOE Group/s: 02.01.01 Physical Sciences: Theoretical Research
CIP Program/s: 400201 Astronomy; 400301 Astrophysics; 400703 Earth and Planetary Sciences
Related DOT Job/s: 021.067-010 ASTRONOMER

24105 CHEMISTS, EXCEPT BIOCHEMISTS. OOH Title/s: Chemists

Conduct qualitative and quantitative chemical analyses or chemical experiments in laboratories for quality or process control or to develop new products or knowledge. Analyzes organic and inorganic compounds to determine chemical and physical properties, composition, structure, relationships, and reactions, utilizing chromatography, spectroscopy, and spectrophotometry techniques. Induces changes in composition of substances by introducing heat, light, energy, and chemical catalysts for quantitative and qualitative analysis. Develops, improves, and customizes products, equipment, formulas, processes, and analytical methods. Compiles and analyzes test information to determine process or equipment operating efficiency and to diagnose malfunctions. Studies effects of various methods of processing, preserving, and packaging on composition and properties of foods. Prepares test solutions, compounds, and reagents for laboratory personnel to conduct test. Confers with scientists and engineers to conduct analyses of research projects, interpret test results, or develop nonstandard tests. Writes technical papers and reports and prepares standards and specifications for processes, facilities, products, and tests. Directs, coordinates, and advises personnel in test procedures for analyzing components and physical properties of materials. Tests, or supervises workers in testing, food and beverage samples to ensure compliance with applicable laws and quality and purity standards.
Yearly Earnings: $39,000
Education: Bachelor's degree
Knowledge: Administration and Management; Production and Processing; Computers and Electronics; Engineering and Technology; Mathematics; Physics; Chemistry; Biology; English Language
Abilities: Oral Comprehension; Written Comprehension; Oral Expression; Written Expression; Problem Sensitivity; Deductive Reasoning; Inductive Reasoning; Information Ordering; Category Flexibility; Mathematical Reasoning; Number Facility; Speed of Closure; Flexibility of Closure; Perceptual Speed; Selective Attention; Time Sharing; Visual Color Discrimination; Speech Clarity
Skills: Reading Comprehension; Active Listening; Writing; Speaking; Mathematics; Science; Critical Thinking; Active Learning; Learning Strategies; Monitoring; Coordination; Instructing; Problem Identification; Information Gathering; Information Organization; Synthesis/Reorganization; Idea Generation; Idea Evaluation; Implementation Planning; Solution Appraisal; Operations Analysis; Technology Design; Equipment Selection; Programming; Testing; Operation Monitoring; Product Inspection; Systems Perception; Identifying Downstream Consequences; Identification of Key Causes; Judgment

and Decision Making; Systems Evaluation; Time Management; Management of Personnel Resources

General Work Activities: Getting Information Needed to Do the Job; Monitoring Processes, Material, or Surroundings; Identifying Objects, Actions, and Events; Inspecting Equipment, Structures, or Material; Estimating Needed Characteristics; Judging Qualities of Things, Services, People; Processing Information; Evaluating Information against Standards; Analyzing Data or Information; Making Decisions and Solving Problems; Thinking Creatively; Updating and Using Job-Relevant Knowledge; Developing Objectives and Strategies; Scheduling Work and Activities; Organizing, Planning, and Prioritizing; Controlling Machines and Processes; Operating Vehicles or Equipment; Drafting and Specifying Technical Devices, etc.; Implementing Ideas, Programs, etc.; Documenting/Recording Information; Interpreting Meaning of Information to Others; Communicating with Other Workers; Coordinating Work and Activities of Others; Developing and Building Teams; Guiding, Directing and Motivating Subordinates; Provide Consultation and Advice to Others; Performing Administrative Activities

Job Characteristics: Objective or Subjective Information; Supervise, Coach, Train Others; Persuade Someone to a Course of Action; Coordinate or Lead Others; Responsibility for Outcomes and Results; Contaminants; Radiation; Diseases/Infections; Hazardous Conditions; Common Protective or Safety Attire; Specialized Protective or Safety Attire; Consequence of Error; Importance of Being Exact or Accurate; Importance of Being Aware of New Events

GOE Group/s: 02.01.01 Physical Sciences: Theoretical Research; 02.02.04 Life Sciences: Food Research; 02.04.01 Laboratory Technology: Physical Sciences

CIP Program/s: 400501 Chemistry, General; 400502 Analytical Chemistry; 400503 Inorganic Chemistry; 400504 Organic Chemistry; 400505 Medicinal/Pharmaceutical Chemistry; 400506 Physical and Theoretical Chemistry; 400801 Physics, General; 400802 Chemical and Atomic/Molecular Physics

Related DOT Job/s: 022.061-010 CHEMIST; 022.061-014 CHEMIST, FOOD; 022.137-010 LABORATORY SUPERVISOR

24108 ATMOSPHERIC AND SPACE SCIENTISTS. OOH Title/s: Meteorologists

Investigate atmospheric phenomena and interpret meteorological data gathered by surface and air stations, satellites, and radar, to prepare reports and forecasts for public and other uses. Include weather analysts and forecasters who work for radio and TV stations and whose functions require the detailed knowledge of a meteorologist. Analyzes and interprets meteorological data gathered by surface and upper air stations, satellites, and radar, to prepare reports and forecasts. Studies and interprets synoptic reports, maps, photographs, and prognostic charts to predict long- and short-range weather conditions. Prepares special forecasts and briefings for air and sea transportation, agriculture, fire prevention, air-pollution control, and school groups. Operates computer graphic equipment to produce weather reports and maps for analysis, distribution, or use in televised weather broadcast. Conducts basic or applied research in meteorology. Issues hurricane and other severe weather warnings. Broadcasts weather forecasts over television or radio. Directs forecasting services at weather station or at radio or television broadcasting facility. Establishes and staffs weather observation stations.

Yearly Earnings: $39,000

Education: Bachelor's degree

Knowledge: Administration and Management; Clerical; Personnel and Human Resources; Computers and Electronics; Mathematics; Physics; Sociology and Anthropology; Geography; Education and Training; English Language; Foreign Language; Telecommunications; Communications and Media

Abilities: Written Expression; Originality; Problem Sensitivity; Deductive Reasoning; Inductive Reasoning; Memorization; Speed of Closure; Flexibility of Closure; Perceptual Speed; Spatial Orientation; Selective Attention; Time Sharing; Glare Sensitivity; Speech Clarity

Skills: Reading Comprehension; Writing; Speaking; Mathematics; Science; Critical Thinking; Active Learning; Learning Strategies; Monitoring; Instructing; Information Gathering; Information Organization; Synthesis/Reorganization; Idea Generation; Idea Evaluation; Implementation Planning; Solution Appraisal; Operations Analysis; Equipment Selection; Visioning; Systems Perception; Identifying Downstream Consequences; Judgment and Decision Making; Systems Evaluation; Time Management; Management of Material Resources; Management of Personnel Resources

General Work Activities: Getting Information Needed to Do the Job; Monitoring Processes, Material, or Surroundings; Identifying Objects, Actions, and Events; Estimating Needed Characteristics; Evaluating Information against Standards; Analyzing Data or Information; Updating and Using Job-Relevant Knowledge; Developing Objectives and Strategies; Operating Vehicles or Equipment; Documenting/Recording Information; Interpreting Meaning of Information to Others; Communicating with Other Workers; Communicating with Persons Outside Organization; Establishing and Maintaining Relationships; Performing for or Working with Public; Provide Consultation and Advice to Others; Staffing Organizational Units

Job Characteristics: Provide a Service to Others; Extremely Bright or Inadequate Lighting; Degree of Automation; Importance of Being Aware of New Events

GOE Group/s: 02.01.01 Physical Sciences: Theoretical Research

CIP Program/s: 400401 Atmospheric Sciences and Meteorology

Related DOT Job/s: 025.062-010 METEOROLOGIST

24111A GEOLOGISTS. OOH Title/s: Geologists and Geophysicists

Study composition, structure, and history of the earth's crust; examine rocks, minerals, and fossil remains to identify and determine the sequence of processes affecting the development of the earth; apply knowledge of chemistry, physics, biology, and mathematics to explain these phenomena and to help locate mineral and petroleum deposits and underground water resources; prepare geologic reports and maps; and interpret research data to recommend further action for study. Studies, examines, measures, and classifies composition, structure, and history of earth's crust, including rocks, minerals, fossils, soil, and ocean floor. Identifies and determines sequence of processes affecting development of earth. Locates and estimates probable gas and oil deposits, using aerial photographs, charts, and research and survey results. Prepares geological reports, maps, charts, and diagrams. Interprets research data, and recommends further study or action. Analyzes engineering problems at construction projects, such as dams, tunnels, and large buildings, applying geological knowledge. Tests industrial diamonds and abrasives, soil, or rocks to determine geological characteristics, using optical, X ray, heat, acid, and precision instruments. Inspects proposed construction site and sets up test equipment and drilling machinery. Measures characteristics of earth, using seismograph, gravimeter, torsion balance, magnetometer, pendulum devices, and electrical resistivity apparatus. Directs field crews drilling exploratory wells and boreholes or collecting samples of rocks and soil. Recommends and prepares reports on foundation design, acquisition, retention, or release of property leases, or areas of further research. Develops instruments for geological work, such as diamond tools and dies, jeweled bearings, and grinding laps and wheels. Repairs diamond and abrasive tools.

Yearly Earnings: $39,000

Education: Bachelor's degree

Knowledge: Administration and Management; Engineering and Technology; Design; Mechanical; Mathematics; Physics; Chemistry; Biology; Psychology; Sociology and Anthropology; Geography; English Language; History and Archeology; Communications and Media
Abilities: Oral Comprehension; Written Comprehension; Written Expression; Deductive Reasoning; Inductive Reasoning; Category Flexibility; Mathematical Reasoning; Number Facility; Memorization; Flexibility of Closure
Skills: Reading Comprehension; Writing; Mathematics; Science; Critical Thinking; Active Learning; Coordination; Problem Identification; Information Gathering; Information Organization; Synthesis/Reorganization; Idea Generation; Idea Evaluation; Implementation Planning; Solution Appraisal; Operations Analysis; Technology Design; Equipment Selection; Installation; Programming; Testing; Product Inspection; Repairing; Visioning; Systems Perception; Identifying Downstream Consequences; Identification of Key Causes; Judgment and Decision Making; Systems Evaluation; Time Management; Management of Personnel Resources
General Work Activities: Getting Information Needed to Do the Job; Monitoring Processes, Material, or Surroundings; Identifying Objects, Actions, and Events; Inspecting Equipment, Structures, or Material; Estimating Needed Characteristics; Judging Qualities of Things, Services, People; Evaluating Information against Standards; Analyzing Data or Information; Making Decisions and Solving Problems; Thinking Creatively; Updating and Using Job-Relevant Knowledge; Developing Objectives and Strategies; Organizing, Planning, and Prioritizing; Controlling Machines and Processes; Operating Vehicles or Equipment; Drafting and Specifying Technical Devices, etc.; Implementing Ideas, Programs, etc.; Documenting/Recording Information; Interpreting Meaning of Information to Others; Communicating with Other Workers; Communicating with Persons Outside Organization; Coordinating Work and Activities of Others; Developing and Building Teams; Coaching and Developing Others; Provide Consultation and Advice to Others
Job Characteristics: Coordinate or Lead Others; Very Hot; Extremely Bright or Inadequate Lighting; Specialized Protective or Safety Attire; Importance of Being Exact or Accurate
GOE Group/s: 02.01.01 Physical Sciences: Theoretical Research; 02.01.02 Physical Sciences: Technology; 05.01.08 Engineering: General Engineering
CIP Program/s: 150901 Mining Tech./Technician; 400601 Geology; 400602 Geochemistry; 400603 Geophysics and Seismology; 400604 Paleontology; 400702 Oceanography; 450201 Anthropology; 450701 Geography
Related DOT Job/s: 024.061-010 CRYSTALLOGRAPHER; 024.061-018 GEOLOGIST; 024.061-022 GEOLOGIST, PETROLEUM; 024.061-026 GEOPHYSICAL PROSPECTOR; 024.061-038 MINERALOGIST; 024.061-042 PALEONTOLOGIST; 024.061-046 PETROLOGIST; 024.061-054 STRATIGRAPHER; 024.161-010 ENGINEER, SOILS; 024.284-010 PROSPECTOR

24111B GEOPHYSICISTS. OOH Title/s: Geologists and Geophysicists

Study physical aspects of the earth, including the atmosphere and hydrosphere. Investigate and measure seismic, gravitational, electrical, thermal, and magnetic forces affecting the earth, utilizing principles of physics, mathematics, and chemistry. Studies and analyzes physical aspects of the earth, including atmosphere and hydrosphere, and interior structure. Studies, measures, and interprets seismic, gravitational, electrical, thermal, and magnetic forces and data affecting the earth. Studies, maps, and charts distribution, disposition, and development of waters of land areas, including form and intensity of precipitation. Studies waters of land areas to determine modes of return to ocean and atmosphere. Investigates origin and activity of glaciers, volcanoes, and earthquakes. Compiles and evaluates data to prepare navigational charts and maps, predict atmospheric conditions, and prepare environmental reports. Evaluates data in reference to project planning, such as flood and drought control, water power and supply, drainage, irrigation, and inland navigation. Prepares and issues maps and reports indicating areas of seismic risk to existing or proposed construction or development.
Yearly Earnings: $39,000
Education: Bachelor's degree
Knowledge: Mathematics; Physics; Chemistry; Geography; English Language; History and Archeology; Communications and Media
Abilities: Oral Comprehension; Written Comprehension; Written Expression; Fluency of Ideas; Deductive Reasoning; Inductive Reasoning; Category Flexibility; Mathematical Reasoning; Number Facility; Flexibility of Closure
Skills: Reading Comprehension; Writing; Mathematics; Science; Critical Thinking; Active Learning; Problem Identification; Information Gathering; Information Organization; Synthesis/Reorganization; Idea Generation; Idea Evaluation; Implementation Planning; Solution Appraisal; Operations Analysis; Programming; Visioning; Systems Perception; Identifying Downstream Consequences; Identification of Key Causes; Judgment and Decision Making
General Work Activities: Getting Information Needed to Do the Job; Monitoring Processes, Material, or Surroundings; Identifying Objects, Actions, and Events; Estimating Needed Characteristics; Processing Information; Evaluating Information against Standards; Analyzing Data or Information; Making Decisions and Solving Problems; Thinking Creatively; Updating and Using Job-Relevant Knowledge; Developing Objectives and Strategies; Organizing, Planning, and Prioritizing; Operating Vehicles or Equipment; Implementing Ideas, Programs, etc.; Documenting/Recording Information; Interpreting Meaning of Information to Others; Communicating with Other Workers; Provide Consultation and Advice to Others
Job Characteristics: Very Hot
GOE Group/s: 02.01.01 Physical Sciences: Theoretical Research; 02.04.01 Laboratory Technology: Physical Sciences
CIP Program/s: 400601 Geology; 400603 Geophysics and Seismology; 400702 Oceanography
Related DOT Job/s: 024.061-030 GEOPHYSICIST; 024.061-034 HYDROLOGIST; 024.061-050 SEISMOLOGIST; 024.167-010 GEOPHYSICAL-LABORATORY CHIEF

24199A GEOGRAPHERS. OOH Title/s: Social Scientists

Study nature and use of areas of earth's surface, relating and interpreting interactions of physical and cultural phenomena. Conduct research on physical aspects of a region, including land forms, climates, soils, plants, and animals; and conduct research on the spatial implications of human activities within a given area, including social characteristics, economic activities, and political organization, as well as researching interdependence between regions at scales ranging from local to global. Collects data on physical characteristics of specified area, such as geological formation, climate, and vegetation, using surveying or meteorological equipment. Studies population characteristics within area, such as ethnic distribution and economic activity. Constructs and interprets maps, graphs, and diagrams. Uses surveying equipment to assess geology, physics, and biology within given area. Prepares environmental impact reports based on results of study. Advises governments and organizations on ethnic and natural boundaries between nation or administrative areas.
Yearly Earnings: $37,960
Education: Master's degree
Knowledge: Physics; Biology; Sociology and Anthropology; Geography; Foreign Language; History and Archeology

Abilities: Written Expression; Flexibility of Closure; Spatial Orientation; Far Vision; Visual Color Discrimination; Night Vision; Depth Perception
Skills: Reading Comprehension; Writing; Mathematics; Critical Thinking; Information Gathering; Information Organization
General Work Activities: Estimating Needed Characteristics; Evaluating Information against Standards; Documenting/Recording Information; Communicating with Persons Outside Organization
Job Characteristics: None above average
GOE Group/s: 02.01.01 Physical Sciences: Theoretical Research
CIP Program/s: 450701 Geography
Related DOT Job/s: 029.067-010 GEOGRAPHER; 029.067-014 GEOGRAPHER, PHYSICAL

24199B ENVIRONMENTAL SCIENTISTS. OOH Title/s: Foresters and Conservation Scientists
Conduct research to develop methods of abating, controlling, or remediating sources of environmental pollutants, utilizing knowledge of various scientific disciplines. Identify and analyze sources of pollution to determine their effects. Collect and synthesize data derived from pollution-emission measurements, atmospheric monitoring, meteorological and mineralogical information, or soil and water samples. Exclude wildlife conservationists and natural resource scientists. Plans and develops research models using knowledge of mathematical and statistical concepts. Collects, identifies, and analyzes data to assess sources of pollution, determine their effects, and establish standards. Determines data collection methods to be employed in research projects and surveys. Prepares graphs or charts from data samples, and advises enforcement personnel on proper standards and regulations.
Yearly Earnings: $39,000
Education: Bachelor's degree
Knowledge: Mathematics; Physics; Chemistry; Biology
Abilities: Deductive Reasoning; Mathematical Reasoning; Number Facility
Skills: Reading Comprehension; Writing; Mathematics; Science; Critical Thinking; Active Learning; Information Gathering; Information Organization; Synthesis/Reorganization; Idea Generation; Idea Evaluation; Solution Appraisal; Operations Analysis; Visioning; Systems Perception; Identifying Downstream Consequences; Identification of Key Causes; Systems Evaluation
General Work Activities: Getting Information Needed to Do the Job; Monitoring Processes, Material, or Surroundings; Identifying Objects, Actions, and Events; Estimating Needed Characteristics; Processing Information; Evaluating Information against Standards; Analyzing Data or Information; Making Decisions and Solving Problems; Thinking Creatively; Updating and Using Job-Relevant Knowledge; Developing Objectives and Strategies; Operating Vehicles or Equipment; Implementing Ideas, Programs, etc.; Documenting/Recording Information; Interpreting Meaning of Information to Others; Communicating with Other Workers
Job Characteristics: Objective or Subjective Information; Contaminants; Radiation; Diseases/Infections; Specialized Protective or Safety Attire; Importance of Being Sure All is Done; Importance of Being Aware of New Events
GOE Group/s: 02.01.02 Physical Sciences: Technology
CIP Program/s: 030101 Natural Resources Conservation, General; 030102 Environmental Science/Studies
Related DOT Job/s: 019.081-018 POLLUTION-CONTROL ENGINEER; 029.081-010 ENVIRONMENTAL ANALYST

24199C MATERIALS SCIENTISTS. OOH Title/s: Indirectly related to Physical Scientists
Research and study the structures and chemical properties of various natural and manmade materials, including metals, alloys, rubber, ceramics, semiconductors, polymers, and glass. Determine ways to strengthen or combine materials, or develop new materials with new or specific properties for use in a variety of products and applications. Include glass scientists, ceramic scientists, metallurgical scientists, and polymer scientists. Plans laboratory experiments to confirm feasibility of processes and techniques to produce materials having special characteristics. Studies structures and properties of materials, such as metals, alloys, polymers, and ceramics, to obtain research data. Reports materials study findings for other scientists and requesters. Guides technical staff engaged in developing materials for specific use in projected product or device.
Yearly Earnings: $39,000
Education: Bachelor's degree
Knowledge: Administration and Management; Engineering and Technology; Mathematics; Physics; Chemistry; English Language; Foreign Language; Communications and Media
Abilities: Oral Comprehension; Written Comprehension; Oral Expression; Written Expression; Fluency of Ideas; Originality; Deductive Reasoning; Mathematical Reasoning; Number Facility; Speed of Closure
Skills: Reading Comprehension; Writing; Mathematics; Science; Active Learning; Operations Analysis; Testing; Product Inspection
General Work Activities: Getting Information Needed to Do the Job; Monitoring Processes, Material, or Surroundings; Identifying Objects, Actions, and Events; Estimating Needed Characteristics; Evaluating Information against Standards; Analyzing Data or Information; Thinking Creatively; Updating and Using Job-Relevant Knowledge; Controlling Machines and Processes; Operating Vehicles or Equipment; Implementing Ideas, Programs, etc.; Repairing and Maintaining Electrical Equipment; Documenting/Recording Information; Interpreting Meaning of Information to Others; Communicating with Other Workers; Guiding, Directing and Motivating Subordinates
Job Characteristics: Supervise, Coach, Train Others; Coordinate or Lead Others; Sitting; Frustrating Circumstances; Importance of Being Exact or Accurate
GOE Group/s: 02.01.02 Physical Sciences: Technology
CIP Program/s: 143101 Materials Science
Related DOT Job/s: 029.081-014 MATERIALS SCIENTIST

Life Scientists

24302A FORESTERS. OOH Title/s: Foresters and Conservation Scientists
Plan, develop, and control environmental factors affecting forests and their resources for economic and recreation purposes. Plans and directs forestation and reforestation projects. Investigates adaptability of different tree species to new environmental conditions, such as soil type, climate, and altitude. Determines methods of cutting and removing timber with minimum waste and environmental damage. Plans cutting programs to assure continuous production or to assist timber companies to achieve production goals. Researches forest propagation and culture affecting tree growth rates, yield, and duration and seed production, growth viability, and germination of different species. Analyzes forest conditions to determine reason for prevalence of different variety of trees. Studies classification, life history, light and soil requirements, and resistance to disease and insects of different tree species. Maps forest areas and estimates standing timber and future growth. Manages tree nurseries and thins forest to encourage natural growth of sprouts or seedlings of desired varieties. Participates in

environmental studies and prepares environmental reports. Assists in planning and implementing projects for control of floods, soil erosion, tree diseases, infestation, and forest fires. Plans and directs construction and maintenance of recreation facilities, fire towers, trails, roads, and fire breaks. Develops techniques for measuring and identifying trees. Patrols forests and enforces laws. Directs suppression of forest fires and fights forest fires. Advises landowners on forestry management techniques. Conducts public educational programs on forest care and conservation. Suggests methods of processing wood for various uses. Manages timber sales for government agency or landowner, and administers budgets. Supervises activities of other forestry workers.
Yearly Earnings: $39,000
Education: Bachelor's degree
Knowledge: Administration and Management; Economics and Accounting; Sales and Marketing; Personnel and Human Resources; Production and Processing; Engineering and Technology; Design; Building and Construction; Mathematics; Physics; Chemistry; Biology; Sociology and Anthropology; Geography; Education and Training; English Language; History and Archeology; Philosophy and Theology; Public Safety and Security; Law, Government, and Jurisprudence; Telecommunications; Communications and Media; Transportation
Abilities: Written Comprehension; Written Expression; Fluency of Ideas; Originality; Problem Sensitivity; Deductive Reasoning; Inductive Reasoning; Category Flexibility; Memorization; Speed of Closure; Flexibility of Closure; Spatial Orientation; Visualization; Time Sharing; Stamina; Far Vision; Night Vision; Speech Clarity
Skills: Reading Comprehension; Active Listening; Writing; Speaking; Mathematics; Science; Critical Thinking; Active Learning; Learning Strategies; Monitoring; Social Perceptiveness; Coordination; Persuasion; Negotiation; Instructing; Problem Identification; Information Gathering; Information Organization; Synthesis/Reorganization; Idea Generation; Idea Evaluation; Implementation Planning; Solution Appraisal; Operations Analysis; Visioning; Systems Perception; Identifying Downstream Consequences; Identification of Key Causes; Judgment and Decision Making; Systems Evaluation; Time Management; Management of Financial Resources; Management of Material Resources; Management of Personnel Resources
General Work Activities: Getting Information Needed to Do the Job; Monitoring Processes, Material, or Surroundings; Identifying Objects, Actions, and Events; Estimating Needed Characteristics; Judging Qualities of Things, Services, People; Evaluating Information against Standards; Analyzing Data or Information; Making Decisions and Solving Problems; Thinking Creatively; Updating and Using Job-Relevant Knowledge; Developing Objectives and Strategies; Scheduling Work and Activities; Organizing, Planning, and Prioritizing; Drafting and Specifying Technical Devices, etc.; Implementing Ideas, Programs, etc.; Documenting/Recording Information; Interpreting Meaning of Information to Others; Communicating with Other Workers; Communicating with Persons Outside Organization; Establishing and Maintaining Relationships; Performing for or Working with Public; Coordinating Work and Activities of Others; Developing and Building Teams; Teaching Others; Guiding, Directing and Motivating Subordinates; Coaching and Developing Others; Provide Consultation and Advice to Others; Monitoring and Controlling Resources
Job Characteristics: Supervise, Coach, Train Others; Persuade Someone to a Course of Action; Provide a Service to Others; Take a Position Opposed to Others; Deal with External Customers; Coordinate or Lead Others; Very Hot; Extremely Bright or Inadequate Lighting; High Places; Hazardous Situations; Climbing Ladders, Scaffolds, Poles, etc.; Keeping or Regaining Balance; Special Uniform; Specialized Protective or Safety Attire; Importance of Being Aware of New Events
GOE Group/s: 02.02.02 Life Sciences: Plant Specialization; 03.01.04 Managerial Work: Plants and Animals: Forestry and Logging
CIP Program/s: 010601 Horticulture Services Operations and Management, General; 010606 Nursery Operations and Management; 030101 Natural Resources Conservation, General; 030401 Forest Harvesting and Production Technologists and Technicians; 030501 Forestry, General; 030502 Forestry Sciences; 030506 Forest Management
Related DOT Job/s: 040.061-030 FOREST ECOLOGIST; 040.061-050 SILVICULTURIST; 040.167-010 FORESTER

24302B SOIL CONSERVATIONISTS. OOH Title/s: Foresters and Conservation Scientists

Plan and develop coordinated practices for soil erosion control, soil and water conservation, and sound land use. Plans soil management practices, such as crop rotation, reforestation, permanent vegetation, contour plowing, or terracing, to maintain soil and conserve water. Develops plans for conservation, such as conservation cropping systems, woodlands management, pasture planning, and engineering systems. Analyzes results of investigations to determine measures needed to maintain or restore proper soil management. Conducts surveys and investigations of various land uses, such as rural or urban, agriculture, construction, forestry, or mining. Computes design specification for implementation of conservation practices, using survey and field information technical guides, engineering manuals, and calculator. Develops or participates in environmental studies. Monitors projects during and after construction to ensure projects conform to design specifications. Computes cost estimates of different conservation practices based on needs of land users, maintenance requirements, and life expectancy of practices. Surveys property to mark locations and measurements, using surveying instruments. Discusses conservation plans, problems, and alternative solutions with land users, applying knowledge of agronomy, soil science, forestry, or agricultural sciences. Revisits land users to view implemented land use practices and plans.
Yearly Earnings: $39,000
Education: Bachelor's degree
Knowledge: Administration and Management; Economics and Accounting; Food Production; Engineering and Technology; Design; Building and Construction; Mathematics; Physics; Chemistry; Biology; Geography; Education and Training; English Language; History and Archeology; Philosophy and Theology
Abilities: Oral Expression; Written Expression; Fluency of Ideas; Originality; Problem Sensitivity; Deductive Reasoning; Inductive Reasoning; Information Ordering; Number Facility; Memorization; Speed of Closure; Flexibility of Closure; Spatial Orientation; Far Vision; Depth Perception
Skills: Reading Comprehension; Active Listening; Writing; Speaking; Mathematics; Science; Critical Thinking; Active Learning; Learning Strategies; Monitoring; Persuasion; Negotiation; Problem Identification; Information Gathering; Information Organization; Synthesis/Reorganization; Idea Generation; Idea Evaluation; Implementation Planning; Solution Appraisal; Operations Analysis; Product Inspection; Visioning; Systems Perception; Identifying Downstream Consequences; Identification of Key Causes; Judgment and Decision Making; Systems Evaluation; Time Management
General Work Activities: Getting Information Needed to Do the Job; Monitoring Processes, Material, or Surroundings; Identifying Objects, Actions, and Events; Estimating Needed Characteristics; Processing Information; Evaluating Information against Standards; Analyzing Data or Information; Making Decisions and Solving Problems; Thinking Creatively; Updating and Using Job-Relevant Knowledge; Developing Objectives and Strategies; Organizing, Planning, and Prioritizing; Drafting and Specifying Technical Devices, etc.; Implementing Ideas, Programs, etc.; Documenting/Recording Information; Interpreting Meaning of Information to Others; Communicating with Other Workers; Communicating with Persons Outside Organization; Establishing and Maintaining Relationships; Selling or Influencing

Others; Teaching Others; Provide Consultation and Advice to Others; Monitoring and Controlling Resources
Job Characteristics: Objective or Subjective Information; Persuade Someone to a Course of Action; Provide a Service to Others; Take a Position Opposed to Others; Deal with External Customers; Frequency in Conflict Situations; Deal with Unpleasant or Angry People; Very Hot; Extremely Bright or Inadequate Lighting; Frustrating Circumstances; Importance of Being Aware of New Events
GOE Group/s: 02.02.02 Life Sciences: Plant Specialization
CIP Program/s: 020501 Soil Sciences; 030101 Natural Resources Conservation, General; 030501 Forestry, General; 030502 Forestry Sciences; 030506 Forest Management
Related DOT Job/s: 040.061-054 SOIL CONSERVATIONIST; 040.261-010 SOIL-CONSERVATION TECHNICIAN

24302C WOOD TECHNOLOGISTS. OOH Title/s: Foresters and Conservation Scientists
Conduct research to determine composition, properties, behavior, utilization, development, treatments, and processing methods of wood and wood products. Studies methods of curing wood to determine best and most economical procedure. Investigates processes for converting wood into commodities such as alcohol, veneer, plywood, wood plastics, and other uses. Investigates methods of turning waste wood materials into useful products. Analyzes physical, chemical, and biological properties of wood. Develops and improves methods of preserving and treating wood with substances to increase resistance to wear, fire, fungi, and infestation. Conducts test to determine stability, strength, hardness, and crystallinity of wood under variety of conditions. Determines best types of wood for specific applications. Conducts tests to determine ability of wood adhesives to withstand water, oil penetration, and temperature extremes. Evaluates and improves effectiveness of industrial equipment and production processes for wood.
Yearly Earnings: $39,000
Education: Bachelor's degree
Knowledge: Production and Processing; Engineering and Technology; Building and Construction; Mathematics; Physics; Chemistry; Biology; Geography; English Language
Abilities: Fluency of Ideas; Originality; Inductive Reasoning; Information Ordering; Category Flexibility; Speed of Closure
Skills: Reading Comprehension; Mathematics; Science; Critical Thinking; Active Learning; Learning Strategies; Problem Identification; Information Gathering; Information Organization; Synthesis/Reorganization; Idea Generation; Idea Evaluation; Implementation Planning; Solution Appraisal; Operations Analysis; Technology Design; Equipment Selection; Testing; Product Inspection; Visioning; Systems Perception; Identifying Downstream Consequences; Identification of Key Causes; Judgment and Decision Making; Systems Evaluation
General Work Activities: Getting Information Needed to Do the Job; Monitoring Processes, Material, or Surroundings; Inspecting Equipment, Structures, or Material; Estimating Needed Characteristics; Judging Qualities of Things, Services, People; Processing Information; Evaluating Information against Standards; Analyzing Data or Information; Making Decisions and Solving Problems; Thinking Creatively; Updating and Using Job-Relevant Knowledge; Developing Objectives and Strategies; Organizing, Planning, and Prioritizing; Implementing Ideas, Programs, etc.; Provide Consultation and Advice to Others
Job Characteristics: Objective or Subjective Information; Take a Position Opposed to Others; Contaminants; Hazardous Conditions
GOE Group/s: 02.02.02 Life Sciences: Plant Specialization
CIP Program/s: 030404 Forest Products Technologists and Technicians; 030501 Forestry, General; 030509 Wood Science and Pulp/Paper Technology
Related DOT Job/s: 040.061-062 WOOD TECHNOLOGIST

24302D RANGE MANAGERS. OOH Title/s: Foresters and Conservation Scientists
Research or study rangeland management practices to provide sustained production of forage, livestock, and wildlife. Studies rangelands to determine best grazing seasons. Studies rangelands to determine number and kind of livestock that can be most profitably grazed. Studies forage plants and their growth requirements to determine varieties best suited to particular range. Develops improved practices for range reseeding. Develops methods for controlling poisonous plants in rangelands. Develops methods for protecting range from fire and rodent damage. Plans and directs maintenance of range improvements. Plans and directs construction of range improvements, such as fencing, corrals, stock-watering reservoirs and soil-erosion control structures.
Yearly Earnings: $39,000
Education: Bachelor's degree
Knowledge: Administration and Management; Economics and Accounting; Food Production; Building and Construction; Biology; Geography; Law, Government, and Jurisprudence
Abilities: Spatial Orientation
Skills: Science; Critical Thinking; Active Learning; Problem Identification; Information Gathering; Synthesis/Reorganization; Idea Generation; Idea Evaluation; Implementation Planning; Solution Appraisal; Operations Analysis; Technology Design; Equipment Selection; Visioning; Systems Perception; Identifying Downstream Consequences; Identification of Key Causes; Judgment and Decision Making; Systems Evaluation; Management of Material Resources; Management of Personnel Resources
General Work Activities: Getting Information Needed to Do the Job; Monitoring Processes, Material, or Surroundings; Identifying Objects, Actions, and Events; Estimating Needed Characteristics; Judging Qualities of Things, Services, People; Evaluating Information against Standards; Analyzing Data or Information; Making Decisions and Solving Problems; Thinking Creatively; Updating and Using Job-Relevant Knowledge; Developing Objectives and Strategies; Scheduling Work and Activities; Organizing, Planning, and Prioritizing; Drafting and Specifying Technical Devices, etc.; Provide Consultation and Advice to Others; Monitoring and Controlling Resources
Job Characteristics: Objective or Subjective Information; Supervise, Coach, Train Others; Persuade Someone to a Course of Action; Take a Position Opposed to Others; Coordinate or Lead Others; Responsible for Others' Health and Safety; Responsibility for Outcomes and Results; Walking or Running; Frustrating Circumstances
GOE Group/s: 02.02.02 Life Sciences: Plant Specialization
CIP Program/s: 020401 Plant Sciences, General; 020409 Range Science and Management; 030101 Natural Resources Conservation, General
Related DOT Job/s: 040.061-046 RANGE MANAGER

24302E PARK NATURALISTS. OOH Title/s: Foresters and Conservation Scientists
Plan, develop, and conduct programs to inform public of historical, natural, and scientific features of national, state, or local park. Conducts field trips to point out scientific, historic, and natural features of park. Plans and develops audio-visual devices for public programs. Interviews specialists in desired fields to obtain and develop data for park information programs. Confers with park staff to determine subjects to be presented to public. Prepares and presents illustrated lectures of park features. Constructs historical, scientific, and nature visitor-center displays. Takes photographs and motion pictures to illustrate lectures and publications and to develop displays. Surveys park to determine forest conditions. Surveys park to determine

distribution and abundance of fauna and flora. Plans and organizes activities of seasonal staff members. Maintains official park photographic and information files. Performs emergency duties to protect human life, government property, and natural features of park.
Yearly Earnings: $39,000
Education: Bachelor's degree
Knowledge: Administration and Management; Biology; Geography; Education and Training; English Language; Fine Arts; History and Archeology; Communications and Media
Abilities: Spatial Orientation; Time Sharing; Stamina; Gross Body Equilibrium
Skills: Speaking; Service Orientation; Implementation Planning; Operations Analysis; Technology Design; Systems Perception; Identifying Downstream Consequences; Time Management; Management of Material Resources; Management of Personnel Resources
General Work Activities: Thinking Creatively; Scheduling Work and Activities; Communicating with Persons Outside Organization; Establishing and Maintaining Relationships; Assisting and Caring for Others; Performing for or Working with Public; Teaching Others
Job Characteristics: Objective or Subjective Information; Job-Required Social Interaction; Provide a Service to Others; Deal with External Customers; Responsible for Others' Health and Safety; Very Hot; Extremely Bright or Inadequate Lighting; Hazardous Situations; Walking or Running; Special Uniform
GOE Group/s: 11.07.03 Services Administration: Education Services
CIP Program/s: 020401 Plant Sciences, General; 020409 Range Science and Management
Related DOT Job/s: 049.127-010 PARK NATURALIST

24305A ANIMAL SCIENTISTS. OOH Title/s: Agricultural Scientists

Research or study selection, breeding, feeding, management, and marketing of livestock, pets, or other economically important animals. Studies nutritional requirements of animals and nutritive value of feed materials for animals and poultry. Studies effects of management practices, processing methods, feed, and environmental conditions on quality and quantity of animal products, such as eggs and milk. Researches and controls selection and breeding practices to increase efficiency of production and improve quality of animals. Develops improved practices in incubation, brooding, and artificial insemination. Develops improved practices in feeding, housing, sanitation, and parasite and disease control of animals and poultry. Determines generic composition of animal population and heritability of traits, utilizing principles of genetics. Crossbreeds animals with existing strains, or crosses strains to obtain new combinations of desirable characteristics.
Yearly Earnings: $39,000
Education: Bachelor's degree
Knowledge: Food Production; Chemistry; Biology; Medicine and Dentistry; History and Archeology
Abilities: Oral Comprehension; Written Comprehension; Written Expression; Fluency of Ideas; Originality; Problem Sensitivity; Deductive Reasoning; Inductive Reasoning; Information Ordering; Category Flexibility; Mathematical Reasoning; Number Facility; Memorization; Flexibility of Closure
Skills: Reading Comprehension; Writing; Mathematics; Science; Critical Thinking; Active Learning; Monitoring; Problem Identification; Information Gathering; Information Organization; Synthesis/Reorganization; Idea Generation; Idea Evaluation; Implementation Planning; Solution Appraisal; Operations Analysis; Technology Design; Equipment Selection; Programming; Testing; Product Inspection; Visioning; Systems Perception; Identifying Downstream Consequences; Identification of Key Causes; Judgment and Decision Making; Systems Evaluation
General Work Activities: Getting Information Needed to Do the Job; Monitoring Processes, Material, or Surroundings; Identifying Objects, Actions, and Events; Estimating Needed Characteristics; Judging Qualities of Things, Services, People; Evaluating Information against Standards; Analyzing Data or Information; Making Decisions and Solving Problems; Thinking Creatively; Updating and Using Job-Relevant Knowledge; Developing Objectives and Strategies; Operating Vehicles or Equipment; Implementing Ideas, Programs, etc.; Interpreting Meaning of Information to Others; Provide Consultation and Advice to Others
Job Characteristics: Diseases/Infections; Specialized Protective or Safety Attire
GOE Group/s: 02.02.01 Life Sciences: Animal Specialization
CIP Program/s: 020101 Agriculture/Agricultural Sciences, General; 020201 Animal Sciences, General; 020202 Agricultural Animal Breeding and Genetics; 020203 Agricultural Animal Health; 020204 Agricultural Animal Nutrition; 020206 Dairy Science; 020209 Poultry Science
Related DOT Job/s: 040.061-014 ANIMAL SCIENTIST; 040.061-018 DAIRY SCIENTIST; 040.061-042 POULTRY SCIENTIST; 041.061-014 ANIMAL BREEDER

24305B PLANT SCIENTISTS. OOH Title/s: Agricultural Scientists

Conduct research in breeding, production, and yield of plants or crops, and control of pests. Conducts research to determine best methods of planting, spraying, cultivating, and harvesting horticultural products. Experiments to develop new or improved varieties of products having specific features, such as higher yield, resistance to disease, size, or maturity. Studies crop production to discover effects of various climatic and soil conditions on crops. Develops methods for control of noxious weeds, crop diseases, and insect pests. Conducts experiments and investigations to determine methods of storing, processing, and transporting horticultural products. Studies insect distribution and habitat, and recommends methods to prevent importation and spread of injurious species. Aids in control and elimination of agricultural, structural, and forest pests by developing new and improved pesticides. Conducts experiments regarding causes of bee diseases and factors affecting yields of nectar pollen on various plants visited by bees. Identifies and classifies species of insects and allied forms, such as mites and spiders. Prepares articles and gives lectures on horticultural subjects. Improves bee strains, utilizing selective breeding by artificial insemination.
Yearly Earnings: $39,000
Education: Bachelor's degree
Knowledge: Food Production; Chemistry; Biology; Geography; Education and Training; English Language; History and Archeology; Communications and Media
Abilities: Oral Comprehension; Written Comprehension; Written Expression; Fluency of Ideas; Deductive Reasoning; Inductive Reasoning; Information Ordering; Category Flexibility; Mathematical Reasoning; Number Facility; Memorization; Flexibility of Closure
Skills: Reading Comprehension; Writing; Speaking; Mathematics; Science; Critical Thinking; Active Learning; Problem Identification; Information Gathering; Information Organization; Synthesis/Reorganization; Idea Generation; Idea Evaluation; Implementation Planning; Solution Appraisal; Operations Analysis; Testing; Product Inspection; Visioning; Identifying Downstream Consequences; Judgment and Decision Making; Time Management
General Work Activities: Getting Information Needed to Do the Job; Monitoring Processes, Material, or Surroundings; Identifying Objects, Actions, and Events; Estimating Needed Characteristics; Judging Qualities of Things, Services, People; Processing Information; Evaluating Information against Standards; Analyzing Data or Information;

Making Decisions and Solving Problems; Thinking Creatively; Updating and Using Job-Relevant Knowledge; Developing Objectives and Strategies; Organizing, Planning, and Prioritizing; Operating Vehicles or Equipment; Implementing Ideas, Programs, etc.; Documenting/Recording Information; Interpreting Meaning of Information to Others; Communicating with Persons Outside Organization; Teaching Others; Provide Consultation and Advice to Others
Job Characteristics: Specialized Protective or Safety Attire
GOE Group/s: 02.02.01 Life Sciences: Animal Specialization; 02.02.02 Life Sciences: Plant Specialization
CIP Program/s: 020101 Agriculture/Agricultural Sciences, General; 020201 Animal Sciences, General; 020202 Agricultural Animal Breeding and Genetics; 020401 Plant Sciences, General; 020402 Agronomy and Crop Science; 020403 Horticulture Science; 020405 Plant Breeding and Genetics; 020406 Agricultural Plant Pathology; 020408 Plant Protection (Pest Management); 260701 Zoology, General; 260702 Entomology
Related DOT Job/s: 040.061-010 AGRONOMIST; 040.061-038 HORTICULTURIST; 041.061-018 APICULTURIST; 041.061-046 ENTOMOLOGIST; 041.061-082 PLANT BREEDER

24305C FOOD SCIENTISTS. OOH Title/s: Agricultural Scientists

Apply scientific and engineering principles in research, development, production, packaging, and processing of foods. Conducts research on new products and development of foods, applying scientific and engineering principles. Develops new and improved methods and systems for food processing, production, quality control, packaging, and distribution. Studies methods to improve quality of foods, such as flavor, color, texture, nutritional value, and convenience. Studies methods to improve physical, chemical, and microbiological composition of foods. Develops food standards, safety and sanitary regulations, and waste management and water supply specifications. Confers with process engineers, flavor experts, and packaging and marketing specialists to resolve problems in product development. Tests new products in test kitchen.
Yearly Earnings: $39,000
Education: Bachelor's degree
Knowledge: Production and Processing; Food Production; Chemistry; Biology; Law, Government, and Jurisprudence
Abilities: Written Comprehension; Fluency of Ideas; Originality; Deductive Reasoning; Inductive Reasoning; Category Flexibility
Skills: Reading Comprehension; Mathematics; Science; Critical Thinking; Active Learning; Information Gathering; Synthesis/Reorganization; Idea Generation; Idea Evaluation; Implementation Planning; Solution Appraisal; Operations Analysis; Technology Design; Equipment Selection; Programming; Testing; Product Inspection; Visioning; Identifying Downstream Consequences; Identification of Key Causes; Judgment and Decision Making
General Work Activities: Getting Information Needed to Do the Job; Monitoring Processes, Material, or Surroundings; Inspecting Equipment, Structures, or Material; Estimating Needed Characteristics; Judging Qualities of Things, Services, People; Processing Information; Evaluating Information against Standards; Analyzing Data or Information; Making Decisions and Solving Problems; Thinking Creatively; Updating and Using Job-Relevant Knowledge; Implementing Ideas, Programs, etc.; Documenting/Recording Information; Interpreting Meaning of Information to Others; Provide Consultation and Advice to Others
Job Characteristics: None above average
GOE Group/s: 02.02.04 Life Sciences: Food Research
CIP Program/s: 020101 Agriculture/Agricultural Sciences, General; 020301 Food Sciences and Technology; 190501 Foods and Nutrition Studies, General; 190502 Foods and Nutrition Science
Related DOT Job/s: 041.081-010 FOOD TECHNOLOGIST

24305D SOIL SCIENTISTS. OOH Title/s: Agricultural Scientists

Research or study soil characteristics, map soil types, and investigate responses of soils to known management practices to determine use capabilities of soils and effects of alternative practices on soil productivity. Studies soil characteristics and classifies soils according to standard types. Investigates responses of specific soil types to soil management practices, such as fertilization, crop rotation, and industrial waste control. Conducts experiments on farms or experimental stations to determine best soil types for different plants. Performs chemical analysis on micro-organism content of soil to determine microbial reactions and chemical mineralogical relationship to plant growth. Provides advice on rural or urban land use.
Yearly Earnings: $39,000
Education: Bachelor's degree
Knowledge: Food Production; Chemistry; Biology; Geography
Abilities: Oral Comprehension; Written Comprehension; Fluency of Ideas; Originality; Deductive Reasoning; Inductive Reasoning; Category Flexibility; Mathematical Reasoning; Number Facility; Flexibility of Closure
Skills: Reading Comprehension; Writing; Speaking; Mathematics; Science; Critical Thinking; Active Learning; Information Gathering; Information Organization; Idea Generation; Idea Evaluation; Solution Appraisal; Operations Analysis; Programming; Testing; Identification of Key Causes
General Work Activities: Getting Information Needed to Do the Job; Monitoring Processes, Material, or Surroundings; Identifying Objects, Actions, and Events; Estimating Needed Characteristics; Judging Qualities of Things, Services, People; Processing Information; Evaluating Information against Standards; Analyzing Data or Information; Making Decisions and Solving Problems; Thinking Creatively; Updating and Using Job-Relevant Knowledge; Developing Objectives and Strategies; Operating Vehicles or Equipment; Implementing Ideas, Programs, etc.; Documenting/Recording Information; Interpreting Meaning of Information to Others; Communicating with Persons Outside Organization; Provide Consultation and Advice to Others
Job Characteristics: None above average
GOE Group/s: 02.02.02 Life Sciences: Plant Specialization
CIP Program/s: 020501 Soil Sciences
Related DOT Job/s: 040.061-058 SOIL SCIENTIST

24308A BIOCHEMISTS. OOH Title/s: Biological and Medical Scientists

Research or study chemical composition and processes of living organisms that affect vital processes such as growth and aging, to determine chemical actions and effects on organisms, such as the action of foods, drugs, or other substances on body functions and tissues. Studies chemistry of living processes, such as cell development, breathing, and digestion, and living energy changes, such as growth, aging, and death. Researches methods of transferring characteristics, such as resistance to disease, from one organism to another. Researches and determines chemical action of substances, such as drugs, serums, hormones, and food, on tissues and vital processes. Examines chemical aspects of formation of antibodies, and researches chemistry of cells and blood corpuscles. Isolates, analyzes, and identifies hormones, vitamins, allergens, minerals, and enzymes, and determines their effects on body functions. Develops and executes tests to detect disease, genetic disorders, or other abnormalities. Develops methods to process, store, and use food, drugs, and chemical compounds. Develops and tests new drugs and medications used for commercial distribution. Prepares reports and recommendations based

upon research outcomes. Designs and builds laboratory equipment needed for special research projects. Cleans, purifies, refines, and otherwise prepares pharmaceutical compounds for commercial distribution. Analyzes foods to determine nutritional value and effects of cooking, canning, and processing on this value.
Yearly Earnings: $39,000
Education: Doctor's degree
Knowledge: Building and Construction; Mathematics; Chemistry; Biology
Abilities: Oral Comprehension; Written Comprehension; Oral Expression; Written Expression; Originality; Problem Sensitivity; Deductive Reasoning; Inductive Reasoning; Information Ordering; Category Flexibility; Number Facility; Memorization; Speed of Closure; Near Vision
Skills: Reading Comprehension; Writing; Mathematics; Science; Critical Thinking; Active Learning; Problem Identification; Information Gathering; Information Organization; Synthesis/Reorganization; Idea Generation; Idea Evaluation; Solution Appraisal; Operations Analysis; Equipment Selection; Programming; Testing; Visioning; Systems Perception; Identifying Downstream Consequences; Identification of Key Causes
General Work Activities: Getting Information Needed to Do the Job; Monitoring Processes, Material, or Surroundings; Identifying Objects, Actions, and Events; Inspecting Equipment, Structures, or Material; Estimating Needed Characteristics; Judging Qualities of Things, Services, People; Processing Information; Evaluating Information against Standards; Analyzing Data or Information; Making Decisions and Solving Problems; Thinking Creatively; Updating and Using Job-Relevant Knowledge; Developing Objectives and Strategies; Organizing, Planning, and Prioritizing; Controlling Machines and Processes; Operating Vehicles or Equipment; Drafting and Specifying Technical Devices, etc.; Implementing Ideas, Programs, etc.; Documenting/Recording Information; Interpreting Meaning of Information to Others; Communicating with Other Workers; Provide Consultation and Advice to Others; Performing Administrative Activities; Monitoring and Controlling Resources
Job Characteristics: Radiation; Diseases/Infections; Frustrating Circumstances; Importance of Being Exact or Accurate; Importance of Being Sure All is Done
GOE Group/s: 02.02.03 Life Sciences: Plant and Animal Specialization
CIP Program/s: 260202 Biochemistry; 260203 Biophysics; 260616 Biotechnology Research; 260701 Zoology, General; 260705 Pharmacology, Human and Animal; 511302 Medical Biochemistry
Related DOT Job/s: 041.061-026 BIOCHEMIST

24308B BIOLOGISTS. OOH Title/s: Biological and Medical Scientists

Study the relationship among organisms and between organisms and their environment. Studies basic principles of plant and animal life, such as origin, relationship, development, anatomy, and functions. Studies aquatic plants and animals and environmental conditions affecting them, such as radioactivity or pollution. Collects and analyzes biological data about relationship among and between organisms and their environment. Studies reactions of plants, animals, and marine species to parasites. Identifies, classifies, and studies structure, behavior, ecology, physiology, nutrition, culture, and distribution of plant and animal species. Measures salinity, acidity, light, oxygen content, and other physical conditions of water to determine their relationship to aquatic life. Studies and manages wild animal populations. Develops methods and apparatus for securing representative plant, animal, aquatic, or soil samples. Investigates and develops pest management and control measures. Communicates test results to state and federal representatives and general public. Prepares environmental impact reports for industry, government, or publication. Cultivates, breeds, and grows aquatic life, such as lobsters, clams, or fish farming. Plans and administers biological research programs for government, research firms, medical industries, or manufacturing firms. Researches environmental effects of present and potential uses of land and water areas, and determines methods of improving environment or crop yields. Develops methods of extracting drugs from aquatic plants and animals.
Yearly Earnings: $39,000
Education: Doctor's degree
Knowledge: Food Production; Mathematics; Physics; Chemistry; Biology; English Language
Abilities: Oral Comprehension; Written Comprehension; Oral Expression; Written Expression; Originality; Problem Sensitivity; Deductive Reasoning; Inductive Reasoning; Information Ordering; Category Flexibility; Memorization; Speed of Closure; Flexibility of Closure; Near Vision
Skills: Reading Comprehension; Writing; Mathematics; Science; Critical Thinking; Active Learning; Learning Strategies; Problem Identification; Information Gathering; Information Organization; Synthesis/Reorganization; Idea Generation; Idea Evaluation; Implementation Planning; Programming; Systems Perception; Identification of Key Causes
General Work Activities: Getting Information Needed to Do the Job; Monitoring Processes, Material, or Surroundings; Identifying Objects, Actions, and Events; Inspecting Equipment, Structures, or Material; Estimating Needed Characteristics; Judging Qualities of Things, Services, People; Processing Information; Evaluating Information against Standards; Analyzing Data or Information; Making Decisions and Solving Problems; Thinking Creatively; Updating and Using Job-Relevant Knowledge; Developing Objectives and Strategies; Scheduling Work and Activities; Organizing, Planning, and Prioritizing; Controlling Machines and Processes; Operating Vehicles or Equipment; Drafting and Specifying Technical Devices, etc.; Implementing Ideas, Programs, etc.; Documenting/Recording Information; Interpreting Meaning of Information to Others; Communicating with Other Workers; Communicating with Persons Outside Organization; Selling or Influencing Others; Coordinating Work and Activities of Others; Developing and Building Teams; Teaching Others; Provide Consultation and Advice to Others; Performing Administrative Activities; Monitoring and Controlling Resources
Job Characteristics: Radiation; Diseases/Infections; Specialized Protective or Safety Attire; Importance of Being Exact or Accurate; Importance of Being Sure All is Done
GOE Group/s: 02.02.01 Life Sciences: Animal Specialization; 02.02.03 Life Sciences: Plant and Animal Specialization
CIP Program/s: 260607 Marine/Aquatic Biology; 260701 Zoology, General; 511399 Basic Medical Sciences, Other
Related DOT Job/s: 041.061-022 AQUATIC BIOLOGIST; 041.061-030 BIOLOGIST; 041.061-066 NEMATOLOGIST

24308C BIOPHYSICISTS. OOH Title/s: Biological and Medical Scientists

Research or study physical principles of living cells and organisms, their electrical and mechanical energy, and related phenomena. Studies physical principles of living cells and organisms and their electrical and mechanical energy. Researches manner in which characteristics of plants and animals are carried through successive generations. Researches transformation of substances in cells, using atomic isotopes. Investigates damage to cells and tissues caused by X rays and nuclear particles. Studies spatial configuration of submicroscopic molecules, such as proteins, using X ray and electron microscope. Investigates transmission of electrical impulses along nerves and muscles. Investigates dynamics of seeing and hearing. Analyzes

functions of electronic and human brains, such as learning, thinking, and memory. Researches cancer treatment, using radiation and nuclear particles. Studies absorption of light by chlorophyll in photosynthesis or by pigments of eye involved in vision.
Yearly Earnings: $39,000
Education: Doctor's degree
Knowledge: Mathematics; Physics; Chemistry; Biology
Abilities: Oral Comprehension; Written Comprehension; Written Expression; Originality; Problem Sensitivity; Deductive Reasoning; Inductive Reasoning; Information Ordering; Category Flexibility; Mathematical Reasoning; Number Facility; Memorization; Speed of Closure; Flexibility of Closure; Near Vision
Skills: Reading Comprehension; Writing; Mathematics; Science; Critical Thinking; Active Learning; Information Gathering; Information Organization; Idea Generation; Idea Evaluation; Solution Appraisal; Programming
General Work Activities: Getting Information Needed to Do the Job; Monitoring Processes, Material, or Surroundings; Identifying Objects, Actions, and Events; Inspecting Equipment, Structures, or Material; Estimating Needed Characteristics; Judging Qualities of Things, Services, People; Processing Information; Evaluating Information against Standards; Analyzing Data or Information; Making Decisions and Solving Problems; Thinking Creatively; Updating and Using Job-Relevant Knowledge; Developing Objectives and Strategies; Organizing, Planning, and Prioritizing; Controlling Machines and Processes; Operating Vehicles or Equipment; Implementing Ideas, Programs, etc.; Documenting/Recording Information; Interpreting Meaning of Information to Others; Provide Consultation and Advice to Others; Monitoring and Controlling Resources
Job Characteristics: Radiation; Diseases/Infections; Importance of Being Exact or Accurate; Importance of Being Sure All is Done
GOE Group/s: 02.02.03 Life Sciences: Plant and Animal Specialization
CIP Program/s: 260202 Biochemistry; 260203 Biophysics; 511304 Medical Physics/Biophysics
Related DOT Job/s: 041.061-034 BIOPHYSICIST

24308D BOTANISTS. OOH Title/s: Biological and Medical Scientists

Research or study development of life processes, physiology, heredity, environment, distribution, morphology, and economic value of plants for application in such fields as agronomy, forestry, horticulture, and pharmacology. Studies development, life processes, and economic value of plants and fungi for application in such fields as horticulture and pharmacology. Studies behavior, internal and external structure, mechanics, and biochemistry of plant or fungi cells, using microscope and scientific equipment. Investigates effect of rainfall, deforestation, pollution, acid rain, temperature, climate, soil, and elevation on plant or fungi growth. Studies and compares healthy and diseased plants to determine agents responsible for diseased conditions. Investigates comparative susceptibility of different varieties of plants to disease, and develops plant varieties immune to disease. Studies rates of spread and intensity of plant diseases under different environmental conditions, and predicts disease outbreaks. Inspects flower and vegetable seed stocks and flowering bulbs, to determine presence of diseases, infections, and insect infestation. Identifies and classifies plants or fungi based on study and research. Tests disease control measures under laboratory and field conditions for comparative effectiveness, practicality, and economy. Plans and administers environmental research programs for government, research firms, medical industries, or manufacturing firms. Devises methods of destroying or controlling disease-causing agents. Prepares reports and recommendations based upon research outcomes. Develops drugs, medicines, molds, yeasts, or foods from plants or fungi, or develops new types of plants. Develops practices to prevent or reduce deterioration of perishable plant products in transit or storage. Develops improved methods of propagating and growing edible fungi.
Yearly Earnings: $39,000
Education: Doctor's degree
Knowledge: Chemistry; Biology
Abilities: Oral Comprehension; Written Comprehension; Written Expression; Originality; Problem Sensitivity; Deductive Reasoning; Inductive Reasoning; Information Ordering; Category Flexibility; Speed of Closure; Flexibility of Closure; Near Vision
Skills: Reading Comprehension; Writing; Mathematics; Science; Critical Thinking; Active Learning; Information Gathering; Information Organization; Synthesis/Reorganization; Idea Generation; Solution Appraisal; Programming; Identifying Downstream Consequences; Identification of Key Causes
General Work Activities: Getting Information Needed to Do the Job; Monitoring Processes, Material, or Surroundings; Identifying Objects, Actions, and Events; Inspecting Equipment, Structures, or Material; Estimating Needed Characteristics; Judging Qualities of Things, Services, People; Processing Information; Evaluating Information against Standards; Analyzing Data or Information; Making Decisions and Solving Problems; Thinking Creatively; Updating and Using Job-Relevant Knowledge; Developing Objectives and Strategies; Organizing, Planning, and Prioritizing; Operating Vehicles or Equipment; Implementing Ideas, Programs, etc.; Documenting/Recording Information; Interpreting Meaning of Information to Others; Communicating with Other Workers; Communicating with Persons Outside Organization; Teaching Others; Provide Consultation and Advice to Others; Monitoring and Controlling Resources
Job Characteristics: None above average
GOE Group/s: 02.02.02 Life Sciences: Plant Specialization
CIP Program/s: 020401 Plant Sciences, General; 020406 Agricultural Plant Pathology; 020408 Plant Protection (Pest Management); 260202 Biochemistry; 260301 Botany, General; 260305 Plant Pathology; 260307 Plant Physiology; 260399 Botany, Other; 260610 Parasitology; 511399 Basic Medical Sciences, Other
Related DOT Job/s: 041.061-038 BOTANIST; 041.061-062 MYCOLOGIST; 041.061-086 PLANT PATHOLOGIST

24308E MICROBIOLOGISTS. OOH Title/s: Biological and Medical Scientists

Research or study growth, structure, development, and general characteristics of bacteria and other micro-organisms. Studies growth, structure, development, and general characteristics of bacteria and other micro-organisms. Examines physiological, morphological, and cultural characteristics, using microscope, to identify micro-organisms. Studies growth structure and development of viruses and rickettsiae. Observes action of micro-organisms upon living tissues of plants, higher animals, and other micro- organisms, and on dead organic matter. Isolates and makes cultures of bacteria or other micro-organisms in prescribed media, controlling moisture, aeration, temperature, and nutrition. Conducts chemical analyses of substances, such as acids, alcohols, and enzymes. Researches use of bacteria and micro-organisms to develop vitamins, antibiotics, amino acids, grain alcohol, sugars, and polymers. Prepares technical reports and recommendations based upon research outcomes. Plans and administers biological research program for government, private research centers, or medical industry.
Yearly Earnings: $39,000
Education: Doctor's degree
Knowledge: Mathematics; Chemistry; Biology; English Language
Abilities: Oral Comprehension; Written Comprehension; Oral Expression; Written Expression; Fluency of Ideas; Originality; Problem Sensitivity; Deductive Reasoning; Inductive Reasoning; Information

Ordering; Category Flexibility; Mathematical Reasoning; Number Facility; Memorization; Speed of Closure; Flexibility of Closure; Perceptual Speed; Visualization; Selective Attention; Near Vision
Skills: Reading Comprehension; Writing; Mathematics; Science; Active Learning; Problem Identification; Information Gathering; Synthesis/Reorganization; Idea Evaluation; Equipment Selection; Programming
General Work Activities: Getting Information Needed to Do the Job; Monitoring Processes, Material, or Surroundings; Identifying Objects, Actions, and Events; Judging Qualities of Things, Services, People; Processing Information; Evaluating Information against Standards; Analyzing Data or Information; Making Decisions and Solving Problems; Thinking Creatively; Updating and Using Job-Relevant Knowledge; Developing Objectives and Strategies; Scheduling Work and Activities; Organizing, Planning, and Prioritizing; Controlling Machines and Processes; Operating Vehicles or Equipment; Implementing Ideas, Programs, etc.; Documenting/Recording Information; Interpreting Meaning of Information to Others; Communicating with Other Workers; Communicating with Persons Outside Organization; Guiding, Directing and Motivating Subordinates; Provide Consultation and Advice to Others; Performing Administrative Activities; Monitoring and Controlling Resources
Job Characteristics: Diseases/Infections; Common Protective or Safety Attire; Specialized Protective or Safety Attire; Importance of Being Exact or Accurate; Importance of Being Sure All is Done
GOE Group/s: 02.02.03 Life Sciences: Plant and Animal Specialization
CIP Program/s: 260202 Biochemistry; 260401 Cell Biology; 260501 Microbiology/Bacteriology; 260619 Virology; 511308 Medical Microbiology
Related DOT Job/s: 041.061-058 MICROBIOLOGIST

24308F GENETICISTS. OOH Title/s: Biological and Medical Scientists

Research or study inheritance and variation of characteristics on forms of life to determine laws, mechanisms, and environmental factors in origin, transmission, and development of inherited traits. Conducts experiments to determine laws, mechanisms, and environmental factors in origin, transmission, and development of inherited traits. Analyses determinants responsible for specific inherited traits, such as color differences, size, and disease resistance. Studies genetic determinants to understand relationship of heredity to maturity, fertility, or other factors. Devises methods for altering or producing new traits, using chemicals, heat, light, or other means. Prepares technical reports and recommendations based upon research outcomes. Counsels clients in human and medical genetics. Plans and administers genetic research program for government, private research centers, or medical industry.
Yearly Earnings: $39,000
Education: Doctor's degree
Knowledge: Administration and Management; Mathematics; Chemistry; Biology; Medicine and Dentistry; Therapy and Counseling; Foreign Language
Abilities: Oral Comprehension; Written Comprehension; Oral Expression; Written Expression; Originality; Deductive Reasoning; Inductive Reasoning; Information Ordering; Category Flexibility; Mathematical Reasoning; Flexibility of Closure; Near Vision
Skills: Reading Comprehension; Active Listening; Writing; Speaking; Mathematics; Science; Critical Thinking; Active Learning; Learning Strategies; Persuasion; Instructing; Problem Identification; Information Gathering; Information Organization; Synthesis/Reorganization; Idea Generation; Idea Evaluation; Solution Appraisal; Equipment Selection; Programming; Visioning; Systems Perception; Management of Financial Resources; Management of Personnel Resources
General Work Activities: Getting Information Needed to Do the Job; Monitoring Processes, Material, or Surroundings; Identifying Objects, Actions, and Events; Inspecting Equipment, Structures, or Material; Estimating Needed Characteristics; Judging Qualities of Things, Services, People; Processing Information; Evaluating Information against Standards; Analyzing Data or Information; Making Decisions and Solving Problems; Thinking Creatively; Updating and Using Job-Relevant Knowledge; Developing Objectives and Strategies; Scheduling Work and Activities; Organizing, Planning, and Prioritizing; Operating Vehicles or Equipment; Drafting and Specifying Technical Devices, etc.; Implementing Ideas, Programs, etc.; Documenting/Recording Information; Interpreting Meaning of Information to Others; Communicating with Other Workers; Communicating with Persons Outside Organization; Establishing and Maintaining Relationships; Performing for or Working with Public; Coordinating Work and Activities of Others; Teaching Others; Provide Consultation and Advice to Others; Monitoring and Controlling Resources
Job Characteristics: Radiation; Diseases/Infections; Consequence of Error; Importance of Being Exact or Accurate; Importance of Being Sure All is Done
GOE Group/s: 02.02.01 Life Sciences: Animal Specialization
CIP Program/s: 260202 Biochemistry; 260401 Cell Biology; 260402 Molecular Biology; 260613 Genetics, Plant and Animal; 260616 Biotechnology Research; 260617 Evolutionary Biology; 511306 Medical Genetics
Related DOT Job/s: 041.061-050 GENETICIST

24308G PHYSIOLOGISTS AND CYTOLOGISTS.

OOH Title/s: Biological and Medical Scientists

Research or study cellular structure and functions, or organ-system functions, of plants and animals. Studies cells, cellular structure, cell division, and organ-system functions of plants and animals. Studies functions of plants and animals, such as growth, respiration, movement, and reproduction, under normal and abnormal conditions. Conducts experiments to determine effects of internal and external environmental factors on life processes and functions. Studies physiology of plants, animals, or particular human body area, function, organ, or system. Utilizes microscope, X ray equipment, spectroscope, and other equipment to study cell structure and function and to perform experiments. Studies glands and their relationship to bodily functions. Analyzes reproductive cells and methods by which chromosomes divide or unite. Studies formation of sperm and eggs in animal sex glands, and studies origin of blood and tissue cells. Researches physiology of unicellular organisms, such as protozoa, to ascertain physical and chemical factors of growth. Studies influence of physical and chemical factors on malignant and normal cells. Assesses and evaluates hormonal status and presence of atypical or malignant changes in exfoliated, aspirated, or abraded cells. Selects and sections minute particles of animal or plant tissue for microscopic study, using microtome and other equipment. Stains tissue sample to make cell structures visible or to differentiate parts. Prepares technical reports and recommendations based upon research outcomes. Plans and administers biological research programs for government, private research centers, or medical industry.
Yearly Earnings: $39,000
Education: Doctor's degree
Knowledge: Administration and Management; Chemistry; Biology
Abilities: Oral Comprehension; Written Comprehension; Oral Expression; Written Expression; Fluency of Ideas; Originality; Problem Sensitivity; Deductive Reasoning; Inductive Reasoning; Information Ordering; Category Flexibility; Memorization; Speed of Closure; Flexibility of Closure; Near Vision
Skills: Reading Comprehension; Writing; Mathematics; Science; Critical Thinking; Active Learning; Problem Identification; Informa-

tion Gathering; Information Organization; Synthesis/Reorganization; Idea Generation; Idea Evaluation; Implementation Planning; Solution Appraisal; Equipment Selection; Programming; Operation Monitoring; Operation and Control; Visioning; Identifying Downstream Consequences; Identification of Key Causes
General Work Activities: Getting Information Needed to Do the Job; Monitoring Processes, Material, or Surroundings; Identifying Objects, Actions, and Events; Inspecting Equipment, Structures, or Material; Estimating Needed Characteristics; Judging Qualities of Things, Services, People; Processing Information; Evaluating Information against Standards; Analyzing Data or Information; Making Decisions and Solving Problems; Thinking Creatively; Updating and Using Job-Relevant Knowledge; Developing Objectives and Strategies; Scheduling Work and Activities; Organizing, Planning, and Prioritizing; Controlling Machines and Processes; Operating Vehicles or Equipment; Implementing Ideas, Programs, etc.; Documenting/Recording Information; Interpreting Meaning of Information to Others; Communicating with Other Workers; Communicating with Persons Outside Organization; Selling or Influencing Others; Developing and Building Teams; Guiding, Directing and Motivating Subordinates; Provide Consultation and Advice to Others; Performing Administrative Activities; Staffing Organizational Units; Monitoring and Controlling Resources
Job Characteristics: Radiation; Diseases/Infections; Importance of Being Exact or Accurate; Importance of Being Sure All is Done
GOE Group/s: 02.02.03 Life Sciences: Plant and Animal Specialization
CIP Program/s: 020401 Plant Sciences, General; 020407 Agricultural Plant Physiology; 260202 Biochemistry; 260301 Botany, General; 260307 Plant Physiology; 260401 Cell Biology; 260601 Anatomy; 260608 Neuroscience; 260616 Biotechnology Research; 260701 Zoology, General; 260706 Physiology, Human and Animal; 511305 Medical Cell Biology; 511313 Medical Physiology
Related DOT Job/s: 041.061-042 CYTOLOGIST; 041.061-078 PHYSIOLOGIST

24308H ZOOLOGISTS. OOH Title/s: Biological and Medical Scientists

Research or study origins, interrelationships, classification, habits, life histories, life processes, diseases, relation to environment, growth, development, genetics, and distribution of animals. Studies origins, interrelationships, classification, life histories, diseases, development, genetics, and distribution of animals. Analyzes characteristics of animals to identify and classify animals. Studies animals in their natural habitats, and assesses effects of environment on animals. Collects and dissects animal specimens and examines specimens under microscope. Prepares collections of preserved specimens or microscopic slides for species identification and study of species development or animal disease. Conducts experimental studies, using chemicals and various types of scientific equipment. Raises specimens for study and observation or for use in experiments.
Yearly Earnings: $39,000
Education: Doctor's degree
Knowledge: Chemistry; Biology
Abilities: Oral Comprehension; Written Comprehension; Written Expression; Fluency of Ideas; Originality; Problem Sensitivity; Deductive Reasoning; Inductive Reasoning; Information Ordering; Category Flexibility; Memorization; Speed of Closure; Flexibility of Closure; Perceptual Speed; Spatial Orientation; Selective Attention; Time Sharing; Response Orientation; Gross Body Equilibrium; Far Vision; Night Vision; Glare Sensitivity; Hearing Sensitivity; Auditory Attention; Sound Localization
Skills: Reading Comprehension; Writing; Mathematics; Science; Critical Thinking; Active Learning; Learning Strategies; Problem Identification; Information Gathering; Information Organization; Synthesis/Reorganization; Idea Generation; Idea Evaluation; Equipment Selection; Identifying Downstream Consequences
General Work Activities: Getting Information Needed to Do the Job; Monitoring Processes, Material, or Surroundings; Judging Qualities of Things, Services, People; Processing Information; Evaluating Information against Standards; Analyzing Data or Information; Thinking Creatively; Updating and Using Job-Relevant Knowledge; Organizing, Planning, and Prioritizing; Operating Vehicles or Equipment; Documenting/Recording Information; Interpreting Meaning of Information to Others; Monitoring and Controlling Resources
Job Characteristics: Radiation; Diseases/Infections; Hazardous Situations; Importance of Being Sure All is Done
GOE Group/s: 02.02.01 Life Sciences: Animal Specialization
CIP Program/s: 260701 Zoology, General
Related DOT Job/s: 041.061-090 ZOOLOGIST

24308J TOXICOLOGISTS. OOH Title/s: Biological and Medical Scientists

Research or study the effects of toxic substances on physiological functions of humans, animals, and plants. Researches effects of toxic substances on physiological functions of humans, animals, and plants for consumer protection and industrial safety programs. Designs and conducts studies to determine physiological effects of various substances on laboratory animals, plants, and human tissue. Interprets results of studies in terms of toxicological properties of substances and hazards associated with their misuse. Collects and prepares samples of toxic materials for analysis or examination. Dissects dead animals, using surgical instruments, and examines organs for toxic substances. Applies cosmetic or ingredient onto skin, or injects substance into animal, and observes animal for abnormalities, inflammation, or irritation. Analyzes samples of toxic materials to identify compound and develop treatment. Tests and analyzes blood samples for presence of toxic conditions, using microscope and laboratory test equipment. Reviews toxicological data for accuracy, and suggests clarifications or corrections to data. Writes and maintains records and reports of studies and tests for use as toxicological resource material. Informs regulatory agency personnel and industrial firms concerning toxicological properties of products and materials. Advises governmental and industrial personnel on degree of hazard of toxic materials and on precautionary labeling. Testifies as expert witness on toxicology in hearings and court proceedings.
Yearly Earnings: $39,000
Education: Doctor's degree
Knowledge: Mathematics; Chemistry; Biology; English Language
Abilities: Oral Comprehension; Written Comprehension; Oral Expression; Written Expression; Fluency of Ideas; Originality; Problem Sensitivity; Deductive Reasoning; Inductive Reasoning; Information Ordering; Category Flexibility; Mathematical Reasoning; Number Facility; Memorization; Speed of Closure; Flexibility of Closure; Perceptual Speed; Visualization; Selective Attention; Time Sharing; Manual Dexterity; Near Vision; Far Vision; Visual Color Discrimination; Peripheral Vision; Glare Sensitivity; Speech Clarity
Skills: Reading Comprehension; Writing; Mathematics; Science; Critical Thinking; Active Learning; Learning Strategies; Problem Identification; Information Gathering; Idea Evaluation; Equipment Selection; Programming; Testing; Identification of Key Causes
General Work Activities: Getting Information Needed to Do the Job; Monitoring Processes, Material, or Surroundings; Identifying Objects, Actions, and Events; Inspecting Equipment, Structures, or Material; Estimating Needed Characteristics; Judging Qualities of Things, Services, People; Processing Information; Evaluating Information against Standards; Analyzing Data or Information; Making Decisions and Solving Problems; Thinking Creatively; Updating and Using Job-Relevant Knowledge; Developing Objectives and Strategies; Organizing,

Planning, and Prioritizing; Operating Vehicles or Equipment; Implementing Ideas, Programs, etc.; Documenting/Recording Information; Interpreting Meaning of Information to Others; Communicating with Other Workers; Communicating with Persons Outside Organization; Selling or Influencing Others; Teaching Others; Provide Consultation and Advice to Others; Performing Administrative Activities; Monitoring and Controlling Resources
Job Characteristics: Responsible for Others' Health and Safety; Contaminants; Radiation; Diseases/Infections; Common Protective or Safety Attire; Specialized Protective or Safety Attire; Consequence of Error; Importance of Being Exact or Accurate; Importance of Being Sure All is Done
GOE Group/s: 02.02.01 Life Sciences: Animal Specialization; 02.04.02 Laboratory Technology: Life Sciences
CIP Program/s: 260202 Biochemistry; 260612 Toxicology; 400501 Chemistry, General; 400505 Medicinal/Pharmaceutical Chemistry; 511314 Medical Toxicology; 512202 Environmental Health
Related DOT Job/s: 022.081-010 TOXICOLOGIST; 041.061-094 STAFF TOXICOLOGIST

24311 MEDICAL SCIENTISTS. OOH Title/s: Biological and Medical Scientists

Conduct research dealing with the understanding of human diseases and the improvement of human health. Engage in clinical investigation or other research, production, technical writing, or related activities. Include medical scientists such as physicians, dentists, public health specialists, pharmacologists, and medical pathologists. Exclude practitioners who provide medical care or dispense drugs. Plans and directs studies to investigate human or animal disease, preventive methods, and treatments for disease. Analyzes data, applying statistical techniques and scientific knowledge, prepares reports, and presents findings. Investigates cause, progress, life cycle, or mode of transmission of diseases or parasites. Studies effects of drugs, gases, pesticides, parasites, or micro-organisms, or health and physiological processes of animals and humans. Conducts research to develop methodologies, instrumentation, or identification, diagnosing, and treatment procedures for medical application. Plans methodological design of research study and arranges for data collection. Examines organs, tissues, cell structures, or micro-organisms by systematic observation or using microscope. Consults with and advises physicians, educators, researchers, and others regarding medical applications of sciences, such as physics, biology, and chemistry. Prepares and analyzes samples for toxicity, bacteria, or micro-organisms or to study cell structure and properties. Confers with health department, industry personnel, physicians, and others to develop health safety standards and programs to improve public health. Standardizes drug dosages, methods of immunization, and procedures for manufacture of drugs and medicinal compounds. Teaches principles of medicine and medical and laboratory procedures to physicians, residents, students, and technicians. Supervises activities of clerical and statistical or laboratory personnel.
Yearly Earnings: $39,000
Education: Doctor's degree
Knowledge: Food Production; Mathematics; Physics; Chemistry; Biology; Psychology; Medicine and Dentistry; Therapy and Counseling; Education and Training; Foreign Language; History and Archeology; Public Safety and Security; Law, Government, and Jurisprudence; Telecommunications; Communications and Media; Transportation
Abilities: Oral Comprehension; Written Comprehension; Oral Expression; Written Expression; Fluency of Ideas; Originality; Problem Sensitivity; Deductive Reasoning; Inductive Reasoning; Information Ordering; Category Flexibility; Mathematical Reasoning; Number Facility; Speed of Closure; Flexibility of Closure; Perceptual Speed; Time Sharing; Arm-Hand Steadiness; Finger Dexterity; Near Vision; Night Vision; Speech Clarity
Skills: Reading Comprehension; Active Listening; Writing; Speaking; Mathematics; Science; Critical Thinking; Active Learning; Learning Strategies; Monitoring; Social Perceptiveness; Coordination; Persuasion; Negotiation; Instructing; Service Orientation; Problem Identification; Information Gathering; Information Organization; Synthesis/Reorganization; Idea Generation; Idea Evaluation; Implementation Planning; Solution Appraisal; Operations Analysis; Equipment Selection; Programming; Testing; Visioning; Systems Perception; Identifying Downstream Consequences; Identification of Key Causes; Judgment and Decision Making; Systems Evaluation; Time Management; Management of Financial Resources; Management of Material Resources; Management of Personnel Resources
General Work Activities: Getting Information Needed to Do the Job; Monitoring Processes, Material, or Surroundings; Identifying Objects, Actions, and Events; Inspecting Equipment, Structures, or Material; Estimating Needed Characteristics; Judging Qualities of Things, Services, People; Processing Information; Evaluating Information against Standards; Analyzing Data or Information; Making Decisions and Solving Problems; Thinking Creatively; Updating and Using Job-Relevant Knowledge; Developing Objectives and Strategies; Scheduling Work and Activities; Organizing, Planning, and Prioritizing; Operating Vehicles or Equipment; Implementing Ideas, Programs, etc.; Documenting/Recording Information; Interpreting Meaning of Information to Others; Communicating with Other Workers; Communicating with Persons Outside Organization; Selling or Influencing Others; Coordinating Work and Activities of Others; Teaching Others; Guiding, Directing and Motivating Subordinates; Coaching and Developing Others; Provide Consultation and Advice to Others; Performing Administrative Activities
Job Characteristics: Supervise, Coach, Train Others; Responsible for Others' Health and Safety; Responsibility for Outcomes and Results; Radiation; Diseases/Infections; Special Uniform; Common Protective or Safety Attire; Specialized Protective or Safety Attire; Consequence of Error; Frustrating Circumstances; Importance of Being Exact or Accurate; Importance of Being Sure All is Done
GOE Group/s: 02.02.01 Life Sciences: Animal Specialization; 02.04.02 Laboratory Technology: Life Sciences
CIP Program/s: 260202 Biochemistry; 260203 Biophysics; 260501 Microbiology/Bacteriology; 260601 Anatomy; 260610 Parasitology; 260612 Toxicology; 260616 Biotechnology Research; 260618 Biological Immunology; 260701 Zoology, General; 260705 Pharmacology, Human and Animal; 511301 Medical Anatomy; 511304 Medical Physics/Biophysics; 511312 Medical Pathology; 511399 Basic Medical Sciences, Other; 512003 Medical Pharmacology and Pharmaceutical Sciences; 512202 Environmental Health; 512203 Epidemiology; 512205 Health Physics/Radiologic Health
Related DOT Job/s: 041.061-010 ANATOMIST; 041.061-054 HISTOPATHOLOGIST; 041.061-070 PARASITOLOGIST; 041.061-074 PHARMACOLOGIST; 041.067-010 MEDICAL COORDINATOR, PESTICIDE USE; 041.167-010 ENVIRONMENTAL EPIDEMIOLOGIST; 041.261-010 PUBLIC-HEALTH MICROBIOLOGIST; 079.021-014 MEDICAL PHYSICIST

Life and Physical Sciences Technologists and Technicians

24502A BIOLOGICAL AND AGRICULTURAL TECHNOLOGISTS. OOH Title/s: Science Technicians

Study and apply biological and agricultural principles to experiment, test, and develop new and improved methods in production, preservation, and processing of plant and animal life.

Applies scientific principles to devise new or improved methods of production, preservation, and processing of plant and animal life. Develops improved manufacturing methods for natural and synthetic fibers. Analyses the nature and use of animal, plant, and synthetic fibers. Tests the quality control of plant, animal, and synthetic products. Experiments with methods of handling, processing, and packaging dairy products.
Yearly Earnings: $26,728
Education: Associate degree
Knowledge: Production and Processing; Food Production; Mathematics; Chemistry; Biology
Abilities: Originality; Deductive Reasoning; Inductive Reasoning; Mathematical Reasoning; Memorization
Skills: Reading Comprehension; Mathematics; Science; Critical Thinking; Active Learning; Information Gathering; Information Organization; Synthesis/Reorganization; Idea Generation; Idea Evaluation; Operations Analysis; Technology Design; Equipment Selection; Testing; Visioning; Identifying Downstream Consequences; Systems Evaluation
General Work Activities: Monitoring Processes, Material, or Surroundings; Evaluating Information against Standards; Analyzing Data or Information; Making Decisions and Solving Problems; Thinking Creatively; Updating and Using Job-Relevant Knowledge; Operating Vehicles or Equipment
Job Characteristics: Diseases/Infections
GOE Group/s: 02.02.04 Life Sciences: Food Research; 05.01.08 Engineering: General Engineering
CIP Program/s: 020201 Animal Sciences, General; 020206 Dairy Science; 410101 Biological Technologists and Technicians
Related DOT Job/s: 040.061-022 DAIRY TECHNOLOGIST; 040.061-026 FIBER TECHNOLOGIST

24502B ARTIFICIAL BREEDING TECHNICIANS. OOH Title/s: Science Technicians

Collect, inject, measure, or test animal semen to breed livestock or to develop improved artificial insemination methods. Attaches vial or sheath to genitals of animal to collect semen sample. Examines semen sample to determine its quality, using microscope and other devices. Measures and transfers semen into insemination containers. Injects semen samples into animals, using syringe. Adds chemicals to semen, and refrigerates semen samples to preserve them. Experiments with tests to improve sample purity and preservation. Records information on semen collection and artificial insemination. Observes animals to determine best times for artificial insemination. Cleans and sterilizes laboratory equipment.
Yearly Earnings: $26,728
Education: Associate degree
Knowledge: Food Production; Chemistry; Biology; Medicine and Dentistry
Abilities: None above average
Skills: None above average
General Work Activities: None above average
Job Characteristics: Specialized Protective or Safety Attire; Importance of Being Exact or Accurate
GOE Group/s: 02.04.02 Laboratory Technology: Life Sciences; 03.02.04 General Supervision: Plants and Animals: Services; 03.04.05 Elemental Work: Plants and Animals: Services
CIP Program/s: 010301 Agricultural Production Workers and Managers, General; 010302 Agricultural Animal Husbandry and Production Management; 010501 Agricultural Supplies Retailing and Wholesaling; 020201 Animal Sciences, General; 020202 Agricultural Animal Breeding and Genetics
Related DOT Job/s: 040.361-010 LABORATORY TECHNICIAN, ARTIFICIAL BREEDING; 411.384-010 POULTRY INSEMINATOR; 418.384-010 ARTIFICIAL INSEMINATOR; 418.384-014 ARTIFICIAL-BREEDING TECHNICIAN

24502C BIOLOGICAL AND AGRICULTURAL TECHNICIANS. OOH Title/s: Science Technicians

Set up and maintain laboratory, and collect and record data to assist scientists in biology, plant pathology, and related agricultural science experiments. Sets up laboratory and field equipment to assist research workers. Cleans and maintains laboratory and field equipment and work areas. Plants seeds in specified area, and counts plants that grow, to determine germination rate of seeds. Examines animals and specimens to determine presence of disease or other problems. Pricks animals, and collects blood samples for testing, using hand-held devices. Waters and feeds rations to livestock and laboratory animals. Records production and test data for evaluation by personnel. Adjusts testing equipment and prepares culture media, following standard procedures. Measures or weighs ingredients used in testing or as animal feed.
Yearly Earnings: $26,728
Education: Associate degree
Knowledge: Food Production; Biology
Abilities: None above average
Skills: None above average
General Work Activities: None above average
Job Characteristics: Diseases/Infections; Kneeling, Crouching, or Crawling; Keeping or Regaining Balance
GOE Group/s: 02.04.02 Laboratory Technology: Life Sciences; 03.04.05 Elemental Work: Plants and Animals: Services
CIP Program/s: 010301 Agricultural Production Workers and Managers, General; 010302 Agricultural Animal Husbandry and Production Management; 010304 Crop Production Operations and Management; 020201 Animal Sciences, General; 020204 Agricultural Animal Nutrition; 020401 Plant Sciences, General; 020402 Agronomy and Crop Science; 410101 Biological Technologists and Technicians
Related DOT Job/s: 040.361-014 SEED ANALYST; 049.364-010 FEED-RESEARCH AIDE; 049.364-018 BIOLOGICAL AIDE; 411.364-010 BLOOD TESTER, FOWL; 559.384-010 LABORATORY ASSISTANT, CULTURE MEDIA

24502D BIOLOGY SPECIMEN TECHNICIANS. OOH Title/s: Science Technicians

Prepare biological specimens of plant and animal life for use as instructional aids in schools, museums, and other institutions. Dissects, trims, and stains section of plant or animal to display desired features. Selects specimens of plant or animal life to prepare as instructional aids. Assembles and positions components of specimen in mold, using pins and holding devices. Embeds biological specimens of plant and animal life in plastic, using molding techniques. Arranges specimens between sheets of paper to protect them and to stack them in pressing frame. Mounts dried specimens on heavy paper, using glue or other materials. Mixes one of various types of plastic to embed specimen in mold. Records information to identify specimens and method of preservation, and to maintain specimen file. Tightens frame section with screws to compress stacks and to press dry specimens into desired configuration. Turns valves to release fumes that fumigate plant specimens.
Yearly Earnings: $26,728
Education: Associate degree
Knowledge: Chemistry; Biology
Abilities: Category Flexibility; Finger Dexterity
Skills: None above average
General Work Activities: None above average
Job Characteristics: Radiation; Diseases/Infections
GOE Group/s: 02.04.02 Laboratory Technology: Life Sciences

CIP Program/s: 410101 Biological Technologists and Technicians
Related DOT Job/s: 041.381-010 BIOLOGY SPECIMEN TECHNICIAN; 041.384-010 HERBARIUM WORKER

24505A CHEMICAL TECHNICIANS AND TECHNOLOGISTS. OOH Title/s: Science Technicians

Conduct chemical and physical laboratory tests to assist scientists in making qualitative and quantitative analyses of solids, liquids, and gaseous materials. Tests and analyzes chemical and physical properties of liquids, solids, gases, radioactive and biological materials, and products such as perfumes. Prepares chemical solutions for products and processes, following standardized formulas, or creates experimental formulas. Sets up and calibrates laboratory equipment and instruments used for testing, process control, product development, and research. Cleans and sterilizes laboratory equipment. Documents results of tests and analyses, and writes technical reports or prepares graphs and charts. Reviews process paperwork for products to ensure compliance to standards and specifications. Directs other workers in compounding and distilling chemicals.
Yearly Earnings: $26,728
Education: Associate degree
Knowledge: Mathematics; Chemistry; Biology; English Language
Abilities: Written Comprehension; Written Expression; Deductive Reasoning; Information Ordering; Category Flexibility; Mathematical Reasoning; Number Facility; Memorization; Perceptual Speed; Arm-Hand Steadiness; Control Precision; Visual Color Discrimination
Skills: Mathematics; Science; Critical Thinking; Monitoring; Equipment Selection; Programming; Testing
General Work Activities: Monitoring Processes, Material, or Surroundings; Identifying Objects, Actions, and Events; Inspecting Equipment, Structures, or Material; Evaluating Information against Standards; Updating and Using Job-Relevant Knowledge; Controlling Machines and Processes; Operating Vehicles or Equipment; Drafting and Specifying Technical Devices, etc.; Repairing and Maintaining Electrical Equipment; Documenting/Recording Information; Interpreting Meaning of Information to Others; Communicating with Other Workers; Assisting and Caring for Others; Guiding, Directing and Motivating Subordinates
Job Characteristics: Contaminants; Radiation; Hazardous Conditions; Common Protective or Safety Attire
GOE Group/s: 02.01.02 Physical Sciences: Technology; 02.04.01 Laboratory Technology: Physical Sciences
CIP Program/s: 020301 Food Sciences and Technology; 150702 Quality Control Technologists and Technicians; 150803 Automotive Engineering Technologists and Technicians; 150903 Petroleum Technologists and Technicians; 410301 Chemical Technologists and Technicians; 510802 Medical Laboratory Assistant
Related DOT Job/s: 019.261-030 LABORATORY TECHNICIAN; 022.161-018 PERFUMER; 022.261-010 CHEMICAL LABORATORY TECHNICIAN; 029.261-010 LABORATORY TESTER

24505B FOOD SCIENCE TECHNICIANS AND TECHNOLOGISTS. OOH Title/s: Science Technicians

Perform standardized qualitative and quantitative tests to determine physical or chemical properties of food or beverage products. Conducts standardized tests on food, beverages, additives, and preservatives to ensure compliance to standards, for factors such as color, texture, nutrients, and coloring. Tastes or smells food or beverages to ensure flavor meets specifications or to select samples with specific characteristics. Analyzes test results to classify product, or compares results with standard tables. Computes moisture or salt content, percentage of ingredients, formulas, or other product factors, using mathematical and chemical procedures. Examines chemical and biological samples to identify cell structure, bacteria, or extraneous material, using microscope. Mixes, blends, or cultivates ingredients to make reagents or to manufacture food or beverage products. Records and compiles test results, and prepares graphs, charts, and reports. Prepares slides and incubates slides with cell cultures. Measures, tests, and weighs bottles, cans, and other containers to ensure that hardness, strength, and dimensions meet specifications. Orders supplies to maintain inventory in laboratory or in storage facility of food or beverage processing plant. Cleans and sterilizes laboratory equipment.
Yearly Earnings: $26,728
Education: Associate degree
Knowledge: Production and Processing; Food Production; Mathematics; Chemistry; Biology; English Language
Abilities: Information Ordering; Category Flexibility; Mathematical Reasoning; Number Facility; Visual Color Discrimination
Skills: Reading Comprehension; Writing; Mathematics; Science; Critical Thinking; Active Learning; Information Gathering; Equipment Selection; Programming; Testing; Operation Monitoring; Product Inspection
General Work Activities: Monitoring Processes, Material, or Surroundings; Judging Qualities of Things, Services, People; Evaluating Information against Standards; Analyzing Data or Information; Documenting/Recording Information; Interpreting Meaning of Information to Others
Job Characteristics: Importance of Being Exact or Accurate
GOE Group/s: 02.04.02 Laboratory Technology: Life Sciences; 05.02.03 Managerial Work: Mechanical: Processing and Manufacturing
CIP Program/s: 020301 Food Sciences and Technology; 150701 Occupational Safety and Health Technologists and Technicians; 410301 Chemical Technologists and Technicians
Related DOT Job/s: 022.261-014 MALT-SPECIFICATIONS-CONTROL ASSISTANT; 022.381-010 YEAST-CULTURE DEVELOPER; 029.361-010 BOTTLE-HOUSE QUALITY-CONTROL TECHNICIAN; 029.361-014 FOOD TESTER; 199.251-010 TESTER, FOOD PRODUCTS; 526.381-018 BAKER, TEST

24505C ASSAYERS. OOH Title/s: Science Technicians

Test ores and minerals and analyze results to determine value and properties. Performs dry-method processes, such as applying heat in furnace to form slags of lead, borax, or other impurities, to test ores and minerals. Analyzes test results to determine value and properties of ores and minerals, using spectroscope and other instruments and laboratory equipment. Separates metals from dross materials by liquid processes, such as flotation or solution, to test ores and minerals. Weighs ore residues to determine proportion of gold, silver, platinum, or other metals, using balance scale.
Yearly Earnings: $26,728
Education: Associate degree
Knowledge: History and Archeology
Abilities: Category Flexibility; Flexibility of Closure; Near Vision; Visual Color Discrimination
Skills: Science; Operation and Control
General Work Activities: Controlling Machines and Processes
Job Characteristics: None above average
GOE Group/s: 02.04.01 Laboratory Technology: Physical Sciences
CIP Program/s: 410301 Chemical Technologists and Technicians
Related DOT Job/s: 022.281-010 ASSAYER

24505D TEXTILE SCIENCE TECHNICIANS AND TECHNOLOGISTS. OOH Title/s: Science Technicians; Textile Machinery Operators

Conduct tests to determine characteristics of textile products, fibers, and related materials and adherence to specifications. May develop and test color formulas. Performs standardized tests

to determine chemical characteristics of fiber, such as shrinkage, absorbency, color value, fading, or fire retardancy. Measures physical characteristics of fiber, such as tensile and tear strength, using testing equipment. Photographs, develops, and prints samples of fibers, using microphotographic and photographic equipment. Examines photographs or fiber and cloth samples under microscope to determine characteristics, such as fiber type, weave, structure, or threads per inch. Prepares fiber or cloth samples for microscopic or photographic analysis and chemical and physical testing. Compares printed cloth specimen with customer sample or with test results. Inspects finished material for conformance to plant and customer specifications. Classifies textiles and fibers according to quality. Tests related textile items, such as buckles, buttons, bindings, laces, or oil and soap products. Prepares reports of test findings or file folders containing color formulas. Selects dyes and develops color formulas and color charts to match textile product to customer specifications. Mixes colors for dyes or chemicals for use in removing stains. Inventories and requisitions supplies. Coordinates activities of department with other departments.
Yearly Earnings: $26,728
Education: Associate degree
Knowledge: Production and Processing; Chemistry; Fine Arts
Abilities: Category Flexibility; Perceptual Speed; Near Vision; Visual Color Discrimination
Skills: Science; Testing; Operation Monitoring
General Work Activities: Drafting and Specifying Technical Devices, etc.
Job Characteristics: Hazardous Conditions
GOE Group/s: 02.04.01 Laboratory Technology: Physical Sciences
CIP Program/s: 410301 Chemical Technologists and Technicians
Related DOT Job/s: 022.161-014 COLORIST; 022.281-018 LABORATORY TESTER; 029.381-010 CLOTH TESTER; 029.381-014 LABORATORY ASSISTANT; 582.384-010 DYE-LAB TECHNICIAN

24505E ENVIRONMENTAL SCIENCE TECHNICIANS. OOH Title/s: Science Technicians

Perform laboratory and field tests to monitor environmental resources and determine sources of pollution, under direction of environmental scientist. Collect samples of gases, soil, water, and other materials for testing. May recommend remediation treatment to resolve pollution problems. Collects samples of gases, soils, water, industrial wastewater, and asbestos products to conduct tests on pollutant levels. Performs chemical and physical laboratory and field tests on collected samples to assess compliance with pollution standards, using test instruments. Conducts standardized tests to ensure materials and supplies used throughout power-supply system meet processing and safety specifications. Examines and analyzes material for presence and concentration of contaminants such as asbestos in environment, using variety of microscopes. Weighs, analyzes, and measures collected sample particles, such as lead, coal dust, or rock, to determine concentration of pollutants. Calculates amount of pollutant in samples or computes air pollution or gas flow in industrial processes, using chemical and mathematical formulas. Prepares samples or photomicrographs for testing and analysis. Determines amounts and kinds of chemicals to use in destroying harmful organisms and removing impurities from purification systems. Sets up equipment or station to monitor and collect pollutants from sites, such as smoke stacks, manufacturing plants, or mechanical equipment. Records test data and prepares reports, summaries, and charts that interpret test results and recommend changes. Develops procedures and directs activities of workers in laboratory. Calibrates microscopes and test instruments. Discusses test results and analyses with customers.
Yearly Earnings: $26,728
Education: Associate degree
Knowledge: Mathematics; Physics; Chemistry; Biology; English Language; Public Safety and Security; Communications and Media
Abilities: Oral Comprehension; Written Comprehension; Oral Expression; Written Expression; Problem Sensitivity; Deductive Reasoning; Inductive Reasoning; Information Ordering; Category Flexibility; Mathematical Reasoning; Number Facility; Memorization; Speed of Closure; Flexibility of Closure; Perceptual Speed; Arm-Hand Steadiness; Finger Dexterity; Control Precision; Gross Body Equilibrium; Near Vision; Far Vision
Skills: Writing; Mathematics; Science; Critical Thinking; Information Gathering; Equipment Selection; Installation; Programming; Testing; Operation Monitoring; Operation and Control
General Work Activities: Identifying Objects, Actions, and Events; Inspecting Equipment, Structures, or Material; Estimating Needed Characteristics; Processing Information; Evaluating Information against Standards; Analyzing Data or Information; Updating and Using Job-Relevant Knowledge; Developing Objectives and Strategies; Controlling Machines and Processes; Operating Vehicles or Equipment; Drafting and Specifying Technical Devices, etc.; Implementing Ideas, Programs, etc.; Documenting/Recording Information; Interpreting Meaning of Information to Others; Communicating with Other Workers; Communicating with Persons Outside Organization; Guiding, Directing and Motivating Subordinates; Provide Consultation and Advice to Others
Job Characteristics: Take a Position Opposed to Others; Responsible for Others' Health and Safety; Responsibility for Outcomes and Results; Deal with Unpleasant or Angry People; Contaminants; Radiation; Hazardous Conditions; Climbing Ladders, Scaffolds, Poles, etc.; Specialized Protective or Safety Attire
GOE Group/s: 02.01.01 Physical Sciences: Theoretical Research; 02.04.02 Laboratory Technology: Life Sciences
CIP Program/s: 150599 Environmental Control Technologists and Technicians, Other; 410301 Chemical Technologists and Technicians
Related DOT Job/s: 012.261-010 AIR ANALYST; 012.281-010 SMOKE TESTER; 022.261-018 CHEMIST, INSTRUMENTATION; 022.261-022 CHEMIST, WASTEWATER-TREATMENT PLANT; 022.281-014 CHEMIST, WATER PURIFICATION; 029.261-014 POLLUTION-CONTROL TECHNICIAN; 029.261-030 ; 029.361-018 LABORATORY ASSISTANT

24508A NUCLEAR EQUIPMENT OPERATION TECHNICIANS. OOH Title/s: Science Technicians

Operate equipment used for the release, control, and utilization of nuclear energy to assist scientists in laboratory and production activities. Sets control panel switches and activates equipment, such as nuclear reactor, particle accelerator, or gamma radiation equipment, according to specifications. Calculates equipment operating factors, such as radiation time, dosage, temperature, and pressure, using standard formulas and conversion tables. Monitors instruments, gauges, and recording devices in control room during operation of equipment, under direction of nuclear experimenter. Adjusts controls of equipment to control particle beam, chain reaction, or radiation, according to specifications. Reviews experiment schedule to determine specifications, such as subatomic particle parameters, radiation time, dosage, and gamma intensity. Installs instrumentation leads in reactor core to measure operating temperature and pressure according to mockups, blueprints, and diagrams. Positions fuel elements in reactor or environmental chamber, according to specified configuration, using slave manipulators or extension tools. Controls laboratory compounding equipment enclosed in protective hot cell to prepare radioisotopes and other radioactive materials. Transfers experimental materials to and from specified containers and to tube, chamber, or tunnel, using slave manipulators or extension tools. Sets up and operates machines to saw fuel elements to size or to cut and polish test pieces, following blueprints and other specifications. Withdraws radioactive sample for

analysis, fills container with prescribed quantity of material for shipment, or removes spent fuel elements. Tests physical, chemical, or metallurgical properties of experimental materials, according to standardized procedures, using test equipment and measuring instruments. Communicates with maintenance personnel to ensure readiness of support systems and to warn of radiation hazards. Writes summary of activities or records experiment data in log for further analysis by engineers, scientists, or customers, or for future reference. Disassembles, cleans, and decontaminates hot cells and reactor parts during maintenance shutdown, using slave manipulators, crane, and hand tools. Modifies, devises, and maintains equipment used in operations.
Yearly Earnings: $26,728
Education: Associate degree
Knowledge: Production and Processing; Engineering and Technology; Design; Mathematics; Physics; Chemistry; Public Safety and Security
Abilities: Problem Sensitivity; Information Ordering; Mathematical Reasoning; Number Facility; Memorization; Perceptual Speed; Time Sharing; Arm-Hand Steadiness; Manual Dexterity; Finger Dexterity; Control Precision; Response Orientation; Rate Control; Reaction Time
Skills: Mathematics; Science; Installation; Testing; Operation Monitoring; Operation and Control; Equipment Maintenance; Troubleshooting
General Work Activities: Identifying Objects, Actions, and Events; Inspecting Equipment, Structures, or Material; Evaluating Information against Standards; Updating and Using Job-Relevant Knowledge; Controlling Machines and Processes; Implementing Ideas, Programs, etc.; Repairing and Maintaining Mechanical Equipment; Documenting/Recording Information
Job Characteristics: Responsible for Others' Health and Safety; Contaminants; Radiation; Hazardous Conditions; Hazardous Equipment; Common Protective or Safety Attire; Specialized Protective or Safety Attire; Consequence of Error; Degree of Automation; Importance of Being Exact or Accurate; Importance of Being Sure All is Done; Importance of Being Aware of New Events; Pace Determined by Speed of Equipment
GOE Group/s: 02.04.01 Laboratory Technology: Physical Sciences
CIP Program/s: 410204 Industrial Radiologic Technologists and Technicians; 410299 Nuclear and Industrial Radiologic Technologists and Technicians, Other
Related DOT Job/s: 015.362-010 ACCELERATOR OPERATOR; 015.362-014 GAMMA-FACILITIES OPERATOR; 015.362-018 HOT-CELL TECHNICIAN; 015.362-022 RADIOISOTOPE-PRODUCTION OPERATOR; 015.362-026 REACTOR OPERATOR, TEST-AND-RESEARCH

24508B NUCLEAR MONITORING TECHNICIANS.

OOH Title/s: Science Technicians

Collect and test samples to monitor results of nuclear experiments and contamination of humans, facilities, and environment. Measures intensity and identifies type of radiation in work areas, equipment, and materials, using radiation detectors and other instruments. Collects samples of air, water, gases, and solids to determine radioactivity levels of contamination. Assists in setting up equipment that automatically detects area radiation deviations, and tests detection equipment to ensure accuracy. Calculates safe radiation exposure time for personnel, using plant contamination readings and prescribed safe levels of radiation. Observes projected photographs to locate particle tracks and events, and compiles lists of events from particle detectors. Scans photographic emulsions exposed to direct radiation to compute track properties from standard formulas, using microscope with scales and protractors. Monitors personnel for length and intensity of exposure to radiation for health and safety purposes. Calibrates and maintains chemical instrumentation sensing elements and sampling system equipment, using calibration instruments and hand tools. Informs supervisors to take action when individual exposures or area radiation levels approach maximum permissible limits. Prepares reports on contamination tests, material and equipment decontaminated, and methods used in decontamination process. Confers with scientist directing project to determine significant events to watch for during test. Instructs personnel in radiation safety procedures, and demonstrates use of protective clothing and equipment. Determines or recommends radioactive decontamination procedures, according to size and nature of equipment and degree of contamination. Weighs and mixes decontamination chemical solutions in tank, and immerses objects in solution for specified time, using hoist. Enters data into computer to record characteristics of nuclear events and locating coordinates of particles. Decontaminates objects by cleaning with soap or solvents or by abrading, using wire brush, buffing wheel, or sandblasting machine. Places radioactive waste, such as sweepings and broken sample bottles, into containers for disposal.
Yearly Earnings: $26,728
Education: Associate degree
Knowledge: Computers and Electronics; Engineering and Technology; Mathematics; Physics; Chemistry; Biology; Medicine and Dentistry; Education and Training; English Language; Public Safety and Security; Communications and Media
Abilities: Oral Comprehension; Written Comprehension; Oral Expression; Problem Sensitivity; Deductive Reasoning; Inductive Reasoning; Information Ordering; Category Flexibility; Mathematical Reasoning; Number Facility; Speed of Closure; Selective Attention; Manual Dexterity; Finger Dexterity; Control Precision; Dynamic Flexibility; Gross Body Equilibrium; Near Vision; Speech Clarity
Skills: Speaking; Mathematics; Science; Information Gathering; Installation; Testing; Operation Monitoring; Operation and Control
General Work Activities: Monitoring Processes, Material, or Surroundings; Identifying Objects, Actions, and Events; Inspecting Equipment, Structures, or Material; Estimating Needed Characteristics; Judging Qualities of Things, Services, People; Processing Information; Evaluating Information against Standards; Analyzing Data or Information; Making Decisions and Solving Problems; Updating and Using Job-Relevant Knowledge; Controlling Machines and Processes; Operating Vehicles or Equipment; Implementing Ideas, Programs, etc.; Documenting/Recording Information; Interpreting Meaning of Information to Others; Communicating with Other Workers; Teaching Others
Job Characteristics: Coordinate or Lead Others; Responsible for Others' Health and Safety; Contaminants; Radiation; Hazardous Conditions; Hazardous Equipment; Climbing Ladders, Scaffolds, Poles, etc.; Common Protective or Safety Attire; Specialized Protective or Safety Attire; Consequence of Error; Degree of Automation; Importance of Being Exact or Accurate; Importance of Being Sure All is Done; Importance of Being Aware of New Events
GOE Group/s: 02.04.01 Laboratory Technology: Physical Sciences; 05.03.08 Engineering Technology: Environmental Control; 11.10.03 Regulations Enforcement: Health and Safety
CIP Program/s: 410205 Nuclear/Nuclear Power Technologists and Technicians; 410299 Nuclear and Industrial Radiologic Technologists and Technicians, Other; 512205 Health Physics/Radiologic Health
Related DOT Job/s: 015.261-010 CHEMICAL-RADIATION TECHNICIAN; 015.384-010 SCANNER; 199.167-010 RADIATION MONITOR; 199.384-010 DECONTAMINATOR

24511B GEOLOGICAL DATA TECHNICIANS.

OOH Title/s: Science Technicians; Engineering Technicians

Measure, record, and evaluate geological data, such as core samples and cuttings, used in prospecting for oil or gas. Measures geological characteristics used in prospecting for oil or gas, using measuring instruments. Records readings to obtain data used in pros-

pecting for oil or gas. Evaluates and interprets core samples and cuttings, and other geological data used in prospecting for oil or gas. Operates and adjusts equipment and apparatus to obtain geological data. Reads and studies reports to compile information and data for geological and geophysical prospecting. Sets up, or directs set-up, of instruments used to collect geological data. Collects samples and cuttings, using equipment and hand tools. Interviews individuals and researches public databases to obtain information Assembles, maintains, and distributes information for library or record system. Plans and directs activities of workers who operate equipment to collect data, or operates equipment. Develops and prints photographic recordings of information, using equipment. Diagnoses and repairs malfunctioning instruments and equipment, using manufacturers' manuals and hand tools. Develops and designs packing materials and handling procedures for shipping of objects. Prepares and attaches packing instructions to shipping container.
Yearly Earnings: $26,728
Education: Associate degree
Knowledge: Administration and Management; Clerical; Production and Processing; Engineering and Technology; Physics
Abilities: Written Comprehension; Fluency of Ideas; Deductive Reasoning; Information Ordering; Mathematical Reasoning; Number Facility; Speed of Closure; Flexibility of Closure; Time Sharing; Control Precision; Gross Body Equilibrium; Far Vision; Visual Color Discrimination; Speech Clarity
Skills: Reading Comprehension; Science; Information Gathering; Information Organization; Programming
General Work Activities: Estimating Needed Characteristics; Analyzing Data or Information; Updating and Using Job-Relevant Knowledge; Repairing and Maintaining Mechanical Equipment; Coordinating Work and Activities of Others
Job Characteristics: Responsibility for Outcomes and Results; Extremely Bright or Inadequate Lighting
GOE Group/s: 02.04.01 Laboratory Technology: Physical Sciences; 05.03.04 Engineering Technology: Petroleum
CIP Program/s: 150903 Petroleum Technologists and Technicians
Related DOT Job/s: 010.161-018 OBSERVER, SEISMIC PROSPECTING; 010.261-014 OBSERVER, ELECTRICAL PROSPECTING; 010.261-018 OBSERVER, GRAVITY PROSPECTING; 010.261-022 SURVEYOR, OIL-WELL DIRECTIONAL; 010.267-010 SCOUT; 024.267-010 GEOLOGICAL AIDE; 194.382-010 SECTION-PLOTTER OPERATOR; 930.167-010 TECHNICAL OPERATOR

24511E GEOLOGICAL SAMPLE TEST TECHNICIANS. OOH Title/s: Science Technicians; Engineering Technicians

Test and analyze geological samples, crude oil, or petroleum products to detect presence of petroleum, gas, or mineral deposits indicating potential for exploration and production, or to determine physical and chemical properties to ensure that products meet quality standards. Tests samples for content and characteristics, using laboratory apparatus and testing equipment. Analyzes samples to determine presence, quantity, and quality of products, such as oil or gases. Records testing and operational data for review and further analysis. Collects solid and fluid samples from oil or gas bearing formations for analysis. Assembles and disassembles testing, measuring, and mechanical equipment and devices. Adjusts and repairs testing, electrical, and mechanical equipment and devices. Inspects engines for wear and defective parts, using equipment and measuring devices. Supervises and coordinates activities of workers, including initiating and recommending personnel actions.
Yearly Earnings: $26,728
Education: Associate degree
Knowledge: Personnel and Human Resources; Mechanical; Physics; Chemistry
Abilities: Inductive Reasoning; Information Ordering; Mathematical Reasoning; Number Facility; Flexibility of Closure; Wrist-Finger Speed; Visual Color Discrimination
Skills: Science; Programming; Testing; Equipment Maintenance; Management of Personnel Resources
General Work Activities: Analyzing Data or Information; Repairing and Maintaining Mechanical Equipment; Repairing and Maintaining Electrical Equipment; Staffing Organizational Units
Job Characteristics: Supervise, Coach, Train Others; Coordinate or Lead Others; Responsibility for Outcomes and Results; Extremely Bright or Inadequate Lighting; Radiation; Hazardous Conditions; Walking or Running; Pace Determined by Speed of Equipment
GOE Group/s: 02.04.01 Laboratory Technology: Physical Sciences; 05.03.07 Engineering Technology: Mechanical
CIP Program/s: 150903 Petroleum Technologists and Technicians; 410301 Chemical Technologists and Technicians; 410399 Physical Science Technologists and Technicians, Other
Related DOT Job/s: 010.131-010 WELL-LOGGING CAPTAIN, MUD ANALYSIS; 010.261-010 FIELD ENGINEER, SPECIALIST; 010.261-026 TEST-ENGINE EVALUATOR; 010.281-022 WELL-LOGGING OPERATOR, MUD ANALYSIS; 024.381-010 LABORATORY ASSISTANT; 029.261-018 TEST-ENGINE OPERATOR; 029.261-022 TESTER

24599A METEOROLOGICAL TECHNICIANS. OOH Title/s: Science Technicians

Analyze and record oceanographic and meteorological data to forecast changes in weather or sea conditions, and to determine trends in movement and utilization of water. Analyzes oceanographic and meteorological data to forecast changes in water, weather, and sea conditions. Observes general weather conditions and visibility, and reads test or measuring instruments to collect meteorological and oceanographic data. Prepares maps, charts, graphs, and technical reports describing surface weather, upper air, and sea conditions. Recommends or positions equipment and instruments used to test, manipulate, or adjust for environmental conditions. Prepares warnings or briefings regarding current or predicted environmental conditions, using teletype machine. Pilots and controls submersible craft to conduct research, salvage, or rescue operations, in accordance with plans. Plans and develops operational procedures or techniques to conduct underwater research. Installs, maintains, and conducts operational tests of watercraft, equipment, and facilities.
Yearly Earnings: $26,728
Education: Associate degree
Knowledge: Computers and Electronics; Design; Mathematics; Physics; Geography; English Language; Communications and Media; Transportation
Abilities: Written Comprehension; Written Expression; Problem Sensitivity; Deductive Reasoning; Inductive Reasoning; Information Ordering; Category Flexibility; Number Facility; Memorization; Speed of Closure; Flexibility of Closure; Perceptual Speed; Spatial Orientation; Selective Attention; Time Sharing; Response Orientation; Rate Control; Wrist-Finger Speed; Gross Body Equilibrium; Near Vision; Far Vision; Night Vision; Depth Perception; Glare Sensitivity
Skills: Mathematics; Science; Information Gathering; Installation; Testing; Operation and Control
General Work Activities: Getting Information Needed to Do the Job; Monitoring Processes, Material, or Surroundings; Identifying Objects, Actions, and Events; Estimating Needed Characteristics; Evaluating Information against Standards; Analyzing Data or Information; Updating and Using Job-Relevant Knowledge; Interacting with Computers; Documenting/Recording Information; Interpreting Meaning of Information to Others; Provide Consultation and Advice to Others

Job Characteristics: Extremely Bright or Inadequate Lighting; Sitting; Climbing Ladders, Scaffolds, Poles, etc.; Degree of Automation; Importance of Being Aware of New Events
GOE Group/s: 02.04.01 Laboratory Technology: Physical Sciences; 05.04.02 Air and Water Vehicle Operation: Water
CIP Program/s: 030101 Natural Resources Conservation, General; 410399 Physical Science Technologists and Technicians, Other; 490304 Diver (Professional)
Related DOT Job/s: 025.264-010 HYDROGRAPHER; 025.267-010 OCEANOGRAPHER, ASSISTANT; 025.267-014 WEATHER OBSERVER; 029.383-010 PILOT, SUBMERSIBLE

24599B CRIMINALISTS AND BALLISTICS EXPERTS. OOH Title/s: Science Technicians

Examine, identify, classify, and analyze evidence related to criminology. Examines, tests, and analyzes tissue samples, chemical substances, physical materials, and ballistics evidence, using recording, measuring, and testing equipment. Interprets laboratory findings and test results to identify and classify substances, materials, and other evidence collected at crime scene. Collects and preserves criminal evidence used to solve cases. Confers with ballistics, fingerprinting, handwriting, documents, electronics, medical, chemical, or metallurgical experts concerning evidence and its interpretation. Reconstructs crime scene to determine relationships among pieces of evidence. Prepares reports or presentations of findings, investigative methods, or laboratory techniques. Testifies as expert witness on evidence or laboratory techniques in trials or hearings.
Yearly Earnings: $26,728
Education: Associate degree
Knowledge: Computers and Electronics; Chemistry; Biology; Medicine and Dentistry; English Language; Public Safety and Security; Law, Government, and Jurisprudence
Abilities: Oral Expression; Written Expression; Fluency of Ideas; Originality; Inductive Reasoning; Information Ordering; Category Flexibility; Number Facility; Memorization; Speed of Closure; Flexibility of Closure; Spatial Orientation; Visualization; Near Vision; Visual Color Discrimination; Night Vision; Peripheral Vision; Depth Perception; Glare Sensitivity; Speech Clarity
Skills: Speaking; Mathematics; Science; Critical Thinking; Information Gathering; Information Organization; Synthesis/Reorganization; Equipment Selection; Programming; Testing; Visioning; Systems Perception
General Work Activities: Getting Information Needed to Do the Job; Monitoring Processes, Material, or Surroundings; Judging Qualities of Things, Services, People; Analyzing Data or Information; Making Decisions and Solving Problems; Documenting/Recording Information; Interpreting Meaning of Information to Others; Communicating with Other Workers; Communicating with Persons Outside Organization
Job Characteristics: Take a Position Opposed to Others; Frequency in Conflict Situations; Diseases/Infections; Frustrating Circumstances; Importance of Being Exact or Accurate; Importance of Being Sure All is Done
GOE Group/s: 02.04.01 Laboratory Technology: Physical Sciences
CIP Program/s: 430106 Forensic Tech./Technician; 450401 Criminology
Related DOT Job/s: 029.261-026 CRIMINALIST; 199.267-010 BALLISTICS EXPERT, FORENSIC

24599C SCIENTIFIC HELPERS. OOH Title/s: Science Technicians

Assist supervising scientists to research problems and conduct experiments and tests. Prepares and tests mineralogical or geophysical samples for analysis or examination. Compiles and records mineralogical or geophysical sample data specifications. Joins scientists on mineralogical or geophysical expeditions to collect samples. Packs and labels mineralogical or geophysical specimens.
Yearly Earnings: $26,728
Education: Associate degree
Knowledge: Production and Processing; Physics; Geography; History and Archeology
Abilities: Information Ordering; Category Flexibility; Memorization; Flexibility of Closure; Manual Dexterity; Stamina; Gross Body Coordination; Gross Body Equilibrium; Visual Color Discrimination
Skills: Science; Testing
General Work Activities: Evaluating Information against Standards; Updating and Using Job-Relevant Knowledge
Job Characteristics: Extremely Bright or Inadequate Lighting; Cramped Work Space, Awkward Positions
GOE Group/s: 02.04.01 Laboratory Technology: Physical Sciences
CIP Program/s: 030404 Forest Products Technologists and Technicians; 150702 Quality Control Technologists and Technicians; 150903 Petroleum Technologists and Technicians; 410101 Biological Technologists and Technicians; 410204 Industrial Radiologic Technologists and Technicians; 410205 Nuclear/Nuclear Power Technologists and Technicians; 410301 Chemical Technologists and Technicians; 410399 Physical Science Technologists and Technicians, Other
Related DOT Job/s: 024.364-010 PALEONTOLOGICAL HELPER; 049.364-014 VECTOR CONTROL ASSISTANT; 199.364-014 SCIENTIFIC HELPER; 850.684-010 EXCAVATOR

Computer Scientists

25102 SYSTEMS ANALYSTS, ELECTRONIC DATA PROCESSING. OOH Title/s: Computer Scientists and Systems Analysts

Analyze business, scientific, and technical problems for application to electronic data processing systems. Exclude persons working primarily as engineers, mathematicians, or scientists. Analyzes, plans, and tests computer programs, using programming and system techniques. Consults with staff and users to identify operating procedure problems. Formulates and reviews plans outlining steps required to develop programs to meet staff and user requirements. Devises flowcharts and diagrams to illustrate steps and to describe logical operational steps of program. Writes documentation to describe and develop installation and operating procedures of programs. Coordinates installation of computer programs and operating systems, and tests, maintains, and monitors computer system. Reads manuals, periodicals, and technical reports to learn how to develop programs to meet staff and user requirements. Sets up computer test to find and correct program or system errors. Writes and revises quality standards and test procedures, and modifies existing procedures for program and system design for evaluation. Reviews and analyzes computer printouts and performance indications to locate code problems. Modifies program to correct errors by correcting computer codes. Enters instructions into computer to test program or system for conformance to standards. Assists staff and users to solve computer-related problems, such as malfunctions and program problems. Trains staff and users to use computer system and its programs.
Yearly Earnings: $43,940
Education: Bachelor's degree
Knowledge: Clerical; Customer and Personal Service; Computers and Electronics; Mathematics; Education and Training; English Language; Telecommunications; Communications and Media
Abilities: Oral Comprehension; Written Comprehension; Oral Expression; Written Expression; Fluency of Ideas; Originality; Problem Sensitivity; Deductive Reasoning; Inductive Reasoning; Information

Ordering; Category Flexibility; Mathematical Reasoning; Number Facility; Memorization; Speed of Closure; Flexibility of Closure; Perceptual Speed; Visualization; Selective Attention; Wrist-Finger Speed; Near Vision; Visual Color Discrimination; Speech Recognition; Speech Clarity
Skills: Reading Comprehension; Active Listening; Writing; Speaking; Mathematics; Science; Critical Thinking; Active Learning; Learning Strategies; Monitoring; Instructing; Service Orientation; Problem Identification; Information Gathering; Information Organization; Synthesis/Reorganization; Idea Generation; Idea Evaluation; Implementation Planning; Solution Appraisal; Operations Analysis; Technology Design; Equipment Selection; Installation; Programming; Testing; Operation Monitoring; Operation and Control; Product Inspection; Equipment Maintenance; Troubleshooting; Visioning; Systems Perception; Identifying Downstream Consequences; Identification of Key Causes; Systems Evaluation; Time Management; Management of Material Resources
General Work Activities: Getting Information Needed to Do the Job; Monitoring Processes, Material, or Surroundings; Inspecting Equipment, Structures, or Material; Estimating Needed Characteristics; Processing Information; Evaluating Information against Standards; Analyzing Data or Information; Making Decisions and Solving Problems; Thinking Creatively; Updating and Using Job-Relevant Knowledge; Developing Objectives and Strategies; Organizing, Planning, and Prioritizing; Operating Vehicles or Equipment; Drafting and Specifying Technical Devices, etc.; Implementing Ideas, Programs, etc.; Repairing and Maintaining Electrical Equipment; Documenting/Recording Information; Interpreting Meaning of Information to Others; Communicating with Other Workers; Communicating with Persons Outside Organization; Teaching Others; Coaching and Developing Others; Provide Consultation and Advice to Others
Job Characteristics: Supervise, Coach, Train Others; Sitting; Degree of Automation; Importance of Being Exact or Accurate; Importance of Being Sure All is Done
GOE Group/s: 11.01.01 Mathematics and Statistics: Data Processing Design
CIP Program/s: 110101 Computer and Information Sciences, General; 110201 Computer Programming; 110501 Computer Systems Analysis; 521201 Management Information Systems and Business Data Processing; 521202 Business Computer Programming/Programmer; 521203 Business Systems Analysis and Design
Related DOT Job/s: 030.162-014 PROGRAMMER-ANALYST; 030.162-022 SYSTEMS PROGRAMMER; 030.167-014 SYSTEMS ANALYST; 033.262-010 QUALITY ASSURANCE ANALYST

25103A DATABASE ADMINISTRATORS. OOH Title/s: Computer Scientists and Systems Analysts

Coordinate changes to computer databases; test and implement the database, applying knowledge of database management systems. May plan, coordinate, and implement security measures to safeguard computer databases. Writes logical and physical database descriptions, including location, space, access method, and security. Establishes and calculates optimum values for database parameters, using manuals and calculator. Develops data model describing data elements and how they are used, following procedures using pen, template, or computer software. Codes database descriptions and specifies identifiers of database to management system, or directs others in coding descriptions. Tests, corrects errors, and modifies changes to programs or to database. Reviews project request describing database user needs, estimating time and cost required to accomplish project. Selects and enters codes to monitor database performance and to create production database. Directs programmers and analysts to make changes to database management system. Reviews workflow charts developed by programmer analyst to understand tasks computer will perform, such as updating records. Reviews procedures in database management system manuals for making changes to database. Confers with coworkers to determine scope and limitations of project. Revises company definition of data as defined in data dictionary. Specifies user and user access levels for each segment of database. Trains users and answers questions.
Yearly Earnings: $43,472
Education: Bachelor's degree
Knowledge: Administration and Management; Computers and Electronics; Mathematics; Education and Training
Abilities: Written Comprehension; Written Expression; Fluency of Ideas; Originality; Problem Sensitivity; Deductive Reasoning; Inductive Reasoning; Information Ordering; Category Flexibility; Mathematical Reasoning; Number Facility; Memorization; Speed of Closure; Flexibility of Closure; Perceptual Speed; Time Sharing; Wrist-Finger Speed; Near Vision
Skills: Mathematics; Critical Thinking; Monitoring; Instructing; Information Organization; Synthesis/Reorganization; Idea Generation; Solution Appraisal; Operations Analysis; Technology Design; Installation; Programming; Testing; Troubleshooting; Visioning; Systems Perception; Identifying Downstream Consequences; Identification of Key Causes; Systems Evaluation; Management of Personnel Resources
General Work Activities: Getting Information Needed to Do the Job; Identifying Objects, Actions, and Events; Estimating Needed Characteristics; Evaluating Information against Standards; Analyzing Data or Information; Making Decisions and Solving Problems; Thinking Creatively; Updating and Using Job-Relevant Knowledge; Operating Vehicles or Equipment; Implementing Ideas, Programs, etc.; Communicating with Other Workers; Teaching Others
Job Characteristics: Supervise, Coach, Train Others; Take a Position Opposed to Others; Coordinate or Lead Others; Responsibility for Outcomes and Results; Sitting; Frustrating Circumstances; Degree of Automation; Importance of Being Sure All is Done
GOE Group/s: 11.01.01 Mathematics and Statistics: Data Processing Design
CIP Program/s: 110101 Computer and Information Sciences, General; 110201 Computer Programming; 110401 Information Sciences and Systems; 521201 Management Information Systems and Business Data Processing; 521202 Business Computer Programming/Programmer; 521203 Business Systems Analysis and Design
Related DOT Job/s: 039.162-010 DATA BASE ADMINISTRATOR; 039.162-014 DATA BASE DESIGN ANALYST; 109.067-010 INFORMATION SCIENTIST

25103B GEOGRAPHIC INFORMATION SYSTEM SPECIALISTS. OOH Title/s: Social Scientists

Design and coordinate development of integrated geographical information system database of spatial and nonspatial data; develop analyses and presentation of this data, applying knowledge of geographic information system. Designs database and coordinates physical changes to database, applying additional knowledge of spatial feature representations. Chooses and applies analysis procedures for spatial and nonspatial data. Determines how to analyze spatial relationships, including adjacency, containment, and proximity. Decides effective presentation of information, and selects cartographic and additional elements. Determines information to be queried, such as location, characteristics of location, trend, pattern, routing, and modeling various series of events. Meets with users to develop system or project requirements. Creates maps and graphs, using computer and geographic information system software and related equipment. Reviews existing and incoming data for currency, accuracy, usefulness, quality, and documentation. Selects or verifies designations of cartographic symbols. Presents information to users and answers questions.

Oversees entry of data into database, including applications, keyboard entry, manual digitizing, scanning, and automatic conversion. Recommends procedures to increase data accessibility and ease of use. Discusses problems in development of transportation planning and modeling, marketing and demographic mapping, or assessment of geologic and environmental factors.
Yearly Earnings: $43,940
Education: Bachelor's degree
Knowledge: Administration and Management; Sales and Marketing; Computers and Electronics; Design; Mathematics; Physics; Sociology and Anthropology; Geography; English Language; Transportation
Abilities: Written Expression; Fluency of Ideas; Originality; Inductive Reasoning; Information Ordering; Category Flexibility; Mathematical Reasoning; Number Facility; Perceptual Speed; Spatial Orientation; Visualization; Selective Attention; Speech Clarity
Skills: Active Listening; Speaking; Mathematics; Critical Thinking; Active Learning; Monitoring; Information Organization; Synthesis/Reorganization; Idea Generation; Implementation Planning; Operations Analysis; Technology Design; Installation; Programming; Troubleshooting; Systems Perception; Identification of Key Causes; Systems Evaluation
General Work Activities: Getting Information Needed to Do the Job; Processing Information; Evaluating Information against Standards; Analyzing Data or Information; Making Decisions and Solving Problems; Operating Vehicles or Equipment; Drafting and Specifying Technical Devices, etc.; Implementing Ideas, Programs, etc.; Documenting/Recording Information; Interpreting Meaning of Information to Others; Communicating with Other Workers; Communicating with Persons Outside Organization
Job Characteristics: Responsibility for Outcomes and Results; Degree of Automation; Importance of Being Exact or Accurate

25104 COMPUTER SUPPORT SPECIALISTS. OOH

Title/s: Computer Programmers; Adult Education Teachers

Provide technical assistance and training to system users. Investigate and resolve computer software and hardware problems of users. Answer clients' inquiries in person and via telephone concerning the use of computer hardware and software, including printing, word processing, programming languages, electronic mail, and operating systems. Installs and performs minor repairs to hardware, software, and peripheral equipment, following design or installation specifications. Confers with staff, users, and management to determine requirements for new systems or modifications. Reads technical manuals, confers with users, and conducts computer diagnostics to determine nature of problems and provide technical assistance. Develops training materials and procedures, and conducts training programs. Enters commands and observes system functioning to verify correct operations and detect errors. Tests and monitors software, hardware, and peripheral equipment to evaluate use, effectiveness, and adequacy of product for user. Prepares evaluations of software and hardware, and submits recommendations to management for review. Refers major hardware or software problems or defective products to vendors or technicians for service. Maintains record of daily data communication transactions, problems and remedial action taken, and installation activities. Conducts office automation feasibility studies, including workflow analysis, space design, and cost comparison analysis. Reads trade magazines and technical manuals, and attends conferences and seminars to maintain knowledge of hardware and software. Supervises and coordinates workers engaged in problem-solving, monitoring, and installing data communication equipment and software. Inspects equipment and reads order sheets to prepare for delivery to users.
Yearly Earnings: $38,220
Education: Bachelor's degree
Knowledge: Administration and Management; Economics and Accounting; Sales and Marketing; Customer and Personal Service; Computers and Electronics; Mathematics; Education and Training; Telecommunications
Abilities: Written Comprehension; Oral Expression; Written Expression; Originality; Deductive Reasoning; Mathematical Reasoning; Number Facility; Speed of Closure; Visualization; Selective Attention; Time Sharing; Finger Dexterity; Near Vision; Visual Color Discrimination; Speech Recognition; Speech Clarity
Skills: Reading Comprehension; Active Listening; Writing; Speaking; Mathematics; Science; Critical Thinking; Active Learning; Learning Strategies; Monitoring; Social Perceptiveness; Coordination; Persuasion; Negotiation; Instructing; Service Orientation; Problem Identification; Information Gathering; Information Organization; Idea Generation; Idea Evaluation; Implementation Planning; Solution Appraisal; Operations Analysis; Technology Design; Equipment Selection; Installation; Programming; Testing; Troubleshooting; Visioning; Systems Perception; Identifying Downstream Consequences; Identification of Key Causes; Judgment and Decision Making; Systems Evaluation; Time Management; Management of Financial Resources; Management of Material Resources; Management of Personnel Resources
General Work Activities: Identifying Objects, Actions, and Events; Inspecting Equipment, Structures, or Material; Updating and Using Job-Relevant Knowledge; Operating Vehicles or Equipment; Drafting and Specifying Technical Devices, etc.; Repairing and Maintaining Electrical Equipment; Coordinating Work and Activities of Others; Teaching Others; Coaching and Developing Others; Provide Consultation and Advice to Others
Job Characteristics: Supervise, Coach, Train Others; Persuade Someone to a Course of Action; Provide a Service to Others; Take a Position Opposed to Others; Coordinate or Lead Others; Responsibility for Outcomes and Results; Sitting; Frustrating Circumstances; Degree of Automation
GOE Group/s: 05.05.05 Craft Technology: Electrical-Electronic Systems Installation and Repair; 11.01.01 Mathematics and Statistics: Data Processing Design
CIP Program/s: 110401 Information Sciences and Systems; 110701 Computer Science; 470101 Electrical and Electronics Equipment Installer and Repairer; 470104 Computer Installer and Repairer; 521201 Management Information Systems and Business Data Processing; 521203 Business Systems Analysis and Design; 521204 Business Systems Networking and Telecommunications
Related DOT Job/s: 031.132-010 SUPERVISOR, NETWORK CONTROL OPERATORS; 031.262-014 NETWORK CONTROL OPERATOR; 032.132-010 USER SUPPORT ANALYST SUPERVISOR; 032.262-010 USER SUPPORT ANALYST; 033.162-018 TECHNICAL SUPPORT SPECIALIST; 039.264-010 MICROCOMPUTER SUPPORT SPECIALIST

25105 COMPUTER PROGRAMMERS. OOH Title/s: Computer Programmers

Convert project specifications and statements of problems and procedures to detailed logical flowcharts for coding into computer language. Develop and write computer programs to store, locate, and retrieve specific documents, data, and information. Analyzes, reviews, and rewrites programs, using workflow chart and diagram, applying knowledge of computer capabilities, subject matter, and symbolic logic. Converts detailed logical flowchart to language processible by computer. Resolves symbolic formulations, prepares flowcharts and block diagrams, and encodes resultant equations for processing. Develops programs from workflow charts or diagrams, considering computer storage capacity, speed, and intended use of output data. Prepares or receives detailed workflow chart and diagram

to illustrate sequence of steps to describe input, output, and logical operation. Compiles and writes documentation of program development and subsequent revisions. Revises or directs revision of existing programs to increase operating efficiency or adapt to new requirements. Consults with managerial and engineering and technical personnel to clarify program intent, identify problems, and suggest changes. Enters program and test data into computer, using keyboard. Writes instructions to guide operating personnel during production runs. Observes computer monitor screen to interpret program operating codes. Prepares records and reports. Collaborates with computer manufacturers and other users to develop new programming methods. Assists computer operators or system analysts to resolve problems in running computer program. Assigns, coordinates, and reviews work of programming personnel. Trains subordinates in programming and program coding. Directs and coordinates activities of computer programmers working as part of project team.
Yearly Earnings: $38,220
Education: Bachelor's degree
Knowledge: Administration and Management; Clerical; Personnel and Human Resources; Computers and Electronics; Design; Mathematics; Education and Training; English Language; Communications and Media
Abilities: Oral Comprehension; Written Comprehension; Oral Expression; Written Expression; Fluency of Ideas; Originality; Problem Sensitivity; Deductive Reasoning; Inductive Reasoning; Information Ordering; Category Flexibility; Mathematical Reasoning; Number Facility; Memorization; Speed of Closure; Flexibility of Closure; Perceptual Speed; Visualization; Selective Attention; Finger Dexterity; Wrist-Finger Speed; Near Vision
Skills: Reading Comprehension; Active Listening; Writing; Speaking; Mathematics; Critical Thinking; Active Learning; Learning Strategies; Monitoring; Coordination; Instructing; Problem Identification; Information Organization; Synthesis/Reorganization; Idea Generation; Idea Evaluation; Implementation Planning; Solution Appraisal; Operations Analysis; Technology Design; Equipment Selection; Programming; Testing; Product Inspection; Troubleshooting; Visioning; Systems Perception; Identifying Downstream Consequences; Identification of Key Causes; Systems Evaluation; Time Management; Management of Personnel Resources
General Work Activities: Monitoring Processes, Material, or Surroundings; Processing Information; Evaluating Information against Standards; Analyzing Data or Information; Making Decisions and Solving Problems; Thinking Creatively; Updating and Using Job-Relevant Knowledge; Developing Objectives and Strategies; Scheduling Work and Activities; Organizing, Planning, and Prioritizing; Operating Vehicles or Equipment; Drafting and Specifying Technical Devices, etc.; Implementing Ideas, Programs, etc.; Documenting/Recording Information; Interpreting Meaning of Information to Others; Communicating with Other Workers; Resolving Conflicts, Negotiating with Others; Coordinating Work and Activities of Others; Developing and Building Teams; Teaching Others; Guiding, Directing and Motivating Subordinates; Coaching and Developing Others; Provide Consultation and Advice to Others; Performing Administrative Activities; Staffing Organizational Units
Job Characteristics: Supervise, Coach, Train Others; Coordinate or Lead Others; Responsibility for Outcomes and Results; Sitting; Frustrating Circumstances; Degree of Automation; Importance of Being Exact or Accurate; Importance of Being Sure All is Done
GOE Group/s: 11.01.01 Mathematics and Statistics: Data Processing Design
CIP Program/s: 110201 Computer Programming; 521201 Management Information Systems and Business Data Processing; 521202 Business Computer Programming/Programmer
Related DOT Job/s: 030.162-010 COMPUTER PROGRAMMER; 030.162-018 PROGRAMMER, ENGINEERING AND SCIENTIFIC; 030.167-010 CHIEF, COMPUTER PROGRAMMER

25111 PROGRAMMERS—NUMERICAL, TOOL, AND PROCESS CONTROL. OOH Title/s: Machinists and Tool Programmers

Develop numerical control tape programs to control machining or processing of parts by automatic machine tools, equipment, or systems. Prepares geometric layout from graphic displays, using computer-assisted drafting software or drafting instruments and graph paper. Writes instruction sheets, cutter lists, and machine instruction programs to guide set-up and encode numerical control tape. Analyzes drawings, specifications, printed circuit board pattern film, and design data to calculate dimensions, tool selection, machine speeds, and feed rates. Determines reference points, machine cutting paths, or hole locations, and computes angular and linear dimensions, radii, and curvatures. Compares encoded tape or computer printout with original program sheet to verify accuracy of instructions. Draws machine tool paths on pattern film, using colored markers and following guidelines for tool speed and efficiency. Revises numerical control machine tape programs to eliminate instruction errors and omissions. Enters computer commands to store or retrieve parts patterns, graphic displays, or programs to transfer data to other media. Aligns and secures pattern film on reference table of optical programmer, and observes enlarger scope view of printed circuit board. Moves reference table to align pattern film over circuit board holes with reference marks on enlarger scope. Depresses pedal or button of programmer to enter coordinates of each hole location into program memory. Loads and unloads disks or tapes, and observes operation of machine on trial run to test taped or programmed instructions. Reviews shop orders to determine job specifications and requirements. Sorts shop orders into groups to maximize materials utilization and minimize machine set-up.
Yearly Earnings: $33,540
Education: Work experience in a related occupation
Knowledge: Production and Processing; Computers and Electronics; Design; Mathematics; Foreign Language
Abilities: Deductive Reasoning; Information Ordering; Mathematical Reasoning; Number Facility; Speed of Closure; Near Vision
Skills: Mathematics; Information Organization; Synthesis/Reorganization; Operations Analysis; Technology Design; Equipment Selection; Installation; Programming; Testing; Operation Monitoring; Operation and Control; Product Inspection; Troubleshooting; Identifying Downstream Consequences
General Work Activities: Operating Vehicles or Equipment; Drafting and Specifying Technical Devices, etc.
Job Characteristics: Sitting; Frustrating Circumstances; Degree of Automation; Importance of Being Exact or Accurate; Pace Determined by Speed of Equipment
GOE Group/s: 05.01.06 Engineering: Work Planning and Utilization; 05.03.02 Engineering Technology: Drafting
CIP Program/s: 110201 Computer Programming; 110301 Data Processing Technologists and Technicians; 110501 Computer Systems Analysis; 480501 Machinist/Machine Technologist; 521201 Management Information Systems and Business Data Processing; 521202 Business Computer Programming/Programmer
Related DOT Job/s: 007.167-018 TOOL PROGRAMMER, NUMERICAL CONTROL; 007.362-010 NESTING OPERATOR, NUMERICAL CONTROL; 609.262-010 TOOL PROGRAMMER, NUMERICAL CONTROL

25199A DATA COMMUNICATIONS ANALYSTS. OOH Title/s: Systems Analysts

Research, test, evaluate, and recommend data communications hardware and software. Analyzes test data and recommends hard-

ware or software for purchase. Identifies areas of operation which need upgraded equipment, such as modems, fiber optic cables, and telephone wires. Tests and evaluates hardware and software to determine efficiency, reliability, and compatibility with existing system. Reads technical manuals and brochures to determine equipment which meets establishment requirements. Monitors system performance. Conducts survey to determine user needs. Develops and writes procedures for installation, use, and solving problems of communications hardware and software. Visits vendors to learn about available products or services. Assists users to identify and solve data communication problems. Trains users in use of equipment.
Yearly Earnings: $43,940
Education: Bachelor's degree
Knowledge: Sales and Marketing; Customer and Personal Service; Computers and Electronics; Mathematics; Psychology; Education and Training; Telecommunications; Communications and Media
Abilities: Oral Comprehension; Written Comprehension; Oral Expression; Written Expression; Fluency of Ideas; Originality; Deductive Reasoning; Inductive Reasoning; Mathematical Reasoning; Number Facility; Selective Attention; Near Vision; Speech Clarity
Skills: Reading Comprehension; Active Listening; Writing; Speaking; Science; Critical Thinking; Active Learning; Learning Strategies; Monitoring; Persuasion; Negotiation; Instructing; Service Orientation; Problem Identification; Information Organization; Synthesis/Reorganization; Idea Generation; Idea Evaluation; Implementation Planning; Solution Appraisal; Operations Analysis; Technology Design; Equipment Selection; Installation; Programming; Testing; Troubleshooting; Visioning; Systems Perception; Identifying Downstream Consequences; Judgment and Decision Making; Systems Evaluation; Management of Financial Resources; Management of Material Resources
General Work Activities: Getting Information Needed to Do the Job; Monitoring Processes, Material, or Surroundings; Identifying Objects, Actions, and Events; Inspecting Equipment, Structures, or Material; Judging Qualities of Things, Services, People; Evaluating Information against Standards; Analyzing Data or Information; Updating and Using Job-Relevant Knowledge; Operating Vehicles or Equipment; Drafting and Specifying Technical Devices, etc.; Implementing Ideas, Programs, etc.; Repairing and Maintaining Electrical Equipment; Selling or Influencing Others; Teaching Others; Provide Consultation and Advice to Others
Job Characteristics: Supervise, Coach, Train Others; Radiation; Sitting; Keeping or Regaining Balance; Frustrating Circumstances; Degree of Automation
GOE Group/s: 11.01.01 Mathematics and Statistics: Data Processing Design
CIP Program/s: 110301 Data Processing Technologists and Technicians; 521201 Management Information Systems and Business Data Processing; 521204 Business Systems Networking and Telecommunications
Related DOT Job/s: 031.262-010 DATA COMMUNICATIONS ANALYST

Mathematical Scientists and Technicians

25302 OPERATIONS AND SYSTEMS RESEARCHERS AND ANALYSTS, EXCEPT COMPUTER. OOH Title/s: Operations Research Analysts

Conduct analyses of management and operational problems in terms of management information and concepts. Formulate mathematical or simulation models of the problem for solution by computer or other method. May develop and supply time and cost networks, such as program evaluation and review techniques. Analyzes problem in terms of management information, and conceptualizes and defines problem. Prepares model of problem in form of one or several equations that relate constants and variables, restrictions, alternatives, conflicting objectives, and their numerical parameters. Specifies manipulative or computational methods to be applied to model. Performs validation and testing of model to ensure adequacy, or determines need for reformulation. Evaluates implementation and effectiveness of research. Designs, conducts, and evaluates experimental operational models where insufficient data exists to formulate model. Develops and applies time and cost networks to plan and control large projects. Defines data requirements and gathers and validates information, applying judgment and statistical tests. Studies information and selects plan from competitive proposals that afford maximum probability of profit or effectiveness relating to cost or risk. Prepares for management reports defining problem, evaluation, and possible solution.
Yearly Earnings: $40,456
Education: Master's degree
Knowledge: Administration and Management; Clerical; Economics and Accounting; Sales and Marketing; Personnel and Human Resources; Production and Processing; Computers and Electronics; Mathematics; Communications and Media
Abilities: Oral Comprehension; Written Comprehension; Oral Expression; Written Expression; Fluency of Ideas; Deductive Reasoning; Mathematical Reasoning; Number Facility
Skills: Reading Comprehension; Active Listening; Writing; Speaking; Mathematics; Science; Critical Thinking; Active Learning; Learning Strategies; Monitoring; Coordination; Persuasion; Problem Identification; Information Gathering; Information Organization; Synthesis/Reorganization; Idea Generation; Idea Evaluation; Implementation Planning; Solution Appraisal; Operations Analysis; Programming; Visioning; Systems Perception; Identifying Downstream Consequences; Identification of Key Causes; Judgment and Decision Making; Systems Evaluation; Time Management; Management of Financial Resources
General Work Activities: Getting Information Needed to Do the Job; Monitoring Processes, Material, or Surroundings; Estimating Needed Characteristics; Judging Qualities of Things, Services, People; Processing Information; Evaluating Information against Standards; Analyzing Data or Information; Making Decisions and Solving Problems; Thinking Creatively; Updating and Using Job-Relevant Knowledge; Developing Objectives and Strategies; Organizing, Planning, and Prioritizing; Operating Vehicles or Equipment; Implementing Ideas, Programs, etc.; Interpreting Meaning of Information to Others; Communicating with Other Workers; Provide Consultation and Advice to Others
Job Characteristics: Deal with Physical, Aggressive People; Sitting; Consequence of Error; Importance of Being Exact or Accurate; Importance of Being Sure All is Done
GOE Group/s: 11.01.01 Mathematics and Statistics: Data Processing Design
CIP Program/s: 270301 Applied Mathematics, General; 270302 Operations Research; 521301 Management Science
Related DOT Job/s: 020.067-018 OPERATIONS-RESEARCH ANALYST

25312 STATISTICIANS. OOH Title/s: Statisticians

Plan surveys and collect, organize, interpret, summarize, and analyze numerical data, applying statistical theory and methods to provide usable information in scientific, business, economic, and other fields. Data derived from surveys may represent either complete enumeration or statistical samples. Include mathe-

matical statisticians who are engaged in the development of mathematical theory associated with the application of statistical techniques. Conducts research into mathematical theories and proofs that form basis of science of statistics. Plans data collection, and analyzes and interprets numerical data from experiments, studies, surveys, and other sources. Applies statistical methodology to provide information for scientific research and statistical analysis. Plans methods to collect information and develops questionnaire techniques according to survey design. Conducts surveys utilizing sampling techniques or complete enumeration bases. Analyzes and interprets statistics to point up significant differences in relationships among sources of information, and prepares conclusions and forecasts. Develops and tests experimental designs, sampling techniques, and analytical methods, and prepares recommendations concerning their use. Investigates, evaluates, and reports on applicability, efficiency, and accuracy of statistical methods used to obtain and evaluate data. Evaluates reliability of source information, adjusts and weighs raw data, and organizes results into form compatible with analysis by computers or other methods. Develops statistical methodology. Examines theories, such as those of probability and inference, to discover mathematical bases for new or improved methods of obtaining and evaluating numerical data. Presents numerical information by computer readouts, graphs, charts, tables, written reports, or other methods. Describes sources of information, and limitations on reliability and usability.

Yearly Earnings: $43,212

Education: Bachelor's degree

Knowledge: Administration and Management; Economics and Accounting; Computers and Electronics; Mathematics; English Language; Philosophy and Theology

Abilities: Written Comprehension; Written Expression; Fluency of Ideas; Originality; Deductive Reasoning; Inductive Reasoning; Information Ordering; Category Flexibility; Mathematical Reasoning; Number Facility; Memorization; Speed of Closure; Flexibility of Closure; Perceptual Speed; Finger Dexterity

Skills: Reading Comprehension; Active Listening; Writing; Speaking; Mathematics; Science; Critical Thinking; Active Learning; Learning Strategies; Monitoring; Problem Identification; Information Gathering; Information Organization; Synthesis/Reorganization; Idea Generation; Idea Evaluation; Implementation Planning; Solution Appraisal; Operations Analysis; Programming; Testing; Visioning; Systems Perception; Identifying Downstream Consequences; Identification of Key Causes; Judgment and Decision Making; Systems Evaluation

General Work Activities: Getting Information Needed to Do the Job; Monitoring Processes, Material, or Surroundings; Estimating Needed Characteristics; Judging Qualities of Things, Services, People; Processing Information; Evaluating Information against Standards; Analyzing Data or Information; Making Decisions and Solving Problems; Thinking Creatively; Updating and Using Job-Relevant Knowledge; Developing Objectives and Strategies; Organizing, Planning, and Prioritizing; Operating Vehicles or Equipment; Implementing Ideas, Programs, etc.; Documenting/Recording Information; Interpreting Meaning of Information to Others; Communicating with Other Workers; Communicating with Persons Outside Organization; Provide Consultation and Advice to Others

Job Characteristics: Take a Position Opposed to Others; Sitting; Importance of Being Exact or Accurate

GOE Group/s: 11.01.01 Mathematics and Statistics: Data Processing Design; 11.01.02 Mathematics and Statistics: Data Analysis

CIP Program/s: 260615 Biostatistics; 270101 Mathematics; 270301 Applied Mathematics, General; 270501 Mathematical Statistics; 450501 Demography/Population Studies; 450601 Economics, General; 450603 Econometrics and Quantitative Economics; 511303 Medical Biomathematics and Biometrics; 512204 Health and Medical Biostatistics; 521302 Business Statistics

Related DOT Job/s: 020.067-022 STATISTICIAN, MATHEMATICAL; 020.167-026 STATISTICIAN, APPLIED

25313 ACTUARIES. OOH Title/s: Actuaries

Apply knowledge of mathematics, probability, statistics, and principles of finance and business to problems in life, health, social, and casualty insurance, annuities, and pensions. Determines mortality, accident, sickness, disability, and retirement rates. Constructs probability tables regarding fire, natural disasters, and unemployment, based on analysis of statistical data and other pertinent information. Designs or reviews insurance and pension plans and calculates premiums. Determines equitable basis for distributing surplus earnings under participating insurance and annuity contracts in mutual companies. Ascertains premium rates required and cash reserves and liabilities necessary to ensure payment of future benefits.

Yearly Earnings: $43,212

Education: Bachelor's degree

Knowledge: Clerical; Economics and Accounting; Mathematics; Sociology and Anthropology; History and Archeology; Philosophy and Theology; Law, Government, and Jurisprudence

Abilities: Written Expression; Deductive Reasoning; Mathematical Reasoning; Number Facility; Speed of Closure; Flexibility of Closure

Skills: Reading Comprehension; Writing; Mathematics; Critical Thinking; Active Learning; Monitoring; Information Gathering; Information Organization; Synthesis/Reorganization; Idea Generation; Idea Evaluation; Implementation Planning; Solution Appraisal; Programming; Visioning; Systems Perception; Identifying Downstream Consequences; Identification of Key Causes; Judgment and Decision Making; Systems Evaluation; Management of Financial Resources

General Work Activities: Getting Information Needed to Do the Job; Monitoring Processes, Material, or Surroundings; Judging Qualities of Things, Services, People; Processing Information; Evaluating Information against Standards; Analyzing Data or Information; Making Decisions and Solving Problems; Developing Objectives and Strategies; Organizing, Planning, and Prioritizing; Operating Vehicles or Equipment; Implementing Ideas, Programs, etc.; Documenting/Recording Information; Interpreting Meaning of Information to Others; Performing Administrative Activities; Monitoring and Controlling Resources

Job Characteristics: Deal with Physical, Aggressive People; Sitting; Importance of Being Exact or Accurate

GOE Group/s: 11.01.02 Mathematics and Statistics: Data Analysis

CIP Program/s: 520801 Finance, General; 520802 Actuarial Science

Related DOT Job/s: 020.167-010 ACTUARY

25315 FINANCIAL ANALYSTS, STATISTICAL. OOH Title/s: Statisticians

Conduct statistical analyses of information affecting investment programs of public or private institutions and private individuals. Analyzes financial information to forecast business, industry, and economic conditions, for use in making investment decisions. Interprets data concerning price, yield, stability, and future trends in investment risks and economic influences pertinent to investments. Gathers information such as industry, regulatory, and economic information, company financial statements, financial periodicals, and newspapers. Recommends investment timing and buy-and-orders to company or to staff of investment establishment of advising clients. Draws charts and graphs to illustrate reports, using computer. Calls brokers and purchases investments for company, according to company policy.

Yearly Earnings: $43,212

Education: Bachelor's degree

Knowledge: Economics and Accounting; Sales and Marketing; Computers and Electronics; Mathematics; Foreign Language; History and Archeology; Law, Government, and Jurisprudence
Abilities: Oral Comprehension; Written Comprehension; Oral Expression; Written Expression; Fluency of Ideas; Originality; Deductive Reasoning; Inductive Reasoning; Category Flexibility; Mathematical Reasoning; Number Facility; Memorization; Speed of Closure; Selective Attention; Near Vision; Speech Recognition
Skills: Reading Comprehension; Writing; Speaking; Mathematics; Critical Thinking; Active Learning; Monitoring; Information Gathering; Information Organization; Synthesis/Reorganization; Idea Evaluation; Solution Appraisal; Programming; Visioning; Systems Perception; Identifying Downstream Consequences; Identification of Key Causes; Judgment and Decision Making; Systems Evaluation; Management of Financial Resources
General Work Activities: Getting Information Needed to Do the Job; Monitoring Processes, Material, or Surroundings; Identifying Objects, Actions, and Events; Estimating Needed Characteristics; Judging Qualities of Things, Services, People; Processing Information; Evaluating Information against Standards; Analyzing Data or Information; Making Decisions and Solving Problems; Updating and Using Job-Relevant Knowledge; Developing Objectives and Strategies; Operating Vehicles or Equipment; Documenting/Recording Information; Interpreting Meaning of Information to Others; Communicating with Other Workers; Communicating with Persons Outside Organization; Establishing and Maintaining Relationships; Selling or Influencing Others; Provide Consultation and Advice to Others; Performing Administrative Activities; Monitoring and Controlling Resources
Job Characteristics: Persuade Someone to a Course of Action; Take a Position Opposed to Others; Frequency in Conflict Situations; Sitting; Consequence of Error; Degree of Automation; Importance of Being Exact or Accurate; Importance of Being Sure All is Done; Importance of Being Aware of New Events
GOE Group/s: 11.06.03 Finance: Risk and Profit Analysis
CIP Program/s: 520801 Finance, General; 520804 Financial Planning; 520805 Insurance and Risk Management; 520807 Investments and Securities
Related DOT Job/s: 160.267-026 INVESTMENT ANALYST

25319A MATHEMATICIANS. OOH Title/s: Mathematicians

Conduct research in fundamental mathematics or in application of mathematical techniques to science, management, and other fields. Solve or direct solutions to problems in various fields by mathematical methods. Conducts research in fundamental mathematics and in application of mathematical techniques to science, management, and other fields. Conceives or directs ideas for application of mathematics to wide variety of fields, including science, engineering, military planning, electronic data processing, and management. Conducts research in such branches of mathematics as algebra, geometry, number theory, logic, and topology. Performs computations and applies methods of numerical analysis. Studies and tests hypotheses and alternative theories. Applies mathematics or mathematical methods of numerical analysis, and operates or directs operation of desk calculators and mechanical and other functional areas. Utilizes knowledge of such subjects or fields as physics, engineering, astronomy, biology, economics, business and industrial management, or cryptography. Operates or directs operation of desk calculators and mechanical and electronic computation machines, analyzers, and plotters in solving problem support of mathematical, scientific, or industrial research. Acts as advisor or consultant to research personnel concerning mathematical methods and applications.
Yearly Earnings: $43,212
Education: Doctor's degree
Knowledge: Administration and Management; Economics and Accounting; Computers and Electronics; Engineering and Technology; Mathematics; Physics
Abilities: Oral Comprehension; Written Expression; Fluency of Ideas; Originality; Deductive Reasoning; Inductive Reasoning; Information Ordering; Mathematical Reasoning; Number Facility; Memorization
Skills: Mathematics; Critical Thinking; Active Learning; Learning Strategies; Information Gathering; Information Organization; Synthesis/Reorganization; Idea Generation; Solution Appraisal; Programming
General Work Activities: Getting Information Needed to Do the Job; Monitoring Processes, Material, or Surroundings; Estimating Needed Characteristics; Evaluating Information against Standards; Analyzing Data or Information; Thinking Creatively; Updating and Using Job-Relevant Knowledge; Operating Vehicles or Equipment; Interpreting Meaning of Information to Others
Job Characteristics: Sitting
GOE Group/s: 02.01.01 Physical Sciences: Theoretical Research
CIP Program/s: 270101 Mathematics; 270301 Applied Mathematics, General; 400801 Physics, General; 400810 Theoretical and Mathematical Physics
Related DOT Job/s: 020.067-014 MATHEMATICIAN

25319B WEIGHT ANALYSTS. OOH Title/s: Mathematicians

Analyze and calculate weight data of structural assemblies, components, and loads for purposes of weight, balance, loading, and operational functions of ships, aircraft, space vehicles, missiles, research instrumentation, and commercial and industrial products and systems. Studies weight factors involved in new designs or modifications, utilizing computer techniques for analysis and simulation. Analyzes data and prepares reports of weight distribution estimates for use in design studies. Weighs parts, assemblies, or completed products; estimates weight of parts from engineering drawings; and calculates weight distribution to determine balance. Confers with design engineering personnel to ensure coordination of weight, balance, and load specification with other phases of product development. May analyze various systems, structures, and support equipment designs to obtain information on most efficient compromise between weight, operations, and cost. May prepare cargo and equipment loading sequences to maintain balance of aircraft or space vehicle within specified load limits. Prepares reports or graphic data for designers when weight and balance require engineering changes. Prepares technical reports on inertia, static and dynamic balance, dead weight distribution, cargo and fuselage compartments, and fuel center of gravity travel. May conduct research and analysis to develop new techniques for weight-estimating criteria.
Yearly Earnings: $43,212
Education: Doctor's degree
Knowledge: Production and Processing; Computers and Electronics; Engineering and Technology; Design; Mathematics; Physics; Transportation
Abilities: Oral Comprehension; Written Expression; Deductive Reasoning; Inductive Reasoning; Mathematical Reasoning; Number Facility
Skills: Mathematics; Science; Information Gathering; Operations Analysis
General Work Activities: Monitoring Processes, Material, or Surroundings; Estimating Needed Characteristics; Evaluating Information against Standards; Analyzing Data or Information; Making Decisions and Solving Problems; Updating and Using Job-Relevant Knowledge; Operating Vehicles or Equipment; Drafting and Specifying Technical Devices, etc.; Communicating with Other Workers
Job Characteristics: Sitting

GOE Group/s: 07.02.03 Mathematical Detail: Statistical Reporting and Analysis
CIP Program/s: 270301 Applied Mathematics, General
Related DOT Job/s: 020.167-030 WEIGHT ANALYST

25319C ALL OTHER MATHEMATICAL SCIENTISTS. OOH Title/s: Mathematicians

All other mathematical scientists not classified separately above.
Yearly Earnings: $43,212
Education: Doctor's degree
GOE Group/s: 11.08.04 Communications: Translating and Interpreting
CIP Program/s: 270101 Mathematics; 270301 Applied Mathematics, General
Related DOT Job/s: 199.267-014 CRYPTANALYST

25323 MATHEMATICAL TECHNICIANS. OOH Title/s: Science Technicians

Apply standardized mathematical formulas, principles, and methodologies to technical problems in engineering and physical science in relation to specific industrial and research objectives, processes, equipment, and products. Selects most feasible combination and sequence of computational methods to reduce raw data to meaningful and manageable terms. Analyzes raw data from computer or recorded on photographic film or other media. Selects most economical and reliable combination of manual, mechanical, or data processing methods and equipment consistent with data reduction requirements. Calculates data for analysis, using computer or calculator. Translates data into numerical values, equations, flowcharts, graphs, or other media. Modifies standard formulas to conform to data processing method selected. Analyzes processed data to detect errors. Confers with professional, scientific, and engineering personnel to plan project.
Yearly Earnings: $26,728
Education: Associate degree
Knowledge: Computers and Electronics; Engineering and Technology; Mathematics; English Language
Abilities: Oral Comprehension; Fluency of Ideas; Deductive Reasoning; Mathematical Reasoning; Number Facility
Skills: Reading Comprehension; Active Listening; Speaking; Mathematics; Science; Critical Thinking; Active Learning; Learning Strategies; Monitoring; Problem Identification; Information Gathering; Information Organization; Synthesis/Reorganization; Idea Generation; Idea Evaluation; Implementation Planning; Solution Appraisal; Operations Analysis; Equipment Selection; Programming; Testing; Identification of Key Causes; Judgment and Decision Making
General Work Activities: Getting Information Needed to Do the Job; Monitoring Processes, Material, or Surroundings; Estimating Needed Characteristics; Processing Information; Evaluating Information against Standards; Analyzing Data or Information; Making Decisions and Solving Problems; Thinking Creatively; Updating and Using Job-Relevant Knowledge; Organizing, Planning, and Prioritizing; Operating Vehicles or Equipment; Implementing Ideas, Programs, etc.; Documenting/Recording Information; Interpreting Meaning of Information to Others; Communicating with Other Workers
Job Characteristics: Sitting; Importance of Being Exact or Accurate
GOE Group/s: 11.01.02 Mathematics and Statistics: Data Analysis
CIP Program/s: 270301 Applied Mathematics, General
Related DOT Job/s: 020.162-010 MATHEMATICAL TECHNICIAN

Social Scientists

27102A ECONOMISTS. OOH Title/s: Economists and Marketing Research Analysts

Conduct research, prepare reports, or formulate plans to aid in solution of economic problems arising from production and distribution of goods and services. May collect and process economic and statistical data using econometric and sampling techniques. Exclude market research analysts. Studies economic and statistical data in area of specialization, such as finance, labor, or agriculture. Reviews and analyzes data to prepare reports, to forecast future marketing trends, and to stay abreast of economic changes. Organizes research data into report format, including graphic illustrations of research findings. Compiles data relating to research area, such as employment, productivity, and wages and hours. Formulates recommendations, policies, or plans to interpret markets or solve economic problems. Devises methods and procedures for collecting and processing data, using various econometric and sampling techniques. Develops economic guidelines and standards in preparing points of view used in forecasting trends and formulating economic policy. Supervises research projects and students' study projects. Provides advice and consultation to business and public and private agencies. Testifies at regulatory or legislative hearings to present recommendations. Teaches theories, principles, and methods of economics. Assigns work to staff.
Yearly Earnings: $45,812
Education: Bachelor's degree
Knowledge: Economics and Accounting; Personnel and Human Resources; Production and Processing; Food Production; Computers and Electronics; Mathematics; Geography; Education and Training; History and Archeology; Philosophy and Theology; Law, Government, and Jurisprudence
Abilities: Oral Comprehension; Written Comprehension; Oral Expression; Written Expression; Fluency of Ideas; Originality; Problem Sensitivity; Deductive Reasoning; Inductive Reasoning; Category Flexibility; Mathematical Reasoning; Number Facility; Speed of Closure; Near Vision; Speech Recognition; Speech Clarity
Skills: Reading Comprehension; Active Listening; Writing; Speaking; Mathematics; Science; Critical Thinking; Active Learning; Learning Strategies; Monitoring; Social Perceptiveness; Coordination; Persuasion; Negotiation; Instructing; Service Orientation; Problem Identification; Information Gathering; Information Organization; Synthesis/Reorganization; Idea Generation; Idea Evaluation; Implementation Planning; Solution Appraisal; Operations Analysis; Programming; Visioning; Systems Perception; Identifying Downstream Consequences; Identification of Key Causes; Judgment and Decision Making; Systems Evaluation; Time Management; Management of Financial Resources; Management of Material Resources; Management of Personnel Resources
General Work Activities: Getting Information Needed to Do the Job; Monitoring Processes, Material, or Surroundings; Evaluating Information against Standards; Analyzing Data or Information; Making Decisions and Solving Problems; Thinking Creatively; Updating and Using Job-Relevant Knowledge; Organizing, Planning, and Prioritizing; Operating Vehicles or Equipment; Interpreting Meaning of Information to Others; Teaching Others; Guiding, Directing and Motivating Subordinates; Provide Consultation and Advice to Others
Job Characteristics: Supervise, Coach, Train Others; Persuade Someone to a Course of Action; Take a Position Opposed to Others; Responsibility for Outcomes and Results; Sitting; Importance of Being Aware of New Events
GOE Group/s: 11.03.05 Social Research: Economic

CIP Program/s: 010101 Agricultural Business and Management, General; 010103 Agricultural Economics; 450601 Economics, General; 450602 Applied and Resource Economics; 450603 Econometrics and Quantitative Economics; 450604 Development Economics and International Development; 450605 International Economics; 450699 Economics, Other; 520601 Business/Managerial Economics
Related DOT Job/s: 050.067-010 ECONOMIST

27102B MARKET RESEARCH ANALYSTS. OOH

Title/s: Economists and Marketing Research Analysts

Research market conditions in local, regional, or national areas to determine potential sales of a product or service. May gather information on competitors, prices, sales, and methods of marketing and distribution. May use survey results to create a marketing campaign based on regional preferences and buying habits. Examines and analyzes statistical data to forecast future marketing trends and to identify potential markets. Gathers data on competitors, and analyzes prices, sales, and method of marketing and distribution. Establishes research methodology and designs format for data gathering, such as surveys, opinion polls, or questionnaires. Collects data on customer preferences and buying habits. Checks consumer reaction to new or improved products or services. Prepares reports and graphic illustrations of findings. Attends staff conferences to submit findings and proposals to management for consideration. Translates complex numerical data into nontechnical, written text.
Yearly Earnings: $45,812
Education: Bachelor's degree
Knowledge: Economics and Accounting; Sales and Marketing; Customer and Personal Service; Food Production; Computers and Electronics; Mathematics; Psychology; Geography; Philosophy and Theology
Abilities: Written Expression; Deductive Reasoning; Inductive Reasoning; Mathematical Reasoning; Number Facility; Speed of Closure; Selective Attention; Near Vision; Auditory Attention
Skills: Reading Comprehension; Active Listening; Writing; Speaking; Mathematics; Critical Thinking; Active Learning; Learning Strategies; Monitoring; Social Perceptiveness; Persuasion; Information Gathering; Information Organization; Synthesis/Reorganization; Idea Generation; Idea Evaluation; Implementation Planning; Solution Appraisal; Operations Analysis; Programming; Visioning; Systems Perception; Identifying Downstream Consequences; Identification of Key Causes; Systems Evaluation; Management of Material Resources
General Work Activities: Getting Information Needed to Do the Job; Monitoring Processes, Material, or Surroundings; Evaluating Information against Standards; Analyzing Data or Information; Organizing, Planning, and Prioritizing; Operating Vehicles or Equipment; Documenting/Recording Information; Interpreting Meaning of Information to Others; Communicating with Other Workers
Job Characteristics: Objective or Subjective Information; Take a Position Opposed to Others; Sitting
GOE Group/s: 11.06.03 Finance: Risk and Profit Analysis
CIP Program/s: 450601 Economics, General; 450602 Applied and Resource Economics; 450603 Econometrics and Quantitative Economics; 521402 Marketing Research
Related DOT Job/s: 050.067-014 MARKET-RESEARCH ANALYST I; 169.267-034 RESEARCH ANALYST

27105 URBAN AND REGIONAL PLANNERS. OOH

Title/s: Urban and Regional Planners

Develop comprehensive plans and programs for use of land and physical facilities of cities, counties, and metropolitan areas. Develops alternative plans with recommendations for program or project. Compiles, organizes, and analyzes data on economic, social, and physical factors affecting land use, using statistical methods. Reviews and evaluates environmental impact reports applying to specific private and public planning projects and programs. Evaluates information to determine feasibility of proposals or to identify factors requiring amendment. Recommends governmental measures affecting land use, public utilities, community facilities, housing, and transportation. Discusses purpose of land use projects, such as transportation, conservation, residential, commercial, industrial, and community use, with planning officials. Prepares or requisitions graphic and narrative report on land use data. Determines regulatory limitations on project. Conducts field investigations, economic or public opinion surveys, demographic studies, or other research to gather required information. Advises planning officials on feasibility, cost effectiveness, regulatory conformance, and alternative recommendations for project. Maintains collection of socioeconomic, environmental, and regulatory data related to land use for governmental and private sectors.
Yearly Earnings: $37,960
Education: Master's degree
Knowledge: Administration and Management; Clerical; Economics and Accounting; Sales and Marketing; Computers and Electronics; Engineering and Technology; Design; Building and Construction; Mathematics; Biology; Sociology and Anthropology; Geography; Education and Training; English Language; History and Archeology; Philosophy and Theology; Public Safety and Security; Law, Government, and Jurisprudence; Communications and Media; Transportation
Abilities: Oral Comprehension; Written Comprehension; Oral Expression; Written Expression; Fluency of Ideas; Originality; Problem Sensitivity; Deductive Reasoning; Inductive Reasoning; Category Flexibility; Mathematical Reasoning; Number Facility; Speed of Closure; Speech Clarity
Skills: Reading Comprehension; Active Listening; Writing; Speaking; Mathematics; Critical Thinking; Active Learning; Learning Strategies; Monitoring; Social Perceptiveness; Coordination; Persuasion; Negotiation; Problem Identification; Information Gathering; Information Organization; Synthesis/Reorganization; Idea Generation; Idea Evaluation; Implementation Planning; Solution Appraisal; Operations Analysis; Visioning; Systems Perception; Identifying Downstream Consequences; Identification of Key Causes; Judgment and Decision Making; Systems Evaluation; Time Management; Management of Financial Resources; Management of Material Resources
General Work Activities: Getting Information Needed to Do the Job; Monitoring Processes, Material, or Surroundings; Estimating Needed Characteristics; Judging Qualities of Things, Services, People; Processing Information; Evaluating Information against Standards; Analyzing Data or Information; Making Decisions and Solving Problems; Thinking Creatively; Developing Objectives and Strategies; Organizing, Planning, and Prioritizing; Operating Vehicles or Equipment; Implementing Ideas, Programs, etc.; Documenting/Recording Information; Interpreting Meaning of Information to Others; Communicating with Other Workers; Communicating with Persons Outside Organization; Establishing and Maintaining Relationships; Provide Consultation and Advice to Others; Performing Administrative Activities
Job Characteristics: Objective or Subjective Information; Persuade Someone to a Course of Action; Provide a Service to Others; Take a Position Opposed to Others; Deal with External Customers; Coordinate or Lead Others; Frequency in Conflict Situations; Sitting; Frustrating Circumstances
GOE Group/s: 11.03.02 Social Research: Sociological
CIP Program/s: 040301 City/Urban, Community and Regional Planning; 040701 Architectural Urban Design and Planning; 440501 Public Policy Analysis
Related DOT Job/s: 188.167-110 PLANNER, PROGRAM SERVICES; 199.167-014 URBAN PLANNER

27108A DEVELOPMENTAL PSYCHOLOGISTS. OOH

Title/s: Psychologists

Study and research the emotional, mental, physical, and social growth and development of individuals, from birth to death, to increase understanding of human behavior and processes of human growth and decline. Formulates hypothesis or researches problem regarding growth, development, and decline of emotional, mental, physical, and social processes in individuals. Selects or develops method of investigation to test hypothesis. Studies behavior of children to analyze processes of learning, language development, and parental influence on children's behavior. Analyzes growth or change of social values and attitudes, using information obtained from observation, questionnaires, and interviews. Administers intelligence and performance tests to establish and measure human patterns of intellectual and psychological growth, development, and decline. Observes and records behavior of infants to establish patterns of social, motor, and sensory development. Formulates theories based on research findings for application in such fields as juvenile delinquency, education, parenting, and gerontology. Experiments with animals to conduct cross-species comparative studies to contribute to understanding of human behavior.

Yearly Earnings: $32,708

Education: Master's degree

Knowledge: Mathematics; Biology; Psychology; Sociology and Anthropology; Therapy and Counseling; Education and Training; English Language; Philosophy and Theology

Abilities: Oral Comprehension; Written Comprehension; Written Expression; Fluency of Ideas; Originality; Problem Sensitivity; Deductive Reasoning; Inductive Reasoning; Information Ordering; Category Flexibility; Mathematical Reasoning; Number Facility; Memorization; Speed of Closure; Flexibility of Closure; Perceptual Speed; Selective Attention; Speech Recognition; Speech Clarity

Skills: Reading Comprehension; Active Listening; Writing; Speaking; Mathematics; Science; Critical Thinking; Active Learning; Learning Strategies; Monitoring; Social Perceptiveness; Service Orientation; Problem Identification; Information Gathering; Information Organization; Synthesis/Reorganization; Idea Generation; Idea Evaluation; Implementation Planning; Solution Appraisal; Programming; Visioning; Systems Perception; Identifying Downstream Consequences; Identification of Key Causes; Judgment and Decision Making; Systems Evaluation

General Work Activities: Getting Information Needed to Do the Job; Monitoring Processes, Material, or Surroundings; Identifying Objects, Actions, and Events; Judging Qualities of Things, Services, People; Evaluating Information against Standards; Analyzing Data or Information; Making Decisions and Solving Problems; Thinking Creatively; Updating and Using Job-Relevant Knowledge; Developing Objectives and Strategies; Organizing, Planning, and Prioritizing; Implementing Ideas, Programs, etc.; Documenting/Recording Information; Interpreting Meaning of Information to Others; Communicating with Persons Outside Organization; Performing for or Working with Public

Job Characteristics: Objective or Subjective Information; Take a Position Opposed to Others; Frustrating Circumstances

GOE Group/s: 11.03.01 Social Research: Psychological

CIP Program/s: 420101 Psychology, General; 420301 Cognitive Psychology and Psycholinguistics; 420701 Developmental and Child Psychology

Related DOT Job/s: 045.061-010 PSYCHOLOGIST, DEVELOPMENTAL

27108C EXPERIMENTAL PSYCHOLOGISTS. OOH

Title/s: Psychologists

Plan, design, and conduct, laboratory experiments to investigate animal or human physiology, perception, memory, learning, personality, and cognitive processes. Conduct interdisciplinary studies with scientists in such fields as physiology, biology, and sociology. Formulates hypotheses and experimental designs to investigate problems of perception, memory, learning, personality, and cognitive processes. Selects, controls, and modifies variables in human or animal laboratory experiments, and observes and records behavior in relation to variables. Analyzes test results, using statistical techniques, and evaluates significance of data in relation to original hypotheses. Conducts research in areas such as aesthetics, learning, emotion, motivation, electroencephalography, motor skills, autonomic functions, and the relationship of behavior to physiology. Designs and constructs equipment and apparatus for laboratory study. Writes scientific papers describing experiments and interpreting research results for publication or presentation. Studies animal behavior to develop theories on comparison of animal and human behavior. Collaborates with scientists in such fields as physiology, biology, and sociology to conduct interdisciplinary studies and formulate theories of behavior.

Yearly Earnings: $32,708

Education: Master's degree

Knowledge: Mathematics; Biology; Psychology; Sociology and Anthropology; English Language

Abilities: Oral Comprehension; Written Comprehension; Oral Expression; Written Expression; Fluency of Ideas; Originality; Deductive Reasoning; Inductive Reasoning; Information Ordering; Category Flexibility; Mathematical Reasoning; Number Facility; Memorization; Speed of Closure; Speech Clarity

Skills: Reading Comprehension; Active Listening; Writing; Speaking; Mathematics; Science; Critical Thinking; Active Learning; Monitoring; Social Perceptiveness; Problem Identification; Information Gathering; Information Organization; Synthesis/Reorganization; Idea Generation; Idea Evaluation; Implementation Planning; Solution Appraisal; Operations Analysis; Technology Design; Programming; Systems Perception; Judgment and Decision Making; Systems Evaluation

General Work Activities: Getting Information Needed to Do the Job; Monitoring Processes, Material, or Surroundings; Identifying Objects, Actions, and Events; Estimating Needed Characteristics; Judging Qualities of Things, Services, People; Evaluating Information against Standards; Analyzing Data or Information; Making Decisions and Solving Problems; Thinking Creatively; Updating and Using Job-Relevant Knowledge; Developing Objectives and Strategies; Organizing, Planning, and Prioritizing; Operating Vehicles or Equipment; Implementing Ideas, Programs, etc.; Documenting/Recording Information; Interpreting Meaning of Information to Others; Communicating with Other Workers; Communicating with Persons Outside Organization; Establishing and Maintaining Relationships

Job Characteristics: Objective or Subjective Information; Diseases/Infections; Sitting; Importance of Being Sure All is Done

GOE Group/s: 11.03.01 Social Research: Psychological

CIP Program/s: 420101 Psychology, General; 420301 Cognitive Psychology and Psycholinguistics; 420801 Experimental Psychology; 421101 Physiological Psychology/Psychobiology

Related DOT Job/s: 045.061-018 PSYCHOLOGIST, EXPERIMENTAL

27108D EDUCATIONAL PSYCHOLOGISTS. OOH

Title/s: Psychologists

Investigate processes of learning and teaching, and develop psychological principles and techniques applicable to educational problems. Conducts experiments to study educational problems, such as motivation, adjustment, teacher training, and individual differences in mental abilities. Conducts research to aid introduction of programs in schools to meet current psychological, educational, and sociological needs of children. Investigates traits, attitudes, and feelings of teachers to predict conditions that affect teachers' mental health and success with students. Formulates achievement, diagnostic, and predictive tests to aid teachers in planning methods and content of instruction. Interprets and explains test results—in terms of norms, reliability, and validity—to teachers, counselors, students, and other entitled parties. Plans remedial classes and testing programs designed to meet needs of special students. Advises teachers and other school personnel on methods to enhance school and classroom atmosphere to maximize student learning and motivation. Analyzes characteristics and adjustment needs of students having various mental abilities, and recommends educational program to promote maximum adjustment. Evaluates needs, limitations, and potentials of child, through observation, review of school records, and consultation with parents and school personnel. Administers standardized tests to evaluate intelligence, achievement, and personality, and to diagnose disabilities and difficulties among students. Collaborates with education specialists in developing curriculum content and methods of organizing and conducting classroom work. Recommends placement of students in classes and treatment programs based on individual needs. Counsels pupils individually and in groups, to assist pupils to achieve personal, social, and emotional adjustment. Advises school board, superintendent, administrative committees, and parent-teacher groups regarding provision of psychological services within educational system or school. Refers individuals to community agencies to obtain medical, vocational, or social services for child or family.

Yearly Earnings: $32,708

Education: Master's degree

Knowledge: Administration and Management; Mathematics; Psychology; Sociology and Anthropology; Therapy and Counseling; Education and Training; English Language

Abilities: Oral Comprehension; Written Comprehension; Oral Expression; Written Expression; Fluency of Ideas; Originality; Problem Sensitivity; Deductive Reasoning; Inductive Reasoning; Information Ordering; Category Flexibility; Mathematical Reasoning; Number Facility; Memorization; Speed of Closure; Flexibility of Closure; Perceptual Speed; Auditory Attention

Skills: Reading Comprehension; Active Listening; Writing; Speaking; Mathematics; Science; Critical Thinking; Active Learning; Learning Strategies; Monitoring; Social Perceptiveness; Coordination; Persuasion; Negotiation; Instructing; Service Orientation; Problem Identification; Information Gathering; Information Organization; Synthesis/Reorganization; Idea Generation; Idea Evaluation; Implementation Planning; Solution Appraisal; Operations Analysis; Programming; Visioning; Systems Perception; Identifying Downstream Consequences; Identification of Key Causes; Judgment and Decision Making; Systems Evaluation

General Work Activities: Getting Information Needed to Do the Job; Monitoring Processes, Material, or Surroundings; Identifying Objects, Actions, and Events; Judging Qualities of Things, Services, People; Processing Information; Evaluating Information against Standards; Analyzing Data or Information; Making Decisions and Solving Problems; Thinking Creatively; Updating and Using Job-Relevant Knowledge; Developing Objectives and Strategies; Scheduling Work and Activities; Organizing, Planning, and Prioritizing; Implementing Ideas, Programs, etc.; Interpreting Meaning of Information to Others; Communicating with Other Workers; Communicating with Persons Outside Organization; Establishing and Maintaining Relationships; Assisting and Caring for Others; Selling or Influencing Others; Resolving Conflicts, Negotiating with Others; Performing for or Working with Public; Teaching Others; Coaching and Developing Others; Provide Consultation and Advice to Others

Job Characteristics: Objective or Subjective Information; Job-Required Social Interaction; Persuade Someone to a Course of Action; Provide a Service to Others; Deal with External Customers; Coordinate or Lead Others; Frequency in Conflict Situations; Deal with Unpleasant or Angry People; Deal with Physical, Aggressive People; Sitting; Consequence of Error; Frustrating Circumstances; Importance of Being Exact or Accurate; Importance of Being Sure All is Done; Importance of Being Aware of New Events

GOE Group/s: 10.01.02 Social Services: Counseling and Social Work; 11.03.01 Social Research: Psychological

CIP Program/s: 130604 Educational Assessment, Testing and Measurement; 130802 Educational Psychology; 420101 Psychology, General; 420201 Clinical Psychology; 420301 Cognitive Psychology and Psycholinguistics; 420601 Counseling Psychology; 420901 Industrial and Organizational Psychology; 421601 Social Psychology; 421701 School Psychology

Related DOT Job/s: 045.067-010 PSYCHOLOGIST, EDUCATIONAL; 045.067-018 PSYCHOMETRIST; 045.107-034 PSYCHOLOGIST, SCHOOL

27108E SOCIAL PSYCHOLOGISTS. OOH Title/s: Psychologists

Investigate psychological aspects of human interrelationships to gain understanding of individual and group thought, feeling, and behavior. Conduct research to analyze attitude, motivation, opinion, and group behavior, using behavioral observation, experimentation, or survey techniques. Observes and analyzes individual relationships, behavior, and attitudes within and toward religious, racial, political, occupational, and other groups. Researches variables, such as prejudice, values transmission, motivation, morals, leadership, and the contribution of social factors to behavior. Conducts surveys and polls, using statistical sampling techniques, to measure and analyze attitudes and opinions. Utilizes research findings to predict economic, political, and other behavior of groups. Develops techniques, such as rating scales and sampling methods, to collect and measure behavioral data. Prepares reports documenting research methods and findings.

Yearly Earnings: $32,708

Education: Master's degree

Knowledge: Administration and Management; Mathematics; Psychology; Sociology and Anthropology; English Language; Philosophy and Theology

Abilities: Oral Comprehension; Written Comprehension; Oral Expression; Written Expression; Fluency of Ideas; Originality; Problem Sensitivity; Deductive Reasoning; Inductive Reasoning; Information Ordering; Mathematical Reasoning; Memorization; Speed of Closure; Flexibility of Closure; Speech Clarity

Skills: Reading Comprehension; Active Listening; Writing; Speaking; Mathematics; Science; Critical Thinking; Active Learning; Social Perceptiveness; Information Gathering; Information Organization; Synthesis/Reorganization; Implementation Planning; Programming; Systems Perception; Identifying Downstream Consequences; Systems Evaluation

General Work Activities: Getting Information Needed to Do the Job; Monitoring Processes, Material, or Surroundings; Estimating Needed Characteristics; Evaluating Information against Standards; Analyzing Data or Information; Making Decisions and Solving Problems; Thinking Creatively; Updating and Using Job-Relevant Knowledge; Devel-

oping Objectives and Strategies; Operating Vehicles or Equipment; Implementing Ideas, Programs, etc.; Documenting/Recording Information; Interpreting Meaning of Information to Others; Communicating with Persons Outside Organization
Job Characteristics: Objective or Subjective Information; Sitting; Consequence of Error; Frustrating Circumstances; Importance of Being Sure All is Done
GOE Group/s: 11.03.01 Social Research: Psychological
CIP Program/s: 420101 Psychology, General; 420401 Community Psychology; 420901 Industrial and Organizational Psychology; 421601 Social Psychology
Related DOT Job/s: 045.067-014 PSYCHOLOGIST, SOCIAL

27108G CLINICAL PSYCHOLOGISTS. OOH Title/s: Psychologists; Counselors

Diagnose or evaluate mental and emotional disorders of individuals through observation, interview, and psychological tests; formulate and administer programs of treatment. Observes individual at play, in group interactions, or other situations to detect indications of mental deficiency, abnormal behavior, or maladjustment. Develops treatment plan, including type, frequency, intensity, and duration of therapy, in collaboration with psychiatrists and other specialists. Analyzes information to assess client problems, determine advisability of counseling, and refer client to other specialists, institutions, or support services. Conducts individual and group counseling sessions regarding psychological or emotional problems, such as stress, substance abuse, and family situations. Responds to client reactions, evaluates effectiveness of counseling or treatment, and modifies plan as needed. Interviews individuals, couples, or families, and reviews records to obtain information on medical, psychological, emotional, relationship, or other problems. Selects, administers, scores, and interprets psychological tests to obtain information on individual's intelligence, achievement, interest, and personality. Utilizes treatment methods, such as psychotherapy, hypnosis, behavior modification, stress reduction therapy, psychodrama, and play therapy. Plans and develops accredited psychological service programs in psychiatric center or hospital, in collaboration with psychiatrists and other professional staff. Consults reference material, such as textbooks, manuals, and journals, to identify symptoms, make diagnoses, and develop approach to treatment. Assists clients to gain insight, define goals, and plan action to achieve effective personal, social, educational, and vocational development and adjustment. Provides occupational, educational, and other information to enable individual to formulate realistic educational and vocational plans. Plans, supervises, and conducts psychological research in fields such as personality development and diagnosis, treatment, and prevention of mental disorders. Directs, coordinates, and evaluates activities of psychological staff and student interns engaged in patient evaluation and treatment in psychiatric facility. Provides psychological services and advice to private firms and community agencies on individual cases or mental health programs. Develops, directs, and participates in staff training programs.
Yearly Earnings: $32,708
Education: Master's degree
Knowledge: Administration and Management; Customer and Personal Service; Personnel and Human Resources; Biology; Psychology; Sociology and Anthropology; Medicine and Dentistry; Therapy and Counseling; Education and Training; English Language
Abilities: Oral Comprehension; Written Comprehension; Oral Expression; Written Expression; Fluency of Ideas; Originality; Problem Sensitivity; Deductive Reasoning; Inductive Reasoning; Information Ordering; Category Flexibility; Memorization; Speed of Closure; Flexibility of Closure; Near Vision; Speech Recognition; Speech Clarity
Skills: Reading Comprehension; Active Listening; Writing; Speaking; Science; Critical Thinking; Active Learning; Learning Strategies; Monitoring; Social Perceptiveness; Coordination; Persuasion; Negotiation; Instructing; Service Orientation; Problem Identification; Information Gathering; Information Organization; Synthesis/Reorganization; Idea Generation; Idea Evaluation; Implementation Planning; Solution Appraisal; Visioning; Systems Perception; Identifying Downstream Consequences; Identification of Key Causes; Judgment and Decision Making; Systems Evaluation; Time Management; Management of Personnel Resources
General Work Activities: Getting Information Needed to Do the Job; Monitoring Processes, Material, or Surroundings; Identifying Objects, Actions, and Events; Judging Qualities of Things, Services, People; Evaluating Information against Standards; Analyzing Data or Information; Making Decisions and Solving Problems; Thinking Creatively; Updating and Using Job-Relevant Knowledge; Developing Objectives and Strategies; Organizing, Planning, and Prioritizing; Operating Vehicles or Equipment; Implementing Ideas, Programs, etc.; Interpreting Meaning of Information to Others; Communicating with Other Workers; Communicating with Persons Outside Organization; Establishing and Maintaining Relationships; Assisting and Caring for Others; Performing for or Working with Public; Coordinating Work and Activities of Others; Teaching Others; Guiding, Directing and Motivating Subordinates; Coaching and Developing Others; Provide Consultation and Advice to Others
Job Characteristics: Objective or Subjective Information; Job-Required Social Interaction; Supervise, Coach, Train Others; Persuade Someone to a Course of Action; Provide a Service to Others; Deal with External Customers; Responsible for Others' Health and Safety; Frequency in Conflict Situations; Deal with Unpleasant or Angry People; Deal with Physical, Aggressive People; Sitting; Consequence of Error; Frustrating Circumstances; Importance of Being Sure All is Done
GOE Group/s: 10.01.02 Social Services: Counseling and Social Work
CIP Program/s: 420101 Psychology, General; 420201 Clinical Psychology; 420601 Counseling Psychology; 512705 Psychoanalysis
Related DOT Job/s: 045.107-022 CLINICAL PSYCHOLOGIST; 045.107-046 PSYCHOLOGIST, CHIEF; 045.107-050 CLINICAL THERAPIST

27108H COUNSELING PSYCHOLOGISTS. OOH Title/s: Psychologists; Counselors

Assess and evaluate individuals' problems through the use of case histories, interviews, and observation, and provide individual or group counseling services to assist individuals in achieving more effective personal, social, educational, and vocational development and adjustment. Counsels clients to assist them in understanding personal or interactive problems, defining goals, and developing realistic action plans. Collects information about individuals or clients, using interviews, case histories, observational techniques, and other assessment methods. Develops therapeutic and treatment plans based on individual interests, abilities, or needs of clients. Selects, administers, or interprets psychological tests to assess intelligence, aptitude, ability, or interests. Advises clients on the potential benefits of counseling, or makes referrals to specialists or other institutions for noncounseling problems. Analyzes data, such as interview notes, test results, and reference manuals and texts to identify symptoms and diagnose the nature of client's problems. Evaluates results of counseling methods to determine the reliability and validity of treatments. Consults with other professionals to discuss therapy or treatment, counseling resources or techniques, and to share occupational information. Conducts research to develop or improve diagnostic or therapeutic counseling techniques.
Yearly Earnings: $32,708
Education: Master's degree

Knowledge: Psychology; Sociology and Anthropology; Therapy and Counseling; Education and Training; Philosophy and Theology
Abilities: Oral Comprehension; Written Comprehension; Oral Expression; Written Expression; Originality; Problem Sensitivity; Deductive Reasoning; Inductive Reasoning; Memorization; Speed of Closure; Speech Recognition; Speech Clarity
Skills: Reading Comprehension; Active Listening; Writing; Speaking; Science; Critical Thinking; Active Learning; Learning Strategies; Monitoring; Social Perceptiveness; Persuasion; Negotiation; Instructing; Service Orientation; Problem Identification; Information Gathering; Information Organization; Synthesis/Reorganization; Idea Generation; Idea Evaluation; Implementation Planning; Solution Appraisal; Visioning; Identifying Downstream Consequences; Identification of Key Causes; Judgment and Decision Making
General Work Activities: Monitoring Processes, Material, or Surroundings; Evaluating Information against Standards; Analyzing Data or Information; Making Decisions and Solving Problems; Thinking Creatively; Updating and Using Job-Relevant Knowledge; Developing Objectives and Strategies; Operating Vehicles or Equipment; Documenting/Recording Information; Interpreting Meaning of Information to Others; Communicating with Persons Outside Organization; Establishing and Maintaining Relationships; Assisting and Caring for Others; Resolving Conflicts, Negotiating with Others; Performing for or Working with Public; Coaching and Developing Others; Provide Consultation and Advice to Others
Job Characteristics: Objective or Subjective Information; Job-Required Social Interaction; Provide a Service to Others; Take a Position Opposed to Others; Deal with External Customers; Responsible for Others' Health and Safety; Frequency in Conflict Situations; Deal with Unpleasant or Angry People; Deal with Physical, Aggressive People; Sitting; Consequence of Error; Frustrating Circumstances; Importance of Being Aware of New Events
GOE Group/s: 10.01.02 Social Services: Counseling and Social Work
CIP Program/s: 131101 Counselor Education Counseling and Guidance Services; 131102 College/Postsecondary Student Counseling and Personnel Services; 420101 Psychology, General; 420201 Clinical Psychology; 420601 Counseling Psychology; 512705 Psychoanalysis
Related DOT Job/s: 045.107-026 PSYCHOLOGIST, COUNSELING; 045.107-054 COUNSELOR, MARRIAGE AND FAMILY

27108J INDUSTRIAL-ORGANIZATIONAL PSYCHOLOGISTS. OOH Title/s: Psychologists

Apply principles of psychology and human behavior to personnel, administration, management, sales, and marketing problems. Develop personnel policies, instruments, and programs for the selection, placement, training and development, and evaluation of employees. Conduct organizational analysis and programs for organizational development. Conduct research studies of leadership, supervision, morale, motivation, and worker productivity. Develops interview techniques, rating scales, and psychological tests to assess skills, abilities, and interests as aids in selection, placement, and promotion. Conducts research studies of physical work environments, organizational structure, communication systems, group interaction, morale, and motivation to assess organizational functioning. Analyzes data, using statistical methods and applications, to evaluate and measure the effectiveness of program implementation or training. Advises management in strategic changes to personnel, managerial, and marketing policies and practices to improve organizational effectiveness and efficiency. Studies consumer reaction to new products and package designs, using surveys and tests, and measures the effectiveness of advertising media. Plans, develops, and organizes training programs, applying principles of learning and individual differences. Analyzes job requirements to establish criteria for classification, selection, training, and other related personnel functions. Observes and interviews workers to identify the physical, mutual, and educational requirements of job.
Yearly Earnings: $32,708
Education: Master's degree
Knowledge: Administration and Management; Sales and Marketing; Personnel and Human Resources; Mathematics; Psychology; Sociology and Anthropology; Therapy and Counseling; Education and Training; Philosophy and Theology
Abilities: Oral Comprehension; Written Comprehension; Oral Expression; Written Expression; Fluency of Ideas; Originality; Problem Sensitivity; Inductive Reasoning; Mathematical Reasoning; Speech Clarity
Skills: Reading Comprehension; Active Listening; Writing; Speaking; Mathematics; Science; Critical Thinking; Active Learning; Learning Strategies; Monitoring; Social Perceptiveness; Coordination; Persuasion; Negotiation; Instructing; Problem Identification; Information Gathering; Information Organization; Synthesis/Reorganization; Idea Generation; Idea Evaluation; Implementation Planning; Solution Appraisal; Operations Analysis; Visioning; Systems Perception; Identifying Downstream Consequences; Identification of Key Causes; Judgment and Decision Making; Systems Evaluation; Management of Personnel Resources
General Work Activities: Getting Information Needed to Do the Job; Monitoring Processes, Material, or Surroundings; Estimating Needed Characteristics; Evaluating Information against Standards; Analyzing Data or Information; Making Decisions and Solving Problems; Thinking Creatively; Updating and Using Job-Relevant Knowledge; Developing Objectives and Strategies; Scheduling Work and Activities; Organizing, Planning, and Prioritizing; Operating Vehicles or Equipment; Implementing Ideas, Programs, etc.; Documenting/Recording Information; Interpreting Meaning of Information to Others; Communicating with Other Workers; Communicating with Persons Outside Organization; Selling or Influencing Others; Developing and Building Teams; Teaching Others; Guiding, Directing and Motivating Subordinates; Coaching and Developing Others; Provide Consultation and Advice to Others; Performing Administrative Activities; Staffing Organizational Units
Job Characteristics: Objective or Subjective Information; Job-Required Social Interaction; Supervise, Coach, Train Others; Persuade Someone to a Course of Action; Provide a Service to Others; Take a Position Opposed to Others; Deal with External Customers; Coordinate or Lead Others; Responsibility for Outcomes and Results; Frequency in Conflict Situations; Deal with Unpleasant or Angry People; Frustrating Circumstances; Importance of Being Aware of New Events
GOE Group/s: 11.03.01 Social Research: Psychological
CIP Program/s: 420101 Psychology, General; 420901 Industrial and Organizational Psychology; 421601 Social Psychology
Related DOT Job/s: 045.061-014 PSYCHOLOGIST, ENGINEERING; 045.107-030 PSYCHOLOGIST, INDUSTRIAL-ORGANIZATIONAL

27199A POLITICAL SCIENTISTS. OOH Title/s: Social Scientists

Study the origin, development, and operation of political systems. Research a wide range of subjects, such as relations between the United States and foreign countries, the beliefs and institutions of foreign nations, or the politics of small towns or a major metropolis. May study topics such as public opinion, political decision making, and ideology. May analyze the structure and operation of governments as well as various political entities. May conduct public opinion surveys, analyze election results, or analyze public documents. Conducts research into political philosophy and theories of political systems, such as governmen-

tal institutions, public laws, and international law. Analyzes and interprets results of studies, and prepares reports detailing findings, recommendations, or conclusions. Consults with government officials, civic bodies, research agencies, and political parties. Organizes and conducts public opinion surveys, and interprets results. Recommends programs and policies to institutions and organizations. Prepares reports detailing findings and conclusions.
Yearly Earnings: $37,960
Education: Master's degree
Knowledge: Psychology; Sociology and Anthropology; Geography; English Language; Foreign Language; History and Archeology; Philosophy and Theology; Law, Government, and Jurisprudence; Communications and Media
Abilities: Oral Comprehension; Written Comprehension; Oral Expression; Written Expression; Fluency of Ideas; Deductive Reasoning; Inductive Reasoning; Speech Recognition
Skills: Reading Comprehension; Active Listening; Writing; Speaking; Mathematics; Critical Thinking; Active Learning; Social Perceptiveness; Information Gathering; Information Organization; Synthesis/Reorganization; Idea Generation; Idea Evaluation; Implementation Planning; Operations Analysis; Programming; Visioning; Systems Perception; Identifying Downstream Consequences; Identification of Key Causes; Judgment and Decision Making
General Work Activities: Getting Information Needed to Do the Job; Monitoring Processes, Material, or Surroundings; Estimating Needed Characteristics; Judging Qualities of Things, Services, People; Processing Information; Evaluating Information against Standards; Analyzing Data or Information; Making Decisions and Solving Problems; Developing Objectives and Strategies; Organizing, Planning, and Prioritizing; Operating Vehicles or Equipment; Implementing Ideas, Programs, etc.; Documenting/Recording Information; Interpreting Meaning of Information to Others; Communicating with Other Workers; Communicating with Persons Outside Organization; Resolving Conflicts, Negotiating with Others; Teaching Others; Provide Consultation and Advice to Others
Job Characteristics: Objective or Subjective Information; Take a Position Opposed to Others; Sitting; Importance of Being Aware of New Events
GOE Group/s: 11.03.02 Social Research: Sociological
CIP Program/s: 450901 International Relations and Affairs; 451001 Political Science, General; 451002 American Government and Politics; 451099 Political Science and Government, Other
Related DOT Job/s: 051.067-010 POLITICAL SCIENTIST

27199B SOCIOLOGISTS. OOH Title/s: Social Scientists

Conduct research into the development, structure, and behavior of groups of human beings and patterns of culture and social organization. Collects and analyzes scientific data concerning social phenomena, such as community, associations, social institutions, ethnic minorities, and social change. Plans and directs research on crime and prevention, group relations in industrial organization, urban communities, and physical environment and technology. Observes group interaction, and interviews group members to identify problems and collect data related to factors such as group organization and authority relationships. Develops research designs on basis of existing knowledge and evolving theory. Develops approaches to solution of group's problems, based on findings and incorporating sociological research and study in related disciplines. Constructs and tests methods of data collection. Collects information and makes judgments through observation, interview, and review of documents. Analyzes and evaluates data. Develops intervention procedures, utilizing techniques such as interviews, consultations, role-playing, and participant observation of group interaction, to facilitate solution. Monitors group interaction and role affiliations to evaluate progress and to determine need for additional change. Consults with lawmakers, administrators, and other officials who deal with problems of social change. Interprets methods employed and findings to individuals within agency and community. Prepares publications and reports on subjects, such as social factors which affect health, demographic characteristics, and social and racial discrimination in society. Collaborates with research workers in other disciplines. Directs work of statistical clerks, statisticians, and others.
Yearly Earnings: $37,960
Education: Master's degree
Knowledge: Administration and Management; Psychology; Sociology and Anthropology; Geography; Education and Training; English Language; Foreign Language; History and Archeology; Philosophy and Theology; Law, Government, and Jurisprudence; Communications and Media
Abilities: Oral Comprehension; Written Comprehension; Oral Expression; Written Expression; Fluency of Ideas; Originality; Problem Sensitivity; Deductive Reasoning; Inductive Reasoning; Category Flexibility; Mathematical Reasoning; Number Facility; Memorization; Speech Recognition; Speech Clarity
Skills: Reading Comprehension; Active Listening; Writing; Speaking; Mathematics; Critical Thinking; Active Learning; Learning Strategies; Social Perceptiveness; Coordination; Instructing; Problem Identification; Information Gathering; Information Organization; Synthesis/Reorganization; Idea Generation; Idea Evaluation; Implementation Planning; Solution Appraisal; Operations Analysis; Programming; Visioning; Systems Perception; Identifying Downstream Consequences; Identification of Key Causes; Judgment and Decision Making; Systems Evaluation; Time Management; Management of Personnel Resources
General Work Activities: Getting Information Needed to Do the Job; Monitoring Processes, Material, or Surroundings; Estimating Needed Characteristics; Judging Qualities of Things, Services, People; Processing Information; Evaluating Information against Standards; Analyzing Data or Information; Making Decisions and Solving Problems; Thinking Creatively; Updating and Using Job-Relevant Knowledge; Developing Objectives and Strategies; Organizing, Planning, and Prioritizing; Operating Vehicles or Equipment; Implementing Ideas, Programs, etc.; Documenting/Recording Information; Interpreting Meaning of Information to Others; Communicating with Other Workers; Communicating with Persons Outside Organization; Performing for or Working with Public; Coordinating Work and Activities of Others; Teaching Others; Provide Consultation and Advice to Others
Job Characteristics: Objective or Subjective Information; Deal with Physical, Aggressive People; Sitting; Importance of Being Aware of New Events
GOE Group/s: 11.03.02 Social Research: Sociological
CIP Program/s: 430104 Criminal Justice Studies; 450201 Anthropology; 450401 Criminology; 450501 Demography/Population Studies; 451001 Political Science, General; 451101 Sociology; 451201 Urban Affairs/Studies
Related DOT Job/s: 054.067-010 RESEARCH WORKER, SOCIAL WELFARE; 054.067-014 SOCIOLOGIST; 054.107-010 CLINICAL SOCIOLOGIST

27199C ANTHROPOLOGISTS. OOH Title/s: Social Scientists

Research or study the origins and physical, social, and cultural development and behavior of humans, and the cultures and organizations they have created. Gathers, analyzes, and reports data on human physique, social customs, and artifacts, such as weapons, tools, pottery, and clothing. Studies museum collections of skeletal remains and human fossils to determine their meaning in terms of long-range human evolution. Studies physical and physiological adaptations to differing environments and hereditary characteristics of

living populations. Studies growth patterns, sexual differences, and aging phenomena of human groups, current and past. Studies cultures, particularly preindustrial and non-Western societies, including religion, economics, mythology and traditions, and intellectual and artistic life. Observes and measures bodily variations and physical attributes of existing human types. Studies relationships between language and culture and sociolinguistic studies, relationship between individual personality and culture, or complex industrialized societies. Formulates general laws of cultural development, general rules of social and cultural behavior, or general value orientations. Applies anthropological data and techniques to solution of problems in human relations. Applies anthropological concepts to current problems. Writes for professional journals and other publications. Supervises field research projects and student study programs.
Yearly Earnings: $37,960
Education: Master's degree
Knowledge: Administration and Management; Biology; Psychology; Sociology and Anthropology; Geography; Education and Training; English Language; Foreign Language; Fine Arts; History and Archeology; Philosophy and Theology; Communications and Media
Abilities: Oral Comprehension; Written Comprehension; Written Expression; Fluency of Ideas; Deductive Reasoning; Inductive Reasoning; Category Flexibility; Number Facility; Speed of Closure; Flexibility of Closure; Speech Recognition; Speech Clarity
Skills: Reading Comprehension; Writing; Speaking; Mathematics; Science; Critical Thinking; Active Learning; Learning Strategies; Monitoring; Social Perceptiveness; Coordination; Instructing; Problem Identification; Information Gathering; Information Organization; Synthesis/Reorganization; Idea Generation; Idea Evaluation; Implementation Planning; Solution Appraisal; Programming; Visioning; Management of Personnel Resources
General Work Activities: Getting Information Needed to Do the Job; Monitoring Processes, Material, or Surroundings; Estimating Needed Characteristics; Judging Qualities of Things, Services, People; Evaluating Information against Standards; Analyzing Data or Information; Making Decisions and Solving Problems; Developing Objectives and Strategies; Organizing, Planning, and Prioritizing; Operating Vehicles or Equipment; Implementing Ideas, Programs, etc.; Documenting/Recording Information; Interpreting Meaning of Information to Others; Communicating with Other Workers; Coordinating Work and Activities of Others; Developing and Building Teams; Teaching Others; Guiding, Directing and Motivating Subordinates; Coaching and Developing Others; Provide Consultation and Advice to Others
Job Characteristics: Supervise, Coach, Train Others; Coordinate or Lead Others; Sitting; Importance of Being Aware of New Events
GOE Group/s: 02.02.01 Life Sciences: Animal Specialization; 11.03.03 Social Research: Historical
CIP Program/s: 450201 Anthropology; 450301 Archeology; 450501 Demography/Population Studies; 450901 International Relations and Affairs; 451101 Sociology; 500901 Music, General; 500905 Musicology and Ethnomusicology
Related DOT Job/s: 055.067-010 ANTHROPOLOGIST; 055.067-014 ANTHROPOLOGIST, PHYSICAL; 055.067-022 ETHNOLOGIST

27199D LINGUISTIC SCIENTISTS. OOH Title/s: Social Scientists

Study the structure and development of a specific language or language group. Traces origin and evolution of words and syntax through comparative analysis of ancient parent languages and modern language groups. Studies words and structural characteristics, such as morphology, semantics, phonology, accent, grammar, and literature. Identifies and classifies obscure languages, both ancient and modern, according to family and origin. Reconstructs and deciphers ancient languages from examples found in archeological remains of past civilizations. Prepares description of sounds, forms, and vocabulary of language. Develops improved methods in translation, including computerization. Reduces previously unwritten languages to standardized written form. Prepares descriptions of comparative languages to facilitate improvement of teaching and translation. Contributes to development of linguistic theory. Prepares tests for language-learning aptitudes and language proficiency. Prepares language-teaching materials, such as dictionaries and handbooks. Prepares literacy materials. Teaches language to other than native speakers. Consults with government agencies regarding language programs.
Yearly Earnings: $37,960
Education: Master's degree
Knowledge: Sociology and Anthropology; Geography; Education and Training; English Language; Foreign Language; History and Archeology; Philosophy and Theology
Abilities: Oral Comprehension; Written Comprehension; Oral Expression; Written Expression; Fluency of Ideas; Originality; Memorization; Sound Localization; Speech Recognition; Speech Clarity
Skills: Reading Comprehension; Active Listening; Writing; Speaking; Critical Thinking; Active Learning; Learning Strategies; Social Perceptiveness; Instructing; Information Gathering; Information Organization; Synthesis/Reorganization; Idea Generation; Idea Evaluation; Implementation Planning; Visioning
General Work Activities: Getting Information Needed to Do the Job; Monitoring Processes, Material, or Surroundings; Judging Qualities of Things, Services, People; Evaluating Information against Standards; Analyzing Data or Information; Making Decisions and Solving Problems; Thinking Creatively; Operating Vehicles or Equipment; Implementing Ideas, Programs, etc.; Documenting/Recording Information; Interpreting Meaning of Information to Others; Teaching Others; Provide Consultation and Advice to Others
Job Characteristics: None above average
GOE Group/s: 11.03.02 Social Research: Sociological
CIP Program/s: 160101 Foreign Languages and Literatures, General; 160102 Linguistics; 450201 Anthropology; 450301 Archeology; 450901 International Relations and Affairs
Related DOT Job/s: 059.067-010 PHILOLOGIST; 059.067-014 SCIENTIFIC LINGUIST

27199E HISTORIANS. OOH Title/s: Social Scientists

Research, analyze, record, and interpret the past as recorded in sources such as government and institutional records, newspapers and other periodicals, photographs, interviews, films, and unpublished manuscripts, such as personal diaries and letters. Conducts historical research on subjects of import to society, and presents finding and theories in textbooks, journals, and other publications. Assembles historical data by consulting sources, such as archives, court records, diaries, news files, and miscellaneous published and unpublished materials. Traces historical development within restricted field of research, such as economics, sociology, or philosophy. Organizes and evaluates data on basis of authenticity and relative significance. Reviews and collects data, such as books, pamphlets, periodicals, and rare newspapers, to provide source material for research. Consults experts or witnesses of historical events. Consults with or advises other individuals on historical authenticity of various materials. Reviews publications and exhibits prepared by staff prior to public release in order to ensure historical accuracy of presentations. Advises or consults with individuals, institutions, and commercial organizations on technological evolution or customs peculiar to certain historical period. Approves or recommends purchase of library reference materials for department. Translates or requests translation of reference materials. Directs and coordinates activities of research staff. Speaks before various groups, organizations, and clubs to promote societal aims and activities. Performs administrative duties, such as

budget preparation, employee evaluation, and program planning. Edits society publications. Coordinates activities of workers engaged in cataloging and filing materials. Conducts campaigns to raise funds for society programs and projects.
Yearly Earnings: $37,960
Education: Master's degree
Knowledge: Administration and Management; Economics and Accounting; Sales and Marketing; Personnel and Human Resources; Sociology and Anthropology; Geography; Education and Training; English Language; Foreign Language; Fine Arts; History and Archeology; Philosophy and Theology; Communications and Media
Abilities: Oral Comprehension; Written Comprehension; Oral Expression; Written Expression; Deductive Reasoning; Inductive Reasoning; Memorization; Speech Clarity
Skills: Reading Comprehension; Writing; Speaking; Critical Thinking; Active Learning; Coordination; Information Gathering; Information Organization; Synthesis/Reorganization; Idea Generation; Idea Evaluation; Implementation Planning; Time Management; Management of Financial Resources; Management of Material Resources; Management of Personnel Resources
General Work Activities: Getting Information Needed to Do the Job; Monitoring Processes, Material, or Surroundings; Judging Qualities of Things, Services, People; Evaluating Information against Standards; Analyzing Data or Information; Making Decisions and Solving Problems; Developing Objectives and Strategies; Organizing, Planning, and Prioritizing; Operating Vehicles or Equipment; Documenting/Recording Information; Interpreting Meaning of Information to Others; Communicating with Other Workers; Communicating with Persons Outside Organization; Performing for or Working with Public; Coordinating Work and Activities of Others; Developing and Building Teams; Teaching Others; Guiding, Directing and Motivating Subordinates; Coaching and Developing Others; Provide Consultation and Advice to Others; Performing Administrative Activities; Staffing Organizational Units; Monitoring and Controlling Resources
Job Characteristics: Coordinate or Lead Others; Sitting
GOE Group/s: 11.03.03 Social Research: Historical
CIP Program/s: 450801 History, General; 450802 American (United States) History; 450803 European History; 450804 History and Philosophy of Science and Technology; 450805 Public/Applied History and Archival Administration; 450901 International Relations and Affairs; 451001 Political Science, General; 500501 Drama/Theater Arts, General; 500505 Drama/Theater Literature, History and Criticism; 500701 Art, General; 500704 Arts Management; 520201 Business Administration and Management, General
Related DOT Job/s: 052.067-014 DIRECTOR, STATE-HISTORICAL SOCIETY; 052.067-022 HISTORIAN; 052.067-026 HISTORIAN, DRAMATIC ARTS; 052.167-010 DIRECTOR, RESEARCH

27199F INTELLIGENCE SPECIALISTS. OOH Title/s: Social Scientists

Collect, record, analyze, and disseminate tactical, political, strategic, or technical intelligence information to facilitate development of military or political strategies. Evaluates results of research and prepares recommendations for implementing or rejecting proposed solution to plans. Segregates and records incoming intelligence data according to type of data to facilitate comparison, study, and accessibility. Prepares and analyzes information concerning strength, equipment, location, disposition, organization, and movement of enemy forces. Compiles intelligence information to be used in preparing situation maps, charts, visual aids, briefing papers, reports, and publications. Examines intelligence source materials. Compiles terrain intelligence, such as condition of land routes, port facilities, and sources of water, sand, gravel, rock, and timbers. Evaluates data concerning subversive activities, enemy propaganda, and military or political conditions in foreign countries to facilitate counteraction. Briefs and debriefs ground or aviation personnel prior to and after missions. Confers with military leaders and supporting personnel to determine dimensions of problem and to discuss proposals for solution. Develops plans for predicting factors, such as cost and probable success of solutions, according to research techniques and computer formulations. Maintains familiarity with geography; cultural traditions; and social, political, and economic structure of countries from which subversive data originates. Maintains intelligence libraries, including maps, charts, documents, and other items. Assists intelligence officers in analysis and selection of aerial bombardment targets. Plans or assists superiors in planning and supervising intelligence activities of unit assigned.
Yearly Earnings: $37,960
Education: Master's degree
Knowledge: Administration and Management; Clerical; Economics and Accounting; Psychology; Sociology and Anthropology; Geography; Education and Training; Foreign Language; History and Archeology; Philosophy and Theology; Public Safety and Security; Law, Government, and Jurisprudence; Telecommunications; Communications and Media; Transportation
Abilities: Oral Comprehension; Written Comprehension; Oral Expression; Written Expression; Fluency of Ideas; Originality; Problem Sensitivity; Deductive Reasoning; Inductive Reasoning; Information Ordering; Category Flexibility; Number Facility; Memorization; Speed of Closure; Flexibility of Closure; Visualization; Speech Recognition
Skills: Reading Comprehension; Active Listening; Writing; Speaking; Critical Thinking; Active Learning; Learning Strategies; Monitoring; Social Perceptiveness; Coordination; Persuasion; Negotiation; Problem Identification; Information Gathering; Information Organization; Synthesis/Reorganization; Idea Generation; Idea Evaluation; Implementation Planning; Solution Appraisal; Operations Analysis; Systems Perception; Identifying Downstream Consequences; Identification of Key Causes; Judgment and Decision Making; Time Management
General Work Activities: Getting Information Needed to Do the Job; Monitoring Processes, Material, or Surroundings; Identifying Objects, Actions, and Events; Estimating Needed Characteristics; Judging Qualities of Things, Services, People; Processing Information; Evaluating Information against Standards; Analyzing Data or Information; Making Decisions and Solving Problems; Thinking Creatively; Updating and Using Job-Relevant Knowledge; Developing Objectives and Strategies; Scheduling Work and Activities; Organizing, Planning, and Prioritizing; Operating Vehicles or Equipment; Implementing Ideas, Programs, etc.; Documenting/Recording Information; Interpreting Meaning of Information to Others; Communicating with Other Workers; Communicating with Persons Outside Organization; Establishing and Maintaining Relationships; Selling or Influencing Others; Developing and Building Teams; Guiding, Directing and Motivating Subordinates; Provide Consultation and Advice to Others
Job Characteristics: Deal with Physical, Aggressive People; Sitting; Consequence of Error; Importance of Being Exact or Accurate; Importance of Being Aware of New Events
GOE Group/s: 04.01.02 Safety and Law Enforcement: Investigating; 11.03.02 Social Research: Sociological
CIP Program/s: 450901 International Relations and Affairs; 451001 Political Science, General; 451101 Sociology
Related DOT Job/s: 059.167-010 INTELLIGENCE RESEARCH SPECIALIST; 059.267-010 INTELLIGENCE SPECIALIST; 059.267-014 INTELLIGENCE SPECIALIST

27199G GENEALOGISTS. OOH Title/s: Social Scientists

Research genealogical background of individual or family to establish descent from specific ancestor or to identify forebears

of individual or family. Consults American and foreign genealogical tables, publications, and documents to trace lines of descent or succession. References materials, such as church and county records, for evidence of births, baptisms, marriages, deaths, and legacies. Organizes and evaluates data on basis of significance and authenticity. Gathers and appraises available physical evidence, such as drawings and photographs. Constructs chart showing lines of descent and family relationships. Prepares history of family in narrative form, or writes brief sketches emphasizing points of interest in family background.
Yearly Earnings: $37,960
Education: Master's degree
Knowledge: Sociology and Anthropology; Geography; English Language; Foreign Language; History and Archeology
Abilities: Inductive Reasoning
Skills: Information Gathering; Information Organization
General Work Activities: Evaluating Information against Standards; Analyzing Data or Information; Documenting/Recording Information; Interpreting Meaning of Information to Others
Job Characteristics: Sitting
GOE Group/s: 11.03.03 Social Research: Historical
CIP Program/s: 450801 History, General; 450805 Public/Applied History and Archival Administration
Related DOT Job/s: 052.067-018 GENEALOGIST

27199H ARCHEOLOGISTS. OOH Title/s: Social Scientists
Conduct research to reconstruct record of past human life and culture from human remains, artifacts, architectural features, and structures recovered through excavation, underwater recovery, or other means of discovery. Studies artifacts, architectural features, and types of structures recovered by excavation in order to determine age and cultural identity. Classifies and interprets artifacts, architectural features, and types of structures recovered by excavation to determine age and cultural identity. Establishes chronological sequence of development of each culture from simpler to more advanced levels.
Yearly Earnings: $37,960
Education: Master's degree
Knowledge: Sociology and Anthropology; Geography; Foreign Language; History and Archeology; Philosophy and Theology
Abilities: Written Comprehension; Deductive Reasoning; Inductive Reasoning; Category Flexibility
Skills: Reading Comprehension; Writing; Science; Critical Thinking; Active Learning; Information Gathering; Information Organization; Synthesis/Reorganization; Idea Generation; Idea Evaluation
General Work Activities: Getting Information Needed to Do the Job; Monitoring Processes, Material, or Surroundings; Estimating Needed Characteristics; Judging Qualities of Things, Services, People; Evaluating Information against Standards; Analyzing Data or Information; Making Decisions and Solving Problems; Developing Objectives and Strategies; Organizing, Planning, and Prioritizing; Documenting/Recording Information; Interpreting Meaning of Information to Others
Job Characteristics: Very Hot; Extremely Bright or Inadequate Lighting; Cramped Work Space, Awkward Positions; Kneeling, Crouching, or Crawling; Bending or Twisting the Body; Importance of Being Aware of New Events
GOE Group/s: 11.03.03 Social Research: Historical
CIP Program/s: 450201 Anthropology; 450301 Archeology
Related DOT Job/s: 055.067-018 ARCHEOLOGIST

Social Services Workers

27302 SOCIAL WORKERS, MEDICAL AND PSYCHIATRIC. OOH Title/s: Social Workers
Counsel and aid individuals and families with problems that may arise during or following the recovery from physical or mental illness, by providing supportive services designed to help the persons understand, accept, and follow medical recommendations. Include chemical dependency counselors. Counsels clients and patients, individually and in group sessions, to assist in overcoming dependencies, adjusting to life, and making changes. Counsels family members to assist in understanding, dealing with, and supporting client or patient. Interviews client, reviews records, and confers with other professionals to evaluate mental or physical condition of client or patient. Formulates or coordinates program plan for treatment, care, and rehabilitation of client or patient, based on social work experience and knowledge. Monitors, evaluates, and records client progress according to measurable goals described in treatment and care plan. Modifies treatment plan to comply with changes in client's status. Refers patient, client, or family to community resources to assist in recovery from mental or physical illness. Intervenes as advocate for client or patient to resolve emergency problems in crisis situation. Plans and conducts programs to prevent substance abuse or improve health and counseling services in community. Develops and monitors budgetary expenditures for program. Supervises and directs other workers providing services to client or patient.
Yearly Earnings: $33,332
Education: Bachelor's degree
Knowledge: Customer and Personal Service; Personnel and Human Resources; Psychology; Sociology and Anthropology; Medicine and Dentistry; Therapy and Counseling; Education and Training; Philosophy and Theology; Communications and Media
Abilities: Oral Expression; Fluency of Ideas; Originality; Problem Sensitivity; Time Sharing; Speech Recognition; Speech Clarity
Skills: Reading Comprehension; Active Listening; Writing; Speaking; Critical Thinking; Active Learning; Learning Strategies; Monitoring; Social Perceptiveness; Coordination; Persuasion; Negotiation; Instructing; Service Orientation; Problem Identification; Idea Generation; Idea Evaluation; Implementation Planning; Solution Appraisal; Visioning; Systems Perception; Identifying Downstream Consequences; Identification of Key Causes; Judgment and Decision Making; Systems Evaluation; Time Management; Management of Financial Resources; Management of Personnel Resources
General Work Activities: Monitoring Processes, Material, or Surroundings; Making Decisions and Solving Problems; Organizing, Planning, and Prioritizing; Communicating with Persons Outside Organization; Establishing and Maintaining Relationships; Assisting and Caring for Others; Selling or Influencing Others; Resolving Conflicts, Negotiating with Others; Coordinating Work and Activities of Others; Developing and Building Teams; Guiding, Directing and Motivating Subordinates; Coaching and Developing Others; Monitoring and Controlling Resources
Job Characteristics: Objective or Subjective Information; Job-Required Social Interaction; Persuade Someone to a Course of Action; Provide a Service to Others; Deal with External Customers; Coordinate or Lead Others; Responsible for Others' Health and Safety; Frequency in Conflict Situations; Deal with Unpleasant or Angry People; Deal with Physical, Aggressive People; Sitting; Importance of Being Aware of New Events
GOE Group/s: 10.01.02 Social Services: Counseling and Social Work

CIP Program/s: 420201 Clinical Psychology; 420601 Counseling Psychology; 440701 Social Work; 511501 Alcohol/Drug Abuse Counseling; 511503 Clinical and Medical Social Work
Related DOT Job/s: 045.107-058 SUBSTANCE ABUSE COUNSELOR; 195.107-030 SOCIAL WORKER, MEDICAL; 195.107-034 SOCIAL WORKER, PSYCHIATRIC; 195.107-050 ; 195.167-050

27305A COMMUNITY ORGANIZATION SOCIAL WORKERS. OOH Title/s: Social Workers; Human Services Workers; School Teachers—Kindergarten, Elementary, and Secondary

Plan, organize, and work with community groups to help solve social problems and deliver specialized social services. Organizes projects, such as discussion groups, and conducts consumer problem surveys to stimulate civic responsibility and promote group work concepts. Investigates problems of assigned community and individuals disadvantaged because of income, age, or economic or personal handicaps, to determine needs. Develops, organizes, and directs customized programs, such as physical, educational, recreational, or cultural activities, for individuals and groups. Reviews and evaluates available resources and services from local agencies to provide social assistance for clients. Secures and coordinates community social service assistance, such as health, welfare, and education for individuals and families. Assists communities in establishing new local affiliates or programs. Initiates and maintains liaison between housing authority and local agencies to promote development and management of public housing. Speaks before groups to explain supportive services and resources available to persons needing special assistance. Facilitates establishment of constructive relationships between tenants and housing management, and among tenants. Interprets standards and program goals of national or state agencies to assist local organizations in establishing goals and standards. Coordinates work activities of individuals to improve vocational skills. Writes proposals to obtain government or private funding for projects designed to meet needs of community. Maintains records and prepares reports on community topics, such as work activities, local conditions, and developing trends. Assesses complexity level of individual's capacity to perform work activities. Identifies individual's behavior deviations and assists individual to resolve work-related difficulties. Demonstrates and instructs participants in activities, such as sports, dances, games, arts, crafts, and dramatics. Demonstrates job duties to individuals, oversees and monitors work performance, and examines workpiece to verify adherence to specifications. Recruits, trains, and supervises paid staff and volunteers in specific assignments. Prepares and presents budgets.
Yearly Earnings: $26,312
Education: Bachelor's degree
Knowledge: Administration and Management; Sales and Marketing; Customer and Personal Service; Personnel and Human Resources; Psychology; Sociology and Anthropology; Therapy and Counseling; Education and Training; English Language; Communications and Media
Abilities: Time Sharing; Speech Recognition
Skills: Reading Comprehension; Active Listening; Writing; Speaking; Critical Thinking; Learning Strategies; Monitoring; Social Perceptiveness; Coordination; Persuasion; Negotiation; Instructing; Service Orientation; Problem Identification; Information Gathering; Synthesis/Reorganization; Idea Generation; Idea Evaluation; Implementation Planning; Solution Appraisal; Visioning; Systems Perception; Identification of Key Causes; Judgment and Decision Making; Time Management; Management of Financial Resources; Management of Material Resources; Management of Personnel Resources
General Work Activities: Getting Information Needed to Do the Job; Monitoring Processes, Material, or Surroundings; Estimating Needed Characteristics; Judging Qualities of Things, Services, People; Analyzing Data or Information; Making Decisions and Solving Problems; Thinking Creatively; Developing Objectives and Strategies; Scheduling Work and Activities; Organizing, Planning, and Prioritizing; Implementing Ideas, Programs, etc.; Documenting/Recording Information; Interpreting Meaning of Information to Others; Communicating with Other Workers; Communicating with Persons Outside Organization; Establishing and Maintaining Relationships; Assisting and Caring for Others; Selling or Influencing Others; Resolving Conflicts, Negotiating with Others; Performing for or Working with Public; Coordinating Work and Activities of Others; Developing and Building Teams; Teaching Others; Guiding, Directing and Motivating Subordinates; Coaching and Developing Others; Provide Consultation and Advice to Others; Performing Administrative Activities; Staffing Organizational Units; Monitoring and Controlling Resources
Job Characteristics: Objective or Subjective Information; Job-Required Social Interaction; Supervise, Coach, Train Others; Persuade Someone to a Course of Action; Deal with External Customers; Coordinate or Lead Others
GOE Group/s: 09.01.01 Hospitality Services: Social and Recreational Activities; 10.01.02 Social Services: Counseling and Social Work; 11.07.01 Services Administration: Social Services; 11.07.03 Services Administration: Education Services
CIP Program/s: 130101 Education, General; 131001 Special Education, General; 131005 Education of the Emotionally Handicapped; 131006 Education of the Mentally Handicapped; 131007 Education of the Multiple Handicapped; 131008 Education of the Physically Handicapped; 131011 Education of the Specific Learning Disabled; 131012 Education of the Speech Impaired; 440201 Community Organization, Resources and Services; 440701 Social Work
Related DOT Job/s: 187.134-010 SUPERVISOR, CONTRACT-SHELTERED WORKSHOP; 187.137-014 SUPERVISOR, VOLUNTEER SERVICES; 189.267-010 FIELD REPRESENTATIVE; 195.164-010 GROUP WORKER; 195.167-010 COMMUNITY ORGANIZATION WORKER; 195.167-014 COMMUNITY-RELATIONS-AND-SERVICES ADVISOR, PUBLIC HOUSING; 195.367-018 COMMUNITY WORKER

27305B SOCIAL WORKERS. OOH Title/s: Social Workers

Counsel and aid individuals and families with problems relating to personal and family adjustments, finances, employment, food, clothing, housing, or other human needs and conditions. Counsels individuals or family members regarding behavior modifications, rehabilitation, social adjustments, financial assistance, vocational training, child care, or medical care. Counsels parents with child-rearing problems and children and youth with difficulties in social adjustments. Interviews individuals to assess social and emotional capabilities, physical and mental impairments, and financial needs. Refers client to community resources for needed assistance. Arranges for daycare, homemaker service, prenatal care, and child planning programs for clients in need of such services. Leads group counseling sessions to provide support in such areas as grief, stress, or chemical dependency. Counsels students whose behavior, school progress, or mental or physical impairment indicates need for assistance. Arranges for medical, psychiatric, and other tests that may disclose cause of difficulties and indicate remedial measures. Consults with parents, teachers, and other school personnel to determine causes of problems and effect solutions. Serves as liaison between student, home, school, family service agencies, child guidance clinics, courts, protective services, doctors, and clergy members. Investigates home conditions to determine suitability of foster or adoptive home, or to protect children from harmful environment. Develops program content and organizes and leads activities planned to enhance social development of individual members and accomplishment of group goals. Determines client's eligibility for financial assistance. Reviews service plan

and performs follow-up to determine quantity and quality of service provided to client. Places children in foster or adoptive homes, institutions, or medical treatment centers. Evaluates personal characteristics of foster home or adoption applicants. Maintains case history records and prepares reports. Collects supplementary information, such as employment, medical records, or school reports. Assists travelers, including runaways, migrants, transients, refugees, repatriated Americans, and problem families.
Yearly Earnings: $26,312
Education: Bachelor's degree
Knowledge: Administration and Management; Clerical; Customer and Personal Service; Psychology; Sociology and Anthropology; Therapy and Counseling; Foreign Language; Philosophy and Theology; Law, Government, and Jurisprudence
Abilities: Oral Comprehension; Oral Expression
Skills: Reading Comprehension; Active Listening; Writing; Speaking; Critical Thinking; Active Learning; Learning Strategies; Monitoring; Social Perceptiveness; Coordination; Persuasion; Negotiation; Instructing; Service Orientation; Problem Identification; Information Gathering; Information Organization; Synthesis/Reorganization; Idea Generation; Idea Evaluation; Implementation Planning; Solution Appraisal; Visioning; Identification of Key Causes; Judgment and Decision Making; Time Management
General Work Activities: Getting Information Needed to Do the Job; Monitoring Processes, Material, or Surroundings; Identifying Objects, Actions, and Events; Estimating Needed Characteristics; Judging Qualities of Things, Services, People; Processing Information; Analyzing Data or Information; Making Decisions and Solving Problems; Updating and Using Job-Relevant Knowledge; Developing Objectives and Strategies; Organizing, Planning, and Prioritizing; Implementing Ideas, Programs, etc.; Documenting/Recording Information; Interpreting Meaning of Information to Others; Communicating with Persons Outside Organization; Establishing and Maintaining Relationships; Assisting and Caring for Others; Selling or Influencing Others; Resolving Conflicts, Negotiating with Others; Performing for or Working with Public; Coordinating Work and Activities of Others; Developing and Building Teams; Coaching and Developing Others; Provide Consultation and Advice to Others; Performing Administrative Activities
Job Characteristics: Objective or Subjective Information; Job-Required Social Interaction; Provide a Service to Others; Deal with External Customers; Frequency in Conflict Situations; Deal with Unpleasant or Angry People; Deal with Physical, Aggressive People; Sitting; Frustrating Circumstances
GOE Group/s: 10.01.02 Social Services: Counseling and Social Work
CIP Program/s: 420201 Clinical Psychology; 440701 Social Work
Related DOT Job/s: 195.107-010 CASEWORKER; 195.107-014 CASEWORKER, CHILD WELFARE; 195.107-018 CASEWORKER, FAMILY; 195.107-022 SOCIAL GROUP WORKER; 195.107-026 SOCIAL WORKER, DELINQUENCY PREVENTION; 195.107-038 SOCIAL WORKER, SCHOOL; 195.137-010 CASEWORK SUPERVISOR

27305C PROBATION AND CORRECTIONAL TREATMENT SPECIALISTS. OOH Title/s: Social Workers; Personnel, Training, and Labor Relations Specialists and Managers

Provide social services to assist in rehabilitation of law offenders in custody or on probation. Include probation and parole officers. Counsels offender and refers offender to social resources of community for assistance. Provides guidance to inmates or offenders, such as development of vocational and educational plans and available social services. Formulates rehabilitation plan for each assigned offender or inmate. Interviews offender or inmate to determine social progress and individual problems, needs, interests, and attitude. Consults with attorneys, judges, and institution personnel to evaluate inmate's social progress. Conducts follow-up interview with offender or inmate to ascertain progress made. Determines nature and extent of inmate's or offender's criminal record and current and prospective social problems. Reviews and evaluates legal and social history and progress of offender or inmate. Informs offender or inmate of requirements of conditional release, such as office visits, restitution payments, or educational and employment stipulations. Confers with inmate's or offender's family to identify needs and problems, and to ensure that family and business are attended to. Makes recommendations concerning conditional release or institutionalization of offender or inmate. Assists offender or inmate with matters concerning detainers, sentences in other jurisdictions, writs, and applications for social assistance. Develops and prepares informational packets of social agencies and assistance organizations and programs for inmate or offender. Prepares and maintains case folder for each assigned inmate or offender. Conducts prehearing or presentencing investigations, and testifies in court.
Yearly Earnings: $26,312
Education: Bachelor's degree
Knowledge: Psychology; Sociology and Anthropology; Therapy and Counseling; Public Safety and Security; Law, Government, and Jurisprudence
Abilities: None above average
Skills: Active Listening; Speaking; Social Perceptiveness; Persuasion; Negotiation; Service Orientation; Problem Identification; Idea Evaluation; Implementation Planning; Identifying Downstream Consequences; Identification of Key Causes; Judgment and Decision Making; Systems Evaluation
General Work Activities: Getting Information Needed to Do the Job; Monitoring Processes, Material, or Surroundings; Identifying Objects, Actions, and Events; Estimating Needed Characteristics; Judging Qualities of Things, Services, People; Making Decisions and Solving Problems; Developing Objectives and Strategies; Organizing, Planning, and Prioritizing; Documenting/Recording Information; Interpreting Meaning of Information to Others; Communicating with Other Workers; Communicating with Persons Outside Organization; Establishing and Maintaining Relationships; Assisting and Caring for Others; Selling or Influencing Others; Resolving Conflicts, Negotiating with Others; Performing for or Working with Public; Coaching and Developing Others; Provide Consultation and Advice to Others; Performing Administrative Activities
Job Characteristics: Objective or Subjective Information; Job-Required Social Interaction; Persuade Someone to a Course of Action; Take a Position Opposed to Others; Deal with External Customers; Frequency in Conflict Situations; Deal with Unpleasant or Angry People; Deal with Physical, Aggressive People; Importance of Being Aware of New Events
GOE Group/s: 10.01.02 Social Services: Counseling and Social Work
CIP Program/s: 440701 Social Work
Related DOT Job/s: 166.267-022 PRISONER-CLASSIFICATION INTERVIEWER; 195.107-042 CORRECTIONAL-TREATMENT SPECIALIST; 195.107-046 PROBATION-AND-PAROLE OFFICER; 195.367-026 PREPAROLE-COUNSELING AIDE

27307 RESIDENTIAL COUNSELORS. OOH Title/s: Human Services Workers

Coordinate activities for residents of care and treatment institutions, boarding schools, college fraternities or sororities, children's homes, or similar establishments. Work includes developing or assisting in the development of program plans for individuals, maintaining household records, and assigning rooms. Counsel residents in identifying and resolving social or other problems. Order supplies and determine need for maintenance, repairs, and furnishings. Assigns room, assists in planning

recreational activities, and supervises work and study programs. Counsels residents in identifying and resolving social and other problems. Orders supplies and determines need for maintenance, repairs, and furnishings. Compiles records of daily activities of residents. Ascertains need for and secures service of physician. Escorts individuals on trips outside establishment for shopping or to obtain medical or dental services. Chaperons group-sponsored trips and social functions. Hires and supervises activities of housekeeping personnel. Plans menus of meals for residents of establishment. Answers telephone. Sorts and distributes mail.
Yearly Earnings: $36,088
Education: Bachelor's degree
Knowledge: Administration and Management; Customer and Personal Service; Personnel and Human Resources; Psychology; Sociology and Anthropology; Medicine and Dentistry; Therapy and Counseling; Philosophy and Theology; Transportation
Abilities: Originality; Night Vision
Skills: Active Listening; Speaking; Learning Strategies; Social Perceptiveness; Coordination; Persuasion; Negotiation; Service Orientation; Idea Generation; Implementation Planning; Solution Appraisal; Time Management; Management of Financial Resources; Management of Material Resources; Management of Personnel Resources
General Work Activities: Scheduling Work and Activities; Establishing and Maintaining Relationships; Assisting and Caring for Others; Resolving Conflicts, Negotiating with Others; Coordinating Work and Activities of Others; Guiding, Directing and Motivating Subordinates; Coaching and Developing Others; Provide Consultation and Advice to Others; Staffing Organizational Units; Monitoring and Controlling Resources
Job Characteristics: Objective or Subjective Information; Job-Required Social Interaction; Supervise, Coach, Train Others; Persuade Someone to a Course of Action; Provide a Service to Others; Take a Position Opposed to Others; Deal with External Customers; Coordinate or Lead Others; Responsible for Others' Health and Safety; Responsibility for Outcomes and Results; Frequency in Conflict Situations; Deal with Unpleasant or Angry People; Deal with Physical, Aggressive People; Diseases/Infections; Walking or Running; Frustrating Circumstances; Importance of Being Aware of New Events
GOE Group/s: 11.07.01 Services Administration: Social Services
CIP Program/s: 200201 Child Care and Guidance Workers and Managers, General; 200202 Child Care Provider/Assistant; 200203 Child Care Services Manager
Related DOT Job/s: 187.167-186 RESIDENCE SUPERVISOR

27308 HUMAN SERVICES WORKERS. OOH Title/s: Human Services Workers

Assist social group workers and caseworkers with developing, organizing, and conducting programs to prevent and resolve problems relevant to substance abuse and human relationships. Aid families and clients in obtaining information on the use of social and community services. May recommend additional services. Exclude residential counselors and psychiatric technicians. Visits individuals in homes or attends group meetings to provide information on agency services, requirements, and procedures. Advises clients regarding food stamps, child care, food, money management, sanitation, and housekeeping. Interviews individuals and family members to compile information on social, educational, criminal, institutional, or drug history. Provides information on and refers individuals to public or private agencies and community services for assistance. Assists clients with preparation of forms, such as tax or rent forms. Assists in locating housing for displaced individuals. Assists in planning of food budget, utilizing charts and sample budgets. Monitors free, supplementary meal program to ensure cleanliness of facility and that eligibility guidelines are met for persons receiving meals. Meets with youth groups to acquaint them with consequences of delinquent acts. Observes clients' food selections, and recommends alternate economical and nutritional food choices. Observes and discusses meal preparation, and suggests alternate methods of food preparation. Consults with supervisor concerning programs for individual families. Oversees day-to-day group activities of residents in institution. Transports and accompanies clients to shopping area and to appointments, using automobile. Explains rules established by owner or management, such as sanitation and maintenance requirements, and parking regulations. Demonstrates use and care of equipment for tenant use. Informs tenants of facilities, such as laundries and playgrounds. Submits to and reviews reports and problems with superior. Keeps records and prepares reports for owner or management concerning visits with clients. Cares for children in client's home during client's appointments.
Yearly Earnings: $13,416
Education: Moderate-term O-J-T
Knowledge: Administration and Management; Clerical; Customer and Personal Service; Food Production; Psychology; Sociology and Anthropology; Therapy and Counseling; Education and Training; Philosophy and Theology; Transportation
Abilities: Oral Expression; Time Sharing
Skills: Active Listening; Speaking; Learning Strategies; Social Perceptiveness; Persuasion; Negotiation; Instructing; Service Orientation; Identification of Key Causes
General Work Activities: Developing Objectives and Strategies; Interacting with Computers; Documenting/Recording Information; Establishing and Maintaining Relationships; Assisting and Caring for Others; Selling or Influencing Others; Performing for or Working with Public; Coaching and Developing Others; Performing Administrative Activities
Job Characteristics: Objective or Subjective Information; Job-Required Social Interaction; Persuade Someone to a Course of Action; Provide a Service to Others; Deal with External Customers; Coordinate or Lead Others; Frequency in Conflict Situations; Deal with Unpleasant or Angry People; Deal with Physical, Aggressive People; Diseases/Infections; Frustrating Circumstances
GOE Group/s: 07.01.01 Administrative Detail: Interviewing; 10.01.02 Social Services: Counseling and Social Work
CIP Program/s: 200601 Custodial, Housekeeping and Home Services Workers and Managers; 200602 Elder Care Provider/Companion; 200606 Homemaker's Aide
Related DOT Job/s: 195.367-010 CASE AIDE; 195.367-014 MANAGEMENT AIDE; 195.367-022 FOOD-MANAGEMENT AIDE; 195.367-034 SOCIAL-SERVICES AIDE

27311 RECREATION WORKERS. OOH Title/s: Recreation Workers

Conduct recreation activities with groups in public, private, or volunteer agencies or recreation facilities. Organize and promote activities such as arts and crafts, sports, games, music, dramatics, social recreation, camping, and hobbies, taking into account needs and interests of individual members. Organizes, leads, and promotes interest in facility activities, such as arts, crafts, sports, games, camping, and hobbies. Conducts recreational activities and instructs participants to develop skills in provided activities. Arranges for activity requirements, such as entertainment and setting up equipment and decorations. Schedules facility activities and maintains record of programs. Explains principles, techniques, and safety procedures of facility activities to participants, and demonstrates use of material and equipment. Ascertains and interprets group interests, evaluates equipment and facilities, and adapts activities to meet participant needs. Meets and collaborates with agency personnel, community organizations, and other professional personnel to plan balanced

recreational programs for participants. Enforces rules and regulations of facility, maintains discipline, and ensures safety. Greets and introduces new arrivals to other guests, acquaints arrivals with facilities, and encourages group participation. Tests and documents content of swimming pool water, and schedules maintenance and use of facilities. Supervises and coordinates work activities of personnel, trains staff, and assigns duties. Schedules maintenance and use of facilities. Evaluates staff performance and records reflective information on performance evaluation forms. Completes and maintains time and attendance forms and inventory lists. Meets with staff to discuss rules, regulations, and work-related problems. Administers first aid, according to prescribed procedures, or notifies emergency medical personnel when necessary. Assists management to resolve complaints.
Yearly Earnings: $25,636
Education: Bachelor's degree
Knowledge: Administration and Management; Customer and Personal Service; Personnel and Human Resources; Psychology; Sociology and Anthropology; Medicine and Dentistry; Therapy and Counseling; Education and Training; Foreign Language; Fine Arts; Public Safety and Security; Law, Government, and Jurisprudence; Communications and Media
Abilities: Oral Expression; Fluency of Ideas; Originality; Category Flexibility; Memorization; Spatial Orientation; Time Sharing; Gross Body Coordination; Gross Body Equilibrium; Far Vision; Night Vision; Speech Recognition; Speech Clarity
Skills: Learning Strategies; Social Perceptiveness; Coordination; Instructing; Service Orientation; Implementation Planning; Time Management; Management of Material Resources; Management of Personnel Resources
General Work Activities: Judging Qualities of Things, Services, People; Thinking Creatively; Developing Objectives and Strategies; Scheduling Work and Activities; Organizing, Planning, and Prioritizing; Communicating with Other Workers; Communicating with Persons Outside Organization; Establishing and Maintaining Relationships; Assisting and Caring for Others; Selling or Influencing Others; Resolving Conflicts, Negotiating with Others; Performing for or Working with Public; Coordinating Work and Activities of Others; Developing and Building Teams; Teaching Others; Guiding, Directing and Motivating Subordinates; Coaching and Developing Others; Provide Consultation and Advice to Others; Performing Administrative Activities; Staffing Organizational Units; Monitoring and Controlling Resources
Job Characteristics: Objective or Subjective Information; Job-Required Social Interaction; Supervise, Coach, Train Others; Provide a Service to Others; Deal with External Customers; Coordinate or Lead Others; Responsible for Others' Health and Safety; Responsibility for Outcomes and Results; Deal with Unpleasant or Angry People; Walking or Running
GOE Group/s: 09.01.01 Hospitality Services: Social and Recreational Activities; 10.02.02 Nursing, Therapy, and Specialized Teaching Services: Therapy and Rehabilitation; 11.07.04 Services Administration: Recreation Services; 11.11.02 Business Management: Recreation and Amusement
CIP Program/s: 200201 Child Care and Guidance Workers and Managers, General; 200202 Child Care Provider/Assistant; 310101 Parks, Recreation and Leisure Studies; 310301 Parks, Recreation and Leisure Facilities Management; 520901 Hospitality/Administration Management
Related DOT Job/s: 159.124-010 COUNSELOR, CAMP; 187.167-238 RECREATION SUPERVISOR; 195.167-026 DIRECTOR, RECREATION CENTER; 195.227-010 PROGRAM AIDE, GROUP WORK; 195.227-014 RECREATION LEADER; 352.167-010 DIRECTOR, SOCIAL

Religious Workers

27502 CLERGY. OOH Title/s: Protestant Ministers; Roman Catholic Priests; Rabbis

Conduct religious worship and perform other spiritual functions associated with beliefs and practices of religious faith or denomination, as delegated by ordinance, license, or other authorization. Provide spiritual and moral guidance and assistance to members. Leads congregation in worship services. Conducts wedding and funeral services. Administers religious rites or ordinances. Counsels those in spiritual need. Interprets doctrine of religion. Instructs people who seek conversion to faith. Prepares and delivers sermons and other talks. Visits sick and shut-ins, and helps poor. Engages in interfaith, community, civic, educational, and recreational activities sponsored by or related to interest of denomination. Writes articles for publication. Teaches in seminaries and universities.
Yearly Earnings: $27,092
Education: First professional degree
Knowledge: Psychology; Sociology and Anthropology; Therapy and Counseling; Education and Training; English Language; History and Archeology; Philosophy and Theology; Communications and Media
Abilities: Oral Expression; Written Expression; Fluency of Ideas; Speech Clarity
Skills: Reading Comprehension; Active Listening; Writing; Speaking; Active Learning; Learning Strategies; Monitoring; Social Perceptiveness; Persuasion; Negotiation; Instructing; Service Orientation; Idea Generation; Implementation Planning; Visioning
General Work Activities: Developing Objectives and Strategies; Organizing, Planning, and Prioritizing; Interpreting Meaning of Information to Others; Communicating with Persons Outside Organization; Establishing and Maintaining Relationships; Assisting and Caring for Others; Selling or Influencing Others; Performing for or Working with Public; Developing and Building Teams; Teaching Others; Guiding, Directing and Motivating Subordinates; Coaching and Developing Others; Provide Consultation and Advice to Others
Job Characteristics: Objective or Subjective Information; Job-Required Social Interaction; Persuade Someone to a Course of Action; Frequency in Conflict Situations; Special Uniform
GOE Group/s: 10.01.01 Social Services: Religious
CIP Program/s: 390201 Bible/Biblical Studies; 390301 Missions/Missionary Studies and Misology; 390602 Divinity/Ministry (B.D., M.Div.); 390701 Pastoral Counseling and Specialized Ministries
Related DOT Job/s: 120.107-010 CLERGY

27505 DIRECTORS, RELIGIOUS ACTIVITIES AND EDUCATION. OOH Title/s: Directors, Religious Activities and Education

Direct and coordinate activities of a denominational group to meet religious needs of students. Plan, organize, and direct church school programs designed to promote religious education among church membership. Provide counseling and guidance relative to marital, health, financial, and religious problems. Coordinates activities with religious advisers, councils, and university officials to meet religious needs of students. Counsels individuals regarding marital, health, financial, and religious problems. Plans congregational activities and projects to encourage participation in religious education programs. Develops, organizes, and directs study courses and religious education programs within congregation. Supervises instructional staff in religious education program. Promotes student participation in extracurricular congregational activities. Assists and advises groups in promoting interfaith understanding. Plans

and conducts conferences dealing with interpretation of religious ideas and convictions. Solicits support, participation, and interest in religious education programs from congregation members, organizations, officials, and clergy. Analyzes member participation and changes in congregation emphasis to determine needs for religious education. Interprets policies of university to community religious workers. Interprets religious education to public through speaking, leading discussions, and writing articles for local and national publications. Analyzes revenue and program cost data to determine budget priorities. Orders and distributes school supplies.
Yearly Earnings: $25,636
Education: Bachelor's degree
Knowledge: Administration and Management; Economics and Accounting; Psychology; Sociology and Anthropology; Therapy and Counseling; Education and Training; English Language; Philosophy and Theology; Communications and Media
Abilities: Oral Expression; Speech Clarity
Skills: Reading Comprehension; Active Listening; Writing; Speaking; Critical Thinking; Learning Strategies; Monitoring; Social Perceptiveness; Coordination; Persuasion; Instructing; Service Orientation; Idea Evaluation; Implementation Planning; Solution Appraisal; Visioning; Systems Perception; Identifying Downstream Consequences; Identification of Key Causes; Judgment and Decision Making; Systems Evaluation; Time Management; Management of Financial Resources; Management of Material Resources; Management of Personnel Resources
General Work Activities: Getting Information Needed to Do the Job; Thinking Creatively; Developing Objectives and Strategies; Scheduling Work and Activities; Organizing, Planning, and Prioritizing; Interpreting Meaning of Information to Others; Communicating with Other Workers; Communicating with Persons Outside Organization; Establishing and Maintaining Relationships; Assisting and Caring for Others; Selling or Influencing Others; Resolving Conflicts, Negotiating with Others; Performing for or Working with Public; Coordinating Work and Activities of Others; Developing and Building Teams; Teaching Others; Guiding, Directing and Motivating Subordinates; Coaching and Developing Others; Provide Consultation and Advice to Others; Staffing Organizational Units; Monitoring and Controlling Resources
Job Characteristics: Objective or Subjective Information; Job-Required Social Interaction; Supervise, Coach, Train Others; Persuade Someone to a Course of Action; Provide a Service to Others; Take a Position Opposed to Others; Deal with External Customers; Coordinate or Lead Others; Responsibility for Outcomes and Results
GOE Group/s: 10.01.01 Social Services: Religious; 11.07.03 Services Administration: Education Services
CIP Program/s: 390201 Bible/Biblical Studies; 390301 Missions/Missionary Studies and Misology; 390401 Religious Education; 390701 Pastoral Counseling and Specialized Ministries
Related DOT Job/s: 129.107-018 DIRECTOR OF RELIGIOUS ACTIVITIES; 129.107-022 DIRECTOR, RELIGIOUS EDUCATION

27599 ALL OTHER RELIGIOUS WORKERS. OOH Title/s: Directors, Religious Activities and Education

All other religious workers not classified separately above.
Yearly Earnings: $25,636
Education: Bachelor's degree
GOE Group/s: 10.01.01 Social Services: Religious; 10.01.02 Social Services: Counseling and Social Work; 10.03.02 Child and Adult Care: Patient Care; 11.07.03 Services Administration: Education Services
CIP Program/s: 390401 Religious Education; 390501 Religious/Sacred Music; 390701 Pastoral Counseling and Specialized Ministries
Related DOT Job/s: 129.027-010 CANTOR; 129.107-010 CHRISTIAN SCIENCE NURSE; 129.107-014 CHRISTIAN SCIENCE PRACTITIONER; 129.107-026 PASTORAL ASSISTANT; 129.271-010 MOHEL; 199.207-010 DIANETIC COUNSELOR

Lawyers and Judges

28102 JUDGES AND MAGISTRATES. OOH Title/s: Lawyers and Judges

Judges arbitrate, advise, and administer justice in a court of law. Sentence defendant in criminal cases according to statutes of state or federal government. May determine liability of defendant in civil cases. Magistrates adjudicate criminal cases not involving penitentiary sentences and civil cases concerning damages below a sum specified by state law. May issue marriage licenses and perform wedding ceremonies. Listens to presentation of case, rules on admissibility of evidence and methods of conducting testimony, and settles disputes between opposing attorneys. Instructs jury on applicable law, and directs jury to deduce facts from evidence presented. Sentences defendant in criminal cases, on conviction by jury, according to statutes of state or federal government. Adjudicates cases involving motor vehicle laws. Establishes rules of procedure on questions for which standard procedures have not been established by law or by superior court. Conducts preliminary hearings in felony cases to determine reasonable and probable cause to hold defendant for further proceedings or trial. Reads or listens to allegations made by plaintiff in civil suits to determine their sufficiency. Awards judicial relief to litigants in civil cases in relation to findings by jury or by court. Examines evidence in criminal cases to determine if evidence will support charges. Performs wedding ceremonies.
Yearly Earnings: $58,864
Education: Work experience, plus degree
Knowledge: Economics and Accounting; Personnel and Human Resources; Psychology; Sociology and Anthropology; Geography; English Language; History and Archeology; Philosophy and Theology; Public Safety and Security; Law, Government, and Jurisprudence; Communications and Media
Abilities: Oral Comprehension; Written Comprehension; Oral Expression; Originality; Problem Sensitivity; Deductive Reasoning; Inductive Reasoning; Information Ordering; Memorization; Speed of Closure; Flexibility of Closure; Selective Attention; Time Sharing; Speech Clarity
Skills: Reading Comprehension; Active Listening; Writing; Speaking; Critical Thinking; Active Learning; Learning Strategies; Monitoring; Social Perceptiveness; Coordination; Persuasion; Negotiation; Problem Identification; Information Gathering; Information Organization; Synthesis/Reorganization; Idea Generation; Idea Evaluation; Implementation Planning; Solution Appraisal; Visioning; Systems Perception; Identifying Downstream Consequences; Identification of Key Causes; Judgment and Decision Making; Systems Evaluation; Time Management
General Work Activities: Getting Information Needed to Do the Job; Monitoring Processes, Material, or Surroundings; Identifying Objects, Actions, and Events; Judging Qualities of Things, Services, People; Processing Information; Evaluating Information against Standards; Analyzing Data or Information; Making Decisions and Solving Problems; Thinking Creatively; Updating and Using Job-Relevant Knowledge; Developing Objectives and Strategies; Scheduling Work and Activities; Organizing, Planning, and Prioritizing; Implementing Ideas, Programs, etc.; Interpreting Meaning of Information to Others; Communicating with Other Workers; Communicating with Persons Outside Organization; Resolving Conflicts, Negotiating with Others; Performing for or Working with Public; Performing Administrative Activities

Job Characteristics: Objective or Subjective Information; Job-Required Social Interaction; Take a Position Opposed to Others; Deal with External Customers; Coordinate or Lead Others; Frequency in Conflict Situations; Deal with Unpleasant or Angry People; Deal with Physical, Aggressive People; Sitting; Special Uniform; Consequence of Error; Frustrating Circumstances
GOE Group/s: 11.04.01 Law: Justice Administration
CIP Program/s: 220101 Law (LL.B., J.D.)
Related DOT Job/s: 111.107-010 JUDGE; 111.107-014 MAGISTRATE

28105 ADJUDICATORS, HEARINGS OFFICERS, AND JUDICIAL REVIEWERS. OOH Title/s: Lawyers and Judges

Conduct hearings to review and decide claims filed by the government against individuals or organizations, or individual eligibility issues concerning social programs, disability, or unemployment benefits. Determine the existence and the amount of liability; recommend the acceptance or rejection of claims; or compromise settlements according to laws, regulations, policies, and precedent decisions. Confer with persons or organizations involved, and prepare written decisions. Arranges and conducts hearings to obtain information and evidence relative to disposition of claim. Determines existence and amount of liability, according to law, administrative and judicial precedents, and evidence. Counsels parties, and recommends acceptance or rejection of compromise settlement offers. Prepares written opinions and decisions. Analyzes evidence and applicable law, regulations, policy, and precedent decisions to determine conclusions. Interviews or corresponds with claimants or agents to elicit information. Questions witnesses to obtain information. Reviews and evaluates data on documents, such as claim applications, birth or death certificates, and physician or employer records. Rules on exceptions, motions, and admissibility of evidence. Researches laws, regulations, policies, and precedent decisions to prepare for hearings. Participates in court proceedings. Issues subpoenas and administers oaths to prepare for formal hearing. Obtains additional information to clarify evidence. Authorizes payment of valid claims. Notifies claimant of denied claim and appeal rights. Conducts studies of appeals procedures in field agencies to ensure adherence to legal requirements and to facilitate determination of cases.
Yearly Earnings: $58,864
Education: Work experience, plus degree
Knowledge: Administration and Management; Psychology; Sociology and Anthropology; Therapy and Counseling; English Language; History and Archeology; Philosophy and Theology; Law, Government, and Jurisprudence
Abilities: Oral Comprehension; Written Comprehension; Written Expression; Deductive Reasoning; Inductive Reasoning; Memorization; Speech Clarity
Skills: Reading Comprehension; Active Listening; Writing; Speaking; Critical Thinking; Active Learning; Social Perceptiveness; Negotiation; Information Gathering; Information Organization; Synthesis/Reorganization; Idea Generation; Idea Evaluation; Judgment and Decision Making
General Work Activities: Getting Information Needed to Do the Job; Monitoring Processes, Material, or Surroundings; Judging Qualities of Things, Services, People; Processing Information; Evaluating Information against Standards; Analyzing Data or Information; Making Decisions and Solving Problems; Updating and Using Job-Relevant Knowledge; Organizing, Planning, and Prioritizing; Documenting/Recording Information; Interpreting Meaning of Information to Others; Communicating with Other Workers; Communicating with Persons Outside Organization; Establishing and Maintaining Relationships; Selling or Influencing Others; Resolving Conflicts, Negotiating with Others; Performing for or Working with Public; Provide Consultation and Advice to Others; Performing Administrative Activities
Job Characteristics: Objective or Subjective Information; Take a Position Opposed to Others; Frequency in Conflict Situations; Deal with Unpleasant or Angry People; Deal with Physical, Aggressive People; Sitting; Frustrating Circumstances; Importance of Being Sure All is Done; Importance of Being Aware of New Events
GOE Group/s: 11.04.01 Law: Justice Administration; 11.04.03 Law: Conciliation; 11.12.01 Contracts and Claims: Claims and Settlement
CIP Program/s: 220101 Law (LL.B., J.D.); 440701 Social Work
Related DOT Job/s: 119.107-010 HEARING OFFICER; 119.117-010 APPEALS REVIEWER, VETERAN; 119.167-010 ADJUDICATOR; 119.267-014 APPEALS REFEREE; 169.267-010 CLAIMS ADJUDICATOR

28108 LAWYERS. OOH Title/s: Lawyers and Judges

Conduct criminal and civil lawsuits, draw up legal documents, advise clients as to legal rights, and practice other phases of law. May represent client in court or before quasi-judicial or administrative agencies of government. May specialize in a single area of law, such as patent law, corporate law, or criminal law. Conducts case, examining and cross-examining witnesses, and summarizes case to judge or jury. Represents client in court or before government agency, or prosecutes or defends defendant in civil or criminal litigation. Advises client concerning business transactions, claim liability, advisability of prosecuting or defending law suits, or legal rights and obligations. Interviews client and witnesses to ascertain facts of case. Gathers evidence to formulate defense or to initiate legal actions. Examines legal data to determine advisability of defending or prosecuting lawsuit. Evaluates findings and develops strategy and arguments in preparation for presentation of case. Studies Constitution, statutes, decisions, regulations, and ordinances of quasi-judicial bodies. Confers with colleagues with specialty in area of legal issue to establish and verify basis for legal proceeding. Interprets laws, rulings, and regulations for individuals and business. Prepares and files legal briefs. Presents evidence to grand jury for indictment or release of accused. Prepares and drafts legal documents, such as wills, deeds, patent applications, mortgages, leases, and contracts. Prepares opinions on legal issues. Probates wills and represents and advises executors and administrators of estates. Acts as agent, trustee, guardian, or executor for business or individual. Searches for and examines public and other legal records to write opinions or establish ownership.
Yearly Earnings: $58,812
Education: First professional degree
Knowledge: Administration and Management; Clerical; Computers and Electronics; Psychology; Sociology and Anthropology; Therapy and Counseling; Education and Training; English Language; Public Safety and Security; Law, Government, and Jurisprudence
Abilities: Oral Comprehension; Written Comprehension; Oral Expression; Written Expression; Originality; Deductive Reasoning; Inductive Reasoning; Time Sharing; Speech Clarity
Skills: Reading Comprehension; Active Listening; Writing; Speaking; Critical Thinking; Active Learning; Learning Strategies; Monitoring; Social Perceptiveness; Coordination; Persuasion; Negotiation; Instructing; Problem Identification; Information Gathering; Information Organization; Synthesis/Reorganization; Idea Generation; Idea Evaluation; Implementation Planning; Solution Appraisal; Visioning; Systems Perception; Identifying Downstream Consequences; Identification of Key Causes; Judgment and Decision Making; Systems Evaluation; Time Management; Management of Financial Resources
General Work Activities: Getting Information Needed to Do the Job; Monitoring Processes, Material, or Surroundings; Estimating Needed Characteristics; Judging Qualities of Things, Services, People; Processing Information; Evaluating Information against Standards; Analyzing Data or Information; Making Decisions and Solving Problems;

Updating and Using Job-Relevant Knowledge; Developing Objectives and Strategies; Organizing, Planning, and Prioritizing; Implementing Ideas, Programs, etc.; Documenting/Recording Information; Interpreting Meaning of Information to Others; Communicating with Other Workers; Communicating with Persons Outside Organization; Establishing and Maintaining Relationships; Assisting and Caring for Others; Selling or Influencing Others; Resolving Conflicts, Negotiating with Others; Performing for or Working with Public; Developing and Building Teams; Teaching Others; Provide Consultation and Advice to Others; Performing Administrative Activities; Staffing Organizational Units; Monitoring and Controlling Resources
Job Characteristics: Persuade Someone to a Course of Action; Take a Position Opposed to Others; Deal with External Customers; Frequency in Conflict Situations; Deal with Unpleasant or Angry People; Consequence of Error; Frustrating Circumstances; Importance of Being Exact or Accurate; Importance of Being Sure All is Done
GOE Group/s: 11.04.02 Law: Legal Practice
CIP Program/s: 220101 Law (LL.B., J.D.); 220104 Juridical Science/Legal Specialization(LL.M.,M.C.L.,J.S.D./S)
Related DOT Job/s: 110.107-010 LAWYER; 110.107-014 LAWYER, CRIMINAL; 110.117-010 DISTRICT ATTORNEY; 110.117-014 INSURANCE ATTORNEY; 110.117-018 LAWYER, ADMIRALTY; 110.117-022 LAWYER, CORPORATION; 110.117-026 LAWYER, PATENT; 110.117-030 LAWYER, PROBATE; 110.117-034 LAWYER, REAL ESTATE; 110.117-038 TAX ATTORNEY; 110.117-042 TITLE ATTORNEY

Legal Assistants

28302 LAW CLERKS. OOH Title/s: Paralegals

Research legal data for brief or argument based on statutory law or decisions. Search for and study legal records and documents to obtain data applicable to case under consideration. Prepare rough drafts of briefs or arguments. File pleadings for firm with court clerk. Serve copies of pleading on opposing counsel. Prepare affidavits of documents and keep document file and correspondence of cases. Researches and analyzes law sources to prepare legal documents for review, approval, and use by attorney. Files pleadings with court clerk. Prepares affidavits of documents, and maintains document file. Investigates facts and law of case to determine causes of action and to prepare case accordingly. Delivers or directs delivery of subpoenas to witness and parties to action. Searches patent files to ascertain originality of parent application. Stores, catalogs, and maintains currency of legal volumes. Appraises and inventories real and personal property for estate planning. Directs and coordinates activities of law office employees. Prepares real estate closing statement, and assists in closing process. Communicates and arbitrates disputes between disputing parties. Prepares office accounts and tax returns.
Yearly Earnings: $42,952
Education: Associate degree
Knowledge: Administration and Management; Clerical; Economics and Accounting; Personnel and Human Resources; English Language; Law, Government, and Jurisprudence; Communications and Media
Abilities: Written Comprehension; Number Facility; Near Vision; Speech Recognition; Speech Clarity
Skills: Reading Comprehension; Active Listening; Writing; Speaking; Critical Thinking; Active Learning; Persuasion; Negotiation; Problem Identification; Information Gathering; Information Organization; Synthesis/Reorganization; Idea Generation; Idea Evaluation; Implementation Planning; Identification of Key Causes; Judgment and Decision Making; Time Management
General Work Activities: Getting Information Needed to Do the Job; Monitoring Processes, Material, or Surroundings; Processing Information; Analyzing Data or Information; Making Decisions and Solving Problems; Updating and Using Job-Relevant Knowledge; Documenting/Recording Information; Interpreting Meaning of Information to Others; Communicating with Other Workers; Resolving Conflicts, Negotiating with Others; Coordinating Work and Activities of Others; Guiding, Directing and Motivating Subordinates; Performing Administrative Activities
Job Characteristics: Sitting; Importance of Being Sure All is Done
GOE Group/s: 11.04.02 Law: Legal Practice
CIP Program/s: 220103 Paralegal/Legal Assistant
Related DOT Job/s: 119.267-026 PARALEGAL

28305 PARALEGALS AND LEGAL ASSISTANTS.

OOH Title/s: Paralegals
Assist lawyers by researching legal precedent, investigating facts, or preparing legal documents. Conduct research to support a legal proceeding, to formulate a defense, or to initiate legal action. Gathers and analyzes research data, such as statutes, decisions, and legal articles, codes, and documents. Prepares legal documents, including briefs, pleadings, appeals, wills, and contracts. Investigates facts and law of cases to determine causes of action and to prepare cases. Prepares affidavits or other documents, maintains document file, and files pleadings with court clerk. Appraises and inventories real and personal property for estate planning. Arbitrates disputes between parties, and assists in real estate closing process. Calls upon witnesses to testify at hearing. Answers questions regarding legal issues pertaining to civil service hearings. Directs and coordinates law office activity, including delivery of subpoenas. Completes office accounts, tax returns, and real estate closing statements. Keeps and monitors legal volumes to ensure that law library is up-to-date. Presents arguments and evidence to support appeal at appeal hearing.
Yearly Earnings: $25,792
Education: Associate degree
Knowledge: Administration and Management; Clerical; Economics and Accounting; Personnel and Human Resources; Computers and Electronics; Sociology and Anthropology; English Language; Law, Government, and Jurisprudence
Abilities: Oral Comprehension; Written Comprehension; Oral Expression; Written Expression; Deductive Reasoning
Skills: Reading Comprehension; Active Listening; Writing; Speaking; Mathematics; Critical Thinking; Active Learning; Monitoring; Coordination; Persuasion; Negotiation; Problem Identification; Information Gathering; Information Organization; Synthesis/Reorganization; Idea Generation; Implementation Planning; Visioning; Identification of Key Causes; Judgment and Decision Making; Time Management; Management of Financial Resources
General Work Activities: Getting Information Needed to Do the Job; Monitoring Processes, Material, or Surroundings; Identifying Objects, Actions, and Events; Estimating Needed Characteristics; Judging Qualities of Things, Services, People; Processing Information; Evaluating Information against Standards; Analyzing Data or Information; Making Decisions and Solving Problems; Updating and Using Job-Relevant Knowledge; Scheduling Work and Activities; Organizing, Planning, and Prioritizing; Documenting/Recording Information; Interpreting Meaning of Information to Others; Communicating with Other Workers; Resolving Conflicts, Negotiating with Others; Coordinating Work and Activities of Others; Guiding, Directing and Motivating Subordinates; Performing Administrative Activities
Job Characteristics: Sitting; Consequence of Error; Importance of Being Exact or Accurate; Importance of Being Sure All is Done
GOE Group/s: 11.04.02 Law: Legal Practice
CIP Program/s: 220103 Paralegal/Legal Assistant
Related DOT Job/s: 119.167-014 PATENT AGENT; 119.267-022 LEGAL INVESTIGATOR; 119.267-026

28308 TITLE SEARCHERS. OOH Title/s: Title Examiners and Searchers

Compile list of mortgages, deeds, contracts, judgments, and other instruments pertaining to title, by searching public and private records of real estate or title insurance company. Searches lot books, geographic and general indices, and assessor's rolls to compile lists of transactions pertaining to property. Reads search request to ascertain type of title evidence required, and to obtain description of property and names of involved parties. Compares legal description of property with legal description contained in records and indices, to verify such factors as deed ownership. Compiles information and documents required for title binder. Requisitions maps or drawings delineating property from company title plant, county surveyor, or assessor's office. Examines title to determine if there are restrictions limiting use of property, lists restrictions, and indicates action needed for clear title. Uses computerized system to retrieve additional documentation needed to complete real estate transaction. Confers with realtors, lending institution personnel, buyers, sellers, contractors, surveyors, and courthouse personnel to obtain additional information. Retrieves and examines closing files for accuracy and to ensure that information included is recorded and executed according to regulations. Prepares title commitment and final policy of title insurance based on information compiled from title search. Prepares closing statement, utilizing knowledge and expertise in real estate procedures.

Yearly Earnings: $25,792

Education: Moderate-term O-J-T

Knowledge: Clerical; Economics and Accounting; Computers and Electronics; Sociology and Anthropology; Geography; English Language; History and Archeology; Law, Government, and Jurisprudence

Abilities: Written Comprehension; Written Expression

Skills: Writing; Speaking; Information Gathering; Information Organization

General Work Activities: Getting Information Needed to Do the Job; Processing Information; Evaluating Information against Standards; Operating Vehicles or Equipment; Documenting/Recording Information; Communicating with Persons Outside Organization

Job Characteristics: Provide a Service to Others; Deal with External Customers; Sitting

GOE Group/s: 07.05.02 Records Processing: Record Verification and Proofing

CIP Program/s: 220103 Paralegal/Legal Assistant

Related DOT Job/s: 209.367-046 TITLE SEARCHER

28311 TITLE EXAMINERS AND ABSTRACTORS. OOH Title/s: Title Examiners and Searchers

Title examiners search public records and examine titles to determine legal condition of property title. Copy or summarize (abstract) recorded documents which affect condition of title to property (e.g., mortgages, trust deeds, and contracts). May prepare and issue policy that guarantees legality of title. Abstractors summarize pertinent legal or insurance details or sections of statutes or case law from reference books for purpose of examination, proof, or ready reference. Search out titles to determine if title deed is correct. Copies or summarizes recorded documents, such as mortgages, trust deeds, and contracts, affecting title to property. Examines mortgages, liens, judgments, easements, vital statistics, plat books, and maps to verify property legal description, ownership, and restrictions. Analyzes encumbrances to title, statutes and case law, and prepares report outlining encumbrances and actions required to clear title. Prepares and issues title insurance policy. Searches records to determine if delinquent taxes are due. Prepares correspondence and other records. Confers with interested parties to resolve problems and impart information. Directs activities of workers searching records and examining titles to real property. Verifies computations of fees, rentals, bonuses, commissions, and other expenses.

Yearly Earnings: $25,792

Education: Moderate-term O-J-T

Knowledge: Administration and Management; Clerical; Economics and Accounting; Geography; English Language; Law, Government, and Jurisprudence

Abilities: Written Comprehension; Written Expression; Near Vision

Skills: Reading Comprehension; Active Listening; Writing; Speaking; Critical Thinking; Information Gathering; Information Organization; Synthesis/Reorganization; Time Management; Management of Personnel Resources

General Work Activities: Getting Information Needed to Do the Job; Monitoring Processes, Material, or Surroundings; Processing Information; Evaluating Information against Standards; Analyzing Data or Information; Scheduling Work and Activities; Documenting/Recording Information; Interpreting Meaning of Information to Others; Communicating with Persons Outside Organization; Resolving Conflicts, Negotiating with Others; Performing for or Working with Public; Coordinating Work and Activities of Others; Guiding, Directing and Motivating Subordinates; Performing Administrative Activities

Job Characteristics: Provide a Service to Others; Sitting

GOE Group/s: 07.01.05 Administrative Detail: Certifying; 11.04.04 Law: Abstracting, Document Preparation

CIP Program/s: 220103 Paralegal/Legal Assistant; 520201 Business Administration and Management, General; 520204 Office Supervision and Management

Related DOT Job/s: 119.167-018 TITLE SUPERVISOR; 119.267-010 ABSTRACTOR; 119.287-010 TITLE EXAMINER; 162.267-010 TITLE CLERK

28399 ALL OTHER LEGAL ASSISTANTS AND TECHNICIANS, EXCEPT CLERICAL. OOH Title/s: Paralegals

All other legal assistants and technicians not classified separately above.

Yearly Earnings: $42,952

Education: Associate degree

GOE Group/s: 07.01.04 Administrative Detail: Financial Work; 07.01.05 Administrative Detail: Certifying

CIP Program/s: 220103 Paralegal/Legal Assistant; 520201 Business Administration and Management, General; 520202 Purchasing, Procurement and Contracts Management; 521501 Real Estate

Related DOT Job/s: 119.267-018 CONTRACT CLERK; 119.367-010 ESCROW OFFICER; 186.167-074 CLOSER

Section 3
Professional and Support Specialties—Educators, Librarians, Counselors, Health Care Workers, Artists, Writers, Performers, and Other Professional Workers

College and University Faculty

31114 NURSING INSTRUCTORS—POSTSECONDARY. OOH Title/s: College and University Faculty

Demonstrate and teach patient care in classroom and clinical units to nursing students. Instruct students in principles and application of physical, biological, and psychological subjects related to nursing. Conduct and supervise laboratory experiments. Issue assignments, direct seminars, etc. Participate in planning curriculum with medical and nursing personnel and in evaluating and improving teaching and nursing practices. May specialize in specific subjects, such as anatomy or chemistry, or in a type of nursing activity, such as nursing of surgical patients. Instructs and lectures nursing students in principles and application of physical, biological, and psychological subjects related to nursing. Conducts and supervises laboratory work. Issues assignments to students. Participates in planning curriculum, teaching schedule, and course outline with medical and nursing personnel. Directs seminars and panels. Supervises student nurses and demonstrates patient care in clinical units of hospital. Cooperates with medical and nursing personnel in evaluating and improving teaching and nursing practices. Prepares and administers examinations to nursing students. Evaluates student progress and maintains records of student classroom and clinical experience. Conducts classes for patients in health practices and procedures.

Yearly Earnings: $43,888

Education: Doctor's degree

Knowledge: Administration and Management; Customer and Personal Service; Personnel and Human Resources; Chemistry; Biology; Psychology; Sociology and Anthropology; Medicine and Dentistry; Therapy and Counseling; Education and Training; English Language; Philosophy and Theology; Public Safety and Security; Law, Government, and Jurisprudence

Abilities: Oral Comprehension; Written Comprehension; Oral Expression; Written Expression; Fluency of Ideas; Originality; Problem Sensitivity; Deductive Reasoning; Inductive Reasoning; Information Ordering; Category Flexibility; Mathematical Reasoning; Number Facility; Memorization; Speed of Closure; Visualization; Time Sharing; Arm-Hand Steadiness; Response Orientation; Reaction Time; Static Strength; Gross Body Equilibrium; Near Vision; Far Vision; Visual Color Discrimination; Night Vision; Sound Localization; Speech Recognition; Speech Clarity

Skills: Reading Comprehension; Active Listening; Writing; Speaking; Science; Critical Thinking; Active Learning; Learning Strategies; Monitoring; Social Perceptiveness; Coordination; Persuasion; Instructing; Service Orientation; Information Organization; Idea Generation; Idea Evaluation; Implementation Planning; Solution Appraisal; Testing; Visioning; Systems Perception; Identification of Key Causes; Judgment and Decision Making; Time Management; Management of Personnel Resources

General Work Activities: Getting Information Needed to Do the Job; Monitoring Processes, Material, or Surroundings; Identifying Objects, Actions, and Events; Judging Qualities of Things, Services, People; Processing Information; Analyzing Data or Information; Making Decisions and Solving Problems; Thinking Creatively; Updating and Using Job-Relevant Knowledge; Developing Objectives and Strategies; Scheduling Work and Activities; Organizing, Planning, and Prioritizing; Operating Vehicles or Equipment; Implementing Ideas, Programs, etc.; Documenting/Recording Information; Interpreting Meaning of Information to Others; Communicating with Other Workers; Communicating with Persons Outside Organization; Establishing and Maintaining Relationships; Assisting and Caring for Others; Resolving Conflicts, Negotiating with Others; Performing for or Working with Public; Coordinating Work and Activities of Others; Developing and Building Teams; Teaching Others; Guiding, Directing and Motivating Subordinates; Coaching and Developing Others; Provide Consultation and Advice to Others; Performing Administrative Activities; Monitoring and Controlling Resources

Job Characteristics: Job-Required Social Interaction; Supervise, Coach, Train Others; Coordinate or Lead Others; Responsible for Others' Health and Safety; Responsibility for Outcomes and Results; Frequency in Conflict Situations; Deal with Unpleasant or Angry People; Deal with Physical, Aggressive People; Diseases/Infections; Special Uniform; Consequence of Error; Importance of Being Exact or Accurate; Importance of Being Sure All is Done

GOE Group/s: 10.02.01 Nursing, Therapy, and Specialized Teaching Services: Nursing

CIP Program/s: 511601 Nursing (R.N. Training); 511603 Nursing, Adult Health (Post-R.N.); 511604 Nursing Anesthetist (Post-R.N.); 511605 Nursing, Family Practice (Post-R.N.); 511606 Nursing, Maternal/Child Health (Post-R.N.); 511607 Nursing Midwifery (Post-R.N.); 511608 Nursing Science (Post-R.N.); 511609 Nursing, Pediatric (Post-R.N.); 511610 Nursing, Psychiatric/Mental Health (Post-R.N.); 511611 Nursing, Public Health (Post-R.N.); 511612 Nursing, Surgical (Post-R.N.)

Related DOT Job/s: 075.124-018 NURSE, INSTRUCTOR

31117 GRADUATE ASSISTANTS, TEACHING. OOH Title/s: Indirectly related to College and University Faculty

Assist department chairperson, faculty members, or other professional staff members in college or university by performing teaching or teaching-related duties, such as teaching lower-level courses, developing teaching materials, preparing and giving examinations, and grading examinations or papers. Graduate assistants who primarily perform nonteaching duties, such as laboratory research, are included in the occupational category related to the work performed. Develops teaching materials, such as syllabi and visual aids. Prepares and gives examinations. Grades examinations and papers. Teaches lower-level courses. Assists faculty member or staff with student conferences. Assists faculty member or staff with laboratory or field research. Assists library staff in maintaining library collection.

Yearly Earnings: NA

Education: Bachelor's degree

Knowledge: Clerical; Education and Training; English Language

Abilities: Oral Comprehension; Written Comprehension; Oral Expression; Written Expression; Fluency of Ideas; Speech Clarity

Skills: Reading Comprehension; Active Listening; Writing; Speaking; Mathematics; Science; Critical Thinking; Active Learning; Learning Strategies; Monitoring; Persuasion; Instructing; Service Orientation; Information Organization; Synthesis/Reorganization; Idea Evaluation; Implementation Planning

General Work Activities: Getting Information Needed to Do the Job; Developing Objectives and Strategies; Interpreting Meaning of Information to Others; Teaching Others

Job Characteristics: None above average

GOE Group/s: 11.02.01 Educational and Library Services: Teaching and Instructing, General

CIP Program/s: 130101 Education, General

Related DOT Job/s: 090.227-014 GRADUATE ASSISTANT

31202 LIFE SCIENCES TEACHERS—POSTSECONDARY. OOH Title/s: College and University Faculty

Teach courses pertaining to living organisms, such as biological sciences, agricultural sciences, and medical sciences. Include teachers of subjects such as botany, zoology, agronomy, biochemistry, biophysics, soil conservation, forestry, psychiatry, surgery, and obstetrics. Prepares and delivers lectures to students. Stimulates class discussions. Compiles bibliographies of specialized materials for outside reading assignments. Compiles, administers, and grades examinations, or assigns this work to others. Advises students on academic and vocational curricula. Directs research of other teachers or graduate students working for advanced academic degrees. Conducts research in particular field of knowledge and publishes findings in professional journals. Acts as adviser to student organizations. Serves on faculty committee providing professional consulting services to government and industry.

Yearly Earnings: $43,888

Education: Doctor's degree

Knowledge: Administration and Management; Clerical; Food Production; Computers and Electronics; Mathematics; Physics; Chemistry; Biology; Psychology; Medicine and Dentistry; Therapy and Counseling; Education and Training; English Language; Communications and Media

Abilities: Oral Comprehension; Written Comprehension; Oral Expression; Written Expression; Fluency of Ideas; Mathematical Reasoning; Number Facility; Speech Recognition; Speech Clarity

Skills: Reading Comprehension; Active Listening; Writing; Speaking; Mathematics; Science; Critical Thinking; Active Learning; Learning Strategies; Monitoring; Social Perceptiveness; Instructing; Problem Identification; Information Gathering; Information Organization; Synthesis/Reorganization; Idea Generation; Idea Evaluation; Implementation Planning; Solution Appraisal; Programming; Visioning; Systems Perception; Identification of Key Causes; Judgment and Decision Making; Time Management; Management of Financial Resources

General Work Activities: Getting Information Needed to Do the Job; Evaluating Information against Standards; Analyzing Data or Information; Developing Objectives and Strategies; Scheduling Work and Activities; Implementing Ideas, Programs, etc.; Documenting/Recording Information; Interpreting Meaning of Information to Others; Establishing and Maintaining Relationships; Developing and Building Teams; Teaching Others; Guiding, Directing and Motivating Subordinates; Coaching and Developing Others; Provide Consultation and Advice to Others

Job Characteristics: Job-Required Social Interaction; Supervise, Coach, Train Others

GOE Group/s: 11.02.01 Educational and Library Services: Teaching and Instructing, General

CIP Program/s: 020101 Agriculture/Agricultural Sciences, General; 020201 Animal Sciences, General; 020202 Agricultural Animal Breeding and Genetics; 020203 Agricultural Animal Health; 020204 Agricultural Animal Nutrition; 020205 Agricultural Animal Physiology; 020206 Dairy Science; 020209 Poultry Science; 020301 Food Sciences and Technology; 020401 Plant Sciences, General; 020402 Agronomy and Crop Science; 020403 Horticulture Science; 020405 Plant Breeding and Genetics; 020406 Agricultural Plant Pathology; 020407 Agricultural Plant Physiology; 020408 Plant Protection (Pest Management); 020409 Range Science and Management; 020501 Soil Sciences; 030101 Natural Resources Conservation, General; 030102 Environmental Science/Studies; 030201 Natural Resources Management and Policy; 030301 Fishing and Fisheries Sciences and Management; 030501 Forestry, General; 030502 Forestry Sciences; 030506 Forest Management; 030601 Wildlife and Wildlands Management; 260101 Biology, General; 260202 Biochemistry; 260203 Biophysics; 260301 Botany, General; 260305 Plant Pathology; 260307 Plant Physiology; 260401 Cell Biology; 260402 Molecular Biology; 260501 Microbiology/Bacteriology; 260601 Anatomy; 260603 Ecology; 260607 Marine/Aquatic Biology; 260608 Neuroscience; 260609 Nutritional Sciences; 260610 Parasitology; 260611 Radiation Biology/Radiobiology; 260612 Toxicology; 260613 Genetics, Plant and Animal; 260614 Biometrics; 260616 Biotechnology Research; 260617 Evolutionary Biology; 260618 Biological Immunology; 260619 Virology; 260701 Zoology, General; 260702 Entomology; 260704 Pathology, Human and Animal; 260705 Pharmacology, Human and Animal; 260706 Physiology, Human and Animal; 300101 Biological and Physical Sciences; 301001 Biopsychology; 301101 Gerontology; 511201 Medicine (M.D.); 511301 Medical Anatomy; 511302 Medical Biochemistry; 511303 Medical Biomathematics and Biometrics; 511304 Medical Physics/Biophysics; 511305 Medical Cell Biology; 511306 Medical Genetics; 511307 Medical Immunology; 511308 Medical Microbiology; 511309 Medical Molecular Biology; 511310 Medical Neurobiology; 511311 Medical Nutrition; 511312 Medical Pathology; 511313 Medical Physiology; 511314 Medical Toxicology; 511399 Basic Medical Sciences, Other; 511401 Medical Clinical Sciences (M.S., Ph.D.); 512203 Epidemiology; 512901 Aerospace Medicine Residency; 512902 Allergies and Immunology Residency; 512903 Anesthesiology Residency; 512904 Blood Banking Residency; 512905 Cardiology Residency; 512906 Chemical Pathology Residency; 512907 Child/Pediatric Neurology Residency; 512908 Child Psychiatry Residency; 512909 Colon and Rectal Surgery Residency; 512910 Critical Care Anesthesiology Residency; 512911 Critical Care Medicine Residency; 512912 Critical Care Surgery Residency; 512913 Dermatology Residency; 512914 Dermatopathology Residency; 512915 Diagnostic Radiology Residency; 512916 Emergency Medicine Residency; 512917 Endocrinology and Metabolism Residency; 512918 Family Medicine Residency; 512919 Forensic Pathology Residency; 512920 Gastroenterology Residency; 512921 General Surgery Residency; 512922 Geriatric Medicine Residency; 512923 Hand Surgery Residency; 512924 Hematology Residency; 512925 Hematological Pathology Residency; 512926 Immunopathology Residency; 512927 Infectious Disease Residency; 512928 Internal Medicine Residency; 512929 Laboratory Medicine Residency; 512930 Musculoskeletal Oncology Residency; 512931 Neonatal-Perinatal Medicine Residency; 512932 Nephrology Residency; 512933 Neurological Surgery/Neurosurgery Residency; 512934 Neurology Residency; 512935 Neuropathology Residency; 512936 Nuclear Medicine Residency; 512937 Nuclear Radiology Residency; 512938 Obstetrics and Gynecology Residency; 512939 Occupational Medicine Residency; 512940 Oncology Residency; 512941 Ophthalmology Residency; 512942 Orthopedics/Orthopedic Surgery Residency; 512943 Otolaryngology Residency; 512944 Pathology Residency; 512945 Pediatric Cardiology Residency; 512946 Pediatric Endocrinology Residency; 512947 Pediatric Hemato-Oncology Residency; 512948 Pediatric Nephrology Residency; 512949 Pediatric Orthopedics Residency; 512950 Pediatric Surgery Residency; 512951 Pediatrics Residency; 512952 Physical and Rehabilitation Medicine Residency; 512953 Plastic Surgery Residency; 512954 Preventive Medicine Residency; 512955 Psychiatry Residency; 512956 Public Health Medicine Residency; 512957 Pulmonary Disease Residency; 512958 Radiation Oncology Residency; 512959 Radioisotopic Pathology Residency; 512960 Rheumatology Residency; 512961 Sports Medicine Residency; 512962 Thoracic Surgery Residency; 512963 Urology Residency; 512964 Vascular Surgery Residency

Related DOT Job/s: 090.227-010 FACULTY MEMBER, COLLEGE OR UNIVERSITY

31204 CHEMISTRY TEACHERS—POSTSECONDARY. OOH Title/s: College and University Faculty

Teach courses pertaining to the chemical and physical properties and compositional changes of substances. Work may include instruction in the methods of qualitative and quantitative chemical analysis. Prepares and delivers lectures to students. Stimulates class discussions. Compiles, administers, and grades examinations, or assigns this work to others. Compiles bibliographies of specialized materials for outside reading assignments. Directs research of other teachers or graduate students working for advanced academic degrees. Advises students on academic and vocational curricula. Conducts research in particular field of knowledge and publishes findings in professional journals. Acts as adviser to student organizations. Serves on faculty committee providing professional consulting services to government and industry.

Yearly Earnings: $43,888

Education: Doctor's degree

Knowledge: Administration and Management; Computers and Electronics; Engineering and Technology; Mathematics; Physics; Chemistry; Biology; Psychology; Sociology and Anthropology; Education and Training; English Language; Foreign Language

Abilities: Oral Comprehension; Written Comprehension; Oral Expression; Written Expression; Fluency of Ideas; Originality; Deductive Reasoning; Inductive Reasoning; Information Ordering; Category Flexibility; Mathematical Reasoning; Number Facility; Memorization; Speed of Closure; Perceptual Speed; Selective Attention; Finger Dexterity; Far Vision; Night Vision; Speech Clarity

Skills: Reading Comprehension; Active Listening; Writing; Speaking; Mathematics; Science; Critical Thinking; Active Learning; Learning Strategies; Monitoring; Social Perceptiveness; Coordination; Negotiation; Instructing; Information Gathering; Information Organization; Synthesis/Reorganization; Idea Generation; Idea Evaluation; Implementation Planning; Solution Appraisal; Equipment Selection; Visioning; Identification of Key Causes; Judgment and Decision Making; Time Management; Management of Personnel Resources

General Work Activities: Getting Information Needed to Do the Job; Monitoring Processes, Material, or Surroundings; Processing Information; Evaluating Information against Standards; Analyzing Data or Information; Making Decisions and Solving Problems; Thinking Creatively; Updating and Using Job-Relevant Knowledge; Developing Objectives and Strategies; Scheduling Work and Activities; Organizing, Planning, and Prioritizing; Operating Vehicles or Equipment; Implementing Ideas, Programs, etc.; Documenting/Recording Information; Interpreting Meaning of Information to Others; Communicating with Other Workers; Communicating with Persons Outside Organization; Establishing and Maintaining Relationships; Performing for or Working with Public; Teaching Others; Guiding, Directing and Motivating Subordinates; Coaching and Developing Others; Provide Consultation and Advice to Others

Job Characteristics: Objective or Subjective Information; Job-Required Social Interaction; Supervise, Coach, Train Others; Persuade Someone to a Course of Action; Provide a Service to Others; Take a Position Opposed to Others; Coordinate or Lead Others; Responsibility for Outcomes and Results; Diseases/Infections; Hazardous Conditions; Frustrating Circumstances

GOE Group/s: 11.02.01 Educational and Library Services: Teaching and Instructing, General

CIP Program/s: 400101 Physical Sciences, General; 400501 Chemistry, General; 400502 Analytical Chemistry; 400503 Inorganic Chemistry; 400504 Organic Chemistry; 400505 Medicinal/Pharmaceutical Chemistry; 400506 Physical and Theoretical Chemistry; 400507 Polymer Chemistry

Related DOT Job/s: 090.227-010 FACULTY MEMBER, COLLEGE OR UNIVERSITY

31206 PHYSICS TEACHERS—POSTSECONDARY. OOH Title/s: College and University Faculty

Teach courses pertaining to the laws of matter and energy. Prepares and delivers lectures to students. Stimulates class discussions. Compiles, administers, and grades examinations, or assigns this work to others. Compiles bibliographies of specialized materials for outside reading assignments. Advises students on academic and vocational curricula. Directs research of other teachers or graduate students working for advanced academic degrees. Conducts research in particular field of knowledge and publishes findings in professional journals. Serves on faculty committee providing professional consulting services to government and industry. Acts as adviser to student organizations.

Yearly Earnings: $43,888

Education: Doctor's degree

Knowledge: Administration and Management; Engineering and Technology; Mathematics; Physics; Chemistry; Psychology; Sociology and Anthropology; Therapy and Counseling; Education and Training; English Language; Foreign Language; History and Archeology; Philosophy and Theology

Abilities: Oral Comprehension; Written Comprehension; Oral Expression; Written Expression; Fluency of Ideas; Originality; Problem Sensitivity; Deductive Reasoning; Inductive Reasoning; Information Ordering; Category Flexibility; Mathematical Reasoning; Number Facility; Memorization; Speed of Closure; Flexibility of Closure; Selective Attention; Time Sharing; Far Vision; Night Vision; Sound Localization; Speech Clarity

Skills: Reading Comprehension; Active Listening; Writing; Speaking; Mathematics; Science; Critical Thinking; Active Learning; Learning Strategies; Monitoring; Social Perceptiveness; Coordination; Instructing; Information Gathering; Information Organization; Synthesis/Reorganization; Idea Generation; Idea Evaluation; Implementation Planning; Solution Appraisal; Testing; Visioning; Identifying Downstream Consequences; Identification of Key Causes; Judgment and Decision Making; Time Management; Management of Personnel Resources

General Work Activities: Getting Information Needed to Do the Job; Monitoring Processes, Material, or Surroundings; Estimating Needed Characteristics; Judging Qualities of Things, Services, People; Processing Information; Evaluating Information against Standards; Analyzing Data or Information; Making Decisions and Solving Problems; Thinking Creatively; Updating and Using Job-Relevant Knowledge; Developing Objectives and Strategies; Scheduling Work and Activities; Organizing, Planning, and Prioritizing; Operating Vehicles or Equipment; Implementing Ideas, Programs, etc.; Documenting/Recording Information; Interpreting Meaning of Information to Others; Communicating with Other Workers; Communicating with Persons Outside Organization; Establishing and Maintaining Relationships; Performing for or Working with Public; Coordinating Work and Activities of Others; Teaching Others; Guiding, Directing and Motivating Subordinates; Coaching and Developing Others; Provide Consultation and Advice to Others

Job Characteristics: Objective or Subjective Information; Job-Required Social Interaction; Supervise, Coach, Train Others; Persuade Someone to a Course of Action; Provide a Service to Others; Take a Position Opposed to Others; Coordinate or Lead Others; Responsibility for Outcomes and Results; Frustrating Circumstances

GOE Group/s: 11.02.01 Educational and Library Services: Teaching and Instructing, General

CIP Program/s: 300101 Biological and Physical Sciences; 400101 Physical Sciences, General; 400801 Physics, General; 400802 Chemi-

cal and Atomic/Molecular Physics; 400804 Elementary Particle Physics; 400805 Plasma and High-Temperature Physics; 400806 Nuclear Physics; 400807 Optics; 400808 Solid State and Low-Temperature Physics; 400809 Acoustics; 400810 Theoretical and Mathematical Physics
Related DOT Job/s: 090.227-010 FACULTY MEMBER, COLLEGE OR UNIVERSITY

31209 ALL OTHER PHYSICAL SCIENCE TEACHERS—POSTSECONDARY. OOH Title/s: College and University Faculty
Teach courses in the physical sciences, except chemistry and physics. Include teachers of subjects such as astronomy, atmospheric and space sciences, geology, and geography.
Yearly Earnings: $43,888
Education: Doctor's degree
GOE Group/s: 11.02.01 Educational and Library Services: Teaching and Instructing, General
CIP Program/s: 400101 Physical Sciences, General; 400201 Astronomy; 400301 Astrophysics; 400401 Atmospheric Sciences and Meteorology; 400601 Geology; 400602 Geochemistry; 400603 Geophysics and Seismology; 400604 Paleontology; 400701 Metallurgy; 400702 Oceanography; 400703 Earth and Planetary Sciences; 450701 Geography; 511304 Medical Physics/Biophysics
Related DOT Job/s: 090.227-010 FACULTY MEMBER, COLLEGE OR UNIVERSITY

31210 SOCIAL SCIENCE TEACHERS—POSTSECONDARY. OOH Title/s: College and University Faculty
Teach courses pertaining to human society and its characteristic elements, with economic and social relations and with scientific data relating to human behavior and mental processes. Include teachers of subjects such as psychology, economics, history, political science, and sociology. Prepares and delivers lectures to students. Stimulates class discussions. Compiles, administers, and grades examinations, or assigns this work to others. Compiles bibliographies of specialized materials for outside reading assignments. Advises students on academic and vocational curricula. Directs research of other teachers or graduate students working for advanced academic degrees. Conducts research in particular field of knowledge and publishes findings in professional journals. Serves on faculty committee providing professional consulting services to government and industry. Acts as adviser to student organizations.
Yearly Earnings: $43,888
Education: Doctor's degree
Knowledge: Administration and Management; Clerical; Economics and Accounting; Personnel and Human Resources; Computers and Electronics; Mathematics; Psychology; Sociology and Anthropology; Geography; Therapy and Counseling; Education and Training; English Language; History and Archeology; Philosophy and Theology; Law, Government, and Jurisprudence; Communications and Media
Abilities: Oral Comprehension; Written Comprehension; Oral Expression; Written Expression; Fluency of Ideas; Deductive Reasoning; Mathematical Reasoning; Speech Clarity
Skills: Reading Comprehension; Active Listening; Writing; Speaking; Mathematics; Science; Critical Thinking; Active Learning; Learning Strategies; Monitoring; Social Perceptiveness; Persuasion; Negotiation; Instructing; Service Orientation; Problem Identification; Information Gathering; Information Organization; Synthesis/Reorganization; Idea Generation; Idea Evaluation; Implementation Planning; Solution Appraisal; Programming; Visioning; Identification of Key Causes; Time Management; Management of Financial Resources
General Work Activities: Getting Information Needed to Do the Job; Evaluating Information against Standards; Analyzing Data or Information; Developing Objectives and Strategies; Scheduling Work and Activities; Organizing, Planning, and Prioritizing; Documenting/Recording Information; Interpreting Meaning of Information to Others; Establishing and Maintaining Relationships; Developing and Building Teams; Teaching Others; Guiding, Directing and Motivating Subordinates; Coaching and Developing Others; Provide Consultation and Advice to Others
Job Characteristics: Job-Required Social Interaction; Supervise, Coach, Train Others; Deal with External Customers
GOE Group/s: 11.02.01 Educational and Library Services: Teaching and Instructing, General
CIP Program/s: 010101 Agricultural Business and Management, General; 010103 Agricultural Economics; 050101 African Studies; 050102 American Studies/Civilization; 050103 Asian Studies; 050104 East Asian Studies; 050105 Eastern European Area Studies; 050106 European Studies; 050107 Latin American Studies; 050108 Middle Eastern Studies; 050109 Pacific Area Studies; 050110 Russian and Slavic Area Studies; 050111 Scandinavian Area Studies; 050112 South Asian Studies; 050113 Southeast Asian Studies; 050114 Western European Studies; 050115 Canadian Studies; 050201 Afro-American (Black) Studies; 050202 American Indian/Native American Studies; 050203 Hispanic-American Studies; 050204 Islamic Studies; 050205 Jewish/Judaic Studies; 050206 Asian-American Studies; 050207 Women's Studies; 300501 Peace and Conflict Studies; 301101 Gerontology; 301301 Medieval and Renaissance Studies; 301501 Science, Tech. and Society; 310501 Health and Physical Education, General; 310506 Socio-Psychological Sports Studies; 420101 Psychology, General; 420201 Clinical Psychology; 420301 Cognitive Psychology and Psycholinguistics; 420401 Community Psychology; 420601 Counseling Psychology; 420701 Developmental and Child Psychology; 420801 Experimental Psychology; 420901 Industrial and Organizational Psychology; 421101 Physiological Psychology/Psychobiology; 421601 Social Psychology; 421701 School Psychology; 430102 Corrections/Correctional Administration; 430103 Criminal Justice/Law Enforcement Administration; 430104 Criminal Justice Studies; 450101 Social Sciences, General; 450201 Anthropology; 450301 Archeology; 450401 Criminology; 450501 Demography/Population Studies; 450601 Economics, General; 450602 Applied and Resource Economics; 450603 Econometrics and Quantitative Economics; 450604 Development Economics and International Development; 450605 International Economics; 450801 History, General; 450802 American (United States) History; 450803 European History; 450804 History and Philosophy of Science and Technology; 450805 Public/Applied History and Archival Administration; 450901 International Relations and Affairs; 451001 Political Science, General; 451002 American Government and Politics; 451101 Sociology; 451201 Urban Affairs/Studies; 520601 Business/Managerial Economics
Related DOT Job/s: 090.227-010 FACULTY MEMBER, COLLEGE OR UNIVERSITY

31212 HEALTH SPECIALTIES TEACHERS—POSTSECONDARY. OOH Title/s: College and University Faculty
Teach courses in health specialties such as veterinary medicine, dentistry, pharmacy, therapy, laboratory technology, and public health. Exclude nursing instructors and medical sciences teachers. Prepares and delivers lectures to students. Compiles bibliographies of specialized materials for outside reading assignments. Stimulates class discussions. Compiles, administers, and grades examinations, or assigns this work to others. Advises students on academic and vocational curricula. Directs research of other teachers or graduate

students working for advanced academic degrees. Conducts research in particular field of knowledge and publishes findings in professional journals. Acts as adviser to student organizations. Serves on faculty committee providing professional consulting services to government and industry.
Yearly Earnings: $43,888
Education: Doctor's degree
Knowledge: Administration and Management; Clerical; Computers and Electronics; Mathematics; Chemistry; Biology; Psychology; Sociology and Anthropology; Medicine and Dentistry; Therapy and Counseling; Education and Training; English Language; Philosophy and Theology; Law, Government, and Jurisprudence; Communications and Media
Abilities: Oral Comprehension; Written Comprehension; Oral Expression; Written Expression; Mathematical Reasoning; Speech Clarity
Skills: Reading Comprehension; Active Listening; Writing; Speaking; Mathematics; Science; Critical Thinking; Active Learning; Learning Strategies; Monitoring; Social Perceptiveness; Coordination; Persuasion; Negotiation; Instructing; Service Orientation; Problem Identification; Information Gathering; Information Organization; Synthesis/Reorganization; Idea Generation; Idea Evaluation; Implementation Planning; Solution Appraisal; Operations Analysis; Equipment Selection; Visioning; Systems Perception; Identifying Downstream Consequences; Identification of Key Causes; Time Management; Management of Financial Resources; Management of Personnel Resources
General Work Activities: Getting Information Needed to Do the Job; Identifying Objects, Actions, and Events; Evaluating Information against Standards; Analyzing Data or Information; Thinking Creatively; Updating and Using Job-Relevant Knowledge; Developing Objectives and Strategies; Scheduling Work and Activities; Organizing, Planning, and Prioritizing; Interpreting Meaning of Information to Others; Communicating with Other Workers; Communicating with Persons Outside Organization; Establishing and Maintaining Relationships; Performing for or Working with Public; Developing and Building Teams; Teaching Others; Guiding, Directing and Motivating Subordinates; Coaching and Developing Others; Provide Consultation and Advice to Others
Job Characteristics: Job-Required Social Interaction; Supervise, Coach, Train Others; Coordinate or Lead Others; Responsibility for Outcomes and Results; Radiation; Diseases/Infections
GOE Group/s: 11.02.01 Educational and Library Services: Teaching and Instructing, General
CIP Program/s: 301101 Gerontology; 310501 Health and Physical Education, General; 310502 Adapted Physical Education/Therapeutic Recreation; 310503 Athletic Training and Sports Medicine; 310505 Exercise Sciences/Physiology and Movement Studies; 510101 Chiropractic (D.C., D.C.M.); 510201 Communication Disorders, General; 510202 Audiology/Hearing Sciences; 510203 Speech-Language Pathology; 510204 Speech-Language Pathology and Audiology; 510205 Sign Language Interpreter; 510301 Community Health Liaison; 510401 Dentistry (D.D.S., D.M.D.); 510501 Dental Clinical Sciences/Graduate Dentistry (M.S., Ph.D.); 510602 Dental Hygienist; 510603 Dental Laboratory Technician; 510701 Health System/Health Services Administration; 510702 Hospital/Health Facilities Administration; 510807 Physician Assistant; 510901 Cardiovascular Technologists and Technicians; 510902 Electrocardiograph Technologists and Technicians; 510903 Electroencephalograph Technologists and Technicians; 510904 Emergency Medical Technologists and Technicians; 510905 Nuclear Medical Technologists and Technicians; 510906 Perfusion Technologists and Technicians; 510907 Medical Radiologic Technologists and Technicians; 510908 Respiratory Therapy Technician; 510909 Surgical/Operating Room Technician; 510910 Diagnostic Medical Sonography; 511005 Medical Technology; 511502 Psychiatric/Mental Health Services Technician; 511503 Clinical and Medical Social Work; 511701 Optometry (O.D.); 511901 Osteopathic Medicine (D.O.); 512001 Pharmacy (B. Pharm., Pharm.D.); 512002 Pharmacy Administration and Pharmaceutics; 512003 Medical Pharmacology and Pharmaceutical Sciences; 512101 Podiatry (D.P.M., D.P., Pod.D.); 512201 Public Health, General; 512202 Environmental Health; 512203 Epidemiology; 512205 Health Physics/Radiologic Health; 512206 Occupational Health and Industrial Hygiene; 512207 Public Health Education and Promotion; 512301 Art Therapy; 512302 Dance Therapy; 512303 Hypnotherapy; 512304 Movement Therapy; 512305 Music Therapy; 512306 Occupational Therapy; 512307 Orthotics/Prosthetics; 512308 Physical Therapy; 512309 Recreational Therapy; 512310 Vocational Rehabilitation Counseling; 512399 Rehabilitation/Therapeutic Services, Other; 512401 Veterinary Medicine (D.V.M.); 512501 Veterinary Clinical Sciences (M.S., Ph.D.); 512701 Acupuncture and Oriental Medicine; 512702 Medical Dietician; 512703 Medical Illustrating; 512704 Naturopathic Medicine; 512705 Psychoanalysis; 512801 Dental/Oral Surgery Specialty; 512802 Dental Public Health Specialty; 512803 Endodontics Specialty; 512804 Oral Pathology Specialty; 512805 Orthodontics Specialty; 512806 Pedodontics Specialty; 512807 Periodontics Specialty; 512808 Prosthodontics Specialty; 513001 Veterinary Anesthesiology; 513002 Veterinary Dentistry; 513003 Veterinary Dermatology; 513004 Veterinary Emergency and Critical Care Medicine; 513005 Veterinary Internal Medicine; 513006 Laboratory Animal Medicine; 513007 Veterinary Microbiology; 513008 Veterinary Nutrition; 513009 Veterinary Ophthalmology; 513010 Veterinary Pathology; 513011 Veterinary Practice; 513012 Veterinary Preventive Medicine; 513013 Veterinary Radiology; 513014 Veterinary Surgery; 513015 Theriogenology; 513016 Veterinary Toxicology; 513017 Zoological Medicine
Related DOT Job/s: 090.227-010 FACULTY MEMBER, COLLEGE OR UNIVERSITY

31216 ENGLISH AND FOREIGN LANGUAGE TEACHERS—POSTSECONDARY. OOH Title/s: College and University Faculty

Teach courses in English language and literature or in foreign languages and literature. Include teachers of subjects such as journalism, classics, and linguistics. Prepares and delivers lectures to students. Compiles, administers, and grades examinations, or assigns this work to others. Compiles bibliographies of specialized materials for outside reading assignments. Stimulates class discussions. Advises students on academic and vocational curricula. Directs research of other teachers or graduate students working for advanced academic degrees. Conducts research in particular field of knowledge and publishes findings in professional journals. Acts as adviser to student organizations. Serves on faculty committee providing professional consulting services to government and industry.
Yearly Earnings: $43,888
Education: Doctor's degree
Knowledge: Clerical; Computers and Electronics; Sociology and Anthropology; Therapy and Counseling; Education and Training; English Language; Foreign Language; History and Archeology; Philosophy and Theology; Communications and Media
Abilities: Oral Comprehension; Written Comprehension; Oral Expression; Written Expression; Fluency of Ideas; Speech Recognition; Speech Clarity
Skills: Reading Comprehension; Active Listening; Writing; Speaking; Critical Thinking; Active Learning; Learning Strategies; Monitoring; Social Perceptiveness; Persuasion; Negotiation; Instructing; Service Orientation; Information Gathering; Information Organization; Synthesis/Reorganization; Idea Generation; Idea Evaluation; Implementation Planning; Solution Appraisal; Visioning; Systems Perception;

Identifying Downstream Consequences; Identification of Key Causes; Systems Evaluation; Time Management; Management of Financial Resources; Management of Personnel Resources
General Work Activities: Getting Information Needed to Do the Job; Evaluating Information against Standards; Analyzing Data or Information; Thinking Creatively; Developing Objectives and Strategies; Operating Vehicles or Equipment; Implementing Ideas, Programs, etc.; Interpreting Meaning of Information to Others; Communicating with Other Workers; Communicating with Persons Outside Organization; Establishing and Maintaining Relationships; Performing for or Working with Public; Teaching Others; Guiding, Directing and Motivating Subordinates; Coaching and Developing Others; Provide Consultation and Advice to Others; Performing Administrative Activities
Job Characteristics: Objective or Subjective Information; Job-Required Social Interaction; Supervise, Coach, Train Others; Coordinate or Lead Others; Responsibility for Outcomes and Results
GOE Group/s: 11.02.01 Educational and Library Services: Teaching and Instructing, General
CIP Program/s: 090401 Journalism; 160101 Foreign Languages and Literatures, General; 160102 Linguistics; 160103 Foreign Language Interpretation and Translation; 160301 Chinese Language and Literature; 160302 Japanese Language and Literature; 160399 East and Southeast Asian Languages and Literatures, Other; 160402 Russian Language and Literature; 160403 Slavic Languages and Literatures (Other Than Russian); 160499 East European Languages and Literatures, Other; 160501 German Language and Literature; 160502 Scandinavian Languages and Literatures; 160599 Germanic Languages and Literatures, Other; 160601 Greek Language and Literature (Modern); 160703 South Asian Languages and Literatures; 160901 French Language and Literature; 160902 Italian Language and Literature; 160904 Portuguese Language and Literature; 160905 Spanish Language and Literature; 160999 Romance Languages and Literatures, Other; 161101 Arabic Language and Literature; 161102 Hebrew Language and Literature; 161199 Middle Eastern Languages and Literatures, Other; 161201 Classics and Classical Languages and Literatures; 161202 Greek Language and Literature (Ancient and Medieval); 161203 Latin Language and Literature (Ancient and Medieval); 161299 Classical and Ancient Near Eastern Languages and Literatures; 230101 English Language and Literature, General; 230301 Comparative Literature; 230401 English Composition; 230501 English Creative Writing; 230701 American Literature (United States); 230801 English Literature (British and Commonwealth); 231001 Speech and Rhetorical Studies; 231101 English Technical and Business Writing
Related DOT Job/s: 090.227-010 FACULTY MEMBER, COLLEGE OR UNIVERSITY

31218 ART, DRAMA, AND MUSIC TEACHERS—POSTSECONDARY. OOH Title/s: College and University Faculty

Teach courses in art, drama, and music, including painting and sculpture. Prepares and delivers lectures to students. Stimulates class discussions. Compiles bibliographies of specialized materials for outside reading assignments. Compiles, administers, and grades examinations, or assigns this work to others. Advises students on academic and vocational curricula. Directs research of other teachers or graduate students working for advanced academic degrees. Conducts research in particular field of knowledge and publishes findings in professional journals. Serves on faculty committee providing professional consulting services to government and industry. Acts as adviser to student organizations.
Yearly Earnings: $43,888
Education: Doctor's degree
Knowledge: Administration and Management; Clerical; Sociology and Anthropology; Therapy and Counseling; Education and Training; English Language; Fine Arts; History and Archeology; Philosophy and Theology; Communications and Media
Abilities: Oral Comprehension; Written Comprehension; Oral Expression; Written Expression; Fluency of Ideas; Originality; Flexibility of Closure; Far Vision; Visual Color Discrimination; Hearing Sensitivity; Speech Clarity
Skills: Reading Comprehension; Active Listening; Writing; Speaking; Critical Thinking; Active Learning; Learning Strategies; Monitoring; Social Perceptiveness; Persuasion; Negotiation; Instructing; Service Orientation; Information Gathering; Information Organization; Synthesis/Reorganization; Idea Generation; Idea Evaluation; Implementation Planning; Solution Appraisal; Programming; Visioning; Identification of Key Causes; Time Management; Management of Personnel Resources
General Work Activities: Getting Information Needed to Do the Job; Analyzing Data or Information; Thinking Creatively; Developing Objectives and Strategies; Scheduling Work and Activities; Interpreting Meaning of Information to Others; Establishing and Maintaining Relationships; Developing and Building Teams; Teaching Others; Guiding, Directing and Motivating Subordinates; Coaching and Developing Others; Provide Consultation and Advice to Others
Job Characteristics: Job-Required Social Interaction; Supervise, Coach, Train Others
GOE Group/s: 11.02.01 Educational and Library Services: Teaching and Instructing, General
CIP Program/s: 500201 Crafts, Folk Art and Artisanry; 500301 Dance; 500501 Drama/Theater Arts, General; 500502 Technical Theater/Theater Design and Stagecraft; 500503 Acting and Directing; 500504 Playwriting and Screenwriting; 500505 Drama/Theater Literature, History and Criticism; 500601 Film/Cinema Studies; 500602 Film-Video Making/Cinematography and Production; 500605 Photography; 500701 Art, General; 500702 Fine/Studio Arts; 500703 Art History, Criticism and Conservation; 500704 Arts Management; 500705 Drawing; 500706 Intermedia; 500708 Painting; 500709 Sculpture; 500710 Printmaking; 500711 Ceramics Arts and Ceramics; 500712 Fiber, Textile and Weaving Arts; 500713 Metal and Jewelry Arts; 500901 Music, General; 500902 Music History and Literature; 500903 Music - General Performance; 500904 Music Theory and Composition; 500905 Musicology and Ethnomusicology; 500906 Music Conducting; 500907 Music - Piano and Organ Performance; 500908 Music - Voice and Choral/Opera Performance; 500909 Music Business Management and Merchandising
Related DOT Job/s: 090.227-010 FACULTY MEMBER, COLLEGE OR UNIVERSITY

31222 ENGINEERING TEACHERS—POSTSECONDARY. OOH Title/s: College and University Faculty

Teach courses pertaining to the application of physical laws and principles of engineering for the development of machines, materials, instruments, processes, and services. Include teachers of subjects such as chemical, civil, electrical, industrial, mechanical, mineral, and petroleum engineering. Prepares and delivers lectures to students. Stimulates class discussions. Compiles bibliographies of specialized materials for outside reading assignments. Compiles, administers, and grades examinations, or assigns this work to others. Advises students on academic and vocational curricula. Directs research of other teachers or graduate students working for advanced academic degrees. Conducts research in particular field of knowledge and publishes findings in professional journals. Serves on faculty committee providing professional consulting services to government and industry. Acts as adviser to student organizations.
Yearly Earnings: $43,888
Education: Doctor's degree

Knowledge: Administration and Management; Clerical; Computers and Electronics; Engineering and Technology; Design; Building and Construction; Mathematics; Physics; Chemistry; Therapy and Counseling; Education and Training; English Language; Telecommunications; Communications and Media
Abilities: Oral Comprehension; Written Comprehension; Oral Expression; Written Expression; Fluency of Ideas; Originality; Deductive Reasoning; Mathematical Reasoning; Number Facility; Time Sharing; Speech Clarity
Skills: Reading Comprehension; Active Listening; Writing; Speaking; Mathematics; Science; Critical Thinking; Active Learning; Learning Strategies; Monitoring; Social Perceptiveness; Instructing; Problem Identification; Information Gathering; Information Organization; Synthesis/Reorganization; Idea Generation; Idea Evaluation; Implementation Planning; Solution Appraisal; Operations Analysis; Technology Design; Equipment Selection; Programming; Troubleshooting; Visioning; Systems Perception; Identifying Downstream Consequences; Identification of Key Causes; Judgment and Decision Making; Systems Evaluation; Time Management; Management of Financial Resources; Management of Material Resources
General Work Activities: Getting Information Needed to Do the Job; Evaluating Information against Standards; Analyzing Data or Information; Updating and Using Job-Relevant Knowledge; Developing Objectives and Strategies; Operating Vehicles or Equipment; Interpreting Meaning of Information to Others; Communicating with Other Workers; Developing and Building Teams; Teaching Others; Guiding, Directing and Motivating Subordinates; Coaching and Developing Others; Provide Consultation and Advice to Others
Job Characteristics: Job-Required Social Interaction; Supervise, Coach, Train Others; Coordinate or Lead Others; Responsibility for Outcomes and Results
GOE Group/s: 11.02.01 Educational and Library Services: Teaching and Instructing, General
CIP Program/s: 140101 Engineering, General; 140201 Aerospace, Aeronautical and Astronautical Engineering; 140301 Agricultural Engineering; 140401 Architectural Engineering; 140501 Bioengineering and Biomedical Engineering; 140601 Ceramic Sciences and Engineering; 140701 Chemical Engineering; 140801 Civil Engineering, General; 140802 Geotechnical Engineering; 140803 Structural Engineering; 140804 Transportation and Highway Engineering; 140805 Water Resources Engineering; 140901 Computer Engineering; 141001 Electrical, Electronics and Communication Engineering; 141101 Engineering Mechanics; 141201 Engineering Physics; 141301 Engineering Science; 141401 Environmental/Environmental Health Engineering; 141501 Geological Engineering; 141601 Geophysical Engineering; 141701 Industrial/Manufacturing Engineering; 141801 Material Engineering; 141901 Mechanical Engineering; 142001 Metallurgical Engineering; 142101 Mining and Mineral Engineering; 142201 Naval Architecture and Marine Engineering; 142301 Nuclear Engineering; 142401 Ocean Engineering; 142501 Petroleum Engineering; 142701 Systems Engineering; 142801 Textile Sciences and Engineering; 142901 Engineering Design; 143001 Engineering/Industrial Management; 143101 Materials Science; 143201 Polymer/Plastics Engineering; 151101 Engineering-Related Technologists and Technicians, General
Related DOT Job/s: 090.227-010 FACULTY MEMBER, COLLEGE OR UNIVERSITY

31224 MATHEMATICAL SCIENCES TEACHERS—POSTSECONDARY. OOH Title/s: College and University Faculty

Teach courses pertaining to mathematical concepts, statistics, and actuarial science and to the application of original and standardized mathematical techniques in solving specific problems and situations. Prepares and delivers lectures to students. Compiles, administers, and grades examinations, or assigns this work to others. Stimulates class discussions. Directs research of other teachers or graduate students working for advanced academic degrees. Compiles bibliographies of specialized materials for outside reading assignments. Conducts research in particular field of knowledge and publishes findings in professional journals. Advises students on academic and vocational curricula. Acts as adviser to student organizations. Serves on faculty committee providing professional consulting services to government and industry.
Yearly Earnings: $43,888
Education: Doctor's degree
Knowledge: Administration and Management; Clerical; Computers and Electronics; Mathematics; Education and Training; English Language; Philosophy and Theology; Communications and Media
Abilities: Oral Comprehension; Written Comprehension; Oral Expression; Written Expression; Fluency of Ideas; Originality; Mathematical Reasoning; Number Facility; Speech Clarity
Skills: Reading Comprehension; Active Listening; Writing; Speaking; Mathematics; Science; Critical Thinking; Active Learning; Learning Strategies; Monitoring; Instructing; Problem Identification; Information Gathering; Information Organization; Synthesis/Reorganization; Idea Generation; Idea Evaluation; Implementation Planning; Solution Appraisal; Operations Analysis; Programming; Identifying Downstream Consequences; Judgment and Decision Making; Systems Evaluation; Time Management
General Work Activities: Getting Information Needed to Do the Job; Judging Qualities of Things, Services, People; Evaluating Information against Standards; Analyzing Data or Information; Updating and Using Job-Relevant Knowledge; Developing Objectives and Strategies; Operating Vehicles or Equipment; Implementing Ideas, Programs, etc.; Interpreting Meaning of Information to Others; Communicating with Other Workers; Establishing and Maintaining Relationships; Developing and Building Teams; Teaching Others; Guiding, Directing and Motivating Subordinates; Coaching and Developing Others; Provide Consultation and Advice to Others
Job Characteristics: Job-Required Social Interaction; Supervise, Coach, Train Others; Coordinate or Lead Others
GOE Group/s: 11.02.01 Educational and Library Services: Teaching and Instructing, General
CIP Program/s: 260615 Biostatistics; 270101 Mathematics; 270301 Applied Mathematics, General; 270302 Operations Research; 270501 Mathematical Statistics; 300801 Mathematics and Computer Science; 511303 Medical Biomathematics and Biometrics; 512204 Health and Medical Biostatistics; 520801 Finance, General; 520802 Actuarial Science; 521302 Business Statistics
Related DOT Job/s: 090.227-010 FACULTY MEMBER, COLLEGE OR UNIVERSITY

31226 COMPUTER SCIENCE TEACHERS—POSTSECONDARY. OOH Title/s: College and University Faculty

Teach courses in computer science. May specialize in a field of computer science, such as the design and function of computers or operations and research analysis. Prepares and delivers lectures to students. Stimulates class discussions. Compiles bibliographies of specialized materials for outside reading assignments. Compiles, administers, and grades examinations, or assigns this work to others. Directs research of other teachers or graduate students working for advanced academic degrees. Conducts research in particular field of knowledge and publishes findings in professional journals. Advises students on academic and vocational curricula. Acts as adviser to student organizations. Serves on faculty committee providing professional consulting services to government and industry.

Yearly Earnings: $43,888
Education: Doctor's degree
Knowledge: Administration and Management; Clerical; Computers and Electronics; Engineering and Technology; Design; Mathematics; Physics; Psychology; Sociology and Anthropology; Therapy and Counseling; Education and Training; English Language; Philosophy and Theology; Telecommunications; Communications and Media
Abilities: Oral Comprehension; Written Comprehension; Oral Expression; Written Expression; Fluency of Ideas; Originality; Deductive Reasoning; Inductive Reasoning; Category Flexibility; Memorization; Speed of Closure; Flexibility of Closure; Far Vision; Night Vision; Speech Clarity
Skills: Reading Comprehension; Active Listening; Writing; Speaking; Mathematics; Science; Critical Thinking; Active Learning; Learning Strategies; Monitoring; Social Perceptiveness; Coordination; Persuasion; Instructing; Service Orientation; Problem Identification; Information Gathering; Information Organization; Synthesis/Reorganization; Idea Generation; Idea Evaluation; Implementation Planning; Solution Appraisal; Operations Analysis; Technology Design; Equipment Selection; Programming; Testing; Troubleshooting; Visioning; Systems Perception; Identifying Downstream Consequences; Identification of Key Causes; Judgment and Decision Making; Time Management; Management of Material Resources; Management of Personnel Resources
General Work Activities: Getting Information Needed to Do the Job; Judging Qualities of Things, Services, People; Evaluating Information against Standards; Analyzing Data or Information; Thinking Creatively; Updating and Using Job-Relevant Knowledge; Operating Vehicles or Equipment; Interpreting Meaning of Information to Others; Communicating with Persons Outside Organization; Establishing and Maintaining Relationships; Developing and Building Teams; Teaching Others; Guiding, Directing and Motivating Subordinates; Coaching and Developing Others; Provide Consultation and Advice to Others
Job Characteristics: Objective or Subjective Information; Job-Required Social Interaction; Supervise, Coach, Train Others; Persuade Someone to a Course of Action; Provide a Service to Others; Take a Position Opposed to Others; Deal with External Customers; Coordinate or Lead Others; Responsibility for Outcomes and Results; Sitting; Frustrating Circumstances
GOE Group/s: 11.02.01 Educational and Library Services: Teaching and Instructing, General
CIP Program/s: 110101 Computer and Information Sciences, General; 110201 Computer Programming; 110401 Information Sciences and Systems; 110501 Computer Systems Analysis; 110701 Computer Science; 300801 Mathematics and Computer Science; 521201 Management Information Systems and Business Data Processing; 521202 Business Computer Programming/Programmer; 521203 Business Systems Analysis and Design; 521204 Business Systems Networking and Telecommunications
Related DOT Job/s: 090.227-010 FACULTY MEMBER, COLLEGE OR UNIVERSITY

31299 ALL OTHER POSTSECONDARY TEACHERS.

OOH Title/s: College and University Faculty
All other postsecondary teachers not elsewhere classified. Include teachers of subjects such as business, physical education, education, theology, law, and home economics.
Yearly Earnings: $43,888
Education: Doctor's degree
GOE Group/s: 11.02.01 Educational and Library Services: Teaching and Instructing, General
CIP Program/s: 010101 Agricultural Business and Management, General; 010301 Agricultural Production Workers and Managers, General; 010507 Equestrian/Equine Studies, Horse Management and Training; 010601 Horticulture Services Operations and Management, General; 040201 Architecture; 040301 City/Urban, Community and Regional Planning; 040501 Interior Architecture; 040601 Landscape Architecture; 040701 Architectural Urban Design and Planning; 080101 Apparel and Accessories Marketing Operations, General; 080301 Entrepreneurship; 080901 Hospitality and Recreation Marketing Operations, General; 090101 Communications, General; 090201 Advertising; 090402 Broadcast Journalism; 090403 Mass Communications; 090501 Public Relations and Organizational Communications; 090701 Radio and Television Broadcasting; 120501 Baker/Pastry Chef; 120503 Culinary Arts/Chef Training; 120504 Food and Beverage/Restaurant Operations Manager; 130101 Education, General; 130201 Bilingual/Bicultural Education; 130301 Curriculum and Instruction; 130401 Education Administration and Supervision, General; 130402 Administration of Special Education; 130403 Adult and Continuing Education Administration; 130404 Educational Supervision; 130405 Elementary, Middle and Secondary Education Administration; 130406 Higher Education Administration; 130407 Community and Junior College Administration; 130501 Educational/Instructional Media Design; 130601 Educational Evaluation and Research; 130603 Educational Statistics and Research Methods; 130604 Educational Assessment, Testing and Measurement; 130701 International and Comparative Education; 130802 Educational Psychology; 130901 Social and Philosophical Foundations of Education; 131001 Special Education, General; 131003 Education of the Deaf and Hearing Impaired; 131004 Education of the Gifted and Talented; 131005 Education of the Emotionally Handicapped; 131006 Education of the Mentally Handicapped; 131007 Education of the Multiple Handicapped; 131008 Education of the Physically Handicapped; 131009 Education of the Blind and Visually Handicapped; 131011 Education of the Specific Learning Disabled; 131012 Education of the Speech Impaired; 131013 Education of the Autistic; 131101 Counselor Education Counseling and Guidance Services; 131102 College/Postsecondary Student Counseling and Personnel Services; 131201 Adult and Continuing Teacher Education; 131202 Elementary Teacher Education; 131203 Junior High/Intermediate/Middle School Teacher Education; 131204 Pre-Elementary/Early Childhood/Kindergarten Teacher Education; 131205 Secondary Teacher Education; 131206 Teacher Education, Multiple Levels; 131299 General Teacher Education, Other; 131301 Agricultural Teacher Education (Vocational); 131302 Art Teacher Education; 131303 Business Teacher Education (Vocational); 131304 Driver and Safety Teacher Education; 131305 English Teacher Education; 131306 Foreign Languages Teacher Education; 131307 Health Teacher Education; 131308 Home Economics Teacher Education (Vocational); 131309 Technology Teacher Education/Industrial Arts Teacher Education; 131310 Marketing Operations Teacher Ed./Mkt. & Distribution Teacher; 131311 Mathematics Teacher Education; 131312 Music Teacher Education; 131314 Physical Education Teaching and Coaching; 131315 Reading Teacher Education; 131316 Science Teacher Education, General; 131317 Social Science Teacher Education; 131318 Social Studies Teacher Education; 131319 Technical Teacher Education (Vocational); 131320 Trade and Industrial Teacher Education (Vocational); 131321 Computer Teacher Education; 131322 Biology Teacher Education; 131323 Chemistry Teacher Education; 131324 Drama and Dance Teacher Education; 131325 French Language Teacher Education; 131326 German Language Teacher Education; 131327 Health Occupations Teacher Education (Vocational); 131328 History Teacher Education; 131329 Physics Teacher Education; 131330 Spanish Language Teacher Education; 131331 Speech Teacher Education; 151102 Surveying; 190101 Home Economics, General; 190201 Business Home Economics; 190202 Home Economics Communications; 190301 Family and Community Studies; 190402 Consumer Economics and Science; 190501 Foods and Nutrition Studies, General; 190503 Dietetics/Human Nutri-

tional Services; 190601 Housing Studies, General; 190603 Interior Environments; 190701 Individual and Family Development Studies, General; 190703 Family and Marriage Counseling; 190705 Gerontological Services; 190901 Clothing/Apparel and Textile Studies; 220101 Law (LL.B., J.D.); 220104 Juridical Science/Legal Specialization(LL.M.,M.C.L.,J.S.D./S); 240101 Liberal Arts and Sciences/Liberal Studies; 240102 General Studies; 240103 Humanities/Humanistic Studies; 250101 Library Science/Librarianship; 290101 Military Technologies; 301201 Historic Preservation, Conservation, and Architectural History; 301401 Museology/Museum Studies; 310101 Parks, Recreation and Leisure Studies; 310301 Parks, Recreation and Leisure Facilities Management; 310501 Health and Physical Education, General; 310504 Sport and Fitness Administration/Management; 380101 Philosophy; 380201 Religion/Religious Studies; 389999 Philosophy and Religion; 390101 Biblical and Other Theological Languages and Literatures; 390201 Bible/Biblical Studies; 390301 Missions/Missionary Studies and Misology; 390401 Religious Education; 390501 Religious/Sacred Music; 390601 Theology/Theological Studies; 390602 Divinity/Ministry (B.D., M.Div.); 390604 Rabbinical and Talmudic Studies (M.H.L./Rav); 390605 Pre-Theological/Pre-Ministerial Studies; 430102 Corrections/Correctional Administration; 430103 Criminal Justice/Law Enforcement Administration; 430104 Criminal Justice Studies; 440201 Community Organization, Resources and Services; 440401 Public Administration; 440501 Public Policy Analysis; 440701 Social Work; 450702 Cartography; 470609 Aviation Systems and Avionics Maintenance Technologists and Technicians; 480101 Drafting, General; 490101 Aviation and Airway Science; 490309 Marine Science/Merchant Marine Officer; 500401 Design and Visual Communications; 500402 Graphic Design, Commercial Art and Illustration; 500404 Industrial Design; 500406 Commercial Photography; 500407 Fashion Design and Illustration; 500408 Interior Design; 500701 Art, General; 500704 Arts Management; 511501 Alcohol/Drug Abuse Counseling; 520101 Business, General; 520201 Business Administration and Management, General; 520301 Accounting; 520401 Administrative Assistant/Secretarial Science, General; 520501 Business Communications; 520801 Finance, General; 520804 Financial Planning; 520805 Insurance and Risk Management; 520806 International Finance; 520807 Investments and Securities; 520808 Public Finance; 520901 Hospitality/Administration Management; 520902 Hotel/Motel and Restaurant Management; 520903 Travel-Tourism Management; 521001 Human Resources Management; 521002 Labor/Personnel Relations and Studies; 521003 Organizational Behavior Studies; 521101 International Business; 521201 Management Information Systems and Business Data Processing; 521202 Business Computer Programming/Programmer; 521203 Business Systems Analysis and Design; 521204 Business Systems Networking and Telecommunications; 521301 Management Science; 521401 Business Marketing and Marketing Management; 521402 Marketing Research; 521403 International Business Marketing; 521501 Real Estate; 521601 Taxation

Related DOT Job/s: 090.227-010 FACULTY MEMBER, COLLEGE OR UNIVERSITY

Preschool, Kindergarten, Elementary, Secondary, and Special Education Teachers and Instructors

31303 TEACHERS—PRESCHOOL. OOH Title/s: Preschool Teachers and Child-Care Workers

Instruct children (normally up to 5 years of age) in activities designed to promote social, physical, and intellectual growth needed for primary school in preschool, daycare center, or other child development facility. May be required to hold state certification. Instructs children in activities designed to promote social, physical, and intellectual growth in a facility such as preschool or daycare center. Plans individual and group activities for children, such as learning to listen to instructions, playing with others, and using play equipment. Demonstrates activity. Structures play activities to instill concepts of respect and concern for others. Monitors individual and/or group activities to prevent accidents and promote social skills. Reads books to entire class or to small groups. Confers with parents to explain preschool program and to discuss ways they can develop their child's interest. Plans instructional activities for teacher aide. Administers tests to determine each child's level of development according to design of test. Attends staff meetings.

Yearly Earnings: $19,552

Education: Bachelor's degree

Knowledge: Customer and Personal Service; Psychology; Sociology and Anthropology; Therapy and Counseling; Education and Training; Foreign Language; Fine Arts; History and Archeology; Philosophy and Theology

Abilities: Fluency of Ideas; Originality; Memorization; Time Sharing; Far Vision; Peripheral Vision; Speech Recognition

Skills: Learning Strategies; Monitoring; Social Perceptiveness; Instructing

General Work Activities: Thinking Creatively; Developing Objectives and Strategies; Scheduling Work and Activities; Organizing, Planning, and Prioritizing; Establishing and Maintaining Relationships; Assisting and Caring for Others; Selling or Influencing Others; Resolving Conflicts, Negotiating with Others; Coordinating Work and Activities of Others; Developing and Building Teams; Teaching Others; Guiding, Directing and Motivating Subordinates; Coaching and Developing Others; Performing Administrative Activities; Monitoring and Controlling Resources

Job Characteristics: Objective or Subjective Information; Job-Required Social Interaction; Responsible for Others' Health and Safety; Frequency in Conflict Situations; Deal with Unpleasant or Angry People; Deal with Physical, Aggressive People

GOE Group/s: 10.02.03 Nursing, Therapy, and Specialized Teaching Services: Specialized Teach

CIP Program/s: 130101 Education, General; 130201 Bilingual/Bicultural Education; 130401 Education Administration and Supervision, General; 130404 Educational Supervision; 131204 Pre-Elementary/Early Childhood/Kindergarten Teacher Education; 131206 Teacher Education, Multiple Levels; 131302 Art Teacher Education; 131305 English Teacher Education; 131306 Foreign Languages Teacher Education; 131311 Mathematics Teacher Education; 131312 Music Teacher Education; 131314 Physical Education Teaching and Coaching; 131315 Reading Teacher Education; 131316 Science Teacher Education, General; 131318 Social Studies Teacher Education; 131324 Drama and Dance Teacher Education; 131325 French

Language Teacher Education; 131326 German Language Teacher Education; 131330 Spanish Language Teacher Education; 131331 Speech Teacher Education; 131399 Teacher Education, Specific Academic and Vocational Programs; 200201 Child Care and Guidance Workers and Managers, General; 200203 Child Care Services Manager
Related DOT Job/s: 092.227-018 TEACHER, PRESCHOOL

31304 TEACHERS—KINDERGARTEN. OOH Title/s: School Teachers—Kindergarten, Elementary, and Secondary

Teach elemental natural and social science, personal hygiene, music, art, and literature to children from 4 to 6 years old. Promote physical, mental, and social development. May be required to hold state certification. Teaches elemental science, personal hygiene, and humanities to children to promote physical, mental, and social development. Supervises student activities, such as field visits, to stimulate student interest and broaden understanding of physical and social environment. Organizes and conducts games and group projects to develop cooperative behavior and assist children in forming satisfying relationships. Encourages students in activities, such as singing, dancing, and rhythmic activities, to promote self-expression and appreciation of aesthetic experience. Instructs children in practices of personal cleanliness and self-care. Observes children to detect signs of ill health or emotional disturbance, and to evaluate progress. Discusses student problems and progress with parents. Alternates periods of strenuous activity with periods of rest or light activity to avoid overstimulation and fatigue.
Yearly Earnings: $19,552
Education: Bachelor's degree
Knowledge: Customer and Personal Service; Psychology; Sociology and Anthropology; Geography; Medicine and Dentistry; Therapy and Counseling; Education and Training; English Language; Foreign Language; Fine Arts; History and Archeology; Philosophy and Theology; Law, Government, and Jurisprudence; Communications and Media
Abilities: Fluency of Ideas; Originality; Problem Sensitivity; Deductive Reasoning; Category Flexibility; Memorization; Speed of Closure; Flexibility of Closure; Spatial Orientation; Selective Attention; Time Sharing; Far Vision; Night Vision; Peripheral Vision; Hearing Sensitivity; Auditory Attention; Sound Localization; Speech Recognition; Speech Clarity
Skills: Learning Strategies; Monitoring; Social Perceptiveness; Instructing; Service Orientation
General Work Activities: Getting Information Needed to Do the Job; Thinking Creatively; Developing Objectives and Strategies; Scheduling Work and Activities; Organizing, Planning, and Prioritizing; Communicating with Persons Outside Organization; Establishing and Maintaining Relationships; Assisting and Caring for Others; Resolving Conflicts, Negotiating with Others; Performing for or Working with Public; Developing and Building Teams; Teaching Others; Coaching and Developing Others; Provide Consultation and Advice to Others; Monitoring and Controlling Resources
Job Characteristics: Objective or Subjective Information; Job-Required Social Interaction; Responsible for Others' Health and Safety; Frequency in Conflict Situations; Deal with Unpleasant or Angry People; Deal with Physical, Aggressive People; Diseases/Infections
GOE Group/s: 10.02.03 Nursing, Therapy, and Specialized Teaching Services: Specialized Teach
CIP Program/s: 130101 Education, General; 130201 Bilingual/Bicultural Education; 130401 Education Administration and Supervision, General; 130404 Educational Supervision; 131202 Elementary Teacher Education; 131204 Pre-Elementary/Early Childhood/Kindergarten Teacher Education; 131206 Teacher Education, Multiple Levels; 131302 Art Teacher Education; 131305 English Teacher Education; 131306 Foreign Languages Teacher Education; 131311 Mathematics Teacher Education; 131312 Music Teacher Education; 131314 Physical Education Teaching and Coaching; 131315 Reading Teacher Education; 131316 Science Teacher Education, General; 131318 Social Studies Teacher Education; 131324 Drama and Dance Teacher Education; 131325 French Language Teacher Education; 131326 German Language Teacher Education; 131330 Spanish Language Teacher Education; 131331 Speech Teacher Education; 131399 Teacher Education, Specific Academic and Vocational Programs
Related DOT Job/s: 092.227-014 TEACHER, KINDERGARTEN

31305 TEACHERS—ELEMENTARY SCHOOL. OOH Title/s: School Teachers—Kindergarten, Elementary, and Secondary

Teach elementary pupils in public or private schools basic academic, social, and other formulative skills. Exclude special education teachers of the handicapped. Lectures, demonstrates, and uses audio-visual aids and computers to present academic, social, and motor skill subject matter to class. Teaches subjects such as math, science, or social studies. Prepares course objectives and outline for course of study, following curriculum guidelines or requirements of state and school. Prepares, administers, and corrects tests, and records results. Assigns lessons, corrects papers, and hears oral presentations. Teaches rules of conduct and maintains discipline and suitable learning environment in classroom and on playground. Evaluates student performance and discusses pupil academic and behavioral attitudes and achievements with parents. Keeps attendance and grade records and prepares reports as required by school. Counsels pupils when adjustment and academic problems arise. Supervises outdoor and indoor play activities. Teaches combined grade classes. Attends staff meetings, serves on committees, and attends workshops or in-service training activities. Coordinates class field trips. Prepares bulletin boards.
Yearly Earnings: $32,604
Education: Bachelor's degree
Knowledge: Administration and Management; Clerical; Customer and Personal Service; Mathematics; Chemistry; Biology; Psychology; Sociology and Anthropology; Geography; Medicine and Dentistry; Therapy and Counseling; Education and Training; English Language; Foreign Language; Fine Arts; History and Archeology; Philosophy and Theology; Law, Government, and Jurisprudence; Transportation
Abilities: Oral Comprehension; Written Comprehension; Oral Expression; Written Expression; Fluency of Ideas; Originality; Category Flexibility; Mathematical Reasoning; Number Facility; Memorization; Speed of Closure; Spatial Orientation; Time Sharing; Gross Body Equilibrium; Far Vision; Night Vision; Peripheral Vision; Auditory Attention; Speech Recognition; Speech Clarity
Skills: Speaking; Active Learning; Learning Strategies; Monitoring; Social Perceptiveness; Coordination; Persuasion; Instructing; Service Orientation; Information Organization; Implementation Planning; Time Management
General Work Activities: Getting Information Needed to Do the Job; Identifying Objects, Actions, and Events; Judging Qualities of Things, Services, People; Thinking Creatively; Updating and Using Job-Relevant Knowledge; Developing Objectives and Strategies; Scheduling Work and Activities; Organizing, Planning, and Prioritizing; Operating Vehicles or Equipment; Implementing Ideas, Programs, etc.; Communicating with Persons Outside Organization; Establishing and Maintaining Relationships; Assisting and Caring for Others; Resolving Conflicts, Negotiating with Others; Coordinating Work and Activities of Others; Developing and Building Teams; Teaching Others; Guiding, Directing and Motivating Subordinates; Coaching and Developing Others; Provide Consultation and Advice to Others; Performing Administrative Activities
Job Characteristics: Job-Required Social Interaction; Provide a Service to Others; Frequency in Conflict Situations; Deal with Unpleasant or Angry People; Deal with Physical, Aggressive People

GOE Group/s: 11.02.01 Educational and Library Services: Teaching and Instructing, General
CIP Program/s: 130101 Education, General; 130201 Bilingual/Bicultural Education; 130401 Education Administration and Supervision, General; 130404 Educational Supervision; 131202 Elementary Teacher Education; 131203 Junior High/Intermediate/Middle School Teacher Education; 131204 Pre-Elementary/Early Childhood/Kindergarten Teacher Education; 131206 Teacher Education, Multiple Levels; 131301 Agricultural Teacher Education (Vocational); 131302 Art Teacher Education; 131303 Business Teacher Education (Vocational); 131305 English Teacher Education; 131306 Foreign Languages Teacher Education; 131307 Health Teacher Education; 131308 Home Economics Teacher Education (Vocational); 131309 Technology Teacher Education/Industrial Arts Teacher Education; 131311 Mathematics Teacher Education; 131312 Music Teacher Education; 131314 Physical Education Teaching and Coaching; 131315 Reading Teacher Education; 131316 Science Teacher Education, General; 131317 Social Science Teacher Education; 131318 Social Studies Teacher Education; 131321 Computer Teacher Education; 131324 Drama and Dance Teacher Education; 131325 French Language Teacher Education; 131326 German Language Teacher Education; 131328 History Teacher Education; 131330 Spanish Language Teacher Education; 131331 Speech Teacher Education; 131399 Teacher Education, Specific Academic and Vocational Programs
Related DOT Job/s: 092.227-010 TEACHER, ELEMENTARY SCHOOL

31308 TEACHERS—SECONDARY SCHOOL. OOH Title/s: School Teachers—Kindergarten, Elementary, and Secondary

Instruct students in public or private schools in one or more subjects, such as English, mathematics, or social studies. May be designated according to subject matter specialty, such as typing instructors, commercial teachers, or English teachers. Include vocational high school teachers. Instructs students, using various teaching methods, such as lecture and demonstration. Assigns lessons and corrects homework. Develops and administers tests. Prepares course outlines and objectives according to curriculum guidelines or state and local requirements. Uses audio-visual aids and other materials to supplement presentations. Evaluates, records, and reports student progress. Confers with students, parents, and school counselors to resolve behavioral and academic problems. Maintains discipline in classroom. Participates in faculty and professional meetings, educational conferences, and teacher training workshops. Selects, stores, orders, issues, and inventories classroom equipment, materials, and supplies. Keeps attendance records. Performs advisory duties, such as sponsoring student organizations or clubs, helping students select courses, and counseling students with problems.
Yearly Earnings: $35,880
Education: Bachelor's degree
Knowledge: Administration and Management; Clerical; Psychology; Sociology and Anthropology; Geography; Therapy and Counseling; Education and Training; English Language; Foreign Language; History and Archeology; Philosophy and Theology
Abilities: Oral Comprehension; Written Comprehension; Oral Expression; Written Expression; Originality; Memorization; Time Sharing; Speech Recognition; Speech Clarity
Skills: Reading Comprehension; Active Listening; Writing; Speaking; Mathematics; Active Learning; Learning Strategies; Monitoring; Social Perceptiveness; Instructing; Service Orientation; Information Organization; Synthesis/Reorganization; Implementation Planning; Operations Analysis; Time Management
General Work Activities: Getting Information Needed to Do the Job; Judging Qualities of Things, Services, People; Thinking Creatively; Updating and Using Job-Relevant Knowledge; Developing Objectives and Strategies; Organizing, Planning, and Prioritizing; Interpreting Meaning of Information to Others; Communicating with Persons Outside Organization; Establishing and Maintaining Relationships; Assisting and Caring for Others; Performing for or Working with Public; Developing and Building Teams; Teaching Others; Guiding, Directing and Motivating Subordinates; Coaching and Developing Others; Provide Consultation and Advice to Others
Job Characteristics: Job-Required Social Interaction; Coordinate or Lead Others; Frequency in Conflict Situations; Deal with Unpleasant or Angry People; Deal with Physical, Aggressive People
GOE Group/s: 11.02.01 Educational and Library Services: Teaching and Instructing, General; 11.02.02 Educational and Library Services: Teaching, Vocational and Industrial
CIP Program/s: 130101 Education, General; 130201 Bilingual/Bicultural Education; 130401 Education Administration and Supervision, General; 130404 Educational Supervision; 131203 Junior High/Intermediate/Middle School Teacher Education; 131205 Secondary Teacher Education; 131206 Teacher Education, Multiple Levels; 131301 Agricultural Teacher Education (Vocational); 131302 Art Teacher Education; 131303 Business Teacher Education (Vocational); 131304 Driver and Safety Teacher Education; 131305 English Teacher Education; 131306 Foreign Languages Teacher Education; 131307 Health Teacher Education; 131308 Home Economics Teacher Education (Vocational); 131309 Technology Teacher Education/Industrial Arts Teacher Education; 131310 Marketing Operations Teacher Ed./Mkt. & Distribution Teacher; 131311 Mathematics Teacher Education; 131312 Music Teacher Education; 131314 Physical Education Teaching and Coaching; 131315 Reading Teacher Education; 131316 Science Teacher Education, General; 131317 Social Science Teacher Education; 131318 Social Studies Teacher Education; 131319 Technical Teacher Education (Vocational); 131320 Trade and Industrial Teacher Education (Vocational); 131321 Computer Teacher Education; 131322 Biology Teacher Education; 131323 Chemistry Teacher Education; 131324 Drama and Dance Teacher Education; 131325 French Language Teacher Education; 131326 German Language Teacher Education; 131327 Health Occupations Teacher Education (Vocational); 131328 History Teacher Education; 131329 Physics Teacher Education; 131330 Spanish Language Teacher Education; 131331 Speech Teacher Education; 131399 Teacher Education, Specific Academic and Vocational Programs
Related DOT Job/s: 091.221-010 TEACHER, INDUSTRIAL ARTS; 091.227-010 TEACHER, SECONDARY SCHOOL; 099.224-010 INSTRUCTOR, PHYSICAL EDUCATION; 099.227-022 INSTRUCTOR, MILITARY SCIENCE

31311A SPECIAL EDUCATION VOCATIONAL TRAINING TEACHERS. OOH Title/s: Special Education Teachers; Blue Collar Worker Supervisors

Plan and conduct special education work and study programs or teach vocational skills to handicapped students. Counsels and instructs students in matters such as vocational choices, job readiness, and job retention skills and behaviors. Instructs students in areas such as personal-social skills and work-related attitudes and behaviors. Confers with students, parents, school personnel, and other individuals to plan vocational training that meet needs, interests, and abilities of students. Develops work opportunities that allow students to experience success in performing tasks of increasing difficulty and that teach work values. Confers with potential employers to obtain cooperation, adapting work situations to special needs of students. Confers with employers and visits worksite to monitor progress of students. Establishes contacts with employers and employment agencies and surveys newspapers and other sources to locate work opportunities for students. Evaluates and selects program participants according to specified criteria. Determines support needed to meet employer requirements

and fulfill program goals. Assists students in applying for jobs and accompanies students to employment interviews. Conducts field trips to enable students to learn about job activities and to explore work environments.
Yearly Earnings: $33,644
Education: Bachelor's degree
Knowledge: Administration and Management; Sales and Marketing; Customer and Personal Service; Personnel and Human Resources; Psychology; Sociology and Anthropology; Therapy and Counseling; Education and Training; Philosophy and Theology
Abilities: Written Comprehension; Oral Expression
Skills: Speaking; Learning Strategies; Social Perceptiveness; Coordination; Persuasion; Instructing; Service Orientation; Idea Generation; Implementation Planning; Management of Personnel Resources
General Work Activities: Judging Qualities of Things, Services, People; Developing Objectives and Strategies; Organizing, Planning, and Prioritizing; Communicating with Other Workers; Communicating with Persons Outside Organization; Establishing and Maintaining Relationships; Assisting and Caring for Others; Performing for or Working with Public; Developing and Building Teams; Teaching Others; Guiding, Directing and Motivating Subordinates; Coaching and Developing Others
Job Characteristics: Job-Required Social Interaction; Coordinate or Lead Others
GOE Group/s: 10.02.03 Nursing, Therapy, and Specialized Teaching Services: Specialized Teach
CIP Program/s: 130101 Education, General; 130401 Education Administration and Supervision, General; 130402 Administration of Special Education; 131001 Special Education, General; 131003 Education of the Deaf and Hearing Impaired; 131005 Education of the Emotionally Handicapped; 131006 Education of the Mentally Handicapped; 131007 Education of the Multiple Handicapped; 131008 Education of the Physically Handicapped; 131009 Education of the Blind and Visually Handicapped; 131011 Education of the Specific Learning Disabled; 131012 Education of the Speech Impaired
Related DOT Job/s: 094.107-010 WORK-STUDY COORDINATOR, SPECIAL EDUCATION; 094.227-026 TEACHER, VOCATIONAL TRAINING; 365.131-010 SHOE-REPAIR SUPERVISOR

31311B TEACHERS—EMOTIONALLY IMPAIRED, MENTALLY IMPAIRED, AND LEARNING DISABLED. OOH Title/s: Special Education Teachers

Teach basic academic and living skills to students with emotional or mental impairments or learning disabilities. Teaches socially acceptable behavior, employing techniques such as behavior modification and positive reinforcement. Instructs students, using special educational strategies and techniques to improve sensory-motor and perceptual-motor development, memory, language, and cognition. Instructs students in academic subjects, utilizing various teaching techniques, such as phonetics, multisensory learning, and repetition, to reinforce learning. Instructs students in daily living skills required for independent maintenance and economic self-sufficiency, such as hygiene, safety, and food preparation. Plans curriculum and other instructional materials to meet student's needs, considering such factors as physical, emotional, and educational abilities. Selects and teaches reading material and math problems related to everyday life of individual student. Administers and interprets results of ability and achievement tests. Confers with parents, administrators, testing specialists, social workers, and others to develop individual educational plan for student. Confers with other staff members to plan programs designed to promote educational, physical, and social development of students. Works with students to increase motivation. Provides consistent reinforcement to learning, and continuous feedback to students. Observes, evaluates, and prepares reports on progress of students. Meets with parents to provide support, guidance in using community resources, and skills in dealing with students' learning impairments.
Yearly Earnings: $33,644
Education: Bachelor's degree
Knowledge: Customer and Personal Service; Psychology; Sociology and Anthropology; Medicine and Dentistry; Therapy and Counseling; Education and Training; English Language; Foreign Language
Abilities: Written Comprehension; Oral Expression; Written Expression; Speech Clarity
Skills: Active Listening; Writing; Speaking; Learning Strategies; Monitoring; Social Perceptiveness; Persuasion; Instructing; Service Orientation; Idea Generation; Idea Evaluation; Implementation Planning; Solution Appraisal; Identification of Key Causes
General Work Activities: Judging Qualities of Things, Services, People; Making Decisions and Solving Problems; Thinking Creatively; Updating and Using Job-Relevant Knowledge; Developing Objectives and Strategies; Implementing Ideas, Programs, etc.; Interpreting Meaning of Information to Others; Establishing and Maintaining Relationships; Assisting and Caring for Others; Performing for or Working with Public; Developing and Building Teams; Teaching Others; Guiding, Directing and Motivating Subordinates; Coaching and Developing Others; Provide Consultation and Advice to Others
Job Characteristics: Objective or Subjective Information; Job-Required Social Interaction; Take a Position Opposed to Others; Coordinate or Lead Others; Deal with Unpleasant or Angry People; Deal with Physical, Aggressive People; Importance of Being Aware of New Events
GOE Group/s: 10.02.03 Nursing, Therapy, and Specialized Teaching Services: Specialized Teach; 11.02.01 Educational and Library Services: Teaching and Instructing, General
CIP Program/s: 130101 Education, General; 130201 Bilingual/Bicultural Education; 130401 Education Administration and Supervision, General; 130402 Administration of Special Education; 130404 Educational Supervision; 131001 Special Education, General; 131003 Education of the Deaf and Hearing Impaired; 131005 Education of the Emotionally Handicapped; 131006 Education of the Mentally Handicapped; 131007 Education of the Multiple Handicapped; 131008 Education of the Physically Handicapped; 131009 Education of the Blind and Visually Handicapped; 131011 Education of the Specific Learning Disabled; 131012 Education of the Speech Impaired; 131013 Education of the Autistic
Related DOT Job/s: 094.227-010 TEACHER, EMOTIONALLY IMPAIRED; 094.227-022 TEACHER, MENTALLY IMPAIRED; 094.227-030 TEACHER, LEARNING DISABLED; 099.227-042 TEACHER, RESOURCE

31311C TEACHERS—PHYSICALLY, VISUALLY, AND HEARING IMPAIRED. OOH Title/s: Special Education Teachers

Teach elementary and secondary school subjects to physically, visually, and hearing impaired students. Teaches academic subjects, daily living skills, and vocational skills to students, adapting teaching techniques to meet individual needs of students. Plans curriculum and prepares lessons and other materials, considering such factors as individual needs and learning levels and physical limitations of students. Instructs students in various forms of communication, such as gestures, sign language, finger spelling, and cues. Instructs students in reading and writing, using magnification equipment and large-print material or Braille system. Confers with parents, administrators, testing specialists, social workers, and others to develop individual educational program. Encourages students' participation in verbal and sensory classroom experiences to ensure comprehension of subject matter and development of social and communication skills. Attends and interprets lectures and instructions for students enrolled in regular classes, using sign language. Transcribes lessons and other materials

into Braille for blind students or large print for low-vision students. Arranges for and conducts field trips designed to promote experiential learning. Discusses with parents how parents can encourage students' independence and well-being and to provide guidance in using community resources. Tests students' hearing aids to ensure hearing aids are functioning. Arranges and adjusts tools, work aids, and equipment utilized by students in classroom, such as specially equipped work tables, computers, and typewriters. Devises special teaching tools, techniques, and equipment.
Yearly Earnings: $33,644
Education: Bachelor's degree
Knowledge: Administration and Management; Clerical; Customer and Personal Service; Biology; Psychology; Sociology and Anthropology; Therapy and Counseling; Education and Training; English Language; Foreign Language; History and Archeology; Philosophy and Theology
Abilities: Oral Comprehension; Written Comprehension; Oral Expression; Originality; Auditory Attention; Speech Recognition; Speech Clarity
Skills: Reading Comprehension; Active Listening; Writing; Speaking; Learning Strategies; Monitoring; Social Perceptiveness; Instructing; Service Orientation; Idea Generation; Implementation Planning; Solution Appraisal; Operations Analysis; Technology Design; Identification of Key Causes; Time Management
General Work Activities: Getting Information Needed to Do the Job; Judging Qualities of Things, Services, People; Evaluating Information against Standards; Making Decisions and Solving Problems; Thinking Creatively; Updating and Using Job-Relevant Knowledge; Developing Objectives and Strategies; Interpreting Meaning of Information to Others; Communicating with Other Workers; Communicating with Persons Outside Organization; Establishing and Maintaining Relationships; Assisting and Caring for Others; Resolving Conflicts, Negotiating with Others; Performing for or Working with Public; Developing and Building Teams; Teaching Others; Guiding, Directing and Motivating Subordinates; Coaching and Developing Others
Job Characteristics: Objective or Subjective Information; Job-Required Social Interaction; Supervise, Coach, Train Others; Coordinate or Lead Others; Deal with Unpleasant or Angry People; Deal with Physical, Aggressive People
GOE Group/s: 10.02.03 Nursing, Therapy, and Specialized Teaching Services: Specialized Teaching
CIP Program/s: 130101 Education, General; 130401 Education Administration and Supervision, General; 130402 Administration of Special Education; 131001 Special Education, General; 131003 Education of the Deaf and Hearing Impaired; 131008 Education of the Physically Handicapped; 131009 Education of the Blind and Visually Handicapped
Related DOT Job/s: 094.224-010 TEACHER, HEARING IMPAIRED; 094.224-014 TEACHER, PHYSICALLY IMPAIRED; 094.224-018 TEACHER, VISUALLY IMPAIRED

31311D SPECIAL EDUCATION EVALUATORS. OOH

Title/s: Special Education Teachers

Assess type and degree of disability of handicapped children to aid in determining special programs and services required to meet educational needs. Observes student behavior and rates strength and weakness of factors, such as motivation, cooperativeness, aggression, and task completion. Tests children to detect learning limitations, and recommends follow-up activities, consultation, or services. Selects, administers, and scores tests to measure individual's aptitudes, educational achievements, perceptual motor skills, vision, and hearing. Evaluates student's readiness to transfer from special classes to regular classroom. Determines evaluation procedures for children having or suspected of having learning disabilities, mental retardation, behavior disorders, or physical handicaps. Confers with school or other personnel and studies records to obtain additional information on nature and severity of disability. Administers work-related tests and reviews records and other data to assess student vocational interests and abilities. Reports findings for staff consideration in placement of children in educational programs. Provides supportive services to regular classroom teacher.
Yearly Earnings: $33,644
Education: Bachelor's degree
Knowledge: Customer and Personal Service; Psychology; Sociology and Anthropology; Therapy and Counseling; Education and Training
Abilities: Oral Comprehension; Written Comprehension; Oral Expression; Written Expression
Skills: Reading Comprehension; Active Listening; Writing; Speaking; Critical Thinking; Learning Strategies; Monitoring; Social Perceptiveness; Service Orientation; Problem Identification; Synthesis/Reorganization; Idea Generation; Idea Evaluation; Implementation Planning; Solution Appraisal; Identification of Key Causes; Judgment and Decision Making
General Work Activities: Getting Information Needed to Do the Job; Monitoring Processes, Material, or Surroundings; Judging Qualities of Things, Services, People; Evaluating Information against Standards; Analyzing Data or Information; Making Decisions and Solving Problems; Updating and Using Job-Relevant Knowledge; Developing Objectives and Strategies; Interpreting Meaning of Information to Others; Communicating with Other Workers; Communicating with Persons Outside Organization; Establishing and Maintaining Relationships; Assisting and Caring for Others; Teaching Others; Coaching and Developing Others; Provide Consultation and Advice to Others
Job Characteristics: Job-Required Social Interaction; Sitting
GOE Group/s: 10.02.03 Nursing, Therapy, and Specialized Teaching Services: Specialized Teaching
CIP Program/s: 130101 Education, General; 130401 Education Administration and Supervision, General; 130402 Administration of Special Education; 130604 Educational Assessment, Testing and Measurement; 131001 Special Education, General; 131003 Education of the Deaf and Hearing Impaired; 131005 Education of the Emotionally Handicapped; 131006 Education of the Mentally Handicapped; 131007 Education of the Multiple Handicapped; 131008 Education of the Physically Handicapped; 131009 Education of the Blind and Visually Handicapped; 131011 Education of the Specific Learning Disabled; 131012 Education of the Speech Impaired
Related DOT Job/s: 094.267-010 EVALUATOR

31311E PARENT INSTRUCTORS—CHILD DEVELOPMENT AND REHABILITATION. OOH

Title/s: Special Education Teachers

Instruct parents of mentally and physically handicapped children in therapy techniques and behavior modification. Instructs parents in behavior modification, physical development, language development, and conceptual learning exercises and activities. Develops individual teaching plan covering self-help, motor, social, cognitive, and language skills development for parents to implement in home. Evaluates child's responses to determine level of physical and mental development. Determines parent's ability to comprehend and apply therapeutic and behavior modification techniques. Revises teaching plan to correspond with child's rate of development. Counsels parents and organizes groups of parents in similar situations to provide social and emotional support to parents. Consults and coordinates plans with other professionals. Teaches preschool subjects, such as limited-vocabulary sign language and color recognition, to children capable of learning such subjects. Refers parents and children to social services agencies for additional services and financial assistance.
Yearly Earnings: $33,644
Education: Bachelor's degree

Knowledge: Customer and Personal Service; Psychology; Sociology and Anthropology; Medicine and Dentistry; Therapy and Counseling; Education and Training
Abilities: Oral Comprehension; Fluency of Ideas; Speech Clarity
Skills: Reading Comprehension; Active Listening; Speaking; Critical Thinking; Active Learning; Learning Strategies; Monitoring; Social Perceptiveness; Coordination; Persuasion; Instructing; Service Orientation; Problem Identification; Synthesis/Reorganization; Idea Generation; Idea Evaluation; Implementation Planning; Solution Appraisal; Identification of Key Causes; Judgment and Decision Making; Time Management
General Work Activities: Monitoring Processes, Material, or Surroundings; Identifying Objects, Actions, and Events; Judging Qualities of Things, Services, People; Making Decisions and Solving Problems; Developing Objectives and Strategies; Organizing, Planning, and Prioritizing; Implementing Ideas, Programs, etc.; Interpreting Meaning of Information to Others; Communicating with Persons Outside Organization; Establishing and Maintaining Relationships; Assisting and Caring for Others; Teaching Others; Coaching and Developing Others; Provide Consultation and Advice to Others
Job Characteristics: Objective or Subjective Information; Job-Required Social Interaction; Provide a Service to Others; Deal with External Customers; Coordinate or Lead Others
GOE Group/s: 10.02.03 Nursing, Therapy, and Specialized Teaching Services: Specialized Teaching
CIP Program/s: 130101 Education, General; 131001 Special Education, General; 131003 Education of the Deaf and Hearing Impaired; 131005 Education of the Emotionally Handicapped; 131006 Education of the Mentally Handicapped; 131007 Education of the Multiple Handicapped; 131008 Education of the Physically Handicapped; 131009 Education of the Blind and Visually Handicapped; 131011 Education of the Specific Learning Disabled; 131012 Education of the Speech Impaired; 190701 Individual and Family Development Studies, General; 190706 Child Growth, Care and Development Studies
Related DOT Job/s: 195.227-018 TEACHER, HOME THERAPY

31314 TEACHERS AND INSTRUCTORS—VOCATIONAL EDUCATION AND TRAINING. OOH

Title/s: Adult Education Teachers

Teach or instruct vocational and/or occupational subjects at the postsecondary level (but at less than the baccalaureate) to students who have graduated or left high school. Subjects include business, secretarial science, data processing, trades, and practical nursing. Include correspondence school instructors; industrial, commercial, and government training instructors; and adult education teachers and instructors who prepare persons to operate industrial machinery and equipment and transportation and communications equipment. Teaching may take place in public or private schools whose primary business is education or in a school associated with an organization whose primary business is other than education. Conducts on-the-job training, classes, or training sessions to teach and demonstrate principles, techniques, procedures, or methods of designated subjects. Presents lectures and conducts discussions to increase students' knowledge and competence, using visual aids, such as graphs, charts, videotapes, and slides. Observes and evaluates students' work to determine progress, provide feedback, and make suggestions for improvement. Develops training programs, teaching aids, and study materials for instruction in vocational or occupational subjects. Plans course content and method of instruction. Prepares outline of instructional program and training schedule, and establishes course goals. Selects and assembles books, materials, supplies, and equipment for training, courses, or projects. Administers oral, written, or performance tests to measure progress and to evaluate effectiveness of training. Determines training needs of students or workers. Corrects, grades, and comments on lesson assignments. Develops instructional software, multimedia visual aids, and computer tutorials. Prepares reports and maintains records, such as student grades, attendance, training activities, production records, and supply or equipment inventories. Reviews enrollment applications and corresponds with applicants. Arranges for lectures by subject matter experts in designated fields. Recommends advancement, transfer, or termination of student or trainee based on mastery of subject. Participates in meetings, seminars, and training sessions, and integrates relevant information into training program. Solves operational problems and provides technical assistance with equipment and process techniques.
Yearly Earnings: $27,560
Education: Work experience in a related occupation
Knowledge: Sociology and Anthropology; Education and Training; English Language; History and Archeology; Philosophy and Theology
Abilities: Oral Expression; Fluency of Ideas; Originality; Speech Clarity
Skills: Reading Comprehension; Active Listening; Writing; Speaking; Critical Thinking; Learning Strategies; Social Perceptiveness; Instructing; Service Orientation; Information Organization; Idea Generation; Idea Evaluation; Implementation Planning; Solution Appraisal; Technology Design; Equipment Selection; Programming; Identification of Key Causes; Judgment and Decision Making; Management of Material Resources
General Work Activities: Getting Information Needed to Do the Job; Judging Qualities of Things, Services, People; Thinking Creatively; Updating and Using Job-Relevant Knowledge; Developing Objectives and Strategies; Scheduling Work and Activities; Organizing, Planning, and Prioritizing; Operating Vehicles or Equipment; Implementing Ideas, Programs, etc.; Interpreting Meaning of Information to Others; Communicating with Persons Outside Organization; Establishing and Maintaining Relationships; Assisting and Caring for Others; Selling or Influencing Others; Performing for or Working with Public; Developing and Building Teams; Teaching Others; Coaching and Developing Others; Provide Consultation and Advice to Others
Job Characteristics: Objective or Subjective Information; Job-Required Social Interaction; Persuade Someone to a Course of Action; Provide a Service to Others; Take a Position Opposed to Others; Deal with External Customers; Coordinate or Lead Others; Responsibility for Outcomes and Results; Frequency in Conflict Situations; Deal with Physical, Aggressive People; Walking or Running; Importance of Being Aware of New Events
GOE Group/s: 01.06.03 Craft Arts: Hand Lettering, Painting and Decorating; 04.01.01 Safety and Law Enforcement: Managing; 05.05.09 Craft Technology: Mechanical Work; 05.06.04 Systems Operation: Processing; 06.02.01 Production Work: Supervision; 06.04.15 Elemental Work: Industrial: Equipment Operation, Food Processing; 07.04.02 Oral Communications: Order, Complaint, and Claims Handling; 07.04.05 Oral Communications: Information Transmitting and Receiving; 09.03.03 Passenger Services: Instruction and Supervision; 10.02.01 Nursing, Therapy, and Specialized Teaching Services: Nursing; 11.02.01 Educational and Library Services: Teaching and Instructing, General; 11.02.02 Educational and Library Services: Teaching, Vocational and Industrial
CIP Program/s: 010401 Agricultural and Food Products Processing Operations and Management; 130101 Education, General; 130401 Education Administration and Supervision, General; 130404 Educational Supervision; 131201 Adult and Continuing Teacher Education; 131205 Secondary Teacher Education; 131206 Teacher Education, Multiple Levels; 131301 Agricultural Teacher Education (Vocational); 131303 Business Teacher Education (Vocational); 131308 Home Economics Teacher Education (Vocational); 131310 Marketing Opera-

tions Teacher Ed./Mkt. & Distribution Teacher; 131319 Technical Teacher Education (Vocational); 131320 Trade and Industrial Teacher Education (Vocational); 131327 Health Occupations Teacher Education (Vocational); 430107 Law Enforcement/Police Science; 470408 Watch, Clock and Jewelry Repairer; 470608 Aircraft Mechanic/Technician, Powerplant; 490205 Truck, Bus and Other Commercial Vehicle Operator; 521001 Human Resources Management

Related DOT Job/s: 075.127-010 INSTRUCTOR, PSYCHIATRIC AIDE; 090.222-010 INSTRUCTOR, BUSINESS EDUCATION; 097.221-010 INSTRUCTOR, VOCATIONAL TRAINING; 099.227-014 INSTRUCTOR, CORRESPONDENCE SCHOOL; 099.227-018 INSTRUCTOR, GROUND SERVICES; 166.221-010 INSTRUCTOR, TECHNICAL TRAINING; 166.227-010 TRAINING REPRESENTATIVE; 235.222-010 PRIVATE-BRANCH-EXCHANGE SERVICE ADVISER; 239.227-010 CUSTOMER-SERVICE-REPRESENTATIVE INSTRUCTOR; 375.227-010 POLICE-ACADEMY INSTRUCTOR; 378.227-010 MARKSMANSHIP INSTRUCTOR; 522.264-010 TRAINING TECHNICIAN; 621.221-010 FIELD-SERVICE REPRESENTATIVE; 683.222-010 INSTRUCTOR, WEAVING; 689.324-010 INSTRUCTOR; 715.221-010 INSTRUCTOR, WATCH ASSEMBLY; 740.221-010 INSTRUCTOR, DECORATING; 788.222-010 INSTRUCTOR; 789.222-010 INSTRUCTOR, APPAREL MANUFACTURE; 919.223-010 INSTRUCTOR, BUS, TROLLEY, AND TAXI; 955.222-010 INSTRUCTOR, WASTEWATER-TREATMENT PLANT

31317 INSTRUCTORS—NONVOCATIONAL EDUCATION. OOH Title/s: Adult Education Teachers

Teach or instruct out-of-school youths and adults in courses other than those that normally lead to an occupational objective and are less than the baccalaureate level. Subjects may include self-improvement and nonvocational courses such as Americanization, basic education, art, drama, music, bridge, homemaking, stock market analysis, languages, modeling, flying, dancing, and automobile driving. Teaching may take place in public or private schools or in an organization whose primary business is other than education. Conducts classes, workshops, and demonstrations to teach principles, techniques, procedures, or methods of designated subject. Presents lectures and conducts discussions to increase students' knowledge and competence. Administers oral, written, and performance tests and issues grades in accordance with performance. Plans course content and method of instruction. Prepares outline of instructional program and lesson plans, and establishes course goals. Selects and assembles books, materials, and supplies for courses or projects. Observes students to determine and evaluate qualifications, limitations, abilities, interests, aptitudes, temperament, and individual characteristics. Observes and evaluates students' work to determine progress, and makes suggestions for improvement. Adapts course of study and training methods to meet students' needs and abilities. Conducts seminars or workshops for other teachers to demonstrate methods of using institution facilities and collections to enhance school programs. Directs and supervises student project activities, performances, tournaments, exhibits, contests, or plays. Evaluates success of instruction, based on number and enthusiasm of participants, and recommends retaining or eliminating course in future. Plans and conducts field trips to enrich instructional programs. Confers with leaders of government and other groups to coordinate training or to assist students to fulfill required criteria. Maintains records, such as student grades, attendance, and supply inventory. Confers with parents of students or students to resolve problems. Writes instructional articles on designated subjects. Orders, stores, and inventories books, materials, and supplies.

Yearly Earnings: $27,560

Education: Work experience in a related occupation

Knowledge: Economics and Accounting; Sociology and Anthropology; Education and Training; English Language; Foreign Language; Fine Arts; History and Archeology; Philosophy and Theology

Abilities: Oral Comprehension; Oral Expression; Written Expression; Speech Clarity

Skills: Active Listening; Writing; Speaking; Learning Strategies; Monitoring; Social Perceptiveness; Instructing; Service Orientation; Information Organization; Idea Generation; Idea Evaluation; Implementation Planning; Operations Analysis; Identification of Key Causes; Judgment and Decision Making; Time Management; Management of Material Resources

General Work Activities: Getting Information Needed to Do the Job; Monitoring Processes, Material, or Surroundings; Identifying Objects, Actions, and Events; Estimating Needed Characteristics; Judging Qualities of Things, Services, People; Analyzing Data or Information; Making Decisions and Solving Problems; Thinking Creatively; Updating and Using Job-Relevant Knowledge; Developing Objectives and Strategies; Scheduling Work and Activities; Organizing, Planning, and Prioritizing; Implementing Ideas, Programs, etc.; Interpreting Meaning of Information to Others; Communicating with Other Workers; Communicating with Persons Outside Organization; Establishing and Maintaining Relationships; Assisting and Caring for Others; Selling or Influencing Others; Performing for or Working with Public; Coordinating Work and Activities of Others; Developing and Building Teams; Teaching Others; Guiding, Directing and Motivating Subordinates; Coaching and Developing Others; Provide Consultation and Advice to Others; Monitoring and Controlling Resources

Job Characteristics: Objective or Subjective Information; Job-Required Social Interaction; Persuade Someone to a Course of Action; Provide a Service to Others; Take a Position Opposed to Others; Deal with External Customers; Coordinate or Lead Others; Deal with Physical, Aggressive People

GOE Group/s: 01.02.01 Visual Arts: Instructing and Appraising; 01.03.01 Performing Arts:Drama: Instructing and Directing; 01.04.01 Performing Arts:Music: Instructing and Directing; 01.05.01 Performing Arts:Dance: Instructing and Choreography; 01.08.01 Modeling: Personal Appearance; 05.04.01 Air and Water Vehicle Operation: Air; 09.01.01 Hospitality Services: Social and Recreational Activities; 09.03.03 Passenger Services: Instruction and Supervision; 10.02.03 Nursing, Therapy, and Specialized Teaching Services: Specialized Teaching; 11.02.01 Educational and Library Services: Teaching and Instructing, General; 11.07.02 Services Administration: Health and Safety Services

CIP Program/s: 130101 Education, General; 130201 Bilingual/Bicultural Education; 131201 Adult and Continuing Teacher Education; 131206 Teacher Education, Multiple Levels; 131302 Art Teacher Education; 131304 Driver and Safety Teacher Education; 131310 Marketing Operations Teacher Ed./Mkt. & Distribution Teacher; 131312 Music Teacher Education; 131324 Drama and Dance Teacher Education; 131399 Teacher Education, Specific Academic and Vocational Programs; 131401 Teaching English as a Second Language/Foreign Language; 430203 Fire Science/Firefighting; 500501 Drama/Theater Arts, General; 500503 Acting and Directing; 500901 Music, General; 500903 Music - General Performance

Related DOT Job/s: 090.227-018 INSTRUCTOR, EXTENSION WORK; 097.227-010 INSTRUCTOR, FLYING II; 099.223-010 INSTRUCTOR, DRIVING; 099.224-014 TEACHER, ADVENTURE EDUCATION; 099.227-026 INSTRUCTOR, MODELING; 099.227-030 TEACHER, ADULT EDUCATION; 099.227-038 TEACHER; 149.021-010 TEACHER, ART; 150.027-014 TEACHER, DRAMA; 151.027-014 INSTRUCTOR, DANCING; 152.021-010 TEACHER, MUSIC; 159.227-010 INSTRUCTOR, BRIDGE; 169.127-010 CIVIL PREPAREDNESS TRAINING OFFICER

31321 INSTRUCTORS AND COACHES, SPORTS AND PHYSICAL TRAINING. OOH Title/s: Instructors and Coaches, Sports and Physical Training

Instruct or coach groups or individuals in the fundamentals of sports. Demonstrate techniques and methods of participation. Observe and inform participants of corrective measures necessary to improve their skills. Those required to hold teaching degrees are included in the appropriate teaching category. Teaches individual and team sports to participants, utilizing knowledge of sports techniques and of physical capabilities of participants. Organizes, leads, instructs, and referees indoor and outdoor games, such as volleyball, baseball, and basketball. Plans physical education program to promote development of participant physical attributes and social skills. Explains and enforces safety rules and regulations. Teaches and demonstrates use of gymnastic and training apparatus, such as trampolines and weights. Organizes and conducts competitions and tournaments. Selects, stores, orders, issues, and inventories equipment, materials, and supplies. Advises participants in use of heat or ultraviolet treatments and hot baths.

Yearly Earnings: $27,560

Education: Moderate-term O-J-T

Knowledge: Customer and Personal Service; Psychology; Sociology and Anthropology; Medicine and Dentistry; Therapy and Counseling; Education and Training; History and Archeology

Abilities: Oral Comprehension; Oral Expression; Fluency of Ideas; Memorization; Spatial Orientation; Visualization; Selective Attention; Time Sharing; Manual Dexterity; Multilimb Coordination; Response Orientation; Rate Control; Reaction Time; Speed of Limb Movement; Static Strength; Explosive Strength; Dynamic Strength; Trunk Strength; Stamina; Extent Flexibility; Dynamic Flexibility; Gross Body Coordination; Gross Body Equilibrium; Far Vision; Night Vision; Peripheral Vision; Depth Perception; Glare Sensitivity; Auditory Attention; Sound Localization; Speech Recognition; Speech Clarity

Skills: Speaking; Learning Strategies; Monitoring; Social Perceptiveness; Coordination; Persuasion; Instructing; Service Orientation; Implementation Planning; Time Management; Management of Material Resources; Management of Personnel Resources

General Work Activities: Developing Objectives and Strategies; Scheduling Work and Activities; Organizing, Planning, and Prioritizing; Performing General Physical Activities; Establishing and Maintaining Relationships; Assisting and Caring for Others; Selling or Influencing Others; Resolving Conflicts, Negotiating with Others; Coordinating Work and Activities of Others; Developing and Building Teams; Teaching Others; Guiding, Directing and Motivating Subordinates; Coaching and Developing Others; Provide Consultation and Advice to Others; Monitoring and Controlling Resources

Job Characteristics: Job-Required Social Interaction; Supervise, Coach, Train Others; Persuade Someone to a Course of Action; Responsible for Others' Health and Safety; Deal with Physical, Aggressive People; Extremely Bright or Inadequate Lighting; Standing; Walking or Running; Kneeling, Crouching, or Crawling; Keeping or Regaining Balance; Bending or Twisting the Body; Special Uniform; Importance of Being Aware of New Events

GOE Group/s: 10.02.02 Nursing, Therapy, and Specialized Teaching Services: Therapy and Rehabilitation; 11.02.01 Educational and Library Services: Teaching and Instructing, General; 12.01.01 Sports: Coaching and Instructing

CIP Program/s: 130101 Education, General; 130401 Education Administration and Supervision, General; 130404 Educational Supervision; 131201 Adult and Continuing Teacher Education; 131314 Physical Education Teaching and Coaching; 310501 Health and Physical Education, General

Related DOT Job/s: 099.224-010 INSTRUCTOR, PHYSICAL EDUCATION; 153.227-014 INSTRUCTOR, PHYSICAL; 153.227-018 INSTRUCTOR, SPORTS

31323 FARM AND HOME MANAGEMENT ADVISORS. OOH Title/s: Farm and Home Management Advisors

Advise, instruct, and assist individuals and families engaged in agriculture, agricultural-related processes, or home economics activities. Demonstrate procedures and apply research findings to solve problems; instruct and train in product development, sales, and the utilization of machinery and equipment to promote general welfare. Include county agricultural agents, feed and farm management advisers, home economists, and extension service advisers. Advises farmers in matters such as feeding and health maintenance of livestock, cultivation, growing and harvesting practices, and budgeting. Advises individuals and families on home management practices, such as budget planning, meal preparation, energy conservation, clothing, and home furnishings. Conducts classes to educate others in subjects such as nutrition, home management, home furnishing, child care, and farming techniques. Plans, develops, organizes, and evaluates training programs in subjects such as home management, horticulture, and consumer information. Collects and evaluates data to ascertain needs and develop programs beneficial to community. Delivers lectures to organizations or talks over radio and television to disseminate information and promote objectives of program. Organizes, advises, and participates in community activities and organizations, such as county and state fair events and 4-H clubs. Prepares leaflets, pamphlets, and other material, such as visual aids for educational and informational purposes.

Yearly Earnings: $27,560

Education: Bachelor's degree

Knowledge: Administration and Management; Economics and Accounting; Sales and Marketing; Personnel and Human Resources; Food Production; Computers and Electronics; Mathematics; Chemistry; Biology; Education and Training; Communications and Media; Transportation

Abilities: Oral Expression; Originality; Mathematical Reasoning; Number Facility; Near Vision; Far Vision; Speech Recognition; Speech Clarity

Skills: Reading Comprehension; Active Listening; Writing; Speaking; Active Learning; Learning Strategies; Monitoring; Persuasion; Negotiation; Instructing; Service Orientation; Problem Identification; Information Gathering; Idea Generation; Idea Evaluation; Implementation Planning; Solution Appraisal; Operations Analysis; Programming; Visioning; Systems Perception; Identifying Downstream Consequences; Identification of Key Causes; Systems Evaluation; Management of Financial Resources

General Work Activities: Organizing, Planning, and Prioritizing; Communicating with Persons Outside Organization; Establishing and Maintaining Relationships; Assisting and Caring for Others; Teaching Others; Coaching and Developing Others; Provide Consultation and Advice to Others

Job Characteristics: Objective or Subjective Information; Job-Required Social Interaction; Supervise, Coach, Train Others; Persuade Someone to a Course of Action; Provide a Service to Others; Deal with External Customers; Coordinate or Lead Others; Frequency in Conflict Situations

GOE Group/s: 11.02.03 Educational and Library Services: Teaching, Home Economics, Agriculture

CIP Program/s: 010101 Agricultural Business and Management, General; 010104 Farm and Ranch Management; 010301 Agricultural Production Workers and Managers, General; 010302 Agricultural

Animal Husbandry and Production Management; 010304 Crop Production Operations and Management; 010501 Agricultural Supplies Retailing and Wholesaling; 020102 Agricultural Extension; 020201 Animal Sciences, General; 020204 Agricultural Animal Nutrition; 130101 Education, General; 131301 Agricultural Teacher Education (Vocational); 131308 Home Economics Teacher Education (Vocational); 190501 Foods and Nutrition Studies, General; 190503 Dietetics/Human Nutritional Services; 190901 Clothing/Apparel and Textile Studies
Related DOT Job/s: 096.121-010 COUNTY HOME-DEMONSTRATION AGENT; 096.121-014 HOME ECONOMIST; 096.127-010 COUNTY-AGRICULTURAL AGENT; 096.127-014 EXTENSION SERVICE SPECIALIST; 096.127-018 FEED AND FARM MANAGEMENT ADVISER; 096.127-022 FOUR-H CLUB AGENT

31399 ALL OTHER TEACHERS AND INSTRUCTORS. OOH Title/s: Indirectly related to Teachers, Librarians, and Counselors

All other teachers and instructors not classified separately above.
Yearly Earnings: $31,720
Education: Master's degree
GOE Group/s: 11.02.01 Educational and Library Services: Teaching and Instructing, General
CIP Program/s: 130101 Education, General; 130201 Bilingual/Bicultural Education; 131001 Special Education, General; 131003 Education of the Deaf and Hearing Impaired; 131206 Teacher Education, Multiple Levels; 131399 Teacher Education, Specific Academic and Vocational Programs
Related DOT Job/s: 099.227-022 INSTRUCTOR, MILITARY SCIENCE; 099.227-034 TUTOR

Librarians, Curators, and Counselors

31502A LIBRARIANS. OOH Title/s: Librarians

Administer library services; provide library patrons access to or instruction in accessing library resources; and select, acquire, process, and organize library materials and collections for patron use. Organizes collections of books, publications, documents, audio-visual aids, and other reference materials for convenient access. Reviews and evaluates resource material to select and order books, periodicals, audio-visual aids, and other materials for acquisition. Assists patrons in selecting books and informational material and in research problems. Codes, classifies, and catalogs books, publications, films, audio-visual aids, and other library materials. Researches, retrieves, and disseminates information from books, periodicals, reference materials, or commercial databases in response to requests. Manages library resources stored in files, on film, or in computer data bases for research information. Reviews, compiles, and publishes listing of library materials, including bibliographies and book reviews, to notify users. Explains use of library facilities, resources, equipment, and services and provides information governing library use and policies. Manages library program for children and other special groups. Assembles and arranges display materials. Directs and trains library staff in duties, including receiving, shelving, researching, cataloging, and equipment use. Keys information into computer to store or search for selected material or databases. Compiles lists of overdue materials and notifies borrowers. Confers with teachers, parents, and community organizations to develop, plan, and conduct programs in reading, viewing, and communication skills.
Yearly Earnings: $31,252
Education: Master's degree
Knowledge: Administration and Management; Clerical; Sales and Marketing; Customer and Personal Service; Personnel and Human Resources; Computers and Electronics; Psychology; Sociology and Anthropology; Geography; Education and Training; English Language; Foreign Language; Fine Arts; History and Archeology; Philosophy and Theology; Communications and Media
Abilities: Oral Comprehension; Written Comprehension; Oral Expression; Written Expression; Fluency of Ideas; Originality; Deductive Reasoning; Inductive Reasoning; Category Flexibility; Memorization; Speed of Closure; Perceptual Speed; Wrist-Finger Speed; Gross Body Equilibrium; Near Vision; Far Vision; Speech Recognition; Speech Clarity
Skills: Reading Comprehension; Active Listening; Speaking; Learning Strategies; Social Perceptiveness; Instructing; Service Orientation; Information Gathering; Information Organization; Synthesis/Reorganization; Implementation Planning; Time Management; Management of Material Resources; Management of Personnel Resources
General Work Activities: Estimating Needed Characteristics; Evaluating Information against Standards; Developing Objectives and Strategies; Scheduling Work and Activities; Interpreting Meaning of Information to Others; Communicating with Persons Outside Organization; Establishing and Maintaining Relationships; Resolving Conflicts, Negotiating with Others; Performing for or Working with Public; Coordinating Work and Activities of Others; Developing and Building Teams; Teaching Others; Guiding, Directing and Motivating Subordinates; Coaching and Developing Others; Provide Consultation and Advice to Others; Performing Administrative Activities; Staffing Organizational Units; Monitoring and Controlling Resources
Job Characteristics: Job-Required Social Interaction; Supervise, Coach, Train Others; Provide a Service to Others; Deal with External Customers; Responsibility for Outcomes and Results
GOE Group/s: 11.02.04 Educational and Library Services: Library Services; 11.07.04 Services Administration: Recreation Services
CIP Program/s: 130501 Educational/Instructional Media Design; 250101 Library Science/Librarianship
Related DOT Job/s: 100.117-010 LIBRARY DIRECTOR; 100.127-010 CHIEF LIBRARIAN, BRANCH OR DEPARTMENT; 100.127-014 LIBRARIAN; 100.167-010 AUDIOVISUAL LIBRARIAN; 100.167-014 BOOKMOBILE LIBRARIAN; 100.167-018 CHILDREN'S LIBRARIAN; 100.167-022 INSTITUTION LIBRARIAN; 100.167-026 LIBRARIAN, SPECIAL LIBRARY; 100.167-030 MEDIA SPECIALIST, SCHOOL LIBRARY; 100.167-034 YOUNG-ADULT LIBRARIAN; 100.167-038 NEWS LIBRARIAN; 100.267-010 ACQUISITIONS LIBRARIAN; 100.267-014 LIBRARIAN, SPECIAL COLLECTIONS; 100.367-022 MUSIC LIBRARIAN; 100.367-026 MUSIC LIBRARIAN, INTERNATIONAL BROADCAST

31502B LIBRARY RESEARCH WORKERS. OOH Title/s: Librarians

Research specific subjects and make information available to library patrons on an individual basis. Researches and retrieves information on specified subjects in response to inquiries from library patrons. Compiles and analyzes information on specified subjects from books, periodicals, reference materials, or commercial databases. Prepares summary of research and analysis and transmits information to inquirers.
Yearly Earnings: $31,252
Education: Master's degree
Knowledge: Customer and Personal Service; English Language; Foreign Language; Philosophy and Theology; Communications and Media
Abilities: Oral Comprehension; Written Comprehension; Written Expression; Fluency of Ideas; Inductive Reasoning; Category Flexibility; Memorization; Near Vision; Speech Recognition

Skills: Reading Comprehension; Writing; Active Learning; Information Gathering; Information Organization; Synthesis/Reorganization
General Work Activities: Getting Information Needed to Do the Job; Evaluating Information against Standards; Analyzing Data or Information; Updating and Using Job-Relevant Knowledge; Interpreting Meaning of Information to Others
Job Characteristics: Provide a Service to Others; Sitting
GOE Group/s: 11.08.02 Communications: Writing
CIP Program/s: 250301 Library Assistant
Related DOT Job/s: 109.267-014 RESEARCH WORKER, ENCYCLOPEDIA

31505 TECHNICAL ASSISTANTS, LIBRARY. OOH Title/s: Library Technicians

Assist librarians by furnishing information on library sciences, facilities, and rules; by assisting readers in the use of card catalogs and indexes to locate books and other materials; and by answering questions that require only brief consultation of standard reference. May catalog books or train and supervise clerical staff. Assists patrons in operating equipment, and obtaining library materials and services, and explains use of reference tools. Reviews subject matter of materials to be classified and selects classification numbers and headings according to Dewey Decimal, Library of Congress, or other classification systems. Processes print and nonprint library materials, and classifies and catalogs materials. Files catalog cards according to system used. Verifies bibliographical data, including author, title, publisher, publication date, and edition, on computer terminal. Issues identification card to borrowers and checks materials in and out. Directs activities of library clerks and aides. Compiles and maintains records relating to circulation, materials, and equipment. Prepares order slips for materials, follows up on orders, and compiles lists of materials acquired or withdrawn. Composes explanatory summaries of contents of books or other reference materials. Designs posters and special displays to promote use of library facilities or specific reading program at library.
Yearly Earnings: $33,540
Education: Short-term O-J-T
Knowledge: Clerical; Customer and Personal Service; English Language; Communications and Media
Abilities: Category Flexibility; Perceptual Speed
Skills: Service Orientation; Information Organization
General Work Activities: Performing for or Working with Public; Developing and Building Teams
Job Characteristics: Supervise, Coach, Train Others; Persuade Someone to a Course of Action; Provide a Service to Others; Coordinate or Lead Others; Climbing Ladders, Scaffolds, Poles, etc.; Walking or Running; Bending or Twisting the Body
GOE Group/s: 11.02.04 Educational and Library Services: Library Services
CIP Program/s: 250301 Library Assistant
Related DOT Job/s: 100.367-010 BIBLIOGRAPHER; 100.367-014 CLASSIFIER; 100.367-018 LIBRARY TECHNICAL ASSISTANT; 100.387-010 CATALOG LIBRARIAN

31508 AUDIO-VISUAL SPECIALISTS. OOH Title/s: Library Technicians

Plan and prepare audio-visual teaching aids and methods for use in school system. Plans and develops preproduction ideas into outlines, scripts, continuity, story boards, and graphics, or directs assistants to develop ideas. Sets up, adjusts, and operates equipment such as cameras, sound mixers, and recorders during production. Constructs and positions properties, sets, lighting equipment, and other equipment. Determines format, approach, content, level, and medium to meet objectives most effectively within budgetary constraints, utilizing research, knowledge, and training. Locates and secures settings, properties, effects, and other production necessities. Develops production ideas based on assignment or generates own ideas based on objectives and interest. Develops manuals, texts, workbooks, or related materials for use in conjunction with production materials. Executes, or directs assistants to execute, rough and finished graphics and graphic designs. Performs narration or presents announcements. Reviews, evaluates, and directs modifications to material produced independently by other personnel. Directs and coordinates activities of assistants and other personnel during production. Conducts training sessions on selection, use, and design of audio-visual materials, and operation of presentation equipment.
Yearly Earnings: $33,540
Education: Short-term O-J-T
Knowledge: Administration and Management; Economics and Accounting; Personnel and Human Resources; Computers and Electronics; Building and Construction; Psychology; Education and Training; English Language; Fine Arts; History and Archeology; Telecommunications; Communications and Media
Abilities: Written Expression; Fluency of Ideas; Originality; Information Ordering; Category Flexibility; Memorization; Visualization; Selective Attention; Time Sharing; Rate Control; Gross Body Equilibrium; Night Vision; Peripheral Vision; Depth Perception; Glare Sensitivity; Hearing Sensitivity; Sound Localization; Speech Recognition; Speech Clarity
Skills: Reading Comprehension; Active Listening; Writing; Speaking; Critical Thinking; Active Learning; Learning Strategies; Monitoring; Social Perceptiveness; Coordination; Instructing; Information Gathering; Information Organization; Synthesis/Reorganization; Idea Generation; Idea Evaluation; Implementation Planning; Solution Appraisal; Operations Analysis; Technology Design; Equipment Selection; Product Inspection; Visioning; Identification of Key Causes; Judgment and Decision Making; Time Management; Management of Financial Resources; Management of Material Resources; Management of Personnel Resources
General Work Activities: Making Decisions and Solving Problems; Thinking Creatively; Updating and Using Job-Relevant Knowledge; Developing Objectives and Strategies; Scheduling Work and Activities; Organizing, Planning, and Prioritizing; Drafting and Specifying Technical Devices, etc.; Implementing Ideas, Programs, etc.; Communicating with Other Workers; Establishing and Maintaining Relationships; Coordinating Work and Activities of Others; Developing and Building Teams; Teaching Others; Guiding, Directing and Motivating Subordinates; Coaching and Developing Others
Job Characteristics: Supervise, Coach, Train Others; Provide a Service to Others; Coordinate or Lead Others; Responsibility for Outcomes and Results; Degree of Automation
GOE Group/s: 01.02.03 Visual Arts: Commercial Art
CIP Program/s: 100101 Educational/Instructional Media Technologists and Technicians; 130501 Educational/Instructional Media Design
Related DOT Job/s: 149.061-010 AUDIOVISUAL PRODUCTION SPECIALIST

31511A CURATORS. OOH Title/s: Archivists and Curators

Plan, direct, and coordinate activities of exhibiting institution, such as museum, art gallery, botanical garden, zoo, or historic site. Direct instructional, acquisition, exhibitory, safekeeping, research, and public service activities of institution. Plans and organizes acquisition, storage, and exhibition of collections and related educational materials. Develops and maintains institution's registration, cataloging, and basic recordkeeping systems. Studies, examines, and tests acquisitions to authenticate their origin, composition, history, and current value. Negotiates and authorizes purchase, sale, exchange, or loan of collections. Directs and coordinates activities of curatorial, personnel, fiscal, technical, research, and clerical staff. Confers with institution's board of directors to formulate and interpret policies, determine budget requirements, and plan overall operations. Arranges insurance coverage for objects on loan or special exhibits, and recommends changes in coverage for entire collection. Plans and conducts special research projects. Writes and reviews grant proposals, journal articles, institutional reports, and publicity materials. Attends meetings, conventions, and civic events to promote use of institution's services, seek financing, and maintain community alliances. Conducts or organizes tours, workshops, and instructional sessions to acquaint individuals with use of institution's facilities and materials. Reserves facilities for group tours and social events and collects admission fees. Inspects premises for evidence of deterioration and need for repair. Schedules special events at facility and organizes details such as refreshment, entertainment, and decorations.

Yearly Earnings: $30,836

Education: Master's degree

Knowledge: Administration and Management; Clerical; Economics and Accounting; Sales and Marketing; Sociology and Anthropology; Geography; English Language; Foreign Language; Fine Arts; History and Archeology; Philosophy and Theology; Communications and Media

Abilities: Category Flexibility; Memorization; Speech Clarity

Skills: Reading Comprehension; Active Listening; Writing; Speaking; Critical Thinking; Active Learning; Learning Strategies; Monitoring; Social Perceptiveness; Coordination; Persuasion; Negotiation; Instructing; Service Orientation; Problem Identification; Information Gathering; Information Organization; Synthesis/Reorganization; Idea Generation; Idea Evaluation; Implementation Planning; Solution Appraisal; Operations Analysis; Product Inspection; Visioning; Systems Perception; Identifying Downstream Consequences; Identification of Key Causes; Judgment and Decision Making; Systems Evaluation; Time Management; Management of Financial Resources; Management of Material Resources; Management of Personnel Resources

General Work Activities: Getting Information Needed to Do the Job; Monitoring Processes, Material, or Surroundings; Inspecting Equipment, Structures, or Material; Estimating Needed Characteristics; Judging Qualities of Things, Services, People; Processing Information; Evaluating Information against Standards; Analyzing Data or Information; Making Decisions and Solving Problems; Thinking Creatively; Developing Objectives and Strategies; Scheduling Work and Activities; Organizing, Planning, and Prioritizing; Implementing Ideas, Programs, etc.; Interpreting Meaning of Information to Others; Communicating with Other Workers; Communicating with Persons Outside Organization; Establishing and Maintaining Relationships; Selling or Influencing Others; Resolving Conflicts, Negotiating with Others; Performing for or Working with Public; Coordinating Work and Activities of Others; Developing and Building Teams; Teaching Others; Guiding, Directing and Motivating Subordinates; Coaching and Developing Others; Provide Consultation and Advice to Others; Performing Administrative Activities; Staffing Organizational Units; Monitoring and Controlling Resources

Job Characteristics: Objective or Subjective Information; Job-Required Social Interaction; Supervise, Coach, Train Others; Persuade Someone to a Course of Action; Take a Position Opposed to Others; Deal with External Customers; Coordinate or Lead Others; Responsibility for Outcomes and Results

GOE Group/s: 07.01.02 Administrative Detail: Administration; 11.02.01 Educational and Library Services: Teaching and Instructing, General; 11.05.03 Business Administration: Management Services: Government; 11.07.03 Services Administration: Education Services; 11.07.04 Services Administration: Recreation Services

CIP Program/s: 130101 Education, General; 130301 Curriculum and Instruction; 130501 Educational/Instructional Media Design; 301401 Museology/Museum Studies; 450801 History, General; 450805 Public/Applied History and Archival Administration; 500701 Art, General; 500703 Art History, Criticism and Conservation

Related DOT Job/s: 099.167-030 EDUCATIONAL RESOURCE COORDINATOR; 102.017-010 CURATOR; 102.117-010 SUPERVISOR, HISTORIC SITES; 102.117-014 DIRECTOR, MUSEUM-OR-ZOO; 102.167-014 HISTORIC-SITE ADMINISTRATOR; 102.167-018 REGISTRAR, MUSEUM

31511B ARCHIVISTS. OOH Title/s: Archivists and Curators

Appraise, edit, and direct safekeeping of permanent records and historically valuable documents. Participate in research activities based on archival materials. Directs activities of workers engaged in cataloging and safekeeping of valuable materials and disposition of worthless materials. Directs filing and cross-indexing of selected documents in alphabetical and chronological order. Prepares document descriptions and reference aids for use of archives, such as accession lists, bibliographies, abstracts, and microfilmed documents. Directs acquisition and physical arrangement of new materials. Analyzes documents by ascertaining date of writing, author, or original recipient of letter to appraise value to posterity. Establishes policy guidelines concerning public access and use of materials. Selects and edits documents for publication and display, according to knowledge of subject, literary expression, and techniques for presentation and display. Requests or recommends pertinent materials available in libraries, private collections, or other archives. Advises government agencies, scholars, journalists, and others conducting research by supplying available materials and information.

Yearly Earnings: $30,836

Education: Master's degree

Knowledge: Administration and Management; Clerical; Sociology and Anthropology; English Language; History and Archeology; Philosophy and Theology; Communications and Media

Abilities: Category Flexibility; Memorization

Skills: Reading Comprehension; Active Listening; Writing; Speaking; Coordination; Service Orientation; Information Gathering; Information Organization; Synthesis/Reorganization; Implementation Planning; Operations Analysis; Product Inspection; Identification of Key Causes; Judgment and Decision Making; Time Management; Management of Material Resources; Management of Personnel Resources

General Work Activities: Monitoring Processes, Material, or Surroundings; Estimating Needed Characteristics; Judging Qualities of Things, Services, People; Evaluating Information against Standards; Analyzing Data or Information; Updating and Using Job-Relevant Knowledge; Scheduling Work and Activities; Interpreting Meaning of Information to Others; Communicating with Persons Outside Organization; Assisting and Caring for Others; Coordinating Work and Activities of Others; Developing and Building Teams; Teaching Others; Guiding, Directing and Motivating Subordinates; Coaching and Developing Others; Provide Consultation and Advice to Others; Monitoring and Controlling Resources

Job Characteristics: Job-Required Social Interaction; Supervise, Coach, Train Others; Persuade Someone to a Course of Action; Deal with External Customers; Coordinate or Lead Others; Responsibility for Outcomes and Results; Sitting; Importance of Being Exact or Accurate

GOE Group/s: 11.03.03 Social Research: Historical

CIP Program/s: 301401 Museology/Museum Studies; 450801 History, General; 450805 Public/Applied History and Archival Administration; 500701 Art, General; 500703 Art History, Criticism and Conservation

Related DOT Job/s: 101.167-010 ARCHIVIST

31511C MUSEUM RESEARCH WORKERS. OOH Title/s: Archivists and Curators

Plan, organize, and conduct research in scientific, historical, cultural, or artistic fields to document or support exhibits in museums and museum publications. Conducts research on historic monuments, buildings, and scenes to construct exhibits. Develops plans for project or studies guidelines for project prepared by professional staff member to outline research procedures. Plans schedule according to variety of methods to be used, availability and quantity of resources, and number of personnel assigned. Conducts research, utilizing institution library, archives, and collections, and other sources of information, to collect, record, analyze, and evaluate facts. Discusses findings with other personnel to evaluate validity of findings. Prepares reports of completed projects for publication, for presentation to agency requesting project, or for use in other research activities. Monitors construction of exhibits to ensure authenticity of proportion, color, and costumes.

Yearly Earnings: $30,836

Education: Master's degree

Knowledge: Administration and Management; Computers and Electronics; Mathematics; Psychology; Sociology and Anthropology; Geography; English Language; Foreign Language; Fine Arts; History and Archeology; Philosophy and Theology; Telecommunications; Communications and Media

Abilities: Written Comprehension; Written Expression

Skills: Reading Comprehension; Active Listening; Writing; Speaking; Mathematics; Science; Critical Thinking; Active Learning; Learning Strategies; Monitoring; Problem Identification; Information Gathering; Information Organization; Synthesis/Reorganization; Idea Generation; Idea Evaluation; Implementation Planning; Solution Appraisal; Operations Analysis; Programming; Visioning; Systems Perception; Identifying Downstream Consequences; Identification of Key Causes; Judgment and Decision Making; Systems Evaluation; Time Management; Management of Personnel Resources

General Work Activities: Getting Information Needed to Do the Job; Monitoring Processes, Material, or Surroundings; Estimating Needed Characteristics; Judging Qualities of Things, Services, People; Evaluating Information against Standards; Analyzing Data or Information; Making Decisions and Solving Problems; Thinking Creatively; Updating and Using Job-Relevant Knowledge; Developing Objectives and Strategies; Scheduling Work and Activities; Organizing, Planning, and Prioritizing; Operating Vehicles or Equipment; Drafting and Specifying Technical Devices, etc.; Implementing Ideas, Programs, etc.; Documenting/Recording Information; Interpreting Meaning of Information to Others; Communicating with Other Workers; Communicating with Persons Outside Organization; Coordinating Work and Activities of Others; Developing and Building Teams; Provide Consultation and Advice to Others

Job Characteristics: Objective or Subjective Information; Persuade Someone to a Course of Action; Take a Position Opposed to Others; Importance of Being Exact or Accurate

GOE Group/s: 11.03.03 Social Research: Historical

CIP Program/s: 301401 Museology/Museum Studies; 450801 History, General; 450805 Public/Applied History and Archival Administration; 500701 Art, General; 500703 Art History, Criticism and Conservation

Related DOT Job/s: 109.067-014 RESEARCH ASSOCIATE; 109.267-010 RESEARCH ASSISTANT I

31511D MUSEUM TECHNICIANS AND CONSERVATORS. OOH Title/s: Archivists and Curators

Prepare specimens, such as fossils, skeletal parts, and textiles, for museum collection and exhibits. May restore documents or install, arrange, and exhibit materials. Preserves or directs preservation of objects, using plaster, resin, sealants, hardeners, and shellac. Repairs and restores surfaces of artifacts to original appearance and to prevent deterioration, according to accepted procedures. Evaluates need for repair and determines safest and most effective method of treating surface of object. Cleans objects, such as paper, textiles, wood, metal, glass, rock, pottery, and furniture, using cleansers, solvents, soap solutions, and polishes. Constructs skeletal mounts of fossils, replicas of archaeological artifacts, or duplicate specimens, using variety of materials and hand tools. Repairs or reassembles broken objects, using glue, solder, hand tools, power tools, and small machines. Studies descriptive information on object or conducts standard chemical and physical tests to determine age, composition, and original appearance. Designs and fabricates missing or broken parts. Cuts and welds metal sections in reconstruction or renovation of exterior structural sections and accessories of exhibits. Recommends preservation measures, such as control of temperature, humidity, and exposure to light, to curatorial and building maintenance staff. Installs, arranges, assembles, and prepares artifacts for exhibition. Plans and conducts research to develop and improve methods of restoring and preserving specimens. Records methods and treatment taken to repair, preserve, and restore each artifact, and maintains museum files. Prepares reports of activities. Notifies superior when restoration of artifact requires outside experts. Directs curatorial and technical staff in handling, mounting, care, and storage of art objects. Estimates cost of restoration work. Builds, repairs, and installs wooden steps, scaffolds, and walkways to gain access to or permit improved view of exhibited equipment.

Yearly Earnings: $30,836

Education: Master's degree

Knowledge: Building and Construction; Chemistry; Sociology and Anthropology; Fine Arts; History and Archeology; Philosophy and Theology

Abilities: Flexibility of Closure; Visualization; Wrist-Finger Speed; Visual Color Discrimination

Skills: Writing; Information Organization; Operations Analysis; Equipment Selection; Installation; Product Inspection; Repairing; Management of Material Resources; Management of Personnel Resources

General Work Activities: Getting Information Needed to Do the Job; Inspecting Equipment, Structures, or Material; Estimating Needed Characteristics; Judging Qualities of Things, Services, People; Evaluating Information against Standards; Analyzing Data or Information; Making Decisions and Solving Problems; Thinking Creatively; Updating and Using Job-Relevant Knowledge; Developing Objectives and Strategies; Scheduling Work and Activities; Organizing, Planning, and Prioritizing; Drafting and Specifying Technical Devices, etc.; Implementing Ideas, Programs, etc.; Interpreting Meaning of Information to Others; Communicating with Other Workers; Teaching Others

Job Characteristics: Objective or Subjective Information; Supervise, Coach, Train Others; Coordinate or Lead Others; Responsible for Others' Health and Safety; Climbing Ladders, Scaffolds, Poles, etc.; Kneeling, Crouching, or Crawling; Keeping or Regaining Balance

GOE Group/s: 01.06.02 Craft Arts: Arts and Crafts; 01.06.03 Craft Arts: Hand Lettering, Painting and Decorating

CIP Program/s: 301401 Museology/Museum Studies; 450801 History, General; 450805 Public/Applied History and Archival Administration; 500201 Crafts, Folk Art and Artisanry; 500701 Art, General; 500703 Art History, Criticism and Conservation; 500711 Ceramics Arts and Ceramics

Related DOT Job/s: 055.381-010 CONSERVATOR, ARTIFACTS; 102.167-010 ART CONSERVATOR; 102.261-010 CONSERVATION TECHNICIAN; 102.361-010 RESTORER, LACE AND TEXTILES; 102.361-014 RESTORER, CERAMIC; 102.367-010 FINE ARTS PACKER; 102.381-010 MUSEUM TECHNICIAN; 109.281-010 ARMORER TECHNICIAN; 109.361-010 RESTORER, PAPER-AND-PRINTS; 779.381-018 REPAIRER, ART OBJECTS; 899.384-010 TRANSPORTATION-EQUIPMENT-MAINTENANCE WORKER; 979.361-010 DOCUMENT RESTORER

31511E CRAFT DEMONSTRATORS. OOH Title/s: Archivists and Curators

Demonstrate and explain techniques and purposes of historic crafts. Engages in activities such as molding candles, shoeing horses, operating looms, or working in appropriate period setting to demonstrate craft. Describes craft techniques and explains the relationship of craft to traditional lifestyle of time and area. Practices techniques involved in handicraft to ensure accurate and skillful demonstrations. Answers visitor questions, or refers visitors to other sources for information. Studies historical and technical literature to acquire information about time period and lifestyle depicted in display and craft techniques. Drafts outline of talk, assisted by research personnel, to acquaint visitors with customs and crafts associated with folk life depicted.
Yearly Earnings: $30,836
Education: Master's degree
Knowledge: Sociology and Anthropology; Geography; Fine Arts; History and Archeology; Philosophy and Theology
Abilities: Multilimb Coordination; Speech Clarity
Skills: Instructing; Service Orientation
General Work Activities: Interpreting Meaning of Information to Others; Communicating with Persons Outside Organization; Performing for or Working with Public; Teaching Others
Job Characteristics: Objective or Subjective Information; Job-Required Social Interaction; Provide a Service to Others; Deal with External Customers; Kneeling, Crouching, or Crawling; Making Repetitive Motions; Special Uniform
GOE Group/s: 09.01.02 Hospitality Services: Guide Services
CIP Program/s: 500201 Crafts, Folk Art and Artisanry
Related DOT Job/s: 109.364-010 CRAFT DEMONSTRATOR

31514 VOCATIONAL AND EDUCATIONAL COUNSELORS. OOH Title/s: Counselors

Counsel individuals and provide group educational and vocational guidance services. Advises counselees to assist them in developing their educational and vocational objectives. Advises counselees to assist them in understanding and overcoming personal and social problems. Collects and evaluates information about counselees' abilities, interests, and personality characteristics, using records, tests, and interviews. Compiles and studies occupational, educational, and economic information to assist counselees in making and carrying out vocational and educational objectives. Interprets program regulations or benefit requirements and assists counselees in obtaining needed supportive services. Refers qualified counselees to employer or employment service for placement. Conducts follow-up interviews with counselees and maintains case records. Establishes and maintains relationships with employers and personnel from supportive service agencies to develop opportunities for counselees. Plans and conducts orientation programs and group conferences to promote adjustment of individuals to new life experiences. Teaches vocational and educational guidance classes. Addresses community groups and faculty members to explain counseling services.
Yearly Earnings: $36,088
Education: Master's degree
Knowledge: Personnel and Human Resources; Psychology; Sociology and Anthropology; Therapy and Counseling; Education and Training; English Language
Abilities: Oral Expression
Skills: Reading Comprehension; Active Listening; Writing; Speaking; Critical Thinking; Active Learning; Learning Strategies; Monitoring; Social Perceptiveness; Coordination; Persuasion; Negotiation; Instructing; Service Orientation; Problem Identification; Information Gathering; Information Organization; Synthesis/Reorganization; Idea Generation; Idea Evaluation; Implementation Planning; Solution Appraisal; Visioning; Identification of Key Causes; Judgment and Decision Making; Systems Evaluation
General Work Activities: Getting Information Needed to Do the Job; Judging Qualities of Things, Services, People; Analyzing Data or Information; Making Decisions and Solving Problems; Developing Objectives and Strategies; Documenting/Recording Information; Interpreting Meaning of Information to Others; Communicating with Persons Outside Organization; Establishing and Maintaining Relationships; Assisting and Caring for Others; Selling or Influencing Others; Performing for or Working with Public; Teaching Others; Coaching and Developing Others; Provide Consultation and Advice to Others
Job Characteristics: Objective or Subjective Information; Job-Required Social Interaction; Provide a Service to Others; Deal with External Customers; Sitting
GOE Group/s: 07.01.01 Administrative Detail: Interviewing; 10.01.02 Social Services: Counseling and Social Work; 11.07.03 Services Administration: Education Services
CIP Program/s: 130201 Bilingual/Bicultural Education; 130401 Education Administration and Supervision, General; 130406 Higher Education Administration; 130407 Community and Junior College Administration; 131101 Counselor Education Counseling and Guidance Services; 131102 College/Postsecondary Student Counseling and Personnel Services; 421701 School Psychology
Related DOT Job/s: 045.107-010 COUNSELOR; 045.107-014 COUNSELOR, NURSES' ASSOCIATION; 045.107-018 DIRECTOR OF COUNSELING; 045.107-038 RESIDENCE COUNSELOR; 045.107-042 VOCATIONAL REHABILITATION COUNSELOR; 045.117-010 DIRECTOR OF GUIDANCE IN PUBLIC SCHOOLS; 090.107-010 FOREIGN-STUDENT ADVISER; 169.267-026 SUPERVISOR, SPECIAL SERVICES; 187.167-198 VETERANS CONTACT REPRESENTATIVE

31517A PUBLIC HEALTH EDUCATORS. OOH Title/s: Adult Education Teachers

Plan, organize, and direct health education programs for group and community needs. Plans and provides educational opportunities for health personnel. Collaborates with health specialists and civic groups to ascertain community health needs, determine availability of services, and develop goals. Promotes health discussions in schools, industry, and community agencies. Conducts community surveys to ascertain health needs, develop desirable health goals, and determine availability of professional health services. Prepares and disseminates educational and informational materials. Develops and maintains cooperation between public, civic, professional, and voluntary agencies.
Yearly Earnings: $31,720
Education: Master's degree
Knowledge: Administration and Management; Sales and Marketing; Customer and Personal Service; Biology; Psychology; Sociology and Anthropology; Medicine and Dentistry; Therapy and Counseling; Education and Training; English Language; Philosophy and Theology; Communications and Media
Abilities: Oral Expression; Originality; Inductive Reasoning; Speech Clarity
Skills: Active Listening; Writing; Speaking; Active Learning; Learning Strategies; Social Perceptiveness; Coordination; Persuasion; In-

structing; Service Orientation; Information Gathering; Information Organization; Synthesis/Reorganization; Idea Generation; Idea Evaluation; Implementation Planning; Visioning; Systems Perception; Systems Evaluation
General Work Activities: Getting Information Needed to Do the Job; Monitoring Processes, Material, or Surroundings; Estimating Needed Characteristics; Developing Objectives and Strategies; Implementing Ideas, Programs, etc.; Interpreting Meaning of Information to Others; Communicating with Other Workers; Communicating with Persons Outside Organization; Establishing and Maintaining Relationships; Assisting and Caring for Others; Performing for or Working with Public; Developing and Building Teams; Teaching Others; Coaching and Developing Others; Provide Consultation and Advice to Others
Job Characteristics: Persuade Someone to a Course of Action; Coordinate or Lead Others; Sitting
GOE Group/s: 11.07.02 Services Administration: Health and Safety Services
CIP Program/s: 130301 Curriculum and Instruction; 510301 Community Health Liaison
Related DOT Job/s: 079.117-014 PUBLIC HEALTH EDUCATOR

31517B VOCATIONAL REHABILITATION COORDINATORS. OOH Title/s: Counselors; Education Administrators
Develop and coordinate implementation of vocational rehabilitation programs. Develops proposals for rehabilitation programs to provide needed services, utilizing knowledge of program funding sources and government regulations. Consults with community groups and personnel from rehabilitation agencies to identify need for new or modified vocational rehabilitation programs. Collects and analyzes data to define and resolve rehabilitation problems, utilizing knowledge of vocational rehabilitation theory and practice. Monitors program operations and recommends additional measures to ensure that programs meet defined needs. Negotiates contracts for rehabilitation program equipment and supplies. Plans and provides training for vocational rehabilitation staff.
Yearly Earnings: $36,088
Education: Master's degree
Knowledge: Administration and Management; Personnel and Human Resources; Psychology; Sociology and Anthropology; Therapy and Counseling; Education and Training; English Language; Philosophy and Theology; Law, Government, and Jurisprudence
Skills: Reading Comprehension; Active Listening; Writing; Speaking; Mathematics; Critical Thinking; Active Learning; Monitoring; Coordination; Negotiation; Instructing; Service Orientation; Problem Identification; Information Gathering; Information Organization; Idea Generation; Idea Evaluation; Implementation Planning; Solution Appraisal; Operations Analysis; Visioning; Systems Perception; Identifying Downstream Consequences; Identification of Key Causes; Judgment and Decision Making; Systems Evaluation; Time Management; Management of Financial Resources; Management of Material Resources; Management of Personnel Resources
General Work Activities: Getting Information Needed to Do the Job; Monitoring Processes, Material, or Surroundings; Identifying Objects, Actions, and Events; Estimating Needed Characteristics; Judging Qualities of Things, Services, People; Processing Information; Evaluating Information against Standards; Analyzing Data or Information; Making Decisions and Solving Problems; Thinking Creatively; Developing Objectives and Strategies; Scheduling Work and Activities; Organizing, Planning, and Prioritizing; Implementing Ideas, Programs, etc.; Documenting/Recording Information; Interpreting Meaning of Information to Others; Communicating with Other Workers; Communicating with Persons Outside Organization; Selling or Influencing Others; Resolving Conflicts, Negotiating with Others; Performing for or Working with Public; Coordinating Work and Activities of Others; Developing and Building Teams; Teaching Others; Guiding, Directing and Motivating Subordinates; Coaching and Developing Others; Provide Consultation and Advice to Others; Performing Administrative Activities; Staffing Organizational Units; Monitoring and Controlling Resources
Job Characteristics: Objective or Subjective Information; Job-Required Social Interaction; Supervise, Coach, Train Others; Persuade Someone to a Course of Action; Deal with External Customers; Coordinate or Lead Others; Frustrating Circumstances
GOE Group/s: 11.07.03 Services Administration: Education Services
CIP Program/s: 130401 Education Administration and Supervision, General; 130402 Administration of Special Education; 131001 Special Education, General
Related DOT Job/s: 094.117-018 VOCATIONAL REHABILITATION CONSULTANT

31517C LABORATORY MANAGERS. OOH Title/s: Education, Science, and Data Processing Managers
Coordinate activities of university science laboratory to assist faculty in teaching and research programs. Prepares and puts in place equipment scheduled for use during laboratory teaching sessions. Confers with teaching staff to evaluate new equipment and methods. Consults with laboratory coordinator to determine equipment purchase priorities based on budget allowances, condition of existing equipment, and scheduled activities. Demonstrates care and use of equipment to teaching assistants. Trains teaching staff and students in application and use of new equipment. Develops methods of laboratory experimentation, applying knowledge of scientific theory and computer capability. Builds prototype equipment, applying electromechanical knowledge and using hand tools and power tools. Diagnoses and repairs malfunctioning equipment, applying knowledge of shop mechanics and using gauges, meters, hand tools, and power tools. Teaches laboratory sessions in absence of teaching assistant.
Yearly Earnings: $39,936
Education: Work experience, plus degree
Knowledge: Administration and Management; Economics and Accounting; Computers and Electronics; Engineering and Technology; Mathematics; Physics; Chemistry; Biology; Education and Training; English Language
Abilities: Speech Recognition
Skills: Reading Comprehension; Active Listening; Speaking; Science; Active Learning; Learning Strategies; Coordination; Instructing; Service Orientation; Information Gathering; Idea Generation; Idea Evaluation; Implementation Planning; Operations Analysis; Technology Design; Equipment Selection; Installation; Programming; Testing; Equipment Maintenance; Troubleshooting; Repairing; Judgment and Decision Making; Time Management; Management of Financial Resources; Management of Material Resources; Management of Personnel Resources
General Work Activities: Thinking Creatively; Drafting and Specifying Technical Devices, etc.; Repairing and Maintaining Mechanical Equipment; Repairing and Maintaining Electrical Equipment; Teaching Others; Coaching and Developing Others; Monitoring and Controlling Resources
Job Characteristics: Supervise, Coach, Train Others; Persuade Someone to a Course of Action; Coordinate or Lead Others; Responsible for Others' Health and Safety; Responsibility for Outcomes and Results; Radiation; Diseases/Infections
GOE Group/s: 11.07.03 Services Administration: Education Services
CIP Program/s: 000000 NO CIP ASSIGNED
Related DOT Job/s: 090.164-010 LABORATORY MANAGER

31517D INSTRUCTIONAL COORDINATORS. OOH

Title/s: Education Administrators

Develop instructional material, educational content, and instructional methods to provide guidelines to educators and instructors for developing curricula, conducting courses, and incorporating current technology. Researches, evaluates, and prepares recommendations on curricula, instructional methods, and materials for school system. Develops tests, questionnaires, and procedures to measure effectiveness of curriculum and to determine if program objectives are being met. Prepares or approves manuals, guidelines, and reports on state educational policies and practices for distribution to school districts. Orders or authorizes purchase of instructional materials, supplies, equipment, and visual aids designed to meet educational needs of students. Confers with school officials, teachers, and administrative staff to plan and develop curricula and establish guidelines for educational programs. Confers with educational committees and advisory groups to gather information on instructional methods and materials related to specific academic subjects. Advises teaching and administrative staff in assessment, curriculum development, management of student behavior, and use of materials and equipment. Observes, evaluates, and recommends changes in work of teaching staff to strengthen teaching skills in classroom. Plans, conducts, and evaluates training programs and conferences for teachers to study new classroom procedures, instructional materials, and teaching aids. Advises school officials on implementation of state and federal programs and procedures. Conducts or participates in workshops, committees, and conferences designed to promote intellectual, social, and physical welfare of students. Coordinates activities of workers engaged in cataloging, distributing, and maintaining educational materials and equipment in curriculum library and laboratory. Interprets and enforces provisions of state education codes and rules and regulations of state board of education. Prepares or assists in preparation of grant proposals, budgets, and program policies and goals. Addresses public audiences to explain and elicit support for program objectives. Recruits, interviews, and recommends hiring of teachers. Reviews student files and confers with educators, parents, and other concerned parties to decide student placement and provision of services. Inspects and authorizes repair of instructional equipment, such as musical instruments.

Yearly Earnings: $39,208

Education: Work experience, plus degree

Knowledge: Administration and Management; Economics and Accounting; Sales and Marketing; Personnel and Human Resources; Psychology; Sociology and Anthropology; Therapy and Counseling; Education and Training; English Language; Foreign Language; Fine Arts; History and Archeology; Philosophy and Theology; Law, Government, and Jurisprudence; Communications and Media

Abilities: Oral Comprehension; Written Comprehension; Oral Expression; Written Expression; Fluency of Ideas; Originality; Memorization; Speech Recognition; Speech Clarity

Skills: Reading Comprehension; Active Listening; Writing; Speaking; Critical Thinking; Active Learning; Learning Strategies; Monitoring; Social Perceptiveness; Coordination; Persuasion; Negotiation; Instructing; Information Gathering; Information Organization; Synthesis/Reorganization; Idea Generation; Idea Evaluation; Implementation Planning; Solution Appraisal; Operations Analysis; Equipment Selection; Visioning; Systems Perception; Identifying Downstream Consequences; Identification of Key Causes; Judgment and Decision Making; Systems Evaluation; Time Management; Management of Financial Resources; Management of Material Resources; Management of Personnel Resources

General Work Activities: Getting Information Needed to Do the Job; Monitoring Processes, Material, or Surroundings; Estimating Needed Characteristics; Judging Qualities of Things, Services, People; Evaluating Information against Standards; Analyzing Data or Information; Making Decisions and Solving Problems; Thinking Creatively; Developing Objectives and Strategies; Organizing, Planning, and Prioritizing; Operating Vehicles or Equipment; Implementing Ideas, Programs, etc.; Interpreting Meaning of Information to Others; Communicating with Other Workers; Communicating with Persons Outside Organization; Establishing and Maintaining Relationships; Selling or Influencing Others; Coordinating Work and Activities of Others; Developing and Building Teams; Teaching Others; Guiding, Directing and Motivating Subordinates; Coaching and Developing Others; Provide Consultation and Advice to Others; Staffing Organizational Units; Monitoring and Controlling Resources

Job Characteristics: Objective or Subjective Information; Job-Required Social Interaction; Supervise, Coach, Train Others; Coordinate or Lead Others; Frequency in Conflict Situations; Sitting

GOE Group/s: 10.02.03 Nursing, Therapy, and Specialized Teaching Services: Specialized Teaching; 11.07.03 Services Administration: Education Services

CIP Program/s: 130101 Education, General; 130201 Bilingual/Bicultural Education; 130301 Curriculum and Instruction; 130401 Education Administration and Supervision, General; 130402 Administration of Special Education; 130404 Educational Supervision; 130405 Elementary, Middle and Secondary Education Administration; 130501 Educational/Instructional Media Design; 130601 Educational Evaluation and Research; 130603 Educational Statistics and Research Methods; 130604 Educational Assessment, Testing and Measurement; 130701 International and Comparative Education; 131001 Special Education, General; 131003 Education of the Deaf and Hearing Impaired; 131004 Education of the Gifted and Talented; 131005 Education of the Emotionally Handicapped; 131006 Education of the Mentally Handicapped; 131007 Education of the Multiple Handicapped; 131008 Education of the Physically Handicapped; 131009 Education of the Blind and Visually Handicapped; 131011 Education of the Specific Learning Disabled; 131012 Education of the Speech Impaired

Related DOT Job/s: 094.167-010 SUPERVISOR, SPECIAL EDUCATION; 099.117-026 SUPERVISOR, EDUCATION; 099.167-014 CONSULTANT, EDUCATION; 099.167-018 DIRECTOR, INSTRUCTIONAL MATERIAL; 099.167-022 EDUCATIONAL SPECIALIST; 099.167-026 MUSIC SUPERVISOR

31521 TEACHER AIDES, PARAPROFESSIONAL.

OOH Title/s: Teacher Aides

Perform duties that are instructional in nature, or deliver direct services to students and/or parents. Serve in a position for which a teacher or another professional has ultimate responsibility for the design and implementation of educational programs and services. Presents subject matter to students, using lecture, discussion, or supervised role-playing methods. Helps students, individually or in groups, with lesson assignments to present or reinforce learning concepts. Prepares lesson outline and plan in assigned area and submits outline to teacher for review. Plans, prepares, and develops various teaching aids, such as bibliographies, charts, and graphs. Discusses assigned teaching area with classroom teacher to coordinate instructional efforts. Prepares, administers, and grades examinations. Confers with parents on progress of students.

Yearly Earnings: $12,376

Education: Short-term O-J-T

Knowledge: Psychology; Sociology and Anthropology; Education and Training; English Language; History and Archeology; Philosophy and Theology

Skills: Active Listening; Speaking; Learning Strategies; Social Perceptiveness; Instructing; Service Orientation

General Work Activities: Thinking Creatively; Developing Objectives and Strategies; Scheduling Work and Activities; Establishing and Maintaining Relationships; Assisting and Caring for Others; Selling or Influencing Others; Resolving Conflicts, Negotiating with Others; Developing and Building Teams; Teaching Others; Coaching and Developing Others
Job Characteristics: Objective or Subjective Information; Job-Required Social Interaction; Persuade Someone to a Course of Action; Provide a Service to Others; Deal with External Customers; Frequency in Conflict Situations; Deal with Unpleasant or Angry People; Deal with Physical, Aggressive People; Frustrating Circumstances
GOE Group/s: 11.02.01 Educational and Library Services: Teaching and Instructing, General
CIP Program/s: 130101 Education, General; 130201 Bilingual/Bicultural Education; 131501 Teacher Assistant/Aide
Related DOT Job/s: 099.327-010 TEACHER AIDE I

Diagnosing and Treating Practitioners

32102A DOCTORS OF MEDICINE (MD). OOH Title/s: Physicians

Diagnose illness and prescribe and administer treatment for injury and disease. Exclude doctors of osteopathy, psychiatrists, anesthesiologists, surgeons, and pathologists. Examines or conducts tests on patient to provide information on medical condition. Analyzes records, reports, test results, or examination information to diagnose medical condition of patient. Prescribes or administers treatment, therapy, medication, vaccination, and other specialized medical care to treat or prevent illness, disease, or injury. Monitors patient's condition and progress and reevaluates treatments as necessary. Explains procedures and discusses test results on prescribed treatments with patients. Operates on patients to remove, repair, or improve functioning of diseased or injured body parts and systems, and delivers babies. Collects, records, and maintains patient information, such as medical history, reports, and examination results. Refers patients to medical specialist or other practitioner when necessary. Advises patients and community concerning diet, activity, hygiene, and disease prevention. Plans, implements, or administers health programs or standards in hospital, business, or community for information, prevention, or treatment of injury or illness. Directs and coordinates activities of nurses, students, assistants, specialists, therapists, and other medical staff. Prepares reports for government or management of birth, death, and disease statistics, workforce evaluations, or medical status of individuals. Conducts research to study anatomy and develop or test medications, treatments, or procedures to prevent or control disease or injury.
Yearly Earnings: $54,080
Education: First professional degree
Knowledge: Administration and Management; Personnel and Human Resources; Mathematics; Physics; Chemistry; Biology; Psychology; Sociology and Anthropology; Medicine and Dentistry; Therapy and Counseling; Education and Training; English Language; Foreign Language; Law, Government, and Jurisprudence
Abilities: Oral Comprehension; Written Comprehension; Oral Expression; Written Expression; Fluency of Ideas; Problem Sensitivity; Deductive Reasoning; Inductive Reasoning; Information Ordering; Mathematical Reasoning; Number Facility; Speed of Closure; Flexibility of Closure; Perceptual Speed; Selective Attention; Time Sharing; Arm-Hand Steadiness; Manual Dexterity; Finger Dexterity; Control Precision; Multilimb Coordination; Response Orientation; Reaction Time; Wrist-Finger Speed; Near Vision; Visual Color Discrimination; Hearing Sensitivity; Auditory Attention; Speech Clarity
Skills: Reading Comprehension; Active Listening; Writing; Speaking; Mathematics; Science; Critical Thinking; Active Learning; Learning Strategies; Monitoring; Social Perceptiveness; Coordination; Persuasion; Negotiation; Instructing; Service Orientation; Problem Identification; Information Gathering; Information Organization; Synthesis/Reorganization; Idea Generation; Idea Evaluation; Implementation Planning; Solution Appraisal; Equipment Selection; Programming; Testing; Product Inspection; Troubleshooting; Systems Perception; Identifying Downstream Consequences; Identification of Key Causes; Judgment and Decision Making; Systems Evaluation; Time Management; Management of Personnel Resources
General Work Activities: Getting Information Needed to Do the Job; Monitoring Processes, Material, or Surroundings; Identifying Objects, Actions, and Events; Estimating Needed Characteristics; Judging Qualities of Things, Services, People; Processing Information; Evaluating Information against Standards; Analyzing Data or Information; Making Decisions and Solving Problems; Thinking Creatively; Updating and Using Job-Relevant Knowledge; Developing Objectives and Strategies; Scheduling Work and Activities; Implementing Ideas, Programs, etc.; Documenting/Recording Information; Interpreting Meaning of Information to Others; Communicating with Other Workers; Communicating with Persons Outside Organization; Assisting and Caring for Others; Performing for or Working with Public; Coordinating Work and Activities of Others; Provide Consultation and Advice to Others
Job Characteristics: Job-Required Social Interaction; Supervise, Coach, Train Others; Persuade Someone to a Course of Action; Provide a Service to Others; Take a Position Opposed to Others; Deal with External Customers; Coordinate or Lead Others; Responsible for Others' Health and Safety; Responsibility for Outcomes and Results; Frequency in Conflict Situations; Deal with Unpleasant or Angry People; Radiation; Diseases/Infections; Walking or Running; Bending or Twisting the Body; Special Uniform; Common Protective or Safety Attire; Consequence of Error; Frustrating Circumstances; Importance of Being Exact or Accurate; Importance of Being Sure All is Done
GOE Group/s: 02.03.01 Medical Sciences: Medicine and Surgery
CIP Program/s: 511201 Medicine (M.D.); 511307 Medical Immunology; 511310 Medical Neurobiology; 511401 Medical Clinical Sciences (M.S., Ph.D.); 512902 Allergies and Immunology Residency; 512905 Cardiology Residency; 512907 Child/Pediatric Neurology Residency; 512909 Colon and Rectal Surgery Residency; 512911 Critical Care Medicine Residency; 512913 Dermatology Residency; 512915 Diagnostic Radiology Residency; 512916 Emergency Medicine Residency; 512918 Family Medicine Residency; 512922 Geriatric Medicine Residency; 512926 Immunopathology Residency; 512928 Internal Medicine Residency; 512931 Neonatal-Perinatal Medicine Residency; 512933 Neurological Surgery/Neurosurgery Residency; 512934 Neurology Residency; 512937 Nuclear Radiology Residency; 512938 Obstetrics and Gynecology Residency; 512939 Occupational Medicine Residency; 512941 Ophthalmology Residency; 512943 Otolaryngology Residency; 512945 Pediatric Cardiology Residency; 512946 Pediatric Endocrinology Residency; 512947 Pediatric Hemato-Oncology Residency; 512948 Pediatric Nephrology Residency; 512951 Pediatrics Residency; 512952 Physical and Rehabilitation Medicine Residency; 512956 Public Health Medicine Residency; 512957 Pulmonary Disease Residency; 512958 Radiation Oncology Residency; 512959 Radioisotopic Pathology Residency; 512962 Thoracic Surgery Residency; 512963 Urology Residency; 512999 Medical Residency Programs, Other
Related DOT Job/s: 070.101-014 CARDIOLOGIST; 070.101-018 DERMATOLOGIST; 070.101-022 GENERAL PRACTITIONER; 070.101-026 FAMILY PRACTITIONER; 070.101-034 GYNECOLOGIST; 070.101-042 INTERNIST; 070.101-046 PUBLIC HEALTH PHYSICIAN; 070.101-050 NEUROLOGIST; 070.101-054 OBSTETRICIAN; 070.101-058 OPHTHAL-

MOLOGIST; 070.101-062 OTOLARYNGOLOGIST; 070.101-066 PEDIATRICIAN; 070.101-070 PHYSIATRIST; 070.101-078 PHYSICIAN, OCCUPATIONAL; 070.101-082 POLICE SURGEON; 070.101-086 PROCTOLOGIST; 070.101-090 RADIOLOGIST; 070.101-098 UROLOGIST; 070.101-102 ALLERGIST-IMMUNOLOGIST

32102B DOCTORS OF OSTEOPATHY (DO). OOH

Title/s: Physicians

Diagnose illness and prescribe and administer treatment for injury and disease with emphasis on body's musculoskeletal system. Prescribes and administers medical, surgical, or manipulative therapy treatments to correct disorders or injuries of bones, muscles, or nerves. Examines or conducts test on patient to provide information on musculoskeletal system, using diagnostic images, drugs, and other aids. Analyzes reports and test or examination findings to diagnose musculoskeletal system impairment. Operates on patient to repair injuries or improve functions of musculoskeletal system. Advises patient and community of prevention and treatment of injury of musculoskeletal system. Conducts research to develop and test medications or medical techniques to cure or control disease or injury of musculoskeletal system. Directs and coordinates activities of nurses, assistants, and other medical staff.

Yearly Earnings: $54,080

Education: First professional degree

Knowledge: Customer and Personal Service; Mathematics; Chemistry; Biology; Psychology; Sociology and Anthropology; Medicine and Dentistry; Therapy and Counseling; English Language

Abilities: Oral Comprehension; Written Comprehension; Oral Expression; Written Expression; Problem Sensitivity; Deductive Reasoning; Inductive Reasoning; Information Ordering; Memorization; Speed of Closure; Flexibility of Closure; Selective Attention; Time Sharing; Arm-Hand Steadiness; Manual Dexterity; Finger Dexterity; Reaction Time; Wrist-Finger Speed; Near Vision; Speech Clarity

Skills: Reading Comprehension; Active Listening; Writing; Speaking; Science; Critical Thinking; Active Learning; Learning Strategies; Monitoring; Coordination; Persuasion; Service Orientation; Problem Identification; Information Gathering; Information Organization; Synthesis/Reorganization; Idea Generation; Idea Evaluation; Implementation Planning; Solution Appraisal; Equipment Selection; Visioning; Systems Perception; Identifying Downstream Consequences; Identification of Key Causes; Judgment and Decision Making; Systems Evaluation; Time Management; Management of Material Resources; Management of Personnel Resources

General Work Activities: Getting Information Needed to Do the Job; Monitoring Processes, Material, or Surroundings; Identifying Objects, Actions, and Events; Estimating Needed Characteristics; Judging Qualities of Things, Services, People; Processing Information; Evaluating Information against Standards; Analyzing Data or Information; Making Decisions and Solving Problems; Thinking Creatively; Updating and Using Job-Relevant Knowledge; Developing Objectives and Strategies; Scheduling Work and Activities; Organizing, Planning, and Prioritizing; Handling and Moving Objects; Controlling Machines and Processes; Implementing Ideas, Programs, etc.; Documenting/Recording Information; Interpreting Meaning of Information to Others; Communicating with Other Workers; Communicating with Persons Outside Organization; Establishing and Maintaining Relationships; Assisting and Caring for Others; Selling or Influencing Others; Performing for or Working with Public; Coordinating Work and Activities of Others; Developing and Building Teams; Teaching Others; Guiding, Directing and Motivating Subordinates; Coaching and Developing Others; Provide Consultation and Advice to Others; Performing Administrative Activities; Staffing Organizational Units

Job Characteristics: Objective or Subjective Information; Job-Required Social Interaction; Supervise, Coach, Train Others; Persuade Someone to a Course of Action; Provide a Service to Others; Take a Position Opposed to Others; Deal with External Customers; Coordinate or Lead Others; Responsible for Others' Health and Safety; Responsibility for Outcomes and Results; Radiation; Diseases/Infections; Bending or Twisting the Body; Special Uniform; Common Protective or Safety Attire; Consequence of Error; Importance of Being Exact or Accurate; Importance of Being Sure All is Done

GOE Group/s: 02.03.01 Medical Sciences: Medicine and Surgery

CIP Program/s: 511901 Osteopathic Medicine (D.O.)

Related DOT Job/s: 071.101-010 OSTEOPATHIC PHYSICIAN

32102E PSYCHIATRISTS. OOH Title/s: Physicians

Diagnose mental, emotional, and behavioral disorders and prescribe medication or administer psychotherapeutic treatments to treat disorders. Analyzes and evaluates patient data and test or examination findings to diagnose nature and extent of mental disorder. Prescribes, directs, and administers psychotherapeutic treatments or medications to treat mental, emotional, or behavioral disorders. Examines or conducts laboratory or diagnostic tests on patient to provide information on general physical condition and mental disorder. Gathers and maintains patient information and records, including social and medical history obtained from patient, relatives, and other professionals. Reviews and evaluates treatment procedures and outcomes of other psychiatrists and medical professionals. Advises and informs guardians, relatives, and significant others of patient's condition and treatment. Prepares case reports and summaries for government agencies. Teaches, conducts research, and publishes findings to increase understanding of mental, emotional, and behavioral states and disorders.

Yearly Earnings: $54,080

Education: First professional degree

Knowledge: Customer and Personal Service; Chemistry; Biology; Psychology; Sociology and Anthropology; Medicine and Dentistry; Therapy and Counseling; Education and Training; English Language; Philosophy and Theology; Law, Government, and Jurisprudence; Communications and Media

Abilities: Oral Comprehension; Written Comprehension; Oral Expression; Written Expression; Problem Sensitivity; Deductive Reasoning; Inductive Reasoning; Information Ordering; Memorization; Speed of Closure; Selective Attention; Speech Recognition; Speech Clarity

Skills: Reading Comprehension; Active Listening; Writing; Speaking; Science; Critical Thinking; Active Learning; Learning Strategies; Monitoring; Social Perceptiveness; Coordination; Persuasion; Negotiation; Instructing; Service Orientation; Problem Identification; Information Gathering; Information Organization; Synthesis/Reorganization; Idea Generation; Idea Evaluation; Implementation Planning; Solution Appraisal; Programming; Visioning; Systems Perception; Identifying Downstream Consequences; Identification of Key Causes; Judgment and Decision Making; Systems Evaluation

General Work Activities: Getting Information Needed to Do the Job; Monitoring Processes, Material, or Surroundings; Identifying Objects, Actions, and Events; Estimating Needed Characteristics; Judging Qualities of Things, Services, People; Processing Information; Evaluating Information against Standards; Analyzing Data or Information; Making Decisions and Solving Problems; Thinking Creatively; Updating and Using Job-Relevant Knowledge; Developing Objectives and Strategies; Documenting/Recording Information; Interpreting Meaning of Information to Others; Communicating with Other Workers; Communicating with Persons Outside Organization; Establishing and Maintaining Relationships; Assisting and Caring for Others; Selling or Influencing Others; Resolving Conflicts, Negotiating with Others; Performing for or Working with Public; Teaching Others; Coaching and Developing Others; Provide Consultation and Advice to Others; Performing Administrative Activities

Job Characteristics: Objective or Subjective Information; Job-Required Social Interaction; Persuade Someone to a Course of Action; Provide a Service to Others; Take a Position Opposed to Others; Deal with External Customers; Responsible for Others' Health and Safety; Frequency in Conflict Situations; Deal with Unpleasant or Angry People; Deal with Physical, Aggressive People; Sitting; Consequence of Error; Frustrating Circumstances; Importance of Being Exact or Accurate; Importance of Being Sure All is Done; Importance of Being Aware of New Events
GOE Group/s: 02.03.01 Medical Sciences: Medicine and Surgery
CIP Program/s: 512705 Psychoanalysis; 512908 Child Psychiatry Residency; 512955 Psychiatry Residency
Related DOT Job/s: 070.107-014 PSYCHIATRIST

32102F ANESTHESIOLOGISTS. OOH Title/s: Physicians
Administer anesthetic during surgery or other medical procedures. Administers anesthetic or sedation during medical procedures, using local, intravenous, spinal, or caudal methods. Monitors patient before, during, and after anesthesia and counteracts adverse reactions or complications. Examines patient to determine risk during surgical, obstetrical, and other medical procedures. Confers with medical professional to determine type and method of anesthetic or sedation to render patient insensible to pain. Records type and amount of anesthesia and patient condition throughout procedure. Positions patient on operating table to maximize patient comfort and surgical accessibility. Informs students and staff of types and methods of anesthesia administration, signs of complications, and emergency methods to counteract reactions.
Yearly Earnings: $54,080
Education: First professional degree
Knowledge: Chemistry; Biology; Medicine and Dentistry; English Language
Abilities: Problem Sensitivity; Time Sharing; Control Precision; Speech Clarity
Skills: Reading Comprehension; Active Listening; Speaking; Science; Critical Thinking; Active Learning; Monitoring; Coordination; Instructing; Problem Identification; Information Gathering; Information Organization; Idea Generation; Idea Evaluation; Implementation Planning; Solution Appraisal; Equipment Selection; Testing; Operation Monitoring; Operation and Control; Troubleshooting; Visioning; Systems Perception; Identification of Key Causes; Judgment and Decision Making; Systems Evaluation
General Work Activities: Getting Information Needed to Do the Job; Monitoring Processes, Material, or Surroundings; Identifying Objects, Actions, and Events; Inspecting Equipment, Structures, or Material; Estimating Needed Characteristics; Judging Qualities of Things, Services, People; Processing Information; Evaluating Information against Standards; Analyzing Data or Information; Making Decisions and Solving Problems; Updating and Using Job-Relevant Knowledge; Controlling Machines and Processes; Interpreting Meaning of Information to Others; Communicating with Other Workers; Establishing and Maintaining Relationships; Assisting and Caring for Others; Developing and Building Teams; Teaching Others; Guiding, Directing and Motivating Subordinates; Coaching and Developing Others; Provide Consultation and Advice to Others; Performing Administrative Activities
Job Characteristics: Objective or Subjective Information; Job-Required Social Interaction; Provide a Service to Others; Take a Position Opposed to Others; Responsible for Others' Health and Safety; Responsibility for Outcomes and Results; Frequency in Conflict Situations; Radiation; Diseases/Infections; Special Uniform; Common Protective or Safety Attire; Consequence of Error; Importance of Being Exact or Accurate; Importance of Being Sure All is Done; Importance of Being Aware of New Events
GOE Group/s: 02.03.01 Medical Sciences: Medicine and Surgery
CIP Program/s: 511401 Medical Clinical Sciences (M.S., Ph.D.); 512903 Anesthesiology Residency; 512910 Critical Care Anesthesiology Residency
Related DOT Job/s: 070.101-010 ANESTHESIOLOGIST

32102J SURGEONS. OOH Title/s: Physicians
Perform surgery to repair injuries; remove or repair diseased organs, bones, or tissue; correct deformities, or improve function in patients. Operates on patient to correct deformities, repair injuries, prevent diseases, or improve or restore patient's functions. Analyzes patient's medical history, medication allergies, physical condition, and examination results to verify operation's necessity and to determine best procedure. Examines patient to provide information on medical condition and patient's surgical risk. Refers patient to medical specialist or other practitioners when necessary. Conducts research to develop and test surgical techniques to improve operating procedures and outcomes. Examines instruments, equipment, and operating room to ensure sterility. Directs and coordinates activities of nurses, assistants, specialists, and other medical staff.
Yearly Earnings: $54,080
Education: First professional degree
Knowledge: Administration and Management; Physics; Chemistry; Biology; Psychology; Medicine and Dentistry; Therapy and Counseling; English Language
Abilities: Written Comprehension; Oral Expression; Written Expression; Fluency of Ideas; Originality; Problem Sensitivity; Deductive Reasoning; Inductive Reasoning; Information Ordering; Category Flexibility; Mathematical Reasoning; Number Facility; Memorization; Speed of Closure; Flexibility of Closure; Perceptual Speed; Spatial Orientation; Visualization; Selective Attention; Time Sharing; Arm-Hand Steadiness; Manual Dexterity; Finger Dexterity; Control Precision; Multilimb Coordination; Response Orientation; Rate Control; Reaction Time; Wrist-Finger Speed; Speed of Limb Movement; Explosive Strength; Dynamic Strength; Trunk Strength; Stamina; Gross Body Equilibrium; Near Vision; Depth Perception; Sound Localization; Speech Clarity
Skills: Reading Comprehension; Active Listening; Writing; Speaking; Science; Critical Thinking; Active Learning; Monitoring; Social Perceptiveness; Coordination; Persuasion; Negotiation; Instructing; Service Orientation; Problem Identification; Information Gathering; Synthesis/Reorganization; Idea Generation; Idea Evaluation; Implementation Planning; Solution Appraisal; Operations Analysis; Equipment Selection; Testing; Operation and Control; Product Inspection; Troubleshooting; Visioning; Systems Perception; Identifying Downstream Consequences; Identification of Key Causes; Judgment and Decision Making; Systems Evaluation; Time Management; Management of Personnel Resources
General Work Activities: Getting Information Needed to Do the Job; Monitoring Processes, Material, or Surroundings; Identifying Objects, Actions, and Events; Inspecting Equipment, Structures, or Material; Judging Qualities of Things, Services, People; Processing Information; Evaluating Information against Standards; Analyzing Data or Information; Making Decisions and Solving Problems; Thinking Creatively; Updating and Using Job-Relevant Knowledge; Developing Objectives and Strategies; Performing General Physical Activities; Implementing Ideas, Programs, etc.; Interpreting Meaning of Information to Others; Communicating with Other Workers; Communicating with Persons Outside Organization; Establishing and Maintaining Relationships; Assisting and Caring for Others; Coordinating Work and Activities of Others; Developing and Building Teams; Guiding, Directing and Motivating Subordinates
Job Characteristics: Objective or Subjective Information; Supervise, Coach, Train Others; Persuade Someone to a Course of Action; Provide

a Service to Others; Take a Position Opposed to Others; Deal with External Customers; Coordinate or Lead Others; Responsible for Others' Health and Safety; Responsibility for Outcomes and Results; Frequency in Conflict Situations; Radiation; Diseases/Infections; Standing; Special Uniform; Common Protective or Safety Attire; Specialized Protective or Safety Attire; Consequence of Error; Frustrating Circumstances; Importance of Being Exact or Accurate; Importance of Being Sure All is Done; Importance of Being Aware of New Events
GOE Group/s: 02.03.01 Medical Sciences: Medicine and Surgery
CIP Program/s: 512912 Critical Care Surgery Residency; 512921 General Surgery Residency; 512923 Hand Surgery Residency; 512942 Orthopedics/Orthopedic Surgery Residency; 512949 Pediatric Orthopedics Residency; 512950 Pediatric Surgery Residency; 512953 Plastic Surgery Residency; 512962 Thoracic Surgery Residency; 512964 Vascular Surgery Residency
Related DOT Job/s: 070.101-094 SURGEON

32102U PATHOLOGISTS. OOH Title/s: Physicians

Research or study the nature, cause, effects, and development of diseases; and determine presence and extent of disease in body tissue, fluids, secretions, and other specimens. Conducts research to gain knowledge of nature, cause, and development of diseases, and resulting structural and functional body changes. Examines, collects tissue or fluid samples, and conducts tests on patient to provide information on patient's disease. Diagnoses nature, cause, and development of disease and resulting changes of patient's body, using results of sample analyses and tests. Performs autopsies to determine nature and extent of disease, cause of death, and effects of treatment. Advises other medical practitioners on nature, cause, and development of diseases. Directs and coordinates activities of nurses, students, and other staff in medical school, hospital, medical examiner's office, or research institute.
Yearly Earnings: $54,080
Education: First professional degree
Knowledge: Administration and Management; Mathematics; Chemistry; Biology; Medicine and Dentistry; Therapy and Counseling; Education and Training; English Language
Abilities: Oral Comprehension; Written Comprehension; Oral Expression; Written Expression; Fluency of Ideas; Originality; Problem Sensitivity; Deductive Reasoning; Inductive Reasoning; Information Ordering; Category Flexibility; Mathematical Reasoning; Memorization; Speed of Closure; Flexibility of Closure; Perceptual Speed; Arm-Hand Steadiness; Manual Dexterity; Finger Dexterity; Control Precision; Multilimb Coordination; Wrist-Finger Speed; Speed of Limb Movement; Near Vision; Visual Color Discrimination
Skills: Reading Comprehension; Writing; Speaking; Mathematics; Science; Critical Thinking; Active Learning; Monitoring; Coordination; Problem Identification; Information Gathering; Information Organization; Synthesis/Reorganization; Idea Generation; Idea Evaluation; Implementation Planning; Visioning; Systems Perception; Identifying Downstream Consequences; Identification of Key Causes; Judgment and Decision Making; Systems Evaluation; Time Management; Management of Personnel Resources
General Work Activities: Getting Information Needed to Do the Job; Monitoring Processes, Material, or Surroundings; Judging Qualities of Things, Services, People; Processing Information; Analyzing Data or Information; Making Decisions and Solving Problems; Scheduling Work and Activities; Interpreting Meaning of Information to Others; Communicating with Other Workers; Communicating with Persons Outside Organization; Coordinating Work and Activities of Others; Guiding, Directing and Motivating Subordinates; Provide Consultation and Advice to Others
Job Characteristics: Supervise, Coach, Train Others; Take a Position Opposed to Others; Coordinate or Lead Others; Frequency in Conflict Situations; Radiation; Diseases/Infections; Hazardous Conditions; Special Uniform; Common Protective or Safety Attire; Consequence of Error; Frustrating Circumstances; Importance of Being Exact or Accurate; Importance of Being Sure All is Done
GOE Group/s: 02.03.01 Medical Sciences: Medicine and Surgery
CIP Program/s: 260701 Zoology, General; 260704 Pathology, Human and Animal; 511401 Medical Clinical Sciences (M.S., Ph.D.); 512906 Chemical Pathology Residency; 512919 Forensic Pathology Residency; 512925 Hematological Pathology Residency; 512935 Neuropathology Residency; 512944 Pathology Residency; 512959 Radioisotopic Pathology Residency
Related DOT Job/s: 070.061-010 PATHOLOGIST

32105A ORAL PATHOLOGISTS. OOH Title/s: Dentists

Research or study nature, cause, effects, and development of diseases associated with mouth. Examine oral tissue specimens of patients to determine pathological conditions such as tumors and lesions. Examines oral tissue specimen to determine pathological conditions, such as tumors and lesions, using microscope and other laboratory equipment. Determines nature and cause of oral condition. Evaluates previous and future development of oral condition. Examines patient's mouth, jaw, face, and associated areas. Obtains oral tissue specimen from patient, using medical instruments. Discusses diagnosis with patient and referring practitioner.
Yearly Earnings: $50,076
Education: First professional degree
Knowledge: Chemistry; Biology; Psychology; Medicine and Dentistry; Therapy and Counseling; English Language
Abilities: Problem Sensitivity; Arm-Hand Steadiness; Finger Dexterity
Skills: Reading Comprehension; Active Listening; Writing; Speaking; Mathematics; Science; Critical Thinking; Active Learning; Learning Strategies; Monitoring; Persuasion; Service Orientation; Problem Identification; Information Gathering; Information Organization; Synthesis/Reorganization; Idea Generation; Idea Evaluation; Implementation Planning; Solution Appraisal; Equipment Selection; Identification of Key Causes; Judgment and Decision Making
General Work Activities: Getting Information Needed to Do the Job; Monitoring Processes, Material, or Surroundings; Judging Qualities of Things, Services, People; Processing Information; Analyzing Data or Information; Making Decisions and Solving Problems; Updating and Using Job-Relevant Knowledge; Interpreting Meaning of Information to Others; Establishing and Maintaining Relationships; Assisting and Caring for Others; Performing for or Working with Public; Provide Consultation and Advice to Others
Job Characteristics: Responsible for Others' Health and Safety; Diseases/Infections; Special Uniform; Importance of Being Exact or Accurate; Importance of Being Sure All is Done
GOE Group/s: 02.03.02 Medical Sciences: Dentistry
CIP Program/s: 512804 Oral Pathology Specialty
Related DOT Job/s: 072.061-010 ORAL PATHOLOGIST

32105B DENTISTS. OOH Title/s: Dentists

Diagnose, prevent, and treat problems of the teeth and tissue of the mouth. Exclude orthodontists; prosthodontists; oral and maxillofacial surgeons; and oral pathologists. Fills, extracts, and replaces teeth, using rotary and hand instruments, dental appliances, medications, and surgical implements. Applies fluoride and sealants to teeth. Treats exposure of pulp by pulp capping, removal of pulp from pulp chamber, or root canal, using dental instruments. Treats infected root canal and related tissues. Fills pulp chamber and canal with endodontic materials. Eliminates irritating margins of fillings and corrects occlusions, using dental instruments. Examines teeth, gums, and related tissues to determine condition, using dental instruments, X

ray, and other diagnostic equipment. Formulates plan of treatment for patient's teeth and mouth tissue. Removes pathologic tissue or diseased tissue using surgical instruments. Restores natural color of teeth by bleaching, cleaning, and polishing. Analyzes and evaluates dental needs to determine changes and trends in patterns of dental disease. Counsels and advises patients about growth and development of dental problems and preventive oral health care services. Fabricates prosthodontic appliances, such as space maintainers, bridges, dentures, and obturating appliances. Fits and adjusts prosthodontic appliances in patient's mouth. Produces and evaluates dental health educational materials. Plans, organizes, and maintains dental health programs.
Yearly Earnings: $50,076
Education: First professional degree
Knowledge: Chemistry; Biology; Medicine and Dentistry; English Language
Abilities: Oral Expression; Problem Sensitivity; Arm-Hand Steadiness; Manual Dexterity; Finger Dexterity; Control Precision
Skills: Reading Comprehension; Science; Critical Thinking; Active Learning; Learning Strategies; Monitoring; Service Orientation; Problem Identification; Idea Generation; Idea Evaluation; Implementation Planning; Solution Appraisal; Judgment and Decision Making; Management of Financial Resources
General Work Activities: Monitoring Processes, Material, or Surroundings; Making Decisions and Solving Problems; Updating and Using Job-Relevant Knowledge; Handling and Moving Objects; Implementing Ideas, Programs, etc.; Establishing and Maintaining Relationships; Assisting and Caring for Others
Job Characteristics: Job-Required Social Interaction; Provide a Service to Others; Deal with External Customers; Responsible for Others' Health and Safety; Deal with Unpleasant or Angry People; Radiation; Diseases/Infections; Special Uniform; Common Protective or Safety Attire; Importance of Being Exact or Accurate; Importance of Being Sure All is Done
GOE Group/s: 02.03.02 Medical Sciences: Dentistry
CIP Program/s: 510401 Dentistry (D.D.S., D.M.D.); 510501 Dental Clinical Sciences/Graduate Dentistry (M.S., Ph.D.); 512802 Dental Public Health Specialty; 512803 Endodontics Specialty; 512806 Pedodontics Specialty; 512807 Periodontics Specialty
Related DOT Job/s: 072.101-010 DENTIST; 072.101-014 ENDODONTIST; 072.101-026 PEDIATRIC DENTIST; 072.101-030 PERIODONTIST; 072.101-038 PUBLIC-HEALTH DENTIST

32105D ORTHODONTISTS. OOH Title/s: Dentists

Examine, diagnose, and treat dental malocclusions and oral cavity anomalies. Design and fabricate appliances to realign teeth and jaws to produce and maintain normal function and to improve appearance. Diagnoses teeth and jaw or other dental-facial abnormalities. Plans treatment, using cephalometric, height, and weight records, dental X rays and front and lateral dental photographs. Examines patient's mouth to determine position of teeth and jaw development. Fits dental appliances in patient's mouth to alter position and relationship of teeth and jaws and to realign teeth. Adjusts dental appliances periodically to produce and maintain normal function. Designs and fabricates appliances, such as space maintainers, retainers, and labial and lingual arch wires.
Yearly Earnings: $50,076
Education: First professional degree
Knowledge: Customer and Personal Service; Chemistry; Biology; Medicine and Dentistry; Therapy and Counseling
Abilities: Arm-Hand Steadiness; Manual Dexterity; Finger Dexterity; Control Precision
Skills: Reading Comprehension; Active Listening; Science; Critical Thinking; Active Learning; Learning Strategies; Monitoring; Service Orientation; Problem Identification; Synthesis/Reorganization; Idea Generation; Idea Evaluation; Implementation Planning; Solution Appraisal; Operations Analysis; Technology Design; Equipment Selection; Installation; Identification of Key Causes; Judgment and Decision Making; Management of Financial Resources
General Work Activities: Getting Information Needed to Do the Job; Monitoring Processes, Material, or Surroundings; Identifying Objects, Actions, and Events; Making Decisions and Solving Problems; Updating and Using Job-Relevant Knowledge; Developing Objectives and Strategies; Handling and Moving Objects; Drafting and Specifying Technical Devices, etc.; Establishing and Maintaining Relationships; Assisting and Caring for Others; Performing for or Working with Public; Teaching Others; Guiding, Directing and Motivating Subordinates; Coaching and Developing Others; Staffing Organizational Units; Monitoring and Controlling Resources
Job Characteristics: Provide a Service to Others; Radiation; Diseases/Infections; Special Uniform; Common Protective or Safety Attire; Importance of Being Exact or Accurate
GOE Group/s: 02.03.02 Medical Sciences: Dentistry
CIP Program/s: 512805 Orthodontics Specialty
Related DOT Job/s: 072.101-022 ORTHODONTIST

32105F PROSTHODONTISTS. OOH Title/s: Dentists

Construct oral prostheses to replace missing teeth and other oral structures; to correct natural and acquired deformation of mouth and jaws; to restore and maintain oral function, such as chewing and speaking; and to improve appearance. Designs and fabricates dental prostheses. Corrects natural and acquired deformation of mouth and jaws through use of prosthetic appliances. Records physiologic position of jaws to determine shape and size of dental prostheses, using face bows, dental articulators, and recording devices. Adjusts prostheses to fit patient. Replaces missing teeth and associated oral structures with artificial teeth to improve chewing, speech, and appearance.
Yearly Earnings: $50,076
Education: First professional degree
Knowledge: Chemistry; Biology; Medicine and Dentistry
Abilities: Finger Dexterity
Skills: Reading Comprehension; Mathematics; Science; Critical Thinking; Active Learning; Learning Strategies; Service Orientation; Problem Identification; Synthesis/Reorganization; Solution Appraisal; Operations Analysis; Technology Design; Equipment Selection; Product Inspection; Judgment and Decision Making
General Work Activities: Making Decisions and Solving Problems; Updating and Using Job-Relevant Knowledge; Documenting/Recording Information; Establishing and Maintaining Relationships; Assisting and Caring for Others
Job Characteristics: Special Uniform; Importance of Being Exact or Accurate; Importance of Being Sure All is Done
GOE Group/s: 02.03.02 Medical Sciences: Dentistry
CIP Program/s: 512808 Prosthodontics Specialty
Related DOT Job/s: 072.101-034 PROSTHODONTIST

32105G ORAL AND MAXILLOFACIAL SURGEONS. OOH Title/s: Dentists

Perform surgery on mouth, jaws, and related head and neck structure to execute difficult and multiple extractions of teeth, to remove tumors and other abnormal growths; to correct abnormal jaw relations by mandibular or maxillary revision; to prepare mouth for insertion of dental prosthesis; or to treat fractured jaws. Executes difficult and multiple extraction of teeth. Removes tumors and other abnormal growths, using surgical instruments. Performs preprosthetic surgery to prepare mouth for insertion of dental prosthesis. Corrects abnormal jaw relations by mandibular or

maxillary revision. Treats fractures of jaws. Administers general and local anesthetics.
Yearly Earnings: $50,076
Education: First professional degree
Knowledge: Chemistry; Biology; Psychology; Medicine and Dentistry; Therapy and Counseling; English Language
Abilities: Problem Sensitivity; Visualization; Arm-Hand Steadiness; Manual Dexterity; Finger Dexterity; Control Precision; Reaction Time; Near Vision
Skills: Reading Comprehension; Active Listening; Writing; Speaking; Mathematics; Science; Critical Thinking; Active Learning; Learning Strategies; Monitoring; Service Orientation; Problem Identification; Idea Generation; Idea Evaluation; Implementation Planning; Solution Appraisal; Visioning; Identification of Key Causes; Judgment and Decision Making
General Work Activities: Getting Information Needed to Do the Job; Monitoring Processes, Material, or Surroundings; Identifying Objects, Actions, and Events; Estimating Needed Characteristics; Judging Qualities of Things, Services, People; Analyzing Data or Information; Making Decisions and Solving Problems; Updating and Using Job-Relevant Knowledge; Organizing, Planning, and Prioritizing; Implementing Ideas, Programs, etc.; Assisting and Caring for Others; Provide Consultation and Advice to Others
Job Characteristics: Job-Required Social Interaction; Provide a Service to Others; Deal with External Customers; Responsible for Others' Health and Safety; Diseases/Infections; Special Uniform; Common Protective or Safety Attire; Consequence of Error; Importance of Being Exact or Accurate; Importance of Being Sure All is Done
GOE Group/s: 02.03.02 Medical Sciences: Dentistry
CIP Program/s: 512801 Dental/Oral Surgery Specialty
Related DOT Job/s: 072.101-018 ORAL AND MAXILLOFACIAL SURGEON

32108 OPTOMETRISTS. OOH Title/s: Optometrists

Diagnose, manage, and treat conditions and diseases of the human eye and visual system. Examine eyes to determine visual efficiency and performance by use of instruments and observation. Prescribe corrective procedures. Prescribes eyeglasses, contact lenses, and other vision aids or therapeutic procedures to correct or conserve vision. Examines eyes to determine visual acuity and perception and to diagnose diseases and other abnormalities, such as glaucoma and color blindness. Consults with and refers patients to ophthalmologist or other health care practitioner if additional medical treatment is determined necessary. Prescribes medications to treat eye diseases if state laws permit. Conducts research, instructs in college or university, acts as consultant, or works in public health field.
Yearly Earnings: $50,076
Education: First professional degree
Knowledge: Chemistry; Biology; Medicine and Dentistry; Therapy and Counseling; Education and Training; Foreign Language
Abilities: Oral Comprehension; Written Comprehension; Oral Expression; Written Expression; Problem Sensitivity; Deductive Reasoning; Inductive Reasoning; Flexibility of Closure; Near Vision
Skills: Reading Comprehension; Active Listening; Writing; Speaking; Mathematics; Science; Learning Strategies; Monitoring; Social Perceptiveness; Instructing; Synthesis/Reorganization; Idea Evaluation; Solution Appraisal; Technology Design
General Work Activities: Getting Information Needed to Do the Job; Monitoring Processes, Material, or Surroundings; Processing Information; Evaluating Information against Standards; Analyzing Data or Information; Making Decisions and Solving Problems; Updating and Using Job-Relevant Knowledge; Organizing, Planning, and Prioritizing; Operating Vehicles or Equipment; Implementing Ideas, Programs, etc.; Interpreting Meaning of Information to Others; Communicating with Persons Outside Organization; Establishing and Maintaining Relationships; Assisting and Caring for Others; Performing for or Working with Public; Teaching Others; Guiding, Directing and Motivating Subordinates; Coaching and Developing Others; Provide Consultation and Advice to Others
Job Characteristics: Provide a Service to Others; Deal with External Customers; Special Uniform; Specialized Protective or Safety Attire; Importance of Being Exact or Accurate; Importance of Being Sure All is Done
GOE Group/s: 02.03.04 Medical Sciences: Health Specialties
CIP Program/s: 511701 Optometry (O.D.)
Related DOT Job/s: 079.101-018 OPTOMETRIST

32111 PODIATRISTS. OOH Title/s: Podiatrists

Diagnose and treat diseases and deformities of the human foot. Diagnoses ailments, such as tumors, ulcers, fractures, skin or nail diseases, and deformities, utilizing urinalysis, blood tests, and X rays. Treats conditions such as corns, calluses, ingrown nails, tumors, shortened tendons, bunions, cysts, and abscesses by surgical methods. Corrects deformities by means of plaster casts and strapping. Treats bone, muscle, and joint disorders. Treats deformities by mechanical and electrical methods, such as whirlpool or paraffin baths and shortwave and low-voltage currents. Prescribes corrective footwear. Prescribes drugs. Makes and fits prosthetic appliances. Performs surgery. Treats children's foot diseases. Advises patients concerning continued treatment of disorders and foot care to prevent recurrence of disorders. Refers patients to physician when symptoms indicative of systemic disorders, such as arthritis or diabetes, are observed in feet and legs.
Yearly Earnings: $50,076
Education: First professional degree
Knowledge: Customer and Personal Service; Physics; Chemistry; Biology; Psychology; Sociology and Anthropology; Medicine and Dentistry; Therapy and Counseling; English Language; Philosophy and Theology
Abilities: Fluency of Ideas; Problem Sensitivity; Deductive Reasoning; Inductive Reasoning; Memorization; Speed of Closure; Flexibility of Closure; Perceptual Speed; Selective Attention; Time Sharing; Arm-Hand Steadiness; Manual Dexterity; Finger Dexterity; Control Precision; Response Orientation; Reaction Time; Wrist-Finger Speed; Speed of Limb Movement; Near Vision; Night Vision; Depth Perception; Glare Sensitivity
Skills: Reading Comprehension; Active Listening; Speaking; Science; Critical Thinking; Active Learning; Learning Strategies; Monitoring; Social Perceptiveness; Persuasion; Instructing; Service Orientation; Problem Identification; Information Gathering; Information Organization; Synthesis/Reorganization; Idea Generation; Idea Evaluation; Implementation Planning; Solution Appraisal; Technology Design; Equipment Selection; Visioning; Systems Perception; Identifying Downstream Consequences; Identification of Key Causes; Judgment and Decision Making; Systems Evaluation; Time Management; Management of Personnel Resources
General Work Activities: Getting Information Needed to Do the Job; Monitoring Processes, Material, or Surroundings; Identifying Objects, Actions, and Events; Judging Qualities of Things, Services, People; Processing Information; Evaluating Information against Standards; Analyzing Data or Information; Making Decisions and Solving Problems; Updating and Using Job-Relevant Knowledge; Organizing, Planning, and Prioritizing; Implementing Ideas, Programs, etc.; Interpreting Meaning of Information to Others; Communicating with Persons Outside Organization; Establishing and Maintaining Relationships; Assisting and Caring for Others; Performing for or Working with Public; Provide Consultation and Advice to Others
Job Characteristics: Job-Required Social Interaction; Persuade Someone to a Course of Action; Provide a Service to Others; Take a

Position Opposed to Others; Deal with External Customers; Responsible for Others' Health and Safety; Radiation; Diseases/Infections; Special Uniform; Common Protective or Safety Attire; Consequence of Error; Importance of Being Exact or Accurate; Importance of Being Sure All is Done
GOE Group/s: 02.03.01 Medical Sciences: Medicine and Surgery
CIP Program/s: 512101 Podiatry (D.P.M., D.P., Pod.D.)
Related DOT Job/s: 079.101-022 PODIATRIST

32113 CHIROPRACTORS. OOH Title/s: Chiropractors
Adjust spinal column and other articulations of the body to prevent disease and correct abnormalities of the human body believed to be caused by interference with the nervous system. Examine patient to determine nature and extent of disorder. Manipulate spine or other involved area. May utilize supplementary measures such as exercise, rest, water, light, heat, and nutritional therapy. Examines patient to determine nature and extent of disorder. Manipulates spinal column and other extremities to adjust, align, or correct abnormalities caused by neurologic and kinetic articular dysfunction. Utilizes supplementary measures, such as exercise, rest, water, light, heat, and nutritional therapy. Performs diagnostic procedures, including physical, neurologic, and orthopedic examinations, and laboratory tests, using instruments and equipment such as X ray machine and electrocardiograph.
Yearly Earnings: $50,076
Education: First professional degree
Knowledge: Customer and Personal Service; Physics; Chemistry; Biology; Psychology; Sociology and Anthropology; Medicine and Dentistry; Therapy and Counseling; English Language; Philosophy and Theology
Abilities: Problem Sensitivity; Deductive Reasoning; Inductive Reasoning; Perceptual Speed; Manual Dexterity; Finger Dexterity; Multilimb Coordination; Wrist-Finger Speed; Speed of Limb Movement; Dynamic Strength
Skills: Reading Comprehension; Active Listening; Speaking; Science; Critical Thinking; Active Learning; Learning Strategies; Monitoring; Social Perceptiveness; Persuasion; Instructing; Service Orientation; Problem Identification; Information Gathering; Information Organization; Synthesis/Reorganization; Idea Generation; Idea Evaluation; Implementation Planning; Solution Appraisal; Equipment Selection; Visioning; Systems Perception; Identifying Downstream Consequences; Identification of Key Causes; Judgment and Decision Making; Systems Evaluation; Time Management
General Work Activities: Getting Information Needed to Do the Job; Monitoring Processes, Material, or Surroundings; Processing Information; Analyzing Data or Information; Making Decisions and Solving Problems; Updating and Using Job-Relevant Knowledge; Developing Objectives and Strategies; Handling and Moving Objects; Establishing and Maintaining Relationships; Assisting and Caring for Others; Performing for or Working with Public
Job Characteristics: Objective or Subjective Information; Job-Required Social Interaction; Persuade Someone to a Course of Action; Provide a Service to Others; Take a Position Opposed to Others; Deal with External Customers; Responsible for Others' Health and Safety; Deal with Unpleasant or Angry People; Radiation; Diseases/Infections; Bending or Twisting the Body; Special Uniform; Consequence of Error
GOE Group/s: 02.03.04 Medical Sciences: Health Specialties
CIP Program/s: 510101 Chiropractic (D.C., D.C.M.)
Related DOT Job/s: 079.101-010 CHIROPRACTOR

32114A VETERINARY PATHOLOGISTS. OOH Title/s: Veterinarians
Study nature, cause, and development of animal diseases; form and structure of animals; or drugs related to veterinary medicine. Performs biopsies, and tests and analyzes body tissue and fluids to diagnose presence, source, and stage of disease in animals. Investigates efficiency of vaccines, antigens, antibiotics, and other materials in prevention, diagnosis, and cure of animal diseases. Studies drugs, including material medical and therapeutics, as related to veterinary medicine. Conducts research on animal parasites in domestic animals to determine control and preventive measures, utilizing chemicals, heat, electricity, and methods. Studies factors influencing existence and spread of diseases among humans and animals, particularly those diseases transmissible from animals to humans. Conducts further research to expand scope of findings, or recommends treatment to consulting veterinary personnel. Identifies laboratory cultures of micro-organisms taken from diseased animals by microscopic examination and bacteriological tests. Tests virulence of pathogenic organisms by observing effects of inoculations on laboratory and other animals. Studies form and structure of animals, both gross and microscopic. Studies function and mechanism of systems and organs in healthy and diseased animals. Prepares laboratory cultures of micro-organisms taken from body fluids and tissues of diseased animals for additional study. Directs activities of veterinary pathology department in educational institution or industrial establishment.
Yearly Earnings: $50,076
Education: First professional degree
Knowledge: Administration and Management; Food Production; Mathematics; Chemistry; Biology; Medicine and Dentistry; Therapy and Counseling; Education and Training; English Language; Philosophy and Theology; Public Safety and Security
Abilities: Oral Comprehension; Written Comprehension; Oral Expression; Written Expression; Fluency of Ideas; Originality; Problem Sensitivity; Deductive Reasoning; Inductive Reasoning; Information Ordering; Category Flexibility; Memorization; Speed of Closure; Flexibility of Closure; Perceptual Speed; Finger Dexterity; Control Precision; Near Vision
Skills: Reading Comprehension; Active Listening; Writing; Speaking; Mathematics; Science; Critical Thinking; Active Learning; Learning Strategies; Monitoring; Coordination; Persuasion; Instructing; Problem Identification; Information Gathering; Information Organization; Synthesis/Reorganization; Idea Generation; Idea Evaluation; Implementation Planning; Solution Appraisal; Equipment Selection; Programming; Testing; Product Inspection; Visioning; Systems Perception; Identifying Downstream Consequences; Identification of Key Causes; Judgment and Decision Making; Systems Evaluation; Time Management; Management of Material Resources; Management of Personnel Resources
General Work Activities: Getting Information Needed to Do the Job; Monitoring Processes, Material, or Surroundings; Identifying Objects, Actions, and Events; Estimating Needed Characteristics; Judging Qualities of Things, Services, People; Processing Information; Evaluating Information against Standards; Analyzing Data or Information; Making Decisions and Solving Problems; Thinking Creatively; Updating and Using Job-Relevant Knowledge; Developing Objectives and Strategies; Scheduling Work and Activities; Organizing, Planning, and Prioritizing; Implementing Ideas, Programs, etc.; Documenting/Recording Information; Interpreting Meaning of Information to Others; Communicating with Other Workers; Communicating with Persons Outside Organization; Coordinating Work and Activities of Others; Developing and Building Teams; Teaching Others; Guiding, Directing and Motivating Subordinates; Coaching and Developing Others; Provide Consultation and Advice to Others
Job Characteristics: Objective or Subjective Information; Frequency in Conflict Situations; Contaminants; Radiation; Diseases/Infections; Hazardous Situations; Special Uniform; Common Protective or Safety Attire; Consequence of Error; Frustrating Circumstances; Importance of Being Exact or Accurate; Importance of Being Sure All is Done

GOE Group/s: 02.02.01 Life Sciences: Animal Specialization
CIP Program/s: 512401 Veterinary Medicine (D.V.M.); 513007 Veterinary Microbiology; 513010 Veterinary Pathology; 513012 Veterinary Preventive Medicine
Related DOT Job/s: 073.061-014 VETERINARY ANATOMIST; 073.061-018 VETERINARY MICROBIOLOGIST; 073.061-022 VETERINARY EPIDEMIOLOGIST; 073.061-026 VETERINARY PARASITOLOGIST; 073.061-030 VETERINARY PATHOLOGIST; 073.061-034 VETERINARY PHARMACOLOGIST; 073.061-038 VETERINARY PHYSIOLOGIST

32114B VETERINARIANS. OOH Title/s: Veterinarians

Diagnose and treat medical problems in animals. Exclude veterinary inspectors and veterinary pathologists. Examines animal to determine nature of disease or injury, and treats animal surgically or medically. Inspects and tests horses, sheep, poultry flocks, and other animals for diseases, and inoculates animals against various diseases, including rabies. Examines laboratory animals to detect indications of disease or injury, and treats animals to prevent spread of disease. Conducts postmortem studies and analyzes results to determine cause of death. Establishes and conducts quarantine and testing procedures for incoming animals to prevent spread of disease and compliance with governmental regulations. Inspects housing and advises animal owners regarding sanitary measures, feeding, and general care to promote health of animals. Consults with veterinarians in general practice seeking advice in treatment of exotic animals. Participates in research projects, plans procedures, and selects animals for scientific research based on knowledge of species and research principles. Ensures compliance with regulations governing humane and ethical treatment of animals used in scientific research. Oversees activities concerned with feeding, care, and maintenance of animal quarters to ensure compliance with laboratory regulations. Participates in planning and executing nutrition and reproduction programs for animals, particularly animals on endangered species list. Trains zoo personnel in handling and care of animals. Exchanges information with zoos and aquariums concerning care, transfer, sale, or trade of animals to maintain all-species nationwide inventory. Teaches or conducts research in universities or in commercial setting.
Yearly Earnings: $50,076
Education: First professional degree
Knowledge: Mathematics; Chemistry; Biology; Psychology; Medicine and Dentistry; Therapy and Counseling; Education and Training; English Language; Philosophy and Theology; Public Safety and Security
Abilities: Oral Comprehension; Written Comprehension; Oral Expression; Written Expression; Fluency of Ideas; Originality; Problem Sensitivity; Deductive Reasoning; Inductive Reasoning; Information Ordering; Category Flexibility; Memorization; Speed of Closure; Flexibility of Closure; Perceptual Speed; Selective Attention; Time Sharing; Arm-Hand Steadiness; Manual Dexterity; Finger Dexterity; Control Precision; Multilimb Coordination; Response Orientation; Rate Control; Wrist-Finger Speed; Speed of Limb Movement; Near Vision; Visual Color Discrimination; Glare Sensitivity; Hearing Sensitivity; Speech Clarity
Skills: Reading Comprehension; Active Listening; Writing; Speaking; Mathematics; Science; Critical Thinking; Active Learning; Learning Strategies; Monitoring; Social Perceptiveness; Coordination; Persuasion; Negotiation; Instructing; Problem Identification; Information Gathering; Information Organization; Synthesis/Reorganization; Idea Generation; Idea Evaluation; Implementation Planning; Solution Appraisal; Operations Analysis; Equipment Selection; Testing; Visioning; Systems Perception; Identifying Downstream Consequences; Identification of Key Causes; Judgment and Decision Making; Systems Evaluation; Time Management; Management of Material Resources; Management of Personnel Resources
General Work Activities: Getting Information Needed to Do the Job; Monitoring Processes, Material, or Surroundings; Identifying Objects, Actions, and Events; Processing Information; Evaluating Information against Standards; Analyzing Data or Information; Making Decisions and Solving Problems; Thinking Creatively; Updating and Using Job-Relevant Knowledge; Developing Objectives and Strategies; Scheduling Work and Activities; Organizing, Planning, and Prioritizing; Implementing Ideas, Programs, etc.; Interpreting Meaning of Information to Others; Communicating with Other Workers; Communicating with Persons Outside Organization; Establishing and Maintaining Relationships; Assisting and Caring for Others; Performing for or Working with Public; Coordinating Work and Activities of Others; Teaching Others; Guiding, Directing and Motivating Subordinates; Coaching and Developing Others; Provide Consultation and Advice to Others; Monitoring and Controlling Resources
Job Characteristics: Persuade Someone to a Course of Action; Provide a Service to Others; Deal with External Customers; Coordinate or Lead Others; Responsible for Others' Health and Safety; Responsibility for Outcomes and Results; Frequency in Conflict Situations; Deal with Unpleasant or Angry People; Contaminants; Radiation; Diseases/Infections; Hazardous Conditions; Hazardous Situations; Kneeling, Crouching, or Crawling; Special Uniform; Common Protective or Safety Attire; Consequence of Error; Frustrating Circumstances
GOE Group/s: 02.02.01 Life Sciences: Animal Specialization; 02.03.03 Medical Sciences: Veterinary Medicine
CIP Program/s: 512401 Veterinary Medicine (D.V.M.); 513001 Veterinary Anesthesiology; 513002 Veterinary Dentistry; 513003 Veterinary Dermatology; 513004 Veterinary Emergency and Critical Care Medicine; 513005 Veterinary Internal Medicine; 513006 Laboratory Animal Medicine; 513008 Veterinary Nutrition; 513009 Veterinary Ophthalmology; 513011 Veterinary Practice; 513013 Veterinary Radiology; 513014 Veterinary Surgery; 513015 Theriogenology; 513016 Veterinary Toxicology; 513017 Zoological Medicine
Related DOT Job/s: . **Related DOT Jobs:** 073.061-010 VETERINARIAN, LABORATORY ANIMAL CARE; 073.101-010 VETERINARIAN; 073.101-014 VETERINARIAN, POULTRY; 073.101-018 ZOO VETERINARIAN

32114C VETERINARY INSPECTORS. OOH Title/s: Veterinarians

Inspect animals for presence of disease in facilities such as laboratories, livestock sites, and livestock slaughter or meat-processing facilities. Examines animals used in production process to determine presence of disease. Examines animal and carcass before and after slaughtering to detect evidence of disease or other abnormal conditions. Tests animals and submits specimens of tissue and other parts for laboratory analysis. Inspects processing areas where livestock and poultry are slaughtered and processed to ensure compliance with governmental standards. Reports existence of disease conditions to state and federal authorities. Inspects facilities engaged in processing milk and milk products to ensure compliance with governmental standards. Inspects facilities where serums and other products used in treatment of animals are manufactured to ensure governmental standards are maintained. Institutes and enforces quarantine or other regulations governing import, export, and interstate movement of livestock. Determines that ingredients used in processing and marketing meat and meat products comply with governmental standards of purity and grading. Advises livestock owners of economic aspects of disease eradication. Advises consumers and public health officials of implications of diseases transmissible from animals to humans.
Yearly Earnings: $50,076
Education: First professional degree
Knowledge: Economics and Accounting; Production and Processing; Food Production; Chemistry; Biology; Geography; Medicine and Den-

tistry; English Language; Philosophy and Theology; Public Safety and Security; Law, Government, and Jurisprudence
Abilities: Problem Sensitivity; Inductive Reasoning; Speed of Closure; Flexibility of Closure; Perceptual Speed; Visual Color Discrimination; Auditory Attention
Skills: Reading Comprehension; Active Listening; Writing; Speaking; Science; Critical Thinking; Active Learning; Learning Strategies; Monitoring; Persuasion; Problem Identification; Information Gathering; Information Organization; Synthesis/Reorganization; Idea Generation; Idea Evaluation; Implementation Planning; Solution Appraisal; Testing; Product Inspection; Visioning; Systems Perception; Identifying Downstream Consequences; Identification of Key Causes; Judgment and Decision Making; Systems Evaluation; Time Management
General Work Activities: Getting Information Needed to Do the Job; Monitoring Processes, Material, or Surroundings; Identifying Objects, Actions, and Events; Inspecting Equipment, Structures, or Material; Estimating Needed Characteristics; Processing Information; Documenting/Recording Information; Interpreting Meaning of Information to Others; Communicating with Other Workers; Communicating with Persons Outside Organization; Performing for or Working with Public; Teaching Others; Provide Consultation and Advice to Others
Job Characteristics: Persuade Someone to a Course of Action; Provide a Service to Others; Take a Position Opposed to Others; Deal with External Customers; Responsible for Others' Health and Safety; Frequency in Conflict Situations; Deal with Unpleasant or Angry People; Very Hot; Extremely Bright or Inadequate Lighting; Contaminants; Cramped Work Space, Awkward Positions; Diseases/Infections; Hazardous Situations; Walking or Running; Kneeling, Crouching, or Crawling; Common Protective or Safety Attire; Consequence of Error
GOE Group/s: 02.03.03 Medical Sciences: Veterinary Medicine
CIP Program/s: 512401 Veterinary Medicine (D.V.M.)
Related DOT Job/s: 073.161-010 VETERINARY LIVESTOCK INSPECTOR; 073.261-010 VETERINARY VIRUS-SERUM INSPECTOR; 073.264-010 VETERINARY MEAT-INSPECTOR

32199 ALL OTHER HEALTH DIAGNOSING AND TREATING PRACTITIONERS. OOH Title/s: Health Diagnosing and Treating Occupations

All other health diagnosing and treating practitioners not classified separately above.
Yearly Earnings: $26,156
Education: Degree varies
GOE Group/s: 02.03.04 Medical Sciences: Health Specialties; 10.02.02 Nursing, Therapy, and Specialized Teaching Services: Therapy and Rehabilitation
CIP Program/s: 512303 Hypnotherapy; 512701 Acupuncture and Oriental Medicine; 512704 Naturopathic Medicine
Related DOT Job/s: 078.384-010 CEPHALOMETRIC ANALYST; 079.101-014 DOCTOR, NATUROPATHIC; 079.157-010 HYPNOTHERAPIST; 079.271-010 ACUPUNCTURIST; 079.271-014 ACUPRESSURIST; 354.377-010 BIRTH ATTENDANT; 354.677-010 FIRST-AID ATTENDANT

Medical Therapists

32302 RESPIRATORY THERAPISTS. OOH Title/s: Respiratory Therapists

Set up and operate various types of equipment, such as ventilators, oxygen tents, resuscitators, and incubators, to administer oxygen and other gases to patients. Sets up and operates devices, such as mechanical ventilators, therapeutic gas administration apparatus, environmental control systems, and aerosol generators. Operates equipment to administer medicinal gases and aerosol drugs to patients following specified parameters of treatment. Reads prescription, measures arterial blood gases, and reviews patient information to assess patient condition. Monitors patient's physiological responses to therapy, such as vital signs, arterial blood gases, and blood chemistry changes. Performs pulmonary function and adjusts equipment to obtain optimum results to therapy. Inspects and tests respiratory therapy equipment to ensure equipment is functioning safely and efficiently. Determines requirements for treatment, such as type and duration of therapy, and medication and dosages. Determines most suitable method of administering inhalants, precautions to be observed, and potential modifications needed, compatible with physician's orders. Performs bronchopulmonary drainage and assists patient in performing breathing exercises. Consults with physician in event of adverse reactions. Maintains patient's chart which contains pertinent identification and therapy information. Orders repairs when necessary. Demonstrates respiratory care procedures to trainees and other health care personnel.
Yearly Earnings: $33,332
Education: Associate degree
Knowledge: Chemistry; Biology; Psychology; Medicine and Dentistry; Therapy and Counseling; Education and Training
Skills: Reading Comprehension; Active Listening; Speaking; Science; Critical Thinking; Active Learning; Learning Strategies; Monitoring; Social Perceptiveness; Instructing; Service Orientation; Problem Identification; Solution Appraisal; Equipment Selection; Testing; Operation Monitoring; Operation and Control; Identification of Key Causes; Judgment and Decision Making
General Work Activities: Identifying Objects, Actions, and Events; Establishing and Maintaining Relationships; Assisting and Caring for Others
Job Characteristics: Provide a Service to Others; Deal with External Customers; Responsible for Others' Health and Safety; Deal with Unpleasant or Angry People; Diseases/Infections; Special Uniform; Consequence of Error; Importance of Being Exact or Accurate; Importance of Being Sure All is Done
GOE Group/s: 10.02.02 Nursing, Therapy, and Specialized Teaching Services: Therapy and Rehabilitation
CIP Program/s: 510908 Respiratory Therapy Technician
Related DOT Job/s: 076.361-014 RESPIRATORY THERAPIST

32305 OCCUPATIONAL THERAPISTS. OOH Title/s: Occupational Therapists

Plan, organize, and participate in medically-oriented occupational programs in hospital or similar institution to rehabilitate patients who are physically or mentally ill. Plans, organizes, and conducts occupational therapy program in hospital, institutional, or community setting. Plans programs and social activities to help patients learn work skills and adjust to handicaps. Selects activities which will help individual learn work skills within limits of individual's mental and physical capabilities. Teaches individual skills and techniques required for participation in activities, and evaluates individual's progress. Recommends changes in individual's work or living environment, consistent with needs and capabilities. Consults with rehabilitation team to select activity programs and coordinate occupational therapy with other therapeutic activities. Arranges salaried employment for mentally ill patients within hospital environment. Lays out materials for individual's use, and cleans and repairs tools after therapy sessions. Requisitions supplies and equipment, and designs and constructs special equipment, such as splints and braces. Trains nurses and other medical staff in therapy techniques and objectives. Processes payroll, distributes salaries, and completes and maintains necessary records.
Yearly Earnings: $33,332
Education: Bachelor's degree

Knowledge: Administration and Management; Clerical; Economics and Accounting; Customer and Personal Service; Personnel and Human Resources; Biology; Psychology; Sociology and Anthropology; Medicine and Dentistry; Therapy and Counseling; Education and Training; Foreign Language
Skills: Active Listening; Speaking; Learning Strategies; Social Perceptiveness; Coordination; Instructing; Service Orientation; Idea Generation; Implementation Planning; Solution Appraisal; Technology Design; Equipment Selection; Time Management; Management of Material Resources
General Work Activities: Getting Information Needed to Do the Job; Monitoring Processes, Material, or Surroundings; Identifying Objects, Actions, and Events; Analyzing Data or Information; Making Decisions and Solving Problems; Updating and Using Job-Relevant Knowledge; Developing Objectives and Strategies; Organizing, Planning, and Prioritizing; Interpreting Meaning of Information to Others; Communicating with Other Workers; Establishing and Maintaining Relationships; Assisting and Caring for Others; Performing for or Working with Public; Developing and Building Teams; Teaching Others; Guiding, Directing and Motivating Subordinates; Coaching and Developing Others; Provide Consultation and Advice to Others; Performing Administrative Activities; Monitoring and Controlling Resources
Job Characteristics: Job-Required Social Interaction; Provide a Service to Others; Coordinate or Lead Others; Diseases/Infections; Sitting; Bending or Twisting the Body; Special Uniform; Frustrating Circumstances; Importance of Being Aware of New Events
GOE Group/s: 10.02.02 Nursing, Therapy, and Specialized Teaching Services: Therapy and Rehabilitation
CIP Program/s: 512306 Occupational Therapy
Related DOT Job/s: 076.121-010 OCCUPATIONAL THERAPIST; 076.167-010 INDUSTRIAL THERAPIST

32308 PHYSICAL THERAPISTS. OOH Title/s: Physical Therapists

Apply techniques and treatments that help relieve pain, increase the patient's strength, and decrease or prevent deformity and crippling. Administers manual exercises to improve and maintain function. Administers treatment involving application of physical agents, using equipment, moist packs, ultraviolet and infrared lamps, and ultrasound machines. Administers massage, applying knowledge of massage techniques and body physiology. Administers traction to relieve pain, using traction equipment. Instructs, motivates, and assists patient to perform various physical activities and use supportive devices, such as crutches, canes, and prostheses. Evaluates effects of treatment at various stages and adjusts treatment to achieve maximum benefit. Tests and measures patient's strength, motor development, sensory perception, functional capacity, and respiratory and circulatory efficiency, and records data. Reviews physician's referral and patient's condition and medical records to determine physical therapy treatment required. Plans and prepares written treatment program based on evaluation of patient data. Instructs patient and family in treatment procedures to be continued at home. Evaluates, fits, and adjusts prosthetic and orthotic devices and recommends modification to orthotist. Confers with medical practitioners to obtain additional information, suggest revisions in treatment, and integrate physical therapy into patient's care. Records treatment, response, and progress in patient's chart, or enters information into computer. Plans, directs, and coordinates physical therapy program. Orients, instructs, and directs work activities of assistants, aides, and students. Plans and develops physical therapy research programs and participates in conducting research. Writes technical articles and reports for publications. Plans and conducts lectures and training programs on physical therapy and related topics for medical staff, students, and community groups.
Yearly Earnings: $33,332
Education: Bachelor's degree
Knowledge: Administration and Management; Customer and Personal Service; Biology; Psychology; Medicine and Dentistry; Therapy and Counseling; Education and Training; English Language
Abilities: Speech Clarity
Skills: Reading Comprehension; Active Listening; Writing; Speaking; Science; Critical Thinking; Active Learning; Learning Strategies; Monitoring; Social Perceptiveness; Instructing; Service Orientation; Problem Identification; Information Gathering; Synthesis/Reorganization; Idea Generation; Idea Evaluation; Implementation Planning; Solution Appraisal; Technology Design; Equipment Selection; Identification of Key Causes; Judgment and Decision Making; Management of Financial Resources; Management of Material Resources
General Work Activities: Getting Information Needed to Do the Job; Monitoring Processes, Material, or Surroundings; Identifying Objects, Actions, and Events; Estimating Needed Characteristics; Judging Qualities of Things, Services, People; Processing Information; Making Decisions and Solving Problems; Updating and Using Job-Relevant Knowledge; Developing Objectives and Strategies; Scheduling Work and Activities; Performing General Physical Activities; Operating Vehicles or Equipment; Implementing Ideas, Programs, etc.; Communicating with Other Workers; Communicating with Persons Outside Organization; Establishing and Maintaining Relationships; Assisting and Caring for Others; Coordinating Work and Activities of Others; Developing and Building Teams; Teaching Others; Guiding, Directing and Motivating Subordinates; Coaching and Developing Others; Provide Consultation and Advice to Others; Staffing Organizational Units
Job Characteristics: Job-Required Social Interaction; Deal with Unpleasant or Angry People; Special Uniform; Importance of Being Sure All is Done
GOE Group/s: 10.02.02 Nursing, Therapy, and Specialized Teaching Services: Therapy and Rehabilitation
CIP Program/s: 310501 Health and Physical Education, General; 310505 Exercise Sciences/Physiology and Movement Studies; 512304 Movement Therapy; 512308 Physical Therapy
Related DOT Job/s: 076.121-014 PHYSICAL THERAPIST

32311A MANUAL ARTS THERAPISTS. OOH Title/s: Physical Therapists

Instruct patients in prescribed manual arts activities, such as woodworking, photography, or graphic arts, to prevent anatomical and physiological deconditioning and to assist in maintaining, improving, or developing work skills. Teaches patient manual arts activities, such as woodworking, graphic arts, or photography. Observes and interacts with patient to evaluate progress of patient in meeting physical and mental demands of employment. Confers with other rehabilitation team members to develop treatment plan to prevent physical deconditioning and enhance work skills of patient. Plans and organizes work activities according to patients' capabilities and disabilities. Prepares reports showing development of patient's work tolerance and emotional and social adjustment.
Yearly Earnings: $33,332
Education: Bachelor's degree
Knowledge: Customer and Personal Service; Psychology; Therapy and Counseling; Education and Training; Fine Arts
Abilities: Oral Comprehension; Written Expression; Originality; Problem Sensitivity; Time Sharing; Arm-Hand Steadiness; Multilimb Coordination
Skills: Social Perceptiveness; Instructing; Service Orientation
General Work Activities: Judging Qualities of Things, Services, People; Developing Objectives and Strategies; Scheduling Work and Activities; Organizing, Planning, and Prioritizing; Implementing Ideas, Programs, etc.; Documenting/Recording Information; Communicating with Other Workers; Communicating with Persons Outside

Organization; Establishing and Maintaining Relationships; Assisting and Caring for Others; Selling or Influencing Others; Teaching Others; Coaching and Developing Others
Job Characteristics: Objective or Subjective Information; Job-Required Social Interaction; Persuade Someone to a Course of Action; Provide a Service to Others; Deal with External Customers; Coordinate or Lead Others; Responsible for Others' Health and Safety; Frequency in Conflict Situations; Frustrating Circumstances
GOE Group/s: 10.02.02 Nursing, Therapy, and Specialized Teaching Services: Therapy and Rehabilitation
CIP Program/s: 512306 Occupational Therapy
Related DOT Job/s: 076.124-010 MANUAL-ARTS THERAPIST

32311B CORRECTIVE THERAPISTS. OOH Title/s: Physical Therapists

Apply techniques and treatments designed to prevent muscular deconditioning resulting from long convalescence or inactivity due to chronic illness. Applies skin lubricant and massages client's body to relax muscles, stimulate nerves, promote range of motion, and release tissue. Plans and organizes program treatment procedures with client, or in collaboration with others on rehabilitation team. Demonstrates and directs client to participate in body movements designed to improve muscular function and flexibility and to reduce tension. Teaches client spatial and body awareness, new movement skills, and effective and expressive body habits. Instructs patient in use of prostheses, devices such as canes, crutches, and braces, and walking skills for sightless patients. Observes and/or photographs client's arm and leg movements, posture, and flexibility to evaluate client in relation to established norms. Observes and evaluates client's progress during treatment program and modifies treatment as required. Teaches client stress management, relaxation, and hygiene techniques to compensate for disabilities. Interviews patient or consults client's questionnaire to determine client's medical history and physical condition. Prepares reports describing client's treatment, progress, emotional reactions, and response to treatment. Consults with client to establish rapport, discuss program goals, and motivate patient.
Yearly Earnings: $33,332
Education: Bachelor's degree
Knowledge: Customer and Personal Service; Biology; Psychology; Medicine and Dentistry; Therapy and Counseling; Education and Training; Communications and Media
Abilities: Fluency of Ideas; Originality; Problem Sensitivity; Deductive Reasoning; Inductive Reasoning; Memorization; Arm-Hand Steadiness; Finger Dexterity; Multilimb Coordination; Wrist-Finger Speed; Speed of Limb Movement; Dynamic Strength; Trunk Strength; Stamina; Dynamic Flexibility; Gross Body Coordination; Gross Body Equilibrium
Skills: Active Listening; Writing; Speaking; Monitoring; Social Perceptiveness; Service Orientation; Problem Identification; Judgment and Decision Making
General Work Activities: Getting Information Needed to Do the Job; Identifying Objects, Actions, and Events; Updating and Using Job-Relevant Knowledge; Developing Objectives and Strategies; Organizing, Planning, and Prioritizing; Communicating with Persons Outside Organization; Establishing and Maintaining Relationships; Assisting and Caring for Others; Selling or Influencing Others; Performing for or Working with Public; Teaching Others; Coaching and Developing Others
Job Characteristics: Objective or Subjective Information; Job-Required Social Interaction; Persuade Someone to a Course of Action; Provide a Service to Others; Deal with External Customers; Responsible for Others' Health and Safety; Frequency in Conflict Situations; Deal with Unpleasant or Angry People; Deal with Physical, Aggressive People; Diseases/Infections; Bending or Twisting the Body; Special Uniform; Consequence of Error; Importance of Being Aware of New Events
GOE Group/s: 10.02.02 Nursing, Therapy, and Specialized Teaching Services: Therapy and Rehabilitation
CIP Program/s: 310501 Health and Physical Education, General; 310502 Adapted Physical Education/Therapeutic Recreation; 310505 Exercise Sciences/Physiology and Movement Studies; 512308 Physical Therapy; 512399 Rehabilitation/Therapeutic Services, Other
Related DOT Job/s: 076.264-010 PHYSICAL-INTEGRATION PRACTITIONER; 076.361-010 CORRECTIVE THERAPIST

32314 SPEECH-LANGUAGE PATHOLOGISTS AND AUDIOLOGISTS. OOH Title/s: Speech-Language Pathologists and Audiologists

Examine and provide remedial services for persons with speech and hearing disorders. Perform research related to speech and language problems. Administers hearing or speech/language evaluations, tests, or examinations to patients to collect information on type and degree of impairment. Conducts or directs research and reports findings on speech or hearing topics to develop procedures, technology, or treatments. Evaluates hearing and speech/language test results and medical or background information to determine hearing or speech impairment and treatment. Counsels and instructs clients in techniques to improve speech or hearing impairment, including sign language or lip-reading. Plans and conducts prevention and treatment programs for clients' hearing or speech problems. Records and maintains reports of speech or hearing research or treatments. Refers clients to additional medical or educational services if needed. Advises educators or other medical staff on speech or hearing topics. Participates in conferences or training to update or share knowledge of new hearing or speech disorder treatment methods or technology. Teaches staff or students about hearing or speech disorders, including explaining new treatments or equipment. Directs and coordinates staff activities of speech or hearing clinic, and hires, trains, and evaluates personnel. Prepares budget requesting funding for specific projects, including equipment, supplies, and staff.
Yearly Earnings: $33,332
Education: Master's degree
Knowledge: Administration and Management; Economics and Accounting; Customer and Personal Service; Personnel and Human Resources; Biology; Psychology; Medicine and Dentistry; Therapy and Counseling; Education and Training; English Language; Foreign Language; Telecommunications
Abilities: Oral Comprehension; Written Comprehension; Oral Expression; Written Expression; Hearing Sensitivity; Auditory Attention; Sound Localization; Speech Recognition; Speech Clarity
Skills: Reading Comprehension; Active Listening; Writing; Speaking; Science; Critical Thinking; Active Learning; Learning Strategies; Monitoring; Social Perceptiveness; Coordination; Instructing; Service Orientation; Problem Identification; Information Gathering; Information Organization; Synthesis/Reorganization; Idea Generation; Idea Evaluation; Implementation Planning; Solution Appraisal; Operations Analysis; Technology Design; Visioning; Identifying Downstream Consequences; Identification of Key Causes; Systems Evaluation; Time Management; Management of Financial Resources; Management of Material Resources; Management of Personnel Resources
General Work Activities: Getting Information Needed to Do the Job; Monitoring Processes, Material, or Surroundings; Identifying Objects, Actions, and Events; Estimating Needed Characteristics; Judging Qualities of Things, Services, People; Processing Information; Evaluating Information against Standards; Analyzing Data or Information; Making Decisions and Solving Problems; Thinking Creatively; Updating and Using Job-Relevant Knowledge; Developing Objectives and Strategies; Organizing, Planning, and Prioritizing; Operating Vehicles

or Equipment; Implementing Ideas, Programs, etc.; Documenting/Recording Information; Interpreting Meaning of Information to Others; Communicating with Persons Outside Organization; Establishing and Maintaining Relationships; Assisting and Caring for Others; Resolving Conflicts, Negotiating with Others; Performing for or Working with Public; Coordinating Work and Activities of Others; Developing and Building Teams; Teaching Others; Guiding, Directing and Motivating Subordinates; Coaching and Developing Others; Provide Consultation and Advice to Others; Performing Administrative Activities; Staffing Organizational Units; Monitoring and Controlling Resources
Job Characteristics: Job-Required Social Interaction; Coordinate or Lead Others
GOE Group/s: 02.03.04 Medical Sciences: Health Specialties
CIP Program/s: 510201 Communication Disorders, General; 510202 Audiology/Hearing Sciences; 510203 Speech-Language Pathology; 510204 Speech-Language Pathology and Audiology
Related DOT Job/s: 076.101-010 AUDIOLOGIST; 076.104-010 VOICE PATHOLOGIST; 076.107-010 SPEECH PATHOLOGIST

32317 RECREATIONAL THERAPISTS. OOH Title/s: Recreational Therapists

Plan, organize, and direct medically-approved recreation programs for patients in hospitals, nursing homes, or other institutions. Activities include sports, trips, dramatics, social activities, and arts and crafts. Organizes and participates in activities to assist patient in developing needed skills and to make patient aware of available recreational resources. Instructs patient in activities and techniques, such as sports, dance, gardening, music, or art, designed to meet specific physical or psychological needs. Observes and confers with patient to assess patient's needs, capabilities, and interests and to devise treatment plan. Develops treatment plan to meet needs of patient, based on needs assessment and objectives of therapy. Analyzes patient's reactions to treatment experiences to assess progress and effectiveness of treatment plan. Modifies content of patient's treatment program based on observation and evaluation of progress. Confers with members of treatment team to determine patient's needs, capabilities, and interests, and to determine objectives of therapy. Counsels and encourages patient to develop leisure activities. Prepares and submits reports and charts to treatment team to reflect patients' reactions and evidence of progress or regression. Attends and participates in professional conferences and workshops to enhance efficiency and knowledge. Maintains and repairs art materials and equipment.
Yearly Earnings: $33,332
Education: Bachelor's degree
Knowledge: Administration and Management; Customer and Personal Service; Biology; Psychology; Sociology and Anthropology; Medicine and Dentistry; Therapy and Counseling; Education and Training; English Language; Philosophy and Theology
Abilities: Originality; Memorization; Time Sharing; Gross Body Equilibrium; Night Vision; Peripheral Vision; Speech Clarity
Skills: Active Listening; Writing; Speaking; Critical Thinking; Active Learning; Learning Strategies; Monitoring; Social Perceptiveness; Coordination; Persuasion; Instructing; Service Orientation; Problem Identification; Information Gathering; Synthesis/Reorganization; Idea Generation; Idea Evaluation; Implementation Planning; Solution Appraisal; Visioning; Systems Perception; Identification of Key Causes; Judgment and Decision Making; Time Management; Management of Material Resources
General Work Activities: Monitoring Processes, Material, or Surroundings; Judging Qualities of Things, Services, People; Developing Objectives and Strategies; Scheduling Work and Activities; Organizing, Planning, and Prioritizing; Performing General Physical Activities; Establishing and Maintaining Relationships; Assisting and Caring for Others; Teaching Others; Coaching and Developing Others
Job Characteristics: Objective or Subjective Information; Job-Required Social Interaction; Persuade Someone to a Course of Action; Provide a Service to Others; Take a Position Opposed to Others; Deal with External Customers; Coordinate or Lead Others; Responsible for Others' Health and Safety; Frequency in Conflict Situations; Deal with Unpleasant or Angry People; Deal with Physical, Aggressive People; Diseases/Infections; Walking or Running; Special Uniform; Frustrating Circumstances
GOE Group/s: 10.02.02 Nursing, Therapy, and Specialized Teaching Services: Therapy and Rehabilitation
CIP Program/s: 310501 Health and Physical Education, General; 310502 Adapted Physical Education/Therapeutic Recreation; 512301 Art Therapy; 512302 Dance Therapy; 512305 Music Therapy; 512309 Recreational Therapy
Related DOT Job/s: 076.124-014 RECREATIONAL THERAPIST; 076.124-018 HORTICULTURAL THERAPIST; 076.127-010 ART THERAPIST; 076.127-014 MUSIC THERAPIST; 076.127-018 DANCE THERAPIST

32399A EXERCISE PHYSIOLOGISTS. OOH Title/s: Physical Therapists

Develop, implement, and coordinate exercise programs and administer medical tests, under physician's supervision, to program participants to promote physical fitness. Records heart activity, using electrocardiograph (EKG) machine, while participant undergoes stress test on treadmill, under physician's supervision. Measures oxygen consumption and lung functioning, using spirometer. Measures amount of fat in body, using hydrostatic scale, skinfold calipers, and tape measure to assess body composition. Performs routine laboratory tests of blood samples for cholesterol level and glucose tolerance. Conducts individual and group aerobic, strength, and flexibility exercises. Writes initial and follow-up exercise prescriptions for participants, following physician's recommendation, specifying equipment, such as treadmill, track, or bike. Demonstrates correct use of exercise equipment and exercise routines. Interprets test results. Observes participants during exercise for signs of stress. Teaches behavior modification classes, such as stress management, weight control, and related subjects. Interviews participants to obtain vital statistics and medical history and records information. Explains program and test procedures to participants. Schedules other examinations and tests, such as physical examination, chest X ray, and urinalysis. Records test data in participant's record. Orders material and supplies. Adjusts and calibrates exercise equipment, using hand tools.
Yearly Earnings: $33,332
Education: Bachelor's degree
Knowledge: Customer and Personal Service; Chemistry; Biology; Psychology; Medicine and Dentistry; Therapy and Counseling; Education and Training; Foreign Language
Abilities: Written Comprehension; Multilimb Coordination; Stamina; Dynamic Flexibility; Gross Body Coordination; Gross Body Equilibrium
Skills: Active Listening; Speaking; Learning Strategies; Social Perceptiveness; Instructing; Service Orientation; Implementation Planning
General Work Activities: Identifying Objects, Actions, and Events; Repairing and Maintaining Electrical Equipment; Interpreting Meaning of Information to Others; Assisting and Caring for Others; Performing for or Working with Public; Teaching Others; Coaching and Developing Others
Job Characteristics: Provide a Service to Others; Deal with External Customers; Coordinate or Lead Others; Responsible for Others' Health and Safety; Bending or Twisting the Body; Importance of Being Aware of New Events
GOE Group/s: 10.02.02 Nursing, Therapy, and Specialized Teaching Services: Therapy and Rehabilitation

CIP Program/s: 310501 Health and Physical Education, General; 310502 Adapted Physical Education/Therapeutic Recreation; 310503 Athletic Training and Sports Medicine; 310505 Exercise Sciences/Physiology and Movement Studies
Related DOT Job/s: 076.121-018 EXERCISE PHYSIOLOGIST

32399B ORIENTATION AND MOBILITY THERAPISTS. OOH Title/s: Physical Therapists
Train blind and visually impaired clients in the techniques of daily living to maximize independence and personal adjustment. Trains clients in awareness of physical environment through sense of smell, hearing, and touch. Teaches clients personal skills, such as eating, grooming, dressing, and use of bathroom facilities. Teaches clients home management skills, such as cooking and coin and money identification. Teaches clients communication skills, such as use of telephone. Teaches clients to protect body, using hands and arms to detect obstacles. Teaches clients to read and write Braille. Trains clients to travel alone, with or without cane, through use of variety of actual or simulated travel situations and exercises. Instructs clients in use of reading machines and common electrical devices, and in development of effective listening techniques. Administers assessment tests to clients to determine present and required or desired orientation and mobility skills. Instructs clients in arts, crafts, and recreational skills, such as macrame, leatherworking, sewing, ceramics, and piano playing. Interviews clients to obtain information concerning medical history, lifestyle, or other pertinent information. Instructs clients in group activities, such as swimming, dancing, or playing modified sports activities. Prepares progress report for use of rehabilitation team to evaluate clients' ability to perform varied activities essential to daily living.
Yearly Earnings: $33,332
Education: Bachelor's degree
Knowledge: Customer and Personal Service; Psychology; Medicine and Dentistry; Therapy and Counseling; Education and Training; Foreign Language; Fine Arts; Telecommunications
Skills: Active Listening; Speaking; Learning Strategies; Monitoring; Social Perceptiveness; Persuasion; Instructing; Service Orientation; Synthesis/Reorganization; Implementation Planning
General Work Activities: Interpreting Meaning of Information to Others; Communicating with Other Workers; Establishing and Maintaining Relationships; Assisting and Caring for Others; Teaching Others; Coaching and Developing Others
Job Characteristics: Job-Required Social Interaction; Deal with External Customers; Responsible for Others' Health and Safety; Deal with Unpleasant or Angry People; Deal with Physical, Aggressive People; Importance of Being Aware of New Events
GOE Group/s: 10.02.02 Nursing, Therapy, and Specialized Teaching Services: Therapy and Rehabilitation
CIP Program/s: 131001 Special Education, General; 131009 Education of the Blind and Visually Handicapped; 440701 Social Work; 510806 Physical Therapy Assistant; 512308 Physical Therapy; 512310 Vocational Rehabilitation Counseling
Related DOT Job/s: 076.224-014 ORIENTATION AND MOBILITY THERAPIST FOR THE BLIND

Health Care Providers

32502 REGISTERED NURSES. OOH Title/s: Registered Nurses
Administer nursing care to ill or injured persons. Licensing or registration required. Include administrative, public health, industrial, private duty, and surgical nurses. Provides health care, first aid, and immunization in facilities such as schools, hospitals, and industry. Observes patient's skin color, dilation of pupils, and computerized equipment to monitor vital signs. Records patient's medical information and vital signs. Administers local, inhalation, intravenous, and other anesthetics. Prepares patients for and assists with examinations. Orders, interprets, and evaluates diagnostic tests to identify and assess patient's condition. Prepares rooms, sterile instruments, equipment, and supplies, and hands items to surgeon. Prescribes or recommends drugs or other forms of treatment, such as physical therapy, inhalation therapy, or related therapeutic procedures. Contracts independently to render nursing care, usually to one patient, in hospital or private home. Provides prenatal and postnatal care to obstetrical patients under supervision of obstetrician. Discusses cases with physician or obstetrician. Informs physician of patient's condition during anesthesia. Administers stipulated emergency measures, and contacts obstetrician when deviations from standard are encountered during pregnancy or delivery. Advises and consults with specified personnel concerning necessary precautions to be taken to prevent possible contamination or infection. Instructs on topics, such as health education, disease prevention, childbirth, and home nursing, and develops health improvement programs. Delivers infants and performs postpartum examinations and treatment. Refers students or patients to community agencies furnishing assistance, and cooperates with agencies. Conducts specified laboratory tests. Maintains stock of supplies. Directs and coordinates infection-control program in hospital.
Yearly Earnings: $35,620
Education: Associate degree
Knowledge: Administration and Management; Clerical; Customer and Personal Service; Personnel and Human Resources; Chemistry; Biology; Psychology; Sociology and Anthropology; Medicine and Dentistry; Therapy and Counseling; Education and Training; English Language; Foreign Language; Philosophy and Theology; Public Safety and Security; Law, Government, and Jurisprudence; Communications and Media
Abilities: Oral Comprehension; Written Comprehension; Oral Expression; Written Expression; Fluency of Ideas; Originality; Problem Sensitivity; Deductive Reasoning; Inductive Reasoning; Information Ordering; Category Flexibility; Mathematical Reasoning; Memorization; Speed of Closure; Perceptual Speed; Spatial Orientation; Selective Attention; Time Sharing; Arm-Hand Steadiness; Manual Dexterity; Finger Dexterity; Response Orientation; Reaction Time; Wrist-Finger Speed; Static Strength; Gross Body Equilibrium; Near Vision; Visual Color Discrimination; Night Vision; Peripheral Vision; Hearing Sensitivity; Auditory Attention; Sound Localization; Speech Recognition; Speech Clarity
Skills: Reading Comprehension; Active Listening; Speaking; Science; Critical Thinking; Active Learning; Learning Strategies; Monitoring; Social Perceptiveness; Coordination; Instructing; Service Orientation; Problem Identification; Information Organization; Solution Appraisal; Systems Perception; Judgment and Decision Making; Systems Evaluation; Time Management; Management of Material Resources; Management of Personnel Resources
General Work Activities: Monitoring Processes, Material, or Surroundings; Identifying Objects, Actions, and Events; Judging Qualities of Things, Services, People; Processing Information; Making Decisions and Solving Problems; Updating and Using Job-Relevant Knowledge; Developing Objectives and Strategies; Scheduling Work and Activities; Performing General Physical Activities; Operating Vehicles or Equipment; Implementing Ideas, Programs, etc.; Documenting/Recording Information; Communicating with Other Workers; Communicating with Persons Outside Organization; Establishing and Maintaining Relationships; Assisting and Caring for Others; Selling or Influencing Others; Resolving Conflicts, Negotiating with Others; Performing for or Working with Public; Coordinating Work and Activities of Others; Developing and Building Teams; Teaching Others;

Guiding, Directing and Motivating Subordinates; Coaching and Developing Others; Provide Consultation and Advice to Others; Performing Administrative Activities; Staffing Organizational Units; Monitoring and Controlling Resources
Job Characteristics: Job-Required Social Interaction; Provide a Service to Others; Take a Position Opposed to Others; Deal with External Customers; Responsible for Others' Health and Safety; Frequency in Conflict Situations; Deal with Unpleasant or Angry People; Deal with Physical, Aggressive People; Radiation; Diseases/Infections; Standing; Walking or Running; Special Uniform; Common Protective or Safety Attire; Consequence of Error; Frustrating Circumstances; Degree of Automation; Importance of Being Exact or Accurate; Importance of Being Sure All is Done; Importance of Being Aware of New Events
GOE Group/s: 10.02.01 Nursing, Therapy, and Specialized Teaching Services: Nursing
CIP Program/s: 511601 Nursing (R.N. Training); 511602 Nursing Administration (Post-R.N.); 511603 Nursing, Adult Health (Post-R.N.); 511604 Nursing Anesthetist (Post-R.N.); 511605 Nursing, Family Practice (Post-R.N.); 511606 Nursing, Maternal/Child Health (Post-R.N.); 511607 Nursing Midwifery (Post-R.N.); 511608 Nursing Science (Post-R.N.); 511609 Nursing, Pediatric (Post-R.N.); 511610 Nursing, Psychiatric/Mental Health (Post-R.N.); 511611 Nursing, Public Health (Post-R.N.); 511612 Nursing, Surgical (Post-R.N.); 511699 Nursing, Other
Related DOT Job/s: 075.124-010 NURSE, SCHOOL; 075.124-014 NURSE, STAFF, COMMUNITY HEALTH; 075.127-014 NURSE, CONSULTANT; 075.127-026 NURSE, SUPERVISOR, COMMUNITY-HEALTH NURSING; 075.127-030 NURSE, SUPERVISOR, EVENING-OR-NIGHT; 075.127-034 NURSE, INFECTION CONTROL; 075.137-010 NURSE, SUPERVISOR, OCCUPATIONAL HEALTH NURSING; 075.137-014 NURSE, HEAD; 075.167-010 NURSE, SUPERVISOR; 075.264-010 NURSE PRACTITIONER; 075.264-014 NURSE-MIDWIFE; 075.364-010 NURSE, GENERAL DUTY; 075.371-010 NURSE ANESTHETIST; 075.374-014 NURSE, OFFICE; 075.374-018 NURSE, PRIVATE DUTY; 075.374-022 NURSE, STAFF, OCCUPATIONAL HEALTH NURSING

32505 LICENSED PRACTICAL NURSES. OOH Title/s: Licensed Practical Nurses

Care for ill, injured, convalescent, and handicapped persons in hospitals, clinics, private homes, sanitariums, and similar institutions. Administers specified medication, orally or by subcutaneous or intramuscular injection, and notes time and amount on patients' charts. Provides medical treatment and personal care to patients in private home settings. Takes and records patients' vital signs. Dresses wounds and gives enemas, douches, alcohol rubs, and massages. Applies compresses, ice bags, and hot water bottles. Observes patients and reports adverse reactions to medication or treatment to medical personnel in charge. Bathes, dresses, and assists patients in walking and turning. Assembles and uses such equipment as catheters, tracheotomy tubes, and oxygen suppliers. Collects samples, such as urine, blood, and sputum, from patients for testing, and performs routine laboratory tests on samples. Sterilizes equipment and supplies, using germicides, sterilizer, or autoclave. Records food and fluid intake and output. Prepares or examines food trays for prescribed diet and feeds patients. Assists in delivery, care, and feeding of infants. Cleans rooms, makes beds, and answers patients' calls. Washes and dresses bodies of deceased persons. Inventories and requisitions supplies.
Yearly Earnings: $23,400
Education: Postsecondary vocational training
Knowledge: Customer and Personal Service; Chemistry; Biology; Psychology; Sociology and Anthropology; Medicine and Dentistry; Therapy and Counseling
Abilities: Reaction Time
Skills: Reading Comprehension; Monitoring; Social Perceptiveness; Service Orientation
General Work Activities: Identifying Objects, Actions, and Events; Performing General Physical Activities; Documenting/Recording Information; Establishing and Maintaining Relationships; Assisting and Caring for Others; Performing for or Working with Public
Job Characteristics: Job-Required Social Interaction; Provide a Service to Others; Deal with External Customers; Responsible for Others' Health and Safety; Deal with Unpleasant or Angry People; Diseases/Infections; Standing; Special Uniform; Consequence of Error; Frustrating Circumstances; Importance of Being Exact or Accurate; Importance of Being Sure All is Done
GOE Group/s: 10.02.01 Nursing, Therapy, and Specialized Teaching Services: Nursing
CIP Program/s: 511613 Practical Nurse (L.P.N. Training)
Related DOT Job/s: 079.374-014 NURSE, LICENSED PRACTICAL

32508 EMERGENCY MEDICAL TECHNICIANS.

OOH Title/s: Emergency Medical Technicians

Administer first-aid treatment and transport sick or injured persons to medical facility, working as members of an emergency medical team. Administers first-aid treatment and life-support care to sick or injured persons in prehospital setting. Assists in removal and transport of victims to treatment center. Assesses nature and extent of illness or injury to establish and prioritize medical procedures. Observes, records, and reports patient's condition and reactions to drugs and treatment, to physician. Monitors cardiac patient, using electrocardiograph. Communicates with treatment center personnel to arrange reception of victims and to receive instructions for further treatment. Assists treatment center personnel to obtain and record victim's vital statistics, and to administer emergency treatment. Assists treatment center personnel to obtain information relating to circumstances of emergency. Drives mobile intensive care unit to specified location, following instructions from emergency medical dispatcher. Maintains vehicles and medical and communication equipment, and replenishes first-aid equipment and supplies.
Yearly Earnings: $23,972
Education: Postsecondary vocational training
Knowledge: Chemistry; Biology; Psychology; Geography; Medicine and Dentistry; Therapy and Counseling; Foreign Language; Telecommunications; Transportation
Abilities: Problem Sensitivity; Speed of Closure; Selective Attention; Time Sharing; Response Orientation; Rate Control; Reaction Time; Static Strength; Stamina; Gross Body Equilibrium; Night Vision; Peripheral Vision; Glare Sensitivity
Skills: Active Listening; Social Perceptiveness; Coordination; Service Orientation; Problem Identification; Implementation Planning; Operation Monitoring; Operation and Control; Equipment Maintenance; Judgment and Decision Making; Time Management
General Work Activities: Getting Information Needed to Do the Job; Monitoring Processes, Material, or Surroundings; Identifying Objects, Actions, and Events; Making Decisions and Solving Problems; Updating and Using Job-Relevant Knowledge; Organizing, Planning, and Prioritizing; Interacting with Computers; Repairing and Maintaining Mechanical Equipment; Repairing and Maintaining Electrical Equipment; Interpreting Meaning of Information to Others; Establishing and Maintaining Relationships; Assisting and Caring for Others; Performing for or Working with Public
Job Characteristics: Responsible for Others' Health and Safety; Frequency in Conflict Situations; Deal with Unpleasant or Angry People; Deal with Physical, Aggressive People; Very Hot; Cramped Work Space, Awkward Positions; Diseases/Infections; Walking or Running; Kneeling, Crouching, or Crawling; Bending or Twisting the Body; Special Uniform; Common Protective or Safety Attire; Special-

ized Protective or Safety Attire; Consequence of Error; Importance of Being Exact or Accurate; Importance of Being Sure All is Done; Importance of Being Aware of New Events
GOE Group/s: 10.03.02 Child and Adult Care: Patient Care
CIP Program/s: 510904 Emergency Medical Technologists and Technicians
Related DOT Job/s: 079.364-026 PARAMEDIC; 079.374-010 EMERGENCY MEDICAL TECHNICIAN

32511 PHYSICIAN'S ASSISTANTS. OOH Title/s: Physician Assistants
Provide patient services under direct supervision and responsibility of doctor of medicine or osteopathy. Elicit detailed patient histories and make complete physical examinations. Reach tentative diagnoses and order appropriate laboratory tests. Require substantial educational preparation, usually at junior or four-year colleges. Most physician's assistants complete two years of formal training, but training may vary from one to five years depending on the nature of the training and previous education and experience. May require certification. Exclude nurses and ambulance attendants, whose training is limited to the application of first aid. Examines patient. Administers or orders diagnostic tests, such as X ray, electrocardiogram, and laboratory tests. Compiles patient medical data, including health history and results of physical examination. Interprets diagnostic test results for deviations from normal. Performs therapeutic procedures, such as injections, immunizations, suturing and wound care, and managing infection. Counsels patients regarding prescribed therapeutic regimens, normal growth and development, family planning, emotional problems of daily living, and health maintenance. Develops and implements patient management plans, records progress notes, and assists in provision of continuity of care.
Yearly Earnings: $35,620
Education: Bachelor's degree
Knowledge: Chemistry; Biology; Psychology; Medicine and Dentistry; Therapy and Counseling
Abilities: Problem Sensitivity; Inductive Reasoning; Information Ordering; Speed of Closure; Arm-Hand Steadiness
Skills: Reading Comprehension; Active Listening; Writing; Speaking; Science; Critical Thinking; Active Learning; Learning Strategies; Monitoring; Social Perceptiveness; Persuasion; Service Orientation; Problem Identification; Information Gathering; Synthesis/Reorganization; Idea Generation; Solution Appraisal; Judgment and Decision Making
General Work Activities: Getting Information Needed to Do the Job; Monitoring Processes, Material, or Surroundings; Identifying Objects, Actions, and Events; Judging Qualities of Things, Services, People; Evaluating Information against Standards; Updating and Using Job-Relevant Knowledge; Documenting/Recording Information; Establishing and Maintaining Relationships; Assisting and Caring for Others; Selling or Influencing Others; Performing for or Working with Public
Job Characteristics: Job-Required Social Interaction; Provide a Service to Others; Deal with External Customers; Responsible for Others' Health and Safety; Deal with Unpleasant or Angry People; Radiation; Diseases/Infections; Standing; Special Uniform; Common Protective or Safety Attire; Consequence of Error; Importance of Being Exact or Accurate
GOE Group/s: 10.02.01 Nursing, Therapy, and Specialized Teaching Services: Nursing
CIP Program/s: 510807 Physician Assistant
Related DOT Job/s: 079.364-018 PHYSICIAN ASSISTANT; 079.367-018 MEDICAL-SERVICE TECHNICIAN

32514 OPTICIANS, DISPENSING AND MEASURING. OOH Title/s: Dispensing Opticians
Design, measure, fit, and adapt lenses and frames for client, according to written optical prescription or specification. Assist client with selecting frames. Measure customer for size of eyeglasses and coordinate frames with facial and eye measurements and optical prescription. Prepare work order for optical laboratory containing instructions for grinding and mounting lenses in frames. Verify exactness of finished lens spectacles. Adjust frame and lens position to fit client. May shape or reshape frames. Include contact lens opticians. Measures client's bridge and eye size, temple length, vertex distance, pupillary distance, and optical centers of eyes, using measuring devices. Prepares work order and instructions for grinding lenses and fabricating eyeglasses. Verifies finished lenses are ground to specification. Determines client's current lens prescription, when necessary, using lensometer or lens analyzer and client's eyeglasses. Recommends specific lenses, lens coatings, and frames to suit client needs. Assists client in selecting frames according to style and color, coordinating frames with facial and eye measurements and optical prescription. Heats, shapes, or bends plastic or metal frames to adjust eyeglasses to fit client, using pliers and hands. Evaluates prescription in conjunction with client's vocational and avocational visual requirements. Repairs damaged frames. Fabricates lenses to prescription specifications. Instructs clients in adapting to wearing and caring for eyeglasses. Grinds lens edges or applies coating to lenses. Selects and orders frames for display. Manages one or more optical shops. Sells optical goods, such as binoculars, sunglasses, magnifying glasses, and low-vision aids. Computes amount of sale and collects payment for services.
Yearly Earnings: $18,044
Education: Long-term O-J-T
Knowledge: Administration and Management; Economics and Accounting; Sales and Marketing; Customer and Personal Service; Personnel and Human Resources
Skills: Service Orientation; Problem Identification; Technology Design; Time Management; Management of Financial Resources; Management of Material Resources; Management of Personnel Resources
General Work Activities: Establishing and Maintaining Relationships; Assisting and Caring for Others; Selling or Influencing Others; Performing for or Working with Public; Monitoring and Controlling Resources
Job Characteristics: Persuade Someone to a Course of Action; Provide a Service to Others; Deal with External Customers; Sitting; Importance of Being Exact or Accurate
GOE Group/s: 05.10.01 Crafts: Structural
CIP Program/s: 511801 Opticianry/Dispensing Optician
Related DOT Job/s: 299.361-010 OPTICIAN, DISPENSING; 299.361-014 OPTICIAN APPRENTICE, DISPENSING

32517 PHARMACISTS. OOH Title/s: Pharmacists; Health Services Managers
Compound and dispense medications following prescriptions issued by physicians, dentists, or other authorized medical practitioners. Compounds medications, using standard formulas and processes, such as weighing, measuring, and mixing ingredients. Compounds radioactive substances and reagents to prepare radiopharmaceuticals, following radiopharmacy laboratory procedures. Plans and implements procedures in pharmacy, such as mixing, packaging, and labeling pharmaceuticals according to policies and legal requirements. Reviews prescription to assure accuracy and determine ingredients needed and suitability of radiopharmaceutical prescriptions. Answers questions and provides information to pharmacy customers on drug interactions, side effects, dosage, and storage of pharmaceuti-

cals. Assays prepared radiopharmaceutical, using instruments and equipment to verify rate of drug disintegration and to ensure patient receives required dose. Calculates volume of radioactive pharmaceutical required to provide patient with desired level of radioactivity at prescribed time. Consults medical staff to advise on drug applications and characteristics and to review and evaluate quality and effectiveness of radiopharmaceuticals. Maintains established procedures concerning quality assurance, security of controlled substances, and disposal of hazardous waste. Maintains records, such as pharmacy files, charge system, inventory, and control records for radioactive nuclei. Oversees preparation and dispensation of experimental drugs. Verifies that specified radioactive substance and reagent will give desired results in examination or treatment procedures. Analyzes records to indicate prescribing trends and excessive usage. Directs and coordinates, through subordinate supervisory personnel, activities and functions of pharmacy. Directs pharmacy personnel programs, such as hiring, training, and intern programs. Prepares pharmacy budget. Observes pharmacy personnel at work to develop quality assurance techniques to ensure safe, legal, and ethical practices. Participates in development of computer programs for pharmacy information-management systems, patient and department charge systems, and inventory control. Conducts research to develop or improve radiopharmaceuticals. Instructs students, interns, and other medical personnel on matters pertaining to pharmacy or concerning radiopharmacy use, characteristics, and compounding procedures.
Yearly Earnings: $35,620
Education: Bachelor's degree
Knowledge: Administration and Management; Clerical; Economics and Accounting; Personnel and Human Resources; Computers and Electronics; Chemistry; Biology; Medicine and Dentistry; Therapy and Counseling; Education and Training; English Language; Foreign Language; Law, Government, and Jurisprudence
Abilities: Oral Comprehension; Written Comprehension; Oral Expression; Information Ordering; Mathematical Reasoning
Skills: Reading Comprehension; Active Listening; Writing; Speaking; Mathematics; Science; Critical Thinking; Active Learning; Learning Strategies; Monitoring; Instructing; Service Orientation; Problem Identification; Solution Appraisal; Operations Analysis; Programming; Product Inspection; Visioning; Identifying Downstream Consequences; Identification of Key Causes; Judgment and Decision Making; Systems Evaluation; Time Management; Management of Financial Resources; Management of Material Resources; Management of Personnel Resources
General Work Activities: Getting Information Needed to Do the Job; Monitoring Processes, Material, or Surroundings; Identifying Objects, Actions, and Events; Estimating Needed Characteristics; Judging Qualities of Things, Services, People; Processing Information; Evaluating Information against Standards; Making Decisions and Solving Problems; Updating and Using Job-Relevant Knowledge; Developing Objectives and Strategies; Scheduling Work and Activities; Operating Vehicles or Equipment; Drafting and Specifying Technical Devices, etc.; Implementing Ideas, Programs, etc.; Documenting/Recording Information; Interpreting Meaning of Information to Others; Assisting and Caring for Others; Performing for or Working with Public; Coordinating Work and Activities of Others; Teaching Others; Guiding, Directing and Motivating Subordinates; Coaching and Developing Others; Provide Consultation and Advice to Others; Performing Administrative Activities; Staffing Organizational Units; Monitoring and Controlling Resources
Job Characteristics: Supervise, Coach, Train Others; Coordinate or Lead Others; Responsible for Others' Health and Safety; Responsibility for Outcomes and Results; Radiation; Special Uniform; Consequence of Error; Importance of Being Exact or Accurate; Importance of Being Sure All is Done
GOE Group/s: 02.04.01 Laboratory Technology: Physical Sciences
CIP Program/s: 512001 Pharmacy (B. Pharm., Pharm.D.); 512002 Pharmacy Administration and Pharmaceutics
Related DOT Job/s: 074.161-010 PHARMACIST; 074.161-014 RADIOPHARMACIST; 074.167-010 DIRECTOR, PHARMACY SERVICES

32518 PHARMACY TECHNICIANS. OOH Title/s: Pharmacy Technicians

Fill orders for unit doses and prepackaged pharmaceuticals and perform other related duties under the supervision and direction of a pharmacy supervisor or staff pharmacist. Duties include keeping records of drugs delivered to the pharmacy, storing incoming merchandise in proper locations, and informing the supervisor of stock needs and shortages. May clean equipment used in the performance of duties and assist in the care and maintenance of equipment and supplies. Assists pharmacist to prepare and dispense medication. Mixes pharmaceutical preparations, fills bottles with prescribed tablets and capsules, and types labels for bottles. Processes records of medication and equipment dispensed to hospital patient, computes charges, and enters data in computer. Receives and stores incoming supplies. Counts stock and enters data in computer to maintain inventory records. Prepares intravenous (IV) packs, using sterile technique, under supervision of hospital pharmacist. Cleans equipment and sterilizes glassware according to prescribed methods.
Yearly Earnings: $23,972
Education: Moderate-term O-J-T
Knowledge: Clerical; Chemistry; Medicine and Dentistry
Skills: None above average
General Work Activities: None above average
Job Characteristics: Special Uniform; Consequence of Error; Importance of Being Exact or Accurate
GOE Group/s: 05.09.01 Material Control: Shipping, Receiving, and Stock Checking
CIP Program/s: 000000 NO CIP ASSIGNED
Related DOT Job/s: 074.381-010 PHARMACIST ASSISTANT; 074.382-010 PHARMACY TECHNICIAN

32521 DIETITIANS AND NUTRITIONISTS. OOH Title/s: Dietitians and Nutritionists; Health Services Managers

Organize, plan, and conduct food service or nutritional programs to assist in promotion of health and control of disease. May administer activities of department providing quantity food service. May plan, organize, and conduct programs in nutritional research. Develops and implements dietary-care plans based on assessments of nutritional needs, diet restrictions, and other current health plans. Consults with physicians and health care personnel to determine nutritional needs and diet restrictions of patients or clients. Instructs patients and their families in nutritional principles, dietary plans, and food selection and preparation. Monitors food service operations and ensures conformance to nutritional and quality standards. Plans, organizes, and conducts training programs in dietetics, nutrition, and institutional management and administration for medical students and hospital personnel. Supervises activities of workers engaged in planning, preparing, and serving meals. Evaluates nutritional care plans and provides follow-up on continuity of care. Plans, conducts, and evaluates dietary, nutritional, and epidemiological research, and analyzes findings for practical applications. Inspects meals served for conformance to prescribed diets and standards of palatability and appearance. Develops curriculum and prepares manuals, visual aids, course outlines, and other materials used in teaching. Writes research reports and other publications to document and communicate research findings. Plans and prepares grant proposals to request program fund-

ing. Confers with design, building, and equipment personnel to plan for construction and remodeling of food service units.
Yearly Earnings: $28,392
Education: Bachelor's degree
Knowledge: Food Production; Computers and Electronics; Chemistry; Biology; Psychology; Medicine and Dentistry; Education and Training; English Language; History and Archeology
Abilities: Written Comprehension; Oral Expression; Written Expression; Fluency of Ideas; Originality; Speed of Closure; Near Vision; Auditory Attention; Speech Clarity
Skills: Reading Comprehension; Active Listening; Writing; Speaking; Science; Critical Thinking; Active Learning; Learning Strategies; Monitoring; Social Perceptiveness; Coordination; Persuasion; Negotiation; Instructing; Service Orientation; Problem Identification; Information Gathering; Information Organization; Synthesis/Reorganization; Idea Generation; Idea Evaluation; Implementation Planning; Solution Appraisal; Operations Analysis; Programming; Visioning; Systems Perception; Identifying Downstream Consequences; Identification of Key Causes; Judgment and Decision Making; Systems Evaluation; Time Management; Management of Financial Resources; Management of Material Resources; Management of Personnel Resources
General Work Activities: Analyzing Data or Information; Organizing, Planning, and Prioritizing; Documenting/Recording Information; Communicating with Other Workers; Communicating with Persons Outside Organization; Establishing and Maintaining Relationships; Assisting and Caring for Others; Selling or Influencing Others; Coordinating Work and Activities of Others; Teaching Others; Guiding, Directing and Motivating Subordinates; Coaching and Developing Others
Job Characteristics: Objective or Subjective Information; Job-Required Social Interaction; Supervise, Coach, Train Others; Persuade Someone to a Course of Action; Coordinate or Lead Others; Responsible for Others' Health and Safety; Responsibility for Outcomes and Results; Diseases/Infections; Special Uniform
GOE Group/s: 02.02.04 Life Sciences: Food Research; 05.05.17 Craft Technology: Food Preparation; 11.02.02 Educational and Library Services: Teaching, Vocational and Industrial; 11.02.03 Educational and Library Services: Teaching, Home Economics, Agriculture; 11.05.02 Business Administration: Administrative Specialization
CIP Program/s: 190501 Foods and Nutrition Studies, General; 190502 Foods and Nutrition Science; 190503 Dietetics/Human Nutritional Services; 190505 Food Systems Administration; 200401 Institutional Food Workers and Administrators, General; 200409 Institutional Food Services Administrator; 511311 Medical Nutrition; 511312 Medical Pathology; 512702 Medical Dietician
Related DOT Job/s: 077.061-010 DIETITIAN, RESEARCH; 077.117-010 DIETITIAN, CHIEF; 077.127-010 COMMUNITY DIETITIAN; 077.127-014 DIETITIAN, CLINICAL; 077.127-018 DIETITIAN, CONSULTANT; 077.127-022 DIETITIAN, TEACHING

32523 DIETETIC TECHNICIANS. OOH Title/s: Dietitians and Nutritionists

Provide service in assigned areas of food service management. Teach principles of food and nutrition and provide dietary counseling under direction of dietitians. Guides individuals and families in food selection, preparation, and menu planning, based upon nutritional needs. Plans menus based on established guidelines. Obtains and evaluates dietary histories of individuals to plan nutritional programs. Selects, schedules, and conducts orientation and in-service education programs. Standardizes recipes and tests new products for use in facility. Supervises food production and service. Assists in referrals for continuity of patient care. Assists in implementing established cost control procedures. Develops job specifications, job descriptions, and work schedules.
Yearly Earnings: $26,156
Education: Associate degree
Knowledge: Administration and Management; Economics and Accounting; Customer and Personal Service; Personnel and Human Resources; Food Production; Chemistry; Biology; Psychology; Sociology and Anthropology; Medicine and Dentistry; Education and Training
Abilities: Fluency of Ideas; Originality; Speech Clarity
Skills: Reading Comprehension; Active Listening; Writing; Speaking; Active Learning; Learning Strategies; Monitoring; Social Perceptiveness; Coordination; Persuasion; Negotiation; Instructing; Service Orientation; Synthesis/Reorganization; Idea Generation; Idea Evaluation; Implementation Planning; Solution Appraisal; Product Inspection; Identification of Key Causes; Time Management; Management of Personnel Resources
General Work Activities: Scheduling Work and Activities; Assisting and Caring for Others; Performing for or Working with Public; Coordinating Work and Activities of Others; Teaching Others; Guiding, Directing and Motivating Subordinates; Coaching and Developing Others; Staffing Organizational Units; Monitoring and Controlling Resources
Job Characteristics: Job-Required Social Interaction; Supervise, Coach, Train Others; Persuade Someone to a Course of Action; Provide a Service to Others; Deal with External Customers; Coordinate or Lead Others; Diseases/Infections; Hazardous Situations; Special Uniform
GOE Group/s: 05.05.17 Craft Technology: Food Preparation
CIP Program/s: 190501 Foods and Nutrition Studies, General; 190502 Foods and Nutrition Science; 190503 Dietetics/Human Nutritional Services; 200401 Institutional Food Workers and Administrators, General; 200404 Dietician Assistant
Related DOT Job/s: 077.124-010 DIETETIC TECHNICIAN

Medical Technologists and Technicians

32902 MEDICAL AND CLINICAL LABORATORY TECHNOLOGISTS. OOH Title/s: Clinical Laboratory Technologists and Technicians; Health Services Managers

Perform a wide range of complex procedures in the general area of the clinical laboratory, or perform specialized procedures in such areas as cytology, histology, and microbiology. Duties may include supervising and coordinating activities of workers engaged in laboratory testing. Include workers who teach medical technology when teaching is not their primary activity. Cuts, stains, and mounts biological material on slides for microscopic study and diagnosis, following standard laboratory procedures. Examines slides under microscope to detect deviations from norm and to report abnormalities for further study. Analyzes samples of biological material for chemical content or reaction. Selects and prepares specimen and media for cell culture, using aseptic technique and knowledge of medium components and cell requirements. Harvests cell culture at optimum time sequence based on knowledge of cell cycle differences and culture conditions. Prepares slide of cell culture to identify chromosomes, views and photographs slide under photomicroscope, and prints picture. Cultivates, isolates, and assists in identifying microbial organisms, and performs various tests on these micro-organisms. Examines and tests human, animal, or other materials for microbial organisms. Conducts chemical analysis of body fluids, including blood, urine, and spinal fluid, to determine presence of normal and abnormal components. Performs tests to determine blood

group, type, and compatibility for transfusion purposes. Studies blood cells, number of blood cells, and morphology, using microscopic technique. Cuts images of chromosomes from photograph and identifies and arranges them in numbered pairs on karyotype chart, using standard practices. Conducts research under direction of microbiologist or biochemist. Communicates with physicians, family members, and researchers requesting technical information regarding test results. Calibrates and maintains equipment used in quantitative and qualitative analysis, such as spectrophotometers, calorimeters, flame photometers, and computer-controlled analyzers. Enters analysis of medical tests and clinical results into computer for storage. Sets up, cleans, and maintains laboratory equipment.
Yearly Earnings: $27,196
Education: Bachelor's degree
Knowledge: Clerical; Personnel and Human Resources; Chemistry; Biology; Psychology; Medicine and Dentistry; Therapy and Counseling; Education and Training; English Language; Philosophy and Theology; Communications and Media
Abilities: Oral Comprehension; Written Comprehension; Oral Expression; Written Expression; Fluency of Ideas; Originality; Problem Sensitivity; Deductive Reasoning; Inductive Reasoning; Information Ordering; Category Flexibility; Mathematical Reasoning; Number Facility; Memorization; Speed of Closure; Flexibility of Closure; Perceptual Speed; Visualization; Selective Attention; Time Sharing; Arm-Hand Steadiness; Near Vision; Far Vision; Visual Color Discrimination; Speech Recognition; Speech Clarity
Skills: Reading Comprehension; Active Listening; Writing; Speaking; Science; Critical Thinking; Active Learning; Learning Strategies; Monitoring; Instructing; Problem Identification; Information Gathering; Information Organization; Synthesis/Reorganization; Solution Appraisal; Equipment Selection; Systems Evaluation; Time Management; Management of Financial Resources; Management of Material Resources; Management of Personnel Resources
General Work Activities: Getting Information Needed to Do the Job; Monitoring Processes, Material, or Surroundings; Identifying Objects, Actions, and Events; Judging Qualities of Things, Services, People; Processing Information; Analyzing Data or Information; Updating and Using Job-Relevant Knowledge; Scheduling Work and Activities; Organizing, Planning, and Prioritizing; Operating Vehicles or Equipment; Repairing and Maintaining Electrical Equipment; Documenting/Recording Information; Interpreting Meaning of Information to Others; Communicating with Other Workers; Communicating with Persons Outside Organization; Establishing and Maintaining Relationships; Resolving Conflicts, Negotiating with Others; Coordinating Work and Activities of Others; Developing and Building Teams; Teaching Others; Guiding, Directing and Motivating Subordinates; Coaching and Developing Others; Provide Consultation and Advice to Others; Performing Administrative Activities; Monitoring and Controlling Resources
Job Characteristics: Deal with Physical, Aggressive People; Diseases/Infections; Special Uniform; Common Protective or Safety Attire; Degree of Automation; Importance of Being Exact or Accurate; Importance of Being Sure All is Done
GOE Group/s: 02.04.02 Laboratory Technology: Life Sciences
CIP Program/s: 511002 Cytotechnologist; 511004 Medical Laboratory Technician; 511005 Medical Technology; 511099 Health and Medical Laboratory Technologists and Technicians, Other
Related DOT Job/s: 078.121-010 MEDICAL TECHNOLOGIST, TEACHING SUPERVISOR; 078.161-010 MEDICAL TECHNOLOGIST, CHIEF; 078.261-010 BIOCHEMISTRY TECHNOLOGIST; 078.261-014 MICROBIOLOGY TECHNOLOGIST; 078.261-026 CYTOGENETIC TECHNOLOGIST; 078.261-030 HISTOTECHNOLOGIST; 078.261-038 MEDICAL TECHNOLOGIST; 078.261-046 IMMUNOHEMATOLOGIST; 078.281-010 CYTOTECHNOLOGIST

32905 MEDICAL AND CLINICAL LABORATORY TECHNICIANS. OOH Title/s: Clinical Laboratory Technologists and Technicians

Perform routine tests in medical laboratory for use in treatment and diagnosis of disease. Prepare vaccines, biologicals, and serums for prevention of disease. Prepare tissue samples for pathologists, take blood samples, and execute such laboratory tests as urinalysis and blood counts. May work under the general supervision of a medical laboratory technologist. Conducts quantitative and qualitative chemical analyses of body fluids, such as blood, urine, and spinal fluid. Performs blood counts, using microscope. Incubates bacteria for specified period and prepares vaccines and serums by standard laboratory methods. Conducts blood tests for transfusion purposes. Inoculates fertilized eggs, broths, or other bacteriological media with organisms. Tests vaccines for sterility and virus inactivity. Prepares standard volumetric solutions and reagents used in testing. Draws blood from patient, observing principles of asepsis to obtain blood sample.
Yearly Earnings: $27,196
Education: Bachelor's degree
Knowledge: Mathematics; Chemistry; Biology; Medicine and Dentistry; Philosophy and Theology
Abilities: Oral Comprehension; Inductive Reasoning; Information Ordering; Category Flexibility; Number Facility; Memorization; Speed of Closure; Flexibility of Closure; Perceptual Speed; Selective Attention; Arm-Hand Steadiness; Finger Dexterity; Wrist-Finger Speed; Near Vision; Visual Color Discrimination
Skills: Science; Testing
General Work Activities: Monitoring Processes, Material, or Surroundings; Processing Information; Controlling Machines and Processes
Job Characteristics: Radiation; Diseases/Infections; Special Uniform; Common Protective or Safety Attire; Specialized Protective or Safety Attire; Consequence of Error; Degree of Automation; Importance of Being Exact or Accurate; Importance of Being Sure All is Done
GOE Group/s: 02.04.02 Laboratory Technology: Life Sciences
CIP Program/s: 511003 Hematology Tech./Technician; 511004 Medical Laboratory Technician
Related DOT Job/s: 078.381-014 MEDICAL-LABORATORY TECHNICIAN; 078.687-010 LABORATORY ASSISTANT, BLOOD AND PLASMA; 559.361-010 LABORATORY TECHNICIAN, PHARMACEUTICAL

32908 DENTAL HYGIENISTS. OOH Title/s: Dental Hygienists

Perform dental prophylactic treatments and instruct groups and individuals in the care of the teeth and mouth. Cleans calcareous deposits, accretions, and stains from teeth and beneath margins of gums, using dental instruments. Applies fluorides and other cavity-preventing agents to arrest dental decay. Provides clinical services and health education to improve and maintain oral health of school children. Conducts dental health clinics for community groups to augment services of dentist. Removes excess cement from coronal surfaces of teeth. Charts conditions of decay and disease for diagnosis and treatment by dentist. Places and removes rubber dams, matrices, and temporary restorations. Examines gums, using probes, to locate periodontal recessed gums and signs of gum disease. Feels lymph nodes under patient's chin to detect swelling or tenderness that could indicate presence of oral cancer. Feels and visually examines gums for sores and signs of disease. Places, carves, and finishes amalgam restorations. Makes impressions for study casts. Removes sutures and dressings. Exposes and develops X ray film. Administers local anesthetic agents.
Yearly Earnings: $23,972

Education: Associate degree
Knowledge: Biology; Medicine and Dentistry
Abilities: Arm-Hand Steadiness
Skills: Reading Comprehension; Science; Service Orientation
General Work Activities: Establishing and Maintaining Relationships; Assisting and Caring for Others; Performing for or Working with Public
Job Characteristics: Deal with External Customers; Deal with Unpleasant or Angry People; Radiation; Diseases/Infections; Special Uniform; Common Protective or Safety Attire; Importance of Being Sure All is Done
GOE Group/s: 10.02.02 Nursing, Therapy, and Specialized Teaching Services: Therapy and Rehabilitation
CIP Program/s: 510602 Dental Hygienist
Related DOT Job/s: 078.361-010 DENTAL HYGIENIST

32911 MEDICAL RECORDS TECHNICIANS. OOH Title/s: Medical Record Technicians

Compile and maintain medical records of hospital and clinic patients. Compiles and maintains medical records of patients to document condition and treatment and to provide data for research studies. Compiles medical care and census data for statistical reports on diseases treated, surgery performed, and use of hospital beds. Maintains variety of health record indexes and storage and retrieval systems. Reviews records for completeness and to abstract and code data, using standard classification systems, and to identify and compile patient data. Enters data such as demographic characteristics, history and extent of disease, diagnostic procedures, and treatment into computer. Contacts discharge patients, their families, and physicians to maintain registry with follow-up information, such as quality of life and length of survival of cancer patients. Prepares statistical reports, narrative reports, and graphic presentations of tumor registry data for use by hospital staff, researchers, and other users. Assists in special studies or research, as needed.
Yearly Earnings: $23,972
Education: Associate degree
Knowledge: Clerical; Computers and Electronics; Mathematics; Medicine and Dentistry
Abilities: Wrist-Finger Speed
Skills: Information Organization
General Work Activities: Operating Vehicles or Equipment; Guiding, Directing and Motivating Subordinates; Performing Administrative Activities
Job Characteristics: Supervise, Coach, Train Others; Sitting; Special Uniform; Importance of Being Exact or Accurate
GOE Group/s: 07.05.03 Records Processing: Record Preparation and Maintenance
CIP Program/s: 510707 Medical Records Tech./Technician; 510999 Health and Medical Diagnostic and Treatment Services, Other
Related DOT Job/s: 079.362-014 MEDICAL RECORD TECHNICIAN; 079.362-018 TUMOR REGISTRAR; 169.167-046 PUBLIC HEALTH REGISTRAR

32913 RADIATION THERAPISTS. OOH Title/s: Radiologic Technologists

Provide radiation therapy to patients as prescribed by a radiologist, according to established practices and standards. Duties may include reviewing prescription and diagnosis; acting as liaison with physician and supportive care personnel; preparing equipment, such as immobilization, treatment, and protection devices; and maintaining records, reports, and files. May assist in dosimetry procedures and tumor localization. Reviews prescription, diagnosis, patient chart, and identification. Acts as liaison with physician and supportive care personnel. Maintains records, reports, and files as required. Prepares equipment, such as immobilization, treatment, and protection devices, and positions patient according to prescription. Enters data into computer and sets controls to operate and adjust equipment and regulate dosage. Follows principles of radiation protection for patient, self, and others. Observes and reassures patient during treatment and reports unusual reactions to physician. Photographs treated area of patient and processes film.
Yearly Earnings: $29,224
Education: Associate degree
Knowledge: Clerical; Customer and Personal Service; Computers and Electronics; Biology; Medicine and Dentistry; Therapy and Counseling
Abilities: Category Flexibility; Speed of Closure; Flexibility of Closure; Selective Attention; Response Orientation; Gross Body Equilibrium; Speech Clarity
Skills: Science; Operation Monitoring; Operation and Control
General Work Activities: Identifying Objects, Actions, and Events; Operating Vehicles or Equipment; Assisting and Caring for Others
Job Characteristics: Provide a Service to Others; Deal with External Customers; Responsible for Others' Health and Safety; Radiation; Diseases/Infections; Special Uniform; Common Protective or Safety Attire; Specialized Protective or Safety Attire; Consequence of Error; Importance of Being Exact or Accurate; Importance of Being Sure All is Done
GOE Group/s: 10.02.02 Nursing, Therapy, and Specialized Teaching Services: Therapy and Rehabilitation
CIP Program/s: 510905 Nuclear Medical Technologists and Technicians
Related DOT Job/s: 078.361-034 RADIATION-THERAPY TECHNOLOGIST

32914 NUCLEAR MEDICINE TECHNOLOGISTS. OOH Title/s: Health Services Managers

Prepare, administer, and measure radioactive isotopes in therapeutic, diagnostic, and tracer studies utilizing a variety of radioisotope equipment. Prepare stock solutions of radioactive materials and calculate doses to be administered by radiologist. Subject patients to radiation. Execute blood volume, red cell survival, and fat absorption studies following standard laboratory techniques. Administers radiopharmaceuticals or radiation to patient to detect or treat diseases, using radioisotope equipment, under direction of physician. Calculates, measures, prepares, and records radiation dosage or radiopharmaceuticals, using computer and following physician's prescription and X rays. Measures glandular activity, blood volume, red cell survival, and radioactivity of patient, using scanners, Geiger counters, scintillometers, and other laboratory equipment. Positions radiation fields, radiation beams, and patient to develop most effective treatment of patient's disease, using computer. Maintains and calibrates radioisotope and laboratory equipment. Develops computer protocols and treatment procedures for nuclear medicine studies and treatment programs. Disposes of radioactive materials and stores radiopharmaceuticals, following radiation safety procedures. Trains, coordinates, and monitors nuclear medicine technologists' activities to ensure accuracy and safety.
Yearly Earnings: $29,224
Education: Associate degree
Knowledge: Clerical; Computers and Electronics; Physics; Chemistry; Biology; Medicine and Dentistry; Therapy and Counseling
Abilities: Oral Comprehension; Written Comprehension; Problem Sensitivity; Deductive Reasoning; Information Ordering

Skills: Reading Comprehension; Mathematics; Science; Instructing; Programming; Operation Monitoring; Operation and Control; Equipment Maintenance; Management of Personnel Resources
General Work Activities: Getting Information Needed to Do the Job; Monitoring Processes, Material, or Surroundings; Identifying Objects, Actions, and Events; Inspecting Equipment, Structures, or Material; Estimating Needed Characteristics; Judging Qualities of Things, Services, People; Processing Information; Evaluating Information against Standards; Analyzing Data or Information; Making Decisions and Solving Problems; Thinking Creatively; Updating and Using Job-Relevant Knowledge; Developing Objectives and Strategies; Controlling Machines and Processes; Operating Vehicles or Equipment; Implementing Ideas, Programs, etc.; Repairing and Maintaining Electrical Equipment; Interpreting Meaning of Information to Others; Assisting and Caring for Others; Performing for or Working with Public; Coordinating Work and Activities of Others; Developing and Building Teams; Teaching Others; Guiding, Directing and Motivating Subordinates; Coaching and Developing Others
Job Characteristics: Responsible for Others' Health and Safety; Radiation; Diseases/Infections; Special Uniform; Common Protective or Safety Attire; Specialized Protective or Safety Attire; Consequence of Error; Importance of Being Exact or Accurate; Importance of Being Sure All is Done; Importance of Being Aware of New Events
GOE Group/s: 02.04.02 Laboratory Technology: Life Sciences; 10.02.02 Nursing, Therapy, and Specialized Teaching Services: Therapy and Rehabilitation
CIP Program/s: 510905 Nuclear Medical Technologists and Technicians; 510907 Medical Radiologic Technologists and Technicians
Related DOT Job/s: 078.131-010 CHIEF TECHNOLOGIST, NUCLEAR MEDICINE; 078.261-034 MEDICAL RADIATION DOSIMETRIST; 078.361-018 NUCLEAR MEDICINE TECHNOLOGIST

32919 RADIOLOGIC TECHNOLOGISTS. OOH Title/s: Radiologic Technologists; Health Services Managers

Take X rays and CAT scans or administer nonradioactive materials into patient's blood stream for diagnostic purposes. Include technologists who specialize in other modalities, such as computed tomography, ultrasound, and magnetic resonance. Include workers whose primary duties are to demonstrate portions of the human body on X ray film or fluoroscopic screen. Operates or oversees operation of radiologic and magnetic imaging equipment to produce photographs of the body for diagnostic purposes. Administers oral or injected contrast media to patients. Operates fluoroscope to aid physician to view and guide wire or catheter through blood vessels to area of interest. Positions imaging equipment and adjusts controls to set exposure time and distance, according to specification of examination. Keys commands and data into computer to document and specify scan sequences, adjust transmitters and receivers, or photograph certain images. Monitors video display of area being, scanned and adjusts density or contrast to improve picture quality. Monitors use of radiation safety measures to comply with government regulations and to ensure safety of patients and staff. Positions and immobilizes patient on examining table. Reviews and evaluates developed X rays, videotape, or computer-generated information for technical quality. Explains procedures and observes patients to ensure safety and comfort during scan. Demonstrates new equipment, procedures, and techniques, and provides technical assistance to staff. Assigns duties to radiologic staff to maintain patient flows and achieve production goals. Develops departmental operating budget and coordinates purchase of supplies and equipment. Evaluates radiologic staff and recommends or implements personnel actions, such as promotions or disciplinary procedures.
Yearly Earnings: $29,224
Education: Associate degree
Knowledge: Computers and Electronics; Chemistry; Biology; Psychology; Medicine and Dentistry
Skills: Reading Comprehension; Equipment Selection; Operation Monitoring; Operation and Control
General Work Activities: Identifying Objects, Actions, and Events; Updating and Using Job-Relevant Knowledge; Handling and Moving Objects; Controlling Machines and Processes; Operating Vehicles or Equipment; Assisting and Caring for Others
Job Characteristics: Supervise, Coach, Train Others; Responsible for Others' Health and Safety; Radiation; Diseases/Infections; Special Uniform; Specialized Protective or Safety Attire; Importance of Being Exact or Accurate; Importance of Being Sure All is Done
GOE Group/s: 02.04.01 Laboratory Technology: Physical Sciences; 10.02.02 Nursing, Therapy, and Specialized Teaching Services: Therapy and Rehabilitation
CIP Program/s: 510907 Medical Radiologic Technologists and Technicians; 510910 Diagnostic Medical Sonography; 510999 Health and Medical Diagnostic and Treatment Services, Other
Related DOT Job/s: 078.162-010 RADIOLOGIC TECHNOLOGIST, CHIEF; 078.362-026 RADIOLOGIC TECHNOLOGIST; 078.362-046 SPECIAL PROCEDURES TECHNOLOGIST, ANGIOGRAM; 078.362-054 SPECIAL PROCEDURES TECHNOLOGIST, CT SCAN; 078.362-058 SPECIAL PROCEDURES TECHNOLOGIST, MAGNETIC RESONANCE IMAGING (MRI); 078.364-010 ULTRASOUND TECHNOLOGIST

32921 RADIOLOGIC TECHNICIANS. OOH Title/s: Radiologic Technologists

Maintain and use equipment and supplies necessary to demonstrate portions of the human body on X ray film or fluoroscopic screen for diagnostic purposes. Uses beam-restrictive devices and patient-shielding skills to minimize radiation exposure to patient and staff. Moves X ray equipment into position and adjusts controls to set exposure factors, such as time and distance. Operates mobile X ray equipment in operating room, emergency room, or at patient's bedside. Positions patient on examining table and adjusts equipment to obtain optimum view of specific body area requested by physician. Explains procedures to patient to reduce anxieties and obtain patient cooperation.
Yearly Earnings: $29,224
Education: Associate degree
Knowledge: Customer and Personal Service; Biology; Medicine and Dentistry
Abilities: Gross Body Coordination
Skills: None above average
General Work Activities: Assisting and Caring for Others; Performing for or Working with Public
Job Characteristics: Responsible for Others' Health and Safety; Radiation; Diseases/Infections; Special Uniform; Specialized Protective or Safety Attire; Consequence of Error; Importance of Being Exact or Accurate
GOE Group/s: 10.02.02 Nursing, Therapy, and Specialized Teaching Services: Therapy and Rehabilitation
CIP Program/s: 510907 Medical Radiologic Technologists and Technicians
Related DOT Job/s: 078.362-026 RADIOLOGIC TECHNOLOGIST

32923 ELECTRONEURODIAGNOSTIC TECHNOLOGISTS. OOH Title/s: Electroneurodiagnostic Technologists

Record electrical activity of the brain and other nervous system functions using a variety of techniques and equipment. May prepare patients for the test, obtain medical history, calculate results, and maintain equipment. Measures electrical activity of

brain and nerves, using electroencephalograph (EEG), polysomnograph, or electromyograph to diagnose brain, sleep, and nervous system disorders. Operates recording instruments and supplemental equipment and chooses settings for optimal viewing of nervous system. Attaches electrodes to predetermined locations, and verifies functioning of electrodes and recording instrument. Records montage (electrode combination) and instrument settings, and observes and notes patient's behavior during test. Performs other physiological tests, such as electrocardiogram, electrooculogram, and ambulatory electroencephalogram. Measures patient's head and other body parts, using tape measure, and marks points where electrodes are to be placed. Conducts visual, auditory, and somatosensory-evoked-potential response tests to measure latency of response to stimuli. Writes technical reports summarizing test results to assist physician in diagnosis of brain disorders. Monitors patient during surgery, using EEG or evoked-potential instrument. Performs video monitoring of patient's actions during test.
Yearly Earnings: $23,972
Education: Moderate-term O-J-T
Knowledge: Computers and Electronics; Biology; Medicine and Dentistry; English Language
Abilities: Written Expression; Selective Attention
Skills: Writing; Operation and Control
General Work Activities: Monitoring Processes, Material, or Surroundings; Identifying Objects, Actions, and Events; Evaluating Information against Standards; Analyzing Data or Information; Updating and Using Job-Relevant Knowledge; Documenting/Recording Information; Interpreting Meaning of Information to Others; Communicating with Other Workers; Assisting and Caring for Others; Performing for or Working with Public
Job Characteristics: Responsible for Others' Health and Safety; Diseases/Infections; Special Uniform; Specialized Protective or Safety Attire; Consequence of Error; Importance of Being Exact or Accurate; Importance of Being Sure All is Done; Importance of Being Aware of New Events
GOE Group/s: 10.03.01 Child and Adult Care: Data Collection
CIP Program/s: 510903 Electroencephalograph Technologists and Technicians
Related DOT Job/s: 078.362-022 ELECTROENCEPHALOGRAPHIC TECHNOLOGIST; 078.362-038 ELECTROMYOGRAPHIC TECHNICIAN; 078.362-042 POLYSOMNOGRAPHIC TECHNICIAN

32925 CARDIOLOGY TECHNOLOGISTS. OOH Title/s: Cardiovascular Technologists and Technicians; Health Services Managers; Medical Assistants

Conduct tests on pulmonary and/or cardiovascular systems of patients for diagnostic purposes. May conduct or assist in electrocardiograms, cardiac catheterizations, and pulmonary function, lung capacity and similar tests. Operates diagnostic imaging equipment to produce contrast-enhanced radiographs of heart and cardiovascular system. Injects contrast medium into blood vessels of patient. Activates fluoroscope and 35 mm motion picture camera to produce images used to guide catheter through cardiovascular system. Conducts electrocardiogram, phonocardiogram, echocardiogram, stress testing, and other cardiovascular tests, using specialized electronic test equipment, recording devices, and laboratory instruments. Conducts tests of pulmonary system, using spirometer and other respiratory testing equipment. Observes gauges, recorder, and video screens of multichannel data analysis system, during imaging of cardiovascular system. Operates multichannel physiologic monitor to measure and record functions of cardiovascular and pulmonary systems, as part of cardiac catheterization team. Records variations in action of heart muscle, using electrocardiograph. Records two-dimensional ultrasonic and Doppler flow analyses of heart and related structures, using ultrasound equipment. Observes ultrasound display screen and listens to Doppler signals to acquire data for measurement of blood flow velocities. Compares measurements of heart wall thickness and chamber sizes to standard norms to identify abnormalities. Assesses cardiac physiology and calculates valve areas from blood flow velocity measurements. Enters factors such as amount and quality of radiation beam, and filming sequence, into computer. Alerts physician to abnormalities or changes in patient responses. Adjusts equipment and controls according to physicians' orders or established protocol. Explains testing procedures to patient to obtain cooperation and reduce anxiety. Reviews test results with physician. Records test results and other data into patient's record. Prepares and positions patients for testing.
Yearly Earnings: $23,972
Education: Associate degree
Knowledge: Clerical; Computers and Electronics; Physics; Chemistry; Biology; Psychology; Medicine and Dentistry; Therapy and Counseling; English Language; Foreign Language
Abilities: Hearing Sensitivity
Skills: Science; Testing; Operation Monitoring; Operation and Control
General Work Activities: Monitoring Processes, Material, or Surroundings; Identifying Objects, Actions, and Events; Processing Information; Evaluating Information against Standards; Updating and Using Job-Relevant Knowledge; Documenting/Recording Information; Interpreting Meaning of Information to Others; Establishing and Maintaining Relationships; Assisting and Caring for Others; Performing for or Working with Public; Provide Consultation and Advice to Others
Job Characteristics: Radiation; Diseases/Infections; Special Uniform; Specialized Protective or Safety Attire; Consequence of Error; Importance of Being Exact or Accurate; Importance of Being Sure All is Done; Importance of Being Aware of New Events
GOE Group/s: 02.04.02 Laboratory Technology: Life Sciences; 10.02.02 Nursing, Therapy, and Specialized Teaching Services: Therapy and Rehabilitation; 10.03.01 Child and Adult Care: Data Collection
CIP Program/s: 510901 Cardiovascular Technologists and Technicians; 510910 Diagnostic Medical Sonography
Related DOT Job/s: 078.161-014 CARDIOPULMONARY TECHNOLOGIST, CHIEF; 078.262-010 PULMONARY-FUNCTION TECHNICIAN; 078.264-010 HOLTER SCANNING TECHNICIAN; 078.362-030 CARDIOPULMONARY TECHNOLOGIST; 078.362-034 PERFUSIONIST; 078.362-050 SPECIAL PROCEDURES TECHNOLOGIST, CARDIAC CATHETERIZATION; 078.362-062 STRESS TEST TECHNICIAN; 078.364-014 ECHOCARDIOGRAPH TECHNICIAN

32926 ELECTROCARDIOGRAPH TECHNICIANS. OOH Title/s: Cardiovascular Technologists and Technicians

Record electromotive variations in heart muscle using electrocardiograph, to provide data for diagnosis of heart ailments. Moves electrodes along specified area of chest to produce electrocardiogram and record electromotive variations occurring in different areas of heart muscle. Connects electrode leads to EKG machine and starts machine to record pulse from electrodes. Monitors electrocardiogram to identify abnormal heart rhythm patterns. Keys information into machine or presses button to mark tracing paper to indicate positions of chest electrodes. Obtains information from patient for electrocardiograph (EKG) records, including patient identification, brief history, and medication used. Attaches electrodes to specified locations on patient, such as chest, arms, and legs. Enters patient data into computer for analysis of tracing. Attaches electrodes of Holter monitor (electrocardiograph) to patient to record data over extended period of time. Explains test procedures and gives instructions to patient. Directs patient to perform physical exercise as specified by physician. Edits and forwards final test results to attending physician for analysis and interpretation. Maintains patient comfort and privacy, using such meth-

ods as draping and bed screens. Pastes and labels tracings on mounting cards. Notifies physicians of emergencies and assists physicians in emergencies. Escorts patient to treatment room or wheels equipment to patient bedside. Cleans and maintains equipment and supplies.
Yearly Earnings: $23,972
Education: Associate degree
Knowledge: Clerical; Customer and Personal Service; Computers and Electronics; Biology; Psychology; Medicine and Dentistry; Therapy and Counseling; Philosophy and Theology
Abilities: Oral Comprehension; Oral Expression; Problem Sensitivity; Inductive Reasoning; Information Ordering; Memorization; Speed of Closure; Flexibility of Closure; Perceptual Speed; Spatial Orientation; Selective Attention; Finger Dexterity; Response Orientation; Reaction Time; Hearing Sensitivity; Speech Recognition
Skills: Speaking; Science; Service Orientation; Operation Monitoring; Operation and Control; Equipment Maintenance
General Work Activities: Identifying Objects, Actions, and Events; Processing Information; Controlling Machines and Processes; Repairing and Maintaining Electrical Equipment; Establishing and Maintaining Relationships; Assisting and Caring for Others
Job Characteristics: Job-Required Social Interaction; Responsible for Others' Health and Safety; Deal with Unpleasant or Angry People; Diseases/Infections; Walking or Running; Special Uniform; Consequence of Error; Degree of Automation; Importance of Being Sure All is Done; Importance of Being Aware of New Events
GOE Group/s: 10.03.01 Child and Adult Care: Data Collection
CIP Program/s: 510902 Electrocardiograph Technologists and Technicians
Related DOT Job/s: 078.362-018 ELECTROCARDIOGRAPH TECHNICIAN

32928 SURGICAL TECHNOLOGISTS AND TECHNICIANS. OOH Title/s: Surgical Technologists

Perform any combination of the following tasks, either before, during, or after an operation: prepare patient by washing, shaving, etc.; place equipment and supplies in operating room according to surgeon's instructions; arrange instruments under direction of nurse; maintain specified supply of fluids for use during operation; adjust lights and equipment as directed; hand instruments and supplies to surgeon, hold retractors, and cut sutures as directed; count sponges, needles, and instruments used during operation; and clean operating room. Places equipment and supplies in operating room and arranges instruments, according to instruction. Maintains supply of fluids, such as plasma, saline, blood, and glucose, for use during operation. Hands instruments and supplies to surgeon, holds retractors and cuts sutures, and performs other tasks as directed by surgeon during operation. Cleans operating room. Counts sponges, needles, and instruments before and after operation. Washes and sterilizes equipment, using germicides and sterilizers. Assists team members to place and position patient on table. Puts dressings on patient following surgery. Scrubs arms and hands and dons gown and gloves. Aids team to don gowns and gloves.
Yearly Earnings: $23,972
Education: Postsecondary vocational training
Knowledge: Biology; Medicine and Dentistry
Skills: Active Listening
General Work Activities: Assisting and Caring for Others
Job Characteristics: Diseases/Infections; Standing; Special Uniform; Consequence of Error; Importance of Being Sure All is Done
GOE Group/s: 10.03.02 Child and Adult Care: Patient Care
CIP Program/s: 510909 Surgical/Operating Room Technician
Related DOT Job/s: 079.374-022 SURGICAL TECHNICIAN

32931 PSYCHIATRIC TECHNICIANS. OOH Title/s: Psychiatric technicians

Provide nursing care to mentally ill, emotionally disturbed, or mentally retarded patients. Participate in rehabilitation and treatment programs. Help with personal hygiene. Administer oral medications and hypodermic injections, following physician's prescriptions and hospital procedures. Monitor patient's physical and emotional well-being and report to medical staff. Helps patients with their personal hygiene, such as bathing and keeping beds, clothing, and living areas clean. Administers oral medications and hypodermic injections, following physician's prescriptions and hospital procedures. Takes and records measures of patient's general physical condition, such as pulse, temperature, and respiration, to provide daily information. Observes patients to detect behavior patterns and reports observations to medical staff. Issues medications from dispensary and maintains records in accordance with specified procedures. Leads prescribed individual or group therapy sessions as part of specific therapeutic procedures. Intervenes to restrain violent or potentially violent or suicidal patients by verbal or physical means as required. Contacts patient's relatives by telephone to arrange family conferences. Completes initial admittance forms for new patients.
Yearly Earnings: $14,456
Education: Associate degree
Knowledge: Clerical; Customer and Personal Service; Biology; Psychology; Medicine and Dentistry; Therapy and Counseling
Skills: Reading Comprehension; Active Listening; Speaking; Learning Strategies; Monitoring; Social Perceptiveness; Service Orientation
General Work Activities: Establishing and Maintaining Relationships; Assisting and Caring for Others; Resolving Conflicts, Negotiating with Others
Job Characteristics: Job-Required Social Interaction; Provide a Service to Others; Deal with External Customers; Responsible for Others' Health and Safety; Frequency in Conflict Situations; Deal with Unpleasant or Angry People; Deal with Physical, Aggressive People; Diseases/Infections; Special Uniform
GOE Group/s: 10.02.02 Nursing, Therapy, and Specialized Teaching Services: Therapy and Rehabilitation
CIP Program/s: 511502 Psychiatric/Mental Health Services Technician
Related DOT Job/s: 079.374-026 PSYCHIATRIC TECHNICIAN

32996A HEALTH SERVICE COORDINATORS. OOH Title/s: Health Technologists and Technicians

Conduct or coordinate health programs or services in hospitals, private homes, businesses, or other institutions. Monitors medical records to schedule services or to determine patient review dates according to established criteria. Analyzes utilization of health care program and legitimacy of admission and treatment to ensure quality or compliance with reimbursement policies. Formulates and negotiates health program contracts between insurance companies and health care providers, utilizing standard agreement procedures and insurance company policies. Presents health care program to participating parties and discusses program modifications or health and nutritional issues. Interviews individuals to obtain participant medical histories and maintains health records. Evaluates services and prepares reports. Investigates and resolves claims reimbursement and program procedural problems. Reviews application for patient admission, according to insurance and governmental standards, and approves admission or refers for review. Abstracts or compiles information and data and maintains statistics. Oversees and coordinates activities of staff or in hospital services. Conducts information and training workshops on resolving claim processing errors. Participates in health advisory committee or quality assurance reviews.

Yearly Earnings: $26,156
Education: Associate degree
Knowledge: Administration and Management; Clerical; Customer and Personal Service; Personnel and Human Resources; Medicine and Dentistry; Therapy and Counseling; Education and Training
Abilities: Oral Comprehension; Written Comprehension; Oral Expression; Written Expression; Problem Sensitivity; Deductive Reasoning; Inductive Reasoning; Mathematical Reasoning; Number Facility; Memorization; Perceptual Speed; Time Sharing
Skills: Reading Comprehension; Active Listening; Writing; Speaking; Social Perceptiveness; Negotiation; Instructing; Information Gathering; Synthesis/Reorganization; Implementation Planning; Programming; Visioning; Systems Perception; Identifying Downstream Consequences; Systems Evaluation; Management of Financial Resources
General Work Activities: Getting Information Needed to Do the Job; Monitoring Processes, Material, or Surroundings; Identifying Objects, Actions, and Events; Judging Qualities of Things, Services, People; Processing Information; Evaluating Information against Standards; Analyzing Data or Information; Making Decisions and Solving Problems; Updating and Using Job-Relevant Knowledge; Developing Objectives and Strategies; Scheduling Work and Activities; Implementing Ideas, Programs, etc.; Documenting/Recording Information; Interpreting Meaning of Information to Others; Communicating with Other Workers; Communicating with Persons Outside Organization; Establishing and Maintaining Relationships; Assisting and Caring for Others; Selling or Influencing Others; Resolving Conflicts, Negotiating with Others; Performing for or Working with Public; Coordinating Work and Activities of Others; Teaching Others; Guiding, Directing and Motivating Subordinates; Provide Consultation and Advice to Others; Performing Administrative Activities
Job Characteristics: Supervise, Coach, Train Others; Take a Position Opposed to Others; Deal with External Customers; Coordinate or Lead Others; Responsibility for Outcomes and Results; Frequency in Conflict Situations; Deal with Unpleasant or Angry People; Diseases/Infections; Sitting; Frustrating Circumstances
Related DOT Job/s: See Individual Specialists

32996B TRANSPLANT COORDINATORS. OOH

Title/s: Health Services Managers

Plan and coordinate organ and tissue services and solicit medical and community groups for organ and tissue donors. Assists medical team in retrieval of organs for transplantation, using medical instruments. Solicits medical and community groups for organ donors. Coordinates in-hospital services. Communicates with donors, patients, and health team members to ensure comprehensive documentation. Analyzes medical data of organ donors and recipients from medical and social records, physical examination, and consultation with health team. Compares collected data to normal values and correlates. Correlates and summarizes laboratory reports, X rays, and office test to assist physician to determine medical suitability for procedure. Schedules recipient and donor laboratory tests to determine histocompatibility of blood or tissue of recipient donor. Counsels recipient and donor to alleviate anxieties and assists recipient and donor throughout procedure. Assesses progress of patient and offers advice and assistance to patient following transplant. Advises post-operative patients on therapies for managing health after transplant and serves as team member monitor.
Yearly Earnings: $26,156
Education: Associate degree
Knowledge: Administration and Management; Clerical; Customer and Personal Service; Mathematics; Biology; Psychology; Medicine and Dentistry; Therapy and Counseling
Abilities: Oral Comprehension; Written Comprehension; Oral Expression; Written Expression; Problem Sensitivity; Inductive Reasoning; Information Ordering; Memorization; Speed of Closure; Flexibility of Closure; Perceptual Speed; Time Sharing; Arm-Hand Steadiness; Manual Dexterity; Finger Dexterity; Response Orientation; Reaction Time; Wrist-Finger Speed; Near Vision; Depth Perception; Speech Recognition; Speech Clarity
Skills: Reading Comprehension; Active Listening; Writing; Speaking; Mathematics; Science; Critical Thinking; Active Learning; Monitoring; Social Perceptiveness; Coordination; Persuasion; Negotiation; Service Orientation; Information Gathering; Information Organization; Programming; Visioning; Systems Perception; Identifying Downstream Consequences; Judgment and Decision Making; Management of Material Resources
General Work Activities: Getting Information Needed to Do the Job; Monitoring Processes, Material, or Surroundings; Identifying Objects, Actions, and Events; Inspecting Equipment, Structures, or Material; Judging Qualities of Things, Services, People; Evaluating Information against Standards; Analyzing Data or Information; Making Decisions and Solving Problems; Updating and Using Job-Relevant Knowledge; Developing Objectives and Strategies; Scheduling Work and Activities; Organizing, Planning, and Prioritizing; Documenting/Recording Information; Communicating with Other Workers; Communicating with Persons Outside Organization; Establishing and Maintaining Relationships; Assisting and Caring for Others; Selling or Influencing Others; Performing for or Working with Public; Coordinating Work and Activities of Others; Teaching Others; Coaching and Developing Others; Provide Consultation and Advice to Others; Performing Administrative Activities
Job Characteristics: Job-Required Social Interaction; Persuade Someone to a Course of Action; Provide a Service to Others; Deal with External Customers; Coordinate or Lead Others; Responsible for Others' Health and Safety; Frequency in Conflict Situations; Diseases/Infections; Special Uniform; Specialized Protective or Safety Attire; Consequence of Error; Frustrating Circumstances; Importance of Being Exact or Accurate; Importance of Being Sure All is Done; Importance of Being Aware of New Events
GOE Group/s: 10.02.01 Nursing, Therapy, and Specialized Teaching Services: Nursing
CIP Program/s: 510999 Health and Medical Diagnostic and Treatment Services, Other
Related DOT Job/s: 079.151-010 TRANSPLANT COORDINATOR

32996C OCCUPATIONAL HEALTH AND SAFETY SPECIALISTS. OOH Title/s: Inspectors and Compliance Officers, Except Construction; Health Technologists and Technicians

Review, evaluate, and analyze work environments and design programs and procedures to control, eliminate, and prevent disease or injury caused by chemical, physical, and biological agents or ergonomic factors. Investigates adequacy of ventilation, exhaust equipment, lighting, and other conditions which may affect employee health, comfort, or efficiency. Conducts evaluations of exposure to ionizing and nonionizing radiation and to noise. Collects samples of dust, gases, vapors, and other potentially toxic materials for analysis. Recommends measures to ensure maximum employee protection. Collaborates with engineers and physicians to institute control and remedial measures for hazardous and potentially hazardous conditions of equipment. Participates in educational meetings to instruct employees in matters pertaining to occupational health and prevention of accidents. Prepares reports, including observations, analysis of contaminants, and recommendation for control and correction of hazards. Reviews physicians' reports and conducts worker studies to

determine if diseases or illnesses are job-related. Prepares and calibrates equipment used to collect and analyze samples. Prepares documents to be used in legal proceedings and gives testimony in court proceedings. Uses cost-benefit analysis to justify money spent.
Yearly Earnings: $26,156
Education: Associate degree
Knowledge: Economics and Accounting; Physics; Chemistry; Biology; Medicine and Dentistry; Education and Training; Public Safety and Security; Law, Government, and Jurisprudence
Abilities: Written Comprehension; Oral Expression; Written Expression; Originality; Problem Sensitivity; Deductive Reasoning; Inductive Reasoning; Mathematical Reasoning; Number Facility; Memorization; Speed of Closure; Flexibility of Closure
Skills: Reading Comprehension; Active Listening; Writing; Speaking; Mathematics; Science; Persuasion; Negotiation; Instructing; Problem Identification; Information Gathering; Operations Analysis; Testing; Operation Monitoring; Systems Perception; Identifying Downstream Consequences; Management of Financial Resources
General Work Activities: Getting Information Needed to Do the Job; Monitoring Processes, Material, or Surroundings; Identifying Objects, Actions, and Events; Inspecting Equipment, Structures, or Material; Judging Qualities of Things, Services, People; Processing Information; Evaluating Information against Standards; Analyzing Data or Information; Making Decisions and Solving Problems; Updating and Using Job-Relevant Knowledge; Developing Objectives and Strategies; Drafting and Specifying Technical Devices, etc.; Implementing Ideas, Programs, etc.; Documenting/Recording Information; Interpreting Meaning of Information to Others; Communicating with Other Workers; Communicating with Persons Outside Organization; Selling or Influencing Others; Teaching Others; Provide Consultation and Advice to Others; Performing Administrative Activities; Monitoring and Controlling Resources
Job Characteristics: Persuade Someone to a Course of Action; Take a Position Opposed to Others; Deal with External Customers; Responsible for Others' Health and Safety; Frequency in Conflict Situations; Contaminants; Radiation; Diseases/Infections; Hazardous Conditions; Walking or Running; Common Protective or Safety Attire; Specialized Protective or Safety Attire; Importance of Being Sure All is Done
GOE Group/s: 11.10.03 Regulations Enforcement: Health and Safety
CIP Program/s: 150701 Occupational Safety and Health Technologists and Technicians
Related DOT Job/s: 079.161-010 INDUSTRIAL HYGIENIST

32999A ORTHOTISTS AND PROSTHETISTS. OOH Title/s: Health Technologists and Technicians

Fabricate and fit orthopedic braces or prostheses to assist patients with disabling conditions of limbs and spine, or with partial or total absence of limb. Fits patients for device, using static and dynamic alignments. Assists physician in formulating specifications and prescription for orthopedic and/or prosthetic devices. Designs orthopedic and prosthetic devices, according to physician's prescription. Selects materials and components, and makes cast measurements, model modifications, and layouts, using measuring equipment. Evaluates device on patient and makes adjustments to assure fit, function, comfort, and quality. Instructs patients in use of orthopedic or prosthetic devices. Examines, measures, and evaluates patients' needs in relation to disease and functional loss. Maintains patients' records. Repairs and maintains orthopedic prosthetic devices, using hand tools. Supervises laboratory activities or activities of prosthetic assistants and support staff relating to development of orthopedic or prosthetic devices. Lectures and demonstrates to colleagues and other professionals concerned with orthopedics or prosthetics. Participates in research to modify design, fit, and function of orthopedic or prosthetic devices.
Yearly Earnings: $26,156
Education: Associate degree
Knowledge: Customer and Personal Service; Engineering and Technology; Design; Building and Construction; Psychology; Medicine and Dentistry; Therapy and Counseling; Education and Training
Abilities: Oral Comprehension; Written Comprehension; Oral Expression; Fluency of Ideas; Originality; Problem Sensitivity; Deductive Reasoning; Inductive Reasoning; Category Flexibility; Speed of Closure; Visualization; Time Sharing; Arm-Hand Steadiness; Finger Dexterity; Control Precision; Near Vision; Speech Clarity
Skills: Active Listening; Speaking; Science; Social Perceptiveness; Instructing; Service Orientation; Solution Appraisal; Operations Analysis; Technology Design; Installation; Programming; Product Inspection; Time Management; Management of Personnel Resources
General Work Activities: Inspecting Equipment, Structures, or Material; Drafting and Specifying Technical Devices, etc.; Assisting and Caring for Others; Performing for or Working with Public; Guiding, Directing and Motivating Subordinates
Job Characteristics: Job-Required Social Interaction; Supervise, Coach, Train Others; Provide a Service to Others; Coordinate or Lead Others; Responsible for Others' Health and Safety; Responsibility for Outcomes and Results; Diseases/Infections; Kneeling, Crouching, or Crawling; Bending or Twisting the Body; Special Uniform; Frustrating Circumstances; Importance of Being Exact or Accurate; Importance of Being Sure All is Done
GOE Group/s: 05.05.11 Craft Technology: Scientific, Medical, & Technical Equip. Fabric. & Related; 10.03.02 Child and Adult Care: Patient Care
CIP Program/s: 510801 Medical Assistant; 512307 Orthotics/Prosthetics
Related DOT Job/s: 078.261-018 ORTHOTIST; 078.261-022 PROSTHETIST; 078.361-022 ORTHOTICS ASSISTANT; 078.361-026 PROSTHETICS ASSISTANT; 078.664-010 ORTHOPEDIC ASSISTANT

32999B PHERESIS TECHNICIANS. OOH Title/s: Health Technologists and Technicians

Collect blood components and provide therapeutic treatment, such as replacement of plasma or removal of white blood cells or platelets, using blood cell separator equipment. Punctures vein of donor/patient with needle to connect donor or patient to tubing of equipment in preparation for procedure. Adjusts equipment settings for blood collection or replacement. Monitors equipment and observes warning lights indicating equipment problems. Connects and installs tubing, fluid containers, and other components to set up equipment. Compiles and evaluates donor/patient information, such as blood pressure and weight, to ensure that screening criteria are met. Explains procedures to patient to reduce anxieties and obtain cooperation. Talks to and observes patient for distress or side effects, such as nausea or fainting, during procedure. Records information such as flow rate, anticoagulant rate, temperature, and blood pressure following blood collection or treatment. Forwards collection bag to laboratory for testing or further processing.
Yearly Earnings: $26,156
Education: Associate degree
Knowledge: Biology; Psychology; Medicine and Dentistry; Therapy and Counseling
Abilities: Perceptual Speed; Arm-Hand Steadiness; Manual Dexterity; Finger Dexterity; Control Precision; Response Orientation; Reaction Time; Wrist-Finger Speed; Near Vision
Skills: Operation Monitoring
General Work Activities: Assisting and Caring for Others; Performing for or Working with Public
Job Characteristics: Job-Required Social Interaction; Provide a Service to Others; Deal with External Customers; Responsible for Others' Health and Safety; Diseases/Infections; Special Uniform; Common

Protective or Safety Attire; Frustrating Circumstances; Importance of Being Exact or Accurate; Importance of Being Sure All is Done
GOE Group/s: 10.02.02 Nursing, Therapy, and Specialized Teaching Services: Therapy and Rehabilitation
CIP Program/s: 510999 Health and Medical Diagnostic and Treatment Services, Other
Related DOT Job/s: 078.261-042 PHERESIS SPECIALIST

32999C OPTOMETRIC AND OPHTHALMIC TECHNICIANS. OOH Title/s: Medical Assistants

Test and measure eye function to assist with diagnosis and treatment of disease. Tests and measures patient's acuity, peripheral vision, depth perception, focus, ocular movement and color, as requested by physician. Measures intraocular pressure of eyes, using glaucoma test. Measures axial length of eye, using ultrasound equipment. Examines eye for abnormalities of cornea and anterior or posterior chambers, using slit lamp. Applies drops to anesthetize, dilate, or medicate eyes. Instructs patient in eye care and use of glasses or contact lenses. Instructs patient in vision therapy, using eye exercises. Obtains and records patient's preliminary case history. Adjusts and repairs glasses, using screwdrivers and pliers. Assists patient in frame selection. Assists in fabrication of eye glasses or contact lenses. Develops visual skills, near-visual discrimination, and depth perception, using developmental glasses. Maintains records, schedules appointments, and performs bookkeeping, correspondence, and filing. Maintains inventory of materials and cleans instruments.
Yearly Earnings: $26,156
Education: Associate degree
Knowledge: Customer and Personal Service; Biology; Medicine and Dentistry; Therapy and Counseling
Abilities: Near Vision; Peripheral Vision; Depth Perception
Skills: Service Orientation
General Work Activities: Performing for or Working with Public
Job Characteristics: Provide a Service to Others; Deal with External Customers; Diseases/Infections; Sitting; Importance of Being Exact or Accurate; Importance of Being Sure All is Done
GOE Group/s: 10.02.02 Nursing, Therapy, and Specialized Teaching Services: Therapy and Rehabilitation; 10.03.01 Child and Adult Care: Data Collection; 10.03.02 Child and Adult Care: Patient Care
CIP Program/s: 510804 Ophthalmic Medical Assistant; 510899 Health and Medical Assistants, Other; 511803 Ophthalmic Medical Technologist; 511804 Orthoptics
Related DOT Job/s: 078.361-038 OPHTHALMIC TECHNICIAN; 079.364-014 OPTOMETRIC ASSISTANT; 079.371-014 ORTHOPTIST

32999D AUDIOMETRISTS. OOH Title/s: Health Technologists and Technicians

Administer audiometric screening and threshold tests under supervision of audiologist or otolaryngologist and refer individual to audiologist or other health professional for test interpretation or further examination. Fits earphones on individuals and provides instruction on procedures to be followed. Adjusts audiometer to control sound emitted and records subjects' responses. Refers individuals to audiologist for interpretation of test results and more definitive hearing examination, or to physician for medical examination.
Yearly Earnings: $26,156
Education: Associate degree
Knowledge: None above average
Skills: None above average
General Work Activities: None above average
Job Characteristics: Job-Required Social Interaction; Provide a Service to Others; Sitting; Making Repetitive Motions; Importance of Being Exact or Accurate; Importance of Being Sure All is Done
GOE Group/s: 10.03.01 Child and Adult Care: Data Collection
CIP Program/s: 512601 Health Aide
Related DOT Job/s: 078.362-010 AUDIOMETRIST

32999E DIALYSIS TECHNICIANS. OOH Title/s: Health Technologists and Technicians

Set up and operate hemodialysis machine to provide dialysis treatment for patients with kidney failure. Starts blood flow at prescribed rate. Inspects equipment settings, including pressure, conductivity, and temperature, to ensure conformance to safety standards. Attaches tubing to assemble machine for use. Mixes solution according to formula and primes equipment. Calculates fluid removal or replacement to be achieved during dialysis procedure. Monitors patient for adverse reaction and machine malfunction. Cleans area of access with antiseptic solution. Connects patient to machine, using needle or catheter. Records patient's predialysis and postdialysis weight, temperature, and blood pressure. Explains procedures and operation of equipment to patient. Transports patient to and from treatment room.
Yearly Earnings: $26,156
Education: Associate degree
Knowledge: Customer and Personal Service; Chemistry; Biology; Medicine and Dentistry; Therapy and Counseling
Abilities: Information Ordering
Skills: Operation Monitoring
General Work Activities: Identifying Objects, Actions, and Events; Controlling Machines and Processes; Assisting and Caring for Others
Job Characteristics: Job-Required Social Interaction; Deal with External Customers; Responsible for Others' Health and Safety; Deal with Unpleasant or Angry People; Diseases/Infections; Special Uniform; Consequence of Error; Importance of Being Exact or Accurate; Importance of Being Sure All is Done; Importance of Being Aware of New Events; Pace Determined by Speed of Equipment
GOE Group/s: 10.02.02 Nursing, Therapy, and Specialized Teaching Services: Therapy and Rehabilitation
CIP Program/s: 510999 Health and Medical Diagnostic and Treatment Services, Other
Related DOT Job/s: 078.362-014 DIALYSIS TECHNICIAN

Artistic, Creative, and Entertainment Providers

34002A COLUMNISTS, CRITICS, AND COMMENTATORS. OOH Title/s: Writers and Editors; Radio and Television Announcers and Newscasters

Write commentaries or critical reviews based on analysis of news items or literary, musical, or artistic works and performances. Analyzes and interprets news, current issues, and personal experiences to formulate ideas and other materials for column or commentary. Analyzes factors such as theme, expression, and technique, and forms critical opinions of literary, musical, dramatic, or visual art works and performances. Writes column, editorial, commentary, or review to stimulate or influence public opinion. Gathers information and develops perspective through research, interview, experience, and attendance at political, news, sports, artistic, social, and other functions. Revises text to meet editorial approval or to fit time or space requirements. Selects and organizes material pertinent to presentation into appropriate media form and format. Enters information into computer to prepare commentary or review. Discusses issues with editor of publication or broadcast facility editorial board to establish priorities and positions. Presents commentary live or in recorded form when working in broadcast medium.
Yearly Earnings: $32,916
Education: Bachelor's degree

Knowledge: Computers and Electronics; English Language; Fine Arts; Communications and Media
Abilities: Written Expression; Fluency of Ideas; Originality; Category Flexibility; Speed of Closure; Perceptual Speed
Skills: Reading Comprehension; Writing; Speaking; Critical Thinking; Active Learning; Persuasion; Information Gathering; Synthesis/Reorganization; Idea Generation; Idea Evaluation; Visioning
General Work Activities: Getting Information Needed to Do the Job; Monitoring Processes, Material, or Surroundings; Judging Qualities of Things, Services, People; Thinking Creatively; Organizing, Planning, and Prioritizing; Operating Vehicles or Equipment; Interpreting Meaning of Information to Others; Communicating with Other Workers; Communicating with Persons Outside Organization; Establishing and Maintaining Relationships; Selling or Influencing Others; Performing for or Working with Public; Provide Consultation and Advice to Others
Job Characteristics: Objective or Subjective Information; Take a Position Opposed to Others; Sitting
GOE Group/s: 01.01.02 Literary Arts: Creative Writing; 01.01.03 Literary Arts: Critiquing; 11.08.03 Communications: Writing and Broadcasting
CIP Program/s: 090401 Journalism; 090402 Broadcast Journalism; 230501 English Creative Writing; 500501 Drama/Theater Arts, General; 500505 Drama/Theater Literature, History and Criticism; 500601 Film/Cinema Studies; 500901 Music, General; 500902 Music History and Literature
Related DOT Job/s: 131.067-010 COLUMNIST/COMMENTATOR; 131.067-018 CRITIC; 131.067-022 EDITORIAL WRITER

34002B POETS AND LYRICISTS. OOH Title/s: Writers and Editors

Write poetry or song lyrics for publication or performance. Writes words to fit musical compositions, including lyrics for operas, musical plays, and choral works. Writes narrative, dramatic, lyric, or other types of poetry for publication. Adapts text to accommodate musical requirements of composer and singer. Chooses subject matter and suitable form to express personal feeling and experience or ideas or to narrate story or event.
Yearly Earnings: $32,916
Education: Bachelor's degree
Knowledge: English Language; Fine Arts; Communications and Media
Abilities: Written Expression; Fluency of Ideas; Originality; Hearing Sensitivity
Skills: Writing
General Work Activities: Thinking Creatively
Job Characteristics: Objective or Subjective Information; Sitting
GOE Group/s: 01.01.02 Literary Arts: Creative Writing
CIP Program/s: 230501 English Creative Writing
Related DOT Job/s: 131.067-030 LIBRETTIST; 131.067-034 LYRICIST; 131.067-042 POET

34002C CREATIVE WRITERS. OOH Title/s: Writers and Editors; Social Scientists

Create original written works, such as plays or prose, for publication or performance. Writes fiction or nonfiction prose work, such as short story, novel, biography, article, descriptive or critical analysis, or essay. Writes play or script for moving pictures or television, based on original ideas or adapted from fictional, historical, or narrative sources. Writes humorous material for publication or performance, such as comedy routines, gags, comedy shows, or scripts for entertainers. Organizes material for project, plans arrangement or outline, and writes synopsis. Develops factors, such as theme, plot, characterization, psychological analysis, historical environment, action, and dialogue, to create material. Selects subject or theme for writing project based on personal interest and writing specialty, or on assignment from publisher, client, producer, or director. Reviews, submits for approval, and revises written material to meet personal standards and satisfy needs of client, publisher, director, or producer. Conducts research to obtain factual information and authentic detail, utilizing sources such as newspaper accounts, diaries, and interviews. Confers with client, publisher, or producer to discuss development changes or revisions. Collaborates with other writers on specific projects.
Yearly Earnings: $32,916
Education: Bachelor's degree
Knowledge: Sociology and Anthropology; English Language; Fine Arts; Communications and Media
Abilities: Oral Comprehension; Written Comprehension; Written Expression; Fluency of Ideas; Originality; Inductive Reasoning; Near Vision
Skills: Reading Comprehension; Writing; Critical Thinking; Coordination; Idea Generation; Idea Evaluation
General Work Activities: Judging Qualities of Things, Services, People; Thinking Creatively; Organizing, Planning, and Prioritizing; Communicating with Persons Outside Organization; Selling or Influencing Others
Job Characteristics: Objective or Subjective Information; Sitting
GOE Group/s: 01.01.02 Literary Arts: Creative Writing
CIP Program/s: 090401 Journalism; 090402 Broadcast Journalism; 090701 Radio and Television Broadcasting; 230501 English Creative Writing; 231101 English Technical and Business Writing; 500501 Drama/Theater Arts, General; 500504 Playwriting and Screenwriting
Related DOT Job/s: 052.067-010 BIOGRAPHER; 131.067-026 HUMORIST; 131.067-038 PLAYWRIGHT; 131.067-046 WRITER, PROSE, FICTION AND NONFICTION; 131.067-050 SCREEN WRITER; 131.087-010 CONTINUITY WRITER; 139.087-010 CROSSWORD-PUZZLE MAKER

34002D EDITORS. OOH Title/s: Writers and Editors

Perform variety of editorial duties, such as laying out, indexing, and revising content of written materials in preparation for final publication. Exclude managing editors, programming and script editors, book editors, and film editors. Plans and prepares page layouts to position and space articles and photographs or illustrations. Reads and evaluates manuscripts or other materials submitted for publication, and confers with authors regarding changes or publication. Writes and rewrites headlines, captions, columns, articles, and stories to conform to publication's style, editorial policy, and publishing requirements. Determines placement of stories based on relative significance, available space, and knowledge of layout principles. Confers with management and editorial staff members regarding placement of developing news stories. Reads copy or proof to detect and correct errors in spelling, punctuation, and syntax, and indicates corrections, using standard proofreading and typesetting symbols. Selects and crops photographs and illustrative materials to conform to space and subject matter requirements. Reviews and approves proofs submitted by composing room. Reads material to determine items to be included in index of book or other publication. Arranges topical or alphabetical list of index items, according to page or chapter, indicating location of item in text. Verifies facts, dates, and statistics, using standard reference sources. Compiles index cross-references and related items, such as glossaries, bibliographies, and footnotes. Selects local, state, national, and international news items received by wire from press associations.
Yearly Earnings: $32,916
Education: Bachelor's degree
Knowledge: English Language; Communications and Media
Abilities: Written Comprehension; Written Expression; Originality; Problem Sensitivity; Deductive Reasoning; Information Ordering; Memorization; Flexibility of Closure; Visualization; Near Vision

Skills: Reading Comprehension; Writing; Persuasion; Product Inspection

General Work Activities: Getting Information Needed to Do the Job; Monitoring Processes, Material, or Surroundings; Judging Qualities of Things, Services, People; Thinking Creatively; Organizing, Planning, and Prioritizing; Drafting and Specifying Technical Devices, etc.; Communicating with Other Workers; Establishing and Maintaining Relationships; Selling or Influencing Others; Resolving Conflicts, Negotiating with Others; Guiding, Directing and Motivating Subordinates; Provide Consultation and Advice to Others; Staffing Organizational Units; Monitoring and Controlling Resources

Job Characteristics: Objective or Subjective Information; Importance of Being Exact or Accurate; Importance of Being Sure All is Done

GOE Group/s: 01.01.01 Literary Arts: Editing; 11.08.01 Communications: Editing

CIP Program/s: 090401 Journalism; 090402 Broadcast Journalism; 090701 Radio and Television Broadcasting; 230501 English Creative Writing; 231101 English Technical and Business Writing; 520501 Business Communications

Related DOT Job/s: 132.067-022 EDITOR, GREETING CARD; 132.067-026 EDITOR, NEWS; 132.267-010 EDITOR, TELEGRAPH; 132.267-014 EDITORIAL ASSISTANT; 132.367-010 EDITOR, INDEX

34002E MANAGING EDITORS. OOH Title/s: Writers and Editors

Direct and coordinate editorial operations of newspaper, newspaper department, or magazine. Include workers who formulate editorial policy. Formulates editorial and publication policies in consultation and negotiation with owner's representative, executives, editorial policy committee, and department heads. Directs and coordinates editorial departments and activities of personnel engaged in selecting, gathering, and editing news and photography for radio, television station, or print. Assigns research, writing, and editorial duties to staff members and reviews work products. Confers with management and staff to relay information, develop operating procedures and schedules, allocate space or time, and solve problems. Originates or approves story ideas or themes, sets priorities, and assigns coverage to members of reporting and photography staff. Directs page make-up of publication, organizes material, plans page layouts, and selects type. Edits copy or reviews edited copy to ensure that writing meets establishment standards and slanderous, libelous, and profane statements are avoided. Reviews final proofs, approves or makes changes, and performs other editorial duties. Coordinates and tracks assignments, using computer and two-way radio. Writes leading or policy editorials, headlines, articles, and other materials. Reads and selects submitted material, such as letters and articles, for publication. Secures graphic material from picture sources and assigns artists and photographers to produce pictures, illustrations, and cartoons. Interviews individuals and attends gatherings to obtain items for publication, verify facts, and clarify information. Represents organization at professional and community functions and maintains contact with outside agencies. Performs personnel-related activities, such as hiring, reviewing work, and terminating employment.

Yearly Earnings: $32,916

Education: Bachelor's degree

Knowledge: Administration and Management; Personnel and Human Resources; Computers and Electronics; English Language; Communications and Media

Abilities: Oral Comprehension; Written Comprehension; Oral Expression; Written Expression; Fluency of Ideas; Originality; Deductive Reasoning; Category Flexibility; Memorization; Speed of Closure; Flexibility of Closure; Perceptual Speed; Selective Attention; Time Sharing

Skills: Reading Comprehension; Active Listening; Writing; Speaking; Critical Thinking; Active Learning; Learning Strategies; Monitoring; Social Perceptiveness; Coordination; Negotiation; Instructing; Problem Identification; Information Gathering; Information Organization; Synthesis/Reorganization; Idea Evaluation; Programming; Visioning; Judgment and Decision Making; Systems Evaluation; Time Management; Management of Material Resources; Management of Personnel Resources

General Work Activities: Getting Information Needed to Do the Job; Monitoring Processes, Material, or Surroundings; Judging Qualities of Things, Services, People; Processing Information; Making Decisions and Solving Problems; Thinking Creatively; Updating and Using Job-Relevant Knowledge; Developing Objectives and Strategies; Scheduling Work and Activities; Organizing, Planning, and Prioritizing; Operating Vehicles or Equipment; Drafting and Specifying Technical Devices, etc.; Interpreting Meaning of Information to Others; Communicating with Other Workers; Communicating with Persons Outside Organization; Establishing and Maintaining Relationships; Selling or Influencing Others; Resolving Conflicts, Negotiating with Others; Performing for or Working with Public; Coordinating Work and Activities of Others; Developing and Building Teams; Teaching Others; Guiding, Directing and Motivating Subordinates; Coaching and Developing Others; Provide Consultation and Advice to Others; Performing Administrative Activities; Staffing Organizational Units; Monitoring and Controlling Resources

Job Characteristics: Objective or Subjective Information; Job-Required Social Interaction; Supervise, Coach, Train Others; Persuade Someone to a Course of Action; Coordinate or Lead Others; Responsibility for Outcomes and Results; Sitting

GOE Group/s: 01.01.01 Literary Arts: Editing; 11.05.01 Business Administration: Management Services: Non-Government; 11.08.01 Communications: Editing

CIP Program/s: 090401 Journalism; 090402 Broadcast Journalism; 230501 English Creative Writing; 231101 English Technical and Business Writing

Related DOT Job/s: 132.017-010 EDITOR, MANAGING, NEWSPAPER; 132.017-014 EDITOR, NEWSPAPER; 132.037-014 EDITOR, CITY; 132.037-018 EDITOR, DEPARTMENT; 132.037-022 EDITOR, PUBLICATIONS; 132.067-010 BUREAU CHIEF; 132.132-010 ASSIGNMENT EDITOR

34002F PROGRAMMING AND SCRIPT EDITORS AND COORDINATORS. OOH Title/s: Writers and Editors

Direct and coordinate activities of workers who prepare scripts for radio, television, or motion picture productions. Include workers who develop, write, and edit proposals for new radio or television programs. Reviews writers' work and gives instruction and direction regarding changes, additions, and corrections. Hires, assigns work to, and supervises staff and freelance writers or other employees. Writes or edits proposals for original program concepts, and submits proposals for review by programming, financial, and other departmental personnel. Evaluates stories, proposals, or other materials to determine potential and feasibility of development into scripts or programs. Reads and evaluates written material to select writers and stories for radio, television, or motion picture production. Edits material to ensure conformance with company policy and standards, copyright laws, and federal regulations. Rewrites, combines, and polishes draft scripts, as necessary, to prepare scripts for production. Participates in selection of researchers, consultants, producers, and on-air personalities to facilitate development of program ideas. Maintains liaison between program production department and proposal originators to ensure timely exchange of information regarding project. Recommends purchasing material for use in developing scripts, in consultation with production head. Authorizes budget preparation for final proposals.

Yearly Earnings: $32,916
Education: Bachelor's degree
Knowledge: Administration and Management; Economics and Accounting; Personnel and Human Resources; English Language; Fine Arts; Communications and Media
Abilities: Oral Comprehension; Written Comprehension; Written Expression; Fluency of Ideas; Originality; Inductive Reasoning
Skills: Reading Comprehension; Writing; Critical Thinking; Active Learning; Learning Strategies; Coordination; Persuasion; Negotiation; Idea Generation; Idea Evaluation; Management of Financial Resources; Management of Personnel Resources
General Work Activities: Judging Qualities of Things, Services, People; Thinking Creatively; Developing Objectives and Strategies; Scheduling Work and Activities; Organizing, Planning, and Prioritizing; Communicating with Other Workers; Establishing and Maintaining Relationships; Selling or Influencing Others; Resolving Conflicts, Negotiating with Others; Coordinating Work and Activities of Others; Developing and Building Teams; Guiding, Directing and Motivating Subordinates; Coaching and Developing Others; Provide Consultation and Advice to Others; Performing Administrative Activities; Staffing Organizational Units; Monitoring and Controlling Resources
Job Characteristics: Objective or Subjective Information; Supervise, Coach, Train Others; Coordinate or Lead Others; Sitting; Importance of Being Sure All is Done
GOE Group/s: 01.01.01 Literary Arts: Editing; 11.05.02 Business Administration: Administrative Specialization
CIP Program/s: 090402 Broadcast Journalism; 090701 Radio and Television Broadcasting; 230501 English Creative Writing; 500501 Drama/Theater Arts, General; 500504 Playwriting and Screenwriting
Related DOT Job/s: 132.037-010 CONTINUITY DIRECTOR; 132.037-026 STORY EDITOR; 132.067-030 PROGRAM PROPOSALS COORDINATOR

34002G BOOK EDITORS. OOH Title/s: Writers and Editors

Secure, select, and coordinate publication of manuscripts in book form. Confers with author and publisher to arrange purchase and details such as publication date, royalties, and quantity to be printed. Coordinates book design and production activities. Makes recommendations regarding procurement and revision of manuscript. Contracts design and production or personally designs and produces book. Reviews submitted book manuscript and determines market demand based on consumer trends and personal knowledge. Assigns and supervises editorial staff work activities.
Yearly Earnings: $32,916
Education: Bachelor's degree
Knowledge: Administration and Management; Sales and Marketing; English Language; Communications and Media
Abilities: Written Comprehension; Fluency of Ideas; Originality; Category Flexibility; Speed of Closure; Flexibility of Closure; Selective Attention
Skills: Reading Comprehension; Writing; Coordination; Persuasion; Negotiation; Idea Evaluation; Operations Analysis; Judgment and Decision Making; Management of Personnel Resources
General Work Activities: Getting Information Needed to Do the Job; Monitoring Processes, Material, or Surroundings; Judging Qualities of Things, Services, People; Making Decisions and Solving Problems; Thinking Creatively; Developing Objectives and Strategies; Scheduling Work and Activities; Organizing, Planning, and Prioritizing; Communicating with Other Workers; Communicating with Persons Outside Organization; Establishing and Maintaining Relationships; Selling or Influencing Others; Resolving Conflicts, Negotiating with Others; Coordinating Work and Activities of Others; Developing and Building Teams; Guiding, Directing and Motivating Subordinates; Coaching and Developing Others; Provide Consultation and Advice to Others; Performing Administrative Activities; Staffing Organizational Units; Monitoring and Controlling Resources
Job Characteristics: Objective or Subjective Information; Supervise, Coach, Train Others; Persuade Someone to a Course of Action; Coordinate or Lead Others; Sitting
GOE Group/s: 01.01.01 Literary Arts: Editing
CIP Program/s: 230501 English Creative Writing; 231101 English Technical and Business Writing
Related DOT Job/s: 132.067-014 EDITOR, BOOK

34002H READERS. OOH Title/s: Writers and Editors

Read books, plays, or scripts to prepare synopses for review by editorial staff or to recommend content revisions. Reads novels, stories, and plays and prepares synopses for review by editorial department or film, radio, or television producer. Recommends revisions to or disallows broadcast of materials violating federal regulations or station standards. Reads and listens to material to be broadcast on radio or television to detect vulgar, libelous, or misleading statements. Prepares recommended editorial revisions in script, using computer or typewriter. Suggests possible treatment of selected materials in film or program. Confers with sales or advertising agency personnel to report on revised or disallowed commercials.
Yearly Earnings: $32,916
Education: Bachelor's degree
Knowledge: English Language; Communications and Media
Abilities: Written Comprehension; Written Expression; Originality; Flexibility of Closure; Wrist-Finger Speed; Near Vision
Skills: Reading Comprehension; Writing; Critical Thinking; Active Learning; Idea Evaluation
General Work Activities: Judging Qualities of Things, Services, People; Processing Information
Job Characteristics: Objective or Subjective Information; Take a Position Opposed to Others; Sitting
GOE Group/s: 01.01.01 Literary Arts: Editing; 07.05.02 Records Processing: Record Verification and Proofing
CIP Program/s: 090402 Broadcast Journalism; 090701 Radio and Television Broadcasting
Related DOT Job/s: 131.087-014 READER; 131.267-022 SCRIPT READER

34002J CAPTION WRITERS. OOH Title/s: Writers and Editors

Write caption phrases of dialogue for hearing-impaired and foreign language-speaking viewers of movie or television productions. Writes captions to describe music and background noises. Watches production and reviews captions simultaneously to determine which caption phrases require editing. Translates foreign-language dialogue into English-language captions or English dialogue into foreign-language captions. Enters commands to synchronize captions with dialogue and place on the screen. Operates computerized captioning system for movies or television productions for hearing-impaired and foreign-language speaking viewers. Edits translations for correctness of grammar, punctuation, and clarity of expression. Oversees encoding of captions to master tape of television production. Discusses captions with directors or producers of movie and television productions.
Yearly Earnings: $32,916
Education: Bachelor's degree
Knowledge: Computers and Electronics; English Language; Foreign Language; Communications and Media
Abilities: Wrist-Finger Speed; Near Vision
Skills: Writing

General Work Activities: Operating Vehicles or Equipment; Interpreting Meaning of Information to Others
Job Characteristics: Sitting
GOE Group/s: 07.05.03 Records Processing: Record Preparation and Maintenance
CIP Program/s: 160101 Foreign Languages and Literatures, General; 160103 Foreign Language Interpretation and Translation
Related DOT Job/s: 203.362-026 CAPTION WRITER

34002L COPY WRITERS. OOH Title/s: Writers and Editors

Write advertising copy for use by publication or broadcast media to promote sale of goods and services. Writes advertising copy for use by publication or broadcast media and revises copy according to supervisor's instructions. Writes articles, bulletins, sales letters, speeches, and other related informative and promotional material. Prepares advertising copy, using computer. Consults with sales media and marketing representatives to obtain information on product or service and discuss style and length of advertising copy. Obtains additional background and current development information through research and interviews. Reviews advertising trends, consumer surveys, and other data regarding marketing of goods and services to formulate approach.
Yearly Earnings: $32,916
Education: Bachelor's degree
Knowledge: Sales and Marketing; Computers and Electronics; English Language; Communications and Media
Abilities: Oral Comprehension; Written Comprehension; Written Expression; Fluency of Ideas; Originality; Wrist-Finger Speed; Near Vision
Skills: Reading Comprehension; Writing; Active Learning; Social Perceptiveness; Persuasion; Idea Generation; Idea Evaluation; Programming
General Work Activities: Judging Qualities of Things, Services, People; Thinking Creatively; Selling or Influencing Others
Job Characteristics: Objective or Subjective Information; Provide a Service to Others; Sitting; Importance of Being Sure All is Done
GOE Group/s: 01.01.02 Literary Arts: Creative Writing
CIP Program/s: 090201 Advertising
Related DOT Job/s: 131.067-014 COPY WRITER

34002M DICTIONARY EDITORS. OOH Title/s: Writers and Editors

Research information about words, and write and review definitions for publication in dictionary. Conducts or directs research to discover origin, spelling, syllabication, pronunciation, meaning, and usage of words. Organizes research material and writes definitions for general or specialized dictionary. Studies frequency of use for specific words and other factors to select words for inclusion in dictionary. Edits and reviews definitions written by other staff prior to publication. Selects drawings or other graphic material to illustrate word meaning.
Yearly Earnings: $32,916
Education: Bachelor's degree
Knowledge: English Language
Abilities: Written Expression; Category Flexibility; Speed of Closure; Perceptual Speed; Selective Attention
Skills: Reading Comprehension; Writing; Information Gathering; Information Organization; Synthesis/Reorganization
General Work Activities: Getting Information Needed to Do the Job; Interpreting Meaning of Information to Others
Job Characteristics: Sitting
GOE Group/s: 11.08.01 Communications: Editing
CIP Program/s: 230501 English Creative Writing; 231101 English Technical and Business Writing
Related DOT Job/s: 132.067-018 EDITOR, DICTIONARY

34005 TECHNICAL WRITERS. OOH Title/s: Writers and Editors; Engineering Technicians

Write or edit technical materials, such as equipment manuals, appendices, and operating and maintenance instructions. May oversee preparation of illustrations, photographs, diagrams, and charts; and assist in layout work. Organizes material and completes writing assignment according to set standards regarding order, clarity, conciseness, style, and terminology. Writes speeches, articles, and public or employee relations releases. Studies drawings, specifications, mock ups, and product samples to integrate and delineate technology, operating procedure, and production sequence and detail. Reviews published materials and recommends revisions or changes in scope, format, content, and methods of reproduction and binding. Assists in laying out material for publication. Interviews production and engineering personnel and reads journals and other material to become familiar with product technologies and production methods. Reviews manufacturer's and trade catalogs, drawings, and other data relative to operation, maintenance, and service of equipment. Edits, standardizes, or makes changes to material prepared by other writers or establishment personnel. Analyzes developments in specific field to determine need for revisions in previously published materials and development of new material. Observes production, developmental, and experimental activities to determine operating procedure and detail. Selects photographs, drawings, sketches, diagrams, and charts to illustrate material. Maintains records and files of work and revisions. Draws sketches to illustrate specified materials or assembly sequence. Arranges for typing, duplication, and distribution of material. Assigns work to other writers and oversees and edits their work.
Yearly Earnings: $32,916
Education: Bachelor's degree
Knowledge: Administration and Management; Clerical; Computers and Electronics; Engineering and Technology; Design; Sociology and Anthropology; Education and Training; English Language; Telecommunications; Communications and Media
Abilities: Oral Comprehension; Written Comprehension; Written Expression; Fluency of Ideas; Originality; Inductive Reasoning; Information Ordering; Speed of Closure; Perceptual Speed
Skills: Reading Comprehension; Active Listening; Writing; Speaking; Critical Thinking; Active Learning; Learning Strategies; Monitoring; Coordination; Instructing; Information Gathering; Information Organization; Synthesis/Reorganization; Idea Generation; Idea Evaluation; Implementation Planning; Solution Appraisal; Operations Analysis; Product Inspection; Visioning; Systems Perception; Identification of Key Causes; Judgment and Decision Making; Time Management; Management of Personnel Resources
General Work Activities: Getting Information Needed to Do the Job; Identifying Objects, Actions, and Events; Evaluating Information against Standards; Thinking Creatively; Updating and Using Job-Relevant Knowledge; Scheduling Work and Activities; Organizing, Planning, and Prioritizing; Drafting and Specifying Technical Devices, etc.; Documenting/Recording Information; Interpreting Meaning of Information to Others; Communicating with Other Workers; Coordinating Work and Activities of Others; Guiding, Directing and Motivating Subordinates; Coaching and Developing Others
Job Characteristics: Supervise, Coach, Train Others; Sitting
GOE Group/s: 11.08.02 Communications: Writing
CIP Program/s: 230501 English Creative Writing; 231101 English Technical and Business Writing; 520501 Business Communications
Related DOT Job/s: 019.267-010 SPECIFICATION WRITER; 131.267-026 WRITER, TECHNICAL PUBLICATIONS; 132.017-018 EDITOR, TECHNICAL AND SCIENTIFIC PUBLICATIONS

34008 PUBLIC RELATIONS SPECIALISTS AND PUBLICITY WRITERS. OOH Title/s: Public Relations Specialists

Engage in promoting or creating goodwill for individuals, groups, or organizations by writing or selecting favorable publicity material and releasing it through various communications media. Prepare and arrange displays, make speeches, and perform related publicity efforts. Plans and directs development and communication of informational programs designed to keep public informed of client's products, accomplishments, or agenda. Prepares and distributes fact sheets, news releases, photographs, scripts, motion pictures, or tape recordings to media representatives and others. Promotes sales and/or creates goodwill for client's products, services, or persona by coordinating exhibits, lectures, contests, or public appearances. Prepares or edits organizational publications, such as newsletters to employees or public or stockholders' reports, to favorably present client's viewpoint. Studies needs, objectives, and policies of organization or individual seeking to influence public opinion or promote specific products. Conducts market and public opinion research to introduce or test specific products or measure public opinion. Counsels clients in effective ways of communicating with public. Consults with advertising agencies or staff to arrange promotional campaigns in all types of media for products, organizations, or individuals. Purchases advertising space and time as required to promote client's product or agenda. Arranges for and conducts public-contact programs designed to meet client's objectives. Confers with production and support personnel to coordinate production of advertisements and promotions. Represents client during community projects and at public, social, and business gatherings.

Yearly Earnings: $30,004

Education: Bachelor's degree

Knowledge: Clerical; Sales and Marketing; Personnel and Human Resources; Computers and Electronics; Psychology; Sociology and Anthropology; Therapy and Counseling; Education and Training; Communications and Media

Abilities: Oral Expression; Written Expression; Fluency of Ideas; Originality; Deductive Reasoning; Mathematical Reasoning; Number Facility; Speed of Closure; Near Vision; Auditory Attention; Speech Recognition; Speech Clarity

Skills: Active Listening; Writing; Speaking; Critical Thinking; Active Learning; Learning Strategies; Monitoring; Social Perceptiveness; Coordination; Persuasion; Negotiation; Instructing; Service Orientation; Problem Identification; Information Gathering; Information Organization; Synthesis/Reorganization; Idea Generation; Idea Evaluation; Implementation Planning; Solution Appraisal; Programming; Visioning; Systems Perception; Identifying Downstream Consequences; Identification of Key Causes; Systems Evaluation; Time Management; Management of Financial Resources; Management of Material Resources; Management of Personnel Resources

General Work Activities: Getting Information Needed to Do the Job; Judging Qualities of Things, Services, People; Thinking Creatively; Scheduling Work and Activities; Organizing, Planning, and Prioritizing; Communicating with Other Workers; Communicating with Persons Outside Organization; Establishing and Maintaining Relationships; Selling or Influencing Others; Performing for or Working with Public; Provide Consultation and Advice to Others

Job Characteristics: Objective or Subjective Information; Job-Required Social Interaction; Supervise, Coach, Train Others; Persuade Someone to a Course of Action; Take a Position Opposed to Others; Deal with External Customers; Coordinate or Lead Others; Responsibility for Outcomes and Results; Frequency in Conflict Situations

GOE Group/s: 11.09.01 Promotion: Sales; 11.09.03 Promotion: Public Relations

CIP Program/s: 080204 Business Services Marketing Operations; 090501 Public Relations and Organizational Communications

Related DOT Job/s: 165.017-010 LOBBYIST; 165.167-010 SALES-SERVICE PROMOTER; 165.167-014 PUBLIC-RELATIONS REPRESENTATIVE

34011 REPORTERS AND CORRESPONDENTS. OOH Title/s: Reporters and Correspondents; Writers and Editors

Collect and analyze facts about newsworthy events by interview, investigation, or observation. Report and write stories for newspaper, news magazine, radio, or television. Exclude correspondents who broadcast news for radio and television. Gathers and verifies factual information regarding story through interview, observation, and research. Organizes material and determines slant or emphasis. Writes news stories for publication or broadcast from written or recorded notes provided by reporting staff, following prescribed editorial style and format standards. Reviews and evaluates notes to isolate pertinent facts and details. Monitors police and fire department radio communications to obtain story leads. Conducts taped or filmed interviews or narratives. Receives assignment or evaluates news leads and news tips to develop story idea. Reports live from site of event or mobile broadcast unit. Transmits information to writing staff to write story. Edits or assists in editing videos for broadcast. Takes photographs or shoots video to illustrate stories.

Yearly Earnings: $32,240

Education: Bachelor's degree

Knowledge: Computers and Electronics; Sociology and Anthropology; Geography; English Language; Telecommunications; Communications and Media

Abilities: Written Expression; Time Sharing; Speech Recognition

Skills: Reading Comprehension; Active Listening; Writing; Speaking; Critical Thinking; Active Learning; Social Perceptiveness; Persuasion; Information Gathering; Information Organization; Synthesis/Reorganization; Idea Generation

General Work Activities: Getting Information Needed to Do the Job; Monitoring Processes, Material, or Surroundings; Identifying Objects, Actions, and Events; Judging Qualities of Things, Services, People; Analyzing Data or Information; Thinking Creatively; Updating and Using Job-Relevant Knowledge; Organizing, Planning, and Prioritizing; Documenting/Recording Information; Interpreting Meaning of Information to Others; Communicating with Persons Outside Organization; Establishing and Maintaining Relationships; Selling or Influencing Others; Performing for or Working with Public

Job Characteristics: Objective or Subjective Information; Frequency in Conflict Situations; Deal with Unpleasant or Angry People; Frustrating Circumstances; Importance of Being Exact or Accurate; Importance of Being Aware of New Events

GOE Group/s: 11.08.02 Communications: Writing

CIP Program/s: 090401 Journalism; 090402 Broadcast Journalism

Related DOT Job/s: 131.262-014 NEWSWRITER; 131.262-018 REPORTER

34014 BROADCAST NEWS ANALYSTS. OOH Title/s: Radio and Television Announcers and Newscasters

Analyze, interpret, and broadcast news received from various sources. Gathers information and develops subject perspective through research, interview, observation, and experience. Analyzes and interprets information to formulate and outline story ideas. Records commentary or presents commentary or news live when working in broadcast medium. Examines news items of local, national, and international significance to determine selection, or is assigned items for broadcast by editorial staff. Selects material most pertinent to presentation and organizes material into acceptable media form and format. Writes commentary, column, or script, using computer. Edits material

for available time or space. Introduces broadcasters who specialize in particular fields, such as sports or weather.
Yearly Earnings: $30,004
Education: Long-term O-J-T
Knowledge: Computers and Electronics; Sociology and Anthropology; Geography; English Language; Foreign Language; Fine Arts; History and Archeology; Philosophy and Theology; Telecommunications; Communications and Media
Abilities: Oral Comprehension; Written Comprehension; Oral Expression; Written Expression; Speech Clarity
Skills: Reading Comprehension; Active Listening; Writing; Speaking; Critical Thinking; Social Perceptiveness; Information Gathering; Information Organization; Synthesis/Reorganization
General Work Activities: Getting Information Needed to Do the Job; Organizing, Planning, and Prioritizing; Documenting/Recording Information; Interpreting Meaning of Information to Others; Communicating with Persons Outside Organization; Establishing and Maintaining Relationships; Performing for or Working with Public
Job Characteristics: Objective or Subjective Information; Take a Position Opposed to Others; Deal with Physical, Aggressive People; Sitting; Importance of Being Aware of New Events
GOE Group/s: 11.08.03 Communications: Writing and Broadcasting
CIP Program/s: 090401 Journalism; 090402 Broadcast Journalism; 230501 English Creative Writing
Related DOT Job/s: 131.067-010 COLUMNIST/COMMENTATOR; 131.262-010 NEWSCASTER

34017 ANNOUNCERS, RADIO AND TELEVISION. OOH Title/s: Radio and Television Announcers and Newscasters; Actors, Directors, and Producers

Introduce various types of radio or television programs, interview or question guests, or act as master of ceremonies. Read news flashes and identify station by giving call letters. Announces musical selections, station breaks, commercials, or public service information, and accepts listening audience requests. Interviews show guests about their lives, their work, or topics of current interest. Reads news flashes to inform audience of important events. Asks questions of contestants, or manages play or game, to enable contestants to win prizes. Interviews guest, such as musical, sports, or public personality, and moderates panel or discussion show to entertain audience. Memorizes script and reads, interviews, or ad-libs to identify station, introduce and close shows. Comments on music and other matters, such as weather, time, or traffic conditions. Describes public event, such as parade or convention. Discusses various topics over telephone with viewers or listeners. Hosts civic, charitable, or promotional events that are broadcast over television or radio. Cues worker to transmit program from network central station or other pick-up points, according to schedule. Discusses and prepares program content with producer and assistants. Selects recordings to be played, based on program specialty, knowledge of audience taste, or listening audience requests. Describes or demonstrates products that viewers may purchase by telephoning show, by mail, or by purchase in stores. Rewrites news bulletin from wire service teletype to fit specific time slot. Keeps daily program log to provide information on all elements aired during broadcast, such as musical selections and station promotions. Operates control console.
Yearly Earnings: $30,004
Education: Long-term O-J-T
Knowledge: Sales and Marketing; Computers and Electronics; English Language; Telecommunications; Communications and Media
Abilities: Oral Expression; Memorization; Speech Clarity
Skills: Active Listening; Writing; Speaking; Social Perceptiveness; Persuasion; Synthesis/Reorganization; Time Management
General Work Activities: Communicating with Persons Outside Organization; Selling or Influencing Others; Performing for or Working with Public
Job Characteristics: Objective or Subjective Information; Sitting
GOE Group/s: 01.03.03 Performing Arts:Drama: Narrating and Announcing
CIP Program/s: 090402 Broadcast Journalism; 090701 Radio and Television Broadcasting
Related DOT Job/s: 159.147-010 ANNOUNCER; 159.147-014 DISC JOCKEY; 159.147-018 SHOW HOST/HOSTESS

34021 ANNOUNCERS, EXCEPT RADIO AND TELEVISION. OOH Title/s: Actors, Directors, and Producers

Announce information to patrons of sporting and other entertainment events using public address system. Announces program and substitutions or other changes to patrons. Informs patrons of coming events or emergency calls. Observes event to provide running commentary of activities, such as play-by-play description, or explanation of official decisions. Speaks extemporaneously to audience on items of interest, such as background and history of event or past record of participants. Reads prepared script to describe acts or tricks during performance. Furnishes information concerning play to scoreboard operator. Provides information about event to cue operation of scoreboard or control board.
Yearly Earnings: $30,004
Education: Long-term O-J-T
Knowledge: Communications and Media
Abilities: Selective Attention; Time Sharing; Far Vision; Night Vision; Peripheral Vision; Glare Sensitivity; Auditory Attention; Speech Recognition; Speech Clarity
Skills: Social Perceptiveness
General Work Activities: Performing for or Working with Public
Job Characteristics: Objective or Subjective Information; Provide a Service to Others; Extremely Bright or Inadequate Lighting; High Places; Sitting; Importance of Being Aware of New Events
GOE Group/s: 01.07.02 Elemental Arts: Announcing
CIP Program/s: 090101 Communications, General
Related DOT Job/s: 159.347-010 ANNOUNCER

34023A PROFESSIONAL PHOTOGRAPHERS. OOH Title/s: Photographers and Camera Operators

Photograph subjects or newsworthy events, using still cameras, color or black-and-white film, and variety of photographic accessories. Exclude scientific photographers. Photographs subjects or newsworthy events, using still cameras, to produce pictures, related to an area of interest. Sights camera and takes pictures of subjects or newsworthy events. Adjusts camera based on lighting, subject material, distance, and film speed. Estimates or measures light level, distance, and number of exposures needed, using measuring devices and formulas. Selects and assembles equipment and required background properties, according to subject, materials, and conditions. Observes and arranges subject material in desired position. Confers with personnel to discuss subject material or newsworthy events and conditions of shoot. Removes and develops exposed film, using chemicals, touch-up tools, and equipment. Travels to assigned location to set up equipment and take photograph. Directs activities of workers in setting up equipment used to photograph subjects or newsworthy events.
Yearly Earnings: $24,648
Education: Moderate-term O-J-T
Knowledge: Chemistry; Geography; Fine Arts; History and Archeology; Communications and Media
Abilities: Fluency of Ideas; Originality; Information Ordering; Category Flexibility; Memorization; Flexibility of Closure; Perceptual

Speed; Spatial Orientation; Visualization; Selective Attention; Time Sharing; Arm-Hand Steadiness; Finger Dexterity; Control Precision; Response Orientation; Rate Control; Reaction Time; Wrist-Finger Speed; Gross Body Equilibrium; Near Vision; Far Vision; Visual Color Discrimination; Night Vision; Peripheral Vision; Depth Perception; Glare Sensitivity
Skills: Equipment Selection; Visioning; Management of Material Resources
General Work Activities: Estimating Needed Characteristics; Judging Qualities of Things, Services, People; Thinking Creatively; Controlling Machines and Processes
Job Characteristics: Objective or Subjective Information; Extremely Bright or Inadequate Lighting; Standing; Climbing Ladders, Scaffolds, Poles, etc.; Keeping or Regaining Balance; Frustrating Circumstances
GOE Group/s: 01.02.03 Visual Arts: Commercial Art; 01.06.01 Craft Arts: Graphics Arts and Related Crafts; 05.10.05 Crafts: Reproduction
CIP Program/s: 500406 Commercial Photography; 500605 Photography
Related DOT Job/s: 143.062-014 PHOTOGRAPHER, AERIAL; 143.062-018 PHOTOGRAPHER, APPRENTICE; 143.062-030 PHOTOGRAPHER, STILL; 143.062-034 PHOTOJOURNALIST; 143.382-014 PHOTOGRAPHER, FINISH

34023B PHOTOGRAPHERS, SCIENTIFIC. OOH Title/s: Photographers and Camera Operators

Photograph variety of subject materials to illustrate or record scientific/medical data or phenomena, utilizing knowledge of scientific procedures and photographic technology and techniques. Photographs variety of subject materials to illustrate or record scientific or medical data or phenomena, related to an area of interest. Sights and focuses camera to take picture of subject material to illustrate or record scientific or medical data or phenomena. Plans methods and procedures for photographing subject material, and sets up required equipment. Observes and arranges subject material to desired position. Removes exposed film and develops film, using chemicals, touch-up tools, and equipment. Engages in research to develop new photographic procedure, materials, and scientific data.
Yearly Earnings: $24,648
Education: Moderate-term O-J-T
Knowledge: Engineering and Technology; Physics; Chemistry; Medicine and Dentistry; Fine Arts; Communications and Media
Abilities: Fluency of Ideas; Originality; Information Ordering; Category Flexibility; Memorization; Speed of Closure; Flexibility of Closure; Perceptual Speed; Spatial Orientation; Time Sharing; Response Orientation; Rate Control; Reaction Time; Gross Body Equilibrium; Near Vision; Far Vision; Visual Color Discrimination; Night Vision; Peripheral Vision; Depth Perception; Glare Sensitivity
Skills: Reading Comprehension; Science; Technology Design; Equipment Selection
General Work Activities: Thinking Creatively; Organizing, Planning, and Prioritizing; Drafting and Specifying Technical Devices, etc.
Job Characteristics: Extremely Bright or Inadequate Lighting; Hazardous Conditions; Frustrating Circumstances; Degree of Automation; Importance of Being Exact or Accurate; Importance of Being Sure All is Done
GOE Group/s: 02.04.01 Laboratory Technology: Physical Sciences; 02.04.02 Laboratory Technology: Life Sciences
CIP Program/s: 500406 Commercial Photography; 500605 Photography; 511803 Ophthalmic Medical Technologist
Related DOT Job/s: 029.280-010 PHOTO-OPTICS TECHNICIAN; 143.062-026 PHOTOGRAPHER, SCIENTIFIC; 143.362-010 BIOLOGICAL PHOTOGRAPHER; 143.362-014 OPHTHALMIC PHOTOGRAPHER

34026 CAMERA OPERATORS, TELEVISION AND MOTION PICTURE. OOH Title/s: Photographers and Camera Operators; Photographic Process Workers

Operate television or motion picture camera to photograph scenes for TV broadcasts, advertising, or motion pictures. Sets up cameras, optical printers and related equipment to produce photographs and special effects. Adjusts position and controls of camera, printer, and related equipment to produce desired effects, using precision measuring instruments. Selects cameras, accessories, equipment, and film stock to use during filming, using knowledge of filming techniques, requirements, and computations. Observes set or location for potential problems and to determine filming and lighting requirements. Views film to resolve problems of exposure control, subject and camera movement, changes in subject distance, and related variables. Reads work order to determine specifications and location of subject material. Analyzes specifications to determine work procedures, sequence of operations, and machine set-up. Confers with director and electrician regarding interpretation of scene, desired effects, and filming and lighting requirements. Reads charts and computes ratios to determine variables, such as lighting, shutter angles, filter factors, and camera distance. Exposes frames of film in sequential order and regulates exposures and aperture to obtain special effects. Instructs camera operators regarding camera set-up, angles, distances, movement, and other variables and cues for starting and stopping filming.
Yearly Earnings: $22,412
Education: Long-term O-J-T
Knowledge: Physics; Fine Arts; Telecommunications; Communications and Media
Abilities: Flexibility of Closure; Spatial Orientation; Visualization; Selective Attention; Time Sharing; Arm-Hand Steadiness; Rate Control; Far Vision; Visual Color Discrimination; Peripheral Vision; Depth Perception
Skills: Technology Design
General Work Activities: Thinking Creatively; Controlling Machines and Processes; Communicating with Other Workers; Guiding, Directing and Motivating Subordinates
Job Characteristics: Objective or Subjective Information; Supervise, Coach, Train Others; Persuade Someone to a Course of Action; Take a Position Opposed to Others; Coordinate or Lead Others; Frequency in Conflict Situations; Extremely Bright or Inadequate Lighting; High Places; Climbing Ladders, Scaffolds, Poles, etc.; Frustrating Circumstances; Importance of Being Aware of New Events; Importance of Repeating Same Tasks
GOE Group/s: 01.02.03 Visual Arts: Commercial Art; 05.10.05 Crafts: Reproduction
CIP Program/s: 100103 Photographic Technologists and Technicians; 500406 Commercial Photography; 500602 Film-Video Making/Cinematography and Production; 500605 Photography
Related DOT Job/s: 143.062-010 DIRECTOR OF PHOTOGRAPHY; 143.062-022 CAMERA OPERATOR; 143.260-010 OPTICAL-EFFECTS-CAMERA OPERATOR; 143.382-010 CAMERA OPERATOR, ANIMATION; 976.382-010 CAMERA OPERATOR, TITLE

34028B BROADCAST TECHNICIANS. OOH Title/s: Broadcast Technicians; Engineering Technicians

Set up, operate, and maintain electrical and electronic equipment used in radio and television broadcasts. Lays electrical cord and audio and video cables between vehicle, microphone, camera, and reporter or person to be interviewed. Aligns antennae with receiving dish to obtain clearest signal for transmission of news event to station. Sets up, operates, and maintains radio and television production equipment to broadcast programs or events. Monitors transmission of news event to station and adjusts equipment as needed to maintain quality

broadcast. Previews scheduled program to ensure that signal is functioning and program is ready for transmission. Performs preventive and minor equipment maintenance, using hand tools. Observes monitors and converses with station personnel to set audio and video levels and to verify station is on-air. Selects source, such as satellite or studio, from which program will be recorded. Reads television programming log to ascertain program to be recorded or aired. Maintains log, as required by station management and Federal Communications Commission. Edits manuals, schedules programs, and prepares reports outlining past and future programs, including content. Instructs trainees in how to use television production equipment, to film events, and to copy/edit graphics or sound onto videotape. Produces educational and training films and videotapes, including selection of equipment and preparation of script. Drives news van to location of news events.
Yearly Earnings: $33,540
Education: Postsecondary vocational training
Knowledge: Computers and Electronics; Geography; Education and Training; Telecommunications; Communications and Media; Transportation
Abilities: Deductive Reasoning; Information Ordering; Selective Attention; Time Sharing; Control Precision; Response Orientation; Rate Control; Reaction Time; Gross Body Coordination; Gross Body Equilibrium; Far Vision; Visual Color Discrimination; Night Vision; Peripheral Vision; Depth Perception; Glare Sensitivity; Hearing Sensitivity; Auditory Attention; Sound Localization; Speech Recognition
Skills: Writing; Learning Strategies; Monitoring; Instructing; Technology Design; Installation; Operation Monitoring; Operation and Control; Equipment Maintenance; Troubleshooting; Repairing; Visioning; Systems Perception; Management of Material Resources; Management of Personnel Resources
General Work Activities: Interacting with Computers; Repairing and Maintaining Electrical Equipment; Teaching Others
Job Characteristics: Extremely Bright or Inadequate Lighting; High Places; Standing; Climbing Ladders, Scaffolds, Poles, etc.; Frustrating Circumstances; Degree of Automation; Importance of Being Aware of New Events
GOE Group/s: 01.02.03 Visual Arts: Commercial Art; 05.03.05 Engineering Technology: Electrical-Electronic; 05.10.05 Crafts: Reproduction
CIP Program/s: 100103 Photographic Technologists and Technicians; 100104 Radio and Television Broadcasting Technologists and Technicians
Related DOT Job/s: 193.167-014 FIELD SUPERVISOR, BROADCAST; 193.262-018 FIELD ENGINEER; 194.062-010 TELEVISION TECHNICIAN; 194.122-010 ACCESS COORDINATOR, CABLE TELEVISION; 194.262-010 AUDIO OPERATOR; 194.262-022 MASTER CONTROL OPERATOR; 194.282-010 VIDEO OPERATOR; 194.362-018 TELECINE OPERATOR; 194.362-022 TECHNICIAN, NEWS GATHERING; 194.381-010 TECHNICAL TESTING ENGINEER; 194.382-018 VIDEOTAPE OPERATOR

34028C TRANSMITTER ENGINEERS. OOH Title/s: Broadcast Technicians

Operate and maintain radio transmitter to broadcast radio and television programs. Operates and maintains radio transmitter to broadcast radio and television programs. Monitors console panel and signal emission and makes adjustments as needed to maintain quality of transmission. Operates microwave transmitter and receiver to receive or send program to and from other broadcast stations. Tests components of malfunctioning transmitter to diagnose trouble, using test equipment, such as oscilloscope, voltmeters, and ammeters. Disassembles and repairs equipment, using hand tools. Notifies broadcast studio when ready to transmit. Converses with studio personnel to determine cause of equipment failure and to solve problem. Maintains log of programs transmitted, as required by Federal Communications Commission.
Yearly Earnings: $33,540
Education: Postsecondary vocational training
Knowledge: Computers and Electronics; Telecommunications; Communications and Media
Abilities: Problem Sensitivity; Selective Attention; Time Sharing; Response Orientation; Rate Control; Reaction Time; Hearing Sensitivity; Auditory Attention; Sound Localization
Skills: Testing; Operation Monitoring; Operation and Control; Troubleshooting; Repairing
General Work Activities: Controlling Machines and Processes; Repairing and Maintaining Electrical Equipment
Job Characteristics: Radiation; High Places; Degree of Automation; Importance of Being Aware of New Events
GOE Group/s: 05.03.05 Engineering Technology: Electrical-Electronic
CIP Program/s: 100104 Radio and Television Broadcasting Technologists and Technicians
Related DOT Job/s: 193.262-038 TRANSMITTER OPERATOR

34032 FILM EDITORS. OOH Title/s: Photographic Process Workers; Actors, Directors, and Producers

Edit motion picture film and sound tracks. Edits film and video tape to insert music, dialogue, and sound effects, and to correct errors, using editing equipment. Trims film segments to specified lengths and reassembles segments in sequence that presents story with maximum effect. Reviews assembled film or edited video tape on screen or monitor and makes corrections. Evaluates and selects scenes in terms of dramatic and entertainment value and story continuity. Studies script and confers with producers and directors concerning layout or editing to increase dramatic or entertainment value of production. Supervises and coordinates activities of workers engaged in editing and assembling filmed scenes photographed by others. Operates studio or portable, shoulder-mounted camera.
Yearly Earnings: $30,004
Education: Long-term O-J-T
Knowledge: Computers and Electronics; English Language; Fine Arts; Telecommunications; Communications and Media
Abilities: Fluency of Ideas; Originality; Information Ordering; Category Flexibility; Speed of Closure; Perceptual Speed; Visualization; Time Sharing; Rate Control; Gross Body Equilibrium; Far Vision; Visual Color Discrimination; Night Vision; Peripheral Vision; Glare Sensitivity; Hearing Sensitivity; Auditory Attention; Sound Localization; Speech Recognition
Skills: Active Listening; Speaking; Critical Thinking; Active Learning; Monitoring; Social Perceptiveness; Coordination; Persuasion; Negotiation; Information Organization; Synthesis/Reorganization; Idea Generation; Idea Evaluation; Solution Appraisal; Operations Analysis; Operation and Control; Product Inspection; Visioning; Identification of Key Causes; Judgment and Decision Making; Time Management; Management of Personnel Resources
General Work Activities: Monitoring Processes, Material, or Surroundings; Identifying Objects, Actions, and Events; Judging Qualities of Things, Services, People; Making Decisions and Solving Problems; Thinking Creatively; Organizing, Planning, and Prioritizing; Controlling Machines and Processes; Implementing Ideas, Programs, etc.; Communicating with Other Workers; Coordinating Work and Activities of Others; Guiding, Directing and Motivating Subordinates
Job Characteristics: Objective or Subjective Information; Supervise, Coach, Train Others; Take a Position Opposed to Others; Frequency in Conflict Situations; Sitting
GOE Group/s: 01.01.01 Literary Arts: Editing

CIP Program/s: 100104 Radio and Television Broadcasting Technologists and Technicians; 500602 Film-Video Making/Cinematography and Production

Related DOT Job/s: 962.132-010 SUPERVISING FILM-OR-VIDEOTAPE EDITOR; 962.262-010 FILM OR VIDEOTAPE EDITOR; 962.361-010 OPTICAL-EFFECTS LAYOUT PERSON; 962.382-014 SOUND CUTTER

34035A PAINTERS AND ILLUSTRATORS. OOH Title/s: Visual Artists

Paint or draw subject material to produce original artwork or provide illustrations to explain or adorn written or spoken word, using watercolors, oils, acrylics, tempera, or other paint mediums. Renders drawings, illustrations, and sketches of buildings, manufactured products, or models, working from sketches, blueprints, memory, or reference materials. Paints scenic backgrounds, murals, and portraiture for motion picture and television production sets, glass artworks, and exhibits. Etches, carves, paints, or draws artwork on material, such as stone, glass, canvas, wood, and linoleum. Develops drawings, paintings, diagrams, and models of medical or biological subjects for use in publications, exhibits, consultations, research, and teaching. Integrates and develops visual elements, such as line, space, mass, color, and perspective, to produce desired effect. Brushes or sprays protective or decorative finish on completed background panels, informational legends, exhibit accessories, or finished painting. Confers with professional personnel or client to discuss objectives of museum exhibits, develop illustration ideas, and theme to be portrayed. Selects colored glass, cuts glass, and arranges pieces in design pattern for painting. Integrates knowledge of glass cutting, stresses, portraiture, symbolism, heraldry, ornamental and historical styles, and related factors with functional requirements to conceptualize idea. Photographs person, artifacts, scenes, plants, or other objects, and develops negatives to obtain prints to be used in exhibits. Studies style, techniques, colors, textures, and materials used by artist to maintain consistency in reconstruction or retouching procedures. Cuts, carves, scrapes, molds, or otherwise shapes material to fashion exhibit accessories from clay, plastic, wood, fiberglass, and papier-mache. Performs tests to determine factors, such as age, structure, pigment stability, and probable reaction to various cleaning agents and solvents. Removes painting from frame or paint layer from canvas to restore artwork, following specified technique and equipment. Applies select solvents and cleaning agents to clean surface of painting and remove accretions, discolorations, and deteriorated varnish. Examines surfaces of paintings and proofs of artwork, using magnifying device, to determine method of restoration or needed corrections. Assembles, leads, and solders finished glass to fabricate stained glass article. Installs finished stained glass in window or door frame.

Yearly Earnings: $29,900

Education: Work experience, plus degree

Knowledge: Design; Chemistry; Fine Arts; History and Archeology

Abilities: Fluency of Ideas; Originality; Visualization; Gross Body Equilibrium; Visual Color Discrimination

Skills: Idea Generation; Operations Analysis

General Work Activities: Thinking Creatively; Drafting and Specifying Technical Devices, etc.

Job Characteristics: Objective or Subjective Information; Making Repetitive Motions

GOE Group/s: 01.02.02 Visual Arts: Studio Art; 01.02.03 Visual Arts: Commercial Art

CIP Program/s: 500402 Graphic Design, Commercial Art and Illustration; 500501 Drama/Theater Arts, General; 500502 Technical Theater/Theater Design and Stagecraft; 500701 Art, General; 500702 Fine/Studio Arts; 500705 Drawing; 500708 Painting; 500710 Printmaking; 512703 Medical Illustrating

Related DOT Job/s: 102.261-014 PAINTINGS RESTORER; 141.061-014 FASHION ARTIST; 141.061-022 ILLUSTRATOR; 141.061-026 ILLUSTRATOR, MEDICAL AND SCIENTIFIC; 141.061-030 ILLUSTRATOR, SET; 144.061-010 PAINTER; 144.061-014 PRINTMAKER; 149.261-010 EXHIBIT ARTIST; 970.281-014 DELINEATOR

34035B SKETCH ARTISTS. OOH Title/s: Visual Artists

Sketch likenesses of subjects according to observation or descriptions either to assist law enforcement agencies in identifying suspects or for entertainment purposes of patrons, using mediums such as pencil, charcoal, and pastels. Draws sketch, profile, or likeness of posed subject or photograph, using pencil, charcoal, pastels, or other medium. Assembles and arranges outlines of features to form composite image, according to information provided by witness or victim. Alters copy of composite image until witness or victim is satisfied that composite is best possible representation of suspect. Interviews crime victims and witnesses to obtain descriptive information concerning physical build, sex, nationality, and facial features of unidentified suspect. Prepares series of simple line drawings conforming to description of suspect and presents drawings to informant for selection of sketch. Poses subject to accentuate most pleasing features or profile. Classifies and codes components of image, using established system, to help identify suspect. Measures distances and develops sketches of crime scene from photograph and measurements. Adjusts strong lights to cast subject's shadow on backdrop to aid in viewing subject's profile. Cuts profile from photograph or cuts freehand outline of profile from paper. Glues silhouette on paper of contrasting color or mounts silhouette in frame or folder. Operates photocopy or similar machine to reproduce composite image. Searches police photograph records, using classification and coding system, to determine if existing photograph of suspect is available.

Yearly Earnings: $29,900

Education: Work experience, plus degree

Knowledge: Design; Fine Arts

Abilities: Visualization; Arm-Hand Steadiness; Finger Dexterity

Skills: Active Listening; Information Organization

General Work Activities: None above average

Job Characteristics: Objective or Subjective Information; Sitting; Making Repetitive Motions

GOE Group/s: 01.02.02 Visual Arts: Studio Art; 01.02.03 Visual Arts: Commercial Art; 01.06.01 Craft Arts: Graphics Arts and Related Crafts

CIP Program/s: 430106 Forensic Tech./Technician; 500402 Graphic Design, Commercial Art and Illustration; 500701 Art, General; 500705 Drawing; 500708 Painting

Related DOT Job/s: 141.061-034 POLICE ARTIST; 149.041-010 QUICK SKETCH ARTIST; 149.051-010 SILHOUETTE ARTIST; 970.361-018 ARTIST, SUSPECT

34035C GRAPHIC DESIGNERS. OOH Title/s: Visual Artists

Design art and copy layouts for material to be presented by visual communications media, such as books, magazines, newspapers, television, and packaging. Draws sample of finished layout and presents sample to art director for approval. Draws and prints charts, graphs, illustrations, and other artwork, using computer. Arranges layout based upon available space, knowledge of layout principles, and aesthetic design concepts. Marks up, pastes, and assembles final layouts to prepare layouts for printer. Keys information into computer equipment to create layouts for client or supervisor. Determines size and arrangement of illustrative material and copy, and selects style and size of type. Prepares illustrations or rough sketches of material according to instructions of client or supervisor. Produces still and animated graphic formats for on-air and taped portions of

television news broadcasts, using electronic video equipment. Studies illustrations and photographs to plan presentation of material, product, or service. Reviews final layout and suggests improvements as needed. Prepares series of drawings to illustrate sequence and timing of story development for television production. Confers with client regarding layout design. Photographs layouts, using camera, to make layout prints for supervisor or client. Prepares notes and instructions for workers who assemble and prepare final layouts for printing. Develops negatives and prints, using negative and print developing equipment and tools and work aids, to produce layout photographs.
Yearly Earnings: $29,900
Education: Work experience, plus degree
Knowledge: Computers and Electronics; Design; Fine Arts; Telecommunications; Communications and Media
Abilities: Fluency of Ideas; Originality; Visualization; Visual Color Discrimination; Speech Recognition
Skills: Idea Generation; Programming
General Work Activities: Thinking Creatively; Operating Vehicles or Equipment; Drafting and Specifying Technical Devices, etc.
Job Characteristics: Objective or Subjective Information; Sitting
GOE Group/s: 01.02.03 Visual Arts: Commercial Art
CIP Program/s: 500402 Graphic Design, Commercial Art and Illustration; 500701 Art, General; 500710 Printmaking
Related DOT Job/s: 141.061-018 GRAPHIC DESIGNER

34035D CARTOONISTS AND ANIMATORS. OOH Title/s: Visual Artists

Draw cartoons or other animated images by hand for publication, motion pictures, or television. May specialize in creating storyboards, laying out scenes, painting, in-betweening, developing characters, or clean up. Sketches and submits cartoon or animation for approval. Renders sequential drawings of characters or other subject material which, when photographed and projected at specific speed, becomes animated. Creates and prepares sketches and model drawings of characters, providing details from memory, live models, manufactured products, or reference material. Develops personal ideas for cartoons, comic strips, or animations, or reads written material to develop ideas. Makes changes and corrections to cartoon, comic strip, or animation as necessary. Develops color patterns and moods and paints background layouts to dramatize action for animated cartoon scenes. Labels each section with designated colors when colors are used. Discusses ideas for cartoons, comic strips, or animations with editor or publisher's representative.
Yearly Earnings: $29,900
Education: Work experience, plus degree
Knowledge: Sales and Marketing; Fine Arts; Communications and Media
Abilities: Fluency of Ideas; Originality; Visualization; Arm-Hand Steadiness; Visual Color Discrimination
Skills: Idea Generation
General Work Activities: Thinking Creatively
Job Characteristics: Objective or Subjective Information; Sitting
GOE Group/s: 01.02.03 Visual Arts: Commercial Art
CIP Program/s: 500201 Crafts, Folk Art and Artisanry; 500402 Graphic Design, Commercial Art and Illustration
Related DOT Job/s: 141.061-010 CARTOONIST; 141.081-010 CARTOONIST, MOTION PICTURES

34035E SCULPTORS. OOH Title/s: Visual Artists

Design and construct three-dimensional artworks, using materials such as stone, wood, plaster, and metal and employing various manual and tool techniques. Carves objects from stone, concrete, plaster, wood, or other material, using abrasives and tools such as chisels, gouges, and mall. Constructs artistic forms from metal or stone, using metal-working, welding, or masonry tools and equipment. Cuts, bends, laminates, arranges, and fastens individual or mixed raw and manufactured materials and products to form works of art. Models substances, such as clay or wax, using fingers and small hand tools to form objects.
Yearly Earnings: $29,900
Education: Work experience, plus degree
Knowledge: Design; Fine Arts
Abilities: Originality; Visualization; Manual Dexterity
Skills: None above average
General Work Activities: Thinking Creatively; Implementing Ideas, Programs, etc.
Job Characteristics: Objective or Subjective Information
GOE Group/s: 01.02.02 Visual Arts: Studio Art
CIP Program/s: 500701 Art, General; 500702 Fine/Studio Arts; 500709 Sculpture
Related DOT Job/s: 144.061-018 SCULPTOR

34038A FASHION DESIGNERS. OOH Title/s: Designers

Design clothing and accessories. Create original garments or design garments that follow well-established fashion trends. May develop the line of color and kinds of materials. Designs custom garments for clients. Integrates findings of analysis and discussion, and personal tastes and knowledge of design, to originate design ideas. Sketches rough and detailed drawings of apparel or accessories, and writes specifications, such as color scheme, construction, or material type. Draws pattern for article designed, cuts pattern, and cuts material according to pattern, using measuring and drawing instruments, and scissors. Examines sample garment on and off model, and modifies design to achieve desired effect. Attends fashion shows and reviews garment magazines and manuals to analyze fashion trends, predictions, and consumer preferences. Confers with sales and management executives or with clients regarding design ideas. Sews together sections to form mockup or sample of garment or article, using sewing equipment. Arranges for showing of sample garments at sales meetings or fashion shows. Directs and coordinates workers who draw and cut patterns, and constructs sample or finished garment.
Yearly Earnings: $30,680
Education: Bachelor's degree
Knowledge: Sales and Marketing; Customer and Personal Service; Production and Processing; Design; Education and Training; Fine Arts
Abilities: Fluency of Ideas; Originality; Visualization; Time Sharing; Arm-Hand Steadiness; Manual Dexterity; Finger Dexterity; Wrist-Finger Speed; Visual Color Discrimination
Skills: Active Learning; Social Perceptiveness; Coordination; Persuasion; Negotiation; Service Orientation; Synthesis/Reorganization; Idea Generation; Idea Evaluation; Operations Analysis; Product Inspection; Systems Perception; Identifying Downstream Consequences; Identification of Key Causes; Judgment and Decision Making; Systems Evaluation; Time Management; Management of Financial Resources; Management of Material Resources; Management of Personnel Resources
General Work Activities: Judging Qualities of Things, Services, People; Thinking Creatively; Drafting and Specifying Technical Devices, etc.
Job Characteristics: Objective or Subjective Information; Supervise, Coach, Train Others; Persuade Someone to a Course of Action; Coordinate or Lead Others; Responsibility for Outcomes and Results; Kneeling, Crouching, or Crawling
GOE Group/s: 01.02.03 Visual Arts: Commercial Art
CIP Program/s: 200301 Clothing, Apparel and Textile Workers and Managers, General; 200305 Custom Tailor; 500402 Graphic Design, Commercial Art and Illustration; 500407 Fashion Design and Illustration

Related DOT Job/s: 142.061-018 FASHION DESIGNER; 142.081-014 FUR DESIGNER; 142.281-010 COPYIST

34038B COMMERCIAL AND INDUSTRIAL DESIGNERS. OOH Title/s: Designers

Develop and design manufactured products, such as cars, home appliances, and children's toys. Combine artistic talent with research on product use, marketing, and materials, to create the most functional and appealing product design. Confers with engineering, marketing, production, or sales department, or with customer, to establish design concepts for manufactured products. Integrates findings and concepts and sketches design ideas. Prepares detailed drawings, illustrations, artwork, or blueprints, using drawing instruments or paints and brushes. Designs packaging and containers for products, such as foods, beverages, toiletries, or medicines. Evaluates design ideas for feasibility based on factors such as appearance, function, serviceability, budget, production costs/methods, and market characteristics. Creates and designs graphic material for use as ornamentation, illustration, or advertising on manufactured materials and packaging. Presents design to customer or design committee for approval and discusses need for modification. Modifies design to conform with customer specifications, production limitations, or changes in design trends. Reads publications, attends showings, and studies traditional, period, and contemporary design styles and motifs to obtain perspective and design concepts. Directs and coordinates preparation of detailed drawings from sketches or fabrication of models or samples. Fabricates model or sample in paper, wood, glass, fabric, plastic, or metal, using hand and power tools. Prepares itemized production requirements to produce item.
Yearly Earnings: $30,680
Education: Bachelor's degree
Knowledge: Sales and Marketing; Production and Processing; Design; Education and Training; Fine Arts; History and Archeology
Abilities: Oral Comprehension; Written Comprehension; Oral Expression; Fluency of Ideas; Originality; Deductive Reasoning; Information Ordering; Mathematical Reasoning; Number Facility; Visualization; Arm-Hand Steadiness; Near Vision; Visual Color Discrimination; Speech Recognition
Skills: Reading Comprehension; Active Listening; Speaking; Critical Thinking; Active Learning; Monitoring; Social Perceptiveness; Coordination; Persuasion; Negotiation; Instructing; Service Orientation; Information Organization; Synthesis/Reorganization; Idea Generation; Idea Evaluation; Implementation Planning; Solution Appraisal; Operations Analysis; Technology Design; Equipment Selection; Programming; Visioning; Identifying Downstream Consequences; Identification of Key Causes; Judgment and Decision Making; Systems Evaluation; Time Management; Management of Financial Resources
General Work Activities: Thinking Creatively; Organizing, Planning, and Prioritizing; Drafting and Specifying Technical Devices, etc.; Communicating with Persons Outside Organization
Job Characteristics: Objective or Subjective Information; Persuade Someone to a Course of Action; Take a Position Opposed to Others; Coordinate or Lead Others; Frustrating Circumstances
GOE Group/s: 01.02.02 Visual Arts: Studio Art; 01.02.03 Visual Arts: Commercial Art; 01.06.01 Craft Arts: Graphics Arts and Related Crafts; 05.01.07 Engineering: Design
CIP Program/s: 200501 Home Furnishings and Equipment Installers and Consultants, General; 500402 Graphic Design, Commercial Art and Illustration; 500404 Industrial Design; 500407 Fashion Design and Illustration
Related DOT Job/s: 141.061-038 COMMERCIAL DESIGNER; 142.061-010 BANK-NOTE DESIGNER; 142.061-014 CLOTH DESIGNER; 142.061-022 FURNITURE DESIGNER; 142.061-026 INDUSTRIAL DESIGNER; 142.061-030 MEMORIAL DESIGNER; 142.061-034 ORNAMENTAL-METALWORK DESIGNER; 142.061-038 SAFETY-CLOTHING-AND-EQUIPMENT DEVELOPER; 142.061-054 STAINED GLASS ARTIST; 142.081-018 PACKAGE DESIGNER

34038C SET DESIGNERS. OOH Title/s: Designers

Design sets for theatrical, motion picture, and television productions. Integrates requirements including script, research, budget, and available locations to develop design. Prepares rough draft and scale working drawings of sets, including floor plans, scenery, and properties to be constructed. Presents drawings for approval and makes changes and corrections as directed. Designs and builds scale models of set design or miniature sets used in filming backgrounds or special effects. Selects furniture, draperies, pictures, lamps, and rugs for decorative quality and appearance. Researches and consults experts to determine architectural and furnishing styles to depict given periods or locations. Confers with heads of production and direction to establish budget and schedules, and to discuss design ideas. Estimates costs of design materials and construction, or rental of location or props. Directs and coordinates set construction, erection, or decoration activities to ensure conformance to design, budget, and schedule requirements. Reads script to determine location, set, or decoration requirements. Examines dressed set to ensure props and scenery do not interfere with movements of cast or view of camera. Assigns staff to complete design ideas and prepare sketches, illustrations, and detailed drawings of sets, or graphics and animation.
Yearly Earnings: $30,680
Education: Bachelor's degree
Knowledge: Design; Building and Construction; Geography; Fine Arts; History and Archeology; Communications and Media
Abilities: Fluency of Ideas; Originality; Speed of Closure; Spatial Orientation; Visualization; Selective Attention; Time Sharing; Gross Body Equilibrium; Far Vision; Visual Color Discrimination; Night Vision; Auditory Attention; Sound Localization
Skills: Active Listening; Speaking; Critical Thinking; Active Learning; Monitoring; Social Perceptiveness; Coordination; Persuasion; Negotiation; Information Gathering; Synthesis/Reorganization; Idea Generation; Implementation Planning; Solution Appraisal; Operations Analysis; Technology Design; Equipment Selection; Product Inspection; Visioning; Identification of Key Causes; Systems Evaluation; Time Management; Management of Financial Resources; Management of Material Resources; Management of Personnel Resources
General Work Activities: Estimating Needed Characteristics; Thinking Creatively; Scheduling Work and Activities; Organizing, Planning, and Prioritizing; Drafting and Specifying Technical Devices, etc.; Implementing Ideas, Programs, etc.; Establishing and Maintaining Relationships; Coordinating Work and Activities of Others; Monitoring and Controlling Resources
Job Characteristics: Objective or Subjective Information; Supervise, Coach, Train Others; Coordinate or Lead Others; Responsibility for Outcomes and Results; High Places; Climbing Ladders, Scaffolds, Poles, etc.; Walking or Running; Keeping or Regaining Balance; Bending or Twisting the Body; Frustrating Circumstances
GOE Group/s: 01.02.03 Visual Arts: Commercial Art
CIP Program/s: 500408 Interior Design; 500501 Drama/Theater Arts, General; 500502 Technical Theater/Theater Design and Stagecraft; 500599 Dramatic/Theater Arts and Stagecraft, Other
Related DOT Job/s: 142.061-042 SET DECORATOR; 142.061-046 SET DESIGNER; 142.061-050 SET DESIGNER; 142.061-062 ART DIRECTOR; 149.031-010 SUPERVISOR, SCENIC ARTS

34038D EXHIBIT DESIGNERS. OOH Title/s: Designers

Plan, design, and oversee construction and installation of permanent and temporary exhibits and displays. Prepares preliminary drawings of proposed exhibit, including detailed construction,

layout, material specifications, or special effects diagrams. Designs display to decorate streets, fairgrounds, buildings, or other places for celebrations, using paper, cloth, plastic, or other materials. Designs, draws, paints, or sketches backgrounds and fixtures for use in windows or interior displays. Oversees preparation of artwork, construction of exhibit components, and placement of collection to ensure intended interpretation of concepts and conformance to specifications. Confers with client or staff regarding theme, interpretative or informational purpose, planned location, budget, materials, or promotion. Submits plans for approval, and adapts plan to serve intended purpose or to conform to budget or fabrication restrictions. Arranges for acquisition of specimens or graphics, or building of exhibit structures by outside contractors to complete exhibit. Inspects installed exhibit for conformance to specifications and satisfactory operation of special effects components.
Yearly Earnings: $30,680
Education: Bachelor's degree
Knowledge: Sales and Marketing; Customer and Personal Service; Computers and Electronics; Design; Building and Construction; Fine Arts
Abilities: Fluency of Ideas; Originality; Visualization; Time Sharing; Arm-Hand Steadiness; Wrist-Finger Speed; Far Vision; Visual Color Discrimination
Skills: Social Perceptiveness; Coordination; Persuasion; Negotiation; Service Orientation; Information Organization; Synthesis/Reorganization; Idea Evaluation; Implementation Planning; Operations Analysis; Installation; Visioning; Identification of Key Causes; Systems Evaluation; Time Management; Management of Financial Resources; Management of Material Resources; Management of Personnel Resources
General Work Activities: Thinking Creatively; Organizing, Planning, and Prioritizing; Drafting and Specifying Technical Devices, etc.; Coordinating Work and Activities of Others; Monitoring and Controlling Resources
Job Characteristics: Objective or Subjective Information; Persuade Someone to a Course of Action; Coordinate or Lead Others; Responsibility for Outcomes and Results; High Places; Climbing Ladders, Scaffolds, Poles, etc.; Walking or Running; Keeping or Regaining Balance
GOE Group/s: 01.02.03 Visual Arts: Commercial Art
CIP Program/s: 200501 Home Furnishings and Equipment Installers and Consultants, General; 500402 Graphic Design, Commercial Art and Illustration; 500408 Interior Design; 500501 Drama/Theater Arts, General; 500502 Technical Theater/Theater Design and Stagecraft
Related DOT Job/s: 142.051-010 DISPLAY DESIGNER; 142.061-058 EXHIBIT DESIGNER

34038E ART DIRECTORS. OOH Title/s: Designers; Marketing, Advertising, and Public Relations Managers; Visual Artists

Formulate design concepts and presentation approaches, and direct workers engaged in artwork, layout design, and copy writing for visual communications media, such as magazines, books, newspapers, and packaging. Assigns and directs staff members to develop design concepts into art layouts or prepare layouts for printing. Formulates basic layout design or presentation approach, and conceives material details, such as style and size of type, photographs, graphics, and arrangement. Reviews and approves art and copy materials developed by staff, and proofs of printed copy. Reviews illustrative material and confers with client concerning objectives, budget, background information, and presentation approaches, styles, and techniques. Confers with creative, art, copy writing, or production department heads to discuss client requirements, outline presentation concepts, and coordinate creative activities. Presents final layouts to client for approval. Prepares detailed storyboard showing sequence and timing of story development for television production. Writes typography instructions, such as margin widths and type sizes, and submits for typesetting or printing. Marks up, pastes, and completes layouts to prepare for printing. Draws custom illustrations for project.
Yearly Earnings: $30,680
Education: Bachelor's degree
Knowledge: Administration and Management; Sales and Marketing; Production and Processing; Design; Psychology; Fine Arts; Communications and Media
Abilities: Oral Expression; Fluency of Ideas; Originality; Visualization; Time Sharing; Near Vision; Visual Color Discrimination; Night Vision; Speech Recognition; Speech Clarity
Skills: Active Listening; Speaking; Critical Thinking; Active Learning; Learning Strategies; Monitoring; Social Perceptiveness; Coordination; Persuasion; Negotiation; Service Orientation; Information Organization; Synthesis/Reorganization; Idea Generation; Idea Evaluation; Implementation Planning; Solution Appraisal; Operations Analysis; Equipment Selection; Visioning; Systems Perception; Identifying Downstream Consequences; Identification of Key Causes; Systems Evaluation; Time Management; Management of Financial Resources; Management of Material Resources; Management of Personnel Resources
General Work Activities: Thinking Creatively; Organizing, Planning, and Prioritizing; Drafting and Specifying Technical Devices, etc.; Communicating with Persons Outside Organization; Coordinating Work and Activities of Others; Developing and Building Teams; Guiding, Directing and Motivating Subordinates
Job Characteristics: Objective or Subjective Information; Persuade Someone to a Course of Action; Take a Position Opposed to Others; Deal with External Customers; Coordinate or Lead Others; Responsibility for Outcomes and Results; Sitting
GOE Group/s: 01.02.03 Visual Arts: Commercial Art
CIP Program/s: 090201 Advertising; 500402 Graphic Design, Commercial Art and Illustration
Related DOT Job/s: 141.031-010 ART DIRECTOR; 141.067-010 CREATIVE DIRECTOR; 141.137-010 PRODUCTION MANAGER, ADVERTISING

34038F FLORAL DESIGNERS. OOH Title/s: Designers

Design and fashion live, cut, dried, and artificial floral and foliar arrangements for events, such as holidays, anniversaries, weddings, balls, and funerals. Plans arrangement according to client's requirements, utilizing knowledge of design and properties of materials, or selects appropriate standard design pattern. Selects flora and foliage for arrangement. Trims material and arranges bouquets, wreaths, terrariums, and other items using trimmers, shapers, wire, pin, floral tape, foam, and other materials. Confers with client regarding price and type of arrangement desired. Decorates buildings, halls, churches, or other facilities where events are planned. Packs and wraps completed arrangements. Estimates costs and prices arrangements. Conducts classes, demonstrations, or trains other workers.
Yearly Earnings: $30,680
Education: Bachelor's degree
Knowledge: Customer and Personal Service; Fine Arts
Abilities: Gross Body Equilibrium; Visual Color Discrimination
Skills: Negotiation; Service Orientation; Management of Financial Resources; Management of Material Resources
General Work Activities: None above average
Job Characteristics: Objective or Subjective Information; Supervise, Coach, Train Others; Provide a Service to Others; Deal with External Customers
GOE Group/s: 01.02.03 Visual Arts: Commercial Art
CIP Program/s: 080503 Floristry Marketing Operations; 200501 Home Furnishings and Equipment Installers and Consultants, General

Related DOT Job/s: 142.081-010 FLORAL DESIGNER; 899.364-014 ARTIFICIAL-FOLIAGE ARRANGER

34041 INTERIOR DESIGNERS. OOH Title/s: Designers

Plan, design, and furnish interiors of residential, commercial, or industrial buildings. Formulate design which is practical, aesthetic, and conducive to intended purposes, such as raising productivity, selling merchandise, or improving lifestyle. May specialize in a particular field, style, or phase of interior design. Exclude merchandise display designers. Formulates environmental plan to be practical, aesthetic, and conducive to intended purposes, such as raising productivity or selling merchandise. Selects or designs and purchases furnishings, artworks, and accessories. Confers with client to determine factors affecting planning interior environments, such as budget, architectural preferences, and purpose and function. Plans and designs interior environments for boats, planes, buses, trains, and other enclosed spaces. Advises client on interior design factors, such as space planning, layout and utilization of furnishings and equipment, and color coordination. Renders design ideas in form of paste-ups or drawings. Estimates material requirements and costs, and presents design to client for approval. Subcontracts fabrication, installation, and arrangement of carpeting, fixtures, accessories, draperies, paint and wall coverings, artwork, furniture, and related items.

Yearly Earnings: $30,680

Education: Bachelor's degree

Knowledge: Administration and Management; Sales and Marketing; Customer and Personal Service; Design; Fine Arts

Abilities: Fluency of Ideas; Originality; Visualization; Visual Color Discrimination

Skills: Active Listening; Speaking; Mathematics; Coordination; Persuasion; Negotiation; Service Orientation; Synthesis/Reorganization; Idea Generation; Idea Evaluation; Implementation Planning; Operations Analysis; Visioning; Identification of Key Causes; Time Management; Management of Financial Resources; Management of Material Resources

General Work Activities: Estimating Needed Characteristics; Thinking Creatively; Drafting and Specifying Technical Devices, etc.; Establishing and Maintaining Relationships; Selling or Influencing Others; Coordinating Work and Activities of Others; Monitoring and Controlling Resources

Job Characteristics: Objective or Subjective Information; Persuade Someone to a Course of Action; Deal with External Customers

GOE Group/s: 01.02.03 Visual Arts: Commercial Art

CIP Program/s: 040501 Interior Architecture; 190601 Housing Studies, General; 190603 Interior Environments; 200501 Home Furnishings and Equipment Installers and Consultants, General; 500408 Interior Design

Related DOT Job/s: 141.051-010 COLOR EXPERT; 142.051-014 INTERIOR DESIGNER

34044 MERCHANDISE DISPLAYERS AND WINDOW TRIMMERS. OOH Title/s: Designers

Plan and erect commercial displays, such as those in windows and interiors of retail stores and at trade exhibitions. Constructs or assembles prefabricated display properties from fabric, glass, paper, and plastic, using hand tools and woodworking power tools, according to specifications. Originates ideas for merchandise display or window decoration. Develops layout and selects theme, lighting, colors, and props to be used. Prepares sketches or floor plans of proposed displays. Installs booths, exhibits, displays, carpets, and drapes, as guided by floor plan of building and specifications. Consults with advertising and sales staff to determine type of merchandise to be featured and time and place for each display. Cuts out designs on cardboard, hardboard, and plywood, according to motif of event. Arranges properties, furniture, merchandise, backdrop, and other accessories, as shown in prepared sketch. Installs decorations, such as flags, banners, festive lights, and bunting, on or in building, street, exhibit hall, or booth. Places price and descriptive signs on backdrop, fixtures, merchandise, or floor. Dresses mannequins for use in displays.

Yearly Earnings: $30,680

Education: Bachelor's degree

Knowledge: Sales and Marketing; Design; Sociology and Anthropology; Fine Arts; Communications and Media

Abilities: Originality; Visualization; Extent Flexibility; Dynamic Flexibility; Gross Body Equilibrium; Visual Color Discrimination; Depth Perception

Skills: Idea Generation; Idea Evaluation; Installation

General Work Activities: Thinking Creatively; Drafting and Specifying Technical Devices, etc.

Job Characteristics: Objective or Subjective Information; Extremely Bright or Inadequate Lighting; Cramped Work Space, Awkward Positions; High Places; Hazardous Situations; Climbing Ladders, Scaffolds, Poles, etc.; Kneeling, Crouching, or Crawling; Keeping or Regaining Balance; Bending or Twisting the Body

GOE Group/s: 01.02.03 Visual Arts: Commercial Art; 01.06.02 Craft Arts: Arts and Crafts

CIP Program/s: 200501 Home Furnishings and Equipment Installers and Consultants, General; 500401 Design and Visual Communications

Related DOT Job/s: 142.031-014 MANAGER, DISPLAY; 298.081-010 DISPLAYER, MERCHANDISE; 298.381-010 DECORATOR

34047A MUSIC DIRECTORS. OOH Title/s: Musicians

Direct and conduct instrumental or vocal performances by musical groups, such as orchestras or choirs. Directs group at rehearsals and live or recorded performances to achieve desired effects, such as tonal and harmonic balance dynamics, rhythm, and tempo. Selects vocal, instrumental, and recorded music suitable to type of performance requirements to accommodate ability of group. Issues assignments and reviews work of staff in such areas as scoring, arranging, and copying music, lyric, and vocal coaching. Positions members within group to obtain balance among instrumental sections. Auditions and selects vocal and instrumental groups for musical presentations. Transcribes musical compositions and melodic lines to adapt them to or create particular style for group. Engages services of composer to write score of motion picture television program. Schedules tours and performances and arranges for transportation and lodging. Evaluates subordinates' job performance and initiates and recommends personnel actions.

Yearly Earnings: $21,424

Education: Long-term O-J-T

Knowledge: Administration and Management; Personnel and Human Resources; Foreign Language; Fine Arts

Abilities: Oral Comprehension; Oral Expression; Fluency of Ideas; Originality; Flexibility of Closure; Hearing Sensitivity; Auditory Attention; Sound Localization; Speech Recognition

Skills: Learning Strategies; Monitoring; Social Perceptiveness; Coordination; Negotiation; Instructing; Synthesis/Reorganization; Implementation Planning; Operations Analysis; Visioning; Time Management; Management of Personnel Resources

General Work Activities: Thinking Creatively; Scheduling Work and Activities; Organizing, Planning, and Prioritizing; Establishing and Maintaining Relationships; Coordinating Work and Activities of Others; Developing and Building Teams; Guiding, Directing and Motivating Subordinates; Coaching and Developing Others; Staffing Organizational Units

Job Characteristics: Objective or Subjective Information; Supervise, Coach, Train Others; Coordinate or Lead Others; Responsibility for Outcomes and Results; Importance of Repeating Same Tasks
GOE Group/s: 01.04.01 Performing Arts:Music: Instructing and Directing
CIP Program/s: 390501 Religious/Sacred Music; 500901 Music, General; 500903 Music - General Performance; 500905 Musicology and Ethnomusicology; 500906 Music Conducting; 500908 Music - Voice and Choral/Opera Performance
Related DOT Job/s: 152.047-010 CHORAL DIRECTOR; 152.047-014 CONDUCTOR, ORCHESTRA; 152.047-018 DIRECTOR, MUSIC

34047B MUSIC ARRANGERS AND ORCHESTRATORS. OOH Title/s: Musicians

Write and transcribe musical scores. Composes musical scores for orchestra, band, choral group, or individual instrumentalist or vocalist, using knowledge of music theory and instrumental and vocal capabilities. Transposes music from one voice or instrument to another to accommodate particular musician in musical group. Adapts musical composition for orchestra, band, choral group, or individual to style for which it was not originally written. Transcribes musical parts from score written by arranger or orchestrator for each instrument or voice, using knowledge of music composition. Copies parts from score for individual performers. Determines voice, instrument, harmonic structure, rhythm, tempo, and tone balance to achieve desired effect.
Yearly Earnings: $21,424
Education: Long-term O-J-T
Knowledge: Foreign Language; Fine Arts
Abilities: Fluency of Ideas; Originality; Hearing Sensitivity; Auditory Attention; Sound Localization
Skills: Coordination; Synthesis/Reorganization; Idea Generation
General Work Activities: Thinking Creatively; Implementing Ideas, Programs, etc.
Job Characteristics: Objective or Subjective Information; Sitting
GOE Group/s: 01.04.02 Performing Arts:Music: Composing and Arranging
CIP Program/s: 500901 Music, General; 500904 Music Theory and Composition
Related DOT Job/s: 152.067-010 ARRANGER; 152.067-022 ORCHESTRATOR; 152.267-010 COPYIST

34047C SINGERS. OOH Title/s: Musicians

Sing songs on stage, radio, television, or motion pictures. Sings before audience or recipient of message as soloist, or in group, as member of vocal ensemble. Sings *a cappella* or with musical accompaniment. Memorizes musical selections and routines, or sings following printed text, musical notation, or customer instructions. Interprets or modifies music, applying knowledge of harmony, melody, rhythm, and voice production, to individualize presentation and maintain audience interest. Observes choral leader or prompter for cues or directions in vocal presentation. Practices songs and routines to maintain and improve vocal skills.
Yearly Earnings: $21,424
Education: Long-term O-J-T
Knowledge: Foreign Language; Fine Arts
Abilities: Originality; Memorization; Hearing Sensitivity; Auditory Attention; Sound Localization; Speech Clarity
Skills: None above average
General Work Activities: Thinking Creatively; Performing for or Working with Public
Job Characteristics: Objective or Subjective Information
GOE Group/s: 01.04.03 Performing Arts:Music: Vocal Performing
CIP Program/s: 500901 Music, General; 500903 Music - General Performance; 500908 Music - Voice and Choral/Opera Performance
Related DOT Job/s: 152.047-022 SINGER; 230.647-010 SINGING MESSENGER

34047E COMPOSERS. OOH Title/s: Musicians

Compose music for orchestra, choral group, or band. Creates original musical form or writes within circumscribed musical form, such as sonata, symphony, or opera. Creates musical and tonal structure, applying elements of music theory, such as instrumental and vocal capabilities. Develops pattern of harmony, applying knowledge of music theory. Synthesizes ideas for melody of musical scores for choral group or band. Determines basic pattern of melody, applying knowledge of music theory. Transcribes or records musical ideas into notes on scored music paper.
Yearly Earnings: $21,424
Education: Long-term O-J-T
Knowledge: Fine Arts; History and Archeology
Abilities: Fluency of Ideas; Originality; Flexibility of Closure; Hearing Sensitivity; Auditory Attention; Sound Localization
Skills: Idea Generation; Idea Evaluation
General Work Activities: Thinking Creatively; Implementing Ideas, Programs, etc.
Job Characteristics: Objective or Subjective Information; Sitting
GOE Group/s: 01.04.02 Performing Arts:Music: Composing and Arranging
CIP Program/s: 500901 Music, General; 500904 Music Theory and Composition
Related DOT Job/s: 152.067-014 COMPOSER

34047F PROMPTERS. OOH Title/s: Musicians

Prompt performers in stage productions. Speaks or signs in language required by opera to prompt performers. Marks copy of vocal score to note cues. Observes orchestra conductor and follows vocal score to time cues accurately.
Yearly Earnings: $21,424
Education: Long-term O-J-T
Knowledge: Foreign Language; Fine Arts
Abilities: Hearing Sensitivity; Auditory Attention; Sound Localization
Skills: None above average
General Work Activities: None above average
Job Characteristics: Job-Required Social Interaction; Coordinate or Lead Others; Importance of Being Aware of New Events; Importance of Repeating Same Tasks
GOE Group/s: 01.04.02 Performing Arts:Music: Composing and Arranging
CIP Program/s: 500901 Music, General; 500904 Music Theory and Composition
Related DOT Job/s: 152.367-010 PROMPTER

34051 MUSICIANS, INSTRUMENTAL. OOH Title/s: Musicians

Play one or more musical instruments in recital, in accompaniment, or as members of an orchestra, band, or other musical group. Plays musical instrument as soloist or as member of musical group, such as orchestra or band, to entertain audience. Plays from memory or by following score. Studies and rehearses music to learn and interpret score. Improvises music during performance. Practices performance on musical instrument to maintain and improve skills. Memorizes musical scores. Transposes music to play in alternate key or to fit individual style or purposes. Composes new musical scores. Teaches music for specific instruments. Directs band or orchestra.
Yearly Earnings: $21,424
Education: Long-term O-J-T
Knowledge: Psychology; Education and Training; Fine Arts; History and Archeology

Abilities: Oral Comprehension; Oral Expression; Fluency of Ideas; Originality; Category Flexibility; Memorization; Speed of Closure; Flexibility of Closure; Perceptual Speed; Selective Attention; Time Sharing; Manual Dexterity; Finger Dexterity; Multilimb Coordination; Response Orientation; Reaction Time; Wrist-Finger Speed; Speed of Limb Movement; Near Vision; Far Vision; Night Vision; Peripheral Vision; Glare Sensitivity; Hearing Sensitivity; Auditory Attention; Sound Localization; Speech Recognition; Speech Clarity
Skills: Active Learning; Learning Strategies; Monitoring; Coordination; Instructing; Visioning; Management of Personnel Resources
General Work Activities: Thinking Creatively; Performing for or Working with Public; Coordinating Work and Activities of Others; Developing and Building Teams; Teaching Others; Guiding, Directing and Motivating Subordinates; Coaching and Developing Others
Job Characteristics: Objective or Subjective Information; Supervise, Coach, Train Others; Responsibility for Outcomes and Results; Sitting; Making Repetitive Motions; Importance of Being Exact or Accurate
GOE Group/s: 01.04.04 Performing Arts:Music: Instrumental Performing
CIP Program/s: 390501 Religious/Sacred Music; 500901 Music, General; 500903 Music - General Performance; 500907 Music - Piano and Organ Performance
Related DOT Job/s: 152.041-010 MUSICIAN, INSTRUMENTAL

34053A DANCERS. OOH Title/s: Dancers and Choreographers

Dance alone, with partners, or in a group to entertain audience. Performs classical, modern, or acrobatic dances in productions. Harmonizes body movements to rhythm of musical accompaniment. Studies and practices dance moves required in role. Rehearses solo or with partners or troupe members. Coordinates dancing with that of partner or dance ensemble. Works with choreographer to refine or modify dance steps. Devises and choreographs dance for self or others. Auditions for parts in productions.
Yearly Earnings: $30,004
Education: Postsecondary vocational training
Knowledge: Fine Arts
Abilities: Fluency of Ideas; Originality; Memorization; Spatial Orientation; Multilimb Coordination; Speed of Limb Movement; Static Strength; Explosive Strength; Dynamic Strength; Trunk Strength; Stamina; Extent Flexibility; Dynamic Flexibility; Gross Body Coordination; Gross Body Equilibrium; Peripheral Vision; Depth Perception; Auditory Attention
Skills: None above average
General Work Activities: Thinking Creatively; Performing General Physical Activities; Performing for or Working with Public; Coordinating Work and Activities of Others; Developing and Building Teams
Job Characteristics: Objective or Subjective Information; Standing; Walking or Running; Kneeling, Crouching, or Crawling; Keeping or Regaining Balance; Bending or Twisting the Body; Making Repetitive Motions; Importance of Repeating Same Tasks
GOE Group/s: 01.05.02 Performing Arts:Dance: Performing
CIP Program/s: 500301 Dance
Related DOT Job/s: 151.047-010 DANCER

34053B CHOREOGRAPHERS. OOH Title/s: Dancers and Choreographers

Create and teach original dances for ballet, musical, or revue to be performed for stage, television, motion picture, or nightclub production. Determines dance movements designed to suggest story, interpret emotion, or enliven show. Creates original dance routines for ballets, musicals, or other forms of entertainment. Instructs cast in dance movements at rehearsals to achieve desired effect. Studies story line and music to envision and devise dance movements. Directs and stages dance presentations for various forms of entertainment. Auditions performers for one or more dance parts.
Yearly Earnings: $30,004
Education: Postsecondary vocational training
Knowledge: Personnel and Human Resources; Education and Training; Fine Arts; Communications and Media
Abilities: Fluency of Ideas; Originality; Memorization; Spatial Orientation; Visualization; Time Sharing; Multilimb Coordination; Speed of Limb Movement; Explosive Strength; Dynamic Strength; Trunk Strength; Stamina; Extent Flexibility; Dynamic Flexibility; Gross Body Coordination; Gross Body Equilibrium; Peripheral Vision; Depth Perception
Skills: Coordination; Instructing; Idea Generation
General Work Activities: Identifying Objects, Actions, and Events; Judging Qualities of Things, Services, People; Thinking Creatively; Organizing, Planning, and Prioritizing; Performing General Physical Activities; Implementing Ideas, Programs, etc.; Interpreting Meaning of Information to Others; Coordinating Work and Activities of Others; Developing and Building Teams; Teaching Others; Guiding, Directing and Motivating Subordinates; Coaching and Developing Others; Staffing Organizational Units
Job Characteristics: Objective or Subjective Information; Job-Required Social Interaction; Supervise, Coach, Train Others; Take a Position Opposed to Others; Coordinate or Lead Others; Responsibility for Outcomes and Results; Standing; Walking or Running; Kneeling, Crouching, or Crawling; Keeping or Regaining Balance; Bending or Twisting the Body; Making Repetitive Motions
GOE Group/s: 01.05.01 Performing Arts:Dance: Instructing and Choreography
CIP Program/s: 500301 Dance
Related DOT Job/s: 151.027-010 CHOREOGRAPHER

34056A ACTORS AND PERFORMERS. OOH Title/s: Actors, Directors, and Producers

Perform dramatic roles, comedic routines, or tricks of illusion to entertain audiences. Portrays and interprets role, using speech, gestures, and body movements, to entertain radio, film, television, or live audience. Performs original and stock tricks of illusion to entertain and mystify audience, occasionally including audience members as participants. Tells jokes, performs comic dances and songs, impersonates mannerisms and voices of others, contorts face, and uses other devices to amuse audience. Performs humorous and serious interpretations of emotions, actions, and situations, using only body movements, facial expressions, and gestures. Reads and rehearses role from script to learn lines, stunts, and cues as directed. Reads from script or book to narrate action, inform, or entertain audience, utilizing few or no stage props. Dresses in comical clown costume and make-up and performs comedy routines to entertain audience. Prepares for and performs action stunts for motion picture, television, or stage production. Sings or dances during dramatic or comedy performance. Manipulates string, wire, rod, or fingers to animate puppet or dummy in synchronization to talking, singing, or recorded program. Signals start and introduces performers to stimulate excitement and to coordinate smooth transition of acts during circus performance. Writes original or adapted material for drama, comedy, puppet show, narration, or other performance. Constructs puppets and ventriloquist dummies, and sews accessory clothing, using hand tools and machines. Designs, builds, and repairs equipment for stunts.
Yearly Earnings: $30,004
Education: Long-term O-J-T
Knowledge: Fine Arts; Communications and Media
Abilities: Originality; Memorization; Spatial Orientation; Reaction Time; Speed of Limb Movement; Dynamic Flexibility; Gross Body Coordination; Gross Body Equilibrium; Near Vision; Speech Clarity

Skills: Speaking; Monitoring; Social Perceptiveness
General Work Activities: Thinking Creatively; Performing General Physical Activities; Communicating with Persons Outside Organization; Performing for or Working with Public
Job Characteristics: Objective or Subjective Information; Special Uniform
GOE Group/s: 01.03.02 Performing Arts:Drama: Performing; 01.03.03 Performing Arts:Drama: Narrating and Announcing; 01.07.02 Elemental Arts: Announcing; 12.02.01 Physical Feats: Performing
CIP Program/s: 500501 Drama/Theater Arts, General; 500503 Acting and Directing
Related DOT Job/s: 150.047-010 ACTOR; 150.147-010 NARRATOR; 159.041-010 MAGICIAN; 159.041-014 PUPPETEER; 159.044-010 VENTRILOQUIST; 159.047-010 CLOWN; 159.047-014 COMEDIAN; 159.047-018 IMPERSONATOR; 159.047-022 MIME; 159.341-014 STUNT PERFORMER; 159.367-010 RING CONDUCTOR

34056B EXTRAS/STAND-INS. OOH Title/s: Actors, Directors, and Producers

Perform as nonspeaking member of scene in stage, motion picture, or television productions. Performs as nonspeaking member of scene in stage, motion picture, or television production. Portrays image and imitates gestures and mannerisms of star performer in motion picture or television performance. Parades across stage to display costumes and provide background for chorus line in stage or film production. Substitutes for star performer to determine desired angle, lighting effects, and background prior to actual filming. Dresses in costume of star performer to perform roles or act as photographic double. Performs activities that require special skills, such as dancing, swimming, skating, handling livestock, or riding. Rehearses and performs pantomime, portraying points essential in staging of scenes.
Yearly Earnings: $30,004
Education: Long-term O-J-T
Knowledge: Fine Arts
Abilities: Speed of Limb Movement; Explosive Strength; Dynamic Flexibility; Gross Body Coordination; Gross Body Equilibrium
Skills: None above average
General Work Activities: None above average
Job Characteristics: Objective or Subjective Information; Extremely Bright or Inadequate Lighting; Special Uniform
GOE Group/s: 01.08.01 Modeling: Personal Appearance
CIP Program/s: 500501 Drama/Theater Arts, General; 500503 Acting and Directing
Related DOT Job/s: 159.647-014 EXTRA; 159.647-022 SHOW GIRL; 961.364-010 DOUBLE; 961.667-014 STAND-IN

34056D AMUSEMENT ENTERTAINERS. OOH Title/s: Actors, Directors, and Producers

Entertain audiences by exhibiting special skills, such as juggling, diving, swimming, acrobatics, or by performing daredevil feats. Performs daredevil feats, such as being shot from cannon, parachuting from airplane, or diving from platform, at carnivals, fairs, and circuses. Juggles and balances objects, such as balls, knives, plates, tenpins, and hats, to entertain audience. Performs synchronized swimming, water-ballet, and underwater swimming routines to entertain audience. Performs specialty act, such as fire eating, sword swallowing, or snake charming, in sideshow or amusement park. Hypnotizes others to entertain audience at nightclub, live variety show, television, or other venue. Dives to bottom of fish tank in diving suit to feed, describe, and identify fish to inform and entertain audience. Sells tickets or performs other duties when not performing for audience. Cleans fish tank bottom and windows, using suction hose and scrubbing brush. Observes, reports, and treats diseased fish in tank during underwater activity.
Yearly Earnings: $30,004
Education: Long-term O-J-T
Knowledge: None above average
Abilities: Spatial Orientation; Multilimb Coordination; Rate Control; Wrist-Finger Speed; Speed of Limb Movement; Explosive Strength; Dynamic Strength; Trunk Strength; Stamina; Extent Flexibility; Dynamic Flexibility; Gross Body Coordination; Gross Body Equilibrium; Peripheral Vision; Depth Perception
Skills: None above average
General Work Activities: Performing General Physical Activities; Performing for or Working with Public
Job Characteristics: Objective or Subjective Information; Job-Required Social Interaction; Provide a Service to Others; Deal with External Customers; Cramped Work Space, Awkward Positions; High Places; Standing; Climbing Ladders, Scaffolds, Poles, etc.; Keeping or Regaining Balance; Bending or Twisting the Body; Special Uniform; Specialized Protective or Safety Attire; Importance of Repeating Same Tasks
GOE Group/s: 01.07.02 Elemental Arts: Announcing; 01.07.03 Elemental Arts: Entertaining; 12.02.01 Physical Feats: Performing
CIP Program/s: 490304 Diver (Professional)
Related DOT Job/s: 159.247-010 ACROBAT; 159.247-014 AERIALIST; 159.341-010 JUGGLER; 159.347-014 AQUATIC PERFORMER; 159.347-018 THRILL PERFORMER; 159.347-022 WIRE WALKER; 159.647-010 AMUSEMENT PARK ENTERTAINER; 349.247-010 DIVER

34056E EQUESTRIAN PERFORMERS. OOH Title/s: Actors, Directors, and Producers

Ride horses at circus, carnival, exhibition, or rodeo, performing feats of equestrian skills and daring to entertain audiences. Performs acrobatic stunts on horseback to entertain audience at circus, exhibition, or horse show. Demonstrates skill in bronco riding, calf roping, steer wrestling, or other rodeo events to entertain and compete for prize money. Rides bareback to perform feats of skill and daring. Rides or leads horse at horse show to display best points of animal before judges and audience.
Yearly Earnings: $30,004
Education: Long-term O-J-T
Knowledge: None above average
Abilities: Spatial Orientation; Multilimb Coordination; Response Orientation; Rate Control; Reaction Time; Speed of Limb Movement; Static Strength; Explosive Strength; Dynamic Strength; Trunk Strength; Stamina; Extent Flexibility; Dynamic Flexibility; Gross Body Coordination; Gross Body Equilibrium; Peripheral Vision; Depth Perception
Skills: Monitoring
General Work Activities: Thinking Creatively; Performing General Physical Activities; Performing for or Working with Public
Job Characteristics: Whole Body Vibration; Hazardous Situations; Keeping or Regaining Balance; Bending or Twisting the Body; Special Uniform; Specialized Protective or Safety Attire
GOE Group/s: 12.02.01 Physical Feats: Performing
CIP Program/s: 010507 Equestrian/Equine Studies, Horse Management and Training
Related DOT Job/s: 159.344-010 EQUESTRIAN; 159.344-014 RODEO PERFORMER; 159.344-018 SHOW-HORSE DRIVER

34056F PRODUCERS. OOH Title/s: Actors, Directors, and Producers

Plan and coordinate various aspects of radio, television, stage, or motion picture production, such as selecting script, coordinating writing, directing, and editing; and arranging financing. Coordinates various aspects of production, such as audio and camera work, music, timing, writing, and staging. Conducts meetings with staff to discuss production progress and to ensure production objectives are attained. Selects and hires cast and staff members and arbitrates personnel disputes. Directs activities of one or more departments of motion picture studio and prepares rehearsal call sheets and reports of activities and operating costs. Reviews film, recordings, or rehearsals to ensure conformance to production and broadcast standards. Produces shows for special occasions, such as holiday or testimonial. Composes and edits script, or outlines story for screenwriter to write script. Obtains and distributes costumes, props, music, and studio equipment to complete production. Establishes management policies, production schedules, and operating budgets for production. Distributes rehearsal call sheets and copies of script, arranges for rehearsal quarters, and contacts cast members to verify readiness for rehearsal. Times scene and calculates program timing. Reads manuscript and selects play for stage performance. Selects scenes from taped program to be used for promotional purposes. Represents network or company in negotiations with independent producers.

Yearly Earnings: $30,004

Education: Long-term O-J-T

Knowledge: Administration and Management; Economics and Accounting; Personnel and Human Resources; English Language; Fine Arts; Communications and Media

Abilities: Oral Comprehension; Written Comprehension; Oral Expression; Written Expression; Fluency of Ideas; Originality; Problem Sensitivity; Information Ordering; Memorization; Time Sharing; Speech Recognition; Speech Clarity

Skills: Reading Comprehension; Active Listening; Writing; Speaking; Critical Thinking; Active Learning; Learning Strategies; Monitoring; Social Perceptiveness; Coordination; Persuasion; Negotiation; Instructing; Synthesis/Reorganization; Idea Generation; Idea Evaluation; Implementation Planning; Operations Analysis; Visioning; Identifying Downstream Consequences; Judgment and Decision Making; Time Management; Management of Financial Resources; Management of Material Resources; Management of Personnel Resources

General Work Activities: Getting Information Needed to Do the Job; Judging Qualities of Things, Services, People; Processing Information; Making Decisions and Solving Problems; Thinking Creatively; Developing Objectives and Strategies; Scheduling Work and Activities; Organizing, Planning, and Prioritizing; Drafting and Specifying Technical Devices, etc.; Implementing Ideas, Programs, etc.; Communicating with Other Workers; Communicating with Persons Outside Organization; Establishing and Maintaining Relationships; Selling or Influencing Others; Resolving Conflicts, Negotiating with Others; Performing for or Working with Public; Coordinating Work and Activities of Others; Developing and Building Teams; Guiding, Directing and Motivating Subordinates; Coaching and Developing Others; Provide Consultation and Advice to Others; Performing Administrative Activities; Staffing Organizational Units; Monitoring and Controlling Resources

Job Characteristics: Objective or Subjective Information; Job-Required Social Interaction; Supervise, Coach, Train Others; Persuade Someone to a Course of Action; Coordinate or Lead Others; Responsibility for Outcomes and Results; Frustrating Circumstances

GOE Group/s: 01.01.01 Literary Arts: Editing; 01.03.01 Performing Arts:Drama: Instructing and Directing; 11.05.02 Business Administration: Administrative Specialization

CIP Program/s: 090701 Radio and Television Broadcasting; 500501 Drama/Theater Arts, General; 500502 Technical Theater/Theater Design and Stagecraft; 500503 Acting and Directing; 500602 Film-Video Making/Cinematography and Production

Related DOT Job/s: 159.117-010 PRODUCER; 187.167-174 PRODUCER; 187.167-178 PRODUCER; 187.167-182 PRODUCER, ASSISTANT; 962.167-014 PROGRAM ASSISTANT

34056G DIRECTORS—STAGE, MOTION PICTURE, TELEVISION, AND RADIO. OOH Title/s: Actors, Directors, and Producers

Interpret script, conduct rehearsals, and direct activities of cast and technical crew for stage, motion picture, television, or radio programs. Reads and rehearses cast to develop performance based on script interpretations. Directs cast, crew, and technicians during production or recording and filming in studio or on location. Directs live broadcasts, films and recordings, or nonbroadcast programming for public entertainment or education. Confers with technical directors, managers, and writers to discuss details of production, such as photography, script, music, sets, and costumes. Establishes pace of program and sequences of scenes according to time requirements and cast and set accessibility. Coaches performers in acting techniques to develop and improve performance and image. Approves equipment and elements required for production, such as scenery, lights, props, costumes, choreography, and music. Interprets stage-set diagrams to determine stage layout, and supervises placement of equipment and scenery. Auditions and selects cast and technical staff. Compiles cue words and phrases and cues announcers, cast members, and technicians during performances. Cuts and edits film or tape to integrate component parts of film into desired sequence. Writes and compiles letters, memos, notes, scripts, and other program material, using computer. Reviews educational material to gather information for scripts. Coordinates animal performances at amusement park to educate visitors.

Yearly Earnings: $30,004

Education: Long-term O-J-T

Knowledge: Administration and Management; Fine Arts; Communications and Media

Abilities: Oral Expression; Fluency of Ideas; Originality; Category Flexibility; Memorization; Speed of Closure; Visualization; Selective Attention; Time Sharing; Gross Body Equilibrium; Far Vision; Auditory Attention; Sound Localization; Speech Clarity

Skills: Reading Comprehension; Speaking; Critical Thinking; Active Learning; Learning Strategies; Social Perceptiveness; Coordination; Persuasion; Negotiation; Instructing; Synthesis/Reorganization; Idea Generation; Idea Evaluation; Implementation Planning; Equipment Selection; Operation and Control; Visioning; Identification of Key Causes; Systems Evaluation; Time Management; Management of Financial Resources; Management of Material Resources; Management of Personnel Resources

General Work Activities: Monitoring Processes, Material, or Surroundings; Judging Qualities of Things, Services, People; Making Decisions and Solving Problems; Thinking Creatively; Developing Objectives and Strategies; Scheduling Work and Activities; Organizing, Planning, and Prioritizing; Drafting and Specifying Technical Devices, etc.; Communicating with Other Workers; Establishing and Maintaining Relationships; Selling or Influencing Others; Resolving Conflicts, Negotiating with Others; Performing for or Working with Public; Coordinating Work and Activities of Others; Developing and Building Teams; Guiding, Directing and Motivating Subordinates; Coaching and Developing Others; Provide Consultation and Advice to Others; Staffing Organizational Units; Monitoring and Controlling Resources

Job Characteristics: Objective or Subjective Information; Job-Required Social Interaction; Supervise, Coach, Train Others; Persuade Someone to a Course of Action; Take a Position Opposed to Others; Coordinate or Lead Others; Responsibility for Outcomes and Results; Extremely Bright or Inadequate Lighting; Radiation

GOE Group/s: 01.03.01 Performing Arts:Drama: Instructing and Directing; 01.03.03 Performing Arts:Drama: Narrating and Announcing

CIP Program/s: 090701 Radio and Television Broadcasting; 310301 Parks, Recreation and Leisure Facilities Management; 500501 Drama/Theater Arts, General; 500502 Technical Theater/Theater Design and Stagecraft; 500503 Acting and Directing; 500602 Film-Video Making/Cinematography and Production
Related DOT Job/s: 139.167-010 PROGRAM COORDINATOR; 150.027-010 DRAMATIC COACH; 150.067-010 DIRECTOR, STAGE; 159.067-010 DIRECTOR, MOTION PICTURE; 159.067-014 DIRECTOR, TELEVISION; 159.167-014 DIRECTOR, RADIO; 159.167-018 MANAGER, STAGE

34056H PROGRAM DIRECTORS. OOH Title/s: Actors, Directors, and Producers
Direct and coordinate activities of personnel engaged in preparation of radio or television station program schedules and programs, such as sports or news. Directs and coordinates activities of personnel engaged in broadcast news, sports, or programming. Plans and schedules programming and event coverage based on length of broadcast and available station or network time. Evaluates length, content, and suitability of programs for broadcast. Reviews, corrects, and advises member stations concerning programs and schedules. Coordinates activities between departments, such as news and programming. Confers with directors and production staff to discuss issues, such as production and casting problems, budget, policy, and news coverage. Directs set-up of remote facilities and installs or cancels programs at remote stations. Establishes work schedules and hires, assigns, and evaluates staff. Monitors and reviews news and programming copy and film, using audio or video equipment. Originates feature ideas and researches program topics for implementation. Examines expenditures to ensure programming and broadcasting activities are within budget. Writes news copy, notes, letters, and memos, using computer. Arranges for office space and equipment.
Yearly Earnings: $30,004
Education: Long-term O-J-T
Knowledge: Administration and Management; Economics and Accounting; Personnel and Human Resources; Communications and Media
Abilities: Oral Comprehension; Oral Expression; Written Expression; Fluency of Ideas; Originality; Deductive Reasoning; Memorization; Perceptual Speed; Near Vision
Skills: Writing; Active Learning; Coordination; Negotiation; Instructing; Idea Generation; Idea Evaluation; Implementation Planning; Programming; Visioning; Time Management; Management of Financial Resources; Management of Material Resources; Management of Personnel Resources
General Work Activities: Getting Information Needed to Do the Job; Monitoring Processes, Material, or Surroundings; Estimating Needed Characteristics; Judging Qualities of Things, Services, People; Making Decisions and Solving Problems; Thinking Creatively; Developing Objectives and Strategies; Scheduling Work and Activities; Organizing, Planning, and Prioritizing; Operating Vehicles or Equipment; Communicating with Other Workers; Establishing and Maintaining Relationships; Selling or Influencing Others; Resolving Conflicts, Negotiating with Others; Coordinating Work and Activities of Others; Developing and Building Teams; Guiding, Directing and Motivating Subordinates; Coaching and Developing Others; Provide Consultation and Advice to Others; Performing Administrative Activities; Staffing Organizational Units; Monitoring and Controlling Resources
Job Characteristics: Supervise, Coach, Train Others; Coordinate or Lead Others; Responsibility for Outcomes and Results
GOE Group/s: 11.05.02 Business Administration: Administrative Specialization; 11.08.01 Communications: Editing; 11.09.03 Promotion: Public Relations
CIP Program/s: 500501 Drama/Theater Arts, General; 500503 Acting and Directing; 500602 Film-Video Making/Cinematography and Production
Related DOT Job/s: 184.117-010 DIRECTOR, PUBLIC SERVICE; 184.167-014 DIRECTOR, NEWS; 184.167-022 DIRECTOR, OPERATIONS, BROADCAST; 184.167-030 DIRECTOR, PROGRAM; 184.167-034 DIRECTOR, SPORTS

34056J TALENT DIRECTORS. OOH Title/s: Actors, Directors, and Producers; Personnel, Training, and Labor Relations Specialists and Managers
Audition and interview performers to select most appropriate talent for parts in stage, television, radio, or motion picture productions. Auditions and interviews performers to identify most suitable talent for broadcasting, stage, or musical production. Selects performer or submits list of suitable performers to producer or director for final selection. Arranges for screen tests or auditions for new performers. Maintains talent file, including information about personalities, such as specialties, past performances, and availability. Negotiates contract agreements with performers. Directs recording sessions for musical artists. Promotes record sales by personal appearances and contacts with broadcasting personalities.
Yearly Earnings: $30,004
Education: Long-term O-J-T
Knowledge: Administration and Management; Sales and Marketing; Personnel and Human Resources; Fine Arts; Communications and Media
Abilities: Memorization; Hearing Sensitivity
Skills: Active Listening; Speaking; Social Perceptiveness; Persuasion; Negotiation; Management of Personnel Resources
General Work Activities: Monitoring Processes, Material, or Surroundings; Judging Qualities of Things, Services, People; Thinking Creatively; Scheduling Work and Activities; Organizing, Planning, and Prioritizing; Communicating with Persons Outside Organization; Establishing and Maintaining Relationships; Selling or Influencing Others; Resolving Conflicts, Negotiating with Others; Performing for or Working with Public; Coordinating Work and Activities of Others; Provide Consultation and Advice to Others; Performing Administrative Activities; Staffing Organizational Units; Monitoring and Controlling Resources
Job Characteristics: Objective or Subjective Information; Job-Required Social Interaction; Supervise, Coach, Train Others; Persuade Someone to a Course of Action; Deal with External Customers
GOE Group/s: 01.03.01 Performing Arts:Drama: Instructing and Directing; 01.04.01 Performing Arts:Music: Instructing and Directing
CIP Program/s: 500501 Drama/Theater Arts, General; 500503 Acting and Directing
Related DOT Job/s: 159.167-010 ARTIST AND REPERTOIRE MANAGER; 159.267-010 DIRECTOR, CASTING; 166.167-010 CONTESTANT COORDINATOR

34056K TECHNICAL DIRECTORS/MANAGERS. OOH Title/s: Actors, Directors, and Producers
Coordinate activities of technical departments, such as taping, editing, engineering, and maintenance, to produce radio or television programs. Coordinates activities of radio or television studio and control-room personnel to ensure technical quality of programs. Supervises and assigns duties to workers engaged in technical control and production of radio and television programs. Observes picture through monitor and directs camera and video staff concerning shading and composition. Coordinates elements of program, such as audio, camera, special effects, timing, and script, to ensure production objectives are met. Schedules use of studio and editing facilities for producers and engineering and maintenance staff. Monitors broadcast

to ensure that programs conform with station or network policies and regulations. Directs personnel in auditioning talent and programs. Trains workers in use of equipment, such as switcher, camera, monitor, microphones, and lights. Operates equipment to produce programs or broadcast live programs from remote locations.
Yearly Earnings: $30,004
Education: Long-term O-J-T
Knowledge: Administration and Management; Personnel and Human Resources; Education and Training; Fine Arts; Telecommunications; Communications and Media
Abilities: Memorization; Speed of Closure; Perceptual Speed; Selective Attention; Time Sharing; Reaction Time; Gross Body Equilibrium; Near Vision; Far Vision; Visual Color Discrimination; Hearing Sensitivity; Auditory Attention; Sound Localization
Skills: Speaking; Learning Strategies; Monitoring; Coordination; Persuasion; Negotiation; Instructing; Idea Evaluation; Operations Analysis; Equipment Selection; Operation Monitoring; Operation and Control; Systems Perception; Identification of Key Causes; Time Management; Management of Material Resources; Management of Personnel Resources
General Work Activities: Judging Qualities of Things, Services, People; Scheduling Work and Activities; Organizing, Planning, and Prioritizing; Communicating with Other Workers; Establishing and Maintaining Relationships; Resolving Conflicts, Negotiating with Others; Coordinating Work and Activities of Others; Developing and Building Teams; Guiding, Directing and Motivating Subordinates; Coaching and Developing Others; Staffing Organizational Units
Job Characteristics: Job-Required Social Interaction; Supervise, Coach, Train Others; Coordinate or Lead Others; Responsibility for Outcomes and Results
GOE Group/s: 05.02.04 Managerial Work: Mechanical: Communications; 11.05.02 Business Administration: Administrative Specialization
CIP Program/s: 090701 Radio and Television Broadcasting; 500602 Film-Video Making/Cinematography and Production
Related DOT Job/s: 184.162-010 MANAGER, PRODUCTION; 962.162-010 DIRECTOR, TECHNICAL

34058A COACHES AND SCOUTS. OOH Title/s: Athletes, Coaches, Umpires, and Referees

Analyze performance or instruct athletes of professional sporting events. May evaluate athletes' strengths and weaknesses as possible recruits or to improve the athletes' technique to prepare them for competition. Analyzes athletes' performance and reviews game statistics or records to determine fitness and potential for professional sports. Plans and directs physical conditioning program for athletes to achieve maximum athletic performance. Observes athletes to determine areas of deficiency and need for individual or team improvement. Evaluates team and opposition capabilities to develop and plan game strategy. Instructs athletes, individually or in groups, demonstrating sport techniques and game strategies. Evaluates athletes' skills and discusses or recommends acquisition, trade, or position assignment of players. Prepares scouting reports detailing information, such as selection or rejection of athletes and locations identified for future recruitment. Negotiates with professional athletes or representatives to obtain services and arrange contracts.
Yearly Earnings: $30,004
Education: Long-term O-J-T
Knowledge: Administration and Management; Sales and Marketing; Personnel and Human Resources; Psychology; Therapy and Counseling; Education and Training
Abilities: Oral Expression; Fluency of Ideas; Originality; Problem Sensitivity; Deductive Reasoning; Inductive Reasoning; Category Flexibility; Memorization; Speed of Closure; Flexibility of Closure; Perceptual Speed; Spatial Orientation; Visualization; Selective Attention; Time Sharing; Response Orientation; Reaction Time; Speed of Limb Movement; Explosive Strength; Stamina; Dynamic Flexibility; Gross Body Coordination; Gross Body Equilibrium; Far Vision; Night Vision; Peripheral Vision; Depth Perception; Glare Sensitivity; Auditory Attention; Sound Localization
Skills: Social Perceptiveness; Persuasion; Negotiation; Instructing; Idea Generation; Implementation Planning; Visioning; Systems Perception; Identification of Key Causes; Systems Evaluation; Time Management; Management of Financial Resources; Management of Personnel Resources
General Work Activities: Developing Objectives and Strategies; Scheduling Work and Activities; Selling or Influencing Others; Resolving Conflicts, Negotiating with Others; Developing and Building Teams; Teaching Others; Guiding, Directing and Motivating Subordinates; Coaching and Developing Others; Staffing Organizational Units
Job Characteristics: Objective or Subjective Information; Job-Required Social Interaction; Supervise, Coach, Train Others; Persuade Someone to a Course of Action; Take a Position Opposed to Others; Coordinate or Lead Others; Responsible for Others' Health and Safety; Responsibility for Outcomes and Results; Frequency in Conflict Situations; Deal with Unpleasant or Angry People; Very Hot; Walking or Running; Keeping or Regaining Balance; Frustrating Circumstances; Importance of Being Aware of New Events
GOE Group/s: 12.01.01 Sports: Coaching and Instructing
CIP Program/s: 131314 Physical Education Teaching and Coaching
Related DOT Job/s: 153.117-010 HEAD COACH; 153.117-018 SCOUT, PROFESSIONAL SPORTS; 153.227-010 COACH, PROFESSIONAL ATHLETES

34058B ATHLETIC TRAINERS. OOH Title/s: Athletes, Coaches, Umpires, and Referees

Evaluate, advise, and treat athletes to maintain physical fitness. Evaluates physical condition of athletes and advises or prescribes routines and corrective exercises to strengthen muscles. Recommends special diets to improve health, increase stamina, and reduce weight of athletes. Wraps ankles, fingers, wrists, or other body parts with synthetic skin, gauze, or adhesive tape to support muscles and ligaments. Administers emergency first aid, treats minor chronic disabilities, or refers injured person to physician. Massages body parts to relieve soreness, strains, and bruises.
Yearly Earnings: $30,004
Education: Long-term O-J-T
Knowledge: Customer and Personal Service; Biology; Psychology; Medicine and Dentistry; Therapy and Counseling
Abilities: Problem Sensitivity; Speed of Closure; Speed of Limb Movement; Static Strength; Stamina; Extent Flexibility; Dynamic Flexibility; Gross Body Coordination; Gross Body Equilibrium
Skills: Persuasion; Service Orientation
General Work Activities: Assisting and Caring for Others; Coaching and Developing Others
Job Characteristics: Objective or Subjective Information; Job-Required Social Interaction; Supervise, Coach, Train Others; Persuade Someone to a Course of Action; Provide a Service to Others; Take a Position Opposed to Others; Coordinate or Lead Others; Responsible for Others' Health and Safety; Diseases/Infections; Standing; Walking or Running; Kneeling, Crouching, or Crawling; Keeping or Regaining Balance; Frustrating Circumstances
GOE Group/s: 10.02.02 Nursing, Therapy, and Specialized Teaching Services: Therapy and Rehabilitation
CIP Program/s: 310501 Health and Physical Education, General; 310503 Athletic Training and Sports Medicine
Related DOT Job/s: 153.224-010 ATHLETIC TRAINER

34058C PROFESSIONAL ATHLETES. OOH Title/s: Athletes, Coaches, Umpires, and Referees

Participate in physical, competitive athletic events. Participates in athletic events and competitive sports, according to established rules and regulations. Plays professional sport and is identified according to sport played, such as football, basketball, baseball, hockey, or boxing. Exercises and practices under direction of athletic trainer or professional coach to prepare and train for competitive events. Represents team or professional sports club, speaking to groups involved in activities, such as sports clinics and fund raisers.
Yearly Earnings: $30,004
Education: Long-term O-J-T
Knowledge: None above average
Abilities: Spatial Orientation; Visualization; Selective Attention; Time Sharing; Arm-Hand Steadiness; Manual Dexterity; Multilimb Coordination; Response Orientation; Rate Control; Reaction Time; Speed of Limb Movement; Static Strength; Explosive Strength; Dynamic Strength; Trunk Strength; Stamina; Extent Flexibility; Dynamic Flexibility; Gross Body Coordination; Gross Body Equilibrium; Far Vision; Peripheral Vision; Depth Perception; Glare Sensitivity; Auditory Attention; Sound Localization; Speech Recognition
Skills: Monitoring
General Work Activities: Performing General Physical Activities; Performing for or Working with Public
Job Characteristics: Objective or Subjective Information; Job-Required Social Interaction; Frequency in Conflict Situations; Deal with Unpleasant or Angry People; Deal with Physical, Aggressive People; Sounds, Noise Levels are Distracting, etc.; Very Hot; Hazardous Situations; Standing; Walking or Running; Keeping or Regaining Balance; Bending or Twisting the Body; Special Uniform; Frustrating Circumstances; Importance of Being Aware of New Events; Importance of Repeating Same Tasks
GOE Group/s: 12.01.03 Sports: Performing
CIP Program/s: 000000 NO CIP ASSIGNED
Related DOT Job/s: 153.341-010 PROFESSIONAL ATHLETE

34058E MOTOR RACERS. OOH Title/s: Athletes, Coaches, Umpires, and Referees

Drive automobiles or ride motorcycles in competitive races. Drives car or motorcycle over track, course, or natural terrain to participate in trial, qualifying, and competitive races. Maneuvers vehicle to avoid accident, barrier, or other emergency situation. Watches for warning flags and other signals indicating emergency situation and responds to instructions given by track officials. Listens to engine and observes fuel, oil, compression, and other gauges to ensure vehicle is operating efficiently. Evaluates speed, maneuverability, and position of other vehicles during competitive race to determine appropriate racing strategy. Performs maintenance work on car or motorcycle.
Yearly Earnings: $30,004
Education: Long-term O-J-T
Knowledge: Mechanical; Transportation
Abilities: Perceptual Speed; Spatial Orientation; Visualization; Selective Attention; Time Sharing; Arm-Hand Steadiness; Manual Dexterity; Control Precision; Multilimb Coordination; Response Orientation; Rate Control; Reaction Time; Speed of Limb Movement; Stamina; Extent Flexibility; Gross Body Coordination; Far Vision; Peripheral Vision; Depth Perception; Glare Sensitivity; Hearing Sensitivity; Auditory Attention; Sound Localization
Skills: Equipment Maintenance; Repairing
General Work Activities: Handling and Moving Objects; Interacting with Computers; Repairing and Maintaining Mechanical Equipment
Job Characteristics: Responsible for Others' Health and Safety; Deal with Physical, Aggressive People; Sounds, Noise Levels are Distracting, etc.; Very Hot; Extremely Bright or Inadequate Lighting; Contaminants; Cramped Work Space, Awkward Positions; Whole Body Vibration; Hazardous Conditions; Hazardous Equipment; Sitting; Using Hands on Objects, Tools, or Controls; Special Uniform; Common Protective or Safety Attire; Specialized Protective or Safety Attire; Consequence of Error; Frustrating Circumstances; Importance of Being Aware of New Events; Importance of Repeating Same Tasks; Pace Determined by Speed of Equipment
GOE Group/s: 12.01.03 Sports: Performing
CIP Program/s: 000000 NO CIP ASSIGNED
Related DOT Job/s: 153.243-010 AUTOMOBILE RACER; 153.243-014 MOTORCYCLE RACER

34058F JOCKEYS AND SULKY DRIVERS. OOH Title/s: Athletes, Coaches, Umpires, and Referees

Ride racehorses or drive sulkies in horse or harness race. Drives and controls speed of horse or horse-drawn sulky to race from starting gate to finish line. Monitors speed and position of horses or sulkies to determine how to challenge for lead position in race. Mounts horse after weighing-in, and rides horse to specified numbered stall of starting gate. Studies performance record of competing horses to plan race strategy. Confers with training personnel to discuss ability and peculiarities of horses, and to analyze performance of horses for competitive races. Trains or directs other workers involved in training and grooming, feeding, stabling, handling, and transporting race horses.
Yearly Earnings: $30,004
Education: Long-term O-J-T
Knowledge: None above average
Abilities: Spatial Orientation; Visualization; Selective Attention; Time Sharing; Multilimb Coordination; Response Orientation; Rate Control; Reaction Time; Speed of Limb Movement; Dynamic Strength; Trunk Strength; Stamina; Gross Body Coordination; Gross Body Equilibrium; Far Vision; Peripheral Vision; Depth Perception; Glare Sensitivity
Skills: Instructing
General Work Activities: Performing General Physical Activities; Teaching Others
Job Characteristics: Objective or Subjective Information; Supervise, Coach, Train Others; Very Hot; Extremely Bright or Inadequate Lighting; Cramped Work Space, Awkward Positions; Whole Body Vibration; Radiation; Keeping or Regaining Balance; Bending or Twisting the Body; Special Uniform; Frustrating Circumstances; Importance of Being Aware of New Events; Importance of Repeating Same Tasks
GOE Group/s: 12.01.03 Sports: Performing
CIP Program/s: 000000 NO CIP ASSIGNED
Related DOT Job/s: 153.244-010 JOCKEY; 153.244-014 SULKY DRIVER

34058G HORSE RIDERS/EXERCISERS. OOH Title/s: Athletes, Coaches, Umpires, and Referees

Ride horses to exercise, condition, or lead other horses. Rides horse to exercise, condition, and train horse for racing, following specific instructions of training personnel. Leads procession of riders in post position order onto track to starting gate area. Leads horses to and from receiving barn or paddock before and after race. Informs trainer of horse's behavior and physical condition to modify training or conditioning in preparation for race. Rides horse to chase and restrain runaway horses to prevent disruption of race and injury to horse or thrown rider. Grooms and feeds horses. Diverts riders from competitor involved in accident on racetrack. Assists horse ambulance workers to remove injured horse from track, using block and tackle.
Yearly Earnings: $30,004
Education: Long-term O-J-T
Knowledge: Medicine and Dentistry

Abilities: Rate Control; Speed of Limb Movement; Dynamic Strength; Trunk Strength; Stamina; Gross Body Coordination; Gross Body Equilibrium; Far Vision; Peripheral Vision
Skills: None above average
General Work Activities: Performing General Physical Activities
Job Characteristics: Objective or Subjective Information; Very Hot; Contaminants; Whole Body Vibration; Radiation; Hazardous Situations; Keeping or Regaining Balance; Bending or Twisting the Body; Importance of Repeating Same Tasks
GOE Group/s: 03.03.01 Animal Training and Service: Animal Training; 12.01.02 Sports: Officiating
CIP Program/s: 010507 Equestrian/Equine Studies, Horse Management and Training
Related DOT Job/s: 153.384-010 MARSHAL; 153.674-010 EXERCISER, HORSE; 153.674-014 LEAD PONY RIDER

34058L UMPIRES, REFEREES, AND OTHER SPORTS OFFICIALS. OOH Title/s: Athletes, Coaches, Umpires, and Referees

Officiate at competitive athletic or sporting events. Detect infractions of rules and decide penalties according to established regulations. Include all sporting officials, referees, and competition judges. Observes actions of participants at athletic and sporting events to regulate competition and detect infractions of rules. Resolves claims of rule infractions, or complaints lodged by participants, and assesses penalties based on established regulations. Clocks events according to established standards for play, or to measure performance of participants. Makes qualifying determinations regarding participants, such as qualifying order or handicap. Signals participants or other officials to facilitate identification of infractions or otherwise regulate play or competition. Directs participants to assigned areas such as starting blocks or penalty areas. Inspects sporting equipment or examines participants to ensure compliance to regulations and safety of participants and spectators. Records and maintains information regarding participants and sporting activities. Confers with other sporting officials and facility managers to provide information, coordinate activities, and discuss problems. Prepares reports to regulating organization concerning sporting activities, complaints, and actions taken or needed, such as fines or other disciplinary actions.
Yearly Earnings: $30,004
Education: Long-term O-J-T
Knowledge: None above average
Abilities: Memorization; Perceptual Speed; Selective Attention; Time Sharing; Response Orientation; Rate Control; Reaction Time; Speed of Limb Movement; Stamina; Gross Body Coordination; Gross Body Equilibrium; Far Vision; Peripheral Vision; Depth Perception; Glare Sensitivity; Hearing Sensitivity; Auditory Attention; Speech Clarity
Skills: None above average
General Work Activities: Resolving Conflicts, Negotiating with Others
Job Characteristics: Objective or Subjective Information; Job-Required Social Interaction; Take a Position Opposed to Others; Coordinate or Lead Others; Frequency in Conflict Situations; Deal with Unpleasant or Angry People; Deal with Physical, Aggressive People; Sounds, Noise Levels are Distracting, etc.; Very Hot; Standing; Walking or Running; Bending or Twisting the Body; Special Uniform; Importance of Being Aware of New Events; Importance of Repeating Same Tasks
GOE Group/s: 03.03.02 Animal Training and Service: Animal Service; 11.06.03 Finance: Risk and Profit Analysis; 12.01.02 Sports: Officiating
CIP Program/s: 010505 Animal Trainer; 010507 Equestrian/Equine Studies, Horse Management and Training; 120204 Umpires and Other Sports Officials
Related DOT Job/s: 153.117-022 STEWARD, RACETRACK; 153.167-010 PADDOCK JUDGE; 153.167-014 PIT STEWARD; 153.167-018 RACING SECRETARY AND HANDICAPPER; 153.267-010 HORSE-RACE STARTER; 153.267-014 PATROL JUDGE; 153.267-018 UMPIRE; 153.287-010 HOOF AND SHOE INSPECTOR; 153.367-010 CLOCKER; 153.367-014 HORSE-RACE TIMER; 153.387-010 IDENTIFIER, HORSE; 153.387-014 SCORER; 153.467-010 CLERK-OF-SCALES; 153.667-010 STARTER; 219.267-010 HANDICAPPER, HARNESS RACING; 349.367-010 KENNEL MANAGER, DOG TRACK; 349.367-014 RECEIVING-BARN CUSTODIAN; 349.665-010 SCOREBOARD OPERATOR

Other Professional, Paraprofessional, and Technical Workers

39002 AIRPLANE DISPATCHERS AND AIR TRAFFIC CONTROLLERS. OOH Title/s: Air Traffic Controllers

Control air traffic on and within vicinity of airport and movement of air traffic between altitude sectors and control centers, according to established procedures and policies. Authorize, regulate, and control commercial airline flights, according to government or company regulations, to expedite and ensure flight safety. Communicates with, relays flight plans to, and coordinates movement of air traffic between control centers. Determines timing of and procedure for flight vector changes in sector. Issues landing and take-off authorizations and instructions, and communicates other information to aircraft. Controls air traffic at and within vicinity of airport. Recommends flight path changes to planes traveling in storms or fog or in emergency situations. Relays air traffic information, such as altitude, expected time of arrival, and course of aircraft, to control centers. Transfers control of departing flights to traffic control center and accepts control of arriving flights from air traffic control center. Analyzes factors, such as weather reports, fuel requirements, and maps, to determine flights and air routes. Directs radio searches for aircraft, and alerts control centers emergency facilities of flight difficulties. Inspects, adjusts, and controls radio equipment and airport lights. Completes daily activity report and keeps record of messages from aircraft. Reviews records and reports for clarity and completeness and maintains records and reports.
Yearly Earnings: $33,540
Education: Long-term O-J-T
Knowledge: Computers and Electronics; Physics; Geography; Telecommunications; Transportation
Abilities: Number Facility; Memorization; Speed of Closure; Flexibility of Closure; Perceptual Speed; Spatial Orientation; Selective Attention; Time Sharing; Response Orientation; Reaction Time; Gross Body Equilibrium; Near Vision; Hearing Sensitivity; Auditory Attention; Sound Localization; Speech Clarity
Skills: Active Listening; Critical Thinking; Coordination; Idea Evaluation; Operation Monitoring; Operation and Control; Systems Perception
General Work Activities: Getting Information Needed to Do the Job; Monitoring Processes, Material, or Surroundings; Identifying Objects, Actions, and Events; Inspecting Equipment, Structures, or Material; Estimating Needed Characteristics; Processing Information; Evaluating Information against Standards; Analyzing Data or Information; Making Decisions and Solving Problems; Thinking Creatively; Communicating with Other Workers; Assisting and Caring for Others; Coordinating Work and Activities of Others

Job Characteristics: Job-Required Social Interaction; Coordinate or Lead Others; Responsible for Others' Health and Safety; Responsibility for Outcomes and Results; Sitting; Consequence of Error; Degree of Automation; Importance of Being Exact or Accurate; Importance of Being Sure All is Done; Importance of Being Aware of New Events; Importance of Repeating Same Tasks
GOE Group/s: 05.03.03 Engineering Technology: Expediting and Coordinating
CIP Program/s: 490105 Air Traffic Controller
Related DOT Job/s: 193.162-010 AIR-TRAFFIC COORDINATOR; 193.162-014 AIR-TRAFFIC-CONTROL SPECIALIST, STATION; 193.162-018 AIR-TRAFFIC-CONTROL SPECIALIST, TOWER; 193.167-010 CHIEF CONTROLLER; 912.167-010 DISPATCHER

39005 TRAFFIC TECHNICIANS. OOH Title/s: Engineering Technicians

Conduct field studies to determine traffic volume and speed, effectiveness of signals, adequacy of lighting, and other factors influencing traffic conditions, under direction of traffic engineer. Observes factors affecting traffic conditions, such as lighting, visibility of signs and pavement markings, traffic signals, and width of street. Analyzes traffic volume and interviews motorists at intersections or areas where congestion exists or disproportionate number of accidents has occurred. Determines average speed of vehicles, using electrical timing devices or radar equipment. Conducts statistical studies of traffic conditions. Times stoplight or other delays, using stopwatch. Draws graphs, charts, diagrams, and similar aids to illustrate observations and conclusions. Computes mathematical factors for adjusting timing of traffic signals, speed restrictions, and related data, using standard formulas. Prepares drawings of proposed signal installations or other control devices, using drafting instruments. Recommends changes in traffic control devices and regulations on basis of findings.
Yearly Earnings: $28,808
Education: Associate degree
Knowledge: Computers and Electronics; Engineering and Technology; Design; Mathematics; Sociology and Anthropology; Geography; Public Safety and Security; Law, Government, and Jurisprudence; Telecommunications; Transportation
Abilities: Fluency of Ideas; Number Facility; Flexibility of Closure; Selective Attention; Reaction Time; Glare Sensitivity
Skills: Active Listening; Writing; Speaking; Mathematics; Critical Thinking; Active Learning; Monitoring; Persuasion; Problem Identification; Information Gathering; Information Organization; Synthesis/Reorganization; Idea Generation; Idea Evaluation; Implementation Planning; Solution Appraisal; Operations Analysis; Equipment Selection; Testing; Visioning; Systems Perception; Identifying Downstream Consequences; Identification of Key Causes
General Work Activities: Identifying Objects, Actions, and Events; Evaluating Information against Standards; Analyzing Data or Information; Operating Vehicles or Equipment; Drafting and Specifying Technical Devices, etc.
Job Characteristics: Very Hot; Extremely Bright or Inadequate Lighting; Importance of Being Aware of New Events
GOE Group/s: 05.03.06 Engineering Technology: Industrial and Safety
CIP Program/s: 150201 Civil Engineering/Civil Tech./Technician
Related DOT Job/s: 199.267-030 TRAFFIC TECHNICIAN

39008 RADIO OPERATORS. OOH Title/s: Broadcast Technicians

Receive and transmit communications using radiotelegraph or radiotelephone equipment, in accordance with government regulations. May repair equipment. Communicates by radio with test pilots, engineering personnel, and others during flight testing to relay information. Communicates with receiving operator to give and receive instruction for transmission. Turns controls or throws switches to activate power, adjust voice volume and modulation, and set transmitter on specified frequency. Repairs transmitting equipment, using electronic testing equipment, hand tools, and power tools, to maintain communication system in operative condition. Determines and obtains bearings of source from which signal originated, using direction-finding procedures and equipment. Monitors emergency frequency for distress calls and dispatches emergency equipment. Operates sound-recording equipment to record signals and preserve broadcast for analysis by intelligence personnel. Coordinates radio searches for overdue or lost airplanes. Examines and operates new equipment prior to installation in airport radio stations. Establishes and maintains standards of operation by periodic inspections of equipment and routine tests. Reviews company and Federal Aviation Authority regulations regarding radio communications, and reports violations. Maintains station log of messages transmitted and received for activities such as flight testing and fire locations.
Yearly Earnings: $31,148
Education: Associate degree
Knowledge: Computers and Electronics; Geography; Telecommunications; Communications and Media
Abilities: Oral Expression; Flexibility of Closure; Selective Attention; Time Sharing; Control Precision; Response Orientation; Reaction Time; Hearing Sensitivity; Auditory Attention; Sound Localization; Speech Recognition; Speech Clarity
Skills: Operation Monitoring
General Work Activities: Identifying Objects, Actions, and Events; Repairing and Maintaining Electrical Equipment
Job Characteristics: Job-Required Social Interaction; Deal with Unpleasant or Angry People; Sitting; Importance of Being Aware of New Events; Importance of Repeating Same Tasks
GOE Group/s: 05.03.05 Engineering Technology: Electrical-Electronic; 07.04.05 Oral Communications: Information Transmitting and Receiving
CIP Program/s: 470101 Electrical and Electronics Equipment Installer and Repairer; 470103 Communication Systems Installer and Repairer
Related DOT Job/s: 193.162-022 AIRLINE-RADIO OPERATOR, CHIEF; 193.262-010 AIRLINE-RADIO OPERATOR; 193.262-014 DISPATCHER; 193.262-022 RADIO OFFICER; 193.262-026 RADIO STATION OPERATOR; 193.262-030 RADIOTELEGRAPH OPERATOR; 193.262-034 RADIOTELEPHONE OPERATOR; 193.362-010 PHOTORADIO OPERATOR; 193.362-014 RADIO-INTELLIGENCE OPERATOR; 193.382-010 ELECTRONIC INTELLIGENCE OPERATIONS SPECIALIST

39011 FUNERAL DIRECTORS AND MORTICIANS. OOH Title/s: Funeral Directors

Perform various tasks to arrange and direct funeral services, such as coordinating transportation of body to mortuary for embalming, interviewing family or other authorized persons to arrange details, selecting pallbearers, procuring official for religious rites, and providing transportation for mourners. Arranges and directs funeral services. Interviews family or other authorized persons to arrange details, such as selection of casket and location and time of burial. Directs placement and removal of casket from hearse. Closes casket and leads funeral cortege to church or burial site. Directs preparations and shipment of body for out-of-state burial. Plans placement of casket in parlor or chapel and adjusts lights, fixtures, and floral displays.
Yearly Earnings: $36,088
Education: Long-term O-J-T

Knowledge: Administration and Management; Sales and Marketing; Customer and Personal Service; Psychology; Transportation
Skills: Social Perceptiveness; Coordination; Negotiation; Service Orientation; Management of Financial Resources; Management of Material Resources; Management of Personnel Resources
General Work Activities: None above average
Job Characteristics: Provide a Service to Others; Deal with External Customers; Deal with Unpleasant or Angry People
GOE Group/s: 11.11.04 Business Management: Services
CIP Program/s: 120301 Funeral Services and Mortuary Science
Related DOT Job/s: 187.167-030 DIRECTOR, FUNERAL

39014 EMBALMERS. OOH Title/s: Science Technicians; Funeral Directors

Prepare bodies for interment in conformity with legal requirements. Packs body orifices with cotton saturated with embalming fluid to prevent escape of gases or waste matter. Makes incision in arm or thigh and drains blood from circulatory system, and replaces blood with embalming fluid, using pump. Incises stomach and abdominal walls and probes internal organs, using trocar, to withdraw blood and waste matter from organs. Attaches trocar to pump-tube, starts pump, and repeats probing to force embalming fluid into organs. Closes incisions, using needle and suture. Reshapes or reconstructs disfigured or maimed bodies, using materials such as clay, cotton, plaster of paris, and wax. Applies cosmetics to impart lifelike appearance. Presses diaphragm to evacuate air from lungs. Joins lips, using needle and thread or wire. Washes and dries body, using germicidal soap and towels or hot air drier. Inserts convex celluloid or cotton between eyeball and eyelid to prevent slipping and sinking of eyelid. Maintains records, such as itemized list of clothing or valuables delivered with body and names of persons embalmed. Dresses and places body in casket. Arranges funeral details, such as type of casket or burial dress and place of interment.
Yearly Earnings: $36,088
Education: Long-term O-J-T
Knowledge: Customer and Personal Service; Chemistry; Biology; Sociology and Anthropology; Medicine and Dentistry; Philosophy and Theology; Law, Government, and Jurisprudence
Abilities: Arm-Hand Steadiness; Finger Dexterity; Static Strength; Visual Color Discrimination
Skills: None above average
General Work Activities: Assisting and Caring for Others
Job Characteristics: Provide a Service to Others; Contaminants; Diseases/Infections; Hazardous Conditions; Common Protective or Safety Attire
GOE Group/s: 02.04.02 Laboratory Technology: Life Sciences
CIP Program/s: 120301 Funeral Services and Mortuary Science
Related DOT Job/s: 338.371-010 EMBALMER APPRENTICE; 338.371-014 EMBALMER

39999A INTERPRETERS AND TRANSLATORS. OOH Title/s: Indirectly related to Public Relations Specialists

Translate and interpret written or spoken communications from one language to another or from spoken to manual sign language used by hearing-impaired. Translates approximate or exact message of speaker into specified language, orally or by using hand signs for hearing-impaired. Translates responses from second language to first. Reads written material, such as legal documents, scientific works, or news reports, and rewrites material into specified language, according to established rules of grammar. Listens to statements of speaker to ascertain meaning and to remember what is said, using electronic audio system. Receives information on subject to be discussed prior to interpreting session.
Yearly Earnings: $31,460
Education: Bachelor's degree
Knowledge: Sociology and Anthropology; English Language; Foreign Language; History and Archeology; Communications and Media
Abilities: Oral Comprehension; Written Comprehension; Oral Expression; Written Expression; Memorization; Selective Attention; Auditory Attention; Speech Recognition; Speech Clarity
Skills: Reading Comprehension; Active Listening; Writing; Speaking; Service Orientation
General Work Activities: Evaluating Information against Standards; Interpreting Meaning of Information to Others
Job Characteristics: Objective or Subjective Information; Job-Required Social Interaction; Importance of Being Exact or Accurate
GOE Group/s: 01.03.02 Performing Arts:Drama: Performing; 11.08.04 Communications: Translating and Interpreting
CIP Program/s: 160101 Foreign Languages and Literatures, General; 160103 Foreign Language Interpretation and Translation; 510201 Communication Disorders, General; 510205 Sign Language Interpreter
Related DOT Job/s: 137.267-010 INTERPRETER; 137.267-014 INTERPRETER, DEAF; 137.267-018 TRANSLATOR

39999B AGENTS AND BUSINESS MANAGERS OF ARTISTS, PERFORMERS, AND ATHLETES. OOH Title/s: Marketing, Advertising, and Public Relations Managers; Public Relations Specialists

Represent and promote artists, performers, and athletes to prospective employers. May handle contract negotiations and other business matters for clients. Negotiates with management, promoters, union officials, and other persons, to obtain contracts for clients such as entertainers, artists, and athletes. Manages business affairs for clients, such as obtaining travel and lodging accommodations, selling tickets, marketing and advertising, and paying expenses. Schedules promotional or performance engagements for clients. Advises clients on financial and legal matters, such as investments and taxes. Collects fees, commission, or other payment, according to contract terms. Obtains information and inspects facilities, equipment, and accommodations of potential performance venue. Hires trainer or coach to advise client on performance matters, such as training techniques or presentation of act. Prepares periodic accounting statements for clients concerning financial affairs. Conducts auditions or interviews new clients.
Yearly Earnings: $43,784
Education: Work experience, plus degree
Knowledge: Administration and Management; Economics and Accounting; Sales and Marketing; Personnel and Human Resources; Fine Arts; Law, Government, and Jurisprudence
Abilities: Speech Recognition; Speech Clarity
Skills: Speaking; Coordination; Persuasion; Negotiation; Service Orientation; Implementation Planning; Time Management; Management of Financial Resources; Management of Personnel Resources
General Work Activities: Developing Objectives and Strategies; Scheduling Work and Activities; Organizing, Planning, and Prioritizing; Communicating with Persons Outside Organization; Establishing and Maintaining Relationships; Selling or Influencing Others; Resolving Conflicts, Negotiating with Others; Provide Consultation and Advice to Others; Performing Administrative Activities; Staffing Organizational Units; Monitoring and Controlling Resources
Job Characteristics: Objective or Subjective Information; Job-Required Social Interaction; Supervise, Coach, Train Others; Persuade Someone to a Course of Action; Provide a Service to Others; Take a Position Opposed to Others; Deal with External Customers; Coordinate or Lead Others; Responsibility for Outcomes and Results; Frequency in Conflict Situations; Deal with Unpleasant or Angry People; Deal with Physical, Aggressive People; Frustrating Circumstances

GOE Group/s: 11.11.04 Business Management: Services; 11.12.03 Contracts and Claims: Booking
CIP Program/s: 080299 Business and Personal Services Marketing Operations, Other; 080901 Hospitality and Recreation Marketing Operations, General; 080903 Recreation Products/Services Marketing Operations; 090501 Public Relations and Organizational Communications; 500901 Music, General; 500909 Music Business Management and Merchandising
Related DOT Job/s: 153.117-014 MANAGER, ATHLETE; 191.117-010 ARTIST'S MANAGER; 191.117-014 BOOKING MANAGER; 191.117-018 BUSINESS MANAGER; 191.117-022 CIRCUS AGENT; 191.117-026 JOCKEY AGENT; 191.117-034 LITERARY AGENT; 191.117-038 MANAGER, TOURING PRODUCTION; 191.167-010 ADVANCE AGENT

39999C CITY PLANNING AIDES. OOH Title/s: Urban and Regional Planners

Compile data from various sources, such as maps, reports, and field and file investigations, for use by city planner in making planning studies. Summarizes information from maps, reports, investigations, and books. Prepares reports, using statistics, charts, and graphs, to illustrate planning studies in areas such as population, land use, or zoning. Prepares and updates files and records. Conducts interviews and surveys and observes conditions which affect land usage. Answers public inquiries.
Yearly Earnings: $31,460
Education: Bachelor's degree
Knowledge: Clerical; Mathematics; Geography
Skills: Writing; Mathematics
General Work Activities: None above average
Job Characteristics: Sitting
GOE Group/s: 11.03.02 Social Research: Sociological
CIP Program/s: 150201 Civil Engineering/Civil Tech./Technician
Related DOT Job/s: 199.364-010 CITY PLANNING AIDE

39999D STUDIO, STAGE, AND SPECIAL EFFECTS TECHNICIANS. OOH Title/s: Indirectly related to Actors, Directors, and Producers; Engineering Technicians

Install, operate, and maintain special equipment used in stage, television, or motion picture production. Modifies lighting and sound equipment and adjusts controls to achieve desired effects, according to specifications, using hand tools. Installs special effects properties, lighting fixtures, and sound equipment in specified locations in theater, using hand tools and power tools. Connects wiring for light and sound equipment to power source and control panel, using hand tools and power tools. Repairs and maintains equipment, using hand tools and precision instruments, according to preventive maintenance schedule and knowledge of electronics. Constructs and assembles special effects properties, using hand tools, power tools, and materials such as wood, metal, or plastic. Studies blueprint or layout of stage to determine type and placement of equipment needed for specified event. Reads script and confers with production personnel to determine specified effects. Selects and synchronizes music with visual display and other recorded commentary. Directs crew in setting up, arranging, and operating equipment for use in theater.
Yearly Earnings: $30,004
Education: Long-term O-J-T
Knowledge: Computers and Electronics; Design; Building and Construction; Physics; Fine Arts
Abilities: Fluency of Ideas; Originality; Finger Dexterity; Gross Body Equilibrium
Skills: Operations Analysis; Technology Design; Installation; Equipment Maintenance; Repairing
General Work Activities: Thinking Creatively; Repairing and Maintaining Mechanical Equipment; Repairing and Maintaining Electrical Equipment; Guiding, Directing and Motivating Subordinates
Job Characteristics: Supervise, Coach, Train Others; Coordinate or Lead Others; Responsibility for Outcomes and Results; High Places; Climbing Ladders, Scaffolds, Poles, etc.
GOE Group/s: 01.03.01 Performing Arts:Drama: Instructing and Directing; 01.06.02 Craft Arts: Arts and Crafts; 05.10.03 Crafts: Electrical-Electronic; 05.10.04 Crafts: Structural-Mechanical-Electrical-Electronic; 05.10.05 Crafts: Reproduction; 05.12.16 Elemental Work: Mechanical: Electrical Work
CIP Program/s: 100101 Educational/Instructional Media Technologists and Technicians; 100104 Radio and Television Broadcasting Technologists and Technicians; 460201 Carpenter; 460301 Electrical and Power Transmission Installer, General; 460302 Electrician; 500501 Drama/Theater Arts, General; 500502 Technical Theater/Theater Design and Stagecraft; 500602 Film-Video Making/Cinematography and Production
Related DOT Job/s: 159.042-010 LASERIST; 962.261-010 PLANETARIUM TECHNICIAN; 962.261-014 STAGE TECHNICIAN; 962.267-010 SIGHT-EFFECTS SPECIALIST; 962.281-014 SOUND-EFFECTS TECHNICIAN; 962.281-018 SPECIAL EFFECTS SPECIALIST; 962.362-010 COMMUNICATIONS TECHNICIAN; 962.362-014 LIGHT TECHNICIAN; 962.381-014 LIGHTING-EQUIPMENT OPERATOR

39999E TAXIDERMISTS. OOH Title/s: Indirectly related to Science Technicians; Visual Artists

Prepare, stuff, and mount skins of birds, fish, or mammals in lifelike form. Removes skin from animal, using knives, scissors, and pliers, and rubs preservative solutions into skin. Constructs wire foundation or plaster mold, and forms body, using papier-mache and tape, to display lifelike from. Covers foundation with skin, using adhesive or modeling clay. Affixes eyes, teeth, and claws to specimen, using adhesive. Dresses feathers and brushes fur to enhance lifelike appearance. Mounts specimen in case to present animal in its natural environment. Prepares animal carcasses for scientific or exhibition purposes.
Yearly Earnings: $26,728
Education: Associate degree
Knowledge: Biology
Abilities: Visualization; Arm-Hand Steadiness
Skills: None above average
General Work Activities: None above average
Job Characteristics: None above average
GOE Group/s: 01.06.02 Craft Arts: Arts and Crafts
CIP Program/s: 000000 NO CIP ASSIGNED
Related DOT Job/s: 199.261-010 TAXIDERMIST

39999G POLYGRAPH EXAMINERS. OOH Title/s: Indirectly related to Police, Detectives, and Special Agents; Private Detectives and Investigators

Interrogate and screen individuals to detect deception, using polygraph equipment. Interrogates individual and interprets, diagnoses, and evaluates individual's emotional responses and other reactions to questions posed. Attaches apparatus to individual's skin to measure and record changes in respiration, blood pressure, and perspiration. Prepares reports and keeps records of examinations. Conducts investigation, when assigned to criminal case, to gather information for use in interrogation. Testifies in court on matters relating to polygraph examinations. Teaches classes on interrogation techniques, methods, and uses.
Yearly Earnings: $33,904
Education: Work experience in a related occupation
Knowledge: Biology; Psychology; Education and Training; Law, Government, and Jurisprudence

Abilities: Oral Expression; Inductive Reasoning; Speed of Closure; Flexibility of Closure
Skills: Active Listening; Speaking; Critical Thinking; Social Perceptiveness; Instructing; Operation Monitoring
General Work Activities: Analyzing Data or Information; Documenting/Recording Information; Teaching Others; Coaching and Developing Others
Job Characteristics: Objective or Subjective Information; Job-Required Social Interaction; Supervise, Coach, Train Others; Take a Position Opposed to Others; Frequency in Conflict Situations; Deal with Unpleasant or Angry People; Deal with Physical, Aggressive People; Sitting; Consequence of Error; Frustrating Circumstances; Importance of Being Exact or Accurate; Importance of Being Aware of New Events
GOE Group/s: 02.04.02 Laboratory Technology: Life Sciences
CIP Program/s: 430106 Forensic Tech./Technician
Related DOT Job/s: 199.267-026 POLYGRAPH EXAMINER

39999H ALL OTHER PROFESSIONAL, PARAPROFESSIONAL, AND TECHNICAL WORKERS. OOH Title/s: Indirectly related to Professional Specialties
All other professional, paraprofessional, and technical workers not classified separately above.
Yearly Earnings: $31,460
Education: Degree varies
GOE Group/s: 02.04.01 Laboratory Technology: Physical Sciences; 05.10.06 Crafts: Blasting
CIP Program/s: 430106 Forensic Tech./Technician
Related DOT Job/s: 152.067-018 CUE SELECTOR; 199.267-022 EXAMINER, QUESTIONED DOCUMENTS; 199.267-038 GRAPHOLOGIST; 851.362-010 SEWER-LINE PHOTO-INSPECTOR; 969.664-010 FIREWORKS DISPLAY SPECIALIST

Section 4
Sales Workers

Sales Supervisors and Managers

41002 FIRST-LINE SUPERVISORS AND MANAGER/SUPERVISORS—SALES AND RELATED WORKERS. OOH Title/s: Retail Sales Worker Supervisors and Managers; Retail Sales Workers; Services Sales Representatives

Directly supervise and coordinate activities of marketing, sales, and related workers. May perform management functions, such as budgeting, accounting, marketing, and personnel work, in addition to their supervisory duties. Directs and supervises employees engaged in sales, inventory-taking, reconciling cash receipts, or performing specific service such as pumping gasoline for customers. Plans and prepares work schedules and assigns employees to specific duties. Hires, trains, and evaluates personnel in sales or marketing establishment. Coordinates sales promotion activities and prepares merchandise displays and advertising copy. Confers with company officials to develop methods and procedures to increase sales, expand markets, and promote business. Keeps records of employees' work schedules and time cards. Prepares sales and inventory reports for management and budget departments. Assists sales staff in completing complicated and difficult sales. Listens to and resolves customer complaints regarding service, product, or personnel. Keeps records pertaining to purchases, sales, and requisitions. Examines merchandise to ensure that it is correctly priced and displayed and functions as advertised. Formulates pricing policies on merchandise according to requirements for profitability of store operations. Analyzes customers' wants and needs by observing which items sell most rapidly. Inventories stock and reorders when inventories drop to specified level. Prepares rental or lease agreement, specifying charges and payment procedures, for use of machinery, tools, or other such items. Examines products purchased for resale or received for storage to determine condition of product or item.

Yearly Earnings: $25,948

Education: Work experience in a related occupation

Knowledge: Administration and Management; Economics and Accounting; Sales and Marketing; Customer and Personal Service; Personnel and Human Resources; Mathematics; Psychology; Education and Training; Communications and Media

Abilities: Fluency of Ideas; Originality; Number Facility; Time Sharing

Skills: Learning Strategies; Social Perceptiveness; Coordination; Negotiation; Instructing; Implementation Planning; Systems Perception; Systems Evaluation; Time Management; Management of Financial Resources; Management of Material Resources; Management of Personnel Resources

General Work Activities: Developing Objectives and Strategies; Scheduling Work and Activities; Communicating with Other Workers; Establishing and Maintaining Relationships; Selling or Influencing Others; Resolving Conflicts, Negotiating with Others; Performing for or Working with Public; Coordinating Work and Activities of Others; Developing and Building Teams; Teaching Others; Guiding, Directing and Motivating Subordinates; Coaching and Developing Others; Performing Administrative Activities; Staffing Organizational Units; Monitoring and Controlling Resources

Job Characteristics: Job-Required Social Interaction; Supervise, Coach, Train Others; Persuade Someone to a Course of Action; Deal with External Customers; Coordinate or Lead Others; Responsibility for Outcomes and Results; Frequency in Conflict Situations; Deal with Unpleasant or Angry People; Importance of Being Aware of New Events

GOE Group/s: 07.07.02 Clerical Handling: Sorting and Distrubtion; 08.02.01 General Sales: Wholesale; 08.02.08 General Sales: Soliciting-Selling; 09.04.01 Customer Services: Food Services; 09.04.02 Customer Services: Sales Services; 11.05.04 Business Administration: Sales and Purchasing Management; 11.09.02 Promotion: Fund and Membership Solicitation; 11.11.04 Business Management: Services; 11.11.05 Business Management: Wholesale-Retail

CIP Program/s: 010201 Agricultural Mechanization, General; 010204 Agricultural Power Machinery Operator; 010501 Agricultural Supplies Retailing and Wholesaling; 080101 Apparel and Accessories Marketing Operations, General; 080204 Business Services Marketing Operations; 080299 Business and Personal Services Marketing Operations, Other; 080601 Food Products Retailing and Wholesaling Operations; 080705 General Retailing Operations; 080706 General Selling Skills and Sales Operations; 080708 General Marketing Operations; 080709 General Distribution Operations; 080809 Home Products Marketing Operations; 080810 Office Products Marketing Operations; 080901 Hospitality and Recreation Marketing Operations, General; 080903 Recreation Products/Services Marketing Operations; 081001 Insurance Marketing Operations; 081203 Vehicle Parts and Accessories Marketing Operations; 081209 Petroleum Products Retailing Operations; 081301 Health Products and Services Marketing Operations; 120504 Food and Beverage/Restaurant Operations Manager; 190901 Clothing/Apparel and Textile Studies; 200301 Clothing, Apparel and Textile Workers and Managers, General; 520902 Hotel/Motel and Restaurant Management; 521101 International Business; 521403 International Business Marketing

Related DOT Job/s: 163.167-014 MANAGER, CIRCULATION; 169.167-038 ORDER DEPARTMENT SUPERVISOR; 180.167-010 ARTIFICIAL-BREEDING DISTRIBUTOR; 185.157-018 WHOLESALER II; 185.167-010 COMMISSARY MANAGER; 185.167-014 MANAGER, AUTOMOBILE SERVICE STATION; 185.167-022 MANAGER, FOOD CONCESSION; 185.167-026 MANAGER, MACHINERY-OR-EQUIPMENT, RENTAL AND LEASING; 185.167-030 MANAGER, MEAT SALES AND STORAGE; 185.167-038 MANAGER, PARTS; 185.167-046 MANAGER, RETAIL STORE; 185.167-050 MANAGER, TEXTILE CONVERSION; 185.167-054 MANAGER, TOBACCO WAREHOUSE; 185.167-066 VENDING-STAND SUPERVISOR; 185.167-070 WHOLESALER I; 186.167-034 MANAGER, INSURANCE OFFICE; 187.167-098 MANAGER, EMPLOYMENT AGENCY; 187.167-138 MANAGER, SALES; 230.137-010 SUPERVISOR, ADVERTISING-MATERIAL DISTRIBUTORS; 291.157-010 SUBSCRIPTION CREW LEADER; 293.137-010 SUPERVISOR, BLOOD-DONOR RECRUITERS; 299.137-010 MANAGER, DEPARTMENT; 299.137-014 SALES SUPERVISOR, MALT LIQUORS; 299.137-022 SUPERVISOR, ICE STORAGE, SALE, AND DELIVERY; 299.137-026 SUPERVISOR, MARINA SALES AND SERVICE

Sales Agents

43002 SALES AGENTS AND PLACERS, INSURANCE. OOH Title/s: Insurance Agents and Brokers

Sell or advise clients on life, endowments, fire, accident, and other types of insurance. May refer clients to independent brokers, work as independent brokers, or be employed by an insurance company. Advises clients of broker (independent agent) in selecting casualty, life, or property insurance. Calls on policy holders to deliver and explain policy, to suggest additions or changes in insurance program, or to change beneficiaries. Discusses advantages and disadvantages of various policies. Explains group insurance programs to promote sale of insurance plan. Selects company that offers type of coverage requested by client to underwrite policy. Explains

necessary bookkeeping requirements for customer to implement and provide group insurance program. Contacts underwriter and submits forms to obtain binder coverage. Establishes client's method of payment. Plans and oversees incorporation of insurance program into bookkeeping system of company. Installs bookkeeping systems and resolves system problems.
Yearly Earnings: $31,200
Education: Long-term O-J-T
Knowledge: Clerical; Economics and Accounting; Sales and Marketing
Abilities: Written Comprehension; Oral Expression; Speech Recognition
Skills: Active Listening; Speaking; Critical Thinking; Social Perceptiveness; Persuasion; Negotiation; Visioning; Identification of Key Causes; Judgment and Decision Making; Management of Financial Resources
General Work Activities: Operating Vehicles or Equipment; Interpreting Meaning of Information to Others; Establishing and Maintaining Relationships; Selling or Influencing Others; Performing for or Working with Public; Provide Consultation and Advice to Others
Job Characteristics: Job-Required Social Interaction; Persuade Someone to a Course of Action; Deal with External Customers; Sitting; Importance of Being Sure All is Done
GOE Group/s: 08.01.02 Sales Technology: Intangible Sales
CIP Program/s: 081001 Insurance Marketing Operations; 520801 Finance, General; 520805 Insurance and Risk Management
Related DOT Job/s: 169.167-050 SPECIAL AGENT, GROUP INSURANCE; 186.167-010 ESTATE PLANNER; 239.267-010 PLACER; 250.257-010 SALES AGENT, INSURANCE

43008 SALES AGENTS, REAL ESTATE. OOH Title/s: Real Estate Agents, Brokers, and Appraisers

Rent, buy, and sell property to clients. Perform duties such as studying property listings, interviewing prospective clients, accompanying clients to property site, discussing conditions of sale, and drawing up real estate contracts. Displays and explains features of property to client, and discusses conditions of sale or terms of lease. Answers client's questions regarding work under construction, financing, maintenance, repairs, and appraisals. Interviews prospective tenants and records information to ascertain needs and qualifications. Solicits and compiles listings of available rental property. Prepares real estate contracts, such as closing statements, deeds, leases, and mortgages, and negotiates loans on property. Reviews plans and recommends to client construction features. Enumerates options on new home sales. Oversees signing of real estate documents, disburses funds, and coordinates closing activities. Collects rental deposit. Locates and appraises undeveloped areas for building sites, based on evaluation of area market conditions. Appraises client's unimproved property to determine loan value. Plans and organizes sales promotion programs and materials, including newspaper advertisements and real estate promotional booklets. Investigates client's financial and credit status to determine eligibility for financing. Searches public records to ascertain that client has clear title to property. Reviews trade journals and relevant literature and attends staff and association meetings to remain knowledgeable about real estate market. Inspects condition of premises and arranges for or notifies owner of necessary maintenance. Secures construction financing with own firm or mortgage company. Contacts utility companies for service hook-up to client's property. Conducts seminars and training sessions for sales agents to improve sales techniques.
Yearly Earnings: $30,888
Education: Postsecondary vocational training
Knowledge: Economics and Accounting; Sales and Marketing; Mathematics; Sociology and Anthropology; Geography; Law, Government, and Jurisprudence; Communications and Media
Abilities: Number Facility; Spatial Orientation; Speech Recognition
Skills: Active Listening; Speaking; Mathematics; Social Perceptiveness; Persuasion; Negotiation; Service Orientation; Idea Generation; Identifying Downstream Consequences; Identification of Key Causes; Judgment and Decision Making; Management of Financial Resources
General Work Activities: Judging Qualities of Things, Services, People; Processing Information; Organizing, Planning, and Prioritizing; Documenting/Recording Information; Communicating with Persons Outside Organization; Establishing and Maintaining Relationships; Assisting and Caring for Others; Selling or Influencing Others; Performing for or Working with Public; Teaching Others; Coaching and Developing Others; Performing Administrative Activities
Job Characteristics: Objective or Subjective Information; Job-Required Social Interaction; Persuade Someone to a Course of Action; Deal with External Customers
GOE Group/s: 08.02.04 General Sales: Real Estate
CIP Program/s: 080706 General Selling Skills and Sales Operations; 521501 Real Estate
Related DOT Job/s: 250.157-010 SUPERINTENDENT, SALES; 250.357-010 BUILDING CONSULTANT; 250.357-014 LEASING AGENT, RESIDENCE; 250.357-018 SALES AGENT, REAL ESTATE

43011 APPRAISERS, REAL ESTATE. OOH Title/s: Real Estate Agents, Brokers, and Appraisers

Appraise real property to determine its value for purchase, sales, investment, mortgage, or loan purposes. Considers such factors as depreciation, value comparison of similar property, and income potential, when computing final estimation of property value. Inspects property for construction, condition, and functional design and takes property measurements. Considers location and trends or impending changes that could influence future value of property. Interviews persons familiar with property and immediate surroundings, such as contractors, home owners, and other realtors to obtain pertinent information. Prepares written report, utilizing data collected, and submits report to corroborate value established. Searches public records for transactions, such as sales, leases, and assessments. Photographs interiors and exteriors of property to assist in estimating property value, to substantiate finding, and to complete appraisal report.
Yearly Earnings: $30,888
Education: Work experience in a related occupation
Knowledge: Administration and Management; Clerical; Economics and Accounting; Personnel and Human Resources; Building and Construction; Geography; Public Safety and Security; Law, Government, and Jurisprudence; Communications and Media
Abilities: Deductive Reasoning; Number Facility
Skills: Writing; Mathematics; Information Gathering; Time Management; Management of Personnel Resources
General Work Activities: Monitoring Processes, Material, or Surroundings; Inspecting Equipment, Structures, or Material; Judging Qualities of Things, Services, People; Processing Information; Analyzing Data or Information; Updating and Using Job-Relevant Knowledge; Communicating with Other Workers; Coordinating Work and Activities of Others; Guiding, Directing and Motivating Subordinates; Coaching and Developing Others; Performing Administrative Activities
Job Characteristics: Supervise, Coach, Train Others; Importance of Being Exact or Accurate
GOE Group/s: 11.06.03 Finance: Risk and Profit Analysis
CIP Program/s: 521501 Real Estate
Related DOT Job/s: 191.267-010 APPRAISER, REAL ESTATE

43014A SALES AGENTS, SECURITIES AND COMMODITIES. OOH Title/s: Purchasers and Buyers; Securities and Financial Services Sales Representatives

Buy and sell securities in investment and trading firms and develop and implement financial plans for individuals, businesses, and organizations. Develops financial plan based on analysis of client's financial status, and discusses financial options with client. Contacts exchange or brokerage firm to execute order or buys and sells securities based on market quotation and competition in market. Records transactions accurately and keeps client informed about transactions. Analyzes market conditions to determine optimum time to execute securities transactions. Keeps informed about political and economic trends that influence stock prices. Reads corporate reports and calculates ratios to determine best prospects for profit on stock purchase and to monitor client account. Interviews client to determine client's assets, liabilities, cash flow, insurance coverage, tax status, and financial objectives. Reviews all securities transactions to ensure accuracy of information and that trades conform to regulations of governing agencies. Prepares documents to implement plan selected by client. Completes sales order tickets and submits for processing of client-requested transaction. Informs and advises concerned parties regarding fluctuations and securities transactions affecting plan or account. Prepares financial reports to monitor client or corporate finances. Identifies potential clients, using advertising campaigns, mailing lists, and personal contacts, and solicits business.

Yearly Earnings: $37,388

Education: Long-term O-J-T

Knowledge: Economics and Accounting; Sales and Marketing; Customer and Personal Service; Personnel and Human Resources; Computers and Electronics; Mathematics

Abilities: Written Comprehension; Written Expression; Fluency of Ideas; Deductive Reasoning; Mathematical Reasoning; Number Facility; Speed of Closure; Near Vision; Speech Recognition; Speech Clarity

Skills: Reading Comprehension; Active Listening; Writing; Speaking; Mathematics; Critical Thinking; Active Learning; Learning Strategies; Monitoring; Social Perceptiveness; Coordination; Persuasion; Negotiation; Instructing; Service Orientation; Problem Identification; Information Gathering; Information Organization; Synthesis/Reorganization; Idea Generation; Idea Evaluation; Implementation Planning; Solution Appraisal; Operations Analysis; Programming; Visioning; Systems Perception; Identifying Downstream Consequences; Identification of Key Causes; Judgment and Decision Making; Systems Evaluation; Management of Financial Resources

General Work Activities: Getting Information Needed to Do the Job; Monitoring Processes, Material, or Surroundings; Judging Qualities of Things, Services, People; Evaluating Information against Standards; Analyzing Data or Information; Making Decisions and Solving Problems; Updating and Using Job-Relevant Knowledge; Developing Objectives and Strategies; Organizing, Planning, and Prioritizing; Documenting/Recording Information; Interpreting Meaning of Information to Others; Communicating with Persons Outside Organization; Selling or Influencing Others; Provide Consultation and Advice to Others; Performing Administrative Activities; Monitoring and Controlling Resources

Job Characteristics: Objective or Subjective Information; Job-Required Social Interaction; Persuade Someone to a Course of Action; Provide a Service to Others; Take a Position Opposed to Others; Deal with External Customers; Frequency in Conflict Situations; Deal with Unpleasant or Angry People; Sitting; Frustrating Circumstances; Importance of Being Aware of New Events

GOE Group/s: 08.01.02 Sales Technology: Intangible Sales; 11.06.03 Finance: Risk and Profit Analysis; 11.06.04 Finance: Brokering

CIP Program/s: 080401 Financial Services Marketing Operations; 520801 Finance, General; 520804 Financial Planning; 520807 Investments and Securities; 521601 Taxation

Related DOT Job/s: 162.157-010 BROKER-AND-MARKET OPERATOR, GRAIN; 162.167-034 FLOOR BROKER; 162.167-038 SECURITIES TRADER; 250.257-014 FINANCIAL PLANNER; 250.257-018 REGISTERED REPRESENTATIVE

43014B SALES AGENTS, FINANCIAL SERVICES. OOH Title/s: Securities and Financial Services Sales Representatives

Sell financial services, such as loan, tax, and securities counseling, to customers of financial institutions and business establishments. Sells services and equipment, such as trust, investment, and check processing services. Develops prospects from current commercial customers, referral leads, and sales and trade meetings. Contacts prospective customers to present information and explain available services. Determines customers' financial services needs and prepares proposals to sell services. Reviews business trends and advises customers regarding expected fluctuations. Makes presentations on financial services to groups to attract new clients. Prepares forms or agreement to complete sale. Evaluates costs and revenue of agreements to determine continued profitability.

Yearly Earnings: $37,388

Education: Long-term O-J-T

Knowledge: Economics and Accounting; Sales and Marketing; Customer and Personal Service; Computers and Electronics; Law, Government, and Jurisprudence

Abilities: Written Comprehension; Deductive Reasoning; Mathematical Reasoning; Number Facility; Near Vision; Speech Recognition; Speech Clarity

Skills: Active Listening; Speaking; Mathematics; Critical Thinking; Active Learning; Learning Strategies; Monitoring; Social Perceptiveness; Persuasion; Negotiation; Service Orientation; Problem Identification; Information Gathering; Information Organization; Idea Generation; Idea Evaluation; Implementation Planning; Solution Appraisal; Operations Analysis; Visioning; Systems Perception; Identifying Downstream Consequences; Identification of Key Causes; Judgment and Decision Making; Systems Evaluation; Management of Financial Resources

General Work Activities: Interpreting Meaning of Information to Others; Communicating with Persons Outside Organization; Establishing and Maintaining Relationships; Selling or Influencing Others; Performing for or Working with Public; Provide Consultation and Advice to Others

Job Characteristics: Objective or Subjective Information; Job-Required Social Interaction; Persuade Someone to a Course of Action; Provide a Service to Others; Deal with External Customers; Deal with Unpleasant or Angry People; Sitting; Importance of Being Aware of New Events

GOE Group/s: 08.01.02 Sales Technology: Intangible Sales

CIP Program/s: 080204 Business Services Marketing Operations; 080401 Financial Services Marketing Operations; 520801 Finance, General; 520804 Financial Planning

Related DOT Job/s: 250.257-022 SALES REPRESENTATIVE, FINANCIAL SERVICES; 250.357-026 SALES AGENT, FINANCIAL-REPORT SERVICE

43017 SALES AGENTS, SELECTED BUSINESS SERVICES. OOH Title/s: Services Sales Representatives

Sell selected services, such as building maintenance, credit reporting, bookkeeping, security, printing, and storage space, to businesses. Exclude advertising, insurance, financial, and

real estate sales agents. Personally visits, telephones, or writes prospective and current customers to explain benefits of service or expanded service. Consults with customers concerning needs; inspects buildings and equipment; and reviews building plans to determine services to be offered. Writes orders or service contracts for new and current customers, and schedules initiation or discontinuance of services. Analyzes information obtained from prospective client and writes prospectus or recommendations for service. Computes and quotes prices, fares, and rates and explains details such as routes, regulations, and schedules to customer. Explains methods for using service or equipment to customer, or assists customer in developing operating procedures for use with service. Develops prospective customer list from business and telephone directories, telephone inquiries received, and business associates, and by observing business establishments. Reviews past orders and current accounts to generate ideas on expanding services to customers. Consults with technical staff to obtain information on special problems or current price quotes. Confers with customers to verify service satisfaction or investigate and resolve customer complaints and other problems. Writes and distributes sales pamphlets, promotional letters or materials, and other advertising aids. Collects payments on account and records or directs staff to record customer payments received. Speaks to individuals or groups on behalf of customer to stimulate interest in or use of customer services or products. Reviews customer accounts and prepares written reports of services rendered, including problems encountered. Reviews customer inventory records to determine charges for replacement of damaged rental articles, and recommends discontinuance of service when necessary. Serves as advertiser or coordinator during hotel function, such as convention or meeting.

Yearly Earnings: $26,312

Education: Moderate-term O-J-T

Knowledge: Administration and Management; Clerical; Economics and Accounting; Sales and Marketing; Customer and Personal Service; English Language; Communications and Media

Abilities: Written Comprehension; Oral Expression; Written Expression; Fluency of Ideas; Originality; Memorization

Skills: Active Listening; Writing; Speaking; Persuasion; Negotiation; Service Orientation

General Work Activities: Judging Qualities of Things, Services, People; Developing Objectives and Strategies; Organizing, Planning, and Prioritizing; Communicating with Persons Outside Organization; Establishing and Maintaining Relationships; Assisting and Caring for Others; Selling or Influencing Others; Resolving Conflicts, Negotiating with Others; Performing for or Working with Public; Provide Consultation and Advice to Others

Job Characteristics: Job-Required Social Interaction; Persuade Someone to a Course of Action; Provide a Service to Others; Deal with External Customers; Deal with Physical, Aggressive People; Sitting; Frustrating Circumstances

GOE Group/s: 05.02.06 Managerial Work: Mechanical: Services; 08.01.01 Sales Technology: Technical Sales; 08.01.02 Sales Technology: Intangible Sales; 08.02.06 General Sales: Services; 08.02.08 General Sales: Soliciting-Selling

CIP Program/s: 010501 Agricultural Supplies Retailing and Wholesaling; 020401 Plant Sciences, General; 020408 Plant Protection (Pest Management); 080204 Business Services Marketing Operations; 080706 General Selling Skills and Sales Operations; 080901 Hospitality and Recreation Marketing Operations, General; 080902 Hotel/Motel Services Marketing Operations; 520702 Franchise Operation; 520902 Hotel/Motel and Restaurant Management

Related DOT Job/s: 165.157-010 SONG PLUGGER; 236.252-010 REPRESENTATIVE, PERSONAL SERVICE; 250.357-022 SALES REPRESENTATIVE; 251.157-014 SALES REPRESENTATIVE, DATA PROCESSING SERVICES; 251.257-014 SALES AGENT, PSYCHOLOGICAL TESTS AND INDUSTRIAL RELATIONS; 251.357-010 SALES AGENT, BUSINESS SERVICES; 251.357-018 SALES AGENT, PEST CONTROL SERVICE; 251.357-022 SALES REPRESENTATIVE, FRANCHISE; 251.357-026 SALES REPRESENTATIVE, HERBICIDE SERVICE; 252.257-010 TRAFFIC AGENT; 252.357-010 CRATING-AND-MOVING ESTIMATOR; 252.357-014 SALES REPRESENTATIVE, SHIPPING SERVICES; 253.157-010 COMMUNICATIONS CONSULTANT; 253.257-010 SALES REPRESENTATIVE, TELEPHONE SERVICES; 253.357-010 SALES REPRESENTATIVE, PUBLIC UTILITIES; 254.357-018 SALES REPRESENTATIVE, PRINTING; 259.157-014 SALES REPRESENTATIVE, HOTEL SERVICES; 259.257-018 SERVICE REPRESENTATIVE, ELEVATORS, ESCALATORS, AND DUMBWAITERS; 259.257-022 SALES REPRESENTATIVE, SECURITY SYSTEMS; 259.357-030 SALES REPRESENTATIVE, WEATHER-FORECASTING SERVICE; 259.357-038 TOBACCO-WAREHOUSE AGENT; 299.357-010 LINEN CONTROLLER

43021 TRAVEL AGENTS. OOH Title/s: Travel Agents

Plan trips for travel agency customers. Duties include determining destination, modes of transportation, travel dates, costs, and accommodations required; and planning, describing, or selling itinerary package tours. May specialize in foreign or domestic service, individual or group travel, specific geographical area, airplane charters, or package tours. Plans, describes, arranges, and sells itinerary tour packages and promotional travel incentives offered by various travel carriers. Converses with customer to determine destination, mode of transportation, travel dates, financial considerations, and accommodations required. Computes cost of travel and accommodations, using calculator, computer, carrier tariff books, and hotel rate books, or quotes package tour's costs. Books transportation and hotel reservations, using computer terminal or telephone. Provides customer with brochures and publications containing travel information, such as local customs, points of interest, or foreign country regulations. Prints or requests transportation carrier tickets, using computer printer system or system link to travel carrier. Collects payment for transportation and accommodations from customer.

Yearly Earnings: $16,848

Education: Postsecondary vocational training

Knowledge: Clerical; Sales and Marketing; Customer and Personal Service; Sociology and Anthropology; Geography; Foreign Language; Transportation

Abilities: None above average

Skills: Persuasion; Service Orientation

General Work Activities: Establishing and Maintaining Relationships; Assisting and Caring for Others; Selling or Influencing Others; Performing for or Working with Public

Job Characteristics: Job-Required Social Interaction; Persuade Someone to a Course of Action; Provide a Service to Others; Deal with External Customers; Sitting; Importance of Being Exact or Accurate; Importance of Being Sure All is Done

GOE Group/s: 08.02.06 General Sales: Services

CIP Program/s: 081105 Travel Services Marketing Operations

Related DOT Job/s: 252.152-010 TRAVEL AGENT

43023A SITE LEASING AND PROMOTION AGENTS. OOH Title/s: Services Sales Representatives

Promote products by obtaining leases for outdoor advertising sites or permission to display product promotional items in establishments. Persuades property owners to lease sites for erection of billboard signs used in outdoor advertising. Visits retail establishments and clubs to persuade customers to use display items to promote sale of company products. Arranges price and draws up lease. Arranges display of items in customer's establishment. Locates potential billboard sites, using automobile to travel through assigned district. Searches legal records for land ownership. Delivers promotion items,

such as posters, glasses, napkins, and samples of product. Takes sales order from customer.
Yearly Earnings: $26,312
Education: Moderate-term O-J-T
Knowledge: Sales and Marketing; Psychology; Geography; Law, Government, and Jurisprudence; Communications and Media
Abilities: None above average
Skills: Persuasion; Negotiation; Management of Financial Resources
General Work Activities: Interacting with Computers; Communicating with Persons Outside Organization; Establishing and Maintaining Relationships; Selling or Influencing Others; Resolving Conflicts, Negotiating with Others; Performing for or Working with Public
Job Characteristics: Persuade Someone to a Course of Action; Deal with External Customers; Sitting
GOE Group/s: 08.02.01 General Sales: Wholesale; 11.12.02 Contracts and Claims: Rental and Leasing
CIP Program/s: 080706 General Selling Skills and Sales Operations; 090201 Advertising
Related DOT Job/s: 254.357-010 LEASING AGENT, OUTDOOR ADVERTISING; 269.357-018 SALES-PROMOTION REPRESENTATIVE

43023B SALES AGENTS, ADVERTISING. OOH Title/s: Services Sales Representatives

Sell or solicit advertising, such as graphic art, advertising space in publications, custom-made signs, and air time on TV and radio. Advises customer on advantages of various types of programming and methods of composing layouts and designs for signs and displays. Exhibits prepared layouts with mats and copy with headings. Visits advertisers to point out advantages of publication. Draws up contract covering arrangements for designing, fabricating, erecting, and maintaining sign or display. Sells signs to be made according to customers' specifications, utilizing knowledge of lettering, color harmony, and sign-making processes. Calls on prospects and presents outlines of various programs or commercial announcements. Informs customer of types of artwork available by providing samples. Prepares list of prospects for classified and display space for publication from leads in other papers and from old accounts. Obtains pertinent information concerning prospect's past and current advertising for use in sales presentation. Calls on advertisers and sales promotion people to obtain information concerning prospects for current advertising and sales promotion. Prepares promotional plans, sales literature, and sales contracts, using computer. Plans and sketches layouts to meet customer needs. Computes job costs. Writes copy as part of layout. Collects payments due. Delivers advertising or illustration proofs to customer for approval. Arranges for and accompanies prospect to commercial taping sessions.
Yearly Earnings: $26,312
Education: Moderate-term O-J-T
Knowledge: Sales and Marketing; Psychology; English Language; Fine Arts; Communications and Media
Abilities: Oral Expression; Originality; Speech Recognition
Skills: Active Listening; Writing; Speaking; Social Perceptiveness; Persuasion; Negotiation; Synthesis/Reorganization; Idea Generation; Implementation Planning; Solution Appraisal; Identification of Key Causes; Management of Financial Resources
General Work Activities: Thinking Creatively; Developing Objectives and Strategies; Scheduling Work and Activities; Organizing, Planning, and Prioritizing; Operating Vehicles or Equipment; Drafting and Specifying Technical Devices, etc.; Communicating with Persons Outside Organization; Establishing and Maintaining Relationships; Selling or Influencing Others; Resolving Conflicts, Negotiating with Others; Performing for or Working with Public; Provide Consultation and Advice to Others
Job Characteristics: Job-Required Social Interaction; Persuade Someone to a Course of Action; Deal with External Customers; Sitting
GOE Group/s: 08.01.01 Sales Technology: Technical Sales; 08.01.02 Sales Technology: Intangible Sales
CIP Program/s: 080204 Business Services Marketing Operations; 080706 General Selling Skills and Sales Operations; 090201 Advertising
Related DOT Job/s: 254.251-010 SALES REPRESENTATIVE, GRAPHIC ART; 254.257-010 SALES REPRESENTATIVE, SIGNS AND DISPLAYS; 254.357-014 SALES REPRESENTATIVE, ADVERTISING; 254.357-022 SALES REPRESENTATIVE, SIGNS; 259.357-018 SALES REPRESENTATIVE, RADIO AND TELEVISION TIME

43099A SALES REPRESENTATIVES, SERVICE.

OOH Title/s: Services Sales Representatives

Contact prospective customers to sell services, such as educational courses, dance instructions, cable television, furniture repair, auto leasing, and burial needs. Interviews customer to ascertain and evaluate needs and wishes of customer. Explains advantages and features of service being rented or sold to stimulate customer's interest. Answers customer's questions pertaining to service being offered. Advises customer on variables and options to assist customer in making decision. Computes estimate or final cost of sale and presents information to customer. Compiles list of prospective customers for use as sales leads, using newspapers, directories and other sources. Confers with other company personnel to convey customer's needs and to plan program to meet customer's needs. Compiles and records sales and lease information and records of expenses incurred. Prepares and sends leasing contract to leasing agency. Evaluates advertising campaigns and administrative procedures to increase sales and efficiency. Receives payments. Purchases items and prices items for profitable resale.
Yearly Earnings: $26,312
Education: Moderate-term O-J-T
Knowledge: Administration and Management; Economics and Accounting; Sales and Marketing; Customer and Personal Service
Abilities: Oral Expression; Mathematical Reasoning; Speech Recognition
Skills: Active Listening; Speaking; Social Perceptiveness; Persuasion; Negotiation; Service Orientation; Solution Appraisal; Identification of Key Causes
General Work Activities: Organizing, Planning, and Prioritizing; Interpreting Meaning of Information to Others; Communicating with Persons Outside Organization; Establishing and Maintaining Relationships; Selling or Influencing Others; Performing for or Working with Public
Job Characteristics: Job-Required Social Interaction; Persuade Someone to a Course of Action; Deal with External Customers; Deal with Unpleasant or Angry People; Frustrating Circumstances
GOE Group/s: 08.01.02 Sales Technology: Intangible Sales; 08.02.02 General Sales: Retail; 08.02.05 General Sales: Demonstration and Sales; 08.02.06 General Sales: Services; 08.02.08 General Sales: Soliciting-Selling; 11.06.04 Finance: Brokering
CIP Program/s: 080204 Business Services Marketing Operations; 080205 Personal Services Marketing Operations; 080299 Business and Personal Services Marketing Operations, Other; 080705 General Retailing Operations; 080706 General Selling Skills and Sales Operations; 080901 Hospitality and Recreation Marketing Operations, General; 080903 Recreation Products/Services Marketing Operations; 081104 Tourism Promotion Operations; 081208 Vehicle Marketing Operations; 120301 Funeral Services and Mortuary Science; 200501 Home Furnishings and Equipment Installers and Consultants, General
Related DOT Job/s: 259.157-010 SALES REPRESENTATIVE, AUDIOVISUAL PROGRAM PRODUCTIONS; 259.257-010 SALES REP-

RESENTATIVE, EDUCATION COURSES; 259.357-010 GROUP-SALES REPRESENTATIVE; 259.357-014 SALES REPRESENTATIVE, DANCING INSTRUCTIONS; 259.357-022 SALES REPRESENTATIVE, TELEVISION CABLE SERVICE; 259.357-026 SALES REPRESENTATIVE, UPHOLSTERY AND FURNITURE REPAIR; 259.357-034 TICKET BROKER; 273.357-014 SALES REPRESENTATIVE, AUTOMOTIVE-LEASING; 279.357-042 SALESPERSON, BURIAL NEEDS

43099B FUND RAISERS AND SOLICITORS. OOH Title/s: Services Sales Representatives

Solicit contributions to support nonprofit organization, such as charity or university. May encourage individuals to join or participate in activities of organization. Writes, visits, or telephones potential blood donors, contributors, and members to explain blood program or to solicit contributions or membership in organization. Collects pledges, funds, or gifts-in-kind from contributors, or membership dues or payments for publications. Compiles and analyzes information about potential contributors to develop mailing or contact lists and to prepare promotional campaign. Prepares brochures for mail-solicitation programs. Schedules appointments for blood donations or for pick-up of gifts-in-kind. Sells emblems or other tokens of organization represented. Plans social functions to generate interest and enthusiasm for activity being promoted. Records and maintains records of activities, such as members enrolled, funds pledged or collected, expenses incurred, and donors enlisted. Writes letter to express appreciation for donation. Trains volunteers to perform certain duties to assist fund raising. Consults blood bank records to answer questions, monitor activity, or resolve problems of blood donor group.

Yearly Earnings: $26,312

Education: Moderate-term O-J-T

Knowledge: Administration and Management; Clerical; Economics and Accounting; Sales and Marketing; Psychology; Sociology and Anthropology; Education and Training; Communications and Media

Abilities: None above average

Skills: Speaking; Social Perceptiveness; Persuasion; Instructing; Idea Generation; Idea Evaluation; Implementation Planning; Visioning; Management of Financial Resources; Management of Personnel Resources

General Work Activities: Developing Objectives and Strategies; Scheduling Work and Activities; Implementing Ideas, Programs, etc.; Communicating with Persons Outside Organization; Establishing and Maintaining Relationships; Selling or Influencing Others; Performing for or Working with Public; Developing and Building Teams

Job Characteristics: Objective or Subjective Information; Job-Required Social Interaction; Supervise, Coach, Train Others; Persuade Someone to a Course of Action; Deal with External Customers; Coordinate or Lead Others

GOE Group/s: 08.02.08 General Sales: Soliciting-Selling; 11.09.02 Promotion: Fund and Membership Solicitation

CIP Program/s: 080299 Business and Personal Services Marketing Operations, Other; 080706 General Selling Skills and Sales Operations; 080901 Hospitality and Recreation Marketing Operations, General; 080903 Recreation Products/Services Marketing Operations; 500701 Art, General; 500704 Arts Management

Related DOT Job/s: 293.157-010 FUND RAISER I; 293.357-010 BLOOD-DONOR RECRUITER; 293.357-014 FUND RAISER II; 293.357-022 MEMBERSHIP SOLICITOR

Technical, Wholesale, and Retail Sales Workers

49002 SALES ENGINEERS. OOH Title/s: Manufacturers' and Wholesale Sales Representatives; Retail Sales Workers

Sell business goods or services that require a technical background equivalent to a baccalaureate degree in engineering. Exclude engineers whose primary function is not marketing or sales. Calls on management representatives at commercial, industrial, and other establishments to convince prospective clients to buy products or services offered. Assists sales force in sale of company products. Demonstrates and explains product or service to customer representatives, such as engineers, architects, and other professionals. Draws up sales or service contract for products or services. Provides technical services to clients relating to use, operation, and maintenance of equipment. Arranges for trial installations of equipment. Designs draft variations of standard products in order to meet customer needs. Reviews customer documents to develop and prepare cost estimates or projected production increases from use of proposed equipment or services. Draws up or proposes changes in equipment, processes, materials, or services resulting in cost reduction or improvement in customer operations. Assists in development of custom-made machinery. Diagnoses problems with equipment installed. Provides technical training to employees of client.

Yearly Earnings: $26,312

Education: Moderate-term O-J-T

Knowledge: Economics and Accounting; Sales and Marketing; Customer and Personal Service; Production and Processing; Computers and Electronics; Engineering and Technology; Design; Mechanical; Mathematics; Physics; Psychology; Education and Training; English Language; History and Archeology; Telecommunications

Abilities: Oral Comprehension; Written Comprehension; Oral Expression; Written Expression; Fluency of Ideas; Originality; Problem Sensitivity; Deductive Reasoning; Inductive Reasoning; Information Ordering; Category Flexibility; Mathematical Reasoning; Number Facility; Memorization; Speed of Closure; Visualization; Selective Attention; Time Sharing; Response Orientation; Rate Control; Reaction Time; Extent Flexibility; Gross Body Equilibrium; Near Vision; Far Vision; Visual Color Discrimination; Night Vision; Peripheral Vision; Hearing Sensitivity; Auditory Attention; Sound Localization; Speech Recognition; Speech Clarity

Skills: Reading Comprehension; Active Listening; Speaking; Mathematics; Science; Critical Thinking; Active Learning; Learning Strategies; Monitoring; Social Perceptiveness; Persuasion; Negotiation; Instructing; Service Orientation; Problem Identification; Synthesis/Reorganization; Idea Generation; Implementation Planning; Solution Appraisal; Operations Analysis; Technology Design; Equipment Selection; Installation; Testing; Operation Monitoring; Troubleshooting; Systems Perception; Identifying Downstream Consequences; Identification of Key Causes; Systems Evaluation; Management of Material Resources

General Work Activities: Inspecting Equipment, Structures, or Material; Estimating Needed Characteristics; Judging Qualities of Things, Services, People; Processing Information; Evaluating Information against Standards; Analyzing Data or Information; Making Decisions and Solving Problems; Thinking Creatively; Updating and Using Job-Relevant Knowledge; Developing Objectives and Strategies; Organizing, Planning, and Prioritizing; Operating Vehicles or Equipment; Drafting and Specifying Technical Devices, etc.; Implementing Ideas, Programs, etc.; Documenting/Recording Information; Interpreting Meaning of Information to Others; Communicating with Other Work-

ers; Communicating with Persons Outside Organization; Establishing and Maintaining Relationships; Selling or Influencing Others; Resolving Conflicts, Negotiating with Others; Teaching Others; Coaching and Developing Others; Provide Consultation and Advice to Others; Performing Administrative Activities
Job Characteristics: Objective or Subjective Information; Job-Required Social Interaction; Supervise, Coach, Train Others; Persuade Someone to a Course of Action; Provide a Service to Others; Deal with External Customers; Coordinate or Lead Others; Deal with Unpleasant or Angry People; Frustrating Circumstances; Degree of Automation
GOE Group/s: 05.01.05 Engineering: Sales Engineering
CIP Program/s: 140201 Aerospace, Aeronautical and Astronautical Engineering; 140301 Agricultural Engineering; 140601 Ceramic Sciences and Engineering; 140701 Chemical Engineering; 141001 Electrical, Electronics and Communication Engineering; 141901 Mechanical Engineering; 142101 Mining and Mineral Engineering; 142201 Naval Architecture and Marine Engineering; 142301 Nuclear Engineering; 142701 Systems Engineering
Related DOT Job/s: 002.151-010 SALES ENGINEER, AERONAUTICAL PRODUCTS; 003.151-010 SALES-ENGINEER, ELECTRICAL PRODUCTS; 003.151-014 SALES-ENGINEER, ELECTRONICS PRODUCTS AND SYSTEMS; 006.151-010 SALES ENGINEER, CERAMIC PRODUCTS; 007.151-010 SALES ENGINEER, MECHANICAL EQUIPMENT; 008.151-010 CHEMICAL-EQUIPMENT SALES ENGINEER; 010.151-010 SALES ENGINEER, MINING-AND-OIL-WELL EQUIPMENT AND SERVICES; 013.151-010 SALES ENGINEER, AGRICULTURAL EQUIPMENT; 014.151-010 SALES ENGINEER, MARINE EQUIPMENT; 015.151-010 SALES ENGINEER, NUCLEAR EQUIPMENT

49005A SALES REPRESENTATIVES, AGRICULTURAL. OOH Title/s: Manufacturers' and Wholesale Sales Representatives

Sell agricultural products and services, such as animal feeds, farm and garden equipment, and dairy, poultry, and veterinarian supplies. Solicits orders from customers in person or by phone. Displays or shows customer agricultural-related products. Quotes prices and credit terms. Compiles lists of prospective customers for use as sales leads. Prepares sales contracts for orders obtained. Consults with customer regarding installation, set-up, or layout of agricultural equipment and machines. Informs customer of estimated delivery schedule, service contracts, warranty, or other information pertaining to purchased products. Demonstrates use of agricultural equipment or machines. Prepares reports of business transactions. Recommends changes in customer use of agricultural products to improve production.
Yearly Earnings: $26,312
Education: Moderate-term O-J-T
Knowledge: Economics and Accounting; Sales and Marketing; Customer and Personal Service; Food Production
Abilities: Speech Recognition
Skills: Persuasion; Negotiation
General Work Activities: Controlling Machines and Processes; Communicating with Persons Outside Organization; Selling or Influencing Others; Performing for or Working with Public
Job Characteristics: Job-Required Social Interaction; Persuade Someone to a Course of Action; Deal with External Customers
GOE Group/s: 08.02.01 General Sales: Wholesale; 08.02.02 General Sales: Retail; 08.02.03 General Sales: Wholesale and Retail
CIP Program/s: 010501 Agricultural Supplies Retailing and Wholesaling; 020201 Animal Sciences, General; 020204 Agricultural Animal Nutrition; 020209 Poultry Science; 080706 General Selling Skills and Sales Operations; 510808 Veterinarian Assistant/Animal Health Technician
Related DOT Job/s: 272.357-010 SALES REPRESENTATIVE, ANIMAL-FEED PRODUCTS; 272.357-014 SALES REPRESENTATIVE, FARM AND GARDEN EQUIPMENT AND SUPPLIES; 272.357-018 SALES REPRESENTATIVE, POULTRY EQUIPMENT AND SUPPLIES; 274.357-030 SALES REPRESENTATIVE, DAIRY SUPPLIES; 276.357-018 SALES REPRESENTATIVE, VETERINARIAN SUPPLIES; 299.251-010 SALES-SERVICE REPRESENTATIVE, MILKING MACHINES

49005B SALES REPRESENTATIVES, CHEMICAL AND PHARMACEUTICAL. OOH Title/s: Manufacturers' and Wholesale Sales Representatives

Sell chemical or pharmaceutical products or services, such as acids, industrial chemicals, agricultural chemicals, medicines, drugs, and water treatment supplies. Promotes and sells pharmaceutical and chemical products to potential customers. Explains water treatment package benefits to customer, and sells chemicals to treat and resolve water process problems. Distributes drug samples to customer and takes orders for pharmaceutical supply items from customer. Discusses characteristics and clinical studies pertaining to pharmaceutical products with physicians, dentists, hospitals, and retail/wholesale establishments. Estimates and advises customer of service costs to correct water-treatment process problems. Inspects, tests, and observes chemical changes in water system equipment, utilizing test kit, reference manual, and knowledge of chemical treatment.
Yearly Earnings: $26,312
Education: Moderate-term O-J-T
Knowledge: Sales and Marketing; Chemistry
Abilities: Oral Expression
Skills: Social Perceptiveness; Persuasion
General Work Activities: Inspecting Equipment, Structures, or Material; Communicating with Persons Outside Organization; Establishing and Maintaining Relationships; Selling or Influencing Others; Performing for or Working with Public
Job Characteristics: Job-Required Social Interaction; Persuade Someone to a Course of Action; Deal with External Customers
GOE Group/s: 08.01.01 Sales Technology: Technical Sales; 08.02.01 General Sales: Wholesale
CIP Program/s: 010501 Agricultural Supplies Retailing and Wholesaling; 080706 General Selling Skills and Sales Operations; 150506 Water Quality and Wastewater Treatment Technologists and Technicians; 410301 Chemical Technologists and Technicians; 510805 Pharmacy Technician/Assistant
Related DOT Job/s: 262.157-010 PHARMACEUTICAL DETAILER; 262.357-010 SALES REPRESENTATIVE, CHEMICALS AND DRUGS; 262.357-022 SALES REPRESENTATIVE, WATER-TREATMENT CHEMICALS

49005C SALES REPRESENTATIVES, ELECTRICAL/ELECTRONIC. OOH Title/s: Manufacturers' and Wholesale Sales Representatives

Sell electrical, electronic, or related products or services, such as communication equipment, radiographic-inspection equipment and services, ultrasonic equipment, electronics parts, computers, and EDP systems. Analyzes communication needs of customer and consults with staff engineers regarding technical problems. Recommends equipment to meet customer requirements, considering salable features, such as flexibility, cost, capacity, and economy of operation. Sells electrical or electronic equipment, such as computers and data-processing and radiographic equipment to businesses and industrial establishments. Negotiates terms of sale and services with customer. Trains establishment personnel in equipment use, utilizing knowledge of electronics and product sold.
Yearly Earnings: $26,312

Education: Moderate-term O-J-T
Knowledge: Economics and Accounting; Sales and Marketing; Computers and Electronics; Psychology; Education and Training; Telecommunications
Abilities: None above average
Skills: Persuasion; Negotiation; Instructing; Operations Analysis
General Work Activities: Communicating with Persons Outside Organization; Establishing and Maintaining Relationships; Selling or Influencing Others; Resolving Conflicts, Negotiating with Others; Performing for or Working with Public
Job Characteristics: Job-Required Social Interaction; Persuade Someone to a Course of Action; Provide a Service to Others; Deal with External Customers
GOE Group/s: 08.01.01 Sales Technology: Technical Sales
CIP Program/s: 080706 General Selling Skills and Sales Operations; 080810 Office Products Marketing Operations; 150301 Computer Engineering Tech./Technician; 150303 Electrical, Electronic and Communications Engineering Technologists and Technicians; 150402 Computer Maintenance Technologists and Technicians; 150404 Instrumentation Technologists and Technicians; 150611 Metallurgical Technologists and Technicians
Related DOT Job/s: 271.257-010 SALES REPRESENTATIVE, COMMUNICATION EQUIPMENT; 271.352-010 SALES REPRESENTATIVE, RADIOGRAPHIC-INSPECTION EQUIPMENT AND SERVICES; 271.352-014 SALES REPRESENTATIVE, ULTRASONIC EQUIPMENT; 271.357-010 SALES REPRESENTATIVE, ELECTRONICS PARTS; 275.257-010 SALES REPRESENTATIVE, COMPUTERS AND EDP SYSTEMS

49005D SALES REPRESENTATIVES, MECHANICAL EQUIPMENT AND SUPPLIES. OOH Title/s: Manufacturers' and Wholesale Sales Representatives

Sell mechanical equipment, machinery, materials, and supplies, such as aircraft and railroad equipment and parts, construction machinery, material-handling equipment, industrial machinery, and welding equipment. Recommends and sells textile, industrial, construction, railroad, and oilfield machinery, equipment, materials, and supplies, and services utilizing knowledge of machine operations. Contacts current and potential customers, visits establishments to evaluate needs, and promotes sale of products and services. Computes installation or production costs, estimates savings, and prepares and submits bid specifications to customer for review and approval. Submits orders for product and follows up on order to verify material list accuracy and that delivery schedule meets project deadline. Arranges for installation and test-operation of machinery and recommends solutions to product-related problems. Appraises equipment and verifies customer credit rating to establish trade-in value and contract terms. Demonstrates and explains use of installed equipment and production processes. Reviews existing machinery/equipment placement and diagrams proposal to illustrate efficient space utilization, using standard measuring devices and templates. Inspects establishment premises to verify installation feasibility, and obtains building blueprints and elevator specifications to submit to engineering department for bid. Attends sales and trade meetings and reads related publications to obtain current market condition information, business trends, and industry developments.
Yearly Earnings: $26,312
Education: Moderate-term O-J-T
Knowledge: Economics and Accounting; Sales and Marketing; Customer and Personal Service; Mathematics
Abilities: Oral Expression; Problem Sensitivity; Memorization; Speech Recognition; Speech Clarity
Skills: Active Listening; Speaking; Persuasion; Negotiation; Instructing; Operations Analysis; Equipment Selection
General Work Activities: Inspecting Equipment, Structures, or Material; Estimating Needed Characteristics; Evaluating Information against Standards; Controlling Machines and Processes; Communicating with Persons Outside Organization; Establishing and Maintaining Relationships; Selling or Influencing Others; Performing for or Working with Public
Job Characteristics: Objective or Subjective Information; Job-Required Social Interaction; Persuade Someone to a Course of Action; Provide a Service to Others; Deal with External Customers; Frequency in Conflict Situations; Deal with Unpleasant or Angry People; Deal with Physical, Aggressive People; Walking or Running
GOE Group/s: 08.01.01 Sales Technology: Technical Sales; 08.02.01 General Sales: Wholesale
CIP Program/s: 010501 Agricultural Supplies Retailing and Wholesaling; 080706 General Selling Skills and Sales Operations; 150603 Industrial/Manufacturing Technologists and Technicians; 150607 Plastics Technologists and Technicians; 150611 Metallurgical Technologists and Technicians; 150801 Aeronautical and Aerospace Engineering Technologists and Technicians; 150903 Petroleum Technologists and Technicians; 151001 Construction/Building Tech./Technician; 470303 Industrial Machinery Maintenance and Repair; 480501 Machinist/Machine Technologist; 480508 Welder/Welding Technologist; 490202 Construction Equipment Operator
Related DOT Job/s: 259.257-014 SALES REPRESENTATIVE, ELECTROPLATING; 273.253-010 SALES REPRESENTATIVE, AIRCRAFT; 273.357-010 SALES REPRESENTATIVE, AIRCRAFT EQUIPMENT AND PARTS; 273.357-026 SALES REPRESENTATIVE, RAILROAD EQUIPMENT AND SUPPLIES; 274.157-010 SALES REPRESENTATIVE, ELEVATORS, ESCALATORS, AND DUMBWAITERS; 274.257-010 SALES REPRESENTATIVE, FOUNDRY AND MACHINE SHOP PRODUCTS; 274.357-010 SALES REPRESENTATIVE, ABRASIVES; 274.357-018 SALES REPRESENTATIVE, BUILDING EQUIPMENT AND SUPPLIES; 274.357-022 SALES REPRESENTATIVE, CONSTRUCTION MACHINERY; 274.357-038 SALES REPRESENTATIVE, INDUSTRIAL MACHINERY; 274.357-046 SALES REPRESENTATIVE, LUBRICATING EQUIPMENT; 274.357-050 SALES REPRESENTATIVE, MATERIAL-HANDLING EQUIPMENT; 274.357-054 SALES REPRESENTATIVE, METALS; 274.357-058 SALES REPRESENTATIVE, OIL FIELD SUPPLIES AND EQUIPMENT; 274.357-070 SALES REPRESENTATIVE, TEXTILE MACHINERY; 274.357-074 SALES REPRESENTATIVE, WELDING EQUIPMENT; 274.357-078 SALES REPRESENTATIVE, WIRE ROPE

49005F SALES REPRESENTATIVES, MEDICAL. OOH Title/s: Manufacturers' and Wholesale Sales Representatives

Sell medical equipment, products, and services. Does not include pharmaceutical sales representatives. Promotes sale of medical and dental equipment, supplies, and services to doctors, dentists, hospitals, medical schools, and retail establishments. Selects surgical appliances from stock, and fits and sells appliances to customer. Studies data describing new products to accurately recommend purchase of equipment and supplies. Writes specifications to order custom-made surgical appliances, using customer measurements and physician prescriptions. Advises customer regarding office layout, legal and insurance regulations, cost analysis, and collection methods. Designs and fabricates custom-made medical appliances.
Yearly Earnings: $26,312
Education: Moderate-term O-J-T
Knowledge: Economics and Accounting; Sales and Marketing; Design; Mathematics; Medicine and Dentistry
Abilities: Speech Recognition
Skills: Active Listening; Persuasion; Negotiation; Operations Analysis; Technology Design

General Work Activities: Drafting and Specifying Technical Devices, etc.; Communicating with Persons Outside Organization; Establishing and Maintaining Relationships; Selling or Influencing Others; Resolving Conflicts, Negotiating with Others; Performing for or Working with Public
Job Characteristics: Job-Required Social Interaction; Persuade Someone to a Course of Action; Deal with External Customers
GOE Group/s: 08.01.01 Sales Technology: Technical Sales; 08.02.02 General Sales: Retail
CIP Program/s: 080706 General Selling Skills and Sales Operations; 081301 Health Products and Services Marketing Operations; 150401 Biomedical Engineering-Related Technologists and Technicians
Related DOT Job/s: 276.257-010 SALES REPRESENTATIVE, DENTAL AND MEDICAL EQUIPMENT AND SUPPLIES; 276.257-022 SALESPERSON, SURGICAL APPLIANCES

49005G SALES REPRESENTATIVES, INSTRUMENTS. OOH Title/s: Manufacturers' and Wholesale Sales Representatives

Sell precision instruments, such as dynamometers and spring scales, and laboratory, navigation, and surveying instruments. Assists customer with product selection, utilizing knowledge of engineering specifications and catalog resources. Sells weighing and other precision instruments, such as spring scales and dynamometers, and laboratory, navigational, and surveying instruments to customer. Evaluates customer needs and emphasizes product features based on technical knowledge of product capabilities and limitations.
Yearly Earnings: $26,312
Education: Moderate-term O-J-T
Knowledge: Sales and Marketing
Abilities: None above average
Skills: Persuasion
General Work Activities: Communicating with Persons Outside Organization; Establishing and Maintaining Relationships; Selling or Influencing Others; Provide Consultation and Advice to Others
Job Characteristics: Job-Required Social Interaction; Persuade Someone to a Course of Action; Deal with External Customers
GOE Group/s: 08.01.01 Sales Technology: Technical Sales
CIP Program/s: 080706 General Selling Skills and Sales Operations; 150404 Instrumentation Technologists and Technicians
Related DOT Job/s: 276.257-014 SALES REPRESENTATIVE, WEIGHING AND FORCE-MEASUREMENT INSTRUMENTS; 276.357-014 SALES REPRESENTATIVE, PRECISION INSTRUMENTS

49008 SALES REPRESENTATIVES, EXCEPT RETAIL AND SCIENTIFIC AND RELATED PRODUCTS AND SERVICES. OOH Title/s: Manufacturers' and Wholesale Sales Representatives

Sell goods or services for wholesalers or manufacturers to businesses or groups of individuals. Solicit orders from established clients or secure new customers. Work requires substantial knowledge of items sold. Contacts regular and prospective customers to solicit orders. Recommends products to customers, based on customers' specific needs and interests. Answers questions about products, prices, durability, and credit terms. Meets with customers to demonstrate and explain features of products. Prepares lists of prospective customers. Reviews sales records and current market information to determine value or sales potential of product. Estimates delivery dates and arranges delivery schedules. Completes sales contracts or forms to record sales information. Instructs customers in use of products. Assists and advises retail dealers in use of sales promotion techniques. Investigates and resolves customer complaints. Forwards orders to manufacturer. Assembles and stocks product displays in retail stores. Writes reports on sales and products. Prepares drawings, estimates, and bids to meet specific needs of customer. Obtains credit information on prospective customers. Oversees delivery or installation of products or equipment.
Yearly Earnings: $26,312
Education: Moderate-term O-J-T
Knowledge: Economics and Accounting; Sales and Marketing; Customer and Personal Service; Mathematics; Psychology; Sociology and Anthropology; Education and Training; Foreign Language; Philosophy and Theology; Communications and Media; Transportation
Abilities: Fluency of Ideas; Originality; Category Flexibility; Mathematical Reasoning; Number Facility; Memorization; Response Orientation; Speech Recognition; Speech Clarity
Skills: Active Listening; Writing; Speaking; Active Learning; Social Perceptiveness; Persuasion; Negotiation; Instructing; Service Orientation; Problem Identification; Information Gathering; Idea Generation; Implementation Planning; Operations Analysis; Identifying Downstream Consequences; Identification of Key Causes; Management of Material Resources
General Work Activities: Estimating Needed Characteristics; Developing Objectives and Strategies; Organizing, Planning, and Prioritizing; Drafting and Specifying Technical Devices, etc.; Communicating with Other Workers; Communicating with Persons Outside Organization; Establishing and Maintaining Relationships; Selling or Influencing Others; Resolving Conflicts, Negotiating with Others; Performing for or Working with Public; Provide Consultation and Advice to Others; Performing Administrative Activities
Job Characteristics: Objective or Subjective Information; Job-Required Social Interaction; Persuade Someone to a Course of Action; Provide a Service to Others; Deal with External Customers; Frequency in Conflict Situations; Deal with Unpleasant or Angry People; Frustrating Circumstances
GOE Group/s: 08.01.03 Sales Technology: Purchasing and Sales; 08.02.01 General Sales: Wholesale; 08.02.03 General Sales: Wholesale and Retail; 11.09.01 Promotion: Sales
CIP Program/s: 010501 Agricultural Supplies Retailing and Wholesaling; 080101 Apparel and Accessories Marketing Operations, General; 080102 Fashion Merchandising; 080199 Apparel and Accessories Marketing Operations, Other; 080299 Business and Personal Services Marketing Operations, Other; 080503 Floristry Marketing Operations; 080601 Food Products Retailing and Wholesaling Operations; 080705 General Retailing Operations; 080706 General Selling Skills and Sales Operations; 080810 Office Products Marketing Operations; 080901 Hospitality and Recreation Marketing Operations, General; 080903 Recreation Products/Services Marketing Operations; 089999 Marketing Operations/Marketing and Distribution, Other; 150101 Architectural Engineering Technologists and Technicians; 200301 Clothing, Apparel and Textile Workers and Managers, General; 200306 Fashion and Fabric Consultant
Related DOT Job/s: 162.157-026 COMMISSION AGENT, LIVESTOCK; 260.257-010 SALES REPRESENTATIVE, LIVESTOCK; 260.357-010 COMMISSION AGENT, AGRICULTURAL PRODUCE; 260.357-014 SALES REPRESENTATIVE, FOOD PRODUCTS; 260.357-018 SALES REPRESENTATIVE, MALT LIQUORS; 260.357-022 SALES REPRESENTATIVE, TOBACCO PRODUCTS AND SMOKING SUPPLIES; 261.357-010 SALES REPRESENTATIVE, APPAREL TRIMMINGS; 261.357-014 SALES REPRESENTATIVE, CANVAS PRODUCTS; 261.357-018 SALES REPRESENTATIVE, FOOTWEAR; 261.357-022 SALES REPRESENTATIVE, MEN'S AND BOYS' APPAREL; 261.357-026 SALES REPRESENTATIVE, SAFETY APPAREL AND EQUIPMENT; 261.357-030 SALES REPRESENTATIVE, TEXTILES; 261.357-034 SALES REPRESENTATIVE, UNIFORMS; 261.357-038 SALES REPRESENTATIVE, WOMEN'S AND GIRLS' APPAREL; 262.357-014 SALES REPRESENTATIVE, TOILET PREPARATIONS; 269.357-010 SALES REPRESENTATIVE, FUELS;

269.357-014 SALES REPRESENTATIVE, PETROLEUM PRODUCTS; 270.357-010 SALES REPRESENTATIVE, HOME FURNISHINGS; 270.357-014 SALES REPRESENTATIVE, HOUSEHOLD APPLIANCES; 271.357-014 SALES REPRESENTATIVE, VIDEOTAPE; 273.357-022 SALES REPRESENTATIVE, MOTOR VEHICLES AND SUPPLIES; 274.357-014 SALES REPRESENTATIVE, BOTTLES AND BOTTLING EQUIPMENT; 274.357-026 SALES REPRESENTATIVE, CONTAINERS; 274.357-034 SALES REPRESENTATIVE, HARDWARE SUPPLIES; 274.357-042 SALES REPRESENTATIVE, INDUSTRIAL RUBBER GOODS; 274.357-062 SALES REPRESENTATIVE, PRINTING SUPPLIES; 274.357-066 SALES REPRESENTATIVE, TEXTILE DESIGNS; 275.357-010 SALES REPRESENTATIVE, BARBER AND BEAUTY EQUIPMENT AND SUPPLIES; 275.357-014 SALES REPRESENTATIVE, CHURCH FURNITURE AND RELIGIOUS SUPPLIES; 275.357-018 SALES REPRESENTATIVE, COMMERCIAL EQUIPMENT AND SUPPLIES; 275.357-022 SALES REPRESENTATIVE, CORDAGE; 275.357-026 SALES REPRESENTATIVE, HOTEL AND RESTAURANT EQUIPMENT AND SUPPLIES; 275.357-030 SALES REPRESENTATIVE, MORTICIAN SUPPLIES; 275.357-034 SALES REPRESENTATIVE, OFFICE MACHINES; 275.357-038 SALES REPRESENTATIVE, PRESSURE-SENSITIVE TAPE; 275.357-042 SALES REPRESENTATIVE, SCHOOL EQUIPMENT AND SUPPLIES; 275.357-046 SALES REPRESENTATIVE, SHOE LEATHER AND FINDINGS; 275.357-050 SALES REPRESENTATIVE, VENDING AND COIN MACHINES; 275.357-054 SALESPERSON, FLORIST SUPPLIES; 276.357-010 SALES REPRESENTATIVE, ARCHITECTURAL AND ENGINEERING SUPPLIES; 277.357-010 SALES REPRESENTATIVE, HOBBIES AND CRAFTS; 277.357-014 SALES REPRESENTATIVE, MUSICAL INSTRUMENTS AND ACCESSORIES; 277.357-018 SALES REPRESENTATIVE, NOVELTIES; 277.357-022 SALES REPRESENTATIVE, PUBLICATIONS; 277.357-026 SALES REPRESENTATIVE, RECREATION AND SPORTING GOODS; 277.357-030 SALES REPRESENTATIVE, WRITING AND MARKING PENS; 279.157-010 MANUFACTURER'S REPRESENTATIVE; 279.357-014 SALES REPRESENTATIVE, GENERAL MERCHANDISE; 279.357-018 SALES REPRESENTATIVE, JEWELRY; 279.357-022 SALES REPRESENTATIVE, LEATHER GOODS; 279.357-026 SALES REPRESENTATIVE, PAPER AND PAPER PRODUCTS; 279.357-030 SALES REPRESENTATIVE, PLASTIC PRODUCTS; 279.357-034 SALES REPRESENTATIVE, WATER-SOFTENING EQUIPMENT; 299.167-010 CIRCULATION-SALES REPRESENTATIVE

49011 SALESPERSONS, RETAIL. OOH Title/s: Retail Sales Workers

Sell to the public any of a wide variety of merchandise, such as furniture, motor vehicles, appliances, or apparel. Include workers who sell less expensive merchandise, where a knowledge of the item sold is not a primary requirement. Exclude cashiers. Prepares sales slip or sales contract. Computes sale price of merchandise. Describes merchandise and explains use, operation, and care of merchandise to customers. Sells or arranges for delivery, insurance, financing, or service contracts for merchandise. Totals purchases, receives payment, makes change, or processes credit transaction. Recommends, selects, and obtains merchandise based on customer needs and desires. Demonstrates use or operation of merchandise. Greets customer. Fits or assists customers in trying on merchandise. Estimates quantity and cost of merchandise required, such as paint or floor covering. Tickets, arranges, and displays merchandise to promote sales. Maintains records related to sales. Estimates and quotes trade-in allowances. Estimates cost of repair or alteration of merchandise. Wraps merchandise. Rents merchandise to customers. Inventories stock. Requisitions new stock. Cleans shelves, counters, and tables. Repairs or alters merchandise.

Yearly Earnings: $18,304

Education: Short-term O-J-T

Knowledge: Economics and Accounting; Sales and Marketing; Customer and Personal Service

Abilities: Memorization; Gross Body Equilibrium; Visual Color Discrimination; Speech Recognition

Skills: Service Orientation

General Work Activities: Establishing and Maintaining Relationships; Selling or Influencing Others; Performing for or Working with Public

Job Characteristics: Job-Required Social Interaction; Persuade Someone to a Course of Action; Provide a Service to Others; Deal with External Customers; Deal with Unpleasant or Angry People; Standing; Walking or Running

GOE Group/s: 07.03.01 Financial Detail: Paying and Receiving; 08.02.02 General Sales: Retail; 08.02.03 General Sales: Wholesale and Retail; 09.04.02 Customer Services: Sales Services

CIP Program/s: 010501 Agricultural Supplies Retailing and Wholesaling; 010601 Horticulture Services Operations and Management, General; 010603 Ornamental Horticulture Operations and Management; 010604 Greenhouse Operations and Management; 010606 Nursery Operations and Management; 080101 Apparel and Accessories Marketing Operations, General; 080102 Fashion Merchandising; 080199 Apparel and Accessories Marketing Operations, Other; 080503 Floristry Marketing Operations; 080705 General Retailing Operations; 080706 General Selling Skills and Sales Operations; 080809 Home Products Marketing Operations; 080901 Hospitality and Recreation Marketing Operations, General; 080903 Recreation Products/Services Marketing Operations; 081203 Vehicle Parts and Accessories Marketing Operations; 081208 Vehicle Marketing Operations; 081301 Health Products and Services Marketing Operations; 089999 Marketing Operations/Marketing and Distribution, Other; 200301 Clothing, Apparel and Textile Workers and Managers, General; 200306 Fashion and Fabric Consultant; 200501 Home Furnishings and Equipment Installers and Consultants, General

Related DOT Job/s: 260.357-026 SALESPERSON, FLOWERS; 261.351-010 SALESPERSON, WIGS; 261.354-010 SALESPERSON, CORSETS; 261.357-042 SALESPERSON, FURS; 261.357-046 SALESPERSON, INFANTS' AND CHILDREN'S WEAR; 261.357-050 SALESPERSON, MEN'S AND BOYS' CLOTHING; 261.357-054 SALESPERSON, MEN'S FURNISHINGS; 261.357-058 SALESPERSON, MILLINERY; 261.357-062 SALESPERSON, SHOES; 261.357-066 SALESPERSON, WOMEN'S APPAREL AND ACCESSORIES; 261.357-070 SALESPERSON, YARD GOODS; 261.357-074 SALESPERSON, LEATHER-AND-SUEDE APPAREL-AND-ACCESSORIES; 262.357-018 SALESPERSON, COSMETICS AND TOILETRIES; 270.352-010 SALESPERSON, SEWING MACHINES; 270.357-018 SALESPERSON, CHINA AND SILVERWARE; 270.357-022 SALESPERSON, CURTAINS AND DRAPERIES; 270.357-026 SALESPERSON, FLOOR COVERINGS; 270.357-030 SALESPERSON, FURNITURE; 270.357-034 SALESPERSON, HOUSEHOLD APPLIANCES; 270.357-038 SALESPERSON, STEREO EQUIPMENT; 271.354-010 SALESPERSON, ELECTRIC MOTORS; 272.357-022 SALESPERSON, HORTICULTURAL AND NURSERY PRODUCTS; 273.353-010 SALESPERSON, AUTOMOBILES; 273.357-018 SALES REPRESENTATIVE, BOATS AND MARINE SUPPLIES; 273.357-030 SALESPERSON, AUTOMOBILE ACCESSORIES; 273.357-034 SALESPERSON, TRAILERS AND MOTOR HOMES; 276.257-018 SALESPERSON, ORTHOPEDIC SHOES; 276.354-010 HEARING AID SPECIALIST; 277.354-010 SALESPERSON, PIANOS AND ORGANS; 277.357-034 SALESPERSON, BOOKS; 277.357-038 SALESPERSON, MUSICAL INSTRUMENTS AND ACCESSORIES; 277.357-042 SALESPERSON, PETS AND PET SUPPLIES; 277.357-046 SALESPERSON, PHONOGRAPH RECORDS AND TAPE RECORDINGS; 277.357-050 SALESPERSON, PHOTOGRAPHIC SUPPLIES AND EQUIPMENT; 277.357-054 SALESPERSON, SHEET MUSIC; 277.357-058 SALESPERSON, SPORTING GOODS; 277.357-062 SALESPERSON, STAMPS OR COINS; 277.357-066 SALESPERSON, TOY TRAINS AND ACCESSORIES;

277.457-010 SALESPERSON, ART OBJECTS; 279.357-046 SALESPERSON, FLYING SQUAD; 279.357-050 SALESPERSON, GENERAL HARDWARE; 279.357-054 SALESPERSON, GENERAL MERCHANDISE; 279.357-058 SALESPERSON, JEWELRY; 290.477-014 SALES CLERK; 299.377-010 PLATFORM ATTENDANT; 299.467-010 LAYAWAY CLERK; 299.677-010 SALES ATTENDANT

49014 SALESPERSONS, PARTS. OOH Title/s: Retail Sales Workers

Sell spare and replaceable parts and equipment from behind counter in agency, repair shop, or parts store. Determine make, year, and type of part needed by observing damaged part or listening to a description of malfunction. Read catalog to find stock number, price, etc., and fill customer's order from stock. Exclude workers whose primary responsibilities are to receive, store, and issue materials, equipment, and other items from stockroom. Determines replacement part required, according to inspection of old part, customer request, or customer description of malfunction. Reads catalog, microfiche viewer, or computer display to determine replacement part stock number and price. Fills customer orders from stock. Advises customer on substitution or modification of part when identical replacement is not available. Examines returned part for defects, and exchanges defective part or refunds money. Prepares sales slip or sales contract. Receives payment or obtains credit authorization. Receives and fills telephone orders for parts. Demonstrates equipment to customer and explains functioning of equipment. Discusses use and features of various parts, based on knowledge of machine or equipment. Measures parts, using precision measuring instruments to determine whether similar parts may be machined to required size. Places new merchandise on display. Marks and stores parts in stockroom according to prearranged system. Takes inventory of stock. Repairs parts or equipment.

Yearly Earnings: $18,304

Education: Short-term O-J-T

Knowledge: Sales and Marketing; Customer and Personal Service; Mechanical; Telecommunications

Abilities: Memorization; Visualization; Gross Body Equilibrium; Visual Color Discrimination; Auditory Attention; Speech Recognition

Skills: Service Orientation; Product Inspection; Troubleshooting; Repairing

General Work Activities: Inspecting Equipment, Structures, or Material; Selling or Influencing Others; Performing for or Working with Public

Job Characteristics: Job-Required Social Interaction; Persuade Someone to a Course of Action; Provide a Service to Others; Deal with External Customers; Deal with Unpleasant or Angry People; Standing

GOE Group/s: 08.02.03 General Sales: Wholesale and Retail

CIP Program/s: 010501 Agricultural Supplies Retailing and Wholesaling; 080705 General Retailing Operations; 080706 General Selling Skills and Sales Operations; 081203 Vehicle Parts and Accessories Marketing Operations

Related DOT Job/s: 279.357-062 SALESPERSON, PARTS

49017 COUNTER AND RENTAL CLERKS. OOH Title/s: Counter and Rental Clerks; Retail Sales Workers; Handlers, Equipment Cleaners, Helpers, and Laborers

Receive orders for services, such as rentals, repairs, dry-cleaning, and storage. May compute cost and accept payment. Rents item or arranges for provision of service to customer. Prepares rental forms, obtains customer signature, and collects deposit. Computes charges based on rental. Receives, examines, and tags articles to be altered, cleaned, stored, or repaired. Explains rental fees and provides information about rented items, such as operation or description. Receives payment or records credit charges. Answers telephone and receives orders by phone. Recommends to customer items offered by rental facility that meet customer needs. Reserves items for requested time and keeps record of items rented. Greets customers of agency that rents items, such as apparel, tools, and conveyances, or that provide services, such as rug cleaning. Requests license for car or plane rental. Receives film for processing and loads film into automatic processing equipment. Inspects and adjusts rental items to meet needs of customer. Files processed film and photographic prints, according to name.

Yearly Earnings: $13,936

Education: Short-term O-J-T

Knowledge: Clerical; Sales and Marketing; Customer and Personal Service; Telecommunications

Abilities: Category Flexibility; Speech Recognition

Skills: Service Orientation

General Work Activities: Establishing and Maintaining Relationships; Assisting and Caring for Others; Selling or Influencing Others; Performing for or Working with Public

Job Characteristics: Job-Required Social Interaction; Persuade Someone to a Course of Action; Provide a Service to Others; Deal with External Customers; Frequency in Conflict Situations; Deal with Unpleasant or Angry People; Standing

GOE Group/s: 05.09.01 Material Control: Shipping, Receiving, and Stock Checking; 05.09.02 Material Control: Estimating, Scheduling, and Record Keeping; 07.02.04 Mathematical Detail: Billing and Rate Computation; 07.03.01 Financial Detail: Paying and Receiving; 07.04.03 Oral Communications: Registration; 09.04.02 Customer Services: Sales Services

CIP Program/s: 080705 General Retailing Operations; 080706 General Selling Skills and Sales Operations; 081105 Travel Services Marketing Operations; 081299 Vehicle and Petroleum Products Marketing Operations, Other; 200301 Clothing, Apparel and Textile Workers and Managers, General; 200309 Drycleaner and Launderer (Commercial); 470408 Watch, Clock and Jewelry Repairer

Related DOT Job/s: 216.482-030 LAUNDRY PRICING CLERK; 249.362-010 COUNTER CLERK; 249.366-010 COUNTER CLERK; 290.477-010 COUPON-REDEMPTION CLERK; 290.477-018 SALES CLERK, FOOD; 295.357-010 APPAREL-RENTAL CLERK; 295.357-014 TOOL-AND-EQUIPMENT-RENTAL CLERK; 295.357-018 FURNITURE-RENTAL CONSULTANT; 295.367-010 AIRPLANE-CHARTER CLERK; 295.367-014 BABY-STROLLER AND WHEELCHAIR RENTAL CLERK; 295.367-026 STORAGE-FACILITY RENTAL CLERK; 295.467-010 BICYCLE-RENTAL CLERK; 295.467-014 BOAT-RENTAL CLERK; 295.467-018 HOSPITAL-TELEVISION-RENTAL CLERK; 295.467-022 TRAILER-RENTAL CLERK; 295.467-026 AUTOMOBILE RENTAL CLERK; 299.367-018 WATCH-AND-CLOCK-REPAIR CLERK; 369.367-010 FUR-STORAGE CLERK; 369.367-014 RUG MEASURER; 369.467-010 MANAGER, BRANCH STORE; 369.477-010 CURB ATTENDANT; 369.477-014 SERVICE-ESTABLISHMENT ATTENDANT; 369.587-010 VAULT CUSTODIAN; 369.677-010 SELF-SERVICE-LAUNDRY-AND-DRY-CLEANING ATTENDANT

49021 STOCK CLERKS, SALES FLOOR. OOH Title/s: Stock Clerks

Receive, store, and issue sales floor merchandise. Stock shelves, racks, cases, bins, and tables with merchandise, and arrange merchandise displays to attract customers. May periodically take physical count of stock or check and mark merchandise. Receives, opens, and unpacks cartons or crates of merchandise and checks invoice against items received. Stocks storage areas and displays with new or transferred merchandise. Sets up advertising signs and displays merchandise on shelves, counters, or tables to attract customers and promote sales. Takes inventory or examines merchandise to identify items to be reordered or replenished. Stamps, attaches,

or changes price tags on merchandise, referring to price list. Requisitions merchandise from supplier based on available space, merchandise on hand, customer demand, or advertised specials. Cleans display cases, shelves, and aisles. Itemizes and totals customer merchandise selection at check-out counter, using cash register, and accepts cash or charge card for purchases. Answers questions and advises customer in selection of merchandise. Cuts lumber, screening, glass, and related materials to size requested by customer. Packs customer purchases in bags or cartons. Transports packages to customer vehicle.
Yearly Earnings: $20,696
Education: Short-term O-J-T
Knowledge: Clerical; Sales and Marketing
Abilities: Category Flexibility; Memorization; Perceptual Speed; Spatial Orientation; Visualization; Manual Dexterity; Multilimb Coordination; Speed of Limb Movement; Static Strength; Dynamic Strength; Trunk Strength; Extent Flexibility; Dynamic Flexibility; Gross Body Equilibrium; Far Vision; Speech Recognition
Skills: None above average
General Work Activities: Handling and Moving Objects; Interacting with Computers; Establishing and Maintaining Relationships; Selling or Influencing Others; Performing for or Working with Public
Job Characteristics: Persuade Someone to a Course of Action; Provide a Service to Others; Deal with External Customers; Standing; Climbing Ladders, Scaffolds, Poles, etc.; Walking or Running
GOE Group/s: 05.09.01 Material Control: Shipping, Receiving, and Stock Checking; 09.04.02 Customer Services: Sales Services
CIP Program/s: 080601 Food Products Retailing and Wholesaling Operations; 080705 General Retailing Operations; 089999 Marketing Operations/Marketing and Distribution, Other
Related DOT Job/s: 299.367-014 STOCK CLERK; 299.677-014 SALES ATTENDANT, BUILDING MATERIALS

49023A CASHIERS, GENERAL. OOH Title/s: Cashiers
Receive payments, issue receipts, handle credit transactions, account for the amounts received, and perform related clerical duties in a wide variety of business establishments. Receives sales slip, cash, check, voucher, or charge payments, and issues refunds or credits to customer. Issues receipt and change due. Operates cash register or electronic scanner. Computes and records totals of transactions. Cashes checks. Keeps periodic balance sheet of amount and number of transactions. Sells tickets and other items to customer. Sorts, counts, and wraps currency and coins. Learns prices, stocks shelves, marks prices, weighs items, issues trading stamps, and redeems food stamps and coupons. Answers questions and provides information to customers. Bags, boxes, or wraps merchandise. Compiles and maintains nonmonetary reports and records. Resolves customers' complaints. Accepts bets and computes and pays winnings in gambling establishment. Monitors check-out stations, issues and removes cash as needed, and assigns workers to reduce customer delay.
Yearly Earnings: $12,064
Education: Short-term O-J-T
Knowledge: Clerical; Sales and Marketing; Customer and Personal Service
Abilities: Memorization; Perceptual Speed; Finger Dexterity; Wrist-Finger Speed; Speech Recognition
Skills: None above average
General Work Activities: Establishing and Maintaining Relationships; Selling or Influencing Others; Performing for or Working with Public
Job Characteristics: Job-Required Social Interaction; Provide a Service to Others; Deal with External Customers; Frequency in Conflict Situations; Deal with Unpleasant or Angry People; Special Uniform
GOE Group/s: 07.02.02 Mathematical Detail: Accounting; 07.03.01 Financial Detail: Paying and Receiving; 07.07.02 Clerical Handling: Sorting and Distrubtion; 09.04.02 Customer Services: Sales Services
CIP Program/s: 080601 Food Products Retailing and Wholesaling Operations; 080705 General Retailing Operations; 520801 Finance, General; 520803 Banking and Financial Support Services
Related DOT Job/s: 211.367-010 PAYMASTER OF PURSES; 211.462-010 CASHIER II; 211.462-014 CASHIER-CHECKER; 211.462-018 CASHIER-WRAPPER; 211.462-022 CASHIER, GAMBLING; 211.462-026 CHECK CASHIER; 211.462-030 DRIVERS'-CASH CLERK; 211.462-034 TELLER; 211.462-038 TOLL COLLECTOR; 211.467-010 CASHIER, COURTESY BOOTH; 211.467-014 MONEY COUNTER; 211.467-018 PARIMUTUEL-TICKET CASHIER; 211.467-022 PARIMUTUEL-TICKET SELLER; 211.467-026 SHEET WRITER; 211.467-030 TICKET SELLER; 211.467-034 CHANGE PERSON; 211.482-010 CASHIER, TUBE ROOM; 211.482-014 FOOD CHECKER; 249.467-010 INFORMATION CLERK-CASHIER; 294.567-010 AUCTION CLERK

49023B CASH ACCOUNTING CLERKS. OOH Title/s: Cashiers
Receive payments, issue receipts, handle credit transactions, account for the amounts received, and perform related clerical duties in a wide variety of business establishments. Operate office machines, such as typewriter; computer terminal; and adding, calculating, bookkeeping, and check-writing machines. Receives cash or checks or completes credit card transactions. Counts money to verify amounts and issues receipts for funds received. Issues change and cashes checks. Compares totals on cash register with amount of currency in register to verify balances. Endorses checks, lists and totals cash and checks, and prepares bank deposit slips. Operates office machines, such as typewriter; computer terminal; and adding, calculating, bookkeeping, and check-writing machines. Issues itemized statements to customers. Disburses cash and writes vouchers and checks in payment of company expenses. Posts data and balances accounts. Withdraws cash from bank accounts and keeps custody of cash fund. Compiles collection, disbursement, and bank-reconciliation reports. Prepares payroll paychecks. Authorizes various plant expenditures and purchases.
Yearly Earnings: $12,064
Education: Short-term O-J-T
Knowledge: Clerical; Economics and Accounting; Computers and Electronics
Abilities: Mathematical Reasoning; Number Facility; Perceptual Speed; Wrist-Finger Speed; Near Vision
Skills: Management of Financial Resources
General Work Activities: Monitoring and Controlling Resources
Job Characteristics: Provide a Service to Others; Deal with External Customers; Deal with Unpleasant or Angry People; Degree of Automation; Importance of Being Exact or Accurate; Importance of Repeating Same Tasks
GOE Group/s: 07.03.01 Financial Detail: Paying and Receiving
CIP Program/s: 080705 General Retailing Operations; 520801 Finance, General; 520803 Banking and Financial Support Services
Related DOT Job/s: 211.362-010 CASHIER I

49026 TELEMARKETERS, DOOR-TO-DOOR SALES WORKERS, NEWS AND STREET VENDERS, AND OTHER RELATED WORKERS. OOH Title/s: Retail Sales Workers
Solicit orders for goods or services over the telephone; sell goods or services door-to-door or on the street. Contacts customers by phone, mail, or in person to offer or persuade them to purchase merchandise or services. Explains products or services and prices and

demonstrates use of products. Writes orders for merchandise or enters orders into computer. Circulates among potential customers or travels by foot, truck, automobile, or bicycle to deliver or sell merchandise or services. Arranges buying party and solicits sponsorship of parties to sell merchandise. Delivers merchandise, serves customer, collects money, and makes change. Distributes product samples or literature that details products or services. Maintains records of accounts and orders and develops prospect lists. Orders or purchases supplies and stocks cart or stand. Sets up and displays sample merchandise at parties or stands.
Yearly Earnings: $18,304
Education: Short-term O-J-T
Knowledge: Sales and Marketing; Customer and Personal Service
Abilities: None above average
Skills: Persuasion; Service Orientation
General Work Activities: Interacting with Computers; Communicating with Persons Outside Organization; Establishing and Maintaining Relationships; Selling or Influencing Others; Performing for or Working with Public; Monitoring and Controlling Resources
Job Characteristics: Objective or Subjective Information; Job-Required Social Interaction; Persuade Someone to a Course of Action; Provide a Service to Others; Deal with External Customers; Frequency in Conflict Situations; Deal with Unpleasant or Angry People; Deal with Physical, Aggressive People; Walking or Running
GOE Group/s: 08.02.05 General Sales: Demonstration and Sales; 08.02.08 General Sales: Soliciting-Selling; 08.03.01 Vending: Peddling and Hawking; 09.04.02 Customer Services: Sales Services
CIP Program/s: 080705 General Retailing Operations; 080708 General Marketing Operations; 080809 Home Products Marketing Operations
Related DOT Job/s: 279.357-038 SALESPERSON-DEMONSTRATOR, PARTY PLAN; 291.357-010 SALES REPRESENTATIVE, DOOR-TO-DOOR; 291.454-010 LEI SELLER; 291.457-010 CIGARETTE VENDOR; 291.457-014 LOUNGE-CAR ATTENDANT; 291.457-018 PEDDLER; 291.457-022 VENDOR; 292.457-010 NEWSPAPER CARRIER; 299.357-014 TELEPHONE SOLICITOR

49032A DEMONSTRATORS AND PROMOTERS.

OOH Title/s: Retail Sales Workers

Demonstrate merchandise and answer questions for the purpose of creating public interest in buying the products. Demonstrates and explains products, methods, or services to persuade customers to purchase products or utilize services available, and answers questions. Visits homes, community organizations, stores, and schools to demonstrate products or services. Attends trade, traveling, promotional, educational, or amusement exhibits to answer visitors' questions and to protect exhibit against theft or damage. Sets up and arranges display to attract attention of prospective customers. Suggests product improvements to employer and product to purchase to customer. Gives product samples or token gifts to customers, and distributes handbills, brochures, or gift certificates to passersby. Answers telephone and written requests from customers for information about product use, and writes articles and pamphlets on product. Lectures and shows slides to users of company product. Advises customers on homemaking problems related to products or services offered by company. Wears costume or sign boards and walks in public to attract attention to advertise merchandise, services, or belief. Contacts businesses and civic establishments and arranges to exhibit and sell merchandise made by disadvantaged persons. Instructs customers in alteration of products. Represents utility company as guest on radio or television programs to discuss proper use and conservation of company's product. Develops list of prospective clients from sources, such as newspaper items, company records, local merchants, and customers. Solicits new organization membership. Trains demonstrators to present company's products or services. Conducts guided tours of plant where product is made. Prepares reports of services rendered and visits made for parent organization and member firms. Drives truck and trailer to transport exhibit. Collects fees or accepts donations.
Yearly Earnings: $18,304
Education: Short-term O-J-T
Knowledge: Clerical; Sales and Marketing; Customer and Personal Service; Sociology and Anthropology; Education and Training; English Language; Communications and Media
Abilities: Oral Expression; Written Expression; Fluency of Ideas; Originality; Memorization; Response Orientation; Night Vision; Speech Clarity
Skills: Speaking; Active Learning; Learning Strategies; Social Perceptiveness; Persuasion; Instructing; Idea Generation; Implementation Planning; Identification of Key Causes
General Work Activities: Scheduling Work and Activities; Interacting with Computers; Communicating with Persons Outside Organization; Establishing and Maintaining Relationships; Selling or Influencing Others; Performing for or Working with Public; Coaching and Developing Others
Job Characteristics: Objective or Subjective Information; Job-Required Social Interaction; Persuade Someone to a Course of Action; Provide a Service to Others; Deal with External Customers; Deal with Unpleasant or Angry People; Walking or Running; Special Uniform
GOE Group/s: 01.06.03 Craft Arts: Hand Lettering, Painting and Decorating; 08.02.02 General Sales: Retail; 08.02.05 General Sales: Demonstration and Sales; 08.03.02 Vending: Promoting; 09.01.02 Hospitality Services: Guide Services; 11.09.01 Promotion: Sales
CIP Program/s: 080299 Business and Personal Services Marketing Operations, Other; 080705 General Retailing Operations; 080706 General Selling Skills and Sales Operations; 080809 Home Products Marketing Operations; 200301 Clothing, Apparel and Textile Workers and Managers, General; 200306 Fashion and Fabric Consultant; 200501 Home Furnishings and Equipment Installers and Consultants, General; 500701 Art, General; 500708 Painting; 500712 Fiber, Textile and Weaving Arts
Related DOT Job/s: 279.357-010 SALES EXHIBITOR; 293.357-018 GOODWILL AMBASSADOR; 297.354-010 DEMONSTRATOR; 297.354-014 DEMONSTRATOR, KNITTING; 297.357-010 DEMONSTRATOR, ELECTRIC-GAS APPLIANCES; 297.367-010 EXHIBIT-DISPLAY REPRESENTATIVE; 297.451-010 INSTRUCTOR, PAINTING; 297.454-010 DEMONSTRATOR, SEWING TECHNIQUES; 299.687-014 SANDWICH-BOARD CARRIER

49032B MODELS. OOH Title/s: Actors, Directors, and Producers

Model for photographers or artists, or display merchandise or depict characters. Poses as subject for paintings, sculptures, and other types of art for translation into plastic or pictorial values. Poses as directed or strikes suitable interpretive poses for promoting and selling merchandise or fashions during photo session. Wears character costumes and impersonates characters portrayed to amuse children and adults. Impersonates holiday or storybook characters to promote sales or to entertain at conventions and in stores, hospitals, parks, and private homes. Stands, turns, and walks to demonstrate features of garment to observers at fashion shows, private showings, and retail establishments. Hands out samples or presents, demonstrates toys, and converses with children and adults while dressed in costume. Dresses in sample or completed garments and selects own accessories. Appears in costume parade. Applies make-up to face and styles hair to enhance appearance, considering such factors as color, camera techniques, and facial features. Informs prospective purchasers as to model, number, and price of garments and department where garment can be purchased. Solicits donations on street for charitable purposes.

Yearly Earnings: $30,004
Education: Long-term O-J-T
Knowledge: Sales and Marketing; Sociology and Anthropology; Fine Arts; Communications and Media
Abilities: Gross Body Coordination; Gross Body Equilibrium; Glare Sensitivity
Skills: None above average
General Work Activities: Establishing and Maintaining Relationships; Selling or Influencing Others; Performing for or Working with Public
Job Characteristics: Objective or Subjective Information; Job-Required Social Interaction; Persuade Someone to a Course of Action; Deal with External Customers; Extremely Bright or Inadequate Lighting; Standing; Walking or Running; Keeping or Regaining Balance; Special Uniform
GOE Group/s: 01.07.02 Elemental Arts: Announcing; 01.08.01 Modeling: Personal Appearance
CIP Program/s: 080101 Apparel and Accessories Marketing Operations, General; 080102 Fashion Merchandising; 080103 Fashion Modeling
Related DOT Job/s: 297.667-014 MODEL; 299.647-010 IMPERSONATOR, CHARACTER; 961.367-010 MODEL, PHOTOGRAPHERS'; 961.667-010 MODEL, ARTISTS'

Sales Consultants and Estimators

49999A MERCHANDISE APPRAISERS AND AUCTIONEERS. OOH Title/s: Manufacturers' and Wholesale Sales Representatives

Appraise and estimate value of items, such as paintings, antiques, jewelry, cameras, musical instruments, machinery, and fixtures for loan, insurance, or sale purposes. May sell merchandise at auction. Examines items and estimates values, based on knowledge of specific article, current market values, and economic trends. Examines and assigns value to item based on knowledge of values or accepted listing of wholesale prices. Tests art works and antiques, using X rays and chemicals, to detect forgery or to otherwise authenticate item. Weighs gold or silver articles on coin scales or employs acid tests to determine carat content and purity to verify value of articles. Inspects diamonds and other gems for flaws and color, using loupe (magnifying glass). Prepares and submits reports of estimates to clients, such as insurance firms, lending agencies, government offices, creditors, courts, or attorneys. Illuminates artworks, using quartz light, to examine color quality, brushstroke style, and other characteristics to identify artist or period. Selects item and describes and provides information about merchandise to be auctioned, such as history and ownership, to encourage bidding. Continues to ask for bids, attempting to stimulate buying desire of bidders, and closes sale to highest bidder. Issues pawn or pledge tickets, keeps record of loans, and computes interest when pledges are redeemed or extended.
Yearly Earnings: $26,312
Education: Moderate-term O-J-T
Knowledge: Economics and Accounting; Sales and Marketing; Fine Arts; History and Archeology; Law, Government, and Jurisprudence
Abilities: Number Facility; Memorization; Near Vision; Visual Color Discrimination; Speech Clarity
Skills: Persuasion; Information Organization; Product Inspection; Judgment and Decision Making
General Work Activities: Monitoring Processes, Material, or Surroundings; Judging Qualities of Things, Services, People; Processing Information; Implementing Ideas, Programs, etc.; Interpreting Meaning of Information to Others; Communicating with Persons Outside Organization; Selling or Influencing Others; Performing for or Working with Public; Provide Consultation and Advice to Others
Job Characteristics: Objective or Subjective Information; Persuade Someone to a Course of Action
GOE Group/s: 01.02.01 Visual Arts: Instructing and Appraising; 08.01.03 Sales Technology: Purchasing and Sales; 08.02.03 General Sales: Wholesale and Retail; 11.06.03 Finance: Risk and Profit Analysis
CIP Program/s: 010501 Agricultural Supplies Retailing and Wholesaling; 080701 Auctioneering; 080705 General Retailing Operations; 080706 General Selling Skills and Sales Operations; 080708 General Marketing Operations; 500701 Art, General; 500704 Arts Management
Related DOT Job/s: 191.157-010 PAWNBROKER; 191.287-010 APPRAISER; 191.287-014 APPRAISER, ART; 294.257-010 AUCTIONEER

49999B HOME FURNISHINGS ESTIMATORS. OOH Title/s: Retail Sales Workers

Measure dimensions and estimate price of making and installing household accessories. Measures windows for draperies and shades, furniture for upholstery, and window and door frames for doors, windows, and screen. Computes cost of fabric and hardware, according to measurements, work specifications, and type of fabric to be used, using calculator and price listings. Itemizes labor in fabrication and installation of goods and records total price on sales check or contract. Discusses selection of fabric and other materials with customer, using material samples. Draws sketches to scale of work to be done. Confers with architects and interior decorators to obtain additional information when computing cost estimates on commercial orders.
Yearly Earnings: $26,312
Education: Moderate-term O-J-T
Knowledge: Sales and Marketing; Customer and Personal Service; Design; Building and Construction
Abilities: Gross Body Equilibrium; Visual Color Discrimination
Skills: Service Orientation
General Work Activities: None above average
Job Characteristics: Objective or Subjective Information; Persuade Someone to a Course of Action; Provide a Service to Others; Deal with External Customers
GOE Group/s: 05.09.02 Material Control: Estimating, Scheduling, and Record Keeping
CIP Program/s: 200501 Home Furnishings and Equipment Installers and Consultants, General; 200502 Window Treatment Maker and Installer; 480303 Upholsterer
Related DOT Job/s: 299.364-010 DRAPERY AND UPHOLSTERY MEASURER; 299.387-010 DRAPERY AND UPHOLSTERY ESTIMATOR; 869.367-014 MEASURER

49999C SALES CONSULTANTS. OOH Title/s: Retail Sales Workers

Select, recommend, or purchase merchandise or services for customers shopping either in person or by telephone at department or specialty stores. Include personal shoppers and wedding consultants. Accompanies customer when shopping or shops for customer to purchase specific merchandise. Recommends, displays, and sells trousseau for bride, and attire for attendants, and advises on selection of tableware, stationery, flowers, and caterers. Provides customers with catalogs, promotional material and information, price of merchandise, shipping time and costs, and store services. Takes orders and prepares special order worksheet for such items as decorated cakes, cut flowers, personalized stationery, and merchandise rentals. Answers customers' telephone, mail, and in-person inquiries and di-

rects customers to appropriate sales area. Resolves customer complaints and requests for refunds, exchanges, repairs, replacements, and adjustments. Issues temporary customer identification cards in group buying stores, such as military shops and special discount stores. Arranges for gift wrapping, monogramming, printing, and fabrication of such items as desk nameplates or rubber stamps. Approves customers' checks and provides checking service according to exchange policy. Keeps record of services in progress, notifies customer when service is completed, and accepts payment for services. Arranges for photographers to take pictures, and attends rehearsals to advise wedding party regarding etiquette. Keeps records of items in layaway, receives and posts customer payments, and prepares and forwards delinquent notices.
Yearly Earnings: $26,312
Education: Moderate-term O-J-T
Knowledge: Sales and Marketing; Customer and Personal Service
Abilities: Visual Color Discrimination; Speech Recognition
Skills: Persuasion; Negotiation; Service Orientation
General Work Activities: Selling or Influencing Others; Performing for or Working with Public
Job Characteristics: Objective or Subjective Information; Job-Required Social Interaction; Persuade Someone to a Course of Action; Provide a Service to Others; Deal with External Customers; Frequency in Conflict Situations; Deal with Unpleasant or Angry People; Walking or Running
GOE Group/s: 08.02.06 General Sales: Services; 09.04.02 Customer Services: Sales Services
CIP Program/s: 080101 Apparel and Accessories Marketing Operations, General; 080102 Fashion Merchandising; 080205 Personal Services Marketing Operations; 080705 General Retailing Operations; 080706 General Selling Skills and Sales Operations; 200301 Clothing, Apparel and Textile Workers and Managers, General; 200306 Fashion and Fabric Consultant; 200601 Custodial, Housekeeping and Home Services Workers and Managers; 200606 Homemaker's Aide
Related DOT Job/s: 296.357-010 PERSONAL SHOPPER; 299.357-018 WEDDING CONSULTANT; 299.367-010 CUSTOMER-SERVICE CLERK

49999D ALL OTHER SALES AND RELATED WORKERS. OOH Title/s: Retail Sales Workers

All other sales and related workers not classified separately above.
Yearly Earnings: $26,312
Education: Moderate-term O-J-T
GOE Group/s: 01.06.03 Craft Arts: Hand Lettering, Painting and Decorating; 05.09.01 Material Control: Shipping, Receiving, and Stock Checking; 05.09.03 Material Control: Verifying, Recording, and Marking; 07.05.03 Records Processing: Record Preparation and Maintenance; 08.01.03 Sales Technology: Purchasing and Sales
CIP Program/s: 081203 Vehicle Parts and Accessories Marketing Operations; 081208 Vehicle Marketing Operations; 200301 Clothing, Apparel and Textile Workers and Managers, General; 200306 Fashion and Fabric Consultant
Related DOT Job/s: 296.367-010 AUTOMOBILE LOCATOR; 296.367-014 COMPARISON SHOPPER; 299.364-014 GIFT WRAPPER; 299.387-018 STAMP CLASSIFIER; 299.667-014 STOCK CHECKER, APPAREL

Section 5
Administrative Support Workers

Administrative Supervisors

51002A FIRST-LINE SUPERVISORS, CUSTOMER SERVICE. OOH Title/s: Clerical Supervisors and Managers; Material Recording, Scheduling, Dispatching, and Distributing Occupations

Supervise and coordinate activities of workers involved in providing customer service. Supervises and coordinates activities of workers engaged in clerical, administrative support, or service activities. Schedules workers according to workload to meet necessary deadlines. Observes and evaluates workers' performance. Issues instructions and assigns duties to workers. Trains and instructs employees. Hires and discharges workers. Communicates with other departments and management to resolve problems and expedite work. Interprets and communicates work procedures and company policies to staff. Helps workers in resolving problems and completing work. Resolves complaints and answers questions of customers regarding services and procedures. Reviews and checks work of subordinates, such as reports, records, and applications, for accuracy and content, and corrects errors. Prepares, maintains, and submits reports and records, such as budgets and operational and personnel reports. Makes recommendations to management concerning staff and improvement of procedures. Plans and develops improved procedures. Requisitions or purchases supplies.

Yearly Earnings: $27,976

Education: Work experience in a related occupation

Knowledge: Administration and Management; Clerical; Economics and Accounting; Customer and Personal Service; Personnel and Human Resources; Psychology; Sociology and Anthropology; Therapy and Counseling; Education and Training; Law, Government, and Jurisprudence; Communications and Media

Abilities: Written Expression; Fluency of Ideas; Originality; Mathematical Reasoning; Number Facility; Memorization; Perceptual Speed; Near Vision; Speech Recognition; Speech Clarity

Skills: Speaking; Critical Thinking; Learning Strategies; Monitoring; Social Perceptiveness; Coordination; Persuasion; Negotiation; Instructing; Service Orientation; Problem Identification; Idea Evaluation; Implementation Planning; Visioning; Systems Perception; Identification of Key Causes; Systems Evaluation; Time Management; Management of Financial Resources; Management of Material Resources; Management of Personnel Resources

General Work Activities: Developing Objectives and Strategies; Scheduling Work and Activities; Documenting/Recording Information; Communicating with Other Workers; Establishing and Maintaining Relationships; Resolving Conflicts, Negotiating with Others; Performing for or Working with Public; Coordinating Work and Activities of Others; Developing and Building Teams; Teaching Others; Guiding, Directing and Motivating Subordinates; Coaching and Developing Others; Provide Consultation and Advice to Others; Performing Administrative Activities; Staffing Organizational Units; Monitoring and Controlling Resources

Job Characteristics: Job-Required Social Interaction; Supervise, Coach, Train Others; Provide a Service to Others; Take a Position Opposed to Others; Deal with External Customers; Coordinate or Lead Others; Responsibility for Outcomes and Results; Frequency in Conflict Situations; Deal with Unpleasant or Angry People; Walking or Running; Frustrating Circumstances

GOE Group/s: 05.07.05 Quality Control: Petroleum; 05.09.01 Material Control: Shipping, Receiving, and Stock Checking; 05.12.01 Elemental Work: Mechanical: Supervision; 07.01.02 Administrative Detail: Administration; 07.01.04 Administrative Detail: Financial Work; 07.02.02 Mathematical Detail: Accounting; 07.02.04 Mathematical Detail: Billing and Rate Computation; 07.03.01 Financial Detail: Paying and Receiving; 07.04.01 Oral Communications: Interviewing; 07.04.02 Oral Communications: Order, Complaint, and Claims Handling; 07.04.04 Oral Communications: Reception and Information Giving; 07.04.05 Oral Communications: Information Transmitting and Receiving; 07.04.06 Oral Communications: Switchboard Services; 07.05.01 Records Processing: Coordinating and Scheduling; 07.05.02 Records Processing: Record Verification and Proofing; 07.05.03 Records Processing: Record Preparation and Maintenance; 07.05.04 Records Processing: Routing and Distribution; 09.05.04 Attendant Services: Doorkeeping Services; 11.12.01 Contracts and Claims: Claims and Settlement

CIP Program/s: 080709 General Distribution Operations; 081104 Tourism Promotion Operations; 081105 Travel Services Marketing Operations; 120504 Food and Beverage/Restaurant Operations Manager; 430103 Criminal Justice/Law Enforcement Administration; 510704 Health Unit Manager/Ward Supervisor; 520201 Business Administration and Management, General; 520203 Logistics and Materials Management; 520204 Office Supervision and Management; 520205 Operations Management and Supervision; 520902 Hotel/Motel and Restaurant Management; 520903 Travel-Tourism Management

Related DOT Job/s: 168.167-058 MANAGER, CUSTOMER SERVICE; 205.137-014 SUPERVISOR, SURVEY WORKERS; 205.162-010 ADMITTING OFFICER; 209.132-014 TECHNICAL COORDINATOR; 209.137-014 METER READER, CHIEF; 211.132-010 TELLER, HEAD; 211.137-010 SUPERVISOR, CASHIERS; 211.137-014 SUPERVISOR, FOOD CHECKERS AND CASHIERS; 211.137-022 SUPERVISOR, TELLERS; 214.137-010 DOCUMENTATION SUPERVISOR; 214.137-014 SUPERVISOR, STATEMENT CLERKS; 214.137-022 SUPERVISOR, ACCOUNTS RECEIVABLE; 216.137-014 TRANSFER CLERK, HEAD; 222.137-014 LINEN-ROOM SUPERVISOR; 222.137-026 PETROLEUM-INSPECTOR SUPERVISOR; 230.137-018 SUPERVISOR, MAIL CARRIERS; 235.132-010 CENTRAL-OFFICE-OPERATOR SUPERVISOR; 237.137-010 SUPERVISOR, TELEPHONE INFORMATION; 237.137-014 SUPERVISOR, TRAVEL-INFORMATION CENTER; 238.137-010 MANAGER, RESERVATIONS; 238.137-014 SENIOR RESERVATIONS AGENT; 238.137-018 SUPERVISOR, GATE SERVICES; 238.137-022 SUPERVISOR, TICKET SALES; 239.137-014 CUSTOMER SERVICE REPRESENTATIVE SUPERVISOR; 241.137-010 SUPERVISOR, CREDIT AND LOAN COLLECTIONS; 241.137-014 SUPERVISOR, CUSTOMER-COMPLAINT SERVICE; 241.137-018 SUPERVISOR, CLAIMS; 247.137-010 SUPERVISOR, ADVERTISING-DISPATCH CLERKS; 247.137-014 SUPERVISOR, CLASSIFIED ADVERTISING; 248.137-018 SUPERVISOR, CUSTOMER SERVICES; 249.137-010 OFFICE SUPERVISOR, ANIMAL HOSPITAL; 249.137-014 SUPERVISOR, CONTACT AND SERVICE CLERKS; 249.137-018 SUPERVISOR, CORRESPONDENCE SECTION; 249.137-022 SUPERVISOR, CUSTOMER RECORDS DIVISION; 249.137-026 SUPERVISOR, ORDER TAKERS; 249.137-034 SUPERVISOR, LENDING ACTIVITIES; 249.167-010 AUTOMOBILE-CLUB-SAFETY-PROGRAM COORDINATOR; 295.137-010 SUPERVISOR, SAFETY DEPOSIT; 375.137-038 COMPLAINT EVALUATION SUPERVISOR; 379.132-010 SUPERVISOR, TELECOMMUNICATOR; 910.137-010 BAGGAGE-AND-MAIL AGENT; 910.137-038 STATION AGENT I; 939.137-010 CHIEF DISPATCHER; 959.137-014 DISPATCHER, SERVICE, CHIEF; 959.137-022 SUPERVISOR, HOME-ENERGY CONSULTANT

51002B FIRST-LINE SUPERVISORS, ADMINISTRATIVE SUPPORT. OOH Title/s: Clerical Supervisors and Managers; Material Recording, Scheduling, Dispatching, and Distributing Occupations

Supervise and coordinate activities of workers involved in providing administrative support. Supervises and coordinates activities of workers engaged in clerical, administrative support, or service activities. Directs workers in such activities as maintaining files, compiling and preparing reports, computing figures, or moving shipments. Plans, prepares, and revises work schedules and duty assignments according to budget allotments, customer needs, problems, workloads, and statistical forecasts. Evaluates subordinate job performance and conformance to regulations, and recommends appropriate personnel action. Oversees, coordinates, or performs activities associated with shipping, receiving, distribution, and transportation. Verifies completeness and accuracy of subordinates' work, computations, and records. Interviews, selects, and discharges employees. Consults with supervisor and other personnel to resolve problems, such as equipment performance, output quality, and work schedules. Reviews records and reports pertaining to such activities as production, operation, payroll, customer accounts, and shipping. Trains employees in work and safety procedures and company policies. Participates in work of subordinates to facilitate productivity or overcome difficult aspects of work. Examines procedures and recommends changes to save time, labor, and other costs and to improve quality control and operating efficiency. Maintains records of such matters as inventory, personnel, orders, supplies, and machine maintenance. Identifies and resolves discrepancies or errors. Compiles reports and information required by management or governmental agencies. Plans layout of stockroom, warehouse, or other storage areas, considering turnover, size, weight, and related factors pertaining to items stored. Inspects equipment for defects and notifies maintenance personnel or outside service contractors for repairs. Analyzes financial activities of establishment or department and assists in planning budget. Computes figures, such as balances, totals, and commissions. Requisitions supplies.

Yearly Earnings: $27,976

Education: Work experience in a related occupation

Knowledge: Administration and Management; Clerical; Economics and Accounting; Customer and Personal Service; Personnel and Human Resources; Mathematics; Psychology; Education and Training; Philosophy and Theology; Public Safety and Security; Law, Government, and Jurisprudence; Transportation

Abilities: Oral Comprehension; Written Comprehension; Oral Expression; Written Expression; Inductive Reasoning; Category Flexibility; Mathematical Reasoning; Number Facility; Memorization; Perceptual Speed; Time Sharing; Wrist-Finger Speed; Gross Body Equilibrium; Near Vision; Speech Recognition; Speech Clarity

Skills: Active Listening; Writing; Speaking; Learning Strategies; Monitoring; Social Perceptiveness; Coordination; Persuasion; Negotiation; Instructing; Information Organization; Idea Generation; Idea Evaluation; Implementation Planning; Systems Perception; Systems Evaluation; Time Management; Management of Financial Resources; Management of Material Resources; Management of Personnel Resources

General Work Activities: Estimating Needed Characteristics; Processing Information; Evaluating Information against Standards; Making Decisions and Solving Problems; Developing Objectives and Strategies; Scheduling Work and Activities; Organizing, Planning, and Prioritizing; Operating Vehicles or Equipment; Communicating with Other Workers; Establishing and Maintaining Relationships; Resolving Conflicts, Negotiating with Others; Coordinating Work and Activities of Others; Developing and Building Teams; Guiding, Directing and Motivating Subordinates; Coaching and Developing Others; Performing Administrative Activities; Staffing Organizational Units; Monitoring and Controlling Resources

Job Characteristics: Job-Required Social Interaction; Supervise, Coach, Train Others; Take a Position Opposed to Others; Coordinate or Lead Others; Responsibility for Outcomes and Results; Frequency in Conflict Situations; Deal with Unpleasant or Angry People; Sitting; Frustrating Circumstances; Importance of Being Aware of New Events

GOE Group/s: 05.09.01 Material Control: Shipping, Receiving, and Stock Checking; 05.09.02 Material Control: Estimating, Scheduling, and Record Keeping; 05.09.03 Material Control: Verifying, Recording, and Marking; 05.10.05 Crafts: Reproduction; 05.12.01 Elemental Work: Mechanical: Supervision; 06.02.01 Production Work: Supervision; 07.01.02 Administrative Detail: Administration; 07.01.04 Administrative Detail: Financial Work; 07.02.01 Mathematical Detail: Bookkeeping and Auditing; 07.02.02 Mathematical Detail: Accounting; 07.02.03 Mathematical Detail: Statistical Reporting and Analysis; 07.02.05 Mathematical Detail: Payroll and Timekeeping; 07.04.05 Oral Communications: Information Transmitting and Receiving; 07.04.06 Oral Communications: Switchboard Services; 07.05.01 Records Processing: Coordinating and Scheduling; 07.05.03 Records Processing: Record Preparation and Maintenance; 07.05.04 Records Processing: Routing and Distribution; 07.06.01 Clerical Machine Operation: Computer Operation; 07.06.02 Clerical Machine Operation: Keyboard Machine Operation; 07.07.02 Clerical Handling: Sorting and Distrubtion; 07.07.03 Clerical Handling: General Clerical Work; 11.02.04 Educational and Library Services: Library Services

CIP Program/s: 080709 General Distribution Operations; 110301 Data Processing Technologists and Technicians; 200301 Clothing, Apparel and Textile Workers and Managers, General; 200303 Commercial Garment and Apparel Worker; 430103 Criminal Justice/Law Enforcement Administration; 520201 Business Administration and Management, General; 520203 Logistics and Materials Management; 520204 Office Supervision and Management; 520205 Operations Management and Supervision; 521201 Management Information Systems and Business Data Processing; 521205 Business Computer Facilities Operator

Related DOT Job/s: 109.137-010 SHELVING SUPERVISOR; 202.132-010 SUPERVISOR, STENO POOL; 203.132-010 SUPERVISOR, TELEGRAPHIC-TYPEWRITER OPERATORS; 203.132-014 SUPERVISOR, TRANSCRIBING OPERATORS; 203.137-010 SUPERVISOR, WORD PROCESSING; 203.137-014 TYPING SECTION CHIEF; 206.137-010 SUPERVISOR, FILES; 207.137-010 CHIEF CLERK, PRINT SHOP; 209.132-010 SUPERVISOR, PERSONNEL CLERKS; 209.137-010 MAILROOM SUPERVISOR; 209.137-018 SUPERVISOR, AGENCY APPOINTMENTS; 209.137-026 SUPERVISOR, MARKING ROOM; 210.132-010 SUPERVISOR, AUDIT CLERKS; 211.137-018 SUPERVISOR, MONEY-ROOM; 213.132-010 SUPERVISOR, COMPUTER OPERATIONS; 214.137-018 RATE SUPERVISOR; 215.137-010 CREW SCHEDULER, CHIEF; 215.137-014 SUPERVISOR, PAYROLL; 215.137-018 SUPERVISOR, FORCE ADJUSTMENT; 216.132-010 SUPERVISOR, ACCOUNTING CLERKS; 216.132-014 SUPERVISOR, SECURITIES VAULT; 216.137-010 COST-AND-SALES-RECORD SUPERVISOR; 217.132-010 PROOF-MACHINE-OPERATOR SUPERVISOR; 219.132-010 SUPERVISOR, POLICY-CHANGE CLERKS; 219.132-014 SUPERVISOR, TRUST ACCOUNTS; 219.132-022 SUPERVISOR, UNDERWRITING CLERKS; 219.137-010 FIELD CASHIER; 221.132-010 CHIEF CLERK, MEASUREMENT DEPARTMENT; 221.137-010 CONTROL CLERK, HEAD; 221.137-014 SUPERVISOR, PRODUCTION CLERKS; 221.137-018 SUPERVISOR, PRODUCTION CONTROL; 222.137-010 FILM-VAULT SUPERVISOR; 222.137-018 MAGAZINE SUPERVISOR; 222.137-022 MAILROOM SUPERVISOR; 222.137-030 SHIPPING-AND-RECEIVING SUPERVISOR; 222.137-034 STOCK SUPERVISOR; 222.137-038 STOCK-CONTROL SUPERVISOR; 222.137-042 SUPERVISOR, ASSEMBLY STOCK; 222.137-046 TOOL-CRIB SUPERVISOR; 222.137-050 VAULT CASHIER; 229.137-010 SACK-DEPARTMENT SUPERVISOR; 229.137-014 YARD SUPERVISOR; 230.137-014 SUPERVISOR, DELIVERY DEPARTMENT; 235.132-014 COMMUNICATION-CENTER COORDINATOR; 235.137-010 TELEPHONE OPERATOR, CHIEF; 239.132-010 SUPERVISOR, TELEPHONE CLERKS; 239.137-018 ROUTE SUPERVISOR; 239.137-022 SERVICE OBSERVER, CHIEF; 239.137-026 SUPERVISOR, PUBLIC MESSAGE SERVICE; 243.137-010 SUPERVISOR, MAILS; 248.137-010 BOOKING SUPERVISOR; 248.137-014 PURCHASING-AND-CLAIMS SUPERVISOR; 249.137-030 SUPERVISOR, REAL-ESTATE OFFICE; 292.137-010 COIN-MACHINE-COLLECTOR

SUPERVISOR; 375.137-022 SECRETARY OF POLICE; 381.137-014 SUPERVISOR, CENTRAL SUPPLY; 789.137-010 BOXING-AND-PRESSING SUPERVISOR; 922.137-010 SENIOR-COMMISSARY AGENT; 959.137-010 DISPATCHER, CHIEF, SERVICE OR WORK; 959.137-018 ORDER DISPATCHER, CHIEF

Financial Transaction Workers

53102 TELLERS. OOH Title/s: Bank Tellers

Receive and pay out money. Keep records of money and negotiable instruments involved in a financial institution's various transactions. Receives checks and cash for deposit, verifies amount, and examines checks for endorsements. Cashes checks and pays out money after verification of signatures and customer balances. Counts currency, coins, and checks received for deposit, shipment to branch banks, or Federal Reserve Bank, by hand or currency-counting machine. Prepares daily inventory of currency, drafts, and travelers' checks. Examines coupons and bills presented for payment to verify issue, payment date, and amount due. Enters customers' transactions into computer to record transactions and issues computer-generated receipts. Issues checks to bond owners in settlement of transactions. Balances currency, coin, and checks in cash drawer at end of shift and calculates daily transactions. Quotes unit exchange rate, following daily international rate sheet or computer display. Removes deposits from automated teller machines and night depository, and counts and balances cash in them. Gives information to customer about foreign currency regulations, and computes exchange value and transaction fee for currency exchange. Explains, promotes, or sells products or services, such as travelers' checks, savings bonds, money orders, and cashier's checks. Composes, types, and mails correspondence relating to discrepancies, errors, and outstanding unpaid items.

Yearly Earnings: $15,392
Education: Short-term O-J-T
Knowledge: Clerical; Economics and Accounting; Sales and Marketing; Customer and Personal Service; Foreign Language; Law, Government, and Jurisprudence
Abilities: Number Facility; Memorization; Perceptual Speed; Wrist-Finger Speed; Near Vision; Speech Recognition
Skills: Service Orientation
General Work Activities: Evaluating Information against Standards; Establishing and Maintaining Relationships; Selling or Influencing Others; Performing for or Working with Public; Performing Administrative Activities; Monitoring and Controlling Resources
Job Characteristics: Job-Required Social Interaction; Provide a Service to Others; Deal with External Customers; Deal with Unpleasant or Angry People; Making Repetitive Motions; Degree of Automation; Importance of Being Exact or Accurate; Importance of Being Sure All is Done
GOE Group/s: 07.02.02 Mathematical Detail: Accounting; 07.03.01 Financial Detail: Paying and Receiving; 08.01.03 Sales Technology: Purchasing and Sales
CIP Program/s: 080401 Financial Services Marketing Operations; 520801 Finance, General; 520803 Banking and Financial Support Services; 521403 International Business Marketing
Related DOT Job/s: 211.362-014 FOREIGN BANKNOTE TELLER-TRADER; 211.362-018 TELLER; 211.382-010 TELLER, VAULT; 219.462-010 COUPON CLERK

53105 NEW ACCOUNTS CLERKS. OOH Title/s: Interviewing and New Accounts Clerks

Interview persons desiring to open bank accounts. Explain banking services available to prospective customers and assist them in preparing application form. Interviews customer to obtain information needed to open account or rent safe-deposit box. Assists customer in completing application forms for loans, accounts, or safe-deposit boxes, using typewriter or computer, and obtains signature. Answers customer questions and explains available services, such as deposit accounts, bonds, and securities. Enters account information in computer, and files forms or other documents. Collects and records fees and funds for deposit from customer, and issues receipt, using computer. Issues initial and replacement safe-deposit key to customer, and admits customer to vault. Investigates and corrects errors upon customer request, according to customer and bank records, using calculator or computer. Executes wire transfers of funds. Obtains credit records from reporting agency. Schedules repairs for locks on safe-deposit box.

Yearly Earnings: $18,876
Education: Work experience in a related occupation
Knowledge: Clerical; Economics and Accounting; Sales and Marketing; Customer and Personal Service; Computers and Electronics
Abilities: Number Facility; Memorization
Skills: None above average
General Work Activities: Performing for or Working with Public
Job Characteristics: Job-Required Social Interaction; Provide a Service to Others; Deal with External Customers; Deal with Unpleasant or Angry People; Sitting
GOE Group/s: 07.04.01 Oral Communications: Interviewing
CIP Program/s: 520801 Finance, General; 520803 Banking and Financial Support Services
Related DOT Job/s: 205.362-026 CUSTOMER SERVICE REPRESENTATIVE; 295.367-022 SAFE-DEPOSIT-BOX RENTAL CLERK

53108 TRANSIT CLERKS. OOH Title/s: Billing Clerks and Billing Machine Operators

Sort, record, prove, and prepare transit items for mailing to or from out-of-city banks to ensure correct routing and prompt collection. Operates machines to encode, add, cancel, photocopy, and sort checks, drafts, and money orders for collection and prove records of transactions. Places checks into machine that encodes amounts in magnetic ink, adds amounts, and cancels checks. Enters amount of each check, using keyboard. Places encoded checks in sorter and activates machine to automatically microfilm, sort, and total checks according to bank drawn on. Reads check and enters data, such as amount, bank, or account number, using keyboard. Records, sorts, and proves other transaction documents, such as deposit and withdrawal slips, using proof machine. Encodes correct amount, or prepares transaction correction record if error is found. Observes panel light to note check machine cannot read. Compares machine totals to listing received with batch of checks, and rechecks each item if totals differ. Enters commands to transfer data from machine to computer. Manually sorts and lists items for proof or collection. Bundles sorted check with tape listing each item to prepare checks, drawn on other banks, for collection. Cleans equipment and replaces printer ribbons, film, and tape. Operates separate photocopying machine.

Yearly Earnings: $22,360
Education: Short-term O-J-T
Knowledge: Clerical; Computers and Electronics
Abilities: None above average
Skills: None above average
General Work Activities: None above average
Job Characteristics: Making Repetitive Motions; Importance of Repeating Same Tasks
GOE Group/s: 07.06.02 Clerical Machine Operation: Keyboard Machine Operation
CIP Program/s: 520302 Accounting Technician; 520801 Finance, General; 520803 Banking and Financial Support Services
Related DOT Job/s: 217.382-010 PROOF-MACHINE OPERATOR

53114 CREDIT AUTHORIZERS. OOH Title/s: Credit Clerks and Authorizers

Authorize credit charges against customers' accounts. Verifies credit standing of customer from information in files, and approves or disapproves credit, based on predetermined standards. Receives charge slip or credit application by mail, or receives information from salespeople or merchants by phone. Files sales slips in customer's ledger for billing purposes. Prepares credit cards or charge account plates. Keeps record of customer's charges and payments, and mails charge statement to customer.

Yearly Earnings: $21,944
Education: Short-term O-J-T
Knowledge: Clerical
Abilities: None above average
Skills: None above average
General Work Activities: None above average
Job Characteristics: Provide a Service to Others; Deal with External Customers; Deal with Unpleasant or Angry People; Sitting
GOE Group/s: 07.05.02 Records Processing: Record Verification and Proofing
CIP Program/s: 520801 Finance, General; 520803 Banking and Financial Support Services
Related DOT Job/s: 249.367-022 CREDIT AUTHORIZER

53117 CREDIT CHECKERS. OOH Title/s: Credit Clerks and Authorizers

Investigate history and credit standing of individuals or business establishments applying for credit. Telephone or write to credit departments of business and service establishments to obtain information about applicant's credit standing. Interviews credit applicant by telephone or in person to obtain financial and personal data for credit report. Obtains information from banks, credit bureaus, and other credit services, and provides reciprocal information if requested. Contacts former employers and other acquaintances to verify references, employment, health history, and social behavior. Compiles and analyzes credit information gathered by investigation. Examines city directories and public records to verify residence property ownership, bankruptcies, liens, arrest record, or unpaid taxes of applicant. Telephones subscriber to relay requested information or sends subscriber typewritten or credit report. Prepares reports of findings and recommendations, using typewriter or computer.

Yearly Earnings: $21,216
Education: Short-term O-J-T
Knowledge: None above average
Abilities: Gross Body Equilibrium; Speech Clarity
Skills: Active Listening; Speaking
General Work Activities: Getting Information Needed to Do the Job
Job Characteristics: Job-Required Social Interaction; Deal with External Customers; Frequency in Conflict Situations; Deal with Unpleasant or Angry People; Sitting; Frustrating Circumstances
GOE Group/s: 07.05.02 Records Processing: Record Verification and Proofing; 07.05.03 Records Processing: Record Preparation and Maintenance
CIP Program/s: 000000 NO CIP ASSIGNED
Related DOT Job/s: 209.362-018 CREDIT REFERENCE CLERK; 237.367-014 CALL-OUT OPERATOR; 241.267-030 INVESTIGATOR

53121 LOAN AND CREDIT CLERKS. OOH Title/s: Adjusters, Investigators, and Collectors

Assemble documents, prepare papers, process applications, and complete transactions of individuals applying for loans and credit. Loan clerks review loan papers to ensure completeness; operate typewriters to prepare correspondence, reports, and loan documents from draft; and complete transactions between loan establishment, borrowers, and sellers upon approval of loan. Credit clerks interview applicants to obtain personal and financial data; determine credit worthiness; process applications; and notify customer of acceptance or rejection of credit. Exclude loan interviewers. Verifies and examines information and accuracy of loan application and closing documents. Prepares and types loan applications, closing documents, legal documents, letters, forms, government notices, and checks, using computer. Interviews loan applicant to obtain personal and financial data and to assist in filling out application. Assembles and compiles documents for closing, such as title abstract, insurance form, loan form, and tax receipt. Records applications for loan and credit, loan information, and disbursement of funds, using computer. Submits loan application with recommendation for underwriting approval. Contacts customer by mail, telephone, or in person concerning acceptance or rejection of application. Contacts credit bureaus, employers, and other sources to check applicant credit and personal references. Checks value of customer collateral to be held as loan security. Calculates, reviews, and corrects errors on interest, principal, payment, and closing costs, using computer or calculator. Answers questions and advises customer regarding loans and transactions. Schedules and conducts closing of mortgage transaction. Presents loan and repayment schedule to customer. Establishes credit limit and grants extension of credit on overdue accounts. Files and maintains loan records. Orders property insurance or mortgage insurance policies to ensure protection against loss on mortgaged property. Accepts payment on accounts. Reviews customer accounts to determine whether payments are made on time and that other loan terms are being followed.

Yearly Earnings: $20,904
Education: Short-term O-J-T
Knowledge: Clerical; Economics and Accounting; Customer and Personal Service; Law, Government, and Jurisprudence
Abilities: Mathematical Reasoning; Number Facility; Perceptual Speed; Wrist-Finger Speed; Near Vision; Speech Recognition
Skills: None above average
General Work Activities: Operating Vehicles or Equipment; Performing Administrative Activities
Job Characteristics: Provide a Service to Others; Deal with External Customers; Deal with Unpleasant or Angry People; Sitting
GOE Group/s: 07.01.04 Administrative Detail: Financial Work; 07.04.01 Oral Communications: Interviewing; 07.05.02 Records Processing: Record Verification and Proofing
CIP Program/s: 520801 Finance, General; 520803 Banking and Financial Support Services
Related DOT Job/s: 205.367-022 CREDIT CLERK; 219.362-038 MORTGAGE-CLOSING CLERK; 219.367-046 DISBURSEMENT CLERK; 249.362-014 MORTGAGE CLERK; 249.362-018 MORTGAGE LOAN CLOSER; 249.362-022 MORTGAGE LOAN PROCESSOR

53123 ADJUSTMENT CLERKS. OOH Title/s: Adjusters, Investigators, and Collectors; Material Recording, Scheduling, Dispatching, and Distributing Occupations

Investigate and resolve customers' inquiries concerning merchandise, service, billing, or credit rating. Examine pertinent information to determine accuracy of customers' complaints and responsibility for errors. Notify customers and appropriate personnel of findings, adjustments, and recommendations, such as exchange of merchandise, refund of money, credit to customers' accounts, or adjustment to customers' bills. Reviews claims adjustments with dealer, examines parts claimed to be defective, and approves or disapproves of dealer's claim. Notifies customer and designated personnel of findings and recommendations, such as ex-

changing merchandise or refunding money, or adjustment of bill. Examines weather conditions and number of days in billing period, and reviews meter accounts for errors which might explain high utility charges. Writes work order. Prepares reports showing volume, types, and disposition of claims handled. Compares merchandise with original requisition and information on invoice, and prepares invoice for returned goods. Orders tests to detect product malfunction, and determines if defect resulted from faulty construction. Trains dealers or service personnel in construction of products, service operations, and customer service.
Yearly Earnings: $21,216
Education: Short-term O-J-T
Knowledge: Economics and Accounting
Abilities: None above average
Skills: Instructing
General Work Activities: Resolving Conflicts, Negotiating with Others; Performing for or Working with Public
Job Characteristics: Supervise, Coach, Train Others; Take a Position Opposed to Others; Deal with External Customers; Frequency in Conflict Situations; Deal with Unpleasant or Angry People; Sitting
GOE Group/s: 05.09.01 Material Control: Shipping, Receiving, and Stock Checking; 07.05.02 Records Processing: Record Verification and Proofing; 11.12.01 Contracts and Claims: Claims and Settlement
CIP Program/s: 081203 Vehicle Parts and Accessories Marketing Operations; 520401 Administrative Assistant/Secretarial Science, General; 520408 General Office/Clerical and Typing Services
Related DOT Job/s: 191.167-022 SERVICE REPRESENTATIVE; 209.587-042 RETURN-TO-FACTORY CLERK; 221.387-014 COMPLAINT CLERK; 241.267-034 INVESTIGATOR, UTILITY-BILL COMPLAINTS; 241.367-014 CUSTOMER-COMPLAINT CLERK; 241.367-034 TIRE ADJUSTER; 241.387-010 CLAIMS CLERK

53126 STATEMENT CLERKS. OOH Title/s: Brokerage Clerks and Statement Clerks

Prepare and distribute bank statements to customers, answer inquiries, and reconcile discrepancies in records and accounts. Compares previously prepared bank statements with canceled checks, prepares statements for distribution to customers, and reconciles discrepancies in records and accounts. Recovers checks returned to customer in error, adjusts customer account, and answers inquiries. Matches statements with batches of canceled checks by account numbers. Inserts statements and canceled checks in envelopes and affixes postage, or stuffs envelopes and meters postage. Routes statements for mailing or over-the-counter delivery to customers. Keeps canceled checks and customer signature files. Posts stop-payment notices to prevent payment of protested checks. Encodes and cancels checks, using machine. Takes orders for imprinted checks.
Yearly Earnings: $20,748
Education: Short-term O-J-T
Knowledge: Clerical; Economics and Accounting; Computers and Electronics
Abilities: Perceptual Speed
Skills: None above average
General Work Activities: None above average
Job Characteristics: Provide a Service to Others; Deal with External Customers; Frequency in Conflict Situations; Deal with Unpleasant or Angry People; Sitting
GOE Group/s: 07.02.02 Mathematical Detail: Accounting
CIP Program/s: 520302 Accounting Technician
Related DOT Job/s: 214.362-046 STATEMENT CLERK

53128 BROKERAGE CLERKS. OOH Title/s: Brokerage Clerks and Statement Clerks

Perform clerical duties involving the purchase or sale of securities. Duties include writing orders for stock purchases and sales, computing transfer taxes, verifying stock transactions, accepting and delivering securities, informing customers of stock price fluctuations, computing equity, distributing dividends, and keeping records of daily transactions and holdings. Records and documents security transactions, such as purchases, sales, conversions, redemptions, and payments, using computers, accounting ledgers, and certificate records. Prepares reports summarizing daily transactions and earnings for individual customer accounts. Computes total holdings, dividends, interest, transfer taxes, brokerage fees, and commissions, and allocates appropriate payments to customers. Prepares forms, such as receipts, withdrawal orders, transmittal papers, and transfer confirmations, based on transaction requests from stockholders. Corresponds with customers and confers with coworkers to answer inquiries, discuss market fluctuations, and resolve account problems. Schedules and coordinates transfer and delivery of security certificates between companies, departments, and customers. Monitors daily stock prices and computes fluctuations to determine the need for additional collateral to secure loans. Verifies ownership and transaction information and dividend distribution instructions to ensure conformance with governmental regulations, using stock records and reports. Files, types, and operates standard office machines.
Yearly Earnings: $20,748
Education: Short-term O-J-T
Knowledge: Clerical; Economics and Accounting; Sales and Marketing; Computers and Electronics; Mathematics; Communications and Media
Abilities: Written Comprehension; Mathematical Reasoning; Number Facility; Wrist-Finger Speed
Skills: Active Listening; Service Orientation
General Work Activities: Getting Information Needed to Do the Job; Monitoring Processes, Material, or Surroundings; Scheduling Work and Activities; Operating Vehicles or Equipment; Communicating with Persons Outside Organization; Performing for or Working with Public; Performing Administrative Activities
Job Characteristics: Persuade Someone to a Course of Action; Provide a Service to Others; Deal with External Customers; Frequency in Conflict Situations; Sitting; Consequence of Error; Frustrating Circumstances; Importance of Being Aware of New Events
GOE Group/s: 07.01.04 Administrative Detail: Financial Work; 07.02.02 Mathematical Detail: Accounting
CIP Program/s: 520302 Accounting Technician; 520401 Administrative Assistant/Secretarial Science, General; 520407 Information Processing/Data Entry Technician
Related DOT Job/s: 216.362-046 TRANSFER CLERK; 216.382-046 MARGIN CLERK II; 216.482-034 DIVIDEND CLERK; 219.362-018 BROKERAGE CLERK II; 219.362-054 SECURITIES CLERK; 219.482-010 BROKERAGE CLERK I

Insurance Specialists

53302 INSURANCE ADJUSTERS, EXAMINERS, AND INVESTIGATORS. OOH Title/s: Adjusters, Investigators, and Collectors

Investigate, analyze, and determine the extent of insurance company's liability concerning personal, casualty, or property loss or damages, and attempt to effect settlement with claimants. Correspond with or interview medical specialists, agents, witnesses, or claimants to compile information. Calculate benefit payments and approve payment of claims within a certain monetary limit. Exclude insurance sales agents, insurance policy processing clerks, and claims clerks. Investigates and assesses damage to property. Interviews or corresponds with claimant and witnesses, consults police and hospital records, and inspects property damage to determine extent of liability. Interviews or corresponds with agents and claimants to correct errors or omissions and to investigate questionable entries. Analyzes information gathered by investigation and reports findings and recommendations. Negotiates claim settlements and recommends litigation when settlement cannot be negotiated. Examines titles to property to determine validity and acts as company agent in transactions with property owners. Examines claims form and other records to determine insurance coverage. Collects evidence to support contested claims in court. Prepares report of findings of investigation. Communicates with former associates to verify employment record and to obtain background information regarding persons or businesses applying for credit. Refers questionable claims to investigator or claims adjuster for investigation or settlement. Obtains credit information from banks and other credit services.

Yearly Earnings: $23,764
Education: Long-term O-J-T
Knowledge: Economics and Accounting; Personnel and Human Resources; Public Safety and Security; Law, Government, and Jurisprudence
Abilities: Written Comprehension; Oral Expression; Written Expression; Inductive Reasoning; Mathematical Reasoning; Number Facility; Near Vision
Skills: Reading Comprehension; Active Listening; Writing; Speaking; Critical Thinking; Persuasion; Negotiation; Information Gathering; Information Organization; Synthesis/Reorganization; Solution Appraisal; Identification of Key Causes; Judgment and Decision Making; Systems Evaluation; Management of Financial Resources
General Work Activities: Getting Information Needed to Do the Job; Monitoring Processes, Material, or Surroundings; Judging Qualities of Things, Services, People; Processing Information; Evaluating Information against Standards; Documenting/Recording Information; Communicating with Other Workers; Communicating with Persons Outside Organization; Resolving Conflicts, Negotiating with Others; Monitoring and Controlling Resources
Job Characteristics: Objective or Subjective Information; Job-Required Social Interaction; Take a Position Opposed to Others; Deal with External Customers; Frequency in Conflict Situations; Deal with Unpleasant or Angry People; Deal with Physical, Aggressive People; Radiation; Frustrating Circumstances
GOE Group/s: 11.12.01 Contracts and Claims: Claims and Settlement
CIP Program/s: 081001 Insurance Marketing Operations; 520801 Finance, General; 520803 Banking and Financial Support Services; 520805 Insurance and Risk Management; 521501 Real Estate
Related DOT Job/s: 191.167-014 CLAIM AGENT; 241.217-010 CLAIM ADJUSTER; 241.267-018 CLAIM EXAMINER

53305 INSURANCE APPRAISERS, AUTO DAMAGE. OOH Title/s: Adjusters, Investigators, and Collectors

Appraise automobile or other vehicle damage to determine cost of repair for insurance claim settlement and seek agreement with automotive repair shop on cost of repair. Prepare insurance forms to indicate repair cost or cost estimates and recommendations. Estimates parts and labor to repair damage, using standard automotive labor and parts-cost manuals and knowledge of automotive repair. Reviews repair-cost estimates with automobile-repair shop to secure agreement on cost of repairs. Examines damaged vehicle to determine extent of structural, body, mechanical, electrical, or interior damage. Prepares insurance forms to indicate repair-cost estimates and recommendations. Evaluates practicality of repair as opposed to payment of market value of vehicle before accident. Determines salvage value on total-loss vehicle. Arranges to have damage appraised by another appraiser to resolve disagreement with shop on repair cost.

Yearly Earnings: $23,764
Education: Long-term O-J-T
Knowledge: Economics and Accounting
Abilities: Mathematical Reasoning; Number Facility
Skills: Negotiation
General Work Activities: Estimating Needed Characteristics
Job Characteristics: Take a Position Opposed to Others; Deal with External Customers; Frequency in Conflict Situations; Deal with Unpleasant or Angry People; Deal with Physical, Aggressive People
GOE Group/s: 11.12.01 Contracts and Claims: Claims and Settlement
CIP Program/s: 081001 Insurance Marketing Operations
Related DOT Job/s: 241.267-014 APPRAISER, AUTOMOBILE DAMAGE

53311 INSURANCE CLAIMS CLERKS. OOH Title/s: Adjusters, Investigators, and Collectors

Obtain information from insured or designated persons for purpose of settling claim with insurance carrier. Contacts insured or other involved persons for missing information. Prepares and reviews insurance-claim forms and related documents for completeness. Reviews insurance policy to determine coverage. Posts or attaches information to claim file. Transmits claims for payment or further investigation. Calculates amount of claim.

Yearly Earnings: $20,904
Education: Short-term O-J-T
Knowledge: Clerical; Economics and Accounting; Law, Government, and Jurisprudence
Abilities: Number Facility; Near Vision; Speech Recognition
Skills: None above average
General Work Activities: Processing Information; Evaluating Information against Standards; Performing Administrative Activities
Job Characteristics: Frequency in Conflict Situations; Deal with Unpleasant or Angry People; Sitting
GOE Group/s: 07.04.02 Oral Communications: Order, Complaint, and Claims Handling; 07.05.02 Records Processing: Record Verification and Proofing
CIP Program/s: 520801 Finance, General; 520803 Banking and Financial Support Services
Related DOT Job/s: 205.367-018 CLAIMS CLERK II; 241.362-010 CLAIMS CLERK I

53314 INSURANCE POLICY PROCESSING CLERKS. OOH Title/s: Adjusters, Investigators, and Collectors

Process applications for, changes to, reinstatement of, and cancellation of insurance policies. Duties include reviewing insurance applications to ensure that all questions have been answered, compiling data on insurance policy changes, changing policy records to conform to insured party's specifications, compiling data on lapsed insurance policies to determine automatic reinstatement according to company policies, canceling insurance policies as requested by agents, and verifying the accuracy of insurance company records. Exclude insurance claims clerks and banking insurance clerks. Reviews and verifies data, such as age, name, address, and principal sum and value of property on insurance applications and policies. Compares information from application to criteria for policy reinstatement, and approves reinstatement when criteria are met. Examines letters from policy

holders or agents, original insurance applications, and other company documents to determine changes are needed and effects of changes. Computes refund and prepares and mails cancellation letter with canceled policy to policy holder. Checks computations of interest accrued, premiums due, and settlement surrender on loan values. Calculates premiums, commissions, adjustments, and new reserve requirements, using insurance rate standards. Corresponds with insured or agent to obtain information or inform them of status or changes to application of account. Notifies insurance agent and accounting department of policy cancellation. Receives computer printout of policy cancellations or obtains cancellation card from file. Transcribes data to worksheets and enters data into computer for use in preparing documents and adjusting accounts. Collects initial premiums, issues receipts, and compiles periodic reports for management.
Yearly Earnings: $20,904
Education: Short-term O-J-T
Knowledge: Clerical
Abilities: Mathematical Reasoning; Number Facility; Speech Clarity
Skills: None above average
General Work Activities: None above average
Job Characteristics: Deal with External Customers; Sitting
GOE Group/s: 07.02.02 Mathematical Detail: Accounting; 07.05.02 Records Processing: Record Verification and Proofing; 07.05.03 Records Processing: Record Preparation and Maintenance
CIP Program/s: 520401 Administrative Assistant/Secretarial Science, General; 520408 General Office/Clerical and Typing Services; 520801 Finance, General; 520803 Banking and Financial Support Services
Related DOT Job/s: 203.382-014 CANCELLATION CLERK; 209.382-014 SPECIAL-CERTIFICATE DICTATOR; 209.687-018 REVIEWER; 219.362-042 POLICY-CHANGE CLERK; 219.362-050 REVIVAL CLERK; 219.482-014 INSURANCE CHECKER

Investigators and Collectors

53502 WELFARE ELIGIBILITY WORKERS AND INTERVIEWERS. OOH Title/s: Adjusters, Investigators, and Collectors; Social Workers; Inspectors and Compliance Officers, Except Construction

Interview and investigate applicants and recipients to determine eligibility for use of social programs and agency resources. Duties include recording and evaluating personal and financial data obtained from individuals; initiating procedures to grant, modify, deny, or terminate eligibility for various aid programs; authorizing grant amounts; and preparing reports. These workers generally receive specialized training and assist social service caseworkers. Interviews and investigates applicants for public assistance to gather information pertinent to their application. Selects and refers eligible applicants to public assistance or public housing agencies. Records and evaluates personal and financial data to determine initial or continuing eligibility. Initiates procedures to grant, modify, deny, or terminate eligibility and grants for various assistance programs. Authorizes amounts of grants, money payments, food stamps, medical care, or other general assistance. Prepares regular and special reports, keeps records of assigned cases, and submits individual recommendations. Computes public housing rent in proportion to eligible tenant's income. Prepares and assists applicants in completion of routine intake and personnel forms. Conducts annual, interim, and special housing reviews and home visits to ensure conformance to regulations. Explains eligibility requirements, form completion requirements, community resources for financial assistance, housing opportunities, and tenant selection methods. Reviews training approval forms and payment vouchers for completeness and accuracy. Interprets and explains rules and regulations governing eligibility and grants, payment methods, and applicant's legal rights. Receives and records security deposits and advance rents from selected tenants.
Yearly Earnings: $23,608
Education: Moderate-term O-J-T
Knowledge: Clerical; Psychology; Sociology and Anthropology; Therapy and Counseling; Law, Government, and Jurisprudence
Abilities: None above average
Skills: Active Listening; Speaking; Social Perceptiveness; Service Orientation; Information Gathering; Identification of Key Causes; Judgment and Decision Making; Systems Evaluation; Management of Financial Resources
General Work Activities: Evaluating Information against Standards; Developing Objectives and Strategies; Communicating with Persons Outside Organization; Establishing and Maintaining Relationships; Assisting and Caring for Others; Selling or Influencing Others; Performing for or Working with Public; Performing Administrative Activities; Monitoring and Controlling Resources
Job Characteristics: Objective or Subjective Information; Job-Required Social Interaction; Persuade Someone to a Course of Action; Provide a Service to Others; Deal with External Customers; Frequency in Conflict Situations; Deal with Unpleasant or Angry People; Deal with Physical, Aggressive People; Sitting; Frustrating Circumstances
GOE Group/s: 07.01.01 Administrative Detail: Interviewing; 07.04.01 Oral Communications: Interviewing
CIP Program/s: 440201 Community Organization, Resources and Services; 440701 Social Work; 520401 Administrative Assistant/Secretarial Science, General
Related DOT Job/s: 168.267-038 ELIGIBILITY-AND-OCCUPANCY INTERVIEWER; 169.167-018 CONTACT REPRESENTATIVE; 195.267-010 ELIGIBILITY WORKER; 195.267-018 PATIENT-RESOURCES-AND-REIMBURSEMENT AGENT; 205.367-046 REHABILITATION CLERK

53505 INVESTIGATORS, CLERICAL. OOH Title/s: Administrative Support Occupations

Contact persons or businesses by telephone to verify employment records, health history, and moral and social behavior. Examine city directories and public records. Write reports on findings and recommendations. Exclude insurance, credit, and welfare investigators. Contacts individuals and businesses to gather information to process employment or other applications or to evaluate business practices. Locates and examines directories and business or public records to ascertain or verify information relevant to subject being investigated. Interviews individuals to ascertain information relevant to subject being investigated. Prepares reports of findings and recommendations, using typewriter or computer. Analyzes information to arrive at decision and make recommendation relevant to subject being investigated. Locates and examines merchandise or other physical objects to verify against inventory or other business records.
Yearly Earnings: $22,256
Education: Moderate-term O-J-T
Knowledge: Clerical; Computers and Electronics
Abilities: None above average
Skills: Speaking
General Work Activities: None above average
Job Characteristics: Objective or Subjective Information; Job-Required Social Interaction; Persuade Someone to a Course of Action; Deal with External Customers; Frequency in Conflict Situations; Deal with Unpleasant or Angry People; Deal with Physical, Aggressive People; Sitting; Frustrating Circumstances
GOE Group/s: 07.05.02 Records Processing: Record Verification and Proofing; 11.06.03 Finance: Risk and Profit Analysis; 11.10.01 Regulations Enforcement: Finance

CIP Program/s: 010501 Agricultural Supplies Retailing and Wholesaling; 081001 Insurance Marketing Operations; 520401 Administrative Assistant/Secretarial Science, General; 520408 General Office/Clerical and Typing Services; 520801 Finance, General; 520803 Banking and Financial Support Services
Related DOT Job/s: 214.362-034 TARIFF INSPECTOR; 241.267-030 INVESTIGATOR; 241.367-038 INVESTIGATOR, DEALER ACCOUNTS; 249.387-018 PEDIGREE TRACER

53508 BILL AND ACCOUNT COLLECTORS. OOH Title/s: Adjusters, Investigators, and Collectors

Locate and notify customers of delinquent accounts by mail, telephone, or personal visit to solicit payment. Duties include receiving payment and posting amount to customers' account; preparing statements to credit department if customer fails to respond; initiating repossession proceedings or service disconnection; and keeping records of collection and status of accounts. Exclude workers who collect money from coin boxes. Mails form letters to customers to encourage payment of delinquent accounts. Persuades customers to pay amount due on credit account, damage claim, or nonpayable check, or negotiates extension of credit. Notifies credit department, orders merchandise repossession or service disconnection, or turns over account to attorney if customer fails to respond. Receives payments and posts amount paid to customer account, using computer or paper records. Records information about financial status of customer and status of collection efforts. Confers with customer by telephone or in person to determine reason for overdue payment and review terms of sales, service, or credit contract. Traces delinquent customer to new address by inquiring at post office or questioning neighbors. Drives vehicle to visit customer, return merchandise to creditor, or deliver bills. Sorts and files correspondence, and performs miscellaneous clerical duties.
Yearly Earnings: $19,760
Education: Short-term O-J-T
Knowledge: Clerical; Economics and Accounting; Law, Government, and Jurisprudence
Abilities: Rate Control; Speech Recognition
Skills: Active Listening; Persuasion
General Work Activities: Interacting with Computers; Selling or Influencing Others; Resolving Conflicts, Negotiating with Others; Performing for or Working with Public
Job Characteristics: Objective or Subjective Information; Job-Required Social Interaction; Persuade Someone to a Course of Action; Take a Position Opposed to Others; Deal with External Customers; Frequency in Conflict Situations; Deal with Unpleasant or Angry People; Deal with Physical, Aggressive People; Frustrating Circumstances
GOE Group/s: 04.02.03 Security Services: Law and Order; 07.03.01 Financial Detail: Paying and Receiving; 07.04.02 Oral Communications: Order, Complaint, and Claims Handling
CIP Program/s: 520401 Administrative Assistant/Secretarial Science, General; 520408 General Office/Clerical and Typing Services; 520801 Finance, General; 520803 Banking and Financial Support Services
Related DOT Job/s: 241.357-010 COLLECTION CLERK; 241.367-010 COLLECTOR; 241.367-022 REPOSSESSOR

Government Clerks

53702 COURT CLERKS. OOH Title/s: Court Clerks

Perform clerical duties in court of law; prepare docket of cases to be called; secure information for judges; and contact witnesses, attorneys, and litigants to obtain information for court. Prepares docket or calendar of cases to be called, using typewriter or computer. Secures information for judges, and contacts witnesses, attorneys, and litigants to obtain information for court. Prepares case folders, and posts, files, or routes documents. Instructs parties when to appear in court. Examines legal documents submitted to court for adherence to law or court procedures. Explains procedures or forms to parties in case. Notifies district attorney's office of cases prosecuted by district attorney. Records minutes of court proceedings, using stenotype machine or shorthand, and transcribes testimony, using typewriter or computer. Records case disposition, court orders, and arrangement for payment of court fees. Collects court fees or fines, and records amounts collected. Administers oath to witnesses.
Yearly Earnings: $22,360
Education: Short-term O-J-T
Knowledge: Clerical; Law, Government, and Jurisprudence
Abilities: Wrist-Finger Speed; Near Vision
Skills: Information Organization; Time Management
General Work Activities: Documenting/Recording Information; Performing for or Working with Public; Performing Administrative Activities
Job Characteristics: Deal with Physical, Aggressive People; Sitting; Importance of Being Exact or Accurate; Importance of Repeating Same Tasks
GOE Group/s: 07.01.02 Administrative Detail: Administration
CIP Program/s: 520401 Administrative Assistant/Secretarial Science, General; 520405 Court Reporter
Related DOT Job/s: 243.362-010 COURT CLERK

53705 MUNICIPAL CLERKS. OOH Title/s: Municipal Clerks

Draft agendas and bylaws for town or city council, record minutes of council meetings, answer official correspondence, keep fiscal records and accounts, and prepare reports on civic needs. Prepares agendas and bylaws for town council. Records minutes of council meetings. Answers official correspondence. Keeps fiscal records and accounts. Prepares reports on civic needs.
Yearly Earnings: $22,360
Education: Short-term O-J-T
Knowledge: Administration and Management; Clerical; Economics and Accounting; Mathematics; Sociology and Anthropology; Geography; English Language; History and Archeology; Philosophy and Theology; Law, Government, and Jurisprudence; Communications and Media
Abilities: Selective Attention; Wrist-Finger Speed; Night Vision
Skills: Active Listening; Writing
General Work Activities: Documenting/Recording Information; Performing Administrative Activities
Job Characteristics: Provide a Service to Others; Deal with External Customers; Frequency in Conflict Situations; Deal with Unpleasant or Angry People; Sitting
GOE Group/s: 07.01.02 Administrative Detail: Administration
CIP Program/s: 520401 Administrative Assistant/Secretarial Science, General; 520402 Executive Assistant/Secretary
Related DOT Job/s: 243.367-018 TOWN CLERK

53708 LICENSE CLERKS. OOH Title/s: Adjusters, Investigators, and Collectors; Municipal Clerks

Issue licenses or permits to qualified applicants. Obtain necessary information, record data, advise applicants on requirements, collect fees, and issue licenses. May conduct oral, written, visual, or performance testing. Questions applicant to obtain information, such as name, address, and age, and records data on prescribed forms. Issues driver's, automobile, marriage, dog, or

other license. Evaluates information obtained to determine applicant qualification for licensure. Collects prescribed fee. Conducts oral, visual, written, or performance test to determine applicant qualifications. Counts collected fees and applications. Submits fees and reports to government for record.
Yearly Earnings: $22,360
Education: Short-term O-J-T
Knowledge: Clerical; Law, Government, and Jurisprudence
Abilities: None above average
Skills: None above average
General Work Activities: Performing for or Working with Public
Job Characteristics: Job-Required Social Interaction; Provide a Service to Others; Deal with External Customers; Frequency in Conflict Situations; Deal with Unpleasant or Angry People; Diseases/Infections
GOE Group/s: 07.04.03 Oral Communications: Registration
CIP Program/s: 520401 Administrative Assistant/Secretarial Science, General; 520408 General Office/Clerical and Typing Services
Related DOT Job/s: 205.367-034 LICENSE CLERK; 249.367-030 DOG LICENSER; 379.137-014 SUPERVISOR, DOG LICENSE OFFICER

Travel and Hotel Clerks

53802 TRAVEL CLERKS. OOH Title/s: Reservation and Transportation Ticket Agents and Travel Clerks; Receptionists
Provide tourists with travel information, such as points of interest, restaurants, rates, and emergency service. Duties include answering inquiries; offering suggestions; and providing literature pertaining to trips, excursions, sporting events, concerts, and plays. May make reservations, deliver tickets, arrange for visas, or contact individuals and groups to inform them of package tours. Exclude travel agents. Provides customers with travel suggestions and information such as guides, directories, brochures, and maps. Confers with customers by telephone, writing, or in person to answer questions regarding services and to determine travel preferences. Provides information concerning fares, availability of travel, and accommodations, either orally or by using guides, brochures, and maps. Informs client of travel dates, times, connections, baggage limits, medical and visa requirements, and emergency information. Obtains reservations for air, train, or car travel and hotel or other housing accommodations. Confirms travel arrangements and reservations. Plans itinerary for travel and accommodations, using knowledge of routes, types of carriers, and regulations. Assists client in preparing required documents and forms for travel, such as visa. Calculates estimated travel rates and expenses, using items such as rate tables and calculators. Studies maps, directories, routes, and rate tables to determine travel route and cost and availability of accommodations. Contacts motel, hotel, resort, and travel operators by mail or telephone to obtain advertising literature.
Yearly Earnings: $16,848
Education: Short-term O-J-T
Knowledge: Customer and Personal Service; Geography; Transportation
Abilities: Fluency of Ideas; Wrist-Finger Speed
Skills: Service Orientation
General Work Activities: Scheduling Work and Activities; Establishing and Maintaining Relationships; Assisting and Caring for Others; Selling or Influencing Others; Performing for or Working with Public
Job Characteristics: Job-Required Social Interaction; Provide a Service to Others; Deal with External Customers; Sitting
GOE Group/s: 07.04.04 Oral Communications: Reception and Information Giving; 07.05.01 Records Processing: Coordinating and Scheduling
CIP Program/s: 081104 Tourism Promotion Operations; 081105 Travel Services Marketing Operations
Related DOT Job/s: 214.362-030 RATE CLERK, PASSENGER; 237.367-050 TOURIST-INFORMATION ASSISTANT; 238.167-010 TRAVEL CLERK; 238.167-014 TRAVEL COUNSELOR, AUTOMOBILE CLUB; 238.362-014 RESERVATION CLERK; 238.367-030 TRAVEL CLERK

53805 RESERVATION AND TRANSPORTATION TICKET AGENTS. OOH Title/s: Reservation and Transportation Ticket Agents and Travel Clerks
Make and confirm reservations for passengers and sell tickets for transportation agencies such as airlines, bus companies, railroads, and steamship lines. May check baggage and direct passengers to designated concourse, pier, or track. Exclude workers selling tickets for subways, city buses, ferry boats, and street railways. Arranges reservations and routing for passengers at request of ticket agent. Assigns specified space to customers and maintains computerized inventory of passenger space available. Determines whether space is available on travel dates requested by customer. Checks baggage and directs passenger to designated location for loading. Examines passenger ticket or pass to direct passenger to specified area for loading. Answers inquiries made to travel agencies or transportation firms, such as airlines, bus companies, railroad companies, and steamship lines. Plans route and computes ticket cost, using schedules, rate books, and computer. Sells and assembles tickets for transmittal or mailing to customers. Reads coded data on tickets to ascertain destination, marks tickets, and assigns boarding pass. Telephones customer or ticket agent to advise of changes with travel conveyance or to confirm reservation. Assists passengers requiring special assistance to board or depart conveyance. Announces arrival and departure information, using public-address system. Informs travel agents in other locations of space reserved or available. Sells travel insurance.
Yearly Earnings: $16,848
Education: Short-term O-J-T
Knowledge: Clerical; Sales and Marketing; Customer and Personal Service; Computers and Electronics; Geography; Foreign Language; Philosophy and Theology; Transportation
Abilities: Memorization; Near Vision; Auditory Attention; Speech Recognition; Speech Clarity
Skills: Service Orientation
General Work Activities: Scheduling Work and Activities; Assisting and Caring for Others; Selling or Influencing Others; Performing for or Working with Public
Job Characteristics: Job-Required Social Interaction; Persuade Someone to a Course of Action; Provide a Service to Others; Deal with External Customers; Frequency in Conflict Situations; Deal with Unpleasant or Angry People; Special Uniform; Degree of Automation
GOE Group/s: 07.02.04 Mathematical Detail: Billing and Rate Computation; 07.03.01 Financial Detail: Paying and Receiving; 07.04.03 Oral Communications: Registration; 07.05.01 Records Processing: Coordinating and Scheduling; 09.05.04 Attendant Services: Doorkeeping Services
CIP Program/s: 081105 Travel Services Marketing Operations; 490106 Flight Attendant
Related DOT Job/s: 238.367-010 GATE AGENT; 238.367-014 RESERVATION CLERK; 238.367-018 RESERVATIONS AGENT; 238.367-026 TICKET AGENT; 248.382-010 TICKETING CLERK

53808 HOTEL DESK CLERKS. OOH Title/s: Hotel and Motel Desk Clerks
Accommodate hotel patrons by registering and assigning rooms to guests, issuing room keys, transmitting and receiving mes-

sages, keeping records of occupied rooms and guests' accounts, making and confirming reservations, and presenting statements to and collecting payments from departing guests. Greets, registers, and assigns rooms to guests of hotel or motel. Keeps records of room availability and guests' accounts, manually or using computer. Computes bill, collects payment, and makes change for guests. Makes and confirms reservations. Posts charges, such as room, food, liquor, or telephone, to ledger, manually or using computer. Transmits and receives messages, using telephone or telephone switchboard. Issues room key and escort instructions to bellhop. Date-stamps, sorts, and racks incoming mail and messages. Answers inquiries pertaining to hotel services; registration of guests; and shopping, dining, entertainment, and travel directions. Makes restaurant, transportation, or entertainment reservations, and arranges for tours. Deposits guests' valuables in hotel safe or safe-deposit box. Orders complimentary flowers or champagne for guests.
Yearly Earnings: $16,744
Education: Short-term O-J-T
Knowledge: Clerical; Customer and Personal Service; Transportation
Abilities: None above average
Skills: Service Orientation
General Work Activities: Assisting and Caring for Others; Performing for or Working with Public
Job Characteristics: Job-Required Social Interaction; Provide a Service to Others; Deal with External Customers; Standing; Special Uniform
GOE Group/s: 07.04.03 Oral Communications: Registration
CIP Program/s: 080901 Hospitality and Recreation Marketing Operations, General; 080902 Hotel/Motel Services Marketing Operations
Related DOT Job/s: 238.367-038 HOTEL CLERK

Other Clerical Workers

53902 LIBRARY ASSISTANTS AND BOOKMOBILE DRIVERS. OOH Title/s: Library Assistants and Bookmobile Drivers; Stock Clerks

Library assistants compile records; sort and shelve books; issue and receive library materials, such as pictures, cards, slides, phonograph records, and microfilm; and handle tape decks. Locate library materials for loan, and replace materials in shelving area (stacks) or files according to identification number and title. Register patrons to permit them to borrow books, periodicals, and other library materials. Bookmobile drivers operate a bookmobile or light truck that pulls a book trailer to specific locations on a predetermined schedule and assist with providing services in mobile library. Issues borrower's identification card according to established procedures. Drives bookmobile to specified locations following library services schedule and to garage for preventive maintenance and repairs. Issues books to patrons and records information on borrower's card, by hand or using photographic equipment. Sorts books, publications, and other items according to procedure and returns them to shelves, files, or other designated storage area. Locates library materials for patrons, such as books, periodicals, tape cassettes, Braille volumes, and pictures. Classifies and catalogs items according to contents and purpose, and prepares index cards for file reference. Maintains records of items received, stored, issued, and returned and files catalog cards according to system used. Answers routine inquiries and refers patrons who need professional assistance to librarian. Delivers and retrieves items to and from departments by hand or pushcart. Prepares, stores, and retrieves classification and catalog information, lecture notes, or other documents related to document stored, using computer. Reviews records, such as microfilm and issue cards, to determine title of overdue materials and to identify borrower. Inspects returned books for damage, verifies due-date, and computes and receives overdue fines. Selects substitute titles, following criteria such as age, education, and interest, when requested materials are unavailable. Places books in mailing container, affixes address label, and secures container with straps for mailing to blind library patrons. Operates and maintains audio-visual equipment and explains use of reference equipment to patrons. Prepares address labels for books to be mailed, overdue notices, and duty schedules, using computer or typewriter. Repairs books, using mending tape and paste and brush, and places plastic covers on new books.
Yearly Earnings: $18,772
Education: Short-term O-J-T
Knowledge: Clerical; Customer and Personal Service; History and Archeology
Abilities: Category Flexibility; Memorization; Time Sharing; Reaction Time; Wrist-Finger Speed
Skills: Service Orientation; Information Organization
General Work Activities: Interacting with Computers; Assisting and Caring for Others; Performing for or Working with Public
Job Characteristics: Provide a Service to Others; Deal with External Customers; Climbing Ladders, Scaffolds, Poles, etc.; Kneeling, Crouching, or Crawling; Bending or Twisting the Body
GOE Group/s: 05.09.01 Material Control: Shipping, Receiving, and Stock Checking; 07.04.03 Oral Communications: Registration; 07.05.04 Records Processing: Routing and Distribution; 07.07.02 Clerical Handling: Sorting and Distrubtion; 11.02.04 Educational and Library Services: Library Services
CIP Program/s: 250301 Library Assistant; 520401 Administrative Assistant/Secretarial Science, General; 520408 General Office/Clerical and Typing Services
Related DOT Job/s: 209.387-026 LIBRARY CLERK, TALKING BOOKS; 222.367-026 FILM-OR-TAPE LIBRARIAN; 222.587-014 BRAILLE-AND-TALKING BOOKS CLERK; 249.363-010 BOOKMOBILE DRIVER; 249.365-010 REGISTRATION CLERK; 249.367-046 LIBRARY ASSISTANT; 249.687-014 PAGE

53905 TEACHER AIDES AND EDUCATIONAL ASSISTANTS, CLERICAL. OOH Title/s: Teacher Aides

Arrange work materials, supervise students at play, and operate audio-visual equipment under guidance of a teacher. Distributes teaching materials to students, such as textbooks, workbooks, or paper and pencils. Operates learning aids, such as film and slide projectors and tape recorders. Activates audio-visual receiver and monitors classroom viewing of live or recorded courses transmitted by communication satellite. Maintains order within school and school grounds. Takes class attendance and maintains class attendance records. Types material and operates duplicating equipment to reproduce instructional materials. Grades homework and tests and computes and records results, using answer sheets or electronic marking devices. Requisitions teaching materials and stockroom supplies. Collects completed assignments and tests and mails to training center or institute of higher learning. Stimulates classroom discussion following broadcast of seminar, and consolidates and transmits students' questions for direct response via satellite.
Yearly Earnings: $12,376
Education: Short-term O-J-T
Knowledge: Clerical; Customer and Personal Service; Psychology; Sociology and Anthropology; Therapy and Counseling; Education and Training; English Language; Foreign Language; History and Archeology; Telecommunications; Communications and Media
Abilities: Category Flexibility; Memorization; Speed of Closure; Time Sharing; Response Orientation; Reaction Time; Far Vision; Peripheral Vision; Auditory Attention; Sound Localization; Speech Recognition; Speech Clarity

Skills: None above average
General Work Activities: Establishing and Maintaining Relationships; Assisting and Caring for Others; Resolving Conflicts, Negotiating with Others; Teaching Others
Job Characteristics: Job-Required Social Interaction; Deal with Unpleasant or Angry People; Deal with Physical, Aggressive People
GOE Group/s: 07.01.02 Administrative Detail: Administration; 07.02.03 Mathematical Detail: Statistical Reporting and Analysis
CIP Program/s: 130101 Education, General; 130201 Bilingual/Bicultural Education; 131501 Teacher Assistant/Aide
Related DOT Job/s: 219.467-010 GRADING CLERK; 249.367-074 TEACHER AIDE II; 249.367-086 SATELLITE-INSTRUCTION FACILITATOR

53908 ADVERTISING CLERKS. OOH Title/s: Order Clerks

Receive orders for classified advertising in a newspaper or magazine from customers in person or by telephone. Examine and mark classified advertisements according to copy sheet specifications to guide composing room in assembling type. Verify conformance of published advertisements to specifications for billing purposes. Receives and solicits orders from customers and reviews content, publication dates, and specifications. Writes classified order forms, according to customer's specification, and compiles and submits advertising orders to publishers. Examines, counts, and records expired lines and computes new advertisement line space required to guide composing room in assembling type. Reads and marks expired advertisements and indicates time remaining for continued advertisements, using daily classified file copy and copy sheet. Measures and draws outlines of advertisement in specified sizes onto dummy copy sheets, using ruler, pencil, or transparent calibrated overlay. Scans publication to locate published advertisement and verifies conformance to order specifications. Computes customer cost based on rates and order specifications, such as size, date, and position, using rate schedule and calculator. Positions and views advertisements on dummy sheet to ensure page balance and to prevent inclusion of competitive advertisements on page. Records identifying data onto dummy copy and worksheets, such as advertiser name, outlined advertisement dimensions, cost, date, and page number. Extracts and transfers guide data from dummy copy and worksheets onto production worksheets for production workers. Delivers or transmits orders, dummy copy, and production worksheets to production department for publication or to administrative personnel for review. Records transactions, such as payments and customer requests for corrections/cancellations to advertisement, and assigns box numbers to anonymous advertisements. Types and mails orders and specifications to designated publishers and files order data pending receipt of publication. Computes and posts cost differential onto order controls for advertisement variance, and routes tear sheet with order to billing department. Separates tear sheet from designated publication and types and attaches identifying information onto tear sheet to clarify billing modification. Collects payments from and issues receipts to customers for cost of advertisement.
Yearly Earnings: $24,336
Education: Short-term O-J-T
Knowledge: Clerical; Economics and Accounting; Sales and Marketing; Production and Processing
Abilities: Near Vision; Speech Recognition
Skills: Service Orientation
General Work Activities: None above average
Job Characteristics: Persuade Someone to a Course of Action; Provide a Service to Others; Deal with External Customers; Deal with Unpleasant or Angry People; Sitting; Frustrating Circumstances; Importance of Repeating Same Tasks
GOE Group/s: 01.06.01 Craft Arts: Graphics Arts and Related Crafts; 07.02.04 Mathematical Detail: Billing and Rate Computation; 07.04.02 Oral Communications: Order, Complaint, and Claims Handling; 07.05.02 Records Processing: Record Verification and Proofing
CIP Program/s: 090201 Advertising
Related DOT Job/s: 247.367-010 CLASSIFIED-AD CLERK I; 247.387-010 ADVERTISING CLERK; 247.387-018 ADVERTISING-SPACE CLERK; 247.387-022 CLASSIFIED-AD CLERK II

53911 PROOFREADERS AND COPY MARKERS. OOH Title/s: Proofreaders and Copy Markers

Read transcript or proof type set-up to detect and mark for correction any grammatical, typographical, or compositional errors. Exclude workers whose primary duty is editing copy. Include proofreaders of Braille. Marks proofs to correct errors, using standard printers' marks. Reads proofs against copy and corrects errors in type, arrangement, grammar, punctuation, or spelling, using proofreader marks. Corrects or records omissions, errors, or inconsistencies found. Compares information or figures on one record against same data on other records or with original copy to detect errors. Routes proofs with marked corrections to be reprinted, and reads corrected copies or proofs. Calls attention to discrepancies between copy and proof. Consults reference books or secures aid of reader to check references to rules of grammar and composition. Reads proofsheet aloud, calling out punctuation marks and spelling unusual words and proper names. Measures dimensions, spacing, and positioning of page elements (copy and illustrations) to verify conformance to specifications, using printer's ruler. Places proof and copy side by side on reading board.
Yearly Earnings: $19,188
Education: Short-term O-J-T
Knowledge: English Language
Abilities: Written Comprehension; Memorization; Perceptual Speed; Near Vision
Skills: Reading Comprehension
General Work Activities: None above average
Job Characteristics: Sitting; Importance of Being Exact or Accurate; Importance of Repeating Same Tasks
GOE Group/s: 07.05.02 Records Processing: Record Verification and Proofing
CIP Program/s: 520401 Administrative Assistant/Secretarial Science, General; 520408 General Office/Clerical and Typing Services; 520501 Business Communications
Related DOT Job/s: 209.387-030 PROOFREADER; 209.667-010 COPY HOLDER; 209.687-010 CHECKER II; 247.667-010 PRODUCTION PROOFREADER

53914 REAL ESTATE CLERKS. OOH Title/s: Real Estate Clerks

Perform duties concerned with rental, sale, and management of real estate, such as typing copies of listings, computing interest or penalty owed, holding collateral in escrow, and checking due notices on taxes and renewal dates of insurance and mortgage loans. Types copies of listings of rentals and sales for distribution to trade publications, and for use as reference data. Computes interest owed, penalty payment, amount of principal, and taxes due on mortgage loans, using calculating machine. Checks due notices on taxes and renewal dates of insurance and mortgage loans to take follow-up action. Holds in escrow collateral posted to ensure fulfillment of contracts in transferring real estate and property titles. Scans records to identify dates requiring action, such as insurance premium due dates, tax due notices, and lease expiration dates. Sends rent notices to tenants. Writes checks in payment of bills due, keeps record of disbursements, and

examines canceled returned checks for endorsement. Composes and prepares routine correspondence, rental notices, letters, and material for advertisement. Maintains and balances bank accounts for sales transactions and operating expenses. Compiles list of prospects from leads in newspapers and trade periodicals to locate prospective purchasers of real estate. Maintains log of sales and commissions received by real estate sales staff. Submits photographs and descriptions of property to newspaper for publication. Secures estimates from contractors for building repairs. Opens, sorts, and distributes mail.
Yearly Earnings: $19,396
Education: Short-term O-J-T
Knowledge: Clerical; Economics and Accounting; Sales and Marketing; Computers and Electronics; Mathematics; Geography; English Language; Law, Government, and Jurisprudence; Communications and Media
Abilities: Number Facility; Wrist-Finger Speed
Skills: Management of Financial Resources
General Work Activities: Performing Administrative Activities
Job Characteristics: Sitting
GOE Group/s: 07.01.04 Administrative Detail: Financial Work
CIP Program/s: 520401 Administrative Assistant/Secretarial Science, General; 520408 General Office/Clerical and Typing Services
Related DOT Job/s: 219.362-046 REAL-ESTATE CLERK

Secretaries

55102 LEGAL SECRETARIES. OOH Title/s: Secretaries
Prepare legal papers and correspondence, such as summonses, complaints, motions, and subpoenas. May review law journals and other legal publications to identify court decisions pertinent to pending cases and submit articles to company officials. Must be familiar with legal terminology, procedures, and documents, as well as legal research. Prepares and processes legal documents and papers, such as summonses, subpoenas, complaints, appeals, motions, and pretrial agreements. Reviews legal publications and performs database searches to identify laws and court decisions relevant to pending cases. Submits articles and information from searches to attorneys for review and approval for use. Assists attorneys in collecting information such as employment, medical, and other records. Organizes and maintains law libraries and document and case files. Completes various forms, such as accident reports, trial and courtroom requests, and applications for clients. Mails, faxes, or arranges for delivery of legal correspondence to clients, witnesses, and court officials. Attends legal meetings, such as client interviews, hearings, or depositions, and takes notes. Drafts and types office memos. Receives and places telephone calls. Schedules and makes appointments. Makes photocopies of correspondence, documents, and other printed matter.
Yearly Earnings: $19,968
Education: Postsecondary vocational training
Knowledge: Clerical; Economics and Accounting; Computers and Electronics; Law, Government, and Jurisprudence
Abilities: Written Comprehension; Time Sharing; Wrist-Finger Speed; Near Vision; Speech Recognition
Skills: Reading Comprehension; Active Listening; Writing; Service Orientation; Information Organization; Programming
General Work Activities: Communicating with Other Workers; Performing Administrative Activities
Job Characteristics: Job-Required Social Interaction; Sitting; Importance of Being Sure All is Done; Importance of Repeating Same Tasks
GOE Group/s: 07.01.03 Administrative Detail: Secretarial Work
CIP Program/s: 520401 Administrative Assistant/Secretarial Science, General; 520403 Legal Administrative Assistant/Secretary
Related DOT Job/s: 201.362-010 LEGAL SECRETARY

55105 MEDICAL SECRETARIES. OOH Title/s: Secretaries
Perform secretarial duties utilizing specific knowledge of medical terminology and hospital, clinic, or laboratory procedures. Duties include taking dictation and compiling and recording medical charts, reports, and correspondence, using a typewriter or computer. Duties also may include preparing and sending bills to patients or recording appointments. Compiles and records medical charts, reports, and correspondence, using typewriter, personal computer, or word processor. Performs secretarial duties, utilizing knowledge of medical terminology and hospital, clinic, or laboratory procedures. Takes dictation, using shorthand or dictaphone. Answers telephone, schedules appointments, and greets and directs visitors. Maintains files.
Yearly Earnings: $19,968
Education: Postsecondary vocational training
Knowledge: Clerical; Computers and Electronics
Abilities: Wrist-Finger Speed
Skills: Active Listening
General Work Activities: Performing Administrative Activities
Job Characteristics: Deal with External Customers; Sitting; Importance of Being Sure All is Done
GOE Group/s: 07.01.03 Administrative Detail: Secretarial Work
CIP Program/s: 510705 Medical Office Management; 510708 Medical Transcription; 520401 Administrative Assistant/Secretarial Science, General; 520404 Medical Administrative Assistant/Secretary
Related DOT Job/s: 201.362-010 LEGAL SECRETARY

55108 SECRETARIES, EXCEPT LEGAL AND MEDICAL. OOH Title/s: Secretaries
Relieve officials of clerical work and minor administrative and business details by scheduling appointments, giving information to callers, taking dictation, composing and typing routine correspondence (using typewriter or computer), reading and routing incoming mail, filing correspondence and other records, and other assigned clerical duties. Exclude executive secretaries. Answers telephone and gives information to callers, takes messages, or transfers calls to appropriate individuals. Opens incoming mail and routes mail to appropriate individuals. Answers routine correspondence. Composes and distributes meeting notes, correspondence, and reports. Schedules appointments. Maintains calendar and coordinates conferences and meetings. Takes dictation, in shorthand or by machine, and transcribes information. Locates and attaches appropriate file to incoming correspondence requiring reply. Files correspondence and other records. Makes copies of correspondence and other printed matter. Arranges travel schedules and reservations. Greets and welcomes visitors, determines nature of business, and conducts visitors to employer or appropriate person. Compiles and maintains lists and records, using typewriter or computer. Records and types minutes of meetings, using typewriter or computer. Compiles and types statistical reports, using typewriter or computer. Mails newsletters, promotional material, and other information. Orders and dispenses supplies. Prepares and mails checks. Collects and disburses funds from cash account and keeps records. Provides customer services such as order placement and account information.
Yearly Earnings: $19,968
Education: Postsecondary vocational training
Knowledge: Clerical; Economics and Accounting; Customer and Personal Service; Computers and Electronics; Geography; English Language; Communications and Media; Transportation
Abilities: Category Flexibility; Memorization; Speed of Closure; Perceptual Speed; Finger Dexterity; Wrist-Finger Speed; Near Vision; Speech Recognition

Skills: Service Orientation
General Work Activities: Scheduling Work and Activities; Operating Vehicles or Equipment; Establishing and Maintaining Relationships; Performing Administrative Activities
Job Characteristics: Deal with External Customers; Deal with Unpleasant or Angry People; Sitting; Importance of Repeating Same Tasks
GOE Group/s: 01.03.01 Performing Arts:Drama: Instructing and Directing; 07.01.02 Administrative Detail: Administration; 07.01.03 Administrative Detail: Secretarial Work
CIP Program/s: 520401 Administrative Assistant/Secretarial Science, General
Related DOT Job/s: 201.162-010 SOCIAL SECRETARY; 201.362-018 MEMBERSHIP SECRETARY; 201.362-022 SCHOOL SECRETARY; 201.362-026 SCRIPT SUPERVISOR; 201.362-030 SECRETARY; 219.362-074 TRUST OPERATIONS ASSISTANT

General Office Support Workers

55302A STENOTYPE OPERATORS. OOH Title/s: Stenographers, Court Reporters, and Medical Transcriptionists

Operate stenotype machine to take dictation, record proceedings, or provide captions. Listens to and records proceedings, dialogue, or dictation of reports, correspondence, and other matter using stenotype machine. Transcribes recorded material, using word processor or typewriter, or dictates material into recording machine. Directs speakers to clarify inaudible statements. Devises stenographic equivalents of new words or terms, and adds to stenographic glossary. Reads portions of transcript aloud, as requested. Reviews glossary items for words and terms likely to be used during proceedings or program.
Yearly Earnings: $19,968
Education: Postsecondary vocational training
Knowledge: Clerical; Computers and Electronics
Abilities: Memorization; Perceptual Speed; Selective Attention; Wrist-Finger Speed; Auditory Attention; Speech Recognition
Skills: Active Listening
General Work Activities: None above average
Job Characteristics: Sitting; Making Repetitive Motions; Importance of Repeating Same Tasks
GOE Group/s: 07.05.03 Records Processing: Record Preparation and Maintenance
CIP Program/s: 090701 Radio and Television Broadcasting; 520401 Administrative Assistant/Secretarial Science, General; 520405 Court Reporter
Related DOT Job/s: 202.362-010 SHORTHAND REPORTER; 202.362-022 STENOTYPE OPERATOR; 202.382-010 STENOCAPTIONER

55302B STENOGRAPHERS. OOH Title/s: Stenographers, Court Reporters, and Medical Transcriptionists

Take dictation in shorthand and transcribe dictated material. Takes dictation in shorthand of correspondence, reports, and other narrated information. Operates typewriter or word processing computer to transcribe dictated material. Drafts and types narrative from rough drafts, dictation, and tape-recorded notes. Prepares letters and packages for shipping.
Yearly Earnings: $19,968
Education: Postsecondary vocational training
Knowledge: Clerical
Abilities: Memorization; Wrist-Finger Speed; Auditory Attention; Sound Localization; Speech Recognition
Skills: None above average
General Work Activities: None above average
Job Characteristics: Sitting; Making Repetitive Motions; Importance of Repeating Same Tasks
GOE Group/s: 07.05.03 Records Processing: Record Preparation and Maintenance
CIP Program/s: 510708 Medical Transcription; 520401 Administrative Assistant/Secretarial Science, General
Related DOT Job/s: 202.362-014 STENOGRAPHER; 202.362-018 STENOGRAPHER, PRINT SHOP

55305 RECEPTIONISTS AND INFORMATION CLERKS. OOH Title/s: Receptionists

Answer inquiries and obtain information for general public (e.g., customers, visitors, and other interested parties). Provide information regarding activities conducted at establishment; location of departments, offices, and employees within organization; or services in a hotel. May perform other clerical duties as assigned. Exclude receptionists who operate switchboards. Greets persons entering establishment, determines nature and purpose of visit, and directs visitor to specific destination, or answers questions and provides information. Provides information to public regarding tours, classes, workshops, and other programs. Answers telephone to schedule future appointments, provide information, or forward call. Provides information to public concerning available land leases, land classification, or mineral resources. Registers visitors of public facility, such as national park or military base, collects fees, explains regulations, and assigns sites. Transmits information or documents to customer, using computer, mail, or facsimile. Analyzes data to determine answer to customer or public inquiry. Records, compiles, enters, and retrieves information, by hand or using computer. Collects and distributes messages for employees of organization. Calculates and quotes rates for tours, stocks, insurance policies, and other products and services. Types memos, correspondence, travel vouchers, or other documents. Enrolls individuals to participate in programs, prepares lists, notifies individuals of acceptance in programs, and arranges and schedules space and equipment for participants. Files and maintains records. Hears and resolves complaints from customers and public. Conducts tours or delivers talks describing features of public facility, such as historic site or national park. Receives payment and records receipts for services. Examines, completes, and processes land use documents, and collects fees. Monitors public facilities, such as campgrounds, to ensure compliance with regulations. Participates in activities at national park or other public facility, such as first-aid treatment, fire suppression, conservation, or restoration of buildings. Performs duties such as taking care of plants and straightening magazines to maintain lobby or reception area. Operates telephone switchboard to receive incoming calls.
Yearly Earnings: $16,536
Education: Short-term O-J-T
Knowledge: Clerical; Customer and Personal Service; Geography; Foreign Language; History and Archeology; Telecommunications
Abilities: Memorization; Spatial Orientation; Wrist-Finger Speed; Speech Recognition; Speech Clarity
Skills: Service Orientation
General Work Activities: Scheduling Work and Activities; Performing for or Working with Public
Job Characteristics: Job-Required Social Interaction; Provide a Service to Others; Deal with External Customers; Deal with Unpleasant or Angry People
GOE Group/s: 07.04.02 Oral Communications: Order, Complaint, and Claims Handling; 07.04.03 Oral Communications: Registration; 07.04.04 Oral Communications: Reception and Information Giving; 07.05.01 Records Processing: Coordinating and Scheduling; 07.06.01 Clerical Machine Operation: Computer Operation

CIP Program/s: 081104 Tourism Promotion Operations; 520401 Administrative Assistant/Secretarial Science, General; 520406 Receptionist; 520407 Information Processing/Data Entry Technician; 520408 General Office/Clerical and Typing Services

Related DOT Job/s: 203.362-014 CREDIT REPORTING CLERK; 205.367-038 REGISTRAR; 237.267-010 INFORMATION CLERK, AUTOMOBILE CLUB; 237.367-010 APPOINTMENT CLERK; 237.367-018 INFORMATION CLERK; 237.367-022 INFORMATION CLERK; 237.367-038 RECEPTIONIST; 237.367-042 REFERRAL-AND-INFORMATION AIDE; 237.367-046 TELEPHONE QUOTATION CLERK; 238.367-022 SPACE SCHEDULER; 238.367-034 SCHEDULER; 239.367-034 UTILITY CLERK; 249.262-010 POLICYHOLDER-INFORMATION CLERK; 249.367-082 PARK AIDE

55307 TYPISTS, INCLUDING WORD PROCESSING.

OOH Title/s: Typists, Word Processors, and Data Entry Keyers

Use typewriter or computer to type letters, reports, forms, or other straight copy material from rough draft, corrected copy, or voice recording. May perform other clerical duties as assigned. Exclude keypunchers, secretaries, and stenographers. Types from rough draft, corrected copy, or previous version displayed on screen, using computer or typewriter. Types from recorded dictation. Addresses envelopes or prepares envelope labels, using typewriter or computer. Gathers and arranges material to be typed, following instructions. Adjusts settings for format, page layout, line spacing, and other style requirements. Checks completed work for spelling, grammar, punctuation, and format. Stores completed documents on computer hard drive or data storage medium, such as disk. Transcribes stenotyped notes of court proceedings. Prints and makes copy of work. Files and stores completed documents. Collates pages of reports and other documents prepared. Sorts and distributes mail. Answers telephone. Operates duplicating machine. Transmits work electronically to other locations. Computes and verifies totals on report forms, requisitions, or bills, using adding machine or calculator. Keeps records of work performed. Uses data entry device, such as optical scanner, to input data into computer for revision or editing.

Yearly Earnings: $19,292

Education: Moderate-term O-J-T

Knowledge: Clerical; Computers and Electronics; English Language

Abilities: Category Flexibility; Perceptual Speed; Wrist-Finger Speed; Near Vision; Auditory Attention; Speech Recognition

Skills: None above average

General Work Activities: None above average

Job Characteristics: Sitting; Making Repetitive Motions; Degree of Automation; Importance of Repeating Same Tasks

GOE Group/s: 07.05.03 Records Processing: Record Preparation and Maintenance; 07.06.02 Clerical Machine Operation: Keyboard Machine Operation

CIP Program/s: 520401 Administrative Assistant/Secretarial Science, General; 520405 Court Reporter; 520408 General Office/Clerical and Typing Services

Related DOT Job/s: 203.362-010 CLERK-TYPIST; 203.382-030 WORD PROCESSING MACHINE OPERATOR; 203.582-058 TRANSCRIBING-MACHINE OPERATOR; 203.582-066 TYPIST; 203.582-078 NOTEREADER; 209.382-010 CONTINUITY CLERK; 209.587-010 ADDRESSER

55314 PERSONNEL CLERKS, EXCEPT PAYROLL AND TIMEKEEPING. OOH Title/s: Personnel Clerks

Compile and keep personnel records. Record data for each employee, such as address, weekly earnings, absences, amount of sales or production, supervisory reports on ability, and date of and reason for termination. Compile and type reports from employment records. File employment records. Search employee files and furnish information to authorized persons. Examines employee files to answer inquiries and provide information for personnel actions. Records employee data, such as address, rate of pay, absences, and benefits, using personal computer. Compiles and types reports from employment records. Maintains and updates employee records to document personnel actions and changes in employee status. Processes and reviews employment application to evaluate qualifications or eligibility of applicant. Interviews applicants to obtain and verify information. Answers questions regarding examinations, eligibility, salaries, benefits, and other pertinent information. Prepares listing of vacancies and notifies eligible workers of position availability. Administers and scores employee aptitude, skills, personality, and interests tests. Communicates with employees or applicants to explain company personnel policies and procedures. Explains company insurance policies and options to employees and files claim and cancellation forms. Selects applicants having specified job requirements and refers to employing official. Requests information from law enforcement officials, previous employers, and other references to determine applicant's employment acceptability.

Yearly Earnings: $24,544

Education: Short-term O-J-T

Knowledge: Clerical; Personnel and Human Resources

Abilities: Gross Body Equilibrium

Skills: Equipment Selection; Programming

General Work Activities: Establishing and Maintaining Relationships; Performing Administrative Activities; Staffing Organizational Units; Monitoring and Controlling Resources

Job Characteristics: Sitting; Importance of Repeating Same Tasks

GOE Group/s: 07.01.05 Administrative Detail: Certifying; 07.04.01 Oral Communications: Interviewing; 07.04.04 Oral Communications: Reception and Information Giving; 07.05.03 Records Processing: Record Preparation and Maintenance

CIP Program/s: 521001 Human Resources Management

Related DOT Job/s: 205.362-010 CIVIL-SERVICE CLERK; 205.362-014 EMPLOYMENT CLERK; 205.362-022 IDENTIFICATION CLERK; 205.367-062 REFERRAL CLERK, TEMPORARY HELP AGENCY; 205.567-010 BENEFITS CLERK II; 209.362-026 PERSONNEL CLERK; 241.267-010 AGENT-CONTRACT CLERK; 249.367-090 ASSIGNMENT CLERK

55317 CORRESPONDENCE CLERKS. OOH Title/s: Secretaries; File Clerks

Compose letters in reply to requests for merchandise, damage claims, credit and other information, delinquent accounts, incorrect billings, or unsatisfactory services. Duties may include gathering data to formulate reply and typing correspondence. Composes letter in response to request or problem identified by correspondence. Reads incoming correspondence to ascertain nature of writer's concern and determine disposition of correspondence. Gathers data to formulate reply. Completes form letters in response to request or problem identified by correspondence. Types acknowledgment letter to person sending correspondence. Reviews records pertinent to resolution of problem for completeness and accuracy, and attaches records to correspondence for reply by others. Processes orders for goods requested in correspondence. Compiles data pertinent to manufacture of special products for customers. Routes correspondence to other departments for reply. Maintains files and control records to show status of action in processing correspondence. Confers with company personnel regarding feasibility of complying with writer's request, such as to design and manufacture special product. Investigates discrepancies in reports and records and confers with personnel in affected departments to ensure accuracy and compliance with procedures. Compiles data from records to prepare periodic reports.

Yearly Earnings: $19,968

Education: Postsecondary vocational training
Knowledge: Clerical
Abilities: Wrist-Finger Speed
Skills: None above average
General Work Activities: Performing Administrative Activities
Job Characteristics: Objective or Subjective Information; Frequency in Conflict Situations; Deal with Unpleasant or Angry People; Sitting
GOE Group/s: 05.09.02 Material Control: Estimating, Scheduling, and Record Keeping; 07.04.02 Oral Communications: Order, Complaint, and Claims Handling; 07.05.04 Records Processing: Routing and Distribution
CIP Program/s: 520401 Administrative Assistant/Secretarial Science, General; 520408 General Office/Clerical and Typing Services
Related DOT Job/s: 209.362-034 CORRESPONDENCE CLERK; 209.367-018 CORRESPONDENCE-REVIEW CLERK; 209.387-034 SUGGESTION CLERK; 221.367-062 SALES CORRESPONDENT

55321 FILE CLERKS. OOH Title/s: File Clerks

File correspondence, cards, invoices, receipts, and other records in alphabetical or numerical order or according to the filing system used. Locate and remove material from file when requested. May be required to classify and file new material. Sorts or classifies information, according to content, purpose, user criteria, or chronological, alphabetical, or numerical order. Locates and retrieves files upon request from authorized users. Places materials into storage receptacles, such as file cabinets, boxes, bins, or drawers, according to classification and identification information. Removes or destroys outdated materials in accordance with file maintenance schedules or legal requirements. Scans or reads incoming materials to determine filing order or location. Assigns and records or stamps identification numbers or codes to index materials for filing. Inspects or examines materials or files for accuracy, legibility, or damage. Inserts additional data on file records. Authorizes or documents material movement, using logbook or computer, and traces missing files. Photographs or makes copies of data and records, using photocopying or microfilming equipment.
Yearly Earnings: $16,224
Education: Short-term O-J-T
Knowledge: Clerical
Abilities: None above average
Skills: None above average
General Work Activities: None above average
Job Characteristics: Sitting; Importance of Being Exact or Accurate; Importance of Repeating Same Tasks
GOE Group/s: 07.05.03 Records Processing: Record Preparation and Maintenance; 07.07.01 Clerical Handling: Filing
CIP Program/s: 520401 Administrative Assistant/Secretarial Science, General; 520408 General Office/Clerical and Typing Services
Related DOT Job/s: 206.367-014 FILE CLERK II; 206.367-018 TAPE LIBRARIAN; 206.387-010 CLASSIFICATION CLERK; 206.387-014 FINGERPRINT CLERK II; 206.387-022 RECORD CLERK; 206.387-034 FILE CLERK I

55323 ORDER CLERKS—MATERIALS, MERCHANDISE, AND SERVICE. OOH Title/s: Order Clerks; Cashiers

Receive and process incoming orders for materials, merchandise, or services such as repairs, installations, or rental of facilities. Duties include informing customers of order receipt, prices, shipping dates, and delays; preparing contracts; and handling complaints. Exclude workers who dispatch as well as take orders for services. Receives and handles customer complaints. Informs customer by mail or phone of information, such as unit price, shipping date, anticipated delay, and additional information needed. Prepares invoices and shipping documents. Writes or types information on form to record customer's requests and specifications. Routes or relays orders to specified department or unit to prepare and ship orders to designated locations. Computes total charge for merchandise or services and shipping charges. Confers with production, sales, shipping, warehouse, or common carrier personnel to expedite or trace merchandise or delayed shipments. Reviews orders for completeness, according to reporting procedures, and forwards incomplete orders for further processing. Files copies of orders received or posts order on records. Calculates and compiles statistics and prepares reports for management. Checks inventory control to determine availability of merchandise, and notifies department of order that would deplete stock. Collects charge vouchers and cash for service and keeps record of transaction. Inspects outgoing work for compliance with customer's specifications. Recommends type of packing or labeling needed on order. Attempts to sell additional merchandise or service to prospective or current customers by phone or through visits. Recommends merchandise or services to customer.
Yearly Earnings: $24,336
Education: Short-term O-J-T
Knowledge: Clerical; Economics and Accounting; Sales and Marketing; Transportation
Abilities: Problem Sensitivity; Mathematical Reasoning; Number Facility; Speech Recognition
Skills: Persuasion; Service Orientation
General Work Activities: Communicating with Other Workers; Selling or Influencing Others; Resolving Conflicts, Negotiating with Others; Performing for or Working with Public
Job Characteristics: Job-Required Social Interaction; Persuade Someone to a Course of Action; Provide a Service to Others; Deal with External Customers; Frequency in Conflict Situations; Deal with Unpleasant or Angry People; Sitting
GOE Group/s: 05.10.05 Crafts: Reproduction; 07.04.05 Oral Communications: Information Transmitting and Receiving; 07.05.03 Records Processing: Record Preparation and Maintenance; 07.05.04 Records Processing: Routing and Distribution; 11.02.04 Educational and Library Services: Library Services
CIP Program/s: 520401 Administrative Assistant/Secretarial Science, General; 520408 General Office/Clerical and Typing Services
Related DOT Job/s: 209.387-018 CONTACT CLERK; 209.567-014 ORDER CLERK, FOOD AND BEVERAGE; 245.367-026 ORDER-CONTROL CLERK, BLOOD BANK; 249.362-026 ORDER CLERK; 249.367-042 GAS-DISTRIBUTION-AND-EMERGENCY CLERK; 295.367-018 FILM-RENTAL CLERK; 659.462-010 ELECTROTYPE SERVICER

55326 PROCUREMENT CLERKS. OOH Title/s: Material Recording, Scheduling, Dispatching, and Distributing Occupations

Compile information and records to draw up purchase orders for procurement of materials. Verifies terminology and specifications of purchase requests. Reads catalogs and interviews suppliers to obtain prices and specifications. Compiles records of items purchased or transferred between departments. Types or writes purchase order and sends copy to supplier and department originating request. Computes total cost of items purchased, using calculator. Verifies bills from suppliers with bids and purchase orders. Types or writes invitation-of-bid forms and mails forms to supplier firms or distributes forms for public posting. Compares prices, specifications, and delivery dates, and awards contract to supplier with best bid. Determines if material is on hand in sufficient quantity. Approves bills for payment. Confers with suppliers concerning late deliveries.
Yearly Earnings: $20,696
Education: Short-term O-J-T

Knowledge: Clerical; Economics and Accounting; Transportation
Abilities: None above average
Skills: Persuasion; Negotiation; Management of Financial Resources; Management of Material Resources
General Work Activities: Establishing and Maintaining Relationships; Monitoring and Controlling Resources
Job Characteristics: Deal with Unpleasant or Angry People; Sitting
GOE Group/s: 07.01.02 Administrative Detail: Administration; 07.07.03 Clerical Handling: General Clerical Work
CIP Program/s: 520499 Administrative and Secretarial Services, Other
Related DOT Job/s: 249.367-066 PROCUREMENT CLERK; 976.567-010 FILM-REPLACEMENT ORDERER

55328A STATISTICAL DATA CLERKS. OOH Title/s: Statistical Clerks

Compile and compute data for use in statistical studies. Compiles statistics from source materials, such as production, sales, and personnel records, surveys, and questionnaires. Computes statistical data according to formulas, using computer or calculator. Assembles and classifies statistics, following prescribed procedures. Operates computer to enter and retrieve data and prepare correspondence and reports. Prepares reports and graphs to show comparisons or survey results of statistical information obtained. Verifies completeness and accuracy of source data. Posts and files charts.
Yearly Earnings: $21,112
Education: Moderate-term O-J-T
Knowledge: Clerical; Computers and Electronics; Mathematics
Abilities: Category Flexibility; Mathematical Reasoning; Number Facility; Wrist-Finger Speed
Skills: Mathematics; Information Organization
General Work Activities: Evaluating Information against Standards; Analyzing Data or Information; Operating Vehicles or Equipment
Job Characteristics: Sitting; Making Repetitive Motions; Importance of Being Exact or Accurate; Importance of Repeating Same Tasks
GOE Group/s: 05.09.03 Material Control: Verifying, Recording, and Marking; 07.02.03 Mathematical Detail: Statistical Reporting and Analysis; 07.02.04 Mathematical Detail: Billing and Rate Computation; 07.05.03 Records Processing: Record Preparation and Maintenance; 07.07.03 Clerical Handling: General Clerical Work
CIP Program/s: 520401 Administrative Assistant/Secretarial Science, General; 520408 General Office/Clerical and Typing Services
Related DOT Job/s: 209.387-014 COMPILER; 214.487-010 CHART CALCULATOR; 216.382-062 STATISTICAL CLERK; 216.382-066 STATISTICAL CLERK, ADVERTISING; 219.387-022 PLANIMETER OPERATOR; 221.382-010 CHART CLERK; 221.584-010 CHART CHANGER

55328B MEDICAL RECORD CLERKS. OOH Title/s: Record Clerks

Compile medical statistical data, such as diagnoses, treatments, deaths, and births. Compiles statistical data, such as admissions, discharges, deaths, births, and types of treatment given. Prepares folders and maintains records of newly admitted patients. Reviews medical records for completeness and assembles records into standard order. Posts results of laboratory tests to records. Files records in designated areas according to applicable alphabetic and numeric filing system. Operates computer to enter and retrieve data and type correspondence and reports. Locates, signs out, and delivers medical records requested by hospital departments. Assists other workers with coding of records.
Yearly Earnings: $16,224
Education: Short-term O-J-T
Knowledge: Clerical
Abilities: Category Flexibility; Wrist-Finger Speed
Skills: None above average
General Work Activities: None above average
Job Characteristics: Sitting; Making Repetitive Motions; Importance of Being Sure All is Done; Importance of Repeating Same Tasks
GOE Group/s: 07.05.03 Records Processing: Record Preparation and Maintenance
CIP Program/s: 510707 Medical Records Tech./Technician
Related DOT Job/s: 245.362-010 MEDICAL-RECORD CLERK

55332 INTERVIEWING CLERKS, EXCEPT PERSONNEL AND SOCIAL WELFARE. OOH Title/s: Interviewing and New Accounts Clerks

Interview public to obtain information. Contact persons by telephone, mail, or in person for the purpose of completing forms, applications, or questionnaires. Ask specific questions, record answers, and assist persons with completing forms. May sort, classify, and file forms. Exclude workers whose primary duty is processing applications. Contacts persons at home, place of business, or field location, by telephone, mail, or in person. Asks questions to obtain various specified information, such as person's name, address, age, religion, and state of residency. Records results and data from interview or survey, using computer or specified form. Assists person in filling out application or questionnaire. Compiles and sorts data from interview, and reviews to correct errors. Explains reason for questioning, and other specified information.
Yearly Earnings: $18,876
Education: Short-term O-J-T
Knowledge: Clerical; Personnel and Human Resources
Abilities: None above average
Skills: Speaking
General Work Activities: None above average
Job Characteristics: Job-Required Social Interaction; Deal with External Customers; Sitting
GOE Group/s: 07.04.01 Oral Communications: Interviewing
CIP Program/s: 520401 Administrative Assistant/Secretarial Science, General; 520406 Receptionist
Related DOT Job/s: 205.362-018 HOSPITAL-ADMITTING CLERK; 205.367-014 CHARGE-ACCOUNT CLERK; 205.367-026 CREEL CLERK; 205.367-042 REGISTRATION CLERK; 205.367-054 SURVEY WORKER; 205.367-058 TRAFFIC CHECKER

55335 CUSTOMER SERVICE REPRESENTATIVES, UTILITIES. OOH Title/s: Customer Service Representatives, Utilities

Interview applicants for water, gas, electric, or telephone service. Talk with customer by phone or in person, and receive orders for installation, turn-on, discontinuance, or change in services. Confers with customer by phone or in person to receive orders for installation, turn-on, discontinuance, or change in service. Completes contract forms, prepares change-of-address records, and issues discontinuance orders, using computer. Resolves billing or service complaints and refers grievances to designated departments for investigation. Determines charges for service requested and collects deposits. Solicits sale of new or additional utility services.
Yearly Earnings: $24,336
Education: Short-term O-J-T
Knowledge: Sales and Marketing; Customer and Personal Service
Abilities: None above average
Skills: Active Listening; Service Orientation
General Work Activities: Resolving Conflicts, Negotiating with Others; Performing for or Working with Public
Job Characteristics: Job-Required Social Interaction; Persuade Someone to a Course of Action; Provide a Service to Others; Deal with

External Customers; Frequency in Conflict Situations; Deal with Unpleasant or Angry People; Sitting; Importance of Repeating Same Tasks
GOE Group/s: 07.04.01 Oral Communications: Interviewing
CIP Program/s: 520401 Administrative Assistant/Secretarial Science, General; 520406 Receptionist
Related DOT Job/s: 239.362-014 CUSTOMER SERVICE REPRESENTATIVE

55338A BOOKKEEPERS. OOH Title/s: Bookkeeping, Accounting, and Auditing Clerks

Classify, record, and summarize numerical data to compile and maintain financial records. Computes and/or records financial transactions and other account information (such as interest) to update or maintain accounting records. Classifies items on reports for bookkeeping purposes. Posts records. Compiles statistical reports of cash receipts, expenditures, accounts payable and receivable, profit and loss, and other items pertinent to business operation. Examines accuracy of balances, figures, calculations, postings, and other records pertaining to business or operating transactions, and reconciles or notes any discrepancies. Calculates such items as amounts due, balances, costs, discounts, dividends, equity, interest, net charges, outstanding balances, principal, profits, ratios, taxes, and wages. Debits or credits accounts. Compiles information from financial records into reports for organizational and regulatory personnel or customers. Complies with federal, state, and company policies, procedures, and regulations. Receives, processes, or transfers negotiable instruments, such as checks, drafts, coupons, and vouchers. Files and sorts documents. Types vouchers, invoices, account statements, and reports, using typewriter or computer. Prepares and processes billing statements and investigates billing irregularities. Prepares budgets and compiles budgetary reports containing statistics and other data. Verifies terms of credit, such as amount, insurance coverage, and shipping conditions, to determine compliance with standards. Handles inquiries and complaints, using account information and transition records. Coordinates customer credit information and collateral papers, complying with bank credit standards. Prepares letters. Examines collateral or appraises retirement value of equipment.
Yearly Earnings: $19,500
Education: Moderate-term O-J-T
Knowledge: Clerical; Economics and Accounting; Computers and Electronics; Mathematics; Law, Government, and Jurisprudence
Abilities: Written Expression; Deductive Reasoning; Category Flexibility; Mathematical Reasoning; Number Facility; Memorization; Perceptual Speed; Wrist-Finger Speed; Near Vision; Speech Recognition
Skills: Mathematics; Information Organization; Management of Financial Resources
General Work Activities: Processing Information; Evaluating Information against Standards; Operating Vehicles or Equipment; Documenting/Recording Information; Performing Administrative Activities
Job Characteristics: Sitting; Frustrating Circumstances; Degree of Automation; Importance of Being Exact or Accurate; Importance of Being Sure All is Done; Importance of Repeating Same Tasks
GOE Group/s: 07.01.04 Administrative Detail: Financial Work; 07.02.01 Mathematical Detail: Bookkeeping and Auditing; 07.02.02 Mathematical Detail: Accounting; 07.02.03 Mathematical Detail: Statistical Reporting and Analysis; 07.03.01 Financial Detail: Paying and Receiving; 07.05.02 Records Processing: Record Verification and Proofing
CIP Program/s: 120504 Food and Beverage/Restaurant Operations Manager; 520302 Accounting Technician; 520801 Finance, General; 520803 Banking and Financial Support Services
Related DOT Job/s: 210.362-010 DISTRIBUTION-ACCOUNTING CLERK; 210.367-010 ACCOUNT-INFORMATION CLERK; 210.367-014 FOREIGN-EXCHANGE-POSITION CLERK; 210.382-010 AUDIT CLERK; 210.382-014 BOOKKEEPER; 210.382-042 FIXED-CAPITAL CLERK; 210.382-046 GENERAL-LEDGER BOOKKEEPER; 210.382-054 NIGHT AUDITOR; 210.382-062 SECURITIES CLERK; 216.362-014 COLLECTION CLERK; 216.362-022 FOOD-AND-BEVERAGE CONTROLLER; 216.362-034 RESERVES CLERK; 216.362-038 ELECTRONIC FUNDS TRANSFER COORDINATOR; 216.362-042 MARGIN CLERK I; 216.367-014 TRUST-VAULT CLERK; 216.382-022 BUDGET CLERK; 216.482-010 ACCOUNTING CLERK; 219.367-042 CANCELING AND CUTTING CONTROL CLERK; 219.367-050 LETTER-OF-CREDIT CLERK

55338B ACCOUNTING CLERKS. OOH Title/s: Bookkeeping, Accounting, and Auditing Clerks

Compute, calculate, and post financial, statistical, and numerical data to maintain accounting records. Computes and/or records financial transactions and other account information (such as interest) to update or maintain accounting records. Calculates such items as amounts due, balances, costs, discounts, dividends, equity, interest, net charges, outstanding balances, principal, profits, ratios, taxes, and wages. Posts records. Examines accuracy of balances, calculations, postings, and other records pertaining to business or operating transactions, and reconciles or notes discrepancies. Classifies items on reports for bookkeeping purposes. Compiles statistical reports of cash receipts, expenditures, accounts payable and receivable, profit and loss, and other items pertinent to business operation. Compiles information from financial records into reports for organizational and regulatory personnel or customers. Receives, processes, or transfers negotiable instruments, such as checks, drafts, coupons, and vouchers. Prepares financial application forms. Files and sorts documents. Types vouchers, invoices, account statements, and reports, using typewriter or computer. Prepares letters.
Yearly Earnings: $19,500
Education: Moderate-term O-J-T
Knowledge: Clerical; Economics and Accounting; Computers and Electronics; Mathematics; English Language
Abilities: Written Expression; Deductive Reasoning; Category Flexibility; Mathematical Reasoning; Number Facility; Memorization; Speed of Closure; Perceptual Speed; Wrist-Finger Speed; Near Vision
Skills: Mathematics; Information Organization
General Work Activities: Operating Vehicles or Equipment; Performing Administrative Activities
Job Characteristics: Sitting; Degree of Automation; Importance of Being Exact or Accurate; Importance of Repeating Same Tasks
GOE Group/s: 07.02.01 Mathematical Detail: Bookkeeping and Auditing; 07.02.02 Mathematical Detail: Accounting; 07.02.04 Mathematical Detail: Billing and Rate Computation; 07.05.02 Records Processing: Record Verification and Proofing
CIP Program/s: 520302 Accounting Technician
Related DOT Job/s: 210.382-030 CLASSIFICATION-CONTROL CLERK; 210.382-038 CREDIT-CARD CLERK; 210.382-050 MORTGAGE-LOAN-COMPUTATION CLERK; 216.362-026 MORTGAGE-ACCOUNTING CLERK; 216.382-026 CLEARING-HOUSE CLERK; 216.382-058 RETURNED-ITEM CLERK; 216.482-026 DIVIDEND-DEPOSIT-VOUCHER CLERK; 219.362-066 VOUCHER CLERK; 219.382-010 CHECK WRITER; 219.487-010 TAX CLERK; 219.587-010 PARIMUTUEL-TICKET CHECKER

55341 PAYROLL AND TIMEKEEPING CLERKS. OOH Title/s: Payroll and Timekeeping Clerks

Compute wages and post wage data to payroll records. Keep daily records showing time of arrival and departure from work of employees. Compute earnings from timesheets and work tickets using calculator. Operate posting machine to compute and subtract payroll deductions. Enter net wages on earnings record card, check stub, and payroll sheet. Compiles employee time, production, and payroll data from timesheets and other records. Verifies attendance, hours worked, and pay adjustments, and posts information onto designated records. Calculates or computes wages and deductions and enters data into computer. Reviews timesheets, work charts, timecards, and union agreements for completeness and to determine payroll factors and pay rates. Compares wage computations, logs, and timesheets to detect and reconcile payroll discrepancies. Records employee information, such as exemptions, transfers, leave pay, and insurance coverage, to maintain and update payroll records. Compiles and submits payroll status and other reports to designated departments. Processes and issues paychecks to employees. Prorates departmental debit or credit expenses for cost accounting records.

Yearly Earnings: $21,320

Education: Short-term O-J-T

Knowledge: Clerical; Economics and Accounting; Personnel and Human Resources

Abilities: Mathematical Reasoning; Number Facility

Skills: None above average

General Work Activities: None above average

Job Characteristics: Sitting; Importance of Being Exact or Accurate; Importance of Being Sure All is Done

GOE Group/s: 07.02.05 Mathematical Detail: Payroll and Timekeeping

CIP Program/s: 520302 Accounting Technician

Related DOT Job/s: 215.362-018 FLIGHT-CREW-TIME CLERK; 215.362-022 TIMEKEEPER; 215.382-014 PAYROLL CLERK

55344 BILLING, COST, AND RATE CLERKS. OOH Title/s: Billing Clerks and Billing Machine Operators

Compile data, compute fees and charges, and prepare invoices for billing purposes. Duties include computing costs and calculating rates for goods, services, and shipment of goods; posting data; and keeping other relevant records. May involve use of computer or typewriter, calculator, and adding and bookkeeping machines. Exclude workers whose primary duty is operation of special office machines or workers who calculate charges for passenger transportation. Computes amounts due from such documents as purchase orders, sales tickets, and charge slips. Compiles and computes credit terms, discounts, and purchase prices for billing documents. Keeps records of invoices and support documents. Consults manuals which include rates, rules, regulations, and government tax and tariff information. Compiles cost factor reports, such as labor, production, storage, and equipment. Verifies compiled data from vendor invoices to ensure accuracy, and revises billing data when errors are found. Types billing documents, shipping labels, credit memorandums, and credit forms, using typewriter or computer. Resolves discrepancies on accounting records. Answers mail and telephone inquiries regarding rates, routing, and procedures. Estimates market value of product or services. Updates manuals when rates, rules, or regulations are amended.

Yearly Earnings: $22,204

Education: Short-term O-J-T

Knowledge: Clerical; Economics and Accounting; Mathematics; Law, Government, and Jurisprudence; Transportation

Abilities: Written Expression; Category Flexibility; Mathematical Reasoning; Number Facility; Perceptual Speed; Wrist-Finger Speed; Near Vision; Speech Recognition

Skills: None above average

General Work Activities: Operating Vehicles or Equipment; Performing Administrative Activities

Job Characteristics: Deal with External Customers; Sitting; Degree of Automation; Importance of Repeating Same Tasks

GOE Group/s: 05.09.02 Material Control: Estimating, Scheduling, and Record Keeping; 07.01.04 Administrative Detail: Financial Work; 07.02.02 Mathematical Detail: Accounting; 07.02.03 Mathematical Detail: Statistical Reporting and Analysis; 07.02.04 Mathematical Detail: Billing and Rate Computation; 07.07.03 Clerical Handling: General Clerical Work; 11.06.03 Finance: Risk and Profit Analysis

CIP Program/s: 080709 General Distribution Operations; 520302 Accounting Technician; 520401 Administrative Assistant/Secretarial Science, General; 520408 General Office/Clerical and Typing Services; 520499 Administrative and Secretarial Services, Other; 520801 Finance, General; 520803 Banking and Financial Support Services; 521403 International Business Marketing

Related DOT Job/s: 184.387-010 WHARFINGER; 191.367-010 PERSONAL PROPERTY ASSESSOR; 214.267-010 RATE ANALYST, FREIGHT; 214.362-010 DEMURRAGE CLERK; 214.362-014 DOCUMENTATION-BILLING CLERK; 214.362-022 INSURANCE CLERK; 214.362-026 INVOICE-CONTROL CLERK; 214.362-038 TRAFFIC-RATE CLERK; 214.362-042 BILLING CLERK; 214.382-014 BILLING TYPIST; 214.382-018 C.O.D. CLERK; 214.382-022 INTERLINE CLERK; 214.382-026 REVISING CLERK; 214.382-030 SETTLEMENT CLERK; 214.387-010 BILLING-CONTROL CLERK; 214.387-014 RATE REVIEWER; 214.387-018 SERVICES CLERK; 214.467-010 FOREIGN CLERK; 214.467-014 PRICER, MESSAGE AND DELIVERY SERVICE; 214.482-014 DEPOSIT-REFUND CLERK; 214.482-018 MEDICAL-VOUCHER CLERK; 214.482-022 RATER; 214.587-010 TELEGRAPH-SERVICE RATER; 216.382-034 COST CLERK; 216.382-050 POLICY-VALUE CALCULATOR; 216.382-054 RECEIPT-AND-REPORT CLERK; 221.382-026 SAMPLE CLERK; 237.367-030 MANAGER, TRAFFIC II; 241.267-026 DEPOSIT CLERK; 248.387-014 TONNAGE-COMPILATION CLERK; 249.367-034 EVALUATOR

55347 GENERAL OFFICE CLERKS. OOH Title/s: General Office Clerks; Material Recording, Scheduling, Dispatching, and Distributing Occupations

Perform duties too varied and diverse to be classified in any specific office clerical occupation. Clerical duties may be assigned in accordance with the office procedures of individual establishments and may include a combination of bookkeeping, typing, stenography, office machine operation, and filing. Compiles, copies, sorts, and files records of office activities, business transactions, and other activities. Computes, records, and proofreads data and other information, such as records or reports. Operates office machines, such as photocopier, telecopier, and personal computer. Completes and mails bills, contracts, policies, invoices, or checks. Stuffs envelopes and addresses, stamps, sorts, and distributes mail, packages, and other materials. Transcribes dictation and composes and types letters and other correspondence, using typewriter or computer. Orders materials, supplies, and services, and completes records and reports. Answers telephone, responds to requests, delivers messages, and runs errands. Reviews files, records, and other documents to obtain information to respond to requests. Completes work schedules and arranges appointments for staff and students. Collects, counts, and disburses money, completes banking transactions, and processes payroll. Communicates with customers, employees, and other individuals to disseminate or explain information.

Yearly Earnings: $19,396

Education: Short-term O-J-T

Knowledge: Clerical; Economics and Accounting; Customer and Personal Service; Telecommunications

Abilities: Number Facility; Perceptual Speed; Wrist-Finger Speed; Near Vision; Speech Recognition

Skills: None above average

General Work Activities: Operating Vehicles or Equipment

Job Characteristics: Deal with Unpleasant or Angry People; Sitting; Importance of Repeating Same Tasks

GOE Group/s: 07.01.02 Administrative Detail: Administration; 07.02.02 Mathematical Detail: Accounting; 07.04.01 Oral Communications: Interviewing; 07.04.03 Oral Communications: Registration; 07.04.04 Oral Communications: Reception and Information Giving; 07.04.05 Oral Communications: Information Transmitting and Receiving; 07.05.01 Records Processing: Coordinating and Scheduling; 07.05.03 Records Processing: Record Preparation and Maintenance; 07.07.03 Clerical Handling: General Clerical Work; 11.02.04 Educational and Library Services: Library Services
CIP Program/s: 510703 Health Unit Coordinator/Ward Clerk; 520401 Administrative Assistant/Secretarial Science, General; 520408 General Office/Clerical and Typing Services
Related DOT Job/s: 162.167-026 PRIZE COORDINATOR; 205.367-010 ADMISSIONS EVALUATOR; 205.367-030 ELECTION CLERK; 209.362-010 CIRCULATION CLERK; 209.362-014 CONTROL CLERK, AUDITING; 209.362-022 IDENTIFICATION CLERK; 209.362-030 CONGRESSIONAL-DISTRICT AIDE; 209.367-010 AGENT-LICENSING CLERK; 209.367-026 FINGERPRINT CLERK I; 209.367-034 LOST-CHARGE-CARD CLERK; 209.367-038 NEWS ASSISTANT; 209.367-050 TRIP FOLLOWER; 209.367-054 YARD CLERK; 209.382-022 TRAFFIC CLERK; 209.387-022 DATA-EXAMINATION CLERK; 209.562-010 CLERK, GENERAL; 209.587-014 CREDIT-CARD CLERK; 209.587-022 HISTORY-CARD CLERK; 209.587-030 MAP CLERK; 209.587-050 WRONG-ADDRESS CLERK; 209.667-014 ORDER CALLER; 209.667-018 CODE AND TEST CLERK; 209.687-022 SORTER; 219.362-010 ADMINISTRATIVE CLERK; 219.362-014 ATTENDANCE CLERK; 219.362-022 CLERK, TELEGRAPH SERVICE; 219.362-026 CONTRACT CLERK, AUTOMOBILE; 219.367-038 UNDERWRITING CLERK; 219.387-014 INSURANCE CLERK; 219.462-014 TRAIN CLERK; 219.482-018 REINSURANCE CLERK; 221.387-038 LAUNDRY CLERK; 221.387-042 MELTER CLERK; 222.367-030 FLOOR-SPACE ALLOCATOR; 222.367-034 LOST-AND-FOUND CLERK; 222.367-054 PROPERTY CLERK; 222.387-046 RETURNED-TELEPHONE-EQUIPMENT APPRAISER; 222.587-026 LABORATORY CLERK; 222.587-038 ROUTER; 222.687-034 STUBBER; 229.587-010 GREIGE-GOODS MARKER; 235.387-010 RADIO-MESSAGE ROUTER; 241.367-030 THROW-OUT CLERK; 241.367-042 PROPERTY-ASSESSMENT MONITOR; 243.362-014 POLICE AIDE; 245.362-014 UNIT CLERK; 245.367-014 BLOOD-DONOR-UNIT ASSISTANT; 245.367-018 CALENDAR-CONTROL CLERK, BLOOD BANK; 245.367-022 CREDIT CLERK, BLOOD BANK; 245.587-010 DIET CLERK; 247.382-010 MEDIA CLERK; 248.362-014 WEATHER CLERK; 249.267-010 COPYRIGHT EXPERT; 249.367-010 ANIMAL-SHELTER CLERK; 249.367-014 CAREER-GUIDANCE TECHNICIAN; 249.367-018 CHARTER; 249.367-026 CREDIT CARD CONTROL CLERK; 249.367-062 PROCESS SERVER; 249.367-078 TEST TECHNICIAN; 249.387-010 BROADCAST CHECKER; 249.387-022 READER; 249.587-010 BOARD ATTENDANT; 249.587-014 CUTTER-AND-PASTER, PRESS CLIPPINGS; 249.587-018 DOCUMENT PREPARER, MICROFILMING; 294.667-010 AUCTION ASSISTANT; 375.362-010 POLICE CLERK; 910.367-014 CAR DISTRIBUTOR; 962.167-018 PROPERTY COORDINATOR

Office Machine Operators

56002 BILLING, POSTING, AND CALCULATING MACHINE OPERATORS. OOH Title/s: Billing Clerks and Billing Machine Operators
Operate machines that automatically perform mathematical processes, such as addition, subtraction, multiplication, and division, to calculate and record billing, accounting, statistical, and other numerical data. Duties include operating special billing machines to prepare statements, bills, and invoices; and operating bookkeeping machines to copy and post data, make computations, and compile records of transactions. Calculates accounting and other numerical data, such as amounts customers owe, sales totals, and inventory data, using calculating machine. Encodes and adds amounts of transaction documents, such as checks or money orders, using encoding machine. Posts totals to records and prepares bills or invoices to be sent to customers, using billing machine. Sorts and microfilms transaction documents, such as checks, using sorting machine. Transcribes data from office records, using specified forms, billing machine, and transcribing machine. Compares machine totals to records for errors, and encodes correct amount, or prepares correction record if error is found. Transfers data from machine, such as encoding machine, to computer. Observes operation of sorter to note documents machine cannot read, and manually records amount, using keyboard. Bundles sorted documents to prepare those drawn on other banks for collection. Manually sorts and lists items for proof or collection. Cleans machines, such as encoding or sorting machines, and replaces ribbons, film, and tape.
Yearly Earnings: $24,336
Education: Short-term O-J-T
Knowledge: Clerical; Economics and Accounting
Abilities: Selective Attention; Wrist-Finger Speed
Skills: Mathematics
General Work Activities: None above average
Job Characteristics: Sitting; Making Repetitive Motions; Importance of Being Exact or Accurate; Importance of Repeating Same Tasks; Pace Determined by Speed of Equipment
GOE Group/s: 07.02.02 Mathematical Detail: Accounting; 07.02.04 Mathematical Detail: Billing and Rate Computation; 07.06.02 Clerical Machine Operation: Keyboard Machine Operation
CIP Program/s: 520302 Accounting Technician; 520801 Finance, General; 520803 Banking and Financial Support Services
Related DOT Job/s: 214.462-010 ACCOUNTS-ADJUSTABLE CLERK; 214.482-010 BILLING-MACHINE OPERATOR; 216.482-018 AUDIT-MACHINE OPERATOR; 216.482-022 CALCULATING-MACHINE OPERATOR; 217.382-010 PROOF-MACHINE OPERATOR

56005 DUPLICATING MACHINE OPERATORS. OOH Title/s: Duplicating, Mail, and Other Office Machine Operators
Operate one of a variety of office machines, such as photocopying, photographic, mimeograph, and duplicating machines, to make copies. Exclude blueprinting machine operators and operators of offset printing machines and presses. Sets controls for number of copies and presses buttons to start machine. Selects type, embossed plate, or paper stock, according to size, color, thickness, and quantity specified. Places original copy in feed tray, feeds originals into feed rolls, or positions originals on table beneath camera lens. Adjusts machine to regulate ink flow, speed, paper size, focus, exposure, and camera distance from document. Loads machine with blank paper or film and places paper roll in holding tray or rack of machine. Moves heat unit and clamping frame over screen bed to form Braille impression on page. Cuts copies apart and writes identifying information on copies. Cleans, oils, and repairs machine and printing plate. Records number of copies and receives payment.
Yearly Earnings: $16,328
Education: Short-term O-J-T
Knowledge: None above average
Abilities: Visual Color Discrimination
Skills: Repairing
General Work Activities: None above average
Job Characteristics: Making Repetitive Motions; Degree of Automation; Pace Determined by Speed of Equipment
GOE Group/s: 05.10.05 Crafts: Reproduction; 05.12.19 Elemental Work: Mechanical: Reproduction Services
CIP Program/s: 520401 Administrative Assistant/Secretarial Science, General; 520408 General Office/Clerical and Typing Services

Related DOT Job/s: 207.682-010 DUPLICATING-MACHINE OPERATOR I; 207.682-014 DUPLICATING-MACHINE OPERATOR II; 207.682-018 OFFSET-DUPLICATING-MACHINE OPERATOR; 207.685-010 BRAILLE-DUPLICATING-MACHINE OPERATOR; 207.685-014 PHOTOCOPYING-MACHINE OPERATOR; 207.685-018 PHOTOGRAPHIC-MACHINE OPERATOR

56008 MAIL MACHINE OPERATORS, PREPARATION AND HANDLING. OOH Title/s: Duplicating, Mail, and Other Office Machine Operators

Operate machines that emboss names, addresses, and other matter onto metal plates for use in addressing machines; print names, addresses, and similar information onto items such as envelopes, accounting forms, and advertising literature; address, fold, stuff, seal, and stamp mail; and open envelopes. Exclude workers who prepare incoming and outgoing mail for distribution by hand. Inserts material for printing or addressing into loading rack on machine. Starts machine. Operates embossing machine or typewriter to make corrections, additions, and changes on address plates. Removes printed material from machine, such as labeled articles, postmarked envelopes or tape, and folded sheets. Selects type of die size. Adjusts machine guides, rollers, and card insert prior to starting machine. Changes machine ribbon. Checks ink level, adds ink, and fills paste reservoir. Observes machine operation to detect evidence of malfunctions during production run. Makes adjustments to machine and inspects output for defects. Positions plates, stencils, or tapes in machine magazine. Places folded sheets into envelopes preparatory to mailing. Reads production order to determine type and size of items scheduled for printing and mailing.
Yearly Earnings: $16,328
Education: Short-term O-J-T
Knowledge: None above average
Abilities: Rate Control
Skills: None above average
General Work Activities: None above average
Job Characteristics: Making Repetitive Motions; Degree of Automation; Importance of Repeating Same Tasks; Pace Determined by Speed of Equipment
GOE Group/s: 05.12.19 Elemental Work: Mechanical: Reproduction Services; 06.04.38 Elemental Work: Industrial: Wrapping and Packaging
CIP Program/s: 520401 Administrative Assistant/Secretarial Science, General; 520408 General Office/Clerical and Typing Services
Related DOT Job/s: 208.462-010 MAILING-MACHINE OPERATOR; 208.582-010 ADDRESSING-MACHINE OPERATOR; 208.685-014 FOLDING-MACHINE OPERATOR; 208.685-018 INSERTING-MACHINE OPERATOR; 208.685-026 SEALING-AND-CANCELING-MACHINE OPERATOR; 208.685-034 WING-MAILER-MACHINE OPERATOR

56011 COMPUTER OPERATORS, EXCEPT PERIPHERAL EQUIPMENT. OOH Title/s: Computer and Peripheral Equipment Operators

Monitor and control electronic computer to process business, scientific, engineering, and other data according to operating instructions. Exclude operators who control peripheral equipment only. Enters commands, using computer terminal, and activates controls on computer and peripheral equipment to integrate and operate equipment. Enters commands to clear computer system and start operation, using keyboard of computer terminal. Loads peripheral equipment with selected materials for operating runs, or oversees loading of peripheral equipment by peripheral equipment operators. Observes peripheral equipment operation and error messages displayed on terminal monitor to detect faulty output or machine stoppage. Diagnoses reasons for equipment malfunction and enters commands to correct error or stoppage and resume operations. Clears equipment at end of operating run and reviews schedule to determine next assignment. Records information such as computer operating time and problems which occurred, such as down time, and actions taken. Reads job set-up instructions to determine equipment to be used and order of use. Answers telephone calls to assist computer users encountering problems. Notifies supervisor of errors or equipment stoppage. Separates output, when needed, and sends data to specified users. Assists workers in classifying, cataloging, and maintaining tapes.
Yearly Earnings: $21,268
Education: Moderate-term O-J-T
Knowledge: Clerical; Customer and Personal Service; Computers and Electronics; Telecommunications
Abilities: Information Ordering; Category Flexibility; Memorization; Speed of Closure; Selective Attention; Wrist-Finger Speed; Near Vision; Sound Localization; Speech Recognition
Skills: Reading Comprehension; Active Listening; Equipment Selection; Programming; Troubleshooting
General Work Activities: Operating Vehicles or Equipment; Repairing and Maintaining Electrical Equipment
Job Characteristics: Sitting; Degree of Automation; Pace Determined by Speed of Equipment
GOE Group/s: 07.06.01 Clerical Machine Operation: Computer Operation
CIP Program/s: 110301 Data Processing Technologists and Technicians; 521201 Management Information Systems and Business Data Processing; 521205 Business Computer Facilities Operator
Related DOT Job/s: 213.362-010 COMPUTER OPERATOR

56014 PERIPHERAL EDP EQUIPMENT OPERATORS. OOH Title/s: Computer and Peripheral Equipment Operators

Operate computer peripheral equipment, such as tape or disk drives, printers, card-to-tape or tabulating machines, sorters, or interpreters. Exclude computer operators and data entry keyers. Operates computer peripheral equipment to transfer data to and from computer and to convert data from one format to another. Operates encoding machine to trace coordinates on documents, such as maps or drawings, and to encode document points into computer. Mounts reels and cartridges of magnetic tape in tape drives. Loads paper in printer and loads checks or other documents in magnetic ink reader-sorter or optical character reader. Types command on keyboard to transfer encoded data from memory unit to magnetic tape. Sets controls and enters commands into computer, using computer terminal, and performs other tasks to start and operate peripheral machines. Unloads and labels magnetic tape for delivery to other worker or tape library. Observes machine operation and error lights on machines to detect malfunction. Removes faulty materials and notifies supervisor of error or machine stoppage. Separates, sorts, and distributes output. Reads instructions and schedule, such as schedule of documents to be printed, or receives oral instructions regarding work for shift. Observes printed materials for defects, such as creases and tears. Keeps record of work orders, time, and tape production. Cleans and supplies equipment operated with paper, ink, film, developing solution, and other material. Guides digitizer cursor over document to trace coordinates, stops at specified points, and punches cursor key to digitize points into computer memory unit.
Yearly Earnings: $21,216
Education: Moderate-term O-J-T
Knowledge: Computers and Electronics; Telecommunications
Abilities: None above average
Skills: Operation Monitoring; Operation and Control
General Work Activities: Operating Vehicles or Equipment

Job Characteristics: Degree of Automation
GOE Group/s: 07.06.01 Clerical Machine Operation: Computer Operation
CIP Program/s: 110301 Data Processing Technologists and Technicians; 521201 Management Information Systems and Business Data Processing; 521205 Business Computer Facilities Operator; 521299 Business Information and Data Processing Services, Other
Related DOT Job/s: 213.382-010 COMPUTER PERIPHERAL EQUIPMENT OPERATOR; 213.582-010 DIGITIZER OPERATOR

56017 DATA ENTRY KEYERS, EXCEPT COMPOSING. OOH Title/s: Typists, Word Processors, and Data Entry Keyers

Operate keyboard or other data entry devices to prepare data processing input on cards, disk, or tape. Duties include coding and verifying alphabetic or numeric data. Enters data from source documents into computer or onto tape or disk for subsequent entry, using keyboard or scanning device. Compiles, sorts, and verifies accuracy of data to be entered. Compares data entered with source documents. Deletes incorrectly entered data. Reenters data in verification format to detect errors. Keeps record of completed work. Selects materials needed to complete work assignment. Loads machine with required input or output media, such as paper, cards, disk, tape or Braille media. Resolves garbled or indecipherable messages, using cryptographic procedures and equipment. Files completed documents.
Yearly Earnings: $18,928
Education: Postsecondary vocational training
Knowledge: Clerical; Computers and Electronics
Abilities: Wrist-Finger Speed
Skills: None above average
General Work Activities: None above average
Job Characteristics: Sitting; Making Repetitive Motions; Importance of Being Exact or Accurate; Importance of Being Sure All is Done; Importance of Repeating Same Tasks; Pace Determined by Speed of Equipment
GOE Group/s: 07.06.01 Clerical Machine Operation: Computer Operation; 07.06.02 Clerical Machine Operation: Keyboard Machine Operation
CIP Program/s: 520401 Administrative Assistant/Secretarial Science, General; 520407 Information Processing/Data Entry Technician
Related DOT Job/s: 203.582-010 BRAILLE OPERATOR; 203.582-014 BRAILLE TYPIST; 203.582-018 CRYPTOGRAPHIC-MACHINE OPERATOR; 203.582-038 PERFORATOR TYPIST; 203.582-054 DATA ENTRY CLERK

56021 DATA KEYERS, COMPOSING. OOH Title/s: Typists, Word Processors, and Data Entry Keyers

Operate photocomposing perforator or comparable data entry composing machines (similar in operation to an electric typewriter) to prepare materials for printing or publication. Operates keyboards on computers and recording, composing, or typing machines to enter and retrieve information and control codes. Inserts blank stationary, coated paper, tape cartridges, or rolls onto machine and presses buttons to start machine and feeder. Selects and installs type fonts and platen gears or sets spacing and margin controls on typesetting or composing machine. Reads instructions, manuscripts, and proof sheets to determine information targeted for storage, retrieval, or modification and to obtain computer control codes. Examines proof copy or tapes for errors and marks error or makes corrections. Designs layout of page elements, such as illustrations, charts, text, justification, spacing, and margins, using typesetting, design, and drafting knowledge. Calculates dimensions for enlargements and reductions of copy. Removes copy or completed tapes from machine. Positions copy and instructions in copy holder. Draws decorative or illustrative designs on copy. Maintains log of activities.
Yearly Earnings: $18,928
Education: Postsecondary vocational training
Knowledge: Clerical; Computers and Electronics
Abilities: Wrist-Finger Speed
Skills: None above average
General Work Activities: None above average
Job Characteristics: Sitting; Making Repetitive Motions; Degree of Automation; Importance of Repeating Same Tasks; Pace Determined by Speed of Equipment
GOE Group/s: 07.06.01 Clerical Machine Operation: Computer Operation; 07.06.02 Clerical Machine Operation: Keyboard Machine Operation
CIP Program/s: 480201 Graphic and Printing Equipment Operator, General; 480205 Mechanical Typesetter and Composer; 480211 Computer Typography and Composition Equipment Operator
Related DOT Job/s: 203.382-018 MAGNETIC-TAPE-COMPOSER OPERATOR; 203.382-026 VARITYPE OPERATOR; 203.582-042 PHOTOCOMPOSING-PERFORATOR-MACHINE OPERATOR; 203.582-046 PHOTOCOMPOSITION-KEYBOARD OPERATOR; 203.582-062 TYPESETTER-PERFORATOR OPERATOR; 208.382-010 TERMINAL-MAKEUP OPERATOR

56099 ALL OTHER OFFICE MACHINE OPERATORS. OOH Title/s: Photographic Process Workers; Duplicating, Mail, and Other Office Machine Operators

All other office machine operators not classified separately above.
Yearly Earnings: $16,328
Education: Short-term O-J-T
GOE Group/s: 05.09.03 Material Control: Verifying, Recording, and Marking; 05.12.19 Elemental Work: Mechanical: Reproduction Services; 06.02.02 Production Work: Machine Work, Metal and Plastics
CIP Program/s: 520401 Administrative Assistant/Secretarial Science, General; 520408 General Office/Clerical and Typing Services; 520801 Finance, General; 520803 Banking and Financial Support Services
Related DOT Job/s: 208.582-014 EMBOSSING-MACHINE OPERATOR I; 208.682-010 EMBOSSING-MACHINE OPERATOR II; 208.685-010 COLLATOR OPERATOR; 208.685-022 MICROFILM MOUNTER; 216.685-010 GAS USAGE METER CLERK; 217.485-010 CURRENCY COUNTER; 217.585-010 COIN-COUNTER-AND-WRAPPER; 976.682-022 MICROFILM-CAMERA OPERATOR

Communications Equipment Operators

57102 SWITCHBOARD OPERATORS. OOH Title/s: Telephone Operators

Operate cord or cordless switchboard to relay incoming, outgoing, and interoffice calls. May supply information to callers and record messages. May also act as receptionist, perform routine clerical work, and type. Operates communication system, such as telephone, switchboard, intercom, two-way radio, or public address. Greets caller, furnishes information to caller or visitor, and relays calls. Places telephone calls, using telephone directories and card indexes to locate telephone numbers. Records messages, suggesting rewording for clarity and conciseness. Relays and routes messages, spelling misunderstood words, using phonetic alphabet. Performs clerical duties, such as typing, proofreading, accepting orders, scheduling appointments, and sorting mail. Keeps records of calls placed and toll

charges. Receives visitors and obtains name and nature of business. Telephones for ambulances or fire-fighting equipment when requested. Date-stamps and files messages. Quotes rates to customer from rate book and records rate for customer billing.
Yearly Earnings: $20,696
Education: Short-term O-J-T
Knowledge: Clerical; Foreign Language; Telecommunications
Abilities: Wrist-Finger Speed; Auditory Attention; Speech Recognition
Skills: None above average
General Work Activities: None above average
Job Characteristics: Job-Required Social Interaction; Deal with External Customers; Deal with Unpleasant or Angry People; Sitting
GOE Group/s: 07.04.05 Oral Communications: Information Transmitting and Receiving; 07.04.06 Oral Communications: Switchboard Services
CIP Program/s: 520401 Administrative Assistant/Secretarial Science, General; 520406 Receptionist
Related DOT Job/s: 235.562-014 SWITCHBOARD OPERATOR, POLICE DISTRICT; 235.662-014 COMMUNICATION-CENTER OPERATOR; 235.662-022 TELEPHONE OPERATOR; 235.662-026 TELEPHONE-ANSWERING-SERVICE OPERATOR; 239.362-010 TELEPHONE CLERK, TELEGRAPH OFFICE

57105 DIRECTORY ASSISTANCE OPERATORS.

OOH Title/s: Telephone Operators

Provide telephone information from central office switchboard. Refer to alphabetical or geographical reels or directories to answer questions or suggest answer sources. Refers to alphabetical or geographical reels or directories to answer questions and provide telephone information. Types location and spelling of name on computer terminal keyboard, and scans directory or microfilm viewer to locate number. Suggests alternate locations and spellings under which number could be listed. Plugs in headphones when signal light flashes on cord switchboard, or pushes switch keys on cordless switchboard to make connections. Maintains record of calls received. Keeps reels and directories up-to-date.
Yearly Earnings: $20,696
Education: Moderate-term O-J-T
Knowledge: Clerical; Customer and Personal Service; Computers and Electronics; Geography; Foreign Language; Telecommunications
Abilities: Perceptual Speed; Response Orientation; Reaction Time; Wrist-Finger Speed; Auditory Attention; Speech Recognition; Speech Clarity
Skills: None above average
General Work Activities: None above average
Job Characteristics: Job-Required Social Interaction; Provide a Service to Others; Deal with External Customers; Deal with Unpleasant or Angry People; Sitting; Degree of Automation; Importance of Repeating Same Tasks
GOE Group/s: 07.04.06 Oral Communications: Switchboard Services
CIP Program/s: 000000 NO CIP ASSIGNED
Related DOT Job/s: 235.662-018 DIRECTORY-ASSISTANCE OPERATOR

57108 CENTRAL OFFICE OPERATORS. OOH Title/s: Telephone Operators

Operate telephone switchboard to establish or assist customers in establishing local or long-distance telephone connections. Observes signal light on switchboard, plugs cords into trunk-jack, and dials or presses button to make connections. Consults charts to determine charges for pay-telephone calls. Inserts tickets in calculagraph (time-stamping device) to record time of toll calls. Requests coin deposits for calls. Gives information regarding subscribers' telephone numbers. Calculates and quotes charges on long-distance connections.
Yearly Earnings: $20,696
Education: Short-term O-J-T
Knowledge: Telecommunications
Abilities: Speech Recognition
Skills: None above average
General Work Activities: None above average
Job Characteristics: Provide a Service to Others; Deal with External Customers; Sitting
GOE Group/s: 07.04.06 Oral Communications: Switchboard Services
CIP Program/s: 520401 Administrative Assistant/Secretarial Science, General; 520406 Receptionist
Related DOT Job/s: 235.462-010 CENTRAL-OFFICE OPERATOR

57111 TELEGRAPH AND TELETYPE OPERATORS.

OOH Title/s: Indirectly related to Dispatchers

Operate telegraphic typewriter, telegraph key, teletype machine facsimile, and related equipment to transmit and receive signals or messages. Prepare messages according to prescribed formats. Verify and correct errors in messages. May adjust equipment for proper operation. Routes messages to customers, according to procedures, using various types of equipment. Turns on equipment and enters information into computer to begin start-up. Types and transmits outgoing messages. Types requests for clarification when messages are garbled. Reads messages to determine errors and marks for distribution. Records time and date messages were received or transmitted, using computer. Sorts messages for delivery. Receives requests for message pick-up within area served by telegraph office. Replaces paper in equipment as required. Receives and records remittances returned for messages picked up. Verifies or assigns code number to telecommunication messages. Folds and places messages in envelopes for delivery.
Yearly Earnings: $20,020
Education: Moderate-term O-J-T
Knowledge: Clerical; Computers and Electronics; Telecommunications
Abilities: Wrist-Finger Speed
Skills: None above average
General Work Activities: None above average
Job Characteristics: Sitting; Making Repetitive Motions; Degree of Automation; Importance of Repeating Same Tasks; Pace Determined by Speed of Equipment
GOE Group/s: 07.04.05 Oral Communications: Information Transmitting and Receiving; 07.05.04 Records Processing: Routing and Distribution; 07.06.02 Clerical Machine Operation: Keyboard Machine Operation
CIP Program/s: 520401 Administrative Assistant/Secretarial Science, General; 520406 Receptionist
Related DOT Job/s: 203.562-010 WIRE-TRANSFER CLERK; 203.582-050 TELEGRAPHIC-TYPEWRITER OPERATOR; 235.562-010 CLERK, ROUTE; 236.562-010 TELEGRAPHER; 236.562-014 TELEGRAPHER AGENT

57199 ALL OTHER COMMUNICATIONS EQUIPMENT OPERATORS. OOH Title/s: Telephone Operators; Dispatchers

All other communications equipment operators not classified separately above.
Yearly Earnings: $20,020
Education: Moderate-term O-J-T

GOE Group/s: 05.10.05 Crafts: Reproduction; 07.04.05 Oral Communications: Information Transmitting and Receiving; 09.04.02 Customer Services: Sales Services
CIP Program/s: 520401 Administrative Assistant/Secretarial Science, General; 520406 Receptionist
Related DOT Job/s: 237.367-034 PAY-STATION ATTENDANT; 239.367-026 SERVICE OBSERVER; 239.382-010 WIRE-PHOTO OPERATOR, NEWS; 372.167-010 DISPATCHER, SECURITY GUARD

Mail Clerks, Carriers, and Messengers

57302 MAIL CLERKS, EXCEPT MAIL MACHINE OPERATORS AND POSTAL SERVICE. OOH Title/s: Mail Clerks and Messengers

Prepare incoming and outgoing mail for distribution. Duties include time-stamping, opening, reading, sorting, and routing incoming mail; sealing, stamping, and affixing postage to outgoing mail or packages; and keeping necessary records and completed forms. Exclude workers whose primary duty is mail distribution or operation of mail-preparing and mail-handling machines. Sorts letters or packages into sacks or bins, and places identifying tag on sack or bin, according to destination and type. Affixes postage to packages or letter by hand, or stamps with postage meter, and dispatches mail. Stamps date and time of receipt of incoming mail, and distributes and collects mail. Seals or opens envelopes by hand or machine. Records and maintains records of information such as charges and destination of insured, registered, or c.o.d. packages. Wraps packages or bundles by hand or using tying machine. Weighs packages or letters, computes charges, and accepts payment, using weight scale and rate chart. Inspects wrapping, address, and appearance of outgoing package or letter for conformance to standards and accuracy. Addresses packages or letters by hand, or using addressing machine, label, or stamp. Stacks bundles of bulk-printed matter for shipment, and loads and unloads from trucks and conveyors. Releases packages or letters to customer upon presentation of written notice or other identification. Receives request for merchandise samples or promotional literature, prepares shipping slips, and mails samples or literature. Answers inquiries regarding shipping or mailing policies.
Yearly Earnings: $16,796
Education: Short-term O-J-T
Knowledge: Clerical; Geography
Abilities: Gross Body Equilibrium
Skills: Service Orientation
General Work Activities: None above average
Job Characteristics: Making Repetitive Motions; Importance of Repeating Same Tasks
GOE Group/s: 05.09.01 Material Control: Shipping, Receiving, and Stock Checking; 07.03.01 Financial Detail: Paying and Receiving; 07.05.04 Records Processing: Routing and Distribution; 07.07.02 Clerical Handling: Sorting and Distrubtion
CIP Program/s: 520401 Administrative Assistant/Secretarial Science, General; 520408 General Office/Clerical and Typing Services
Related DOT Job/s: 209.587-018 DIRECT-MAIL CLERK; 209.687-026 MAIL CLERK; 222.367-022 EXPRESS CLERK; 222.387-038 PARCEL POST CLERK; 222.567-018 SLOT-TAG INSERTER; 222.587-030 MAILER; 222.587-032 MAILER APPRENTICE; 249.687-010 OFFICE COPY SELECTOR

57305 POSTAL MAIL CARRIERS. OOH Title/s: Postal Clerks and Mail Carriers

Sort mail for delivery. Deliver mail on established route by vehicle or on foot. Inserts mail into slots of mail rack to sort mail for delivery. Delivers mail to residences and business establishments along route. Drives vehicle over established route. Completes delivery forms, collects charges, and obtains signatures on receipts for delivery of specified types of mail. Enters changes of address in route book and readdresses mail to be forwarded. Picks up outgoing mail. Sells stamps and issues money orders.
Yearly Earnings: $33,644
Education: Short-term O-J-T
Knowledge: Geography; Transportation
Abilities: Spatial Orientation
Skills: None above average
General Work Activities: Performing General Physical Activities; Handling and Moving Objects; Interacting with Computers
Job Characteristics: Very Hot; Walking or Running; Special Uniform; Importance of Being Exact or Accurate
GOE Group/s: 07.05.04 Records Processing: Routing and Distribution
CIP Program/s: 000000 NO CIP ASSIGNED
Related DOT Job/s: 230.363-010 RURAL MAIL CARRIER; 230.367-010 MAIL CARRIER

57308 POSTAL SERVICE CLERKS. OOH Title/s: Postal Clerks and Mail Carriers

Perform any combination of tasks in a post office, such as receive letters and parcels; sell postage and revenue stamps, postal cards, and stamped envelopes; fill out and sell money orders; place mail in pigeon holes of mail rack or in bags according to state, address, or other scheme; and examine mail for correct postage. Collects payment for postage stamps, postal cards, stamped envelopes, metered postage, and money orders. Weighs, registers, insures, and computes mailing costs of letters and parcels based on type, weight, and destination. Sorts mail according to groups and destination, by hand or by operating electronic mail-sorting or scanning device. Examines mail for correct postage. Answers questions pertaining to mail regulations, procedures, postage rates, and mail delivery. Transports mail from one work station to another within same postal office. Feeds mail into electric-electronic postage canceling device, or hand stamps to cancel postage. Calibrates postage meters. Receives, registers, and refers for investigation complaints regarding mail theft, delivery, lost mail, and damaged mail. Posts announcements on centrally located bulletin board to distribute government-related information to general public. Assists public in complying with federal regulations of Postal Service and other federal agencies, such as registration of aliens.
Yearly Earnings: $32,656
Education: Short-term O-J-T
Knowledge: Clerical; Customer and Personal Service; Geography
Abilities: None above average
Skills: None above average
General Work Activities: Handling and Moving Objects; Assisting and Caring for Others; Performing for or Working with Public
Job Characteristics: Provide a Service to Others; Deal with External Customers; Deal with Unpleasant or Angry People; Deal with Physical, Aggressive People; Standing; Making Repetitive Motions; Special Uniform; Importance of Being Sure All is Done; Importance of Repeating Same Tasks
GOE Group/s: 07.03.01 Financial Detail: Paying and Receiving; 07.05.04 Records Processing: Routing and Distribution
CIP Program/s: 000000 NO CIP ASSIGNED

Related DOT Job/s: 209.687-014 MAIL HANDLER; 243.367-014 POST-OFFICE CLERK

57311A COURIERS AND MESSENGERS. OOH Title/s: Mail Clerks and Messengers

Pick up and carry messages, documents, packages, and other items between offices or departments within an establishment or to other business concerns, traveling by foot, bicycle, motorcycle, automobile, or public conveyance. Delivers messages and items, such as documents, packages, and food, between establishment departments and to other establishments and private homes. Receives message or materials to be delivered, and information on recipient, such as name, address, and telephone number. Walks, rides bicycle, drives vehicle, or uses public conveyance to reach destination to deliver message or materials in person. Calls by telephone to deliver verbal messages. Records information, such as items received and delivered and recipient's reply to message. Obtains signature, receipt, or payment from recipient for articles delivered. Monitors fluid levels and replenishes fuel to maintain delivery vehicle.

Yearly Earnings: $17,888

Education: Short-term O-J-T

Knowledge: None above average

Abilities: Spatial Orientation; Response Orientation; Rate Control; Reaction Time; Speed of Limb Movement; Stamina; Gross Body Coordination; Gross Body Equilibrium; Far Vision; Night Vision; Glare Sensitivity; Speech Recognition

Skills: None above average

General Work Activities: Performing General Physical Activities; Interacting with Computers

Job Characteristics: Provide a Service to Others; Walking or Running

GOE Group/s: 07.07.02 Clerical Handling: Sorting and Distrubtion; 07.07.03 Clerical Handling: General Clerical Work

CIP Program/s: 000000 NO CIP ASSIGNED

Related DOT Job/s: 215.563-010 CALLER; 230.663-010 DELIVERER, OUTSIDE; 239.567-010 OFFICE HELPER; 239.677-010 MESSENGER, COPY; 239.687-010 ROUTE AIDE; 239.687-014 TUBE OPERATOR; 299.477-010 DELIVERER, MERCHANDISE

Material Recording, Scheduling, and Distributing Workers

58002 DISPATCHERS—POLICE, FIRE, AND AMBULANCE. OOH Title/s: Dispatchers

Receive complaints from public concerning crimes and police emergencies. Broadcast orders to police radio patrol units in vicinity of complaint to investigate. Operate radio and telephone equipment to receive reports of fires and medical emergencies, and relay information or orders to proper officials. Receives incoming calls by telephone or alarm system. Coordinates emergency requests, and dispatches response units to emergency, using radio or alarm system. Operates telecommunication equipment to relay information and messages to and from emergency site and between law enforcement agencies. Contacts officers to verify assignment locations. Monitors alarm system to detect fires, illegal entry into establishments, or other emergencies. Questions caller to determine nature of problem and type and number of personnel and equipment needed. Determines response needed to emergency. Questions caller, observes alarm register, and scans map to determine if emergency is within service area. Provides instructions to caller, utilizing knowledge of emergency medical care. Scans status charts and computer screen to determine emergency units available for response. Records details of calls, dispatches, and messages, and maintains logs and files, using computer. Tests and adjusts communication and alarm systems, and reports malfunctions to maintenance units.

Yearly Earnings: $21,112

Education: Moderate-term O-J-T

Knowledge: Computers and Electronics; Geography; Therapy and Counseling; Public Safety and Security; Telecommunications

Abilities: Oral Comprehension; Memorization; Speed of Closure; Selective Attention; Time Sharing; Speech Recognition; Speech Clarity

Skills: Active Listening; Coordination; Instructing; Service Orientation; Problem Identification

General Work Activities: Getting Information Needed to Do the Job; Identifying Objects, Actions, and Events; Estimating Needed Characteristics; Repairing and Maintaining Electrical Equipment; Communicating with Persons Outside Organization; Assisting and Caring for Others; Resolving Conflicts, Negotiating with Others; Performing for or Working with Public; Coordinating Work and Activities of Others

Job Characteristics: Objective or Subjective Information; Job-Required Social Interaction; Persuade Someone to a Course of Action; Deal with External Customers; Coordinate or Lead Others; Responsibility for Outcomes and Results; Frequency in Conflict Situations; Deal with Unpleasant or Angry People; Sitting; Consequence of Error; Frustrating Circumstances; Importance of Being Aware of New Events

GOE Group/s: 07.04.05 Oral Communications: Information Transmitting and Receiving

CIP Program/s: 520401 Administrative Assistant/Secretarial Science, General; 520406 Receptionist

Related DOT Job/s: 379.162-010 ALARM OPERATOR; 379.362-010 DISPATCHER, RADIO; 379.362-014 PROTECTIVE-SIGNAL OPERATOR; 379.362-018 TELECOMMUNICATOR

58005 DISPATCHERS—EXCEPT POLICE, FIRE, AND AMBULANCE. OOH Title/s: Dispatchers

Schedule and dispatch workers, work crews, equipment, or service vehicles for conveyance of materials, freight, or passengers or for normal installation, service, or emergency repairs rendered outside the place of business. Duties may include use of radio or telephone to transmit assignments and compiling statistics and reports on work progress. Routes or assigns workers or equipment to appropriate location, according to customer request, specifications, or needs. Determines types or amount of equipment, vehicles, materials, or personnel required, according to work order or specifications. Relays work orders, messages, and information to or from work crews, supervisors, and field inspectors, using telephone or two-way radio. Receives or prepares work orders, according to customer request or specifications. Records and maintains files and records regarding customer requests, work or services performed, charges, expenses, inventory, and other dispatch information. Confers with customer or supervising personnel regarding questions, problems, and requests for service or equipment. Orders supplies and equipment, and issues to personnel.

Yearly Earnings: $21,112

Education: Moderate-term O-J-T

Knowledge: Customer and Personal Service; Geography; Telecommunications; Transportation

Abilities: None above average

Skills: Time Management; Management of Material Resources

General Work Activities: Performing for or Working with Public; Coordinating Work and Activities of Others; Monitoring and Controlling Resources

Job Characteristics: Job-Required Social Interaction; Provide a Service to Others; Deal with External Customers; Coordinate or Lead

Others; Frequency in Conflict Situations; Deal with Unpleasant or Angry People; Sitting; Importance of Repeating Same Tasks
GOE Group/s: 05.02.01 Managerial Work: Mechanical: Systems; 05.06.03 Systems Operation: Oil, Gas, and Water Distribution; 05.09.02 Material Control: Estimating, Scheduling, and Record Keeping; 06.01.01 Production Technology: Supervision and Instruction; 07.04.05 Oral Communications: Information Transmitting and Receiving; 07.05.01 Records Processing: Coordinating and Scheduling; 07.05.03 Records Processing: Record Preparation and Maintenance; 07.05.04 Records Processing: Routing and Distribution
CIP Program/s: 080709 General Distribution Operations; 410205 Nuclear/Nuclear Power Technologists and Technicians; 470501 Stationary Energy Sources Installer and Operator; 490399 Water Transportation Workers, Other; 520401 Administrative Assistant/Secretarial Science, General; 520406 Receptionist
Related DOT Job/s: 215.167-010 CAR CLERK, PULLMAN; 215.367-018 TAXICAB COORDINATOR; 221.362-014 DISPATCHER, RELAY; 221.367-070 SERVICE CLERK; 221.367-082 WORK-ORDER-SORTING CLERK; 239.167-014 DISPATCHER; 239.367-014 DISPATCHER, MAINTENANCE SERVICE; 239.367-022 RECEIVER-DISPATCHER; 239.367-030 DISPATCHER, STREET DEPARTMENT; 248.367-026 DISPATCHER, SHIP PILOT; 249.167-014 DISPATCHER, MOTOR VEHICLE; 249.367-070 ROUTING CLERK; 910.167-014 TRAIN DISPATCHER, ASSISTANT CHIEF; 910.367-018 ENGINE DISPATCHER; 911.167-010 DISPATCHER, TUGBOAT; 913.167-010 BUS DISPATCHER, INTERSTATE; 913.367-010 TAXICAB STARTER; 914.167-014 DISPATCHER, OIL; 919.162-010 DISPATCHER, TRAFFIC OR SYSTEM; 932.167-010 DISPATCHER; 939.362-010 DISPATCHER, OIL WELL SERVICES; 952.167-010 DISPATCHER, SERVICE OR WORK; 953.167-010 GAS DISPATCHER; 954.367-010 WATER-SERVICE DISPATCHER; 955.167-010 DISPATCHER, RADIOACTIVE-WASTE-DISPOSAL; 959.167-010 DISPATCHER, SERVICE

58008 PRODUCTION, PLANNING, AND EXPEDITING CLERKS. OOH Title/s: Material Recording, Scheduling, Dispatching, and Distributing Occupations
Coordinate and expedite the flow of work and materials within or between departments of an establishment, according to production schedule. Duties, which are primarily clerical in nature, include reviewing and distributing production schedules and work orders; conferring with department supervisors to determine progress of work and completion dates; and compiling reports on progress of work and production problems. Work may also include scheduling workers and estimating costs; routing and delivering parts to ensure production quotas are met; scheduling shipment of parts; keeping inventory of material in departments; ensuring vendors ship merchandise on promised date; and writing special orders for services and merchandise. Reviews documents such as production schedules, staffing tables, and specifications to obtain information, such as materials, priorities, and personnel requirements. Confers with establishment personnel, vendors, and customers to coordinate processing and shipping, and to resolve complaints. Completes status reports, such as production progress, customer information, and materials inventory. Compiles schedules and orders, such as personnel assignments, production, work flow, transportation, and maintenance and repair. Examines documents, materials, and products, and monitors work processes for completeness, accuracy, and conformance to standards and specifications. Monitors work progress; provides services, such as furnishing permits, tickets, and union information; and directs workers to expedite work flow. Arranges for delivery and distributes supplies and parts to expedite flow of materials to meet production schedules. Requisitions and maintains inventory of materials and supplies to meet production demands. Maintains files, such as maintenance records, bills of lading, and cost reports. Calculates figures, such as labor and materials amounts, manufacturing costs, and wages, using pricing schedules, adding machine, or calculator.
Yearly Earnings: $23,868
Education: Short-term O-J-T
Knowledge: Clerical; Economics and Accounting; Production and Processing; Computers and Electronics; Mathematics
Abilities: Near Vision
Skills: Monitoring; Persuasion; Negotiation; Service Orientation; Information Organization; Implementation Planning; Systems Perception; Identifying Downstream Consequences; Systems Evaluation; Time Management; Management of Financial Resources; Management of Material Resources; Management of Personnel Resources
General Work Activities: Performing Administrative Activities; Monitoring and Controlling Resources
Job Characteristics: Coordinate or Lead Others; Sitting; Importance of Repeating Same Tasks
GOE Group/s: 05.03.02 Engineering Technology: Drafting; 05.03.03 Engineering Technology: Expediting and Coordinating; 05.09.02 Material Control: Estimating, Scheduling, and Record Keeping; 05.09.03 Material Control: Verifying, Recording, and Marking; 05.10.05 Crafts: Reproduction; 07.01.02 Administrative Detail: Administration; 07.02.05 Mathematical Detail: Payroll and Timekeeping; 07.04.05 Oral Communications: Information Transmitting and Receiving; 07.05.01 Records Processing: Coordinating and Scheduling; 07.05.03 Records Processing: Record Preparation and Maintenance; 07.07.03 Clerical Handling: General Clerical Work
CIP Program/s: 200301 Clothing, Apparel and Textile Workers and Managers, General; 200303 Commercial Garment and Apparel Worker; 470408 Watch, Clock and Jewelry Repairer; 480201 Graphic and Printing Equipment Operator, General; 480205 Mechanical Typesetter and Composer; 520201 Business Administration and Management, General; 520202 Purchasing, Procurement and Contracts Management; 520203 Logistics and Materials Management; 520302 Accounting Technician; 520401 Administrative Assistant/Secretarial Science, General; 520407 Information Processing/Data Entry Technician; 520408 General Office/Clerical and Typing Services; 521201 Management Information Systems and Business Data Processing; 521205 Business Computer Facilities Operator
Related DOT Job/s: 199.382-010 TELEVISION-SCHEDULE COORDINATOR; 215.362-010 CREW SCHEDULER; 215.362-014 DISPATCHER CLERK; 215.367-010 ASSIGNMENT CLERK; 215.367-014 PERSONNEL SCHEDULER; 219.362-030 EXTENSION CLERK; 219.387-010 ASSIGNMENT CLERK; 221.162-010 PRODUCTION SCHEDULER, PAPERBOARD PRODUCTS; 221.167-010 COPY CUTTER; 221.167-014 MATERIAL COORDINATOR; 221.167-018 PRODUCTION COORDINATOR; 221.167-022 RETORT-LOAD EXPEDITER; 221.167-026 CUSTOMER SERVICES COORDINATOR; 221.362-018 ESTIMATOR, PAPERBOARD BOXES; 221.362-022 PROGRESS CLERK; 221.362-030 COMPUTER PROCESSING SCHEDULER; 221.367-010 ALTERATIONS WORKROOM CLERK; 221.367-014 ESTIMATOR, PRINTING; 221.367-018 FOLLOW-UP CLERK; 221.367-026 LINE-UP WORKER; 221.367-030 LOCOMOTIVE LUBRICATING-SYSTEMS CLERK; 221.367-034 MACHINE-STOPPAGE-FREQUENCY CHECKER; 221.367-038 MAINTENANCE DATA ANALYST; 221.367-042 MATERIAL EXPEDITER; 221.367-046 MILL RECORDER, COMPUTERIZED MILL; 221.367-050 RECORDER; 221.367-054 RELAY-RECORD CLERK; 221.367-058 REPRODUCTION ORDER PROCESSOR; 221.367-066 SCHEDULER, MAINTENANCE; 221.367-078 TRAFFIC CLERK; 221.367-086 CLERK, TELEVISION PRODUCTION; 221.367-090 FORMULA CLERK; 221.382-018 PRODUCTION CLERK; 221.382-022 REPAIR-ORDER CLERK; 221.387-010 BACK-SHOE WORKER; 221.387-018 CONTROL CLERK; 221.387-022 ESTIMATOR, JEWELRY; 221.387-026 EXPEDITER CLERK; 221.387-030 JACKET PREPARER; 221.387-034 JOB TRACER; 221.387-046 ORDER DETAILER;

221.387-050 PRODUCTION ASSISTANT; 221.387-054 BATCH-RECORDS CLERK; 221.482-010 FABRIC-AND-ACCESSORIES ESTIMATOR; 221.482-014 LUMBER ESTIMATOR; 221.484-010 YARDAGE ESTIMATOR; 221.587-014 CHECKER-IN; 221.587-038 TICKET SCHEDULER; 221.587-042 WEAVE-DEFECT-CHARTING CLERK; 221.587-050 YARDAGE-CONTROL CLERK; 221.667-010 WORK-TICKET DISTRIBUTOR; 222.167-010 METAL-CONTROL COORDINATOR; 222.367-018 EXPEDITER; 222.367-070 EXPEDITER, SERVICE ORDER; 229.387-010 MATERIAL LISTER; 247.387-014 ADVERTISING-DISPATCH CLERK; 248.167-010 SUPERCARGO; 248.367-010 AIRPLANE-DISPATCH CLERK; 249.167-018 LABOR EXPEDITER; 912.367-010 FLIGHT-INFORMATION EXPEDITER; 913.167-018 SCHEDULE MAKER; 976.564-010 DETAILER, SCHOOL PHOTOGRAPHS

58011 TRANSPORTATION AGENTS. OOH Title/s: Material Recording, Scheduling, Dispatching, and Distributing Occupations

Expedite movement of freight, mail, baggage, and passengers through airline terminals. Route inbound and outbound air freight shipments. May prepare airway bill of lading on freight and record baggage, mail, freight, weights, and number of passengers on airplane. Prepares airway bill of lading on freight from consignors, and routes freight on first available flight. Prepares manifest showing baggage, mail, freight weights, and number of passengers on airplane, and teletypes data to destination. Obtains flight number, airplane number, and names of crew members from dispatcher and records data on flight papers of airplane. Oversees or participates in loading cargo to ensure completeness of load and even distribution of weight. Verifies passengers' tickets as they board plane. Unloads inbound freight and baggage and notifies consignees of arrival of shipments. Positions ramp for loading of airplane. Arranges for delivery of freight and baggage to consignees. Removes ramp and signals pilot that personnel and equipment are clear of plane. Forces conditioned air into interior of plane for passenger comfort prior to departure, using mobile aircraft-air-conditioning unit.
Yearly Earnings: $20,800
Education: Short-term O-J-T
Knowledge: Clerical; Customer and Personal Service; Geography; Telecommunications; Transportation
Abilities: Static Strength
Skills: Service Orientation
General Work Activities: None above average
Job Characteristics: Sounds, Noise Levels are Distracting, etc.; Walking or Running; Special Uniform
GOE Group/s: 05.09.01 Material Control: Shipping, Receiving, and Stock Checking; 07.05.01 Records Processing: Coordinating and Scheduling
CIP Program/s: 080709 General Distribution Operations
Related DOT Job/s: 248.367-018 CARGO AGENT; 912.367-014 TRANSPORTATION AGENT

58014 METER READERS, UTILITIES. OOH Title/s: Material Recording, Scheduling, Dispatching, and Distributing Occupations

Read electric, gas, water, or steam consumption meters and record volume used by residential and commercial customers. Walks or drives truck over established route and takes readings of meter dials. Reads electric meter. Reads gas meter. Reads steam meter. Reads water meter. Indicates irregularities on forms for necessary action by service department. Verifies readings to locate abnormal consumption, and records reasons for fluctuations. Returns route book to business office for billing purposes. Collects bills in arrears. Inspects meters for defects, damage, and unauthorized connections Turns service off for nonpayment of charges in vacant premises, or on for new occupants.
Yearly Earnings: $20,956
Education: Short-term O-J-T
Knowledge: None above average
Abilities: None above average
Skills: None above average
General Work Activities: Performing General Physical Activities; Interacting with Computers
Job Characteristics: Very Hot; Standing; Walking or Running; Special Uniform; Importance of Being Exact or Accurate
GOE Group/s: 05.09.03 Material Control: Verifying, Recording, and Marking
CIP Program/s: 000000 NO CIP ASSIGNED
Related DOT Job/s: 248.367-018 CARGO AGENT; 912.367-014 TRANSPORTATION AGENT

58017 WEIGHERS, MEASURERS, CHECKERS, AND SAMPLERS—RECORDKEEPING. OOH Title/s: Material Recording, Scheduling, Dispatching, and Distributing Occupations; Traffic, Shipping, and Receiving Clerks

Weigh, measure, and check materials, supplies, and equipment for the purpose of keeping relevant records. Duties are primarily clerical in nature. Include workers who collect and keep records of samples of products or materials. Exclude production samplers and weighers. Weighs or measures materials or products, using volume meters, scales, rules, and calipers. Documents quantity, quality, type, weight, and value of materials or products to maintain shipping, receiving, and production records and files. Counts or estimates quantities of materials, parts, or products received or shipped. Examines products or materials, parts, and subassemblies for damage, defects, or shortages, using specification sheets, gauges, and standards charts. Collects, prepares, or attaches measurement, weight, or identification labels or tickets to products. Compares product labels, tags, or tickets; shipping manifests; purchase orders; and bills of lading to verify that the contents, quantity, or weight of shipments is accurate. Computes product totals and charges for shipments, using calculator. Prepares measurement tables and conversion charts, using standard formulae. Sorts products or materials into predetermined sequence or groupings for packing, shipping, or storage. Maintains perpetual inventory of samples and replenishes stock to maintain required levels. Collects and prepares product samples for laboratory analysis or testing. Fills orders for products and samples, following order tickets, and forwards or mails items. Unloads or unpacks incoming shipments, or arranges, packs, or prepares materials and products for display, distribution, outgoing shipment, or storage. Transports materials, products, or samples to processing, shipping, or storage areas, manually or by using conveyors, pumps, or handtrucks. Removes products or loads not meeting quality standards from stock, and notifies supervisor or appropriate department of discrepancy or shortage. Examines blueprints and prepares plans, layouts, or drawings of facility or finished products to identify storage locations or verify parts assemblies. Collects fees and issues receipts for payments. Operates or tends machines to clean or sanitize equipment, or manually washes equipment, using detergent, brushes, and hoses. Communicates with customers and vendors to exchange information regarding products, materials, and services. Works with, signals, or instructs other workers to weigh, move, or check products.
Yearly Earnings: $19,188
Education: Short-term O-J-T
Knowledge: Clerical; Design; Transportation
Abilities: Selective Attention; Manual Dexterity; Multilimb Coordination; Dynamic Flexibility; Gross Body Coordination; Gross Body

Equilibrium; Depth Perception; Hearing Sensitivity; Sound Localization
Skills: None above average
General Work Activities: None above average
Job Characteristics: Using Hands on Objects, Tools, or Controls; Making Repetitive Motions; Importance of Repeating Same Tasks
GOE Group/s: 03.04.05 Elemental Work: Plants and Animals: Services; 05.09.01 Material Control: Shipping, Receiving, and Stock Checking; 05.09.02 Material Control: Estimating, Scheduling, and Record Keeping; 05.09.03 Material Control: Verifying, Recording, and Marking; 06.04.26 Elemental Work: Industrial: Manual Work, Paper; 06.04.27 Elemental Work: Industrial: Manual Work, Textile, Fabric and Leather; 06.04.38 Elemental Work: Industrial: Wrapping and Packaging; 07.07.02 Clerical Handling: Sorting and Distrubtion; 09.04.02 Customer Services: Sales Services
CIP Program/s: 080705 General Retailing Operations; 520401 Administrative Assistant/Secretarial Science, General; 520408 General Office/Clerical and Typing Services
Related DOT Job/s: 206.587-010 BRAND RECORDER; 209.587-046 SAMPLE CLERK, PAPER; 216.462-010 BOOKING PRIZER; 219.367-010 CHECKER, DUMP GROUNDS; 221.467-010 GIN CLERK; 221.482-018 TICKET WORKER; 221.487-010 LUMBER SCALER; 221.587-010 CHECKER; 221.587-026 RECORDER; 221.587-030 TALLIER; 221.587-034 TARE WEIGHER; 221.587-046 WHEEL-PRESS CLERK; 221.687-014 TICKET PULLER; 222.367-010 CARGO CHECKER; 222.387-010 AIRCRAFT-SHIPPING CHECKER; 222.387-066 SAMPLE CLERK; 222.387-074 SHIPPING-AND-RECEIVING WEIGHER; 222.485-010 MILK-RECEIVER, TANK TRUCK; 222.585-010 MILK RECEIVER; 222.587-042 SAMPLER, WOOL; 222.587-046 STACKER; 222.587-050 SWATCH CLERK; 222.687-010 CHECKER I; 222.687-018 RECEIVING CHECKER; 222.687-026 SAMPLE DISPLAY PREPARER; 229.387-014 TANK CALIBRATOR; 229.687-010 SAMPLE CHECKER; 299.587-010 PRODUCE WEIGHER; 410.357-010 MILK SAMPLER; 789.587-026 SAMPLE CLERK; 919.687-010 CHECKER; 920.687-154 SAMPLE WORKER; 922.687-042 COTTON SAMPLER

58021 MARKING CLERKS. OOH Title/s: Material Recording, Scheduling, Dispatching, and Distributing Occupations

Print and attach price tickets to articles of merchandise using one of several methods, such as marking price on tickets by hand or using ticket-printing machine. Marks selling price by hand on boxes containing merchandise or on price tickets. Presses lever or plunger of mechanism that pins, pastes, ties, or staples ticket to article. Prints information on tickets, using ticket-printing machine. Records price, buyer, and grade of tobacco on tickets attached to piles or baskets of tobacco as tobacco is auctioned. Pastes, staples, sews, or otherwise fastens tickets, tags, labels, or shipping documents to cloth or carpeting. Attaches price ticket to each article, and signals purchaser to raise bids that are below government support price. Indicates price, size, style, color, and inspection results on tags, tickets, and labels, using rubber stamp or writing instrument. Compares printed price tickets with entries on purchase order to verify accuracy, and notifies supervisor of discrepancies. Records number and types of articles marked and packs articles in boxes. Performs other clerical tasks during periods between auction sales. Computes number of rolls of cloth to be produced from each lot to determine required number of tags or labels. Trims excess threads from selvage (finished edge) of cloth, using scissors or shears. Keeps records of production, returned goods, and personnel transactions.
Yearly Earnings: $20,800
Education: Short-term O-J-T
Knowledge: Clerical
Abilities: None above average
Skills: None above average
General Work Activities: None above average
Job Characteristics: Making Repetitive Motions; Importance of Repeating Same Tasks
GOE Group/s: 05.09.03 Material Control: Verifying, Recording, and Marking
CIP Program/s: 000000 NO CIP ASSIGNED
Related DOT Job/s: 209.587-034 MARKER; 216.567-010 TICKET MARKER; 222.387-054 SORTER-PRICER; 229.587-018 TICKETER

58023 STOCK CLERKS—STOCKROOM, WAREHOUSE, OR STORAGE YARD. OOH Title/s: Stock Clerks

Receive, store, and issue materials, equipment, and other items from stockroom, warehouse, or storage yard. Keep records and compile stock reports. Exclude stockroom laborers and workers whose primary duties involve shipping, weighing, and checking. Receives, counts, and stores stock items and records data, manually or using computer. Records nature, quantity, value, or location of material, supplies, or equipment received, shipped, used, or issued to workers. Compares office inventory records with sales orders, invoices, or requisitions to verify accuracy and receipt of items. Locates and selects material, supplies, tools, equipment, or other articles from stock, or issues stock item to workers. Compiles, reviews, and maintains data from contracts, purchase orders, requisitions, and other documents to determine supply needs. Packs, unpacks, and marks stock items, using identification tag, stamp, electric marking tool, or other labeling equipment. Determines method of storage, identification, and stock location based on turnover, environmental factors, and physical capacity of facility. Delivers products, supplies, and equipment to designated area, and determines sequence and release of back orders according to stock availability. Verifies computations against physical count of stock, adjusts for errors, or investigates discrepancies. Prepares documents, such as inventory balance, price lists, shortages, expenditures, and periodic reports, using computer, typewriter, or calculator. Receives and fills orders or sells supplies, materials, and products to customers. Purchases or prepares documents to purchase new or additional stock and recommends disposal of excess, defective, or obsolete stock. Confers with engineering and purchasing personnel and vendors regarding procurement and stock availability. Examines and inspects stock items for wear or defects, reports damage to supervisor, and disposes of or returns items to vendor. Adjusts, repairs, assembles, or prepares products, supplies, equipment, or other items, according to specifications or customer requirements. Assists or directs other stockroom, warehouse, or storage yard workers. Cleans and maintains supplies, tools, equipment, instruments, and storage areas to ensure compliance to safety regulations. Drives truck to pick up incoming stock or deliver parts to designated locations.
Yearly Earnings: $20,696
Education: Short-term O-J-T
Knowledge: Clerical; Computers and Electronics
Abilities: Category Flexibility; Spatial Orientation; Trunk Strength; Extent Flexibility; Dynamic Flexibility; Gross Body Coordination; Gross Body Equilibrium
Skills: None above average
General Work Activities: Interacting with Computers; Monitoring and Controlling Resources
Job Characteristics: Climbing Ladders, Scaffolds, Poles, etc.; Walking or Running; Kneeling, Crouching, or Crawling; Keeping or Regaining Balance
GOE Group/s: 05.09.01 Material Control: Shipping, Receiving, and Stock Checking; 05.09.02 Material Control: Estimating, Scheduling, and Record Keeping; 05.09.03 Material Control: Verifying, Recording, and Marking; 05.12.18 Elemental Work: Mechanical: Cleaning

and Maintenance; 05.12.19 Elemental Work: Mechanical: Reproduction Services; 07.02.03 Mathematical Detail: Statistical Reporting and Analysis; 07.05.03 Records Processing: Record Preparation and Maintenance; 07.05.04 Records Processing: Routing and Distribution; 07.07.02 Clerical Handling: Sorting and Distrubtion

CIP Program/s: 080709 General Distribution Operations; 081203 Vehicle Parts and Accessories Marketing Operations; 520499 Administrative and Secretarial Services, Other

Related DOT Job/s: 219.367-018 MERCHANDISE DISTRIBUTOR; 219.387-026 SPACE-AND-STORAGE CLERK; 219.387-030 STOCK CONTROL CLERK; 221.587-018 ODD-PIECE CHECKER; 221.587-022 OUTSOLE SCHEDULER; 222.367-014 CUT-FILE CLERK; 222.367-038 MAGAZINE KEEPER; 222.367-042 PARTS CLERK; 222.367-050 PRESCRIPTION CLERK, LENS-AND-FRAMES; 222.367-062 TOOL-CRIB ATTENDANT; 222.387-018 FUEL-OIL CLERK; 222.387-026 INVENTORY CLERK; 222.387-030 LINEN-ROOM ATTENDANT; 222.387-034 MATERIAL CLERK; 222.387-042 PROPERTY CUSTODIAN; 222.387-058 STOCK CLERK; 222.387-062 STOREKEEPER; 222.487-010 CHECKER, BAKERY PRODUCTS; 222.587-022 KITCHEN CLERK; 222.587-054 TRANSFORMER-STOCK CLERK; 222.684-010 MEAT CLERK; 222.687-038 TOOTH CLERK; 222.687-046 PROTECTIVE-CLOTHING ISSUER; 229.367-010 FIELD RECORDER; 229.367-014 PARTS LISTER; 229.587-014 QUALITY-CONTROL CLERK; 249.367-058 PARTS-ORDER-AND-STOCK CLERK; 339.687-010 SUPPLY CLERK; 381.687-010 CENTRAL-SUPPLY WORKER; 969.367-010 CUSTODIAN, ATHLETIC EQUIPMENT

58026 ORDER FILLERS, WHOLESALE AND RETAIL SALES. OOH Title/s: Stock Clerks

Fill customers' mail and telephone orders from stored merchandise in accordance with specifications on sales slips or order forms. Duties include computing prices of items, completing order receipts, keeping records of outgoing orders, and requisitioning additional materials, supplies, and equipment. Exclude laborers, stock clerks, and workers whose primary duties involve weighing and checking. Computes price of each group of items. Reads order to ascertain catalog number, size, color, and quantity of merchandise. Obtains merchandise from bins or shelves. Places merchandise on conveyor leading to wrapping area.

Yearly Earnings: $20,696

Education: Short-term O-J-T

Knowledge: None above average

Abilities: None above average

Skills: None above average

General Work Activities: None above average

Job Characteristics: Standing; Climbing Ladders, Scaffolds, Poles, etc.; Making Repetitive Motions

GOE Group/s: 05.09.01 Material Control: Shipping, Receiving, and Stock Checking

CIP Program/s: 000000 NO CIP ASSIGNED

Related DOT Job/s: 222.487-014 ORDER FILLER; 299.387-014 STAMP ANALYST

58028 SHIPPING, RECEIVING, AND TRAFFIC CLERKS. OOH Title/s: Traffic, Shipping, and Receiving Clerks

Verify and keep records on incoming and outgoing shipments. Prepare items for shipment. Duties include assembling, addressing, stamping, and shipping merchandise or material; receiving, unpacking, verifying, and recording incoming merchandise or material; and arranging for the transportation of products. Exclude laborers, stock clerks, and workers whose primary duties involve weighing and checking. Examines contents and compares with records, such as manifests, invoices, or orders, to verify accuracy of incoming or outgoing shipment. Records shipment data, such as weight, charges, space availability, damages, and discrepancies, for reporting, accounting, and recordkeeping purposes. Determines shipping method for materials, using knowledge of shipping procedures, routes, and rates. Contacts carrier representative to make arrangements and to issue instructions for shipping and delivery of materials. Packs, seals, labels, and affixes postage to prepare materials for shipping, using work devices such as hand tools, power tools, and postage meter. Prepares documents, such as work orders, bills of lading, and shipping orders to route materials. Computes amounts, such as space available and shipping, storage, and demurrage charges, using calculator or price list. Confers and corresponds with establishment representatives to rectify problems such as damages, shortages, and nonconformance to specifications. Delivers or routes materials to departments, using work devices such as handtruck, conveyor, or sorting bins. Requisitions and stores shipping materials and supplies to maintain inventory of stock.

Yearly Earnings: $19,812

Education: Short-term O-J-T

Knowledge: Clerical; Economics and Accounting; Philosophy and Theology; Transportation

Abilities: Stamina; Gross Body Equilibrium; Speech Recognition

Skills: Negotiation; Service Orientation

General Work Activities: Handling and Moving Objects

Job Characteristics: Importance of Repeating Same Tasks

GOE Group/s: 05.09.01 Material Control: Shipping, Receiving, and Stock Checking; 05.09.03 Material Control: Verifying, Recording, and Marking; 06.03.02 Quality Control: Inspecting, Grading, Sorting, Weighing, and Recording; 07.02.03 Mathematical Detail: Statistical Reporting and Analysis; 07.02.04 Mathematical Detail: Billing and Rate Computation; 07.05.01 Records Processing: Coordinating and Scheduling; 07.05.04 Records Processing: Routing and Distribution; 07.07.02 Clerical Handling: Sorting and Distrubtion

CIP Program/s: 520499 Administrative and Secretarial Services, Other

Related DOT Job/s: 209.367-042 RECONSIGNMENT CLERK; 214.587-014 TRAFFIC CLERK; 219.367-022 PAPER-CONTROL CLERK; 219.367-030 SHIPPING-ORDER CLERK; 221.367-022 INDUSTRIAL-ORDER CLERK; 222.367-066 TRUCKLOAD CHECKER; 222.387-014 CAR CHECKER; 222.387-022 GUN-REPAIR CLERK; 222.387-050 SHIPPING AND RECEIVING CLERK; 222.567-010 GRAIN ELEVATOR CLERK; 222.567-014 SHIP RUNNER; 222.587-018 DISTRIBUTING CLERK; 222.587-034 ROUTE-DELIVERY CLERK; 222.587-058 VAULT WORKER; 222.687-022 ROUTING CLERK; 222.687-030 SHIPPING CHECKER; 248.362-010 INCOMING-FREIGHT CLERK; 248.367-014 BOOKING CLERK; 248.367-022 CONTAINER COORDINATOR; 976.687-018 PHOTOFINISHING LABORATORY WORKER

58099A ENGINEERING CLERKS. OOH Title/s: Material Recording, Scheduling, Dispatching, and Distributing Occupations

Compile, maintain, check, release, and distribute engineering control records, such as blueprints, drawings, engineering documents, parts listings, and catalogs. Releases data and documentation to authorized departments and organizations. Prepares or maintains manual or computerized record systems. Examines engineering drawings, blueprints, orders, and other documentation for completeness and accuracy. Confers with document originators or engineering liaison personnel to resolve discrepancies and update documents. Reviews engineering data and compiles list of materials, parts, and equipment required for manufacturing product. Determines material requirements for fabricating parts, considering size, cutting, and forming involved. Operates reproduction equipment. Prepares

reports and memorandums. Assists in determining spare parts inventory requirements for customers.
Yearly Earnings: $20,800
Education: Short-term O-J-T
Knowledge: Clerical
Abilities: Near Vision
Skills: Programming
General Work Activities: Operating Vehicles or Equipment
Job Characteristics: Sitting
GOE Group/s: 05.03.02 Engineering Technology: Drafting; 07.05.03 Records Processing: Record Preparation and Maintenance
CIP Program/s: 520401 Administrative Assistant/Secretarial Science, General; 520408 General Office/Clerical and Typing Services; 520499 Administrative and Secretarial Services, Other
Related DOT Job/s: 206.367-010 ENGINEERING-DOCUMENT-CONTROL CLERK; 229.267-010 PARTS CATALOGER

58099B TRANSPORTATION MAINTENANCE CLERKS. OOH Title/s: Material Recording, Scheduling, Dispatching, and Distributing Occupations

Compile and record information, such as amount of equipment usage, time between inspections, repairs made, materials used, and hours of work expended, to document maintenance of transportation equipment. Compiles data from flight schedules to compute usage of airplanes, gasoline, and individual parts. Compiles and records information regarding track and right-of-way repair and maintenance by railroad section crews. Maintains file for individual parts with notations of time used and inspection results. Records work notations onto inspection report forms. Notifies inspection department when parts and airplanes approach date for inspection, including accumulated time and routing schedule. Prepares reports for Federal Aviation Administration on schedule delays caused by mechanical difficulties. Requisitions needed materials. Keeps employee time records.
Yearly Earnings: $20,800
Education: Short-term O-J-T
Knowledge: Clerical; Transportation
Abilities: None above average
Skills: None above average
General Work Activities: Performing Administrative Activities
Job Characteristics: Importance of Being Exact or Accurate; Importance of Repeating Same Tasks
GOE Group/s: 07.05.03 Records Processing: Record Preparation and Maintenance
CIP Program/s: 520401 Administrative Assistant/Secretarial Science, General; 520408 General Office/Clerical and Typing Services
Related DOT Job/s: 221.362-010 AIRCRAFT-LOG CLERK; 221.362-026 RAILROAD-MAINTENANCE CLERK

58099C ALL OTHER MATERIAL RECORDING, SCHEDULING, AND DISTRIBUTING WORKERS. OOH Title/s: Material Recording, Scheduling, and Distribution Workers

All other material recording, scheduling, and distributing workers not classified separately above.
Yearly Earnings: NA
Education: Unknown
GOE Group/s: 05.09.02 Material Control: Estimating, Scheduling, and Record Keeping
CIP Program/s: 520302 Accounting Technician
Related DOT Job/s: 216.587-010 BOOKING CLERK

59999 ALL OTHER CLERICAL AND ADMINISTRATIVE SUPPORT WORKERS. OOH Title/s: Mail Clerks and Messengers; Adjusters, Investigators, and Collectors; Credit Clerks and Authorizers; Receptionists

All other clerical and administrative support workers not classified separately above.
Yearly Earnings: $22,360
Education: Short-term O-J-T
GOE Group/s: 07.01.07 Administrative Detail: Test Administration; 07.04.01 Oral Communications: Interviewing; 07.04.04 Oral Communications: Reception and Information Giving; 07.04.05 Oral Communications: Information Transmitting and Receiving; 07.05.02 Records Processing: Record Verification and Proofing; 07.05.03 Records Processing: Record Preparation and Maintenance
CIP Program/s: 520401 Administrative Assistant/Secretarial Science, General; 520408 General Office/Clerical and Typing Services; 520501 Business Communications; 520801 Finance, General; 520803 Banking and Financial Support Services
Related DOT Job/s: 199.267-018 EXAMINATION PROCTOR; 209.367-014 BRAILLE PROOFREADER; 219.367-014 INSURANCE CLERK; 237.367-026 LAND-LEASING EXAMINER; 241.367-018 LOAN INTERVIEWER, MORTGAGE; 243.367-010 MAIL CENSOR; 248.367-030 WATERWAY TRAFFIC CHECKER

Section 6
Service Workers

Service Supervisors and Managers

61002A MUNICIPAL FIRE FIGHTING AND PREVENTION SUPERVISORS. OOH Title/s: Firefighting Occupations

Supervise fire fighters who control and extinguish municipal fires, protect life and property, and conduct rescue efforts. Coordinates and supervises fire-fighting and rescue activities, and reports events to supervisor, using two-way radio. Assesses nature and extent of fire, condition of building, danger to adjacent buildings, and water supply to determine crew or company requirements. Evaluates efficiency and performance of employees, and recommends awards for service. Directs investigation of cases of suspected arson, hazards, and false alarms. Trains subordinates in use of equipment, methods of extinguishing fires, and rescue operations. Directs building inspections to ensure compliance with fire and safety regulations. Inspects fire stations, equipment, and records to ensure efficiency and enforcement of departmental regulations. Keeps equipment and personnel records. Confers with civic representatives, and plans talks and demonstrations of fire safety to direct fire prevention information program. Oversees review of new building plans to ensure compliance with laws, ordinances, and administrative rules for public fire safety. Orders and directs fire drills for occupants of buildings. Writes and submits proposals for new equipment or modification of existing equipment. Studies and interprets fire safety codes to establish procedures for issuing permits regulating storage or use of hazardous or flammable substances. Compiles report of fire call, listing location, type, probable cause, estimated damage, and disposition.

Yearly Earnings: $36,920

Education: Work experience in a related occupation

Knowledge: Administration and Management; Personnel and Human Resources; Building and Construction; Geography; Medicine and Dentistry; Education and Training; Public Safety and Security; Telecommunications

Abilities: Oral Expression; Fluency of Ideas; Originality; Problem Sensitivity; Deductive Reasoning; Inductive Reasoning; Information Ordering; Speed of Closure; Flexibility of Closure; Spatial Orientation; Selective Attention; Time Sharing; Multilimb Coordination; Response Orientation; Rate Control; Reaction Time; Speed of Limb Movement; Static Strength; Explosive Strength; Dynamic Strength; Trunk Strength; Stamina; Dynamic Flexibility; Gross Body Coordination; Gross Body Equilibrium; Near Vision; Far Vision; Night Vision; Peripheral Vision; Depth Perception; Glare Sensitivity; Hearing Sensitivity; Auditory Attention; Sound Localization; Speech Recognition; Speech Clarity

Skills: Reading Comprehension; Active Listening; Writing; Science; Critical Thinking; Active Learning; Learning Strategies; Monitoring; Social Perceptiveness; Coordination; Persuasion; Negotiation; Instructing; Service Orientation; Problem Identification; Information Gathering; Idea Generation; Idea Evaluation; Implementation Planning; Solution Appraisal; Operations Analysis; Equipment Selection; Testing; Product Inspection; Equipment Maintenance; Troubleshooting; Visioning; Systems Perception; Identifying Downstream Consequences; Identification of Key Causes; Judgment and Decision Making; Systems Evaluation; Time Management; Management of Financial Resources; Management of Material Resources; Management of Personnel Resources

General Work Activities: Inspecting Equipment, Structures, or Material; Estimating Needed Characteristics; Processing Information; Analyzing Data or Information; Scheduling Work and Activities; Interacting with Computers; Coordinating Work and Activities of Others; Developing and Building Teams; Teaching Others; Guiding, Directing and Motivating Subordinates

Job Characteristics: Job-Required Social Interaction; Supervise, Coach, Train Others; Persuade Someone to a Course of Action; Take a Position Opposed to Others; Deal with External Customers; Coordinate or Lead Others; Responsible for Others' Health and Safety; Responsibility for Outcomes and Results; Frequency in Conflict Situations; Deal with Unpleasant or Angry People; Deal with Physical, Aggressive People; Sounds, Noise Levels are Distracting, etc.; Very Hot; Extremely Bright or Inadequate Lighting; Contaminants; Cramped Work Space, Awkward Positions; Whole Body Vibration; Radiation; High Places; Hazardous Conditions; Hazardous Situations; Climbing Ladders, Scaffolds, Poles, etc.; Walking or Running; Kneeling, Crouching, or Crawling; Keeping or Regaining Balance; Bending or Twisting the Body; Special Uniform; Common Protective or Safety Attire; Specialized Protective or Safety Attire; Consequence of Error; Frustrating Circumstances; Importance of Being Sure All is Done; Importance of Being Aware of New Events; Importance of Repeating Same Tasks

GOE Group/s: 04.01.01 Safety and Law Enforcement: Managing

CIP Program/s: 430201 Fire Protection and Safety Tech./Technician; 430202 Fire Services Administration

Related DOT Job/s: 373.134-010 FIRE CAPTAIN; 373.167-010 BATTALION CHIEF; 373.167-014 CAPTAIN, FIRE-PREVENTION BUREAU; 373.167-018 FIRE MARSHAL

61002B FOREST FIRE FIGHTING AND PREVENTION SUPERVISORS. OOH Title/s: Firefighting Occupations

Supervise fire fighters who control and suppress fires in forests or on vacant public land. Dispatches crews according to reported size, location, and condition of forest fires. Directs loading of fire-suppression equipment into aircraft and parachuting of equipment to crews on ground. Observes fire and crews from air to determine force requirements and note changing conditions. Maintains radio communication with crews at fire scene to inform crews and base of changing conditions and learn of casualties. Parachutes to major fire locations and directs fire containment and suppression activities. Trains workers in parachute jumping, fire suppression, aerial observation, and radio communication.

Yearly Earnings: $36,920

Education: Work experience in a related occupation

Knowledge: Administration and Management; Chemistry; Geography; Education and Training; Public Safety and Security; Transportation

Abilities: Oral Expression; Fluency of Ideas; Problem Sensitivity; Speed of Closure; Flexibility of Closure; Spatial Orientation; Selective Attention; Time Sharing; Response Orientation; Rate Control; Reaction Time; Speed of Limb Movement; Static Strength; Explosive Strength; Dynamic Strength; Trunk Strength; Stamina; Dynamic Flexibility; Gross Body Coordination; Gross Body Equilibrium; Far Vision; Night Vision; Peripheral Vision; Depth Perception; Glare Sensitivity; Hearing Sensitivity; Auditory Attention; Sound Localization; Speech Recognition; Speech Clarity

Skills: Learning Strategies; Monitoring; Social Perceptiveness; Coordination; Persuasion; Instructing; Service Orientation; Idea Evaluation; Implementation Planning; Solution Appraisal; Visioning; Systems Perception; Identifying Downstream Consequences; Identification of Key Causes; Judgment and Decision Making; Systems Evaluation; Time Management; Management of Material Resources; Management of Personnel Resources

General Work Activities: Monitoring Processes, Material, or Surroundings; Identifying Objects, Actions, and Events; Estimating

Needed Characteristics; Making Decisions and Solving Problems; Scheduling Work and Activities; Performing General Physical Activities; Interacting with Computers; Communicating with Other Workers; Coordinating Work and Activities of Others; Developing and Building Teams; Teaching Others; Guiding, Directing and Motivating Subordinates; Coaching and Developing Others
Job Characteristics: Job-Required Social Interaction; Supervise, Coach, Train Others; Take a Position Opposed to Others; Coordinate or Lead Others; Responsible for Others' Health and Safety; Responsibility for Outcomes and Results; Sounds, Noise Levels are Distracting, etc.; Very Hot; Extremely Bright or Inadequate Lighting; Contaminants; Cramped Work Space, Awkward Positions; Radiation; High Places; Hazardous Conditions; Hazardous Situations; Climbing Ladders, Scaffolds, Poles, etc.; Walking or Running; Kneeling, Crouching, or Crawling; Keeping or Regaining Balance; Bending or Twisting the Body; Special Uniform; Common Protective or Safety Attire; Specialized Protective or Safety Attire; Consequence of Error; Frustrating Circumstances; Importance of Being Sure All is Done; Importance of Being Aware of New Events; Importance of Repeating Same Tasks
GOE Group/s: 04.02.04 Security Services: Emergency Responding
CIP Program/s: 030203 Natural Resources Law Enforcement and Protective Services; 430202 Fire Services Administration; 430203 Fire Science/Firefighting
Related DOT Job/s: 452.134-010 SMOKE JUMPER SUPERVISOR

61005 POLICE AND DETECTIVE SUPERVISORS.

OOH Title/s: Police, Detectives, and Special Agents; Visual Artists

Supervise and coordinate activities of members of police force. Prepares work schedules, assigns duties, and develops and revises departmental procedures. Supervises and coordinates investigation of criminal cases. Monitors and evaluates job performance of subordinates. Disciplines staff for violation of department rules and regulations. Directs collection, preparation, and handling of evidence and personal property of prisoners. Assists subordinates in performing job duties. Investigates and resolves personnel problems within organization. Investigates charges of misconduct against staff. Prepares reports and directs preparation, handling, and maintenance of departmental records. Trains staff. Prepares budgets and manages expenditures of department funds. Inspects facilities, supplies, vehicles, and equipment to ensure conformance to standards. Requisitions and issues department equipment and supplies. Directs release or transfer of prisoners. Reviews contents of written orders to ensure adherence to legal requirements. Prepares news releases and responds to police correspondence. Cooperates with court personnel and officials from other law enforcement agencies, and testifies in court. Conducts raids and orders detention of witnesses and suspects for questioning. Meets with civic, educational, and community groups to develop community programs and events, and addresses groups concerning law enforcement subjects.
Yearly Earnings: $36,920
Education: Work experience in a related occupation
Knowledge: Administration and Management; Clerical; Economics and Accounting; Sales and Marketing; Customer and Personal Service; Personnel and Human Resources; Psychology; Sociology and Anthropology; Geography; Medicine and Dentistry; Therapy and Counseling; Education and Training; English Language; Foreign Language; Philosophy and Theology; Public Safety and Security; Law, Government, and Jurisprudence; Telecommunications; Communications and Media; Transportation
Abilities: Oral Comprehension; Written Comprehension; Oral Expression; Written Expression; Fluency of Ideas; Originality; Problem Sensitivity; Deductive Reasoning; Inductive Reasoning; Information Ordering; Category Flexibility; Mathematical Reasoning; Number Facility; Memorization; Speed of Closure; Flexibility of Closure; Spatial Orientation; Visualization; Selective Attention; Time Sharing; Multilimb Coordination; Response Orientation; Rate Control; Reaction Time; Wrist-Finger Speed; Speed of Limb Movement; Static Strength; Explosive Strength; Dynamic Strength; Trunk Strength; Stamina; Extent Flexibility; Gross Body Coordination; Gross Body Equilibrium; Near Vision; Far Vision; Night Vision; Peripheral Vision; Depth Perception; Hearing Sensitivity; Auditory Attention; Sound Localization; Speech Recognition; Speech Clarity
Skills: Active Listening; Writing; Speaking; Critical Thinking; Active Learning; Learning Strategies; Monitoring; Social Perceptiveness; Coordination; Persuasion; Negotiation; Instructing; Service Orientation; Problem Identification; Information Gathering; Information Organization; Idea Generation; Idea Evaluation; Implementation Planning; Visioning; Systems Perception; Identifying Downstream Consequences; Identification of Key Causes; Judgment and Decision Making; Systems Evaluation; Time Management; Management of Financial Resources; Management of Material Resources; Management of Personnel Resources
General Work Activities: Getting Information Needed to Do the Job; Monitoring Processes, Material, or Surroundings; Identifying Objects, Actions, and Events; Estimating Needed Characteristics; Judging Qualities of Things, Services, People; Processing Information; Evaluating Information against Standards; Analyzing Data or Information; Making Decisions and Solving Problems; Thinking Creatively; Developing Objectives and Strategies; Scheduling Work and Activities; Organizing, Planning, and Prioritizing; Performing General Physical Activities; Operating Vehicles or Equipment; Interacting with Computers; Implementing Ideas, Programs, etc.; Documenting/Recording Information; Interpreting Meaning of Information to Others; Communicating with Other Workers; Communicating with Persons Outside Organization; Establishing and Maintaining Relationships; Assisting and Caring for Others; Selling or Influencing Others; Resolving Conflicts, Negotiating with Others; Performing for or Working with Public; Coordinating Work and Activities of Others; Developing and Building Teams; Teaching Others; Guiding, Directing and Motivating Subordinates; Coaching and Developing Others; Provide Consultation and Advice to Others; Performing Administrative Activities; Staffing Organizational Units; Monitoring and Controlling Resources
Job Characteristics: Objective or Subjective Information; Job-Required Social Interaction; Supervise, Coach, Train Others; Persuade Someone to a Course of Action; Take a Position Opposed to Others; Deal with External Customers; Coordinate or Lead Others; Responsible for Others' Health and Safety; Responsibility for Outcomes and Results; Frequency in Conflict Situations; Deal with Unpleasant or Angry People; Deal with Physical, Aggressive People; Extremely Bright or Inadequate Lighting; Keeping or Regaining Balance; Special Uniform; Specialized Protective or Safety Attire; Consequence of Error; Frustrating Circumstances; Importance of Being Sure All is Done; Importance of Being Aware of New Events
GOE Group/s: 04.01.01 Safety and Law Enforcement: Managing; 07.01.06 Administrative Detail: Investigating; 11.09.03 Promotion: Public Relations
CIP Program/s: 430102 Corrections/Correctional Administration; 430103 Criminal Justice/Law Enforcement Administration
Related DOT Job/s: 372.137-010 CORRECTION OFFICER, HEAD; 372.167-018 JAILER, CHIEF; 375.133-010 POLICE SERGEANT, PRECINCT I; 375.137-010 COMMANDER, IDENTIFICATION AND RECORDS; 375.137-014 DESK OFFICER; 375.137-018 POLICE LIEUTENANT, COMMUNITY RELATIONS; 375.137-026 TRAFFIC SERGEANT; 375.137-030 COMMANDER, POLICE RESERVES; 375.137-034 COMMANDING OFFICER, POLICE; 375.163-010 COMMANDING OFFICER, MOTORIZED SQUAD; 375.167-010 COMMANDING OFFICER, HOMICIDE SQUAD; 375.167-014 COMMANDING OFFICER, INVESTIGATION DIVISION; 375.167-022 DETECTIVE CHIEF; 375.167-030

LAUNCH COMMANDER, HARBOR POLICE; 375.167-034 POLICE CAPTAIN, PRECINCT; 375.167-038 POLICE LIEUTENANT, PATROL; 375.167-046 TRAFFIC LIEUTENANT; 375.167-050 COMMANDER, INTERNAL AFFAIRS; 377.134-010 SUPERVISOR, IDENTIFICATION AND COMMUNICATIONS; 377.137-010 DEPUTY SHERIFF, COMMANDER, CIVIL DIVISION; 377.137-014 DEPUTY SHERIFF, COMMANDER, CRIMINAL AND PATROL DIVISION; 377.137-018 DEPUTY, COURT; 377.167-010 DEPUTY SHERIFF, CHIEF; 970.131-014 SUPERVISOR, ARTIST, SUSPECT

61008 HOUSEKEEPING SUPERVISORS. OOH Title/s: Janitors and Cleaners and Cleaning Supervisors; Hotel Managers and Assistants

Supervise work activities of cleaning personnel to ensure clean, orderly, and attractive rooms in hotels, hospitals, educational institutions, and similar establishments. Assign duties, inspect work, and investigate complaints regarding housekeeping service and equipment, and take corrective action. May purchase housekeeping supplies and equipment, take periodic inventories, screen applicants, train new employees, and recommend dismissals. Assigns workers their duties and inspects work for conformance to prescribed standards of cleanliness. Investigates complaints regarding housekeeping service and equipment, and takes corrective action. Obtains list of rooms to be cleaned immediately and list of prospective check-outs or discharges to prepare work assignments. Coordinates work activities among departments. Screens job applicants, hires new employees, and recommends promotions, transfers, and dismissals. Records data regarding work assignments, personnel actions, and time cards, and prepares periodic reports. Advises manager, desk clerk, or admitting personnel of rooms ready for occupancy. Conducts orientation training and in-service training to explain policies and work procedures and to demonstrate use and maintenance of equipment. Establishes standards and procedures for work of housekeeping staff. Inventories stock to ensure adequate supplies. Issues supplies and equipment to workers. Evaluates records to forecast department personnel requirements. Attends staff meetings to discuss company policies and patrons' complaints. Makes recommendations to improve service and ensure more efficient operation. Examines building to determine need for repairs or replacement of furniture or equipment, and makes recommendations to management. Attends training seminars to improve housekeeping techniques and procedures and to enhance supervisory skills. Prepares reports concerning room occupancy, payroll, and department expenses. Performs cleaning duties in cases of emergency or staff shortage. Selects and purchases new furnishings. Reads trade journals to keep informed of new and improved cleaning products, supplies, and equipment.

Yearly Earnings: $18,876

Education: Work experience in a related occupation

Knowledge: Administration and Management; Clerical; Customer and Personal Service; Personnel and Human Resources; Education and Training; Foreign Language

Abilities: None above average

Skills: Coordination; Time Management; Management of Financial Resources; Management of Material Resources; Management of Personnel Resources

General Work Activities: Scheduling Work and Activities; Communicating with Other Workers; Establishing and Maintaining Relationships; Resolving Conflicts, Negotiating with Others; Coordinating Work and Activities of Others; Developing and Building Teams; Teaching Others; Guiding, Directing and Motivating Subordinates; Coaching and Developing Others; Performing Administrative Activities; Staffing Organizational Units; Monitoring and Controlling Resources

Job Characteristics: Supervise, Coach, Train Others; Coordinate or Lead Others; Responsibility for Outcomes and Results

GOE Group/s: 05.12.01 Elemental Work: Mechanical: Supervision

CIP Program/s: 200601 Custodial, Housekeeping and Home Services Workers and Managers; 200605 Executive Housekeeper

Related DOT Job/s: 187.167-046 EXECUTIVE HOUSEKEEPER; 321.137-010 HOUSEKEEPER

61099A CHEFS AND HEAD COOKS. OOH Title/s: Restaurant and Food Service Managers; Chefs, Cooks, and Other Kitchen Workers

Direct preparation, seasoning, and cooking of salads, soups, fish, meats, vegetables, desserts, or other foods. May plan and price menu items, order supplies, and keep records and accounts. May participate in cooking. Supervises and coordinates activities of cooks and workers engaged in food preparation. Observes workers and work procedures to ensure compliance with established standards. Trains and otherwise instructs cooks and workers in proper food preparation procedures. Helps cooks and workers cook and prepare food on demand. Estimates amounts and costs, and requisitions supplies and equipment to ensure efficient operation. Determines production schedules and worker-time requirements to ensure timely delivery of services. Collaborates with specified personnel, and plans and develops recipes and menus. Inspects supplies, equipment, and work areas to ensure conformance to established standards. Records production and operational data on specified forms. Evaluates and solves procedural problems to ensure safe and efficient operations.

Yearly Earnings: $21,580

Education: Work experience in a related occupation

Knowledge: Administration and Management; Economics and Accounting; Personnel and Human Resources; Food Production; Education and Training

Abilities: Originality; Perceptual Speed; Time Sharing; Manual Dexterity; Finger Dexterity; Wrist-Finger Speed

Skills: Coordination; Instructing; Implementation Planning; Time Management; Management of Financial Resources; Management of Material Resources; Management of Personnel Resources

General Work Activities: Scheduling Work and Activities; Guiding, Directing and Motivating Subordinates

Job Characteristics: Objective or Subjective Information; Job-Required Social Interaction; Supervise, Coach, Train Others; Persuade Someone to a Course of Action; Take a Position Opposed to Others; Coordinate or Lead Others; Responsibility for Outcomes and Results; Sounds, Noise Levels are Distracting, etc.; Very Hot; Hazardous Situations; Standing; Using Hands on Objects, Tools, or Controls; Making Repetitive Motions; Special Uniform

GOE Group/s: 05.05.17 Craft Technology: Food Preparation; 05.10.08 Crafts: Food Preparation

CIP Program/s: 120501 Baker/Pastry Chef; 120503 Culinary Arts/Chef Training; 200401 Institutional Food Workers and Administrators, General

Related DOT Job/s: 313.131-010 BAKER, HEAD; 313.131-014 CHEF; 313.131-018 COOK, HEAD, SCHOOL CAFETERIA; 313.131-022 PASTRY CHEF; 313.131-026 SOUS CHEF; 315.131-010 COOK, CHIEF; 315.131-014 PASTRY CHEF; 315.137-010 CHEF, PASSENGER VESSEL; 315.137-014 SOUS CHEF

61099B FIRST-LINE SUPERVISORS/MANAGERS OF FOOD PREPARATION AND SERVING WORKERS. OOH Title/s: Restaurant and Food Service Managers; Chefs, Cooks, and Other Kitchen Workers

Supervise workers engaged in serving and preparing food. Supervises and coordinates activities of workers engaged in preparing and serving food and other related duties. Observes and evaluates workers and work procedures to ensure quality standards and service. Assigns duties, responsibilities, and work stations to employees, following work requirements. Collaborates with specified personnel to plan menus, serving arrangements, and other related details. Specifies food portions and courses, production and time sequences, and work station and equipment arrangements. Inspects supplies, equipment, and work areas to ensure efficient service and conformance to standards. Trains workers in proper food preparation and service procedures. Recommends measures to improve work procedures and worker performance, to increase quality of services and job safety. Records production and operational data on specified forms. Purchases or requisitions supplies and equipment to ensure quality and timely delivery of services. Resolves customer complaints regarding food service. Initiates personnel actions, such as hires and discharges, to ensure proper staffing. Receives, issues, and takes inventory of supplies and equipment, and reports shortages to designated personnel. Analyzes operational problems, such as theft and wastage, and establishes controls. Schedules parties and reservations, and greets and escorts guests to seating arrangements.

Yearly Earnings: $21,580

Education: Work experience in a related occupation

Knowledge: Administration and Management; Customer and Personal Service; Personnel and Human Resources; Production and Processing; Food Production

Abilities: Originality; Deductive Reasoning; Time Sharing; Auditory Attention; Speech Recognition; Speech Clarity

Skills: Speaking; Social Perceptiveness; Coordination; Persuasion; Negotiation; Instructing; Service Orientation; Implementation Planning; Systems Perception; Identifying Downstream Consequences; Identification of Key Causes; Systems Evaluation; Time Management; Management of Financial Resources; Management of Material Resources; Management of Personnel Resources

General Work Activities: Scheduling Work and Activities; Resolving Conflicts, Negotiating with Others; Performing for or Working with Public; Coordinating Work and Activities of Others; Guiding, Directing and Motivating Subordinates; Performing Administrative Activities; Staffing Organizational Units; Monitoring and Controlling Resources

Job Characteristics: Objective or Subjective Information; Job-Required Social Interaction; Supervise, Coach, Train Others; Persuade Someone to a Course of Action; Provide a Service to Others; Take a Position Opposed to Others; Deal with External Customers; Coordinate or Lead Others; Responsibility for Outcomes and Results; Frequency in Conflict Situations; Diseases/Infections; Hazardous Situations; Walking or Running; Keeping or Regaining Balance

GOE Group/s: 05.10.08 Crafts: Food Preparation; 05.12.01 Elemental Work: Mechanical: Supervision; 07.01.02 Administrative Detail: Administration; 09.01.03 Hospitality Services: Food Services; 09.05.02 Attendant Services: Food Services; 11.11.04 Business Management: Services

CIP Program/s: 120507 Waiter/Waitress and Dining Room Manager; 190501 Foods and Nutrition Studies, General; 190505 Food Systems Administration; 200401 Institutional Food Workers and Administrators, General; 200404 Dietician Assistant; 200405 Food Caterer; 200409 Institutional Food Services Administrator

Related DOT Job/s: 310.137-018 STEWARD/STEWARDESS; 310.137-022 STEWARD/STEWARDESS, BANQUET; 310.137-026 STEWARD/STEWARDESS, RAILROAD DINING CAR; 311.137-010 COUNTER SUPERVISOR; 311.137-014 WAITER/WAITRESS, BANQUET, HEAD; 311.137-018 WAITER/WAITRESS, CAPTAIN; 311.137-022 WAITER/WAITRESS, HEAD; 318.137-010 KITCHEN STEWARD/STEWARDESS; 319.137-010 FOOD-SERVICE SUPERVISOR; 319.137-022 SUPERVISOR, COMMISSARY PRODUCTION; 319.137-026 SUPERVISOR, KOSHER DIETARY SERVICE; 319.137-030 KITCHEN SUPERVISOR; 350.137-010 HEADWAITER/HEADWAITRESS; 350.137-014 STEWARD/STEWARDESS, CHIEF, CARGO VESSEL

61099C FIRST-LINE SUPERVISORS/HOSPITALITY AND PERSONAL SERVICE WORKERS. OOH Title/s: Hotel Managers and Assistants

Supervise workers engaged in providing hospitality and personal services. Supervises and coordinates activities of workers engaged in lodging and personal services. Observes and evaluates workers' appearance and performance to ensure quality service and compliance with specifications. Assigns work schedules, following work requirements, to ensure quality and timely delivery of services. Trains workers in proper operational procedures and functions, and explains company policy. Resolves customer complaints regarding worker performance and services rendered. Collaborates with personnel to plan and develop programs of events, schedules of activities, and menus. Analyzes and records personnel and operational data and writes activity reports. Inspects work areas and operating equipment to ensure conformance to established standards. Requisitions supplies, equipment, and designated services, to ensure quality and timely service and efficient operations. Informs workers about interests of specific groups. Furnishes customers with information on events and activities.

Yearly Earnings: $21,580

Education: Work experience in a related occupation

Knowledge: Administration and Management; Customer and Personal Service; Personnel and Human Resources; Psychology; Education and Training

Abilities: Time Sharing

Skills: Active Listening; Speaking; Learning Strategies; Monitoring; Social Perceptiveness; Coordination; Persuasion; Negotiation; Instructing; Service Orientation; Identification of Key Causes; Time Management; Management of Financial Resources; Management of Material Resources; Management of Personnel Resources

General Work Activities: Scheduling Work and Activities; Organizing, Planning, and Prioritizing; Resolving Conflicts, Negotiating with Others; Coordinating Work and Activities of Others; Teaching Others; Guiding, Directing and Motivating Subordinates; Coaching and Developing Others

Job Characteristics: Job-Required Social Interaction; Supervise, Coach, Train Others; Provide a Service to Others; Deal with External Customers; Coordinate or Lead Others; Responsibility for Outcomes and Results; Deal with Unpleasant or Angry People; Importance of Being Sure All is Done

GOE Group/s: 05.12.01 Elemental Work: Mechanical: Supervision; 09.01.02 Hospitality Services: Guide Services; 09.01.04 Hospitality Services: Safety and Comfort Services; 09.05.03 Attendant Services: Portering and Baggage Services; 09.05.08 Attendant Services: Ticket Taking, Ushering; 09.05.09 Attendant Services: Elevator Services

CIP Program/s: 081104 Tourism Promotion Operations; 200601 Custodial, Housekeeping and Home Services Workers and Managers; 200604 Custodian/Caretaker; 200605 Executive Housekeeper; 490106 Flight Attendant; 520902 Hotel/Motel and Restaurant Management

Related DOT Job/s: 321.137-014 INSPECTOR; 323.137-010 SUPERVISOR, HOUSECLEANER; 324.137-010 BAGGAGE PORTER, HEAD; 324.137-014 BELL CAPTAIN; 329.137-010 SUPERINTENDENT, SERVICE; 344.137-010 USHER, HEAD; 350.137-018 STEWARD/STEWARDESS, CHIEF, PASSENGER SHIP; 350.137-022 STEWARD/STEWARDESS, SECOND; 350.137-026 STEWARD/STEWARDESS, THIRD; 352.137-010 SUPERVISOR, AIRPLANE-FLIGHT ATTENDANT; 353.137-010 GUIDE, CHIEF AIRPORT; 358.137-010 CHECKROOM CHIEF; 388.367-010 ELEVATOR STARTER

61099D FIRST-LINE SUPERVISORS/MANAGERS OF HOUSEKEEPING AND JANITORIAL WORKERS.

OOH Title/s: Janitors and Cleaners and Cleaning Supervisors

Supervise work activities of cleaning personnel in hotels, hospitals, offices, and other establishments. Supervises and coordinates activities of workers engaged in janitorial services. Assigns janitorial work to employees, following material and work requirements. Trains workers in janitorial methods and procedures and proper operation of equipment. Inspects work performed to ensure conformance to specifications and established standards. Confers with staff to resolve production and personnel problems. Recommends personnel actions, such as hires and discharges, to ensure proper staffing. Records personnel data on specified forms. Issues janitorial supplies and equipment to workers to ensure quality and timely delivery of services.

Yearly Earnings: $18,876

Education: Work experience in a related occupation

Knowledge: Administration and Management; Customer and Personal Service; Personnel and Human Resources

Abilities: None above average

Skills: Social Perceptiveness; Coordination; Persuasion; Negotiation; Instructing; Time Management; Management of Personnel Resources

General Work Activities: Scheduling Work and Activities; Resolving Conflicts, Negotiating with Others; Coordinating Work and Activities of Others; Guiding, Directing and Motivating Subordinates; Staffing Organizational Units

Job Characteristics: Supervise, Coach, Train Others; Coordinate or Lead Others; Responsibility for Outcomes and Results; Standing; Walking or Running

GOE Group/s: 05.12.01 Elemental Work: Mechanical: Supervision; 05.12.18 Elemental Work: Mechanical: Cleaning and Maintenance

CIP Program/s: 200601 Custodial, Housekeeping and Home Services Workers and Managers; 200604 Custodian/Caretaker

Related DOT Job/s: 381.137-010 SUPERVISOR, JANITORIAL SERVICES; 382.137-010 SUPERVISOR, MAINTENANCE; 389.137-010 SUPERVISOR, HOME RESTORATION SERVICE

61099E ALL OTHER SERVICE SUPERVISORS AND MANAGER/SUPERVISORS. OOH Title/s: Indirectly related to Executive, Administrative, and Managerial Occupations

All other supervisors and manager/supervisors of service workers not classified separately above.

Yearly Earnings: $37,076

Education: Work experience, plus degree

GOE Group/s: 05.10.02 Crafts: Mechanical; 09.05.06 Attendant Services: Individualized Services

CIP Program/s: 000000 NO CIP ASSIGNED

Related DOT Job/s: 341.137-010 CADDIE SUPERVISOR; 342.137-010 SUPERVISOR, RIDES

Private Household Workers

62031 HOUSEKEEPERS, PRIVATE HOUSEHOLD.

OOH Title/s: Private Household Workers

Manage, maintain, and clean private home and render personal services to family members. Cleans furnishings, floors, windows, and lavatories, using vacuum cleaner, mops, brooms, cloths, and cleaning solutions. Changes linens and removes and hangs draperies. Washes dishes and cleans kitchen, cooking utensils, and silverware. Sorts clothing and other articles, loads washing machine, and irons and folds dried items. Plans menus and cooks and serves meals and refreshments, according to employer's instructions or following own methods. Purchases or orders foodstuffs and household supplies, and records expenditures. Answers telephone and doorbell. Oversees activities of children or other household employees. Grooms, exercises, or feeds pets. Assigns duties to household employees and gives instructions in work methods and routines.

Yearly Earnings: $10,296

Education: Moderate-term O-J-T

Knowledge: Customer and Personal Service; Food Production

Abilities: Extent Flexibility; Dynamic Flexibility; Gross Body Equilibrium

Skills: Service Orientation

General Work Activities: Establishing and Maintaining Relationships; Assisting and Caring for Others

Job Characteristics: Provide a Service to Others; Standing; Kneeling, Crouching, or Crawling; Bending or Twisting the Body; Special Uniform

GOE Group/s: 05.12.01 Elemental Work: Mechanical: Supervision; 05.12.18 Elemental Work: Mechanical: Cleaning and Maintenance; 09.01.03 Hospitality Services: Food Services

CIP Program/s: 200601 Custodial, Housekeeping and Home Services Workers and Managers; 200604 Custodian/Caretaker; 200605 Executive Housekeeper; 200606 Homemaker's Aide

Related DOT Job/s: 301.137-010 HOUSEKEEPER, HOME; 301.474-010 HOUSE WORKER, GENERAL; 301.687-010 CARETAKER; 301.687-014 DAY WORKER; 302.685-010 LAUNDRY WORKER, DOMESTIC; 302.687-010 IRONER; 309.137-010 BUTLER; 309.674-010 BUTLER, SECOND

62041 CHILD MONITORS, PRIVATE HOUSEHOLD.

OOH Title/s: Private Household Workers

Attend to and care for children in private home. Observes and monitors play activities of children. Prepares and serves meals or formulas. Dresses or assists children to dress and bathe. Entertains children by reading to or playing games with them. Accompanies children on walks and other outings. Keeps children's quarters clean and washes clothing.

Yearly Earnings: $8,372

Education: Short-term O-J-T

Knowledge: Customer and Personal Service; Psychology

Abilities: None above average

Skills: None above average

General Work Activities: Establishing and Maintaining Relationships; Assisting and Caring for Others

Job Characteristics: Objective or Subjective Information; Job-Required Social Interaction; Provide a Service to Others; Coordinate or Lead Others; Responsible for Others' Health and Safety; Frequency in Conflict Situations; Deal with Unpleasant or Angry People; Deal with Physical, Aggressive People; Diseases/Infections; Kneeling, Crouching, or Crawling

GOE Group/s: 10.03.03 Child and Adult Care: Care of Others

CIP Program/s: 130101 Education, General; 200201 Child Care and Guidance Workers and Managers, General; 200202 Child Care Provider/Assistant; 200601 Custodial, Housekeeping and Home Services Workers and Managers; 200604 Custodian/Caretaker; 200606 Homemaker's Aide

Related DOT Job/s: 099.227-010 CHILDREN'S TUTOR; 301.677-010 CHILD MONITOR; 309.677-014 FOSTER PARENT

62061 PERSONAL ATTENDANTS, PRIVATE HOUSEHOLD. OOH Title/s: Private Household Workers

Provide personal services and companionship to persons in private household. Draws bath, lays out clothing, and assists employer to dress. Performs grooming services, such as shampooing hair, shaving face, manicuring nails, and applying cosmetics. Mends, cleans, presses, and packs clothing. Performs errands or handles employer's social or business affairs. Cleans employer's quarters, changes linens,

and makes bed. Reads aloud, plays cards or other games, and accompanies employer on outings. Prepares and serves meals and drinks. Purchases clothing and accessories for employer.
Yearly Earnings: $10,296
Education: Moderate-term O-J-T
Knowledge: Customer and Personal Service; Food Production
Abilities: None above average
Skills: Service Orientation
General Work Activities: Establishing and Maintaining Relationships; Assisting and Caring for Others
Job Characteristics: Job-Required Social Interaction; Provide a Service to Others; Deal with External Customers; Deal with Unpleasant or Angry People; Diseases/Infections; Walking or Running; Bending or Twisting the Body; Importance of Being Aware of New Events
GOE Group/s: 05.10.08 Crafts: Food Preparation; 09.05.06 Attendant Services: Individualized Services; 10.03.03 Child and Adult Care: Care of Others
CIP Program/s: 200301 Clothing, Apparel and Textile Workers and Managers, General; 200601 Custodial, Housekeeping and Home Services Workers and Managers; 200602 Elder Care Provider/Companion; 200604 Custodian/Caretaker; 200606 Homemaker's Aide
Related DOT Job/s: 305.281-010 COOK; 309.674-014 PERSONAL ATTENDANT; 309.677-010 COMPANION

Protective Service Workers

63002A FIRE INSPECTORS. OOH Title/s: Firefighting Occupations; Construction and Building Inspectors

Inspect buildings and equipment to detect fire hazards and enforce state and local regulations. Inspects interiors and exteriors of buildings to detect hazardous conditions or violations of fire codes. Tests equipment, such as gasoline storage tanks, air compressors, and fire-extinguishing and fire protection equipment, to ensure conformance to fire and safety codes. Discusses violations and unsafe conditions with facility representative, makes recommendations, and instructs in fire safety practices. Issues permits and summons, and enforces fire codes. Prepares reports, such as inspections performed, code violations, and recommendations for eliminating fire hazards. Collects fees for permits and licenses. Gives first aid in emergencies.
Yearly Earnings: $33,228
Education: Work experience in a related occupation
Knowledge: Medicine and Dentistry; Therapy and Counseling; Education and Training; Public Safety and Security; Law, Government, and Jurisprudence
Abilities: Problem Sensitivity; Flexibility of Closure; Spatial Orientation; Response Orientation; Reaction Time; Speed of Limb Movement; Explosive Strength; Stamina; Gross Body Coordination; Gross Body Equilibrium; Far Vision; Visual Color Discrimination; Night Vision; Peripheral Vision; Auditory Attention; Sound Localization
Skills: Writing; Learning Strategies; Persuasion; Instructing; Service Orientation; Problem Identification; Idea Evaluation; Testing; Troubleshooting; Identifying Downstream Consequences
General Work Activities: Inspecting Equipment, Structures, or Material; Assisting and Caring for Others; Teaching Others; Provide Consultation and Advice to Others
Job Characteristics: Take a Position Opposed to Others; Deal with External Customers; Responsible for Others' Health and Safety; Frequency in Conflict Situations; Very Hot; Cramped Work Space, Awkward Positions; Radiation; High Places; Hazardous Conditions; Standing; Climbing Ladders, Scaffolds, Poles, etc.; Walking or Running; Kneeling, Crouching, or Crawling; Keeping or Regaining Balance; Bending or Twisting the Body; Special Uniform; Consequence of Error; Importance of Being Exact or Accurate; Importance of Being Sure All is Done
GOE Group/s: 04.02.02 Security Services: Property and People; 05.07.01 Quality Control: Structural; 11.10.03 Regulations Enforcement: Health and Safety
CIP Program/s: 430201 Fire Protection and Safety Tech./Technician
Related DOT Job/s: 168.267-010 BUILDING INSPECTOR; 373.267-010 FIRE INSPECTOR; 373.367-010 FIRE INSPECTOR; 379.687-010 FIRE-EXTINGUISHER-SPRINKLER INSPECTOR

63002B FIRE INVESTIGATORS. OOH Title/s: Firefighting Occupations

Conduct investigations to determine causes of fires and explosions. Examines site and collects evidence to gather information relating to cause of fire, explosion, or false alarm. Photographs damage and evidence relating to cause of fire or explosion, for future reference. Tests site and materials to establish facts, such as burn patterns and flash points of materials, using test equipment. Analyzes evidence and other information to determine probable cause of fire or explosion. Subpoenas and interviews witnesses, property owners, and building occupants to obtain information and sworn testimony. Conducts internal investigation to determine negligence and violation of laws and regulations by fire department employees. Prepares and maintains reports of investigation results and records of convicted arsonists and arson suspects. Testifies in court for cases involving fires, suspected arson, and false alarms. Swears out warrants and arrests, logs, fingerprints, and detains suspected arsonists. Instructs children about dangers of fire.
Yearly Earnings: $33,228
Education: Work experience in a related occupation
Knowledge: Building and Construction; Chemistry; Psychology; Education and Training; Public Safety and Security; Law, Government, and Jurisprudence; Telecommunications
Abilities: Oral Expression; Written Expression; Fluency of Ideas; Problem Sensitivity; Deductive Reasoning; Inductive Reasoning; Information Ordering; Category Flexibility; Speed of Closure; Flexibility of Closure; Spatial Orientation; Visualization; Selective Attention; Time Sharing; Stamina; Gross Body Equilibrium; Far Vision; Visual Color Discrimination; Night Vision; Auditory Attention; Speech Clarity
Skills: Active Listening; Writing; Speaking; Science; Critical Thinking; Active Learning; Learning Strategies; Social Perceptiveness; Persuasion; Instructing; Service Orientation; Problem Identification; Information Gathering; Information Organization; Synthesis/Reorganization; Visioning; Identification of Key Causes; Judgment and Decision Making; Systems Evaluation
General Work Activities: Inspecting Equipment, Structures, or Material; Documenting/Recording Information
Job Characteristics: Responsible for Others' Health and Safety; Very Hot; Extremely Bright or Inadequate Lighting; Contaminants; Cramped Work Space, Awkward Positions; Radiation; High Places; Climbing Ladders, Scaffolds, Poles, etc.; Walking or Running; Kneeling, Crouching, or Crawling; Keeping or Regaining Balance; Special Uniform; Specialized Protective or Safety Attire; Frustrating Circumstances; Importance of Being Aware of New Events
GOE Group/s: 04.01.02 Safety and Law Enforcement: Investigating; 11.10.03 Regulations Enforcement: Health and Safety
CIP Program/s: 430109 Security and Loss Prevention Services; 430201 Fire Protection and Safety Tech./Technician; 430202 Fire Services Administration; 430203 Fire Science/Firefighting
Related DOT Job/s: 373.267-014 FIRE MARSHAL; 373.267-018 FIRE-INVESTIGATION LIEUTENANT

63005 FOREST FIRE INSPECTORS AND PREVENTION SPECIALISTS. OOH Title/s: Firefighting Occupations

Administer fire regulations. Locate and report forest fires and weather conditions, usually from remote locations within forest or logging area. Inspect area for fire hazards and equipment for serviceability. May work from a station or patrol area. Inspects forest tracts and logging areas for fire hazards, such as accumulated wastes, mishandling of combustibles, or defective exhaust systems. Inspects campsites to ensure camper compliance with forest use regulations. Patrols and maintains surveillance, looking for forest fires, hazardous conditions, and weather phenomena. Locates forest fires on area map, using azimuth sighter and known landmarks. Relays messages relative to emergencies, accidents, location of crew and personnel, weather forecasts, and fire hazard conditions. Estimates size and characteristics of fire, and reports findings to base camp by radio or telephone. Examines and inventories fire-fighting equipment, such as axes, fire hoses, shovels, pumps, buckets, and fire extinguishers, to determine amount and condition. Gives instructions regarding sanitation, fire prevention, violation corrections, and related forest regulations. Observes instruments and reports meteorological data, such as temperature, relative humidity, wind direction and velocity, and types of cloud formations. Restricts public access and recreational use of forest lands during critical fire season. Directs maintenance and repair of fire-fighting equipment and requisitions new equipment. Maintains records and logbooks. Extinguishes smaller fires with portable extinguisher, shovel, and ax. Gives directions to crew on fireline during forest fire. Renders assistance or first aid to lost or injured persons. Participates in search for lost travelers or campers.

Yearly Earnings: $33,228

Education: Work experience in a related occupation

Knowledge: Customer and Personal Service; Physics; Chemistry; Biology; Sociology and Anthropology; Geography; Medicine and Dentistry; Education and Training; Public Safety and Security; Law, Government, and Jurisprudence; Telecommunications

Abilities: Problem Sensitivity; Memorization; Speed of Closure; Flexibility of Closure; Perceptual Speed; Spatial Orientation; Time Sharing; Multilimb Coordination; Response Orientation; Rate Control; Reaction Time; Speed of Limb Movement; Static Strength; Explosive Strength; Dynamic Strength; Trunk Strength; Stamina; Dynamic Flexibility; Gross Body Coordination; Gross Body Equilibrium; Far Vision; Night Vision; Peripheral Vision; Depth Perception; Glare Sensitivity; Sound Localization; Speech Recognition; Speech Clarity

Skills: Critical Thinking; Active Learning; Learning Strategies; Monitoring; Coordination; Instructing; Service Orientation; Idea Generation; Implementation Planning; Solution Appraisal; Equipment Selection; Equipment Maintenance; Systems Perception; Identifying Downstream Consequences; Identification of Key Causes; Judgment and Decision Making; Time Management; Management of Material Resources; Management of Personnel Resources

General Work Activities: Getting Information Needed to Do the Job; Identifying Objects, Actions, and Events; Inspecting Equipment, Structures, or Material; Estimating Needed Characteristics; Judging Qualities of Things, Services, People; Performing General Physical Activities; Interacting with Computers; Establishing and Maintaining Relationships; Assisting and Caring for Others; Performing for or Working with Public; Coordinating Work and Activities of Others

Job Characteristics: Supervise, Coach, Train Others; Provide a Service to Others; Take a Position Opposed to Others; Deal with External Customers; Coordinate or Lead Others; Responsible for Others' Health and Safety; Frequency in Conflict Situations; Deal with Physical, Aggressive People; Very Hot; Extremely Bright or Inadequate Lighting; Contaminants; Diseases/Infections; High Places; Hazardous Conditions; Hazardous Situations; Climbing Ladders, Scaffolds, Poles, etc.; Walking or Running; Special Uniform; Common Protective or Safety Attire; Specialized Protective or Safety Attire; Consequence of Error; Frustrating Circumstances; Importance of Being Aware of New Events

GOE Group/s: 04.01.02 Safety and Law Enforcement: Investigating; 04.02.02 Security Services: Property and People; 07.04.05 Oral Communications: Information Transmitting and Receiving

CIP Program/s: 030203 Natural Resources Law Enforcement and Protective Services; 430202 Fire Services Administration; 430203 Fire Science/Firefighting

Related DOT Job/s: 452.167-010 FIRE WARDEN; 452.367-010 FIRE LOOKOUT; 452.367-014 FIRE RANGER

63008A MUNICIPAL FIRE FIGHTERS. OOH Title/s: Firefighting Occupations

Control and extinguish municipal fires, protect life and property, and conduct rescue efforts. Positions and climbs ladders to gain access to upper levels of buildings, or to rescue individuals from burning structures. Creates openings in buildings for ventilation or entrance, using ax, chisel, crowbar, electric saw, or core cutter. Selects hose nozzle, depending on type of fire, and directs stream of water or chemicals onto fire. Protects property from water and smoke, using waterproof salvage covers, smoke ejectors, and deodorants. Administers first aid and cardiopulmonary resuscitation to injured persons and those overcome by fire and smoke. Sprays foam onto runway, extinguishes fire, and rescues aircraft crew and passengers in air-crash emergency. Responds to fire alarms and other emergency calls. Assesses fire and situation, reports to superior, and receives instructions, using two-way radio. Establishes firelines to prevent unauthorized persons from entering area. Drives and operates fire-fighting vehicles and equipment. Maintains fire-fighting equipment and apparatus, vehicles, hydrants, and fire station. Participates in fire drills and demonstrations of fire-fighting techniques. Participates in courses in hydraulics, pump operation, and fire-fighting techniques. Inspects buildings for fire hazards and compliance with fire prevention ordinances.

Yearly Earnings: $33,020

Education: Long-term O-J-T

Knowledge: Geography; Medicine and Dentistry; Therapy and Counseling; Public Safety and Security; Telecommunications; Transportation

Abilities: Information Ordering; Speed of Closure; Flexibility of Closure; Spatial Orientation; Selective Attention; Time Sharing; Manual Dexterity; Control Precision; Multilimb Coordination; Response Orientation; Rate Control; Reaction Time; Speed of Limb Movement; Static Strength; Explosive Strength; Dynamic Strength; Trunk Strength; Stamina; Extent Flexibility; Dynamic Flexibility; Gross Body Coordination; Gross Body Equilibrium; Far Vision; Visual Color Discrimination; Night Vision; Peripheral Vision; Depth Perception; Glare Sensitivity; Auditory Attention; Sound Localization

Skills: Coordination; Service Orientation; Equipment Maintenance; Repairing; Systems Perception

General Work Activities: Inspecting Equipment, Structures, or Material; Performing General Physical Activities; Handling and Moving Objects; Interacting with Computers; Repairing and Maintaining Mechanical Equipment; Assisting and Caring for Others

Job Characteristics: Objective or Subjective Information; Job-Required Social Interaction; Persuade Someone to a Course of Action; Provide a Service to Others; Deal with External Customers; Coordinate or Lead Others; Responsible for Others' Health and Safety; Frequency in Conflict Situations; Deal with Physical, Aggressive People; Sounds, Noise Levels are Distracting, etc.; Very Hot; Extremely Bright or Inadequate Lighting; Contaminants; Cramped Work Space, Awkward

Positions; Whole Body Vibration; Radiation; Diseases/Infections; High Places; Hazardous Conditions; Hazardous Situations; Climbing Ladders, Scaffolds, Poles, etc.; Walking or Running; Kneeling, Crouching, or Crawling; Keeping or Regaining Balance; Bending or Twisting the Body; Special Uniform; Common Protective or Safety Attire; Specialized Protective or Safety Attire; Consequence of Error; Frustrating Circumstances; Importance of Being Sure All is Done; Importance of Being Aware of New Events; Importance of Repeating Same Tasks; Pace Determined by Speed of Equipment
GOE Group/s: 04.02.04 Security Services: Emergency Responding
CIP Program/s: 430203 Fire Science/Firefighting
Related DOT Job/s: 373.363-010 FIRE CHIEF'S AIDE; 373.364-010 FIRE FIGHTER; 373.663-010 FIRE FIGHTER, CRASH, FIRE, AND RESCUE

63008B FOREST FIRE FIGHTERS. OOH Title/s: Firefighting Occupations

Control and suppress fires in forests or on vacant public land. Fells trees, cuts and clears brush, and digs trenches to contain fire, using ax, chainsaw, or shovel. Extinguishes flames and embers to suppress fire, using shovel or engine- or hand-driven water or chemical pumps. Ascertains best method for attacking fire, and communicates plan to airplane or base camp, using two-way radio. Patrols burned area after fire to watch for hot spots that may restart fire. Works as member of fire-fighting crew. Orients self in relation to fire, using compass and map, and collects supplies and equipment dropped by parachute. Parachutes from aircraft and guides direction of fall toward clear landing area near scene of fire. Packs parachutes.
Yearly Earnings: $33,020
Education: Long-term O-J-T
Knowledge: Geography; Therapy and Counseling; Public Safety and Security; Telecommunications; Transportation
Abilities: Problem Sensitivity; Speed of Closure; Flexibility of Closure; Spatial Orientation; Selective Attention; Time Sharing; Multilimb Coordination; Response Orientation; Rate Control; Reaction Time; Wrist-Finger Speed; Speed of Limb Movement; Static Strength; Explosive Strength; Dynamic Strength; Trunk Strength; Stamina; Extent Flexibility; Dynamic Flexibility; Gross Body Coordination; Gross Body Equilibrium; Far Vision; Night Vision; Peripheral Vision; Depth Perception; Glare Sensitivity; Auditory Attention; Sound Localization
Skills: Coordination; Service Orientation; Technology Design
General Work Activities: Identifying Objects, Actions, and Events; Performing General Physical Activities; Interacting with Computers
Job Characteristics: Responsible for Others' Health and Safety; Sounds, Noise Levels are Distracting, etc.; Very Hot; Extremely Bright or Inadequate Lighting; Contaminants; Cramped Work Space, Awkward Positions; Whole Body Vibration; Radiation; High Places; Hazardous Conditions; Hazardous Equipment; Hazardous Situations; Standing; Climbing Ladders, Scaffolds, Poles, etc.; Walking or Running; Keeping or Regaining Balance; Bending or Twisting the Body; Special Uniform; Common Protective or Safety Attire; Specialized Protective or Safety Attire; Consequence of Error; Frustrating Circumstances; Importance of Being Sure All is Done; Importance of Being Aware of New Events; Importance of Repeating Same Tasks
GOE Group/s: 03.04.02 Elemental Work: Plants and Animals: Forestry and Logging; 04.02.04 Security Services: Emergency Responding
CIP Program/s: 030203 Natural Resources Law Enforcement and Protective Services; 430203 Fire Science/Firefighting
Related DOT Job/s: 452.364-014 SMOKE JUMPER; 452.687-014 FOREST-FIRE FIGHTER

63011A POLICE DETECTIVES. OOH Title/s: Police, Detectives, and Special Agents

Conduct investigations to prevent crimes or to solve criminal cases. Examines scene of crime to obtain clues and gather evidence. Interviews complainant, witnesses, and accused persons to obtain facts or statements; and records interviews, using recording device. Investigates establishments or persons to establish facts supporting complainant or accused, using supportive information from witnesses or tangible evidence. Maintains surveillance of establishments to attain identifying information on suspects. Arrests or assists in arrest of criminals or suspects. Records progress of investigation, maintains informational files on suspects, and submits reports to commanding officer or magistrate to authorize warrants. Observes and photographs narcotics purchase transaction to compile evidence and protect undercover investigators. Reviews governmental agency files to obtain identifying data pertaining to suspects or establishments suspected of violating anti-vice laws. Prepares assigned cases for court and charges or responses to charges, according to formalized procedures. Compiles identifying information on suspects charged with selling narcotics. Examines prescriptions in pharmacies and physicians' records to ascertain legality of sale and distribution of narcotics, and determines drug stock. Testifies before court and grand jury and appears in court as witness. Schedules polygraph test for consenting parties, and records results of test interpretations for presentation with findings. Selects undercover officer best suited to contact suspect and purchase narcotics. Obtains police funds required to make purchase.
Yearly Earnings: $33,904
Education: Work experience in a related occupation
Knowledge: Clerical; Psychology; Sociology and Anthropology; Geography; Foreign Language; Public Safety and Security; Law, Government, and Jurisprudence; Telecommunications
Abilities: Oral Comprehension; Deductive Reasoning; Inductive Reasoning; Speed of Closure; Flexibility of Closure; Selective Attention; Reaction Time; Explosive Strength; Gross Body Coordination; Gross Body Equilibrium; Night Vision; Peripheral Vision; Glare Sensitivity; Auditory Attention; Sound Localization
Skills: Active Listening; Speaking; Critical Thinking; Active Learning; Social Perceptiveness; Coordination; Persuasion; Problem Identification; Information Gathering; Information Organization; Synthesis/Reorganization; Idea Generation; Idea Evaluation; Implementation Planning
General Work Activities: Judging Qualities of Things, Services, People; Processing Information; Analyzing Data or Information; Making Decisions and Solving Problems; Developing Objectives and Strategies; Documenting/Recording Information; Interpreting Meaning of Information to Others; Assisting and Caring for Others; Selling or Influencing Others; Resolving Conflicts, Negotiating with Others; Performing for or Working with Public
Job Characteristics: Take a Position Opposed to Others; Deal with External Customers; Frequency in Conflict Situations; Deal with Unpleasant or Angry People; Deal with Physical, Aggressive People; Extremely Bright or Inadequate Lighting; Special Uniform; Specialized Protective or Safety Attire; Frustrating Circumstances; Importance of Being Aware of New Events
GOE Group/s: 04.01.02 Safety and Law Enforcement: Investigating; 07.01.06 Administrative Detail: Investigating
CIP Program/s: 430107 Law Enforcement/Police Science
Related DOT Job/s: 375.267-010 DETECTIVE; 375.267-014 DETECTIVE, NARCOTICS AND VICE; 375.267-018 INVESTIGATOR, NARCOTICS; 375.267-022 INVESTIGATOR, VICE; 375.267-034 INVESTIGATOR, INTERNAL AFFAIRS

63011B POLICE IDENTIFICATION AND RECORDS OFFICERS. OOH Title/s: Police, Detectives, and Special Agents

Collect evidence at crime scene, classify and identify fingerprints, and photograph evidence for use in criminal and civil cases. Dusts selected areas of crime scene to locate and reveal latent fingerprints. Lifts prints from crime site, using special tape. Photographs crime or accident scene to obtain record of evidence. Photographs, records physical description, and fingerprints homicide victims and suspects for identification. Classifies and files fingerprints. Develops film and prints, using photographic developing equipment. Submits evidence to supervisor.

Yearly Earnings: $33,904

Education: Work experience in a related occupation

Knowledge: Clerical; Chemistry; Public Safety and Security; Law, Government, and Jurisprudence

Abilities: Category Flexibility

Skills: None above average

General Work Activities: None above average

Job Characteristics: High Places; Climbing Ladders, Scaffolds, Poles, etc.; Kneeling, Crouching, or Crawling; Special Uniform; Importance of Being Exact or Accurate; Importance of Being Sure All is Done

GOE Group/s: 07.01.06 Administrative Detail: Investigating

CIP Program/s: 430107 Law Enforcement/Police Science

Related DOT Job/s: 375.384-010 POLICE OFFICER, IDENTIFICATION AND RECORDS; 375.387-010 FINGERPRINT CLASSIFIER

63014A POLICE INVESTIGATORS—PATROLLERS. OOH Title/s: Police, Detectives, and Special Agents; Inspectors and Compliance Officers, Except Construction

Patrol assigned area to enforce laws and ordinances, regulate traffic, control crowds, prevent crime, and arrest violators. Patrols specific area on foot, horseback, or motorized conveyance. Maintains order, responds to emergencies, protects people and property, and enforces motor vehicle and criminal laws. Arrests perpetrators of criminal acts or submits citations or warnings to violators of motor vehicle ordinances. Monitors traffic to ensure motorists observe traffic regulations and exhibit safe driving procedures. Directs traffic flow and reroutes traffic in case of emergencies. Reviews facts to determine if criminal act or statute violation is involved. Evaluates complaint and emergency-request information to determine response requirements. Investigates traffic accidents and other accidents to determine causes and to determine if crime has been committed. Provides road information to assist motorists. Relays complaint and emergency-request information to appropriate agency dispatcher. Records facts, photographs and diagrams crime or accident scene, and interviews principal and eye witnesses. Expedites processing of prisoners, and prepares and maintains records of prisoner bookings and prisoner status during booking and pretrial process. Testifies in court to present evidence or to act as witness in traffic and criminal cases. Prepares reports to document activities. Renders aid to accident victims and other persons requiring first aid for physical injuries.

Yearly Earnings: $33,904

Education: Long-term O-J-T

Knowledge: Clerical; Customer and Personal Service; Psychology; Sociology and Anthropology; Geography; Medicine and Dentistry; Therapy and Counseling; Foreign Language; Philosophy and Theology; Public Safety and Security; Law, Government, and Jurisprudence; Telecommunications; Transportation

Abilities: Oral Comprehension; Oral Expression; Written Expression; Fluency of Ideas; Originality; Problem Sensitivity; Deductive Reasoning; Inductive Reasoning; Memorization; Speed of Closure; Flexibility of Closure; Perceptual Speed; Spatial Orientation; Selective Attention; Time Sharing; Multilimb Coordination; Response Orientation; Rate Control; Reaction Time; Speed of Limb Movement; Static Strength; Explosive Strength; Dynamic Strength; Stamina; Dynamic Flexibility; Gross Body Coordination; Gross Body Equilibrium; Far Vision; Visual Color Discrimination; Night Vision; Peripheral Vision; Depth Perception; Glare Sensitivity; Hearing Sensitivity; Sound Localization; Speech Recognition; Speech Clarity

Skills: Active Listening; Speaking; Critical Thinking; Monitoring; Social Perceptiveness; Persuasion; Negotiation; Service Orientation; Problem Identification; Information Gathering; Information Organization; Judgment and Decision Making

General Work Activities: Processing Information; Performing General Physical Activities; Interacting with Computers; Documenting/Recording Information; Interpreting Meaning of Information to Others; Communicating with Other Workers; Communicating with Persons Outside Organization; Establishing and Maintaining Relationships; Assisting and Caring for Others; Selling or Influencing Others; Resolving Conflicts, Negotiating with Others; Performing for or Working with Public; Developing and Building Teams; Performing Administrative Activities

Job Characteristics: Objective or Subjective Information; Job-Required Social Interaction; Persuade Someone to a Course of Action; Take a Position Opposed to Others; Deal with External Customers; Responsible for Others' Health and Safety; Frequency in Conflict Situations; Deal with Unpleasant or Angry People; Deal with Physical, Aggressive People; Sounds, Noise Levels are Distracting, etc.; Very Hot; Extremely Bright or Inadequate Lighting; Diseases/Infections; High Places; Walking or Running; Bending or Twisting the Body; Special Uniform; Consequence of Error; Frustrating Circumstances; Importance of Being Aware of New Events

GOE Group/s: 04.01.02 Safety and Law Enforcement: Investigating; 04.02.01 Security Services: Dentention; 04.02.02 Security Services: Property and People; 04.02.03 Security Services: Law and Order; 07.04.05 Oral Communications: Information Transmitting and Receiving

CIP Program/s: 430107 Law Enforcement/Police Science

Related DOT Job/s: 168.167-010 CUSTOMS PATROL OFFICER; 169.167-042 PARK RANGER; 372.363-010 PROTECTIVE OFFICER; 375.263-010 ACCIDENT-PREVENTION-SQUAD POLICE OFFICER; 375.263-014 POLICE OFFICER I; 375.263-018 STATE-HIGHWAY POLICE OFFICER; 375.264-010 POLICE OFFICER, CRIME PREVENTION; 375.267-030 POLICE INSPECTOR II; 375.267-042 POLICE OFFICER, SAFETY INSTRUCTION; 375.363-010 BORDER GUARD; 375.367-014 COMPLAINT EVALUATION OFFICER; 375.367-018 POLICE OFFICER, BOOKING; 379.263-014 PUBLIC-SAFETY OFFICER

63014B HIGHWAY PATROL PILOTS. OOH Title/s: Police, Detectives, and Special Agents

Pilot aircraft to patrol highway and enforce traffic laws. Pilots airplane to maintain order, respond to emergencies, enforce traffic and criminal laws, and apprehend criminals. Informs ground personnel of traffic congestion or unsafe driving conditions to ensure traffic flow and reduce incidence of accidents. Informs ground personnel where to reroute traffic in case of emergencies. Arrests perpetrator of criminal act or submits citation or warning to violator of motor vehicle ordinance. Investigates traffic accidents and other accidents to determine causes and to determine if crime was committed. Reviews facts to determine if criminal act or statute violation is involved. Records facts, photographs and diagrams crime or accident scene, and interviews witnesses to gather information for possible use in legal action or safety programs. Testifies in court to present evidence or to act as witness in traffic and criminal cases. Renders aid to accident victims and other persons requiring first aid for physical injuries. Evaluates complaint

and emergency-request information to determine response requirements. Relays complaint and emergency-request information to appropriate agency dispatcher. Prepares reports to document activities. Expedites processing of prisoners, prepares and maintains records of prisoner bookings, and maintains record of prisoner status during booking and pretrial process. Contacts health and social agencies to refer persons for assistance.
Yearly Earnings: $33,904
Education: Long-term O-J-T
Knowledge: Customer and Personal Service; Psychology; Sociology and Anthropology; Geography; Medicine and Dentistry; Therapy and Counseling; Foreign Language; Philosophy and Theology; Public Safety and Security; Law, Government, and Jurisprudence; Telecommunications; Transportation
Abilities: Oral Expression; Fluency of Ideas; Problem Sensitivity; Deductive Reasoning; Inductive Reasoning; Information Ordering; Category Flexibility; Memorization; Speed of Closure; Flexibility of Closure; Perceptual Speed; Spatial Orientation; Selective Attention; Time Sharing; Control Precision; Multilimb Coordination; Response Orientation; Rate Control; Reaction Time; Wrist-Finger Speed; Speed of Limb Movement; Static Strength; Explosive Strength; Dynamic Strength; Trunk Strength; Extent Flexibility; Dynamic Flexibility; Gross Body Coordination; Gross Body Equilibrium; Near Vision; Far Vision; Night Vision; Peripheral Vision; Depth Perception; Glare Sensitivity; Hearing Sensitivity; Auditory Attention; Sound Localization; Speech Recognition; Speech Clarity
Skills: Reading Comprehension; Active Listening; Speaking; Critical Thinking; Social Perceptiveness; Persuasion; Negotiation; Service Orientation; Problem Identification; Operation Monitoring; Operation and Control; Judgment and Decision Making
General Work Activities: Identifying Objects, Actions, and Events; Judging Qualities of Things, Services, People; Processing Information; Analyzing Data or Information; Making Decisions and Solving Problems; Thinking Creatively; Updating and Using Job-Relevant Knowledge; Performing General Physical Activities; Operating Vehicles or Equipment; Interacting with Computers; Documenting/Recording Information; Interpreting Meaning of Information to Others; Communicating with Other Workers; Communicating with Persons Outside Organization; Establishing and Maintaining Relationships; Assisting and Caring for Others; Selling or Influencing Others; Resolving Conflicts, Negotiating with Others; Performing for or Working with Public; Coordinating Work and Activities of Others; Performing Administrative Activities
Job Characteristics: Job-Required Social Interaction; Provide a Service to Others; Deal with External Customers; Responsible for Others' Health and Safety; Frequency in Conflict Situations; Deal with Unpleasant or Angry People; Deal with Physical, Aggressive People; Sounds, Noise Levels are Distracting, etc.; Very Hot; Extremely Bright or Inadequate Lighting; Cramped Work Space, Awkward Positions; Whole Body Vibration; High Places; Sitting; Keeping or Regaining Balance; Special Uniform; Common Protective or Safety Attire; Specialized Protective or Safety Attire; Consequence of Error; Frustrating Circumstances; Degree of Automation; Importance of Being Sure All is Done; Importance of Being Aware of New Events
GOE Group/s: 04.01.02 Safety and Law Enforcement: Investigating
CIP Program/s: 490102 Aircraft Pilot and Navigator (Professional)
Related DOT Job/s: 375.163-014 PILOT, HIGHWAY PATROL

63017 CORRECTION OFFICERS AND JAILERS.

OOH Title/s: Correctional Officers

Guard inmates in penal or rehabilitative institution, in accordance with established regulations and procedures. May guard prisoners in transit between jail, courtroom, prison, or other point, traveling by automobile or public transportation. Include deputy sheriffs who spend the majority of their time guarding prisoners in county correctional institutions. Monitors conduct of prisoners, according to established policies, regulations, and procedures, to prevent escape or violence. Takes prisoner into custody and escorts to locations within and outside of facility, such as visiting room, courtroom, or airport. Inspects locks, window bars, grills, doors, and gates at correctional facility, to prevent escape. Uses weapons, handcuffs, and physical force to maintain discipline and order among prisoners. Searches prisoners, cells, and vehicles for weapons, valuables, or drugs. Guards facility entrance to screen visitors. Records information, such as prisoner identification, charges, and incidences of inmate disturbance. Questions and investigates prisoner and crime to obtain information to solve crime and make recommendations concerning disposition of case. Serves meals and distributes commissary items to prisoners. Administers medical aid to injured or ill prisoners.
Yearly Earnings: $25,220
Education: Long-term O-J-T
Knowledge: Psychology; Sociology and Anthropology; Medicine and Dentistry; Public Safety and Security; Law, Government, and Jurisprudence
Abilities: Problem Sensitivity; Spatial Orientation; Selective Attention; Time Sharing; Response Orientation; Reaction Time; Speed of Limb Movement; Static Strength; Explosive Strength; Dynamic Strength; Stamina; Gross Body Coordination; Gross Body Equilibrium; Far Vision; Night Vision; Peripheral Vision; Glare Sensitivity; Hearing Sensitivity; Sound Localization
Skills: Social Perceptiveness
General Work Activities: Performing General Physical Activities; Assisting and Caring for Others; Resolving Conflicts, Negotiating with Others; Performing for or Working with Public
Job Characteristics: Objective or Subjective Information; Job-Required Social Interaction; Persuade Someone to a Course of Action; Take a Position Opposed to Others; Coordinate or Lead Others; Responsible for Others' Health and Safety; Frequency in Conflict Situations; Deal with Unpleasant or Angry People; Deal with Physical, Aggressive People; Climbing Ladders, Scaffolds, Poles, etc.; Walking or Running; Special Uniform; Consequence of Error; Frustrating Circumstances; Importance of Being Aware of New Events
GOE Group/s: 04.02.01 Security Services: Dentention
CIP Program/s: 430102 Corrections/Correctional Administration; 430107 Law Enforcement/Police Science; 430199 Criminal Justice and Corrections, Other
Related DOT Job/s: 372.367-014 JAILER; 372.567-014 GUARD, IMMIGRATION; 372.667-018 CORRECTION OFFICER; 372.677-010 PATROL CONDUCTOR; 375.367-010 POLICE OFFICER II

63021 PARKING ENFORCEMENT OFFICERS. OOH

Title/s: Police, Detectives, and Special Agents

Patrol assigned area such as public parking lot or section of city, to issue tickets to overtime parking violators and illegally parked vehicles. Chalks tires of vehicles parked in unmetered spaces, records time, and returns at specific intervals to ticket vehicles illegally parked. Winds parking meter clocks. Surrenders ticket book at end of shift to supervisor to facilitate preparation of violation records. Reports missing traffic signals or signs to superior at end of shift. Collects coins deposited in meters.
Yearly Earnings: $25,064
Education: Moderate-term O-J-T
Knowledge: None above average
Abilities: None above average
Skills: None above average
General Work Activities: None above average

Job Characteristics: Deal with Unpleasant or Angry People; Deal with Physical, Aggressive People; Very Hot; Extremely Bright or Inadequate Lighting; Standing; Walking or Running; Special Uniform
GOE Group/s: 04.02.02 Security Services: Property and People
CIP Program/s: 000000 NO CIP ASSIGNED
Related DOT Job/s: 375.587-010 PARKING ENFORCEMENT OFFICER

63023 BAILIFFS. OOH Title/s: Police, Detectives, and Special Agents

Open court by announcing entrance of judge. Seat witnesses and jurors in specified areas of courtroom. Eject or arrest individuals disturbing proceedings. Maintains order in courtroom during trial and guards jury from outside contact. Enforces courtroom rules of behavior and warns persons not to smoke or disturb court procedure. Announces entrance of judge. Stops people from entering courtroom while judge charges jury. Collects and retains unauthorized firearms from persons entering courtroom Provides jury escort to restaurant and other areas outside of courtroom to prevent jury contact with public. Checks courtroom for security and cleanliness, and assures availability of sundry supplies for use of judge. Guards lodging of sequestered jury. Reports need for police or medical assistance to sheriff's office. Advises attorneys of dress required of witnesses.
Yearly Earnings: $25,064
Education: Moderate-term O-J-T
Knowledge: Psychology; Sociology and Anthropology; Public Safety and Security; Law, Government, and Jurisprudence
Abilities: Selective Attention; Response Orientation; Reaction Time; Speed of Limb Movement; Far Vision; Night Vision; Peripheral Vision; Sound Localization
Skills: Social Perceptiveness
General Work Activities: Resolving Conflicts, Negotiating with Others; Performing for or Working with Public
Job Characteristics: Job-Required Social Interaction; Persuade Someone to a Course of Action; Take a Position Opposed to Others; Deal with External Customers; Responsible for Others' Health and Safety; Frequency in Conflict Situations; Deal with Unpleasant or Angry People; Deal with Physical, Aggressive People; Special Uniform; Importance of Being Aware of New Events
GOE Group/s: 04.02.03 Security Services: Law and Order
CIP Program/s: 430107 Law Enforcement/Police Science
Related DOT Job/s: 377.667-010 BAILIFF

63026 UNITED STATES MARSHALS. OOH Title/s: Police, Detectives, and Special Agents

Perform such law enforcement activities as serve civil writs and criminal warrants issued by federal courts; trace and arrest persons wanted under court warrants; seize and dispose of property under court orders; safeguard and transport prisoners and jurors; and maintain order in courtroom. Escorts prisoners to and from jails and courts. Provides protection to court personnel, jurors, and witnesses or their families. Serves civil and criminal writs. Traces and arrests individuals named in criminal warrants. Seizes property pursuant to court orders. Maintains order in courtroom. Receives prisoners into federal custody. Assists federal agencies in matters such as investigations, raids, and arrests. Guards prisoners during hospitalization. Reviews records and gathers information.
Yearly Earnings: $30,368
Education: Long-term O-J-T
Knowledge: Psychology; Sociology and Anthropology; Geography; Philosophy and Theology; Public Safety and Security; Law, Government, and Jurisprudence; Transportation
Abilities: Speed of Closure; Flexibility of Closure; Selective Attention; Time Sharing; Response Orientation; Rate Control; Reaction Time; Speed of Limb Movement; Static Strength; Explosive Strength; Stamina; Gross Body Coordination; Gross Body Equilibrium; Far Vision; Night Vision; Peripheral Vision; Glare Sensitivity; Auditory Attention; Sound Localization; Speech Recognition; Speech Clarity
Skills: Active Listening; Social Perceptiveness; Coordination; Persuasion; Negotiation; Information Gathering; Information Organization; Synthesis/Reorganization; Idea Generation; Idea Evaluation; Implementation Planning; Judgment and Decision Making
General Work Activities: Performing General Physical Activities; Establishing and Maintaining Relationships; Assisting and Caring for Others; Resolving Conflicts, Negotiating with Others; Performing for or Working with Public
Job Characteristics: Job-Required Social Interaction; Persuade Someone to a Course of Action; Provide a Service to Others; Take a Position Opposed to Others; Deal with External Customers; Responsible for Others' Health and Safety; Frequency in Conflict Situations; Deal with Unpleasant or Angry People; Deal with Physical, Aggressive People; Very Hot; Extremely Bright or Inadequate Lighting; Special Uniform; Consequence of Error; Frustrating Circumstances; Importance of Being Sure All is Done; Importance of Being Aware of New Events
GOE Group/s: 04.01.02 Safety and Law Enforcement: Investigating
CIP Program/s: 430107 Law Enforcement/Police Science
Related DOT Job/s: 377.267-010 DEPUTY UNITED STATES MARSHAL

63028A CRIMINAL INVESTIGATORS AND SPECIAL AGENTS. OOH Title/s: Police, Detectives, and Special Agents

Investigate alleged or suspected criminal violations of federal, state, or local laws to determine if evidence is sufficient to recommend prosecution. Obtains and verifies evidence or establishes facts by interviewing, observing, and interrogating suspects and witnesses and analyzing records. Analyzes charge, complaint, or allegation of law violation to identify issues involved and types of evidence needed. Assists in determining scope, timing, and direction of investigation. Examines records to detect links in chain of evidence or information. Searches for evidence, dusts surfaces to reveal latent fingerprints, and records evidence and documents, using cameras and investigative equipment. Obtains and uses search and arrest warrants. Vacuums site to collect physical evidence, and submits evidence to supervisor for verification. Compares crime scene fingerprints with those of suspect or with fingerprint files to identify perpetrator, using computer. Develops and uses informants to get leads to information. Maintains surveillance and performs undercover assignments. Lifts print on tape and transfers print to permanent record card. Presents findings in reports. Reports critical information to and coordinates activities with other offices or agencies when applicable. Prepares and photographs plastic moulage of footprints and tire tracks. Photographs, fingerprints, and measures height and weight of arrested suspect, noting physical characteristics, and posts data on record for filing. Manipulates mask mirror on specialized equipment to prepare montage of suspect according to description from witnesses. Serves subpoenas or other official papers. Testifies before grand juries. Fingerprints applicant for employment or federal clearance, and forwards prints to other law enforcement agencies.
Yearly Earnings: $33,904
Education: Work experience in a related occupation
Knowledge: Psychology; Sociology and Anthropology; Geography; Philosophy and Theology; Public Safety and Security; Law, Government, and Jurisprudence; Telecommunications
Abilities: Oral Expression; Written Expression; Fluency of Ideas; Inductive Reasoning; Memorization; Flexibility of Closure; Perceptual Speed; Selective Attention; Near Vision; Far Vision; Night Vision;

Peripheral Vision; Glare Sensitivity; Sound Localization; Speech Recognition; Speech Clarity
Skills: Active Listening; Writing; Speaking; Critical Thinking; Active Learning; Social Perceptiveness; Coordination; Persuasion; Negotiation; Problem Identification; Information Gathering; Information Organization; Synthesis/Reorganization; Idea Generation; Idea Evaluation; Implementation Planning; Judgment and Decision Making
General Work Activities: Getting Information Needed to Do the Job; Monitoring Processes, Material, or Surroundings; Identifying Objects, Actions, and Events; Estimating Needed Characteristics; Judging Qualities of Things, Services, People; Analyzing Data or Information; Making Decisions and Solving Problems; Thinking Creatively; Developing Objectives and Strategies; Organizing, Planning, and Prioritizing; Implementing Ideas, Programs, etc.; Documenting/Recording Information; Interpreting Meaning of Information to Others; Communicating with Other Workers; Establishing and Maintaining Relationships; Selling or Influencing Others; Resolving Conflicts, Negotiating with Others; Performing for or Working with Public; Developing and Building Teams
Job Characteristics: Objective or Subjective Information; Persuade Someone to a Course of Action; Take a Position Opposed to Others; Deal with External Customers; Coordinate or Lead Others; Frequency in Conflict Situations; Deal with Unpleasant or Angry People; Deal with Physical, Aggressive People; Walking or Running; Kneeling, Crouching, or Crawling; Specialized Protective or Safety Attire; Frustrating Circumstances; Importance of Being Sure All is Done; Importance of Being Aware of New Events
GOE Group/s: 04.01.02 Safety and Law Enforcement: Investigating; 07.01.06 Administrative Detail: Investigating
CIP Program/s: 430107 Law Enforcement/Police Science
Related DOT Job/s: 375.167-042 SPECIAL AGENT; 377.264-010 IDENTIFICATION OFFICER

63028B CHILD SUPPORT, MISSING PERSONS, AND UNEMPLOYMENT INSURANCE FRAUD INVESTIGATORS. OOH Title/s: Police, Detectives, and Special Agents; Social Workers

Conduct investigations to locate, arrest, and return fugitives and persons wanted for nonpayment of child support and unemployment insurance fraud, and to locate missing persons. Serves warrants and makes arrests to return persons sought in connection with crimes or for nonpayment of child support. Contacts employers, neighbors, relatives, and law enforcement agencies to locate person sought and verify information gathered about case. Interviews client to obtain information, such as relocation of absent parent, amount of child support awarded, and names of witnesses. Interviews and discusses case with parent charged with nonpayment of support to resolve issues in lieu of filing court proceedings. Reviews files and criminal records to develop possible leads, such as previous addresses and aliases. Obtains extradition papers to bring about return of fugitive. Prepares file indicating data, such as wage records of accused, witnesses, and blood test results. Confers with prosecuting attorney to prepare court case and with court clerk to obtain arrest warrant and schedule court date. Determines types of court jurisdiction, according to facts and circumstances surrounding case, and files court action. Monitors child support payments awarded by court to ensure compliance and enforcement of child support laws. Completes reports to document information acquired during criminal and child support cases, and actions taken. Examines case file to determine that divorce decree and court-ordered judgment for payment are in order. Examines medical and dental X rays, fingerprints, and other information to identify bodies held in morgue. Testifies in court to present evidence regarding cases. Computes amount of child support payments.
Yearly Earnings: $25,064
Education: Moderate-term O-J-T
Knowledge: Sociology and Anthropology; Geography; Therapy and Counseling; Public Safety and Security; Law, Government, and Jurisprudence
Abilities: Speech Clarity
Skills: Active Listening; Speaking; Critical Thinking; Persuasion; Negotiation; Service Orientation; Information Gathering
General Work Activities: Getting Information Needed to Do the Job; Organizing, Planning, and Prioritizing; Documenting/Recording Information; Communicating with Persons Outside Organization; Establishing and Maintaining Relationships; Selling or Influencing Others; Resolving Conflicts, Negotiating with Others
Job Characteristics: Objective or Subjective Information; Job-Required Social Interaction; Persuade Someone to a Course of Action; Take a Position Opposed to Others; Deal with External Customers; Frequency in Conflict Situations; Deal with Unpleasant or Angry People; Deal with Physical, Aggressive People; Frustrating Circumstances; Importance of Being Aware of New Events
GOE Group/s: 04.01.02 Safety and Law Enforcement: Investigating; 10.01.02 Social Services: Counseling and Social Work
CIP Program/s: 430107 Law Enforcement/Police Science; 440701 Social Work
Related DOT Job/s: 195.267-022 CHILD SUPPORT OFFICER; 375.267-038 POLICE OFFICER III

63032 SHERIFFS AND DEPUTY SHERIFFS. OOH Title/s: Police, Detectives, and Special Agents

Enforce law and order in rural or unincorporated districts or serve legal processes of courts. May patrol courthouse, guard court or grand jury, or escort defendants. Exclude deputy sheriffs who spend the majority of their time guarding prisoners in county correctional institutions. Serves subpoenas and summonses. Executes arrest warrants, locating and taking persons into custody and issues citations. Transports or escorts prisoners or defendants between courtroom, prison, jail, district attorney's offices, or medical facilities. Patrols and guards courthouse, grand jury room, district attorney's offices, or other areas to provide security and maintain order. Investigates illegal or suspicious activities of persons. Takes control of accident scene to maintain traffic flow, assist accident victims, and investigate causes. Confiscates real or personal property by court order, and posts notices in public places. Questions individuals entering secured areas to determine purpose of business, and directs or reroutes individuals to destinations. Notifies patrol units to take violators into custody or provide needed assistance or medical aid. Arranges delivery of prisoner's arrest records from criminal investigation unit, at district attorney's request. Maintains records, submits reports of dispositions, and logs daily activities. Collects money from garnishee (debtor), and issues receipt. Prepares and validates receipts to reimburse witnesses for travel expenses.
Yearly Earnings: $30,368
Education: Long-term O-J-T
Knowledge: Administration and Management; Clerical; Psychology; Sociology and Anthropology; Geography; Therapy and Counseling; Foreign Language; Philosophy and Theology; Public Safety and Security; Law, Government, and Jurisprudence; Telecommunications; Transportation
Abilities: Inductive Reasoning; Selective Attention; Multilimb Coordination; Response Orientation; Rate Control; Stamina; Gross Body Coordination; Night Vision; Glare Sensitivity
Skills: Active Listening; Social Perceptiveness; Service Orientation
General Work Activities: Getting Information Needed to Do the Job; Judging Qualities of Things, Services, People; Interacting with Computers; Assisting and Caring for Others; Resolving Conflicts, Negoti-

ating with Others; Performing for or Working with Public; Performing Administrative Activities
Job Characteristics: Deal with External Customers; Responsible for Others' Health and Safety; Frequency in Conflict Situations; Deal with Unpleasant or Angry People; Deal with Physical, Aggressive People; Special Uniform; Specialized Protective or Safety Attire; Importance of Being Aware of New Events
GOE Group/s: 04.01.02 Safety and Law Enforcement: Investigating; 04.02.03 Security Services: Law and Order
CIP Program/s: 430107 Law Enforcement/Police Science
Related DOT Job/s: 377.263-010 SHERIFF, DEPUTY; 377.363-010 DEPUTY SHERIFF, GRAND JURY; 377.667-014 DEPUTY SHERIFF, BUILDING GUARD; 377.667-018 DEPUTY SHERIFF, CIVIL DIVISION

63035 DETECTIVES AND INVESTIGATORS, EXCEPT PUBLIC. OOH Title/s: Private Detectives and Investigators

Protect property, merchandise, and money of store or similar establishment by detecting theft, shoplifting, or other unlawful practices by public or employees. Perform necessary action to preserve order and enforce standards of decorum established by management. Include investigators who conduct private investigations, such as obtaining confidential information, seeking missing persons, or investigating crimes and thefts. Enforces conformance to establishment rules and protects persons or property. Observes employees or customers and patrols premises to detect violations and obtain evidence, using binoculars, cameras, and television. Questions persons to obtain evidence for cases of divorce, child custody, or missing persons, or individuals' character or financial status. Examines crime scene for clues or fingerprints, and submits evidence to laboratory for analysis. Warns and ejects troublemakers from premises, and apprehends and releases suspects to authorities or security personnel. Obtains and analyzes information on suspects, crimes, and disturbances to solve cases, identify criminal activity, and maintain public peace and order. Counts cash and reviews transactions, sales checks, and register tapes to verify amount of cash and shortages. Confers with establishment officials, security department, police, or postal officials to identify problems, provide information, and receive instructions. Alerts staff and superiors of presence of suspect in establishment. Writes reports and case summaries to document investigations or inform supervisors. Testifies at hearings and court trials to present evidence. Locates persons using phone or mail directories to collect money owed or to serve legal papers. Evaluates performance and honesty of employees by posing as customer or employee and comparing employee to standards. Assists victims, police, fire department, and others during emergencies.
Yearly Earnings: $17,732
Education: Moderate-term O-J-T
Knowledge: Psychology; Therapy and Counseling; Public Safety and Security; Law, Government, and Jurisprudence; Telecommunications
Abilities: Fluency of Ideas; Originality; Inductive Reasoning; Speed of Closure; Flexibility of Closure; Selective Attention; Time Sharing; Response Orientation; Rate Control; Reaction Time; Speed of Limb Movement; Explosive Strength; Stamina; Gross Body Coordination; Gross Body Equilibrium; Far Vision; Night Vision; Peripheral Vision; Auditory Attention; Sound Localization; Speech Recognition
Skills: Active Listening; Writing; Speaking; Critical Thinking; Social Perceptiveness; Persuasion; Negotiation; Service Orientation; Problem Identification; Systems Perception; Identifying Downstream Consequences; Identification of Key Causes; Judgment and Decision Making; Systems Evaluation
General Work Activities: Judging Qualities of Things, Services, People; Documenting/Recording Information; Assisting and Caring for Others
Job Characteristics: Job-Required Social Interaction; Take a Position Opposed to Others; Responsible for Others' Health and Safety; Frequency in Conflict Situations; Deal with Unpleasant or Angry People; Deal with Physical, Aggressive People; Standing; Climbing Ladders, Scaffolds, Poles, etc.; Walking or Running; Keeping or Regaining Balance; Consequence of Error; Frustrating Circumstances; Importance of Being Aware of New Events
GOE Group/s: 04.01.02 Safety and Law Enforcement: Investigating; 04.02.02 Security Services: Property and People; 04.02.03 Security Services: Law and Order; 04.02.04 Security Services: Emergency Responding; 11.10.01 Regulations Enforcement: Finance; 11.10.05 Regulations Enforcement: Company Policy
CIP Program/s: 120203 Card Dealer; 430109 Security and Loss Prevention Services
Related DOT Job/s: 186.267-010 BONDING AGENT; 241.367-026 SKIP TRACER; 343.367-014 GAMBLING MONITOR; 376.267-010 INVESTIGATOR, CASH SHORTAGE; 376.267-014 INVESTIGATOR, FRAUD; 376.267-018 INVESTIGATOR, PRIVATE; 376.267-022 SHOPPING INVESTIGATOR; 376.367-010 ALARM INVESTIGATOR; 376.367-014 DETECTIVE I; 376.367-018 HOUSE OFFICER; 376.367-022 INVESTIGATOR; 376.367-026 UNDERCOVER OPERATOR; 376.667-014 DETECTIVE II

63038 RAILROAD AND TRANSIT POLICE AND SPECIAL AGENTS. OOH Title/s: Police, Detectives, and Special Agents

Protect and police railroad and transit property, employees, or passengers. Include workers who coordinate security staff. Directs security activities at derailments, fires, floods, and strikes involving railroad property. Examines credentials of unauthorized persons attempting to enter secured areas. Guards, patrols, and polices railroad yards, cars, stations, and other facilities to protect company property and shipments and to maintain order. Investigates or directs investigations of freight theft, suspicious damage or loss of passenger's valuables, and other crimes on railroad property. Apprehends or coordinates with local enforcement personnel to apprehend or remove trespassers or thieves from rail property. Plans and implements special safety and preventive programs, such as fire and accident prevention. Prepares reports documenting the results and activities concerned with investigations. Interviews neighbors, associates, and former employers of job applicants to verify personal references and obtain work history data. Records and verifies seal numbers from boxcars containing high pilferage items, such as cigarettes and liquor, to detect tampering. Directs and coordinates the daily activities and training of security staff. Seals empty boxcars by twisting nails in door hasps, using nail twister.
Yearly Earnings: $25,064
Education: Moderate-term O-J-T
Knowledge: Public Safety and Security; Law, Government, and Jurisprudence; Transportation
Abilities: Inductive Reasoning; Speed of Closure; Flexibility of Closure; Spatial Orientation; Selective Attention; Time Sharing; Response Orientation; Speed of Limb Movement; Static Strength; Explosive Strength; Stamina; Gross Body Coordination; Gross Body Equilibrium; Far Vision; Night Vision; Peripheral Vision; Glare Sensitivity; Hearing Sensitivity; Auditory Attention; Sound Localization
Skills: Active Listening; Speaking; Social Perceptiveness; Instructing; Management of Personnel Resources
General Work Activities: Performing General Physical Activities; Coordinating Work and Activities of Others; Guiding, Directing and Motivating Subordinates

Job Characteristics: Objective or Subjective Information; Job-Required Social Interaction; Supervise, Coach, Train Others; Coordinate or Lead Others; Responsible for Others' Health and Safety; Responsibility for Outcomes and Results; Frequency in Conflict Situations; Deal with Unpleasant or Angry People; Deal with Physical, Aggressive People; Extremely Bright or Inadequate Lighting; Climbing Ladders, Scaffolds, Poles, etc.; Walking or Running; Keeping or Regaining Balance; Bending or Twisting the Body; Special Uniform; Importance of Being Aware of New Events
GOE Group/s: 04.01.01 Safety and Law Enforcement: Managing; 04.02.02 Security Services: Property and People
CIP Program/s: 430109 Security and Loss Prevention Services
Related DOT Job/s: 372.267-010 SPECIAL AGENT; 376.167-010 SPECIAL AGENT-IN-CHARGE; 376.667-018 PATROLLER

63041 FISH AND GAME WARDENS. OOH Title/s: Police, Detectives, and Special Agents

Patrol assigned area to prevent game law violations. Investigate reports of damage to crops or property by wildlife. Compile biological data. Patrols assigned area by car, boat, airplane, horse, or on foot to observe persons engaged in taking fish and game. Ensures that method and equipment used are lawful, and apprehends violators. Investigates reports of fish and game law violations, and issues warnings or citations. Collects and reports information on condition of fish and wildlife in their habitat, availability of game food and cover, and suspected pollution. Searches area of reported property damage for animal tracks, leavings, and other evidence to identify species of animal responsible. Serves warrants, makes arrests, and prepares and presents evidence in court actions. Investigates hunting accidents and files reports of findings. Conducts on-site surveys to estimate number of birds and animals in designated areas and availability of game food and cover. Seizes equipment used in fish and game law violations, and arranges for disposition of fish and game illegally taken or possessed. Resurveys area and totals bag counts of hunters to determine effectiveness of control measures. Recommends revised hunting and trapping regulations and other control measures and release of birds for restocking. Recommends changes in hunting and trapping seasons and relocation of animals in overpopulated areas to obtain balance of wildlife. Assists in promoting hunter safety training by arranging for materials and instructors. Traps beavers, dynamites beaver dams, and tranquilizes animals to implement approved control measures. Advises owner of methods to remedy future damages, and implements measures, such as erecting fences and spraying repellents. Photographs extent of damage, documents other evidence, estimates financial loss, and recommends compensation. Addresses schools and civic groups to disseminate wildlife information and promote public relations. Enlists aid of sporting groups in such programs as lake and stream rehabilitation and game habitat improvement.
Yearly Earnings: $25,064
Education: Moderate-term O-J-T
Knowledge: Administration and Management; Economics and Accounting; Food Production; Chemistry; Biology; Sociology and Anthropology; Geography; Medicine and Dentistry; Education and Training; History and Archeology; Philosophy and Theology; Public Safety and Security; Law, Government, and Jurisprudence; Communications and Media; Transportation
Abilities: Fluency of Ideas; Originality; Problem Sensitivity; Inductive Reasoning; Memorization; Flexibility of Closure; Spatial Orientation; Selective Attention; Time Sharing; Multilimb Coordination; Response Orientation; Rate Control; Reaction Time; Speed of Limb Movement; Static Strength; Explosive Strength; Dynamic Strength; Trunk Strength; Stamina; Gross Body Equilibrium; Far Vision; Night Vision; Peripheral Vision; Depth Perception; Glare Sensitivity; Auditory Attention; Sound Localization; Speech Clarity
Skills: Active Listening; Speaking; Critical Thinking; Active Learning; Monitoring; Social Perceptiveness; Persuasion; Negotiation; Instructing; Problem Identification; Information Gathering; Information Organization; Synthesis/Reorganization; Idea Generation; Idea Evaluation; Implementation Planning; Solution Appraisal; Visioning; Systems Perception; Identifying Downstream Consequences; Identification of Key Causes; Judgment and Decision Making; Systems Evaluation
General Work Activities: Estimating Needed Characteristics; Organizing, Planning, and Prioritizing; Performing General Physical Activities; Interacting with Computers; Documenting/Recording Information; Interpreting Meaning of Information to Others; Communicating with Other Workers; Communicating with Persons Outside Organization; Establishing and Maintaining Relationships; Assisting and Caring for Others; Resolving Conflicts, Negotiating with Others; Performing for or Working with Public; Teaching Others
Job Characteristics: Job-Required Social Interaction; Persuade Someone to a Course of Action; Provide a Service to Others; Take a Position Opposed to Others; Deal with External Customers; Responsible for Others' Health and Safety; Frequency in Conflict Situations; Deal with Unpleasant or Angry People; Deal with Physical, Aggressive People; Very Hot; Extremely Bright or Inadequate Lighting; Diseases/Infections; Hazardous Conditions; Hazardous Situations; Walking or Running; Special Uniform; Importance of Being Aware of New Events
GOE Group/s: 04.01.02 Safety and Law Enforcement: Investigating
CIP Program/s: 030203 Natural Resources Law Enforcement and Protective Services; 030301 Fishing and Fisheries Sciences and Management; 030601 Wildlife and Wildlands Management
Related DOT Job/s: 379.167-010 FISH AND GAME WARDEN; 379.267-010 WILDLIFE CONTROL AGENT

63044 CROSSING GUARDS. OOH Title/s: Crossing Guards

Guide or control vehicular or pedestrian traffic at such places as street and railroad crossings and construction sites. Directs actions of pedestrians and traffic at intersections. Escorts pedestrians across street. Directs movement of traffic through site, using signs, flags, and hand signals. Activates warning signal lights, lowers crossing gates until train passes, and raises gate when crossing is clear. Distributes traffic control and caution signs and markers at designated points. Waves flags, signs, or lanterns in emergencies. Informs drivers of detour routes through construction sites. Discusses traffic routing plans, and type and location of control points with superior. Records license numbers of vehicles disregarding traffic signals, and reports infractions to police. Warns construction workers when approaching vehicle driver fails to heed signals to prevent accident and injury to workers.
Yearly Earnings: $17,472
Education: Short-term O-J-T
Knowledge: None above average
Abilities: Spatial Orientation; Selective Attention; Time Sharing; Reaction Time; Stamina; Dynamic Flexibility; Gross Body Coordination; Gross Body Equilibrium; Far Vision; Night Vision; Peripheral Vision; Depth Perception; Glare Sensitivity; Hearing Sensitivity; Sound Localization
Skills: None above average
General Work Activities: None above average
Job Characteristics: Job-Required Social Interaction; Persuade Someone to a Course of Action; Deal with External Customers; Responsible for Others' Health and Safety; Deal with Unpleasant or Angry People; Deal with Physical, Aggressive People; Sounds, Noise Levels are Distracting, etc.; Very Hot; Extremely Bright or Inadequate Lighting; Contaminants; Standing; Walking or Running; Making Re-

petitive Motions; Special Uniform; Common Protective or Safety Attire; Consequence of Error; Importance of Being Aware of New Events; Importance of Repeating Same Tasks
GOE Group/s: 05.12.20 Elemental Work: Mechanical: Signaling; 10.03.03 Child and Adult Care: Care of Others
CIP Program/s: 430109 Security and Loss Prevention Services
Related DOT Job/s: 371.567-010 GUARD, SCHOOL-CROSSING; 371.667-010 CROSSING TENDER; 372.667-022 FLAGGER

63047 GUARDS AND WATCH GUARDS. OOH Title/s: Guards

Stand guard at entrance gate or walk about premises of business or industrial establishment to prevent theft, violence, or infractions of rules. Guard property against fire, theft, vandalism, and illegal entry. Direct patrons or employees and answer questions relative to services of establishment. Control traffic to and from buildings and grounds. Include workers who perform these functions using a car patrol. Patrols industrial and commercial premises to prevent and detect signs of intrusion and ensure security of doors, windows, and gates. Monitors and authorizes entrance and departure of employees, visitors, and other persons to guard against theft and to maintain security of premises. Warns persons of rule infractions or violations, and apprehends or evicts violators from premises, using force when necessary. Answers alarms and investigates disturbances. Circulates among visitors, patrons, and employees to preserve order and protect property. Calls police or fire departments in cases of emergency, such as fire or presence of unauthorized persons. Inspects and adjusts security systems, equipment, and machinery to ensure operational use and to detect evidence of tampering. Operates detecting devices to screen individuals and prevent passage of prohibited articles into restricted areas. Drives and guards armored vehicle to transport money and valuables to prevent theft and ensure safe delivery. Answers telephone calls to take messages, answer questions, and provide information during nonbusiness hours or when switchboard is closed. Writes reports of daily activities and irregularities, such as equipment or property damage, theft, presence of unauthorized persons, or unusual occurrences. Escorts or drives motor vehicle to transport individuals to specified locations and to provide personal protection. Monitors and adjusts controls that regulate building systems, such as air-conditioning, furnace, or boiler. Picks up and removes garbage, mows lawns, and sweeps gate areas to maintain grounds and premises.
Yearly Earnings: $17,732
Education: Short-term O-J-T
Knowledge: Customer and Personal Service; Psychology; Geography; Public Safety and Security; Law, Government, and Jurisprudence; Telecommunications; Transportation
Abilities: Memorization; Flexibility of Closure; Perceptual Speed; Spatial Orientation; Selective Attention; Time Sharing; Multilimb Coordination; Response Orientation; Rate Control; Reaction Time; Speed of Limb Movement; Static Strength; Explosive Strength; Dynamic Strength; Trunk Strength; Stamina; Gross Body Coordination; Gross Body Equilibrium; Far Vision; Night Vision; Peripheral Vision; Depth Perception; Glare Sensitivity; Hearing Sensitivity; Auditory Attention; Sound Localization; Speech Recognition
Skills: None above average
General Work Activities: Performing General Physical Activities; Interacting with Computers; Resolving Conflicts, Negotiating with Others; Performing for or Working with Public; Monitoring and Controlling Resources
Job Characteristics: Responsible for Others' Health and Safety; Frequency in Conflict Situations; Deal with Unpleasant or Angry People; Deal with Physical, Aggressive People; Walking or Running; Special Uniform; Consequence of Error; Importance of Being Aware of New Events
GOE Group/s: 04.02.02 Security Services: Property and People; 04.02.03 Security Services: Law and Order; 12.01.02 Sports: Officiating
CIP Program/s: 430109 Security and Loss Prevention Services
Related DOT Job/s: 372.563-010 ARMORED-CAR GUARD AND DRIVER; 372.567-010 ARMORED-CAR GUARD; 372.667-010 AIRLINE SECURITY REPRESENTATIVE; 372.667-014 BODYGUARD; 372.667-030 GATE GUARD; 372.667-034 GUARD, SECURITY; 372.667-038 MERCHANT PATROLLER; 376.667-010 BOUNCER; 379.667-010 GOLF-COURSE RANGER

63099B PROTECTIVE SERVICE WORKERS, RECREATIONAL. OOH Title/s: Guards

Monitor recreational areas, such as pools, beaches, or ski slopes, to provide assistance and protection to participants. Patrols or monitors recreational areas, such as trails, slopes, and swimming areas, on foot, in vehicle, or from tower. Cautions recreational participant regarding inclement weather, unsafe areas, or illegal conduct. Rescues distressed persons, using rescue techniques and equipment. Observes activities in assigned area with binoculars to detect hazards, disturbances, or safety infractions. Contacts emergency medical services in case of serious injury. Examines injured persons and administers first aid or cardiopulmonary resuscitation, utilizing training and medical supplies and equipment. Inspects facilities for cleanliness and maintains order in recreational areas. Inspects recreational equipment, such as rope tows, T-bar, J-bar, and chairlifts, for safety hazards and damage or wear. Maintains information on emergency medical treatment and weather and beach conditions, using report forms. Instructs participants in skiing, swimming, or other recreational activity. Participates in recreational demonstrations to entertain resort guests.
Yearly Earnings: $15,184
Education: Short-term O-J-T
Knowledge: Medicine and Dentistry; Public Safety and Security
Abilities: Flexibility of Closure; Spatial Orientation; Selective Attention; Time Sharing; Multilimb Coordination; Response Orientation; Reaction Time; Speed of Limb Movement; Static Strength; Explosive Strength; Dynamic Strength; Trunk Strength; Stamina; Extent Flexibility; Dynamic Flexibility; Gross Body Coordination; Gross Body Equilibrium; Far Vision; Night Vision; Peripheral Vision; Depth Perception; Glare Sensitivity; Hearing Sensitivity; Auditory Attention; Sound Localization; Speech Clarity
Skills: Learning Strategies; Social Perceptiveness; Persuasion; Instructing; Service Orientation
General Work Activities: Performing General Physical Activities; Assisting and Caring for Others; Performing for or Working with Public
Job Characteristics: Job-Required Social Interaction; Provide a Service to Others; Deal with External Customers; Coordinate or Lead Others; Responsible for Others' Health and Safety; Deal with Unpleasant or Angry People; Deal with Physical, Aggressive People; Very Hot; Extremely Bright or Inadequate Lighting; Radiation; Diseases/Infections; High Places; Hazardous Situations; Climbing Ladders, Scaffolds, Poles, etc.; Walking or Running; Keeping or Regaining Balance; Special Uniform; Specialized Protective or Safety Attire; Consequence of Error; Importance of Being Aware of New Events; Importance of Repeating Same Tasks
GOE Group/s: 04.02.03 Security Services: Law and Order
CIP Program/s: 430199 Criminal Justice and Corrections, Other
Related DOT Job/s: 379.364-014 BEACH LIFEGUARD; 379.664-010 SKI PATROLLER; 379.667-014 LIFEGUARD

63099C ANIMAL CONTROL WORKERS. OOH Title/s: Protective Service Occupations

Handle animals for the purpose of investigations of mistreatment, or control of abandoned or unattended animals. Captures or removes stray, uncontrolled, or abused animals from undesirable conditions and transports to shelter. Trains police officers in dog-handling and training techniques for tracking, crowd control, and narcotics and bomb detection. Examines animals for injuries or malnutrition, and arranges for medical treatment. Instructs handlers in dog health care and handlers' responsibilities. Investigates animal bites and alleged violations, interviews witnesses, and reports violations to police, or requests arrest of violators. Conducts tours of facility, demonstrates dog-handling techniques, and explains use of dogs in police work, using trained dog. Removes animal from vehicle and places animal in shelter cage or other enclosure. Euthanatizes rabid, unclaimed, or severely injured animals. Examines animal licenses and inspects establishments housing animals for compliance with laws, and issues warnings or summonses to violators. Supplies animals with food, water, and personal care. Writes reports of activities, and maintains files of impoundment and disposition of animals.
Yearly Earnings: $25,064
Education: Moderate-term O-J-T
Knowledge: Biology; Education and Training
Abilities: Rate Control; Reaction Time; Speed of Limb Movement; Explosive Strength; Dynamic Strength; Stamina; Gross Body Coordination; Gross Body Equilibrium; Far Vision; Auditory Attention; Sound Localization
Skills: Learning Strategies; Social Perceptiveness; Instructing; Service Orientation
General Work Activities: Assisting and Caring for Others; Teaching Others
Job Characteristics: Supervise, Coach, Train Others; Frequency in Conflict Situations; Deal with Unpleasant or Angry People; Deal with Physical, Aggressive People; Diseases/Infections; Hazardous Situations; Walking or Running; Kneeling, Crouching, or Crawling; Keeping or Regaining Balance
GOE Group/s: 03.03.01 Animal Training and Service: Animal Training; 03.04.05 Elemental Work: Plants and Animals: Services; 11.10.03 Regulations Enforcement: Health and Safety
CIP Program/s: 010505 Animal Trainer; 430107 Law Enforcement/Police Science; 430199 Criminal Justice and Corrections, Other; 439999 Protective Services, Other
Related DOT Job/s: 379.137-010 SUPERVISOR, ANIMAL CRUELTY INVESTIGATION; 379.227-010 INSTRUCTOR-TRAINER, CANINE SERVICE; 379.263-010 ANIMAL TREATMENT INVESTIGATOR; 379.673-010 DOG CATCHER

63099D AUTOMATIC TELLER MACHINE SERVICERS. OOH Title/s: Indirectly related to Protective Services Occupations

Collect deposits and replenish automatic teller machines with cash and supplies. Removes money canisters from ATMs, and replenishes machine supplies, such as deposit envelopes, receipt paper, and cash. Counts cash and items deposited by customers, and compares to transactions indicated on transaction tape from ATM. Records transaction information on form or log, and notifies designated personnel of discrepancies. Tests machine functions, and balances machine cash account, using electronic keypad. Corrects malfunctions, such as jammed cash or paper, or calls repair personnel when ATM needs repair.
Yearly Earnings: $15,184
Education: Short-term O-J-T
Knowledge: Philosophy and Theology
Abilities: None above average
Skills: None above average
General Work Activities: None above average
Job Characteristics: Standing; Importance of Being Exact or Accurate; Importance of Repeating Same Tasks

63099E ALL OTHER PROTECTIVE SERVICE WORKERS. OOH Title/s: Police, Detectives, and Special Agents; Private Household Workers

All other protective service workers not classified separately above.
Yearly Earnings: $15,184
Education: Short-term O-J-T
GOE Group/s: 04.02.03 Security Services: Law and Order
CIP Program/s: 000000 NO CIP ASSIGNED
Related DOT Job/s: 309.367-010 HOUSE SITTER; 372.367-010 COMMUNITY SERVICE OFFICER, PATROL; 372.667-042 SCHOOL BUS MONITOR; 379.367-010 SURVEILLANCE-SYSTEM MONITOR

Food Service Workers

65002 HOSTS AND HOSTESSES—RESTAURANT, LOUNGE OR COFFEE SHOP. OOH Title/s: Food and Beverage Service Occupations

Welcome patrons, seat them at tables or in lounge, and ensure quality of facilities and service. Greets and escorts guests to tables, and provides menus. Resolves complaints of patrons. Schedules dining reservations, and arranges parties or special service for diners. Inspects dining room serving stations for neatness and cleanliness, and requisitions table linens and other supplies for tables and serving stations. Assigns work tasks and coordinates activities of dining room personnel to ensure prompt and courteous service to patrons. Supervises and coordinates activities of dining room personnel to provide fast and courteous service to patrons. Trains dining room employees. Prepares beverages and expedites food orders. Totals receipts at end of shift to verify sales and clear cash register. Interviews, hires, and discharges dining room personnel. Schedules work hours and keeps time records of dining room workers. Assists in planning menus. Collects payment from customers.
Yearly Earnings: $16,900
Education: Short-term O-J-T
Knowledge: Administration and Management; Customer and Personal Service; Personnel and Human Resources
Abilities: None above average
Skills: Service Orientation; Time Management; Management of Personnel Resources
General Work Activities: Scheduling Work and Activities; Establishing and Maintaining Relationships; Performing for or Working with Public; Coordinating Work and Activities of Others; Developing and Building Teams; Guiding, Directing and Motivating Subordinates; Coaching and Developing Others; Staffing Organizational Units
Job Characteristics: Job-Required Social Interaction; Supervise, Coach, Train Others; Provide a Service to Others; Deal with External Customers; Coordinate or Lead Others; Responsibility for Outcomes and Results; Frequency in Conflict Situations; Deal with Unpleasant or Angry People; Standing; Walking or Running; Special Uniform
GOE Group/s: 09.01.03 Hospitality Services: Food Services
CIP Program/s: 120507 Waiter/Waitress and Dining Room Manager
Related DOT Job/s: 310.137-010 HOST/HOSTESS, RESTAURANT

65005 BARTENDERS. OOH Title/s: Food and Beverage Service Occupations

Mix and serve to patrons alcoholic and nonalcoholic drinks, following standard recipes. Mixes ingredients, such as liquor, soda water, sugar, and bitters, to prepare cocktails and other drinks. Serves wine and draft or bottled beer. Collects money for drinks served. Arranges bottles and glasses to make attractive display. Slices and pits fruit for garnishing drinks. Orders or requisitions liquors and supplies. Cleans glasses, utensils, and bar equipment. Prepares appetizers, such as pickles, cheese, and cold meats.
Yearly Earnings: $15,704
Education: Short-term O-J-T
Knowledge: Sales and Marketing; Customer and Personal Service; Psychology; Philosophy and Theology; Law, Government, and Jurisprudence
Abilities: Memorization; Wrist-Finger Speed; Speed of Limb Movement; Trunk Strength; Stamina; Extent Flexibility; Gross Body Equilibrium; Visual Color Discrimination; Night Vision; Peripheral Vision; Auditory Attention; Speech Recognition
Skills: None above average
General Work Activities: Establishing and Maintaining Relationships; Selling or Influencing Others; Performing for or Working with Public; Monitoring and Controlling Resources
Job Characteristics: Job-Required Social Interaction; Provide a Service to Others; Deal with External Customers; Deal with Unpleasant or Angry People; Deal with Physical, Aggressive People; Sounds, Noise Levels are Distracting, etc.; Extremely Bright or Inadequate Lighting; Standing; Walking or Running; Special Uniform
GOE Group/s: 09.04.01 Customer Services: Food Services; 09.05.02 Attendant Services: Food Services
CIP Program/s: 120502 Bartender/Mixologist
Related DOT Job/s: 312.474-010 BARTENDER; 312.477-010 BAR ATTENDANT; 312.677-010 TAPROOM ATTENDANT

65008A WAITERS/WAITRESSES. OOH Title/s: Food and Beverage Service Occupations

Take food orders and serve food and beverages to patrons in dining establishments. Takes order from patron for food or beverage, writing order down or memorizing it. Relays order to kitchen, or enters order into computer. Serves meals or beverages to patrons. Observes patrons to respond to additional requests and to determine when meal has been completed or beverage consumed. Presents menu to patron, suggests food or beverage selections, and answers questions regarding preparation and service. Obtains and replenishes supplies of food, tableware, and linen. Serves, or assists patrons to serve themselves at buffet or smorgasbord table. Computes cost of meal or beverage. Accepts payment and returns change, or refers patron to cashier. Removes dishes and glasses from table or counter and takes them to kitchen for cleaning. Prepares hot, cold, and mixed drinks for patrons, and chills bottles of wine. Garnishes and decorates dishes preparatory to serving. Cleans and arranges assigned station, including side stands, chairs, and table pieces, such as linen, silverware, and glassware. Carves meats, bones fish and fowl, and prepares special dishes and desserts at work station or patron's table. Prepares salads, appetizers, and cold dishes, portions desserts, brews coffee, and performs other services as determined by establishment's size and practices. Fills salt, pepper, sugar, cream, condiment, and napkin containers. Washes glassware and silverware. Delivers messages to patrons.
Yearly Earnings: $13,416
Education: Short-term O-J-T
Knowledge: Sales and Marketing; Customer and Personal Service; Food Production; Foreign Language
Abilities: Memorization; Response Orientation; Reaction Time; Wrist-Finger Speed; Speed of Limb Movement; Trunk Strength; Stamina; Dynamic Flexibility; Gross Body Coordination; Gross Body Equilibrium; Night Vision; Peripheral Vision; Auditory Attention; Speech Recognition
Skills: None above average
General Work Activities: Establishing and Maintaining Relationships; Selling or Influencing Others; Performing for or Working with Public
Job Characteristics: Job-Required Social Interaction; Provide a Service to Others; Deal with External Customers; Deal with Unpleasant or Angry People; Standing; Walking or Running; Special Uniform
GOE Group/s: 09.04.01 Customer Services: Food Services; 09.05.02 Attendant Services: Food Services
CIP Program/s: 120507 Waiter/Waitress and Dining Room Manager
Related DOT Job/s: 311.477-018 WAITER/WAITRESS, BAR; 311.477-022 WAITER/WAITRESS, DINING CAR; 311.477-026 WAITER/WAITRESS, FORMAL; 311.477-030 WAITER/WAITRESS, INFORMAL; 311.674-018 WAITER/WAITRESS, BUFFET; 350.677-010 MESS ATTENDANT; 350.677-026 STEWARD/STEWARDESS, WINE; 350.677-030 WAITER/WAITRESS; 352.677-018 WAITER/WAITRESS, CLUB

65008B WINE STEWARDS/STEWARDESSES. OOH Title/s: Food and Beverage Service Occupations

Select, requisition, store, and serve wines in restaurant. Assist patrons making wine selections to accompany meals. Replenish stock and maintain storage conditions for wine inventory. Discusses wines with patrons and assists patrons to make wine selection, applying knowledge of wines. Serves wines to patrons. Maintains inventory of wine in stock. Selects and orders wine to replenish stock. Stores wine on racks or shelves. Tastes wine prior to serving.
Yearly Earnings: $13,416
Education: Short-term O-J-T
Knowledge: Sales and Marketing; Customer and Personal Service; Food Production; Geography; Foreign Language
Abilities: Category Flexibility; Memorization; Night Vision; Speech Recognition
Skills: Service Orientation
General Work Activities: Selling or Influencing Others; Performing for or Working with Public; Monitoring and Controlling Resources
Job Characteristics: Job-Required Social Interaction; Persuade Someone to a Course of Action; Provide a Service to Others; Deal with External Customers; Deal with Unpleasant or Angry People; Standing; Walking or Running; Special Uniform
GOE Group/s: 09.05.02 Attendant Services: Food Services
CIP Program/s: 120507 Waiter/Waitress and Dining Room Manager
Related DOT Job/s: 310.357-010 WINE STEWARD/STEWARDESS

65011 FOOD SERVERS, OUTSIDE. OOH Title/s: Food and Beverage Service Occupations

Serve food to patrons outside of a restaurant environment, such as in hotels, hospital rooms, or cars. Exclude food vendors. Serves food and refreshments to patrons in automobiles and rooms. Prepares and delivers food trays. Places filled order on tray and fastens tray to car door, and removes equipment from room or automobile. Apportions and places food servings on plates and trays according to diet list on menu card. Examines filled tray for completeness and places on cart, dumbwaiter, or conveyor belt. Takes order and relays order to kitchen or serving counter to be filled. Carries silverware, linen, and food on tray or uses cart. Pushes carts to halls or ward kitchen, and serves trays to patients. Removes tray and stacks dishes for return to kitchen. Reads production orders on color-coded menu cards on trays to determine items to place on food tray. Prepares food items, such as sandwiches, salads, soups, and beverages, and places items, such as

eating utensils, napkins, and condiments, on trays. Prepares fountain drinks, such as sodas, milkshakes, and malted milks. Records amount and types of special food items served to customers. Places servings in blender to make foods for soft or liquid diets. Totals and presents check to customer and accepts payment for service. Restocks service counter with items, such as ice, napkins, and straws. Washes dishes and cleans work area, tables, cabinets, and ovens. Sweeps service area with broom.
Yearly Earnings: $11,700
Education: Short-term O-J-T
Knowledge: None above average
Abilities: None above average
Skills: None above average
General Work Activities: None above average
Job Characteristics: Job-Required Social Interaction; Provide a Service to Others; Deal with External Customers; Standing; Walking or Running; Special Uniform
GOE Group/s: 09.04.01 Customer Services: Food Services; 09.05.02 Attendant Services: Food Services
CIP Program/s: 120507 Waiter/Waitress and Dining Room Manager
Related DOT Job/s: 311.477-010 CAR HOP; 311.477-034 WAITER/WAITRESS, ROOM SERVICE; 319.677-014 FOOD-SERVICE WORKER, HOSPITAL

65014 DINING ROOM AND CAFETERIA ATTENDANTS, AND BARTENDER HELPERS. OOH Title/s: Food and Beverage Service Occupations
Perform any combination of the following duties to facilitate food service: carry dirty dishes from dining room to kitchen; replace soiled table linens; set tables with silverware and glassware; replenish supply of clean linens, silverware, glassware, and dishes; supply service bar with food, such as soups, salads, and desserts; and serve ice water, butter, and coffee to patrons. May wash tables. Carries dirty dishes to kitchen and wipes tables and seats with dampened cloth. Carries food, dishes, trays, and silverware from kitchen and supply departments to serving counters. Replenishes supply of clean linens, silverware, glassware, and dishes in dining room. Replenishes food and equipment at steamtables and serving counters of cafeteria to facilitate service to patrons. Sets tables with clean linens, sugar bowls, and condiments. Cleans bar and equipment, and replenishes bar supplies, such as liquor, fruit, ice, and dishes. Carries trays from food counters to tables for cafeteria patrons, and serves ice water and butter to patrons. Keeps assigned area and equipment clean, makes coffee, fills fruit juice dispensers, and stocks vending machines with food in automat. Stocks refrigerating units with wines and bottled beer, replaces empty beer kegs, and slices and pits fruit used to garnish drinks. Washes glasses, bar, and equipment, polishes bar fixtures, mops floors, and removes empty bottles and trash. Circulates among diners and serves coffee. Garnishes and positions foods on table to ensure visibility to patrons and convenience in serving. Mixes and prepares flavors for mixed drinks. Transfers food and dishes between floors of establishment, using dumbwaiter. Runs errands and delivers food orders to offices.
Yearly Earnings: $11,908
Education: Short-term O-J-T
Knowledge: None above average
Abilities: None above average
Skills: None above average
General Work Activities: None above average
Job Characteristics: Standing; Walking or Running; Special Uniform; Importance of Repeating Same Tasks
GOE Group/s: 05.12.18 Elemental Work: Mechanical: Cleaning and Maintenance; 09.05.02 Attendant Services: Food Services
CIP Program/s: 000000 NO CIP ASSIGNED
Related DOT Job/s: 311.677-010 CAFETERIA ATTENDANT; 311.677-018 DINING ROOM ATTENDANT; 312.687-010 BARTENDER HELPER; 319.687-010 COUNTER-SUPPLY WORKER

65017 COUNTER ATTENDANTS—LUNCHROOM, COFFEE SHOP, OR CAFETERIA. OOH Title/s: Food and Beverage Service Occupations
Serve food to diners at counter or from a steamtable. Exclude counter attendants who also wait tables. Serves food, beverages, or desserts to customers in variety of settings, such as take-out counter of restaurant or lunchroom. Serves salads, vegetables, meat, breads, and cocktails; ladles soups and sauces; portions desserts; and fills beverage cups and glasses. Calls order to kitchen and picks up and serves order when it is ready. Writes items ordered on tickets, totals orders, passes orders to cook, and gives ticket stubs to customers to identify filled orders. Serves sandwiches, salads, beverages, desserts, and candies to employees in industrial establishment. Replenishes foods at serving stations. Prepares and serves soft drinks and ice cream dishes, such as sundaes, using memorized formulas and methods of following directions. Brews coffee and tea and fills containers with requested beverages. Wraps menu items, such as sandwiches, hot entrees, and desserts. Accepts payment for food, using cash register or adding machine to total check. Prepares sandwiches, salads, and other short-order items. Carves meat. Serves employees from mobile canteen. Adds relishes and garnishes according to instructions. Scrubs and polishes counters, steamtables, and other equipment; cleans glasses, dishes, and fountain equipment; and polishes metalwork on fountain. Sells cigars and cigarettes. Orders items to replace stocks.
Yearly Earnings: $11,960
Education: Short-term O-J-T
Knowledge: Sales and Marketing; Customer and Personal Service
Abilities: None above average
Skills: None above average
General Work Activities: Performing for or Working with Public
Job Characteristics: Job-Required Social Interaction; Provide a Service to Others; Deal with External Customers; Standing; Walking or Running; Special Uniform
GOE Group/s: 09.04.01 Customer Services: Food Services; 09.05.02 Attendant Services: Food Services
CIP Program/s: 080901 Hospitality and Recreation Marketing Operations, General; 080906 Food Sales Operations; 120507 Waiter/Waitress and Dining Room Manager
Related DOT Job/s: 311.477-014 COUNTER ATTENDANT, LUNCHROOM OR COFFEE SHOP; 311.477-038 WAITER/WAITRESS, TAKE OUT; 311.674-010 CANTEEN OPERATOR; 311.677-014 COUNTER ATTENDANT, CAFETERIA; 319.474-010 FOUNTAIN SERVER

65021 BAKERS, BREAD AND PASTRY. OOH Title/s: Chefs, Cooks, and Other Kitchen Workers
Mix and bake ingredients according to recipes to produce small quantities of breads, pastries, and other baked goods for consumption on premises or for sale as specialty baked goods. Weighs and measures ingredients, using measuring cups and spoons. Mixes ingredients to form dough or batter by hand, or using electric mixer. Rolls and shapes dough, using rolling pin, and cuts dough in uniform portions with knife, divider, and cookie cutter. Molds dough in desired shapes, places dough in greased or floured pans, and trims overlapping edges with knife. Mixes and cooks pie fillings, pours fillings into pie shells, and tops filling with meringue or cream. Checks production schedule to determine variety and quantity of goods to bake. Spreads or sprinkles toppings on loaves or specialties and places dough in oven, using long-handled paddle (peel). Covers filling with top crust; places pies in oven; and adjust drafts or thermostatic controls to regulate oven temperatures. Mixes ingredients to make icings, deco-

rates cakes and pastries, and blends colors for icings, shaped ornaments, and statuaries. Cuts, peels, and prepares fruit for pie fillings.
Yearly Earnings: $13,312
Education: Moderate-term O-J-T
Knowledge: Food Production
Abilities: None above average
Skills: None above average
General Work Activities: Handling and Moving Objects
Job Characteristics: Standing; Making Repetitive Motions; Special Uniform
GOE Group/s: 05.10.08 Crafts: Food Preparation
CIP Program/s: 120501 Baker/Pastry Chef
Related DOT Job/s: 313.361-010 BAKER, SECOND; 313.361-038 PIE MAKER; 313.381-010 BAKER; 313.381-018 COOK APPRENTICE, PASTRY; 313.381-026 COOK, PASTRY

65023 BUTCHERS AND MEAT CUTTERS. OOH Title/s: Chefs, Cooks, and Other Kitchen Workers; Butchers and Meat, Poultry, and Fish Cutters

Cut, trim, and prepare carcasses and consumer-sized portions of meat for sale or for use in food service establishments. Exclude butchers working in slaughtering, meat-packing, or prepared-meat establishments. Cuts, trims, bones, ties, and grinds meats, such as beef, pork, poultry, and fish, to prepare meat in cooking form. Shapes, laces, and ties roasts, using boning knife, skewer, and twine. Wraps and weighs meat for customers and collects money for sales. Places meat on trays in display counter. Receives, inspects, and stores meat upon delivery. Estimates requirements and requisitions or orders meat supply. Records quantity of meat received and issued to cooks.
Yearly Earnings: $17,108
Education: Long-term O-J-T
Knowledge: Food Production
Abilities: None above average
Skills: None above average
General Work Activities: Handling and Moving Objects; Performing for or Working with Public; Monitoring and Controlling Resources
Job Characteristics: Hazardous Situations; Standing; Making Repetitive Motions; Special Uniform
GOE Group/s: 05.10.08 Crafts: Food Preparation
CIP Program/s: 120506 Meatcutter
Related DOT Job/s: 316.681-010 BUTCHER, MEAT; 316.684-018 MEAT CUTTER; 316.684-022 MEAT-CUTTER APPRENTICE

65026 COOKS, RESTAURANT. OOH Title/s: Chefs, Cooks, and Other Kitchen Workers

Prepare, season, and cook soups, meats, vegetables, desserts, and other foodstuffs in restaurants. May order supplies, keep records and accounts, price items on menu, or plan menu. Weighs, measures, and mixes ingredients according to recipe or personal judgment, using various kitchen utensils and equipment. Bakes, roasts, broils, and steams meats, fish, vegetables, and other foods. Observes and tests food to determine that it is cooked, by tasting, smelling, or piercing, and turns or stirs food if necessary. Seasons and cooks food according to recipes or personal judgment and experience. Regulates temperature of ovens, broilers, grills, and roasters. Prepares, seasons, and barbecues pork, beef, chicken, and other types of meat. Bakes bread, rolls, cakes, and pastry. Inspects food preparation and serving areas to ensure observance of safe, sanitary food-handling practices. Washes, peels, cuts, and seeds fruits and vegetables to prepare fruits and vegetables for use. Portions, arranges, and garnishes food, and serves food to waiter or patron. Prepares dishes, such as meat loaves, casseroles, and salads. Prepares appetizers, sauces, dressings, relishes, and hors d'oeuvres. Prepares sandwiches. Prepares frozen dessert items. Plans items on menu. Carves and trims meats, such as beef, veal, ham, pork, and lamb, for hot or cold service or for sandwiches. Butchers and dresses animals, fowl, or shellfish, or cuts and bones meat prior to cooking. Estimates food consumption and requisitions or purchases supplies, or procures food from storage. Designs and prepares decorated foods and artistic food arrangements. Hires, trains, and supervises other cooks and kitchen staff. Carves decorations out of ice, using chisels and ice picks. Participates in or attends culinary exhibitions and conferences.
Yearly Earnings: $13,312
Education: Long-term O-J-T
Knowledge: Administration and Management; Sales and Marketing; Customer and Personal Service; Personnel and Human Resources; Food Production; Education and Training; Foreign Language; Fine Arts; Public Safety and Security; Law, Government, and Jurisprudence
Abilities: Fluency of Ideas; Originality; Deductive Reasoning; Information Ordering; Category Flexibility; Memorization; Perceptual Speed; Time Sharing; Response Orientation; Wrist-Finger Speed; Gross Body Equilibrium; Visual Color Discrimination; Night Vision; Peripheral Vision
Skills: Management of Personnel Resources
General Work Activities: Thinking Creatively; Scheduling Work and Activities; Coordinating Work and Activities of Others; Developing and Building Teams; Guiding, Directing and Motivating Subordinates; Coaching and Developing Others; Staffing Organizational Units; Monitoring and Controlling Resources
Job Characteristics: Supervise, Coach, Train Others; Provide a Service to Others; Responsible for Others' Health and Safety; Responsibility for Outcomes and Results; Hazardous Situations; Standing; Making Repetitive Motions; Special Uniform
GOE Group/s: 05.05.17 Craft Technology: Food Preparation; 05.10.08 Crafts: Food Preparation
CIP Program/s: 120503 Culinary Arts/Chef Training; 120505 Kitchen Personnel/Cook and Assistant Training
Related DOT Job/s: 313.281-010 CHEF DE FROID; 313.361-014 COOK; 313.361-018 COOK APPRENTICE; 313.361-030 COOK, SPECIALTY, FOREIGN FOOD; 313.361-034 GARDE MANGER; 313.381-022 COOK, BARBECUE; 313.381-034 ICE-CREAM CHEF; 315.361-022 COOK, STATION; 315.381-014 COOK, LARDER; 315.381-018 COOK, RAILROAD

65028 COOKS, INSTITUTION OR CAFETERIA. OOH Title/s: Chefs, Cooks, and Other Kitchen Workers

Prepare and cook family-style meals for institutions such as schools, hospitals, or cafeterias. Usually prepare meals in large quantities rather than to individual order. May cook for employees in office building or other large facility. Cooks foodstuffs according to menu, special dietary or nutritional restrictions, and number of persons to be served. Prepares and cooks vegetables, salads, dressings, and desserts. Cleans, cuts, and cooks meat, fish, and poultry. Bakes breads, rolls, and other pastries. Plans menus, taking advantage of foods in season and local availability. Requisitions food supplies, kitchen equipment and appliances, and other supplies, and receives deliveries. Cleans and inspects galley equipment, kitchen appliances, and work areas for cleanliness and functional operation. Apportions and serves food to residents, employees, or patrons. Compiles and maintains food cost records and accounts. Washes pots, pans, dishes, utensils, and other cooking equipment. Directs activities of one or more workers who assist in preparing and serving meals.
Yearly Earnings: $13,312
Education: Long-term O-J-T
Knowledge: Administration and Management; Economics and Accounting; Customer and Personal Service; Food Production
Abilities: None above average

Skills: Management of Financial Resources; Management of Personnel Resources
General Work Activities: Handling and Moving Objects; Monitoring and Controlling Resources
Job Characteristics: Very Hot; Standing; Special Uniform
GOE Group/s: 05.10.08 Crafts: Food Preparation
CIP Program/s: 120501 Baker/Pastry Chef; 120505 Kitchen Personnel/Cook and Assistant Training
Related DOT Job/s: 313.381-030 COOK, SCHOOL CAFETERIA; 315.361-010 COOK; 315.371-010 COOK, MESS; 315.381-010 COOK; 315.381-022 COOK, THIRD; 315.381-026 SECOND COOK AND BAKER

65032 COOKS, SPECIALTY FAST FOOD. OOH Title/s: Chefs, Cooks, and Other Kitchen Workers

Prepare and cook food in a fast-food restaurant with a limited menu. Duties of the cooks are limited to one or two basic items, such as hamburgers, chicken, pizza, tacos, or fish and chips, and normally involve operating large-volume single-purpose cooking equipment. Prepares specialty foods, such as pizzas, fish and chips, sandwiches, and tacos, following specific methods, usually requiring short preparation time. Reads food order slip or receives verbal instructions as to food required by patron, and prepares and cooks food according to instructions. Measures required ingredients needed for specific food item being prepared. Slices meats, cheeses, and vegetables, using knives and food-slicing machines. Prepares dough, following recipe. Cleans work area and food preparation equipment. Prepares and serves beverage, such as coffee and fountain drinks. Serves orders to customers at window or counter.
Yearly Earnings: $13,312
Education: Short-term O-J-T
Knowledge: Customer and Personal Service
Abilities: None above average
Skills: None above average
General Work Activities: None above average
Job Characteristics: Hazardous Situations; Standing; Making Repetitive Motions; Special Uniform
GOE Group/s: 05.10.08 Crafts: Food Preparation
CIP Program/s: 120505 Kitchen Personnel/Cook and Assistant Training
Related DOT Job/s: 313.361-026 COOK, SPECIALTY; 313.374-010 COOK, FAST FOOD; 313.381-014 BAKER, PIZZA

65035 COOKS, SHORT ORDER. OOH Title/s: Chefs, Cooks, and Other Kitchen Workers

Prepare and cook to order a variety of foods that require only a short preparation time. May take orders from customers and serve patrons at counters or tables. Exclude cooks, specialty fast foods. Takes order from customer and cooks foods requiring short preparation time, according to customer requirements. Completes order from steamtable and serves customer at table or counter. Carves meats, makes sandwiches, and brews coffee. Cleans food preparation equipment, work area, and counter or tables. Accepts payment and makes change, or writes charge slip.
Yearly Earnings: $13,312
Education: Long-term O-J-T
Knowledge: Customer and Personal Service; Food Production
Abilities: None above average
Skills: None above average
General Work Activities: Performing for or Working with Public
Job Characteristics: Provide a Service to Others; Hazardous Situations; Standing; Special Uniform
GOE Group/s: 05.10.08 Crafts: Food Preparation
CIP Program/s: 000000 NO CIP ASSIGNED
Related DOT Job/s: 313.374-014 COOK, SHORT ORDER

65038A FOOD PREPARATION WORKERS. OOH Title/s: Chefs, Cooks, and Other Kitchen Workers

Perform a variety of food preparation duties other than cooking, such as preparing cold foods and shellfish, slicing meat, and brewing coffee or tea. Cleans and portions, and cuts or peels various foods to prepare for cooking or serving. Prepares variety of foods according to customers' orders or instructions of superior, following approved procedures. Portions and arranges food on serving dishes, trays, carts, or conveyor belts. Cleans, cuts, slices, or disjoints meats and poultry to prepare for cooking. Prepares and serves variety of beverages, such as coffee, tea, and soft drinks. Carries food supplies, equipment, and utensils to and from storage and work areas. Stores food in designated containers and storage areas to prevent spoilage. Distributes food to waiters and waitresses to serve to customers. Cleans and maintains work areas, equipment, and utensils. Requisitions, stores, and distributes food supplies, equipment, and utensils. Butchers and cleans fowl, fish, poultry, and shellfish to prepare for cooking or serving. Serves food to customers.
Yearly Earnings: $12,428
Education: Short-term O-J-T
Knowledge: Customer and Personal Service; Food Production
Abilities: Manual Dexterity; Reaction Time; Wrist-Finger Speed; Trunk Strength; Extent Flexibility; Gross Body Equilibrium; Hearing Sensitivity
Skills: None above average
General Work Activities: Handling and Moving Objects
Job Characteristics: Provide a Service to Others; Deal with External Customers; Responsible for Others' Health and Safety; Deal with Unpleasant or Angry People; Diseases/Infections; Standing; Special Uniform
GOE Group/s: 05.10.08 Crafts: Food Preparation; 05.12.17 Elemental Work: Mechanical: Food Preparation; 09.05.02 Attendant Services: Food Services
CIP Program/s: 120505 Kitchen Personnel/Cook and Assistant Training; 120506 Meatcutter; 200401 Institutional Food Workers and Administrators, General; 200405 Food Caterer
Related DOT Job/s: 311.674-014 RAW SHELLFISH PREPARER; 313.684-010 BAKER HELPER; 313.687-010 COOK HELPER, PASTRY; 316.661-010 CARVER; 316.684-010 BUTCHER, CHICKEN AND FISH; 316.684-014 DELI CUTTER-SLICER; 317.384-010 SALAD MAKER; 317.664-010 SANDWICH MAKER; 317.684-010 COFFEE MAKER; 317.684-014 PANTRY GOODS MAKER; 317.687-010 COOK HELPER; 319.484-010 FOOD ASSEMBLER, KITCHEN; 319.677-010 CATERER HELPER

65038B KITCHEN HELPERS. OOH Title/s: Chefs, Cooks, and Other Kitchen Workers

Maintain and clean kitchen work areas, equipment, and utensils. Cleans and maintains work areas, equipment, and utensils. Removes garbage and trash and places refuse in designated pick-up area. Carries or transfers by handtruck supplies and equipment between storage and work areas. Stocks serving stations with food and utensils. Prepares and packages individual place settings. Loads or unloads trucks used in delivering or picking up food and supplies. Cleans and prepares various foods for cooking or serving. Sets up banquet tables.
Yearly Earnings: $12,428
Education: Short-term O-J-T
Knowledge: Food Production
Abilities: Wrist-Finger Speed; Dynamic Strength; Trunk Strength; Extent Flexibility; Dynamic Flexibility; Gross Body Equilibrium; Peripheral Vision
Skills: None above average

General Work Activities: None above average
Job Characteristics: Standing; Walking or Running; Special Uniform
GOE Group/s: 05.12.18 Elemental Work: Mechanical: Cleaning and Maintenance
CIP Program/s: 000000 NO CIP ASSIGNED
Related DOT Job/s: 318.687-010 KITCHEN HELPER; 318.687-014 SCULLION; 318.687-018 SILVER WRAPPER

65041 COMBINED FOOD PREPARATION AND SERVICE WORKERS. OOH Title/s: Food and Beverage Service Occupations
Perform duties which combine both food preparation and food service. Workers who spend more than 80 percent of their time in one job are classified in that occupation. Selects food items from serving or storage areas and places food and beverage items on serving tray or in take-out bag. Makes and serves hot and cold beverages or desserts. Cooks or reheats food items, such as french fries. Requests and records customer order and computes bill. Notifies kitchen personnel of shortages or special orders. Receives payment.
Yearly Earnings: $12,428
Education: Short-term O-J-T
Knowledge: Sales and Marketing; Customer and Personal Service; Food Production
Abilities: Reaction Time; Wrist-Finger Speed; Gross Body Equilibrium
Skills: None above average
General Work Activities: Performing for or Working with Public
Job Characteristics: Job-Required Social Interaction; Provide a Service to Others; Deal with External Customers; Deal with Unpleasant or Angry People; Standing; Walking or Running; Special Uniform
GOE Group/s: 09.04.01 Customer Services: Food Services
CIP Program/s: 080901 Hospitality and Recreation Marketing Operations, General; 080906 Food Sales Operations
Related DOT Job/s: 311.472-010 FAST-FOODS WORKER

65099A VENDING MACHINE ATTENDANTS. OOH Title/s: Vending Machine Servicers and Repairers
Stock vending machine with food and beverages. May make minor adjustments to machines to correct jams or similar malfunctions, or to adjust temperature of refrigerated machines. Include workers who stock mini-bars in hotel rooms. Places foods and beverages into vending machine, cart, or hotel room mini-bar and labels items. Removes money from vending machines, keeps records of receipts, or records items consumed for billing purposes. Observes thermometer and adjusts temperature gauges in vending machine to maintain items at specified temperatures. Makes change for customers and answers questions about selections. Maintains storeroom inventory and prepares requisitions for food and beverage supplies, using inventory list. Performs minor repairs or adjustments on machines to correct jams or other malfunctions, using hand tools. Removes trash from tables and cleans and dusts tables and vending machines with damp cloth to keep eating area clean.
Yearly Earnings: $25,220
Education: Long-term O-J-T
Knowledge: None above average
Abilities: None above average
Skills: None above average
General Work Activities: Monitoring and Controlling Resources
Job Characteristics: Standing; Special Uniform
GOE Group/s: 09.04.01 Customer Services: Food Services
CIP Program/s: 000000 NO CIP ASSIGNED
Related DOT Job/s: 319.464-010 AUTOMAT-CAR ATTENDANT; 319.464-014 VENDING-MACHINE ATTENDANT

65099B FOOD ORDER EXPEDITERS. OOH Title/s: Food and Beverage Service Occupations
Expedite food preparation by calling out customers' orders to cooks and food preparation workers. Inspect portions and presentation of prepared orders, and notify wait staff when orders are ready to be served. Calls out and verifies food orders to cooks and kitchen workers. Notifies serving personnel when order is ready. Reviews orders for accuracy and tabulates check. Examines portioning and garnishing of completed food orders. Assists in preparation and cooking of food that can be completed in a short period of time. Records supplies used to accumulate food control data.
Yearly Earnings: $11,700
Education: Short-term O-J-T
Knowledge: Food Production
Abilities: Memorization; Perceptual Speed
Skills: None above average
General Work Activities: None above average
Job Characteristics: Standing
GOE Group/s: 05.09.03 Material Control: Verifying, Recording, and Marking
CIP Program/s: 000000 NO CIP ASSIGNED
Related DOT Job/s: 211.482-018 FOOD-AND-BEVERAGE CHECKER; 319.467-010 FOOD ORDER EXPEDITER

Medical Assistants and Aides

66002 DENTAL ASSISTANTS. OOH Title/s: Dental Assistants
Assist dentist at chair, set up patient and equipment, keep records, and perform related duties as required. Prepares patient, sterilizes and disinfects instruments, sets up instrument trays, prepares materials, and assists dentist during dental procedures. Takes and records medical and dental histories and vital signs of patients. Records treatment information in patient records. Assists dentist in management of medical and dental emergencies. Exposes dental diagnostic X rays. Applies protective coating of fluoride to teeth. Provides postoperative instructions prescribed by dentist. Makes preliminary impressions for study casts and occlusal registrations for mounting study casts. Pours, trims, and polishes study casts. Cleans and polishes removable appliances. Instructs patients in oral hygiene and plaque-control programs. Schedules appointments, prepares bills and receives payment for dental services, completes insurance forms, and maintains records, manually or using computer. Cleans teeth, using dental instruments. Fabricates temporary restorations and custom impressions from preliminary impressions.
Yearly Earnings: $17,056
Education: Moderate-term O-J-T
Knowledge: Clerical; Medicine and Dentistry
Abilities: Control Precision
Skills: Service Orientation
General Work Activities: Assisting and Caring for Others
Job Characteristics: Provide a Service to Others; Radiation; Diseases/Infections; Special Uniform; Common Protective or Safety Attire; Importance of Being Exact or Accurate; Importance of Being Sure All is Done
GOE Group/s: 10.03.02 Child and Adult Care: Patient Care
CIP Program/s: 510601 Dental Assistant
Related DOT Job/s: 079.361-018 DENTAL ASSISTANT

66005 MEDICAL ASSISTANTS. OOH Title/s: Medical Assistants
Perform various duties under the direction of physician in examination and treatment of patients. Prepare treatment room,

inventory supplies and instruments, and set up patient for attention of physician. Hand instruments and materials to physician as directed. Schedule appointments, keep medical records, and perform secretarial duties. Prepares treatment rooms for examination of patients. Hands instruments and materials to physician. Schedules appointments. Maintains medical records. Interviews patients; measures vital signs, weight, and height; and records information. Inventories and orders medical supplies and materials. Cleans and sterilizes instruments. Contacts medical facility or department to schedule patients for tests. Computes and mails monthly statements to patients and records transactions. Lifts and turns patients. Completes insurance forms. Gives physiotherapy treatments, such as diathermy, galvanics, and hydrotherapy. Operates X ray, electrocardiograph (EKG), and other equipment to administer routine diagnostic tests. Receives payment for bills. Gives injections or treatments to patients. Performs routine laboratory tests.
Yearly Earnings: $23,972
Education: Moderate-term O-J-T
Knowledge: Clerical; Economics and Accounting; Customer and Personal Service; Chemistry; Biology; Psychology; Medicine and Dentistry; Therapy and Counseling; English Language; Foreign Language; Public Safety and Security; Law, Government, and Jurisprudence
Abilities: Problem Sensitivity; Information Ordering; Category Flexibility; Number Facility; Memorization; Speed of Closure; Flexibility of Closure; Selective Attention; Arm-Hand Steadiness; Finger Dexterity; Control Precision; Response Orientation; Reaction Time; Near Vision; Visual Color Discrimination; Night Vision; Peripheral Vision; Hearing Sensitivity; Auditory Attention; Sound Localization; Speech Recognition
Skills: Active Listening; Service Orientation
General Work Activities: Scheduling Work and Activities; Establishing and Maintaining Relationships; Assisting and Caring for Others; Performing for or Working with Public
Job Characteristics: Job-Required Social Interaction; Provide a Service to Others; Deal with External Customers; Responsible for Others' Health and Safety; Deal with Unpleasant or Angry People; Deal with Physical, Aggressive People; Radiation; Diseases/Infections; Special Uniform; Common Protective or Safety Attire; Specialized Protective or Safety Attire; Consequence of Error; Degree of Automation; Importance of Being Exact or Accurate; Importance of Being Sure All is Done
GOE Group/s: 10.03.02 Child and Adult Care: Patient Care
CIP Program/s: 510705 Medical Office Management; 510801 Medical Assistant; 510899 Health and Medical Assistants, Other
Related DOT Job/s: 079.362-010 MEDICAL ASSISTANT; 079.364-010 CHIROPRACTOR ASSISTANT; 079.374-018 PODIATRIC ASSISTANT

66008 NURSING AIDES, ORDERLIES, AND ATTENDANTS. OOH Title/s: Nursing Aides and Psychiatric Aides

Work under the direction of nursing or medical staff to provide auxiliary services in the care of patients. Perform duties such as answering patient's call bell, serving and collecting food trays, and feeding patients. Orderlies are primarily concerned with setting up equipment and relieving nurses of heavier work. Exclude psychiatric aides and home health aides. Feeds patients unable to feed themselves. Sets up equipment, such as oxygen tents, portable x-ray machines, and overhead irrigation bottles. Prepares food trays. Bathes, grooms, and dresses patients. Assists patient to walk. Turns and repositions bedfast patients, alone or with assistance, to prevent bedsores. Transports patient to areas, such as operating and X ray rooms. Measures and records food and liquid intake and output. Administers massages and alcohol rubs. Measures and records vital signs. Sterilizes equipment and supplies. Administers medication as directed by physician or nurse. Administers catheterizations, bladder irrigations, enemas, and douches. Cleans room and changes linen. Stores, prepares, and issues dressing packs, treatment trays, and other supplies.
Yearly Earnings: $14,456
Education: Short-term O-J-T
Knowledge: Customer and Personal Service; Chemistry; Psychology; Medicine and Dentistry; Therapy and Counseling; Foreign Language; Philosophy and Theology
Abilities: Memorization; Perceptual Speed; Spatial Orientation; Selective Attention; Arm-Hand Steadiness; Manual Dexterity; Multilimb Coordination; Response Orientation; Reaction Time; Static Strength; Dynamic Strength; Trunk Strength; Extent Flexibility; Dynamic Flexibility; Gross Body Equilibrium; Visual Color Discrimination; Night Vision; Peripheral Vision; Hearing Sensitivity; Sound Localization; Speech Recognition
Skills: Social Perceptiveness; Service Orientation
General Work Activities: Performing General Physical Activities; Establishing and Maintaining Relationships; Assisting and Caring for Others
Job Characteristics: Job-Required Social Interaction; Provide a Service to Others; Responsible for Others' Health and Safety; Deal with Unpleasant or Angry People; Deal with Physical, Aggressive People; Radiation; Diseases/Infections; Standing; Walking or Running; Special Uniform; Common Protective or Safety Attire; Consequence of Error
GOE Group/s: 10.03.02 Child and Adult Care: Patient Care
CIP Program/s: 511614 Nurse Assistant/Aide; 511615 Home Health Aide; 512601 Health Aide
Related DOT Job/s: 354.374-010 NURSE, PRACTICAL; 355.374-014 CERTIFIED MEDICATION TECHNICIAN; 355.674-014 NURSE ASSISTANT; 355.674-018 ORDERLY

66011 HOME HEALTH AIDES. OOH Title/s: Homemaker-Home Health Aides

Care for elderly, convalescent, or handicapped person in home of patient. Perform duties for patient such as changing bed linen; preparing meals; assisting in and out of bed; bathing, dressing, and grooming; and administering oral medications under doctors' orders or direction of nurse. Exclude nursing aides and homemakers. Changes bed linens, washes and irons patient's laundry, and cleans patient's quarters. Assists patients into and out of bed, automobile, or wheelchair, to lavatory, and up and down stairs. Administers prescribed oral medication under written direction of physician or as directed by home care nurse and aide. Purchases, prepares, and serves food for patient and other members of family, following special prescribed diets. Massages patient and applies preparations and treatment, such as liniment or alcohol rubs and heat-lamp stimulation. Visits several households to provide daily health care to patients. Maintains records of services performed and of apparent condition of patient. Entertains patient, reads aloud, and plays cards and other games with patient. Performs variety of miscellaneous duties as requested, such as obtaining household supplies and running errands.
Yearly Earnings: $14,456
Education: Short-term O-J-T
Knowledge: Customer and Personal Service; Psychology; Medicine and Dentistry; Therapy and Counseling
Abilities: Static Strength
Skills: Social Perceptiveness; Service Orientation
General Work Activities: Performing General Physical Activities; Establishing and Maintaining Relationships; Assisting and Caring for Others

Job Characteristics: Objective or Subjective Information; Job-Required Social Interaction; Provide a Service to Others; Responsible for Others' Health and Safety; Diseases/Infections; Special Uniform
GOE Group/s: 10.03.03 Child and Adult Care: Care of Others
CIP Program/s: 200601 Custodial, Housekeeping and Home Services Workers and Managers; 200602 Elder Care Provider/Companion; 200606 Homemaker's Aide; 511614 Nurse Assistant/Aide; 511615 Home Health Aide; 512601 Health Aide
Related DOT Job/s: 354.377-014 HOME ATTENDANT

66014 PSYCHIATRIC AIDES. OOH Title/s: Nursing Aides and Psychiatric Aides

Assist mentally ill patients, working under direction of nursing and medical staff. Monitors patients to ensure patients remain in assigned areas, and aids or restrains patients to prevent injuries. Assists patients in becoming accustomed to hospital routine. Demonstrates and assists patients in bathing, dressing, and grooming. Accompanies patients to and from wards for medical and dental treatments, shopping trips, and to religious and recreational events. Encourages patients to participate in social, educational, and recreational activities. Notes and maintains records of patients' activities, such as vital signs, eating habits, and daily behavior. Serves meals and feeds patients needing assistance. Administers prescribed medications, measures vital signs, and performs other nursing duties, such as collecting specimens and drawing blood samples.
Yearly Earnings: $14,456
Education: Short-term O-J-T
Knowledge: Customer and Personal Service; Chemistry; Biology; Psychology; Medicine and Dentistry; Therapy and Counseling; Transportation
Abilities: Time Sharing; Speed of Limb Movement; Static Strength; Trunk Strength; Stamina; Dynamic Flexibility; Gross Body Coordination; Gross Body Equilibrium; Peripheral Vision; Speech Recognition
Skills: Social Perceptiveness; Persuasion; Service Orientation
General Work Activities: Identifying Objects, Actions, and Events; Establishing and Maintaining Relationships; Assisting and Caring for Others; Coaching and Developing Others
Job Characteristics: Job-Required Social Interaction; Persuade Someone to a Course of Action; Provide a Service to Others; Responsible for Others' Health and Safety; Frequency in Conflict Situations; Deal with Unpleasant or Angry People; Deal with Physical, Aggressive People; Diseases/Infections; Walking or Running; Special Uniform; Frustrating Circumstances; Importance of Being Aware of New Events
GOE Group/s: 10.03.02 Child and Adult Care: Patient Care
CIP Program/s: 511502 Psychiatric/Mental Health Services Technician; 511599 Mental Health Services, Other; 511614 Nurse Assistant/Aide; 512601 Health Aide
Related DOT Job/s: 355.377-014 PSYCHIATRIC AIDE; 355.377-018 MENTAL-RETARDATION AIDE

66017 PHYSICAL AND CORRECTIVE THERAPY ASSISTANTS AND AIDES. OOH Title/s: Physical Therapy Assistants and Aides

Prepare patient and/or administer physical therapy treatment, such as massages, traction, and heat, light, and sound treatment. Instruct, motivate, and assist patients with learning and improving functional activities. Normally work under the direction of a physical or corrective therapist. Administers active and passive manual therapeutic exercises; therapeutic massage; and heat, light, sound, water, and electrical modality treatments, such as ultrasound. Instructs, motivates, and assists patients to learn and improve functional activities, such as perambulation, transfer, ambulation, and daily-living activities. Safeguards, motivates, and assists patients practicing exercises and functional activities under direction of professional staff. Administers traction to relieve neck and back pain, using intermittent and static traction equipment. Trains patients in use and care of orthopedic braces, prostheses, and supportive devices, such as crutches. Provides routine treatments, such as hydrotherapy, hot and cold packs, and paraffin bath. Adjusts fit of supportive devices for patients, as instructed. Observes patients during treatments, compiles and evaluates data on patients' responses to treatments and progress, and reports to physical therapist. Secures patients into or onto therapy equipment. Confers with physical therapy staff and others to discuss and evaluate patient information for planning, modifying, and coordinating treatment. Measures patient's range-of-joint motion, body parts, and vital signs to determine effects of treatments or for patient evaluations. Assists patients to dress, undress, and put on and remove supportive devices, such as braces, splints, and slings. Records treatment given and equipment used. Fits patients for orthopedic braces, prostheses, and supportive devices, such as crutches. Monitors treatments administered by physical therapy aides. Transports patients to and from treatment area. Gives orientation to new physical therapist assistants and directs and gives instruction to physical therapy aides. Cleans work area and equipment after treatment. Performs clerical duties, such as taking inventory, ordering supplies, answering telephone, taking messages, and filling out forms.
Yearly Earnings: $15,392
Education: Moderate-term O-J-T
Knowledge: Clerical; Customer and Personal Service; Biology; Psychology; Medicine and Dentistry; Therapy and Counseling; Education and Training
Abilities: None above average
Skills: Learning Strategies; Social Perceptiveness; Instructing; Service Orientation
General Work Activities: Performing General Physical Activities; Documenting/Recording Information; Establishing and Maintaining Relationships; Assisting and Caring for Others; Teaching Others; Guiding, Directing and Motivating Subordinates; Coaching and Developing Others
Job Characteristics: Job-Required Social Interaction; Persuade Someone to a Course of Action; Provide a Service to Others; Deal with External Customers; Responsible for Others' Health and Safety; Deal with Unpleasant or Angry People; Diseases/Infections; Standing; Special Uniform
GOE Group/s: 10.02.02 Nursing, Therapy, and Specialized Teaching Services: Therapy and Rehabilitation; 10.03.02 Child and Adult Care: Patient Care
CIP Program/s: 510806 Physical Therapy Assistant; 512601 Health Aide
Related DOT Job/s: 076.224-010 PHYSICAL THERAPIST ASSISTANT; 355.354-010 PHYSICAL THERAPY AIDE

66021 OCCUPATIONAL THERAPY ASSISTANTS AND AIDES. OOH Title/s: Occupational Therapy Assistants and Aides

Assist occupational therapists in administering medically-oriented occupational programs to assist in rehabilitating patients in hospitals and similar institutions. Assists occupational therapist to plan, implement, and administer educational, vocational, and recreational activities to restore, reinforce, and enhance task performances. Assists in evaluation of physically, developmentally, mentally retarded, or emotionally disabled client's daily living skills and capacities. Instructs or assists in instructing patient and family in home programs and basic living skills as well as care and use of adaptive equipment. Reports information and observations to supervisor verbally. Helps professional staff demonstrate therapy techniques, such as manual and creative arts and games. Transports patient to and from

occupational therapy work area. Designs and adapts equipment and working-living environment. Maintains observed information in client records and prepares written reports. Assists educational specialist or clinical psychologist in administering situational or diagnostic tests to measure client's abilities or progress. Fabricates splints and other assistant devices. Prepares work material, assembles and maintains equipment, and orders supplies.
Yearly Earnings: $22,620
Education: Moderate-term O-J-T
Knowledge: Clerical; Customer and Personal Service; Biology; Psychology; Medicine and Dentistry; Therapy and Counseling; Education and Training; Foreign Language
Abilities: Gross Body Coordination; Gross Body Equilibrium
Skills: Social Perceptiveness; Instructing; Service Orientation; Technology Design
General Work Activities: Establishing and Maintaining Relationships; Assisting and Caring for Others; Performing for or Working with Public; Teaching Others
Job Characteristics: Job-Required Social Interaction; Deal with Unpleasant or Angry People; Diseases/Infections; Kneeling, Crouching, or Crawling; Special Uniform; Importance of Being Aware of New Events
GOE Group/s: 10.02.02 Nursing, Therapy, and Specialized Teaching Services: Therapy and Rehabilitation; 10.03.02 Child and Adult Care: Patient Care
CIP Program/s: 510803 Occupational Therapy Assistant; 512601 Health Aide
Related DOT Job/s: 076.364-010 OCCUPATIONAL THERAPY ASSISTANT; 355.377-010 OCCUPATIONAL THERAPY AIDE

66023 AMBULANCE DRIVERS AND ATTENDANTS, EXCEPT EMERGENCY MEDICAL TECHNICIANS.

OOH Title/s: Ambulance Drivers and Attendants, Except Emergency Medical Technicians

Drive ambulance or assist ambulance driver in transporting sick, injured, or convalescent persons. Assist in lifting patients and rendering first aid. May be required to have Red Cross first-aid training certificate. Transports sick or injured persons to hospital, or convalescents to destination, avoiding sudden motions detrimental to patients. Places patient on stretcher and loads stretcher into ambulance, usually with help of ambulance attendant. Administers first aid as needed. Reports facts concerning accident or emergency to hospital personnel or law enforcement officials. Changes soiled linens on stretcher. Shackles violent patients.
Yearly Earnings: $15,392
Education: Short-term O-J-T
Knowledge: Customer and Personal Service; Biology; Geography; Medicine and Dentistry; Therapy and Counseling; Foreign Language; Transportation
Abilities: Memorization; Speed of Closure; Flexibility of Closure; Spatial Orientation; Selective Attention; Time Sharing; Control Precision; Multilimb Coordination; Response Orientation; Rate Control; Reaction Time; Wrist-Finger Speed; Speed of Limb Movement; Static Strength; Explosive Strength; Stamina; Dynamic Flexibility; Gross Body Coordination; Gross Body Equilibrium; Far Vision; Night Vision; Peripheral Vision; Depth Perception; Glare Sensitivity; Hearing Sensitivity; Auditory Attention; Sound Localization
Skills: Service Orientation
General Work Activities: Performing General Physical Activities; Interacting with Computers; Assisting and Caring for Others; Performing for or Working with Public
Job Characteristics: Job-Required Social Interaction; Provide a Service to Others; Deal with External Customers; Responsible for Others' Health and Safety; Frequency in Conflict Situations; Deal with Unpleasant or Angry People; Deal with Physical, Aggressive People; Sounds, Noise Levels are Distracting, etc.; Extremely Bright or Inadequate Lighting; Contaminants; Cramped Work Space, Awkward Positions; Whole Body Vibration; Diseases/Infections; High Places; Hazardous Conditions; Kneeling, Crouching, or Crawling; Keeping or Regaining Balance; Bending or Twisting the Body; Special Uniform; Consequence of Error; Frustrating Circumstances
GOE Group/s: 05.08.03 Land and Water Vehicle Operation: Services Requiring Driving; 10.03.02 Child and Adult Care: Patient Care
CIP Program/s: 000000 NO CIP ASSIGNED
Related DOT Job/s: 355.374-010 AMBULANCE ATTENDANT; 913.683-010 AMBULANCE DRIVER

66097 HEALTH EQUIPMENT SERVICE WORKERS.

OOH Title/s: Indirectly related to Health Service Occupations

Prepare, sterilize, install, and/or clean laboratory or health care equipment. May perform routine laboratory tasks and operate or inspect equipment. Examines equipment to detect leaks, worn or loose parts, or other indications of disrepair. Disinfects, and sterilizes equipment, such as respirators, hospital beds, wheelchairs, and oxygen and dialysis equipment, using cleansing and sterilizing solutions. Installs and sets up equipment, using hand tools. Starts equipment and observes gauges and equipment operation to detect malfunctions and assure equipment is operating to prescribed standards. Connects equipment to water source and flushes water through system to purge equipment of wastes. Delivers equipment to specified hospital location or to patient's private residence. Maintains inventory and equipment usage records.
Yearly Earnings: $15,392
Education: Short-term O-J-T
Knowledge: None above average
Abilities: None above average
Skills: Technology Design; Installation; Equipment Maintenance; Troubleshooting
General Work Activities: Repairing and Maintaining Mechanical Equipment
Job Characteristics: Diseases/Infections
GOE Group/s: 05.08.03 Land and Water Vehicle Operation: Services Requiring Driving; 10.03.02 Child and Adult Care: Patient Care
CIP Program/s: 150401 Biomedical Engineering-Related Technologists and Technicians; 510908 Respiratory Therapy Technician
Related DOT Job/s: 355.674-022 RESPIRATORY-THERAPY AIDE; 359.363-010 HEALTH-EQUIPMENT SERVICER

66099A MORGUE ATTENDANTS. OOH Title/s: Medical Assistants

Assist pathologist by preparing bodies and organ specimens for postmortem examinations. May maintain morgue room, laboratory supplies, instruments, and equipment. Lays out surgical instruments and laboratory supplies for postmortem examination by pathologist. Washes table, storage trays, and instruments, sharpens knives, and replaces soiled linens. Places body on autopsy table or in refrigerated compartment, using portable hoist and stretcher. Mixes preserving fluids according to formulas, preserves specimens, and stains slides. Closes postmortem incisions, using surgical needle and thread, and fills cranium with plaster. Records identifying information for morgue file. Photographs specimens, using camera. Releases body to authorized person, according to established procedure. Waters, feeds, and cleans quarters for animals used in medical research.
Yearly Earnings: $23,972
Education: Moderate-term O-J-T
Knowledge: Chemistry; Biology
Abilities: Selective Attention; Depth Perception

Skills: None above average
General Work Activities: None above average
Job Characteristics: Diseases/Infections; Special Uniform
GOE Group/s: 02.04.02 Laboratory Technology: Life Sciences
CIP Program/s: 510801 Medical Assistant; 510909 Surgical/Operating Room Technician
Related DOT Job/s: 355.667-010 MORGUE ATTENDANT

66099B PATIENT TRANSPORTERS. OOH Title/s: Nursing Aides and Psychiatric Aides

Transport medical patients in bed, wheeled cart, or wheelchair to designated areas within medical facility during patient stay, or assist ambulatory patients in walking to prevent falling accidents. Directs or escorts patient from admitting office or reception desk to designated area of hospital or medical facility. Assists patient in walking to destination to prevent accidents by falling. Transports nonambulatory patient in wheelchair, bed, or gurney to designated area within hospital or medical facility. Reads or listens to instructions to determine patient name, destination, mode of travel, time, and other data. Carries patient's personal belongings to destination. Delivers mail, messages, medical records, or other items within facility.
Yearly Earnings: $14,456
Education: Short-term O-J-T
Knowledge: Customer and Personal Service
Abilities: Stamina
Skills: Service Orientation
General Work Activities: Performing General Physical Activities; Assisting and Caring for Others
Job Characteristics: Job-Required Social Interaction; Provide a Service to Others; Deal with External Customers; Deal with Physical, Aggressive People; Diseases/Infections; Standing; Walking or Running; Special Uniform
GOE Group/s: 10.03.03 Child and Adult Care: Care of Others
CIP Program/s: 000000 NO CIP ASSIGNED
Related DOT Job/s: 355.677-014 TRANSPORTER, PATIENTS

66099D PHLEBOTOMISTS. OOH Title/s: Clinical Laboratory Technologists and Technicians; Medical Assistants

Draw blood from patients or donors in hospital, blood bank, or similar facility for analysis or other medical purposes. Assembles equipment for drawing blood, such as needles, tourniquet, gauze, blood collection devices, cotton, and alcohol, according to test or procedure requirements. Applies tourniquet, inserts needle into vein or pricks finger, draws blood into collection bag or tube, and applies treatment to puncture site. Labels and stores blood containers. Examines patients to take vital signs. Conducts medical testing procedures to screen blood samples. Conducts interviews to gather and record patient information, such as medical and personal history. Converses with patient or donor to explain and allay fears of procedure.
Yearly Earnings: $23,972
Education: Moderate-term O-J-T
Knowledge: Medicine and Dentistry
Abilities: Selective Attention; Arm-Hand Steadiness; Response Orientation; Visual Color Discrimination; Hearing Sensitivity; Auditory Attention; Sound Localization
Skills: Science
General Work Activities: Assisting and Caring for Others
Job Characteristics: Deal with External Customers; Responsible for Others' Health and Safety; Diseases/Infections; Standing; Special Uniform; Common Protective or Safety Attire; Consequence of Error; Importance of Being Sure All is Done
GOE Group/s: 02.04.02 Laboratory Technology: Life Sciences
CIP Program/s: 511001 Blood Bank Technologists and Technicians
Related DOT Job/s: 079.364-022 PHLEBOTOMIST

Cleaning and Building Service Workers

67002 MAIDS AND HOUSEKEEPING CLEANERS. OOH Title/s: Janitors and Cleaners and Cleaning Supervisors

Perform any combination of tasks to maintain private households or commercial establishments, such as hotels, restaurants, and hospitals, in a clean and orderly manner. Duties include making beds, replenishing linens, cleaning rooms and halls, and arranging furniture. Cleans rooms, hallways, lobbies, lounges, restrooms, corridors, elevators, stairways, locker rooms, and other work areas. Cleans rugs, carpets, upholstered furniture, and draperies, using vacuum cleaner. Dusts furniture and equipment. Empties wastebaskets, and empties and cleans ashtrays. Sweeps, scrubs, waxes, and polishes floors, using brooms, mops, and powered scrubbing and waxing machines. Collects soiled linens for laundering, and receives and stores linen supplies in linen closet. Polishes metalwork, such as fixtures and fittings. Washes walls, ceiling, and woodwork. Washes windows, door panels, and sills. Transports trash and waste to disposal area. Replenishes supplies, such as drinking glasses, writing supplies, and bathroom items. Moves and arranges furniture, turns mattresses, hangs draperies, dusts venetian blinds, and polishes metalwork to ready hotel facilities for occupancy. Washes beds and mattresses, and remakes beds after dismissal of hospital patients. Replaces light bulbs. Arranges decorations, apparatus, or furniture for banquets and social functions. Cleans and removes debris from driveway and garage areas. Prepares sample rooms for sales meetings. Delivers television sets, ironing boards, baby cribs, and rollaway beds to guests rooms. Cleans swimming pool with vacuum.
Yearly Earnings: $14,716
Education: Short-term O-J-T
Knowledge: Customer and Personal Service
Abilities: None above average
Skills: None above average
General Work Activities: Performing General Physical Activities
Job Characteristics: Provide a Service to Others; Standing; Walking or Running; Kneeling, Crouching, or Crawling; Making Repetitive Motions; Special Uniform
GOE Group/s: 05.12.18 Elemental Work: Mechanical: Cleaning and Maintenance
CIP Program/s: 000000 NO CIP ASSIGNED
Related DOT Job/s: 323.687-010 CLEANER, HOSPITAL; 323.687-014 CLEANER, HOUSEKEEPING; 323.687-018 HOUSECLEANER

67005 JANITORS AND CLEANERS, EXCEPT MAIDS AND HOUSEKEEPING CLEANERS. OOH Title/s: Janitors and Cleaners and Cleaning Supervisors

Keep building in clean and orderly condition. Perform heavy cleaning duties, such as operating motor-driven cleaning equipment, mopping floors, washing walls and glass, and removing rubbish. Duties may include tending furnace and boiler, performing routine maintenance activities, notifying management of need for repairs and additions, and cleaning snow or debris from sidewalk. Sweeps, mops, scrubs, and vacuums floors of buildings, using cleaning solutions, tools,and equipment. Cleans or polishes walls, ceilings, windows, plant equipment,and building fixtures, using-steam cleaning equipment, scrapers, brooms, and variety of hand and power tools. Applies waxes or sealers to wood or concrete floors. Gathers and empties trash. Tends, cleans, adjusts, and services furnaces, air-conditioners, boilers, and other building heating and cooling systems. Notifies management personnel concerning need for major

repairs or additions to building operating systems. Removes snow from sidewalks, driveways, and parking areas, using snowplow, snowblower, and snow shovel, and spreads snow-melting chemicals. Dusts furniture, walls, machines, and equipment. Services and repairs cleaning and maintenance equipment and machinery and performs minor routine painting, plumbing, electrical, and related activities. Cleans and restores building interiors damaged by fire, smoke, or water, using commercial cleaning equipment. Cleans chimneys, flues, and connecting pipes, using power and hand tools. Drives vehicles, such as vans, industrial trucks, or industrial vacuum cleaners. Mixes water and detergents or acids in container to prepare cleaning solutions, according to specifications. Mows and trims lawns and shrubbery, using mowers and hand and power trimmers, and clears debris from grounds. Cleans laboratory equipment, such as glassware and metal instruments, using solvents, brushes, rags, and power cleaning equipment. Sprays insecticides and fumigants to prevent insect and rodent infestation. Requisitions supplies and equipment used in cleaning and maintenance duties. Sets up, arranges, and removes decorations, tables, chairs, ladders, and scaffolding for events such as banquets and social functions. Moves items between departments, manually or using handtruck.
Yearly Earnings: $14,716
Education: Short-term O-J-T
Knowledge: Building and Construction; Mechanical; Chemistry; Transportation
Abilities: Information Ordering; Spatial Orientation; Manual Dexterity; Multilimb Coordination; Response Orientation; Rate Control; Reaction Time; Wrist-Finger Speed; Speed of Limb Movement; Static Strength; Explosive Strength; Dynamic Strength; Trunk Strength; Stamina; Extent Flexibility; Dynamic Flexibility; Gross Body Coordination; Gross Body Equilibrium; Night Vision; Depth Perception; Glare Sensitivity; Hearing Sensitivity; Sound Localization
Skills: Equipment Maintenance; Repairing
General Work Activities: Performing General Physical Activities; Handling and Moving Objects; Interacting with Computers; Repairing and Maintaining Mechanical Equipment
Job Characteristics: Very Hot; Extremely Bright or Inadequate Lighting; Contaminants; High Places; Hazardous Conditions; Standing; Climbing Ladders, Scaffolds, Poles, etc.; Walking or Running; Kneeling, Crouching, or Crawling; Bending or Twisting the Body; Special Uniform
GOE Group/s: 05.11.01 Equipment Operation: Construction; 05.12.18 Elemental Work: Mechanical: Cleaning and Maintenance; 06.04.40 Elemental Work: Industrial: Loading, Moving, Hoisting, and Conveying
CIP Program/s: 200601 Custodial, Housekeeping and Home Services Workers and Managers; 200604 Custodian/Caretaker; 460401 Building/Property Maintenance and Management
Related DOT Job/s: 358.687-010 CHANGE-HOUSE ATTENDANT; 381.687-014 CLEANER, COMMERCIAL OR INSTITUTIONAL; 381.687-018 CLEANER, INDUSTRIAL; 381.687-022 CLEANER, LABORATORY EQUIPMENT; 381.687-026 CLEANER, WALL; 381.687-030 PATCH WORKER; 381.687-034 WAXER, FLOOR; 382.664-010 JANITOR; 389.664-010 CLEANER, HOME RESTORATION SERVICE; 389.667-010 SEXTON; 389.683-010 SWEEPER-CLEANER, INDUSTRIAL; 389.687-014 CLEANER, WINDOW; 891.684-018 SWIMMING-POOL SERVICER; 891.687-010 CHIMNEY SWEEP; 891.687-018 PROJECT-CREW WORKER

67008 PEST CONTROLLERS AND ASSISTANTS. OOH Title/s: Pest Controllers and Assistants

Spray or release chemical solutions or toxic gases and set mechanical traps to kill pests and vermin such as mice, termites, and roaches that infest buildings and surrounding areas. Sprays or dusts chemical solutions, powders, or gases into rooms; onto clothing, furnishings or wood; and over marshlands, ditches, and catch-basins. Sets mechanical traps and places poisonous paste or bait in sewers, burrows, and ditches. Inspects premises to identify infestation source and extent of damage to property, wall, and roof porosity, and access to infested locations. Cuts or bores openings in building or surrounding concrete, accesses infested areas, inserts nozzle, and injects pesticide to impregnate ground. Studies preliminary reports and diagrams of infested area, and determines treatment type required to eliminate and prevent recurrence of infestation. Directs and/or assists other workers in treatment and extermination processes to eliminate and control rodents, insects, and weeds. Measures area dimensions requiring treatment, using rule, calculates fumigant requirements, and estimates cost for service. Cleans and removes blockages from infested areas to facilitate spraying procedure and provide drainage, using broom, mop, shovel, and rake. Positions and fastens edges of tarpaulins over building and tapes vents to ensure air-tight environment. Holds halide lamp near tarpaulin seams and building vents to detect leaking fumigant. Posts warning signs and locks building doors to secure area to be fumigated. Drives truck equipped with power spraying equipment. Records work activities performed. Cleans worksite after completion of job. Digs up and burns or sprays weeds with herbicides.
Yearly Earnings: $15,080
Education: Moderate-term O-J-T
Knowledge: Chemistry
Abilities: Gross Body Equilibrium
Skills: None above average
General Work Activities: Interacting with Computers
Job Characteristics: Contaminants; Cramped Work Space, Awkward Positions; Hazardous Conditions; Hazardous Situations; Climbing Ladders, Scaffolds, Poles, etc.; Kneeling, Crouching, or Crawling; Specialized Protective or Safety Attire
GOE Group/s: 03.04.05 Elemental Work: Plants and Animals: Services; 05.10.09 Crafts: Environmental; 05.12.03 Elemental Work: Mechanical: Loading, Moving
CIP Program/s: 010501 Agricultural Supplies Retailing and Wholesaling
Related DOT Job/s: 379.687-014 MOSQUITO SPRAYER; 383.361-010 FUMIGATOR; 383.364-010 EXTERMINATOR, TERMITE; 383.684-010 EXTERMINATOR HELPER; 383.687-010 EXTERMINATOR HELPER, TERMITE; 389.684-010 EXTERMINATOR

67011 ELEVATOR OPERATORS. OOH Title/s: Personal and Building Service Occupations

Operate elevator to transport passengers and/or freight between floors of such buildings as offices, apartment houses, hotels, and stores. Pushes buttons or moves control levers to control movement of elevator. Opens and closes safety gate and door of elevator at each floor where stop is made. Transports freight from elevator to designated area, using handtruck. Loads and unloads elevator. Supplies information to passengers, such as location of offices, merchandise, and individuals. Prevents unauthorized persons from entering building. Sweeps or vacuums elevator.
Yearly Earnings: $14,820
Education: Short-term O-J-T
Knowledge: None above average
Abilities: Gross Body Equilibrium
Skills: None above average
General Work Activities: None above average
Job Characteristics: Provide a Service to Others; Deal with External Customers; Frequency in Conflict Situations; Deal with Unpleasant or Angry People; Whole Body Vibration; High Places; Keeping or Regaining Balance; Special Uniform; Degree of Automation; Pace Determined by Speed of Equipment
GOE Group/s: 05.12.04 Elemental Work: Mechanical: Hoisting, Conveying; 09.05.09 Attendant Services: Elevator Services

CIP Program/s: 000000 NO CIP ASSIGNED
Related DOT Job/s: 388.663-010 ELEVATOR OPERATOR; 921.683-038 ELEVATOR OPERATOR, FREIGHT

67099 ALL OTHER CLEANING AND BUILDING SERVICE WORKERS. OOH Title/s: Personal and Building Service Occupations
All other cleaning and building service workers not classified separately above.
Yearly Earnings: $14,820
Education: Short-term O-J-T
GOE Group/s: 05.12.12 Elemental Work: Mechanical: Structural Work; 05.12.18 Elemental Work: Mechanical: Cleaning and Maintenance
CIP Program/s: 000000 NO CIP ASSIGNED
Related DOT Job/s: 329.683-010 ATTENDANT, CAMPGROUND; 389.687-010 AIR PURIFIER SERVICER; 389.687-018 LIGHT-FIXTURE SERVICER

Personal Service Workers

68002 BARBERS. OOH Title/s: Barbers and Cosmetologists
Provide customers with barbering services, including cutting, trimming, shampooing, and styling hair. Give shaves and shape contour of hairline. May sell lotions, tonics, and other cosmetic supplies. Cuts, shapes, trims, and tapers hair, using clippers, comb, blow-out gun, and scissors. Applies lather and shaves beard or shapes hair contour (outline) on temple and neck, using razor. Performs other tonsorial services, such as applying hairdressings or lotions, dyeing, shampooing, singeing, or styling hair, and massaging face, neck, or scalp. Questions patron regarding services and style of haircut desired. Sells lotions, tonics, or other cosmetic supplies. Drapes and pins protective cloth around customer's shoulders. Records service on ticket or receives payment. Orders supplies. Cleans work area and works tools.
Yearly Earnings: $14,196
Education: Postsecondary vocational training
Knowledge: Sales and Marketing; Customer and Personal Service
Abilities: Arm-Hand Steadiness; Finger Dexterity
Skills: None above average
General Work Activities: Performing for or Working with Public
Job Characteristics: Objective or Subjective Information; Job-Required Social Interaction; Persuade Someone to a Course of Action; Provide a Service to Others; Deal with External Customers; Hazardous Situations; Standing; Making Repetitive Motions
GOE Group/s: 09.02.02 Barber and Beauty Services: Barbering
CIP Program/s: 120402 Barber/Hairstylist
Related DOT Job/s: 330.371-010 BARBER; 330.371-014 BARBER APPRENTICE

68005A HAIRDRESSERS, HAIRSTYLISTS, AND COSMETOLOGISTS. OOH Title/s: Barbers and Cosmetologists
Provide beauty services, such as shampooing, cutting, coloring, and styling hair, and massaging and treating scalp. May also apply make-up, dress wigs, perform hair removal, and provide nail and skin care services. Cuts, trims, and shapes hair or hair pieces, using clippers, scissors, trimmers, and razors. Shampoos, rinses, and dries hair and scalp orhair pieces with water, liquid soap, or other solutions. Bleaches, dyes, or tints hair, using applicator or brush. Applies water, setting, or waving solutions to hair and winds hair on curlers or rollers. Combs, brushes, and sprays hair or wigs to set style. Attaches wig or hairpiece to model head and dresses wigs and hairpieces according to instructions, samples, sketches, or photographs. Analyzes patron's hair and other physical features or reads make-up instructions to determine and recommend beauty treatment. Massages and treats scalp for hygienic and remedial purposes, using hands, fingers, or vibrating equipment. Administers therapeutic medication and advises patron to seek medical treatment for chronic or contagious scalp conditions. Recommends and applies cosmetics, lotions, and creams to patron to soften and lubricate skin and enhance and restore natural appearance. Shapes and colors eyebrows or eyelashes and removes facial hair, using depilatory cream and tweezers. Cleans, shapes, and polishes fingernails and toenails, using files and nail polish. Updates and maintains customer information records, such as beauty services provided or personal effects of deceased patron.
Yearly Earnings: $15,236
Education: Postsecondary vocational training
Knowledge: Customer and Personal Service
Abilities: Originality; Arm-Hand Steadiness; Manual Dexterity; Finger Dexterity; Dynamic Flexibility; Gross Body Equilibrium; Visual Color Discrimination
Skills: Service Orientation
General Work Activities: Handling and Moving Objects; Establishing and Maintaining Relationships; Assisting and Caring for Others; Selling or Influencing Others; Performing for or Working with Public
Job Characteristics: Objective or Subjective Information; Job-Required Social Interaction; Persuade Someone to a Course of Action; Provide a Service to Others; Deal with External Customers; Frequency in Conflict Situations; Deal with Unpleasant or Angry People; Contaminants; Hazardous Conditions; Standing; Using Hands on Objects, Tools, or Controls; Making Repetitive Motions
GOE Group/s: 01.06.02 Craft Arts: Arts and Crafts; 09.02.01 Barber and Beauty Services: Cosmetology
CIP Program/s: 120301 Funeral Services and Mortuary Science; 120402 Barber/Hairstylist; 120403 Cosmetologist
Related DOT Job/s: 332.271-010 COSMETOLOGIST; 332.271-014 COSMETOLOGIST APPRENTICE; 332.271-018 HAIR STYLIST; 332.361-010 WIG DRESSER; 339.361-010 MORTUARY BEAUTICIAN

68005B MAKE-UP ARTISTS, THEATRICAL AND PERFORMANCE. OOH Title/s: Barbers and Cosmetologists
Apply make-up to performers to reflect period, setting, and situation of their role. Applies make-up to performers to alter their appearance to accord with their roles. Selects desired makeup shades from stock, or mixes oil, grease, and coloring to achieve special color effects. Attaches prostheses to performer and applies make-up to change physical features and depict desired character. Designs rubber or plastic prostheses and requisitions materials, such as wigs, beards, and special cosmetics. Studies production information, such as character, period settings, and situations to determine make-up requirements. Confers with stage or motion picture officials and performers to determine dress or make-up alterations. Examines sketches, photographs, and plaster models to obtain desired character image depiction. Creates character drawings or models, based upon independent research to augment period production files.
Yearly Earnings: $15,236
Education: Postsecondary vocational training
Knowledge: Sociology and Anthropology; Fine Arts; History and Archeology
Abilities: Originality; Visualization; Arm-Hand Steadiness; Manual Dexterity; Finger Dexterity; Visual Color Discrimination
Skills: None above average
General Work Activities: Thinking Creatively; Drafting and Specifying Technical Devices, etc.; Assisting and Caring for Others

Job Characteristics: Objective or Subjective Information; Job-Required Social Interaction; Using Hands on Objects, Tools, or Controls
GOE Group/s: 01.06.02 Craft Arts: Arts and Crafts
CIP Program/s: 120403 Cosmetologist; 120406 Make-Up Artist
Related DOT Job/s: 333.071-010 MAKE-UP ARTIST; 333.271-010 BODY-MAKE-UP ARTIST

68005C ELECTROLOGISTS. OOH Title/s: Barbers and Cosmetologists

Remove unwanted hair from patrons for cosmetic purposes using electrolysis equipment. Swabs skin area with antiseptic solution and inserts needle into hair follicle and papilla. Presses switch and adjusts timing and controls of equipment to regulate flow of electricity through needles to decompose papilla cells. Removes needle or needles and pulls hair from follicle, using tweezers. Positions sterile bulbous or round-tipped needles into electrodes of galvanic or short-wave electrical equipment. Places secondary electrode in patron's hand to complete circuit and stabilize amount of electricity during equipment operation.
Yearly Earnings: $15,236
Education: Postsecondary vocational training
Knowledge: Customer and Personal Service
Abilities: Arm-Hand Steadiness; Manual Dexterity; Finger Dexterity; Control Precision; Wrist-Finger Speed; Near Vision
Skills: None above average
General Work Activities: Performing for or Working with Public
Job Characteristics: Job-Required Social Interaction; Provide a Service to Others; Deal with External Customers; Responsible for Others' Health and Safety; Diseases/Infections; Using Hands on Objects, Tools, or Controls; Making Repetitive Motions; Importance of Repeating Same Tasks
GOE Group/s: 09.05.01 Attendant Services: Physical Conditioning
CIP Program/s: 120404 Electrolysis Technician
Related DOT Job/s: 339.371-010 ELECTROLOGIST

68008 MANICURISTS. OOH Title/s: Barbers and Cosmetologists

Clean, shape, and polish customers' fingernails and toenails. Removes previously applied nail polish, using liquid remover and swabs. Shapes and smooths ends of nails, using scissors, files, and emery boards. Cleans customers' nails in soapy water, using swabs, files, and orange sticks. Applies clear or colored liquid polish onto nails with brush. Forms artificial fingernails on customer's fingers. Roughens surfaces of fingernails, using abrasive wheel. Polishes nails, using powdered polish and buffer. Brushes additional powder and solvent onto new growth between cuticles and nails to maintain nail appearance. Attaches paper forms to tips of customer's fingers to support and shape artificial nails. Brushes coats of powder and solvent onto nails and paper forms with handbrush to extend nails to desired length. Softens nail cuticles with water and oil, pushes back cuticles, using cuticle knife, and trims cuticles, using scissors or nippers. Removes paper forms and shapes and smooths edges of nails, using rotary abrasive wheel. Whitens underside of nails with white paste or pencil.
Yearly Earnings: $15,236
Education: Postsecondary vocational training
Knowledge: Customer and Personal Service
Abilities: Arm-Hand Steadiness; Finger Dexterity; Visual Color Discrimination; Glare Sensitivity
Skills: None above average
General Work Activities: Performing for or Working with Public
Job Characteristics: Job-Required Social Interaction; Provide a Service to Others; Deal with External Customers; Diseases/Infections; Hazardous Conditions; Sitting; Using Hands on Objects, Tools, or Controls
GOE Group/s: 09.05.01 Attendant Services: Physical Conditioning
CIP Program/s: 120403 Cosmetologist
Related DOT Job/s: 331.674-010 MANICURIST; 331.674-014 FINGERNAIL FORMER

68014A AMUSEMENT AND RECREATION ATTENDANTS. OOH Title/s: Amusement and Recreation Attendants

Perform variety of attending duties at amusement or recreation facility. May schedule use of recreation facilities, maintain and provide equipment to participants of sporting events or recreational pursuits, or operate amusement concessions and rides. Schedules use of recreation facilities, such as golf courses, tennis courts, bowling alleys, and softball diamonds. Rents, sells, and issues sports equipment and supplies, such as bowling shoes, golf balls, swimming suits, and beach chairs. Sells tickets and collects fees from customers, and collects or punches tickets. Operates or drives mechanical riding devices in amusement parks or carnivals, or explains use of devices. Receives, retrieves, replaces, and stores sports equipment and supplies; arranges items in designated areas; and erects or removes equipment. Provides information about facilities, entertainment options, and rules and regulations. Assists patrons on and off amusement rides, boats, or ski lifts, and in mounting and riding animals; and fastens or directs patrons to fasten safety devices. Directs patrons of establishment to rides, seats, or attractions, or escorts patrons on tours of points of interest. Monitors activities to ensure adherence to rules and safety procedures to protect environment and maintain order, and ejects unruly patrons. Tends automatic equipment in funhouse to amuse, excite, or mystify patrons, and ski-lift to transport skiers. Launches, moors, and demonstrates use of boats, such as rowboats, canoes, and motorboats, or caddies for golfers. Provides entertainment services, such as guessing patron's weight, conducting games, or explaining use of arcade game machines, and photographing patrons. Announces and describes amusement park attractions to patrons to entice customers to games and other entertainment. Sells and serves refreshments to customers. Verifies winning bingo cards and awards prizes or pays money to winning players. Cleans sporting equipment, vehicles, rides, booths, facilities, and grounds. Inspects, repairs, adjusts, tests, fuels, and oils sporting and recreation equipment, game machines, and amusement rides. Records details of attendance, sales, receipts, reservations, and repair activities. Attends animals, performing such tasks as harnessing, saddling, feeding, watering, and grooming, and drives horse-drawn vehicle for entertainment or advertising purposes.
Yearly Earnings: $17,264
Education: Short-term O-J-T
Knowledge: Sales and Marketing; Customer and Personal Service; Mechanical; Public Safety and Security
Abilities: Perceptual Speed; Spatial Orientation; Time Sharing; Control Precision; Response Orientation; Rate Control; Reaction Time; Static Strength; Dynamic Strength; Trunk Strength; Stamina; Extent Flexibility; Dynamic Flexibility; Gross Body Coordination; Gross Body Equilibrium; Far Vision; Night Vision; Peripheral Vision; Depth Perception; Glare Sensitivity; Hearing Sensitivity; Auditory Attention; Sound Localization; Speech Recognition
Skills: None above average
General Work Activities: Scheduling Work and Activities; Interacting with Computers; Repairing and Maintaining Mechanical Equipment; Assisting and Caring for Others; Selling or Influencing Others; Performing for or Working with Public
Job Characteristics: Job-Required Social Interaction; Persuade Someone to a Course of Action; Provide a Service to Others; Deal with External Customers; Responsible for Others' Health and Safety; Deal with Unpleasant or Angry People; Sounds, Noise Levels are Distracting, etc.; Very Hot; Extremely Bright or Inadequate Lighting; High

Places; Climbing Ladders, Scaffolds, Poles, etc.; Walking or Running; Special Uniform; Degree of Automation
GOE Group/s: 01.07.02 Elemental Arts: Announcing; 01.07.03 Elemental Arts: Entertaining; 03.03.02 Animal Training and Service: Animal Service; 05.10.02 Crafts: Mechanical; 05.12.15 Elemental Work: Mechanical: Mechanical Work; 05.12.18 Elemental Work: Mechanical: Cleaning and Maintenance; 07.04.03 Oral Communications: Registration; 09.01.01 Hospitality Services: Social and Recreational Activities; 09.04.02 Customer Services: Sales Services; 09.05.05 Attendant Services: Card and Game Room Services; 09.05.06 Attendant Services: Individualized Services; 09.05.08 Attendant Services: Ticket Taking, Ushering; 12.01.02 Sports: Officiating
CIP Program/s: 000000 NO CIP ASSIGNED
Related DOT Job/s: 195.367-030 RECREATION AIDE; 340.367-010 DESK CLERK, BOWLING FLOOR; 340.477-010 RACKER; 341.367-010 RECREATION-FACILITY ATTENDANT; 341.464-010 SKATE-SHOP ATTENDANT; 341.665-010 SKI-TOW OPERATOR; 341.677-010 CADDIE; 341.683-010 GOLF-RANGE ATTENDANT; 342.357-010 WEIGHT GUESSER; 342.657-010 BARKER; 342.657-014 GAME ATTENDANT; 342.663-010 RIDE OPERATOR; 342.665-010 FUN-HOUSE OPERATOR; 342.667-010 WHARF ATTENDANT; 342.667-014 ATTENDANT, ARCADE; 342.677-010 RIDE ATTENDANT; 343.467-014 FLOOR ATTENDANT; 343.577-010 CARDROOM ATTENDANT II; 349.477-010 JINRIKISHA DRIVER; 349.664-010 AMUSEMENT PARK WORKER; 349.674-010 ANIMAL-RIDE ATTENDANT; 349.677-010 CABANA ATTENDANT; 349.677-014 COACH DRIVER; 352.667-010 HOST/HOSTESS; 372.667-026 FLAGGER

68014B GAMES-OF-CHANCE ATTENDANTS. OOH Title/s: Ushers, Lobby Attendants, and Ticket Takers

Perform a variety of duties associated with games of chance. Conduct gambling tables, such as dice, roulette, or cards, collect fees, pay winnings, and explain rules. Conducts gambling table or game, such as dice, roulette, cards, or keno, and ensures that game rules are followed. Exchanges paper currency for playing chips or coin money, and collects game fees or wagers. Verifies, computes, and pays out winnings. Participates in card game for gambling establishment to provide minimum complement of players at table. Prepares collection report for submission to supervisor. Seats cardroom patrons at tables. Sells food, beverages, and tobacco to players.
Yearly Earnings: $17,264
Education: Short-term O-J-T
Knowledge: Sales and Marketing; Customer and Personal Service; Foreign Language; Law, Government, and Jurisprudence
Abilities: Memorization; Perceptual Speed; Selective Attention; Time Sharing; Response Orientation; Wrist-Finger Speed; Night Vision; Peripheral Vision; Auditory Attention; Sound Localization; Speech Recognition
Skills: Service Orientation
General Work Activities: Selling or Influencing Others; Performing for or Working with Public
Job Characteristics: Job-Required Social Interaction; Provide a Service to Others; Deal with External Customers; Deal with Unpleasant or Angry People; Making Repetitive Motions; Special Uniform; Importance of Being Exact or Accurate
GOE Group/s: 09.04.02 Customer Services: Sales Services
CIP Program/s: 120203 Card Dealer
Related DOT Job/s: 343.367-010 CARD PLAYER; 343.464-010 GAMBLING DEALER; 343.467-010 CARDROOM ATTENDANT I; 343.467-022 KENO WRITER

68017A TRAVEL GUIDES. OOH Title/s: Travel Agents

Plan, organize, and conduct cruises, tours, and expeditions for individuals and groups. Plans tour itinerary, applying knowledge of travel routes and destination sites. Arranges for transportation, accommodations, activity equipment, and services of medical personnel. Selects activity tour sites, and leads individuals or groups to location, and describes points of interest. Verifies quantity and quality of equipment to ensure that prerequisite needs for expeditions and tours have been met. Instructs novices in climbing techniques, mountaineering, and wilderness survival, and demonstrates use of hunting, fishing, and climbing equipment. Obtains or assists tourists to obtain permits and documents, such as visas, passports, and health certificates, and to convert currency. Pitches camp and prepares meals for tour group members. Explains hunting and fishing laws to group to ensure compliance. Pilots airplane or drives land and water vehicles to transport tourists to activity/tour site. Administers first aid to injured group participants. Sells or rents equipment, clothing, and supplies.
Yearly Earnings: $16,848
Education: Postsecondary vocational training
Knowledge: Administration and Management; Sales and Marketing; Customer and Personal Service; Sociology and Anthropology; Geography; Medicine and Dentistry; Foreign Language; History and Archeology; Public Safety and Security; Law, Government, and Jurisprudence; Communications and Media; Transportation
Abilities: Memorization; Spatial Orientation; Time Sharing; Multilimb Coordination; Response Orientation; Rate Control; Reaction Time; Dynamic Strength; Trunk Strength; Stamina; Gross Body Coordination; Gross Body Equilibrium; Night Vision; Peripheral Vision; Depth Perception; Glare Sensitivity; Auditory Attention; Sound Localization; Speech Recognition; Speech Clarity
Skills: Persuasion; Instructing; Service Orientation; Implementation Planning; Operation and Control; Time Management; Management of Material Resources
General Work Activities: Scheduling Work and Activities; Performing General Physical Activities; Interacting with Computers; Assisting and Caring for Others; Selling or Influencing Others; Performing for or Working with Public; Teaching Others; Coaching and Developing Others
Job Characteristics: Objective or Subjective Information; Job-Required Social Interaction; Persuade Someone to a Course of Action; Provide a Service to Others; Deal with External Customers; Responsible for Others' Health and Safety; Deal with Unpleasant or Angry People; Deal with Physical, Aggressive People; High Places; Climbing Ladders, Scaffolds, Poles, etc.; Walking or Running; Keeping or Regaining Balance; Specialized Protective or Safety Attire; Importance of Being Aware of New Events
GOE Group/s: 07.05.01 Records Processing: Coordinating and Scheduling; 09.01.01 Hospitality Services: Social and Recreational Activities
CIP Program/s: 080901 Hospitality and Recreation Marketing Operations, General; 080903 Recreation Products/Services Marketing Operations; 081105 Travel Services Marketing Operations; 310301 Parks, Recreation and Leisure Facilities Management
Related DOT Job/s: 353.161-010 GUIDE, HUNTING AND FISHING; 353.164-010 GUIDE, ALPINE; 353.167-010 GUIDE, TRAVEL; 353.364-010 DUDE WRANGLER

68017B TOUR GUIDES AND ESCORTS. OOH Title/s: Indirectly related to Ushers, Lobby Attendants, and Ticket Takers

Escort individuals or groups on sightseeing tours or through places of interest, such as industrial establishments, public buildings, and art galleries. Escorts group on city and establishment tours, describes points of interest, and responds to questions. Drives motor vehicle to transport visitors to establishments and tour site locations. Provides directions and other pertinent information to visitors. Distributes brochures, conveys background information, and ex-

plains establishment processes and operations at tour site. Monitors visitors' activities and cautions visitors not complying with establishment regulations. Greets and registers visitors and issues identification badges and safety devices. Assumes responsibility for safety of group. Plans rest stops and refreshment items. Speaks foreign language to communicate with foreign visitors. Solicits tour patronage and collects fees and tickets from group members. Carries equipment, luggage, or sample cases for visitors and provides errand service. Performs clerical duties, such as filing, typing, operating switchboard, and delivering and collection of mail and messages. Monitors facilities and notifies establishment personnel of need for maintenance.
Yearly Earnings: $17,264
Education: Short-term O-J-T
Knowledge: Sales and Marketing; Customer and Personal Service; Geography; Foreign Language; Fine Arts; History and Archeology; Communications and Media; Transportation
Abilities: Memorization; Spatial Orientation; Time Sharing; Rate Control; Reaction Time; Night Vision; Speech Recognition; Speech Clarity
Skills: Service Orientation
General Work Activities: Interacting with Computers; Communicating with Persons Outside Organization; Establishing and Maintaining Relationships; Assisting and Caring for Others; Selling or Influencing Others; Performing for or Working with Public
Job Characteristics: Objective or Subjective Information; Job-Required Social Interaction; Persuade Someone to a Course of Action; Provide a Service to Others; Deal with External Customers; Responsible for Others' Health and Safety; Frequency in Conflict Situations; Deal with Unpleasant or Angry People; Walking or Running; Special Uniform; Importance of Being Aware of New Events
GOE Group/s: 09.01.02 Hospitality Services: Guide Services; 09.05.08 Attendant Services: Ticket Taking, Ushering
CIP Program/s: 080901 Hospitality and Recreation Marketing Operations, General; 080903 Recreation Products/Services Marketing Operations; 081104 Tourism Promotion Operations; 310101 Parks, Recreation and Leisure Studies
Related DOT Job/s: 109.367-010 MUSEUM ATTENDANT; 353.363-010 GUIDE, SIGHTSEEING; 353.367-010 GUIDE; 353.367-014 GUIDE, ESTABLISHMENT; 353.367-018 GUIDE, PLANT; 353.367-022 PAGE; 353.667-010 ESCORT

68021 USHERS, LOBBY ATTENDANTS, AND TICKET TAKERS. OOH Title/s: Ushers, Lobby Attendants, and Ticket Takers

Assist patrons at entertainment events, such as sporting events, motion pictures, or theater performances. Collect admission tickets and passes from patrons. May assist in finding seats, searching for lost articles, and locating such facilities as restrooms and telephones. Collects admission tickets and passes from patrons at entertainment events. Assists patrons to find seats, search for lost articles, and locate facilities, such as restrooms and telephones. Verifies credentials of patrons desiring entrance into press-box, and permits only authorized persons to enter. Examines ticket or pass to verify authenticity, using criteria such as color and date issued. Refuses admittance to patrons without ticket or pass, or those who are undesirable for reasons such as intoxication or improper attire. Distributes programs to patrons, or door checks to patrons temporarily leaving establishment. Greets patrons desiring to attend entertainment events. Counts and records number of tickets collected. Monitors patrons' activities to prevent disorderly conduct and rowdiness and to detect infractions of rules. Serves patrons at refreshment stand during intermission. Runs errand for patrons of press-box, such as obtaining refreshments and carrying news releases. Parks car or directs patron to parking space at drive-in theater, indicating available space with flashlight. Attaches loudspeaker to automobile door and turns controls to adjust volume. Assists other workers to change advertising display.
Yearly Earnings: $17,264
Education: Short-term O-J-T
Knowledge: Customer and Personal Service; Foreign Language
Abilities: None above average
Skills: None above average
General Work Activities: Performing for or Working with Public
Job Characteristics: Provide a Service to Others; Deal with External Customers; Frequency in Conflict Situations; Deal with Unpleasant or Angry People; Standing; Walking or Running; Special Uniform
GOE Group/s: 09.05.04 Attendant Services: Doorkeeping Services; 09.05.08 Attendant Services: Ticket Taking, Ushering
CIP Program/s: 000000 NO CIP ASSIGNED
Related DOT Job/s: 344.667-010 TICKET TAKER; 344.677-010 PRESS-BOX CUSTODIAN; 344.677-014 USHER; 349.673-010 DRIVE-IN THEATER ATTENDANT; 349.677-018 CHILDREN'S ATTENDANT

68023 BAGGAGE PORTERS AND BELLHOPS. OOH Title/s: Baggage Porters and Bellhops

Carry baggage for travelers at transportation terminals or for guests at hotels or similar establishments. Additional duties include assisting handicapped persons, running errands, delivering ice, and directing people to their desired destinations. Delivers, carries, or transfers luggage, trunks, and packages to and from rooms, loading areas, vehicles, or transportation terminals. Sets up display tables, racks, or shelves, and arranges merchandise display for sales personnel. Supplies guests or travelers with directions, travel information, and other information, such as available services and points of interest. Escorts incoming hotel guests to their rooms. Inspects guest's room and explains features, such as night-lock and operation of television. Transports guests about premises and local area, or calls taxicabs. Computes and completes charge slips for services rendered and maintains records. Pages guests in hotel lobby, dining room, or other areas, delivers messages and room service orders. Arranges for clothing of hotel guests to be cleaned, laundered, or repaired. Runs errands for guests. Completes and attaches baggage claim checks and completes baggage insurance forms. Weighs and bills baggage and parcels for shipment, and arranges for freight to be shipped.
Yearly Earnings: $14,196
Education: Short-term O-J-T
Knowledge: Customer and Personal Service; Geography
Abilities: Static Strength; Stamina
Skills: Service Orientation
General Work Activities: Performing General Physical Activities; Handling and Moving Objects; Assisting and Caring for Others; Performing for or Working with Public
Job Characteristics: Job-Required Social Interaction; Provide a Service to Others; Deal with External Customers; Deal with Unpleasant or Angry People; Standing; Walking or Running; Special Uniform
GOE Group/s: 09.05.03 Attendant Services: Portering and Baggage Services
CIP Program/s: 000000 NO CIP ASSIGNED
Related DOT Job/s: 324.477-010 PORTER, BAGGAGE; 324.677-010 BELLHOP; 357.477-010 BAGGAGE CHECKER; 357.677-010 PORTER

68026 FLIGHT ATTENDANTS. OOH Title/s: Flight Attendants

Provide personal services to ensure the safety and comfort of airline passengers during flight. Greet passengers, verify tickets, record destinations, and assign seats. Explain use of safety equipment. Serve meals and beverages. Greets passengers, verifies tickets, records destinations, and directs passengers to assigned seats.

Explains use of safety equipment to passengers. Serves prepared meals and beverages. Assists passengers to store carry-on luggage in overhead, garment, or under-seat storage. Walks aisle of plane to verify that passengers have complied with federal regulations prior to take off. Administers first aid to passengers in distress, when needed. Collects money for meals and beverages. Prepares reports showing place of departure and destination, passenger ticket numbers, meal and beverages inventories, and lost and found articles.
Yearly Earnings: $23,712
Education: Long-term O-J-T
Knowledge: Customer and Personal Service; Psychology; Geography; Medicine and Dentistry; Therapy and Counseling; Public Safety and Security; Transportation
Abilities: Reaction Time; Gross Body Equilibrium; Speech Recognition
Skills: Social Perceptiveness; Service Orientation
General Work Activities: Assisting and Caring for Others; Performing for or Working with Public
Job Characteristics: Job-Required Social Interaction; Provide a Service to Others; Deal with External Customers; Responsible for Others' Health and Safety; Deal with Unpleasant or Angry People; Whole Body Vibration; High Places; Standing; Walking or Running; Keeping or Regaining Balance; Special Uniform
GOE Group/s: 09.01.04 Hospitality Services: Safety and Comfort Services
CIP Program/s: 490106 Flight Attendant
Related DOT Job/s: 352.367-010 AIRPLANE-FLIGHT ATTENDANT; 352.367-014 FLIGHT ATTENDANT, RAMP

68028 TRANSPORTATION ATTENDANTS, EXCEPT FLIGHT ATTENDANTS AND BAGGAGE PORTERS.

OOH Title/s: No related OOH occupation

Provide personal services to ensure the safety and comfort of passengers aboard ship, bus, or train. Greet passengers, explain use of safety equipment, serve meals and beverages, and answer questions related to travel. Exclude flight attendants. Greets passengers boarding mode of transportation, announces stops, and responds to passengers' questions concerning schedules, routes, and fares. Demonstrates safety procedures, such as use of life jackets, and provides information on points of interest to passengers. Provides seating arrangements, and straightens and adjusts window shades and seat cushions to accommodate requests of passengers. Activates tape recorder to provide music to passengers, and serves snacks, lunch, and refreshments during entertainment. Responds to stateroom request signals from passengers, and delivers food and beverages. Distributes sports and game equipment, magazines, newspapers, pillows, blankets, and other items to passengers and guests. Investigates passenger complaints, assists ill passengers, warms baby bottles, and provides care for children. Carries baggage to assigned rooms or to station platform. Mails letters or arranges for dispatch of telegrams to assist passengers. Issues and collects passenger boarding passes and transfers and tears or punches tickets to prevent reuse. Counts and verifies tickets and seat reservations, and records number of passengers boarding and leaving mode of transportation. Signals transportation operator to stop or proceed, opens and closes doors, and establishes order among passengers. Inspects kitchen and dining area to ensure adherence to sanitation requirements. Cleans rooms, changes linens, and replenishes supplies to washroom. Cleans public areas of mode of transportation, such as showers, sinks, lavatory equipment, and other bathroom facilities. Records names of passengers on manifest and inventories food supplies to account for food served and on-hand.
Yearly Earnings: NA
Education: Unknown
Knowledge: Customer and Personal Service; Foreign Language; Transportation
Abilities: Gross Body Equilibrium; Glare Sensitivity
Skills: Service Orientation
General Work Activities: Establishing and Maintaining Relationships; Assisting and Caring for Others; Resolving Conflicts, Negotiating with Others; Performing for or Working with Public
Job Characteristics: Job-Required Social Interaction; Persuade Someone to a Course of Action; Provide a Service to Others; Deal with External Customers; Responsible for Others' Health and Safety; Frequency in Conflict Situations; Deal with Unpleasant or Angry People; Deal with Physical, Aggressive People; Whole Body Vibration; Walking or Running; Keeping or Regaining Balance; Bending or Twisting the Body; Special Uniform; Importance of Being Aware of New Events
GOE Group/s: 05.12.18 Elemental Work: Mechanical: Cleaning and Maintenance; 09.01.04 Hospitality Services: Safety and Comfort Services; 09.05.02 Attendant Services: Food Services; 09.05.08 Attendant Services: Ticket Taking, Ushering
CIP Program/s: 081105 Travel Services Marketing Operations
Related DOT Job/s: 350.677-014 PASSENGER ATTENDANT; 350.677-018 STEWARD/STEWARDESS, BATH; 350.677-022 STEWARD/STEWARDESS; 351.677-010 SERVICE ATTENDANT, SLEEPING CAR; 352.577-010 BUS ATTENDANT; 352.677-010 PASSENGER SERVICE REPRESENTATIVE I; 910.367-026 PASSENGER REPRESENTATIVE; 910.667-014 CONDUCTOR; 910.677-010 PASSENGER SERVICE REPRESENTATIVE II

68032A LOCKER ROOM, COATROOM, AND DRESSING ROOM ATTENDANTS.

OOH Title/s: Indirectly related to Ushers, Lobby Attendants, and Ticket Takers

Provide personal items to patrons or customers in locker rooms, dressing rooms, or coatrooms. Seats patrons, massages body or gives baths, and furnishes towel or dries patron. Selects and fits clothing or costume for patrons. Issues or distributes clothing articles and assists patron to dress. Procures beverage, food, and other items as requested. Turns controls to regulate temperature or room environment. Examines dress, accessories, or equipment to ensure conformance with specifications. Collects and organizes clothing, accessories, or linens. Maintains and cleans dressing and bathing areas or lavatories. Alters, mends, presses, and spot-cleans costumes, clothing, or wardrobe accessories. Sends out clothing articles for major repair or cleaning.
Yearly Earnings: $17,264
Education: Short-term O-J-T
Knowledge: Customer and Personal Service
Abilities: None above average
Skills: Service Orientation
General Work Activities: Assisting and Caring for Others; Performing for or Working with Public
Job Characteristics: Job-Required Social Interaction; Provide a Service to Others; Deal with External Customers; Standing
GOE Group/s: 09.05.01 Attendant Services: Physical Conditioning; 09.05.06 Attendant Services: Individualized Services; 09.05.07 Attendant Services: General Wardrobe Services; 12.01.02 Sports: Officiating
CIP Program/s: 000000 NO CIP ASSIGNED
Related DOT Job/s: 335.677-010 COOLING-ROOM ATTENDANT; 335.677-014 HOT-ROOM ATTENDANT; 346.667-010 JOCKEY-ROOM CUSTODIAN; 346.677-010 JOCKEY VALET; 346.677-014 RIDING-SILKS CUSTODIAN; 346.677-018 SECOND; 358.677-018 REST ROOM ATTENDANT

68032B COSTUMERS AND WARDROBE SPECIALISTS. OOH Title/s: Apparel Workers

Select, fit, and maintain costumes and wardrobes for entertainers. Inventories stock to determine types and condition of costuming available, and selects costumes based on historical analysis and studies. Examines costume fit on cast member, and sketches or writes notes for alterations. Repairs, alters, cleans, presses, and refits costume prior to performance, and cleans and stores costume following performance. Analyzes or reviews analysis of script to determine locale of story, period, number of characters, and costumes required per character. Designs and constructs costume, or sends it to tailor for construction or major repairs and alterations. Studies books, pictures, and examples of period clothing to determine styles worn during specific period in history. Arranges or directs cast dresser to arrange costumes on clothing racks in sequence of appearance. Assists cast in donning costumes, or assigns cast dresser to assist specific cast members with costume changes. Purchases or rents costumes and other wardrobe accessories from vendor.

Yearly Earnings: $16,484

Education: Work experience in a related occupation

Knowledge: Design; Sociology and Anthropology; Fine Arts; History and Archeology

Abilities: Category Flexibility; Selective Attention; Arm-Hand Steadiness; Wrist-Finger Speed; Dynamic Flexibility; Gross Body Equilibrium; Visual Color Discrimination

Skills: None above average

General Work Activities: Thinking Creatively; Monitoring and Controlling Resources

Job Characteristics: Objective or Subjective Information; Job-Required Social Interaction; Provide a Service to Others

GOE Group/s: 01.06.02 Craft Arts: Arts and Crafts; 09.05.07 Attendant Services: General Wardrobe Services

CIP Program/s: 200301 Clothing, Apparel and Textile Workers and Managers, General; 200305 Custom Tailor

Related DOT Job/s: 346.261-010 COSTUMER; 346.361-010 WARDROBE SUPERVISOR

68035 PERSONAL AND HOME CARE AIDES. OOH Title/s: Homemaker-Home Health Aides

Perform a variety of tasks at places of residence. Duties include keeping house and advising families having problems with such things as nutrition, cleanliness, and household utilities. Exclude nursing aides and home health aides. Advises and assists family members in planning nutritious meals, purchasing and preparing foods, and utilizing commodities from surplus food programs. Explains fundamental hygiene principles. Evaluates needs of individuals served and plans for continuing services. Assists in training children. Prepares and maintains records of assistance rendered. Gives bedside care to incapacitated individuals and trains family members to provide bedside care. Assists client with dressing, undressing, and toilet activities. Assigns housekeeping duties according to children's capabilities. Assists parents in establishing good study habits for children. Obtains information for clients, for personal and business purposes. Drives motor vehicle to transport clients to specified locations. Types correspondence and reports.

Yearly Earnings: $13,416

Education: Short-term O-J-T

Knowledge: Clerical; Customer and Personal Service; Food Production; Psychology; Sociology and Anthropology; Medicine and Dentistry; Therapy and Counseling; Education and Training; Transportation

Abilities: None above average

Skills: Learning Strategies; Social Perceptiveness; Persuasion; Negotiation; Service Orientation; Time Management; Management of Financial Resources

General Work Activities: Interacting with Computers; Establishing and Maintaining Relationships; Assisting and Caring for Others; Selling or Influencing Others; Teaching Others; Coaching and Developing Others

Job Characteristics: Objective or Subjective Information; Job-Required Social Interaction; Provide a Service to Others; Coordinate or Lead Others; Responsible for Others' Health and Safety; Deal with Unpleasant or Angry People; Diseases/Infections; Walking or Running

GOE Group/s: 10.03.03 Child and Adult Care: Care of Others; 11.02.03 Educational and Library Services: Teaching, Home Economics, Agriculture

CIP Program/s: 200201 Child Care and Guidance Workers and Managers, General; 200202 Child Care Provider/Assistant; 200601 Custodial, Housekeeping and Home Services Workers and Managers; 200602 Elder Care Provider/Companion; 200606 Homemaker's Aide

Related DOT Job/s: 309.354-010 HOMEMAKER; 359.573-010 BLIND AIDE

68038 CHILD CARE WORKERS. OOH Title/s: Preschool Teachers and Child-Care Workers

Attend to children at schools, businesses, and institutions. Perform variety of tasks, such as dressing, feeding, bathing, and overseeing play. Exclude preschool teachers and teacher aides. Cares for children in institutional setting, such as group homes, nursery schools, private businesses, or schools for the handicapped. Organizes and participates in recreational activities, such as games. Disciplines children and recommends or initiates other measures to control behavior, such as caring for own clothing and picking up toys and books. Places or hoists children into baths or pools. Instructs children regarding desirable health and personal habits, such as eating, resting, and toilet habits. Assists in preparing food for children, serves meals and refreshments to children, and regulates rest periods. Reads to children, and teaches them simple painting, drawing, handwork, and songs. Wheels handicapped children to classes or other areas of facility, secure in equipment, such as chairs and slings. Monitors children on life-support equipment to detect malfunctioning of equipment and calls for medical assistance when needed.

Yearly Earnings: $12,844

Education: Short-term O-J-T

Knowledge: Customer and Personal Service; Psychology; Therapy and Counseling

Abilities: Time Sharing; Sound Localization

Skills: Service Orientation

General Work Activities: Performing General Physical Activities; Establishing and Maintaining Relationships; Assisting and Caring for Others

Job Characteristics: Objective or Subjective Information; Job-Required Social Interaction; Provide a Service to Others; Deal with External Customers; Responsible for Others' Health and Safety; Deal with Unpleasant or Angry People; Deal with Physical, Aggressive People; Diseases/Infections

GOE Group/s: 10.03.03 Child and Adult Care: Care of Others

CIP Program/s: 200201 Child Care and Guidance Workers and Managers, General; 200202 Child Care Provider/Assistant

Related DOT Job/s: 355.674-010 CHILD-CARE ATTENDANT, SCHOOL; 359.677-010 ATTENDANT, CHILDREN'S INSTITUTION; 359.677-018 NURSERY SCHOOL ATTENDANT; 359.677-026 PLAYROOM ATTENDANT

68041 FUNERAL ATTENDANTS. OOH Title/s: Personal and Building Service Occupations

Perform variety of tasks during funeral, such as placing casket in parlor or chapel prior to service, arranging floral offerings or lights around casket, directing or escorting mourners, closing casket, and issuing and storing funeral equipment. Places casket in parlor or chapel prior to wake or funeral. Arranges floral offerings or lights around casket. Directs or escorts mourners to parlor or chapel in which wake or funeral is being held. Assists in closing casket. Issues and stores funeral equipment. Carries flowers to hearse or limousine for transportation to place of interment. Assists mourners in and out of limousines. Assists in carrying casket.

Yearly Earnings: $18,720

Education: Work experience in a related occupation

Knowledge: Customer and Personal Service; Psychology; Sociology and Anthropology

Abilities: Static Strength; Gross Body Equilibrium

Skills: Social Perceptiveness; Service Orientation

General Work Activities: Assisting and Caring for Others

Job Characteristics: Provide a Service to Others; Deal with External Customers; Walking or Running

GOE Group/s: 09.01.04 Hospitality Services: Safety and Comfort Services

CIP Program/s: 000000 NO CIP ASSIGNED

Related DOT Job/s: 359.677-014 FUNERAL ATTENDANT; 359.687-010 PALLBEARER

69999A PASSENGER SERVICE REPRESENTATIVES. OOH Title/s: Personal and Building Service Occupations

Render specialized personal service such as assisting elderly persons, unaccompanied children, distinguished persons and other special passengers to facilitate movement of passengers through terminal and to create goodwill. Greets passengers and guests and answers questions concerning flight schedules, terminal facilities, seat selection, fares, travel itineraries, and accommodations. Directs or escorts passengers to lounge, departure gates, and other terminal facilities. Transports special passengers, such as unaccompanied children, injured persons, and elderly people, to boarding area, using electric cart. Contacts other stations to reserve special services for arriving passengers. Arranges for air and ground transportation. Assembles and forwards luggage to departing aircraft. Verifies passenger reservations. Admits members and guests to airline lounge, and serves refreshments, such as cocktails, coffee, and snacks, using serving tray. Provides first aid to ill or injured passengers and obtains medical help. Removes trash and dishes from lounge area.

Yearly Earnings: $18,720

Education: Work experience in a related occupation

Knowledge: Customer and Personal Service; Medicine and Dentistry; Foreign Language; Transportation

Abilities: Spatial Orientation; Gross Body Equilibrium; Auditory Attention; Sound Localization; Speech Recognition; Speech Clarity

Skills: Service Orientation

General Work Activities: Assisting and Caring for Others; Performing for or Working with Public

Job Characteristics: Job-Required Social Interaction; Provide a Service to Others; Deal with External Customers; Frequency in Conflict Situations; Deal with Unpleasant or Angry People; Walking or Running; Special Uniform; Importance of Being Aware of New Events

GOE Group/s: 09.01.03 Hospitality Services: Food Services; 09.01.04 Hospitality Services: Safety and Comfort Services

CIP Program/s: 000000 NO CIP ASSIGNED

Related DOT Job/s: 352.377-010 HOST/HOSTESS, GROUND; 352.677-014 RECEPTIONIST, AIRLINE LOUNGE; 359.677-022 PASSENGER SERVICE REPRESENTATIVE

69999B PERSONAL ATTENDANTS. OOH Title/s: Personal and Building Service Occupations

Perform a variety of personal services such as arranging for or providing valet services, issuing locker room supplies, or checking hats and coats for customers in club, restaurant, recreational facility, hotel, or other hospitality establishment. Explains nature and cost of services and facilities available, demonstrates use of equipment, and answers customer inquiries. Interviews, evaluates, and advises client to develop personal improvement plan, such as weight loss, using scales, measures, and recommended guidelines. Conducts body-conditioning therapy, such as steam or electric shock, using physical or visual stimuli. Assists customers in tub or steam room, bathes or massages them, using water, brush, mitt, sponge, and towel, to clean skin. Packs equipment and uniforms and attends to needs of individual athletes in clubhouse. Arranges, supervises, and provides valet services such as clothes pressing, shoe shining, sending and receiving mail, and car parking. Cleans and polishes footwear, using brush, sponge, cleaning fluid, polish, wax, liquid or sole dressing, and dauber. Schedules appointments for client sessions, registers guests, and assigns accommodations. Issues keys, athletic equipment, or supplies, such as soap, towels, and weight loss aids. Stores personal possessions for patrons, issues a claim check for articles stored, and returns articles on receipt of check. Assists persons in establishments such as apartments, hotels, or hospitals, by opening doors, carrying bags, and performing related services. Transports customers and baggage, using motor vehicle. Records and reviews client's activities to assure program is followed. Sells service-related products and collects fees for services, rent, products, or supplies. Secures boat to dock, using mooring lines, connects utility lines to boat, and pumps water from boat for patrons. Performs general cleaning and maintenance of facilities and equipment, using mop, broom, lawn mower, and other cleaning aids. Inspects building and grounds, and reports or removes unauthorized or undesirable persons.

Yearly Earnings: $18,720

Education: Work experience in a related occupation

Knowledge: Sales and Marketing; Customer and Personal Service; Transportation

Abilities: Gross Body Equilibrium; Night Vision; Glare Sensitivity; Auditory Attention; Speech Recognition

Skills: Social Perceptiveness; Service Orientation

General Work Activities: Assisting and Caring for Others; Performing for or Working with Public

Job Characteristics: Objective or Subjective Information; Job-Required Social Interaction; Persuade Someone to a Course of Action; Provide a Service to Others; Deal with External Customers; Deal with Unpleasant or Angry People; Standing; Walking or Running; Bending or Twisting the Body; Special Uniform

GOE Group/s: 09.05.01 Attendant Services: Physical Conditioning; 09.05.03 Attendant Services: Portering and Baggage Services; 09.05.04 Attendant Services: Doorkeeping Services; 09.05.07 Attendant Services: General Wardrobe Services

CIP Program/s: 120405 Massage; 190501 Foods and Nutrition Studies, General; 190503 Dietetics/Human Nutritional Services; 200401 Institutional Food Workers and Administrators, General; 200404 Dietician Assistant

Related DOT Job/s: 324.577-010 ROOM-SERVICE CLERK; 324.677-014 DOORKEEPER; 329.467-010 ATTENDANT, LODGING FACILITIES; 329.677-010 PORTER, MARINA; 334.374-010 MASSEUR/MASSEUSE; 334.677-010 RUBBER; 358.677-010 CHECKROOM ATTENDANT; 358.677-014 LOCKER-ROOM ATTENDANT; 359.367-014 WEIGHT-RE-

DUCTION SPECIALIST; 359.567-010 REDUCING-SALON ATTENDANT; 366.677-010 SHOE SHINER

69999D SOCIAL ESCORTS. OOH Title/s: Personal and Building Service Occupations

Attend functions as a social partner to enable accompanied individual to attend and engage in social functions requiring a partner, or to provide companionship while visiting public establishments. Accompanies persons to public establishments and social functions to provide companionship, partner, or protection. Suggests places of entertainment and arranges for transportation and tickets. Introduces unaccompanied persons to hosts or hostesses to distribute patrons among them. Explains procedure for engaging social partner to unaccompanied persons at establishment. Collects tickets or fees for time spent with person. Counts tickets collected from patrons and submits tickets to management at end of shift. Inspects clothing of hosts or hostesses to ensure clean, pleasing personal appearance.
Yearly Earnings: $18,720
Education: Work experience in a related occupation
Knowledge: Sales and Marketing; Customer and Personal Service
Abilities: Auditory Attention; Sound Localization; Speech Recognition
Skills: Active Listening; Social Perceptiveness; Service Orientation
General Work Activities: Establishing and Maintaining Relationships; Performing for or Working with Public
Job Characteristics: Objective or Subjective Information; Job-Required Social Interaction; Persuade Someone to a Course of Action; Provide a Service to Others; Deal with External Customers; Coordinate or Lead Others; Diseases/Infections; Walking or Running
GOE Group/s: 09.01.01 Hospitality Services: Social and Recreational Activities
CIP Program/s: 000000 NO CIP ASSIGNED
Related DOT Job/s: 349.667-010 HOST/HOSTESS, DANCE HALL; 349.667-014 HOST/HOSTESS, HEAD; 359.367-010 ESCORT

69999E ALL OTHER SERVICE WORKERS. OOH Title/s: Personal and Building Service Occupations

All other service workers not classified separately above.
Yearly Earnings: $18,720
Education: Work experience in a related occupation
GOE Group/s: 01.06.02 Craft Arts: Arts and Crafts; 01.07.01 Elemental Arts: Psychic Science; 02.04.02 Laboratory Technology: Life Sciences; 04.02.03 Security Services: Law and Order; 06.04.19 Elemental Work: Industrial: Equipment Operation, Assorted Materials Processing; 09.01.01 Hospitality Services: Social and Recreational Activities; 09.05.06 Attendant Services: Individualized Services
CIP Program/s: 000000 NO CIP ASSIGNED
Related DOT Job/s: 143.457-010 PHOTOGRAPHER; 159.207-010 ASTROLOGER; 159.647-018 PSYCHIC READER; 339.371-014 SCALP-TREATMENT OPERATOR; 339.571-010 TATTOO ARTIST; 346.374-010 COSTUMER ASSISTANT; 346.674-010 DRESSER; 352.667-014 PARLOR CHAPERONE; 355.687-014 GRAVES REGISTRATION SPECIALIST; 359.667-010 CHAPERON; 359.677-030 RESEARCH SUBJECT; 359.685-010 CREMATOR

Section 7
Agricultural, Forestry, and Fishing Workers

Agriculture, Forestry, and Fishing Supervisors

72002A AGRICULTURAL CROP SUPERVISORS. OOH Title/s: Supervisors, Farming, Forestry, and Agricultural-Related Occupations

Supervise and coordinate the activities of agricultural workers engaged in planting, maintaining, and harvesting crops. Assigns duties—such as tilling soil; planting, irrigating, and storing crops; and maintaining machines—and assigns fields or rows to workers. Determines number and kind of workers needed to perform required work, and schedules activities. Observes workers to detect inefficient and unsafe work procedures or identify problems, and initiates actions to correct improper procedure or solve problem. Inspects crops and fields to determine maturity, yield, infestation, or work requirements, such as cultivating, spraying, weeding, or harvesting. Issues farm implements and machinery, ladders, or containers to workers and collects them at end of workday. Recruits, hires, and discharges workers. Investigates grievances and settles disputes to maintain harmony among workers. Contracts with seasonal workers and farmers to provide employment, and arranges for transportation, equipment, and living quarters. Trains workers in methods of field work and safety regulations, and briefs them on identifying characteristic of insects and diseases. Directs or assists in adjustment, repair, and maintenance of farm machinery and equipment. Prepares time, payroll, and production reports, such as farm conditions, amount of yield, machinery breakdowns, and labor problems. Confers with manager to evaluate weather and soil conditions and to develop and revise plans and procedures. Requisitions and purchases farm supplies, such as insecticides, machine parts or lubricants, and tools. Drives and operates farm machinery, such as trucks, tractors, or self-propelled harvesters, to transport workers or to cultivate and harvest fields. Opens gate to permit entry of water into ditches or pipes, and signals worker to start flow of water to irrigate fields.

Yearly Earnings: $16,640

Education: Work experience, plus degree

Knowledge: Administration and Management; Personnel and Human Resources; Food Production; Chemistry; Biology; Education and Training; Transportation

Abilities: Control Precision; Multilimb Coordination

Skills: Speaking; Coordination; Negotiation; Instructing; Implementation Planning; Equipment Selection; Product Inspection; Equipment Maintenance; Repairing; Time Management; Management of Financial Resources; Management of Material Resources; Management of Personnel Resources

General Work Activities: Scheduling Work and Activities; Interacting with Computers; Repairing and Maintaining Mechanical Equipment; Resolving Conflicts, Negotiating with Others; Coordinating Work and Activities of Others; Developing and Building Teams; Guiding, Directing and Motivating Subordinates; Staffing Organizational Units

Job Characteristics: Job-Required Social Interaction; Supervise, Coach, Train Others; Coordinate or Lead Others; Responsibility for Outcomes and Results; Frequency in Conflict Situations; Hazardous Equipment; Standing; Frustrating Circumstances

GOE Group/s: 03.01.01 Managerial Work: Plants and Animals: Farming; 03.02.01 General Supervision: Plants and Animals: Farming; 03.02.04 General Supervision: Plants and Animals: Services; 03.04.01 Elemental Work: Plants and Animals: Farming; 03.04.05 Elemental Work: Plants and Animals: Services; 05.12.01 Elemental Work: Mechanical: Supervision

CIP Program/s: 010299 Agricultural Mechanization, Other; 010301 Agricultural Production Workers and Managers, General; 010302 Agricultural Animal Husbandry and Production Management; 010304 Crop Production Operations and Management; 010501 Agricultural Supplies Retailing and Wholesaling; 020401 Plant Sciences, General; 020403 Horticulture Science; 020408 Plant Protection (Pest Management)

Related DOT Job/s: 180.167-014 FIELD SUPERVISOR, SEED PRODUCTION; 180.167-022 GROUP LEADER; 180.167-050 MIGRANT LEADER; 401.137-010 SUPERVISOR, AREA; 401.137-014 SUPERVISOR, DETASSELING CREW; 402.131-010 SUPERVISOR, VEGETABLE FARMING; 403.131-010 SUPERVISOR, TREE-FRUIT-AND-NUT FARMING; 403.131-014 SUPERVISOR, VINE-FRUIT FARMING; 404.131-010 SUPERVISOR, FIELD-CROP FARMING; 404.131-014 SUPERVISOR, SHED WORKERS; 407.131-010 SUPERVISOR, DIVERSIFIED CROPS; 408.137-010 SUPERVISOR, INSECT AND DISEASE INSPECTION; 409.117-010 HARVEST CONTRACTOR; 409.131-010 SUPERVISOR, PICKING CREW; 409.137-010 IRRIGATOR, HEAD; 409.137-014 ROW BOSS, HOEING; 929.137-034 YARD SUPERVISOR, COTTON GIN

72002B LIVESTOCK SUPERVISORS. OOH Title/s: Supervisors, Farming, Forestry, and Agricultural-Related Occupations

Supervise and coordinate the activities of workers engaged in animal husbandry. Assigns workers to tasks, such as feeding and treating animals, cleaning quarters, transferring animals, and maintaining facilities. Oversees animal care, maintenance, breeding, or packing and transfer activities to ensure work is done correctly and to identify and solve problems. Plans and prepares work schedules. Studies feed, weight, health, genetic, or milk production records to determine feed formula and rations or breeding schedule. Recruits, hires, and pays workers. Confers with manager to discuss and ascertain production requirements, condition of equipment and supplies, and work schedules. Inspects buildings, fences, fields or range, supplies, and equipment to determine work to be done. Observes animals, such as cattle, sheep, poultry, or game animals, for signs of illness, injury, nervousness, or unnatural behavior. Notifies veterinarian and manager of serious illnesses or injuries to animals. Trains workers in animal care, artificial insemination techniques, egg candling and sorting, and transfer of animals. Prepares animal condition, production, feed consumption, and worker attendance reports. Requisitions equipment, materials, and supplies. Transports or arranges for transport of animals, equipment, food, animal feed, and other supplies to and from worksite. Inseminates livestock artificially to produce desired offspring and to demonstrate techniques to farmers. Treats animal illness or injury, following experience or instructions of veterinarian. Monitors eggs and adjusts incubator thermometer and gauges, to ascertain hatching progress and maintain specified conditions.

Yearly Earnings: $16,640

Education: Work experience, plus degree

Knowledge: Administration and Management; Personnel and Human Resources; Production and Processing; Food Production; Biology; Medicine and Dentistry; Transportation

Abilities: Problem Sensitivity; Information Ordering; Category Flexibility; Memorization; Flexibility of Closure; Perceptual Speed; Spatial Orientation; Time Sharing; Dynamic Strength; Dynamic Flexibility; Gross Body Coordination; Gross Body Equilibrium; Peripheral Vision

Skills: Social Perceptiveness; Coordination; Persuasion; Instructing; Implementation Planning; Equipment Selection; Troubleshooting; Identifying Downstream Consequences; Systems Evaluation; Time Management; Management of Financial Resources; Management of Material Resources; Management of Personnel Resources

General Work Activities: Scheduling Work and Activities; Coordinating Work and Activities of Others; Teaching Others; Guiding, Directing and Motivating Subordinates; Staffing Organizational Units
Job Characteristics: Supervise, Coach, Train Others; Take a Position Opposed to Others; Coordinate or Lead Others; Responsible for Others' Health and Safety; Responsibility for Outcomes and Results; Frequency in Conflict Situations; Sounds, Noise Levels are Distracting, etc.; Very Hot; Extremely Bright or Inadequate Lighting; Contaminants; Cramped Work Space, Awkward Positions; Diseases/Infections; Walking or Running; Keeping or Regaining Balance; Frustrating Circumstances; Importance of Being Sure All is Done; Importance of Being Aware of New Events
GOE Group/s: 03.01.01 Managerial Work: Plants and Animals: Farming; 03.02.01 General Supervision: Plants and Animals: Farming; 03.02.04 General Supervision: Plants and Animals: Services; 03.04.01 Elemental Work: Plants and Animals: Farming
CIP Program/s: 010301 Agricultural Production Workers and Managers, General; 010302 Agricultural Animal Husbandry and Production Management; 010501 Agricultural Supplies Retailing and Wholesaling; 010507 Equestrian/Equine Studies, Horse Management and Training; 020201 Animal Sciences, General; 020206 Dairy Science; 020401 Plant Sciences, General; 020409 Range Science and Management
Related DOT Job/s: 410.131-010 BARN BOSS; 410.131-014 SUPERVISOR, ARTIFICIAL BREEDING RANCH; 410.131-018 SUPERVISOR, DAIRY FARM; 410.131-022 SUPERVISOR, STOCK RANCH; 410.134-010 SUPERVISOR, LIVESTOCK-YARD; 410.134-014 SUPERVISOR, WOOL-SHEARING; 410.134-022 SUPERVISOR, RESEARCH DAIRY FARM; 410.137-010 CAMP TENDER; 410.137-014 TOP SCREW; 411.131-010 SUPERVISOR, POULTRY FARM; 411.137-010 SUPERVISOR, POULTRY HATCHERY; 412.131-010 SUPERVISOR, GAME FARM

72002C ANIMAL CARE SUPERVISORS, EXCEPT LIVESTOCK. OOH Title/s: Supervisors, Farming, Forestry, and Agricultural-Related Occupations

Supervise and coordinate the activities of workers engaged in providing care to animals in kennels, zoos, research facilities, or other nonagricultural establishments. Assigns workers to tasks, such as feeding and treatment of animals and cleaning and maintenance of animal quarters. Establishes work schedule and procedures of animal care. Monitors animal care, inspects facilities to identify problems, and discusses solutions with workers. Trains workers in animal care procedures, maintenance duties, and safety precautions. Directs and assists workers in maintenance and repair of facilities. Plans budget and arranges for purchase of animals, feed, or supplies. Observes and examines animals to detect signs of illness and determine need of services from veterinarian. Prepares reports concerning activity of facility, employees' time records, and animal treatment. Investigates complaints of animal neglect or cruelty, and follows up on complaints appearing to justify prosecution. Operates euthanasia equipment to destroy animals. Delivers lectures to public to stimulate interest in animals and to communicate humane philosophy to public.
Yearly Earnings: $16,640
Education: Work experience, plus degree
Knowledge: Administration and Management; Economics and Accounting; Personnel and Human Resources; Biology; Medicine and Dentistry; Education and Training
Abilities: Problem Sensitivity; Speed of Closure; Manual Dexterity; Gross Body Coordination; Gross Body Equilibrium; Peripheral Vision
Skills: Writing; Speaking; Coordination; Negotiation; Instructing; Service Orientation; Implementation Planning; Systems Perception; Identification of Key Causes; Systems Evaluation; Time Management; Management of Financial Resources; Management of Material Resources; Management of Personnel Resources
General Work Activities: Scheduling Work and Activities; Assisting and Caring for Others; Resolving Conflicts, Negotiating with Others; Performing for or Working with Public; Coordinating Work and Activities of Others; Teaching Others; Guiding, Directing and Motivating Subordinates; Coaching and Developing Others; Monitoring and Controlling Resources
Job Characteristics: Job-Required Social Interaction; Supervise, Coach, Train Others; Persuade Someone to a Course of Action; Take a Position Opposed to Others; Coordinate or Lead Others; Responsible for Others' Health and Safety; Responsibility for Outcomes and Results; Frequency in Conflict Situations; Deal with Unpleasant or Angry People; Diseases/Infections; Hazardous Conditions; Hazardous Situations; Kneeling, Crouching, or Crawling; Importance of Being Aware of New Events
GOE Group/s: 02.04.02 Laboratory Technology: Life Sciences; 03.02.01 General Supervision: Plants and Animals: Farming; 03.02.04 General Supervision: Plants and Animals: Services; 03.03.02 Animal Training and Service: Animal Service
CIP Program/s: 010301 Agricultural Production Workers and Managers, General; 010302 Agricultural Animal Husbandry and Production Management; 020201 Animal Sciences, General; 020204 Agricultural Animal Nutrition
Related DOT Job/s: 180.167-038 MANAGER, GAME PRESERVE; 187.167-218 MANAGER, ANIMAL SHELTER; 410.134-018 SUPERVISOR, KENNEL; 410.137-018 SUPERVISOR, ANIMAL MAINTENANCE; 412.137-010 ANIMAL KEEPER, HEAD; 418.137-010 SUPERVISOR, LABORATORY ANIMAL FACILITY; 418.137-014 SUPERVISOR, RESEARCH KENNEL

72002D LANDSCAPE SUPERVISORS. OOH Title/s: Supervisors, Farming, Forestry, and Agricultural-Related Occupations

Supervise and coordinate the activities of landscape workers. Directs workers in maintenance and repair of driveways, walkways, benches, graves, and mausoleums. Observes ongoing work to ascertain if work is being performed according to instructions and will be completed on time. Determines work priority and crew and equipment requirements, and assigns workers tasks, such as planting, fertilizing, irrigating, and mowing. Directs and assists workers engaged in maintenance and repair of equipment such as power mower and backhoe, using hand tools and power tools. Mixes and prepares spray and dust solutions, and directs application of fertilizer, insecticide, and fungicide. Confers with manager to develop plans and schedules for maintenance and improvement of grounds. Trains workers in tasks, such as transplanting and pruning trees and shrubs, finishing cement, using equipment, and caring for turf. Keeps employee time records and records daily work performed. Tours grounds, such as park, botanical garden, cemetery, or golf course, to inspect conditions. Assists workers in performing work when completion is critical. Interviews, hires, and discharges workers.
Yearly Earnings: $16,640
Education: Work experience, plus degree
Knowledge: Administration and Management; Personnel and Human Resources; Chemistry; Biology; Education and Training
Abilities: Information Ordering; Spatial Orientation; Time Sharing; Static Strength; Gross Body Coordination; Gross Body Equilibrium; Visual Color Discrimination
Skills: Coordination; Instructing; Implementation Planning; Systems Perception; Systems Evaluation; Time Management; Management of Material Resources; Management of Personnel Resources
General Work Activities: Scheduling Work and Activities; Interacting with Computers; Coordinating Work and Activities of Others; Guiding, Directing and Motivating Subordinates; Staffing Organizational Units

Job Characteristics: Objective or Subjective Information; Job-Required Social Interaction; Supervise, Coach, Train Others; Take a Position Opposed to Others; Coordinate or Lead Others; Responsibility for Outcomes and Results; Very Hot; Extremely Bright or Inadequate Lighting; Contaminants; Radiation; Hazardous Situations; Standing; Walking or Running
GOE Group/s: 03.01.03 Managerial Work: Plants and Animals: Specialty Cropping; 03.02.03 General Supervision: Plants and Animals: Nursery and Groundskeeping; 03.04.04 Elemental Work: Plants and Animals: Nursery and Groundskeeping; 03.04.05 Elemental Work: Plants and Animals: Services
CIP Program/s: 010601 Horticulture Services Operations and Management, General; 010603 Ornamental Horticulture Operations and Management; 010605 Landscaping Operations and Management; 010607 Turf Management; 010699 Horticulture Services Operations and Management, Other
Related DOT Job/s: 406.134-010 SUPERVISOR, CEMETERY WORKERS; 406.134-014 SUPERVISOR, LANDSCAPE; 406.137-010 GREENSKEEPER I; 406.137-014 SUPERINTENDENT, GREENS; 408.137-014 SUPERVISOR, TREE-TRIMMING

72002E HORTICULTURAL SUPERVISORS. OOH Title/s: Supervisors, Farming, Forestry, and Agricultural-Related Occupations

Supervise and coordinate the activities of horticultural workers. Assigns workers to duties, such as cultivation, harvesting, maintenance, grading and packing products, or altering greenhouse environmental conditions. Reviews employees' work to ascertain quality and quantity of work performed. Estimates work-hour requirements to plant, cultivate, or harvest, and prepares work schedule. Reads inventory records, customer orders, and shipping schedules to ascertain day's activities. Confers with management to report conditions, to plan planting and harvesting schedules, and to discuss changes in fertilizer, herbicides, or cultivating techniques. Observes plants, flowers, shrubs, and trees in greenhouses, cold frames, or fields to ascertain condition. Inspects facilities to determine maintenance needs, such as malfunctioning environmental-control system, clogged sprinklers, or missing glass panes in greenhouse. Trains employees in horticultural techniques, such as transplanting and weeding, shearing and harvesting trees, and grading and packing flowers. Prepares and submits written or oral reports of personnel actions, such as performance evaluations, hires, promotions, and discipline. Maintains records of employees' hours worked and work completed. Drives and operates heavy machinery, such as dump truck, tractor, or growth-media tiller, to transport materials and supplies.
Yearly Earnings: $16,640
Education: Work experience, plus degree
Knowledge: Administration and Management; Clerical; Personnel and Human Resources; Food Production; Chemistry; Biology
Abilities: Control Precision; Multilimb Coordination; Glare Sensitivity
Skills: Learning Strategies; Coordination; Persuasion; Instructing; Implementation Planning; Troubleshooting; Time Management; Management of Material Resources; Management of Personnel Resources
General Work Activities: Scheduling Work and Activities; Interacting with Computers; Coordinating Work and Activities of Others; Teaching Others; Guiding, Directing and Motivating Subordinates; Coaching and Developing Others; Performing Administrative Activities; Staffing Organizational Units
Job Characteristics: Objective or Subjective Information; Job-Required Social Interaction; Supervise, Coach, Train Others; Take a Position Opposed to Others; Coordinate or Lead Others; Responsibility for Outcomes and Results; Very Hot; Extremely Bright or Inadequate Lighting; Radiation
GOE Group/s: 03.02.01 General Supervision: Plants and Animals: Farming; 03.02.02 General Supervision: Plants and Animals: Forestry and Logging; 03.02.03 General Supervision: Plants and Animals: Nursery and Groundskeeping; 03.04.04 Elemental Work: Plants and Animals: Nursery and Groundskeeping
CIP Program/s: 010301 Agricultural Production Workers and Managers, General; 010304 Crop Production Operations and Management; 010601 Horticulture Services Operations and Management, General; 010603 Ornamental Horticulture Operations and Management; 010604 Greenhouse Operations and Management; 010606 Nursery Operations and Management; 020401 Plant Sciences, General; 020403 Horticulture Science; 030401 Forest Harvesting and Production Technologists and Technicians
Related DOT Job/s: 405.131-010 SUPERVISOR, HORTICULTURAL-SPECIALTY FARMING; 405.137-010 SUPERVISOR, ROSE-GRADING; 451.137-010 FOREST NURSERY SUPERVISOR; 451.137-014 SUPERVISOR, CHRISTMAS-TREE FARM

72002F LOGGING SUPERVISORS. OOH Title/s: Supervisors, Farming, Forestry, and Agricultural-Related Occupations; Industrial Production Managers

Supervise and coordinate the activities of logging workers. Plans and schedules logging operations, such as felling and bucking trees, grading and sorting logs, and yarding and loading logs. Assigns workers to duties, such as trees to be cut, cutting sequence and specifications, and loading of trucks, railcars, or rafts. Oversees logging operations to identify and solve problems and to ensure that safety and company regulations are being followed. Coordinates dismantling, moving, and setting up equipment at new worksite. Determines methods for logging operations, size of crew, and equipment requirements. Coordinates selection and movement of logs from storage areas, according to transportation schedules or production requirements of wood products plant. Changes logging operations or methods to eliminate unsafe conditions, and warns or disciplines workers disregarding safety regulations. Confers with mill, company, and government forestry officials to determine safest and most efficient method of logging tract. Trains workers in felling and bucking trees, operating tractors and loading machines, yarding and loading techniques, and safety regulations. Prepares production and personnel time records for management.
Yearly Earnings: $16,640
Education: Work experience, plus degree
Knowledge: Administration and Management; Personnel and Human Resources; Production and Processing; Education and Training; Public Safety and Security; Transportation
Abilities: Originality; Spatial Orientation; Time Sharing; Multilimb Coordination; Response Orientation; Rate Control; Speed of Limb Movement; Static Strength; Explosive Strength; Dynamic Strength; Stamina; Dynamic Flexibility; Gross Body Coordination; Gross Body Equilibrium; Far Vision; Depth Perception; Glare Sensitivity; Auditory Attention; Sound Localization
Skills: Social Perceptiveness; Coordination; Persuasion; Negotiation; Instructing; Problem Identification; Implementation Planning; Equipment Selection; Operation and Control; Troubleshooting; Systems Perception; Identifying Downstream Consequences; Identification of Key Causes; Systems Evaluation; Time Management; Management of Material Resources; Management of Personnel Resources
General Work Activities: Developing Objectives and Strategies; Scheduling Work and Activities; Performing General Physical Activities; Interacting with Computers; Coordinating Work and Activities of Others; Guiding, Directing and Motivating Subordinates; Coaching and Developing Others
Job Characteristics: Job-Required Social Interaction; Supervise, Coach, Train Others; Take a Position Opposed to Others; Coordinate or Lead Others; Responsible for Others' Health and Safety; Responsi-

bility for Outcomes and Results; Sounds, Noise Levels are Distracting, etc.; Very Hot; Extremely Bright or Inadequate Lighting; Whole Body Vibration; Radiation; High Places; Hazardous Equipment; Hazardous Situations; Standing; Climbing Ladders, Scaffolds, Poles, etc.; Walking or Running; Keeping or Regaining Balance; Common Protective or Safety Attire
GOE Group/s: 03.02.02 General Supervision: Plants and Animals: Forestry and Logging; 03.04.02 Elemental Work: Plants and Animals: Forestry and Logging; 05.12.04 Elemental Work: Mechanical: Hoisting, Conveying
CIP Program/s: 000000 NO CIP ASSIGNED
Related DOT Job/s: 183.167-038 SUPERINTENDENT, LOGGING; 454.134-010 SUPERVISOR, FELLING-BUCKING; 455.134-010 SUPERVISOR, LOG SORTING; 459.133-010 SUPERVISOR, LOGGING; 459.137-010 WOODS BOSS; 921.131-010 HOOK TENDER

72002G FISHERY SUPERVISORS. OOH Title/s: Supervisors, Farming, Forestry, and Agricultural-Related Occupations
Supervise and coordinate activities of workers engaged in spawning fish or cultivating shellfish. Assigns workers to duties, such as fertilizing and incubating spawn, feeding and transferring fish, and planting, cultivating, and harvesting shellfish beds. Oversees worker activities, such as treatment and rearing of fingerlings, maintenance of equipment, and harvesting of fish or shellfish. Directs workers to correct deviations or problems, such as disease, quality of seed distribution, or adequacy of cultivation. Plans work schedules according to availability of personnel and equipment, tidal levels, feeding schedules, or need for transfer or harvest. Trains workers in spawning, rearing, cultivating, and harvesting methods, and use of equipment. Observes fish and beds or ponds to detect diseases, determine quality of fish, or determine completeness of harvesting. Confers with manager to determine time and place of seed planting, and cultivating, feeding, or harvesting of fish or shellfish. Records number and type of fish or shellfish reared and harvested, and keeps workers' time records.
Yearly Earnings: $16,640
Education: Work experience, plus degree
Knowledge: Administration and Management; Personnel and Human Resources; Production and Processing; Food Production; Biology
Abilities: Deductive Reasoning; Category Flexibility; Speed of Closure; Flexibility of Closure; Perceptual Speed; Time Sharing; Wrist-Finger Speed; Gross Body Equilibrium; Far Vision; Depth Perception; Glare Sensitivity
Skills: Instructing; Implementation Planning; Time Management; Management of Material Resources; Management of Personnel Resources
General Work Activities: Scheduling Work and Activities; Coordinating Work and Activities of Others; Teaching Others; Coaching and Developing Others
Job Characteristics: Job-Required Social Interaction; Supervise, Coach, Train Others; Persuade Someone to a Course of Action; Take a Position Opposed to Others; Coordinate or Lead Others; Responsible for Others' Health and Safety; Responsibility for Outcomes and Results; Extremely Bright or Inadequate Lighting; Diseases/Infections; Walking or Running; Frustrating Circumstances; Importance of Being Aware of New Events
GOE Group/s: 03.02.01 General Supervision: Plants and Animals: Farming
CIP Program/s: 010301 Agricultural Production Workers and Managers, General; 010303 Aquaculture Operations and Production Management; 030301 Fishing and Fisheries Sciences and Management
Related DOT Job/s: 446.133-010 SUPERVISOR, SHELLFISH FARMING; 446.134-010 SUPERVISOR, FISH HATCHERY

Timber Cutting and Related Logging Workers

73002 FALLERS AND BUCKERS. OOH Title/s: Forestry and Logging Workers
Fell trees and saw into specified log lengths, working alone or as members of a team. Scores cutting lines with ax, saws undercut along scored lines with chainsaw, and knocks slabs from cuts with ax. Saws back-cuts, leaving sufficient sound wood to control direction of fall. Inserts jacks or drives wedge behind saw to prevent binding of saw and start tree falling. Cuts limbs from felled trees, using chainsaw or ax. Cuts felled trees into log lengths, using chainsaw and ax. Determines position, direction, and depth of cuts to be made, and placement of wedges or jacks. Stops saw engine as tree falls, pulls cutting bar from cut, and runs to safe location to avoid injury. Measures and marks felled trees for cutting into log lengths. Splits logs, using ax, wedges, and maul, and stacks wood in rick or cord lots. Places supporting limbs or poles under felled tree to avoid splitting underside and to prevent log from rolling. Clears brush from work area and escape route, and cuts sapling and other trees from direction of fall, using ax and chainsaw. Appraises tree for characteristics, such as twist, rot, and heavy limb growth, and gauges amount and direction of lean. Secures cables to logs, and drives tractor to drag logs to landing. Loads logs or wood onto trucks, by hand or using winch. Tags unsafe trees with high-visibility ribbon.
Yearly Earnings: $19,812
Education: Short-term O-J-T
Knowledge: Public Safety and Security
Abilities: Spatial Orientation; Time Sharing; Arm-Hand Steadiness; Control Precision; Multilimb Coordination; Response Orientation; Rate Control; Reaction Time; Wrist-Finger Speed; Speed of Limb Movement; Static Strength; Explosive Strength; Dynamic Strength; Trunk Strength; Stamina; Extent Flexibility; Dynamic Flexibility; Gross Body Coordination; Gross Body Equilibrium; Far Vision; Peripheral Vision; Depth Perception; Sound Localization
Skills: None above average
General Work Activities: Performing General Physical Activities; Handling and Moving Objects; Interacting with Computers
Job Characteristics: Responsible for Others' Health and Safety; Sounds, Noise Levels are Distracting, etc.; Very Hot; Extremely Bright or Inadequate Lighting; Cramped Work Space, Awkward Positions; Whole Body Vibration; Radiation; High Places; Hazardous Equipment; Hazardous Situations; Standing; Climbing Ladders, Scaffolds, Poles, etc.; Walking or Running; Keeping or Regaining Balance; Making Repetitive Motions; Specialized Protective or Safety Attire; Importance of Being Aware of New Events; Importance of Repeating Same Tasks
GOE Group/s: 03.04.02 Elemental Work: Plants and Animals: Forestry and Logging
CIP Program/s: 030405 Logging/Timber Harvesting
Related DOT Job/s: 454.384-010 FALLER I; 454.684-010 BUCKER; 454.684-014 FALLER II; 454.684-018 LOGGER, ALL-ROUND; 454.684-026 TREE CUTTER; 454.687-010 CHAIN SAW OPERATOR

73005 CHOKE SETTERS. OOH Title/s: Forestry and Logging Workers
Fasten chokers around logs, preparing to yard them from felling and bucking area to storage or loading landing. Secures end of cable to bell (sliding fastener) to form noose. Pulls choker cables from tractor winch or mainline of yarding machine, passes ball (one end) under and around log. Assists rigging slinger in installing and disman-

tling rigging of high lead or similar yarding system. Clears brush and earth from under log, using ax and shovel.
Yearly Earnings: $19,812
Education: Short-term O-J-T
Knowledge: None above average
Abilities: Multilimb Coordination; Explosive Strength; Trunk Strength; Stamina; Extent Flexibility; Gross Body Coordination; Gross Body Equilibrium
Skills: None above average
General Work Activities: Performing General Physical Activities
Job Characteristics: Very Hot; Standing; Importance of Repeating Same Tasks
GOE Group/s: 05.12.04 Elemental Work: Mechanical: Hoisting, Conveying
CIP Program/s: 000000 NO CIP ASSIGNED
Related DOT Job/s: 921.687-014 CHOKE SETTER

73011 LOGGING TRACTOR OPERATORS. OOH Title/s: Forestry and Logging Workers

Drive tractor equipped with one or more accessories—such as bulldozer blade, frontal hydraulic shear, grapple, logging arch, cable winches, hoisting rack, or crane boom—to fell trees, to skid, load and unload, or stack logs; or to pull stumps or clear brush. Drives and maneuvers tractor and activates shear to cut and fell trees. Controls hydraulic tractor equipped with tree clamp and boom to lift, swing, and bunch sheared trees. Controls equipment to load, unload, or stack logs, pull stumps, and clear brush. Drives tractor to build or repair logging and skid roads. Saws felled trees into lengths. Gives or receives signals from coworkers to move logs.
Yearly Earnings: $22,100
Education: Short-term O-J-T
Knowledge: None above average
Abilities: Control Precision; Multilimb Coordination; Reaction Time; Trunk Strength; Gross Body Equilibrium; Peripheral Vision; Depth Perception
Skills: Operation and Control
General Work Activities: Performing General Physical Activities; Controlling Machines and Processes; Interacting with Computers
Job Characteristics: Whole Body Vibration; Hazardous Equipment; Sitting; Climbing Ladders, Scaffolds, Poles, etc.; Importance of Repeating Same Tasks
GOE Group/s: 03.04.02 Elemental Work: Plants and Animals: Forestry and Logging
CIP Program/s: 030405 Logging/Timber Harvesting
Related DOT Job/s: 454.683-010 TREE-SHEAR OPERATOR; 929.663-010 LOGGING-TRACTOR OPERATOR

73099A TREE, LOG, AND BRUSH CUTTERS. OOH Title/s: Forestry and Logging Workers

Trim trees and brush and split logs, using saws and axes. Removes branches interfering with communication or electric powerlines, using climbing equipment or bucket of extended truck boom. Prunes trees and trims jagged stumps, using saws or pruning shears. Rives (splits) logs or wooden blocks into bolts, pickets, posts, or stakes, using hand tools such as ax wedges, sledgehammer, and mallet. Fells trees and cuts limbs from felled trees, using portable power saw or ax. Removes broken limbs from wires, using hooked extension pole. Hoists tools and equipment to tree trimmer, and lowers branches with rope or block and tackle. Harvests tanbark by cutting rings and slits in bark and stripping bark from tree, using spud or ax. Piles up wood debris and brush or loads onto truck, using winch. Feeds brush into shredding or chipping machine.
Yearly Earnings: $19,812
Education: Short-term O-J-T
Knowledge: None above average
Abilities: Spatial Orientation; Manual Dexterity; Multilimb Coordination; Rate Control; Speed of Limb Movement; Static Strength; Explosive Strength; Dynamic Strength; Trunk Strength; Stamina; Extent Flexibility; Dynamic Flexibility; Gross Body Coordination; Gross Body Equilibrium; Peripheral Vision; Depth Perception
Skills: None above average
General Work Activities: Performing General Physical Activities; Handling and Moving Objects; Controlling Machines and Processes; Interacting with Computers
Job Characteristics: Sounds, Noise Levels are Distracting, etc.; Very Hot; Extremely Bright or Inadequate Lighting; Contaminants; Whole Body Vibration; Radiation; High Places; Hazardous Conditions; Hazardous Equipment; Standing; Climbing Ladders, Scaffolds, Poles, etc.; Kneeling, Crouching, or Crawling; Keeping or Regaining Balance; Using Hands on Objects, Tools, or Controls; Bending or Twisting the Body; Common Protective or Safety Attire; Specialized Protective or Safety Attire; Pace Determined by Speed of Equipment
GOE Group/s: 03.04.02 Elemental Work: Plants and Animals: Forestry and Logging; 03.04.05 Elemental Work: Plants and Animals: Services
CIP Program/s: 010699 Horticulture Services Operations and Management, Other; 030405 Logging/Timber Harvesting
Related DOT Job/s: 408.664-010 TREE TRIMMER; 408.667-010 TREE-TRIMMER HELPER; 454.684-022 RIVER; 454.687-014 LABORER, TANBARK; 459.687-010 LABORER, BRUSH CLEARING

73099B LOG SORTERS, MARKERS, MOVERS, AND DEBARKERS. OOH Title/s: Forestry and Logging Workers; Handlers, Equipment Cleaners, Helpers, and Laborers

Sort, mark, and move logs, based on species, size, and ownership, and tend machine that debarks logs. Starts conveyor and turns valves, controls, and levers to remove bark and dirt from logs. Sorts logs according to species, size, and owner's markings into designated storage areas, using pike pole. Marks logs in river or pond to designate ownership, cutting origin, species, or intended use, using branding hammer, spray can, or saw. Binds logs with chain or cable, and bores holes into side and cross poles to thread chain and assemble logs into rafts for towing to mill. Guides, rolls, or lifts logs or log blocks onto skids, conveyors, or log-haul chain for further processing. Measures and marks cutting locations on trees to obtain maximum yield of standard lengths. Loads and unloads logs from railroad cars and log trucks, using peavey, cant hook, or other loading equipment. Raises sunken logs, using hoist or powered winch. Secures tongs, slings, or other attachments to log loads. Selects seasoned logs, following specifications on work ticket, and examines wood for moisture content, using moisture gauge. Guides workers loading or moving logs, using hand signals. Positions railcars or connects trailer to trucks, using power winches and pinchbar, to prepare for loading logs. Trims protruding limbs and knots, using ax and chainsaw.
Yearly Earnings: $19,812
Education: Short-term O-J-T
Knowledge: Production and Processing; Mechanical; Transportation
Abilities: Spatial Orientation; Time Sharing; Manual Dexterity; Control Precision; Multilimb Coordination; Response Orientation; Rate Control; Speed of Limb Movement; Static Strength; Explosive Strength; Dynamic Strength; Trunk Strength; Stamina; Extent Flexibility; Dynamic Flexibility; Gross Body Coordination; Gross Body Equilibrium; Peripheral Vision
Skills: Operation and Control
General Work Activities: Performing General Physical Activities; Handling and Moving Objects; Controlling Machines and Processes; Interacting with Computers

Job Characteristics: Sounds, Noise Levels are Distracting, etc.; Very Hot; Extremely Bright or Inadequate Lighting; Contaminants; Whole Body Vibration; Hazardous Equipment; Standing; Walking or Running; Kneeling, Crouching, or Crawling; Using Hands on Objects, Tools, or Controls; Bending or Twisting the Body; Common Protective or Safety Attire
GOE Group/s: 03.04.02 Elemental Work: Plants and Animals: Forestry and Logging; 05.12.03 Elemental Work: Mechanical: Loading, Moving; 05.12.04 Elemental Work: Mechanical: Hoisting, Conveying; 06.04.03 Elemental Work: Industrial: Machine Work, Wood
CIP Program/s: 000000 NO CIP ASSIGNED
Related DOT Job/s: 454.687-018 LOG MARKER; 455.664-010 RAFTER; 455.684-010 LOG SORTER; 455.687-010 LOG MARKER; 669.485-010 POWER-BARKER OPERATOR; 669.687-022 PICKER; 921.686-018 LOG-HAUL CHAIN FEEDER; 921.686-022 POND WORKER; 921.687-022 LOG LOADER HELPER; 921.687-030 RIGGER, THIRD; 922.687-082 PULP PILER

73099C RIGGING SLINGERS AND CHASERS. OOH Title/s: Forestry and Logging Workers

Rig blocks and attach guy lines and choker cables to tree trunks, and signal yarding engineer or other logging equipment operators where to haul or drop logs. Issues directions to crew regarding logs to be yarded, positioning and securing of chokers, and position of crew during movement of logs. Signals others to control position of choker cables and placement of logs, or to inform others of fire, injuries, or other conditions. Leads workers in stalling, moving, and dismantling yarder rigging. Determines sequence of logs to be yarded, according to established guidelines. Attaches equipment, such as chokers, lines, blocks, and fire equipment, to outbound rigging, as indicated by whistle signals. Trains new workers in choker-setting techniques, safety practices, and whistle signals. Cuts knots and limbs from logs, using ax and chainsaw.
Yearly Earnings: $19,812
Education: Short-term O-J-T
Knowledge: None above average
Abilities: Spatial Orientation; Time Sharing; Manual Dexterity; Multilimb Coordination; Rate Control; Reaction Time; Speed of Limb Movement; Static Strength; Explosive Strength; Dynamic Strength; Trunk Strength; Stamina; Extent Flexibility; Dynamic Flexibility; Gross Body Coordination; Gross Body Equilibrium; Peripheral Vision; Depth Perception
Skills: None above average
General Work Activities: Performing General Physical Activities; Handling and Moving Objects; Controlling Machines and Processes; Coordinating Work and Activities of Others; Teaching Others; Guiding, Directing and Motivating Subordinates
Job Characteristics: Supervise, Coach, Train Others; Coordinate or Lead Others; Responsible for Others' Health and Safety; Responsibility for Outcomes and Results; Very Hot; Extremely Bright or Inadequate Lighting; Hazardous Equipment; Standing; Climbing Ladders, Scaffolds, Poles, etc.; Walking or Running; Keeping or Regaining Balance; Bending or Twisting the Body; Common Protective or Safety Attire; Importance of Being Aware of New Events; Pace Determined by Speed of Equipment
GOE Group/s: 05.12.04 Elemental Work: Mechanical: Hoisting, Conveying
CIP Program/s: 030405 Logging/Timber Harvesting
Related DOT Job/s: 921.364-010 RIGGING SLINGER; 921.667-014 CHASER

73099D CRUISERS. OOH Title/s: Forestry and Logging Workers

Estimate volume of marketable timber on forest land and collect data for appraisal, sales, administration, logging, land use, and forest management. Sights over scale stick to estimate height and diameter of each tree in sample. Estimates loss of marketable volume due to defects in each tree, such as rot and bends, and computes quantity of usable wood. Walks forest area in established pattern and applies sampling techniques. Prepares report of timber types, sizes, conditions, and outstanding features of area, such as roads, streams, lakes, and communication facilities. Marks trees with spray paint for cutting or to denote trails or boundaries.
Yearly Earnings: $19,812
Education: Short-term O-J-T
Knowledge: None above average
Abilities: Category Flexibility; Flexibility of Closure; Spatial Orientation; Stamina; Gross Body Coordination; Gross Body Equilibrium; Far Vision; Peripheral Vision; Depth Perception; Glare Sensitivity
Skills: None above average
General Work Activities: Monitoring Processes, Material, or Surroundings; Estimating Needed Characteristics; Judging Qualities of Things, Services, People; Evaluating Information against Standards; Performing General Physical Activities
Job Characteristics: Very Hot; Extremely Bright or Inadequate Lighting; Walking or Running
GOE Group/s: 03.02.02 General Supervision: Plants and Animals: Forestry and Logging
CIP Program/s: 030101 Natural Resources Conservation, General; 030404 Forest Products Technologists and Technicians
Related DOT Job/s: 459.387-010 CRUISER

73099E ALL OTHER TIMBER CUTTING AND RELATED LOGGING WORKERS. OOH Title/s: Forestry and Logging Workers

All other timber cutting and related logging workers not classified separately above.
Yearly Earnings: $19,812
Education: Short-term O-J-T
GOE Group/s: 03.04.02 Elemental Work: Plants and Animals: Forestry and Logging
CIP Program/s: 030405 Logging/Timber Harvesting
Related DOT Job/s: 929.663-010 LOGGING-TRACTOR OPERATOR

Plant and Animal Workers

79002A FOREST AND CONSERVATION WORKERS. OOH Title/s: Forestry and Logging Workers

Develop, maintain, and protect forest, forested areas, and woodlands through activities such as raising and transporting tree seedlings and combating insects, pests, and diseases harmful to trees. Plants, cultivates, and harvests trees and tree seedlings to reforest land. Sprays or injects trees, brush, and weeds with herbicides to combat insects, pests, and harmful diseases. Sorts and separates tree seedlings, discarding substandard seedlings, according to standard chart and verbal instructions. Identifies and cuts diseased, weak, and other undesirable trees to protect forested areas. Prunes or shears tree tops and limbs to control growth, increase density, and improve shape. Fells trees, clears brush from fire breaks, and extinguishes flames and embers to suppress fires. Selects and cuts trees according to markings or size, species, and grade. Examines and grades trees according to standard chart, and staples color-coded grade tags to limbs. Helps forest survey crews by clearing site-lines, holding measuring tools, and setting stakes. Clears and piles brush, limbs, and other debris from

roadside, fire trails, camping areas, and planting areas. Drags cut trees from cutting area and loads trees onto truck. Erects signs and fences, using posthole digger, shovel, or other hand tools. Maintains campsites and recreational areas, replenishing firewood and other supplies and cleaning kitchens and restrooms. Gathers, bundles or sacks, and delivers forest products to buyer. Cuts or bores tap in tree face to collect sugar and other tree saps.
Yearly Earnings: $19,812
Education: Short-term O-J-T
Knowledge: Food Production; Chemistry; Biology; Public Safety and Security
Abilities: Spatial Orientation; Speed of Limb Movement; Static Strength; Explosive Strength; Dynamic Strength; Trunk Strength; Stamina; Dynamic Flexibility; Gross Body Equilibrium
Skills: None above average
General Work Activities: Performing General Physical Activities; Handling and Moving Objects
Job Characteristics: Very Hot; Extremely Bright or Inadequate Lighting; Hazardous Situations; Standing; Walking or Running; Special Uniform; Common Protective or Safety Attire
GOE Group/s: 03.04.01 Elemental Work: Plants and Animals: Farming; 03.04.02 Elemental Work: Plants and Animals: Forestry and Logging; 03.04.04 Elemental Work: Plants and Animals: Nursery and Groundskeeping
CIP Program/s: 030401 Forest Harvesting and Production Technologists and Technicians
Related DOT Job/s: 451.687-010 CHRISTMAS-TREE FARM WORKER; 451.687-014 CHRISTMAS-TREE GRADER; 451.687-018 SEEDLING PULLER; 451.687-022 SEEDLING SORTER; 452.687-010 FOREST WORKER; 452.687-018 TREE PLANTER; 453.687-010 FOREST-PRODUCTS GATHERER; 453.687-014 LABORER, TREE TAPPING

79002B FORESTER AIDES. OOH Title/s: Forestry and Logging Workers

Compile data pertaining to size, content, condition, and other characteristics of forest tracts, and lead workers in forest propagation, fire prevention and suppression, and facilities maintenance. Gathers information on size, content, and condition of forest lands, including fire and harvest potential. Collects and records data from instruments, such as rain gauge, thermometer, and soil-moisture gauge. Selects and marks trees for thinning or logging according to specified species, condition, and size. Helps survey crews by measuring distances, recording data, and cleaning site-lines. Trains conservation workers to plant tree seedlings, suppress fires, clear fire breaks, and clean recreational areas. Informs visitors of camping, vehicle, fire, sanitation, and other regulations, and enforces regulations.
Yearly Earnings: $19,812
Education: Short-term O-J-T
Knowledge: Biology; Geography; Public Safety and Security
Abilities: Stamina
Skills: Instructing
General Work Activities: Coaching and Developing Others
Job Characteristics: Supervise, Coach, Train Others; Very Hot; Walking or Running; Special Uniform
GOE Group/s: 03.02.02 General Supervision: Plants and Animals: Forestry and Logging
CIP Program/s: 030101 Natural Resources Conservation, General; 030203 Natural Resources Law Enforcement and Protective Services; 030401 Forest Harvesting and Production Technologists and Technicians
Related DOT Job/s: 452.364-010 FORESTER AIDE

79005 NURSERY WORKERS. OOH Title/s: Nursery Workers

Work in nursery facilities or at customer locations planting, cultivating, harvesting, and transplanting trees, shrubs, or plants. Hauls and spreads topsoil, fertilizer, peat moss, and other materials to condition soil, using wheelbarrow or cart and shovel. Digs, rakes, and screens soil and fills cold frames and hot beds to prepare them for planting. Sows grass seed or plants plugs of grass and cuts, rolls, and stacks sod. Plants, sprays, weeds, and waters plants, shrubs, and trees, using hand tools and gardening tools. Cuts and opens incision in rootstock, using budding knife, and inserts and ties bud. Fills growing tanks with water. Inspects bud tie to ensure quality. Moves containerized shrubs, plants, and trees, using wheelbarrow. Traps and destroys pests, such as moles, gophers, and mice, using pesticides. Ties, bunches and wraps roots, and packs flowers, plants, shrubs, and trees to fill orders. Folds and staples corrugated forms to make boxes used for packing horticultural products. Dips rose cuttings into vat to disinfect prior to storage.
Yearly Earnings: $13,520
Education: Short-term O-J-T
Knowledge: None above average
Abilities: Flexibility of Closure; Speed of Limb Movement; Dynamic Strength; Trunk Strength; Stamina; Extent Flexibility; Dynamic Flexibility; Gross Body Equilibrium; Glare Sensitivity; Hearing Sensitivity
Skills: None above average
General Work Activities: Performing General Physical Activities
Job Characteristics: Very Hot; Hazardous Situations; Standing; Kneeling, Crouching, or Crawling; Keeping or Regaining Balance; Using Hands on Objects, Tools, or Controls; Bending or Twisting the Body; Common Protective or Safety Attire
GOE Group/s: 03.04.04 Elemental Work: Plants and Animals: Nursery and Groundskeeping
CIP Program/s: 000000 NO CIP ASSIGNED
Related DOT Job/s: 405.684-010 BUDDER; 405.687-014 HORTICULTURAL WORKER II

79008 LOG GRADERS AND SCALERS. OOH Title/s: Forestry and Logging Workers

Grade logs or estimate the marketable content or value of logs or pulpwood in sorting yard, millpond, log deck, or similar locations. Inspect logs for defects, or measure logs to determine volume. Exclude log inspectors who are primarily buyers. Estimates and calculates total volume, waste volume, and marketable volume of log, using measurements and conversion table, and records results. Measures wood to determine dimensions or quantity, using measuring device and conversion table. Jabs log with scale stick and inspects log for defects and to ascertain characteristics. Evaluates log's characteristics and determines grade, using established criteria. Paints mark on log to identify grade and species, or calls out grade. Weighs log trucks before and after unloading, and records weight and identity of supplier. Tends conveyor chain to move logs to and from scaling station.
Yearly Earnings: $19,812
Education: Short-term O-J-T
Knowledge: None above average
Abilities: Gross Body Equilibrium
Skills: Product Inspection
General Work Activities: None above average
Job Characteristics: Whole Body Vibration; High Places; Climbing Ladders, Scaffolds, Poles, etc.
GOE Group/s: 05.07.06 Quality Control: Logging and Lumber
CIP Program/s: 030404 Forest Products Technologists and Technicians

Related DOT Job/s: 455.367-010 LOG GRADER; 455.487-010 LOG SCALER

79011 GRADERS AND SORTERS, AGRICULTURAL PRODUCTS. OOH Title/s: Fishers, Hunters, and Trappers
Grade, sort, or classify unprocessed food and other agricultural products by size, weight, color, or condition. Exclude inspectors and graders of processed agricultural products. Grades and sorts products according to factors, such as color, length, width, appearance, feel, and smell. Segregates products on conveyor belt or table, according to grade, color, size, fiber quality, species, deformities, and sex. Weighs and places products in containers according to grade, and marks grade on containers. Estimates weight of product visually and by feel. Records grade on tag or shipping, receiving, or sales sheet. Examines product fibers through microscope to determine maturity and spirality of fibers. Pulls product sample apart between fingers to determine fiber quality. Discards inferior or defective products and foreign matter, and places acceptable products in containers for further processing.
Yearly Earnings: $26,416
Education: Short-term O-J-T
Knowledge: Production and Processing; Food Production
Abilities: Category Flexibility; Speed of Closure; Flexibility of Closure; Perceptual Speed; Selective Attention; Time Sharing; Finger Dexterity; Rate Control; Speed of Limb Movement; Gross Body Equilibrium; Depth Perception; Hearing Sensitivity
Skills: None above average
General Work Activities: Handling and Moving Objects
Job Characteristics: Using Hands on Objects, Tools, or Controls; Making Repetitive Motions; Importance of Repeating Same Tasks; Pace Determined by Speed of Equipment
GOE Group/s: 03.04.01 Elemental Work: Plants and Animals: Farming; 03.04.03 Elemental Work: Plants and Animals: Hunting and Fishing; 06.01.05 Production Technology: Inspection; 06.02.28 Production Work: Manual Work, Food Processing; 06.03.01 Quality Control: Inspecting, Testing, and Repairing; 06.03.02 Quality Control: Inspecting, Grading, Sorting, Weighing, and Recording
CIP Program/s: 010401 Agricultural and Food Products Processing Operations and Management
Related DOT Job/s: 409.687-010 INSPECTOR-GRADER, AGRICULTURAL ESTABLISHMENT; 410.687-026 WOOL-FLEECE SORTER; 411.687-010 CHICK GRADER; 411.687-014 CHICK SEXER; 429.387-010 COTTON CLASSER; 429.587-010 COTTON CLASSER AIDE; 446.687-010 CLAM SORTER; 522.384-010 FISH ROE TECHNICIAN; 529.687-074 EGG CANDLER; 529.687-186 SORTER, AGRICULTURAL PRODUCE; 589.387-014 WOOL SORTER; 589.687-054 WOOL-FLEECE GRADER

79015 ANIMAL BREEDERS. OOH Title/s: Farm Operators and Managers
Breed livestock or pets, such as cattle, goats, horses, sheep, swine, dogs, and cats. Breed animals for purposes such as riding, working, or show; and for products such as milk, wool, meat, and hair. Select and breed animals according to knowledge of animals' genealogy, characteristics, and offspring. Selects animals to be bred, according to knowledge of animals' genealogy, traits, and offspring desired. Examines animals to detect symptoms of illness or injury. Records weight, diet, and other breeding data. Feeds and waters animals, and cleans pens, cages, yards, and hutches. Brands, tags, dehorns, tattoos, or castrates animals. Treats minor injuries and ailments and engages veterinarian to treat animals with serious illnesses or injuries. Milks cows and goats. Clips or shears hair on animals. Adjusts controls to maintain specific temperature in building. Arranges for sale of animals to hospitals, research centers, pet shops, and food processing plants. Builds and maintains hutches, pens, and fenced yards. Exhibits animals at shows. Kills animals, removes their pelts, and arranges for sale of pelts.
Yearly Earnings: $37,596
Education: Bachelor's degree
Knowledge: Sales and Marketing; Food Production; Biology; Medicine and Dentistry
Abilities: Gross Body Equilibrium
Skills: None above average
General Work Activities: Selling or Influencing Others; Monitoring and Controlling Resources
Job Characteristics: Sounds, Noise Levels are Distracting, etc.; Hazardous Situations; Kneeling, Crouching, or Crawling; Bending or Twisting the Body
GOE Group/s: 03.01.02 Managerial Work: Plants and Animals: Specialty Breeding
CIP Program/s: 010301 Agricultural Production Workers and Managers, General; 010302 Agricultural Animal Husbandry and Production Management
Related DOT Job/s: 410.161-010 ANIMAL BREEDER; 410.161-014 FUR FARMER; 410.161-018 LIVESTOCK RANCHER; 410.161-022 HOG-CONFINEMENT-SYSTEM MANAGER; 411.161-010 CANARY BREEDER; 411.161-014 POULTRY BREEDER; 413.161-014 REPTILE FARMER

79016 ANIMAL TRAINERS. OOH Title/s: Animal Breeders and Trainers
Train animals for riding, harness, security, or obedience. Accustom animals to human voice and contact, and condition animals to respond to oral, hand, spur, and reign commands. Train animals according to prescribed standards for show or competition. May train animals to carry pack loads or work as part of pack team. Trains animals to obey commands, compete in shows, or perform tricks to entertain audience. Conducts training program to develop desired behavior. Trains horses for riding, show, work, or racing. Rehearses animal according to script for motion picture, television film, stage, or circus program. Evaluates animal to determine temperament, ability, and aptitude for training. Cues or signals animal during performance. Trains guard dog to protect property, and teaches guide dog and its master to function as team. Trains horses as independent operator, and advises owners regarding purchase of horses. Observes animal's physical condition to detect illness or unhealthy condition requiring medical care. Organizes format show. Feeds, exercises, and gives general care to animal. Arranges for mating of stallions and mares, and assists mares during foaling.
Yearly Earnings: $37,596
Education: Bachelor's degree
Knowledge: Sales and Marketing; Customer and Personal Service; Biology; Therapy and Counseling; Education and Training
Abilities: Memorization; Flexibility of Closure; Speed of Limb Movement; Dynamic Flexibility; Gross Body Equilibrium; Peripheral Vision
Skills: Learning Strategies; Monitoring; Persuasion; Instructing; Solution Appraisal
General Work Activities: Judging Qualities of Things, Services, People; Thinking Creatively; Developing Objectives and Strategies; Performing General Physical Activities; Performing for or Working with Public; Provide Consultation and Advice to Others
Job Characteristics: Objective or Subjective Information; Persuade Someone to a Course of Action; Provide a Service to Others; Deal with External Customers; Deal with Physical, Aggressive People; Contaminants; Diseases/Infections; Hazardous Situations; Standing; Walking or Running; Kneeling, Crouching, or Crawling; Keeping or Regaining Balance; Bending or Twisting the Body; Frustrating Circumstances
GOE Group/s: 03.03.01 Animal Training and Service: Animal Training

CIP Program/s: 010505 Animal Trainer; 010507 Equestrian/Equine Studies, Horse Management and Training
Related DOT Job/s: 159.224-010 ANIMAL TRAINER; 419.224-010 HORSE TRAINER

79017A ANIMAL CARETAKERS, EXCEPT FARM. OOH Title/s: Animal Caretakers, Except Farm

Feed, water, and exercise or otherwise care for small or large animals in establishments such as zoos, pounds, animal hospitals, or kennels. Feeds and waters animals according to schedule and feeding instructions. Mixes food, liquid formulas, medications, or food supplements according to instructions, prescriptions, and knowledge of animal species. Exercises animals to maintain their fitness and health, or trains animals to perform certain tasks. Adjusts controls to regulate specified temperature and humidity of animal quarters, nursery, or exhibit area. Examines and observes animals for signs of illness, disease, or injury, and provides treatment or informs veterinarian. Washes, brushes, clips, trims, and grooms animals. Cleans and disinfects animal quarters, such as pens, stables, cages, and yards, and surgical or other equipment, such as saddles and bridles. Anesthetizes and inoculates animals, according to instructions. Transfers animals between enclosures for breeding, birthing, shipping, or rearranging exhibits. Records information about animals, such as weight, size, physical condition, diet, medications, and food intake. Orders, unloads, and stores feed and supplies. Saddles and shoes animals. Responds to questions from patrons and provides information about animals, such as behavior, habitat, breeding habits, or facility activities. Observes and cautions children petting and feeding animals in designated area. Installs equipment in animal care facility, such as infrared lights, feeding devices, or cribs. Repairs fences, cages, or pens.
Yearly Earnings: $14,300
Education: Short-term O-J-T
Knowledge: Medicine and Dentistry
Abilities: Dynamic Strength
Skills: None above average
General Work Activities: Performing General Physical Activities
Job Characteristics: Sounds, Noise Levels are Distracting, etc.; Contaminants; Diseases/Infections; Kneeling, Crouching, or Crawling
GOE Group/s: 03.03.02 Animal Training and Service: Animal Service
CIP Program/s: 010301 Agricultural Production Workers and Managers, General; 010302 Agricultural Animal Husbandry and Production Management; 010501 Agricultural Supplies Retailing and Wholesaling
Related DOT Job/s: 410.674-010 ANIMAL CARETAKER; 410.674-022 STABLE ATTENDANT; 412.674-010 ANIMAL KEEPER; 412.674-014 ANIMAL-NURSERY WORKER

79017B FARRIERS. OOH Title/s: Animal Caretakers, Except Farm

Fit, shape, and nail protective shoes to animals' hooves. Trims and shapes hoof, using knife and snippers. Shapes shoe to fit hoof, using swage, forge, and hammer. Nails shoe to hoof and files hoof flush with shoe. Removes worn or defective shoe from animal's hoof, using nail snippers and pincers. Examines hoof to detect bruises and cracks and to determine trimming required. Measures hoof, using calipers and steel tape. Selects aluminum or steel shoe from stock, according to hoof measurements and purpose and requirements of use. Places leather pad, sponge, or pine tar mixture onto bruised or cracked hoof for protection.
Yearly Earnings: $14,300
Education: Short-term O-J-T
Knowledge: None above average
Abilities: Wrist-Finger Speed; Speed of Limb Movement; Explosive Strength; Dynamic Strength; Gross Body Equilibrium; Peripheral Vision
Skills: None above average
General Work Activities: Performing General Physical Activities; Handling and Moving Objects
Job Characteristics: Cramped Work Space, Awkward Positions; Kneeling, Crouching, or Crawling; Keeping or Regaining Balance; Bending or Twisting the Body; Making Repetitive Motions
GOE Group/s: 03.03.02 Animal Training and Service: Animal Service
CIP Program/s: 010501 Agricultural Supplies Retailing and Wholesaling; 010507 Equestrian/Equine Studies, Horse Management and Training
Related DOT Job/s: 418.381-010 HORSESHOER

79017C ANIMAL GROOMERS AND BATHERS. OOH Title/s: Animal Caretakers, Except Farm

Comb, clip, trim, bathe, and shape animals' coats to groom animals. Trims animal's toenails, and clips hair and fur according to determined pattern, using clippers, comb, and shears. Combs and brushes animal to remove matting, dead skin, and burrs, and to shape coat, using animal brush and comb. Draws and regulates water for bath, and washes animal, using perfumed soap or shampoo and handbrush. Places and secures animal on grooming table and studies proportions of animal to determine cutting pattern that will achieve desired style. Dries animal, using towel and electric dryer. Determines desired clipping pattern for animal, according to written or oral instructions. Calms animal by talking or employing other techniques. Cleans animal quarters.
Yearly Earnings: $14,300
Education: Short-term O-J-T
Knowledge: None above average
Abilities: Speed of Limb Movement
Skills: None above average
General Work Activities: None above average
Job Characteristics: Provide a Service to Others; Deal with External Customers; Hazardous Situations; Kneeling, Crouching, or Crawling; Bending or Twisting the Body; Making Repetitive Motions
GOE Group/s: 03.03.02 Animal Training and Service: Animal Service
CIP Program/s: 010501 Agricultural Supplies Retailing and Wholesaling
Related DOT Job/s: 418.674-010 DOG GROOMER; 418.677-010 DOG BATHER

79017D AQUARISTS. OOH Title/s: Indirectly related to Animal Caretakers, Except Farm

Perform a variety of duties, such as feeding, cleaning tanks, monitoring temperature, and treating sick or injured fish, to care for aquatic life in aquarium exhibits. Prepares food and feeds fish and other aquatic life according to schedule. Monitors thermometers to determine water temperature in tanks, and adjusts thermostats to maintain specified temperature. Collects water samples, compares samples to chart for acid analysis, and adds chemicals to maintain specified water conditions. Cleans tanks and removes algae from tank windows. Observes fish and aquatic life to detect and treat disease, injury, and illness, according to instructions. Maintains aquatic plants and decorations in aquatic displays. Fires sedation gun and assists crew in collection of aquatic specimens during expeditions.
Yearly Earnings: $14,300
Education: Short-term O-J-T
Knowledge: Chemistry; Biology
Abilities: None above average

Skills: None above average
General Work Activities: None above average
Job Characteristics: Walking or Running; Kneeling, Crouching, or Crawling; Bending or Twisting the Body
GOE Group/s: 03.03.02 Animal Training and Service: Animal Service
CIP Program/s: 030301 Fishing and Fisheries Sciences and Management
Related DOT Job/s: 449.674-010 AQUARIST

79021 FARM EQUIPMENT OPERATORS. OOH

Title/s: Farm Workers

Drive and control farm equipment to till soil and to plant, cultivate, and harvest crops. Drives tractor with implements to plow, plant, cultivate, or harvest crops and to move trailers for crop harvest. Manipulates controls to set, activate, and regulate mechanisms on machinery such as self-propelled machines, conveyors, separators, cleaners, and dryers. Drives truck to haul harvested crops, supplies, tools, or farm workers. Drives truck, or tractor with trailer attached, alongside crew loading crop or adjacent to harvesting machine. Sprays fertilizer or pesticide solutions, using hand sprayer, to control insects, fungus and weed growth, and diseases. Observes and listens to machinery operation to detect equipment malfunction, and removes obstruction to avoid damage to product or machinery. Attaches farm implements, such as plow, disc, sprayer, or harvester, to tractor, using bolts and mechanic's hand tools. Drives horses or mules to tow farm equipment and plant, cultivate, or harvest crops. Discards diseased or rotting product, and guides product on conveyor to regulate flow through machine. Positions boxes or attaches bags at discharge end of machinery to catch products, places lids on boxes, and closes sacks. Thins, hoes, weeds, or prunes row crops, fruit trees, or vines, using hand implements. Loads hoppers, containers, or conveyors to feed machine with products, using suction gates, shovel, or pitchfork. Adjusts, repairs, lubricates, and services farm machinery, and notifies supervisor or appropriate personnel when machinery malfunctions. Walks beside or rides on planting machine while inserting plants in planter mechanism at specified intervals. Irrigates soil, using portable pipe or ditch system, and maintains ditch or pipe and pumps. Mixes specified materials or chemicals and dumps solutions, powders, or seeds into planter or sprayer machinery. Loads and unloads crops or containers of materials, manually or using conveyors, handtruck, forklift, or transfer auger. Weighs crop-filled containers and records weights and other identifying information. Hand-picks fruit, such as apples, oranges, or strawberries. Oversees work crew engaged in planting, weeding, or harvesting activities.
Yearly Earnings: $13,520
Education: Short-term O-J-T
Knowledge: Food Production; Mechanical; Chemistry; Foreign Language; Transportation
Abilities: Information Ordering; Spatial Orientation; Time Sharing; Manual Dexterity; Finger Dexterity; Control Precision; Multilimb Coordination; Response Orientation; Rate Control; Reaction Time; Speed of Limb Movement; Static Strength; Explosive Strength; Dynamic Strength; Trunk Strength; Stamina; Extent Flexibility; Dynamic Flexibility; Gross Body Equilibrium; Far Vision; Night Vision; Peripheral Vision; Hearing Sensitivity; Sound Localization
Skills: Operation Monitoring; Operation and Control; Equipment Maintenance; Repairing; Time Management
General Work Activities: Performing General Physical Activities; Controlling Machines and Processes; Interacting with Computers; Repairing and Maintaining Mechanical Equipment
Job Characteristics: Very Hot; Extremely Bright or Inadequate Lighting; Contaminants; Cramped Work Space, Awkward Positions; Whole Body Vibration; Radiation; High Places; Hazardous Conditions; Hazardous Equipment; Hazardous Situations; Climbing Ladders, Scaffolds, Poles, etc.; Walking or Running; Kneeling, Crouching, or Crawling; Keeping or Regaining Balance; Bending or Twisting the Body; Making Repetitive Motions; Frustrating Circumstances; Degree of Automation; Importance of Repeating Same Tasks; Pace Determined by Speed of Equipment
GOE Group/s: 03.04.01 Elemental Work: Plants and Animals: Farming; 03.04.04 Elemental Work: Plants and Animals: Nursery and Groundskeeping; 05.12.07 Elemental Work: Mechanical: Crushing, Mixing, Separating, and Chipping
CIP Program/s: 010204 Agricultural Power Machinery Operator; 010301 Agricultural Production Workers and Managers, General; 010304 Crop Production Operations and Management; 010501 Agricultural Supplies Retailing and Wholesaling
Related DOT Job/s: 401.683-010 FARMWORKER, GRAIN I; 401.683-014 FARMWORKER, RICE; 402.663-010 FARMWORKER, VEGETABLE I; 403.683-010 FARMWORKER, FRUIT I; 404.663-010 FARMWORKER, FIELD CROP I; 404.685-010 SEED-POTATO ARRANGER; 405.683-010 FARMWORKER, BULBS; 405.683-014 GROWTH-MEDIA MIXER, MUSHROOM; 407.663-010 FARMWORKER, DIVERSIFIED CROPS I; 409.683-010 FARM-MACHINE OPERATOR; 409.683-014 FIELD HAULER; 409.685-010 FARM-MACHINE TENDER; 409.686-010 FARMWORKER, MACHINE; 421.683-010 FARMWORKER, GENERAL I; 429.685-010 GINNER; 429.685-014 THRESHER, BROOMCORN

79030B GARDENERS AND GROUNDSKEEPERS.

OOH Title/s: Gardeners and Groundskeepers

Mow, water, and fertilize grass and shrubs; prune trees and hedges; and remove debris, litter, or snow, using hand and power tools or equipment to maintain grounds of private or public property. Plants grass, flowers, trees, and shrubs, using gardening tools. Prunes and trims trees, shrubs, and hedges, using shears, pruners, or chainsaw. Mows grass or turf, using hand or power mower. Mixes and sprays or spreads fertilizer, herbicides, or insecticides onto grass, shrubs, and trees, using hand or automatic sprayer or spreader. Repairs and maintains walks, fences, benches, burial sites, buildings, and tools and equipment, using hand tools and power tools. Waters grass, shrubs, or trees, using hose or by activating fixed or portable sprinkler system. Weeds and grubs around trees, bushes, and flower beds. Conditions and prepares soil for planting, using gardening tools. Removes leaves and other debris or litter from grounds, using rake, broom, or leaf blower. Shovels snow and spreads salt on walks and driveways. Cultivates grass or lawn, using power aerator and thatcher. Operates tractor or backhoe, using attachments, to till, dig, cultivate, grade, spray fertilizer or herbicide, mow, or remove snow. Records lawn-care services rendered, materials used, and charges assessed on appropriate forms.
Yearly Earnings: $14,976
Education: Short-term O-J-T
Knowledge: Chemistry
Abilities: Static Strength; Explosive Strength; Dynamic Strength; Trunk Strength; Stamina; Extent Flexibility; Dynamic Flexibility; Gross Body Coordination; Gross Body Equilibrium
Skills: None above average
General Work Activities: Performing General Physical Activities; Interacting with Computers; Repairing and Maintaining Mechanical Equipment
Job Characteristics: Very Hot; Hazardous Situations; Kneeling, Crouching, or Crawling
GOE Group/s: 03.04.04 Elemental Work: Plants and Animals: Nursery and Groundskeeping
CIP Program/s: 010601 Horticulture Services Operations and Management, General; 010603 Ornamental Horticulture Operations and Management; 010604 Greenhouse Operations and Management;

010605 Landscaping Operations and Management; 010607 Turf Management
Related DOT Job/s: 406.683-010 GREENSKEEPER II; 406.684-010 CEMETERY WORKER; 406.684-014 GROUNDSKEEPER, INDUSTRIAL-COMMERCIAL; 406.684-018 GARDEN WORKER; 406.687-010 LANDSCAPE SPECIALIST; 408.161-010 LANDSCAPE GARDENER; 408.684-010 LAWN-SERVICE WORKER

79033 PRUNERS. OOH Title/s: Gardeners and Groundskeepers; Science Technicians

Prune and treat ornamental and shade trees and shrubs in yards and parks to improve their appearance, health, and value. Cut away dead and excess branches from trees, using handsaws, pruning hooks, sheers, and clippers. May use truck-mounted hydraulic lifts and power pruners. May scrape decayed matter from cavities in trees and fill holes with cement to promote healing and prevent further deterioration. Exclude workers who also perform duties of sprayers/applicators or lawn maintenance workers. Cuts away dead and excess branches from trees, using handsaws, pruning hooks, sheers, and clippers. Uses truck-mounted hydraulic lifts and pruners and power pruners. Scrapes decayed matter from cavities in trees, and fills holes with cement to promote healing and to prevent further deterioration. Applies tar or other protective substances to cut surfaces to seal surfaces against insects. Prunes, cuts down, fertilizes, and sprays trees, as directed by tree surgeon. Climbs trees, using climbing hooks and belts, or climbs ladders to gain access to work area.
Yearly Earnings: $14,300
Education: Short-term O-J-T
Knowledge: Chemistry; Biology
Abilities: Multilimb Coordination; Speed of Limb Movement; Explosive Strength; Dynamic Strength; Stamina; Extent Flexibility; Dynamic Flexibility; Gross Body Coordination; Gross Body Equilibrium
Skills: None above average
General Work Activities: Performing General Physical Activities
Job Characteristics: Very Hot; Extremely Bright or Inadequate Lighting; Cramped Work Space, Awkward Positions; Whole Body Vibration; High Places; Hazardous Situations; Climbing Ladders, Scaffolds, Poles, etc.; Keeping or Regaining Balance; Making Repetitive Motions; Specialized Protective or Safety Attire
GOE Group/s: 03.04.05 Elemental Work: Plants and Animals: Services
CIP Program/s: 010301 Agricultural Production Workers and Managers, General; 010304 Crop Production Operations and Management; 010699 Horticulture Services Operations and Management, Other
Related DOT Job/s: 408.181-010 TREE SURGEON; 408.684-018 TREE PRUNER

79036 SPRAYERS/APPLICATORS. OOH Title/s: Gardeners and Groundskeepers

Spray herbicides, pesticides, and fungicides on trees, shrubs, and lawns, using hoses and truck-mounted tank. Fill sprayer tank with water and chemicals, according to prescribed formula. May use portable spray equipment. Exclude workers who also perform duties of lawn maintenance workers or pruners. Lifts, pushes, and swings nozzle, hose, and tube to direct spray over designated area. Covers area to specified depth, applying knowledge of weather conditions, droplet size, elevation-to-distance ratio, and obstructions. Fills sprayer tank with water and chemicals, according to formula. Connects hoses and nozzles, selected according to terrain, distribution pattern requirements, type of infestation, and velocity. Starts motor and engages machinery, such as sprayer agitator and pump. Gives driving instructions to truck driver, using hand and horn signals, to ensure complete coverage of designated area. Cleans and services machinery to ensure operating efficiency, using water, gasoline, lubricants, and hand tools. Sprays livestock with pesticides. Plants grass with seed spreader and operates straw blower to cover seeded area with asphalt and straw mixture.
Yearly Earnings: $14,976
Education: Moderate-term O-J-T
Knowledge: Food Production; Chemistry
Abilities: Explosive Strength; Dynamic Strength; Stamina; Dynamic Flexibility
Skills: None above average
General Work Activities: Performing General Physical Activities; Repairing and Maintaining Mechanical Equipment
Job Characteristics: Very Hot; Extremely Bright or Inadequate Lighting; Contaminants; Hazardous Conditions; Standing; Specialized Protective or Safety Attire
GOE Group/s: 03.04.04 Elemental Work: Plants and Animals: Nursery and Groundskeeping
CIP Program/s: 010204 Agricultural Power Machinery Operator; 010301 Agricultural Production Workers and Managers, General; 010304 Crop Production Operations and Management; 010601 Horticulture Services Operations and Management, General; 010605 Landscaping Operations and Management; 010606 Nursery Operations and Management; 010607 Turf Management
Related DOT Job/s: 408.662-010 HYDRO-SPRAYER OPERATOR; 408.684-014 SPRAYER, HAND

79041 LABORERS, LANDSCAPING AND GROUNDSKEEPING. OOH Title/s: Gardeners and Groundskeepers; Janitors and Cleaners and Cleaning Supervisors

Landscape and/or maintain grounds of public or private property, using hand and power tools or equipment. May work in nursery facility or at customer location. Workers typically perform a variety of tasks, which may include any combination of the following: sod laying, mowing, trimming, planting, watering, fertilizing, digging, raking, and sprinkler installation. May help brick and stone masons. Exclude workers who also perform duties of pruners or sprayers/applicators. Mows lawns, using power mower. Trims and picks flowers and cleans flower beds. Digs holes for plants, mixes fertilizer or lime with dirt in holes, inserts plants, and fills holes with dirt. Hauls or spreads topsoil, and spreads straw over seeded soil to hold soil in place. Waters lawns, trees, and plants, using portable sprinkler system, hose, or watering can. Decorates garden with stones and plants. Applies herbicides, fungicides, fertilizers, and pesticides, using spreaders or spray equipment. Attaches wires from planted trees to support stakes. Seeds and fertilizes lawns. Maintains tools and equipment. Builds forms and mixes and pours cement to form garden borders. Shovels snow from walks and driveways.
Yearly Earnings: $14,976
Education: Short-term O-J-T
Knowledge: Chemistry
Abilities: Speed of Limb Movement; Static Strength; Explosive Strength; Dynamic Strength; Trunk Strength; Stamina; Dynamic Flexibility; Gross Body Equilibrium
Skills: None above average
General Work Activities: Performing General Physical Activities; Interacting with Computers
Job Characteristics: Very Hot; Contaminants; Hazardous Conditions; Hazardous Situations; Walking or Running; Kneeling, Crouching, or Crawling; Bending or Twisting the Body; Making Repetitive Motions

GOE Group/s: 03.04.04 Elemental Work: Plants and Animals: Nursery and Groundskeeping; 03.04.05 Elemental Work: Plants and Animals: Services; 05.12.18 Elemental Work: Mechanical: Cleaning and Maintenance
CIP Program/s: 010601 Horticulture Services Operations and Management, General; 010603 Ornamental Horticulture Operations and Management; 010604 Greenhouse Operations and Management; 010606 Nursery Operations and Management
Related DOT Job/s: 405.684-014 HORTICULTURAL WORKER I; 405.687-010 FLOWER PICKER; 405.687-018 TRANSPLANTER, ORCHID; 408.364-010 PLANT-CARE WORKER; 408.687-014 LABORER, LANDSCAPE; 408.687-018 TREE-SURGEON HELPER II; 952.687-010 HYDRO-ELECTRIC-PLANT MAINTAINER

Farm Workers

79806 VETERINARY ASSISTANTS. OOH Title/s: Veterinary Assistants
Examine animals for veterinarian, prepare animals for surgery, perform post-operational medical treatment as needed, and give medications to animals. Usually work directly under veterinarian. Receive extensive training on the job and may also have some postsecondary education, such as trade school or junior college. Assists veterinarian in variety of animal health care duties, including injections, venipunctures, and wound dressings. Prepares examination or treatment room, and holds or restrains animal during procedures. Prepares patient, medications, equipment, and instruments for surgical procedures, using specialized knowledge. Assists veterinarian during surgical procedures, passing instruments and materials in accordance with oral instructions. Completes routine laboratory tests and cares for and feeds laboratory animals. Assists professional personnel with research projects in commercial, public health, or research laboratories. Inspects products or carcasses to ensure compliance with health standards, when employed in food processing plant.
Yearly Earnings: $14,300
Education: Short-term O-J-T
Knowledge: Food Production; Biology; Medicine and Dentistry; Therapy and Counseling
Abilities: Oral Comprehension; Speed of Closure; Flexibility of Closure; Perceptual Speed; Selective Attention; Arm-Hand Steadiness; Finger Dexterity; Response Orientation; Speed of Limb Movement; Gross Body Equilibrium; Visual Color Discrimination; Peripheral Vision
Skills: Social Perceptiveness
General Work Activities: Assisting and Caring for Others
Job Characteristics: Provide a Service to Others; Deal with Physical, Aggressive People; Cramped Work Space, Awkward Positions; Radiation; Diseases/Infections; Hazardous Conditions; Hazardous Situations; Kneeling, Crouching, or Crawling; Special Uniform; Common Protective or Safety Attire
GOE Group/s: 02.03.03 Medical Sciences: Veterinary Medicine
CIP Program/s: 510808 Veterinarian Assistant/Animal Health Technician
Related DOT Job/s: 079.361-014 VETERINARY TECHNICIAN

79855 GENERAL FARMWORKERS. OOH Title/s: Farm Workers
Apply pesticides, herbicides, and fertilizer to crops and livestock; plant, maintain, and harvest food crops; and tend livestock and poultry. Repair farm buildings and fences. Duties may include operating milking machines and other dairy processing equipment, supervising seasonal help, irrigating crops, and hauling livestock products to market. Operates tractors, tractor-drawn machinery, and self-propelled machinery to plow, harrow, and fertilize soil and plant, cultivate, spray, and harvest crops. Feeds, waters, grooms, and otherwise cares for livestock and poultry. Harvests fruits and vegetables by hand. Digs and transplants seedlings by hand. Repairs farm buildings, fences, and other structures. Sets up and operates irrigation equipment. Clears and maintains irrigation ditches. Operates truck to haul livestock and products to market. Loads agricultural products into trucks for transport. Cleans barns, stables, pens, and kennels. Administers simple medications to animals and fowls. Repairs and maintains farm vehicles, implements, and mechanical equipment. Oversees casual and seasonal help during planting and harvesting.
Yearly Earnings: $13,520
Education: Short-term O-J-T
Knowledge: Food Production; Building and Construction; Mechanical; Chemistry; Biology; Foreign Language; Transportation
Abilities: Spatial Orientation; Manual Dexterity; Control Precision; Multilimb Coordination; Response Orientation; Rate Control; Reaction Time; Wrist-Finger Speed; Speed of Limb Movement; Static Strength; Explosive Strength; Dynamic Strength; Trunk Strength; Stamina; Extent Flexibility; Dynamic Flexibility; Gross Body Coordination; Gross Body Equilibrium; Night Vision; Peripheral Vision; Depth Perception; Glare Sensitivity; Hearing Sensitivity; Auditory Attention; Sound Localization
Skills: Operation Monitoring; Operation and Control; Equipment Maintenance; Repairing; Management of Personnel Resources
General Work Activities: Performing General Physical Activities; Handling and Moving Objects; Interacting with Computers; Repairing and Maintaining Mechanical Equipment; Developing and Building Teams
Job Characteristics: Responsibility for Outcomes and Results; Sounds, Noise Levels are Distracting, etc.; Very Hot; Extremely Bright or Inadequate Lighting; Contaminants; Cramped Work Space, Awkward Positions; Whole Body Vibration; Diseases/Infections; High Places; Hazardous Equipment; Hazardous Situations; Standing; Climbing Ladders, Scaffolds, Poles, etc.; Walking or Running; Kneeling, Crouching, or Crawling; Keeping or Regaining Balance; Bending or Twisting the Body; Frustrating Circumstances; Importance of Repeating Same Tasks; Pace Determined by Speed of Equipment
GOE Group/s: 03.04.01 Elemental Work: Plants and Animals: Farming
CIP Program/s: 010204 Agricultural Power Machinery Operator; 010301 Agricultural Production Workers and Managers, General; 010302 Agricultural Animal Husbandry and Production Management; 010304 Crop Production Operations and Management
Related DOT Job/s: 421.683-010 FARMWORKER, GENERAL I; 421.687-010 FARMWORKER, GENERAL II

79856 FARMWORKERS, FOOD AND FIBER CROPS. OOH Title/s: Farm Workers
Plant, cultivate, and harvest food and fiber products, such as grains, vegetables, fruits, nuts, and field crops (e.g., cotton, mint, hops, and tobacco). Use hand tools, such as shovels, trowels, hoes, tampers, pruning hooks, shears, and knives. Duties may include tilling soil and applying fertilizers; transplanting, weeding, thinning, or pruning crops; applying fungicides, herbicides, or pesticides; and packing and loading harvested products. May construct trellises, repair fences and farm building, or participate in irrigation activities. Include workers involved in expediting pollination and those who cut seed tuber crops into sections for planting. Plants seeds or digs up and transplants seedlings and sets, using hand tools such as hoes. Pulls, cuts, or chops out weeds and surplus seedlings. Cuts and trims away leaves,

plant tops, and unwanted branches from plants to promote growth of produce. Grooves dirt along row to facilitate irrigation, and mounds dirt around plant to protect roots. Cuts or pulls tops and other foliage from harvested crops. Loads produce in containers or onto trucks or field conveyors, or lays bunches of produce along row for collection. Sprays plants with prescribed herbicides, fungicides, and pesticides to control diseases and insects. Repairs fences and buildings, using carpenter's tools. Sets up poles and strings wire or twine to build trellises or fences for vines or running plants. Picks produce from plant, pulls produce from soil, cuts produce from stem or root, or shakes produce from vine or tree. Ties harvested produce in bundles, using twine, wire, or rubber bands. Moves supplies, equipment, seedlings, and harvested crops from one place to another, and loads and unloads trucks. Carries and positions irrigation pipes and clears irrigation ditches, using shovel. Picks out debris, such as vines and culls, to clean harvested crops, and cleans up area around harvesting machines. Cleans, lubricates, sharpens, or otherwise maintains farm machines and equipment.
Yearly Earnings: $13,520
Education: Short-term O-J-T
Knowledge: Food Production
Abilities: Manual Dexterity; Wrist-Finger Speed; Static Strength; Explosive Strength; Dynamic Strength; Trunk Strength; Stamina; Dynamic Flexibility; Gross Body Coordination; Gross Body Equilibrium; Glare Sensitivity
Skills: None above average
General Work Activities: Performing General Physical Activities; Handling and Moving Objects; Repairing and Maintaining Mechanical Equipment
Job Characteristics: Very Hot; Extremely Bright or Inadequate Lighting; Contaminants; Hazardous Situations; Walking or Running; Kneeling, Crouching, or Crawling; Keeping or Regaining Balance; Using Hands on Objects, Tools, or Controls; Bending or Twisting the Body; Making Repetitive Motions; Importance of Repeating Same Tasks
GOE Group/s: 03.04.01 Elemental Work: Plants and Animals: Farming
CIP Program/s: 000000 NO CIP ASSIGNED
Related DOT Job/s: 401.687-010 FARMWORKER, GRAIN II; 402.687-010 FARMWORKER, VEGETABLE II; 402.687-014 HARVEST WORKER, VEGETABLE; 403.687-010 FARMWORKER, FRUIT II; 403.687-014 FIG CAPRIFIER; 403.687-018 HARVEST WORKER, FRUIT; 403.687-022 VINE PRUNER; 404.686-010 SEED CUTTER; 404.687-010 FARMWORKER, FIELD CROP II; 404.687-014 HARVEST WORKER, FIELD CROP; 407.687-010 FARMWORKER, DIVERSIFIED CROPS II; 409.687-018 WEEDER-THINNER; 421.687-010 FARMWORKER, GENERAL II

79858 FARMWORKERS, FARM AND RANCH ANIMALS. OOH Title/s: Farm Workers

Attend to live farm or ranch animals, including cattle, sheep, swine, goats, and poultry produced for animal products, such as meat, fur, skins, feathers, milk, and eggs. Duties may include feeding, watering, herding, grazing, castrating, branding, debeaking, weighing, catching, and loading animals. May maintain records on animals, examine animals to detect diseases and injuries, assist in birth deliveries, and administer medications, vaccinations, or insecticides as appropriate. May clean and maintain animal housing areas. Include workers who tend dairy milking machines, shear wool from sheep, collect eggs in hatcheries, place shoes on animals' hooves, and tend bee colonies. Waters livestock. Herds livestock to pasture for grazing or to scales, trucks, or other enclosures. Examines animals to detect disease and injuries. Applies or administers medications and vaccinates animals. Sprays livestock with disinfectants and insecticides. Cleans stalls, pens, and equipment, using disinfectant solutions, brushes, shovels and water hoses. Castrates or docks ears and tails of animals. Marks livestock to identify ownership and grade, using brands, tags, paint, or tattoos. Assists with birthing of animals. Debeaks and trims wings of poultry. Fills feed troughs with feed. Milks farm animals, such as cows and goats, by hand or using milking machine. Collects, inspects, packs, or places eggs in incubator. Mixes feed, additives, and medicines in prescribed portions. Maintains growth, feeding, production, and cost records. Inspects and repairs fences, stalls, and pens. Moves equipment, poultry, or livestock manually from one location to another using truck or cart. Grooms, clips, and trims animals. Segregates animals according to weight, age, color, and physical condition. Maintains equipment and machinery.
Yearly Earnings: $13,520
Education: Short-term O-J-T
Knowledge: Food Production; Biology
Abilities: Manual Dexterity; Multilimb Coordination; Rate Control; Reaction Time; Speed of Limb Movement; Static Strength; Explosive Strength; Dynamic Strength; Trunk Strength; Stamina; Dynamic Flexibility; Gross Body Coordination; Gross Body Equilibrium
Skills: Equipment Maintenance; Repairing
General Work Activities: Performing General Physical Activities; Handling and Moving Objects; Interacting with Computers
Job Characteristics: Very Hot; Cramped Work Space, Awkward Positions; Diseases/Infections; Hazardous Situations; Standing; Walking or Running; Kneeling, Crouching, or Crawling; Keeping or Regaining Balance; Bending or Twisting the Body; Making Repetitive Motions
GOE Group/s: 03.01.01 Managerial Work: Plants and Animals: Farming; 03.04.01 Elemental Work: Plants and Animals: Farming
CIP Program/s: 010301 Agricultural Production Workers and Managers, General; 010302 Agricultural Animal Husbandry and Production Management; 010501 Agricultural Supplies Retailing and Wholesaling
Related DOT Job/s: 410.364-010 LAMBER; 410.664-010 FARMWORKER, LIVESTOCK; 410.674-014 COWPUNCHER; 410.674-018 LIVESTOCK-YARD ATTENDANT; 410.684-010 FARMWORKER, DAIRY; 410.684-014 SHEEP SHEARER; 410.685-010 MILKER, MACHINE; 410.687-010 FLEECE TIER; 410.687-014 GOAT HERDER; 410.687-022 SHEEP HERDER; 411.161-018 POULTRY FARMER; 411.364-014 POULTRY TENDER; 411.584-010 FARMWORKER, POULTRY; 411.684-010 CAPONIZER; 411.684-014 POULTRY VACCINATOR; 411.687-018 LABORER, POULTRY FARM; 411.687-022 LABORER, POULTRY HATCHERY; 411.687-026 POULTRY DEBEAKER; 412.684-010 GAME-FARM HELPER; 413.687-014 WORM-FARM LABORER; 413.687-018 BEE WORKER; 421.687-010 FARMWORKER, GENERAL II; 920.687-202 WORM PACKER

Other Agricultural Workers

79999A WEED, DISEASE, AND INSECT CONTROL INSPECTORS. OOH Title/s: Farm Workers

Inspect fields, roadsides, and ditches to detect presence of noxious insects and plant diseases. Searches sample areas to locate plant pests, such as noxious weeds and insects and plant diseases. Identifies pests, applying knowledge of insect, weed, and plant disease characteristics. Counts numbers of insects on examined plants or number of diseased plants within sample area. Collects samples of infected soil, diseased plants, or insects for laboratory analysis or supervisor's identification. Records results of inspections and treatments. Marks infested area to determine effectiveness of treatment. Notifies landowners in area where suspected pests are located. Mixes exterminating agents, such as herbicides, insecticides, and fungicides, according to type of infection or infestation to be treated. Applies solution to infected area, using spraying equipment.

Yearly Earnings: $14,144
Education: Short-term O-J-T
Knowledge: Chemistry; Biology
Abilities: Flexibility of Closure; Sound Localization
Skills: None above average
General Work Activities: Interacting with Computers
Job Characteristics: Hazardous Conditions; Hazardous Situations; Standing; Kneeling, Crouching, or Crawling; Common Protective or Safety Attire; Specialized Protective or Safety Attire
GOE Group/s: 03.02.04 General Supervision: Plants and Animals: Services; 03.04.05 Elemental Work: Plants and Animals: Services
CIP Program/s: 010301 Agricultural Production Workers and Managers, General; 010304 Crop Production Operations and Management
Related DOT Job/s: 408.381-010 SCOUT; 408.381-014 WEED INSPECTOR; 408.687-010 FIELD INSPECTOR, DISEASE AND INSECT CONTROL

79999B IRRIGATION WORKERS. OOH Title/s: Farm Workers

Irrigate crops, using sprinklers or gravity flow system. Operates gates, checks, turnouts, and wasteways to regulate water flow into canals and laterals. Removes plugs from portholes to release water, and replugs when area is filled with water. Starts motor that pumps water through system, and opens valves to direct water. Observes rate of flow, and adjusts valves to ensure uniform distribution of water. Disassembles portable system, and moves to next location after specified time interval. Lays out pipe along designated settings, and attaches sprinkler heads at specified points. Connects pipe to gate or pipe system, using hand tools. Measures or estimates quantity of water required and delivered and duration of delivery. Shovels and packs dirt in low spots of embankment, or cuts trenches in high areas to direct water flow. Patrols area to detect leaks, breaks, weak areas, or obstructions and damage to irrigation system. Writes reports and keeps records of deliveries, users, quantity of water used, condition of system and equipment, or repairs needed. Lubricates, adjusts, and repairs or replaces parts to maintain system, using hand tools.
Yearly Earnings: $13,520
Education: Short-term O-J-T
Knowledge: Food Production; Building and Construction
Abilities: Dynamic Strength; Trunk Strength; Gross Body Equilibrium
Skills: Installation
General Work Activities: Repairing and Maintaining Mechanical Equipment
Job Characteristics: Kneeling, Crouching, or Crawling; Using Hands on Objects, Tools, or Controls
GOE Group/s: 03.04.05 Elemental Work: Plants and Animals: Services; 05.06.03 Systems Operation: Oil, Gas, and Water Distribution
CIP Program/s: 010201 Agricultural Mechanization, General; 010204 Agricultural Power Machinery Operator; 010301 Agricultural Production Workers and Managers, General; 010304 Crop Production Operations and Management
Related DOT Job/s: 409.684-010 IRRIGATOR, VALVE PIPE; 409.685-014 IRRIGATOR, SPRINKLING SYSTEM; 409.687-014 IRRIGATOR, GRAVITY FLOW; 954.362-010 DITCH RIDER

79999C HORTICULTURAL SPECIALTY GROWERS. OOH Title/s: Nursery Workers

Grow horticultural specialty products and crops, such as flowers and ornamental plants and shrubs. Bends, covers, cuts and binds, or buries branches of parent plant in soil to initiate new plant growth. Inspects growing area to ascertain temperature and humidity conditions, nutrient deficiencies, disease, or foreign plant growth. Selects materials, such as fertilizers, herbicides, or growth media, according to type of plant. Plants seeds or places cuttings from parent plant in growth media to initiate new growth. Prunes, trains, or grafts developing plants to promote altered growth characteristics, such as disease resistance, bonsai shape, or color brilliance. Monitors timing and metering devices and regulates environmental conditions to ensure conformance with specifications. Determines type and quantity of plantings or seedlings to grow. Plans growing area utilization and schedules activities according to knowledge of climate and market conditions. Removes substandard plants to maintain quality control and prunes plants to enhance development. Arranges plantings to artistically display products, and adds decorative materials, such as rocks, moss, and mirrors. Operates farm equipment, such as tractor or harvesting machine, to till soil or plant, cultivate, or harvest crop. Arranges for sale of products and services to customers, or purchases supplies and materials from vendors. Explains and demonstrates care-taking techniques or transplanting and cultivation to coworkers and subordinates. Hires workers, assigns duties, and monitors activities to assure adherence to established procedures.
Yearly Earnings: $13,520
Education: Short-term O-J-T
Knowledge: Administration and Management; Sales and Marketing; Personnel and Human Resources; Food Production; Education and Training
Abilities: Deductive Reasoning; Inductive Reasoning; Dynamic Strength; Trunk Strength; Stamina; Dynamic Flexibility; Gross Body Equilibrium
Skills: Management of Material Resources
General Work Activities: Interacting with Computers; Selling or Influencing Others; Resolving Conflicts, Negotiating with Others; Coordinating Work and Activities of Others; Developing and Building Teams; Teaching Others; Guiding, Directing and Motivating Subordinates; Coaching and Developing Others; Staffing Organizational Units; Monitoring and Controlling Resources
Job Characteristics: Supervise, Coach, Train Others; Hazardous Situations; Standing; Kneeling, Crouching, or Crawling; Using Hands on Objects, Tools, or Controls; Bending or Twisting the Body
GOE Group/s: 03.01.03 Managerial Work: Plants and Animals: Specialty Cropping; 03.04.04 Elemental Work: Plants and Animals: Nursery and Groundskeeping
CIP Program/s: 010301 Agricultural Production Workers and Managers, General; 010304 Crop Production Operations and Management; 010601 Horticulture Services Operations and Management, General; 010603 Ornamental Horticulture Operations and Management; 010604 Greenhouse Operations and Management; 010606 Nursery Operations and Management; 010607 Turf Management
Related DOT Job/s: 405.161-010 BONSAI CULTURIST; 405.161-014 HORTICULTURAL-SPECIALTY GROWER, FIELD; 405.161-018 HORTICULTURAL-SPECIALTY GROWER, INSIDE; 405.361-010 PLANT PROPAGATOR

79999D FARMERS. OOH Title/s: Farm Operators and Managers

Grow and harvest fruits, vegetables, grains, or specialty crops, such as honey. Harvests crops and collects specialty products, such as royal jelly from queen bee cells and honey from honeycombs. Sets up and operates farm machinery to till soil, plant, prune, fertilize, apply herbicides and pesticides, and haul harvested crops. Inspects growing environment to maintain optimum growing or breeding conditions. Plans harvesting, considering ripeness and maturity of crop and weather conditions. Determines kind and quantity of crops or livestock to be raised, according to market conditions, weather, and farm size. Destroys diseased or superfluous crops, such as queen bee cells, bee colonies, parasites, and vermin. Selects and purchases supplies and equipment, such as seed, tree stock, fertilizers, farm machinery, implements, livestock, and feed. Breeds and raises stock, such as animals,

poultry, honeybees, or earthworms. Grows out-of-season crops in greenhouse or early crops in cold-frame bed, or buds and grafts plant stock. Arranges with buyers for sale and shipment of crops. Installs irrigation systems and irrigates fields. Hires and directs workers engaged in planting, cultivating, irrigating, harvesting, and marketing crops and raising livestock. Demonstrates and explains farmwork techniques and safety regulations to workers. Assembles, positions, and secures structures, such as trellises or beehives, using hand tools. Grades and packages crop for marketing. Lubricates, adjusts, and makes minor repairs on farm equipment, using oilcan, grease gun, and hand tools. Maintains employee and financial records.
Yearly Earnings: $11,596
Education: Long-term O-J-T
Knowledge: Administration and Management; Economics and Accounting; Sales and Marketing; Personnel and Human Resources; Production and Processing; Food Production; Transportation
Abilities: Deductive Reasoning; Information Ordering; Control Precision; Multilimb Coordination; Static Strength; Dynamic Strength; Trunk Strength; Stamina; Gross Body Equilibrium
Skills: Instructing; Equipment Selection; Installation; Operation and Control; Product Inspection; Equipment Maintenance; Management of Financial Resources; Management of Material Resources; Management of Personnel Resources
General Work Activities: Developing Objectives and Strategies; Scheduling Work and Activities; Organizing, Planning, and Prioritizing; Performing General Physical Activities; Interacting with Computers; Drafting and Specifying Technical Devices, etc.; Repairing and Maintaining Mechanical Equipment; Selling or Influencing Others; Resolving Conflicts, Negotiating with Others; Coordinating Work and Activities of Others; Developing and Building Teams; Guiding, Directing and Motivating Subordinates; Coaching and Developing Others; Performing Administrative Activities; Staffing Organizational Units; Monitoring and Controlling Resources
Job Characteristics: Supervise, Coach, Train Others; Contaminants; Hazardous Equipment; Hazardous Situations; Standing; Kneeling, Crouching, or Crawling; Using Hands on Objects, Tools, or Controls; Bending or Twisting the Body; Specialized Protective or Safety Attire; Frustrating Circumstances
GOE Group/s: 03.01.01 Managerial Work: Plants and Animals: Farming; 03.01.02 Managerial Work: Plants and Animals: Specialty Breeding
CIP Program/s: 010301 Agricultural Production Workers and Managers, General; 010302 Agricultural Animal Husbandry and Production Management; 010304 Crop Production Operations and Management
Related DOT Job/s: 401.161-010 FARMER, CASH GRAIN; 402.161-010 FARMER, VEGETABLE; 403.161-010 FARMER, TREE-FRUIT-AND-NUT CROPS; 403.161-014 FARMER, FRUIT CROPS, BUSH AND VINE; 404.161-010 FARMER, FIELD CROP; 407.161-010 FARMER, DIVERSIFIED CROPS; 413.161-010 BEEKEEPER; 413.161-018 WORM GROWER; 421.161-010 FARMER, GENERAL

79999E COMMERCIAL FISHERY WORKERS. OOH Title/s: Fishers, Hunters, and Trappers

Catch finfish, shellfish, and other marine life, using equipment such as nets, traps, or dredges. Cultivates and harvests or gathers marine life, such as sponges, abalone, or oysters, from sea bottom, using diving or dredging equipment or barge. Connects accessories, such as floats, weights, flags, lights, or markers, to nets, lines, or traps. Puts fishing equipment into water and anchors or tows equipment, according to method of fishing. Pulls and guides nets, traps, and lines onto vessel, by hand or using hoisting equipment. Attaches nets, slings, hooks, blades, and lifting devices to cables, booms, hoists, and dredges. Hits fish with club or hooks fish with gaff to assist in hauling large fish from water. Removes catch from fishing equipment and uses measuring equipment to ensure compliance with legal size. Loads and unloads equipment and supplies aboard vessel, by hand or using hoisting equipment. Stands lookout for schools of fish and for steering and engine-room watches. Sorts and cleans marine life, and returns undesirable or illegal catch to sea. Signals other workers to move, hoist, and position loads. Places catch in containers and stows in hold with salt and ice. Steers vessel in fishing area. Rows boats and dinghies and operates skiffs to transport fishers, divers, and sponge hookers and to tow and position fishing equipment. Records date, harvest area, and yield in logbook. Washes deck, conveyors, knives, and other equipment, using brush, detergent, and water. Lubricates, adjusts, and makes minor repairs to engines and fishing equipment. Negotiates with buyers for sale of catch.
Yearly Earnings: $26,416
Education: Short-term O-J-T
Knowledge: Food Production; Biology; Transportation
Abilities: Spatial Orientation; Manual Dexterity; Multilimb Coordination; Response Orientation; Rate Control; Wrist-Finger Speed; Speed of Limb Movement; Static Strength; Dynamic Strength; Trunk Strength; Stamina; Extent Flexibility; Gross Body Equilibrium; Far Vision; Glare Sensitivity
Skills: Negotiation; Equipment Maintenance; Repairing
General Work Activities: Performing General Physical Activities; Interacting with Computers; Repairing and Maintaining Mechanical Equipment; Selling or Influencing Others; Resolving Conflicts, Negotiating with Others
Job Characteristics: Contaminants; Hazardous Situations; Standing; Kneeling, Crouching, or Crawling; Keeping or Regaining Balance; Using Hands on Objects, Tools, or Controls; Bending or Twisting the Body; Importance of Repeating Same Tasks
GOE Group/s: 03.01.02 Managerial Work: Plants and Animals: Specialty Breeding; 03.04.03 Elemental Work: Plants and Animals: Hunting and Fishing; 05.10.01 Crafts: Structural
CIP Program/s: 010301 Agricultural Production Workers and Managers, General; 010303 Aquaculture Operations and Production Management; 030301 Fishing and Fisheries Sciences and Management; 490303 Fishing Technology/Commercial Fishing
Related DOT Job/s: 441.132-010 BOATSWAIN, OTTER TRAWLER; 441.683-010 SKIFF OPERATOR; 441.684-010 FISHER, NET; 441.684-014 FISHER, POT; 441.684-018 FISHER, TERRAPIN; 441.684-022 FISHER, WEIR; 442.684-010 FISHER, LINE; 443.664-010 FISHER, DIVING; 443.684-010 FISHER, SPEAR; 446.161-014 SHELLFISH GROWER; 446.663-010 SHELLFISH DREDGE OPERATOR; 446.684-014 SHELLFISH-BED WORKER; 449.664-010 NET REPAIRER; 449.667-010 DECKHAND, FISHING VESSEL; 449.687-010 OYSTER FLOATER

79999F HUNTERS AND TRAPPERS. OOH Title/s: Fishers, Hunters, and Trappers

Hunt and trap wild animals for human consumption, fur, feed, bait, or other purposes. Traps or captures quarry alive for identification, relocation, or live sale. Select, baits, and sets traps according to species, size, habits, and environs of bird or animal and reason for trapping. Drives quarry into traps, nets, or killing area, using dogs or prods. Kills quarry for pelts or bounty, using club, poison, gun, or drowning method. Patrols trapline or nets to inspect settings, remove catch, and reset or relocate traps. Restrains quarry with arms or nets, and rigs net or sling under catch to permit hoisting without bodily injury. Releases quarry from trap or net and transfers it to cage, or secures identification tag to quarry and releases it. Skins quarry, using knife, and stretches pelts on frames to be cured. Scrapes fat, blubber, or flesh from skin-side of pelt, using knife or hand scraper, and cures pelts with salt and boric acid. Washes and sorts pelts according to species, color, and quality. Packs pelts in containers and loads containers onto trucks for transporting. Removes designated parts, such as ears or tail, from slain quarry as evidence for killing bounty, using knife. Trains dogs for hunting. Stands watch to observe behavior of captured quarry.

Yearly Earnings: $14,144
Education: Short-term O-J-T
Knowledge: None above average
Abilities: Flexibility of Closure; Spatial Orientation; Rate Control; Wrist-Finger Speed; Speed of Limb Movement; Static Strength; Explosive Strength; Dynamic Strength; Trunk Strength; Stamina; Extent Flexibility; Dynamic Flexibility; Gross Body Coordination; Gross Body Equilibrium; Far Vision; Visual Color Discrimination; Night Vision; Peripheral Vision; Depth Perception; Hearing Sensitivity; Sound Localization
Skills: None above average
General Work Activities: Performing General Physical Activities; Handling and Moving Objects
Job Characteristics: Diseases/Infections; Hazardous Situations; Kneeling, Crouching, or Crawling; Bending or Twisting the Body; Specialized Protective or Safety Attire
GOE Group/s: 03.04.03 Elemental Work: Plants and Animals: Hunting and Fishing
CIP Program/s: 000000 NO CIP ASSIGNED
Related DOT Job/s: 461.134-010 EXPEDITION SUPERVISOR; 461.661-010 PREDATORY-ANIMAL HUNTER; 461.664-010 UNDERWATER HUNTER-TRAPPER; 461.684-010 SEALER; 461.684-014 TRAPPER, ANIMAL; 461.684-018 TRAPPER, BIRD

79999G AQUA-CULTURISTS. OOH Title/s: Fishers, Hunters, and Trappers

Cultivate and harvest finfish, shellfish, or other aquatic or marine life in ponds or tanks. Collects marine life, such as finfish or shellfish, using net, lines, pots, shovel, tongs, or dredge baskets. Strips eggs from female finfish, adds milt from male finfish of same species, and places mixture in moist containers. Fills hatchery trays with fertilized eggs, and places trays in incubation troughs, or sows spat on sea bottom. Inspects eggs and discards dead, infertile, and off-color eggs, using suction syringe. Observes appearance and actions of developing fish to detect disease, and adds medications to food and water, according to instructions. Sorts finfish or shellfish according to size, coloring, and species, and transfers fingerlings to rearing areas, using nets, buckets, or tank truck. Adjusts controls of pumps and baffles to regulate volume, depth, velocity, temperature, and aeration of tank or pond water. Removes mature fish from pond and transfers to rivers and lakes. Selects marketable marine life, such as soft-shell crabs, and places them in containers for shipment. Patrols ponds and tidal pens on foot or by motorboat to detect presence of predators and for harvesting. Performs standard tests on water samples to determine water content, using water-testing equipment. Stakes or fences ponds and growing areas, following specified pattern to lay out planting bed. Scatters food over surface of water by hand, or activates blower to automatically scatter food over water to feed fish. Counts and weighs fish, records field data, and prepares reports of hatchery activities. Observes shellfish to determine shedding of outer shells, and assists during molting. Arranges with buyers for sale of fish. Drains and cleans ponds, tanks, and troughs, using brushes, chemicals, and water, and removes debris, seaweed, and predators. Makes minor repairs on screens, retaining walls, fences, and hatchery equipment.

Yearly Earnings: $26,416
Education: Short-term O-J-T
Knowledge: Sales and Marketing; Food Production; Biology
Abilities: Speed of Closure; Flexibility of Closure; Perceptual Speed; Spatial Orientation; Selective Attention; Rate Control; Speed of Limb Movement; Explosive Strength; Dynamic Strength; Gross Body Coordination; Gross Body Equilibrium; Far Vision; Peripheral Vision; Depth Perception; Glare Sensitivity; Hearing Sensitivity; Auditory Attention; Sound Localization
Skills: None above average
General Work Activities: Interacting with Computers; Selling or Influencing Others; Monitoring and Controlling Resources
Job Characteristics: Diseases/Infections; Hazardous Situations; Kneeling, Crouching, or Crawling; Keeping or Regaining Balance; Using Hands on Objects, Tools, or Controls; Bending or Twisting the Body; Making Repetitive Motions; Common Protective or Safety Attire; Importance of Repeating Same Tasks
GOE Group/s: 03.01.02 Managerial Work: Plants and Animals: Specialty Breeding; 03.04.03 Elemental Work: Plants and Animals: Hunting and Fishing
CIP Program/s: 010301 Agricultural Production Workers and Managers, General; 010303 Aquaculture Operations and Production Management; 030301 Fishing and Fisheries Sciences and Management
Related DOT Job/s: 446.161-010 FISH FARMER; 446.684-010 FISH HATCHERY WORKER; 446.684-018 SOFT CRAB SHEDDER; 446.687-014 LABORER, AQUATIC LIFE

79999H UNDERWATER GATHERERS. OOH Title/s: Fishers, Hunters, and Trappers

Gather marine life, such as kelp, Irish moss, and sponges, from sea bottom. Uses tools, such as rakes, mowers, and other hand tools, to gather marine life from sea bottom. Lowers mower into water from boat and retrieves marine life, such as kelp or Irish moss. Attaches grabhook of winch to help maintain an evenly distributed load in boat. Transfers marine life to beach, where it is washed, dried, and bleached. Pours saltwater over marine life in order to bleach it. Cleans marine life of foreign particles and sorts according to size for packing. Clips torn or irregular parts from marine life, using cutting shears or serrated knives.

Yearly Earnings: $26,416
Education: Short-term O-J-T
Knowledge: Food Production
Abilities: Spatial Orientation; Static Strength; Dynamic Strength; Trunk Strength; Gross Body Equilibrium; Glare Sensitivity
Skills: None above average
General Work Activities: Performing General Physical Activities; Handling and Moving Objects; Interacting with Computers
Job Characteristics: Radiation; Standing; Keeping or Regaining Balance; Using Hands on Objects, Tools, or Controls; Making Repetitive Motions; Importance of Repeating Same Tasks
GOE Group/s: 03.04.03 Elemental Work: Plants and Animals: Hunting and Fishing
CIP Program/s: 000000 NO CIP ASSIGNED
Related DOT Job/s: 447.684-010 SPONGE HOOKER; 447.687-010 DULSER; 447.687-014 IRISH-MOSS BLEACHER; 447.687-018 IRISH-MOSS GATHERER; 447.687-022 KELP CUTTER; 447.687-026 SPONGE CLIPPER

79999J GAMEKEEPERS. OOH Title/s: Farm Operators and Managers

Breed, raise, and protect game animals and birds on state game farm or private game preserve. Selects pairs of animals or birds for mating on basis of size, color, vigor, or desired characteristics. Breeds game animals or birds, or crossbreeds to improve strain and to develop new types. Gathers bird eggs for artificial incubations, and transfers young to rearing pens or cages. Sets and maintains traps for predatory and noxious animals and birds that may prey upon or carry disease to breeding stock. Examines stock to detect signs of illness, and inoculates stock with antibiotics. Clips birds' wings to prevent flight and trims birds' bills to prevent injury. Mixes food according to formulas, and cleans and fills feeding stations and water containers. Releases birds

and animals in designated areas. Builds, repairs, and cleans pens, yards, and cages. Drives stock into coops to prepare them for transportation.
Yearly Earnings: $16,640
Education: Work experience, plus degree
Knowledge: Food Production; Biology
Abilities: Trunk Strength; Visual Color Discrimination
Skills: None above average
General Work Activities: Performing General Physical Activities
Job Characteristics: Cramped Work Space, Awkward Positions; Diseases/Infections; Hazardous Situations; Standing; Kneeling, Crouching, or Crawling
GOE Group/s: 03.01.02 Managerial Work: Plants and Animals: Specialty Breeding
CIP Program/s: 010301 Agricultural Production Workers and Managers, General; 010302 Agricultural Animal Husbandry and Production Management; 030601 Wildlife and Wildlands Management
Related DOT Job/s: 169.171-010 GAMEKEEPER; 412.161-010 GAME-BIRD FARMER

79999K AGRICULTURAL CROP FARM MANAGERS. OOH Title/s: Farm Operators and Managers
Direct and coordinate, through subordinate supervisory personnel, activities of workers engaged in agricultural crop production for corporations, cooperatives, or other owners. Directs and coordinates worker activities, such as planting, irrigation, chemical application, harvesting, grading, payroll, and record keeping. Contracts with farmers or independent owners for raising of crops or for management of crop production. Coordinates growing activities with those of engineering, equipment maintenance, packing houses, and other related departments. Analyzes market conditions to determine acreage allocations. Evaluates financial statements and makes budget proposals. Negotiates with bank officials to obtain credit from bank. Hires, discharges, transfers, and promotes workers; enforces safety regulations; and interprets policies. Confers with purchasers and arranges for sale of crops. Purchases machinery, equipment, and supplies, such as tractors, seed, fertilizer, and chemicals. Records information, such as production, farm management practices, and parent stock, and prepares financial and operational reports. Plans and directs development and production of hybrid plant varieties with high-yield or disease- and insect-resistant characteristics. Determines procedural changes in drying, grading, storage, and shipment for greater efficiency and accuracy. Inspects orchards and fields to determine maturity dates of crops or to estimate potential crop damage from weather. Analyzes soil to determine type and quantity of fertilizer required for maximum production. Inspects equipment to ensure proper functioning.
Yearly Earnings: $16,640
Education: Work experience, plus degree
Knowledge: Administration and Management; Economics and Accounting; Sales and Marketing; Personnel and Human Resources; Production and Processing; Food Production; Mathematics; Chemistry; Public Safety and Security; Transportation
Abilities: Written Comprehension; Written Expression; Originality; Deductive Reasoning; Inductive Reasoning; Mathematical Reasoning; Number Facility; Spatial Orientation; Near Vision
Skills: Speaking; Learning Strategies; Coordination; Persuasion; Negotiation; Instructing; Idea Generation; Idea Evaluation; Equipment Selection; Product Inspection; Identifying Downstream Consequences; Management of Financial Resources; Management of Material Resources; Management of Personnel Resources
General Work Activities: Getting Information Needed to Do the Job; Monitoring Processes, Material, or Surroundings; Inspecting Equipment, Structures, or Material; Estimating Needed Characteristics; Analyzing Data or Information; Making Decisions and Solving Problems; Thinking Creatively; Developing Objectives and Strategies; Scheduling Work and Activities; Organizing, Planning, and Prioritizing; Operating Vehicles or Equipment; Communicating with Other Workers; Communicating with Persons Outside Organization; Establishing and Maintaining Relationships; Selling or Influencing Others; Resolving Conflicts, Negotiating with Others; Coordinating Work and Activities of Others; Developing and Building Teams; Guiding, Directing and Motivating Subordinates; Coaching and Developing Others; Provide Consultation and Advice to Others; Performing Administrative Activities; Staffing Organizational Units; Monitoring and Controlling Resources
Job Characteristics: Supervise, Coach, Train Others; Persuade Someone to a Course of Action; Coordinate or Lead Others; Responsibility for Outcomes and Results
GOE Group/s: 03.01.01 Managerial Work: Plants and Animals: Farming
CIP Program/s: 010101 Agricultural Business and Management, General; 010102 Agricultural Business/Agribusiness Operations; 010104 Farm and Ranch Management; 010301 Agricultural Production Workers and Managers, General; 010302 Agricultural Animal Husbandry and Production Management; 010304 Crop Production Operations and Management; 020401 Plant Sciences, General; 020403 Horticulture Science
Related DOT Job/s: 180.161-010 MANAGER, PRODUCTION, SEED CORN; 180.167-018 GENERAL MANAGER, FARM; 180.167-058 SUPERINTENDENT, PRODUCTION; 180.167-066 MANAGER, ORCHARD

79999L LIVESTOCK PRODUCTION MANAGERS. OOH Title/s: Farm Operators and Managers
Direct and coordinate, through subordinate supervisory personnel, activities of workers engaged in livestock production for corporations, cooperatives, or other owners. Directs and coordinates livestock farm activities, such as breeding, rearing, maintenance, and shipment of livestock. Plans and implements policies and procedures to attain profitability and to ensure compliance with government regulations. Reviews production and storage records to determine productivity. Prepares breeding or hatching schedules based on customer orders, market forecasts, and available facilities and equipment. Examines livestock for illness or disease, and advises designated personnel of action to be taken or secures veterinarian services. Inspects facilities and equipment to ensure compliance with sanitation standards and to determine maintenance and repair requirements. Prepares farm activity reports, such as livestock production, sales, and reports required by government regulations. Researches technical literature for data on breeding, rearing, habits, diets, diseases, and treatment of various species of birds and animals. Purchases supplies and equipment, such as eggs, feed, sanitation chemicals, incubators, and brooders. Arranges for sale of livestock. Interprets genetic data and advises customers regarding breeding, brooding, feeding, and sanitation practices.
Yearly Earnings: $16,640
Education: Work experience, plus degree
Knowledge: Administration and Management; Economics and Accounting; Sales and Marketing; Food Production; Biology; Law, Government, and Jurisprudence
Abilities: Written Comprehension; Problem Sensitivity; Deductive Reasoning; Inductive Reasoning; Number Facility; Near Vision
Skills: Reading Comprehension; Science; Critical Thinking; Learning Strategies; Persuasion; Negotiation; Instructing; Idea Generation; Idea Evaluation; Operations Analysis; Programming; Management of Financial Resources; Management of Material Resources; Management of Personnel Resources
General Work Activities: Inspecting Equipment, Structures, or Material; Estimating Needed Characteristics; Analyzing Data or Information; Making Decisions and Solving Problems; Developing Objectives

and Strategies; Scheduling Work and Activities; Organizing, Planning, and Prioritizing; Interpreting Meaning of Information to Others; Communicating with Other Workers; Establishing and Maintaining Relationships; Selling or Influencing Others; Resolving Conflicts, Negotiating with Others; Coordinating Work and Activities of Others; Developing and Building Teams; Guiding, Directing and Motivating Subordinates; Coaching and Developing Others; Provide Consultation and Advice to Others; Performing Administrative Activities; Staffing Organizational Units; Monitoring and Controlling Resources
Job Characteristics: Supervise, Coach, Train Others; Coordinate or Lead Others; Responsibility for Outcomes and Results; Diseases/Infections
GOE Group/s: 03.01.01 Managerial Work: Plants and Animals: Farming; 03.01.02 Managerial Work: Plants and Animals: Specialty Breeding
CIP Program/s: 010101 Agricultural Business and Management, General; 010102 Agricultural Business/Agribusiness Operations; 010104 Farm and Ranch Management; 010301 Agricultural Production Workers and Managers, General; 010302 Agricultural Animal Husbandry and Production Management
Related DOT Job/s: 180.167-026 MANAGER, DAIRY FARM; 180.167-034 MANAGER, GAME BREEDING FARM; 180.167-046 MANAGER, POULTRY HATCHERY

79999M FISH HATCHERY MANAGERS. OOH Title/s: Farm Operators and Managers

Direct and coordinate, through subordinate supervisory personnel, activities of workers engaged in fish hatchery production for corporations, cooperatives, or other owners. Determines, administers, and executes policies relating to administration, standards of hatchery operations, and facility maintenance. Oversees trapping and spawning of fish, egg incubation, and fry rearing, applying knowledge of management and fish culturing techniques. Oversees movement of mature fish to lakes, ponds, streams, or commercial tanks. Confers with biologists and other fishery personnel to obtain data concerning fish habits, food, and environmental requirements. Collects information regarding techniques for collecting, fertilizing, incubating spawn, and treatment of spawn and fry. Prepares budget reports. Prepares reports required by state and federal laws. Accounts for and dispenses funds. Approves employment and discharge of employees, signs payrolls, and performs personnel duties.
Yearly Earnings: $16,640
Education: Work experience, plus degree
Knowledge: Administration and Management; Economics and Accounting; Personnel and Human Resources; Food Production; Biology
Abilities: Flexibility of Closure; Selective Attention; Gross Body Equilibrium; Far Vision
Skills: Time Management; Management of Financial Resources; Management of Material Resources; Management of Personnel Resources
General Work Activities: Getting Information Needed to Do the Job; Processing Information; Evaluating Information against Standards; Making Decisions and Solving Problems; Developing Objectives and Strategies; Scheduling Work and Activities; Organizing, Planning, and Prioritizing; Communicating with Other Workers; Establishing and Maintaining Relationships; Resolving Conflicts, Negotiating with Others; Coordinating Work and Activities of Others; Developing and Building Teams; Guiding, Directing and Motivating Subordinates; Coaching and Developing Others; Performing Administrative Activities; Staffing Organizational Units; Monitoring and Controlling Resources
Job Characteristics: Supervise, Coach, Train Others; Coordinate or Lead Others; Responsibility for Outcomes and Results
GOE Group/s: 03.01.02 Managerial Work: Plants and Animals: Specialty Breeding
CIP Program/s: 010101 Agricultural Business and Management, General; 010102 Agricultural Business/Agribusiness Operations; 010104 Farm and Ranch Management; 010301 Agricultural Production Workers and Managers, General; 010303 Aquaculture Operations and Production Management; 030301 Fishing and Fisheries Sciences and Management
Related DOT Job/s: 180.167-030 MANAGER, FISH HATCHERY

79999N YARD WORKERS, PRIVATE HOUSEHOLD. OOH Title/s: Gardeners and Groundskeepers

Maintain and keep grounds of private residence in neat and orderly condition. Plants, transplants, fertilizes, sprays with pesticides, prunes, cultivates, and waters flowers, shrubbery, and trees. Seeds and mows lawns, rakes leaves, and keeps ground free of debris. Cleans patio furniture and garage, and shovels snow from walks. Whitewashes or paints fences. Washes and polishes automobiles.
Yearly Earnings: $14,976
Education: Short-term O-J-T
Knowledge: None above average
Abilities: Static Strength; Dynamic Strength; Trunk Strength; Stamina; Dynamic Flexibility
Skills: None above average
General Work Activities: Performing General Physical Activities
Job Characteristics: Very Hot; Extremely Bright or Inadequate Lighting; Hazardous Situations; Standing; Climbing Ladders, Scaffolds, Poles, etc.; Kneeling, Crouching, or Crawling; Bending or Twisting the Body; Making Repetitive Motions; Importance of Repeating Same Tasks
GOE Group/s: 03.04.04 Elemental Work: Plants and Animals: Nursery and Groundskeeping
CIP Program/s: 000000 NO CIP ASSIGNED
Related DOT Job/s: 301.687-018 YARD WORKER

79999P ALL OTHER AGRICULTURAL, FORESTRY, FISHING, AND RELATED WORKERS. OOH Title/s: Gardeners and Groundskeepers

All other agricultural, forestry, fishing, and related workers, not classified separately above.
Yearly Earnings: $16,640
Education: Work experience, plus degree
GOE Group/s: 03.04.01 Elemental Work: Plants and Animals: Farming
CIP Program/s: 000000 NO CIP ASSIGNED
Related DOT Job/s: 406.381-010 GARDENER, SPECIAL EFFECTS AND INSTRUCTION MODELS; 413.687-010 WORM PICKER; 919.664-010 TEAMSTER

Section 8
Mechanics, Installers, Repairers, Construction Trades, Extractive Trades, Metal and Plastics Working, Woodworking, Apparel, Precision Printing, and Food Processing Workers

Blue Collar Worker Supervisors

81002 FIRST LINE SUPERVISORS AND MANAGER/SUPERVISORS—MECHANICS, INSTALLERS, AND REPAIRERS. OOH Title/s:

Blue-Collar Worker Supervisors; Management Analysts and Consultants

Directly supervise and coordinate activities of mechanics, repairers, and installers and their helpers. Managers/supervisors are generally found in smaller establishments, where they perform both supervisory and management functions, such as accounting, marketing, and personnel work, and may also engage in the same repair work as the workers they supervise. Exclude work leaders who spend 20 percent or more of their time at tasks similar to those of employees under their supervision. These are included in the occupations which are most closely related to their specific work duties. Assigns workers to perform activities, such as service appliances, repair and maintain vehicles, and install machinery and equipment. Directs, coordinates, and assists in performance of workers' activities, such as engine tune-up, hydroelectric turbine repair, or circuit breaker installation. Recommends or initiates personnel actions, such as employment, performance evaluations, promotions, transfers, discharges, and disciplinary measures. Confers with personnel—such as management, engineering, quality control, customers, and workers' representatives—to coordinate work activities and resolve problems. Examines object, system, or facilities—such as telephone, air-conditioning, or industrial plant—and analyzes information to determine installation, service, or repair needed. Interprets specifications, blueprints, and job orders, and constructs templates and lays out reference points for workers. Monitors operations, and inspects, tests, and measures completed work, such as hand tools, gauges, and specifications to verify conformance to standards. Establishes or adjusts work methods and procedures to meet production schedules, using knowledge of capacities of machines, equipment, and personnel. Computes estimates and actual costs of factors, such as materials, labor, and outside contractors, and prepares budgets. Requisitions materials and supplies, such as tools, equipment, and replacement parts for work activities. Completes and maintains reports, such as time and production records, inventories, and test results. Trains workers in methods, procedures, and use of equipment and work aids, such as blueprints, hand tools, and test equipment. Recommends measures, such as procedural changes, service manual revisions, and equipment purchases, to improve work performance and minimize operating costs. Patrols work area and examines tools and equipment to detect unsafe conditions or violations of safety rules.

Yearly Earnings: $32,136

Education: Work experience in a related occupation

Knowledge: Administration and Management; Economics and Accounting; Sales and Marketing; Personnel and Human Resources; Design; Building and Construction; Mechanical; Public Safety and Security

Abilities: Information Ordering

Skills: Active Listening; Speaking; Learning Strategies; Monitoring; Social Perceptiveness; Coordination; Persuasion; Negotiation; Instructing; Idea Generation; Idea Evaluation; Implementation Planning; Operations Analysis; Installation; Operation Monitoring; Product Inspection; Equipment Maintenance; Troubleshooting; Repairing; Visioning; Systems Perception; Identifying Downstream Consequences; Identification of Key Causes; Systems Evaluation; Time Management; Management of Financial Resources; Management of Material Resources; Management of Personnel Resources

General Work Activities: Identifying Objects, Actions, and Events; Inspecting Equipment, Structures, or Material; Scheduling Work and Activities; Organizing, Planning, and Prioritizing; Repairing and Maintaining Mechanical Equipment; Establishing and Maintaining Relationships; Resolving Conflicts, Negotiating with Others; Coordinating Work and Activities of Others; Guiding, Directing and Motivating Subordinates; Coaching and Developing Others; Performing Administrative Activities; Staffing Organizational Units; Monitoring and Controlling Resources

Job Characteristics: Objective or Subjective Information; Job-Required Social Interaction; Supervise, Coach, Train Others; Take a Position Opposed to Others; Coordinate or Lead Others; Responsibility for Outcomes and Results; Sounds, Noise Levels are Distracting, etc.; High Places; Hazardous Conditions; Importance of Being Sure All is Done

GOE Group/s: 05.02.02 Managerial Work: Mechanical: Maintenance and Construction; 05.02.06 Managerial Work: Mechanical: Services; 05.05.03 Craft Technology: Plumbing and Pipefitting; 05.05.05 Craft Technology: Electrical-Electronic Systems Installation and Repair; 05.05.06 Craft Technology: Metal Fabrication and Repair; 05.05.07 Craft Technology: Machining; 05.05.09 Craft Technology: Mechanical Work; 05.05.10 Craft Technology: Electrical-Electronic Equipment Repair; 05.06.03 Systems Operation: Oil, Gas, and Water Distribution; 05.10.01 Crafts: Structural; 05.10.02 Crafts: Mechanical; 05.10.03 Crafts: Electrical-Electronic; 05.10.04 Crafts: Structural-Mechanical-Electrical-Electronic; 05.12.01 Elemental Work: Mechanical: Supervision; 05.12.18 Elemental Work: Mechanical: Cleaning and Maintenance; 06.01.01 Production Technology: Supervision and Instruction; 06.04.01 Elemental Work: Industrial: Supervision; 11.05.03 Business Administration: Management Services: Government; 11.11.04 Business Management: Services

CIP Program/s: 081203 Vehicle Parts and Accessories Marketing Operations; 520201 Business Administration and Management, General; 520203 Logistics and Materials Management; 520205 Operations Management and Supervision

Related DOT Job/s: 169.167-074 PREVENTIVE MAINTENANCE COORDINATOR; 184.167-050 MAINTENANCE SUPERVISOR; 184.167-194 SUPERINTENDENT, METERS; 185.164-010 SERVICE MANAGER; 185.167-058 SERVICE MANAGER; 185.167-074 MANAGER, AUTO SPECIALTY SERVICES; 187.167-010 APPLIANCE-SERVICE SUPERVISOR; 187.167-130 MANAGER, MARINE SERVICE; 187.167-142 MANAGER, SERVICE DEPARTMENT; 189.167-046 SUPERINTENDENT, MAINTENANCE; 375.167-018 COMMANDING OFFICER, MOTOR EQUIPMENT; 620.131-010 SUPERVISOR, ENDLESS TRACK VEHICLE; 620.131-014 SUPERVISOR, GARAGE; 620.131-018 SUPERVISOR, MOTORCYCLE REPAIR SHOP; 620.137-010 TANK AND AMPHIBIAN TRACTOR OPERATIONS CHIEF; 621.131-010 SUPERCHARGER-REPAIR SUPERVISOR; 621.131-014 SUPERVISOR, AIRCRAFT MAINTENANCE; 622.131-010 SUPERVISOR, RAILROAD CAR REPAIR; 622.131-014 SUPERVISOR, ROUNDHOUSE; 622.131-018 SUPERVISOR, WHEEL SHOP; 622.137-010 SUPERVISOR, BRAKE REPAIR; 622.137-014 SUPERVISOR, CAR AND YARD; 623.131-014 SUPERVISOR, GEAR REPAIR; 624.131-010 SUPERVISOR, FARM-EQUIPMENT MAINTENANCE; 625.131-010 ENGINE-TESTING SUPERVISOR; 625.131-014 SUPERVISOR, ENGINE-REPAIR; 625.137-010 SUPERVISOR, LOCOMOTIVE; 626.137-010 SUPERVISOR, WELDING EQUIPMENT REPAIRER; 629.131-010 BAKERY-MACHINE-MECHANIC SUPERVISOR; 629.131-014 OIL-FIELD EQUIPMENT MECHANIC SUPERVISOR; 630.131-010 PUMP-SERVICER SUPERVISOR; 631.131-010 POWERHOUSE-MECHANIC SUPERVISOR; 632.131-010 ARTILLERY-MAINTENANCE SUPERVISOR; 633.131-010 OFFICE-MACHINE-SERVICE SUPERVISOR; 637.131-010 SUPERVISOR, COOLER SERVICE; 638.131-010 FUEL-SYSTEM-MAINTENANCE SUPERVISOR;

638.131-018 MAINTENANCE SUPERVISOR, FIRE-FIGHTING-EQUIPMENT; 638.131-022 MAINTENANCE-MECHANIC SUPERVISOR; 638.131-026 MECHANICAL-MAINTENANCE SUPERVISOR; 638.131-030 MILLWRIGHT SUPERVISOR; 638.131-034 MAINTENANCE SUPERVISOR, MOBILE BATTERY EQUIPMENT; 710.131-010 SUPERVISOR, GAS METER REPAIR; 710.131-018 SUPERVISOR, INSTRUMENT MECHANICS; 710.131-022 SUPERVISOR, INSTRUMENT REPAIR; 710.131-026 SUPERVISOR, METER REPAIR SHOP; 710.131-030 SUPERVISOR, METER SHOP; 710.137-014 SUPERVISOR, METER-AND-REGULATOR SHOP; 721.131-010 ELECTRIC MOTOR REPAIRING SUPERVISOR; 722.131-010 INSTRUMENT-SHOP SUPERVISOR; 805.131-010 SUPERVISOR, BOILERMAKING; 805.137-010 SUPERVISOR, BOILER REPAIR; 806.131-030 SUPERVISOR, RIGGER; 807.137-010 SUPERVISOR, AUTOMOBILE BODY REPAIR; 820.131-010 ELECTRICIAN SUPERVISOR, SUBSTATION; 821.131-010 ELECTRICAL-INSTALLATION SUPERVISOR; 821.131-014 LINE SUPERVISOR; 821.131-018 SERVICE SUPERVISOR II; 821.131-026 WIREWORKER SUPERVISOR; 822.131-010 CENTRAL-OFFICE-REPAIRER SUPERVISOR; 822.131-014 CUSTOMER-FACILITIES SUPERVISOR; 822.131-018 LINE SUPERVISOR; 822.131-022 PROTECTIVE-SIGNAL SUPERINTENDENT; 822.131-026 SIGNAL SUPERVISOR; 822.131-030 TEST-DESK SUPERVISOR; 823.131-010 COMMUNICATIONS ELECTRICIAN SUPERVISOR; 823.131-014 RIGGER SUPERVISOR; 823.131-018 SUPERVISOR, AVIONICS SHOP; 823.131-022 SUPERVISOR, RADIO INTERFERENCE; 823.131-026 SUPERVISOR, SOUND TECHNICIAN; 824.137-014 STREET-LIGHT-SERVICER SUPERVISOR; 825.131-014 ELEVATOR-CONSTRUCTOR SUPERVISOR; 825.137-010 SUPERVISOR, LINE DEPARTMENT; 826.131-010 ELECTRICAL SUPERVISOR; 827.131-010 ELECTRICAL-APPLIANCE-SERVICER SUPERVISOR; 827.131-018 SUPERVISOR, AIR-CONDITIONING INSTALLER; 828.131-010 SUPERVISOR, ELECTRONIC CONTROLS REPAIRER; 828.161-010 SUPERVISOR, ELECTRONICS SYSTEMS MAINTENANCE; 829.131-010 CABLE SUPERVISOR; 829.131-018 INSTALLATION SUPERINTENDENT, PIN-SETTING MACHINE; 829.131-022 SUPERVISOR, ELECTRICAL REPAIR AND TELEPHONE LINE MAINTENANCE; 861.134-010 SUPERVISOR, SMOKE CONTROL; 862.134-014 SUPERVISOR, WATER SOFTENER SERVICE; 862.137-014 STEAM-DISTRIBUTION SUPERVISOR; 869.131-010 CABIN-EQUIPMENT SUPERVISOR; 891.131-010 DOCK SUPERVISOR; 891.137-010 MAINTENANCE SUPERVISOR; 899.130-010 SUPERVISOR, CANAL-EQUIPMENT MAINTENANCE; 899.131-014 LOCK MAINTENANCE SUPERVISOR; 899.137-018 SUPERVISOR, MAINTENANCE; 915.134-010 TIRE-SERVICE SUPERVISOR; 929.131-010 SUPERVISOR, SALVAGE; 952.137-018 SUPERINTENDENT, LOCAL; 953.137-018 SERVICE SUPERVISOR I; 962.137-010 GRIP BOSS

81005A FIRST LINE SUPERVISORS AND MANAGER/SUPERVISORS—CONSTRUCTION TRADES. OOH Title/s: Blue-Collar Worker Supervisors

Directly supervise and coordinate activities of construction trades workers. Supervises and coordinates activities of construction trades workers. Directs and leads workers engaged in construction activities. Assigns work to employees, using material and worker requirements data. Confers with staff and workers to ensure production and personnel problems are resolved. Suggests and initiates personnel actions, such as promotions, transfers, and hires. Analyzes and resolves worker problems and recommends motivational plans. Examines and inspects work progress, equipment, and construction sites to verify safety and ensure that specifications are met. Estimates material and worker requirements to complete job. Reads specifications, such as blueprints and data, to determine construction requirements. Analyzes and plans installation and construction of equipment and structures. Locates, measures, and marks location and placement of structures and equipment. Records information, such as personnel, production, and operational data, on specified forms and reports. Trains workers in construction methods and operation of equipment. Recommends measures to improve production methods and equipment performance to increase efficiency and safety. Assists workers engaged in construction activities, using hand tools and equipment.

Yearly Earnings: $32,136

Education: Work experience in a related occupation

Knowledge: Administration and Management; Personnel and Human Resources; Design; Building and Construction; Psychology

Abilities: Originality; Problem Sensitivity; Information Ordering; Category Flexibility; Memorization; Speed of Closure; Flexibility of Closure; Perceptual Speed; Spatial Orientation; Visualization; Time Sharing; Arm-Hand Steadiness; Manual Dexterity; Finger Dexterity; Control Precision; Multilimb Coordination; Response Orientation; Rate Control; Reaction Time; Wrist-Finger Speed; Speed of Limb Movement; Static Strength; Explosive Strength; Dynamic Strength; Trunk Strength; Stamina; Extent Flexibility; Dynamic Flexibility; Gross Body Coordination; Gross Body Equilibrium; Peripheral Vision; Glare Sensitivity

Skills: Social Perceptiveness; Coordination; Persuasion; Negotiation; Instructing; Implementation Planning; Operations Analysis; Equipment Selection; Installation; Product Inspection; Equipment Maintenance; Troubleshooting; Systems Perception; Identifying Downstream Consequences; Systems Evaluation; Time Management; Management of Financial Resources; Management of Material Resources; Management of Personnel Resources

General Work Activities: Inspecting Equipment, Structures, or Material; Developing Objectives and Strategies; Scheduling Work and Activities; Performing General Physical Activities; Establishing and Maintaining Relationships; Resolving Conflicts, Negotiating with Others; Coordinating Work and Activities of Others; Guiding, Directing and Motivating Subordinates; Performing Administrative Activities; Staffing Organizational Units; Monitoring and Controlling Resources

Job Characteristics: Job-Required Social Interaction; Supervise, Coach, Train Others; Persuade Someone to a Course of Action; Take a Position Opposed to Others; Coordinate or Lead Others; Responsible for Others' Health and Safety; Responsibility for Outcomes and Results; Frequency in Conflict Situations; Deal with Unpleasant or Angry People; Sounds, Noise Levels are Distracting, etc.; Very Hot; Extremely Bright or Inadequate Lighting; Contaminants; Cramped Work Space, Awkward Positions; Whole Body Vibration; High Places; Hazardous Equipment; Standing; Climbing Ladders, Scaffolds, Poles, etc.; Walking or Running; Kneeling, Crouching, or Crawling; Keeping or Regaining Balance; Bending or Twisting the Body; Common Protective or Safety Attire; Specialized Protective or Safety Attire; Frustrating Circumstances; Importance of Being Sure All is Done; Importance of Being Aware of New Events; Importance of Repeating Same Tasks

GOE Group/s: 05.02.02 Managerial Work: Mechanical: Maintenance and Construction; 05.05.01 Craft Technology: Masonry, Stone, and Brick Work; 05.05.02 Craft Technology: Construction and Maintenance; 05.05.03 Craft Technology: Plumbing and Pipefitting; 05.05.04 Craft Technology: Painting, Plastering, and Paperhanging; 05.05.05 Craft Technology: Electrical-Electronic Systems Installation and Repair; 05.05.06 Craft Technology: Metal Fabrication and Repair; 05.06.02 Systems Operation: Stationary Engineering; 05.10.01 Crafts: Structural; 05.10.07 Crafts: Painting, Dyeing, and Coating; 05.11.01 Equipment Operation: Construction; 05.11.02 Equipment Operation: Mining, Quarrying, Drilling; 05.12.01 Elemental Work: Mechanical: Supervision; 06.01.01 Production Technology: Supervision and Instruction

CIP Program/s: 520201 Business Administration and Management, General; 520205 Operations Management and Supervision

Related DOT Job/s: 184.167-234 SUPERVISOR OF WAY; 801.131-010 SUPERVISOR, CHIMNEY CONSTRUCTION; 801.134-010 SUPERVISOR,

REINFORCED-STEEL-PLACING; 809.131-014 SUPERVISOR, ORNAMENTAL IRONWORKING; 809.131-018 SUPERVISOR, STRUCTURAL-STEEL ERECTION; 821.131-022 STEEL-POST-INSTALLER SUPERVISOR; 824.137-010 ELECTRICIAN, CHIEF; 825.131-010 ELECTRICIAN SUPERVISOR; 829.131-014 ELECTRICIAN SUPERVISOR; 840.131-010 SUPERVISOR, PAINTING; 840.131-014 SUPERVISOR, PAINTING, SHIPYARD; 841.137-010 SUPERVISOR, BILLPOSTING; 842.131-010 SUPERVISOR, DRY-WALL APPLICATION; 842.131-014 SUPERVISOR, LATHING; 842.131-018 SUPERVISOR, PLASTERING; 842.134-010 SUPERVISOR, TAPING; 843.134-010 SUPERVISOR, DOPING; 843.137-010 SUPERVISOR, WATERPROOFING; 850.133-010 SUPERVISOR, RECLAMATION; 850.137-014 SUPERVISOR, LABOR GANG; 850.137-018 SUPERVISOR, RIPRAP PLACING; 851.137-010 BANK BOSS; 851.137-014 SUPERVISOR, SEWER MAINTENANCE; 853.133-010 SUPERVISOR, ASPHALT PAVING; 853.137-010 SUPERVISOR, MIXING PLACE; 859.133-010 SUPERVISOR, RIGHT-OF-WAY MAINTENANCE; 859.137-014 SUPERVISOR, PILE DRIVING; 859.137-018 SUPERVISOR, TUNNEL HEADING; 860.131-010 SUPERVISOR, ACOUSTICAL TILE CARPENTERS; 860.131-014 SUPERVISOR, BOATBUILDERS, WOOD; 860.131-018 SUPERVISOR, CARPENTERS; 860.131-022 SUPERVISOR, JOINERS; 860.131-026 SUPERVISOR, MOLD CONSTRUCTION; 861.131-010 BRICKLAYER SUPERVISOR; 861.131-014 CHIMNEY SUPERVISOR, BRICK; 861.131-018 STONEMASON SUPERVISOR; 861.131-022 SUPERVISOR, MARBLE; 861.131-026 SUPERVISOR, TERRAZZO; 862.131-010 PIPE-FITTER SUPERVISOR; 862.131-014 PIPE-FITTER SUPERVISOR; 862.131-018 PLUMBER SUPERVISOR; 862.131-022 SUPERVISOR, PIPELINES; 862.137-010 MAINS-AND-SERVICE SUPERVISOR; 863.134-010 BUILDING-INSULATION SUPERVISOR; 863.134-014 SUPERVISOR, INSULATION; 865.131-010 GLAZIER SUPERVISOR; 866.131-010 ROOFING SUPERVISOR; 869.131-014 CONCRETING SUPERVISOR; 869.131-018 FIELD-ASSEMBLY SUPERVISOR; 869.131-022 HOUSE-MOVER SUPERVISOR; 869.131-034 TANKAGE SUPERVISOR; 869.131-038 SUPERVISOR, SWIMMING-POOL MAINTENANCE; 869.133-010 CLEARING SUPERVISOR; 869.134-010 FENCE-ERECTOR SUPERVISOR; 869.134-014 SUPERVISOR, ADJUSTABLE-STEEL-JOIST-SETTING; 869.134-018 SUPERVISOR, PIPELINE MAINTENANCE; 869.134-022 TRACK-LAYING SUPERVISOR; 869.134-026 SUPERVISOR, ASBESTOS REMOVAL; 869.367-010 ASSISTANT CONSTRUCTION SUPERINTENDENT; 899.131-010 LABOR-CREW SUPERVISOR; 899.131-018 UTILITIES-AND-MAINTENANCE SUPERVISOR; 899.133-010 SUPERVISOR, LABOR GANG; 899.134-010 HIGHWAY-MAINTENANCE SUPERVISOR; 899.137-010 AIRPORT-MAINTENANCE CHIEF; 899.137-014 SUPERINTENDENT, TRACK; 921.130-010 RIGGING SUPERVISOR

81005B FIRST LINE SUPERVISORS AND MANAGER/SUPERVISORS—EXTRACTIVE WORKERS. OOH Title/s: Blue-Collar Worker Supervisors

Directly supervise and coordinate activities of extractive workers. Supervises and coordinates activities of workers engaged in the extraction of geological materials. Directs and leads workers engaged in extraction of geological materials. Assigns work to employees, using material and worker requirements data. Confers with staff and workers to ensure production personnel problems are resolved. Analyzes and resolves worker problems and recommends motivational plans. Analyzes and plans extraction process of geological materials. Trains workers in construction methods and operation of equipment. Examines and inspects equipment, site, and materials to verify specifications are met. Recommends measures to improve production methods and equipment performance to increase efficiency and safety. Suggests and initiates personnel actions, such as promotions, transfers, and hires. Records information, such as personnel, production, and operational data on specified forms. Assists workers engaged in extraction activities, using hand tools and equipment. Locates, measures, and marks materials and site location, using measuring and marking equipment. Orders materials, supplies, and repair of equipment and machinery.
Yearly Earnings: $32,136
Education: Work experience in a related occupation
Knowledge: Administration and Management; Personnel and Human Resources; Engineering and Technology; Education and Training
Abilities: Problem Sensitivity; Deductive Reasoning; Information Ordering
Skills: Monitoring; Social Perceptiveness; Coordination; Persuasion; Negotiation; Instructing; Implementation Planning; Solution Appraisal; Operations Analysis; Equipment Selection; Operation Monitoring; Systems Perception; Identifying Downstream Consequences; Systems Evaluation; Time Management; Management of Financial Resources; Management of Material Resources; Management of Personnel Resources
General Work Activities: Scheduling Work and Activities; Resolving Conflicts, Negotiating with Others; Coordinating Work and Activities of Others; Developing and Building Teams; Teaching Others; Guiding, Directing and Motivating Subordinates; Performing Administrative Activities; Staffing Organizational Units
Job Characteristics: Job-Required Social Interaction; Supervise, Coach, Train Others; Take a Position Opposed to Others; Coordinate or Lead Others; Responsibility for Outcomes and Results; Whole Body Vibration; Common Protective or Safety Attire; Specialized Protective or Safety Attire; Consequence of Error; Frustrating Circumstances
GOE Group/s: 05.02.05 Managerial Work: Mechanical: Mining, Logging, and Petroleum Production; 05.11.01 Equipment Operation: Construction; 05.11.02 Equipment Operation: Mining, Quarrying, Drilling; 05.11.03 Equipment Operation: Drilling and Oil Exploration; 05.11.04 Equipment Operation: Material Handling; 05.12.01 Elemental Work: Mechanical: Supervision
CIP Program/s: 000000 NO CIP ASSIGNED
Related DOT Job/s: 850.137-010 SUPERVISOR, CORE DRILLING; 930.130-010 TOOL PUSHER; 930.131-010 FIELD SUPERVISOR, OIL-WELL SERVICES; 930.134-010 QUARRY SUPERVISOR, DIMENSION STONE; 932.132-010 BANK BOSS; 939.131-010 QUARRY SUPERVISOR, OPEN PIT; 939.132-010 DREDGE OPERATOR SUPERVISOR; 939.132-014 OIL-WELL-SERVICES SUPERVISOR; 939.137-014 PIT SUPERVISOR; 939.137-018 SECTION SUPERVISOR; 939.137-022 SUPERVISOR, HARVESTING

81008 FIRST LINE SUPERVISORS AND MANAGER/SUPERVISORS—PRODUCTION AND OPERATING WORKERS. OOH Title/s: Blue-Collar Worker Supervisors

Directly supervise and coordinate activities of production and operating workers, such as testers, precision workers, machine setters and operators, assemblers, fabricators, or plant and system operators. Manager/supervisors are generally found in smaller establishments, where they perform both supervisory and management functions, such as accounting, marketing, and personnel work, and may also engage in the same production work as the workers they supervise. Exclude work leaders who spend 20 percent or more of their time at tasks similar to those of employees under their supervision. These are included in the occupations which are most closely related to their specific work duties. Directs and coordinates the activities of employees engaged in production or processing of goods. Plans and establishes work schedules, assignments, and production sequences to meet production goals. Calculates labor and equipment requirements and production specifications, using standard formulae. Determines standards, production, and rates based on company policy, equipment and labor availability, and workload. Reviews operations and accounting records or reports to determine feasibility of production estimates and to evaluate current production. Confers with management or subordinates to resolve worker problems, complaints, or grievances. Confers with other supervisors to coordinate operations and activities within departments or between departments. Reads and analyzes charts, work orders, or production schedules to determine production requirements. Maintains operations data, such as time, production, and cost records and prepares management reports. Recommends or implements measures to motivate employees and improve production methods, equipment performance, product quality, or efficiency. Requisitions materials, supplies, equipment parts, or repair services. Interprets specifications, blueprints, job orders, and company policies and procedures for workers. Inspects materials, products, or equipment to detect defects or malfunctions. Demonstrates equipment operations or work procedures to new employees, or assigns employees to experienced workers for training. Monitors or patrols work area and enforces safety or sanitation regulations. Monitors gauges, dials, and other indicators to ensure operators conform to production or processing standards. Sets up and adjusts machines and equipment.

Yearly Earnings: $32,136

Education: Work experience in a related occupation

Knowledge: Administration and Management; Economics and Accounting; Sales and Marketing; Personnel and Human Resources; Production and Processing; Mathematics; Psychology; Education and Training

Abilities: Oral Comprehension; Problem Sensitivity; Number Facility; Selective Attention; Time Sharing; Response Orientation; Auditory Attention; Sound Localization; Speech Clarity

Skills: Social Perceptiveness; Coordination; Persuasion; Negotiation; Instructing; Idea Evaluation; Implementation Planning; Operations Analysis; Operation Monitoring; Product Inspection; Visioning; Systems Perception; Identifying Downstream Consequences; Systems Evaluation; Time Management; Management of Financial Resources; Management of Material Resources; Management of Personnel Resources

General Work Activities: Identifying Objects, Actions, and Events; Inspecting Equipment, Structures, or Material; Estimating Needed Characteristics; Scheduling Work and Activities; Organizing, Planning, and Prioritizing; Controlling Machines and Processes; Communicating with Other Workers; Establishing and Maintaining Relationships; Resolving Conflicts, Negotiating with Others; Coordinating Work and Activities of Others; Developing and Building Teams; Guiding, Directing and Motivating Subordinates; Coaching and Developing Others; Performing Administrative Activities; Staffing Organizational Units; Monitoring and Controlling Resources

Job Characteristics: Objective or Subjective Information; Job-Required Social Interaction; Supervise, Coach, Train Others; Persuade Someone to a Course of Action; Take a Position Opposed to Others; Coordinate or Lead Others; Responsible for Others' Health and Safety; Responsibility for Outcomes and Results; Frequency in Conflict Situations; Deal with Unpleasant or Angry People; Deal with Physical, Aggressive People; Walking or Running

GOE Group/s: 01.02.03 Visual Arts: Commercial Art; 01.06.01 Craft Arts: Graphics Arts and Related Crafts; 01.06.02 Craft Arts: Arts and Crafts; 01.06.03 Craft Arts: Hand Lettering, Painting and Decorating; 03.02.02 General Supervision: Plants and Animals: Forestry and Logging; 05.02.01 Managerial Work: Mechanical: Systems; 05.02.02 Managerial Work: Mechanical: Maintenance and Construction; 05.02.07 Managerial Work: Mechanical: Materials Handling; 05.03.02 Engineering Technology: Drafting; 05.05.01 Craft Technology: Masonry, Stone, and Brick Work; 05.05.03 Craft Technology: Plumbing and Pipefitting; 05.05.06 Craft Technology: Metal Fabrication and Repair; 05.05.07 Craft Technology: Machining; 05.05.08 Craft Technology: Woodworking; 05.05.09 Craft Technology: Mechanical Work; 05.05.10 Craft Technology: Electrical-Electronic Equipment Repair; 05.05.11 Craft Technology: Scientific, Medical, & Technical Equip. Fabric. & Related; 05.05.13 Craft Technology: Printing; 05.05.14 Craft Technology: Gem Cutting and Finishing; 05.05.15 Craft Technology: Custom Sewing, Tailoring, and Upholstering; 05.06.01 Systems Operation: Electricity Generation and Transmission; 05.06.02 Systems Operation: Stationary Engineering; 05.06.03 Systems Operation: Oil, Gas, and Water Distribution; 05.06.04 Systems Operation: Processing; 05.09.01 Material Control: Shipping, Receiving, and Stock Checking; 05.09.02 Material Control: Estimating, Scheduling, and Record Keeping; 05.10.01 Crafts: Structural; 05.10.02 Crafts: Mechanical; 05.10.04 Crafts: Structural-Mechanical-Electrical-Electronic; 05.10.05 Crafts: Reproduction; 05.10.07 Crafts: Painting, Dyeing, and Coating; 05.11.01 Equipment Operation: Construction; 05.12.01 Elemental Work: Mechanical: Supervision; 05.12.15 Elemental Work: Mechanical: Mechanical Work; 06.01.01 Production Technology: Supervision and Instruction; 06.02.01 Production Work: Supervision; 06.02.02 Production Work: Machine Work, Metal and Plastics; 06.02.03 Production Work: Machine Work, Wood; 06.02.04 Production Work: Machine Work, Paper; 06.02.09 Production Work: Machine Work, Assorted Materials; 06.02.10 Production Work: Equipment Operation, Metal Processing; 06.02.11 Production Work: Equipment Operation, Chemical Processing; 06.02.15 Production Work: Equipment Operation, Food Processing; 06.03.02 Quality Control: Inspecting, Grading, Sorting, Weighing, and Recording; 06.04.01 Elemental Work: Industrial: Supervision; 07.06.02 Clerical Machine Operation: Keyboard Machine Operation; 11.10.03 Regulations Enforcement: Health and Safety; 11.11.04 Business Management: Services

CIP Program/s: 010401 Agricultural and Food Products Processing Operations and Management; 020301 Food Sciences and Technology; 150702 Quality Control Technologists and Technicians; 200301 Clothing, Apparel and Textile Workers and Managers, General; 200305 Custom Tailor; 200309 Drycleaner and Launderer (Commercial); 470101 Electrical and Electronics Equipment Installer and Repairer; 470102 Business Machine Repairer; 480501 Machinist/Machine Technologist; 520201 Business Administration and Management, General; 520203 Logistics and Materials Management; 520205 Operations Management and Supervision

Related DOT Job/s: 184.167-046 INCINERATOR-PLANT-GENERAL SUPERVISOR; 184.167-142 SUPERINTENDENT, COLD STORAGE; 299.137-018 SAMPLE-ROOM SUPERVISOR; 361.137-010 SUPERVISOR, LAUNDRY; 369.137-010 SUPERVISOR, DRY CLEANING; 369.137-014 SUPERVISOR, RUG CLEANING; 369.167-010 MANAGER, LAUNDROMAT; 500.131-010 SUPERVISOR; 500.132-010 SUPERVISOR, SHEET MANUFACTURING; 500.134-010 SUPERVISOR, MATRIX; 501.130-010 SUPERVISOR, HOT-DIP-TINNING; 501.137-010 SUPERVISOR, HOT-DIP PLATING; 502.130-010 SUPERVISOR, CASTING-AND-PASTING; 503.137-010 SUPERVISOR, SANDBLASTER; 504.131-010 HEAT-TREAT SUPERVISOR; 505.130-010 SUPERVISOR, METALIZING; 505.130-014 SUPERVISOR, VACUUM METALIZING; 509.130-010 SUPERVISOR, POWDERED METAL; 509.130-014 SUPERVISOR, POWER-REACTOR; 509.132-010 SUPERVISOR, SOAKING PITS; 511.130-010 ALUMINA-PLANT SUPERVISOR; 511.132-010 PRECIPITATOR SUPERVISOR; 511.135-010 FILTER-PLANT SUPERVISOR; 512.130-010 REDUCTION-PLANT SUPERVISOR; 512.132-010 MELTER SUPERVISOR; 512.132-014 RECLAMATION SUPERVISOR; 512.132-018 REMELT-FURNACE EXPEDITER; 512.132-022 SUPERVISOR, BLAST FURNACE; 512.135-010 POT-ROOM SUPERVISOR; 513.132-010 CONVERTER SUPERVISOR; 514.130-010 PERMANENT-MOLD SUPERVISOR; 514.130-014 SUPERVISOR, DIE CASTING; 514.131-010 INSPECTOR, CHIEF; 514.134-010 TAPPER SUPERVISOR; 514.137-010 SUPERVISOR, PIG-MACHINE; 514.137-014 SUPERVISOR, PIT-AND-AUXILIARIES; 515.130-010 MILL SUPERVISOR; 515.132-010 CRUSHER SUPERVISOR; 519.130-010 CELL-

FEED-DEPARTMENT SUPERVISOR; 519.130-014 SAMPLER, HEAD; 519.130-018 SUPERVISOR, LEAD REFINERY; 519.130-022 SUPERVISOR, REVERBERATORY FURNACE; 519.130-026 SUPERVISOR, SINTERING PLANT; 519.130-030 SUPERVISOR, URANIUM PROCESSING; 519.131-010 FOUNDRY SUPERVISOR; 519.131-014 MILL-LABOR SUPERVISOR; 519.132-010 SUPERVISOR, BLAST FURNACE; 519.132-014 SUPERVISOR, BLAST-FURNACE-AUXILIARIES; 519.132-018 SUPERVISOR, CELL OPERATION; 519.132-022 SUPERVISOR, SOLDER MAKING; 519.134-010 POT-LINING SUPERVISOR; 519.137-010 SUPERVISOR, MOLD YARD; 520.132-010 BLENDING SUPERVISOR; 520.132-014 SUPERVISOR, COMPRESSED YEAST; 520.136-010 BLENDING SUPERVISOR; 520.137-010 SUPERVISOR, LUMP ROOM; 521.130-010 MILLER SUPERVISOR; 521.130-014 SUPERVISOR, POWDERED SUGAR; 521.131-010 SUPERVISOR, RICE MILLING; 521.132-010 MILL PLATFORM SUPERVISOR; 521.132-014 SUPERVISOR, THRESHING DEPARTMENT; 521.137-010 SUPERVISOR, PICKING; 522.130-010 SUPERVISOR, MELT HOUSE; 522.131-010 DISTILLING-DEPARTMENT SUPERVISOR; 522.132-010 SUPERVISOR, MALT HOUSE; 522.134-010 SUPERVISOR, BRINEYARD; 523.131-010 TESTING AND ANALYSIS DEPARTMENT SUPERVISOR; 523.132-010 SUPERVISOR, CHAR HOUSE; 523.137-010 SUPERVISOR, ICE HOUSE; 525.131-010 SUPERVISOR, ABATTOIR; 525.131-014 SUPERVISOR, CUTTING AND BONING; 525.132-010 SUPERVISOR, CURED MEATS; 525.132-014 SUPERVISOR, TANK HOUSE; 525.134-010 SUPERVISOR, FISH PROCESSING; 525.134-014 SUPERVISOR, POULTRY PROCESSING; 526.131-010 BAKERY SUPERVISOR; 526.134-010 COOK, MEXICAN FOOD; 526.137-010 POTATO-CHIP-PROCESSING SUPERVISOR; 529.130-010 SUPERVISOR, CANDY; 529.130-014 SUPERVISOR, CHOCOLATE-AND-COCOA PROCESSING; 529.130-018 SUPERVISOR, COFFEE; 529.130-022 SUPERVISOR, FILTRATION; 529.130-026 SUPERVISOR, NUT PROCESSING; 529.130-030 SUPERVISOR, PULP HOUSE; 529.130-034 SUPERVISOR, REFINING; 529.130-038 SUPERVISOR, SOFT SUGAR; 529.130-042 SUPERVISOR, WHITE SUGAR; 529.131-010 CELLAR SUPERVISOR; 529.131-014 SUPERVISOR, DAIRY PROCESSING; 529.132-010 CUSTOM-FEED-MILL OPERATOR; 529.132-014 PLANT SUPERVISOR; 529.132-018 SUPERVISOR, BEET END; 529.132-022 SUPERVISOR, BOTTLE-HOUSE CLEANERS; 529.132-026 SUPERVISOR, BREW HOUSE; 529.132-030 SUPERVISOR, CEREAL; 529.132-034 SUPERVISOR, CIGAR-MAKING MACHINE; 529.132-038 SUPERVISOR, COOK ROOM; 529.132-042 SUPERVISOR, DRIED YEAST; 529.132-046 SUPERVISOR, DRY-STARCH; 529.132-050 SUPERVISOR, FEED HOUSE; 529.132-054 SUPERVISOR, FEED MILL; 529.132-058 SUPERVISOR, FERMENTING CELLARS; 529.132-062 SUPERVISOR, GRAIN AND YEAST PLANTS; 529.132-066 SUPERVISOR, LIQUID YEAST; 529.132-070 SUPERVISOR, MALTED MILK; 529.132-074 SUPERVISOR, MILL HOUSE; 529.132-078 SUPERVISOR, NUTRITIONAL YEAST; 529.132-082 SUPERVISOR, SOAKERS; 529.132-086 SUPERVISOR, STEFFEN HOUSE; 529.132-090 SUPERVISOR, SUGAR HOUSE; 529.132-094 SUPERVISOR, SUGAR REFINERY; 529.132-098 SUPERVISOR, TANK STORAGE; 529.132-102 SUPERVISOR, TEA AND SPICE; 529.132-106 SUPERVISOR, WASH HOUSE; 529.132-110 SUPERVISOR; 529.135-010 COOKING, CASING, AND DRYING SUPERVISOR; 529.135-014 SUPERVISOR, CURED-MEAT PACKING; 529.137-010 PREPARATION SUPERVISOR; 529.137-014 SANITARIAN; 529.137-018 SUGAR-REPROCESS OPERATOR, HEAD; 529.137-022 SUPERINTENDENT, GRAIN ELEVATOR; 529.137-026 SUPERVISOR; 529.137-030 SUPERVISOR; 529.137-034 SUPERVISOR, CIGAR TOBACCO PROCESSING; 529.137-038 SUPERVISOR, CURING ROOM; 529.137-042 SUPERVISOR, EGG PROCESSING; 529.137-046 SUPERVISOR, FRUIT GRADING; 529.137-050 SUPERVISOR, MAPLE PRODUCTS; 529.137-054 SUPERVISOR, READY-MIXED FOOD PREPARATION; 529.137-058 SUPERVISOR, SYRUP SHED; 529.137-062 SUPERVISOR, SPECIALTY FOOD PRODUCTS; 529.137-066 SUPERVISOR,

81011 FIRST LINE SUPERVISORS AND MANAGER/SUPERVISORS—TRANSPORTATION AND MATERIAL MOVING MACHINE AND VEHICLE OPERATORS. OOH Title/s: Blue-Collar Worker Supervisors

Directly supervise and coordinate activities of transportation and material-moving machine and vehicle operators. May supervise helpers assigned to these workers. Manager/supervisors are generally found in smaller establishments where they perform both supervisory and management functions, such as accounting, marketing, and personnel work, and may also engage in the same work as the workers they supervise. Exclude work leaders who spend 20 percent or more of their time at tasks similar to those of employees under their supervision. These are included in the occupations which are most closely related to their specific work duties. Reviews orders, production schedules, and shipping/receiving notices to determine work sequence and material shipping dates, type, volume, and destinations. Plans and establishes transportation routes, work schedules, and assignments and allocates equipment to meet transportation, operations, or production goals. Directs workers in transportation or related services, such as pumping, moving, storing, and loading/unloading of materials or people. Maintains or verifies time, transportation, financial, inventory, and personnel records. Explains and demonstrates work tasks to new workers, or assigns workers to experienced workers for further training. Resolves worker problems or assists workers in solving problems. Computes and estimates cash, payroll, transportation, personnel, and storage requirements, using calculator. Requisitions needed personnel, supplies, equipment, parts, or repair services. Recommends and implements measures to improve worker motivation, equipment performance, work methods, and customer service. Prepares, compiles, and submits reports on work activities, operations, production, and work-related accidents. Inspects or tests materials, stock, vehicles, equipment, and facilities to locate defects, meet maintenance or production specifications, and verify safety standards. Interprets transportation and tariff regulations, shipping orders, safety regulations, and company policies and procedures for workers. Recommends or implements personnel actions, such as hiring, firing, and performance evaluations. Receives telephone or radio reports of emergencies, and dispatches personnel and vehicle in response to request. Confers with customers, supervisors, contractors, and other personnel to exchange information and resolve problems. Assists workers in performing tasks, such as coupling railroad cars or loading vehicles. Repairs or schedules repair and preventive maintenance of vehicles and other equipment. Examines, measures, and weighs cargo or materials to determine specific handling requirements. Drives vehicles or operates machines or equipment.

Yearly Earnings: $32,136

Education: Work experience in a related occupation

Knowledge: Administration and Management; Economics and Accounting; Sales and Marketing; Personnel and Human Resources; Production and Processing; Mathematics; Physics; Psychology; Geography; Education and Training; Public Safety and Security; Transportation

Abilities: Mathematical Reasoning; Number Facility; Speech Recognition

Skills: Learning Strategies; Social Perceptiveness; Coordination; Negotiation; Instructing; Implementation Planning; Operations Analysis; Equipment Maintenance; Repairing; Visioning; Systems Perception; Identifying Downstream Consequences; Systems Evaluation; Time Management; Management of Financial Resources; Management of Material Resources; Management of Personnel Resources

General Work Activities: Inspecting Equipment, Structures, or Material; Estimating Needed Characteristics; Processing Information; Developing Objectives and Strategies; Scheduling Work and Activities; Organizing, Planning, and Prioritizing; Interacting with Computers; Repairing and Maintaining Mechanical Equipment; Documenting/Recording Information; Communicating with Other Workers; Establishing and Maintaining Relationships; Resolving Conflicts, Negotiating with Others; Coordinating Work and Activities of Others; Developing and Building Teams; Teaching Others; Guiding, Directing and Motivating Subordinates; Coaching and Developing Others; Performing Administrative Activities; Staffing Organizational Units; Monitoring and Controlling Resources
Job Characteristics: Supervise, Coach, Train Others; Take a Position Opposed to Others; Coordinate or Lead Others; Responsibility for Outcomes and Results; Frequency in Conflict Situations; Deal with Unpleasant or Angry People; Deal with Physical, Aggressive People
GOE Group/s: 05.02.01 Managerial Work: Mechanical: Systems; 05.06.03 Systems Operation: Oil, Gas, and Water Distribution; 05.08.01 Land and Water Vehicle Operation: Truck Driving; 05.08.02 Land and Water Vehicle Operation: Rail Vehicle Operation; 05.08.03 Land and Water Vehicle Operation: Services Requiring Driving; 05.09.01 Material Control: Shipping, Receiving, and Stock Checking; 05.11.01 Equipment Operation: Construction; 05.11.02 Equipment Operation: Mining, Quarrying, Drilling; 05.11.04 Equipment Operation: Material Handling; 05.12.01 Elemental Work: Mechanical: Supervision; 05.12.02 Elemental Work: Mechanical: Mining, Quarrying, Drilling; 05.12.18 Elemental Work: Mechanical: Cleaning and Maintenance; 06.01.01 Production Technology: Supervision and Instruction; 07.04.05 Oral Communications: Information Transmitting and Receiving; 08.02.07 General Sales: Driving-Selling; 09.03.03 Passenger Services: Instruction and Supervision; 09.04.02 Customer Services: Sales Services; 11.11.03 Business Management: Transportation
CIP Program/s: 080709 General Distribution Operations; 490309 Marine Science/Merchant Marine Officer; 520201 Business Administration and Management, General; 520203 Logistics and Materials Management
Related DOT Job/s: 185.167-018 MANAGER, DISTRIBUTION WAREHOUSE; 187.167-150 MANAGER, STORAGE GARAGE; 292.137-014 SUPERVISOR, ROUTE SALES-DELIVERY DRIVERS; 579.137-030 DISPATCHER, CONCRETE PRODUCTS; 859.137-010 SUPERVISOR, GRADING; 909.137-010 DRIVER SUPERVISOR; 909.137-014 GARBAGE-COLLECTION SUPERVISOR; 909.137-018 TRUCK SUPERVISOR; 910.137-022 CONDUCTOR, YARD; 910.137-034 ROAD SUPERVISOR OF ENGINES; 910.137-046 YARD MANAGER; 911.131-010 BOATSWAIN; 911.137-018 HEADER; 911.137-022 SUPERINTENDENT, STEVEDORING; 911.137-026 SUPERVISOR, FERRY TERMINAL; 913.133-010 ROAD SUPERVISOR; 913.133-014 SUPERVISOR, CAB; 913.167-014 DISPATCHER, BUS AND TROLLEY; 914.131-010 SUPERVISOR, PUMPING; 914.132-010 COMPRESSOR-STATION ENGINEER, CHIEF; 914.132-014 STATION ENGINEER, CHIEF; 914.132-018 SUPERVISOR, CELLARS; 914.132-022 SUPERVISOR, FIELD PIPELINES; 914.134-010 GAUGER, CHIEF; 914.137-010 DISTRIBUTION SUPERVISOR; 914.137-014 LOADING-RACK SUPERVISOR; 914.137-018 SUPERVISOR, DOCK; 915.133-010 SUPERVISOR, PARKING LOT; 921.132-010 TRACK SUPERVISOR; 921.133-010 CRANE-CREW SUPERVISOR; 921.133-014 LOAD-OUT SUPERVISOR; 921.133-018 MATERIAL-HANDLING SUPERVISOR; 921.137-014 MATERIAL-CREW SUPERVISOR; 922.137-026 WAREHOUSE TRAFFIC SUPERVISOR; 929.132-010 SUPERVISOR, REACTOR FUELING; 929.133-010 YARD SUPERVISOR; 929.137-030 YARD SUPERVISOR, BUILDING MATERIALS OR LUMBER; 932.132-014 SURFACE SUPERVISOR; 939.131-018 WELL PULLER, HEAD; 953.137-010 GAS-PUMPING-STATION SUPERVISOR; 955.133-010 SANITARY-LANDFILL SUPERVISOR; 955.137-010 SNOW-REMOVING SUPERVISOR

81017 FIRST LINE SUPERVISORS AND MANAGER/SUPERVISORS—HELPERS, LABORERS, AND MATERIAL MOVERS, HAND. OOH Title/s: Blue-Collar Worker Supervisors

Directly supervise and coordinate activities of helpers, laborers, and material movers. Manager/supervisors are generally found in smaller establishments, where they perform both supervisory and management functions, such as accounting, marketing, and personnel work, and may also engage in the same hand labor as the workers they supervise. Exclude work leaders who spend 20 percent or more of theirtime at tasks similar to those of employees under their supervision. These are included in the occupations which are most closely related to their specific work duties. Supervises and coordinates activities of workers performing assigned tasks. Assigns duties and work schedules. Determines work sequence and equipment needed, according to work order, shipping records, and experience. Observes work procedures to ensure quality of work. Trains and instructs workers. Records information, such as daily receipts, employee time and wage data, description of freight, and inspection results. Verifies materials loaded or unloaded against work order, and schedules times of shipment and mode of transportation. Examines freight to determine sequence of loading and equipment to determine compliance with specifications. Inspects equipment for wear and completed work for conformance to standards. Inventories and orders supplies. Informs designated employees or department of items loaded, or reports loading deficiencies. Quotes prices to customers. Resolves customer complaints.
Yearly Earnings: $32,136
Education: Work experience in a related occupation
Knowledge: Administration and Management; Economics and Accounting; Sales and Marketing; Customer and Personal Service; Personnel and Human Resources; Production and Processing; Mathematics; Psychology; Education and Training
Abilities: None above average
Skills: Learning Strategies; Social Perceptiveness; Instructing; Implementation Planning; Systems Perception; Systems Evaluation; Time Management; Management of Personnel Resources
General Work Activities: Scheduling Work and Activities; Resolving Conflicts, Negotiating with Others; Teaching Others; Guiding, Directing and Motivating Subordinates; Coaching and Developing Others
Job Characteristics: Supervise, Coach, Train Others; Coordinate or Lead Others; Responsibility for Outcomes and Results; Frequency in Conflict Situations
GOE Group/s: 05.12.01 Elemental Work: Mechanical: Supervision; 06.01.01 Production Technology: Supervision and Instruction; 06.04.01 Elemental Work: Industrial: Supervision
CIP Program/s: 520201 Business Administration and Management, General; 520205 Operations Management and Supervision
Related DOT Job/s: 189.167-042 SUPERINTENDENT, LABOR UTILIZATION; 519.137-014 SUPERVISOR, SCRAP PREPARATION; 559.137-050 SUPERVISOR, TANK CLEANING; 570.132-022 SUPERVISOR; 699.137-010 SUPERVISOR, CLEANING; 860.137-010 CARPENTER-LABOR SUPERVISOR; 891.137-014 SUPERVISOR, AIRCRAFT CLEANING; 891.137-018 SUPERVISOR, TANK CLEANING; 899.131-022 UTILITY SUPERVISOR, BOAT AND PLANT; 910.137-014 CAR-CLEANING SUPERVISOR; 910.137-018 CIRCUS-TRAIN SUPERVISOR; 910.137-026 FREIGHT-LOADING SUPERVISOR; 915.137-010 CAR-WASH SUPERVISOR; 922.137-018 SUPERVISOR, LOADING AND UNLOADING

Inspectors, Testers, and Graders

83002A MATERIALS INSPECTORS. OOH Title/s: Inspectors, Testers, and Graders

Examine and inspect materials and finished parts and products for defects and wear, and to ensure conformance with work orders, diagrams, blueprints, and template specifications. Usually specialize in a single phase of inspection. Inspects materials, products, and work in progress for conformance to specifications, and adjusts process or assembly equipment to meet standards. Tests and measures finished products, components, or assemblies for functioning, operation, accuracy, or assembly to verify adherence to functional specifications. Analyzes and interprets blueprints, sample data, and other materials to determine, change, or measure specifications or inspection and testing procedures. Collects samples for testing, and computes findings. Reads dials and meters to verify functioning of equipment according to specifications. Observes and monitors production operations and equipment to ensure proper assembly of parts, or assists in testing and monitoring activities. Fabricates, installs, positions, or connects components, parts, finished products, or instruments for testing or operational purposes. Marks items for acceptance or rejection, records test results and inspection data, and compares findings with specifications to ensure conformance to standards. Operates or tends machinery and equipment, and uses hand tools. Supervises testing or drilling activities, and adjusts equipment to obtain sample fluids or to direct drilling. Confers with vendors and others regarding inspection results, recommends corrective procedures, and compiles reports of results. Recommendations, and needed repairs.

Yearly Earnings: $22,932

Education: Work experience in a related occupation

Knowledge: Production and Processing; Engineering and Technology; Design; Mechanical; Physics; Public Safety and Security

Abilities: Problem Sensitivity; Inductive Reasoning; Information Ordering; Category Flexibility; Mathematical Reasoning; Memorization; Flexibility of Closure; Perceptual Speed; Visualization; Selective Attention; Time Sharing; Manual Dexterity; Finger Dexterity; Response Orientation; Rate Control; Reaction Time; Wrist-Finger Speed; Static Strength; Explosive Strength; Dynamic Flexibility; Gross Body Equilibrium; Near Vision; Visual Color Discrimination; Peripheral Vision; Hearing Sensitivity; Auditory Attention; Sound Localization

Skills: Mathematics; Solution Appraisal; Operations Analysis; Technology Design; Installation; Testing; Operation Monitoring; Operation and Control; Product Inspection; Troubleshooting; Repairing; Management of Personnel Resources

General Work Activities: Identifying Objects, Actions, and Events; Inspecting Equipment, Structures, or Material; Processing Information; Updating and Using Job-Relevant Knowledge; Controlling Machines and Processes; Operating Vehicles or Equipment; Drafting and Specifying Technical Devices, etc.; Repairing and Maintaining Mechanical Equipment; Repairing and Maintaining Electrical Equipment; Provide Consultation and Advice to Others

Job Characteristics: Degree of Automation; Importance of Being Sure All is Done; Pace Determined by Speed of Equipment

GOE Group/s: 05.05.07 Craft Technology: Machining; 05.05.11 Craft Technology: Scientific, Medical, & Technical Equip. Fabric. & Related; 05.05.14 Craft Technology: Gem Cutting and Finishing; 05.07.01 Quality Control: Structural; 05.07.05 Quality Control: Petroleum; 06.01.05 Production Technology: Inspection; 06.03.01 Quality Control: Inspecting, Testing, and Repairing

CIP Program/s: 020301 Food Sciences and Technology; 150603 Industrial/Manufacturing Technologists and Technicians; 150607 Plastics Technologists and Technicians; 150611 Metallurgical Technologists and Technicians; 150801 Aeronautical and Aerospace Engineering Technologists and Technicians; 150903 Petroleum Technologists and Technicians; 460201 Carpenter; 460403 Construction/Building Inspector; 460501 Plumber and Pipefitter; 470101 Electrical and Electronics Equipment Installer and Repairer; 470102 Business Machine Repairer; 470201 Heating, Air Conditioning and Refrigeration Mechanics and Repairers; 470303 Industrial Machinery Maintenance and Repair; 470402 Gunsmith; 470408 Watch, Clock and Jewelry Repairer; 470604 Auto/Automotive Mechanic/Technician; 470605 Diesel Engine Mechanic and Repairer; 470607 Aircraft Mechanic/Technician, Airframe; 480501 Machinist/Machine Technologist; 480503 Machine Shop Assistant; 480507 Tool and Die Maker/Technologist; 480508 Welder/Welding Technologist; 480599 Precision Metal Workers, Other; 489999 Precision Production Trades, Other; 490306 Marine Maintenance and Repair

Related DOT Job/s: 199.361-010 RADIOGRAPHER; 504.281-010 HEAT-TREAT INSPECTOR; 526.381-022 CAKE TESTER; 529.281-010 TASTER; 549.261-010 MECHANICAL INSPECTOR; 559.381-010 INSPECTOR; 559.381-014 RUBBER TESTER; 572.360-010 FURNACE-COMBUSTION ANALYST; 600.281-014 LAY-OUT INSPECTOR; 601.261-010 INSPECTOR, SET-UP AND LAY-OUT; 601.281-022 INSPECTOR, TOOL; 609.361-010 INSPECTOR, FLOOR; 612.261-010 INSPECTOR; 616.361-010 SPRING INSPECTOR I; 619.261-010 INSPECTOR, METAL FABRICATING; 619.364-010 INSPECTOR I; 619.381-010 INSPECTOR; 619.381-014 EDDY-CURRENT INSPECTOR; 622.381-038 SALVAGE INSPECTOR; 632.381-014 INSPECTOR, FIREARMS; 701.261-010 QUALITY-CONTROL INSPECTOR; 706.381-022 INSPECTOR, TYPEWRITER ASSEMBLY AND PARTS; 736.281-010 GUN EXAMINER; 739.281-014 ULTRASONIC TESTER; 739.381-026 EXPERIMENTAL ASSEMBLER; 739.484-010 CHRONOGRAPH OPERATOR; 750.382-010 TIRE TECHNICIAN; 759.381-010 RUBBER-GOODS TESTER; 770.267-010 DIAMOND EXPERT; 770.687-014 DIAMOND SIZER AND SORTER; 770.687-018 JEWEL GAUGER; 777.381-046 SAND TESTER; 806.261-034 INSPECTOR, MATERIAL DISPOSITION; 806.261-042 INSPECTOR, OUTSIDE PRODUCTION; 806.261-046 INSPECTOR, PLASTICS AND COMPOSITES; 806.261-050 OPERATIONAL TEST MECHANIC; 806.264-014 INSPECTOR, AIRCRAFT LAUNCHING AND ARRESTING SYSTEMS; 806.283-014 TEST DRIVER I; 806.361-018 FINAL INSPECTOR, TRUCK TRAILER; 806.361-022 INSPECTOR, FABRICATION; 806.381-074 INSPECTOR, PROCESSING; 819.281-018 WELD INSPECTOR I; 827.361-010 AIR-CONDITIONING-UNIT TESTER; 860.261-010 CARPENTER INSPECTOR; 862.381-038 THREAD INSPECTOR; 869.281-018 YARD INSPECTOR; 930.261-014 FORMATION-TESTING OPERATOR; 930.267-010 OIL-PIPE INSPECTOR

83002B MECHANICAL INSPECTORS. OOH Title/s: Inspectors, Testers, and Graders

Inspect and test mechanical assemblies and systems—such as motors, vehicles, and transportation equipment—for defects and wear to ensure compliance with specifications. Tests and measures finished products, components, or assemblies for functioning, operation, accuracy, or assembly to verify adherence to functional specifications. Inspects materials, products, and work in progress for conformance to specifications, and adjusts process or assembly equipment to meet standards. Starts and operates finished products for testing or inspection. Reads dials and meters to ensure that equipment is operating according to specifications. Collects samples for testing, and computes findings. Marks items for acceptance or rejection, records test results and inspection data, and compares findings with specifications to ensure conformance to standards. Discards or rejects products, materials, and equipment not meeting specifications. Reads and interprets materials, such as work orders, inspection manuals, and blueprints, to determine inspection and test procedures. Analyzes and interprets sample data. Installs and positions new or replacement parts, components, and instruments. Estimates and records operational data. Completes necessary procedures to satisfy licensing requirements, and indicates concurrence with acceptance or rejection decisions. Confers with vendors and others regarding inspection results, recommends corrective procedures, and compiles reports of results, recommendations, and needed repairs. Cleans and maintains test equipment and instruments to ensure proper functioning.

Yearly Earnings: $22,932

Education: Work experience in a related occupation

Knowledge: Production and Processing; Engineering and Technology; Design; Mechanical; Physics; Public Safety and Security; Law, Government, and Jurisprudence

Abilities: Written Comprehension; Inductive Reasoning; Information Ordering; Category Flexibility; Mathematical Reasoning; Number Facility; Memorization; Speed of Closure; Flexibility of Closure; Perceptual Speed; Visualization; Selective Attention; Manual Dexterity; Finger Dexterity; Control Precision; Response Orientation; Rate Control; Reaction Time; Extent Flexibility; Gross Body Equilibrium; Near Vision; Far Vision; Visual Color Discrimination; Depth Perception; Hearing Sensitivity; Auditory Attention; Sound Localization

Skills: Science; Installation; Testing; Operation Monitoring; Operation and Control; Product Inspection; Equipment Maintenance; Troubleshooting

General Work Activities: Inspecting Equipment, Structures, or Material; Processing Information; Interacting with Computers; Drafting and Specifying Technical Devices, etc.; Repairing and Maintaining Mechanical Equipment; Repairing and Maintaining Electrical Equipment

Job Characteristics: Sounds, Noise Levels are Distracting, etc.; Importance of Being Exact or Accurate; Importance of Being Aware of New Events

GOE Group/s: 05.05.09 Craft Technology: Mechanical Work; 05.07.01 Quality Control: Structural; 05.07.02 Quality Control: Mechincal; 06.01.05 Production Technology: Inspection

CIP Program/s: 010201 Agricultural Mechanization, General; 010204 Agricultural Power Machinery Operator; 150801 Aeronautical and Aerospace Engineering Technologists and Technicians; 470603 Auto/Automotive Body Repairer; 470604 Auto/Automotive Mechanic/Technician; 470605 Diesel Engine Mechanic and Repairer; 470607 Aircraft Mechanic/Technician, Airframe; 470608 Aircraft Mechanic/Technician, Powerplant; 470611 Motorcycle Mechanic and Repairer

Related DOT Job/s: 602.362-010 GEAR INSPECTOR; 620.261-014 AUTOMOBILE TESTER; 620.261-018 AUTOMOBILE-REPAIR-SERVICE ESTIMATOR; 620.281-014 AUTOMOTIVE TECHNICIAN, EXHAUST EMISSIONS; 620.281-030 BUS INSPECTOR; 621.261-010 AIRPLANE INSPECTOR; 621.261-014 ENGINE TESTER; 622.281-010 LOCOMOTIVE INSPECTOR; 622.381-034 RAILROAD WHEELS AND AXLE INSPECTOR; 624.361-010 INSPECTOR AND TESTER; 625.261-010 DIESEL-ENGINE TESTER; 710.384-014 INSPECTOR; 736.381-018 PROCESS INSPECTOR; 801.381-018 MAJOR-ASSEMBLY INSPECTOR; 806.261-010 INTERNAL-COMBUSTION-ENGINE INSPECTOR; 806.261-022 TESTER, ROCKET MOTOR; 806.261-030 INSPECTOR, ASSEMBLIES AND INSTALLATIONS; 806.261-038 INSPECTOR, MISSILE; 806.281-010 DYNAMOMETER TESTER, ENGINE; 806.281-018 FINAL INSPECTOR, MOTORCYLES; 806.281-026 INSPECTOR, PRECISION ASSEMBLY; 806.387-014 WHEEL INSPECTOR

83002C PRECISION DEVICES INSPECTORS AND TESTERS. OOH Title/s: Inspectors, Testers, and Graders; Precision Assemblers

Verify accuracy of and adjust precision devices—such as meters and gauges, testing instruments, and clock and watch mechanisms—to ensure operation of device is in accordance with design specifications. Inspects materials, products, and work in progress for conformance to specifications, and adjusts process or assembly equipment to meet standards. Reads dials and meters to verify functioning of equipment according to specifications. Tests and measures finished products, components, or assemblies for functioning, operation, accuracy, or assembly to verify adherence to functional specifications. Cleans and maintains test equipment and instruments, and certifies that precision instruments meet standards. Marks items for acceptance or rejection, records test results and inspection data, and compares findings with specifications to ensure conformance to standards. Fabricates, installs, positions, or connects components, parts, finished products, or instruments for testing or operational purposes. Analyzes and interprets blueprints, sample data, and other materials to determine, change, or measure specifications or inspection and testing procedures. Discards or rejects products, materials, and equipment not meeting specifications. Operates or tends machinery and equipment, and uses hand tools. Estimates operational data to meet acceptable standards. Disassembles defective parts and components. Confers with vendors and others regarding inspection results and recommends corrective procedures. Computes or calculates data and other information. Completes necessary procedures to satisfy licensing requirements.

Yearly Earnings: $22,932

Education: Work experience in a related occupation

Knowledge: Production and Processing; Engineering and Technology; Design; Mechanical; Mathematics

Abilities: Problem Sensitivity; Inductive Reasoning; Information Ordering; Category Flexibility; Mathematical Reasoning; Number Facility; Memorization; Speed of Closure; Flexibility of Closure; Perceptual Speed; Spatial Orientation; Visualization; Selective Attention; Arm-Hand Steadiness; Finger Dexterity; Control Precision; Multilimb Coordination; Response Orientation; Rate Control; Reaction Time; Wrist-Finger Speed; Speed of Limb Movement; Extent Flexibility; Gross Body Equilibrium; Near Vision; Visual Color Discrimination; Hearing Sensitivity; Auditory Attention; Sound Localization

Skills: Science; Technology Design; Installation; Testing; Operation Monitoring; Product Inspection; Equipment Maintenance; Troubleshooting

General Work Activities: Inspecting Equipment, Structures, or Material; Processing Information; Updating and Using Job-Relevant Knowledge; Handling and Moving Objects; Operating Vehicles or Equipment; Drafting and Specifying Technical Devices, etc.; Implementing Ideas, Programs, etc.; Repairing and Maintaining Mechanical Equipment; Repairing and Maintaining Electrical Equipment

Job Characteristics: Degree of Automation; Importance of Being Exact or Accurate; Importance of Being Sure All is Done

GOE Group/s: 02.04.01 Laboratory Technology: Physical Sciences; 05.05.10 Craft Technology: Electrical-Electronic Equipment Repair; 06.01.04 Production Technology: Precision Hand Work; 06.01.05 Production Technology: Inspection; 06.03.01 Quality Control: Inspecting, Testing, and Repairing

CIP Program/s: 150401 Biomedical Engineering-Related Technologists and Technicians; 150403 Electromechanical Technologists and Technicians; 150699 Industrial Production Technologists and Technicians, Other; 150801 Aeronautical and Aerospace Engineering Technologists and Technicians; 470401 Instrument Calibration and Repairer; 470408 Watch, Clock and Jewelry Repairer; 470499 Miscellaneous Mechanics and Repairers, Other; 470609 Aviation Systems and Avionics Maintenance Technologists and Technicians; 480503 Machine Shop Assistant

Related DOT Job/s: 601.281-018 INSPECTOR, GAUGE AND INSTRUMENT; 710.381-014 BALANCER, SCALE; 710.381-030 HYDROMETER CALIBRATOR; 710.381-034 CALIBRATOR; 710.381-042 CALIBRATOR, BAROMETERS; 710.384-022 METER INSPECTOR; 711.281-010 INSPECTOR, OPTICAL INSTRUMENT; 714.381-014 INSPECTOR, PHOTOGRAPHIC EQUIPMENT; 715.261-010 MECHANICAL TECHNICIAN, LABORATORY; 715.381-050 FINAL INSPECTOR; 715.381-058 HAIRSPRING TRUER; 715.381-066 INSPECTOR, HAIRSPRING I; 715.381-070 INSPECTOR, WATCH ASSEMBLY; 715.381-074 INSPECTOR, WATCH TRAIN; 715.381-078 LOCATION-AND-MEASUREMENT TECHNICIAN; 715.384-022 INSPECTOR, WATCH PARTS; 716.381-010 INSPECTOR, PRECISION; 722.381-014 INSTRUMENT INSPECTOR; 729.281-046 X-RAY-EQUIPMENT TESTER; 729.361-010 INSPECTOR, ELECTROMECHANICAL; 821.381-010 ELECTRIC-METER TESTER

83002D ELECTRICAL AND ELECTRONIC INSPECTORS AND TESTERS. OOH Title/s: Inspectors, Testers, and Graders

Inspect and test electrical and electronic systems—such as radar navigational equipment, computer memory units, and television and radio transmitters—using precision measuring instruments. Usually designated according to product inspected. Tests and measures finished products, components, or assemblies for functioning, operation, accuracy, or assembly to verify adherence to functional specifications. Inspects materials, products, and work in progress for conformance to specifications, and adjusts process or assembly equipment to meet standards. Marks items for acceptance or rejection, records test results and inspection data, and compares findings with specifications to ensure conformance to standards. Reads dials and meters to verify functioning of equipment according to specifications. Analyzes and interprets blueprints, sample data, and other materials to determine, change, or measure specifications or inspection and testing procedures. Computes or calculates sample data and test results. Examines and adjusts or repairs finished products and components or parts. Assists supervisor and other workers in testing and monitoring activities. Confers with vendors and others regarding inspection results, recommends corrective procedures, and compiles reports of results, recommendations, and needed repairs. Operates or tends machinery and equipment, and uses hand tools. Positions or directs other workers to position products, components, or parts for testing. Cleans and maintains test equipment and instruments to ensure proper functioning. Disassembles defective parts and components. Reviews maintenance records to ensure that plant equipment functions properly. Supervises testing or drilling activities. Installs, positions, or connects new or replacement parts, components, and instruments. Writes and installs computer programs to control test equipment.

Yearly Earnings: $22,932

Education: Work experience in a related occupation

Knowledge: Production and Processing; Computers and Electronics; Engineering and Technology; Design; Mechanical; Mathematics; Physics; English Language; Telecommunications

Abilities: Fluency of Ideas; Deductive Reasoning; Information Ordering; Category Flexibility; Mathematical Reasoning; Number Facility; Memorization; Speed of Closure; Flexibility of Closure; Perceptual Speed; Spatial Orientation; Visualization; Selective Attention; Time Sharing; Manual Dexterity; Finger Dexterity; Control Precision; Multilimb Coordination; Response Orientation; Rate Control; Reaction Time; Wrist-Finger Speed; Explosive Strength; Trunk Strength; Extent Flexibility; Gross Body Equilibrium; Near Vision; Visual Color Discrimination; Peripheral Vision; Depth Perception; Hearing Sensitivity; Auditory Attention; Sound Localization; Speech Recognition

Skills: Mathematics; Science; Problem Identification; Operations Analysis; Technology Design; Equipment Selection; Installation; Programming; Testing; Operation Monitoring; Operation and Control; Product Inspection; Equipment Maintenance; Troubleshooting; Repairing

General Work Activities: Identifying Objects, Actions, and Events; Inspecting Equipment, Structures, or Material; Processing Information; Updating and Using Job-Relevant Knowledge; Controlling Machines and Processes; Operating Vehicles or Equipment; Drafting and Specifying Technical Devices, etc.; Implementing Ideas, Programs, etc.; Repairing and Maintaining Electrical Equipment; Documenting/Recording Information

Job Characteristics: Supervise, Coach, Train Others; Responsibility for Outcomes and Results; Hazardous Conditions; Degree of Automation

GOE Group/s: 05.05.05 Craft Technology: Electrical-Electronic Systems Installation and Repair; 05.06.01 Systems Operation: Electricity Generation and Transmission; 05.07.03 Quality Control: Electrical; 05.10.03 Crafts: Electrical-Electronic; 06.01.05 Production Technology: Inspection; 06.03.01 Quality Control: Inspecting, Testing, and Repairing; 06.03.02 Quality Control: Inspecting, Grading, Sorting, Weighing, and Recording

CIP Program/s: 150403 Electromechanical Technologists and Technicians; 150702 Quality Control Technologists and Technicians; 460301 Electrical and Power Transmission Installer, General; 460302 Electrician; 460303 Lineworker; 470101 Electrical and Electronics Equipment Installer and Repairer; 470103 Communication Systems Installer and Repairer; 470105 Industrial Electronics Installer and Repairer; 470199 Electrical and Electronics Equipment Installer and Repairer; 470401 Instrument Calibration and Repairer; 470501 Stationary Energy Sources Installer and Operator; 470607 Aircraft Mechanic/Technician, Airframe; 470609 Aviation Systems and Avionics Maintenance Technologists and Technicians

Related DOT Job/s: 710.381-046 TESTER, ELECTRONIC SCALE; 721.261-014 FINAL TESTER; 721.281-030 TESTER, MOTORS AND CONTROLS; 721.361-010 INSPECTOR, MOTORS AND GENERATORS; 724.281-010 TRANSFORMER TESTER; 724.364-010 WINDING INSPECTOR AND TESTER; 724.384-010 ARMATURE TESTER I; 726.261-018 ELECTRONICS TESTER; 726.361-018 GROUP LEADER, PRINTED CIRCUIT BOARD QUALITY CONTROL; 726.362-010 GROUP LEADER, SEMICONDUCTOR TESTING; 726.364-010 LEAD HAND, INSPECTING AND TESTING; 726.381-010 ELECTRONICS INSPECTOR; 726.384-014 INSPECTOR, CIRCUITRY NEGATIVE; 726.384-018 INSPECTOR, SEMICONDUCTOR WAFER PROCESSING; 726.384-022 PHOTO MASK INSPECTOR; 726.682-018 COORDINATE MEASURING EQUIPMENT OPERATOR; 727.381-018 DRY-CELL TESTER; 727.381-022 STORAGE BATTERY INSPECTOR AND TESTER; 729.281-038 RELAY TESTER; 729.381-010 ELECTRICAL-EQUIPMENT TESTER; 820.361-018 REGULATOR INSPECTOR; 821.381-014 VOLTAGE TESTER; 822.261-018 MAINTENANCE INSPECTOR; 822.261-026 TESTING-AND-REGULATING TECHNICIAN; 822.361-010 CABLE TESTER; 822.361-026 TRANSMISSION TESTER; 822.361-030 TROUBLE LOCATOR, TEST DESK; 824.281-014 ELECTRIC-DISTRIBUTION CHECKER; 825.361-014 VIBRATOR-EQUIPMENT TESTER; 825.381-026 ELECTRICAL INSPECTOR; 827.381-010 CONTROL-PANEL TESTER; 829.261-010 COMPLAINT INSPECTOR; 829.361-018 CIRCULATING PROCESS INSPECTOR; 952.261-010 SUBSTATION INSPECTOR

83005A PRODUCTION INSPECTORS, TESTERS, GRADERS, SORTERS, SAMPLERS, AND WEIGHERS. OOH Title/s: Inspectors, Testers, and Graders

Inspect, test, grade, sort, sample, or weigh nonagricultural raw materials or processed, machined, fabricated, or assembled parts or products. Work may be performed before, during, or

after processing. Weighs materials, products, containers, or samples to verify packaging weight, to determine percentage of each ingredient, or to determine sorting. Examines product or monitors processing of product, using any or all of five senses, to determine defects or grade. Measures dimensions of product, using measuring instruments—such as rulers, calipers, gauges, or micrometers, to verify conformance to specifications. Compares color, shape, texture, or grade of product or material with color chart, template, or sample, to verify conformance to standards. Tests samples, materials, or products—using test equipment such as thermometer, voltmeter, moisture meter, or tensiometer—for conformance to specifications. Grades, classifies, and sorts products according to size, weight, color, or other specifications. Marks, affixes, or stamps product or container to identify defects or to denote grade or size information. Records inspection or test data, such as weight, temperature, grade, or moisture content, and number inspected or graded. Collects or selects samples for testing or for use as model. Discards or routes defective products or contaminants for rework or reuse. Notifies supervisor or specified personnel of deviations from specifications, machine malfunctions, or need for equipment maintenance. Reads work order to determine inspection criteria and to verify identification numbers and product type. Uses or operates product to test functional performance. Computes percentages or averages, using formulas and calculator, and prepares reports of inspection or test findings. Sets controls, starts machine, and observes machine which automatically sorts or inspects products. Counts number of product tested or inspected, and stacks or arranges for further processing, shipping, or packing. Cleans, trims, makes adjustments, or repairs product or processing equipment to correct defects found during inspection. Transports inspected or tested products to other work stations, using handtruck or lift truck. Wraps and packages products for shipment or delivery.

Yearly Earnings: $22,932

Education: Work experience in a related occupation

Knowledge: Production and Processing

Abilities: Category Flexibility; Flexibility of Closure; Perceptual Speed; Selective Attention; Control Precision; Dynamic Flexibility; Near Vision; Visual Color Discrimination; Auditory Attention

Skills: Testing; Operation Monitoring; Product Inspection

General Work Activities: Inspecting Equipment, Structures, or Material

Job Characteristics: Take a Position Opposed to Others; Importance of Repeating Same Tasks; Pace Determined by Speed of Equipment

GOE Group/s: 01.06.01 Craft Arts: Graphics Arts and Related Crafts; 02.04.01 Laboratory Technology: Physical Sciences; 03.04.02 Elemental Work: Plants and Animals: Forestry and Logging; 05.03.09 Engineering Technology: Packaging and Storing; 05.05.15 Craft Technology: Custom Sewing, Tailoring, and Upholstering; 05.07.01 Quality Control: Structural; 05.07.02 Quality Control: Mechincal; 05.07.04 Quality Control: Environmental; 05.07.05 Quality Control: Petroleum; 05.07.06 Quality Control: Logging and Lumber; 05.08.03 Land and Water Vehicle Operation: Services Requiring Driving; 05.09.01 Material Control: Shipping, Receiving, and Stock Checking; 05.09.02 Material Control: Estimating, Scheduling, and Record Keeping; 05.09.03 Material Control: Verifying, Recording, and Marking; 05.10.05 Crafts: Reproduction; 05.12.03 Elemental Work: Mechanical: Loading, Moving; 05.12.07 Elemental Work: Mechanical: Crushing, Mixing, Separating, and Chipping; 05.12.12 Elemental Work: Mechanical: Structural Work; 06.01.04 Production Technology: Precision Hand Work; 06.01.05 Production Technology: Inspection; 06.02.02 Production Work: Machine Work, Metal and Plastics; 06.02.06 Production Work: Machine Work, Textiles; 06.02.09 Production Work: Machine Work, Assorted Materials; 06.02.27 Production Work: Manual Work, Textile, Fabric and Leather; 06.02.30 Production Work: Manual Work, Stone, Glass, and Clay; 06.02.31 Production Work: Manual Work, Laying Out and Marking; 06.03.01 Quality Control: Inspecting, Testing, and Repairing; 06.03.02 Quality Control: Inspecting, Grading, Sorting, Weighing, and Recording; 06.04.01 Elemental Work: Industrial: Supervision; 06.04.02 Elemental Work: Industrial: Machine Work, Metal and Plastics; 06.04.08 Elemental Work: Industrial: Machine Work, Stone, Glass, and Clay; 06.04.10 Elemental Work: Industrial: Equipment Operation, Metal Processing; 06.04.14 Elemental Work: Industrial: Equipment Operation, Paper Making; 06.04.15 Elemental Work: Industrial: Equipment Operation, Food Processing; 06.04.17 Elemental Work: Industrial: Equipment Operation, Clay Processing; 06.04.24 Elemental Work: Industrial: Manual Work, Metal and Plastics; 06.04.25 Elemental Work: Industrial: Manual Work, Wood; 06.04.26 Elemental Work: Industrial: Manual Work, Paper; 06.04.27 Elemental Work: Industrial: Manual Work, Textile, Fabric and Leather; 06.04.28 Elemental Work: Industrial: Manual Work, Food Processing; 06.04.29 Elemental Work: Industrial: Manual Work, Rubber; 06.04.34 Elemental Work: Industrial: Manual Work, Assorted Materials; 06.04.35 Elemental Work: Industrial: Laundering, Dry Cleaning; 06.04.37 Elemental Work: Industrial: Manual Work, Stamping, Marking, Labeling, and Ticketing; 06.04.38 Elemental Work: Industrial: Wrapping and Packaging; 06.04.40 Elemental Work: Industrial: Loading, Moving, Hoisting, and Conveying; 07.07.03 Clerical Handling: General Clerical Work

CIP Program/s: 010204 Agricultural Power Machinery Operator; 010401 Agricultural and Food Products Processing Operations and Management; 030404 Forest Products Technologists and Technicians; 030501 Forestry, General; 030509 Wood Science and Pulp/Paper Technology; 100103 Photographic Technologists and Technicians; 120402 Barber/Hairstylist; 120501 Baker/Pastry Chef; 150607 Plastics Technologists and Technicians; 150699 Industrial Production Technologists and Technicians, Other; 150702 Quality Control Technologists and Technicians; 150801 Aeronautical and Aerospace Engineering Technologists and Technicians; 150803 Automotive Engineering Technologists and Technicians; 150903 Petroleum Technologists and Technicians; 200301 Clothing, Apparel and Textile Workers and Managers, General; 200303 Commercial Garment and Apparel Worker; 200305 Custom Tailor; 200309 Drycleaner and Launderer (Commercial); 410205 Nuclear/Nuclear Power Technologists and Technicians; 410301 Chemical Technologists and Technicians; 460101 Mason and Tile Setter; 460301 Electrical and Power Transmission Installer, General; 460303 Lineworker; 460403 Construction/Building Inspector; 460408 Painter and Wall Coverer; 460499 Construction and Building Finishers and Managers, Other; 460501 Plumber and Pipefitter; 469999 Construction Trades, Other; 470101 Electrical and Electronics Equipment Installer and Repairer; 470102 Business Machine Repairer; 470105 Industrial Electronics Installer and Repairer; 470199 Electrical and Electronics Equipment Installer and Repairer; 470201 Heating, Air Conditioning and Refrigeration Mechanics and Repairers; 470302 Heavy Equipment Maintenance and Repair; 470303 Industrial Machinery Maintenance and Repair; 470401 Instrument Calibration and Repairer; 470402 Gunsmith; 470404 Musical Instrument Repairer; 470408 Watch, Clock and Jewelry Repairer; 470499 Miscellaneous Mechanics and Repairers, Other; 470501 Stationary Energy Sources Installer and Operator; 470603 Auto/Automotive Body Repairer; 470604 Auto/Automotive Mechanic/Technician; 470606 Small Engine Mechanic and Repairer; 470608 Aircraft Mechanic/Technician, Powerplant; 470611 Motorcycle Mechanic and Repairer; 480201 Graphic and Printing Equipment Operator, General; 480206 Lithographer and Platemaker; 480208 Printing Press Operator; 480299 Graphic and Printing Equipment Operators, Other; 480303 Upholsterer; 480304 Shoe, Boot and Leather Repairer; 480399 Leatherworkers and Upholsterers, Other; 480501 Machinist/Machine Technologist; 480503 Machine Shop Assistant; 480506 Sheet Metal Worker; 480507 Tool and Die Maker/Technologist; 480508 Welder/Welding Technologist; 480599 Precision Metal Workers, Other; 480701 Woodworkers, General; 480702 Furniture Designer and Maker; 489999 Precision Production Trades, Other; 490306 Marine Maintenance and Repair; 511006 Optometric/Ophthalmic Laboratory Technician

Related DOT Job/s: 194.387-010 QUALITY-CONTROL INSPECTOR; 194.387-014 RECORD TESTER; 199.171-010 PROOF TECHNICIAN; 222.367-046 PETROLEUM INSPECTOR; 222.384-010 INSPECTOR, RECEIVING; 222.687-042 INSPECTOR, HANDBAG FRAMES; 343.687-010 PLASTIC-CARD GRADER, CARDROOM; 361.587-010 FLATWORK TIER; 361.687-010 ASSEMBLER, WET WASH; 361.687-014 CLASSIFIER; 361.687-022 LINEN GRADER; 369.687-010 ASSEMBLER; 369.687-014 CHECKER; 369.687-022 INSPECTOR; 369.687-026 MARKER; 369.687-030 RUG INSPECTOR; 500.287-010 INSPECTOR, PLATING; 502.382-014 FLUOROSCOPE OPERATOR; 504.387-010 HARDNESS INSPECTOR; 509.584-010 TEST PREPARER; 509.686-018 SCRAP SORTER; 509.687-022 WEIGHER, ALLOY; 511.667-014 COLOR TESTER; 512.467-010 POTLINE MONITOR; 512.487-010 METAL CONTROL WORKER; 512.667-010 TEMPERATURE REGULATOR, PYROMETER; 514.687-010 CASTING INSPECTOR; 515.567-010 WEIGHER-AND-CRUSHER; 518.687-010 CORE CHECKER; 519.387-010 MANOMETER TECHNICIAN; 519.484-014 RAW SAMPLER; 519.585-010 HARDNESS TESTER; 519.585-018 SAMPLE TESTER-GRINDER; 519.687-042 TEST WORKER; 520.387-010 BLENDER; 520.487-010 CHEESE BLENDER; 520.487-018 PANTRY WORKER; 520.686-026 GLUCOSE-AND-SYRUP WEIGHER; 520.687-026 CASING-MATERIAL WEIGHER; 520.687-042 HOP WEIGHER; 521.687-018 BINDER SELECTOR; 521.687-022 BONE PICKER; 521.687-062 FISH-LIVER SORTER; 521.687-086 NUT SORTER; 521.687-094 PEELED-POTATO INSPECTOR; 522.584-010 OLIVE BRINE TESTER; 522.587-010 CARBONATION TESTER; 522.667-010 LIQUOR INSPECTOR; 523.687-010 COFFEE-ROASTER HELPER; 525.387-010 GRADER, MEAT; 525.687-042 HIDE INSPECTOR; 525.687-102 SKIN GRADER; 526.687-010 POTATO-CHIP SORTER; 529.167-010 FRUIT COORDINATOR; 529.367-010 CIGARETTE-AND-FILTER CHIEF INSPECTOR; 529.367-014 HOGSHEAD INSPECTOR; 529.367-018 QUALITY-CONTROL INSPECTOR; 529.367-022 QUALITY-CONTROL TECHNICIAN; 529.367-026 ROUGH-RICE GRADER; 529.367-030 YIELD-LOSS INSPECTOR; 529.367-034 QUALITY CONTROL INSPECTOR; 529.387-010 CHEESE GRADER; 529.387-014 CIGARETTE TESTER; 529.387-018 FRUIT-BUYING GRADER; 529.387-022 GAUGER; 529.387-026 INSPECTOR, GRAIN MILL PRODUCTS; 529.387-030 QUALITY-CONTROL TECHNICIAN; 529.387-034 SAMPLER; 529.467-010 TIP-LENGTH CHECKER; 529.485-026 WEIGH-TANK OPERATOR; 529.487-010 SPECIAL TESTER; 529.567-010 CIGARETTE INSPECTOR; 529.567-014 MARKER, COMPANY; 529.587-010 BOTTLE GAUGER; 529.587-014 SAUSAGE INSPECTOR; 529.587-018 SCRAP SEPARATOR; 529.587-022 TOBACCO-SAMPLE PULLER; 529.666-010 CATCHER, FILTER TIP; 529.666-014 CIGARETTE-MAKING-MACHINE CATCHER; 529.667-010 INSPECTOR, FILTER TIP; 529.684-014 INGREDIENT SCALER; 529.685-026 BOTTLED-BEVERAGE INSPECTOR; 529.685-194 RAW-JUICE WEIGHER; 529.685-274 X-RAY INSPECTOR; 529.687-026 CASING GRADER; 529.687-042 CIGAR INSPECTOR; 529.687-046 COFFEE WEIGHER; 529.687-058 DEFLECTOR OPERATOR; 529.687-082 FISH-BIN TENDER; 529.687-090 FRESH-WORK INSPECTOR; 529.687-098 GRADER; 529.687-102 GRADER, DRESSED POULTRY; 529.687-106 GRADER, GREEN MEAT; 529.687-110 GRAIN PICKER; 529.687-114 INSPECTOR; 529.687-118 INSPECTOR, CANNED FOOD RECONDITIONING; 529.687-126 KOSHER INSPECTOR; 529.687-134 LEAF SORTER; 529.687-142 LEAF-SIZE PICKER; 529.687-146 LIGHTOUT EXAMINER; 529.687-162 MOISTURE-METER OPERATOR; 529.687-174 SALVAGE INSPECTOR; 529.687-178 SAMPLER; 529.687-198 SUMATRA OPENER; 529.687-202 TEMPERATURE INSPECTOR; 529.687-218 WRAPPER SELECTOR; 529.687-226 INSPECTOR, PROCESSING; 530.687-010 RAG INSPECTOR; 539.364-010 PULP-AND-PAPER TESTER; 539.367-010 FINAL INSPECTOR, PAPER; 539.367-014 WATER-QUALITY TESTER; 539.387-010 CHIP TESTER; 539.485-010 WEIGHT TESTER; 539.487-010 INSPECTOR, FIBROUS WALLBOARD; 539.667-010 CONTROL INSPECTOR; 542.567-010 COKE INSPECTOR; 543.684-010 QUALITY-CONTROL TESTER; 549.364-010 TESTER, COMPRESSED GASES; 549.367-010 INSPECTOR; 549.387-010 CARGO INSPECTOR; 549.587-014 SAMPLER; 549.587-018 SAMPLER; 550.584-014 SAMPLE-COLOR MAKER; 550.587-014 SAMPLE COLLECTOR; 553.364-010 SAMPLE TESTER; 554.587-010 ROLL INSPECTOR; 555.687-010 SCALE OPERATOR; 556.684-010 CELL INSPECTOR; 557.564-014 PUMP TESTER; 558.584-010 CELL TESTER; 559.364-010 FURNACE-STOCK INSPECTOR; 559.367-010 QUALITY-CONTROL TESTER; 559.387-010 INSPECTOR IV; 559.387-014 INSPECTOR; 559.467-010 TEMPERATURE-CONTROL INSPECTOR; 559.567-014 WEIGHER AND GRADER; 559.584-010 ROLL-TENSION TESTER; 559.584-014 VARNISH INSPECTOR; 559.667-010 TABLET TESTER; 559.687-010 AMPOULE EXAMINER; 559.687-058 SOAP INSPECTOR; 559.687-066 TUBE SORTER; 559.687-070 WEIGHER OPERATOR; 559.687-074 INSPECTOR AND HAND PACKAGER; 560.587-010 COMPOUNDER, CORK; 561.587-010 POLE INSPECTOR; 563.687-014 MOISTURE TESTER; 569.367-010 TREATING INSPECTOR; 569.384-010 QUALITY-CONTROL TESTER; 569.686-046 LAMINATING-MACHINE OFFBEARER; 569.687-022 SORTER I; 569.687-030 QUALITY CONTROL INSPECTOR; 569.687-034 VENEER GRADER; 570.682-010 ABRASIVE GRADER; 573.687-034 SORTER; 573.687-038 TILE SORTER; 574.367-010 TILE SHADER; 575.687-022 MAT INSPECTOR; 575.687-034 INSPECTOR I; 579.364-010 QUALITY CONTROL TECHNICIAN; 579.367-010 QUALITY-CONTROL INSPECTOR; 579.367-014 QUALITY-CONTROL TECHNICIAN; 579.384-0

83005B CONSTRUCTION CHECKERS. OOH Title/s: Inspectors, Testers, and Graders

Inspect worksite and work in progress to ensure completed work meets work order specifications and to ensure work practices safeguard workers onsite. Inspects completed construction work for defects, decay, or conformance to specifications or safety regulations. Observes construction work in progress to ensure that specifications are followed, and to prevent excessive damage to existing facilities. Inspects equipment, tools, safety equipment, and working conditions to ensure safety of workers engaged in construction or maintenance. Verifies depth of alignment of trenches, roads, or bridges, using gauging instruments such as tape measure or level. Examines construction materials, such as pipe, masonry, or timbers, for defects. Investigates and observes preparation of right-of-way for conformance to contract agreement. Determines need for repair or improvement of construction or utility delivery system, and consults with supervisor concerning advisability of improvement. Examines power lines, pole installations, or underground cables to determine maintenance needs or need for improvements. Removes or rejects faulty materials or equipment, and marks status with chalk or label. Prepares report of findings, noting location, type of construction, defect, decay, or extent of damage. Examines and verifies accuracy of electric, gas, or steam meter, to investigate reports of meter tampering. Makes repairs or adjustments to correct problems found during inspection, such as loose connections, blown fuses, or meter adjustment.

Yearly Earnings: $22,932

Education: Work experience in a related occupation

Knowledge: Engineering and Technology; Building and Construction; Mechanical; Public Safety and Security

Abilities: Problem Sensitivity; Inductive Reasoning; Speed of Closure; Flexibility of Closure; Spatial Orientation; Selective Attention; Gross Body Equilibrium; Far Vision; Visual Color Discrimination; Auditory Attention; Sound Localization

Skills: Operation Monitoring; Product Inspection; Troubleshooting

General Work Activities: Inspecting Equipment, Structures, or Material; Performing General Physical Activities
Job Characteristics: Take a Position Opposed to Others; Responsible for Others' Health and Safety; Frequency in Conflict Situations; Sounds, Noise Levels are Distracting, etc.; Very Hot; Extremely Bright or Inadequate Lighting; Contaminants; High Places; Hazardous Conditions; Standing; Climbing Ladders, Scaffolds, Poles, etc.; Walking or Running; Kneeling, Crouching, or Crawling; Keeping or Regaining Balance; Bending or Twisting the Body; Common Protective or Safety Attire; Consequence of Error; Importance of Being Exact or Accurate; Importance of Being Sure All is Done
GOE Group/s: 05.03.06 Engineering Technology: Industrial and Safety; 05.05.05 Craft Technology: Electrical-Electronic Systems Installation and Repair; 05.07.01 Quality Control: Structural; 05.07.03 Quality Control: Electrical; 05.10.02 Crafts: Mechanical; 06.03.02 Quality Control: Inspecting, Grading, Sorting, Weighing, and Recording
CIP Program/s: 150701 Occupational Safety and Health Technologists and Technicians; 460301 Electrical and Power Transmission Installer, General; 460303 Lineworker; 460403 Construction/Building Inspector; 470401 Instrument Calibration and Repairer; 470501 Stationary Energy Sources Installer and Operator; 480501 Machinist/Machine Technologist; 480508 Welder/Welding Technologist
Related DOT Job/s: 575.687-030 PRESS-PIPE INSPECTOR; 703.687-018 METAL-FINISH INSPECTOR; 821.364-010 UTILITIES SERVICE INVESTIGATOR; 821.367-010 CONSTRUCTION CHECKER; 821.367-014 SAFETY INSPECTOR; 822.267-010 LINE INSPECTOR; 850.387-010 INSPECTOR OF DREDGING; 859.267-010 STREET-OPENINGS INSPECTOR; 869.287-010 BRIDGE INSPECTOR; 869.367-018 PIPELINE CONSTRUCTION INSPECTOR; 956.267-010 INSPECTOR, CHIEF; 956.387-010 BUILDING-EQUIPMENT INSPECTOR

83008A RAILROAD INSPECTORS. OOH Title/s: Inspectors, Testers, and Graders; Inspectors and Compliance Officers, Except Construction

Inspect railroad equipment, roadbed, and track to ensure safe transport of people or cargo. Inspects signals and track wiring to determine continuity of electrical connections. Examines roadbed, switches, fishplates, rails, and ties to detect damage or wear. Examines locomotives and cars to detect damage or structural defects. Inspects and tests completed work. Operates switches to determine working conditions. Tests and synchronizes rail-flaw-detection machine, using circuit tester and hand tools, and reloads machine with paper and ink. Starts machine and signals workers to operate rail-detector car. Prepares reports on repairs made and equipment, railcars, or roadbed needing repairs. Tags railcars needing immediate repair. Fills paint container on rail-detector car used to mark sections of defective rail with paint. Directs crews to repair or replace defective equipment or to reballast roadbed. Places lanterns or flags in front and rear of train to signal that inspection is being performed. Seals leaks found during inspection that can be sealed with caulking compound. Replaces defective brake rod pins and tightens safety appliances. Notifies train dispatcher of railcar to be moved to shop for repair. Makes minor repairs. Packs brake bearings with grease.
Yearly Earnings: $22,932
Education: Work experience in a related occupation
Knowledge: Engineering and Technology; Building and Construction; Mechanical; Public Safety and Security; Transportation
Abilities: Flexibility of Closure; Arm-Hand Steadiness; Control Precision; Multilimb Coordination; Response Orientation; Reaction Time; Extent Flexibility; Gross Body Coordination; Gross Body Equilibrium; Night Vision; Hearing Sensitivity
Skills: Testing; Operation Monitoring; Product Inspection; Equipment Maintenance; Troubleshooting; Repairing; Systems Perception; Identifying Downstream Consequences; Time Management; Management of Personnel Resources
General Work Activities: Inspecting Equipment, Structures, or Material; Interacting with Computers; Repairing and Maintaining Mechanical Equipment
Job Characteristics: Take a Position Opposed to Others; Responsible for Others' Health and Safety; Responsibility for Outcomes and Results; Sounds, Noise Levels are Distracting, etc.; Very Hot; Extremely Bright or Inadequate Lighting; Cramped Work Space, Awkward Positions; Radiation; High Places; Standing; Climbing Ladders, Scaffolds, Poles, etc.; Walking or Running; Kneeling, Crouching, or Crawling; Keeping or Regaining Balance; Bending or Twisting the Body; Consequence of Error; Importance of Being Exact or Accurate; Importance of Being Sure All is Done
GOE Group/s: 05.07.01 Quality Control: Structural; 05.10.02 Crafts: Mechanical
CIP Program/s: 470302 Heavy Equipment Maintenance and Repair
Related DOT Job/s: 168.287-018 INSPECTOR, RAILROAD; 910.263-010 RAIL-FLAW-DETECTOR OPERATOR; 910.367-030 WAY INSPECTOR; 910.384-010 TANK-CAR INSPECTOR; 910.387-014 RAILROAD-CAR INSPECTOR; 910.667-010 CAR INSPECTOR

83008C AUTOMOBILE AND TRUCK INSPECTORS. OOH Title/s: Inspectors, Testers, and Graders; Inspectors and Compliance Officers, Except Construction

Inspect automotive vehicles to ensure compliance with government regulations and safety standards. Inspects truck accessories, air lines, and electric circuits, and reports needed repairs. Examines vehicle for damage, and drives vehicle to detect malfunctions. Tests vehicle components for wear, damage, or improper adjustment, using mechanical or electrical devices. Applies inspection stickers to vehicles that pass inspection, and rejection sticker to vehicles that fail. Prepares report on each vehicle for follow-up action by owner or police. Prepares and keeps record of vehicles delivered. Positions trailer and drives car onto truck trailer. Notifies authorities of owners having illegal equipment installed on vehicle. Services vehicles with fuel and water.
Yearly Earnings: $22,932
Education: Work experience in a related occupation
Knowledge: Computers and Electronics; Public Safety and Security
Abilities: Flexibility of Closure; Control Precision; Multilimb Coordination; Response Orientation; Extent Flexibility; Gross Body Equilibrium; Visual Color Discrimination; Hearing Sensitivity; Sound Localization
Skills: Testing; Troubleshooting
General Work Activities: Interacting with Computers
Job Characteristics: Frequency in Conflict Situations; Cramped Work Space, Awkward Positions; Standing; Kneeling, Crouching, or Crawling; Keeping or Regaining Balance; Bending or Twisting the Body
GOE Group/s: 05.07.01 Quality Control: Structural; 06.03.01 Quality Control: Inspecting, Testing, and Repairing
CIP Program/s: 470604 Auto/Automotive Mechanic/Technician; 470605 Diesel Engine Mechanic and Repairer
Related DOT Job/s: 168.267-058 INSPECTOR, MOTOR VEHICLES; 379.364-010 AUTOMOBILE TESTER; 919.363-010 NEW-CAR INSPECTOR; 919.687-018 SAFETY INSPECTOR, TRUCK

83008D FREIGHT INSPECTORS. OOH Title/s: Inspectors, Testers, and Graders

Inspect freight for proper storage, according to specifications. Inspects shipment to ascertain that freight is securely braced and blocked. Observes loading of freight to ensure that crews comply with procedures. Monitors temperature and humidity of freight storage area. Records freight condition and handling, and notifies crews to reload

freight or insert additional bracing or packing. Measures height and width of loads that will pass over bridges or through tunnels. Notifies workers of special treatment required for shipments. Prepares and submits report after trip. Posts warning signs on vehicles containing explosives or inflammatory or radioactive materials.
Yearly Earnings: $22,932
Education: Work experience in a related occupation
Knowledge: Public Safety and Security; Transportation
Abilities: Category Flexibility; Gross Body Equilibrium
Skills: None above average
General Work Activities: None above average
Job Characteristics: Take a Position Opposed to Others; Cramped Work Space, Awkward Positions; Radiation; High Places; Standing; Climbing Ladders, Scaffolds, Poles, etc.; Keeping or Regaining Balance
GOE Group/s: 05.07.01 Quality Control: Structural; 05.10.08 Crafts: Food Preparation; 05.12.01 Elemental Work: Mechanical: Supervision
CIP Program/s: 520201 Business Administration and Management, General; 520203 Logistics and Materials Management
Related DOT Job/s: 910.387-010 PERISHABLE-FRUIT INSPECTOR; 910.667-018 LOADING INSPECTOR; 910.667-022 PERISHABLE-FREIGHT INSPECTOR

83099 ALL OTHER INSPECTORS, TESTERS AND RELATED WORKERS. OOH Title/s: Line Installers and Cable Splicers; Handlers, Equipment Cleaners, Helpers, and Laborers

All other inspectors, testers, and related workers not classified separately above.
Yearly Earnings: $22,932
Education: Work experience in a related occupation
GOE Group/s: 05.07.01 Quality Control: Structural
CIP Program/s: 000000 NO CIP ASSIGNED
Related DOT Job/s: 823.261-014 RADIO INTERFERENCE INVESTIGATOR; 930.364-010 OIL-PIPE-INSPECTOR HELPER; 959.367-010 ELECTRIC POWER LINE EXAMINER

Industrial Equipment Mechanics

85112 MACHINERY MAINTENANCE MECHANICS, TEXTILE MACHINES. OOH Title/s: Industrial Machinery Repairers

Adjust and repair one or a variety of textile machines. Machines may be of one group or type called a section. Dismantles equipment and removes worn or defective parts, using hand tools. Replaces defective parts, such as plugs, reeds, needles, points, shuttles, cots, chains, heddles, slide rods, and side or frame hooks. Adjusts parts and tension on parts such as rollers, chains, and cylinders, using hand tools and gauges. Repairs defective parts, such as flats, wires, shuttles, collars, frames, chains, and rollers, using hand tools and soldering and welding equipment. Aligns, straightens, spaces, and levels parts, using hand tools, straightedge, level, and plumb bob. Replaces worn covering (rubber, cork, leather, cloth, felt) on cylinders, rollers, and roller arbors, using hand tools and arbor press. Inspects and examines textile machines and equipment to detect defects, by observing or listening to machine or using micrometers and feeler gauges. Verifies accuracy of part repair or replacement, adjustment, or alignment. Installs special attachments to equipment. Lubricates machinery and equipment. Smooths and polishes equipment, using abrasives and buffing, sanding, and grinding machines. Cleans equipment with solvent, brushes, and air hose to remove dirt, lint, oil, and rust. Maintains parts and equipment inventory, receipt, and transfer records. Cuts fur, bristles, cord, leather, or cloth, according to specifications. Moves equipment and machine components, using hoists, rollers, and handtrucks. Traces outline and engraves surfaces, following pattern and using gravers and magnifying lens. Sorts and stores parts and equipment according to type or size.
Yearly Earnings: $27,612
Education: Long-term O-J-T
Knowledge: Mechanical
Abilities: Finger Dexterity; Control Precision; Multilimb Coordination; Wrist-Finger Speed; Speed of Limb Movement; Static Strength; Explosive Strength; Dynamic Strength; Trunk Strength; Gross Body Equilibrium; Hearing Sensitivity; Auditory Attention; Sound Localization
Skills: Installation; Equipment Maintenance; Troubleshooting; Repairing
General Work Activities: Performing General Physical Activities; Handling and Moving Objects; Repairing and Maintaining Mechanical Equipment
Job Characteristics: Cramped Work Space, Awkward Positions; Hazardous Equipment; Climbing Ladders, Scaffolds, Poles, etc.; Kneeling, Crouching, or Crawling; Bending or Twisting the Body; Pace Determined by Speed of Equipment
GOE Group/s: 05.05.09 Craft Technology: Mechanical Work; 05.10.01 Crafts: Structural; 05.10.02 Crafts: Mechanical; 05.10.04 Crafts: Structural-Mechanical-Electrical-Electronic; 06.01.04 Production Technology: Precision Hand Work; 06.02.02 Production Work: Machine Work, Metal and Plastics; 06.02.09 Production Work: Machine Work, Assorted Materials; 06.02.24 Production Work: Manual Work, Metal and Plastics; 06.02.32 Production Work: Manual Work, Assorted Materials
CIP Program/s: 470303 Industrial Machinery Maintenance and Repair
Related DOT Job/s: 628.261-010 OVERHAULER; 628.281-010 MACHINE FIXER; 628.381-010 CARD CLOTHIER; 628.382-010 FLAT CLOTHIER; 628.484-010 REED REPAIRER; 628.682-010 ROLLER COVERER; 628.684-018 NEEDLE STRAIGHTENER; 628.684-026 SHUTTLE FIXER; 628.684-030 SPINDLE PLUMBER; 628.684-034 UTILITY WORKER, ROLLER SHOP; 628.684-038 WIRE REPAIRER; 683.380-010 HARNESS BUILDER; 683.684-010 CHAIN REPAIRER; 979.381-026 ROLLER REPAIRER

85113 MACHINERY MAINTENANCE MECHANICS, SEWING MACHINES. OOH Title/s: Industrial Machinery Repairers

Repair, adjust, and maintain sewing machines in sewing departments of industrial establishments, homes, or shops. Adjusts machine parts, using hand tools. Dismantles machines and replaces or repairs broken or worn parts, using hand tools. Installs attachments on machines. Inspects machines, shafts, and belts. Operates machine tools, such as lathes and drill presses, to make new parts. Orders new machines or parts.
Yearly Earnings: $27,612
Education: Long-term O-J-T
Knowledge: Mechanical
Abilities: Finger Dexterity
Skills: Technology Design; Installation; Operation and Control; Equipment Maintenance; Troubleshooting; Repairing
General Work Activities: Repairing and Maintaining Mechanical Equipment
Job Characteristics: Sounds, Noise Levels are Distracting, etc.; Hazardous Equipment; Using Hands on Objects, Tools, or Controls
GOE Group/s: 05.10.02 Crafts: Mechanical
CIP Program/s: 470199 Electrical and Electronics Equipment Installer and Repairer

Related DOT Job/s: 639.281-018 SEWING-MACHINE REPAIRER

85116A MARINE MACHINISTS, MAINTENANCE.

OOH Title/s: Industrial Machinery Repairers

Repair and install mechanical equipment aboard marine craft and related harbor and dock machinery. Dismantles, repairs, or replaces defective parts, and reassembles machinery, using machinist's tools, chain hoists, and steel rollers. Installs ship machinery, such as propelling machinery and steering gear, working from blueprints and using hand tools, calipers, and micrometers. Installs below-deck auxiliary equipment—such as evaporators, stills, heaters, pumps, condensers, and boilers—and connects them to steampipe systems. Operates machinery, such as cargo winches and windlasses, to determine causes of malfunctioning. Lays out passage holes on bulkheads, decks, and other surfaces for connections, such as shafting and steam lines. Fabricates replacement parts, using machine shop tools such as lathe, boring mill, planer, shaper, slotter, and milling machine. Tests and inspects installed machinery and equipment during dock and sea trials.

Yearly Earnings: $27,612

Education: Long-term O-J-T

Knowledge: Design; Building and Construction; Mechanical; Transportation

Abilities: Spatial Orientation; Arm-Hand Steadiness; Manual Dexterity; Control Precision; Multilimb Coordination; Response Orientation; Rate Control; Wrist-Finger Speed; Speed of Limb Movement; Explosive Strength; Stamina; Extent Flexibility; Dynamic Flexibility; Gross Body Equilibrium; Peripheral Vision; Depth Perception

Skills: Technology Design; Equipment Selection; Installation; Testing; Operation Monitoring; Equipment Maintenance; Troubleshooting; Repairing

General Work Activities: Inspecting Equipment, Structures, or Material; Handling and Moving Objects; Controlling Machines and Processes; Interacting with Computers; Implementing Ideas, Programs, etc.; Repairing and Maintaining Mechanical Equipment

Job Characteristics: Sounds, Noise Levels are Distracting, etc.; Very Hot; Extremely Bright or Inadequate Lighting; Cramped Work Space, Awkward Positions; Whole Body Vibration; Hazardous Conditions; Hazardous Equipment; Climbing Ladders, Scaffolds, Poles, etc.; Kneeling, Crouching, or Crawling; Keeping or Regaining Balance; Using Hands on Objects, Tools, or Controls; Bending or Twisting the Body

GOE Group/s: 05.05.09 Craft Technology: Mechanical Work

CIP Program/s: 490306 Marine Maintenance and Repair; 490309 Marine Science/Merchant Marine Officer

Related DOT Job/s: 623.281-010 DECK ENGINEER; 623.281-022 MACHINIST APPRENTICE, OUTSIDE; 623.281-030 MACHINIST, OUTSIDE

85116B MARINE ENGINE MECHANICS. OOH Title/s: Industrial Machinery Repairers

Repair and maintain propulsion, diesel, and other engines and engine parts aboard ship. Dismantles and repairs defective equipment or engine, or replaces defective parts, and reassembles equipment, using hand tools. Examines engine equipment—such as pumps, circulators, condensers, and steering engines—to locate malfunctions. Positions engine over mounting, bolts engine to mount, and straps fuel tank to cradle, using chain hoist and hand tools. Connects fuel, oil, and water lines to engine, and installs engine controls, propeller shaft, and propeller. Starts and tests engines, using tachometer and voltmeter. Stands watch in engine room; observes temperature, pressure, and rpm gauges; and adjusts controls to maintain specified operating conditions. Fabricates engine replacement parts, such as valves, stay rods, and bolts, using metal-working machinery. Records gauge readings and test data, such as revolutions per minutes and voltage output, in engineering log.

Yearly Earnings: $27,612

Education: Long-term O-J-T

Knowledge: Production and Processing; Engineering and Technology; Mechanical; Transportation

Abilities: Arm-Hand Steadiness; Manual Dexterity; Finger Dexterity; Control Precision; Wrist-Finger Speed; Speed of Limb Movement; Explosive Strength; Dynamic Strength; Trunk Strength; Extent Flexibility; Dynamic Flexibility; Gross Body Coordination; Gross Body Equilibrium; Hearing Sensitivity

Skills: Installation; Equipment Maintenance; Troubleshooting; Repairing

General Work Activities: Interacting with Computers; Repairing and Maintaining Mechanical Equipment

Job Characteristics: Sounds, Noise Levels are Distracting, etc.; Very Hot; Contaminants; Cramped Work Space, Awkward Positions; High Places; Hazardous Conditions; Hazardous Equipment; Climbing Ladders, Scaffolds, Poles, etc.; Kneeling, Crouching, or Crawling; Using Hands on Objects, Tools, or Controls; Bending or Twisting the Body

GOE Group/s: 05.05.09 Craft Technology: Mechanical Work

CIP Program/s: 490306 Marine Maintenance and Repair

Related DOT Job/s: 623.281-018 MACHINIST APPRENTICE, MARINE ENGINE; 623.281-026 MACHINIST, MARINE ENGINE; 623.281-034 MAINTENANCE MECHANIC, ENGINE

85116C MARINE SERVICES TECHNICIANS. OOH Title/s: Industrial Machinery Repairers; Electricians

Assemble, repair, and maintain marine and related equipment, including body work, components, parts, and accessories. Removes flaked paint, barnacles, and encrusted debris from hulls or vessel, using scrapers, scrubbers, power washers, and sandblasting equipment. Removes damaged or rotted sections from wooden or fiberglass vessels, using drill, saw, and hand tools. Repairs defective components or fabricates and installs replacement parts, using drawings, measuring instruments, hand tools, power tools, or woodworking machines. Caulks wooden hulls with cotton to prevent leaks. Grinds and sands edges around removed fiberglass sections of vessels. Mixes and applies paint or gels to boats with hand or spray equipment, utilizing knowledge of color mixing and matching. Tests engine, transmission, rigging, propeller, navigational, and related systems to diagnose malfunctions, using measuring instruments. Examines repair or installation orders, drawings, and vessel to determine repairs or modifications required for equipment, accessory, and hardware installation. Layers cloth over damaged area, and smooths area to match contour of hull, using rollers, squeegee, and power sander. Installs and tests sanitation, refrigeration, and electrical systems and accessories, cabinetry, hardware, trim, and related components, following manufacturer's specifications. Consults with supervisor regarding installation or repair problems, sequence of operations, and time required to complete repair or installation. Removes vessels from water, using movable lift crane or marine railway. Positions and secures blocking around vessels, according to size and weight distribution of vessels, using fasteners, hand tools, and power tools. Mixes fiberglass bonding resin and catalyst, cuts fiberglass cloth to size, and soaks cloth with mixture.

Yearly Earnings: $27,612

Education: Long-term O-J-T

Knowledge: Design; Building and Construction; Mechanical; Transportation

Abilities: Spatial Orientation; Arm-Hand Steadiness; Manual Dexterity; Finger Dexterity; Control Precision; Multilimb Coordination; Rate Control; Wrist-Finger Speed; Speed of Limb Movement; Static Strength; Explosive Strength; Dynamic Strength; Trunk Strength; Stamina; Extent Flexibility; Dynamic Flexibility; Gross Body Coordi-

nation; Gross Body Equilibrium; Visual Color Discrimination; Peripheral Vision; Depth Perception; Glare Sensitivity
Skills: Installation; Testing; Operation Monitoring; Equipment Maintenance; Troubleshooting; Repairing
General Work Activities: Inspecting Equipment, Structures, or Material; Performing General Physical Activities; Handling and Moving Objects; Controlling Machines and Processes; Interacting with Computers; Implementing Ideas, Programs, etc.; Repairing and Maintaining Mechanical Equipment; Repairing and Maintaining Electrical Equipment
Job Characteristics: Very Hot; Extremely Bright or Inadequate Lighting; Contaminants; Cramped Work Space, Awkward Positions; High Places; Hazardous Conditions; Standing; Climbing Ladders, Scaffolds, Poles, etc.; Kneeling, Crouching, or Crawling; Keeping or Regaining Balance; Using Hands on Objects, Tools, or Controls; Bending or Twisting the Body; Making Repetitive Motions; Importance of Repeating Same Tasks
GOE Group/s: 05.05.02 Craft Technology: Construction and Maintenance
CIP Program/s: 490306 Marine Maintenance and Repair
Related DOT Job/s: 623.281-014 DEEP SUBMERGENCE VEHICLE CREWMEMBER; 806.261-026 MARINE-SERVICES TECHNICIAN; 806.381-062 INSTALLER, ELECTRICAL, PLUMBING, MECHANICAL

85118 MACHINERY MAINTENANCE MECHANICS, WATER OR POWER GENERATION PLANTS. OOH Title/s: Industrial Machinery Repairers

Install, adjust, repair, and maintain machinery in power-generating stations and water treatment plants. Duties include the repair and maintenance of mechanical elements of generators, waterwheels, piping, and water-inlet controls in generating stations; steam boilers, condensers, pumps, compressors, and similar equipment in gas manufacturing plants; and equipment used to process and distribute water for human consumption and industrial use. Dismantles machinery and equipment to repair or replace faulty parts, using hand and power tools. Sets up and operates machine tools to repair or reproduce mechanical elements, using blueprint or defective part. Fabricates special tools and replacement parts for equipment.
Yearly Earnings: $27,612
Education: Long-term O-J-T
Knowledge: Engineering and Technology; Design; Mechanical
Abilities: Gross Body Equilibrium
Skills: Technology Design; Installation; Testing; Operation and Control; Equipment Maintenance; Troubleshooting; Repairing
General Work Activities: Repairing and Maintaining Mechanical Equipment
Job Characteristics: Sounds, Noise Levels are Distracting, etc.; Very Hot; Cramped Work Space, Awkward Positions; Whole Body Vibration; Hazardous Conditions; Kneeling, Crouching, or Crawling; Bending or Twisting the Body
GOE Group/s: 05.05.09 Craft Technology: Mechanical Work; 05.10.02 Crafts: Mechanical
CIP Program/s: 470303 Industrial Machinery Maintenance and Repair; 470501 Stationary Energy Sources Installer and Operator
Related DOT Job/s: 630.281-038 TREATMENT-PLANT MECHANIC; 631.261-010 HYDROELECTRIC-MACHINERY MECHANIC; 631.261-014 POWERHOUSE MECHANIC; 631.261-018 POWERHOUSE-MECHANIC APPRENTICE

85119A MACHINERY MAINTENANCE MECHANICS. OOH Title/s: Industrial Machinery Repairers

Diagnose malfunctions in production machinery and equipment. Repair and maintain machinery and equipment in accordance with blueprints, schematic drawings, operations manuals, and manufacturer's specifications. May set up and operate metal-working machinery and tools, such as lathe, drill press, and grinder, to make and repair parts. Confers with operators and observes, tests, and evaluates operation of machinery and equipment to diagnose cause of malfunction. Disassembles machinery and equipment to remove parts and make repairs. Examines parts for defects, such as breakage or excessive wear. Repairs, replaces, adjusts, and aligns components of machinery and equipment. Cleans and lubricates parts, equipment, and machinery. Test-runs repaired machinery and equipment to verify adequacy of repairs. Fabricates replacement parts. Welds to repair broken metal parts, fabricate new parts, and assemble new equipment. Orders or requisitions parts and materials. Repairs and replaces electrical wiring and components of machinery. Enters codes and instructions to program computer-controlled machinery. Records repairs and maintenance performed.
Yearly Earnings: $27,612
Education: Long-term O-J-T
Knowledge: Computers and Electronics; Engineering and Technology; Mechanical; Physics; Public Safety and Security
Abilities: Information Ordering; Category Flexibility; Memorization; Spatial Orientation; Visualization; Manual Dexterity; Finger Dexterity; Control Precision; Multilimb Coordination; Response Orientation; Reaction Time; Wrist-Finger Speed; Speed of Limb Movement; Static Strength; Explosive Strength; Dynamic Strength; Trunk Strength; Extent Flexibility; Dynamic Flexibility; Gross Body Coordination; Gross Body Equilibrium; Visual Color Discrimination; Night Vision; Peripheral Vision; Depth Perception; Hearing Sensitivity; Auditory Attention; Sound Localization
Skills: Problem Identification; Technology Design; Installation; Programming; Testing; Operation Monitoring; Operation and Control; Product Inspection; Equipment Maintenance; Troubleshooting; Repairing
General Work Activities: Inspecting Equipment, Structures, or Material; Performing General Physical Activities; Controlling Machines and Processes; Operating Vehicles or Equipment; Drafting and Specifying Technical Devices, etc.; Repairing and Maintaining Mechanical Equipment; Repairing and Maintaining Electrical Equipment
Job Characteristics: Sounds, Noise Levels are Distracting, etc.; Cramped Work Space, Awkward Positions; Hazardous Equipment; Kneeling, Crouching, or Crawling; Using Hands on Objects, Tools, or Controls; Bending or Twisting the Body; Common Protective or Safety Attire
GOE Group/s: 05.05.01 Craft Technology: Masonry, Stone, and Brick Work; 05.05.09 Craft Technology: Mechanical Work; 05.10.01 Crafts: Structural; 05.10.02 Crafts: Mechanical; 06.01.04 Production Technology: Precision Hand Work
CIP Program/s: 010204 Agricultural Power Machinery Operator; 470201 Heating, Air Conditioning and Refrigeration Mechanics and Repairers; 470303 Industrial Machinery Maintenance and Repair; 470399 Industrial Equipment Maintenance and Repair, Other; 470501 Stationary Energy Sources Installer and Operator; 480507 Tool and Die Maker/Technologist
Related DOT Job/s: 601.281-030 TOOL AND FIXTURE REPAIRER; 620.281-018 AUTOMOTIVE-MAINTENANCE-EQUIPMENT SERVICER; 626.261-010 FORGE-SHOP-MACHINE REPAIRER; 626.261-014 REPAIRER, WELDING SYSTEMS AND EQUIPMENT; 626.361-010 REPAIRER, WELDING, BRAZING, AND BURNING MACHINES; 626.381-014 GAS-WELDING-EQUIPMENT MECHANIC; 626.381-018 HY-

DRAULIC-PRESS SERVICER; 626.384-010 REPAIRER, WELDING EQUIPMENT; 627.261-010 COMPOSING-ROOM MACHINIST; 627.261-014 MACHINIST APPRENTICE, COMPOSING ROOM; 627.261-018 MACHINIST APPRENTICE, LINOTYPE; 627.261-022 MACHINIST, LINOTYPE; 629.261-010 LAUNDRY-MACHINE MECHANIC; 629.261-014 MILLER, HEAD, WET PROCESS; 629.261-018 POWDER-LINE REPAIRER; 629.261-022 ELECTRONIC-PRODUCTION-LINE-MAINTENANCE MECHANIC; 629.280-010 MAINTENANCE MECHANIC; 629.281-010 BAKERY-MACHINE MECHANIC; 629.281-014 CELLOPHANE-CASTING-MACHINE REPAIRER; 629.281-030 MAINTENANCE MECHANIC; 629.281-034 PUMP MECHANIC; 630.261-010 MAINTENANCE MECHANIC, COMPRESSED-GAS PLANT; 630.261-014 OVEN-EQUIPMENT REPAIRER; 630.261-018 REPAIRER I; 630.281-010 PNEUMATIC-TOOL REPAIRER; 630.281-014 PNEUMATIC-TUBE REPAIRER; 630.281-018 PUMP SERVICER; 630.281-022 REPAIRER; 630.281-026 REPAIRER; 630.281-030 RUBBERIZING MECHANIC; 630.281-034 SERVICE MECHANIC, COMPRESSED-GAS EQUIPMENT; 630.381-010 CONVEYOR-MAINTENANCE MECHANIC; 630.381-018 LEAD OPERATOR; 630.381-022 LUBRICATION-EQUIPMENT SERVICER; 630.381-026 SPRAY-GUN REPAIRER; 637.281-014 STOKER ERECTOR-AND-SERVICER; 638.261-030 MACHINE REPAIRER, MAINTENANCE; 638.281-014 MAINTENANCE MECHANIC; 638.281-026 PARTS SALVAGER; 638.281-030 HYDRAULIC-RUBBISH-COMPACTOR MECHANIC; 638.281-034 HYDRAULIC REPAIRER; 638.381-010 FUEL-SYSTEM-MAINTENANCE WORKER; 899.281-010 CANAL-EQUIPMENT MECHANIC

85119B MACHINERY MAINTENANCE REPAIRERS. OOH Title/s: Industrial Machinery Repairers

Adjust and make minor repairs to maintain operation of machines and equipment to determine cause of malfunction or defect, and repair or replace worn, damaged, or defective part. Reassembles or installs machinery, adjusting and aligning parts as needed. Dismantles machinery or equipment. Inspects machines and equipment to diagnose cause of malfunction or determine need for routine maintenance. Clears jams from machinery. Cleans and lubricates parts and equipment. Welds, solders, and brazes parts together. Fabricates, modifies, and cleans parts, using hand tools, power tools, and machine shop equipment. Examines product to determine if machine is operating within specifications. Drills and taps holes. Signals crane operator to move machinery. Maintains records.

Yearly Earnings: $27,612

Education: Long-term O-J-T

Knowledge: Engineering and Technology; Mechanical

Abilities: Perceptual Speed; Spatial Orientation; Visualization; Manual Dexterity; Finger Dexterity; Control Precision; Multilimb Coordination; Response Orientation; Reaction Time; Wrist-Finger Speed; Static Strength; Explosive Strength; Trunk Strength; Extent Flexibility; Gross Body Equilibrium; Visual Color Discrimination; Peripheral Vision; Hearing Sensitivity; Auditory Attention; Sound Localization

Skills: Installation; Testing; Operation Monitoring; Product Inspection; Equipment Maintenance; Troubleshooting; Repairing

General Work Activities: Inspecting Equipment, Structures, or Material; Performing General Physical Activities; Handling and Moving Objects; Controlling Machines and Processes; Repairing and Maintaining Mechanical Equipment

Job Characteristics: Sounds, Noise Levels are Distracting, etc.; Cramped Work Space, Awkward Positions; Hazardous Equipment; Standing; Kneeling, Crouching, or Crawling; Bending or Twisting the Body; Common Protective or Safety Attire

GOE Group/s: 05.10.01 Crafts: Structural; 05.10.02 Crafts: Mechanical; 05.12.12 Elemental Work: Mechanical: Structural Work; 06.01.02 Production Technology: Machine Set-up; 06.01.04 Production Technology: Precision Hand Work; 06.04.25 Elemental Work: Industrial: Manual Work, Wood

CIP Program/s: 470303 Industrial Machinery Maintenance and Repair; 470399 Industrial Equipment Maintenance and Repair, Other; 480501 Machinist/Machine Technologist

Related DOT Job/s: 626.381-010 CASE-FINISHING-MACHINE ADJUSTER; 629.281-026 FORMING-MACHINE ADJUSTER; 629.361-010 MACHINE-CLOTHING REPLACER; 629.381-010 FOILING-MACHINE ADJUSTER; 630.384-010 FIXTURE REPAIRER-FABRICATOR; 630.664-014 SCREEN-AND-CYCLONE REPAIRER; 630.684-010 ANODE REBUILDER; 630.684-014 BELT REPAIRER; 630.684-026 REPAIRER II; 630.684-030 SCREEN REPAIRER, CRUSHER; 630.684-038 WHEEL-AND-CASTER REPAIRER; 632.380-010 INSPECTING-MACHINE ADJUSTER; 638.261-022 PINSETTER MECHANIC, AUTOMATIC; 739.684-134 NEEDLE-BOARD REPAIRER; 769.664-010 SHAKER REPAIRER; 776.684-014 POLISHING-WHEEL SETTER; 779.684-026 GLASS-LINED TANK REPAIRER; 829.381-010 PINSETTER ADJUSTER, AUTOMATIC; 979.684-038 SILK-SCREEN REPAIRER

85119C ALL OTHER MACHINERY MAINTENANCE MECHANICS. OOH Title/s: Industrial Machinery Repairers

All other machinery maintenance mechanics not classified separately above.

Yearly Earnings: $27,612

Education: Long-term O-J-T

GOE Group/s: 05.05.06 Craft Technology: Metal Fabrication and Repair

CIP Program/s: 470399 Industrial Equipment Maintenance and Repair, Other

Related DOT Job/s: 622.381-030 MINE-CAR REPAIRER

85123A EQUIPMENT SERVICERS AND TECHNICIANS. OOH Title/s: Millwrights; Inspectors, Testers, and Graders

Install new machinery and heavy equipment, including robots and related equipment, according to layout plans, blueprints, and other drawings in customer's establishment. Consult with engineering staff to resolve problems of machine design and deviation of machine operation. Operate machine or equipment through trial run to ensure conformance to specifications. May train customer's personnel in adjusting, maintaining, and repairing machinery or equipment. Installs and repairs machinery or equipment in customer's establishment, utilizing knowledge of mechanical, hydraulic, and electrical machinery. Consults with personnel in engineering department to resolve problems of machine design and deviation of machine operation from original specifications. Operates machine or equipment through trial run at customer's establishment to ensure that quality and rate of production meet specifications. Trains customer's personnel in adjusting, maintaining, and repairing machinery or equipment. Arranges machine parts according to sequence of assembly and effective use of floor space. Directs workers in positioning equipment, following floor plans and manufacturer's instructions. Modifies previously installed equipment to ensure compatibility with new units. Explains reasons for design changes to avoid construction problems in customer's establishment. Repairs or supervises repair of worn or defective machinery or equipment in customer's plant. Installs safety devices or attachments to old equipment.

Yearly Earnings: $36,140

Education: Long-term O-J-T

Knowledge: Customer and Personal Service; Production and Processing; Computers and Electronics; Engineering and Technology; Design;

Building and Construction; Mechanical; Physics; Education and Training; Public Safety and Security
Abilities: Problem Sensitivity; Inductive Reasoning; Information Ordering; Memorization; Flexibility of Closure; Perceptual Speed; Spatial Orientation; Visualization; Selective Attention; Time Sharing; Arm-Hand Steadiness; Manual Dexterity; Finger Dexterity; Control Precision; Multilimb Coordination; Response Orientation; Rate Control; Reaction Time; Wrist-Finger Speed; Static Strength; Explosive Strength; Dynamic Strength; Trunk Strength; Extent Flexibility; Dynamic Flexibility; Gross Body Equilibrium; Near Vision; Visual Color Discrimination; Peripheral Vision; Depth Perception; Hearing Sensitivity; Auditory Attention; Sound Localization; Speech Recognition
Skills: Learning Strategies; Coordination; Instructing; Operations Analysis; Technology Design; Installation; Testing; Operation Monitoring; Operation and Control; Product Inspection; Equipment Maintenance; Troubleshooting; Repairing
General Work Activities: Inspecting Equipment, Structures, or Material; Estimating Needed Characteristics; Processing Information; Updating and Using Job-Relevant Knowledge; Performing General Physical Activities; Handling and Moving Objects; Controlling Machines and Processes; Interacting with Computers; Drafting and Specifying Technical Devices, etc.; Implementing Ideas, Programs, etc.; Repairing and Maintaining Mechanical Equipment; Repairing and Maintaining Electrical Equipment; Communicating with Persons Outside Organization; Coordinating Work and Activities of Others; Developing and Building Teams; Teaching Others; Guiding, Directing and Motivating Subordinates; Coaching and Developing Others; Provide Consultation and Advice to Others
Job Characteristics: Supervise, Coach, Train Others; Provide a Service to Others; Coordinate or Lead Others; Responsible for Others' Health and Safety; Responsibility for Outcomes and Results; Deal with Physical, Aggressive People; Cramped Work Space, Awkward Positions; Whole Body Vibration; Hazardous Equipment; Bending or Twisting the Body; Common Protective or Safety Attire; Degree of Automation
GOE Group/s: 05.05.05 Craft Technology: Electrical-Electronic Systems Installation and Repair; 05.05.09 Craft Technology: Mechanical Work
CIP Program/s: 110101 Computer and Information Sciences, General; 470101 Electrical and Electronics Equipment Installer and Repairer; 470105 Industrial Electronics Installer and Repairer; 470303 Industrial Machinery Maintenance and Repair
Related DOT Job/s: 638.261-010 AUTOMATED EQUIPMENT ENGINEER-TECHNICIAN; 638.261-018 MANUFACTURER'S SERVICE REPRESENTATIVE; 638.261-026 FIELD SERVICE TECHNICIAN; 869.261-014 MECHANICAL-TEST TECHNICIAN

85123B MILLWRIGHTS AND MACHINERY ERECTORS. OOH Title/s: Millwrights

Install new machinery and heavy equipment according to layout plans, blueprints, and other drawings in customer's establishment. Dismantle and move machinery and heavy equipment when changes in plant layout are required. Dismantles machines, using hammers, wrenches, crowbars, and other hand tools. Assembles and installs equipment, using hand tools and power tools. Bolts parts, such as side and deck plates, jaw plates, and journals, to basic assembly unit. Attaches moving parts and subassemblies to basic assembly unit, using hand tools and power tools. Assembles machines, and bolts, welds, rivets, or otherwise fastens them to foundation or other structures, using hand tools and power tools. Dismantles machinery and equipment for shipment to installation site, usually performing installation and maintenance work as part of team. Moves machinery and equipment, using hoists, dollies, rollers, and trucks. Aligns machines and equipment, using hoists, jacks, hand tools, squares, rules, micrometers, and plumb bobs. Connects power unit to machines or steam piping to equipment, and tests unit to evaluate its mechanical operation. Positions steel beams to support bedplates of machines and equipment, using blueprints and schematic drawings, to determine work procedures. Lays out mounting holes, using measuring instruments, and drills holes with power drill. Inserts shims, adjusts tension on nuts and bolts, or positions parts, using hand tools and measuring instruments, to set specified clearances between moving and stationary parts. Levels bedplate and establishes centerline, using straightedge, levels, and transit. Shrink-fits bushings, sleeves, rings, liners, gears, and wheels to specified items, using portable gas heating equipment. Installs robot and modifies its program, using teach pendant. Constructs foundation for machines, using hand tools and building materials such as wood, cement, and steel. Signals crane operator to lower basic assembly units to bedplate, and aligns unit to centerline. Operates engine lathe to grind, file, and turn machine parts to dimensional specifications. Repairs and lubricates machines and equipment. Replaces defective parts of machine, or adjusts clearances and alignment of moving parts.
Yearly Earnings: $36,140
Education: Long-term O-J-T
Knowledge: Engineering and Technology; Design; Building and Construction; Mechanical; Physics; Transportation
Abilities: Information Ordering; Perceptual Speed; Spatial Orientation; Visualization; Selective Attention; Time Sharing; Arm-Hand Steadiness; Manual Dexterity; Finger Dexterity; Control Precision; Multilimb Coordination; Response Orientation; Rate Control; Reaction Time; Wrist-Finger Speed; Speed of Limb Movement; Static Strength; Explosive Strength; Dynamic Strength; Trunk Strength; Stamina; Extent Flexibility; Dynamic Flexibility; Gross Body Coordination; Gross Body Equilibrium; Far Vision; Visual Color Discrimination; Peripheral Vision; Depth Perception; Hearing Sensitivity; Auditory Attention; Sound Localization
Skills: Installation; Testing; Product Inspection; Equipment Maintenance; Troubleshooting; Repairing
General Work Activities: Inspecting Equipment, Structures, or Material; Performing General Physical Activities; Handling and Moving Objects; Controlling Machines and Processes; Interacting with Computers; Implementing Ideas, Programs, etc.; Repairing and Maintaining Mechanical Equipment
Job Characteristics: Responsible for Others' Health and Safety; Sounds, Noise Levels are Distracting, etc.; Extremely Bright or Inadequate Lighting; Cramped Work Space, Awkward Positions; Whole Body Vibration; Hazardous Equipment; Kneeling, Crouching, or Crawling; Keeping or Regaining Balance; Using Hands on Objects, Tools, or Controls; Bending or Twisting the Body; Common Protective or Safety Attire; Importance of Being Sure All is Done; Pace Determined by Speed of Equipment
GOE Group/s: 05.05.06 Craft Technology: Metal Fabrication and Repair; 05.05.09 Craft Technology: Mechanical Work
CIP Program/s: 010201 Agricultural Mechanization, General; 470303 Industrial Machinery Maintenance and Repair
Related DOT Job/s: 638.261-014 MACHINERY ERECTOR; 638.281-018 MILLWRIGHT; 638.281-022 MILLWRIGHT APPRENTICE

85126 REFRACTORY MATERIALS REPAIRERS, EXCEPT BRICK MASONS. OOH Title/s: Industrial Machinery Repairers

Build or repair furnaces, kilns, cupolas, boilers, converters, ladles, soaking pits, ovens, etc., using refractory materials. May pack insulation or repair casings and linings. Exclude refractory brick masons. Relines or repairs ladle and pouring spout with refractory clay, using trowel. Dries and bakes new lining by placing inverted lining over burner, building fire in ladle, or using blowtorch. Drills holes in furnace wall, bolts overlapping layers of plastic to walls, and hammers surface to compress layers into solid sheets. Fastens stopper head to rod with metal pin, to assemble refractory stopper used to plug pouring nozzles of steel ladles. Spreads mortar on stopper head and rod, using trowel, and slides brick sleeves over rod to form refractory jacket. Tightens locknuts holding assembly together, spreads mortar on jacket to seal sleeve joints, and dries mortar in oven. Mixes specified amounts of sand, clay, mortar powder, and water to form refractory clay or mortar, using shovel or mixing machine. Dumps and tamps clay in mold, using tamping tool. Disassembles mold, and cuts, chips, and smoothes clay structures, such as floaters, drawbars, and L-blocks, using square rule and hand tools. Removes worn or damaged plastic block refractory lining of furnace, using hand tools. Bolts sections of wooden mold together, using wrench, and lines mold with paper to prevent adherence of clay to mold. Measures furnace wall, and cuts required number of sheets from plastic block, using saw. Installs clay structures in melting tanks and drawing kilns to control flow and temperature of molten glass, using hoists and hand tools. Climbs scaffolding with hose, and sprays surfaces of cupola with refractory mixture, using spray equipment. Transfers clay structures to curing ovens, melting tanks, and drawing kilns, using electric forklift truck. Chips slag from lining of ladle, or entire lining when beyond repair, using hammer and chisel. Installs preformed metal scaffolding in interior of cupola, using hand tools.

Yearly Earnings: $27,612

Education: Long-term O-J-T

Knowledge: Building and Construction

Abilities: Multilimb Coordination; Wrist-Finger Speed; Speed of Limb Movement; Static Strength; Explosive Strength; Dynamic Strength; Trunk Strength; Stamina; Extent Flexibility; Dynamic Flexibility; Gross Body Coordination; Gross Body Equilibrium; Depth Perception

Skills: Installation; Repairing

General Work Activities: Performing General Physical Activities; Handling and Moving Objects; Interacting with Computers; Repairing and Maintaining Mechanical Equipment

Job Characteristics: Sounds, Noise Levels are Distracting, etc.; Very Hot; Extremely Bright or Inadequate Lighting; Contaminants; Cramped Work Space, Awkward Positions; Whole Body Vibration; High Places; Hazardous Conditions; Hazardous Equipment; Hazardous Situations; Climbing Ladders, Scaffolds, Poles, etc.; Kneeling, Crouching, or Crawling; Keeping or Regaining Balance; Bending or Twisting the Body; Making Repetitive Motions; Common Protective or Safety Attire; Importance of Repeating Same Tasks

GOE Group/s: 05.10.01 Crafts: Structural; 05.12.14 Elemental Work: Mechanical: Painting, Caulking, and Coating; 06.02.30 Production Work: Manual Work, Stone, Glass, and Clay; 06.04.30 Elemental Work: Industrial: Manual Work, Stone, Glass, and Clay

CIP Program/s: 000000 NO CIP ASSIGNED

Related DOT Job/s: 519.684-010 LADLE LINER; 519.684-022 STOPPER MAKER; 579.664-010 CLAY-STRUCTURE BUILDER AND SERVICER; 849.484-010 BOILER RELINER, PLASTIC BLOCK; 899.684-010 BONDACTOR-MACHINE OPERATOR

85128A MACHINERY MAINTENANCE SERVICERS.

OOH Title/s: Industrial Machinery Repairers

Perform basic maintenance activities, such as cleaning, adjusting, and lubricating, to maintain equipment and machinery. Replace worn or defective parts, such as filters and lining, and replenish machine fluids. Sets up and operates machine and adjusts controls that regulate operational functions to ensure conformance to specifications. Installs, replaces, or changes machine parts and attachments, according to production specifications. Lubricates, oils, or applies adhesive or other material to machines, machine parts, or other equipment, according to specified procedures. Starts machine and observes mechanical operation to determine efficiency and to detect defects, malfunctions, or other machine damage. Replaces or repairs metal, wood, leather, glass, or other lining in machine or equipment compartments or containers. Inspects or tests damaged machine parts, and marks defective area or advises supervisor of need for repair. Dismantles machine, removes machine parts, and reassembles machine, using hand tools, chain falls, jack, crane, or hoist. Cuts, shapes, smooths, attaches, or assembles pieces of metal, wood, rubber, or other material to repair and maintenance machines and equipment. Cleans machine and machine parts, using cleaning solvent, cloth, air gun, hose, vacuum, or other equipment. Reads work orders and specifications to determine machines and equipment requiring repair or maintenance. Removes hardened material from machine or machine parts, using abrasives, power and hand tools, jackhammer, sledgehammer, or other equipment. Replaces, empties, or replenishes empty machine and equipment containers, such as gas tanks or boxes. Communicates with or assists other workers to repair or move machines, machine parts or equipment. Measures, mixes, prepares, and tests chemical solutions used to clean or repair machinery and equipment, according to product specifications. Marks, separates, ties, aligns, threads, attaches, or inserts material or product preparatory to machine operation or to identify machine process. Records and maintains production, repair, and machine maintenance information. Inventories and requisitions machine parts, equipment, and other supplies to replenish and maintain stock. Transports machine parts, tools, equipment, and other material between work areas and storage, using crane, hoist, or dolly. Collects and discards worn machine parts and other garbage to maintain machinery and work areas.

Yearly Earnings: $27,612

Education: Long-term O-J-T

Knowledge: Production and Processing; Mechanical; Chemistry; Transportation

Abilities: Rate Control; Reaction Time; Extent Flexibility; Gross Body Equilibrium

Skills: Technology Design; Installation; Testing; Operation Monitoring; Operation and Control; Equipment Maintenance; Troubleshooting; Repairing

General Work Activities: Inspecting Equipment, Structures, or Material; Performing General Physical Activities; Controlling Machines and Processes; Interacting with Computers; Repairing and Maintaining Mechanical Equipment

Job Characteristics: Sounds, Noise Levels are Distracting, etc.; Extremely Bright or Inadequate Lighting; Contaminants; Cramped Work Space, Awkward Positions; Whole Body Vibration; High Places; Hazardous Equipment; Hazardous Situations; Standing; Climbing Ladders, Scaffolds, Poles, etc.; Kneeling, Crouching, or Crawling; Keeping or Regaining Balance; Bending or Twisting the Body; Making Repetitive Motions; Common Protective or Safety Attire; Specialized Protective or Safety Attire; Pace Determined by Speed of Equipment

GOE Group/s: 05.09.01 Material Control: Shipping, Receiving, and Stock Checking; 05.10.01 Crafts: Structural; 05.10.02 Crafts: Mechanical; 05.12.12 Elemental Work: Mechanical: Structural Work; 05.12.15 Elemental Work: Mechanical: Mechanical Work; 06.01.02 Production Technology: Machine Set-up; 06.03.02 Quality Control: Inspecting, Grading, Sorting, Weighing, and Recording; 06.04.05 Elemental Work: Industrial: Machine Work, Fabric and Leather; 06.04.06 Elemental Work: Industrial: Machine Work, Textiles; 06.04.15 Elemental Work: Industrial: Equipment Operation, Food Processing; 06.04.24 Elemental Work: Industrial: Manual Work, Metal and Plastics; 06.04.27 Elemental Work: Industrial: Manual Work, Textile, Fabric and Leather; 06.04.34 Elemental Work: Industrial: Manual Work, Assorted Materials; 06.04.39 Elemental Work: Industrial: Cleaning

CIP Program/s: 470101 Electrical and Electronics Equipment Installer and Repairer; 470105 Industrial Electronics Installer and Repairer; 470303 Industrial Machinery Maintenance and Repair
Related DOT Job/s: 514.684-018 NOZZLE-AND-SLEEVE WORKER; 519.664-014 POT LINER; 519.667-010 CARBON SETTER; 519.684-014 LEAF COVERER; 529.667-014 MASH-FILTER-CLOTH CHANGER; 564.684-010 KNIFE SETTER, GRINDER MACHINE; 590.384-014 PRODUCTION TECHNICIAN, SEMICONDUCTOR PROCESSING EQUIPMENT; 622.684-018 SWITCH REPAIRER; 628.684-010 BINDER AND BOX BUILDER; 628.684-014 FRAME BANDER; 628.684-022 OVERHEAD CLEANER MAINTAINER; 628.684-042 SPINDLE REPAIRER; 628.684-046 TEXTURING-MACHINE FIXER; 628.687-010 FLYER REPAIRER; 629.684-010 CURING-PRESS MAINTAINER; 630.584-010 EQUIPMENT CLEANER-AND-TESTER; 638.684-010 KNIFE CHANGER; 638.684-014 KNIFE SETTER; 652.385-010 PRINTING-ROLLER HANDLER; 680.684-010 CARD GRINDER HELPER; 682.684-010 ROLLER CHECKER; 683.684-022 LEASE-OUT WORKER; 683.685-014 CARD CHANGER, JACQUARD LOOM; 683.687-034 WARP-TENSION TESTER; 685.685-014 PATTERN ASSEMBLER; 689.686-026 FRAME CHANGER; 689.687-070 SHUTTLER; 801.664-010 LINER REPLACER; 801.664-014 UTILITY WORKER, MERCHANT MILL; 828.281-018 MISSILE FACILITIES REPAIRER; 891.564-010 PIPE CHANGER

85128B OILERS. OOH Title/s: Industrial Machinery Repairers; Farm Equipment Mechanics

Lubricate moving parts of friction surfaces of mechanical equipment. Heats, sprays, pours, and applies lubricant onto gears and other moving parts of machine or mechanical equipment. Fills container—such as oilcan, grease gun, or tank—or wells and sumps of lubricating systems with specified lubricant. Observes panel to determine efficiency of automatic lubricant system and turns or adjusts valves to regulate flow of oil. Inspects moving parts of mechanical equipment to detect wear and determine need for lubrication. Reports machinery defects or malfunctions to supervisor. Records and maintains production, repair, and machine and equipment maintenance information. Cleans machines, sweeps floors, and transports stock to maintain work area.
Yearly Earnings: $27,612
Education: Long-term O-J-T
Knowledge: None above average
Abilities: None above average
Skills: None above average
General Work Activities: Repairing and Maintaining Mechanical Equipment
Job Characteristics: Sounds, Noise Levels are Distracting, etc.; Very Hot; Contaminants; Cramped Work Space, Awkward Positions; Hazardous Equipment; Climbing Ladders, Scaffolds, Poles, etc.; Kneeling, Crouching, or Crawling; Keeping or Regaining Balance; Bending or Twisting the Body; Making Repetitive Motions; Degree of Automation; Importance of Being Aware of New Events; Importance of Repeating Same Tasks; Pace Determined by Speed of Equipment
GOE Group/s: 05.12.08 Elemental Work: Mechanical: Lubricating
CIP Program/s: 470303 Industrial Machinery Maintenance and Repair; 470399 Industrial Equipment Maintenance and Repair, Other
Related DOT Job/s: 624.684-010 GREASER; 630.687-010 PULLEY MAINTAINER; 699.687-018 OILER; 850.684-018 STRIPPING-SHOVEL OILER; 932.667-014 LOADING-SHOVEL OILER

85132 MAINTENANCE REPAIRERS, GENERAL UTILITY. OOH Title/s: General Maintenance Mechanics

Perform work involving two or more maintenance skills to keep machines, mechanical equipment, or structure of an establishment in repair. Duties may involve pipefitting, boilermaking, insulating, welding, machining, machine and equipment repairing, carpentry, and electrical work. May also include planning and laying out of work relating to repairs; repairing electrical or mechanical equipment; installing, aligning, and balancing new equipment; and repairing buildings, floors, or stairs. This occupation is generally found in small establishments, where specialization in maintenance work is impractical. Inspects and tests machinery and equipment to diagnose machine malfunctions. Dismantles and reassembles defective machines and equipment. Installs new or repaired parts. Cleans and lubricates shafts, bearings, gears, and other parts of machinery. Installs or repairs wiring and electrical and electronic components. Assembles, installs, or repairs pipe systems and hydraulic and pneumatic equipment. Installs machinery and equipment. Assembles, installs, or repairs plumbing. Paints and repairs woodwork and plaster. Lays brick to repair and maintain physical structure of establishment. Sets up and operates machine tools to repair or fabricate machine parts, jigs and fixtures, and tools. Operates cutting torch or welding equipment to cut or join metal parts. Fabricates and repairs counters, benches, partitions, and other wooden structures, such as sheds and outbuildings. Records repairs made and costs. Estimates costs of repairs.
Yearly Earnings: $25,220
Education: Long-term O-J-T
Knowledge: Engineering and Technology; Design; Building and Construction; Mechanical; Public Safety and Security
Abilities: Problem Sensitivity; Information Ordering; Category Flexibility; Memorization; Speed of Closure; Flexibility of Closure; Perceptual Speed; Spatial Orientation; Visualization; Selective Attention; Arm-Hand Steadiness; Manual Dexterity; Finger Dexterity; Control Precision; Multilimb Coordination; Response Orientation; Reaction Time; Wrist-Finger Speed; Speed of Limb Movement; Static Strength; Explosive Strength; Dynamic Strength; Trunk Strength; Stamina; Extent Flexibility; Dynamic Flexibility; Gross Body Coordination; Gross Body Equilibrium; Far Vision; Visual Color Discrimination; Night Vision; Peripheral Vision; Depth Perception; Glare Sensitivity; Hearing Sensitivity; Auditory Attention; Sound Localization
Skills: Equipment Selection; Installation; Testing; Operation Monitoring; Equipment Maintenance; Troubleshooting; Repairing
General Work Activities: Inspecting Equipment, Structures, or Material; Performing General Physical Activities; Interacting with Computers; Repairing and Maintaining Mechanical Equipment; Repairing and Maintaining Electrical Equipment
Job Characteristics: Sounds, Noise Levels are Distracting, etc.; Cramped Work Space, Awkward Positions; High Places; Hazardous Equipment; Climbing Ladders, Scaffolds, Poles, etc.; Kneeling, Crouching, or Crawling; Keeping or Regaining Balance; Bending or Twisting the Body; Common Protective or Safety Attire
GOE Group/s: 05.05.09 Craft Technology: Mechanical Work; 05.10.01 Crafts: Structural
CIP Program/s: 010201 Agricultural Mechanization, General; 460401 Building/Property Maintenance and Management; 479999 Mechanics and Repairers, Other
Related DOT Job/s: 638.281-010 FIRE-FIGHTING-EQUIPMENT SPECIALIST; 899.261-014 MAINTENANCE REPAIRER, INDUSTRIAL; 899.381-010 MAINTENANCE REPAIRER, BUILDING; 899.484-010 MOBILE-HOME-LOT UTILITY WORKER; 912.364-010 AIRPORT ATTENDANT

Motor Vehicle Mechanics

85302A AUTOMOTIVE MASTER MECHANICS. OOH Title/s: Automotive Mechanics

Repair automobiles, trucks, buses, and other vehicles. Master mechanics repair virtually any part on the vehicle or specialize

in the transmission system. Repairs and overhauls defective automotive units, such as engines, transmissions, or differentials. Repairs or replaces parts, such as pistons, rods, gears, valves, and bearings. Overhauls or replaces carburetors, blowers, generators, distributors, starts, and pumps. Repairs manual and automatic transmissions. Repairs, relines, replaces, and adjusts brakes. Rewires ignition system, lights, and instrument panel. Repairs or replaces shock absorbers. Installs and repairs accessories, such as radios, heaters, mirrors, and windshield wipers. Repairs radiator leaks. Replaces and adjusts headlights. Examines vehicles and discusses extent of damage or malfunction with customer. Aligns front end. Rebuilds parts, such as crankshafts and cylinder blocks. Repairs damaged automobile bodies.
Yearly Earnings: $22,828
Education: Long-term O-J-T
Knowledge: Computers and Electronics; Engineering and Technology; Mechanical
Abilities: Originality; Problem Sensitivity; Inductive Reasoning; Information Ordering; Memorization; Perceptual Speed; Spatial Orientation; Visualization; Selective Attention; Time Sharing; Manual Dexterity; Finger Dexterity; Control Precision; Response Orientation; Rate Control; Reaction Time; Wrist-Finger Speed; Speed of Limb Movement; Static Strength; Explosive Strength; Trunk Strength; Extent Flexibility; Dynamic Flexibility; Gross Body Equilibrium; Visual Color Discrimination; Depth Perception; Hearing Sensitivity; Auditory Attention; Sound Localization
Skills: Problem Identification; Technology Design; Installation; Operation Monitoring; Product Inspection; Equipment Maintenance; Troubleshooting; Repairing
General Work Activities: Inspecting Equipment, Structures, or Material; Estimating Needed Characteristics; Updating and Using Job-Relevant Knowledge; Performing General Physical Activities; Handling and Moving Objects; Interacting with Computers; Repairing and Maintaining Mechanical Equipment; Repairing and Maintaining Electrical Equipment
Job Characteristics: Deal with Unpleasant or Angry People; Sounds, Noise Levels are Distracting, etc.; Extremely Bright or Inadequate Lighting; Contaminants; Cramped Work Space, Awkward Positions; Hazardous Equipment; Standing; Kneeling, Crouching, or Crawling; Bending or Twisting the Body; Special Uniform; Common Protective or Safety Attire
GOE Group/s: 05.05.09 Craft Technology: Mechanical Work; 05.10.02 Crafts: Mechanical
CIP Program/s: 470604 Auto/Automotive Mechanic/Technician
Related DOT Job/s: 620.261-010 AUTOMOBILE MECHANIC; 620.261-012 AUTOMOBILE-MECHANIC APPRENTICE; 620.281-062 TRANSMISSION MECHANIC; 620.364-010 SQUEAK, RATTLE, AND LEAK REPAIRER; 620.381-022 REPAIRER, HEAVY

85302B AUTOMOTIVE SPECIALTY TECHNICIANS. OOH Title/s: Automotive Mechanics; Metalworking and Plastics-Working Machine Operators

Repair only one system or component on a vehicle, such as brakes, suspension, or radiator. Repairs, installs, and adjusts hydraulic and electromagnetic automatic lift mechanisms used to raise and lower automobile windows, seats, and tops. Repairs and replaces automobile leaf springs. Removes and replaces defective mufflers and tailpipes from automobiles. Repairs and aligns defective wheels of automobiles. Repairs and rebuilds clutch systems. Repairs, overhauls, and adjusts automobile brake systems. Installs and repairs automotive air-conditioning units. Rebuilds, repairs, and tests automotive injection units. Converts vehicle fuel systems from gasoline to butane gas operations, and repairs and services operating butane fuel units. Aligns and repairs wheels, axles, frames, torsion bars, and steering mechanisms of automobiles. Repairs, replaces, and adjusts defective carburetor parts and gasoline filters. Repairs and replaces defective balljoint suspension, brakeshoes, and wheel bearings. Inspects and tests new vehicles for damage, records findings, and makes repairs. Inspects, tests, repairs, and replaces automotive cooling systems and fuel tanks. Tunes automobile engines and tests electronic computer components. Examines vehicle, compiles estimate of repair costs, and secures customer approval to perform repairs.
Yearly Earnings: $22,828
Education: Long-term O-J-T
Knowledge: Customer and Personal Service; Computers and Electronics; Engineering and Technology; Design; Mechanical; Physics; Chemistry
Abilities: Information Ordering; Flexibility of Closure; Perceptual Speed; Visualization; Manual Dexterity; Multilimb Coordination; Response Orientation; Rate Control; Reaction Time; Wrist-Finger Speed; Static Strength; Explosive Strength; Trunk Strength; Extent Flexibility; Dynamic Flexibility; Gross Body Equilibrium; Visual Color Discrimination; Peripheral Vision; Hearing Sensitivity; Auditory Attention; Sound Localization
Skills: Installation; Equipment Maintenance; Troubleshooting; Repairing
General Work Activities: Inspecting Equipment, Structures, or Material; Performing General Physical Activities; Handling and Moving Objects; Interacting with Computers; Repairing and Maintaining Mechanical Equipment; Repairing and Maintaining Electrical Equipment
Job Characteristics: Provide a Service to Others; Deal with External Customers; Deal with Unpleasant or Angry People; Sounds, Noise Levels are Distracting, etc.; Extremely Bright or Inadequate Lighting; Contaminants; Cramped Work Space, Awkward Positions; Standing; Kneeling, Crouching, or Crawling; Bending or Twisting the Body; Special Uniform; Common Protective or Safety Attire
GOE Group/s: 05.05.09 Craft Technology: Mechanical Work; 05.10.01 Crafts: Structural; 05.10.02 Crafts: Mechanical; 05.10.03 Crafts: Electrical-Electronic; 05.12.12 Elemental Work: Mechanical: Structural Work; 05.12.15 Elemental Work: Mechanical: Mechanical Work; 06.02.02 Production Work: Machine Work, Metal and Plastics
CIP Program/s: 470201 Heating, Air Conditioning and Refrigeration Mechanics and Repairers; 470604 Auto/Automotive Mechanic/Technician; 480501 Machinist/Machine Technologist
Related DOT Job/s: 619.380-018 SPRING REPAIRER, HAND; 620.261-030 AUTOMOBILE-SERVICE-STATION MECHANIC; 620.261-034 AUTOMOTIVE-COOLING-SYSTEM DIAGNOSTIC TECHNICIAN; 620.281-010 AIR-CONDITIONING MECHANIC; 620.281-026 BRAKE REPAIRER; 620.281-034 CARBURETOR MECHANIC; 620.281-038 FRONT-END MECHANIC; 620.281-066 TUNE-UP MECHANIC; 620.281-070 VEHICLE-FUEL-SYSTEMS CONVERTER; 620.381-010 AUTOMOBILE-RADIATOR MECHANIC; 620.682-010 BRAKE-DRUM-LATHE OPERATOR; 620.684-018 BRAKE ADJUSTER; 620.684-022 CLUTCH REBUILDER; 625.281-022 FUEL-INJECTION SERVICER; 706.381-046 WHEELWRIGHT; 806.361-026 NEW-CAR GET-READY MECHANIC; 807.664-010 MUFFLER INSTALLER; 807.684-022 FLOOR SERVICE WORKER, SPRING; 825.381-014 AUTOMATIC-WINDOW-SEAT-AND-TOP-LIFT REPAIRER

85305A AUTOMOTIVE GLASS INSTALLERS AND REPAIRERS. OOH Title/s: Automotive Body Repairers

Replace or repair broken windshields and window glass in motor vehicles. Installs precut replacement glass to replace curved or custom-shaped windows. Removes broken or damaged glass windshield or window glass from motor vehicles, using hand tools to remove screws from frame holding glass. Applies moisture-proofing compound along glass edges and installs glass into windshield- or glass-frame in door or side panel of vehicle. Installs rubber-channeling strip around edge of glass or frame to weather-proof and to prevent rattling.

Cuts flat safety glass according to specified pattern, using glass-cutter. Holds cut or uneven edge of glass against automated abrasive belt to shape or smooth edges. Obtains windshield for specific automobile make and model from stock and examines for defects prior to installation. Replaces or adjusts motorized or manual window-raising mechanisms.
Yearly Earnings: $23,712
Education: Long-term O-J-T
Knowledge: None above average
Abilities: Arm-Hand Steadiness; Static Strength; Trunk Strength; Stamina; Extent Flexibility; Dynamic Flexibility; Gross Body Coordination; Gross Body Equilibrium
Skills: Installation; Repairing
General Work Activities: None above average
Job Characteristics: Hazardous Situations; Standing; Keeping or Regaining Balance; Common Protective or Safety Attire
GOE Group/s: 05.10.01 Crafts: Structural
CIP Program/s: 470603 Auto/Automotive Body Repairer
Related DOT Job/s: 865.684-010 GLASS INSTALLER

85305B AUTOMOTIVE BODY REPAIRERS. OOH Title/s: Automotive Body Repairers

Repair and customize automotive bodies and frames. Positions dolly block against surface of dented area and beats opposite surface to remove dents, using hammer. Straightens bent automobile or other vehicle frames, using pneumatic frame-straightening machine. Fills depressions with body filler and files, grinds, and sands repaired surfaces, using power tools and hand tools. Paints and sands repaired surface, using paint spraygun and motorized sander. Cuts opening in vehicle body for installation of customized windows, using templates and power shears or chisel. Fits and secures windows, vinyl roof, and metal trim to vehicle body, using caulking gun, adhesive brush, and mallet. Removes damaged fenders and panels, using wrenches and cutting torch, and installs replacement parts, using wrenches or welding equipment. Measures and marks vinyl material and cuts material to size for roof installation, using rule, straightedge, and hand shears. Cuts away damaged fiberglass from automobile body, using air grinder. Soaks fiberglass matting in resin mixture and applies layers of matting over repair area to specified thickness. Mixes polyester resin and hardener to be used in restoring damaged area. Peels separating film from repair area and washes repaired surface with water. Examines vehicle to determine extent and type of damage. Cuts and tapes plastic separating film to outside repair area to avoid damaging surrounding surfaces during repair procedure. Removes upholstery, accessories, electrical window- and seat-operating equipment, and trim to gain access to vehicle body and fenders. Reads specifications or confers with customer to determine custom modifications to alter appearance of vehicle. Adjusts or aligns headlights, wheels, and brake system. Cleans work area, using air hose to remove damaged material and discarded fiberglass strips used in repair procedures.
Yearly Earnings: $23,712
Education: Long-term O-J-T
Knowledge: Engineering and Technology; Mechanical; Foreign Language
Abilities: Visualization; Selective Attention; Finger Dexterity; Wrist-Finger Speed; Speed of Limb Movement; Static Strength; Dynamic Strength; Trunk Strength; Stamina; Extent Flexibility; Dynamic Flexibility; Gross Body Equilibrium; Visual Color Discrimination
Skills: Technology Design; Installation; Product Inspection; Repairing
General Work Activities: Performing General Physical Activities; Handling and Moving Objects; Repairing and Maintaining Mechanical Equipment; Repairing and Maintaining Electrical Equipment
Job Characteristics: Deal with Unpleasant or Angry People; Deal with Physical, Aggressive People; Sounds, Noise Levels are Distracting, etc.; Very Hot; Extremely Bright or Inadequate Lighting; Contaminants; Cramped Work Space, Awkward Positions; Whole Body Vibration; Hazardous Conditions; Hazardous Equipment; Kneeling, Crouching, or Crawling; Keeping or Regaining Balance; Bending or Twisting the Body; Common Protective or Safety Attire; Pace Determined by Speed of Equipment
GOE Group/s: 05.05.06 Craft Technology: Metal Fabrication and Repair; 05.10.01 Crafts: Structural
CIP Program/s: 470603 Auto/Automotive Body Repairer
Related DOT Job/s: 807.361-010 AUTOMOBILE-BODY CUSTOMIZER; 807.381-010 AUTOMOBILE-BODY REPAIRER; 807.381-030 AUTO-BODY REPAIRER, FIBERGLASS

85305C TRUCK AND TRAILER BODY REPAIRERS. OOH Title/s: Automotive Body Repairers

Repair and service truck bodies and trailers. Replaces and repairs worn and defective parts on used metal trailers. Constructs and repairs metal truck bodies and trailers, using hand tools and power tools. Overhauls used and wrecked trailer bodies, following shop orders or specifications. Installs metal or wood flooring on trailers. Installs interiors, insulation, and fixtures, using hand tools—such as hammer, file, and screwdriver—and power tools, such as bandsaw, sander, and drill. Installs electrical wiring for dome lights, tail lights, brake lights, and other equipment, according to specified procedures. Fits and assembles components, using hand tools and portable power tools, such as drill, riveter, and welding apparatus. Installs, adjusts, and services motor-cooling systems in refrigerated trailers. Lays out dimensions on metal stock according to specifications, using square, rule, and punch. Sprays or brushes paint, primer, or protective coating on wood and metal surfaces. Examines completed new trailers and tests, adjusts, and repairs wheel alignments, bearings, lights, and brake assemblies.
Yearly Earnings: $23,712
Education: Long-term O-J-T
Knowledge: Mechanical
Abilities: Visualization; Finger Dexterity; Multilimb Coordination; Speed of Limb Movement; Stamina; Extent Flexibility; Dynamic Flexibility; Gross Body Coordination; Gross Body Equilibrium; Visual Color Discrimination; Hearing Sensitivity
Skills: Technology Design; Installation; Equipment Maintenance; Troubleshooting; Repairing
General Work Activities: Repairing and Maintaining Mechanical Equipment
Job Characteristics: Extremely Bright or Inadequate Lighting; Cramped Work Space, Awkward Positions; Climbing Ladders, Scaffolds, Poles, etc.; Kneeling, Crouching, or Crawling; Keeping or Regaining Balance; Bending or Twisting the Body
GOE Group/s: 05.05.06 Craft Technology: Metal Fabrication and Repair; 05.10.01 Crafts: Structural
CIP Program/s: 470603 Auto/Automotive Body Repairer
Related DOT Job/s: 807.281-010 TRUCK-BODY BUILDER; 807.381-022 SERVICE MECHANIC

85305D AUTOMOTIVE BODY REPAIR ESTIMATORS. OOH Title/s: Automotive Body Repairers

Estimate cost of repairing damaged automobile and truck bodies. Examines damaged vehicle for dents, scratches, broken glass, and other areas requiring repair, replacement, or repainting. Examines interior for evidence of fire or water damage to upholstery and appointments. Determines feasibility of repair or replacement of parts, such as bumpers, fenders, and doors, according to relative costs and damage. Computes cost of replacement parts and labor to restore vehicle, using standard labor and parts cost manuals. Estimates cost of repainting, converting vehicles to special purposes, or customizing undamaged vehicles, depending on specialty of shop. Sights along fenders to detect

frame damage, or positions vehicle in frame-aligning rig to locate misalignment. Explains estimate to customer, and answers customer's questions regarding estimate. Enters itemized estimate on job order card or estimate form.
Yearly Earnings: $23,712
Education: Long-term O-J-T
Knowledge: None above average
Abilities: Gross Body Equilibrium; Near Vision
Skills: None above average
General Work Activities: None above average
Job Characteristics: Deal with External Customers; Frequency in Conflict Situations; Deal with Unpleasant or Angry People; Cramped Work Space, Awkward Positions; Standing; Kneeling, Crouching, or Crawling; Keeping or Regaining Balance; Bending or Twisting the Body
GOE Group/s: 05.07.01 Quality Control: Structural
CIP Program/s: 470603 Auto/Automotive Body Repairer
Related DOT Job/s: 807.267-010 SHOP ESTIMATOR

85308 MOTORCYCLE REPAIRERS. OOH Title/s: Motorcycle, Boat, and Small Engine Mechanics; Automotive Body Repairers

Repair and overhaul motorcycles, motor scooters, mopeds, or similar motorized vehicles. Dismantles engine and repairs or replaces defective parts, such as magneto, carburetor, and generator. Removes cylinder heads, grinds valves, scrapes off carbon, and replaces defective valves, pistons, cylinders and rings, using hand tools and power tools. Hammers out dents and bends in frame, welds tears and breaks, reassembles frame, and reinstalls engine. Repairs or replaces other parts, such as headlight, horn, handlebar controls, gasoline and oil tanks, starter, and muffler. Repairs and adjusts motorcycle subassemblies, such as forks, transmissions, brakes, and drive chain, according to specifications. Replaces defective parts, using hand tools, arbor press, flexible power press, or power tools. Reassembles and tests subassembly unit. Disassembles subassembly unit and examines condition, movement, or alignment of parts visually or using gauges. Listens to engine, examines vehicle's frame, and confers with customer to determine nature and extent of malfunction or damage. Connects test panel to engine and measures generator output, ignition timing, and other engine performance indicators.
Yearly Earnings: $25,272
Education: Long-term O-J-T
Knowledge: Engineering and Technology; Mechanical
Abilities: None above average
Skills: Technology Design; Installation; Testing; Equipment Maintenance; Troubleshooting; Repairing
General Work Activities: Inspecting Equipment, Structures, or Material; Repairing and Maintaining Mechanical Equipment; Repairing and Maintaining Electrical Equipment
Job Characteristics: Deal with Unpleasant or Angry People; Contaminants; Cramped Work Space, Awkward Positions; Kneeling, Crouching, or Crawling
GOE Group/s: 05.05.09 Craft Technology: Mechanical Work; 05.10.02 Crafts: Mechanical
CIP Program/s: 470611 Motorcycle Mechanic and Repairer
Related DOT Job/s: 620.281-054 MOTORCYCLE REPAIRER; 620.684-026 MOTORCYCLE SUBASSEMBLY REPAIRER; 807.381-018 FRAME REPAIRER; 807.484-010 FRAME STRAIGHTENER

85311A BUS AND TRUCK MECHANICS AND DIESEL ENGINE SPECIALISTS. OOH Title/s: Diesel Mechanics; Industrial Machinery Repairers

Inspect, repair, and maintain diesel engines used to power machines. Inspects defective equipment and diagnoses malfunctions, using test instruments, such as motor analyzers, chassis charts, and pressure gauges. Inspects and verifies dimensions and clearances of parts to ensure conformance to factory specifications. Inspects, repairs, and maintains automotive and mechanical equipment and machinery, such as pumps and compressors. Disassembles and overhauls internal combustion engines, pumps, generators, transmissions, clutches, and rear ends. Reconditions and replaces parts, pistons, bearings, gears, and valves. Reads job orders and observes and listens to operating equipment to ensure conformance to specifications or to determine malfunctions. Attaches test instruments to equipment and reads dials and gauges to diagnose malfunctions. Adjusts brakes, aligns wheels, tightens bolts and screws, and reassembles equipment. Changes oil, checks batteries, repairs tires and tubes, and lubricates equipment and machinery. Operates valve-grinding machine to grind and reset valves. Examines and adjusts protective guards, loose bolts, and specified safety devices.
Yearly Earnings: $25,376
Education: Long-term O-J-T
Knowledge: Mechanical
Abilities: Hearing Sensitivity
Skills: Installation; Testing; Equipment Maintenance; Troubleshooting; Repairing
General Work Activities: Inspecting Equipment, Structures, or Material; Performing General Physical Activities; Handling and Moving Objects; Interacting with Computers; Repairing and Maintaining Mechanical Equipment; Repairing and Maintaining Electrical Equipment
Job Characteristics: Very Hot; Cramped Work Space, Awkward Positions; Standing; Kneeling, Crouching, or Crawling; Special Uniform
GOE Group/s: 05.05.09 Craft Technology: Mechanical Work
CIP Program/s: 010204 Agricultural Power Machinery Operator; 470302 Heavy Equipment Maintenance and Repair; 470604 Auto/Automotive Mechanic/Technician; 470605 Diesel Engine Mechanic and Repairer
Related DOT Job/s: 620.281-046 MAINTENANCE MECHANIC; 620.281-050 MECHANIC, INDUSTRIAL TRUCK; 620.281-058 TRACTOR MECHANIC; 625.281-010 DIESEL MECHANIC; 625.281-014 DIESEL-MECHANIC APPRENTICE; 629.381-014 OIL-FIELD EQUIPMENT MECHANIC

85311B DIESEL ENGINE ERECTORS. OOH Title/s: Diesel Mechanics

Position, fit, and secure engine parts to erect diesel engines according to specifications. Positions engine parts and assemblies, such as valve lever assembly, pistons, rods, crankshaft, and camshaft housing. Aligns and secures vertical columns with tie rods to form engine frame. Files, scrapes, drills, taps, dowels, and shins parts such as cylinder liners, keys, and matching parts. Measures clearances and dimension, using scales, micrometers, and other instruments. Adjusts fuel rack and governor and aligns timing marks, using hand tools. Installs and connects fuel, lubrication, and cooling piping, using pipe benders, cutters, and threaders. Connects engine to test equipment and runs engine for specified time to test horsepower at designated revolutions per minute.
Yearly Earnings: $25,376
Education: Long-term O-J-T
Knowledge: Mechanical
Abilities: Manual Dexterity; Finger Dexterity; Wrist-Finger Speed; Static Strength; Dynamic Strength; Dynamic Flexibility; Gross Body Equilibrium
Skills: Installation; Troubleshooting
General Work Activities: Performing General Physical Activities; Handling and Moving Objects; Drafting and Specifying Technical Devices, etc.; Repairing and Maintaining Mechanical Equipment

Job Characteristics: Sounds, Noise Levels are Distracting, etc.; Cramped Work Space, Awkward Positions; Kneeling, Crouching, or Crawling
GOE Group/s: 05.05.09 Craft Technology: Mechanical Work
CIP Program/s: 470605 Diesel Engine Mechanic and Repairer
Related DOT Job/s: 625.361-010 DIESEL-ENGINE ERECTOR

85314 MOBILE HEAVY EQUIPMENT MECHANICS, EXCEPT ENGINES. OOH Title/s: Mobile Heavy Equipment Mechanics

Repair and maintain mobile mechanical, hydraulic, and pneumatic equipment—such as cranes, bulldozers, graders, and conveyors—used in construction, logging, and surface mining. Exclude railcar repairers and diesel engine specialists. Repairs and replaces damaged or worn parts. Adjusts, maintains, and repairs or replaces engines and subassemblies, including transmissions and crawler heads, using hand tools, jacks, and cranes. Dismantles and reassembles heavy equipment, using hoists and hand tools. Overhauls and tests machines or equipment to ensure operating efficiency. Examines parts for damage or excessive wear, using micrometers and gauges. Operates and inspects machines or heavy equipment to diagnose defects. Welds or cuts metal, and welds broken parts and structural members, using electric or gas welder. Immerses parts in tanks of solvent or sprays parts with grease solvent to clean. Directs workers engaged in cleaning parts and assisting with assembly or disassembly of equipment.
Yearly Earnings: $28,808
Education: Long-term O-J-T
Knowledge: Mechanical
Abilities: Control Precision; Multilimb Coordination; Explosive Strength; Trunk Strength; Extent Flexibility; Gross Body Coordination; Gross Body Equilibrium
Skills: Testing; Operation and Control; Equipment Maintenance; Troubleshooting; Repairing
General Work Activities: Inspecting Equipment, Structures, or Material; Performing General Physical Activities; Controlling Machines and Processes; Interacting with Computers; Repairing and Maintaining Mechanical Equipment; Repairing and Maintaining Electrical Equipment
Job Characteristics: Very Hot; Cramped Work Space, Awkward Positions; Whole Body Vibration; Hazardous Equipment; Climbing Ladders, Scaffolds, Poles, etc.; Kneeling, Crouching, or Crawling; Bending or Twisting the Body
GOE Group/s: 05.05.09 Craft Technology: Mechanical Work
CIP Program/s: 470302 Heavy Equipment Maintenance and Repair
Related DOT Job/s: 620.261-022 CONSTRUCTION-EQUIPMENT MECHANIC; 620.281-042 LOGGING-EQUIPMENT MECHANIC; 620.381-014 MECHANIC, ENDLESS TRACK VEHICLE

85317 RAILCAR REPAIRERS. OOH Title/s: Mobile Heavy Equipment Mechanics

Repair and rebuild railroad rolling stock, mine cars, and trolley or subway cars, according to federal and company regulations and specifications. Exclude engine specialists. Repairs, reassembles, and replaces defective parts following diagrams. Repairs structural metal sections, such as panels, underframing, and piping, using torch, wrench, hand tools, power tools, and welding equipment. Examines car roof for wear and damage and repairs defective sections, using roofing material, cement, nails, and waterproof paint. Installs and repairs interior flooring, walls, plumbing, steps, and platforms. Inspects components such as bearings, seals, gaskets, wheels, truck and brake assemblies, air cylinder reservoirs, valves, and coupler assemblies. Aligns car sides for installation of car ends and crossties, using width gauge, turnbuckle, and wrench. Repairs signage, using hand tools. Replaces defective wiring and insulation, and tightens electrical connections, using hand tools. Disassembles units, such as water pump, control valve, governor, distributor, windshield wiper motor, compressor and roller bearings. Tests units before and after repairs for operability. Adjusts repaired or replaced units as needed, following diagrams. Repairs window sash frames, attaches weather stripping and channels to frame, and replaces window glass, using hand tools. Measures sections and drills holes to prepare replacement sections for reassembly. Measures diameter of axle wheel seats, using micrometer, and marks dimension on axle for boring of wheels to specified dimensions. Tests electric systems of cars, using ammeter and by operating light and signal switches. Fabricates and installs interior fixtures, such as cabinets and other wood fixtures, using carpentry tools. Removes locomotive, car mechanical unit, or other component, using pneumatic hoist and jack, pinch bar, hand tools, and cutting torch. Records condition of cars, repairs made, and other repair work to be performed. Cleans units and components, using compressed air blower.
Yearly Earnings: $25,480
Education: Long-term O-J-T
Knowledge: Engineering and Technology; Building and Construction; Mechanical; Transportation
Abilities: Multilimb Coordination; Static Strength; Explosive Strength; Extent Flexibility; Gross Body Equilibrium; Night Vision; Peripheral Vision; Depth Perception; Glare Sensitivity
Skills: Installation; Product Inspection; Equipment Maintenance; Troubleshooting; Repairing
General Work Activities: Performing General Physical Activities; Handling and Moving Objects; Repairing and Maintaining Mechanical Equipment; Repairing and Maintaining Electrical Equipment
Job Characteristics: Sounds, Noise Levels are Distracting, etc.; Very Hot; Extremely Bright or Inadequate Lighting; Contaminants; Cramped Work Space, Awkward Positions; High Places; Hazardous Conditions; Hazardous Equipment; Hazardous Situations; Climbing Ladders, Scaffolds, Poles, etc.; Kneeling, Crouching, or Crawling; Keeping or Regaining Balance; Using Hands on Objects, Tools, or Controls; Bending or Twisting the Body; Common Protective or Safety Attire
GOE Group/s: 05.05.06 Craft Technology: Metal Fabrication and Repair; 05.05.09 Craft Technology: Mechanical Work; 05.10.01 Crafts: Structural; 05.10.02 Crafts: Mechanical; 05.10.04 Crafts: Structural-Mechanical-Electrical-Electronic
CIP Program/s: 470302 Heavy Equipment Maintenance and Repair; 470401 Instrument Calibration and Repairer
Related DOT Job/s: 620.381-018 MECHANICAL-UNIT REPAIRER; 622.381-014 CAR REPAIRER; 622.381-018 CAR REPAIRER, PULLMAN; 622.381-022 CAR-REPAIRER APPRENTICE; 622.684-010 AIR-COMPRESSOR MECHANIC; 807.381-026 STREETCAR REPAIRER

85321 FARM EQUIPMENT MECHANICS. OOH Title/s: Farm Equipment Mechanics

Maintain, repair, and overhaul farm machinery and vehicles, such as tractors, harvesters, and irrigation systems. Include repairers of dairy equipment. Exclude engine specialists. Repairs or replaces defective parts, using hand tools, milling and woodworking machines, lathes, welding equipment, grinders, or saws. Reassembles, adjusts, and lubricates machines and equipment, using hand tools. Dismantles defective machines, using hand tools. Installs and repairs agricultural plumbing systems. Installs and maintains self-propelled irrigation system, using truck-mounted crane, wrenches, tube cutter, and pipe threader. Tests and replaces electrical components and wiring, using test meter, soldering equipment, and wire strippers. Examines and listens to machines, motors, gas and diesel engines, and equipment to detect malfunctioning. Reads inspection reports and

examines equipment to determine type and extent of defect. Fabricates new metal parts, using drill press, engine lathe, and other machine tools. Drives truck to haul tools and equipment to worksite. Records type and cause of defect on agricultural equipment.
Yearly Earnings: $28,808
Education: Long-term O-J-T
Knowledge: Engineering and Technology; Mechanical; Foreign Language; Transportation
Abilities: Arm-Hand Steadiness; Finger Dexterity; Control Precision; Multilimb Coordination; Response Orientation; Rate Control; Static Strength; Explosive Strength; Trunk Strength; Stamina; Extent Flexibility; Gross Body Equilibrium; Visual Color Discrimination; Hearing Sensitivity; Auditory Attention; Sound Localization
Skills: Technology Design; Installation; Testing; Operation Monitoring; Equipment Maintenance; Troubleshooting; Repairing
General Work Activities: Inspecting Equipment, Structures, or Material; Performing General Physical Activities; Handling and Moving Objects; Controlling Machines and Processes; Interacting with Computers; Repairing and Maintaining Mechanical Equipment; Repairing and Maintaining Electrical Equipment
Job Characteristics: Extremely Bright or Inadequate Lighting; Cramped Work Space, Awkward Positions; Radiation; Hazardous Equipment; Hazardous Situations; Kneeling, Crouching, or Crawling; Keeping or Regaining Balance; Using Hands on Objects, Tools, or Controls; Bending or Twisting the Body
GOE Group/s: 05.05.09 Craft Technology: Mechanical Work; 05.10.01 Crafts: Structural; 05.10.02 Crafts: Mechanical; 06.02.24 Production Work: Manual Work, Metal and Plastics
CIP Program/s: 010204 Agricultural Power Machinery Operator
Related DOT Job/s: 624.281-010 FARM-EQUIPMENT MECHANIC I; 624.281-014 FARM-EQUIPMENT-MECHANIC APPRENTICE; 624.361-014 SPRINKLER-IRRIGATION-EQUIPMENT MECHANIC; 624.381-010 ASSEMBLY REPAIRER; 624.381-014 FARM-EQUIPMENT MECHANIC II; 629.281-018 DAIRY-EQUIPMENT REPAIRER; 809.381-018 MILKING-SYSTEM INSTALLER

85323A AIRCRAFT MECHANICS. OOH Title/s: Aircraft Mechanics, Including Engine Specialists

Inspect, test, repair, maintain, and service aircraft. Adjusts, aligns, and calibrates aircraft systems, using hand tools, gauges, and test equipment. Examines and inspects engines or other components for cracks, breaks, or leaks. Tests engine and system operations, using testing equipment, and listens to engine sounds to detect and diagnose malfunctions. Disassembles and inspects parts for wear, warping, or other defects. Repairs, replaces, and rebuilds aircraft structures, functional components, and parts, such as wings and fuselage, rigging, and hydraulic units. Services and maintains aircraft systems by performing tasks, such as flushing crankcase, cleaning screens, greasing moving parts, and checking brakes. Assembles and installs electrical, plumbing, mechanical, hydraulic, and structural components and accessories, using hand tools and power tools. Removes engine from aircraft or installs engine, using hoist or forklift truck. Reads and interprets aircraft maintenance manuals and specifications to determine feasibility and method of repairing or replacing malfunctioning or damaged components. Modifies aircraft structures, space vehicles, systems, or components, following drawings, engineering orders, and technical publications.
Yearly Earnings: $36,712
Education: Postsecondary vocational training
Knowledge: Engineering and Technology; Design; Building and Construction; Mechanical
Abilities: Deductive Reasoning; Memorization; Speed of Closure; Flexibility of Closure; Perceptual Speed; Arm-Hand Steadiness; Manual Dexterity; Finger Dexterity; Control Precision; Multilimb Coordination; Rate Control; Reaction Time; Wrist-Finger Speed; Speed of Limb Movement; Static Strength; Explosive Strength; Dynamic Strength; Trunk Strength; Stamina; Extent Flexibility; Dynamic Flexibility; Gross Body Coordination; Gross Body Equilibrium; Visual Color Discrimination; Depth Perception; Hearing Sensitivity; Sound Localization
Skills: Equipment Selection; Installation; Testing; Operation Monitoring; Product Inspection; Equipment Maintenance; Troubleshooting; Repairing
General Work Activities: Identifying Objects, Actions, and Events; Inspecting Equipment, Structures, or Material; Updating and Using Job-Relevant Knowledge; Handling and Moving Objects; Controlling Machines and Processes; Interacting with Computers; Drafting and Specifying Technical Devices, etc.; Implementing Ideas, Programs, etc.; Repairing and Maintaining Mechanical Equipment; Repairing and Maintaining Electrical Equipment
Job Characteristics: Deal with Physical, Aggressive People; Sounds, Noise Levels are Distracting, etc.; Very Hot; Extremely Bright or Inadequate Lighting; Cramped Work Space, Awkward Positions; High Places; Hazardous Conditions; Hazardous Equipment; Climbing Ladders, Scaffolds, Poles, etc.; Kneeling, Crouching, or Crawling; Keeping or Regaining Balance; Using Hands on Objects, Tools, or Controls; Bending or Twisting the Body; Common Protective or Safety Attire; Consequence of Error
GOE Group/s: 05.05.09 Craft Technology: Mechanical Work
CIP Program/s: 470607 Aircraft Mechanic/Technician, Airframe; 470608 Aircraft Mechanic/Technician, Powerplant
Related DOT Job/s: 621.261-022 EXPERIMENTAL AIRCRAFT MECHANIC; 621.281-014 AIRFRAME-AND-POWER-PLANT MECHANIC; 621.281-018 AIRFRAME-AND-POWER-PLANT-MECHANIC APPRENTICE

85323B AIRCRAFT BODY AND BONDED STRUCTURE REPAIRERS. OOH Title/s: Aircraft Mechanics, Including Engine Specialists

Repair body or structure of aircraft according to specifications. Reinstalls repaired or replacement parts for subsequent riveting or welding, using clamps and wrenches. Repairs or fabricates defective section or part, using metal fabricating machines, saws, brakes, shears, and grinders. Trims and shapes replacement section to specified size, and fits and secures section in place, using adhesives, hand tools, and power tools. Reads work orders, blueprints, and specifications, or examines sample or damaged part to determine repair or fabrication procedures and sequence of operations. Locates and marks dimension and reference lines on defective or replacement part, using templates, scribes, compass, and steel rule. Removes or cuts out defective part, or drills holes to gain access to internal defect or damage, using drill and punch. Positions and secures damaged part or structure, and examines to determine location and extent of damage or defect. Communicates with other workers to fit and align heavy parts or to expedite processing of repair parts. Cleans, strips, primes, and sands structural surfaces and materials prior to bonding. Cures bonded structure, using portable or stationary curing equipment. Spreads plastic film over area to be repaired to prevent damage to surrounding area.
Yearly Earnings: $36,712
Education: Postsecondary vocational training
Knowledge: Design; Building and Construction; Mechanical
Abilities: Information Ordering; Manual Dexterity; Finger Dexterity; Multilimb Coordination; Rate Control; Wrist-Finger Speed; Speed of Limb Movement; Explosive Strength; Dynamic Strength; Trunk Strength; Stamina; Extent Flexibility; Dynamic Flexibility; Gross Body Coordination; Gross Body Equilibrium; Depth Perception
Skills: Installation; Equipment Maintenance; Repairing

General Work Activities: Inspecting Equipment, Structures, or Material; Repairing and Maintaining Mechanical Equipment
Job Characteristics: Sounds, Noise Levels are Distracting, etc.; Cramped Work Space, Awkward Positions; High Places; Hazardous Conditions; Hazardous Equipment; Climbing Ladders, Scaffolds, Poles, etc.; Kneeling, Crouching, or Crawling; Keeping or Regaining Balance; Using Hands on Objects, Tools, or Controls; Specialized Protective or Safety Attire; Degree of Automation
GOE Group/s: 05.05.06 Craft Technology: Metal Fabrication and Repair; 06.02.32 Production Work: Manual Work, Assorted Materials
CIP Program/s: 470607 Aircraft Mechanic/Technician, Airframe
Related DOT Job/s: 807.261-010 AIRCRAFT BODY REPAIRER; 807.381-014 BONDED STRUCTURES REPAIRER

85326 AIRCRAFT ENGINE SPECIALISTS. OOH Title/s: Aircraft Mechanics, Including Engine Specialists

Repair and maintain the operating condition of aircraft engines. Include helicopter engine mechanics. Exclude electrical system specialists and aircraft mechanics whose primary duties do not involve engine repair. Replaces or repairs worn, defective, or damaged components, using hand tools, gauges, and testing equipment. Disassembles and inspects engine parts, such as turbine blades and cylinders, for wear, warping, cracks, and leaks. Reassembles engine and installs engine in aircraft. Listens to operating engine to detect and diagnose malfunctions, such as sticking or burned valves. Tests engine operation—using test equipment such as ignition analyzer, compression checker, distributor timer, and ammeter—to identify malfunction. Removes engine from aircraft, using hoist or forklift truck. Services and maintains aircraft and related apparatus by performing activities such as flushing crankcase, cleaning screens, and lubricating moving parts. Reads and interprets manufacturers' maintenance manuals, service bulletins, and other specifications to determine feasibility and methods of repair. Adjusts, repairs, or replaces electrical wiring system and aircraft accessories. Services, repairs, and rebuilds aircraft structures, such as wings, fuselage, rigging, and surface and hydraulic controls, using hand or power tools and equipment.
Yearly Earnings: $36,712
Education: Postsecondary vocational training
Knowledge: Engineering and Technology; Building and Construction; Mechanical; Physics
Abilities: Written Comprehension; Problem Sensitivity; Inductive Reasoning; Information Ordering; Speed of Closure; Flexibility of Closure; Finger Dexterity; Multilimb Coordination; Static Strength; Explosive Strength; Extent Flexibility; Dynamic Flexibility; Gross Body Equilibrium; Night Vision; Peripheral Vision; Depth Perception; Hearing Sensitivity; Auditory Attention; Sound Localization
Skills: Problem Identification; Equipment Selection; Installation; Testing; Operation Monitoring; Product Inspection; Equipment Maintenance; Troubleshooting; Repairing; Systems Perception; Judgment and Decision Making
General Work Activities: Getting Information Needed to Do the Job; Inspecting Equipment, Structures, or Material; Updating and Using Job-Relevant Knowledge; Handling and Moving Objects; Interacting with Computers; Repairing and Maintaining Mechanical Equipment; Repairing and Maintaining Electrical Equipment
Job Characteristics: Responsible for Others' Health and Safety; Sounds, Noise Levels are Distracting, etc.; Extremely Bright or Inadequate Lighting; Cramped Work Space, Awkward Positions; High Places; Hazardous Conditions; Hazardous Equipment; Hazardous Situations; Climbing Ladders, Scaffolds, Poles, etc.; Keeping or Regaining Balance; Using Hands on Objects, Tools, or Controls; Bending or Twisting the Body; Importance of Being Sure All is Done
GOE Group/s: 05.05.09 Craft Technology: Mechanical Work
CIP Program/s: 470607 Aircraft Mechanic/Technician, Airframe; 470608 Aircraft Mechanic/Technician, Powerplant
Related DOT Job/s: 621.281-014 AIRFRAME-AND-POWER-PLANT MECHANIC; 621.281-030 ROCKET-ENGINE-COMPONENT MECHANIC; 825.281-038 EXPERIMENTAL-ROCKET-SLED MECHANIC

85328A MOTORBOAT MECHANICS. OOH Title/s: Motorcycle, Boat, and Small Engine Mechanics

Test, repair, and rebuild electrical and mechanical equipment of gasoline- or diesel-powered inboard or outboard boat engines. Tests motor for conformance to specifications and operations, while motor is running in tank, using tachometer, monometer, voltmeter, ammeter, and stroboscope. Replaces parts, such as gears, magneto points, piston rings, and spark plugs, and reassembles engine. Repairs mechanical equipment of engines, such as power-tilt, bilge pumps, or power take-offs. Idles motor and observes thermometer to determine effectiveness of cooling system. Analyzes test results, and disassembles and inspects motor for defective parts, using mechanic's hand tools and gauges. Examines propeller and propeller shafts, and aligns, repairs, or replaces defective parts. Adjusts generator and replaces faulty wiring, using hand tools and soldering iron. Starts motor and listens to and inspects it for signs of malfunctioning, such as smoke, excessive vibration, misfiring, and missing or broken parts. Adjusts carburetor mixture, electrical point settings, and timing while motor is running in water-filled test tank. Operates machine tools—such as lathes, mills, drills, and grinders—to repair or rework parts, such as cams, rods, crankshaft, and propeller. Sets starter lock, and aligns and repairs steering or throttle controls, using gauges, screwdrivers, and wrenches. Mounts motor to boat and operates boat at various speeds on waterway to conduct operational tests. Writes test report to indicate acceptance or reason for rejection of motor.
Yearly Earnings: $25,272
Education: Long-term O-J-T
Knowledge: Engineering and Technology; Mechanical
Abilities: Hearing Sensitivity
Skills: Installation; Testing; Equipment Maintenance; Troubleshooting; Repairing
General Work Activities: Inspecting Equipment, Structures, or Material; Repairing and Maintaining Mechanical Equipment; Repairing and Maintaining Electrical Equipment
Job Characteristics: Cramped Work Space, Awkward Positions; Kneeling, Crouching, or Crawling
GOE Group/s: 05.05.09 Craft Technology: Mechanical Work; 06.01.05 Production Technology: Inspection
CIP Program/s: 490306 Marine Maintenance and Repair
Related DOT Job/s: 623.261-010 EXPERIMENTAL MECHANIC, OUTBOARD MOTORS; 623.261-014 OUTBOARD-MOTOR TESTER; 623.281-038 MOTORBOAT MECHANIC; 623.281-042 OUTBOARD-MOTOR MECHANIC

85328B SMALL ENGINE MECHANICS. OOH Title/s: Motorcycle, Boat, and Small Engine Mechanics

Repair engines of snowmobiles, lawn mowers, chain saws, and other small gasoline- or diesel-powered engines. Repairs or replaces defective parts, such as water pump, carburetor, thermostat, gears, solenoid, pistons, valves, and crankshaft, using hand tools. Adjusts points, valves, carburetor, distributor, and spark plug gaps, using feeler gauges. Repairs fractional-horsepower gasoline engines used to power lawn mowers, garden tractors, and similar machines. Tests and repairs magnetos used in gasoline and diesel engines, using meters, gauges, and hand tools. Repairs and maintains portable saws powered by internal combustion engines, following manufacturers' repair manuals and using hand tools. Dismantles engines, using hand tools, examines parts for defects, and cleans parts. Tests and repairs

turbo- or superchargers. Reassembles engines and listens to engines in action to detect operational difficulties. Repairs engines in factory service departments, according to company specifications, charts, or test rejection tag. Repairs and maintains gas internal-combustion engines that power electric generators, compressors, and similar equipment. Tests and inspects engines to determine malfunctions and to locate missing and broken parts, using diagnostic instruments. Grinds, reams, rebores, and retaps parts to obtain specified clearances, using grinders, lathes, taps, reamers, boring machines, and micrometers. Positions and bolts engine to engine stand. Records repairs made, time spent, and parts used.
Yearly Earnings: $25,272
Education: Long-term O-J-T
Knowledge: Engineering and Technology; Mechanical
Abilities: Extent Flexibility
Skills: Installation; Testing; Equipment Maintenance; Troubleshooting; Repairing
General Work Activities: Repairing and Maintaining Mechanical Equipment; Repairing and Maintaining Electrical Equipment
Job Characteristics: Sounds, Noise Levels are Distracting, etc.; Contaminants; Cramped Work Space, Awkward Positions; Kneeling, Crouching, or Crawling
GOE Group/s: 05.05.05 Craft Technology: Electrical-Electronic Systems Installation and Repair; 05.05.09 Craft Technology: Mechanical Work; 06.01.04 Production Technology: Precision Hand Work
CIP Program/s: 010201 Agricultural Mechanization, General; 010204 Agricultural Power Machinery Operator; 470199 Electrical and Electronics Equipment Installer and Repairer; 470606 Small Engine Mechanic and Repairer
Related DOT Job/s: 625.281-018 ENGINE REPAIRER, SERVICE; 625.281-026 GAS-ENGINE REPAIRER; 625.281-030 POWER-SAW MECHANIC; 625.281-034 SMALL-ENGINE MECHANIC; 625.381-010 ENGINE REPAIRER, PRODUCTION; 721.281-022 MAGNETO REPAIRER

Communications Equipment Mechanics

85502 CENTRAL OFFICE AND PBX INSTALLERS AND REPAIRERS. OOH Title/s: Communications Equipment Mechanics

Test, analyze, and repair telephone or telegraph circuits and equipment at a central office location using test meters and hand tools. Analyze and repair defects in communications equipment on customers' premises using circuit diagrams, polarity probes, meters, and a telephone test set. May install equipment. Tests circuits and components of malfunctioning telecommunication equipment to isolate source of malfunction, using test instruments and circuit diagrams. Analyzes test readings, computer printouts, and trouble reports to determine method of repair. Repairs or replaces defective components, such as switches, relays, amplifiers, and circuit boards, using hand tools and soldering iron. Tests and adjusts installed equipment to ensure circuit continuity and operational performance, using test instruments. Retests repaired equipment to ensure that malfunction has been corrected. Installs preassembled or partially assembled switching equipment, switchboards, wiring frames, and power apparatus, according to floor plans. Connects wires to equipment, using hand tools, soldering iron, or wire wrap gun. Removes and remakes connections on wire distributing frame to change circuit layout, following diagrams. Enters codes to correct programming of electronic switching systems. Routes cables and trunklines from entry points to specified equipment, following diagrams.
Yearly Earnings: $35,152
Education: Postsecondary vocational training
Knowledge: Computers and Electronics; Design; Telecommunications
Abilities: Flexibility of Closure; Finger Dexterity
Skills: Technology Design; Installation; Testing; Operation Monitoring; Equipment Maintenance; Troubleshooting; Repairing
General Work Activities: Inspecting Equipment, Structures, or Material; Repairing and Maintaining Electrical Equipment
Job Characteristics: None above average
GOE Group/s: 05.05.05 Craft Technology: Electrical-Electronic Systems Installation and Repair
CIP Program/s: 470101 Electrical and Electronics Equipment Installer and Repairer; 470103 Communication Systems Installer and Repairer
Related DOT Job/s: 822.281-014 CENTRAL-OFFICE REPAIRER; 822.281-022 PRIVATE-BRANCH-EXCHANGE REPAIRER; 822.361-014 CENTRAL-OFFICE INSTALLER; 822.381-018 PRIVATE-BRANCH-EXCHANGE INSTALLER; 822.381-022 TELEGRAPH-PLANT MAINTAINER

85505 FRAME WIRERS, CENTRAL OFFICE. OOH Title/s: Communications Equipment Mechanics

Connect wires from telephone lines and cables to distributing frames in telephone company central office, using soldering iron and other hand tools. Solders connections, following diagram or oral instructions. Strings distributing frames with connecting wires. Removes and remakes connections to change circuit layouts. Tests circuit connections, using voltmeter or ammeter. Cleans switches and replaces contact points, using vacuum hose, solvents, and hand tools. Lubricates moving switch parts. Assists in locating and correcting malfunction in wiring on distributing frame.
Yearly Earnings: $32,136
Education: Postsecondary vocational training
Knowledge: Engineering and Technology; Telecommunications
Abilities: None above average
Skills: Installation; Testing; Troubleshooting
General Work Activities: Inspecting Equipment, Structures, or Material; Repairing and Maintaining Electrical Equipment
Job Characteristics: Cramped Work Space, Awkward Positions; High Places; Hazardous Conditions; Climbing Ladders, Scaffolds, Poles, etc.
GOE Group/s: 05.10.03 Crafts: Electrical-Electronic
CIP Program/s: 470101 Electrical and Electronics Equipment Installer and Repairer; 470103 Communication Systems Installer and Repairer
Related DOT Job/s: 822.684-010 FRAME WIRER

85508 TELEGRAPH AND TELETYPE INSTALLERS AND MAINTAINERS. OOH Title/s: Communications Equipment Mechanics

Install and repair telegraphic transmitting and receiving equipment, following floor plan sketches and wiring diagrams. Analyzes problems and repairs manual and automatic telegraphic transmitting and receiving apparatus, such as teletypewriters, facsimile-recording devices, and switching equipment. Installs equipment, following floor-plan sketches and wiring diagrams, using hand tools and soldering iron. Tests and adjusts equipment, using testing devices such as voltmeters and ohmmeters, following blueprints and schematics and using hand tools. Tests and regulates telegraph repeaters. Wires and assembles equipment prior to installation.
Yearly Earnings: $32,136
Education: Postsecondary vocational training
Knowledge: Computers and Electronics; Design; Telecommunications
Abilities: None above average

Skills: Installation; Testing; Troubleshooting; Repairing
General Work Activities: Repairing and Maintaining Electrical Equipment
Job Characteristics: None above average
GOE Group/s: 05.05.05 Craft Technology: Electrical-Electronic Systems Installation and Repair
CIP Program/s: 470101 Electrical and Electronics Equipment Installer and Repairer; 470103 Communication Systems Installer and Repairer
Related DOT Job/s: 822.281-010 AUTOMATIC-EQUIPMENT TECHNICIAN; 822.381-010 EQUIPMENT INSTALLER822.281-010 AUTOMATIC-EQUIPMENT TECHNICIAN; 822.381-010 EQUIPMENT INSTALLER

85511 SIGNAL OR TRACK SWITCH MAINTAINERS. OOH Title/s: Communications Equipment Mechanics

Install, inspect, test, and repair electric gate crossings, signals, signal equipment, track switches, section lines, and intercommunication systems within a railroad system, following blueprints and work orders. Installs and inspects switch-controlling mechanism on trolley wire and switch in bed of track bed, using hand tools and test equipment. Inspects and tests gate crossings, signals, and signal equipment, such as interlocks and hotbox detectors. Inspects electrical units of railroad grade crossing gates to detect loose bolts and defective electrical connections and parts. Tests signal circuit connections, using standard electrical testing equipment. Replaces defective wiring, broken lenses, or burned-out light bulbs. Tightens loose bolts, using wrench, and tests circuits and connections by opening and closing gate. Inspects mechanical gate crossings and repairs defective cables on hand-operated gates. Tests air lines and air cylinders on pneumatically operated gates. Inspects batteries to ensure that batteries are filled with battery water or to determine need for replacement. Lubricates moving parts on gate crossing mechanisms and swinging signals. Maintains high-tension lines, deenergizing lines for power company as repairs are requested. Cleans lenses of lamps with cloths and solvent. Compiles reports indicating mileage or track inspected, repairs made, and equipment requiring replacement.
Yearly Earnings: $32,136
Education: Postsecondary vocational training
Knowledge: Engineering and Technology; Mechanical; Physics; Geography; Public Safety and Security; Telecommunications; Transportation
Abilities: Finger Dexterity; Gross Body Equilibrium; Peripheral Vision; Depth Perception; Sound Localization
Skills: Installation; Testing; Operation Monitoring; Product Inspection; Equipment Maintenance; Troubleshooting; Repairing
General Work Activities: Inspecting Equipment, Structures, or Material; Performing General Physical Activities; Repairing and Maintaining Mechanical Equipment; Repairing and Maintaining Electrical Equipment
Job Characteristics: Responsible for Others' Health and Safety; Sounds, Noise Levels are Distracting, etc.; Very Hot; Extremely Bright or Inadequate Lighting; High Places; Hazardous Conditions; Hazardous Equipment; Hazardous Situations; Standing; Kneeling, Crouching, or Crawling; Keeping or Regaining Balance; Bending or Twisting the Body; Common Protective or Safety Attire; Consequence of Error
GOE Group/s: 05.05.05 Craft Technology: Electrical-Electronic Systems Installation and Repair
CIP Program/s: 460301 Electrical and Power Transmission Installer, General; 460302 Electrician; 460303 Lineworker
Related DOT Job/s: 822.281-026 SIGNAL MAINTAINER; 825.261-010 ELECTRIC-TRACK-SWITCH MAINTAINER

85514 RADIO MECHANICS. OOH Title/s: Communications Equipment Mechanics; Commercial and Industrial Electronic Machinery Repairers

Test and repair stationary, mobile, and portable radio transmitting and receiving equipment and two-way radio communication systems, used in ship-to-shore communications and found in service and emergency vehicles, in accordance with diagrams and manufacturers' specifications. Examine equipment for damaged components and loose or broken connections and wires; replace defective components and parts. Involves use of hand tools and electrical measuring instruments. May repair intercommunication telephone systems. Occupation may require Federal Communications Commission Radiotelephone Operator's License, depending on the nature of repairs performed. Locates defects, such as loose connections, broken wires, or burned-out components, using schematic diagrams, test equipment, and inspection tags. Inspects wiring and soldering, and performs repairs, using soldering iron, wire cutters, pliers, and wiring diagram. Tests equipment for power output, frequency, and calibration, using oscilloscope, circuit analyzer, frequency meter, wattmeter, ammeter, and voltmeter. Replaces defective components—such as conductors, resistors, semiconductors, and integrated circuits—using soldering iron, wire cutters, and hand tools. Tests batteries with hydrometer and ammeter, and charges batteries. Tests noise level and audio quality, using audiometer. Monitors radio range station to detect flaws in transmission, and adjusts controls to eliminate flaws. Applies touch-up paint to abrasions on equipment case and varnish to exposed wiring. Removes and replaces defective units that are not repairable. Adjusts receivers for maximum sensitivity and transmitters for maximum output, using frequency meter. Installs, tests, adjusts, modifies, and repairs intercommunication systems. Inserts plugs into receptacles, and bolts or screws leads to terminals to connect equipment to power source, using hand tools. Tests emergency transmitter to ensure readiness for immediate use.
Yearly Earnings: $32,136
Education: Postsecondary vocational training
Knowledge: Computers and Electronics; Engineering and Technology; Design; Mechanical; Physics; Telecommunications
Abilities: Speed of Closure; Flexibility of Closure; Finger Dexterity; Visual Color Discrimination; Hearing Sensitivity
Skills: Installation; Testing; Operation Monitoring; Equipment Maintenance; Troubleshooting; Repairing
General Work Activities: Identifying Objects, Actions, and Events; Inspecting Equipment, Structures, or Material; Handling and Moving Objects; Repairing and Maintaining Electrical Equipment
Job Characteristics: Cramped Work Space, Awkward Positions; Hazardous Situations; Using Hands on Objects, Tools, or Controls
GOE Group/s: 05.05.05 Craft Technology: Electrical-Electronic Systems Installation and Repair; 05.05.10 Craft Technology: Electrical-Electronic Equipment Repair; 05.10.03 Crafts: Electrical-Electronic
CIP Program/s: 470101 Electrical and Electronics Equipment Installer and Repairer; 470103 Communication Systems Installer and Repairer
Related DOT Job/s: 726.381-014 ELECTRONIC EQUIPMENT REPAIRER; 823.261-018 RADIO MECHANIC; 823.281-014 ELECTRICIAN, RADIO

85599A COMMUNICATION EQUIPMENT MECHANICS, INSTALLERS, AND REPAIRERS. OOH Title/s: Communications Equipment Mechanics

Install, maintain, test, and repair communication cables and equipment. Examines and tests malfunctioning equipment to deter-

mine defects, using blueprints and electrical measuring instruments. Disassembles equipment to adjust, repair, or replace parts, using hand tools. Repairs, replaces, or adjusts defective components. Assembles and installs communication equipment, such as data communication lines and equipment, computer systems, and antennas and towers, using hand tools. Tests installed equipment for conformance to specifications, using test equipment. Evaluates quality of performance of installed equipment by observance and using test equipment. Measures, cuts, splices, connects, solders, and installs wires and cables. Performs routine maintenance on equipment, which includes adjustment, repair, and painting. Adjusts or modifies equipment in accordance with customer request or to enhance performance of equipment. Reviews work orders, building permits, manufacturers' instructions, and ordinances to move, change, install, repair, or remove communication equipment. Plans layout and installation of data communications equipment. Climbs poles and ladders; constructs pole, roof mounts, or reinforcements; and mixes concrete to enable equipment installation. Measures distance from landmarks to identify exact installation site. Determines viability of site through observation, and discusses site location and construction requirements with customer. Demonstrates equipment and instructs customer in use of equipment. Communicates with base, using telephone or two-way radio to receive instructions or technical advise, or to report unauthorized use of equipment. Cleans and maintains tools, test equipment, and motor vehicle. Answers customers' inquiries or complaints. Digs holes or trenches.
Yearly Earnings: $32,136
Education: Postsecondary vocational training
Knowledge: Computers and Electronics; Design; Telecommunications
Abilities: Response Orientation; Explosive Strength; Dynamic Strength; Trunk Strength; Stamina; Gross Body Coordination; Gross Body Equilibrium; Depth Perception
Skills: Technology Design; Installation; Testing; Equipment Maintenance; Troubleshooting; Repairing
General Work Activities: Inspecting Equipment, Structures, or Material; Performing General Physical Activities; Repairing and Maintaining Electrical Equipment
Job Characteristics: Deal with External Customers; High Places; Hazardous Conditions; Climbing Ladders, Scaffolds, Poles, etc.; Kneeling, Crouching, or Crawling; Keeping or Regaining Balance; Bending or Twisting the Body; Common Protective or Safety Attire
GOE Group/s: 05.05.05 Craft Technology: Electrical-Electronic Systems Installation and Repair; 05.05.06 Craft Technology: Metal Fabrication and Repair; 05.05.10 Craft Technology: Electrical-Electronic Equipment Repair
CIP Program/s: 460301 Electrical and Power Transmission Installer, General; 460302 Electrician; 460303 Lineworker; 470101 Electrical and Electronics Equipment Installer and Repairer; 470103 Communication Systems Installer and Repairer; 470104 Computer Installer and Repairer
Related DOT Job/s: 722.281-010 INSTRUMENT REPAIRER; 821.261-010 CABLE TELEVISION LINE TECHNICIAN; 822.261-010 ELECTRICIAN, OFFICE; 822.281-030 TECHNICIAN, PLANT AND MAINTENANCE; 822.281-034 TECHNICIAN, SUBMARINE CABLE EQUIPMENT; 823.261-022 ANTENNA INSTALLER, SATELLITE COMMUNICATIONS; 823.261-030 DATA COMMUNICATIONS TECHNICIAN; 823.281-022 RIGGER

85599B TELECOMMUNICATIONS FACILITY EXAMINERS. OOH Title/s: Telephone Installers and Repairers

Examine telephone transmission facilities to determine equipment requirements for providing subscribers with new or additional telephone services. Examines telephone transmission facilities to determine requirements for new or additional telephone services. Climbs telephone poles or stands on truck-mounted boom to examine terminal boxes for available connections. Designates cables available for use. Visits subscribers' premises to arrange for new installations, such as telephone booths and telephone poles.
Yearly Earnings: $32,136
Education: Postsecondary vocational training
Knowledge: Computers and Electronics; Telecommunications
Abilities: Dynamic Strength; Stamina; Extent Flexibility; Gross Body Coordination; Gross Body Equilibrium; Night Vision
Skills: None above average
General Work Activities: Performing General Physical Activities; Interacting with Computers
Job Characteristics: Persuade Someone to a Course of Action; Provide a Service to Others; Deal with External Customers; Very Hot; Extremely Bright or Inadequate Lighting; Cramped Work Space, Awkward Positions; High Places; Hazardous Conditions; Climbing Ladders, Scaffolds, Poles, etc.; Walking or Running; Keeping or Regaining Balance; Bending or Twisting the Body; Common Protective or Safety Attire
GOE Group/s: 05.05.05 Craft Technology: Electrical-Electronic Systems Installation and Repair
CIP Program/s: 470101 Electrical and Electronics Equipment Installer and Repairer; 470103 Communication Systems Installer and Repairer
Related DOT Job/s: 959.367-014 FACILITY EXAMINER

85599C SOUND TECHNICIANS. OOH Title/s: Communications Equipment Mechanics

Install, maintain, and repair sound and intercommunication systems, multiple antenna systems, closed circuit TV systems, and associated apparatus. Installs coaxial cable and interconnecting cable and wiring for sound-amplifying systems, intercommunication systems, and associated sound systems. Installs and repairs mobile sound-amplifying system in sound truck. Installs sound components or systems for playing musical records in homes or business establishments. Positions loudspeakers and microphones. Tests and repairs equipment, using hand tools, soldering iron, and electronic test meters. Tests installation to verify proper functioning, by listening to sound and testing output. Drives sound truck.
Yearly Earnings: $32,136
Education: Postsecondary vocational training
Knowledge: Computers and Electronics; Telecommunications; Transportation
Abilities: Hearing Sensitivity; Auditory Attention; Sound Localization
Skills: Technology Design; Installation; Testing; Troubleshooting; Repairing
General Work Activities: Interacting with Computers; Repairing and Maintaining Electrical Equipment
Job Characteristics: Cramped Work Space, Awkward Positions; High Places; Hazardous Conditions; Climbing Ladders, Scaffolds, Poles, etc.; Kneeling, Crouching, or Crawling; Bending or Twisting the Body; Specialized Protective or Safety Attire
GOE Group/s: 05.05.05 Craft Technology: Electrical-Electronic Systems Installation and Repair; 05.05.10 Craft Technology: Electrical-Electronic Equipment Repair
CIP Program/s: 470101 Electrical and Electronics Equipment Installer and Repairer; 470103 Communication Systems Installer and Repairer
Related DOT Job/s: 823.261-010 PUBLIC-ADDRESS SERVICER; 829.281-022 SOUND TECHNICIAN

Line Installers and Electronic Equipment Repairers

85702 TELEPHONE AND CABLE TELEVISION LINE INSTALLERS AND REPAIRERS. OOH Title/s: Line Installers and Cable Splicers

String and repair telephone and television cable and other equipment for transmitting messages or TV programming. Duties include locating and repairing defects in existing systems; placing, rearranging, and removing underground or aerial cables; installing supports, insulation, or guy wire systems; and other auxiliary tasks necessary to maintain lines and cables. Installs terminal boxes and strings lead-in wires, using electrician's tools. Repairs cable system, defective lines, and auxiliary equipment. Ascends poles or enters tunnels and sewers to string lines and install terminal boxes, auxiliary equipment, and appliances, according to diagrams. Pulls lines through ducts by hand or with use of winch. Computes impedance of wire from pole to house to determine additional resistance needed for reducing signal to desired level. Connects television set to cable system, evaluates incoming signal, and adjusts system to ensure optimum reception. Measures television signal strength at utility pole, using electronic test equipment. Installs and removes plant equipment, such as call boxes and clocks. Digs holes, using power auger or shovel, and hoists poles upright into holes, using truck-mounted winch. Fills and tamps holes, using cement, earth, and tamping device. Cleans and maintains tools and test equipment. Communicates with supervisor to receive instructions and technical advice and to report problems. Explains cable service to subscriber. Collects installation fees.

Yearly Earnings: $35,048

Education: Long-term O-J-T

Knowledge: Computers and Electronics; Telecommunications

Abilities: Manual Dexterity; Gross Body Coordination; Gross Body Equilibrium

Skills: Installation; Equipment Maintenance; Troubleshooting; Repairing

General Work Activities: Performing General Physical Activities; Repairing and Maintaining Electrical Equipment

Job Characteristics: Very Hot; Extremely Bright or Inadequate Lighting; Cramped Work Space, Awkward Positions; High Places; Climbing Ladders, Scaffolds, Poles, etc.; Kneeling, Crouching, or Crawling; Bending or Twisting the Body

GOE Group/s: 05.05.05 Craft Technology: Electrical-Electronic Systems Installation and Repair; 05.10.03 Crafts: Electrical-Electronic

CIP Program/s: 460301 Electrical and Power Transmission Installer, General; 460303 Lineworker

Related DOT Job/s: 821.281-010 CABLE TELEVISION INSTALLER; 822.381-014 LINE INSTALLER-REPAIRER

85705 DATA PROCESSING EQUIPMENT REPAIRERS. OOH Title/s: Commercial and Industrial Electronic Equipment Repairers

Repair, maintain, and install electronic computers (mainframes, minis, and micros), peripheral equipment, and word-processing systems. Replaces defective components and wiring. Tests faulty equipment and applies knowledge of functional operation of electronic units and systems to diagnose cause of malfunction. Tests electronic components and circuits to locate defects, using oscilloscopes, signal generators, ammeters, and voltmeters. Aligns, adjusts, and calibrates equipment according to specifications. Converses with equipment operators to ascertain problems with equipment before breakdown or cause of breakdown. Adjusts mechanical parts, using hand tools and soldering iron. Calibrates testing instruments. Maintains records of repairs, calibrations, and tests. Enters information into computer to copy program from one electronic component to another, or to draw, modify, or store schematics. Operates equipment, such as communication equipment or missile control systems in ground and flight test.

Yearly Earnings: $30,056

Education: Postsecondary vocational training

Knowledge: Customer and Personal Service; Computers and Electronics; Engineering and Technology; Design; Mechanical; Physics; Telecommunications

Abilities: Written Comprehension; Fluency of Ideas; Originality; Problem Sensitivity; Deductive Reasoning; Inductive Reasoning; Information Ordering; Mathematical Reasoning; Memorization; Speed of Closure; Perceptual Speed; Visualization; Selective Attention; Manual Dexterity; Finger Dexterity; Control Precision; Response Orientation; Wrist-Finger Speed; Explosive Strength; Extent Flexibility; Gross Body Equilibrium; Near Vision; Visual Color Discrimination; Hearing Sensitivity; Auditory Attention; Sound Localization

Skills: Reading Comprehension; Science; Problem Identification; Solution Appraisal; Technology Design; Equipment Selection; Installation; Programming; Testing; Operation Monitoring; Operation and Control; Product Inspection; Equipment Maintenance; Troubleshooting; Repairing

General Work Activities: Inspecting Equipment, Structures, or Material; Updating and Using Job-Relevant Knowledge; Operating Vehicles or Equipment; Repairing and Maintaining Electrical Equipment

Job Characteristics: Hazardous Conditions; Frustrating Circumstances; Degree of Automation; Importance of Being Sure All is Done

GOE Group/s: 05.05.10 Craft Technology: Electrical-Electronic Equipment Repair

CIP Program/s: 150402 Computer Maintenance Technologists and Technicians

Related DOT Job/s: 828.261-022 ELECTRONICS MECHANIC; 828.261-026 ELECTRONICS-MECHANIC APPRENTICE

85708 ELECTRONIC HOME ENTERTAINMENT EQUIPMENT REPAIRERS. OOH Title/s: Electronic Home Entertainment Equipment Repairers

Adjust and repair radio and television receivers, phonographs, stereo systems, tape recorders, video systems, and other electronic home entertainment equipment. Disassembles equipment and repairs or replaces loose, worn, or defective components and wiring, using hand tools and soldering iron. Tunes or adjusts equipment and instruments, according to specifications, to obtain optimum visual or auditory reception. Analyzes and tests products and parts to locate defects or source of trouble. Tests circuits, using schematic diagrams, service manuals, and testing instruments such as voltmeters, oscilloscopes, and audiogenerators. Confers with customers to determine nature of problem or to explain repairs. Makes service calls and repairs units in customers' homes, or returns unit to shop for major repair. Installs electronic equipment or instruments, such as televisions, radios, audio-visual equipment, and organs, using hand tools. Computes cost estimates for labor and materials. Positions or mounts speakers, and wires speakers to console.

Yearly Earnings: $28,080

Education: Postsecondary vocational training

Knowledge: Customer and Personal Service; Computers and Electronics; Design; Telecommunications

Abilities: Speed of Closure; Visualization; Arm-Hand Steadiness; Finger Dexterity; Static Strength; Gross Body Equilibrium; Visual Color Discrimination; Hearing Sensitivity; Sound Localization

Skills: Science; Service Orientation; Technology Design; Installation; Testing; Equipment Maintenance; Troubleshooting; Repairing
General Work Activities: Inspecting Equipment, Structures, or Material; Repairing and Maintaining Electrical Equipment
Job Characteristics: Provide a Service to Others; Deal with External Customers; Frequency in Conflict Situations; Deal with Unpleasant or Angry People; Cramped Work Space, Awkward Positions; Climbing Ladders, Scaffolds, Poles, etc.; Kneeling, Crouching, or Crawling; Keeping or Regaining Balance; Bending or Twisting the Body; Frustrating Circumstances
GOE Group/s: 05.05.10 Craft Technology: Electrical-Electronic Equipment Repair; 05.05.12 Craft Technology: Musical Instrument Fabrication and Repair; 05.10.03 Crafts: Electrical-Electronic
CIP Program/s: 470101 Electrical and Electronics Equipment Installer and Repairer; 470103 Communication Systems Installer and Repairer; 470404 Musical Instrument Repairer
Related DOT Job/s: 720.281-010 RADIO REPAIRER; 720.281-014 TAPE-RECORDER REPAIRER; 720.281-018 TELEVISION-AND-RADIO REPAIRER; 729.281-010 AUDIO-VIDEO REPAIRER; 730.281-018 ELECTRIC-ORGAN INSPECTOR AND REPAIRER; 823.361-010 TELEVISION INSTALLER; 828.261-010 ELECTRONIC-ORGAN TECHNICIAN

85711A ELECTRIC HOME APPLIANCE AND POWER TOOL REPAIRERS. OOH Title/s: Home Appliance and Power Tool Repairers

Repair, adjust, and install all types of electric household appliances. Disassembles appliance to examine specific mechanical and electrical parts to diagnose problem. Replaces worn and defective parts, such as switches, bearings, transmissions, belts, gears, circuit boards, or defective wiring. Reassembles unit, making necessary adjustments to ensure efficient operation. Connects appliance to power source and uses test instruments to calibrate timers and thermostats and to adjust contact points. Observes and examines appliance during operation to detect specific malfunction, such as loose parts or leaking fluid. Traces electrical circuits, following diagram, to locate shorts and grounds, using electrical circuit testers. Instructs customer regarding operation and care of appliance, and provides emergency service number. Cleans, lubricates, and touches up minor scratches on newly installed or repaired appliances. Maintains stock of parts used in on-site installation, maintenance, and repair of appliance. Records nature of maintenance or repair in log, and returns to business office for further assignments. Measures and performs minor carpentry procedures to area where appliance is to be installed.
Yearly Earnings: $31,252
Education: Long-term O-J-T
Knowledge: Building and Construction; Mechanical
Abilities: None above average
Skills: Technology Design; Installation; Operation Monitoring; Equipment Maintenance; Troubleshooting; Repairing
General Work Activities: Inspecting Equipment, Structures, or Material; Repairing and Maintaining Mechanical Equipment; Repairing and Maintaining Electrical Equipment
Job Characteristics: Special Uniform
GOE Group/s: 05.05.09 Craft Technology: Mechanical Work; 05.05.10 Craft Technology: Electrical-Electronic Equipment Repair; 05.10.03 Crafts: Electrical-Electronic
CIP Program/s: 470101 Electrical and Electronics Equipment Installer and Repairer; 470106 Major Appliance Installer and Repairer; 470199 Electrical and Electronics Equipment Installer and Repairer; 470201 Heating, Air Conditioning and Refrigeration Mechanics and Repairers
Related DOT Job/s: 637.261-010 AIR-CONDITIONING INSTALLER-SERVICER, WINDOW UNIT; 723.381-010 ELECTRICAL-APPLIANCE REPAIRER; 723.381-014 VACUUM CLEANER REPAIRER; 723.584-010 APPLIANCE REPAIRER; 729.281-022 ELECTRIC-TOOL REPAIRER; 827.261-010 ELECTRICAL-APPLIANCE SERVICER; 827.261-014 ELECTRICAL-APPLIANCE-SERVICER APPRENTICE

85711B HOME APPLIANCE INSTALLERS. OOH Title/s: Home Appliance and Power Tool Repairers

Install household appliances—such as refrigerators, washing machines, and stoves—in mobile homes or customers' homes. Observes and tests operation of appliances, such as refrigerators, washers, and dryers, and makes initial installation adjustments accordingly. Levels refrigerators, adjusts doors, and connects water lines to water pipes for ice-makers and water dispensers, using hand tools. Levels washing machines and connects hoses to water pipes, using plumbing and other hand tools. Lights and adjusts pilot lights on gas stoves and examines valves and burners for gas leakage and specified flame. Advises customers regarding use and care of appliance, and provides emergency service number. Disassembles and reinstalls existing kitchen cabinets, and assembles and installs prefabricated kitchen cabinets in conjunction with appliance installation.
Yearly Earnings: $31,252
Education: Long-term O-J-T
Knowledge: Building and Construction; Mechanical
Abilities: Static Strength; Dynamic Strength
Skills: Installation; Troubleshooting
General Work Activities: None above average
Job Characteristics: Cramped Work Space, Awkward Positions; Standing; Kneeling, Crouching, or Crawling; Using Hands on Objects, Tools, or Controls; Bending or Twisting the Body; Special Uniform
GOE Group/s: 05.10.04 Crafts: Structural-Mechanical-Electrical-Electronic
CIP Program/s: 470101 Electrical and Electronics Equipment Installer and Repairer; 470106 Major Appliance Installer and Repairer
Related DOT Job/s: 827.661-010 HOUSEHOLD-APPLIANCE INSTALLER

85714A ELECTRIC MOTOR AND SWITCH ASSEMBLERS AND REPAIRERS. OOH Title/s: Industrial Machinery Repairers

Test, repair, rebuild, and assemble electric motors, generators, and equipment. Assembles electrical parts, such as alternators, generators, starting devices, and switches, following schematic drawings, using hand, machine, and power tools. Repairs and rebuilds defective mechanical parts in electric motors, generators, and related equipment, using hand tools and power tools. Tests for overheating, using speed gauges and thermometers. Rewinds coils on core while core is in slots, or makes replacement coils, using coil-winding machine. Replaces defective parts, such as coil leads, carbon brushes, and connecting wires, using soldering equipment. Installs, secures, and aligns parts, using hand tools, welding equipment, and electrical meters. Rewires electrical systems and repairs or replaces electrical accessories. Reassembles repaired electric motors to specified requirements and ratings, using hand tools and electrical meters. Disassembles defective unit, using hand tools. Measures velocity, horsepower, rpm, amperage, circuitry, and voltage of unit or parts, using electrical meters and mechanical testing devices. Cuts and removes parts, such as defective coils and insulation. Adjusts working parts, such as fan belt tension, voltage output, contacts, and springs, using hand tools, and verifies corrections, using gauges. Tests charges and replaces batteries. Inspects parts for wear or damage, or reads work order or schematic drawings to determine required repairs. Cuts and forms insulation and inserts insulation into armature, rotor, or stator slots. Refaces, reams, and polishes commutators and machine parts to specified tolerances, using machine tools. Records repairs required, parts used, and labor time. Scrapes and cleans units or parts, using cleaning solvent, and

lubricates moving parts. Lifts units or parts, such as motors or generators, using crane or chain hoist.
Yearly Earnings: $27,612
Education: Long-term O-J-T
Knowledge: Computers and Electronics; Engineering and Technology; Design; Mechanical; Foreign Language; Public Safety and Security
Abilities: Speed of Closure; Arm-Hand Steadiness; Finger Dexterity; Multilimb Coordination; Response Orientation; Speed of Limb Movement; Explosive Strength; Stamina; Extent Flexibility; Gross Body Equilibrium; Visual Color Discrimination; Hearing Sensitivity; Sound Localization
Skills: Science; Technology Design; Installation; Testing; Operation Monitoring; Operation and Control; Product Inspection; Equipment Maintenance; Troubleshooting; Repairing
General Work Activities: Inspecting Equipment, Structures, or Material; Repairing and Maintaining Mechanical Equipment; Repairing and Maintaining Electrical Equipment
Job Characteristics: Hazardous Conditions; Hazardous Equipment; Using Hands on Objects, Tools, or Controls
GOE Group/s: 05.05.05 Craft Technology: Electrical-Electronic Systems Installation and Repair; 05.05.10 Craft Technology: Electrical-Electronic Equipment Repair; 05.07.02 Quality Control: Mechincal; 05.10.03 Crafts: Electrical-Electronic; 06.02.23 Production Work: Manual Work, Assembly Small Parts
CIP Program/s: 460301 Electrical and Power Transmission Installer, General; 460302 Electrician; 470101 Electrical and Electronics Equipment Installer and Repairer; 470105 Industrial Electronics Installer and Repairer; 470199 Electrical and Electronics Equipment Installer and Repairer; 470501 Stationary Energy Sources Installer and Operator; 470604 Auto/Automotive Mechanic/Technician
Related DOT Job/s: 620.261-026 ELECTRIC-GOLF-CART REPAIRER; 721.261-010 ELECTRIC-MOTOR ANALYST; 721.281-010 AUTOMOTIVE-GENERATOR-AND-STARTER REPAIRER; 721.281-014 ELECTRIC-MOTOR ASSEMBLER AND TESTER; 721.281-018 ELECTRIC-MOTOR REPAIRER; 721.281-026 PROPULSION-MOTOR-AND-GENERATOR REPAIRER; 721.381-010 ELECTRIC-MOTOR FITTER; 724.381-010 ADJUSTER, ELECTRICAL CONTACTS; 729.684-038 REPAIRER, SWITCHGEAR; 821.381-018 WIND-GENERATING-ELECTRIC-POWER INSTALLER

85714B BATTERY REPAIRERS. OOH Title/s: Industrial Machinery Repairers; Handlers, Equipment Cleaners, Helpers, and Laborers

Inspect, repair, recharge, and replace batteries. Inspects electrical connections, wiring charging relays, charging resistance box, and storage batteries, following wiring diagram. Inspects battery for defects, such as dented cans, damaged carbon rods and terminals, and defective seals. Removes and disassembles cells and cathode assembly, using tension handles, prybars, and hoist, and cuts wires to faulty cells. Tests condition, fluid level, and specific gravity of electrolyte cells, using voltmeter, hydrometer, and thermometer. Connects battery to battery charger and adjusts rheostat to start flow of electricity into battery. Replaces defective parts, such as cell plates, fuses, lead parts, switches, wires, anodes, cathodes, and rheostat. Repairs or adjusts defective parts, using hand tools or power tools. Adds water and acid to battery cells to obtain specified concentration. Disconnects electrical leads and removes battery, using hand tools and hoist. Cleans cells, cell assemblies, glassware, leads, electrical connections, and battery poles, using scraper, steam, water, emery cloth, power grinder, or acid. Installs recharged or repaired battery or cells, using hand tools. Positions and levels, or signals worker to position and level, cell, anode, or cathode, using hoist and leveling jacks. Secures cell on rocker mechanism or attaches assemblies, using bolts or cement. Measures cathode blade and anode, using ruler, and rate of mercury flow, using stopwatch. Repairs battery-charging equipment. Seals joints with putty, mortar, and asbestos, using putty extruder and knife. Compiles operating and maintenance records. Fabricates and assembles electrolytic cell parts for storage batteries.
Yearly Earnings: $27,612
Education: Long-term O-J-T
Knowledge: Computers and Electronics
Abilities: Explosive Strength; Dynamic Strength; Dynamic Flexibility; Gross Body Equilibrium
Skills: Installation; Product Inspection; Equipment Maintenance; Troubleshooting; Repairing
General Work Activities: Handling and Moving Objects; Repairing and Maintaining Electrical Equipment
Job Characteristics: Contaminants; Cramped Work Space, Awkward Positions; Hazardous Conditions; Hazardous Situations; Kneeling, Crouching, or Crawling; Bending or Twisting the Body
GOE Group/s: 05.10.03 Crafts: Electrical-Electronic; 05.12.16 Elemental Work: Mechanical: Electrical Work; 06.02.32 Production Work: Manual Work, Assorted Materials; 06.04.34 Elemental Work: Industrial: Manual Work, Assorted Materials
CIP Program/s: 460301 Electrical and Power Transmission Installer, General; 460302 Electrician; 470101 Electrical and Electronics Equipment Installer and Repairer
Related DOT Job/s: 727.381-014 BATTERY REPAIRER; 727.684-018 CELL REPAIRER; 820.381-010 BATTERY MAINTAINER, LARGE EMERGENCY STORAGE; 825.684-018 BATTERY CHARGER; 826.384-010 CELL REPAIRER; 826.684-014 CELL CHANGER; 826.684-018 CELL INSTALLER; 829.684-010 BATTERY INSPECTOR

85714C TRANSFORMER REPAIRERS. OOH Title/s: Commercial and Industrial Electronic Equipment Repairers

Clean and repair electrical transformers. Cleans transformer case, using scrapers and solvent. Disassembles distribution, streetlight, or instrument transformers. Drains and filters transformer oil. Reassembles transformer. Fills reassembled transformer with oil until coils are submerged. Replaces worn or defective parts, using hand tools. Dismantles lamination assembly, preparatory to cleaning and inspection. Inspects transformer for defects, such as cracked weldments. Secures input and output wires in position. Signals crane operator to raise heavy transformer component subassemblies. Winds replacement coils, using coil-winding machine.
Yearly Earnings: $28,080
Education: Postsecondary vocational training
Knowledge: Mechanical; Telecommunications
Abilities: Manual Dexterity; Dynamic Strength; Dynamic Flexibility; Gross Body Equilibrium
Skills: Installation; Equipment Maintenance; Troubleshooting; Repairing
General Work Activities: Performing General Physical Activities; Handling and Moving Objects; Repairing and Maintaining Mechanical Equipment; Repairing and Maintaining Electrical Equipment
Job Characteristics: Very Hot; Cramped Work Space, Awkward Positions; High Places; Hazardous Conditions; Climbing Ladders, Scaffolds, Poles, etc.; Walking or Running; Common Protective or Safety Attire; Specialized Protective or Safety Attire; Consequence of Error
GOE Group/s: 05.05.05 Craft Technology: Electrical-Electronic Systems Installation and Repair; 05.10.03 Crafts: Electrical-Electronic
CIP Program/s: 460301 Electrical and Power Transmission Installer, General; 460302 Electrician; 470199 Electrical and Electronics Equipment Installer and Repairer; 470501 Stationary Energy Sources Installer and Operator

Related DOT Job/s: 724.381-018 TRANSFORMER REPAIRER; 821.361-034 POWER-TRANSFORMER REPAIRER

85714D ARMATURE AND SALVAGE REPAIRERS. OOH Title/s: Commercial and Industrial Electronic Equipment Repairers

Recondition and rebuild salvaged electrical parts of equipment, and wind new coils on armatures of used generators and motors. Solders, wraps, and coats wires to ensure proper insulation. Replaces broken and defective parts. Cuts insulating material to fit slots on armature core, and places material in bottom of core slots. Winds new coils on armatures of generators and motors. Disassembles salvaged equipment used in electric-power systems, such as air circuit breakers and lightning arresters, using hand tools, and discards nonrepairable parts. Inserts and hammers ready-made coils into place. Cleans and polishes parts, using solvent and buffing wheel. Bolts porcelain insulators to wood parts to assemble hot stools. Solders ends of coils to commutator segments. Tests armatures and motors to ensure proper operation.

Yearly Earnings: $28,080

Education: Postsecondary vocational training

Knowledge: Mechanical

Abilities: None above average

Skills: Installation; Testing; Equipment Maintenance; Repairing

General Work Activities: Handling and Moving Objects; Repairing and Maintaining Mechanical Equipment; Repairing and Maintaining Electrical Equipment

Job Characteristics: Making Repetitive Motions

GOE Group/s: 05.10.03 Crafts: Electrical-Electronic; 06.02.24 Production Work: Manual Work, Metal and Plastics

CIP Program/s: 470101 Electrical and Electronics Equipment Installer and Repairer; 470199 Electrical and Electronics Equipment Installer and Repairer

Related DOT Job/s: 724.684-018 ARMATURE WINDER, REPAIR; 729.384-018 SALVAGE REPAIRER II

85717A ELECTRONICS MECHANICS AND TECHNICIANS. OOH Title/s: Commercial and Industrial Electronic Equipment Repairers; Precision Assemblers

Install, maintain, and repair electronic equipment, such as industrial controls, telemetering and missile control systems, radar systems, transmitters, and antennae. Analyzes technical requirements of customer desiring to utilize electronic equipment, and performs installation and maintenance duties. Replaces or repairs defective components, using hand tools and technical documents. Adjusts defective components, using hand tools and technical documents. Installs equipment in industrial or military establishments and in aircraft and missiles. Calibrates testing instruments and installed or repaired equipment to prescribed specifications. Tests faulty equipment, using test equipment and applying knowledge of functional operation of electronic unit and systems, to diagnose malfunction. Inspects components of equipment for defects, such as loose connections and frayed wire, and for accuracy of assembly and installation. Determines feasibility of using standardized equipment, and develops specifications for equipment required to perform additional functions. Operates equipment to demonstrate use of equipment and to analyze malfunctions. Services electrical radioactivity-detecting instruments used to locate radioactive formations in oil- or gas-well boreholes, using special testing apparatus. Studies blueprints, schematics, manuals, and other specifications to determine installation procedures. Converses with equipment operators to ascertain whether mechanical or human error contributed to equipment breakdown. Maintains records of repairs, calibrations, and tests. Enters information into computer to copy program or to draw, modify, or store schematics, applying knowledge of software package used. Consults with customer, supervisor, and engineers to plan layout of equipment and to resolve problems in system operation and maintenance. Signs overhaul documents for equipment replaced or repaired. Advises management regarding customer satisfaction, product performance, and suggestions for product improvements. Accompanies flight crew to perform in-flight adjustments and to determine and record required post-flight repair work. Supervises workers in installing, testing, tuning, and adjusting equipment to obtain optimum operating performance. Instructs workers in electronic theory.

Yearly Earnings: $28,080

Education: Postsecondary vocational training

Knowledge: Administration and Management; Personnel and Human Resources; Computers and Electronics; Engineering and Technology; Design; Mathematics; Physics; Education and Training; Telecommunications

Abilities: Oral Comprehension; Oral Expression; Deductive Reasoning; Information Ordering; Mathematical Reasoning; Visualization; Finger Dexterity

Skills: Reading Comprehension; Mathematics; Science; Active Learning; Learning Strategies; Coordination; Instructing; Problem Identification; Synthesis/Reorganization; Idea Evaluation; Operations Analysis; Technology Design; Equipment Selection; Installation; Testing; Operation Monitoring; Operation and Control; Product Inspection; Equipment Maintenance; Troubleshooting; Repairing; Visioning; Systems Perception

General Work Activities: Identifying Objects, Actions, and Events; Inspecting Equipment, Structures, or Material; Processing Information; Updating and Using Job-Relevant Knowledge; Handling and Moving Objects; Controlling Machines and Processes; Operating Vehicles or Equipment; Drafting and Specifying Technical Devices, etc.; Repairing and Maintaining Electrical Equipment; Interpreting Meaning of Information to Others; Teaching Others; Guiding, Directing and Motivating Subordinates; Provide Consultation and Advice to Others

Job Characteristics: Supervise, Coach, Train Others; Cramped Work Space, Awkward Positions; Radiation; Special Uniform; Consequence of Error; Importance of Being Exact or Accurate; Importance of Being Sure All is Done

GOE Group/s: 05.05.05 Craft Technology: Electrical-Electronic Systems Installation and Repair; 05.05.10 Craft Technology: Electrical-Electronic Equipment Repair; 05.05.11 Craft Technology: Scientific, Medical, & Technical Equip. Fabric. & Related

CIP Program/s: 150402 Computer Maintenance Technologists and Technicians; 410204 Industrial Radiologic Technologists and Technicians; 470101 Electrical and Electronics Equipment Installer and Repairer; 470102 Business Machine Repairer; 470103 Communication Systems Installer and Repairer; 470104 Computer Installer and Repairer; 470105 Industrial Electronics Installer and Repairer; 470609 Aviation Systems and Avionics Maintenance Technologists and Technicians

Related DOT Job/s: 823.261-026 AVIONICS TECHNICIAN; 828.251-010 ELECTRONIC-SALES-AND-SERVICE TECHNICIAN; 828.261-014 FIELD SERVICE ENGINEER; 828.261-022 ELECTRONICS MECHANIC; 828.261-026 ELECTRONICS-MECHANIC APPRENTICE; 828.281-022 RADIOACTIVITY-INSTRUMENT MAINTENANCE TECHNICIAN; 828.281-026 COMPUTERIZED ENVIRONMENTAL CONTROL INSTALLER

85717B TEST CARD AND CIRCUIT BOARD REPAIRERS. OOH Title/s: Commercial and Industrial Electronic Equipment Repairers

Replace and realign broken, worn, or misaligned probes on probe test cards, and repair defective surfaces and circuitry on printed circuit boards. Repairs defective circuitry and board surface

faults, using hand tools and soldering or welding equipment. Removes, replaces, and resolders defective wiring and probes, using tweezers and soldering iron. Cuts and removes defective wires on PCBs, using knife. Observes probe card through microscope and aligns probes in specified position over test wafer, using tweezers. Aligns probes on even plane, using tweezers and test equipment. Positions replacement wire on circuit, using magnetic tweezers, and positions PCB's under microscope to examine circuitry. Reads specification sheets, manuals, and diagrams to determine probe card wiring and probe positions. Inspects probe cards, using microscope, to detect defects, and examines boards to determine that repairs meet specifications. Reads work orders to determine number of PCBs to be repaired, type of repairs, and method and tools required. Washes solder or liquid gold over specified areas to restore board surfaces. Cleans repaired boards with solvent, using brush and rags. Places PCBs in industrial oven to cure solder mask. Removes and stacks repaired boards on racks for movement to next work station. Maintains repair, replacement, probe, and inventory records, using computer. Prepares production reports.
Yearly Earnings: $28,080
Education: Postsecondary vocational training
Knowledge: Computers and Electronics
Abilities: Arm-Hand Steadiness; Finger Dexterity; Control Precision; Near Vision
Skills: Science; Installation; Testing; Product Inspection; Repairing
General Work Activities: Inspecting Equipment, Structures, or Material; Repairing and Maintaining Electrical Equipment
Job Characteristics: Sitting; Importance of Being Exact or Accurate; Importance of Being Sure All is Done
GOE Group/s: 06.01.04 Production Technology: Precision Hand Work; 06.02.23 Production Work: Manual Work, Assembly Small Parts
CIP Program/s: 470101 Electrical and Electronics Equipment Installer and Repairer; 470105 Industrial Electronics Installer and Repairer
Related DOT Job/s: 726.361-022 REPAIRER, PROBE TEST CARD, SEMICONDUCTOR WAFERS; 726.684-090 REWORKER, PRINTED CIRCUIT BOARD

85721 POWERHOUSE, SUBSTATION, AND RELAY ELECTRICIANS. OOH Title/s: Commercial and Industrial Electronic Equipment Repairers

Inspect, test, repair, and maintain electrical equipment in generating stations or powerhouses; substation equipment, such as oil circuit breakers and transformers; and in-service relays, to prevent and remedy abnormal behavior of transmission and distribution lines and equipment. Repairs, replaces, and cleans equipment, such as brushes, commutators, windings, bearings, relays, switches, controls, and instruments. Repairs or rebuilds circuit breakers, transformers, and lightning arresters by replacing worn parts. Inspects and tests equipment and circuits to identify malfunction or defect, using wiring diagrams and testing devices such as ohmmeters, voltmeters, or ammeters. Tests oil in circuit breakers and transformers for dielectric strength, and periodically refills. Tests insulators and bushings of equipment by inducing voltage across insulation, using testing apparatus and calculating insulation loss. Disconnects voltage regulators, bolts, and screws, and connects replacement regulators to high-voltage lines. Analyzes test data to diagnose malfunctions and evaluate effect of system modifications. Prepares reports of work performed. Notifies personnel of need for equipment shutdown requiring changes from normal operation to maintain service. Paints, repairs, and maintains buildings, and sets forms and pours concrete footings for installation of heavy equipment.
Yearly Earnings: $28,080
Education: Postsecondary vocational training
Knowledge: Computers and Electronics; Engineering and Technology; Mechanical; Physics
Abilities: Perceptual Speed; Selective Attention; Reaction Time; Dynamic Strength; Extent Flexibility; Dynamic Flexibility; Gross Body Equilibrium; Visual Color Discrimination; Hearing Sensitivity; Auditory Attention; Sound Localization
Skills: Science; Equipment Selection; Installation; Testing; Operation Monitoring; Equipment Maintenance; Troubleshooting; Repairing
General Work Activities: Identifying Objects, Actions, and Events; Inspecting Equipment, Structures, or Material; Repairing and Maintaining Mechanical Equipment; Repairing and Maintaining Electrical Equipment
Job Characteristics: Cramped Work Space, Awkward Positions; High Places; Hazardous Conditions; Climbing Ladders, Scaffolds, Poles, etc.; Bending or Twisting the Body
GOE Group/s: 05.05.05 Craft Technology: Electrical-Electronic Systems Installation and Repair
CIP Program/s: 460301 Electrical and Power Transmission Installer, General; 460302 Electrician; 470501 Stationary Energy Sources Installer and Operator
Related DOT Job/s: 820.261-010 ELECTRICIAN APPRENTICE, POWERHOUSE; 820.261-014 ELECTRICIAN, POWERHOUSE; 820.261-018 ELECTRICIAN, SUBSTATION; 821.261-018 RELAY TECHNICIAN

85723 ELECTRICAL POWER LINE INSTALLERS AND REPAIRERS. OOH Title/s: Line Installers and Cable Splicers

Install and repair cables or wires used in electrical power or distribution systems. Install insulators and erect wooden poles and light or heavy duty transmission towers. Include cable splicers and troubleshooters. Exclude repairers of transformers and substation equipment, and telephone and telegraph communications workers. Repairs electrical power cables and auxiliary equipment for electrical power lines. Installs and repairs conduits, cables, wires, and auxiliary equipment following blueprints. Splices cables together or to overhead transmission line, customer service line, or street light line. Splices, solders, and insulates conductors and wiring to join sections of power line, and to connect transformers and electrical accessories. Tests electric power lines and auxiliary equipment, using direct reading and testing instruments to identify cause of disturbances. Strings wire conductors and cable between erected poles and adjusts slack, using winch. Climbs poles and removes and installs hardware, wires, and other equipment. Opens switches or clamps grounding device to deenergize disturbed or fallen lines to facilitate repairs or to remove electrical hazards. Replaces and straightens poles and attaches crossarms, insulators, and auxiliary equipment to wood poles preparatory to erection. Cuts and peels lead sheath and insulation from defective or newly installed cables and conducts prior to splicing. Cleans, tins, and splices corresponding conductors by twisting ends together or by joining ends with metal clamps and soldering connection. Tests conductors to identify corresponding conductors and to prevent incorrect connections, according to electrical diagrams and specifications. Installs watt-hour meters and connects service drops between power line and consumer. Covers conductors with insulating or fireproofing materials. Works on energized lines to avoid interruption of service. Drives conveyance equipped with tools and materials to job site.
Yearly Earnings: $37,960
Education: Long-term O-J-T
Knowledge: Computers and Electronics; Engineering and Technology; Design; Building and Construction; Mechanical; Foreign Language; Public Safety and Security
Abilities: Information Ordering; Flexibility of Closure; Perceptual Speed; Spatial Orientation; Visualization; Selective Attention; Arm-

Hand Steadiness; Manual Dexterity; Finger Dexterity; Control Precision; Multilimb Coordination; Response Orientation; Wrist-Finger Speed; Speed of Limb Movement; Static Strength; Explosive Strength; Dynamic Strength; Trunk Strength; Stamina; Extent Flexibility; Dynamic Flexibility; Gross Body Coordination; Gross Body Equilibrium; Visual Color Discrimination
Skills: Technology Design; Installation; Testing; Product Inspection; Equipment Maintenance; Troubleshooting; Repairing
General Work Activities: Inspecting Equipment, Structures, or Material; Performing General Physical Activities; Handling and Moving Objects; Interacting with Computers; Repairing and Maintaining Electrical Equipment
Job Characteristics: Very Hot; Extremely Bright or Inadequate Lighting; Cramped Work Space, Awkward Positions; Radiation; High Places; Hazardous Conditions; Climbing Ladders, Scaffolds, Poles, etc.; Keeping or Regaining Balance; Using Hands on Objects, Tools, or Controls; Common Protective or Safety Attire; Specialized Protective or Safety Attire; Consequence of Error; Frustrating Circumstances; Importance of Being Exact or Accurate; Importance of Being Sure All is Done
GOE Group/s: 05.05.05 Craft Technology: Electrical-Electronic Systems Installation and Repair; 05.10.04 Crafts: Structural-Mechanical-Electrical-Electronic
CIP Program/s: 460301 Electrical and Power Transmission Installer, General; 460303 Lineworker
Related DOT Job/s: 821.261-014 LINE MAINTAINER; 821.261-022 SERVICE RESTORER, EMERGENCY; 821.261-026 TROUBLE SHOOTER II; 821.361-010 CABLE INSTALLER-REPAIRER; 821.361-018 LINE ERECTOR; 821.361-022 LINE INSTALLER, STREET RAILWAY; 821.361-026 LINE REPAIRER; 821.361-030 LINE-ERECTOR APPRENTICE; 821.361-038 TOWER ERECTOR; 821.684-022 TROLLEY-WIRE INSTALLER; 825.381-038 THIRD-RAIL INSTALLER; 829.361-010 CABLE SPLICER; 829.361-014 CABLE-SPLICER APPRENTICE

85726 STATION INSTALLERS AND REPAIRERS, TELEPHONE. OOH Title/s: Telephone Installers and Repairers

Install and repair telephone station equipment, such as telephones, coin collectors, telephone booths, and switching-key equipment. Installs communication equipment, such as intercommunication systems and related apparatus, using schematic diagrams, testing devices, and hand tools. Assembles telephone equipment, mounts brackets, and connects wire leads, using hand tools and following installation diagrams or work order. Repairs cables, lays out plans for new equipment, and estimates material required. Analyzes equipment operation, using testing devices to locate and diagnose nature of malfunction and ascertain needed repairs. Disassembles components and replaces, cleans, adjusts, and repairs parts, wires, switches, relays, circuits, or signaling units, using hand tools. Operates and tests equipment to ensure elimination of malfunction. Climbs poles to install or repair outside service lines.
Yearly Earnings: $28,080
Education: Postsecondary vocational training
Knowledge: Computers and Electronics; Mechanical; Telecommunications
Abilities: Dynamic Strength; Stamina; Gross Body Coordination; Gross Body Equilibrium
Skills: Installation; Testing; Equipment Maintenance; Troubleshooting; Repairing
General Work Activities: Performing General Physical Activities; Handling and Moving Objects; Repairing and Maintaining Electrical Equipment
Job Characteristics: High Places; Climbing Ladders, Scaffolds, Poles, etc.; Keeping or Regaining Balance; Special Uniform; Common Protective or Safety Attire; Importance of Being Exact or Accurate; Importance of Being Sure All is Done
GOE Group/s: 05.05.05 Craft Technology: Electrical-Electronic Systems Installation and Repair
CIP Program/s: 470101 Electrical and Electronics Equipment Installer and Repairer; 470103 Communication Systems Installer and Repairer
Related DOT Job/s: 822.261-022 STATION INSTALLER-AND-REPAIRER; 822.281-018 MAINTENANCE MECHANIC, TELEPHONE

85728A AIRCRAFT ELECTRICIANS. OOH Title/s: Commercial and Industrial Electronic Equipment Repairers

Lay out, install, repair, test, and maintain electrical systems in aircraft. Assembles components, such as switches, electrical controls, and junction boxes, using hand tools and soldering iron. Connects components to assemblies, such as radio systems, instruments, magnetos, inverters, and in-flight refueling systems, using hand tools and soldering iron. Tests components or assemblies, using circuit tester, oscilloscope, and voltmeter. Adjusts, repairs, or replaces malfunctioning components or assemblies, using hand tools and soldering iron. Lays out installation of assemblies and systems in aircraft, according to blueprints and wiring diagrams, using scribe, scale, and protractor. Installs electrical and electronic components, assemblies, and systems in aircraft, using hand tools, power tools, and soldering iron. Sets up and operates ground support and test equipment to perform functional flight test of electrical and electronic systems. Interprets flight test data to diagnose malfunctions and systemic performance problems. Fabricates parts and test aids as required.
Yearly Earnings: $28,080
Education: Postsecondary vocational training
Knowledge: Computers and Electronics; Engineering and Technology; Design; Physics; Telecommunications
Abilities: Information Ordering; Spatial Orientation; Visualization; Arm-Hand Steadiness; Manual Dexterity; Finger Dexterity; Multilimb Coordination; Wrist-Finger Speed; Speed of Limb Movement; Explosive Strength; Extent Flexibility; Dynamic Flexibility; Gross Body Coordination; Gross Body Equilibrium; Visual Color Discrimination
Skills: Science; Equipment Selection; Installation; Testing; Operation Monitoring; Operation and Control; Equipment Maintenance; Troubleshooting; Repairing; Systems Perception
General Work Activities: Identifying Objects, Actions, and Events; Inspecting Equipment, Structures, or Material; Drafting and Specifying Technical Devices, etc.; Implementing Ideas, Programs, etc.; Repairing and Maintaining Electrical Equipment
Job Characteristics: Sounds, Noise Levels are Distracting, etc.; Cramped Work Space, Awkward Positions; Hazardous Conditions; Climbing Ladders, Scaffolds, Poles, etc.; Kneeling, Crouching, or Crawling; Using Hands on Objects, Tools, or Controls; Importance of Being Exact or Accurate; Importance of Being Sure All is Done
GOE Group/s: 05.05.05 Craft Technology: Electrical-Electronic Systems Installation and Repair; 06.02.23 Production Work: Manual Work, Assembly Small Parts
CIP Program/s: 460301 Electrical and Power Transmission Installer, General; 460302 Electrician; 470607 Aircraft Mechanic/Technician, Airframe; 470608 Aircraft Mechanic/Technician, Powerplant
Related DOT Job/s: 825.261-018 ELECTRICIAN, AIRCRAFT; 825.381-010 AIRCRAFT MECHANIC, ELECTRICAL AND RADIO; 829.281-018 IN-FLIGHT REFUELING SYSTEM REPAIRER

85728B GROUND TRANSPORTATION ELECTRICIANS. OOH Title/s: Commercial and Industrial Electronic Equipment Repairers

Install and repair electrical wiring equipment and systems in automobiles, locomotives, buses, trucks, and travel trailers.

Adjusts, repairs, or replaces defective wiring and relays in ignition, lighting, air-conditioning, and safety control systems, using electrician's tools. Repairs or rebuilds starters, generators, distributors, or door controls, using electrician's tools. Installs electrical equipment, such as air-conditioning, heating, or ignition systems, generator brushes, and commutators, using hand tools. Installs fixtures, outlets, terminal boards, switches, and wall boxes, using hand tools. Measures, cuts, and installs framework and conduit to support and connect wiring, control panels, and junction boxes, using hand tools. Splices wires with knife or cutting pliers, and solders connections to fixtures, outlets, and equipment. Visually inspects and tests electrical system or equipment, using testing devices such as oscilloscope, voltmeter, and ammeter, to determine malfunctions. Cuts openings and drills holes for fixtures, outlet boxes, and fuse holders, using electric drill and router. Confers with customer to determine nature of malfunction. Estimates cost of repairs based on parts and labor charges.
Yearly Earnings: $28,080
Education: Postsecondary vocational training
Knowledge: Computers and Electronics; Building and Construction; Mechanical
Abilities: Arm-Hand Steadiness; Manual Dexterity; Finger Dexterity; Control Precision; Multilimb Coordination; Wrist-Finger Speed; Speed of Limb Movement; Explosive Strength; Trunk Strength; Stamina; Extent Flexibility; Dynamic Flexibility; Gross Body Coordination; Gross Body Equilibrium; Visual Color Discrimination
Skills: Equipment Selection; Installation; Repairing
General Work Activities: Inspecting Equipment, Structures, or Material; Repairing and Maintaining Mechanical Equipment; Repairing and Maintaining Electrical Equipment
Job Characteristics: Sounds, Noise Levels are Distracting, etc.; Cramped Work Space, Awkward Positions; Hazardous Conditions; Hazardous Equipment; Hazardous Situations; Kneeling, Crouching, or Crawling; Using Hands on Objects, Tools, or Controls; Bending or Twisting the Body; Making Repetitive Motions
GOE Group/s: 05.05.05 Craft Technology: Electrical-Electronic Systems Installation and Repair; 05.05.10 Craft Technology: Electrical-Electronic Equipment Repair; 05.10.04 Crafts: Structural-Mechanical-Electrical-Electronic
CIP Program/s: 460301 Electrical and Power Transmission Installer, General; 460302 Electrician; 470604 Auto/Automotive Mechanic/Technician
Related DOT Job/s: 825.281-022 ELECTRICIAN, AUTOMOTIVE; 825.281-026 ELECTRICIAN, LOCOMOTIVE; 825.381-018 CONTROLLER REPAIRER-AND-TESTER; 828.381-010 EQUIPMENT INSTALLER; 829.684-014 BODY WIRER

85799 ALL OTHER ELECTRICAL AND ELECTRONIC EQUIPMENT MECHANICS, INSTALLERS, AND REPAIRERS. OOH Title/s: Electronic Equipment Repairers
All other electrical and electronic equipment mechanics, installers, and repairers not classified separately above.
Yearly Earnings: $28,080
Education: Postsecondary vocational training
GOE Group/s: 05.05.12 Craft Technology: Musical Instrument Fabrication and Repair; 05.09.01 Material Control: Shipping, Receiving, and Stock Checking; 05.10.03 Crafts: Electrical-Electronic; 06.04.34 Elemental Work: Industrial: Manual Work, Assorted Materials
CIP Program/s: 470101 Electrical and Electronics Equipment Installer and Repairer; 470103 Communication Systems Installer and Repairer; 470199 Electrical and Electronics Equipment Installer and Repairer; 470399 Industrial Equipment Maintenance and Repair, Other; 470404 Musical Instrument Repairer; 470607 Aircraft Mechanic/Technician, Airframe
Related DOT Job/s: 719.381-014 HEARING-AID REPAIRER; 729.684-042 SAFETY-LAMP KEEPER; 730.381-050 PLAYER-PIANO TECHNICIAN; 731.684-022 TOY-ELECTRIC-TRAIN REPAIRER; 759.684-026 DEICER REPAIRER

Other Mechanics, Installers, and Repairers

85902A HEATING AND AIR-CONDITIONING MECHANICS. OOH Title/s: Heating, Air-Conditioning, and Refrigeration Technicians
Install, service, and repair heating and air-conditioning systems in residences and commercial establishments. Installs, connects, and adjusts thermostats, humidistats, and timers, using hand tools. Repairs or replaces defective equipment, components, or wiring. Joins pipes or tubing to equipment and to fuel, water, or refrigerant source, to form complete circuit. Fabricates, assembles, and installs duct work and chassis parts, using portable metal-working tools and welding equipment. Tests electrical circuits and components for continuity, using electrical test equipment. Disassembles system and cleans and oils parts. Assembles, positions, and mounts heating or cooling equipment, following blueprints. Tests pipe or tubing joints and connections for leaks, using pressure gauge or soap-and-water solution. Installs auxiliary components to heating-cooling equipment, such as expansion and discharge valves, air ducts, pipes, blowers, dampers, flues, and stokers, following blueprints. Adjusts system controls to setting recommended by manufacturer to balance system, using hand tools. Inspects and tests system to verify system compliance with plans and specifications and to detect malfunctions. Discusses heating-cooling system malfunctions with users to isolate problems or to verify malfunctions have been corrected. Inspects inoperative equipment to locate source of trouble. Studies blueprints to determine configuration of heating or cooling equipment components. Wraps pipes in insulation and secures it in place with cement or wire bands. Lays out and connects electrical wiring between controls and equipment according to wiring diagram, using electrician's hand tools. Reassembles equipment and starts unit to test operation. Measures, cuts, threads, and bends pipe or tubing, using pipefitter's tools. Cuts and drills holes in floors, walls, and roof to install equipment, using power saws and drills.
Yearly Earnings: $25,844
Education: Long-term O-J-T
Knowledge: Engineering and Technology; Design; Building and Construction; Mechanical
Abilities: Arm-Hand Steadiness; Manual Dexterity; Finger Dexterity; Multilimb Coordination; Extent Flexibility; Gross Body Equilibrium
Skills: Technology Design; Installation; Testing; Equipment Maintenance; Troubleshooting; Repairing
General Work Activities: Inspecting Equipment, Structures, or Material; Drafting and Specifying Technical Devices, etc.; Repairing and Maintaining Mechanical Equipment; Repairing and Maintaining Electrical Equipment
Job Characteristics: Very Hot; Extremely Bright or Inadequate Lighting; Cramped Work Space, Awkward Positions; Climbing Ladders, Scaffolds, Poles, etc.; Kneeling, Crouching, or Crawling
GOE Group/s: 05.05.03 Craft Technology: Plumbing and Pipefitting; 05.05.05 Craft Technology: Electrical-Electronic Systems Installation and Repair; 05.05.09 Craft Technology: Mechanical Work; 05.10.04 Crafts: Structural-Mechanical-Electrical-Electronic
CIP Program/s: 470201 Heating, Air Conditioning and Refrigeration Mechanics and Repairers
Related DOT Job/s: 637.261-014 HEATING-AND-AIR-CONDITIONING INSTALLER-SERVICER; 637.261-030 SOLAR-ENERGY-SYSTEM

INSTALLER; 637.261-034 AIR AND HYDRONIC BALANCING TECHNICIAN; 637.381-010 EVAPORATIVE-COOLER INSTALLER; 862.281-018 OIL-BURNER-SERVICER-AND-INSTALLER; 862.361-010 FURNACE INSTALLER; 869.281-010 FURNACE INSTALLER-AND-REPAIRER, HOT AIR

85902B REFRIGERATION MECHANICS. OOH Title/s: Heating, Air-Conditioning, and Refrigeration Technicians

Install and repair industrial and commercial refrigerating systems. Mounts compressor, condenser, and other components in specified location on frame, using hand tools and acetylene welding equipment. Assembles structural and functional components, such as controls, switches, gauges, wiring harnesses, valves, pumps, compressors, condensers, cores, and pipes. Installs expansion and control valves, using acetylene torch and wrenches. Replaces or adjusts defective or worn parts to repair system, and reassembles system. Cuts, bends, threads, and connects pipe to functional components and water, power, or refrigeration system. Brazes or solders parts to repair defective joints and leaks. Fabricates and assembles components and structural portions of refrigeration system, using hand tools, power tools, and welding equipment. Drills holes and installs mounting brackets and hangers into floor and walls of building. Lifts and aligns components into position, using hoist or block and tackle. Adjusts valves according to specifications, and charges system with specified type of refrigerant. Observes system operation, using gauges and instruments, and adjusts or replaces mechanisms and parts, according to specifications. Dismantles malfunctioning systems and tests components, using electrical, mechanical, and pneumatic testing equipment. Lays out reference points for installation of structural and functional components, using measuring instruments. Tests lines, components, and connections for leaks. Reads blueprints to determine location, size, capacity, and type of components needed to build refrigeration system. Keeps records of repairs and replacements made and causes of malfunctions.
Yearly Earnings: $25,844
Education: Long-term O-J-T
Knowledge: Engineering and Technology; Design; Building and Construction; Mechanical
Abilities: Static Strength; Explosive Strength; Extent Flexibility; Gross Body Equilibrium
Skills: Installation; Testing; Operation Monitoring; Product Inspection; Equipment Maintenance; Troubleshooting; Repairing
General Work Activities: Repairing and Maintaining Mechanical Equipment; Repairing and Maintaining Electrical Equipment
Job Characteristics: Cramped Work Space, Awkward Positions; Hazardous Conditions; Hazardous Equipment; Kneeling, Crouching, or Crawling
GOE Group/s: 05.05.09 Craft Technology: Mechanical Work; 05.10.02 Crafts: Mechanical
CIP Program/s: 470201 Heating, Air Conditioning and Refrigeration Mechanics and Repairers
Related DOT Job/s: 637.261-026 REFRIGERATION MECHANIC; 637.381-014 REFRIGERATION UNIT REPAIRER; 827.361-014 REFRIGERATION MECHANIC

85905 PRECISION INSTRUMENT REPAIRERS. OOH Title/s: Precision Instrument Repairers

Install, test, repair, maintain, and adjust indicating, recording, telemetering, and controlling instruments used to measure and control variables such as pressure, flow, temperature, motion, force, and chemical composition. Include instrument repairers who repair, calibrate, and test instruments such as voltmeters, ammeters, and galvanometers. Inspects gauges, meters, and indicators to detect abnormal fluctuations or defects. Tests accuracy of meters, gauges, indicators, or other recording or controlling instruments to locate defective components and for conformance to standards. Calculates adjustment and calibrates instruments or scales, using hand tools, computer, or electronic devices. Traces out and tests electronic solid state components to locate defective parts, using test equipment, schematics, and manuals. Installs scales, equipment, or instruments, using blueprints and diagrams. Adjusts scales, gears, equipment, or fit of parts. Disassembles malfunctioning instrument and repairs, or replaces damaged or worn parts, using hand tools and power tools. Reassembles instrument or equipment, adjusts parts, and replaces in system. Cleans and lubricates parts and instruments. Cuts or fabricates replacement parts for instruments, using lathe, drill press, or glass cutter. Maintains record of repairs, calibration, test results, parts and components used, and inventory. Prepares schematic drawings, sketches, or reports to demonstrate changes or alterations made in instruments or system.
Yearly Earnings: $26,052
Education: Long-term O-J-T
Knowledge: Computers and Electronics; Engineering and Technology; Mechanical
Abilities: Speed of Closure; Flexibility of Closure; Perceptual Speed; Visualization; Selective Attention; Arm-Hand Steadiness; Finger Dexterity; Control Precision; Wrist-Finger Speed; Dynamic Flexibility; Visual Color Discrimination; Hearing Sensitivity; Sound Localization
Skills: Science; Technology Design; Equipment Selection; Installation; Testing; Operation Monitoring; Operation and Control; Equipment Maintenance; Troubleshooting; Repairing
General Work Activities: Inspecting Equipment, Structures, or Material; Processing Information; Operating Vehicles or Equipment; Drafting and Specifying Technical Devices, etc.; Repairing and Maintaining Mechanical Equipment; Repairing and Maintaining Electrical Equipment
Job Characteristics: Cramped Work Space, Awkward Positions; Climbing Ladders, Scaffolds, Poles, etc.; Using Hands on Objects, Tools, or Controls; Making Repetitive Motions
GOE Group/s: 05.05.09 Craft Technology: Mechanical Work; 05.05.10 Craft Technology: Electrical-Electronic Equipment Repair; 05.05.11 Craft Technology: Scientific, Medical, & Technical Equip. Fabric. & Related
CIP Program/s: 470401 Instrument Calibration and Repairer
Related DOT Job/s: 633.281-026 SCALE MECHANIC; 710.261-010 INSTRUMENT REPAIRER; 710.281-026 INSTRUMENT MECHANIC; 710.281-030 INSTRUMENT TECHNICIAN; 710.281-038 TAXIMETER REPAIRER; 710.281-042 INSTRUMENT-TECHNICIAN APPRENTICE; 710.381-054 REPAIRER, GYROSCOPE; 711.281-014 INSTRUMENT MECHANIC, WEAPONS SYSTEM; 729.281-026 ELECTRICAL-INSTRUMENT REPAIRER; 823.281-018 METEOROLOGICAL-EQUIPMENT REPAIRER

85908 ELECTROMEDICAL AND BIOMEDICAL EQUIPMENT REPAIRERS. OOH Title/s: Electromedical and Biomedical Equipment Repairers

Test, adjust, and repair electromedical equipment, using hand tools and meters. Inspects and tests malfunctioning medical and related equipment, using test and analysis instruments and following manufacturers' specifications. Repairs and replaces defective parts, such as motors, clutches, tubes, transformers, resistors, condensers, and switches, using hand tools. Calibrates and adjusts components and equipment, using hand tools, power tools, measuring devices, and following manufacturers' manuals and troubleshooting techniques. Disassembles malfunctioning equipment and removes defective components. Safety-tests medical equipment and facility's structural environment to ensure patient and staff safety from electrical or mechanical hazards. Solders loose connections, using soldering iron. Maintains

various equipment and apparatus, such as patient monitors, electrocardiographs, x-ray units, defibrillators, electrosurgical units, anesthesia apparatus, pacemakers, and sterilizers. Installs medical, dental, and related technical equipment in medical and research facilities. Fabricates hardware, using machine and power tools and hand tools. Modifies or develops instruments or devices, under supervision of medical or engineering staff. Cleans and lubricates equipment, using solvents, rags, and lubricants. Logs records of maintenance and repair work and approved updates of equipment as required by manufacturer. Consults with medical or research staff to ensure that equipment functions properly and safely. Demonstrates and explains correct operation of equipment to medical personnel. Represents equipment manufacturer as salesperson or service technician.
Yearly Earnings: $25,220
Education: Long-term O-J-T
Knowledge: Sales and Marketing; Computers and Electronics; Engineering and Technology; Design; Mechanical; Chemistry; Medicine and Dentistry; Telecommunications
Abilities: Written Comprehension; Visualization; Selective Attention; Finger Dexterity; Explosive Strength; Hearing Sensitivity; Sound Localization; Speech Clarity
Skills: Persuasion; Instructing; Technology Design; Installation; Testing; Operation Monitoring; Equipment Maintenance; Troubleshooting; Repairing
General Work Activities: Identifying Objects, Actions, and Events; Inspecting Equipment, Structures, or Material; Updating and Using Job-Relevant Knowledge; Repairing and Maintaining Mechanical Equipment; Repairing and Maintaining Electrical Equipment; Selling or Influencing Others; Teaching Others
Job Characteristics: Persuade Someone to a Course of Action; Provide a Service to Others; Responsible for Others' Health and Safety; Radiation; Diseases/Infections; Hazardous Conditions; Hazardous Equipment; Hazardous Situations; Kneeling, Crouching, or Crawling; Using Hands on Objects, Tools, or Controls; Importance of Being Sure All is Done
GOE Group/s: 02.04.02 Laboratory Technology: Life Sciences; 05.05.11 Craft Technology: Scientific, Medical, & Technical Equip. Fabric. & Related; 05.10.02 Crafts: Mechanical
CIP Program/s: 150401 Biomedical Engineering-Related Technologists and Technicians
Related DOT Job/s: 019.261-010 BIOMEDICAL EQUIPMENT TECHNICIAN; 639.281-022 MEDICAL-EQUIPMENT REPAIRER; 719.261-014 RADIOLOGICAL-EQUIPMENT SPECIALIST; 729.281-030 ELECTROMEDICAL-EQUIPMENT REPAIRER; 829.261-014 DENTAL-EQUIPMENT INSTALLER AND SERVICER

85911 ELECTRIC METER INSTALLERS AND REPAIRERS. OOH Title/s: Electric Meter Installers and Repairers

Install electric meters on customers' premises or on pole. Test meters and perform necessary repairs. Turn current on or off by connecting or disconnecting service drop. Mounts and installs meters and other electric equipment, such as time clocks, transformers, and circuit breakers, using electrician's hand tools. Inspects and tests electric meters, relays, and power, to detect cause of malfunction and inaccuracy, using hand tools and testing equipment. Repairs electric meters and components, such as transformers and relays, and changes faulty or incorrect wiring, using hand tools. Splices and connects cable from meter or current transformer to pull box or switchboard, using hand tools, to provide power. Makes adjustments to meter components, such as setscrews or timing mechanism, to conform to specifications. Disconnects and removes electric power meters when defective or when customer accounts are in default, using hand tools. Cleans meter parts, using chemical solutions, brushes, sandpaper, and soap and water. Records meter reading and installation data on meter cards, work orders, or field service orders.
Yearly Earnings: $26,052
Education: Long-term O-J-T
Knowledge: Computers and Electronics; Engineering and Technology; Mechanical
Abilities: Information Ordering; Spatial Orientation; Arm-Hand Steadiness; Manual Dexterity; Finger Dexterity; Multilimb Coordination; Reaction Time; Speed of Limb Movement; Explosive Strength; Trunk Strength; Stamina; Extent Flexibility; Dynamic Flexibility; Gross Body Coordination; Gross Body Equilibrium; Far Vision; Visual Color Discrimination; Glare Sensitivity
Skills: Technology Design; Installation; Testing; Equipment Maintenance; Troubleshooting; Repairing
General Work Activities: Repairing and Maintaining Electrical Equipment
Job Characteristics: Cramped Work Space, Awkward Positions; Radiation; High Places; Hazardous Conditions; Hazardous Situations; Standing; Climbing Ladders, Scaffolds, Poles, etc.; Kneeling, Crouching, or Crawling; Keeping or Regaining Balance; Special Uniform; Specialized Protective or Safety Attire; Importance of Being Sure All is Done
GOE Group/s: 05.05.05 Craft Technology: Electrical-Electronic Systems Installation and Repair; 05.05.10 Craft Technology: Electrical-Electronic Equipment Repair; 05.10.03 Crafts: Electrical-Electronic
CIP Program/s: 470401 Instrument Calibration and Repairer
Related DOT Job/s: 729.281-014 ELECTRIC-METER REPAIRER; 729.281-018 ELECTRIC-METER-REPAIRER APPRENTICE; 729.281-034 INSIDE-METER TESTER; 821.361-014 ELECTRIC-METER INSTALLER I; 821.684-010 ELECTRIC-METER INSTALLER II

85914 CAMERA AND PHOTOGRAPHIC EQUIPMENT REPAIRERS. OOH Title/s: Camera and Photographic Equipment Repairers

Repair and adjust cameras and photographic equipment, including motion picture cameras and equipment, using specialized tools and testing devices. Measures parts to verify specified dimensions/settings, such as camera shutter speed and light meter reading accuracy, using measuring instruments. Examines cameras, equipment, processed film, and laboratory reports to diagnose malfunction, using work aids and specifications. Disassembles equipment to gain access to defect, using hand tools. Adjusts cameras, photographic mechanisms, and equipment, such as range and view finders, shutters, light meters, and lens systems, using hand tools. Calibrates and verifies accuracy of light meters, shutter diaphragm operation, and lens carriers, using timing instruments. Fabricates or modifies defective electronic, electrical, and mechanical components, using bench lathe, milling machine, shaper, grinder, and precision hand tools, according to specifications. Tests equipment performance, focus of lens system, alignment of diaphragm, lens mounts, and film transport, using precision gauges. Reads and interprets engineering drawings, diagrams, instructions, and specifications to determine needed repairs, fabrication method, and operation sequence. Assembles aircraft cameras, still and motion picture cameras, photographic equipment, and frames, using diagrams, blueprints, bench machines, hand tools, and power tools. Installs film in aircraft camera and electrical assemblies and wiring in camera housing, following blueprints and using hand tools and soldering equipment. Lays out reference points and dimensions on parts and metal stock to be machined, using precision measuring instruments. Cleans and lubricates cameras and polishes camera lenses, using cleaning materials and work aids. Records test data and documents fabrication techniques on reports. Requisitions parts and materials. Demonstrates operation and servicing of equipment to customers. Recommends design changes or upgrades of micro-filming, film-de-

veloping, and photographic equipment. Schedules service calls according to customer location and priority. Interviews prospective buyers and provides informational leads to sales personnel.
Yearly Earnings: $26,052
Education: Moderate-term O-J-T
Knowledge: Sales and Marketing; Computers and Electronics; Engineering and Technology; Design; Mechanical; Physics; Chemistry; Fine Arts
Abilities: Written Comprehension; Arm-Hand Steadiness; Finger Dexterity; Control Precision; Dynamic Flexibility; Gross Body Equilibrium; Near Vision; Visual Color Discrimination; Night Vision; Depth Perception; Glare Sensitivity; Hearing Sensitivity; Sound Localization; Speech Clarity
Skills: Speaking; Active Learning; Instructing; Problem Identification; Solution Appraisal; Technology Design; Installation; Testing; Operation Monitoring; Equipment Maintenance; Troubleshooting; Repairing
General Work Activities: Inspecting Equipment, Structures, or Material; Controlling Machines and Processes; Drafting and Specifying Technical Devices, etc.; Repairing and Maintaining Mechanical Equipment; Repairing and Maintaining Electrical Equipment; Communicating with Persons Outside Organization
Job Characteristics: Provide a Service to Others; Deal with External Customers; Extremely Bright or Inadequate Lighting; Using Hands on Objects, Tools, or Controls
GOE Group/s: 05.05.09 Craft Technology: Mechanical Work; 05.05.11 Craft Technology: Scientific, Medical, & Technical Equip. Fabric. & Related; 05.05.13 Craft Technology: Printing
CIP Program/s: 470101 Electrical and Electronics Equipment Installer and Repairer; 470104 Computer Installer and Repairer; 470105 Industrial Electronics Installer and Repairer; 470499 Miscellaneous Mechanics and Repairers, Other
Related DOT Job/s: 714.281-010 AIRCRAFT-PHOTOGRAPHIC-EQUIPMENT MECHANIC; 714.281-014 CAMERA REPAIRER; 714.281-018 MACHINIST, MOTION-PICTURE EQUIPMENT; 714.281-022 PHOTOGRAPHIC EQUIPMENT TECHNICIAN; 714.281-026 PHOTOGRAPHIC-EQUIPMENT-MAINTENANCE TECHNICIAN; 714.281-030 SERVICE TECHNICIAN, COMPUTERIZED-PHOTOFINISHING EQUIPMENT; 826.261-010 FIELD-SERVICE ENGINEER

85917 WATCHMAKERS. OOH Title/s: Watchmakers

Repair, clean, and adjust mechanisms of instruments such as watches, time clocks, and timing switches, using hand tools and measuring instruments. Exclude workers who perform a specialized operation. Repairs or replaces broken, damaged, or worn parts, using watchmaker's lathe, drill press, and hand tools. Assembles mechanism, oils moving parts, and demagnetizes mechanism, using demagnetizing machine. Cleans, rinses, and dries parts, using watch-cleaning machine. Tests accuracy of balance wheel assembly and adjusts timing regulator, using truing calipers, watch-rate recorder, and tweezers. Removes mechanism from case and disassembles parts, such as hands, springs, or wheels, using hand tools. Tests and replaces batteries and other electronic components. Examines watch mechanism, case, and parts for defects or foreign matter, using loupe (magnifier). Repairs watch cases, surface defects of clocks, and watch bands. Estimates cost of watch for repair. Records quantity and type of clocks repaired.
Yearly Earnings: $26,052
Education: Long-term O-J-T
Knowledge: None above average
Abilities: Arm-Hand Steadiness; Finger Dexterity; Near Vision
Skills: Equipment Maintenance; Troubleshooting; Repairing
General Work Activities: Repairing and Maintaining Mechanical Equipment; Repairing and Maintaining Electrical Equipment
Job Characteristics: Sitting; Using Hands on Objects, Tools, or Controls; Making Repetitive Motions; Importance of Being Exact or Accurate
GOE Group/s: 05.05.11 Craft Technology: Scientific, Medical, & Technical Equip. Fabric. & Related; 06.04.34 Elemental Work: Industrial: Manual Work, Assorted Materials
CIP Program/s: 470408 Watch, Clock and Jewelry Repairer
Related DOT Job/s: 715.281-010 WATCH REPAIRER; 715.281-014 WATCH REPAIRER APPRENTICE; 715.584-014 REPAIRER, AUTO CLOCKS

85921A KEYBOARD INSTRUMENT REPAIRERS AND TUNERS. OOH Title/s: Musical Instrument Repairers and Tuners

Repair, adjust, refinish, and tune musical keyboard instruments. Repairs or replaces defective, broken, or worn parts, using hand tools, power tools, glue, and nails. Adjusts lips, reeds, or toe hole of organ pipes, using hand tools, to regulate air flow and loudness of sound. Adjusts felt hammers on piano to increase tonal mellowness or brilliance, using sanding paddle, lacquer, or needles. Adjusts alignment, string spacing, and striking point of hammers of piano, using wrench, burner, shims, and bushings. Disassembles and reassembles instruments and parts to tune and repair, using hand tools and power tools. Compares pitch of instruments with specified pitch of tuning tool to tune instrument. Removes irregularities from tuning pins, strings, and hammers of piano, using wood block or filing tool. Inspects and tests parts of pianos, pipe organs, accordions, and concertinas to determine defects, using hand tools, gauges, and electronic testing equipment. Assembles and installs new pipe organs and pianos in buildings. Makes wood replacement parts for accordions, using woodworking machines and hand tools. Mixes and measures glue. Cleans instruments, using vacuum cleaner.
Yearly Earnings: $26,052
Education: Long-term O-J-T
Knowledge: Mechanical; Fine Arts
Abilities: Finger Dexterity; Wrist-Finger Speed; Extent Flexibility; Dynamic Flexibility; Hearing Sensitivity; Auditory Attention; Sound Localization
Skills: Installation; Repairing
General Work Activities: Repairing and Maintaining Mechanical Equipment
Job Characteristics: Provide a Service to Others; Cramped Work Space, Awkward Positions; Using Hands on Objects, Tools, or Controls; Making Repetitive Motions
GOE Group/s: 05.05.12 Craft Technology: Musical Instrument Fabrication and Repair; 06.01.04 Production Technology: Precision Hand Work; 06.02.32 Production Work: Manual Work, Assorted Materials; 06.04.34 Elemental Work: Industrial: Manual Work, Assorted Materials
CIP Program/s: 470404 Musical Instrument Repairer
Related DOT Job/s: 730.281-014 ACCORDION REPAIRER; 730.281-038 PIANO TECHNICIAN; 730.361-010 PIANO TUNER; 730.361-014 PIPE-ORGAN TUNER AND REPAIRER; 730.381-010 ACCORDION TUNER; 730.381-038 ORGAN-PIPE VOICER; 730.681-010 PIANO REGULATOR-INSPECTOR; 730.684-026 CHIP TUNER; 730.684-094 TONE REGULATOR

85921B STRINGED INSTRUMENT REPAIRERS AND TUNERS. OOH Title/s: Musical Instrument Repairers and Tuners

Repair, adjust, refinish, and tune musical stringed instruments. Repairs broken parts, using glue, clamp, and handpress. Refinishes instruments to protect and decorate them, using hand tools, buffing tools, and varnish. Strings instrument and adjusts truss and bridge of instrument to obtain specified string tension and height. Adjusts string

tension to tune instrument, using hand tools and electronic tuning device. Reassembles instrument or bow with new or repaired parts, using glue, hairs, yarn, resin, and clamps. Disassembles instrument or bow, using hand tools. Inspects musical instruments, such as cellos, violins, guitars, and mandolins, to determine defects. Removes cracked, worn, or broken parts of instrument, using heated knife and hand tools. Carves wood replacement parts, such as wedges or plugs, according to the shape and dimensions of the instrument or bow. Assembles instrument according to specifications, using hand tools. Plays instrument to determine pitch. Tests tubes and pickups in electronic amplifier units, and solders parts and connections.
Yearly Earnings: $26,052
Education: Long-term O-J-T
Knowledge: Fine Arts
Abilities: Flexibility of Closure; Visualization; Speed of Limb Movement; Hearing Sensitivity; Auditory Attention; Sound Localization
Skills: Repairing
General Work Activities: Repairing and Maintaining Electrical Equipment
Job Characteristics: Using Hands on Objects, Tools, or Controls
GOE Group/s: 05.05.12 Craft Technology: Musical Instrument Fabrication and Repair; 06.02.23 Production Work: Manual Work, Assembly Small Parts
CIP Program/s: 470404 Musical Instrument Repairer
Related DOT Job/s: 730.281-026 FRETTED-INSTRUMENT REPAIRER; 730.281-050 VIOLIN REPAIRER; 730.381-026 HARP REGULATOR; 730.684-022 BOW REHAIRER

85921C REED OR WIND INSTRUMENT REPAIRERS AND TUNERS. OOH Title/s: Musical Instrument Repairers and Tuners
Repair, adjust, refinish, and tune musical reed and wind instruments. Disassembles instrument parts, such as keys, pistons, and other parts, to tune or repair, using gas torch and hand tools. Repairs cracks in wood or metal instruments, using wire, lathe, filler, clamps, or soldering iron. Files reed until pitch corresponds with standard pitch of tuning bar. Replaces worn pads and springs, using hand tools. Lubricates and reassembles instrument, using hand tools and soldering iron or torch. Inspects mechanical parts of instrument to determine defects. Removes dents and burrs from metal instruments, using mallet and burnishing tool. Shapes old parts and replacement parts to improve tone or intonation, using hand tools, lathe, or soldering iron. Operates bellows to sound metal reed and ascertain its pitch. Compares pitch of reed with pitch of tuning bar. Polishes instrument, using rag and polishing compound, buffing wheel, or burnishing tool. Washes metal instruments in lacquer-stripping and cyanide solution to remove lacquer and tarnish.
Yearly Earnings: $26,052
Education: Long-term O-J-T
Knowledge: None above average
Abilities: Flexibility of Closure; Finger Dexterity; Speed of Limb Movement; Depth Perception; Hearing Sensitivity; Auditory Attention; Sound Localization
Skills: Repairing
General Work Activities: Repairing and Maintaining Mechanical Equipment
Job Characteristics: Using Hands on Objects, Tools, or Controls
GOE Group/s: 05.05.12 Craft Technology: Musical Instrument Fabrication and Repair
CIP Program/s: 470404 Musical Instrument Repairer
Related DOT Job/s: 730.281-054 WIND-INSTRUMENT REPAIRER; 730.381-034 METAL-REED TUNER

85921D PERCUSSION INSTRUMENT REPAIRERS AND TUNERS. OOH Title/s: Musical Instrument Repairers and Tuners
Repair and tune musical percussion instruments. Stretches skin over rim hoop, using hand-tucking tool. Places rim hoop back onto drum shell to allow drumhead to dry and become taut. Repairs breaks in percussion instruments, such as drums and cymbals, using drill press, power saw, glues, clamps, or other hand tools. Strikes wood, fiberglass, or metal bars of instruments, such as xylophone or vibraharp, to ascertain tone. Compares tone of bar with tuned block, stroboscope, or electronic tuner. Removes dents in tympani, using steel block and hammer. Removes drumhead, using drum key and cutting tools. Cuts new drumhead from animal skin, using scissors. Soaks drumhead in water to make it pliable. Removes material from bar, using bandsaw, sanding machine, machine grinder, or hand files and scrapers, to obtain the specified tone. Assembles bar onto instruments. Solders or welds frames of mallet instruments and metal drum parts. Cleans, sands, and paints parts of percussion instruments to maintain their condition, in accordance to blueprints and shop drawings.
Yearly Earnings: $26,052
Education: Long-term O-J-T
Knowledge: Fine Arts
Abilities: Hearing Sensitivity
Skills: Testing; Repairing
General Work Activities: None above average
Job Characteristics: Using Hands on Objects, Tools, or Controls
GOE Group/s: 05.05.12 Craft Technology: Musical Instrument Fabrication and Repair
CIP Program/s: 470404 Musical Instrument Repairer
Related DOT Job/s: 730.381-042 PERCUSSION-INSTRUMENT REPAIRER; 730.381-058 TUNER, PERCUSSION

85923 LOCKSMITHS AND SAFE REPAIRERS. OOH Title/s: Locksmiths and Safe Repairers
Repair and open locks, make keys, and change locks and safe combinations. May install and repair safes. Disassembles mechanical or electrical locking devices and repairs or replaces worn tumblers, springs, and other parts, using hand tools. Inserts new or repaired tumblers into lock to change combination. Repairs and adjusts safes, vault doors, and vault components, using hand tools, lathe, drill press, and welding and acetylene cutting apparatus. Cuts new or duplicate keys, using key-cutting machine. Installs safes, vault doors, and deposit boxes according to blueprints, using equipment such as power drill, tap, die, truck crane, and dolly. Opens safe locks by drilling. Moves picklock in cylinder to open door locks without keys. Removes interior and exterior finishes on safes and vaults and sprays on new finishes. Keeps record of company locks and keys.
Yearly Earnings: $26,052
Education: Moderate-term O-J-T
Knowledge: Mechanical
Abilities: Arm-Hand Steadiness; Finger Dexterity
Skills: Installation; Repairing
General Work Activities: Repairing and Maintaining Mechanical Equipment
Job Characteristics: None above average
GOE Group/s: 05.05.06 Craft Technology: Metal Fabrication and Repair; 05.05.09 Craft Technology: Mechanical Work
CIP Program/s: 470403 Locksmith and Safe Repairer
Related DOT Job/s: 709.281-010 LOCKSMITH; 709.281-014 LOCKSMITH APPRENTICE; 869.381-022 SAFE-AND-VAULT SERVICE MECHANIC

85926 OFFICE MACHINE AND CASH REGISTER SERVICERS. OOH Title/s: Computer and Office Machine Repairers

Repair and service office machines, such as adding, accounting, calculating, duplicating, and typewriting machines. Include worker s who repair manual, electrical, and electronic office machines. Exclude those who repair computerized systems and word processing systems. Tests machine to locate cause of electrical problems, using testing devices such as voltmeter, ohmmeter, and circuit test equipment. Disassembles machine and examines parts, such as wires, gears, and bearings, for wear and defects, using hand tools, power tools, and measuring devices. Repairs, adjusts, or replaces electrical and mechanical components and parts, using hand tools, power tools, and soldering or welding equipment. Operates machine, such as typewriter, cash register, or adding machine, to test functioning of parts and mechanisms. Reads specifications, such as blueprints, charts, and schematics, to determine machine settings and adjustments. Cleans and oils mechanical parts to maintain machine. Assembles and installs machine according to specifications, using hand tools, power tools, and measuring devices. Fabricates and reshapes parts, such as shims or bolts, on bench lathe or grinder. Instructs operators and servicers in operation, maintenance, assembly, and repair of machine.

Yearly Earnings: $25,896

Education: Long-term O-J-T

Knowledge: Computers and Electronics; Engineering and Technology; Design; Mechanical; Education and Training; Foreign Language; Telecommunications

Abilities: Visualization; Arm-Hand Steadiness; Finger Dexterity; Visual Color Discrimination; Speech Clarity

Skills: Instructing; Technology Design; Installation; Testing; Equipment Maintenance; Troubleshooting; Repairing

General Work Activities: Repairing and Maintaining Mechanical Equipment; Repairing and Maintaining Electrical Equipment

Job Characteristics: Using Hands on Objects, Tools, or Controls

GOE Group/s: 05.05.09 Craft Technology: Mechanical Work; 06.01.04 Production Technology: Precision Hand Work; 06.02.24 Production Work: Manual Work, Metal and Plastics

CIP Program/s: 470101 Electrical and Electronics Equipment Installer and Repairer; 470102 Business Machine Repairer; 470104 Computer Installer and Repairer

Related DOT Job/s: 633.261-010 ASSEMBLY TECHNICIAN; 633.261-014 MAIL-PROCESSING-EQUIPMENT MECHANIC; 633.281-010 CASH-REGISTER SERVICER; 633.281-014 DICTATING-TRANSCRIBING-MACHINE SERVICER; 633.281-018 OFFICE-MACHINE SERVICER; 633.281-022 OFFICE-MACHINE-SERVICER APPRENTICE; 633.281-030 STATISTICAL-MACHINE SERVICER; 706.381-010 ALIGNER, TYPEWRITER; 706.381-030 REPAIRER, TYPEWRITER

85928A VALVE AND REGULATOR REPAIRERS. OOH Title/s: Industrial Machinery Repairers

Test, repair, and adjust mechanical regulators and valves. Replaces, repairs, or adjusts defective valve or regulator parts, and tightens attachments, using hand tools, power tools, and welder. Tests valves and regulators for leaks, temperature, and pressure settings, using precision testing equipment. Disassembles mechanical control devices or valves, such as regulators, thermostats, or hydrants, using power tools, hand tools, and cutting torch. Examines valves or mechanical control device parts for defects, dents, or loose attachments. Lubricates wearing surfaces of mechanical parts, using oils or other lubricants. Measures salvageable parts removed from mechanical control devices for conformance to standards or specifications, using gauges, micrometers, and calipers. Cleans corrosives and other deposits from serviceable parts, using solvents, wire brushes, or sandblaster. Dips valves and regulators in molten lead to prevent leakage, and paints valves, fittings, and other devices, using spray gun. Correlates testing data, performs technical calculations, and writes test reports to record data. Records repair work, inventories parts, and orders new parts. Advises customers on proper installation of valves or regulators and related equipment.

Yearly Earnings: $28,080

Education: Postsecondary vocational training

Knowledge: Mechanical; Physics

Abilities: Arm-Hand Steadiness; Manual Dexterity; Finger Dexterity; Wrist-Finger Speed; Extent Flexibility; Dynamic Flexibility; Gross Body Equilibrium

Skills: Installation; Equipment Maintenance; Repairing

General Work Activities: Repairing and Maintaining Mechanical Equipment

Job Characteristics: Sounds, Noise Levels are Distracting, etc.; Very Hot; Extremely Bright or Inadequate Lighting; Contaminants; Cramped Work Space, Awkward Positions; Whole Body Vibration; High Places; Hazardous Conditions; Hazardous Equipment; Standing; Climbing Ladders, Scaffolds, Poles, etc.; Kneeling, Crouching, or Crawling; Keeping or Regaining Balance; Using Hands on Objects, Tools, or Controls; Bending or Twisting the Body; Making Repetitive Motions

GOE Group/s: 05.05.09 Craft Technology: Mechanical Work; 05.05.11 Craft Technology: Scientific, Medical, & Technical Equip. Fabric. & Related; 05.10.02 Crafts: Mechanical

CIP Program/s: 470303 Industrial Machinery Maintenance and Repair; 470399 Industrial Equipment Maintenance and Repair, Other; 470401 Instrument Calibration and Repairer; 470501 Stationary Energy Sources Installer and Operator

Related DOT Job/s: 622.381-010 AIR-VALVE REPAIRER; 630.381-030 VALVE REPAIRER; 637.261-022 INDUSTRIAL-GAS SERVICER; 709.684-070 SALVAGER; 710.381-026 GAS-REGULATOR REPAIRER; 710.381-050 THERMOSTAT REPAIRER; 862.684-030 WATER REGULATOR AND VALVE REPAIRER; 953.281-010 FIELD-MECHANICAL-METER TESTER

85928B METER MECHANICS. OOH Title/s: Electric Meter Installers and Repairers

Test, adjust, and repair gas, water, and oil meters. Adjusts meter and repeats test until meter registration is within specified limits. Connects gas, oil, water, or air meter to test apparatus and to detect leaks. Dismantles meter and replaces defective parts—such as case, shafts, gears, disks, and recording mechanisms—using soldering iron and hand tools. Inspects, repairs, and maintains gas meters at wells or processing plants. Reassembles meter and meter parts, using soldering gun, power tools, and hand tools. Analyzes test results to determine cause of persistent meter registration errors. Lubricates moving meter parts, using oil gun. Cleans plant growth, scale, and rust from meter housing, using wire brush, buffer, sandblaster, or cleaning compounds. Records test results, materials used, and meters needing repair on log or card, and segregates meters requiring repair. Caps meter housing and activates controls on paint booth to spray paint meter case.

Yearly Earnings: $26,052

Education: Long-term O-J-T

Knowledge: Mechanical

Abilities: Flexibility of Closure; Arm-Hand Steadiness; Finger Dexterity

Skills: Installation; Testing; Product Inspection; Equipment Maintenance; Repairing

General Work Activities: None above average

Job Characteristics: Extremely Bright or Inadequate Lighting; Cramped Work Space, Awkward Positions; Radiation; Hazardous

Situations; Walking or Running; Kneeling, Crouching, or Crawling; Keeping or Regaining Balance; Bending or Twisting the Body
GOE Group/s: 05.10.02 Crafts: Mechanical; 06.01.05 Production Technology: Inspection
CIP Program/s: 470401 Instrument Calibration and Repairer
Related DOT Job/s: 710.281-022 GAS-METER PROVER; 710.281-034 METER REPAIRER; 710.381-022 GAS-METER MECHANIC I; 710.684-026 GAS-METER MECHANIC II

85928C MECHANICAL DOOR REPAIRERS. OOH Title/s: Industrial Machinery Repairers

Install, service, and repair opening and closing mechanisms of automatic doors and hydraulic door closers. Installs door frames, door closers, and electronic-eye mechanisms, using power tools, hand tools, and electronic test equipment. Removes or disassembles defective automatic mechanical door closers, using hand tools. Sets in and secures floor treadle for door-activating mechanism, and connects powerpack and electrical panelboard to treadle. Repairs, replaces, or fabricates worn or broken parts, using welder, lathe, drill press, and shaping and milling machines. Studies blueprints and schematic diagrams to determine method of installing and repairing automated door openers. Covers treadle with carpeting or other floor-covering materials, and tests system by stepping on treadle. Bores and cuts holes in flooring, using hand tools and power tools. Lubricates door-closer oil chamber and packs spindle with leather washer. Cleans door-closer parts, using caustic soda, rotary brush, and grinding wheel.
Yearly Earnings: $28,080
Education: Postsecondary vocational training
Knowledge: Engineering and Technology; Building and Construction; Mechanical
Abilities: Arm-Hand Steadiness; Speed of Limb Movement; Stamina; Extent Flexibility; Gross Body Equilibrium; Visual Color Discrimination
Skills: Installation; Equipment Maintenance; Repairing
General Work Activities: Performing General Physical Activities; Repairing and Maintaining Mechanical Equipment
Job Characteristics: Cramped Work Space, Awkward Positions; Hazardous Equipment; Standing; Climbing Ladders, Scaffolds, Poles, etc.; Kneeling, Crouching, or Crawling; Keeping or Regaining Balance; Bending or Twisting the Body; Pace Determined by Speed of Equipment
GOE Group/s: 05.10.02 Crafts: Mechanical; 05.10.03 Crafts: Electrical-Electronic
CIP Program/s: 470303 Industrial Machinery Maintenance and Repair
Related DOT Job/s: 630.381-014 DOOR-CLOSER MECHANIC; 829.281-010 AUTOMATIC-DOOR MECHANIC

85928D UTILITIES REPRESENTATIVES. OOH Title/s: Inspectors and Compliance Officers, Except Construction; Electric Meter Installers and Repairers

Install, adjust, and service gas meters, inspect meters and connections for leaks, and record meter readings. Inspects meters, appliance connections, valves, and pipes to determine utility leakage or energy waste. Disconnects or connects utility service, and installs or removes utility meters or regulators in establishments, using hand tools. Reads meter and records readings. Repairs, adjusts, cleans, and tightens gas appliance jets, regulators, and connections, using hand tools. Interviews customer to obtain information on complaints, such as gas leakage, low pressure, or abnormal consumption of gas or electricity. Investigates factors, such as number and type of appliances, temperature settings, loose fitting windows, deficient insulation, or suspected illegal usage. Notifies customer of needed repairs, and recommends energy and utility cost savings tips and programs to customer. Sketches and measures building exterior, interior, and openings, and records dimensions for use in calculating heat loss. Writes work orders for meter installation and specifications for utility distribution changes.
Yearly Earnings: $26,052
Education: Long-term O-J-T
Knowledge: Customer and Personal Service
Abilities: Manual Dexterity; Dynamic Flexibility; Gross Body Equilibrium; Glare Sensitivity
Skills: Service Orientation; Installation; Troubleshooting; Repairing
General Work Activities: Repairing and Maintaining Mechanical Equipment
Job Characteristics: Provide a Service to Others; Deal with External Customers; Very Hot; Extremely Bright or Inadequate Lighting; Cramped Work Space, Awkward Positions; Hazardous Conditions; Standing; Climbing Ladders, Scaffolds, Poles, etc.; Walking or Running; Kneeling, Crouching, or Crawling; Keeping or Regaining Balance; Bending or Twisting the Body; Special Uniform
GOE Group/s: 05.10.01 Crafts: Structural; 05.10.02 Crafts: Mechanical; 05.10.04 Crafts: Structural-Mechanical-Electrical-Electronic
CIP Program/s: 460501 Plumber and Pipefitter; 470501 Stationary Energy Sources Installer and Operator
Related DOT Job/s: 953.364-010 GAS-METER INSTALLER; 959.361-010 CUSTOMER SERVICE REPRESENTATIVE; 959.367-018 ENERGY-CONSERVATION REPRESENTATIVE; 959.574-010 SERVICE REPRESENTATIVE

85932 ELEVATOR INSTALLERS AND REPAIRERS. OOH Title/s: Elevator Installers and Repairers

Assemble, install, repair, and maintain electric and hydraulic freight and passenger elevators, escalators, and dumbwaiters. Assembles and installs electric and hydraulic freight and passenger elevators, escalators, and dumbwaiters. Inspects, tests, and adjusts elevators, escalators, and dumbwaiters to meet factory specifications and safety codes. Repairs or upgrades elevators, escalators, and dumbwaiters to meet safety regulations and building codes. Studies blueprints to determine layout of framework and foundations. Cuts prefabricated sections of framework, rails, and other components to specified dimensions. Completes service reports to verify conformance to prescribed standards.
Yearly Earnings: $26,052
Education: Long-term O-J-T
Knowledge: Engineering and Technology; Building and Construction; Mechanical; Public Safety and Security
Abilities: Information Ordering; Dynamic Strength; Stamina; Extent Flexibility; Gross Body Equilibrium; Night Vision; Peripheral Vision; Depth Perception; Hearing Sensitivity
Skills: Installation; Testing; Operation Monitoring; Product Inspection; Equipment Maintenance; Troubleshooting; Repairing
General Work Activities: Inspecting Equipment, Structures, or Material; Performing General Physical Activities; Handling and Moving Objects; Repairing and Maintaining Mechanical Equipment; Repairing and Maintaining Electrical Equipment
Job Characteristics: Responsible for Others' Health and Safety; Extremely Bright or Inadequate Lighting; Cramped Work Space, Awkward Positions; High Places; Hazardous Conditions; Hazardous Equipment; Hazardous Situations; Climbing Ladders, Scaffolds, Poles, etc.; Kneeling, Crouching, or Crawling; Keeping or Regaining Balance; Using Hands on Objects, Tools, or Controls; Bending or Twisting the Body; Consequence of Error; Importance of Being Sure All is Done
GOE Group/s: 05.05.05 Craft Technology: Electrical-Electronic Systems Installation and Repair; 05.05.06 Craft Technology: Metal Fabrication and Repair; 05.07.03 Quality Control: Electrical
CIP Program/s: 470303 Industrial Machinery Maintenance and Repair

Related DOT Job/s: 825.261-014 ELEVATOR EXAMINER-AND-ADJUSTER; 825.281-030 ELEVATOR REPAIRER; 825.281-034 ELEVATOR-REPAIRER APPRENTICE; 825.361-010 ELEVATOR CONSTRUCTOR

85935 RIGGERS. OOH Title/s: Riggers

Set up or repair rigging for ships and shipyards, manufacturing plants, logging yards, construction projects, and for the entertainment industry. Select cables, ropes, pulleys, winches, blocks, and sheaves according to weight and size of load to be moved. Coordinate and direct other workers and the movement of equipment to accomplish the task. Selects gear—such as cables, pulleys, and winches—according to load weight and size, facilities, and work schedule. Fabricates and repairs rigging, such as slings, tackle, and ladders, using hand and power tools. Assembles and installs supporting structures, rigging, hoists, and pulling gear, using hand and power tools. Attaches pulleys and blocks to fixed overhead structures, such as beams, ceilings, and gin pole booms, with bolts and clamps. Attaches load to rigging, to provide support or prepare for moving, using hand and power tools. Signals or gives verbal directions to workers engaged in hoisting and moving loads, to ensure safety of workers and materials. Tests rigging, to ensure safety and reliability. Dismantles, maintains, and stores rigging equipment. Manipulates rigging lines, hoists, and pulling gear, to move or support materials, such as heavy equipment, ships, or theatrical sets. Aligns, levels, and anchors machinery. Controls movement of heavy equipment through narrow openings or confined spaces. Cleans and dresses machine surfaces and component parts.

Yearly Earnings: $25,220

Education: Long-term O-J-T

Knowledge: Engineering and Technology; Mechanical; Public Safety and Security

Abilities: Spatial Orientation; Visualization; Time Sharing; Manual Dexterity; Multilimb Coordination; Response Orientation; Reaction Time; Wrist-Finger Speed; Speed of Limb Movement; Static Strength; Explosive Strength; Dynamic Strength; Trunk Strength; Stamina; Extent Flexibility; Dynamic Flexibility; Gross Body Coordination; Gross Body Equilibrium; Far Vision; Peripheral Vision; Depth Perception; Glare Sensitivity; Auditory Attention; Sound Localization

Skills: Coordination; Technology Design; Equipment Selection; Installation; Testing; Operation Monitoring; Operation and Control; Repairing; Time Management; Management of Personnel Resources

General Work Activities: Performing General Physical Activities; Handling and Moving Objects; Controlling Machines and Processes; Interacting with Computers; Repairing and Maintaining Mechanical Equipment

Job Characteristics: Responsible for Others' Health and Safety; Very Hot; Extremely Bright or Inadequate Lighting; Cramped Work Space, Awkward Positions; High Places; Climbing Ladders, Scaffolds, Poles, etc.; Walking or Running; Kneeling, Crouching, or Crawling; Keeping or Regaining Balance; Bending or Twisting the Body; Specialized Protective or Safety Attire; Consequence of Error; Importance of Repeating Same Tasks

GOE Group/s: 05.05.06 Craft Technology: Metal Fabrication and Repair; 05.10.01 Crafts: Structural; 05.11.04 Equipment Operation: Material Handling; 05.12.04 Elemental Work: Mechanical: Hoisting, Conveying

CIP Program/s: 030405 Logging/Timber Harvesting; 490202 Construction Equipment Operator; 490306 Marine Maintenance and Repair

Related DOT Job/s: 623.381-010 GEAR REPAIRER; 806.261-014 RIGGER; 806.261-018 RIGGER APPRENTICE; 921.260-010 RIGGER; 921.664-014 RIGGER; 962.664-010 HIGH RIGGER; 962.684-010 ACROBATIC RIGGER; 962.684-014 GRIP

85938 INSTALLERS AND REPAIRERS—MANUFACTURED BUILDINGS, MOBILE HOMES, AND TRAVEL TRAILERS. OOH Title/s: General Maintenance Mechanics

Install, repair, and maintain units and systems in mobile homes, prefabricated buildings, or travel trailers, using hand tools or power tools. Locates and repairs frayed wiring, broken connections, or incorrect wiring, using ohmmeter, soldering iron, tape, and hand tools. Repairs plumbing and propane gas lines, using caulking compounds and plastic or copper pipe. Inspects, examines, and tests operation of parts or systems to be repaired and to verify completeness of work performed. Removes damaged exterior panels, repairs and replaces structural frame members, and seals leaks, using hand tools. Repairs leaks with caulking compound or replaces pipes, using pipe wrench. Connects electrical system to outside power source and activates switches to test operation of appliances and light fixtures. Connects water hose to inlet pipe of plumbing system and tests operation of toilets and sinks. Confers with customer or reads work order to determine nature and extent of damage to unit. Lists parts needed, estimates costs, and plans work procedure, using parts list, technical manuals, and diagrams. Opens and closes doors, windows, and drawers to test their operation and trims edges to fit, using jack plane or drawknife. Refinishes wood surfaces on cabinets, doors, moldings, and floors, using power sander, putty, spray equipment, brush, paints, or varnishes. Resets hardware, using chisel, mallet, and screwdriver. Seals open side of modular units to prepare them for shipment, using polyethylene sheets, nails, and hammer.

Yearly Earnings: $25,480

Education: Long-term O-J-T

Knowledge: Building and Construction; Mechanical

Abilities: Control Precision; Trunk Strength; Extent Flexibility; Gross Body Equilibrium

Skills: Installation; Troubleshooting; Repairing

General Work Activities: Performing General Physical Activities; Repairing and Maintaining Mechanical Equipment; Repairing and Maintaining Electrical Equipment

Job Characteristics: Cramped Work Space, Awkward Positions; Whole Body Vibration; Hazardous Conditions; Standing; Climbing Ladders, Scaffolds, Poles, etc.; Kneeling, Crouching, or Crawling; Keeping or Regaining Balance

GOE Group/s: 05.10.01 Crafts: Structural

CIP Program/s: 460401 Building/Property Maintenance and Management

Related DOT Job/s: 806.381-070 CUSTOM VAN CONVERTER; 869.261-022 REPAIRER, RECREATIONAL VEHICLE; 869.384-010 REPAIRER, MANUFACTURED BUILDINGS; 869.684-074 UTILITY WORKER

85944 GAS APPLIANCE REPAIRERS. OOH Title/s: Home Appliance and Power Tool Repairers

Repair and install gas appliances and equipment, such as ovens, dryers, and hot water heaters. Measures, cuts, and threads pipe and connects it to feeder lines and equipment or appliance, using rule and hand tools. Dismantles meters and regulators, and replaces defective pipes, thermocouples, thermostats, valves, and indicator spindles, using hand tools. Assembles new or reconditioned appliances. Tests and examines pipelines and equipment to locate leaks and faulty connections and to determine pressure and flow of gas. Collects payment for service.

Yearly Earnings: $31,252

Education: Long-term O-J-T

Knowledge: Mechanical

Abilities: Depth Perception; Sound Localization

Skills: Installation; Operation Monitoring; Equipment Maintenance; Troubleshooting; Repairing
General Work Activities: Performing General Physical Activities; Handling and Moving Objects; Repairing and Maintaining Mechanical Equipment
Job Characteristics: Provide a Service to Others; Extremely Bright or Inadequate Lighting; Contaminants; Cramped Work Space, Awkward Positions; Hazardous Conditions; Hazardous Situations; Kneeling, Crouching, or Crawling; Keeping or Regaining Balance; Using Hands on Objects, Tools, or Controls; Bending or Twisting the Body
GOE Group/s: 05.10.02 Crafts: Mechanical
CIP Program/s: 470101 Electrical and Electronics Equipment Installer and Repairer; 470106 Major Appliance Installer and Repairer
Related DOT Job/s: 637.261-018 GAS-APPLIANCE SERVICER

85947 COIN AND VENDING MACHINE SERVICERS AND REPAIRERS. OOH Title/s: Vending Machine Servicers and Repairers

Install, service, adjust, and repair coin or vending machines placed in establishments on a concessional basis, using hand or power tools. Exclude repairers of electronic video games and other specialized electronic vending machines. Adjusts and repairs vending machines and meters, and replaces defective mechanical and electrical parts, using hand tools, soldering iron, and diagrams. Tests dispensing, coin-handling, electrical, refrigeration, carbonation, or ice-making systems of machine. Examines and inspects vending machines and meters to determine cause of malfunction. Disassembles and assembles machines, following specifications and using hand tools and power tools. Cleans and oils parts with soap and water, gasoline, kerosene, or carbon tetrachloride. Replenishes vending machines with ingredients or products. Shellacs or paints dial markings or mechanism's exterior, using brush or spray gun. Collects coins from machine and makes settlements with concessionaires. Keeps records of machine maintenance and repair.
Yearly Earnings: $25,220
Education: Long-term O-J-T
Knowledge: None above average
Abilities: Finger Dexterity; Wrist-Finger Speed; Trunk Strength; Dynamic Flexibility; Gross Body Equilibrium
Skills: Installation; Equipment Maintenance; Troubleshooting; Repairing
General Work Activities: Repairing and Maintaining Mechanical Equipment; Repairing and Maintaining Electrical Equipment
Job Characteristics: Kneeling, Crouching, or Crawling; Bending or Twisting the Body; Making Repetitive Motions
GOE Group/s: 05.10.02 Crafts: Mechanical
CIP Program/s: 470199 Electrical and Electronics Equipment Installer and Repairer
Related DOT Job/s: 349.680-010 TICKET-DISPENSER CHANGER; 639.281-014 COIN-MACHINE-SERVICE REPAIRER; 710.384-026 PARKING-METER SERVICER; 710.681-018 REGISTER REPAIRER; 729.381-014 PIN-GAME-MACHINE INSPECTOR; 729.384-014 FARE-REGISTER REPAIRER

85951 BICYCLE REPAIRERS. OOH Title/s: Bicycle Repairers

Repair and service bicycles, using hand tools. Installs, repairs, and replaces equipment or accessories, such as handle bars, stands, lights, and seats. Aligns wheels. Disassembles axle to repair, adjust, and replace defective parts, using hand tools. Installs and adjusts speed and gear mechanisms. Welds broken or cracked frame together, using oxyacetylene torch and welding rods. Repairs holes in tire tubes, using scraper and patch. Paints bicycle frame, using spray gun or brush. Shapes replacement parts, using bench grinder. Assembles new bicycles. Sells new bicycles and accessories.
Yearly Earnings: $25,220
Education: Moderate-term O-J-T
Knowledge: Sales and Marketing; Engineering and Technology; Mechanical
Abilities: Finger Dexterity; Gross Body Equilibrium
Skills: Technology Design; Installation; Repairing
General Work Activities: Repairing and Maintaining Mechanical Equipment; Selling or Influencing Others; Performing for or Working with Public
Job Characteristics: Provide a Service to Others; Hazardous Equipment; Kneeling, Crouching, or Crawling; Using Hands on Objects, Tools, or Controls
GOE Group/s: 05.10.02 Crafts: Mechanical
CIP Program/s: 470610 Bicycle Mechanic and Repairer
Related DOT Job/s: 639.681-010 BICYCLE REPAIRER

85953 TIRE REPAIRERS AND CHANGERS. OOH Title/s: Tire Repairers and Changers

Repair and replace tires, tubes, treads, and related products on automobiles, buses, trucks, and other vehicles. Duties include mounting tires on wheels, balancing tires and wheels, and testing and repairing damaged tires and inner tubes. Remounts wheel onto vehicle. Removes wheel from vehicle by hand or by use of power hoist. Locates puncture in tubeless tire by visual inspection or by immersing inflated tire in water bath and observing air bubbles. Seals puncture in tubeless tire by inserting adhesive material and expanding rubber plug into puncture, using hand tools. Separates tubed tire from wheel, using rubber mallet and metal bar or mechanical tire changer. Removes inner tube from tire and inspects tire casing for defects, such as holes and tears. Patches tube with adhesive rubber patch, or seals rubber patch to tube, using hot vulcanizing plate. Reassembles tire onto wheel. Unbolts wheel, using lug wrench. Glues boot (tire patch) over rupture in tire casing, using rubber cement. Inflates inner tube and immerses it in water to locate leak. Places wheel on balancing machine to determine counterweights required to balance wheel. Rotates tires to different positions on vehicle, using hand tools. Hammers required counterweights onto rim of wheel. Raises vehicle, using hydraulic jack. Buffs defective area of inner tube, using scraper. Responds to emergency calls to make repairs or replacements of damaged tires at customer's home or on road. Cleans sides of white wall tires.
Yearly Earnings: $13,364
Education: Short-term O-J-T
Knowledge: None above average
Abilities: None above average
Skills: Repairing
General Work Activities: Performing General Physical Activities; Handling and Moving Objects
Job Characteristics: Sounds, Noise Levels are Distracting, etc.; Cramped Work Space, Awkward Positions; Whole Body Vibration; Standing; Kneeling, Crouching, or Crawling; Using Hands on Objects, Tools, or Controls; Special Uniform
GOE Group/s: 05.12.15 Elemental Work: Mechanical: Mechanical Work
CIP Program/s: 000000 NO CIP ASSIGNED
Related DOT Job/s: 750.681-010 TIRE REPAIRER; 915.684-010 TIRE REPAIRER

85956A TEXTILE MENDERS. OOH Title/s: Apparel Workers

Hand- or machine-sew holes and tears in textile articles. Operates sewing machine to restitch defective seams, sew up holes, or

replace garment pockets or blanket-binding ribbons. Patches holes, sews tears and ripped seams, or darns defects in items, using needle and thread or sewing machine. Reknits runs and replaces broken threads, using latch needle. Repairs holes by weaving thread over them, using needle. Pulls knots to wrong side of garment, using hook. Spreads out articles or material and examines for holes, tears, worn areas, and other marked or unmarked defects. Replaces defective shrouds, and splices connections between shrouds and harness, using hand tools. Trims edges of cut or torn fabric, using scissors or knife, and stitches together. Sews fringe, tassels, and ruffles onto drapes and curtains, and buttons and trimming onto garments. Measures and hems curtains, garments, and canvas coverings to size, using tape measure. Sews labels and emblems on articles for identification. Stamps grommets into canvas, using mallet and punch or eyelet machine. Cleans stains from fabric or garment, using spray gun and cleaning fluid.
Yearly Earnings: $14,664
Education: Long-term O-J-T
Knowledge: None above average
Abilities: Arm-Hand Steadiness; Manual Dexterity; Finger Dexterity; Wrist-Finger Speed; Near Vision; Visual Color Discrimination
Skills: None above average
General Work Activities: None above average
Job Characteristics: Sitting; Making Repetitive Motions; Importance of Repeating Same Tasks; Pace Determined by Speed of Equipment
GOE Group/s: 05.10.04 Crafts: Structural-Mechanical-Electrical-Electronic; 06.02.05 Production Work: Machine Work, Leather and Fabrics; 06.02.27 Production Work: Manual Work, Textile, Fabric and Leather; 06.04.27 Elemental Work: Industrial: Manual Work, Textile, Fabric and Leather; 06.04.34 Elemental Work: Industrial: Manual Work, Assorted Materials
CIP Program/s: 200301 Clothing, Apparel and Textile Workers and Managers, General; 200303 Commercial Garment and Apparel Worker; 490306 Marine Maintenance and Repair
Related DOT Job/s: 782.684-010 CANVAS REPAIRER; 782.684-046 MENDER, KNIT GOODS; 784.684-046 MENDER; 787.682-030 MENDER; 789.684-038 PARACHUTE MENDER

85956C HAND WEAVERS. OOH Title/s: Apparel Workers
Weave threads or patches into fabric articles to repair holes, tears, or worn places. Reweaves loose thread ends of patch into fabric, and fabric into patch, and turns article over and repeats, to repair. Threads needle and interlaces between threads, across hole or worn area, and pulls through fabric, leaving thread ends projecting, to fill hole. Ravels threads from edge of hole and patch, and pins or bastes patch under hole. Pulls strands back and forth with fingers until woven part matches article. Cuts off thread ends, and marks repaired area with thread to facilitate inspection. Pins article to padded block, cuts patch from article, using scissors, and pulls threads from patch, to obtain reweaving material. Presses article, using steam iron or damp cloth and dry iron.
Yearly Earnings: $14,664
Education: Long-term O-J-T
Knowledge: None above average
Abilities: Arm-Hand Steadiness; Finger Dexterity; Wrist-Finger Speed; Visual Color Discrimination
Skills: None above average
General Work Activities: None above average
Job Characteristics: Hazardous Situations; Sitting; Making Repetitive Motions; Importance of Repeating Same Tasks
GOE Group/s: 05.05.15 Craft Technology: Custom Sewing, Tailoring, and Upholstering
CIP Program/s: 200301 Clothing, Apparel and Textile Workers and Managers, General
Related DOT Job/s: 782.381-022 WEAVER, HAND

85998 PRODUCT REPAIRERS. OOH Title/s: Mechanics, Installers, and Repairers
Repair, mend, or install a wide variety of nonelectrical, manufactured products. May use hand tools and machines. Replaces or repairs worn, damaged, or defective parts according to specifications or customer needs. Disassembles and inspects item to remove or adjust parts. Attaches or installs new section or part, using hand or power tools and following prescribed procedure. Fills and patches cracks, holes, and chips to repair product surface. Smooths repaired section and paints, stains, shellacs, or oils surfaces of item to restore original appearance. Tests item before and after repairs, to verify conformance to specifications. Examines product to determine damage or defects and needed repairs. Reviews customer or manufacturer specifications to determine method of repairing item. Makes parts from materials, such as wood, metal, rubber, leather, fabric, or plastic. Places item being repaired in jigs or heat device to facilitate repairs. Cleans and polishes item, using power tools such as buffing machine and sandblasting equipment. Measures item and verifies shape to facilitate repairs. Wipes, washes, or cleans product, using cloth and cleaning solution. Reweighs item to achieve specified weight. Stamps identifying information on repaired item. Stacks or packages repaired items for shipment or storage. Keeps and maintains records of inventory and customer data. Sells items.
Yearly Earnings: $25,480
Education: Long-term O-J-T
Knowledge: Sales and Marketing; Production and Processing; Engineering and Technology; Building and Construction; Mechanical
Abilities: Visualization; Arm-Hand Steadiness; Finger Dexterity; Visual Color Discrimination
Skills: Technology Design; Installation; Product Inspection; Repairing
General Work Activities: Repairing and Maintaining Mechanical Equipment
Job Characteristics: Hazardous Equipment; Making Repetitive Motions
GOE Group/s: 01.06.02 Craft Arts: Arts and Crafts; 05.07.01 Quality Control: Structural; 05.10.01 Crafts: Structural; 05.10.04 Crafts: Structural-Mechanical-Electrical-Electronic; 05.12.15 Elemental Work: Mechanical: Mechanical Work; 05.12.18 Elemental Work: Mechanical: Cleaning and Maintenance; 05.12.19 Elemental Work: Mechanical: Reproduction Services; 06.02.24 Production Work: Manual Work, Metal and Plastics; 06.02.25 Production Work: Manual Work, Wood; 06.02.29 Production Work: Manual Work, Rubber; 06.02.32 Production Work: Manual Work, Assorted Materials; 06.03.02 Quality Control: Inspecting, Grading, Sorting, Weighing, and Recording; 06.04.24 Elemental Work: Industrial: Manual Work, Metal and Plastics; 06.04.25 Elemental Work: Industrial: Manual Work, Wood; 06.04.29 Elemental Work: Industrial: Manual Work, Rubber; 06.04.34 Elemental Work: Industrial: Manual Work, Assorted Materials
CIP Program/s: 470402 Gunsmith; 470499 Miscellaneous Mechanics and Repairers, Other; 470603 Auto/Automotive Body Repairer; 470607 Aircraft Mechanic/Technician, Airframe; 480501 Machinist/Machine Technologist
Related DOT Job/s: 369.684-018 UMBRELLA REPAIRER; 705.684-042 MOTHER REPAIRER; 709.364-014 TOWEL-CABINET REPAIRER; 709.384-010 FIRE-EXTINGUISHER REPAIRER; 709.684-034 CIGARETTE-LIGHTER REPAIRER; 709.684-062 REPAIRER; 731.684-014 DOLL REPAIRER; 732.364-014 SKI-BINDING FITTER-AND-REPAIRER; 732.381-022 GOLF-CLUB REPAIRER; 732.684-102 ROLLER-SKATE REPAIRER; 732.684-118 SKI REPAIRER, PRODUCTION; 732.684-122 SPORTS-EQUIPMENT REPAIRER; 733.384-010 REPAIRER, PENS AND PENCILS; 733.684-014 PEN-AND-PENCIL REPAIRER; 739.381-034 FIGURE REFINISHER AND REPAIRER; 739.381-054 SURVIVAL-EQUIPMENT REPAIRER; 739.484-014 FIRE-EQUIPMENT INSPECTOR;

739.484-018 SMOKING-PIPE REPAIRER; 739.684-106 LAST REMODELER-REPAIRER; 739.684-110 LAST REPAIRER; 739.684-186 PIPE STEM REPAIRER; 739.687-198 VENETIAN-BLIND CLEANER AND REPAIRER; 754.684-046 PLASTICS REPAIRER; 759.384-010 SELF-SEALING-FUEL-TANK REPAIRER; 759.684-042 MAT REPAIRER; 759.684-054 RUBBER-GOODS REPAIRER; 761.684-042 STOCK PATCHER; 769.684-014 BASKET PATCHER; 769.684-058 REPAIRER, VENEER SHEET; 809.684-034 REPAIRER, FINISHED METAL; 977.684-010 BOOK REPAIRER

85999A HAND AND PORTABLE POWER TOOL REPAIRERS. OOH Title/s: Home Appliance and Power Tool Repairers

Repair and adjust hand and power tools. Repairs or replaces tools and defective parts—such as handles, vises, pliers, or metal buckets—using soldering tool, gas torch, power tools, or hand tools. Examines and tests tools to determine defects or cause of malfunction, using hand and power tools, observation, and experience. Disassembles and reassembles tools, using hand tools, power tools, or arbor press. Verifies and adjusts alignment and dimensions of parts, using gauges and tracing lathe. Sharpens tools, such as picks, shovels, screwdrivers, and scoops, using bench grinder and emery wheel. Sprays, brushes, or recoats surface of polishing wheel, and places it in oven to dry. Cleans polishing and buffing wheels, using steam cleaning machine, to remove abrasives and bonding materials, and salvages cloth from wheel. Records nature and extent of repairs performed. Maintains stock of parts.
Yearly Earnings: $31,252
Education: Long-term O-J-T
Knowledge: Mechanical
Abilities: Manual Dexterity; Finger Dexterity; Wrist-Finger Speed
Skills: Repairing
General Work Activities: Repairing and Maintaining Mechanical Equipment
Job Characteristics: Hazardous Equipment; Using Hands on Objects, Tools, or Controls; Making Repetitive Motions; Common Protective or Safety Attire; Importance of Repeating Same Tasks
GOE Group/s: 05.10.02 Crafts: Mechanical; 06.02.24 Production Work: Manual Work, Metal and Plastics; 06.02.32 Production Work: Manual Work, Assorted Materials; 06.04.24 Elemental Work: Industrial: Manual Work, Metal and Plastics; 06.04.34 Elemental Work: Industrial: Manual Work, Assorted Materials
CIP Program/s: 010201 Agricultural Mechanization, General; 470401 Instrument Calibration and Repairer; 480599 Precision Metal Workers, Other
Related DOT Job/s: 519.684-026 TOOL REPAIRER; 701.381-010 REPAIRER, HANDTOOLS; 701.384-010 TOOL-MAINTENANCE WORKER; 701.684-010 CALIBRATOR; 739.684-030 BUFFING-AND-POLISHING-WHEEL REPAIRER

85999B PUMP INSTALLERS AND SERVICERS. OOH Title/s: Industrial Machinery Repairers

Erect, install, and repair electric, gasoline, diesel, or turbine pumps, according to diagrams or specifications, using hand and power tools. Cuts, threads, and tightens pump parts to assemble pump section, using hand tools and power tools. Installs pump section vertically in well casing, using rig loadline and winch, hand tools, power tools, and diagrams. Dismantles, cleans, repairs, and replaces defective pump parts. Aligns pump parts to minimize friction, using hand tools and gauges. Verifies alignment of pump shaft by visually inspecting or using dial indicator. Lubricates moving parts, and adjusts valves to prevent overloading. Pumps air into well to measure water levels and capacity of well, using pressure gauge and orifice meter. Recommends repair or adjustment of motor to improve operation of pumps. Extends hoisting mast of rig, and stabilizes, using guy wires and struts. Drives rig (truck-mounted hoisting equipment) adjacent to well.
Yearly Earnings: $28,080
Education: Postsecondary vocational training
Knowledge: Building and Construction; Mechanical; Transportation
Abilities: Spatial Orientation; Arm-Hand Steadiness; Manual Dexterity; Control Precision; Multilimb Coordination; Rate Control; Reaction Time; Speed of Limb Movement; Static Strength; Explosive Strength; Dynamic Strength; Trunk Strength; Stamina; Extent Flexibility; Dynamic Flexibility; Gross Body Coordination; Gross Body Equilibrium; Depth Perception; Glare Sensitivity
Skills: Installation; Equipment Maintenance; Troubleshooting; Repairing
General Work Activities: Performing General Physical Activities; Interacting with Computers; Repairing and Maintaining Mechanical Equipment
Job Characteristics: Sounds, Noise Levels are Distracting, etc.; Very Hot; Extremely Bright or Inadequate Lighting; Whole Body Vibration; High Places; Hazardous Conditions; Hazardous Equipment; Standing; Climbing Ladders, Scaffolds, Poles, etc.; Kneeling, Crouching, or Crawling; Keeping or Regaining Balance; Using Hands on Objects, Tools, or Controls; Bending or Twisting the Body; Making Repetitive Motions
GOE Group/s: 05.05.09 Craft Technology: Mechanical Work; 05.10.01 Crafts: Structural
CIP Program/s: 010204 Agricultural Power Machinery Operator; 470303 Industrial Machinery Maintenance and Repair
Related DOT Job/s: 630.684-018 PUMP INSTALLER; 637.281-010 PUMP ERECTOR

85999C BLACKSMITHS. OOH Title/s: Mechanics, Installers, and Repairers

Forge and repair metal products, according to work order, diagram, or sample, using furnace or forge and hand tools. Heats metal stock or parts in furnace or forge, and tempers forged articles. Hammers stock into specified size and shape, using hammer and anvil or power hammer. Repairs metal articles and farm machinery, such as tongs, hooks, or chains, according to work orders, diagrams, or sample parts. Designs jigs and fixtures, and forges tools and tool parts, such as hammers, chisels, or angle heads. Repairs castings and forgings, using special cold process that requires no welding. Cuts, assembles, and welds metal parts, using welding equipment. Calculates extent of fracture and tensile strength and distribution of strain in material for use in cold repair process. Inserts holding and locking devices in casting and smooths finish using air-powered tools, punches, and strippers. Records repair or fabrication of tools or machine parts.
Yearly Earnings: $25,480
Education: Long-term O-J-T
Knowledge: Production and Processing; Building and Construction
Abilities: Arm-Hand Steadiness; Wrist-Finger Speed; Speed of Limb Movement; Static Strength; Explosive Strength; Dynamic Strength; Trunk Strength; Stamina; Extent Flexibility; Dynamic Flexibility; Gross Body Coordination; Gross Body Equilibrium
Skills: Technology Design; Equipment Maintenance; Repairing
General Work Activities: Performing General Physical Activities; Handling and Moving Objects; Repairing and Maintaining Mechanical Equipment
Job Characteristics: Sounds, Noise Levels are Distracting, etc.; Very Hot; Extremely Bright or Inadequate Lighting; Contaminants; Hazardous Equipment; Hazardous Situations; Using Hands on Objects, Tools, or Controls; Making Repetitive Motions; Common Protective or Safety Attire; Importance of Repeating Same Tasks; Pace Determined by Speed of Equipment

GOE Group/s: 05.05.06 Craft Technology: Metal Fabrication and Repair; 05.10.01 Crafts: Structural
CIP Program/s: 480501 Machinist/Machine Technologist; 480599 Precision Metal Workers, Other
Related DOT Job/s: 610.381-010 BLACKSMITH; 610.381-014 BLACKSMITH APPRENTICE; 619.281-010 CASTING REPAIRER

85999D GUNSMITHS. OOH Title/s: Mechanics, Installers, and Repairers

Repair and modify firearms to blueprint and customer specifications, using hand tools and machines, such as grinders, planers, and millers. Operates metal-working machines to enlarge caliber of bore, cut rifling in barrel, and grind and polish metal parts of firearms. Installs and aligns parts of gun, such as action sights, barrel, or choke device, using screws and hand tools. Refinishes wooden stocks for guns, using sanding and rubbing tools, finishing oil, and lacquer. Immerses metal parts in bluing salt bath to rust-proof surface and impart blue color to metal. Fires gun to determine strength characteristics, correct alignment, and assembly of piece. Designs and fabricates tools, testing equipment, and parts for guns according to blueprint or customer specifications, using hand tools and machines. Develops plans and calculates details—such as bullet-flight arcs, projectile velocity, and sight positions—to design new gun.
Yearly Earnings: $25,480
Education: Long-term O-J-T
Knowledge: Design; Physics
Abilities: Originality; Visualization; Arm-Hand Steadiness; Manual Dexterity; Finger Dexterity; Wrist-Finger Speed; Speed of Limb Movement; Explosive Strength; Dynamic Strength
Skills: Technology Design; Installation; Product Inspection; Repairing
General Work Activities: Controlling Machines and Processes; Repairing and Maintaining Mechanical Equipment
Job Characteristics: Hazardous Equipment
GOE Group/s: 05.05.07 Craft Technology: Machining
CIP Program/s: 470402 Gunsmith
Related DOT Job/s: 609.260-010 GUNSMITH, BALLISTICS LABORATORY; 632.281-010 GUNSMITH

85999E AUTOMOBILE WRECKERS. OOH Title/s: Mechanics, Installers, and Repairers

Salvage usable parts from wrecked vehicles, using hand tools and cutting torch. Dismantles wrecked vehicles, using hand tools, bolt cutters, and welding torch, and removes usable parts. Cleans salvaged parts, using solvents and brush, or vapor-degreasing machine. Stores parts in bins according to condition and part number. Sorts, piles, and loads scrap onto railroad cars or trucks. Drives tow truck. Sells usable parts, such as automobile glass and tires.
Yearly Earnings: $25,480
Education: Long-term O-J-T
Knowledge: Sales and Marketing
Abilities: Arm-Hand Steadiness; Manual Dexterity; Multilimb Coordination; Rate Control; Reaction Time; Speed of Limb Movement; Static Strength; Explosive Strength; Dynamic Strength; Trunk Strength; Stamina; Extent Flexibility; Dynamic Flexibility; Gross Body Coordination; Gross Body Equilibrium
Skills: None above average
General Work Activities: Performing General Physical Activities; Interacting with Computers; Selling or Influencing Others
Job Characteristics: Sounds, Noise Levels are Distracting, etc.; Contaminants; Cramped Work Space, Awkward Positions; Hazardous Equipment; Hazardous Situations; Kneeling, Crouching, or Crawling; Keeping or Regaining Balance; Using Hands on Objects, Tools, or Controls; Bending or Twisting the Body
GOE Group/s: 05.12.15 Elemental Work: Mechanical: Mechanical Work
CIP Program/s: 000000 NO CIP ASSIGNED
Related DOT Job/s: 620.684-010 AUTOMOBILE WRECKER

85999F DIVERS. OOH Title/s: No related OOH occupation

Dive below surface of water, using diving suit or scuba gear. Descends into water with aid of diver helper, using scuba gear or diving suit. Communicates with surface while underwater by signal line or telephone. Searches for lost or sunken objects, such as bodies, torpedoes, equipment, and ships. Recovers objects by placing rigging around sunken objects and hooking rigging to crane lines. Inspects docks, hulls and propellers of ships, underwater pipelines, cables, and sewers. Repairs ships and other structures below the water line, using caulk, bolts, and hand tools. Cuts and welds steel, using underwater welding equipment. Removes obstructions from strainers and marine railways or launching ways, using pneumatic and power hand tools. Sets or guides placement of pilings and sandbags to provide support for structures, such as docks, bridges, cofferdams, and platforms. Drills holes in rock, and rigs explosives for underwater demolitions. Photographs underwater structures or marine life. Levels rails, using wedges and maul or sledgehammer.
Yearly Earnings: NA
Education: Unknown
Knowledge: Building and Construction; Mechanical; Physics; Fine Arts
Abilities: Flexibility of Closure; Perceptual Speed; Spatial Orientation; Arm-Hand Steadiness; Manual Dexterity; Finger Dexterity; Multilimb Coordination; Response Orientation; Rate Control; Reaction Time; Wrist-Finger Speed; Speed of Limb Movement; Static Strength; Explosive Strength; Dynamic Strength; Trunk Strength; Stamina; Extent Flexibility; Dynamic Flexibility; Gross Body Coordination; Gross Body Equilibrium; Far Vision; Visual Color Discrimination; Night Vision; Peripheral Vision; Depth Perception
Skills: Repairing
General Work Activities: Performing General Physical Activities; Repairing and Maintaining Mechanical Equipment
Job Characteristics: Very Hot; Extremely Bright or Inadequate Lighting; Cramped Work Space, Awkward Positions; Hazardous Conditions; Hazardous Situations; Kneeling, Crouching, or Crawling; Keeping or Regaining Balance; Bending or Twisting the Body; Making Repetitive Motions; Common Protective or Safety Attire; Specialized Protective or Safety Attire; Consequence of Error; Importance of Being Aware of New Events
GOE Group/s: 05.10.01 Crafts: Structural
CIP Program/s: 490304 Diver (Professional)
Related DOT Job/s: 379.384-010 SCUBA DIVER; 899.261-010 DIVER

85999G ALL OTHER MECHANICS, INSTALLERS, AND REPAIRERS. OOH Title/s: All Other Mechanics, Installers, and Repairers

All other mechanics, installers, and repairers not classified separately above.
Yearly Earnings: $25,480
Education: Long-term O-J-T
GOE Group/s: 05.12.12 Elemental Work: Mechanical: Structural Work; 06.02.24 Production Work: Manual Work, Metal and Plastics; 06.04.24 Elemental Work: Industrial: Manual Work, Metal and Plastics
CIP Program/s: 470607 Aircraft Mechanic/Technician, Airframe; 470608 Aircraft Mechanic/Technician, Powerplant
Related DOT Job/s: 621.684-014 RECLAMATION WORKER; 806.384-038 PRESSURE SEALER-AND-TESTER; 807.684-018 AIRCRAFT SKIN BURNISHER

Carpenters, Drywall Workers, and Lathers

87102A CONSTRUCTION CARPENTERS. OOH

Title/s: Carpenters

Construct, erect, install, and repair structures and fixtures of wood, plywood, and wallboard, using carpenter's hand tools and power tools. Shapes or cuts materials to specified measurements, using hand tools, machines, or power saw. Assembles and fastens materials, using hand tools and wood screws, nails, dowel pins, or glue, to make framework or props. Builds or repairs cabinets, doors, frameworks, floors, and other wooden fixtures used in buildings, using woodworking machines, carpenter's hand tools, and power tools. Installs structures and fixtures (such as windows, frames, floorings, and trim), or hardware, using carpenter's hand and power tools. Fills cracks and other defects in plaster or plasterboard and sands patch, using patching plaster, trowel, and sanding tool. Finishes surfaces of woodworking or wallboard in houses and buildings, using paint, hand tools, and paneling. Removes damaged or defective parts or sections of structure, and repairs or replaces, using hand tools. Measures and marks cutting lines on materials, using ruler, pencil, chalk, and marking gauge. Verifies trueness of structure, using plumb bob and level. Studies specifications in blueprints, sketches, or building plans to determine materials required and dimensions of structure to be fabricated. Prepares layout according to blueprint or oral instructions, using rule, framing square, and calipers. Inspects ceiling or floor tile, wall coverings, siding, glass, or woodwork to detect broken or damaged structures. Estimates amount and kind of lumber or other materials required, and selects and orders them.

Yearly Earnings: $22,360

Education: Long-term O-J-T

Knowledge: Design; Building and Construction

Abilities: Spatial Orientation; Visualization; Arm-Hand Steadiness; Manual Dexterity; Finger Dexterity; Control Precision; Multilimb Coordination; Wrist-Finger Speed; Speed of Limb Movement; Static Strength; Explosive Strength; Dynamic Strength; Trunk Strength; Stamina; Extent Flexibility; Dynamic Flexibility; Gross Body Coordination; Gross Body Equilibrium; Peripheral Vision; Depth Perception; Glare Sensitivity

Skills: Installation; Repairing; Management of Material Resources

General Work Activities: Performing General Physical Activities

Job Characteristics: Sounds, Noise Levels are Distracting, etc.; Very Hot; Extremely Bright or Inadequate Lighting; Contaminants; Cramped Work Space, Awkward Positions; Whole Body Vibration; High Places; Hazardous Equipment; Standing; Climbing Ladders, Scaffolds, Poles, etc.; Kneeling, Crouching, or Crawling; Keeping or Regaining Balance; Using Hands on Objects, Tools, or Controls; Bending or Twisting the Body; Making Repetitive Motions; Common Protective or Safety Attire

GOE Group/s: 01.06.02 Craft Arts: Arts and Crafts; 05.05.02 Craft Technology: Construction and Maintenance; 05.10.04 Crafts: Structural-Mechanical-Electrical-Electronic

CIP Program/s: 460201 Carpenter

Related DOT Job/s: 860.281-010 CARPENTER, MAINTENANCE; 860.381-022 CARPENTER; 860.381-026 CARPENTER APPRENTICE; 860.381-034 CARPENTER, MOLD; 860.381-038 CARPENTER, RAILCAR; 869.381-010 HOUSE REPAIRER; 962.281-010 PROP MAKER

87102B ROUGH CARPENTERS. OOH Title/s: Carpenters

Build rough wooden structures—such as concrete forms, scaffolds; tunnel, bridge, or sewer supports; billboard signs; and temporary frame shelters—according to sketches, blueprints, or oral instructions. Assembles and fastens material together to construct wood or metal framework of structure, using bolts, nails, or screws. Studies blueprints and diagrams to determine dimensions of structure or form to be constructed or erected. Measures materials or distances—using square, measuring tape, or rule—to lay out work. Cuts or saws boards, timbers, or plywood to required size, using handsaw, power saw, or woodworking machine. Bores bolt-holes in timber with masonry or concrete walls, using power drill. Erects prefabricated forms, framework, scaffolds, hoists, roof supports, or chutes, using hand tools, plumb rule, and level. Installs rough door and window frames, subflooring, fixtures, or temporary supports in structures undergoing construction or repair. Anchors and braces forms and other structures in place, using nails, bolts, anchor rods, steel cables, planks, wedges, and timbers. Examines structural timbers and supports to detect decay, and replaces timber, using hand tools, nuts, and bolts. Fabricates parts, using woodworking and metal-working machines. Digs or directs digging of post holes, and sets pole to support structure.

Yearly Earnings: $22,360

Education: Long-term O-J-T

Knowledge: Building and Construction

Abilities: Visualization; Manual Dexterity; Speed of Limb Movement; Static Strength; Trunk Strength; Gross Body Equilibrium

Skills: Installation

General Work Activities: Performing General Physical Activities

Job Characteristics: Cramped Work Space, Awkward Positions; High Places; Hazardous Equipment; Standing; Climbing Ladders, Scaffolds, Poles, etc.; Kneeling, Crouching, or Crawling; Keeping or Regaining Balance; Using Hands on Objects, Tools, or Controls; Bending or Twisting the Body; Making Repetitive Motions; Common Protective or Safety Attire; Importance of Being Exact or Accurate; Importance of Being Sure All is Done

GOE Group/s: 05.05.02 Craft Technology: Construction and Maintenance; 05.05.06 Craft Technology: Metal Fabrication and Repair

CIP Program/s: 010201 Agricultural Mechanization, General; 460201 Carpenter

Related DOT Job/s: 860.381-030 CARPENTER, BRIDGE; 860.381-042 CARPENTER, ROUGH; 860.381-046 FORM BUILDER; 869.361-018 SIGN ERECTOR-AND-REPAIRER; 869.381-034 TIMBER FRAMER

87102C TANK BUILDERS AND COOPERS. OOH

Title/s: Carpenters

Construct or assemble and erect wooden tanks for storing liquids. Determines dimensions of wooden parts of tank from blueprints, diagrams, and other specifications, using measuring instruments. Cuts tank parts from lumber, using power tools and carpenter's hand tools. Assembles and fastens cut or precut parts together, using hammer and staple gun. Shapes parts, using hand tools to trim and bevel edges and to form bottoms, headings, and ends of tanks. Positions hoops or rods around tank and tightens them, using hand tools, to secure them in place. Measures or marks position of wooden parts on foundation. Levels parts, using leveling shims, carpenter's level, and hand tools. Places or directs placement of assembled tank on foundation, using powered hoist, and secures it on foundation, using hand tools. Tests tanks to determine leaks and holding properties, and adjusts tank sections to repair lead, using caulking. Removes and replaces defective parts of tank or hogshead mat, using windlass to compress staves and loosen hoops, and hand tools. Inspects parts for fit or to detect damage or defect. Plugs holes with wooden plugs.

Yearly Earnings: $22,360

Education: Long-term O-J-T

Knowledge: Building and Construction

Abilities: Arm-Hand Steadiness; Manual Dexterity; Finger Dexterity; Control Precision; Multilimb Coordination; Wrist-Finger Speed;

Speed of Limb Movement; Static Strength; Explosive Strength; Dynamic Strength; Trunk Strength; Stamina; Dynamic Flexibility; Gross Body Coordination; Gross Body Equilibrium
Skills: Technology Design; Product Inspection; Repairing
General Work Activities: None above average
Job Characteristics: Sounds, Noise Levels are Distracting, etc.; Very Hot; Extremely Bright or Inadequate Lighting; High Places; Hazardous Equipment; Standing; Climbing Ladders, Scaffolds, Poles, etc.; Kneeling, Crouching, or Crawling; Keeping or Regaining Balance; Using Hands on Objects, Tools, or Controls; Bending or Twisting the Body; Making Repetitive Motions
GOE Group/s: 05.05.02 Craft Technology: Construction and Maintenance
CIP Program/s: 460201 Carpenter
Related DOT Job/s: 764.684-022 COOPER; 764.684-026 HOGSHEAD COOPER I; 860.381-066 TANK BUILDER AND ERECTOR; 860.381-070 TANK ERECTOR

87102D CARPENTER ASSEMBLERS AND REPAIRERS. OOH Title/s: Carpenters

Perform a variety of tasks requiring a limited knowledge of carpentry, such as applying siding and weatherboard to building exteriors or assembling and erecting prefabricated buildings. Measures and marks location of studs, leaders, and receptacle openings, using tape measure, template, and marker. Cuts sidings and moldings, sections of weatherboard, and openings in platerboard, and lumber, using hand tools and power tools. Aligns and fastens materials together, using hand tools and power tools, to form building or bracing. Lays out and aligns materials on work table or in assembly jig according to specified instructions. Installs prefabricated windows and doors, insulation, walls, and ceiling and floor panels or siding, using adhesives, hoists, hand tools, and power tools. Trims overlapping edges of wood, and weatherboard, using portable router or power saw and hand tools. Removes surface defects, using knife, scraper, wet sponge, electric iron, and sanding tools. Repairs or replaces defective locks, hinges, cranks, and pieces of wood, using glue, hand tools, and power tools. Realigns windows and screens to fit casements, and oils moving parts. Measures cut materials to determine conformance to specifications, using tape measure. Examines wood surfaces for defects, such as nicks, cracks, or blisters. Fills cracks, seams, depressions, and nail holes with filler. Studies blueprints, specification sheets, and drawings to determine style and type of window or wall panel required. Moves panel or roof section to other work stations or to storage or shipping area, using electric hoist. Directs crane operator in positioning floor, wall, ceiling, and roof panels on house foundation. Applies stain, paints or crayons to defects and filter to touch up the repaired area.
Yearly Earnings: $22,360
Education: Long-term O-J-T
Knowledge: Building and Construction
Abilities: Spatial Orientation; Visualization; Arm-Hand Steadiness; Manual Dexterity; Multilimb Coordination; Speed of Limb Movement; Static Strength; Explosive Strength; Dynamic Strength; Trunk Strength; Stamina; Extent Flexibility; Dynamic Flexibility; Gross Body Coordination; Gross Body Equilibrium; Depth Perception; Glare Sensitivity
Skills: Installation; Repairing
General Work Activities: Performing General Physical Activities
Job Characteristics: Sounds, Noise Levels are Distracting, etc.; Very Hot; Extremely Bright or Inadequate Lighting; Contaminants; Cramped Work Space, Awkward Positions; Whole Body Vibration; High Places; Hazardous Conditions; Hazardous Equipment; Standing; Climbing Ladders, Scaffolds, Poles, etc.; Kneeling, Crouching, or Crawling; Keeping or Regaining Balance; Using Hands on Objects, Tools, or Controls; Bending or Twisting the Body; Making Repetitive Motions; Common Protective or Safety Attire; Importance of Repeating Same Tasks
GOE Group/s: 05.10.01 Crafts: Structural; 05.12.12 Elemental Work: Mechanical: Structural Work; 06.02.22 Production Work: Manual Work, Assembly Large Parts; 06.02.31 Production Work: Manual Work, Laying Out and Marking; 06.04.22 Elemental Work: Industrial: Manual Work, Assembly Large Parts; 06.04.25 Elemental Work: Industrial: Manual Work, Wood
CIP Program/s: 460201 Carpenter
Related DOT Job/s: 769.684-038 REPAIRER, ASSEMBLED WOOD PRODUCTS; 860.664-010 CARPENTER I; 860.681-010 CARPENTER II; 860.684-010 BUILDER, BEAM; 860.684-014 SIDER; 863.684-010 COMPOSITION-WEATHERBOARD APPLIER; 863.684-014 SIDER; 869.684-018 ASSEMBLER, SUBASSEMBLY; 869.684-034 LAY-OUT WORKER; 869.684-038 PANEL INSTALLER; 869.684-042 ROOF ASSEMBLER I; 869.684-062 STULL INSTALLER; 869.684-066 TRIMMER; 899.684-042 WINDOW REPAIRER; 920.684-010 CRATER

87102E BOAT AND SHIP BUILDERS. OOH Title/s: Carpenters

Construct and repair ships or boats, according to blueprints. Cuts and forms parts, such as keel, ribs, sidings, and support structures and blocks, using woodworking hand tools and power tools. Constructs and shapes wooden frames, structures, and other parts according to blueprint specifications, using hand tools, power tools, and measuring instruments. Assembles and installs hull timbers and other structures in ship, using adhesive, measuring instruments, and hand tools or power tools. Attaches metal part—such as fittings, plates, and bulkheads—to ship, using brace and bits, augers, and wrenches. Cuts out defect, using power tools and hand tools, and fits and secures replacement part, using caulking gun, adhesive, or hand tools. Smooths and finishes ship surfaces, using power sander, broadax, adze, and paint, and waxes and buffs surface to specified finish. Establishes dimensional reference points on layout and hull to make template of parts and to locate machinery and equipment. Measures and marks dimensional lines on lumber, following template and using scriber. Positions and secures support structures on construction area. Inspects boat to determine location and extent of defect. Marks outline of boat on building dock, shipway, or mold loft according to blueprint specifications, using measuring instruments and crayon. Attaches hoist to sections of hull, and directs hoist operator to align parts over blocks, according to layout of boat. Consults with customer or supervisor, and reads blueprint to determine necessary repairs.
Yearly Earnings: $22,360
Education: Long-term O-J-T
Knowledge: Production and Processing; Engineering and Technology; Design; Building and Construction; Mechanical
Abilities: Information Ordering; Visualization; Arm-Hand Steadiness; Manual Dexterity; Speed of Limb Movement; Static Strength; Dynamic Strength; Extent Flexibility; Gross Body Equilibrium
Skills: Operations Analysis; Installation; Repairing
General Work Activities: Performing General Physical Activities
Job Characteristics: Very Hot; Cramped Work Space, Awkward Positions; High Places; Standing; Climbing Ladders, Scaffolds, Poles, etc.; Kneeling, Crouching, or Crawling; Keeping or Regaining Balance; Using Hands on Objects, Tools, or Controls; Bending or Twisting the Body; Making Repetitive Motions; Importance of Being Sure All is Done
GOE Group/s: 05.05.02 Craft Technology: Construction and Maintenance
CIP Program/s: 460201 Carpenter; 490306 Marine Maintenance and Repair

Related DOT Job/s: 807.361-014 BOAT REPAIRER; 860.361-010 BOATBUILDER, WOOD; 860.361-014 BOATBUILDER APPRENTICE, WOOD; 860.381-058 SHIPWRIGHT; 860.381-062 SHIPWRIGHT APPRENTICE

87102F SHIP CARPENTERS AND JOINERS. OOH Title/s: Carpenters

Fabricate, assemble, install, or repair wooden furnishings in ships or boats. Reads blueprints to determine dimensions of furnishings in ships or boats. Shapes and laminates wood to form parts of ship, using steam chambers, clamps, glue, and jigs. Assembles and installs hardware, gaskets, floors, furnishings, or insulation, using adhesive, hand tools, and power tools. Repairs structural woodwork and replaces defective parts and equipment, using hand tools and power tools. Cuts wood or glass to specified dimensions, using hand tools and power tools. Constructs floors, doors, and partitions, using woodworking machines, hand tools, and power tools. Shapes irregular parts and trims excess material from bulkhead and furnishings to ensure that fit meets specifications. Transfers dimensions or measurements of wood parts or bulkhead on plywood, using measuring instruments and marking devices. Greases gears and other moving parts of machines on ship.
Yearly Earnings: $22,360
Education: Long-term O-J-T
Knowledge: Design; Building and Construction
Abilities: Visualization; Manual Dexterity; Speed of Limb Movement; Stamina; Dynamic Flexibility; Gross Body Equilibrium
Skills: Installation; Repairing
General Work Activities: Performing General Physical Activities
Job Characteristics: Cramped Work Space, Awkward Positions; High Places; Hazardous Equipment; Hazardous Situations; Standing; Climbing Ladders, Scaffolds, Poles, etc.; Kneeling, Crouching, or Crawling; Keeping or Regaining Balance; Using Hands on Objects, Tools, or Controls; Bending or Twisting the Body; Making Repetitive Motions; Common Protective or Safety Attire; Specialized Protective or Safety Attire; Importance of Being Sure All is Done
GOE Group/s: 05.05.02 Craft Technology: Construction and Maintenance
CIP Program/s: 460201 Carpenter; 490306 Marine Maintenance and Repair
Related DOT Job/s: 806.281-058 CARPENTER, PROTOTYPE; 860.281-014 CARPENTER, SHIP; 860.381-050 JOINER; 860.381-054 JOINER APPRENTICE

87105 CEILING TILE INSTALLERS AND ACOUSTICAL CARPENTERS. OOH Title/s: Carpenters

Apply or mount acoustical tiles or blocks, strips, or sheets of shock-absorbing materials to ceilings and walls of buildings to reduce or reflect sound. Materials may be of decorative quality. Exclude carpet, wood, or hard tile installers. Applies acoustical tiles or shock-absorbing materials to ceilings and walls of buildings to reduce or reflect sound and to decorate rooms. Applies cement to back of tile and presses tile into place, aligning with layout marks and joints of previously laid tile. Nails or screws molding to wall to support, and seals joint between ceiling tile and wall. Scribes and cuts edges of tile to fit wall where wall molding is not specified. Nails channels or wood furring strips to surfaces to provide mounting for tile. Cuts tiles for fixture and borders, using keyhole saw, and inserts tiles into supporting framework. Measures and marks surface to lay out work according to blueprints and drawings. Hangs dry lines (stretched string) to wall molding to guide positioning of main runners. Inspects furrings, mechanical mountings, and masonry surface for plumbness and level, using spirit or water level. Washes concrete surfaces with washing soda and zinc sulfate solution before mounting tile to increase adhesive qualities of surfaces.
Yearly Earnings: $22,360
Education: Moderate-term O-J-T
Knowledge: Building and Construction
Abilities: Extent Flexibility; Dynamic Flexibility; Gross Body Equilibrium
Skills: None above average
General Work Activities: Performing General Physical Activities
Job Characteristics: Sounds, Noise Levels are Distracting, etc.; Contaminants; Cramped Work Space, Awkward Positions; High Places; Hazardous Conditions; Hazardous Equipment; Hazardous Situations; Standing; Climbing Ladders, Scaffolds, Poles, etc.; Kneeling, Crouching, or Crawling; Keeping or Regaining Balance; Using Hands on Objects, Tools, or Controls; Bending or Twisting the Body; Common Protective or Safety Attire
GOE Group/s: 05.05.02 Craft Technology: Construction and Maintenance
CIP Program/s: 460201 Carpenter
Related DOT Job/s: 860.381-010 ACOUSTICAL CARPENTER

87108 DRYWALL INSTALLERS. OOH Title/s: Drywall Workers and Lathers

Apply plasterboard or other wallboard to ceilings and interior walls of buildings. Scribes cutting lines on drywall, using straightedge and utility knife, and breaks board along cut lines. Trims rough edges from wallboard to maintain even joints, using knife. Fits and fastens wallboard or pasterboard into specified position, using hand tools, portable power tools, or adhesive. Measures and marks cutting lines on framing, drywall, and trim, using tape measure, straightedge or square, and marking devices. Cuts openings into board for electrical outlets, windows, vents, or fixtures, using keyhole saw or other cutting tools. Cuts metal or wood framing, angle and channel iron, and trim to size, using cutting tools. Installs horizontal and vertical metal or wooden studs for attachment of wallboard on interior walls, using hand tools. Suspends angle iron grid and channel iron from ceiling, using wire. Lays out reference lines and points, computes position of framing and furring channels, and marks position, using chalkline. Reads blueprints and other specifications to determine method of installation, work procedures, and material and tool requirements. Assembles and installs metal framing and decorative trim for windows, doorways, and bents. Removes plaster, drywall, or paneling, using crowbar and hammer. Installs blanket insulation between studs, and tacks plastic moisture barrier over insulation.
Yearly Earnings: $22,100
Education: Moderate-term O-J-T
Knowledge: Design; Building and Construction
Abilities: Gross Body Equilibrium
Skills: Installation
General Work Activities: Performing General Physical Activities
Job Characteristics: Very Hot; Contaminants; Cramped Work Space, Awkward Positions; High Places; Climbing Ladders, Scaffolds, Poles, etc.; Keeping or Regaining Balance; Importance of Repeating Same Tasks
GOE Group/s: 05.05.04 Craft Technology: Painting, Plastering, and Paperhanging; 05.10.01 Crafts: Structural; 06.04.34 Elemental Work: Industrial: Manual Work, Assorted Materials
CIP Program/s: 469999 Construction Trades, Other
Related DOT Job/s: 842.361-030 DRY-WALL APPLICATOR; 842.684-014 DRY-WALL APPLICATOR; 869.684-050 SHEETROCK APPLICATOR

87111 TAPERS. OOH Title/s: Drywall Workers and Lathers

Seal joints between plasterboard or other wallboard to prepare wall surface for painting or papering. Spreads sealing compound between boards, using trowel, broadknife, or spatula. Presses paper tape over joint to embed tape into sealing compound and seal joint. Tapes joint, using mechanical applicator that spreads compound and

embeds tape in one operation. Spreads and smooths cementing material over tape, using trowel or floating machine to blend joint with wall surface. Sands rough spots after cement has dried. Fills cracks and holes in walls and ceiling with sealing compound. Installs metal molding at corners in lieu of sealant and tape. Mixes sealing compound by hand or with portable electric mixer. Applies texturizing compound and primer to walls and ceiling preparatory to final finishing, using brushes, roller, or spray gun. Countersinks nails or screws below surface of wall prior to applying sealing compound, using hammer or screwdriver.
Yearly Earnings: $22,100
Education: Moderate-term O-J-T
Knowledge: Building and Construction
Abilities: Gross Body Equilibrium
Skills: None above average
General Work Activities: Performing General Physical Activities
Job Characteristics: Sounds, Noise Levels are Distracting, etc.; Contaminants; Cramped Work Space, Awkward Positions; High Places; Hazardous Conditions; Hazardous Situations; Standing; Climbing Ladders, Scaffolds, Poles, etc.; Kneeling, Crouching, or Crawling; Keeping or Regaining Balance; Using Hands on Objects, Tools, or Controls; Bending or Twisting the Body; Common Protective or Safety Attire
GOE Group/s: 05.10.01 Crafts: Structural
CIP Program/s: 469999 Construction Trades, Other
Related DOT Job/s: 842.664-010 TAPER

87114 LATHERS. OOH Title/s: Drywall Workers and Lathers

Fasten wooden, metal, or plasterboard lath to walls, ceilings, and partitions of buildings to provide supporting base for plaster, or fire-proofing or acoustical material. Wires, nails, clips, or staples lath to framework, ceiling joints, and flat concrete surfaces. Bends metal lath to fit corners, or attaches preformed corner reinforcements. Erects horizontal metal framework to which laths are fastened, using nails, bolts, and studgun. Wires plasterer's channels to overhead structural framework to provide support for plaster or acoustical ceiling tile. Drives end of wooden or metal studs into holes to provide anchor for furring or pasterboard lath. Wires horizontal strips to furring to stiffen framework. Drills holes in floor and ceiling, using portable electric tools. Cuts lath to fit openings and projections, using hand tools or portable power tools. Installs metal casings around openings, metal window stools, and metal trim and plaster grounds nailed to studding. Welds metal frame supports to steel structural members.
Yearly Earnings: $22,100
Education: Moderate-term O-J-T
Knowledge: Building and Construction
Abilities: Multilimb Coordination; Explosive Strength; Stamina; Extent Flexibility; Gross Body Equilibrium
Skills: Installation
General Work Activities: None above average
Job Characteristics: Whole Body Vibration; High Places; Standing; Climbing Ladders, Scaffolds, Poles, etc.; Kneeling, Crouching, or Crawling; Bending or Twisting the Body
GOE Group/s: 05.10.01 Crafts: Structural
CIP Program/s: 469999 Construction Trades, Other
Related DOT Job/s: 842.361-010 LATHER; 842.361-014 LATHER APPRENTICE

87121 BRATTICE BUILDERS. OOH Title/s: Carpenters

Build doors or brattices (ventilation walls or partitions) in underground passageways to control the proper circulation of air through the passageways and to work areas. Installs rigid and flexible air ducts to transport air to work areas. Erects partitions to support roof in areas unsuited to timbering or bolting. Drills and blasts obstructing boulders to reopen ventilation shafts.
Yearly Earnings: $22,360
Education: Long-term O-J-T
Knowledge: Building and Construction
Abilities: Explosive Strength; Dynamic Strength; Trunk Strength; Stamina; Extent Flexibility; Gross Body Equilibrium
Skills: Technology Design; Installation
General Work Activities: Performing General Physical Activities
Job Characteristics: Sounds, Noise Levels are Distracting, etc.; Very Hot; Cramped Work Space, Awkward Positions; Whole Body Vibration; Hazardous Conditions; Standing; Climbing Ladders, Scaffolds, Poles, etc.; Keeping or Regaining Balance; Specialized Protective or Safety Attire
GOE Group/s: 05.10.01 Crafts: Structural
CIP Program/s: 460201 Carpenter
Related DOT Job/s: 869.684-058 STOPPING BUILDER

Electricians

87202A ELECTRICIANS. OOH Title/s: Electricians

Install, maintain, and repair electrical wiring, equipment, and fixtures. Installs electrical wiring, equipment, apparatus, and fixtures, using hand tools and power tools. Maintains and repairs or replaces wiring, equipment, and fixtures, using hand tools. Plans layout and installation of electrical wiring, equipment, and fixtures consistent with specifications and local codes. Inspects systems and electrical parts to detect hazards, defects, and need for adjustments or repair. Tests electrical systems and continuity of circuits in electrical wiring, equipment, and fixtures, using testing devices, such as ohmmeter, voltmeter, and oscilloscope. Diagnoses malfunctioning systems, apparatus, and components, using test equipment and hand tools. Readies and assembles electrical wiring, equipment, and fixtures, using specifications and hand tools. Prepares sketches of location of wiring and equipment, or follows blueprints to determine location of equipment and conformance to safety codes. Climbs ladder to install, maintain, or repair electrical wiring, equipment, and fixtures. Constructs and fabricates parts, using hand tools and specifications. Possesses electrician's license or identification card to meet governmental regulations. Directs and trains workers to install, maintain, or repair electrical wiring, equipment, and fixtures. Drives vehicle, operates floodlights, and places flares during power failure or emergency.
Yearly Earnings: $30,472
Education: Long-term O-J-T
Knowledge: Computers and Electronics; Engineering and Technology; Design; Building and Construction; Physics; Education and Training; Public Safety and Security
Abilities: Memorization; Arm-Hand Steadiness; Manual Dexterity; Finger Dexterity; Multilimb Coordination; Rate Control; Wrist-Finger Speed; Speed of Limb Movement; Trunk Strength; Extent Flexibility; Dynamic Flexibility; Gross Body Equilibrium; Near Vision; Visual Color Discrimination; Night Vision; Depth Perception
Skills: Instructing; Equipment Selection; Installation; Testing; Equipment Maintenance; Troubleshooting; Repairing
General Work Activities: Identifying Objects, Actions, and Events; Inspecting Equipment, Structures, or Material; Performing General Physical Activities; Interacting with Computers; Drafting and Specifying Technical Devices, etc.; Implementing Ideas, Programs, etc.; Repairing and Maintaining Electrical Equipment; Coordinating Work and Activities of Others; Teaching Others; Guiding, Directing and Motivating Subordinates; Coaching and Developing Others
Job Characteristics: Supervise, Coach, Train Others; Responsibility for Outcomes and Results; Sounds, Noise Levels are Distracting, etc.; Cramped Work Space, Awkward Positions; High Places; Hazardous

Conditions; Hazardous Equipment; Climbing Ladders, Scaffolds, Poles, etc.; Keeping or Regaining Balance; Using Hands on Objects, Tools, or Controls; Bending or Twisting the Body; Common Protective or Safety Attire; Specialized Protective or Safety Attire
GOE Group/s: 05.05.05 Craft Technology: Electrical-Electronic Systems Installation and Repair; 05.05.10 Craft Technology: Electrical-Electronic Equipment Repair
CIP Program/s: 010204 Agricultural Power Machinery Operator; 460301 Electrical and Power Transmission Installer, General; 460302 Electrician; 490306 Marine Maintenance and Repair
Related DOT Job/s: 729.381-018 STREET-LIGHT REPAIRER; 822.361-018 PROTECTIVE-SIGNAL INSTALLER; 822.361-022 PROTECTIVE-SIGNAL REPAIRER; 824.261-010 ELECTRICIAN; 824.261-014 ELECTRICIAN APPRENTICE; 824.281-010 AIRPORT ELECTRICIAN; 824.281-018 NEON-SIGN SERVICER; 824.381-010 STREET-LIGHT SERVICER; 824.681-010 ELECTRICIAN; 825.281-014 ELECTRICIAN; 825.381-030 ELECTRICIAN; 825.381-034 ELECTRICIAN APPRENTICE; 829.261-018 ELECTRICIAN, MAINTENANCE

87202C ELECTRICAL UTILITY TROUBLESHOOTERS. OOH Title/s: Electricians

Answer trouble or service calls of customers and attempt to locate source of problem. Troubleshoots electrical interruptions and makes minor repairs or replaces defective parts. Inspects automatic light switches to detect defects, using hand tools. Tests circuits, switches, or meters to locate short circuits or presence of current, using testing device. Climbs pole to reach switch or meter controls, using ladder. Turns power on or off to meter or light switches. Reports or notifies worker or customer of malfunctioning equipment.
Yearly Earnings: $30,472
Education: Long-term O-J-T
Knowledge: Computers and Electronics; Engineering and Technology; Telecommunications
Abilities: Flexibility of Closure; Spatial Orientation; Arm-Hand Steadiness; Manual Dexterity; Finger Dexterity; Multilimb Coordination; Response Orientation; Speed of Limb Movement; Explosive Strength; Dynamic Strength; Stamina; Extent Flexibility; Dynamic Flexibility; Gross Body Coordination; Gross Body Equilibrium; Visual Color Discrimination; Glare Sensitivity
Skills: Testing; Equipment Maintenance; Troubleshooting; Repairing
General Work Activities: Inspecting Equipment, Structures, or Material; Performing General Physical Activities; Repairing and Maintaining Electrical Equipment
Job Characteristics: Provide a Service to Others; Deal with External Customers; Very Hot; Extremely Bright or Inadequate Lighting; Cramped Work Space, Awkward Positions; High Places; Hazardous Conditions; Climbing Ladders, Scaffolds, Poles, etc.; Keeping or Regaining Balance; Bending or Twisting the Body; Special Uniform; Common Protective or Safety Attire; Specialized Protective or Safety Attire
GOE Group/s: 05.10.03 Crafts: Electrical-Electronic
CIP Program/s: 460301 Electrical and Power Transmission Installer, General; 460302 Electrician; 460303 Lineworker
Related DOT Job/s: 952.364-010 TROUBLE SHOOTER I; 952.381-010 SWITCH INSPECTOR

Masons, Concrete Workers, Tile Setters, and Reinforcing Metal Workers

87302 BRICK MASONS. OOH Title/s: Bricklayers and Stonemasons

Lay building materials—such as brick, structural tile, concrete, cinder, glass, gypsum, and terra cotta block (except stone)—to construct or repair walls, partitions, arches, sewers, and other structures. Include refractory brick masons. Lays and aligns bricks, blocks, or tiles to build or repair structures or high-temperature equipment, such as cupolas, kilns, ovens, or furnaces. Applies and smooths mortar or other mixture over work surface and removes excess, using trowel and hand tools. Examines brickwork or structure to determine need for repair. Measures distance from reference points and marks guidelines to lay out work, using plumb bobs and levels. Calculates angles and courses, and determines vertical and horizontal alignment of courses. Mixes specified amount of sand, clay, dirt, or mortar powder with water to form refractory mixture. Applies primer to work surface and fuses plastic liner to primed surface, using torch. Fastens or fuses brick or other building material to structure with wire clamps, anchor holes, torch, or cement. Breaks or cuts bricks, tiles, or blocks to size, using edge of trowel, hammer, or power saw. Positions frame over casings on kiln frame to lay arches or to build new kilns. Cleans working surface to remove scale, dust, soot, or chips of brick and mortar, using broom, wire brush, or scraper. Removes burned or damaged brick or mortar, using sledgehammer, crowbar, chipping gun, or chisel. Sprays or spreads refractories over brickwork to protect against deterioration.
Yearly Earnings: $25,480
Education: Long-term O-J-T
Knowledge: Building and Construction
Abilities: Information Ordering; Visualization; Manual Dexterity; Static Strength; Explosive Strength; Dynamic Strength; Trunk Strength; Stamina; Extent Flexibility; Dynamic Flexibility; Gross Body Equilibrium
Skills: None above average
General Work Activities: Performing General Physical Activities; Handling and Moving Objects
Job Characteristics: Very Hot; Contaminants; Cramped Work Space, Awkward Positions; High Places; Standing; Climbing Ladders, Scaffolds, Poles, etc.; Kneeling, Crouching, or Crawling; Keeping or Regaining Balance; Using Hands on Objects, Tools, or Controls; Bending or Twisting the Body; Making Repetitive Motions
GOE Group/s: 05.05.01 Craft Technology: Masonry, Stone, and Brick Work; 05.10.01 Crafts: Structural; 05.12.08 Elemental Work: Mechanical: Lubricating; 05.12.09 Elemental Work: Mechanical: Masonry
CIP Program/s: 460101 Mason and Tile Setter
Related DOT Job/s: 573.684-010 KILN-DOOR BUILDER; 709.684-046 HOT-TOP LINER; 861.381-010 ACID-TANK LINER; 861.381-014 BRICKLAYER; 861.381-018 BRICKLAYER; 861.381-022 BRICKLAYER APPRENTICE; 861.381-026 BRICKLAYER, FIREBRICK AND REFRACTORY TILE; 861.684-010 CUPOLA PATCHER; 861.684-014 PATCHER; 861.684-022 REPAIRER, KILN CAR; 899.364-010 CHIMNEY REPAIRER

87305B STONE MASONS. OOH Title/s: Bricklayers and Stonemasons

Build stone structures, such as piers, walls, and abutments. Lay walks, curbstones, or special types of masonry for vats, tanks, and floors. Shapes, trims, faces, and cuts marble or stone preparatory to setting, using power saws, cutting equipment, and hand tools. Sets stone or marble in place, according to layout or pattern. Aligns and levels stone or marble, using measuring devices such as rule, square, and plumbline. Lays out wall pattern or foundation of monument, using straightedge, rule, or staked lines. Mixes mortar or grout and pours or spreads mortar or grout on marble slabs, stone, or foundation. Finishes joints between stones, using trowel. Cleans excess mortar or grout from surface of marble, stone, or monument, using sponge, brush, water, or acid. Smooths, polishes, and bevels surfaces, using hand tools and power tools. Lines interiors of molds with treated paper and fills molds with composition-stone mixture. Positions mold along guidelines of wall, presses mold in place, and removes mold and paper from wall. Repairs cracked or chipped areas of ornamental stone or marble surface, using blow-torch and mastic. Removes sections of monument from truck bed, and guides stone onto foundation, using skids, hoist, or truck crane. Drills holes in marble or ornamental stone and anchors bracket. Digs trench for foundation of monument, using pick and shovel.

Yearly Earnings: $25,480

Education: Long-term O-J-T

Knowledge: Building and Construction

Abilities: Wrist-Finger Speed; Speed of Limb Movement; Static Strength; Explosive Strength; Dynamic Strength; Trunk Strength; Stamina; Dynamic Flexibility; Gross Body Equilibrium

Skills: None above average

General Work Activities: Performing General Physical Activities; Handling and Moving Objects; Controlling Machines and Processes; Interacting with Computers

Job Characteristics: Sounds, Noise Levels are Distracting, etc.; Contaminants; Cramped Work Space, Awkward Positions; Whole Body Vibration; High Places; Climbing Ladders, Scaffolds, Poles, etc.; Walking or Running; Kneeling, Crouching, or Crawling; Bending or Twisting the Body; Making Repetitive Motions; Common Protective or Safety Attire; Specialized Protective or Safety Attire

GOE Group/s: 05.05.01 Craft Technology: Masonry, Stone, and Brick Work

CIP Program/s: 460101 Mason and Tile Setter

Related DOT Job/s: 861.361-010 COMPOSITION-STONE APPLICATOR; 861.361-014 MONUMENT SETTER; 861.381-030 MARBLE SETTER; 861.381-038 STONEMASON; 861.381-042 STONEMASON APPRENTICE

87308 HARD TILE SETTERS. OOH Title/s: Tilesetters

Apply tile to walls, floors, ceilings, and promenade roof decks following design specifications. Positions and presses or taps tile with trowel handle to affix tile to plaster or adhesive base. Measures and marks surfaces to be tiled and lays out work, following blueprints. Cuts tile backing to required size, using shears. Spreads plaster or concrete over surface to form tile base and levels to specified thickness, using brush, trowel, and screed. Spreads mastic or other adhesive base on roof deck to form base for promenade tile, using serrated spreader. Cuts and shapes tile, using tile cutters and biters. Selects tile and other items to be installed, such as bathroom accessories, walls, panels, and cabinets, according to specifications. Measures and cuts metal lath to size for walls and ceilings, using tin snips. Tacks lath to wall and ceiling surfaces, using staple gun or hammer. Wipes grout between tiles and removes excess, using wet sponge. Mixes and applies mortar or cement to edges and ends of drain tiles to seal halves and joints. Brushes glue onto manila paper on which design has been drawn, and positions tile's finished side down onto paper. Installs and anchors fixtures in designated positions, using hand tools. Splits and places drain tiles on runners to form insulating conduit for water or steam pipes, according to specified procedures. Applies completed units to cement surface and removes paper to form mosaic. Lays runners in trench and adjusts slope, using carpenter's level, shovel, and loose soil.

Yearly Earnings: $24,856

Education: Long-term O-J-T

Knowledge: Design; Building and Construction

Abilities: Gross Body Equilibrium

Skills: Installation

General Work Activities: Performing General Physical Activities; Handling and Moving Objects

Job Characteristics: Extremely Bright or Inadequate Lighting; Contaminants; Cramped Work Space, Awkward Positions; High Places; Hazardous Conditions; Hazardous Equipment; Hazardous Situations; Climbing Ladders, Scaffolds, Poles, etc.; Kneeling, Crouching, or Crawling; Keeping or Regaining Balance; Using Hands on Objects, Tools, or Controls; Bending or Twisting the Body; Making Repetitive Motions

GOE Group/s: 05.05.01 Craft Technology: Masonry, Stone, and Brick Work; 05.10.01 Crafts: Structural; 05.12.09 Elemental Work: Mechanical: Masonry

CIP Program/s: 460101 Mason and Tile Setter

Related DOT Job/s: 779.381-014 MOSAIC WORKER; 861.381-054 TILE SETTER; 861.381-058 TILE SETTER APPRENTICE; 861.381-062 TILE-CONDUIT LAYER; 861.684-018 TILE SETTER

87311 CONCRETE AND TERRAZZO FINISHERS. OOH Title/s: Concrete Masons and Terrazzo Workers

Apply cement, sand, pigment, or marble chips to floors, stairways, and cabinet fixtures to finish and attain durable and decorative surfaces, according to specifications and drawings. Finish surfaces to remove imperfections from freshly poured concrete walls, roads, walkways, and ornamental stone facings of concrete structural products. Include concrete rubbers. Chips, scrapes, and grinds high spots, ridges, and rough projections to finish concrete, using pneumatic chisel, hand chisel, or hand tools. Cleans chipped area, using wire brush, and feels and observes surface to detect rough or uneven surface. Wets surface to prepare for bonding, fills holes and cracks with grout or slurry, and smooths, using trowel. Wets concrete surface and rubs with stone to smooth surface and obtain specified finish. Sprinkles colored marble or stone chips, powdered steel, or coloring powder over surface to produce prescribed finish. Pushes roller over surface to embed chips in surface. Polishes surface, using polishing or surfacing machine. Spreads, levels, and smooths concrete, using rake, shovel, hand or power trowel, hand or power screed, and float. Produces rough concrete surface, using broom. Spreads roofing paper on surface of foundation, and spreads concrete onto roofing paper with trowel to form terrazzo base. Cuts metal division strips, and presses them into terrazzo base so that top edges form desired design or pattern. Applies muriatic acid to clean surface, and rinses with water. Molds expansion joints and edges, using edging tools, jointers, and straightedge. Mixes cement, sand, and water to produce concrete, grout, or slurry, using hoe, trowel, tamper, scraper, or concrete-mixing machine. Cuts out damaged areas, drills holes for reinforcing rods, and positions reinforcing rods to repair concrete, using power saw and drill. Builds wooden molds, and clamps molds around area to be repaired, using hand tools. Signals truck driver to position truck to facilitate pouring concrete, and moves chute to direct concrete on forms.

Yearly Earnings: $21,788

Education: Long-term O-J-T

Knowledge: Building and Construction

Abilities: Manual Dexterity; Multilimb Coordination; Wrist-Finger Speed; Speed of Limb Movement; Static Strength; Explosive Strength; Dynamic Strength; Trunk Strength; Stamina; Extent Flexibility; Dynamic Flexibility; Gross Body Coordination; Gross Body Equilibrium
Skills: None above average
General Work Activities: Performing General Physical Activities
Job Characteristics: Sounds, Noise Levels are Distracting, etc.; Very Hot; Cramped Work Space, Awkward Positions; Radiation; High Places; Climbing Ladders, Scaffolds, Poles, etc.; Kneeling, Crouching, or Crawling; Keeping or Regaining Balance; Bending or Twisting the Body; Making Repetitive Motions; Specialized Protective or Safety Attire; Importance of Repeating Same Tasks; Pace Determined by Speed of Equipment
GOE Group/s: 05.05.01 Craft Technology: Masonry, Stone, and Brick Work; 05.10.01 Crafts: Structural
CIP Program/s: 460499 Construction and Building Finishers and Managers, Other
Related DOT Job/s: 844.364-010 CEMENT MASON; 844.364-014 CEMENT-MASON APPRENTICE; 844.461-010 CONCRETE-STONE FINISHER; 844.684-010 CONCRETE RUBBER; 861.381-046 TERRAZZO WORKER; 861.381-050 TERRAZZO-WORKER APPRENTICE

87314 REINFORCING METAL WORKERS. OOH

Title/s: Structural and Reinforcing Ironworkers

Position and secure metal bars in concrete forms to reinforce concrete. Determine number, size, shape, and location of reinforcing rods from blueprints, sketches, or oral instructions. Determines number, sizes, shapes, and locations of reinforcing rods from blueprints, sketches, or oral instructions. Selects and places rods in forms, spacing and fastening them together, using wire and pliers. Welds reinforcing bars together, using arch-welding equipment. Bends steel rods with hand tools and rod-bending machine. Reinforces concrete with wire mesh. Cuts rods to required lengths, using hacksaw, bar cutters, or acetylene torch.
Yearly Earnings: $29,900
Education: Long-term O-J-T
Knowledge: Building and Construction
Abilities: Static Strength; Explosive Strength; Dynamic Flexibility; Gross Body Equilibrium; Glare Sensitivity
Skills: None above average
General Work Activities: Performing General Physical Activities; Handling and Moving Objects
Job Characteristics: Sounds, Noise Levels are Distracting, etc.; Very Hot; Extremely Bright or Inadequate Lighting; Contaminants; Cramped Work Space, Awkward Positions; High Places; Hazardous Equipment; Hazardous Situations; Climbing Ladders, Scaffolds, Poles, etc.; Kneeling, Crouching, or Crawling; Keeping or Regaining Balance; Using Hands on Objects, Tools, or Controls; Bending or Twisting the Body; Common Protective or Safety Attire
GOE Group/s: 05.05.06 Craft Technology: Metal Fabrication and Repair
CIP Program/s: 460499 Construction and Building Finishers and Managers, Other
Related DOT Job/s: 801.684-026 REINFORCING-METAL WORKER

87317 PLASTERERS AND STUCCO MASONS. OOH

Title/s: Plasterers

Apply coats of plaster onto interior or exterior walls, ceilings, or partitions of buildings to produce finished surface according to blueprints, architect's drawings, or oral instructions. Applies coats of plaster or stucco to walls, ceilings, or partitions of buildings. Creates decorative textures in finish coat, using sand, pebbles, or stones. Mixes mortar to desired consistency and puts up scaffolds. Installs guidewires on exterior surface of buildings to indicate thickness of plaster or stucco. Applies weatherproof, decorative covering to exterior surfaces of building. Molds and installs ornamental plaster pieces, panels, and trim. Directs workers to mix plaster to desired consistency and to erect scaffolds.
Yearly Earnings: $24,856
Education: Long-term O-J-T
Knowledge: Building and Construction
Abilities: Dynamic Strength; Dynamic Flexibility; Gross Body Equilibrium; Glare Sensitivity
Skills: None above average
General Work Activities: Performing General Physical Activities; Handling and Moving Objects
Job Characteristics: Supervise, Coach, Train Others; Extremely Bright or Inadequate Lighting; Contaminants; Cramped Work Space, Awkward Positions; High Places; Climbing Ladders, Scaffolds, Poles, etc.; Kneeling, Crouching, or Crawling; Keeping or Regaining Balance; Using Hands on Objects, Tools, or Controls; Bending or Twisting the Body; Common Protective or Safety Attire
GOE Group/s: 05.05.04 Craft Technology: Painting, Plastering, and Paperhanging
CIP Program/s: 469999 Construction Trades, Other
Related DOT Job/s: 842.361-018 PLASTERER; 842.361-022 PLASTERER APPRENTICE; 842.361-026 PLASTERER, MOLDING; 842.381-014 STUCCO MASON

Painters and Paperhangers

87402A PAINTERS, CONSTRUCTION AND MAINTENANCE. OOH Title/s: Painters and Paperhangers

Paint walls, equipment, buildings, bridges, and other structural surfaces, using brushes, rollers, and spray guns. May remove old paint to prepare surface prior to painting. May mix colors or oils to obtain desired color or consistency. Exclude workers who specialize in hanging wallpaper. Paints surfaces, using brushes, spray gun, or rollers. Applies paint to simulate wood grain, marble, brick, or stonework. Bakes finish on painted and enameled articles in baking oven. Sands surfaces between coats, and polishes final coat to specified finish. Cuts stencils, and brushes and sprays lettering and decorations on surfaces. Washes and treats surfaces with oil, turpentine, mildew remover, or other preparations. Smooths surfaces, using sandpaper, scrapers, brushes, steel wool, or sanding machine. Mixes and matches colors of paint, stain, or varnish. Sprays or brushes hot plastics or pitch onto surfaces. Fills cracks, holes, and joints with caulk putty, plaster, or other filler, using caulking gun or putty knife. Removes fixtures, such as pictures and electric switch covers, from walls prior to painting. Burns off old paint, using blowtorch. Covers surfaces with drop cloths or masking tape and paper to protect surface during painting. Erects scaffolding or sets up ladders to work above ground level. Reads work order or receives instructions from supervisor or homeowner. Cuts glass and installs window and door panes.
Yearly Earnings: $24,440
Education: Moderate-term O-J-T
Knowledge: Building and Construction
Abilities: Wrist-Finger Speed; Dynamic Strength; Stamina; Gross Body Equilibrium; Visual Color Discrimination
Skills: None above average
General Work Activities: Performing General Physical Activities; Handling and Moving Objects
Job Characteristics: Very Hot; Extremely Bright or Inadequate Lighting; Contaminants; High Places; Standing; Climbing Ladders, Scaffolds, Poles, etc.; Keeping or Regaining Balance; Making Repetitive Motions; Special Uniform

GOE Group/s: 01.06.03 Craft Arts: Hand Lettering, Painting and Decorating; 05.10.07 Crafts: Painting, Dyeing, and Coating
CIP Program/s: 460408 Painter and Wall Coverer; 490306 Marine Maintenance and Repair
Related DOT Job/s: 840.381-010 PAINTER; 840.381-014 PAINTER APPRENTICE, SHIPYARD; 840.381-018 PAINTER, SHIPYARD; 840.681-010 PAINTER, STAGE SETTINGS

87402B PAPERHANGERS. OOH Title/s: Painters and Paperhangers
Cover interior walls and ceilings of rooms with decorative wallpaper or fabric, or attach advertising posters on surfaces, such as walls and billboards. Duties include removing old materials from surface to be papered. Applies thinned glue to waterproof, porous surfaces, using brush, roller, or pasting machine. Measures and cuts strips from roll of wallpaper or fabric, using shears or razor. Mixes paste, using paste-powder and water, and brushes paste onto surface. Trims rough edges from strips, using straightedge and trimming knife. Aligns and places strips or poster sections of billboard on surface to match adjacent edges. Smooths strips or poster sections with brush or roller to remove wrinkles and bubbles and to smooth joints. Trims excess material at ceiling or baseboard, using knife. Marks vertical guideline on wall to align first strip, using plumb bob and chalkline. Applies acetic acid to damp plaster to prevent lime from bleeding through paper. Staples or tacks advertising posters onto fences, walls, or poles. Measures walls and ceiling to compute number and length of strips required to cover surface. Smooths rough spots on walls and ceilings, using sandpaper. Fills holes and cracks with plaster, using trowel. Removes old paper, using water, steam machine, or chemical remover and scraper. Removes paint, varnish, and grease from surfaces, using paint remover and water soda solution. Erects and works from scaffold.
Yearly Earnings: $24,440
Education: Moderate-term O-J-T
Knowledge: Building and Construction
Abilities: Stamina; Extent Flexibility; Gross Body Equilibrium
Skills: None above average
General Work Activities: Performing General Physical Activities; Handling and Moving Objects
Job Characteristics: High Places; Standing; Climbing Ladders, Scaffolds, Poles, etc.; Keeping or Regaining Balance; Making Repetitive Motions; Importance of Repeating Same Tasks
GOE Group/s: 05.05.04 Craft Technology: Painting, Plastering, and Paperhanging; 05.12.14 Elemental Work: Mechanical: Painting, Caulking, and Coating
CIP Program/s: 460408 Painter and Wall Coverer
Related DOT Job/s: 841.381-010 PAPERHANGER; 841.684-010 BILLPOSTER

Plumbing Workers

87502A PIPE FITTERS. OOH Title/s: Plumbers and Pipefitters
Lay out, assemble, install, and maintain pipe systems, pipe supports, and related hydraulic and pneumatic equipment for steam, hot water, heating, cooling, lubricating, sprinkling, and industrial production and processing systems. Plans pipe system layout, installation, or repair according to specifications. Cuts, threads, and hammers pipe to specifications, using tools such as saws, cutting torches, and pipe threaders and benders. Attaches pipes to walls, structures, and fixtures such as radiators or tanks, using brackets, clamps, tools, or welding equipment. Modifies and maintains pipe systems and related machines and equipment components following specifications, using hand tools and power tools. Selects pipe sizes and types and related materials, such as supports, hangers, and hydraulic cylinders, according to specifications. Measures and marks pipes for cutting and threading. Assembles pipes, tubes, and fittings, according to specifications. Inspects, examines, and tests installed systems and pipe lines, using pressure gauge, hydrostatic testing, observation, or other methods. Lays out full-scale drawings of pipe systems, supports, and related equipment, following blueprints. Inspects worksite to determine presence of obstructions and to ensure that holes will not cause structure weakness. Coats nonferrous piping materials by dipping in mixture of molten tin and lead to prevent erosion or galvanic and electrolytic action. Cuts and bores holes in structures, such as bulkheads, decks, walls, and mains, using hand and power tools, prior to pipe installation. Turns valve to shut off steam, water, or other gases or liquids from pipe section, using valve key or wrenches. Operates motorized pump to remove water from flooded manholes, basements, or facility floors.
Yearly Earnings: $27,924
Education: Long-term O-J-T
Knowledge: Design; Building and Construction; Mechanical
Abilities: Information Ordering; Flexibility of Closure; Perceptual Speed; Spatial Orientation; Visualization; Selective Attention; Arm-Hand Steadiness; Finger Dexterity; Multilimb Coordination; Wrist-Finger Speed; Speed of Limb Movement; Static Strength; Explosive Strength; Dynamic Strength; Trunk Strength; Stamina; Extent Flexibility; Gross Body Equilibrium
Skills: Installation; Product Inspection; Equipment Maintenance
General Work Activities: Inspecting Equipment, Structures, or Material; Performing General Physical Activities
Job Characteristics: Sounds, Noise Levels are Distracting, etc.; Very Hot; Extremely Bright or Inadequate Lighting; Contaminants; Cramped Work Space, Awkward Positions; Hazardous Equipment; Kneeling, Crouching, or Crawling; Using Hands on Objects, Tools, or Controls; Bending or Twisting the Body; Common Protective or Safety Attire; Frustrating Circumstances; Importance of Being Exact or Accurate; Importance of Being Sure All is Done
GOE Group/s: 05.05.03 Craft Technology: Plumbing and Pipefitting; 05.10.01 Crafts: Structural
CIP Program/s: 460501 Plumber and Pipefitter
Related DOT Job/s: 862.261-010 PIPE FITTER; 862.281-010 COPPERSMITH; 862.281-014 COPPERSMITH APPRENTICE; 862.281-022 PIPE FITTER; 862.281-026 PIPE-FITTER APPRENTICE; 862.361-014 GAS-MAIN FITTER; 862.361-018 PIPE FITTER, DIESEL ENGINE I; 862.361-022 STEAM SERVICE INSPECTOR; 862.381-014 INDUSTRIAL-GAS FITTER; 862.381-022 PIPE FITTER, DIESEL ENGINE II

87502B PLUMBERS. OOH Title/s: Plumbers and Pipefitters
Assemble, install, and repair pipes, fittings, and fixtures of heating, water, and drainage systems, according to specifications and plumbing codes. Repairs and maintains plumbing by replacing defective washers, replacing or mending broken pipes, and opening clogged drains. Assembles pipe sections, tubing, and fittings, using screws, bolts, solder, plastic solvent, and caulking. Installs pipe assemblies, fittings, valves, and fixtures such as sinks, toilets and tubs, using hand and power tools. Studies building plans and inspects structure to determine required materials and equipment and sequence of pipe installations. Cuts opening in structures to accommodate pipe and pipe fittings, using hand and power tools. Locates and marks position of pipe installations and passage holes in structures, using measuring instruments such as ruler and level. Cuts, threads, and bends pipe to required angle, using pipe cutters, pipe-threading machine, and pipe-bending machine. Fills pipes or plumbing fixtures with water or air and observes pressure gauges to detect and locate leaks. Directs

workers engaged in pipe-cutting and preassembly and installation of plumbing systems and components.
Yearly Earnings: $27,924
Education: Long-term O-J-T
Knowledge: Design; Building and Construction; Mechanical
Abilities: Flexibility of Closure; Perceptual Speed; Visualization; Arm-Hand Steadiness; Manual Dexterity; Finger Dexterity; Multilimb Coordination; Wrist-Finger Speed; Speed of Limb Movement; Static Strength; Explosive Strength; Dynamic Strength; Trunk Strength; Stamina; Extent Flexibility; Gross Body Equilibrium; Near Vision; Night Vision
Skills: Technology Design; Installation; Equipment Maintenance; Repairing; Management of Personnel Resources
General Work Activities: Performing General Physical Activities
Job Characteristics: Extremely Bright or Inadequate Lighting; Cramped Work Space, Awkward Positions; Hazardous Conditions; Standing; Kneeling, Crouching, or Crawling; Using Hands on Objects, Tools, or Controls; Bending or Twisting the Body; Importance of Being Sure All is Done
GOE Group/s: 05.05.03 Craft Technology: Plumbing and Pipefitting
CIP Program/s: 460501 Plumber and Pipefitter
Related DOT Job/s: 862.381-030 PLUMBER; 862.381-034 PLUMBER APPRENTICE; 862.681-010 PLUMBER

87505 PIPELAYING FITTERS. OOH Title/s: Pipelayers and Pipelaying Fitters
Align pipeline section in preparation of welding. Signal tractor driver for placement of pipeline sections in proper alignment. Insert steel spacer. Guides pipe into trench and signals hoist operator to move pipe until specified alignment with other pipes is achieved. Inserts spacers between pipe ends. Inspects joint to verify uniformity of spacing and alignment of pipe surfaces. Corrects misalignment of pipe, using sledgehammer.
Yearly Earnings: $21,372
Education: Moderate-term O-J-T
Knowledge: None above average
Abilities: Spatial Orientation; Speed of Limb Movement; Explosive Strength; Trunk Strength; Stamina; Dynamic Flexibility; Gross Body Coordination; Gross Body Equilibrium; Peripheral Vision; Depth Perception
Skills: None above average
General Work Activities: Performing General Physical Activities; Handling and Moving Objects
Job Characteristics: Sounds, Noise Levels are Distracting, etc.; Very Hot; Extremely Bright or Inadequate Lighting; Contaminants; Cramped Work Space, Awkward Positions; Hazardous Equipment; Standing; Walking or Running; Kneeling, Crouching, or Crawling; Keeping or Regaining Balance; Bending or Twisting the Body; Making Repetitive Motions; Common Protective or Safety Attire; Importance of Repeating Same Tasks
GOE Group/s: 05.10.01 Crafts: Structural
CIP Program/s: 460408 Painter and Wall Coverer; 469999 Construction Trades, Other; 470201 Heating, Air Conditioning and Refrigeration Mechanics and Repairers
Related DOT Job/s: 869.664-014 CONSTRUCTION WORKER I

87508 PIPELAYERS. OOH Title/s: Pipelayers and Pipelaying Fitters
Lay glazed or unglazed clay, concrete, plastic, or cast-iron pipe for storm or sanitation sewers, drains, water mains, and oil or gas lines. Perform any combination of the following tasks: grade trenches or culverts, position pipe, or seal joints. Grades and levels base of trench, using tamping machine and hand tools. Lays pipe in trench and welds, cements, glues, or otherwise connects pieces together. Lays out route of pipe, following written instructions or blueprints. Checks slope, using carpenter's level or lasers. Digs trench to desired or required depth by hand or using trenching tool. Taps and drills holes into pipe to introduce auxiliary lines or devices. Covers pipe with earth or other materials.
Yearly Earnings: $21,372
Education: Moderate-term O-J-T
Knowledge: Building and Construction
Abilities: Spatial Orientation; Manual Dexterity; Multilimb Coordination; Speed of Limb Movement; Static Strength; Explosive Strength; Dynamic Strength; Trunk Strength; Stamina; Extent Flexibility; Dynamic Flexibility; Gross Body Coordination; Gross Body Equilibrium; Glare Sensitivity
Skills: None above average
General Work Activities: Performing General Physical Activities; Handling and Moving Objects
Job Characteristics: Sounds, Noise Levels are Distracting, etc.; Very Hot; Extremely Bright or Inadequate Lighting; Contaminants; Cramped Work Space, Awkward Positions; Hazardous Equipment; Hazardous Situations; Standing; Kneeling, Crouching, or Crawling; Using Hands on Objects, Tools, or Controls; Bending or Twisting the Body; Making Repetitive Motions; Common Protective or Safety Attire; Importance of Repeating Same Tasks
GOE Group/s: 05.10.01 Crafts: Structural; 05.11.01 Equipment Operation: Construction
CIP Program/s: 010204 Agricultural Power Machinery Operator; 460408 Painter and Wall Coverer; 469999 Construction Trades, Other; 470201 Heating, Air Conditioning and Refrigeration Mechanics and Repairers
Related DOT Job/s: 851.383-010 IRRIGATION SYSTEM INSTALLER; 869.664-014 CONSTRUCTION WORKER I

87511 SEPTIC TANK SERVICERS AND SEWER PIPE CLEANERS. OOH Title/s: Plumbers and Pipefitters
Clean and repair septic tanks, sewer lines, or drains. May patch walls and partitions of tank, replace damaged drain tile, or repair breaks in underground piping. Rotates cleaning rods manually with turning pin. Operates sewer-cleaning equipment, including power rodder, high-velocity water jet, sewer flusher, bucket machine, wayne ball, and vac-all. Cleans sewage collection points and sanitary lines, and repairs catch basins, manholes, culverts, and storm drains. Cuts damaged section of pipe with cutters, removes broken section from ditch, and replaces pipe section, using pipe sleeve. Starts machine to feed revolving cable or rods into opening, stopping machine and changing knives to conform to pipe size. Withdraws cable and observes residue for evidence of mud, roots, grease, and other deposits indicating broken or clogged sewer line. Cleans and disinfects domestic basements and other areas flooded as result of sewer stoppages. Installs rotary knives on flexible cable, mounted on reel of machine, according to diameter of pipe to be cleaned. Measures distance of excavation site, using plumber's snake, tapeline, or length of cutting head within sewer, and marks trenching area. Inspects manholes to locate stoppage of sewer line and repaired sewer line joints to ensure tightness, prior to backfilling. Covers repaired pipe with dirt and packs backfilled excavation, using air and gasoline tamper. Breaks asphalt and other pavement, using air hammer, pick, and shovel. Notifies coworkers to dig out ruptured line or digs out shallow sewers, using shovel. Requisitions tools and equipment, and prepares records showing actions taken, human resources and equipment used, and disposition of material. Taps mainline sewers to install sewer saddles. Drives pickup trucks to haul crew, materials, and equipment. Services, adjusts, and makes minor repairs to equipment, machines, and attachments. Updates sewer maps and manhole charting. Communicates with supervisor and other workers, using radio telephone. Estimates cost of service to customer.

Yearly Earnings: $27,924
Education: Long-term O-J-T
Knowledge: Building and Construction; Mechanical
Abilities: Static Strength; Explosive Strength; Trunk Strength; Extent Flexibility; Gross Body Coordination; Gross Body Equilibrium
Skills: Installation; Operation and Control; Repairing
General Work Activities: Performing General Physical Activities; Interacting with Computers; Repairing and Maintaining Mechanical Equipment
Job Characteristics: Very Hot; Contaminants; Cramped Work Space, Awkward Positions; Whole Body Vibration; Hazardous Conditions; Climbing Ladders, Scaffolds, Poles, etc.; Kneeling, Crouching, or Crawling; Bending or Twisting the Body; Common Protective or Safety Attire; Specialized Protective or Safety Attire
GOE Group/s: 05.12.12 Elemental Work: Mechanical: Structural Work
CIP Program/s: 460501 Plumber and Pipefitter
Related DOT Job/s: 869.664-018 SEWER-LINE REPAIRER; 899.664-014 SEWER-PIPE CLEANER

Flooring Installers

87602 CARPET INSTALLERS. OOH Title/s: Carpet Installers

Lay carpets or rugs in homes or buildings. Exclude workers who lay linoleum. Stretches carpet to ensure smooth surface and presses carpet in place over tack strips. Installs carpet on some floors using adhesive, following prescribed method. Cuts carpet padding to size, and installs padding, following prescribed method. Measures and cuts carpeting to size according to floor sketches, using carpet knife. Cuts and trims carpet to fit along wall edges, openings, and projections. Joins edges of carpet that meet at openings, using tape with glue and heated carpet iron. Studies floor sketches to determine area to be carpeted and amount of material needed to complete job. Sews sections of carpeting together by hand, when necessary. Nails tack strips around area to be carpeted, or uses old strips to attach edges of new carpet. Fastens metal treads across door openings or where carpet meets flooring to hold carpet in place. Moves furniture from area to be carpeted and removes old carpet and padding.
Yearly Earnings: $21,892
Education: Moderate-term O-J-T
Knowledge: None above average
Abilities: Arm-Hand Steadiness; Multilimb Coordination; Speed of Limb Movement; Static Strength; Explosive Strength; Dynamic Strength; Trunk Strength; Stamina; Extent Flexibility; Dynamic Flexibility; Gross Body Coordination; Gross Body Equilibrium
Skills: Installation
General Work Activities: Performing General Physical Activities
Job Characteristics: Cramped Work Space, Awkward Positions; Hazardous Situations; Kneeling, Crouching, or Crawling; Keeping or Regaining Balance; Bending or Twisting the Body; Making Repetitive Motions; Importance of Repeating Same Tasks
GOE Group/s: 05.10.01 Crafts: Structural
CIP Program/s: 469999 Construction Trades, Other
Related DOT Job/s: 864.381-010 CARPET LAYER

87605 FLOOR LAYERS—EXCEPT CARPET, WOOD, AND HARD TILES. OOH Title/s: Indirectly related to Construction Trades

Apply blocks, strips, or sheets of shock-absorbing, sound-deadening, or decorative coverings to floors and cabinets. Include soft tile setters. Exclude acoustical carpenters and installers of carpets, wood, or hard tile. Lays out, positions, and applies tile and other decorative material to floors, walls, and cabinets. Cuts covering and foundation materials, according to blueprints and sketches, and cuts pattern around floor obstructions. Rolls and presses sheet wall and floor covering into cement base to smooth and finish surface, using hand roller. Trims excess covering materials, tacks edges, and joins sections of covering material to form tight joint. Brushes waterproof compound onto surface and fills cracks with plaster, putty, or grout to seal pores and form smooth foundation. Applies adhesive cement onto floor or wall material to join and adhere foundation material. Heats and softens floor covering materials to patch cracks and form floor coverings around irregular surfaces, using blowtorch. Measures and marks guidelines on surfaces or foundations, using chalklines and dividers. Removes excess cement to clean finished surface and applies grout to seal joints of tile. Sweeps, scrapes, sands, or chips dirt and irregularities to clean base surfaces. Disconnects and removes appliances, light fixtures, and worn floor and wall covering from floors, walls, and cabinets.
Yearly Earnings: $21,788
Education: Moderate-term O-J-T
Knowledge: Building and Construction
Abilities: Extent Flexibility
Skills: None above average
General Work Activities: None above average
Job Characteristics: Cramped Work Space, Awkward Positions; Kneeling, Crouching, or Crawling; Bending or Twisting the Body
GOE Group/s: 05.05.01 Craft Technology: Masonry, Stone, and Brick Work; 05.10.01 Crafts: Structural
CIP Program/s: 460101 Mason and Tile Setter; 469999 Construction Trades, Other
Related DOT Job/s: 622.381-026 FLOOR-COVERING LAYER; 861.381-034 SOFT-TILE SETTER; 864.481-010 FLOOR LAYER; 864.481-014 FLOOR-LAYER APPRENTICE

87608 FLOOR-SANDING MACHINE OPERATORS. OOH Title/s: Handlers, Equipment Cleaners, Helpers, and Laborers

Scrape and sand wooden floors to smooth surfaces, using floor scraper and floor sanding machine. Guides machine over surface of floor until surface is smooth. Scrapes and sands floor edges and areas inaccessible to floor sander, using scraper and disk-type sander. Attaches sandpaper to roller of sanding machine. Applies filler compound to floor to seal wood.
Yearly Earnings: $14,768
Education: Short-term O-J-T
Knowledge: None above average
Abilities: Manual Dexterity; Multilimb Coordination; Rate Control; Speed of Limb Movement; Static Strength; Explosive Strength; Dynamic Strength; Trunk Strength; Stamina; Dynamic Flexibility; Gross Body Coordination; Gross Body Equilibrium
Skills: None above average
General Work Activities: None above average
Job Characteristics: Sounds, Noise Levels are Distracting, etc.; Contaminants; Whole Body Vibration; Standing; Walking or Running; Kneeling, Crouching, or Crawling; Using Hands on Objects, Tools, or Controls; Bending or Twisting the Body; Making Repetitive Motions; Common Protective or Safety Attire; Degree of Automation; Importance of Repeating Same Tasks; Pace Determined by Speed of Equipment
GOE Group/s: 05.10.01 Crafts: Structural
CIP Program/s: 460408 Painter and Wall Coverer; 469999 Construction Trades, Other; 470201 Heating, Air Conditioning and Refrigeration Mechanics and Repairers
Related DOT Job/s: 869.664-014 CONSTRUCTION WORKER I

Highway and Rail Workers

87702 AIR HAMMER OPERATORS. OOH Title/s: Handlers, Equipment Cleaners, Helpers, and Laborers

Use air hammer to break asphalt, concrete, stone, or other pavement; loosen earth; dig clay; break rock; trim bottom or sides of trenches or other excavations; drill holes in concrete; reduce size of large stones; or tamp earth in backfills. Inserts drill in chuck, trips trigger to start hammer, and leans on hammer to force drill into solid mass. Connects steam or compressed-air and water lines to hammer. Changes drill or adds lengths as depth of hole increases. Replaces or sharpens bits. Lays steam, compressed-air, or water pipelines used to power jackhammer. Lubricates hammer.

Yearly Earnings: $14,768
Education: Short-term O-J-T
Knowledge: Mechanical
Abilities: Multilimb Coordination; Static Strength; Explosive Strength; Dynamic Strength; Trunk Strength; Stamina; Gross Body Coordination; Gross Body Equilibrium
Skills: None above average
General Work Activities: Performing General Physical Activities; Handling and Moving Objects; Controlling Machines and Processes
Job Characteristics: Sounds, Noise Levels are Distracting, etc.; Very Hot; Contaminants; Cramped Work Space, Awkward Positions; Whole Body Vibration; Standing; Keeping or Regaining Balance; Making Repetitive Motions; Common Protective or Safety Attire; Importance of Repeating Same Tasks; Pace Determined by Speed of Equipment
GOE Group/s: 05.12.02 Elemental Work: Mechanical: Mining, Quarrying, Drilling
CIP Program/s: 000000 NO CIP ASSIGNED
Related DOT Job/s: 930.684-018 JACKHAMMER OPERATOR

87705 PILE DRIVING OPERATORS. OOH Title/s: Material Moving Equipment Operators

Operate pile drivers mounted on skids, barges, crawler treads, or locomotive cranes to drive pilings for foundations of structures, such as buildings, bridges, and piers. Moves hand and foot levers to control hoisting equipment to position piling leads, hoist piling into leads, and position hammer over piling. Moves levers and turns valves to activate power hammer or raise and lower drop hammer, which drives piles to required depth.

Yearly Earnings: $24,440
Education: Moderate-term O-J-T
Knowledge: Engineering and Technology; Building and Construction
Abilities: Multilimb Coordination; Far Vision; Peripheral Vision; Depth Perception; Glare Sensitivity
Skills: Operation Monitoring; Operation and Control
General Work Activities: Controlling Machines and Processes; Interacting with Computers
Job Characteristics: Sounds, Noise Levels are Distracting, etc.; Very Hot; Extremely Bright or Inadequate Lighting; Cramped Work Space, Awkward Positions; Whole Body Vibration; High Places; Hazardous Equipment; Sitting; Keeping or Regaining Balance; Using Hands on Objects, Tools, or Controls; Common Protective or Safety Attire; Degree of Automation; Pace Determined by Speed of Equipment
GOE Group/s: 05.11.01 Equipment Operation: Construction
CIP Program/s: 490202 Construction Equipment Operator
Related DOT Job/s: 859.682-018 PILE-DRIVER OPERATOR

87708 PAVING, SURFACING, AND TAMPING EQUIPMENT OPERATORS. OOH Title/s: Material Moving Equipment Operators; Paving, Surfacing, and Tamping Equipment Operators

Operate equipment used for applying concrete, asphalt, or other materials to roadbeds, parking lots, or airport runways and taxiways, or equipment used for tamping gravel, dirt, or other materials. Include concrete and asphalt paving machine operators, form tampers, tamping machine operators, and stone spreader operators. Operates machine or manually rolls surfaces to compact earth fills, foundation forms, and finished road materials, according to grade specifications. Operates machine to spread, smooth, or steel-reinforce stone, concrete, or asphalt. Operates machine to mix and spray binding, waterproofing, and curing compounds. Operates machine to clean or cut expansion joints in concrete or asphalt and to rout out cracks in pavement. Drives and operates curbing machine to extrude concrete or asphalt curbing. Starts machine, engages clutch, pushes and moves levers, and turns wheels to control and guide machine along forms or guidelines. Monitors machine operation and observes distribution of paving material to adjust machine settings or material flow. Lights burner or starts heating unit of machine and regulates temperature. Drives machine onto truck trailer and drives truck to transport machine to and from job site. Installs dies, cutters, and extensions to screed onto machine, using hand tools. Fills tank, hopper, or machine with paving materials. Cleans, maintains, and repairs equipment, according to specifications, using mechanic's hand tools, or reports malfunction to supervisor. Sets up forms and lays out guidelines for curbs, according to written specifications, using string, spray paint, and concrete/water mix.

Yearly Earnings: $24,856
Education: Moderate-term O-J-T
Knowledge: Mechanical; Transportation
Abilities: Manual Dexterity; Control Precision; Multilimb Coordination; Response Orientation; Rate Control; Reaction Time; Speed of Limb Movement; Static Strength; Explosive Strength; Dynamic Strength; Trunk Strength; Stamina; Dynamic Flexibility; Gross Body Coordination; Gross Body Equilibrium; Far Vision; Peripheral Vision; Depth Perception; Glare Sensitivity
Skills: Equipment Maintenance
General Work Activities: Controlling Machines and Processes; Interacting with Computers; Repairing and Maintaining Mechanical Equipment
Job Characteristics: Responsible for Others' Health and Safety; Sounds, Noise Levels are Distracting, etc.; Very Hot; Extremely Bright or Inadequate Lighting; Contaminants; Whole Body Vibration; Radiation; High Places; Hazardous Conditions; Hazardous Equipment; Climbing Ladders, Scaffolds, Poles, etc.; Using Hands on Objects, Tools, or Controls; Degree of Automation; Pace Determined by Speed of Equipment
GOE Group/s: 05.11.01 Equipment Operation: Construction
CIP Program/s: 490202 Construction Equipment Operator
Related DOT Job/s: 853.663-010 ASPHALT-PAVING-MACHINE OPERATOR; 853.663-014 CONCRETE-PAVING-MACHINE OPERATOR; 853.663-018 ROAD-OILING-TRUCK DRIVER; 853.663-022 STONE-SPREADER OPERATOR; 853.683-010 CURB-MACHINE OPERATOR; 853.683-014 HEATER-PLANER OPERATOR; 853.683-018 JOINT-CLEANING-AND-GROOVING-MACHINE OPERATOR; 859.683-022 REINFORCING-STEEL-MACHINE OPERATOR; 859.683-026 ROAD-MIXER OPERATOR; 859.683-030 ROAD-ROLLER OPERATOR; 869.683-010 FORM-TAMPER OPERATOR; 869.683-018 TAMPING-MACHINE OPERATOR

87711 HIGHWAY MAINTENANCE WORKERS. OOH

Title/s: Highway Maintenance Workers

Maintain highways, municipal and rural roads, airport runways, and rights-of-way in safe condition. Duties include patching broken or eroded pavement, and erecting and repairing guardrails, highway markers, and snow fences, using a posthole digger, shovel, axe, saw, hammer and nails, or power tools, May also clear brush or plant trees along rights-of-way. Erects, installs, and repairs guardrails, highway markers, button-type lane markers, and snow fences, using hand tools and power tools. Dumps, spreads, and tamps asphalt, using pneumatic tamper to patch broken pavement. Measures and marks locations for installation of markers, using tape, string, or chalk. Drives truck or tractor equipped with adjustable snowplow and blower unit. Drives tractor with mower attachment to cut grass. Sets signs and cones around work area to divert traffic. Blends compounds to form adhesive mixture, using spoon. Verifies alignment of markers by sight. Drives truck to transport crew and equipment to worksite.

Yearly Earnings: $21,372

Education: Short-term O-J-T

Knowledge: Building and Construction

Abilities: Multilimb Coordination; Response Orientation; Rate Control; Reaction Time; Static Strength; Dynamic Strength; Trunk Strength; Stamina; Glare Sensitivity

Skills: Installation; Repairing

General Work Activities: Performing General Physical Activities; Interacting with Computers

Job Characteristics: Sounds, Noise Levels are Distracting, etc.; Very Hot; Extremely Bright or Inadequate Lighting; Contaminants; Whole Body Vibration; Hazardous Situations; Standing; Walking or Running; Common Protective or Safety Attire

GOE Group/s: 05.12.12 Elemental Work: Mechanical: Structural Work

CIP Program/s: 000000 NO CIP ASSIGNED

Related DOT Job/s: 859.684-010 LANE-MARKER INSTALLER; 899.684-014 HIGHWAY-MAINTENANCE WORKER

87714A RAIL-TRACK LAYING AND MAINTENANCE EQUIPMENT OPERATORS. OOH

Title/s: Material Moving Equipment Operators

Operate track-mounted equipment used to lay, repair, and maintain railroad tracks. Drives vehicle that automatically moves and lays track or rails over section of track to be constructed, repaired, or maintained. Pushes control to close grasping device on track or rail section, to raise or move section to specified location. Engages mechanism that lays track or rail to specified gauge. Adjusts controls of machines that spread, shape, raise, level, and align track, according to specifications. Turns wheels of machine, using lever controls, to adjust guidelines for track alignments and grades, following specifications. Strings and attaches wire-guidelines machine to rails to level or align track or rails. Drives graders, tamping machines, brooms, and ballast-cleaning-spreading machines to redistribute gravel and ballast between rails. Observes leveling indicator arms to verify levelness and alignment of track. Lubricates machines, changes oil, and fills hydraulic reservoirs to specified levels.

Yearly Earnings: $24,440

Education: Moderate-term O-J-T

Knowledge: Building and Construction; Mechanical; Transportation

Abilities: Control Precision; Multilimb Coordination; Rate Control; Peripheral Vision; Depth Perception; Glare Sensitivity; Sound Localization

Skills: Operation Monitoring; Operation and Control; Equipment Maintenance

General Work Activities: Interacting with Computers

Job Characteristics: Responsible for Others' Health and Safety; Sounds, Noise Levels are Distracting, etc.; Very Hot; Extremely Bright or Inadequate Lighting; Contaminants; Cramped Work Space, Awkward Positions; Whole Body Vibration; Hazardous Equipment; Hazardous Situations; Sitting; Using Hands on Objects, Tools, or Controls; Common Protective or Safety Attire; Consequence of Error; Degree of Automation; Pace Determined by Speed of Equipment

GOE Group/s: 05.11.01 Equipment Operation: Construction

CIP Program/s: 490202 Construction Equipment Operator

Related DOT Job/s: 859.683-018 RAILWAY-EQUIPMENT OPERATOR; 910.663-010 TRACK-MOVING-MACHINE OPERATOR; 910.683-018 TRACK-SURFACING-MACHINE OPERATOR

87714B RAIL-TRACK MAINTENANCE WORKERS. OOH Title/s: Indirectly related to Highway Maintenance Workers

Install and repair railroad track, using hand and power tools. Tightens or loosens bolts at joints that hold ensd of rails together, using hand tools. Grinds ends of both newly laid and worn rails, using portable metal grinder. Holds grinding wheel against steel rail parts to remove imperfections and impart appropriate shape, restoring rail for safe, smooth operation. Raises rail, using hydraulic jack, to facilitate removal of old ties and installation of new rail. Pulls old spikes from tie, using single- or multiple-head spike puller. Operates tie-adzing machine to cut portion of tie in order that tie plate can be inserted to hold rail. Drills holes through rails, tie plates, and fishplates for insertion of bolts and spike, using power drill. Operates single- or multiple-head spike driving machine to drive spike into tie and secure rail. Sprays ties, fishplates, and joints with oil to protect them from weather. Repairs and adjusts track switches, using wrenches and specified replacement parts. Changes worn or chipped grinding wheels, and lubricates portable grinding wheel. Paints railroad signs, such as speed limits and gate-crossing warnings.

Yearly Earnings: $21,372

Education: Short-term O-J-T

Knowledge: Building and Construction

Abilities: Manual Dexterity; Speed of Limb Movement; Static Strength; Explosive Strength; Dynamic Strength; Trunk Strength; Stamina; Dynamic Flexibility; Gross Body Equilibrium

Skills: Installation; Equipment Maintenance; Repairing

General Work Activities: Performing General Physical Activities; Handling and Moving Objects

Job Characteristics: Responsible for Others' Health and Safety; Sounds, Noise Levels are Distracting, etc.; Very Hot; Extremely Bright or Inadequate Lighting; Whole Body Vibration; Hazardous Equipment; Walking or Running; Kneeling, Crouching, or Crawling; Bending or Twisting the Body; Making Repetitive Motions; Common Protective or Safety Attire

GOE Group/s: 05.10.01 Crafts: Structural; 05.12.12 Elemental Work: Mechanical: Structural Work

CIP Program/s: 480503 Machine Shop Assistant; 490202 Construction Equipment Operator

Related DOT Job/s: 910.684-010 GRINDING-MACHINE OPERATOR, PORTABLE; 910.684-014 TRACK REPAIRER

87714C RAILROAD BRAKE REPAIRERS. OOH

Title/s: Industrial Machinery Repairers

Repair and maintain braking devices on railroad tracks. Removes designated part, places new part in braking device, and adjusts fit to ensure accurate placement. Greases fittings of brake device to maintain and prevent excessive wear of parts. Loosens and lifts braking device from rail, using hand tools and crane, and replaces broken or deteriorated track beams. Adjusts and measures distances between

brake shoes to specified standards, using hand tools, gauge, and steel rule. Removes bolts, screws, and metal plates to access parts of braking device, following blueprints. Examines broken device to isolate defect or verify repairs needed. Replaces bolts, screws, and metal parts, using hand and pneumatic tools. Inspects braking device for conformance to standards. Inspects and secures couplings and air hoses, and tests air and hand brakes before train leaves. Watches for smoke, sparks, and signs of sticking brakes, overheated axle bearings, and other faulty equipment while train is moving. Sets warning signals, such as flares or lanterns, at both ends of train during emergency stops. Informs conductor of needed repairs.
Yearly Earnings: $27,612
Education: Long-term O-J-T
Knowledge: Mechanical
Abilities: Gross Body Equilibrium
Skills: Installation; Operation Monitoring; Equipment Maintenance; Troubleshooting; Repairing
General Work Activities: Handling and Moving Objects; Repairing and Maintaining Mechanical Equipment
Job Characteristics: Take a Position Opposed to Others; Responsible for Others' Health and Safety; Sounds, Noise Levels are Distracting, etc.; Very Hot; Cramped Work Space, Awkward Positions; Standing; Kneeling, Crouching, or Crawling; Bending or Twisting the Body; Making Repetitive Motions
GOE Group/s: 05.05.09 Craft Technology: Mechanical Work
CIP Program/s: 470302 Heavy Equipment Maintenance and Repair
Related DOT Job/s: 622.261-010 BRAKE REPAIRER, RAILROAD

Other Construction Workers

87802 INSULATION WORKERS. OOH Title/s: Insulation Workers

Cover and line structures with asbestos, cork, canvas, tar paper, magnesia, and related materials, using saws, knives, rasps, trowels, and other tools and implements. May also specialize in providing blown-in insulation. Fits, wraps, or attaches insulating materials to structures of surfaces, using hand tools or wires, following blueprint specifications. Evenly distributes insulating materials into small spaces within floors, ceilings, or walls, using blower and hose attachments or cement mortar. Covers, seals or finishes insulated surfaces or access holes with plastic covers, canvas ships, sealant, tape, cement, or asphalt mastic. Prepares surfaces for insulation application by brushing or spreading on adhesives, cement, or asphalt or by attaching metal pins to surfaces. Reads blueprints and selects appropriate insulation, based on the heat-retaining or excluding characteristics of the material. Measures and cuts insulation for covering surfaces, using tape measure, handsaw, knife, or scissors. Moves controls, buttons, or levers to start blower and regulate flow of materials through nozzle. Fills blower hopper with insulating materials.
Yearly Earnings: $25,792
Education: Moderate-term O-J-T
Knowledge: Building and Construction
Abilities: None above average
Skills: None above average
General Work Activities: Performing General Physical Activities; Handling and Moving Objects
Job Characteristics: Contaminants; Cramped Work Space, Awkward Positions; High Places; Standing; Climbing Ladders, Scaffolds, Poles, etc.; Keeping or Regaining Balance; Bending or Twisting the Body; Common Protective or Safety Attire
GOE Group/s: 05.10.01 Crafts: Structural; 05.11.01 Equipment Operation: Construction; 05.12.14 Elemental Work: Mechanical: Painting, Caulking, and Coating
CIP Program/s: 469999 Construction Trades, Other
Related DOT Job/s: 863.364-010 INSULATION-WORKER APPRENTICE; 863.364-014 INSULATION WORKER; 863.381-010 CORK INSULATOR, REFRIGERATION PLANT; 863.381-014 PIPE COVERER AND INSULATOR; 863.664-010 BLOWER INSULATOR; 863.685-010 INSULATION-POWER-UNIT TENDER

87808 ROOFERS. OOH Title/s: Roofers

Cover roofs of structures with slate, asphalt, aluminum, wood, and related materials, using brushes, knives, punches, hammers, and other tools. May spray roofs, sidings, and walls with material to bind, seal, insulate, or soundproof sections of structures. Fastens composition shingles or sheets to roof with asphalt, cement, or nails. Applies alternate layers of hot asphalt or tar and roofing paper until roof covering is completed as specified. Aligns roofing material with edge of roof. Overlaps successive layers, determining distance of overlap, using chalkline, gauge on shingling hatchet, or the lines on shingles. Cuts strips of flashing and fits them into angles formed by walls, vents, and intersecting roof surfaces. Mops or pours hot asphalt or tar onto roof base when applying asphalt or tar and gravel to roof. Applies gravel or pebbles over top layer, using rake or stiff-bristled broom. Cuts roofing paper to size and nails or staples paper to roof in overlapping strips to form base for roofing materials. Punches holes in slate, tile, terra cotta, or wooden shingles, using punch and hammer. Attaches shingles to exterior walls and applies roofing paper and tar to shower pans, decks, and promenade waterproof surfaces. Constructs and attaches prefabricated roof sections to rafters. Insulates, soundproofs, and seals buildings with foam, using spray gun, air compressor, and heater. Injects nitrogen from secondary tank into supply tank to prevent crystallization of foam in tank when spraying is completed. Removes snow, water, or ice from roofs prior to applying roofing materials.
Yearly Earnings: $20,020
Education: Moderate-term O-J-T
Knowledge: Building and Construction
Abilities: Speed of Limb Movement; Static Strength; Explosive Strength; Dynamic Strength; Trunk Strength; Stamina; Extent Flexibility; Dynamic Flexibility; Gross Body Coordination; Gross Body Equilibrium
Skills: None above average
General Work Activities: Performing General Physical Activities; Handling and Moving Objects
Job Characteristics: Sounds, Noise Levels are Distracting, etc.; Very Hot; Extremely Bright or Inadequate Lighting; Cramped Work Space, Awkward Positions; High Places; Hazardous Situations; Climbing Ladders, Scaffolds, Poles, etc.; Kneeling, Crouching, or Crawling; Keeping or Regaining Balance; Bending or Twisting the Body; Making Repetitive Motions; Common Protective or Safety Attire; Specialized Protective or Safety Attire; Importance of Repeating Same Tasks
GOE Group/s: 05.10.01 Crafts: Structural; 05.12.14 Elemental Work: Mechanical: Painting, Caulking, and Coating
CIP Program/s: 469999 Construction Trades, Other
Related DOT Job/s: 866.381-010 ROOFER; 866.381-014 ROOFER APPRENTICE; 866.684-010 ROOFER APPLICATOR

87811 GLAZIERS. OOH Title/s: Glaziers

Install glass in windows, skylights, storefronts, and display cases, or on surfaces such as building fronts, interior walls, ceilings, and tabletops. Exclude glaziers who work primarily on production lines. Fastens glass panes into wood sash, and spreads and smooths putty around edge of pane with knife to seal joints. Installs preassembled framework for windows or doors designed to be fitted with glass panels, including stained glass windows, using hand tools. Attaches backing and leveling devices to wall surface, using nails and

screws, and cuts mounting strips and moldings to required lengths. Marks outline or pattern on glass, cuts glass, and breaks off excess glass by hand or with notched tool. Sets glass doors into frame, and bolts metal hinges, handles, locks, and other hardware onto glass doors. Assembles, fits, and attaches metal-framed glass enclosures for showers or bathtubs to framing around bath enclosure. Measures mirror and dimensions of area to be covered and determines plumb of walls or ceilings, using plumbline and level. Attaches mounting strips and moldings to surface and applies mastic, cement, putty, or screws to secure mirrors into position. Measures, cuts, fits, and presses antiglare adhesive film to glass, or sprays glass with tinting solution to prevent light glare. Covers mirrors with protective material to prevent damage. Loads and arranges mirrors on truck, following sequence of deliveries. Drives truck to installation site and unloads mirrors, equipment, and tools. Moves furniture to clear worksite and covers floors and furnishings with drop cloths.
Yearly Earnings: $24,856
Education: Long-term O-J-T
Knowledge: Building and Construction
Abilities: Spatial Orientation; Multilimb Coordination; Reaction Time; Speed of Limb Movement; Static Strength; Explosive Strength; Dynamic Strength; Trunk Strength; Stamina; Extent Flexibility; Dynamic Flexibility; Gross Body Coordination; Gross Body Equilibrium; Peripheral Vision; Glare Sensitivity
Skills: Technology Design; Installation
General Work Activities: Interacting with Computers
Job Characteristics: High Places; Hazardous Situations; Standing; Climbing Ladders, Scaffolds, Poles, etc.; Kneeling, Crouching, or Crawling; Keeping or Regaining Balance; Bending or Twisting the Body; Importance of Repeating Same Tasks
GOE Group/s: 05.10.01 Crafts: Structural
CIP Program/s: 469999 Construction Trades, Other
Related DOT Job/s: 865.361-010 MIRROR INSTALLER; 865.381-010 GLAZIER; 865.381-014 GLAZIER APPRENTICE

87814 STRUCTURAL METAL WORKERS. OOH Title/s: Structural and Reinforcing Ironworkers

Raise, place, and unite girders, columns, and other structural steel members to form completed structures or structural frameworks. Include workers who erect metal storage tanks and assemble prefabricated metal buildings. Exclude reinforcing metal workers. Guides structural-steel member, using tab line (rope), or rides on member in order to guide it into position. Pulls, pushes, or pries structural-steel member into approximate position while member is supported by hoisting device. Forces structural-steel members into final position, using turnbuckles, crowbars, jacks, and hand tools. Drives drift pins through rivet holes to align rivet holes in structural-steel member with corresponding holes in previously placed member. Bolts aligned structural-steel members in position until they can be permanently riveted, bolted, or welded in place. Fastens structural-steel members to cable of hoist, using chain, cable, or rope. Verifies vertical and horizontal alignment of structural-steel members, using plumb bob and level. Signals worker operating hoisting equipment to lift and place structural-steel member. Catches hot rivets tossed by rivet heater in bucket and inserts rivets in holes, using tongs. Bucks (holds) rivets while pneumatic riveter uses air hammer to form heads on rivets. Cuts and welds steel members to make alterations, using oxyacetylene welding equipment. Inserts sealing strips, wiring, insulating material, ladders, flanges, gauges, and valves, depending on type of structure being assembled. Sets up hoisting equipment for raising and placing structural-steel members.
Yearly Earnings: $29,900
Education: Long-term O-J-T
Knowledge: Building and Construction; Mechanical; Public Safety and Security
Abilities: Spatial Orientation; Visualization; Manual Dexterity; Multilimb Coordination; Response Orientation; Rate Control; Reaction Time; Wrist-Finger Speed; Speed of Limb Movement; Static Strength; Explosive Strength; Dynamic Strength; Trunk Strength; Stamina; Extent Flexibility; Dynamic Flexibility; Gross Body Coordination; Gross Body Equilibrium; Far Vision; Night Vision; Peripheral Vision; Depth Perception; Glare Sensitivity; Sound Localization
Skills: Installation
General Work Activities: Performing General Physical Activities; Handling and Moving Objects; Controlling Machines and Processes; Interacting with Computers
Job Characteristics: Responsible for Others' Health and Safety; Sounds, Noise Levels are Distracting, etc.; Very Hot; Extremely Bright or Inadequate Lighting; Cramped Work Space, Awkward Positions; Radiation; High Places; Hazardous Conditions; Standing; Climbing Ladders, Scaffolds, Poles, etc.; Kneeling, Crouching, or Crawling; Keeping or Regaining Balance; Bending or Twisting the Body; Common Protective or Safety Attire; Specialized Protective or Safety Attire
GOE Group/s: 05.05.06 Craft Technology: Metal Fabrication and Repair
CIP Program/s: 469999 Construction Trades, Other
Related DOT Job/s: 801.361-014 STRUCTURAL-STEEL WORKER; 801.361-018 STRUCTURAL-STEEL-WORKER APPRENTICE; 801.361-022 TANK SETTER; 801.381-010 ASSEMBLER, METAL BUILDING

87817 FENCE ERECTORS. OOH Title/s: Construction Trade Occupations

Erect and repair metal and wooden fences and fence gates around highways, industrial establishments, residences, or farms, using hand and power tools. Sets metal or wooden post in upright position in posthole. Attaches fence rail support to post, using hammer and pliers. Inserts metal tubing through rail supports. Completes top fence rail of metal fence by connecting tube sections, using metal sleeves. Attaches rails or tension wire along bottoms of posts to form fencing frame. Stretches wire, wire mesh, or chain-link fencing between posts. Attaches fencing to frame. Nails top and bottom rails to fence posts, or inserts them in slots on posts. Nails pointed slats to rails to construct picket fence. Erects alternate panel, basket weave, and louvered fences. Mixes and pours concrete around base of post, or tamps soil into posthole to embed post. Assembles gate and fastens gate in position, using hand tools. Saws required lengths of lumber to make rails for wooden fence. Digs postholes with spade, posthole digger, or power-driven auger. Aligns posts, using line or by sighting, and verifies vertical alignment of posts with plumb bob or spirit level. Lays out fence line, using tape measure, and marks positions for postholes. Cuts metal tubing, using pipe cutter. Welds metal parts together, using portable gas welding equipment. Blasts rock formations with dynamite to facilitate digging of postholes.
Yearly Earnings: $21,788
Education: Moderate-term O-J-T
Knowledge: Building and Construction
Abilities: Speed of Limb Movement; Static Strength; Explosive Strength; Dynamic Strength; Trunk Strength; Stamina; Extent Flexibility; Dynamic Flexibility; Depth Perception; Glare Sensitivity
Skills: Repairing
General Work Activities: Performing General Physical Activities; Handling and Moving Objects
Job Characteristics: Sounds, Noise Levels are Distracting, etc.; Very Hot; Extremely Bright or Inadequate Lighting; Whole Body Vibration; Hazardous Conditions; Hazardous Situations; Standing; Kneeling, Crouching, or Crawling; Using Hands on Objects, Tools, or Controls; Bending or Twisting the Body

GOE Group/s: 05.10.01 Crafts: Structural
CIP Program/s: 010201 Agricultural Mechanization, General
Related DOT Job/s: 869.684-022 FENCE ERECTOR

87899A CONSTRUCTION INSTALLATION WORKERS. OOH Title/s: Construction Trade Occupations

Install variety of equipment or home improvement products, such as awnings, antennae, and lawn-sprinkler systems, using hand and portable power tools. Cuts materials and components to size, using power saw or hand saw. Joins component parts together or attaches components to structure or building, using screws, bolts, nails, hand tools, and power tools. Examines installation site and studies sketches or blueprints to determine materials, dimensions, position, tools, and assembly methods required. Lays out components needed to assemble unit to organize fabrication and assembly procedure. Measures and marks buildings, piping, and components to determine assembly and installation requirements and procedures. Drills holes in components or structure to facilitate installation or assembly. Installs electrical and mechanical control mechanisms. Installs piping and other plumbing-related components, using wrenches, sealants, torches, solder, and pipe cutting, threading, and bending equipment. Mixes and places cement around bases of standards. Performs necessary carpentry work. Operates completed unit to ensure proper operation and identify malfunctions. Digs trenches or excavates building site, using shovel or ditching machine.
Yearly Earnings: $21,788
Education: Moderate-term O-J-T
Knowledge: Design; Building and Construction; Mechanical
Abilities: Multilimb Coordination; Static Strength; Explosive Strength; Dynamic Strength; Trunk Strength; Stamina; Extent Flexibility; Gross Body Equilibrium
Skills: Installation; Repairing
General Work Activities: Performing General Physical Activities
Job Characteristics: Very Hot; Cramped Work Space, Awkward Positions; Whole Body Vibration; High Places; Standing; Climbing Ladders, Scaffolds, Poles, etc.; Keeping or Regaining Balance
GOE Group/s: 05.10.01 Crafts: Structural; 05.12.12 Elemental Work: Mechanical: Structural Work; 05.12.16 Elemental Work: Mechanical: Electrical Work; 06.02.22 Production Work: Manual Work, Assembly Large Parts
CIP Program/s: 010601 Horticulture Services Operations and Management, General; 010605 Landscaping Operations and Management; 460201 Carpenter; 460501 Plumber and Pipefitter; 469999 Construction Trades, Other; 470101 Electrical and Electronics Equipment Installer and Repairer; 470103 Communication Systems Installer and Repairer
Related DOT Job/s: 801.684-018 PLAYGROUND-EQUIPMENT ERECTOR; 809.664-010 ALUMINUM-POOL INSTALLER; 820.361-010 CORROSION-CONTROL FITTER; 821.684-018 WIRER, STREET LIGHT; 823.684-010 ANTENNA INSTALLER; 862.682-010 PIPE CUTTER; 862.684-026 PLUMBING ASSEMBLER-INSTALLER; 862.684-034 WATER-SOFTENER SERVICER-AND-INSTALLER; 869.381-014 LABORATORY-EQUIPMENT INSTALLER; 869.381-018 PIPE INSTALLER; 869.481-010 AWNING MAKER-AND-INSTALLER; 869.484-010 AWNING HANGER; 869.684-030 LAWN-SPRINKLER INSTALLER; 954.564-010 WATER-METER INSTALLER

87899B WINDOW TREATMENT INSTALLERS. OOH Title/s: Construction Trade Occupations

Install venetian blinds and draperies. Hangs and arranges drapes and venetian blinds to enhance appearance of room. Measures installation site to obtain specifications for fabrication of draperies or venetian blinds. Measures and marks location for hanging brackets, using rule and pencil. Drills bracket holes in cement, plaster, or wood brackets, using hand or electric drill. Screws and bolts brackets and hangers onto wall, using hand tools. Pulls lowering, raising, and tilting cords to detect and adjust functioning defects. Delivers finished draperies to customers' homes.
Yearly Earnings: $21,788
Education: Moderate-term O-J-T
Knowledge: None above average
Abilities: None above average
Skills: None above average
General Work Activities: None above average
Job Characteristics: Provide a Service to Others; High Places; Standing; Climbing Ladders, Scaffolds, Poles, etc.; Keeping or Regaining Balance
GOE Group/s: 05.10.01 Crafts: Structural
CIP Program/s: 200501 Home Furnishings and Equipment Installers and Consultants, General; 200502 Window Treatment Maker and Installer
Related DOT Job/s: 869.484-014 DRAPERY HANGER; 869.484-018 VENETIAN-BLIND INSTALLER

87899C SWIMMING POOL INSTALLERS AND SERVICERS. OOH Title/s: Construction Trade Occupations

Install and service swimming pools. Assembles and aligns wall panel sections, edging, and drain tiles, using nuts, bolts, electric air gun, and transit. Lays out and connects pipelines for water inlets, return valves, and filters, using hand tools. Mixes, pours, spreads, and smooths concrete evenly throughout foundation, walls, and deck surrounding pool. Installs liner into pool. Assembles heater parts; connects gas, oil, or electric lines; and starts heater to verify working order of unit. Maintains and repairs pool and equipment, advises customers, and sells chemicals to prevent pool water problems. Plots length and width of pool site, according to specifications, and marks corners of site, using stakes and sledgehammer. Starts pump to fill pool with water, installs return valves, and checks pool for leaks. Dumps and spreads gravel into hollow foundation to form drain field, using wheelbarrow, shovel, and rake. Operates backhoe to dig, shape, and grade walls for pool. Confers with customer to ensure that pool location and dimensions meet customer's demands.
Yearly Earnings: $21,788
Education: Moderate-term O-J-T
Knowledge: Sales and Marketing; Customer and Personal Service; Engineering and Technology; Design; Building and Construction; Physics; Chemistry
Abilities: Static Strength; Explosive Strength; Dynamic Strength; Trunk Strength; Stamina; Extent Flexibility; Gross Body Coordination; Gross Body Equilibrium
Skills: Installation; Repairing
General Work Activities: Performing General Physical Activities; Controlling Machines and Processes; Interacting with Computers; Selling or Influencing Others
Job Characteristics: Very Hot; Extremely Bright or Inadequate Lighting; Cramped Work Space, Awkward Positions; Whole Body Vibration; Climbing Ladders, Scaffolds, Poles, etc.; Kneeling, Crouching, or Crawling; Bending or Twisting the Body
GOE Group/s: 05.10.01 Crafts: Structural
CIP Program/s: 469999 Construction Trades, Other
Related DOT Job/s: 869.463-010 SWIMMING POOL INSTALLER-AND-SERVICER

87899D CONSTRUCTION WORKERS, EXCEPT TRADE. OOH Title/s: Metalworking and Plastics-Working Machine Operators; Construction and Building Inspectors; Insulation Workers

Perform a variety of tasks in support of construction trade workers, such as cleaning, demolition, and equipment tending. Tends pumps, compressors, and generators to provide power for tools, machinery, and equipment or to heat and move materials such as asphalt. Mops, brushes, or spreads paints, cleaning solutions, or other compounds over surfaces to clean or provide protection. Cleans construction site to eliminate possible hazards. Tends machine that pumps concrete, grout, cement, sand, plaster, or stucco through spray gun for application to ceilings and walls. Lubricates, cleans, and repairs machinery, equipment, and tools. Sprays materials such as water, sand, steam, vinyl, paint, or stucco through hose to clean, coat, or seal surfaces. Mixes ingredients to create compounds used to cover or clean surfaces. Razes buildings and salvages useful materials. Loads and unloads trucks and hauls and hoists materials. Mixes concrete, using portable mixer. Erects and disassembles scaffolding, shoring, braces, and other temporary structures. Grinds, scrapes, sands, or polishes surfaces, such as concrete, marble, terrazzo, or wood flooring, using abrasive tools or machines. Builds and positions forms for pouring concrete and dismantles forms after use, using saws, hammers, nails, or bolts. Signals equipment operators to facilitate alignment, movement, and adjustment of machinery, equipment, and materials. Digs ditches and levels earth to grade specifications, using pick and shovel. Positions, joins, aligns, and seals structural components, such as concrete wall sections and pipes. Applies caulking compounds by hand or with caulking gun to seal crevices. Smooths and finishes freshly poured cement or concrete, using float, trowel, screed, or powered cement finishing tool. Measures, marks, and records openings and distances to lay out area to be graded or to erect building structures.

Yearly Earnings: $21,788
Education: Moderate-term O-J-T
Knowledge: Building and Construction; Mechanical
Abilities: Speed of Limb Movement; Static Strength; Dynamic Strength; Trunk Strength; Stamina; Gross Body Equilibrium
Skills: None above average
General Work Activities: Performing General Physical Activities; Handling and Moving Objects; Controlling Machines and Processes; Interacting with Computers
Job Characteristics: Sounds, Noise Levels are Distracting, etc.; Very Hot; Extremely Bright or Inadequate Lighting; Contaminants; Whole Body Vibration; High Places; Hazardous Equipment; Hazardous Situations; Standing; Climbing Ladders, Scaffolds, Poles, etc.; Keeping or Regaining Balance; Making Repetitive Motions; Importance of Repeating Same Tasks; Pace Determined by Speed of Equipment
GOE Group/s: 05.09.02 Material Control: Estimating, Scheduling, and Record Keeping; 05.10.01 Crafts: Structural; 05.10.07 Crafts: Painting, Dyeing, and Coating; 05.11.01 Equipment Operation: Construction; 05.12.06 Elemental Work: Mechanical: Pumping; 05.12.12 Elemental Work: Mechanical: Structural Work; 06.04.32 Elemental Work: Industrial: Manual Work, Casting and Molding
CIP Program/s: 200601 Custodial, Housekeeping and Home Services Workers and Managers; 200604 Custodian/Caretaker; 460408 Painter and Wall Coverer; 469999 Construction Trades, Other; 470201 Heating, Air Conditioning and Refrigeration Mechanics and Repairers; 470501 Stationary Energy Sources Installer and Operator
Related DOT Job/s: 800.684-010 RIVETER; 800.684-014 RIVETER, PNEUMATIC; 842.665-010 PLASTER-MACHINE TENDER; 849.665-010 PUMP TENDER, CEMENT BASED MATERIALS; 850.467-010 GRADE CHECKER; 853.665-010 ASPHALT-DISTRIBUTOR TENDER; 853.685-010 ASPHALT-HEATER TENDER; 864.684-010 FLOOR AND WALL APPLIER, LIQUID; 869.487-010 MEASURER; 869.664-010 CONCRETE-BUILDING ASSEMBLER; 869.664-014 CONSTRUCTION WORKER I; 869.665-010 AUXILIARY-EQUIPMENT TENDER; 869.667-010 COLUMN PRECASTER; 869.684-082 ASBESTOS REMOVAL WORKER; 891.684-022 BUILDING CLEANER; 891.685-010 STEAM-CLEANING-MACHINE OPERATOR; 899.684-046 MAINTENANCE WORKER, MUNICIPAL

87899E CONCRETE AND UTILITY CUTTERS AND DRILLERS. OOH Title/s: Construction Trade Occupations

Operate machines to cut and drill concrete or asphalt to facilitate installation and maintenance of utilities. Positions and lowers saw or drill over marked cutting or drilling mark. Starts motor and begins cutting or drilling operation. Guides saw along line, using handle bars attached to saw. Observes pressure gauge to maintain specified pressure on drill bit with crank. Locates and marks cutting or drilling position, using rule and chalk. Attaches diamond-edged circular blade or diamond-tipped core drill to equipment, using hand tools. Assembles components of drilling equipment and connects water hose to supply coolant to cutting blade or drill, using hand tools. Lubricates equipment, changes worn cutting blades and core drills, and makes minor repairs, using grease gun and hand tools.

Yearly Earnings: $21,788
Education: Moderate-term O-J-T
Knowledge: Building and Construction
Abilities: None above average
Skills: None above average
General Work Activities: Performing General Physical Activities; Handling and Moving Objects; Controlling Machines and Processes; Repairing and Maintaining Mechanical Equipment
Job Characteristics: Sounds, Noise Levels are Distracting, etc.; Contaminants; Cramped Work Space, Awkward Positions; Whole Body Vibration; Hazardous Equipment; Standing; Using Hands on Objects, Tools, or Controls; Common Protective or Safety Attire; Importance of Repeating Same Tasks; Pace Determined by Speed of Equipment
GOE Group/s: 05.10.01 Crafts: Structural; 05.11.03 Equipment Operation: Drilling and Oil Exploration
CIP Program/s: 490202 Construction Equipment Operator
Related DOT Job/s: 869.682-010 CIRCULAR SAW OPERATOR; 869.682-014 CORE-DRILL OPERATOR

87899F CONDUIT MECHANICS. OOH Title/s: Construction Trade Occupations

Build and repair concrete underground vaults and manholes, and install ducts to provide installation and maintenance facilities for underground power cables. Installs sheeting, shoring, and bracing for excavation. Builds wooden forms and erects steel reinforcing for concrete vaults and manholes. Installs brackets and braces, and cuts apertures required for installation of electric equipment and ducts. Demolishes or trims vaults and manholes, using pneumatic tools, working in proximity to high-voltage electric cables and equipment. Cuts, threads, bends, and installs metal conduit. Lays drain pipe and connects it to sewer system. Cuts and lays tile or fiber ducts, using portable saw and grinder and brick mason's hand tools. Forces air through ducts to test for obstructions, using air compressor. Directs workers engaged in pouring concrete into forms, and removes forms after concrete has set.

Yearly Earnings: $21,788
Education: Moderate-term O-J-T
Knowledge: Engineering and Technology; Building and Construction; Mechanical; Physics
Abilities: Arm-Hand Steadiness; Multilimb Coordination; Static Strength; Explosive Strength; Dynamic Strength; Trunk Strength; Stamina; Gross Body Equilibrium
Skills: Installation

General Work Activities: Performing General Physical Activities; Controlling Machines and Processes
Job Characteristics: Sounds, Noise Levels are Distracting, etc.; Extremely Bright or Inadequate Lighting; Contaminants; Cramped Work Space, Awkward Positions; Whole Body Vibration; Hazardous Conditions; Hazardous Equipment; Standing; Climbing Ladders, Scaffolds, Poles, etc.; Kneeling, Crouching, or Crawling; Keeping or Regaining Balance; Bending or Twisting the Body; Common Protective or Safety Attire
GOE Group/s: 05.05.06 Craft Technology: Metal Fabrication and Repair
CIP Program/s: 469999 Construction Trades, Other
Related DOT Job/s: 869.361-010 CONDUIT MECHANIC

87899G HYDRAULIC JACK SETTERS AND OPERATORS. OOH Title/s: Construction Trade Occupations

Set up and operate hydraulic jacks to raise precast concrete floors or roof slabs. Attaches precast concrete slabs to jacks, using threaded metal rods and nuts. Mounts motor to jacks, attaches hoses and electrical wiring, and sets tension on chain drive to prepare for lifting operation. Connects pump and jacks to control panel, and positions panel so that jacks and grade marks may be observed simultaneously. Starts pump and moves levers and valves on control panel to regulate action of jacks. Adjusts control valves when slab has reached predetermined position. Observes performance of jacks during lifting operation to detect malfunction. Measures and marks grade lines on support columns. Signals worker to verify grade with rule. Directs welding crew to weld supporting collars or brackets to column.
Yearly Earnings: $21,788
Education: Moderate-term O-J-T
Knowledge: Engineering and Technology; Building and Construction
Abilities: Gross Body Equilibrium
Skills: Operation Monitoring; Operation and Control
General Work Activities: Performing General Physical Activities; Controlling Machines and Processes
Job Characteristics: Very Hot; Whole Body Vibration; High Places; Standing; Climbing Ladders, Scaffolds, Poles, etc.; Kneeling, Crouching, or Crawling; Keeping or Regaining Balance; Bending or Twisting the Body; Common Protective or Safety Attire
GOE Group/s: 05.05.06 Craft Technology: Metal Fabrication and Repair; 05.12.04 Elemental Work: Mechanical: Hoisting, Conveying
CIP Program/s: 490202 Construction Equipment Operator
Related DOT Job/s: 869.361-014 HYDRAULIC-JACK ADJUSTER; 869.662-010 LIFT-SLAB OPERATOR

87899H PIPELINE MAINTENANCE WORKERS. OOH Title/s: Pipelayers and Pipelaying Fitters

Perform a variety of duties required in the cleaning and maintenance of pipelines. Starts engine and moves levers to control cleaning, coating, and wrapping operation. Opens valve to start flow of hot coating compounds onto pipe surface. Removes rust and foreign substances from meters and valves, using sandblasting equipment. Pours corrosion-resistant material over pipe or applies material with brush or spray gun. Wraps pipe with strips of paper or fabric to prevent corrosion and leakage. Selects, assembles, and installs scraping, brushing, coating, and wrapping apparatus. Inspects paper holders, observes flow of hot compounds into reservoir, and makes adjustments to ensure proper operation. Dismantles and restores fences, gates, water lines, and other obstructions that inhibit pipeline work. Cuts or clears brush, trees, weeds, and trash from pipeline right-of-ways, using axes and hoes. Installs connections to pipes, using wrenches and pipe tongs. Signals tractor operator to lift and move assembled apparatus into position at end of pipe. Drives and operates equipment, such as backhoes, bulldozers, and side booms, to dig ditches and lay pipe. Cleans storage tanks, using squeegees and rakes. Digs drainage ditches, using shovel. Spreads chemical pellets along right-of-way for control of tree growth. Loads and unloads trucks, and moves and positions materials and equipment for other workers.
Yearly Earnings: $21,788
Education: Moderate-term O-J-T
Knowledge: Building and Construction; Mechanical; Physics
Abilities: Control Precision; Multilimb Coordination; Rate Control; Static Strength; Explosive Strength; Dynamic Strength; Stamina; Gross Body Equilibrium
Skills: Installation
General Work Activities: Performing General Physical Activities; Handling and Moving Objects; Controlling Machines and Processes; Interacting with Computers; Repairing and Maintaining Mechanical Equipment
Job Characteristics: Sounds, Noise Levels are Distracting, etc.; Very Hot; Extremely Bright or Inadequate Lighting; Contaminants; Cramped Work Space, Awkward Positions; Whole Body Vibration; Hazardous Equipment; Climbing Ladders, Scaffolds, Poles, etc.; Kneeling, Crouching, or Crawling; Keeping or Regaining Balance; Bending or Twisting the Body; Making Repetitive Motions; Common Protective or Safety Attire; Importance of Repeating Same Tasks
GOE Group/s: 05.10.04 Crafts: Structural-Mechanical-Electrical-Electronic; 05.11.01 Equipment Operation: Construction
CIP Program/s: 470303 Industrial Machinery Maintenance and Repair; 490202 Construction Equipment Operator
Related DOT Job/s: 851.262-010 SEWER-LINE REPAIRER, TELE-GROUT; 862.662-010 PIPE-CLEANING-AND-PRIMING-MACHINE OPERATOR; 862.682-014 PIPE-WRAPPING-MACHINE OPERATOR; 899.684-026 PIPELINER

87899J SIGN ERECTORS. OOH Title/s: Line Installers and Cable Splicers; Construction Trade Occupations

Erect, assemble, and maintain signs and steel posts. Places wood or metal post in hole, and secures post in vertical position with cement. Mounts sign post onto previously constructed base, using shims, carpenter's level, and wrench. Bolts, screws, or nails plywood or metal sign panels to sign post or frame, using hand tools. Attaches poles and guy wires for hanging signs to buildings, using bolts, hammers, wrenches, and other hand tools and power tools. Raises signs and poles into position using truck-mounted hoist or hydraulic boom. Secures sign to hanging pole with hooks. Operates airhammer to drive metal post into ground. Paints or replaces worn or damaged signs. Measures, marks, and drills holes for mounting sign, using tape measure, chalk, and drill. Digs hole with posthole digger or shovel. Makes electrical connections to power source and tests sign for correct operation.
Yearly Earnings: $21,788
Education: Moderate-term O-J-T
Knowledge: Building and Construction
Abilities: Static Strength; Explosive Strength; Dynamic Strength; Stamina; Gross Body Equilibrium
Skills: None above average
General Work Activities: Performing General Physical Activities; Controlling Machines and Processes; Interacting with Computers
Job Characteristics: Very Hot; Extremely Bright or Inadequate Lighting; Whole Body Vibration; High Places; Standing; Climbing Ladders, Scaffolds, Poles, etc.; Keeping or Regaining Balance; Bending or Twisting the Body; Common Protective or Safety Attire
GOE Group/s: 05.10.01 Crafts: Structural
CIP Program/s: 000000 NO CIP ASSIGNED
Related DOT Job/s: 821.687-010 STEEL-POST INSTALLER; 869.381-026 SIGN ERECTOR I; 869.684-054 SIGN ERECTOR II

87899K ORNAMENTAL IRON WORKERS. OOH Title/s: Structural and Reinforcing Ironworkers

Install prefabricated ornamental ironwork other than structural ironwork. Welds brackets to lintels, sills, columns, and other structural framework. Cuts, miters, and bevels metal trim and cover plates to size, using handsaws or portable power saws. Bolts, clips, welds, or solders ironwork together and to brackets or anchors. Fastens cover plates and molding in place with metal screws to finish and trim work. Drills holes in metal, concrete, and masonry structure, using portable power drill, air hammer, and hand tools. Measures and marks layout for installation, according to blueprints, using rule, template, square, and compass. Verifies level and plumbness, using level or plumb bob.
Yearly Earnings: $29,900
Education: Long-term O-J-T
Knowledge: Design; Building and Construction
Abilities: None above average
Skills: None above average
General Work Activities: Handling and Moving Objects
Job Characteristics: Sounds, Noise Levels are Distracting, etc.; Whole Body Vibration; Hazardous Equipment; Standing
GOE Group/s: 05.05.06 Craft Technology: Metal Fabrication and Repair
CIP Program/s: 480501 Machinist/Machine Technologist
Related DOT Job/s: 809.381-022 ORNAMENTAL-IRON WORKER; 809.381-026 ORNAMENTAL-IRON-WORKER APPRENTICE

87899L HOUSE MOVERS. OOH Title/s: Material Moving Equipment Operators

Prepare buildings for moving from one site to another on trailer truck or rollers. Cuts large buildings into sections, using carpentry tools, to facilitate moving building and to comply with permit regulations. Breaks holes in foundation or removes underpinning, using steel cutters and carpentry tools. Positions jacks under beams and raises house. Attaches beams, winches, and cables to structure to facilitate towing of structure. Rolls pneumatic-tired dollies under beams, lowers house onto dollies, and fastens dollies to beams, using chains. Observes size, shape, and position of building to determine placement of beams and route of travel. Directs workers in positioning timbers or steel beams under house. Directs truck driver in moving building to new location and position on new site.
Yearly Earnings: $24,440
Education: Moderate-term O-J-T
Knowledge: Engineering and Technology; Building and Construction; Physics; Geography; Transportation
Abilities: Static Strength; Explosive Strength; Trunk Strength
Skills: None above average
General Work Activities: Estimating Needed Characteristics; Performing General Physical Activities; Handling and Moving Objects; Controlling Machines and Processes; Interacting with Computers
Job Characteristics: Coordinate or Lead Others; Sounds, Noise Levels are Distracting, etc.; Very Hot; Whole Body Vibration; Hazardous Equipment; Hazardous Situations; Standing; Climbing Ladders, Scaffolds, Poles, etc.; Consequence of Error; Importance of Being Sure All is Done
GOE Group/s: 05.10.01 Crafts: Structural
CIP Program/s: 460201 Carpenter
Related DOT Job/s: 869.261-010 HOUSE MOVER

87899M ALL OTHER CONSTRUCTION TRADES WORKERS. OOH Title/s: Construction Trade Occupations

All other construction trades workers not classified separately above.
Yearly Earnings: $21,788
Education: Moderate-term O-J-T
GOE Group/s: 05.05.01 Craft Technology: Masonry, Stone, and Brick Work; 05.05.02 Craft Technology: Construction and Maintenance; 05.05.06 Craft Technology: Metal Fabrication and Repair; 05.10.01 Crafts: Structural
CIP Program/s: 460101 Mason and Tile Setter; 460201 Carpenter; 469999 Construction Trades, Other
Related DOT Job/s: 779.684-058 STONE REPAIRER; 869.261-018 POURED-CONCRETE-WALL TECHNICIAN; 869.281-014 HOUSE BUILDER; 869.381-030 STEEPLE JACK; 869.681-010 CONCRETE-FENCE BUILDER

Extractive Trades Workers

87902A CONSTRUCTION DRILLERS. OOH Title/s: Mining, Quarrying, and Tunneling Occupations

Operate machine to drill or bore through earth or rock. Starts, stops, and controls drilling speed of machine and insertion of casing into hole. Monitors drilling operation and strata being drilled to determine need to adjust drilling or insert casing into hole. Retracts auger to force discharge dirt from hole. Operates machine to flush earth cuttings, or blows dust from hole. Assembles and positions machine, augers, and casing pipes. Verifies depth and level of boring position. Operates hoist to lift powerline poles into position. Signals crane operator to move equipment. Drives truck or tractor to worksite.
Yearly Earnings: $33,852
Education: Long-term O-J-T
Knowledge: Mechanical; Public Safety and Security; Transportation
Abilities: Spatial Orientation; Manual Dexterity; Control Precision; Multilimb Coordination; Response Orientation; Rate Control; Reaction Time; Speed of Limb Movement; Static Strength; Explosive Strength; Dynamic Strength; Trunk Strength; Stamina; Extent Flexibility; Dynamic Flexibility; Gross Body Coordination; Gross Body Equilibrium; Far Vision; Night Vision; Peripheral Vision; Depth Perception; Glare Sensitivity; Hearing Sensitivity; Auditory Attention; Sound Localization
Skills: Operation Monitoring
General Work Activities: Performing General Physical Activities; Controlling Machines and Processes; Interacting with Computers; Repairing and Maintaining Mechanical Equipment
Job Characteristics: Sounds, Noise Levels are Distracting, etc.; Very Hot; Extremely Bright or Inadequate Lighting; Contaminants; Cramped Work Space, Awkward Positions; Whole Body Vibration; Hazardous Equipment; Standing; Bending or Twisting the Body; Common Protective or Safety Attire; Degree of Automation; Pace Determined by Speed of Equipment
GOE Group/s: 05.11.01 Equipment Operation: Construction
CIP Program/s: 490202 Construction Equipment Operator; 490299 Vehicle and Equipment Operators, Other
Related DOT Job/s: 850.662-010 HORIZONTAL-EARTH-BORING-MACHINE OPERATOR; 850.662-014 ROCK-DRILL OPERATOR II; 850.683-034 ROCK-DRILL OPERATOR I; 859.682-010 EARTH-BORING-MACHINE OPERATOR; 859.682-014 FOUNDATION-DRILL OPERATOR

87902B WELL AND CORE DRILL OPERATORS. OOH Title/s: Mining, Quarrying, and Tunneling Occupations

Operate machine to drill wells and take samples or cores for analysis of strata. Starts and controls drilling action and lowering of well casing into well bore. Monitors operation of drilling equipment to determine changes in strata or variations in drilling. Withdraws drill rod from hole and extracts core sample. Couples additional lengths of drill rod as bit advances. Assembles non-truck-mounted drilling equipment, using hand tools and power tools. Changes drill bits as needed.

Inspects core samples to determine nature of strata, or takes samples to laboratory for analysis. Pours water into well or pumps water or slush into well to cool drill bit and remove drillings. Drives or guides truck-mounted equipment into position, levels and stabilizes rig, and extends telescoping derrick. Retrieves lost equipment from bore holes, using retrieval tools and equipment. Lubricates machine, splices worn or broken cables, replaces parts, and builds up and repairs drill bits. Records drilling progress and geological data. Fabricates well casings.
Yearly Earnings: $33,852
Education: Long-term O-J-T
Knowledge: Engineering and Technology; Mechanical; Physics; Geography; History and Archeology; Transportation
Abilities: Information Ordering; Category Flexibility; Flexibility of Closure; Perceptual Speed; Spatial Orientation; Selective Attention; Arm-Hand Steadiness; Manual Dexterity; Finger Dexterity; Control Precision; Multilimb Coordination; Response Orientation; Rate Control; Reaction Time; Speed of Limb Movement; Static Strength; Explosive Strength; Dynamic Strength; Trunk Strength; Stamina; Extent Flexibility; Dynamic Flexibility; Gross Body Coordination; Gross Body Equilibrium; Far Vision; Visual Color Discrimination; Night Vision; Peripheral Vision; Depth Perception; Glare Sensitivity; Hearing Sensitivity; Auditory Attention; Sound Localization
Skills: Operation Monitoring; Operation and Control; Equipment Maintenance; Repairing
General Work Activities: Performing General Physical Activities; Handling and Moving Objects; Controlling Machines and Processes; Interacting with Computers; Repairing and Maintaining Mechanical Equipment
Job Characteristics: Sounds, Noise Levels are Distracting, etc.; Very Hot; Extremely Bright or Inadequate Lighting; Whole Body Vibration; Radiation; Hazardous Equipment; Standing; Common Protective or Safety Attire; Pace Determined by Speed of Equipment
GOE Group/s: 05.11.03 Equipment Operation: Drilling and Oil Exploration
CIP Program/s: 490202 Construction Equipment Operator
Related DOT Job/s: 859.362-010 WELL-DRILL OPERATOR

87905 BLASTERS AND EXPLOSIVES WORKERS.
OOH Title/s: Mining, Quarrying, and Tunneling Occupations
Place explosives in holes or other spots, and detonate the explosives to demolish structures or to loosen, remove, or displace earth, rock, or other materials. Include tier-detonator blasters, perforator operators, and seismograph shooters. Assembles equipment, primer, explosives, and blasting cap, or loads perforating gun with explosives. Loads specified amount of explosives into blast holes, manually or using rope or hoist. Lights fuse, drops detonating device into well, or connects wires to firing device and activates device to set off blast. Plants explosive charges in structures or outside, using rope and safety harness for climbing. Cuts specified lengths of primacord and attaches primer to end of cord. Lays primacord between rows of charged blast holes and ties cord into main line to form blast pattern. Ties specified lengths of delaying fuses into pattern to time sequence of explosions. Fills and tamps blasting hole. Observes control panel to verify detonation of charges or listens for sound of blast. Examines blast area to determine amount and kind of explosive needed and to ensure safety prior to detonation. Marks location and depth of charge holes for drilling, and measures depth of drilled blast holes. Sets up and operates pneumatic drilling equipment to dill blast holes. Operates equipment, such as hoist, jackhammer, or drill, to bore charge holes. Sets up and operates radio or telephone equipment to receive blast information. Signals workers to clear area and hoist operator to raise equipment and sample from blast hole after detonation. Places safety cones around blast area to alert other workers. Drives truck to transport explosives and blasting equipment to blasting site. Moves, stores, and maintains inventories of high explosives. Repairs and services blasting and automotive equipment and electrical instruments, using hand tools.
Yearly Earnings: $33,852
Education: Long-term O-J-T
Knowledge: Engineering and Technology; Building and Construction; Physics; Chemistry; Public Safety and Security; Telecommunications; Transportation
Abilities: Information Ordering; Spatial Orientation; Selective Attention; Time Sharing; Arm-Hand Steadiness; Multilimb Coordination; Response Orientation; Rate Control; Reaction Time; Wrist-Finger Speed; Speed of Limb Movement; Static Strength; Explosive Strength; Dynamic Strength; Trunk Strength; Stamina; Extent Flexibility; Dynamic Flexibility; Gross Body Coordination; Gross Body Equilibrium; Far Vision; Visual Color Discrimination; Depth Perception; Glare Sensitivity; Sound Localization
Skills: Operation Monitoring; Operation and Control; Equipment Maintenance
General Work Activities: Performing General Physical Activities; Controlling Machines and Processes; Interacting with Computers; Drafting and Specifying Technical Devices, etc.; Repairing and Maintaining Mechanical Equipment; Repairing and Maintaining Electrical Equipment
Job Characteristics: Responsible for Others' Health and Safety; Sounds, Noise Levels are Distracting, etc.; Very Hot; Extremely Bright or Inadequate Lighting; Contaminants; Cramped Work Space, Awkward Positions; Whole Body Vibration; Radiation; High Places; Hazardous Conditions; Hazardous Equipment; Climbing Ladders, Scaffolds, Poles, etc.; Walking or Running; Kneeling, Crouching, or Crawling; Keeping or Regaining Balance; Bending or Twisting the Body; Common Protective or Safety Attire; Specialized Protective or Safety Attire; Consequence of Error; Frustrating Circumstances; Importance of Being Exact or Accurate; Importance of Being Sure All is Done; Importance of Repeating Same Tasks; Pace Determined by Speed of Equipment
GOE Group/s: 05.10.06 Crafts: Blasting; 05.11.01 Equipment Operation: Construction; 05.11.03 Equipment Operation: Drilling and Oil Exploration; 05.12.02 Elemental Work: Mechanical: Mining, Quarrying, Drilling
CIP Program/s: 490202 Construction Equipment Operator; 490299 Vehicle and Equipment Operators, Other
Related DOT Job/s: 850.381-010 MINER; 859.261-010 BLASTER; 931.261-010 BLASTER; 931.361-010 SAMPLE-TAKER OPERATOR; 931.361-014 SHOOTER; 931.361-018 SHOOTER, SEISMOGRAPH; 931.382-010 PERFORATOR OPERATOR, OIL WELL; 931.664-010 TIER-AND-DETONATOR; 931.667-010 POWDER LOADER

87908 ROCK SPLITTERS, QUARRY. OOH Title/s: Mining, Quarrying, and Tunneling Occupations
Separate blocks of rough dimension stone from quarry mass using jackhammer, wedges, and feathers. Inserts wedges and feathers into holes and drives wedges with sledgehammer to split stone from mass. Marks desired dimensions on stone, using rule and chalkline. Cuts groove along outline, using chisel. Drills holes along outline with jackhammer. Drills holes into side of stone broken from mass, inserts dogs or attaches sling, and directs movement of stone from area. Sets charges of explosives to split rock.
Yearly Earnings: $33,852
Education: Long-term O-J-T
Knowledge: Public Safety and Security
Abilities: Speed of Limb Movement; Static Strength; Explosive Strength; Dynamic Strength; Trunk Strength; Stamina; Gross Body Equilibrium; Peripheral Vision; Depth Perception; Glare Sensitivity
Skills: None above average

General Work Activities: Performing General Physical Activities; Handling and Moving Objects
Job Characteristics: Responsible for Others' Health and Safety; Sounds, Noise Levels are Distracting, etc.; Very Hot; Extremely Bright or Inadequate Lighting; Contaminants; Cramped Work Space, Awkward Positions; Whole Body Vibration; High Places; Hazardous Conditions; Hazardous Equipment; Hazardous Situations; Standing; Climbing Ladders, Scaffolds, Poles, etc.; Kneeling, Crouching, or Crawling; Keeping or Regaining Balance; Using Hands on Objects, Tools, or Controls; Bending or Twisting the Body; Common Protective or Safety Attire; Specialized Protective or Safety Attire; Consequence of Error
GOE Group/s: 05.12.02 Elemental Work: Mechanical: Mining, Quarrying, Drilling
CIP Program/s: 490299 Vehicle and Equipment Operators, Other
Related DOT Job/s: 930.684-022 QUARRY PLUG-AND-FEATHER DRILLER

87911 ROTARY DRILL OPERATORS, OIL AND GAS EXTRACTION. OOH Title/s: Indirectly related to Roustabouts

Set up or operate a variety of drills to remove petroleum products from the earth and to remove core samples for testing during oil and gas exploration. Include core and rotary drillers and well and prospecting drillers. Observes pressure gauge and moves control to regulate speed of rotary table and pressure of tools at bottom of borehole. Selects and changes drill bits according to nature of strata, using hand tools. Pushes levers and brake pedals to control draw works, which lowers and raises drill pipe and casing in and out of well. Withdraws core barrel from hole and extracts core from barrel. Connects sections of drill pipe, using hand tools and powered wrenches and tongs. Counts sections of drill rod to determine depth of borehole. Positions truck-mounted derrick at drilling area specified on field map. Examines operation of slush pumps to ensure circulation and consistency of mud (drilling fluid) in well. Examines drillings or core samples from bottom of well to determine nature of strata. Fishes for and recovers lost or broken bits, casing, and drill pipes from well, using special tools. Caps well or turns valves to regulate outflow of oil from well. Keeps record of footage drilled, location and nature of strata penetrated, and materials used. Repairs or replaces defective parts of machinery, using hand tools. Lowers and explodes charge in borehole to start flow of oil from well.
Yearly Earnings: $33,852
Education: Moderate-term O-J-T
Knowledge: Engineering and Technology; Building and Construction; Mechanical; Physics; Geography; Transportation
Abilities: Flexibility of Closure; Spatial Orientation; Control Precision; Multilimb Coordination; Response Orientation; Rate Control; Speed of Limb Movement; Static Strength; Gross Body Equilibrium; Far Vision; Peripheral Vision; Depth Perception
Skills: Operation Monitoring; Operation and Control; Equipment Maintenance; Repairing
General Work Activities: Performing General Physical Activities; Handling and Moving Objects; Controlling Machines and Processes; Interacting with Computers; Repairing and Maintaining Mechanical Equipment
Job Characteristics: Sounds, Noise Levels are Distracting, etc.; Very Hot; Extremely Bright or Inadequate Lighting; Contaminants; Whole Body Vibration; High Places; Hazardous Conditions; Hazardous Equipment; Hazardous Situations; Climbing Ladders, Scaffolds, Poles, etc.; Keeping or Regaining Balance; Common Protective or Safety Attire; Frustrating Circumstances; Degree of Automation; Importance of Being Aware of New Events
GOE Group/s: 05.11.03 Equipment Operation: Drilling and Oil Exploration
CIP Program/s: 490299 Vehicle and Equipment Operators, Other
Related DOT Job/s: 930.382-018 PROSPECTING DRILLER; 930.382-026 ROTARY DRILLER; 950.382-022 ROTARY-RIG ENGINE OPERATOR

87914 DERRICK OPERATORS, OIL AND GAS EXTRACTION. OOH Title/s: Indirectly related to Roustabouts

Rig derrick equipment and operate pumps to circulate mud through drill hole. Starts pumps that circulate mud through drill pipe and borehole to cool drill bit and flush out drillcuttings. Sets and bolts crown block to posts at top of derrick. Strings cables through pulleys and blocks. Clamps holding fixture on end of hoisting cable. Mixes drilling mud, using portable power mixer. Weighs clay. Cleans and oils pulleys, blocks, and cables. Repairs pumps.
Yearly Earnings: $33,852
Education: Moderate-term O-J-T
Knowledge: Mechanical; Physics
Abilities: Static Strength; Extent Flexibility; Gross Body Equilibrium
Skills: Operation and Control; Equipment Maintenance; Troubleshooting; Repairing
General Work Activities: Performing General Physical Activities; Handling and Moving Objects; Controlling Machines and Processes; Repairing and Maintaining Mechanical Equipment
Job Characteristics: Sounds, Noise Levels are Distracting, etc.; Very Hot; Extremely Bright or Inadequate Lighting; Contaminants; Cramped Work Space, Awkward Positions; Whole Body Vibration; High Places; Hazardous Conditions; Hazardous Equipment; Hazardous Situations; Standing; Climbing Ladders, Scaffolds, Poles, etc.; Keeping or Regaining Balance; Bending or Twisting the Body; Common Protective or Safety Attire; Specialized Protective or Safety Attire; Degree of Automation
GOE Group/s: 05.11.03 Equipment Operation: Drilling and Oil Exploration
CIP Program/s: 490299 Vehicle and Equipment Operators, Other
Related DOT Job/s: 930.382-022 ROTARY DERRICK OPERATOR

87917 SERVICE UNIT OPERATORS. OOH Title/s: Indirectly related to Roustabouts

Operate equipment to increase oil flow from producing wells or to remove stuck pipe, casing, tools, or other obstructions from drilling wells. Include fishing-tool technicians. Operates equipment to increase oil flow from producing wells. Operates equipment to remove stuck pipe, casing, tools, or other obstructions from drilling wells, using specialized subsurface tools and instruments. Starts pumps that circulate water, oil, or other fluid through well, removing sand and other materials obstructing free flow of oil. Moves controls to back off pipe or to sever pipe at point of obstruction. Operates hoist to lower and raise tools. Analyzes conditions of unserviceable oil or gas wells and directs recovery of lost equipment and other obstacles from boreholes. Plans fishing methods and selects tools for removing obstacles, such as liners, broken casing, screens, and drill pipe from wells. Assembles and lowers detection instruments into wells having drill pipe, drilling tools, or other obstructions wedged in well. Interprets instrument readings to ascertain depth of obstruction. Assembles and operates sound wave generating and detecting mechanisms for determining fluid level in wells. Confers with superintendent to gather information regarding size of pipes and tools and borehole conditions in wells. Perforates well casing or sidewall of borehole with explosive charge. Observes variations on gauges, mud pumps, and pressure indicators, and listens to equipment to detect faulty operations or unusual conditions. Directs lowering of specialized equipment to point of obstruction. Directs drilling crew in installation of well-bottom

equipment. Directs other workers to assemble and connect pipe and hydraulic lines of flushing equipment to wellhead. Directs activities of preparing for and drilling around lodged obstacles or specified earth formations with specialized tools and whipstocks. Quotes prices to customer and prepares reports of services rendered, tools used, and time required, to serve as basis for billing customer.
Yearly Earnings: $33,852
Education: Moderate-term O-J-T
Knowledge: Administration and Management; Economics and Accounting; Engineering and Technology; Mechanical; Physics; Geography; Public Safety and Security
Abilities: Flexibility of Closure; Control Precision; Multilimb Coordination; Response Orientation; Rate Control; Reaction Time; Dynamic Flexibility; Gross Body Equilibrium; Night Vision; Peripheral Vision; Depth Perception; Glare Sensitivity; Hearing Sensitivity; Auditory Attention; Sound Localization
Skills: Monitoring; Coordination; Solution Appraisal; Equipment Selection; Operation Monitoring; Operation and Control; Troubleshooting; Systems Perception; Identification of Key Causes; Time Management; Management of Personnel Resources
General Work Activities: Getting Information Needed to Do the Job; Monitoring Processes, Material, or Surroundings; Identifying Objects, Actions, and Events; Inspecting Equipment, Structures, or Material; Performing General Physical Activities; Controlling Machines and Processes; Interacting with Computers; Coordinating Work and Activities of Others; Developing and Building Teams; Guiding, Directing and Motivating Subordinates
Job Characteristics: Supervise, Coach, Train Others; Provide a Service to Others; Deal with External Customers; Coordinate or Lead Others; Responsible for Others' Health and Safety; Responsibility for Outcomes and Results; Frequency in Conflict Situations; Sounds, Noise Levels are Distracting, etc.; Very Hot; Extremely Bright or Inadequate Lighting; Contaminants; Whole Body Vibration; High Places; Hazardous Conditions; Hazardous Equipment; Hazardous Situations; Climbing Ladders, Scaffolds, Poles, etc.; Keeping or Regaining Balance; Specialized Protective or Safety Attire; Frustrating Circumstances; Degree of Automation; Importance of Being Aware of New Events
GOE Group/s: 05.03.04 Engineering Technology: Petroleum; 05.11.03 Equipment Operation: Drilling and Oil Exploration
CIP Program/s: 490299 Vehicle and Equipment Operators, Other
Related DOT Job/s: 930.261-010 FISHING-TOOL TECHNICIAN, OIL WELL; 930.361-010 SERVICE-UNIT OPERATOR, OIL WELL

87921 ROUSTABOUTS. OOH Title/s: Roustabouts
Assemble or repair oil field equipment using hand and power tools. Perform other tasks as needed. Bolts or nails together wood or steel framework to erect derrick. Dismantles and assembles boilers and steam engine parts, using hand tools and power tools. Connects tanks and flow lines, using wrenches. Bolts together pump and engine parts. Unscrews or tightens pipe, casing, tubing, and pump rods, using hand and power wrenches and tongs. Digs holes, sets forms, and mixes and pours concrete into forms to make foundations for wood or steel derricks.
Yearly Earnings: $33,852
Education: Short-term O-J-T
Knowledge: Engineering and Technology; Building and Construction; Mechanical
Abilities: Static Strength; Explosive Strength; Dynamic Strength; Trunk Strength; Stamina; Dynamic Flexibility; Gross Body Equilibrium
Skills: Installation; Troubleshooting; Repairing
General Work Activities: Performing General Physical Activities; Repairing and Maintaining Mechanical Equipment
Job Characteristics: Sounds, Noise Levels are Distracting, etc.; Very Hot; Extremely Bright or Inadequate Lighting; Contaminants; Cramped Work Space, Awkward Positions; Whole Body Vibration; High Places; Hazardous Conditions; Hazardous Equipment; Hazardous Situations; Standing; Kneeling, Crouching, or Crawling; Keeping or Regaining Balance; Using Hands on Objects, Tools, or Controls; Bending or Twisting the Body; Common Protective or Safety Attire
GOE Group/s: 05.10.01 Crafts: Structural
CIP Program/s: 470399 Industrial Equipment Maintenance and Repair, Other
Related DOT Job/s: 869.684-046 ROUSTABOUT

87923 ROOF BOLTERS. OOH Title/s: Mining, Quarrying, and Tunneling Occupations
Operate self-propelled machine to install roof support bolts in underground mine. Drills hole into roof, according to specifications. Removes drill bit from chuck and inserts bolt into chuck. Forces bolt into hole, using hydraulic mechanism of self-propelled bolting machine. Rotates chuck to turn bolt and open expansion head against rock formation. Installs truss bolts traversing entire ceiling span. Positions self-propelled bolting machine, inserts drill bit in chuck, and starts drill. Tightens ends of anchored truss bolts, using turnbuckle. Tests bolt for specified tension, using torque wrench. Positions safety jack to support underground mine roof until bolts can be installed.
Yearly Earnings: $33,852
Education: Long-term O-J-T
Knowledge: Building and Construction; Mechanical
Abilities: Extent Flexibility; Gross Body Equilibrium
Skills: None above average
General Work Activities: Performing General Physical Activities
Job Characteristics: Sounds, Noise Levels are Distracting, etc.; Very Hot; Extremely Bright or Inadequate Lighting; Contaminants; Cramped Work Space, Awkward Positions; Whole Body Vibration; High Places; Hazardous Conditions; Standing; Climbing Ladders, Scaffolds, Poles, etc.; Kneeling, Crouching, or Crawling; Keeping or Regaining Balance; Common Protective or Safety Attire; Specialized Protective or Safety Attire; Consequence of Error; Importance of Repeating Same Tasks
GOE Group/s: 05.11.02 Equipment Operation: Mining, Quarrying, Drilling
CIP Program/s: 490299 Vehicle and Equipment Operators, Other
Related DOT Job/s: 930.683-026 ROOF BOLTER

87941 CONTINUOUS MINING MACHINE OPERATORS. OOH Title/s: Mining, Quarrying, and Tunneling Occupations
Operate self-propelled mining machines that rip coal, metal and nonmetal ores, rock, stone, or sand from the face and load it onto conveyors or into shuttle cars in a continuous operation. Moves levers to sump (advance) ripper bar or boring head into face of coal seam. Starts machine to gather coal and convey it to floor or shuttle car. Moves lever to raise and lower hydraulic safety bar that supports roof above machine until other workers complete their framing. Drives machine into position at working face. Repairs, oils, and adjusts machine and changes cutting teeth, using wrench.
Yearly Earnings: $33,852
Education: Long-term O-J-T
Knowledge: Mechanical
Abilities: Multilimb Coordination; Night Vision; Peripheral Vision; Depth Perception
Skills: Operation and Control; Equipment Maintenance; Repairing
General Work Activities: Controlling Machines and Processes; Interacting with Computers; Repairing and Maintaining Mechanical Equipment

Job Characteristics: Responsible for Others' Health and Safety; Sounds, Noise Levels are Distracting, etc.; Very Hot; Extremely Bright or Inadequate Lighting; Contaminants; Cramped Work Space, Awkward Positions; Whole Body Vibration; Hazardous Conditions; Hazardous Equipment; Hazardous Situations; Keeping or Regaining Balance; Using Hands on Objects, Tools, or Controls; Common Protective or Safety Attire; Specialized Protective or Safety Attire; Consequence of Error; Degree of Automation; Importance of Being Aware of New Events; Pace Determined by Speed of Equipment
GOE Group/s: 05.11.02 Equipment Operation: Mining, Quarrying, Drilling
CIP Program/s: 490299 Vehicle and Equipment Operators, Other
Related DOT Job/s: 930.683-010 CONTINUOUS-MINING-MACHINE OPERATOR

87943 MINE CUTTING AND CHANNELING MACHINE OPERATORS. OOH Title/s: Mining, Quarrying, and Tunneling Occupations

Operate machines that cut or channel along the face or seams of coal mines, stone quarries, or other mining surfaces to facilitate blasting, separating, or removing minerals or materials from mines or from the earth's surface. Include shale planers. Moves controls to start and position drill cutter or torch, and to advance tool into mine or quarry face. Repositions machine and moves controls to make additional holes or cuts. Observes and listens to operation to detect binding or stoppage of tool or equipment malfunction. Determines location, boundaries, and depth of holes or channels to be cut. Drives mobile, truck-mounted, or track-mounted drilling or cutting machine in mine, quarry, or construction site. Moves controls to start and regulate movement of conveyors to move or load material. Replaces worn or broken tools and machine parts, and lubricates machine. Signals crew members to adjust speed of equipment movement. Guides and assists crew laying track for machine and resetting supports and blocking, using jacks, shovel, sledge, and pinch bar. Installs casing to prevent cave-ins. Charges and sets off explosives in blasting holes.
Yearly Earnings: $33,852
Education: Long-term O-J-T
Knowledge: Building and Construction; Mechanical; Public Safety and Security; Transportation
Abilities: Spatial Orientation; Multilimb Coordination; Rate Control; Speed of Limb Movement; Explosive Strength; Gross Body Equilibrium; Night Vision; Peripheral Vision; Depth Perception; Glare Sensitivity; Hearing Sensitivity; Auditory Attention
Skills: Operation Monitoring; Operation and Control; Equipment Maintenance; Repairing
General Work Activities: Performing General Physical Activities; Controlling Machines and Processes; Interacting with Computers; Repairing and Maintaining Mechanical Equipment
Job Characteristics: Coordinate or Lead Others; Responsible for Others' Health and Safety; Sounds, Noise Levels are Distracting, etc.; Very Hot; Extremely Bright or Inadequate Lighting; Contaminants; Cramped Work Space, Awkward Positions; Whole Body Vibration; Hazardous Conditions; Hazardous Equipment; Hazardous Situations; Kneeling, Crouching, or Crawling; Keeping or Regaining Balance; Using Hands on Objects, Tools, or Controls; Bending or Twisting the Body; Common Protective or Safety Attire; Specialized Protective or Safety Attire; Consequence of Error; Degree of Automation; Importance of Being Aware of New Events; Pace Determined by Speed of Equipment
GOE Group/s: 05.11.02 Equipment Operation: Mining, Quarrying, Drilling
CIP Program/s: 490202 Construction Equipment Operator; 490299 Vehicle and Equipment Operators, Other
Related DOT Job/s: 930.382-010 DRILLER, MACHINE; 930.383-010 CHANNELING-MACHINE RUNNER; 930.482-010 DRILLING-MACHINE OPERATOR; 930.662-010 LONG-WALL SHEAR OPERATOR; 930.663-010 SHALE PLANER OPERATOR; 930.683-014 CUTTER OPERATOR; 930.684-010 FLAME CHANNELER

87949A MINING MACHINE OPERATORS AND TENDERS. OOH Title/s: Mining, Quarrying, and Tunneling Occupations

Operate or tend a variety of mining machines or equipment used to extract minerals or aggregate from the earth. Controls hydraulic valves that advance jacks used to push forward mine tunnel shield that supports overlying ground. Operates and adjusts feed conveyor of trailer-mounted machine to recover gold from sand. Controls plow blade advancing through coal strata by remote control on electronic or radio signal. Adjusts speed of bellows to force air through sand and float it over riffles, allowing gold-bearing particles to collect. Opens valves to transfer ore residues (sand) from mill and admit water to mixing tank. Opens valves to transfer slurry to excavations (slopes) and to flush distribution lines. Observes indicator lights and gauges on control panel to detect machine malfunction. Listens for unusual sounds that would indicate equipment malfunctions. Observes flow of fine sand from conveyor to screen and inclined riffle tables. Starts mixer that blends slurry to specified consistency. Assists in routine maintenance or repair of mining machinery. Adds measured amounts of cement to slurry when hard-surface fill is specified. Washes residue from tanks and records amount of slurry produced and deposited in mine.
Yearly Earnings: $33,852
Education: Long-term O-J-T
Knowledge: Mechanical
Abilities: Control Precision; Multilimb Coordination; Rate Control; Reaction Time; Night Vision; Peripheral Vision; Depth Perception; Hearing Sensitivity; Auditory Attention; Sound Localization
Skills: Operation Monitoring; Operation and Control; Equipment Maintenance; Repairing
General Work Activities: Controlling Machines and Processes; Interacting with Computers
Job Characteristics: Responsible for Others' Health and Safety; Sounds, Noise Levels are Distracting, etc.; Very Hot; Extremely Bright or Inadequate Lighting; Contaminants; Cramped Work Space, Awkward Positions; Whole Body Vibration; Hazardous Conditions; Hazardous Equipment; Keeping or Regaining Balance; Using Hands on Objects, Tools, or Controls; Common Protective or Safety Attire; Specialized Protective or Safety Attire; Degree of Automation; Importance of Being Aware of New Events; Pace Determined by Speed of Equipment
GOE Group/s: 05.11.01 Equipment Operation: Construction; 05.11.02 Equipment Operation: Mining, Quarrying, Drilling; 05.12.07 Elemental Work: Mechanical: Crushing, Mixing, Separating, and Chipping
CIP Program/s: 490202 Construction Equipment Operator; 490299 Vehicle and Equipment Operators, Other
Related DOT Job/s: 850.682-010 SHIELD RUNNER; 930.665-010 LONG-WALL-MINING-MACHINE TENDER; 939.382-010 DRY-PLACER-MACHINE OPERATOR; 939.485-010 SANDFILL OPERATOR

87949B SERVICE UNIT OPERATORS—OIL, GAS, AND MINING. OOH Title/s: Mining, Quarrying, and Tunneling Occupations

Operate equipment to increase oil flow from producing wells or to remove stuck pipe, casing, tools, or other obstructions from drilling wells. May also perform similar services in mining

exploration operations. Include fishing-tool technicians. Observes meters and pressure gauges to regulate quantity and consistency of materials. Observes meters and gauges to control pump pressure. Determines well condition, pipe sizes, and amount of acid, cement, or fracturing chemicals to be used. Mixes acid, chemicals, or dry cement according to specifications of customer. Adjusts pipes between pumps and well, using hand tools. Directs unloading of pipes, fittings, and chemicals. Performs routine maintenance on vehicles and equipment.
Yearly Earnings: $33,852
Education: Long-term O-J-T
Knowledge: None above average
Abilities: Reaction Time; Dynamic Strength; Gross Body Equilibrium
Skills: Operation Monitoring; Operation and Control; Equipment Maintenance; Troubleshooting; Repairing
General Work Activities: None above average
Job Characteristics: Contaminants; Whole Body Vibration; Hazardous Equipment; Climbing Ladders, Scaffolds, Poles, etc.; Kneeling, Crouching, or Crawling; Bending or Twisting the Body; Common Protective or Safety Attire
GOE Group/s: 05.11.03 Equipment Operation: Drilling and Oil Exploration
CIP Program/s: 470399 Industrial Equipment Maintenance and Repair, Other
Related DOT Job/s: 939.462-010 OIL-WELL-SERVICE OPERATOR

87989A MINERS AND PETROLEUM AND GAS EXTRACTIVE WORKERS. OOH Title/s: Mining, Quarrying, and Tunneling Occupations

Perform a variety of duties, such as erecting and repairing shaft supports, operating mining machines, and setting explosives, to extract minerals or oil and gas from the earth. Operates cutting or drilling machine, uses pick, or sets off explosives to mine ore, coal, or rock in underground mine. Connects and disconnects rod and tubing sections as they move to and from wellhole, using hand wrenches and power tongs. Mines precious metals from sand and gravel, using inclined trough with riffles or cleats at bottom. Inserts and places waterproof sealer, bullet, igniting charge, and fuse in gun port and assembles cylinders. Dumps sand and cement over shot of nitroglycerin in oil or gas well, using special bailer and hoist. Advances coal conveyors and jack units forward to facilitate making new cuts in coal strata, using horizontal jacks. Tightens or unscrews wellhead connections, using pipe wrench, and replaces or removes dumping unit head. Guides tubing sections being moved to and from wellhole to derrick or ground rack, using tubing lifting clamp. Operates pneumatic jack in coordination with other jacks to raise or lower offshore oil-drilling barge. Pulls lever to position jacks, and fastens or unfastens guy lines to support and level derrick and pulling machine. Loads sand, tamping materials, and cement into bailer; lowers bailer and tools into borehole; and dumps cement, using hoist. Performs mine development, such as opening new passageways, air vents, auxiliary tunnels, and rooms to facilitate mining operations. Installs timbering, roof bolts, cribs, or hydraulic jacks to support walls and roof. Cleans, gauges, and lubricates gun ports and barrel, and assembles perforators, using special hand tools. Determines amount and consistency of tamping materials and cement, and selects tools, according to characteristics of borehole. Shovels shattered materials into mine cars or onto conveyor. Lays track for mine cars or track-mounted equipment. Inspects, repairs, and replaces mine shaft parts, such as timbers, cage guides, guardrails, and cable, using hand tools. Stores loaded guns, explosives, and related materials, and keeps inventory records, in compliance with local and federal laws. Cleans, maintains, and repairs tools and equipment.
Yearly Earnings: $33,852
Education: Long-term O-J-T
Knowledge: Production and Processing; Engineering and Technology; Building and Construction; Mechanical; Physics; Public Safety and Security; Law, Government, and Jurisprudence
Abilities: Perceptual Speed; Spatial Orientation; Arm-Hand Steadiness; Manual Dexterity; Control Precision; Multilimb Coordination; Rate Control; Speed of Limb Movement; Static Strength; Explosive Strength; Dynamic Strength; Trunk Strength; Stamina; Extent Flexibility; Dynamic Flexibility; Gross Body Coordination; Gross Body Equilibrium; Night Vision; Peripheral Vision; Depth Perception; Glare Sensitivity
Skills: Operation Monitoring; Operation and Control; Equipment Maintenance
General Work Activities: Performing General Physical Activities; Handling and Moving Objects; Controlling Machines and Processes; Interacting with Computers; Repairing and Maintaining Mechanical Equipment
Job Characteristics: Responsible for Others' Health and Safety; Sounds, Noise Levels are Distracting, etc.; Very Hot; Extremely Bright or Inadequate Lighting; Contaminants; Cramped Work Space, Awkward Positions; Whole Body Vibration; Hazardous Conditions; Hazardous Equipment; Standing; Climbing Ladders, Scaffolds, Poles, etc.; Kneeling, Crouching, or Crawling; Keeping or Regaining Balance; Using Hands on Objects, Tools, or Controls; Bending or Twisting the Body; Making Repetitive Motions; Common Protective or Safety Attire; Specialized Protective or Safety Attire; Frustrating Circumstances; Importance of Being Aware of New Events; Importance of Repeating Same Tasks; Pace Determined by Speed of Equipment
GOE Group/s: 05.10.01 Crafts: Structural; 05.10.06 Crafts: Blasting; 05.11.02 Equipment Operation: Mining, Quarrying, Drilling; 05.11.03 Equipment Operation: Drilling and Oil Exploration; 05.12.02 Elemental Work: Mechanical: Mining, Quarrying, Drilling
CIP Program/s: 470399 Industrial Equipment Maintenance and Repair, Other; 490299 Vehicle and Equipment Operators, Other
Related DOT Job/s: 899.684-034 SHAFT MECHANIC; 930.684-014 FLOOR WORKER, WELL SERVICE; 931.384-010 GUN-PERFORATOR LOADER; 931.684-010 DUMPER-BAILER OPERATOR; 939.281-010 MINER I; 939.682-014 PNEUMATIC-JACK OPERATOR; 939.684-010 JACK SETTER; 939.684-014 MINER, PLACER

87989B ALL OTHER EXTRACTIVE WORKERS, EXCEPT HELPERS. OOH Title/s: Mining, Quarrying, and Tunneling Occupations

All other extractive workers, except helpers, not classified separately above.
Yearly Earnings: $33,852
Education: Long-term O-J-T
GOE Group/s: 05.12.03 Elemental Work: Mechanical: Loading, Moving; 05.12.12 Elemental Work: Mechanical: Structural Work; 05.12.14 Elemental Work: Mechanical: Painting, Caulking, and Coating; 06.01.02 Production Technology: Machine Set-up
CIP Program/s: 000000 NO CIP ASSIGNED
Related DOT Job/s: 930.664-010 CASER; 933.664-010 CRUSHER SETTER; 939.667-014 QUARRY WORKER; 939.687-026 ROCK-DUST SPRAYER

87999 ALL OTHER CONSTRUCTION AND EXTRACTIVE WORKERS, EXCEPT HELPERS. OOH Title/s: Mining, Quarrying, and Tunneling Occupations

All other construction and extractive workers, except helpers, not classified separately above.
Yearly Earnings: $33,852
Education: Long-term O-J-T
GOE Group/s: 05.12.03 Elemental Work: Mechanical: Loading, Moving

CIP Program/s: 000000 NO CIP ASSIGNED
Related DOT Job/s: 869.687-026 CONSTRUCTION WORKER II

Metalworking and Plastics Working Occupations

89102 TOOL AND DIE MAKERS. OOH Title/s: Tool and Die Makers

Analyze specifications, lay out metal stock, set up and operate machine tools, and fit and assemble parts to make and repair dies, cutting tools, jigs, fixtures, gauges, and machinist's hand tools. Include paper die makers and die sinkers. Exclude die setters. Studies blueprints or specifications and visualizes shape of die, part, or tool. Computes dimensions of assembly and plans sequence of operations. Measures, marks, and scribes metal or plastic stock to lay out machining, using instruments such as protractors, micrometers, scribes, and rulers. Sets up and operates machine tools, such as lathes, milling machines, shapers, and grinders, to machine parts. Lifts, positions, and secures machined parts on surface plate or work table, using hoist, vises, v-blocks, or angle plates. Smooths and polishes flat and contoured surfaces of parts or tools, using scrapers, abrasive stones, files, emery cloth, or power grinder. Verifies dimensions, alignments, and clearances of finished parts, using measuring instruments such as calipers, gauge blocks, micrometers, and dial indicators. Fits and assembles parts, using bolts, glue, and other fasteners, and hand tools, such as hammers and wrenches. Sets pyrometer controls of heat-treating furnace, and feeds or places parts, tools, or assemblies into furnace to harden. Repairs or modifies tools and dies, using machine tools and hand tools. Designs tools, jigs, fixtures, and templates for use as work aids. Cuts, shapes, and trims blank or block to specified length or shape, using power saws, power shears, rule, and hand tools. Casts plastic tools or parts, or tungsten-carbide cutting tips, using premade molds. Sets up and operates drill press to drill and tap holes in parts for assembly. Operates power press to test completed dies, and applies pigment to die to indicate high spots that require reworking. Inspects die for smoothness, contour conformity, and defects by touch or visually, using loupe or microscope. Connects wiring and hydraulic lines to install electrical and hydraulic components. Fabricates sawblades, using power roller to straighten blade stock, punch press to cut teeth, and power grinder to sharpen teeth.
Yearly Earnings: $34,944
Education: Long-term O-J-T
Knowledge: Production and Processing; Building and Construction; Mechanical
Abilities: Mathematical Reasoning; Number Facility; Manual Dexterity; Control Precision; Wrist-Finger Speed
Skills: Technology Design; Equipment Selection; Installation; Operation and Control; Equipment Maintenance; Repairing
General Work Activities: Performing General Physical Activities; Handling and Moving Objects; Controlling Machines and Processes; Repairing and Maintaining Mechanical Equipment
Job Characteristics: Hazardous Equipment; Using Hands on Objects, Tools, or Controls; Making Repetitive Motions; Importance of Repeating Same Tasks; Pace Determined by Speed of Equipment
GOE Group/s: 05.05.06 Craft Technology: Metal Fabrication and Repair; 05.05.07 Craft Technology: Machining; 05.05.09 Craft Technology: Mechanical Work; 06.01.04 Production Technology: Precision Hand Work
CIP Program/s: 480501 Machinist/Machine Technologist; 480507 Tool and Die Maker/Technologist
Related DOT Job/s: 601.260-010 TOOL-AND-DIE MAKER; 601.260-014 TOOL-AND-DIE-MAKER APPRENTICE; 601.280-010 DIE MAKER, STAMPING; 601.280-014 DIE MAKER, TRIM; 601.280-018 DIE MAKER, WIRE DRAWING; 601.280-022 DIE SINKER; 601.280-030 MOLD MAKER, DIE-CASTING AND PLASTIC MOLDING; 601.280-034 TAP-AND-DIE-MAKER TECHNICIAN; 601.280-042 TOOL MAKER; 601.280-058 TOOL-MAKER APPRENTICE; 601.281-010 DIE MAKER, BENCH, STAMPING; 601.281-014 DIE-TRY-OUT WORKER, STAMPING; 601.281-026 TOOL MAKER, BENCH; 601.380-010 CARBIDE OPERATOR; 601.381-010 DIE FINISHER; 601.381-014 DIE MAKER; 601.381-022 DIE-MAKER APPRENTICE; 601.381-026 PLASTIC TOOL MAKER; 601.381-030 PLASTIC-FIXTURE BUILDER; 601.381-034 SAW MAKER; 601.381-042 DIE MAKER, ELECTRONIC; 739.381-018 DIE MAKER; 739.381-022 DIE-MAKER APPRENTICE

89105 PRECISION INSTRUMENT MAKERS. OOH Title/s: Precision Assemblers

Fabricate, modify, or repair mechanical instruments or mechanical assemblies of electrical or electronic instruments, such as chronometric timing devices, thermostats, seismographs, and servomechanisms. Set up and operate machine tools to remodel electrical and electronic instruments used in electrical logging, subsurface surveying, and other oil, gas, or borehole prospecting, testing, and servicing operations. Fits and installs components, such as timing devices, springs, balance mechanisms, and gear trains, using jeweler's lathe, loupe, and hand tools. Sets up and operates machine tools to remodel electrical and electronic instruments, following engineering orders and specifications. Measures, marks, and scribes stock, such as silver, platinum, steel, and plastic, following drawings to lay out workpiece for matching. Anneals and tempers metal parts. Assembles parts in jig and brazes or welds parts. Verifies dimensions of parts and installation of components, using measuring instruments such as micrometer, calipers, and electronic gauges. Connects circuit components, such as tubes, coils, and switches, using wire strippers and soldering iron and following circuit diagrams. Tests instruments to determine conformance to specifications, using equipment such as voltmeters and ohmmeters. Sets up and operates machines to fabricate dies for punch presses. Coats assembled instrument with protective finish, such as lacquer or enamel, using spray gun. Installs electrical and electronic parts, such as sockets, switches, and rheostats, in chassis. Installs wiring and electrical components to specifications.
Yearly Earnings: $34,944
Education: Long-term O-J-T
Knowledge: Production and Processing; Computers and Electronics; Engineering and Technology; Design; Mechanical
Abilities: Arm-Hand Steadiness; Finger Dexterity; Control Precision; Wrist-Finger Speed; Visual Color Discrimination; Glare Sensitivity; Hearing Sensitivity; Sound Localization
Skills: Technology Design; Equipment Selection; Installation; Testing; Operation Monitoring; Operation and Control; Product Inspection; Troubleshooting; Repairing
General Work Activities: Identifying Objects, Actions, and Events; Inspecting Equipment, Structures, or Material; Controlling Machines and Processes; Repairing and Maintaining Mechanical Equipment; Repairing and Maintaining Electrical Equipment
Job Characteristics: Sounds, Noise Levels are Distracting, etc.; Hazardous Conditions; Hazardous Equipment; Hazardous Situations; Kneeling, Crouching, or Crawling; Using Hands on Objects, Tools, or Controls; Bending or Twisting the Body; Consequence of Error; Importance of Being Exact or Accurate
GOE Group/s: 05.05.10 Craft Technology: Electrical-Electronic Equipment Repair; 05.05.11 Craft Technology: Scientific, Medical, & Technical Equip. Fabric. & Related
CIP Program/s: 480503 Machine Shop Assistant

Related DOT Job/s: 600.280-014 INSTRUMENT-MAKER AND REPAIRER; 600.280-018 INSTRUMENT-MAKER APPRENTICE

89108 MACHINISTS. OOH Title/s: Machinists and Tool Programmers; Engineering Technicians; Aircraft Mechanics, Including Engine Specialists

Set up and operate variety of machine tools. Fit and assemble parts to make or repair machine tools, and maintain industrial machines, applying knowledge of mechanics, shop mathematics, metal properties, layout, and machining procedures. Study specifications, such as blueprints, sketch, or description of part to be replaced, and plan sequence of operations. Studies sample parts, blueprints, drawings, and engineering information to determine methods and sequence of operations to fabricate product. Operates metal-working machine tools, such as lathe, milling machine, shaper, or grinder, to machine parts to specifications. Assembles parts into completed units, using jigs, fixtures, hand tools, and power tools. Fabricates, assembles, and modifies tooling, such as jigs, fixtures, templates, and molds or dies, to produce parts and assemblies. Lays out and verifies dimensions of parts, using precision measuring and marking instruments and knowledge of trigonometry. Calculates and sets controls to regulate machining, or enters commands to retrieve, input, or edit computerized machine control media. Selects, aligns, and secures holding fixtures, cutting tools, attachments, accessories, and materials onto machines. Measures, examines, and tests completed units to detect defects and ensure conformance to specifications. Installs repaired part into equipment and operates equipment to verify operational efficiency. Operates brazing, heat-treating, and welding equipment to cut, solder, and braze metal. Dismantles machine or equipment, using hand tools and power tools, to examine parts for defect or to remove defective parts. Cleans, lubricates, and maintains machines, tools, and equipment to remove grease, rust, stains, and foreign matter. Observes and listens to operating machines or equipment to diagnose machine malfunction and determine need for adjustment or repair. Cuts and shapes sheet metal, and heats and bends metal to specified shape. Installs experimental parts and assemblies, such as hydraulic systems, electrical wiring, lubricants, and batteries, into machines and mechanisms. Establishes work procedures for fabricating new structural products, using variety of metal working machines. Confers with engineering, supervisory, and manufacturing personnel to exchange technical information. Designs fixtures, tooling, and experimental parts to meet special engineering needs. Tests experimental models under simulated operating conditions for such purposes as development, standardization, and feasibility of design. Evaluates experimental procedures and recommends changes or modifications for efficiency and adaptability to set-up and production.

Yearly Earnings: $26,988

Education: Long-term O-J-T

Knowledge: Production and Processing; Engineering and Technology; Design; Mechanical; Physics; Chemistry

Abilities: Oral Comprehension; Oral Expression; Fluency of Ideas; Originality; Deductive Reasoning; Inductive Reasoning; Information Ordering; Category Flexibility; Mathematical Reasoning; Number Facility; Memorization; Speed of Closure; Perceptual Speed; Spatial Orientation; Visualization; Selective Attention; Time Sharing; Arm-Hand Steadiness; Manual Dexterity; Finger Dexterity; Control Precision; Multilimb Coordination; Response Orientation; Rate Control; Reaction Time; Wrist-Finger Speed; Speed of Limb Movement; Explosive Strength; Dynamic Strength; Trunk Strength; Extent Flexibility; Dynamic Flexibility; Gross Body Equilibrium; Near Vision; Visual Color Discrimination; Peripheral Vision; Hearing Sensitivity; Auditory Attention; Sound Localization; Speech Recognition

Skills: Mathematics; Science; Critical Thinking; Problem Identification; Synthesis/Reorganization; Solution Appraisal; Operations Analysis; Technology Design; Equipment Selection; Installation; Testing; Operation Monitoring; Operation and Control; Product Inspection; Equipment Maintenance; Troubleshooting; Repairing; Management of Material Resources

General Work Activities: Inspecting Equipment, Structures, or Material; Performing General Physical Activities; Handling and Moving Objects; Controlling Machines and Processes; Drafting and Specifying Technical Devices, etc.; Implementing Ideas, Programs, etc.; Repairing and Maintaining Mechanical Equipment; Repairing and Maintaining Electrical Equipment

Job Characteristics: Sounds, Noise Levels are Distracting, etc.; Cramped Work Space, Awkward Positions; Hazardous Equipment; Bending or Twisting the Body; Making Repetitive Motions; Common Protective or Safety Attire; Degree of Automation; Pace Determined by Speed of Equipment

GOE Group/s: 05.05.07 Craft Technology: Machining

CIP Program/s: 480501 Machinist/Machine Technologist; 480503 Machine Shop Assistant

Related DOT Job/s: 019.161-014 TEST TECHNICIAN; 600.260-022 MACHINIST, EXPERIMENTAL; 600.280-022 MACHINIST; 600.280-026 MACHINIST APPRENTICE; 600.280-030 MACHINIST APPRENTICE, AUTOMOTIVE; 600.280-034 MACHINIST, AUTOMOTIVE; 600.280-042 MAINTENANCE MACHINIST; 600.281-010 FLUID-POWER MECHANIC; 600.380-010 FIXTURE MAKER; 693.261-014 DEVELOPMENT MECHANIC; 693.261-022 ROCKET-MOTOR MECHANIC; 806.281-014 EXPERIMENTAL MECHANIC, ELECTRICAL

89111 TOOL GRINDERS, FILERS, SHARPENERS, AND OTHER PRECISION GRINDERS. OOH Title/s: Industrial Machinery Repairers; Metalworking and Plastics-Working Machine Operators

Perform such operations as precision smoothing, sharpening, polishing, and grinding of metal objects by the wearing action of abrasive materials or machine files. Include tool, cylinder, and card grinders and grinder operators, saw filers, and filer-finishers. Sets up, operates, and adjusts grinding or polishing machines to grind metal workpieces, such as dies, parts, and tools. Dresses grinding wheel, according to specifications. Tends machine that grinds, files, or polishes workpiece. Files or finishes surface of workpiece, using prescribed hand tool. Observes and listens to machine operation to determine whether adjustments are necessary to ensure that workpiece meets specifications. Selects and mounts grinding wheels on machines, according to specifications, using hand tools and applying knowledge of abrasive and grinding procedures. Examines and feels surface of workpiece to verify grinding meets specifications. Straightens workpiece and removes dents in workpiece, using straightening press and hammers. Turns valves to direct flow of coolant against cutting wheel and workpiece. Computes number, width, and angle of cutting tool, micrometer, scales, and gauges, and adjusts tool to produce specified cuts. Measures and examines workpiece to verify that dimensions meet specifications. Studies blueprint or layout of metal workpiece to visualize grinding procedure and plan sequences of operations. Places workpiece in electroplating solution, or applies pigment to surfaces of workpiece to highlight ridges and grooves. Duplicates workpiece contours, using tracer attachment. Removes and replaces machine parts, using hand tools. Forms specified section of workpiece and repairs cracks in workpiece, using welding or brazing equipment. Fits parts together in preassembly to ensure dimensions are accurate. Inspects dies to detect defects, assess wear, and verify specifications, using micrometers, steel gauge pins, and loupe. Removes finished

workpiece from machine and places in boxes or racks, depending on size of workpiece. Cleans and lubricates machine parts.
Yearly Earnings: $20,332
Education: Moderate-term O-J-T
Knowledge: Design; Mechanical; Foreign Language
Abilities: Wrist-Finger Speed; Speed of Limb Movement; Gross Body Equilibrium; Hearing Sensitivity; Auditory Attention; Sound Localization
Skills: Technology Design; Equipment Selection; Testing; Operation Monitoring; Operation and Control; Product Inspection; Equipment Maintenance; Repairing
General Work Activities: Repairing and Maintaining Mechanical Equipment
Job Characteristics: Sounds, Noise Levels are Distracting, etc.; Hazardous Equipment; Hazardous Situations; Keeping or Regaining Balance; Common Protective or Safety Attire; Degree of Automation; Importance of Repeating Same Tasks; Pace Determined by Speed of Equipment
GOE Group/s: 05.05.06 Craft Technology: Metal Fabrication and Repair; 05.05.07 Craft Technology: Machining; 05.10.05 Crafts: Reproduction; 06.01.02 Production Technology: Machine Set-up; 06.01.03 Production Technology: Machine Set-up and Operation; 06.01.04 Production Technology: Precision Hand Work
CIP Program/s: 010201 Agricultural Mechanization, General; 470402 Gunsmith; 480503 Machine Shop Assistant; 480507 Tool and Die Maker/Technologist
Related DOT Job/s: 500.381-010 CYLINDER GRINDER; 601.381-018 DIE POLISHER; 603.280-010 GRINDER OPERATOR, EXTERNAL, TOOL; 603.280-014 GRINDER OPERATOR, SURFACE, TOOL; 603.280-018 GRINDER OPERATOR, TOOL; 603.280-022 GRINDER SET-UP OPERATOR, INTERNAL; 603.280-030 GRINDER SET-UP OPERATOR, UNIVERSAL; 603.280-038 TOOL-GRINDER OPERATOR; 680.380-010 CARD GRINDER; 701.381-014 SAW FILER; 701.381-018 TOOL GRINDER I; 701.684-030 TOOL FILER; 705.381-010 DIE BARBER; 705.481-010 FILER, FINISH; 705.481-014 LAPPER, HAND, TOOL

89114A MODEL MAKERS, METAL AND PLASTIC. OOH Title/s: Metalworking and Plastics-Working Machine Operators

Set up and operate machines, such as lathes, milling and engraving machines, and jig borers to make working models of metal or plastic objects. Include template makers. Sets up and operates machines, such as lathes, drill presses, punch presses, or bandsaws, to fabricate prototypes or models. Determines fixtures, machines, tooling, and sequence of operations to fabricate parts, dies, and tooling, according to drawings and sketches. Drills, countersinks, and reams holes in parts and assemblies for bolts, screws, and other fasteners, using power tools. Lays out and marks reference points and dimensions on materials, using measuring instruments and drawing or scribing tools. Cuts, shapes, and forms metal parts, using lathe, power saw, snips, power brakes and shear, files, and mallets. Grinds, files, and sands parts to finished dimensions. Studies blueprint, drawings, or sketches, and computes dimensions for laying out materials and planning model production. Fabricates metal or plastic parts, using hand tools. Aligns, fits, and joins parts, using bolts or screws or by welding or gluing. Assembles mechanical, electrical, and electronic components into models or prototypes, using hand tools, power tools, and fabricating machines. Wires and solders electrical and electronic connections and components. Reworks or alters component model or parts as required to ensure performance of equipment or that parts meet standards. Inspects and tests model or other product to verify conformance to specifications, using precision measuring instruments or circuit tester. Devises and constructs own tools, dies, molds, jigs, and fixtures, or modifies existing tools and equipment. Makes bridges, plates, wheels, cutting teeth on wheels and pinions, and threaded screws. Consults and confers with engineering personnel to discuss developmental problems and to recommend modifications to correct or improve performance of product. Records specifications, production operations, and final dimensions of model for use in establishing operating standards and machinery procedures.
Yearly Earnings: $20,332
Education: Moderate-term O-J-T
Knowledge: Computers and Electronics; Engineering and Technology; Design; Building and Construction; Mechanical; Foreign Language
Abilities: Originality; Information Ordering; Mathematical Reasoning; Number Facility; Visualization; Arm-Hand Steadiness; Finger Dexterity; Control Precision; Reaction Time; Gross Body Equilibrium; Visual Color Discrimination; Auditory Attention
Skills: Problem Identification; Synthesis/Reorganization; Operations Analysis; Technology Design; Equipment Selection; Installation; Testing; Operation Monitoring; Operation and Control; Product Inspection; Troubleshooting; Repairing; Systems Perception; Identifying Downstream Consequences
General Work Activities: Controlling Machines and Processes; Drafting and Specifying Technical Devices, etc.; Repairing and Maintaining Mechanical Equipment; Repairing and Maintaining Electrical Equipment
Job Characteristics: Hazardous Equipment; Hazardous Situations; Bending or Twisting the Body; Making Repetitive Motions; Pace Determined by Speed of Equipment
GOE Group/s: 05.05.06 Craft Technology: Metal Fabrication and Repair; 05.05.07 Craft Technology: Machining; 05.05.11 Craft Technology: Scientific, Medical, & Technical Equip. Fabric. & Related
CIP Program/s: 470401 Instrument Calibration and Repairer; 470408 Watch, Clock and Jewelry Repairer; 480501 Machinist/Machine Technologist; 480503 Machine Shop Assistant
Related DOT Job/s: 600.260-014 EXPERIMENTAL MECHANIC; 600.260-018 MODEL MAKER, FIREARMS; 600.280-054 SAMPLE MAKER, APPLIANCES; 693.260-018 ENGINEERING MODEL MAKER; 693.361-014 MOCK-UP BUILDER; 693.380-010 MODEL MAKER; 709.381-014 MODEL BUILDER; 710.361-010 MODEL MAKER, SCALE; 723.361-010 MODEL MAKER, FLUORESCENT LIGHTING

89114B PATTERN MAKERS, METAL AND PLASTIC. OOH Title/s: Tool and Die Makers

Lay out, machine, fit, and assemble castings and parts to metal or plastic foundry patterns, core boxes, or match plates. Sets up and operates machine tools, such as milling machines, lathes, drill presses, and grinders, to machine castings or patterns. Cuts, trims, shapes, and forms pattern or template, using hand tools and power tools. Designs and develops template or pattern according to work orders, sample parts, or mockups. Lays out and draws or scribes pattern onto material, using compass, protractor, ruler, scribe, or other instruments. Verifies conformance of pattern or template dimensions to specifications, using measuring instruments such as calipers, scales, and micrometers. Studies blueprint of part to be cast or pattern to be made, computes dimensions, and plans sequence of operations. Operates welding equipment to weld pattern together. Assembles pattern sections, using hand tools, bolts, screws, rivets, or glue. Cleans and fine finishes pattern or template, using emery cloth, files, scrapers, and power grinders. Repairs and reworks templates and patterns. Marks identification numbers or symbols onto pattern or template. Makes templates or files for own use in inspection and finishing of particular shape. Constructs platforms, fixtures, and jigs for holding and placing patterns. Covers or sprays pattern used in producing plastic with plastic-impregnated fabric or coat of sealing lacquer or wax.
Yearly Earnings: $34,944

Education: Long-term O-J-T
Knowledge: Production and Processing; Design; Foreign Language
Abilities: Visualization; Arm-Hand Steadiness; Finger Dexterity; Wrist-Finger Speed; Gross Body Equilibrium; Near Vision; Auditory Attention
Skills: Technology Design; Operation Monitoring; Operation and Control; Product Inspection; Repairing
General Work Activities: Handling and Moving Objects; Controlling Machines and Processes; Drafting and Specifying Technical Devices, etc.
Job Characteristics: Sounds, Noise Levels are Distracting, etc.; Hazardous Equipment; Hazardous Situations; Common Protective or Safety Attire; Pace Determined by Speed of Equipment
GOE Group/s: 01.06.01 Craft Arts: Graphics Arts and Related Crafts; 05.05.06 Craft Technology: Metal Fabrication and Repair; 05.05.07 Craft Technology: Machining; 06.01.04 Production Technology: Precision Hand Work
CIP Program/s: 150607 Plastics Technologists and Technicians; 480501 Machinist/Machine Technologist; 480507 Tool and Die Maker/Technologist
Related DOT Job/s: 600.280-046 PATTERNMAKER APPRENTICE, METAL; 600.280-050 PATTERNMAKER, METAL; 601.280-038 TEMPLATE MAKER, EXTRUSION DIE; 601.381-038 TEMPLATE MAKER; 693.281-014 PATTERNMAKER; 693.281-018 PATTERNMAKER, METAL, BENCH; 693.281-022 PATTERNMAKER, SAMPLE; 703.381-010 PATTERNMAKER; 709.381-034 PATTERNMAKER; 751.381-010 PATTERNMAKER; 754.381-014 PATTERNMAKER, PLASTICS

89117 PRECISION LAYOUT WORKERS, METAL. OOH Title/s: Tool and Die Makers

Lay out reference points and dimensions on metal stock or workpieces, such as sheets, plates, tubes, structural shapes, castings, or machine parts, for further processing, such as machining, fabricating, welding, and assembling. Details location and sequence of cutting, drilling, bending, rolling, punching, and welding operations, using compass, protractor, dividers, and rule. Marks curves, lines, holes, dimensions, and welding symbols onto workpiece, using scribes, soapstone, punches, and hand drill. Determines reference points and computes layout dimensions and works to tolerances, as close as 0.001 inch. Locates center line and verifies template position, using measuring instruments, including gauge blocks, height gauges, and dial indicators. Examines workpiece and verifies such requirements as dimensions and squareness, using rule, square, and straightedge. Plans and develops layout from blueprints and templates, applying knowledge of trigonometry, design, effects of heat, and properties of metal. Lifts and positions workpiece in relation to surface plate manually or with hoist, using parallel blocks and angle plates. Adds dimensional details to blueprints or drawings by other workers and designs templates of wood, paper, or metal. Fits and aligns fabricated parts for welding or assembly operations. Inspects machined parts to verify conformance to specifications. Applies pigment to layout surfaces, using paint brush.
Yearly Earnings: $34,944
Education: Long-term O-J-T
Knowledge: Production and Processing; Design
Abilities: Mathematical Reasoning; Visualization; Arm-Hand Steadiness; Finger Dexterity; Multilimb Coordination
Skills: Mathematics; Technology Design; Product Inspection
General Work Activities: Drafting and Specifying Technical Devices, etc.
Job Characteristics: Standing; Using Hands on Objects, Tools, or Controls
GOE Group/s: 05.05.06 Craft Technology: Metal Fabrication and Repair; 05.05.07 Craft Technology: Machining; 06.02.31 Production Work: Manual Work, Laying Out and Marking
CIP Program/s: 480501 Machinist/Machine Technologist; 480503 Machine Shop Assistant
Related DOT Job/s: 600.281-018 LAY-OUT WORKER; 809.281-010 LAY-OUT WORKER I; 809.381-014 LAY-OUT WORKER II

89121 SHIPFITTERS. OOH Title/s: Shipfitters

Lay out and fabricate metal structural parts, such as plates, bulkheads, and frames. Brace them in position within hull or ship for riveting or welding. May prepare molds and templates for fabrication of nonstandard parts. Lays out position of parts on metal, working from blueprints or templates and using scribe and hand tools. Locates and marks reference lines, such as center, buttock, and frame lines. Positions parts in hull of ship, assisted by rigger. Aligns parts in relation to each other, using jacks, turnbuckles, clips, wedges, and mauls. Marks location of holes to be drilled and installs temporary fasteners to hold part in place for welding or riveting. Prepares molds and templates for fabrication of nonstandard parts. Rolls, bends, flanges, cuts, and shapes plates, beams, and other heavy metal parts, using shop machinery such as plate rolls, presses, bending brakes, and joggle machine. Installs packing, gaskets, liners, and structural accessories and members, such as doors, hatches, brackets, and clips. Tacks weld clips and brackets in place prior to permanent welding.
Yearly Earnings: $28,392
Education: Long-term O-J-T
Knowledge: Design; Building and Construction; Mechanical
Abilities: Multilimb Coordination; Extent Flexibility; Dynamic Flexibility; Gross Body Equilibrium; Peripheral Vision; Depth Perception; Auditory Attention
Skills: Installation
General Work Activities: Performing General Physical Activities; Handling and Moving Objects; Controlling Machines and Processes; Drafting and Specifying Technical Devices, etc.
Job Characteristics: Sounds, Noise Levels are Distracting, etc.; Very Hot; Extremely Bright or Inadequate Lighting; Contaminants; Cramped Work Space, Awkward Positions; Whole Body Vibration; Hazardous Equipment; Hazardous Situations; Kneeling, Crouching, or Crawling; Keeping or Regaining Balance; Bending or Twisting the Body; Common Protective or Safety Attire; Consequence of Error
GOE Group/s: 05.05.06 Craft Technology: Metal Fabrication and Repair
CIP Program/s: 490306 Marine Maintenance and Repair
Related DOT Job/s: 806.381-046 SHIPFITTER; 806.381-050 SHIPFITTER APPRENTICE

89123A JEWELERS. OOH Title/s: Jewelers

Fabricate and repair jewelry articles. Cuts and shapes metal into jewelry pieces, using cutting and carving tools. Arranges jewelry pieces into specified design, softens metal by heating with gas torch, and shapes, using hammer and die. Solders pieces of jewelry together and enlarges or reduces size of rings, using soldering torch or iron. Repairs, reshapes, and restyles jewelry by replacing broken parts or using hand tools and machines. Ties or twists gold or silver wires together, and bends to form rings. Smooths soldered joints and rough spots, using hand file and emery paper, and polishes with polishing wheel or buffing wire. Immerses jewelry in cleaning solution or acid to remove stains, or in solution of gold or other metal to color jewelry. Forms model of article from wax or metal, using carving tools. Places model in casting ring, and pours plaster into ring to form mold. Casts metal model from plaster mold, and forms mold of sand or rubber from model for casting article. Pours molten metal into mold, or operates centrifugal casting machine to cast article. Examines gemstone surfaces and internal

structure to evaluate their genuineness, quality, and value, using polariscope, refractometer, and other optical instruments. Immerses gemstones in chemical solutions to determine specific gravities and key properties for gem identification, quality determination, and appraisal. Grades stones for color, perfection, and quality of cut. Estimates wholesale and retail value of gemstones, following price guides and market fluctuations.
Yearly Earnings: $28,392
Education: Long-term O-J-T
Knowledge: Production and Processing; Fine Arts
Abilities: Category Flexibility; Visualization; Arm-Hand Steadiness; Manual Dexterity; Finger Dexterity; Control Precision; Wrist-Finger Speed; Near Vision; Visual Color Discrimination
Skills: Product Inspection; Repairing
General Work Activities: Judging Qualities of Things, Services, People; Thinking Creatively
Job Characteristics: Hazardous Conditions; Sitting; Using Hands on Objects, Tools, or Controls; Making Repetitive Motions
GOE Group/s: 01.06.02 Craft Arts: Arts and Crafts; 06.01.04 Production Technology: Precision Hand Work
CIP Program/s: 470408 Watch, Clock and Jewelry Repairer; 500201 Crafts, Folk Art and Artisanry; 500701 Art, General; 500713 Metal and Jewelry Arts
Related DOT Job/s: 199.281-010 GEMOLOGIST; 700.281-010 JEWELER; 700.281-014 JEWELER APPRENTICE; 700.381-030 LOCKET MAKER; 700.381-042 RING MAKER; 700.381-046 SAMPLE MAKER I

89123B SILVERSMITHS. OOH Title/s: Jewelers

Anneal, solder, hammer, shape, and glue silver articles. Anneals silverware, such as coffeepots, tea sets, and trays, in gas oven for prescribed time to soften metal for reworking. Solders parts together, and fills holes and cracks with silver solder, using gas torch. Hammers out deformations, selecting and using hammer and dollies with head corresponding in curvature with surface of article. Forms concavity in bottom of article to improve stability, using tracing punches and hammer. Shapes and straightens damaged or twisted articles by hand, or using pliers. Strikes article with small tools, or punches with hammer, to indent or restore embossing. Glues plastic separators to handles of coffee- and teapots. Outlines design from photographs or drawings onto surface of article, using hand tools. Positions article over snarling tool and raises design area, using foot-powered hammer. Peens edges of scratches or holes to repair defect, using peening hammer. Wires parts, such as legs, spouts, and handles, to body to prepare article for soldering. Pierces and cuts open design in ornamentation, using hand drill and scroll saw. Examines article to determine nature of defects, such as dents, uneven bottom, scratches, or holes, to repair. Verifies levelness of bottom edges of article, using straightedge or by rocking back and forth on flat surface.
Yearly Earnings: $28,392
Education: Long-term O-J-T
Knowledge: Production and Processing; Mechanical; Fine Arts
Abilities: Arm-Hand Steadiness; Manual Dexterity; Finger Dexterity; Explosive Strength; Gross Body Equilibrium
Skills: None above average
General Work Activities: Handling and Moving Objects
Job Characteristics: Sounds, Noise Levels are Distracting, etc.; Very Hot; Hazardous Equipment
GOE Group/s: 01.06.02 Craft Arts: Arts and Crafts
CIP Program/s: 500201 Crafts, Folk Art and Artisanry
Related DOT Job/s: 700.281-022 SILVERSMITH II; 700.381-022 HAMMERSMITH; 704.381-010 CHASER

89126C MODEL AND MOLD MAKERS, JEWELRY. OOH Title/s: Jewelers

Make models or molds to create jewelry items. Carves, chisels, scrapes, and files plaster, wax or other plastic materials to make mold or model, according to design specifications. Fits, secures, and solders halves of molds together, and drills holes in mold to attach handles and allow gases to escape during casting. Lays out design on metal stock, and cuts along markings to fabricate pieces used to cast metal molds. Builds sand mold in flask, following pattern, and heats flask, using furnace or torch to dry and harden mold. Cuts design in mold or other material to be used as model to fabricate metal and jewelry products. Constructs preliminary model of wax, metal, clay or plaster; forms sample casting in mold, and measures casting to verify dimensions. Mixes or melts clay, metal, plaster, wax, or other material and pours material into mold to cast model or mold. Examines and measures metal parts for conformance to design specifications on scale drawing. Writes or modifies design specifications, such as content, weight, and material to be used to cast article. Presses model into clay, and builds up clay around exposed parts of model to retain plaster. Removes mold from cast article, cleans mold, and applies shellac and dry powder to preserve mold for reuse. Polishes metal surfaces and products, using abrasive wheel. Modifies, sharpens, repairs or fabricates jigs, fixtures, and hand tools, such as scrapers, cutter, gougers, and shapers. Computes cost of labor and material to determine production cost of products and articles.
Yearly Earnings: $28,392
Education: Long-term O-J-T
Knowledge: Design; Fine Arts
Abilities: Arm-Hand Steadiness; Finger Dexterity; Wrist-Finger Speed; Near Vision
Skills: None above average
General Work Activities: Drafting and Specifying Technical Devices, etc.
Job Characteristics: Objective or Subjective Information; Hazardous Situations; Using Hands on Objects, Tools, or Controls; Importance of Repeating Same Tasks; Pace Determined by Speed of Equipment
GOE Group/s: 01.06.02 Craft Arts: Arts and Crafts; 05.03.02 Engineering Technology: Drafting; 06.01.04 Production Technology: Precision Hand Work
CIP Program/s: 470408 Watch, Clock and Jewelry Repairer; 480501 Machinist/Machine Technologist; 500701 Art, General; 500713 Metal and Jewelry Arts
Related DOT Job/s: 518.381-010 BENCH-MOLDER APPRENTICE; 518.381-022 MOLDER, BENCH; 700.281-018 MODEL MAKER I; 700.381-034 MOLD MAKER I; 700.381-038 MOLD-MAKER APPRENTICE; 709.381-018 MODEL MAKER II; 709.381-022 MODEL-MAKER APPRENTICE; 735.381-018 SAMPLE MAKER II; 777.381-022 MOLD MAKER II

89126E BENCH WORKERS, JEWELRY. OOH Title/s: Metalworking and Plastics-Working Machine Operators

Cut, file, form, and solder parts for jewelry. Cuts, trims, shapes, and smooths jewelry stones, pearls, and metal pieces, using abrasives, grinding stone, and power and hand tools. Weighs, mixes, and melts metal alloys or material, and pours molten material into mold to cast models of jewelry. Forms, joins, or assembles metal pieces, articles, or wire, using soldering iron, gas torch, and hand tools. Disassembles mold casting from metal or jewelry workpiece, and places workpiece in water or on tray to cool. Marks and drills holes in jewelry mounting to center stones according to design specifications. Positions and aligns stones and metal pieces, and sets, mounts, and secures item in place, using setting and hand tools. Manually rotates mold to distribute molten material and prevent formation of air pockets in mold. Marks, engraves, or embosses designs on metal pieces, such as castings, wire, or jewelry, following samples, sketches, or other specifications. Plates articles,

such as jewelry pieces and clock and watch dials, with silver, gold, nickel, or other metals. Examines assembled or finished product, using magnifying glass or precision measuring instruments, to ensure conformance to specifications. Repairs existing jewelry mountings to reposition jewels or adjust mounting. Sands inside mold pieces, using emery cloth and chalkdust. Assembles and secures mold sections used to cast metal articles and pieces. Brushes, buffs, cleans, and polishes metal items and jewelry pieces, using jeweler's tools, polishing wheel, and chemical bath. Operates machines, such as centrifugal-casting, routing, and lathe, to fabricate casting molds, metal parts, or wax models of products. Weighs completed pieces to determine deviation from specifications, and records weight and processing time on production records. Designs and fabricates molds, models, and machine accessories, and modifies hand tools used to cast metal and jewelry pieces. Researches and analyzes reference materials and consults with interested parties to develop new or modify existing products.
Yearly Earnings: $28,392
Education: Long-term O-J-T
Knowledge: Production and Processing; Fine Arts
Abilities: Visualization; Arm-Hand Steadiness; Manual Dexterity; Finger Dexterity; Control Precision; Wrist-Finger Speed; Near Vision; Visual Color Discrimination
Skills: Product Inspection
General Work Activities: Thinking Creatively
Job Characteristics: Sitting; Using Hands on Objects, Tools, or Controls; Making Repetitive Motions; Importance of Being Exact or Accurate
GOE Group/s: 01.06.01 Craft Arts: Graphics Arts and Related Crafts; 01.06.02 Craft Arts: Arts and Crafts; 05.05.14 Craft Technology: Gem Cutting and Finishing; 06.01.04 Production Technology: Precision Hand Work; 06.02.23 Production Work: Manual Work, Assembly Small Parts; 06.02.24 Production Work: Manual Work, Metal and Plastics
CIP Program/s: 470408 Watch, Clock and Jewelry Repairer; 500701 Art, General; 500711 Ceramics Arts and Ceramics; 500713 Metal and Jewelry Arts
Related DOT Job/s: 502.381-010 CASTER; 502.682-018 CENTRIFUGAL-CASTING-MACHINE OPERATOR; 700.381-010 CHAIN MAKER, HAND; 700.381-014 FANCY-WIRE DRAWER; 700.381-018 GOLD-BEATER; 700.381-026 LAY-OUT WORKER; 700.381-050 SOLDERER; 700.381-054 STONE SETTER; 700.381-058 STONE-SETTER APPRENTICE; 704.381-018 ENGINE TURNER; 715.381-046 DIAL MAKER; 735.381-010 BENCH HAND; 735.381-014 PEARL RESTORER; 735.681-010 BRACELET AND BROOCH MAKER; 770.381-010 BEAD MAKER

89126K PEWTER CASTERS AND FINISHERS. OOH Title/s: No related OOH occupation

Cast and finish pewter alloy to form parts for goblets, candlesticks, and other pewterware. Fills casting mold to form parts. Secures molded item in chuck of lathe, activates lathe, and finishes inner and outer surfaces of item. Rotates mold to distribute alloy in mold and to prevent formation of air pockets. Heats ingots or alloy mixture and skims off impurities. Weighs and mixes alloy ingredients. Engraves decorative lines on item, using engraving tool. Routs out location of part and solder path where part is joined to item, using routing machine. Positions and aligns auxiliary part in jig and joins parts, using solder and blowtorch. Sands inside of mold parts, applies glaze to inside surface of mold, and assembles mold. Strikes mold to separate dried casting from mold. Determines placement of auxiliary parts, such as handle and spout, and marks locations of parts. Weighs completed item to determine deviation from specified weight, and records weight. Designs, drafts, and fabricates models of new casting molds and chipping and turning tools used to finish surface of products. Carries castings or finished items to storage area or next work station. Researches reference materials, analyzes production data, and consults with interested parties to develop ideas for new products.
Yearly Earnings: $28,392
Education: Long-term O-J-T
Knowledge: Production and Processing; Design; Fine Arts
Abilities: Originality; Visualization; Arm-Hand Steadiness; Control Precision; Speed of Limb Movement; Auditory Attention
Skills: Technology Design; Operation and Control
General Work Activities: Drafting and Specifying Technical Devices, etc.
Job Characteristics: Very Hot; Extremely Bright or Inadequate Lighting; Hazardous Situations; Importance of Repeating Same Tasks; Pace Determined by Speed of Equipment
GOE Group/s: 01.06.02 Craft Arts: Arts and Crafts; 06.02.24 Production Work: Manual Work, Metal and Plastics
CIP Program/s: 480501 Machinist/Machine Technologist; 500701 Art, General; 500713 Metal and Jewelry Arts
Related DOT Job/s: 502.384-010 PEWTER CASTER; 700.261-010 PEWTERER; 700.281-026 PEWTER FINISHER

89128 PRECISION ETCHERS AND ENGRAVERS, HAND OR MACHINE. OOH Title/s: Prepress Workers

Engrave or etch flat or curved metal, wood, rubber, or other materials by hand or machine for printing, identification, or decorative purposes. Include etchers and engravers of both hard and soft metals or materials, and jewelry and seal engravers. Exclude photoengravers, pantographers, and glass etchers and engravers. Engraves or cuts lettering, design, or characters in workpiece surface, using hand tools and engraving tool. Sketches, traces, or scribes layout lines and design on workpiece, plates, dies, or rollers, using compass, scriber, graver, or pencil. Determines machine settings and moves bars or levers to reproduce designs on rollers or plates. Operates machine to engrave design into steel rollers or plates. Trims precut designs or cuts around design to remove undesirable part, using graver. Reviews sketches, diagrams, blueprints, or photographs to determine design to be cut or engraved. Measures and computes dimensions of lettering, designs, or patterns to be engraved. Prints proof or examines design to verify accuracy, and reworks engraving as required. Sketches original design or pattern for use in printing or engraving. Transfers design from sleet or film to die or roller by decimal staining. Casts male die from engraved female die for use in seals. Positions and clamps workpiece, plate, or roller in holding fixture. Scrapes plate or die to remove imperfections and smooth surface. Sharpens and forms cutting edge of gravers or cutter grinders. Polishes and oils surface of plate or die, or brushes with acid-proof paint.
Yearly Earnings: $22,412
Education: Long-term O-J-T
Knowledge: Design; Fine Arts
Abilities: Arm-Hand Steadiness; Finger Dexterity; Control Precision; Depth Perception
Skills: None above average
General Work Activities: None above average
Job Characteristics: Making Repetitive Motions
GOE Group/s: 01.06.01 Craft Arts: Graphics Arts and Related Crafts; 05.10.05 Crafts: Reproduction
CIP Program/s: 470408 Watch, Clock and Jewelry Repairer; 480201 Graphic and Printing Equipment Operator, General; 480205 Mechanical Typesetter and Composer
Related DOT Job/s: 704.381-022 ENGRAVER APPRENTICE, DECORATIVE; 704.381-026 ENGRAVER, HAND, HARD METALS; 704.381-030 ENGRAVER, HAND, SOFT METALS; 704.381-034 ENGRAVER, SEALS; 972.381-018 SKETCH MAKER II; 972.681-010 MUSIC ENGRAVER; 979.281-010 DIE MAKER; 979.281-014 ENGRAVER, BLOCK; 979.281-018

ENGRAVER, PICTURE; 979.381-010 ENGRAVER I; 979.381-030 SIDEROGRAPHER

89132 SHEET-METAL WORKERS. OOH Title/s: Sheetmetal Workers

Fabricate, assemble, install, and repair sheet-metal products and equipment, such as control boxes, drainpipes, and furnace casings. Work may involve any of the following: set up and operate fabricating machines to cut, bend, and straighten sheet metal; shape metal over anvils, blocks, or forms using hammer; operate soldering and welding equipment to join sheet metal parts; inspect, assemble, andsmooth seams and joints of burred surfaces. Sets up and operates fabricating machines, such as shears, brakes, presses, and routers, to cut, bend, block, and form materials. Welds, solders, bolts, rivets, screws, clips, caulks, or bonds component parts to assemble products, using hand tools, power tools, and equipment. Shapes metal material over anvil, block, or other form, using hand tools. Trims, files, grinds, deburrs, buffs, and smooths surfaces, using hand tools and portable power tools. Installs assemblies in supportive framework according to blueprints, using hand tools, power tools, and lifting and handling devices. Lays out and marks dimensions and reference lines on material, using scribes, dividers, squares, and rulers. Determines sequence and methods of fabricating, assembling, and installing sheet-metal products, using blueprints, sketches, or product specifications. Selects gauge and type of sheet metal or non-metallic material, according to product specifications. Inspects assemblies and installation for conformance to specifications, using measuring instruments, such as calipers, scales, dial indicators, gauges, and micrometers. Operates laser-beam cutter or plasma-arc cutter to cut patterns from sheet metal. Operates computer-aided drafting (CAD) equipment to develop scale drawings of product or system.

Yearly Earnings: $28,340

Education: Moderate-term O-J-T

Knowledge: Production and Processing; Computers and Electronics; Design; Building and Construction; Mechanical

Abilities: None above average

Skills: Technology Design; Equipment Selection; Installation

General Work Activities: Performing General Physical Activities; Handling and Moving Objects; Controlling Machines and Processes; Operating Vehicles or Equipment

Job Characteristics: Sounds, Noise Levels are Distracting, etc.; Hazardous Equipment; Common Protective or Safety Attire; Pace Determined by Speed of Equipment

GOE Group/s: 05.05.06 Craft Technology: Metal Fabrication and Repair

CIP Program/s: 469999 Construction Trades, Other; 480506 Sheet Metal Worker

Related DOT Job/s: 804.281-010 SHEET-METAL WORKER; 804.281-014 SHEET-METAL-WORKER APPRENTICE; 804.481-010 HOOD MAKER

89135 BOILERMAKERS. OOH Title/s: Boilermakers

Construct, assemble, maintain, and repair stationary steam boilers and boiler house auxiliaries. Align structures or plate sections to assemble boiler frame tanks or vats, following blueprints. Work involves use of hand and power tools, plumb bobs, levels, wedges, dogs, or turnbuckles. Assist in testing assembled vessels. Direct cleaning of boilers and boiler furnaces. Inspect and repair boiler fittings, such as safety valves, regulators, automatic-control mechanisms, water columns, and auxiliary machines. Positions, aligns, and secures structural parts and related assemblies of pressure vessels, using plumb bobs, levels, wedges, and turnbuckles. Bolts or arc-welds pressure vessel structures and parts together, using wrenches and welding equipment. Straightens or reshapes bent pressure vessel plates and structure parts, using hammer, jacks, and torch. Bells, beads with power hammer, or welds pressure vessel tube ends to ensure leak-proof joints. Installs manholes, handholes, valves, gauges, and feedwater connections in drums of water tube boilers, using hand tools. Inspects assembled vessels for faulty accessories and pressure tests for leakage. Repairs or replaces defective pressure vessel parts, using torch, jacks, caulking hammers, power saw, threading die, and welding equipment. Maintains and repairs stationary steam boilers and boiler house auxiliaries, using hand tools and power tools. Shapes seams, joints, and irregular edges of pressure vessel sections and structural parts to attain specified fit, using cutting torch, file, and power grinder. Repairs insulation of pressure vessel with cement. Studies blueprints to determine location, relationship and dimensions of parts, to assemble pressure vessels, such as boilers, tanks, and vats. Locates and marks reference points for columns or plates on foundation, using master straightedge, square, transit, and measuring instruments. Installs refractory brick and other heat resistant materials in firebox of pressure vessel. Fabricates parts, such as stacks, uptakes, and chutes, to adapt pressure vessel to premises. Cleans pressure vessel equipment, using scrapers, wire brush, and cleaning solvent. Attaches rigging and signals crane operator to lift pressure vessel parts to specified position.

Yearly Earnings: $28,392

Education: Long-term O-J-T

Knowledge: Engineering and Technology; Building and Construction; Mechanical; Physics; Public Safety and Security

Abilities: Manual Dexterity; Finger Dexterity; Multilimb Coordination; Speed of Limb Movement; Static Strength; Explosive Strength; Dynamic Strength; Extent Flexibility; Dynamic Flexibility; Gross Body Equilibrium; Night Vision; Peripheral Vision; Depth Perception; Glare Sensitivity; Auditory Attention; Sound Localization

Skills: Technology Design; Installation; Testing; Product Inspection; Equipment Maintenance; Troubleshooting; Repairing

General Work Activities: Inspecting Equipment, Structures, or Material; Performing General Physical Activities; Handling and Moving Objects; Repairing and Maintaining Mechanical Equipment

Job Characteristics: Sounds, Noise Levels are Distracting, etc.; Very Hot; Extremely Bright or Inadequate Lighting; Cramped Work Space, Awkward Positions; Whole Body Vibration; High Places; Hazardous Conditions; Hazardous Equipment; Hazardous Situations; Standing; Climbing Ladders, Scaffolds, Poles, etc.; Kneeling, Crouching, or Crawling; Keeping or Regaining Balance; Using Hands on Objects, Tools, or Controls; Bending or Twisting the Body; Common Protective or Safety Attire

GOE Group/s: 05.05.06 Craft Technology: Metal Fabrication and Repair

CIP Program/s: 470303 Industrial Machinery Maintenance and Repair

Related DOT Job/s: 805.261-010 BOILERMAKER APPRENTICE; 805.261-014 BOILERMAKER I; 805.361-010 BOILERHOUSE MECHANIC; 805.361-014 BOILERMAKER FITTER; 805.381-010 BOILERMAKER II

89199 ALL OTHER PRECISION METAL WORKERS. OOH Title/s: Tool and Die Makers

All other precision metal workers not classified separately above.

Yearly Earnings: $34,944

Education: Long-term O-J-T

GOE Group/s: 05.05.06 Craft Technology: Metal Fabrication and Repair; 06.01.04 Production Technology: Precision Hand Work; 06.02.02 Production Work: Machine Work, Metal and Plastics; 06.02.24 Production Work: Manual Work, Metal and Plastics; 06.04.24 Elemental Work: Industrial: Manual Work, Metal and Plastics

CIP Program/s: 480501 Machinist/Machine Technologist; 480507 Tool and Die Maker/Technologist; 490306 Marine Maintenance and Repair
Related DOT Job/s: 616.681-010 WEAVER, BENCH LOOM; 619.260-010 ORNAMENTAL-METAL-WORKER APPRENTICE; 619.260-014 ORNAMENTAL-METAL WORKER; 619.361-010 FORMER, HAND; 704.381-014 CHEMICAL-ETCHING PROCESSOR; 705.381-014 EXTRUSION-DIE REPAIRER; 706.381-014 BENCH HAND; 709.381-042 SPRING FORMER, HAND; 709.381-046 WIRE-MESH-FILTER FABRICATOR; 732.381-018 GOLF-CLUB HEAD FORMER; 734.481-010 WIRE-FRAME MAKER; 809.381-030 PNEUMATIC-TOOL OPERATOR

Woodworking Occupations

89302A PATTERN MAKERS, WOOD. OOH Title/s: Woodworking Occupations

Plan, lay out, and construct wooden unit or sectional patterns used in forming sand molds for castings, according to blueprint specifications. Plans, lays out, and draws outline of unit, sectional patterns, or full-scale mock-up of products. Fits, fastens, and assembles wood parts together to form pattern, model, or section, using glue, nails, dowels, bolts, and screws. Sets up, operates, and adjusts variety of woodworking machines to cut and shape sections, parts, and patterns, according to specifications. Trims, smooths and shapes surfaces, and planes, shaves, files, scrapes, and sands models to attain specified shapes, using hand tools. Constructs wooden models, templates, full-scale mock-up, and molds for parts of products. Reads blueprints, drawing, or written specifications to determine size and shape of pattern and required machine set-up. Trims, smoothes and shapes surfaces, and planes, shaves, files, scrapes, and sands models to attain specified shapes, using hand tools. Shellacs, lacquers, or waxes finished pattern or model. Marks identifying information, such as colors or codes, on patterns, parts, and templates to indicate assembly method. Issues patterns to designated machine operators, and maintains pattern record for reference.
Yearly Earnings: $21,528
Education: Long-term O-J-T
Knowledge: Design; Building and Construction
Abilities: None above average
Skills: Product Inspection
General Work Activities: Drafting and Specifying Technical Devices, etc.
Job Characteristics: Hazardous Situations
GOE Group/s: 05.05.08 Craft Technology: Woodworking
CIP Program/s: 480701 Woodworkers, General; 480702 Furniture Designer and Maker; 480703 Cabinet Maker and Millworker
Related DOT Job/s: 661.280-010 PATTERNMAKER; 661.281-010 LOFT WORKER; 661.281-014 LOFT WORKER APPRENTICE; 661.281-018 PATTERNMAKER APPRENTICE, WOOD; 661.281-022 PATTERNMAKER, WOOD; 661.380-010 MODEL MAKER, WOOD

89302C JIG BUILDERS. OOH Title/s: Woodworking Occupations

Build jigs used as guides for assembling wooden containers. Assembles jigs to be used as guides for assembling barrels or boxes. Measures and marks positions of stops on work table, following blueprints. Nails stops to work table as indicated on blueprint. Reads blueprints to determine size and shape of wooden container.
Yearly Earnings: $21,528
Education: Long-term O-J-T
Knowledge: Building and Construction
Abilities: None above average
Skills: None above average
General Work Activities: None above average
Job Characteristics: Bending or Twisting the Body
GOE Group/s: 05.10.01 Crafts: Structural
CIP Program/s: 480701 Woodworkers, General; 480703 Cabinet Maker and Millworker
Related DOT Job/s: 761.381-014 JIG BUILDER

89305 WOODWORKING LAYOUT WORKERS. OOH Title/s: Woodworking Occupations

Lay out outline of frames and furniture parts on woodstock to guide machine operators working from blueprints, job orders, or models. Measures and marks with rule, square, and pencil or crayon, outlines of cuts to be made by various machine operators. Traces outlines from blueprints for decorative or irregular cutting on bandsaw. Traces around patterns to indicate cutting lines. Calibrates and records machining dimensions on stock or pattern for use in production as guide for machining parts. Studies architectural drawing or blueprint of part or full assembly to be made. Selects stock lumber of necessary size.
Yearly Earnings: $21,528
Education: Long-term O-J-T
Knowledge: Design; Building and Construction
Abilities: None above average
Skills: None above average
General Work Activities: None above average
Job Characteristics: Sounds, Noise Levels are Distracting, etc.; Contaminants; Using Hands on Objects, Tools, or Controls; Importance of Being Exact or Accurate
GOE Group/s: 06.02.31 Production Work: Manual Work, Laying Out and Marking
CIP Program/s: 480701 Woodworkers, General; 480703 Cabinet Maker and Millworker
Related DOT Job/s: 149.281-010 FURNITURE REPRODUCER; 761.381-022 PATTERN MARKER I

89308 WOOD MACHINISTS. OOH Title/s: Woodworking Occupations

Set up and operate a variety of woodworking machines to surface, cut, and shape lumber, and to fabricate parts for wood products, such as door and window frames, furniture, and sashes, according to specifications. Exclude workers primarily concerned with one or a limited number of machine phases and include them with their specialty. Operates variety of machines to saw, smooth, shape, bore holes in, and cut slots, grooves, and designs in woodstock. Selects, installs, and adjusts saw blades, cutter heads, boring bits, and sanding belts in respective machines, using hand tools and rule. Starts machine and makes trial cut. Periodically verifies dimensions of parts for adherence to specifications, using gauges and templates. Assembles fabricated parts to make millwork products, such as doors, sashes, and door and window frames.
Yearly Earnings: $21,528
Education: Long-term O-J-T
Knowledge: Production and Processing; Building and Construction
Abilities: None above average
Skills: None above average
General Work Activities: Handling and Moving Objects; Controlling Machines and Processes
Job Characteristics: Sounds, Noise Levels are Distracting, etc.; Whole Body Vibration; Hazardous Equipment; Standing; Making Repetitive Motions; Common Protective or Safety Attire; Degree of Automation; Importance of Being Exact or Accurate; Pace Determined by Speed of Equipment
GOE Group/s: 05.05.08 Craft Technology: Woodworking

CIP Program/s: 480701 Woodworkers, General; 480703 Cabinet Maker and Millworker
Related DOT Job/s: 669.380-010 MACHINIST APPRENTICE, WOOD; 669.380-014 MACHINIST, WOOD

89311 CABINETMAKERS AND BENCH CARPENTERS. OOH Title/s: Woodworking Occupations
Cut, shape, and assemble wooden articles, such as store fixtures, office equipment, cabinets, and-high grade furniture. Set up and operate variety of machines, such as power saws, jointers, mortisers, tenoners, molders, and shapers, to cut and shape parts from woodstock. Exclude workers primarily concerned with one or a limited number of machine phases and include them with their specialty. Sets up and operates machines, including power saws, jointers, mortisers, tenoners, molders, and shapers, to cut and shape woodstock. Trims component parts of joints to ensure snug fit, using hand tools such as planes, chisels, or wood files. Glues, fits, and clamps parts and subassemblies together to form complete unit. Drives nails or other fasteners to joints of articles to prepare articles for finishing. Bores holes for insertion of screws or dowel by hand or using boring machine. Marks dimensions of parts on paper or lumber stock, following blueprints, and matches lumber for color, grain, and texture. Sands and scrapes surfaces and joints of articles to prepare articles for finishing. Studies blueprints, drawings, and written specifications of articles to be constructed or repaired, and plans sequence of performing such operations. Dips, brushes, or sprays assembled articles with protective or decorative materials, such as stain, varnish, or lacquer. Installs hardware, such as hinges, catches, and drawer pulls, using hand tools.
Yearly Earnings: $20,020
Education: Long-term O-J-T
Knowledge: Production and Processing; Engineering and Technology; Design; Building and Construction
Abilities: None above average
Skills: Installation
General Work Activities: None above average
Job Characteristics: Cramped Work Space, Awkward Positions; Whole Body Vibration; Kneeling, Crouching, or Crawling; Using Hands on Objects, Tools, or Controls; Bending or Twisting the Body
GOE Group/s: 05.05.08 Craft Technology: Woodworking
CIP Program/s: 480701 Woodworkers, General; 480703 Cabinet Maker and Millworker
Related DOT Job/s: 660.280-010 CABINETMAKER; 660.280-014 CABINETMAKER APPRENTICE

89314 FURNITURE FINISHERS. OOH Title/s: Woodworking Occupations
Shape, finish, and refinish damaged, worn, or used furniture or new high-grade furniture to specified color or finish, utilizing knowledge of wood properties, finishes, and furniture style. Disassembles items, masks areas adjacent to those items being refinished, and removes accessories, using hand tools, to prepare for finishing. Removes old finish and damaged or deteriorated parts, using hand tools, abrasives, or solvents. Fills cracks, blemishes, or depressions and repairs broken parts, using plastic or wood putty, glue, nails, or screws. Treats warped or stained surfaces to restore original contour and color. Smooths and shapes surfaces with sandpaper, pumice stone, steel wool, or chisel. Washes or bleaches surface to return to natural color or prepare for application of finish. Brushes, sprays, or hand rubs finishing ingredients onto and into grain of wood. Finishes surfaces of new furniture pieces to replicate antiques by distressing surfaces with abrasives before staining. Examines furniture to determine extent of damage or deterioration, and determines method of repair or restoration. Selects appropriate finishing ingredients, such as paint, stain, lacquer, shellac, or varnish, for wood surface. Mixes finish ingredients to obtain desired color or shade of existing finish. Stencils, gilds, embosses, or paints designs or borders on restored pieces to reproduce original appearance. Polishes, sprays, or waxes finished pieces to match surrounding finish. Replaces and refurbishes upholstery of item, using tacks, adhesives, softeners, solvents, stains, or polish. Spreads graining ink over metal portions of furniture to simulate wood-grain finish.
Yearly Earnings: $20,020
Education: Long-term O-J-T
Knowledge: Building and Construction; Chemistry; Fine Arts
Abilities: Speed of Limb Movement; Dynamic Flexibility; Visual Color Discrimination
Skills: Equipment Selection
General Work Activities: None above average
Job Characteristics: Contaminants; Hazardous Conditions; Hazardous Situations; Kneeling, Crouching, or Crawling; Using Hands on Objects, Tools, or Controls
GOE Group/s: 05.05.08 Craft Technology: Woodworking; 05.10.01 Crafts: Structural
CIP Program/s: 480701 Woodworkers, General; 480702 Furniture Designer and Maker; 500201 Crafts, Folk Art and Artisanry
Related DOT Job/s: 763.380-010 FURNITURE RESTORER; 763.381-010 FURNITURE FINISHER; 763.381-014 FURNITURE-FINISHER APPRENTICE; 763.681-010 FRAME REPAIRER; 763.684-022 CANER II; 763.684-034 FINISH PATCHER

89397A CUSTOM PRECISION WOODWORKERS, MUSICAL INSTRUMENTS. OOH Title/s: Woodworking Occupations; Electronic Home Entertainment Equipment Repairers
Lay out, construct, and assemble wooden musical instruments or components, using hand tools and operating variety of woodworking machines. Products may contain additional materials, including metal or strings. Operates woodworking machines and uses hand tools to cut and shape wooden components of instrument. Fits and assembles electrical, wooden, and metal parts in instrument. Fastens components together with screws, nails, or glue, using hand tools or portable power tools. Measures and marks woodstock to lay out wooden parts according to blueprint or specifications. Sands and scrapes wooden parts to prepare for finishing. Bends wooden components using steam and clamps. Fits and glues inlay materials to decorate instrument. Applies varnish, stain, oil, or lacquer to finish surfaces. Examines completed instrument for defects. Tunes instrument to specified pitch.
Yearly Earnings: $20,020
Education: Long-term O-J-T
Knowledge: Production and Processing; Design; Fine Arts
Abilities: Arm-Hand Steadiness; Finger Dexterity; Speed of Limb Movement; Hearing Sensitivity
Skills: None above average
General Work Activities: None above average
Job Characteristics: None above average
GOE Group/s: 05.05.12 Craft Technology: Musical Instrument Fabrication and Repair
CIP Program/s: 470404 Musical Instrument Repairer
Related DOT Job/s: 730.281-010 ACCORDION MAKER; 730.281-022 FRETTED-INSTRUMENT MAKER, HAND; 730.281-030 HARP MAKER; 730.281-042 PIPE-ORGAN BUILDER; 730.281-046 VIOLIN MAKER, HAND; 730.281-058 BOW MAKER

89397B CUSTOM PRECISION WOODWORKERS.

OOH Title/s: Woodworking Occupations

Design, carve, and fabricate custom wood products or patterns that are unique to specifications of individual job assignments. Exclude musical instrument makers. Cuts and shapes woodstock to desired dimensions using woodworking machines such as bandsaw or lathe. Draws or sketches design for wood carving, checkering, or marquetry. Shapes contours or carves design using hand tools such as drawknife, chisels, or rasps. Lays out dimensions on woodstock according to design or template. Selects special woods for carving or marquetry according to color, strength, and grain. Sands and scrapes workpiece to prepare for finishing. Applies varnish, stain, oil or lacquer to finish surfaces. Inspects finished workpiece for irregularities and conformance to specifications or pattern. Sharpens and maintains woodworking tools.

Yearly Earnings: $20,020
Education: Long-term O-J-T
Knowledge: Production and Processing; Design; Building and Construction; Fine Arts
Abilities: Visualization; Arm-Hand Steadiness
Skills: None above average
General Work Activities: Thinking Creatively
Job Characteristics: Hazardous Equipment
GOE Group/s: 01.06.02 Craft Arts: Arts and Crafts; 05.05.08 Craft Technology: Woodworking
CIP Program/s: 470402 Gunsmith; 480701 Woodworkers, General; 480702 Furniture Designer and Maker; 500201 Crafts, Folk Art and Artisanry
Related DOT Job/s: 761.281-010 CARVER, HAND; 761.281-018 MARQUETRY WORKER; 761.381-034 STOCK CHECKERER I; 761.381-038 STOCK MAKER, CUSTOM

89398 STANDARD PRECISION WOODWORKERS.

OOH Title/s: Woodworking Occupations

Fabricate same or similar wood product, or perform similar precision woodwork, such as shaping or cutting, with each job assignment. Components of product may be prefabricated. Fits and assembles components of wood products. Shapes and forms wooden components using hand tools such as files, drawknives, and spokeshaves and vise. Scrapes and sands wooden parts by hand or using portable power sander. Bends wooden components using steam or water and bending frame. Sets up and operates woodworking machines such as lathe, bandsaw, and shaper to cut, shape, form, and saw wooden components. Measures wood blocks, wooden components, and finished wood products to mark areas for removal, lay out components, and verify machining of products according to specifications. Marks layout of wooden components. Inspects finished components or products for irregularities and conformance to specifications or pattern. Inlays veneer into surface of wood products for decoration. Lays out and cuts templates for use in forming wooden components. Draws sketches of wooden components or wood products.

Yearly Earnings: $20,020
Education: Long-term O-J-T
Knowledge: Production and Processing; Design; Building and Construction
Abilities: Visualization; Arm-Hand Steadiness; Wrist-Finger Speed; Speed of Limb Movement; Dynamic Strength; Gross Body Equilibrium
Skills: None above average
General Work Activities: Controlling Machines and Processes; Drafting and Specifying Technical Devices, etc.
Job Characteristics: Sounds, Noise Levels are Distracting, etc.; Hazardous Equipment; Hazardous Situations; Using Hands on Objects, Tools, or Controls; Making Repetitive Motions; Importance of Repeating Same Tasks; Pace Determined by Speed of Equipment
GOE Group/s: 05.05.02 Craft Technology: Construction and Maintenance; 05.05.12 Craft Technology: Musical Instrument Fabrication and Repair; 06.01.04 Production Technology: Precision Hand Work; 06.02.03 Production Work: Machine Work, Wood; 06.02.25 Production Work: Manual Work, Wood
CIP Program/s: 150603 Industrial/Manufacturing Technologists and Technicians; 470404 Musical Instrument Repairer; 480701 Woodworkers, General; 480703 Cabinet Maker and Millworker
Related DOT Job/s: 661.381-010 HAT-BLOCK MAKER; 730.281-034 HARPSICHORD MAKER; 761.281-014 EXPERIMENTAL-BOX TESTER; 761.381-010 BOAT-OAR MAKER; 761.381-018 LAST-MODEL MAKER; 761.381-026 SKI MAKER, WOOD; 761.381-030 SMOKING-PIPE MAKER

Apparel Occupations

89502A FABRIC AND APPAREL PATTERNMAKERS. OOH Title/s: Apparel Workers

Draw and construct sets of precision master patterns or layouts. Mark and cut fabrics and apparel according to blueprints or specifications. Draws outline of pattern parts, using drafting instruments such as calipers, squares, and straight and curved rules. Draws details on outlined parts to indicate guides in joining parts. Draws patterns for range of garment sizes, grading master pattern for each size, using charts or grading device. Draws lines between reference points, producing outline of graded pattern. Positions and cuts out pattern, using scissors and knife. Traces outline of specified pattern onto material and cuts fabric, using scissors. Traces outline of paper onto cardboard pattern, and cuts pattern into parts to make template. Examines sketches or sample articles and design specifications to ascertain number, shape, and size of pattern parts. Calculates dimensions and specifications from sales order and enters data on worksheet. Positions master pattern on paperboard and drafts reference points based on data from charts. Positions master pattern in clamp of grading device, places paperboard under pattern, sets device to specified size, and marks reference points. Computes dimensions of pattern according to size, considering stretching of material, and measures and marks pattern. Makes drawings of garments and patterns, and writes instructions for use in reproducing commercial patterns. Lays out large patterns on floor and cuts material, according to markings. Positions and pins pattern sections onto model form and discusses style lines, details, and revisions with designer. Marks finished pattern with garment size, section, and style information.

Yearly Earnings: $16,796
Education: Long-term O-J-T
Knowledge: Design
Abilities: Visualization; Arm-Hand Steadiness; Wrist-Finger Speed; Near Vision
Skills: None above average
General Work Activities: Drafting and Specifying Technical Devices, etc.
Job Characteristics: Sitting; Importance of Repeating Same Tasks
GOE Group/s: 05.03.02 Engineering Technology: Drafting; 05.05.15 Craft Technology: Custom Sewing, Tailoring, and Upholstering; 06.02.31 Production Work: Manual Work, Laying Out and Marking
CIP Program/s: 200301 Clothing, Apparel and Textile Workers and Managers, General; 200303 Commercial Garment and Apparel Worker; 200501 Home Furnishings and Equipment Installers and Consultants, General; 200502 Window Treatment Maker and Installer; 480304 Shoe, Boot and Leather Repairer; 490306 Marine Maintenance and Repair; 500407 Fashion Design and Illustration
Related DOT Job/s: 781.361-010 ASSISTANT DESIGNER; 781.361-014 PATTERNMAKER; 781.381-022 PATTERN GRADER-CUTTER; 781.381-

030 SAIL-LAY-OUT WORKER; 781.381-034 GRADER MARKER; 781.484-010 PLEAT PATTERNMAKER; 788.281-010 DESIGNER AND PATTERNMAKER; 789.381-014 PATTERN CHART-WRITER; 962.381-010 DRAPER

89502B EMBROIDERY PATTERNMAKERS AND DESIGNERS. OOH Title/s: Apparel Workers

Lay out and draw embroidery patterns and transfer pattern to cloth. Lays out and draws sketch of design according to specifications, using drafting instruments such as triangle, pencils, and crayons. Transfers designs from tracing paper onto cloth to provide guide for embroidery. Looks through eyepiece of enlarger, and traces image of design onto pattern paper to form embroidery pattern. Places customer-approved design in enlarging apparatus. Positions pattern paper on drawing board beneath enlarger, and activates enlarger to illuminate design. Writes specifications on border of pattern, and marks identifying information on outside of pattern. Guides pattern under needle of machine to perforate pattern lines. Rubs wax, powder, or charcoal over perforated lines with wet brush or pouncer to provide guide for embroidery.

Yearly Earnings: $16,796
Education: Long-term O-J-T
Knowledge: Fine Arts
Abilities: Visualization; Arm-Hand Steadiness; Finger Dexterity; Near Vision; Visual Color Discrimination
Skills: None above average
General Work Activities: None above average
Job Characteristics: Sitting; Making Repetitive Motions; Importance of Repeating Same Tasks
GOE Group/s: 01.02.03 Visual Arts: Commercial Art; 01.06.03 Craft Arts: Hand Lettering, Painting and Decorating
CIP Program/s: 200301 Clothing, Apparel and Textile Workers and Managers, General; 200303 Commercial Garment and Apparel Worker
Related DOT Job/s: 781.381-010 CARTOON DESIGNER; 782.361-014 EMBROIDERY PATTERNMAKER

89502D HAT PATTERNMAKERS. OOH Title/s: Apparel Workers

Cast plaster hat-making patterns from sample hat and shape patterns to specified form and dimensions. Whittles, cuts, and scrapes plaster from pattern with hand knife to achieve specified form and dimensions. Presses hat into loose sand to create impression that duplicates dimensions and shape of hat. Compares pattern with hat, using rule and tape, and reworks pattern as necessary. Melts and pours thin, even layer of wax over sample hat to stiffen it. Mixes plaster powder with water, and pours mixture into impression to form pattern. Lifts pattern from sand after pattern hardens.

Yearly Earnings: $16,796
Education: Long-term O-J-T
Knowledge: None above average
Abilities: Arm-Hand Steadiness
Skills: None above average
General Work Activities: None above average
Job Characteristics: Objective or Subjective Information; Using Hands on Objects, Tools, or Controls; Making Repetitive Motions; Importance of Repeating Same Tasks
GOE Group/s: 01.06.02 Craft Arts: Arts and Crafts
CIP Program/s: 200301 Clothing, Apparel and Textile Workers and Managers, General; 200303 Commercial Garment and Apparel Worker
Related DOT Job/s: 784.361-010 PATTERNMAKER

89505A SHOP AND ALTERATION TAILORS. OOH Title/s: Apparel Workers

Make tailored garments from existing patterns. Alter, repair, or fit made-to-measure or ready-to-wear garments. Repairs or replaces defective garment parts, such as pockets, pocket flaps, and linings. Measures and marks alteration lines. Pins altering folds or marks on cloth at seams, darts, or necklines to indicate alterations to be made. Shortens or lengthens garment parts, such as sleeves or legs. Expands or narrows garment parts, such as waist or chest. Raises or lowers garment parts, such as collars or lapels. Resews garment, using needle and thread or sewing machine. Examines tag on garment to ascertain necessary alterations. Fits garment on customer to determine required alterations. Studies garment on customer and measures pieces, such as sleeves, pants, and hems, using tape measure. Removes stitches from garment, using ripper or razor blade. Inserts or eliminates padding in shoulders while maintaining drape and proportions of garment. Records required alterations and instructions. Presses garment, using hand iron or pressing machine.

Yearly Earnings: $16,484
Education: Work experience in a related occupation
Knowledge: Customer and Personal Service
Abilities: Arm-Hand Steadiness; Finger Dexterity
Skills: None above average
General Work Activities: None above average
Job Characteristics: Provide a Service to Others; Sitting; Making Repetitive Motions; Importance of Being Exact or Accurate; Pace Determined by Speed of Equipment
GOE Group/s: 05.05.15 Craft Technology: Custom Sewing, Tailoring, and Upholstering
CIP Program/s: 200301 Clothing, Apparel and Textile Workers and Managers, General; 200303 Commercial Garment and Apparel Worker; 200305 Custom Tailor; 200306 Fashion and Fabric Consultant
Related DOT Job/s: 782.361-010 CORSET FITTER; 785.261-010 ALTERATION TAILOR; 785.261-018 TAILOR APPRENTICE, ALTERATION; 785.361-014 GARMENT FITTER; 785.361-018 SAMPLE STITCHER; 785.361-022 SHOP TAILOR; 785.361-026 SHOP TAILOR APPRENTICE; 969.381-010 WARDROBE-SPECIALTY WORKER

89505B CUSTOM TAILORS. OOH Title/s: Apparel Workers

Design/make tailored garments, applying knowledge of garment design, construction, styling, and fabrics. Develops design for garment, adapts existing design for garment, or copies existing design for garment. Assembles garment parts and joins parts with basting stitches, using needle and thread or sewing machine. Fits basted garment on customer and marks areas requiring alterations. Alters garment and joins parts, using needle and thread or sewing machine, to form finished garment. Measures customer for size, using tape measure and records measurements. Draws individual pattern or alters existing pattern to fit customer's measurements. Positions pattern of garment parts on fabric, and cuts fabric along outlines, using scissors. Sews buttons and buttonholes to finish garment. Confers with customer to determine type of material and garment style desired. Presses garment, using hand iron or pressing machine.

Yearly Earnings: $16,484
Education: Work experience in a related occupation
Knowledge: Customer and Personal Service; Production and Processing; Design; Fine Arts
Abilities: Originality; Arm-Hand Steadiness
Skills: None above average
General Work Activities: Thinking Creatively; Handling and Moving Objects; Drafting and Specifying Technical Devices, etc.

Job Characteristics: Provide a Service to Others; Deal with External Customers; Sitting
GOE Group/s: 05.05.15 Craft Technology: Custom Sewing, Tailoring, and Upholstering
CIP Program/s: 200301 Clothing, Apparel and Textile Workers and Managers, General; 200305 Custom Tailor
Related DOT Job/s: 785.261-014 CUSTOM TAILOR; 785.261-022 TAILOR APPRENTICE, CUSTOM; 785.361-010 DRESSMAKER

89508 UPHOLSTERERS. OOH Title/s: Upholsterers
Make, repair, and replace upholstery for household furniture or transportation vehicles, using knowledge of fabrics and methods of upholstery. Include workers in both manufacturing and nonmanufacturing industries. Exclude workers who perform a specialized operation such as sewing machine operators, assemblers, and hand cutters and trimmers. Measures and cuts new covering material, using pattern and measuring and cutting instruments. Operates sewing machine to seam cushions and join various sections of covering material. Fits, installs, and secures material on workpiece, using hand tools, power tools, glue, cement, or staples. Adjusts or replaces webbing, padding, and springs and secures them in place. Attaches binding or applies solutions to edges of cut material to prevent raveling. Sews rips or tears in material, or creates tufting, using needle and thread. Reads order and applies knowledge and experience with materials to determine type and amount of material required to cover workpiece. Draws cutting lines on material following pattern, templates, sketches, or blueprints, using chalk, pencil, paint, or other method. Attaches fasteners, grommets, buckles, ornamental trim, and other accessories to cover or frame, using hand tools. Examines upholstery to locate defects. Removes covering, webbing, padding, and defective springs from workpiece, using hand tools. Repairs frame of workpiece. Stacks, aligns, and smoothes material on cutting table. Drills or punches holes in material. Designs upholstery cover patterns. Maintains records of time required to perform each job. Refinishes wood surfaces on upholstered or reupholstered furniture. Lifts workpiece, such as household furniture or automotive or aircraft seats and panels, and places workpiece on worktable.
Yearly Earnings: $16,796
Education: Long-term O-J-T
Knowledge: None above average
Abilities: Manual Dexterity; Finger Dexterity; Wrist-Finger Speed; Static Strength; Trunk Strength; Extent Flexibility
Skills: None above average
General Work Activities: None above average
Job Characteristics: Kneeling, Crouching, or Crawling; Using Hands on Objects, Tools, or Controls; Bending or Twisting the Body; Making Repetitive Motions
GOE Group/s: 05.05.15 Craft Technology: Custom Sewing, Tailoring, and Upholstering; 06.02.27 Production Work: Manual Work, Textile, Fabric and Leather; 06.02.32 Production Work: Manual Work, Assorted Materials
CIP Program/s: 200501 Home Furnishings and Equipment Installers and Consultants, General; 480303 Upholsterer
Related DOT Job/s: 780.381-010 AUTOMOBILE UPHOLSTERER; 780.381-014 AUTOMOBILE-UPHOLSTERER APPRENTICE; 780.381-018 FURNITURE UPHOLSTERER; 780.381-022 FURNITURE-UPHOLSTERER APPRENTICE; 780.381-026 UPHOLSTERER, LIMOUSINE AND HEARSE; 780.381-034 SLIPCOVER CUTTER; 780.381-038 UPHOLSTERER, INSIDE; 780.384-014 UPHOLSTERER; 780.684-122 UPHOLSTERY REPAIRER

89511 SHOE AND LEATHER WORKERS AND REPAIRERS—PRECISION. OOH Title/s: Shoe and Leather Workers and Repairers; Handlers, Equipment Cleaners, Helpers, and Laborers
Construct, decorate, or repair precision leather products, such as luggage, shoes, and saddles, using machines and hand tools. Include workers who work with leather-like materials when process is similar. Assembles product according to specifications, utilizing sewing machine, needle and thread, or leather lacing, glue, clamps, or rivets. Attaches accessories or ornamentation to decorate or protect product. Sews rips or patches holes by hand or machine to repair articles, such as purses, shoes, and luggage. Selects material and cuts parts along pattern or outline, with knife, shears, or scissors. Dyes, soaks, paints, stamps, or engraves leather or other materials to obtain desired effect or shape. Inserts and positions padding, foam cushioning, or lining and glues or stitches into place. Fabricates articles such as purses, wallets, belts, luggage frames, and shoes. Repairs and reconditions products such as trunks, luggage, shoes, and saddles. Aligns and stitches or glues materials, such as fabric, fleece, leather, or wood to join parts. Drills or punches holes and inserts metal rings, handles, and hardware. Reads prescription or specifications and measures item, using calipers, tape measures, or rule. Draws pattern, using measurements, plaster cast, or customer specifications, and positions or outlines pattern on workpiece. Trims and buffs, bevels, or flares workpiece to specified size and shape. Inspects article for defects and removes damaged or worn parts, using hand tools.
Yearly Earnings: $16,796
Education: Long-term O-J-T
Knowledge: None above average
Abilities: Arm-Hand Steadiness; Finger Dexterity; Wrist-Finger Speed; Visual Color Discrimination
Skills: None above average
General Work Activities: None above average
Job Characteristics: Sitting; Using Hands on Objects, Tools, or Controls; Making Repetitive Motions; Importance of Repeating Same Tasks
GOE Group/s: 01.06.02 Craft Arts: Arts and Crafts; 05.05.15 Craft Technology: Custom Sewing, Tailoring, and Upholstering; 05.10.01 Crafts: Structural; 06.02.27 Production Work: Manual Work, Textile, Fabric and Leather; 06.02.32 Production Work: Manual Work, Assorted Materials
CIP Program/s: 480304 Shoe, Boot and Leather Repairer; 480399 Leatherworkers and Upholsterers, Other; 500201 Crafts, Folk Art and Artisanry
Related DOT Job/s: 365.361-010 LUGGAGE REPAIRER; 365.361-014 SHOE REPAIRER; 739.684-114 LAST-REPAIRER HELPER; 753.381-010 BOOTMAKER, HAND; 753.684-026 REPAIRER; 780.381-030 PAD HAND; 781.381-018 LEATHER STAMPER; 783.361-010 CUSTOM-LEATHER-PRODUCTS MAKER; 783.381-018 HARNESS MAKER; 783.381-022 LUGGAGE MAKER; 783.381-026 SADDLE MAKER; 788.261-010 ORTHOPEDIC-BOOT-AND-SHOE DESIGNER AND MAKER; 788.381-010 COBBLER; 788.381-014 SHOEMAKER, CUSTOM; 788.684-046 FINGER COBBLER; 788.684-098 SAMPLE SHOE INSPECTOR AND REWORKER

89514 SPOTTERS, DRY CLEANING. OOH Title/s: Laundry and Drycleaning Machine Operators and Tenders, Except Pressers
Identify stains in wool, synthetic, and silk garments and household fabrics and apply chemical solutions to remove stain. Determine spotting procedures on basis of type of fabric and nature of stain. Inspects spots to ascertain composition and select solvent. Sprinkles chemical solvents over stain and pats area with brush

or sponge until stain is removed. Applies bleaching powder to spot, and sprays with steam to remove stains from certain fabrics which do not respond to other cleaning solvents. Applies chemicals to neutralize effect of solvents. Sprays steam, water, or air over spot to flush out chemicals, dry material, raise nap, or brighten color. Cleans fabric using vacuum or airhose. Mixes bleaching agent with hot water in vats and soaks material until it is bleached. Spreads article on worktable and positions stain over vacuum head or on marble slab. Operates drycleaning machine.
Yearly Earnings: $13,364
Education: Moderate-term O-J-T
Knowledge: Chemistry
Abilities: Visual Color Discrimination
Skills: None above average
General Work Activities: None above average
Job Characteristics: Contaminants; Hazardous Conditions; Using Hands on Objects, Tools, or Controls
GOE Group/s: 06.02.27 Production Work: Manual Work, Textile, Fabric and Leather
CIP Program/s: 200301 Clothing, Apparel and Textile Workers and Managers, General; 200309 Drycleaner and Launderer (Commercial)
Related DOT Job/s: 361.684-018 SPOTTER I; 362.381-010 SPOTTER II; 582.684-014 SPOT CLEANER; 780.687-058 UPHOLSTERY CLEANER

89517 PRESSERS, DELICATE FABRICS. OOH Title/s: Laundry and Drycleaning Machine Operators and Tenders, Except Pressers

Press dry-cleaned and wet-cleaned silk and synthetic fiber garments by hand or machine, applying knowledge of fabrics and heat to produce high quality finish. Finish pleated or fancy garments, normally by hand. Operates machine presses to finish parts that can be pressed flat and completes other parts by pressing with hand iron. Finishes velvet garments by steaming them on buck of hot-head press or steamtable, and brushing pile (nap) with handbrush. Finishes fancy garments with hand iron to produce high quality finishes which cannot be obtained on machine presses. Finishes parts difficult to reach, such as flounces, by fitting parts over puff irons. Finishes pleated garments, determining size of pleat from evidence of old pleat or from work order, using machine press or hand iron. Presses ties on small pressing machine. Inserts heated metal form into tie and touches up rough places with hand iron.
Yearly Earnings: $19,500
Education: Short-term O-J-T
Knowledge: None above average
Abilities: None above average
Skills: None above average
General Work Activities: None above average
Job Characteristics: Very Hot; Hazardous Situations; Standing
GOE Group/s: 06.04.35 Elemental Work: Industrial: Laundering, Dry Cleaning
CIP Program/s: 200301 Clothing, Apparel and Textile Workers and Managers, General; 200309 Drycleaner and Launderer (Commercial)
Related DOT Job/s: 363.681-010 SILK FINISHER

89521 PRECISION DYERS. OOH Title/s: Laundry and Drycleaning Machine Operators and Tenders, Except Pressers

Change or restore the color of articles, such as garments, drapes, and slipcovers, by means of dyes. Work requires knowledge of the composition of the textiles being dyed or restored; the chemical properties of bleaches and dyes; and their effects upon such textiles. Include rug dyers. Matches sample color, applying knowledge of bleaching agent and dye properties, and type, construction, condition, and color of article. Examines article to identify fabric and original dye by sight, touch, or by testing sample with fire or chemical reagent. Tests dye on swatch of fabric, to ensure color match. Immerses article in bleaching bath to strip colors. Immerses article in dye solution and stirs with stick, or dyes article in rotary-drum or paddle dyeing machine. Applies dye to article, using spray gun, electrically rotated brush, or handbrush. Rinses article in water and acetic acid solution to remove excess dye and to fix colors. Measures and mixes amounts of bleaches, dyes, oils, and acids, following formulas. Dissolves dye or bleaching chemicals in water. Sprays or brushes article with prepared solution to remove stains. Operates or directs operation of extractor and drier.
Yearly Earnings: $19,500
Education: Short-term O-J-T
Knowledge: Production and Processing; Chemistry
Abilities: Visual Color Discrimination
Skills: None above average
General Work Activities: None above average
Job Characteristics: None above average
GOE Group/s: 05.05.16 Craft Technology: Dyeing
CIP Program/s: 200301 Clothing, Apparel and Textile Workers and Managers, General; 200309 Drycleaner and Launderer (Commercial)
Related DOT Job/s: 364.361-010 DYER; 364.361-014 RUG DYER I; 364.684-010 RUG DYER II

89599A RUG REPAIRERS. OOH Title/s: Apparel Workers

Reweave and repair damaged rugs and carpets. Selects rug yarn, and stitches and weaves yarn into backing to form rug pile, using needle. Darns holes in rug-backing by hand. Patches rug by stitching edges of rug and patch together with carpet stitch. Interlaces twine to form rug backing. Stretches rugs to restore shape and remove wrinkles. Cuts tuft yarns and backing twine of damaged area of rug or carpet to be repaired, using scissors or knife. Binds edges of rugs by operating serging machine, or sews edges with needle and thread. Pounds repaired area smooth, when necessary. Examines rug or carpet for tears, defects, or markings that indicate imperfections. Tacks damaged area of rug onto wooden frame. Trims loose thread ends. Remodels rugs by cutting them to required size and shape, using hand shears.
Yearly Earnings: $14,664
Education: Long-term O-J-T
Knowledge: Fine Arts
Abilities: Arm-Hand Steadiness; Finger Dexterity; Wrist-Finger Speed; Speed of Limb Movement; Visual Color Discrimination
Skills: None above average
General Work Activities: None above average
Job Characteristics: Cramped Work Space, Awkward Positions; Kneeling, Crouching, or Crawling; Keeping or Regaining Balance; Using Hands on Objects, Tools, or Controls; Bending or Twisting the Body; Making Repetitive Motions; Importance of Repeating Same Tasks
GOE Group/s: 05.05.15 Craft Technology: Custom Sewing, Tailoring, and Upholstering
CIP Program/s: 000000 NO CIP ASSIGNED
Related DOT Job/s: 782.381-014 ORIENTAL-RUG REPAIRER; 782.381-018 RUG REPAIRER; 782.684-042 MENDER

89599B FUR GARMENT WORKERS. OOH Title/s: Apparel Workers

Design, make, alter, and repair fur garments. Cuts pelts to shape them to garment pattern. Replaces linings and repairs damaged skins. Bastes lining parts together, and sews lining into shell, using sewing machine or needle and thread. Selects fur pelts and matches them for size, color, texture, and quality. Arranges pelts on pattern according to design and color. Slits skin of furs and cuts off inferior or unusable parts, using furrier's knife. Sews interlining to inside of fur skin. Selects

lining pattern, cuts out lining parts, and sews parts together. Numbers pelts to indicate their pattern location. Sews on hooks, rings, hem tape, buttons, monograms, and padding, using needle and thread. Estimates cost of making or repairing garments. Purchases pelts and sells furs.
Yearly Earnings: $14,664
Education: Long-term O-J-T
Knowledge: None above average
Abilities: Arm-Hand Steadiness; Visual Color Discrimination
Skills: None above average
General Work Activities: Drafting and Specifying Technical Devices, etc.
Job Characteristics: Sitting
GOE Group/s: 05.05.15 Craft Technology: Custom Sewing, Tailoring, and Upholstering; 06.02.27 Production Work: Manual Work, Textile, Fabric and Leather
CIP Program/s: 200301 Clothing, Apparel and Textile Workers and Managers, General; 200303 Commercial Garment and Apparel Worker
Related DOT Job/s: 783.261-010 FURRIER; 783.381-010 FUR CUTTER; 783.381-014 FUR FINISHER

89599C CANVAS, NETS, AND RELATED MATERIALS WORKERS. OOH Title/s: Apparel Workers
Lay out and assemble canvas and net goods, such as trawl nets and sails. Fabricate and install surface coverings. Lays out drawing on floor and marks outline on material. Secures rope or cable to finished sail, and wraps and sews parts of rope or cable to prevent chafing. Draws diagram and lays out patterns for net parts on paper, using rule and pencil or marking crayon. Splices, inserts, and hems rope into edges of sail to relieve strain. Hangs net on metering lines or holds seams to align seams, and threads twine through meshes and ties knots to secure seam. Attaches prefabricated bag to truncated end of net. Fastens fabric parts to structure, using cement, needle and thread, or metal strips and screws. Installs grommets, metal fittings, and fasteners, using machine. Marks grommet holes on material, punches holes, and sews galvanized iron ring to hole. Sews material according to markings, using power sewing machine. Sketches design of canvas item, measures boat, and makes pattern from measurements. Installs and adjusts completed sail on ship, and examines sail for conformance to specifications. Fabricates patterns and templates. Cuts material or patterns with shears or power cutter. Reinforces material with cloth tape. Cuts, bends, and joins aluminum framework, attaches sail material, and assembles and installs framework on boat. Applies dope to fabric to color, prime, tighten, strengthen, and preserve, using brush or spray gun. Makes awning frames. Sprays covering with water to smooth surface.
Yearly Earnings: $14,664
Education: Long-term O-J-T
Knowledge: Design; Building and Construction
Abilities: Arm-Hand Steadiness; Manual Dexterity; Finger Dexterity; Wrist-Finger Speed; Dynamic Strength; Dynamic Flexibility; Gross Body Equilibrium
Skills: Technology Design; Installation
General Work Activities: Performing General Physical Activities; Handling and Moving Objects; Drafting and Specifying Technical Devices, etc.
Job Characteristics: Cramped Work Space, Awkward Positions; High Places; Climbing Ladders, Scaffolds, Poles, etc.; Making Repetitive Motions
GOE Group/s: 05.05.15 Craft Technology: Custom Sewing, Tailoring, and Upholstering; 06.01.04 Production Technology: Precision Hand Work
CIP Program/s: 470607 Aircraft Mechanic/Technician, Airframe; 490306 Marine Maintenance and Repair
Related DOT Job/s: 739.381-010 CANVAS WORKER; 739.381-014 CANVAS-WORKER APPRENTICE; 789.261-010 BOAT-CANVAS MAKER-INSTALLER; 789.381-018 TRAWL NET MAKER; 849.381-010 AIRPLANE COVERER

89599D HAT MAKERS AND REPAIRERS. OOH Title/s: Apparel Workers
Fabricate and repair hats. Produces hats in various colors and materials. Cuts pattern, lays pattern on material, and cuts material, following pattern. Molds, drapes, and blocks material, using hat forms and steam iron. Sews sections of hat together and trims hat with ribbons, veils, feathers, or flowers. Stitches leather to hat to form sweatband, by hand or sewing machine. Alters hats by changing ornamentation. Cuts and folds ribbons and leather to form ornaments, and stitches ornaments to hat. Folds ribbon to form binding, and sews linings and ribbons to hat. Removes, scrubs, reshapes, and presses trimmings with iron.
Yearly Earnings: $14,664
Education: Long-term O-J-T
Knowledge: None above average
Abilities: Arm-Hand Steadiness
Skills: None above average
General Work Activities: Handling and Moving Objects
Job Characteristics: Sitting; Making Repetitive Motions
GOE Group/s: 01.06.02 Craft Arts: Arts and Crafts; 06.02.27 Production Work: Manual Work, Textile, Fabric and Leather
CIP Program/s: 200301 Clothing, Apparel and Textile Workers and Managers, General; 200303 Commercial Garment and Apparel Worker; 200305 Custom Tailor
Related DOT Job/s: 782.381-010 HAT TRIMMER; 784.261-010 MILLINER

89599E FUR DRESSERS. OOH Title/s: Apparel Workers
Tan and dress animal pelts. Removes long coarse hair from pelts and evens length of fur, using beaming knife and shaving knife. Removes flesh from pelts and skins, using hand and powered knives. Places pelts in vats containing solutions to clean, soften, and preserve pelts. Oils and clips pelts. Prepares tanning and washing solutions, according to formulas. Examines skins to detect defects. Records defects and sorts furs according to grade. Bends knives to specified angle to facilitate removal of flesh. Sharpens cutting edges of knives.
Yearly Earnings: $14,664
Education: Long-term O-J-T
Knowledge: None above average
Abilities: Arm-Hand Steadiness; Wrist-Finger Speed; Gross Body Equilibrium; Visual Color Discrimination
Skills: None above average
General Work Activities: None above average
Job Characteristics: Hazardous Situations; Using Hands on Objects, Tools, or Controls; Bending or Twisting the Body; Making Repetitive Motions; Importance of Repeating Same Tasks
GOE Group/s: 06.01.04 Production Technology: Precision Hand Work
CIP Program/s: 480399 Leatherworkers and Upholsterers, Other
Related DOT Job/s: 585.681-010 FLESHER; 585.681-014 FUR PLUCKER; 589.361-010 FUR DRESSER

89599F ALL OTHER PRECISION TEXTILE, APPAREL, AND FURNISHINGS WORKERS. OOH Title/s: Apparel Workers
All other precision textile, apparel, and furnishings workers not classified separately above.
Yearly Earnings: $14,664
Education: Long-term O-J-T

GOE Group/s: 05.05.11 Craft Technology: Scientific, Medical, & Technical Equip. Fabric. & Re
CIP Program/s: 200301 Clothing, Apparel and Textile Workers and Managers, General; 200303 Commercial Garment and Apparel Worker
Related DOT Job/s: 712.281-014 DESIGNER

Precision Printing Occupations

89702 HAND COMPOSITORS AND TYPESETTERS. OOH Title/s: Prepress Workers

Set up and arrange type by hand. Assemble and lock setup of type, cuts, and headings. Pull proofs. Exclude phototypesetters or other workers concerned with typesetting by electronic or word processing methods. Inserts spacers between words or units to balance and justify lines. Inserts lead, slugs, or lines of quads between lines to adjust length of setup. Arranges, groups, and locks galley setups of type, cuts, and headings in chases, according to dummy makeup sheet. Selects type from type case and sets it in compositional sequence, reading from copy. Prepares proof copy of setup, using proof press. Arranges galleys of linotype slugs (takes) in sequence on correction table. Measures copy with line gauge to determine length of line. Transfers type from stick to galley when setup is complete. Compares corrected type slugs against proof to detect errors. Compares symbols on proof with galley symbol, and reads portion of text to locate positions for insertion of corrected slugs. Removes incorrect portion and manually inserts corrections. Cleans type after use and distributes it to specified boxes in type case.
Yearly Earnings: $22,412
Education: Long-term O-J-T
Knowledge: Production and Processing; Communications and Media
Abilities: Finger Dexterity
Skills: None above average
General Work Activities: Handling and Moving Objects
Job Characteristics: Sounds, Noise Levels are Distracting, etc.; Using Hands on Objects, Tools, or Controls
GOE Group/s: 05.05.13 Craft Technology: Printing; 05.10.05 Crafts: Reproduction
CIP Program/s: 480201 Graphic and Printing Equipment Operator, General; 480205 Mechanical Typesetter and Composer
Related DOT Job/s: 973.381-010 COMPOSITOR; 973.381-014 COMPOSITOR APPRENTICE; 973.381-026 MAKE-UP ARRANGER; 973.381-030 PROOFSHEET CORRECTOR; 973.681-010 GALLEY STRIPPER

89705 JOB PRINTERS. OOH Title/s: Prepress Workers

Set type according to copy. Operate cylinder or automatic platen press to print job order. Read proof for errors and clarity of impression, and correct imperfections. Job printers are often found in small establishments where work combines several job skills, such as typesetting, printing, reading, and selecting of materials to reproduce copy. Selects type from type case and inserts type in printer's stick to reproduce material in copy. Reads proof for errors and clarity of impression. Runs proof sheet through press and examines sheet for clarity of impression. Inserts spacers between words and leads between lines. Lays form on proof press, inks type, fastens paper to press roller, and pulls roller over form to make proof copy. Corrects errors by resetting type and improves impression by tapping face of type with hammer. Pushes button to start press, examines printed sheets, and adjusts press when printing is defective. Slides type from stick into galley. Places chase over type, inserts quoins, and locks chase to hold type. Removes assembled type from galley and places type on composing stone. Positions form (type in locked chase) on bed of press and tightens clamps, using wrench. Fills ink fountain and moves lever to adjust flow of ink. Sets feed guides according to size and thickness of paper. Cleans ink rollers at end of run.
Yearly Earnings: $22,204
Education: Long-term O-J-T
Knowledge: Production and Processing; English Language; Communications and Media
Abilities: Perceptual Speed; Finger Dexterity; Wrist-Finger Speed
Skills: None above average
General Work Activities: Controlling Machines and Processes
Job Characteristics: Sounds, Noise Levels are Distracting, etc.; Contaminants; Hazardous Conditions; Hazardous Equipment; Bending or Twisting the Body; Frustrating Circumstances; Degree of Automation; Pace Determined by Speed of Equipment
GOE Group/s: 05.05.13 Craft Technology: Printing
CIP Program/s: 480201 Graphic and Printing Equipment Operator, General; 480205 Mechanical Typesetter and Composer
Related DOT Job/s: 973.381-018 JOB PRINTER; 973.381-022 JOB-PRINTER APPRENTICE

89706 PASTE-UP WORKERS. OOH Title/s: Prepress Workers

Arrange and mount typeset material and illustrations into paste-up for printing reproduction, based on artist's or editor's layout. Measures and marks board according to layout to indicate position of artwork, typeset copy, page edges, folds, and colors. Cuts typeset copy and artwork to size, applies adhesive, and aligns artwork and typeset copy on board, following position marks. Measures artwork and layout space of artwork on pasteup. Compares measurements, using ruler and proportion wheel, to determine proportions needed to make reduced or enlarged photographic prints for pasteup. Tapes transparent plastic overlay to board and positions and applies copy to plastic. Operates electronic plotter to draw artwork positions on pasteup. Operates phototypesetter to prepare typeset copy for pasteup. Applies masking film to artwork layout space on overlay to create clear space on negative for subsequent addition of artwork. Indicates crop marks and enlargement or reduction measurements on photographs with grease pencil to facilitate processing. Makes negatives or prints of artwork, using photographic equipment, to prepare artwork for pasteup. Removes excess adhesive from board, using scissors, artist's knife, and drafting instruments. Covers photographs with tissue paper to protect photographs. Tapes tracing paper to board to protect artwork and copy. Draws functional and decorative borders around layout, using marking and measuring instruments. Writes specifications on tracing paper to provide information for other workers.
Yearly Earnings: $20,228
Education: Long-term O-J-T
Knowledge: Design; Fine Arts
Abilities: Arm-Hand Steadiness; Visual Color Discrimination
Skills: None above average
General Work Activities: None above average
Job Characteristics: Contaminants; Hazardous Situations
GOE Group/s: 01.06.01 Craft Arts: Graphics Arts and Related Crafts; 01.06.03 Craft Arts: Hand Lettering, Painting and Decorating
CIP Program/s: 500402 Graphic Design, Commercial Art and Illustration
Related DOT Job/s: 970.381-018 LAY-OUT FORMER; 972.381-030 PASTE-UP ARTIST; 972.381-038 PASTE-UP ARTIST APPRENTICE

89707 ELECTRONIC PAGINATION SYSTEM OPERATORS. OOH Title/s: Prepress Workers

Using a computer screen, call up type and art elements from computer memory and position them into a completed page, using knowledge of type styles and size and composition patterns. The composited page is then transmitted for production

into film or directly into plates. Views monitors for visual representation of work in progress and for instructions and feedback throughout process. Activates options, such as masking or text processing. Enters data, such as background color, shapes, and coordinates of images; and retrieves data from system memory. Activates options, such as masking, pixel (picture element) editing, airbrushing, or image retouching. Enters data, such as coordinates of images and color specifications, into system to retouch and make color corrections. Saves completed work on floppy disks or magnetic tape. Enters digitized data into electronic prepress system computer memory, using scanner, camera, keyboard, or mouse. Studies layout or other instructions to determine work to be done and sequence of operations. Loads floppy disks or tapes containing information into system. Creates special effects, such as vignettes, mosaics, and image combining.
Yearly Earnings: $20,228
Education: Long-term O-J-T
Knowledge: Clerical; Computers and Electronics; English Language; Fine Arts; Telecommunications; Communications and Media
Abilities: Visualization; Wrist-Finger Speed; Near Vision; Visual Color Discrimination
Skills: Equipment Selection
General Work Activities: Thinking Creatively; Updating and Using Job-Relevant Knowledge; Handling and Moving Objects; Operating Vehicles or Equipment
Job Characteristics: Sitting; Degree of Automation
GOE Group/s: 01.06.01 Craft Arts: Graphics Arts and Related Crafts
CIP Program/s: 480201 Graphic and Printing Equipment Operator, General; 480205 Mechanical Typesetter and Composer; 480206 Lithographer and Platemaker; 480211 Computer Typography and Composition Equipment Operator
Related DOT Job/s: 979.282-010 ELECTRONIC PREPRESS SYSTEM OPERATOR

89712 PHOTOENGRAVERS. OOH Title/s: Prepress Workers

Photograph copy, develop negatives, and prepare photosensitized metal plates for use in letterpress and gravure printing. Include photoengraving specialists, such as process-camera operators, printers, etchers, finishers, and proofers. Develops and prints negatives, positives, film, or plates by controlled exposure to light, using exposure equipment, chemical baths, and vacuum. Transfers images, designs, or patterns onto rollers, plates, or film, using photographic or pantographic equipment and techniques, and hand tools. Positions, loads, or mounts copy, plates, film, or rollers and secures into place. Washes rollers and plates preparatory to etching or to remove resistant solution and photographic emulsion, using water, cleaning solution, and brush. Brushes protective solution and powder on plate and starts machine to distribute acid or photosensitizing solution over plate or rollers. Computes camera machine settings for film exposure or reproduction, using equipment meter, computer, worksheets, and standard formulas and tables. Etches designs on metal rollers and plates, using etching machines, hand tools, and acidic chemicals, to produce printing plates and rollers. Mixes caustic or acid solutions. Modifies or repairs plates or film, using etching and artist's brush, acid, and hand tools. Examines developed film, proof, or engravings, using magnifier, chalk, or charcoal to evaluate quality and detect errors. Matches colors with original to produce balanced color values or intensity design. Studies and compares film negatives or positives with originals or design, to determine photographic requirements and verify reproduction.
Yearly Earnings: $22,412
Education: Long-term O-J-T
Knowledge: Computers and Electronics; Chemistry; Fine Arts
Abilities: Flexibility of Closure; Finger Dexterity; Near Vision; Visual Color Discrimination; Night Vision
Skills: None above average
General Work Activities: Controlling Machines and Processes
Job Characteristics: Contaminants; Radiation; Hazardous Conditions
GOE Group/s: 01.06.01 Craft Arts: Graphics Arts and Related Crafts; 05.05.13 Craft Technology: Printing; 05.10.05 Crafts: Reproduction
CIP Program/s: 480201 Graphic and Printing Equipment Operator, General; 480206 Lithographer and Platemaker; 480299 Graphic and Printing Equipment Operators, Other
Related DOT Job/s: 970.361-014 REPEAT CHIEF; 970.381-030 RETOUCHER, PHOTOENGRAVING; 971.261-010 ETCHER, HAND; 971.381-010 ETCHER APPRENTICE, PHOTOENGRAVING; 971.381-014 ETCHER, PHOTOENGRAVING; 971.381-022 PHOTOENGRAVER; 971.381-026 PHOTOENGRAVER APPRENTICE; 971.381-030 PHOTOENGRAVING FINISHER; 971.381-034 PHOTOENGRAVING PRINTER; 971.381-038 PHOTOENGRAVING PROOFER; 971.381-040 PHOTOENGRAVING-PROOFER APPRENTICE; 971.382-014 PHOTOGRAPHER, PHOTOENGRAVING; 971.382-018 REPEAT-PHOTOCOMPOSING-MACHINE OPERATOR; 972.382-018 PHOTO MASK MAKER, ELECTRON-BEAM

89713 CAMERA OPERATORS. OOH Title/s: Prepress Workers

Operate process camera and related darkroom equipment to photograph and develop negatives of material to be printed. Feeds film into automatic film processor that develops, fixes, washes, and dries film. Adjusts camera settings, lights, and lens. Selects and installs screens and filters in camera to produce desired effects. Exposes high contrast film for predetermined exposure time. Immerses film in series of chemical baths to develop images and hangs film on rack to dry. Performs exposure tests to determine line, halftone, and color reproduction exposure lengths for various photographic factors. Measures density of continuous tone images to be photographed to set exposure time for halftone images. Mounts material to be photographed on copyboard of camera. Measures original layouts and determines proportions needed to make reduced or enlarged photographic prints for pasteup.
Yearly Earnings: $22,412
Education: Long-term O-J-T
Knowledge: Chemistry; Fine Arts
Abilities: Visual Color Discrimination
Skills: Technology Design
General Work Activities: None above average
Job Characteristics: None above average
GOE Group/s: 01.06.01 Craft Arts: Graphics Arts and Related Crafts
CIP Program/s: 480201 Graphic and Printing Equipment Operator, General; 480206 Lithographer and Platemaker; 500406 Commercial Photography
Related DOT Job/s: 972.382-010 PHOTOGRAPHER APPRENTICE, LITHOGRAPHIC; 972.382-014 PHOTOGRAPHER, LITHOGRAPHIC

89715 SCANNER OPERATORS. OOH Title/s: Prepress Workers

Operate electronic or computerized scanning equipment to produce and screen film separations of photographs or art for use in producing lithographic printing plates. Evaluate and correct for deficiencies in the film. Activates scanner to produce positive or negative films for each primary color and black in original copy. Types on scanner keyboard or touches mouse to symbols on scanner video display unit to input software, or moves controls to set scanner to specific color density, size, screen ruling, and exposure adjustments. Loads film into holder, places holder in exposing chamber, and starts mechanism that loads and secures film on scanner drum. Unloads exposed film from scanner and places film in automatic processor to

develop image on film. Inspects developed film for specified results and quality and forwards acceptable negatives or positives to other workers or customer. Analyzes original to evaluate color density, gradation highlights, middle tones, and shadows, using densitometer and knowledge of light and color. Performs tests to determine exposure adjustments on scanner and adjusts scanner controls until specified results are obtained. Positions color transparency, negative, or reflection copy on scanning drum and mounts drum and head on scanner.
Yearly Earnings: $22,412
Education: Long-term O-J-T
Knowledge: Production and Processing; Computers and Electronics; Fine Arts
Abilities: Perceptual Speed; Visual Color Discrimination; Night Vision
Skills: Testing; Product Inspection
General Work Activities: Handling and Moving Objects; Controlling Machines and Processes; Operating Vehicles or Equipment
Job Characteristics: Objective or Subjective Information; Extremely Bright or Inadequate Lighting; Sitting; Using Hands on Objects, Tools, or Controls; Degree of Automation; Pace Determined by Speed of Equipment
GOE Group/s: 05.10.05 Crafts: Reproduction
CIP Program/s: 480201 Graphic and Printing Equipment Operator, General; 480206 Lithographer and Platemaker
Related DOT Job/s: 972.282-010 SCANNER OPERATOR

89717 STRIPPERS. OOH Title/s: Prepress Workers

Cut and arrange film into flats (layout sheets resembling a film negative of text in its final form) which are used to make plates. Prepare separate flat for each color. Cuts image window area to allow exposure to plate or film, using razor or artist's knife. Applies rubber solution and collodion to toughen negative, cuts to size, and immerses in acid bath to prepare negative for stripping. Positions film negatives or positives on light table according to art layout, blueprint, and color register to form film flat. Selects and inserts screen tints in film flat, using knowledge of dot percentages required to obtain specific colors. Cuts masks and arranges negatives to prepare for contact printing, plate exposure, or proof making. Aligns negatives and masks over unexposed film in vacuum frame to make negatives or positives for final film of each color. Assembles and aligns negatives or positives to assure register and fit with units of color. Strips negative from base. Examines pasteup, artwork, film, prints, and instructions to determine size and dimensions, number of job colors, and camera work needed. Makes proof from film flat to determine accuracy of flat. Determines proportions needed to reduce or enlarge photographs and graphics to fit in designated area, using calculator or proportion scale. Examines negatives and photographs to detect defective areas, using lighted viewing table. Determines or approves plans and page sequences to lay out job for specific printing press. Touches up imperfections, using opaque and brush on negatives, and needle and crayon pencil on photographs. Examines proof returned by customer and makes corrections according to customer specifications. Sends completed flat to proofing area or platemaking area for preparation of final proof or lithographic plate. Draws ruled lines and borders around negatives or positives.
Yearly Earnings: $22,412
Education: Long-term O-J-T
Knowledge: Fine Arts
Abilities: Visualization; Visual Color Discrimination
Skills: None above average
General Work Activities: None above average
Job Characteristics: Importance of Being Sure All is Done
GOE Group/s: 01.06.01 Craft Arts: Graphics Arts and Related Crafts
CIP Program/s: 480201 Graphic and Printing Equipment Operator, General; 480206 Lithographer and Platemaker
Related DOT Job/s: 971.381-050 STRIPPER; 971.381-054 STRIPPER APPRENTICE; 972.281-022 STRIPPER, LITHOGRAPHIC I; 972.381-022 STRIPPER, LITHOGRAPHIC II

89718 PLATEMAKERS. OOH Title/s: Prepress Workers

Produce printing plates by exposing sensitized metal sheets to special light through a photographic negative. May operate machines that process plates automatically. Mounts negative and plate in camera that exposes exposed plate to artificial light through photographic negative, thus transferring image. Transfers image from master plate to unexposed plate and immerses plate in developing solution to develop image on plate. Transfers images by hand and covers surface of plates with photosensitive chemical, using brush, and allows plate to dry. Lowers vacuum frame onto plate-film assembly to establish contact between positive-negative film and plate, and sets timer to expose plate. Removes plate-film assembly from vacuum frame and places exposed plate in automatic processor to develop image and dry plate. Mixes and applies chemical-based developing solution to plates and replenishes solution in processor to maintain it in working order. Examines unexposed photographic plate to detect flaws or foreign particles prior to printing pattern of aperture masks on sensitized steel. Examines plate, using light-box and microscope to detect flaws, verify conformity with master plate, and measure dot size and center. Installs and aligns plates in printing case. Repairs defective plates with missing dots, using photographic touch-up tool and ink. Punches holes in light-sensitive plate and inserts pins in holes to prepare plate for contact with positive or negative film. Places plate in vacuum frame to align positives or negatives with each other and places masking paper over uncovered areas. Performs tests to determine time required for exposure by exposing plates and compares exposure to scale which measures tone ranges.
Yearly Earnings: $22,412
Education: Long-term O-J-T
Knowledge: Production and Processing; Chemistry; Fine Arts
Abilities: None above average
Skills: Testing; Product Inspection
General Work Activities: None above average
Job Characteristics: None above average
GOE Group/s: 01.06.01 Craft Arts: Graphics Arts and Related Crafts; 05.10.05 Crafts: Reproduction
CIP Program/s: 480201 Graphic and Printing Equipment Operator, General; 480206 Lithographer and Platemaker
Related DOT Job/s: 714.381-018 PHOTOGRAPHIC-PLATE MAKER; 972.381-010 LITHOGRAPHIC PLATEMAKER; 972.381-014 LITHOGRAPHIC-PLATE-MAKER APPRENTICE; 972.381-026 TRANSFERRER

89719A DOT ETCHERS. OOH Title/s: Prepress Workers

Increase or reduce size of photographic dots by chemical or photomechanical methods to make color corrections on halftone negatives or positives to be used in preparation of lithographic printing plates. Places masks over separation negatives or positives and exposes film for specified time, using contact frame and automatic film processor to reduce size of photographic dots to increase or reduce color. Prepares dyes and other chemical solutions according to standard and applies solution to inaccurately colored areas of film to correct color by chemical method. Blocks out or modifies color shades of film, using template, brushes, and opaque. Prepares photographic masks to protect areas of film not needing correction, using contact frame and automatic film processor or by manually cutting masking material, to correct color by photomechanical method. Determines extent of correction and exposure length needed based on experience or predetermined exposure and color charts. Compares

proof print of color separation negative or positive with customer's original copy and standard color chart to determine accuracy of reproduction. Applies opaque to defective areas of film to block out blemishes and pinholes. Examines film on light table to determine specified color and color balance, using magnifying glass or densitometer. Identifies and marks color discrepancies on print and film.
Yearly Earnings: $22,412
Education: Long-term O-J-T
Knowledge: Chemistry; Fine Arts
Abilities: Flexibility of Closure; Visual Color Discrimination; Night Vision
Skills: None above average
General Work Activities: Controlling Machines and Processes
Job Characteristics: Extremely Bright or Inadequate Lighting; Radiation; Pace Determined by Speed of Equipment
GOE Group/s: 01.06.01 Craft Arts: Graphics Arts and Related Crafts
CIP Program/s: 480201 Graphic and Printing Equipment Operator, General; 480206 Lithographer and Platemaker
Related DOT Job/s: 972.281-010 DOT ETCHER; 972.281-018 DOT ETCHER APPRENTICE

89719B ELECTRONIC MASKING SYSTEM OPERATORS. OOH Title/s: Prepress Workers

Operate computerized masking system to produce stripping masks used in production of offset lithographic printing plates. Views monitors for feedback and error prompts, for visual representations of work in progress, and for numerical information such as width of line and last point plotted. Selects options on menu of electronic masking system, such as shape, dimensions of designs to be drawn, register marks, and retrieval of stored designs. Touches symbol of option selected on menu and activates option with mouse. Touches reference points of designs on layout sheet, using mouse, and presses button of mouse to enter coordinates of design in system memory. Presses button to activate vacuum to hold masking in place and to activate drafting unit that scores masking material with programmed figures. Activates plotting drum to make photographic mask exposures. Presses button to transfer data from system memory to disk. Loads drafting unit with masking material to prepare for plotting and scoring of programmed figures or loads film into plotting drum to make photographic mask exposure. Studies layout sheet to determine shapes of windows drawn on layout sheet. Positions artist's layout on digitizing tables of electronic masking system to prepare for data entry in system memory. Removes film from plotting drum and puts film in automatic film processor to create masks. Removes scored masking material from drafting table. Places material on light table and peels scored figures from masking material, using needle and tape.
Yearly Earnings: $22,412
Education: Long-term O-J-T
Knowledge: Computers and Electronics; Design; Fine Arts
Abilities: None above average
Skills: None above average
General Work Activities: Operating Vehicles or Equipment
Job Characteristics: Sitting; Degree of Automation
GOE Group/s: 01.06.01 Craft Arts: Graphics Arts and Related Crafts
CIP Program/s: 480201 Graphic and Printing Equipment Operator, General; 480206 Lithographer and Platemaker
Related DOT Job/s: 972.282-018 ELECTRONIC MASKING SYSTEM OPERATOR; 972.382-022 PHOTO MASK TECHNICIAN, ELECTRON-BEAM

89721 BOOKBINDERS. OOH Title/s: Bindery Workers

Cut, saw, and glue component parts to bind new books. Perform other finishing operations, such as grooving, decorating, and lettering. Primarily use hand tools but may also employ other precision processing methods or new technology. This occupation normally requires an apprenticeship program (usually 2 years or more) or equivalent training and more extensive experience than that of bindery workers. Exclude book repairers. Applies glue to back of book, using brush or glue machine, and attaches cloth backing and headband. Cuts binder board to specified dimension, using board shears, hand cutter, or cutting machine. Cuts cover material to specified dimensions and fits and glues material to binder board manually or by machine. Glues outside endpapers to cover. Attaches endpapers to top and bottom of book body, using sewing machine, or glues endpapers and signatures together along spine, using brush or glue machine. Trims edges of book to size, using cutting or book trimming machine or hand cutter. Inserts book body in device that forms back edge of book into convex shape and produces grooves to facilitate attachment of cover. Applies color to edges of signatures, using brush, pad, or atomizer. Imprints and embosses lettering, designs, or numbers on cover, using gold, silver, or colored foil and stamping machine. Compresses sewed or glued signatures to reduce book to required thickness, using handpress or smashing machine. Folds printed sheets to form signatures (pages) and assembles signatures in numerical order to form book body. Places bound book in press that exerts pressure on cover until glue dries. Packs, weighs, and stacks books on pallet for shipment.
Yearly Earnings: $18,044
Education: Moderate-term O-J-T
Knowledge: Production and Processing
Abilities: None above average
Skills: None above average
General Work Activities: Handling and Moving Objects
Job Characteristics: Contaminants; Hazardous Conditions; Hazardous Situations; Degree of Automation; Pace Determined by Speed of Equipment
GOE Group/s: 05.05.15 Craft Technology: Custom Sewing, Tailoring, and Upholstering
CIP Program/s: 480299 Graphic and Printing Equipment Operators, Other
Related DOT Job/s: 977.381-010 BOOKBINDER; 977.381-014 BOOKBINDER APPRENTICE

89799A PRECISION PRINTING WORKERS. OOH Title/s: Prepress Workers; Inspectors, Testers, and Graders; Photographic Process Workers

Perform variety of precision printing activities, such as duplication of microfilm and reproduction of graphic arts materials. Operates automatic processor to develop photographs, plates, or base material used in single or multicolor proofs. Sets up and operates various types of cameras to produce negatives, photostats, or plastic or paper printing plates. Immerses exposed materials into chemical solutions to hand develop single or multicolor proofs, or printing plates. Operates offset-duplicating machine or small printing press to reproduce single or multicolor copies of line, drawings, graphs, or similar materials. Prepares microfiche duplicates of microfilm, using contact printer and developing machine. Positions and aligns negatives to assemble flats for reproduction. Puts flats into vacuum frame to produce aluminum plate, microfiche print, or single or multicolor proof. Compares test exposures to quality control color guides or exposure guides to determine data for exposure settings. Hand rubs paper against printing plate to transfer specified design onto paper for use in etching glassware. Enters, positions, and alters size of text, using computer, to make up and arrange pages to produce printed materials. Scans artwork, using optical scanner, which changes image into computer-readable form. Prints paper or film copies of completed material from computer. Measures density levels of colors or color guides on proofs, using

densitometer, and compares readings to set standards. Reviews layout and customer order to determine size and style of type. Mixes powdered ink pigments, using matching book and measuring and mixing tools. Examines and inspects printed material for clarity of print and specified color. Maintains printing machinery and equipment. Sets up and operates bindery equipment to cut, assemble, staple, or bind materials.
Yearly Earnings: $22,412
Education: Long-term O-J-T
Knowledge: None above average
Abilities: Visual Color Discrimination
Skills: None above average
General Work Activities: Operating Vehicles or Equipment
Job Characteristics: Radiation; Making Repetitive Motions; Degree of Automation; Importance of Repeating Same Tasks; Pace Determined by Speed of Equipment
GOE Group/s: 01.06.01 Craft Arts: Graphics Arts and Related Crafts; 05.10.05 Crafts: Reproduction
CIP Program/s: 100103 Photographic Technologists and Technicians; 480201 Graphic and Printing Equipment Operator, General; 480205 Mechanical Typesetter and Composer; 480206 Lithographer and Platemaker; 480208 Printing Press Operator; 480211 Computer Typography and Composition Equipment Operator; 480212 Desktop Publishing Equipment Operator; 500402 Graphic Design, Commercial Art and Illustration
Related DOT Job/s: 971.381-046 SCREEN MAKER, TEXTILE; 972.381-034 PROOFER, PREPRESS; 976.381-014 MICROFICHE DUPLICATOR; 979.381-014 LINE-UP EXAMINER; 979.382-018 PRINTER; 979.382-026 COMPUTER TYPESETTER-KEYLINER; 979.384-010 SCREEN MAKER, PHOTOGRAPHIC PROCESS; 979.681-014 PRINTER

89799B ELECTROTYPERS AND STEREOTYPERS.

OOH Title/s: Prepress Workers

Fabricate and finish electrotype and stereotype printing plates. Inserts pins in base to register stereotype plates to key plate for mat molding. Pours metal into casting box or plated mold by hand to produce electrotype or stereotype printing plates. Drills matching holes in series of mounted color stereotype plates to be duplicated. Forms mold of composed type, using plastic sheet-molding or wood-fiber mat, and hydraulic press. Operates automatic casting machine to produce electrotype or stereotype printing plates. Corrects defects on plate, using engraver's hand tools, punches, and hammers. Removes excess metal from edges, back, and nonprinting surface areas of plate, using power shear, milling machines, or routing machine. Aligns and notches mats of color series with key color mat, using matching machine with monocolor magnifier attachment. Trims mat, using trimming machine, by aligning notches of mat with pins on trimming machine. Sprays plastic mold with silver solution and immerses mold in plating tank. Examines plate to detect imperfect formation of lines, type, and halftone dots, using magnifier. Operates proof press to obtain proof of plate reproduction and registration. Cuts and pastes pieces of paper-felt or cardboard in nonprinting areas of wood-fiber mat to prevent collapse during casting. Curves plates for cylinder presses, using plate-curving machine. Mounts finished plates on wood or metal blocks for flatbed presses, using hammer, nails, or bonding press.
Yearly Earnings: $22,412
Education: Long-term O-J-T
Knowledge: None above average
Abilities: Arm-Hand Steadiness; Manual Dexterity; Finger Dexterity; Rate Control; Visual Color Discrimination
Skills: Operation and Control
General Work Activities: Handling and Moving Objects; Controlling Machines and Processes
Job Characteristics: Deal with Physical, Aggressive People; Sounds, Noise Levels are Distracting, etc.; Hazardous Equipment; Keeping or Regaining Balance; Using Hands on Objects, Tools, or Controls; Making Repetitive Motions; Common Protective or Safety Attire; Importance of Repeating Same Tasks; Pace Determined by Speed of Equipment
GOE Group/s: 05.05.13 Craft Technology: Printing
CIP Program/s: 480201 Graphic and Printing Equipment Operator, General; 480205 Mechanical Typesetter and Composer
Related DOT Job/s: 974.381-010 ELECTROTYPER; 974.381-014 ELECTROTYPER APPRENTICE; 974.382-010 STEREOTYPER APPRENTICE; 974.382-014 STEREOTYPER

Food Processing Occupations

89802 SLAUGHTERERS AND BUTCHERS. OOH

Title/s: Butchers and Meat, Poultry, and Fish Cutters

Work in a slaughtering or meat packing establishment to prepare meat for sale by performing precision tasks, such as stunning, skinning and trimming; cutting standard cuts of meat for marketing; cleaning and salting hides; making sausage; preparing meats for salting; and wrapping meats. Trims headmeat and otherwise severs or removes parts of animals heads or skulls. Wraps dressed carcasses and/or meat cuts. Trims, cleans, and/or cures animal hides. Removes bone and cuts meat into standard cuts to prepare meat for marketing. Skins sections of animals or whole animals. Grinds meat into sausage. Stuns animals prior to slaughtering. Slaughters animals in accordance with religious law and determines that carcasses meet specified religious standards when slaughtering is performed for religious purposes. Saws, splits, or scribes slaughtered animals to reduce carcasses. Slits open, eviscerates, and trims carcasses of slaughtered animals. Severs jugular vein to drain blood and facilitate slaughtering. Cuts, trims, skins, sorts, and washes viscera of slaughtered animals to separate edible portions from offal. Shackles hind legs of animals to raise them for slaughtering or skinning. Washes and/or shaves carcasses.
Yearly Earnings: $17,108
Education: Long-term O-J-T
Knowledge: Food Production; Biology; Philosophy and Theology; Public Safety and Security
Abilities: Arm-Hand Steadiness; Manual Dexterity; Multilimb Coordination; Rate Control; Reaction Time; Wrist-Finger Speed; Speed of Limb Movement; Static Strength; Explosive Strength; Dynamic Strength; Trunk Strength; Stamina; Extent Flexibility; Dynamic Flexibility; Gross Body Equilibrium; Visual Color Discrimination; Peripheral Vision
Skills: None above average
General Work Activities: Performing General Physical Activities; Handling and Moving Objects
Job Characteristics: Deal with Physical, Aggressive People; Sounds, Noise Levels are Distracting, etc.; Contaminants; Diseases/Infections; Hazardous Situations; Climbing Ladders, Scaffolds, Poles, etc.; Making Repetitive Motions; Special Uniform; Common Protective or Safety Attire; Importance of Repeating Same Tasks
GOE Group/s: 03.04.05 Elemental Work: Plants and Animals: Services; 06.02.28 Production Work: Manual Work, Food Processing; 06.03.01 Quality Control: Inspecting, Testing, and Repairing
CIP Program/s: 120506 Meatcutter
Related DOT Job/s: 525.361-010 SLAUGHTERER, RELIGIOUS RITUAL; 525.381-010 BUTCHER APPRENTICE; 525.381-014 BUTCHER, ALL-ROUND; 525.664-010 MEAT DRESSER

89805 BAKERS, MANUFACTURING. OOH Title/s: Bakers, Manufacturing
Mix and bake ingredients according to recipes to produce breads, pastries, and other baked goods. Goods are produced in large quantities for sale through establishments such as grocery stores. Generally, high volume production equipment is used. Measures flour and other ingredients to prepare batters, dough, fillings, and icings, using scale and graduated containers. Places dough in pans, molds, or on sheets, and bakes dough in oven or on grill. Observes color of products being baked and adjusts oven temperature. Dumps ingredients into mixing-machine bowl or steam kettle to mix or cook ingredients according to specific instructions. Rolls, cuts, and shapes dough to form sweet rolls, pie crusts, tarts, cookies, and related products prior to baking. Applies glace, icing, or other topping to baked goods, using spatula or brush. Decorates cakes. Develops new recipes for cakes and icings.
Yearly Earnings: $17,420
Education: Moderate-term O-J-T
Knowledge: Production and Processing; Food Production
Abilities: None above average
Skills: None above average
General Work Activities: None above average
Job Characteristics: Very Hot; Hazardous Situations; Standing; Special Uniform; Importance of Repeating Same Tasks; Pace Determined by Speed of Equipment
GOE Group/s: 06.02.15 Production Work: Equipment Operation, Food Processing
CIP Program/s: 120501 Baker/Pastry Chef
Related DOT Job/s: 520.384-010 BENCH HAND; 526.381-010 BAKER; 526.381-014 BAKER APPRENTICE

89808 FOOD BATCHMAKERS. OOH Title/s: Food Processing Occupations
Set up and operate equipment that mixes, blends, or cooks ingredients used in the manufacturing of food products, according to formulas or recipes. May modify or reformulate recipes to produce products of specific flavor, texture, and color. This occupation requires at least 1 year (and often more) of training or experience. Include candy makers, almond paste mixers, cheesemakers, flavorings compounders, and honey graders and blenders. Calculates ingredient amounts to formulate or modify recipes to produce food product of specific flavor, texture, clarity, bouquet, and color. Fills processing or cooking container, such as water-cooled kettle, steam-jacketed rotating cooker, pressure cooker, or vat, with ingredients, following recipe. Mixes or blends ingredients, according to recipe, using paddle or agitator. Determines mixing sequence, based on knowledge of temperature effects and solubility and miscibility properties of specific ingredients. Stirs and cooks ingredients at specified temperatures. Operates refining machine to reduce size of cooked batch. Measures and weighs ingredients, using English or metric measures and balance scales. Separates, spreads, kneads, spins, casts, cuts, or rolls food product by hand or using machine. Homogenizes or pasteurizes material to prevent separation of substances or to obtain prescribed butterfat content. Examines, feels, and tastes product to evaluate color, texture, flavor, and bouquet. Tests food product sample for moisture content, acidity level, or butter-fat content. Cools food product batch on slabs or in water-cooled kettle. Grades food product according to government regulations or according to type, color, bouquet, and moisture content. Records amounts of ingredients used, test results, and time cycles. Gives directions to other workers who are assisting in batchmaking process.
Yearly Earnings: $17,004
Education: Long-term O-J-T
Knowledge: Food Production
Abilities: Information Ordering; Memorization
Skills: None above average
General Work Activities: Monitoring Processes, Material, or Surroundings
Job Characteristics: Standing; Making Repetitive Motions; Special Uniform
GOE Group/s: 06.01.04 Production Technology: Precision Hand Work; 06.02.28 Production Work: Manual Work, Food Processing
CIP Program/s: 010401 Agricultural and Food Products Processing Operations and Management; 200401 Institutional Food Workers and Administrators, General
Related DOT Job/s: 520.361-010 HONEY GRADER-AND-BLENDER; 529.361-010 ALMOND-PASTE MIXER; 529.361-014 CANDY MAKER; 529.361-018 CHEESEMAKER; 529.381-010 COMPOUNDER, FLAVORINGS

89899 ALL OTHER PRECISION FOOD AND TOBACCO WORKERS. OOH Title/s: Food Processing Occupations
All other precision food and tobacco workers not classified separately above.
Yearly Earnings: $17,004
Education: Long-term O-J-T
GOE Group/s: 05.10.08 Crafts: Food Preparation
CIP Program/s: 000000 NO CIP ASSIGNED
Related DOT Job/s: 520.487-014 FORMULA-ROOM WORKER; 790.381-010 TOBACCO BLENDER

Other Precision Occupations

89902 PRECISION FOUNDRY MOLD AND CORE MAKERS. OOH Title/s: Foundry, Mold Assembly and Shakeout Workers
Make and form wax or sand cores and molds used in the production of metal castings in foundries. Work involves using hand and power tools and applying knowledge of variables such as metal characteristics, molding sand, contour of patterns, reinforcing, and pouring procedures. Forms and assembles slab cores around pattern and positions wire in mold sections to reinforce mold, using hand tools and glue. Sifts sand and packs sand into mold sections, core box, and pattern contours, using hand or pneumatic ramming tools. Positions cores into lower section of mold and reassembles mold for pouring. Cuts spouts, runner holes, and sprue holes into mold. Sprinkles or sprays parting agent onto pattern and mold sections, to facilitate removal of pattern from mold. Positions patterns inside mold sections and clamps sections together. Operates ovens to bake cores or furnaces to melt, skim, and flux metal. Lifts upper mold section from lower and removes molded patterns. Rotates sweep board around spindle to make symmetrical molds for convex impressions. Cleans and smoothes molds, cores, and core boxes, and repairs surface imperfections. Pours molten metal into mold, manually or using crane ladle. Moves and positions workpieces, such as mold sections, patterns, and bottom boards, using cranes, or signals others to move workpieces.
Yearly Earnings: $18,772
Education: Moderate-term O-J-T
Knowledge: Building and Construction; Mechanical
Abilities: Arm-Hand Steadiness; Multilimb Coordination; Speed of Limb Movement; Static Strength; Stamina; Gross Body Equilibrium
Skills: None above average
General Work Activities: Handling and Moving Objects
Job Characteristics: Sounds, Noise Levels are Distracting, etc.; Very Hot; Extremely Bright or Inadequate Lighting; Contaminants; Hazard-

ous Equipment; Hazardous Situations; Standing; Making Repetitive Motions; Common Protective or Safety Attire; Importance of Repeating Same Tasks; Pace Determined by Speed of Equipment
GOE Group/s: 06.01.04 Production Technology: Precision Hand Work
CIP Program/s: 480599 Precision Metal Workers, Other
Related DOT Job/s: 518.361-010 MOLDER; 518.361-014 MOLDER APPRENTICE; 518.361-018 MOLDER, SWEEP; 518.381-014 COREMAKER; 518.381-018 COREMAKER APPRENTICE

89905A MOLDERS AND CASTERS. OOH Title/s: Foundry, Mold Assembly and Shakeout Workers

Cast molds and patterns according to blueprints, sketches, and instructions. Pours, packs, spreads, or presses plaster, concrete, liquid plastic, or other materials into or around model, figure, flask, or mold. Applies reinforcing strips of hemp fiber and additional layers of plaster, mesh, or liquid plastic to form pattern of model. Reviews specifications, blueprint, or sketch, to plan and lay out work. Applies lubricant, parting agent, or shellac to part, mold, pattern, or flask. Constructs or assembles wooden mold, using clamps and bolts, hand tools, and power tools. Locates and scribes parting line on wood, metal, or plastic patterns, using measuring instruments, such as calipers, square, and depth gauge. Positions and secures reinforcing structure or materials, flask, mold, model, or pattern. Measures, melts, combines, and kneads putty ingredients to attain specified viscosity and shape. Tamps concrete mixtures and facing aggregate, using hand tools, measuring instruments, hoist, hopper, and pneumatic vibrator. Removes casting from mold after specified time, using tools and equipment such as hand tools, power tools, and crane. Verifies dimensions, using measuring instruments, such as calipers, vernier gauge, and protractor. Mixes ingredients for plaster according to standard formula. Trims or removes excess material, using scraper, knife, or bandsaw. Patches broken edges and fractures, using clay or plaster and molders hand tools. Brushes and scrapes concrete from mold preparatory to next casting.
Yearly Earnings: $18,772
Education: Moderate-term O-J-T
Knowledge: Production and Processing; Design; Building and Construction
Abilities: Wrist-Finger Speed
Skills: None above average
General Work Activities: None above average
Job Characteristics: Sounds, Noise Levels are Distracting, etc.; Standing
GOE Group/s: 01.06.02 Craft Arts: Arts and Crafts; 06.01.04 Production Technology: Precision Hand Work; 06.02.30 Production Work: Manual Work, Stone, Glass, and Clay; 06.02.32 Production Work: Manual Work, Assorted Materials
CIP Program/s: 460101 Mason and Tile Setter; 469999 Construction Trades, Other
Related DOT Job/s: 575.461-010 CONCRETE-STONE FABRICATOR; 739.381-046 MANNEQUIN-MOLD MAKER; 769.381-010 COMPO CASTER; 777.081-010 MODELER; 777.381-034 PLASTER MOLDER I; 777.381-038 PLASTER-PATTERN CASTER

89905B MOLDERS AND CASTERS, NONFERROUS METALS. OOH Title/s: Foundry, Mold Assembly and Shakeout Workers

Cast molds and patterns from nonferrous metals according to specifications. Shapes mold to specified contours with sand, using trowel and related tools. Tilts melting pot or uses ladle to pour molten alloy, bronze, or other nonferrous metal into sand mold. Preheats dies or patterns, using blowtorch or other equipment, and applies parting compound. Lowers metal jig into molten metal in prescribed manner to attach anchor bolts to punch. Clamps metal and plywood strips around die or pattern to form mold. Operates foundry furnaces and ovens. Constructs wood patterns used to form sand molds for metal casts. Operates hoist to position dies or patterns on foundry floor. Machines metal patterns to exact dimensions.
Yearly Earnings: $18,772
Education: Moderate-term O-J-T
Knowledge: None above average
Abilities: Manual Dexterity; Reaction Time; Explosive Strength; Dynamic Strength; Depth Perception; Glare Sensitivity
Skills: Operation and Control
General Work Activities: Controlling Machines and Processes
Job Characteristics: Sounds, Noise Levels are Distracting, etc.; Very Hot; Extremely Bright or Inadequate Lighting; Contaminants; Hazardous Conditions; Hazardous Equipment; Hazardous Situations; Making Repetitive Motions; Common Protective or Safety Attire; Specialized Protective or Safety Attire; Pace Determined by Speed of Equipment
GOE Group/s: 06.02.24 Production Work: Manual Work, Metal and Plastics
CIP Program/s: 480501 Machinist/Machine Technologist; 480599 Precision Metal Workers, Other
Related DOT Job/s: 502.381-014 MOLDER, PUNCH; 693.381-022 MOLDER, PATTERN

89905C STONE CUTTERS AND CARVERS. OOH Title/s: Indirectly related to Bricklayers and Stone Masons; Visual Artists

Cut or carve stone according to diagrams and patterns. Guides nozzle over stone following stencil outline or chips along marks to create design or work surface down to desired finish. Drills holes, or cuts molding and grooves in stone. Studies artistic objects or graphic materials, such as models, sketches, or blueprints and plans carving or cutting technique. Lays out designs or dimensions on stone surface, by freehand or transfer from tracing paper, using scribe or chalk and measuring instruments. Selects chisels, pneumatic or surfacing tools, or sandblasting nozzles and determines sequence of their use according to intricacy of design or figure. Removes or adds stencil during blasting to create differences in depth of cuts, intricate designs, or rough, pitted finish. Loads sandblasting equipment with abrasive, attaches nozzle to hose, and turns valves to admit compressed air and activate jet. Verifies depth and dimensions of cut or carving, using measuring instruments, to ensure adherence to specifications. Moves fingers over surface of carving to ensure smoothness of finish.
Yearly Earnings: $25,480
Education: Long-term O-J-T
Knowledge: Design; Building and Construction; Physics; Fine Arts
Abilities: Visualization; Arm-Hand Steadiness; Depth Perception
Skills: None above average
General Work Activities: Thinking Creatively; Controlling Machines and Processes
Job Characteristics: Sounds, Noise Levels are Distracting, etc.; Contaminants; Whole Body Vibration; Common Protective or Safety Attire; Importance of Repeating Same Tasks
GOE Group/s: 01.06.02 Craft Arts: Arts and Crafts; 05.05.01 Craft Technology: Masonry, Stone, and Brick Work; 05.10.01 Crafts: Structural
CIP Program/s: 460101 Mason and Tile Setter; 500201 Crafts, Folk Art and Artisanry
Related DOT Job/s: 673.382-010 SANDBLASTER, STONE; 673.382-014 SANDBLASTER, STONE APPRENTICE; 771.281-014 STONE CARVER; 771.381-010 STONECUTTER APPRENTICE, HAND; 771.381-014 STONECUTTER, HAND

89905D GLASS BLOWERS, MOLDERS, BENDERS, AND FINISHERS. OOH Title/s: Indirectly related to Visual Artists

Shape molten glass according to patterns. Shapes, bends, or joins sections of glass, using paddles, pressing and flattening hand tools, or cork. Blows tubing into specified shape, using compressed air or own breath. Places glass into die or mold of press and controls press to form products, such as, glassware components or optical blanks. Dips end of blowpipe into molten glass to collect gob on pipe head or cuts gob from molten glass, using sheers. Preheats or melts glass pieces or anneals or cools glass products and components, using ovens and refractory powder. Heats glass to pliable stage, using gas flame or oven. Cuts length of tubing to specified size, using file or cutting wheel. Inspects and measures product to verify conformance to specifications, using instruments, such as micrometers, calipers, magnifier, and ruler. Examines gob of molten glass for imperfections, utilizing knowledge of molten glass characteristics. Strikes neck of finished article to separate article from blowpipe. Determines type and quantity of glass required to fabricate product. Adjusts press stroke length and pressure, and regulates oven temperatures according to glass type processed. Develops sketch of glass product into blueprint specifications, applying knowledge of glass technology and glass blowing.

Yearly Earnings: $29,900
Education: Work experience, plus degree
Knowledge: Production and Processing
Abilities: None above average
Skills: None above average
General Work Activities: Handling and Moving Objects
Job Characteristics: Very Hot; Hazardous Situations; Standing; Making Repetitive Motions; Importance of Repeating Same Tasks
GOE Group/s: 01.06.02 Craft Arts: Arts and Crafts; 05.05.11 Craft Technology: Scientific, Medical, & Technical Equip. Fabric. & Related; 06.01.04 Production Technology: Precision Hand Work; 06.02.30 Production Work: Manual Work, Stone, Glass, and Clay
CIP Program/s: 150304 Laser and Optical Technologists and Technicians; 500201 Crafts, Folk Art and Artisanry
Related DOT Job/s: 006.261-010 SCIENTIFIC GLASS BLOWER; 575.381-010 MOLDER; 772.281-010 GLASS BLOWER, LABORATORY APPARATUS; 772.381-010 GLASS BENDER; 772.381-018 WARE FINISHER; 772.381-022 GLASS BLOWER

89905F THROWERS. OOH Title/s: Indirectly related to Visual Artists

Mold clay into ware as clay revolves on potter's wheel. Raises and shapes clay into ware, such as vases, saggers, and pitchers, on revolving wheel, using hands, fingers, and thumbs. Smoothes surfaces of finished piece, using rubber scrapers and wet sponge. Adjusts speed of wheel according to feel of changing firmness of clay. Positions ball of clay in center of potters wheel. Starts motor, or pumps treadle with foot to revolve wheel. Pulls wire through base of article and wheel to separate finished piece. Verifies size and form, using calipers and templates. Moves piece from wheel to dry.

Yearly Earnings: $29,900
Education: Work experience, plus degree
Knowledge: Fine Arts
Abilities: Arm-Hand Steadiness; Manual Dexterity; Rate Control
Skills: None above average
General Work Activities: None above average
Job Characteristics: Sitting; Using Hands on Objects, Tools, or Controls; Bending or Twisting the Body; Making Repetitive Motions; Importance of Repeating Same Tasks; Pace Determined by Speed of Equipment
GOE Group/s: 06.02.30 Production Work: Manual Work, Stone, Glass, and Clay
CIP Program/s: 500701 Art, General; 500711 Ceramics Arts and Ceramics
Related DOT Job/s: 774.381-010 THROWER

89908A PATTERNMAKERS AND MODEL BUILDERS. OOH Title/s: Indirectly related to Tool and Die Makers

Plan, layout, and construct precision parts, models, and patterns. Marks layout, dimensions, and cutting lines on stock, using measuring and marking instruments, such as calipers, dividers, and straightedges. Reads blueprints and engineering information to determine sequence of operations and design specifications. Shapes parts of model or pattern from pliable stock, using hands and hand tools, to mold material. Assembles parts or components together, using hand tools, bolts, screws, clamps, or glue, to form models, mockups, or patterns. Drills holes in parts and assemblies for fasteners, such as bolts and screws. Abrades parts to attain specified fit and finish, using hand tools and power tools. Sets up and operates machine tools to cut and fabricate models, patterns, templates, and other parts. Applies finish, such as enamel, paint, or lacquer, to completed model. Installs completed parts to assembly, using hand tools and power tools. Modifies model, mockup, pattern, or template as necessary to conform with specifications or engineering instructions. Verifies finished dimensions of model or pattern, using precision instruments and testing equipment, such as scales, calipers, micrometer, and protractor. Selects stock materials, such as aluminum, wood, styrene, and fiberglass, according to design specifications. Develops templates, patterns, and molds for fabricating, laying out, or inspecting parts. Repairs broken or damaged models or patterns. Collaborates with engineering, tooling, production, and other personnel to resolve developmental, assembly, and installation problems.

Yearly Earnings: $28,184
Education: Long-term O-J-T
Knowledge: Production and Processing; Engineering and Technology; Design; Building and Construction
Abilities: Written Comprehension; Deductive Reasoning; Information Ordering; Visualization; Arm-Hand Steadiness; Finger Dexterity; Control Precision; Gross Body Equilibrium; Auditory Attention
Skills: Technology Design; Installation
General Work Activities: Handling and Moving Objects; Controlling Machines and Processes; Drafting and Specifying Technical Devices, etc.
Job Characteristics: Hazardous Equipment; Hazardous Situations
GOE Group/s: 01.06.02 Craft Arts: Arts and Crafts; 05.05.07 Craft Technology: Machining; 05.05.15 Craft Technology: Custom Sewing, Tailoring, and Upholstering; 06.01.04 Production Technology: Precision Hand Work
CIP Program/s: 150801 Aeronautical and Aerospace Engineering Technologists and Technicians; 480501 Machinist/Machine Technologist; 480503 Machine Shop Assistant; 480507 Tool and Die Maker/Technologist; 489999 Precision Production Trades, Other; 500501 Drama/Theater Arts, General; 500502 Technical Theater/Theater Design and Stagecraft
Related DOT Job/s: 693.261-010 DEVELOPER PROVER, INTERIOR ASSEMBLIES; 693.261-018 MODEL MAKER; 693.280-014 PATTERNMAKER, ALL-AROUND; 693.281-030 TOOL BUILDER; 693.380-014 MODEL MAKER; 693.381-018 MOCK-UP BUILDER; 731.280-010 MODEL MAKER; 777.261-010 MODEL MAKER I; 777.281-018 PATTERNMAKER, PLASTER; 962.381-018 MINIATURE-SET CONSTRUCTOR

89908B CUTTERS AND LAYOUT WORKERS. OOH

Title/s: Indirectly related to Tool and Die Makers

Layout and cut designs or patterns on a variety of materials. Draws layout and dimensions of pattern on material to be used as stencil, using drafting tools and aids, such as sketch. Cuts out stencils or templates, by hand or by machine, for use in creating detailed reproduction of patterns and designs. Cuts out pattern or design along cutting lines, using knife, cutting tool, or cutting machines. Transfers shape of stencil onto material to create cutting lines, using tracing, projection, marking, or drafting instruments. Aligns stencil on stock or multiple layers of stock, using straightedge or T-square. Scales size of pattern and repeats cutting for additional stencils or patterns according to work order. Determines size, number, color, and types of materials required from work order or customer specifications. Attaches pattern stock to worktable for cutting. Compares pattern or design cut-out to template or original pattern size and shape to verify. Assembles cut out pattern sections to form completed or sample design. Tests completed design, proof copy, or sample to determine suitability for intended use and records results. Determines machines, tools, and sequence of operation to cut product following patterns or designs, utilizing knowledge of machine tools and equipment. Brushes paint or shellac on stencils or patterns. Inspects rolls of materials received and stores on shelves.

Yearly Earnings: $28,184
Education: Long-term O-J-T
Knowledge: Production and Processing; Fine Arts
Abilities: Arm-Hand Steadiness; Control Precision; Wrist-Finger Speed; Speed of Limb Movement; Gross Body Equilibrium
Skills: None above average
General Work Activities: Drafting and Specifying Technical Devices, etc.
Job Characteristics: Hazardous Situations; Using Hands on Objects, Tools, or Controls; Making Repetitive Motions; Importance of Repeating Same Tasks; Pace Determined by Speed of Equipment
GOE Group/s: 01.06.01 Craft Arts: Graphics Arts and Related Crafts; 01.06.02 Craft Arts: Arts and Crafts; 01.06.03 Craft Arts: Hand Lettering, Painting and Decorating; 05.03.02 Engineering Technology: Drafting; 06.01.04 Production Technology: Precision Hand Work; 06.02.04 Production Work: Machine Work, Paper
CIP Program/s: 150603 Industrial/Manufacturing Technologists and Technicians; 460101 Mason and Tile Setter; 480501 Machinist/Machine Technologist; 500402 Graphic Design, Commercial Art and Illustration; 500404 Industrial Design
Related DOT Job/s: 649.361-010 PATTERNMAKER, ENVELOPE; 693.382-010 LAST-PATTERN GRADER; 739.281-010 PACKAGING TECHNICIAN; 739.381-038 INSET CUTTER; 751.684-026 PREFORM PLATE MAKER; 771.281-010 STENCIL CUTTER; 772.381-014 PATTERNMAKER; 979.381-038 STENCIL MAKER; 979.681-022 SILK-SCREEN CUTTER

89908C MODEL AND MOLD MAKERS. OOH Title/s:

Indirectly related to Visual Artists

Construct molds or models, using fiberglass, plaster, or clay. Shapes sculptured clay surfaces to form details of mold or model, using various sculptor's tools, hands, and scrapers. Pours plaster or compound over model and spreads evenly over surface, using brush or spatula. Builds layers of material, such as fiberglass, resin, or rubber paint around model to form mold or cast, and shield around cast. Cuts and removes sections of hardened mold or cast, using hand or power tools. Reassembles sections of shield and cast to form complete mold, using shellac or concrete. Mixes water and powder or catalytic compound, and clay, according to specifications, to form plaster or other compound. Punches holes in surface of model to assure plaster will adhere. Smoothes surface of cast to remove excess materials, using electric grinder, polishing wheel, file, or sandpaper. Cuts templates of model according to blueprints or layout drawings. Constructs frame to support figure while modeling. Verifies uniformity and smoothness of curved surfaces. Brushes liquid soap or wax onto model or frame to prevent adhesion of plaster or fiberglass. Duplicates completed model half to make measurements of unfinished half symmetrical. Covers specified portions of model with aluminum foil or transparent media trim to identify or detail. Repairs molds using carpenter tools.

Yearly Earnings: $29,900
Education: Work experience, plus degree
Knowledge: Building and Construction; Fine Arts
Abilities: Visualization; Arm-Hand Steadiness; Manual Dexterity; Wrist-Finger Speed; Speed of Limb Movement; Explosive Strength
Skills: None above average
General Work Activities: None above average
Job Characteristics: Contaminants; Using Hands on Objects, Tools, or Controls; Making Repetitive Motions
GOE Group/s: 01.06.02 Craft Arts: Arts and Crafts; 05.05.11 Craft Technology: Scientific, Medical, & Technical Equip. Fabric. & Related
CIP Program/s: 150607 Plastics Technologists and Technicians; 151102 Surveying; 460499 Construction and Building Finishers and Managers, Other; 489999 Precision Production Trades, Other
Related DOT Job/s: 777.281-010 CONCRETE SCULPTOR; 777.281-014 MODEL MAKER; 777.361-010 EAR-MOLD LABORATORY TECHNICIAN; 777.381-010 MODEL MAKER, FIBERGLASS; 777.381-014 MODEL-AND-MOLD MAKER; 777.381-018 MODEL-AND-MOLD MAKER, PLASTER; 777.381-042 RELIEF-MAP MODELER; 779.281-010 CLAY MODELER

89908D EXHIBIT BUILDERS. OOH Title/s: Carpenters

Construct and install exhibits or displays for museums or other commercial exhibitions. Sets up display in designated site, such as exhibit gallery or commercial location. Cuts glass, wood, plastic, plexiglas, or sheet metal parts for framework of exhibit or display, using hand and power tools. Assembles parts with nails, screws, bolts, and glue, to fabricate panels, shelves, and other exhibit components, using hand tools. Installs electrical wiring for illumination, audio, video, or control equipment in framework of exhibit or display, according to design specifications. Paints enamel, varnish, or other finish on structures of exhibit, using spray, brush, cloth, sponge, or fingers. Designs displays or exhibits according to pictures, sketches or verbal instructions from customer. Affixes murals, photographs, mounted legend materials, and graphics in framework or on fixtures. Studies sketches or scale drawings for displays or exhibits to determine type, amount, and cost of material needed. Tests electrical, electronic, and mechanical components of exhibit structure to verify operation. Disassembles and reassembles display to make working drawings for production, or to send to prospective customers. Confers with exhibit personnel, designer, customer, or salesperson to discuss refinement, additions, or adjustments to exhibit or display. Maintains inventory of building materials, tools, and equipment, and orders supplies. Supervises assigned duties of carpentry, electrical, and other workers assisting in construction of exhibit or display.

Yearly Earnings: $22,360
Education: Long-term O-J-T
Knowledge: Administration and Management; Personnel and Human Resources; Engineering and Technology; Design; Building and Construction; Fine Arts
Abilities: Originality; Spatial Orientation; Visualization; Arm-Hand Steadiness; Manual Dexterity; Finger Dexterity; Wrist-Finger Speed; Speed of Limb Movement; Static Strength; Explosive Strength; Dynamic Strength; Trunk Strength; Stamina; Extent Flexibility; Dynamic Flexibility; Gross Body Coordination; Gross Body Equilibrium; Visual Color Discrimination; Peripheral Vision; Depth Perception

Skills: Mathematics; Coordination; Operations Analysis; Technology Design; Installation; Time Management; Management of Financial Resources; Management of Material Resources; Management of Personnel Resources
General Work Activities: Performing General Physical Activities; Drafting and Specifying Technical Devices, etc.; Repairing and Maintaining Electrical Equipment; Coordinating Work and Activities of Others
Job Characteristics: Supervise, Coach, Train Others; Coordinate or Lead Others; Responsibility for Outcomes and Results; Sounds, Noise Levels are Distracting, etc.; Extremely Bright or Inadequate Lighting; Cramped Work Space, Awkward Positions; Radiation; High Places; Hazardous Conditions; Hazardous Equipment; Climbing Ladders, Scaffolds, Poles, etc.; Kneeling, Crouching, or Crawling; Keeping or Regaining Balance; Bending or Twisting the Body; Making Repetitive Motions
GOE Group/s: 01.06.02 Craft Arts: Arts and Crafts
CIP Program/s: 080299 Business and Personal Services Marketing Operations, Other; 460201 Carpenter
Related DOT Job/s: 739.261-010 EXHIBIT BUILDER; 739.361-010 DISPLAY MAKER

89911A PRECISION PAINTERS. OOH Title/s: Indirectly related to Visual Artists

Paint decorative free-hand designs on objects, such as pottery, cigarette cases, and lampshades, using hand brushes. Applies paint or metallic leaf to workpiece, using handbrush, airbrush, or roller. Sketches or traces design or lettering onto workpiece or pattern material to prepare pattern or stencil, using measuring and drawing instruments. Designs pattern or lettering to paint workpieces, such as signs, glassware, pottery, or zinc plates, using measuring and drawing instruments. Removes excess paint, using brush or cotton swab. Mixes paint according to established formulas to obtain specified color and desired consistency. Examines workpiece to compare with pattern and to detect imperfections. Applies preservative coating to workpiece. Reads work order to determine work procedures and materials required. Positions and aligns workpiece on work area. Uses wheel equipment to hold and revolve workpiece while applying paint. Cuts out letters or designs using hand or powered cutting tools. Hangs workpieces on rack to dry or places workpieces on conveyor. Maintains daily production records.
Yearly Earnings: $29,900
Education: Work experience, plus degree
Knowledge: Design; Fine Arts
Abilities: Originality; Arm-Hand Steadiness; Manual Dexterity; Finger Dexterity; Wrist-Finger Speed; Visual Color Discrimination
Skills: None above average
General Work Activities: Thinking Creatively
Job Characteristics: Contaminants; Hazardous Conditions; Sitting; Using Hands on Objects, Tools, or Controls; Making Repetitive Motions
GOE Group/s: 01.06.03 Craft Arts: Hand Lettering, Painting and Decorating
CIP Program/s: 500402 Graphic Design, Commercial Art and Illustration; 500701 Art, General; 500711 Ceramics Arts and Ceramics
Related DOT Job/s: 740.381-010 DECORATOR; 740.381-014 LUSTER APPLICATOR; 740.381-018 PAINTER; 740.681-010 LINER; 970.281-022 SIGN WRITER, HAND; 970.381-014 DECORATOR, MANNEQUIN; 970.381-022 PAINTER, HAND; 970.381-026 PAINTER, SIGN; 970.681-026 PAINTER, ANIMATED CARTOONS; 970.681-030 PAINTER, PLATE

89911B SILK SCREEN PROCESS DECORATORS. OOH Title/s: Indirectly related to Visual Artists

Apply lettering, designs, or coloring to products, using silk screen process. Applies ink or glaze to screen or pattern over drawing or plate and prints design. Positions mask or applies protective coating over parts not to be shaded. Selects and prepares color glaze or ink. Cleans ink, glaze, or protective coating from parts of drawing not to be shaded. Cuts stencil by hand, using cutting tools, or photographs design on film. Reads job order and examines drawing or design to determine method of making stencil. Catalogs and stores screens for future orders.
Yearly Earnings: $29,900
Education: Work experience, plus degree
Knowledge: Production and Processing; Fine Arts
Abilities: Arm-Hand Steadiness; Visual Color Discrimination
Skills: None above average
General Work Activities: None above average
Job Characteristics: Hazardous Conditions; Using Hands on Objects, Tools, or Controls; Making Repetitive Motions
GOE Group/s: 01.06.03 Craft Arts: Hand Lettering, Painting and Decorating
CIP Program/s: 500402 Graphic Design, Commercial Art and Illustration
Related DOT Job/s: 773.381-010 TILE DECORATOR; 970.681-010 BEN-DAY ARTIST

89911C ENGRAVERS/CARVERS. OOH Title/s: Indirectly related to Visual Artists

Engrave or carve designs or lettering onto objects, using hand-held power tools. Holds workpiece against outer edge of wheel and twists and turns workpiece to grind glass according to marked design. Carves design on workpiece, using electric hand tool. Cuts outline of impression with graver and removes excess material with knife. Traces, sketches, or presses design or facsimile signature on workpiece by hand, or by using artist equipment. Selects and mounts wheel and miter on lathe, and equips lathe with water to cool wheel and prevent dust. Polishes engravings using felt and cork wheels. Prepares workpiece to be engraved or carved, such as glassware, rubber, or plastic product. Attaches engraved workpiece to mount, using cement. Dresses and shapes cutting wheels by holding dressing stone against rotating wheel. Suggests original designs to customer or management.
Yearly Earnings: $29,900
Education: Work experience, plus degree
Knowledge: Production and Processing; Fine Arts
Abilities: Originality; Arm-Hand Steadiness; Manual Dexterity; Finger Dexterity; Rate Control; Wrist-Finger Speed; Dynamic Flexibility; Near Vision; Depth Perception
Skills: None above average
General Work Activities: Thinking Creatively
Job Characteristics: Hazardous Equipment; Using Hands on Objects, Tools, or Controls; Making Repetitive Motions; Importance of Being Exact or Accurate
GOE Group/s: 01.06.01 Craft Arts: Graphics Arts and Related Crafts; 05.10.05 Crafts: Reproduction; 06.01.04 Production Technology: Precision Hand Work
CIP Program/s: 500201 Crafts, Folk Art and Artisanry; 500402 Graphic Design, Commercial Art and Illustration
Related DOT Job/s: 733.381-010 ENGRAVER, RUBBER; 754.381-010 INTERNAL CARVER; 775.381-010 ENGRAVER

89911D ETCHERS. OOH Title/s: Indirectly related to Visual Artists

Etch or cut artistic designs in glass articles, using acid solutions, sandblasting equipment, and design patterns. Immerses waxed ware in hydrofluoric acid to etch design on glass surface. Sandblasts exposed area of glass, using spray gun, to cut design in surface. Places template against glassware surface and sprays with sand to cut design in surface. Positions pattern against waxed or taped ware and sprays ink through pattern to transfer design to wax or tape.

Removes wax or tape, using stylus or knife, to expose glassware surface to be etched. Coats glass in molten wax or masks glassware with tape. Immerses ware in hot water to remove wax or peels off tape.
Yearly Earnings: $29,900
Education: Work experience, plus degree
Knowledge: Production and Processing; Chemistry; Fine Arts
Abilities: Arm-Hand Steadiness; Manual Dexterity; Wrist-Finger Speed; Gross Body Equilibrium
Skills: None above average
General Work Activities: None above average
Job Characteristics: Contaminants; Hazardous Conditions; Hazardous Equipment; Using Hands on Objects, Tools, or Controls; Making Repetitive Motions; Common Protective or Safety Attire; Importance of Repeating Same Tasks
GOE Group/s: 01.06.01 Craft Arts: Graphics Arts and Related Crafts
CIP Program/s: 500701 Art, General; 500711 Ceramics Arts and Ceramics
Related DOT Job/s: 775.381-014 GLASS DECORATOR

89911E TRACERS AND LETTERERS. OOH Title/s: Prepress Workers; Indirectly related to Visual Artists

Lay out and trace lettering and designs on various surfaces, using stylus or writing instruments and master copies. Draws designs, letters, and lines by hand, according to specifications, using artist and drafting tools. Traces lettering or designs on workpiece, using light box, opaque projector, and artist and drafting equipment. Designs letters, borders, scrollwork, characters, or script, according to specifications. Positions design on workpiece and lays out reference points on design, using measuring instruments. Reads work order or manuscript to determine words and symbols needed. Measures width, thickness, and spacing of characters and design, using optical or measuring instruments. Cuts out letters or designs, using cutting tools. Applies colors to patterns, using stylus, pen, brush, sponge, opaque, India ink, and paints. Applies coatings to workpiece, such as metallic leaf, shellac, oil, glue, or lacquer, using brush, spray, roller, or hand tools. Positions and secures work piece. Rubs metallic leaf with burnishing agate, cotton pad, or gloved hand to polish leaf or simulate worn metal finish. Assembles composite design to determine accuracy for final approved form. Corrects errors in design to make ready for printing. Determines availability of characters specified on order. Reproduces reference copies, using automatic film developer or duplication equipment. Types lines and characters, such as letters, musical notations, Braille symbols, using typewriter or computer. Maintains detailed records of jobs and reference sources.
Yearly Earnings: $29,900
Education: Work experience, plus degree
Knowledge: Production and Processing; Design; Fine Arts
Abilities: Visualization; Arm-Hand Steadiness; Manual Dexterity; Finger Dexterity; Visual Color Discrimination
Skills: None above average
General Work Activities: None above average
Job Characteristics: Sitting; Using Hands on Objects, Tools, or Controls; Making Repetitive Motions
GOE Group/s: 01.02.03 Visual Arts: Commercial Art; 01.06.01 Craft Arts: Graphics Arts and Related Crafts; 01.06.02 Craft Arts: Arts and Crafts; 01.06.03 Craft Arts: Hand Lettering, Painting and Decorating
CIP Program/s: 480201 Graphic and Printing Equipment Operator, General; 480211 Computer Typography and Composition Equipment Operator; 500402 Graphic Design, Commercial Art and Illustration
Related DOT Job/s: 209.582-010 MUSIC COPYIST; 209.584-010 BRAILLE TRANSCRIBER, HAND; 779.381-022 TRACER; 970.281-026 SKETCH MAKER, PHOTOENGRAVING; 970.361-010 FORM DESIGNER; 970.381-038 STENCIL CUTTER; 970.381-042 TYPE COPYIST; 970.581-010 MUSIC GRAPHER; 970.661-010 ENGROSSER; 970.661-014 LETTERER; 970.681-018 INKER AND OPAQUER; 970.681-022 MANUGRAPHER; 979.381-034 SKETCH MAKER I; 979.681-010 LETTERER

89911G GILDERS. OOH Title/s: Indirectly related to Visual Artists

Cover surfaces of items, such as books, furniture, and signs, with metal leaf, using hand tools. Picks up leaf with brush or felt-edged tool and lays leaf over sizing. Smoothes leaf over surface and removes excess, using brush. Presses sheets or ribbons of leaf onto sizing by hand. Brushes sizing (thin glue) on sections of items to be covered with leaf, according to design. Rubs leaf with polished burnishing agent or cotton pad to polish leaf or simulate worn metal finish. Transfers leaf from supply book onto pallet.
Yearly Earnings: $29,900
Education: Work experience, plus degree
Knowledge: Fine Arts
Abilities: Arm-Hand Steadiness; Manual Dexterity; Wrist-Finger Speed; Dynamic Strength
Skills: None above average
General Work Activities: None above average
Job Characteristics: Sitting; Using Hands on Objects, Tools, or Controls; Making Repetitive Motions
GOE Group/s: 01.06.03 Craft Arts: Hand Lettering, Painting and Decorating
CIP Program/s: 500402 Graphic Design, Commercial Art and Illustration
Related DOT Job/s: 749.381-010 GILDER

89914A PHOTOGRAPHIC RETOUCHERS AND RESTORERS. OOH Title/s: Photographic Process Workers

Retouch or restore photographic negatives and prints to accentuate desirable features of subject, using pencils, watercolors, or airbrushes. Applies paint to retouch or enhance negative or photograph, using airbrush, pen, artist's brush, cotton swab, or gloved finger. Shades negative or photograph with pencil to smooth facial contours, conceal blemishes, stray hairs, or wrinkles, and soften highlights. Rubs eraser or cloth over photograph to reduce gloss, remove debris, or prepare specified areas of illustration for highlighting. Paints negative with retouching medium, to ensure retouching pencil will mark surface of negative. Inks borders or lettering on illustration, using pen, brush, or drafting instruments. Wipes excess color from portrait to produce specified shade, using cotton swab. Examines drawing, negative, or photographic print to determine coloring, shading, accenting, and changes required to retouch or restore. Cuts out masking template, using shears, and positions templates on picture to mask selected areas. Mixes ink or paint solutions, according to color specifications, color chart, and consistency desired. Trims edges of print to enhance appearance, using scissors or paper cutter.
Yearly Earnings: $16,848
Education: Long-term O-J-T
Knowledge: Fine Arts
Abilities: Visualization; Arm-Hand Steadiness; Manual Dexterity; Finger Dexterity; Wrist-Finger Speed; Visual Color Discrimination
Skills: None above average
General Work Activities: None above average
Job Characteristics: Deal with Physical, Aggressive People; Using Hands on Objects, Tools, or Controls; Importance of Being Exact or Accurate
GOE Group/s: 01.06.03 Craft Arts: Hand Lettering, Painting and Decorating
CIP Program/s: 100103 Photographic Technologists and Technicians; 500402 Graphic Design, Commercial Art and Illustration

Related DOT Job/s: 970.281-010 AIRBRUSH ARTIST; 970.281-018 PHOTOGRAPH RETOUCHER; 970.381-010 COLORIST, PHOTOGRAPHY; 970.381-034 SPOTTER, PHOTOGRAPHIC

89914B PHOTOGRAPHIC REPRODUCTION TECHNICIANS. OOH Title/s: Photographic Process Workers
Duplicate materials to produce prints on sensitized paper, cloth, or film, using photographic equipment. Starts exposure to duplicate original, photograph, or negative. Estimates exposure time, according to size of lens aperture, grade of sensitized paper, and intensity of light. Places filter over lens to make color separation when copying color work. Sets automatic timer, lens opening, and carriage of printer to specified focus and exposure time. Reprints original to enlarge, or in sections to be pieced together. Examines negative for contrast to determine grade of sensitized paper required for print. Selects lens assembly according to size and type of negative or photograph to be printed. Measures material to be copied and computes percentage of enlargement or reproduction necessary, using rule, chart, or percentage scale. Mounts original photograph, negative, or other printed material in holder or vacuum frame beneath light. Mounts camera on tripod or stand, and loads prescribed type and size film in camera. Reads work order to determine required processes, techniques. materials, and equipment. Places sensitized paper in frame of projection printer, photostat, or other reproduction machine. Rinses developed print in water and places in heated drying cabinet. Retouches defects in print, using chemicals, inks, brushes, and pens. Rolls exposed section of sensitized paper into developer tank inside machine. Develops exposed paper or material. Examines developed print for defects, such as broken lines, spots, and blurs. Mixes developing and processing solutions, for use in developing, processing, and rinsing prints.
Yearly Earnings: $16,848
Education: Long-term O-J-T
Knowledge: Chemistry; Fine Arts
Abilities: Information Ordering; Arm-Hand Steadiness; Near Vision; Visual Color Discrimination; Night Vision
Skills: None above average
General Work Activities: None above average
Job Characteristics: Extremely Bright or Inadequate Lighting; Hazardous Conditions; Pace Determined by Speed of Equipment
GOE Group/s: 05.10.05 Crafts: Reproduction
CIP Program/s: 100103 Photographic Technologists and Technicians
Related DOT Job/s: 976.361-010 REPRODUCTION TECHNICIAN; 976.381-018 PROJECTION PRINTER; 976.381-022 TEMPLATE REPRODUCTION TECHNICIAN; 976.382-022 PHOTOSTAT OPERATOR

89914C PHOTOGRAPHIC HAND DEVELOPERS. OOH Title/s: Photographic Process Workers
Develop exposed photographic film or sensitized paper in series of chemical and water baths to produce negative or positive prints. Immerses exposed film or photographic paper in developer solution, to bring out latent image. Immerses negative paper, film, or print in stop bath to arrest developer action. Immerses negative paper, film, or print in hyposolution to fix image. Immerses negative paper, film, or print in water to remove chemicals. Dries prints or negatives, using sponge, squeegee, or mechanical air dryer. Mixes developing and fixing solutions, following formula. Produces color photographs, negatives, and slides, using color reproduction processes.
Yearly Earnings: $16,848
Education: Long-term O-J-T
Knowledge: Chemistry; Fine Arts
Abilities: Visual Color Discrimination; Night Vision
Skills: None above average
General Work Activities: None above average
Job Characteristics: Extremely Bright or Inadequate Lighting; Contaminants; Hazardous Conditions; Standing; Using Hands on Objects, Tools, or Controls
GOE Group/s: 05.10.05 Crafts: Reproduction
CIP Program/s: 100103 Photographic Technologists and Technicians
Related DOT Job/s: 976.681-010 DEVELOPER

89914D FILM LABORATORY TECHNICIANS. OOH Title/s: Photographic Process Workers
Evaluate motion picture film to determine characteristics, such as sensitivity to light, density, and exposure time required for printing. Computes amount of light intensity needed to compensate for density of film, using standardized formulas. Exposes film strip to progressively timed lights to compare effects of various exposure times. Examines developed film strip to determine optimal exposure time and light intensity required for printing. Reads gauges on sensitometer to determine film's sensitivity to light. Threads film strip through densitometer and exposes film to light to determine density of film. Threads film strip through sensitometer and exposes film to light. Records test data and routes film to film developer and film printer for further processing.
Yearly Earnings: $16,848
Education: Long-term O-J-T
Knowledge: None above average
Abilities: Visual Color Discrimination; Night Vision
Skills: None above average
General Work Activities: None above average
Job Characteristics: Extremely Bright or Inadequate Lighting
GOE Group/s: 02.04.01 Laboratory Technology: Physical Sciences
CIP Program/s: 100103 Photographic Technologists and Technicians
Related DOT Job/s: 976.381-010 FILM LABORATORY TECHNICIAN I

89917A PRECISION LENS GRINDERS AND POLISHERS. OOH Title/s: Ophthalmic Laboratory Technicians
Set up and operate variety of machines and equipment to grind and polish lens and other optical elements. Sets up and operates machines to polish, bevel, edge, and grind lenses, flats, blanks, and other precision optical elements. Mounts and secures lens blanks or optical lens in holding tool or chuck of cutting, polishing, grinding, or coating machine. Holds lens against rotating wheel to grind or polish lens manually or using machine. Cleans and polishes finished lenses and eyeglasses, using cloth, solvent, and equipment. Positions and adjusts cutting tool to specified curvature, dimensions, and depth of cut. Examines prescription, work order, or broken or used eyeglasses to determine specifications for lenses, contact lens, and other optical elements. Selects lens blank, molds, tools, or polishing or grinding wheel, according to production specifications. Inspects and measures mounted or unmounted lenses to verify alignment and conformance to specifications, using precision measuring instruments. Controls equipment to coat lenses to alter reflective quality of lens. Cuts or blocks lenses, optical glass, and blanks, using cutting machinery or precision hand tools. Inspects lens blank to detect flaws, verify smoothness of surface, and ensure thickness of coating on lens. Inspects, weighs, and measures lens blanks or lens to verify compliance to specifications, using precision instruments. Lays out lenses and traces lens outline on glass, using template or assembles molds to cast contact lenses. Marks lenses and writes specifications to guide fabricators. Removes lenses from molds and separates lenses in containers for further processing or storage. Adjusts lenses and frames to correct alignment and repairs broken parts, using precision hand tools and soldering iron. Immerses eyeglass frames in solutions to harden, soften, or dye frames. Assembles eyeglass frame, and attaches shields, nose pads, and temple pieces, using pliers, screwdriver, and drill. Mounts, secures, and aligns lenses

in frames or optical assemblies, using precision hand tools. Adjusts lenses and frames to correct alignment and repairs broken parts, using precision hand tools and soldering iron.
Yearly Earnings: $19,396
Education: Long-term O-J-T
Knowledge: Production and Processing; Mechanical; Physics
Abilities: Arm-Hand Steadiness; Manual Dexterity; Finger Dexterity; Control Precision; Rate Control; Near Vision
Skills: Equipment Selection; Operation and Control
General Work Activities: None above average
Job Characteristics: Using Hands on Objects, Tools, or Controls; Degree of Automation; Importance of Being Exact or Accurate
GOE Group/s: 05.05.11 Craft Technology: Scientific, Medical, & Technical Equip. Fabric. & Related; 06.01.04 Production Technology: Precision Hand Work; 06.02.08 Production Work: Machine Work, Stone, Glass, and Clay; 06.02.21 Production Work: Coating and Plating; 06.02.23 Production Work: Manual Work, Assembly Small Parts
CIP Program/s: 511006 Optometric/Ophthalmic Laboratory Technician; 511801 Opticianry/Dispensing Optician; 511802 Optical Technician/Assistant
Related DOT Job/s: 713.381-010 LENS-MOLD SETTER; 713.681-010 LENS MOUNTER II; 716.280-010 OPTICIAN APPRENTICE; 716.280-014 OPTICIAN; 716.381-014 LAY-OUT TECHNICIAN; 716.382-010 LATHE OPERATOR, CONTACT LENS; 716.382-014 OPTICAL-ELEMENT COATER; 716.382-018 PRECISION-LENS GRINDER; 716.382-022 PRECISION-LENS-GRINDER APPRENTICE; 716.462-010 PRECISION-LENS CENTERER AND EDGER; 716.681-010 BLOCKER AND CUTTER, CONTACT LENS; 716.681-014 GLASS CUTTER, HAND; 716.681-018 LENS POLISHER, HAND; 716.682-010 EYEGLASS-LENS CUTTER; 716.682-014 PRECISION-LENS GENERATOR; 716.682-018 PRECISION-LENS POLISHER

89917D OPTICAL INSTRUMENT ASSEMBLERS. OOH Title/s: Ophthalmic Laboratory Technicians

Assemble optical instruments, such as telescopes, level-transits, and gunsights. Assembles structural, mechanical, and optical parts of instrument, using hand tools and cement. Mixes holding compounds, and mounts workpiece or optical element on holding fixture and machine. Measures and marks dimensions and reference points, and lays out stock for machining. Studies work orders, blueprints, and sketches to formulate plans and sequences for fabricating optical elements, instruments, and systems. Paints parts, using brush and spray gun. Computes distance of sighting instruments, using trigonometric formulas. Coats optical elements according to specifications, using coating equipment. Grinds and polishes optics, using hand tools and polishing cloths. Measures and tests optics, using precision measuring and testing instruments. Tests and sights instruments to verify compliance to specifications, using precision testing instruments. Cleans elements and parts, using tissue, cleaning solution, and air compressor. Sets up and operates machines to fabricate fixtures, optics, and tools. Records production, inspection, and test data in logs.
Yearly Earnings: $19,396
Education: Long-term O-J-T
Knowledge: Mechanical; Mathematics; Physics
Abilities: Number Facility; Arm-Hand Steadiness; Manual Dexterity; Finger Dexterity; Rate Control; Gross Body Equilibrium; Near Vision
Skills: Mathematics; Equipment Selection; Testing; Operation Monitoring
General Work Activities: Inspecting Equipment, Structures, or Material; Controlling Machines and Processes
Job Characteristics: Using Hands on Objects, Tools, or Controls; Degree of Automation; Pace Determined by Speed of Equipment
GOE Group/s: 05.05.11 Craft Technology: Scientific, Medical, & Technical Equip. Fabric. & Related; 06.01.04 Production Technology: Precision Hand Work
CIP Program/s: 150304 Laser and Optical Technologists and Technicians; 511801 Opticianry/Dispensing Optician; 511802 Optical Technician/Assistant
Related DOT Job/s: 711.381-010 OPTICAL-INSTRUMENT ASSEMBLER; 716.280-018 OPTICIAN

89921 PRECISION DENTAL LABORATORY TECHNICIANS. OOH Title/s: Dental Laboratory Technicians

Construct and repair full or partial dentures or dental appliances or apparatus, following prescriptions or specifications of dentists or orthodontists. May also provide analytical and diagnostic services. Include dental ceramists, crown and bridge technicians, and orthodontic technicians. Exclude assistants, bite-block makers, opaquers, and denture and coiler packers. Fabricates dental appliances or apparatus, such as dentures, retainers, or metal bands. Rebuilds or replaces linings, wire sections, and missing teeth to repair dentures. Casts plastic, plaster, and metal framework and removes mold from frame. Reads prescription or specifications and examines models and impressions to determine design of dental products to be constructed. Melts metals or mixes plaster, porcelain, or acrylic paste, and pours material into molds or over framework to form dental apparatus or prosthesis. Shapes and solders wire and metal frames or bands for dental products, using soldering iron and hand tools. Applies investments or mixtures, such as porcelain paste or wax, over prosthesis framework or setup, using brushes and spatula. Removes excess mixture and investment and polishes surface of prosthesis or framework, using polishing machine. Fills chipped or low spots in surface with acrylic resin. Assembles, carves, grinds, and polishes metal and plastic appliances, using pliers, spatula, grinders, and polishes. Tests appliance for conformance to specifications and accuracy of occlusion, using articulator and micrometer.
Yearly Earnings: $18,044
Education: Long-term O-J-T
Knowledge: Medicine and Dentistry
Abilities: Visualization; Arm-Hand Steadiness; Manual Dexterity; Finger Dexterity; Control Precision; Wrist-Finger Speed; Near Vision; Visual Color Discrimination
Skills: Science; Operations Analysis; Technology Design; Testing; Product Inspection
General Work Activities: None above average
Job Characteristics: Sitting; Using Hands on Objects, Tools, or Controls; Importance of Being Sure All is Done; Importance of Repeating Same Tasks
GOE Group/s: 05.05.11 Craft Technology: Scientific, Medical, & Technical Equip. Fabric. & Related; 06.02.32 Production Work: Manual Work, Assorted Materials
CIP Program/s: 510603 Dental Laboratory Technician
Related DOT Job/s: 712.381-014 CONTOUR WIRE SPECIALIST, DENTURE; 712.381-018 DENTAL-LABORATORY TECHNICIAN; 712.381-022 DENTAL-LABORATORY-TECHNICIAN APPRENTICE; 712.381-026 ORTHODONTIC BAND MAKER; 712.381-030 ORTHODONTIC TECHNICIAN; 712.381-042 DENTAL CERAMIST; 712.381-046 DENTURE WAXER; 712.381-050 FINISHER, DENTURE; 712.664-010 DENTAL CERAMIST ASSISTANT

89923 MEDICAL APPLIANCE MAKERS. OOH Title/s: Precision Assemblers

Construct, fit, maintain, and repair medical supportive devices, such as braces, artificial limbs, and arch supports, and other surgical and medical appliances, following the prescriptions

and specifications of orthotists, prosthetists, or podiatrists. May instruct patients in the use of the device. Carves, cuts, grinds, and welds wood, plastic, or metal material to fabricate medical supportive devices, using hand and power tools. Repairs and maintains medical supportive devices, such as artificial limbs, braces, and surgical supports, according to specifications. Lays out and marks dimensions of parts, using templates and precision measuring instruments. Drills and taps holes for rivets, and glues, welds, bolts, and rivets parts together to form prosthetic or orthotic device. Bends, forms, and shapes fabric or material to conform to measurements for prescribed contours to fabricate structural components. Instructs patient in use of prosthetic or orthotic device. Fits appliance onto patient and adjusts appliance as necessary. Fabricates wax or plastic impression of amputated area and prepares mold from impression to form artificial cosmetic ear, nose, or hand. Covers or pads metal or plastic structures and devices, using coverings such as rubber, leather, felt, plastic, or fiberglass. Tests medical supportive device for body fit, alignment, movement, and biomechanical stability, using meters and alignment fixtures. Constructs or receives plaster cast of patient's torso or limbs to use as pattern for cutting and fabricating supportive devices. Reads specifications to determine type of product or device to be fabricated and selects required materials and tools. Mixes pigments according to formula to match skin coloring of patient and applies mixture to prosthetic or orthotic device. Polishes artificial limbs, braces, and supports, using grinding and buffing wheels.
Yearly Earnings: $28,392
Education: Work experience in a related occupation
Knowledge: Engineering and Technology; Design; Mechanical; Medicine and Dentistry; Therapy and Counseling
Abilities: Visualization; Manual Dexterity; Finger Dexterity; Visual Color Discrimination
Skills: Instructing; Operations Analysis; Technology Design; Equipment Selection; Product Inspection; Equipment Maintenance; Repairing
General Work Activities: Handling and Moving Objects; Controlling Machines and Processes; Drafting and Specifying Technical Devices, etc.; Repairing and Maintaining Mechanical Equipment; Assisting and Caring for Others; Teaching Others
Job Characteristics: Radiation; Making Repetitive Motions
GOE Group/s: 05.05.11 Craft Technology: Scientific, Medical, & Technical Equip. Fabric. & Related; 05.10.01 Crafts: Structural
CIP Program/s: 512307 Orthotics/Prosthetics
Related DOT Job/s: 712.381-010 ARCH-SUPPORT TECHNICIAN; 712.381-034 ORTHOTICS TECHNICIAN; 712.381-038 PROSTHETICS TECHNICIAN

89926A GEM AND DIAMOND WORKERS. OOH Title/s: Indirectly related to Jewelers

Split, saw, cut, shape, polish, or drill gems and diamonds used in jewelry or industrial tools. Holds stone, gem, die, or stylus, attached to holder or lapidary stick, against rotating plates or wheels to shape, grind, and polish. Bores, laps, and polishes holes in industrial diamonds used for dies, using drill, lathe, lapping machine, and hand tools. Splits gem along premarked lines to remove imperfections, using blade and jeweler's hammer. Grinds, drills, and finishes jewel bearings for use in precision instruments, such as compasses and chronometers. Laps girdle on rough diamonds, using diamond girdling lathe. Locates and marks drilling position on surface of diamond dies, using diamond chip and power hand drill. Measures size of stone's bore holes and cuts to ensure adherence to specifications, using precision measuring instruments. Positions gem or diamond against edge of revolving saw, lathe saw, or lapidary slitter to cut, block, or slit stone. Selects shaping wheel, mixes, and applies abrasive, bort, or polishing compound. Examines diamond or gem to determine shape, cut, and width of stone. Secures gem or diamond in holder, chuck, dop, lapidary stick, or block for cutting, polishing, grinding, drilling, or shaping. Examines gem during processing to ensure accuracy of angle and position of cut or bore, using magnifying glass, loupe, or shadowgraph. Replaces, trues, and sharpens blades, drills, and plates. Lubricates, dismantles, and cleans lapping, boring, cutting, polishing, and shaping equipment and machinery.
Yearly Earnings: $28,392
Education: Long-term O-J-T
Knowledge: None above average
Abilities: Selective Attention; Arm-Hand Steadiness; Manual Dexterity; Finger Dexterity; Control Precision; Wrist-Finger Speed; Near Vision; Visual Color Discrimination; Depth Perception
Skills: None above average
General Work Activities: None above average
Job Characteristics: Hazardous Equipment; Hazardous Situations; Sitting; Using Hands on Objects, Tools, or Controls; Importance of Being Exact or Accurate; Importance of Repeating Same Tasks
GOE Group/s: 05.05.14 Craft Technology: Gem Cutting and Finishing; 06.01.04 Production Technology: Precision Hand Work; 06.02.08 Production Work: Machine Work, Stone, Glass, and Clay
CIP Program/s: 470408 Watch, Clock and Jewelry Repairer; 500701 Art, General; 500713 Metal and Jewelry Arts
Related DOT Job/s: 770.261-010 BRILLIANDEER-LOPPER; 770.261-014 GIRDLER; 770.281-014 GEM CUTTER; 770.381-014 DIAMOND CLEAVER; 770.381-018 DIAMOND DRILLER; 770.381-022 DIAMOND-DIE POLISHER; 770.381-026 JEWEL BLOCKER AND SAWYER; 770.381-030 JEWEL-BEARING MAKER; 770.381-034 OLIVING-MACHINE OPERATOR; 770.381-038 SAPPHIRE-STYLUS GRINDER; 770.381-042 SPOTTER; 770.382-010 LATHE OPERATOR; 770.382-014 PHONOGRAPH-NEEDLE-TIP MAKER

89999A COLOR MATCHERS AND DYE FORMULATORS. OOH Title/s: Indirectly related to Painting and Coating Machine Operators; Apparel Workers

Formulate, mix, and match coloring solutions used in paints and dyeing materials. Determines composition and compares color with color sample visually, with colorimeter or spectrophometer charts. Develops formula to prepare coloring solutions. Weighs and mixes pigments to prepare dye according to specifications and makes sample. Calculates weights and proportions of pigments and other materials required to make production batch of dye. Examines color of dispersed pigment, using color-checking lamps. Observes procedures in mixing dye with other formulas and reviews laboratory reports to investigate causes of substandard color. Prepares directions for batch production of the desired color and records specifications. Removes foreign matter from batch, using centrifuge. Determines specific gravity, using hydrometer. Consults with and advises production staff regarding technical problems, formulas, and methods to improve production methods for mixing colors. Prepares sample for laboratory testing.
Yearly Earnings: $19,136
Education: Moderate-term O-J-T
Knowledge: Production and Processing; Chemistry; Fine Arts
Abilities: Category Flexibility; Visual Color Discrimination
Skills: Mathematics; Operations Analysis
General Work Activities: None above average
Job Characteristics: Deal with Physical, Aggressive People; Contaminants; Hazardous Conditions
GOE Group/s: 02.04.01 Laboratory Technology: Physical Sciences; 06.02.11 Production Work: Equipment Operation, Chemical Processing; 06.02.32 Production Work: Manual Work, Assorted Materials
CIP Program/s: 150603 Industrial/Manufacturing Technologists and Technicians; 150607 Plastics Technologists and Technicians
Related DOT Job/s: 530.261-010 COLOR DEVELOPER; 550.381-010 COLOR MATCHER; 550.381-014 TINTER

89999B WIG MAKERS. OOH Title/s: Precision Assemblers
Lay out, sew, and fasten materials and hair strands to make wigs. Folds, glues, and pins hair strands to secure position on foundation. Hooks strands of hair into foundation holes, using ventilating needle. Arranges, weaves and sews hair in specified position to form hairpieces, such as braids, switches, and chignons. Selects strands of hair and combs, cuts, and blends them, according to specified length and color. Draws or pins wig pattern on model head. Places sections of foundation material over pattern and molds it to model or sews sections together to form wig foundation. Designs wig style according to specifications, using tape, pins, comb, and rods. Dries hair under electric drier and sprays wig with lacquer to set a hair style. Repairs damaged or worn wigs and hairpieces.
Yearly Earnings: $19,916
Education: Long-term O-J-T
Knowledge: None above average
Abilities: Arm-Hand Steadiness; Finger Dexterity; Wrist-Finger Speed; Visual Color Discrimination
Skills: None above average
General Work Activities: None above average
Job Characteristics: Objective or Subjective Information; Sitting; Using Hands on Objects, Tools, or Controls; Making Repetitive Motions; Importance of Repeating Same Tasks
GOE Group/s: 05.05.15 Craft Technology: Custom Sewing, Tailoring, and Upholstering; 06.01.04 Production Technology: Precision Hand Work
CIP Program/s: 120402 Barber/Hairstylist
Related DOT Job/s: 739.381-042 MANNEQUIN WIG MAKER; 739.381-058 WIG MAKER

89999C ALL OTHER PRECISION WORKERS. OOH Title/s: Precision Assemblers
All other precision workers not classified separately above.
Yearly Earnings: $19,916
Education: Long-term O-J-T
GOE Group/s: 06.02.24 Production Work: Manual Work, Metal and Plastics
CIP Program/s: 470402 Gunsmith
Related DOT Job/s: 713.261-010 ARTIFICIAL-GLASS-EYE MAKER; 713.261-014 ARTIFICIAL-PLASTIC-EYE MAKER; 732.281-010 CUSTOM SKI MAKER; 732.381-010 BOW MAKER, CUSTOM; 736.381-014 FITTER, VENTILATED RIB; 736.481-010 SIGHT MOUNTER; 770.281-010 DIAMOND SELECTOR; 779.381-010 GLAZIER, STAINED GLASS

Section 9
Machine Setters, Operators, and Tenders, Production Workers, Hand Workers, Plant and System Workers, Transportation Workers, and Helpers

Machine Cutting, Turning, Drilling, Grinding, and Polishing Setters, Operators, and Tenders

91102 SAWING MACHINE TOOL SETTERS AND SET-UP OPERATORS, METAL AND PLASTIC. OOH Title/s: Metalworking and Plastics-Working Machine Operators
Set up or set up and operate metal or plastic sawing machines to cut straight, curved, irregular, or internal patterns in metal or plastic stock or to trim edges of metal or plastic objects. Involves the use of such machines as band saws, circular saws, friction saws, hacksawing machines, and jigsaws. Turns controls to set cutting speed, feed rate, and table angle for specified operation. Starts machine and feeds workpiece against blade, guiding along layout lines, to cut workpiece to specified dimensions. Sets blade tension, height, and angle to perform prescribed cut, using wrench. Turns valves to start flow of coolant against cutting area and to start airflow which blows cuttings away from kerf. Selects blade according to specifications and installs on machine, using hand tools. Positions guides, stops, holding blocks, or other fixtures to secure and direct workpiece, using hand tools and measuring devices. Scribes reference lines on workpiece as guide for sawing operations, according to blueprints, templates, sample parts, or specifications. Reads work order for specifications, such as materials to be used, location of cutting lines, and dimensions and tolerances. Replaces defective blades or wheels, using hand tools. Measures completed workpiece to verify conformance to specifications, using micrometers, gauges, calipers, templates, or rulers. Places workpiece on cutting table, manually or using hoist, and clamps workpiece into position. Sharpens dulled blades, using bench grinder, abrasive wheel, or lathe. Removes housings, feed tubes, tool holders, and other accessories to replace worn or broken parts, such as springs and bushings. Examines completed workpieces for defects, such as chipped edges and marred surfaces, and sorts defective pieces according to defect. Marks identifying data on workpieces.
Yearly Earnings: $21,476
Education: Moderate-term O-J-T
Knowledge: Production and Processing
Abilities: Arm-Hand Steadiness; Manual Dexterity; Finger Dexterity; Control Precision; Rate Control; Explosive Strength; Stamina
Skills: Operation Monitoring; Equipment Maintenance
General Work Activities: Controlling Machines and Processes; Repairing and Maintaining Mechanical Equipment
Job Characteristics: Sounds, Noise Levels are Distracting, etc.; Contaminants; Whole Body Vibration; Hazardous Equipment; Hazardous Situations; Standing; Using Hands on Objects, Tools, or Controls; Making Repetitive Motions; Common Protective or Safety Attire; Degree of Automation; Pace Determined by Speed of Equipment
GOE Group/s: 06.01.02 Production Technology: Machine Set-up; 06.02.02 Production Work: Machine Work, Metal and Plastics
CIP Program/s: 150607 Plastics Technologists and Technicians; 480501 Machinist/Machine Technologist
Related DOT Job/s: 607.382-010 CONTOUR-BAND-SAW OPERATOR, VERTICAL; 607.382-014 SAW OPERATOR; 607.682-010 CUT-OFF-SAW OPERATOR, METAL; 609.280-010 TRIM-MACHINE ADJUSTER; 690.482-010 SAWYER; 700.682-018 PROFILE-SAW OPERATOR

91105 LATHE AND TURNING MACHINE TOOL SETTERS AND SET-UP OPERATORS, METAL AND PLASTIC. OOH Title/s: Metalworking and Plastics-Working Machine Operators
Set up or set up and operate plastic or metal lathe and turning machines to turn, bore, thread, form, or face plastic or metal materials, such as wire, rod, or bar stock according to specifications. Moves controls to set cutting speeds, depths, and feed rates, and to position tool in relation to workplace. Cranks machine through cycle, stopping to adjust tool positions and machine controls, to ensure specified timing, clearance, and tolerances. Starts machine and turns valve handle to direct flow of coolant on work area, or coats disk with spinning compound. Installs holding fixtures, cams, gears, and stops to control stock and tool movement, using hand tools, power tools, and measuring instruments. Moves toolholder manually or by turning handwheel, or engages automatic feeding mechanism, to feed tools to and along workpiece. Selects cutting tools and tooling instructions, according to knowledge of metal properties and shop mathematics, or written specifications. Positions, secures, and aligns cutting tools in toolholders on machine, using hand tools, and verifies their position with measuring instruments. Observes operation and stops machine to inspect finished workpiece and verify conformance with specifications of first run, using measuring instruments. Mounts attachments, such as relieving or tracing attachments, to perform operations, such as duplicating contours of template or trimming workpiece. Studies blueprint, layout, or chart to visualize work and determine materials needed, sequence of operations, dimensions, and tooling instructions. Computes unspecified dimensions and machine settings, using knowledge of metal properties and shop mathematics. Lifts metal stock or workpiece manually or using hoist, and positions and secures it in machine, using fasteners and hand tools. Replaces worn tools and sharpens dull cutting tools and dies.
Yearly Earnings: $21,892
Education: Moderate-term O-J-T
Knowledge: Production and Processing; Engineering and Technology; Mechanical
Abilities: Visualization; Control Precision; Stamina
Skills: Technology Design; Installation; Equipment Maintenance
General Work Activities: Controlling Machines and Processes; Repairing and Maintaining Mechanical Equipment
Job Characteristics: Sounds, Noise Levels are Distracting, etc.; Hazardous Equipment; Using Hands on Objects, Tools, or Controls; Common Protective or Safety Attire; Degree of Automation; Importance of Being Exact or Accurate; Importance of Being Sure All is Done; Pace Determined by Speed of Equipment
GOE Group/s: 06.01.02 Production Technology: Machine Set-up; 06.01.03 Production Technology: Machine Set-up and Operation; 06.02.02 Production Work: Machine Work, Metal and Plastics
CIP Program/s: 470408 Watch, Clock and Jewelry Repairer; 480501 Machinist/Machine Technologist
Related DOT Job/s: 604.260-010 SCREW-MACHINE SET-UP OPERATOR, SWISS-TYPE; 604.280-010 ENGINE-LATHE SET-UP OPERATOR, TOOL; 604.280-014 SCREW-MACHINE SET-UP OPERATOR, MULTIPLE SPINDLE; 604.280-018 SCREW-MACHINE SET-UP OPERATOR, SINGLE SPINDLE; 604.280-022 TURRET-LATHE SET-UP OPERATOR, TOOL; 604.360-010 SETTER, AUTOMATIC-SPINNING LATHE; 604.380-010 CHUCKING-MACHINE SET-UP OPERATOR; 604.380-014 CHUCKING-MACHINE SET-UP OPERATOR, MULTIPLE SPINDLE, VERTICAL; 604.380-018 ENGINE-LATHE SET-UP OPERATOR; 604.380-022 SCREW-MACHINE SET-UP OPERATOR; 604.380-026 TURRET-LATHE SET-UP OPERATOR; 604.682-014 THREADING-MACHINE OPERATOR; 609.380-014 THREADING-MACHINE SETTER; 619.362-018 SPINNER, HAND; 619.362-022 SPINNER, HYDRAULIC

91108 DRILLING AND BORING MACHINE TOOL SETTERS AND SET-UP OPERATORS, METAL AND PLASTIC. OOH Title/s: Metalworking and Plastics-Working Machine Operators

Set up or set up and operate drilling machines to drill, bore, ream, mill, and countersink metal or plastic workpieces according to specifications. Operates single- or multiple-spindle drill press to bore holes to perform machining operations on metal, nonmetallic, or plastic workpieces. Installs tool in spindle. Studies machining instructions to determine dimensional and finish specifications, sequence of operation, set-up, and tooling requirements. Lays out reference lines and machining locations on work, applying knowledge of shop math and layout techniques, using layout tools. Selects cutting tool according to instructions and knowledge of metal properties. Positions and secures workpiece on table with bolts, jigs, clamps, shims, or other holding devices, using machining hand tools. Operates tracing attachment to duplicate contours from templates or models. Verifies conformance of machined work to specifications, using measuring instruments such as calipers, micrometers, and fixed and telescoping gauges. Lifts workpiece either manually or with hoist onto machine table, or directs crane operator to lift and position workpiece.

Yearly Earnings: $21,892
Education: Moderate-term O-J-T
Knowledge: Building and Construction; Mechanical; Foreign Language
Abilities: Visualization; Selective Attention; Arm-Hand Steadiness; Multilimb Coordination; Static Strength; Dynamic Strength; Stamina; Gross Body Equilibrium
Skills: Installation; Operation Monitoring; Operation and Control; Product Inspection
General Work Activities: None above average
Job Characteristics: Sounds, Noise Levels are Distracting, etc.; Hazardous Equipment; Hazardous Situations; Standing; Making Repetitive Motions; Common Protective or Safety Attire; Degree of Automation; Importance of Repeating Same Tasks; Pace Determined by Speed of Equipment
GOE Group/s: 06.01.03 Production Technology: Machine Set-up and Operation; 06.02.02 Production Work: Machine Work, Metal and Plastics
CIP Program/s: 480501 Machinist/Machine Technologist
Related DOT Job/s: 606.280-010 BORING-MACHINE SET-UP OPERATOR, JIG; 606.280-014 BORING-MILL SET-UP OPERATOR, HORIZONTAL; 606.380-010 DRILL-PRESS SET-UP OPERATOR, MULTIPLE SPINDLE; 606.380-014 DRILL-PRESS SET-UP OPERATOR, RADIAL; 606.380-018 DRILL-PRESS SET-UP OPERATOR, RADIAL, TOOL; 606.382-022 BORING-MACHINE OPERATOR; 606.682-018 DRILL-PRESS SET-UP OPERATOR, SINGLE SPINDLE; 606.682-022 TAPPER OPERATOR; 676.382-010 DRILL-PRESS OPERATOR, PRINTED CIRCUIT BOARDS; 731.381-010 DICE MAKER

91111 MILLING AND PLANING MACHINE SETTERS AND SET-UP OPERATORS, METAL AND PLASTIC. OOH Title/s: Metalworking and Plastics-Working Machine Operators

Set up or set up and operate milling or planing machines to mill, plane, shape, groove, or profile metal or plastic workpieces according to specifications. Selects and installs cutting tool, stylus, and other accessories according to specifications, using hand tools or power tools. Moves controls to set cutting specifications, position cutting tool and workpiece in relation to each other, and start machine. Moves cutter or material manually or by turning handwheel, or engages automatic feeding mechanism to mill workpiece to specifications. Observes machine operation and adjusts controls to ensure conformance with specified tolerances. Selects cutting speed, feed rate, and depth of cut, applying knowledge of metal properties and shop mathematics. Verifies alignment of workpiece on machine, using measuring instruments such as rules, gauges, or calipers. Turns valve to begin and regulate the flow of coolant on work area. Studies blueprint, layout, sketch, or other specifications to determine materials needed, sequence of operations, dimensions, and tooling instructions. Computes dimensions, tolerances, and angles, of workpiece or machine according to specifications and knowledge of metal properties and shop mathematics. Positions and secures workpiece on machine, using holding devices, measuring instruments, hand tools, and hoists. Verifies conformance of finished workpiece to specifications, using measuring instruments such as microscopes, gauges, calipers, and micrometers. Removes workpiece and template or model from machine. Mounts attachments and other tools, such as pantograph, engraver, or router, to perform other operations, such as drilling or boring. Replaces worn tools, using hand tools. Sharpens dull tools, using bench grinder. Makes templates or cutting tools. Records production output.

Yearly Earnings: $18,772
Education: Moderate-term O-J-T
Knowledge: Production and Processing
Abilities: None above average
Skills: Technology Design; Operation and Control; Equipment Maintenance
General Work Activities: Controlling Machines and Processes
Job Characteristics: Sounds, Noise Levels are Distracting, etc.; Hazardous Equipment; Standing; Making Repetitive Motions; Common Protective or Safety Attire; Degree of Automation; Pace Determined by Speed of Equipment
GOE Group/s: 06.01.03 Production Technology: Machine Set-up and Operation; 06.02.02 Production Work: Machine Work, Metal and Plastics
CIP Program/s: 470408 Watch, Clock and Jewelry Repairer; 480501 Machinist/Machine Technologist
Related DOT Job/s: 605.280-010 MILLING-MACHINE SET-UP OPERATOR I; 605.280-014 PROFILING-MACHINE SET-UP OPERATOR I; 605.280-018 PROFILING-MACHINE SET-UP OPERATOR, TOOL; 605.282-010 MILLING-MACHINE SET-UP OPERATOR II; 605.282-014 PLANER SET-UP OPERATOR, TOOL; 605.282-018 PLANER-TYPE-MILLING-MACHINE SET-UP OPERATOR; 605.382-010 BROACHING-MACHINE SET-UP OPERATOR; 605.382-014 ENGRAVER, TIRE MOLD; 605.382-018 KEYSEATING-MACHINE SET-UP OPERATOR; 605.382-022 PANTOGRAPH-MACHINE SET-UP OPERATOR; 605.382-026 PROFILING-MACHINE SET-UP OPERATOR II; 605.382-030 ROTARY-HEAD-MILLING-MACHINE SET-UP OPERATOR; 605.382-034 ROUTER OPERATOR; 605.382-038 SHAPER SET-UP OPERATOR, TOOL; 605.382-042 THREAD-MILLING-MACHINE SET-UP OPERATOR; 605.482-010 STEEL-WOOL-MACHINE OPERATOR; 605.682-010 BARREL-RIB MATTING-MACHINE OPERATOR; 605.682-022 SCALPER OPERATOR; 605.682-026 TOOTH CUTTER, ESCAPE WHEEL

91114A GRINDING, HONING, LAPPING, AND DEBURRING MACHINE SET-UP OPERATORS. OOH Title/s: Metalworking and Plastics-Working Machine Operators

Set up and operate grinding, honing, lapping, or deburring machines to remove excess materials or burrs from internal and external surfaces. Moves machine controls to index workpiece and adjust machine for preselected operational settings. Activates machine start-up switches to grind, lap, hone, debar, shear, or cut workpiece according to specifications. Threads and hand-feeds materials through machine cutters or abraders. Computes machine indexing and settings for specified dimension and base reference points. Selects machine tooling to be used in machine operation, utilizing knowledge of machine and production requirements. Observes and adjusts machine

operation. Studies blueprints, work orders, or machining instructions to determine product dimensions, tooling, and to plan operational sequence. Mounts and positions tools in machine chuck, spindle, or other tool-holding device to specifications, using hand tools. Measures workpieces and lays out work, using precision measuring devices. Grinds, sharpens, or hones tools, dies, and products to prescribed dimensions, using power tools, hand tools, and precision measuring instruments. Inspects or measures workpiece using measuring instruments, such as gauges or micrometers for conformance to specifications. Lifts and positions workpiece manually or with hoist, and secures in hopper, on machine table, faceplate, or chuck, using clamps. Brushes or sprays lubricating compound on workpiece or turns valve handle and directs flow of coolant against tool and workpiece. Repairs or replaces machine parts, using hand tools, or notifies engineering personnel when corrective action is required. Maintains stock of machine parts and machining tools.
Yearly Earnings: $20,332
Education: Moderate-term O-J-T
Knowledge: Production and Processing
Abilities: Visualization; Selective Attention; Control Precision; Static Strength
Skills: Installation; Operation and Control; Equipment Maintenance
General Work Activities: Controlling Machines and Processes; Repairing and Maintaining Mechanical Equipment
Job Characteristics: Sounds, Noise Levels are Distracting, etc.; Hazardous Equipment; Using Hands on Objects, Tools, or Controls; Making Repetitive Motions; Degree of Automation; Importance of Repeating Same Tasks; Pace Determined by Speed of Equipment
GOE Group/s: 05.05.07 Craft Technology: Machining; 06.01.02 Production Technology: Machine Set-up; 06.01.03 Production Technology: Machine Set-up and Operation; 06.02.02 Production Work: Machine Work, Metal and Plastics
CIP Program/s: 470408 Watch, Clock and Jewelry Repairer; 480501 Machinist/Machine Technologist; 480507 Tool and Die Maker/Technologist
Related DOT Job/s: 601.482-010 PROFILE-GRINDER TECHNICIAN; 602.360-010 GRINDER SET-UP OPERATOR, GEAR, TOOL; 602.382-034 GRINDER, GEAR; 602.482-010 GEAR-LAPPING-MACHINE OPERATOR; 603.260-010 GRINDER SET-UP OPERATOR, THREAD TOOL; 603.280-026 GRINDER SET-UP OPERATOR, JIG; 603.280-034 JOB SETTER, HONING; 603.380-010 GRINDER MACHINE SETTER; 603.382-014 GRINDER SET-UP OPERATOR, CENTERLESS; 603.382-018 HONING-MACHINE SET-UP OPERATOR; 603.382-022 HONING-MACHINE SET-UP OPERATOR, TOOL; 603.382-026 LAPPING-MACHINE SET-UP OPERATOR; 603.382-034 GRINDER SET-UP OPERATOR; 603.382-038 KNIFE GRINDER; 603.482-010 DEBURRER, STRIP; 609.682-026 NICKING-MACHINE OPERATOR; 628.382-014 SHEAR-GRINDER OPERATOR; 629.682-010 ROLL GRINDER; 690.280-010 DEBURRING-AND-TOOLING-MACHINE OPERATOR

91114B BUFFING AND POLISHING SET-UP OPERATORS. OOH Title/s: Metalworking and Plastics-Working Machine Operators

Set up and operate buffing or polishing machine. Sets and adjusts machine controls according to product specifications, utilizing knowledge of machine operation. Starts and observes machine operation for conformance to specifications. Selects buffing or polishing tools and positions and mounts tools to machine tool, chuck, or jig, using hand tools. Reads work order to determine parts to be buffed or polished. Selects and attaches workpiece-holding fixture to drive mechanism, and positions or clamps workpiece to fixture. Holds stick of buffing compound or turns valve and depresses pedal to administer coolant to workpiece surface. Removes workpiece and examines finish or luster to ensure surface meets specifications. Repairs or replaces machine parts to maintain machine in operational condition.
Yearly Earnings: $20,332
Education: Moderate-term O-J-T
Knowledge: None above average
Abilities: Control Precision; Rate Control; Speed of Limb Movement; Stamina; Dynamic Flexibility; Gross Body Equilibrium
Skills: Repairing
General Work Activities: None above average
Job Characteristics: Sounds, Noise Levels are Distracting, etc.; Hazardous Equipment; Standing; Using Hands on Objects, Tools, or Controls; Making Repetitive Motions; Degree of Automation; Pace Determined by Speed of Equipment
GOE Group/s: 06.01.02 Production Technology: Machine Set-up; 06.02.02 Production Work: Machine Work, Metal and Plastics
CIP Program/s: 480501 Machinist/Machine Technologist
Related DOT Job/s: 603.360-010 BUFFING-LINE SET-UP WORKER; 603.382-010 BUFFING-MACHINE OPERATOR; 603.682-010 BUFFING-MACHINE OPERATOR, SILVERWARE; 603.682-022 MIRROR-FINISHING-MACHINE OPERATOR; 603.682-026 POLISHING-MACHINE OPERATOR

91117 MACHINE TOOL CUTTING OPERATORS AND TENDERS, METAL AND PLASTIC. OOH Title/s: Metalworking and Plastics-Working Machine Operators

Operate or tend one type of cutting machine tool that has previously been set up. Exclude workers who operate or tend more than one type of cutting machine. Types of cutting machine tools include sawing machines, grinding machines, lathe and turning machines, buffing and polishing machines, drilling and boring machines, lapping and honing machines, and milling and planing machines. Activates automatic machine operation and observes machine to detect malfunction or excessive tool wear. Turns controls to bring workpiece into contact with tool to cut, drill, bore, ream, or lap. Manually guides tool against workpiece or vice versa to cut, shape, chamfer, grind, sharpen, or polish. Adjusts controls and changes tool settings to keep dimensions within specified tolerances. Positions and secures workpiece in machine, such as lathe or drill press, using hand tools. Reads job order or blueprint for such information as dimensions, tolerances, and number of workpieces to be machined. Sets controls, engages automatic feeding mechanism, or places workpieces in machine such as milling, polishing, screwing, or routing machines. Selects and installs or changes tools such as drill or router bits, abrasive or polishing wheels, and reamer fixtures, using hand tools. Removes and inspects workpiece to verify conformance to standards, using such instruments as gauges, calipers, micrometers, and templates. Removes and stacks workpieces for further processing or shipping. Applies abrasive compound, lubricant, or coolant to workpiece or tool to facilitate cutting, polishing, or grinding. Files, burnishes, or polishes workpiece by hand to remove defects, using hand file, burnishing tool, or whetstone. Replaces worn or damaged tools on machine, using hand tools. Cleans machined workpiece using cleaning solution, brush, or air hose.
Yearly Earnings: $21,476
Education: Moderate-term O-J-T
Knowledge: Production and Processing
Abilities: Control Precision; Multilimb Coordination; Wrist-Finger Speed; Depth Perception
Skills: Equipment Maintenance
General Work Activities: Handling and Moving Objects; Controlling Machines and Processes; Repairing and Maintaining Mechanical Equipment

Job Characteristics: Sounds, Noise Levels are Distracting, etc.; Hazardous Equipment; Standing; Using Hands on Objects, Tools, or Controls; Making Repetitive Motions; Common Protective or Safety Attire; Degree of Automation; Importance of Repeating Same Tasks; Pace Determined by Speed of Equipment
GOE Group/s: 05.12.02 Elemental Work: Mechanical: Mining, Quarrying, Drilling; 06.01.04 Production Technology: Precision Hand Work; 06.02.01 Production Work: Supervision; 06.02.02 Production Work: Machine Work, Metal and Plastics; 06.02.09 Production Work: Machine Work, Assorted Materials; 06.02.24 Production Work: Manual Work, Metal and Plastics; 06.04.02 Elemental Work: Industrial: Machine Work, Metal and Plastics; 06.04.09 Elemental Work: Industrial: Machine Work, Assorted Materials; 06.04.24 Elemental Work: Industrial: Manual Work, Metal and Plastics
CIP Program/s: 470408 Watch, Clock and Jewelry Repairer; 480503 Machine Shop Assistant
Related DOT Job/s: 603.382-030 PRINTING-ROLLER POLISHER; 603.482-030 GRINDER I; 603.482-034 HONING-MACHINE OPERATOR, PRODUCTION; 603.664-010 TOOL GRINDER II; 603.665-010 BUFFING-MACHINE TENDER; 603.682-018 LINTER-SAW SHARPENER; 603.682-030 DRILL-BIT SHARPENER; 603.685-010 BAND-REAMER-MACHINE OPERATOR; 603.685-014 BARREL POLISHER, INSIDE; 603.685-022 BEVEL POLISHER; 603.685-026 BIT SHARPENER; 603.685-030 BIT-SHARPENER OPERATOR; 603.685-034 BOTTOM POLISHER; 603.685-038 BRUSH POLISHER; 603.685-042 BURNISHER; 603.685-046 BURRER, MACHINE; 603.685-050 DEBURRER; 603.685-054 FLAT POLISHER; 603.685-058 GRINDER OPERATOR, AUTOMATIC; 603.685-062 GRINDING MACHINE TENDER; 603.685-066 GRINDER, LAP; 603.685-070 LAPPING-MACHINE OPERATOR, PRODUCTION; 603.685-074 SHOT-GRINDER OPERATOR; 603.685-078 SNAILER; 603.685-082 STONER AND POLISHER, BEVEL FACE; 604.382-010 SCREW-MACHINE OPERATOR, MULTIPLE SPINDLE; 604.382-014 SCREW-MACHINE OPERATOR, SINGLE SPINDLE; 604.682-010 SCREW-MACHINE OPERATOR, SWISS-TYPE; 604.685-010 BALANCE RECESSER; 604.685-014 FACING-MACHINE OPERATOR; 604.685-018 KNURLING-MACHINE OPERATOR; 604.685-022 LAP CUTTER-TRUER OPERATOR; 604.685-026 LATHE TENDER; 604.685-030 RIM-TURNING FINISHER; 604.685-034 SCREW-MACHINE TENDER; 604.685-038 THREADING-MACHINE OPERATOR; 604.685-042 TURRET-LATHE OPERATOR, TUMBLE TAILSTOCK; 605.682-014 BROACHING-MACHINE OPERATOR, PRODUCTION; 605.682-030 WHEEL CUTTER; 605.682-034 ROUTER, PRINTED CIRCUIT BOARDS; 605.685-010 BARREL RIFLER; 605.685-014 FILE CUTTER; 605.685-018 HOOKING-MACHINE OPERATOR; 605.685-022 JEWEL STRIPPER; 605.685-026 LEVER MILLER; 605.685-030 MILLING-MACHINE TENDER; 605.685-034 PLANING-MACHINE OPERATOR; 605.685-038 PROFILING-MACHINE OPERATOR; 605.685-042 SCRIBING-MACHINE OPERATOR; 605.685-046 SQUARING-MACHINE OPERATOR; 605.685-050 TOOTH CUTTER; 605.685-054 ROUTER MACHINE OPERATOR; 606.382-010 DRILLER-AND-REAMER, AUTOMATIC; 606.682-014 DRILL-PRESS OPERATOR; 606.685-010 BORING-MACHINE OPERATOR, PRODUCTION; 606.685-014 CHAMFERING-MACHINE OPERATOR I; 606.685-018 CHAMFERING-MACHINE OPERATOR II; 606.685-022 CHOKE REAMER; 606.685-026 DRILL PRESS TENDER; 606.685-030 DRILLING-MACHINE OPERATOR, AUTOMATIC; 606.685-034 REAMING-MACHINE TENDER; 607.682-014 PROFILE TRIMMER; 607.685-010 CUT-OFF SAW TENDER, METAL; 607.685-014 DEBRIDGING-MACHINE OPERATOR; 607.686-010 MAGNESIUM-MILL OPERATOR; 615.685-018 CUP-TRIMMING-MACHINE OPERATOR; 619.382-014 FITTINGS FINISHER; 619.685-094 CUT-OFF-MACHINE OPERATOR; 690.685-142 EDGE GRINDER; 690.685-170 FINISHER, MACHINE; 690.685-190 FOUNTAIN PEN TURNER; 690.685-202 GROOVING-LATHE TENDER; 690.685-262 LAST SAWYER; 690.685-510 TRADE MARKER; 699.682-034 BEVELER, PRINTED CIRCUIT BOARDS; 699.685-046 PINNER, PRINTED CIRCUIT BOARDS; 699.685-054 TRIMMER, PRINTED CIRCUIT BOARD PANELS; 700.682-014 LATHE HAND; 700.684-026 DRILLER; 700.684-046 JIGSAWYER; 700.687-066 SCRAPER; 703.684-010 BENCH-SHEAR OPERATOR; 705.582-010 BLADE GROOVER; 705.682-010 GOLD-NIB GRINDER; 705.682-014 TRIMMER; 705.684-010 BENCH GRINDER; 705.684-014 BUFFER I; 705.684-058 POLISHER; 705.684-066 POLISHER APPRENTICE; 705.684-070 POLISHER, SAND; 705.684-074 SNAG GRINDER; 709.684-082 STAB SETTER AND DRILLER; 713.684-038 POLISHER, EYEGLASS FRAMES; 715.381-034 BLOCKER AND POLISHER, GOLD WHEEL; 715.381-090 SCREWHEAD POLISHER; 715.682-010 BARREL FINISHER; 715.682-014 COUNTERSINKER; 715.682-018 POLISHER; 715.682-026 TOOTH POLISHER; 715.684-062 COLLET DRILLER; 715.684-158 PALLET RECTIFIER; 715.685-014 CUTTER, V-GROOVE; 715.685-018 DEBURRER, MACHINE; 715.685-022 DRILLER AND BROACHER; 715.685-026 END POLISHER; 715.685-042 PINION POLISHER; 715.685-046 POLISHER, BALANCE SCREWHEAD; 715.685-062 TAPPER II; 726.682-026 SAW OPERATOR; 733.685-026 SMOOTHER; 734.584-010 NEEDLE GRINDER

Punching, Pressing, Extruding, Rolling, and Forming Machine Setters and Operators

91302 PUNCHING MACHINE SETTERS AND SET-UP OPERATORS, METAL AND PLASTIC. OOH

Title/s: Metalworking and Plastics-Working Machine Operators
Set up or set up and operate machines to punch, crimp, cut blanks, or notch metal or plastic workpieces between preset dies, according to specifications. Activates machine and observes operation to detect misalignment or machine malfunctions. Installs, aligns, and locks specified punches, dies, and cutting blades in ram or bed of machine, using gauges and hand tools. Adjusts ram stroke of press to specified length, using hand tools. Sets stops or guides or installs jigs or fixtures for positioning successive workpieces. Sets controls or installs gears to synchronize action of feed bar or rollers. Reads job order to determine location of holes or cutting lines. Measures workpiece with rule or tape, or traces from template and marks location with scribe, soapstone, or centerpunch. Positions, aligns, and secures workpiece against fixtures or stops on machine bed or on die. Inspects workpieces for conformance to specifications—visually or using gauges or templates, scale, or compass—and adjusts machine to correct errors. Cleans and lubricates machines.
Yearly Earnings: $20,488
Education: Moderate-term O-J-T
Knowledge: None above average
Abilities: Control Precision
Skills: Equipment Maintenance
General Work Activities: None above average
Job Characteristics: Hazardous Equipment; Standing; Using Hands on Objects, Tools, or Controls; Making Repetitive Motions; Importance of Repeating Same Tasks; Pace Determined by Speed of Equipment
GOE Group/s: 06.01.02 Production Technology: Machine Set-up; 06.02.02 Production Work: Machine Work, Metal and Plastics
CIP Program/s: 480501 Machinist/Machine Technologist; 480506 Sheet Metal Worker
Related DOT Job/s: 615.382-010 PUNCH-PRESS OPERATOR I; 615.482-014 DUPLICATOR-PUNCH OPERATOR; 615.482-018 IRONWORKER-MACHINE OPERATOR; 615.482-026 PUNCH-PRESS OPERATOR, AUTOMATIC; 619.380-014 PUNCH-PRESS SETTER; 699.380-010 DIE SET-UP OPERATOR, PRINTED CIRCUIT BOARDS

91305 PRESS AND PRESS BRAKE MACHINE SETTERS AND SET-UP OPERATORS, METAL AND PLASTIC. OOH Title/s: Metalworking and Plastics-Working Machine Operators; Automotive Body Repairers

Set up or set up and operate power-press machines or power-brake machines to bend, form, stretch, notch, punch, or straighten metal or plastic plate and structural shapes, as specified by work order ,blueprint, drawing, template, or layout. Sets stops on machine bed, changes dies, and adjusts components such as ram or power press when making multiple or successive passes. Operates power press, power brake, apron brake, swaging machine, foot-powered press, hydraulic press, or arbor press according to specifications. Selects and positions flat, block, radius, or special purpose die sets into ram and bed of machine, using hoist, crane, measuring instruments, and hand tools. Installs, aligns, and secures gears, holding fixtures, and dies to machine bed, using gauges, templates, feelers, shims, and hand tools. Measures workpiece and verifies dimensions and weight, using micrometer, template, straightedge, and scale. Inspects workpiece for defects. Plans sequence of operations, applying knowledge of physical properties of metal. Preheats workpiece, using heating furnace or hand torch. Lifts, positions, and secures workpiece between dies of machine, using crane and sledge. Lubricates workpiece with oil. Grinds out burrs and sharp edges, using portable grinder, speed lathe, and polishing jack. Hand-forms or finishes workpiece, using tools such as table saw, hand sledge anvil, flaring tool, and gauge.

Yearly Earnings: $20,280

Education: Moderate-term O-J-T

Knowledge: Building and Construction; Mechanical; Foreign Language

Abilities: Information Ordering; Visualization; Arm-Hand Steadiness; Manual Dexterity; Control Precision; Multilimb Coordination; Static Strength; Explosive Strength; Dynamic Strength; Trunk Strength; Stamina; Extent Flexibility; Gross Body Equilibrium; Depth Perception

Skills: Science; Technology Design; Installation; Testing; Operation Monitoring; Operation and Control; Equipment Maintenance

General Work Activities: Handling and Moving Objects; Controlling Machines and Processes; Repairing and Maintaining Mechanical Equipment

Job Characteristics: Sounds, Noise Levels are Distracting, etc.; Whole Body Vibration; Hazardous Equipment; Hazardous Situations; Common Protective or Safety Attire; Importance of Repeating Same Tasks; Pace Determined by Speed of Equipment

GOE Group/s: 06.01.02 Production Technology: Machine Set-up; 06.02.02 Production Work: Machine Work, Metal and Plastics; 06.02.20 Production Work: Machine Assembling

CIP Program/s: 480501 Machinist/Machine Technologist; 480506 Sheet Metal Worker

Related DOT Job/s: 616.682-010 ARBOR-PRESS OPERATOR I; 616.682-026 KICK-PRESS OPERATOR I; 617.260-010 PRESS OPERATOR, HEAVY DUTY; 617.360-010 BRAKE OPERATOR I; 617.360-014 SWAGING-MACHINE ADJUSTER; 617.380-010 KICK PRESS SETTER; 617.382-010 TUBE BENDER, BRASS-WIND INSTRUMENTS; 617.480-014 PRESS SETTER; 617.482-010 BENDING-MACHINE OPERATOR I; 807.684-010 AUTOMOBILE-BUMPER STRAIGHTENER

91308 SHEAR AND SLITTER MACHINE SETTERS AND SET-UP OPERATORS, METAL AND PLASTIC. OOH Title/s: Metalworking and Plastics-Working Machine Operators

Set up or set up and operate power-shear or slitting machines to cut metal or plastic material, such as plates, sheets, slabs, billets, or bars, to specified dimensions and angles. Installs and aligns knives, disk cutters, or fixtures to shear, bevel, or trim fabricated items. Starts machine; adjusts blade and controls using wrenches, rule, gauge, or template; and monitors operation. Tests and adjusts cutting speed and action, according to specified length of product, using gauges and hand tools. Selects, cleans, and installs spacers, rubber sleeves, and cutter on arbors. Operates shear or slitter that cuts or shears to size metal, such as plate, sheets, slabs, billets, or bars. Reads production schedule to determine setup or adjustment of equipment. Threads ends of metal coil from reel through slitter and secures ends on recoiler. Observes machine operation and examines cut strips for flatness, holes, burrs, and surface defects. Hones cutters with oilstone to remove nicks. Measures dimensions of workpiece, using tape, gauge, template, or rule and square, for conformance to specifications. Lays out cutting lines on metal stock to obtain maximum number of pieces from stock. Lifts workpiece manually or by hoist, and positions and secures against guides and stops. Lubricates and cleans machine.

Yearly Earnings: $21,476

Education: Moderate-term O-J-T

Knowledge: Production and Processing; Mechanical

Abilities: Visualization; Selective Attention; Arm-Hand Steadiness; Finger Dexterity; Control Precision; Multilimb Coordination; Reaction Time; Speed of Limb Movement; Static Strength; Stamina; Extent Flexibility; Gross Body Equilibrium

Skills: Technology Design; Installation; Testing; Operation Monitoring; Operation and Control; Product Inspection; Equipment Maintenance; Troubleshooting

General Work Activities: Controlling Machines and Processes

Job Characteristics: Sounds, Noise Levels are Distracting, etc.; Whole Body Vibration; Hazardous Equipment; Hazardous Situations; Standing; Keeping or Regaining Balance; Bending or Twisting the Body; Making Repetitive Motions; Common Protective or Safety Attire; Frustrating Circumstances; Degree of Automation; Pace Determined by Speed of Equipment

GOE Group/s: 06.01.02 Production Technology: Machine Set-up; 06.02.02 Production Work: Machine Work, Metal and Plastics

CIP Program/s: 480501 Machinist/Machine Technologist; 480506 Sheet Metal Worker

Related DOT Job/s: 615.280-010 SLITTER SERVICE AND SETTER; 615.380-010 SHEAR SETTER; 615.482-010 ANGLE SHEAR OPERATOR; 615.662-010 SLITTING-MACHINE OPERATOR II; 615.682-010 FLYING-SHEAR OPERATOR; 615.682-018 SHEAR OPERATOR I

91311 EXTRUDING AND DRAWING MACHINE SETTERS AND SET-UP OPERATORS, METAL AND PLASTIC. OOH Title/s: Metalworking and Plastics-Working Machine Operators

Set up or set up and operate machines to extrude or draw thermoplastic or metal materials, forming such products as tubes, rods, hoses, or wire; or to shape hot billets into products such as bars and structural shapes. Installs dies, machine screws, and sizing rings on machine extruding thermoplastic or metal materials. Starts machine and sets controls to regulate vacuum, air pressure, sizing rings, and temperature, and synchronizes speed of extrusion. Selects coating (extruding) nozzles, spacers, and wire guides, according to diameter and length of rod. Loads machine hopper with mixed materials, using auger, or stuffs rolls of plastic dough into machine cylinders. Adjusts controls to draw or press metal into specified shape and diameter. Studies specifications, determines set-up procedures, and selects machine dies and parts. Operates shearing mechanism to cut rods to specified length. Weighs and mixes pelletized, granular, or powdered thermoplastic materials and coloring pigments. Replaces worn dies when products vary from specifications. Examines extruded product for defects such as wrinkles, bubbles, and splits. Measures

extruded articles for conformance to specifications, and adjusts controls to obtain product of specified dimensions. Tests physical properties of product with testing devices such as acid-bath tester, burst tester, and impact tester. Reels extruded product into rolls of specified length and weight.
Yearly Earnings: $20,280
Education: Moderate-term O-J-T
Knowledge: Production and Processing; Mechanical
Abilities: None above average
Skills: Installation; Testing; Operation Monitoring; Operation and Control; Product Inspection; Equipment Maintenance; Repairing
General Work Activities: Handling and Moving Objects; Controlling Machines and Processes
Job Characteristics: Sounds, Noise Levels are Distracting, etc.; Hazardous Equipment; Standing; Common Protective or Safety Attire; Degree of Automation; Pace Determined by Speed of Equipment
GOE Group/s: 06.01.02 Production Technology: Machine Set-up; 06.02.02 Production Work: Machine Work, Metal and Plastics; 06.02.13 Production Work: Equipment Operation, Rubber, Plastics, and Glass Processing; 06.02.18 Production Work: Equipment Operation, Assorted Materials Processing
CIP Program/s: 150607 Plastics Technologists and Technicians; 480501 Machinist/Machine Technologist
Related DOT Job/s: 557.382-010 EXTRUDER OPERATOR; 614.380-010 EXTRUSION-PRESS ADJUSTER; 614.382-010 WIRE DRAWER; 614.482-010 DRAW-BENCH OPERATOR; 614.482-014 EXTRUDER OPERATOR; 614.482-018 EXTRUSION-PRESS OPERATOR I

91314 ROLLING MACHINE SETTERS AND SET-UP OPERATORS, METAL AND PLASTIC. OOH Title/s: Metalworking and Plastics-Working Machine Operators

Set up or set up and operate machines to roll steel or plastic material—such as strips, bars, and flats—to form bends, beads, knurls, rolls, or plate, or to flatten, temper, and reduce gauge of material. Work involves using measuring instruments and following rolling orders or blueprints. Starts operation of rolling and milling machines to flatten, temper, form, and reduce sheet metal sections and produce steel strips. Manipulates controls and observes dial indicators to monitor, adjust, and regulate speed of machine mechanisms. Resets, adjusts, and corrects machine set-up to reduce thickness, reshape products, and eliminate product defects. Monitors machine cycles and mill operation to detect jamming and to ensure that fabricated products conform to specifications. Selects rolls, dies, roll stands, and chucks from data charts to form specified contours and to fabricate products. Sets distance points between rolls, guides, meters, and stops, according to specifications. Positions, aligns, and secures arbor, spindle, coils, mandrel, dies, and slitting knives onto machine. Installs equipment such as guides, guards, gears, cooling equipment, and rolls, using hand tools. Fills oil cups, adjusts valves, and observes gauges to control flow of metal coolant and lubricants onto workpiece. Examines, inspects, measures, and feels raw materials and finished product to verify conformance to specifications, visually or using measurement instruments. Reads rolling order and mill schedules to determine set-up specifications, work sequence, product dimensions, and installation procedures. Calculates draft space and roll speed for each mill stand to plan rolling sequence and specified dimensions and temper. Threads or feeds sheets or rods through rolling mechanism, or starts and controls mechanism that automatically feeds steel into rollers. Activates shear and grinder to trim workpiece, cut steel strips, and monitor forming of gears to specified length and diameter. Disassembles sizing mills removed from rolling line, and sorts and stores parts. Removes scratches and polishes roll surface, using polishing stone and electric buffer. Records mill production on schedule sheet. Directs and trains other workers to change rolls, operate mill equipment, remove coils and cobbles, and band and load material. Signals and assists other workers to remove and position equipment, fill hoppers, and feed materials into machine.
Yearly Earnings: $20,280
Education: Moderate-term O-J-T
Knowledge: Production and Processing
Abilities: Perceptual Speed; Spatial Orientation; Time Sharing; Arm-Hand Steadiness; Manual Dexterity; Control Precision; Multilimb Coordination; Response Orientation; Rate Control; Reaction Time; Speed of Limb Movement; Static Strength; Explosive Strength; Dynamic Strength; Trunk Strength; Stamina; Extent Flexibility; Dynamic Flexibility; Gross Body Coordination; Gross Body Equilibrium
Skills: Installation; Operation Monitoring; Operation and Control; Product Inspection; Equipment Maintenance
General Work Activities: Handling and Moving Objects; Controlling Machines and Processes
Job Characteristics: Supervise, Coach, Train Others; Sounds, Noise Levels are Distracting, etc.; Whole Body Vibration; Hazardous Equipment; Standing; Kneeling, Crouching, or Crawling; Using Hands on Objects, Tools, or Controls; Bending or Twisting the Body; Degree of Automation; Pace Determined by Speed of Equipment
GOE Group/s: 06.01.02 Production Technology: Machine Set-up; 06.01.03 Production Technology: Machine Set-up and Operation; 06.02.02 Production Work: Machine Work, Metal and Plastics; 06.02.10 Production Work: Equipment Operation, Metal Processing
CIP Program/s: 480501 Machinist/Machine Technologist; 480506 Sheet Metal Worker; 480599 Precision Metal Workers, Other
Related DOT Job/s: 613.360-010 ROLL-FORMING-MACHINE SET-UP MECHANIC; 613.360-014 ROLL-TUBE SETTER; 613.360-018 TIN ROLLER, HOT MILL; 613.361-010 GUIDE SETTER; 613.382-014 FINISHER; 613.462-018 ROLLING-MILL OPERATOR; 613.482-014 PIERCING-MACHINE OPERATOR; 613.662-018 COLD-MILL OPERATOR; 613.682-014 REELING-MACHINE OPERATOR; 613.682-022 STRIP ROLLER; 613.682-030 MILL OPERATOR, ROLLS; 617.480-010 JOB SETTER, SPLINE-ROLLING MACHINE; 617.482-014 FORMING-ROLL OPERATOR I; 617.482-018 ROLL-FORMING-MACHINE OPERATOR I; 617.682-022 SETTER, COLD-ROLLING MACHINE; 619.462-010 ROLL-THREADER OPERATOR

91317 FORGING MACHINE SETTERS AND SET-UP OPERATORS, METAL AND PLASTIC. OOH Title/s: Metalworking and Plastics-Working Machine Operators

Set up or set up and operate forging machines—such as forging presses, coining presses, drop hammers, forging rolls, or upsetters—to taper, shape, or form metal or plastic parts, following work order or blueprint specifications. Starts machine, produces sample workpiece, and observes operations to detect machine malfunction and ensure that set-up conforms to specifications. Selects, aligns, and bolts positioning fixtures and stops and specified dies to ram and anvil, forging rolls, or presses and hammers. Turns handles or knobs to set pressure and depth of ram stroke and synchronize machine operations. Installs and adjusts or removes and replaces dies, synchronizing cams, forging hammer, and stop guides, according to specifications. Reads blueprints to determine specified tolerances and sequence of operations to set up machines. Marks layout; verifies dimensions; and measures, weighs, and inspects machined parts to ensure conformance to product specifications. Positions and moves metal wire or workpiece through series of dies to compress and shape stock to form die impressions. Trims and compresses finished forgings to specified tolerances. Adjusts temperature controls of furnace in which rods are heated. Sharpens cutting tools and drill bits, using bench grinder. Confers with other workers regarding set-up and operational specifications of machines.
Yearly Earnings: $20,280

Education: Moderate-term O-J-T
Knowledge: Design; Mechanical
Abilities: Visualization; Control Precision; Gross Body Equilibrium
Skills: Installation; Operation Monitoring; Operation and Control
General Work Activities: Repairing and Maintaining Mechanical Equipment
Job Characteristics: Sounds, Noise Levels are Distracting, etc.; Using Hands on Objects, Tools, or Controls; Common Protective or Safety Attire; Degree of Automation; Importance of Repeating Same Tasks; Pace Determined by Speed of Equipment
GOE Group/s: 06.01.02 Production Technology: Machine Set-up; 06.01.03 Production Technology: Machine Set-up and Operation; 06.02.02 Production Work: Machine Work, Metal and Plastics
CIP Program/s: 480501 Machinist/Machine Technologist; 480507 Tool and Die Maker/Technologist
Related DOT Job/s: 610.362-010 DROPHAMMER OPERATOR; 611.482-010 FORGING-PRESS OPERATOR I; 611.662-010 UPSETTER; 611.682-010 STEEL-SHOT-HEADER OPERATOR; 612.260-010 FASTENER TECHNOLOGIST; 612.360-010 DIE SETTER; 612.361-010 HEAVY FORGER; 612.462-010 MULTI-OPERATION-MACHINE OPERATOR; 612.462-014 NUT FORMER; 612.662-010 SPIKE-MACHINE OPERATOR; 612.682-010 BUCKSHOT-SWAGE OPERATOR; 612.682-014 FORGING-ROLL OPERATOR

91321 MACHINE FORMING OPERATORS AND TENDERS, METAL AND PLASTIC. OOH Title/s: Metalworking and Plastics-Working Machine Operators

Operate or tend one type of forming machine that has previously been set up. Exclude workers who operate more than one type of forming machine. Types of forming machines include punching machines, shear and slitter machines, rolling machines, press and press brake machines, extruding and drawing machines, and forging machines. Starts and monitors machine—such as shear, roller, lathe, extruder, punch-press, hammer, or deburrer—that stamps, cuts, or otherwise forms workpiece. Sets and adjusts controls, pumps, guides, and switches to regulate speed, pressure, heat, thickness, clearance, hardness, or other machining variables. Observes machine operation and adjusts controls to correct imperfections and attain specified dimensions and shape. Positions workpiece on table of forming machine manually or using crane. Threads workpiece or wire into machine feed mechanism. Stops motor and shuts down machine to change set-up, repair malfunctions, and remove clogs or finished workpiece. Inspects and measures completed piece to verify conformance to specifications, using precision measuring instruments and templates. Traces or positions layout lines on workpiece, using compass or template. Reads and reviews work orders and blueprints to determine machine set-up, sequences of operations, and specifications. Preheats or anneals workpiece using hand torch or heating furnace. Tempers, trims, finishes, shapes, or aligns piece using hand tools and hand-held power tools. Adjusts, installs, or scribes guides, blades, punches, dies, stops, or fixtures on forming machine, using hand tools, thumbscrews, or handwheels. Directs other workers in activities such as changing rolls, regulating speed of conveyors, or positioning workpiece. Cleans and lubricates machines and workpieces. Records production and inspection information such as date, materials used, and number of pieces completed.
Yearly Earnings: $18,772
Education: Moderate-term O-J-T
Knowledge: Production and Processing; Physics
Abilities: None above average
Skills: Operation Monitoring; Equipment Maintenance; Repairing
General Work Activities: Controlling Machines and Processes
Job Characteristics: Sounds, Noise Levels are Distracting, etc.; Hazardous Equipment; Standing; Degree of Automation; Pace Determined by Speed of Equipment
GOE Group/s: 05.05.06 Craft Technology: Metal Fabrication and Repair; 06.02.02 Production Work: Machine Work, Metal and Plastics; 06.02.10 Production Work: Equipment Operation, Metal Processing; 06.02.24 Production Work: Manual Work, Metal and Plastics; 06.03.02 Quality Control: Inspecting, Grading, Sorting, Weighing, and Recording; 06.04.02 Elemental Work: Industrial: Machine Work, Metal and Plastics; 06.04.10 Elemental Work: Industrial: Equipment Operation, Metal Processing; 06.04.13 Elemental Work: Industrial: Equipment Operation, Rubber, Plastics, Glass Processing; 06.04.20 Elemental Work: Industrial: Machine Assembling; 06.04.21 Elemental Work: Industrial: Machine Work, Brushing, Spraying, and Coating; 06.04.24 Elemental Work: Industrial: Manual Work, Metal and Plastics
CIP Program/s: 470404 Musical Instrument Repairer; 470408 Watch, Clock and Jewelry Repairer; 480503 Machine Shop Assistant; 480506 Sheet Metal Worker; 480599 Precision Metal Workers, Other
Related DOT Job/s: 559.685-186 WET-END OPERATOR I; 610.684-014 SPRING SALVAGE WORKER; 611.482-014 ROLLER-MACHINE OPERATOR; 611.682-014 AUTOMATIC CASTING-FORGING MACHINE OPERATOR; 611.685-010 FORGING-PRESS OPERATOR II; 611.685-014 HYDRAULIC OPERATOR; 612.685-010 LEVER TENDER; 612.685-014 SPRING TESTER I; 613.362-014 ROLLER, PRIMARY MILL; 613.362-018 ROUGHER; 613.362-022 SPEED OPERATOR; 613.382-018 SCREWDOWN OPERATOR; 613.662-014 ROUGHER OPERATOR; 613.662-022 STRAIGHTENING-ROLL OPERATOR; 613.682-010 MANIPULATOR; 613.682-018 ROLLER; 613.682-026 TABLE OPERATOR; 613.685-018 PIERCING-MILL OPERATOR; 613.685-022 ROLLER-LEVELER OPERATOR; 613.685-030 TUBING-MACHINE OPERATOR; 614.382-014 WIRE DRAWER; 614.382-018 WIRE DRAWING MACHINE OPERATOR; 614.682-010 DRAW-BENCH OPERATOR; 614.685-010 EXTRUDING-PRESS OPERATOR; 614.685-014 EXTRUSION-PRESS OPERATOR II; 614.685-018 REDUCING-MACHINE OPERATOR; 614.685-022 TUBE DRAWER; 614.685-026 WIRE-DRAWING-MACHINE TENDER; 615.482-030 ROTARY-SHEAR OPERATOR; 615.482-038 TURRET-PUNCH-PRESS OPERATOR; 615.682-014 PUNCH-PRESS OPERATOR III; 615.685-010 BURRING-MACHINE OPERATOR; 615.685-014 CLEARANCE CUTTER; 615.685-022 CUT-OFF-MACHINE OPERATOR; 615.685-026 NIBBLER OPERATOR; 615.685-030 PUNCH-PRESS OPERATOR II; 615.685-034 SHEAR OPERATOR II; 615.685-038 STRIP-METAL-PUNCH-AND-STRAIGHTENER OPERATOR; 615.685-042 TURRET-PUNCH-PRESS OPERATOR, TAPE-CONTROL; 616.685-066 SLAT TWISTER; 616.685-086 WIRE COINER; 617.382-014 HAMMER OPERATOR; 617.482-026 STRAIGHTENING-PRESS OPERATOR II; 617.685-010 BENDING-MACHINE OPERATOR II; 617.685-014 CORNER FORMER; 617.685-026 POWER-PRESS TENDER; 617.685-034 ROLL-FORMING-MACHINE OPERATOR II; 617.685-038 SINTERING-PRESS OPERATOR; 617.685-042 SWAGE TENDER; 619.362-014 ROLL OPERATOR I; 619.485-014 TWISTING-MACHINE OPERATOR; 619.662-014 SKELP PROCESSOR; 619.682-010 BELL SPINNER; 619.682-026 HOOP BENDER, TANK; 619.685-014 BANDING-MACHINE OPERATOR; 619.685-018 BANDING-MACHINE OPERATOR; 619.685-026 BRAKE OPERATOR II; 619.685-034 DRUM STRAIGHTENER I; 619.685-046 FORMING-ROLL OPERATOR II; 619.685-070 METALLIC-YARN-SLITTING-MACHINE OPERATOR; 619.685-082 SPINNING-LATHE OPERATOR, AUTOMATIC; 619.685-086 WINDING-LATHE OPERATOR; 690.585-014 MOTTLE-LAY-UP OPERATOR; 690.665-010 SLASHER; 690.685-078 CENTER-PUNCH OPERATOR; 700.687-054 PLANISHER; 715.684-030 BEVELER; 715.685-050 PRESS OPERATOR, PIERCE AND SHAVE; 715.685-070 TUBING-MACHINE TENDER; 724.684-022 COIL SHAPER; 727.685-010 PLATE SLITTER-AND-INSPECTOR; 730.684-070 SEAM HAMMERER

91502 NUMERICAL CONTROL MACHINE TOOL OPERATORS AND TENDERS, METAL AND PLASTIC. OOH Title/s: Metalworking and Plastics-Working Machine Operators

Set up and operate numerical control (magnetic- or punched-tape-controlled) machine tools that automatically mill, drill, broach, and ream metal and plastic parts. May adjust machine feed and speed, change cutting tools, or adjust machine controls when automatic programming is faulty or if machine malfunctions. Selects, measures, assembles, and sets machine tools, such as drill bits and milling or cutting tools, using precision gauges and instruments. Mounts, installs, aligns, and secures tools, attachments, fixtures, and workpiece on machine, using hand tools and precision measuring instruments. Loads control media, such as tape, card, or disk, in machine controller, or enters commands to retrieve programmed instructions. Determines specifications or procedures for tooling set-up, machine operation, workpiece dimensions, or numerical control sequences, using blueprints, instructions, and machine knowledge. Positions and secures workpiece on machine bed, indexing table, fixture, or dispensing or holding device. Lays out and marks areas of part to be shot-peened, and fills hopper with shot. Calculates and sets machine controls to position tools, synchronize tape and tool, or regulate cutting depth, speed, feed, or coolant flow. Starts automatic operation of numerical control machine to machine parts or test set-up, workpiece dimensions, or programming. Monitors machine operation and control panel displays to detect malfunctions and compare readings to specifications. Stops machine to remove finished workpiece or change tooling, set-up, or workpiece placement, according to required machining sequence. Enters commands or manually adjusts machine controls to correct malfunctions or tolerances. Lifts workpiece to machine manually, with hoist or crane, or with tweezers. Measures dimensions of finished workpiece to ensure conformance to specifications, using precision measuring instruments, templates, and fixtures. Operates lathe, drill-press, jig-boring machine, or other machines manually or semiautomatically. Examines electronic components for defects and completeness of laser-beam trimming, using microscope. Maintains machines and removes and replaces broken or worn machine tools, using hand tools. Confers with supervisor or programmer to resolve machine malfunctions and production errors, and obtains approval to continue production. Cleans machine, tooling, and parts, using solvent or solution and rag.

Yearly Earnings: $21,892

Education: Moderate-term O-J-T

Knowledge: Production and Processing; Engineering and Technology; Design

Abilities: Rate Control; Reaction Time; Wrist-Finger Speed; Dynamic Strength; Dynamic Flexibility

Skills: Equipment Selection; Programming; Operation Monitoring; Operation and Control; Product Inspection; Equipment Maintenance

General Work Activities: Inspecting Equipment, Structures, or Material; Handling and Moving Objects; Controlling Machines and Processes; Repairing and Maintaining Mechanical Equipment; Repairing and Maintaining Electrical Equipment

Job Characteristics: Sounds, Noise Levels are Distracting, etc.; Hazardous Equipment; Standing; Degree of Automation; Pace Determined by Speed of Equipment

GOE Group/s: 06.01.03 Production Technology: Machine Set-up and Operation; 06.02.02 Production Work: Machine Work, Metal and Plastics; 06.02.09 Production Work: Machine Work, Assorted Materials

CIP Program/s: 480503 Machine Shop Assistant

Related DOT Job/s: 604.362-010 LATHE OPERATOR, NUMERICAL CONTROL; 605.360-010 ROUTER SET-UP OPERATOR, NUMERICAL CONTROL; 605.380-010 MILLING-MACHINE SET-UP OPERATOR, NUMERICAL CONTROL; 605.382-046 NUMERICAL-CONTROL ROUTER OPERATOR; 606.362-010 DRILL-PRESS OPERATOR, NUMERICAL CONTROL; 606.382-014 JIG-BORING MACHINE OPERATOR, NUMERICAL CONTROL; 606.382-018 NUMERICAL-CONTROL DRILL OPERATOR, PRINTED CIRCUIT BOARDS; 606.382-026 ROBOTIC MACHINE OPERATOR; 609.360-010 NUMERICAL CONTROL MACHINE SET-UP OPERATOR; 609.362-010 NUMERICAL CONTROL MACHINE OPERATOR; 617.280-010 SHOT-PEENING OPERATOR; 699.362-010 AUTOMATED CUTTING MACHINE OPERATOR; 726.682-010 LASER-BEAM-TRIM OPERATOR

91505 COMBINATION MACHINE TOOL SETTERS AND SET-UP OPERATORS, METAL AND PLASTIC. OOH Title/s: Metalworking and Plastics-Working Machine Operators

Set up or set up and operate more than one type of cutting or forming machine tool, such as gear hobbers, lathes, press brakes, shearing, and boring machines. Exclude workers who set up or set up and operate only one type of metal or plastic working machine. Sets up and operates lathes, cutters, borers, millers, grinders, presses, drills, and auxiliary machines to make metallic and plastic workpieces. Moves controls or mounts gears, cams, or templates in machine to set feed rate and cutting speed, depth, and angle. Monitors machine operation and moves controls to align and adjust position of workpieces and action of cutting tools. Selects, installs, and adjusts alignment of drills, cutters, dies, guides, and holding devices, using template, measuring instruments, and hand tools. Starts machine and turns handwheels or valves to engage feeding, cooling, and lubricating mechanisms. Reads blueprint or job order to determine product specifications and tooling instructions and to plan operational sequences. Measures and marks reference points and cutting lines on workpiece, using traced templates, compasses, and rules. Computes data, such as gear dimensions and machine settings, applying knowledge of shop mathematics. Inspects first-run workpieces and verifies conformance to specifications to check accuracy of machine set-up. Lifts, positions, and secures workpieces in holding devices, using hoists and hand tools. Makes minor electrical and mechanical repairs and adjustments, and notifies supervisor when major service is required. Records operational data such as pressure readings, length of stroke, feeds, and speeds. Instructs operators or other workers in machine set-up and operation.

Yearly Earnings: $21,892

Education: Moderate-term O-J-T

Knowledge: Production and Processing; Design; Mechanical; Foreign Language

Abilities: Perceptual Speed; Visualization; Selective Attention; Time Sharing; Control Precision; Reaction Time; Speed of Limb Movement; Static Strength; Extent Flexibility; Gross Body Equilibrium; Visual Color Discrimination; Auditory Attention

Skills: Mathematics; Instructing; Installation; Testing; Operation Monitoring; Operation and Control; Product Inspection; Equipment Maintenance; Troubleshooting; Repairing

General Work Activities: Controlling Machines and Processes; Repairing and Maintaining Mechanical Equipment; Repairing and Maintaining Electrical Equipment

Job Characteristics: Supervise, Coach, Train Others; Sounds, Noise Levels are Distracting, etc.; Hazardous Equipment; Hazardous Situations; Standing; Common Protective or Safety Attire; Degree of Automation; Importance of Repeating Same Tasks; Pace Determined by Speed of Equipment

GOE Group/s: 05.05.07 Craft Technology: Machining; 06.01.02 Production Technology: Machine Set-up; 06.01.03 Production Technology: Machine Set-up and Operation; 06.01.05 Production Technology:

Inspection; 06.02.02 Production Work: Machine Work, Metal and Plastics; 06.03.01 Quality Control: Inspecting, Testing, and Repairing
CIP Program/s: 470408 Watch, Clock and Jewelry Repairer; 480501 Machinist/Machine Technologist; 480507 Tool and Die Maker/Technologist
Related DOT Job/s: 600.360-010 MACHINE TRY-OUT SETTER; 600.360-014 MACHINE SETTER; 600.380-018 MACHINE SET-UP OPERATOR; 600.380-022 MACHINE SETTER; 601.280-054 TOOL-MACHINE SET-UP OPERATOR; 602.280-010 GEAR-CUTTING-MACHINE SET-UP OPERATOR, TOOL; 602.380-010 GEAR-CUTTING-MACHINE SET-UP OPERATOR; 602.382-010 GEAR HOBBER SET-UP OPERATOR; 602.382-014 GEAR-GENERATOR SET-UP OPERATOR, SPIRAL BEVEL; 602.382-018 GEAR-GENERATOR SET-UP OPERATOR, STRAIGHT BEVEL; 602.382-022 GEAR-MILLING-MACHINE SET-UP OPERATOR; 602.382-026 GEAR-SHAPER SET-UP OPERATOR; 602.382-030 GEAR-SHAVER SET-UP OPERATOR; 616.360-022 MACHINE SETTER; 616.380-018 MACHINE OPERATOR I; 692.682-034 ELECTRODE TURNER-AND-FINISHER

91508 COMBINATION MACHINE TOOL OPERATORS AND TENDERS, METAL AND PLASTIC. OOH Title/s: Metalworking and Plastics-Working Machine Operators

Operate or tend more than one type of cutting or forming machine tool that has been previously set up. Includes such machine tools as band saws, press brakes, slitting machines, drills, lathes, and boring machines. Exclude workers who operate or tend only one type of cutting or forming machine. Activates and tends or operates machines to cut, shape, thread, bore, drill, tap, bend, or mill metal or non-metallic material. Observes machine operation to detect workpiece defects or machine malfunction. Positions, adjusts, and secures workpiece against stops, on arbor, or in chuck, fixture, or automatic feeding mechanism manually or using hoist. Reads job specifications to determine machine adjustments and material requirements. Aligns layout marks with die or blade. Extracts or lifts jammed pieces from machine, using fingers, wire hooks, or lift bar. Inspects workpiece for defects and measures workpiece, using rule, template, or other measuring instruments, to determine accuracy of machine operation. Adjusts machine components and changes worn accessories, such as cutting tools and brushes, using hand tools. Sets machine stops or guides to specified length as indicated by scale, rule, or template. Installs machine components, such as chucks, boring bars, or cutting tools, according to specifications, using hand tools. Removes burrs, sharp edges, rust, or scale from workpiece, using file, hand grinder, wire brush, or power tools. Performs minor machine maintenance, such as oiling or cleaning machines, dies, or workpieces, or adding coolant to machine reservoir.
Yearly Earnings: $21,892
Education: Moderate-term O-J-T
Knowledge: Production and Processing
Abilities: Manual Dexterity; Control Precision; Multilimb Coordination; Rate Control; Speed of Limb Movement; Dynamic Flexibility; Gross Body Equilibrium
Skills: Installation; Operation Monitoring; Operation and Control; Equipment Maintenance
General Work Activities: Controlling Machines and Processes; Repairing and Maintaining Mechanical Equipment
Job Characteristics: Sounds, Noise Levels are Distracting, etc.; Hazardous Equipment; Hazardous Situations; Standing; Using Hands on Objects, Tools, or Controls; Making Repetitive Motions; Common Protective or Safety Attire; Degree of Automation; Pace Determined by Speed of Equipment
GOE Group/s: 06.02.02 Production Work: Machine Work, Metal and Plastics; 06.04.02 Elemental Work: Industrial: Machine Work, Metal and Plastics
CIP Program/s: 480503 Machine Shop Assistant
Related DOT Job/s: 602.685-010 GEAR-CUTTING-MACHINE OPERATOR, PRODUCTION; 609.682-010 AUTOMATIC-WHEEL-LINE OPERATOR; 609.682-022 MACHINE OPERATOR, CENTRIFUGAL-CONTROL SWITCHES; 609.685-018 PRODUCTION MACHINE TENDER; 609.685-022 TRANSFER-MACHINE OPERATOR; 609.685-026 TRIM-MACHINE OPERATOR; 619.685-062 MACHINE OPERATOR II

Metal Fabricating Machine Setters, Operators, and Related Workers

91702 WELDING MACHINE SETTERS AND SET-UP OPERATORS. OOH Title/s: Welders, Cutters, and Welding Machine Operators

Set up or set up and operate welding machines that join or bond together components to fabricate metal products or assemblies, according to specifications and blueprints. Include workers who set up or set up and operate laser cutters or laser-beam machines. Sets up and operates welding machines that join or bond components to fabricate metal products or assemblies. Turns and presses controls—such as cranks, knobs, and buttons—to adjust and activate welding process. Feeds workpiece into welding machine to join or bond components. Observes and listens to welding machine and its gauges to ensure welding process meets specifications. Operates welding machine to produce trial workpieces, used to examine and test. Positions and adjusts fixtures, attachments, or workpieces on machine, using hand tools. Lays out, fits, or tacks workpieces together, using hand tools. Stops and opens holding device on welding machine, using hand tools. Examines metal product or assemblies to ensure specifications are met. Adds components, chemicals, and solutions to welding machine, using hand tools. Tends auxiliary equipment used in welding process. Cleans and maintains workpieces and welding machine parts, using hand tools and equipment. Devises and builds fixtures used to bond components during the welding process. Tests products and records test results and operational data on specified forms.
Yearly Earnings: $23,868
Education: Moderate-term O-J-T
Knowledge: Production and Processing; Mechanical
Abilities: Arm-Hand Steadiness; Manual Dexterity; Finger Dexterity; Multilimb Coordination; Response Orientation; Rate Control; Reaction Time; Dynamic Flexibility; Gross Body Equilibrium; Depth Perception; Hearing Sensitivity; Auditory Attention; Sound Localization
Skills: Equipment Selection; Testing; Operation Monitoring; Equipment Maintenance
General Work Activities: Inspecting Equipment, Structures, or Material; Handling and Moving Objects; Controlling Machines and Processes; Repairing and Maintaining Mechanical Equipment
Job Characteristics: Sounds, Noise Levels are Distracting, etc.; Hazardous Conditions; Hazardous Equipment; Standing; Using Hands on Objects, Tools, or Controls; Common Protective or Safety Attire; Degree of Automation; Pace Determined by Speed of Equipment
GOE Group/s: 06.01.02 Production Technology: Machine Set-up; 06.02.19 Production Work: Equipment Operation, Welding, Brazing and Soldering
CIP Program/s: 480508 Welder/Welding Technologist
Related DOT Job/s: 727.662-010 LEAD BURNER, MACHINE; 810.382-010 WELDING-MACHINE OPERATOR, ARC; 811.482-010 WELDING-

MACHINE OPERATOR, GAS; 812.360-010 WELDER SETTER, RESISTANCE MACHINE; 812.682-010 WELDING-MACHINE OPERATOR, RESISTANCE; 815.380-010 WELDER SETTER, ELECTRON-BEAM MACHINE; 815.382-010 WELDING-MACHINE OPERATOR, ELECTRON BEAM

91705 WELDING MACHINE OPERATORS AND TENDERS. OOH Title/s: Welders, Cutters, and Welding Machine Operators

Operate or tend welding machines that join or bond together components to fabricate metal products and assemblies, according to specifications and blueprints. Include laser cutters and laser-beam machine operators. Operates or tends welding machines that join or bond components to fabricate metal products and assemblies. Turns and presses knobs and buttons to adjust and start welding machine. Observes and listens to welding machine and its controls to ensure welding process meets specifications. Enters operating instructions into computer to adjust and start welding machine. Positions and adjusts fixtures, attachments, or workpiece on machine, using hand tools and measuring devices. Reads production schedule and specifications to ascertain product to be fabricated. Stops and opens holding device on welding machine, using hand tools. Inspects metal workpiece to ensure specifications are met, using measuring devices. Tends auxiliary equipment used in the welding process. Adds chemicals or solutions to welding machine to join or bind components. Cleans and maintains workpieces and welding machine parts, using hand tools and equipment. Transfers components, metal products, and assemblies, using moving equipment.

Yearly Earnings: $23,868

Education: Moderate-term O-J-T

Knowledge: Production and Processing

Abilities: Arm-Hand Steadiness; Manual Dexterity; Control Precision; Rate Control; Reaction Time; Speed of Limb Movement; Hearing Sensitivity

Skills: Operation Monitoring; Operation and Control; Equipment Maintenance

General Work Activities: Controlling Machines and Processes; Repairing and Maintaining Mechanical Equipment

Job Characteristics: Sounds, Noise Levels are Distracting, etc.; Very Hot; Contaminants; Hazardous Conditions; Hazardous Equipment; Hazardous Situations; Standing; Using Hands on Objects, Tools, or Controls; Common Protective or Safety Attire; Degree of Automation; Pace Determined by Speed of Equipment

GOE Group/s: 05.10.01 Crafts: Structural; 06.02.19 Production Work: Equipment Operation, Welding, Brazing and Soldering; 06.02.22 Production Work: Manual Work, Assembly Large Parts; 06.02.24 Production Work: Manual Work, Metal and Plastics; 06.04.02 Elemental Work: Industrial: Machine Work, Metal and Plastics

CIP Program/s: 480508 Welder/Welding Technologist

Related DOT Job/s: 614.684-010 BILLET ASSEMBLER; 814.382-010 WELDING-MACHINE OPERATOR, FRICTION; 814.682-010 WELDING-MACHINE OPERATOR, ULTRASONIC; 814.684-010 WELDER, EXPLOSION; 815.382-014 WELDING-MACHINE OPERATOR, ELECTROSLAG; 815.682-010 LASER-BEAM-MACHINE OPERATOR; 815.682-014 WELDING-MACHINE OPERATOR, THERMIT; 819.685-010 WELDING-MACHINE TENDER

91708 SOLDERING AND BRAZING MACHINE SETTERS AND SET-UP OPERATORS. OOH Title/s: Solderers and Brazers

Set up or set up and operate soldering or brazing machines to braze, solder, heat-treat, or spot-weld fabricated metal products or components as specified by work orders, blueprints, and layout specifications. Selects torch tips, alloy, flux, coil, tubing, and wire, according to metal type and thickness, data charts, and records. Connects, forms, and installs parts to braze, heat-treat, and spot-weld workpiece, metal parts, and components. Sets dials and timing controls to regulate electrical current, gas-flow pressure, heating/cooling cycles, and shut-off. Positions, aligns, and bolts holding fixtures, guides, and stops onto or into brazing machine to position and hold workpieces. Fills hoppers and positions spout to direct flow of flux, or manually brushes flux onto seams of workpieces. Starts machine to complete trial run, readjusts machine, and records set-up data. Assembles, aligns, and clamps workpieces into holding fixture to bond, heat-treat, or solder fabricated metal components. Manipulates levers to synchronize brazing action or to move workpiece through brazing process. Operates and trains workers to operate heat-treating equipment to bond fabricated metal components according to blueprints, work orders, or specifications. Disconnects electrical current, and removes and immerses workpiece into water or acid bath to cool and clean component. Examines workpiece for defective seams, solidification, and adherence to specifications, and anneals finished workpiece to relieve internal stress. Cleans, lubricates, and adjusts equipment to maintain efficient operation, using air hose, cleaning fluid, and hand tools.

Yearly Earnings: $19,500

Education: Moderate-term O-J-T

Knowledge: Building and Construction; Mechanical

Abilities: None above average

Skills: Instructing; Installation; Operation Monitoring; Operation and Control; Product Inspection

General Work Activities: Handling and Moving Objects; Controlling Machines and Processes; Repairing and Maintaining Mechanical Equipment; Teaching Others; Coaching and Developing Others

Job Characteristics: Sounds, Noise Levels are Distracting, etc.; Very Hot; Extremely Bright or Inadequate Lighting; Contaminants; Cramped Work Space, Awkward Positions; Hazardous Conditions; Hazardous Equipment; Common Protective or Safety Attire; Specialized Protective or Safety Attire; Pace Determined by Speed of Equipment

GOE Group/s: 06.01.02 Production Technology: Machine Set-up; 06.02.10 Production Work: Equipment Operation, Metal Processing; 06.02.19 Production Work: Equipment Operation, Welding, Brazing and Soldering

CIP Program/s: 480508 Welder/Welding Technologist

Related DOT Job/s: 813.360-010 BRAZING-MACHINE SETTER; 813.360-014 SETTER, INDUCTION-HEATING EQUIPMENT; 813.382-010 BRAZER, INDUCTION; 813.382-014 BRAZING-MACHINE OPERATOR

91711 SOLDERING AND BRAZING MACHINE OPERATORS AND TENDERS. OOH Title/s: Solderers and Brazers

Operate or tend soldering and brazing machines that braze, solder, or spot-weld fabricated metal products or components as specified by work orders, blueprints, and layout specifications. Operates or tends soldering and brazing machines that braze, solder, or spot-weld fabricated products or components. Moves controls to activate and adjust soldering and brazing machines. Observes meters, gauges, and machine to ensure solder or brazing process meets specifications. Loads and adjusts workpieces, clamps, and parts onto machine, using hand tools. Adds chemicals and materials to workpieces or machines, using hand tools. Removes workpieces and parts from machinery, using hand tools. Cleans and maintains workpieces and machines, using equipment and hand tools. Examines and tests soldered or brazed products or components, using testing devices. Reads and records operational information on specified production reports.

Yearly Earnings: $19,500
Education: Moderate-term O-J-T
Knowledge: None above average
Abilities: Perceptual Speed; Control Precision
Skills: Equipment Selection; Operation Monitoring; Operation and Control; Product Inspection; Equipment Maintenance; Repairing
General Work Activities: None above average
Job Characteristics: Very Hot; Hazardous Equipment; Using Hands on Objects, Tools, or Controls; Common Protective or Safety Attire; Importance of Repeating Same Tasks; Pace Determined by Speed of Equipment
GOE Group/s: 06.02.10 Production Work: Equipment Operation, Metal Processing; 06.02.19 Production Work: Equipment Operation, Welding, Brazing and Soldering; 06.04.02 Elemental Work: Industrial: Machine Work, Metal and Plastics; 06.04.10 Elemental Work: Industrial: Equipment Operation, Metal Processing; 06.04.19 Elemental Work: Industrial: Equipment Operation, Assorted Materials Processing; 06.04.20 Elemental Work: Industrial: Machine Assembling
CIP Program/s: 480508 Welder/Welding Technologist
Related DOT Job/s: 706.685-010 TYPE-SOLDERING-MACHINE TENDER; 715.685-058 SOLDERER; 726.362-014 WAVE-SOLDERING MACHINE OPERATOR; 726.684-094 SOLDER DEPOSIT OPERATOR; 726.685-038 REFLOW OPERATOR; 813.482-010 BRAZER, FURNACE; 813.685-010 BRAZER, CONTROLLED ATMOSPHERIC FURNACE

91714 METAL FABRICATORS, STRUCTURAL METAL PRODUCTS. **OOH Title/s: Metalworking and Plastics-Working Machine Operators**
Fabricate and assemble structural metal products, such as frameworks or shells for machinery, ovens, tanks, and stacks, and metal parts for buildings and bridges, according to job order or blueprints. Develops layout and plans sequence of operations for fabricating and assembling structural metal products, applying trigonometry and knowledge of metal. Locates and marks bending and cutting lines onto workpiece, allowing for stock thickness and machine and welding shrinkage, Sets up and operates fabricating machines, such as brakes, rolls, shears, flame cutters, and drill presses. Hammers, chips, and grinds workpiece to cut, bend, and straighten metal. Positions, aligns, fits, and welds together parts, using jigs, welding torch, and hand tools. Preheats workpieces to render them malleable, using hand torch or furnace. Verifies conformance of workpiece to specifications, using square, ruler, and measuring tape. Sets up and operates machine tools associated with fabricating shops, such as radial drill, end mill, and edge planer. Designs and constructs templates and fixtures, using hand tools.
Yearly Earnings: $21,892
Education: Moderate-term O-J-T
Knowledge: Production and Processing; Engineering and Technology; Design; Building and Construction; Mechanical
Abilities: Control Precision; Static Strength; Explosive Strength; Extent Flexibility
Skills: Mathematics; Operation and Control; Product Inspection
General Work Activities: Controlling Machines and Processes; Drafting and Specifying Technical Devices, etc.
Job Characteristics: Sounds, Noise Levels are Distracting, etc.; Whole Body Vibration; Hazardous Equipment; Standing
GOE Group/s: 05.05.06 Craft Technology: Metal Fabrication and Repair
CIP Program/s: 480501 Machinist/Machine Technologist
Related DOT Job/s: 619.361-014 METAL FABRICATOR; 619.361-018 METAL-FABRICATOR APPRENTICE

Molding, Casting, Plating, and Heating Machine Setters and Operators

91902 PLASTIC MOLDING AND CASTING MACHINE SETTERS AND SET-UP OPERATORS.
OOH Title/s: Metalworking and Plastics-Working Machine Operators
Set up or set up and operate plastic molding machines, such as compression or injection molding machines, to mold, form, or cast thermoplastic materials to specified shape. Positions, aligns, and secures assembled mold, mold components, and machine accessories onto machine press bed, and attaches connecting lines. Installs dies onto machine or press and coats dies with parting agent, according to work order specifications. Sets machine controls to regulate molding temperature, volume, pressure, and time, according to knowledge of plastics and molding procedures. Presses button or pulls lever to activate machine to inject dies and compress compounds to form and cure specified products. Reads specifications to determine set-up and prescribed temperature and time settings to mold, form, or cast plastic materials. Weighs premixed compounds and dumps compound into die well, or fills hoppers of machines that automatically supply compound to die. Observes and adjusts machine set-up and operations to eliminate production of defective parts and products. Mixes catalysts, thermoplastic materials, and coloring pigments according to formula, using paddle and mixing machine. Measures and visually inspects products for surface and dimension defects, using precision measuring instruments, to ensure conformance to specifications. Removes finished or cured product from dies or mold, using hand tools and airhose. Trims excess material from part, using knife, and grinds scrap plastic into powder for reuse. Repairs and maintains machines and auxiliary equipment, using hand tools and power tools.
Yearly Earnings: $21,892
Education: Moderate-term O-J-T
Knowledge: Production and Processing; Mechanical
Abilities: Control Precision; Wrist-Finger Speed; Explosive Strength; Dynamic Flexibility
Skills: Operation Monitoring; Operation and Control; Product Inspection; Equipment Maintenance; Repairing
General Work Activities: Repairing and Maintaining Mechanical Equipment
Job Characteristics: Sounds, Noise Levels are Distracting, etc.; Contaminants; Hazardous Conditions; Hazardous Equipment; Common Protective or Safety Attire; Degree of Automation; Pace Determined by Speed of Equipment
GOE Group/s: 06.01.02 Production Technology: Machine Set-up; 06.02.13 Production Work: Equipment Operation, Rubber, Plastics, and Glass Processing
CIP Program/s: 150607 Plastics Technologists and Technicians
Related DOT Job/s: 556.380-010 MOLD SETTER; 556.382-014 INJECTION-MOLDING-MACHINE OPERATOR; 556.682-014 COMPRESSION-MOLDING-MACHINE OPERATOR

91905 PLASTIC MOLDING AND CASTING MACHINE OPERATORS AND TENDERS. **OOH Title/s: Metalworking and Plastics-Working Machine Operators**
Operate or tend plastic molding machines, such as compression or injection molding machines, to mold, form, or cast thermoplastic materials to specified shape. Starts machine that automatically liquefies plastic material in heating chamber, injects liquefied

material into mold, and ejects molded product. Turns valves and dials of machines to regulate pressure and temperature, to set press-cycle time, and to close press. Observes meters and gauges to verify specified temperatures, pressures, and press-cycle times. Observes continuous operation of automatic machine and width and alignment of plastic sheeting to ensure side flanges. Dumps plastic powder, preformed plastic pellets, or preformed rubber slugs into hopper of molding machine. Pulls level and toggle latches to fill mold and regulate tension on sheeting and to release mold covers. Mixes and pours liquid plastic into rotating drum of machine that spreads, hardens, and shapes mixture. Fills tubs, molds, or cavities of machine with plastic material in solid or liquid form prior to activating machine. Examines molded product for surface defects, such as dents, bubbles, thin areas, and cracks. Positions mold frame to correct alignment and tubs containing mixture on top of mold to facilitate loading of molds. Removes product from mold or conveyor, and cleans and reloads mold. Weighs prescribed amounts of material for molded part and finished product to ensure specifications are maintained. Heats plastic material prior to forming product, or cools product after processing to prevent distortion. Breaks seals that hold plastic product in molds, using hand tool, and removes product from mold. Feels stiffness and consistency of molded sheeting to detect machinery malfunction. Stacks molded parts in boxes or on conveyor for subsequent processing, or leaves parts in mold to cool. Reports defect in molds to supervisor. Throws flash and rejected parts into grinder machine to be recycled. Signals coworker to synchronize feed of materials into molding process. Trims flashing from product.
Yearly Earnings: $18,772
Education: Moderate-term O-J-T
Knowledge: Production and Processing; Mechanical
Abilities: Perceptual Speed; Control Precision; Rate Control; Reaction Time; Speed of Limb Movement; Static Strength; Dynamic Strength; Trunk Strength; Stamina; Dynamic Flexibility; Gross Body Coordination; Gross Body Equilibrium
Skills: Operation Monitoring; Operation and Control
General Work Activities: Controlling Machines and Processes
Job Characteristics: Sounds, Noise Levels are Distracting, etc.; Hazardous Conditions; Hazardous Equipment; Standing; Using Hands on Objects, Tools, or Controls; Bending or Twisting the Body; Degree of Automation; Pace Determined by Speed of Equipment
GOE Group/s: 06.04.10 Elemental Work: Industrial: Equipment Operation, Metal Processing; 06.04.13 Elemental Work: Industrial: Equipment Operation, Rubber, Plastics, Glass Processing; 06.04.19 Elemental Work: Industrial: Equipment Operation, Assorted Materials Processing
CIP Program/s: 150607 Plastics Technologists and Technicians
Related DOT Job/s: 556.385-010 CENTRIFUGAL-CASTING-MACHINE TENDER; 556.665-010 CAKE-PRESS OPERATOR; 556.665-014 CORRUGATOR OPERATOR; 556.665-018 MOLDER, PIPE COVERING; 556.685-022 COMPRESSION-MOLDING-MACHINE TENDER; 556.685-038 INJECTION-MOLDING-MACHINE TENDER; 556.685-082 VACUUM PLASTIC-FORMING-MACHINE OPERATOR; 556.685-086 BLOW-MOLDING-MACHINE TENDER; 556.685-090 CENTRIFUGAL-CASTING-MACHINE TENDER; 690.685-090 CONTACT-LENS MOLDER

91908 METAL MOLDING, COREMAKING, AND CASTING MACHINE SETTERS AND SET-UP OPERATORS. OOH Title/s: Metalworking and Plastics-Working Machine Operators

Set up or set up and operate metal casting, molding, and coremaking machines to mold or cast metal parts and products, such as tubes, rods, automobile trim, carburetor housings, and motor parts. Machines include die casting and continuous casting machines, and roll-over, squeeze, and shell-molding machines. Moves controls to start, set, or adjust casting, molding, or pressing machines. Loads die sections into machine, using equipment such as chain fall or hoist, and secures in position, using hand tools. Pours molten metal into cold-chamber machine or cylinders, using hand ladle. Connects water hose to cooling system of die, using hand tools. Loads metal ingots or aluminum bars into melting furnace, and transfers molten metal to reservoir of die casting machine. Lines cylinder pot with asbestos strips and disk to prevent chilling. Stacks and mounts rotor core laminations over keyed mandrel of casting machine, and removes and stamps rotor with identifying data. Preheats die sections with torch or electric heater. Removes castings from dies and dips castings in water to cool, using pliers or tongs. Obtains and moves specified pattern to work station, manually or using hoist, and secures pattern to machine, using wrenches. Repairs or replaces worn or defective machine parts and dies. Inspects castings and core slots for defects, using fixed gauges. Cleans and lubricates casting machine and dies, using air hose and brushes.
Yearly Earnings: $18,772
Education: Moderate-term O-J-T
Knowledge: Production and Processing; Mechanical
Abilities: Arm-Hand Steadiness; Manual Dexterity; Control Precision; Rate Control; Reaction Time; Static Strength; Explosive Strength; Dynamic Strength; Trunk Strength; Stamina; Extent Flexibility; Dynamic Flexibility; Gross Body Coordination; Gross Body Equilibrium; Depth Perception
Skills: Equipment Selection; Installation; Operation Monitoring; Operation and Control; Equipment Maintenance
General Work Activities: Handling and Moving Objects; Controlling Machines and Processes; Repairing and Maintaining Mechanical Equipment
Job Characteristics: Sounds, Noise Levels are Distracting, etc.; Very Hot; Contaminants; Hazardous Equipment; Hazardous Situations; Using Hands on Objects, Tools, or Controls; Common Protective or Safety Attire; Specialized Protective or Safety Attire; Degree of Automation; Pace Determined by Speed of Equipment
GOE Group/s: 06.01.02 Production Technology: Machine Set-up; 06.02.10 Production Work: Equipment Operation, Metal Processing
CIP Program/s: 480599 Precision Metal Workers, Other
Related DOT Job/s: 502.482-018 ROTOR CASTING-MACHINE OPERATOR; 502.682-014 CASTING-MACHINE OPERATOR; 514.360-010 DIE-CASTING-MACHINE SETTER; 514.382-010 DIE-CASTING-MACHINE OPERATOR I; 518.380-010 SETTER, MOLDING-AND-COREMAKING MACHINES

91911 METAL MOLDING, COREMAKING, AND CASTING MACHINE OPERATORS AND TENDERS. OOH Title/s: Metalworking and Plastics-Working Machine Operators

Operate or tend metal molding, casting, or coremaking machines to mold or cast metal products—such as pipes, brake drums, and rods—and metal parts—such as automobile trim, carburetor housings, and motor parts. Machines include centrifugal casting machines, vacuum casting machines, turnover draw-type coremaking machines, conveyor-screw coremaking machines, and die casting machines. Starts and operates furnace, oven, diecasting, coremaking, metal molding, or rotating machines to pour metal or create molds and casts. Positions ladles or pourers and adjusts controls to regulate the flow of metal, sand, or coolant into mold. Positions, aligns, and secures molds or core boxes in holding devices or under pouring spouts and tubes, using hand tools. Removes casting from mold, mold from press, or core from core box, using tongs, pliers, or hydraulic ram, or by inversion. Observes and records data

from pyrometers, lights, and gauges to monitor molding process and adjust furnace temperature. Pours or loads metal or sand into melting pot, furnace, mold, core box, or hopper, using shovel, ladle, or machine. Fills core boxes and mold patterns with sand or powders, using ramming tools or pneumatic hammers, and removes excess. Inspects metal casts and molds for cracks, bubbles, or other defects, and measures castings to ensure that specifications are met. Assembles shell halves, patterns, and foundry flasks, and reinforces core boxes, using glue, clamps, wire, bolts, rams, or machines. Skims or pours dross, slag, or impurities from molten metal, using ladle, rake, hoe, spatula, or spoon. Sprays, smokes, or coats molds with compounds to lubricate or insulate mold, using acetylene torches or sprayers. Smooths and cleans inner surface of mold, using brush, scraper, air hose, or grinding wheel, and fills imperfections with refractory material. Weighs metals and powders and computes amounts of materials necessary to produce mixture of specified content. Requisitions molds and supplies and inventories, and records finished products. Signals or directs other workers to load conveyor, spray molds, or remove ingots. Cuts spouts and pouring holes in molds, and sizes hardened cores, using saws. Cleans, glues, and racks cores, ingots, or finished products for storage. Repairs or replaces damaged molds, pipes, belts, chains, or other equipment, using hand tools, hand-powered press, or jib crane.
Yearly Earnings: $18,772
Education: Moderate-term O-J-T
Knowledge: Production and Processing; Mechanical; Foreign Language
Abilities: Flexibility of Closure; Perceptual Speed; Selective Attention; Time Sharing; Arm-Hand Steadiness; Multilimb Coordination; Response Orientation; Rate Control; Reaction Time; Speed of Limb Movement; Static Strength; Explosive Strength; Dynamic Strength; Trunk Strength; Stamina; Extent Flexibility; Dynamic Flexibility; Gross Body Coordination; Gross Body Equilibrium; Auditory Attention
Skills: Installation; Testing; Operation Monitoring; Operation and Control; Product Inspection; Equipment Maintenance; Repairing
General Work Activities: Performing General Physical Activities; Handling and Moving Objects; Controlling Machines and Processes
Job Characteristics: Sounds, Noise Levels are Distracting, etc.; Very Hot; Contaminants; Hazardous Conditions; Hazardous Equipment; Hazardous Situations; Standing; Keeping or Regaining Balance; Using Hands on Objects, Tools, or Controls; Common Protective or Safety Attire; Degree of Automation; Importance of Repeating Same Tasks; Pace Determined by Speed of Equipment
GOE Group/s: 05.10.05 Crafts: Reproduction; 06.02.10 Production Work: Equipment Operation, Metal Processing; 06.04.08 Elemental Work: Industrial: Machine Work, Stone, Glass, and Clay; 06.04.10 Elemental Work: Industrial: Equipment Operation, Metal Processing; 06.04.17 Elemental Work: Industrial: Equipment Operation, Clay Processing; 06.04.19 Elemental Work: Industrial: Equipment Operation, Assorted Materials Processing; 06.04.32 Elemental Work: Industrial: Manual Work, Casting and Molding
CIP Program/s: 480201 Graphic and Printing Equipment Operator, General; 480206 Lithographer and Platemaker; 480599 Precision Metal Workers, Other
Related DOT Job/s: 502.362-010 SHOT DROPPER; 502.382-010 BULLET-SLUG-CASTING-MACHINE OPERATOR; 502.482-010 CASTER; 502.482-014 CASTING-MACHINE OPERATOR, AUTOMATIC; 502.682-010 BULLET-CASTING OPERATOR; 502.685-010 MOLDER, LEAD INGOT; 502.685-014 REMELTER; 514.362-010 PIG-MACHINE OPERATOR; 514.562-010 CENTRIFUGAL-CASTING-MACHINE OPERATOR III; 514.582-010 VACUUM CASTER; 514.662-010 CASTING OPERATOR; 514.682-010 CASTING-WHEEL OPERATOR; 514.685-010 CENTRIFUGAL-CASTING-MACHINE OPERATOR I; 514.685-014 CENTRIFUGAL-CASTING-MACHINE OPERATOR II; 514.685-018 DIE-CASTING-MACHINE OPERATOR II; 518.682-010 MACHINE MOLDER; 518.685-014 COREMAKER, MACHINE I; 518.685-018 COREMAKER, MACHINE II; 518.685-022 COREMAKER, MACHINE III; 518.685-026 SHELL MOLDER; 590.685-018 DIAMOND BLENDER; 974.682-010 BLOCKER, METAL BASE

91914 FOUNDRY MOLD ASSEMBLY AND SHAKEOUT WORKERS. OOH Title/s: Foundry, Mold Assembly and Shakeout Workers

Prepare molds for pouring. Duties include cleaning and assembling foundry molds, and tending machine that bonds cope and drag together to form completed shell mold. Cleans sand from casting or mold, using air hose and brush. Assembles core to drag and cope. Monitors operation of machines that extract cast core pipe or bond cope and drag to form shell mold. Strikes end of core pipe to loosen baked sand between casting and core pipe, and secures pipe to dolly jaws. Knocks out sprue holes, using iron rod. Positions drag, cope, and bonding agent onto pressure plate of machine. Manipulates controls to start machines, or adjusts temperature or pressure settings.
Yearly Earnings: $18,772
Education: Moderate-term O-J-T
Knowledge: None above average
Abilities: None above average
Skills: Operation Monitoring
General Work Activities: Controlling Machines and Processes
Job Characteristics: Sounds, Noise Levels are Distracting, etc.; Contaminants; Standing; Using Hands on Objects, Tools, or Controls; Making Repetitive Motions; Common Protective or Safety Attire
GOE Group/s: 06.04.02 Elemental Work: Industrial: Machine Work, Metal and Plastics; 06.04.08 Elemental Work: Industrial: Machine Work, Stone, Glass, and Clay
CIP Program/s: 000000 NO CIP ASSIGNED
Related DOT Job/s: 514.685-026 TUBE-CLEANING OPERATOR; 518.685-030 SHELL-MOLD-BONDING-MACHINE OPERATOR

91917 ELECTROLYTIC PLATING AND COATING MACHINE SETTERS AND SET-UP OPERATORS, METAL AND PLASTIC. OOH Title/s: Metalworking and Plastics-Working Machine Operators

Set up or set up and operate electrolytic plating or coating machines, such as continuous multistrand electrogalvanizing machines, to coat metal or plastic products electrolytically with chromium, copper, cadmium, or other metal, to provide protective or decorative surfaces or to build up worn surfaces. Moves controls to permit electrodeposition of metal on object or to regulate movement of wire strand to obtain specified thickness. Adjusts voltage and amperage, based on observations. Determines size and composition of object to be plated and amount of electrical current and time required, following work order. Suspends object, such as part or mold, from cathode rod (negative terminal), and immerses object in plating solution. Suspends stick or piece of plating metal from anode (positive terminal), and immerses metal in plating solution. Mixes chemical solutions, fills tanks, and charges furnaces. Removes plated object from solution at periodic intervals and observes object to ensure conformance to specifications. Plates small objects, such as nuts or bolts, using motor-driven barrel. Immerses object in cleaning and rinsing baths to complete plating process. Examines object at end of process to determine thickness of metal deposit, or measures thickness, using instruments such as micrometers. Measures, marks, and masks areas excluded from plating. Grinds, polishes, or rinses object in water, and dries object to maintain clean, even surface.
Yearly Earnings: $20,176
Education: Moderate-term O-J-T

Knowledge: Chemistry
Abilities: None above average
Skills: Operation Monitoring; Operation and Control
General Work Activities: None above average
Job Characteristics: Common Protective or Safety Attire; Specialized Protective or Safety Attire; Pace Determined by Speed of Equipment
GOE Group/s: 06.02.21 Production Work: Coating and Plating
CIP Program/s: 480599 Precision Metal Workers, Other
Related DOT Job/s: 500.362-010 ELECTROGALVANIZING-MACHINE OPERATOR; 500.380-010 PLATER; 500.380-014 PLATER APPRENTICE

91921 ELECTROLYTIC PLATING AND COATING MACHINE OPERATORS AND TENDERS, METAL AND PLASTIC. OOH Title/s: Metalworking and Plastics-Working Machine Operators

Operate or tend electrolytic plating or coating machines, such as zinc-plating machines and anodizing machines, to coat metal or plastic products electrolytically with chromium, zinc, copper, cadmium, or other metal to provide protective or decorative surfaces or to build up worn surfaces. Measures or estimates amounts of electric current needed and time required to coat objects. Adjusts dials to regulate flow of current and voltage supplied to terminals to control plating process. Positions objects to be plated in frame, or suspends them from positive or negative terminals of power supply. Removes object from plating solution after specified time or when desired thickness of metal is deposited on them. Mixes and tests plating solution to specified formula and turns valves to fill tank with solution. Monitors and measures thickness of electroplating on component part to verify conformance to specifications, using micrometer. Mixes forming acid solution, treats battery plates, and removes and rinses formed plates. Immerses objects to be coated or plated into cleaning solutions, or sprays with conductive solution to prepare object for plating. Rinses coated object in cleansing liquids and dries with cloth or centrifugal driers, or by tumbling in sawdust-filled barrels. Lubricates moving parts of plating conveyor and cleans plating and cleaning solution tanks.
Yearly Earnings: $20,176
Education: Moderate-term O-J-T
Knowledge: Chemistry
Abilities: None above average
Skills: Operation and Control; Product Inspection; Equipment Maintenance
General Work Activities: None above average
Job Characteristics: Hazardous Conditions; Degree of Automation; Pace Determined by Speed of Equipment
GOE Group/s: 06.02.21 Production Work: Coating and Plating; 06.02.32 Production Work: Manual Work, Assorted Materials; 06.04.19 Elemental Work: Industrial: Equipment Operation, Assorted Materials Processing; 06.04.21 Elemental Work: Industrial: Machine Work, Brushing, Spraying, and Coating; 06.04.33 Elemental Work: Industrial: Manual Work, Brushing, Spraying, and Coating
CIP Program/s: 480599 Precision Metal Workers, Other
Related DOT Job/s: 500.362-014 PLATER, BARREL; 500.384-010 MATRIX PLATER; 500.384-014 MATRIX-BATH ATTENDANT; 500.485-010 ZINC-PLATING-MACHINE OPERATOR; 500.682-010 ANODIZER; 500.684-010 ELECTROFORMER; 500.684-018 PLATE FORMER; 500.684-026 PLATER, PRINTED CIRCUIT BOARD PANELS; 500.684-030 PLATER, SEMICONDUCTOR WAFERS AND COMPONENTS; 500.684-034 PLATER; 500.685-014 PLATING EQUIPMENT TENDER

91923 NONELECTROLYTIC PLATING AND COATING MACHINE SETTERS AND SET-UP OPERATORS, METAL AND PLASTIC. OOH Title/s: Metalworking and Plastics-Working Machine Operators

Set up or set up and operate nonelectrolytic plating or coating machines, such as hot-dip lines and metal-spraying machines, to coat metal or plastic products or parts with metal. Measures and sets stops, rolls, brushes, and guides on automatic feeder and conveying equipment or coating machines, using micrometer, rule, and hand tools. Adjusts controls to set temperatures of coating substance, and adjusts speeds of machines and equipment. Attaches nozzle, positions gun, connects hoses, and threads wire to set up metal-spraying machine. Ignites gun and adjusts controls to regulate wire feed, air pressure, and flow of oxygen and fuel to operate metal-spraying machine. Installs gears and holding devices on conveyor equipment. Reads production schedule to determine set-up of equipment and machines. Mixes alodize solution in tank of machine, according to formula, and verifies solution concentration, using gauge. Positions workpieces, starts operation of machines and conveyors, and feeds workpieces into machines to be coated. Adjusts controls to synchronize equipment speed with speed of coating or spraying machine. Operates hoist to place workpieces onto machine feed carriage or spindle. Inspects coated products for defects and specified color and coverage. Operates sandblasting equipment to roughen and clean surface of workpieces. Preheats workpieces in oven.
Yearly Earnings: $20,176
Education: Moderate-term O-J-T
Knowledge: Production and Processing
Abilities: Control Precision; Rate Control; Visual Color Discrimination
Skills: Installation; Operation Monitoring; Operation and Control; Product Inspection
General Work Activities: Controlling Machines and Processes
Job Characteristics: Cramped Work Space, Awkward Positions; Hazardous Equipment; Hazardous Situations; Standing; Common Protective or Safety Attire; Degree of Automation; Pace Determined by Speed of Equipment
GOE Group/s: 06.02.10 Production Work: Equipment Operation, Metal Processing; 06.02.21 Production Work: Coating and Plating
CIP Program/s: 480599 Precision Metal Workers, Other
Related DOT Job/s: 501.362-010 COATING-MACHINE OPERATOR; 505.382-010 METAL-SPRAYING-MACHINE OPERATOR, AUTOMATIC I; 509.462-010 ALODIZE-MACHINE OPERATOR

91926 NONELECTROLYTIC PLATING AND COATING MACHINE OPERATORS AND TENDERS, METAL AND PLASTIC. OOH Title/s: Metalworking and Plastics-Working Machine Operators

Operate or tend nonelectrolytic plating or coating machines, such as metal-spraying machines and vacuum-metalizing machines, to coat metal or plastic products or parts with metal. Observes gauges and adjusts controls of machine to regulate functions, such as speed and temperature, according to specifications. Sprays coating in specified pattern according to instructions, and inspects area for defects, such as air bubbles or uneven coverage. Presses or turns controls to activate and set equipment operation according to specifications. Positions and feeds materials on plate into machine, manually or automatically, for processing. Fills machine receptacle with coating material or solution. Immerses workpieces in coating solution for specified time. Mixes coating material or solution according to formula, or uses premixed solutions. Places materials on racks and transfers to oven to dry for a specified period of time. Removes excess material or impurities from objects, using air hose or grinding machine.

Cuts metal or other materials, using shears or band saw. Measures or weighs materials, using ruler, calculator, and scale. Positions containers to receive parts, and loads or unloads materials in containers, using dolly or handtruck. Cleans and maintains equipment, using water hose and scraper. Solders equipment and visually examines for completeness. Cleans workpieces, using wire brush. Maintains production records. Replaces worn parts and adjusts equipment components, using hand tools.
Yearly Earnings: $20,176
Education: Moderate-term O-J-T
Knowledge: Production and Processing; Chemistry
Abilities: None above average
Skills: Operation Monitoring; Equipment Maintenance
General Work Activities: Controlling Machines and Processes; Repairing and Maintaining Mechanical Equipment
Job Characteristics: Standing; Importance of Repeating Same Tasks; Pace Determined by Speed of Equipment
GOE Group/s: 05.12.14 Elemental Work: Mechanical: Painting, Caulking, and Coating; 06.02.10 Production Work: Equipment Operation, Metal Processing; 06.02.13 Production Work: Equipment Operation, Rubber, Plastics, and Glass Processing; 06.02.18 Production Work: Equipment Operation, Assorted Materials Processing; 06.02.21 Production Work: Coating and Plating; 06.04.10 Elemental Work: Industrial: Equipment Operation, Metal Processing; 06.04.21 Elemental Work: Industrial: Machine Work, Brushing, Spraying, and Coating
CIP Program/s: 480599 Precision Metal Workers, Other
Related DOT Job/s: 501.485-010 WIRE-COATING OPERATOR, METAL; 501.685-010 PLATER, HOT DIP; 501.685-014 TINNING-EQUIPMENT TENDER; 501.685-018 BLACK OXIDE COATING EQUIPMENT TENDER; 501.685-022 ELECTROLESS PLATER, PRINTED CIRCUIT BOARD PANELS; 503.685-010 COATER; 505.382-014 WELDING-ROD COATER; 505.482-010 PASTING-MACHINE OPERATOR; 505.682-010 SPRAYER OPERATOR; 505.685-010 BROWNING PROCESSOR; 505.685-014 METAL-SPRAYING-MACHINE OPERATOR, AUTOMATIC II; 505.685-018 VACUUM-METALIZER OPERATOR; 509.382-010 COATER OPERATOR; 509.685-022 CERAMIC COATER, MACHINE; 509.685-026 GETTERING-FILAMENT-MACHINE OPERATOR; 509.685-030 IMPREGNATOR; 509.685-034 LACQUER-DIPPING-MACHINE OPERATOR; 509.685-038 LUBRICATING-MACHINE TENDER; 554.382-014 PLASTICS-SPREADING-MACHINE OPERATOR; 554.585-014 COATER OPERATOR; 554.685-014 COATING-AND-BAKING OPERATOR; 590.685-046 JEWELRY COATER; 599.685-054 LACQUERER; 599.685-062 OXIDIZED-FINISH PLATER; 599.685-090 SPRAY-MACHINE TENDER; 599.685-102 TUBE COATER; 692.685-238 VACUUM-APPLICATOR OPERATOR; 694.685-018 BULLET-LUBRICATING-MACHINE OPERATOR; 694.685-046 PRIMER-WATERPROOFING-MACHINE OPERATOR; 726.685-050 SOLDER-LEVELER, PRINTED CIRCUIT BOARDS; 843.482-010 METAL SPRAYER, CORROSION PREVENTION

91928 HEATING EQUIPMENT SETTERS AND SET-UP OPERATORS, METAL AND PLASTIC. OOH Title/s: Metalworking and Plastics-Working Machine Operators

Set up or set up and operate heating equipment, such as heat-treating furnaces, flame-hardening machines, and induction machines, that anneal or heat-treat metal objects. Mounts fixtures and industrial coil on machine and workpieces in fixture, using hand tools. Lights gas burners and adjusts flow of gas and coolant water. Sets frequency of current and automatic timer. Starts conveyors and dial feeder plates, and turns setscrews in nozzles to direct flames that anneal specific area of object. Estimates flame temperature and heating cycle based on degree of hardness required and metal to be treated. Reads work order to determine processing specifications. Visually examines or tests objects, using hardness-testing equipment, to determine flame temperature and degree of hardness. Crushes random samples between fingers to determine hardness. Replaces worn dial-feed, burner, and conveyor parts, using hand tools. Instruct new workers in machine operation.
Yearly Earnings: $20,176
Education: Moderate-term O-J-T
Knowledge: Production and Processing; Mechanical; Physics; Education and Training
Abilities: Arm-Hand Steadiness; Manual Dexterity; Control Precision; Rate Control; Explosive Strength; Dynamic Flexibility; Gross Body Equilibrium
Skills: Operation Monitoring; Operation and Control; Product Inspection
General Work Activities: Controlling Machines and Processes; Repairing and Maintaining Mechanical Equipment
Job Characteristics: Sounds, Noise Levels are Distracting, etc.; Very Hot; Contaminants; Hazardous Conditions; Hazardous Equipment; Hazardous Situations; Standing; Using Hands on Objects, Tools, or Controls; Common Protective or Safety Attire; Degree of Automation; Pace Determined by Speed of Equipment
GOE Group/s: 06.01.02 Production Technology: Machine Set-up
CIP Program/s: 480501 Machinist/Machine Technologist
Related DOT Job/s: 504.360-010 FLAME-ANNEALING-MACHINE SETTER; 504.380-010 FLAME-HARDENING-MACHINE SETTER; 504.380-014 INDUCTION-MACHINE SETTER

91932 HEAT TREATING, ANNEALING, AND TEMPERING MACHINE OPERATORS AND TENDERS, METAL AND PLASTIC. OOH Title/s: Metalworking and Plastics-Working Machine Operators

Operate or tend machines—such as furnaces, baths, flame-hardening machines, and electronic induction machines—to harden, anneal, and heat-treat metal products or metal parts. Sets automatic controls, observes gauges, and operates gas or electric furnace used to harden, temper, or anneal metal parts. Positions part in fixture, presses buttons to light burners, and tends flame-hardening machine, according to procedures, to case-harden metal part. Activates and tends electric furnace that anneals base sections of hardened parts for subsequent machining. Adjusts speed and operates continuous furnace through which parts are passed by means of reels and conveyors. Sets up and operates die-quenching machine to prevent parts from warping. Reads production schedule to determine processing sequence and furnace temperature requirements for objects to be heat-treated. Reduces heat and allows parts to cool in furnace. Loads parts into containers, closes furnace door, and inserts parts into furnace when specified temperature is reached. Removes parts from furnace after specified time and air-dries or cools parts in water or oil brine or other baths. Examines parts to ensure that metal shade and color conform to specifications, utilizing knowledge of metal heat-treating. Tests parts for hardness, using hardness-testing equipment, and stamps heat-treatment identification mark on part, using hammer and punch. Signals forklift operator to deposit or extract containers of parts into and from furnaces and quenching rinse tanks. Cleans oxides and scale from parts or fittings, using steam spray or immersing parts in chemical and water baths. Covers parts with charcoal before inserting in furnace to prevent discoloration caused by rapid heating.
Yearly Earnings: $20,176
Education: Moderate-term O-J-T
Knowledge: Production and Processing; Mechanical
Abilities: Rate Control; Speed of Limb Movement; Static Strength; Explosive Strength; Dynamic Strength; Trunk Strength; Stamina; Dynamic Flexibility; Gross Body Coordination; Gross Body Equilibrium; Visual Color Discrimination
Skills: Testing; Operation Monitoring
General Work Activities: Controlling Machines and Processes

Job Characteristics: Sounds, Noise Levels are Distracting, etc.; Very Hot; Contaminants; Hazardous Conditions; Hazardous Equipment; Hazardous Situations; Standing; Making Repetitive Motions; Specialized Protective or Safety Attire; Degree of Automation; Pace Determined by Speed of Equipment
GOE Group/s: 06.02.10 Production Work: Equipment Operation, Metal Processing; 06.04.10 Elemental Work: Industrial: Equipment Operation, Metal Processing
CIP Program/s: 470408 Watch, Clock and Jewelry Repairer; 480503 Machine Shop Assistant; 480599 Precision Metal Workers, Other
Related DOT Job/s: 504.382-010 HARDENER; 504.382-014 HEAT TREATER I; 504.382-018 HEAT-TREATER APPRENTICE; 504.682-010 ANNEALER; 504.682-014 CASE HARDENER; 504.682-018 HEAT TREATER II; 504.682-022 HEAT-TREATING BLUER; 504.682-026 TEMPERER; 504.685-010 BASE-DRAW OPERATOR; 504.685-014 FLAME-HARDENING-MACHINE OPERATOR; 504.685-022 INDUCTION-MACHINE OPERATOR; 504.685-026 PRODUCTION HARDENER; 504.687-010 ANNEALER

91935 FURNACE OPERATORS AND TENDERS. OOH

Title/s: Metalworking and Plastics-Working Machine Operators

Operate or tend furnaces—such as gas, oil, coal, electric-arc or electric induction, open-hearth, or oxygen furnaces—to melt and refine metal before casting or to produce specified types of steel. Exclude heat-treating and related furnace operators. Manipulates controls to ignite burners, adjust fuel mixtures, open and close furnace doors, or load and discharge materials into or from furnace. Observes air and temperature gauges or metal color, and turns fuel valves or adjusts controls to maintain required temperature. Regulates supply of fuel and air or controls flow of electric current and water coolant to heat furnaces. Observes inside of furnace operations by television screen and operates controls to move or discharge metal workpiece. Drains, transfers, or removes molten metal from furnace or into molds by hoist, pumps, or ladles. Observes color and fluidity of molten metal and obtains test sample of metal from furnace or kettle for analysis. Kindles fire and shovels fuels and other materials into furnaces or onto conveyors by hand, with hoists, or by directing crane operator. Sprinkles chemicals over molten metal to bring impurities to surface and removes impurities, using strainers. Analyzes metal test sample, according to specific instructions and for specific and for specific element content. Inspects furnace and equipment for defects and wear and directs work crew in cleaning and repairing furnace walls and flooring. Examines and prepares material to load into furnace, including cleaning, crushing, or applying chemicals, using crushing machine, shovel, rake, or sprayer. Draws smelted metal samples from furnace for analysis and calculates type and amount of material required to correct smelting process. Weighs materials to be charged into furnace or to maintain prescribed weight, using scales. Scrapes accumulations of metal oxides from floors, molds, and crucibles and sifts and stores for reclamation. Records data and maintains production logs.
Yearly Earnings: $26,104
Education: Moderate-term O-J-T
Knowledge: Production and Processing; Mechanical; Physics; Chemistry
Abilities: Manual Dexterity; Control Precision; Multilimb Coordination; Rate Control; Static Strength; Explosive Strength; Dynamic Strength; Trunk Strength; Stamina; Extent Flexibility; Dynamic Flexibility; Gross Body Coordination; Gross Body Equilibrium; Visual Color Discrimination
Skills: Operation Monitoring
General Work Activities: Inspecting Equipment, Structures, or Material; Controlling Machines and Processes; Repairing and Maintaining Mechanical Equipment
Job Characteristics: Sounds, Noise Levels are Distracting, etc.; Very Hot; Extremely Bright or Inadequate Lighting; Contaminants; Hazardous Conditions; Hazardous Equipment; Hazardous Situations; Keeping or Regaining Balance; Specialized Protective or Safety Attire; Degree of Automation; Pace Determined by Speed of Equipment
GOE Group/s: 06.02.10 Production Work: Equipment Operation, Metal Processing; 06.04.10 Elemental Work: Industrial: Equipment Operation, Metal Processing; 06.04.11 Elemental Work: Industrial: Equipment Operation, Chemical Processing
CIP Program/s: 480503 Machine Shop Assistant; 480599 Precision Metal Workers, Other
Related DOT Job/s: 504.665-014 CHARGER OPERATOR; 512.362-010 FIRST HELPER; 512.362-014 FURNACE OPERATOR; 512.362-018 FURNACE OPERATOR; 512.382-010 OXYGEN-FURNACE OPERATOR; 512.382-014 STOVE TENDER; 512.382-018 TIN RECOVERY WORKER; 512.662-010 CUPOLA TENDER; 512.684-014 FURNACE CHARGER; 512.685-010 FURNACE TENDER; 512.685-022 RECLAMATION KETTLE TENDER, METAL; 553.685-114 CADMIUM BURNER

91938 HEATERS, METAL AND PLASTIC. OOH

Title/s: Metalworking and Plastics-Working Machine Operators; Handlers, Equipment Cleaners, Helpers, and Laborers

Operate or tend heating equipment—such as soaking pits, reheating furnaces, and heating and vacuum equipment—to heat metal sheets, blooms, billets, bars, plates, and rods to a specified temperature for rolling or processing, or to heat and cure preformed plastic parts. Ignites furnace with torch, and turns valve to regulate flow of fuel and air to burners. Starts conveyors and opens furnace doors to load stock, or signals crane operator to uncover soaking pits and lower ingots into them. Adjusts controls to maintain temperature and heating time, using thermal instruments and charts, dials and gauges of furnace, and color of stock. Sets oven controls or turns air-pressure valve or autoclave. Adjusts controls to synchronize speed of feed and take-off conveyors of furnace. Inserts vacuum tube into bag and seals bag around tube with tape. Places part on cart, connects vacuum line to tube, and smooths bag around part to ensure vacuum. Positions plastic sheet and mold in plastic bag, heats material under lamps, and forces confrontation of sheet to mold by vacuum pressure. Positions stock in furnace, using tongs, chain hoist, or pry bar. Removes material from furnace, using crane, or signals crane operator to transfer to next station. Removes stock from furnace, using cold rod, tongs, or chain hoist, and places stock on conveyor for transport to work area. Positions part in plastic bag and seals bag with iron. Removes part and cuts away plastic bag. Pushes cart to curing oven or places part in autoclave. Impregnates fabric with plastic resins and cuts fabric into strips. Signals coworker to charge steel into furnace. Records time and production data. Assists workers in repairing, replacing, cleaning, lubricating, or adjusting furnace equipment, using hand tools.
Yearly Earnings: $20,176
Education: Moderate-term O-J-T
Knowledge: Production and Processing
Abilities: None above average
Skills: Equipment Maintenance; Repairing
General Work Activities: Controlling Machines and Processes; Repairing and Maintaining Mechanical Equipment
Job Characteristics: Very Hot; Hazardous Conditions; Hazardous Equipment; Hazardous Situations; Standing; Specialized Protective or Safety Attire
GOE Group/s: 06.02.02 Production Work: Machine Work, Metal and Plastics; 06.02.10 Production Work: Equipment Operation, Metal Processing; 06.04.02 Elemental Work: Industrial: Machine Work,

Metal and Plastics; 06.04.13 Elemental Work: Industrial: Equipment Operation, Rubber, Plastics, Glass Processing
CIP Program/s: 480599 Precision Metal Workers, Other
Related DOT Job/s: 553.685-014 BAGGER; 613.362-010 HEATER I; 613.462-014 FURNACE OPERATOR; 619.682-022 HEATER; 619.686-026 SPIKE-MACHINE HEATER

Other Metal and Plastic Machine Setters and Operators

92197 ALL OTHER METAL AND PLASTIC (CUTTING, FORMING, FABRICATING, OR PROCESSING) MACHINE SETTERS AND SET-UP OPERATORS. OOH Title/s: Metalworking and Plastics-Working Machine Operators

All other metal and plastic machine setters and set-up operators not classified separately above.
Yearly Earnings: $20,176
Education: Moderate-term O-J-T
GOE Group/s: 06.01.02 Production Technology: Machine Set-up; 06.01.03 Production Technology: Machine Set-up and Operation; 06.02.02 Production Work: Machine Work, Metal and Plastics; 06.02.19 Production Work: Equipment Operation, Welding, Brazing and Soldering
CIP Program/s: 470408 Watch, Clock and Jewelry Repairer; 480501 Machinist/Machine Technologist; 480503 Machine Shop Assistant; 480506 Sheet Metal Worker; 480507 Tool and Die Maker/Technologist; 480508 Welder/Welding Technologist
Related DOT Job/s: 505.380-010 METAL SPRAYER, MACHINED PARTS; 553.382-026 METAL-BONDING PRESS OPERATOR; 556.380-014 PREFORM-MACHINE OPERATOR; 609.380-010 ELECTRICAL-DISCHARGE-MACHINE SET-UP OPERATOR; 609.482-014 STRAIGHT-PIN-MAKING-MACHINE OPERATOR; 616.260-010 EMBOSSING TOOLSETTER; 616.260-014 MULTI-OPERATION-FORMING-MACHINE SETTER; 616.260-018 SPRING COILING MACHINE SETTER; 616.260-022 TORSION SPRING COILING MACHINE SETTER; 616.280-010 SPRING MAKER; 616.360-010 BODY-MAKER-MACHINE SETTER; 616.360-014 LOOM SETTER, WIRE WEAVING; 616.360-026 MULTI-OPERATION-FORMING-MACHINE OPERATOR I; 616.360-030 SHOTGUN-SHELL-ASSEMBLY-MACHINE ADJUSTER; 616.360-034 STRAIGHT-LINE-PRESS SETTER; 616.362-010 FABRIC-MACHINE OPERATOR I; 616.380-010 FOUR-SLIDE-MACHINE SETTER; 616.380-014 JOB SETTER; 616.382-014 WIRE WEAVER, CLOTH; 616.460-010 NAIL-MAKING-MACHINE SETTER; 616.482-010 SAFETY-PIN-ASSEMBLING-MACHINE OPERATOR; 616.682-014 BALE-TIE-MACHINE OPERATOR; 616.682-018 CAGE MAKER, MACHINE; 616.682-022 CRIMPING-MACHINE OPERATOR; 616.682-034 STRANDING-MACHINE OPERATOR; 617.482-022 SPRING FORMER, MACHINE; 619.280-010 NEEDLEMAKER; 619.280-018 SPRING-MANUFACTURING SET-UP TECHNICIAN; 619.380-010 HIGH-ENERGY-FORMING EQUIPMENT OPERATOR; 619.382-010 BULLET-GROOVING-SIZING-AND-LUBRICATING-MACHINE OPERATOR; 619.382-018 FOUR-SLIDE-MACHINE OPERATOR I; 619.382-022 TYPE-ROLLING-MACHINE OPERATOR; 619.462-014 TRIMMER OPERATOR; 619.682-018 FISHING ACCESSORIES MAKER; 619.682-042 SEAMLESS-TUBE ROLLER; 690.380-014 MACHINE SETTER-AND-REPAIRER; 694.260-010 LOADING-MACHINE TOOL-SETTER; 694.360-010 PRIMER-CHARGING TOOL SETTER; 694.682-010 BULLET-ASSEMBLY-PRESS SETTER-OPERATOR; 699.482-010 RIVETING-MACHINE OPERATOR I; 710.360-010 SCALE ASSEMBLY SET-UP WORKER; 715.660-010 SET-UP WORKER; 726.380-010 ELECTRONIC EQUIPMENT SET-UP OPERATOR; 806.380-010 RIVETING MACHINE OPERATOR, AUTOMATIC; 816.482-010 THERMAL-CUTTING-MACHINE OPERATOR; 816.682-010 SCARFING MACHINE OPERATOR

92198 ALL OTHER METAL AND PLASTIC (CUTTING, FORMING, FABRICATING, OR PROCESSING) MACHINE OPERATORS AND TENDERS. OOH Title/s: Metalworking and Plastics-Working Machine Operators

All other metal and plastic machine operators and tenders not classified separately above.
Yearly Earnings: $20,176
Education: Moderate-term O-J-T
GOE Group/s: 05.12.13 Elemental Work: Mechanical: Cutting and Finishing; 05.12.18 Elemental Work: Mechanical: Cleaning and Maintenance; 06.02.02 Production Work: Machine Work, Metal and Plastics; 06.02.04 Production Work: Machine Work, Paper; 06.02.09 Production Work: Machine Work, Assorted Materials; 06.02.10 Production Work: Equipment Operation, Metal Processing; 06.02.13 Production Work: Equipment Operation, Rubber, Plastics, and Glass Processing; 06.02.18 Production Work: Equipment Operation, Assorted Materials Processing; 06.02.20 Production Work: Machine Assembling; 06.02.24 Production Work: Manual Work, Metal and Plastics; 06.04.02 Elemental Work: Industrial: Machine Work, Metal and Plastics; 06.04.09 Elemental Work: Industrial: Machine Work, Assorted Materials; 06.04.10 Elemental Work: Industrial: Equipment Operation, Metal Processing; 06.04.12 Elemental Work: Industrial: Equipment Operation, Petroleum, Gas, and Coal Processing; 06.04.13 Elemental Work: Industrial: Equipment Operation, Rubber, Plastics, Glass Processing; 06.04.19 Elemental Work: Industrial: Equipment Operation, Assorted Materials Processing; 06.04.20 Elemental Work: Industrial: Machine Assembling; 06.04.24 Elemental Work: Industrial: Manual Work, Metal and Plastics; 06.04.32 Elemental Work: Industrial: Manual Work, Casting and Molding; 06.04.34 Elemental Work: Industrial: Manual Work, Assorted Materials
CIP Program/s: 150607 Plastics Technologists and Technicians; 470404 Musical Instrument Repairer; 470408 Watch, Clock and Jewelry Repairer; 480503 Machine Shop Assistant; 480506 Sheet Metal Worker; 480599 Precision Metal Workers, Other; 480701 Woodworkers, General
Related DOT Job/s: 500.685-010 ETCHER, ELECTROLYTIC; 503.362-014 SHOTBLAST-EQUIPMENT OPERATOR; 503.685-018 DRIFTER; 503.685-038 SANDBLAST OPERATOR; 503.685-042 SANDBLAST-OR-SHOTBLAST-EQUIPMENT TENDER; 503.685-046 STRIP-TANK TENDER; 509.362-010 MIXER OPERATOR, HOT METAL; 509.382-014 DENTAL-AMALGAM PROCESSOR; 509.384-010 CASE PREPARER-AND-LINER; 509.485-014 SHOT POLISHER AND INSPECTOR; 509.685-042 LUBRICATOR-GRANULATOR; 509.685-054 TANK TENDER; 511.682-010 DUST COLLECTOR, ORE CRUSHING; 512.683-010 CHARGING-MACHINE OPERATOR; 514.682-014 PRESS OPERATOR, CARBON BLOCKS; 519.362-010 NICKEL-PLANT OPERATOR; 519.362-014 TANK-HOUSE OPERATOR; 519.484-010 CARNALLITE-PLANT OPERATOR; 519.582-010 RECOVERY OPERATOR; 519.663-010 DOOR-MACHINE OPERATOR; 519.663-018 PUSHER OPERATOR; 551.582-010 HYDRAULIC-STRAINER OPERATOR; 554.682-018 ROLL OPERATOR; 554.685-010 BULK-SEALER OPERATOR; 556.685-058 PILLING-MACHINE OPERATOR; 559.382-050 SHREDDING-FLOOR-EQUIPMENT OPERATOR; 559.562-010 DRIER OPERATOR I; 559.682-022 FILM-CASTING OPERATOR; 559.682-058 STRETCH-MACHINE OPERATOR; 559.682-070 SCREEN-MACHINE OPERATOR; 559.685-078 FOAM-MACHINE OPERATOR; 590.685-082 STRIPPER-ETCHER, PRINTED CIRCUIT BOARDS; 590.685-094 PLASMA ETCHER, PRINTED CIRCUIT BOARDS; 601.682-010 TOOL DRESSER; 609.462-010 BALANCING-MACHINE OPERATOR; 609.482-010 ELECTRICAL-DISCHARGE-MACHINE OPERATOR, PRODUCTION; 609.682-014 COLLET MAKER; 609.682-018 CROOK

OPERATOR; 609.682-030 SCREWMAKER, AUTOMATIC; 609.685-014 ENGRAVER, AUTOMATIC; 613.382-010 COILER OPERATOR; 613.685-010 COILER; 616.382-010 BARBED-WIRE-MACHINE OPERATOR; 616.485-010 BENCH WORKER; 616.485-014 SPRING COILER; 616.582-010 FENCE-MAKING MACHINE OPERATOR; 616.662-010 HYDRAULIC PRESS OPERATOR; 616.665-010 TENSIONING-MACHINE OPERATOR; 616.682-030 NAIL-ASSEMBLY-MACHINE OPERATOR; 616.685-014 CLINCHING-MACHINE OPERATOR; 616.685-018 COIL ASSEMBLER, MACHINE; 616.685-022 FABRIC-MACHINE OPERATOR II; 616.685-026 HEDDLE-MACHINE OPERATOR; 616.685-030 KNITTER, WIRE MESH; 616.685-038 METAL-SPONGE-MAKING-MACHINE OPERATOR; 616.685-042 MULTI-OPERATION-FORMING-MACHINE OPERATOR II; 616.685-046 PAPERBACK-MACHINE OPERATOR; 616.685-050 POCKET-MACHINE OPERATOR; 616.685-054 RIVETER; 616.685-058 RIVETING-MACHINE OPERATOR; 616.685-062 SCROLL-MACHINE OPERATOR; 616.685-070 SPIRAL SPRING WINDER; 616.685-074 SPIRAL WEAVER; 616.685-078 SWAGER OPERATOR; 616.685-082 SWEEP-PRESS OPERATOR; 616.685-090 ZIPPER CUTTER; 617.585-010 SWAGING-MACHINE OPERATOR; 617.665-010 NAIL-MAKING-MACHINE TENDER; 617.682-010 BARREL-DEDENTING-MACHINE OPERATOR; 617.682-018 HOBBING-PRESS OPERATOR; 617.685-018 EMBOSSING-MACHINE OPERATOR; 617.685-022 EXPANDING MACHINE OPERATOR; 617.685-030 RIPPER; 619.362-010 FLANGING-ROLL OPERATOR; 619.365-010 PRODUCTION-MACHINE TENDER; 619.482-010 LATHE WINDER; 619.485-010 SPOOL WINDER; 619.582-010 STRETCHER-LEVELER OPERATOR; 619.665-010 WINDING-MACHINE OPERATOR; 619.682-014 COUPLING-MACHINE OPERATOR; 619.682-030 HOOP MAKER, MACHINE; 619.682-034 HOOP-FLARING-AND-COILING-MACHINE OPERATOR; 619.685-010 BAND MAKER; 619.685-022 BOBBIN-WINDER TENDER; 619.685-030 COIL-REWIND-MACHINE OPERATOR; 619.685-038 EMBOSSING-MACHINE OPERATOR; 619.685-042 ETCHER, MACHINE; 619.685-050 FOUR-SLIDE-MACHINE OPERATOR II; 619.685-054 HEAD-GAUGE-UNIT OPERATOR; 619.685-058 HEEL-WASHER-STRINGING-MACHINE OPERATOR; 619.685-066 METAL FABRICATOR HELPER; 619.685-074 REPAIRER, SHOE STICKS; 619.685-078 ROD-PULLER AND COILER; 619.685-090 WIRE-WINDING-MACHINE OPERATOR; 669.685-086 STITCHING-MACHINE OPERATOR; 690.382-010 SHEETER OPERATOR; 690.482-014 TRIMMER; 690.682-058 PLANISHING-PRESS OPERATOR; 690.682-062 PRESS OPERATOR; 690.682-074 SPAGHETTI-MACHINE OPERATOR; 690.685-130 DICER OPERATOR; 690.685-154 ELECTRIC-SEALING-MACHINE OPERATOR; 690.685-310 POINTING-MACHINE OPERATOR; 690.685-326 ROLL-OVER-PRESS OPERATOR; 690.685-490 WIRE-WINDING-MACHINE TENDER; 691.685-018 LEAD FORMER; 691.685-022 PAIRING-MACHINE OPERATOR; 691.685-030 UTILITY WORKER, EXTRUSION; 692.485-010 STRINGER-MACHINE TENDER; 692.685-070 DESIGN INSERTER; 692.685-078 DYNAMITE-CARTRIDGE CRIMPER; 692.685-138 PROTECTOR-PLATE ATTACHER; 692.685-206 STOP ATTACHER; 692.685-230 TRIM ATTACHER; 692.685-270 ZIPPER-MACHINE OPERATOR; 694.385-010 SHOTGUN-SHELL-ASSEMBLY-MACHINE OPERATOR; 694.585-010 SHELL-SIEVE OPERATOR; 694.682-014 HYDRAULIC-PRESSURE-AUTO-FRETTAGE-MACHINE OPERATOR; 694.685-010 ANVIL-SEATING-PRESS OPERATOR; 694.685-014 BULLET-ASSEMBLY-PRESS OPERATOR; 694.685-022 FUSE-CUP EXPANDER; 699.685-026 POWER-SCREW-DRIVER OPERATOR; 699.685-030 RIVETING-MACHINE OPERATOR II; 699.685-050 PRODUCTION-MACHINE TENDER; 700.684-066 RING STAMPER; 701.684-026 SAW-EDGE FUSER, CIRCULAR; 709.684-050 KEY CUTTER; 709.684-098 WIRE-FRAME-LAMP-SHADE MAKER; 709.687-058 WIRE BENDER; 713.684-030 FRAME CARVER, SPINDLE; 715.685-030 GRINDER II; 715.685-054 PROFILER, HAND; 723.685-010 HEATING-ELEMENT WINDER; 725.685-010 DISPLAY-SCREEN FABRICATOR; 726.685-026 DIE ATTACHING MACHINE TENDER; 726.685-066 BONDER, SEMICONDUCTOR; 728.685-010 WIRE PREPARATION MACHINE TENDER;

Woodworking Machine Setters and Operators

92302 SAWING MACHINE SETTERS AND SET-UP OPERATORS. OOH Title/s: Woodworking Occupations
Set up or set up and operate wood-sawing machines. Examine blueprints, drawings, work orders, and patterns to determine size and shape of items to be sawed, sawing machines to set up, and sequence of sawing operations. Selects knives to achieve specified diameter of cut, or installs bit and dado saw according to work ticket. Aligns and bolts knives in cutter head and screws it on spindle, using wrenches. Adjusts angle of table by turning handwheel, and bolts or clamps holding jigs to table. Places stock in jig and pushes table containing stock into saw, or lays stock on conveyor that carries it into machine. Pulls table back against stops and depresses pedal to advance cutter head that shapes end of stock.
Yearly Earnings: $16,328
Education: Moderate-term O-J-T
Knowledge: Building and Construction
Abilities: None above average
Skills: None above average
General Work Activities: Handling and Moving Objects; Controlling Machines and Processes
Job Characteristics: Sounds, Noise Levels are Distracting, etc.; Contaminants; Whole Body Vibration; Hazardous Equipment; Hazardous Situations; Standing; Using Hands on Objects, Tools, or Controls; Common Protective or Safety Attire; Degree of Automation; Pace Determined by Speed of Equipment
GOE Group/s: 06.02.03 Production Work: Machine Work, Wood
CIP Program/s: 480701 Woodworkers, General; 480703 Cabinet Maker and Millworker
Related DOT Job/s: 669.682-026 CHUCKING-AND-SAWING-MACHINE OPERATOR; 669.682-030 CORNER-BRACE-BLOCK-MACHINE OPERATOR

92305 HEAD SAWYERS. OOH Title/s: Woodworking Occupations
Operate head saws and feed carriages to saw logs into rough cants or boards from heading bolts. Sets dogs and adjusts carriage blocks to align log for sawing. Sets specified depth of cut and activates carriage that moves log against saw blade. Adjusts setting of carriage blocks as needed. Starts saw to cut log. Starts mechanical log turner or activates automatic log turner to turn log over on carriage for subsequent cuts. Starts conveyor that automatically transfers log to log carriage system, or starts mechanical loader arms that place log on carriage. Observes exposed face of log after first cut to determine grade and size of next cut. Changes saw blades.
Yearly Earnings: $16,328
Education: Moderate-term O-J-T
Knowledge: None above average
Abilities: Auditory Attention
Skills: Operation and Control
General Work Activities: Performing General Physical Activities; Handling and Moving Objects; Controlling Machines and Processes
Job Characteristics: Sounds, Noise Levels are Distracting, etc.; Very Hot; Contaminants; Whole Body Vibration; Hazardous Equipment; Hazardous Situations; Standing; Common Protective or Safety Attire; Degree of Automation; Pace Determined by Speed of Equipment
GOE Group/s: 06.02.03 Production Work: Machine Work, Wood

CIP Program/s: 480701 Woodworkers, General; 480703 Cabinet Maker and Millworker
Related DOT Job/s: 667.662-010 HEAD SAWYER; 667.682-034 HEAD SAWYER, AUTOMATIC; 667.682-038 HEADING-SAW OPERATOR

92308 SAWING MACHINE OPERATORS AND TENDERS. OOH Title/s: Woodworking Occupations

Operate or tend wood-sawing machines, such as circular saws, band saws, multiple-blade sawing machines, scroll saws, ripsaws, equalizer saws, power saws, and crozer machines. Duties include sawing logs to specifications; cutting lumber to specified dimensions; sawing curved or irregular designs; trimming edges and removing defects from lumber; or cutting grooves, bevel, and miter according to specifications or work orders. Operates and tends saws and machines to cut stock and to adjust machine speed and tension, moving levers and handwheels. Guides workpiece against saw, or saw over workpiece, or operates automatic feeding device to guide cuts. Operates panelboard of saw and conveyor system to cut stock to specified dimensions and to move stock through process. Trims defects from stock or workpiece to straighten rough edges of lumber, using circular power saw. Turns knobs, handwheels, setscrews, and panel controls, or uses hand tools to position and adjust cutting stops and guides. Adjusts saw blades by turning handwheels; pressing pedals, levers, and panel buttons; or using wrenches and rulers. Observes approaching lumber on conveyor to determine cut that will produce highest grade. Determines sawing blade, type and grade of stock needed, and cutting procedures, according to work order or supervisor's instructions. Mounts and bolts sawing blade or attachments to machine shaft, and turns handwheels to set blade tension. Positions and clamps stock on table, conveyor, or carriage, using hoists, guides, stops, dogs, wedges, and wrench. Moves machine table to specified angle and height by turning handwheels, cranks, or knobs. Measures workpiece to mark for cuts and to verify accuracy of cuts, using ruler, square, or caliper rule. Clears machine jams, using hand tools. Unclamps and removes finished workpiece from table. Sharpens blades or replaces defective or worn blades and bands, using hand tools. Inspects stock for imperfections, and estimates grade or quality of stock or workpiece. Lubricates and cleans machines, using wrench, grease gun, and solvents. Unloads and rolls logs from truck to sawmill deck or to carriage, or moves logs in pond, using pike pole. Counts, sorts, and stacks finished workpieces and disposes of waste material.
Yearly Earnings: $16,328
Education: Moderate-term O-J-T
Knowledge: Production and Processing; Building and Construction; Mechanical
Abilities: Category Flexibility; Perceptual Speed; Spatial Orientation; Arm-Hand Steadiness; Manual Dexterity; Control Precision; Multilimb Coordination; Response Orientation; Rate Control; Wrist-Finger Speed; Speed of Limb Movement; Static Strength; Explosive Strength; Dynamic Strength; Trunk Strength; Stamina; Extent Flexibility; Dynamic Flexibility; Gross Body Coordination; Gross Body Equilibrium; Peripheral Vision; Depth Perception
Skills: Equipment Maintenance
General Work Activities: Performing General Physical Activities; Handling and Moving Objects
Job Characteristics: Sounds, Noise Levels are Distracting, etc.; Very Hot; Extremely Bright or Inadequate Lighting; Contaminants; Whole Body Vibration; Hazardous Conditions; Hazardous Equipment; Hazardous Situations; Standing; Walking or Running; Keeping or Regaining Balance; Making Repetitive Motions; Common Protective or Safety Attire; Specialized Protective or Safety Attire; Degree of Automation; Pace Determined by Speed of Equipment
GOE Group/s: 03.04.02 Elemental Work: Plants and Animals: Forestry and Logging; 05.05.08 Craft Technology: Woodworking; 06.02.02 Production Work: Machine Work, Metal and Plastics; 06.02.03 Production Work: Machine Work, Wood; 06.04.03 Elemental Work: Industrial: Machine Work, Wood; 06.04.09 Elemental Work: Industrial: Machine Work, Assorted Materials; 06.04.40 Elemental Work: Industrial: Loading, Moving, Hoisting, and Conveying
CIP Program/s: 480701 Woodworkers, General; 480703 Cabinet Maker and Millworker
Related DOT Job/s: 665.685-046 SHAPING MACHINE TENDER; 667.382-010 STOCK GRADER; 667.482-014 POCKET CUTTER; 667.482-018 STOCK CUTTER; 667.485-010 SHINGLE SAWYER; 667.662-014 MACHINE-TANK OPERATOR; 667.682-010 BAND-SCROLL-SAW OPERATOR; 667.682-014 BOTTOM-SAW OPERATOR; 667.682-018 CORNER-TRIMMER OPERATOR; 667.682-022 CUT-OFF-SAW OPERATOR I; 667.682-026 EDGER, AUTOMATIC; 667.682-030 GANG SAWYER; 667.682-042 JIGSAW OPERATOR; 667.682-046 PACKAGER, HEAD; 667.682-050 PONY EDGER; 667.682-054 RADIAL-ARM-SAW OPERATOR; 667.682-058 RESAW OPERATOR; 667.682-062 RIP-AND-GROOVE-MACHINE OPERATOR; 667.682-066 RIPSAW OPERATOR; 667.682-070 SHAKE SAWYER; 667.682-074 STAVE-BOLT EQUALIZER; 667.682-078 STAVE-LOG-CUT-OFF SAW OPERATOR; 667.682-082 STOCK-PATCH SAWYER; 667.682-086 VARIETY-SAW OPERATOR; 667.682-090 LOG-CUT-OFF SAWYER, AUTOMATIC; 667.682-094 TRIMMER SAWYER; 667.685-010 BAND-SAW OPERATOR; 667.685-014 BAND-SAW OPERATOR; 667.685-018 BEADING SAWYER; 667.685-022 BOLTER; 667.685-026 BUZZSAW OPERATOR; 667.685-030 COB SAWYER; 667.685-034 CUT-OFF SAWYER, LOG; 667.685-038 DOWEL POINTER; 667.685-042 KERFER-MACHINE OPERATOR; 667.685-046 SAWYER, CORK SLABS; 667.685-050 SHINGLE TRIMMER; 667.685-054 SLASHER OPERATOR; 667.685-058 STAVE-LOG-RIPSAW OPERATOR; 667.685-062 STAVE-SAW OPERATOR; 667.685-066 TURNING-MACHINE OPERATOR; 667.685-070 AUTOMATIC BANDSAW TENDER; 667.685-074 CUT-OFF-SAW OPERATOR II; 667.687-018 SAWMILL WORKER; 669.682-034 CROZE-MACHINE OPERATOR; 669.682-070 UTILITY OPERATOR; 669.685-026 CIRCLE-CUTTING-SAW OPERATOR

92311 WOODWORKING MACHINE SETTERS AND SET-UP OPERATORS, EXCEPT SAWING. OOH Title/s: Woodworking Occupations

Set up or set up and operate woodworking machines, such as lathes, drill presses, sanders, shapers, and planing machines, to perform woodworking operations. Exclude sawing machine setters and set-up operators. Installs knives, sanding apparatus, cams, cutting heads, bits, chisels, and blades, using hand tools. Attaches and adjusts guides, stops, clamps, chucks, and feed mechanisms, using hand tools. Starts machine and feeds stock into machine through feed mechanisms or conveyors. Monitors operation of automatic machines and makes adjustments as needed to correct problems and ensure conformance to specifications. Examines blueprints, drawings, and work orders to determine characteristics of finished item, materials to be used, and machine set-up requirements. Adjusts machine table or cutting devices to produce specified cut or operation. Pushes or holds workpiece against, under, or through cutting, boring, or shaping mechanism. Selects knives, sanding apparatus, cams, cutting heads, bits, chisels, and blades. Mounts or clamps stock onto machine. Removes and replaces worn machine parts, knives, bits, belts, and sandpaper. Examines workpiece visually, by touch, or using tape rule, calipers, or gauges to ensure product meets desired standards. Unclamps and removes workpiece from machine, and stacks workpiece on pallet or in box. Sharpens knives, bits, and other cutting and shaping tools. Cleans product, machine, or work area, using rags and air hose.
Yearly Earnings: $16,276
Education: Moderate-term O-J-T

Knowledge: Mechanical
Abilities: Arm-Hand Steadiness; Manual Dexterity; Finger Dexterity; Control Precision; Rate Control; Reaction Time; Wrist-Finger Speed; Dynamic Strength; Dynamic Flexibility
Skills: Installation; Operation Monitoring; Operation and Control
General Work Activities: Handling and Moving Objects; Controlling Machines and Processes
Job Characteristics: Hazardous Equipment; Hazardous Situations; Bending or Twisting the Body; Making Repetitive Motions; Common Protective or Safety Attire; Degree of Automation; Pace Determined by Speed of Equipment
GOE Group/s: 05.05.08 Craft Technology: Woodworking; 05.10.01 Crafts: Structural; 06.01.02 Production Technology: Machine Set-up; 06.02.03 Production Work: Machine Work, Wood; 06.02.20 Production Work: Machine Assembling
CIP Program/s: 470402 Gunsmith; 480701 Woodworkers, General; 480703 Cabinet Maker and Millworker
Related DOT Job/s: 662.682-010 MOLDING SANDER; 662.682-014 MULTIPLE-DRUM SANDER; 663.380-010 KNIFE SETTER; 664.382-010 SWING-TYPE-LATHE OPERATOR; 664.382-018 TRIMMING MACHINE SET-UP OPERATOR; 664.662-010 VENEER-LATHE OPERATOR; 665.382-010 CHUCKING-MACHINE OPERATOR; 665.382-018 WOOD-CARVING-MACHINE OPERATOR; 665.482-014 MORTISING-MACHINE OPERATOR; 665.682-010 DOWEL-MACHINE OPERATOR; 665.682-018 MOLDER OPERATOR; 665.682-022 PLANER OPERATOR; 665.682-026 PROFILE-SHAPER OPERATOR, AUTOMATIC; 665.682-030 ROUTER OPERATOR; 665.682-034 SHAPER OPERATOR; 665.682-038 VENEER JOINTER; 665.682-042 JOINTER OPERATOR; 666.382-010 BORING-MACHINE OPERATOR; 669.280-010 MACHINE SETTER; 669.360-010 CHECKERING-MACHINE ADJUSTER; 669.380-018 PIPE-AND-TANK FABRICATOR; 669.382-010 DADO OPERATOR; 669.382-014 RAFTER-CUTTING-MACHINE OPERATOR; 669.382-018 TENONER OPERATOR; 669.382-022 MULTI-PURPOSE MACHINE OPERATOR; 669.382-026 TURNING MACHINE SET-UP OPERATOR; 669.662-010 BOX-BLANK-MACHINE OPERATOR; 669.682-038 DOUBLE-END-TRIMMER-AND-BORING-MACHINE OPERATOR; 669.682-042 DOWEL-INSERTING-MACHINE OPERATOR; 669.682-058 NAILING-MACHINE OPERATOR; 692.380-010 SET-UP MECHANIC; 761.682-018 SPINDLE CARVER

92314 WOODWORKING MACHINE OPERATORS AND TENDERS, EXCEPT SAWING. OOH Title/s: Woodworking Occupations

Operate or tend woodworking machines, such as drill presses, lathes, shapers, routers, sanders, planers, and wood-nailing machines to perform woodworking operations. Exclude sawyers. Starts machine, adjusts controls, and moves lever or depresses pedal to bore, shape, smooth, shave, chip, slice or cut woodstock. Moves lever to engage hydraulic lift to press woodstock into desired form, allows for drying time, and removes. Readjusts and realigns guides of sanding, cutting, or boring machines to correct defects in finished product, using hand tools. Installs and adjusts blades, cutter heads, boring bits, or sanding belts in machines, according to workpiece, machine function, and specifications, using hand tools. Selects knives, blades, cutter heads, boring bits, or sanding belts, according to workpiece, machine function, and specifications. Places or secures woodstock against guide or into holding device prior to feeding into machine. Examines blueprints, drawings, or samples to determine size, type, and setting of machine tools, stops, jigs, and guides to use. Places water-soaked woodstock into form under hydraulic lift to shape for use in making such items as musical instruments. Examines finished workpiece for smoothness, shape, angle, depth of cut, and conformity to specifications, visually and using hands, rule, or other gauges. Examines raw woodstock for defects and to ensure conformity to size and other specification standards. Examines rollers, sanding belts, knives, cutting or boring devises, and conveyor mechanisms, and sharpens or replaces worn parts, using hand tools. Cleans machines, work station, or conveyor, using air hose, wax, solvents, brushes, and rags. Marks or otherwise identifies completed and inspected workpiece. Hand-stacks on pallet or conveyor or controls hoist to remove part or product from work station, following completion.
Yearly Earnings: $16,276
Education: Moderate-term O-J-T
Knowledge: Production and Processing; Building and Construction
Abilities: Visualization; Selective Attention; Arm-Hand Steadiness; Speed of Limb Movement; Static Strength; Trunk Strength; Stamina; Dynamic Flexibility; Gross Body Equilibrium
Skills: Testing; Operation Monitoring; Operation and Control; Product Inspection; Equipment Maintenance
General Work Activities: Handling and Moving Objects; Controlling Machines and Processes
Job Characteristics: Sounds, Noise Levels are Distracting, etc.; Contaminants; Whole Body Vibration; Hazardous Equipment; Hazardous Situations; Keeping or Regaining Balance; Using Hands on Objects, Tools, or Controls; Making Repetitive Motions; Common Protective or Safety Attire; Degree of Automation; Importance of Repeating Same Tasks; Pace Determined by Speed of Equipment
GOE Group/s: 06.02.03 Production Work: Machine Work, Wood; 06.02.09 Production Work: Machine Work, Assorted Materials; 06.02.18 Production Work: Equipment Operation, Assorted Materials Processing; 06.04.03 Elemental Work: Industrial: Machine Work, Wood; 06.04.09 Elemental Work: Industrial: Machine Work, Assorted Materials; 06.04.20 Elemental Work: Industrial: Machine Assembling; 06.04.23 Elemental Work: Industrial: Manual Work, Assembly Small Parts; 06.04.25 Elemental Work: Industrial: Manual Work, Wood; 06.04.34 Elemental Work: Industrial: Manual Work, Assorted Materials
CIP Program/s: 470402 Gunsmith; 480701 Woodworkers, General; 480703 Cabinet Maker and Millworker
Related DOT Job/s: 564.682-010 CHIPPING-MACHINE OPERATOR; 569.662-010 INCISING-MACHINE OPERATOR; 569.685-014 BENDER, MACHINE; 662.682-018 STROKE-BELT-SANDER OPERATOR; 662.685-010 CORK GRINDER; 662.685-014 CYLINDER-SANDER OPERATOR; 662.685-018 LAST SCOURER; 662.685-022 SANDING-MACHINE BUFFER; 662.685-026 SANDING-MACHINE TENDER; 662.685-030 SIZING-MACHINE TENDER; 662.685-034 SPEED-BELT-SANDER TENDER; 662.685-038 TURNING-SANDER TENDER; 662.685-042 WOOD-HEEL BACK-LINER; 663.585-010 CLIPPER, AUTOMATIC; 663.682-010 BARKER OPERATOR; 663.682-018 VENEER-SLICING-MACHINE OPERATOR; 663.685-014 EXCELSIOR-MACHINE TENDER; 663.685-018 MOLDING CUTTER; 663.685-022 PUNCHER; 663.685-026 ROUNDING-MACHINE TENDER; 663.685-030 SHAKE BACKBOARD NOTCHER; 663.685-034 SLICING-MACHINE TENDER; 663.685-038 SPLITTER TENDER; 663.685-042 SPLITTING-MACHINE TENDER; 663.685-046 STAVE-MACHINE TENDER; 663.685-050 VENEER CLIPPER; 664.382-014 WOOD-TURNING-LATHE OPERATOR; 664.682-010 BARREL-LATHE OPERATOR, INSIDE; 664.682-014 BARREL-LATHE OPERATOR, OUTSIDE; 664.682-018 SKIVING-MACHINE OPERATOR; 664.682-022 SPAR-MACHINE OPERATOR; 664.684-010 BOWL TURNER; 664.685-010 BRIAR CUTTER; 664.685-014 BUCKET CHUCKER; 664.685-018 COPY-LATHE TENDER; 664.685-022 FRAZER; 664.685-026 SHUTTLE SPOTTER; 664.685-034 TURNING LATHE TENDER; 665.382-014 LOCK-CORNER-MACHINE OPERATOR; 665.482-018 TIMBER-SIZER OPERATOR; 665.665-010 ROUGH PLANER TENDER; 665.682-014 HEADER; 665.685-010 BOTTOM-TURNING-LATHE TENDER; 665.685-014 END FRAZER; 665.685-018 PLOW-AND-BORING-MACHINE TENDER; 665.685-022 PLYWOOD-SCARFER TENDER; 665.685-026 SCOOPING-MACHINE TENDER; 665.685-030 STAVE JOINTER; 665.685-

034 STOCK CHECKERER II; 665.685-038 RODDING MACHINE TENDER; 665.685-042 ROUTER TENDER; 666.482-010 PULLEY-MORTISER OPERATOR; 666.582-010 PREFITTER, DOORS; 666.684-010 FRAMER; 666.685-010 STEMHOLE BORER; 666.685-014 BORING-MACHINE OPERATOR; 669.662-014 FRAME-TABLE OPERATOR; 669.662-018 TONGUE-AND-GROOVE-MACHINE OPERATOR; 669.682-010 ADZING-AND-BORING-MACHINE OPERATOR; 669.682-018 BUCKET TURNER; 669.682-022 CHUCKING-AND-BORING-MACHINE OPERATOR; 669.682-050 INLETTER; 669.682-054 LAST TRIMMER; 669.682-062 PLUGGING-MACHINE OPERATOR; 669.682-066 TIP INSERTER; 669.685-014 BASKET ASSEMBLER I; 669.685-018 BLIND-SLAT-STAPLING-MACHINE OPERATOR; 669.685-022 BOTTOM-HOOP DRIVER; 669.685-034 COAT-HANGER-SHAPER-MACHINE OPERATOR; 669.685-042 CORRUGATED-FASTENER DRIVER; 669.685-046 DOVETAIL-MACHINE OPERATOR; 669.685-054 END STAPLER; 669.685-062 HEADING-MACHINE OPERATOR; 669.685-066 NAILING-MACHINE OPERATOR, AUTOMATIC; 669.685-070 ROOF-TRUSS-MACHINE TENDER; 669.685-074 SLAT-BASKET MAKER, MACHINE; 669.685-078 SMOKING-PIPE DRILLER AND THREADER; 669.685-082 SQUEEZER OPERATOR; 669.685-094 TURNER; 669.685-102 GROOVER-AND-STRIPER OPERATOR; 669.685-106 PUNCH PRESS OPERATOR; 690.685-226 HEEL-NAILING-MACHINE OPERATOR; 739.684-066 FOOT-MITER OPERATOR; 739.685-034 SHANK THREADER; 761.682-010 LATHE SANDER; 761.682-014 SANDER, MACHINE; 761.684-030 SANDER; 761.684-034 SANDER, PORTABLE MACHINE; 761.684-054 TOUCH-UP CARVER

Printing, Binding, and Related Machine Setters and Operators

92512 OFFSET LITHOGRAPHIC PRESS SETTERS AND SET-UP OPERATORS. OOH Title/s: Printing Press Operators

Set up or set up and operate offset printing press, either sheet- or web-fed, to print single- and multicolor copy from lithographic plates. Examine job order to determine press operating time, quantity to be printed, and stock specifications. Examines job order to determine quantity to be printed, stock specifications, colors, and special printing instructions. Starts press and examines printed copy for ink density, position on paper, and registration. Makes adjustments to press throughout production run to maintain specific registration and color density. Installs and locks plate into position, using hand tools, to achieve pressure required for printing. Measures paper thickness and adjusts space between blanket and impression cylinders according to thickness of paper stock. Measures plate thickness and inserts packing sheets on plate cylinder to build up plate to printing height. Washes plate to remove protective gum coating. Fills ink and dampening solution fountains, and adjusts controls to regulate flow of ink and dampening solution to plate cylinder. Applies packing sheets to blanket cylinder to build up blanket thickness to diameter of plate cylinder. Loads paper into feeder or installs rolls of paper, adjusts feeder and delivery mechanisms, and unloads printed material from delivery mechanism. Removes and cleans plate and cylinders.

Yearly Earnings: $22,464
Education: Moderate-term O-J-T
Knowledge: Production and Processing; Mechanical
Abilities: None above average
Skills: Installation; Operation Monitoring; Operation and Control; Equipment Maintenance
General Work Activities: Controlling Machines and Processes; Guiding, Directing and Motivating Subordinates
Job Characteristics: Sounds, Noise Levels are Distracting, etc.; Standing; Degree of Automation; Pace Determined by Speed of Equipment
GOE Group/s: 05.05.13 Craft Technology: Printing
CIP Program/s: 480201 Graphic and Printing Equipment Operator, General; 480208 Printing Press Operator
Related DOT Job/s: 651.382-042 OFFSET-PRESS OPERATOR I; 651.382-046 OFFSET-PRESS-OPERATOR APPRENTICE

92515 LETTERPRESS SETTERS AND SET-UP OPERATORS. OOH Title/s: Printing Press Operators

Set up or set up and operate direct relief letterpresses, either sheet- or roll- (web) fed, to produce single- or multicolor printed material, such as newspapers, books, and periodicals. Moves controls to set or adjust ink flow, tension rollers, paper guides, and feed controls. Positions and installs printing plates, cylinder packing, die, and type forms in press, according to specifications, using hand tools. Loads, positions, and adjusts unprinted materials on holding fixtures or in feeding mechanism of press. Pushes buttons or moves controls to start printing press and control operation. Monitors feeding and printing operations to maintain specified operating levels and detect malfunctions. Mixes colors or inks and fills reservoirs. Dismantles and reassembles printing unit or parts, using hand tools, to repair, clean, maintain, or adjust press. Operates specially equipped presses and auxiliary equipment, such as cutting, folding, numbering, and pasting devices. Reads work orders and job specifications to select ink and paper stock. Inspects printed materials for irregularities such as off-level areas, variations in ink volume, register slippage, and poor color register. Records and maintains production logsheet. Directs and monitors activities of apprentices and feeding or stacking workers.

Yearly Earnings: $22,464
Education: Moderate-term O-J-T
Knowledge: None above average
Abilities: Perceptual Speed; Visual Color Discrimination
Skills: Installation; Operation Monitoring; Operation and Control; Product Inspection; Equipment Maintenance
General Work Activities: Guiding, Directing and Motivating Subordinates; Coaching and Developing Others
Job Characteristics: Hazardous Equipment; Standing; Using Hands on Objects, Tools, or Controls; Making Repetitive Motions; Degree of Automation; Importance of Repeating Same Tasks; Pace Determined by Speed of Equipment
GOE Group/s: 05.05.13 Craft Technology: Printing; 05.10.05 Crafts: Reproduction
CIP Program/s: 480201 Graphic and Printing Equipment Operator, General; 480208 Printing Press Operator
Related DOT Job/s: 651.362-010 CYLINDER-PRESS OPERATOR; 651.362-014 CYLINDER-PRESS-OPERATOR APPRENTICE; 651.362-018 PLATEN-PRESS OPERATOR; 651.362-022 PLATEN-PRESS-OPERATOR APPRENTICE; 651.362-030 WEB-PRESS OPERATOR; 651.362-034 WEB-PRESS-OPERATOR APPRENTICE; 651.382-034 TAB-CARD-PRESS OPERATOR

92519 ALL OTHER PRINTING PRESS SETTERS AND SET-UP OPERATORS. OOH Title/s: Printing Press Operators

All other printing press setters and set-up operators not classified separately above.

Yearly Earnings: $22,464
Education: Moderate-term O-J-T
GOE Group/s: 05.05.13 Craft Technology: Printing; 05.10.05 Crafts: Reproduction; 06.01.02 Production Technology: Machine Set-up; 06.02.09 Production Work: Machine Work, Assorted Materials

CIP Program/s: 480201 Graphic and Printing Equipment Operator, General; 480208 Printing Press Operator
Related DOT Job/s: 651.362-026 ROTOGRAVURE-PRESS OPERATOR; 651.382-010 ENGRAVING-PRESS OPERATOR; 651.382-030 STEEL-DIE PRINTER; 651.382-038 TRANSFER OPERATOR; 651.384-010 PLATEN BUILDER-UP; 651.682-010 FLEXOGRAPHIC-PRESS OPERATOR; 659.381-010 PLATE SETTER, FLEXOGRAPHIC PRESS

92522A DESIGN PRINTING MACHINE SETTERS AND SET-UP OPERATORS. OOH Title/s: Printing Press Operators

Set up or set up and operate machines to print designs on materials. Installs printing plates, cylinders, or rollers on machine, using hand tools and gauges. Adjusts feed guides, gauges, and rollers, using hand tools. Adjusts and changes gears, using hand tools. Fills reservoirs with paint or ink. Monitors machines and gauges to ensure and maintain standards. Mixes colors of paint according to formulas. Inspects product to detect defects. Cleans and lubricates equipment. Repairs or replaces worn or broken parts, using hand tools. Measures and records amount of product produced.
Yearly Earnings: $22,464
Education: Moderate-term O-J-T
Knowledge: None above average
Abilities: Multilimb Coordination; Rate Control; Dynamic Strength; Dynamic Flexibility; Gross Body Equilibrium; Visual Color Discrimination
Skills: Operation Monitoring; Equipment Maintenance; Repairing
General Work Activities: Handling and Moving Objects; Repairing and Maintaining Mechanical Equipment
Job Characteristics: Hazardous Equipment; Making Repetitive Motions; Degree of Automation; Pace Determined by Speed of Equipment
GOE Group/s: 06.02.02 Production Work: Machine Work, Metal and Plastics; 06.02.04 Production Work: Machine Work, Paper; 06.02.09 Production Work: Machine Work, Assorted Materials
CIP Program/s: 480201 Graphic and Printing Equipment Operator, General; 480208 Printing Press Operator
Related DOT Job/s: 651.382-014 LITHOGRAPH-PRESS OPERATOR, TINWARE; 651.382-026 PRINTER, PLASTIC; 652.382-010 CLOTH PRINTER; 652.662-014 WALLPAPER PRINTER I

92522B MARKING AND IDENTIFICATION PRINTING MACHINE SETTERS AND SET-UP OPERATORS. OOH Title/s: Printing Press Operators

Set up or set up and operate machines to print trademarks, labels, or multicolored identification symbols on materials. Adjusts machine as needed, using hand tools. Selects printing plates, dies, or type according to work order. Mounts printing plates, dies, or type onto machine. Mounts materials to be printed onto feed mechanisms and threads materials through guides on machine. Fills reservoirs with ink or specified coloring agents. Sets rate of flow of coloring agent and speed and spacing of materials to achieve desired product. Monitors printing process to detect machine malfunctions. Examines product to detect defects. Cleans machine and equipment, using solvent and rags.
Yearly Earnings: $22,464
Education: Moderate-term O-J-T
Knowledge: None above average
Abilities: Rate Control; Visual Color Discrimination
Skills: Operation Monitoring; Operation and Control
General Work Activities: None above average
Job Characteristics: Making Repetitive Motions; Degree of Automation; Pace Determined by Speed of Equipment
GOE Group/s: 06.02.09 Production Work: Machine Work, Assorted Materials; 06.04.37 Elemental Work: Industrial: Manual Work, Stamping, Marking, Labeling, and Ticketing
CIP Program/s: 480201 Graphic and Printing Equipment Operator, General; 480208 Printing Press Operator
Related DOT Job/s: 651.682-022 TIP PRINTER; 652.662-010 PRINTING-MACHINE OPERATOR, TAPE RULES; 652.682-010 BOX PRINTER; 652.682-026 STRIPING-MACHINE OPERATOR

92524 SCREEN PRINTING MACHINE SETTERS AND SET-UP OPERATORS. OOH Title/s: Printing Press Operators

Set up or set up and operate screen printing machines to print designs onto articles and materials, such as glass or plasticware, cloth, and paper. Sets and adjusts screws, belts, drive assemblies, pneumatic lifting mechanisms, and bolts on screen printing machine to specifications. Starts dyeing oven and sets thermostat to temperature specified for printing run. Reviews print order to determine settings and adjustments required to set up manually controlled or automatic screen printing machine or decorating equipment. Measures, aligns and positions screen and squeegee attachment, using gauge and hand tools. Determines from orders type and color of designs to print. Mixes paints according to formula, using bench mixer. Examines product for paint smears, position of design, or other defects and adjusts equipment. Compares ink or paint prepared for printing run with master color swatch to confirm accuracy of match. Inspects printing equipment and replaces damaged or defective parts, such as switches, pulleys, fixtures, screws, and bolts. Patrols printing area to monitor production activities and to detect problems, such as mechanical breakdowns or malfunctions. Counts and records quantities printed in production log. Trains workers in use of printing equipment and in quality standards.
Yearly Earnings: $22,464
Education: Moderate-term O-J-T
Knowledge: Production and Processing; Mechanical; Education and Training; Fine Arts
Abilities: Visual Color Discrimination
Skills: Instructing; Operation Monitoring; Operation and Control; Product Inspection; Equipment Maintenance; Troubleshooting; Repairing
General Work Activities: Inspecting Equipment, Structures, or Material; Controlling Machines and Processes; Repairing and Maintaining Mechanical Equipment; Teaching Others
Job Characteristics: Sounds, Noise Levels are Distracting, etc.; Contaminants; Hazardous Conditions; Hazardous Equipment; Degree of Automation
GOE Group/s: 06.01.02 Production Technology: Machine Set-up
CIP Program/s: 480201 Graphic and Printing Equipment Operator, General; 480208 Printing Press Operator; 480299 Graphic and Printing Equipment Operators, Other
Related DOT Job/s: 652.260-010 SECTION LEADER, SCREEN PRINTING; 652.380-010 DECORATING-EQUIPMENT SETTER; 979.360-010 SCREEN-PRINTING-EQUIPMENT SETTER

92525 BINDERY MACHINE SETTERS AND SET-UP OPERATORS. OOH Title/s: Bindery Workers

Set up or set up and operate machines that perform some or all of the following functions in order to produce books, magazines, pamphlets, catalogs, and other printed materials: gathering, folding, cutting, stitching, rounding and backing, supering, casing-in, lining, pressing, and trimming. Installs bindery machine devices, such as knives, guides, and clamps, to accommodate sheets, signatures, or books of specified sizes. Sets machine controls to adjust length and thickness of folds, stitches, or cuts, and to adjust speed and pressure. Mounts and secures rolls or reels of wire, cloth, paper, or other material onto machine spindles and fills paper feed. Positions and

clamps stitching heads on crossarms to space stitches to specified lengths. Starts machines and makes trial runs to verify accuracy of machine set-up. Observes and monitors machine operations to detect malfunctions and makes required adjustments. Fills glue pot and adjusts flow of glue and speed of conveyors. Threads wire into machine to load stitcher head for stapling. Reads work order to determine work instructions. Examines product samples for defects. Cleans and lubricates machinery parts and makes minor repairs. Removes books or products from machine and stacks them. Trains workers to set up, operate, and use automatic bindery machines. Records time spent on specific tasks and number of items produced, for daily production sheet. Manually stocks supplies such as signatures, books, or paper.
Yearly Earnings: $22,412
Education: Moderate-term O-J-T
Knowledge: Production and Processing
Abilities: Perceptual Speed; Arm-Hand Steadiness; Control Precision
Skills: None above average
General Work Activities: None above average
Job Characteristics: Standing; Using Hands on Objects, Tools, or Controls; Making Repetitive Motions; Importance of Repeating Same Tasks; Pace Determined by Speed of Equipment
GOE Group/s: 06.01.02 Production Technology: Machine Set-up; 06.02.04 Production Work: Machine Work, Paper; 06.02.09 Production Work: Machine Work, Assorted Materials; 06.02.20 Production Work: Machine Assembling
CIP Program/s: 480299 Graphic and Printing Equipment Operators, Other
Related DOT Job/s: 653.360-010 CASING-IN-LINE SETTER; 653.360-018 BINDERY-MACHINE SETTER; 653.382-010 FOLDING-MACHINE OPERATOR; 653.382-014 COLLATING-MACHINE OPERATOR; 653.662-010 STITCHING-MACHINE OPERATOR; 653.682-010 BOOK-SEWING-MACHINE OPERATOR II; 653.682-018 HEAD-BANDER-AND-LINER OPERATOR; 653.682-022 TINNING-MACHINE SET-UP OPERATOR

92529A EMBOSSING MACHINE SET-UP OPERATORS. OOH Title/s: Indirectly related to Printing Press Operators

Set up and operate embossing machines. Sets guides to hold cover in position and adjusts table height to obtain correct depth of impression. Starts machine to lower ram and impress cardboard. Stamps embossing design on workpiece, using heated work tools. Positions, installs, and locks embossed plate in chase and locks chase in bed of press. Makes impression of embossing to desired depth in composition on platen, trims off excess, and allows composition to harden. Sets sheets singly in gauge pins and starts press. Mixes embossing composition to putty-like consistency, spreads glue on platen, and applies thin pad of composition over glue. Scrapes high spots on counter die to prevent from puncturing paper. Cuts surface of cardboard leaving design or letters, using hand tools. Removes and stacks embossed covers.
Yearly Earnings: $22,412
Education: Moderate-term O-J-T
Knowledge: Production and Processing
Abilities: None above average
Skills: None above average
General Work Activities: None above average
Job Characteristics: Hazardous Equipment; Using Hands on Objects, Tools, or Controls; Making Repetitive Motions; Degree of Automation; Importance of Repeating Same Tasks; Pace Determined by Speed of Equipment
GOE Group/s: 05.10.05 Crafts: Reproduction; 06.02.04 Production Work: Machine Work, Paper
CIP Program/s: 480201 Graphic and Printing Equipment Operator, General; 480205 Mechanical Typesetter and Composer; 480208 Printing Press Operator
Related DOT Job/s: 659.382-010 EMBOSSER; 659.682-014 EMBOSSING-PRESS OPERATOR; 659.682-018 EMBOSSING-PRESS-OPERATOR APPRENTICE

92529B CASTING MACHINE SET-UP OPERATORS. OOH Title/s: Indirectly related to Printing Press Operators

Set up and operate machines to cast and assemble printing type. Sets up matrices in assembly stick by hand according to specifications. Starts machine and monitors operation for proper functioning. Stops machine when galley is full or when strip is completed. Positions composing stick to length of line specified in casting instructions. Inserts and locks galley or matrix case into place on machine. Places reel of controller paper on holder, threads around reels, and attaches to winding roll. Removes and stores assembly stick, controller reel, and matrix case. Forwards galley to appropriate personnel for proofing.
Yearly Earnings: $22,412
Education: Moderate-term O-J-T
Knowledge: None above average
Abilities: Manual Dexterity
Skills: Operation Monitoring
General Work Activities: None above average
Job Characteristics: Sounds, Noise Levels are Distracting, etc.; Hazardous Equipment; Standing; Using Hands on Objects, Tools, or Controls; Degree of Automation; Pace Determined by Speed of Equipment
GOE Group/s: 05.10.05 Crafts: Reproduction
CIP Program/s: 480201 Graphic and Printing Equipment Operator, General; 480205 Mechanical Typesetter and Composer
Related DOT Job/s: 654.382-010 CASTING-MACHINE OPERATOR; 654.582-010 TYPE-CASTING MACHINE OPERATOR

92529C PLATE FINISHERS. OOH Title/s: Prepress Workers

Set up and operate equipment to trim and mount electrotype or stereotype plates. Selects cutting position and sets controls of saws, milling machines, and routers following specifications. Operates cutting tools to shave and smooth plates to specified thickness. Operates plate-curving machine to cut plates to fit printing press. Mounts finished plates on wood or metal blocks, using hammer and nails or thermoplastic adhesive and heat press. Operates press to print proof of plate, observing printing quality. Rubs surface with finishing material to reveal unevenness. Taps plate with hammer and block to flatten until even. Examines plates with magnifier or microscope to detect flaws, using engraver's tools.
Yearly Earnings: $22,412
Education: Moderate-term O-J-T
Knowledge: Production and Processing
Abilities: Rate Control; Reaction Time; Explosive Strength; Dynamic Strength
Skills: None above average
General Work Activities: None above average
Job Characteristics: Sounds, Noise Levels are Distracting, etc.; Hazardous Equipment; Standing; Using Hands on Objects, Tools, or Controls; Making Repetitive Motions; Degree of Automation; Pace Determined by Speed of Equipment
GOE Group/s: 05.05.07 Craft Technology: Machining
CIP Program/s: 480201 Graphic and Printing Equipment Operator, General; 480206 Lithographer and Platemaker
Related DOT Job/s: 659.360-010 PLATE FINISHER

92529D ENGRAVER SET-UP OPERATORS. OOH Title/s: Prepress Workers

Set up and operate machines to transfer printing designs. Positions machine mechanisms and depresses levers to apply marks on roller. Aligns plate with markings on machine table and tacks to table. Adjusts and tightens levers in position, using hand tools. Turns screws to align machine components. Inserts mandrel through roller and lifts into position on machine. Determines ground setting according to weight of fabric, type of design, and colors in design. Measures depth of engraving and weighs diamond points, using gauges and scales. Examines marks on roller to verify alignment and detect defects. Records ground setting, length of roller, width of engraving, and circumference of roller on production sheet.
Yearly Earnings: $22,412
Education: Moderate-term O-J-T
Knowledge: Production and Processing
Abilities: Control Precision; Visual Color Discrimination
Skills: Operation and Control
General Work Activities: None above average
Job Characteristics: Sounds, Noise Levels are Distracting, etc.; Hazardous Equipment; Hazardous Situations; Degree of Automation; Importance of Repeating Same Tasks; Pace Determined by Speed of Equipment
GOE Group/s: 05.05.13 Craft Technology: Printing; 05.10.05 Crafts: Reproduction
CIP Program/s: 480201 Graphic and Printing Equipment Operator, General; 480206 Lithographer and Platemaker
Related DOT Job/s: 979.380-010 PANTOGRAPH SETTER; 979.382-014 ENGRAVER, MACHINE

92529E ALL OTHER PRINTING RELATED SETTERS AND SET-UP OPERATORS. OOH Title/s: Indirectly related to Printing Press Operators

All other printing related machine setters and set-up operators not classified separately above.
Yearly Earnings: $22,412
Education: Moderate-term O-J-T
GOE Group/s: 06.02.04 Production Work: Machine Work, Paper; 06.02.09 Production Work: Machine Work, Assorted Materials
CIP Program/s: 480201 Graphic and Printing Equipment Operator, General; 480208 Printing Press Operator
Related DOT Job/s: 649.682-046 TAG-PRESS OPERATOR; 659.682-010 CUT-AND-PRINT-MACHINE OPERATOR; 659.682-022 RULING-MACHINE SET-UP OPERATOR; 659.682-026 SIGN WRITER, MACHINE

92541 TYPESETTING AND COMPOSING MACHINE OPERATORS AND TENDERS. OOH Title/s: Prepress Workers

Operate or tend typesetting and composing equipment, such as phototypesetters, linotype or monotype keyboard machines, photocomposers, linocasters, and photoletterers. Exclude data entry keyers of computerized systems. Monitors machines and gauges to ensure and maintain standards. Mounts materials to be printed onto feed mechanisms and threads materials through guides on machine. Adjusts feed guides, gauges, and rollers, using hand tools. Installs printing plates, cylinders, or rollers on machine, using hand tools and gauges. Fills reservoirs with paint or ink. Selects printing plates, dies, or type according to work order. Adjusts and changes gears, using hand tools. Mixes colors of paint according to formulas. Inspects product to detect defects. Measures and records amount of product produced. Cleans and lubricates equipment. Repairs or replaces worn or broken parts, using hand tools.
Yearly Earnings: $20,228
Education: Moderate-term O-J-T
Knowledge: None above average
Abilities: Information Ordering; Arm-Hand Steadiness; Visual Color Discrimination
Skills: None above average
General Work Activities: None above average
Job Characteristics: Hazardous Equipment; Using Hands on Objects, Tools, or Controls; Degree of Automation; Importance of Repeating Same Tasks; Pace Determined by Speed of Equipment
GOE Group/s: 05.10.05 Crafts: Reproduction; 05.12.19 Elemental Work: Mechanical: Reproduction Services; 07.06.02 Clerical Machine Operation: Keyboard Machine Operation
CIP Program/s: 480201 Graphic and Printing Equipment Operator, General; 480205 Mechanical Typesetter and Composer; 480211 Computer Typography and Composition Equipment Operator
Related DOT Job/s: 650.582-010 LINOTYPE OPERATOR; 650.582-014 MONOTYPE-KEYBOARD OPERATOR; 650.582-018 PHOTOCOMPOSING-MACHINE OPERATOR; 650.582-022 PHOTOTYPESETTER OPERATOR; 650.682-010 EQUIPMENT MONITOR, PHOTOTYPESETTING; 650.685-010 TYPESETTING-MACHINE TENDER; 652.585-010 PHOTOLETTERING-MACHINE OPERATOR; 652.685-106 TYPE-PROOF REPRODUCER

92543 PRINTING PRESS MACHINE OPERATORS AND TENDERS. OOH Title/s: Printing Press Operators

Operate or tend various types of printing machines—such as offset lithographic presses, letter or letterset presses, and flexographic or gravure presses—to produce print on paper or other materials such as plastic, cloth, or rubber. Pushes buttons, turns handles, or moves controls and levers to start printing machine, or manually controls equipment operation. Turns, pushes, or moves controls to set and adjust speed, temperature, ink flow, and position and pressure tolerances of press. Selects and installs printing plates, rollers, screens, stencils, type, die, and cylinders in machine according to specifications, using hand tools. Loads, positions and adjusts unprinted materials on holding fixture or in loading and feeding mechanisms of press. Monitors feeding, printing, and racking processes of press to maintain specified operating levels and detect malfunctions. Reviews work order to determine ink, stock, and equipment needed for production. Monitors and controls operation of auxiliary equipment, such as cutters, folders, drying ovens, and sanders to assemble and finish product. Blends and tests paint, inks, stains, and solvents according to type of material being printed and work order specifications. Pours or spreads paint, ink, color compounds, and other materials into reservoirs, troughs, hoppers, or color holders of printing unit. Inspects and examines printed products for print clarity, color accuracy, conformance to specifications, and external defects. Removes printed materials from press, using handtruck, electric lift, or hoist, and transports them to drying, storage, or finishing areas. Cleans and lubricates printing machine and components (e.g., rollers, screens, typesetting, reservoirs) using oil, solvents, brushes, rags, and hoses. Dismantles and reassembles printing unit or parts, using hand and power tools, to repair, maintain, or adjust machine. Discards or corrects misprinted materials, using ink eradicators or solvents. Accepts orders, calculates and quotes prices, and receives payments from customers. Packs and labels cartons, boxes, or bins of finished products. Keeps daily time and materials usage reports and records identifying information printed on manufactured products and parts. Directs and monitors activities of workers feeding, inspecting, and tending printing machines and materials.
Yearly Earnings: $22,464
Education: Moderate-term O-J-T
Knowledge: Production and Processing

Abilities: Category Flexibility; Perceptual Speed; Visualization; Manual Dexterity; Finger Dexterity; Visual Color Discrimination
Skills: Installation; Testing; Operation Monitoring; Operation and Control; Product Inspection; Equipment Maintenance; Repairing; Management of Personnel Resources
General Work Activities: Controlling Machines and Processes; Repairing and Maintaining Mechanical Equipment
Job Characteristics: Supervise, Coach, Train Others; Degree of Automation; Pace Determined by Speed of Equipment
GOE Group/s: 05.05.13 Craft Technology: Printing; 05.10.05 Crafts: Reproduction; 06.02.02 Production Work: Machine Work, Metal and Plastics; 06.02.04 Production Work: Machine Work, Paper; 06.02.06 Production Work: Machine Work, Textiles; 06.02.09 Production Work: Machine Work, Assorted Materials; 06.02.18 Production Work: Equipment Operation, Assorted Materials Processing; 06.04.02 Elemental Work: Industrial: Machine Work, Metal and Plastics; 06.04.03 Elemental Work: Industrial: Machine Work, Wood; 06.04.04 Elemental Work: Industrial: Machine Work, Paper; 06.04.05 Elemental Work: Industrial: Machine Work, Fabric and Leather; 06.04.07 Elemental Work: Industrial: Machine Work, Rubber; 06.04.09 Elemental Work: Industrial: Machine Work, Assorted Materials; 06.04.21 Elemental Work: Industrial: Machine Work, Brushing, Spraying, and Coating; 06.04.37 Elemental Work: Industrial: Manual Work, Stamping, Marking, Labeling, and Ticketing
CIP Program/s: 480201 Graphic and Printing Equipment Operator, General; 480208 Printing Press Operator; 480299 Graphic and Printing Equipment Operators, Other
Related DOT Job/s: 651.582-010 PROOF-PRESS OPERATOR; 651.582-014 LITHOGRAPHIC-PROOFER APPRENTICE; 651.585-010 ASSISTANT-PRESS OPERATOR; 651.682-014 OFFSET-DUPLICATING-MACHINE OPERATOR; 651.682-018 STRIPER; 651.685-010 BAG PRINTER; 651.685-014 DESIGN PRINTER, BALLOON; 651.685-018 OFFSET-PRESS OPERATOR II; 651.685-022 PLATEN-PRESS FEEDER; 651.685-026 ASSISTANT PRESS OPERATOR, OFFSET; 652.462-010 RUBBER-PRINTING-MACHINE OPERATOR; 652.582-010 MARKER; 652.582-014 ROTARY-SCREEN-PRINTING-MACHINE OPERATOR; 652.662-018 PRINT-LINE OPERATOR; 652.682-014 EMBOSSOGRAPH OPERATOR; 652.682-018 SCREEN-PRINTING-MACHINE OPERATOR; 652.682-030 STAMPING-PRESS OPERATOR; 652.685-010 BACK TENDER, CLOTH PRINTING; 652.685-014 BINDING PRINTER; 652.685-018 CARTON MARKER, MACHINE; 652.685-026 DECORATING-MACHINE OPERATOR; 652.685-034 GLOVE PRINTER; 652.685-038 INK PRINTER; 652.685-046 MARKING-MACHINE OPERATOR; 652.685-050 MARKING-MACHINE OPERATOR; 652.685-054 NAME-PLATE STAMPER; 652.685-058 PRESS FEEDER; 652.685-062 PRINTER; 652.685-066 PRINTER, FLOOR COVERING; 652.685-070 PRINTER, MACHINE; 652.685-074 PRINTING-MACHINE OPERATOR, FOLDING RULES; 652.685-078 ROLLER OPERATOR; 652.685-082 STAMPER II; 652.685-090 STRIKE-OFF-MACHINE OPERATOR; 652.685-098 TICKETER; 652.685-102 WAD-PRINTING-MACHINE OPERATOR; 652.685-110 SYMBOL STAMPER, SEMICONDUCTOR PACKAGES; 659.662-010 PRINTER-SLOTTER OPERATOR; 979.362-010 INSTANT PRINT OPERATOR; 979.685-010 SILK-SCREEN PRINTER, MACHINE

92545 PHOTOENGRAVING AND LITHOGRAPHING MACHINE OPERATORS AND TENDERS. OOH Title/s: Prepress Workers

Operate or tend photoengraving and lithographing equipment, such as plate-graining, pantograph, roll-varnishing, and routing machines. Operates machinery such as film processors, graining machines, and varnishing equipment. Cuts excess metal and bevels edges of printing plates, using routing machine. Mounts finished plates on wood, synthetic, or metal blocks, either by hand or using automatic plate-mounting equipment. Immerses and turns printing roller in bath solutions to dissolve coating, develop image, and dye, using electric hoist. Grains printing plates by wet- or dry-sandblasting or using glass marbles. Paints over pinholes, scratches, and reference points on roller, using brush and acid-resistant paint. Applies acid-resistant ink to varnished copper roller, and examines for ink smears or cavities filled with ink. Copies printed materials, such as documents and drawings using blueprint machine. Maintains machinery in working order, such as automatic film processors and exposure machines. Rolls out and hammers used printing plates to remove gripper marks and bent corners. Examines printing plates with magnifier for uniformity, size, and structures of grain, and washes off excess sediment. Cuts printing plates from sheets of aluminum and zinc, using power shears. Examines finished blueprint for specified color, intensity, and sharpness of line.
Yearly Earnings: $22,464
Education: Moderate-term O-J-T
Knowledge: Production and Processing; Chemistry
Abilities: Visual Color Discrimination
Skills: Equipment Maintenance
General Work Activities: Controlling Machines and Processes; Repairing and Maintaining Mechanical Equipment
Job Characteristics: Degree of Automation; Pace Determined by Speed of Equipment
GOE Group/s: 05.10.05 Crafts: Reproduction; 06.02.02 Production Work: Machine Work, Metal and Plastics; 06.02.21 Production Work: Coating and Plating
CIP Program/s: 100103 Photographic Technologists and Technicians; 480201 Graphic and Printing Equipment Operator, General; 480206 Lithographer and Platemaker; 480299 Graphic and Printing Equipment Operators, Other
Related DOT Job/s: 971.685-010 ROLLER-PRINT TENDER; 972.384-014 PLATEMAKER, SEMICONDUCTOR PACKAGES; 972.682-010 PLATE GRAINER; 972.682-014 PLATE-GRAINER APPRENTICE; 979.382-022 PANTOGRAPHER; 979.682-014 BLUEPRINTING-MACHINE OPERATOR; 979.682-022 ROLLER VARNISHER; 979.682-026 ROUTER

92546 BINDERY MACHINE OPERATORS AND TENDERS. OOH Title/s: Bindery Workers

Operate or tend binding machines that round, back, case, line-stitch, press, fold, trim, or perform other binding operations on books and related articles. Exclude hand bindery workers and machine feeders and offbearers. Operates or tends machines that perform binding operations, such as pressing, folding, and trimming on books and related articles. Moves controls to adjust and activate bindery machine to meet specifications. Selects, loads, and adjusts workpieces and machine parts, using hand tools. Feeds books and related articles, such as periodicals and pamphlets, into binding machines, following specifications. Inserts illustrated pages, extra sheets, and collated sets into catalogs, periodicals, directories, and other printed products, and applies labels to envelopes, using hands or machine. Stitches or fastens endpapers or bindings, stitches signatures, and applies glue along binding edge of first and last signatures of books. Opens machine and removes and replaces damaged covers and books, using hand tools. Threads spirals in perforated holes of items to be bound, using spindle or rollers. Removes broken wire pieces from machine and loads machine with spool of wire. Punches holes in paper sheets and fastens sheets, signatures, or other material, using hand or machine punch or stapler. Examines printed material and related products for defects and to ensure conformance to specifications. Creases or compresses signatures before affixing covers, and places paper jackets on finished books. Applies materials on books or related articles, using machine. Removes printed material or finished products from machines or conveyor belts, and stacks material on pallets or skids. Rolls, bends, smooths, and folds sheets, using hands, and stacks sheets to be returned to binding machines. Wraps product in plastic,

using machine, and packs products in boxes. Maintains records of daily production, using specified forms. Cleans work area and maintains equipment and work stations, using hand tools.
Yearly Earnings: $22,412
Education: Moderate-term O-J-T
Knowledge: Production and Processing
Abilities: Arm-Hand Steadiness; Manual Dexterity; Control Precision; Rate Control; Speed of Limb Movement; Explosive Strength; Dynamic Strength; Trunk Strength; Dynamic Flexibility; Gross Body Equilibrium
Skills: Operation Monitoring; Equipment Maintenance
General Work Activities: Controlling Machines and Processes
Job Characteristics: Sounds, Noise Levels are Distracting, etc.; Contaminants; Whole Body Vibration; Hazardous Equipment; Hazardous Situations; Standing; Using Hands on Objects, Tools, or Controls; Making Repetitive Motions; Degree of Automation; Pace Determined by Speed of Equipment
GOE Group/s: 06.02.04 Production Work: Machine Work, Paper; 06.02.09 Production Work: Machine Work, Assorted Materials; 06.02.20 Production Work: Machine Assembling; 06.04.04 Elemental Work: Industrial: Machine Work, Paper; 06.04.09 Elemental Work: Industrial: Machine Work, Assorted Materials
CIP Program/s: 480299 Graphic and Printing Equipment Operators, Other
Related DOT Job/s: 653.682-014 COVERING-MACHINE OPERATOR; 653.685-010 BINDERY WORKER; 653.685-014 BOOK-SEWING-MACHINE OPERATOR I; 653.685-022 MAGAZINE REPAIRER; 653.685-026 ROUNDING-AND-BACKING-MACHINE OPERATOR; 653.685-030 SPIRAL BINDER; 692.685-146 SADDLE-AND-SIDE WIRE STITCHER

92549 ALL OTHER PRINTING, BINDING, AND RELATED MACHINE OPERATORS AND TENDERS.

OOH Title/s: Printing Press Operators; Prepress Workers

All other printing, binding, and related machine operators and tenders not classified separately above.
Yearly Earnings: $22,412
Education: Moderate-term O-J-T
GOE Group/s: 05.05.13 Craft Technology: Printing; 06.02.09 Production Work: Machine Work, Assorted Materials; 06.04.06 Elemental Work: Industrial: Machine Work, Textiles; 06.04.10 Elemental Work: Industrial: Equipment Operation, Metal Processing; 06.04.37 Elemental Work: Industrial: Manual Work, Stamping, Marking, Labeling, and Ticketing
CIP Program/s: 480201 Graphic and Printing Equipment Operator, General; 480205 Mechanical Typesetter and Composer; 480208 Printing Press Operator
Related DOT Job/s: 652.665-014 STRICKLER ATTENDANT; 652.685-042 KEYING-MACHINE OPERATOR; 652.685-086 STENCIL-MACHINE OPERATOR; 652.685-094 TICKET PRINTER AND TAGGER; 659.685-018 SHOTGUN-SHELL-REPRINTING-UNIT OPERATOR; 659.685-022 TRANSFER-MACHINE OPERATOR; 659.685-026 MILL STENCILER; 979.382-010 CLAMPER; 979.682-010 BLOCKER I

Textile and Related Machine Setters, Operators, and Related Workers

92702 TEXTILE MACHINE SETTERS AND SET-UP OPERATORS.

OOH Title/s: Textile Machinery Operators

Set up or set up and operate textile machines that perform textile processing and manufacturing operations, such as winding, twisting, knitting, weaving, bonding, and stretching. Installs, levels, and aligns components—such as gears, chains, guides, dies, cutters, and needles—to set up machinery for operation. Adjusts heating mechanisms, tension, and speed of machine operation to produce product meeting desired specifications. Starts machine, monitors operation, makes adjustments as needed, and stops machine when specified amount of product has been produced. Threads yarn, thread, and fabric through guides, needles, and rollers of machine. Operates machine for test run to verify adjustments and to obtain sample of product. Studies guides, samples, charts, and specification sheets, or confers with supervisor or engineering staff to determine set-up requirements. Inspects product to ensure product meets specifications and to determine need for machine adjustment. Inspects machinery to determine adjustments or repairs needed. Repairs or replaces worn or defective parts or components, using hand tools. Cleans, oils, and lubricates machines, using air hose, cleaning solutions, rags, oilcan, and grease gun.
Yearly Earnings: $13,572
Education: Moderate-term O-J-T
Knowledge: Mechanical
Abilities: Arm-Hand Steadiness; Finger Dexterity; Control Precision; Reaction Time; Extent Flexibility; Gross Body Equilibrium; Hearing Sensitivity; Auditory Attention; Sound Localization
Skills: Installation; Testing; Operation Monitoring; Operation and Control; Product Inspection; Equipment Maintenance; Troubleshooting; Repairing
General Work Activities: Controlling Machines and Processes; Repairing and Maintaining Mechanical Equipment
Job Characteristics: Cramped Work Space, Awkward Positions; Hazardous Equipment; Hazardous Situations; Standing; Kneeling, Crouching, or Crawling; Keeping or Regaining Balance; Bending or Twisting the Body; Making Repetitive Motions; Degree of Automation; Pace Determined by Speed of Equipment
GOE Group/s: 06.01.02 Production Technology: Machine Set-up; 06.01.03 Production Technology: Machine Set-up and Operation; 06.01.04 Production Technology: Precision Hand Work; 06.02.06 Production Work: Machine Work, Textiles; 06.02.18 Production Work: Equipment Operation, Assorted Materials Processing; 06.02.23 Production Work: Manual Work, Assembly Small Parts; 06.02.27 Production Work: Manual Work, Textile, Fabric and Leather
CIP Program/s: 470303 Industrial Machinery Maintenance and Repair
Related DOT Job/s: 580.380-010 FIXER, BOARDING ROOM; 585.380-010 CUTTING-MACHINE FIXER; 589.360-010 BONDING-MACHINE SETTER; 681.380-010 ROPE-MACHINE SETTER; 683.260-010 BRAID-PATTERN SETTER; 683.260-014 CARPET-LOOM FIXER; 683.260-018 LOOM FIXER; 683.360-010 LOOM CHANGER; 683.381-010 CHAIN BUILDER, LOOM CONTROL; 683.680-010 HARNESS PLACER; 683.680-014 HEDDLES TIER, JACQUARD LOOM; 683.682-018 DRAWING-IN-MACHINE TENDER; 685.360-010 KNITTER MECHANIC; 685.380-010 LINK-AND-LINK-KNITTING-MACHINE OPERATOR; 685.381-010 JACQUARD-PLATE MAKER; 685.680-010 THREADER; 689.260-010 MACHINE FIXER; 689.260-014 QUILTER FIXER; 689.260-018 SECTION LEADER AND MACHINE SETTER; 689.260-022 SECTION LEADER AND MACHINE SETTER, POLISHING; 689.260-026 KNITTING-MACHINE FIXER; 689.280-010 BOX TENDER; 689.360-010 NEEDLE-LOOM SETTER; 689.362-010 NEEDLE-FELT-MAKING-MACHINE OPERATOR; 689.380-010 EMBLEM DRAWER-IN; 689.382-010 AUTOMATIC-PAD-MAKING-MACHINE OPERATOR; 689.662-010 NEEDLE-LOOM OPERATOR

92705 TEXTILE MACHINE OPERATORS AND TENDERS—WINDING, TWISTING, KNITTING, WEAVING, AND CUTTING. OOH Title/s: Textile Machinery Operators

Operate or tend textile machines that perform textile processing and manufacturing operations—such as winding, twisting, knitting, weaving, and cutting—using knowledge of machine functions. Exclude textile sewing machine operators and tenders. Starts machine and observes operation to detect malfunctions or defects, such as breaking or twisting of material or thread. Adjusts machine controls, such as width or tension guides, to keep operations within specifications. Mounts, positions, or places roll of material, yarn, line, or bobbin of thread on machine, and threads through guides and rollers. Sets controls on machine according to width, length, or other specifications, and sets counter to record yardage used. Operates machine to cut material into specified lengths. Examines and inspects yarn, lace, or other material for defects, dirt, and conformance to color and size specifications. Measures or weighs product for conformance to specifications, using ruler, measuring tape, or scale. Removes or doffs full packages, rolls, loom beams, spools, or reels from machine, manually or using hoist. Cuts fabric, thread, yarn, or other material to remove defects, or separates from machine using scissors or knife. Replaces defective or worn shuttles, tension springs, needles, or cutting blades, using hand tools. Pieces up or ties breaks in yarn, filling, roving, or sliver. Records production information, such as lot or style number, yardage, number of defects and machine stops, and types of defects. Notifies supervisor or machine fixer of defects or machine malfunctions. Stacks or wraps and packs product for further processing or shipping. Transports product to and from work area, using handtruck. Cleans and lubricates machines.

Yearly Earnings: $13,572

Education: Moderate-term O-J-T

Knowledge: Production and Processing

Abilities: Arm-Hand Steadiness; Control Precision; Rate Control; Gross Body Equilibrium; Visual Color Discrimination; Hearing Sensitivity

Skills: Operation and Control

General Work Activities: None above average

Job Characteristics: Sounds, Noise Levels are Distracting, etc.; Hazardous Equipment; Hazardous Situations; Standing; Using Hands on Objects, Tools, or Controls; Bending or Twisting the Body; Degree of Automation; Importance of Repeating Same Tasks; Pace Determined by Speed of Equipment

GOE Group/s: 06.02.02 Production Work: Machine Work, Metal and Plastics; 06.02.04 Production Work: Machine Work, Paper; 06.02.05 Production Work: Machine Work, Leather and Fabrics; 06.02.06 Production Work: Machine Work, Textiles; 06.02.09 Production Work: Machine Work, Assorted Materials; 06.02.27 Production Work: Manual Work, Textile, Fabric and Leather; 06.04.04 Elemental Work: Industrial: Machine Work, Paper; 06.04.05 Elemental Work: Industrial: Machine Work, Fabric and Leather; 06.04.06 Elemental Work: Industrial: Machine Work, Textiles; 06.04.07 Elemental Work: Industrial: Machine Work, Rubber; 06.04.08 Elemental Work: Industrial: Machine Work, Stone, Glass, and Clay; 06.04.09 Elemental Work: Industrial: Machine Work, Assorted Materials; 06.04.13 Elemental Work: Industrial: Equipment Operation, Rubber, Plastics, Glass Processing; 06.04.16 Elemental Work: Industrial: Equipment Operation, Textile, Fabric, and Leather Processing; 06.04.27 Elemental Work: Industrial: Manual Work, Textile, Fabric and Leather; 06.04.38 Elemental Work: Industrial: Wrapping and Packaging

CIP Program/s: 000000 NO CIP ASSIGNED

Related DOT Job/s: 551.585-022 ROTARY-CUTTER OPERATOR; 554.665-010 CALENDER-WIND-UP TENDER; 557.685-034 TAKE-UP OPERATOR; 580.685-034 HOOKING-MACHINE OPERATOR; 580.685-066 TENTER-FRAME OPERATOR; 581.685-074 WINDING-RACK OPERATOR; 583.685-122 TRIMMING-MACHINE OPERATOR; 585.565-010 CORDUROY-CUTTER OPERATOR; 585.685-026 CLOTH TRIMMER, MACHINE; 585.685-046 FUR-CUTTING-MACHINE OPERATOR; 585.685-062 LABEL PINKER; 585.685-086 ROUNDING-MACHINE OPERATOR; 585.685-102 SHEARING-MACHINE OPERATOR; 585.685-118 STRIPPING CUTTER AND WINDER; 585.685-122 SWEATBAND SEPARATOR; 589.685-086 ROLLING-DOWN-MACHINE OPERATOR; 680.685-022 CHOPPED-STRAND OPERATOR; 680.685-042 FINISHER-CARD TENDER; 680.685-094 SLIVER-LAP-MACHINE TENDER; 680.685-102 STAPLE CUTTER; 681.485-010 ROVING WINDER, FIBERGLASS; 681.585-010 BEAMER; 681.585-014 BOBBIN WINDER, MACHINE; 681.585-018 SINGE WINDER; 681.682-010 DRESSER TENDER; 681.682-014 ROPE-MAKER, ROPEWALK; 681.682-018 RUG SETTER, AXMINSTER; 681.685-010 BALL-WARPER TENDER; 681.685-014 BALLING-MACHINE OPERATOR; 681.685-018 BEAM-WARPER TENDER, AUTOMATIC; 681.685-022 BOBBIN WINDER, MACHINE; 681.685-026 BOBBIN WINDER, SEWING MACHINE; 681.685-030 CARDING-MACHINE OPERATOR; 681.685-034 COILER; 681.685-038 COVERING-MACHINE OPERATOR; 681.685-046 DOUBLING-MACHINE OPERATOR; 681.685-058 LONG-CHAIN BEAMER; 681.685-062 LOOM-WINDER TENDER; 681.685-066 PRECISE WINDER; 681.685-070 QUILLER OPERATOR; 681.685-074 QUILLING-MACHINE OPERATOR, AUTOMATIC; 681.685-078 REELING-MACHINE OPERATOR; 681.685-082 ROPE MAKER, MACHINE; 681.685-086 ROPE-LAYING-MACHINE OPERATOR; 681.685-090 RUBBER-THREAD SPOOLER; 681.685-094 SELVAGE-MACHINE OPERATOR; 681.685-098 SKEIN WINDER; 681.685-102 SKEINER; 681.685-106 SPEEDER TENDER; 681.685-110 SPINNING-MACHINE TENDER; 681.685-114 SPOOLING-MACHINE OPERATOR; 681.685-118 STRAND-FORMING-MACHINE OPERATOR; 681.685-122 THREAD WINDER, AUTOMATIC; 681.685-126 TWISTER; 681.685-130 TWISTER TENDER; 681.685-134 TWISTER TENDER, PAPER; 681.685-138 UPTWISTER TENDER; 681.685-142 WARP SPOOLER; 681.685-146 WARPER; 681.685-150 WINDER OPERATOR, AUTOMATIC; 681.685-154 YARN WINDER; 681.685-158 YARN-TEXTURING-MACHINE OPERATOR I; 682.685-010 SPINNER, FRAME; 682.685-014 SPINNER, MULE; 683.582-010 CARD CUTTER, JACQUARD; 683.662-010 JACQUARD-LOOM WEAVER; 683.665-010 WEAVER, NEEDLE LOOM; 683.682-010 CARPET WEAVER; 683.682-014 CARPET WEAVER, JACQUARD LOOM; 683.682-022 JACQUARD-LOOM WEAVER; 683.682-026 LEVERS-LACE MACHINE OPERATOR; 683.682-030 PLUSH WEAVER; 683.682-034 WEAVER; 683.682-038 WEAVER; 683.682-042 WEAVER APPRENTICE; 683.682-046 WEAVER, NARROW FABRICS; 683.682-050 WEAVER, TIRE CORD; 683.685-030 THREADING-MACHINE TENDER; 683.685-038 WEAVER, AXMINSTER; 684.682-010 KNITTING-MACHINE OPERATOR, FULL-FASHIONED HOSIERY, AUTOMATIC; 684.685-010 SEAMLESS-HOSIERY KNITTER; 685.382-010 SURGICAL-ELASTIC KNITTER, HAND FRAME; 685.665-010 KNITTER, FULL-FASHIONED GARMENT; 685.665-014 KNITTING-MACHINE OPERATOR; 685.665-018 WARP-KNITTING-MACHINE OPERATOR; 685.682-010 CROCHET-MACHINE OPERATOR; 685.684-010 PATTERN WHEEL MAKER; 685.685-010 KNITTING-MACHINE OPERATOR; 685.687-018 LACE WINDER; 686.462-010 DIE-CUTTING-MACHINE OPERATOR, AUTOMATIC; 686.585-010 CUTTING-MACHINE OPERATOR; 686.662-010 RUG CUTTER; 686.682-010 BAND-SAW OPERATOR; 686.682-014 BIAS-CUTTING-MACHINE OPERATOR; 686.682-018 FELT-CUTTING-MACHINE OPERATOR; 686.685-010 CHIN-STRAP CUTTER; 686.685-014 CONTINUOUS PILLOWCASE CUTTER; 686.685-018 CUFF CUTTER; 686.685-022 CUTTER; 686.685-026 FELT CUTTER; 686.685-042 PINKING-MACHINE OPERATOR; 686.685-058 SCALLOP CUTTER, MACHINE; 686.685-066 STRIP-CUTTING-MACHINE OPERATOR; 686.685-074 WELT-TRIMMING-MACHINE OPERATOR; 689.585-010 BLANKET-CUTTING-MACHINE OPERATOR; 689.665-014 THREAD-

CUTTER TENDER; 689.685-014 BLOCKER; 689.685-042 CLOTH REELER; 689.685-046 CLOTH WINDER; 689.685-050 CLOTH-DOUBLING-AND-WINDING-MACHINE OPERATOR; 689.685-066 FISHING-LINE-WINDING-MACHINE OPERATOR; 689.685-086 LABEL-CUTTING-AND-FOLDING-MACHINE OPERATOR, AUTOMATIC; 689.685-114 ROLLING-MACHINE TENDER; 690.682-026 CUTTER, BARREL DRUM; 692.685-250 WINDOW-SHADE CUTTER AND MOUNTER; 699.682-010 BINDING CUTTER, SYNTHETIC CLOTH; 699.682-014 CUTTER; 739.685-030 PAINT-ROLLER WINDER; 759.664-010 BRAIDER SETTER; 781.682-010 TRIMMER, MACHINE; 781.684-038 NYLON-HOT-WIRE CUTTER; 784.685-010 BAND-AND-CUFF CUTTER; 920.685-070 LACE-ROLLER OPERATOR

92708 EXTRUDING AND FORMING MACHINE OPERATORS AND TENDERS, SYNTHETIC OR GLASS FIBERS. OOH Title/s: Textile Machinery Operators

Operate or tend machines that extrude and form continuous filaments from synthetic materials, such as liquid polymer, rayon, and fiberglass, preparatory to further processing. Operates or tends machines that extrude and form filaments from synthetic materials. Loads and adjusts materials into extruding and forming machines, using hand tools. Moves controls to activate and adjust extruding and forming machines. Presses buttons to stop machine when process is completed or malfunction detected. Observes machine operation, control board, and gauges to detect malfunctions. Removes excess or completed filament from machine, using hand tools. Notifies workers of defects and to adjust extruding and forming machines. Cleans and maintains extruding and forming machines, using hand tools. Records operational data on tag and attaches to machine.

Yearly Earnings: $16,120
Education: Moderate-term O-J-T
Knowledge: None above average
Abilities: Perceptual Speed; Control Precision
Skills: Operation Monitoring; Operation and Control; Equipment Maintenance
General Work Activities: Controlling Machines and Processes
Job Characteristics: Using Hands on Objects, Tools, or Controls; Making Repetitive Motions; Common Protective or Safety Attire; Degree of Automation; Pace Determined by Speed of Equipment
GOE Group/s: 06.04.13 Elemental Work: Industrial: Equipment Operation, Rubber, Plastics, Glass Processing; 06.04.16 Elemental Work: Industrial: Equipment Operation, Textile, Fabric, and Leather Processing
CIP Program/s: 000000 NO CIP ASSIGNED
Related DOT Job/s: 557.565-014 SYNTHETIC-FILAMENT EXTRUDER; 557.665-010 SYNTHETIC-STAPLE EXTRUDER; 557.685-018 PROCESSOR; 557.685-022 SECOND-FLOOR OPERATOR; 557.685-026 SPINNER; 575.685-030 FIBER-MACHINE TENDER; 575.685-082 TEST-SKEIN WINDER

92711 TEXTILE DRAW-OUT MACHINE OPERATORS AND TENDERS. OOH Title/s: Textile Machinery Operators

Operate or tend machines, such as slubber machines and drawing frames, that draw out and combine sliver—such as wool, hemp, synthetic, and blended sliver—preparatory to further processing. Sets controls to adjust machine and regulate weight of fiber on conveyer, according to written instructions. Starts and observes machine operation to detect malfunctions while machine stretches, strengthens, mixes, combs, draws, or combines textile fibers. Threads filament, fiber, or sliver through guides, ties filament to previously threaded filaments, or deposits fibers onto automatic feeder of machine. Stops machine to remove processed fibers, unclog rollers, repair breaks in filaments, or replace fiber supply. Positions cans, coils, or balls of textile filament or sliver at feeding area of draw-out or combining machine. Inspects, weighs, sorts, and grades finished fiber. Notifies repair personnel when machine malfunctions. Records production data, marks finished fibers, and writes identification tickets. Cuts, wraps, and packs bundles of batting or fiber. Cleans and lubricates machines, using air hose, brushes, and oil.

Yearly Earnings: $13,728
Education: Moderate-term O-J-T
Knowledge: Production and Processing
Abilities: None above average
Skills: Operation Monitoring
General Work Activities: None above average
Job Characteristics: Contaminants; Standing; Making Repetitive Motions; Degree of Automation; Importance of Repeating Same Tasks; Pace Determined by Speed of Equipment
GOE Group/s: 06.04.06 Elemental Work: Industrial: Machine Work, Textiles
CIP Program/s: 000000 NO CIP ASSIGNED
Related DOT Job/s: 680.585-010 BATTING-MACHINE OPERATOR; 680.585-014 STAPLE-PROCESSING-MACHINE OPERATOR; 680.665-014 DRAW-MACHINE OPERATOR; 680.685-010 BLENDING-MACHINE OPERATOR; 680.685-034 DRAW-FRAME TENDER; 680.685-038 DRAWING-FRAME TENDER; 680.685-058 GILL-BOX TENDER; 680.685-098 SLUBBER TENDER; 689.685-166 UTILITY TENDER, CARDING

92714 TEXTILE BLEACHING AND DYEING MACHINE OPERATORS AND TENDERS. OOH Title/s: Textile Machinery Operators; Handlers, Equipment Cleaners, Helpers, and Laborers

Operate or tend machines, such as padding machines, treating tanks, dye jigs, and vats—to bleach, shrink, wash, dye, and finish textiles—such as cloth, yarn, greige cloth, and fiberglass sliver—preparatory to further processing. Starts machines and equipment to process and finish textile goods prior to further processing, following instructions. Observes display screen, control panel and equipment, and cloth entering or exiting process to determine whether to adjust equipment controls. Presses, pushes, or turns controls to initiate or adjust steps in process. Mixes or adds dyes, water, detergents, or chemicals to tanks to dilute or strengthen solutions as indicated by tests. Mounts roll of cloth on machine, using hoist, or places textile goods in machines or pieces of equipment. Threads ends of cloth or twine through specified sections of equipment prior to processing. Removes items, such as dyed articles, cloth, cones, and bobbins, from tanks and machines for drying and further processing. Creels machine with bobbins or twine. Keys in processing instructions to program electronic equipment. Soaks specified textile products for designated time. Tests solutions used to process textile goods to detect variations from standards, using standard procedures. Weighs ingredient to be mixed together to process textiles. Examines and feels products to determine variation from processing standards. Sews ends of cloth together by hand or using machine to form endless length of cloth to facilitate processing. Positions cloth truck to facilitate processing cloth. Records information, such as fabric yardage processed, temperature readings, fabric tensions, machine speeds, and delays caused by range malfunctions. Notifies supervisor of equipment malfunctions and coworkers to initiate steps in processing of textile goods. Confers with coworkers to ascertain information regarding customer orders, process steps to be completed during shift, or reason for delays. Ravels seams connecting cloth ends after processing is completed. Cleans machines and equipment.

Yearly Earnings: $16,120
Education: Moderate-term O-J-T

Knowledge: Production and Processing; Chemistry
Abilities: Arm-Hand Steadiness; Manual Dexterity; Control Precision; Rate Control; Wrist-Finger Speed; Speed of Limb Movement; Static Strength; Dynamic Strength; Trunk Strength; Stamina; Dynamic Flexibility; Gross Body Coordination; Gross Body Equilibrium; Visual Color Discrimination
Skills: None above average
General Work Activities: Controlling Machines and Processes
Job Characteristics: Sounds, Noise Levels are Distracting, etc.; Contaminants; Hazardous Conditions; Hazardous Equipment; Hazardous Situations; Using Hands on Objects, Tools, or Controls; Making Repetitive Motions; Specialized Protective or Safety Attire; Degree of Automation; Pace Determined by Speed of Equipment
GOE Group/s: 06.02.16 Production Work: Equipment Operation, Textile, Fabric, and Leather Processing; 06.02.18 Production Work: Equipment Operation, Assorted Materials Processing; 06.04.05 Elemental Work: Industrial: Machine Work, Fabric and Leather; 06.04.16 Elemental Work: Industrial: Equipment Operation, Textile, Fabric, and Leather Processing; 06.04.19 Elemental Work: Industrial: Equipment Operation, Assorted Materials Processing; 06.04.33 Elemental Work: Industrial: Manual Work, Brushing, Spraying, and Coating
CIP Program/s: 150699 Industrial Production Technologists and Technicians, Other
Related DOT Job/s: 582.362-010 PANELBOARD OPERATOR; 582.362-014 DYE AUTOMATION OPERATOR; 582.582-010 DYE-RANGE OPERATOR, CLOTH; 582.665-014 DYE-REEL OPERATOR; 582.665-018 JIGGER; 582.685-014 BEAM-DYER OPERATOR; 582.685-018 BLEACH-RANGE OPERATOR; 582.685-022 BOIL-OFF-MACHINE OPERATOR, CLOTH; 582.685-030 CLOTH-WASHER OPERATOR; 582.685-034 COLORING-MACHINE OPERATOR; 582.685-054 DYE-TANK TENDER; 582.685-058 DYED-YARN OPERATOR; 582.685-070 FELT-WASHING-MACHINE TENDER; 582.685-090 JET-DYEING-MACHINE TENDER; 582.685-094 KNIT-GOODS WASHER; 582.685-098 OPEN-DEVELOPER OPERATOR; 582.685-102 PACKAGE-DYEING-MACHINE OPERATOR; 582.685-106 PADDING-MACHINE OPERATOR; 582.685-110 PATCH WASHER; 582.685-114 ROPE-SILICA-MACHINE OPERATOR; 582.685-122 SCRUBBING-MACHINE OPERATOR; 582.685-130 SKEIN-YARN DYER; 582.685-142 STAINING-MACHINE OPERATOR; 582.685-154 TIN-WHIZ-MACHINE OPERATOR; 582.685-158 WARP-DYEING-VAT TENDER; 582.685-162 WASHER; 582.685-166 WOOL-WASHING-MACHINE OPERATOR; 582.685-170 DYE-TUB OPERATOR; 582.687-026 SIZER; 582.687-030 TREATER; 586.687-010 FELT CARBONIZER; 587.685-018 CLOTH-SHRINKING-MACHINE OPERATOR; 589.562-010 CLOTH-FINISHING-RANGE OPERATOR, CHIEF; 589.662-010 SCOURING-TRAIN OPERATOR; 589.662-014 TIRE-FABRIC-IMPREGNATING-RANGE OPERATOR, CHIEF; 589.685-026 CLOTH-FINISHING-RANGE TENDER; 589.685-042 DYER HELPER; 589.685-066 LAUNDRY-MACHINE TENDER; 599.685-034 DYER

92717 SEWING MACHINE OPERATORS, GARMENT. OOH Title/s: Apparel Workers

Operate or tend sewing machines to perform garment sewing operations, such as joining, reinforcing, or decorating garments or garment parts. Include sewing machine operators and tenders who perform specialized or automatic sewing machine functions, such as buttonhole making or tacking. Starts and operates or tends machines that automatically join, reinforce, or decorate material or fabricated articles. Draws thread through guides, tensions, and needles, and adjusts machine functions, according to fabric type. Positions item under needle, using marks on machine, clamp or template, edges of cloth, or markings on cloth as guides. Turns knobs, screws, and dials to adjust settings of machine, according to garment style and observation of operation. Replaces and rethreads needles. Guides garment or garment parts under machine needle and presser foot to sew parts together. Positions material or article in clamps, template, or hoop frame prior to automatic operation of machine. Sews replacement parts or missing stitches, according to repair tickets. Observes sewing machine operation to detect defects in stitching or machine malfunction, and notifies supervisor. Attaches buttons or fasteners to fabric, using feeding hopper or clamp holder. Folds or stretches edges or length of items, while sewing, to facilitate forming specified sections. Attaches tape, trim, or elastic to specified garments or garment parts, according to item specifications. Removes holding devices and finished item from machine. Selects supplies, such as fasteners and thread, according to specifications or characteristics of fabric. Bastes edges of material to align and temporarily secure garment parts for final assembly. Draws markings or pins applique on fabric to obtain variation in design and marks stitching errors with pins or tape. Replaces sewing machine parts and performs basic maintenance, such as oiling machine. Cuts material and threads, using scissors. Inspects garments and examines repair tags and markings on garment to locate defects or damage. Records number of garment parts or complete garments sewn.
Yearly Earnings: $12,324
Education: Moderate-term O-J-T
Knowledge: None above average
Abilities: Selective Attention; Arm-Hand Steadiness; Visual Color Discrimination; Hearing Sensitivity; Sound Localization
Skills: None above average
General Work Activities: None above average
Job Characteristics: Sounds, Noise Levels are Distracting, etc.; Hazardous Equipment; Sitting; Using Hands on Objects, Tools, or Controls; Making Repetitive Motions; Degree of Automation; Importance of Repeating Same Tasks; Pace Determined by Speed of Equipment
GOE Group/s: 06.02.05 Production Work: Machine Work, Leather and Fabrics; 06.03.02 Quality Control: Inspecting, Grading, Sorting, Weighing, and Recording; 06.04.05 Elemental Work: Industrial: Machine Work, Fabric and Leather
CIP Program/s: 200301 Clothing, Apparel and Textile Workers and Managers, General; 200303 Commercial Garment and Apparel Worker
Related DOT Job/s: 684.682-014 SEWER AND INSPECTOR; 689.685-150 WATCHER, AUTOMAT; 689.685-154 WATCHER, PANTOGRAPH; 784.682-010 GLOVE SEWER; 784.682-014 HAT-AND-CAP SEWER; 784.685-014 BRIM STITCHER I; 786.682-010 APPLIQUER, ZIGZAG; 786.682-014 ARMHOLE BASTER, JUMPBASTING; 786.682-018 ARMHOLE FELLER, HANDSTITCHING MACHINE; 786.682-022 ARMHOLE-SEW-AND-TRIM OPERATOR, LOCKSTITCH; 786.682-026 BACK MAKER, LOCKSTITCH; 786.682-030 BASTING-MACHINE OPERATOR; 786.682-034 BINDER, CHAINSTITCH; 786.682-038 BINDER, COVERSTITCH; 786.682-042 BINDER, LOCKSTITCH; 786.682-046 BLINDSTITCH-MACHINE OPERATOR; 786.682-050 CANVAS BASTER, JUMPBASTING; 786.682-054 CHAINSTITCH SEWING MACHINE OPERATOR; 786.682-058 COAT JOINER, LOCKSTITCH; 786.682-062 COLLAR BASTER, JUMPBASTING; 786.682-066 COLLAR FELLER, HANDSTITCHING MACHINE; 786.682-070 COLLAR SETTER, LOCKSTITCH; 786.682-074 COLLAR SETTER, OVERLOCK; 786.682-078 COVERSTITCH-MACHINE OPERATOR; 786.682-082 CUP SETTER, LOCKSTITCH; 786.682-086 ELASTIC ATTACHER, CHAINSTITCH; 786.682-090 ELASTIC ATTACHER, COVERSTITCH; 786.682-094 ELASTIC ATTACHER, OVERLOCK; 786.682-098 ELASTIC ATTACHER, ZIGZAG; 786.682-102 FACING BASTER, JUMPBASTING; 786.682-106 FELLED-SEAM OPERATOR, CHAINSTITCH; 786.682-110 FLATLOCK-SEWING-MACHINE OPERATOR; 786.682-114 FRONT MAKER, LOCKSTITCH; 786.682-118 FRONT-EDGE-TAPE SEWER, LOCKSTITCH; 786.682-122 FUR-MACHINE OPERATOR; 786.682-126 HEMMER, BLINDSTITCH; 786.682-130 HEMMER, CHAINSTITCH; 786.682-134 HEMMER, LOCKSTITCH; 786.682-138 HEMMER, OVERLOCK; 786.682-

142 HEMSTITCHING-MACHINE OPERATOR; 786.682-146 JUMPBASTING-MACHINE OPERATOR; 786.682-150 LAPEL PADDER, BLINDSTITCH; 786.682-154 LINING BASTER, JUMPBASTING; 786.682-158 LINING FELLER, BLINDSTITCH; 786.682-162 LINING MAKER, LOCKSTITCH; 786.682-166 LINING SETTER, LOCKSTITCH; 786.682-170 LOCKSTITCH-MACHINE OPERATOR; 786.682-174 LOCKSTITCH-SEWING-MACHINE OPERATOR, COMPLETE GARMENT; 786.682-178 MULTINEEDLE-CHAINSTITCH-MACHINE OPERATOR; 786.682-182 NECKTIE OPERATOR, POCKETS AND PIECES; 786.682-186 NECKTIE-CENTRALIZING-MACHINE OPERATOR I; 786.682-190 NECKTIE-CENTRALIZING-MACHINE OPERATOR II; 786.682-194 OVERLOCK SEWING MACHINE OPERATOR; 786.682-198 OVERLOCK-MACHINE OPERATOR, COMPLETE GARMENT; 786.682-202 PANTS OUTSEAMER, CHAINSTITCH; 786.682-206 PICKED-EDGE SEWING-MACHINE OPERATOR; 786.682-210 POCKET SETTER, LOCKSTITCH; 786.682-214 REPAIR OPERATOR; 786.682-218 SEAT JOINER, CHAINSTITCH; 786.682-222 SHOULDER JOINER, LOCKSTITCH; 786.682-226 SLEEVE MAKER, LOCKSTITCH; 786.682-230 SLEEVE SETTER, LOCKSTITCH; 786.682-234 SLEEVE SETTER, OVERLOCK; 786.682-238 TOPSTITCHER, LOCKSTITCH; 786.682-242 TOPSTITCHER, ZIGZAG; 786.682-246 TUNNEL-ELASTIC OPERATOR, CHAINSTITCH; 786.682-250 TUNNEL-ELASTIC OPERATOR, LOCKSTITCH; 786.682-254 TUNNEL-ELASTIC OPERATOR, ZIGZAG; 786.682-258 ULTRASONIC-SEAMING-MACHINE OPERATOR; 786.682-262 UTILITY OPERATOR; 786.682-266 WAISTBAND SETTER, LOCKSTITCH; 786.682-270 WAISTLINE JOINER, LOCKSTITCH; 786.682-274 WAISTLINE JOINER, OVERLOCK; 786.682-278 ZIGZAG-MACHINE OPERATOR; 786.682-282 ZIPPER SETTER, CHAINSTITCH; 786.682-286 ZIPPER SETTER, LOCKSTITCH; 786.685-010 BUTTON-SEWING-MACHINE OPERATOR; 786.685-014 BUTTONHOLE-MACHINE OPERATOR; 786.685-018 EMBROIDERY-MACHINE OPERATOR; 786.685-022 PIPED-POCKET-MACHINE OPERATOR; 786.685-026 PROFILE-STITCHING-MACHINE OPERATOR; 786.685-030 SEWING-MACHINE OPERATOR, SEMIAUTOMATIC; 786.685-034 TACKING-MACHINE OPERATOR; 786.685-042 BUTTONHOLE-AND-BUTTON-SEWING-MACHINE OPERATOR; 787.682-022 EMBROIDERY-MACHINE OPERATOR; 787.682-074 SEWING-MACHINE OPERATOR; 787.685-046 TOE-CLOSING-MACHINE TENDER

92721 SEWING MACHINE OPERATORS, NONGARMENT. OOH Title/s: Apparel Workers

Operate or tend sewing machines to join together, reinforce, decorate, or perform related sewing operations in the manufacture of nongarment products, such as upholstery, draperies, linens, carpets, and mattresses. Activates and adjusts machine controls to regulate stitching speed and length, dimensions of gathers and tucks, and material or thread tension. Activates sewing machine to join, gather, hem, reinforce, or decorate materials or fabricated articles, such as linens, toys, or luggage. Monitors machine operation to detect problems, such as defective stitching, breaks in thread, or machine malfunction. Positions materials through feed rollers and guides, or positions and maneuvers under sewing machine presser foot and needle during operation. Mounts attachments, such as needles, cutting blades, or pattern plates, and adjusts machine guides according to specifications. Examines and measures finished articles to verify conformance to standards, using ruler. Selects supplies, such as binding, cord, or thread, according to specifications or color of material. Places spools of thread, cord, or other materials on spindles, inserts bobbin, and threads ends through machine guides and components. Folds or fits together materials, such as cloth, foam rubber, or leather, to prepare for machine sewing. Cuts materials, according to specifications, or cuts excess material or thread from finished product, using blade, scissors, or electric knife. Replaces needles, sands rough areas of needles with sandpaper, and cleans and oils sewing machines to maintain equipment. Positions and marks patterns on materials to prepare for sewing. Tapes or twists together thread or cord to repair breaks. Removes finished materials from sewing machine. Records amount of materials processed in production logs. Sews materials by hand, using needle and thread.

Yearly Earnings: $12,324
Education: Moderate-term O-J-T
Knowledge: Production and Processing
Abilities: Arm-Hand Steadiness; Manual Dexterity; Finger Dexterity; Control Precision; Rate Control; Wrist-Finger Speed; Speed of Limb Movement; Trunk Strength; Dynamic Flexibility; Near Vision; Visual Color Discrimination
Skills: None above average
General Work Activities: Handling and Moving Objects
Job Characteristics: Sounds, Noise Levels are Distracting, etc.; Hazardous Equipment; Sitting; Using Hands on Objects, Tools, or Controls; Making Repetitive Motions; Degree of Automation; Importance of Being Sure All is Done; Importance of Repeating Same Tasks; Pace Determined by Speed of Equipment
GOE Group/s: 06.02.05 Production Work: Machine Work, Leather and Fabrics; 06.04.04 Elemental Work: Industrial: Machine Work, Paper; 06.04.05 Elemental Work: Industrial: Machine Work, Fabric and Leather; 06.04.09 Elemental Work: Industrial: Machine Work, Assorted Materials; 06.04.27 Elemental Work: Industrial: Manual Work, Textile, Fabric and Leather
CIP Program/s: 200301 Clothing, Apparel and Textile Workers and Managers, General; 200303 Commercial Garment and Apparel Worker; 200501 Home Furnishings and Equipment Installers and Consultants, General; 200502 Window Treatment Maker and Installer; 480303 Upholsterer
Related DOT Job/s: 689.662-014 STRIPE MATCHER; 689.682-018 SPLICING-MACHINE OPERATOR; 689.682-022 STITCHER; 689.685-026 BOUFFANT-CURTAIN-MACHINE TENDER; 689.685-106 QUILTING-MACHINE OPERATOR; 689.685-118 SEWING-MACHINE OPERATOR, SPECIAL EQUIPMENT; 689.685-126 STITCH-BONDING-MACHINE TENDER; 692.685-254 WINDOW-SHADE-RING SEWER; 731.685-010 ROOTER OPERATOR; 780.682-010 SEWING-MACHINE OPERATOR; 780.682-014 SLIP-COVER SEWER; 780.682-018 UPHOLSTERY SEWER; 782.687-046 SACK REPAIRER; 783.682-010 FUR-MACHINE OPERATOR; 783.682-014 SEWING MACHINE OPERATOR; 787.682-010 BINDER; 787.682-014 CARPET SEWER; 787.682-018 DRAPERY OPERATOR; 787.682-026 HEMMER; 787.682-034 OVEREDGE SEWER; 787.682-038 ROLL-OR-TAPE-EDGE-MACHINE OPERATOR; 787.682-046 SEWING-MACHINE OPERATOR; 787.682-050 SEWING-MACHINE OPERATOR; 787.682-054 SEWING-MACHINE OPERATOR; 787.682-058 SEWING-MACHINE OPERATOR II; 787.682-066 SEWING MACHINE OPERATOR I; 787.682-078 SHIRRING-MACHINE OPERATOR; 787.682-082 TUCKING-MACHINE OPERATOR; 787.682-086 ZIPPER SETTER; 787.685-010 FASTENER-SEWING-MACHINE OPERATOR; 787.685-014 FOLDER-SEAMER, AUTOMATIC; 787.685-018 HEMMER, AUTOMATIC; 787.685-022 HEMMING-AND-TACKING-MACHINE OPERATOR; 787.685-026 PLEATER; 787.685-030 SERGING-MACHINE OPERATOR, AUTOMATIC; 787.685-034 SEWING-MACHINE OPERATOR, ZIPPER; 787.685-038 SHIRRING-MACHINE OPERATOR, AUTOMATIC; 787.685-042 TACKING-MACHINE OPERATOR; 787.685-050 TRIMMING SEWER, AUTOMATIC; 787.685-054 SEWING-MACHINE OPERATOR, PAPER BAGS

92723 SHOE SEWING MACHINE OPERATORS AND TENDERS. OOH Title/s: Shoe Sewing Machine Operators and Tenders

Operate or tend single-, double-, or multiple-needle stitching machine to join or decorate shoe parts, to reinforce shoe parts, or to attach buckles. Turns setscrew on needle bar and positions

required number of needles in designated stitching machines. Aligns parts to be stitched, following seams, edges, or markings, and positions parts under needles. Draws thread through machine guide slots and needles. Selects and inserts specified cassettes into consoles of stitching machine to stitch decorative designs onto shoe parts. Lowers pressure foot or roller to secure parts and starts machine stitching, using hand, foot, or knee controls. Guides shoe into feeding mechanism that attaches, stitches, joins, or reinforces shoe parts, according to instructions. Selects and places spools of thread or prewound bobbins into shuttles or onto spindles or loopers of stitching machines. Reads shoe part tags to identify appropriate instruction cassette and style and color of thread. Removes and examines shoe parts and design to verify conformance to specifications. Cuts excess thread or material from shoe part, using scissors or knife.
Yearly Earnings: $13,156
Education: Moderate-term O-J-T
Knowledge: None above average
Abilities: Arm-Hand Steadiness; Finger Dexterity; Wrist-Finger Speed
Skills: None above average
General Work Activities: Handling and Moving Objects
Job Characteristics: Hazardous Situations; Sitting; Making Repetitive Motions; Degree of Automation; Importance of Repeating Same Tasks; Pace Determined by Speed of Equipment
GOE Group/s: 06.02.05 Production Work: Machine Work, Leather and Fabrics; 06.04.05 Elemental Work: Industrial: Machine Work, Fabric and Leather
CIP Program/s: 480304 Shoe, Boot and Leather Repairer
Related DOT Job/s: 690.682-078 STITCHER, SPECIAL MACHINE; 690.682-082 STITCHER, STANDARD MACHINE; 690.685-494 STITCHER, TAPE-CONTROLLED MACHINE; 788.684-114 THREAD LASTER

92726 LAUNDRY AND DRY-CLEANING MACHINE OPERATORS AND TENDERS, EXCEPT PRESSING.

OOH Title/s: Laundry and Drycleaning Machine Operators and Tenders, Except Pressers

Operate or tend washing or dry-cleaning machines to wash or dry-clean commercial, industrial, or household articles, such as cloth garments, suede, leather, furs, blankets, draperies, fine linens, rugs, and carpets. Starts washer, dry-cleaner, drier, or extractor, and turns valves or levers to regulate and monitor cleaning or drying operations. Loads or directs other workers to load articles into washer or dry-cleaning machine. Mixes and adds detergents, dyes, bleach, starch, and other solutions and chemicals to clean, color, dry, or stiffen articles. Starts pumps to operate distilling system that drains and reclaims dry-cleaning solvents. Tends variety of automatic machines that comb and polish furs; clean, sterilize, and fluff feathers and blankets; and roll and package towels. Adjusts switches to tend and regulate equipment that fumigates and removes foreign matter from furs. Removes or directs other workers to remove items from washer or dry-cleaning machine and into extractor or tumbler. Cleans machine filters and lubricates equipment. Washes, dry-cleans, or glazes delicate articles or fur garment linings by hand, using mild detergent or dry-cleaning solutions. Presoaks, sterilizes, scrubs, spot-cleans, and dries contaminated or stained articles, using neutralizer solutions and portable machines. Examines and sorts articles to be cleaned into lots, according to color, fabric, dirt content, and cleaning technique required. Sorts and counts articles removed from dryer and folds, wraps, or hangs items for airing out, pick-up, or delivery. Receives and marks articles for laundry or-dry cleaning with identifying code number or name, using hand or machine marker. Irons or presses articles, fabrics, and furs, using hand iron or pressing machine. Hangs curtains, drapes, blankets, pants, and other garments on stretch frames to dry, and transports items between specified locations. Mends and sews articles, using hand stitching, adhesive patch, or power sewing machine.
Yearly Earnings: $13,364
Education: Moderate-term O-J-T
Knowledge: None above average
Abilities: Speed of Limb Movement; Dynamic Strength; Trunk Strength; Stamina; Dynamic Flexibility; Gross Body Coordination; Gross Body Equilibrium
Skills: None above average
General Work Activities: None above average
Job Characteristics: Sounds, Noise Levels are Distracting, etc.; Very Hot; Contaminants; Hazardous Conditions; Hazardous Equipment; Using Hands on Objects, Tools, or Controls; Making Repetitive Motions; Degree of Automation; Pace Determined by Speed of Equipment
GOE Group/s: 05.12.18 Elemental Work: Mechanical: Cleaning and Maintenance; 06.02.16 Production Work: Equipment Operation, Textile, Fabric, and Leather Processing; 06.02.18 Production Work: Equipment Operation, Assorted Materials Processing; 06.02.27 Production Work: Manual Work, Textile, Fabric and Leather; 06.04.16 Elemental Work: Industrial: Equipment Operation, Textile, Fabric, and Leather Processing; 06.04.35 Elemental Work: Industrial: Laundering, Dry Cleaning; 06.04.39 Elemental Work: Industrial: Cleaning
CIP Program/s: 200301 Clothing, Apparel and Textile Workers and Managers, General; 200309 Drycleaner and Launderer (Commercial)
Related DOT Job/s: 361.665-010 WASHER, MACHINE; 361.682-010 RUG CLEANER, MACHINE; 361.684-010 LAUNDERER, HAND; 361.684-014 LAUNDRY WORKER I; 361.685-014 CONTINUOUS-TOWEL ROLLER; 361.685-018 LAUNDRY WORKER II; 362.382-010 DRY-CLEANER APPRENTICE; 362.382-014 DRY CLEANER; 362.684-014 FUR CLEANER; 362.684-026 LEATHER CLEANER; 362.685-010 FEATHER RENOVATOR; 369.684-014 LAUNDRY OPERATOR; 369.685-010 FUR BLOWER; 369.685-014 FUR CLEANER, MACHINE; 369.685-022 FUR-GLAZING-AND-POLISHING-MACHINE OPERATOR; 589.685-038 DRY CLEANER

92728 PRESSING MACHINE OPERATORS AND TENDERS—TEXTILE, GARMENT, AND RELATED MATERIALS.

OOH Title/s: Apparel Workers; Handlers, Equipment Cleaners, Helpers, and Laborers

Operate or tend pressing machines—such as hot-head pressing, steam pressing, automatic pressing, ironing, plunger pressing, and hydraulic pressing machines—to press and shape articles such as leather, fur, and cloth garments, drapes, slipcovers, handkerchiefs, and millinery. Exclude delicate fabric (precision) pressers. Activates pressing machine to remove wrinkles from garments and flatwork items, or to shape, form, or patch articles. Activates and adjusts machine controls to regulate temperature and pressure of rollers, ironing shoe, or plates, according to specifications. Lowers iron, ram, or pressing head of machine into position over material to be pressed. Selects, installs, and adjusts machine components, including pressing forms, rollers, and guides, according to pressing instructions, using hoist and hand tools. Positions materials, such as cloth garments, felt, or straw on table, die, or feeding mechanism of pressing machine. Removes finished pieces from pressing machine and hangs or stacks for cooling, or forwards for additional processing. Presses materials, such as garments, drapes, and slipcovers, using hand iron. Moistens materials to soften, and smooths and straightens materials with hands, to prepare for machine pressing. Examines and measures finished articles to verify conformance to standards, using measuring devices, including tape measure and micrometer. Sews end of new material to leader or to end of material in pressing machine, using sewing machine. Shrinks, stretches, or blocks articles by hand, to conform to original measurements, using forms,

blocks, and steam. Applies cleaning solvents, and brushes materials made of suede, leather, and felt to remove spots, and to raise and smooth nap. Hangs, folds, packages, and tags finished articles for delivery to customers. Cleans and maintains pressing machines, using cleaning solutions and lubricants.
Yearly Earnings: $14,612
Education: Moderate-term O-J-T
Knowledge: None above average
Abilities: Arm-Hand Steadiness; Manual Dexterity; Control Precision; Gross Body Equilibrium
Skills: None above average
General Work Activities: None above average
Job Characteristics: Very Hot; Hazardous Conditions; Hazardous Situations; Making Repetitive Motions; Degree of Automation; Importance of Repeating Same Tasks; Pace Determined by Speed of Equipment
GOE Group/s: 06.02.05 Production Work: Machine Work, Leather and Fabrics; 06.02.27 Production Work: Manual Work, Textile, Fabric and Leather; 06.04.05 Elemental Work: Industrial: Machine Work, Fabric and Leather; 06.04.09 Elemental Work: Industrial: Machine Work, Assorted Materials; 06.04.19 Elemental Work: Industrial: Equipment Operation, Assorted Materials Processing; 06.04.27 Elemental Work: Industrial: Manual Work, Textile, Fabric and Leather; 06.04.35 Elemental Work: Industrial: Laundering, Dry Cleaning
CIP Program/s: 200301 Clothing, Apparel and Textile Workers and Managers, General; 200309 Drycleaner and Launderer (Commercial)
Related DOT Job/s: 361.685-022 PATCHING-MACHINE OPERATOR; 363.682-010 LEATHER FINISHER; 363.682-014 PRESSER, ALL-AROUND; 363.682-018 PRESSER, MACHINE; 363.684-010 BLOCKER; 363.684-014 HAT BLOCKER; 363.685-010 PRESS OPERATOR; 363.685-014 PRESSER, AUTOMATIC; 363.685-018 PRESSER, FORM; 363.685-022 PRESSER, HANDKERCHIEF; 363.685-026 SHIRT PRESSER; 369.685-018 FUR IRONER; 580.685-042 MOLDER; 583.585-010 CALENDER-MACHINE OPERATOR; 583.685-018 BRIM PRESSER I; 583.685-022 BRIM-AND-CROWN PRESSER; 583.685-050 HAT-LINING BLOCKER; 583.685-054 HYDRAULIC-PRESS OPERATOR; 583.685-058 HYDRAULIC-PRESS OPERATOR; 583.685-070 MANGLER; 583.685-086 PRESS OPERATOR; 583.685-090 PRESSER, BUFFING WHEEL; 583.685-098 SEAM PRESSER; 583.685-102 SHAPER AND PRESSER; 583.685-106 STEAM-PRESS TENDER; 583.685-110 STRAW HAT PRESSER, MACHINE; 583.685-114 STRAW-HAT-PLUNGER OPERATOR; 583.685-118 STRIP PRESSER; 686.685-050 PRESS OPERATOR; 689.685-018 BOBBIN PRESSER; 783.685-014 CREASER; 789.687-178 TIE PRESSER

Other Machine Setters, Operators, and Tenders

92902A ELECTRONIC SEMICONDUCTOR PROCESSORS. OOH Title/s: Electronic Semiconductor Processors

Process materials used in manufacture of electronic semiconductors. Measures and weighs amounts of crystal-growing materials, mixes and grinds materials, and loads materials into container, following procedures. Forms seed crystal for crystal growing or locates crystal axis of ingot, using x-ray equipment, drill, and sanding machine. Aligns photomask pattern on photoresist layer, exposes pattern to ultraviolet light, and develops pattern, using specialized equipment. Attaches ampoule to diffusion pump to remove air from ampoule, and seals ampoule, using blowtorch. Places semiconductor wafers in processing containers or equipment holders, using vacuum wand or tweezers. Monitors operation, and adjusts controls of processing machines and equipment, to produce compositions with specific electronic properties. Manipulates valves, switches, and buttons, or keys commands into control panels to start semiconductor processing cycles. Etches, laps, polishes, or grinds wafers or ingots, using etching, lapping, polishing, or grinding equipment. Operates saw to cut remelt into sections of specified size or to cut ingots into wafers. Cleans and dries materials and equipment using solvent, etching or sandblasting equipment, and drying equipment to remove contaminants or photoresist. Studies work order, instructions, formulas, and processing charts to determine specifications and sequence of operations. Loads and unloads equipment chambers and transports finished product to storage or to area for further processing. Inspects materials, components, or products for surface defects and measures circuitry, using electronic test equipment, precision measuring instruments, and standard procedures. Counts, sorts, and weighs processed items. Stamps or etches identifying information on finished component. Maintains processing, production, and inspection information and reports.
Yearly Earnings: $21,164
Education: Moderate-term O-J-T
Knowledge: Production and Processing
Abilities: Control Precision
Skills: Science; Equipment Selection; Operation Monitoring; Operation and Control
General Work Activities: Inspecting Equipment, Structures, or Material; Handling and Moving Objects; Controlling Machines and Processes; Repairing and Maintaining Electrical Equipment
Job Characteristics: Radiation; Using Hands on Objects, Tools, or Controls; Making Repetitive Motions; Importance of Repeating Same Tasks
GOE Group/s: 06.02.18 Production Work: Equipment Operation, Assorted Materials Processing; 06.02.32 Production Work: Manual Work, Assorted Materials; 06.04.19 Elemental Work: Industrial: Equipment Operation, Assorted Materials Processing; 06.04.32 Elemental Work: Industrial: Manual Work, Casting and Molding; 06.04.34 Elemental Work: Industrial: Manual Work, Assorted Materials
CIP Program/s: 470101 Electrical and Electronics Equipment Installer and Repairer; 470105 Industrial Electronics Installer and Repairer
Related DOT Job/s: 590.362-018 GROUP LEADER, SEMICONDUCTOR PROCESSING; 590.382-022 ION IMPLANT MACHINE OPERATOR; 590.384-010 CHARGE PREPARATION TECHNICIAN; 590.684-014 ELECTRONIC-COMPONENT PROCESSOR; 590.684-022 SEMICONDUCTOR PROCESSOR; 590.684-042 INTEGRATED CIRCUIT FABRICATOR; 590.685-070 DIFFUSION FURNACE OPERATOR, SEMICONDUCTOR WAFERS; 590.685-086 METALLIZATION EQUIPMENT TENDER, SEMICONDUCTORS

92902B ELECTRONIC SEMICONDUCTOR WAFER ETCHERS AND ENGRAVERS. OOH Title/s: Electronic Semiconductor Processors

Tend or use equipment to etch or engrave semiconductor wafers. Sets and adjusts equipment controls to activate etch cycle to etch or engrave wafer surface. Places loaded container into air or spin dryer, adjusts controls, and tends machine that rinses and dries etched wafers. Monitors equipment control panels to ensure chemicals and materials meet processing specifications. Immerses containers in chemical and water baths to etch circuitry patterns into or strip excess resist from wafer surfaces. Measures dimensions of wafers, such as thickness, flatness, or diameter, using microscope measuring attachment, micrometer, or flatness or thickness gauge. Calculates etching time based on thickness of material to be removed from wafers or crystals. Scribes identifying information on designated area of wafers, following specifications and using metal stylus. Inspects etched and stripped wafers, using microscope, to detect scratches or contaminants and to ensure

conformance to specifications. Replaces etching and rinsing solutions in equipment and cleans bath containers and work area. Inserts or removes semiconductor wafers from containers, such as boats or cassettes, using vacuum wand or tweezers. Records production details.
Yearly Earnings: $21,164
Education: Moderate-term O-J-T
Knowledge: Chemistry
Abilities: Flexibility of Closure; Selective Attention; Manual Dexterity; Finger Dexterity; Control Precision; Speed of Limb Movement; Gross Body Equilibrium; Depth Perception
Skills: Operation Monitoring; Operation and Control; Product Inspection
General Work Activities: Controlling Machines and Processes; Repairing and Maintaining Electrical Equipment
Job Characteristics: Using Hands on Objects, Tools, or Controls; Making Repetitive Motions; Common Protective or Safety Attire; Importance of Repeating Same Tasks; Pace Determined by Speed of Equipment
GOE Group/s: 06.02.01 Production Work: Supervision; 06.02.09 Production Work: Machine Work, Assorted Materials; 06.04.19 Elemental Work: Industrial: Equipment Operation, Assorted Materials Processing; 06.04.37 Elemental Work: Industrial: Manual Work, Stamping, Marking, Labeling, and Ticketing
CIP Program/s: 470101 Electrical and Electronics Equipment Installer and Repairer; 470105 Industrial Electronics Installer and Repairer
Related DOT Job/s: 590.364-010 LEAD WORKER, WAFER PRODUCTION; 590.684-026 ETCHER-STRIPPER, SEMICONDUCTOR WAFERS; 590.685-074 ETCH OPERATOR, SEMICONDUCTOR WAFERS; 590.685-078 ETCHER; 673.364-010 LEAD WORKER, WAFER POLISHING; 920.587-026 MARKER, SEMICONDUCTOR WAFERS

92902C ELECTRONIC SEMICONDUCTOR TEST AND DEVELOPMENT TECHNICIANS. OOH Title/s: Electronic Semiconductor Processors

Operate variety of machines and equipment used in production and testing of electronic semiconductor wafers and chips. Operates equipment to convert integrated circuit layout designs into working photomasks, using knowledge of microelectronic processing, equipment, procedures, and specifications. Operates equipment to clean, coat, bake, expose, develop, and cure photoresist on wafers. Operates equipment to grow layers of dielectric, metal, and semiconductor material on masked areas of wafers. Operates equipment to clean, etch, or remove materials not covered by photoresist. Operates equipment to implant chemicals to selective areas of wafer substrate to alter substrate characteristics. Inspects and measures test wafer, using electronic measuring equipment and microscope, to ensure wafers meet processing and company specifications. Assembles, dices, cleans, mounts, bonds, and packages integrated circuit devices manually or using special equipment. Analyzes test results, using engineering specifications and calculator. Records test results in logbooks. Discusses production problems with workers. Writes reports on equipment repair, recalibration recommendations, test results, and operator procedure violations. Assists in technical writing of semiconductor processing specifications.
Yearly Earnings: $21,164
Education: Moderate-term O-J-T
Knowledge: Production and Processing; Computers and Electronics; Engineering and Technology; Mathematics
Abilities: Information Ordering; Mathematical Reasoning; Number Facility; Near Vision
Skills: Writing; Science; Equipment Selection; Programming; Testing; Operation Monitoring; Operation and Control; Product Inspection
General Work Activities: Monitoring Processes, Material, or Surroundings; Inspecting Equipment, Structures, or Material; Analyzing Data or Information; Updating and Using Job-Relevant Knowledge; Controlling Machines and Processes; Drafting and Specifying Technical Devices, etc.; Repairing and Maintaining Electrical Equipment; Communicating with Other Workers
Job Characteristics: Using Hands on Objects, Tools, or Controls; Degree of Automation; Importance of Being Exact or Accurate
GOE Group/s: 06.01.03 Production Technology: Machine Set-up and Operation; 06.01.05 Production Technology: Inspection
CIP Program/s: 470101 Electrical and Electronics Equipment Installer and Repairer; 470105 Industrial Electronics Installer and Repairer
Related DOT Job/s: 590.262-014 TEST TECHNICIAN, SEMICONDUCTOR PROCESSING EQUIPMENT; 590.362-022 MICROELECTRONICS TECHNICIAN

92902D ELECTRONIC SEMICONDUCTOR CRYSTAL-GROWING TECHNICIANS AND EQUIPMENT OPERATORS. OOH Title/s: Electronic Semiconductor Processors

Set up and operate furnaces and reactors used to grow crystals from materials—such as silicon, quartz, or gallium arsenide—used in the production of semiconductors. Sets and adjusts computerized or mechanical controls to regulate power level, temperature, vacuum, and rotation speed of furnace, according to crystal-growing specifications. Observes and monitors material meltdown and crystal growth, and readjusts equipment controls as necessary. Connects reactor to computer, using hand tools and power tools. Loads computer-controlled equipment with materials to grow layer of semiconductor material on wafer surface. Inspects wafers for defects, such as scratches, growths, and pits. Activates computer program to clean equipment or cleans by hand, using vacuum cleaner and cleaning supplies Measures and tests thickness and bow of wafer and thickness and photo-luminescence of epitaxial layer, using gauges and test equipment. Inspects equipment for leaks, diagnoses equipment malfunctions, and requests equipment repairs. Analyzes processing procedures and equipment functions to identify and resolve semiconductor crystal-growth problems. Cleans semiconductor wafers, using cleaning equipment such as chemical baths, automatic wafer cleaners, or blow-off wands. Inscribes line on wafer, using metal scribe, and breaks off sample section of wafer. Cuts line on light bar sample to isolate die, using wafer saw, and measures brightness of die, using tester. Computes production statistics, surface area of wafer, or defects per square inch, using calculator. Replaces furnace liners and reactor accessories, such as bell jar and carousel. Constructs sheet metal housing, and installs and repairs wiring, switches, gauges, and lines on reactor, using hand tools and power tools. Records production data in logbook and processing documents. Demonstrates and explains crystal-growing procedures to workers.
Yearly Earnings: $21,164
Education: Moderate-term O-J-T
Knowledge: Computers and Electronics; Mechanical; Mathematics; Physics; Chemistry
Abilities: Flexibility of Closure; Perceptual Speed; Visualization; Selective Attention; Finger Dexterity; Response Orientation; Reaction Time; Gross Body Equilibrium; Hearing Sensitivity; Sound Localization
Skills: Science; Instructing; Equipment Selection; Installation; Testing; Operation Monitoring; Operation and Control; Product Inspection; Equipment Maintenance; Troubleshooting; Repairing
General Work Activities: Identifying Objects, Actions, and Events; Inspecting Equipment, Structures, or Material; Controlling Machines and Processes; Operating Vehicles or Equipment; Repairing and Main-

taining Mechanical Equipment; Repairing and Maintaining Electrical Equipment; Teaching Others
Job Characteristics: Using Hands on Objects, Tools, or Controls; Making Repetitive Motions; Common Protective or Safety Attire; Importance of Repeating Same Tasks; Pace Determined by Speed of Equipment
GOE Group/s: 06.02.18 Production Work: Equipment Operation, Assorted Materials Processing
CIP Program/s: 470101 Electrical and Electronics Equipment Installer and Repairer; 470105 Industrial Electronics Installer and Repairer
Related DOT Job/s: 590.262-010 CRYSTAL GROWING TECHNICIAN; 590.282-010 EPITAXIAL REACTOR TECHNICIAN; 590.382-014 CRYSTAL GROWER; 590.382-018 EPITAXIAL REACTOR OPERATOR

92902E ELECTRONIC SEMICONDUCTOR SAWYERS, ABRADERS, AND POLISHERS. OOH

Title/s: Electronic Semiconductor Processors

Operate equipment to grind, abrade, or scribe semiconductor wafers. Adjusts equipment controls to set speed, angle, and thickness of cut. Monitors equipment cycle to verify accuracy of operation. Positions workpiece in holding fixture of sawing, drilling, grinding, or sanding equipment. Inspects sample workpiece for flaws, using x-ray machine, and measures workpiece with calipers and gauges. Readjusts controls based on inspection and measurements. Determines crystal orientations of ingot sections, using x-ray equipment, and draws orientation lines on ingot. Mounts crystal ingots or wafers on blocks or plastic laminate, using special mounting devices. Removes workpiece from equipment and cleans workpiece, using water, ultrasonic cleaner, or etching equipment. Records production information. Cleans and maintains equipment. Sorts and wraps finished workpieces in protective material.
Yearly Earnings: $21,164
Education: Moderate-term O-J-T
Knowledge: Production and Processing
Abilities: Flexibility of Closure; Perceptual Speed; Selective Attention; Finger Dexterity; Control Precision; Dynamic Flexibility; Hearing Sensitivity; Sound Localization
Skills: Operation Monitoring; Operation and Control; Product Inspection; Equipment Maintenance
General Work Activities: Inspecting Equipment, Structures, or Material; Controlling Machines and Processes; Repairing and Maintaining Electrical Equipment
Job Characteristics: Radiation; Using Hands on Objects, Tools, or Controls; Making Repetitive Motions; Common Protective or Safety Attire; Specialized Protective or Safety Attire; Importance of Repeating Same Tasks; Pace Determined by Speed of Equipment
GOE Group/s: 06.02.09 Production Work: Machine Work, Assorted Materials; 06.04.09 Elemental Work: Industrial: Machine Work, Assorted Materials
CIP Program/s: 470101 Electrical and Electronics Equipment Installer and Repairer; 470105 Industrial Electronics Installer and Repairer
Related DOT Job/s: 677.382-018 CRYSTAL SLICER; 679.362-010 CRYSTAL MACHINING COORDINATOR; 679.384-010 SEED CORE OPERATOR; 726.685-046 SAW OPERATOR, SEMICONDUCTOR WAFERS

92902G ELECTRONIC SEMICONDUCTOR WAFER BREAKERS, MOUNTERS, AND PACKAGERS. OOH

Title/s: Electronic Semiconductor Processors

Break, mount, and package crystals and wafers used in manufacture of electronic semiconductors. Breaks semiconductor wafers into individual dies, using hand tools or chemical solutions and breaking equipment. Positions, secures, and seals lids on semiconductor packages, using tweezers and heated chuck or automatic furnace. Places individual dies in carriers, using vacuum wand or brush. Positions wafers on cushion or waxed template. Tends equipment that attaches, mounts, presses, and disassembles templates and wafers. Attaches crystal ingot to graphite or epoxy backing and mounts on crystal saw block, using adhesive or wax. Sorts semiconductor crystal ingots according to size and crystal orientation. Inspects semiconductors to remove defective devices. Cleans dies and templates, using solutions and cleaning equipment. Maintains production records.
Yearly Earnings: $21,164
Education: Moderate-term O-J-T
Knowledge: Computers and Electronics
Abilities: Finger Dexterity
Skills: None above average
General Work Activities: Repairing and Maintaining Electrical Equipment
Job Characteristics: Using Hands on Objects, Tools, or Controls; Making Repetitive Motions
GOE Group/s: 06.04.09 Elemental Work: Industrial: Machine Work, Assorted Materials; 06.04.23 Elemental Work: Industrial: Manual Work, Assembly Small Parts; 06.04.34 Elemental Work: Industrial: Manual Work, Assorted Materials; 06.04.40 Elemental Work: Industrial: Loading, Moving, Hoisting, and Conveying
CIP Program/s: 000000 NO CIP ASSIGNED
Related DOT Job/s: 677.687-014 CRYSTAL MOUNTER; 726.685-058 WAFER MOUNTER; 726.687-030 LOADER, SEMICONDUCTOR DIES; 726.687-042 SEALER, SEMICONDUCTOR PACKAGES; 726.687-046 WAFER BREAKER, SEMICONDUCTORS

92905 MOTION PICTURE PROJECTIONISTS. OOH

Title/s: Motion Picture Projectionists

Set up and operate motion picture projection and sound-reproducing equipment to produce coordinated effects on screen. Sets up and operates motion picture projection and sound-reproducing equipment to project or produce pictures and sound effects on screen. Inserts film into top magazine reel, or threads film through the projector and onto automatic spool of projector. Regulates and adjusts projection light and focus, volume, tone, and timing of projection equipment. Monitors equipment operation and changes projectors without interruption to showing. Positions, installs, and connects auxiliary equipment, such as microphones, amplifiers, and lights. Operates special-effects equipment, such as stereopticon, to project pictures on screen. Coordinates equipment operation with presentation of supplemental material, such as music, oral commentary, or sound effects. Cleans lenses and maintains and performs minor repairs on projectors and equipment, or notifies maintenance personnel to correct major malfunctions. Inspects and repairs faulty sections of film, and rewinds film onto reels automatically or by hand.
Yearly Earnings: $19,760
Education: Short-term O-J-T
Knowledge: Fine Arts; Communications and Media
Abilities: Arm-Hand Steadiness; Response Orientation; Rate Control; Night Vision; Hearing Sensitivity; Auditory Attention; Sound Localization
Skills: Installation
General Work Activities: Handling and Moving Objects
Job Characteristics: Sounds, Noise Levels are Distracting, etc.; Extremely Bright or Inadequate Lighting; Sitting; Degree of Automation; Pace Determined by Speed of Equipment
GOE Group/s: 05.10.05 Crafts: Reproduction
CIP Program/s: 100101 Educational/Instructional Media Technologists and Technicians; 470499 Miscellaneous Mechanics and Repairers, Other

Related DOT Job/s: 960.362-010 MOTION-PICTURE PROJECTIONIST; 960.382-010 AUDIOVISUAL TECHNICIAN

92908 PHOTOGRAPHIC PROCESSING MACHINE OPERATORS AND TENDERS. OOH Title/s: Photographic Process Workers

Operate or tend photographic processing machines—such as motion picture film printing machines, photographic printing machines, film developing machines, and mounting presses—according to job specifications. Loads circuit boards, racks or rolls of film, negatives, or printing paper into processing or printing machines. Sets and adjusts machine controls, according to specifications, type of operation, and material requirements. Starts and operates machines to prepare circuit boards and expose, develop, etch, fix, wash, dry, and print film or plates. Fills tanks of processing machines with solutions, such as developer, dyes, stop-baths, fixers, bleaches, and washes. Monitors equipment operation to detect malfunctions. Measures and mixes chemicals according to formula to prepare solutions for processing. Removes completed work from equipment and examines circuit boards, plates, film, and prints for conformance to quality standards. Reads work orders and examines negatives and film to determine machine settings and processing requirements. Places film in labeled containers or numbers film for identification, using numbering machine or by hand. Discards or cleans and repairs defective film or circuit patterns on photographic plates, using cleaning solutions and hand tools. Cleans and maintains photoprocessing equipment, using cleaning and rinsing solutions and ultrasonic equipment. Maintains records, such as number and types of processing completed, rate of materials usage, and customer charges.

Yearly Earnings: $21,164
Education: Short-term O-J-T
Knowledge: Production and Processing; Chemistry
Abilities: Rate Control; Visual Color Discrimination; Night Vision
Skills: None above average
General Work Activities: None above average
Job Characteristics: Deal with Physical, Aggressive People; Extremely Bright or Inadequate Lighting; Contaminants; Hazardous Conditions; Standing; Degree of Automation; Pace Determined by Speed of Equipment
GOE Group/s: 05.10.05 Crafts: Reproduction; 05.12.14 Elemental Work: Mechanical: Painting, Caulking, and Coating; 06.02.18 Production Work: Equipment Operation, Assorted Materials Processing; 06.04.19 Elemental Work: Industrial: Equipment Operation, Assorted Materials Processing; 06.04.20 Elemental Work: Industrial: Machine Assembling
CIP Program/s: 100103 Photographic Technologists and Technicians; 480201 Graphic and Printing Equipment Operator, General; 480206 Lithographer and Platemaker
Related DOT Job/s: 976.380-010 COMPUTER-CONTROLLED-COLOR-PHOTOGRAPH-PRINTER OPERATOR; 976.382-014 COLOR-PRINTER OPERATOR; 976.382-018 FILM DEVELOPER; 976.382-030 PHOTOGRAPHIC ALIGNER, SEMICONDUCTOR WAFERS; 976.382-034 STEP-AND-REPEAT REDUCTION CAMERA OPERATOR; 976.382-038 PHOTO MASK PATTERN GENERATOR; 976.384-010 PHOTO TECHNICIAN; 976.384-014 PHOTO MASK PROCESSOR; 976.385-010 MICROFILM PROCESSOR; 976.665-010 TAKE-DOWN SORTER; 976.682-010 FILM PRINTER; 976.682-014 PRINTER OPERATOR, BLACK-AND-WHITE; 976.682-018 RECTIFICATION PRINTER; 976.684-014 FILM LABORATORY TECHNICIAN; 976.684-030 CONTACT PRINTER, PRINTED CIRCUIT BOARDS; 976.684-038 CONTACT WORKER, LITHOGRAPHY; 976.685-014 DEVELOPER, AUTOMATIC; 976.685-018 FILM LABORATORY TECHNICIAN II; 976.685-022 MOUNTER, AUTOMATIC; 976.685-026 PRINT DEVELOPER, AUTOMATIC; 976.685-030 UTILITY WORKER, FILM PROCESSING; 976.685-034 DEVELOPER, PRINTED CIRCUIT BOARD PANELS; 976.685-038 PHOTOGRAPHIC PROCESSOR, SEMICONDUCTOR WAFERS

92911 TIRE BUILDING MACHINE OPERATORS. OOH Title/s: Tire Building Machine Operators

Operate machines such as collapsible drum devices to build pneumatic tires from rubber components, such as beads, ply stock, tread, and sidewalls. Depresses pedal to rotate drum and winds specified number of plies around drum to form tire body. Starts rollers that bond tread and plies as drum revolves. Activates bead setters that press prefabricated beads onto plies and position rollers that turn ply edges under and over beads. Depresses pedal to collapse drum and lifts tire onto conveyor. Aligns tread with guide, starts drum to wind tread onto plies, and slices ends. Turns ends of plies under and over beads with steel rod. Positions ply stitcher rollers and drum according to width of stock, using hand tools and gauges. Brushes solvent onto ply to ensure adhesion and repeats process as specified, alternating direction of each ply to strengthen tire. Winds chafers and breaker onto plies. Rubs cement stick on drum edge to provide adhesive surface for plies. Pulls ply from supply rack and aligns ply with edge of drum. Cuts ply at splice point and presses ends together to form continuous band.

Yearly Earnings: $21,164
Education: Moderate-term O-J-T
Knowledge: Production and Processing
Abilities: None above average
Skills: Operation and Control
General Work Activities: Performing General Physical Activities; Handling and Moving Objects; Controlling Machines and Processes
Job Characteristics: Sounds, Noise Levels are Distracting, etc.; Contaminants; Hazardous Conditions; Hazardous Equipment; Hazardous Situations; Standing; Using Hands on Objects, Tools, or Controls; Common Protective or Safety Attire; Degree of Automation; Pace Determined by Speed of Equipment
GOE Group/s: 06.02.29 Production Work: Manual Work, Rubber; 06.04.07 Elemental Work: Industrial: Machine Work, Rubber
CIP Program/s: 000000 NO CIP ASSIGNED
Related DOT Job/s: 750.384-010 TIRE BUILDER, AUTOMOBILE; 750.684-014 BEAD BUILDER

92914 PAPER GOODS MACHINE SETTERS AND SET-UP OPERATORS. OOH Title/s: Paper Goods Machine Setters and Set-Up Operators

Set up or set up and operate paper goods machines that perform a variety of functions, such as converting, sawing, corrugating, banding, wrapping, boxing, stitching, forming, or sealing paper or paperboard sheets into products, such as toilet tissue, towels, napkins, bags, envelopes, tubing, cartons, wax rolls, and containers. Adjusts guide assembly and folding mechanism according to specifications, using hand tools. Measures, spaces, and sets saw blades, cutters, and perforators, according to product specifications. Starts machine and regulates tension on pressure rolls. Synchronizes speed of machine components and temperature of glue or paraffin. Installs attachments to machines for gluing, folding, printing, or cutting. Places roll of paper or cardboard on machine feedtrack and threads paper through gluing, coating, and slitting rollers. Fills glue and paraffin reservoirs and loads automatic stapling mechanism. Observes operation of various machines to detect machine malfunctions, and makes corrections for product to meet specifications. Examines completed work to detect defects and verify conformance to work orders. Removes finished cores and stacks or places them on conveyor for transfer to other work areas. Disassembles machines to repair or replace broken or worn parts using hand or power tools. Cuts labels to specified dimensions using hand or power cutters.

Yearly Earnings: $19,760
Education: Moderate-term O-J-T
Knowledge: Production and Processing
Abilities: Rate Control
Skills: Installation; Operation Monitoring; Operation and Control; Equipment Maintenance; Troubleshooting; Repairing
General Work Activities: Handling and Moving Objects; Controlling Machines and Processes; Repairing and Maintaining Mechanical Equipment
Job Characteristics: Sounds, Noise Levels are Distracting, etc.; Hazardous Equipment; Standing; Degree of Automation; Pace Determined by Speed of Equipment
GOE Group/s: 06.01.02 Production Technology: Machine Set-up; 06.02.04 Production Work: Machine Work, Paper
CIP Program/s: 470303 Industrial Machinery Maintenance and Repair
Related DOT Job/s: 640.682-010 CONVOLUTE-TUBE WINDER; 640.682-022 SPIRAL-TUBE WINDER; 641.380-010 ENVELOPE-FOLDING-MACHINE ADJUSTER; 649.380-010 MACHINE SET-UP OPERATOR, PAPER GOODS; 649.682-010 BOX-FOLDING-MACHINE OPERATOR

92917 COOKING MACHINE OPERATORS AND TENDERS, FOOD AND TOBACCO. OOH Title/s: Cooking and Roasting Machine Operators and Tenders

Operate or tend cooking equipment, such as steam cooking vats, deep fry cookers, pressure cookers, kettles, and boilers, to prepare food products, such as meats, sugar, cheese, and grain. Exclude food roasting, baking, and drying machine operators and tenders. Starts conveyers, machines, or pumps and sets temperature, pressure, and time controls. Activates agitators and paddles to mix or stir ingredients, and stops machine when ingredients are thoroughly mixed. Operates and controls equipment, such as kettles, cookers, vats, and tanks, to cook ingredients or prepare products for further processing. Observes gauges, dials, and product texture or color and adjusts controls to maintain appropriate temperature, pressure, and flow of ingredients. Admits required amounts of water, steam, cooking oils, or compressed air into equipment. Turns valves or starts pumps to drain product from equipment and transfer to storage, cooling, or further processing areas. Operates auxiliary machines and equipment, such as grinders, canners, and molding presses, to prepare or further process products. Reads recipes or formulae to determine ingredients or quantities of ingredients needed. Places products on conveyor or cart and monitors flow. Listens for malfunction alarms, shuts down equipment, and notifies supervisor. Measures or weighs prescribed ingredients, using scales or measuring containers. Pours, adds, or loads prescribed quantities of ingredients or products into cooking equipment, manually or using hoist. Examines sample of product; tests color, content, consistency, viscosity, acidity, or specific gravity; and removes impurities from product. Notifies or signals other workers to operate equipment or when processing complete. Removes cooked material or products from equipment. Cleans and washes equipment, using water hoses, cleaning or sterilizing solutions, or rinses. Records production and test data, such as processing steps, temperature and steam readings, cooking time, batches processed, and test results.
Yearly Earnings: $20,540
Education: Moderate-term O-J-T
Knowledge: Food Production
Abilities: Response Orientation; Rate Control; Reaction Time; Auditory Attention; Sound Localization
Skills: Operation Monitoring; Operation and Control
General Work Activities: Handling and Moving Objects
Job Characteristics: Very Hot; Hazardous Situations; Standing; Degree of Automation; Pace Determined by Speed of Equipment
GOE Group/s: 06.02.15 Production Work: Equipment Operation, Food Processing; 06.02.28 Production Work: Manual Work, Food Processing; 06.04.15 Elemental Work: Industrial: Equipment Operation, Food Processing; 06.04.19 Elemental Work: Industrial: Equipment Operation, Assorted Materials Processing; 06.04.28 Elemental Work: Industrial: Manual Work, Food Processing
CIP Program/s: 010401 Agricultural and Food Products Processing Operations and Management; 200401 Institutional Food Workers and Administrators, General
Related DOT Job/s: 520.685-082 COOKER, CASING; 521.687-090 NUT STEAMER; 522.362-010 YEAST DISTILLER; 522.382-010 COTTAGE-CHEESE MAKER; 522.382-022 MASH-TUB-COOKER OPERATOR; 522.382-034 SUGAR BOILER; 522.482-010 MASHER; 522.682-010 KETTLE OPERATOR; 522.682-014 ORDERING-MACHINE OPERATOR; 522.685-018 BRINE MAKER I; 522.685-034 CORN COOKER; 522.685-094 STEAM-CONDITIONER OPERATOR; 522.685-102 VACUUM-CONDITIONER OPERATOR; 523.382-022 PROCESSOR, INSTANT POTATO; 523.682-010 CHOCOLATE TEMPERER; 523.682-018 DEXTRINE MIXER; 523.685-014 BLANCHING-MACHINE OPERATOR; 523.685-022 CHOCOLATE TEMPERER; 523.685-030 COOK-BOX FILLER; 523.685-034 COOKER, MEAL; 523.685-114 STERILIZER OPERATOR; 526.381-026 COOK, KETTLE; 526.382-014 CONFECTIONERY COOKER; 526.382-022 MOLASSES AND CARAMEL OPERATOR; 526.665-010 COOKER, PROCESS CHEESE; 526.665-014 KETTLE TENDER; 526.682-014 COOK, DOG-AND-CAT FOOD; 526.682-018 COOK, SYRUP MAKER; 526.682-034 RETORT OPERATOR; 526.685-010 COOK; 526.685-014 COOK, FRY, DEEP FAT; 526.685-018 COOK, VACUUM KETTLE; 526.685-022 COOKER; 526.685-042 POPCORN-CANDY MAKER; 526.685-046 POTATO-CHIP FRIER; 526.685-050 POTATO-PANCAKE FRIER; 526.685-058 THERMOSCREW OPERATOR; 526.685-062 TRIPE COOKER; 529.484-010 STEAK SAUCE MAKER; 529.685-290 COOK, SOYBEAN SPECIALTIES; 553.665-022 COOKER TENDER

92921 ROASTING, BAKING, AND DRYING MACHINE OPERATORS AND TENDERS, FOOD AND TOBACCO. OOH Title/s: Cooking and Roasting Machine Operators and Tenders

Operate or tend roasting, baking, or drying equipment to reduce moisture content of food or tobacco products, such as tobacco, cocoa and coffee beans, macaroni, and grain; roast grain, nuts, or coffee beans; bake bread or other bakery products; or process food preparatory to canning. These machines include hearth ovens, kiln driers, roasters, char kilns, steam ovens, and vacuum drying equipment. Observes temperature, humidity, and pressure gauges, or product, and adjusts controls and turns valves to maintain prescribed operating conditions. Sets temperature and time controls, lights ovens or gas burners, and starts equipment, such as conveyors, blowers, driers, or pumps. Opens valve, discharge gates, or hopper chutes to load or remove product from oven or equipment. Fills or removes product from trays, carts, hoppers, or equipment, using scoop, peel, or shovel, or by hand. Weighs product, using scale hopper or scale conveyor. Observes, feels, or tastes products after processing to ensure products conform to standards. Tests product for moisture content, using moisture meter. Smooths out product in bin, tray, or conveyor, using rake or shovel. Reads work order to determine quantity and type of product to be baked, dried, or roasted. Records production data, such as weight and amount of product processed, type of product, and time and temperature of processing. Observes and listens for machine malfunctions, and notifies supervisor when corrective actions fail. Clears or dislodges blockages in bins, screens, or other equipment, using pole, brush, or mallet. Pushes racks or carts to transfer product to storage or for further processing. Installs equipment, such as spray unit, cutting blades, or screens, using hand tools. Takes sample of

product during or after process for laboratory analysis. Cleans equipment with steam, hot water, and hose.
Yearly Earnings: $20,540
Education: Moderate-term O-J-T
Knowledge: Food Production
Abilities: Selective Attention; Time Sharing; Reaction Time; Static Strength; Trunk Strength; Dynamic Flexibility; Gross Body Equilibrium; Visual Color Discrimination; Hearing Sensitivity; Sound Localization
Skills: Installation; Operation Monitoring; Operation and Control
General Work Activities: None above average
Job Characteristics: Very Hot; Hazardous Equipment; Hazardous Situations; Standing; Common Protective or Safety Attire; Degree of Automation; Importance of Repeating Same Tasks; Pace Determined by Speed of Equipment
GOE Group/s: 06.02.15 Production Work: Equipment Operation, Food Processing; 06.04.15 Elemental Work: Industrial: Equipment Operation, Food Processing
CIP Program/s: 000000 NO CIP ASSIGNED
Related DOT Job/s: 522.662-014 REDRYING-MACHINE OPERATOR; 522.685-038 CURING-BIN OPERATOR; 522.685-066 FISH SMOKER; 523.362-010 COCOA-BEAN ROASTER I; 523.362-014 DRIER OPERATOR; 523.382-010 GUNNER; 523.585-022 DRIER, LONG GOODS; 523.585-030 PULP-DRIER FIRER; 523.585-034 ROASTER, GRAIN; 523.662-010 BONE-CHAR KILN OPERATOR; 523.665-010 SUGAR DRIER; 523.682-014 COFFEE ROASTER; 523.682-022 DRIER OPERATOR; 523.682-026 DRUM DRIER; 523.682-030 KILN OPERATOR, MALT HOUSE; 523.682-038 TOBACCO CURER; 523.685-026 COFFEE ROASTER, CONTINUOUS PROCESS; 523.685-054 DEHYDRATOR TENDER; 523.685-058 DRIER ATTENDANT; 523.685-062 DRIER OPERATOR; 523.685-066 DRIER TENDER; 523.685-070 DRIER TENDER; 523.685-074 DRIER TENDER I; 523.685-078 FIRER, KILN; 523.685-086 GRAIN DRIER; 523.685-090 GRAIN-DRIER OPERATOR; 523.685-094 GRAIN-WAFER-MACHINE OPERATOR; 523.685-098 GRANULATOR OPERATOR; 523.685-106 INSTANTIZER OPERATOR; 523.685-118 TOBACCO-DRIER OPERATOR; 523.685-122 VACUUM DRIER OPERATOR; 523.685-126 WINE PASTEURIZER; 525.682-010 SMOKER; 526.382-026 STEAM-OVEN OPERATOR; 526.585-010 OVEN OPERATOR; 526.682-026 MALT ROASTER; 526.685-026 CORN POPPER; 526.685-030 OVEN TENDER; 526.685-054 PRETZEL COOKER; 526.685-066 WAFER-MACHINE OPERATOR; 526.685-070 OVEN OPERATOR, AUTOMATIC; 529.485-018 DRIER, BELT CONVEYOR; 529.685-098 DRIER OPERATOR, DRUM; 529.685-174 NUT ROASTER

92923 FURNACE, KILN, OVEN, DRIER, OR KETTLE OPERATORS AND TENDERS. OOH Title/s: Furnace, Kiln, or Kettle Operators and Tenders

Operate or tend heating equipment other than basic metal or plastic processing equipment. Oven operators or tenders bake fiberglass or painted products, fuse glass or enamel to metal products, carbonize coal, or cure rubber or other products. Furnace operators or tenders anneal glass, roast sulfur, convert chemicals, or process petroleum. Kettle operators and tenders boil soap, or melt antimony or asphalt materials. Drier operators and tenders remove moisture from paper, chemicals, ore, clay products, or slurry. Loads equipment receptacle or conveyor with material to be processed, manually or using hoist. Presses and adjusts controls to activate, set, and regulate equipment operation according to specifications. Monitors equipment operation, gauges, and panel lights to detect deviation from standards. Stops equipment and clears blockages or jams, using fingers, wire, or hand tools. Weighs or measures specified amount of material or substance to be processed, using devices such as scales and calipers. Reads and interprets work orders and instructions to determine work assignment, process specifications, and production schedule. Removes product from equipment, manually or using hoist, and prepares for storage, shipment, or additional processing. Examines or tests sample of processed substance, or collects sample for laboratory testing, to ensure conformance to specifications. Replaces worn or defective equipment parts, using hand tools. Cleans, lubricates, and adjusts equipment, using items such as scrapers, solvents, air hose, oil, and hand tools. Records gauge readings, test results, and shift production in logbook. Confers with supervisor or other equipment operators to report equipment malfunction or resolve problems resulting from process changes. Transports materials and products to and from work area, manually or using cart, handtruck, or hoist.
Yearly Earnings: $26,104
Education: Moderate-term O-J-T
Knowledge: Production and Processing; Mechanical
Abilities: None above average
Skills: Operation Monitoring; Equipment Maintenance; Repairing
General Work Activities: Controlling Machines and Processes; Repairing and Maintaining Mechanical Equipment
Job Characteristics: Sounds, Noise Levels are Distracting, etc.; Very Hot; Hazardous Conditions; Hazardous Equipment; Standing; Pace Determined by Speed of Equipment
GOE Group/s: 05.06.02 Systems Operation: Stationary Engineering; 05.12.10 Elemental Work: Mechanical: Heating and Melting; 06.02.08 Production Work: Machine Work, Stone, Glass, and Clay; 06.02.10 Production Work: Equipment Operation, Metal Processing; 06.02.11 Production Work: Equipment Operation, Chemical Processing; 06.02.12 Production Work: Equipment Operation, Petroleum and Gas Processing; 06.02.13 Production Work: Equipment Operation, Rubber, Plastics, and Glass Processing; 06.02.14 Production Work: Equipment Operation, Paper and Paper Products Processing; 06.02.15 Production Work: Equipment Operation, Food Processing; 06.02.17 Production Work: Equipment Operation, Clay and Coke Processing; 06.02.18 Production Work: Equipment Operation, Assorted Materials Processing; 06.03.01 Quality Control: Inspecting, Testing, and Repairing; 06.04.05 Elemental Work: Industrial: Machine Work, Fabric and Leather; 06.04.10 Elemental Work: Industrial: Equipment Operation, Metal Processing; 06.04.11 Elemental Work: Industrial: Equipment Operation, Chemical Processing; 06.04.12 Elemental Work: Industrial: Equipment Operation, Petroleum, Gas, and Coal Processing; 06.04.13 Elemental Work: Industrial: Equipment Operation, Rubber, Plastics, Glass Processing; 06.04.14 Elemental Work: Industrial: Equipment Operation, Paper Making; 06.04.16 Elemental Work: Industrial: Equipment Operation, Textile, Fabric, and Leather Processing; 06.04.17 Elemental Work: Industrial: Equipment Operation, Clay Processing; 06.04.18 Elemental Work: Industrial: Equipment Operation, Wood Processing; 06.04.19 Elemental Work: Industrial: Equipment Operation, Assorted Materials Processing; 06.04.21 Elemental Work: Industrial: Machine Work, Brushing, Spraying, and Coating; 06.04.34 Elemental Work: Industrial: Manual Work, Assorted Materials; 06.04.35 Elemental Work: Industrial: Laundering, Dry Cleaning; 06.04.39 Elemental Work: Industrial: Cleaning
CIP Program/s: 000000 NO CIP ASSIGNED
Related DOT Job/s: 361.685-010 CONDITIONER-TUMBLER OPERATOR; 369.685-026 RUG-DRY-ROOM ATTENDANT; 369.685-034 TUMBLER OPERATOR; 503.685-022 FLAME DEGREASER; 504.485-010 RIVET HEATER; 504.685-030 REEL-BLADE-BENDER FURNACE TENDER; 509.565-010 KILN OPERATOR; 509.685-018 BURNING-PLANT OPERATOR; 511.482-010 CONTROL OPERATOR; 511.565-014 DRIER TENDER; 512.685-018 POT TENDER; 513.362-010 CALCINER OPERATOR; 513.462-010 FURNACE OPERATOR; 513.565-010 KILN OPERATOR; 513.682-010 ROTARY-KILN OPERATOR; 518.685-010 CORE-OVEN TENDER; 519.665-014 STANDPIPE TENDER; 519.685-010 BRIQUET-

TING-MACHINE OPERATOR; 519.685-018 KETTLE OPERATOR; 519.685-022 KETTLE TENDER I; 532.585-010 MATRIX-DRIER TENDER; 532.685-010 BACK TENDER, INSULATION BOARD; 532.685-014 COOKER TENDER; 532.687-010 LABEL DRIER; 534.565-010 OVEN TENDER; 542.362-010 HEATER II; 542.562-010 FURNACE OPERATOR; 542.685-010 PLANT OPERATOR, CHANNEL PROCESS; 542.685-018 UNIT OPERATOR; 543.362-010 OIL BOILER; 543.382-010 DRIER OPERATOR; 543.562-010 CARBON-FURNACE OPERATOR; 543.682-010 COKE BURNER; 543.682-014 DRIER OPERATOR; 543.682-018 FURNACE OPERATOR; 543.682-026 STILL OPERATOR; 543.685-014 DRIER TENDER; 543.685-018 OVEN TENDER; 543.685-022 THAW-SHED HEATER TENDER; 551.685-026 CENTRIFUGAL-DRIER OPERATOR; 553.362-014 AUTOCLAVE OPERATOR; 553.382-010 AUTOCLAVE OPERATOR I; 553.382-014 BOILER; 553.382-022 VARNISH MAKER; 553.385-014 PRIMER EXPEDITOR AND DRIER; 553.462-010 FLASH-DRIER OPERATOR; 553.482-010 AGER OPERATOR; 553.582-010 DRIER OPERATOR II; 553.582-014 POT FIRER; 553.585-010 DEBUBBLIZER; 553.585-014 DRY-HOUSE ATTENDANT; 553.585-018 DRYING-ROOM ATTENDANT; 553.665-014 BLACK-MILL OPERATOR; 553.665-018 COOK; 553.665-026 DRIER OPERATOR I; 553.665-030 DRUM-DRIER OPERATOR; 553.665-034 FIRER HELPER; 553.665-038 HEATER TENDER; 553.665-042 PLASTICS-SEASONER OPERATOR; 553.665-054 TRAY-DRIER OPERATOR; 553.682-010 BLACK-ASH-BURNER OPERATOR; 553.682-022 REDUCTION-FURNACE OPERATOR; 553.685-018 BONE-CHAR KILN TENDER; 553.685-022 BONE-DRIER OPERATOR; 553.685-030 CALCINE-FURNACE TENDER; 553.685-034 CONTINUOUS-LINTER-DRIER OPERATOR; 553.685-038 CURING-OVEN TENDER; 553.685-042 DRIER OPERATOR; 553.685-046 DRIER OPERATOR II; 553.685-050 DRIER OPERATOR III; 553.685-054 DRIER OPERATOR IV; 553.685-070 KETTLE WORKER; 553.685-074 LIME-SLUDGE KILN OPERATOR; 553.685-082 OVEN TENDER; 553.685-086 PIGMENT FURNACE TENDER; 553.685-090 RABBLE-FURNACE TENDER; 553.685-094 ROTARY-FURNACE TENDER; 553.685-098 SOAP-DRIER OPERATOR; 553.685-106 VACUUM-DRIER TENDER; 553.685-118 DRIER OPERATOR VI; 556.585-014 POLYMERIZATION-OVEN OPERATOR; 558.482-010 FURNACE OPERATOR; 558.585-030 LEAD-NITRATE PROCESSOR; 558.685-054 RED-LEAD BURNER; 559.662-010 ACID MAKER; 561.362-010 TREATING ENGINEER; 562.665-010 LOG COOKER; 562.665-014 STEAM-BOX OPERATOR; 563.382-010 KILN OPERATOR; 563.585-010 DRIER TENDER; 563.662-010 TREATING-PLANT OPERATOR; 563.682-010 CHARCOAL BURNER, BEEHIVE KILN; 563.685-014 CLOTHESPIN-DRIER OPERATOR; 563.685-018 DRY-HOUSE ATTENDANT; 563.685-022 VENEER DRIER; 563.685-026 VENEER REDRIER; 571.685-010 BURNER TENDER; 572.685-010 GLASS-FURNACE TENDER; 573.362-010 DRY-KILN OPERATOR; 573.382-010 ROTARY-KILN OPERATOR; 573.382-014 SPRAY-DRIER OPERATOR; 573.382-018 TUNNEL-KILN OPERATOR; 573.462-010 LIME-KILN OPERATOR; 573.585-010 OVEN TENDER; 573.662-010 FIRER, KILN; 573.682-010 KILN BURNER; 573.683-010 STEAM-TANK OPERATOR; 573.685-010 ANNEALER; 573.685-014 CLAY ROASTER; 573.685-026 LEHR TENDER; 573.685-030 LENS HARDENER; 573.685-034 REGENERATOR OPERATOR; 573.685-038 BURNER; 573.685-042 OVEN-PRESS TENDER I; 573.685-046 OVEN-PRESS TENDER II; 579.382-014 CUPOLA OPERATOR, INSULATION; 579.685-034 NODULIZER; 580.685-014 CLOTH DRIER; 581.685-014 DRIER; 581.685-018 DRIER OPERATOR III; 581.685-022 DRY-CANS OPERATOR; 581.685-026 DRYING-MACHINE OPERATOR, PACKAGE YARNS; 581.685-030 DRYING-MACHINE TENDER; 581.685-034 DRYING-UNIT-FELTING-MACHINE OPERATOR; 581.685-046 RAW-STOCK-DRIER TENDER; 581.685-050 RUG-DRYING-MACHINE OPERATOR; 581.685-054 SKEIN-YARN DRIER; 581.685-062 TUMBLER TENDER; 581.685-066 VACUUM-DRIER OPERATOR; 581.685-078 FLAT DRIER; 581.685-082 DRUM-DRIER OPERATOR; 581.686-038 TRAY DRIER; 582.685-086 HAIR-BOILER OPERATOR; 587.585-010 AUTOCLAVE OPERATOR; 587.682-010 AUTOCLAVE OPERATOR; 589.485-010 PAD-EXTRACTOR TENDER; 590.382-010 OPERATOR, AUTOMATED PROCESS; 590.662-022 STOVE-CARRIAGE OPERATOR; 590.665-010 OVEN OPERATOR; 590.685-010 BACKING-IN-MACHINE TENDER; 590.685-034 FIRER; 590.685-090 CURING OVEN ATTENDANT; 599.682-014 IMPREGNATOR AND DRIER; 619.662-010 SHRINK-PIT OPERATOR; 709.682-010 AUTOCLAVE OPERATOR II; 869.685-010 KETTLE TENDER; 955.685-010 INCINERATOR OPERATOR I

92926 BOILER OPERATORS AND TENDERS, LOW-PRESSURE. OOH Title/s: Boiler Operators and Tenders, Low Pressure

Operate or tend low-pressure stationary steam boilers and auxiliary steam equipment, such as pumps, compressors, and air-conditioning equipment, to supply steam heat for office buildings, apartment houses, or industrial establishments; to maintain steam at specified pressure aboard marine vessels; or to generate and supply compressed air for operation of pneumatic tools, hoists, and air lances. Tends boilers and equipment to supply and maintain steam or heat for buildings, marine vessels, or operation of pneumatic tools. Moves controls and observes gauges to regulate heat and steam. Ignites fuel in burner using torch or flame. Installs burners and auxiliary equipment, using hand tools. Shovels coal or coke into firebox to feed fuel, using hand tools. Obtains samples from designated location on boiler and carries samples to testing laboratory. Tests ample quantity to ensure sample meets specifications, using testing devices. Cleans and maintains heating and steam boilers and equipment, using hand tools. Records test results on specified form and gives to worker or supervisor.

Yearly Earnings: $30,680
Education: Moderate-term O-J-T
Knowledge: Mechanical
Abilities: Perceptual Speed; Arm-Hand Steadiness; Control Precision; Multilimb Coordination; Response Orientation; Rate Control; Reaction Time; Speed of Limb Movement; Static Strength; Explosive Strength; Dynamic Strength; Trunk Strength; Stamina; Extent Flexibility; Dynamic Flexibility; Gross Body Coordination; Gross Body Equilibrium
Skills: Installation; Equipment Maintenance
General Work Activities: Performing General Physical Activities; Controlling Machines and Processes
Job Characteristics: Sounds, Noise Levels are Distracting, etc.; Very Hot; Extremely Bright or Inadequate Lighting; Contaminants; Cramped Work Space, Awkward Positions; Hazardous Conditions; Hazardous Equipment; Hazardous Situations; Standing; Kneeling, Crouching, or Crawling; Using Hands on Objects, Tools, or Controls; Bending or Twisting the Body; Making Repetitive Motions; Common Protective or Safety Attire; Importance of Repeating Same Tasks
GOE Group/s: 05.06.02 Systems Operation: Stationary Engineering; 06.04.11 Elemental Work: Industrial: Equipment Operation, Chemical Processing
CIP Program/s: 470501 Stationary Energy Sources Installer and Operator
Related DOT Job/s: 553.685-066 FIRER, RETORT; 950.585-014 BOILER-OPERATOR HELPER; 950.685-014 BOILER-ROOM HELPER; 951.685-014 FIRER, LOW PRESSURE; 951.685-018 FIRER, MARINE

92928 COOLING AND FREEZING EQUIPMENT OPERATORS AND TENDERS. OOH Title/s: Indirectly related to Cannery Workers; Dairy Processing Equipment Operators, Including Setters

Operate or tend equipment—such as cooling and freezing units, refrigerators, batch freezers, and freezing tunnels—to cool or

freeze products such as ice cream, meat, blood plasma, and chemicals, preparatory to storage, shipment, or further processing. Starts pumps, agitators, and conveyors, and turns valves to admit or transfer product, refrigerant, or mix. Adjusts machine or freezer speed and air intake to obtain desired consistency and amount of product. Starts equipment to blend contents or mix with air to prevent sticking to vat. Monitors pressure gauges, flowmeters, thermometers, or product, and adjusts controls to maintain specified conditions. Positions molds on conveyor, and measures and adjusts level of fill, using depth gauge. Places or positions containers into equipment and removes containers after cooling or freezing process. Measures or weighs specified amounts of ingredients or material, and adds into tanks, vats, or equipment. Assembles or attaches pipes, fittings, or valves, using hand tools. Inserts forming fixture, and starts machine that cuts frozen product into measured portions or specified shapes. Stirs material with spoon or paddle to mix ingredients or allow even cooling and to prevent coagulation. Draws sample of product and tests for specific gravity, acidity, or sugar content, using hydrometer, pH meter, or refractometer. Flushes lines with solutions or steam to clean and sterilize equipment. Scrapes, dislodges, or breaks excess frost or ice from equipment. Cleans, maintains, and repairs machines. Loads and positions wrapping paper, sticks, bags, or cartons into dispensing machines, and removes jammed sticks, using pliers or picks. Records temperatures, amount of materials processed, or test results on report form.

Yearly Earnings: $20,852
Education: Moderate-term O-J-T
Knowledge: Food Production; Chemistry
Abilities: Perceptual Speed; Manual Dexterity; Finger Dexterity; Reaction Time; Wrist-Finger Speed; Speed of Limb Movement; Stamina; Extent Flexibility; Dynamic Flexibility; Gross Body Coordination; Gross Body Equilibrium
Skills: Testing; Operation Monitoring; Operation and Control; Equipment Maintenance; Troubleshooting; Repairing
General Work Activities: Controlling Machines and Processes; Repairing and Maintaining Mechanical Equipment
Job Characteristics: Very Hot; Cramped Work Space, Awkward Positions; Standing; Keeping or Regaining Balance; Degree of Automation; Importance of Repeating Same Tasks; Pace Determined by Speed of Equipment
GOE Group/s: 06.02.15 Production Work: Equipment Operation, Food Processing; 06.04.11 Elemental Work: Industrial: Equipment Operation, Chemical Processing; 06.04.15 Elemental Work: Industrial: Equipment Operation, Food Processing; 06.04.19 Elemental Work: Industrial: Equipment Operation, Assorted Materials Processing
CIP Program/s: 000000 NO CIP ASSIGNED
Related DOT Job/s: 522.685-014 BREWERY CELLAR WORKER; 523.585-014 CHILLER TENDER; 523.585-018 CRYSTALLIZER OPERATOR; 523.685-010 BATCH FREEZER; 523.685-018 CHILLING-HOOD OPERATOR; 523.685-038 COOLER TENDER; 523.685-042 COOLING-MACHINE OPERATOR; 523.685-046 COOLING-PAN TENDER; 523.685-050 CRYSTALLIZER OPERATOR; 523.685-082 FREEZER TUNNEL OPERATOR; 523.685-102 ICE MAKER; 529.482-010 FREEZER OPERATOR; 529.482-014 NOVELTY MAKER I; 529.482-018 NOVELTY MAKER II; 529.485-010 BARREL FILLER; 529.685-250 VOTATOR-MACHINE OPERATOR; 551.685-042 CHILLER OPERATOR; 556.685-054 PARADICHLOROBENZENE TENDER; 559.685-090 FREEZING-MACHINE OPERATOR; 559.685-170 SPREADING-MACHINE OPERATOR

92932 DAIRY PROCESSING EQUIPMENT OPERATORS, INCLUDING SETTERS. OOH Title/s: Dairy Processing Equipment Operators, Including Setters

Set up, operate, or tend continuous-flow or vat-type equipment to process milk, cream, or other dairy products, following specified methods and formulas. Pumps or pours ingredients, such as salt, into product at specified intervals to make dairy products, such as buttermilk. Starts pumps, agitators, and other equipment, adjusts temperature, and controls flow of product through system. Connects pipes, fittings, valves, bowls, plates, disks, impeller shaft, and other parts to equipment with wrench. Turns control knobs to adjust speed of operation, or adds ingredients to ensure product meets specifications. Starts pump to convey sterile solution through equipment and to admit measured amount of pasteurized cream into churn. Observes and listens to equipment to detect possible malfunctions, and reports malfunctions or product failing to meet specifications to supervisor. Turns valves and observes gauges to regulate temperature and flow of water, refrigerant, and butter oil through chilling vat. Pasteurizes and separates cream to obtain butter oil, using chilling vat and following specified procedures. Observes separation of buttermilk from butter and pumps buttermilk from churn. When making cheese, dumps, presses, salts, curds, pierces, washes, and turns cheese blocks to cure cheese. Adds water, alkali, and coloring to butter oil to achieve specified grade. Opens churn and sprays butter with chlorinated water to remove residue buttermilk to produce butter following churn method. Examines, tastes, and feels butter to detect undesirable flavors and to determine whether texture meets specifications, depending on product. Tests butter or butter oil for moisture, salt content, acidity, and consistency, depending on product being produced, using testing apparatus. Compares butter with color chart and adds coloring to meet specifications. Records production and test data on record sheet.

Yearly Earnings: $32,552
Education: Moderate-term O-J-T
Knowledge: Production and Processing; Food Production; Chemistry
Abilities: Flexibility of Closure; Control Precision; Rate Control; Gross Body Equilibrium; Visual Color Discrimination; Hearing Sensitivity; Auditory Attention; Sound Localization
Skills: Testing; Operation Monitoring; Operation and Control; Product Inspection
General Work Activities: None above average
Job Characteristics: Sounds, Noise Levels are Distracting, etc.; Very Hot; Contaminants; Hazardous Equipment; Common Protective or Safety Attire; Degree of Automation; Pace Determined by Speed of Equipment
GOE Group/s: 06.02.15 Production Work: Equipment Operation, Food Processing
CIP Program/s: 000000 NO CIP ASSIGNED
Related DOT Job/s: 529.362-010 BUTTERMAKER; 529.382-010 BUTTERMAKER, CONTINUOUS CHURN; 529.382-018 DAIRY-PROCESSING-EQUIPMENT OPERATOR; 529.682-014 CHEESEMAKER HELPER

92935 CHEMICAL EQUIPMENT CONTROLLERS AND OPERATORS. OOH Title/s: Chemical Equipment Controllers, Operators, and Tenders

Control or operate equipment to control chemical changes or reactions in the processing of industrial or consumer products. Typical equipment used includes reaction kettles, catalytic converters, continuous or batch-treating equipment, saturator tanks, electrolytic cells, reactor vessels, recovery units, and fermentation chambers. Sets and adjusts indicating, controlling, or timing devices, such as gauging instruments, thermostats, gas analyzers, or recording calorimeters. Starts pumps, agitators, reactors, blowers, or automatic feed of materials. Opens valves or operates pumps to admit or drain specified amounts of materials, impurities, or treating agents to or from equipment. Moves controls to adjust feed and flow of liquids and gases through equipment in specified sequence. Adjusts controls to regulate temperature, pressure, and time of prescribed reaction, according to knowledge of equipment and process. Monitors

gauges, recording instruments, flowmeters, or product to regulate or maintain specified conditions. Operates or tends auxiliary equipment, such as heaters, scrubbers, filters, or driers, to prepare or further process materials. Mixes chemicals according to proportion tables or prescribed formulas. Adds treating or neutralizing agent to product and pumps product through filter or centrifuge to remove impurities of precipitate product. Dumps or scoops prescribed solid, granular, or powdered materials into equipment. Reads plant specifications to ascertain product, ingredient, and prescribed modifications of plant procedures. Weighs or measures specified amounts of materials. Patrols and inspects equipment or unit to detect leaks and malfunctions. Tests sample for specific gravity, chemical characteristics, pH level, concentration, or viscosity. Draws samples of product and sends to laboratory for analysis. Flushes or cleans equipment, using steam hose or mechanical reamer. Records in operating log operational data such as temperature, pressure, ingredients used, processing time, or test results. Makes minor repairs and lubricates and maintains equipment, using hand tools. Directs activities of workers assisting in control or verification of process or in unloading of materials.
Yearly Earnings: $32,552
Education: Moderate-term O-J-T
Knowledge: Mechanical; Chemistry; Foreign Language; Public Safety and Security; Telecommunications
Abilities: Information Ordering; Perceptual Speed; Selective Attention; Time Sharing; Control Precision; Response Orientation; Reaction Time; Gross Body Equilibrium
Skills: Science; Testing; Operation Monitoring; Operation and Control; Product Inspection; Equipment Maintenance; Repairing; Time Management; Management of Personnel Resources
General Work Activities: Identifying Objects, Actions, and Events; Inspecting Equipment, Structures, or Material; Controlling Machines and Processes; Repairing and Maintaining Mechanical Equipment
Job Characteristics: Responsible for Others' Health and Safety; Responsibility for Outcomes and Results; Hazardous Conditions; Hazardous Situations; Keeping or Regaining Balance; Common Protective or Safety Attire; Specialized Protective or Safety Attire; Frustrating Circumstances; Degree of Automation; Importance of Being Aware of New Events; Pace Determined by Speed of Equipment
GOE Group/s: 06.01.03 Production Technology: Machine Set-up and Operation; 06.02.10 Production Work: Equipment Operation, Metal Processing; 06.02.11 Production Work: Equipment Operation, Chemical Processing; 06.02.12 Production Work: Equipment Operation, Petroleum and Gas Processing; 06.02.13 Production Work: Equipment Operation, Rubber, Plastics, and Glass Processing; 06.02.18 Production Work: Equipment Operation, Assorted Materials Processing
CIP Program/s: 410301 Chemical Technologists and Technicians; 480599 Precision Metal Workers, Other
Related DOT Job/s: 511.382-010 TUNGSTEN REFINER; 549.362-014 TREATER; 558.362-010 CATALYTIC-CONVERTER OPERATOR; 558.362-014 CD-REACTOR OPERATOR, HEAD; 558.362-018 SATURATOR OPERATOR; 558.382-014 BURNER OPERATOR; 558.382-018 CAUSTICISER; 558.382-022 CAUSTICISER; 558.382-026 CELL TENDER; 558.382-030 CHLORINATOR OPERATOR; 558.382-034 CUPROUS-CHLORIDE OPERATOR; 558.382-038 KETTLE OPERATOR I; 558.382-046 NITRATOR OPERATOR; 558.382-050 POLYMERIZATION-KETTLE OPERATOR; 558.382-054 SODA-COLUMN OPERATOR; 558.382-058 WET-MIX OPERATOR; 558.582-010 PHOSPHORIC-ACID OPERATOR; 558.682-010 CRACKING-UNIT OPERATOR; 558.682-014 DISSOLVER OPERATOR; 558.682-018 FERMENTATION OPERATOR; 559.362-010 ALUM-PLANT OPERATOR; 559.362-022 MVA-REACTOR OPERATOR, HEAD; 559.382-018 CHEMICAL OPERATOR III; 559.382-030 LINSEED-OIL REFINER; 559.382-034 MAKE-UP OPERATOR; 559.582-014 SPECIALTIES OPERATOR; 559.682-018 CHEMICAL COMPOUNDER

92938 CHEMICAL EQUIPMENT TENDERS. OOH

Title/s: Chemical Equipment Controllers, Operators, and Tenders

Tend equipment in which a chemical change or reaction takes place in the processing of industrial or consumer products. Typical equipment used includes devulcanizers, batch stills, fermenting tanks, steam-jacketed kettles, and reactor vessels. Starts pumps and agitators, turns valves, or moves controls of processing equipment to admit, transfer, filter, or mix chemicals. Adjusts valves or controls to maintain system within specified operating conditions. Observes gauges, meters, and panel lights to monitor operating conditions, such as temperature or pressure. Loads specified amounts of chemicals into processing equipment. Patrols work area to detect leaks and equipment malfunctions and to monitor operating conditions. Weighs, measures, or mixes prescribed quantities of materials. Drains equipment and pumps water or other solution through to flush and clean tanks or equipment. Draws sample of products for analysis to aid in process adjustments and to maintain production standards. Replaces filtering media or makes minor repairs to equipment, using hand tools. Tests samples to determine specific gravity, composition, or acidity, using chemical test equipment such as hydrometer or pH meter. Records data in log from instruments and gauges concerning temperature, pressure, materials used, treating time, and shift production. Notifies maintenance engineer of equipment malfunction. Observes safety precautions to prevent fires and explosions. Assists other workers in preparing and maintaining equipment. Inventories supplies received and consumed.
Yearly Earnings: $32,552
Education: Moderate-term O-J-T
Knowledge: Chemistry; Public Safety and Security
Abilities: Problem Sensitivity; Information Ordering; Selective Attention; Control Precision; Response Orientation; Rate Control; Reaction Time; Speed of Limb Movement; Gross Body Equilibrium
Skills: Science; Testing; Operation Monitoring; Operation and Control; Equipment Maintenance
General Work Activities: Controlling Machines and Processes
Job Characteristics: Responsible for Others' Health and Safety; Contaminants; Radiation; Hazardous Conditions; Hazardous Equipment; Walking or Running; Common Protective or Safety Attire; Specialized Protective or Safety Attire; Degree of Automation; Importance of Being Aware of New Events; Pace Determined by Speed of Equipment
GOE Group/s: 06.02.11 Production Work: Equipment Operation, Chemical Processing; 06.02.12 Production Work: Equipment Operation, Petroleum and Gas Processing; 06.04.10 Elemental Work: Industrial: Equipment Operation, Metal Processing; 06.04.11 Elemental Work: Industrial: Equipment Operation, Chemical Processing; 06.04.13 Elemental Work: Industrial: Equipment Operation, Rubber, Plastics, Glass Processing; 06.04.15 Elemental Work: Industrial: Equipment Operation, Food Processing; 06.04.19 Elemental Work: Industrial: Equipment Operation, Assorted Materials Processing; 06.04.40 Elemental Work: Industrial: Loading, Moving, Hoisting, and Conveying
CIP Program/s: 000000 NO CIP ASSIGNED
Related DOT Job/s: 521.685-190 ION EXCHANGE OPERATOR; 546.385-010 GAS TREATER; 551.465-010 PURIFICATION-OPERATOR HELPER; 551.585-018 PAN HELPER; 551.685-094 LYE TREATER; 553.685-026 CADMIUM-LIQUOR MAKER; 558.385-010 CD-REACTOR OPERATOR; 558.385-014 TOWER HELPER; 558.485-010 CAUSTIC OPERATOR; 558.565-010 ACID-PLANT HELPER; 558.585-010 CATALYTIC-CONVERTER-OPERATOR HELPER; 558.585-018 CONTACT-ACID-PLANT OPERATOR; 558.585-022 CUPROUS-CHLORIDE HELPER; 558.585-026 DEVULCANIZER TENDER; 558.585-034

NEUTRALIZER; 558.585-042 TWITCHELL OPERATOR; 558.685-010 ACID-POLYMERIZATION OPERATOR; 558.685-014 BALL-MILL OPERATOR; 558.685-030 ION-EXCHANGE OPERATOR; 558.685-034 ION-EXCHANGE OPERATOR; 558.685-038 ION-EXCHANGE OPERATOR; 558.685-046 MVA-REACTOR OPERATOR; 558.685-050 NITROGLYCERIN NEUTRALIZER; 558.685-062 CHEMICAL OPERATOR II; 559.664-010 NITROGLYCERIN DISTRIBUTOR; 559.685-014 ALUMINUM-HYDROXIDE-PROCESS OPERATOR; 559.685-070 FERMENTER OPERATOR; 559.685-106 IMPREGNATOR OPERATOR; 559.685-130 PIGMENT PROCESSOR

92941A FIBER PRODUCT MACHINE CUTTERS. OOH Title/s: Production Occupations

Set up and operate machine to cut or slice fiber material, such as paper, wallboard, and insulation material. Adjusts machine controls to position and align and to regulate speed and pressure of components. Activates machine to cut, slice, slit, perforate, or score fiber products, such as paperboard sheets, rubber shoe soles, or plaster wallboard. Selects and installs machine components, such as cutting blades, rollers, and templates, according to specifications, using hand tools. Monitors operation of cutting or slicing machine to detect malfunctions, removes defective or substandard materials, and readjusts machine components to conform to standards. Reviews work orders, blueprints, specifications, or job samples to determine components, settings, and adjustments for cutting and slicing machines. Positions materials, such as rubber, paper, or leather, on feeding mechanism of cutting or slicing machine. Examines, measures, and weighs materials or products to verify conformance to specifications, using measuring devices, such as ruler, micrometer, or scale. Replaces worn or broken parts, and cleans and lubricates cutting or slicing machine to maintain equipment in working order. Removes completed materials or products from cutting or slicing machine and stacks or stores for additional processing. Maintains production records, such as quantity, type, and dimensions of materials produced.

Yearly Earnings: $20,852

Education: Moderate-term O-J-T

Knowledge: Production and Processing

Abilities: Perceptual Speed; Manual Dexterity; Control Precision; Rate Control; Reaction Time; Static Strength; Explosive Strength; Dynamic Flexibility; Gross Body Equilibrium

Skills: Operation Monitoring; Operation and Control

General Work Activities: Controlling Machines and Processes; Repairing and Maintaining Mechanical Equipment

Job Characteristics: Sounds, Noise Levels are Distracting, etc.; Hazardous Equipment; Hazardous Situations; Standing; Using Hands on Objects, Tools, or Controls; Making Repetitive Motions; Degree of Automation; Pace Determined by Speed of Equipment

GOE Group/s: 06.01.02 Production Technology: Machine Set-up; 06.02.04 Production Work: Machine Work, Paper; 06.02.05 Production Work: Machine Work, Leather and Fabrics; 06.02.07 Production Work: Machine Work, Rubber; 06.02.09 Production Work: Machine Work, Assorted Materials

CIP Program/s: 470303 Industrial Machinery Maintenance and Repair; 480501 Machinist/Machine Technologist; 480599 Precision Metal Workers, Other; 489999 Precision Production Trades, Other

Related DOT Job/s: 579.382-018 KNIFE OPERATOR; 640.360-010 PANEL-MACHINE SETTER; 640.682-018 CUTTING-MACHINE OPERATOR; 649.682-026 PLATEN-PRESS OPERATOR; 649.682-038 SLITTER-SCORER-CUT-OFF OPERATOR; 649.682-042 TABLET-MAKING-MACHINE OPERATOR; 677.382-010 BATTING-MACHINE OPERATOR, INSULATION; 677.682-026 TENONER OPERATOR; 690.462-010 OUTSOLE CUTTER, AUTOMATIC; 690.682-010 ARCH-CUSHION-SKIVING-MACHINE OPERATOR; 690.682-038 FOXING-CUTTING-MACHINE OPERATOR, AUTOMATIC; 690.682-042 HEEL BREASTER, LEATHER; 690.682-046 HEEL-SEAT FITTER, MACHINE; 690.682-050 HOT-DIE-PRESS OPERATOR; 692.360-014 BRUSH-MACHINE SETTER; 699.382-010 FLUID JET CUTTER OPERATOR

92941B STONE SAWYERS. OOH Title/s: Production Occupations

Set up and operate gang saws, reciprocating saws, circular saws, or wire saws to cut blocks of stone into specified dimensions. Starts saw and moves blade across surface of material, such as stone, concrete slabs, and asbestos-cement sheets and pipes, to saw. Adjusts blade pressure against stone, using ammeter, and lowers blade in stone as cut depth increases. Starts pump to circulate water and abrasive onto blade or cable during cutting. Changes or replaces saw blades, cables, and grinding wheels, using wrench. Turns crank or presses button to move car under sawing cable or saw frame. Aligns cable or blades with marks on stone, and presses button or turns lever to lower sawing cable or blades to stone. Observes operation to detect uneven sawing and exhausted abrasive supply, and tightens pulleys or adds abrasive to maintain cutting speed. Marks dimensions or traces on stone according to diagram, using chisel and hammer, straightedge, rule, and chalked string. Builds bed of timbers on car, and aligns and levels stone on bed, using crowbar, sledgehammer, wedges, blocks, rule, and spirit level. Washes stone, using water hose, and verifies width or thickness of cut stone, using rule. Operates crane or signals crane operator to position or remove stone from car or saw bed.

Yearly Earnings: $20,852

Education: Moderate-term O-J-T

Knowledge: Building and Construction; Mechanical

Abilities: Manual Dexterity; Control Precision; Multilimb Coordination; Rate Control; Reaction Time; Speed of Limb Movement; Static Strength; Explosive Strength; Dynamic Strength; Trunk Strength; Stamina; Dynamic Flexibility; Gross Body Coordination; Gross Body Equilibrium; Peripheral Vision; Depth Perception

Skills: None above average

General Work Activities: Handling and Moving Objects; Controlling Machines and Processes; Interacting with Computers

Job Characteristics: Sounds, Noise Levels are Distracting, etc.; Very Hot; Contaminants; Whole Body Vibration; Hazardous Equipment; Hazardous Situations; Standing; Kneeling, Crouching, or Crawling; Using Hands on Objects, Tools, or Controls; Bending or Twisting the Body; Making Repetitive Motions; Common Protective or Safety Attire; Specialized Protective or Safety Attire; Degree of Automation; Importance of Repeating Same Tasks; Pace Determined by Speed of Equipment

GOE Group/s: 06.02.08 Production Work: Machine Work, Stone, Glass, and Clay

CIP Program/s: 470303 Industrial Machinery Maintenance and Repair

Related DOT Job/s: 670.362-010 GANG SAWYER, STONE; 677.462-010 CIRCULAR SAWYER, STONE; 677.462-014 WIRE SAWYER

92941D GLASS MACHINE CUTTERS. OOH Title/s: Production Occupations

Set up and operate machines to cut glass. Operates single-cut machine to cut glass. Starts machine to verify set-up and makes adjustments. Adjusts position, height, and stroke of cutting bridges, manually or by turning controls, to score glass to specific dimensions. Adjusts timing mechanism to synchronize breaker bar to snap glass at score. Removes and replaces worn cutter heads, using hand tools. Starts vacuum-cupped crane, to lift and transfer glass. Measures glass with tape to verify dimensions and observes glass to detect defects. Reviews work orders and maintains record of production, using counter. Directs workers on cutting team.

Yearly Earnings: $20,852

Education: Moderate-term O-J-T
Knowledge: Production and Processing
Abilities: Arm-Hand Steadiness; Manual Dexterity; Control Precision; Rate Control; Dynamic Flexibility; Depth Perception
Skills: Operation Monitoring; Operation and Control
General Work Activities: Controlling Machines and Processes; Guiding, Directing and Motivating Subordinates
Job Characteristics: Sounds, Noise Levels are Distracting, etc.; Hazardous Equipment; Hazardous Situations; Using Hands on Objects, Tools, or Controls; Making Repetitive Motions; Degree of Automation; Pace Determined by Speed of Equipment
GOE Group/s: 06.02.08 Production Work: Machine Work, Stone, Glass, and Clay
CIP Program/s: 000000 NO CIP ASSIGNED
Related DOT Job/s: 677.562-010 GLASS-CUTTING-MACHINE OPERATOR, AUTOMATIC

92944 CUTTING AND SLICING MACHINE OPERATORS AND TENDERS. OOH Title/s: Cutting and Slicing Machine Operators and Tenders

Operate or tend machines that cut or slice any of a wide variety of products or materials, such as tobacco, food, paper, roofing slate, glass, stone, rubber, cork, and insulating material. Exclude metal-, wood-, and plastic sawing machine operators and tenders, and textile-cutting machine operators and tenders. Starts cutting machine by pressing button, pulling lever, or depressing pedal to cut stock, following markings or specifications. Stops cutting machine when necessary, by pulling lever, pressing button, or depressing pedal, and removes debris. Adjusts feeding guides, blades, settings, or speed, to regulate specified depth, length, or width of material, using hand tools or hands. Observes cutting machine in operation, to ensure even flow of stock and to detect jamming, improper feeding, or foreign materials. Reads work order or receives oral instructions regarding specifications for stock to be cut. Feeds stock into cutting machine, conveyor, or under cutting blades, by threading, guiding, pushing, or turning handwheel. Positions stock along cutting lines or against stops on bed of scoring or cutting machine. Marks cutting lines or identifying information on stock, using marking pencil, ruler, or scribe. Installs or replaces cutting knives, blades, or wheels in cutting machine, using hand tools. Examines and measures stock to ensure conformance to specifications, using ruler, gauge, micrometer, or scale, and removes defects. Sharpens cutting blades, knives, or saws, using file, bench grinder, or honing stone. Cuts stock manually to prepare for machine cutting, using tools such as knife, cleaver, handsaw, or hammer and chisel. Cleans and lubricates cutting machine, conveyors, blades, saws, or knives, using steam hose, scrapers, brush, or oilcans. Records data on amount and type of stock cut, including weight, length, and width. Moves stock or scrap to and from machine, transporting either manually or using cart, handtruck, or lift truck. Stacks and sorts cut material according to type and size for packaging, further processing, or shipping.
Yearly Earnings: $17,264
Education: Moderate-term O-J-T
Knowledge: Production and Processing; Food Production
Abilities: Reaction Time
Skills: Operation Monitoring
General Work Activities: Handling and Moving Objects; Controlling Machines and Processes; Interacting with Computers; Repairing and Maintaining Mechanical Equipment
Job Characteristics: Hazardous Equipment; Hazardous Situations; Common Protective or Safety Attire; Degree of Automation; Importance of Repeating Same Tasks; Pace Determined by Speed of Equipment
GOE Group/s: 05.12.13 Elemental Work: Mechanical: Cutting and Finishing; 06.02.03 Production Work: Machine Work, Wood; 06.02.04 Production Work: Machine Work, Paper; 06.02.05 Production Work: Machine Work, Leather and Fabrics; 06.02.07 Production Work: Machine Work, Rubber; 06.02.08 Production Work: Machine Work, Stone, Glass, and Clay; 06.02.09 Production Work: Machine Work, Assorted Materials; 06.02.15 Production Work: Equipment Operation, Food Processing; 06.02.32 Production Work: Manual Work, Assorted Materials; 06.04.02 Elemental Work: Industrial: Machine Work, Metal and Plastics; 06.04.03 Elemental Work: Industrial: Machine Work, Wood; 06.04.04 Elemental Work: Industrial: Machine Work, Paper; 06.04.05 Elemental Work: Industrial: Machine Work, Fabric and Leather; 06.04.07 Elemental Work: Industrial: Machine Work, Rubber; 06.04.08 Elemental Work: Industrial: Machine Work, Stone, Glass, and Clay; 06.04.09 Elemental Work: Industrial: Machine Work, Assorted Materials; 06.04.11 Elemental Work: Industrial: Equipment Operation, Chemical Processing; 06.04.15 Elemental Work: Industrial: Equipment Operation, Food Processing; 06.04.16 Elemental Work: Industrial: Equipment Operation, Textile, Fabric, and Leather Processing; 06.04.19 Elemental Work: Industrial: Equipment Operation, Assorted Materials Processing; 06.04.25 Elemental Work: Industrial: Manual Work, Wood; 06.04.34 Elemental Work: Industrial: Manual Work, Assorted Materials
CIP Program/s: 000000 NO CIP ASSIGNED
Related DOT Job/s: 520.682-022 GUM-SCORING-MACHINE OPERATOR; 521.685-018 ALMOND-CUTTING-MACHINE TENDER; 521.685-098 CUTTER, FROZEN MEAT; 521.685-102 CUTTING-MACHINE OPERATOR; 521.685-158 GRANULATING-MACHINE OPERATOR; 521.685-170 HASHER OPERATOR; 521.685-298 SLICE-PLUG-CUTTER OPERATOR; 521.685-302 SLICING-MACHINE OPERATOR; 521.685-306 SLICING-MACHINE OPERATOR; 521.685-310 SMOKING-TOBACCO-CUTTER OPERATOR; 521.685-338 STRIP-CUTTING-MACHINE OPERATOR; 521.685-342 STRIPPER-CUTTER, MACHINE; 521.685-354 SUGAR-CHIPPER-MACHINE OPERATOR; 521.685-386 SCALING MACHINE OPERATOR; 525.685-010 BAND-SAW OPERATOR; 529.585-010 CHEESE CUTTER; 529.685-018 BINDER LAYER; 529.685-082 CUTTER; 529.685-090 DEFECTIVE-CIGARETTE SLITTER; 529.685-110 FILLER SHREDDER, MACHINE; 529.685-118 FISH CLEANER MACHINE TENDER; 529.685-150 ICE CUTTER; 529.685-182 PLUG-CUTTING-MACHINE OPERATOR; 530.665-014 RAG-CUTTING-MACHINE TENDER; 555.585-010 CUTTER OPERATOR; 555.665-010 SHREDDER TENDER; 555.685-010 BEATER OPERATOR; 559.685-134 POWDER-CUTTING OPERATOR; 559.685-142 PRESSER; 559.685-158 RUBBER CUTTER; 564.682-014 FLAKE-CUTTER OPERATOR; 564.685-014 CHIPPER; 579.685-058 BRICK SETTER OPERATOR; 585.685-030 CONCAVING-MACHINE OPERATOR; 585.685-038 CUT-LACE-MACHINE OPERATOR; 585.685-082 ROTARY CUTTER; 585.685-094 SHAVING-MACHINE OPERATOR; 585.685-098 SHEARING-MACHINE FEEDER; 585.685-110 SKIVER, BLOCKERS; 585.685-114 SPLITTER, MACHINE; 585.685-126 TRIMMER, MACHINE; 590.685-050 ROLL-UP-GUIDER OPERATOR; 615.685-046 CUTTER-MACHINE TENDER; 640.565-010 PAPER CUTTER; 640.685-010 BOOK TRIMMER; 640.685-022 COMB-MACHINE OPERATOR; 640.685-026 COMPENSATOR; 640.685-030 CORNER CUTTER; 640.685-034 CUT-OFF-MACHINE OPERATOR; 640.685-038 PANEL-MACHINE OPERATOR; 640.685-066 ROLL-SLICING-MACHINE TENDER; 640.685-074 ROUND-CORNER-CUTTER OPERATOR; 640.685-078 SLOTTER OPERATOR; 640.685-086 TUBE SIZER-AND-CUTTER OPERATOR; 640.685-090 BAND-SAW OPERATOR; 649.682-014 CYLINDER-DIE-MACHINE OPERATOR; 649.685-026 CORE-CUTTER AND REAMER; 649.685-082 PARTITION-MAKING-MACHINE OPERATOR; 649.685-110 STEEL-TIE ADJUSTER, AUTOMATIC; 659.685-014 SAMPLE-BOOK MAKER; 663.682-014 POLE-PEELING-MACHINE OPERATOR; 663.685-010 BLOCK-SPLITTER OPERATOR; 670.685-010 STONE TRIMMER; 677.382-014 SAWYER, OPTICAL GLASS; 677.682-010 HEAD-SAW OP-

ERATOR, INSULATION BOARD; 677.682-014 REFRACTORY-GRINDER OPERATOR; 677.682-018 SINK CUTTER; 677.682-022 STONECUTTER, MACHINE; 677.685-010 ABRASIVE SAWYER; 677.685-014 ASSEMBLER, LAY-UPS; 677.685-018 CARBON CUTTER; 677.685-022 CRAYON SAWYER; 677.685-026 CUT-OFF-SAW OPERATOR, PIPE BLANKS; 677.685-030 GLASS CUT-OFF TENDER; 677.685-034 SAMPLE SAWYER; 677.685-038 SAWYER II; 677.685-042 SPLITTER OPERATOR; 677.685-046 SPLITTING-MACHINE OPERATOR; 677.685-050 STONE SPLITTER; 677.685-054 SAW OPERATOR; 690.485-010 BAND-SAWING-MACHINE OPERATOR; 690.682-022 BIAS-MACHINE OPERATOR; 690.682-086 TRIMMER, MACHINE II; 690.685-026 BAND CUTTER; 690.685-062 BUTTON-DECORATING-MACHINE OPERATOR; 690.685-094 COUNTER CUTTER; 690.685-118 CUTTER I; 690.685-122 CUTTING-MACHINE TENDER; 690.685-126 DESKIDDING-MACHINE OPERATOR; 690.685-150 EDGE TRIMMER; 690.685-166 FEATHEREDGER AND REDUCER, MACHINE; 690.685-198 GROOVER AND TURNER; 690.685-214 HEEL GOUGER; 690.685-238 INSEAM TRIMMER; 690.685-242 INSOLE BEVELER; 690.685-250 JOINT CUTTER, MACHINE; 690.685-274 LIP-OF-SHANK CUTTER; 690.685-290 MOLDED-RUBBER-GOODS CUTTER; 690.685-298 NICKER; 690.685-302 PAD CUTTER; 690.685-306 PLUG CUTTER; 690.685-322 ROLL CUTTER; 690.685-334 ROUGH-ROUNDER, MACHINE; 690.685-338 ROUNDER; 690.685-342 RUBBER-CUTTING-MACHINE TENDER; 690.685-354 SHAPING-MACHINE OPERATOR; 690.685-366 SIZING-MACHINE TENDER; 690.685-370 SKI-TOP TRIMMER; 690.685-374 SKIVER; 690.685-378 SKIVER, MACHINE; 690.685-386 SPLITTING-MACHINE OPERATOR; 690.685-402 STRAP-CUTTING-MACHINE OPERATOR; 690.685-434 TRIMMER, MACHINE I; 690.685-446 TUBER-MACHINE CUTTER; 690.685-458 V-BELT SKIVER; 690.685-478 WELT CUTTER; 690.685-486 WIDTH STRIPPER; 692.682-042 GAUGE OPERATOR; 692.685-130 PINKING-MACHINE OPERATOR; 692.685-174 SLICING-MACHINE OPERATOR; 692.685-222 TILE-POWER-SHEAR OPERATOR; 692.685-258 WIRE-TURNING-MACHINE OPERATOR; 692.685-266 ZIPPER TRIMMER, MACHINE; 699.682-018 CUTTER OPERATOR; 699.682-022 DIE CUTTER; 699.682-026 ROLL-SHEETING CUTTER; 699.682-030 SLITTING-MACHINE OPERATOR I; 699.685-014 CUTTER, MACHINE II; 721.484-018 INSULATION CUTTER AND FORMER; 730.686-010 CUTTER, WOODWIND REEDS; 732.685-014 FEATHER SAWYER; 732.685-038 TRIMMING-MACHINE OPERATOR; 739.685-022 CLIPPER; 775.685-010 CUTTING-MACHINE TENDER, DECORATIVE; 789.382-010 CLICKING-MACHINE OPERATOR; 976.685-010 CUTTER

92947 PAINTERS, TRANSPORTATION EQUIPMENT. OOH Title/s: Painting and Coating Machine Operators

Operate or tend painting machines to paint surfaces of transportation equipment, such as automobiles, buses, trucks, boats, and airplanes. Pours paint into spray gun and sprays specified amount of primer, decorative, or finish coatings onto prepared surfaces. Paints areas inaccessible to spray gun, or retouches painted surface, using brush. Paints designs, lettering, or other identifying information on vehicles, using paint brush or paint sprayer. Mixes, stirs, and thins paint or other coatings, using spatula or power mixing equipment. Selects paint according to company requirements and matches colors of paint following specified color charts. Disassembles sprayer and power equipment, such as sandblaster, and cleans equipment and hand tools, using solvents, wire brushes, and cloths. Regulates controls on portable ventilators and exhaust units to cure and dry paint or other coatings. Lays out logos, symbols, or designs on painted surfaces, according to blueprint specifications, using measuring instruments, stencils, and patterns. Strips grease, dirt, paint, and rust from vehicle surface, using abrasives, solvents, brushes, blowtorch, or sandblaster. Sets up portable ventilators, exhaust units, ladders, and scaffolding. Removes accessories from vehicles, such as chrome or mirrors, and masks other surfaces with tape or paper. Operates lifting and moving devices to move equipment or materials to access areas to be painted.

Yearly Earnings: $19,136
Education: Moderate-term O-J-T
Knowledge: None above average
Abilities: Dynamic Flexibility; Gross Body Equilibrium; Visual Color Discrimination
Skills: None above average
General Work Activities: Interacting with Computers
Job Characteristics: Sounds, Noise Levels are Distracting, etc.; Contaminants; Cramped Work Space, Awkward Positions; High Places; Hazardous Conditions; Standing; Climbing Ladders, Scaffolds, Poles, etc.; Kneeling, Crouching, or Crawling; Keeping or Regaining Balance; Bending or Twisting the Body; Making Repetitive Motions; Common Protective or Safety Attire; Specialized Protective or Safety Attire; Importance of Repeating Same Tasks
GOE Group/s: 01.06.03 Craft Arts: Hand Lettering, Painting and Decorating; 05.10.07 Crafts: Painting, Dyeing, and Coating
CIP Program/s: 460408 Painter and Wall Coverer; 470603 Auto/Automotive Body Repairer
Related DOT Job/s: 845.381-010 PAINTER APPRENTICE, TRANSPORTATION EQUIPMENT; 845.381-014 PAINTER, TRANSPORTATION EQUIPMENT; 845.381-018 PAINT SPRAYER, SANDBLASTER; 845.681-010 RAILROAD-CAR LETTERER

92951 COATING, PAINTING, AND SPRAYING MACHINE SETTERS AND SET-UP OPERATORS. OOH Title/s: Painting and Coating Machine Operators

Set up or set up and operate machines to coat or paint any of a wide variety of products—such as food products, glassware, cloth, ceramic, metal, plastic, paper, and wood products—with lacquer, silver and copper solution, rubber, paint, varnish, glaze, enamel, oil, or rust-proofing materials. Exclude setters and set-up operators who coat or plate metal or plastic with metal using electrolytic or nonelectrolytic processes. Sets up and operates machines to paint or coat products with such materials as silver and copper solution, rubber, paint, glaze, oil, or rust-proofing materials. Selects and loads materials, parts, and workpieces on machine, using hand tools. Turns valves and adjusts controls to regulate speed of conveyor, temperature, air pressure and circulation, and flow or spray of coating or paint. Starts pumps to mix solutions and to activate coating or painting machines. Operates auxiliary machines or equipment used on the coating or painting process. Weighs or measures chemicals, coatings, or paints, and adds to machine. Observes and adjusts loaded workpiece or machine, according to specifications. Removes materials, parts, or workpieces from painting or coating machines, using hand tools. Examines and tests solutions, paints, products, and workpieces to ensure specifications are met. Measures thickness and quality of coating, using micrometer. Cleans and maintains coating and painting machines, using hand tools. Records operational data on specified forms.

Yearly Earnings: $19,136
Education: Moderate-term O-J-T
Knowledge: Production and Processing
Abilities: Manual Dexterity; Rate Control; Explosive Strength; Trunk Strength; Stamina; Dynamic Flexibility; Gross Body Coordination; Visual Color Discrimination
Skills: Operation Monitoring
General Work Activities: Controlling Machines and Processes
Job Characteristics: Sounds, Noise Levels are Distracting, etc.; Contaminants; Hazardous Conditions; Hazardous Equipment; Standing; Common Protective or Safety Attire; Degree of Automation; Pace Determined by Speed of Equipment

GOE Group/s: 06.01.02 Production Technology: Machine Set-up; 06.02.08 Production Work: Machine Work, Stone, Glass, and Clay; 06.02.09 Production Work: Machine Work, Assorted Materials; 06.02.21 Production Work: Coating and Plating
CIP Program/s: 470303 Industrial Machinery Maintenance and Repair; 480501 Machinist/Machine Technologist; 480599 Precision Metal Workers, Other; 489999 Precision Production Trades, Other
Related DOT Job/s: 534.380-010 CARBON-PAPER-COATING-MACHINE SETTER; 574.462-010 ABRASIVE-COATING-MACHINE OPERATOR; 574.582-010 SILVERING APPLICATOR; 574.682-014 SPRAY-MACHINE OPERATOR; 599.382-010 PAINT-SPRAYER OPERATOR, AUTOMATIC; 632.380-018 PRIMER-WATERPROOFING-MACHINE ADJUSTER; 632.380-026 VARNISHING-UNIT TOOL SETTER; 679.682-010 BANDING-MACHINE OPERATOR; 692.682-014 BEAD-FORMING-MACHINE OPERATOR

92953 COATING, PAINTING, AND SPRAYING MACHINE OPERATORS AND TENDERS. OOH Title/s: Painting and Coating Machine Operators

Coating machine operators and tenders operate or tend machines to coat any of a wide variety of items including coating food products with sugar, chocolate, or butter; coating paper and paper products with chemical solutions, wax, or glazes; or coating fabric with rubber or plastic. Painting and spraying machine operators and tenders operate or tend machines to spray or paint decorative, protective, or other coating or finish (such as adhesive, lacquer, paint, stain, latex, preservative, oil, or other solutions). May apply coating or finish to any of a wide variety of items or materials, such as wood and wood products, ceramics, and glass. Include workers who apply coating or finish to materials preparatory to further processing or to consumer use. Observes machine operation and gauges to detect defects or deviations from standards. Turns dial, handwheel, valve, or switch to control and adjust temperature, speed, and flow of product or machine. Starts and stops operation of machine, using lever or button. Fills hopper, reservoir, trough, or pan with material used to coat, paint, or spray, using conveyor or pail. Attaches specified hose or nozzle to machine, using wrench and pliers. Measures and mixes specified quantities of substances to create coatings, paints, or sprays. Aligns or fastens machine parts such as rollers, guides, brushes, and blades to secure roll, using hand tools. Threads or feeds item or product through or around machine rollers and dryers. Places item or product on feed rack, spindle, or reel strand to coat, paint, or spray, using hands, hoist, or trucklift. Examines, measures, weighs, or tests sample product to ensure conformance to specifications. Transfers completed item or product from machine to drying or storage area, using handcart, handtruck, or crane. Cleans machine, equipment, and work area, using water, solvents, and other cleaning aids. Records production data.
Yearly Earnings: $19,136
Education: Moderate-term O-J-T
Knowledge: Food Production; Chemistry
Abilities: Rate Control; Reaction Time; Dynamic Strength; Dynamic Flexibility
Skills: Operation Monitoring; Operation and Control
General Work Activities: Controlling Machines and Processes
Job Characteristics: Sounds, Noise Levels are Distracting, etc.; Contaminants; Hazardous Conditions; Standing; Climbing Ladders, Scaffolds, Poles, etc.; Making Repetitive Motions; Common Protective or Safety Attire; Degree of Automation; Pace Determined by Speed of Equipment
GOE Group/s: 06.02.04 Production Work: Machine Work, Paper; 06.02.09 Production Work: Machine Work, Assorted Materials; 06.02.13 Production Work: Equipment Operation, Rubber, Plastics, and Glass Processing; 06.02.14 Production Work: Equipment Operation, Paper and Paper Products Processing; 06.02.15 Production Work: Equipment Operation, Food Processing; 06.02.16 Production Work: Equipment Operation, Textile, Fabric, and Leather Processing; 06.02.18 Production Work: Equipment Operation, Assorted Materials Processing; 06.02.21 Production Work: Coating and Plating; 06.04.09 Elemental Work: Industrial: Machine Work, Assorted Materials; 06.04.13 Elemental Work: Industrial: Equipment Operation, Rubber, Plastics, Glass Processing; 06.04.14 Elemental Work: Industrial: Equipment Operation, Paper Making; 06.04.15 Elemental Work: Industrial: Equipment Operation, Food Processing; 06.04.16 Elemental Work: Industrial: Equipment Operation, Textile, Fabric, and Leather Processing; 06.04.18 Elemental Work: Industrial: Equipment Operation, Wood Processing; 06.04.19 Elemental Work: Industrial: Equipment Operation, Assorted Materials Processing; 06.04.21 Elemental Work: Industrial: Machine Work, Brushing, Spraying, and Coating
CIP Program/s: 000000 NO CIP ASSIGNED
Related DOT Job/s: 524.382-010 COATING-MACHINE OPERATOR; 524.382-014 ENROBING-MACHINE OPERATOR; 524.665-010 SANDING-MACHINE OPERATOR; 524.682-010 DEPOSITING-MACHINE OPERATOR; 524.685-014 CHEESE SPRAYER; 524.685-018 COATING OPERATOR; 524.685-022 CRACKER SPRAYER; 524.685-026 ENROBING-MACHINE OPERATOR; 524.685-034 ICER, MACHINE; 534.482-010 WAXING-MACHINE OPERATOR; 534.582-010 PAPER-COATING-MACHINE OPERATOR; 534.682-010 AIR-DRIER-MACHINE OPERATOR; 534.682-014 CARBON-COATER-MACHINE OPERATOR; 534.682-018 COATING-MACHINE OPERATOR; 534.682-022 COATING-MACHINE OPERATOR, HARDBOARD; 534.682-038 SUPERCALENDER OPERATOR; 534.685-022 PAPER COATER; 534.685-026 PARAFFIN-MACHINE OPERATOR; 534.685-030 VARNISHING-MACHINE OPERATOR; 539.482-010 CALENDER OPERATOR, INSULATION BOARD; 539.685-014 IMPREGNATION OPERATOR; 554.362-010 CALENDER OPERATOR; 554.382-010 COATER; 554.485-010 BUCKLE-STRAP-DRUM OPERATOR; 554.585-010 CATHODE MAKER; 554.662-010 CALENDER OPERATOR, FOUR-ROLL; 554.682-022 ROOFING-MACHINE OPERATOR; 554.685-026 SIZING-MACHINE OPERATOR; 561.585-010 STAIN APPLICATOR; 562.485-010 WHITING-MACHINE OPERATOR; 562.685-010 GLUE-SIZE-MACHINE OPERATOR; 562.685-014 IMPREGNATOR; 562.685-018 OPERATOR, PREFINISH; 562.685-022 COATER, SMOKING PIPE; 569.685-070 VARNISHER; 573.685-018 GLAZING-MACHINE OPERATOR; 574.682-010 FIBERGLASS-MACHINE OPERATOR; 574.685-010 COATER, BRAKE LININGS; 574.685-014 PAINT-SPRAY TENDER; 575.665-018 SHOT-COAT TENDER; 582.665-026 SIZING-MACHINE-AND-DRIER OPERATOR; 582.685-118 SATURATOR TENDER; 582.685-138 SPRAY-MACHINE OPERATOR; 583.682-010 COATING-AND-EMBOSSING-UNIT OPERATOR; 584.382-010 COATING-MACHINE OPERATOR I; 584.562-010 COATING-MACHINE OPERATOR; 584.685-018 COATING-MACHINE OPERATOR II; 584.685-022 FOXING PAINTER; 584.685-030 KNIFE-MACHINE OPERATOR; 584.685-038 LATEXER I; 584.685-046 TARRING-MACHINE OPERATOR; 584.685-050 WAX-MACHINE OPERATOR; 590.685-014 COATING-MACHINE OPERATOR; 590.685-022 DIPPER; 590.685-038 HEEL SPRAYER, MACHINE; 590.685-054 WAD IMPREGNATOR; 590.685-066 COATING EQUIPMENT OPERATOR, PRINTED CIRCUIT BOARDS; 599.685-026 DIPPER; 599.685-046 IMPREGNATING-TANK OPERATOR; 599.685-066 PAINT-LINE OPERATOR; 599.685-070 PAINTER, TUMBLING BARREL; 599.685-074 PAINTING-MACHINE OPERATOR; 599.685-094 SPRAYER, MACHINE; 599.685-126 SEED PELLETER; 690.682-054 ORNAMENTAL-MACHINE OPERATOR; 692.685-054 COATING-MACHINE OPERATOR; 692.685-142 RIBBON INKER; 692.685-210 TAPE COATER; 733.685-030 TIP BANDER; 741.685-010 SPRAY-PAINTING-MACHINE OPERATOR

92956 CEMENTING AND GLUING MACHINE OPERATORS AND TENDERS. OOH Title/s: Cementing and Gluing Machine Operators and Tenders

Operate or tend cementing and gluing machines to join together items to form a completed product or to form an article for further processing. Processes include joining veneer sheets into plywood; gluing paper to glass wool, cardboard, or paper; joining rubber and rubberized fabric parts, plastic, simulated leather, and other materials. Adjusts machine to apply specified amount of glue, cement, or adhesive. Starts machine and turns valves or moves controls to feed, admit, or transfer materials and adhesive. Adjusts machine components according to specifications, such as width, length, and thickness of materials to be joined. Observes gauges, meters, and control panels to regulate temperature, pressure, or speed of feeder or conveyor. Monitors machine operation to detect malfunctions, remove jammed materials, and readjust machine components to conform to specifications. Monitors and fills machine with glue, cement, or adhesive as needed. Reads work orders and communicates with coworkers to determine machine and equipment settings and adjustments and supply and product specifications. Positions materials being joined to ensure accurate application of adhesive. Mounts or loads material, such as paper, plastic, wood, or rubber, in feeding mechanism of cementing or gluing machine. Measures and mixes ingredients according to specifications to prepare glue. Examines and measures completed materials or products to verify conformance to specifications, using measuring devices such as tape measure, gauge, or calipers. Removes completed materials or products and restocks materials to be joined. Cleans and maintains gluing and cementing machines, using cleaning solutions, lubricants, brushes, and scrapers. Maintains production records, such as number, dimensions, and thickness of materials processed. Transports materials, supplies, and finished products between storage and work areas, using forklift.
Yearly Earnings: $19,760
Education: Moderate-term O-J-T
Knowledge: Production and Processing
Abilities: Arm-Hand Steadiness; Dynamic Flexibility
Skills: Operation Monitoring; Operation and Control; Product Inspection; Equipment Maintenance
General Work Activities: Handling and Moving Objects; Interacting with Computers
Job Characteristics: Sounds, Noise Levels are Distracting, etc.; Contaminants; Hazardous Equipment; Hazardous Situations; Bending or Twisting the Body; Making Repetitive Motions; Common Protective or Safety Attire; Degree of Automation; Importance of Repeating Same Tasks; Pace Determined by Speed of Equipment
GOE Group/s: 05.12.10 Elemental Work: Mechanical: Heating and Melting; 06.02.04 Production Work: Machine Work, Paper; 06.02.20 Production Work: Machine Assembling; 06.02.27 Production Work: Manual Work, Textile, Fabric and Leather; 06.02.29 Production Work: Manual Work, Rubber; 06.04.03 Elemental Work: Industrial: Machine Work, Wood; 06.04.04 Elemental Work: Industrial: Machine Work, Paper; 06.04.05 Elemental Work: Industrial: Machine Work, Fabric and Leather; 06.04.07 Elemental Work: Industrial: Machine Work, Rubber; 06.04.09 Elemental Work: Industrial: Machine Work, Assorted Materials; 06.04.20 Elemental Work: Industrial: Machine Assembling; 06.04.21 Elemental Work: Industrial: Machine Work, Brushing, Spraying, and Coating; 06.04.24 Elemental Work: Industrial: Manual Work, Metal and Plastics; 06.04.27 Elemental Work: Industrial: Manual Work, Textile, Fabric and Leather; 06.04.29 Elemental Work: Industrial: Manual Work, Rubber; 06.04.34 Elemental Work: Industrial: Manual Work, Assorted Materials; 06.04.38 Elemental Work: Industrial: Wrapping and Packaging
CIP Program/s: 480299 Graphic and Printing Equipment Operators, Other
Related DOT Job/s: 554.682-014 MASKING-MACHINE OPERATOR; 554.685-030 LAMINATOR; 569.565-010 CREW LEADER, GLUING; 569.685-018 CORE FEEDER, PLYWOOD LAYUP LINE; 569.685-022 CORE-COMPOSER-MACHINE TENDER; 569.685-026 CORE-LAYING-MACHINE OPERATOR; 569.685-034 EDGE-GLUE-MACHINE TENDER; 569.685-042 GLUE SPREADER, VENEER; 569.685-054 HOT-PLATE-PLYWOOD-PRESS OPERATOR; 569.685-062 SPLICER OPERATOR; 579.685-022 GLASS-WOOL-BLANKET-MACHINE FEEDER; 584.665-014 GLUE-SPREADING-MACHINE OPERATOR; 584.685-026 HAT-STOCK-LAMINATING-MACHINE OPERATOR; 620.685-010 BONDER, AUTOMOBILE BRAKES; 640.685-014 BOOK-JACKET-COVER-MACHINE OPERATOR; 641.662-010 BOX-SEALING-MACHINE OPERATOR; 641.682-010 BLANKET-WINDER OPERATOR; 641.682-014 GLUING-MACHINE OPERATOR, AUTOMATIC; 641.685-014 BOARD-LINER OPERATOR; 641.685-018 BOX-LINING-MACHINE FEEDER; 641.685-030 CHIP-APPLYING-MACHINE TENDER; 641.685-034 COVER STRIPPER; 641.685-042 ENDING-MACHINE OPERATOR; 641.685-046 EXTENSION EDGER; 641.685-058 LINER-MACHINE OPERATOR; 641.685-066 PATCH-MACHINE OPERATOR; 641.685-074 SEALING-MACHINE OPERATOR; 641.685-082 SPOOL MAKER; 641.685-090 STRIPPING-MACHINE OPERATOR; 641.685-098 WRAPPING-MACHINE OPERATOR; 649.685-050 HANDLE-MACHINE OPERATOR; 649.685-126 TAPER OPERATOR; 649.686-014 CARD DECORATOR; 653.685-018 CASE-MAKING-MACHINE OPERATOR; 669.685-050 DOWELING-MACHINE OPERATOR; 689.685-138 TAPE-MAKING-MACHINE OPERATOR; 690.685-070 CEMENTER AND FOLDER, MACHINE; 690.685-134 DUAL-HOSE CEMENTER; 690.686-018 CEMENTER, MACHINE APPLICATOR; 692.685-022 BEAD PREPARER; 692.685-050 CEMENTER, MACHINE; 692.685-062 CROWN-ASSEMBLY-MACHINE OPERATOR; 692.685-094 GLUE-MACHINE OPERATOR; 692.685-098 GLUING-MACHINE OPERATOR; 692.685-106 LAMINATING-MACHINE OPERATOR; 692.685-110 LAMP-SHADE JOINER; 692.685-170 SKI TOPPER; 692.686-070 PASTER, HAT LINING; 715.685-010 COLLET GLUER; 739.685-018 BRUSH-HEAD MAKER; 750.684-010 BAND BUILDER; 759.484-010 ROLL BUILDER; 759.684-066 V-BELT BUILDER; 762.685-010 EDGE BANDER, MACHINE; 783.685-022 LAMINATOR II; 795.687-010 COVERER, LOOSELEAF BINDER

92958 CLEANING, WASHING, AND PICKLING EQUIPMENT OPERATORS AND TENDERS. OOH Title/s: Production Occupations

Operate or tend machines to wash or clean items—such as barrels or kegs, glass products, tin plate surfaces, dried fruit, pulp, animal stock, coal, manufactured articles, plastic, or rubber—to remove impurities preparatory to further processing. Observes machine operation, gauges, or thermometer, and adjusts controls to maintain operation, according to specifications. Sets controls to regulate temperature and length of cycle and starts conveyors, pumps, agitators, and machines. Adds specified amounts of chemicals into equipment at required time to maintain level and concentration of solution. Drains, cleans, and refills machine or tank at designated intervals with cleaning solution or water. Loads and unloads objects to and from machine, conveyor, or rack. Examines and inspects machine for malfunctions, and product for conformance to processing specifications. Draws samples for laboratory analysis or tests solutions for conformance to specifications, such as acidity or specific gravity. Measures, weighs, or mixes specified quantity of cleaning solutions, using measuring tank, calibrated rod, or suction tube. Adjusts, cleans, and lubricates mechanical parts of machine, using hand tools and grease gun. Records gauge readings, materials used, processing time, or test results in production log.
Yearly Earnings: $20,852

Education: Moderate-term O-J-T
Knowledge: None above average
Abilities: Rate Control
Skills: Operation Monitoring; Operation and Control
General Work Activities: Handling and Moving Objects
Job Characteristics: Sounds, Noise Levels are Distracting, etc.; Standing; Making Repetitive Motions; Degree of Automation; Importance of Repeating Same Tasks; Pace Determined by Speed of Equipment
GOE Group/s: 06.02.11 Production Work: Equipment Operation, Chemical Processing; 06.02.14 Production Work: Equipment Operation, Paper and Paper Products Processing; 06.04.02 Elemental Work: Industrial: Machine Work, Metal and Plastics; 06.04.08 Elemental Work: Industrial: Machine Work, Stone, Glass, and Clay; 06.04.09 Elemental Work: Industrial: Machine Work, Assorted Materials; 06.04.10 Elemental Work: Industrial: Equipment Operation, Metal Processing; 06.04.11 Elemental Work: Industrial: Equipment Operation, Chemical Processing; 06.04.13 Elemental Work: Industrial: Equipment Operation, Rubber, Plastics, Glass Processing; 06.04.14 Elemental Work: Industrial: Equipment Operation, Paper Making; 06.04.15 Elemental Work: Industrial: Equipment Operation, Food Processing; 06.04.19 Elemental Work: Industrial: Equipment Operation, Assorted Materials Processing; 06.04.21 Elemental Work: Industrial: Machine Work, Brushing, Spraying, and Coating; 06.04.39 Elemental Work: Industrial: Cleaning
CIP Program/s: 000000 NO CIP ASSIGNED
Related DOT Job/s: 503.685-026 FURNACE-AND-WASH-EQUIPMENT OPERATOR; 503.685-030 METAL-CLEANER, IMMERSION; 503.685-034 METAL-WASHING-MACHINE OPERATOR; 509.685-014 BRANNER-MACHINE TENDER; 511.685-022 DUST-COLLECTOR ATTENDANT; 511.685-066 TROMMEL TENDER; 521.685-110 DRIED FRUIT WASHER; 529.665-014 WASHROOM OPERATOR; 529.685-074 CONTAINER WASHER, MACHINE; 529.685-226 STEAMER; 529.685-254 WASH-HOUSE WORKER; 529.685-258 WASHER, AGRICULTURAL PRODUCE; 529.685-262 WHEAT CLEANER; 529.685-278 YEAST WASHER; 533.362-010 BLEACHER, PULP; 533.665-010 BLOW-PIT OPERATOR; 533.685-010 BLEACH-BOILER FILLER; 533.685-014 BROWN-STOCK WASHER; 533.685-034 WASHER ENGINEER; 549.685-010 AIR-TABLE OPERATOR; 551.682-010 BENZENE-WASHER OPERATOR; 551.685-110 PRECIPITATE WASHER; 558.685-018 BLEACHER OPERATOR; 559.485-010 WASH-MILL OPERATOR; 559.665-042 WASH HELPER; 559.685-022 AMPOULE-WASHING-MACHINE OPERATOR; 559.685-062 ELECTRODE-CLEANING-MACHINE OPERATOR; 559.685-138 PRESS OPERATOR; 559.685-146 PRESSROOM WORKER, FAT; 559.685-182 WASH-TANK TENDER; 579.685-018 GLASS-CLEANING-MACHINE TENDER; 579.685-054 SILVER STRIPPER, MACHINE; 590.685-026 DRY-CHARGE-PROCESS ATTENDANT; 590.685-062 CLEANING MACHINE TENDER, SEMICONDUCTOR WAFERS; 590.685-102 WAFER CLEANER; 599.685-022 DEFINER; 599.685-038 FILTER WASHER AND PRESSER; 599.685-098 TUBBER; 599.685-114 WASHER, MACHINE; 599.685-118 WASHING-MACHINE OPERATOR; 599.685-130 PAINT STRIPPER; 599.685-134 SCRUBBER MACHINE TENDER; 726.685-022 DEFLASH AND WASH OPERATOR

92962 SEPARATING, FILTERING, CLARIFYING, PRECIPITATING, AND STILL MACHINE OPERATORS AND TENDERS. OOH Title/s: Separating and Still Machine Operators and Tenders

Operate or tend machines such as filter presses, shaker screens, centrifuges, condenser tubes, precipitator tanks, fermenting tanks, evaporating tanks, scrubbing towers, and batch stills. These machines extract, sort, or separate liquids, gases, or solid materials from other materials in order to recover a refined product or material. Exclude workers who operate equipment to control chemical changes or reactions. Starts agitators, shakers, conveyors, pumps, or centrifuge machines, turns valves or moves controls to admit, drain, filter, mix, or transfer materials. Sets or adjusts machine controls to regulate conditions, such as material flow, temperature, and pressure, according to specified operating procedures. Monitors material flow and control instruments, such as gauges, indicators, and meters, to ensure optimal processing conditions and results. Dumps, pours, or loads specified amounts of refined or unrefined materials into equipment or containers for further processing or storage. Removes clogs, defects, and impurities from machines, tanks, conveyors, screens, or other processing equipment. Measures or weighs materials to be refined, mixed, transferred, stored, or otherwise processed. Examines samples visually or by hand to verify quality, such as clarity, cleanliness, consistency, dryness, and texture. Inspects machines and equipment for hazards, operating efficiency, mechanical malfunctions, wear, and leaks. Lubricates, connects, installs, replaces, or makes minor adjustments or repairs to hoses, pumps, filters, or screens to maintain processing equipment, using hand tools. Cleans tanks, screens, inflow pipes, and other processing equipment, using hoses, brushes, scrapers, or chemical solutions. Collects samples of material or product for laboratory analysis. Tests samples to determine viscosity, acidity, specific gravity, or degree of concentration, using test equipment, such as viscometer, pH meter, and hydrometer. Removes full bags or containers from discharge outlets and replaces them with empty ones. Maintains log of instrument readings, test results, and shift production. Communicates or signals processing instructions to other workers.
Yearly Earnings: $32,552
Education: Moderate-term O-J-T
Knowledge: Chemistry
Abilities: Control Precision
Skills: Operation Monitoring; Equipment Maintenance
General Work Activities: Repairing and Maintaining Mechanical Equipment
Job Characteristics: Contaminants; Hazardous Conditions; Standing; Using Hands on Objects, Tools, or Controls; Making Repetitive Motions; Common Protective or Safety Attire; Degree of Automation; Importance of Repeating Same Tasks; Pace Determined by Speed of Equipment
GOE Group/s: 03.04.01 Elemental Work: Plants and Animals: Farming; 05.12.06 Elemental Work: Mechanical: Pumping; 05.12.07 Elemental Work: Mechanical: Crushing, Mixing, Separating, and Chipping; 06.02.07 Production Work: Machine Work, Rubber; 06.02.10 Production Work: Equipment Operation, Metal Processing; 06.02.11 Production Work: Equipment Operation, Chemical Processing; 06.02.12 Production Work: Equipment Operation, Petroleum and Gas Processing; 06.02.13 Production Work: Equipment Operation, Rubber, Plastics, and Glass Processing; 06.02.14 Production Work: Equipment Operation, Paper and Paper Products Processing; 06.02.15 Production Work: Equipment Operation, Food Processing; 06.02.17 Production Work: Equipment Operation, Clay and Coke Processing; 06.02.18 Production Work: Equipment Operation, Assorted Materials Processing; 06.03.02 Quality Control: Inspecting, Grading, Sorting, Weighing, and Recording; 06.04.03 Elemental Work: Industrial: Machine Work, Wood; 06.04.07 Elemental Work: Industrial: Machine Work, Rubber; 06.04.08 Elemental Work: Industrial: Machine Work, Stone, Glass, and Clay; 06.04.09 Elemental Work: Industrial: Machine Work, Assorted Materials; 06.04.10 Elemental Work: Industrial: Equipment Operation, Metal Processing; 06.04.11 Elemental Work: Industrial: Equipment Operation, Chemical Processing; 06.04.12 Elemental Work: Industrial: Equipment Operation, Petroleum, Gas, and Coal Processing; 06.04.13 Elemental Work: Industrial: Equipment Operation, Rubber, Plastics, Glass Processing; 06.04.14 Elemental

Work: Industrial: Equipment Operation, Paper Making; 06.04.15 Elemental Work: Industrial: Equipment Operation, Food Processing; 06.04.17 Elemental Work: Industrial: Equipment Operation, Clay Processing; 06.04.18 Elemental Work: Industrial: Equipment Operation, Wood Processing; 06.04.19 Elemental Work: Industrial: Equipment Operation, Assorted Materials Processing; 06.04.40 Elemental Work: Industrial: Loading, Moving, Hoisting, and Conveying

CIP Program/s: 010401 Agricultural and Food Products Processing Operations and Management

Related DOT Job/s: 509.685-050 SCRAP HANDLER; 511.385-010 ZINC-CHLORIDE OPERATOR; 511.462-010 CONCENTRATOR OPERATOR; 511.465-010 TOP-PRECIPITATOR OPERATOR; 511.482-014 CRYOLITE-RECOVERY OPERATOR; 511.485-010 MOLYBDENUM-STEAMER OPERATOR; 511.485-014 THICKENER OPERATOR; 511.562-010 CLASSIFIER OPERATOR; 511.565-010 DEWATERER OPERATOR; 511.565-018 IRON-LAUNDER OPERATOR; 511.582-010 LEACHER; 511.585-010 HYDRATE-CONTROL TENDER; 511.662-010 CLARIFIER OPERATOR; 511.664-010 BOTTOM-PRECIPITATOR OPERATOR; 511.685-010 AMALGAMATOR; 511.685-014 CLASSIFIER TENDER; 511.685-018 CONDENSER-TUBE TENDER; 511.685-026 FLOTATION TENDER; 511.685-030 KETTLE TENDER II; 511.685-034 KETTLE TENDER, PLATINUM AND PALLADIUM; 511.685-038 PRECIPITATOR I; 511.685-042 PRECIPITATOR II; 511.685-050 SCREEN OPERATOR; 511.685-054 SLIME-PLANT OPERATOR II; 511.685-062 TABLE TENDER; 519.665-018 WET-PLANT OPERATOR; 520.485-030 STARCHMAKER; 521.362-010 CONTINUOUS-ABSORPTION-PROCESS OPERATOR; 521.362-018 REFINERY OPERATOR; 521.365-010 CHAR-FILTER OPERATOR; 521.382-010 EVAPORATOR OPERATOR; 521.382-014 SEPARATOR OPERATOR; 521.385-010 CRACKING-AND-FANNING-MACHINE OPERATOR; 521.462-010 REFINERY OPERATOR, ASSISTANT; 521.565-014 MASH-FILTER OPERATOR; 521.565-018 SOFT-SUGAR OPERATOR, HEAD; 521.582-010 SILICA-FILTER OPERATOR; 521.585-010 CENTRIFUGAL-STATION OPERATOR, AUTOMATIC; 521.665-010 CHAR-FILTER-TANK TENDER, HEAD; 521.665-014 EXTRACTOR-MACHINE OPERATOR; 521.665-018 FILTER-PRESS TENDER, HEAD; 521.665-022 RICE CLEANING MACHINE TENDER; 521.665-026 SIEVE-GRADER TENDER; 521.682-010 CENTRIFUGAL OPERATOR; 521.682-014 COCOA-PRESS OPERATOR; 521.682-018 FILTER OPERATOR; 521.682-030 HULLER OPERATOR; 521.685-010 ALMOND HULLER; 521.685-014 ALMOND-BLANCHER OPERATOR; 521.685-022 BATCH-TANK CONTROLLER; 521.685-026 BLEACHER, LARD; 521.685-030 BOLTER; 521.685-038 BRINE-TANK-SEPARATOR OPERATOR; 521.685-042 CENTRIFUGE OPERATOR; 521.685-046 CENTRIFUGE OPERATOR; 521.685-050 CENTRIFUGE OPERATOR; 521.685-054 CLARIFIER; 521.685-058 CLARIFIER; 521.685-062 CLEAN-RICE GRADER AND REEL TENDER; 521.685-066 COCOA-BEAN CLEANER; 521.685-070 COCOA-BUTTER-FILTER OPERATOR; 521.685-106 DETHISTLER OPERATOR; 521.685-114 EGG-BREAKING-MACHINE OPERATOR; 521.685-118 EXTRACTOR OPERATOR; 521.685-126 FILTER OPERATOR; 521.685-130 FILTER-PRESS TENDER; 521.685-134 FILTER-TANK-TENDER HELPER, HEAD; 521.685-138 FILTERING-MACHINE TENDER; 521.685-142 FINISHER OPERATOR; 521.685-146 FRUIT-PRESS OPERATOR; 521.685-150 GLUTEN-SETTLING TENDER; 521.685-154 GRADER TENDER; 521.685-174 HONEY EXTRACTOR; 521.685-178 HOP STRAINER; 521.685-182 HOPPER ATTENDANT; 521.685-186 HOT-WORT SETTLER; 521.685-198 LINTER TENDER; 521.685-206 LYE-PEEL OPERATOR;
521.685-218 MEAT-GRADING-MACHINE OPERATOR; 521.685-230 MONITOR-AND-STORAGE-BIN TENDER; 521.685-238 NUT-SORTER OPERATOR; 521.685-242 OILSEED-MEAT PRESSER; 521.685-246 PEANUT BLANCHER; 521.685-250 POTATO-PEELING-MACHINE OPERATOR; 521.685-254 PROCESSOR, GRAIN; 521.685-258 PULP-PRESS TENDER; 521.685-262 PULPER TENDER; 521.685-270 RIDDLER OPERATOR; 521.685-274 ROUGH-RICE TENDER; 521.685-282 SCREEN-ROOM OPERATOR; 521.685-286 SEPARATOR OPERATOR, SHELLFISH MEATS; 521.685-290 SEPARATOR TENDER II; 521.685-294 SHELLER II; 521.685-318 SORTING-MACHINE OPERATOR; 521.685-322 SPICE CLEANER; 521.685-334 STEMMER, MACHINE; 521.685-362 THRESHING-MACHINE OPERATOR; 521.685-370 WINERY WORKER; 521.685-374 WINTERIZER; 521.685-382 FLAVORING OIL FILTERER; 522.382-014 FERMENTATION OPERATOR; 522.382-018 LIQUOR BLENDER; 522.382-026 STILL OPERATOR II; 522.382-030 STILL OPERATOR I; 522.465-010 STEEP TENDER; 522.585-014 GERMINATION WORKER; 522.665-010 FILTER TENDER; 522.685-042 DE-ALCOHOLIZER; 522.685-046 DEODORIZER; 522.685-050 DORR OPERATOR; 522.685-054 DROPPER, FERMENTING CELLAR; 522.685-058 DRUM LOADER AND UNLOADER; 522.685-070 HONEY PROCESSOR; 522.685-074 MALT-HOUSE OPERATOR; 522.685-078 MOLASSES PREPARER; 522.685-082 NEUTRALIZER; 522.685-090 SEED-YEAST OPERATOR; 522.685-098 STILL OPERATOR; 522.685-106 WRINGER OPERATOR; 522.685-110 YEAST-FERMENTATION ATTENDANT; 522.685-114 BARLEY STEEPER; 523.382-014 MAPLE-SYRUP MAKER; 523.382-018 MELTER OPERATOR; 523.385-010 PRESSURE-TANK OPERATOR; 523.562-010 DIFFUSER OPERATOR; 523.585-010 BUTTER LIQUEFIER; 523.585-026 PASTEURIZER; 523.682-034 PERCOLATOR OPERATOR; 523.685-110 PASTEURIZER; 525.685-022 HIDE PULLER;
525.685-030 SKIN-PEELING-MACHINE OPERATOR; 529.362-014 DRY-STARCH OPERATOR, AUTOMATIC; 529.382-030 IRISH-MOSS OPERATOR; 529.582-010 CARBONATION EQUIPMENT OPERATOR; 529.582-014 FLASH-DRIER OPERATOR; 529.682-010 CENTRIFUGE OPERATOR; 529.682-022 DRIER OPERATOR; 529.682-038 EGG PASTEURIZER; 529.685-094 DEOILING-MACHINE AND PASTEURIZING-MACHINE OPERATOR; 529.685-106 EXPELLER OPERATOR; 529.685-114 FILTER TENDER, JELLY; 529.685-154 LABORER, STARCH FACTORY; 529.685-158 LARD REFINER; 529.685-198 REFINING-MACHINE OPERATOR; 529.687-170 PRESS PULLER; 532.685-018 EVAPORATOR OPERATOR; 533.682-010 DECKER OPERATOR; 533.685-018 SAVE-ALL OPERATOR; 533.685-022 SCREEN TENDER; 533.685-026 SCREEN TENDER, CHIPS; 541.362-010 DESULFURIZER OPERATOR; 541.362-014 PUMP OPERATOR, BYPRODUCTS; 541.382-010 COAL WASHER; 541.382-014 CRUDE-OIL TREATER; 541.585-010 CENTRIFUGE-SEPARATOR TENDER; 541.665-010 SHAKER TENDER; 541.682-010 PARAFFIN-PLANT OPERATOR; 541.685-010 HEAVY-MEDIA OPERATOR; 541.685-014 LEAD RECOVERER, CONTINUOUS-NAPHTHA-TREATING PLANT; 542.685-014 SUBLIMER; 543.682-022 PARAFFIN-PLANT-SWEATER OPERATOR; 549.382-010 NATURAL-GAS-TREATING-UNIT OPERATOR; 549.382-014 OIL-RECOVERY-UNIT OPERATOR; 549.585-010 ACETYLENE-PLANT OPERATOR; 551.362-010 PURIFICATION OPERATOR II; 551.365-010 STRAINER TENDER;551.382-010 ABSORPTION OPERATOR;
551.485-010 WATER-TREATMENT-PLANT OPERATOR; 551.562-010 FILTRATION OPERATOR, POLYETHYLENE CATALYST; 551.585-010 FILTER-TANK OPERATOR; 551.585-014 MERCURY PURIFIER; 551.665-010 NAPHTHALENE OPERATOR; 551.685-014 BOILING-TUB OPERATOR; 551.685-018 BONE-COOKING OPERATOR; 551.685-022 CATALYST-RECOVERY OPERATOR; 551.685-030 CENTRIFUGE OPERATOR; 551.685-034 CENTRIFUGE OPERATOR; 551.685-038 CENTRIFUGE-SEPARATOR OPERATOR; 551.685-050 DUST-COLLECTOR OPERATOR; 551.685-054 EXTRACTOR OPERATOR; 551.685-058 EXTRACTOR OPERATOR; 551.685-062 EXTRACTOR OPERATOR, SOLVENT PROCESS; 551.685-066 EXTRACTOR-AND-WRINGER OPERATOR; 551.685-070 FAT-PURIFICATION WORKER; 551.685-074 FILTER HELPER; 551.685-078 FILTER OPERATOR; 551.685-082 FILTER-PRESS OPERATOR; 551.685-086 GREASE-REFINER OPERATOR; 551.685-090 LEACHER; 551.685-098 MERCURY WASHER; 551.685-102 NITROGLYCERIN-SEPARATOR OPERATOR;

551.685-106 POACHER OPERATOR; 551.685-122 PURIFICATION OPERATOR I; 551.685-126 SALT WASHER; 551.685-130 SCREEN OPERATOR; 551.685-134 SODA DIALYZER; 551.685-146 TETRYL-SCREEN OPERATOR; 551.685-150 VACUUM-PAN OPERATOR I; 551.685-154 VACUUM-PAN OPERATOR II; 551.685-158 WAX BLEACHER; 551.685-162 WRINGER OPERATOR; 552.362-010 MONOMER-PURIFICATION OPERATOR; 552.382-010 PYRIDINE OPERATOR; 552.462-010 DISTILLATION OPERATOR; 552.682-010 DISTILLER I; 552.682-014 DISTILLER II; 552.682-018 EXTRACTOR OPERATOR; 552.685-010 ACETONE-RECOVERY WORKER; 552.685-014 BATCH-STILL OPERATOR I; 552.685-018 BATH-MIX OPERATOR; 552.685-026 STILL TENDER; 552.685-030 STILL-OPERATOR HELPER; 553.382-018 EVAPORATOR OPERATOR I; 553.682-018 EVAPORATOR OPERATOR II; 553.685-010 AMMONIUM-NITRATE CRYSTALLIZER; 558.382-010 ACID EXTRACTOR; 558.382-042 KETTLE OPERATOR; 558.565-014 ELECTRIC-CELL TENDER; 558.682-022 RECOVERY OPERATOR; 558.685-026 DE-IONIZER OPERATOR; 558.685-058 CHEMICAL RECLAMATION EQUIPMENT OPERATOR; 559.382-022 GLUE MAKER, BONE; 559.582-010 COAGULATION OPERATOR; 559.585-022 VACUUM-PAN OPERATOR III; 559.665-018 EXTRACTOR-PLANT OPERATOR; 559.682-026 FLUSHER; 559.682-038 RIPENING-ROOM ATTENDANT; 559.682-054 STERILE-PRODUCTS PROCESSOR; 559.682-062 STRONG-NITRIC OPERATOR; 559.682-066 UTILITY OPERATOR I; 559.685-010 ACID PURIFIER; 559.685-042 CRYSTALLIZER OPERATOR I; 559.685-074 FLAKER OPERATOR; 559.685-118 LIME-KILN OPERATOR; 559.685-166 SEPARATOR OPERATOR; 559.685-190 WET-END OPERATOR II; 559.686-034 OPENER; 571.685-014 GLAZE HANDLER; 579.685-046 ROUGE SIFTER AND MILLER; 589.685-054 FEATHER SEPARATOR; 599.665-010 SEED-CLEANER OPERATOR; 599.685-018 CENTRIFUGE OPERATOR, PLASMA PROCESSING; 599.685-042 FILTER-PRESS TENDER; 599.685-082 SCREENER OPERATOR; 692.685-166 SEPARATOR OPERATOR; 934.685-010 CONE OPERATOR; 934.685-018 SHAKER TENDER; 934.685-022 SPIRAL RUNNER; 939.685-010 POND TENDER; 939.685-014 WASHER-AND-CRUSHER TENDER; 954.385-010 BASIN OPERATOR

92965 CRUSHING, GRINDING, MIXING, AND BLENDING MACHINE OPERATORS AND TENDERS.

OOH Title/s: Crushing and Mixing Machine Operators and Tenders

Crushing, grinding, and polishing machine operators and tenders operate or tend machines that crush or grind any of a wide variety of materials, such as coal, glass, plastic, dried fruit, grain, stone, chemicals, food, or rubber; or operate or tend machines that buff and polish materials or products, such as stone, glass, slate, plastic or metal trim, bowling balls, or eyeglasses. Mixing and blending machine operators and tenders operate or tend machines that mix or blend any of a wide variety of materials, such as spices, dough batter, tobacco, fruit juices, chemicals, livestock feed, food products, color pigments, or explosive ingredients. Operates or tends machines and equipment that crush, grind, polish, or blend materials. Moves controls to start, stop, or adjust machinery and equipment that crushes, grinds, polishes, or blends materials. Observes production monitoring equipment to ensure safety and efficient operation. Loads materials into machinery and equipment, using hand tools. Adds or mixes chemicals and ingredients for processing, using hand tools or other devices. Dislodges and clears jammed materials or other items from machinery and equipment, using hand tools. Tends accessory equipment, such as pumps and conveyors, to move materials or ingredients through production process. Weighs or measures materials, ingredients, and products to ensure conformance to requirements. Reads work orders to ascertain production specifications and information. Examines or feels materials, ingredients, or products to ensure conformance to established standards. Collects samples of materials or products for laboratory testing. Cleans and maintains machinery, equipment, materials, and products, using hand tools. Tests samples of materials or products to ensure compliance with specifications, using test equipment. Transfers materials, supplies, and products between work areas, using moving equipment and hand tools. Records operational and production data on specified forms.

Yearly Earnings: $20,956

Education: Moderate-term O-J-T

Knowledge: Production and Processing

Abilities: Rate Control

Skills: Operation Monitoring; Operation and Control

General Work Activities: Repairing and Maintaining Mechanical Equipment

Job Characteristics: Sounds, Noise Levels are Distracting, etc.; Very Hot; Extremely Bright or Inadequate Lighting; Contaminants; Cramped Work Space, Awkward Positions; Whole Body Vibration; Radiation; Hazardous Equipment; Standing; Bending or Twisting the Body; Making Repetitive Motions; Common Protective or Safety Attire; Specialized Protective or Safety Attire; Degree of Automation; Pace Determined by Speed of Equipment

GOE Group/s: 05.11.03 Equipment Operation: Drilling and Oil Exploration; 05.12.07 Elemental Work: Mechanical: Crushing, Mixing, Separating, and Chipping; 05.12.13 Elemental Work: Mechanical: Cutting and Finishing; 06.02.02 Production Work: Machine Work, Metal and Plastics; 06.02.03 Production Work: Machine Work, Wood; 06.02.08 Production Work: Machine Work, Stone, Glass, and Clay; 06.02.09 Production Work: Machine Work, Assorted Materials; 06.02.10 Production Work: Equipment Operation, Metal Processing; 06.02.11 Production Work: Equipment Operation, Chemical Processing; 06.02.12 Production Work: Equipment Operation, Petroleum and Gas Processing; 06.02.13 Production Work: Equipment Operation, Rubber, Plastics, and Glass Processing; 06.02.14 Production Work: Equipment Operation, Paper and Paper Products Processing; 06.02.15 Production Work: Equipment Operation, Food Processing; 06.02.17 Production Work: Equipment Operation, Clay and Coke Processing; 06.02.18 Production Work: Equipment Operation, Assorted Materials Processing; 06.02.30 Production Work: Manual Work, Stone, Glass, and Clay; 06.02.32 Production Work: Manual Work, Assorted Materials; 06.04.02 Elemental Work: Industrial: Machine Work, Metal and Plastics; 06.04.03 Elemental Work: Industrial: Machine Work, Wood; 06.04.05 Elemental Work: Industrial: Machine Work, Fabric and Leather; 06.04.06 Elemental Work: Industrial: Machine Work, Textiles; 06.04.07 Elemental Work: Industrial: Machine Work, Rubber; 06.04.08 Elemental Work: Industrial: Machine Work, Stone, Glass, and Clay; 06.04.09 Elemental Work: Industrial: Machine Work, Assorted Materials; 06.04.10 Elemental Work: Industrial: Equipment Operation, Metal Processing; 06.04.11 Elemental Work: Industrial: Equipment Operation, Chemical Processing; 06.04.12 Elemental Work: Industrial: Equipment Operation, Petroleum, Gas, and Coal Processing; 06.04.13 Elemental Work: Industrial: Equipment Operation, Rubber, Plastics, Glass Processing; 06.04.14 Elemental Work: Industrial: Equipment Operation, Paper Making; 06.04.15 Elemental Work: Industrial: Equipment Operation, Food Processing; 06.04.16 Elemental Work: Industrial: Equipment Operation, Textile, Fabric, and Leather Processing; 06.04.17 Elemental Work: Industrial: Equipment Operation, Clay Processing; 06.04.19 Elemental Work: Industrial: Equipment Operation, Assorted Materials Processing; 06.04.24 Elemental Work: Industrial: Manual Work, Metal and Plastics; 06.04.25 Elemental Work: Industrial: Manual Work, Wood; 06.04.29 Elemental

Work: Industrial: Manual Work, Rubber; 06.04.30 Elemental Work: Industrial: Manual Work, Stone, Glass, and Clay; 06.04.34 Elemental Work: Industrial: Manual Work, Assorted Materials; 06.04.39 Elemental Work: Industrial: Cleaning

CIP Program/s: 010401 Agricultural and Food Products Processing Operations and Management

Related DOT Job/s: 509.485-010 COMPOUND MIXER; 510.465-010 CARBIDE-POWDER PROCESSOR; 510.465-014 SLURRY-CONTROL TENDER; 510.685-010 DUST MIXER; 510.685-014 MIX-HOUSE TENDER; 510.685-018 MIXER; 510.685-022 PUG-MILL OPERATOR; 510.685-026 SINTER-MACHINE OPERATOR; 510.685-030 SLIME-PLANT OPERATOR I; 511.685-046 REAGENT TENDER; 514.685-022 LIME MIXER TENDER; 515.585-010 SCALE-RECLAMATION TENDER; 515.685-010 BATCH MAKER; 515.685-014 CRUSHER TENDER; 515.685-018 STAMPING-MILL TENDER; 515.687-010 HAMMER-MILL OPERATOR; 519.485-010 GRINDER-MILL OPERATOR; 519.685-026 MUD-MILL TENDER; 519.685-030 ROD-MILL TENDER; 520.362-010 BULK-PLANT OPERATOR; 520.362-014 DRY-STARCH OPERATOR; 520.382-010 CISTERN-ROOM OPERATOR; 520.382-014 LIQUID-SUGAR MELTER; 520.385-010 MIXER, WHIPPED TOPPING; 520.462-010 DOUGH-MIXER OPERATOR; 520.485-010 FLOUR MIXER; 520.485-014 GRAIN MIXER; 520.485-018 MINCEMEAT MAKER; 520.485-022 REFINED-SYRUP OPERATOR; 520.485-026 SYRUP MAKER; 520.565-010 CHURNER; 520.585-010 BLENDER; 520.585-014 BROTH MIXER; 520.585-018 COOLER TENDER; 520.585-022 LIQUID-SUGAR FORTIFIER; 520.585-026 SPICE MIXER; 520.662-010 NOODLE-PRESS OPERATOR; 520.665-010 MINGLER OPERATOR; 520.665-014 MIXING-MACHINE OPERATOR; 520.665-018 STARCH-TREATING ASSISTANT; 520.682-010 BLENDING-PLANT OPERATOR; 520.685-010 BATTER MIXER; 520.685-014 BATTER MIXER; 520.685-018 BLENDER-MACHINE OPERATOR; 520.685-022 BLENDER, SNUFF; 520.685-026 BLENDING-LINE ATTENDANT; 520.685-030 BLENDING-TANK TENDER; 520.685-034 BRINE-MIXER OPERATOR, AUTOMATIC; 520.685-046 CANDY PULLER; 520.685-050 CANDY-MAKER HELPER; 520.685-054 CASING-FLUID TENDER; 520.685-066 CHOPPING-MACHINE OPERATOR; 520.685-070 CHURN OPERATOR, MARGARINE; 520.685-074 COCOA-POWDER-MIXER OPERATOR; 520.685-090 DOUGH-BRAKE-MACHINE OPERATOR; 520.685-094 FEED BLENDER; 520.685-098 FEED MIXER; 520.685-106 FLOUR BLENDER; 520.685-110 GREEN-COFFEE BLENDER; 520.685-114 ICING MIXER; 520.685-118 KETTLE TENDER; 520.685-122 LOZENGE-DOUGH MIXER; 520.685-130 MASH GRINDER; 520.685-134 MILL FEEDER; 520.685-138 MIXER; 520.685-142 MIXER OPERATOR II; 520.685-146 MIXER OPERATOR; 520.685-150 MIXER OPERATOR; 520.685-154 MIXER-AND-BLENDER; 520.685-158 MIXER, CHILI POWDER; 520.685-162 MIXER, DRY-FOOD PRODUCTS; 520.685-166 MIXING-MACHINE OPERATOR; 520.685-170 MIXING-TANK OPERATOR; 520.685-194 RELISH BLENDER; 520.685-202 SAUSAGE MAKER; 520.685-206 SAUSAGE MIXER; 520.685-222 TUMBLER TENDER; 520.685-226 UNLEAVENED-DOUGH MIXER; 520.685-230 MIXER OPERATOR, SNACK FOODS; 520.685-234 DOUGH MIXER; 521.362-014 MILLER, DISTILLERY; 521.585-014 MILLER; 521.585-018 POWDER-MILL OPERATOR; 521.662-010 MILLER, WET PROCESS; 521.682-022 FLAKE MILLER, WHEAT AND OATS; 521.682-026 GRINDER OPERATOR; 521.682-034 REFINING-MACHINE OPERATOR; 521.685-074 COCOA-ROOM OPERATOR; 521.685-078 COFFEE GRINDER; 521.685-082 CORN GRINDER; 521.685-086 CORN-GRINDER OPERATOR, AUTOMATIC; 521.685-090 CRUSHER OPERATOR; 521.685-094 CRUSHING-MACHINE OPERATOR; 521.685-122 FEED GRINDER; 521.685-162 GRATED-CHEESE MAKER; 521.685-166 GRINDER OPERATOR; 521.685-194 LABORATORY MILLER; 521.685-202 LIQUOR-GRINDING-MILL OPERATOR; 521.685-210 MEAL-GRINDER TENDER; 521.685-214 MEAT GRINDER; 521.685-222 MILK-POWDER GRINDER; 521.685-226 MILL OPERATOR; 521.685-234 NUT GRINDER; 521.685-266 PULVERIZER; 521.685-314 SNUFF GRINDER AND SCREENER; 521.685-326 SPICE MILLER; 521.685-346 SUGAR GRINDER; 521.685-358 SWEET-POTATO DISINTEGRATOR; 521.685-378 DEBONER, PET FOOD; 522.382-038 VINEGAR MAKER; 522.485-010 PICKLING SOLUTION MAKER; 522.685-010 BLENDING-MACHINE OPERATOR; 522.685-022 BRINE MAKER II; 522.685-026 CARBONATION EQUIPMENT TENDER; 522.685-062 FERMENTER, WINE; 524.685-010 BREADING MACHINE TENDER; 526.382-010 CONCHE OPERATOR; 529.462-010 SYRUP MIXER; 529.485-014 BLOW-UP OPERATOR; 529.682-034 WHIPPED-TOPPING FINISHER; 529.685-022 BLENDER-CONVEYOR OPERATOR; 529.685-126 FLAVOR EXTRACTOR; 529.685-134 FRUIT-BAR MAKER; 529.685-166 MEAT BLENDER; 529.685-178 PEANUT-BUTTER MAKER; 530.382-010 PULP-REFINER OPERATOR; 530.582-010 PULPER, SYNTHETIC SOIL BLOCKS; 530.662-010 BEATER ENGINEER; 530.662-014 WOOD GRINDER OPERATOR; 530.665-010 BEATER-ENGINEER HELPER; 530.682-010 PULP GRINDER AND BLENDER; 530.685-010 COATING-MIXER TENDER; 530.685-014 PULPER; 539.362-018 SLURRY MIXER; 540.382-010 COMPOUNDER; 540.462-010 BLENDER; 540.585-010 MIXER OPERATOR, CARBON PASTE; 543.685-010 BULLET-LUBRICANT MIXER; 544.565-010 GRINDER, CARBON PLANT; 544.582-010 CRUSHER-AND-BLENDER OPERATOR; 544.585-010 MIX-CRUSHER OPERATOR; 544.662-010 COKE-CRUSHER OPERATOR; 544.665-010 MILL-AND-COAL-TRANSPORT OPERATOR; 544.685-010 BREAKER TENDER; 549.665-010 ACETYLENE-CYLINDER-PACKING MIXER; 549.682-010 GREASE MAKER; 550.362-010 FROTHING-MACHINE OPERATOR; 550.382-010 COLOR MAKER; 550.382-014 COLOR MAKER; 550.382-018 MIXER OPERATOR I; 550.382-026 OPERATOR, CATALYST CONCENTRATION; 550.382-030 ROOF-CEMENT-AND-PAINT MAKER; 550.382-034 SOLUTIONS OPERATOR; 550.485-010 CHEMICAL MIXER; 550.485-018 PAINT MIXER, MACHINE; 550.485-022 POWDER BLENDER AND POURER; 550.485-026 PULVERIZING-AND-SIFTING OPERATOR; 550.564-010 METAL-BONDING CRIB ATTENDANT; 550.565-010 PRIMER-POWDER BLENDER, DRY; 550.582-010 PRIMER-POWDER BLENDER, WET; 550.582-014 WEIGHER-BULKER; 550.585-010 BINDER TECHNICIAN; 550.585-014 CELLOPHANE-BATH MIXER; 550.585-018 CHEMICAL MIXER; 550.585-022 COATING OPERATOR; 550.585-026 LIME-SLUDGE MIXER; 550.585-030 NITRATING-ACID MIXER; 550.585-034 PASTE MIXER; 550.585-038 THINNER; 550.585-042 TRACER-POWDER BLENDER; 550.585-046 WAX BLENDER; 550.662-010 BLEACH-LIQUOR MAKER; 550.665-010 BLENDER II; 550.665-014 COMPOSITION MIXER; 550.665-018 FERTILIZER MIXER; 550.665-022 MOTTLER OPERATOR; 550.682-010 SIZE MAKER; 550.682-014 TANNING-SOLUTION MAKER; 550.684-026 SILVER-SOLUTION MIXER; 550.685-010 BATCH MIXER; 550.685-014 BLENDER I; 550.685-018 BRINE MAKER I; 550.685-022 CD-MIXER; 550.685-026 CEMENT MIXER; 550.685-030 CHEMICAL PREPARER; 550.685-034 CHURN TENDER; 550.685-038 COLOR-PASTE MIXER; 550.685-042 COMPOUND FINISHER; 550.685-046 COMPOUNDER; 550.685-050 COMPOUNDER; 550.685-054 CRUTCHER; 550.685-058 DUSTLESS OPERATOR; 550.685-062 GLUE MIXER; 550.685-066 GROUND MIXER; 550.685-070 INSECTICIDE MIXER; 550.685-074 MIXER I; 550.685-078 MIXER; 550.685-082 MIXER OPERATOR; 550.685-086 MIXER, FOAM RUBBER; 550.685-090 MIXING-MACHINE TENDER; 550.685-094 PEARL-GLUE OPERATOR; 550.685-098 POWERHOUSE HELPER; 550.685-102 RUBBER-MILL TENDER; 550.685-106 SEASONING MIXER; 550.685-110 SWEEPING-COMPOUND BLENDER; 550.685-114 TETRYL-DISSOLVER OPERATOR; 550.685-118 TUMBLER OPERATOR; 550.685-122 WEIGHER AND MIXER; 550.685-126 WET MIXER; 550.685-130 MATERIAL MIXER; 550.685-134 MIXING-MACHINE OPERATOR; 553.682-014 CURER, FOAM RUBBER; 555.382-010 PULVERIZER-MILL OPERATOR; 555.565-010 MILL ATTENDANT I; 555.682-010 MILLER II; 555.682-014 ROLLER-MILL OPERA-

TOR; 555.682-018 SAND-MILL GRINDER; 555.682-022 STONE-MILL OPERATOR; 555.685-014 BONE CRUSHER; 555.685-018 COPRA PROCESSOR; 555.685-022 CRUSHER TENDER; 555.685-026 GRINDER; 555.685-030 GRINDER; 555.685-034 GRINDER OPERATOR; 555.685-038 MILL ATTENDANT II; 555.685-046 PULVERIZER; 555.685-050 SCRATCHER TENDER; 555.685-058 SHREDDER OPERATOR; 555.685-062 SOAP GRINDER; 555.685-066 WHEEL-MILL OPERATOR; 559.382-014 CATALYST OPERATOR, GASOLINE; 559.382-026 GRANULATOR-MACHINE OPERATOR; 559.382-054 SOAP MAKER; 559.665-026 MIXER I; 559.682-030 LACQUER MAKER; 559.682-046 SODA-ROOM OPERATOR; 559.685-034 CD-STORAGE-AND-MATERIALS MAKE-UP HELPER; 559.685-082 FORMULA WEIGHER; 559.685-154 RESTRICTIVE-PREPARATION OPERATOR; 560.465-010 CHIP-MIXING-MACHINE OPERATOR; 560.585-010 MIXING-MACHINE TENDER; 564.662-010 LOG-CHIPPER OPERATOR; 564.682-018 MILLER, WOOD FLOUR; 564.685-010 BREAKER-MACHINE OPERATOR; 564.685-018 HOG TENDER; 569.682-010 GRINDER, HARDBOARD; 570.362-010 BULK-STATION OPERATOR; 570.382-010 MILL OPERATOR; 570.382-014 PLASTER MIXER, MACHINE; 570.382-018 SUPPLY CONTROLLER; 570.482-010 CLAY MAKER; 570.485-010 ABRASIVE MIXER; 570.665-010 DRY-PAN OPERATOR; 570.682-018 SAND MIXER, MACHINE; 570.683-014 SAND-CUTTER OPERATOR; 570.685-010 AUXILIARY-EQUIPMENT TENDER; 570.685-014 CLAY MIXER; 570.685-018 CRUSHER OPERATOR; 570.685-022 CRUSHER TENDER; 570.685-026 CULLET CRUSHER-AND-WASHER; 570.685-030 HAMMER-MILL OPERATOR; 570.685-034 LIME SLAKER; 570.685-038 MILLER; 570.685-042 MILLER I; 570.685-046 MILLER; 570.685-050 MIXER; 570.685-054 MIXER; 570.685-058 MIXER OPERATOR; 570.685-062 MIXER TENDER, BOARD; 570.685-066 MOLDING-MACHINE TENDER; 570.685-070 MUD-MIXER OPERATOR; 570.685-074 PUG-MILL-OPERATOR HELPER; 570.685-078 REFRACTORY MIXER; 570.685-082 ROUGE MIXER; 570.685-086 SAGGER PREPARER; 570.685-090 SILICA-SPRAY MIXER; 570.685-094 SLATE MIXER; 570.685-098 GLAZE MAKER; 579.382-010 CALCINER, GYPSUM; 579.682-010 MIXER, WET POUR; 579.685-014 FRIT-MIXER-AND-BURNER; 579.685-030 MOLD POLISHER; 579.685-074 MIXER; 585.685-018 BUFFER, MACHINE; 586.685-014 CONTINUOUS-CRUSHER OPERATOR; 589.464-010 COLOR MIXER; 589.685-050 FEATHER MIXER; 590.662-018 MIXING-ROLL OPERATOR; 599.685-014 BRAN MIXER; 599.685-058 MILL OPERATOR;
599.685-078 POLISHER; 599.685-106 TUMBLER; 599.685-110 TUMBLER OPERATOR; 673.382-026 CRYSTAL GRINDER; 673.662-010 TOP POLISHER; 673.682-022 FINISH OPENER, JEWEL HOLE; 673.682-030 SLAB GRINDER; 673.685-010 ABRASIVE GRINDER; 673.685-014 BED RUBBER; 673.685-018 BEVELER; 673.685-022 BEVELER; 673.685-026 BLOCKER; 673.685-030 BLOCKER, AUTOMATIC; 673.685-034 CIRCLE BEVELER; 673.685-038 CIRCLE EDGER; 673.685-042 CONVEX-GRINDER OPERATOR; 673.685-054 FINGER-GRIP-MACHINE OPERATOR; 673.685-058 FINISH-MACHINE TENDER; 673.685-062 GROOVER; 673.685-066 LEVEL-VIAL INSIDE GRINDER; 673.685-070 NOTCH GRINDER; 673.685-074 STONE ROUGHER; 673.685-078 STRAIGHT-LINE EDGER; 673.685-082 STRIP POLISHER; 673.685-086 DISC-PAD GRINDER; 673.685-094 POLISHING MACHINE TENDER; 673.685-098 RADIUS CORNER MACHINE OPERATOR; 673.685-102 WAFER ABRADING MACHINE TENDER; 675.682-014 PLANER OPERATOR; 679.685-022 TILE GRINDER; 680.685-062 MIXER; 680.685-066 MIXING-MACHINE OPERATOR; 690.385-010 PLATEN GRINDER; 690.685-038 BOWLING-BALL FINISHER; 690.685-046 BUFFER; 690.685-050 BUFFER, AUTOMATIC; 690.685-054 BUFFER, INFLATED-PAD; 690.685-194 GRINDING-MACHINE OPERATOR, AUTOMATIC; 690.685-330 ROUGH-AND-TRUEING-MACHINE OPERATOR; 690.685-346 SANDER; 690.685-390 SPONGE BUFFER; 690.685-422 TIRE BUFFER; 715.684-078 CRYSTAL CUTTER; 716.685-018 GRINDER, HAND; 716.685-022 LENS-FABRICATING-MACHINE TENDER; 749.684-050 PAINT TRIMMER, PIPE BOWLS; 753.684-010 BUFFING-AND-SUEDING-MACHINE OPERATOR; 759.684-022 BUFFER; 761.684-026 POLISHER; 770.582-010 FACER; 770.682-018 JEWEL-BEARING FACER; 770.685-010 FLAT SURFACER, JEWEL; 770.685-014 JEWEL GRINDER I; 770.685-018 JEWEL-BEARING GRINDER; 770.685-026 JEWEL-CORNER-BRUSHING-MACHINE OPERATOR; 770.685-030 JEWEL-CUPPING-MACHINE OPERATOR; 770.685-034 TURNER, MACHINE; 774.684-042 WARE DRESSER; 775.382-010 GLASS GRINDER, LABORATORY APPARATUS; 775.684-010 BEVELER; 775.684-018 EDGER, TOUCH-UP; 775.684-030 GLASS GRINDER; 775.684-034 GLASS GRINDER; 775.684-042 GLASS SANDER, BELT; 775.684-058 POLISHER; 775.684-062 WATCH-CRYSTAL EDGE GRINDER; 930.685-010 MUD-PLANT OPERATOR

92968 EXTRUDING, FORMING, PRESSING, AND COMPACTING MACHINE SETTERS AND SET-UP OPERATORS. OOH Title/s: Extruding and Forming Machine Setters, Operators, and Tenders

Set up or set up and operate machines—such as glass-forming machines, plodder machines, and tuber machines—to manufacture any of a wide variety of products—such as soap bars, formed rubber, glassware, food, brick, and tile—by means of extruding, compressing, or compacting. Installs dies or molds in machines to produce products from variety of materials, according to work order and specifications. Turns knobs to control machine functions, such as air pressure, vacuum, and coolant flow. Operates machines and notifies supervisor or set-up personnel of needed adjustments to machines. Observes operation of machine and product to detect and diagnose cause of faulty operation, and monitors gauges and recorders. Presses control button to activate machinery and equipment. Synchronizes speed of sections of machine when producing products involving several steps or processes. Selects and measures arbors and dies to verify size specified on work ticket. Installs, aligns, and adjusts neck rings, press plungers, and feeder tubes to molds to deliver material and form product. Couples air and gas lines to machine to maintain plasticity of material and to regulate solidification of final product. Adjusts timer drum to set size of product material and rollers, cutoff knives, and stops to regulate thickness and length. Threads extruded strip through water tank and holddown bars or attaches strands to wire and draws through tube. Pours, scoops, or dumps specified ingredients, metal assemblies, or mixtures into sections of machine prior to starting machine. Feeds product into machine by hand or conveyor. Ignites burner to preheat product or applies heat, using torch. Removes products from discharge belts and molds, mold components, and feeder tubes from machines. Cleans dies, arbors, compression chambers, and molds, using swabs, sponge, or air hose and swabs molds with solution to prevent sticking. Collects, examines, measures, weighs, and tests product to verify machine set-up and conformance of product to specifications. Records product information, such as scrap quantity, machine number, and ingredients, to complete work ticket, and places tickets with product. Routes sample to lab for analysis, according to procedure. Disassembles and repairs machinery and equipment.

Yearly Earnings: $19,760

Education: Moderate-term O-J-T

Knowledge: Production and Processing; Mechanical; Physics; Chemistry

Abilities: Rate Control

Skills: Installation; Operation Monitoring; Equipment Maintenance; Repairing
General Work Activities: Controlling Machines and Processes; Repairing and Maintaining Mechanical Equipment
Job Characteristics: Sounds, Noise Levels are Distracting, etc.; Hazardous Equipment; Degree of Automation; Pace Determined by Speed of Equipment
GOE Group/s: 06.01.02 Production Technology: Machine Set-up; 06.02.07 Production Work: Machine Work, Rubber; 06.02.08 Production Work: Machine Work, Stone, Glass, and Clay; 06.02.11 Production Work: Equipment Operation, Chemical Processing; 06.02.13 Production Work: Equipment Operation, Rubber, Plastics, and Glass Processing; 06.02.15 Production Work: Equipment Operation, Food Processing; 06.02.17 Production Work: Equipment Operation, Clay and Coke Processing; 06.02.18 Production Work: Equipment Operation, Assorted Materials Processing; 06.02.20 Production Work: Machine Assembling; 06.04.13 Elemental Work: Industrial: Equipment Operation, Rubber, Plastics, Glass Processing
CIP Program/s: 470303 Industrial Machinery Maintenance and Repair; 489999 Precision Production Trades, Other
Related DOT Job/s: 520.682-014 CENTER-MACHINE OPERATOR; 556.682-018 PLODDER OPERATOR; 556.682-022 COMPRESSOR; 557.382-014 WINK-CUTTER OPERATOR; 557.682-010 GRAINING-PRESS OPERATOR; 575.380-010 FORMING-MACHINE UPKEEP MECHANIC; 575.382-010 BRICK-AND-TILE-MAKING-MACHINE OPERATOR; 575.382-014 FORMING-MACHINE OPERATOR; 575.382-022 GLASS-ROLLING-MACHINE OPERATOR; 575.682-010 FIBER-GLASS-DOWEL-DRAWING-MACHINE OPERATOR; 575.682-022 RAM-PRESS OPERATOR; 649.582-014 SIZING-MACHINE OPERATOR; 690.662-014 TUBER-MACHINE OPERATOR; 692.362-010 SET-UP MECHANIC, CROWN ASSEMBLY MACHINE

92971 EXTRUDING, FORMING, PRESSING, AND COMPACTING MACHINE OPERATORS AND TENDERS. OOH Title/s: Extruding and Forming Machine Setters, Operators, and Tenders

Operate or tend machines to shape and form any of a wide variety of manufactured products—such as glass bulbs, molded food and candy, rubber goods, clay products, wax products, tobacco plugs, cosmetics, or paper products—by means of extruding, compressing or compacting. Activates machine to shape or form products, such as candy bars, light bulbs, silver spoons, balloons, or insulation panels. Monitors machine operations and observes indicator lights and gauges, such as thermometers, voltage meters, and timers, to detect malfunctions. Adjusts machine components to regulate speed, pressure, and temperature of machine and amount, dimensions, and flow of materials or ingredients. Fills molds or positions ingredients or materials, such as glass rods, candy, or rolls of paper, on machine feeding mechanism. Clears jams, removes defective or substandard materials or products, and readjusts machine components to conform to specifications. Removes materials or products from mold or from extruding, forming, pressing, or compacting machine, and stacks or stores for additional processing. Reviews work orders, specifications, or instructions to determine materials, ingredients, procedures, components, settings, and adjustments for extruding, forming, pressing, or compacting machine. Measures, mixes, cuts, shapes, softens, and joins materials and ingredients, such as powder, cornmeal, or rubber, to prepare for machine processing. Selects and installs machine components, such as dies, molds, and cutters, according to specifications, using hand tools and measuring devices. Examines, measures, and weighs materials or products to verify conformance to standards using measuring devices, such as templates, micrometers, or scales. Moves materials, supplies, components, and finished products between storage and work areas, using racks, hoists, and handtrucks. Replaces worn or broken parts, such as nozzles, punches, and filters, and cleans and lubricates machine components to maintain in working order. Records and maintains production data, such as meter readings and quantity, type, and dimensions of materials produced.
Yearly Earnings: $19,760
Education: Moderate-term O-J-T
Knowledge: Production and Processing
Abilities: Perceptual Speed; Control Precision; Multilimb Coordination; Rate Control; Reaction Time; Speed of Limb Movement; Explosive Strength; Dynamic Strength; Trunk Strength; Dynamic Flexibility; Gross Body Coordination; Gross Body Equilibrium
Skills: Operation Monitoring; Operation and Control; Equipment Maintenance; Repairing
General Work Activities: Repairing and Maintaining Mechanical Equipment
Job Characteristics: Sounds, Noise Levels are Distracting, etc.; Hazardous Conditions; Hazardous Equipment; Standing; Using Hands on Objects, Tools, or Controls; Bending or Twisting the Body; Making Repetitive Motions; Degree of Automation; Importance of Being Aware of New Events; Importance of Repeating Same Tasks; Pace Determined by Speed of Equipment
GOE Group/s: 06.02.02 Production Work: Machine Work, Metal and Plastics; 06.02.04 Production Work: Machine Work, Paper; 06.02.05 Production Work: Machine Work, Leather and Fabrics; 06.02.08 Production Work: Machine Work, Stone, Glass, and Clay; 06.02.09 Production Work: Machine Work, Assorted Materials; 06.02.13 Production Work: Equipment Operation, Rubber, Plastics, and Glass Processing; 06.02.15 Production Work: Equipment Operation, Food Processing; 06.02.17 Production Work: Equipment Operation, Clay and Coke Processing; 06.02.18 Production Work: Equipment Operation, Assorted Materials Processing; 06.04.02 Elemental Work: Industrial: Machine Work, Metal and Plastics; 06.04.03 Elemental Work: Industrial: Machine Work, Wood; 06.04.04 Elemental Work: Industrial: Machine Work, Paper; 06.04.05 Elemental Work: Industrial: Machine Work, Fabric and Leather; 06.04.07 Elemental Work: Industrial: Machine Work, Rubber; 06.04.08 Elemental Work: Industrial: Machine Work, Stone, Glass, and Clay; 06.04.09 Elemental Work: Industrial: Machine Work, Assorted Materials; 06.04.10 Elemental Work: Industrial: Equipment Operation, Metal Processing; 06.04.11 Elemental Work: Industrial: Equipment Operation, Chemical Processing; 06.04.12 Elemental Work: Industrial: Equipment Operation, Petroleum, Gas, and Coal Processing; 06.04.13 Elemental Work: Industrial: Equipment Operation, Rubber, Plastics, Glass Processing; 06.04.14 Elemental Work: Industrial: Equipment Operation, Paper Making; 06.04.15 Elemental Work: Industrial: Equipment Operation, Food Processing; 06.04.17 Elemental Work: Industrial: Equipment Operation, Clay Processing; 06.04.18 Elemental Work: Industrial: Equipment Operation, Wood Processing; 06.04.19 Elemental Work: Industrial: Equipment Operation, Assorted Materials Processing; 06.04.20 Elemental Work: Industrial: Machine Assembling; 06.04.21 Elemental Work: Industrial: Machine Work, Brushing, Spraying, and Coating; 06.04.24 Elemental Work: Industrial: Manual Work, Metal and Plastics; 06.04.30 Elemental Work: Industrial: Manual Work, Stone, Glass, and Clay; 06.04.34 Elemental Work: Industrial: Manual Work, Assorted Materials; 06.04.38 Elemental Work: Industrial: Wrapping and Packaging
CIP Program/s: 470303 Industrial Machinery Maintenance and Repair; 480503 Machine Shop Assistant
Related DOT Job/s: 520.682-030 SPINNER; 520.682-034 CRACKER-AND-COOKIE-MACHINE OPERATOR; 520.685-038 CAKE FORMER; 520.685-058 CASTING-MACHINE OPERATOR; 520.685-062 CASTING-MACHINE OPERATOR; 520.685-078 CONFECTIONERY-DROPS-MACHINE OPERATOR; 520.685-086 DIVIDING-MACHINE OPERATOR;

520.685-102 FLAKING-ROLL OPERATOR; 520.685-178 PELLET-MILL OPERATOR; 520.685-182 PRESS OPERATOR, MEAT; 520.685-186 PRESS TENDER; 520.685-190 PRETZEL-TWISTING-MACHINE OPERATOR; 520.685-198 ROLLING-MACHINE OPERATOR; 520.685-214 SWEET-GOODS-MACHINE OPERATOR; 521.685-330 STEM-ROLLER-OR-CRUSHER OPERATOR; 521.685-350 SUGAR PRESSER; 529.682-026 LOZENGE MAKER; 529.685-014 AUTOMATIC LUMP MAKING MACHINE TENDER; 529.685-042 BUTT MAKER; 529.685-054 CHOCOLATE MOLDER, MACHINE; 529.685-078 CORN-PRESS OPERATOR; 529.685-210 SANDWICH-MACHINE OPERATOR; 529.685-234 SUCKER-MACHINE OPERATOR; 529.685-238 TABLET-MACHINE OPERATOR; 532.685-026 PULP-PRESS TENDER; 534.685-010 DAMPENER OPERATOR; 535.482-010 WAD-COMPRESSOR OPERATOR-ADJUSTER; 535.685-010 PLATE WORKER; 539.565-010 VULCANIZED-FIBER-UNIT OPERATOR; 539.685-010 COATER OPERATOR, INSULATION BOARD; 539.685-018 MOLDING-MACHINE TENDER; 539.685-022 PUMP-PRESS OPERATOR; 539.685-030 WET-MACHINE TENDER; 549.685-018 MOLDER, WAX; 549.685-038 WAX MOLDER; 551.685-046 DEHYDRATING-PRESS OPERATOR; 551.685-114 PRESS OPERATOR; 551.685-118 PRESS OPERATOR II; 551.685-138 STEEPING-PRESS TENDER; 553.585-022 THERMAL MOLDER; 553.665-010 BELT-PRESS OPERATOR II; 553.665-046 STEAM-PRESS TENDER I; 553.665-050 STEAM-PRESS TENDER II; 553.682-026 V-BELT CURER; 554.665-014 LAMINATING-MACHINE TENDER; 554.685-018 COMBINING-MACHINE OPERATOR; 555.685-042 PELLET-PRESS OPERATOR; 556.362-010 ARCH-CUSHION-PRESS OPERATOR; 556.382-018 POLYSTYRENE-BEAD MOLDER; 556.582-010 PLATE MOLDER; 556.585-010 CASTING-ROOM OPERATOR; 556.682-010 BLOW-MOLDING-MACHINE OPERATOR; 556.685-010 AIR-BAG CURER; 556.685-014 BLOCK-PRESS OPERATOR; 556.685-018 BOWLING-BALL MOLDER; 556.685-026 COSMETICS PRESSER; 556.685-030 DIPPER; 556.685-034 DIPPING-MACHINE OPERATOR; 556.685-042 MATTING-PRESS TENDER; 556.685-046 MOLDER, FOAM RUBBER; 556.685-050 MOLDER, MACHINE; 556.685-062 POLYSTYRENE-MOLDING-MACHINE TENDER; 556.685-066 PRESS TENDER; 556.685-070 RECORD-PRESS TENDER; 556.685-074 SLUG-PRESS OPERATOR; 556.685-078 STAMPER; 557.565-010 EXTRUDING-MACHINE OPERATOR; 557.685-010 CORE EXTRUDER; 557.685-014 EXTRUDER TENDER; 559.665-022 FORMING-MACHINE OPERATOR; 559.665-030 PRESS OPERATOR I; 559.682-050 SPONGE-PRESS OPERATOR; 559.685-030 BRIQUETTER OPERATOR; 559.685-038 COMPRESSOR OPERATOR II; 559.685-126 NOODLE-CATALYST MAKER; 559.685-174 TUBE-BUILDING-MACHINE OPERATOR; 563.685-010 BARK-PRESS OPERATOR;
569.382-010 LINE TENDER, FLAKEBOARD; 569.682-014 PRESS OPERATOR, HARDBOARD; 569.685-010 ARTIFICIAL-LOG-MACHINE OPERATOR; 569.685-030 CORK MOLDER; 569.685-038 EXTRUDER OPERATOR; 569.685-046 GLUING-MACHINE OPERATOR; 569.685-050 GLUING-MACHINE OPERATOR, ELECTRONIC; 569.685-058 HYDRAULIC-PRESS OPERATOR; 569.685-078 WOOD-FUEL PELLETIZER; 575.362-010 DRAWING-KILN OPERATOR; 575.362-014 GLASS-RIBBON-MACHINE OPERATOR; 575.365-010 GLASS-RIBBON-MACHINE-OPERATOR ASSISTANT; 575.382-018 GLASS-BULB-MACHINE FORMER, TUBULAR STOCK; 575.382-026 RETORT-OR-CONDENSER PRESS OPERATOR; 575.462-010 AUGER PRESS OPERATOR, MANUAL CONTROL; 575.662-010 DRY-PRESS OPERATOR; 575.662-014 YARDAGE-CONTROL OPERATOR, FORMING; 575.665-010 CONCRETE-PIPE-MAKING-MACHINE OPERATOR; 575.665-014 DIE TRIPPER; 575.682-014 MOLDING-MACHINE OPERATOR; 575.682-018 PRESS OPERATOR; 575.685-010 ABRASIVE-WHEEL MOLDER; 575.685-014 BLOCK-MAKING-MACHINE OPERATOR; 575.685-018 CHALK-EXTRUDING-MACHINE OPERATOR; 575.685-022 CHALK-MOLDING-MACHINE OPERATOR; 575.685-026 DIE PRESSER; 575.685-034 FLOWER-POT-PRESS OPERATOR; 575.685-038 FORMING-MACHINE TENDER; 575.685-042 HOT-PRESS OPERATOR; 575.685-046 HYDRAULIC-BILLET MAKER; 575.685-050 LEAD FORMER; 575.685-054 LENS-MOLDING-EQUIPMENT OPERATOR; 575.685-058 MARBLE-MACHINE TENDER; 575.685-062 MOLDER-MACHINE TENDER; 575.685-066 MOLDER, FIBERGLASS LUGGAGE; 575.685-070 PRESS OPERATOR; 575.685-074 PRESSER; 575.685-078 SYNTHETIC-GEM-PRESS OPERATOR; 579.685-026 MICA-PLATE LAYER; 579.685-066 BRIQUETTE OPERATOR; 590.665-014 PRESS-MACHINE OPERATOR; 590.682-010 CALENDER OPERATOR; 641.685-038 DOMER; 641.685-062 PAPER-CONE-MACHINE TENDER; 649.685-078 PAPER-CUP-MACHINE OPERATOR; 649.685-086 PATTERNMAKER, ACOUSTICAL TILE; 679.685-026 TURNING-AND-BEADING-MACHINE OPERATOR; 690.682-070 SOLE-CONFORMING-MACHINE OPERATOR; 690.685-074 CEMENTER, MACHINE JOINER; 690.685-258 LAMINATOR I; 690.685-318 PRESSER; 690.685-466 VULCANIZING-PRESS OPERATOR; 691.382-010 EXTRUDING-MACHINE OPERATOR; 691.382-014 LEAD-PRESS OPERATOR; 692.462-010 CALENDER-ROLL PRESS OPERATOR; 692.682-026 CANDLE-EXTRUSION-MACHINE OPERATOR; 692.685-030 BROOM BUNDLER; 692.685-034 BUCKLE-FRAME SHAPER; 692.685-038 CANDLE MOLDER, MACHINE; 692.685-058 CORE SHAPER; 692.685-086 FOILING-MACHINE OPERATOR; 692.685-118 LIGHT-BULB ASSEMBLER; 692.685-282 LAMINATOR, PRINTED CIRCUIT BOARDS; 694.685-034 PELLET-PRESS OPERATOR; 694.685-038 PRESS TENDER, PYROTECHNICS; 700.682-010 FLATWARE MAKER; 709.685-014 HOT BOX OPERATOR; 709.685-018 ROLLER, GOLD LEAF; 752.685-010 SECTIONAL-BELT-MOLD ASSEMBLER; 929.685-010 CRATE OPENER

92974 PACKAGING AND FILLING MACHINE OPERATORS AND TENDERS. OOH Title/s: Packaging and Filling Machine Operators and Tenders

Operate or tend machines—such as filling machines, casing-running machines, ham-rolling machines, preservative filling machines, baling machines, wrapping machines, and stuffing machines—to prepare industrial or consumer products—such as gas cylinders, meat and other food products, tobacco, insulation, ammunition, stuffed toys, and athletic equipment—for storage or shipment. Tends or operates machine that packages product. Operates mechanism to cut filler product or packaging material. Regulates machine flow, speed, and temperature. Starts machine by engaging controls. Stops or resets machine when malfunction occurs, and clears machine jams. Adjusts machine tension and pressure and machine components according to size or processing angle of product. Observes machine operations to ensure quality and conformity of filled or packaged products to standards. Removes finished packaged items from machine, and separates rejected items. Inspects and removes defective product and packaging material. Stocks product for packaging or filling machine operation. Stocks packaging material for machine processing. Tests and evaluates product, and verifies product weight or measurement to ensure quality standards. Secures finished packaged items by hand-tying, sewing, or attaching fastener. Cleans, oils, and makes minor repairs to machinery and equipment. Counts and records finished and rejected packaged items. Stacks finished packaged items or packs items in cartons or containers. Attaches identification labels to finished packaged items.

Yearly Earnings: $15,548

Education: Moderate-term O-J-T

Knowledge: Production and Processing; Food Production

Abilities: Perceptual Speed; Manual Dexterity; Finger Dexterity; Control Precision; Response Orientation; Rate Control; Reaction Time; Speed of Limb Movement; Static Strength; Trunk Strength; Extent Flexibility; Dynamic Flexibility; Gross Body Equilibrium; Peripheral Vision; Hearing Sensitivity; Sound Localization

Skills: Operation Monitoring; Operation and Control; Equipment Maintenance; Repairing
General Work Activities: Handling and Moving Objects; Controlling Machines and Processes; Repairing and Maintaining Mechanical Equipment
Job Characteristics: Sounds, Noise Levels are Distracting, etc.; Hazardous Equipment; Standing; Making Repetitive Motions; Special Uniform; Degree of Automation; Importance of Repeating Same Tasks; Pace Determined by Speed of Equipment
GOE Group/s: 03.04.01 Elemental Work: Plants and Animals: Farming; 06.02.09 Production Work: Machine Work, Assorted Materials; 06.02.15 Production Work: Equipment Operation, Food Processing; 06.02.18 Production Work: Equipment Operation, Assorted Materials Processing; 06.04.02 Elemental Work: Industrial: Machine Work, Metal and Plastics; 06.04.04 Elemental Work: Industrial: Machine Work, Paper; 06.04.05 Elemental Work: Industrial: Machine Work, Fabric and Leather; 06.04.07 Elemental Work: Industrial: Machine Work, Rubber; 06.04.08 Elemental Work: Industrial: Machine Work, Stone, Glass, and Clay; 06.04.09 Elemental Work: Industrial: Machine Work, Assorted Materials; 06.04.12 Elemental Work: Industrial: Equipment Operation, Petroleum, Gas, and Coal Processing; 06.04.15 Elemental Work: Industrial: Equipment Operation, Food Processing; 06.04.19 Elemental Work: Industrial: Equipment Operation, Assorted Materials Processing; 06.04.20 Elemental Work: Industrial: Machine Assembling; 06.04.32 Elemental Work: Industrial: Manual Work, Casting and Molding; 06.04.34 Elemental Work: Industrial: Manual Work, Assorted Materials; 06.04.36 Elemental Work: Industrial: Filling; 06.04.37 Elemental Work: Industrial: Manual Work, Stamping, Marking, Labeling, and Ticketing; 06.04.38 Elemental Work: Industrial: Wrapping and Packaging
CIP Program/s: 000000 NO CIP ASSIGNED
Related DOT Job/s: 509.685-046 SCRAP BALLER; 518.683-010 SANDSLINGER OPERATOR; 520.685-174 MOLDER, MEAT; 520.685-210 STUFFER; 520.685-218 TRAY-CASTING-MACHINE OPERATOR; 524.685-030 FILLING MACHINE TENDER; 525.685-014 CASING-RUNNING-MACHINE TENDER; 529.665-010 FRUIT-GRADER OPERATOR; 529.665-022 YEAST-CUTTING-AND-WRAPPING-MACHINE OPERATOR; 529.685-010 AUTO ROLLER; 529.685-038 BUNCH MAKER, MACHINE; 529.685-138 HAM-ROLLING-MACHINE OPERATOR; 529.685-162 LINKING-MACHINE OPERATOR; 529.685-186 PLUG-OVERWRAP-MACHINE TENDER; 529.685-190 PRESERVATIVE FILLER, MACHINE; 529.685-266 WRAPPER LAYER; 529.685-270 WRAPPER-LAYER-AND-EXAMINER, SOFT WORK; 529.685-282 CAN-FILLING-AND-CLOSING-MACHINE TENDER; 529.685-286 CIGAR-WRAPPER TENDER, AUTOMATIC; 554.684-014 FOAM DISPENSER; 559.565-010 CYLINDER FILLER; 559.682-010 CAPSULE-FILLING-MACHINE OPERATOR; 559.685-018 AMPOULE FILLER; 579.685-038 PACKER, INSULATION; 649.685-094 PUNCHBOARD-FILLING-MACHINE OPERATOR; 649.685-122 TAPE-FASTENER-MACHINE OPERATOR; 689.685-102 QUILT STUFFER, MACHINE; 690.685-022 BALER; 692.662-014 GELATIN-DYNAMITE-PACKING OPERATOR; 692.682-038 FILLING-AND-STAPLING-MACHINE OPERATOR; 692.682-058 STRAPPING-MACHINE OPERATOR; 692.685-114 LEVEL-GLASS-VIAL FILLER; 692.685-154 SEAL-EXTRUSION OPERATOR; 694.382-014 TRACER-BULLET-CHARGING-MACHINE OPERATOR; 694.685-026 LOADING-MACHINE OPERATOR; 694.685-030 LOADING-UNIT OPERATOR; 694.685-050 RIM-FIRE-PRIMING OPERATOR; 699.685-038 FILLING-MACHINE OPERATOR; 731.685-014 STUFFER; 732.685-010 BASE-FILLER OPERATOR; 732.685-034 STUFFING-MACHINE OPERATOR; 733.685-014 FILLING-MACHINE OPERATOR; 780.685-014 STUFFING-MACHINE OPERATOR; 827.585-010 FOAM CHARGER; 914.485-010 BARREL FILLER II; 920.482-010 ICICLE-MACHINE OPERATOR; 920.665-010 CARTON-PACKAGING-MACHINE OPERATOR; 920.665-014 RACK-ROOM WORKER; 920.685-010 BALING-MACHINE TENDER; 920.685-014 BANDER-AND-CELLOPHANER, MACHINE; 920.685-018 BB SHOT PACKER; 920.685-026 BOTTLE PACKER; 920.685-030 CANDLE WRAPPING-MACHINE OPERATOR; 920.685-034 CARDER; 920.685-038 CASE PACKER AND SEALER; 920.685-042 CASE-LOADER OPERATOR; 920.685-046 CIGAR BRANDER; 920.685-050 CIGARETTE-PACKING-MACHINE OPERATOR; 920.685-054 COTTON-ROLL PACKER; 920.685-058 FEED WEIGHER; 920.685-062 HYDRAULIC-PRESS OPERATOR; 920.685-066 LABELING-MACHINE OPERATOR; 920.685-074 PACKAGE SEALER, MACHINE; 920.685-078 PACKAGER, MACHINE; 920.685-082 PACKER OPERATOR, AUTOMATIC; 920.685-086 PACKING-MACHINE-PILOT CAN ROUTER; 920.685-090 ROLL FINISHER; 920.685-094 SNUFF-PACKING-MACHINE OPERATOR; 920.685-098 TOBACCO-PACKING-MACHINE OPERATOR; 920.685-106 CUBING-MACHINE TENDER; 920.685-110 BUNDLE TIER AND LABELER; 920.685-114 COTTON BALER; 929.685-014 TYING-MACHINE OPERATOR; 929.685-018 TYING-MACHINE OPERATOR, LUMBER

92997 ALL OTHER MACHINE SETTERS AND SET-UP OPERATORS. OOH Title/s: Industrial Machinery Repairers; Metalworking and Plastics-Working Machine Operators

All other machine setters and set-up operators not classified separately above.
Yearly Earnings: $20,176
Education: Moderate-term O-J-T
GOE Group/s: 02.04.01 Laboratory Technology: Physical Sciences; 05.12.13 Elemental Work: Mechanical: Cutting and Finishing; 06.01.02 Production Technology: Machine Set-up; 06.01.03 Production Technology: Machine Set-up and Operation; 06.02.02 Production Work: Machine Work, Metal and Plastics; 06.02.04 Production Work: Machine Work, Paper; 06.02.05 Production Work: Machine Work, Leather and Fabrics; 06.02.07 Production Work: Machine Work, Rubber; 06.02.08 Production Work: Machine Work, Stone, Glass, and Clay; 06.02.09 Production Work: Machine Work, Assorted Materials; 06.02.10 Production Work: Equipment Operation, Metal Processing; 06.02.13 Production Work: Equipment Operation, Rubber, Plastics, and Glass Processing; 06.02.15 Production Work: Equipment Operation, Food Processing; 06.02.18 Production Work: Equipment Operation, Assorted Materials Processing; 06.02.20 Production Work: Machine Assembling; 06.03.01 Quality Control: Inspecting, Testing, and Repairing
CIP Program/s: 100103 Photographic Technologists and Technicians; 470199 Electrical and Electronics Equipment Installer and Repairer; 470303 Industrial Machinery Maintenance and Repair; 480501 Machinist/Machine Technologist; 489999 Precision Production Trades, Other
Related DOT Job/s: 503.362-010 PICKLER, CONTINUOUS PICKLING LINE; 520.682-026 MOLDING-MACHINE OPERATOR; 521.682-038 SHRIMP-PEELING-MACHINE OPERATOR; 523.380-010 COCOA-BEAN ROASTER II; 526.682-010 BATTER SCALER; 534.682-026 COMBINER OPERATOR; 539.562-010 HIGH-DENSITY FINISHING OPERATOR; 553.362-010 BELT-PRESS OPERATOR I; 559.382-046 PILOT-CONTROL OPERATOR; 559.482-014 PUTTY TINTER-MAKER; 575.360-010 GLASS-BULB-MACHINE ADJUSTER; 579.380-010 BOARD-MACHINE SET-UP OPERATOR; 590.362-014 IMPREGNATING-MACHINE OPERATOR; 599.382-014 EXHAUST EQUIPMENT OPERATOR; 632.360-010 GAUGE-AND-WEIGH-MACHINE ADJUSTER; 632.360-014 LOADING-MACHINE ADJUSTER; 632.360-018 PRIMER-INSERTING-MACHINE ADJUSTER; 632.380-014 LOADING-UNIT TOOL-SETTER; 632.380-022 RIM-FIRE-PRIMING TOOL SETTER; 641.562-010 CORRUGATOR OPERATOR; 649.682-018 DRILL-PRESS OPERATOR, ACOUSTICAL TILE; 649.682-022 EMBOSSER OPERATOR; 649.682-030 SHELL-MACHINE OPERATOR; 649.682-034 SLITTER-CREASER-SLOTTER OPERATOR; 652.682-022 STAMPER, MACHINE; 673.380-010 EDGING-MACHINE

SETTER; 673.382-018 STONE POLISHER, MACHINE; 673.382-022 STONE POLISHER, MACHINE APPRENTICE; 673.682-010 AUTOMATIC PATTERN EDGER; 673.682-014 BEVELING-AND-EDGING-MACHINE OPERATOR; 673.682-018 EDGER-MACHINE OPERATOR; 673.682-026 MITER GRINDER OPERATOR; 674.662-010 STONE-LATHE OPERATOR; 674.682-010 FINISHING-MACHINE OPERATOR; 675.682-010 CONTOUR GRINDER; 675.682-018 PLANER, STONE; 676.462-010 ROUTER OPERATOR; 676.682-010 DRILL OPERATOR, AUTOMATIC; 689.364-010 STROBOSCOPE OPERATOR; 690.360-010 WAD-BLANKING-PRESS ADJUSTER; 690.362-010 LEAD OPERATOR, AUTOMATIC VULCANIZING; 690.380-010 MACHINE SETTER; 690.382-014 WEATHERSTRIP-MACHINE OPERATOR; 690.580-010 HIDE SPLITTER; 690.662-010 TIRE-REGROOVING-MACHINE OPERATOR; 690.680-010 RUBBER-GOODS CUTTER-FINISHER; 690.682-014 BALL-TRUING-MACHINE OPERATOR; 690.682-034 EMBOSSING-PRESS OPERATOR, MOLDED GOODS; 690.682-090 TRIMMING-MACHINE OPERATOR; 691.682-010 ASBESTOS-WIRE FINISHER; 691.682-014 BRAIDER OPERATOR; 692.260-010 MACHINE SETTER; 692.360-010 ASSEMBLY-MACHINE-SET-UP MECHANIC; 692.360-018 FIRESETTER; 692.380-014 SET-UP MECHANIC, AUTOMATIC LINE; 692.382-010 BALLPOINT-PEN-ASSEMBLY-MACHINE OPERATOR; 692.382-014 PLATE STACKER, MACHINE; 692.482-010 CARBON-AND-GRAPHITE-BRUSH-MACHINE OPERATOR; 692.662-010 DYNAMITE-PACKING-MACHINE OPERATOR; 692.682-018 BORING-AND-FILLING-MACHINE OPERATOR; 692.682-046 PAINT-ROLLER-COVER-MACHINE SETTER; 692.682-050 POWER-DRIVEN-BRUSH MAKER; 692.682-070 TWISTING-MACHINE OPERATOR; 694.362-010 CLIP-LOADING-MACHINE ADJUSTER; 694.382-010 SALVAGE-MACHINE OPERATOR; 701.684-022 SAW SETTER; 716.360-010 SIZER, MACHINE; 724.360-010 SET-UP MECHANIC, COIL-WINDING MACHINES; 726.382-010 SEQUENCING-MACHINE OPERATOR; 729.360-010 PROBE TEST EQUIPMENT TECHNICIAN, SEMICONDUCTOR WAFERS; 775.281-010 SURFACE-PLATE FINISHER; 809.382-010 BALANCING-MACHINE SET-UP WORKER; 920.380-010 SETTER, JUICE PACKAGING MACHINES; 920.680-010 FILLING-MACHINE SET-UP MECHANIC; 976.360-010 PRINT CONTROLLER

92998 ALL OTHER MACHINE OPERATORS AND TENDERS. OOH Title/s: Painting and Coating Machine Operators; Metalworking and Plastics-Working Machine Operators; Printing Press Operators; Prepress Workers; Material Moving Equipment Operators; Handlers, Equipment Cleaners, Helpers, and Laborers

All other machine operators and tenders not classified separately above.

Yearly Earnings: $20,852

Education: Moderate-term O-J-T

GOE Group/s: 03.04.01 Elemental Work: Plants and Animals: Farming; 05.10.05 Crafts: Reproduction; 05.12.06 Elemental Work: Mechanical: Pumping; 05.12.07 Elemental Work: Mechanical: Crushing, Mixing, Separating, and Chipping; 05.12.10 Elemental Work: Mechanical: Heating and Melting; 05.12.12 Elemental Work: Mechanical: Structural Work; 06.01.03 Production Technology: Machine Set-up and Operation; 06.01.04 Production Technology: Precision Hand Work; 06.02.02 Production Work: Machine Work, Metal and Plastics; 06.02.03 Production Work: Machine Work, Wood; 06.02.04 Production Work: Machine Work, Paper; 06.02.05 Production Work: Machine Work, Leather and Fabrics; 06.02.06 Production Work: Machine Work, Textiles; 06.02.07 Production Work: Machine Work, Rubber; 06.02.08 Production Work: Machine Work, Stone, Glass, and Clay; 06.02.09 Production Work: Machine Work, Assorted Materials; 06.02.11 Production Work: Equipment Operation, Chemical Processing; 06.02.13 Production Work: Equipment Operation, Rubber, Plastics, and Glass Processing; 06.02.14 Production Work: Equipment Operation, Paper and Paper Products Processing; 06.02.15 Production Work: Equipment Operation, Food Processing; 06.02.16 Production Work: Equipment Operation, Textile, Fabric, and Leather Processing; 06.02.17 Production Work: Equipment Operation, Clay and Coke Processing; 06.02.18 Production Work: Equipment Operation, Assorted Materials Processing; 06.02.20 Production Work: Machine Assembling; 06.02.21 Production Work: Coating and Plating; 06.02.26 Production Work: Manual Work, Paper; 06.02.27 Production Work: Manual Work, Textile, Fabric and Leather; 06.02.32 Production Work: Manual Work, Assorted Materials; 06.03.01 Quality Control: Inspecting, Testing, and Repairing; 06.03.02 Quality Control: Inspecting, Grading, Sorting, Weighing, and Recording; 06.04.02 Elemental Work: Industrial: Machine Work, Metal and Plastics; 06.04.03 Elemental Work: Industrial: Machine Work, Wood; 06.04.04 Elemental Work: Industrial: Machine Work, Paper; 06.04.05 Elemental Work: Industrial: Machine Work, Fabric and Leather; 06.04.06 Elemental Work: Industrial: Machine Work, Textiles; 06.04.07 Elemental Work: Industrial: Machine Work, Rubber; 06.04.08 Elemental Work: Industrial: Machine Work, Stone, Glass, and Clay; 06.04.09 Elemental Work: Industrial: Machine Work, Assorted Materials; 06.04.10 Elemental Work: Industrial: Equipment Operation, Metal Processing; 06.04.11 Elemental Work: Industrial: Equipment Operation, Chemical Processing; 06.04.12 Elemental Work: Industrial: Equipment Operation, Petroleum, Gas, and Coal Processing; 06.04.13 Elemental Work: Industrial: Equipment Operation, Rubber, Plastics, Glass Processing; 06.04.14 Elemental Work: Industrial: Equipment Operation, Paper Making; 06.04.15 Elemental Work: Industrial: Equipment Operation, Food Processing; 06.04.16 Elemental Work: Industrial: Equipment Operation, Textile, Fabric, and Leather Processing; 06.04.18 Elemental Work: Industrial: Equipment Operation, Wood Processing; 06.04.19 Elemental Work: Industrial: Equipment Operation, Assorted Materials Processing; 06.04.20 Elemental Work: Industrial: Machine Assembling; 06.04.21 Elemental Work: Industrial: Machine Work, Brushing, Spraying, and Coating; 06.04.24 Elemental Work: Industrial: Manual Work, Metal and Plastics; 06.04.25 Elemental Work: Industrial: Manual Work, Wood; 06.04.27 Elemental Work: Industrial: Manual Work, Textile, Fabric and Leather; 06.04.28 Elemental Work: Industrial: Manual Work, Food Processing; 06.04.29 Elemental Work: Industrial: Manual Work, Rubber; 06.04.32 Elemental Work: Industrial: Manual Work, Casting and Molding; 06.04.34 Elemental Work: Industrial: Manual Work, Assorted Materials; 06.04.37 Elemental Work: Industrial: Manual Work, Stamping, Marking, Labeling, and Ticketing; 06.04.38 Elemental Work: Industrial: Wrapping and Packaging; 06.04.39 Elemental Work: Industrial: Cleaning; 06.04.40 Elemental Work: Industrial: Loading, Moving, Hoisting, and Conveying

CIP Program/s: 480304 Shoe, Boot and Leather Repairer; 490299 Vehicle and Equipment Operators, Other

Related DOT Job/s: 369.685-030 SHIRT-FOLDING-MACHINE OPERATOR; 503.685-014 DIP-LUBE OPERATOR; 511.482-018 DUST-COLLECTOR OPERATOR; 512.685-014 NOZZLE TENDER; 519.565-010 DIGESTION OPERATOR; 519.585-014 MUD BOSS; 519.665-010 GRANULATOR TENDER; 519.685-014 GROUT-MACHINE TENDER; 520.682-018 EXTRUDER OPERATOR; 520.685-042 CAKE STRIPPER; 520.686-038 TAMALE-MACHINE FEEDER; 521.685-034 BREAKING-MACHINE OPERATOR; 522.685-030 CASING-MACHINE OPERATOR; 522.685-086 PICKLE PUMPER; 524.685-038 MEXICAN-FOOD-MACHINE TENDER; 525.685-018 DEHAIRING-MACHINE TENDER; 525.685-026 POULTRY-PICKING MACHINE TENDER; 526.382-018 CONVERTER OPERATOR; 526.485-010 WORT EXTRACTOR; 526.682-022 DOUGHNUT-MACHINE OPERATOR; 526.685-034 PAN GREASER, MACHINE; 526.685-038 PIE MAKER, MACHINE; 529.382-014 CHOCOLATE-PRODUCTION-MACHINE OPERATOR; 529.382-022 GELATIN MAKER, UTILITY; 529.382-026 HYDROGENATION OPERATOR; 529.385-010 NOODLE MAKER;

529.482-022 SYRUP MAKER; 529.485-022 MATURITY CHECKER; 529.565-010 SUGAR CONTROLLER; 529.665-018 WET-AND-DRY-SUGAR-BIN OPERATOR; 529.682-018 DEPOSITING-MACHINE OPERATOR; 529.685-030 BRINE-TANK TENDER; 529.685-034 BULKER, CUT TOBACCO; 529.685-046 CAN-CONVEYOR FEEDER; 529.685-058 CIGAR-HEAD PIERCER; 529.685-062 CIGARETTE-FILTER-MAKING-MACHINE OPERATOR; 529.685-066 CIGARETTE-MAKING-MACHINE OPERATOR; 529.685-070 COLORER, CITRUS FRUIT; 529.685-086 DECAY-CONTROL OPERATOR; 529.685-122 FISH-CAKE MAKER; 529.685-130 FLAVOR ROOM WORKER; 529.685-142 HORSERADISH MAKER; 529.685-170 MOISTURE-MACHINE TENDER; 529.685-202 RENDERING-EQUIPMENT TENDER; 529.685-206 RESERVE OPERATOR; 529.685-214 SHELLFISH-PROCESSING-MACHINE TENDER; 529.685-218 SPICE FUMIGATOR; 529.685-222 SPREADER OPERATOR, AUTOMATIC; 529.687-158 MELT-HOUSE DRAG OPERATOR; 532.362-010 DIGESTER OPERATOR; 532.685-022 MOISTURE-CONDITIONER OPERATOR; 533.685-030 THRASHER FEEDER; 534.662-010 BACK TENDER, PAPER MACHINE; 534.665-010 SCREEN TENDER; 534.682-030 CREPING-MACHINE OPERATOR; 534.682-034 STRAP-MACHINE OPERATOR; 534.685-014 FRICTION-PAINT-MACHINE TENDER; 534.685-018 OILING-MACHINE OPERATOR; 534.685-034 WET-END HELPER; 539.362-010 CYLINDER-MACHINE OPERATOR; 539.362-014 FOURDRINIER-MACHINE OPERATOR; 539.685-026 SCREEN HANDLER; 539.687-010 WINDER HELPER; 549.662-010 BRIQUETTE-MACHINE OPERATOR; 549.685-014 GRAPHITE PAN-DRIER TENDER; 549.685-022 REELER; 549.685-026 SCREENER-AND-BLENDER OPERATOR; 550.663-010 FORMULA WEIGHER; 551.685-010 BAND TUMBLER; 551.685-142 SULFATE DRIER-MACHINE OPERATOR; 552.685-022 RETORT-CONDENSER ATTENDANT; 553.585-026 TUMBLER OPERATOR; 553.685-062 FIRE-HOSE CURER; 553.685-102 TIRE MOLDER; 553.685-110 WAX-POT TENDER; 554.485-014 STRAP-FOLDING-MACHINE OPERATOR; 554.682-010 CALENDER-LET-OFF OPERATOR; 554.685-022 LINER REROLL TENDER; 554.685-034 PHOTORESIST LAMINATOR, PRINTED CIRCUIT BOARD; 555.685-054 SECOND OPERATOR, MILL TENDER; 558.685-022 CELL-TENDER HELPER; 558.685-042 LEAD-OXIDE-MILL TENDER; 559.362-030 ROLL TENDER; 559.382-042 PHARMACEUTICAL OPERATOR; 559.482-010 COMPOSITION-ROLL MAKER AND CUTTER; 559.585-010 DRY-HOUSE TENDER; 559.585-018 TANKROOM TENDER; 559.665-010 BONE-PROCESS OPERATOR; 559.665-014 DRY-END OPERATOR; 559.665-034 SPLASH-LINE OPERATOR; 559.682-014 CASTING-AND-CURING OPERATOR; 559.682-034 LATEX-RIBBON-MACHINE OPERATOR; 559.682-042 RUBBER-MILL OPERATOR; 559.685-046 DOPE-DRY-HOUSE OPERATOR; 559.685-050 DRIER-AND-PULVERIZER TENDER; 559.685-054 DUSTING-AND-BRUSHING-MACHINE OPERATOR; 559.685-058 EFFERVESCENT-SALTS COMPOUNDER; 559.685-066 FABRIC NORMALIZER; 559.685-086 FRAME STRIPPER; 559.685-094 FUSE MAKER; 559.685-098 GLUE-MILL OPERATOR; 559.685-102 GOLF-BALL-COVER TREATER; 559.685-114 LATEX SPOOLER; 559.685-122 LINSEED-OIL-PRESS TENDER; 559.685-150 REBRANDER; 559.685-162 SCREENER-PERFUMER; 559.685-178 TUMBLER-MACHINE OPERATOR; 561.665-010 TANKER; 562.682-010 HUMIDIFIER OPERATOR; 569.685-074 VENEER TAPER; 574.585-010 PAPERHANGER; 574.665-010 FIBERGLASS-BONDING-MACHINE TENDER;

575.565-010 LINING-MACHINE OPERATOR; 575.664-010 CENTRIFUGAL SPINNER; 579.382-022 BLANKMAKER; 579.662-010 MAT-MACHINE OPERATOR; 579.665-010 BRAKE-LINING FINISHER, ASBESTOS; 579.665-018 WIRE SETTER; 579.685-010 DRIER-AND-GRINDER TENDER; 579.685-070 MARKER MACHINE ATTENDANT; 580.485-010 CALENDERING-MACHINE OPERATOR; 580.682-010 WEFT STRAIGHTENER; 580.685-010 BRIM-STRETCHING-MACHINE OPERATOR; 580.685-018 COLLAR-TURNER OPERATOR; 580.685-022 COTTON-BALL-MACHINE TENDER; 580.685-026 HAT-BLOCKING-MACHINE OPERATOR I; 580.685-030 HAT-BLOCKING-MACHINE OPERATOR II; 580.685-038 HYDRAULIC BLOCKER; 580.685-046 ROLLER OPERATOR; 580.685-050 STAKER, MACHINE; 580.685-054 STRETCHER; 580.685-058 STRETCHING-MACHINE OPERATOR; 580.685-062 TIP STRETCHER; 581.585-010 CARBONIZER; 581.685-010 CLOTH SANDER; 581.685-038 EXTRACTOR OPERATOR; 581.685-042 EXTRACTOR OPERATOR; 581.685-058 STEAM-DRIER TENDER; 581.685-070 WHIZZER; 582.482-010 COLORER, HIDES AND SKINS; 582.482-014 TANNER, ROTARY DRUM, CONTINUOUS PROCESS; 582.482-018 TANNING-DRUM OPERATOR; 582.562-010 SLASHER TENDER; 582.585-010 AGER OPERATOR;

582.665-010 CYLINDER BATCHER; 582.665-022 SATURATION-EQUIPMENT OPERATOR; 582.682-010 FINISHING-MACHINE OPERATOR; 582.685-010 BACK WASHER; 582.685-038 CRABBER; 582.685-042 DECATING-MACHINE OPERATOR; 582.685-046 DESIZING-MACHINE OPERATOR, HEAD-END; 582.685-050 DRUM ATTENDANT; 582.685-062 EXTRACTOR OPERATOR; 582.685-066 FEATHER WASHER; 582.685-074 FUMIGATOR AND STERILIZER; 582.685-078 GARMENT STEAMER; 582.685-082 GREASER OPERATOR; 582.685-126 SHEEPSKIN PICKLER; 582.685-134 SOAKER, HIDES; 582.685-146 STEAMER TENDER; 582.685-150 STEAMING-CABINET TENDER; 583.685-010 BREAKER-MACHINE TENDER; 583.685-014 BRIM CURLER; 583.685-026 CALENDER OPERATOR; 583.685-030 EMBOSSER; 583.685-034 EMBOSSING-MACHINE OPERATOR; 583.685-038 EMBOSSING-MACHINE-OPERATOR HELPER; 583.685-042 FOLDING-MACHINE OPERATOR; 583.685-046 FUSING-MACHINE TENDER; 583.685-062 JACQUARD-TWINE-POLISHER OPERATOR; 583.685-066 LEATHER ETCHER; 583.685-074 NARROW-FABRIC CALENDERER; 583.685-078 PILLOWCASE TURNER; 583.685-082 PLEATING-MACHINE OPERATOR; 583.685-094 ROLLER-MACHINE OPERATOR; 583.685-126 YARN-POLISHING-MACHINE OPERATOR; 583.686-010 BEAD-MACHINE OPERATOR; 584.382-014 QUILTING-MACHINE OPERATOR; 584.665-010 COATER HELPER; 584.665-018 SIZING-MACHINE TENDER; 584.682-010 COATER; 584.682-014 LAMINATING-MACHINE OPERATOR; 584.685-010 CALENDER OPERATOR, ARTIFICIAL LEATHER; 584.685-014 CLOTH-MERCERIZER OPERATOR; 584.685-034 LAMINATOR; 584.685-042 MANGLE TENDER; 584.685-054 YARN-MERCERIZER OPERATOR I; 584.685-058 YARN-MERCERIZER OPERATOR II; 585.665-010 NAPPER TENDER; 585.685-010 BRIM-POUNCING-MACHINE OPERATOR; 585.685-014 BUFFER; 585.685-022 CHINCHILLA-MACHINE OPERATOR; 585.685-034 CORDUROY-BRUSHER OPERATOR; 585.685-042 ELECTRIFIER OPERATOR; 585.685-050 GASSER; 585.685-054 GIG TENDER; 585.685-058 JIGGER-CROWN-POUNCING-MACHINE OPERATOR; 585.685-066 MELLOWING-MACHINE OPERATOR; 585.685-070 NAPPER TENDER; 585.685-074 POUNCING-LATHE OPERATOR; 585.685-078 ROLLING-MACHINE OPERATOR; 585.685-106 SINGER; 586.382-010 FULLING-MACHINE OPERATOR; 586.662-010 FELTING-MACHINE OPERATOR; 586.682-010 FULLER; 586.685-010 CARROTING-MACHINE OPERATOR; 586.685-018 FELT-STRIP FINISHER; 586.685-022 FELTMAKER AND WEIGHER; 586.685-026 HARDENING-MACHINE OPERATOR; 586.685-030 HAT-FORMING-MACHINE OPERATOR; 586.685-034 SHRINKING-MACHINE OPERATOR; 587.685-010 BRUSH OPERATOR; 587.685-014 BRUSHER, MACHINE; 587.685-022 CONDITIONER TENDER; 587.685-026 DUSTER; 587.685-030 STRIKE-OUT-MACHINE OPERATOR; 589.665-010 BONDING-MACHINE TENDER; 589.665-014 CLOTH-FINISHING-RANGE OPERATOR; 589.685-010 BOARDING-MACHINE OPERATOR; 589.685-014 BREAKER-UP-MACHINE OPERATOR; 589.685-018 BURN-OUT TENDER, LACE; 589.685-022 CLOTH MEASURER, MACHINE; 589.685-030 DETACKER; 589.685-034 DRUMMER; 589.685-046 EDGE STAINER I; 589.685-058 FOLDING-MACHINE OPERATOR; 589.685-062 HAT FINISHER; 589.685-070 MEASURING-MACHINE OPERATOR; 589.685-074 PLEATER; 589.685-078 PULLER, MACHINE; 589.685-082 RENOVATOR-MACHINE OPERATOR;

589.685-090 SCUTCHER TENDER; 589.685-094 SHAKER; 589.685-098 WRINGER-MACHINE OPERATOR; 589.685-102 YARN-TEXTURING-

MACHINE OPERATOR; 589.686-022 FUR-FLOOR WORKER; 590.365-010 IRON-PLASTIC BULLET MAKER; 590.662-010 CONTROLS OPERATOR, MOLDED GOODS; 590.662-014 MECHANICAL OXIDIZER; 590.665-018 WINDER OPERATOR; 590.684-010 CERAMIC CAPACITOR PROCESSOR; 590.684-038 POLYSILICON PREPARATION WORKER; 590.685-042 IRONER; 590.685-058 WAD LUBRICATOR; 590.685-098 ROOFING-MACHINE TENDER; 599.585-010 STERILIZER; 599.685-030 DIPPER AND BAKER; 599.685-086 SHREDDER TENDER, PEAT; 599.685-122 WATER TENDER; 609.685-010 BALL SORTER; 616.382-018 TYPING-ELEMENT-MACHINE OPERATOR; 640.385-010 RIBBON-HANKING-MACHINE OPERATOR; 640.682-014 CORE WINDING OPERATOR; 640.685-018 CARBON-PAPER INTERLEAFER; 640.685-042 PAPER-CORE-MACHINE OPERATOR; 640.685-046 PAPER-REEL OPERATOR; 640.685-050 PROCESS-MACHINE OPERATOR; 640.685-054 REELER; 640.685-058 REWINDER OPERATOR; 640.685-062 ROLL RECLAIMER; 640.685-070 ROLLING-MACHINE OPERATOR; 640.685-082 TIGHTENING-MACHINE OPERATOR; 641.662-014 TUBE-MACHINE OPERATOR; 641.685-010 BENDER, MACHINE; 641.685-022 CARTON-FORMING-MACHINE OPERATOR; 641.685-026 CARTON-FORMING-MACHINE TENDER; 641.685-050 FOLDING-MACHINE FEEDER; 641.685-054 FOUR-CORNER-STAYER-MACHINE OPERATOR; 641.685-070 SCORER; 641.685-078 SLIDE-MACHINE TENDER; 641.685-086 STRING-TOP SEALER; 641.685-094 VALVING-MACHINE OPERATOR; 641.686-034 SLEEVER; 649.582-010 PARTITION-ASSEMBLY-MACHINE OPERATOR; 649.685-010 AUTOMATIC-MACHINE ATTENDANT; 649.685-014 BAG-MACHINE OPERATOR; 649.685-018 BINDERY WORKER; 649.685-022 BOTTOMING-MACHINE OPERATOR; 649.685-030 COUNTING-MACHINE OPERATOR; 649.685-034 DRILL-PUNCH OPERATOR; 649.685-038 EMBOSSING-MACHINE TENDER;
649.685-042 ENVELOPE-MACHINE OPERATOR; 649.685-046 FOLDING-MACHINE OPERATOR; 649.685-054 KNOTTING-MACHINE OPERATOR; 649.685-058 LACE-PAPER-MACHINE OPERATOR; 649.685-062 LAUNDRY-BAG-PUNCH OPERATOR; 649.685-066 LAYBOY TENDER; 649.685-070 MACHINE OPERATOR, GENERAL; 649.685-074 MATCH-BOOK ASSEMBLER; 649.685-090 PERFORATING-MACHINE OPERATOR; 649.685-098 RING-MAKING-MACHINE OPERATOR; 649.685-102 SALVAGE WINDER AND INSPECTOR; 649.685-106 SHOT-TUBE-MACHINE TENDER; 649.685-114 STITCHER OPERATOR; 649.685-118 TAG-MACHINE OPERATOR; 652.685-022 CUTTING-AND-PRINTING-MACHINE OPERATOR; 669.682-046 EMBOSSING-MACHINE OPERATOR; 669.685-038 CORE-COMPOSER FEEDER; 669.685-098 VENEER REPAIRER, MACHINE; 673.685-046 DIAMOND-POWDER TECHNICIAN; 673.685-050 ENGRAVER TENDER; 674.382-010 GLASS-LATHE OPERATOR; 676.682-014 STONE DRILLER; 676.685-010 DRILLER, BRAKE LINING; 676.685-014 DRILLER, MACHINE; 677.665-010 GLASS-UNLOADING-EQUIPMENT TENDER; 679.665-010 LEVEL-GLASS-FORMING-MACHINE OPERATOR; 679.685-010 MACHINE OPERATOR, CERAMICS; 679.685-014 PRODUCTION-MACHINE TENDER, GLASS CUTTING-OR-GRINDING; 679.685-018 THERMAL-SURFACING-MACHINE OPERATOR; 680.665-018 MIDDLE-CARD TENDER; 680.685-014 CARD STRIPPER; 680.685-018 CARD TENDER; 680.685-026 CRIMP SETTER; 680.685-030 CRIMPING-MACHINE OPERATOR; 680.685-046 FUR-BLOWER OPERATOR; 680.685-050 GARNETT-MACHINE OPERATOR; 680.685-054 GARNETTER; 680.685-070 OPENER TENDER; 680.685-074 PICKER TENDER; 680.685-078 PICKER-MACHINE OPERATOR; 680.685-082 PICKING-MACHINE OPERATOR; 680.685-086 RIBBON-LAP-MACHINE TENDER; 680.685-090 SILK SPREADER; 680.685-106 STRAND-AND-BINDER CONTROLLER; 680.685-110 STRETCH-BOX TENDER; 680.685-114 WASTE-MACHINE TENDER; 680.685-118 COMBER TENDER; 681.685-050 FLOOR WINDER; 681.685-054 LEASING-MACHINE TENDER; 683.685-010 BRAIDING-MACHINE OPERATOR; 683.685-018 CARD LACER, JACQUARD; 683.685-026 PATTERN DUPLICATOR; 683.685-034 WARP-TYING-MACHINE TENDER; 686.685-030 FOLDER; 686.685-034 HANDLE-AND-VENT-MACHINE OPERATOR; 686.685-038 PERFORATING-MACHINE OPERATOR; 686.685-046 PREPLEATER; 686.685-054 RIVET-HOLE PUNCHER; 686.685-062 SHOELACE-TIPPING-MACHINE OPERATOR; 686.685-070 TUBULAR-SPLITTING-MACHINE TENDER;
687.682-010 FLOWER-MACHINE OPERATOR; 687.682-014 TUFT-MACHINE OPERATOR; 687.685-010 NEEDLE-CONTROL CHENILLER; 687.685-014 TUFTING-MACHINE OPERATOR; 687.685-018 TUFTING-MACHINE OPERATOR; 687.685-022 TUFTING-MACHINE OPERATOR, SINGLE-NEEDLE; 689.582-010 PUNCHER; 689.585-014 FOLDING-MACHINE OPERATOR; 689.585-018 STRINGING-MACHINE TENDER; 689.665-010 STRAP BUCKLER, MACHINE; 689.665-018 VACUUM-TANK TENDER; 689.682-010 LOOPER; 689.682-014 NEEDLE-PUNCH-MACHINE OPERATOR; 689.685-010 BALL-FRINGE-MACHINE OPERATOR; 689.685-022 BOBBIN STRIPPER; 689.685-030 BOW-MAKER-MACHINE TENDER, AUTOMATIC; 689.685-034 BUFFING-WHEEL FORMER, AUTOMATIC; 689.685-054 CRUSHER-AND-BINDER OPERATOR; 689.685-058 DRAWSTRING KNOTTER; 689.685-062 DROP-WIRE ALIGNER; 689.685-070 HEDDLE CLEANER, MACHINE; 689.685-074 HELMET COVERER; 689.685-082 KAPOK-AND-COTTON-MACHINE OPERATOR; 689.685-090 NEEDLE-LOOM TENDER; 689.685-094 PICK-PULLING-MACHINE OPERATOR; 689.685-110 ROLL TURNER; 689.685-122 SPLICING-MACHINE OPERATOR, AUTOMATIC; 689.685-130 SURGICAL-DRESSING MAKER; 689.685-134 TAPE-FOLDING-MACHINE OPERATOR; 689.685-142 TASSEL-MAKING-MACHINE OPERATOR; 689.685-146 TURNING-MACHINE OPERATOR; 689.685-158 YARN-TEXTURING-MACHINE OPERATOR II; 689.685-162 TOE PUNCHER; 690.585-010 MILL-ROLL REWINDER; 690.682-018 BED LASTER; 690.682-030 EMBOSSER; 690.682-066 RING-ROLLING-MACHINE OPERATOR; 690.685-010 ASSEMBLER FOR PULLER-OVER, MACHINE; 690.685-014 ASSEMBLY-PRESS OPERATOR; 690.685-018 BACK-STRIP-MACHINE OPERATOR; 690.685-030 BAND-MACHINE OPERATOR; 690.685-034 BOTTOM PRESSER; 690.685-042 BRANDING-MACHINE TENDER; 690.685-058 BURNISHER; 690.685-066 BUTTON-FACING-MACHINE OPERATOR; 690.685-082 CHANNEL OPENER, OUTSOLES; 690.685-086 CHANNELER, INSOLE; 690.685-098 COUNTER FORMER; 690.685-102 COUNTER MOLDER; 690.685-106 COUNTER ROLLER; 690.685-110 CUT-OUT-AND-MARKING-MACHINE OPERATOR; 690.685-114 CUT-OUT-MACHINE OPERATOR; 690.685-138 EDGE BURNISHER, UPPERS; 690.685-146 EDGE SETTER; 690.685-158 EMBOSSER; 690.685-162 FASTENER, MACHINE; 690.685-174 FOLDER, MACHINE; 690.685-178 FOLDING-MACHINE OPERATOR; 690.685-186 FOREPART LASTER; 690.685-206 HEEL BUILDER, MACHINE; 690.685-210 HEEL COMPRESSOR; 690.685-218 HEEL PRICKER; 690.685-222 HEEL SCORER; 690.685-230 HEEL-SEAT LASTER, MACHINE; 690.685-234 INKER, MACHINE; 690.685-246 INSOLE REINFORCER; 690.685-254 LACER II; 690.685-266 LEATHER-BELT MAKER; 690.685-270 LIP CUTTER AND SCORER; 690.685-278 LUMITE INJECTOR; 690.685-282 MARKER, MACHINE; 690.685-286 MAT PUNCHER; 690.685-294 MOLDER, LABELS; 690.685-314 POUNDER; 690.685-350 SEAM-RUBBING-MACHINE OPERATOR; 690.685-358 SIDE LASTER, CEMENT; 690.685-362 SIDE LASTER, STAPLE; 690.685-382 SOLE LEVELER, MACHINE; 690.685-394 SPORT-SHOE-SPIKE ASSEMBLER;
690.685-398 STAMPING-MACHINE OPERATOR; 690.685-406 STRING LASTER; 690.685-410 TACK PULLER, MACHINE; 690.685-414 TAPER, MACHINE; 690.685-418 TIP FINISHER; 690.685-426 TOE FORMER, STITCHDOWNS; 690.685-430 TOE LASTER, AUTOMATIC; 690.685-438 TUBE MOLDER, FIBERGLASS; 690.685-442 TUBE SPLICER; 690.685-450 V-BELT COVERER; 690.685-454 V-BELT FINISHER; 690.685-462 VULCANIZER; 690.685-470 WELT BEATER; 690.685-474 WELT BUTTER, MACHINE; 690.685-482 WELT WHEELER; 690.685-498 PLASTIC ROLLER; 690.685-502 ROLLER MAKER; 690.685-506 SAMPLE MAKER; 691.682-018 INSULATING-MACHINE OPERATOR; 691.685-010 ARMORING-MACHINE OPERATOR; 691.685-014 LAGGING-MACHINE OPERA-

TOR; 691.685-026 SPOOLING-MACHINE OPERATOR; 692.662-018 WAFER-MACHINE OPERATOR; 692.662-022 WIRE-WRAPPING-MACHINE OPERATOR; 692.665-010 BRAIDING-MACHINE TENDER; 692.665-014 PUNCH-PRESS OPERATOR; 692.665-018 DRY-CELL-ASSEMBLY-MACHINE TENDER; 692.682-010 ANKLE-PATCH MOLDER; 692.682-022 BROOM STITCHER; 692.682-030 COREMAKING-MACHINE OPERATOR; 692.682-054 STACKING-MACHINE OPERATOR I; 692.682-062 STRING-WINDING-MACHINE OPERATOR; 692.682-066 SWEEPER-BRUSH MAKER, MACHINE; 692.685-010 ABRASIVE-BAND WINDER; 692.685-014 ADHESIVE-BANDAGE-MACHINE OPERATOR; 692.685-018 AIR-HOLE DRILLER;
692.685-026 BRASSIERE-SLIDE-MAKING-MACHINE TENDER, AUTOMATIC; 692.685-042 CAPPING-MACHINE OPERATOR; 692.685-046 CELL TUBER, MACHINE; 692.685-066 DEICER-ELEMENT WINDER, MACHINE; 692.685-074 DIELECTRIC-PRESS OPERATOR; 692.685-082 FILM SPOOLER; 692.685-090 GARLAND-MACHINE OPERATOR; 692.685-102 KICK-PRESS OPERATOR; 692.685-122 MAT-MAKING MACHINE TENDER; 692.685-126 MOUNTER II; 692.685-134 POULTICE-MACHINE OPERATOR; 692.685-150 SANITARY-NAPKIN-MACHINE TENDER; 692.685-158 SEALER, DRY CELL; 692.685-162 SEALING-MACHINE OPERATOR; 692.685-178 SLINGER, SEQUINS; 692.685-182 SORTER, MACHINE; 692.685-186 SPIRAL-MACHINE OPERATOR; 692.685-190 SPUN-PASTE-MACHINE OPERATOR; 692.685-194 STAMPING-MACHINE OPERATOR; 692.685-198 STAPLER, MACHINE; 692.685-202 STAPLING-MACHINE OPERATOR; 692.685-214 TAPER, MACHINE; 692.685-218 THERMOSTAT-ASSEMBLY-MACHINE-TENDER, AUTOMATIC; 692.685-226 TINSEL-MACHINE OPERATOR; 692.685-234 TUBE WINDER, HAND; 692.685-242 WICKER, MOLDED CANDLES; 692.685-246 WINDER; 692.685-262 WOOD-WEB-WEAVING-MACHINE OPERATOR; 692.685-274 KEYMODULE-ASSEMBLY-MACHINE TENDER; 692.685-278 DIAPER MACHINE TENDER; 692.685-286 MOLDER, AUTOMOBILE CARPETS; 692.685-290 TRACK LAMINATING MACHINE TENDER; 694.665-010 SHOTGUN-SHELL-LOADING-MACHINE OPERATOR; 694.685-042 PRIMER-INSERTING-MACHINE OPERATOR; 699.685-010 BUTTON-ATTACHING-MACHINE OPERATOR; 699.685-018 EYELET-MACHINE OPERATOR; 699.685-022 EYELET-PUNCH OPERATOR; 703.685-010 PAIL BAILER; 706.685-014 WHEEL-TRUING MACHINE TENDER; 709.684-094 UTILITY OPERATOR II; 709.685-010 GOLD RECLAIMER; 710.685-014 THERMOMETER PRODUCTION WORKER; 715.682-022 TAPPER, BALANCE-WHEEL SCREW HOLE; 716.685-010 BLOCKING-MACHINE TENDER; 716.685-014 DRILLER; 726.685-010 MAGNETIC-TAPE WINDER; 726.685-014 INSERTION MACHINE TENDER, ELECTRONIC COMPONENTS; 726.685-018 BREAK-AND-LOAD OPERATOR; 726.685-042 ROD TAPE OPERATOR; 726.685-062 PROGRAMMING EQUIPMENT OPERATOR; 729.682-010 OPERATOR, CAVITY PUMP; 730.685-010 LOOPER; 731.685-018 TIRE SETTER; 732.685-022 GUIDE-BASE WINDER, MACHINE; 732.685-026 MACHINE SNELLER; 732.685-030 SINKER WINDER; 733.685-022 RIBBON WINDER; 733.685-034 TIPPING-MACHINE OPERATOR; 734.685-010 STAMPER; 734.685-014 BUTTON MAKER AND INSTALLER; 737.685-018 WAX POURER; 739.664-010 CANDLEMAKER; 739.685-010 ASSEMBLER, FINGER BUFFS; 739.685-014 BRUSH MAKER, MACHINE; 739.685-026 MOP MAKER; 739.685-038 STACKING-MACHINE OPERATOR II; 739.685-042 STEM-PROCESSING-MACHINE OPERATOR; 739.685-058 WREATH MACHINE TENDER; 739.687-150 PIPE-SMOKER-MACHINE OPERATOR; 750.685-010 SQUEEGEE TENDER; 750.685-014 TIRE RECAPPER; 752.684-050 SKIN FORMER; 754.685-010 TAB-MACHINE OPERATOR; 759.664-018 ROLLER MAKER; 759.684-018 BELT-BUILDER HELPER; 761.684-058 WIRE BRUSH OPERATOR; 764.684-010 BARREL BRANDER; 769.685-010 PANEL EDGE SEALER; 770.682-014 JEWEL-BEARING DRILLER; 770.682-026 JEWEL-HOLE DRILLER; 772.482-010 GLASS-BLOWING-LATHE OPERATOR; 774.382-010 POTTERY-MACHINE OPERATOR; 781.685-010 SPREADER, MACHINE; 783.685-010 COVERING-MACHINE TENDER; 783.685-018 DISK-AND-TAPE-MACHINE TENDER; 783.685-026 MARKING-MACHINE TENDER; 784.684-058 SIZER, MACHINE; 786.685-038 ULTRASONIC-SEAMING-MACHINE OPERATOR, SEMIAUTOMATIC; 788.684-018 BINDING FOLDER, MACHINE; 788.685-010 FLARE BREAKER; 788.685-014 FOLDING-MACHINE TENDER; 788.685-018 STOCK FITTER; 788.685-022 TONGUE PRESSER; 788.685-026 TOP FORMER; 788.685-030 WRAP TURNER; 789.685-010 ORNAMENT SETTER; 827.485-010 GAS CHARGER; 899.682-010 DIVER PUMPER; 920.685-102 WRAPPER; 934.685-014 SAND PLANT ATTENDANT; 962.665-010 DUBBING-MACHINE OPERATOR; 969.685-010 SNOWMAKER; 979.684-022 MAP-AND-CHART MOUNTER

Precision Production Occupations

93102B AIRCRAFT STRUCTURE ASSEMBLERS, PRECISION. OOH Title/s: Precision Assemblers

Assemble tail, wing, fuselage, or other structural section of aircraft, space vehicles, and missiles from parts, subassemblies, and components; and install functional units, parts, or equipment, such as landing gear, control surfaces, doors, and floorboards. Installs units, parts, equipment, and components in structural assembly, according to blueprints and specifications, using hand tools and power tools. Bolts, screws, or rivets accessories to fasten, support, or hang components and subassemblies. Drills holes in structure and subassemblies, and attaches brackets, hinges, or clips to secure installation or to fasten subassemblies. Locates and marks reference points and holes for installation of parts and components, using jigs, templates, and measuring instruments. Aligns structural assemblies. Cuts, trims, and files parts, and verifies fitting tolerances to prepare for installation. Positions and aligns subassemblies in jigs or fixtures, using measuring instruments, following blueprint lines and index points. Inspects and tests installed units, parts, and equipment for fit, performance, and compliance with standards, using measuring instruments and test equipment.

Yearly Earnings: $28,392

Education: Work experience in a related occupation

Knowledge: Production and Processing; Engineering and Technology; Design; Building and Construction; Mechanical

Abilities: Perceptual Speed; Spatial Orientation; Visualization; Arm-Hand Steadiness; Manual Dexterity; Finger Dexterity; Multilimb Coordination; Rate Control; Wrist-Finger Speed; Speed of Limb Movement; Explosive Strength; Trunk Strength; Stamina; Extent Flexibility; Dynamic Flexibility; Gross Body Coordination; Gross Body Equilibrium; Depth Perception

Skills: Equipment Selection; Installation; Testing; Equipment Maintenance; Troubleshooting

General Work Activities: Inspecting Equipment, Structures, or Material; Handling and Moving Objects; Repairing and Maintaining Mechanical Equipment

Job Characteristics: Sounds, Noise Levels are Distracting, etc.; Very Hot; Extremely Bright or Inadequate Lighting; Cramped Work Space, Awkward Positions; High Places; Standing; Climbing Ladders, Scaffolds, Poles, etc.; Kneeling, Crouching, or Crawling; Using Hands on Objects, Tools, or Controls; Bending or Twisting the Body; Importance of Being Exact or Accurate; Importance of Being Sure All is Done

GOE Group/s: 06.01.04 Production Technology: Precision Hand Work; 06.02.22 Production Work: Manual Work, Assembly Large Parts

CIP Program/s: 470607 Aircraft Mechanic/Technician, Airframe

Related DOT Job/s: 806.361-014 ASSEMBLER-INSTALLER, GENERAL; 806.381-026 ASSEMBLER, AIRCRAFT, STRUCTURES AND SURFACES

93102C AIRCRAFT SYSTEMS ASSEMBLERS, PRECISION. OOH Title/s: Precision Assemblers

Lay out, assemble, install, and test aircraft systems, such as armament, environmental control, plumbing and hydraulic systems. Aligns, fits, and assembles system components, such as armament, structural, and mechanical components, using jigs, fixtures, measuring instruments, hand tools, and power tools. Lays out location of parts and assemblies, according to specifications. Assembles and installs parts, fittings, and assemblies on aircraft, using layout tools, hand tools, power tools, and fasteners. Tests systems and assemblies for functional performance, and adjusts, repairs, or replaces malfunctioning units or parts. Installs mechanical linkages and actuators, and verifies tension of cables, using tensiometer. Examines parts for defects and for conformance to specifications, using precision measuring instruments. Reworks, replaces, realigns, and adjusts parts and assemblies according to specifications. Cleans, oils, assembles, and attaches system components to aircraft, using hand tools, power tools, and measuring instruments. Reads and interprets blueprints, illustrations, and specifications to determine layout, sequence of operations, or identity and relationship of parts. Measures, drills, files, cuts, bends, and smoothes materials to ensure fit and clearance of parts.
Yearly Earnings: $28,392
Education: Work experience in a related occupation
Knowledge: Production and Processing; Engineering and Technology; Design; Building and Construction; Mechanical
Abilities: Visualization; Arm-Hand Steadiness; Manual Dexterity; Multilimb Coordination; Rate Control; Reaction Time; Wrist-Finger Speed; Speed of Limb Movement; Static Strength; Explosive Strength; Dynamic Strength; Trunk Strength; Extent Flexibility; Dynamic Flexibility; Gross Body Equilibrium; Depth Perception
Skills: Technology Design; Equipment Selection; Installation; Testing; Operation Monitoring; Operation and Control; Product Inspection; Equipment Maintenance; Troubleshooting; Repairing; Systems Perception
General Work Activities: Inspecting Equipment, Structures, or Material; Handling and Moving Objects; Implementing Ideas, Programs, etc.; Repairing and Maintaining Mechanical Equipment; Repairing and Maintaining Electrical Equipment
Job Characteristics: Sounds, Noise Levels are Distracting, etc.; Cramped Work Space, Awkward Positions; High Places; Hazardous Equipment; Climbing Ladders, Scaffolds, Poles, etc.; Kneeling, Crouching, or Crawling; Keeping or Regaining Balance; Using Hands on Objects, Tools, or Controls; Bending or Twisting the Body
GOE Group/s: 06.01.04 Production Technology: Precision Hand Work; 06.02.22 Production Work: Manual Work, Assembly Large Parts
CIP Program/s: 470607 Aircraft Mechanic/Technician, Airframe; 470608 Aircraft Mechanic/Technician, Powerplant
Related DOT Job/s: 806.361-030 AIRCRAFT MECHANIC, ARMAMENT; 806.381-014 AIRCRAFT MECHANIC, ENVIRONMENTAL CONTROL SYSTEM; 806.381-018 AIRCRAFT MECHANIC, RIGGING AND CONTROLS; 806.381-066 AIRCRAFT MECHANIC, PLUMBING AND HYDRAULICS; 806.381-082 PRECISION ASSEMBLER

93102D AIRCRAFT RIGGING ASSEMBLERS. OOH Title/s: Precision Assemblers

Fabricate and assemble aircraft tubing or cable components or assemblies. Sets up and operates machines and systems to crimp, cut, bend, form, swage, flare, bead, burr, and straighten tubing, according to specifications. Assembles and attaches fittings onto cable and tubing components, using hand tools. Measures, cuts, and inspects cable and tubing, using master template, measuring instruments, and cable cutter or saw. Welds tubing and fittings, and solders cable ends, using tack-welder, induction brazing chamber, or other equipment. Swages fittings onto cable, using swaging machine. Forms loops or splices in cables, using clamps and fittings, or reweaves cable strands. Marks location of cutouts, holes, and trim lines of parts and relationship of parts, using measuring instruments. Fabricates cable templates. Reads and interprets blueprints, work orders, data charts, and specifications to determine operations, and type, quantity, dimensions, configuration, and finish of tubing, cable, and fittings. Verifies dimensions of cable assembly and position of fittings, using measuring instruments, and repairs and reworks defective assemblies. Selects and installs accessories in swaging machine, using hand tools. Marks identifying information on tubing or cable assemblies, using electro-chemical etching device, label, rubber stamp, or other methods. Tests tubing and cable assemblies for defects, using pressure testing equipment and proofloading machines. Cleans, lubricates, and coats tubing and cable assemblies.
Yearly Earnings: $28,392
Education: Work experience in a related occupation
Knowledge: Production and Processing; Engineering and Technology; Design; Physics
Abilities: Arm-Hand Steadiness; Manual Dexterity; Finger Dexterity; Multilimb Coordination; Rate Control; Speed of Limb Movement; Explosive Strength; Dynamic Strength; Stamina; Dynamic Flexibility; Gross Body Equilibrium
Skills: Installation
General Work Activities: Inspecting Equipment, Structures, or Material; Controlling Machines and Processes; Repairing and Maintaining Mechanical Equipment
Job Characteristics: Hazardous Equipment; Hazardous Situations; Using Hands on Objects, Tools, or Controls; Making Repetitive Motions
GOE Group/s: 06.01.04 Production Technology: Precision Hand Work; 06.02.22 Production Work: Manual Work, Assembly Large Parts
CIP Program/s: 150801 Aeronautical and Aerospace Engineering Technologists and Technicians; 470607 Aircraft Mechanic/Technician, Airframe
Related DOT Job/s: 806.381-034 ASSEMBLER, TUBING; 806.381-042 CABLE ASSEMBLER AND SWAGER

93105 MACHINE BUILDERS AND OTHER PRECISION MACHINE ASSEMBLERS. OOH Title/s: Precision Assemblers

Construct, assemble, or rebuild machines, such as engines, turbines, and office machines, or equipment used in construction, oil fields, rolling mills, textile and paper manufacturing, woodworking, printing, and food wrapping. Fit or assemble components or subassemblies. Install moving parts. Assemble systems of gears by aligning and meshing gears in gearbox. May test or assist in testing of completed product. Fastens components or parts together, using hand tools, rivet gun, and welding equipment. Positions and aligns components for assembly, manually or with hoist. Reworks, repairs, and replaces damaged parts or assemblies. Analyzes assembly blueprint and specifications manual, and plans assembly or building operations. Fastens and installs piping, fixtures, or wiring and electrical components to specifications. Inspects and tests parts and accessories for leakage, defect, or functionality, using test equipment. Sets and verifies clearance of parts. Verifies conformance of parts to stock list and blueprints, using measuring instruments such as calipers, gauges, and micrometers. Lays out and drills, reams, taps, and cuts parts for assembly. Operates machine to verify functioning, machine capabilities, and conformance to customer's specifications. Removes rough spots and smooths surfaces to fit, trim, or clean parts or components, using hand tools and power tools. Sets up and operates metal-working machines, such as milling and grinding machines, to shape or fabricate parts. Maintains and lubricates parts and components.

Yearly Earnings: $28,392

Education: Work experience in a related occupation

Knowledge: Engineering and Technology; Design; Building and Construction; Mechanical; Foreign Language; Public Safety and Security

Abilities: Information Ordering; Visualization; Arm-Hand Steadiness; Finger Dexterity; Control Precision; Multilimb Coordination; Wrist-Finger Speed; Speed of Limb Movement; Static Strength; Explosive Strength; Stamina; Extent Flexibility; Gross Body Equilibrium; Visual Color Discrimination; Hearing Sensitivity

Skills: Technology Design; Equipment Selection; Installation; Testing; Operation Monitoring; Operation and Control; Product Inspection; Equipment Maintenance; Troubleshooting; Repairing

General Work Activities: Inspecting Equipment, Structures, or Material; Controlling Machines and Processes; Repairing and Maintaining Mechanical Equipment

Job Characteristics: Sounds, Noise Levels are Distracting, etc.; Very Hot; Extremely Bright or Inadequate Lighting; Cramped Work Space, Awkward Positions; Hazardous Equipment; Hazardous Situations; Climbing Ladders, Scaffolds, Poles, etc.; Kneeling, Crouching, or Crawling; Keeping or Regaining Balance

GOE Group/s: 05.05.07 Craft Technology: Machining; 05.05.09 Craft Technology: Mechanical Work; 06.01.03 Production Technology: Machine Set-up and Operation; 06.01.04 Production Technology: Precision Hand Work; 06.02.22 Production Work: Manual Work, Assembly Large Parts; 06.02.23 Production Work: Manual Work, Assembly Small Parts; 06.02.24 Production Work: Manual Work, Metal and Plastics

CIP Program/s: 000000 NO CIP ASSIGNED

Related DOT Job/s: 600.261-010 ASSEMBLER, STEAM-AND-GAS TURBINE; 600.281-022 MACHINE BUILDER; 600.380-026 TURBINE-BLADE ASSEMBLER; 624.381-018 FARM-MACHINERY SET-UP MECHANIC; 638.361-010 MACHINE ASSEMBLER; 706.361-010 ASSEMBLER; 706.381-034 SEWING-MACHINE ASSEMBLER; 706.381-038 SUBASSEMBLER; 706.381-042 TURBINE SUBASSEMBLER; 706.481-010 INTERNAL-COMBUSTION-ENGINE SUBASSEMBLER; 801.261-010 ASSEMBLER, MINING MACHINERY; 801.261-018 ROTARY-ENGINE ASSEMBLER; 801.361-010 BLOWER AND COMPRESSOR ASSEMBLER; 806.381-022 ASSEMBLER, AIRCRAFT POWER PLANT; 806.481-014 ASSEMBLER, INTERNAL COMBUSTION ENGINE; 820.361-014 ELECTRIC-MOTOR-AND-GENERATOR ASSEMBLER

93108 FITTERS, STRUCTURAL METAL—PRECISION. OOH Title/s: Precision Assemblers

Lay out, position, align, and fit together fabricated parts of structural metal products preparatory to welding or riveting. Aligns parts, using jack, turnbuckles, wedges, drift pins, pry bars, and hammer. Moves parts into position, manually or by hoist or crane. Marks reference points onto floor or face block and transposes them to workpiece, using measuring devices, squares, chalk, and soapstone. Positions or tightens braces, jacks, clamps, ropes, or bolt straps, or bolts parts in positions for welding or riveting. Tack-welds fitted parts together. Examines blueprints and plans sequence of operation, applying knowledge of geometry, effects of heat, weld shrinkage, machining, and metal thickness. Sets up face block, jigs, and fixtures. Removes high spots and cuts bevels, using hand files, portable grinders, and cutting torch. Locates reference points, using transit, and erects ladders and scaffolding to fit together large assemblies. Straightens warped or bent parts, using sledge, hand torch, straightening press, or bulldozer. Heattreats parts with acetylene torch. Gives directions to welder to build up low spots or short pieces with weld.

Yearly Earnings: $28,392

Education: Work experience in a related occupation

Knowledge: Design; Building and Construction; Mechanical; Mathematics; Physics

Abilities: Control Precision; Multilimb Coordination; Static Strength; Dynamic Flexibility; Gross Body Equilibrium; Night Vision; Peripheral Vision; Depth Perception; Glare Sensitivity

Skills: Mathematics

General Work Activities: Performing General Physical Activities; Handling and Moving Objects; Interacting with Computers

Job Characteristics: Sounds, Noise Levels are Distracting, etc.; Very Hot; Extremely Bright or Inadequate Lighting; Cramped Work Space, Awkward Positions; Whole Body Vibration; High Places; Hazardous Equipment; Hazardous Situations; Climbing Ladders, Scaffolds, Poles, etc.; Kneeling, Crouching, or Crawling; Keeping or Regaining Balance; Using Hands on Objects, Tools, or Controls; Bending or Twisting the Body; Common Protective or Safety Attire

GOE Group/s: 05.05.06 Craft Technology: Metal Fabrication and Repair

CIP Program/s: 480503 Machine Shop Assistant

Related DOT Job/s: 801.261-014 FITTER I; 801.381-014 FITTER; 809.261-010 ASSEMBLER, GROUND SUPPORT EQUIPMENT

93111A ELECTROMECHANICAL EQUIPMENT ASSEMBLERS—PRECISION. OOH Title/s: Precision Assemblers

Assemble, test, and prepare electromechanical equipment or devices, such as servomechanisms, gear trains, gyros, dynamometers, ejection seat mechanisms, wave guides, magnetic drums, tape drives, punched-card reading devices, brakes, control linkage actuators, and gearbox mechanisms, according to specifications. Assembles parts or unit and attaches unit to assembly, subassembly, or frame, using hand tools and power tools. Inspects, tests, and adjusts completed unit to ensure that unit meets specifications, tolerances, and customer order requirements. Connects electrical wiring according to circuit diagram, using soldering iron. Measures parts to determine tolerances, using precision measuring instruments, such as micrometers, calipers, and verniers. Drills, taps, reams, countersinks, and spotfaces bolt holes in parts, using drill press and portable power drill. Positions and aligns parts, using fixtures, jigs, and templates. Reads blueprints and specifications to determine component parts and assembly sequence of electromechanical unit. Files, laps, and buffs parts to fit, using hand tools and power tools. Disassembles unit to replace parts or to crate for shipping. Cleans and lubricates parts and subassemblies. Attaches name plates, and marks identifying information on parts.

Yearly Earnings: $17,316

Education: Work experience in a related occupation

Knowledge: Production and Processing; Computers and Electronics; Design; Mechanical

Abilities: Visualization; Arm-Hand Steadiness; Manual Dexterity; Finger Dexterity; Multilimb Coordination; Wrist-Finger Speed; Speed of Limb Movement; Explosive Strength; Dynamic Strength; Trunk Strength; Dynamic Flexibility; Gross Body Equilibrium; Visual Color Discrimination

Skills: Installation; Testing

General Work Activities: Inspecting Equipment, Structures, or Material; Repairing and Maintaining Electrical Equipment

Job Characteristics: Sounds, Noise Levels are Distracting, etc.; Hazardous Conditions; Hazardous Equipment; Kneeling, Crouching, or

Crawling; Using Hands on Objects, Tools, or Controls; Making Repetitive Motions
GOE Group/s: 06.01.04 Production Technology: Precision Hand Work; 06.02.23 Production Work: Manual Work, Assembly Small Parts
CIP Program/s: 470101 Electrical and Electronics Equipment Installer and Repairer; 470102 Business Machine Repairer; 470199 Electrical and Electronics Equipment Installer and Repairer; 470608 Aircraft Mechanic/Technician, Powerplant
Related DOT Job/s: 706.381-018 FINAL ASSEMBLER; 706.381-050 PRECISION ASSEMBLER, BENCH; 714.381-010 ASSEMBLER, PHOTOGRAPHIC EQUIPMENT; 721.381-018 GOVERNOR ASSEMBLER, HYDRAULIC

93111B ELECTROMECHANICAL TECHNICIANS.

OOH Title/s: Precision Assemblers

Assemble, test, adjust, and fabricate parts, assemblies, instruments, and equipment, such as gyros, radar, temperature probes, and X-ray inspection systems. Operates metal-working machines to fabricate housings, jigs, fittings, and fixtures. Aligns, fits, and assembles component parts, using hand tools, power tools, fixtures, templates, and microscope. Installs electrical and electronic parts and hardware in housing or assembly, using soldering equipment and hand tools. Tests performance of electromechanical assembly, using test instruments such as oscilloscope, electronic voltmeter, and bridge. Repairs, reworks, and calibrates assemblies to meet operational specifications and tolerances. Verifies dimensions and clearances of parts to ensure conformance to specifications, using precision measuring instruments. Inspects parts for surface defects. Analyzes and records test results and prepares written documentation. Reads blueprints, schematics, diagrams, and technical orders to determine method and sequence of assembly.
Yearly Earnings: $17,316
Education: Work experience in a related occupation
Knowledge: Production and Processing; Computers and Electronics; Engineering and Technology; Design; Mechanical
Abilities: Arm-Hand Steadiness; Manual Dexterity; Finger Dexterity; Dynamic Flexibility
Skills: Science; Technology Design; Installation; Testing; Operation Monitoring; Operation and Control; Product Inspection; Equipment Maintenance; Troubleshooting; Repairing
General Work Activities: Inspecting Equipment, Structures, or Material; Controlling Machines and Processes; Repairing and Maintaining Electrical Equipment
Job Characteristics: Sounds, Noise Levels are Distracting, etc.; Radiation; Hazardous Equipment; Using Hands on Objects, Tools, or Controls; Making Repetitive Motions
GOE Group/s: 05.05.11 Craft Technology: Scientific, Medical, & Technical Equip. Fabric. & Related; 06.01.04 Production Technology: Precision Hand Work
CIP Program/s: 150403 Electromechanical Technologists and Technicians; 150405 Robotics Tech./Technician; 470608 Aircraft Mechanic/Technician, Powerplant
Related DOT Job/s: 710.281-018 ELECTROMECHANICAL TECHNICIAN; 828.381-018 ASSEMBLER, ELECTROMECHANICAL

93114 ELECTRICAL AND ELECTRONIC EQUIPMENT ASSEMBLERS—PRECISION. OOH

Title/s: Precision Assemblers

Assemble or modify prototypes or final assemblies of electrical or electronic equipment, such as missile control systems, radio and test equipment, computers, numerical control machine tools, radar, sonar, telemetering systems, or appliances. Include workers who primarily assemble electrical systems for machinery. Assembles systems and support structures, and installs components, units, and printed circuit boards, following specifications and using hand tools and power tools. Reads and interprets schematic drawings, diagrams, blueprints, specifications, work orders, and reports to determine material requirements and assembly instructions. Drills and taps holes in specified locations to mount control units and to provide openings for elements, wiring, and instruments. Inspects units to detect malfunctions, and adjusts, repairs, or replaces component parts to ensure conformance to specifications. Measures and adjusts voltages to specified value to determine operational accuracy of instruments. Fabricates and forms parts, coils, and structures according to specifications, using drill, calipers, cutters, and saws. Tests wiring installations, assemblies, and circuits for resistance factors and operational defects, and records results. Positions, aligns, and adjusts workpieces and electrical parts to facilitate wiring and assembly. Selects or distributes materials, supplies, and subassemblies to work area. Assists or confers with supervisor or engineer to plan and review work activities and to resolve production problems. Completes, reviews, and maintains production, time, and component waste reports. Cleans parts, using cleaning solution, air hose, and cloth. Packs finished assemblies for shipment and transports to storage areas, using hoists or handtrucks. Instructs customers in installation, repair, and maintenance of products and explains assembly procedures or techniques to workers. Paints structures as specified, using paint sprayer. Marks and tags components to track and identify stock inventory.
Yearly Earnings: $17,316
Education: Work experience in a related occupation
Knowledge: Production and Processing; Computers and Electronics; Engineering and Technology; Design; Mechanical
Abilities: Flexibility of Closure; Perceptual Speed; Visualization; Selective Attention; Manual Dexterity; Finger Dexterity; Control Precision; Speed of Limb Movement; Dynamic Flexibility; Gross Body Equilibrium; Visual Color Discrimination; Peripheral Vision; Glare Sensitivity; Hearing Sensitivity; Auditory Attention; Sound Localization
Skills: Science; Instructing; Technology Design; Equipment Selection; Installation; Testing; Operation Monitoring; Operation and Control; Product Inspection; Equipment Maintenance; Repairing
General Work Activities: Inspecting Equipment, Structures, or Material; Updating and Using Job-Relevant Knowledge; Operating Vehicles or Equipment; Drafting and Specifying Technical Devices, etc.; Repairing and Maintaining Electrical Equipment
Job Characteristics: Using Hands on Objects, Tools, or Controls
GOE Group/s: 05.10.01 Crafts: Structural; 05.10.03 Crafts: Electrical-Electronic; 06.01.04 Production Technology: Precision Hand Work; 06.02.23 Production Work: Manual Work, Assembly Small Parts; 06.02.32 Production Work: Manual Work, Assorted Materials
CIP Program/s: 470101 Electrical and Electronics Equipment Installer and Repairer; 470102 Business Machine Repairer; 470103 Communication Systems Installer and Repairer; 470105 Industrial Electronics Installer and Repairer; 470199 Electrical and Electronics Equipment Installer and Repairer; 470303 Industrial Machinery Maintenance and Repair; 470401 Instrument Calibration and Repairer; 470404 Musical Instrument Repairer
Related DOT Job/s: 693.381-026 ELECTRICAL AND RADIO MOCK-UP MECHANIC; 710.281-010 ASSEMBLER AND TESTER, ELECTRONICS; 721.381-014 ELECTRIC-MOTOR-CONTROL ASSEMBLER; 722.381-010 ASSEMBLER; 726.361-014 GROUP LEADER, PRINTED CIRCUIT BOARD ASSEMBLY; 729.281-042 WIRER; 729.381-022 WIRER, CABLE; 730.381-022 ELECTRIC-ORGAN ASSEMBLER AND CHECKER; 759.261-010 PROTOTYPE-DEICER ASSEMBLER; 820.381-014 TRANSFORMER ASSEMBLER I; 826.361-010 ASSEMBLER AND WIRER, INDUSTRIAL EQUIPMENT; 826.381-010 FABRICATOR, INDUSTRIAL FURNACE

93117 WATCH, CLOCK, AND CHRONOMETER ASSEMBLERS, ADJUSTERS, AND CALIBRATORS—PRECISION. OOH Title/s: Precision Assemblers

Perform precision assembling or adjusting, within narrow tolerances, of watches, clocks, or chronometers. Include watch train assemblers and timing adjusters. Adjusts size or positioning of timepiece parts to achieve specified fit or function, using calipers, fixture, and loupe. Assembles and installs components of timepieces, using watchmaker's tools and loupe, to complete mechanism. Disassembles timepieces, such as watches, clocks, and chronometers, to diagnose and repair malfunctions. Replaces specified parts to repair malfunctioning timepieces, using watchmaker's tools, loupe, and holding fixture. Tests operation and fit of timepiece parts and subassemblies, using electronic testing equipment, tweezers, watchmaker's tools, and loupe. Screws parts or assemblies into position. Reviews blueprints, sketches, or work orders to gather information about task to be completed. Examines components of timepieces, such as watches, clocks, or chronometers, for defects, using loupe or microscope. Observes operation of timepiece parts and subassemblies to determine accuracy of movement and to diagnose cause of defects. Bends parts, such as hairsprings, pallets, barrel covers, and bridges, to correct deficiencies in truing or endshake, using tweezers. Cleans and lubricates timepiece parts and assemblies, using solvent, buff stick, and oil.
Yearly Earnings: $28,444
Education: Work experience in a related occupation
Knowledge: Design; Mechanical
Abilities: Visualization; Arm-Hand Steadiness; Manual Dexterity; Finger Dexterity; Wrist-Finger Speed; Near Vision
Skills: Technology Design; Installation; Repairing
General Work Activities: Repairing and Maintaining Mechanical Equipment; Repairing and Maintaining Electrical Equipment
Job Characteristics: Sitting; Using Hands on Objects, Tools, or Controls; Importance of Being Exact or Accurate; Importance of Repeating Same Tasks
GOE Group/s: 06.01.04 Production Technology: Precision Hand Work; 06.02.24 Production Work: Manual Work, Metal and Plastics; 06.02.32 Production Work: Manual Work, Assorted Materials
CIP Program/s: 470408 Watch, Clock and Jewelry Repairer
Related DOT Job/s: 715.381-010 ASSEMBLER; 715.381-014 ASSEMBLER, WATCH TRAIN; 715.381-018 BANKING PIN ADJUSTER; 715.381-022 BARREL ASSEMBLER; 715.381-026 BARREL-BRIDGE ASSEMBLER; 715.381-030 BARREL-ENDSHAKE ADJUSTER; 715.381-038 CHRONOMETER ASSEMBLER AND ADJUSTER; 715.381-042 CHRONOMETER-BALANCE-AND-HAIRSPRING ASSEMBLER; 715.381-054 HAIRSPRING ASSEMBLER; 715.381-062 HAIRSPRING VIBRATOR; 715.381-082 PALLET-STONE INSERTER; 715.381-086 PALLET-STONE POSITIONER; 715.381-094 WATCH ASSEMBLER; 715.681-010 TIMING ADJUSTER

93197A MUSICAL INSTRUMENT MAKERS, METAL. OOH Title/s: Precision Assemblers; Metalworking and Plastics-Working Machine Operators

Fabricate and assemble musical instruments and instrument parts made of metal. Fits and assembles parts to form completed instrument, using hand tools, soldering iron, or riveting machine. Hammers, bends, or rolls metal, using hand tools or torch, to form and finish instrument. Drills holes in tubing, valves, and pistons, using drill press. Solders components, using gas torch or silver or soft solder. Casts metal into sheets and forms metal pipes, using hand tools and knowledge of metal properties. Scrapes edges of metal sheets, using hand tools, to obtain required angle for soldering. Cuts sheet-metal or tubing to specified lengths or shapes, using hand shears or power tools. Installs or mounts and secures components, pipes, or tubing. Sets up and operates machinery, such as lathe, bandsaw, and draw bench, to cut and shape instrument components. Aligns valves and tubes and determines that components are parallel and straight, using gauges. Reviews specifications or blueprints to determine procedures for fabricating and assembling instrument. Brushes sizing or lubricant on metal surfaces of instrument. Cleans instrument and deburrs or removes scratches, using abrasive cloth, sandpaper, or file. Inspects action line and parts to ensure specified tolerances and operation.
Yearly Earnings: $28,444
Education: Work experience in a related occupation
Knowledge: Production and Processing
Abilities: Arm-Hand Steadiness; Manual Dexterity; Finger Dexterity; Rate Control; Explosive Strength; Dynamic Strength
Skills: Installation
General Work Activities: Controlling Machines and Processes
Job Characteristics: Using Hands on Objects, Tools, or Controls; Making Repetitive Motions
GOE Group/s: 05.05.06 Craft Technology: Metal Fabrication and Repair; 05.05.12 Craft Technology: Musical Instrument Fabrication and Repair; 06.01.04 Production Technology: Precision Hand Work; 06.02.24 Production Work: Manual Work, Metal and Plastics
CIP Program/s: 470404 Musical Instrument Repairer
Related DOT Job/s: 709.381-030 ORGAN-PIPE MAKER, METAL; 730.381-014 BELL MAKER; 730.381-018 BRASS-WIND-INSTRUMENT MAKER; 730.381-030 HARP-ACTION ASSEMBLER; 730.381-046 PIPE-ORGAN INSTALLER; 730.381-054 TROMBONE-SLIDE ASSEMBLER; 730.681-014 PISTON MAKER; 730.681-018 VALVE MAKER II

93197C ALL OTHER PRECISION ASSEMBLERS. OOH Title/s: Precision Assemblers

All other precision assemblers not classified separately above.
Yearly Earnings: $28,444
Education: Work experience in a related occupation
GOE Group/s: 06.01.04 Production Technology: Precision Hand Work; 06.02.22 Production Work: Manual Work, Assembly Large Parts; 06.02.23 Production Work: Manual Work, Assembly Small Parts; 06.02.24 Production Work: Manual Work, Metal and Plastics
CIP Program/s: 470402 Gunsmith; 480501 Machinist/Machine Technologist; 480503 Machine Shop Assistant
Related DOT Job/s: 706.381-026 OPERATING-TABLE ASSEMBLER; 709.381-010 ATOMIC-FUEL ASSEMBLER; 709.381-038 REED MAKER; 710.381-010 ASSEMBLER II; 710.681-026 THERMOMETER MAKER; 733.381-014 RUBBER-STAMP MAKER; 736.381-010 ASSEMBLER I; 737.381-010 ASSEMBLER, IGNITER; 739.381-030 FABRICATOR, SHOWER DOORS AND PANELS; 754.381-018 PLASTICS FABRICATOR; 806.381-058 TRAILER ASSEMBLER I; 806.381-078 INSTALLER, INTERIOR ASSEMBLIES; 806.481-010 ASSEMBLER, ALUMINUM BOATS; 809.381-010 FABRICATOR-ASSEMBLER, METAL PRODUCTS; 809.381-034 SOLAR-FABRICATION TECHNICIAN; 809.681-010 ASSEMBLER, UNIT

Hand Workers, Including Assemblers and Fabricators

93902 MACHINE ASSEMBLERS. OOH Title/s: Machine Assemblers

Perform assembly work at a level less than that required of precision assemblers. Include air-conditioning coil assemblers, ball bearing ring assemblers, fuel injection assemblers, and subassemblers. Fastens assemblies or subassemblies together with bolts, screws, and collars, using hand tools, power tools, bench presses,

riveter, and assembly fixtures. Fits and spot-welds, solders, or rivets parts together. Sets and adjusts linkages, tensions, and clearances of assembled components to specifications, using fixed gauges and hand tools. Reads blueprints or written instructions to determine position of assembly components and set-up requirements. Positions parts in assembly fixtures, using holding or clamping device. Joins, bends, and taps parts into alignment or specified shape, using hand tools. Measures finished parts and compares parts with pattern to ensure accuracy. Moves levers to adjust quadrant to degree desired and to bend ends of part to specified angles and clearances. Screws part into testing machine and moves lever to test operation of subcomponent parts. Operates machine to punch, burr, grind, drill, or polish parts following procedures. Files edges and reams holes to fit and align parts, such as gears and housing, using reamer, tap, and file. Tests operation of machine assemblies to detect loose and binding parts and to determine synchronization of related parts. Examines samples of parts under microscope for nicks, grooves, and defects. Stamps identifying numbers on parts, using roll type metal stamper.
Yearly Earnings: $17,472
Education: Short-term O-J-T
Knowledge: Mechanical
Abilities: Manual Dexterity; Rate Control; Dynamic Flexibility
Skills: Testing; Operation and Control; Product Inspection; Troubleshooting
General Work Activities: Handling and Moving Objects; Controlling Machines and Processes; Repairing and Maintaining Mechanical Equipment
Job Characteristics: Sounds, Noise Levels are Distracting, etc.; Hazardous Equipment; Hazardous Situations; Kneeling, Crouching, or Crawling; Using Hands on Objects, Tools, or Controls; Bending or Twisting the Body; Making Repetitive Motions; Common Protective or Safety Attire
GOE Group/s: 06.02.23 Production Work: Manual Work, Assembly Small Parts; 06.04.22 Elemental Work: Industrial: Manual Work, Assembly Large Parts; 06.04.23 Elemental Work: Industrial: Manual Work, Assembly Small Parts
CIP Program/s: 000000 NO CIP ASSIGNED
Related DOT Job/s: 706.684-010 AIR-CONDITIONING-COIL ASSEMBLER; 706.684-014 ASSEMBLER I; 706.684-026 ASSEMBLER, TYPE-BAR-AND-SEGMENT; 706.684-038 BEARING-RING ASSEMBLER; 706.684-046 BENCH HAND; 706.684-062 INJECTOR ASSEMBLER; 706.684-094 SUBASSEMBLER; 724.684-034 MAGNET-VALVE ASSEMBLER; 737.684-010 ASSEMBLER, MECHANICAL ORDNANCE; 801.684-022 PROGRESSIVE ASSEMBLER AND FITTER

93905A BATTERY ASSEMBLERS. OOH Title/s: Electrical and Electronic Assemblers

Assemble cells and other components in container (battery case) to produce storage battery. Inserts cells into container according to prescribed polarity arrangement. Installs covers on cells, fits intercell connectors on posts, and burns fuse connectors to posts. Bolts, welds, solders, cements, and press-fits to join parts into place, using tools, machines, and equipment. Interweaves positive and negative plates in rack, cuts wire to separate positive and negative unit, and aligns units in jig. Threads positive and negative battery plates into connecting bolts, and joins plates into battery case. Wraps insulating material around cell and inserts plastic separating rods on plates. Inserts battery parts, including gaskets and washers, according to color-coded assembly procedures, and applies glue to battery to seal. Attaches terminal cables and removes excess metal around posts, using hand tools. Positions battery plates between teeth of rack, pushes plates under electrode of welding machine, and places terminal assembly on plate edge. Positions or aligns parts in specified relationship to each other in jig, fixture, or other holding device. Adds compounds to fill cavities and to ensure tight seal, and tests sealed units for air leaks, using hand tools. Ladles molten lead into battery cover to form posts and connectors and pours compound over cells to fill cracks and seal. Dips posts in soda solution, or brushes paint or molten wax on posts and connectors to prevent acid corrosion.
Yearly Earnings: $17,472
Education: Short-term O-J-T
Knowledge: Production and Processing; Mechanical
Abilities: Perceptual Speed; Arm-Hand Steadiness; Finger Dexterity; Wrist-Finger Speed; Speed of Limb Movement; Gross Body Equilibrium; Visual Color Discrimination
Skills: Installation
General Work Activities: Handling and Moving Objects
Job Characteristics: Hazardous Conditions; Hazardous Situations; Making Repetitive Motions; Common Protective or Safety Attire
GOE Group/s: 06.02.23 Production Work: Manual Work, Assembly Small Parts; 06.04.23 Elemental Work: Industrial: Manual Work, Assembly Small Parts
CIP Program/s: 470101 Electrical and Electronics Equipment Installer and Repairer
Related DOT Job/s: 727.664-010 BATTERY ASSEMBLER, DRY CELL; 727.684-010 BATTERY ASSEMBLER; 727.684-014 BATTERY ASSEMBLER, PLASTIC; 727.684-026 PLATE ASSEMBLER, SMALL BATTERY; 727.687-022 ASSEMBLER, DRY CELL AND BATTERY; 727.687-038 BATTERY-PARTS ASSEMBLER; 727.687-046 CELL TUBER, HAND; 727.687-082 WAFER-LINE WORKER

93905B ELECTRONIC COMPONENTS ASSEMBLERS. OOH Title/s: Electrical and Electronic Assemblers

Assemble and test electronic components, subassemblies, products, or systems. Inserts cells into container according to prescribed polarity arrangement. Installs covers on cells, fits intercell connectors on posts, and burns fuse connectors to posts. Bolts, welds, solders, cements, and press-fits to join parts into place, using tools, machines, and equipment. Interweaves positive and negative plates in rack, cuts wire to separate positive and negative unit, and aligns units in jig. Threads positive and negative battery plates into connecting bolts, and joins plates into battery case. Wraps insulating material around cell and inserts plastic separating rods on plates. Inserts battery parts, including gaskets and washers, according to color-coded assembly procedures, and applies glue to battery to seal. Attaches terminal cables and removes excess metal around posts, using hand tools. Positions battery plates between teeth of rack, pushes plates under electrode of welding machine, and places terminal assembly on plate edge. Positions or aligns parts in specified relationship to each other in jig, fixture, or other holding device. Adds compounds to fill cavities and to ensure tight seal, and tests sealed units for air leaks, using hand tools. Ladles molten lead into battery cover to form posts and connectors and pours compound over cells to fill cracks and seal. Dips posts in soda solution, or brushes paint or molten wax on posts and connectors to prevent acid corrosion.
Yearly Earnings: $17,472
Education: Short-term O-J-T
Knowledge: Production and Processing; Computers and Electronics; Engineering and Technology; Design; Mechanical; Education and Training; Telecommunications
Abilities: Information Ordering; Category Flexibility; Flexibility of Closure; Perceptual Speed; Visualization; Selective Attention; Arm-Hand Steadiness; Manual Dexterity; Finger Dexterity; Control Precision; Response Orientation; Rate Control; Reaction Time; Wrist-Finger Speed; Explosive Strength; Extent Flexibility; Dynamic Flexibility; Near Vision; Visual Color Discrimination; Hearing Sensitivity; Auditory Attention; Sound Localization

Skills: Instructing; Installation; Testing; Operation Monitoring; Operation and Control; Product Inspection; Equipment Maintenance; Troubleshooting; Repairing
General Work Activities: Inspecting Equipment, Structures, or Material; Handling and Moving Objects; Controlling Machines and Processes; Repairing and Maintaining Electrical Equipment; Coaching and Developing Others
Job Characteristics: Using Hands on Objects, Tools, or Controls; Making Repetitive Motions; Common Protective or Safety Attire; Degree of Automation; Importance of Being Sure All is Done
GOE Group/s: 06.02.23 Production Work: Manual Work, Assembly Small Parts; 06.04.34 Elemental Work: Industrial: Manual Work, Assorted Materials
CIP Program/s: 470101 Electrical and Electronics Equipment Installer and Repairer; 470103 Communication Systems Installer and Repairer
Related DOT Job/s: 725.384-010 TUBE ASSEMBLER, ELECTRON; 725.684-022 TUBE ASSEMBLER, CATHODE RAY; 725.684-026 CATHODE RAY TUBE SALVAGE PROCESSOR; 726.364-018 ELECTRONICS UTILITY WORKER; 726.684-014 ELECTRONIC-SCALE SUBASSEMBLER; 726.684-018 ELECTRONICS ASSEMBLER; 726.684-034 ASSEMBLER, SEMICONDUCTOR; 726.684-042 DIE ATTACHER; 726.684-070 PRINTED CIRCUIT BOARD ASSEMBLER, HAND; 726.684-086 PRINTED CIRCUIT BOARD ASSEMBLY REPAIRER; 726.684-098 TEST FIXTURE ASSEMBLER; 726.687-026 LAMINATION ASSEMBLER, PRINTED CIRCUIT BOARDS

93905C ELECTRIC MOTOR ASSEMBLERS. OOH Title/s: Electrical and Electronic Assemblers

Assemble and test subassemblies and parts of electric motors and generators. Tests windings for motor-housing clearance, grounds, and circuits, using gauge, growler, spring-steel blade, telephone receiver, insulation tester, and resistance bridge. Assembles and attaches end brackets to motor housing, and fastens assembly with screws. Inspects cores to be used in assembling electric motors and generator stators for defects, and files burns from core slots. Winds new coils and rewinds defective coils on armatures, stators, or rotors of used motors and generators. Aligns and slips cover over insulated core and bolts core in place to assemble rotating field for motors and alternators. Drills and taps holes to fasten clamps with bolts to secure connecting cable between coils. Bolts field windings and brush holders into housing of dynamotors, converters, and electric motors, using hand tools and holding device. Presses bushing and bearings into motor head and secures fans and gears to armature shaft, using press, nuts, and washers. Places armature in bearing and solders electrical leads to brushes and switch and cord assembly. Cuts, strips, bends, and twists wire and metal strips used in assembly of electric motors and generator stators, using hand tools. Replaces defective parts in motors and electrical equipment, using wrenches, screwdrivers, holding fixture, nuts, and bolts. Lubricates gears and other moving parts and turns shaft to ensure free movement of assembled parts, using grease gun.
Yearly Earnings: $17,472
Education: Short-term O-J-T
Knowledge: Production and Processing; Mechanical; Telecommunications
Abilities: Perceptual Speed; Visualization; Manual Dexterity; Finger Dexterity; Control Precision; Multilimb Coordination; Reaction Time; Wrist-Finger Speed; Explosive Strength; Extent Flexibility; Visual Color Discrimination; Hearing Sensitivity; Auditory Attention; Sound Localization
Skills: Testing; Product Inspection; Repairing
General Work Activities: Inspecting Equipment, Structures, or Material; Handling and Moving Objects; Repairing and Maintaining Mechanical Equipment; Repairing and Maintaining Electrical Equipment
Job Characteristics: Cramped Work Space, Awkward Positions; Making Repetitive Motions; Special Uniform; Common Protective or Safety Attire; Importance of Repeating Same Tasks; Pace Determined by Speed of Equipment
GOE Group/s: 06.02.23 Production Work: Manual Work, Assembly Small Parts; 06.02.32 Production Work: Manual Work, Assorted Materials; 06.04.23 Elemental Work: Industrial: Manual Work, Assembly Small Parts
CIP Program/s: 470101 Electrical and Electronics Equipment Installer and Repairer
Related DOT Job/s: 721.484-010 ELECTRIC-MOTOR WINDER; 721.484-014 FIELD-RING ASSEMBLER; 721.484-022 SKEIN WINDER; 721.684-014 ASSEMBLER, CARBON BRUSHES; 721.684-022 ELECTRIC-MOTOR ASSEMBLER; 721.684-026 SPIDER ASSEMBLER

93905D ELECTRICAL COMPONENTS ASSEMBLERS. OOH Title/s: Electrical and Electronic Assemblers

Assemble and test electrical instruments and components. Tests function and continuity of electrical assemblies, wiring, and other components, using ohmmeter and other electrical testing devices. Bolts, screws, or fastens subassemblies and parts to electrical assembly block, using metal strips, nuts, bolts, and other fastening devices. Inserts screws, bolts, rivets, wires, and other components into electronic and electrical units, such as transformers, lighting fixtures, appliances, or voltmeters. Connects wiring and terminals to accessories, including relays, circuit breakers, plugs, switches, and condensers, and installs assembly in electrical units. Solders or welds wire and terminal connections at specified locations to attach components to each other and to fixture. Fits covers, parts, and subassemblies into or onto main electrical assembly block or appliance, and attaches them, using hand tools. Applies adhesive inside housing of electrical instruments, such as transformers and small appliances, to hold assembly in place. Inspects wiring, soldered joints, and functioning of components of electrical assemblies, through observation and using electrical testing equipment. Reads and follows work orders, blueprints, guidelines, schematic diagrams, and specifications to determine established assembly methods. Cuts, crimps, strips, twists, and wraps specific electrical components of units, such as appliances, aircraft, missiles, or transformers. Positions electrical components in holding devices for welding, soldering, and assembly and for positioning in housing for completed assembly. Repairs and reworks defective assemblies routed to rework, including coils and transformers. Cleans electrical assemblies, such as coils, to remove material during production process, using solvent, brushes, and other hand tools.
Yearly Earnings: $17,472
Education: Short-term O-J-T
Knowledge: Computers and Electronics; Engineering and Technology; Design; Mechanical; Physics; Telecommunications
Abilities: Information Ordering; Memorization; Speed of Closure; Perceptual Speed; Spatial Orientation; Visualization; Selective Attention; Arm-Hand Steadiness; Manual Dexterity; Finger Dexterity; Multilimb Coordination; Response Orientation; Reaction Time; Wrist-Finger Speed; Explosive Strength; Gross Body Equilibrium; Near Vision; Visual Color Discrimination; Hearing Sensitivity; Sound Localization
Skills: Installation; Testing; Product Inspection; Troubleshooting; Repairing
General Work Activities: Identifying Objects, Actions, and Events; Inspecting Equipment, Structures, or Material; Handling and Moving Objects; Repairing and Maintaining Electrical Equipment
Job Characteristics: Hazardous Conditions; Common Protective or Safety Attire; Importance of Being Exact or Accurate; Importance of Being Sure All is Done; Importance of Repeating Same Tasks

GOE Group/s: 06.02.22 Production Work: Manual Work, Assembly Large Parts; 06.02.23 Production Work: Manual Work, Assembly Small Parts; 06.04.23 Elemental Work: Industrial: Manual Work, Assembly Small Parts
CIP Program/s: 470101 Electrical and Electronics Equipment Installer and Repairer; 470103 Communication Systems Installer and Repairer
Related DOT Job/s: 720.684-014 PHONOGRAPH-CARTRIDGE ASSEMBLER; 720.687-010 RECORD-CHANGER ASSEMBLER; 723.684-010 ASSEMBLER; 723.684-014 ASSEMBLER I; 724.684-030 COMMUTATOR ASSEMBLER; 724.684-038 MOTOR-AND-GENERATOR-BRUSH MAKER; 725.684-014 MOUNTER, HAND; 725.684-018 STEM MOUNTER; 726.687-014 PLUG WIRER; 726.687-022 ENCAPSULATOR; 728.684-010 WIRE HARNESS ASSEMBLER; 729.384-010 ASSEMBLER, ELECTRICAL ACCESSORIES II; 729.384-026 ELECTRICAL ASSEMBLER; 729.684-014 CAPACITOR ASSEMBLER; 729.684-022 ELECTRIC-SIGN ASSEMBLER; 729.684-026 ELECTRICAL-CONTROL ASSEMBLER; 729.684-034 MOTOR-VEHICLE-LIGHT ASSEMBLER; 729.684-046 SPARK-PLUG ASSEMBLER; 729.684-054 SUBASSEMBLER; 729.684-062 WIRER, SUBASSEMBLIES; 729.684-066 LAMINATION ASSEMBLER; 729.687-010 ASSEMBLER, ELECTRICAL ACCESSORIES I; 739.684-050 DEICER ASSEMBLER, ELECTRIC; 820.684-010 TRANSFORMER ASSEMBLER II

93908 COIL WINDERS, TAPERS, AND FINISHERS. OOH Title/s: Precision Assemblers; Coil Winders, Tapers, and Finishers

Wind wire coils used in electrical components, such as resistors and transformers, and in electrical equipment and instruments, such as field cores, bobbins, armature cores, electrical motors, generators, and control equipment. May involve the use of coil-winding and coil-making machines. Operates or tends wire-coiling machine used to wire electrical or electronic components, such as resistors, transformers, electrical equipment, and instruments. Turns or presses controls to adjust and activate wire-coiling machine. Attaches, alters, and trims materials such as wire, insulation, and coils, using hand tools. Reviews work orders and specifications to ascertain material needed and type of part to be processed. Observes gauges and stops machine to remove completed components, using hand tools. Selects and loads materials, such as workpieces, objects, and machine parts onto equipment used in coiling process. Examines and tests wired electrical components, using measuring devices. Applies solutions or paints to wired electrical components, using hand tools. Records production and operational data on specified forms. Repairs and maintains electrical components and machinery parts, using hand tools.
Yearly Earnings: $17,472
Education: Short-term O-J-T
Knowledge: Production and Processing
Abilities: Arm-Hand Steadiness; Manual Dexterity; Control Precision; Rate Control; Speed of Limb Movement; Dynamic Flexibility
Skills: Equipment Maintenance
General Work Activities: Controlling Machines and Processes; Repairing and Maintaining Mechanical Equipment; Repairing and Maintaining Electrical Equipment
Job Characteristics: Sounds, Noise Levels are Distracting, etc.; Hazardous Equipment; Standing; Using Hands on Objects, Tools, or Controls; Degree of Automation; Pace Determined by Speed of Equipment
GOE Group/s: 06.02.02 Production Work: Machine Work, Metal and Plastics; 06.02.09 Production Work: Machine Work, Assorted Materials; 06.02.32 Production Work: Manual Work, Assorted Materials; 06.04.09 Elemental Work: Industrial: Machine Work, Assorted Materials; 06.04.23 Elemental Work: Industrial: Manual Work, Assembly Small Parts
CIP Program/s: 470101 Electrical and Electronics Equipment Installer and Repairer; 470105 Industrial Electronics Installer and Repairer; 470199 Electrical and Electronics Equipment Installer and Repairer
Related DOT Job/s: 721.684-018 COIL CONNECTOR; 724.362-010 WIRE COILER; 724.381-014 COIL WINDER, REPAIR; 724.684-010 ARMATURE BANDER; 724.684-014 ARMATURE CONNECTOR II; 724.684-026 COIL WINDER; 724.685-010 ELEMENT WINDING MACHINE TENDER; 726.682-014 WIRE-WRAPPING-MACHINE OPERATOR

93914A WELDERS, PRODUCTION. OOH Title/s: Welders, Cutters, and Welding Machine Operators

Assemble and weld metal parts on production line, using welding equipment, requiring only a limited knowledge of welding techniques. Welds or tack-welds metal parts together, using spot-welding gun or hand, electric, or gas-welding equipment. Guides and directs flame or electrodes on or across workpiece to straighten, bend, melt, or build up metal. Fuses parts together, seals tension points, and adds metal to build up parts. Connects hoses from torch to tanks of oxygen and fuel gas, and turns valves to release mixture. Ignites torch and regulates flow of gas and air to obtain desired temperature, size, and color of flame. Selects, positions, and secures torch, cutting tips, or welding rod, according to type, thickness, area, and desired temperature of metal. Preheats workpieces preparatory to welding or bending, using torch. Positions and secures workpiece, using hoist, crane, wire, and banding machine, or hand tools. Fills cavities or corrects malformation in lead parts, and hammers out bulges and bends in metal workpieces. Dismantles metal assemblies or cuts scrap metal, using thermal-cutting equipment such as flame-cutting torch or plasma-arc equipment. Examines workpiece for defects and measures workpiece with straightedge or template to ensure conformance to specifications. Signals crane operator to move large workpieces. Learns new or modified methods of performing tasks by periodically attending group session. Climbs ladders or works on scaffolds to disassemble structures.
Yearly Earnings: $23,868
Education: Postsecondary vocational training
Knowledge: Production and Processing
Abilities: Perceptual Speed; Arm-Hand Steadiness; Manual Dexterity; Control Precision; Response Orientation; Rate Control; Wrist-Finger Speed; Speed of Limb Movement; Explosive Strength; Dynamic Strength; Trunk Strength; Stamina; Extent Flexibility; Dynamic Flexibility; Gross Body Coordination; Gross Body Equilibrium; Depth Perception
Skills: None above average
General Work Activities: Handling and Moving Objects; Controlling Machines and Processes
Job Characteristics: Sounds, Noise Levels are Distracting, etc.; Very Hot; Extremely Bright or Inadequate Lighting; Contaminants; Cramped Work Space, Awkward Positions; High Places; Hazardous Conditions; Hazardous Equipment; Standing; Climbing Ladders, Scaffolds, Poles, etc.; Keeping or Regaining Balance; Using Hands on Objects, Tools, or Controls; Bending or Twisting the Body; Making Repetitive Motions; Common Protective or Safety Attire; Specialized Protective or Safety Attire; Degree of Automation; Importance of Repeating Same Tasks; Pace Determined by Speed of Equipment
GOE Group/s: 05.10.01 Crafts: Structural; 05.12.11 Elemental Work: Mechanical: Welding; 06.04.31 Elemental Work: Industrial: Manual Work, Welding and Flame Cutting
CIP Program/s: 480508 Welder/Welding Technologist
Related DOT Job/s: 613.667-010 LINER ASSEMBLER; 709.684-086 TORCH-STRAIGHTENER-AND HEATER; 727.684-022 LEAD BURNER; 810.664-010 WELDER, GUN; 810.684-010 WELDER, TACK; 816.684-010 THERMAL CUTTER, HAND II; 819.684-010 WELDER, PRODUCTION LINE

93914B WELDERS AND CUTTERS. OOH Title/s: Welders, Cutters, and Welding Machine Operators

Use hand welding and flame-cutting equipment to weld together metal components and parts or to cut, trim, or scarf metal objects to dimensions, as specified by layouts, work orders, or blueprints. Welds metal parts or components together, using brazing, gas, or arc welding equipment. Guides electrodes or torch along weld line at specified speed and angle to weld, melt, cut, or trim metal. Reviews layouts, blueprints, diagrams, or work orders in preparation for welding or cutting metal components. Selects and inserts electrode or gas nozzle into holder, and connects hoses and cables to obtain gas or specified amperage, voltage, or polarity. Selects and installs torch, torch tip, filler rod, and flux, according to welding chart specifications or type and thickness of metal. Connects and turns regulator valves to activate and adjust gas flow and pressure to obtain desired flame. Ignites torch or starts power supply and strikes arc. Repairs broken or cracked parts, fills holes, and increases size of metal parts, using welding equipment. Preheats workpiece, using hand torch or heating furnace. Welds in flat, horizontal, vertical, or overhead position. Positions workpieces and clamps together or assembles in jigs or fixtures. Chips or grinds off excess weld, slag, or spatter, using hand scraper or power chipper, portable grinder, or arc-cutting equipment. Inspects finished workpiece for conformance to specifications. Cleans or degreases parts, using wire brush, portable grinder, or chemical bath.
Yearly Earnings: $23,868
Education: Postsecondary vocational training
Knowledge: Production and Processing; Design; Building and Construction; Mechanical
Abilities: Arm-Hand Steadiness; Manual Dexterity; Finger Dexterity; Control Precision; Multilimb Coordination; Rate Control; Wrist-Finger Speed; Speed of Limb Movement; Explosive Strength; Dynamic Strength; Trunk Strength; Stamina; Extent Flexibility; Dynamic Flexibility; Gross Body Equilibrium; Depth Perception; Glare Sensitivity
Skills: Operation Monitoring; Equipment Maintenance
General Work Activities: Handling and Moving Objects
Job Characteristics: Sounds, Noise Levels are Distracting, etc.; Very Hot; Extremely Bright or Inadequate Lighting; Contaminants; Cramped Work Space, Awkward Positions; Hazardous Conditions; Hazardous Equipment; Hazardous Situations; Using Hands on Objects, Tools, or Controls; Making Repetitive Motions; Common Protective or Safety Attire; Specialized Protective or Safety Attire
GOE Group/s: 05.05.06 Craft Technology: Metal Fabrication and Repair; 05.10.01 Crafts: Structural
CIP Program/s: 480508 Welder/Welding Technologist
Related DOT Job/s: 810.384-010 WELDER APPRENTICE, ARC; 810.384-014 WELDER, ARC; 811.684-010 WELDER APPRENTICE, GAS; 811.684-014 WELDER, GAS; 816.364-010 ARC CUTTER; 816.464-010 THERMAL CUTTER, HAND I; 819.384-010 WELDER, COMBINATION; 819.384-014 WELDER APPRENTICE, COMBINATION

93914C WELDER-FITTERS. OOH Title/s: Welders, Cutters, and Welding Machine Operators

Lay out, fit, and fabricate metal components to assemble structural forms, such as machinery frames, bridge parts, and pressure vessels, using knowledge of welding techniques, metallurgy, and engineering requirements. Includes experimental welders who analyze engineering drawings and specifications to plan welding operations where procedural information is unavailable. Lays out, positions, and secures parts and assemblies according to specifications, using straightedge, combination square, calipers, and ruler. Analyzes engineering drawings and specifications to plan layout, assembly, and welding operations. Determines required equipment and welding method, applying knowledge of metallurgy, geometry, and welding techniques. Develops templates and other work aids to hold and align parts. Ignites torch and adjusts valves, amperage, or voltage to obtain desired flame or arc. Tack-welds or welds components and assemblies, using electric, gas, arc, or other welding equipment. Heats, forms, and dresses metal parts, using hand tools, torch, or arc welding equipment. Cuts workpiece, using power saws, hand shears, or chipping knife. Welds components in flat, vertical, or overhead positions. Melts lead bar, wire, or scrap to add lead to joint or to extrude melted scrap into reusable form. Removes rough spots from workpiece, using portable grinder, hand file, or scraper. Installs or repairs equipment, such as lead pipes, valves, floors, and tank linings. Inspects grooves, angles, or gap allowances, using micrometer, caliper, and precision measuring instruments. Observes tests on welded surfaces, such as hydrostatic, x-ray, and dimension tolerance, to evaluate weld quality and conformance to specifications.
Yearly Earnings: $23,868
Education: Postsecondary vocational training
Knowledge: Production and Processing; Engineering and Technology; Design; Building and Construction; Mechanical; Physics; Public Safety and Security
Abilities: Originality; Arm-Hand Steadiness; Multilimb Coordination; Rate Control; Wrist-Finger Speed; Speed of Limb Movement; Dynamic Strength; Trunk Strength; Stamina; Extent Flexibility; Dynamic Flexibility; Gross Body Equilibrium
Skills: Equipment Selection; Installation; Equipment Maintenance; Repairing
General Work Activities: Handling and Moving Objects; Controlling Machines and Processes; Drafting and Specifying Technical Devices, etc.; Repairing and Maintaining Mechanical Equipment
Job Characteristics: Sounds, Noise Levels are Distracting, etc.; Very Hot; Extremely Bright or Inadequate Lighting; Contaminants; Cramped Work Space, Awkward Positions; High Places; Hazardous Conditions; Hazardous Equipment; Hazardous Situations; Climbing Ladders, Scaffolds, Poles, etc.; Keeping or Regaining Balance; Using Hands on Objects, Tools, or Controls; Making Repetitive Motions; Common Protective or Safety Attire; Specialized Protective or Safety Attire
GOE Group/s: 05.05.06 Craft Technology: Metal Fabrication and Repair
CIP Program/s: 480508 Welder/Welding Technologist
Related DOT Job/s: 819.281-010 LEAD BURNER; 819.281-014 LEAD-BURNER APPRENTICE; 819.281-022 WELDER, EXPERIMENTAL; 819.361-010 WELDER-FITTER; 819.361-014 WELDER-FITTER APPRENTICE; 819.381-010 WELDER-ASSEMBLER

93917A SOLDERERS. OOH Title/s: Solderers and Brazers

Solder together components to assemble fabricated metal products, using soldering iron. Melts and applies solder along adjoining edges of workpieces to solder joints, using soldering iron, gas torch, or electric-ultrasonic equipment. Melts and applies solder to fill holes, indentations, and seams of fabricated metal products, using soldering equipment. Heats soldering iron or workpiece to specified temperature for soldering, using gas flame or electric current. Dips workpieces into molten solder or places solder strip between seams and heats seam with iron to band items together. Aligns and clamps workpieces together, using rule, square, or hand tools, or positions items in fixtures, jigs, or vise. Applies flux to workpiece surfaces in preparation for soldering. Grinds, cuts, buffs, or bends edges of workpieces to be joined to ensure snug fit, using power grinder and hand tools. Melts and separates soldered joints to repair misaligned or damaged assemblies, using soldering equipment. Removes workpieces from molten solder and holds parts together until color indicates that solder has set. Cleans tip of soldering iron, using chemical solution or cleaning compound.

Cleans workpieces, using chemical solution, file, wire brush, or grinder.
Yearly Earnings: $19,500
Education: Short-term O-J-T
Knowledge: None above average
Abilities: Arm-Hand Steadiness; Manual Dexterity; Finger Dexterity; Wrist-Finger Speed; Speed of Limb Movement
Skills: Equipment Selection; Operation and Control; Equipment Maintenance
General Work Activities: None above average
Job Characteristics: Contaminants; Hazardous Conditions; Hazardous Situations; Using Hands on Objects, Tools, or Controls; Making Repetitive Motions; Common Protective or Safety Attire; Importance of Repeating Same Tasks
GOE Group/s: 06.02.22 Production Work: Manual Work, Assembly Large Parts; 06.04.31 Elemental Work: Industrial: Manual Work, Welding and Flame Cutting
CIP Program/s: 470402 Gunsmith; 480508 Welder/Welding Technologist
Related DOT Job/s: 736.684-038 SOLDERER, BARREL RIBS; 739.684-054 DEICER FINISHER; 813.684-014 SOLDERER-ASSEMBLER; 813.684-018 SOLDERER-DIPPER; 813.684-022 SOLDERER, PRODUCTION LINE; 813.684-026 SOLDERER, TORCH I; 813.684-030 SOLDERER, ULTRASONIC, HAND

93917B BRAZERS. OOH Title/s: Solderers and Brazers

Braze together components to assemble fabricated metal parts, using torch or welding machine and flux. Guides torch and rod along joint of workpieces to heat to brazing temperature, melt braze alloy, and bond workpieces together. Adjusts electric current and timing cycle of resistance welding machine to heat metal to bonding temperature. Selects torch tip, flux, and brazing alloy from data charts or work order. Connects hoses from torch to regulator valves and cylinders of oxygen and specified fuel gas, acetylene or natural. Turns valves to start flow of gases, lights flame, and adjusts valves to obtain desired color and size of flame. Brushes flux onto joint of workpiece, or dips braze rod into flux to prevent oxidation of metal. Melts and separates brazed joints to remove and straighten damaged or misaligned components, using hand torch or furnace. Aligns and secures workpieces in fixtures, jigs, or vise, using rule, square, or template. Examines seam and rebrazes defective joints or broken parts. Cleans joints of workpieces, using wire brush or by dipping them into cleaning solution. Removes workpiece from fixture, using tongs, and cools workpiece, using air or water. Cuts carbon electrodes to specified size and shape, using cutoff saw.
Yearly Earnings: $19,500
Education: Short-term O-J-T
Knowledge: None above average
Abilities: Glare Sensitivity
Skills: Equipment Selection; Installation; Operation Monitoring; Operation and Control
General Work Activities: None above average
Job Characteristics: Very Hot; Extremely Bright or Inadequate Lighting; Hazardous Conditions; Using Hands on Objects, Tools, or Controls; Making Repetitive Motions; Common Protective or Safety Attire; Specialized Protective or Safety Attire
GOE Group/s: 06.02.19 Production Work: Equipment Operation, Welding, Brazing and Soldering; 06.02.22 Production Work: Manual Work, Assembly Large Parts
CIP Program/s: 480508 Welder/Welding Technologist
Related DOT Job/s: 813.682-010 BRAZER, RESISTANCE; 813.684-010 BRAZER, ASSEMBLER

93921 PRESSERS, HAND. OOH Title/s: Apparel Workers

Press articles to remove wrinkles, flatten seams, and give shape by using hand iron. Articles pressed include drapes, knit goods, millinery parts, parachutes, garments, slip covers, and textiles such as lace, rayon, and silk. May block (shape) knitted garments after cleaning. May press leather goods. Pushes and pulls iron over surface of article, according to type of fabric. Adjusts temperature of iron, according to fabric type, and uses covering cloths to prevent scorching or sheen on delicate fabrics. Fits odd-shaped pieces which cannot be pressed flat over puff iron. Smooths and shapes fabric prior to pressing. Places article in position on ironing board or work table. Measures drapes to specifications, cuts uneven edges with shears, folds material, and presses with iron to form heading. Sprays water over fabric to soften fibers when not using steam iron. Pins, folds, and hangs article after pressing.
Yearly Earnings: $19,500
Education: Short-term O-J-T
Knowledge: None above average
Abilities: None above average
Skills: None above average
General Work Activities: None above average
Job Characteristics: Very Hot; Hazardous Situations; Standing; Using Hands on Objects, Tools, or Controls; Making Repetitive Motions
GOE Group/s: 06.04.27 Elemental Work: Industrial: Manual Work, Textile, Fabric and Leather; 06.04.35 Elemental Work: Industrial: Laundering, Dry Cleaning
CIP Program/s: 000000 NO CIP ASSIGNED
Related DOT Job/s: 363.684-018 PRESSER, HAND; 781.684-030 DRAPERY-HEAD FORMER

93923B SEWERS, HAND. OOH Title/s: Apparel Workers; Handlers, Equipment Cleaners, Helpers, and Laborers

Sew, join, reinforce, or finish, usually with needle and thread, any of a wide variety of manufactured items. Sews using various types of stitches, such as felling, tacking, basting, embroidery, and fagoting. Joins and reinforces parts of articles, such as garments, books, mattresses, toys, and wigs. Selects thread, twine, cord, or yarn, and threads needles. Folds, twists, stretches, or drapes material and secures article in preparation for sewing. Measures and aligns parts, fasteners, or trimmings, following seams, edges, or markings on parts. Trims excess threads or edges of parts, using scissors or knife. Ties, knits, weaves or knots ribbon, yarn or decorative materials. Smooths seams with heated iron, flat bone, or rubbing stick. Attaches trimmings and labels to article with cement, using brush or cement gun. Draws and cuts pattern according to specifications. Waxes thread by drawing it through ball of wax. Softens leather or shoe material with water.
Yearly Earnings: $16,484
Education: Short-term O-J-T
Knowledge: Production and Processing; Fine Arts
Abilities: Arm-Hand Steadiness; Wrist-Finger Speed; Visual Color Discrimination
Skills: None above average
General Work Activities: Handling and Moving Objects
Job Characteristics: Sitting; Using Hands on Objects, Tools, or Controls; Making Repetitive Motions; Importance of Repeating Same Tasks
GOE Group/s: 06.02.27 Production Work: Manual Work, Textile, Fabric and Leather; 06.04.26 Elemental Work: Industrial: Manual Work, Paper; 06.04.27 Elemental Work: Industrial: Manual Work, Textile, Fabric and Leather; 06.04.28 Elemental Work: Industrial: Manual Work, Food Processing; 06.04.34 Elemental Work: Industrial: Manual Work, Assorted Materials; 06.04.38 Elemental Work: Industrial: Wrapping and Packaging

CIP Program/s: 200301 Clothing, Apparel and Textile Workers and Managers, General; 480299 Graphic and Printing Equipment Operators, Other
Related DOT Job/s: 529.687-030 CASING SEWER; 732.684-034 BASEBALL SEWER, HAND; 732.684-050 FEATHER STITCHER; 732.684-090 PELOTA MAKER; 739.384-014 FOUNDATION MAKER; 739.684-162 UMBRELLA TIPPER, HAND; 780.684-070 MATTRESS FINISHER; 782.684-030 HOSIERY MENDER; 782.684-050 PASSEMENTERIE WORKER; 782.684-058 SEWER, HAND; 782.687-018 CLOTH-BALE HEADER; 782.687-058 THREAD MARKER; 784.684-022 DECORATOR; 784.684-042 HAT MAKER; 787.381-010 LAMP-SHADE SEWER; 788.684-054 HAND SEWER, SHOES; 788.684-110 SOLE SEWER, HAND; 789.381-010 BEADWORKER; 789.484-014 FINISHER, HAND; 920.687-022 BALE SEWER; 977.684-022 STITCHER, HAND

93926B ROCK SPLITTERS. OOH Title/s: Indirectly related to Cutting and Slicing Machine Setters, Operators, and Tenders

Split rough dimension stone into smaller units, such as paving blocks, ashlar, or rubble. Splits stone, using airhammer, wedges, and shims. Chips rough edges from stone, using chipping hammer. Splits rough slabs of slate into sheets for use as coping, flooring, and roofing. Scans stone to determine rift and grain lines of splitting, usually at right angles to each other.
Yearly Earnings: $19,500
Education: Short-term O-J-T
Knowledge: None above average
Abilities: Spatial Orientation; Arm-Hand Steadiness; Manual Dexterity; Multilimb Coordination; Speed of Limb Movement; Static Strength; Explosive Strength; Dynamic Strength; Trunk Strength; Stamina; Extent Flexibility; Dynamic Flexibility; Gross Body Coordination; Gross Body Equilibrium; Depth Perception
Skills: None above average
General Work Activities: None above average
Job Characteristics: Sounds, Noise Levels are Distracting, etc.; Very Hot; Extremely Bright or Inadequate Lighting; Whole Body Vibration; Hazardous Equipment; Standing; Kneeling, Crouching, or Crawling; Keeping or Regaining Balance; Using Hands on Objects, Tools, or Controls; Bending or Twisting the Body; Making Repetitive Motions; Common Protective or Safety Attire; Importance of Repeating Same Tasks
GOE Group/s: 05.12.07 Elemental Work: Mechanical: Crushing, Mixing, Separating, and Chipping
CIP Program/s: 460101 Mason and Tile Setter
Related DOT Job/s: 771.684-010 ROCK SPLITTER

93926D GLASS CUTTERS AND FINISHERS. OOH Title/s: Indirectly related to Cutting and Slicing Machine Setters, Operators and Tenders

Lay out, cut, and finish glass to specified size and shape to make a variety of glass products. Positions pattern or drawing on glass, measures dimensions, and marks cutting lines, using glass-cutting tools. Smooths and polishes rough edges, using belt sander or polishing wheels. Transfers pattern for individual stained glass parts from full-size drawing to pattern paper, using stylus to trace drawing. Sandblasts surface within guidelines, using sandblasting tool. Sprays silver solution on glass to provide mirrored surface, using spray gun. Breaks away excess glass by hand or with notched tool or glass pinchers. Assembles glass pieces to make various novelties.
Yearly Earnings: $19,500
Education: Short-term O-J-T
Knowledge: Production and Processing; Fine Arts
Abilities: Arm-Hand Steadiness; Wrist-Finger Speed
Skills: None above average
General Work Activities: None above average
Job Characteristics: Hazardous Situations; Common Protective or Safety Attire; Importance of Repeating Same Tasks
GOE Group/s: 06.02.30 Production Work: Manual Work, Stone, Glass, and Clay; 06.02.31 Production Work: Manual Work, Laying Out and Marking; 06.04.30 Elemental Work: Industrial: Manual Work, Stone, Glass, and Clay
CIP Program/s: 469999 Construction Trades, Other; 500201 Crafts, Folk Art and Artisanry
Related DOT Job/s: 775.684-022 GLASS CUTTER; 775.684-026 GLASS FINISHER; 779.584-010 PATTERNMAKER

93926E CUTTERS AND TRIMMERS, HAND. OOH Title/s: Indirectly related to Cutting and Slicing Machine Setters, Operators, and Tenders; Apparel workers

Use hand tools or hand-held power tools to cut and trim any of a wide variety of items. Cuts materials, such as textiles, food, and metal, using hand tools, portable power tools, or bench-mounted tools. Lowers table-mounted cutter, such as knife blade, cutting wheel, or saw, to cut items to specified size. Adjusts guides and stops to control depth and width of cuts. Routes items to provide cutouts for parts, using portable router, grinder, and hand tools. Positions template or measures material to locate specified point of cut or to obtain maximum yield, using rule, scale, or pattern. Marks cutting lines around pattern or template, or follows layout points, using square, rule, straightedge, and chalk, pencil, or scribe. Reads work order to determine dimensions, cutting locations, and quantity to cut. Unrolls, lays out, attaches, or mounts material or item on cutting table or machine. Folds or shapes materials, preparatory to or after cutting. Observes and marks or discards items with defects, such as spots, stains, scars, snags, chips, scratches, or unacceptable shape or finish. Marks identification numbers, trademark, grade, marketing data, size, or model number on products. Replaces or sharpens dulled cutting tools, such as saws. Separates materials or products according to size, weight, type, condition, color, or shade. Stacks cut items and loads them on racks, conveyors, or onto truck. Cleans, treats, buffs, or polishes finished items, using grinder, brush, chisel, cleaning solutions, and polishing materials. Counts or weighs and bundles items. Transports items to work or storage area by pushing or pulling carts.
Yearly Earnings: $19,500
Education: Short-term O-J-T
Knowledge: None above average
Abilities: Visualization; Manual Dexterity; Wrist-Finger Speed
Skills: None above average
General Work Activities: None above average
Job Characteristics: Hazardous Equipment; Hazardous Situations; Using Hands on Objects, Tools, or Controls; Making Repetitive Motions; Common Protective or Safety Attire; Importance of Repeating Same Tasks
GOE Group/s: 06.02.24 Production Work: Manual Work, Metal and Plastics; 06.02.25 Production Work: Manual Work, Wood; 06.02.27 Production Work: Manual Work, Textile, Fabric and Leather; 06.02.30 Production Work: Manual Work, Stone, Glass, and Clay; 06.03.02 Quality Control: Inspecting, Grading, Sorting, Weighing, and Recording; 06.04.08 Elemental Work: Industrial: Machine Work, Stone, Glass, and Clay; 06.04.14 Elemental Work: Industrial: Equipment Operation, Paper Making; 06.04.16 Elemental Work: Industrial: Equipment Operation, Textile, Fabric, and Leather Processing; 06.04.24 Elemental Work: Industrial: Manual Work, Metal and Plastics; 06.04.25 Elemental Work: Industrial: Manual Work, Wood; 06.04.26 Elemental Work: Industrial: Manual Work, Paper; 06.04.27 Elemental Work: Industrial: Manual Work, Textile, Fabric and Leather; 06.04.28 Elemental Work: Industrial: Manual Work, Food Processing; 06.04.29 Elemental Work: Industrial: Manual Work, Rub-

ber; 06.04.30 Elemental Work: Industrial: Manual Work, Stone, Glass, and Clay; 06.04.34 Elemental Work: Industrial: Manual Work, Assorted Materials; 06.04.39 Elemental Work: Industrial: Cleaning
CIP Program/s: 200301 Clothing, Apparel and Textile Workers and Managers, General; 200303 Commercial Garment and Apparel Worker; 200501 Home Furnishings and Equipment Installers and Consultants, General; 200502 Window Treatment Maker and Installer; 470404 Musical Instrument Repairer; 480304 Shoe, Boot and Leather Repairer; 480399 Leatherworkers and Upholsterers, Other; 480503 Machine Shop Assistant; 490306 Marine Maintenance and Repair
Related DOT Job/s: 521.687-014 BINDER CUTTER, HAND; 521.687-026 BUNCH TRIMMER, MOLD; 521.687-066 FRUIT CUTTER; 524.687-010 CHERRY CUTTER; 525.687-046 HIDE TRIMMER; 539.686-010 CUTTER, WET MACHINE; 569.684-010 LOG PEELER; 569.687-026 WOOD HACKER; 575.684-022 CROSSCUTTER, ROLLED GLASS; 579.684-030 CUTTER; 585.684-010 TRIMMER, HAND; 590.687-022 RUG CUTTER; 673.666-014 STRIPPER; 689.687-090 LAPPER; 700.684-018 BRIGHT CUTTER; 700.684-038 GOLD CUTTER; 700.684-050 MESH CUTTER; 701.687-030 POWER-CHISEL OPERATOR; 703.684-018 TEMPLATE CUTTER; 709.684-074 SHEARER AND TRIMMER, WIRE SCREEN AND FABRIC; 715.684-162 PEARLER; 715.687-038 HAIRSPRING CUTTER I; 715.687-042 HAIRSPRING CUTTER II; 730.684-074 SHEET-METAL-PATTERN CUTTER; 731.687-038 WIRE CUTTER; 732.687-078 TARGET TRIMMER; 733.687-022 CHALK CUTTER; 734.384-010 BUTTON-CUTTING-MACHINE OPERATOR; 734.687-086 SPLITTER, HAND; 739.684-126 MAT CUTTER; 739.687-050 CANDLE CUTTER; 750.684-034 TIRE TRIMMER, HAND; 751.387-010 STOCK PREPARER; 751.684-014 CUTTER, HAND; 751.684-018 CUTTER, HOT KNIFE; 751.684-022 FOXING CUTTER, HOT KNIFE; 751.687-010 HOSE CUTTER, HAND; 753.687-010 CLIPPER; 762.684-022 BASKET MENDER; 763.684-066 SLOT ROUTER; 763.687-030 CANE CUTTER; 769.684-042 SAMPLE MAKER, VENEER; 771.384-010 COPER, HAND; 775.684-046 LEVEL-VIAL MARKER; 779.681-010 MICA SPLITTER; 779.684-022 GLASS CUTTER, OVAL OR CIRCULAR; 779.684-054 SECOND CUTTER; 779.687-030 MICA SIZER; 780.684-038 COTTON DISPATCHER; 781.384-018 SAIL CUTTER; 781.684-018 CUTTER, ROTARY SHEAR; 781.684-034 LAY-OUT-MACHINE OPERATOR; 781.684-046 RUG CLIPPER; 781.684-054 SLITTER; 781.684-070 SAMPLE CUTTER; 781.684-074 CUTTER, HAND I; 781.684-078 CUTTER APPRENTICE, HAND; 781.687-026 CUTTER, HAND II; 781.687-030 CUTTER, HAND III; 781.687-050 RIBBON CUTTER; 781.687-070 TRIMMER, HAND; 782.687-038 RIPPER; 783.684-022 LEATHER CUTTER; 783.687-014 FUR TRIMMER; 784.684-010 BOW MAKER; 784.684-050 ROUNDER, HAND; 784.687-026 ENDBAND CUTTER, HAND; 784.687-054 OPENER I; 788.684-038 BUTTONHOLE MAKER; 788.684-042 CRIPPLE WORKER; 788.684-082 OUTSIDE CUTTER, HAND; 788.687-042 FINISHING TRIMMER; 788.687-074 LACING-STRING CUTTER; 788.687-150 TRIMMER, HAND; 788.687-162 WELT-BUTTER, HAND; 789.684-022 HAIR CLIPPER, POWER; 789.684-050 THREAD CUTTER; 789.687-030 CLIPPER; 789.687-126 POMPOM MAKER; 789.687-150 REMNANTS CUTTER; 790.687-010 CANDY CUTTER, HAND; 794.687-062 TRIMMER, HAND; 804.684-010 CUTTER, ALUMINUM SHEET; 806.684-150 ROUTER OPERATOR, HAND; 809.687-010 DUCT MAKER; 899.684-030 PORTABLE SAWYER; 929.687-010 CUTTER, BANANA ROOM; 976.684-018 MOUNTER, HAND

93928 PORTABLE MACHINE CUTTERS. OOH Title/s: Apparel Workers; Indirectly related to Cutting and Slicing Machine Setters, Operators , and Tenders

Use portable electric cutter to cut multiple layers of fabric into parts for articles, such as awnings, fitted sheets, garments, hats, stuffed toys, and upholstered furniture. Cuts multiple layers of fabrics into parts for articles, such as canvas goods, garments, and upholstered furniture. Spreads fabric on table in single or multiple layers and guides layers around cutter blade. Drills holes through layers of fabric or cuts notches in edges of parts to mark parts for assembly. Sharpens or changes cutter blades when quality of cut indicates blade is dull. Positions pattern over fabric and traces outline of pattern, using chalk or crayon. Separates cutting waste according to material.
Yearly Earnings: $20,852
Education: Moderate-term O-J-T
Knowledge: Production and Processing
Abilities: Arm-Hand Steadiness; Manual Dexterity
Skills: None above average
General Work Activities: None above average
Job Characteristics: Hazardous Situations; Making Repetitive Motions; Importance of Repeating Same Tasks; Pace Determined by Speed of Equipment
GOE Group/s: 06.02.27 Production Work: Manual Work, Textile, Fabric and Leather
CIP Program/s: 000000 NO CIP ASSIGNED
Related DOT Job/s: 781.684-014 CUTTER, MACHINE I

93932 CARPET CUTTERS, DIAGRAMMERS, AND SEAMERS. OOH Title/s: Indirectly related to Cutting and Slicing Machine Setters, Operators ,and Tenders

Measure, mark, cut, and seam carpets or rugs to specific diagrams and dimensions for buildings. Include workers who cut linoleum. Exclude workers who install as well as cut carpet. Measures and marks floor covering according to diagrammed instructions or floor dimensions, using measuring tools and chalkline. Cuts lengths from floor-covering roll, using cutting tool. Seams edges using glue, putty knife, and webbing tape. Positions cut sections upside down to match edges to be seamed. Computes area surface of sections needed to determine cutting lines. Unrolls floor covering on floor. Clips uneven pile yarn along seams, using electric clipper, to make seams invisible. Compares diagram with uncut floor covering to estimate shape of required rug, and visualizes order and manner sections should be joined. Reads instructions to determine floor covering product to be cut. Rerolls floor covering to be returned to storage and rolls up cut floor covering for further handling.
Yearly Earnings: $16,796
Education: Long-term O-J-T
Knowledge: None above average
Abilities: Static Strength
Skills: None above average
General Work Activities: None above average
Job Characteristics: Cramped Work Space, Awkward Positions; Hazardous Situations; Kneeling, Crouching, or Crawling; Keeping or Regaining Balance; Using Hands on Objects, Tools, or Controls
GOE Group/s: 05.10.01 Crafts: Structural; 06.02.27 Production Work: Manual Work, Textile, Fabric and Leather; 06.02.31 Production Work: Manual Work, Laying Out and Marking; 06.04.27 Elemental Work: Industrial: Manual Work, Textile, Fabric and Leather
CIP Program/s: 000000 NO CIP ASSIGNED
Related DOT Job/s: 585.687-014 CARPET CUTTER II; 781.684-010 CARPET CUTTER I; 789.484-010 DIAGRAMMER AND SEAMER; 929.381-010 CARPET CUTTER

93935 CANNERY WORKERS. OOH Title/s: Cannery Workers

Perform any of a variety of routine tasks in canning, freezing, preserving, or packing food products. Duties may include sorting, grading, washing, peeling, trimming, or slicing agricultural produce. Sorts or grades products according to size, color, or quality. Trims, peels, and slices products with knife or paring tool. Feeds products into processing equipment, such as washing, refrigerating, peeling, coring, pitting, trimming, grinding, dicing, cooking, or slicing machines. Fills containers, using scoop or filling form, or packs

by hand. Dumps or places food products in hopper, on sorting table, or on conveyor. Feeds empty containers onto conveyor or forming machines. Places filled containers on trays or racks, or into boxes. Counts, weighs, or tallies processed items according to specifications. Inspects and weighs filled containers to ensure product conforms to quality and weight standards. Loads, moves, or stacks containers by hand or handtruck, and cleans glass containers, using airhose.
Yearly Earnings: $15,548
Education: Short-term O-J-T
Knowledge: Production and Processing; Food Production
Abilities: Manual Dexterity
Skills: None above average
General Work Activities: Handling and Moving Objects
Job Characteristics: Standing; Making Repetitive Motions; Common Protective or Safety Attire; Degree of Automation; Importance of Repeating Same Tasks; Pace Determined by Speed of Equipment
GOE Group/s: 06.04.15 Elemental Work: Industrial: Equipment Operation, Food Processing
CIP Program/s: 000000 NO CIP ASSIGNED
Related DOT Job/s: 529.686-014 CANNERY WORKER

93938 MEAT, POULTRY, AND FISH CUTTERS AND TRIMMERS—HAND. OOH Title/s: Butchers and Meat, Poultry, and Fish Cutters; Handlers, Equipment Cleaners, Helpers, and Laborers

Use hand tools to perform a wide variety of food cutting and trimming tasks that require skills less than that of the precision level. Include meat boners, carcass splitters, poultry eviscerators, fish cleaners and butchers, skinners, and stickers. Trims, slices, and sections carcasses for future processing. Cuts and trims meat to prepare for packing. Removes parts such as skin, feathers, scales, or bones from carcass. Inspects meat products for defects or blemishes. Cleans carcasses and removes waste products or defective portions. Separates meats and byproducts into specified containers. Slaughters live animals. Weighs meats and tags containers for weight and contents. Obtains and distributes specified meat or carcass. Seals containers of meat.
Yearly Earnings: $19,500
Education: Short-term O-J-T
Knowledge: Food Production; Biology
Abilities: Manual Dexterity; Wrist-Finger Speed; Speed of Limb Movement; Static Strength; Dynamic Strength; Trunk Strength; Extent Flexibility; Dynamic Flexibility; Gross Body Equilibrium
Skills: None above average
General Work Activities: Handling and Moving Objects
Job Characteristics: Sounds, Noise Levels are Distracting, etc.; Very Hot; Contaminants; Diseases/Infections; Hazardous Situations; Standing; Making Repetitive Motions; Special Uniform; Common Protective or Safety Attire; Importance of Repeating Same Tasks
GOE Group/s: 06.04.15 Elemental Work: Industrial: Equipment Operation, Food Processing; 06.04.28 Elemental Work: Industrial: Manual Work, Food Processing
CIP Program/s: 120506 Meatcutter
Related DOT Job/s: 521.687-058 FISH CHOPPER, GANG KNIFE; 521.687-106 SAUSAGE-MEAT TRIMMER; 521.687-126 SKIN LIFTER, BACON; 522.687-046 FISH ROE PROCESSOR; 525.684-010 BONER, MEAT; 525.684-014 BUTCHER, FISH; 525.684-018 CARCASS SPLITTER; 525.684-022 CRAB BUTCHER; 525.684-026 FINAL-DRESSING CUTTER; 525.684-030 FISH CLEANER; 525.684-034 HEAD TRIMMER; 525.684-038 OFFAL SEPARATOR; 525.684-042 POULTRY KILLER; 525.684-046 SKINNER; 525.684-050 STICKER, ANIMAL; 525.684-054 TRIMMER, MEAT; 525.684-058 TURKEY-ROLL MAKER; 525.687-010 ANIMAL EVISCERATOR; 525.687-014 CASING SPLITTER; 525.687-030 GAMBRELER; 525.687-066 POULTRY BONER; 525.687-070 POULTRY DRESSER; 525.687-074 POULTRY EVISCERATOR; 525.687-126 CRAB MEAT PROCESSOR; 529.686-022 CUTLET MAKER, PORK

93941 METAL POURERS AND CASTERS, BASIC SHAPES. OOH Title/s: Metalworking and Plastics-Working Machine Operators; Handlers, Equipment Cleaners, Helpers, and Laborers

Operate hand-controlled mechanisms adjunctive to specialized machinery and equipment to pour and regulate the flow of molten metal into molds for producing castings or ingots of specific quality and size. Include steel pourers, casters, and ladle and metal pourers. Pours molten metal into molds and forms, using ladle. Adds metal to molds to compensate for shrinkage. Skims slag or removes excess metal from ingots or equipment, using hand tools, strainers, rakes, or burners, and recycles scrap. Positions equipment or signals workers to position equipment such as ladles, grinding wheels, or crucibles. Reads temperature gauges, observes color changes, and adjusts furnace flame, torch, or electrical heating unit to melt metal. Loads specified amount of metal and flux into furnace or clay crucible. Turns valves to circulate water through core, or sprays water on filled molds to cool and solidify metal. Examines molds to ensure they are clean, smooth, and properly coated. Assembles and embeds cores in casting frames, using hand tools and equipment. Removes metal ingots or cores from molds, using hand tools, cranes, and chain hoists. Collects samples or signals workers to sample metal for analysis. Stencils identifying information on ingots and pigs, using special hand tools. Repairs and maintains metal forms and equipment, using hand tools, sledges, and bars. Transports metal ingots to storage areas, using forklift.
Yearly Earnings: $18,772
Education: Moderate-term O-J-T
Knowledge: Production and Processing
Abilities: Speed of Limb Movement; Explosive Strength; Dynamic Flexibility; Gross Body Equilibrium; Visual Color Discrimination; Depth Perception; Hearing Sensitivity; Sound Localization
Skills: Operation Monitoring; Operation and Control; Equipment Maintenance; Repairing
General Work Activities: Controlling Machines and Processes; Interacting with Computers; Repairing and Maintaining Mechanical Equipment
Job Characteristics: Very Hot; Extremely Bright or Inadequate Lighting; Contaminants; Hazardous Conditions; Hazardous Equipment; Hazardous Situations; Standing; Using Hands on Objects, Tools, or Controls; Common Protective or Safety Attire; Specialized Protective or Safety Attire
GOE Group/s: 06.02.24 Production Work: Manual Work, Metal and Plastics; 06.04.10 Elemental Work: Industrial: Equipment Operation, Metal Processing; 06.04.24 Elemental Work: Industrial: Manual Work, Metal and Plastics; 06.04.32 Elemental Work: Industrial: Manual Work, Casting and Molding
CIP Program/s: 480599 Precision Metal Workers, Other
Related DOT Job/s: 502.664-014 STEEL POURER; 502.687-014 BUSHER; 514.584-010 INGOT HEADER; 514.684-010 CASTER; 514.684-014 LADLE POURER; 514.684-022 POURER, METAL; 518.664-010 MOLD MAKER; 700.687-042 MELTER

93944A MOLD MAKERS, HAND. OOH Title/s: Indirectly related to Tool and Die Makers

Construct or form molds from existing forms for use in casting objects. Constructs molds used for casting metal, clay, or plaster objects, using plaster, fiberglass, rubber, casting machine, patterns and flasks. Assembles hardened molds and seals joints. Places form around

model and separately immerses each half portion of model in plaster, wax, or other mold-making material. Covers portions of model with layers of modeling or casting material treated to harden when allowed to set or dry. Removes excess modeling or mold material, such as plaster, wax, or rubber, using straightedge. Smooths surfaces of mold, using scraping tool and sandpaper. Covers model or pattern of object from which mold is to be made with lubricant or parting agent to prevent mold from sticking to model. Bores holes or cuts grates and risers in mold, using power tools. Separates model or pattern from mold. Examines mold for accuracy. Allows mold to harden or dry in oven, and repeats process until mold is complete. Repairs cracks and broken edges of mold, using hand tools. Mixes modeling material, such as plaster powder and water, or mud, sand, and loam, to specified formula. Melts metal pieces using torch, and casts products, such as inlays and crowns, using centrifugal casting machine.
Yearly Earnings: $18,772
Education: Moderate-term O-J-T
Knowledge: None above average
Abilities: Selective Attention; Dynamic Flexibility; Gross Body Equilibrium; Hearing Sensitivity
Skills: None above average
General Work Activities: Handling and Moving Objects
Job Characteristics: Contaminants; Using Hands on Objects, Tools, or Controls; Making Repetitive Motions; Common Protective or Safety Attire; Specialized Protective or Safety Attire; Importance of Repeating Same Tasks
GOE Group/s: 05.05.11 Craft Technology: Scientific, Medical, & Technical Equip. Fabric. & Related; 06.02.30 Production Work: Manual Work, Stone, Glass, and Clay; 06.04.32 Elemental Work: Industrial: Manual Work, Casting and Molding
CIP Program/s: 489999 Precision Production Trades, Other; 510603 Dental Laboratory Technician
Related DOT Job/s: 518.484-010 PLASTER MOLDER II; 518.684-014 COREMAKER, PIPE; 575.684-038 MOLD MAKER, TERRA COTTA; 712.684-046 DENTURE-MODEL MAKER; 777.684-014 MOLD MAKER; 777.684-018 MOLD MAKER

93944D MOLDERS AND CASTERS. OOH Title/s: Handlers, Equipment Cleaners, Helpers, and Laborers; Metalworking and Plastics-Working Machine Operators; Painters and Paperhangers

Mold and cast, using hand tools or hand-held power tools, any of a wide variety of items. Fills mold with mixed material or applies material to mold to specified thickness. Molds parts or products using vibrator, handpress, or casting equipment, and taps or tilts mold to ensure uniformity. Operates and adjusts controls of heating equipment to melt material or to cure, dry, or bake filled molds according to specifications. Opens mold and removes finished products. Measures ingredients and mixes molding or casting material or sealing compound to prescribed consistency, according to formula. Assembles, inserts, and adjusts wires, tubes, cores, fittings, rods, or patterns into mold, using hand tools and depth gauge. Removes excess material and levels and smooths wet mold mixture. Loads or stacks filled molds in oven, drier, or curing box, or on storage racks or carts. Reads work order or examines part to determine part or section of product to be produced. Selects size and type of mold according to instructions. Installs and secures mold or mold parts together. Brushes or sprays surface of mold with parting agent, or inserts paper to ensure smoothness and to prevent sticking or seepage. Measures and cuts product to specified dimensions, using measuring and cutting instruments. Aligns and assembles parts to produce completed product, using gauges and hand tools. Inspects and tests parts or products for defects and to verify accuracy and adherence to standards. Fastens metal inserts—such as drainage tubes, bolts, or electrical connections—to product, using hand tools and power tools. Cleans, trims, smooths, and polishes products or parts. Cleans and lubricates mold and mold parts. Engraves or stamps identifying symbols, letters, or numbers on product.
Yearly Earnings: $18,772
Education: Moderate-term O-J-T
Knowledge: Production and Processing; Building and Construction
Abilities: None above average
Skills: Operation Monitoring; Operation and Control
General Work Activities: None above average
Job Characteristics: Using Hands on Objects, Tools, or Controls; Bending or Twisting the Body; Making Repetitive Motions; Importance of Repeating Same Tasks
GOE Group/s: 05.05.11 Craft Technology: Scientific, Medical, & Technical Equip. Fabric. & Related; 05.12.12 Elemental Work: Mechanical: Structural Work; 05.12.13 Elemental Work: Mechanical: Cutting and Finishing; 06.02.24 Production Work: Manual Work, Metal and Plastics; 06.02.29 Production Work: Manual Work, Rubber; 06.02.30 Production Work: Manual Work, Stone, Glass, and Clay; 06.02.32 Production Work: Manual Work, Assorted Materials; 06.04.10 Elemental Work: Industrial: Equipment Operation, Metal Processing; 06.04.17 Elemental Work: Industrial: Equipment Operation, Clay Processing; 06.04.19 Elemental Work: Industrial: Equipment Operation, Assorted Materials Processing; 06.04.24 Elemental Work: Industrial: Manual Work, Metal and Plastics; 06.04.28 Elemental Work: Industrial: Manual Work, Food Processing; 06.04.29 Elemental Work: Industrial: Manual Work, Rubber; 06.04.30 Elemental Work: Industrial: Manual Work, Stone, Glass, and Clay; 06.04.32 Elemental Work: Industrial: Manual Work, Casting and Molding; 06.04.34 Elemental Work: Industrial: Manual Work, Assorted Materials
CIP Program/s: 150607 Plastics Technologists and Technicians; 460499 Construction and Building Finishers and Managers, Other; 470101 Electrical and Electronics Equipment Installer and Repairer; 470105 Industrial Electronics Installer and Repairer; 470609 Aviation Systems and Avionics Maintenance Technologists and Technicians; 480501 Machinist/Machine Technologist; 489999 Precision Production Trades, Other; 500201 Crafts, Folk Art and Artisanry; 510603 Dental Laboratory Technician
Related DOT Job/s: 502.684-010 LEAD CASTER; 502.684-014 MILL HELPER; 502.684-022 NEEDLE LEADER; 556.484-010 SCAGLIOLA MECHANIC; 556.684-014 ENCAPSULATOR; 556.684-018 MOLD-FILLING OPERATOR; 556.684-026 RUBBER MOLDER; 556.684-030 LOADER-DEMOLDER; 556.687-022 MOLDER, TOILET PRODUCTS; 556.687-030 MOLD FILLER; 575.684-014 CASTER; 575.684-018 CASTER; 575.684-030 HANDLE MAKER; 575.684-034 LAUNDRY-TUB MAKER; 575.684-042 MOLDER, HAND; 575.684-046 TERRAZZO-TILE MAKER; 575.684-050 CULTURED-MARBLE-PRODUCTS MAKER; 579.684-010 CONCRETE-VAULT MAKER; 579.684-018 KILN-FURNITURE CASTER; 579.684-026 CASTER; 579.685-042 PRECAST MOLDER; 590.687-014 PLASTIC-JOINT MAKER; 712.684-034 PACKER, DENTURE; 719.381-018 BLOCK MAKER; 729.684-030 MOLD OPERATOR; 731.687-026 MOLD FILLER, PLASTIC DOLLS; 739.684-010 ARTIFICIAL-CANDY MAKER; 739.687-054 CANDLE MOLDER, HAND; 739.687-158 POURER; 752.684-026 CATHETER BUILDER; 753.584-010 MACHINE-MADE-SHOE UNIT WORKER; 753.687-030 MOLD FILLER AND DRAINER; 754.684-022 CASTER; 754.684-038 PLASTIC DUPLICATOR; 772.684-022 WATCH-CRYSTAL MOLDER; 774.684-026 PLASTER-DIE MAKER; 779.684-010 CEMENT FITTINGS MAKER; 779.684-014 CONCRETE-PIPE MAKER; 779.684-046 PLASTER MAKER; 779.684-050 PLASTIC MOLDER; 790.687-022 MOLD PRESSER; 844.681-010 CELL MAKER; 869.687-022 CONCRETE-FLOAT MAKER

93947B BAKERY AND CONFECTIONERY DECORATING WORKERS. OOH Title/s: Bakers, Manufacturing

Coat or decorate bakery or confectionery items. Applies coating, such as icing, frosting, or glaze, to baked goods, using brush, spatula, or other instrument. Sprinkles decorative materials, such as chocolate chips, shredded coconut, or chopped nuts, onto baked goods or candy. Applies decorative figures, such as lines, letters, or flowers, to candy or baked goods, using decorating bag. Fills molds with icing or chocolate to form decorative figures, such as flowers or bells. Dips candy centers, fruit, or nuts into coatings to coat, decorate, and identify product. Mixes or cooks ingredients to prepare coating or decorating material, such as chocolate, icing, or pastry creme, to specified consistency. Marks top surface of coated candies with identifying or decorative design.

Yearly Earnings: $17,420
Education: Moderate-term O-J-T
Knowledge: Fine Arts
Abilities: Wrist-Finger Speed; Visual Color Discrimination
Skills: None above average
General Work Activities: None above average
Job Characteristics: Using Hands on Objects, Tools, or Controls; Making Repetitive Motions; Importance of Repeating Same Tasks
GOE Group/s: 06.04.28 Elemental Work: Industrial: Manual Work, Food Processing
CIP Program/s: 120505 Kitchen Personnel/Cook and Assistant Training
Related DOT Job/s: 524.381-010 CAKE DECORATOR; 524.381-014 DECORATOR; 524.684-010 CANDY DIPPER, HAND; 524.684-014 DECORATOR; 524.684-018 ENROBING-MACHINE CORDER; 524.684-022 ICER, HAND

93947E HAND PAINTING, COATING, OR DECORATING WORKERS. OOH Title/s: Painting, Coating, and Decorating Workers, Hand; Visual Artists; ; Painters and Paperhangers; Bindery Workers

Paint, coat, or decorate, using hand tools or power tools, a wide variety of manufactured items. Applies coating, such as paint, ink, or lacquer, to protect or decorate workpiece surface, using spray gun, pen, or brush. Immerses workpiece into coating material for specified time. Positions and glues decorative pieces in cutout section, following pattern. Reads job order and inspects workpiece to determine work procedure and materials required. Conceals blemishes in workpiece, such as nicks and dents, using filler, such as putty. Rinses coated workpiece to remove excess coating material or to facilitate setting of finish coat on workpiece. Drains or wipes workpiece to remove excess coating material or to facilitate setting of finish coat on workpiece. Examines finished surface of workpiece to verify conformance to specifications, and retouches defective areas of surface. Cleans surface of workpiece in preparation for coating, using cleaning fluid, solvent, brushes, scraper, steam, sandpaper, or cloth. Cuts out sections in surface of material to be inlaid with decorative pieces, using pattern and knife or scissors. Places coated workpiece in oven or dryer for specified time to dry or harden finish. Melts or heats coating material to specified temperature. Selects and mixes ingredients to prepare coating substance, according to specifications, using paddle or mechanical mixer. Cleans and maintains tools and equipment, using solvent, brushes, and rags.

Yearly Earnings: $19,500
Education: Short-term O-J-T
Knowledge: None above average
Abilities: Wrist-Finger Speed; Visual Color Discrimination
Skills: None above average
General Work Activities: None above average
Job Characteristics: Contaminants; Using Hands on Objects, Tools, or Controls; Making Repetitive Motions; Common Protective or Safety Attire
GOE Group/s: 01.06.03 Craft Arts: Hand Lettering, Painting and Decorating; 05.10.07 Crafts: Painting, Dyeing, and Coating; 05.12.14 Elemental Work: Mechanical: Painting, Caulking, and Coating; 06.02.21 Production Work: Coating and Plating; 06.02.24 Production Work: Manual Work, Metal and Plastics; 06.02.30 Production Work: Manual Work, Stone, Glass, and Clay; 06.02.32 Production Work: Manual Work, Assorted Materials; 06.03.02 Quality Control: Inspecting, Grading, Sorting, Weighing, and Recording; 06.04.13 Elemental Work: Industrial: Equipment Operation, Rubber, Plastics, Glass Processing; 06.04.24 Elemental Work: Industrial: Manual Work, Metal and Plastics; 06.04.25 Elemental Work: Industrial: Manual Work, Wood; 06.04.27 Elemental Work: Industrial: Manual Work, Textile, Fabric and Leather; 06.04.30 Elemental Work: Industrial: Manual Work, Stone, Glass, and Clay; 06.04.33 Elemental Work: Industrial: Manual Work, Brushing, Spraying, and Coating; 06.04.34 Elemental Work: Industrial: Manual Work, Assorted Materials; 06.04.37 Elemental Work: Industrial: Manual Work, Stamping, Marking, Labeling, and Ticketing
CIP Program/s: 100103 Photographic Technologists and Technicians; 460408 Painter and Wall Coverer; 470408 Watch, Clock and Jewelry Repairer; 470603 Auto/Automotive Body Repairer; 480503 Machine Shop Assistant; 500402 Graphic Design, Commercial Art and Illustration; 500701 Art, General; 500711 Ceramics Arts and Ceramics; 500713 Metal and Jewelry Arts; 510603 Dental Laboratory Technician
Related DOT Job/s: 364.381-010 PAINTER, RUG TOUCH-UP; 500.684-022 SILVER SPRAY WORKER; 505.684-010 ELECTROLESS PLATER; 505.684-014 METAL SPRAYER, PRODUCTION; 509.684-010 ENAMELER; 554.384-010 DYER; 554.684-010 CAUSTIC OPERATOR; 562.687-010 DYER; 562.687-014 RESIN COATER; 574.484-010 OPTICAL-GLASS SILVERER; 574.684-010 GROUND LAYER; 574.684-014 SILVERER; 584.684-010 LATEXER; 584.687-010 LEATHER COATER; 584.687-014 SPRAYER, HAND; 589.687-034 STAINER; 589.687-038 STIFFENER; 599.682-010 PAINTER, ELECTROSTATIC; 599.687-010 BALLOON DIPPER; 700.684-054 OXIDIZER; 700.687-014 BOILER-OUT; 709.684-022 BABBITTER; 712.684-030 OPAQUER; 713.687-010 CLIP COATER; 715.584-010 DIAL REFINISHER; 715.684-138 LACQUERER; 715.687-026 DIPPER, CLOCK AND WATCH HANDS; 715.687-086 MASKER; 715.687-098 PAINTER, CLOCK AND WATCH HANDS; 721.687-010 CLEANER AND PREPARER; 727.687-034 BATTERY-CONTAINER-FINISHING HAND; 729.684-018 DIAL MARKER; 732.687-062 PAINTER AND GRADER, CORK; 733.687-038 DIPPER; 735.687-018 PAINTER; 737.687-130 SHELLACKER; 739.687-170 SMOKING-PIPE LINER; 739.687-174 STAINER; 739.687-178 STARCHER; 740.484-010 STRIPER, HAND; 740.684-010 CHARGER I; 740.684-014 DECORATOR; 740.684-018 ENAMELER; 740.684-022 PAINTER, BRUSH; 740.684-026 TOUCH-UP PAINTER, HAND; 740.687-010 BUTTON SPINDLER; 740.687-018 PAINTER, EMBOSSED OR IMPRESSED LETTERING; 740.687-022 PAINTER, PANEL EDGE; 741.684-010 ARTIST, MANNEQUIN COLORING; 741.684-014 FOAM-GUN OPERATOR; 741.684-018 PAINTER, AIRBRUSH; 741.684-022 PAINTER, MIRROR; 741.684-026 PAINTER, SPRAY I; 741.684-030 PORCELAIN-ENAMEL REPAIRER; 741.687-018 PAINTER, SPRAY II; 741.687-022 STRIPER, SPRAY GUN; 742.684-010 RUBBER; 742.684-014 STAINER; 742.687-010 WIPER; 749.684-010 DECAL APPLIER; 749.684-014 DECORATOR; 749.684-018 DECORATOR, LIGHTING FIXTURES; 749.684-022 EDGE STAINER II; 749.684-026 FINISHER; 749.684-030 FRAME TRIMMER I; 749.684-034 LACQUERER; 749.684-038 PAINTER, TOUCH-UP; 749.684-046 STOVE REFINISHER; 749.684-054 WALL-COVERING TEXTURER; 749.687-010 DIPPER AND DRIER; 749.687-014 KEG VARNISHER; 749.687-022 PAINTER, SKI EDGE; 763.687-022

DRAWER WAXER; 764.687-026 BARREL LINER; 773.684-010 COLORER; 773.684-014 PASTER; 774.684-014 DIPPER; 779.687-018 GLASS-BULB SILVERER; 781.687-054 RUG-BACKING STENCILER; 782.684-054 PINNER; 784.687-014 CARROTER; 784.687-058 POWDERER; 788.684-066 INKER; 788.687-078 LAST CHALKER; 788.687-098 PAINTER, BOTTOM; 788.687-166 WHITE-SHOE RAGGER; 840.684-010 GLASS TINTER; 842.684-010 DRY-WALL SPRAYER; 843.684-014 UNDERCOATER; 920.687-178 STENCILER; 970.681-014 COLORER; 971.684-010 BLOCKER II; 971.684-014 STAGER; 977.684-014 INLAYER

93951A PANTOGRAPH ENGRAVERS. OOH Title/s: Printing Occupations

Affix identifying information onto a variety of materials and products, using engraving machines or equipment. Starts machine and guides stylus over template, causing cutting tool to simultaneously duplicate design or letters on workpiece. Adjusts depth and size of cut by adjusting height of work table or by adjusting gauge on machine arms. Sets stylus at beginning of pattern. Selects and inserts letter or design template beneath stylus attached to machine cutting tool or router, according to work order. Positions and secures workpiece—such as nameplate, stamp, seal, badge, trophy, or bowling ball—in holding fixture, using measuring instruments. Sets reduction scale to obtain required reproduction ratio on workpiece. Inserts cutting tool or bit into machine and secures with wrench. Observes action of cutting tool through microscope, and adjusts movement of stylus to ensure accurate reproduction. Brushes acid over designated engraving to darken or highlight inscription. Verifies conformance to specifications, using micrometers and calipers. Examines engraving for quality of cut, burrs, rough spots, and irregular or incomplete engraving. Sharpens cutting tools on cutter grinder.

Yearly Earnings: $18,044

Education: Short-term O-J-T

Knowledge: None above average

Abilities: Arm-Hand Steadiness; Manual Dexterity; Control Precision; Rate Control; Wrist-Finger Speed; Near Vision; Depth Perception

Skills: None above average

General Work Activities: Controlling Machines and Processes

Job Characteristics: Hazardous Equipment; Hazardous Situations; Using Hands on Objects, Tools, or Controls; Degree of Automation; Pace Determined by Speed of Equipment

GOE Group/s: 05.10.05 Crafts: Reproduction; 06.04.24 Elemental Work: Industrial: Manual Work, Metal and Plastics

CIP Program/s: 500402 Graphic Design, Commercial Art and Illustration

Related DOT Job/s: 704.382-010 ENGRAVER, PANTOGRAPH I; 704.582-010 ENGRAVER, MACHINE II; 704.682-010 ENGRAVER, MACHINE I; 704.682-014 ENGRAVER, PANTOGRAPH II; 732.584-010 BOWLING-BALL ENGRAVER

93951B ETCHERS, HAND. OOH Title/s: Printing Occupations; Visual Artists

Etch patterns, designs, lettering, or figures onto a variety of materials and products. Exposes workpiece to acid to develop etch pattern, such as designs, lettering, or figures. Fills etched characters with opaque paste to improve readability. Prepares workpiece for etching by cutting, sanding, cleaning, or treating with wax, acid resist, lime, etching powder, or light-sensitive enamel. Transfers image to workpiece, using contact printer, pantograph stylus, silkscreen printing device, or stamp pad. Neutralizes workpiece to remove acid, wax, or enamel, using water or solvents. Measures and marks workpiece, such as plastic, fiberglass, epoxy board, metal, or glass, using measuring and calibrating equipment. Prepares etching solution according to formula. Inspects etched work for uniformity, using calibrated microscope and gauge. Positions and secures workpiece to be etched on set-up board. Compares workpiece design—such as lettering, trademark, numerals, or lines—to sample to verify development of pattern. Reduces artwork, using reduction camera.

Yearly Earnings: $18,044

Education: Short-term O-J-T

Knowledge: Production and Processing; Design; Fine Arts

Abilities: Arm-Hand Steadiness; Manual Dexterity; Finger Dexterity

Skills: None above average

General Work Activities: None above average

Job Characteristics: Contaminants; Hazardous Conditions; Hazardous Situations; Using Hands on Objects, Tools, or Controls

GOE Group/s: 01.06.01 Craft Arts: Graphics Arts and Related Crafts; 06.02.30 Production Work: Manual Work, Stone, Glass, and Clay; 06.02.31 Production Work: Manual Work, Laying Out and Marking; 06.02.32 Production Work: Manual Work, Assorted Materials; 06.04.24 Elemental Work: Industrial: Manual Work, Metal and Plastics

CIP Program/s: 470101 Electrical and Electronics Equipment Installer and Repairer; 470105 Industrial Electronics Installer and Repairer; 480201 Graphic and Printing Equipment Operator, General; 480206 Lithographer and Platemaker; 511006 Optometric/Ophthalmic Laboratory Technician; 511802 Optical Technician/Assistant

Related DOT Job/s: 590.684-018 ETCHED-CIRCUIT PROCESSOR; 704.684-010 ETCHER; 704.684-014 SILK-SCREEN ETCHER; 704.687-014 ETCHER, HAND; 716.681-022 OPTICAL-GLASS ETCHER; 775.584-010 GLASS CALIBRATOR

93951C PRINTERS, HAND. OOH Title/s: Printing Occupations

Print patterns, designs, and lettering by hand onto a variety of materials and products. Applies ink, paint, color paste, metallic foil, or carbon tissue to workpiece or printing mechanism. Reads blueprints, work orders, or specifications to determine design or letters to be imprinted and location of imprint on workpiece. Lays out and marks workpiece, using measuring and drawing equipment. Prepares surface of workpiece, using solvents, pumice, photo resist solution, or lacquer. Aligns, positions, and secures workpiece in holding fixture or on work table. Sets guides and positions design template, transfer, screen, stamp, type bar, frame, or heated imprint bar over workpiece in printing mechanism. Operates printing equipment such as screen printer, silk screen press, stamp, or heat imprints, to imprint design on workpiece. Inspects workpiece for defects and uniformity of depth, and to ensure quality of printing. Mixes chemicals, inks, or paints, according to standard formula. Cleans equipment, using spatula, water, or solvent. Fabricates silk screen stencils or prepares photomasks for reticle-making process, using photographic equipment. Affixes gummed labels or decals to workpiece, using automatic equipment or roller.

Yearly Earnings: $18,044

Education: Short-term O-J-T

Knowledge: Production and Processing; Fine Arts

Abilities: Arm-Hand Steadiness; Finger Dexterity; Rate Control; Visual Color Discrimination

Skills: None above average

General Work Activities: Controlling Machines and Processes

Job Characteristics: Using Hands on Objects, Tools, or Controls; Making Repetitive Motions

GOE Group/s: 05.05.11 Craft Technology: Scientific, Medical, & Technical Equip. Fabric. & Related; 05.10.05 Crafts: Reproduction; 06.01.04 Production Technology: Precision Hand Work; 06.02.27 Production Work: Manual Work, Textile, Fabric and Leather; 06.02.31 Production Work: Manual Work, Laying Out and Marking; 06.04.27 Elemental Work: Industrial: Manual Work, Textile, Fabric and Leather; 06.04.34 Elemental Work: Industrial: Manual Work, Assorted Materials; 06.04.37 Elemental Work: Industrial: Manual Work, Stamping, Marking, Labeling, and Ticketing

CIP Program/s: 480299 Graphic and Printing Equipment Operators, Other; 511802 Optical Technician/Assistant
Related DOT Job/s: 709.684-054 MOLD STAMPER; 710.684-018 DIAL MAKER; 713.684-022 EMBOSSER; 715.684-190 TRANSFERRER; 788.684-030 BOTTOM WHEELER; 920.687-126 MARKER II; 976.684-034 CONTACT PRINTER, PHOTORESIST; 979.684-010 CARBON PRINTER; 979.684-030 SCREEN PRINTER; 979.684-034 SCREEN PRINTER

93951D ENGRAVERS, HAND. OOH Title/s: Printing Occupations; Visual Artists

Engrave designs and identifying information onto rollers or plates used in printing. Cuts grooves of specified depth and uniformity into printing roller, following lines of design impression. Cuts around drawn pattern leaving raised design or letters, using cutting tools. Presses sketch on copper printing roller to produce impression of design. Traces pattern of design and letters in reverse on linoleum or on two- or three-ply rubber, using ruler, pencil, drawing instruments, or cutting tools. Cuts strip of engraving gum (two- or three-ply rubber, cemented to cloth backing), using knife. Prepares additional rubber plates for jobs requiring colors by omitting different portions of design or lettering on each plate. Refers to sketch to ensure that lines of only one printing color are engraved into each roller. Glues rubber or linoleum pattern to wood block. Punches holes in plate to fasten plate to press, using hand tools. Inspects designs for defective engraving and re-engraves to meet specifications.
Yearly Earnings: $18,044
Education: Short-term O-J-T
Knowledge: Production and Processing; Design; Fine Arts
Abilities: Arm-Hand Steadiness; Manual Dexterity; Finger Dexterity; Visual Color Discrimination; Depth Perception
Skills: None above average
General Work Activities: None above average
Job Characteristics: Using Hands on Objects, Tools, or Controls; Making Repetitive Motions; Importance of Being Exact or Accurate
GOE Group/s: 01.06.01 Craft Arts: Graphics Arts and Related Crafts
CIP Program/s: 500402 Graphic Design, Commercial Art and Illustration
Related DOT Job/s: 979.581-010 ENGRAVER, RUBBER; 979.681-018 ROLLER ENGRAVER, HAND; 979.684-014 ENGRAVER II

93953 GRINDING AND POLISHING WORKERS, HAND. OOH Title/s: Grinders and Polishers, Hand

Grind and polish, using hand tools or hand-held power tools, a wide variety of metal, stone, clay, plastic, and glass objects or parts. Include grinders and chippers, polishers and buffers, metal sanders and finishers, glass grinders and polishers, and plastic buffers and finishers. Exclude precision-level workers. Grinds, sands, cleans, or polishes objects or parts, using hand tools or equipment. Moves controls to adjust, start, or stop equipment during grinding and polishing process. Trims, scrapes or deburrs objects or parts, using hand tools or equipment. Selects, loads, and adjusts workpiece or abrasive parts onto equipment or work table, using hand tools. Observes and inspects equipment, objects, or parts, to ensure specifications are met. Measures and marks equipment, objects, or parts to ensure grinding and polishing standards are met. Applies solutions and chemicals to equipment, objects, or parts, using hand tools. Removes workpiece from equipment or work table, using hand tools. Repairs and maintains equipment, objects, or parts, using hand tools. Sharpens abrasive grinding tools, using machines and hand tools. Transfers equipment, objects, or parts, to specified work areas, using moving devices. Records product and processing data on specified forms.
Yearly Earnings: $19,500
Education: Short-term O-J-T
Knowledge: Production and Processing; Chemistry
Abilities: Gross Body Equilibrium
Skills: None above average
General Work Activities: Handling and Moving Objects; Repairing and Maintaining Mechanical Equipment
Job Characteristics: Sounds, Noise Levels are Distracting, etc.; Contaminants; Whole Body Vibration; Hazardous Equipment; Making Repetitive Motions; Common Protective or Safety Attire; Importance of Repeating Same Tasks; Pace Determined by Speed of Equipment
GOE Group/s: 05.05.07 Craft Technology: Machining; 05.10.01 Crafts: Structural; 05.12.18 Elemental Work: Mechanical: Cleaning and Maintenance; 06.02.24 Production Work: Manual Work, Metal and Plastics; 06.02.25 Production Work: Manual Work, Wood; 06.02.30 Production Work: Manual Work, Stone, Glass, and Clay; 06.04.08 Elemental Work: Industrial: Machine Work, Stone, Glass, and Clay; 06.04.24 Elemental Work: Industrial: Manual Work, Metal and Plastics; 06.04.25 Elemental Work: Industrial: Manual Work, Wood; 06.04.30 Elemental Work: Industrial: Manual Work, Stone, Glass, and Clay; 06.04.33 Elemental Work: Industrial: Manual Work, Brushing, Spraying, and Coating; 06.04.34 Elemental Work: Industrial: Manual Work, Assorted Materials
CIP Program/s: 460101 Mason and Tile Setter; 470402 Gunsmith; 470404 Musical Instrument Repairer; 470408 Watch, Clock and Jewelry Repairer; 470603 Auto/Automotive Body Repairer; 480503 Machine Shop Assistant; 480507 Tool and Die Maker/Technologist; 480508 Welder/Welding Technologist; 480599 Precision Metal Workers, Other; 480701 Woodworkers, General; 480702 Furniture Designer and Maker; 480799 Woodworkers, Other
Related DOT Job/s: 519.684-018 MOLD DRESSER; 700.684-034 FILER; 700.687-058 POLISHER; 703.687-022 STEEL-BARREL REAMER; 705.384-010 SCRAPER, HAND; 705.484-010 FILER, HAND, TOOL; 705.484-014 FINAL FINISHER, FORGING DIES; 705.684-022 GREASE BUFFER; 705.684-026 GRINDER I; 705.684-030 GRINDER-CHIPPER I; 705.684-034 METAL FINISHER; 705.684-038 MOLD FINISHER; 705.684-046 NEEDLE POLISHER; 705.684-050 NIB FINISHER; 705.684-054 PIPE BUFFER; 705.684-062 POLISHER AND BUFFER II; 705.687-014 LABORER, GRINDING AND POLISHING; 705.687-018 METAL SANDER AND FINISHER; 706.684-098 VALVE GRINDER; 709.381-026 MOLD STAMPER AND REPAIRER; 709.684-058 REAMER, HAND; 713.687-034 POLISHER, IMPLANT; 715.584-018 STONER, HAND; 715.684-038 BURNISHER, BALANCE WHEEL ARM; 715.684-042 BURRER; 715.684-106 HAND FILER, BALANCE WHEEL; 715.684-170 POLISHER, DIAL; 715.687-110 REAMER, CENTER HOLE; 730.684-066 SANDER-AND-BUFFER; 732.584-014 FINISHER; 732.687-074 SPIN-TABLE OPERATOR; 734.687-054 GRINDER, HAND; 735.684-014 STONER; 736.684-018 BARREL FINISHER; 736.684-022 BARREL REPAIRER; 739.684-026 BUFFER; 739.684-074 FRAME REPAIRER; 752.684-022 BUFFER; 754.684-018 BIT SHAVER; 754.684-030 FINISHER, HAND; 761.684-010 GOLF-CLUB FACER; 761.684-038 SHAPER, HAND; 761.684-046 STOCK SHAPER; 761.687-010 SANDER, HAND; 770.682-010 JEWEL-BEARING BROACHER; 770.682-022 JEWEL-BEARING TURNER; 770.684-010 JEWEL GRINDER II; 770.684-014 JEWEL-HOLE CORNERER; 770.684-018 ROUGH OPENER, JEWEL HOLE; 770.685-022 JEWEL-BEARING POLISHER; 771.484-010 BEVELER; 774.687-022 WARE CLEANER; 775.664-010 STONE POLISHER, HAND; 775.684-014 EDGER, HAND; 775.684-038 GLASS POLISHER; 775.684-054 PATCH SANDER; 775.687-022 GOLD BURNISHER; 779.684-018 FETTLER; 779.684-030 INSPECTOR-REPAIRER, SANDSTONE; 788.687-038 DRESSER; 809.684-022 FINISHER, FIBERGLASS BOAT PARTS; 809.684-026 GRINDER-CHIPPER II; 819.664-010 PLATE CONDITIONER; 849.684-010 BOAT BUFFER, PLASTIC

93956 ASSEMBLERS AND FABRICATORS—EXCEPT MACHINE, ELECTRICAL, ELECTRONIC, AND PRECISION. OOH Title/s: Assemblers; Production Occupations; ; Handlers, Equipment Cleaners, Helpers, and Laborers; Automotive Mechanics; Bindery WorkersAssemblers *Assemble or fit together parts to form complete units or subassemblies at a bench or conveyor line, or on the floor. Work may involve the use of hand tools, power tools, and special equipment in order to carry out fitting and assembly operations. Include assemblers whose duties are of a nonprecision nature. Exclude electrical, electronic, machine, and precision assemblers, and workers who perform specialized operations exclusively as part of assembly operations, such as riveting, welding, soldering, machining, or sawing.* Bolts, clips, nails, rivets, screws, welds, or otherwise fastens component parts of assembly together, using hand tools, power tools, or bench machines. Sews, staples, or tacks material together, using sewing machine, staple gun, or hand tools. Positions, fits, or aligns parts on workbench, floor, or machine, following blueprints, diagrams, guides, holes, reference marks, or work orders. Drills, taps, or reams holes to prepare parts for assembly, using arbor or drill press or other bench-mounted drills. Files, grinds, planes, sands, or buffs parts to remove burrs, alter shape, improve fit, or smooth finish, using hand tools or power tools. Applies adhesive, bonding agent, sealant, or paint to surface of material by brushing, spraying, dipping, or rolling. Bends, crimps, or presses materials to specified shape or curvature, using hand tools, bending machine, or pressing machine. Holds parts during assembly, using hands, clamps, pneumatic screw presses, or other work aids. Pours, stuffs, or otherwise fills products or containers with specified amount of material. Measures and marks reference lines and points on parts, according to specifications, using template, rule, or other marking device. Cuts materials, such as fabric, metal, paper, or wood, into specified dimensions or shapes, using cutting machine, scissors, or knife. Reads process charts, work orders, blueprints, or other specifications to determine assembly sequence, machine and tooling requirements, measurements, and tolerances. Inspects, tests, and verifies accuracy of assembled article for conformance to standards, using measuring or testing equipment or by visual examination. Adjusts, repairs, or replaces defective product parts, using hand tools. Cleans dust, dirt, oil, and other foreign matter from material or machine surfaces, using cleaning solution, rags, or air hose. Records production data on paper or in computer. Lifts, loads, sorts, and moves materials, supplies, and finished products between storage and work areas, using pushcart, hoist, or dolly. Packages product in containers for shipment or ties into bundles. Stamps, labels, or otherwise marks product or packages with identifying data.
Yearly Earnings: $18,044
Education: Short-term O-J-T
Knowledge: Production and Processing; Building and Construction
Abilities: Visualization; Arm-Hand Steadiness; Manual Dexterity; Finger Dexterity; Control Precision; Multilimb Coordination; Wrist-Finger Speed; Speed of Limb Movement
Skills: None above average
General Work Activities: None above average
Job Characteristics: Hazardous Equipment; Hazardous Situations; Using Hands on Objects, Tools, or Controls; Making Repetitive Motions; Importance of Repeating Same Tasks
GOE Group/s: 01.06.02 Craft Arts: Arts and Crafts; 05.05.06 Craft Technology: Metal Fabrication and Repair; 05.05.15 Craft Technology: Custom Sewing, Tailoring, and Upholstering; 05.10.01 Crafts: Structural; 05.10.03 Crafts: Electrical-Electronic; 05.12.12 Elemental Work: Mechanical: Structural Work; 05.12.15 Elemental Work: Mechanical: Mechanical Work; 05.12.16 Elemental Work: Mechanical: Electrical Work; 06.01.04 Production Technology: Precision Hand Work; 06.02.20 Production Work: Machine Assembling; 06.02.22 Production Work: Manual Work, Assembly Large Parts; 06.02.23 Production Work: Manual Work, Assembly Small Parts; 06.02.24 Production Work: Manual Work, Metal and Plastics; 06.02.25 Production Work: Manual Work, Wood; 06.02.26 Production Work: Manual Work, Paper; 06.02.27 Production Work: Manual Work, Textile, Fabric and Leather; 06.02.29 Production Work: Manual Work, Rubber; 06.02.30 Production Work: Manual Work, Stone, Glass, and Clay; 06.02.31 Production Work: Manual Work, Laying Out and Marking; 06.02.32 Production Work: Manual Work, Assorted Materials; 06.03.02 Quality Control: Inspecting, Grading, Sorting, Weighing, and Recording; 06.04.02 Elemental Work: Industrial: Machine Work, Metal and Plastics; 06.04.05 Elemental Work: Industrial: Machine Work, Fabric and Leather; 06.04.09 Elemental Work: Industrial: Machine Work, Assorted Materials; 06.04.20 Elemental Work: Industrial: Machine Assembling; 06.04.22 Elemental Work: Industrial: Manual Work, Assembly Large Parts; 06.04.23 Elemental Work: Industrial: Manual Work, Assembly Small Parts; 06.04.24 Elemental Work: Industrial: Manual Work, Metal and Plastics; 06.04.25 Elemental Work: Industrial: Manual Work, Wood; 06.04.26 Elemental Work: Industrial: Manual Work, Paper; 06.04.27 Elemental Work: Industrial: Manual Work, Textile, Fabric and Leather; 06.04.29 Elemental Work: Industrial: Manual Work, Rubber; 06.04.30 Elemental Work: Industrial: Manual Work, Stone, Glass, and Clay; 06.04.31 Elemental Work: Industrial: Manual Work, Welding and Flame Cutting; 06.04.32 Elemental Work: Industrial: Manual Work, Casting and Molding; 06.04.33 Elemental Work: Industrial: Manual Work, Brushing, Spraying, and Coating; 06.04.34 Elemental Work: Industrial: Manual Work, Assorted Materials
CIP Program/s: 150607 Plastics Technologists and Technicians; 200301 Clothing, Apparel and Textile Workers and Managers, General; 200303 Commercial Garment and Apparel Worker; 200501 Home Furnishings and Equipment Installers and Consultants, General; 200502 Window Treatment Maker and Installer; 460201 Carpenter; 460401 Building/Property Maintenance and Management; 469999 Construction Trades, Other; 470101 Electrical and Electronics Equipment Installer and Repairer; 470105 Industrial Electronics Installer and Repairer; 470106 Major Appliance Installer and Repairer; 470401 Instrument Calibration and Repairer; 470402 Gunsmith; 470403 Locksmith and Safe Repairer; 470404 Musical Instrument Repairer; 470408 Watch, Clock and Jewelry Repairer; 470499 Miscellaneous Mechanics and Repairers, Other; 470603 Auto/Automotive Body Repairer; 470607 Aircraft Mechanic/Technician, Airframe; 470610 Bicycle Mechanic and Repairer; 470611 Motorcycle Mechanic and Repairer; 480299 Graphic and Printing Equipment Operators, Other; 480303 Upholsterer; 480304 Shoe, Boot and Leather Repairer; 480399 Leatherworkers and Upholsterers, Other; 480501 Machinist/Machine Technologist; 480503 Machine Shop Assistant; 480701 Woodworkers, General; 480702 Furniture Designer and Maker; 480703 Cabinet Maker and Millworker; 490306 Marine Maintenance and Repair; 500201 Crafts, Folk Art and Artisanry; 500701 Art, General; 500711 Ceramics Arts and Ceramics; 510603 Dental Laboratory Technician; 511006 Optometric/Ophthalmic Laboratory Technician
Related DOT Job/s: 553.684-010 HEAT WELDER, PLASTICS; 585.687-022 PATCHER; 669.364-010 INSPECTOR, ASSEMBLY; 669.682-014 BARREL ASSEMBLER; 700.684-014 ASSEMBLER; 700.684-022 CHAIN MAKER, MACHINE; 700.684-030 EARRING MAKER; 700.684-042 HOLLOW-HANDLE-KNIFE ASSEMBLER; 700.684-070 SILVERWARE ASSEMBLER; 700.684-082 WATCH-BAND ASSEMBLER; 700.687-010 BENCH WORKER, HOLLOW HANDLE; 700.687-026 CHARGER II; 701.684-018 LEVEL-VIAL SETTER; 701.687-010 ASSEMBLER; 703.684-014 CUPBOARD BUILDER; 706.484-010 DRAPERY-ROD ASSEMBLER; 706.684-018 ASSEMBLER, PRODUCT; 706.684-022 ASSEMBLER, SMALL PRODUCTS I; 706.684-030 ATOMIZER ASSEMBLER; 706.684-

034 BAR AND FILLER ASSEMBLER; 706.684-042 BENCH ASSEMBLER; 706.684-050 DRAWER UPFITTER; 706.684-054 FITTER II; 706.684-058 HYDRAULIC-CHAIR ASSEMBLER; 706.684-070 LOCK ASSEMBLER; 706.684-074 LOCK ASSEMBLER; 706.684-078 LOCK INSTALLER; 706.684-082 METAL-BED ASSEMBLER; 706.684-086 PLUMBING-HARDWARE ASSEMBLER; 706.684-090 SPRING ASSEMBLER; 706.684-102 VENDING-MACHINE ASSEMBLER; 706.684-106 WHEEL LACER AND TRUER; 706.687-010 ASSEMBLER, PRODUCTION; 706.687-030 PUSH-CONNECTOR ASSEMBLER; 709.484-010 SILK-SCREEN-FRAME ASSEMBLER; 709.667-010 FABRIC STRETCHER; 709.684-014 ASSEMBLER, METAL FURNITURE; 709.684-026 BIRD-CAGE ASSEMBLER; 709.684-030 CAGE MAKER; 709.684-038 CLIP-BOLTER AND WRAPPER; 709.684-066 RIVETER, HAND; 709.684-078 SPRING FITTER; 709.684-102 WIRE-ROPE-SLING MAKER; 710.584-010 SCROLL ASSEMBLER; 710.684-010 AGATE SETTER; 710.684-038 SEALER; 710.684-042 BELLOWS ASSEMBLER; 710.684-046 INSTRUMENT ASSEMBLER; 711.684-014 CEMENTER; 712.134-010 SUPERVISOR, ARTIFICIAL BREAST FABRICATION; 712.684-010 ASSEMBLER, SURGICAL GARMENT; 712.684-014 BITE-BLOCK MAKER; 712.684-022 GAS-MASK ASSEMBLER; 712.684-042 FABRICATOR, ARTIFICIAL BREAST; 712.684-054 SURGICAL-FORCEPS FABRICATOR; 712.687-010 ASSEMBLER, PLASTIC HOSPITAL PRODUCTS; 713.384-010 ASSEMBLER, GOLD FRAME; 713.684-010 ASSEMBLER, CLIP-ON SUNGLASSES; 713.684-014 ASSEMBLER, MOLDED FRAMES; 713.684-018 BENCH WORKER; 713.684-034 MULTIFOCAL-LENS ASSEMBLER; 713.687-018 FINAL ASSEMBLER; 713.687-026 LENS INSERTER; 713.687-042 SUNGLASS-CLIP ATTACHER; 714.684-010 ASSEMBLER, PRODUCTION LINE; 714.684-014 BELLOWS MAKER; 715.384-010 BALANCE ASSEMBLER; 715.684-014 ASSEMBLER, MOVEMENT; 715.684-022 BALANCE-BRIDGE ASSEMBLER; 715.684-046 CANNON-PINION ADJUSTER; 715.684-050 CAP-JEWEL PLATE ASSEMBLER; 715.684-054 CASER; 715.684-058 CLOCK ASSEMBLER; 715.684-066 COLLETER; 715.684-070 CROWN ATTACHER; 715.684-074 CROWN-WHEEL ASSEMBLER; 715.684-082 DIAL-SCREW ASSEMBLER; 715.684-086 DIALER; 715.684-098 FINER; 715.684-110 HANDS ASSEMBLER; 715.684-130 JEWEL INSERTER; 715.684-134 JEWEL STAKER; 715.684-142 MECHANISM ASSEMBLER; 715.684-150 OVERCOILER; 715.684-154 PALLET ASSEMBLER; 715.684-166 PIN INSERTER, REGULATOR; 715.684-174 PUT-IN-BEAT ADJUSTER; 715.684-178 SET-STAFF FITTER; 715.684-182 STAKER; 715.684-186 STUDDER, HAIRSPRING; 715.685-038 MAINSPRING WINDER AND OILER; 715.687-010 BAND ATTACHER; 715.687-014 BARREL-CAP SETTER; 715.687-018 CRYSTAL ATTACHER; 715.687-114 ROTOR ASSEMBLER; 715.687-118 SET-KEY DRIVER; 722.687-010 SWITCHBOX ASSEMBLER I; 723.684-018 ASSEMBLER II; 723.687-010 PATCHER; 730.384-010 ASSEMBLER, PIANO; 730.684-010 ASSEMBLER, MUSICAL INSTRUMENTS; 730.684-018 BELLY BUILDER; 730.684-030 CONSOLE ASSEMBLER; 730.684-042 KEYBOARD-ACTION ASSEMBLER; 730.684-046 MANUAL WINDER; 730.684-050 MUSICAL-STRING MAKER; 730.684-054 PIANO STRINGER; 730.684-058 PREASSEMBLER AND INSPECTOR; 730.684-062 RACKER, OCTAVE BOARD; 730.684-078 SLIDING-JOINT MAKER; 730.684-082 STOPBOARD ASSEMBLER; 730.684-090 TONE CABINET ASSEMBLER; 730.685-014 MOUTHPIECE MAKER;

731.684-010 COIN-MACHINE ASSEMBLER; 731.684-018 TOY ASSEMBLER; 731.687-010 ASSEMBLER; 731.687-030 PUZZLE ASSEMBLER; 731.687-034 TOY ASSEMBLER; 732.384-010 ASSEMBLER, BILLIARD-TABLE; 732.684-010 ARROWSMITH; 732.684-014 ASSEMBLER; 732.684-018 ASSEMBLER, LIQUID CENTER; 732.684-022 ASSEMBLER, PING-PONG TABLE; 732.684-026 BALL ASSEMBLER; 732.684-038 BOW MAKER, PRODUCTION; 732.684-042 BOW-STRING MAKER; 732.684-046 CELLULOID TRIMMER; 732.684-054 FISH-STRINGER ASSEMBLER; 732.684-058 FISHING-LURE ASSEMBLER; 732.684-062 FISHING-REEL ASSEMBLER; 732.684-066 FISHING-ROD ASSEMBLER; 732.684-070 FISHING-ROD MARKER; 732.684-074 FLY TIER; 732.684-078 GOLF-CLUB ASSEMBLER; 732.684-082 GRIP WRAPPER; 732.684-086 GUIDE WINDER; 732.684-094 RACKET STRINGER; 732.684-098 ROLLER-SKATE ASSEMBLER; 732.684-106 SHAPER, BASEBALL GLOVE; 732.684-110 SKI BASE TRIMMER; 732.684-114 SKI MOLDER; 732.684-126 SURFBOARD MAKER; 732.685-018 FIXING-MACHINE OPERATOR; 732.687-010 ADHESIVE PRIMER; 732.687-014 ASSEMBLER, FISHING FLOATS; 732.687-018 BASE FILLER; 732.687-022 CASTING-PLUG ASSEMBLER; 732.687-026 GOLF-CLUB WEIGHTER; 732.687-034 LACER;

732.687-038 LEADER TIER; 732.687-042 LINING INSERTER; 732.687-050 MOLD STRIPPER; 732.687-058 MOLDER, WAX BALL; 733.684-010 PAINT-BRUSH MAKER; 733.684-018 STAMP MOUNTER; 733.685-010 ASSEMBLER; 733.687-010 ASSEMBLER, MARKING DEVICES; 733.687-014 ASSEMBLER, MECHANICAL PENCILS AND BALLPOINT PENS; 733.687-018 BANDER; 733.687-030 DATER ASSEMBLER; 733.687-034 DESK-PEN-SET ASSEMBLER; 733.687-070 STAMP-PAD MAKER; 734.684-014 FEATHER-DUSTER WINDER; 734.687-010 ACETONE-BUTTON PASTER; 734.687-014 ASSEMBLER; 734.687-018 ASSEMBLER; 734.687-050 COVERED-BUCKLE ASSEMBLER; 734.687-058 HOT-STONE SETTER; 734.687-074 SLIDE-FASTENER-CHAIN ASSEMBLER; 734.687-078 SLIDER ASSEMBLER; 734.687-090 STICKER; 735.684-010 BEAD STRINGER; 735.684-018 TROPHY ASSEMBLER; 735.687-014 LINKER; 735.687-022 PIN-OR-CLIP FASTENER; 735.687-034 STONE SETTER; 735.687-038 SWEDGER; 735.687-042 WIRE DRAWER; 736.684-010 ALIGNER, BARREL AND RECEIVER; 736.684-014 ASSEMBLER II; 736.684-030 FRONT-SIGHT ATTACHER; 736.684-034 GAS-CHECK-PAD MAKER; 737.587-014 FIREWORKS ASSEMBLER; 737.684-014 BOMB LOADER; 737.684-018 FIREWORKS MAKER; 737.684-022 FUSE ASSEMBLER; 737.684-030 POWDER WORKER, TNT; 737.684-034 PRODUCTION ASSEMBLER; 737.684-038 SHELL ASSEMBLER; 737.687-010 ASSEMBLER; 737.687-018 BLASTING-CAP ASSEMBLER; 737.687-022 BOOSTER ASSEMBLER; 737.687-038 DETONATOR ASSEMBLER; 737.687-046 EXPLOSIVE OPERATOR II; 737.687-070 LABORER, AMMUNITION ASSEMBLY I; 737.687-074 LABORER, AMMUNITION ASSEMBLY II; 737.687-098 PRIMER ASSEMBLER; 737.687-102 PRIMER CHARGER; 737.687-110 PROPELLANT-CHARGE-ZONE ASSEMBLER; 737.687-122 SCREW-EYE ASSEMBLER; 739.381-050 SOUVENIR AND NOVELTY MAKER; 739.384-022 VENTILATOR; 739.684-014 ARTIFICIAL-FLOWER MAKER; 739.684-018 BROOMMAKER; 739.684-034 CASE FINISHER; 739.684-038 CLIP-AND-HANGER ATTACHER; 739.684-042 CURTAIN-ROLLER ASSEMBLER; 739.684-046 DECORATOR; 739.684-058 DEICER-ELEMENT WINDER, HAND; 739.684-078 FRAMER; 739.684-082 FURNITURE ASSEMBLER-AND-INSTALLER; 739.684-090 HANDBAG FRAMER; 739.684-094 LAMP-SHADE ASSEMBLER; 739.684-130 MOUNTER, SMOKING PIPE; 739.684-138 OIL-SEAL ASSEMBLER; 739.684-146 PICTURE FRAMER; 739.684-150 SCREEN MAKER; 739.684-154 TICKET-CHOPPER ASSEMBLER; 739.684-158 TIRE MOUNTER; 739.684-166 VENETIAN-BLIND ASSEMBLER; 739.684-170 WEAVER; 739.684-174 WOODEN-SHADE HARDWARE INSTALLER; 739.684-178 WOVEN-WOOD SHADE ASSEMBLER; 739.684-190 CASKET ASSEMBLER; 739.687-010 ASSEMBLER-ARRANGER; 739.687-014 ASSEMBLER, CORNCOB PIPES; 739.687-018 ASSEMBLER, FILTERS; 739.687-022 ASSEMBLER, GARMENT FORM; 739.687-026 ASSEMBLER, FILTERS;

739.687-030 ASSEMBLER, SMALL PRODUCTS II; 739.687-034 BEADER; 739.687-046 BRUSH FILLER, HAND; 739.687-066 COMPACT ASSEMBLER; 739.687-074 DUST-BRUSH ASSEMBLER; 739.687-086 EYE-DROPPER ASSEMBLER; 739.687-122 MOP-HANDLE ASSEMBLER; 739.687-130 ORNAMENT MAKER, HAND; 739.687-134 PAINT-ROLLER ASSEMBLER; 739.687-186 TRAVERSE-ROD ASSEMBLER; 739.687-194 VACUUM-BOTTLE ASSEMBLER; 739.687-202 WICK-AND-BASE ASSEMBLER; 739.687-206 BRUSH LOADER AND HANDLE ATTACHER; 750.384-014 TUBE BUILDER, AIRPLANE; 750.684-042 TIRE-BLADDER MAKER; 750.687-010 INNER-TUBE INSERTER; 752.684-010 BALLOON

MAKER; 752.684-014 BELT BUILDER; 752.684-030 HOSE MAKER; 752.684-038 RUBBER-GOODS ASSEMBLER; 752.684-046 SELF-SEALING-FUEL-TANK BUILDER; 753.684-014 CUT-AND-COVER LINE WORKER; 753.687-022 FITTER-PLACER; 753.687-026 MAKING-LINE WORKER; 754.684-010 ASSEMBLER; 754.684-014 ASSEMBLER-AND-GLUER, LAMINATED PLASTICS; 754.684-042 PLASTICS WORKER; 754.684-050 LAMINATOR, PREFORMS; 759.664-014 EXPANSION-JOINT BUILDER; 759.684-010 AIRPLANE-GAS-TANK-LINER ASSEMBLER; 759.684-014 BASE-PLY HAND; 759.684-030 DEICER-KIT ASSEMBLER; 759.684-038 HOSE WRAPPER; 759.684-050 RUBBER LINER; 759.684-062 TUBE-AND-MANIFOLD BUILDER; 759.687-014 HOSE-COUPLING JOINER; 760.684-010 BENCH CARPENTER; 760.684-014 BOX MAKER, WOOD; 761.684-018 PANEL-LAY-UP WORKER; 762.484-010 REEL ASSEMBLER; 762.684-010 ASSEMBLER; 762.684-014 ASSEMBLER, COMPONENT; 762.684-018 ASSEMBLY OPERATOR; 762.684-026 BOX MAKER; 762.684-030 CURTAIN-STRETCHER ASSEMBLER; 762.684-034 DOOR ASSEMBLER I; 762.684-038 EDGE BANDER, HAND; 762.684-042 GRIP ASSEMBLER; 762.684-046 HARDWARE ASSEMBLER; 762.684-050 NAILER, HAND; 762.684-054 SCARF GLUER; 762.684-058 SIDING STAPLER; 762.684-062 TRUSS ASSEMBLER; 762.684-066 WOODEN-FRAME BUILDER; 762.687-022 CLAMP-JIG ASSEMBLER; 762.687-030 DOOR CORE ASSEMBLER; 762.687-034 GLUER; 762.687-038 GLUER-AND-WEDGER; 762.687-042 HANDLE ASSEMBLER; 762.687-046 HARDWARE ASSEMBLER; 762.687-050 KNOCK-UP ASSEMBLER; 762.687-054 PARTITION ASSEMBLER; 762.687-058 SCREEN TACKER; 762.687-070 WOODENWARE ASSEMBLER; 763.684-014 CABINET ASSEMBLER; 763.684-018 CANER I; 763.684-038 FURNITURE ASSEMBLER; 763.684-042 HARDWARE ASSEMBLER; 763.684-046 LAG SCREWER; 763.684-050 LAMINATOR, HAND;
763.684-058 PIANO CASE AND BENCH ASSEMBLER; 763.684-062 PLASTIC-TOP ASSEMBLER; 763.684-078 WICKER WORKER; 764.684-018 BARREL RAISER; 764.684-030 TANK ASSEMBLER; 764.687-014 ASSEMBLER, FAUCETS; 764.687-058 HEADER; 764.687-062 HEADING MATCHER AND ASSEMBLER; 764.687-070 HOGSHEAD COOPER II; 764.687-074 HOGSHEAD COOPER III; 764.687-082 HOGSHEAD MAT ASSEMBLER; 769.684-010 BASKET ASSEMBLER II; 769.684-034 REELER; 769.684-050 STOCK-PARTS FABRICATOR; 769.684-054 WEAVER; 772.687-010 GLASS-WORKER, PRESSED OR BLOWN; 774.684-022 HANDLER; 774.684-046 PATCHER; 776.684-010 BELT MAKER; 780.384-010 AUTOMOBILE-SEAT-COVER-AND-CONVERTIBLE-TOP INSTALLER; 780.684-010 BACK PADDER; 780.684-014 BAND-TOP MAKER; 780.684-018 BOX-SPRING MAKER I; 780.684-022 BOX-SPRING MAKER II; 780.684-026 CASKET COVERER; 780.684-030 CASKET LINER; 780.684-034 CHAIR UPHOLSTERER; 780.684-046 CUSHION BUILDER; 780.684-054 CUSHION MAKER I; 780.684-058 EDGE ROLLER; 780.684-062 FABRICATOR, FOAM RUBBER; 780.684-066 FILLER; 780.684-074 MATTRESS MAKER; 780.684-078 PADDER, CUSHION; 780.684-082 PANEL COVERER, METAL FURNITURE; 780.684-086 PANEL MAKER; 780.684-090 POCKETED-SPRING ASSEMBLER; 780.684-094 SLIP-SEAT COVERER; 780.684-098 SPRING ASSEMBLER; 780.684-102 SPRING CLIPPER; 780.684-106 SPRINGER; 780.684-114 TRIMMING ASSEMBLER; 780.684-118 UPHOLSTERER, OUTSIDE; 780.684-126 UPHOLSTERY TRIMMER; 780.684-130 WEBBING TACKER; 780.684-134 UPHOLSTERER, ASSEMBLY LINE; 780.685-010 MATTRESS-FILLING-MACHINE TENDER; 780.685-018 WIRE-BORDER ASSEMBLER; 780.687-014 CLIPPER AND TURNER; 780.687-018 HASSOCK MAKER; 780.687-030 MATTRESS-SPRING ENCASER; 780.687-034 PADDING GLUER; 780.687-038 SPRING COVERER; 780.687-042 STAPLER, HAND;
780.687-046 STUFFER; 780.687-062 BACK TUFTER; 780.687-070 SKIRT PANEL ASSEMBLER; 781.684-050 RUG-SAMPLE BEVELER; 782.684-014 CROCHETER, HAND; 783.684-010 ASSEMBLER, LEATHER GOODS I; 783.684-014 FUR NAILER; 783.684-026 LEATHER WORKER; 783.684-030 UTILITY BAG ASSEMBLER; 783.687-010 ASSEMBLER, LEATHER GOODS II; 783.687-026 PASTER, HAND OR MACHINE; 784.684-018 CAP MAKER; 784.684-026 FLANGER; 784.684-030 FOUNDATION MAKER; 784.684-038 HAT BRAIDER; 784.684-070 STEAMER-BLOCKER; 784.684-074 TOP-HAT-BODY MAKER; 784.684-078 TRIMMER; 784.687-022 EAR-MUFF ASSEMBLER; 784.687-082 WIRE INSERTER; 788.684-010 ASSEMBLER FOR PULLER-OVER, HAND; 788.684-014 ASSEMBLER, SANDAL PARTS; 788.684-026 BOTTOM FILLER; 788.684-034 BOW MAKER; 788.684-058 HEEL ATTACHER, WOOD; 788.684-074 LASTER, HAND; 788.684-078 LASTING-MACHINE OPERATOR, HAND METHOD; 788.684-086 PULLER AND LASTER, MACHINE; 788.684-090 PULLER OVER, MACHINE; 788.684-122 UPPER-AND-BOTTOM LACER, HAND; 788.687-030 CEMENTER, HAND; 788.687-054 GOLF-SHOE-SPIKE ASSEMBLER; 788.687-094 MOLDER, SHOE PARTS; 788.687-118 SHANK-PIECE TACKER; 788.687-138 STEEL-BOX-TOE INSERTER; 788.687-154 VAMP CREASER; 789.687-054 FLOCKER; 789.687-082 HARNESS RIGGER; 789.687-102 MONOGRAM-AND-LETTER PASTER; 789.687-154 RIVETER, HAND; 794.684-014 BOX MAKER, PAPERBOARD; 794.684-018 EXPANSION ENVELOPE MAKER, HAND; 794.684-022 PAPER-NOVELTY MAKER; 794.687-010 ASSEMBLER, PRINTED PRODUCTS; 794.687-026 FORWARDER; 794.687-030 GLUER AND SLICER, HAND; 794.687-042 PUNCHBOARD ASSEMBLER I; 794.687-046 PUNCHBOARD ASSEMBLER II; 795.684-026 WADER-BOOT-TOP ASSEMBLER; 795.687-014 GLUER; 795.687-018 GLUER, WET SUIT; 795.687-022 LINING CEMENTER; 795.687-026 TENNIS-BALL COVERER, HAND; 795.687-030 TENNIS-BALL-COVER CEMENTER; 801.384-010 ASSEMBLER, WIRE-MESH GATE; 801.664-018 ROLL BUILDER; 801.684-010 JIG FITTER; 804.684-014 EXTRUSION BENDER; 806.384-030 ASSEMBLER, METAL BONDING; 806.384-034 ASSEMBLER, SUBASSEMBLY; 806.464-010 BOAT RIGGER; 806.684-010 ASSEMBLER, MOTOR VEHICLE; 806.684-014 ASSEMBLER, BICYCLE I; 806.684-018 ASSEMBLER, CAMPER; 806.684-022 ASSEMBLER, DECK AND HULL; 806.684-026 ASSEMBLER, INSULATION AND FLOORING; 806.684-038 AUTOMOBILE-ACCESSORIES INSTALLER; 806.684-046 CAR TRIMMER; 806.684-050 DOOR ASSEMBLER; 806.684-054 FIBERGLASS LAMINATOR; 806.684-070 INSTALLER, METAL FLOORING; 806.684-074 INSTALLER, MOVABLE BULKHEAD; 806.684-082 TRAILER ASSEMBLER II; 806.684-090 MOTORCYCLE ASSEMBLER; 806.684-094 MOTORCYCLE SUBASSEMBLER; 806.684-098 ORDNANCE TRUCK INSTALLATION MECHANIC; 806.684-102 OUTFITTER, CABIN; 806.684-106 OVERLAY PLASTICIAN; 806.684-114 RAILROAD-CAR-TRUCK BUILDER; 806.684-118 REPAIRER, GENERAL; 806.684-126 ROOF FITTER; 806.684-146 BOAT OUTFITTER; 806.687-010 ASSEMBLER, BICYCLE II; 806.687-034 INSTALLER, DOOR FURRING; 806.687-046 ROLLER; 807.684-014 BOAT PATCHER, PLASTIC; 807.684-026 INSTALLER, SOFT TOP; 809.484-010 AWNING-FRAME MAKER; 809.684-010 ASSEMBLER, PRODUCTION LINE; 809.684-014 CASKET ASSEMBLER, METAL; 809.684-030 METAL HANGER; 809.684-038 WHEEL ASSEMBLER; 809.684-042 PANEL LAMINATOR; 826.684-010 ANODE BUILDER; 826.684-022 POT BUILDER; 827.584-010 ELECTRICAL-APPLIANCE PREPARER; 827.684-010 APPLIANCE ASSEMBLER, LINE; 860.684-022 DISPLAY FABRICATOR; 865.684-014 GLASS INSTALLER; 865.684-018 GLAZIER, METAL FURNITURE; 865.684-022 REFRIGERATOR GLAZIER; 869.684-010 ASSEMBLER; 869.684-014 ASSEMBLER, SKYLIGHTS; 869.684-026 INSTALLER; 869.684-078 VENEER STAPLER; 869.687-014 CAMOUFLAGE ASSEMBLER; 899.684-018 LAMINATOR; 915.687-010 AUTOMOBILE-SEAT-COVER INSTALLER; 920.687-082 DENTAL FLOSS PACKER; 977.684-018 PRESSER; 979.684-042 PRINTING SCREEN ASSEMBLER

93997 INTERMEDIATE HAND WORKERS. OOH

Title/s: Assemblers; Production Occupations

Workers who manually perform handwork that usually requires three months to two years to obtain proficiency. Performs the same or similar process for multiple items or the same items.

(Note: Workers do not perform all tasks; job activity is represented by one or two task statements.) Cleans, presses, or dyes articles, such as clothing, rugs, or furnishings, to improve appearance, using hand tools or hand-operated equipment. Assembles parts and materials of metal, wood, and plastic, according to specifications, using hand tools. Shapes material by cumulative addition of material to build up original mass, and presses material into shape. Sorts, weighs, or packages materials. Embroiders or hand-sews designs over stamped or stenciled patterns on fabric. Stretches, bends, straightens, shapes, pounds, or presses metal or plastic, according to specifications, using hand tools. Joins parts together and fastens with sticky substances, such as cement, glue, paste, gum, or other adhesives, or caulks seams. Threads or pulls cables or lines through ducts or fabric seams. Folds fabrics to make pleats or to pack parachutes. Punches symbols in perforated tape or notches in negative film, using electric tape puncher, film footage counter, and hand holder. Smooths and finishes materials such as leather or bisque ware. Stacks or arranges products, such as blocks, bricks, pipe, and roofing tile, in specified patterns. Positions and aligns materials and parts in preparation for assembly or other production processes such as grinding. Mixes or blends materials in solid, fluid, semi-fluid, and gaseous states, according to formula. Determines style and size of standard patterns, and gathers and assembles specified materials and accessories in preparation for next procedure. Sharpens objects, such as buhrstones in grain grinding mills, using sharpening tools. Fills containers, such as thermostat bellows or illuminated sign tubing, with gas or liquid. Converts fiber raw stock into yarn and thread, or interlaces and works yarns to form woven, nonwoven, knitted, and tufted fabrics. Removes metals, such gold, platinum, and palladium, from objects such as dentures and extracted teeth, using furnace, retort, and laboratory equipment. Prepares products for use, such as burning interior of barrel to be used for aging whiskey.

Yearly Earnings: $18,044

Education: Short-term O-J-T

Knowledge: Production and Processing; Building and Construction

Abilities: Perceptual Speed; Selective Attention; Arm-Hand Steadiness; Finger Dexterity; Speed of Limb Movement; Dynamic Flexibility; Gross Body Equilibrium; Visual Color Discrimination; Depth Perception; Hearing Sensitivity

Skills: None above average

General Work Activities: Handling and Moving Objects

Job Characteristics: Using Hands on Objects, Tools, or Controls; Making Repetitive Motions; Importance of Repeating Same Tasks

GOE Group/s: 05.03.02 Engineering Technology: Drafting; 05.05.10 Craft Technology: Electrical-Electronic Equipment Repair; 05.10.03 Crafts: Electrical-Electronic; 05.10.05 Crafts: Reproduction; 05.12.14 Elemental Work: Mechanical: Painting, Caulking, and Coating; 05.12.16 Elemental Work: Mechanical: Electrical Work; 06.02.06 Production Work: Machine Work, Textiles; 06.02.22 Production Work: Manual Work, Assembly Large Parts; 06.02.24 Production Work: Manual Work, Metal and Plastics; 06.02.26 Production Work: Manual Work, Paper; 06.02.27 Production Work: Manual Work, Textile, Fabric and Leather; 06.02.28 Production Work: Manual Work, Food Processing; 06.02.30 Production Work: Manual Work, Stone, Glass, and Clay; 06.02.31 Production Work: Manual Work, Laying Out and Marking; 06.02.32 Production Work: Manual Work, Assorted Materials; 06.03.02 Quality Control: Inspecting, Grading, Sorting, Weighing, and Recording; 06.04.10 Elemental Work: Industrial: Equipment Operation, Metal Processing; 06.04.11 Elemental Work: Industrial: Equipment Operation, Chemical Processing; 06.04.18 Elemental Work: Industrial: Equipment Operation, Wood Processing; 06.04.24 Elemental Work: Industrial: Manual Work, Metal and Plastics; 06.04.26 Elemental Work: Industrial: Manual Work, Paper; 06.04.27 Elemental Work: Industrial: Manual Work, Textile, Fabric and Leather; 06.04.28 Elemental Work: Industrial: Manual Work, Food Processing; 06.04.30 Elemental Work: Industrial: Manual Work, Stone, Glass, and Clay; 06.04.32 Elemental Work: Industrial: Manual Work, Casting and Molding; 06.04.33 Elemental Work: Industrial: Manual Work, Brushing, Spraying, and Coating; 06.04.34 Elemental Work: Industrial: Manual Work, Assorted Materials; 06.04.35 Elemental Work: Industrial: Laundering, Dry Cleaning; 06.04.36 Elemental Work: Industrial: Filling; 06.04.38 Elemental Work: Industrial: Wrapping and Packaging; 06.04.40 Elemental Work: Industrial: Loading, Moving, Hoisting, and Conveying

CIP Program/s: 100103 Photographic Technologists and Technicians; 120501 Baker/Pastry Chef; 120503 Culinary Arts/Chef Training; 120505 Kitchen Personnel/Cook and Assistant Training; 150607 Plastics Technologists and Technicians; 200301 Clothing, Apparel and Textile Workers and Managers, General; 200303 Commercial Garment and Apparel Worker; 200309 Drycleaner and Launderer (Commercial); 410301 Chemical Technologists and Technicians; 460101 Mason and Tile Setter; 460301 Electrical and Power Transmission Installer, General; 460303 Lineworker; 460501 Plumber and Pipefitter; 470101 Electrical and Electronics Equipment Installer and Repairer; 470105 Industrial Electronics Installer and Repairer; 470402 Gunsmith; 470408 Watch, Clock and Jewelry Repairer; 480201 Graphic and Printing Equipment Operator, General; 480208 Printing Press Operator; 480303 Upholsterer; 480304 Shoe, Boot and Leather Repairer; 480399 Leatherworkers and Upholsterers, Other; 480501 Machinist/Machine Technologist; 480503 Machine Shop Assistant; 480599 Precision Metal Workers, Other; 489999 Precision Production Trades, Other; 500201 Crafts, Folk Art and Artisanry; 500701 Art, General; 500711 Ceramics Arts and Ceramics; 500712 Fiber, Textile and Weaving Arts; 510603 Dental Laboratory Technician

Related DOT Job/s: 017.684-010 TAPER, PRINTED CIRCUIT LAYOUT; 362.684-018 FUR CLEANER, HAND; 364.684-018 SPRAYER, LEATHER; 369.384-010 HATTER; 369.384-014 RUG CLEANER, HAND; 502.664-010 BLAST-FURNACE KEEPER; 520.684-010 ALMOND-PASTE MOLDER; 526.684-010 DOUGHNUT MAKER; 529.687-122 KISS SETTER, HAND; 550.584-010 FLUX MIXER; 550.684-010 COAGULATING-BATH MIXER; 559.684-030 HAT-FINISHING-MATERIALS PREPARER; 570.484-010 MIXER, DIAMOND POWDER; 570.683-010 DRY-PAN CHARGER; 573.684-014 SETTER; 575.684-010 BATTER-OUT; 575.684-026 GATHERER; 583.684-010 PLEATER, HAND; 590.464-010 PROCESSOR, SOLID PROPELLANT; 590.684-030 MATERIAL PREPARATION WORKER; 629.684-014 MILLER, HEAD, ASSISTANT, WET PROCESS; 659.684-010 DIE MOUNTER; 683.684-014 DRAWER-IN, HAND; 683.684-030 WEAVER, HAND LOOM; 687.684-010 RUG HOOKER; 700.684-058 PREPARER, MAKING DEPARTMENT; 700.684-062 PREPARER, SAMPLES AND REPAIRS; 700.684-074 SPINNER; 709.484-014 STRAIGHTENER, HAND; 709.684-090 TUBE BENDER, HAND I; 710.684-014 BELLOWS FILLER; 712.684-038 REFINER; 715.684-034 BLOCKER; 726.684-010 CAPACITOR-PACK-PRESS OPERATOR; 728.684-014 ELECTRICAL-LINE SPLICER; 736.684-026 BARREL STRAIGHTENER I; 739.384-010 DIAMOND MOUNTER; 739.684-022 BRUSH MATERIAL PREPARER; 739.684-118 MANNEQUIN MOUNTER; 763.684-054 LEATHER TOOLER; 763.684-074 TABLE-TOP TILE SETTER; 764.684-014 BARREL CHARRER; 774.684-010 BISQUE CLEANER; 774.684-038 TURNER; 780.684-110 TESTER, CONVERTIBLE SOFA BEDSPRING; 781.287-010 CLOTHING-PATTERN PREPARER; 781.684-066 MATERIAL ASSEMBLER; 782.684-018 EMBROIDERER, HAND; 782.684-034 KNITTER, HAND; 784.684-034 HARDENER; 788.684-022 BLEMISH REMOVER; 788.684-062 HEEL-SEAT FITTER, HAND; 789.684-018 CANOPY STRINGER; 790.684-014 CIGAR MAKER; 790.684-022 ROLLER, HAND; 794.684-026 PAPIER MACHE MOLDER; 795.684-014 EDGE STRIPPER; 801.684-014 PATTERN GATER; 806.684-086 MOLD LAMINATOR; 806.684-142 RUNNING RIGGER; 824.684-010 NEON-TUBE PUMPER; 829.684-018 CABLE PULLER; 843.684-010 STEEL-PLATE CAULKER;

862.684-010 JUNCTION MAKER; 912.684-010 PARACHUTE RIGGER; 976.684-010 DENSITY CONTROL PUNCHER

93998 ELEMENTAL HAND WORKERS. OOH Title/s: Assemblers; Production Occupations; ; Bindery Workers

Workers who perform handwork that requires less than three months to obtain proficiency. (Note: Workers do not perform all tasks; job activity is represented by one or two task statements.) Cleans, blocks, dyes, presses, brushes, or treats articles such as shoes, furniture, drapes, leather goods, or ophthalmic or optical elements. Mixes or blends materials in solid, fluid, semi-fluid, and gaseous states, such as chemicals or food products, according to formula. Converts fiber stock into yarn and thread, or braids, interlaces, or works materials to form fabric, decorative designs, or rugs by hand. Fills molds or ladles with molten metal, hot material, or other substances to produce products, and removes products from molds. Stretches, bends, straightens, forms, shapes, pounds, wraps, or folds materials, according to specifications, using hand tools. Assembles or disassembles parts and materials, according to standard patterns, using hand tools. Splices and joins parts together with adhesives, caulks or seals seams, or binds materials, using binding, strapping, crimping, or soldering tools. Smooths, trims, and finishes materials, parts, and products, using sanding or buffing tools, according to specifications. Repairs, replaces, or adjusts parts, either fabric, paper, or metal, according to instructions or specifications, using hand tools. Cuts, saws, splits, or drills material or products in preparation for further processing, according to specifications, using hand tools. Threads materials, such as cable, rope, string, or yarn, through openings to thread machines, wire, or assemble clothes or jewelry. Loads, sorts, weighs, stacks, arranges, or packages materials, parts, or products, according to instructions. Applies coating to material, such as paint, oil, lacquer, chemical(s), or powder, using sprayer, squeeze bottle, brush, or dipping method. Stamps, marks, or traces patterns on products, parts, or materials, using pencil, hand-transfer press, or perforating tool. Screws or hammers nails or pegs into products, using hammer or screwdriver, according to instructions. Repairs, cuts, or softens glass, using torch, hot wire, or furnace, according to instructions. Charges, positions covers, and seals storage batteries. Skims or siphons materials, such as slag or plasma, preparatory to further processing. Combs, brushes, ties, sorts, or cuts human or doll hair or material nap, according to specifications. Positions, aligns, and secures molds, materials, parts, or products in preparation for assembly or other production processes.

Yearly Earnings: $18,044

Education: Short-term O-J-T

Knowledge: None above average

Abilities: Manual Dexterity; Finger Dexterity; Wrist-Finger Speed; Speed of Limb Movement

Skills: None above average

General Work Activities: Handling and Moving Objects

Job Characteristics: Contaminants; Using Hands on Objects, Tools, or Controls; Making Repetitive Motions; Common Protective or Safety Attire; Importance of Repeating Same Tasks

GOE Group/s: 01.02.03 Visual Arts: Commercial Art; 02.04.02 Laboratory Technology: Life Sciences; 03.04.03 Elemental Work: Plants and Animals: Hunting and Fishing; 05.09.03 Material Control: Verifying, Recording, and Marking; 05.10.01 Crafts: Structural; 05.10.05 Crafts: Reproduction; 05.10.08 Crafts: Food Preparation; 05.12.07 Elemental Work: Mechanical: Crushing, Mixing, Separating, and Chipping; 05.12.10 Elemental Work: Mechanical: Heating and Melting; 05.12.12 Elemental Work: Mechanical: Structural Work; 05.12.13 Elemental Work: Mechanical: Cutting and Finishing; 05.12.14 Elemental Work: Mechanical: Painting, Caulking, and Coating; 06.01.02 Production Technology: Machine Set-up; 06.02.24 Production Work: Manual Work, Metal and Plastics; 06.02.27 Production Work: Manual Work, Textile, Fabric and Leather; 06.02.30 Production Work: Manual Work, Stone, Glass, and Clay; 06.02.31 Production Work: Manual Work, Laying Out and Marking; 06.02.32 Production Work: Manual Work, Assorted Materials; 06.03.02 Quality Control: Inspecting, Grading, Sorting, Weighing, and Recording; 06.04.02 Elemental Work: Industrial: Machine Work, Metal and Plastics; 06.04.05 Elemental Work: Industrial: Machine Work, Fabric and Leather; 06.04.06 Elemental Work: Industrial: Machine Work, Textiles; 06.04.08 Elemental Work: Industrial: Machine Work, Stone, Glass, and Clay; 06.04.10 Elemental Work: Industrial: Equipment Operation, Metal Processing; 06.04.11 Elemental Work: Industrial: Equipment Operation, Chemical Processing; 06.04.13 Elemental Work: Industrial: Equipment Operation, Rubber, Plastics, Glass Processing; 06.04.15 Elemental Work: Industrial: Equipment Operation, Food Processing; 06.04.16 Elemental Work: Industrial: Equipment Operation, Textile, Fabric, and Leather Processing; 06.04.19 Elemental Work: Industrial: Equipment Operation, Assorted Materials Processing; 06.04.20 Elemental Work: Industrial: Machine Assembling; 06.04.22 Elemental Work: Industrial: Manual Work, Assembly Large Parts; 06.04.23 Elemental Work: Industrial: Manual Work, Assembly Small Parts; 06.04.24 Elemental Work: Industrial: Manual Work, Metal and Plastics; 06.04.25 Elemental Work: Industrial: Manual Work, Wood; 06.04.26 Elemental Work: Industrial: Manual Work, Paper; 06.04.27 Elemental Work: Industrial: Manual Work, Textile, Fabric and Leather; 06.04.28 Elemental Work: Industrial: Manual Work, Food Processing; 06.04.29 Elemental Work: Industrial: Manual Work, Rubber; 06.04.30 Elemental Work: Industrial: Manual Work, Stone, Glass, and Clay; 06.04.32 Elemental Work: Industrial: Manual Work, Casting and Molding; 06.04.33 Elemental Work: Industrial: Manual Work, Brushing, Spraying, and Coating; 06.04.34 Elemental Work: Industrial: Manual Work, Assorted Materials; 06.04.35 Elemental Work: Industrial: Laundering, Dry Cleaning; 06.04.37 Elemental Work: Industrial: Manual Work, Stamping, Marking, Labeling, and Ticketing; 06.04.38 Elemental Work: Industrial: Wrapping and Packaging; 06.04.39 Elemental Work: Industrial: Cleaning; 06.04.40 Elemental Work: Industrial: Loading, Moving, Hoisting, and Conveying

CIP Program/s: 100103 Photographic Technologists and Technicians; 200301 Clothing, Apparel and Textile Workers and Managers, General; 200303 Commercial Garment and Apparel Worker; 200309 Drycleaner and Launderer (Commercial); 480303 Upholsterer; 480501 Machinist/Machine Technologist; 480503 Machine Shop Assistant; 500406 Commercial Photography; 500701 Art, General; 500711 Ceramics Arts and Ceramics; 500712 Fiber, Textile and Weaving Arts

Related DOT Job/s: 222.687-014 GARMENT SORTER; 362.684-010 DRY CLEANER, HAND; 362.684-022 FURNITURE CLEANER; 364.684-014 SHOE DYER; 369.684-010 FUR GLAZER; 410.687-018 PELTER; 500.684-014 MATRIX WORKER; 502.684-018 MOLD SETTER; 509.687-018 STRINGER; 511.687-022 SKIMMER, REVERBERATORY; 512.687-010 CONDENSER SETTER; 514.664-010 CUPOLA TAPPER; 514.664-014 TAPPER; 519.687-010 CELL PLASTERER; 519.687-018 FLUX-TUBE ATTENDANT; 519.687-034 RODDING-ANODE WORKER; 520.587-010 PRETZEL TWISTER; 520.684-014 ROLLER I; 520.687-030 FILLER MIXER; 520.687-034 FOOD MIXER; 520.687-050 PLUG SHAPER, HAND; 520.687-054 SEASONING MIXER; 520.687-062 SPICE MIXER; 521.687-050 FILTER CHANGER; 521.687-070 HONEYCOMB DECAPPER; 522.684-010 PICKLER; 523.587-014 DRYING-ROOM ATTENDANT; 524.687-022 BAKERY WORKER, CONVEYOR LINE; 525.687-026 DRY CURER; 526.684-014 LUMPIA WRAPPER MAKER; 526.687-014 STARCHMAKER; 529.684-010 FROZEN PIE MAKER; 529.684-018 SIEVE MAKER; 529.687-034 CASING TIER; 529.687-154 MAT SEWER; 543.666-010 FURNACE WORKER; 549.687-014 HOTHOUSE WORKER; 550.684-014 DYE WEIGHER; 550.684-018 PAINT MIXER, HAND; 550.684-022 PRIMING-POWDER-PREMIX BLENDER; 551.687-014 BRINE MAKER II; 553.684-014 NITROCELLULOSE OPERATOR; 556.684-022 NEEDLE-BAR

MOLDER; 556.687-010 BOWLING-BALL-MOLD ASSEMBLER; 557.684-014 JET WIPER; 559.684-010 PACK-ROOM OPERATOR; 559.684-018 RUBBER-MOLD MAKER; 559.687-034 EGG PROCESSOR; 563.687-010 ANTICHECKING-IRON WORKER; 579.584-010 FIBERGLASS-CONTAINER-WINDING OPERATOR; 579.587-010 ROUND-UP-RING HAND; 579.684-022 MICA-PLATE LAYER, HAND; 580.684-010 BLOCKER, HAND I; 580.684-014 BLOCKER, HAND II; 580.687-014 HIDE STRETCHER, HAND; 583.684-014 WAIST PLEATER; 589.687-014 CLOTH FOLDER, HAND; 589.687-030 PAD MAKER; 589.687-046 TUBE COVERER; 599.687-026 SIPHON OPERATOR; 613.687-010 PLUGGER; 619.687-010 COIL BINDER; 619.687-018 PITCH FILLER; 641.687-010 BOX BENDER; 652.687-030 PATTERN HAND; 654.687-014 PAGER; 669.685-030 CLAMPER; 670.587-010 STONE LAYOUT MARKER; 673.687-010 JOINER; 679.664-010 BED SETTER; 682.687-010 TRAVELER CHANGER; 683.684-026 SMASH HAND; 685.687-026 TOPPER; 687.464-010 RUG-FRAME MOUNTER; 687.684-014 TUFTER; 689.587-010 NUMBERER AND WIRER; 689.684-014 DRAWER-IN, STITCH-BONDING MACHINE; 689.684-018 LEASE PICKER; 689.686-050 UTILITY WORKER, WOOLEN MILL; 689.687-026 CLOTH FRAMER; 689.687-034 DROP-WIRE BUILDER; 689.687-054 PEGGER, DOBBY LOOMS; 689.687-078 THREADER; 691.667-010 PNEUMATIC JACKETER; 700.684-010 ARBORER; 700.684-078 STRETCHER; 700.687-018 BRIMER; 700.687-062 PREPARER; 701.687-018 COLD-PRESS LOADER; 701.687-034 WEDGER, MACHINE; 705.684-018 FILER AND SANDER; 706.587-010 CLEANER-TOUCH-UP WORKER; 706.684-110 WRAPPER OPERATOR; 706.687-018 FAN-BLADE ALIGNER; 709.684-010 ADJUSTER; 709.684-042 HAND STAMPER; 709.687-050 TUBE BENDER, HAND II; 709.687-062 WIRE-BASKET MAKER; 711.684-010 ASSEMBLY LOADER;

712.684-018 FLANGER; 712.684-026 GLAZIER; 712.687-014 COILER; 713.684-026 EYEGLASS-FRAME TRUER; 713.687-014 CONTACT-LENS-FLASHING PUNCHER; 713.687-038 SALVAGER; 715.684-010 ADJUSTER, ALARM MECHANISM; 715.684-026 BENCH HAND; 715.684-090 DISASSEMBLER; 715.684-146 OILER; 715.687-022 DIAL BRUSHER; 715.687-030 FOOT STRAIGHTENER; 715.687-046 HAMMER ADJUSTER; 715.687-078 MAINSPRING FORMER, ARBOR END; 715.687-082 MAINSPRING FORMER, BRACE END; 715.687-094 MOUNTER, CLOCK AND WATCH HANDS; 715.687-122 SPRING LAYER; 716.684-010 BLOCKER, HAND; 716.687-010 DEBLOCKER; 725.687-022 GETTERER; 726.687-010 ELECTRONICS WORKER; 726.687-034 MASKER; 726.687-038 PREASSEMBLER, PRINTED CIRCUIT BOARD; 727.484-010 ACID ADJUSTER; 727.587-010 BATTERY CHARGER; 727.684-030 SEALER; 727.687-026 BATTERY CHARGER, CONVEYOR LINE; 727.687-042 CELL COVERER; 727.687-058 FORMING-PROCESS-LINE WORKER; 728.684-022 WIREWORKER; 729.687-022 MICA-WASHER GLUER; 730.684-014 BELL-NECK HAMMERER; 731.687-014 FINISHER; 732.587-010 GOLF-BALL TRIMMER; 732.687-054 MOLDER, INFLATED BALL; 732.687-070 SOFTBALL CORE MOLDER; 733.687-066 STAMP-PAD FINISHER; 734.684-010 FEATHER SHAPER; 734.684-022 SLIDE-FASTENER REPAIRER; 734.684-026 WIRE-FRAME DIPPER; 734.687-034 BUCKLE-WIRE INSERTER; 734.687-046 BUTTON-AND-BUCKLE MAKER; 737.687-042 EXPLOSIVE OPERATOR I; 737.687-078 LACQUER-PIN-PRESS OPERATOR; 737.687-090 MIXER II; 737.687-134 TAPPER, HAND; 737.687-138 VARNISHING-UNIT OPERATOR;

739.684-062 FINISHER, BRUSH; 739.684-070 FORM COVERER; 739.684-086 HAIR WORKER; 739.684-098 LAST IRONER; 739.684-102 LAST MARKER; 739.684-122 MANNEQUIN SANDER AND FINISHER; 739.684-142 PAINT-ROLLER COVERMAKER; 739.684-182 WREATH AND GARLAND MAKER; 739.685-054 UMBRELLA TIPPER, MACHINE; 739.687-070 DIGGER; 739.687-078 DUST-MOP MAKER; 739.687-090 FILLER; 739.687-126 NAILER; 739.687-138 PART MAKER; 739.687-154 POLISHING-PAD MOUNTER; 739.687-162 PULL-OUT OPERATOR; 739.687-190 UMBRELLA FINISHER; 739.687-210 PIPE STEM ALIGNER; 749.687-018 MASKER; 750.684-022 TIRE BUILDER; 750.684-026 TIRE GROOVER; 750.684-038 TIRE VULCANIZER; 750.684-046 TUBE BALANCER; 750.684-050 TUBE REPAIRER; 752.684-018 BIT BENDER; 752.684-034 PADDED-PRODUCTS FINISHER; 752.684-042 RUBBER-TUBING SPLICER; 753.684-018 HOOKER-LASTER; 753.684-022 LASTER; 753.684-030 ROLLER-STITCHER; 753.687-014 DEBRANDER; 754.684-026 DRILLER, HAND; 754.684-034 KNOCK-OUT HAND; 754.687-010 LABORER, GENERAL; 759.684-034 FOLDER-TIER; 759.684-046 PATCHER, BOWLING BALL; 759.684-058 SPLICER; 759.684-070 SPLICER; 761.684-014 JIG BUILDER; 761.684-022 PATTERN MARKER II; 761.684-050 PANEL CUTTER; 762.687-010 BANDER; 762.687-066 VENEER-STOCK LAYER; 763.684-026 CASE FITTER; 763.684-030 DRAWER LINER; 763.687-018 DISTRESSER;

764.687-042 BUNG DRIVER; 764.687-066 HEADING REPAIRER; 764.687-078 HOGSHEAD HOOPER; 764.687-090 LEAK HUNTER; 764.687-094 LEVELER I; 764.687-098 PLUGGER; 769.684-018 BENDER, HAND; 769.684-026 OIL DIPPER; 769.684-030 PATCHER; 769.687-022 FRAME TRIMMER II; 770.687-010 ARTIFICIAL-PEARL MAKER; 770.687-034 ROCK BREAKER; 772.684-010 DEFECT REPAIRER, GLASSWARE; 772.684-014 HOT-WIRE GLASS-TUBE CUTTER; 772.684-018 WARM-IN WORKER; 773.487-010 CLAY-STAIN MIXER; 774.684-018 FINISHER; 774.684-030 SAGGER MAKER; 774.684-034 STICKER-ON; 774.687-014 LACER; 775.684-050 MARK-UP DESIGNER; 775.687-010 FINISHER; 775.687-014 GLASS DRILLER; 776.687-010 BELT-MAKER HELPER; 777.684-010 FORM MAKER, PLASTER; 779.684-034 LEVEL-VIAL SEALER; 779.684-038 MIRROR SPECIALIST; 779.684-042 PIPE FINISHER; 779.687-010 BREAKER; 779.687-014 CARTRIDGE LOADER; 779.687-034 STOCK SHEETS CLEANER-INSPECTOR; 780.684-042 CRUSHER; 780.687-010 BORDER MEASURER AND CUTTER; 780.687-050 TUFTER, HAND; 781.384-014 MARKER I; 781.684-042 PERFORATOR; 781.684-058 TRIM-STENCIL MAKER; 781.687-042 MARKER; 781.687-046 MARKING STITCHER; 782.684-026 FISH-NET STRINGER; 782.684-062 WEAVER, HAND; 782.687-022 ELASTIC-TAPE INSERTER; 782.687-042 RUG BRAIDER, HAND; 782.687-054 TAPE STRINGER; 784.684-014 BRIM IRONER, HAND; 784.684-054 SIZER, HAND; 784.684-062 SLICKER; 784.684-066 SMOOTHER; 784.687-018 CROWN POUNCER, HAND; 784.687-046 LINER; 784.687-062 SINGER; 784.687-070 STICKER; 784.687-074 STRAW-HAT BRUSHER; 784.687-090 SWEATBAND SHAPER; 788.584-014 MARKER, HAND; 788.684-050 FLAMER; 788.684-070 INTERLACER; 788.684-094 RASPER; 788.684-102 SCREW REMOVER; 788.684-106 SLIP LASTER; 788.684-118 TREE DRILLER; 788.684-126 WOOD-HEEL FINISHER; 788.684-130 WRINKLE CHASER; 788.687-010 ANTISQUEAK FILLER; 788.687-014 BOTTOM BLEACHER; 788.687-102 PEGGER; 788.687-142 TABLE WORKER; 788.687-158 VAMP-STRAP IRONER; 789.387-014 SAMPLE SELECTOR; 789.684-010 BOW MAKER; 789.684-014 BUFFING-WHEEL FORMER, HAND; 789.684-026 MOLDER, SHOULDER PAD; 789.684-030 NET MAKER; 789.684-034 PARACHUTE FOLDER; 789.684-042 RAWHIDE-BONE ROLLER; 789.684-046 RIGGER; 789.684-054 ELECTRIC BLANKET WIRER; 789.687-022 BUFFING TURNER-AND-COUNTER; 789.687-098 MIXER II; 789.687-130 QUILT STUFFER; 789.687-170 STEAMER; 790.684-010 BUNCH MAKER, HAND; 790.684-018 PATCH WORKER; 790.687-030 TWISTER, HAND; 794.684-010 BAG REPAIRER; 794.684-030 SAMPLE MAKER, HAND; 794.687-014 COLOR-CARD MAKER; 794.687-022 FOLDER, HAND; 794.687-054 STRINGER; 794.687-058 TABBER; 795.684-018 GLOBE MOUNTER; 795.684-022 TIPPER; 806.684-130 SKIN-LAP BONDER; 809.484-014 TEMPLATE MAKER, TRACK; 809.667-010 HULL AND DECK REMOVER; 809.684-018 DRILLER, HAND; 843.384-010 WOOD CAULKER; 899.684-038 STRIPPER AND TAPER; 920.685-022 BLOCKER; 959.684-010 POLE FRAMER; 976.487-010 PHOTOGRAPH FINISHER; 976.667-010 PHOTOGRAPHER HELPER; 976.684-022 PRINT WASHER; 976.684-026 SPLICER; 977.684-026 BENCH WORKER, BINDING; 979.684-018 LEGEND MAKER

93999 ALL OTHER HAND WORKERS. OOH Title/s: Assemblers; Production Occupations

All other hand workers not classified separately above.

Yearly Earnings: $18,044

Education: Short-term O-J-T

GOE Group/s: 01.06.02 Craft Arts: Arts and Crafts; 05.12.10 Elemental Work: Mechanical: Heating and Melting; 06.02.24 Production Work: Manual Work, Metal and Plastics; 06.02.32 Production Work: Manual Work, Assorted Materials; 06.04.28 Elemental Work: Industrial: Manual Work, Food Processing; 06.04.32 Elemental Work: Industrial: Manual Work, Casting and Molding; 06.04.33 Elemental Work: Industrial: Manual Work, Brushing, Spraying, and Coating; 06.04.39 Elemental Work: Industrial: Cleaning

CIP Program/s: 120402 Barber/Hairstylist

Related DOT Job/s: 503.684-010 CLEANER; 518.684-022 WAX-PATTERN ASSEMBLER; 518.684-026 WAX-PATTERN REPAIRER; 518.687-014 FOUNDRY LABORER, COREROOM; 518.687-022 WAX-PATTERN COATER; 519.687-030 MACHINE-CASTINGS PLASTERER; 520.687-018 CANDY MOLDER, HAND; 700.687-022 CASTER HELPER; 713.684-042 WASHER; 739.384-018 HAIR PREPARER; 749.684-042 PUTTY GLAZER; 749.687-026 PLASTERER; 749.687-030 STRIPPER; 783.681-010 FUR BLENDER

Plant and Systems Occupations

95002A WATER TREATMENT PLANT AND SYSTEM OPERATORS. OOH Title/s: Water and Wastewater Treatment Plant Operators

Operate and control pollution treatment equipment to clean, purify, and neutralize water for human consumption. Operate and control equipment to remove harmful domestic and industrial pollution from wastewater in sewage treatment plants. Operates and adjusts controls on equipment to purify and clarify water, process or dispose of sewage, and generate power. Inspects equipment and monitors operating conditions, meters, and gauges to determine load requirements and detect malfunctions. Adds chemicals, such as ammonia, chlorine, and lime, to disinfect and deodorize water and other liquids. Collects and tests water and sewage samples, using test equipment and color analysis standards. Records operational data, personnel attendance, and meter and gauge readings on specified forms. Cleans and maintains tanks and filter beds, using hand tools and power tools. Maintains, repairs, and lubricates equipment, using hand tools and power tools. Directs and coordinates plant workers engaged in routine operations and maintenance activities.

Yearly Earnings: $31,460

Education: Long-term O-J-T

Knowledge: Production and Processing; Mechanical; Chemistry; Public Safety and Security

Abilities: Information Ordering; Perceptual Speed; Selective Attention; Time Sharing; Control Precision; Rate Control; Dynamic Flexibility; Gross Body Coordination; Gross Body Equilibrium

Skills: Science; Testing; Operation Monitoring; Operation and Control; Systems Perception

General Work Activities: Inspecting Equipment, Structures, or Material; Controlling Machines and Processes; Repairing and Maintaining Mechanical Equipment; Coordinating Work and Activities of Others

Job Characteristics: Responsible for Others' Health and Safety; Responsibility for Outcomes and Results; Sounds, Noise Levels are Distracting, etc.; Very Hot; Extremely Bright or Inadequate Lighting; Contaminants; Diseases/Infections; High Places; Hazardous Conditions; Climbing Ladders, Scaffolds, Poles, etc.; Walking or Running; Keeping or Regaining Balance; Common Protective or Safety Attire; Specialized Protective or Safety Attire; Degree of Automation

GOE Group/s: 05.06.03 Systems Operation: Oil, Gas, and Water Distribution; 05.06.04 Systems Operation: Processing; 06.02.11 Production Work: Equipment Operation, Chemical Processing; 06.02.16 Production Work: Equipment Operation, Textile, Fabric, and Leather Processing

CIP Program/s: 150506 Water Quality and Wastewater Treatment Technologists and Technicians

Related DOT Job/s: 954.382-010 PUMP-STATION OPERATOR, WATERWORKS; 954.382-014 WATER-TREATMENT-PLANT OPERATOR; 955.362-010 WASTEWATER-TREATMENT-PLANT OPERATOR; 955.382-010 CLARIFYING-PLANT OPERATOR; 955.382-014 WASTE-TREATMENT OPERATOR

95002B WATER TREATMENT PLANT ATTENDANTS. OOH Title/s: Water and Wastewater Treatment Plant Operators

Tend pumps, conveyors, blowers, chlorinators, vacuum filters, and other equipment used to decontaminate sewage. Operates and tends equipment—such as pumps, conveyors, blowers, and vacuum filters—that decontaminates wastewater. Adjusts pipe valves to regulate flow velocity to separate sludge by sedimentation. Turns valves to aerate sewage outflow and to control temperatures in tanks. Reads charts, flow meters, and gauges to monitor plant operations and detect equipment malfunctions. Collects samples to test water quality or purity.

Yearly Earnings: $31,460

Education: Long-term O-J-T

Knowledge: Production and Processing

Abilities: Control Precision; Gross Body Equilibrium

Skills: Testing; Operation Monitoring

General Work Activities: Controlling Machines and Processes

Job Characteristics: Contaminants; Diseases/Infections; Hazardous Conditions; Hazardous Equipment; Common Protective or Safety Attire; Specialized Protective or Safety Attire; Degree of Automation; Importance of Being Aware of New Events; Pace Determined by Speed of Equipment

GOE Group/s: 05.12.07 Elemental Work: Mechanical: Crushing, Mixing, Separating, and Chipping

CIP Program/s: 150506 Water Quality and Wastewater Treatment Technologists and Technicians

Related DOT Job/s: 955.585-010 WASTEWATER-TREATMENT-PLANT ATTENDANT

95005A GAS PROCESSING PLANT OPERATORS. OOH Title/s: Gas and Petroleum Plant and Systems Occupations

Control equipment—such as compressors, evaporators, heat exchangers, and refrigeration equipment—to process gas for utility companies and for industrial use. Controls fractioning columns, compressors, purifying towers, heat exchangers, and related equipment, to extract nitrogen and oxygen from air. Adjusts temperature, pressure, vacuum, level, flow rate, or transfer of gas, according to test results and knowledge of process and equipment. Controls operation of compressors, scrubbers, evaporators, and refrigeration equipment to liquefy, compress, or regasify natural gas. Observes pressure, temperature, level, and flow gauges to ensure standard operation. Tests oxygen for purity and moisture content at various stages of process, using burette and moisture meter. Reads logsheet to ascertain demand and disposition of product or to detect equipment malfunctions. Calculates gas ratios, using testing apparatus, to detect deviations from specifications. Records gauge readings and test results. Cleans and repairs equipment, using hand tools. Signals or directs workers tending auxiliary equipment.

Yearly Earnings: $31,460

Education: Long-term O-J-T

Knowledge: Production and Processing; Engineering and Technology; Mechanical; Chemistry
Abilities: None above average
Skills: Testing; Operation Monitoring; Operation and Control; Equipment Maintenance; Troubleshooting; Repairing
General Work Activities: Inspecting Equipment, Structures, or Material; Repairing and Maintaining Mechanical Equipment; Repairing and Maintaining Electrical Equipment
Job Characteristics: Contaminants; Hazardous Conditions; Common Protective or Safety Attire; Specialized Protective or Safety Attire; Consequence of Error; Degree of Automation; Importance of Being Exact or Accurate; Importance of Being Aware of New Events; Pace Determined by Speed of Equipment
GOE Group/s: 05.06.04 Systems Operation: Processing; 06.02.11 Production Work: Equipment Operation, Chemical Processing; 06.02.12 Production Work: Equipment Operation, Petroleum and Gas Processing
CIP Program/s: 410301 Chemical Technologists and Technicians; 470501 Stationary Energy Sources Installer and Operator
Related DOT Job/s: 552.362-014 OXYGEN-PLANT OPERATOR; 559.362-018 LIQUEFACTION-PLANT OPERATOR; 953.362-014 LIQUEFACTION-AND-REGASIFICATION-PLANT OPERATOR

95005B GAS DISTRIBUTION PLANT OPERATORS.
OOH Title/s: Gas and Petroleum Plant and Systems Occupations
Control equipment to regulate flow and pressure of gas for utility companies and industrial use. May control distribution of gas for a municipal or industrial plant or a single process in an industrial plant. Controls equipment to regulate flow and pressure of gas to feedlines of boilers, furnaces, and related steam-generating or heating equipment. Determines required governor adjustments, according to customer-demand estimates. Adjusts governors to maintain specified gas pressure and volume. Observes, records, and reports flow and pressure gauge readings on gas mains and fuel feedlines. Determines causes of abnormal pressure variances and makes corrective recommendations, such as installation of pipe to relieve overloading. Overhauls gas governors. Changes charts in recording meters. Cleans pit housing governors, using suction pump and shovel.
Yearly Earnings: $31,460
Education: Long-term O-J-T
Knowledge: Mechanical; Physics
Abilities: Control Precision
Skills: Operations Analysis; Operation Monitoring; Operation and Control; Equipment Maintenance; Troubleshooting
General Work Activities: Repairing and Maintaining Mechanical Equipment; Repairing and Maintaining Electrical Equipment
Job Characteristics: Contaminants; Hazardous Conditions; Degree of Automation
GOE Group/s: 05.06.02 Systems Operation: Stationary Engineering; 05.06.03 Systems Operation: Oil, Gas, and Water Distribution
CIP Program/s: 470501 Stationary Energy Sources Installer and Operator
Related DOT Job/s: 953.362-010 FUEL ATTENDANT; 953.362-018 PRESSURE CONTROLLER

95008 CHEMICAL PLANT AND SYSTEM OPERATORS. OOH Title/s: Chemical Plant and System Operators
Control or operate an entire chemical process or system of machines, such as reduction pots and heated air towers, through the use of panelboards, control boards, or semi-automatic equipment. Turns valves to regulate flow of product or byproducts through agitator tanks, storage drums, or neutralizer tanks, according to process. Starts pumps to wash and rinse reactor vessels, to exhaust gases and vapors, and to mix product with water. Moves control settings to make control adjustments on equipment units, affecting speed of chemical reactions and quality and yield. Monitors recording instruments, flowmeters, panel lights, and other indicators, and listens for warning signals to verify conformity of process conditions. Interprets chemical reactions visible through sight glasses or on television monitor and reviews laboratory test reports for process adjustments. Adjusts feed valves to regulate flow of liquid and steam to stills and of water to condensers and dephlegmator. Admits natural gas under pressure to exhaust naphtha from reactors. Manually regulates or shuts down equipment during emergency situations, as directed by supervisory personnel. Produces concentrated ammonia liquor by condensing vapors in water-cooled condensers. Records operating data, such as process conditions, test results, and instrument readings, calculating material requirements or yield according to formulas. Determines amount of ammonia in waste liquor and water, using titration test, and adjusts temperatures and pressures to reduce loss. Defrosts frozen valves, using steam hose. Patrols work area to observe level of carbon in thickener tank and wash solutions in overflow troughs to prevent spills. Gauges tank levels, using calibrated rod. Notifies maintenance, stationary-engineering, and other auxiliary personnel to correct equipment malfunction and adjust power, steam, water, or air supply. Inspects equipment for potential and actual hazards, wear, leaks, and other conditions requiring maintenance shutdown. Confers with technical and supervisory personnel to report or resolve conditions affecting safety, efficiency, and product quality. Draws sample of product in beaker and tests for acidity, using pH meter and standard titration test. Compares level of solution in graduated suction tube with conversion chart to determine acidity of sludge.
Yearly Earnings: $31,460
Education: Long-term O-J-T
Knowledge: Production and Processing; Chemistry; Public Safety and Security
Abilities: Information Ordering; Control Precision; Reaction Time
Skills: Mathematics; Science; Problem Identification; Testing; Operation Monitoring; Operation and Control; Product Inspection; Troubleshooting; Systems Perception
General Work Activities: Identifying Objects, Actions, and Events; Inspecting Equipment, Structures, or Material; Processing Information; Controlling Machines and Processes
Job Characteristics: Hazardous Conditions; Consequence of Error; Importance of Being Exact or Accurate; Importance of Being Sure All is Done
GOE Group/s: 06.01.03 Production Technology: Machine Set-up and Operation; 06.02.13 Production Work: Equipment Operation, Rubber, Plastics, and Glass Processing; 06.02.17 Production Work: Equipment Operation, Clay and Coke Processing; 06.02.18 Production Work: Equipment Operation, Assorted Materials Processing
CIP Program/s: 150607 Plastics Technologists and Technicians; 410301 Chemical Technologists and Technicians
Related DOT Job/s: 558.260-010 CHIEF OPERATOR; 559.165-010 CHECKER; 559.382-010 AMMONIA-STILL OPERATOR; 559.382-038 NAPHTHA-WASHING-SYSTEM OPERATOR; 559.662-014 WASH OPERATOR

95011 PETROLEUM PUMP SYSTEM OPERATORS.
OOH Title/s: Gas and Petroleum Plant and Systems Occupations
Control or operate manifold and pumping systems to circulate liquids through a petroleum refinery. Exclude workers who do not operate entire manifold or pumping systems. Starts battery of pumps, observes pressure meters and flowmeters, and turns valves to regulate pumping speeds according to schedules. Turns handwheels to open line valves and direct flow of product. Synchronizes activities

with other pump houses to ensure continuous flow of products and minimum of contamination between products. Plans movement of products through lines to processing, storage, and shipping units, utilizing knowledge of interconnections and capacities system. Reads operating schedules or instructions from dispatcher. Blends oils and gasolines. Signals other workers by telephone or radio to operate pumps, open and close valves, and check temperatures. Repairs pumps, lines, and auxiliary equipment. Records operating data, such as products and quantities pumped, stocks used, gauging results, and operating time.
Yearly Earnings: $31,460
Education: Long-term O-J-T
Knowledge: Mechanical; Chemistry
Abilities: Rate Control
Skills: Coordination; Operation Monitoring; Operation and Control; Troubleshooting; Repairing
General Work Activities: Controlling Machines and Processes; Repairing and Maintaining Mechanical Equipment
Job Characteristics: Degree of Automation
GOE Group/s: 06.02.12 Production Work: Equipment Operation, Petroleum and Gas Processing
CIP Program/s: 470501 Stationary Energy Sources Installer and Operator
Related DOT Job/s: 549.360-010 PUMPER

95014 PETROLEUM REFINERY AND CONTROL PANEL OPERATORS. OOH Title/s: Gas and Petroleum Plant and Systems Occupations

Analyze specifications and control continuous operation of petroleum refining and processing units. Operate control panel to regulate temperature, pressure, rate of flow, and tank level in petroleum refining unit, according to process schedules. Reads and analyzes specifications, schedules, logs, and test results to determine changes to equipment controls required to produce specified product. Operates control panel to coordinate and regulate process variables and to direct product flow rate, according to prescribed schedules. Monitors and adjusts unit controls to ensure safe and efficient operating conditions. Observes instruments, gauges, and meters to verify conformance to specified quality and quantity of product. Operates auxiliary equipment and controls multiple processing units during distilling or treating operations. Inspects equipment and listens for automated warning signals to determine location and nature of malfunction, such as leaks and breakage. Samples and tests liquids and gases for chemical characteristics and color of products, or sends products to laboratory for analysis. Repairs, lubricates, and maintains equipment or reports malfunctioning equipment to supervisor to schedule needed repairs. Cleans interior of processing units by circulating chemicals and solvents within unit. Compiles and records operating data, instrument readings, documents, and results of laboratory analyses.
Yearly Earnings: $31,460
Education: Long-term O-J-T
Knowledge: Production and Processing; Mechanical; Physics; Chemistry
Abilities: Time Sharing; Rate Control; Reaction Time; Auditory Attention; Sound Localization
Skills: Science; Testing; Operation Monitoring; Operation and Control; Product Inspection; Equipment Maintenance; Troubleshooting; Repairing
General Work Activities: Inspecting Equipment, Structures, or Material; Controlling Machines and Processes; Repairing and Maintaining Mechanical Equipment; Repairing and Maintaining Electrical Equipment
Job Characteristics: Hazardous Conditions; Keeping or Regaining Balance; Degree of Automation; Importance of Being Aware of New Events; Pace Determined by Speed of Equipment
GOE Group/s: 06.01.03 Production Technology: Machine Set-up and Operation; 06.02.12 Production Work: Equipment Operation, Petroleum and Gas Processing
CIP Program/s: 470501 Stationary Energy Sources Installer and Operator
Related DOT Job/s: 546.382-010 CONTROL-PANEL OPERATOR; 549.260-010 REFINERY OPERATOR

95017 GAUGERS. OOH Title/s: Gas and Petroleum Plant and Systems Occupations

Gauge and test oil in storage tanks. Regulate flow of oil into pipelines at wells, tank farms, refineries, and marine and rail terminals, following prescribed standards and regulations. Gauges quality of oil in storage tanks before and after delivery, using calibrated steel tape and conversion. Tests oil to determine amount of bottom sediment, water, and foreign materials, using centrifugal tester. Regulates flow of product into pipelines, using automated pumping equipment. Starts pumps and opens valves to regulate flow of oil into and out of tanks, according to delivery schedules. Reads automatic gauges at specified intervals to determine flow rate of oil into or from tanks and amount of oil in tanks. Gauges tanks containing petroleum and natural gas byproducts, such as condensate or natural gasoline. Operates pumps, teletype, and mobile radio. Calculates test results, using standard formulas. Turns bleeder valves or lowers sample container into tank to obtain oil sample. Records readings and test results. Lowers thermometer into tanks to obtain temperature reading. Records meter and pressure readings at gas well. Reports leaks or defective valves to maintenance. Clamps seal around valves to secure tanks. Inspects pipelines, valves, and flanges to detect malfunctions, such as loose connections and leaks. Tightens connections with wrenches, and greases and oils valves, using grease gun and oilcan. Cleans pumps, machinery, and equipment. Issues delivery or receiving tickets.
Yearly Earnings: $31,460
Education: Long-term O-J-T
Knowledge: Mechanical; Physics; Public Safety and Security
Abilities: Perceptual Speed; Response Orientation; Rate Control
Skills: Mathematics; Science; Testing; Operation Monitoring; Operation and Control; Equipment Maintenance; Troubleshooting; Systems Perception
General Work Activities: Inspecting Equipment, Structures, or Material; Repairing and Maintaining Mechanical Equipment
Job Characteristics: Contaminants; High Places; Hazardous Conditions; Climbing Ladders, Scaffolds, Poles, etc.; Keeping or Regaining Balance; Common Protective or Safety Attire
GOE Group/s: 05.06.03 Systems Operation: Oil, Gas, and Water Distribution
CIP Program/s: 470501 Stationary Energy Sources Installer and Operator
Related DOT Job/s: 914.384-010 GAUGER

95021 POWER GENERATING PLANT OPERATORS, EXCEPT AUXILIARY EQUIPMENT OPERATORS. OOH Title/s: Electric Power Generating Plant Operators and Power Distributors and Dispatchers

Control or operate machinery, such as steam-driven turbogenerators, to generate electric power, often through the use of panelboards, control boards, or semi-automatic equipment. Exclude workers operating auxiliary equipment, such as pumps, fans, compressors, filters, feedwater heaters, chlorinators, and condensers. Operates or controls machinery that generates electric

power, using control boards or semiautomatic equipment. Adjusts controls on equipment to generate specified electrical power. Monitors control and switchboard gauges to determine that electrical power distribution meets specifications. Compiles and records operational data on specified forms. Examines and tests electrical power distribution machinery and equipment, using testing devices. Maintains and repairs electrical power distribution machinery and equipment, using hand tools.
Yearly Earnings: $31,460
Education: Long-term O-J-T
Knowledge: Engineering and Technology; Mechanical
Abilities: Perceptual Speed; Selective Attention; Response Orientation; Reaction Time; Gross Body Equilibrium; Hearing Sensitivity; Auditory Attention; Sound Localization
Skills: Testing; Operation Monitoring; Operation and Control; Equipment Maintenance; Troubleshooting; Repairing
General Work Activities: Identifying Objects, Actions, and Events; Inspecting Equipment, Structures, or Material; Controlling Machines and Processes; Repairing and Maintaining Mechanical Equipment; Repairing and Maintaining Electrical Equipment
Job Characteristics: Cramped Work Space, Awkward Positions; High Places; Hazardous Conditions; Climbing Ladders, Scaffolds, Poles, etc.; Keeping or Regaining Balance; Common Protective or Safety Attire; Specialized Protective or Safety Attire; Consequence of Error
GOE Group/s: 05.06.01 Systems Operation: Electricity Generation and Transmission
CIP Program/s: 470501 Stationary Energy Sources Installer and Operator
Related DOT Job/s: 952.362-018 HYDROELECTRIC-STATION OPERATOR; 952.362-042 TURBINE OPERATOR; 952.382-010 DIESEL-PLANT OPERATOR; 952.382-014 POWER OPERATOR; 952.382-018 POWER-PLANT OPERATOR

95023 AUXILIARY EQUIPMENT OPERATORS, POWER. OOH Title/s: Electric Power Generating Plant Operators and Power Distributors and Dispatchers

Control and maintain auxiliary equipment—such as pumps, fans, compressors, condensers, feedwater heaters, filters, and chlorinators—that supply water, fuel, lubricants, air, and auxiliary power for turbines, generators, boilers, and other power-generating plant facilities. Tends portable or stationary high-pressure boilers that supply heat or power for engines, turbines, and steam-powered equipment. Opens and closes valves and switches in sequence upon signal from other worker to start or shut down auxiliary units. Replenishes electrolyte in batteries and oil in voltage transformers, and resets tripped electric relays. Tightens leaking gland and pipe joints and reports need for major equipment repairs. Reads gauges to verify that units are operating at specified capacity, and listens for sounds warning of mechanical malfunction. Cleans and lubricates equipment and collects oil, water, and electrolyte samples for laboratory analysis to prevent equipment failure or deterioration. Assists in making electrical repairs.
Yearly Earnings: $31,460
Education: Long-term O-J-T
Knowledge: Mechanical
Abilities: Control Precision
Skills: Operation Monitoring; Operation and Control; Equipment Maintenance
General Work Activities: Repairing and Maintaining Electrical Equipment
Job Characteristics: Cramped Work Space, Awkward Positions; Hazardous Conditions; Kneeling, Crouching, or Crawling; Degree of Automation; Pace Determined by Speed of Equipment
GOE Group/s: 05.06.01 Systems Operation: Electricity Generation and Transmission; 05.06.02 Systems Operation: Stationary Engineering
CIP Program/s: 470501 Stationary Energy Sources Installer and Operator
Related DOT Job/s: 951.685-010 FIRER, HIGH PRESSURE; 952.362-010 AUXILIARY-EQUIPMENT OPERATOR

95026 POWER REACTOR OPERATORS. OOH Title/s: Electric Power Generating Plant Operators and Power Distributors and Dispatchers

Control nuclear reactor that produces steam for generation of electric power. Coordinate operation of auxiliary equipment. Adjusts controls to start and shut down reactor and to regulate factors that affect reactor power level, following standard practices. Dispatches orders and instructions to personnel through radio telephone, or intercommunication system to coordinate operation of auxiliary equipment. Controls dual-purpose reactors that produce plutonium and steam. Controls operation of auxiliary equipment, such as turbines and generators. Assists in preparing, transferring, loading, and unloading nuclear fuel elements.
Yearly Earnings: $31,460
Education: Long-term O-J-T
Knowledge: Engineering and Technology; Physics; Chemistry; Telecommunications
Abilities: None above average
Skills: Instructing; Operation Monitoring; Operation and Control
General Work Activities: None above average
Job Characteristics: Radiation; Hazardous Conditions; Specialized Protective or Safety Attire; Consequence of Error; Degree of Automation; Importance of Being Exact or Accurate; Importance of Being Aware of New Events; Pace Determined by Speed of Equipment
GOE Group/s: 05.06.01 Systems Operation: Electricity Generation and Transmission
CIP Program/s: 410205 Nuclear/Nuclear Power Technologists and Technicians
Related DOT Job/s: 952.362-022 POWER-REACTOR OPERATOR

95028 POWER DISTRIBUTORS AND DISPATCHERS. OOH Title/s: Electric Power Generating Plant Operators and Power Distributors and Dispatchers

Coordinate, regulate, or distribute electricity or steam in generating stations and substations, and over electric power lines. May work for utility company or in a large industrial establishment. May spend some time generating power. Controls and operates equipment to regulate or distribute electricity or steam, according to data provided by recording or indicating instruments or computers. Adjusts controls to regulate the flow of power between generating stations, substations, and distribution lines. Turns and moves controls to adjust and activate power distribution equipment and machines. Calculates and determines load estimates or equipment requirements to control electrical distribution equipment or stations. Monitors switchboard and control board to ensure equipment operation and electrical and steam distribution. Directs activities of personnel engaged in the controlling and operating of electrical distribution equipment and machinery. Compiles and records operational data, such as chart and meter readings, power demands, and usage and operating times. Tends auxiliary equipment used in the power distribution process. Notifies workers or utilities of electrical and steam distribution process changes. Inspects equipment to ensure specifications are met and to detect defects. Repairs, maintains, and cleans equipment and machines, using hand tools.
Yearly Earnings: $31,460

Education: Long-term O-J-T
Knowledge: Mechanical; Physics
Abilities: Perceptual Speed; Selective Attention; Time Sharing; Response Orientation; Reaction Time; Gross Body Equilibrium; Far Vision; Hearing Sensitivity; Auditory Attention; Sound Localization
Skills: Instructing; Operation Monitoring; Operation and Control; Equipment Maintenance; Troubleshooting; Repairing; Management of Personnel Resources
General Work Activities: Identifying Objects, Actions, and Events; Inspecting Equipment, Structures, or Material; Evaluating Information against Standards; Controlling Machines and Processes; Repairing and Maintaining Mechanical Equipment; Repairing and Maintaining Electrical Equipment; Coordinating Work and Activities of Others; Developing and Building Teams; Guiding, Directing and Motivating Subordinates
Job Characteristics: Coordinate or Lead Others; Cramped Work Space, Awkward Positions; Hazardous Conditions; Consequence of Error; Importance of Being Aware of New Events
GOE Group/s: 05.06.01 Systems Operation: Electricity Generation and Transmission
CIP Program/s: 470501 Stationary Energy Sources Installer and Operator
Related DOT Job/s: 820.662-010 MOTOR-ROOM CONTROLLER; 952.167-014 LOAD DISPATCHER; 952.362-014 FEEDER-SWITCHBOARD OPERATOR; 952.362-026 SUBSTATION OPERATOR; 952.362-030 SUBSTATION OPERATOR APPRENTICE; 952.362-034 SWITCHBOARD OPERATOR; 952.362-038 SWITCHBOARD OPERATOR; 952.367-014 SWITCHBOARD OPERATOR ASSISTANT

95032 STATIONARY ENGINEERS. OOH Title/s: Stationary Engineers

Operate and maintain stationary engines and mechanical equipment to provide utilities for buildings or industrial processes. Operate equipment such as steam engines, generators, motors, turbines, and steam boilers. Adjusts controls and valves on equipment to provide power and regulate and set operations of system and industrial processes. Inspects equipment to determine need for repair, lubrication, or adjustment. Lights burners and opens valves on equipment, such as condensers, pumps, and compressors, to prepare system for operation. Reads dials of temperature, pressure, and ampere gauges and meters to detect malfunctions and to ensure specified operation of equipment. Lubricates, maintains, and repairs equipment, using hand tools and power tools. Adds chemicals or tends equipment to maintain temperature of fluids or atmosphere or to prevent scale build-up. Tests electrical system to determine voltage, using voltage meter. Records temperature, pressure, water levels, fuel consumption, and other data at specified intervals in logbook. Cleans equipment, using air hose, brushes, and rags, and drains water from pipes and air reservoir. Measures and tests moisture content of air, density of brine, or other operating indicators, using hydrometer and other instruments.
Yearly Earnings: $30,680
Education: Long-term O-J-T
Knowledge: Computers and Electronics; Engineering and Technology; Mechanical; Physics
Abilities: None above average
Skills: Testing; Operation Monitoring; Operation and Control; Equipment Maintenance; Troubleshooting; Repairing
General Work Activities: Inspecting Equipment, Structures, or Material; Controlling Machines and Processes; Repairing and Maintaining Mechanical Equipment; Repairing and Maintaining Electrical Equipment
Job Characteristics: Sounds, Noise Levels are Distracting, etc.; Hazardous Conditions; Specialized Protective or Safety Attire
GOE Group/s: 05.06.01 Systems Operation: Electricity Generation and Transmission; 05.06.02 Systems Operation: Stationary Engineering
CIP Program/s: 470201 Heating, Air Conditioning and Refrigeration Mechanics and Repairers; 470501 Stationary Energy Sources Installer and Operator
Related DOT Job/s: 950.362-014 REFRIGERATING ENGINEER; 950.382-010 BOILER OPERATOR; 950.382-018 GAS-ENGINE OPERATOR; 950.382-026 STATIONARY ENGINEER; 950.382-030 STATIONARY-ENGINEER APPRENTICE; 950.485-010 HUMIDIFIER ATTENDANT; 950.685-010 AIR-COMPRESSOR OPERATOR

95099 ALL OTHER PLANT AND SYSTEM OPERATORS. OOH Title/s: Material Moving Equipment Operators

All other plant and system operators not classified separately above.
Yearly Earnings: NA
Education: Unknown
GOE Group/s: 05.06.02 Systems Operation: Stationary Engineering; 05.06.03 Systems Operation: Oil, Gas, and Water Distribution; 05.06.04 Systems Operation: Processing; 05.11.02 Equipment Operation: Mining, Quarrying, Drilling; 06.01.03 Production Technology: Machine Set-up and Operation; 06.02.08 Production Work: Machine Work, Stone, Glass, and Clay; 06.02.11 Production Work: Equipment Operation, Chemical Processing; 06.02.13 Production Work: Equipment Operation, Rubber, Plastics, and Glass Processing; 06.02.18 Production Work: Equipment Operation, Assorted Materials Processing
CIP Program/s: 150506 Water Quality and Wastewater Treatment Technologists and Technicians; 150607 Plastics Technologists and Technicians; 410205 Nuclear/Nuclear Power Technologists and Technicians; 410301 Chemical Technologists and Technicians; 470201 Heating, Air Conditioning and Refrigeration Mechanics and Repairers; 470399 Industrial Equipment Maintenance and Repair, Other; 470501 Stationary Energy Sources Installer and Operator; 489999 Precision Production Trades, Other; 490299 Vehicle and Equipment Operators, Other
Related DOT Job/s: 515.382-010 GRINDING-MILL OPERATOR; 552.362-018 RECOVERY OPERATOR; 552.362-022 STILL OPERATOR, BATCH OR CONTINUOUS; 559.362-014 FINISHING-AREA OPERATOR; 559.362-026 PLANT OPERATOR, FURNACE PROCESS; 559.362-034 TOWER OPERATOR; 570.682-014 PLANT OPERATOR; 572.382-010 BATCH-AND-FURNACE OPERATOR; 590.362-010 FORMING-PROCESS WORKER; 613.662-010 ROLLING ATTENDANT; 914.362-010 COAL PIPELINE OPERATOR; 921.662-014 CHARGE-MACHINE OPERATOR; 939.362-014 PANELBOARD OPERATOR; 950.562-010 PANELBOARD OPERATOR; 950.585-010 VENTILATION EQUIPMENT TENDER; 954.382-018 WATERSHED TENDER; 955.362-014 INCINERATOR OPERATOR II

Motor Vehicle Operators

97102A TRUCK DRIVERS, HEAVY. OOH Title/s: Truckdrivers

Drive trucks with capacity of more than three tons to transport materials to specified destinations. Drives truck with capacity of more than three tons to transport and deliver cargo, materials, or damaged vehicles. Maintains radio or telephone contact with base or supervisor to receive instructions or to be dispatched to a new location. Maintains truck log according to state and federal regulations. Keeps record of materials and products transported. Positions blocks and ties rope around items to secure cargo for transport. Cleans, inspects, and

services vehicle. Operates equipment on vehicle to load, unload, or disperse cargo or materials. Obtains customer signature or collects payment for goods delivered and delivery charges. Assists in loading and unloading truck manually.
Yearly Earnings: $24,284
Education: Short-term O-J-T
Knowledge: Geography; Public Safety and Security; Law, Government, and Jurisprudence; Telecommunications; Transportation
Abilities: Spatial Orientation; Time Sharing; Control Precision; Multilimb Coordination; Response Orientation; Rate Control; Reaction Time; Wrist-Finger Speed; Speed of Limb Movement; Static Strength; Explosive Strength; Dynamic Strength; Trunk Strength; Stamina; Extent Flexibility; Dynamic Flexibility; Gross Body Coordination; Gross Body Equilibrium; Far Vision; Night Vision; Peripheral Vision; Depth Perception; Glare Sensitivity; Hearing Sensitivity; Auditory Attention; Sound Localization
Skills: None above average
General Work Activities: Performing General Physical Activities; Handling and Moving Objects; Interacting with Computers; Repairing and Maintaining Mechanical Equipment
Job Characteristics: Extremely Bright or Inadequate Lighting; Whole Body Vibration; Sitting; Consequence of Error; Degree of Automation
GOE Group/s: 05.08.01 Land and Water Vehicle Operation: Truck Driving; 05.08.03 Land and Water Vehicle Operation: Services Requiring Driving; 05.11.03 Equipment Operation: Drilling and Oil Exploration
CIP Program/s: 010204 Agricultural Power Machinery Operator; 010501 Agricultural Supplies Retailing and Wholesaling; 490205 Truck, Bus and Other Commercial Vehicle Operator
Related DOT Job/s: 900.683-010 CONCRETE-MIXING-TRUCK DRIVER; 902.683-010 DUMP-TRUCK DRIVER; 903.683-010 EXPLOSIVES-TRUCK DRIVER; 903.683-014 POWDER-TRUCK DRIVER; 903.683-018 TANK-TRUCK DRIVER; 905.483-010 MILK DRIVER; 905.663-010 GARBAGE COLLECTOR DRIVER; 905.663-014 TRUCK DRIVER, HEAVY; 905.683-010 WATER-TRUCK DRIVER II; 909.663-010 HOSTLER; 919.663-018 DRIVER-UTILITY WORKER; 919.663-026 TOW-TRUCK OPERATOR; 953.583-010 DRIP PUMPER

97102B TRACTOR-TRAILER TRUCK DRIVERS. OOH Title/s: Truckdrivers

Drive tractor-trailer trucks to transport products, livestock, or materials to specified destinations. Drives tractor-trailer combination, applying knowledge of commercial driving regulations, to transport and deliver products, livestock, or materials, usually over long distances. Maneuvers truck into loading or unloading position, following signals from loading crew as needed. Drives truck to weigh station before and after loading and along route, to document weight and conform to state regulations. Maintains driver log according to I.C.C. regulations. Inspects truck before and after trips and submits report indicating truck condition. Reads bill of lading to determine assignment. Fastens chains or binders to secure load on trailer during transit. Loads or unloads, or assists in loading and unloading truck. Works as member of two-person team driving tractor with sleeper bunk behind cab. Services truck with oil, fuel, and radiator fluid to maintain tractor-trailer. Obtains customer's signature or collects payment for services. Inventories and inspects goods to be moved. Wraps goods using pads, packing paper, and containers, and secures load to trailer wall using straps. Gives directions to helper in packing and moving goods to trailer.
Yearly Earnings: $24,284
Education: Short-term O-J-T
Knowledge: Geography; Public Safety and Security; Law, Government, and Jurisprudence; Transportation
Abilities: Spatial Orientation; Visualization; Time Sharing; Manual Dexterity; Multilimb Coordination; Response Orientation; Rate Control; Reaction Time; Wrist-Finger Speed; Speed of Limb Movement; Static Strength; Explosive Strength; Dynamic Strength; Trunk Strength; Stamina; Extent Flexibility; Dynamic Flexibility; Gross Body Coordination; Gross Body Equilibrium; Far Vision; Night Vision; Peripheral Vision; Depth Perception; Glare Sensitivity; Hearing Sensitivity; Auditory Attention
Skills: Operation and Control; Equipment Maintenance
General Work Activities: Performing General Physical Activities; Handling and Moving Objects; Interacting with Computers; Repairing and Maintaining Mechanical Equipment
Job Characteristics: Provide a Service to Others; Responsible for Others' Health and Safety; Sounds, Noise Levels are Distracting, etc.; Very Hot; Extremely Bright or Inadequate Lighting; Whole Body Vibration; Sitting; Frustrating Circumstances; Degree of Automation; Importance of Being Aware of New Events; Importance of Repeating Same Tasks; Pace Determined by Speed of Equipment
GOE Group/s: 05.08.01 Land and Water Vehicle Operation: Truck Driving
CIP Program/s: 030405 Logging/Timber Harvesting; 490205 Truck, Bus and Other Commercial Vehicle Operator
Related DOT Job/s: 904.383-010 TRACTOR-TRAILER-TRUCK DRIVER; 904.683-010 LOG-TRUCK DRIVER

97105 TRUCK DRIVERS, LIGHT—INCLUDING DELIVERY AND ROUTE WORKERS. OOH Title/s: Truckdrivers

Drive a truck, van, or automobile with a capacity under three tons. May drive light truck to deliver or pick up merchandise. May load and unload truck. Drives truck, van, or automobile with capacity under three tons to transport materials, products, or people. Loads and unloads truck, van, or automobile. Communicates with base or other vehicles using telephone or radio. Maintains records such as vehicle log, record of cargo, or billing statements in accordance with regulations. Inspects and maintains vehicle equipment and supplies. Presents billing invoice and collects receipt or payment. Assists passengers into and out of vehicle. Performs emergency roadside repairs.
Yearly Earnings: $24,284
Education: Short-term O-J-T
Knowledge: Geography; Law, Government, and Jurisprudence; Telecommunications; Transportation
Abilities: Spatial Orientation; Time Sharing; Control Precision; Multilimb Coordination; Response Orientation; Rate Control; Reaction Time; Static Strength; Explosive Strength; Dynamic Strength; Trunk Strength; Stamina; Extent Flexibility; Dynamic Flexibility; Gross Body Coordination; Gross Body Equilibrium; Far Vision; Night Vision; Peripheral Vision; Depth Perception; Glare Sensitivity; Hearing Sensitivity; Auditory Attention; Sound Localization; Speech Recognition
Skills: Equipment Maintenance; Repairing
General Work Activities: Handling and Moving Objects; Interacting with Computers; Repairing and Maintaining Mechanical Equipment
Job Characteristics: Responsible for Others' Health and Safety; Very Hot; Extremely Bright or Inadequate Lighting; Whole Body Vibration; Sitting; Degree of Automation; Importance of Being Aware of New Events
GOE Group/s: 05.08.01 Land and Water Vehicle Operation: Truck Driving; 05.08.03 Land and Water Vehicle Operation: Services Requiring Driving; 09.03.01 Passenger Services: Group Transportation
CIP Program/s: 010501 Agricultural Supplies Retailing and Wholesaling; 490205 Truck, Bus and Other Commercial Vehicle Operator
Related DOT Job/s: 906.683-010 FOOD-SERVICE DRIVER; 906.683-014 LIQUID-FERTILIZER SERVICER; 906.683-018 TELEPHONE-DIREC-

TORY-DISTRIBUTOR DRIVER; 906.683-022 TRUCK DRIVER, LIGHT; 913.663-018 DRIVER; 919.663-022 ESCORT-VEHICLE DRIVER

97108 BUS DRIVERS. OOH Title/s: Busdrivers

Drive bus, transporting passengers over specified routes to local or distant points, according to a time schedule. Assist passengers with baggage. Collect tickets or cash fares. Drives vehicle over specified route or to specified destination, according to time schedule, to transport passengers, complying with traffic regulations. Assists passengers with baggage, and collects tickets or cash fares. Parks vehicle at loading area for passengers to board. Loads and unloads baggage in baggage compartment. Regulates heating, lighting, and ventilating systems for passenger comfort. Advises passengers to be seated and orderly while on vehicle. Records cash receipts and ticket fares. Inspects vehicle and checks gas, oil, and water before departure. Reports delays or accidents. Makes minor repairs to vehicle and changes tires.

Yearly Earnings: $20,852
Education: Moderate-term O-J-T
Knowledge: Geography; Public Safety and Security; Transportation
Abilities: Spatial Orientation; Control Precision; Response Orientation; Reaction Time; Far Vision; Night Vision; Peripheral Vision
Skills: Operation and Control; Repairing
General Work Activities: Interacting with Computers; Repairing and Maintaining Mechanical Equipment; Performing for or Working with Public
Job Characteristics: Provide a Service to Others; Deal with External Customers; Responsible for Others' Health and Safety; Deal with Unpleasant or Angry People; Extremely Bright or Inadequate Lighting; Sitting; Special Uniform; Consequence of Error; Importance of Repeating Same Tasks
GOE Group/s: 09.03.01 Passenger Services: Group Transportation
CIP Program/s: 010501 Agricultural Supplies Retailing and Wholesaling; 490205 Truck, Bus and Other Commercial Vehicle Operator
Related DOT Job/s: 913.363-010 BUS DRIVER, DAY-HAUL OR FARM CHARTER; 913.463-010 BUS DRIVER; 913.663-014 MOBILE-LOUNGE DRIVER

97111 BUS DRIVERS, SCHOOL. OOH Title/s: Busdrivers

Transport students between pick-up points and school. Maintain order during trip and adhere to safety rules when loading and unloading pupils. Drives bus to transport pupils over specified routes. Maintains order among pupils during trip. Complies with local traffic regulations. Reports delays or accidents. Regulates heating, lighting, and ventilating systems for passenger comfort. Inspects bus and checks gas, oil, and water levels. Makes minor repairs to bus.

Yearly Earnings: $20,852
Education: Short-term O-J-T
Knowledge: Customer and Personal Service; Psychology; Geography; Public Safety and Security; Law, Government, and Jurisprudence; Transportation
Abilities: Spatial Orientation; Selective Attention; Time Sharing; Multilimb Coordination; Response Orientation; Rate Control; Reaction Time; Speed of Limb Movement; Far Vision; Night Vision; Peripheral Vision; Depth Perception; Glare Sensitivity; Hearing Sensitivity; Auditory Attention; Sound Localization
Skills: None above average
General Work Activities: Interacting with Computers; Resolving Conflicts, Negotiating with Others; Performing for or Working with Public
Job Characteristics: Job-Required Social Interaction; Responsible for Others' Health and Safety; Deal with Unpleasant or Angry People; Deal with Physical, Aggressive People; Sounds, Noise Levels are Distracting, etc.; Extremely Bright or Inadequate Lighting; Sitting; Consequence of Error; Importance of Being Aware of New Events
GOE Group/s: 09.03.01 Passenger Services: Group Transportation
CIP Program/s: 490205 Truck, Bus and Other Commercial Vehicle Operator
Related DOT Job/s: 913.463-010 BUS DRIVER

97114 TAXI DRIVERS AND CHAUFFEURS. OOH Title/s: Taxi Drivers and Chauffeurs

Drive automobiles, limousines, custom-built sedans, or hearses to transport passengers or cargo. May drive automobiles for delivery. Exclude ambulance drivers and bus drivers. Drives taxicab, limousine, company car, hearse, or privately owned vehicle to transport passengers. Communicates with taxicab dispatcher by radio or telephone to receive requests for passenger service. Collects and documents fees, payments, and deposits determined by rental contracts or taximeter recordings. Assists passengers to enter and exit vehicle, assists with luggage, and holds umbrellas in wet weather. Maintains vehicle by performing such duties as regulating tire pressure and adding gasoline, oil, and water. Delivers automobiles to customers from rental agency, car dealership, or repair shop. Tests performance of vehicle accessories, such as lights, horn, and windshield wipers. Performs errands for customers, such as carrying mail to and from post office. Vacuums, sweeps, and cleans interior, and washes and polishes exterior of automobile. Makes minor repairs on vehicle, such as fixing punctures, cleaning spark plugs, or adjusting carburetor. Drives completed motor vehicle off assembly line in manufacturing plant to specified repair, shipping, or storage area.

Yearly Earnings: $19,500
Education: Short-term O-J-T
Knowledge: Customer and Personal Service; Geography; Transportation
Abilities: Memorization; Spatial Orientation; Time Sharing; Multilimb Coordination; Response Orientation; Rate Control; Reaction Time; Speed of Limb Movement; Far Vision; Night Vision; Peripheral Vision; Depth Perception; Glare Sensitivity; Hearing Sensitivity; Sound Localization; Speech Recognition
Skills: Service Orientation; Operation and Control; Repairing
General Work Activities: Interacting with Computers
Job Characteristics: Job-Required Social Interaction; Provide a Service to Others; Deal with External Customers; Responsible for Others' Health and Safety; Frequency in Conflict Situations; Deal with Unpleasant or Angry People; Deal with Physical, Aggressive People; Special Uniform; Importance of Being Aware of New Events; Pace Determined by Speed of Equipment
GOE Group/s: 05.08.03 Land and Water Vehicle Operation: Services Requiring Driving; 09.03.02 Passenger Services: Individual Transportation
CIP Program/s: 490205 Truck, Bus and Other Commercial Vehicle Operator
Related DOT Job/s: 359.673-010 CHAUFFEUR; 359.673-014 CHAUFFEUR, FUNERAL CAR; 913.463-018 TAXI DRIVER; 913.663-010 CHAUFFEUR; 919.663-010 DELIVERER, CAR RENTAL; 919.683-014 DRIVER

97117 DRIVER/SALES WORKERS. OOH Title/s: Truckdrivers

Drive truck or other vehicle over established routes to deliver and sell goods, such as food products; pick up and deliver items, such as laundry; or refill, service, and collect coins from vending machines. Include newspaper delivery drivers. Drives truck to deliver such items as food, medical supplies, or newspapers. Collects coins from vending machines, refills machines, and removes aged merchandise. Sells food specialties, such as sandwiches and beverages, to office workers and patrons of sports events. Collects money from

customers, makes change, and records transactions on customer receipt. Calls on prospective customers to explain company services and to solicit new business. Records sales or delivery information on daily sales or delivery record. Informs regular customers of new products or services and price changes. Reviews list of dealers, customers, or station drops, and loads truck. Writes customer orders and sales contracts according to company guidelines. Listens to and resolves customers' complaints regarding product or services. Maintains truck and food-dispensing equipment and cleans inside of machines that dispense food or beverages. Arranges merchandise and sales promotion displays, or issues sales promotion materials to customers.
Yearly Earnings: $23,608
Education: Short-term O-J-T
Knowledge: Economics and Accounting; Sales and Marketing; Transportation
Abilities: None above average
Skills: Negotiation
General Work Activities: Interacting with Computers; Establishing and Maintaining Relationships; Selling or Influencing Others; Performing for or Working with Public
Job Characteristics: Persuade Someone to a Course of Action; Provide a Service to Others; Deal with External Customers; Very Hot
GOE Group/s: 05.08.03 Land and Water Vehicle Operation: Services Requiring Driving; 08.02.07 General Sales: Driving-Selling; 09.04.01 Customer Services: Food Services
CIP Program/s: 080705 General Retailing Operations
Related DOT Job/s: 292.353-010 DRIVER, SALES ROUTE; 292.363-010 NEWSPAPER-DELIVERY DRIVER; 292.463-010 LUNCH-TRUCK DRIVER; 292.483-010 COIN COLLECTOR; 292.667-010 DRIVER HELPER, SALES ROUTE; 292.687-010 COIN-MACHINE COLLECTOR

97199 ALL OTHER MOTOR VEHICLE OPERATORS. OOH Title/s: No related OOH occupation

All other motor vehicle operators not classified separately above.
Yearly Earnings: NA
Education: Unknown
GOE Group/s: 05.08.03 Land and Water Vehicle Operation: Services Requiring Driving; 05.11.01 Equipment Operation: Construction
CIP Program/s: 000000 NO CIP ASSIGNED
Related DOT Job/s: 919.683-022 STREET-SWEEPER OPERATOR; 919.683-030 DRIVER, STARTING GATE

Rail Transportation Workers

97302 RAILROAD CONDUCTORS AND YARDMASTERS. OOH Title/s: Rail Transportation Workers

Conductors cordinate activities of train crew engaged in transporting or providing services to passengers on passenger train, or in transporting freight on freight train. Coordinate activities of switch-engine crew engaged in switching railroad cars within yard of railroad, industrial plant, or similar location. Yardmasters coordinate activities of workers engaged in railroad traffic operations, such as the make-up or break-up of trains and switching inbound or outbound traffic of railroad yard on a specified section of line. Review train schedules and switching orders. Directs and instructs workers engaged in yard activities, such as switching track, coupling or uncoupling cars, and routing inbound and outbound traffic. Coordinates crew activities to transport and provide boarding, porter, maid, and meal services to passengers. Signals engineer to begin train run, stop train, or change speed, using radiotelephone, lantern, teletypewriter, or hand movement. Reviews schedules, switching orders, way bills, and shipping records to obtain cargo loading and unloading information. Observes yard traffic to determine tracks available to accommodate inbound and outbound traffic. Instructs workers to set warning signals in front and rear of train during emergency stops to warn oncoming trains. Confers with traffic control personnel, engineer, and other workers engaged in transporting freight to receive and convey instructions. Observes and communicates with passengers and instructs workers to regulate air-conditioning, lighting, and heating to ensure passenger safety and comfort. Observes lights on panelboard to monitor location of trains. Operates controls to electrically activate track switches and traffic signals. Inspects or supervises workers in inspection and maintenance of mechanical equipment to ensure efficient and safe train operation. Collects tickets, fares, or passes from passengers; answers questions concerning train rules, regulations, and schedules; and provides destination information. Inspects freight cars for compliance with sealing procedures, records car and corresponding seal number, and confirms route and destination information. Verifies accuracy of timekeeping instruments with engineer to assure station departure time complies with timetable schedules. Records departure and arrival times, messages, tickets and revenue collected, and passenger accommodations and destinations. Documents and prepares reports of accidents, unscheduled stops, or delays at completion of train run. Charts train movements to estimate arrival times.
Yearly Earnings: $34,996
Education: Work experience in a related occupation
Knowledge: Administration and Management; Geography; Transportation
Abilities: Rate Control; Reaction Time; Gross Body Equilibrium; Far Vision; Night Vision; Speech Clarity
Skills: Coordination; Instructing; Service Orientation; Operation Monitoring; Operation and Control; Equipment Maintenance; Troubleshooting; Systems Perception; Systems Evaluation; Management of Personnel Resources
General Work Activities: Getting Information Needed to Do the Job; Identifying Objects, Actions, and Events; Inspecting Equipment, Structures, or Material; Scheduling Work and Activities; Interacting with Computers; Drafting and Specifying Technical Devices, etc.; Communicating with Other Workers; Coordinating Work and Activities of Others; Developing and Building Teams; Guiding, Directing and Motivating Subordinates; Coaching and Developing Others; Performing Administrative Activities
Job Characteristics: Job-Required Social Interaction; Supervise, Coach, Train Others; Take a Position Opposed to Others; Deal with External Customers; Coordinate or Lead Others; Responsible for Others' Health and Safety; Responsibility for Outcomes and Results; Frequency in Conflict Situations; Deal with Physical, Aggressive People; Sounds, Noise Levels are Distracting, etc.; Hazardous Conditions; Walking or Running; Kneeling, Crouching, or Crawling; Keeping or Regaining Balance; Special Uniform; Degree of Automation; Importance of Being Aware of New Events; Pace Determined by Speed of Equipment
GOE Group/s: 09.01.04 Hospitality Services: Safety and Comfort Services; 11.11.03 Business Management: Transportation
CIP Program/s: 520201 Business Administration and Management, General
Related DOT Job/s: 184.167-262 TRAIN DISPATCHER; 184.167-278 YARD MANAGER; 198.167-010 CONDUCTOR, PASSENGER CAR; 198.167-014 CONDUCTOR, PULLMAN; 198.167-018 CONDUCTOR, ROAD FREIGHT; 910.167-010 CAR CHASER

97305 LOCOMOTIVE ENGINEERS. OOH Title/s: Rail Transportation Workers

Drive electric, diesel-electric, steam, or gas-turbine-electric locomotives to transport passengers or freight. Interpret train

orders, block or semaphore signals, and railroad rules and regulations. Interprets train orders, train signals, and railroad rules and regulations to drive locomotive, following safety regulations and time schedule. Observes track to detect obstructions. Receives starting signal from conductor and moves controls, such as throttle and air brakes, to drive locomotive. Confers with conductor or traffic control center personnel via radiophone to issue or receive information concerning stops, delays, or oncoming trains. Calls out train signals to assistant for verification of meaning to avoid errors in interpretation. Drives diesel-electric rail-detector car to transport rail-flaw-detecting machine over railroad. Inspects locomotive before run to verify specified fuel, sand, water, and other supplies. Synchronizes watch with that of conductor to ensure that departure time from station or terminal is in accordance with time schedule. Inspects locomotive after run to detect damaged or defective equipment. Prepares reports to explain accidents, unscheduled stops, or delays. May lubricate moving parts of locomotive.
Yearly Earnings: $34,996
Education: Work experience in a related occupation
Knowledge: Geography; Public Safety and Security; Telecommunications; Transportation
Abilities: Selective Attention; Time Sharing; Response Orientation; Rate Control; Reaction Time; Gross Body Equilibrium; Far Vision; Night Vision; Peripheral Vision; Depth Perception; Glare Sensitivity; Auditory Attention; Sound Localization; Speech Recognition
Skills: Operation Monitoring; Operation and Control; Equipment Maintenance; Systems Perception
General Work Activities: Inspecting Equipment, Structures, or Material; Interacting with Computers
Job Characteristics: Responsible for Others' Health and Safety; Sounds, Noise Levels are Distracting, etc.; Very Hot; Extremely Bright or Inadequate Lighting; Contaminants; Cramped Work Space, Awkward Positions; Whole Body Vibration; High Places; Hazardous Conditions; Hazardous Equipment; Climbing Ladders, Scaffolds, Poles, etc.; Using Hands on Objects, Tools, or Controls; Special Uniform; Consequence of Error; Frustrating Circumstances; Degree of Automation; Importance of Being Aware of New Events; Pace Determined by Speed of Equipment
GOE Group/s: 05.08.02 Land and Water Vehicle Operation: Rail Vehicle Operation
CIP Program/s: 000000 NO CIP ASSIGNED
Related DOT Job/s: 910.363-014 LOCOMOTIVE ENGINEER

97308 RAIL YARD ENGINEERS, DINKEY OPERATORS, AND HOSTLERS. OOH Title/s: Rail Transportation Workers

Drive switching or other locomotive or dinkey engines within railroad yard, industrial plant, quarry, construction project, or similar location. Drives switching locomotive within railroad yard or other establishment to switch railroad cars. Operates switching diesel engine to switch railroad cars, using remote control. Drives locomotives to and from various stations in roundhouse, to have locomotives cleaned, serviced, repaired, or supplied. Operates and controls dinkey engine to transport and shunt cars at industrial or mine site. Operates flatcar equipped with derrick, or railcar to transport personnel or equipment. Receives switching orders from yard conductor, and talks with conductor and other workers via radiotelephone, to exchange switching information. Reads daily car schedule to determine number of cars needed for next day's run. Inspects engine at start and end of shift, and refuels and lubricates engine as needed. Observes oil, air, and steam pressure gauges and water level, to ensure operating efficiency. Records number of cars available or number of cars sent to repair station and type of service needed. Inspects track for defects, and assists in installation or repair of rails and ties.
Yearly Earnings: $34,996
Education: Work experience in a related occupation
Knowledge: Telecommunications; Transportation
Abilities: Perceptual Speed; Spatial Orientation; Control Precision; Response Orientation; Rate Control; Reaction Time; Night Vision; Peripheral Vision; Depth Perception; Glare Sensitivity
Skills: Operation Monitoring; Operation and Control; Equipment Maintenance
General Work Activities: Interacting with Computers; Repairing and Maintaining Mechanical Equipment
Job Characteristics: Sounds, Noise Levels are Distracting, etc.; Whole Body Vibration; Making Repetitive Motions; Degree of Automation; Pace Determined by Speed of Equipment
GOE Group/s: 05.08.02 Land and Water Vehicle Operation: Rail Vehicle Operation; 05.11.04 Equipment Operation: Material Handling
CIP Program/s: 490299 Vehicle and Equipment Operators, Other
Related DOT Job/s: 910.363-018 YARD ENGINEER; 910.583-010 LABORER, CAR BARN; 910.683-010 HOSTLER; 919.663-014 DINKEY OPERATOR

97311 LOCOMOTIVE FIRERS. OOH Title/s: Rail Transportation Workers

Monitor locomotive instruments and watch for dragging equipment, obstacles on rights-of-way, and train signals during run. Watch for and relay traffic signals from yard workers to yard engineer in railroad yard. Observes oil, temperature, and pressure gauges on dashboard to ascertain if engine is operating safely and efficiently. Observes track from left side of locomotive to detect obstructions on track. Observes train signals along route and verifies their meaning for engineer. Observes train as it goes around curves to detect dragging equipment and smoking journal boxes. Observes signal from workers in rear of train and relays information to engineer. Signals other worker to set brakes and to throw track switches when switching cars from train to way stations. Inspects locomotive to detect damaged or worn parts. Inventories supplies, such as fuel, water, and sand, to ensure safe, efficient operation during run. Operates locomotive during emergency. Starts diesel engine to warm engine before run.
Yearly Earnings: $34,996
Education: Work experience in a related occupation
Knowledge: Geography; Public Safety and Security; Transportation
Abilities: Perceptual Speed; Response Orientation; Rate Control; Reaction Time; Gross Body Equilibrium; Far Vision; Night Vision; Peripheral Vision; Depth Perception; Glare Sensitivity; Auditory Attention
Skills: Operation Monitoring; Operation and Control; Systems Perception
General Work Activities: Interacting with Computers
Job Characteristics: Responsible for Others' Health and Safety; Sounds, Noise Levels are Distracting, etc.; Very Hot; Extremely Bright or Inadequate Lighting; Contaminants; Cramped Work Space, Awkward Positions; Whole Body Vibration; Hazardous Conditions; Hazardous Equipment; Climbing Ladders, Scaffolds, Poles, etc.; Keeping or Regaining Balance; Special Uniform; Common Protective or Safety Attire; Consequence of Error; Degree of Automation; Importance of Being Exact or Accurate; Importance of Being Sure All is Done; Importance of Being Aware of New Events
GOE Group/s: 05.08.02 Land and Water Vehicle Operation: Rail Vehicle Operation
CIP Program/s: 000000 NO CIP ASSIGNED
Related DOT Job/s: 910.363-010 FIRER, LOCOMOTIVE

97314 SUBWAY AND STREETCAR OPERATORS.
OOH Title/s: Rail Transportation Workers
Operate subway or elevated suburban train or electric-powered streetcar to transport passengers. Pilots rail-guided public transportation, such as subways, elevated suburban trains, or electric powered streetcars to transport passengers. Opens and closes doors of train or streetcar to allow passengers to enter or leave vehicle. Answers questions from passengers concerning fares, schedules, and routings. Collects fares from passengers and issues change and transfers. Records readings of coin receptor at beginning and end of shift to verify amount of money received during shift.
Yearly Earnings: $34,996
Education: Moderate-term O-J-T
Knowledge: Customer and Personal Service; Geography; Foreign Language; Transportation
Abilities: Spatial Orientation; Control Precision; Response Orientation; Rate Control; Reaction Time; Night Vision; Glare Sensitivity
Skills: Operation Monitoring; Operation and Control
General Work Activities: Interacting with Computers; Performing for or Working with Public
Job Characteristics: Provide a Service to Others; Deal with External Customers; Deal with Unpleasant or Angry People; Deal with Physical, Aggressive People; Sitting; Special Uniform; Importance of Repeating Same Tasks; Pace Determined by Speed of Equipment
GOE Group/s: 05.08.02 Land and Water Vehicle Operation: Rail Vehicle Operation; 09.03.01 Passenger Services: Group Transportation
CIP Program/s: 490299 Vehicle and Equipment Operators, Other
Related DOT Job/s: 910.683-014 MOTOR OPERATOR; 913.463-014 STREETCAR OPERATOR

97317A TRAIN CREW MEMBERS. OOH Title/s: Rail Transportation Workers
Inspect couplings, air hoses, journal boxes, and handbrakes on trains to ensure that they function properly. Inspects couplings, air hoses, journal boxes, and handbrakes to ensure that they are securely fastened and function properly. Reports to conductor any equipment requiring major repair. Climbs ladder to top of car to set brakes or to ride atop to control its speed when shunted. Makes minor repairs to couplings, air hoses, and journal boxes using hand tools. Signals locomotive engineer to start or stop train when coupling or uncoupling cars. Sets flares, flags, lanterns, or torpedoes in front and at rear of train during emergency stops to warn oncoming trains. Observes signals from other crew members. Pulls or pushes track switch to reroute cars. Collects tickets, fares, and passes from passengers. Answers questions from passengers concerning train rules, station, and timetable information. Assists passengers to board and leave train. Adjusts controls to regulate air-conditioning, heating, and lighting on train for comfort of passengers. Places passengers' baggage in rack above seats on train.
Yearly Earnings: $34,996
Education: Work experience in a related occupation
Knowledge: Customer and Personal Service; Transportation
Abilities: Spatial Orientation; Reaction Time; Dynamic Strength; Stamina; Dynamic Flexibility; Gross Body Coordination; Gross Body Equilibrium; Far Vision; Night Vision; Auditory Attention; Sound Localization
Skills: Service Orientation; Equipment Maintenance; Repairing
General Work Activities: Performing General Physical Activities; Repairing and Maintaining Mechanical Equipment; Performing for or Working with Public
Job Characteristics: Provide a Service to Others; Deal with External Customers; Sounds, Noise Levels are Distracting, etc.; Extremely Bright or Inadequate Lighting; Whole Body Vibration; High Places; Standing; Climbing Ladders, Scaffolds, Poles, etc.; Walking or Running; Keeping or Regaining Balance; Special Uniform
GOE Group/s: 05.12.05 Elemental Work: Mechanical: Braking, Switching, and Coupling; 09.01.04 Hospitality Services: Safety and Comfort Services
CIP Program/s: 470302 Heavy Equipment Maintenance and Repair
Related DOT Job/s: 910.364-010 BRAKER, PASSENGER TRAIN; 910.367-010 BRAKE COUPLER, ROAD FREIGHT

97317B RAILROAD YARD WORKERS. OOH Title/s: Rail Transportation Workers
Perform a variety of activities such as coupling railcars and operating railroad track switches in railroad yard to facilitate the movement of rail cars within the yard. Throws track switches to route cars to different sections of yard. Receives oral or written instructions indicating which cars are to be switched and track assignments. Raises lever to couple and uncouple cars for make-up and break-up of trains. Opens and closes chute gates to load and unload cars. Watches for and relays traffic signals to start and stop cars during shunting, using arm or lantern. Signals engineer to start and stop engine. Rides atop cars that have been shunted and turns handwheel to control speed or stop car at specified position. Attaches cable to cars being hoisted by cable or chain in mines, quarries or industrial plants. Connects air hose to car, using wrench. Opens and closes ventilation doors.
Yearly Earnings: $34,996
Education: Work experience in a related occupation
Knowledge: Transportation
Abilities: Spatial Orientation; Control Precision; Response Orientation; Rate Control; Reaction Time; Speed of Limb Movement; Explosive Strength; Dynamic Strength; Stamina; Gross Body Coordination; Gross Body Equilibrium; Far Vision; Night Vision; Depth Perception; Glare Sensitivity; Auditory Attention; Sound Localization
Skills: Operation and Control
General Work Activities: Performing General Physical Activities; Interacting with Computers
Job Characteristics: Sounds, Noise Levels are Distracting, etc.; Very Hot; Whole Body Vibration; Radiation; High Places; Hazardous Equipment; Climbing Ladders, Scaffolds, Poles, etc.; Keeping or Regaining Balance; Pace Determined by Speed of Equipment
GOE Group/s: 05.12.03 Elemental Work: Mechanical: Loading, Moving; 05.12.05 Elemental Work: Mechanical: Braking, Switching, and Coupling; 05.12.20 Elemental Work: Mechanical: Signaling
CIP Program/s: 000000 NO CIP ASSIGNED
Related DOT Job/s: 910.367-022 LOCOMOTIVE OPERATOR HELPER; 910.664-010 YARD COUPLER; 910.667-026 SWITCH TENDER; 932.664-010 BRAKE HOLDER

97399A ON-TRACK MOBILE EQUIPMENT OPERATORS. OOH Title/s: Rail Transportation Workers
Operate on-track mobile equipment to move railcars or trailers. Drives electric car or trackmobile on rail tracks to transport material to specified areas within work yard. Drives and operates transfer table to transport equipment and material to specified areas. Operates electrically powered locomotive or winch to move railroad cars in and out of material lock pressurized chamber. Operates electric car by remote control from pulpit. Moves levers and controls to position, align, and couple cars. Fastens and engages winch hook to cars to start locomotive. Observes signals to determine when specified air pressure has been reached.
Yearly Earnings: $34,996
Education: Work experience in a related occupation
Knowledge: Transportation

Abilities: Multilimb Coordination; Gross Body Equilibrium; Peripheral Vision; Depth Perception; Glare Sensitivity; Sound Localization
Skills: Operation and Control
General Work Activities: Controlling Machines and Processes; Interacting with Computers
Job Characteristics: Sounds, Noise Levels are Distracting, etc.; Very Hot; Extremely Bright or Inadequate Lighting; Cramped Work Space, Awkward Positions; Whole Body Vibration; Hazardous Conditions; Hazardous Equipment; Consequence of Error; Degree of Automation; Pace Determined by Speed of Equipment
GOE Group/s: 05.08.02 Land and Water Vehicle Operation: Rail Vehicle Operation; 05.11.01 Equipment Operation: Construction; 05.11.04 Equipment Operation: Material Handling
CIP Program/s: 490202 Construction Equipment Operator; 490299 Vehicle and Equipment Operators, Other
Related DOT Job/s: 850.663-018 LOCK TENDER II; 910.683-022 TRANSFER-TABLE OPERATOR; 919.683-018 RAIL-TRACTOR OPERATOR; 919.683-026 TRACKMOBILE OPERATOR

97399B RAILROAD CONTROL TOWER SWITCHING AND CAR RETARDING OPERATORS.

OOH Title/s: Rail Transportation Workers

Control switching and braking equipment from control tower to control movement of rail cars in railyard. Operates track switching equipment in control tower to route train traffic and regulate speed of freight cars in railroad yard. Observes moving trains and controls track switches and car-retarder system to couple freight cars. Reads switching orders and arrival and departure schedules to determine sequence of movement and tracks for routing trains. Receives and transmits switching orders by telephone or telegraph.
Yearly Earnings: $34,996
Education: Work experience in a related occupation
Knowledge: Public Safety and Security; Telecommunications; Transportation
Abilities: Selective Attention; Response Orientation; Rate Control; Reaction Time; Far Vision; Depth Perception; Glare Sensitivity
Skills: Operation Monitoring; Operation and Control
General Work Activities: Controlling Machines and Processes
Job Characteristics: Responsible for Others' Health and Safety; Sitting; Consequence of Error; Degree of Automation; Importance of Being Exact or Accurate; Importance of Being Aware of New Events; Pace Determined by Speed of Equipment
GOE Group/s: 05.03.03 Engineering Technology: Expediting and Coordinating; 05.12.05 Elemental Work: Mechanical: Braking, Switching, and Coupling
CIP Program/s: 490202 Construction Equipment Operator
Related DOT Job/s: 910.362-010 TOWER OPERATOR; 910.382-010 CAR-RETARDER OPERATOR

Water Transportation and Related Workers

97502A SHIP AND BOAT CAPTAINS. OOH Title/s: Water Transportation Occupations; Fishers, Hunters, and Trappers

Command vessels in oceans, bays, lakes, rivers, and coastal waters. Commands water vessels, such as passenger and freight vessels, fishing vessels, yachts, tugboats, barges, deep submergence vehicles, and ferryboats. Directs and coordinates activities of crew or workers, such as loading and unloading, operating signal devices, fishing, and repairing defective equipment. Steers and operates vessel or orders helmsperson to steer vessel, using radio, depth finder, radar, lights, buoys, and lighthouses. Computes position, sets course, and determines speed, using charts, area plotting sheets, compass, sextant, and knowledge of local conditions. Inspects vessel to ensure safety of crew and passengers, efficient and safe operation of vessel and equipment, and conformance to regulations. Signals crew or deckhands to rig tow lines, open or close gates and ramps, and pull guard chains across entry. Monitors sonar and navigational aids and reads gauges to verify sufficient levels of hydraulic fluid, air pressure, and oxygen. Calculates sighting of land, using electronic sounding devices and following contour lines on chart. Maintains records of daily activities, movements, and ports-of-call, and prepares progress and personnel reports. Interviews, hires, and instructs crew, and assigns watches and living quarters. Tows and maneuvers barge or signals tugboat to tow barge to destination. Signals passing vessels, using whistle, flashing lights, flags, and radio. Purchases supplies and equipment, contacts buyers to sell fish, and resolves questions or problems with customs officials. Collects fares from customers or signals ferryboat helper to collect fares.
Yearly Earnings: $32,968
Education: Work experience in a related occupation
Knowledge: Administration and Management; Personnel and Human Resources; Computers and Electronics; Mathematics; Physics; Geography; Foreign Language; Public Safety and Security; Law, Government, and Jurisprudence; Telecommunications; Transportation
Abilities: Spatial Orientation; Selective Attention; Time Sharing; Control Precision; Multilimb Coordination; Response Orientation; Rate Control; Reaction Time; Speed of Limb Movement; Gross Body Equilibrium; Far Vision; Night Vision; Peripheral Vision; Depth Perception; Glare Sensitivity; Hearing Sensitivity; Auditory Attention; Sound Localization; Speech Recognition; Speech Clarity
Skills: Mathematics; Social Perceptiveness; Coordination; Instructing; Problem Identification; Implementation Planning; Equipment Selection; Operation Monitoring; Operation and Control; Equipment Maintenance; Troubleshooting; Systems Perception; Identification of Key Causes; Judgment and Decision Making; Systems Evaluation; Time Management; Management of Financial Resources; Management of Material Resources; Management of Personnel Resources
General Work Activities: Getting Information Needed to Do the Job; Monitoring Processes, Material, or Surroundings; Identifying Objects, Actions, and Events; Inspecting Equipment, Structures, or Material; Estimating Needed Characteristics; Making Decisions and Solving Problems; Developing Objectives and Strategies; Scheduling Work and Activities; Interacting with Computers; Implementing Ideas, Programs, etc.; Repairing and Maintaining Electrical Equipment; Communicating with Other Workers; Coordinating Work and Activities of Others; Developing and Building Teams; Guiding, Directing and Motivating Subordinates; Performing Administrative Activities; Staffing Organizational Units; Monitoring and Controlling Resources
Job Characteristics: Objective or Subjective Information; Job-Required Social Interaction; Supervise, Coach, Train Others; Persuade Someone to a Course of Action; Take a Position Opposed to Others; Deal with External Customers; Coordinate or Lead Others; Responsible for Others' Health and Safety; Responsibility for Outcomes and Results; Very Hot; Extremely Bright or Inadequate Lighting; Whole Body Vibration; Keeping or Regaining Balance; Making Repetitive Motions; Special Uniform; Consequence of Error; Importance of Being Exact or Accurate; Importance of Being Sure All is Done; Importance of Being Aware of New Events; Pace Determined by Speed of Equipment
GOE Group/s: 05.04.02 Air and Water Vehicle Operation: Water; 05.12.01 Elemental Work: Mechanical: Supervision
CIP Program/s: 490303 Fishing Technology/Commercial Fishing; 490309 Marine Science/Merchant Marine Officer; 490399 Water Transportation Workers, Other

Related DOT Job/s: 197.133-010 CAPTAIN, FISHING VESSEL; 197.133-014 MASTER, YACHT; 197.133-030 TUGBOAT CAPTAIN; 197.161-010 DREDGE CAPTAIN; 197.163-010 FERRYBOAT CAPTAIN; 197.163-014 MASTER, PASSENGER BARGE; 197.163-018 MASTER, RIVERBOAT; 197.167-010 MASTER, SHIP; 911.137-010 BARGE CAPTAIN; 911.137-014 DERRICK-BOAT CAPTAIN; 911.263-010 DEEP SUBMERGENCE VEHICLE OPERATOR; 911.363-010 FERRYBOAT OPERATOR

97505 MATES—SHIP, BOAT, AND BARGE. OOH Title/s: Water Transportation Occupations; Fishers, Hunters, and Trappers

Supervise and coordinate activities of crew aboard ships, boats, barges, or dredges. Supervises crew in repair or replacement of defective vessel gear and equipment. Supervises crew in cleaning and maintaining decks, superstructure, and bridge. Observes loading and unloading of cargo and equipment to ensure that handling and storage are according to specifications. Supervises activities of crew engaged in ship's activity, such as barging, towing, dredging, or fishing. Stands watch on vessel during specified periods while vessel is underway. Inspects equipment—such as cargo-handling gear, lifesaving equipment, fishing; towing; or dredging gear; and visual-signaling equipment—for defects. Assumes command of vessel in event ship master becomes incapacitated. Observes water from masthead and advises navigational direction. Determines geographical position of ship, using loran and azimuths of celestial bodies. Steers vessel, utilizing navigation devices, such as compass and sexton, and navigational aids, such as lighthouses and buoys.

Yearly Earnings: $32,968

Education: Work experience in a related occupation

Knowledge: Administration and Management; Personnel and Human Resources; Mechanical; Physics; Geography; Public Safety and Security; Telecommunications; Transportation

Abilities: Spatial Orientation; Control Precision; Rate Control; Gross Body Equilibrium; Far Vision; Night Vision; Peripheral Vision; Depth Perception; Glare Sensitivity

Skills: Coordination; Implementation Planning; Operation Monitoring; Operation and Control; Repairing; Systems Perception; Identifying Downstream Consequences; Time Management; Management of Personnel Resources

General Work Activities: Inspecting Equipment, Structures, or Material; Estimating Needed Characteristics; Interacting with Computers; Repairing and Maintaining Mechanical Equipment; Coordinating Work and Activities of Others; Developing and Building Teams; Guiding, Directing and Motivating Subordinates; Coaching and Developing Others

Job Characteristics: Supervise, Coach, Train Others; Coordinate or Lead Others; Responsibility for Outcomes and Results; Very Hot; Extremely Bright or Inadequate Lighting; Cramped Work Space, Awkward Positions; High Places; Climbing Ladders, Scaffolds, Poles, etc.; Keeping or Regaining Balance

GOE Group/s: 03.04.03 Elemental Work: Plants and Animals: Hunting and Fishing; 05.04.02 Air and Water Vehicle Operation: Water; 05.12.01 Elemental Work: Mechanical: Supervision

CIP Program/s: 490303 Fishing Technology/Commercial Fishing; 490309 Marine Science/Merchant Marine Officer; 490399 Water Transportation Workers, Other

Related DOT Job/s: 197.133-018 MATE, FISHING VESSEL; 197.133-022 MATE, SHIP; 197.133-034 TUGBOAT MATE; 197.137-010 DREDGE MATE; 911.133-010 CADET, DECK

97508 PILOTS, SHIP. OOH Title/s: Water Transportation Occupations

Command ships to steer them into and out of harbors, estuaries, straits, and sounds, and on rivers, lakes, and bays. Must be licensed by U.S. Coast Guard with limitations indicating class and tonnageof vessels for which license is valid and route and waters that may be piloted. Directs course and speed of ship on basis of specialized knowledge of local winds, weather, tides, and current. Orders worker at helm to steer ship. Navigates ship to avoid reefs, outlying shoals, and other hazards, utilizing aids to navigation, such as lighthouses and buoys. Signals tugboat captain to berth and unberth ship.

Yearly Earnings: $32,968

Education: Work experience in a related occupation

Knowledge: Physics; Geography; Public Safety and Security; Law, Government, and Jurisprudence; Transportation

Abilities: Memorization; Flexibility of Closure; Spatial Orientation; Selective Attention; Time Sharing; Control Precision; Response Orientation; Rate Control; Reaction Time; Speed of Limb Movement; Gross Body Equilibrium; Far Vision; Night Vision; Peripheral Vision; Depth Perception; Glare Sensitivity; Auditory Attention; Sound Localization

Skills: Monitoring; Synthesis/Reorganization; Implementation Planning; Operation Monitoring; Operation and Control; Systems Perception; Identifying Downstream Consequences; Judgment and Decision Making; Systems Evaluation; Time Management; Management of Personnel Resources

General Work Activities: Getting Information Needed to Do the Job; Monitoring Processes, Material, or Surroundings; Identifying Objects, Actions, and Events; Estimating Needed Characteristics; Interacting with Computers

Job Characteristics: Supervise, Coach, Train Others; Take a Position Opposed to Others; Coordinate or Lead Others; Responsible for Others' Health and Safety; Responsibility for Outcomes and Results; Sounds, Noise Levels are Distracting, etc.; Very Hot; Extremely Bright or Inadequate Lighting; High Places; Climbing Ladders, Scaffolds, Poles, etc.; Keeping or Regaining Balance; Special Uniform; Consequence of Error; Frustrating Circumstances; Degree of Automation; Importance of Being Aware of New Events; Pace Determined by Speed of Equipment

GOE Group/s: 05.04.02 Air and Water Vehicle Operation: Water

CIP Program/s: 490309 Marine Science/Merchant Marine Officer

Related DOT Job/s: 197.133-026 PILOT, SHIP

97511 MOTORBOAT OPERATORS. OOH Title/s: Water Transportation Occupations

Operate motor-driven boats to carry passengers and freight; take depth soundings in turning basin; serve as liaison between ships, ship to shore, harbor and beach, or area patrol. Starts boat and steers boat with helm or tiller. Casts off securing lines and starts motor. Gives directions for loading and seating in boat. Maintains equipment, such as range markers, fire extinguishers, boat fenders, lines, pumps, and fittings. Services motor by changing oil and lubricating parts. Positions wheeled beaching gear at end of ramp in water, pushes and pulls amphibious plane over ramping gear, and draws plane and gear up ramp onto shore for removal to hanger, using tractor. Cleans boat and amphibious plane and repairs boat hull and superstructure, using hand tools, paint, and brushes. Tunes up, overhauls, or replaces engine.

Yearly Earnings: $32,968

Education: Short-term O-J-T

Knowledge: Mechanical; Geography; Transportation

Abilities: Spatial Orientation; Control Precision; Response Orientation; Rate Control; Reaction Time; Static Strength; Explosive Strength; Extent Flexibility; Dynamic Flexibility; Gross Body Equilibrium; Far Vision; Night Vision; Peripheral Vision; Depth Perception; Glare Sensitivity; Hearing Sensitivity; Auditory Attention; Sound Localization

Skills: Operation Monitoring; Operation and Control; Equipment Maintenance; Troubleshooting; Repairing
General Work Activities: Interacting with Computers; Repairing and Maintaining Mechanical Equipment
Job Characteristics: Provide a Service to Others; Deal with External Customers; Responsible for Others' Health and Safety; Deal with Unpleasant or Angry People; Sounds, Noise Levels are Distracting, etc.; Very Hot; Extremely Bright or Inadequate Lighting; Cramped Work Space, Awkward Positions; Whole Body Vibration; Hazardous Equipment; Hazardous Situations; Kneeling, Crouching, or Crawling; Keeping or Regaining Balance; Bending or Twisting the Body; Common Protective or Safety Attire; Consequence of Error; Frustrating Circumstances; Importance of Being Aware of New Events; Pace Determined by Speed of Equipment
GOE Group/s: 05.08.04 Land and Water Vehicle Operation: Boat Operation
CIP Program/s: 490399 Water Transportation Workers, Other
Related DOT Job/s: 911.663-010 MOTORBOAT OPERATOR; 919.683-010 DOCK HAND

97514 ABLE SEAMEN. OOH Title/s: Water Transportation Occupations

Stand watch at bow or on wing of bridge to look for obstructions in path of vessel. Measure water depth. Turn wheel on bridge or use emergency equipment as directed by mate. Break out, rig, overhaul, and store cargo-handling gear, stationary rigging, and running gear. Chip rust from and paint deck or ship's structure. Must hold government-issued certification. Must hold certification when working aboard liquid-carrying vessels. Measures depth of water in shallow or unfamiliar waters, using leadline, and telephones or shouts information to bridge. Breaks out, rigs, overhauls, and stows cargo-handling gear, stationary rigging, and running gear. Paints and chips rust on deck or superstructure of ship. Stands watch from bow of ship or wing of bridge to look for obstruction in path of ship. Overhauls lifeboats and lifeboat gear, and lowers or raises lifeboats with winch or falls. Steers ship under direction of ship's commander or navigating officer, or directs helmsman to steer, following designated course. Steers ship and maintains visual communication with other ships. Stands by wheel when ship is on automatic pilot and verifies accuracy of course by comparing with magnetic compass. Relays specified signals to ships in vicinity, using visual signaling devices, such as blinker light and semaphore. Stows or removes cargo from ship's hold. Maintains ship's log while in port, and stands gangway watch to prevent unauthorized persons from boarding ship. Gives directions to crew engaged in cleaning wheelhouse and quarter deck.
Yearly Earnings: $32,968
Education: Short-term O-J-T
Knowledge: Mechanical; Geography; Public Safety and Security; Telecommunications; Transportation
Abilities: Spatial Orientation; Selective Attention; Time Sharing; Control Precision; Response Orientation; Rate Control; Reaction Time; Speed of Limb Movement; Static Strength; Explosive Strength; Trunk Strength; Stamina; Extent Flexibility; Dynamic Flexibility; Gross Body Coordination; Gross Body Equilibrium; Far Vision; Night Vision; Peripheral Vision; Depth Perception; Glare Sensitivity; Hearing Sensitivity; Auditory Attention; Sound Localization; Speech Recognition; Speech Clarity
Skills: Operation and Control
General Work Activities: Performing General Physical Activities; Handling and Moving Objects; Interacting with Computers; Repairing and Maintaining Mechanical Equipment
Job Characteristics: Supervise, Coach, Train Others; Take a Position Opposed to Others; Coordinate or Lead Others; Responsible for Others' Health and Safety; Frequency in Conflict Situations; Deal with Unpleasant or Angry People; Sounds, Noise Levels are Distracting, etc.; Very Hot; Extremely Bright or Inadequate Lighting; Cramped Work Space, Awkward Positions; Whole Body Vibration; High Places; Hazardous Conditions; Standing; Climbing Ladders, Scaffolds, Poles, etc.; Keeping or Regaining Balance; Bending or Twisting the Body; Special Uniform; Consequence of Error; Frustrating Circumstances; Importance of Being Aware of New Events
GOE Group/s: 05.04.02 Air and Water Vehicle Operation: Water; 05.12.03 Elemental Work: Mechanical: Loading, Moving
CIP Program/s: 490399 Water Transportation Workers, Other
Related DOT Job/s: 911.363-014 QUARTERMASTER; 911.364-010 ABLE SEAMAN

97517 ORDINARY SEAMEN AND MARINE OILERS.

OOH Title/s: Water Transportation Occupations
Stand deck department watches and perform a variety of tasks to preserve the painted surface of the ship and to maintain lines and ship equipment, such as running and cargo-handling gear. May oil and grease moving parts of engines and auxiliary equipment. Must hold government-issued certification. Must hold certification when working aboard liquid-carrying vessels. Cleans and polishes wood trim, brass, and other metal parts. Chips and cleans rust spots on deck, superstructure, and sides of ship, using wire brush and hand or air chipping machine. Paints or varnishes decks, superstructures, lifeboats, or sides of ship. Lubricates machinery, equipment, and engine parts, such as gears, shafts, and bearings. Sweeps and washes deck, using broom, mops, brushes, and hose. Splices and repairs cables and ropes, using marlinespike, wirecutters, twine, and hand tools. Inspects, repairs, maintains, and adjusts sails and rigging. Handles lines to moor vessel to wharf, tie up vessel to another vessel, or rig towing lines. Stands watch from bow of ship or wing of bridge to look for obstructions in path of ship. Examines machinery for specified pressure and flow of lubricants. Loads or unloads materials from vessel. Reads pressure and temperature gauges or displays, and records data in engineering log. Lowers and mans lifeboat in case of emergency. Assists engineer in overhauling and adjusting machinery. Records data in ship's log such as weather conditions and distance traveled. Makes emergency repairs to auxiliary engine on sailboat. Turns wheel while observing compass to maintain ship on course.
Yearly Earnings: $32,968
Education: Short-term O-J-T
Knowledge: Building and Construction; Mechanical; Geography; Public Safety and Security; Transportation
Abilities: Spatial Orientation; Control Precision; Multilimb Coordination; Rate Control; Speed of Limb Movement; Static Strength; Explosive Strength; Trunk Strength; Stamina; Extent Flexibility; Dynamic Flexibility; Gross Body Coordination; Gross Body Equilibrium; Far Vision; Night Vision; Peripheral Vision; Depth Perception; Glare Sensitivity; Hearing Sensitivity; Auditory Attention; Sound Localization
Skills: Operation Monitoring; Operation and Control; Equipment Maintenance; Repairing
General Work Activities: Performing General Physical Activities; Handling and Moving Objects; Interacting with Computers; Repairing and Maintaining Mechanical Equipment
Job Characteristics: Responsible for Others' Health and Safety; Sounds, Noise Levels are Distracting, etc.; Very Hot; Extremely Bright or Inadequate Lighting; Cramped Work Space, Awkward Positions; Whole Body Vibration; High Places; Hazardous Equipment; Hazardous Situations; Climbing Ladders, Scaffolds, Poles, etc.; Kneeling, Crouching, or Crawling; Keeping or Regaining Balance; Bending or

Twisting the Body; Special Uniform; Common Protective or Safety Attire; Importance of Being Aware of New Events
GOE Group/s: 05.08.04 Land and Water Vehicle Operation: Boat Operation; 05.12.08 Elemental Work: Mechanical: Lubricating; 05.12.18 Elemental Work: Mechanical: Cleaning and Maintenance
CIP Program/s: 490306 Marine Maintenance and Repair; 490399 Water Transportation Workers, Other
Related DOT Job/s: 911.584-010 MARINE OILER; 911.664-014 SAILOR, PLEASURE CRAFT; 911.687-022 DECKHAND; 911.687-030 ORDINARY SEAMAN

97521 SHIP ENGINEERS. OOH Title/s: Water Transportation Occupations

Supervise and coordinate activities of crew engaged in operating and maintaining engines, boilers, deck machinery, and electrical, sanitary, and refrigeration equipment aboard ship. Orders crew to repair or replace defective parts of engines and other equipment. Inspects engines and other equipment. Stands engine-room watch, observing that lubricants and water levels are maintained in machinery and load on generators is within limits. Starts engines to propel ship and regulates engines and power transmission to control speed of ship. Maintains engineering log and bellbook (orders of changes in speed and direction of ship). Repairs machinery, using hand tools and power tools.
Yearly Earnings: $32,968
Education: Work experience in a related occupation
Knowledge: Engineering and Technology; Mechanical; Public Safety and Security; Telecommunications; Transportation
Abilities: Control Precision; Gross Body Equilibrium; Glare Sensitivity
Skills: Coordination; Operation Monitoring; Operation and Control; Equipment Maintenance; Troubleshooting; Repairing; Management of Personnel Resources
General Work Activities: Inspecting Equipment, Structures, or Material; Controlling Machines and Processes; Interacting with Computers; Repairing and Maintaining Mechanical Equipment; Coordinating Work and Activities of Others; Developing and Building Teams; Guiding, Directing and Motivating Subordinates; Coaching and Developing Others
Job Characteristics: Supervise, Coach, Train Others; Responsibility for Outcomes and Results; Very Hot; Extremely Bright or Inadequate Lighting; Cramped Work Space, Awkward Positions; Whole Body Vibration; Climbing Ladders, Scaffolds, Poles, etc.; Kneeling, Crouching, or Crawling; Keeping or Regaining Balance; Special Uniform; Importance of Being Aware of New Events
GOE Group/s: 05.06.02 Systems Operation: Stationary Engineering
CIP Program/s: 490309 Marine Science/Merchant Marine Officer
Related DOT Job/s: 197.130-010 ENGINEER

Air Transportation Workers

97702B AIRPLANE PILOTS, COMMERCIAL. OOH Title/s: Aircraft Pilots

Pilot airplane to transport passengers, mail, or freight for other commercial purposes. Must have commercial pilot's license. Starts engines, operates controls, and pilots airplane to transport passengers, mail, or freight, adhering to flight plan and regulations and procedures. Obtains and reviews data, such as load weight, fuel supply, weather conditions, and flight schedule. Plots flight pattern and files flight plan with appropriate officials. Orders changes in fuel supply, load, route, or schedule to ensure safety of flight. Conducts preflight checks and reads gauges to verify that fluids and pressure are at prescribed levels. Operates radio equipment and contacts control tower for takeoff, clearance, arrival instructions, and other information. Coordinates flight activities with ground crew and air-traffic control, and informs crew members of flight and test procedures. Holds commercial pilot's license issued by Federal Aviation Administration. Conducts in-flight tests and evaluations, at specified altitudes, in all types of weather to determine receptivity and other characteristics of equipment and systems. Logs information, such as flight time, altitude flown, and fuel consumption. Plans and formulates flight activities and test schedules and prepares flight evaluation reports. Gives training and instruction in aircraft operations for students and other pilots.
Yearly Earnings: $52,936
Education: Long-term O-J-T
Knowledge: Computers and Electronics; Engineering and Technology; Mechanical; Physics; Geography; Medicine and Dentistry; Education and Training; Foreign Language; Public Safety and Security; Law, Government, and Jurisprudence; Telecommunications; Transportation
Abilities: Oral Expression; Information Ordering; Mathematical Reasoning; Number Facility; Speed of Closure; Flexibility of Closure; Perceptual Speed; Spatial Orientation; Selective Attention; Time Sharing; Control Precision; Multilimb Coordination; Response Orientation; Rate Control; Reaction Time; Wrist-Finger Speed; Speed of Limb Movement; Far Vision; Visual Color Discrimination; Night Vision; Peripheral Vision; Depth Perception; Glare Sensitivity; Hearing Sensitivity; Auditory Attention; Sound Localization; Speech Recognition; Speech Clarity
Skills: Active Listening; Speaking; Science; Critical Thinking; Learning Strategies; Monitoring; Coordination; Instructing; Implementation Planning; Testing; Operation Monitoring; Operation and Control; Troubleshooting; Systems Perception; Identifying Downstream Consequences; Judgment and Decision Making; Systems Evaluation
General Work Activities: Getting Information Needed to Do the Job; Monitoring Processes, Material, or Surroundings; Identifying Objects, Actions, and Events; Inspecting Equipment, Structures, or Material; Estimating Needed Characteristics; Processing Information; Making Decisions and Solving Problems; Scheduling Work and Activities; Organizing, Planning, and Prioritizing; Interacting with Computers; Coordinating Work and Activities of Others; Teaching Others; Coaching and Developing Others
Job Characteristics: Supervise, Coach, Train Others; Coordinate or Lead Others; Responsible for Others' Health and Safety; Responsibility for Outcomes and Results; Sounds, Noise Levels are Distracting, etc.; Cramped Work Space, Awkward Positions; Whole Body Vibration; Radiation; High Places; Sitting; Special Uniform; Consequence of Error; Frustrating Circumstances; Degree of Automation; Importance of Being Exact or Accurate; Importance of Being Sure All is Done; Importance of Being Aware of New Events; Importance of Repeating Same Tasks
GOE Group/s: 05.04.01 Air and Water Vehicle Operation: Air
CIP Program/s: 490102 Aircraft Pilot and Navigator (Professional)
Related DOT Job/s: 196.263-014 AIRPLANE PILOT, COMMERCIAL; 196.263-030 EXECUTIVE PILOT; 196.263-034 FACILITIES-FLIGHT-CHECK PILOT

97702C SMALL AIRPLANE PILOTS. OOH Title/s: Aircraft Pilots

Pilot airplane or helicopter to perform activities such as crop dusting and aerial photography. Pilots airplane or helicopter to photograph areas of earth's surface or to dust or spray fields. Adjusts controls to hold aircraft on course and to ensure coverage of area to be sprayed or photographed. Holds aircraft in level flight to eliminate forward and lateral tilt of aircraft. Sights along pointers on aircraft to topographical landmarks. Studies maps to become acquainted with topography, obstacles, or hazards, such as air turbulence, hedgerows,

and hills. Notifies livestock owners to move livestock from property to be sprayed or dusted, and arranges for warning signals to be posted.
Yearly Earnings: $52,936
Education: Long-term O-J-T
Knowledge: Food Production; Physics; Geography; Fine Arts; Public Safety and Security; Telecommunications; Transportation
Abilities: Information Ordering; Flexibility of Closure; Perceptual Speed; Spatial Orientation; Selective Attention; Time Sharing; Arm-Hand Steadiness; Control Precision; Multilimb Coordination; Response Orientation; Rate Control; Reaction Time; Gross Body Equilibrium; Far Vision; Night Vision; Peripheral Vision; Depth Perception; Glare Sensitivity; Hearing Sensitivity; Auditory Attention; Sound Localization
Skills: Operation Monitoring; Operation and Control
General Work Activities: Identifying Objects, Actions, and Events; Interacting with Computers
Job Characteristics: Responsible for Others' Health and Safety; Sounds, Noise Levels are Distracting, etc.; Extremely Bright or Inadequate Lighting; Contaminants; Cramped Work Space, Awkward Positions; Whole Body Vibration; Radiation; High Places; Sitting; Climbing Ladders, Scaffolds, Poles, etc.; Keeping or Regaining Balance; Using Hands on Objects, Tools, or Controls; Specialized Protective or Safety Attire; Consequence of Error; Frustrating Circumstances; Degree of Automation; Importance of Being Exact or Accurate; Importance of Being Aware of New Events; Importance of Repeating Same Tasks; Pace Determined by Speed of Equipment
GOE Group/s: 05.04.01 Air and Water Vehicle Operation: Air
CIP Program/s: 010501 Agricultural Supplies Retailing and Wholesaling; 490102 Aircraft Pilot and Navigator (Professional)
Related DOT Job/s: 196.263-010 AIRPLANE PILOT; 196.263-018 AIRPLANE PILOT, PHOTOGRAMMETRY

97702D FLIGHT INSTRUCTORS. OOH Title/s: Aircraft Pilots

Train new and experienced pilots seeking licenses or experience on new aircraft. Instructs new pilots in company regulations and procedures and in operation of company's aircraft. Conducts training and review courses in use of equipment, flight procedures, and techniques. Observes and evaluates performance, knowledge, and skills of pilots, using manuals, check lists, or proficiency tests. Explains operation of aircraft components, such as altimeter, tachometer, rudder, and flaps. Demonstrates techniques for controlling aircraft during taxiing, takeoff, spins, stalls, turns, and landings. Notes pilot's compliance with or infringement of company or Federal Aviation Administration flight regulations. Compiles and issues reports on findings to appropriate company and FAA officials. Holds commercial pilot's certificate, with instructor's rating, issued by Federal Aviation Administration.
Yearly Earnings: $52,936
Education: Long-term O-J-T
Knowledge: Personnel and Human Resources; Computers and Electronics; Geography; Education and Training; Public Safety and Security; Law, Government, and Jurisprudence; Telecommunications; Transportation
Abilities: Written Comprehension; Oral Expression; Information Ordering; Mathematical Reasoning; Number Facility; Speed of Closure; Flexibility of Closure; Perceptual Speed; Spatial Orientation; Selective Attention; Time Sharing; Control Precision; Multilimb Coordination; Response Orientation; Rate Control; Reaction Time; Speed of Limb Movement; Gross Body Equilibrium; Far Vision; Visual Color Discrimination; Night Vision; Peripheral Vision; Depth Perception; Glare Sensitivity; Hearing Sensitivity; Auditory Attention; Sound Localization; Speech Clarity
Skills: Reading Comprehension; Speaking; Science; Critical Thinking; Active Learning; Learning Strategies; Monitoring; Instructing; Service Orientation; Problem Identification; Testing; Operation Monitoring; Operation and Control; Systems Evaluation; Management of Personnel Resources
General Work Activities: Identifying Objects, Actions, and Events; Interacting with Computers; Teaching Others; Coaching and Developing Others
Job Characteristics: Job-Required Social Interaction; Supervise, Coach, Train Others; Coordinate or Lead Others; Responsible for Others' Health and Safety; Responsibility for Outcomes and Results; Sounds, Noise Levels are Distracting, etc.; Cramped Work Space, Awkward Positions; Whole Body Vibration; High Places; Climbing Ladders, Scaffolds, Poles, etc.; Special Uniform; Consequence of Error; Degree of Automation; Importance of Being Exact or Accurate; Importance of Being Sure All is Done; Importance of Being Aware of New Events
GOE Group/s: 05.04.01 Air and Water Vehicle Operation: Air
CIP Program/s: 131399 Teacher Education, Specific Academic and Vocational Programs; 490102 Aircraft Pilot and Navigator (Professional)
Related DOT Job/s: 196.223-010 INSTRUCTOR, FLYING I; 196.223-014 INSTRUCTOR, PILOT; 196.263-022 CHECK PILOT

97702E FLIGHT NAVIGATORS. OOH Title/s: Aircraft Pilots

Locate position and direct course of airplane in flight, using navigational aids such as charts, maps, sextant, and slide rule. Establishes position of airplane, using navigation instruments and charts, celestial observation, or dead reckoning. Directs course of airplane and deviations from course required by weather conditions, such as wind drifts and forecasted atmospheric conditions. Utilizes navigation aids, such as radio beams and beacons, to locate position and direct course of airplane. Records and maintains flight log, including time in flight, altitude flown, and fuel consumed.
Yearly Earnings: $52,936
Education: Long-term O-J-T
Knowledge: Physics; Geography; Foreign Language; Public Safety and Security; Telecommunications; Transportation
Abilities: Deductive Reasoning; Mathematical Reasoning; Number Facility; Speed of Closure; Flexibility of Closure; Perceptual Speed; Spatial Orientation; Selective Attention; Time Sharing; Response Orientation; Rate Control; Near Vision; Far Vision; Night Vision; Peripheral Vision; Depth Perception; Glare Sensitivity; Auditory Attention; Sound Localization; Speech Recognition
Skills: Mathematics; Operation Monitoring; Operation and Control
General Work Activities: Getting Information Needed to Do the Job; Monitoring Processes, Material, or Surroundings; Identifying Objects, Actions, and Events; Estimating Needed Characteristics; Judging Qualities of Things, Services, People; Interacting with Computers
Job Characteristics: Take a Position Opposed to Others; Responsible for Others' Health and Safety; Responsibility for Outcomes and Results; Sounds, Noise Levels are Distracting, etc.; Cramped Work Space, Awkward Positions; Whole Body Vibration; High Places; Sitting; Keeping or Regaining Balance; Special Uniform; Consequence of Error; Frustrating Circumstances; Degree of Automation; Importance of Being Exact or Accurate; Importance of Being Sure All is Done; Importance of Being Aware of New Events
GOE Group/s: 05.03.01 Engineering Technology: Surveying
CIP Program/s: 490102 Aircraft Pilot and Navigator (Professional)
Related DOT Job/s: 196.167-014 NAVIGATOR

97702H FLIGHT ENGINEERS. OOH Title/s: Aircraft Pilots

Make preflight, inflight, and postflight inspections, adjustments, and minor repairs to ensure safe and efficient operation of

aircraft. Inspects aircraft for defects, such as fuel or oil leaks and malfunctions in electrical, hydraulic, and pressurization systems. Adjusts instruments and makes minor repairs, such as replacing fuses and freeing jammed controls, to ensure safe operation of aircraft. Monitors fuel gauges and control panel to verify aircraft performance, and regulates engine speed according to instructions. Verifies passenger and cargo distribution and amount of fuel to ensure conformance to weight and balance specifications. Reports needed repairs to ground maintenance personnel. Keeps log of rate of fuel consumption, engine performance, and uncorrected malfunctions.
Yearly Earnings: $52,936
Education: Long-term O-J-T
Knowledge: Computers and Electronics; Engineering and Technology; Design; Mechanical; Physics; Geography; Public Safety and Security; Telecommunications; Transportation
Abilities: Oral Comprehension; Written Comprehension; Problem Sensitivity; Deductive Reasoning; Mathematical Reasoning; Number Facility; Speed of Closure; Flexibility of Closure; Perceptual Speed; Spatial Orientation; Selective Attention; Time Sharing; Finger Dexterity; Control Precision; Multilimb Coordination; Response Orientation; Rate Control; Reaction Time; Far Vision; Visual Color Discrimination; Night Vision; Peripheral Vision; Hearing Sensitivity; Auditory Attention; Sound Localization
Skills: Science; Testing; Operation Monitoring; Operation and Control; Equipment Maintenance; Troubleshooting; Repairing; Systems Evaluation
General Work Activities: Identifying Objects, Actions, and Events; Inspecting Equipment, Structures, or Material; Repairing and Maintaining Mechanical Equipment
Job Characteristics: Responsible for Others' Health and Safety; Sounds, Noise Levels are Distracting, etc.; Extremely Bright or Inadequate Lighting; Cramped Work Space, Awkward Positions; Whole Body Vibration; Radiation; High Places; Hazardous Conditions; Climbing Ladders, Scaffolds, Poles, etc.; Keeping or Regaining Balance; Special Uniform; Consequence of Error; Frustrating Circumstances; Importance of Being Exact or Accurate; Importance of Being Sure All is Done; Importance of Being Aware of New Events; Importance of Repeating Same Tasks
GOE Group/s: 05.03.06 Engineering Technology: Industrial and Safety
CIP Program/s: 490102 Aircraft Pilot and Navigator (Professional)
Related DOT Job/s: 621.261-018 FLIGHT ENGINEER

97702J HELICOPTER PILOTS. OOH Title/s: Aircraft Pilots

Pilot helicopter for commercial purposes, such as transporting passengers and cargo. Pilots helicopter to transport passengers and cargo, conduct search and rescue missions, fight fires, report traffic conditions, or for other purposes. Plans flight, following government and company regulations, using aeronautical charts and navigation instruments. Inspects helicopter prior to departure to detect malfunctions or unsafe conditions, using check list. Writes specified information in flight record, such as time in flight, altitude flown, and fuel consumption. Instructs students in operation of helicopter and equipment, and flight procedures and techniques.
Yearly Earnings: $52,936
Education: Long-term O-J-T
Knowledge: Computers and Electronics; Engineering and Technology; Geography; Medicine and Dentistry; Therapy and Counseling; Education and Training; Public Safety and Security; Law, Government, and Jurisprudence; Telecommunications; Transportation
Abilities: Number Facility; Flexibility of Closure; Perceptual Speed; Spatial Orientation; Selective Attention; Time Sharing; Arm-Hand Steadiness; Control Precision; Multilimb Coordination; Response Orientation; Rate Control; Reaction Time; Speed of Limb Movement; Gross Body Equilibrium; Far Vision; Night Vision; Peripheral Vision; Depth Perception; Glare Sensitivity; Hearing Sensitivity; Auditory Attention; Sound Localization
Skills: Critical Thinking; Learning Strategies; Coordination; Instructing; Service Orientation; Implementation Planning; Operation Monitoring; Operation and Control; Systems Perception
General Work Activities: Inspecting Equipment, Structures, or Material; Interacting with Computers; Teaching Others
Job Characteristics: Supervise, Coach, Train Others; Responsible for Others' Health and Safety; Sounds, Noise Levels are Distracting, etc.; Extremely Bright or Inadequate Lighting; Cramped Work Space, Awkward Positions; Whole Body Vibration; Radiation; High Places; Sitting; Keeping or Regaining Balance; Special Uniform; Consequence of Error; Frustrating Circumstances; Degree of Automation; Importance of Being Exact or Accurate; Importance of Being Sure All is Done; Importance of Being Aware of New Events; Pace Determined by Speed of Equipment
GOE Group/s: 05.04.01 Air and Water Vehicle Operation: Air
CIP Program/s: 490102 Aircraft Pilot and Navigator (Professional)
Related DOT Job/s: 196.263-038 HELICOPTER PILOT

Other Transportation-Related Workers

97802 BRIDGE, LOCK, AND LIGHTHOUSE TENDERS. OOH Title/s: Material Moving Equipment Operators

Operate and tend bridges, canal locks, and lighthouses to permit marine passage on inland waterways, near shores, and at danger points in waterway passages. May supervise such operations. Include drawbridge operators, lock tenders and operators, and slip bridge operators. Controls machinery to open and close canal locks and dams, railroad or highway drawbridges, or horizontally or vertically adjustable bridges. Moves levers to activate traffic signals, navigation lights, and alarms. Operates gas, steam, and hydroelectric generating units to control mechanisms to open locks or bridge. Observes approaching vessels to determine size and speed, and listens for whistle signal indicating desire to pass. Signals vessels to proceed. Observes positions of vessels to ensure optimum utilization of lock space or bridge opening space. Attaches rope or cable lines to bitt on lock deck or wharf to secure vessel. Relays messages to vessels in waterway. Inspects bridge and bridge or canal auxiliary equipment. Logs data, such as water levels and weather conditions. Prepares accident reports. Cleans, oils, greases, and makes minor repairs and adjustments to equipment. Records names, type, and destinations of vessels passing through bridge opening or locks, and number of trains or vehicles crossing bridge. Writes and submits maintenance work requisitions. Repairs motors, generators, power lines, and other electrical equipment. Installs mechanical and electrical equipment.
Yearly Earnings: $24,440
Education: Moderate-term O-J-T
Knowledge: Engineering and Technology; Mechanical; Transportation
Abilities: Spatial Orientation; Rate Control; Reaction Time; Gross Body Equilibrium; Far Vision; Night Vision; Peripheral Vision; Depth Perception; Glare Sensitivity; Hearing Sensitivity; Sound Localization
Skills: Installation; Operation Monitoring; Operation and Control; Equipment Maintenance; Troubleshooting; Repairing
General Work Activities: Inspecting Equipment, Structures, or Material; Controlling Machines and Processes; Interacting with Comput-

ers; Repairing and Maintaining Mechanical Equipment; Repairing and Maintaining Electrical Equipment
Job Characteristics: Responsible for Others' Health and Safety; Sounds, Noise Levels are Distracting, etc.; Very Hot; Extremely Bright or Inadequate Lighting; High Places; Hazardous Equipment; Climbing Ladders, Scaffolds, Poles, etc.; Keeping or Regaining Balance; Special Uniform; Consequence of Error; Degree of Automation; Importance of Being Aware of New Events
GOE Group/s: 05.05.09 Craft Technology: Mechanical Work; 05.11.04 Equipment Operation: Material Handling
CIP Program/s: 000000 NO CIP ASSIGNED
Related DOT Job/s: 371.362-010 DRAWBRIDGE OPERATOR; 911.131-014 LOCK TENDER, CHIEF OPERATOR; 911.362-010 LOCK OPERATOR; 919.682-010 BRIDGE OPERATOR, SLIP

97805 SERVICE STATION ATTENDANTS. OOH Title/s: Handlers, Equipment Cleaners, Helpers, and Laborers
Service automobiles, buses, trucks, boats, and other automotive or marine vehicles with fuel, lubricants, and accessories. Collect payment for services and supplies. May lubricate vehicle, change motor oil, install antifreeze, or replace lights or other accessories such as windshield wiper blades or fan belts. May repair or replace tires. Fills or allows customer to fill fuel tank of vehicle with gasoline or diesel fuel to specified level. Installs accessories, such as air or oil filter, battery, windshield wiper blades, fan belt, or lights. Collects cash from customer and makes change, or charges purchases to customer's credit card. Services fishing boats and pleasure craft, and drives tow boat vehicle. Greases and lubricates vehicles or specified units, such as springs, universal joints, and steering knuckles, using grease gun or spray lubricant. Changes, tests, and repairs or replaces tires. Checks air pressure in tires and levels of fuel, motor oil, and other fluids, and tests batteries. Adjusts brakes, replaces spark plugs, and makes other minor repairs. Inspects tire pressure and fluid levels of transmission, battery, radiator, crankcase, etc., and adds air, oil, water, and required fluids. Cleans windshield or washes and waxes vehicle. Sells accessories and services, such as batteries, tires, lubrication services, and safety inspections. Assists in arranging merchandise displays and taking inventories. Compiles mileage records, fuel consumption log, and storage tank inventory for company garage. Prepares daily report of fuel, oil, and accessories sold in service station. Maintains customer records and follows up periodically with telephone, mail, or personal reminders of service due. Transports materials, such as oil drums, using forklift. Cleans parking area, offices, and equipment, and removes trash.
Yearly Earnings: $13,364
Education: Short-term O-J-T
Knowledge: Sales and Marketing
Abilities: Rate Control; Extent Flexibility; Hearing Sensitivity
Skills: Repairing
General Work Activities: Repairing and Maintaining Mechanical Equipment; Performing for or Working with Public
Job Characteristics: Job-Required Social Interaction; Persuade Someone to a Course of Action; Provide a Service to Others; Deal with External Customers; Deal with Unpleasant or Angry People; Contaminants; Cramped Work Space, Awkward Positions; Hazardous Conditions; Kneeling, Crouching, or Crawling; Keeping or Regaining Balance; Special Uniform
GOE Group/s: 05.10.02 Crafts: Mechanical; 05.12.06 Elemental Work: Mechanical: Pumping; 05.12.08 Elemental Work: Mechanical: Lubricating; 05.12.18 Elemental Work: Mechanical: Cleaning and Maintenance; 09.04.02 Customer Services: Sales Services
CIP Program/s: 081209 Petroleum Products Retailing Operations; 470302 Heavy Equipment Maintenance and Repair
Related DOT Job/s: 915.467-010 AUTOMOBILE-SERVICE-STATION ATTENDANT; 915.477-010 AUTOMOBILE-SELF-SERVE-SERVICE-STATION ATTENDANT; 915.587-010 GAS-AND-OIL SERVICER; 915.687-014 GARAGE SERVICER, INDUSTRIAL; 915.687-018 LUBRICATION SERVICER; 915.687-030 TAXI SERVICER

97808 PARKING LOT ATTENDANTS. OOH Title/s: Handlers, Equipment Cleaners, Helpers, and Laborers
Park autos or issue tickets for customers in a parking lot or garage. Parks automobiles in parking lot, storage garage, or new car lot. Places numbered tag on windshield of automobile to be parked, and hands customer similar tag to be used in locating parked automobile. Collects parking fee from customer, based on charges for time automobile is parked. Takes numbered tag from customer, locates car, and delivers it to customer, or directs customer to parked car. Patrols area to prevent thefts of parked automobiles or items in automobiles. Assigns stock control numbers to vehicles, and catalogs and stores keys. Compares serial numbers of incoming vehicles against invoice. Signals or directs vehicle drivers with hands or flashlight to parking area. Keeps new car lot in order and maximizes use of space. Lifts, positions, and removes barricades to open or close parking areas. Inspects vehicles to detect damage and to verify presence of accessories listed on invoice. Records description of damages and lists missing items on delivery receipt. Services vehicles with gas, oil, and water. Services cars in storage to protect tires, battery, and finish against deterioration.
Yearly Earnings: $23,504
Education: Short-term O-J-T
Knowledge: None above average
Abilities: None above average
Skills: None above average
General Work Activities: Interacting with Computers
Job Characteristics: Provide a Service to Others; Walking or Running; Special Uniform
GOE Group/s: 05.08.03 Land and Water Vehicle Operation: Services Requiring Driving; 09.04.02 Customer Services: Sales Services
CIP Program/s: 000000 NO CIP ASSIGNED
Related DOT Job/s: 915.473-010 PARKING-LOT ATTENDANT; 915.583-010 LOT ATTENDANT; 915.667-014 PARKING LOT SIGNALER

97899A AIRPORT UTILITY WORKERS. OOH Title/s: Material Moving Equipment Operators
Perform a variety of duties, such as refueling, cleaning, or loading and unloading baggage, while working as member of crew to service aircraft. Operates service vehicles to replenish fuel, water, and waste system chemicals and to remove liquid wastes. Cleans exterior or interior of aircraft, using portable platform, ladders, brushes, rags, water hose, and vacuum. Positions and removes boarding platform to unload or load aircraft passengers. Unloads and loads luggage and cargo from aircraft, using tow truck with luggage carts. Directs incoming and outgoing aircraft near terminal area to assist pilot's maneuvering of aircraft, using visual, hand, or light signals. Traces lost luggage for customers and prepares lost baggage claims.
Yearly Earnings: $23,504
Education: Short-term O-J-T
Knowledge: None above average
Abilities: Multilimb Coordination; Rate Control; Reaction Time; Static Strength; Dynamic Strength; Trunk Strength; Stamina; Extent Flexibility; Dynamic Flexibility; Gross Body Coordination; Gross Body Equilibrium; Far Vision; Night Vision; Peripheral Vision; Glare Sensitivity; Auditory Attention
Skills: Equipment Maintenance
General Work Activities: Performing General Physical Activities; Handling and Moving Objects; Interacting with Computers

Job Characteristics: Responsible for Others' Health and Safety; Sounds, Noise Levels are Distracting, etc.; Very Hot; Extremely Bright or Inadequate Lighting; Contaminants; Cramped Work Space, Awkward Positions; Diseases/Infections; High Places; Standing; Climbing Ladders, Scaffolds, Poles, etc.; Walking or Running; Keeping or Regaining Balance; Bending or Twisting the Body; Special Uniform; Common Protective or Safety Attire; Frustrating Circumstances; Importance of Repeating Same Tasks; Pace Determined by Speed of Equipment
GOE Group/s: 05.12.06 Elemental Work: Mechanical: Pumping
CIP Program/s: 490199 Air Transportation Workers, Other
Related DOT Job/s: 912.663-010 AIRPORT UTILITY WORKER

97899B ALL OTHER TRANSPORTATION AND RELATED WORKERS. OOH Title/s: Handlers, Equipment Cleaners, Helpers, and Laborers; Water Transportation Occupations
All other transportation and related workers not classified separately above.
Yearly Earnings: $23,504
Education: Short-term O-J-T
GOE Group/s: 05.12.03 Elemental Work: Mechanical: Loading, Moving
CIP Program/s: 000000 NO CIP ASSIGNED
Related DOT Job/s: 911.664-010 FERRYBOAT OPERATOR, CABLE; 932.683-010 CAR DROPPER

Material Moving Equipment Operators

97902 LONGSHORE EQUIPMENT OPERATORS. OOH Title/s: Material Moving Equipment Operators
Operate equipment to load crates, containers, and other items on or off ships. Exclude loading and unloading of bulk liquids. Operates crane or winch to move cargo, using hook, magnet, or sling attached in accordance with signals from other workers. Moves controls to start flow of grain from grain trimmer, stopping flow and repositioning spout to fill each hatch in turn. Drives lift truck along dock or aboard ship to transfer bulk items, such as lumber and crated products. Attaches slings, hooks, or other lifting devices to winch for loading or unloading. Drives tractor to transfer loaded trailers from warehouse to dockside. Lashes and stores cargo aboard ship. Signals other workers to move, raise, or lower cargo. Directs activities of cargo gang consisting of stevedores. Positions and fastens hose lines to ships' cargo tanks to load or unload liquid cargo, such as chemicals.
Yearly Earnings: $27,820
Education: Moderate-term O-J-T
Knowledge: Transportation
Abilities: Control Precision; Multilimb Coordination; Response Orientation; Rate Control; Reaction Time; Static Strength; Explosive Strength; Dynamic Strength; Stamina; Dynamic Flexibility; Gross Body Equilibrium; Far Vision; Peripheral Vision; Depth Perception; Glare Sensitivity; Auditory Attention; Sound Localization
Skills: Operation and Control
General Work Activities: Performing General Physical Activities; Handling and Moving Objects; Controlling Machines and Processes; Interacting with Computers
Job Characteristics: Sounds, Noise Levels are Distracting, etc.; Very Hot; Extremely Bright or Inadequate Lighting; Contaminants; Cramped Work Space, Awkward Positions; Whole Body Vibration; High Places; Hazardous Conditions; Hazardous Equipment; Hazardous Situations; Standing; Climbing Ladders, Scaffolds, Poles, etc.; Walking or Running; Kneeling, Crouching, or Crawling; Keeping or Regaining Balance; Bending or Twisting the Body
GOE Group/s: 05.11.04 Equipment Operation: Material Handling
CIP Program/s: 490299 Vehicle and Equipment Operators, Other
Related DOT Job/s: 911.663-014 STEVEDORE I

97905 TANK CAR AND TRUCK LOADERS. OOH Title/s: Material Moving Equipment Operators
Load and unload liquid chemicals, liquid petroleum products, and other liquids into or from tank cars or trucks. May perform a variety of other tasks relating to shipment of product. May gauge or sample shipping tanks and test them for leaks. Starts pumps and adjusts valves to regulate flow of product to vessel, utilizing knowledge of loading procedures. Monitors product movement to and from storage tanks and coordinates with other workers to ensure constant product flow. Unloads cars by connecting hose to outlet plugs and pumping compressed air into car, forcing liquid into storage tank. Verifies tank car, barge, or truck load number to ensure car placement accuracy, based on written or verbal instructions. Weighs and inspects vessels to prevent contamination and to ensure cleanliness and compliance to loading procedures. Tests vessels for leaks, damage, and defects, and repairs or replaces defective parts. Reads meter to verify content, temperature, and volume of liquid load. Copies and tacks load specifications onto tank, and seals outlet valves on tank car, barge, or truck. Records operating data, such as products and quantities pumped, gauge readings, and operating time, manually or using computer. Retrieves liquid sample and performs tests on contents, or delivers sample to laboratory for testing. Operates blenders and heaters to mix, blend, and heat products.
Yearly Earnings: $24,440
Education: Moderate-term O-J-T
Knowledge: Chemistry; Transportation
Abilities: Rate Control; Reaction Time; Static Strength
Skills: Testing; Operation Monitoring; Operation and Control
General Work Activities: Controlling Machines and Processes
Job Characteristics: Contaminants; Hazardous Conditions; Standing; Climbing Ladders, Scaffolds, Poles, etc.; Keeping or Regaining Balance; Common Protective or Safety Attire; Specialized Protective or Safety Attire; Consequence of Error
GOE Group/s: 05.06.04 Systems Operation: Processing; 06.04.40 Elemental Work: Industrial: Loading, Moving, Hoisting, and Conveying
CIP Program/s: 000000 NO CIP ASSIGNED
Related DOT Job/s: 914.382-014 PUMPER-GAUGER; 914.382-018 PUMPER-GAUGER APPRENTICE; 914.667-010 LOADER I

97908 OIL PUMPERS, EXCEPT WELL HEAD. OOH Title/s: Material Moving Equipment Operators
Operate steam, natural gas, gasoline, electric, or diesel pumps and auxiliary equipment to restore and control flow of oil from wells. Opens valves to regulate flow of oil from wells to storage tanks or into pipelines. Turns valve to adjust pressure of separator, which separates natural gas from oil. Reads flowmeters, gauges contents with calibrated steel tape, and prepares reports of amount and quality pumped and in storage. Examines pipelines for leaks. Collects and bottles samples of oil for laboratory analysis. Lubricates and repairs pumps, using grease gun, oilcan, and hand tools. Reports major breakdowns and problems with oil wells.
Yearly Earnings: $24,440
Education: Moderate-term O-J-T
Knowledge: Mechanical
Abilities: None above average
Skills: Operation Monitoring; Operation and Control; Equipment Maintenance; Repairing

General Work Activities: Repairing and Maintaining Mechanical Equipment
Job Characteristics: Very Hot; Contaminants; Hazardous Conditions; Specialized Protective or Safety Attire; Importance of Repeating Same Tasks
GOE Group/s: 05.06.03 Systems Operation: Oil, Gas, and Water Distribution
CIP Program/s: 470399 Industrial Equipment Maintenance and Repair, Other
Related DOT Job/s: 914.382-010 OIL PUMPER

97911 WELL HEAD PUMPERS. OOH Title/s: Material Moving Equipment Operators

Operate power pumps and auxiliary equipment to produce artificial flow of oil or gas from wells in oil field. Starts compressor engines and diverts oil from storage tanks into compressor units and auxiliary equipment to recover natural gas from oil. Operates engines and pumps from central power plant to shut off wells and to switch flow of oil into storage tanks. Starts pumps and opens valves to pump oil from wells into storage tanks. Opens valves to return compressed gas to bottoms of specified wells to repressurize them and force oil to surface. Reads tank gauges and pump meters, and keeps production records.
Yearly Earnings: $24,440
Education: Moderate-term O-J-T
Knowledge: None above average
Abilities: None above average
Skills: Operation Monitoring; Operation and Control
General Work Activities: None above average
Job Characteristics: Sounds, Noise Levels are Distracting, etc.; Very Hot; Extremely Bright or Inadequate Lighting; Contaminants; Hazardous Conditions; Common Protective or Safety Attire; Pace Determined by Speed of Equipment
GOE Group/s: 05.06.03 Systems Operation: Oil, Gas, and Water Distribution
CIP Program/s: 470399 Industrial Equipment Maintenance and Repair, Other
Related DOT Job/s: 914.382-022 PUMPER, HEAD

97914 MAIN-LINE STATION ENGINEERS. OOH Title/s: Material Moving Equipment Operators

Operate electric-, diesel-, or gas-driven pumping equipment to pump and route oil through pipelines at main-line or terminal stations. Turns valves and starts engines to pump oil through station. Turns handwheel or directs others to open or close valves to direct flow of oil through pipeline and storage tank system. Pumps natural gas or natural liquid products. Reads flow- and pressure meters, and turns valves to vary pumping rate and line pressure, according to specifications. Inspects pumping equipment to detect malfunctioning and leaks. Lubricates machinery, and repairs and adjusts pumps and equipment, using hand tools. Records pressures, temperature, and flow rates, and maintains records of oil stock and oil receipts. Gauges and tests oil or directs work of others.
Yearly Earnings: $24,440
Education: Moderate-term O-J-T
Knowledge: Mechanical
Abilities: None above average
Skills: Operation Monitoring; Operation and Control; Equipment Maintenance; Troubleshooting; Repairing
General Work Activities: Inspecting Equipment, Structures, or Material; Repairing and Maintaining Mechanical Equipment
Job Characteristics: Very Hot; Contaminants; Standing; Pace Determined by Speed of Equipment
GOE Group/s: 05.06.03 Systems Operation: Oil, Gas, and Water Distribution
CIP Program/s: 470501 Stationary Energy Sources Installer and Operator
Related DOT Job/s: 914.362-018 STATION ENGINEER, MAIN LINE

97917 GAS PUMPING STATION OPERATORS. OOH Title/s: Material Moving Equipment Operators

Control the operation of steam- ,gas- ,or electric-motor-driven compressor to maintain specified pressures on high- and low-pressure mains dispensing gas from gas holders. Opens valve to allow gas to flow into and out of compressors. Observes pressure gauges to determine consumption rate variations, and turns knobs or switches to regulate pressure. Reads gas meters and records amount of gas received and dispensed from holders. Cleans, lubricates, and adjusts compressors, using hand tools.
Yearly Earnings: $24,440
Education: Moderate-term O-J-T
Knowledge: None above average
Abilities: None above average
Skills: Operation Monitoring
General Work Activities: Repairing and Maintaining Mechanical Equipment
Job Characteristics: Degree of Automation; Pace Determined by Speed of Equipment
GOE Group/s: 05.06.03 Systems Operation: Oil, Gas, and Water Distribution
CIP Program/s: 470501 Stationary Energy Sources Installer and Operator
Related DOT Job/s: 953.382-010 GAS-PUMPING-STATION OPERATOR

97921 GAS COMPRESSOR OPERATORS. OOH Title/s: Material Moving Equipment Operators

Operate steam or internal combustion engines to transmit, compress, or recover gases, such as butane, nitrogen, hydrogen, and natural gas, in various production processes. Moves controls and turns valves to start compressor engines, pumps, and auxiliary equipment. Operates equipment to control transmission of natural gas through pipelines. Observes operation of equipment to detect malfunctions. Tends pumps to mix specified amounts of acids and caustics with water for use in purifying gases. Monitors meters, gauges, and recording instrument charts to ensure specified temperature, pressure, and flow of gas through system. Operates purification tanks (scrubbers) to purify air or byproduct gases. Conducts chemical tests to determine sulfur or moisture content in gas. Records instrument readings and operational changes in operating log. Performs minor repairs on equipment, using hand tools.
Yearly Earnings: $24,440
Education: Moderate-term O-J-T
Knowledge: Mechanical; Physics; Chemistry
Abilities: Control Precision
Skills: Operation Monitoring; Operation and Control; Troubleshooting; Repairing
General Work Activities: Inspecting Equipment, Structures, or Material; Controlling Machines and Processes; Repairing and Maintaining Mechanical Equipment
Job Characteristics: Contaminants; Hazardous Conditions; Climbing Ladders, Scaffolds, Poles, etc.; Specialized Protective or Safety Attire; Degree of Automation; Pace Determined by Speed of Equipment
GOE Group/s: 05.06.02 Systems Operation: Stationary Engineering
CIP Program/s: 470501 Stationary Energy Sources Installer and Operator
Related DOT Job/s: 950.382-014 GAS-COMPRESSOR OPERATOR

97923A EXCAVATING AND LOADING MACHINE OPERATORS. OOH Title/s: Material Moving Equipment Operators

Operate machinery equipped with scoops, shovels, or buckets to excavate and load loose materials. Operates power machinery, such as power shovel, stripping shovel, scraper loader (mucking machine), or backhoe (trench-excavating machine), to excavate and load material. Observes hand signals, grade stakes, and other markings when operating machines. Receives written or oral instructions to move or excavate material. Measures and verifies levels of rock or gravel, base, and other excavated material. Lubricates and repairs machinery and replaces parts, such as gears, bearings, and bucket teeth. Directs ground workers engaged in activities, such as moving stakes or markers.

Yearly Earnings: $23,608

Education: Moderate-term O-J-T

Knowledge: Mechanical

Abilities: Spatial Orientation; Multilimb Coordination; Reaction Time; Trunk Strength; Gross Body Coordination; Gross Body Equilibrium; Depth Perception

Skills: Operation Monitoring; Operation and Control; Equipment Maintenance; Repairing

General Work Activities: Controlling Machines and Processes; Interacting with Computers; Repairing and Maintaining Mechanical Equipment

Job Characteristics: Sounds, Noise Levels are Distracting, etc.; Very Hot; Extremely Bright or Inadequate Lighting; Contaminants; Whole Body Vibration; Hazardous Equipment; Bending or Twisting the Body; Specialized Protective or Safety Attire; Pace Determined by Speed of Equipment

GOE Group/s: 05.11.01 Equipment Operation: Construction; 05.11.02 Equipment Operation: Mining, Quarrying, Drilling; 05.11.04 Equipment Operation: Material Handling

CIP Program/s: 490202 Construction Equipment Operator; 490299 Vehicle and Equipment Operators, Other

Related DOT Job/s: 850.663-026 STRIPPING-SHOVEL OPERATOR; 850.683-026 MUCKING-MACHINE OPERATOR; 850.683-030 POWER-SHOVEL OPERATOR; 850.683-042 TOWER-EXCAVATOR OPERATOR; 851.663-010 SEPTIC-TANK INSTALLER; 921.683-022 COAL-EQUIPMENT OPERATOR; 930.683-022 HARVESTER OPERATOR

97923B AERIAL TRAM TENDERS. OOH Title/s: Material Moving Equipment Operators

Tend aerial tramways to convey refuse, coal, ore, or other materials from plant or mine. Controls movement of tram buckets along cable, using control buttons. Monitors tramway control panel for signal indicating malfunction of equipment. Loads and unloads buckets, using levers and control buttons. Repairs and maintains tram buckets, overhead cables, and pulleys.

Yearly Earnings: $24,232

Education: Moderate-term O-J-T

Knowledge: None above average

Abilities: Rate Control; Glare Sensitivity

Skills: Operation Monitoring; Operation and Control; Equipment Maintenance; Repairing

General Work Activities: Repairing and Maintaining Mechanical Equipment

Job Characteristics: Cramped Work Space, Awkward Positions; High Places; Climbing Ladders, Scaffolds, Poles, etc.; Keeping or Regaining Balance; Specialized Protective or Safety Attire; Degree of Automation; Pace Determined by Speed of Equipment

GOE Group/s: 05.11.04 Equipment Operation: Material Handling

CIP Program/s: 000000 NO CIP ASSIGNED

Related DOT Job/s: 932.685-010 AERIAL-TRAM OPERATOR

97926 DRAGLINE OPERATORS. OOH Title/s: Material Moving Equipment Operators

Operate power-driven crane equipment with dragline bucket to excavate or move sand, gravel, mud, or other materials. Moves controls to position boom, lower and drag bucket through material, and release material at unloading point. Directs workers engaged in placing blocks and outriggers to prevent capsizing of machine when lifting heavy loads. Drives machine to worksite.

Yearly Earnings: $24,232

Education: Moderate-term O-J-T

Knowledge: Building and Construction; Transportation

Abilities: Control Precision; Multilimb Coordination; Response Orientation; Rate Control; Far Vision; Peripheral Vision; Depth Perception

Skills: Operation and Control

General Work Activities: Controlling Machines and Processes; Interacting with Computers

Job Characteristics: Sounds, Noise Levels are Distracting, etc.; Very Hot; Extremely Bright or Inadequate Lighting; Whole Body Vibration; High Places; Hazardous Equipment; Using Hands on Objects, Tools, or Controls; Degree of Automation

GOE Group/s: 05.11.04 Equipment Operation: Material Handling

CIP Program/s: 490202 Construction Equipment Operator; 490299 Vehicle and Equipment Operators, Other

Related DOT Job/s: 850.683-018 DRAGLINE OPERATOR

97928 DREDGE OPERATORS. OOH Title/s: Material Moving Equipment Operators

Operate power-driven dredges to mine sand, gravel, or other materials from lakes, rivers, or streams, and to excavate and maintain navigable channels in waterways. Starts and stops engines to operate equipment. Moves levers to position dredge for excavation, engage hydraulic pump, raise and lower suction boom, and control rotation of cutter head. Starts power winch that draws in or lets out cable to change position of dredge, or pulls in and lets out cable manually. Lowers anchor pole to verify depth of excavation, using winch, or scans depth gauge to determine depth of excavation. Directs workers placing shore anchors and cables, laying additional pipes from dredge to shore, and pumping water from pontoons.

Yearly Earnings: $24,232

Education: Moderate-term O-J-T

Knowledge: Engineering and Technology; Geography; Transportation

Abilities: Static Strength; Gross Body Equilibrium; Peripheral Vision; Depth Perception; Glare Sensitivity; Sound Localization

Skills: Operation Monitoring; Operation and Control; Management of Personnel Resources

General Work Activities: Controlling Machines and Processes; Interacting with Computers

Job Characteristics: Coordinate or Lead Others; Responsible for Others' Health and Safety; Sounds, Noise Levels are Distracting, etc.; Very Hot; Extremely Bright or Inadequate Lighting; Whole Body Vibration; Hazardous Equipment; Hazardous Situations; Keeping or Regaining Balance; Using Hands on Objects, Tools, or Controls; Frustrating Circumstances; Degree of Automation; Importance of Being Aware of New Events

GOE Group/s: 05.11.01 Equipment Operation: Construction

CIP Program/s: 490202 Construction Equipment Operator; 490399 Water Transportation Workers, Other

Related DOT Job/s: 850.663-010 DREDGE OPERATOR

97932 LOADING MACHINE OPERATORS, UNDERGROUND MINING. OOH Title/s: Material Moving Equipment Operators

Operate underground loading machines to load coal, ore, or rock into shuttle or mine cars or onto conveyors. Loading equipment may include power shovels, hoisting engines equipped with cable-drawn scraper or scoop, or machines equipped with gathering arms and conveyor. Moves levers to start, raise, and position conveyor boom and gathering arm; force shovel into pile; and move and dump material. Advances machine to gather material and convey it into car at rear. Stops gathering arms when car is full. Drives machine into pile of material blasted from working face. Pries off loose material from roof and moves it into path of machine with crowbar. Moves trailing electrical cable clear of obstructions, using rubber safety gloves. Replaces hydraulic hoses, headlight bulbs, and gathering-arm teeth.

Yearly Earnings: $24,232

Education: Moderate-term O-J-T

Knowledge: Mechanical

Abilities: Spatial Orientation; Gross Body Equilibrium; Night Vision; Peripheral Vision; Depth Perception; Sound Localization

Skills: Operation and Control; Equipment Maintenance; Repairing

General Work Activities: Handling and Moving Objects; Controlling Machines and Processes; Interacting with Computers

Job Characteristics: Sounds, Noise Levels are Distracting, etc.; Very Hot; Extremely Bright or Inadequate Lighting; Contaminants; Cramped Work Space, Awkward Positions; Whole Body Vibration; Hazardous Conditions; Hazardous Equipment; Hazardous Situations; Keeping or Regaining Balance; Using Hands on Objects, Tools, or Controls; Bending or Twisting the Body; Common Protective or Safety Attire; Specialized Protective or Safety Attire; Degree of Automation; Pace Determined by Speed of Equipment

GOE Group/s: 05.11.02 Equipment Operation: Mining, Quarrying, Drilling

CIP Program/s: 490299 Vehicle and Equipment Operators, Other

Related DOT Job/s: 932.683-014 LOADING-MACHINE OPERATOR; 932.683-018 MECHANICAL-SHOVEL OPERATOR

97935 SHUTTLE CAR OPERATORS. OOH Title/s: Material Moving Equipment Operators

Operate diesel- or electric-powered shuttle cars in underground mine, to transport materials from working face to mine cars or to conveyor. Positions shuttle car under discharge conveyor of loading machine and observes that materials are loaded according to specifications. Controls conveyor, which runs entire length of shuttle car, to apportion load as loading progresses. Drives loaded shuttle car to ramp and moves controls to discharge load into mine car or onto conveyor. Maneuvers shuttle car to keep its nose under discharge conveyor. Moves mine cars into position to be loaded from shuttle car. Charges batteries when operating battery-powered vehicle.

Yearly Earnings: $24,232

Education: Moderate-term O-J-T

Knowledge: Transportation

Abilities: Multilimb Coordination; Rate Control; Night Vision; Peripheral Vision; Depth Perception

Skills: Operation and Control

General Work Activities: Interacting with Computers

Job Characteristics: Sounds, Noise Levels are Distracting, etc.; Very Hot; Extremely Bright or Inadequate Lighting; Contaminants; Cramped Work Space, Awkward Positions; Whole Body Vibration; Hazardous Conditions; Hazardous Equipment; Keeping or Regaining Balance; Using Hands on Objects, Tools, or Controls; Common Protective or Safety Attire; Specialized Protective or Safety Attire; Degree of Automation; Pace Determined by Speed of Equipment

GOE Group/s: 05.11.02 Equipment Operation: Mining, Quarrying, Drilling

CIP Program/s: 490299 Vehicle and Equipment Operators, Other

Related DOT Job/s: 932.683-022 SHUTTLE-CAR OPERATOR

97938 GRADER, BULLDOZER, AND SCRAPER OPERATORS. OOH Title/s: Material Moving Equipment Operators

Operate machines or vehicles equipped with blades to remove, distribute, level, or grade earth. Exclude paving, surfacing, and tamping equipment operators. Starts engine; moves throttle, switches, and levers; and depresses pedals to operate machines, equipment, and attachments. Drives equipment in successive passes over working area to achieve specified result, such as grade terrain or remove, dump, or spread earth and rock. Aligns machine, cutter head, or depth gauge marker with reference stakes and guidelines on ground, or positions equipment following hand signals of assistant. Fastens bulldozer blade or other attachment to tractor, using hitches. Connects hydraulic hoses, belts, mechanical linkage, or power takeoff shaft to tractor. Signals operator to guide movement of tractor-drawn machine. Greases, oils, and performs minor repairs on tractor, using grease gun, oilcan, and hand tools.

Yearly Earnings: $25,844

Education: Moderate-term O-J-T

Knowledge: Mechanical

Abilities: Control Precision; Response Orientation; Rate Control; Reaction Time; Speed of Limb Movement; Static Strength; Explosive Strength; Dynamic Strength; Trunk Strength; Stamina; Gross Body Coordination; Gross Body Equilibrium; Far Vision; Peripheral Vision; Depth Perception; Glare Sensitivity

Skills: Operation and Control

General Work Activities: Controlling Machines and Processes; Interacting with Computers; Repairing and Maintaining Mechanical Equipment

Job Characteristics: Responsible for Others' Health and Safety; Sounds, Noise Levels are Distracting, etc.; Very Hot; Extremely Bright or Inadequate Lighting; Contaminants; Whole Body Vibration; Hazardous Conditions; Hazardous Equipment; Sitting; Using Hands on Objects, Tools, or Controls; Common Protective or Safety Attire; Degree of Automation; Importance of Being Aware of New Events; Importance of Repeating Same Tasks; Pace Determined by Speed of Equipment

GOE Group/s: 05.11.01 Equipment Operation: Construction

CIP Program/s: 490202 Construction Equipment Operator

Related DOT Job/s: 850.663-014 ELEVATING-GRADER OPERATOR; 850.663-022 MOTOR-GRADER OPERATOR; 850.683-010 BULLDOZER OPERATOR I; 850.683-014 DITCHER OPERATOR; 850.683-022 FORM-GRADER OPERATOR; 850.683-038 SCRAPER OPERATOR; 850.683-046 UTILITY-TRACTOR OPERATOR; 955.463-010 SANITARY LANDFILL OPERATOR

97941 HOIST AND WINCH OPERATORS. OOH Title/s: Material Moving Equipment Operators; Handlers, Equipment Cleaners, Helpers, and Laborers

Operate or tend hoists or winches to lift and pull loads using power-operated cable equipment. Exclude crane and tower operators. Operates equipment, such as hoist, winch, or hydraulic boom, to lift and pull loads and materials. Starts engine of hoist or winch to move loads or materials, using controls such as levers, pedals, and buttons. Operates equipment, such as hoist, winch, or hydraulic boom, to lift and pull loads and materials. Observes equipment, gauges,

indicators, and hand signals to verify depth of materials, instruments, or position of load. Moves or repositions hoists, winches, loads, and materials, manually or using equipment and machines such as trucks, cars, and handtrucks. Tends auxiliary equipment, such as jacks, slings, cables, or stop blocks, to facilitate moving items or materials for further processing. Attaches, fastens, and disconnects cables or lines to loads and materials, using hand tools. Selects loads or materials according to weight and size specifications. Climbs ladder to facilitate positioning and set-up of vehicle-mounted derrick. Repairs, maintains, and adjusts equipment, using hand tools.
Yearly Earnings: $27,404
Education: Moderate-term O-J-T
Knowledge: None above average
Abilities: Control Precision; Multilimb Coordination; Response Orientation; Reaction Time; Speed of Limb Movement; Static Strength; Dynamic Strength; Trunk Strength; Stamina; Gross Body Equilibrium; Far Vision; Peripheral Vision; Depth Perception
Skills: Operation Monitoring; Operation and Control; Equipment Maintenance; Troubleshooting; Repairing
General Work Activities: Controlling Machines and Processes; Interacting with Computers; Repairing and Maintaining Mechanical Equipment
Job Characteristics: Sounds, Noise Levels are Distracting, etc.; Very Hot; Extremely Bright or Inadequate Lighting; Cramped Work Space, Awkward Positions; Whole Body Vibration; Radiation; High Places; Hazardous Equipment; Climbing Ladders, Scaffolds, Poles, etc.; Keeping or Regaining Balance; Common Protective or Safety Attire; Pace Determined by Speed of Equipment
GOE Group/s: 03.04.01 Elemental Work: Plants and Animals: Farming; 05.11.01 Equipment Operation: Construction; 05.11.02 Equipment Operation: Mining, Quarrying, Drilling; 05.11.03 Equipment Operation: Drilling and Oil Exploration; 05.11.04 Equipment Operation: Material Handling; 05.12.04 Elemental Work: Mechanical: Hoisting, Conveying; 06.04.03 Elemental Work: Industrial: Machine Work, Wood; 06.04.40 Elemental Work: Industrial: Loading, Moving, Hoisting, and Conveying
CIP Program/s: 030405 Logging/Timber Harvesting; 470399 Industrial Equipment Maintenance and Repair, Other; 490202 Construction Equipment Operator; 490299 Vehicle and Equipment Operators, Other
Related DOT Job/s: 663.686-022 LATHE SPOTTER; 869.683-014 RIGGER; 911.687-018 COAL TRIMMER; 921.662-022 MARINE RAILWAY OPERATOR; 921.663-026 HOIST OPERATOR; 921.663-030 HOISTING ENGINEER; 921.663-046 PNEUMATIC-HOIST OPERATOR; 921.663-050 SCRAPER-LOADER OPERATOR; 921.663-066 YARDING ENGINEER; 921.682-022 TRANSFER CONTROLLER; 921.683-010 BOAT-HOIST OPERATOR; 921.683-030 CUPOLA HOIST OPERATOR; 921.683-046 HYDRAULIC-BOOM OPERATOR; 921.683-054 JAMMER OPERATOR; 921.683-058 LOG LOADER; 921.683-082 WINCH DRIVER; 921.683-086 YARD WORKER; 921.685-010 BOAT LOADER II; 921.685-042 ELECTRIC-FORK OPERATOR; 930.363-010 CLEAN-OUT DRILLER; 930.382-030 WELL PULLER; 930.683-018 DERRICK WORKER, WELL SERVICE; 932.363-010 HOIST OPERATOR

97944 CRANE AND TOWER OPERATORS. OOH Title/s: Material Moving Equipment Operators

Operate mechanical boom and cable, or tower and cable equipment, to lift and move materials, machines, or products in many directions. Exclude dragline operators. Operates cranes, cherry pickers, or other moving equipment to lift and move loads, such as machinery or bulk materials. Loads and unloads bundles from trucks and moves containers to storage bins, using moving equipment. Inspects and adjusts crane mechanisms and accessory equipment to prevent malfunctions and wear. Inspects and compares load weights with lifting capacity to ensure against overload. Cleans, lubricates, and maintains mechanisms, such as cables, pulleys, and grappling devices. Reviews daily truck-delivery schedule to ascertain orders, sequence of deliveries, and special loading instructions. Directs truck drivers backing vehicles into loading bays, and covers, uncovers, and secures loads for delivery. Inspects cables and grappling devices for wear, and installs or replaces cables. Directs helpers engaged in placing blocking and outrigging under crane when lifting loads. Weighs bundles, using floor scale, and records weight for company records. Inspects bundle packaging for conformance to customer requirements, and removes and batches packaging tickets.
Yearly Earnings: $27,820
Education: Moderate-term O-J-T
Knowledge: None above average
Abilities: Spatial Orientation; Control Precision; Multilimb Coordination; Response Orientation; Rate Control; Reaction Time; Speed of Limb Movement; Stamina; Gross Body Equilibrium; Far Vision; Peripheral Vision; Depth Perception; Glare Sensitivity; Auditory Attention
Skills: Installation; Operation and Control; Repairing
General Work Activities: Controlling Machines and Processes; Interacting with Computers
Job Characteristics: Coordinate or Lead Others; Responsible for Others' Health and Safety; Sounds, Noise Levels are Distracting, etc.; Very Hot; Extremely Bright or Inadequate Lighting; Cramped Work Space, Awkward Positions; Whole Body Vibration; Radiation; High Places; Hazardous Equipment; Climbing Ladders, Scaffolds, Poles, etc.; Degree of Automation; Importance of Repeating Same Tasks; Pace Determined by Speed of Equipment
GOE Group/s: 05.11.01 Equipment Operation: Construction; 05.11.04 Equipment Operation: Material Handling; 06.04.10 Elemental Work: Industrial: Equipment Operation, Metal Processing; 06.04.40 Elemental Work: Industrial: Loading, Moving, Hoisting, and Conveying
CIP Program/s: 490202 Construction Equipment Operator; 490299 Vehicle and Equipment Operators, Other
Related DOT Job/s: 519.683-010 DROSS SKIMMER; 921.663-010 OVERHEAD CRANE OPERATOR; 921.663-014 CHERRY-PICKER OPERATOR; 921.663-022 DERRICK OPERATOR; 921.663-038 LOCOMOTIVE-CRANE OPERATOR; 921.663-042 MONORAIL CRANE OPERATOR; 921.663-054 TOWER-CRANE OPERATOR; 921.663-058 TRACTOR-CRANE OPERATOR; 921.663-062 TRUCK-CRANE OPERATOR; 921.663-070 TRUCK LOADER, OVERHEAD CRANE; 921.683-018 CANTILEVER-CRANE OPERATOR; 921.683-034 DERRICK-BOAT OPERATOR; 921.683-066 SORTING-GRAPPLE OPERATOR; 921.683-074 TOWER-LOADER OPERATOR

97947 INDUSTRIAL TRUCK AND TRACTOR OPERATORS. OOH Title/s: Material Moving Equipment Operators

Operate gasoline- or electric-powered industrial trucks or tractors equipped with forklift, elevated platform, or trailer hitch to move materials around a warehouse, storage yard, factory, construction site, or similar location. Exclude logging tractor operators. Moves controls to drive gasoline- or electric-powered trucks, cars, or tractors and to transport materials between loading, processing, and storage areas. Moves levers and controls to operate lifting devices—such as forklifts, lift beams and swivel-hooks, hoists, and elevating platforms—to load, unload, transport, and stack material. Positions lifting device under, over, or around loaded pallets, skids, and boxes, and secures material or products for transport to designated areas. Hooks tow trucks to trailer hitches and fastens attachments—such as graders, plows, rollers, and winch cables—to tractor, using hitchpins. Turns valves and opens chutes to dump, spray, or release materials from dumpcars or storage bins into hoppers. Performs routine

maintenance on vehicles and auxiliary equipment, such as cleaning, lubricating, recharging batteries, fueling, or replacing liquefied-gas tank. Manually loads or unloads materials onto or off pallets, skids, platforms, cars, or lifting devices. Operates or tends automatic stacking, loading, packaging, or cutting machines. Weighs materials or products and records weight and other production data on tags or labels. Signals workers to discharge, dump, or level materials. Operates coke ovens, driers, or other receptacles to process material or products. Inventories, issues, and maintains records of supplies and materials.
Yearly Earnings: $22,100
Education: Short-term O-J-T
Knowledge: Mechanical; Transportation
Abilities: Spatial Orientation; Control Precision; Multilimb Coordination; Response Orientation; Speed of Limb Movement; Static Strength; Trunk Strength; Extent Flexibility; Dynamic Flexibility; Gross Body Equilibrium; Peripheral Vision; Depth Perception
Skills: Operation Monitoring; Operation and Control; Troubleshooting; Repairing
General Work Activities: Performing General Physical Activities; Handling and Moving Objects; Controlling Machines and Processes; Interacting with Computers; Repairing and Maintaining Mechanical Equipment
Job Characteristics: Common Protective or Safety Attire
GOE Group/s: 05.11.04 Equipment Operation: Material Handling; 06.04.40 Elemental Work: Industrial: Loading, Moving, Hoisting, and Conveying
CIP Program/s: 000000 NO CIP ASSIGNED
Related DOT Job/s: 519.663-014 HOT-CAR OPERATOR; 519.683-014 LARRY OPERATOR; 569.683-010 KILN-TRANSFER OPERATOR; 921.583-010 TRANSFER-CAR OPERATOR, DRIER; 921.683-042 FRONT-END LOADER OPERATOR; 921.683-050 INDUSTRIAL-TRUCK OPERATOR; 921.683-070 STRADDLE-TRUCK OPERATOR; 921.683-078 TRANSFER-CAR OPERATOR; 929.583-010 YARD WORKER; 929.683-014 TRACTOR OPERATOR

97951 CONVEYOR OPERATORS AND TENDERS.

OOH Title/s: Material Moving Equipment Operators

Control or tend conveyors or conveyor systems that move materials or products to and from stockpiles, processing stations, departments, vehicles, and underground worksites. May control speed and routing of materials or products. Manipulates controls, levers, and valves to start pumps, auxiliary equipment, or conveyors and to adjust equipment positions, speed, timing, and material flow. Observes conveyor operations and monitors lights, dials, and gauges to maintain specified operating levels and to detect equipment malfunctions. Stops equipment or machinery and clears jams, using poles, bars, and hand tools, or removes damaged materials from conveyors. Reads production and delivery schedules, and confers with supervisor to determine processing procedures. Loads, unloads, or adjusts materials or products on conveyors by hand or using lifts and hoists. Inspects equipment and machinery to prevent loss of materials or products during transit. Signals workers in other departments to move materials, products, or machinery, or notifies work stations of shipments enroute and estimated delivery times. Moves, assembles, and connects hoses or nozzles to material hoppers, storage tanks, conveyor sections or chutes, and pumps. Repairs or replaces equipment components or parts such as blades, rolls, and pumps. Cleans, sterilizes, and maintains equipment, machinery, and work stations, using hand tools, shovels, brooms, chemicals, hoses, and lubricants. Repairs or replaces equipment components or parts such as blades, rolls, and pumps. Weighs or measures materials and products, using scales or other measuring instruments, to verify specified tonnage and prevent overloads. Collects samples of materials or products for laboratory analysis and ensures conformance to specifications. Affixes identifying information to materials or products, using hand tools. Records production data, such as weight, type, quantity, and storage locations of materials, and documents equipment downtime. Distributes materials, supplies, and equipment to work stations, using lifts and trucks.
Yearly Earnings: $24,232
Education: Moderate-term O-J-T
Knowledge: Production and Processing
Abilities: Perceptual Speed; Multilimb Coordination; Rate Control; Trunk Strength
Skills: Operation Monitoring; Operation and Control; Equipment Maintenance; Troubleshooting; Repairing
General Work Activities: Interacting with Computers; Repairing and Maintaining Mechanical Equipment
Job Characteristics: Making Repetitive Motions; Degree of Automation; Pace Determined by Speed of Equipment
GOE Group/s: 05.06.04 Systems Operation: Processing; 05.11.04 Equipment Operation: Material Handling; 05.12.04 Elemental Work: Mechanical: Hoisting, Conveying; 06.02.10 Production Work: Equipment Operation, Metal Processing; 06.04.13 Elemental Work: Industrial: Equipment Operation, Rubber, Plastics, Glass Processing; 06.04.15 Elemental Work: Industrial: Equipment Operation, Food Processing; 06.04.40 Elemental Work: Industrial: Loading, Moving, Hoisting, and Conveying
CIP Program/s: 490299 Vehicle and Equipment Operators, Other
Related DOT Job/s: 524.565-010 TROLLEY OPERATOR; 529.682-030 SILO OPERATOR; 529.685-050 CHAR-CONVEYOR TENDER; 553.685-078 MILLED-RUBBER TENDER; 575.687-038 TIP-OUT WORKER; 579.685-050 SILO TENDER; 579.685-062 BRICK UNLOADER TENDER; 613.685-034 BED OPERATOR; 669.685-090 TIPPLE TENDER; 921.382-010 CONVEYOR OPERATOR, PNEUMATIC SYSTEM; 921.563-010 COKE LOADER; 921.565-010 CEMENT LOADER; 921.662-018 CONVEYOR-SYSTEM OPERATOR; 921.662-026 TIPPLE OPERATOR; 921.682-014 PALLETIZER OPERATOR I; 921.683-014 BOOM-CONVEYOR OPERATOR; 921.685-014 BULL-CHAIN OPERATOR; 921.685-022 CHIP-BIN CONVEYOR TENDER; 921.685-026 CONVEYOR TENDER; 921.685-030 COOKER LOADER; 921.685-034 DRIER-TAKE-OFF TENDER; 921.685-046 FRUIT DISTRIBUTOR; 921.685-050 PRODUCTION-SUPPLY-EQUIPMENT TENDER; 921.685-062 STACKER TENDER; 921.685-066 TRANSFER OPERATOR; 921.685-070 UNSCRAMBLER

97953 PUMP OPERATORS. OOH Title/s: Material Moving Equipment Operators

Tend, control, or operate power-driven, stationary, or portable pumps and manifold systems, to transfer gases, liquids, slurries, or powdered materials to and from various vessels and processes. Operates or tends power-driven, stationary, or portable pumps to transfer substances such as gases, liquids, slurries, or powdered materials. Turns valves and starts pump to commence or regulate flow of substances. Tends vessels that store substances such as gases, liquids, slurries, or powdered materials. Connects hoses and pipes to pumps and vessels, using hand tools. Observes gauges and flowmeter to ascertain that specifications are met, such as tank level, chemical amounts, and pressure. Adds chemicals and solutions to tank to ensure specifications are met. Tends auxiliary equipment such as water treatment and refrigeration units and heat exchanges. Communicates with workers to start flow of materials or substance. Cleans and maintains pumps and vessels, using hand tools and equipment. Collects and delivers sample solutions for laboratory analysis. Tests materials and solutions, using testing equipment. Transfers materials to and from vessels, using moving equipment. Inspects and reports vessel and pump abnormalities such as leaks and pressure and temperature fluctuations. Records information such as type and quantity of material, and operating data.
Yearly Earnings: $24,232

Education: Moderate-term O-J-T
Knowledge: Production and Processing; Mechanical; Physics; Chemistry
Abilities: Control Precision; Rate Control; Speed of Limb Movement; Trunk Strength; Stamina; Dynamic Flexibility; Gross Body Coordination; Gross Body Equilibrium
Skills: Operation Monitoring; Operation and Control; Equipment Maintenance
General Work Activities: Controlling Machines and Processes
Job Characteristics: Sounds, Noise Levels are Distracting, etc.; Whole Body Vibration; Hazardous Conditions; Hazardous Equipment; Standing; Using Hands on Objects, Tools, or Controls; Making Repetitive Motions; Degree of Automation; Importance of Being Aware of New Events; Pace Determined by Speed of Equipment
GOE Group/s: 05.06.03 Systems Operation: Oil, Gas, and Water Distribution; 05.12.06 Elemental Work: Mechanical: Pumping; 06.02.12 Production Work: Equipment Operation, Petroleum and Gas Processing; 06.02.15 Production Work: Equipment Operation, Food Processing; 06.02.17 Production Work: Equipment Operation, Clay and Coke Processing; 06.02.18 Production Work: Equipment Operation, Assorted Materials Processing; 06.04.11 Elemental Work: Industrial: Equipment Operation, Chemical Processing; 06.04.12 Elemental Work: Industrial: Equipment Operation, Petroleum, Gas, and Coal Processing; 06.04.15 Elemental Work: Industrial: Equipment Operation, Food Processing; 06.04.19 Elemental Work: Industrial: Equipment Operation, Assorted Materials Processing; 06.04.40 Elemental Work: Industrial: Loading, Moving, Hoisting, and Conveying
CIP Program/s: 410301 Chemical Technologists and Technicians; 470399 Industrial Equipment Maintenance and Repair, Other; 470501 Stationary Energy Sources Installer and Operator; 490299 Vehicle and Equipment Operators, Other
Related DOT Job/s: 521.565-010 LIQUOR-BRIDGE OPERATOR; 522.662-010 RECEIVER, FERMENTING CELLARS; 529.585-014 TANK TENDER; 529.685-242 TANK PUMPER, PANELBOARD; 529.685-246 TAPPER; 549.362-010 STILL-PUMP OPERATOR; 549.382-018 WASH-OIL-PUMP OPERATOR; 549.685-042 UTILITY OPERATOR III; 559.585-014 GREASE-AND-TALLOW PUMPER; 559.665-038 TANK-FARM ATTENDANT; 559.684-034 UTILITY WORKER, PRODUCTION; 559.685-026 BRINE-WELL OPERATOR; 914.585-010 GAS-TRANSFER OPERATOR; 914.665-010 PIGMENT PUMPER; 914.665-014 PUMPER, BREWERY; 914.682-010 PUMPER; 939.682-010 MONITOR CAR OPERATOR; 950.362-010 ENGINEER, EXHAUSTER; 952.464-010 CABLE MAINTAINER

97956 OPERATING ENGINEERS. OOH Title/s: Material Moving Equipment Operators

Operate several types of power construction equipment—such as compressors, pumps, hoists, derricks, cranes, shovels, tractors, scrapers, or motor graders—that excavates, moves and grades earth, erects structures, or pours concrete or other hard surface pavement. May repair and maintain equipment in addition to other duties. Exclude workers who specialize in operation of a single type of heavy equipment, such as a bulldozer or crane. Adjusts handwheels and depresses pedals to drive machines and control attachments, such as blades, buckets, scrapers, and swing booms. Turns valves to control air and water output of compressors and pumps. Repairs and maintains equipment. Operates machinery on sales lot or customer's property to demonstrate salable features of construction equipment.
Yearly Earnings: $27,404
Education: Moderate-term O-J-T
Knowledge: Sales and Marketing; Building and Construction; Mechanical
Abilities: Multilimb Coordination
Skills: Operation Monitoring; Operation and Control; Equipment Maintenance; Troubleshooting; Repairing
General Work Activities: Handling and Moving Objects; Controlling Machines and Processes; Interacting with Computers; Repairing and Maintaining Mechanical Equipment
Job Characteristics: Sounds, Noise Levels are Distracting, etc.; Very Hot; Extremely Bright or Inadequate Lighting; Whole Body Vibration; Hazardous Equipment; Common Protective or Safety Attire; Pace Determined by Speed of Equipment
GOE Group/s: 05.11.01 Equipment Operation: Construction
CIP Program/s: 490202 Construction Equipment Operator; 490299 Vehicle and Equipment Operators, Other
Related DOT Job/s: 859.683-010 OPERATING ENGINEER; 859.683-014 OPERATING-ENGINEER APPRENTICE

97989A ALL OTHER MATERIAL MOVING EQUIPMENT OPERATORS. OOH Title/s: Material Moving Equipment Operators

All other material-moving equipment operators not classified separately above.
Yearly Earnings: $24,440
Education: Moderate-term O-J-T
GOE Group/s: 03.04.03 Elemental Work: Plants and Animals: Hunting and Fishing; 05.11.04 Equipment Operation: Material Handling; 05.12.02 Elemental Work: Mechanical: Mining, Quarrying, Drilling; 05.12.03 Elemental Work: Mechanical: Loading, Moving; 05.12.04 Elemental Work: Mechanical: Hoisting, Conveying; 05.12.06 Elemental Work: Mechanical: Pumping; 06.04.02 Elemental Work: Industrial: Machine Work, Metal and Plastics; 06.04.03 Elemental Work: Industrial: Machine Work, Wood; 06.04.10 Elemental Work: Industrial: Equipment Operation, Metal Processing; 06.04.11 Elemental Work: Industrial: Equipment Operation, Chemical Processing; 06.04.40 Elemental Work: Industrial: Loading, Moving, Hoisting, and Conveying
CIP Program/s: 490299 Vehicle and Equipment Operators, Other
Related DOT Job/s: 504.665-010 SLAB-DEPILER OPERATOR; 513.685-010 SINTER FEEDER; 521.685-278 ROUTING-EQUIPMENT TENDER; 521.685-366 TIPPLE TENDER; 529.685-102 DUMPING-MACHINE OPERATOR; 557.685-030 SPINNING-BATH PATROLLER; 569.685-066 STACKER, MACHINE; 575.683-010 BUCKET OPERATOR; 612.683-010 MANIPULATOR OPERATOR; 911.364-014 BOAT LOADER I; 914.685-010 FISH BAILER; 921.662-010 CAR-DUMPER OPERATOR; 921.663-018 CHIP UNLOADER; 921.665-010 CEMENT-BOAT-AND-BARGE LOADER; 921.667-018 DUMPER; 921.682-010 LOADER, MALT HOUSE; 921.682-018 STACKER-AND-SORTER OPERATOR; 921.683-062 SKIP OPERATOR; 921.685-018 CAGER OPERATOR; 921.685-038 DUMP OPERATOR; 921.685-058 SPOUT TENDER II; 922.665-010 FLUMER I; 922.665-014 BIN TRIPPER OPERATOR; 932.687-010 CHUTE LOADER; 939.686-010 LOADING-MACHINE-OPERATOR HELPER

97989B IRRADIATED-FUEL HANDLERS. OOH Title/s: Material Moving Equipment Operators

Package, store, and convey irradiated fuels and wastes, using hoists, mechanical arms, shovels, and industrial trucks. Operates machines and equipment to package, store, or transport loads of waste materials. Loads and unloads materials into containers and onto trucks, using hoists or forklifts. Drives truck to convey contaminated waste to designated sea or ground location. Mixes and pours concrete into forms to encase waste material for disposal. Follows prescribed safety procedures and complies with federal laws regulating waste disposal methods. Records number of containers stored at disposal site, and specifies amount and type of equipment and waste disposed. Cleans contaminated equipment for reuse, using detergents and solvents, sandblasters, filter pumps and steam cleaners.

Yearly Earnings: $24,440
Education: Moderate-term O-J-T
Knowledge: Production and Processing; Chemistry; Public Safety and Security; Law, Government, and Jurisprudence; Transportation
Abilities: Control Precision; Static Strength
Skills: None above average
General Work Activities: Controlling Machines and Processes; Interacting with Computers
Job Characteristics: Responsible for Others' Health and Safety; Contaminants; Radiation; Diseases/Infections; Common Protective or Safety Attire; Specialized Protective or Safety Attire; Consequence of Error; Importance of Being Sure All is Done
GOE Group/s: 05.11.04 Equipment Operation: Material Handling; 05.12.03 Elemental Work: Mechanical: Loading, Moving
CIP Program/s: 410205 Nuclear/Nuclear Power Technologists and Technicians
Related DOT Job/s: 921.663-034 IRRADIATED-FUEL HANDLER; 955.383-010 WASTE-DISPOSAL ATTENDANT

Helpers—Mechanics and Repairers

98102 HELPERS—MECHANICS AND REPAIRERS.
OOH Title/s: Handlers, Equipment Cleaners, Helpers, and Laborers

Help mechanics and repairers in maintenance, parts replacement, and repair of vehicles, industrial machinery, and electrical and electronic equipment. Perform duties such as furnishing tools, materials, and supplies to other workers; cleaning work area, machines, and tools; and holding materials or tools for other workers. Helps mechanics and repairers maintain and repair vehicles, industrial machinery, and electrical and electronic equipment. Furnishes tools, parts, equipment, and supplies to other workers. Cleans or lubricates vehicles, machinery, equipment, instruments, tools, work areas, and other objects, using hand tools, power tools, and cleaning equipment. Transfers equipment, tools, parts, and other objects to and from work stations and other areas, using hand tools, power tools, and moving equipment. Assembles and disassembles machinery, equipment, components, and other parts, using hand tools and power tools. Installs or replaces machinery, equipment, and new or replacement parts and instruments, using hand tools or power tools. Adjusts and connects or disconnects wiring, piping, tubing, and other parts, using hand tools or power tools. Applies protective materials to equipment, components, and parts to prevent defects and corrosion. Tends and observes equipment and machinery to verify efficient and safe operation. Positions vehicles, machinery, equipment, physical structures, and other objects for assembly or installation, using hand tools, power tools, and moving equipment. Examines and tests machinery, equipment, components, and parts for defects and to ensure proper functioning. Builds or erects and maintains physical structures, using hand tools or power tools.
Yearly Earnings: $17,160
Education: Short-term O-J-T
Knowledge: Building and Construction; Mechanical
Abilities: Speed of Limb Movement; Static Strength; Explosive Strength; Dynamic Strength; Trunk Strength; Stamina; Extent Flexibility; Dynamic Flexibility; Gross Body Coordination; Gross Body Equilibrium; Visual Color Discrimination; Hearing Sensitivity; Auditory Attention; Sound Localization
Skills: Installation; Equipment Maintenance; Repairing
General Work Activities: Performing General Physical Activities; Handling and Moving Objects; Repairing and Maintaining Mechanical Equipment; Repairing and Maintaining Electrical Equipment
Job Characteristics: Cramped Work Space, Awkward Positions; Hazardous Equipment; Standing; Kneeling, Crouching, or Crawling; Keeping or Regaining Balance; Bending or Twisting the Body; Importance of Repeating Same Tasks
GOE Group/s: 05.05.06 Craft Technology: Metal Fabrication and Repair; 05.07.01 Quality Control: Structural; 05.10.01 Crafts: Structural; 05.10.02 Crafts: Mechanical; 05.10.04 Crafts: Structural-Mechanical-Electrical-Electronic; 05.12.04 Elemental Work: Mechanical: Hoisting, Conveying; 05.12.12 Elemental Work: Mechanical: Structural Work; 05.12.15 Elemental Work: Mechanical: Mechanical Work; 05.12.16 Elemental Work: Mechanical: Electrical Work
CIP Program/s: 460301 Electrical and Power Transmission Installer, General; 460302 Electrician; 470201 Heating, Air Conditioning and Refrigeration Mechanics and Repairers; 470302 Heavy Equipment Maintenance and Repair; 470303 Industrial Machinery Maintenance and Repair
Related DOT Job/s: 620.664-010 CONSTRUCTION-EQUIPMENT-MECHANIC HELPER; 620.664-014 MAINTENANCE MECHANIC HELPER; 620.684-014 AUTOMOBILE-MECHANIC HELPER; 620.684-030 TRACTOR-MECHANIC HELPER; 621.684-010 AIRFRAME-AND-POWER-PLANT-MECHANIC HELPER; 622.684-014 CAR-REPAIRER HELPER; 623.684-010 MOTORBOAT-MECHANIC HELPER; 623.687-010 MACHINIST HELPER, OUTSIDE; 625.684-010 DIESEL-MECHANIC HELPER; 628.664-010 OVERHAULER HELPER; 630.664-010 REPAIRER HELPER; 630.664-018 SERVICE-MECHANIC HELPER, COMPRESSED-GAS EQUIPMENT; 630.684-022 PUMP-SERVICER HELPER; 630.684-034 SPRAY-GUN-REPAIRER HELPER; 631.364-010 HYDROELECTRIC-MACHINERY-MECHANIC HELPER; 631.684-010 POWERHOUSE-MECHANIC HELPER; 632.684-010 ORDNANCE-ARTIFICER HELPER; 637.384-010 INDUSTRIAL-GAS-SERVICER HELPER; 637.664-010 HEATING-AND-AIR-CONDITIONING INSTALLER-SERVICER HELPER; 637.684-010 GAS-APPLIANCE-SERVICER HELPER; 637.687-010 AIR-CONDITIONING INSTALLER-SERVICER HELPER, WINDOW UNIT; 637.687-014 REFRIGERATION-MECHANIC HELPER; 637.687-018 SOLAR-ENERGY-SYSTEM-INSTALLER HELPER; 638.484-010 MILLWRIGHT HELPER; 638.684-018 MAINTENANCE-MECHANIC HELPER; 639.684-010 SEWING-MACHINE-REPAIRER HELPER; 709.687-034 SALVAGER HELPER; 710.384-010 GAS-REGULATOR-REPAIRER HELPER; 710.384-018 INSTRUMENT-REPAIRER HELPER; 710.684-030 INSTRUMENT-TECHNICIAN HELPER; 710.684-034 METER-REPAIRER HELPER; 721.684-010 ARMATURE-WINDER HELPER, REPAIR; 729.684-050 STREET-LIGHT-REPAIRER HELPER; 739.687-094 FIRE-EQUIPMENT-INSPECTOR HELPER; 806.684-122 RIGGER HELPER; 807.687-010 AUTOMOBILE-BODY-REPAIRER HELPER; 807.687-014 STREETCAR-REPAIRER HELPER; 821.564-010 LABORATORY HELPER; 822.684-018 SIGNAL MAINTAINER HELPER; 824.664-010 STREET-LIGHT-SERVICER HELPER; 825.664-010 ELEVATOR-CONSTRUCTOR HELPER; 825.684-014 ELEVATOR-REPAIRER HELPER; 829.667-010 CABLE-SPLICER HELPER; 829.667-014 PINSETTER-MECHANIC HELPER; 862.687-022 OIL-BURNER-SERVICER-AND-INSTALLER HELPER; 869.687-030 FURNACE-INSTALLER-AND-REPAIRER HELPER, HOT AIR; 899.684-022 MAINTENANCE-REPAIRER HELPER, INDUSTRIAL; 921.687-026 RIGGER HELPER; 953.687-010 GAS-METER-INSTALLER HELPER

Helpers—Construction

98311 HELPERS—BRICK AND STONE MASONS, AND HARD TILE SETTERS. OOH Title/s: Handlers, Equipment Cleaners, Helpers, and Laborers

Help brick masons, stone masons, or hard tile setters by performing duties of lesser skill. Duties include supplying or holding materials or tools, and cleaning work area and equipment. Exclude apprentice workers (which are reported with the appropriate construction or maintenance trade occupation). Exclude construction or maintenance laborers who do not primarily assist brick masons, stone masons, or hard tile setters. Assists in the preparation, installation, repair, or rebuilding of tile, brick, or stone surfaces. Removes damaged tile, brick, or mortar, and prepares installation surfaces, using pliers, chipping hammers, chisels, drills, and metal wire anchors. Applies grout between joints of bricks or tiles, using grouting trowel. Removes excess grout and residue from tile or brick joints with wet sponge or trowel. Applies caulk, sealants or other agents to installed surface. Cleans installation surfaces, equipment, tools, worksite, and storage areas, using water, chemical solutions, oxygen lance, or polishing machines. Corrects surface imperfections or fills chipped, cracked, or broken bricks or tiles, using fillers, adhesives, and grouting materials. Modifies material moving, mixing, grouting, grinding, polishing, or cleaning procedures, according to the type of installation or materials required. Transports materials, tools, and machines to installation site, manually or using conveyance equipment. Manually or machine-mixes mortar, plaster, and grout, according to standard formulae. Selects materials for installation, following numbered sequence or drawings. Cuts materials to specified size for installation, using power saw or tile cutter. Moves or positions marble slabs and ingot covers, using crane, hoist, or dolly. Arranges and stores materials, machines, tools and equipment. Erects scaffolding or other installation structures.

Yearly Earnings: $14,768
Education: Short-term O-J-T
Knowledge: Building and Construction
Abilities: Speed of Limb Movement; Static Strength; Dynamic Strength; Stamina; Dynamic Flexibility; Gross Body Equilibrium
Skills: Installation
General Work Activities: Performing General Physical Activities; Handling and Moving Objects; Interacting with Computers
Job Characteristics: Sounds, Noise Levels are Distracting, etc.; Contaminants; Cramped Work Space, Awkward Positions; Whole Body Vibration; High Places; Climbing Ladders, Scaffolds, Poles, etc.; Walking or Running; Kneeling, Crouching, or Crawling; Keeping or Regaining Balance; Bending or Twisting the Body; Making Repetitive Motions
GOE Group/s: 05.05.01 Craft Technology: Masonry, Stone, and Brick Work; 05.12.09 Elemental Work: Mechanical: Masonry
CIP Program/s: 000000 NO CIP ASSIGNED
Related DOT Job/s: 709.687-018 HOT-TOP-LINER HELPER; 861.664-010 MARBLE FINISHER; 861.664-018 TILE FINISHER; 861.687-010 BRICKLAYER HELPER, FIREBRICK AND REFRACTORY TILE; 861.687-014 PATCHER HELPER

98312 HELPERS—CARPENTERS AND RELATED WORKERS. OOH Title/s: Handlers, Equipment Cleaners, Helpers, and Laborers

Help carpenters or carpentry-related craft workers by performing duties of lesser skill. Duties include supplying or holding materials or tools, and cleaning work area and equipment. Exclude apprentice workers (which are reported with the appropriate construction or maintenance trade occupation). Exclude construction or maintenance laborers who do not primarily assist carpenters or carpentry-related craft workers. Holds plumb bobs, sighting rods, and other equipment to aid in establishing reference points and lines. Positions and holds timbers, lumber, and paneling in place for fastening or cutting. Selects needed tools, equipment, and materials from storage and transports items to worksite. Erects scaffolding, shoring, and braces. Hews timbers. Covers surfaces with laminated plastic covering material. Cuts and installs insulating or sound-absorbing material. Drills holes in timbers or lumber. Cuts timbers, lumber, or paneling to specified dimensions. Cuts tile or linoleum to fit. Glues and clamps edges or joints of assembled parts. Smooths and sands surfaces to remove ridges, tool marks, glue, or caulking. Spreads adhesives on flooring to install tile or linoleum. Fastens timbers or lumber with glue, screws, pegs, or nails.

Yearly Earnings: $14,768
Education: Short-term O-J-T
Knowledge: Building and Construction; Mechanical
Abilities: Spatial Orientation; Arm-Hand Steadiness; Manual Dexterity; Multilimb Coordination; Response Orientation; Reaction Time; Wrist-Finger Speed; Speed of Limb Movement; Static Strength; Explosive Strength; Dynamic Strength; Trunk Strength; Stamina; Extent Flexibility; Dynamic Flexibility; Gross Body Equilibrium; Far Vision; Peripheral Vision
Skills: None above average
General Work Activities: Performing General Physical Activities; Handling and Moving Objects; Interacting with Computers
Job Characteristics: Sounds, Noise Levels are Distracting, etc.; Very Hot; Extremely Bright or Inadequate Lighting; Cramped Work Space, Awkward Positions; High Places; Hazardous Equipment; Standing; Climbing Ladders, Scaffolds, Poles, etc.; Walking or Running; Kneeling, Crouching, or Crawling; Keeping or Regaining Balance; Bending or Twisting the Body; Making Repetitive Motions; Common Protective or Safety Attire
GOE Group/s: 05.10.01 Crafts: Structural; 05.12.12 Elemental Work: Mechanical: Structural Work
CIP Program/s: 000000 NO CIP ASSIGNED
Related DOT Job/s: 764.687-050 COOPER HELPER; 860.664-014 JOINER HELPER; 860.664-018 SHIPWRIGHT HELPER; 869.664-014 CONSTRUCTION WORKER I; 869.687-026 CONSTRUCTION WORKER II; 869.687-042 TIMBER-FRAMER HELPER

98313 HELPERS—ELECTRICIANS AND POWERLINE TRANSMISSION INSTALLERS. OOH Title/s: Handlers, Equipment Cleaners, Helpers, and Laborers

Help electricians or powerline transmission installers by performing duties of lesser skill. Duties include supplying or holding materials or tools, and cleaning work area and equipment. Exclude apprentice workers (which are reported with the appropriate construction or maintenance trade occupation). Exclude construction or maintenance laborers who do not primarily assist electricians or powerline transmission installers. Maintains tools and equipment, washes parts, and keeps supplies and parts in order. Transports tools, materials, equipment, and supplies to worksite, manually or using handtruck or by driving truck. Raises, lowers, or positions equipment, tools, and materials for installation or use, using hoist, handline, or block and tackle. Breaks up concrete to facilitate installation or repair of equipment, using air hammer. Trims trees and clears undergrowth along right-of-way. Strips insulation from wire ends, using wire-stripping pliers, and attaches wires to terminals for subsequent soldering. Measures, cuts, and bends wire and conduit, using measuring instruments and hand tools. Drills holes for wiring, using power drill, and pulls or pushes wiring through opening. Bolts

component parts together to form tower assemblies, using hand tools. Solders electrical connections, using soldering iron. Rigs scaffolds, hoists, and shoring, erects barricades, and digs trenches. Traces out short circuits in wiring, using test meter. Examines electrical units for loose connections and broken insulation and tightens connections, using hand tools. Strings transmission lines or cables through ducts or conduits, underground, through equipment, or to towers. Disassembles defective electrical equipment, replaces defective or worn parts, and reassembles equipment, using hand tools. Threads conduit ends, connects couplings, and fabricates and secures conduit support brackets, using hand tools.
Yearly Earnings: $14,768
Education: Short-term O-J-T
Knowledge: Computers and Electronics
Abilities: Spatial Orientation; Arm-Hand Steadiness; Manual Dexterity; Finger Dexterity; Multilimb Coordination; Speed of Limb Movement; Static Strength; Explosive Strength; Dynamic Strength; Trunk Strength; Stamina; Extent Flexibility; Dynamic Flexibility; Gross Body Coordination; Gross Body Equilibrium; Peripheral Vision; Depth Perception
Skills: None above average
General Work Activities: Performing General Physical Activities; Interacting with Computers; Repairing and Maintaining Electrical Equipment; Assisting and Caring for Others
Job Characteristics: Sounds, Noise Levels are Distracting, etc.; Very Hot; Extremely Bright or Inadequate Lighting; Cramped Work Space, Awkward Positions; High Places; Hazardous Conditions; Hazardous Equipment; Climbing Ladders, Scaffolds, Poles, etc.; Walking or Running; Kneeling, Crouching, or Crawling; Keeping or Regaining Balance; Using Hands on Objects, Tools, or Controls; Bending or Twisting the Body; Common Protective or Safety Attire; Specialized Protective or Safety Attire
GOE Group/s: 05.10.01 Crafts: Structural; 05.10.03 Crafts: Electrical-Electronic; 05.12.16 Elemental Work: Mechanical: Electrical Work
CIP Program/s: 000000 NO CIP ASSIGNED
Related DOT Job/s: 821.667-010 HELPER, ELECTRICAL; 821.684-014 TOWER ERECTOR HELPER; 822.664-010 PROTECTIVE-SIGNAL-INSTALLER HELPER; 822.684-014 PROTECTIVE-SIGNAL-REPAIRER HELPER; 825.684-010 ELECTRICIAN HELPER, AUTOMOTIVE; 829.684-022 ELECTRICIAN HELPER; 829.684-026 ELECTRICIAN HELPER

98314 HELPERS—PAINTERS, PAPERHANGERS, PLASTERERS, AND STUCCO MASONS. OOH Title/s: Handlers, Equipment Cleaners, Helpers, and Laborers

Help painters, paperhangers, plasterers, or stucco masons by performing duties of lesser skill. Duties include supplying or holding materials or tools, and cleaning work area and equipment. Exclude apprentice workers (which are reported with the appropriate construction or maintenance trade occupation). Exclude construction or maintenance laborers who do not primarily assist painters, paperhangers, plasterers, or stucco masons. Performs any combination of support duties to assist painter, paperhanger, plasterer, or mason. Pours specified amounts of chemical solutions into stripping tanks. Places articles to be stripped into stripping tanks. Removes articles, such as cabinets, metal furniture, and paint containers, from stripping tanks after prescribed period of time. Covers surfaces of articles not to be painted with masking tape prior to painting. Fills cracks or breaks in surfaces of plaster articles with putty or epoxy compounds. Smooths surfaces of articles to be painted, using sanding and buffing tools and equipment.
Yearly Earnings: $14,768
Education: Short-term O-J-T
Knowledge: None above average
Abilities: Static Strength; Dynamic Strength
Skills: None above average
General Work Activities: None above average
Job Characteristics: Contaminants; Cramped Work Space, Awkward Positions; High Places; Hazardous Conditions; Climbing Ladders, Scaffolds, Poles, etc.; Kneeling, Crouching, or Crawling; Keeping or Regaining Balance; Bending or Twisting the Body; Making Repetitive Motions; Common Protective or Safety Attire
GOE Group/s: 05.12.12 Elemental Work: Mechanical: Structural Work
CIP Program/s: 000000 NO CIP ASSIGNED
Related DOT Job/s: 840.687-010 PAINTER HELPER, SHIPYARD

98315 HELPERS—PLUMBERS, PIPEFITTERS, AND STEAMFITTERS. OOH Title/s: Handlers, Equipment Cleaners, Helpers, and Laborers

Help plumbers, pipefitters, or steamfitters by performing duties of lesser skill. Duties include supplying or holding materials or tools, and cleaning work area and equipment. Exclude apprentice workers (which are reported with the appropriate construction or maintenance trade occupation). Exclude construction or maintenance laborers who do not primarily assist plumbers, pipefitters, or steamfitters. Fits or assists in fitting valves, couplings, or assemblies to tanks, pumps, or systems, using hand tools. Disassembles and removes damaged or worn pipe. Assists in installing gas burners to convert furnaces from wood, coal, or oil. Requisitions tools and equipment and selects type and size of pipe. Fills pipes with sand or resin to prevent distortion, and holds pipes during bending and installation. Immerses pipes in chemical solution to remove dirt, oil, and scale. Cleans shop, work area, and machines, using solvent and rags. Mounts brackets and hangers on walls and ceilings to hold pipes. Cuts or drills holes in walls to accommodate passage of pipes, using pneumatic drill.
Yearly Earnings: $14,768
Education: Short-term O-J-T
Knowledge: Building and Construction
Abilities: Arm-Hand Steadiness; Manual Dexterity; Finger Dexterity; Multilimb Coordination; Static Strength; Explosive Strength; Dynamic Strength; Trunk Strength; Stamina; Extent Flexibility; Dynamic Flexibility; Gross Body Coordination; Gross Body Equilibrium
Skills: Equipment Maintenance
General Work Activities: None above average
Job Characteristics: Sounds, Noise Levels are Distracting, etc.; Extremely Bright or Inadequate Lighting; Contaminants; Cramped Work Space, Awkward Positions; High Places; Hazardous Conditions; Hazardous Equipment; Climbing Ladders, Scaffolds, Poles, etc.; Kneeling, Crouching, or Crawling; Keeping or Regaining Balance; Using Hands on Objects, Tools, or Controls; Bending or Twisting the Body; Common Protective or Safety Attire; Specialized Protective or Safety Attire
GOE Group/s: 05.12.12 Elemental Work: Mechanical: Structural Work
CIP Program/s: 000000 NO CIP ASSIGNED
Related DOT Job/s: 862.684-018 PIPE-FITTER HELPER; 862.684-022 PIPE-FITTER HELPER

98319 HELPERS—ALL OTHER CONSTRUCTION TRADES WORKERS. OOH Title/s: Handlers, Equipment Cleaners, Helpers, and Laborers

All other construction trades helpers not classified separately above.
Yearly Earnings: $14,768
Education: Short-term O-J-T

Knowledge: None above average
Abilities: None above average
Skills: None above average
General Work Activities: None above average
Job Characteristics: None above average
GOE Group/s: 05.05.01 Craft Technology: Masonry, Stone, and Brick Work; 05.10.01 Crafts: Structural; 05.12.02 Elemental Work: Mechanical: Mining, Quarrying, Drilling; 05.12.04 Elemental Work: Mechanical: Hoisting, Conveying; 05.12.05 Elemental Work: Mechanical: Braking, Switching, and Coupling; 05.12.09 Elemental Work: Mechanical: Masonry; 05.12.12 Elemental Work: Mechanical: Structural Work
CIP Program/s: 000000 NO CIP ASSIGNED
Related DOT Job/s: 844.687-010 CEMENT SPRAYER HELPER, NOZZLE; 850.684-014 HORIZONTAL-EARTH-BORING-MACHINE-OPERATOR HELPER; 861.664-014 TERRAZZO FINISHER; 864.687-010 CARPET-LAYER HELPER; 869.567-010 SURVEYOR HELPER; 869.687-010 AWNING-HANGER HELPER; 869.687-034 HOUSE-MOVER HELPER; 899.664-010 DIVER HELPER; 911.667-018 SOUNDER; 930.687-014 CORE-DRILL-OPERATOR HELPER

98323 HELPERS—EXTRACTIVE WORKERS. OOH Title/s: Handlers, Equipment Cleaners, Helpers, and Laborers
Help extractive craft workers—such as earth drillers, blasters and explosives workers, derrick operators, and mining machine operators—by performing duties of lesser skill. Duties include supplyingequipment or cleaning work area. Exclude apprentice workers (which are reported with the appropriate construction or maintenance trade occupation). Exclude laborers who do not primarily assist extractive craft workers. Assists workers to extract geological materials, using hand tools and equipment. Drives moving equipment to transport materials and parts to excavation site. Unloads materials, devices, and machine parts, using hand tools. Sets up and adjusts equipment used to excavate geological materials. Loads materials into gas or well hole or equipment, using hand tools. Organizes materials and prepares site for excavation or boring, using hand tools. Dismantles extracting and boring equipment used for excavation, using hand tools. Observes and monitors equipment operation during extraction process. Repairs and maintains automotive and drilling equipment, using hand tools. Signals workers to start extraction or boring process of geological materials. Examines and collects geological matter, using hand tools and testing devices.
Yearly Earnings: $17,160
Education: Short-term O-J-T
Knowledge: Mechanical; Physics; Transportation
Abilities: Rate Control; Speed of Limb Movement; Static Strength; Explosive Strength; Dynamic Strength; Stamina; Dynamic Flexibility; Gross Body Coordination; Gross Body Equilibrium
Skills: Operation Monitoring; Equipment Maintenance; Repairing
General Work Activities: Performing General Physical Activities; Handling and Moving Objects; Interacting with Computers; Repairing and Maintaining Mechanical Equipment
Job Characteristics: Sounds, Noise Levels are Distracting, etc.; Very Hot; Extremely Bright or Inadequate Lighting; Contaminants; Cramped Work Space, Awkward Positions; Whole Body Vibration; Radiation; Hazardous Conditions; Hazardous Equipment; Hazardous Situations; Climbing Ladders, Scaffolds, Poles, etc.; Walking or Running; Kneeling, Crouching, or Crawling; Keeping or Regaining Balance; Bending or Twisting the Body; Common Protective or Safety Attire; Specialized Protective or Safety Attire; Pace Determined by Speed of Equipment
GOE Group/s: 05.08.03 Land and Water Vehicle Operation: Services Requiring Driving; 05.12.02 Elemental Work: Mechanical: Mining, Quarrying, Drilling; 05.12.03 Elemental Work: Mechanical: Loading, Moving
CIP Program/s: 000000 NO CIP ASSIGNED
Related DOT Job/s: 859.687-010 BLASTER HELPER; 930.664-014 CLEAN-OUT-DRILLER HELPER; 930.666-010 DRILLER HELPER; 930.666-014 TAILER; 930.667-010 SHALE PLANER OPERATOR HELPER; 930.684-026 ROTARY-DRILLER HELPER; 930.687-010 BOTTOM-HOLE-PRESSURE-RECORDING-OPERATOR HELPER; 939.364-010 OBSERVER HELPER, SEISMIC PROSPECTING; 939.663-010 OBSERVER HELPER, GRAVITY PROSPECTING

Helpers—Feeders and Offbearers

98502 MACHINE FEEDERS AND OFFBEARERS. OOH Title/s: Handlers, Equipment Cleaners, Helpers, and Laborers
Feed materials into or remove materials from machines or equipment that is automatic or tended by other workers. Feeds materials into machines and equipment to process and manufacture products. Loads materials and products into machines and equipment, using hand tools and moving devices. Removes materials and products from machines and equipment, using hand tools and moving devices. Offbears materials and products from machines and equipment, using hand tools. Shovels or scoops materials into containers, machines, or equipment for processing, storage, or transport. Adds chemicals, solutions, or ingredients to machines or equipment to ensure manufacturing process meets specifications. Transfers materials and products between storage areas and machinery and equipment. Sorts and selects materials and products and rejects defective pieces, following specified instructions and standards. Fastens, packages, or stacks materials and products, using hand tools and fastening equipment. Inspects materials and products for defects and to ensure conformance to specifications. Weighs or measures materials or products to ensure conformance to specifications. Identifies and marks materials, products, and samples, following instructions. Records production and operational information and data on specified forms. Modifies materials and products during manufacturing process to meet requirements. Moves controls to start, stop, or adjust machinery and equipment. Cleans and maintains machinery, equipment, and work areas to ensure proper functioning and safe working conditions.
Yearly Earnings: $17,108
Education: Short-term O-J-T
Knowledge: Production and Processing
Abilities: Perceptual Speed; Manual Dexterity; Multilimb Coordination; Rate Control; Reaction Time; Speed of Limb Movement; Static Strength; Explosive Strength; Dynamic Strength; Trunk Strength; Stamina; Extent Flexibility; Dynamic Flexibility; Gross Body Coordination; Gross Body Equilibrium
Skills: Equipment Maintenance
General Work Activities: Handling and Moving Objects
Job Characteristics: Sounds, Noise Levels are Distracting, etc.; Hazardous Conditions; Hazardous Equipment; Standing; Using Hands on Objects, Tools, or Controls; Bending or Twisting the Body; Making Repetitive Motions; Degree of Automation; Importance of Being Aware of New Events; Importance of Repeating Same Tasks; Pace Determined by Speed of Equipment
GOE Group/s: 03.04.01 Elemental Work: Plants and Animals: Farming; 05.12.03 Elemental Work: Mechanical: Loading, Moving; 05.12.04 Elemental Work: Mechanical: Hoisting, Conveying; 05.12.19 Elemental Work: Mechanical: Reproduction Services; 06.02.02 Production Work: Machine Work, Metal and Plastics;

06.03.02 Quality Control: Inspecting, Grading, Sorting, Weighing, and Recording; 06.04.02 Elemental Work: Industrial: Machine Work, Metal and Plastics; 06.04.03 Elemental Work: Industrial: Machine Work, Wood; 06.04.04 Elemental Work: Industrial: Machine Work, Paper; 06.04.05 Elemental Work: Industrial: Machine Work, Fabric and Leather; 06.04.06 Elemental Work: Industrial: Machine Work, Textiles; 06.04.07 Elemental Work: Industrial: Machine Work, Rubber; 06.04.08 Elemental Work: Industrial: Machine Work, Stone, Glass, and Clay; 06.04.09 Elemental Work: Industrial: Machine Work, Assorted Materials; 06.04.10 Elemental Work: Industrial: Equipment Operation, Metal Processing; 06.04.11 Elemental Work: Industrial: Equipment Operation, Chemical Processing; 06.04.13 Elemental Work: Industrial: Equipment Operation, Rubber, Plastics, Glass Processing; 06.04.14 Elemental Work: Industrial: Equipment Operation, Paper Making; 06.04.15 Elemental Work: Industrial: Equipment Operation, Food Processing; 06.04.16 Elemental Work: Industrial: Equipment Operation, Textile, Fabric, and Leather Processing; 06.04.17 Elemental Work: Industrial: Equipment Operation, Clay Processing; 06.04.18 Elemental Work: Industrial: Equipment Operation, Wood Processing; 06.04.19 Elemental Work: Industrial: Equipment Operation, Assorted Materials Processing; 06.04.20 Elemental Work: Industrial: Machine Assembling; 06.04.21 Elemental Work: Industrial: Machine Work, Brushing, Spraying, and Coating; 06.04.26 Elemental Work: Industrial: Manual Work, Paper; 06.04.27 Elemental Work: Industrial: Manual Work, Textile, Fabric and Leather; 06.04.28 Elemental Work: Industrial: Manual Work, Food Processing; 06.04.29 Elemental Work: Industrial: Manual Work, Rubber; 06.04.30 Elemental Work: Industrial: Manual Work, Stone, Glass, and Clay; 06.04.31 Elemental Work: Industrial: Manual Work, Welding and Flame Cutting; 06.04.33 Elemental Work: Industrial: Manual Work, Brushing, Spraying, and Coating; 06.04.34 Elemental Work: Industrial: Manual Work, Assorted Materials; 06.04.35 Elemental Work: Industrial: Laundering, Dry Cleaning; 06.04.37 Elemental Work: Industrial: Manual Work, Stamping, Marking, Labeling, and Ticketing; 06.04.38 Elemental Work: Industrial: Wrapping and Packaging; 06.04.39 Elemental Work: Industrial: Cleaning; 06.04.40 Elemental Work: Industrial: Loading, Moving, Hoisting, and Conveying

CIP Program/s: 000000 NO CIP ASSIGNED

Related DOT Job/s: 361.686-010 WASHING-MACHINE LOADER-AND-PULLER; 363.686-010 FLATWORK FINISHER; 369.686-010 FOLDING-MACHINE OPERATOR; 429.686-010 PRESS FEEDER, BROOMCORN; 504.686-014 FURNACE HELPER; 504.686-022 HEAT TREATER; 509.666-010 COMPOUND-COATING-MACHINE OFFBEARER; 509.686-014 PASTING-MACHINE OFFBEARER; 509.687-026 LABORER, GENERAL; 512.686-010 CUPOLA CHARGER; 515.686-010 BATTERY-WRECKER OPERATOR; 519.686-010 LABORER, GENERAL; 520.686-010 BALL-MACHINE OPERATOR; 520.686-014 DESSERT-CUP-MACHINE FEEDER; 520.686-030 MOLDING-MACHINE-OPERATOR HELPER; 520.686-034 PLUG SHAPER, MACHINE; 521.686-014 CAKE PULLER; 521.686-018 CHICLE-GRINDER FEEDER; 521.686-022 COTTON PULLER; 521.686-030 CUT-IN WORKER; 521.686-034 FISH-MACHINE FEEDER; 521.686-038 FLUMER; 521.686-042 FLUMER II; 521.686-046 NUT CHOPPER; 522.686-010 CHIP WASHER; 522.686-014 GENERAL HELPER; 524.686-010 ENROBING-MACHINE FEEDER; 525.686-010 CASING CLEANER; 525.686-014 CONVEYOR LOADER II; 525.686-018 HEAD-MACHINE FEEDER; 525.686-022 SKINNING-MACHINE FEEDER; 529.686-010 BUNDLES HANGER; 529.686-018 CIGARETTE-MAKING-MACHINE-HOPPER FEEDER; 529.686-030 EGG WASHER, MACHINE; 529.686-038 FEEDER-CATCHER, TOBACCO; 529.686-042 FILLER FEEDER; 529.686-054 LABORER, PIE BAKERY; 529.686-062 LONG-GOODS HELPER, MACHINE; 529.686-066 PRESS MACHINE FEEDER; 529.686-070 PRODUCTION HELPER; 529.686-074 RACK LOADER I; 529.686-082 STEAK TENDERIZER, MACHINE; 529.686-086 UTILITY WORKER; 529.687-182 SHREDDED-FILLER HOPPER-FEEDER; 529.687-230 LABORER, SHELLFISH PROCESSING; 530.666-010 RAG-CUTTING-MACHINE FEEDER; 530.686-010 BEATER-AND-PULPER FEEDER; 530.686-014 LOADER, MAGAZINE GRINDER; 530.686-018 WASTE-PAPER-HAMMERMILL OPERATOR; 532.686-010 DIGESTER-OPERATOR HELPER; 532.686-014 PAPER-CONE-DRYING-MACHINE OPERATOR; 549.686-014 FELT HANGER; 550.686-010 BATCH TRUCKER; 550.686-014 COMPOUND FILLER; 550.686-022 GLAZING OPERATOR, BLACK POWDER; 550.686-030 MIXING-MACHINE FEEDER; 550.686-034 MOTTLER-MACHINE FEEDER; 551.666-010 PITCH WORKER; 551.686-010 BEAD PICKER; 551.686-014 EXTRACTOR LOADER AND UNLOADER; 551.686-018 HOPPER FEEDER; 552.686-010 EXTRACTOR-OPERATOR HELPER; 553.486-010 CALCINE FURNACE LOADER; 553.686-010 BONE-CHAR OPERATOR; 553.686-018 CURING-PRESS OPERATOR; 553.686-022 DECKHAND; 553.686-026 DRIER OPERATOR V; 553.686-034 FRAME FEEDER; 553.686-038 ROTARY-DRIER FEEDER; 554.686-010 CALENDER FEEDER; 555.686-010 BLOCK-BREAKER OPERATOR; 555.686-014 SOAP CHIPPER; 556.686-014 CELL STRIPPER; 556.686-018 STRIPPER; 556.686-022 SUPPOSITORY-MOLDING-MACHINE OPERATOR; 558.666-010 DEVULCANIZER CHARGER; 559.686-010 COMPOUND WORKER; 559.686-014 DRIER FEEDER; 559.686-018 HOSE-TUBING BACKER; 559.686-022 LABORER; 559.686-030 LABORER, VAT HOUSE; 559.686-042 SLABBER; 562.686-010 STEAM-TUNNEL FEEDER; 563.686-010 STICKER; 563.686-014 VENEER-DRIER FEEDER; 563.686-018 OFF-BEARER, PIPE SMOKING MACHINE; 564.686-010 WOOD SCRAP HANDLER; 569.686-010 BACK FEEDER, PLYWOOD LAYUP LINE; 569.686-014 CORE LAYER, PLYWOOD LAYUP LINE; 569.686-018 CORK-PRESSING-MACHINE OPERATOR; 569.686-022 GLUING-MACHINE OFFBEARER; 569.686-026 LABORER, HOT-PLATE PLYWOOD PRESS; 569.686-030 PAD-MACHINE OFFBEARER; 569.686-034 RETORT UNLOADER; 569.686-038 GLUING-MACHINE FEEDER; 569.686-042 LAMINATING-MACHINE FEEDER; 569.686-050 PRESS BREAKER; 569.686-054 VENEER-TAPING-MACHINE OFFBEARER; 570.686-010 ABRASIVE-GRADER HELPER; 570.686-018 PREPARATION-ROOM WORKER; 570.687-010 BATCH MIXER; 572.686-010 CUPOLA CHARGER, INSULATION; 573.686-010 BRAKE-LINING CURER; 573.686-014 FUSING-FURNACE LOADER;
573.686-018 GLASS-VIAL-BENDING-CONVEYOR FEEDER; 573.686-022 HACKER; 573.686-026 KILN PLACER; 574.686-010 SPRAY-MACHINE LOADER; 575.686-014 MOLDER HELPER; 575.686-018 PIN MAKER; 579.686-014 MAT PACKER; 579.686-018 MICA-LAMINATING-MACHINE FEEDER; 579.686-022 MIRROR-MACHINE FEEDER; 579.686-026 OFFBEARER, SEWER PIPE; 579.686-030 PRESS OFFBEARER; 581.586-010 HEAT CURER; 581.686-010 BLOWER FEEDER, DYED RAW STOCK; 581.686-014 DRIER; 581.686-018 DRIER ATTENDANT; 581.686-022 DRYING-OVEN ATTENDANT; 581.686-026 DRYING-RACK CHANGER; 581.686-030 DUST-MILL OPERATOR; 581.686-034 FEATHER-DRYING-MACHINE OPERATOR; 581.686-042 WET-COTTON FEEDER; 582.686-010 DYE-HOUSE WORKER; 582.686-018 RAW-STOCK-MACHINE LOADER; 582.686-030 TOP-DYEING-MACHINE LOADER; 582.686-034 TUBE HANDLER; 582.686-038 WARP COILER; 583.686-014 FUSING-MACHINE FEEDER; 583.686-018 GLOVE TURNER AND FORMER, AUTOMATIC; 583.686-022 MANGLE-PRESS CATCHER; 583.686-026 OUTSOLE FLEXER; 583.686-030 PRESS FEEDER; 585.686-010 FEATHER-CUTTING-MACHINE FEEDER; 586.686-010 CARROTING-MACHINE OFFBEARER; 586.686-018 HAT-FORMING-MACHINE FEEDER; 589.686-010 BACK TENDER; 589.686-014 CLOTH FEEDER; 589.686-018 FEATHER-CURLING-MACHINE OPERATOR; 589.686-030 OPENER II; 589.686-034 PACKAGE CRIMPER; 589.686-042 SOCK BOARDER; 589.686-046 TAKER-OFF, HEMP FIBER; 589.686-050 TOBACCO-CLOTH RECLAIMER; 589.687-062 DYE-STAND LOADER; 590.686-014 GUIDER; 590.687-018 RACK LOADER; 599.686-010 MILL-OPERATOR HELPER;

599.686-014 SPRAY-UNIT FEEDER; 603.686-010 POLISHING-MACHINE-OPERATOR HELPER; 603.686-014 DEBURRER, PRINTED CIRCUIT BOARD PANELS; 604.666-010 THREADING-MACHINE FEEDER, AUTOMATIC I; 604.686-010 WIRE THREADER; 612.666-010 SPIKE-MACHINE FEEDER; 613.686-010 CATCHER; 614.586-010 WIRE CHARGER; 614.686-014 TESTER-OPERATOR HELPER; 617.686-010 HOOP COILER; 619.686-010 AUTOMATIC STACKER; 619.686-018 HOPPER FEEDER; 640.686-010 ROTARY-CUTTER FEEDER; 641.686-026 PAPER-BAG-PRESS OPERATOR; 641.686-030 SCORER HELPER; 649.686-022 FINISHING-MACHINE OPERATOR; 649.686-026 PLATING-MACHINE OPERATOR; 649.686-030 SLITTER-CREASER-SLOTTER HELPER; 651.686-010 CYLINDER-PRESS FEEDER; 651.686-014 FEEDER; 651.686-018 JOGGER; 651.686-022 ROLL TENDER; 652.586-010 UTILITY WORKER, CLOTH PRINTING; 652.686-010 CLOTH-PRINTER HELPER; 652.686-014 GRAINER, MACHINE; 652.686-018 GRAY-CLOTH TENDER, PRINTING; 652.686-022 LOADER-UNLOADER, SCREEN-PRINTING MACHINE; 652.686-026 PRINT-LINE FEEDER; 652.686-030 PRINT-LINE TAILER; 652.686-034 RAISED PRINTER; 652.686-046 WARE SERVER; 652.687-038 PRINTER, FLOOR COVERING, ASSISTANT; 653.686-010 CASING-IN-LINE FEEDER; 653.686-026 BINDERY-MACHINE FEEDER-OFFBEARER; 659.686-014 PRINTER-SLOTTER HELPER; 659.687-010 RACKER; 662.686-010 END-TOUCHING-MACHINE OPERATOR; 662.686-014 MULTIPLE-DRUM-SANDER HELPER; 663.686-010 BLOCK FEEDER; 663.686-014 BREAK-OFF WORKER; 663.686-018 GREEN-CHAIN OFFBEARER; 663.686-026 SLICING-MACHINE TENDER; 665.686-010 POLE-PEELING-MACHINE-OPERATOR HELPER; 665.686-014 STAVE-PLANER TENDER; 665.686-022 VENEER-JOINTER OFFBEARER; 667.686-010 CLOTHESPIN-MACHINE OPERATOR; 667.686-018 TRIMMER HELPER; 669.686-010 AUTOMATIC-NAILING-MACHINE FEEDER; 669.686-018 CHAIN OFFBEARER; 669.686-022 REED-PRESS FEEDER; 669.686-030 WOODWORKING-MACHINE FEEDER; 669.686-034 WOODWORKING-MACHINE OFFBEARER; 669.687-010 CLEAT FEEDER; 673.666-010 BELT SANDER, STONE; 673.686-010 BEVELING-AND-EDGING-MACHINE-OPERATOR HELPER; 673.686-014 BURR GRINDER; 673.686-018 EDGER-MACHINE HELPER; 673.686-022 EDGING-MACHINE FEEDER; 673.686-026 LAYER; 673.686-030 DISC-PAD GRINDING MACHINE FEEDER; 676.686-010 STONE-DRILLER HELPER; 676.686-014 DRILLER AND DEBURRER, REFLECTOR; 677.686-010 SAWYER I; 677.686-014 GLASS-CUTTING-MACHINE FEEDER; 679.686-010 ASBESTOS-SHINGLE SHEARING-MACHINE OPERATOR; 680.686-010 CAN DOFFER; 680.686-014 FIRST-BREAKER FEEDER; 680.686-018 MACHINE FEEDER, RAW STOCK; 680.686-022 WASTE-MACHINE OFFBEARER; 681.686-010 BEAM RACKER; 681.686-018 SPOOLER OPERATOR, AUTOMATIC; 683.686-010 BATTERY LOADER; 684.686-010 CLIPPER, MACHINE; 685.686-010 FRINGING-MACHINE OPERATOR; 686.686-010 FELT-TIPPING-MACHINE TENDER; 689.366-010 HEAD DOFFER; 689.686-014 BOBBIN-CLEANING-MACHINE OPERATOR; 689.686-018 CUTTING-MACHINE OFFBEARER; 689.686-022 DOFFER; 689.686-030 HAIR-SPINNING-MACHINE OPERATOR; 689.686-034 NEEDLE-PUNCH-MACHINE-OPERATOR HELPER; 689.686-038 SHUTTLE HAND; 689.686-046 THREAD-PULLING-MACHINE ATTENDANT; 689.686-054 WASTE CHOPPER; 689.686-058 CLOTH DOFFER; 690.686-010 BEVELING-MACHINE OPERATOR; 690.686-022 COATING-MACHINE FEEDER; 690.686-026 CRIMPER; 690.686-034 FOLDING-MACHINE OPERATOR; 690.686-038 INJECTION-MOLDING-MACHINE OFFBEARER; 690.686-042 INJECTION-MOLDING-MACHINE OFFBEARER; 690.686-046 PLASTIC-DESIGN APPLIER; 690.686-050 RUBBER-ROLLER GRINDER; 690.686-054 SPLITTING-MACHINE FEEDER; 690.686-058 SWEATBAND FLANGER; 690.686-062 SWEATBAND-CUTTING-MACHINE OPERATOR; 690.686-066 TOGGLE-PRESS FOLDER-AND-FEEDER; 691.686-010 TWISTING-MACHINE OPERATOR; 692.686-010 ASSEMBLY-MACHINE OPERATOR; 692.686-014 BASE REMOVER; 692.686-018 BROOMCORN SEEDER; 692.686-022 BULB FILLER; 692.686-026 CARBON ROD INSERTER; 692.686-030 CUTTER II; 692.686-034 DESIGN ASSEMBLER; 692.686-038 DYNAMITE-PACKING-MACHINE FEEDER; 692.686-042 GROOVER; 692.686-046 LAMINATED-PLASTIC-TABLETOP-MOLDING WRAPPER; 692.686-050 MOUNTER I; 692.686-054 NAIL-POLISH-BRUSH-MACHINE FEEDER, AUTOMATIC; 692.686-058 NECKER; 692.686-062 STEM SIZER; 692.686-066 THIRD DRY-CELL-ASSEMBLING-MACHINE TENDER; 694.686-010 CLIP-LOADING-MACHINE FEEDER; 699.686-010 MACHINE FEEDER; 715.686-010 DESTATICIZER FEEDER; 715.686-014 MACHINE FEEDER; 726.686-010 WAVE-SOLDER OFFBEARER; 727.687-010 ACID DUMPER; 732.686-010 HAY SORTER; 749.686-010 STRIPER, MACHINE; 751.686-010 HOSE CUTTER, MACHINE; 762.686-010 EDGE-BANDING-MACHINE OFFBEARER; 787.686-010 BAG SEWER; 819.686-010 MACHINE FEEDER; 920.586-010 MASKING-MACHINE FEEDER; 920.686-014 COTTON-BALL BAGGER; 920.686-018 FOLDING-MACHINE FEEDER; 920.686-026 PACKING-FLOOR WORKER; 920.686-030 PACKING-MACHINE CAN FEEDER; 920.686-034 PAD-MACHINE FEEDER; 920.686-038 POLY-PACKER AND HEAT-SEALER; 920.686-042 PRESS BUCKER; 920.686-046 SPOOLER, SEQUINS; 920.686-050 TRAY FILLER; 921.686-010 CARTON-COUNTER FEEDER; 921.686-014 CONVEYOR FEEDER-OFFBEARER; 922.686-010 DUMPER; 922.686-014 LOWERATOR OPERATOR; 929.686-018 CRAYON-SORTING-MACHINE FEEDER; 929.686-022 FEED-IN WORKER; 951.686-010 FUEL-HOUSE ATTENDANT

Helpers—Material Movers

98702 STEVEDORES, EXCEPT EQUIPMENT OPERATORS. OOH Title/s: Handlers, Equipment Cleaners, Helpers, and Laborers

Manually load and unload ship cargo. Stack cargo in transit shed or in hold of ship using pallet or cargo board. Attach and move slings to lift cargo. Guide load lift. Exclude workers who primarily load and unload ship cargo using power equipment, such as power winches, cranes, and lift trucks. Carries or moves cargo by handtruck to wharf, and stacks cargo on pallets to facilitate transfer to and from ship. Stacks cargo in transit shed or in hold of ship as directed. Attaches and moves slings used to lift cargo. Guides load being lifted to prevent swinging. Shores cargo in ship's hold to prevent shifting during voyage.

Yearly Earnings: $17,160

Education: Short-term O-J-T

Knowledge: Transportation

Abilities: Speed of Limb Movement; Static Strength; Explosive Strength; Dynamic Strength; Trunk Strength; Stamina; Extent Flexibility; Dynamic Flexibility; Gross Body Coordination; Gross Body Equilibrium; Peripheral Vision; Depth Perception; Glare Sensitivity

Skills: None above average

General Work Activities: Performing General Physical Activities; Handling and Moving Objects

Job Characteristics: Sounds, Noise Levels are Distracting, etc.; Very Hot; Extremely Bright or Inadequate Lighting; Cramped Work Space, Awkward Positions; High Places; Hazardous Equipment; Standing; Walking or Running; Kneeling, Crouching, or Crawling; Keeping or Regaining Balance; Bending or Twisting the Body

GOE Group/s: 05.12.03 Elemental Work: Mechanical: Loading, Moving

CIP Program/s: 000000 NO CIP ASSIGNED

Related DOT Job/s: 922.687-090 STEVEDORE II

98705 REFUSE AND RECYCLABLE MATERIAL COLLECTORS. OOH Title/s: Handlers, Equipment Cleaners, Helpers, and Laborers

Collect and dump refuse or recyclable materials from containers into truck, on a designated route in a municipality. May drive truck. Drives truck. Starts hoisting device that raises refuse bin attached to rear of truck, and dumps contents into opening in enclosed truck body.

Yearly Earnings: $21,788
Education: Short-term O-J-T
Knowledge: Transportation
Abilities: Rate Control
Skills: None above average
General Work Activities: Performing General Physical Activities; Handling and Moving Objects; Interacting with Computers
Job Characteristics: Sounds, Noise Levels are Distracting, etc.; Very Hot; Extremely Bright or Inadequate Lighting; Contaminants; Standing; Walking or Running; Special Uniform; Importance of Repeating Same Tasks
GOE Group/s: 05.12.03 Elemental Work: Mechanical: Loading, Moving
CIP Program/s: 000000 NO CIP ASSIGNED
Related DOT Job/s: 955.687-022 GARBAGE COLLECTOR

98799A GRIPS AND SET-UP WORKERS—MOTION PICTURE SETS, STUDIOS, AND STAGES. OOH Title/s: Handlers, Equipment Cleaners, Helpers, and Laborers

Arrange equipment; raise and lower scenery; move dollies, cranes, and booms; and perform other duties for motion picture, recording, or television industry. Arranges equipment preparatory to sessions and performances following work order specifications and handles props during performances. Rigs and dismantles stage or set equipment, such as frames, scaffolding, platforms, or backdrops, using carpenter's hand tools. Adjusts controls to raise and lower scenery and stage curtain during performance, following cues. Adjusts controls to guide, position, and move equipment, such as cranes, booms, and cameras. Erects canvas covers to protect equipment from weather. Reads work orders and follows oral instructions to determine specified material and equipment to be moved and its relocation. Connects electrical equipment to power source and tests equipment before performance. Orders equipment and maintains equipment storage areas. Sews and repairs items, using materials and hand tools such as canvas and sewing machines. Produces special lighting and sound effects during performances, using various machines and devices.

Yearly Earnings: $17,160
Education: Short-term O-J-T
Knowledge: Building and Construction
Abilities: Spatial Orientation; Visualization; Static Strength; Trunk Strength; Extent Flexibility; Gross Body Equilibrium; Depth Perception
Skills: Installation
General Work Activities: Performing General Physical Activities
Job Characteristics: High Places; Hazardous Conditions; Standing; Climbing Ladders, Scaffolds, Poles, etc.; Kneeling, Crouching, or Crawling; Keeping or Regaining Balance; Using Hands on Objects, Tools, or Controls; Bending or Twisting the Body
GOE Group/s: 05.12.03 Elemental Work: Mechanical: Loading, Moving; 05.12.04 Elemental Work: Mechanical: Hoisting, Conveying
CIP Program/s: 000000 NO CIP ASSIGNED
Related DOT Job/s: 962.384-010 MICROPHONE-BOOM OPERATOR; 962.664-014 RECORDING STUDIO SET-UP WORKER; 962.684-018 MOTOR-POWER CONNECTOR; 962.684-022 PROP ATTENDANT; 962.687-018 FLYER; 962.687-022 GRIP

98799B FREIGHT, STOCK, AND MATERIAL MOVERS—HAND. OOH Title/s: Handlers, Equipment Cleaners, Helpers, and Laborers

Load, unload and move materials at plant, yard, or other worksite. Loads and unloads materials to and from designated storage areas, such as racks and shelves, or vehicles, such as trucks. Transports receptacles to and from designated areas, by hand or using dollies, handtrucks, and wheelbarrows. Secures lifting attachments to materials and conveys load to destination, using crane or hoist. Directs spouts and positions receptacles, such as bins, carts, and containers, to receive loads. Stacks or piles materials, such as lumber, boards, or pallets. Shovels materials—such as gravel, ice or spilled concrete—into containers and bins or onto conveyors. Bundles and bands material, such as fodder and tobacco leaves, using banding machines. Reads work orders or receives and listens to oral instructions to determine work assignment. Sorts and stores items according to specifications. Installs protective devices, such as bracing, padding, or strapping, to prevent shifting or damage to items being transported. Cleans work area, using brooms, rags, and cleaning compounds. Attaches identifying tags or marks information on containers. Records number of units handled and moved, using daily production sheet or work tickets. Adjusts or replaces equipment parts, such as rollers, belts, plugs, and caps, using hand tools. Assembles product containers and crates, using hand tools and precut lumber.

Yearly Earnings: $16,640
Education: Short-term O-J-T
Knowledge: Production and Processing
Abilities: Multilimb Coordination; Static Strength; Trunk Strength; Stamina; Extent Flexibility; Gross Body Coordination; Gross Body Equilibrium
Skills: None above average
General Work Activities: Performing General Physical Activities; Handling and Moving Objects; Interacting with Computers
Job Characteristics: Standing; Climbing Ladders, Scaffolds, Poles, etc.; Walking or Running; Kneeling, Crouching, or Crawling; Keeping or Regaining Balance; Importance of Repeating Same Tasks
GOE Group/s: 03.03.02 Animal Training and Service: Animal Service; 03.04.05 Elemental Work: Plants and Animals: Services; 05.12.03 Elemental Work: Mechanical: Loading, Moving; 05.12.04 Elemental Work: Mechanical: Hoisting, Conveying; 05.12.06 Elemental Work: Mechanical: Pumping; 05.12.12 Elemental Work: Mechanical: Structural Work; 05.12.19 Elemental Work: Mechanical: Reproduction Services; 06.04.12 Elemental Work: Industrial: Equipment Operation, Petroleum, Gas, and Coal Processing; 06.04.15 Elemental Work: Industrial: Equipment Operation, Food Processing; 06.04.28 Elemental Work: Industrial: Manual Work, Food Processing; 06.04.40 Elemental Work: Industrial: Loading, Moving, Hoisting, and Conveying
CIP Program/s: 000000 NO CIP ASSIGNED
Related DOT Job/s: 412.687-010 COMMISSARY ASSISTANT; 520.687-010 BLENDER LABORER; 520.687-038 GUM PULLER; 523.687-022 FREEZING-ROOM WORKER; 525.687-054 OFFAL ICER, POULTRY; 525.687-086 SHACKLER; 529.687-138 LEAF TIER; 542.667-010 WHARF TENDER; 573.687-030 SETTER HELPER; 575.687-026 PIPE STRIPPER; 579.665-014 LABORER, CONCRETE-MIXING PLANT; 579.687-018 FLOOR ATTENDANT; 669.687-018 LUMBER STRAIGHTENER; 677.687-010 LOG ROLLER; 684.687-022 COLLECTOR; 727.687-030 BATTERY STACKER; 860.684-018 CAR BLOCKER; 905.687-010 TRUCK-DRIVER HELPER; 910.667-030 TRANSFER-TABLE OPERATOR HELPER; 911.667-010 FERRYBOAT-OPERATOR HELPER; 912.687-010 LINE-SERVICE ATTENDANT; 914.687-014 LOADER HELPER; 919.687-022 SUPPLIES PACKER; 921.667-022 LABORER, HOISTING; 921.667-026 WHARF WORKER; 921.687-010 CAR-DUMPER-OPERATOR HELPER; 921.687-018 LOADER; 922.587-010 PRIMING-MIXTURE CARRIER;

922.687-022 BOLT LOADER; 922.687-026 BULL-GANG WORKER; 922.687-034 CAR PINCHER; 922.687-050 INSTALLER; 922.687-070 LUMBER HANDLER; 922.687-078 PAPER STRIPPER; 922.687-098 TIN STACKER; 929.687-030 MATERIAL HANDLER; 929.687-034 MUNITIONS HANDLER; 932.667-010 BOTTOMER I; 939.667-010 CAGER; 939.667-018 SHORE HAND, DREDGE OR BARGE

Helpers—Production, Washing, and Packing

98902A PACKERS AND PACKAGERS—HAND. OOH Title/s: Handlers, Equipment Cleaners, Helpers, and Laborers

Pack or package by hand a wide variety of products and materials. Fastens and wraps products and materials, using hand tools. Seals containers or materials, using glues, fasteners, and hand tools. Assembles and lines cartons, crates, and containers, using hand tools. Places or pours products or materials into containers, using hand tools and equipment. Obtains and sorts products, materials, and orders, using hand tools. Marks and labels containers or products, using marking instruments. Examines and inspects containers, materials, and products to ensure packaging process meets specifications. Loads materials and products into package processing equipment. Records product and packaging information on specified forms and records. Measures, weighs, and counts products and materials, using equipment. Removes and places completed or defective product or materials on moving equipment or specified area. Tends packing machines and equipment that prepare and package materials and products. Cleans containers, materials, or work area, using cleaning solutions and hand tools.
Yearly Earnings: $14,716
Education: Short-term O-J-T
Knowledge: None above average
Abilities: Manual Dexterity; Dynamic Flexibility
Skills: None above average
General Work Activities: Handling and Moving Objects
Job Characteristics: Standing; Climbing Ladders, Scaffolds, Poles, etc.; Making Repetitive Motions; Importance of Repeating Same Tasks
GOE Group/s: 03.04.01 Elemental Work: Plants and Animals: Farming; 05.09.01 Material Control: Shipping, Receiving, and Stock Checking; 05.12.03 Elemental Work: Mechanical: Loading, Moving; 06.03.02 Quality Control: Inspecting, Grading, Sorting, Weighing, and Recording; 06.04.24 Elemental Work: Industrial: Manual Work, Metal and Plastics; 06.04.26 Elemental Work: Industrial: Manual Work, Paper; 06.04.27 Elemental Work: Industrial: Manual Work, Textile, Fabric and Leather; 06.04.28 Elemental Work: Industrial: Manual Work, Food Processing; 06.04.34 Elemental Work: Industrial: Manual Work, Assorted Materials; 06.04.35 Elemental Work: Industrial: Laundering, Dry Cleaning; 06.04.36 Elemental Work: Industrial: Filling; 06.04.38 Elemental Work: Industrial: Wrapping and Packaging; 09.05.10 Attendant Services: Packaging-Wrapping
CIP Program/s: 000000 NO CIP ASSIGNED
Related DOT Job/s: 522.687-010 BARREL FILLER I; 522.687-018 BULKER; 525.687-082 POULTRY-DRESSING WORKER; 525.687-118 TIER; 529.687-022 BULK FILLER; 529.687-086 FISH-EGG PACKER; 529.687-150 LINKER; 559.687-014 AMPOULE SEALER; 585.687-030 SINGER; 700.687-038 LABORER, GOLD LEAF; 710.687-034 TIE-UP WORKER; 737.587-018 PRIMER BOXER; 737.687-014 BAG LOADER; 737.687-030 CORE LOADER; 737.687-094 PACKER-FUSER; 753.687-038 PACKING-LINE WORKER; 784.687-042 INSPECTOR-PACKER; 789.687-106 MOPHEAD TRIMMER-AND-WRAPPER; 794.687-034 PAPER-PATTERN FOLDER; 920.587-010 CLOTH-BOLT BANDER; 920.587-018 PACKAGER, HAND; 920.587-022 SAMPLE CLERK, HANDKERCHIEF; 920.687-010 APPLE-PACKING HEADER; 920.687-014 BAGGER; 920.687-018 BAGGER; 920.687-026 BANDER, HAND; 920.687-030 BANDER, HAND; 920.687-034 BANDOLEER PACKER; 920.687-038 BLUEPRINT TRIMMER; 920.687-042 BOTTLING-LINE ATTENDANT; 920.687-066 CARRIER PACKER; 920.687-074 COTTON TIER; 920.687-078 CRATE LINER; 920.687-086 FISH PACKER; 920.687-090 FLOOR WORKER; 920.687-094 GREENS TIER; 920.687-110 LINE-OUT WORKER I; 920.687-114 LINE-OUT WORKER II; 920.687-118 LINEN-SUPPLY LOAD-BUILDER; 920.687-122 MACHINE-PACK ASSEMBLER; 920.687-130 PACKER; 920.687-134 PACKER, AGRICULTURAL PRODUCE; 920.687-142 PRIZER; 920.687-146 REPACK-ROOM WORKER; 920.687-150 ROSIN-BARREL FILLER; 920.687-158 SHINGLE PACKER; 920.687-166 SHOE PACKER; 920.687-170 SHOT BAGGER; 920.687-174 SNUFF-BOX FINISHER; 920.687-198 WOOL SACKER; 922.684-010 LOCKER-PLANT ATTENDANT; 922.687-010 BIN FILLER; 922.687-014 BINDER-AND-WRAPPER PACKER; 922.687-046 ICER; 922.687-094 TIMBER PACKER; 929.684-010 PACKER; 929.687-042 ROLL COVERER, BURLAP; 929.687-054 PALLETIZER; 929.687-058 BANDER, HAND

98905 VEHICLE WASHERS AND EQUIPMENT CLEANERS. OOH Title/s: Handlers, Equipment Cleaners, Helpers, and Laborers

Wash or otherwise clean vehicles, machinery, and other equipment. Use such materials as water, cleaning agents, brushes, cloths, and hoses. Exclude janitors and building cleaners. Scrubs, scrapes, or sprays machine parts, equipment, or vehicles, using scrapers, brushes, cleaners, disinfectants, insecticides, acid, and abrasives. Presoaks or rinses machine parts, equipment, or vehicles by immersing objects in cleaning solutions or water, manually or using hoists. Presses buttons to activate cleaning equipment or machines. Turns valves or handles on equipment to regulate pressure and flow of water, air, steam, or abrasives from sprayer nozzles. Turns valves or disconnects hoses to eliminate water, cleaning solutions, or vapors from machinery or tanks. Sweeps, shovels, or vacuums loose debris and salvageable scrap into containers, and removes from work area. Mixes cleaning solutions and abrasive compositions and other compounds according to formula. Monitors operation of cleaning machines, and stops machine or notifies supervisor when malfunctions occur. Connects hoses and lines to pumps and other equipment. Disassembles and reassembles machines or equipment, or removes and reattaches vehicle parts and trim, using hand tools. Places objects on drying racks or dyes surfaces, using cloth, squeegees, or air compressors. Examines and inspects parts, equipment, and vehicles for cleanliness, damage, and compliance with standards or regulations. Applies paints, dyes, polishes, reconditioners, and masking materials to vehicles to preserve, protect, or restore color and condition. Lubricates machinery, vehicles, and equipment, and performs minor repairs and adjustments, using hand tools. Transports materials, equipment, or supplies to and from work area, using carts or hoists. Collects and tests samples of cleaning solutions and vapors. Records production and operational data on specified forms. Maintains inventories of supplies.
Yearly Earnings: $14,924
Education: Short-term O-J-T
Knowledge: None above average
Abilities: Speed of Limb Movement; Trunk Strength; Stamina; Extent Flexibility; Dynamic Flexibility; Gross Body Equilibrium
Skills: None above average
General Work Activities: Repairing and Maintaining Mechanical Equipment
Job Characteristics: Very Hot; Contaminants; Cramped Work Space, Awkward Positions; Standing; Kneeling, Crouching, or Crawling; Using Hands on Objects, Tools, or Controls; Bending or Twisting the Body; Making Repetitive Motions; Importance of Repeating Same Tasks
GOE Group/s: 05.12.18 Elemental Work: Mechanical: Cleaning and Maintenance; 06.04.24 Elemental Work: Industrial: Manual Work,

Metal and Plastics; 06.04.27 Elemental Work: Industrial: Manual Work, Textile, Fabric and Leather; 06.04.34 Elemental Work: Industrial: Manual Work, Assorted Materials; 06.04.39 Elemental Work: Industrial: Cleaning; 09.04.02 Customer Services: Sales Services

CIP Program/s: 000000 NO CIP ASSIGNED

Related DOT Job/s: 503.687-010 SANDBLASTER; 511.687-010 BLANKET WASHER; 519.664-010 ASSEMBLY CLEANER; 521.687-030 CHAR PULLER; 521.687-054 FILTER-SCREEN CLEANER; 521.687-114 SHAKER WASHER; 529.685-230 STEM-DRYER MAINTAINER; 529.687-014 BIN CLEANER; 529.687-018 BOX-TRUCK WASHER; 529.687-054 COOKER CLEANER; 529.687-062 DIE CLEANER; 529.687-190 STONE CLEANER; 529.687-194 SUCTION-PLATE-CARRIER CLEANER; 529.687-206 TROLLEY CLEANER; 529.687-210 WASHER; 529.687-214 WASHROOM CLEANER; 557.684-010 JET HANDLER; 559.684-022 TANK CLEANER; 559.687-018 CASTING-MACHINE-SERVICE OPERATOR; 559.687-022 CELL CLEANER; 559.687-038 FILTER CLEANER; 559.687-042 FILTER WASHER; 559.687-062 TANK CLEANER; 569.687-018 SCREEN CLEANER; 573.687-018 KILN CLEANER; 590.684-034 PHOTO MASK CLEANER; 599.684-010 EQUIPMENT CLEANER; 599.687-022 NET WASHER; 599.687-030 WASHER; 599.687-034 DRUM CLEANER; 620.684-034 USED-CAR RENOVATOR; 680.687-014 ROLLER CLEANER; 683.687-026 LINGO CLEANER; 699.687-010 HARNESS CLEANER; 699.687-014 MACHINE CLEANER; 704.687-010 CLEANER; 729.687-030 SALVAGER; 732.687-046 MOLD CLEANER; 739.687-062 CLEANER, SIGNS; 788.687-082 LAST CLEANER; 809.687-026 MOLD PREPARER; 845.684-010 CAR SCRUBBER; 891.687-014 FURNACE CLEANER; 891.687-022 TANK CLEANER; 891.687-030 TUBE CLEANER; 910.687-014 CAR COOPER; 910.687-022 FREIGHT-CAR CLEANER, DELTA SYSTEM; 911.687-014 CLEANER III; 915.667-010 CAR-WASH ATTENDANT, AUTOMATIC; 915.687-022 PORTER, USED-CAR LOT; 915.687-026 STEAM CLEANER; 915.687-034 AUTOMOBILE DETAILER; 919.687-014 CLEANER II; 920.687-182 STERILIZER; 939.687-022 LATRINE CLEANER; 954.587-010 WATER-FILTER CLEANER; 955.687-010 SEWAGE-DISPOSAL WORKER

98999A PRODUCTION LABORERS. OOH Title/s: Handlers, Equipment Cleaners, Helpers, and Laborers

Perform variety of routine tasks to assist in production activities. Carries or handtrucks supplies to work stations. Loads and unloads items from machines, conveyors, and conveyance. Lifts raw materials, final products, and items packed for shipment, manually or using hoist. Breaks up defective products for reprocessing. Attaches slings, ropes, cables, or identification tags to objects, such as pipes, hoses, and bundles. Weighs raw materials for distribution. Ties product in bundles for further processing or shipment, following prescribed procedure. Threads ends of items such as thread, cloth, and lace through needles, rollers, and around take-up tube. Positions spout or chute of storage bin to fill containers during processing. Places product in equipment or on work surface for further processing, inspecting, or wrapping. Cuts or breaks flashing from materials or products. Separates product according to weight, grade, size, and composition of material used to produce product. Folds parts of product and final product during processing. Washes machines, equipment, vehicles, and products, such as prints, rugs, and table linens. Counts finished product to determine completion of production order. Inserts parts into partial assembly, during various stages of assembly to complete product. Feeds items into processing machine. Mixes ingredients, according to formulae. Examines product to verify conformance to company standards. Records information, such as number of product tested, meter readings, and date and time product was placed in oven.

Yearly Earnings: $17,160

Education: Short-term O-J-T

Knowledge: Production and Processing

Abilities: Arm-Hand Steadiness; Manual Dexterity; Multilimb Coordination; Rate Control; Speed of Limb Movement; Static Strength; Explosive Strength; Dynamic Strength; Trunk Strength; Stamina; Extent Flexibility; Dynamic Flexibility; Gross Body Coordination; Gross Body Equilibrium

Skills: None above average

General Work Activities: Performing General Physical Activities; Handling and Moving Objects

Job Characteristics: Sounds, Noise Levels are Distracting, etc.; Very Hot; Extremely Bright or Inadequate Lighting; Cramped Work Space, Awkward Positions; High Places; Hazardous Equipment; Standing; Climbing Ladders, Scaffolds, Poles, etc.; Walking or Running; Keeping or Regaining Balance; Using Hands on Objects, Tools, or Controls; Bending or Twisting the Body; Making Repetitive Motions; Importance of Repeating Same Tasks

GOE Group/s: 03.04.04 Elemental Work: Plants and Animals: Nursery and Groundskeeping; 05.06.01 Systems Operation: Electricity Generation and Transmission; 05.07.01 Quality Control: Structural; 05.09.01 Material Control: Shipping, Receiving, and Stock Checking; 05.09.02 Material Control: Estimating, Scheduling, and Record Keeping; 05.09.03 Material Control: Verifying, Recording, and Marking; 05.12.02 Elemental Work: Mechanical: Mining, Quarrying, Drilling; 05.12.03 Elemental Work: Mechanical: Loading, Moving; 05.12.04 Elemental Work: Mechanical: Hoisting, Conveying; 05.12.06 Elemental Work: Mechanical: Pumping; 05.12.07 Elemental Work: Mechanical: Crushing, Mixing, Separating, and Chipping; 05.12.08 Elemental Work: Mechanical: Lubricating; 05.12.10 Elemental Work: Mechanical: Heating and Melting; 05.12.11 Elemental Work: Mechanical: Welding; 05.12.12 Elemental Work: Mechanical: Structural Work; 05.12.14 Elemental Work: Mechanical: Painting, Caulking, and Coating; 05.12.18 Elemental Work: Mechanical: Cleaning and Maintenance; 05.12.19 Elemental Work: Mechanical: Reproduction Services; 05.12.20 Elemental Work: Mechanical: Signaling; 06.02.06 Production Work: Machine Work, Textiles; 06.02.16 Production Work: Equipment Operation, Textile, Fabric, and Leather Processing; 06.03.02 Quality Control: Inspecting, Grading, Sorting, Weighing, and Recording; 06.04.02 Elemental Work: Industrial: Machine Work, Metal and Plastics; 06.04.03 Elemental Work: Industrial: Machine Work, Wood; 06.04.04 Elemental Work: Industrial: Machine Work, Paper; 06.04.05 Elemental Work: Industrial: Machine Work, Fabric and Leather; 06.04.06 Elemental Work: Industrial: Machine Work, Textiles; 06.04.07 Elemental Work: Industrial: Machine Work, Rubber; 06.04.08 Elemental Work: Industrial: Machine Work, Stone, Glass, and Clay; 06.04.09 Elemental Work: Industrial: Machine Work, Assorted Materials; 06.04.10 Elemental Work: Industrial: Equipment Operation, Metal Processing; 06.04.11 Elemental Work: Industrial: Equipment Operation, Chemical Processing; 06.04.12 Elemental Work: Industrial: Equipment Operation, Petroleum, Gas, and Coal Processing; 06.04.13 Elemental Work: Industrial: Equipment Operation, Rubber, Plastics, Glass Processing; 06.04.14 Elemental Work: Industrial: Equipment Operation, Paper Making; 06.04.15 Elemental Work: Industrial: Equipment Operation, Food Processing; 06.04.16 Elemental Work: Industrial: Equipment Operation, Textile, Fabric, and Leather Processing; 06.04.17 Elemental Work: Industrial: Equipment Operation, Clay Processing; 06.04.18 Elemental Work: Industrial: Equipment Operation, Wood Processing; 06.04.19 Elemental Work: Industrial: Equipment Operation, Assorted Materials Processing; 06.04.20 Elemental Work: Industrial: Machine Assembling; 06.04.21 Elemental Work: Industrial: Machine Work, Brushing, Spraying, and Coating; 06.04.22 Elemental Work: Industrial: Manual Work, Assembly Large Parts; 06.04.23 Elemental Work: Industrial: Manual Work, Assembly Small Parts; 06.04.24 Elemental Work: Industrial: Manual Work, Metal and Plastics; 06.04.25 Elemental Work: Industrial: Manual Work, Wood; 06.04.26 Elemental Work: Industrial: Manual Work,

Paper; 06.04.27 Elemental Work: Industrial: Manual Work, Textile, Fabric and Leather; 06.04.28 Elemental Work: Industrial: Manual Work, Food Processing; 06.04.29 Elemental Work: Industrial: Manual Work, Rubber; 06.04.30 Elemental Work: Industrial: Manual Work, Stone, Glass, and Clay; 06.04.32 Elemental Work: Industrial: Manual Work, Casting and Molding; 06.04.33 Elemental Work: Industrial: Manual Work, Brushing, Spraying, and Coating; 06.04.34 Elemental Work: Industrial: Manual Work, Assorted Materials; 06.04.35 Elemental Work: Industrial: Laundering, Dry Cleaning; 06.04.36 Elemental Work: Industrial: Filling; 06.04.37 Elemental Work: Industrial: Manual Work, Stamping, Marking, Labeling, and Ticketing; 06.04.38 Elemental Work: Industrial: Wrapping and Packaging; 06.04.39 Elemental Work: Industrial: Cleaning; 06.04.40 Elemental Work: Industrial: Loading, Moving, Hoisting, and Conveying; 07.07.02 Clerical Handling: Sorting and Distrubtion; 09.05.06 Attendant Services: Individualized Services

CIP Program/s: 000000 NO CIP ASSIGNED

Related DOT Job/s: 230.667-014 TELEPHONE-DIRECTORY DELIVERER; 230.687-010 ADVERTISING-MATERIAL DISTRIBUTOR; 299.667-010 BILLPOSTER; 299.687-010 PORTER, SAMPLE CASE; 361.687-018 LAUNDRY LABORER; 361.687-026 SHAKER, WEARING APPAREL; 361.687-030 WASHER, HAND; 362.686-010 DRY-CLEANER HELPER; 362.686-014 RUG-CLEANER HELPER; 362.687-010 GLOVE CLEANER, HAND; 362.687-014 LINING SCRUBBER; 362.687-018 SHAVER; 363.687-010 GLOVE FORMER; 363.687-014 IRONER, SOCK; 363.687-018 PUFF IRONER; 363.687-022 STRETCHER-DRIER OPERATOR; 364.687-010 DYER HELPER; 364.687-014 RUG-DYER HELPER; 369.387-010 LAUNDRY WORKER III; 369.687-018 FOLDER; 409.667-010 AIRPLANE-PILOT HELPER; 500.687-010 PLATE-TAKE-OUT WORKER; 502.686-010 CASTING-MACHINE-OPERATOR HELPER; 502.687-010 BLAST-FURNACE-KEEPER HELPER; 502.687-018 LEAD-CASTER HELPER; 504.686-010 CHARGER-OPERATOR HELPER; 504.686-018 HARDENER HELPER; 509.566-010 MIXER OPERATOR HELPER, HOT METAL; 509.687-010 BOTTOM MAKER; 509.687-014 PORCELAIN-ENAMEL LABORER; 511.586-010 TOP-PRECIPITATOR-OPERATOR HELPER; 511.667-010 CLARIFIER-OPERATOR HELPER; 511.686-010 REAGENT TENDER HELPER; 511.687-014 DUST COLLECTOR-TREATER; 511.687-018 FLOTATION-TENDER HELPER; 511.687-026 TAILINGS-DAM LABORER; 512.666-010 FURNACE HELPER; 512.687-014 THIRD HELPER; 513.587-010 KILN-OPERATOR HELPER; 513.667-010 CALCINER-OPERATOR HELPER; 514.567-010 MOLD WORKER; 514.667-010 CASTING-WHEEL-OPERATOR HELPER; 514.667-014 PIG-MACHINE-OPERATOR HELPER; 514.667-018 SPOUT WORKER; 514.687-014 CASTING-HOUSE WORKER; 514.687-018 CASTING-OPERATOR HELPER; 518.684-018 MOLD CLOSER; 518.687-018 MOLD-MAKER HELPER; 519.565-014 TANK-HOUSE-OPERATOR HELPER; 519.667-014 LABORER, SOLDER MAKING; 519.687-014 DUST PULLER; 519.687-022 FOUNDRY WORKER, GENERAL; 519.687-026 LABORER, GENERAL; 519.687-038 STOPPER-MAKER HELPER; 520.686-018 FEED-MIXER HELPER; 520.686-022 FLOUR-BLENDER HELPER; 520.687-014 BLINTZE ROLLER; 520.687-022 CANDY SPREADER; 520.687-046 MEXICAN FOOD MAKER, HAND; 520.687-058 SYRUP-MIXER ASSISTANT; 520.687-066 BLENDING-TANK TENDER HELPER; 521.686-010 BOLTER HELPER; 521.686-026 CUSTOM-FEED-MILL-OPERATOR HELPER; 521.686-050 PROCESSOR HELPER; 521.686-054 SLICE-PLUG-CUTTER-OPERATOR HELPER; 521.687-010 ALMOND BLANCHER, HAND; 521.687-034 CHAR-FILTER-OPERATOR HELPER; 521.687-038 DRIP-BOX TENDER; 521.687-042 EGG BREAKER; 521.687-046 FILLER SPREADER; 521.687-074 LABORER, SYRUP MACHINE; 521.687-078 LIQUOR-BRIDGE-OPERATOR HELPER; 521.687-082 MILLER HELPER, DISTILLERY; 521.687-098 PICKER; 521.687-102 PICKING-TABLE WORKER; 521.687-110 SHAKER; 521.687-118 SHELLER I; 521.687-122 SHELLFISH SHUCKER; 521.687-130 SKULL GRINDER; 521.687-134 STEMMER, HAND; 521.687-138 TABLE HAND; 522.665-014 YEAST PUSHER; 522.687-014 BRINER; 522.687-022 FILLER ROOM ATTENDANT; 522.687-026 LEAF CONDITIONER; 522.687-030 LEAF-CONDITIONER HELPER; 522.687-034 PICKLER; 522.687-038 TURNER; 522.687-042 WRAPPER-HANDS SPRAYER; 523.587-010 DRIER, SHORT GOODS; 523.666-010 COCOA-BEAN-ROASTER HELPER; 523.687-014 FISH DRIER; 523.687-018 KILN LOADER; 524.686-014 NOVELTY WORKER; 524.687-014 GARNISHER; 524.687-018 RACKER; 525.587-010 SHROUDER; 525.587-014 SMOKED MEAT PREPARER; 525.687-018 CONVEYOR LOADER I; 525.687-022 COOLER ROOM WORKER; 525.687-034 GAMBRELER HELPER; 525.687-038 HIDE HANDLER; 525.687-050 NECK SKEWER; 525.687-058 ORDER RUNNER; 525.687-062 PAINTER, DEPILATORY; 525.687-078 POULTRY HANGER; 525.687-090 SHACTOR HELPER; 525.687-094 SHAVER; 525.687-098 SINGER; 525.687-106 SLUNK-SKIN CURER; 525.687-110 STEAMER; 525.687-114 STUNNER, ANIMAL; 525.687-122 WASHER, CARCASS; 526.686-010 BAKER HELPER; 529.486-010 NUT-PROCESS HELPER; 529.686-026 DAIRY HELPER; 529.686-034 FACTORY HELPER; 529.686-046 GENERAL HELPER; 529.686-050 LABORER, CHEESEMAKING; 529.686-078 RAW-CHEESE WORKER; 529.687-010 BASKET FILLER; 529.687-038 CHAR-DUST CLEANER AND SALVAGER; 529.687-050 COOK HELPER; 529.687-066 DISTILLERY WORKER, GENERAL; 529.687-070 DISTRIBUTOR-CLEANER; 529.687-078 FILLER-SHREDDER HELPER; 529.687-094 GENERAL HELPER; 529.687-130 LABORER; 529.687-166 ODD BUNDLE WORKER; 529.687-222 WRAPPING MACHINE HELPER; 530.384-010 MIXER HELPER; 533.686-010 BLOW-PIT HELPER; 533.686-014 WASHER-ENGINEER HELPER; 533.687-010 SCREEN-TENDER HELPER; 534.686-010 PAPER-PROCESSING-MACHINE HELPER; 534.687-010 CONE TREATER; 534.687-014 CREPING-MACHINE-OPERATOR HELPER; 539.587-010 LABORER, RAGS; 540.687-010 SEAL MIXER; 543.687-010 COKE DRAWER, HAND; 543.687-014 OVEN DAUBER; 549.587-010 COMPRESSED-GAS-PLANT WORKER; 549.686-010 BRIQUETTE-MACHINE-OPERATOR HELPER; 549.687-010 CHASER, TAR; 549.687-018 LABORER, PETROLEUM REFINERY; 549.687-022 MUD-MIXER HELPER; 550.586-010 BLENDER HELPER; 550.587-010 MAKE-UP OPERATOR HELPER; 550.686-018 CRUTCHER HELPER; 550.686-026 MIXER HELPER; 550.686-038 ROOF-CEMENT-AND-PAINT-MAKER HELPER; 550.687-010 CHEMICAL-COMPOUNDER HELPER; 550.687-014 COLOR STRAINER; 550.687-018 DYE-WEIGHER HELPER; 551.687-010 BONE PICKER; 551.687-018 DYNAMITE RECLAIMER; 551.687-022 LABORER, COOK HOUSE; 551.687-026 NAPHTHALENE-OPERATOR HELPER; 551.687-030 SIFTER; 551.687-034 SODA-ROOM OPERATOR; 552.687-010 DISTILLATION-OPERATOR HELPER; 553.685-058 DRIER-OPERATOR HELPER; 553.686-014 CD-MIXER HELPER; 553.686-030 DRIER-OPERATOR HELPER; 553.686-042 VARNISH-MAKER HELPER; 553.687-010 DRIER HELPER; 553.687-014 FURNACE HELPER; 554.586-010 FINISHER; 554.686-014 CALENDER-LET-OFF HELPER; 554.686-018 CALENDER-OPERATOR HELPER; 554.686-022 CALENDER-WIND-UP HELPER; 554.687-010 SPREADER; 556.587-010 MOLD PARTER; 556.686-010 CAKE-PRESS-OPERATOR HELPER; 556.687-014 CELL PREPARER; 556.687-018 MOLD CLEANER; 556.687-026 POURER; 558.686-010 FURNACE HELPER; 558.687-010 BLEACH PACKER; 559.587-010 ROD-AND-TUBE STRAIGHTENER; 559.666-010 TOWER ATTENDANT; 559.667-014 LABORER, GENERAL; 559.686-026 LABORER, GENERAL; 559.686-038 REDUCTION-FURNACE-OPERATOR HELPER; 559.687-026 CONTACT-ACID-PLANT-OPERATOR HELPER; 559.687-030 COTTON WASHER; 559.687-046 FRAME STRIPPER; 559.687-050 LABORER, CHEMICAL PROCESSING; 559.687-054 SKEIN-WINDING OPERATOR; 561.685-010 TREATING-ENGINEER HELPER; 561.686-010 LABORER, WOOD-PRESERVING PLANT; 561.687-010 WOOD-POLE TREATER; 564.687-010 CHOPPER; 569.687-010 CLAMP REMOVER; 569.687-014 LOG WASHER; 570.686-014 ABRASIVE-MIXER HELPER; 573.667-010 KILN DRAWER; 573.685-022 KILN-OPERATOR HELPER; 573.687-010 BEDDER; 573.687-014 DRY-KILN OPERATOR HELPER; 573.687-022 KILN WORKER; 573.687-026 KILN-BURNER HELPER; 574.667-010 DUST BOX WORKER;

575.686-010 DRY-PRESS-OPERATOR HELPER; 575.687-010 BALCONY WORKER; 575.687-014 FORMING-MACHINE UPKEEP-MECHANIC HELPER; 575.687-018 LABORER, PRESTRESSED CONCRETE; 579.667-010 LABORER, GENERAL; 579.687-010 BRAKE-LINING-FINISHER HELPER, ASBESTOS; 579.687-034 DISC-PAD KNOCKOUT WORKER; 579.687-038 DISC-PAD-PLATE FILLER; 579.687-042 LABORER, CONCRETE PLANT; 580.687-010 ORIENTAL-RUG STRETCHER; 581.687-010 BURLAP SPREADER; 581.687-014 DRYING-ROOM ATTENDANT; 581.687-018 DRYING-UNIT-FELTING-MACHINE-OPERATOR HELPER; 581.687-022 SPREADER; 582.686-014 DYE-REEL-OPERATOR HELPER; 582.686-022 SKEIN-YARN-DYER HELPER; 582.686-026 SLASHER-TENDER HELPER; 582.687-014 DYER; 582.687-018 FELT-HAT STEAMER; 583.687-010 PRESS HAND; 584.686-010 YARN-MERCERIZER-OPERATOR HELPER; 585.687-018 CLOTH-EDGE SINGER; 585.687-026 SHADE-CLOTH FINISHER; 586.686-014 FELTING-MACHINE-OPERATOR HELPER; 586.686-022 MACHINE HELPER; 587.686-010 CLOTH-SHRINKING-MACHINE-OPERATOR HELPER; 587.687-010 CANVAS SHRINKER; 589.686-026 LABORER, GENERAL; 589.686-038 RUG-INSPECTOR HELPER; 589.687-010 CAKE WRAPPER; 589.687-018 DIPPER; 589.687-022 FABRIC-LAY-OUT WORKER; 589.687-026 LABORER, GENERAL; 589.687-042 TUBE CLEANER; 589.687-058 SHAKER; 590.667-010 STOVE-BOTTOM WORKER; 590.686-010 COATING-MACHINE-OPERATOR HELPER; 590.687-010 LABORER; 599.687-014 BOOKER; 599.687-018 LEAD HANDLER; 612.687-014 HEAVY-FORGER HELPER; 614.686-010 DRAW-BENCH-OPERATOR HELPER; 615.687-010 HELPER, SHEAR OPERATOR; 616.687-010 STRANDING-MACHINE-OPERATOR HELPER; 616.687-014 WIRE-WEAVER HELPER; 619.686-014 HOOP-MAKER HELPER, MACHINE; 619.686-022 METAL-FABRICATING-SHOP HELPER; 619.686-030 STRETCHER-LEVELER-OPERATOR HELPER; 619.686-034 FORGE HELPER; 619.687-014 MACHINE HELPER; 628.687-014 SHEAR-GRINDER-OPERATOR HELPER; 640.686-014 SLOTTER-OPERATOR HELPER; 640.687-014 SPIRAL-TUBE-WINDER HELPER; 641.686-010 BLANKET-WINDER HELPER; 641.686-014 CARTON-FORMING-MACHINE HELPER; 641.686-018 CORRUGATOR-OPERATOR HELPER; 641.686-022 LINER-MACHINE-OPERATOR HELPER; 641.686-038 TUBE-MACHINE-OPERATOR HELPER; 649.686-010 BAG-MACHINE-OPERATOR HELPER; 649.686-018 CYLINDER-DIE-MACHINE HELPER; 651.586-010 PRESS HELPER; 652.686-038 SCREEN-PRINTING-MACHINE-OPERATOR HELPER; 652.687-010 CLOTH SPREADER, SCREEN PRINTING; 652.687-014 COLOR DIPPER; 652.687-018 FILLER-BLOCK INSERTER-REMOVER; 652.687-022 PAINT POURER; 652.687-026 PASTER, SCREEN PRINTING; 652.687-050 WALLPAPER-PRINTER HELPER; 663.686-030 VENEER-CLIPPER HELPER; 665.686-018 VENEER-JOINTER HELPER; 667.686-022 TURNING-MACHINE-OPERATOR HELPER; 667.687-010 BUZZSAW-OPERATOR HELPER; 669.686-014 BOX-BLANK-MACHINE-OPERATOR HELPER; 669.686-026 SLAT-BASKET MAKER HELPER, MACHINE; 677.486-010 CIRCULAR-SAWYER HELPER; 677.666-010 SPLITTING-MACHINE-OPERATOR HELPER; 680.687-010 APRON CLEANER; 681.686-014 BEAMER HELPER; 681.687-014 LOOSE-END FINDER, BOBBIN; 683.687-010 DRAWER-IN HELPER, HAND; 683.687-014 DROP-WIRE HANGER; 683.687-018 HANDER-IN; 683.687-022 HOOK PULLER; 683.687-030 LOOM CHANGEOVER OPERATOR; 685.686-014 KNITTING-MACHINE OPERATOR HELPER; 685.687-014 CUFF FOLDER; 686.686-014 RUG-CUTTER HELPER; 689.686-010 AUTOMATIC-PAD-MAKING-MACHINE OPERATOR HELPER; 689.686-042 STITCH-BONDING-MACHINE-TENDER HELPER; 689.687-010 BAGGING SALVAGER; 689.687-014 BOBBIN CLEANER, HAND; 689.687-018 BUNDLE BREAKER; 689.687-030 CREELER; 689.687-038 END FINDER, ROVING DEPARTMENT; 689.687-042 END FINDER, TWISTING DEPARTMENT; 689.687-046 FRAME HAND; 689.687-050 OIL-SPOT WASHER; 689.687-058 PICK REMOVER; 689.687-066 RUG CLEANER; 689.687-074 SPANNER; 690.686-014 BIAS-MACHINE-OPERATOR HELPER; 690.686-030 CUTTING-MACHINE-TENDER HELPER; 690.686-070 TUBER-MACHINE-OPERATOR HELPER; 691.687-010 PRODUCTION HELPER; 692.687-010 SPLICER;

699.587-010 SLITTING-MACHINE-OPERATOR HELPER I; 699.687-022 ROPE CLEANER; 700.687-030 CUTCH CLEANER; 700.687-046 MOLD SHEET CLEANER; 700.687-050 MOLD-MAKER HELPER; 705.687-010 JIGGER; 709.686-010 LABORER, TIN CAN; 709.687-010 CLEANER AND POLISHER; 709.687-014 CLEANER, FURNITURE; 709.687-046 TIN-CONTAINER STRAIGHTENER; 712.687-030 SUTURE POLISHER; 712.687-034 SUTURE WINDER, HAND; 715.687-090 MOTOR POLARIZER; 715.687-102 PARTS REMOVER; 715.687-106 RACKER; 715.687-126 WASHER; 723.687-022 WIPER; 724.687-010 LACER AND TIER; 727.687-014 ACID FILLER; 727.687-070 LEAD-BURNER HELPER; 729.687-014 ELECTRODE CLEANER; 729.687-018 LAMINATION SPINNER; 729.687-026 PLATE STACKER, HAND; 731.587-010 FINISHER, HAND; 731.687-018 HACKLER, DOLL WIGS; 732.687-030 LABORER; 732.687-066 REVERSER; 732.687-082 WAX-BALL KNOCK-OUT WORKER; 733.687-026 CLAMPER; 733.687-078 WASHER; 734.687-022 BOBBIN DISKER; 735.687-010 DIPPER; 735.687-026 RACKER; 736.587-010 BARREL LOADER AND CLEANER; 736.687-010 GREASER; 737.587-010 BANDOLEER STRAIGHTENER-STAMPER; 737.687-034 DEMOLITION SPECIALIST; 737.687-050 IGNITER CAPPER; 737.687-082 MANUAL-PLATE FILLER; 739.687-058 CLEANER; 739.687-098 FLOOR WORKER; 741.687-014 PAINTER HELPER, SPRAY; 749.587-010 RACKER; 749.687-034 PIPE RACKER; 753.687-034 MOLD-INSERT CHANGER; 753.687-042 STOCK-LAYER; 754.687-014 SEQUINS STRINGER; 762.687-026 CROSSBAND LAYER; 762.687-062 SHEET TURNER; 763.687-010 BLOW-OFF WORKER; 764.687-010 AIR-AND-WATER FILLER; 764.687-018 BARREL DRAINER; 764.687-030 BARREL MARKER; 764.687-034 BARREL-CHARRER HELPER; 764.687-038 BARREL-RAISER HELPER; 764.687-046 CHANNEL INSTALLER; 769.687-038 PUTTY MIXER AND APPLIER; 769.687-054 WOODWORKING-SHOP HAND; 770.687-026 JEWEL STRINGER; 770.687-030 PULVERIZER; 775.687-018 GLASS-CUTTER HELPER; 779.687-038 WAXER; 780.687-026 MATTRESS STRIPPER; 780.687-054 UPHOLSTERER HELPER; 781.687-018 CLOTH TEARER; 781.687-022 CUTTER HELPER; 781.687-038 GOODS LAYER; 781.687-058 SPREADER I; 781.687-062 STAMPER I; 781.687-066 STENCILER; 782.687-010 BASTING PULLER; 782.687-014 BUTTONER; 782.687-026 PINNER; 782.687-030 PULLER-THROUGH; 782.687-034 RAVELER; 783.687-030 TABLE WORKER; 784.687-010 BRIM RAISER; 784.687-038 GLOVE TURNER; 784.687-066 SMOKE-ROOM OPERATOR; 784.687-078 STRAW-HAT-WASHER OPERATOR; 784.687-086 HAT CONDITIONER; 788.687-018 BRUSHER; 788.687-022 BUCKLER AND LACER; 788.687-050 FOLDER, HAND; 788.687-058 HEEL DIPPER; 788.687-062 INSOLE-AND-HEEL-STIFFENER; 788.687-066 LABORER, BOOT AND SHOE; 788.687-070 LACER I; 788.687-086 LAST PULLER; 788.687-090 LEATHER SOFTENER; 788.687-114 SHANK TAPER; 788.687-122 SHOE CLEANER; 788.687-126 SHOE COVERER; 788.687-130 SHOE TURNER; 788.687-134 SOLE SCRAPER; 788.687-146 TACK PULLER; 789.587-018 PARACHUTE MARKER; 789.687-014 BAG LINER; 789.687-018 BONER; 789.687-046 FINAL ASSEMBLER; 789.687-058 FOLDER; 789.687-062 FRINGER; 789.687-066 GARMENT FOLDER; 789.687-074 GARMENT TURNER; 789.687-090 LABORER, CANVAS SHOP; 789.687-094 LACER; 789.687-110 PAIRER; 789.687-118 PARACHUTE-LINE TIER; 789.687-122 PILLOW CLEANER; 789.687-134 RAG SORTER AND CUTTER; 789.687-138 RAKER; 789.687-158 RUG-INSPECTOR HELPER; 789.687-166 SEAM STEAMER; 789.687-174 THREAD SEPARATOR; 789.687-182 TURNER; 794.687-038 PATTERN RULER; 794.687-050 SCRAPPER; 800.687-010 RIVETER HELPER; 801.687-010 ASSEMBLER HELPER, INTERNAL COMBUSTION ENGINE; 801.687-014 FITTER HELPER; 801.687-018 TANK-SETTER HELPER; 805.687-010 BOILERMAKER HELPER I; 806.667-010 HELPER, METAL HANGING; 806.687-022 HELPER, METAL BONDING; 806.687-050 SHIPFITTER HELPER; 807.667-010 FLATCAR WHACKER; 809.687-014 HELPER, MANUFACTURING; 809.687-022 LABORER, SHIPYARD; 819.666-010 MACHINE HELPER; 819.687-014

WELDER HELPER; 869.667-014 SIGNALER; 869.687-018 CLEANER; 899.687-010 DECORATOR, STREET AND BUILDING; 899.687-014 LABORER, AIRPORT MAINTENANCE; 909.687-014 LABORER, GENERAL; 910.687-010 BAGGAGE HANDLER; 910.687-018 CAR ICER; 910.687-026 TRACK OILER; 911.667-014 HATCH TENDER; 911.677-010 TICKET TAKER, FERRYBOAT; 911.687-010 BOAT-LOADER HELPER; 911.687-026 LINES TENDER; 914.687-010 LABORER, PIPELINES; 914.687-018 PUMPER HELPER; 920.587-014 LABEL CODER; 920.686-010 BANDER-AND-CELLOPHANER HELPER, MACHINE; 920.686-022 ORDER FILLER, LINSEED OIL; 920.687-046 BUNDLER, SEASONAL GREENERY; 920.687-062 CARDBOARD INSERTER; 920.687-098 HANDKERCHIEF FOLDER; 920.687-102 HOGSHEAD OPENER; 920.687-106 LABEL REMOVER; 920.687-138 PAPER INSERTER; 920.687-186 TABLE-COVER FOLDER; 920.687-190 TIE BINDER; 921.667-010 BOAT-HOIST-OPERATOR HELPER; 921.687-034 WOOD HANDLER; 922.667-010 YARD WORKER, USED BUILDING MATERIALS; 922.687-030 CAN FILLER; 922.687-058 LABORER, STORES; 922.687-062 LABORER, WHARF; 922.687-066 LAST PUTTER-AWAY; 922.687-102 YARD LABORER; 929.587-010 NUT-AND-BOLT ASSEMBLER; 929.686-014 BAND SALVAGER; 929.687-014 KILN DRAWER; 929.687-018 LABORER, HIGH-DENSITY PRESS; 929.687-022 LABORER, SALVAGE; 929.687-026 LINER INSERTER; 929.687-038 RETURNED-CASE INSPECTOR; 930.687-018 CUTTER-OPERATOR HELPER; 933.687-010 GRIZZLY WORKER; 934.687-010 FOOT WORKER; 939.687-014 COMPANY LABORER; 939.687-018 LABORER; 939.687-034 SAND FILLER; 952.665-010 LABORER, POWERHOUSE; 952.667-010 STREET-LIGHT CLEANER; 952.687-014 SUBSTATION-OPERATOR HELPER; 953.667-010 GAS-LEAK INSPECTOR HELPER; 955.667-010 INCINERATOR PLANT LABORER; 955.687-014 SNOW SHOVELER; 955.687-018 STREET CLEANER; 962.687-010 DOLLY PUSHER; 962.687-014 FILM LOADER; 969.687-010 CIRCUS LABORER; 969.687-014 ICE MAKER, SKATING RINK; 971.687-010 ETCHER HELPER, HAND; 979.687-014 PHOTOSTAT-OPERATOR HELPER; 979.687-022 SCREEN PRINTER HELPER; 979.687-034 GENERAL WORKER, LITHOGRAPHIC

98999B PRODUCTION HELPERS. OOH Title/s: Handlers, Equipment Cleaners, Helpers, and Laborers; Material Moving Equipment Operators

Perform variety of tasks requiring limited knowledge of production processes in support of skilled production workers. Cleans and lubricates equipment. Dumps materials into machine hopper prior to mixing. Loads and unloads processing equipment or conveyance used to receive raw materials or to ship finished products. Marks or tags identification on parts. Observes operation and notifies equipment operator of malfunctions. Places or positions equipment or partially assembled product for further processing, manually or using hoist. Reads gauges and charts, and records data. Removes product, machine attachments, and waste material from machine. Starts machines or equipment to begin process. Turns valves to regulate flow of liquids or air, to reverse machine, to start pump, and to regulate equipment. Mixes ingredients, according to procedure. Tends equipment to facilitate process. Replaces damaged or worn equipment parts. Measures amount of ingredients, length of extruded article, or work to ensure conformance to specifications. Signals coworkers to facilitate moving product during processing.

Yearly Earnings: $17,160

Education: Short-term O-J-T

Knowledge: Production and Processing; Mechanical

Abilities: Reaction Time; Speed of Limb Movement; Static Strength; Stamina; Dynamic Flexibility; Gross Body Equilibrium; Auditory Attention

Skills: Equipment Maintenance; Repairing

General Work Activities: None above average

Job Characteristics: Cramped Work Space, Awkward Positions; High Places; Hazardous Equipment; Hazardous Situations; Standing; Climbing Ladders, Scaffolds, Poles, etc.; Walking or Running; Kneeling, Crouching, or Crawling; Keeping or Regaining Balance; Using Hands on Objects, Tools, or Controls; Bending or Twisting the Body; Importance of Repeating Same Tasks; Pace Determined by Speed of Equipment

GOE Group/s: 01.06.03 Craft Arts: Hand Lettering, Painting and Decorating; 05.05.15 Craft Technology: Custom Sewing, Tailoring, and Upholstering; 05.10.02 Crafts: Mechanical; 05.12.03 Elemental Work: Mechanical: Loading, Moving; 05.12.04 Elemental Work: Mechanical: Hoisting, Conveying; 05.12.07 Elemental Work: Mechanical: Crushing, Mixing, Separating, and Chipping; 05.12.10 Elemental Work: Mechanical: Heating and Melting; 05.12.12 Elemental Work: Mechanical: Structural Work; 05.12.16 Elemental Work: Mechanical: Electrical Work; 05.12.18 Elemental Work: Mechanical: Cleaning and Maintenance; 06.02.12 Production Work: Equipment Operation, Petroleum and Gas Processing; 06.02.21 Production Work: Coating and Plating; 06.02.24 Production Work: Manual Work, Metal and Plastics; 06.03.02 Quality Control: Inspecting, Grading, Sorting, Weighing, and Recording; 06.04.02 Elemental Work: Industrial: Machine Work, Metal and Plastics; 06.04.03 Elemental Work: Industrial: Machine Work, Wood; 06.04.04 Elemental Work: Industrial: Machine Work, Paper; 06.04.05 Elemental Work: Industrial: Machine Work, Fabric and Leather; 06.04.10 Elemental Work: Industrial: Equipment Operation, Metal Processing; 06.04.11 Elemental Work: Industrial: Equipment Operation, Chemical Processing; 06.04.12 Elemental Work: Industrial: Equipment Operation, Petroleum, Gas, and Coal Processing; 06.04.13 Elemental Work: Industrial: Equipment Operation, Rubber, Plastics, Glass Processing; 06.04.15 Elemental Work: Industrial: Equipment Operation, Food Processing; 06.04.18 Elemental Work: Industrial: Equipment Operation, Wood Processing; 06.04.19 Elemental Work: Industrial: Equipment Operation, Assorted Materials Processing; 06.04.21 Elemental Work: Industrial: Machine Work, Brushing, Spraying, and Coating; 06.04.24 Elemental Work: Industrial: Manual Work, Metal and Plastics; 06.04.32 Elemental Work: Industrial: Manual Work, Casting and Molding; 06.04.39 Elemental Work: Industrial: Cleaning

CIP Program/s: 470399 Industrial Equipment Maintenance and Repair, Other

Related DOT Job/s: 365.674-010 SHOE-REPAIRER HELPER; 500.686-010 LABORER, ELECTROPLATING; 502.664-018 STEEL-POURER HELPER; 503.686-010 PICKLER HELPER, CONTINUOUS PICKLING LINE; 504.685-018 HEAT-TREATER HELPER; 509.685-010 ALODIZE-MACHINE HELPER; 511.685-058 SLIME-PLANT-OPERATOR HELPER; 512.684-010 SECOND HELPER; 518.684-010 CORE SETTER; 519.485-014 RECOVERY-OPERATOR HELPER; 529.685-146 ICE CREAM FREEZER ASSISTANT; 540.686-010 COMPOUNDER HELPER; 542.362-014 REFINERY OPERATOR HELPER; 542.665-010 OVEN-HEATER HELPER; 543.664-010 CARBON-FURNACE-OPERATOR HELPER; 549.684-010 PUMPER HELPER; 549.685-030 TREATER HELPER; 549.685-034 WASH-OIL-PUMP OPERATOR HELPER; 557.564-010 EXTRUDER-OPERATOR HELPER; 558.585-038 POLYMERIZATION HELPER; 559.664-014 PILOT-CONTROL-OPERATOR HELPER; 559.684-026 UTILITY WORKER, MOLDING; 559.685-110 LABORER, GENERAL; 599.685-050 IMPREGNATOR-AND-DRIER HELPER; 609.684-014 LABORER, GENERAL; 610.684-010 BLACKSMITH HELPER; 612.684-010 UTILITY WORKER, FORGE; 613.685-014 HEATER HELPER; 613.685-026 ROLLING-MILL-OPERATOR HELPER; 619.484-010 ORNAMENTAL-METAL-WORKER HELPER; 619.684-010 FORMER HELPER, HAND; 620.584-010 SPRING-REPAIRER HELPER, HAND; 649.685-130 TABLET-MAKING-MACHINE-OPERATOR HELPER; 664.685-030 SPAR-MACHINE-OPERATOR HELPER; 669.685-010 BARREL-ASSEMBLER HELPER; 669.685-058 FRAME-TABLE-OPERATOR HELPER; 681.685-042 COVERING-MACHINE-OPERA-

TOR HELPER; 683.685-022 DRAWING-IN-MACHINE-TENDER HELPER; 729.664-010 TEST-DEPARTMENT HELPER; 782.684-038 MATCH-UP WORKER; 801.663-010 ASSEMBLY-INSPECTOR HELPER; 805.664-010 BOILERMAKER HELPER II; 806.384-022 ROCKET-TEST-FIRE WORKER; 845.684-014 PAINTER HELPER, AUTOMOTIVE; 862.684-014 LABORER, CONSTRUCTION OR LEAK GANG; 891.684-010 DOCK HAND; 921.664-010 LINE MOVER; 932.664-014 SPOUT TENDER I; 939.684-018 OIL-WELL-SERVICE-OPERATOR HELPER; 953.584-010 HELPER, LIQUEFACTION-AND-REGASIFICATION; 953.684-010 GAS-PUMPING-STATION HELPER; 970.664-010 PAINTER HELPER, SIGN; 979.684-026 PRINT-SHOP HELPER

Military

99003 MILITARY. OOH Title/s: Not an actual occupation
Protect nation during periods of war and maintain peace and order during times of martial law or civil disobedience. (Occupation may be filled by civilian personnel employed by military. Military specializations with a civilian equivalent are included with the civilian equivalent.)
Yearly Earnings: NA
Education: Varied
Knowledge: None above average
Abilities: None above average
Skills: None above average
General Work Activities: None above average
Job Characteristics: None above average
GOE Group/s: 02.04.02 Laboratory Technology: Life Sciences; 04.01.02 Safety and Law Enforcement: Investigating; 04.02.02 Security Services: Property and People; 05.03.05 Engineering Technology: Electrical-Electronic; 05.05.10 Craft Technology: Electrical-Electronic Equipment Repair; 05.05.11 Craft Technology: Scientific, Medical, & Technical Equip. Fabric. & Related; 05.06.03 Systems Operation: Oil, Gas, and Water Distribution; 05.10.01 Crafts: Structural; 05.10.02 Crafts: Mechanical; 05.11.04 Equipment Operation: Material Handling; 06.01.04 Production Technology: Precision Hand Work; 07.04.05 Oral Communications: Information Transmitting and Receiving; 07.05.03 Records Processing: Record Preparation and Maintenance; 11.02.01 Educational and Library Services: Teaching and Instructing, General
CIP Program/s: 150801 Aeronautical and Aerospace Engineering Technologists and Technicians; 470303 Industrial Machinery Maintenance and Repair; 470401 Instrument Calibration and Repairer; 470402 Gunsmith; 520401 Administrative Assistant/Secretarial Science, General; 520408 General Office/Clerical and Typing Services
Related DOT Job/s: 199.682-010 AEROSPACE PHYSIOLOGICAL TECHNICIAN; 235.662-010 COMMAND AND CONTROL SPECIALIST; 248.387-010 FLIGHT OPERATIONS SPECIALIST; 249.387-014 INTELLIGENCE CLERK; 378.132-010 FIELD ARTILLERY SENIOR SERGEANT; 378.137-010 INFANTRY UNIT LEADER; 378.161-010 COMBAT SURVEILLANCE AND TARGET ACQUISITION NONCOMMISSIONED OFFICER; 378.227-014 RECRUIT INSTRUCTOR; 378.227-018 SURVIVAL SPECIALIST; 378.267-010 COUNTERINTELLIGENCE AGENT; 378.281-010 TARGET AIRCRAFT TECHNICIAN; 378.362-010 SOUND RANGING CREWMEMBER; 378.363-010 ARMOR RECONNAISSANCE SPECIALIST; 378.367-010 ARTILLERY OR NAVAL GUNFIRE OBSERVER; 378.367-014 FIELD ARTILLERY OPERATIONS SPECIALIST; 378.367-018 FLASH RANGING CREWMEMBER; 378.367-022 INFANTRY OPERATIONS SPECIALIST; 378.367-026 OPERATIONS AND INTELLIGENCE ASSISTANT; 378.367-030 RECONNAISSANCE CREWMEMBER; 378.382-010 AIRBORNE SENSOR SPECIALIST; 378.382-014 DEFENSIVE FIRE CONTROL SYSTEMS OPERATOR; 378.382-018 UNATTENDED-GROUND-SENSOR SPECIALIST; 378.464-010 ANTITANK ASSAULT GUNNER; 378.663-010 VULCAN CREWMEMBER; 378.682-010 REDEYE GUNNER; 378.682-014 SMOKE AND FLAME SPECIALIST; 378.683-010 AMPHIBIAN CREWMEMBER; 378.683-014 POWERED BRIDGE SPECIALIST; 378.683-018 TANK CREWMEMBER; 378.684-010 CAMOUFLAGE SPECIALIST; 378.684-014 COMBAT RIFLE CREWMEMBER; 378.684-018 FIELD ARTILLERY CREWMEMBER; 378.684-022 INFANTRY INDIRECT FIRE CREWMEMBER; 378.684-026 INFANTRY WEAPONS CREWMEMBER; 378.684-030 LIGHT AIR DEFENSE ARTILLERY CREWMEMBER; 378.687-010 COMBAT SURVEILLANCE AND TARGET ACQUISITION CREWMEMBER; 632.261-010 AIRCRAFT-ARMAMENT MECHANIC; 632.261-014 FIRE-CONTROL MECHANIC; 632.261-018 ORDNANCE ARTIFICER; 632.381-010 GUN SYNCHRONIZER; 639.281-010 AVIATION SUPPORT EQUIPMENT REPAIRER; 891.684-014 RUBBER AND PLASTICS WORKER; 912.662-010 IN-FLIGHT REFUELING OPERATOR; 912.682-010 AIRCRAFT LAUNCH AND RECOVERY TECHNICIAN

APPENDIX A

Crosswalk Of *Dictionary Of Occupational Titles* (DOT) Numbers To O*NET Occupation Numbers

This appendix presents all 12,741 DOT occupational numbers (from the current DOT) in numerical order and cross-references this DOT number to the related O*NET number.

Keep in mind that each DOT and O*NET number refers to a specific job title. This appendix, then, allows you to go from any "old" DOT job to the more recent O*NET job. This is useful for people who were using information systems based on the DOT, such as some career interest inventories or occupational classification systems.

For an example of how this appendix works, look at the first entry in the appendix, which is "001.061-010 . . 22302." This information provides a cross-reference from the DOT number 001.061-010 (which is for the DOT job "Architect") to the O*NET number 22302 (which is for the O*NET job "Architects, Except Landscape and Marine"). With similar job names, this example is quite straightforward. Some entries are not as logical.

Once you have this DOT to O*NET cross-reference, you can find all sorts of useful information by looking up the O*NET description provided in this book. Because the O*NET information is newer, this appendix provides a way to bridge the older DOT to the newer O*NET systems. For those who need it, this can be a very important cross-reference.

001.061-010 22302
001.061-014 22305
001.061-018 22308
001.167-010 22302
001.261-010 ..... 22514A
001.261-014 ..... 22514A
002.061-010 22102
002.061-014 22102
002.061-018 22102
002.061-022 22102
002.061-026 22102
002.061-030 22102
002.151-010 49002
002.167-010 22102
002.167-014 22102
002.167-018 22102
002.261-010 ..... 22514D
002.261-014 ..... 22599C
002.262-010 ..... 22599C
003.061-010 ..... 22126A
003.061-014 ..... 22126A
003.061-018 ..... 22126A
003.061-022 ..... 22126A
003.061-026 ..... 22126A
003.061-030 ..... 22126B
003.061-034 ..... 22126B
003.061-038 ..... 22126B
003.061-042 ..... 22126B
003.061-046 ..... 22126A
003.061-050 ..... 22126B
003.131-010 ..... 22514B
003.151-010 49002
003.151-014 49002
003.161-010 ...... 22505C
003.161-014 ...... 22505A
003.161-018 ...... 22505A
003.167-010 ...... 22126B
003.167-014 ...... 22126A
003.167-018 ...... 22126A
003.167-022 ...... 22126A
003.167-026 ...... 22126A
003.167-030 ...... 22126B
003.167-034 ...... 13017A
003.167-038 ...... 22126A
003.167-042 ...... 22126B
003.167-046 ...... 22126A
003.167-050 ...... 22126A
003.167-054 ...... 22126A
003.167-058 ...... 22126B
003.167-066 ...... 22126B
003.167-070 ...... 13017A
003.187-010 ...... 22126B
003.187-014 ...... 22126B
003.187-018 ...... 22126B
003.261-010 ...... 22505B
003.261-014 ...... 22514D
003.261-018 ...... 22514B
003.261-022 ...... 22514B
003.281-010 22517
003.281-014 ...... 22514B
003.362-010 ...... 22514B
005.061-010 22121
005.061-014 22121
005.061-018 22121
005.061-022 22121
005.061-026 22121
005.061-030 22121
005.061-034 22121
005.061-038 22121
005.061-042 22117
005.167-010 ...... 13017A
005.167-014 22121
005.167-018 22121
005.167-022 ...... 13017A
005.167-026 22121
005.261-014 22502
005.281-010 ...... 22514C
005.281-014 ...... 22514A
006.061-010 ...... 22105A
006.061-014 ...... 22105A
006.061-018 ...... 22105A
006.061-022 ...... 22105A
006.151-010 49002
006.261-010 ...... 89905D
007.061-010 22135
007.061-014 22135
007.061-018 22135
007.061-022 22135
007.061-026 22135
007.061-030 22135
007.061-034 22135
007.061-038 22135
007.061-042 22135
007.151-010 49002
007.161-010 ...... 22514D
007.161-014 ...... 22514D
007.161-018 ...... 22514D
007.161-022 22135
007.161-026 22511
007.161-030 22511
007.161-034 22135
007.161-038 22135
007.167-010 22511
007.167-014 ..... 13017A
007.167-018 25111
007.181-010 22511
007.261-010 ..... 22599G
007.261-014 ..... 22514D
007.261-018 ..... 22514D
007.261-022 ..... 22514D
007.267-010 22511
007.267-014 22511
007.281-010 ..... 22514D
007.362-010 25111
008.061-010 22114
008.061-014 22114
008.061-018 22114
008.061-022 22114
008.061-026 22114
008.151-010 49002
008.167-010 ..... 13017B
008.261-010 ..... 22599E
010.061-010 22108
010.061-014 22108
010.061-018 22111
010.061-022 22108
010.061-026 22108
010.061-030 22108
010.131-010 ..... 24511E
010.151-010 49002
010.161-010 22111
010.161-014 ..... 13017A
010.161-018 ..... 24511B
010.167-010 22111
010.167-014 22111
010.167-018 ..... 13017A
010.261-010 ..... 24511E
010.261-014 ..... 24511B
010.261-018 ..... 24511B
010.261-022 ..... 24511B
010.261-026 ..... 24511E
010.267-010 ..... 24511B
010.281-010 ..... 22514C
010.281-014 ..... 22514C
010.281-018 ..... 22514C
010.281-022 ..... 24511E
011.061-010 ..... 22105B
011.061-014 ..... 22105B
011.061-018 ..... 22105B
011.061-022 ..... 22105B
011.061-026 ..... 22105C
011.161-010 22128
011.261-010 ..... 22599B
011.261-014 ..... 22599B
011.261-018 ..... 22599B
011.261-022 ..... 22599B
011.281-014 ..... 22599B
011.361-010 ..... 22599B
012.061-010 ..... 22132C
012.061-014 ..... 22132A
012.061-018 22128
012.067-010 22128
012.167-010 22128
012.167-014 22128
012.167-018 22128

012.167-022......22132B
012.167-026......22132B
012.167-030......22128
012.167-034......22132A
012.167-038......22128
012.167-042......22128
012.167-046......22128
012.167-050......22128
012.167-054......22128
012.167-058......22132A
012.167-062......22128
012.167-070......22128
012.167-074......22128
012.167-078......22128
012.167-082......22128
012.187-014......22128
012.261-010......24505E
012.261-014......22508
012.267-010......22508
012.281-010......24505E
013.061-010......22123
013.061-014......22123
013.061-018......22123
013.061-022......22123
013.151-010......49002
013.161-010......22599D
014.061-010......22138
014.061-014......22138
014.061-018......22138
014.061-022......22138
014.151-010......49002
014.167-010......22138
014.167-014......22138
014.281-010......22514A
015.021-010......24102A
015.061-010......22117
015.061-014......22117
015.061-018......22117
015.061-022......22117
015.061-026......22117
015.061-030......22117
015.067-010......22117
015.137-010......22117
015.151-010......49002
015.167-010......22117
015.167-014......22117
015.261-010......24508B
015.362-010......24508A
015.362-014......24508A
015.362-018......24508A
015.362-022......24508A
015.362-026......24508A
015.384-010......24508B
017.161-010......22599G
017.261-010......22511
017.261-014......22514B
017.261-018......22514D
017.261-022......22514D
017.261-026......22514A
017.261-030......22514D
017.261-034......22514A
017.261-038......22514A
017.261-042......22514D
017.281-010......22514D
017.281-014......22514D
017.281-018......22514A
017.281-026......22514D
017.281-030......22514A
017.281-034......22514D
017.684-010......93997
018.131-010......22311A
018.161-010......22311B
018.167-010......22521A
018.167-014......22521B
018.167-018......22311B
018.167-022......13017A
018.167-026......22311B
018.167-030......22521B
018.167-034......22521A
018.167-038......22311B
018.167-042......22311B
018.167-046......22311B
018.261-010......22311A
018.261-018......22521B
018.261-022......22521B
018.261-026......22311A
018.262-010......22311A
018.281-010......22521B
019.061-010......22197
019.061-014......22105D
019.061-018......22197
019.061-022......22199
019.061-026......22197
019.081-010......22197
019.081-014......22197
019.081-018......24199B
019.161-010......22517
019.161-014......89108
019.167-010......22128
019.167-014......13017A
019.167-018......22121
019.187-010......22197
019.261-010......85908
019.261-014......22517
019.261-018......22502
019.261-022......22599D
019.261-026......22502
019.261-030......24505A
019.261-034......22599F
019.267-010......34005
019.281-010......22505B
020.067-014......25319A
020.067-018......25302
020.067-022......25312
020.162-010......25323
020.167-010......25313
020.167-026......25312
020.167-030......25319B
021.067-010......24102B
022.061-010......24105
022.061-014......24105
022.081-010......24308J
022.137-010......24105
022.161-010......13017B
022.161-014......24505D
022.161-018......24505A
022.261-010......24505A
022.261-014......24505B
022.261-018......24505E
022.261-022......24505E
022.281-010......24505C
022.281-014......24505E
022.281-018......24505D
022.381-010......24505B
023.061-010......24102A
023.061-014......24102A
023.067-010......24102A
024.061-010......24111A
024.061-014......22311B
024.061-018......24111A
024.061-022......24111A
024.061-026......24111A
024.061-030......24111B
024.061-034......24111B
024.061-038......24111A
024.061-042......24111A
024.061-046......24111A
024.061-050......24111B
024.061-054......24111A
024.161-010......24111A
024.167-010......24111B
024.267-010......24511B
024.284-010......24111A
024.364-010......24599C
024.381-010......24511E
025.062-010......24108
025.264-010......24599A
025.267-010......24599A
025.267-014......24599A
029.067-010......24199A
029.067-014......24199A
029.081-010......24199B
029.081-014......24199C
029.167-010......22521B
029.167-014......13017B
029.261-010......24505A
029.261-014......24505E
029.261-018......24511E
029.261-022......24511E
029.261-026......24599B
029.280-010......34023B
029.361-010......24505B
029.361-014......24505B
029.361-018......24505E
029.381-010......24505D
029.381-014......24505D
029.383-010......24599A
030.062-010......22127
030.162-010......25105
030.162-014......25102
030.162-018......25105
030.162-022......25102
030.167-010......25105
030.167-014......25102
031.132-010......25104
031.262-010......25199A
031.262-014......25104
032.132-010......25104
032.262-010......25104
033.162-010......21999A
033.162-014......21999A
033.162-018......25104
033.167-010......22127
033.262-010......25102
033.362-010......21999A
039.162-010......25103A
039.162-014......25103A
039.264-010......25104
040.061-010......24305B
040.061-014......24305A
040.061-018......24305A
040.061-022......24502A
040.061-026......24502A
040.061-030......24302A
040.061-038......24305B
040.061-042......24305A
040.061-046......24302D
040.061-050......24302A
040.061-054......24302B
040.061-058......24305D
040.061-062......24302C
040.167-010......24302A
040.261-010......24302B
040.361-010......24502B
040.361-014......24502C
041.061-010......24311
041.061-014......24305A
041.061-018......24305B
041.061-022......24308B
041.061-026......24308A
041.061-030......24308B
041.061-034......24308C
041.061-038......24308D
041.061-042......24308G
041.061-046......24305B
041.061-050......24308F
041.061-054......24311
041.061-058......24308E
041.061-062......24308D
041.061-066......24308B
041.061-070......24311
041.061-074......24311
041.061-078......24308G
041.061-082......24305B
041.061-086......24308D
041.061-090......24308H
041.061-094......24308J
041.067-010......24311
041.081-010......24305C
041.167-010......24311
041.261-010......24311
041.381-010......24502D
041.384-010......24502D
045.061-010......27108A
045.061-014......27108J
045.061-018......27108C
045.067-010......27108D
045.067-014......27108E
045.067-018......27108D
045.107-010......31514
045.107-014......31514
045.107-018......31514
045.107-022......27108G
045.107-026......27108H
045.107-030......27108J
045.107-034......27108D
045.107-038......31514
045.107-042......31514
045.107-046......27108G
045.107-050......27108G
045.107-054......27108H
045.107-058......27302
045.117-010......31514
049.127-010......24302E
049.364-010......24502C
049.364-014......24599C
049.364-018......24502C
050.067-010......27102A
050.067-014......27102B
050.117-010......19005A
051.067-010......27199A
052.067-010......34002C
052.067-014......27199E
052.067-018......27199G
052.067-022......27199E
052.067-026......27199E
052.167-010......27199E
054.067-010......27199B
054.067-014......27199B
054.107-010......27199B
055.067-010......27199C
055.067-014......27199C
055.067-018......27199H
055.067-022......27199C
055.381-010......31511D
059.067-010......27199D
059.067-014......27199D
059.167-010......27199F
059.267-010......27199F
059.267-014......27199F
070.061-010......32102U
070.101-010......32102F
070.101-014......32102A
070.101-018......32102A
070.101-022......32102A
070.101-026......32102A
070.101-034......32102A
070.101-042......32102A
070.101-046......32102A
070.101-050......32102A
070.101-054......32102A
070.101-058......32102A
070.101-062......32102A
070.101-066......32102A
070.101-070......32102A
070.101-078......32102A
070.101-082......32102A
070.101-086......32102A
070.101-090......32102A
070.101-094......32102J
070.101-098......32102A
070.101-102......32102A
070.107-014......32102E
071.101-010......32102B
072.061-010......32105A
072.101-010......32105B
072.101-014......32105B
072.101-018......32105G
072.101-022......32105D
072.101-026......32105B

072.101-030..... 32105B
072.101-034..... 32105F
072.101-038..... 32105B
072.117-010..... 15005B
073.061-010..... 32114B
073.061-014..... 32114A
073.061-018..... 32114A
073.061-022..... 32114A
073.061-026..... 32114A
073.061-030..... 32114A
073.061-034..... 32114A
073.061-038..... 32114A
073.101-010..... 32114B
073.101-014..... 32114B
073.101-018..... 32114B
073.161-010..... 32114C
073.261-010..... 32114C
073.264-010..... 32114C
074.161-010..... 32517
074.161-014..... 32517
074.167-010..... 32517
074.381-010..... 32518
074.382-010..... 32518
075.117-010..... 15005B
075.117-014..... 15008A
075.117-018..... 15005B
075.117-022..... 15008A
075.117-026..... 15008A
075.117-030..... 15008A
075.117-034..... 19999C
075.124-010..... 32502
075.124-014..... 32502
075.124-018..... 31114
075.127-010..... 31314
075.127-014..... 32502
075.127-026..... 32502
075.127-030..... 32502
075.127-034..... 32502
075.137-010..... 32502
075.137-014..... 32502
075.167-010..... 32502
075.264-010..... 32502
075.264-014..... 32502
075.364-010..... 32502
075.371-010..... 32502
075.374-014..... 32502
075.374-018..... 32502
075.374-022..... 32502
076.101-010..... 32314
076.104-010..... 32314
076.107-010..... 32314
076.117-010..... 15008B
076.121-010..... 32305
076.121-014..... 32308
076.121-018..... 32399A
076.124-010..... 32311A
076.124-014..... 32317
076.124-018..... 32317
076.127-010..... 32317
076.127-014..... 32317
076.127-018..... 32317
076.167-010..... 32305
076.224-010..... 66017
076.224-014..... 32399B

076.264-010......32311B
076.361-010......32311B
076.361-014......32302
076.364-010......66021
077.061-010......32521
077.117-010......32521
077.124-010......32523
077.127-010......32521
077.127-014......32521
077.127-018......32521
077.127-022......32521
078.121-010......32902
078.131-010......32914
078.161-010......32902
078.161-014......32925
078.162-010......32919
078.261-010......32902
078.261-014......32902
078.261-018......32999A
078.261-022......32999A
078.261-026......32902
078.261-030......32902
078.261-034......32914
078.261-038......32902
078.261-042......32999B
078.261-046......32902
078.262-010......32925
078.264-010......32925
078.281-010......32902
078.361-010......32908
078.361-018......32914
078.361-022......32999A
078.361-026......32999A
078.361-034......32913
078.361-038......32999C
078.362-010......32999D
078.362-014......32999E
078.362-018......32926
078.362-022......32923
078.362-026......32919
078.362-030......32925
078.362-034......32925
078.362-038......32923
078.362-042......32923
078.362-046......32919
078.362-050......32925
078.362-054......32919
078.362-058......32919
078.362-062......32925
078.364-010......32919
078.364-014......32925
078.381-014......32905
078.384-010......32199
078.664-010......32999A
078.687-010......32905
079.021-014......24311
079.101-010......32113
079.101-014......32199
079.101-018......32108
079.101-022......32111
079.117-010......15008B
079.117-014......31517A
079.117-018......21911A
079.127-010......21511D

079.151-010......32996B
079.157-010......32199
079.161-010......32996C
079.167-010......19005A
079.167-014......15008B
079.271-010......32199
079.271-014......32199
079.361-014......79806
079.361-018......66002
079.362-010......66005
079.362-014......32911
079.362-018......32911
079.364-010......66005
079.364-014......32999C
079.364-018......32511
079.364-022......66099D
079.364-026......32508
079.367-018......32511
079.371-014......32999C
079.374-010......32508
079.374-014......32505
079.374-018......66005
079.374-022......32928
079.374-026......32931
090.107-010......31514
090.117-010......15005A
090.117-014......15005A
090.117-018......15005A
090.117-022......15005A
090.117-026......15005A
090.117-030......15005A
090.117-034......19005B
090.164-010......31517C
090.167-010......15005A
090.167-014......15005A
090.167-018......15005A
090.167-022......15005A
090.167-026......15005A
090.167-030......15005A
090.167-034......15005B
090.222-010......31314
090.227-010......31202
090.227-014......31117
090.227-018......31317
091.107-010......15005B
091.221-010......31308
091.227-010......31308
092.167-010......15005B
092.227-010......31305
092.227-014......31304
092.227-018......31303
094.107-010......31311A
094.117-010......15005B
094.117-018......31517B
094.167-010......31517D
094.167-014......15005B
094.224-010......31311C
094.224-014......31311C
094.224-018......31311C
094.227-010......31311B
094.227-022......31311B
094.227-026......31311A
094.227-030......31311B
094.267-010......31311D

096.121-010..... 31323
096.121-014..... 31323
096.127-010..... 31323
096.127-014..... 31323
096.127-018..... 31323
096.127-022..... 31323
096.161-010..... 15005B
096.167-010..... 15005B
096.167-014..... 15005B
097.167-010..... 15005B
097.221-010..... 31314
097.227-010..... 31317
099.117-010..... 15005B
099.117-014..... 15005B
099.117-018..... 15005B
099.117-022..... 19005B
099.117-026..... 31517D
099.117-030..... 15005B
099.167-010..... 21511E
099.167-014..... 31517D
099.167-018..... 31517D
099.167-022..... 31517D
099.167-026..... 31517D
099.167-030..... 31511A
099.167-034..... 15005B
099.223-010..... 31317
099.224-010..... 31308
099.224-014..... 31317
099.227-010..... 62041
099.227-014..... 31314
099.227-018..... 31314
099.227-022..... 31308
099.227-026..... 31317
099.227-030..... 31317
099.227-034..... 31399
099.227-038..... 31317
099.227-042..... 31311B
099.327-010..... 31521
100.117-010..... 31502A
100.117-014..... 21999J
100.127-010..... 31502A
100.127-014..... 31502A
100.167-010..... 31502A
100.167-014..... 31502A
100.167-018..... 31502A
100.167-022..... 31502A
100.167-026..... 31502A
100.167-030..... 31502A
100.167-034..... 31502A
100.167-038..... 31502A
100.267-010..... 31502A
100.267-014..... 31502A
100.367-010..... 31505
100.367-014..... 31505
100.367-018..... 31505
100.367-022..... 31502A
100.367-026..... 31502A
100.387-010..... 31505
101.167-010..... 31511B
102.017-010..... 31511A
102.117-010..... 31511A
102.117-014..... 31511A
102.167-010..... 31511D
102.167-014..... 31511A

102.167-018..... 31511A
102.261-010..... 31511D
102.261-014..... 34035A
102.361-010..... 31511D
102.361-014..... 31511D
102.367-010..... 31511D
102.381-010..... 31511D
109.067-010..... 25103A
109.067-014..... 31511C
109.137-010..... 51002B
109.267-010..... 31511C
109.267-014..... 31502B
109.281-010..... 31511D
109.361-010..... 31511D
109.364-010..... 31511E
109.367-010..... 68017B
110.107-010..... 28108
110.107-014..... 28108
110.117-010..... 28108
110.117-014..... 28108
110.117-018..... 28108
110.117-022..... 28108
110.117-026..... 28108
110.117-030..... 28108
110.117-034..... 28108
110.117-038..... 28108
110.117-042..... 28108
110.167-010..... 21999J
111.107-010..... 28102
111.107-014..... 28102
119.107-010..... 28105
119.117-010..... 28105
119.167-010..... 28105
119.167-014..... 28305
119.167-018..... 28311
119.267-010..... 28311
119.267-014..... 28105
119.267-018..... 28399
119.267-022..... 28305
119.267-026..... 28302
119.287-010..... 28311
119.367-010..... 28399
129.027-010..... 27599
129.107-010..... 27599
129.107-014..... 27599
129.107-018..... 27505
129.107-022..... 27505
129.107-026..... 27599
129.271-010..... 27599
131.067-010..... 34002A
131.067-014..... 34002L
131.067-018..... 34002A
131.067-022..... 34002A
131.067-026..... 34002C
131.067-030..... 34002B
131.067-034..... 34002B
131.067-038..... 34002C
131.067-042..... 34002B
131.067-046..... 34002C
131.067-050..... 34002C
131.087-010..... 34002C
131.087-014..... 34002H
131.262-010..... 34014
131.262-014..... 34011

131.262-018......34011
131.267-022......34002H
131.267-026......34005
132.017-010......34002E
132.017-014......34002E
132.017-018......34005
132.037-010......34002F
132.037-014......34002E
132.037-018......34002E
132.037-022......34002E
132.037-026......34002F
132.067-010......34002E
132.067-014......34002G
132.067-018......34002M
132.067-022......34002D
132.067-026......34002D
132.067-030......34002F
132.132-010......34002E
132.267-010......34002D
132.267-014......34002D
132.367-010......34002D
137.137-010......19005A
137.267-010......39999A
137.267-014......39999A
137.267-018......39999A
139.087-010......34002C
139.167-010......34056G
141.031-010......34038E
141.051-010......34041
141.061-010......34035D
141.061-014......34035A
141.061-018......34035C
141.061-022......34035A
141.061-026......34035A
141.061-030......34035A
141.061-034......34035B
141.061-038......34038B
141.067-010......34038E
141.081-010......34035D
141.137-010......34038E
142.031-014......34044
142.051-010......34038D
142.051-014......34041
142.061-010......34038B
142.061-014......34038B
142.061-018......34038A
142.061-022......34038B
142.061-026......34038B
142.061-030......34038B
142.061-034......34038B
142.061-038......34038B
142.061-042......34038C
142.061-046......34038C
142.061-050......34038C
142.061-054......34038B
142.061-058......34038D
142.061-062......34038C
142.081-010......34038F
142.081-014......34038A
142.081-018......34038B
142.281-010......34038A
143.062-010......34026
143.062-014......34023A
143.062-018......34023A
143.062-022......34026
143.062-026......34023B
143.062-030......34023A
143.062-034......34023A
143.260-010......34026
143.362-010......34023B
143.362-014......34023B
143.382-010......34026
143.382-014......34023A
143.457-010......69999E
144.061-010......34035A
144.061-014......34035A
144.061-018......34035E
149.021-010......31317
149.031-010......34038C
149.041-010......34035B
149.051-010......34035B
149.061-010......31508
149.261-010......34035A
149.281-010......89305
150.027-010......34056G
150.027-014......31317
150.047-010......34056A
150.067-010......34056G
150.147-010......34056A
151.027-010......34053B
151.027-014......31317
151.047-010......34053A
152.021-010......31317
152.041-010......34051
152.047-010......34047A
152.047-014......34047A
152.047-018......34047A
152.047-022......34047C
152.067-010......34047B
152.067-014......34047E
152.067-018......39999H
152.067-022......34047B
152.267-010......34047B
152.367-010......34047F
153.117-010......34058A
153.117-014......39999B
153.117-018......34058A
153.117-022......34058L
153.137-010......19999A
153.167-010......34058L
153.167-014......34058L
153.167-018......34058L
153.224-010......34058B
153.227-010......34058A
153.227-014......31321
153.227-018......31321
153.243-010......34058E
153.243-014......34058E
153.244-010......34058F
153.244-014......34058F
153.267-010......34058L
153.267-014......34058L
153.267-018......34058L
153.287-010......34058L
153.341-010......34058C
153.367-010......34058L
153.367-014......34058L
153.384-010......34058G
153.387-010.....34058L
153.387-014.....34058L
153.467-010.....34058L
153.667-010.....34058L
153.674-010.....34058G
153.674-014.....34058G
159.041-010.....34056A
159.041-014.....34056A
159.042-010.....39999D
159.044-010.....34056A
159.047-010.....34056A
159.047-014.....34056A
159.047-018.....34056A
159.047-022.....34056A
159.067-010.....34056G
159.067-014.....34056G
159.117-010.....34056F
159.124-010.....27311
159.147-010.....34017
159.147-014.....34017
159.147-018.....34017
159.167-010.....34056J
159.167-014.....34056G
159.167-018.....34056G
159.167-022.....13011A
159.207-010.....69999E
159.224-010.....79016
159.227-010.....31317
159.247-010.....34056D
159.247-014.....34056D
159.267-010.....34056J
159.341-010.....34056D
159.341-014.....34056A
159.344-010.....34056E
159.344-014.....34056E
159.344-018.....34056E
159.347-010.....34021
159.347-014.....34056D
159.347-018.....34056D
159.347-022.....34056D
159.367-010.....34056A
159.647-010.....34056D
159.647-014.....34056B
159.647-018.....69999E
159.647-022.....34056B
160.162-010.....21114A
160.162-018.....21114A
160.162-022.....21114A
160.162-026.....21114A
160.162-030.....21114C
160.167-022.....21114A
160.167-026.....21114A
160.167-030.....21114B
160.167-034.....21114B
160.167-038.....21114B
160.167-042.....21114A
160.167-046.....21911J
160.167-050.....21914
160.167-054.....21114B
160.167-058.....13002A
160.207-010.....21199B
160.267-014.....21114B
160.267-022.....21105
160.267-026.....25315
161.117-010.....21117
161.117-014.....21905
161.117-018.....13002A
161.167-010.....21905
161.167-014.....21905
161.167-018.....21905
161.167-022.....21905
161.267-010.....21905
161.267-018.....21905
161.267-022.....21905
161.267-026.....21905
161.267-030.....21117
162.117-010.....21305A
162.117-014.....13014A
162.117-018.....21308A
162.117-022.....21305A
162.117-026.....21305A
162.117-030.....13017A
162.157-010.....43014A
162.157-018.....21302
162.157-022.....21302
162.157-026.....49008
162.157-030.....21308A
162.157-034.....21308B
162.157-038.....21308A
162.167-010.....21305A
162.167-014.....13008
162.167-018.....21305A
162.167-022.....13008
162.167-026.....55347
162.167-030.....21308C
162.167-034.....43014A
162.167-038.....43014A
162.267-010.....28311
163.117-010.....21308A
163.117-014.....13011B
163.117-018.....13011A
163.117-022.....13011C
163.117-026.....13011D
163.167-010.....13011B
163.167-014.....41002
163.167-018.....13011B
163.167-022.....13011B
163.167-026.....13014A
163.267-010.....13011B
164.117-010.....13011A
164.117-014.....13011A
164.117-018.....13011A
164.167-010.....13011A
165.017-010.....34008
165.117-010.....13011D
165.117-014.....13011D
165.157-010.....43017
165.167-010.....34008
165.167-014.....34008
166.067-010.....21511A
166.117-010.....13005A
166.117-014.....21511C
166.117-018.....13005A
166.167-010.....34056J
166.167-014.....21511B
166.167-018.....13005A
166.167-022.....13005A
166.167-026.....13005B
166.167-030.....13005A
166.167-034.....13005C
166.167-038.....21511D
166.167-042.....21511C
166.167-046.....21505
166.167-050.....13005E
166.167-054.....21511D
166.221-010.....31314
166.227-010.....31314
166.257-010.....21511B
166.267-010.....21508
166.267-014.....21999J
166.267-018.....21511A
166.267-022.....27305C
166.267-026.....21511E
166.267-030.....21511C
166.267-034.....21511B
166.267-038.....21511E
166.267-042.....21511C
166.267-046.....21511C
168.161-010.....21911P
168.161-014.....21911E
168.167-010.....63014A
168.167-014.....21911F
168.167-018.....21911A
168.167-022.....21911C
168.167-026.....21911L
168.167-030.....21908A
168.167-034.....21908A
168.167-038.....21908B
168.167-042.....21911A
168.167-046.....21908A
168.167-050.....21908A
168.167-058.....51002A
168.167-062.....21911E
168.167-066.....21911A
168.167-070.....15023B
168.167-074.....21911D
168.167-078.....21911E
168.167-082.....21911M
168.167-086.....21911E
168.167-090.....19005A
168.261-010.....21911T
168.264-010.....21911K
168.264-014.....21911E
168.264-018.....21911L
168.267-010.....63002A
168.267-014.....21921
168.267-018.....21911C
168.267-022.....21911C
168.267-026.....21999J
168.267-030.....21911A
168.267-034.....21911D
168.267-038.....53502
168.267-042.....21911A
168.267-046.....21911A
168.267-050.....21911H
168.267-054.....21911B
168.267-058.....83008C
168.267-062.....21911H
168.267-066.....21911D
168.267-070.....21911E
168.267-074.....21911E
168.267-078.....21911A

168.267-082 ..... 21911B
168.267-086 ..... 21911B
168.267-090 ..... 21911B
168.267-094 ..... 21911N
168.267-098 ..... 21911B
168.267-102 ..... 21908A
168.267-106 ..... 21911B
168.267-110 ..... 21911B
168.267-114 ..... 21911F
168.287-010 ..... 21911R
168.287-014 ..... 21911H
168.287-018 ..... 83008A
168.367-010 ..... 21999J
168.367-014 ..... 21999J
168.367-018 ..... 21908A
168.367-022 22508
168.387-010 ..... 21911C
169.107-010 ..... 21511F
169.117-010 ..... 19005A
169.117-014 ..... 21999G
169.127-010 31317
169.167-010 ..... 21999C
169.167-014 ..... 21999C
169.167-018 53502
169.167-022 ..... 21999J
169.167-026 ..... 21999J
169.167-030 ..... 13017C
169.167-034 ..... 13014B
169.167-038 41002
169.167-042 ..... 63014A
169.167-046 32911
169.167-050 43002
169.167-054 ..... 21308B
169.167-062 ..... 21511D
169.167-066 ..... 21999B
169.167-070 ..... 15023B
169.167-074 81002
169.167-078 ..... 21999J
169.167-082 ..... 13017C
169.167-086 ..... 13002B
169.171-010 ..... 79999J
169.207-010 ..... 21511F
169.262-010 ..... 21999B
169.267-010 28105
169.267-014 ..... 21911D
169.267-018 ..... 21199B
169.267-022 ..... 15005B
169.267-026 31514
169.267-030 ..... 21911D
169.267-034 ..... 27102B
169.267-038 21902
169.267-042 ..... 21199D
169.267-046 21102
169.284-010 ..... 21911N
169.367-010 21502
180.117-010 15031
180.161-010 ..... 79999K
180.161-014 15031
180.167-010 41002
180.167-014 ..... 72002A
180.167-018 ..... 79999K
180.167-022 ..... 72002A
180.167-026 ..... 79999L
180.167-030 ..... 79999M
180.167-034 ...... 79999L
180.167-038 ...... 72002C
180.167-042 15031
180.167-046 ...... 79999L
180.167-050 ...... 72002A
180.167-054 15014
180.167-058 ...... 79999K
180.167-062 ...... 15023A
180.167-066 ...... 79999K
181.117-010 ...... 15023D
181.117-014 ...... 15021A
181.167-010 ...... 19999G
181.167-014 ...... 15021C
181.167-018 ...... 15021A
182.167-010 ...... 15017B
182.167-014 ...... 15017A
182.167-018 ...... 15017B
182.167-022 15014
182.167-026 ...... 15017B
182.167-030 ...... 15017B
182.167-034 ...... 15017B
182.267-010 ...... 21908A
183.117-010 15014
183.117-014 15014
183.161-014 15014
183.167-010 15014
183.167-014 15014
183.167-018 15014
183.167-022 15014
183.167-026 15014
183.167-030 ...... 19999D
183.167-034 15014
183.167-038 ...... 72002F
184.117-010 ...... 34056H
184.117-014 ...... 15023A
184.117-018 ...... 15023A
184.117-022 ...... 15023D
184.117-026 ...... 15023A
184.117-030 ...... 15023C
184.117-034 ...... 15023A
184.117-038 ...... 15023A
184.117-042 ...... 15023A
184.117-046 ...... 15023C
184.117-050 ...... 15023A
184.117-054 ...... 15023A
184.117-058 ...... 15023A
184.117-062 ...... 15023B
184.117-066 ...... 15023A
184.117-070 ...... 15023B
184.117-074 ...... 15023B
184.117-078 13008
184.117-082 ...... 15023B
184.117-086 ...... 15023A
184.117-090 ...... 15023A
184.161-010 ...... 15023B
184.161-014 ...... 15023C
184.162-010 ...... 34056K
184.163-010 ...... 21911M
184.167-010 ...... 15023A
184.167-014 ...... 34056H
184.167-018 ...... 15023B
184.167-022 ...... 34056H
184.167-026 ...... 22311B
184.167-030 ...... 34056H
184.167-034 ...... 34056H
184.167-038 ...... 15023D
184.167-042 ...... 15023A
184.167-046 81008
184.167-050 81002
184.167-054 ...... 15023A
184.167-058 ...... 15023A
184.167-062 ...... 15023B
184.167-066 ...... 15023A
184.167-070 ...... 15023A
184.167-078 ...... 15023C
184.167-082 ...... 15023A
184.167-086 ...... 15023B
184.167-090 ...... 15023A
184.167-094 ...... 15023A
184.167-098 ...... 15023A
184.167-102 ...... 15023A
184.167-106 ...... 15023A
184.167-110 ...... 15023A
184.167-114 ...... 15023D
184.167-118 ...... 15023D
184.167-122 ...... 15023A
184.167-126 ...... 15023C
184.167-130 ...... 15023A
184.167-134 ...... 15023B
184.167-138 ...... 15023C
184.167-142 81008
184.167-146 ...... 15023D
184.167-150 ...... 15023C
184.167-154 ...... 15023C
184.167-158 ...... 15023A
184.167-162 ...... 15023C
184.167-166 ...... 15023C
184.167-170 ...... 15023A
184.167-174 ...... 15023A
184.167-178 ...... 15023A
184.167-182 ...... 15023A
184.167-186 ...... 15023A
184.167-190 ...... 15023D
184.167-194 81002
184.167-198 ...... 15023C
184.167-202 ...... 15023C
184.167-206 ...... 15023A
184.167-210 ...... 15023C
184.167-214 ...... 15023A
184.167-218 ...... 15023C
184.167-222 ...... 15023C
184.167-226 ...... 15023A
184.167-230 ...... 15023B
184.167-234 ...... 81005A
184.167-238 ...... 15023C
184.167-242 ...... 15023A
184.167-246 ...... 15023C
184.167-250 ...... 21999J
184.167-254 ...... 15023A
184.167-258 ...... 15023B
184.167-262 97302
184.167-266 ...... 15023A
184.167-270 ...... 15023C
184.167-274 ...... 15023A
184.167-278 97302
184.167-282 ...... 15023A
184.167-286 ...... 15023A
184.167-290 ...... 15023A
184.167-294 ..... 15023A
184.267-010 ..... 15023A
184.387-010 55344
185.117-010 ..... 19005B
185.117-014 ..... 13011B
185.137-010 ..... 15026B
185.157-010 ..... 13011C
185.157-014 ..... 13011C
185.157-018 41002
185.164-010 81002
185.167-010 41002
185.167-014 41002
185.167-018 81011
185.167-022 41002
185.167-026 41002
185.167-030 41002
185.167-034 13008
185.167-038 41002
185.167-042 ..... 13011B
185.167-046 41002
185.167-050 41002
185.167-054 41002
185.167-058 81002
185.167-062 ..... 19005A
185.167-066 41002
185.167-070 41002
185.167-074 81002
186.117-010 ..... 15005A
186.117-018 ..... 21999H
186.117-022 ..... 19005A
186.117-030 ..... 15023A
186.117-034 ..... 19005B
186.117-042 ..... 15011A
186.117-046 ..... 15011A
186.117-054 ..... 19005B
186.117-058 ..... 15011A
186.117-062 ..... 15011B
186.117-066 ..... 13002B
186.117-070 ..... 13002A
186.117-074 ..... 13002B
186.117-078 ..... 13002A
186.117-082 ..... 13002B
186.117-086 ..... 13002B
186.137-014 ..... 13002B
186.167-010 43002
186.167-018 ..... 15011B
186.167-030 ..... 15011B
186.167-034 41002
186.167-038 ..... 15011C
186.167-042 ..... 15011B
186.167-046 ..... 15011B
186.167-054 ..... 13002A
186.167-062 ..... 15011B
186.167-066 ..... 15011B
186.167-070 ..... 13002B
186.167-074 28399
186.167-078 21108
186.167-082 ..... 13002B
186.167-086 ..... 13002B
186.167-090 ..... 15011C
186.267-010 63035
186.267-018 21108
186.267-022 21105
186.267-026 21108
187.117-010 ..... 15008B
187.117-018 ..... 19005A
187.117-022 ..... 19999B
187.117-026 ..... 19999B
187.117-030 ..... 19999C
187.117-034 ..... 19999A
187.117-038 ..... 15026A
187.117-042 ..... 19999A
187.117-046 ..... 19999B
187.117-050 ..... 21911A
187.117-054 ..... 19005A
187.117-058 ..... 15008B
187.117-062 ..... 13014B
187.117-066 ..... 19999B
187.134-010 ..... 27305A
187.137-014 ..... 27305A
187.137-018 ..... 15026A
187.161-010 ..... 15026B
187.161-014 ..... 19999A
187.167-010 81002
187.167-014 ..... 19999E
187.167-018 ..... 19999C
187.167-022 ..... 19999B
187.167-026 ..... 15026B
187.167-030 39011
187.167-034 ..... 21511B
187.167-038 ..... 19999B
187.167-042 ..... 19999C
187.167-046 61008
187.167-050 ..... 15026B
187.167-054 ..... 19999A
187.167-058 ..... 19999D
187.167-062 ..... 21999J
187.167-066 ..... 15026B
187.167-070 ..... 19999E
187.167-074 ..... 19005B
187.167-078 ..... 21999F
187.167-082 ..... 19999D
187.167-086 ..... 19999A
187.167-090 15014
187.167-094 ..... 19999A
187.167-098 41002
187.167-102 ..... 19999A
187.167-106 ..... 15026B
187.167-114 ..... 19999A
187.167-118 ..... 19999A
187.167-122 ..... 19999A
187.167-126 ..... 15026B
187.167-130 81002
187.167-134 ..... 19999E
187.167-138 41002
187.167-142 81002
187.167-146 ..... 19999A
187.167-150 81011
187.167-154 ..... 19999A
187.167-158 ..... 19999D
187.167-162 ..... 13011B
187.167-166 ..... 19999A
187.167-170 ..... 13011C
187.167-174 ..... 34056F
187.167-178 ..... 34056F
187.167-182 ..... 34056F
187.167-186 27307
187.167-190 ..... 15011B

187.167-194......19999D
187.167-198......31514
187.167-202......19999A
187.167-206......15026B
187.167-210......15026B
187.167-214......19999B
187.167-218......72002C
187.167-222......19999A
187.167-226......19999D
187.167-230......19999A
187.167-234......19999B
187.167-238......27311
188.117-010......13005B
188.117-014......19005A
188.117-018......19005A
188.117-022......19005A
188.117-026......19005A
188.117-030......19005A
188.117-034......19005A
188.117-038......19005A
188.117-042......19005A
188.117-046......19005A
188.117-050......19005A
188.117-054......19005A
188.117-058......19005A
188.117-062......19005A
188.117-066......19005A
188.117-070......19005A
188.117-074......19005A
188.117-078......19005A
188.117-082......19005A
188.117-086......13005A
188.117-090......19005A
188.117-094......19005A
188.117-098......19005A
188.117-102......19005A
188.117-106......19005A
188.117-110......19005A
188.117-114......19005A
188.117-118......19005A
188.117-122......13014A
188.117-126......19005A
188.117-130......13014B
188.117-134......19005A
188.137-010......19005A
188.167-010......21917
188.167-014......19005A
188.167-018......19005A
188.167-022......19005A
188.167-026......19005A
188.167-030......19005A
188.167-034......19005A
188.167-038......21911J
188.167-042......19005A
188.167-046......19005A
188.167-050......19005A
188.167-054......19005A
188.167-058......19005A
188.167-062......19005A
188.167-066......15002
188.167-070......19005A
188.167-074......21914
188.167-078......19005A
188.167-082......19005A
188.167-086......15002
188.167-090......21911C
188.167-094......15014
188.167-098......19005A
188.167-102......19005A
188.167-106......13014A
188.167-110......27105
188.217-010......13005C
189.117-010......19999C
189.117-014......19999G
189.117-018......13011B
189.117-022......19005B
189.117-026......19005B
189.117-030......19999G
189.117-034......19005B
189.117-038......19005B
189.117-042......19999G
189.117-046......19005B
189.157-010......21999J
189.167-014......13014B
189.167-018......19999G
189.167-022......19005B
189.167-026......19999C
189.167-030......19005B
189.167-034......19999F
189.167-038......15023D
189.167-042......81017
189.167-046......81002
189.167-050......19999F
189.167-054......19999F
189.267-010......27305A
191.117-010......39999B
191.117-014......39999B
191.117-018......39999B
191.117-022......39999B
191.117-026......39999B
191.117-030......21999D
191.117-034......39999B
191.117-038......39999B
191.117-042......21999D
191.117-046......21999D
191.117-050......15011A
191.157-010......49999A
191.167-010......39999B
191.167-014......53302
191.167-018......21999D
191.167-022......53123
191.267-010......43011
191.287-010......49999A
191.287-014......49999A
191.367-010......55344
193.162-010......39002
193.162-014......39002
193.162-018......39002
193.162-022......39008
193.167-010......39002
193.167-014......34028B
193.167-018......15023B
193.262-010......39008
193.262-014......39008
193.262-018......34028B
193.262-022......39008
193.262-026......39008
193.262-030......39008
193.262-034 39008
193.262-038 .....34028C
193.362-010 39008
193.362-014 39008
193.382-010 39008
194.062-010 .....34028B
194.122-010 .....34028B
194.162-010 .....15023B
194.262-010 .....34028B
194.262-014 .....22599A
194.262-018 .....22599A
194.262-022 .....34028B
194.282-010 .....34028B
194.362-010 .....22599A
194.362-014 .....22599A
194.362-018 .....34028B
194.362-022 .....34028B
194.381-010 .....34028B
194.382-010 .....24511B
194.382-014 .....22599A
194.382-018 .....34028B
194.387-010 .....83005A
194.387-014 .....83005A
195.107-010 .....27305B
195.107-014 .....27305B
195.107-018 .....27305B
195.107-022 .....27305B
195.107-026 .....27305B
195.107-030 27302
195.107-034 27302
195.107-038 .....27305B
195.107-042 .....27305C
195.107-046 .....27305C
195.117-010 .....19999B
195.137-010 .....27305B
195.164-010 .....27305A
195.167-010 .....27305A
195.167-014 .....27305A
195.167-018 .....19999A
195.167-022 .....19999B
195.167-026 27311
195.167-038 .....19999B
195.167-042 .....19005A
195.227-010 27311
195.227-014 27311
195.227-018 .....31311E
195.267-010 53502
195.267-018 53502
195.267-022 .....63028B
195.367-010 27308
195.367-014 27308
195.367-018 .....27305A
195.367-022 27308
195.367-026 .....27305C
195.367-030 .....68014A
195.367-034 27308
196.163-010 .....21911D
196.163-014 .....21911K
196.167-010 .....15023A
196.167-014 .....97702E
196.223-010 .....97702D
196.223-014 .....97702D
196.263-010 .....97702C
196.263-014 .....97702B
196.263-018 .....97702C
196.263-022 .....97702D
196.263-026 .....22599G
196.263-030 .....97702B
196.263-034 .....97702B
196.263-038 .....97702J
196.263-042 .....22599G
197.130-010 97521
197.133-010 .....97502A
197.133-014 .....97502A
197.133-018 97505
197.133-022 97505
197.133-026 97508
197.133-030 .....97502A
197.133-034 97505
197.137-010 97505
197.161-010 .....97502A
197.163-010 .....97502A
197.163-014 .....97502A
197.163-018 .....97502A
197.167-010 .....97502A
197.167-014 .....21999J
198.167-010 97302
198.167-014 97302
198.167-018 97302
199.167-010 .....24508B
199.167-014 27105
199.167-018 .....21999J
199.167-022 .....19005A
199.171-010 .....83005A
199.207-010 27599
199.251-010 .....24505B
199.261-010 .....39999E
199.261-014 22502
199.267-010 .....24599B
199.267-014 .....25319C
199.267-018 59999
199.267-022 .....39999H
199.267-026 .....39999G
199.267-030 39005
199.267-034 .....19999G
199.267-038 .....39999H
199.281-010 .....89123A
199.361-010 .....83002A
199.364-010 .....39999C
199.364-014 .....24599C
199.382-010 58008
199.384-010 .....24508B
199.682-010 99003
201.162-010 55108
201.362-010 55102
201.362-014 55105
201.362-018 55108
201.362-022 55108
201.362-026 55108
201.362-030 55108
202.132-010 .....51002B
202.362-010 .....55302A
202.362-014 .....55302B
202.362-018 .....55302B
202.362-022 .....55302A
202.382-010 .....55302A
203.132-010 .....51002B
203.132-014 .....51002B
203.137-010 .....51002B
203.137-014 .....51002B
203.362-010 55307
203.362-014 55305
203.362-026 .....34002J
203.382-014 53314
203.382-018 56021
203.382-026 56021
203.382-030 55307
203.562-010 57111
203.582-010 56017
203.582-014 56017
203.582-018 56017
203.582-038 56017
203.582-042 56021
203.582-046 56021
203.582-050 57111
203.582-054 56017
203.582-058 55307
203.582-062 56021
203.582-066 55307
203.582-078 55307
205.137-014 .....51002A
205.162-010 .....51002A
205.362-010 55314
205.362-014 55314
205.362-018 55332
205.362-022 55314
205.362-026 53105
205.367-010 55347
205.367-014 55332
205.367-018 53311
205.367-022 53121
205.367-026 55332
205.367-030 55347
205.367-034 53708
205.367-038 55305
205.367-042 55332
205.367-046 53502
205.367-050 .....21511E
205.367-054 55332
205.367-058 55332
205.367-062 55314
205.567-010 55314
206.137-010 .....51002B
206.367-010 .....58099A
206.367-014 55321
206.367-018 55321
206.387-010 55321
206.387-014 55321
206.387-022 55321
206.387-034 55321
206.587-010 58017
207.137-010 .....51002B
207.682-010 56005
207.682-014 56005
207.682-018 56005
207.685-010 56005
207.685-014 56005
207.685-018 56005
208.382-010 56021
208.462-010 56008
208.582-010 56008
208.582-014 56099

208.682-010 56099
208.685-010 56099
208.685-014 56008
208.685-018 56008
208.685-022 56099
208.685-026 56008
208.685-034 56008
209.132-010 ..... 51002B
209.132-014 ..... 51002A
209.137-010 ..... 51002B
209.137-014 ..... 51002A
209.137-018 ..... 51002B
209.137-026 ..... 51002B
209.362-010 55347
209.362-014 55347
209.362-018 53117
209.362-022 55347
209.362-026 55314
209.362-030 55347
209.362-034 55317
209.367-010 55347
209.367-014 59999
209.367-018 55317
209.367-026 55347
209.367-034 55347
209.367-038 55347
209.367-042 58028
209.367-046 28308
209.367-050 55347
209.367-054 55347
209.382-010 55307
209.382-014 53314
209.382-022 55347
209.387-014 ..... 55328A
209.387-018 55323
209.387-022 55347
209.387-026 53902
209.387-030 53911
209.387-034 55317
209.562-010 55347
209.567-010 58014
209.567-014 55323
209.582-010 ..... 89911E
209.584-010 ..... 89911E
209.587-010 55307
209.587-014 55347
209.587-018 57302
209.587-022 55347
209.587-030 55347
209.587-034 58021
209.587-042 53123
209.587-046 58017
209.587-050 55347
209.667-010 53911
209.667-014 55347
209.667-018 55347
209.687-010 53911
209.687-014 57308
209.687-018 53314
209.687-022 55347
209.687-026 57302
210.132-010 ..... 51002B
210.362-010 ..... 55338A
210.367-010 ..... 55338A
210.367-014 ...... 55338A
210.382-010 ...... 55338A
210.382-014 ...... 55338A
210.382-030 ...... 55338B
210.382-038 ...... 55338B
210.382-042 ...... 55338A
210.382-046 ...... 55338A
210.382-050 ...... 55338B
210.382-054 ...... 55338A
210.382-062 ...... 55338A
211.132-010 ...... 51002A
211.137-010 ...... 51002A
211.137-014 ...... 51002A
211.137-018 ...... 51002B
211.137-022 ...... 51002A
211.362-010 ...... 49023B
211.362-014 53102
211.362-018 53102
211.367-010 ...... 49023A
211.382-010 53102
211.462-010 ...... 49023A
211.462-014 ...... 49023A
211.462-018 ...... 49023A
211.462-022 ...... 49023A
211.462-026 ...... 49023A
211.462-030 ...... 49023A
211.462-034 ...... 49023A
211.462-038 ...... 49023A
211.467-010 ...... 49023A
211.467-014 ...... 49023A
211.467-018 ...... 49023A
211.467-022 ...... 49023A
211.467-026 ...... 49023A
211.467-030 ...... 49023A
211.467-034 ...... 49023A
211.482-010 ...... 49023A
211.482-014 ...... 49023A
211.482-018 ...... 65099B
213.132-010 ...... 51002B
213.362-010 56011
213.382-010 56014
213.582-010 56014
214.137-010 ...... 51002A
214.137-014 ...... 51002A
214.137-018 ...... 51002B
214.137-022 ...... 51002A
214.267-010 55344
214.362-010 55344
214.362-014 55344
214.362-022 55344
214.362-026 55344
214.362-030 53802
214.362-034 53505
214.362-038 55344
214.362-042 55344
214.362-046 53126
214.382-014 55344
214.382-018 55344
214.382-022 55344
214.382-026 55344
214.382-030 55344
214.387-010 55344
214.387-014 55344
214.387-018 55344
214.462-010 56002
214.467-010 55344
214.467-014 55344
214.482-010 56002
214.482-014 55344
214.482-018 55344
214.482-022 55344
214.487-010 ...... 55328A
214.587-010 55344
214.587-014 58028
215.137-010 ...... 51002B
215.137-014 ...... 51002B
215.137-018 ...... 51002B
215.167-010 58005
215.362-010 58008
215.362-014 58008
215.362-018 55341
215.362-022 55341
215.367-010 58008
215.367-014 58008
215.367-018 58005
215.382-014 55341
215.563-010 ...... 57311A
216.132-010 ...... 51002B
216.132-014 ...... 51002B
216.137-010 ...... 51002B
216.137-014 ...... 51002A
216.362-014 ...... 55338A
216.362-022 ...... 55338A
216.362-026 ...... 55338B
216.362-034 ...... 55338A
216.362-038 ...... 55338A
216.362-042 ...... 55338A
216.362-046 53128
216.367-014 ...... 55338A
216.382-022 ...... 55338A
216.382-026 ...... 55338B
216.382-034 55344
216.382-046 53128
216.382-050 55344
216.382-054 55344
216.382-058 ...... 55338B
216.382-062 ...... 55328A
216.382-066 ...... 55328A
216.462-010 58017
216.482-010 ...... 55338A
216.482-018 56002
216.482-022 56002
216.482-026 ...... 55338B
216.482-030 49017
216.482-034 53128
216.567-010 58021
216.587-010 ...... 58099C
216.685-010 56099
217.132-010 ...... 51002B
217.382-010 53108
217.485-010 56099
217.585-010 56099
219.132-010 ...... 51002B
219.132-014 ...... 51002B
219.132-022 ...... 51002B
219.137-010 ...... 51002B
219.267-010 ...... 34058L
219.362-010 55347
219.362-014 55347
219.362-018 53128
219.362-022 55347
219.362-026 55347
219.362-030 58008
219.362-038 53121
219.362-042 53314
219.362-046 53914
219.362-050 53314
219.362-054 53128
219.362-066 ..... 55338B
219.362-070 21111
219.362-074 55108
219.367-010 58017
219.367-014 59999
219.367-018 58023
219.367-022 58028
219.367-030 58028
219.367-038 55347
219.367-042 ..... 55338A
219.367-046 53121
219.367-050 ..... 55338A
219.382-010 ..... 55338B
219.387-010 58008
219.387-014 55347
219.387-022 ..... 55328A
219.387-026 58023
219.387-030 58023
219.462-010 53102
219.462-014 55347
219.467-010 53905
219.482-010 53128
219.482-014 53314
219.482-018 55347
219.487-010 ..... 55338B
219.587-010 ..... 55338B
221.132-010 ..... 51002B
221.137-010 ..... 51002B
221.137-014 ..... 51002B
221.137-018 ..... 51002B
221.162-010 58008
221.167-010 58008
221.167-014 58008
221.167-018 58008
221.167-022 58008
221.167-026 58008
221.362-010 ..... 58099B
221.362-014 58005
221.362-018 58008
221.362-022 58008
221.362-026 ..... 58099B
221.362-030 58008
221.367-010 58008
221.367-014 58008
221.367-018 58008
221.367-022 58028
221.367-026 58008
221.367-030 58008
221.367-034 58008
221.367-038 58008
221.367-042 58008
221.367-046 58008
221.367-050 58008
221.367-054 58008
221.367-058 58008
221.367-062 55317
221.367-066 58008
221.367-070 58005
221.367-078 58008
221.367-082 58005
221.367-086 58008
221.367-090 58008
221.382-010 ..... 55328A
221.382-018 58008
221.382-022 58008
221.382-026 55344
221.387-010 58008
221.387-014 53123
221.387-018 58008
221.387-022 58008
221.387-026 58008
221.387-030 58008
221.387-034 58008
221.387-038 55347
221.387-042 55347
221.387-046 58008
221.387-050 58008
221.387-054 58008
221.467-010 58017
221.482-010 58008
221.482-014 58008
221.482-018 58017
221.484-010 58008
221.487-010 58017
221.584-010 ..... 55328A
221.587-010 58017
221.587-014 58008
221.587-018 58023
221.587-022 58023
221.587-026 58017
221.587-030 58017
221.587-034 58017
221.587-038 58008
221.587-042 58008
221.587-046 58017
221.587-050 58008
221.667-010 58008
221.687-014 58017
222.137-010 ..... 51002B
222.137-014 ..... 51002A
222.137-018 ..... 51002B
222.137-022 ..... 51002B
222.137-026 ..... 51002A
222.137-030 ..... 51002B
222.137-034 ..... 51002B
222.137-038 ..... 51002B
222.137-042 ..... 51002B
222.137-046 ..... 51002B
222.137-050 ..... 51002B
222.167-010 58008
222.367-010 58017
222.367-014 58023
222.367-018 58008
222.367-022 57302
222.367-026 53902
222.367-030 55347
222.367-034 55347
222.367-038 58023

222.367-042......58023
222.367-046......83005A
222.367-050......58023
222.367-054......55347
222.367-062......58023
222.367-066......58028
222.367-070......58008
222.384-010......83005A
222.387-010......58017
222.387-014......58028
222.387-018......58023
222.387-022......58028
222.387-026......58023
222.387-030......58023
222.387-034......58023
222.387-038......57302
222.387-042......58023
222.387-046......55347
222.387-050......58028
222.387-054......58021
222.387-058......58023
222.387-062......58023
222.387-066......58017
222.387-074......58017
222.485-010......58017
222.487-010......58023
222.487-014......58026
222.567-010......58028
222.567-014......58028
222.567-018......57302
222.585-010......58017
222.587-014......53902
222.587-018......58028
222.587-022......58023
222.587-026......55347
222.587-030......57302
222.587-032......57302
222.587-034......58028
222.587-038......55347
222.587-042......58017
222.587-046......58017
222.587-050......58017
222.587-054......58023
222.587-058......58028
222.684-010......58023
222.687-010......58017
222.687-014......93998
222.687-018......58017
222.687-022......58028
222.687-026......58017
222.687-030......58028
222.687-034......55347
222.687-038......58023
222.687-042......83005A
222.687-046......58023
229.137-010......51002B
229.137-014......51002B
229.267-010......58099A
229.367-010......58023
229.367-014......58023
229.387-010......58008
229.387-014......58017
229.587-010......55347
229.587-014......58023

229.587-018......58021
229.687-010......58017
230.137-010......41002
230.137-014......51002B
230.137-018......51002A
230.363-010......57305
230.367-010......57305
230.647-010......34047C
230.663-010......57311A
230.667-014......98999A
230.687-010......98999A
235.132-010......51002A
235.132-014......51002B
235.137-010......51002B
235.222-010......31314
235.387-010......55347
235.462-010......57108
235.562-010......57111
235.562-014......57102
235.662-010......99003
235.662-014......57102
235.662-018......57105
235.662-022......57102
235.662-026......57102
236.252-010......43017
236.562-010......57111
236.562-014......57111
237.137-010......51002A
237.137-014......51002A
237.267-010......55305
237.367-010......55305
237.367-014......53117
237.367-018......55305
237.367-022......55305
237.367-026......59999
237.367-030......55344
237.367-034......57199
237.367-038......55305
237.367-042......55305
237.367-046......55305
237.367-050......53802
238.137-010......51002A
238.137-014......51002A
238.137-018......51002A
238.137-022......51002A
238.167-010......53802
238.167-014......53802
238.362-014......53802
238.367-010......53805
238.367-014......53805
238.367-018......53805
238.367-022......55305
238.367-026......53805
238.367-030......53802
238.367-034......55305
238.367-038......53808
239.132-010......51002B
239.137-010......21511D
239.137-014......51002A
239.137-018......51002B
239.137-022......51002B
239.137-026......51002B
239.167-010......21999J
239.167-014......58005

239.227-010 31314
239.267-010 43002
239.362-010 57102
239.362-014 55335
239.367-014 58005
239.367-018 ..... 21999J
239.367-022 58005
239.367-026 57199
239.367-030 58005
239.367-034 55305
239.382-010 57199
239.567-010 ..... 57311A
239.677-010 ..... 57311A
239.687-010 ..... 57311A
239.687-014 ..... 57311A
241.137-010 ..... 51002A
241.137-014 ..... 51002A
241.137-018 ..... 51002A
241.217-010 53302
241.267-010 55314
241.267-014 53305
241.267-018 53302
241.267-022 21105
241.267-026 55344
241.267-030 53117
241.267-034 53123
241.357-010 53508
241.362-010 53311
241.367-010 53508
241.367-014 53123
241.367-018 59999
241.367-022 53508
241.367-026 63035
241.367-030 55347
241.367-034 53123
241.367-038 53505
241.367-042 55347
241.387-010 53123
243.137-010 ..... 51002B
243.362-010 53702
243.362-014 55347
243.367-010 59999
243.367-014 57308
243.367-018 53705
245.362-010 ..... 55328B
245.362-014 55347
245.367-014 55347
245.367-018 55347
245.367-022 55347
245.367-026 55323
245.587-010 55347
247.137-010 ..... 51002A
247.137-014 ..... 51002A
247.367-010 53908
247.382-010 55347
247.387-010 53908
247.387-014 58008
247.387-018 53908
247.387-022 53908
247.667-010 53911
248.137-010 ..... 51002B
248.137-014 ..... 51002B
248.137-018 ..... 51002A
248.167-010 58008

248.362-010 58028
248.362-014 55347
248.367-010 58008
248.367-014 58028
248.367-018 58011
248.367-022 58028
248.367-026 58005
248.367-030 59999
248.382-010 53805
248.387-010 99003
248.387-014 55344
249.137-010 ..... 51002A
249.137-014 ..... 51002A
249.137-018 ..... 51002A
249.137-022 ..... 51002A
249.137-026 ..... 51002A
249.137-030 ..... 51002B
249.137-034 ..... 51002A
249.167-010 ..... 51002A
249.167-014 58005
249.167-018 58008
249.262-010 55305
249.267-010 55347
249.362-010 49017
249.362-014 53121
249.362-018 53121
249.362-022 53121
249.362-026 55323
249.363-010 53902
249.365-010 53902
249.366-010 49017
249.367-010 55347
249.367-014 55347
249.367-018 55347
249.367-022 53114
249.367-026 55347
249.367-030 53708
249.367-034 55344
249.367-042 55323
249.367-046 53902
249.367-058 58023
249.367-062 55347
249.367-066 55326
249.367-070 58005
249.367-074 53905
249.367-078 55347
249.367-082 55305
249.367-086 53905
249.367-090 55314
249.387-010 55347
249.387-014 99003
249.387-018 53505
249.387-022 55347
249.467-010 ..... 49023A
249.587-010 55347
249.587-014 55347
249.587-018 55347
249.687-010 57302
249.687-014 53902
250.157-010 43008
250.257-010 43002
250.257-014 ..... 43014A
250.257-018 ..... 43014A
250.257-022 ..... 43014B

250.357-010 43008
250.357-014 43008
250.357-018 43008
250.357-022 43017
250.357-026 ..... 43014B
251.157-014 43017
251.257-014 43017
251.357-010 43017
251.357-018 43017
251.357-022 43017
251.357-026 43017
252.152-010 43021
252.257-010 43017
252.357-010 43017
252.357-014 43017
253.157-010 43017
253.257-010 43017
253.357-010 43017
254.251-010 ..... 43023B
254.257-010 ..... 43023B
254.357-010 ..... 43023A
254.357-014 ..... 43023B
254.357-018 43017
254.357-022 ..... 43023B
259.157-010 ..... 43099A
259.157-014 43017
259.257-010 ..... 43099A
259.257-014 ..... 49005D
259.257-018 43017
259.257-022 43017
259.357-010 ..... 43099A
259.357-014 ..... 43099A
259.357-018 ..... 43023B
259.357-022 ..... 43099A
259.357-026 ..... 43099A
259.357-030 43017
259.357-034 ..... 43099A
259.357-038 43017
260.257-010 49008
260.357-010 49008
260.357-014 49008
260.357-018 49008
260.357-022 49008
260.357-026 49011
261.351-010 49011
261.354-010 49011
261.357-010 49008
261.357-014 49008
261.357-018 49008
261.357-022 49008
261.357-026 49008
261.357-030 49008
261.357-034 49008
261.357-038 49008
261.357-042 49011
261.357-046 49011
261.357-050 49011
261.357-054 49011
261.357-058 49011
261.357-062 49011
261.357-066 49011
261.357-070 49011
261.357-074 49011
262.157-010 ..... 49005B

262.357-010 ..... 49005B
262.357-014 49008
262.357-018 49011
262.357-022 ..... 49005B
269.357-010 49008
269.357-014 49008
269.357-018 ..... 43023A
270.352-010 49011
270.357-010 49008
270.357-014 49008
270.357-018 49011
270.357-022 49011
270.357-026 49011
270.357-030 49011
270.357-034 49011
270.357-038 49011
271.257-010 ..... 49005C
271.352-010 ..... 49005C
271.352-014 ..... 49005C
271.354-010 49011
271.357-010 ..... 49005C
271.357-014 49008
272.357-010 ..... 49005A
272.357-014 ..... 49005A
272.357-018 ..... 49005A
272.357-022 49011
273.253-010 ..... 49005D
273.353-010 49011
273.357-010 ..... 49005D
273.357-014 ..... 43099A
273.357-018 49011
273.357-022 49008
273.357-026 ..... 49005D
273.357-030 49011
273.357-034 49011
274.157-010 ..... 49005D
274.257-010 ..... 49005D
274.357-010 ..... 49005D
274.357-014 49008
274.357-018 ..... 49005D
274.357-022 ..... 49005D
274.357-026 49008
274.357-030 ..... 49005A
274.357-034 49008
274.357-038 ..... 49005D
274.357-042 49008
274.357-046 ..... 49005D
274.357-050 ..... 49005D
274.357-054 ..... 49005D
274.357-058 ..... 49005D
274.357-062 49008
274.357-066 49008
274.357-070 ..... 49005D
274.357-074 ..... 49005D
274.357-078 ..... 49005D
275.257-010 ..... 49005C
275.357-010 49008
275.357-014 49008
275.357-018 49008
275.357-022 49008
275.357-026 49008
275.357-030 49008
275.357-034 49008
275.357-038 49008

275.357-042 49008
275.357-046 49008
275.357-050 49008
275.357-054 49008
276.257-010 ...... 49005F
276.257-014 ...... 49005G
276.257-018 49011
276.257-022 ...... 49005F
276.354-010 49011
276.357-010 49008
276.357-014 ...... 49005G
276.357-018 ...... 49005A
277.354-010 49011
277.357-010 49008
277.357-014 49008
277.357-018 49008
277.357-022 49008
277.357-026 49008
277.357-030 49008
277.357-034 49011
277.357-038 49011
277.357-042 49011
277.357-046 49011
277.357-050 49011
277.357-054 49011
277.357-058 49011
277.357-062 49011
277.357-066 49011
277.457-010 49011
279.157-010 49008
279.357-010 ...... 49032A
279.357-014 49008
279.357-018 49008
279.357-022 49008
279.357-026 49008
279.357-030 49008
279.357-034 49008
279.357-038 49026
279.357-042 ...... 43099A
279.357-046 49011
279.357-050 49011
279.357-054 49011
279.357-058 49011
279.357-062 49014
290.477-010 49017
290.477-014 49011
290.477-018 49017
291.157-010 41002
291.357-010 49026
291.454-010 49026
291.457-010 49026
291.457-014 49026
291.457-018 49026
291.457-022 49026
292.137-010 ...... 51002B
292.137-014 81011
292.353-010 97117
292.363-010 97117
292.457-010 49026
292.463-010 97117
292.483-010 97117
292.667-010 97117
292.687-010 97117
293.137-010 41002

293.157-010 ...... 43099B
293.357-010 ...... 43099B
293.357-014 ...... 43099B
293.357-018 ...... 49032A
293.357-022 ...... 43099B
294.257-010 ...... 49999A
294.567-010 ...... 49023A
294.667-010 55347
295.137-010 ...... 51002A
295.357-010 49017
295.357-014 49017
295.357-018 49017
295.367-010 49017
295.367-014 49017
295.367-018 55323
295.367-022 53105
295.367-026 49017
295.467-010 49017
295.467-014 49017
295.467-018 49017
295.467-022 49017
295.467-026 49017
296.357-010 ...... 49999C
296.367-010 ...... 49999D
296.367-014 ...... 49999D
297.354-010 ...... 49032A
297.354-014 ...... 49032A
297.357-010 ...... 49032A
297.367-010 ...... 49032A
297.451-010 ...... 49032A
297.454-010 ...... 49032A
297.667-014 ...... 49032B
298.081-010 34044
298.381-010 34044
299.137-010 41002
299.137-014 41002
299.137-018 81008
299.137-022 41002
299.137-026 41002
299.167-010 49008
299.251-010 ...... 49005A
299.357-010 43017
299.357-014 49026
299.357-018 ...... 49999C
299.361-010 32514
299.361-014 32514
299.364-010 ...... 49999B
299.364-014 ...... 49999D
299.367-010 ...... 49999C
299.367-014 49021
299.367-018 49017
299.377-010 49011
299.387-010 ...... 49999B
299.387-014 58026
299.387-018 ...... 49999D
299.467-010 49011
299.477-010 ...... 57311A
299.587-010 58017
299.647-010 ...... 49032B
299.667-010 ...... 98999A
299.667-014 ...... 49999D
299.677-010 49011
299.677-014 49021
299.687-010 ...... 98999A

299.687-014 ..... 49032A
301.137-010 62031
301.474-010 62031
301.677-010 62041
301.687-010 62031
301.687-014 62031
301.687-018 ..... 79999N
302.685-010 62031
302.687-010 62031
305.281-010 62061
309.137-010 62031
309.354-010 68035
309.367-010 ..... 63099E
309.674-010 62031
309.674-014 62061
309.677-010 62061
309.677-014 62041
310.137-010 65002
310.137-018 ..... 61099B
310.137-022 ..... 61099B
310.137-026 ..... 61099B
310.267-010 ..... 21999J
310.357-010 ..... 65008B
311.137-010 ..... 61099B
311.137-014 ..... 61099B
311.137-018 ..... 61099B
311.137-022 ..... 61099B
311.472-010 65041
311.477-010 65011
311.477-014 65017
311.477-018 ..... 65008A
311.477-022 ..... 65008A
311.477-026 ..... 65008A
311.477-030 ..... 65008A
311.477-034 65011
311.477-038 65017
311.674-010 65017
311.674-014 ..... 65038A
311.674-018 ..... 65008A
311.677-010 65014
311.677-014 65017
311.677-018 65014
312.474-010 65005
312.477-010 65005
312.677-010 65005
312.687-010 65014
313.131-010 ..... 61099A
313.131-014 ..... 61099A
313.131-018 ..... 61099A
313.131-022 ..... 61099A
313.131-026 ..... 61099A
313.281-010 65026
313.361-010 65021
313.361-014 65026
313.361-018 65026
313.361-026 65032
313.361-030 65026
313.361-034 65026
313.361-038 65021
313.374-010 65032
313.374-014 65035
313.381-010 65021
313.381-014 65032
313.381-018 65021

313.381-022 65026
313.381-026 65021
313.381-030 65028
313.381-034 65026
313.684-010 ..... 65038A
313.687-010 ..... 65038A
315.131-010 ..... 61099A
315.131-014 ..... 61099A
315.137-010 ..... 61099A
315.137-014 ..... 61099A
315.361-010 65028
315.361-022 65026
315.371-010 65028
315.381-010 65028
315.381-014 65026
315.381-018 65026
315.381-022 65028
315.381-026 65028
316.661-010 ..... 65038A
316.681-010 65023
316.684-010 ..... 65038A
316.684-014 ..... 65038A
316.684-018 65023
316.684-022 65023
317.384-010 ..... 65038A
317.664-010 ..... 65038A
317.684-010 ..... 65038A
317.684-014 ..... 65038A
317.687-010 ..... 65038A
318.137-010 ..... 61099B
318.687-010 ..... 65038B
318.687-014 ..... 65038B
318.687-018 ..... 65038B
319.137-010 ..... 61099B
319.137-014 ..... 15026B
319.137-018 ..... 15026B
319.137-022 ..... 61099B
319.137-026 ..... 61099B
319.137-030 ..... 61099B
319.464-010 ..... 65099A
319.464-014 ..... 65099A
319.467-010 ..... 65099B
319.474-010 65017
319.484-010 ..... 65038A
319.677-010 ..... 65038A
319.677-014 65011
319.687-010 65014
320.137-010 ..... 15026B
320.137-014 ..... 15026A
321.137-010 61008
321.137-014 ..... 61099C
323.137-010 ..... 61099C
323.687-010 67002
323.687-014 67002
323.687-018 67002
324.137-010 ..... 61099C
324.137-014 ..... 61099C
324.477-010 68023
324.577-010 ..... 69999B
324.677-010 68023
324.677-014 ..... 69999B
329.137-010 ..... 61099C
329.161-010 ..... 19999A
329.467-010 ..... 69999B

329.677-010......69999B
329.683-010......67099
330.371-010......68002
330.371-014......68002
331.674-010......68008
331.674-014......68008
332.271-010......68005A
332.271-014......68005A
332.271-018......68005A
332.361-010......68005A
333.071-010......68005B
333.271-010......68005B
334.374-010......69999B
334.677-010......69999B
335.677-010......68032A
335.677-014......68032A
338.371-010......39014
338.371-014......39014
339.137-010......19999D
339.361-010......68005A
339.371-010......68005C
339.371-014......69999E
339.571-010......69999E
339.687-010......58023
340.367-010......68014A
340.477-010......68014A
341.137-010......61099E
341.367-010......68014A
341.464-010......68014A
341.665-010......68014A
341.677-010......68014A
341.683-010......68014A
342.137-010......61099E
342.357-010......68014A
342.657-010......68014A
342.657-014......68014A
342.663-010......68014A
342.665-010......68014A
342.667-010......68014A
342.667-014......68014A
342.677-010......68014A
343.137-010......19999E
343.137-014......19999E
343.367-010......68014B
343.367-014......63035
343.464-010......68014B
343.467-010......68014B
343.467-014......68014A
343.467-022......68014B
343.577-010......68014A
343.687-010......83005A
344.137-010......61099C
344.667-010......68021
344.677-010......68021
344.677-014......68021
346.261-010......68032B
346.361-010......68032B
346.374-010......69999E
346.667-010......68032A
346.674-010......69999E
346.677-010......68032A
346.677-014......68032A
346.677-018......68032A
349.224-010......19999A
349.247-010......34056D
349.367-010......34058L
349.367-014......34058L
349.477-010......68014A
349.664-010......68014A
349.665-010......34058L
349.667-010......69999D
349.667-014......69999D
349.673-010......68021
349.674-010......68014A
349.677-010......68014A
349.677-014......68014A
349.677-018......68021
349.680-010......85947
350.137-010......61099B
350.137-014......61099B
350.137-018......61099C
350.137-022......61099C
350.137-026......61099C
350.677-010......65008A
350.677-014......68028
350.677-018......68028
350.677-022......68028
350.677-026......65008A
350.677-030......65008A
351.677-010......68028
352.137-010......61099C
352.167-010......27311
352.367-010......68026
352.367-014......68026
352.377-010......69999A
352.577-010......68028
352.667-010......68014A
352.667-014......69999E
352.677-010......68028
352.677-014......69999A
352.677-018......65008A
353.137-010......61099C
353.161-010......68017A
353.164-010......68017A
353.167-010......68017A
353.363-010......68017B
353.364-010......68017A
353.367-010......68017B
353.367-014......68017B
353.367-018......68017B
353.367-022......68017B
353.667-010......68017B
354.374-010......66008
354.377-010......32199
354.377-014......66011
354.677-010......32199
355.354-010......66017
355.374-010......66023
355.374-014......66008
355.377-010......66021
355.377-014......66014
355.377-018......66014
355.667-010......66099A
355.674-010......68038
355.674-014......66008
355.674-018......66008
355.674-022......66097
355.677-014......66099B
355.687-014.....69999E
357.477-010.....68023
357.677-010.....68023
358.137-010.....61099C
358.677-010.....69999B
358.677-014.....69999B
358.677-018.....68032A
358.687-010.....67005
359.137-010.....19999A
359.363-010.....66097
359.367-010.....69999D
359.367-014.....69999B
359.567-010.....69999B
359.573-010.....68035
359.667-010.....69999E
359.673-010.....97114
359.673-014.....97114
359.677-010.....68038
359.677-014.....68041
359.677-018.....68038
359.677-022.....69999A
359.677-026.....68038
359.677-030.....69999E
359.685-010.....69999E
359.687-010.....68041
361.137-010.....81008
361.587-010.....83005A
361.665-010.....92726
361.682-010.....92726
361.684-010.....92726
361.684-014.....92726
361.684-018.....89514
361.685-010.....92923
361.685-014.....92726
361.685-018.....92726
361.685-022.....92728
361.686-010.....98502
361.687-010.....83005A
361.687-014.....83005A
361.687-018.....98999A
361.687-022.....83005A
361.687-026.....98999A
361.687-030.....98999A
362.381-010.....89514
362.382-010.....92726
362.382-014.....92726
362.684-010.....93998
362.684-014.....92726
362.684-018.....93997
362.684-022.....93998
362.684-026.....92726
362.685-010.....92726
362.686-010.....98999A
362.686-014.....98999A
362.687-010.....98999A
362.687-014.....98999A
362.687-018.....98999A
363.681-010.....89517
363.682-010.....92728
363.682-014.....92728
363.682-018.....92728
363.684-010.....92728
363.684-014.....92728
363.684-018.....93921
363.685-010.....92728
363.685-014.....92728
363.685-018.....92728
363.685-022.....92728
363.685-026.....92728
363.686-010.....98502
363.687-010.....98999A
363.687-014.....98999A
363.687-018.....98999A
363.687-022.....98999A
364.361-010.....89521
364.361-014.....89521
364.381-010.....93947E
364.684-010.....89521
364.684-014.....93998
364.684-018.....93997
364.687-010.....98999A
364.687-014.....98999A
365.131-010.....31311A
365.361-010.....89511
365.361-014.....89511
365.674-010.....98999B
366.677-010.....69999B
369.137-010.....81008
369.137-014.....81008
369.167-010.....81008
369.367-010.....49017
369.367-014.....49017
369.384-010.....93997
369.384-014.....93997
369.387-010.....98999A
369.467-010.....49017
369.477-010.....49017
369.477-014.....49017
369.587-010.....49017
369.677-010.....49017
369.684-010.....93998
369.684-014.....92726
369.684-018.....85998
369.685-010.....92726
369.685-014.....92726
369.685-018.....92728
369.685-022.....92726
369.685-026.....92923
369.685-030.....92998
369.685-034.....92923
369.686-010.....98502
369.687-010.....83005A
369.687-014.....83005A
369.687-018.....98999A
369.687-022.....83005A
369.687-026.....83005A
369.687-030.....83005A
371.362-010.....97802
371.567-010.....63044
371.667-010.....63044
372.137-010.....61005
372.167-010.....57199
372.167-014.....19999F
372.167-018.....61005
372.167-022.....19999F
372.267-010.....63038
372.363-010.....63014A
372.367-010.....63099E
372.367-014.....63017
372.563-010.....63047
372.567-010.....63047
372.567-014.....63017
372.667-010.....63047
372.667-014.....63047
372.667-018.....63017
372.667-022.....63044
372.667-026.....68014A
372.667-030.....63047
372.667-034.....63047
372.667-038.....63047
372.667-042.....63099E
372.677-010.....63017
373.117-010.....19005A
373.134-010.....61002A
373.167-010.....61002A
373.167-014.....61002A
373.167-018.....61002A
373.267-010.....63002A
373.267-014.....63002B
373.267-018.....63002B
373.363-010.....63008A
373.364-010.....63008A
373.367-010.....63002A
373.663-010.....63008A
375.117-010.....19005A
375.133-010.....61005
375.137-010.....61005
375.137-014.....61005
375.137-018.....61005
375.137-022.....51002B
375.137-026.....61005
375.137-030.....61005
375.137-034.....61005
375.137-038.....51002A
375.163-010.....61005
375.163-014.....63014B
375.167-010.....61005
375.167-014.....61005
375.167-018.....81002
375.167-022.....61005
375.167-026.....19005A
375.167-030.....61005
375.167-034.....61005
375.167-038.....61005
375.167-042.....63028A
375.167-046.....61005
375.167-050.....61005
375.167-054.....13005B
375.227-010.....31314
375.263-010.....63014A
375.263-014.....63014A
375.263-018.....63014A
375.264-010.....63014A
375.267-010.....63011A
375.267-014.....63011A
375.267-018.....63011A
375.267-022.....63011A
375.267-026.....21999J
375.267-030.....63014A
375.267-034.....63011A
375.267-038.....63028B
375.267-042.....63014A

375.362-010..... 55347
375.363-010..... 63014A
375.367-010..... 63017
375.367-014..... 63014A
375.367-018..... 63014A
375.384-010..... 63011B
375.387-010..... 63011B
375.587-010..... 63021
376.137-010..... 19999F
376.167-010..... 63038
376.267-010..... 63035
376.267-014..... 63035
376.267-018..... 63035
376.267-022..... 63035
376.367-010..... 63035
376.367-014..... 63035
376.367-018..... 63035
376.367-022..... 63035
376.367-026..... 63035
376.667-010..... 63047
376.667-014..... 63035
376.667-018..... 63038
377.134-010..... 61005
377.137-010..... 61005
377.137-014..... 61005
377.137-018..... 61005
377.167-010..... 61005
377.263-010..... 63032
377.264-010..... 63028A
377.267-010..... 63026
377.363-010..... 63032
377.667-010..... 63023
377.667-014..... 63032
377.667-018..... 63032
378.132-010..... 99003
378.137-010..... 99003
378.161-010..... 99003
378.227-010..... 31314
378.227-014..... 99003
378.227-018..... 99003
378.267-010..... 99003
378.267-014..... 21999J
378.281-010..... 99003
378.362-010..... 99003
378.363-010..... 99003
378.367-010..... 99003
378.367-014..... 99003
378.367-018..... 99003
378.367-022..... 99003
378.367-026..... 99003
378.367-030..... 99003
378.382-010..... 99003
378.382-014..... 99003
378.382-018..... 99003
378.464-010..... 99003
378.663-010..... 99003
378.682-010..... 99003
378.682-014..... 99003
378.683-010..... 99003
378.683-014..... 99003
378.683-018..... 99003
378.684-010..... 99003
378.684-014..... 99003
378.684-018..... 99003
378.684-022......99003
378.684-026......99003
378.684-030......99003
378.687-010......99003
379.132-010......51002A
379.137-010......63099C
379.137-014......53708
379.137-018......19005A
379.137-022......19999F
379.162-010......58002
379.167-010......63041
379.227-010......63099C
379.263-010......63099C
379.263-014......63014A
379.267-010......63041
379.362-010......58002
379.362-014......58002
379.362-018......58002
379.364-010......83008C
379.364-014......63099B
379.367-010......63099E
379.384-010......85999F
379.664-010......63099B
379.667-010......63047
379.667-014......63099B
379.673-010......63099C
379.687-010......63002A
379.687-014......67008
381.137-010......61099D
381.137-014......51002B
381.687-010......58023
381.687-014......67005
381.687-018......67005
381.687-022......67005
381.687-026......67005
381.687-030......67005
381.687-034......67005
382.137-010......61099D
382.664-010......67005
383.361-010......67008
383.364-010......67008
383.684-010......67008
383.687-010......67008
388.367-010......61099C
388.663-010......67011
389.134-010......19999D
389.137-010......61099D
389.664-010......67005
389.667-010......67005
389.683-010......67005
389.684-010......67008
389.687-010......67099
389.687-014......67005
389.687-018......67099
401.137-010......72002A
401.137-014......72002A
401.161-010......79999D
401.683-010......79021
401.683-014......79021
401.687-010......79856
402.131-010......72002A
402.161-010......79999D
402.663-010......79021
402.687-010......79856
402.687-014......79856
403.131-010......72002A
403.131-014......72002A
403.161-010......79999D
403.161-014......79999D
403.683-010......79021
403.687-010......79856
403.687-014......79856
403.687-018......79856
403.687-022......79856
404.131-010......72002A
404.131-014......72002A
404.161-010......79999D
404.663-010......79021
404.685-010......79021
404.686-010......79856
404.687-010......79856
404.687-014......79856
405.131-010......72002E
405.137-010......72002E
405.161-010......79999C
405.161-014......79999C
405.161-018......79999C
405.361-010......79999C
405.683-010......79021
405.683-014......79021
405.684-010......79005
405.684-014......79041
405.687-010......79041
405.687-014......79005
405.687-018......79041
406.134-010......72002D
406.134-014......72002D
406.137-010......72002D
406.137-014......72002D
406.381-010......79999P
406.683-010......79030B
406.684-010......79030B
406.684-014......79030B
406.684-018......79030B
406.687-010......79030B
407.131-010......72002A
407.161-010......79999D
407.663-010......79021
407.687-010......79856
408.131-010......15032
408.137-010......72002A
408.137-014......72002D
408.161-010......79030B
408.181-010......79033
408.364-010......79041
408.381-010......79999A
408.381-014......79999A
408.662-010......79036
408.664-010......73099A
408.667-010......73099A
408.684-010......79030B
408.684-014......79036
408.684-018......79033
408.687-010......79999A
408.687-014......79041
408.687-018......79041
409.117-010......72002A
409.131-010......72002A
409.137-010 ..... 72002A
409.137-014 ..... 72002A
409.667-010 ..... 98999A
409.683-010 79021
409.683-014 79021
409.684-010 ..... 79999B
409.685-010 79021
409.685-014 ..... 79999B
409.686-010 79021
409.687-010 79011
409.687-014 ..... 79999B
409.687-018 79856
410.131-010 ..... 72002B
410.131-014 ..... 72002B
410.131-018 ..... 72002B
410.131-022 ..... 72002B
410.134-010 ..... 72002B
410.134-014 ..... 72002B
410.134-018 ..... 72002C
410.134-022 ..... 72002B
410.137-010 ..... 72002B
410.137-014 ..... 72002B
410.137-018 ..... 72002C
410.161-010 79015
410.161-014 79015
410.161-018 79015
410.161-022 79015
410.357-010 58017
410.364-010 79858
410.664-010 79858
410.674-010 ..... 79017A
410.674-014 79858
410.674-018 79858
410.674-022 ..... 79017A
410.684-010 79858
410.684-014 79858
410.685-010 79858
410.687-010 79858
410.687-014 79858
410.687-018 93998
410.687-022 79858
410.687-026 79011
411.131-010 ..... 72002B
411.137-010 ..... 72002B
411.161-010 79015
411.161-014 79015
411.161-018 79858
411.267-010 ..... 21911R
411.364-010 ..... 24502C
411.364-014 79858
411.384-010 ..... 24502B
411.584-010 79858
411.684-010 79858
411.684-014 79858
411.687-010 79011
411.687-014 79011
411.687-018 79858
411.687-022 79858
411.687-026 79858
412.131-010 ..... 72002B
412.137-010 ..... 72002C
412.161-010 ..... 79999J
412.674-010 ..... 79017A
412.674-014 ..... 79017A
412.684-010..... 79858
412.687-010..... 98799B
413.161-010..... 79999D
413.161-014..... 79015
413.161-018..... 79999D
413.687-010..... 79999P
413.687-014..... 79858
413.687-018..... 79858
418.137-010..... 72002C
418.137-014..... 72002C
418.381-010..... 79017B
418.384-010..... 24502B
418.384-014..... 24502B
418.674-010..... 79017C
418.677-010..... 79017C
419.224-010..... 79016
421.161-010..... 79999D
421.683-010..... 79021
421.687-010..... 79855
429.387-010..... 79011
429.587-010..... 79011
429.685-010..... 79021
429.685-014..... 79021
429.686-010..... 98502
441.132-010..... 79999E
441.683-010..... 79999E
441.684-010..... 79999E
441.684-014..... 79999E
441.684-018..... 79999E
441.684-022..... 79999E
442.684-010..... 79999E
443.664-010..... 79999E
443.684-010..... 79999E
446.133-010..... 72002G
446.134-010..... 72002G
446.161-010..... 79999G
446.161-014..... 79999E
446.663-010..... 79999E
446.684-010..... 79999G
446.684-014..... 79999E
446.684-018..... 79999G
446.687-010..... 79011
446.687-014..... 79999G
447.684-010..... 79999H
447.687-010..... 79999H
447.687-014..... 79999H
447.687-018..... 79999H
447.687-022..... 79999H
447.687-026..... 79999H
449.664-010..... 79999E
449.667-010..... 79999E
449.674-010..... 79017D
449.687-010..... 79999E
451.137-010..... 72002E
451.137-014..... 72002E
451.687-010..... 79002A
451.687-014..... 79002A
451.687-018..... 79002A
451.687-022..... 79002A
452.134-010..... 61002B
452.167-010..... 63005
452.364-010..... 79002B
452.364-014..... 63008B
452.367-010..... 63005

452.367-014......63005
452.687-010......79002A
452.687-014......63008B
452.687-018......79002A
453.687-010......79002A
453.687-014......79002A
454.134-010......72002F
454.384-010......73002
454.683-010......73011
454.684-010......73002
454.684-014......73002
454.684-018......73002
454.684-022......73099A
454.684-026......73002
454.687-010......73002
454.687-014......73099A
454.687-018......73099B
455.134-010......72002F
455.367-010......79008
455.487-010......79008
455.664-010......73099B
455.684-010......73099B
455.687-010......73099B
459.133-010......72002F
459.137-010......72002F
459.387-010......73099D
459.687-010......73099A
461.134-010......79999F
461.661-010......79999F
461.664-010......79999F
461.684-010......79999F
461.684-014......79999F
461.684-018......79999F
500.131-010......81008
500.132-010......81008
500.134-010......81008
500.287-010......83005A
500.362-010......91917
500.362-014......91921
500.380-010......91917
500.380-014......91917
500.381-010......89111
500.384-010......91921
500.384-014......91921
500.485-010......91921
500.682-010......91921
500.684-010......91921
500.684-014......93998
500.684-018......91921
500.684-022......93947E
500.684-026......91921
500.684-030......91921
500.684-034......91921
500.685-010......92198
500.685-014......91921
500.686-010......98999B
500.687-010......98999A
501.130-010......81008
501.137-010......81008
501.362-010......91923
501.485-010......91926
501.685-010......91926
501.685-014......91926
501.685-018......91926
501.685-022......91926
502.130-010......81008
502.362-010......91911
502.381-010......89126E
502.381-014......89905B
502.382-010......91911
502.382-014......83005A
502.384-010......89126K
502.482-010......91911
502.482-014......91911
502.482-018......91908
502.664-010......93997
502.664-014......93941
502.664-018......98999B
502.682-010......91911
502.682-014......91908
502.682-018......89126E
502.684-010......93944D
502.684-014......93944D
502.684-018......93998
502.684-022......93944D
502.685-010......91911
502.685-014......91911
502.686-010......98999A
502.687-010......98999A
502.687-014......93941
502.687-018......98999A
503.137-010......81008
503.362-010......92997
503.362-014......92198
503.684-010......93999
503.685-010......91926
503.685-014......92998
503.685-018......92198
503.685-022......92923
503.685-026......92958
503.685-030......92958
503.685-034......92958
503.685-038......92198
503.685-042......92198
503.685-046......92198
503.686-010......98999B
503.687-010......98905
504.131-010......81008
504.281-010......83002A
504.360-010......91928
504.380-010......91928
504.380-014......91928
504.382-010......91932
504.382-014......91932
504.382-018......91932
504.387-010......83005A
504.485-010......92923
504.665-010......97989A
504.665-014......91935
504.682-010......91932
504.682-014......91932
504.682-018......91932
504.682-022......91932
504.682-026......91932
504.685-010......91932
504.685-014......91932
504.685-018......98999B
504.685-022......91932
504.685-026.....91932
504.685-030.....92923
504.686-010.....98999A
504.686-014.....98502
504.686-018.....98999A
504.686-022.....98502
504.687-010.....91932
505.130-010.....81008
505.130-014.....81008
505.380-010.....92197
505.382-010.....91923
505.382-014.....91926
505.482-010.....91926
505.682-010.....91926
505.684-010.....93947E
505.684-014.....93947E
505.685-010.....91926
505.685-014.....91926
505.685-018.....91926
509.130-010.....81008
509.130-014.....81008
509.132-010.....81008
509.362-010.....92198
509.382-010.....91926
509.382-014.....92198
509.384-010.....92198
509.462-010.....91923
509.485-010.....92965
509.485-014.....92198
509.565-010.....92923
509.566-010.....98999A
509.584-010.....83005A
509.666-010.....98502
509.684-010.....93947E
509.685-010.....98999B
509.685-014.....92958
509.685-018.....92923
509.685-022.....91926
509.685-026.....91926
509.685-030.....91926
509.685-034.....91926
509.685-038.....91926
509.685-042.....92198
509.685-046.....92974
509.685-050.....92962
509.685-054.....92198
509.686-014.....98502
509.686-018.....83005A
509.687-010.....98999A
509.687-014.....98999A
509.687-018.....93998
509.687-022.....83005A
509.687-026.....98502
510.465-010.....92965
510.465-014.....92965
510.685-010.....92965
510.685-014.....92965
510.685-018.....92965
510.685-022.....92965
510.685-026.....92965
510.685-030.....92965
511.130-010.....81008
511.132-010.....81008
511.135-010.....81008
511.382-010.....92935
511.385-010.....92962
511.462-010.....92962
511.465-010.....92962
511.482-010.....92923
511.482-014.....92962
511.482-018.....92998
511.485-010.....92962
511.485-014.....92962
511.562-010.....92962
511.565-010.....92962
511.565-014.....92923
511.565-018.....92962
511.582-010.....92962
511.585-010.....92962
511.586-010.....98999A
511.662-010.....92962
511.664-010.....92962
511.667-010.....98999A
511.667-014.....83005A
511.682-010.....92198
511.685-010.....92962
511.685-014.....92962
511.685-018.....92962
511.685-022.....92958
511.685-026.....92962
511.685-030.....92962
511.685-034.....92962
511.685-038.....92962
511.685-042.....92962
511.685-046.....92965
511.685-050.....92962
511.685-054.....92962
511.685-058.....98999B
511.685-062.....92962
511.685-066.....92958
511.686-010.....98999A
511.687-010.....98905
511.687-014.....98999A
511.687-018.....98999A
511.687-022.....93998
511.687-026.....98999A
512.130-010.....81008
512.132-010.....81008
512.132-014.....81008
512.132-018.....81008
512.132-022.....81008
512.135-010.....81008
512.362-010.....91935
512.362-014.....91935
512.362-018.....91935
512.382-010.....91935
512.382-014.....91935
512.382-018.....91935
512.467-010.....83005A
512.487-010.....83005A
512.662-010.....91935
512.666-010.....98999A
512.667-010.....83005A
512.683-010.....92198
512.684-010.....98999B
512.684-014.....91935
512.685-010.....91935
512.685-014.....92998
512.685-018.....92923
512.685-022.....91935
512.686-010.....98502
512.687-010.....93998
512.687-014.....98999A
513.132-010.....81008
513.362-010.....92923
513.462-010.....92923
513.565-010.....92923
513.587-010.....98999A
513.667-010.....98999A
513.682-010.....92923
513.685-010.....97989A
514.130-010.....81008
514.130-014.....81008
514.131-010.....81008
514.134-010.....81008
514.137-010.....81008
514.137-014.....81008
514.360-010.....91908
514.362-010.....91911
514.382-010.....91908
514.562-010.....91911
514.567-010.....98999A
514.582-010.....91911
514.584-010.....93941
514.662-010.....91911
514.664-010.....93998
514.664-014.....93998
514.667-010.....98999A
514.667-014.....98999A
514.667-018.....98999A
514.682-010.....91911
514.682-014.....92198
514.684-010.....93941
514.684-014.....93941
514.684-018.....85128A
514.684-022.....93941
514.685-010.....91911
514.685-014.....91911
514.685-018.....91911
514.685-022.....92965
514.685-026.....91914
514.687-010.....83005A
514.687-014.....98999A
514.687-018.....98999A
515.130-010.....81008
515.132-010.....81008
515.382-010.....95099
515.567-010.....83005A
515.585-010.....92965
515.685-010.....92965
515.685-014.....92965
515.685-018.....92965
515.686-010.....98502
515.687-010.....92965
518.361-010.....89902
518.361-014.....89902
518.361-018.....89902
518.380-010.....91908
518.381-010.....89126C
518.381-014.....89902
518.381-018.....89902
518.381-022.....89126C

518.484-010 ..... 93944A
518.664-010 93941
518.682-010 91911
518.683-010 92974
518.684-010 ..... 98999B
518.684-014 ..... 93944A
518.684-018 ..... 98999A
518.684-022 93999
518.684-026 93999
518.685-010 92923
518.685-014 91911
518.685-018 91911
518.685-022 91911
518.685-026 91911
518.685-030 91914
518.687-010 ..... 83005A
518.687-014 93999
518.687-018 ..... 98999A
518.687-022 93999
519.130-010 81008
519.130-014 81008
519.130-018 81008
519.130-022 81008
519.130-026 81008
519.130-030 81008
519.131-010 81008
519.131-014 81008
519.132-010 81008
519.132-014 81008
519.132-018 81008
519.132-022 81008
519.134-010 81008
519.137-010 81008
519.137-014 81017
519.362-010 92198
519.362-014 92198
519.387-010 ..... 83005A
519.484-010 92198
519.484-014 ..... 83005A
519.485-010 92965
519.485-014 ..... 98999B
519.565-010 92998
519.565-014 ..... 98999A
519.582-010 92198
519.585-010 ..... 83005A
519.585-014 92998
519.585-018 ..... 83005A
519.663-010 92198
519.663-014 97947
519.663-018 92198
519.664-010 98905
519.664-014 ..... 85128A
519.665-010 92998
519.665-014 92923
519.665-018 92962
519.667-010 ..... 85128A
519.667-014 ..... 98999A
519.683-010 97944
519.683-014 97947
519.684-010 85126
519.684-014 ..... 85128A
519.684-018 93953
519.684-022 85126
519.684-026 ..... 85999A
519.685-010 92923
519.685-014 92998
519.685-018 92923
519.685-022 92923
519.685-026 92965
519.685-030 92965
519.686-010 98502
519.687-010 93998
519.687-014 ...... 98999A
519.687-018 93998
519.687-022 ...... 98999A
519.687-026 ...... 98999A
519.687-030 93999
519.687-034 93998
519.687-038 ...... 98999A
519.687-042 ...... 83005A
520.132-010 81008
520.132-014 81008
520.136-010 81008
520.137-010 81008
520.361-010 89808
520.362-010 92965
520.362-014 92965
520.382-010 92965
520.382-014 92965
520.384-010 89805
520.385-010 92965
520.387-010 ...... 83005A
520.462-010 92965
520.485-010 92965
520.485-014 92965
520.485-018 92965
520.485-022 92965
520.485-026 92965
520.485-030 92962
520.487-010 ...... 83005A
520.487-014 89899
520.487-018 ...... 83005A
520.565-010 92965
520.585-010 92965
520.585-014 92965
520.585-018 92965
520.585-022 92965
520.585-026 92965
520.587-010 93998
520.662-010 92965
520.665-010 92965
520.665-014 92965
520.665-018 92965
520.682-010 92965
520.682-014 92968
520.682-018 92998
520.682-022 92944
520.682-026 92997
520.682-030 92971
520.682-034 92971
520.684-010 93997
520.684-014 93998
520.685-010 92965
520.685-014 92965
520.685-018 92965
520.685-022 92965
520.685-026 92965
520.685-030 92965
520.685-034 92965
520.685-038 92971
520.685-042 92998
520.685-046 92965
520.685-050 92965
520.685-054 92965
520.685-058 92971
520.685-062 92971
520.685-066 92965
520.685-070 92965
520.685-074 92965
520.685-078 92971
520.685-082 92917
520.685-086 92971
520.685-090 92965
520.685-094 92965
520.685-098 92965
520.685-102 92971
520.685-106 92965
520.685-110 92965
520.685-114 92965
520.685-118 92965
520.685-122 92965
520.685-130 92965
520.685-134 92965
520.685-138 92965
520.685-142 92965
520.685-146 92965
520.685-150 92965
520.685-154 92965
520.685-158 92965
520.685-162 92965
520.685-166 92965
520.685-170 92965
520.685-174 92974
520.685-178 92971
520.685-182 92971
520.685-186 92971
520.685-190 92971
520.685-194 92965
520.685-198 92971
520.685-202 92965
520.685-206 92965
520.685-210 92974
520.685-214 92971
520.685-218 92974
520.685-222 92965
520.685-226 92965
520.685-230 92965
520.685-234 92965
520.686-010 98502
520.686-014 98502
520.686-018 ...... 98999A
520.686-022 ...... 98999A
520.686-026 ...... 83005A
520.686-030 98502
520.686-034 98502
520.686-038 92998
520.687-010 ...... 98799B
520.687-014 ...... 98999A
520.687-018 93999
520.687-022 ...... 98999A
520.687-026 ...... 83005A
520.687-030 93998
520.687-034 93998
520.687-038 ..... 98799B
520.687-042 ..... 83005A
520.687-046 ..... 98999A
520.687-050 93998
520.687-054 93998
520.687-058 ..... 98999A
520.687-062 93998
520.687-066 ..... 98999A
521.130-010 81008
521.130-014 81008
521.131-010 81008
521.132-010 81008
521.132-014 81008
521.137-010 81008
521.362-010 92962
521.362-014 92965
521.362-018 92962
521.365-010 92962
521.382-010 92962
521.382-014 92962
521.385-010 92962
521.462-010 92962
521.565-010 97953
521.565-014 92962
521.565-018 92962
521.582-010 92962
521.585-010 92962
521.585-014 92965
521.585-018 92965
521.662-010 92965
521.665-010 92962
521.665-014 92962
521.665-018 92962
521.665-022 92962
521.665-026 92962
521.682-010 92962
521.682-014 92962
521.682-018 92962
521.682-022 92965
521.682-026 92965
521.682-030 92962
521.682-034 92965
521.682-038 92997
521.685-010 92962
521.685-014 92962
521.685-018 92944
521.685-022 92962
521.685-026 92962
521.685-030 92962
521.685-034 92998
521.685-038 92962
521.685-042 92962
521.685-046 92962
521.685-050 92962
521.685-054 92962
521.685-058 92962
521.685-062 92962
521.685-066 92962
521.685-070 92962
521.685-074 92965
521.685-078 92965
521.685-082 92965
521.685-086 92965
521.685-090 92965
521.685-094 92965
521.685-098 92944
521.685-102 92944
521.685-106 92962
521.685-110 92958
521.685-114 92962
521.685-118 92962
521.685-122 92965
521.685-126 92962
521.685-130 92962
521.685-134 92962
521.685-138 92962
521.685-142 92962
521.685-146 92962
521.685-150 92962
521.685-154 92962
521.685-158 92944
521.685-162 92965
521.685-166 92965
521.685-170 92944
521.685-174 92962
521.685-178 92962
521.685-182 92962
521.685-186 92962
521.685-190 92938
521.685-194 92965
521.685-198 92962
521.685-202 92965
521.685-206 92962
521.685-210 92965
521.685-214 92965
521.685-218 92962
521.685-222 92965
521.685-226 92965
521.685-230 92962
521.685-234 92965
521.685-238 92962
521.685-242 92962
521.685-246 92962
521.685-250 92962
521.685-254 92962
521.685-258 92962
521.685-262 92962
521.685-266 92965
521.685-270 92962
521.685-274 92962
521.685-278 ..... 97989A
521.685-282 92962
521.685-286 92962
521.685-290 92962
521.685-294 92962
521.685-298 92944
521.685-302 92944
521.685-306 92944
521.685-310 92944
521.685-314 92965
521.685-318 92962
521.685-322 92962
521.685-326 92965
521.685-330 92971
521.685-334 92962
521.685-338 92944
521.685-342 92944

521.685-346......92965
521.685-350......92971
521.685-354......92944
521.685-358......92965
521.685-362......92962
521.685-366......97989A
521.685-370......92962
521.685-374......92962
521.685-378......92965
521.685-382......92962
521.685-386......92944
521.686-010......98999A
521.686-014......98502
521.686-018......98502
521.686-022......98502
521.686-026......98999A
521.686-030......98502
521.686-034......98502
521.686-038......98502
521.686-042......98502
521.686-046......98502
521.686-050......98999A
521.686-054......98999A
521.687-010......98999A
521.687-014......93926E
521.687-018......83005A
521.687-022......83005A
521.687-026......93926E
521.687-030......98905
521.687-034......98999A
521.687-038......98999A
521.687-042......98999A
521.687-046......98999A
521.687-050......93998
521.687-054......98905
521.687-058......93938
521.687-062......83005A
521.687-066......93926E
521.687-070......93998
521.687-074......98999A
521.687-078......98999A
521.687-082......98999A
521.687-086......83005A
521.687-090......92917
521.687-094......83005A
521.687-098......98999A
521.687-102......98999A
521.687-106......93938
521.687-110......98999A
521.687-114......98905
521.687-118......98999A
521.687-122......98999A
521.687-126......93938
521.687-130......98999A
521.687-134......98999A
521.687-138......98999A
522.130-010......81008
522.131-010......81008
522.132-010......81008
522.134-010......81008
522.264-010......31314
522.362-010......92917
522.382-010......92917
522.382-014......92962
522.382-018......92962
522.382-022......92917
522.382-026......92962
522.382-030......92962
522.382-034......92917
522.382-038......92965
522.384-010......79011
522.465-010......92962
522.482-010......92917
522.485-010......92965
522.584-010......83005A
522.585-014......92962
522.587-010......83005A
522.662-010......97953
522.662-014......92921
522.665-010......92962
522.665-014......98999A
522.667-010......83005A
522.682-010......92917
522.682-014......92917
522.684-010......93998
522.685-010......92965
522.685-014......92928
522.685-018......92917
522.685-022......92965
522.685-026......92965
522.685-030......92998
522.685-034......92917
522.685-038......92921
522.685-042......92962
522.685-046......92962
522.685-050......92962
522.685-054......92962
522.685-058......92962
522.685-062......92965
522.685-066......92921
522.685-070......92962
522.685-074......92962
522.685-078......92962
522.685-082......92962
522.685-086......92998
522.685-090......92962
522.685-094......92917
522.685-098......92962
522.685-102......92917
522.685-106......92962
522.685-110......92962
522.685-114......92962
522.686-010......98502
522.686-014......98502
522.687-010......98902A
522.687-014......98999A
522.687-018......98902A
522.687-022......98999A
522.687-026......98999A
522.687-030......98999A
522.687-034......98999A
522.687-038......98999A
522.687-042......98999A
522.687-046......93938
523.131-010......81008
523.132-010......81008
523.137-010......81008
523.362-010......92921
523.362-014 92921
523.380-010 92997
523.382-010 92921
523.382-014 92962
523.382-018 92962
523.382-022 92917
523.385-010 92962
523.562-010 92962
523.585-010 92962
523.585-014 92928
523.585-018 92928
523.585-022 92921
523.585-026 92962
523.585-030 92921
523.585-034 92921
523.587-010 ..... 98999A
523.587-014 93998
523.662-010 92921
523.665-010 92921
523.666-010 ..... 98999A
523.682-010 92917
523.682-014 92921
523.682-018 92917
523.682-022 92921
523.682-026 92921
523.682-030 92921
523.682-034 92962
523.682-038 92921
523.685-010 92928
523.685-014 92917
523.685-018 92928
523.685-022 92917
523.685-026 92921
523.685-030 92917
523.685-034 92917
523.685-038 92928
523.685-042 92928
523.685-046 92928
523.685-050 92928
523.685-054 92921
523.685-058 92921
523.685-062 92921
523.685-066 92921
523.685-070 92921
523.685-074 92921
523.685-078 92921
523.685-082 92928
523.685-086 92921
523.685-090 92921
523.685-094 92921
523.685-098 92921
523.685-102 92928
523.685-106 92921
523.685-110 92962
523.685-114 92917
523.685-118 92921
523.685-122 92921
523.685-126 92921
523.687-010 ..... 83005A
523.687-014 ..... 98999A
523.687-018 ..... 98999A
523.687-022 ..... 98799B
524.381-010 ..... 93947B
524.381-014 ..... 93947B
524.382-010 92953
524.382-014 92953
524.565-010 97951
524.665-010 92953
524.682-010 92953
524.684-010 ..... 93947B
524.684-014 ..... 93947B
524.684-018 ..... 93947B
524.684-022 ..... 93947B
524.685-010 92965
524.685-014 92953
524.685-018 92953
524.685-022 92953
524.685-026 92953
524.685-030 92974
524.685-034 92953
524.685-038 92998
524.686-010 98502
524.686-014 ..... 98999A
524.687-010 ..... 93926E
524.687-014 ..... 98999A
524.687-018 ..... 98999A
524.687-022 93998
525.131-010 81008
525.131-014 81008
525.132-010 81008
525.132-014 81008
525.134-010 81008
525.134-014 81008
525.361-010 89802
525.381-010 89802
525.381-014 89802
525.387-010 ..... 83005A
525.587-010 ..... 98999A
525.587-014 ..... 98999A
525.664-010 89802
525.682-010 92921
525.684-010 93938
525.684-014 93938
525.684-018 93938
525.684-022 93938
525.684-026 93938
525.684-030 93938
525.684-034 93938
525.684-038 93938
525.684-042 93938
525.684-046 93938
525.684-050 93938
525.684-054 93938
525.684-058 93938
525.685-010 92944
525.685-014 92974
525.685-018 92998
525.685-022 92962
525.685-026 92998
525.685-030 92962
525.686-010 98502
525.686-014 98502
525.686-018 98502
525.686-022 98502
525.687-010 93938
525.687-014 93938
525.687-018 ..... 98999A
525.687-022 ..... 98999A
525.687-026 93998
525.687-030 93938
525.687-034 ..... 98999A
525.687-038 ..... 98999A
525.687-042 ..... 83005A
525.687-046 ..... 93926E
525.687-050 ..... 98999A
525.687-054 ..... 98799B
525.687-058 ..... 98999A
525.687-062 ..... 98999A
525.687-066 93938
525.687-070 93938
525.687-074 93938
525.687-078 ..... 98999A
525.687-082 ..... 98902A
525.687-086 ..... 98799B
525.687-090 ..... 98999A
525.687-094 ..... 98999A
525.687-098 ..... 98999A
525.687-102 ..... 83005A
525.687-106 ..... 98999A
525.687-110 ..... 98999A
525.687-114 ..... 98999A
525.687-118 ..... 98902A
525.687-122 ..... 98999A
525.687-126 93938
526.131-010 81008
526.134-010 81008
526.137-010 81008
526.381-010 89805
526.381-014 89805
526.381-018 ..... 24505B
526.381-022 ..... 83002A
526.381-026 92917
526.382-010 92965
526.382-014 92917
526.382-018 92998
526.382-022 92917
526.382-026 92921
526.485-010 92998
526.585-010 92921
526.665-010 92917
526.665-014 92917
526.682-010 92997
526.682-014 92917
526.682-018 92917
526.682-022 92998
526.682-026 92921
526.682-034 92917
526.684-010 93997
526.684-014 93998
526.685-010 92917
526.685-014 92917
526.685-018 92917
526.685-022 92917
526.685-026 92921
526.685-030 92921
526.685-034 92998
526.685-038 92998
526.685-042 92917
526.685-046 92917
526.685-050 92917
526.685-054 92921
526.685-058 92917

526.685-062..... 92917
526.685-066..... 92921
526.685-070..... 92921
526.686-010..... 98999A
526.687-010..... 83005A
526.687-014..... 93998
529.130-010..... 81008
529.130-014..... 81008
529.130-018..... 81008
529.130-022..... 81008
529.130-026..... 81008
529.130-030..... 81008
529.130-034..... 81008
529.130-038..... 81008
529.130-042..... 81008
529.131-010..... 81008
529.131-014..... 81008
529.132-010..... 81008
529.132-014..... 81008
529.132-018..... 81008
529.132-022..... 81008
529.132-026..... 81008
529.132-030..... 81008
529.132-034..... 81008
529.132-038..... 81008
529.132-042..... 81008
529.132-046..... 81008
529.132-050..... 81008
529.132-054..... 81008
529.132-058..... 81008
529.132-062..... 81008
529.132-066..... 81008
529.132-070..... 81008
529.132-074..... 81008
529.132-078..... 81008
529.132-082..... 81008
529.132-086..... 81008
529.132-090..... 81008
529.132-094..... 81008
529.132-098..... 81008
529.132-102..... 81008
529.132-106..... 81008
529.132-110..... 81008
529.135-010..... 81008
529.135-014..... 81008
529.137-010..... 81008
529.137-014..... 81008
529.137-018..... 81008
529.137-022..... 81008
529.137-026..... 81008
529.137-030..... 81008
529.137-034..... 81008
529.137-038..... 81008
529.137-042..... 81008
529.137-046..... 81008
529.137-050..... 81008
529.137-054..... 81008
529.137-058..... 81008
529.137-062..... 81008
529.137-066..... 81008
529.137-070..... 81008
529.137-074..... 81008
529.137-078..... 81008
529.137-082..... 81008
529.167-010......83005A
529.281-010......83002A
529.361-010......89808
529.361-014......89808
529.361-018......89808
529.362-010......92932
529.362-014......92962
529.367-010......83005A
529.367-014......83005A
529.367-018......83005A
529.367-022......83005A
529.367-026......83005A
529.367-030......83005A
529.367-034......83005A
529.381-010......89808
529.382-010......92932
529.382-014......92998
529.382-018......92932
529.382-022......92998
529.382-026......92998
529.382-030......92962
529.385-010......92998
529.387-010......83005A
529.387-014......83005A
529.387-018......83005A
529.387-022......83005A
529.387-026......83005A
529.387-030......83005A
529.387-034......83005A
529.462-010......92965
529.467-010......83005A
529.482-010......92928
529.482-014......92928
529.482-018......92928
529.482-022......92998
529.484-010......92917
529.485-010......92928
529.485-014......92965
529.485-018......92921
529.485-022......92998
529.485-026......83005A
529.486-010......98999A
529.487-010......83005A
529.565-010......92998
529.567-010......83005A
529.567-014......83005A
529.582-010......92962
529.582-014......92962
529.585-010......92944
529.585-014......97953
529.587-010......83005A
529.587-014......83005A
529.587-018......83005A
529.587-022......83005A
529.665-010......92974
529.665-014......92958
529.665-018......92998
529.665-022......92974
529.666-010......83005A
529.666-014......83005A
529.667-010......83005A
529.667-014......85128A
529.682-010......92962
529.682-014......92932
529.682-018......92998
529.682-022......92962
529.682-026......92971
529.682-030......97951
529.682-034......92965
529.682-038......92962
529.684-010......93998
529.684-014......83005A
529.684-018......93998
529.685-010......92974
529.685-014......92971
529.685-018......92944
529.685-022......92965
529.685-026......83005A
529.685-030......92998
529.685-034......92998
529.685-038......92974
529.685-042......92971
529.685-046......92998
529.685-050......97951
529.685-054......92971
529.685-058......92998
529.685-062......92998
529.685-066......92998
529.685-070......92998
529.685-074......92958
529.685-078......92971
529.685-082......92944
529.685-086......92998
529.685-090......92944
529.685-094......92962
529.685-098......92921
529.685-102......97989A
529.685-106......92962
529.685-110......92944
529.685-114......92962
529.685-118......92944
529.685-122......92998
529.685-126......92965
529.685-130......92998
529.685-134......92965
529.685-138......92974
529.685-142......92998
529.685-146......98999B
529.685-150......92944
529.685-154......92962
529.685-158......92962
529.685-162......92974
529.685-166......92965
529.685-170......92998
529.685-174......92921
529.685-178......92965
529.685-182......92944
529.685-186......92974
529.685-190......92974
529.685-194......83005A
529.685-198......92962
529.685-202......92998
529.685-206......92998
529.685-210......92971
529.685-214......92998
529.685-218......92998
529.685-222......92998
529.685-226......92958
529.685-230..... 98905
529.685-234..... 92971
529.685-238..... 92971
529.685-242..... 97953
529.685-246..... 97953
529.685-250..... 92928
529.685-254..... 92958
529.685-258..... 92958
529.685-262..... 92958
529.685-266..... 92974
529.685-270..... 92974
529.685-274..... 83005A
529.685-278..... 92958
529.685-282..... 92974
529.685-286..... 92974
529.685-290..... 92917
529.686-010..... 98502
529.686-014..... 93935
529.686-018..... 98502
529.686-022..... 93938
529.686-026..... 98999A
529.686-030..... 98502
529.686-034..... 98999A
529.686-038..... 98502
529.686-042..... 98502
529.686-046..... 98999A
529.686-050..... 98999A
529.686-054..... 98502
529.686-062..... 98502
529.686-066..... 98502
529.686-070..... 98502
529.686-074..... 98502
529.686-078..... 98999A
529.686-082..... 98502
529.686-086..... 98502
529.687-010..... 98999A
529.687-014..... 98905
529.687-018..... 98905
529.687-022..... 98902A
529.687-026..... 83005A
529.687-030..... 93923B
529.687-034..... 93998
529.687-038..... 98999A
529.687-042..... 83005A
529.687-046..... 83005A
529.687-050..... 98999A
529.687-054..... 98905
529.687-058..... 83005A
529.687-062..... 98905
529.687-066..... 98999A
529.687-070..... 98999A
529.687-074..... 79011
529.687-078..... 98999A
529.687-082..... 83005A
529.687-086..... 98902A
529.687-090..... 83005A
529.687-094..... 98999A
529.687-098..... 83005A
529.687-102..... 83005A
529.687-106..... 83005A
529.687-110..... 83005A
529.687-114..... 83005A
529.687-118..... 83005A
529.687-122..... 93997
529.687-126..... 83005A
529.687-130..... 98999A
529.687-134..... 83005A
529.687-138..... 98799B
529.687-142..... 83005A
529.687-146..... 83005A
529.687-150..... 98902A
529.687-154..... 93998
529.687-158..... 92998
529.687-162..... 83005A
529.687-166..... 98999A
529.687-170..... 92962
529.687-174..... 83005A
529.687-178..... 83005A
529.687-182..... 98502
529.687-186..... 79011
529.687-190..... 98905
529.687-194..... 98905
529.687-198..... 83005A
529.687-202..... 83005A
529.687-206..... 98905
529.687-210..... 98905
529.687-214..... 98905
529.687-218..... 83005A
529.687-222..... 98999A
529.687-226..... 83005A
529.687-230..... 98502
530.132-010..... 81008
530.132-014..... 81008
530.132-018..... 81008
530.132-022..... 81008
530.261-010..... 89999A
530.382-010..... 92965
530.384-010..... 98999A
530.582-010..... 92965
530.662-010..... 92965
530.662-014..... 92965
530.665-010..... 92965
530.665-014..... 92944
530.666-010..... 98502
530.682-010..... 92965
530.685-010..... 92965
530.685-014..... 92965
530.686-010..... 98502
530.686-014..... 98502
530.686-018..... 98502
530.687-010..... 83005A
532.362-010..... 92998
532.585-010..... 92923
532.685-010..... 92923
532.685-014..... 92923
532.685-018..... 92962
532.685-022..... 92998
532.685-026..... 92971
532.686-010..... 98502
532.686-014..... 98502
532.687-010..... 92923
533.362-010..... 92958
533.665-010..... 92958
533.682-010..... 92962
533.685-010..... 92958
533.685-014..... 92958
533.685-018..... 92962
533.685-022..... 92962

533.685-026......92962
533.685-030......92998
533.685-034......92958
533.686-010......98999A
533.686-014......98999A
533.687-010......98999A
534.130-010......81008
534.132-010......81008
534.132-014......81008
534.137-010......81008
534.380-010......92951
534.482-010......92953
534.565-010......92923
534.582-010......92953
534.662-010......92998
534.665-010......92998
534.682-010......92953
534.682-014......92953
534.682-018......92953
534.682-022......92953
534.682-026......92997
534.682-030......92998
534.682-034......92998
534.682-038......92953
534.685-010......92971
534.685-014......92998
534.685-018......92998
534.685-022......92953
534.685-026......92953
534.685-030......92953
534.685-034......92998
534.686-010......98999A
534.687-010......98999A
534.687-014......98999A
535.482-010......92971
535.685-010......92971
539.130-010......81008
539.130-014......81008
539.131-010......81008
539.132-010......81008
539.132-014......81008
539.132-018......81008
539.134-010......81008
539.137-010......81008
539.137-014......81008
539.362-010......92998
539.362-014......92998
539.362-018......92965
539.364-010......83005A
539.367-010......83005A
539.367-014......83005A
539.387-010......83005A
539.482-010......92953
539.485-010......83005A
539.487-010......83005A
539.562-010......92997
539.565-010......92971
539.587-010......98999A
539.667-010......83005A
539.685-010......92971
539.685-014......92953
539.685-018......92971
539.685-022......92971
539.685-026......92998
539.685-030......92971
539.686-010......93926E
539.687-010......92998
540.382-010......92965
540.462-010......92965
540.585-010......92965
540.686-010......98999B
540.687-010......98999A
541.362-010......92962
541.362-014......92962
541.382-010......92962
541.382-014......92962
541.585-010......92962
541.665-010......92962
541.682-010......92962
541.685-010......92962
541.685-014......92962
542.130-010......81008
542.130-014......81008
542.132-010......81008
542.132-014......81008
542.362-010......92923
542.362-014......98999B
542.562-010......92923
542.567-010......83005A
542.665-010......98999B
542.667-010......98799B
542.685-010......92923
542.685-014......92962
542.685-018......92923
543.362-010......92923
543.382-010......92923
543.562-010......92923
543.664-010......98999B
543.666-010......93998
543.682-010......92923
543.682-014......92923
543.682-018......92923
543.682-022......92962
543.682-026......92923
543.684-010......83005A
543.685-010......92965
543.685-014......92923
543.685-018......92923
543.685-022......92923
543.687-010......98999A
543.687-014......98999A
544.565-010......92965
544.582-010......92965
544.585-010......92965
544.662-010......92965
544.665-010......92965
544.685-010......92965
546.382-010......95014
546.385-010......92938
549.130-010......81008
549.131-010......81008
549.132-010......81008
549.132-014......81008
549.132-018......81008
549.132-022......81008
549.132-026......81008
549.132-030......81008
549.132-034......81008
549.137-010 81008
549.137-014 81008
549.137-018 81008
549.260-010 95014
549.261-010 ..... 83002A
549.360-010 95011
549.362-010 97953
549.362-014 92935
549.364-010 ..... 83005A
549.367-010 ..... 83005A
549.382-010 92962
549.382-014 92962
549.382-018 97953
549.387-010 ..... 83005A
549.585-010 92962
549.587-010 ..... 98999A
549.587-014 ..... 83005A
549.587-018 ..... 83005A
549.662-010 92998
549.665-010 92965
549.682-010 92965
549.684-010 ..... 98999B
549.685-010 92958
549.685-014 92998
549.685-018 92971
549.685-022 92998
549.685-026 92998
549.685-030 ..... 98999B
549.685-034 ..... 98999B
549.685-038 92971
549.685-042 97953
549.686-010 ..... 98999A
549.686-014 98502
549.687-010 ..... 98999A
549.687-014 93998
549.687-018 ..... 98999A
549.687-022 ..... 98999A
550.131-010 81008
550.132-010 81008
550.132-014 81008
550.135-010 81008
550.135-014 81008
550.137-010 81008
550.137-014 81008
550.137-018 81008
550.362-010 92965
550.381-010 ..... 89999A
550.381-014 ..... 89999A
550.382-010 92965
550.382-014 92965
550.382-018 92965
550.382-026 92965
550.382-030 92965
550.382-034 92965
550.485-010 92965
550.485-018 92965
550.485-022 92965
550.485-026 92965
550.564-010 92965
550.565-010 92965
550.582-010 92965
550.582-014 92965
550.584-010 93997
550.584-014 ..... 83005A
550.585-010 92965
550.585-014 92965
550.585-018 92965
550.585-022 92965
550.585-026 92965
550.585-030 92965
550.585-034 92965
550.585-038 92965
550.585-042 92965
550.585-046 92965
550.586-010 ..... 98999A
550.587-010 ..... 98999A
550.587-014 ..... 83005A
550.662-010 92965
550.663-010 92998
550.665-010 92965
550.665-014 92965
550.665-018 92965
550.665-022 92965
550.682-010 92965
550.682-014 92965
550.684-010 93997
550.684-014 93998
550.684-018 93998
550.684-022 93998
550.684-026 92965
550.685-010 92965
550.685-014 92965
550.685-018 92965
550.685-022 92965
550.685-026 92965
550.685-030 92965
550.685-034 92965
550.685-038 92965
550.685-042 92965
550.685-046 92965
550.685-050 92965
550.685-054 92965
550.685-058 92965
550.685-062 92965
550.685-066 92965
550.685-070 92965
550.685-074 92965
550.685-078 92965
550.685-082 92965
550.685-086 92965
550.685-090 92965
550.685-094 92965
550.685-098 92965
550.685-102 92965
550.685-106 92965
550.685-110 92965
550.685-114 92965
550.685-118 92965
550.685-122 92965
550.685-126 92965
550.685-130 92965
550.685-134 92965
550.686-010 98502
550.686-014 98502
550.686-018 ..... 98999A
550.686-022 98502
550.686-026 ..... 98999A
550.686-030 98502
550.686-034 98502
550.686-038 ..... 98999A
550.687-010 ..... 98999A
550.687-014 ..... 98999A
550.687-018 ..... 98999A
551.130-010 81008
551.362-010 92962
551.365-010 92962
551.382-010 92962
551.465-010 92938
551.485-010 92962
551.562-010 92962
551.582-010 92198
551.585-010 92962
551.585-014 92962
551.585-018 92938
551.585-022 92705
551.665-010 92962
551.666-010 98502
551.682-010 92958
551.685-010 92998
551.685-014 92962
551.685-018 92962
551.685-022 92962
551.685-026 92923
551.685-030 92962
551.685-034 92962
551.685-038 92962
551.685-042 92928
551.685-046 92971
551.685-050 92962
551.685-054 92962
551.685-058 92962
551.685-062 92962
551.685-066 92962
551.685-070 92962
551.685-074 92962
551.685-078 92962
551.685-082 92962
551.685-086 92962
551.685-090 92962
551.685-094 92938
551.685-098 92962
551.685-102 92962
551.685-106 92962
551.685-110 92958
551.685-114 92971
551.685-118 92971
551.685-122 92962
551.685-126 92962
551.685-130 92962
551.685-134 92962
551.685-138 92971
551.685-142 92998
551.685-146 92962
551.685-150 92962
551.685-154 92962
551.685-158 92962
551.685-162 92962
551.686-010 98502
551.686-014 98502
551.686-018 98502
551.687-010 ..... 98999A
551.687-014 93998

551.687-018 ..... 98999A
551.687-022 ..... 98999A
551.687-026 ..... 98999A
551.687-030 ..... 98999A
551.687-034 ..... 98999A
552.132-010 81008
552.362-010 92962
552.362-014 ..... 95005A
552.362-018 95099
552.362-022 95099
552.382-010 92962
552.462-010 92962
552.682-010 92962
552.682-014 92962
552.682-018 92962
552.685-010 92962
552.685-014 92962
552.685-018 92962
552.685-022 92998
552.685-026 92962
552.685-030 92962
552.686-010 98502
552.687-010 ..... 98999A
553.132-010 81008
553.362-010 92997
553.362-014 92923
553.364-010 ..... 83005A
553.382-010 92923
553.382-014 92923
553.382-018 92962
553.382-022 92923
553.382-026 92197
553.385-014 92923
553.462-010 92923
553.482-010 92923
553.486-010 98502
553.582-010 92923
553.582-014 92923
553.585-010 92923
553.585-014 92923
553.585-018 92923
553.585-022 92971
553.585-026 92998
553.665-010 92971
553.665-014 92923
553.665-018 92923
553.665-022 92917
553.665-026 92923
553.665-030 92923
553.665-034 92923
553.665-038 92923
553.665-042 92923
553.665-046 92971
553.665-050 92971
553.665-054 92923
553.682-010 92923
553.682-014 92965
553.682-018 92962
553.682-022 92923
553.682-026 92971
553.684-010 93956
553.684-014 93998
553.685-010 92962
553.685-014 91938
553.685-018 92923
553.685-022 92923
553.685-026 92938
553.685-030 92923
553.685-034 92923
553.685-038 92923
553.685-042 92923
553.685-046 92923
553.685-050 92923
553.685-054 92923
553.685-058 ...... 98999A
553.685-062 92998
553.685-066 92926
553.685-070 92923
553.685-074 92923
553.685-078 97951
553.685-082 92923
553.685-086 92923
553.685-090 92923
553.685-094 92923
553.685-098 92923
553.685-102 92998
553.685-106 92923
553.685-110 92998
553.685-114 91935
553.685-118 92923
553.686-010 98502
553.686-014 ...... 98999A
553.686-018 98502
553.686-022 98502
553.686-026 98502
553.686-030 ...... 98999A
553.686-034 98502
553.686-038 98502
553.686-042 ...... 98999A
553.687-010 ...... 98999A
553.687-014 ...... 98999A
554.137-010 81008
554.137-014 81008
554.362-010 92953
554.382-010 92953
554.382-014 91926
554.384-010 ...... 93947E
554.485-010 92953
554.485-014 92998
554.585-010 92953
554.585-014 91926
554.586-010 ...... 98999A
554.587-010 ...... 83005A
554.662-010 92953
554.665-010 92705
554.665-014 92971
554.682-010 92998
554.682-014 92956
554.682-018 92198
554.682-022 92953
554.684-010 ...... 93947E
554.684-014 92974
554.685-010 92198
554.685-014 91926
554.685-018 92971
554.685-022 92998
554.685-026 92953
554.685-030 92956
554.685-034 92998
554.686-010 98502
554.686-014 ...... 98999A
554.686-018 ...... 98999A
554.686-022 ...... 98999A
554.687-010 ...... 98999A
555.382-010 92965
555.565-010 92965
555.585-010 92944
555.665-010 92944
555.682-010 92965
555.682-014 92965
555.682-018 92965
555.682-022 92965
555.685-010 92944
555.685-014 92965
555.685-018 92965
555.685-022 92965
555.685-026 92965
555.685-030 92965
555.685-034 92965
555.685-038 92965
555.685-042 92971
555.685-046 92965
555.685-050 92965
555.685-054 92998
555.685-058 92965
555.685-062 92965
555.685-066 92965
555.686-010 98502
555.686-014 98502
555.687-010 ...... 83005A
556.130-010 81008
556.130-014 81008
556.130-018 81008
556.362-010 92971
556.380-010 91902
556.380-014 92197
556.382-014 91902
556.382-018 92971
556.385-010 91905
556.484-010 ...... 93944D
556.582-010 92971
556.585-010 92971
556.585-014 92923
556.587-010 ...... 98999A
556.665-010 91905
556.665-014 91905
556.665-018 91905
556.682-010 92971
556.682-014 91902
556.682-018 92968
556.682-022 92968
556.684-010 ...... 83005A
556.684-014 ...... 93944D
556.684-018 ...... 93944D
556.684-022 93998
556.684-026 ...... 93944D
556.684-030 ...... 93944D
556.685-010 92971
556.685-014 92971
556.685-018 92971
556.685-022 91905
556.685-026 92971
556.685-030 92971
556.685-034 92971
556.685-038 91905
556.685-042 92971
556.685-046 92971
556.685-050 92971
556.685-054 92928
556.685-058 92198
556.685-062 92971
556.685-066 92971
556.685-070 92971
556.685-074 92971
556.685-078 92971
556.685-082 91905
556.685-086 91905
556.685-090 91905
556.686-010 ..... 98999A
556.686-014 98502
556.686-018 98502
556.686-022 98502
556.687-010 93998
556.687-014 ..... 98999A
556.687-018 ..... 98999A
556.687-022 ..... 93944D
556.687-026 ..... 98999A
556.687-030 ..... 93944D
557.130-010 81008
557.130-014 81008
557.382-010 91311
557.382-014 92968
557.564-010 ..... 98999B
557.564-014 ..... 83005A
557.565-010 92971
557.565-014 92708
557.665-010 92708
557.682-010 92968
557.684-010 98905
557.684-014 93998
557.685-010 92971
557.685-014 92971
557.685-018 92708
557.685-022 92708
557.685-026 92708
557.685-030 ..... 97989A
557.685-034 92705
558.130-010 81008
558.132-010 81008
558.132-014 81008
558.132-018 81008
558.134-010 81008
558.134-014 81008
558.134-018 81008
558.134-022 81008
558.260-010 95008
558.362-010 92935
558.362-014 92935
558.362-018 92935
558.382-010 92962
558.382-014 92935
558.382-018 92935
558.382-022 92935
558.382-026 92935
558.382-030 92935
558.382-034 92935
558.382-038 92935
558.382-042 92962
558.382-046 92935
558.382-050 92935
558.382-054 92935
558.382-058 92935
558.385-010 92938
558.385-014 92938
558.482-010 92923
558.485-010 92938
558.565-010 92938
558.565-014 92962
558.582-010 92935
558.584-010 ..... 83005A
558.585-010 92938
558.585-018 92938
558.585-022 92938
558.585-026 92938
558.585-030 92923
558.585-034 92938
558.585-038 ..... 98999B
558.585-042 92938
558.666-010 98502
558.682-010 92935
558.682-014 92935
558.682-018 92935
558.682-022 92962
558.685-010 92938
558.685-014 92938
558.685-018 92958
558.685-022 92998
558.685-026 92962
558.685-030 92938
558.685-034 92938
558.685-038 92938
558.685-042 92998
558.685-046 92938
558.685-050 92938
558.685-054 92923
558.685-058 92962
558.685-062 92938
558.686-010 ..... 98999A
558.687-010 ..... 98999A
559.130-010 81008
559.130-014 81008
559.130-018 81008
559.130-022 81008
559.131-010 81008
559.131-014 81008
559.131-018 81008
559.132-010 81008
559.132-014 81008
559.132-018 81008
559.132-022 81008
559.132-026 81008
559.132-030 81008
559.132-034 81008
559.132-038 81008
559.132-042 81008
559.132-046 81008
559.132-050 81008
559.132-054 81008
559.132-058 81008
559.132-062 81008

559.132-066......81008
559.132-070......81008
559.132-074......81008
559.132-078......81008
559.132-082......81008
559.132-086......81008
559.132-090......81008
559.132-094......81008
559.132-098......81008
559.132-102......81008
559.132-106......81008
559.132-110......81008
559.132-114......81008
559.132-118......81008
559.132-122......81008
559.132-126......81008
559.132-130......81008
559.132-134......81008
559.132-138......81008
559.134-010......81008
559.134-014......81008
559.137-010......81008
559.137-014......81008
559.137-018......81008
559.137-022......81008
559.137-026......81008
559.137-030......81008
559.137-034......81008
559.137-038......81008
559.137-042......81008
559.137-046......81008
559.137-050......81017
559.165-010......95008
559.167-010......81008
559.361-010......32905
559.362-010......92935
559.362-014......95099
559.362-018......95005A
559.362-022......92935
559.362-026......95099
559.362-030......92998
559.362-034......95099
559.364-010......83005A
559.367-010......83005A
559.381-010......83002A
559.381-014......83002A
559.382-010......95008
559.382-014......92965
559.382-018......92935
559.382-022......92962
559.382-026......92965
559.382-030......92935
559.382-034......92935
559.382-038......95008
559.382-042......92998
559.382-046......92997
559.382-050......92198
559.382-054......92965
559.384-010......24502C
559.387-010......83005A
559.387-014......83005A
559.467-010......83005A
559.482-010......92998
559.482-014......92997
559.485-010......92958
559.562-010......92198
559.565-010......92974
559.567-014......83005A
559.582-010......92962
559.582-014......92935
559.584-010......83005A
559.584-014......83005A
559.585-010......92998
559.585-014......97953
559.585-018......92998
559.585-022......92962
559.587-010......98999A
559.662-010......92923
559.662-014......95008
559.664-010......92938
559.664-014......98999B
559.665-010......92998
559.665-014......92998
559.665-018......92962
559.665-022......92971
559.665-026......92965
559.665-030......92971
559.665-034......92998
559.665-038......97953
559.665-042......92958
559.666-010......98999A
559.667-010......83005A
559.667-014......98999A
559.682-010......92974
559.682-014......92998
559.682-018......92935
559.682-022......92198
559.682-026......92962
559.682-030......92965
559.682-034......92998
559.682-038......92962
559.682-042......92998
559.682-046......92965
559.682-050......92971
559.682-054......92962
559.682-058......92198
559.682-062......92962
559.682-066......92962
559.682-070......92198
559.684-010......93998
559.684-018......93998
559.684-022......98905
559.684-026......98999B
559.684-030......93997
559.684-034......97953
559.685-010......92962
559.685-014......92938
559.685-018......92974
559.685-022......92958
559.685-026......97953
559.685-030......92971
559.685-034......92965
559.685-038......92971
559.685-042......92962
559.685-046......92998
559.685-050......92998
559.685-054......92998
559.685-058......92998
559.685-062 92958
559.685-066 92998
559.685-070 92938
559.685-074 92962
559.685-078 92198
559.685-082 92965
559.685-086 92998
559.685-090 92928
559.685-094 92998
559.685-098 92998
559.685-102 92998
559.685-106 92938
559.685-110 .....98999B
559.685-114 92998
559.685-118 92962
559.685-122 92998
559.685-126 92971
559.685-130 92938
559.685-134 92944
559.685-138 92958
559.685-142 92944
559.685-146 92958
559.685-150 92998
559.685-154 92965
559.685-158 92944
559.685-162 92998
559.685-166 92962
559.685-170 92928
559.685-174 92971
559.685-178 92998
559.685-182 92958
559.685-186 91321
559.685-190 92962
559.686-010 98502
559.686-014 98502
559.686-018 98502
559.686-022 98502
559.686-026 .....98999A
559.686-030 98502
559.686-034 92962
559.686-038 .....98999A
559.686-042 98502
559.687-010 .....83005A
559.687-014 .....98902A
559.687-018 98905
559.687-022 98905
559.687-026 .....98999A
559.687-030 .....98999A
559.687-034 93998
559.687-038 98905
559.687-042 98905
559.687-046 .....98999A
559.687-050 .....98999A
559.687-054 .....98999A
559.687-058 .....83005A
559.687-062 98905
559.687-066 .....83005A
559.687-070 .....83005A
559.687-074 .....83005A
560.465-010 92965
560.585-010 92965
560.587-010 .....83005A
561.131-010 81008
561.362-010 92923
561.585-010 92953
561.587-010 .....83005A
561.665-010 92998
561.685-010 .....98999A
561.686-010 .....98999A
561.687-010 .....98999A
562.485-010 92953
562.665-010 92923
562.665-014 92923
562.682-010 92998
562.685-010 92953
562.685-014 92953
562.685-018 92953
562.685-022 92953
562.686-010 98502
562.687-010 .....93947E
562.687-014 .....93947E
563.135-010 81008
563.137-010 81008
563.382-010 92923
563.585-010 92923
563.662-010 92923
563.682-010 92923
563.685-010 92971
563.685-014 92923
563.685-018 92923
563.685-022 92923
563.685-026 92923
563.686-010 98502
563.686-014 98502
563.686-018 98502
563.687-010 93998
563.687-014 .....83005A
564.132-010 81008
564.662-010 92965
564.682-010 92314
564.682-014 92944
564.682-018 92965
564.684-010 .....85128A
564.685-010 92965
564.685-014 92944
564.685-018 92965
564.686-010 98502
564.687-010 .....98999A
569.130-010 81008
569.132-010 81008
569.135-010 81008
569.367-010 .....83005A
569.382-010 92971
569.384-010 .....83005A
569.565-010 92956
569.662-010 92314
569.682-010 92965
569.682-014 92971
569.683-010 97947
569.684-010 .....93926E
569.685-010 92971
569.685-014 92314
569.685-018 92956
569.685-022 92956
569.685-026 92956
569.685-030 92971
569.685-034 92956
569.685-038 92971
569.685-042 92956
569.685-046 92971
569.685-050 92971
569.685-054 92956
569.685-058 92971
569.685-062 92956
569.685-066 .....97989A
569.685-070 92953
569.685-074 92998
569.685-078 92971
569.686-010 98502
569.686-014 98502
569.686-018 98502
569.686-022 98502
569.686-026 98502
569.686-030 98502
569.686-034 98502
569.686-038 98502
569.686-042 98502
569.686-046 .....83005A
569.686-050 98502
569.686-054 98502
569.687-010 .....98999A
569.687-014 .....98999A
569.687-018 98905
569.687-022 .....83005A
569.687-026 .....93926E
569.687-030 .....83005A
569.687-034 .....83005A
570.130-010 81008
570.132-010 81008
570.132-014 81008
570.132-018 81008
570.132-022 81017
570.137-010 81008
570.362-010 92965
570.382-010 92965
570.382-014 92965
570.382-018 92965
570.482-010 92965
570.484-010 93997
570.485-010 92965
570.665-010 92965
570.682-010 .....83005A
570.682-014 95099
570.682-018 92965
570.683-010 93997
570.683-014 92965
570.685-010 92965
570.685-014 92965
570.685-018 92965
570.685-022 92965
570.685-026 92965
570.685-030 92965
570.685-034 92965
570.685-038 92965
570.685-042 92965
570.685-046 92965
570.685-050 92965
570.685-054 92965
570.685-058 92965
570.685-062 92965
570.685-066 92965
570.685-070 92965

570.685-074..... 92965
570.685-078..... 92965
570.685-082..... 92965
570.685-086..... 92965
570.685-090..... 92965
570.685-094..... 92965
570.685-098..... 92965
570.686-010..... 98502
570.686-014..... 98999A
570.686-018..... 98502
570.687-010..... 98502
571.685-010..... 92923
571.685-014..... 92962
572.360-010..... 83002A
572.382-010..... 95099
572.685-010..... 92923
572.686-010..... 98502
573.132-010..... 81008
573.362-010..... 92923
573.382-010..... 92923
573.382-014..... 92923
573.382-018..... 92923
573.462-010..... 92923
573.585-010..... 92923
573.662-010..... 92923
573.667-010..... 98999A
573.682-010..... 92923
573.683-010..... 92923
573.684-010..... 87302
573.684-014..... 93997
573.685-010..... 92923
573.685-014..... 92923
573.685-018..... 92953
573.685-022..... 98999A
573.685-026..... 92923
573.685-030..... 92923
573.685-034..... 92923
573.685-038..... 92923
573.685-042..... 92923
573.685-046..... 92923
573.686-010..... 98502
573.686-014..... 98502
573.686-018..... 98502
573.686-022..... 98502
573.686-026..... 98502
573.687-010..... 98999A
573.687-014..... 98999A
573.687-018..... 98905
573.687-022..... 98999A
573.687-026..... 98999A
573.687-030..... 98799B
573.687-034..... 83005A
573.687-038..... 83005A
574.130-010..... 81008
574.132-010..... 81008
574.132-014..... 81008
574.134-010..... 81008
574.367-010..... 83005A
574.462-010..... 92951
574.484-010..... 93947E
574.582-010..... 92951
574.585-010..... 92998
574.665-010..... 92998
574.667-010..... 98999A
574.682-010......92953
574.682-014......92951
574.684-010......93947E
574.684-014......93947E
574.685-010......92953
574.685-014......92953
574.686-010......98502
575.130-010......81008
575.130-014......81008
575.130-018......81008
575.131-010......81008
575.131-014......81008
575.137-010......81008
575.137-014......81008
575.360-010......92997
575.362-010......92971
575.362-014......92971
575.365-010......92971
575.380-010......92968
575.381-010......89905D
575.382-010......92968
575.382-014......92968
575.382-018......92971
575.382-022......92968
575.382-026......92971
575.461-010......89905A
575.462-010......92971
575.565-010......92998
575.662-010......92971
575.662-014......92971
575.664-010......92998
575.665-010......92971
575.665-014......92971
575.665-018......92953
575.682-010......92968
575.682-014......92971
575.682-018......92971
575.682-022......92968
575.683-010......97989A
575.684-010......93997
575.684-014......93944D
575.684-018......93944D
575.684-022......93926E
575.684-026......93997
575.684-030......93944D
575.684-034......93944D
575.684-038......93944A
575.684-042......93944D
575.684-046......93944D
575.684-050......93944D
575.685-010......92971
575.685-014......92971
575.685-018......92971
575.685-022......92971
575.685-026......92971
575.685-030......92708
575.685-034......92971
575.685-038......92971
575.685-042......92971
575.685-046......92971
575.685-050......92971
575.685-054......92971
575.685-058......92971
575.685-062......92971
575.685-066......92971
575.685-070......92971
575.685-074......92971
575.685-078......92971
575.685-082......92708
575.686-010......98999A
575.686-014......98502
575.686-018......98502
575.687-010......98999A
575.687-014......98999A
575.687-018......98999A
575.687-022......83005A
575.687-026......98799B
575.687-030......83005B
575.687-034......83005A
575.687-038......97951
579.130-010......81008
579.130-014......81008
579.130-018......81008
579.130-022......81008
579.131-010......81008
579.132-010......81008
579.132-014......81008
579.134-010......81008
579.134-014......81008
579.134-018......81008
579.137-010......81008
579.137-014......81008
579.137-018......81008
579.137-022......81008
579.137-026......81008
579.137-030......81011
579.364-010......83005A
579.367-010......83005A
579.367-014......83005A
579.380-010......92997
579.382-010......92965
579.382-014......92923
579.382-018......92941A
579.382-022......92998
579.384-010......83005A
579.384-014......83005A
579.384-018......83005A
579.387-010......83005A
579.484-010......83005A
579.584-010......93998
579.585-010......83005A
579.587-010......93998
579.662-010......92998
579.664-010......85126
579.664-014......83005A
579.665-010......92998
579.665-014......98799B
579.665-018......92998
579.667-010......98999A
579.682-010......92965
579.684-010......93944D
579.684-014......83005A
579.684-018......93944D
579.684-022......93998
579.684-026......93944D
579.684-030......93926E
579.685-010......92998
579.685-014......92965
579.685-018 92958
579.685-022 92956
579.685-026 92971
579.685-030 92965
579.685-034 92923
579.685-038 92974
579.685-042 ..... 93944D
579.685-046 92962
579.685-050 97951
579.685-054 92958
579.685-058 92944
579.685-062 97951
579.685-066 92971
579.685-070 92998
579.685-074 92965
579.686-014 98502
579.686-018 98502
579.686-022 98502
579.686-026 98502
579.686-030 98502
579.687-010 ..... 98999A
579.687-014 ..... 83005A
579.687-018 ..... 98799B
579.687-022 ..... 83005A
579.687-026 ..... 83005A
579.687-030 ..... 83005A
579.687-034 ..... 98999A
579.687-038 ..... 98999A
579.687-042 ..... 98999A
580.380-010 92702
580.485-010 92998
580.682-010 92998
580.684-010 93998
580.684-014 93998
580.685-010 92998
580.685-014 92923
580.685-018 92998
580.685-022 92998
580.685-026 92998
580.685-030 92998
580.685-034 92705
580.685-038 92998
580.685-042 92728
580.685-046 92998
580.685-050 92998
580.685-054 92998
580.685-058 92998
580.685-062 92998
580.685-066 92705
580.687-010 ..... 98999A
580.687-014 93998
581.585-010 92998
581.586-010 98502
581.685-010 92998
581.685-014 92923
581.685-018 92923
581.685-022 92923
581.685-026 92923
581.685-030 92923
581.685-034 92923
581.685-038 92998
581.685-042 92998
581.685-046 92923
581.685-050 92923
581.685-054..... 92923
581.685-058..... 92998
581.685-062..... 92923
581.685-066..... 92923
581.685-070..... 92998
581.685-074..... 92705
581.685-078..... 92923
581.685-082..... 92923
581.686-010..... 98502
581.686-014..... 98502
581.686-018..... 98502
581.686-022..... 98502
581.686-026..... 98502
581.686-030..... 98502
581.686-034..... 98502
581.686-038..... 92923
581.686-042..... 98502
581.687-010..... 98999A
581.687-014..... 98999A
581.687-018..... 98999A
581.687-022..... 98999A
582.130-010..... 81008
582.131-010..... 81008
582.131-014..... 81008
582.132-010..... 81008
582.132-014..... 81008
582.132-018..... 81008
582.132-022..... 81008
582.261-010..... 83005A
582.362-010..... 92714
582.362-014..... 92714
582.384-010..... 24505D
582.387-010..... 83005A
582.482-010..... 92998
582.482-014..... 92998
582.482-018..... 92998
582.562-010..... 92998
582.582-010..... 92714
582.585-010..... 92998
582.587-010..... 83005A
582.665-010..... 92998
582.665-014..... 92714
582.665-018..... 92714
582.665-022..... 92998
582.665-026..... 92953
582.682-010..... 92998
582.684-010..... 83005A
582.684-014..... 89514
582.685-010..... 92998
582.685-014..... 92714
582.685-018..... 92714
582.685-022..... 92714
582.685-026..... 83005A
582.685-030..... 92714
582.685-034..... 92714
582.685-038..... 92998
582.685-042..... 92998
582.685-046..... 92998
582.685-050..... 92998
582.685-054..... 92714
582.685-058..... 92714
582.685-062..... 92998
582.685-066..... 92998
582.685-070..... 92714

582.685-074......92998
582.685-078......92998
582.685-082......92998
582.685-086......92923
582.685-090......92714
582.685-094......92714
582.685-098......92714
582.685-102......92714
582.685-106......92714
582.685-110......92714
582.685-114......92714
582.685-118......92953
582.685-122......92714
582.685-126......92998
582.685-130......92714
582.685-134......92998
582.685-138......92953
582.685-142......92714
582.685-146......92998
582.685-150......92998
582.685-154......92714
582.685-158......92714
582.685-162......92714
582.685-166......92714
582.685-170......92714
582.686-010......98502
582.686-014......98999A
582.686-018......98502
582.686-022......98999A
582.686-026......98999A
582.686-030......98502
582.686-034......98502
582.686-038......98502
582.687-010......83005A
582.687-014......98999A
582.687-018......98999A
582.687-022......83005A
582.687-026......92714
582.687-030......92714
583.132-010......81008
583.137-010......81008
583.585-010......92728
583.682-010......92953
583.684-010......93997
583.684-014......93998
583.685-010......92998
583.685-014......92998
583.685-018......92728
583.685-022......92728
583.685-026......92998
583.685-030......92998
583.685-034......92998
583.685-038......92998
583.685-042......92998
583.685-046......92998
583.685-050......92728
583.685-054......92728
583.685-058......92728
583.685-062......92998
583.685-066......92998
583.685-070......92728
583.685-074......92998
583.685-078......92998
583.685-082......92998
583.685-086......92728
583.685-090......92728
583.685-094......92998
583.685-098......92728
583.685-102......92728
583.685-106......92728
583.685-110......92728
583.685-114......92728
583.685-118......92728
583.685-122......92705
583.685-126......92998
583.686-010......92998
583.686-014......98502
583.686-018......98502
583.686-022......98502
583.686-026......98502
583.686-030......98502
583.687-010......98999A
584.382-010......92953
584.382-014......92998
584.562-010......92953
584.665-010......92998
584.665-014......92956
584.665-018......92998
584.682-010......92998
584.682-014......92998
584.684-010......93947E
584.685-010......92998
584.685-014......92998
584.685-018......92953
584.685-022......92953
584.685-026......92956
584.685-030......92953
584.685-034......92998
584.685-038......92953
584.685-042......92998
584.685-046......92953
584.685-050......92953
584.685-054......92998
584.685-058......92998
584.686-010......98999A
584.687-010......93947E
584.687-014......93947E
585.130-010......81008
585.380-010......92702
585.565-010......92705
585.665-010......92998
585.681-010......89599E
585.681-014......89599E
585.684-010......93926E
585.685-010......92998
585.685-014......92998
585.685-018......92965
585.685-022......92998
585.685-026......92705
585.685-030......92944
585.685-034......92998
585.685-038......92944
585.685-042......92998
585.685-046......92705
585.685-050......92998
585.685-054......92998
585.685-058......92998
585.685-062......92705
585.685-066 92998
585.685-070 92998
585.685-074 92998
585.685-078 92998
585.685-082 92944
585.685-086 92705
585.685-090 .....83005A
585.685-094 92944
585.685-098 92944
585.685-102 92705
585.685-106 92998
585.685-110 92944
585.685-114 92944
585.685-118 92705
585.685-122 92705
585.685-126 92944
585.686-010 98502
585.687-010 .....83005A
585.687-014 93932
585.687-018 .....98999A
585.687-022 93956
585.687-026 .....98999A
585.687-030 .....98902A
586.130-010 81008
586.382-010 92998
586.662-010 92998
586.682-010 92998
586.685-010 92998
586.685-014 92965
586.685-018 92998
586.685-022 92998
586.685-026 92998
586.685-030 92998
586.685-034 92998
586.685-038 .....83005A
586.686-010 98502
586.686-014 .....98999A
586.686-018 98502
586.686-022 .....98999A
586.687-010 92714
587.384-010 .....83005A
587.585-010 92923
587.682-010 92923
587.685-010 92998
587.685-014 92998
587.685-018 92714
587.685-022 92998
587.685-026 92998
587.685-030 92998
587.686-010 .....98999A
587.687-010 .....98999A
589.130-010 81008
589.130-014 81008
589.130-018 81008
589.130-022 81008
589.130-026 81008
589.130-030 81008
589.132-010 81008
589.132-014 81008
589.134-010 81008
589.135-010 81008
589.137-010 81008
589.137-014 81008
589.360-010 92702
589.361-010 .....89599E
589.384-010 .....83005A
589.387-010 .....83005A
589.387-014 79011
589.387-018 .....83005A
589.387-022 .....83005A
589.464-010 92965
589.485-010 92923
589.487-010 .....83005A
589.562-010 92714
589.662-010 92714
589.662-014 92714
589.665-010 92998
589.665-014 92998
589.684-010 .....83005A
589.685-010 92998
589.685-014 92998
589.685-018 92998
589.685-022 92998
589.685-026 92714
589.685-030 92998
589.685-034 92998
589.685-038 92726
589.685-042 92714
589.685-046 92998
589.685-050 92965
589.685-054 92962
589.685-058 92998
589.685-062 92998
589.685-066 92714
589.685-070 92998
589.685-074 92998
589.685-078 92998
589.685-082 92998
589.685-086 92705
589.685-090 92998
589.685-094 92998
589.685-098 92998
589.685-102 92998
589.686-010 98502
589.686-014 98502
589.686-018 98502
589.686-022 92998
589.686-026 .....98999A
589.686-030 98502
589.686-034 98502
589.686-038 .....98999A
589.686-042 98502
589.686-046 98502
589.686-050 98502
589.687-010 .....98999A
589.687-014 93998
589.687-018 .....98999A
589.687-022 .....98999A
589.687-026 .....98999A
589.687-030 93998
589.687-034 .....93947E
589.687-038 .....93947E
589.687-042 .....98999A
589.687-046 93998
589.687-050 .....83005A
589.687-054 79011
589.687-058 .....98999A
589.687-062 98502
590.130-010 81008
590.130-014 81008
590.130-018 81008
590.131-010 81008
590.132-010 81008
590.134-010 81008
590.262-010 .....92902D
590.262-014 .....92902C
590.282-010 .....92902D
590.362-010 95099
590.362-014 92997
590.362-018 .....92902A
590.362-022 .....92902C
590.364-010 .....92902B
590.365-010 92998
590.367-010 .....83005A
590.382-010 92923
590.382-014 .....92902D
590.382-018 .....92902D
590.382-022 .....92902A
590.384-010 .....92902A
590.384-014 .....85128A
590.464-010 93997
590.487-010 .....83005A
590.662-010 92998
590.662-014 92998
590.662-018 92965
590.662-022 92923
590.665-010 92923
590.665-014 92971
590.665-018 92998
590.667-010 .....98999A
590.682-010 92971
590.684-010 92998
590.684-014 .....92902A
590.684-018 .....93951B
590.684-022 .....92902A
590.684-026 .....92902B
590.684-030 93997
590.684-034 98905
590.684-038 92998
590.684-042 .....92902A
590.685-010 92923
590.685-014 92953
590.685-018 91911
590.685-022 92953
590.685-026 92958
590.685-034 92923
590.685-038 92953
590.685-042 92998
590.685-046 91926
590.685-050 92944
590.685-054 92953
590.685-058 92998
590.685-062 92958
590.685-066 92953
590.685-070 .....92902A
590.685-074 .....92902B
590.685-078 .....92902B
590.685-082 92198
590.685-086 .....92902A
590.685-090 92923
590.685-094 92198
590.685-098 92998

590.685-102 92958
590.686-010 ..... 98999A
590.686-014 98502
590.687-010 ..... 98999A
590.687-014 ..... 93944D
590.687-018 98502
590.687-022 ..... 93926E
599.132-010 81008
599.137-010 81008
599.382-010 92951
599.382-014 92997
599.585-010 92998
599.665-010 92962
599.682-010 ..... 93947E
599.682-014 92923
599.684-010 98905
599.684-014 ..... 83005A
599.685-014 92965
599.685-018 92962
599.685-022 92958
599.685-026 92953
599.685-030 92998
599.685-034 92714
599.685-038 92958
599.685-042 92962
599.685-046 92953
599.685-050 ..... 98999B
599.685-054 91926
599.685-058 92965
599.685-062 91926
599.685-066 92953
599.685-070 92953
599.685-074 92953
599.685-078 92965
599.685-082 92962
599.685-086 92998
599.685-090 91926
599.685-094 92953
599.685-098 92958
599.685-102 91926
599.685-106 92965
599.685-110 92965
599.685-114 92958
599.685-118 92958
599.685-122 92998
599.685-126 92953
599.685-130 92958
599.685-134 92958
599.686-010 98502
599.686-014 98502
599.687-010 ..... 93947E
599.687-014 ..... 98999A
599.687-018 ..... 98999A
599.687-022 98905
599.687-026 93998
599.687-030 98905
599.687-034 98905
599.687-038 ..... 83005A
600.130-010 81008
600.131-014 81008
600.260-014 ..... 89114A
600.260-018 ..... 89114A
600.260-022 89108
600.261-010 93105
600.280-014 89105
600.280-018 89105
600.280-022 89108
600.280-026 89108
600.280-030 89108
600.280-034 89108
600.280-042 89108
600.280-046 ...... 89114B
600.280-050 ...... 89114B
600.280-054 ...... 89114A
600.281-010 89108
600.281-014 ...... 83002A
600.281-018 89117
600.281-022 93105
600.360-010 91505
600.360-014 91505
600.380-010 89108
600.380-018 91505
600.380-022 91505
600.380-026 93105
601.130-010 81008
601.260-010 89102
601.260-014 89102
601.261-010 ...... 83002A
601.280-010 89102
601.280-014 89102
601.280-018 89102
601.280-022 89102
601.280-030 89102
601.280-034 89102
601.280-038 ...... 89114B
601.280-042 89102
601.280-054 91505
601.280-058 89102
601.281-010 89102
601.281-014 89102
601.281-018 ...... 83002C
601.281-022 ...... 83002A
601.281-026 89102
601.281-030 ...... 85119A
601.380-010 89102
601.381-010 89102
601.381-014 89102
601.381-018 89111
601.381-022 89102
601.381-026 89102
601.381-030 89102
601.381-034 89102
601.381-038 ...... 89114B
601.381-042 89102
601.482-010 ...... 91114A
601.682-010 92198
602.280-010 91505
602.360-010 ...... 91114A
602.362-010 ...... 83002B
602.362-014 ...... 83005A
602.380-010 91505
602.382-010 91505
602.382-014 91505
602.382-018 91505
602.382-022 91505
602.382-026 91505
602.382-030 91505
602.382-034 ...... 91114A
602.482-010 ...... 91114A
602.685-010 91508
603.130-010 81008
603.137-010 81008
603.260-010 ...... 91114A
603.280-010 89111
603.280-014 89111
603.280-018 89111
603.280-022 89111
603.280-026 ...... 91114A
603.280-030 89111
603.280-034 ...... 91114A
603.280-038 89111
603.360-010 ...... 91114B
603.380-010 ...... 91114A
603.382-010 ...... 91114B
603.382-014 ...... 91114A
603.382-018 ...... 91114A
603.382-022 ...... 91114A
603.382-026 ...... 91114A
603.382-030 91117
603.382-034 ...... 91114A
603.382-038 ...... 91114A
603.482-010 ...... 91114A
603.482-030 91117
603.482-034 91117
603.664-010 91117
603.665-010 91117
603.682-010 ...... 91114B
603.682-018 91117
603.682-022 ...... 91114B
603.682-026 ...... 91114B
603.682-030 91117
603.685-010 91117
603.685-014 91117
603.685-022 91117
603.685-026 91117
603.685-030 91117
603.685-034 91117
603.685-038 91117
603.685-042 91117
603.685-046 91117
603.685-050 91117
603.685-054 91117
603.685-058 91117
603.685-062 91117
603.685-066 91117
603.685-070 91117
603.685-074 91117
603.685-078 91117
603.685-082 91117
603.686-010 98502
603.686-014 98502
604.130-010 81008
604.260-010 91105
604.280-010 91105
604.280-014 91105
604.280-018 91105
604.280-022 91105
604.360-010 91105
604.362-010 91502
604.380-010 91105
604.380-014 91105
604.380-018 91105
604.380-022 91105
604.380-026 91105
604.382-010 91117
604.382-014 91117
604.666-010 98502
604.682-010 91117
604.682-014 91105
604.685-010 91117
604.685-014 91117
604.685-018 91117
604.685-022 91117
604.685-026 91117
604.685-030 91117
604.685-034 91117
604.685-038 91117
604.685-042 91117
604.686-010 98502
605.280-010 91111
605.280-014 91111
605.280-018 91111
605.282-010 91111
605.282-014 91111
605.282-018 91111
605.360-010 91502
605.380-010 91502
605.382-010 91111
605.382-014 91111
605.382-018 91111
605.382-022 91111
605.382-026 91111
605.382-030 91111
605.382-034 91111
605.382-038 91111
605.382-042 91111
605.382-046 91502
605.482-010 91111
605.682-010 91111
605.682-014 91117
605.682-022 91111
605.682-026 91111
605.682-030 91117
605.682-034 91117
605.685-010 91117
605.685-014 91117
605.685-018 91117
605.685-022 91117
605.685-026 91117
605.685-030 91117
605.685-034 91117
605.685-038 91117
605.685-042 91117
605.685-046 91117
605.685-050 91117
605.685-054 91117
606.280-010 91108
606.280-014 91108
606.362-010 91502
606.380-010 91108
606.380-014 91108
606.380-018 91108
606.382-010 91117
606.382-014 91502
606.382-018 91502
606.382-022 91108
606.382-026 91502
606.682-014 91117
606.682-018 91108
606.682-022 91108
606.685-010 91117
606.685-014 91117
606.685-018 91117
606.685-022 91117
606.685-026 91117
606.685-030 91117
606.685-034 91117
607.382-010 91102
607.382-014 91102
607.682-010 91102
607.682-014 91117
607.685-010 91117
607.685-014 91117
607.686-010 91117
609.130-010 81008
609.130-014 81008
609.130-018 81008
609.130-022 81008
609.130-026 81008
609.131-010 81008
609.131-014 81008
609.131-018 81008
609.132-010 81008
609.260-010 ..... 85999D
609.262-010 25111
609.280-010 91102
609.360-010 91502
609.361-010 ..... 83002A
609.362-010 91502
609.380-010 92197
609.380-014 91105
609.462-010 92198
609.482-010 92198
609.482-014 92197
609.682-010 91508
609.682-014 92198
609.682-018 92198
609.682-022 91508
609.682-026 ..... 91114A
609.682-030 92198
609.684-010 ..... 83005A
609.684-014 ..... 98999B
609.685-010 92998
609.685-014 92198
609.685-018 91508
609.685-022 91508
609.685-026 91508
610.362-010 91317
610.381-010 ..... 85999C
610.381-014 ..... 85999C
610.684-010 ..... 98999B
610.684-014 91321
611.482-010 91317
611.482-014 91321
611.662-010 91317
611.682-010 91317
611.682-014 91321
611.685-010 91321
611.685-014 91321
612.130-010 81008

612.131-010......81008
612.260-010......91317
612.261-010......83002A
612.360-010......91317
612.361-010......91317
612.384-010......83005A
612.462-010......91317
612.462-014......91317
612.662-010......91317
612.666-010......98502
612.682-010......91317
612.682-014......91317
612.683-010......97989A
612.684-010......98999B
612.685-010......91321
612.685-014......91321
612.687-010......83005A
612.687-014......98999A
613.130-010......81008
613.130-014......81008
613.130-018......81008
613.132-010......81008
613.360-010......91314
613.360-014......91314
613.360-018......91314
613.361-010......91314
613.362-010......91938
613.362-014......91321
613.362-018......91321
613.362-022......91321
613.382-010......92198
613.382-014......91314
613.382-018......91321
613.462-014......91938
613.462-018......91314
613.482-014......91314
613.662-010......95099
613.662-014......91321
613.662-018......91314
613.662-022......91321
613.667-010......93914A
613.667-014......83005A
613.682-010......91321
613.682-014......91314
613.682-018......91321
613.682-022......91314
613.682-026......91321
613.682-030......91314
613.685-010......92198
613.685-014......98999B
613.685-018......91321
613.685-022......91321
613.685-026......98999B
613.685-030......91321
613.685-034......97951
613.686-010......98502
613.687-010......93998
614.132-010......81008
614.132-014......81008
614.380-010......91311
614.382-010......91311
614.382-014......91321
614.382-018......91321
614.482-010......91311
614.482-014......91311
614.482-018......91311
614.586-010......98502
614.682-010......91321
614.684-010......91705
614.684-014......83005A
614.685-010......91321
614.685-014......91321
614.685-018......91321
614.685-022......91321
614.685-026......91321
614.686-010......98999A
614.686-014......98502
615.130-010......81008
615.130-014......81008
615.132-010......81008
615.280-010......91308
615.380-010......91308
615.382-010......91302
615.482-010......91308
615.482-014......91302
615.482-018......91302
615.482-026......91302
615.482-030......91321
615.482-038......91321
615.662-010......91308
615.682-010......91308
615.682-014......91321
615.682-018......91308
615.685-010......91321
615.685-014......91321
615.685-018......91117
615.685-022......91321
615.685-026......91321
615.685-030......91321
615.685-034......91321
615.685-038......91321
615.685-042......91321
615.685-046......92944
615.687-010......98999A
616.130-010......81008
616.130-014......81008
616.130-018......81008
616.130-022......81008
616.260-010......92197
616.260-014......92197
616.260-018......92197
616.260-022......92197
616.280-010......92197
616.360-010......92197
616.360-014......92197
616.360-022......91505
616.360-026......92197
616.360-030......92197
616.360-034......92197
616.361-010......83002A
616.362-010......92197
616.380-010......92197
616.380-014......92197
616.380-018......91505
616.382-010......92198
616.382-014......92197
616.382-018......92998
616.460-010......92197
616.482-010......92197
616.484-010......83005A
616.485-010......92198
616.485-014......92198
616.582-010......92198
616.662-010......92198
616.665-010......92198
616.681-010......89199
616.682-010......91305
616.682-014......92197
616.682-018......92197
616.682-022......92197
616.682-026......91305
616.682-030......92198
616.682-034......92197
616.685-010......83005A
616.685-014......92198
616.685-018......92198
616.685-022......92198
616.685-026......92198
616.685-030......92198
616.685-034......83005A
616.685-038......92198
616.685-042......92198
616.685-046......92198
616.685-050......92198
616.685-054......92198
616.685-058......92198
616.685-062......92198
616.685-066......91321
616.685-070......92198
616.685-074......92198
616.685-078......92198
616.685-082......92198
616.685-086......91321
616.685-090......92198
616.687-010......98999A
616.687-014......98999A
617.130-010......81008
617.130-014......81008
617.260-010......91305
617.280-010......91502
617.360-010......91305
617.360-014......91305
617.380-010......91305
617.382-010......91305
617.382-014......91321
617.480-010......91314
617.480-014......91305
617.482-010......91305
617.482-014......91314
617.482-018......91314
617.482-022......92197
617.482-026......91321
617.585-010......92198
617.665-010......92198
617.682-010......92198
617.682-018......92198
617.682-022......91314
617.685-010......91321
617.685-014......91321
617.685-018......92198
617.685-022......92198
617.685-026......91321
617.685-030......92198
617.685-034......91321
617.685-038......91321
617.685-042......91321
617.686-010......98502
619.130-010......81008
619.130-014......81008
619.130-018......81008
619.130-022......81008
619.130-026......81008
619.130-030......81008
619.130-034......81008
619.130-038......81008
619.130-042......81008
619.130-046......81008
619.131-010......81008
619.131-014......81008
619.131-018......81008
619.132-010......81008
619.132-014......81008
619.132-018......81008
619.132-022......81008
619.132-026......81008
619.132-030......81008
619.134-010......81008
619.137-010......81008
619.260-010......89199
619.260-014......89199
619.261-010......83002A
619.280-010......92197
619.280-018......92197
619.281-010......85999C
619.361-010......89199
619.361-014......91714
619.361-018......91714
619.362-010......92198
619.362-014......91321
619.362-018......91105
619.362-022......91105
619.364-010......83002A
619.365-010......92198
619.380-010......92197
619.380-014......91302
619.380-018......85302B
619.381-010......83002A
619.381-014......83002A
619.382-010......92197
619.382-014......91117
619.382-018......92197
619.382-022......92197
619.387-010......83005A
619.462-010......91314
619.462-014......92197
619.482-010......92198
619.484-010......98999B
619.485-010......92198
619.485-014......91321
619.582-010......92198
619.662-010......92923
619.662-014......91321
619.665-010......92198
619.682-010......91321
619.682-014......92198
619.682-018......92197
619.682-022......91938
619.682-026......91321
619.682-030......92198
619.682-034......92198
619.682-038......83005A
619.682-042......92197
619.684-010......98999B
619.685-010......92198
619.685-014......91321
619.685-018......91321
619.685-022......92198
619.685-026......91321
619.685-030......92198
619.685-034......91321
619.685-038......92198
619.685-042......92198
619.685-046......91321
619.685-050......92198
619.685-054......92198
619.685-058......92198
619.685-062......91508
619.685-066......92198
619.685-070......91321
619.685-074......92198
619.685-078......92198
619.685-082......91321
619.685-086......91321
619.685-090......92198
619.685-094......91117
619.686-010......98502
619.686-014......98999A
619.686-018......98502
619.686-022......98999A
619.686-026......91938
619.686-030......98999A
619.686-034......98999A
619.687-010......93998
619.687-014......98999A
619.687-018......93998
620.131-010......81002
620.131-014......81002
620.131-018......81002
620.137-010......81002
620.261-010......85302A
620.261-012......85302A
620.261-014......83002B
620.261-018......83002B
620.261-022......85314
620.261-026......85714A
620.261-030......85302B
620.261-034......85302B
620.281-010......85302B
620.281-014......83002B
620.281-018......85119A
620.281-026......85302B
620.281-030......83002B
620.281-034......85302B
620.281-038......85302B
620.281-042......85314
620.281-046......85311A
620.281-050......85311A
620.281-054......85308
620.281-058......85311A
620.281-062......85302A

620.281-066 ..... 85302B
620.281-070 ..... 85302B
620.364-010 ..... 85302A
620.381-010 ..... 85302B
620.381-014 85314
620.381-018 85317
620.381-022 ..... 85302A
620.384-010 ..... 83005A
620.584-010 ..... 98999B
620.664-010 98102
620.664-014 98102
620.682-010 ..... 85302B
620.684-010 ..... 85999E
620.684-014 98102
620.684-018 ..... 85302B
620.684-022 ..... 85302B
620.684-026 85308
620.684-030 98102
620.684-034 98905
620.685-010 92956
621.131-010 81002
621.131-014 81002
621.137-010 81008
621.221-010 31314
621.261-010 ..... 83002B
621.261-014 ..... 83002B
621.261-018 ..... 97702H
621.261-022 ..... 85323A
621.281-014 ..... 85323A
621.281-018 ..... 85323A
621.281-030 85326
621.684-010 98102
621.684-014 ..... 85999G
622.131-010 81002
622.131-014 81002
622.131-018 81002
622.137-010 81002
622.137-014 81002
622.261-010 ..... 87714C
622.281-010 ..... 83002B
622.381-010 ..... 85928A
622.381-014 85317
622.381-018 85317
622.381-022 85317
622.381-026 87605
622.381-030 ..... 85119C
622.381-034 ..... 83002B
622.381-038 ..... 83002A
622.382-010 ..... 83005A
622.684-010 85317
622.684-014 98102
622.684-018 ..... 85128A
622.684-022 ..... 83005A
623.131-010 81008
623.131-014 81002
623.261-010 ..... 85328A
623.261-014 ..... 85328A
623.281-010 ..... 85116A
623.281-014 ..... 85116C
623.281-018 ..... 85116B
623.281-022 ..... 85116A
623.281-026 ..... 85116B
623.281-030 ..... 85116A
623.281-034 ..... 85116B
623.281-038 ...... 85328A
623.281-042 ...... 85328A
623.381-010 85935
623.684-010 98102
623.687-010 98102
624.131-010 81002
624.281-010 85321
624.281-014 85321
624.361-010 ...... 83002B
624.361-014 85321
624.381-010 85321
624.381-014 85321
624.381-018 93105
624.684-010 ...... 85128B
625.131-010 81002
625.131-014 81002
625.137-010 81002
625.261-010 ...... 83002B
625.281-010 ...... 85311A
625.281-014 ...... 85311A
625.281-018 ...... 85328B
625.281-022 ...... 85302B
625.281-026 ...... 85328B
625.281-030 ...... 85328B
625.281-034 ...... 85328B
625.361-010 ...... 85311B
625.381-010 ...... 85328B
625.684-010 98102
626.137-010 81002
626.261-010 ...... 85119A
626.261-014 ...... 85119A
626.361-010 ...... 85119A
626.381-010 ...... 85119B
626.381-014 ...... 85119A
626.381-018 ...... 85119A
626.384-010 ...... 85119A
627.261-010 ...... 85119A
627.261-014 ...... 85119A
627.261-018 ...... 85119A
627.261-022 ...... 85119A
628.261-010 85112
628.281-010 85112
628.381-010 85112
628.382-010 85112
628.382-014 ...... 91114A
628.484-010 85112
628.664-010 98102
628.682-010 85112
628.684-010 ...... 85128A
628.684-014 ...... 85128A
628.684-018 85112
628.684-022 ...... 85128A
628.684-026 85112
628.684-030 85112
628.684-034 85112
628.684-038 85112
628.684-042 ...... 85128A
628.684-046 ...... 85128A
628.687-010 ...... 85128A
628.687-014 ...... 98999A
629.131-010 81002
629.131-014 81002
629.261-010 ...... 85119A
629.261-014 ...... 85119A
629.261-018 ...... 85119A
629.261-022 ...... 85119A
629.280-010 ...... 85119A
629.281-010 ...... 85119A
629.281-014 ...... 85119A
629.281-018 85321
629.281-026 ...... 85119B
629.281-030 ...... 85119A
629.281-034 ...... 85119A
629.361-010 ...... 85119B
629.381-010 ...... 85119B
629.381-014 ...... 85311A
629.382-010 ...... 83005A
629.682-010 ...... 91114A
629.684-010 ...... 85128A
629.684-014 93997
630.131-010 81002
630.134-010 81008
630.261-010 ...... 85119A
630.261-014 ...... 85119A
630.261-018 ...... 85119A
630.281-010 ...... 85119A
630.281-014 ...... 85119A
630.281-018 ...... 85119A
630.281-022 ...... 85119A
630.281-026 ...... 85119A
630.281-030 ...... 85119A
630.281-034 ...... 85119A
630.281-038 85118
630.381-010 ...... 85119A
630.381-014 ...... 85928C
630.381-018 ...... 85119A
630.381-022 ...... 85119A
630.381-026 ...... 85119A
630.381-030 ...... 85928A
630.384-010 ...... 85119B
630.584-010 ...... 85128A
630.664-010 98102
630.664-014 ...... 85119B
630.664-018 98102
630.684-010 ...... 85119B
630.684-014 ...... 85119B
630.684-018 ...... 85999B
630.684-022 98102
630.684-026 ...... 85119B
630.684-030 ...... 85119B
630.684-034 98102
630.684-038 ...... 85119B
630.687-010 ...... 85128B
631.131-010 81002
631.261-010 85118
631.261-014 85118
631.261-018 85118
631.364-010 98102
631.684-010 98102
632.131-010 81002
632.261-010 99003
632.261-014 99003
632.261-018 99003
632.281-010 ...... 85999D
632.360-010 92997
632.360-014 92997
632.360-018 92997
632.380-010 ...... 85119B
632.380-014 92997
632.380-018 92951
632.380-022 92997
632.380-026 92951
632.381-010 99003
632.381-014 ..... 83002A
632.684-010 98102
633.131-010 81002
633.261-010 85926
633.261-014 85926
633.281-010 85926
633.281-014 85926
633.281-018 85926
633.281-022 85926
633.281-026 85905
633.281-030 85926
637.131-010 81002
637.261-010 ..... 85711A
637.261-014 ..... 85902A
637.261-018 85944
637.261-022 ..... 85928A
637.261-026 ..... 85902B
637.261-030 ..... 85902A
637.261-034 ..... 85902A
637.281-010 ..... 85999B
637.281-014 ..... 85119A
637.381-010 ..... 85902A
637.381-014 ..... 85902B
637.384-010 98102
637.664-010 98102
637.684-010 98102
637.684-014 ..... 83005A
637.687-010 98102
637.687-014 98102
637.687-018 98102
638.131-010 81002
638.131-014 81008
638.131-018 81002
638.131-022 81002
638.131-026 81002
638.131-030 81002
638.131-034 81002
638.261-010 ..... 85123A
638.261-014 ..... 85123B
638.261-018 ..... 85123A
638.261-022 ..... 85119B
638.261-026 ..... 85123A
638.261-030 ..... 85119A
638.281-010 85132
638.281-014 ..... 85119A
638.281-018 ..... 85123B
638.281-022 ..... 85123B
638.281-026 ..... 85119A
638.281-030 ..... 85119A
638.281-034 ..... 85119A
638.361-010 93105
638.381-010 ..... 85119A
638.484-010 98102
638.684-010 ..... 85128A
638.684-014 ..... 85128A
638.684-018 98102
639.281-010 99003
639.281-014 85947
639.281-018 85113
639.281-022 85908
639.681-010 85951
639.684-010 98102
640.132-010 81008
640.360-010 ..... 92941A
640.385-010 92998
640.565-010 92944
640.682-010 92914
640.682-014 92998
640.682-018 ..... 92941A
640.682-022 92914
640.685-010 92944
640.685-014 92956
640.685-018 92998
640.685-022 92944
640.685-026 92944
640.685-030 92944
640.685-034 92944
640.685-038 92944
640.685-042 92998
640.685-046 92998
640.685-050 92998
640.685-054 92998
640.685-058 92998
640.685-062 92998
640.685-066 92944
640.685-070 92998
640.685-074 92944
640.685-078 92944
640.685-082 92998
640.685-086 92944
640.685-090 92944
640.686-010 98502
640.686-014 ..... 98999A
640.687-010 ..... 83005A
640.687-014 ..... 98999A
641.380-010 92914
641.562-010 92997
641.662-010 92956
641.662-014 92998
641.682-010 92956
641.682-014 92956
641.685-010 92998
641.685-014 92956
641.685-018 92956
641.685-022 92998
641.685-026 92998
641.685-030 92956
641.685-034 92956
641.685-038 92971
641.685-042 92956
641.685-046 92956
641.685-050 92998
641.685-054 92998
641.685-058 92956
641.685-062 92971
641.685-066 92956
641.685-070 92998
641.685-074 92956
641.685-078 92998
641.685-082 92956
641.685-086 92998
641.685-090 92956
641.685-094 92998

641.685-098......92956
641.686-010......98999A
641.686-014......98999A
641.686-018......98999A
641.686-022......98999A
641.686-026......98502
641.686-030......98502
641.686-034......92998
641.686-038......98999A
641.687-010......93998
641.687-014......83005A
649.130-010......81008
649.361-010......89908B
649.367-010......83005A
649.380-010......92914
649.487-010......83005A
649.582-010......92998
649.582-014......92968
649.665-010......83005A
649.682-010......92914
649.682-014......92944
649.682-018......92997
649.682-022......92997
649.682-026......92941A
649.682-030......92997
649.682-034......92997
649.682-038......92941A
649.682-042......92941A
649.682-046......92529E
649.685-010......92998
649.685-014......92998
649.685-018......92998
649.685-022......92998
649.685-026......92944
649.685-030......92998
649.685-034......92998
649.685-038......92998
649.685-042......92998
649.685-046......92998
649.685-050......92956
649.685-054......92998
649.685-058......92998
649.685-062......92998
649.685-066......92998
649.685-070......92998
649.685-074......92998
649.685-078......92971
649.685-082......92944
649.685-086......92971
649.685-090......92998
649.685-094......92974
649.685-098......92998
649.685-102......92998
649.685-106......92998
649.685-110......92944
649.685-114......92998
649.685-118......92998
649.685-122......92974
649.685-126......92956
649.685-130......98999B
649.686-010......98999A
649.686-014......92956
649.686-018......98999A
649.686-022......98502
649.686-026......98502
649.686-030......98502
649.687-010......83005A
649.687-014......83005A
649.687-018......83005A
650.132-010......81008
650.582-010......92541
650.582-014......92541
650.582-018......92541
650.582-022......92541
650.682-010......92541
650.685-010......92541
651.130-010......81008
651.362-010......92515
651.362-014......92515
651.362-018......92515
651.362-022......92515
651.362-026......92519
651.362-030......92515
651.362-034......92515
651.382-010......92519
651.382-014......92522A
651.382-026......92522A
651.382-030......92519
651.382-034......92515
651.382-038......92519
651.382-042......92512
651.382-046......92512
651.384-010......92519
651.582-010......92543
651.582-014......92543
651.585-010......92543
651.586-010......98999A
651.682-010......92519
651.682-014......92543
651.682-018......92543
651.682-022......92522B
651.685-010......92543
651.685-014......92543
651.685-018......92543
651.685-022......92543
651.685-026......92543
651.686-010......98502
651.686-014......98502
651.686-018......98502
651.686-022......98502
651.687-010......83005A
652.130-010......81008
652.130-014......81008
652.130-018......81008
652.132-010......81008
652.137-010......81008
652.137-014......81008
652.260-010......92524
652.380-010......92524
652.382-010......92522A
652.385-010......85128A
652.462-010......92543
652.567-010......83005A
652.582-010......92543
652.582-014......92543
652.585-010......92541
652.586-010......98502
652.662-010......92522B
652.662-014.....92522A
652.662-018.....92543
652.665-014.....92549
652.682-010.....92522B
652.682-014.....92543
652.682-018.....92543
652.682-022.....92997
652.682-026.....92522B
652.682-030.....92543
652.685-010.....92543
652.685-014.....92543
652.685-018.....92543
652.685-022.....92998
652.685-026.....92543
652.685-034.....92543
652.685-038.....92543
652.685-042.....92549
652.685-046.....92543
652.685-050.....92543
652.685-054.....92543
652.685-058.....92543
652.685-062.....92543
652.685-066.....92543
652.685-070.....92543
652.685-074.....92543
652.685-078.....92543
652.685-082.....92543
652.685-086.....92549
652.685-090.....92543
652.685-094.....92549
652.685-098.....92543
652.685-102.....92543
652.685-106.....92541
652.685-110.....92543
652.686-010.....98502
652.686-014.....98502
652.686-018.....98502
652.686-022.....98502
652.686-026.....98502
652.686-030.....98502
652.686-034.....98502
652.686-038.....98999A
652.686-042.....83005A
652.686-046.....98502
652.687-010.....98999A
652.687-014.....98999A
652.687-018.....98999A
652.687-022.....98999A
652.687-026.....98999A
652.687-030.....93998
652.687-034.....83005A
652.687-038.....98502
652.687-042.....83005A
652.687-046.....83005A
652.687-050.....98999A
653.131-010.....81008
653.360-010.....92525
653.360-018.....92525
653.382-010.....92525
653.382-014.....92525
653.662-010.....92525
653.667-010.....83005A
653.682-010.....92525
653.682-014.....92546
653.682-018.....92525
653.682-022.....92525
653.685-010.....92546
653.685-014.....92546
653.685-018.....92956
653.685-022.....92546
653.685-026.....92546
653.685-030.....92546
653.686-010.....98502
653.686-026.....98502
653.687-010.....83005A
654.382-010.....92529B
654.582-010.....92529B
654.687-010.....83005A
654.687-014.....93998
659.360-010.....92529C
659.381-010.....92519
659.382-010.....92529A
659.462-010.....55323
659.662-010.....92543
659.667-010.....83005A
659.682-010.....92529E
659.682-014.....92529A
659.682-018.....92529A
659.682-022.....92529E
659.682-026.....92529E
659.684-010.....93997
659.685-014.....92944
659.685-018.....92549
659.685-022.....92549
659.685-026.....92549
659.686-014.....98502
659.687-010.....98502
659.687-014.....83005A
660.130-010.....81008
660.280-010.....89311
660.280-014.....89311
661.131-010.....81008
661.137-010.....81008
661.280-010.....89302A
661.281-010.....89302A
661.281-014.....89302A
661.281-018.....89302A
661.281-022.....89302A
661.380-010.....89302A
661.381-010.....89398
662.132-010.....81008
662.682-010.....92311
662.682-014.....92311
662.682-018.....92314
662.685-010.....92314
662.685-014.....92314
662.685-018.....92314
662.685-022.....92314
662.685-026.....92314
662.685-030.....92314
662.685-034.....92314
662.685-038.....92314
662.685-042.....92314
662.686-010.....98502
662.686-014.....98502
663.132-010.....81008
663.380-010.....92311
663.585-010.....92314
663.682-010.....92314
663.682-014.....92944
663.682-018.....92314
663.685-010.....92944
663.685-014.....92314
663.685-018.....92314
663.685-022.....92314
663.685-026.....92314
663.685-030.....92314
663.685-034.....92314
663.685-038.....92314
663.685-042.....92314
663.685-046.....92314
663.685-050.....92314
663.686-010.....98502
663.686-014.....98502
663.686-018.....98502
663.686-022.....97941
663.686-026.....98502
663.686-030.....98999A
663.687-010.....83005A
664.382-010.....92311
664.382-014.....92314
664.382-018.....92311
664.662-010.....92311
664.682-010.....92314
664.682-014.....92314
664.682-018.....92314
664.682-022.....92314
664.684-010.....92314
664.685-010.....92314
664.685-014.....92314
664.685-018.....92314
664.685-022.....92314
664.685-026.....92314
664.685-030.....98999B
664.685-034.....92314
665.382-010.....92311
665.382-014.....92314
665.382-018.....92311
665.482-014.....92311
665.482-018.....92314
665.665-010.....92314
665.682-010.....92311
665.682-014.....92314
665.682-018.....92311
665.682-022.....92311
665.682-026.....92311
665.682-030.....92311
665.682-034.....92311
665.682-038.....92311
665.682-042.....92311
665.685-010.....92314
665.685-014.....92314
665.685-018.....92314
665.685-022.....92314
665.685-026.....92314
665.685-030.....92314
665.685-034.....92314
665.685-038.....92314
665.685-042.....92314
665.685-046.....92308
665.686-010.....98502
665.686-014.....98502

665.686-018 ..... 98999A
665.686-022 98502
666.382-010 92311
666.482-010 92314
666.582-010 92314
666.684-010 92314
666.685-010 92314
666.685-014 92314
667.137-010 81008
667.382-010 92308
667.482-014 92308
667.482-018 92308
667.485-010 92308
667.662-010 92305
667.662-014 92308
667.682-010 92308
667.682-014 92308
667.682-018 92308
667.682-022 92308
667.682-026 92308
667.682-030 92308
667.682-034 92305
667.682-038 92305
667.682-042 92308
667.682-046 92308
667.682-050 92308
667.682-054 92308
667.682-058 92308
667.682-062 92308
667.682-066 92308
667.682-070 92308
667.682-074 92308
667.682-078 92308
667.682-082 92308
667.682-086 92308
667.682-090 92308
667.682-094 92308
667.685-010 92308
667.685-014 92308
667.685-018 92308
667.685-022 92308
667.685-026 92308
667.685-030 92308
667.685-034 92308
667.685-038 92308
667.685-042 92308
667.685-046 92308
667.685-050 92308
667.685-054 92308
667.685-058 92308
667.685-062 92308
667.685-066 92308
667.685-070 92308
667.685-074 92308
667.686-010 98502
667.686-018 98502
667.686-022 ..... 98999A
667.687-010 ..... 98999A
667.687-014 ..... 83005A
667.687-018 92308
669.130-010 81008
669.130-014 81008
669.130-018 81008
669.130-022 81008
669.130-026 81008
669.130-030 81008
669.130-034 81008
669.130-038 81008
669.132-010 81008
669.137-010 81008
669.280-010 92311
669.360-010 92311
669.364-010 93956
669.380-010 89308
669.380-014 89308
669.380-018 92311
669.382-010 92311
669.382-014 92311
669.382-018 92311
669.382-022 92311
669.382-026 92311
669.485-010 ..... 73099B
669.662-010 92311
669.662-014 92314
669.662-018 92314
669.682-010 92314
669.682-014 93956
669.682-018 92314
669.682-022 92314
669.682-026 92302
669.682-030 92302
669.682-034 92308
669.682-038 92311
669.682-042 92311
669.682-046 92998
669.682-050 92314
669.682-054 92314
669.682-058 92311
669.682-062 92314
669.682-066 92314
669.682-070 92308
669.685-010 ..... 98999B
669.685-014 92314
669.685-018 92314
669.685-022 92314
669.685-026 92308
669.685-030 93998
669.685-034 92314
669.685-038 92998
669.685-042 92314
669.685-046 92314
669.685-050 92956
669.685-054 92314
669.685-058 ..... 98999B
669.685-062 92314
669.685-066 92314
669.685-070 92314
669.685-074 92314
669.685-078 92314
669.685-082 92314
669.685-086 92198
669.685-090 97951
669.685-094 92314
669.685-098 92998
669.685-102 92314
669.685-106 92314
669.686-010 98502
669.686-014 ..... 98999A
669.686-018 98502
669.686-022 98502
669.686-026 ..... 98999A
669.686-030 98502
669.686-034 98502
669.687-010 98502
669.687-014 ..... 83005A
669.687-018 ..... 98799B
669.687-022 ..... 73099B
669.687-026 ..... 83005A
669.687-030 ..... 83005A
670.362-010 ..... 92941B
670.384-010 ..... 83005A
670.587-010 93998
670.685-010 92944
673.130-010 81008
673.364-010 ..... 92902B
673.380-010 92997
673.382-010 ..... 89905C
673.382-014 ..... 89905C
673.382-018 92997
673.382-022 92997
673.382-026 92965
673.662-010 92965
673.666-010 98502
673.666-014 ..... 93926E
673.682-010 92997
673.682-014 92997
673.682-018 92997
673.682-022 92965
673.682-026 92997
673.682-030 92965
673.685-010 92965
673.685-014 92965
673.685-018 92965
673.685-022 92965
673.685-026 92965
673.685-030 92965
673.685-034 92965
673.685-038 92965
673.685-042 92965
673.685-046 92998
673.685-050 92998
673.685-054 92965
673.685-058 92965
673.685-062 92965
673.685-066 92965
673.685-070 92965
673.685-074 92965
673.685-078 92965
673.685-082 92965
673.685-086 92965
673.685-094 92965
673.685-098 92965
673.685-102 92965
673.686-010 98502
673.686-014 98502
673.686-018 98502
673.686-022 98502
673.686-026 98502
673.686-030 98502
673.687-010 93998
674.382-010 92998
674.662-010 92997
674.682-010 92997
675.682-010 92997
675.682-014 92965
675.682-018 92997
676.382-010 91108
676.462-010 92997
676.682-010 92997
676.682-014 92998
676.685-010 92998
676.685-014 92998
676.686-010 98502
676.686-014 98502
677.131-010 81008
677.382-010 ..... 92941A
677.382-014 92944
677.382-018 ..... 92902E
677.462-010 ..... 92941B
677.462-014 ..... 92941B
677.486-010 ..... 98999A
677.562-010 ..... 92941D
677.665-010 92998
677.666-010 ..... 98999A
677.682-010 92944
677.682-014 92944
677.682-018 92944
677.682-022 92944
677.682-026 ..... 92941A
677.685-010 92944
677.685-014 92944
677.685-018 92944
677.685-022 92944
677.685-026 92944
677.685-030 92944
677.685-034 92944
677.685-038 92944
677.685-042 92944
677.685-046 92944
677.685-050 92944
677.685-054 92944
677.686-010 98502
677.686-014 98502
677.687-010 ..... 98799B
677.687-014 ..... 92902G
679.130-010 81008
679.130-014 81008
679.130-018 81008
679.137-010 81008
679.137-014 81008
679.362-010 ..... 92902E
679.384-010 ..... 92902E
679.567-010 ..... 83005A
679.664-010 93998
679.665-010 92998
679.682-010 92951
679.685-010 92998
679.685-014 92998
679.685-018 92998
679.685-022 92965
679.685-026 92971
679.686-010 98502
679.687-010 ..... 83005A
680.130-010 81008
680.130-014 81008
680.135-010 81008
680.367-010 ..... 83005A
680.380-010 89111
680.585-010 92711
680.585-014 92711
680.665-014 92711
680.665-018 92998
680.684-010 ..... 85128A
680.685-010 92711
680.685-014 92998
680.685-018 92998
680.685-022 92705
680.685-026 92998
680.685-030 92998
680.685-034 92711
680.685-038 92711
680.685-042 92705
680.685-046 92998
680.685-050 92998
680.685-054 92998
680.685-058 92711
680.685-062 92965
680.685-066 92965
680.685-070 92998
680.685-074 92998
680.685-078 92998
680.685-082 92998
680.685-086 92998
680.685-090 92998
680.685-094 92705
680.685-098 92711
680.685-102 92705
680.685-106 92998
680.685-110 92998
680.685-114 92998
680.685-118 92998
680.686-010 98502
680.686-014 98502
680.686-018 98502
680.686-022 98502
680.687-010 ..... 98999A
680.687-014 98905
680.687-018 ..... 83005A
681.130-010 81008
681.130-014 81008
681.380-010 92702
681.387-010 ..... 83005A
681.485-010 92705
681.585-010 92705
681.585-014 92705
681.585-018 92705
681.682-010 92705
681.682-014 92705
681.682-018 92705
681.685-010 92705
681.685-014 92705
681.685-018 92705
681.685-022 92705
681.685-026 92705
681.685-030 92705
681.685-034 92705
681.685-038 92705
681.685-042 ..... 98999B
681.685-046 92705
681.685-050 92998

681.685-054......92998
681.685-058......92705
681.685-062......92705
681.685-066......92705
681.685-070......92705
681.685-074......92705
681.685-078......92705
681.685-082......92705
681.685-086......92705
681.685-090......92705
681.685-094......92705
681.685-098......92705
681.685-102......92705
681.685-106......92705
681.685-110......92705
681.685-114......92705
681.685-118......92705
681.685-122......92705
681.685-126......92705
681.685-130......92705
681.685-134......92705
681.685-138......92705
681.685-142......92705
681.685-146......92705
681.685-150......92705
681.685-154......92705
681.685-158......92705
681.686-010......98502
681.686-014......98999A
681.686-018......98502
681.687-010......83005A
681.687-014......98999A
681.687-018......83005A
681.687-022......83005A
681.687-026......83005A
681.687-030......83005A
682.130-010......81008
682.684-010......85128A
682.685-010......92705
682.685-014......92705
682.687-010......93998
683.130-010......81008
683.130-014......81008
683.130-018......81008
683.130-022......81008
683.132-010......81008
683.222-010......31314
683.260-010......92702
683.260-014......92702
683.260-018......92702
683.260-022......83005A
683.360-010......92702
683.360-014......83005A
683.380-010......85112
683.381-010......92702
683.384-010......83005A
683.487-010......83005A
683.582-010......92705
683.662-010......92705
683.665-010......92705
683.680-010......92702
683.680-014......92702
683.682-010......92705
683.682-014......92705
683.682-018......92702
683.682-022......92705
683.682-026......92705
683.682-030......92705
683.682-034......92705
683.682-038......92705
683.682-042......92705
683.682-046......92705
683.682-050......92705
683.684-010......85112
683.684-014......93997
683.684-018......83005A
683.684-022......85128A
683.684-026......93998
683.684-030......93997
683.684-034......83005A
683.685-010......92998
683.685-014......85128A
683.685-018......92998
683.685-022......98999B
683.685-026......92998
683.685-030......92705
683.685-034......92998
683.685-038......92705
683.686-010......98502
683.687-010......98999A
683.687-014......98999A
683.687-018......98999A
683.687-022......98999A
683.687-026......98905
683.687-030......98999A
683.687-034......85128A
684.137-010......81008
684.384-010......83005A
684.682-010......92705
684.682-014......92717
684.684-010......83005A
684.684-014......83005A
684.685-010......92705
684.686-010......98502
684.687-010......83005A
684.687-014......83005A
684.687-022......98799B
685.130-010......81008
685.360-010......92702
685.380-010......92702
685.381-010......92702
685.382-010......92705
685.665-010......92705
685.665-014......92705
685.665-018......92705
685.680-010......92702
685.682-010......92705
685.684-010......92705
685.685-010......92705
685.685-014......85128A
685.686-010......98502
685.686-014......98999A
685.687-010......83005A
685.687-014......98999A
685.687-018......92705
685.687-022......83005A
685.687-026......93998
686.462-010......92705
686.585-010 92705
686.662-010 92705
686.682-010 92705
686.682-014 92705
686.682-018 92705
686.685-010 92705
686.685-014 92705
686.685-018 92705
686.685-022 92705
686.685-026 92705
686.685-030 92998
686.685-034 92998
686.685-038 92998
686.685-042 92705
686.685-046 92998
686.685-050 92728
686.685-054 92998
686.685-058 92705
686.685-062 92998
686.685-066 92705
686.685-070 92998
686.685-074 92705
686.686-010 98502
686.686-014 ..... 98999A
687.132-010 81008
687.464-010 93998
687.682-010 92998
687.682-014 92998
687.684-010 93997
687.684-014 93998
687.685-010 92998
687.685-014 92998
687.685-018 92998
687.685-022 92998
689.130-010 81008
689.130-014 81008
689.130-018 81008
689.130-022 81008
689.130-026 81008
689.130-030 81008
689.130-034 81008
689.130-038 81008
689.132-010 81008
689.132-014 81008
689.134-010 81008
689.134-014 81008
689.134-018 81008
689.134-022 81008
689.134-026 81008
689.137-010 81008
689.137-014 81008
689.260-010 92702
689.260-014 92702
689.260-018 92702
689.260-022 92702
689.260-026 92702
689.280-010 92702
689.324-010 31314
689.360-010 92702
689.362-010 92702
689.364-010 92997
689.364-014 ..... 83005A
689.366-010 98502
689.380-010 92702
689.382-010 92702
689.384-010 ..... 83005A
689.384-014 ..... 83005A
689.387-010 ..... 83005A
689.564-010 ..... 83005A
689.582-010 92998
689.585-010 92705
689.585-014 92998
689.585-018 92998
689.587-010 93998
689.662-010 92702
689.662-014 92721
689.665-010 92998
689.665-014 92705
689.665-018 92998
689.667-010 ..... 83005A
689.682-010 92998
689.682-014 92998
689.682-018 92721
689.682-022 92721
689.684-010 ..... 83005A
689.684-014 93998
689.684-018 93998
689.685-010 92998
689.685-014 92705
689.685-018 92728
689.685-022 92998
689.685-026 92721
689.685-030 92998
689.685-034 92998
689.685-038 ..... 83005A
689.685-042 92705
689.685-046 92705
689.685-050 92705
689.685-054 92998
689.685-058 92998
689.685-062 92998
689.685-066 92705
689.685-070 92998
689.685-074 92998
689.685-078 ..... 83005A
689.685-082 92998
689.685-086 92705
689.685-090 92998
689.685-094 92998
689.685-098 ..... 83005A
689.685-102 92974
689.685-106 92721
689.685-110 92998
689.685-114 92705
689.685-118 92721
689.685-122 92998
689.685-126 92721
689.685-130 92998
689.685-134 92998
689.685-138 92956
689.685-142 92998
689.685-146 92998
689.685-150 92717
689.685-154 92717
689.685-158 92998
689.685-162 92998
689.685-166 92711
689.686-010 ..... 98999A
689.686-014 98502
689.686-018 98502
689.686-022 98502
689.686-026 ..... 85128A
689.686-030 98502
689.686-034 98502
689.686-038 98502
689.686-042 ..... 98999A
689.686-046 98502
689.686-050 93998
689.686-054 98502
689.686-058 98502
689.687-010 ..... 98999A
689.687-014 ..... 98999A
689.687-018 ..... 98999A
689.687-022 ..... 83005A
689.687-026 93998
689.687-030 ..... 98999A
689.687-034 93998
689.687-038 ..... 98999A
689.687-042 ..... 98999A
689.687-046 ..... 98999A
689.687-050 ..... 98999A
689.687-054 93998
689.687-058 ..... 98999A
689.687-062 ..... 83005A
689.687-066 ..... 98999A
689.687-070 ..... 85128A
689.687-074 ..... 98999A
689.687-078 93998
689.687-082 ..... 83005A
689.687-086 ..... 83005A
689.687-090 ..... 93926E
690.130-010 81008
690.130-014 81008
690.130-018 81008
690.130-022 81008
690.280-010 ..... 91114A
690.360-010 92997
690.362-010 92997
690.380-010 92997
690.380-014 92197
690.382-010 92198
690.382-014 92997
690.385-010 92965
690.462-010 ..... 92941A
690.482-010 91102
690.482-014 92198
690.485-010 92944
690.580-010 92997
690.585-010 92998
690.585-014 91321
690.662-010 92997
690.662-014 92968
690.665-010 91321
690.680-010 92997
690.682-010 ..... 92941A
690.682-014 92997
690.682-018 92998
690.682-022 92944
690.682-026 92705
690.682-030 92998
690.682-034 92997
690.682-038 ..... 92941A

690.682-042 ..... 92941A
690.682-046 ..... 92941A
690.682-050 ..... 92941A
690.682-054 92953
690.682-058 92198
690.682-062 92198
690.682-066 92998
690.682-070 92971
690.682-074 92198
690.682-078 92723
690.682-082 92723
690.682-086 92944
690.682-090 92997
690.685-010 92998
690.685-014 92998
690.685-018 92998
690.685-022 92974
690.685-026 92944
690.685-030 92998
690.685-034 92998
690.685-038 92965
690.685-042 92998
690.685-046 92965
690.685-050 92965
690.685-054 92965
690.685-058 92998
690.685-062 92944
690.685-066 92998
690.685-070 92956
690.685-074 92971
690.685-078 91321
690.685-082 92998
690.685-086 92998
690.685-090 91905
690.685-094 92944
690.685-098 92998
690.685-102 92998
690.685-106 92998
690.685-110 92998
690.685-114 92998
690.685-118 92944
690.685-122 92944
690.685-126 92944
690.685-130 92198
690.685-134 92956
690.685-138 92998
690.685-142 91117
690.685-146 92998
690.685-150 92944
690.685-154 92198
690.685-158 92998
690.685-162 92998
690.685-166 92944
690.685-170 91117
690.685-174 92998
690.685-178 92998
690.685-182 ..... 83005A
690.685-186 92998
690.685-190 91117
690.685-194 92965
690.685-198 92944
690.685-202 91117
690.685-206 92998
690.685-210 92998
690.685-214 92944
690.685-218 92998
690.685-222 92998
690.685-226 92314
690.685-230 92998
690.685-234 92998
690.685-238 92944
690.685-242 92944
690.685-246 92998
690.685-250 92944
690.685-254 92998
690.685-258 92971
690.685-262 91117
690.685-266 92998
690.685-270 92998
690.685-274 92944
690.685-278 92998
690.685-282 92998
690.685-286 92998
690.685-290 92944
690.685-294 92998
690.685-298 92944
690.685-302 92944
690.685-306 92944
690.685-310 92198
690.685-314 92998
690.685-318 92971
690.685-322 92944
690.685-326 92198
690.685-330 92965
690.685-334 92944
690.685-338 92944
690.685-342 92944
690.685-346 92965
690.685-350 92998
690.685-354 92944
690.685-358 92998
690.685-362 92998
690.685-366 92944
690.685-370 92944
690.685-374 92944
690.685-378 92944
690.685-382 92998
690.685-386 92944
690.685-390 92965
690.685-394 92998
690.685-398 92998
690.685-402 92944
690.685-406 92998
690.685-410 92998
690.685-414 92998
690.685-418 92998
690.685-422 92965
690.685-426 92998
690.685-430 92998
690.685-434 92944
690.685-438 92998
690.685-442 92998
690.685-446 92944
690.685-450 92998
690.685-454 92998
690.685-458 92944
690.685-462 92998
690.685-466 92971
690.685-470 92998
690.685-474 92998
690.685-478 92944
690.685-482 92998
690.685-486 92944
690.685-490 92198
690.685-494 92723
690.685-498 92998
690.685-502 92998
690.685-506 92998
690.685-510 91117
690.686-010 98502
690.686-014 ...... 98999A
690.686-018 92956
690.686-022 98502
690.686-026 98502
690.686-030 ...... 98999A
690.686-034 98502
690.686-038 98502
690.686-042 98502
690.686-046 98502
690.686-050 98502
690.686-054 98502
690.686-058 98502
690.686-062 98502
690.686-066 98502
690.686-070 ...... 98999A
691.130-010 81008
691.130-014 81008
691.367-010 ...... 83005A
691.382-010 92971
691.382-014 92971
691.387-010 ...... 83005A
691.667-010 93998
691.682-010 92997
691.682-014 92997
691.682-018 92998
691.685-010 92998
691.685-014 92998
691.685-018 92198
691.685-022 92198
691.685-026 92998
691.685-030 92198
691.686-010 98502
691.687-010 ...... 98999A
692.130-010 81008
692.130-014 81008
692.130-018 81008
692.130-022 81008
692.130-026 81008
692.130-030 81008
692.130-034 81008
692.130-038 81008
692.130-042 81008
692.132-010 81008
692.132-014 81008
692.132-018 81008
692.137-010 81008
692.137-014 81008
692.260-010 92997
692.360-010 92997
692.360-014 ...... 92941A
692.360-018 92997
692.362-010 92968
692.380-010 92311
692.380-014 92997
692.382-010 92997
692.382-014 92997
692.462-010 92971
692.482-010 92997
692.485-010 92198
692.662-010 92997
692.662-014 92974
692.662-018 92998
692.662-022 92998
692.665-010 92998
692.665-014 92998
692.665-018 92998
692.682-010 92998
692.682-014 92951
692.682-018 92997
692.682-022 92998
692.682-026 92971
692.682-030 92998
692.682-034 91505
692.682-038 92974
692.682-042 92944
692.682-046 92997
692.682-050 92997
692.682-054 92998
692.682-058 92974
692.682-062 92998
692.682-066 92998
692.682-070 92997
692.685-010 92998
692.685-014 92998
692.685-018 92998
692.685-022 92956
692.685-026 92998
692.685-030 92971
692.685-034 92971
692.685-038 92971
692.685-042 92998
692.685-046 92998
692.685-050 92956
692.685-054 92953
692.685-058 92971
692.685-062 92956
692.685-066 92998
692.685-070 92198
692.685-074 92998
692.685-078 92198
692.685-082 92998
692.685-086 92971
692.685-090 92998
692.685-094 92956
692.685-098 92956
692.685-102 92998
692.685-106 92956
692.685-110 92956
692.685-114 92974
692.685-118 92971
692.685-122 92998
692.685-126 92998
692.685-130 92944
692.685-134 92998
692.685-138 92198
692.685-142 92953
692.685-146 92546
692.685-150 92998
692.685-154 92974
692.685-158 92998
692.685-162 92998
692.685-166 92962
692.685-170 92956
692.685-174 92944
692.685-178 92998
692.685-182 92998
692.685-186 92998
692.685-190 92998
692.685-194 92998
692.685-198 92998
692.685-202 92998
692.685-206 92198
692.685-210 92953
692.685-214 92998
692.685-218 92998
692.685-222 92944
692.685-226 92998
692.685-230 92198
692.685-234 92998
692.685-238 91926
692.685-242 92998
692.685-246 92998
692.685-250 92705
692.685-254 92721
692.685-258 92944
692.685-262 92998
692.685-266 92944
692.685-270 92198
692.685-274 92998
692.685-278 92998
692.685-282 92971
692.685-286 92998
692.685-290 92998
692.686-010 98502
692.686-014 98502
692.686-018 98502
692.686-022 98502
692.686-026 98502
692.686-030 98502
692.686-034 98502
692.686-038 98502
692.686-042 98502
692.686-046 98502
692.686-050 98502
692.686-054 98502
692.686-058 98502
692.686-062 98502
692.686-066 98502
692.686-070 92956
692.687-010 ..... 98999A
693.130-010 81008
693.131-010 81008
693.132-010 81008
693.260-018 ..... 89114A
693.261-010 ..... 89908A
693.261-014 89108
693.261-018 ..... 89908A
693.261-022 89108
693.280-014 ..... 89908A
693.281-014 ..... 89114B

693.281-018......89114B
693.281-022......89114B
693.281-030......89908A
693.361-014......89114A
693.380-010......89114A
693.380-014......89908A
693.381-018......89908A
693.381-022......89905B
693.381-026......93114
693.382-010......89908B
694.131-010......81008
694.132-010......81008
694.260-010......92197
694.360-010......92197
694.362-010......92997
694.382-010......92997
694.382-014......92974
694.385-010......92198
694.585-010......92198
694.665-010......92998
694.682-010......92197
694.682-014......92198
694.685-010......92198
694.685-014......92198
694.685-018......91926
694.685-022......92198
694.685-026......92974
694.685-030......92974
694.685-034......92971
694.685-038......92971
694.685-042......92998
694.685-046......91926
694.685-050......92974
694.686-010......98502
699.130-010......81008
699.131-010......81008
699.137-010......81017
699.362-010......91502
699.380-010......91302
699.382-010......92941A
699.384-010......83005A
699.482-010......92197
699.587-010......98999A
699.682-010......92705
699.682-014......92705
699.682-018......92944
699.682-022......92944
699.682-026......92944
699.682-030......92944
699.682-034......91117
699.685-010......92998
699.685-014......92944
699.685-018......92998
699.685-022......92998
699.685-026......92198
699.685-030......92198
699.685-038......92974
699.685-046......91117
699.685-050......92198
699.685-054......91117
699.686-010......98502
699.687-010......98905
699.687-014......98905
699.687-018......85128B

699.687-022......98999A
700.130-010......81008
700.131-010......81008
700.131-014......81008
700.131-018......81008
700.261-010......89126K
700.281-010......89123A
700.281-014......89123A
700.281-018......89126C
700.281-022......89123B
700.281-026......89126K
700.381-010......89126E
700.381-014......89126E
700.381-018......89126E
700.381-022......89123B
700.381-026......89126E
700.381-030......89123A
700.381-034......89126C
700.381-038......89126C
700.381-042......89123A
700.381-046......89123A
700.381-050......89126E
700.381-054......89126E
700.381-058......89126E
700.682-010......92971
700.682-014......91117
700.682-018......91102
700.684-010......93998
700.684-014......93956
700.684-018......93926E
700.684-022......93956
700.684-026......91117
700.684-030......93956
700.684-034......93953
700.684-038......93926E
700.684-042......93956
700.684-046......91117
700.684-050......93926E
700.684-054......93947E
700.684-058......93997
700.684-062......93997
700.684-066......92198
700.684-070......93956
700.684-074......93997
700.684-078......93998
700.684-082......93956
700.687-010......93956
700.687-014......93947E
700.687-018......93998
700.687-022......93999
700.687-026......93956
700.687-030......98999A
700.687-034......83005A
700.687-038......98902A
700.687-042......93941
700.687-046......98999A
700.687-050......98999A
700.687-054......91321
700.687-058......93953
700.687-062......93998
700.687-066......91117
701.137-010......81008
701.261-010......83002A
701.381-010......85999A

701.381-014 89111
701.381-018 89111
701.384-010 .....85999A
701.684-010 .....85999A
701.684-014 .....83005A
701.684-018 93956
701.684-022 92997
701.684-026 92198
701.684-030 89111
701.687-010 93956
701.687-014 .....83005A
701.687-018 93998
701.687-022 .....83005A
701.687-026 .....83005A
701.687-030 .....93926E
701.687-034 93998
703.132-010 81008
703.381-010 .....89114B
703.684-010 91117
703.684-014 93956
703.684-018 .....93926E
703.685-010 92998
703.685-014 .....83005A
703.687-010 .....83005A
703.687-014 .....83005A
703.687-018 .....83005B
703.687-022 93953
704.131-010 81008
704.131-014 81008
704.381-010 .....89123B
704.381-014 89199
704.381-018 .....89126E
704.381-022 89128
704.381-026 89128
704.381-030 89128
704.381-034 89128
704.382-010 .....93951A
704.582-010 .....93951A
704.682-010 .....93951A
704.682-014 .....93951A
704.684-010 .....93951B
704.684-014 .....93951B
704.687-010 98905
704.687-014 .....93951B
705.381-010 89111
705.381-014 89199
705.384-010 93953
705.481-010 89111
705.481-014 89111
705.484-010 93953
705.484-014 93953
705.582-010 91117
705.682-010 91117
705.682-014 91117
705.684-010 91117
705.684-014 91117
705.684-018 93998
705.684-022 93953
705.684-026 93953
705.684-030 93953
705.684-034 93953
705.684-038 93953
705.684-042 85998
705.684-046 93953

705.684-050 93953
705.684-054 93953
705.684-058 91117
705.684-062 93953
705.684-066 91117
705.684-070 91117
705.684-074 91117
705.687-010 .....98999A
705.687-014 93953
705.687-018 93953
706.130-010 81008
706.131-010 81008
706.131-014 81008
706.131-018 81008
706.361-010 93105
706.361-014 .....83005A
706.381-010 85926
706.381-014 89199
706.381-018 .....93111A
706.381-022 .....83002A
706.381-026 .....93197C
706.381-030 85926
706.381-034 93105
706.381-038 93105
706.381-042 93105
706.381-046 .....85302B
706.381-050 .....93111A
706.382-010 .....83005A
706.382-014 .....83005A
706.384-010 .....83005A
706.387-010 .....83005A
706.387-014 .....83005A
706.481-010 93105
706.484-010 93956
706.587-010 93998
706.587-014 .....83005A
706.684-010 93902
706.684-014 93902
706.684-018 93956
706.684-022 93956
706.684-026 93902
706.684-030 93956
706.684-034 93956
706.684-038 93902
706.684-042 93956
706.684-046 93902
706.684-050 93956
706.684-054 93956
706.684-058 93956
706.684-062 93902
706.684-070 93956
706.684-074 93956
706.684-078 93956
706.684-082 93956
706.684-086 93956
706.684-090 93956
706.684-094 93902
706.684-098 93953
706.684-102 93956
706.684-106 93956
706.684-110 93998
706.685-010 91711
706.685-014 92998
706.687-010 93956

706.687-018 93998
706.687-022 .....83005A
706.687-026 .....83005A
706.687-030 93956
706.687-034 .....83005A
709.134-010 81008
709.137-010 81008
709.281-010 85923
709.281-014 85923
709.364-010 .....83005A
709.364-014 85998
709.367-010 .....83005A
709.381-010 .....93197C
709.381-014 .....89114A
709.381-018 .....89126C
709.381-022 .....89126C
709.381-026 93953
709.381-030 .....93197A
709.381-034 .....89114B
709.381-038 .....93197C
709.381-042 89199
709.381-046 89199
709.382-010 .....83005A
709.384-010 85998
709.484-010 93956
709.484-014 93997
709.587-010 .....83005A
709.587-014 .....83005A
709.667-010 93956
709.682-010 92923
709.684-010 93998
709.684-014 93956
709.684-018 .....83005A
709.684-022 .....93947E
709.684-026 93956
709.684-030 93956
709.684-034 85998
709.684-038 93956
709.684-042 93998
709.684-046 87302
709.684-050 92198
709.684-054 .....93951C
709.684-058 93953
709.684-062 85998
709.684-066 93956
709.684-070 .....85928A
709.684-074 .....93926E
709.684-078 93956
709.684-082 91117
709.684-086 .....93914A
709.684-090 93997
709.684-094 92998
709.684-098 92198
709.684-102 93956
709.685-010 92998
709.685-014 92971
709.685-018 92971
709.686-010 .....98999A
709.687-010 .....98999A
709.687-014 .....98999A
709.687-018 98311
709.687-022 .....83005A
709.687-026 .....83005A
709.687-030 .....83005A

709.687-034 98102
709.687-038 ..... 83005A
709.687-042 ..... 83005A
709.687-046 ..... 98999A
709.687-050 93998
709.687-054 ..... 83005A
709.687-058 92198
709.687-062 93998
710.131-010 81002
710.131-014 81008
710.131-018 81002
710.131-022 81002
710.131-026 81002
710.131-030 81002
710.131-034 81008
710.131-038 81008
710.131-042 81008
710.137-010 81008
710.137-014 81002
710.261-010 85905
710.281-010 93114
710.281-018 ..... 93111B
710.281-022 ..... 85928B
710.281-026 85905
710.281-030 85905
710.281-034 ..... 85928B
710.281-038 85905
710.281-042 85905
710.360-010 92197
710.361-010 ..... 89114A
710.361-014 ..... 22599C
710.381-010 ..... 93197C
710.381-014 ..... 83002C
710.381-022 ..... 85928B
710.381-026 ..... 85928A
710.381-030 ..... 83002C
710.381-034 ..... 83002C
710.381-042 ..... 83002C
710.381-046 ..... 83002D
710.381-050 ..... 85928A
710.381-054 85905
710.384-010 98102
710.384-014 ..... 83002B
710.384-018 98102
710.384-022 ..... 83002C
710.384-026 85947
710.384-030 ..... 83005A
710.387-010 ..... 83005A
710.584-010 93956
710.681-018 85947
710.681-026 ..... 93197C
710.684-010 93956
710.684-014 93997
710.684-018 ..... 93951C
710.684-026 ..... 85928B
710.684-030 98102
710.684-034 98102
710.684-038 93956
710.684-042 93956
710.684-046 93956
710.684-050 ..... 83005A
710.685-014 92998
710.687-014 ..... 83005A
710.687-034 ..... 98902A
711.137-010 81008
711.281-010 ...... 83002C
711.281-014 85905
711.381-010 ...... 89917D
711.684-010 93998
711.684-014 93956
712.131-010 81008
712.132-010 81008
712.134-010 93956
712.137-010 81008
712.137-014 81008
712.281-014 ...... 89599F
712.381-010 89923
712.381-014 89921
712.381-018 89921
712.381-022 89921
712.381-026 89921
712.381-030 89921
712.381-034 89923
712.381-038 89923
712.381-042 89921
712.381-046 89921
712.381-050 89921
712.487-010 ...... 83005A
712.664-010 89921
712.684-010 93956
712.684-014 93956
712.684-018 93998
712.684-022 93956
712.684-026 93998
712.684-030 ...... 93947E
712.684-034 ...... 93944D
712.684-038 93997
712.684-042 93956
712.684-046 ...... 93944A
712.684-050 ...... 83005A
712.684-054 93956
712.687-010 93956
712.687-014 93998
712.687-018 ...... 83005A
712.687-022 ...... 83005A
712.687-030 ...... 98999A
712.687-034 ...... 98999A
712.687-038 ...... 83005A
713.261-010 ...... 89999C
713.261-014 ...... 89999C
713.381-010 ...... 89917A
713.384-010 93956
713.384-014 ...... 83005A
713.667-010 ...... 83005A
713.681-010 ...... 89917A
713.684-010 93956
713.684-014 93956
713.684-018 93956
713.684-022 ...... 93951C
713.684-026 93998
713.684-030 92198
713.684-034 93956
713.684-038 91117
713.684-042 93999
713.687-010 ...... 93947E
713.687-014 93998
713.687-018 93956
713.687-022 ...... 83005A
713.687-026 93956
713.687-030 ...... 83005A
713.687-034 93953
713.687-038 93998
713.687-042 93956
714.131-010 81008
714.281-010 85914
714.281-014 85914
714.281-018 85914
714.281-022 85914
714.281-026 85914
714.281-030 85914
714.381-010 ...... 93111A
714.381-014 ...... 83002C
714.381-018 89718
714.667-010 ...... 83005A
714.684-010 93956
714.684-014 93956
714.687-010 ...... 83005A
715.131-010 81008
715.131-014 81008
715.131-018 81008
715.131-022 81008
715.131-026 81008
715.131-030 81008
715.221-010 31314
715.261-010 ...... 83002C
715.281-010 85917
715.281-014 85917
715.381-010 93117
715.381-014 93117
715.381-018 93117
715.381-022 93117
715.381-026 93117
715.381-030 93117
715.381-034 91117
715.381-038 93117
715.381-042 93117
715.381-046 ...... 89126E
715.381-050 ...... 83002C
715.381-054 93117
715.381-058 ...... 83002C
715.381-062 93117
715.381-066 ...... 83002C
715.381-070 ...... 83002C
715.381-074 ...... 83002C
715.381-078 ...... 83002C
715.381-082 93117
715.381-086 93117
715.381-090 91117
715.381-094 93117
715.384-010 93956
715.384-014 ...... 83005A
715.384-018 ...... 83005A
715.384-022 ...... 83002C
715.584-010 ...... 93947E
715.584-014 85917
715.584-018 93953
715.660-010 92197
715.681-010 93117
715.682-010 91117
715.682-014 91117
715.682-018 91117
715.682-022 92998
715.682-026 91117
715.684-010 93998
715.684-014 93956
715.684-018 ..... 83005A
715.684-022 93956
715.684-026 93998
715.684-030 91321
715.684-034 93997
715.684-038 93953
715.684-042 93953
715.684-046 93956
715.684-050 93956
715.684-054 93956
715.684-058 93956
715.684-062 91117
715.684-066 93956
715.684-070 93956
715.684-074 93956
715.684-078 92965
715.684-082 93956
715.684-086 93956
715.684-090 93998
715.684-094 ..... 83005A
715.684-098 93956
715.684-102 ..... 83005A
715.684-106 93953
715.684-110 93956
715.684-114 ..... 83005A
715.684-118 ..... 83005A
715.684-122 ..... 83005A
715.684-126 ..... 83005A
715.684-130 93956
715.684-134 93956
715.684-138 ..... 93947E
715.684-142 93956
715.684-146 93998
715.684-150 93956
715.684-154 93956
715.684-158 91117
715.684-162 ..... 93926E
715.684-166 93956
715.684-170 93953
715.684-174 93956
715.684-178 93956
715.684-182 93956
715.684-186 93956
715.684-190 ..... 93951C
715.684-194 ..... 83005A
715.685-010 92956
715.685-014 91117
715.685-018 91117
715.685-022 91117
715.685-026 91117
715.685-030 92198
715.685-034 ..... 83005A
715.685-038 93956
715.685-042 91117
715.685-046 91117
715.685-050 91321
715.685-054 92198
715.685-058 91711
715.685-062 91117
715.685-066 ..... 83005A
715.685-070 91321
715.686-010 98502
715.686-014 98502
715.687-010 93956
715.687-014 93956
715.687-018 93956
715.687-022 93998
715.687-026 ..... 93947E
715.687-030 93998
715.687-034 ..... 83005A
715.687-038 ..... 93926E
715.687-042 ..... 93926E
715.687-046 93998
715.687-050 ..... 83005A
715.687-054 ..... 83005A
715.687-058 ..... 83005A
715.687-062 ..... 83005A
715.687-066 ..... 83005A
715.687-070 ..... 83005A
715.687-074 ..... 83005A
715.687-078 93998
715.687-082 93998
715.687-086 ..... 93947E
715.687-090 ..... 98999A
715.687-094 93998
715.687-098 ..... 93947E
715.687-102 ..... 98999A
715.687-106 ..... 98999A
715.687-110 93953
715.687-114 93956
715.687-118 93956
715.687-122 93998
715.687-126 ..... 98999A
715.687-130 ..... 83005A
716.130-010 81008
716.280-010 ..... 89917A
716.280-014 ..... 89917A
716.280-018 ..... 89917D
716.360-010 92997
716.381-010 ..... 83002C
716.381-014 ..... 89917A
716.382-010 ..... 89917A
716.382-014 ..... 89917A
716.382-018 ..... 89917A
716.382-022 ..... 89917A
716.462-010 ..... 89917A
716.681-010 ..... 89917A
716.681-014 ..... 89917A
716.681-018 ..... 89917A
716.681-022 ..... 93951B
716.682-010 ..... 89917A
716.682-014 ..... 89917A
716.682-018 ..... 89917A
716.684-010 93998
716.685-010 92998
716.685-014 92998
716.685-018 92965
716.685-022 92965
716.687-010 93998
716.687-014 ..... 83005A
716.687-018 ..... 83005A
716.687-022 ..... 83005A
716.687-026 ..... 83005A
716.687-030 ..... 83005A
716.687-034 ..... 83005A

719.261-014......85908
719.381-014......85799
719.381-018......93944D
720.281-010......85708
720.281-014......85708
720.281-018......85708
720.684-010......83005A
720.684-014......93905D
720.687-010......93905D
720.687-014......83005A
721.131-010......81002
721.131-014......81008
721.261-010......85714A
721.261-014......83002D
721.281-010......85714A
721.281-014......85714A
721.281-018......85714A
721.281-022......85328B
721.281-026......85714A
721.281-030......83002D
721.361-010......83002D
721.381-010......85714A
721.381-014......93114
721.381-018......93111A
721.484-010......93905C
721.484-014......93905C
721.484-018......92944
721.484-022......93905C
721.684-010......98102
721.684-014......93905C
721.684-018......93908
721.684-022......93905C
721.684-026......93905C
721.687-010......93947E
722.131-010......81002
722.281-010......85599A
722.381-010......93114
722.381-014......83002C
722.687-010......93956
723.131-010......81008
723.132-010......81008
723.361-010......89114A
723.381-010......85711A
723.381-014......85711A
723.584-010......85711A
723.684-010......93905D
723.684-014......93905D
723.684-018......93956
723.684-022......83005A
723.685-010......92198
723.687-010......93956
723.687-014......83005A
723.687-018......83005A
723.687-022......98999A
724.130-010......81008
724.131-010......81008
724.131-014......81008
724.281-010......83002D
724.360-010......92997
724.362-010......93908
724.364-010......83002D
724.381-010......85714A
724.381-014......93908
724.381-018......85714C
724.384-010......83002D
724.384-014......83005A
724.684-010......93908
724.684-014......93908
724.684-018......85714D
724.684-022......91321
724.684-026......93908
724.684-030......93905D
724.684-034......93902
724.684-038......93905D
724.685-010......93908
724.685-014......83005A
724.687-010......98999A
725.381-010......22505A
725.384-010......93905B
725.684-010......83005A
725.684-014......93905D
725.684-018......93905D
725.684-022......93905B
725.684-026......93905B
725.685-010......92198
725.687-010......83005A
725.687-014......83005A
725.687-018......83005A
725.687-022......93998
725.687-026......83005A
726.130-010......81008
726.131-014......81008
726.131-018......81008
726.134-010......81008
726.261-010......22505A
726.261-014......22505C
726.261-018......83002D
726.361-014......93114
726.361-018......83002D
726.361-022......85717B
726.362-010......83002D
726.362-014......91711
726.364-010......83002D
726.364-014......22514B
726.364-018......93905B
726.367-010......83005A
726.380-010......92197
726.381-010......83002D
726.381-014......85514
726.382-010......92997
726.384-014......83002D
726.384-018......83002D
726.384-022......83002D
726.682-010......91502
726.682-014......93908
726.682-018......83002D
726.682-026......91117
726.684-010......93997
726.684-014......93905B
726.684-018......93905B
726.684-022......83005A
726.684-026......83005A
726.684-034......93905B
726.684-042......93905B
726.684-050......83005A
726.684-054......83005A
726.684-058......83005A
726.684-062......83005A
726.684-066......83005A
726.684-070......93905B
726.684-074......83005A
726.684-078......83005A
726.684-082......83005A
726.684-086......93905B
726.684-090......85717B
726.684-094......91711
726.684-098......93905B
726.684-102......83005A
726.684-106......83005A
726.684-110......83005A
726.685-010......92998
726.685-014......92998
726.685-018......92998
726.685-022......92958
726.685-026......92198
726.685-030......83005A
726.685-034......83005A
726.685-038......91711
726.685-042......92998
726.685-046......92902E
726.685-050......91926
726.685-054......83005A
726.685-058......92902G
726.685-062......92998
726.685-066......92198
726.686-010......98502
726.687-010......93998
726.687-014......93905D
726.687-022......93905D
726.687-026......93905B
726.687-030......92902G
726.687-034......93998
726.687-038......93998
726.687-042......92902G
726.687-046......92902G
727.130-010......81008
727.137-010......81008
727.381-010......83005A
727.381-014......85714B
727.381-018......83002D
727.381-022......83002D
727.384-010......83005A
727.484-010......93998
727.587-010......93998
727.662-010......91702
727.664-010......93905A
727.684-010......93905A
727.684-014......93905A
727.684-018......85714B
727.684-022......93914A
727.684-026......93905A
727.684-030......93998
727.685-010......91321
727.687-010......98502
727.687-014......98999A
727.687-018......83005A
727.687-022......93905A
727.687-026......93998
727.687-030......98799B
727.687-034......93947E
727.687-038......93905A
727.687-042......93998
727.687-046......93905A
727.687-050......83005A
727.687-054......83005A
727.687-058......93998
727.687-062......83005A
727.687-066......83005A
727.687-070......98999A
727.687-074......83005A
727.687-078......83005A
727.687-082......93905A
728.684-010......93905D
728.684-014......93997
728.684-018......83005A
728.684-022......93998
728.685-010......92198
729.130-010......81008
729.131-010......81008
729.131-014......81008
729.281-010......85708
729.281-014......85911
729.281-018......85911
729.281-022......85711A
729.281-026......85905
729.281-030......85908
729.281-034......85911
729.281-038......83002D
729.281-042......93114
729.281-046......83002C
729.360-010......92997
729.361-010......83002C
729.381-010......83002D
729.381-014......85947
729.381-018......87202A
729.381-022......93114
729.384-010......93905D
729.384-014......85947
729.384-018......85714D
729.384-022......83005A
729.384-026......93905D
729.387-010......83005A
729.387-014......83005A
729.387-018......83005A
729.387-022......83005A
729.387-026......83005A
729.664-010......98999B
729.682-010......92998
729.684-010......83005A
729.684-014......93905D
729.684-018......93947E
729.684-022......93905D
729.684-026......93905D
729.684-030......93944D
729.684-034......93905D
729.684-038......85714A
729.684-042......85799
729.684-046......93905D
729.684-050......98102
729.684-054......93905D
729.684-058......83005A
729.684-062......93905D
729.684-066......93905D
729.687-010......93905D
729.687-014......98999A
729.687-018......98999A
729.687-022......93998
729.687-026......98999A
729.687-030......98905
730.131-010......81008
730.281-010......89397A
730.281-014......85921A
730.281-018......85708
730.281-022......89397A
730.281-026......85921B
730.281-030......89397A
730.281-034......89398
730.281-038......85921A
730.281-042......89397A
730.281-046......89397A
730.281-050......85921B
730.281-054......85921C
730.281-058......89397A
730.361-010......85921A
730.361-014......85921A
730.367-010......83005A
730.381-010......85921A
730.381-014......93197A
730.381-018......93197A
730.381-022......93114
730.381-026......85921B
730.381-030......93197A
730.381-034......85921C
730.381-038......85921A
730.381-042......85921D
730.381-046......93197A
730.381-050......85799
730.381-054......93197A
730.381-058......85921D
730.384-010......93956
730.681-010......85921A
730.681-014......93197A
730.681-018......93197A
730.682-010......92198
730.684-010......93956
730.684-014......93998
730.684-018......93956
730.684-022......85921B
730.684-026......85921A
730.684-030......93956
730.684-034......83005A
730.684-038......83005A
730.684-042......93956
730.684-046......93956
730.684-050......93956
730.684-054......93956
730.684-058......93956
730.684-062......93956
730.684-066......93953
730.684-070......91321
730.684-074......93926E
730.684-078......93956
730.684-082......93956
730.684-086......83005A
730.684-090......93956
730.684-094......85921A
730.685-010......92998
730.685-014......93956
730.686-010......92944
731.131-010......81008

731.280-010..... 89908A
731.381-010..... 91108
731.587-010..... 98999A
731.684-010..... 93956
731.684-014..... 85998
731.684-018..... 93956
731.684-022..... 85799
731.685-010..... 92721
731.685-014..... 92974
731.685-018..... 92998
731.687-010..... 93956
731.687-014..... 93998
731.687-018..... 98999A
731.687-022..... 83005A
731.687-026..... 93944D
731.687-030..... 93956
731.687-034..... 93956
731.687-038..... 93926E
732.130-010..... 81008
732.281-010..... 89999C
732.364-014..... 85998
732.381-010..... 89999C
732.381-014..... 83005A
732.381-018..... 89199
732.381-022..... 85998
732.384-010..... 93956
732.384-014..... 83005A
732.487-010..... 83005A
732.567-010..... 83005A
732.584-010..... 93951A
732.584-014..... 93953
732.587-010..... 93998
732.587-014..... 83005A
732.684-010..... 93956
732.684-014..... 93956
732.684-018..... 93956
732.684-022..... 93956
732.684-026..... 93956
732.684-030..... 83005A
732.684-034..... 93923B
732.684-038..... 93956
732.684-042..... 93956
732.684-046..... 93956
732.684-050..... 93923B
732.684-054..... 93956
732.684-058..... 93956
732.684-062..... 93956
732.684-066..... 93956
732.684-070..... 93956
732.684-074..... 93956
732.684-078..... 93956
732.684-082..... 93956
732.684-086..... 93956
732.684-090..... 93923B
732.684-094..... 93956
732.684-098..... 93956
732.684-102..... 85998
732.684-106..... 93956
732.684-110..... 93956
732.684-114..... 93956
732.684-118..... 85998
732.684-122..... 85998
732.684-126..... 93956
732.684-130..... 83005A

732.685-010......92974
732.685-014......92944
732.685-018......93956
732.685-022......92998
732.685-026......92998
732.685-030......92998
732.685-034......92974
732.685-038......92944
732.686-010......98502
732.687-010......93956
732.687-014......93956
732.687-018......93956
732.687-022......93956
732.687-026......93956
732.687-030......98999A
732.687-034......93956
732.687-038......93956
732.687-042......93956
732.687-046......98905
732.687-050......93956
732.687-054......93998
732.687-058......93956
732.687-062......93947E
732.687-066......98999A
732.687-070......93998
732.687-074......93953
732.687-078......93926E
732.687-082......98999A
732.687-086......83005A
733.130-010......81008
733.131-010......81008
733.137-010......81008
733.137-014......81008
733.137-018......81008
733.281-010......83005A
733.364-010......83005A
733.381-010......89911C
733.381-014......93197C
733.384-010......85998
733.684-010......93956
733.684-014......85998
733.684-018......93956
733.685-010......93956
733.685-014......92974
733.685-018......92198
733.685-022......92998
733.685-026......91117
733.685-030......92953
733.685-034......92998
733.687-010......93956
733.687-014......93956
733.687-018......93956
733.687-022......93926E
733.687-026......98999A
733.687-030......93956
733.687-034......93956
733.687-038......93947E
733.687-042......83005A
733.687-046......83005A
733.687-050......83005A
733.687-054......83005A
733.687-058......83005A
733.687-062......83005A
733.687-066......93998

733.687-070......93956
733.687-074......83005A
733.687-078......98999A
734.131-010......81008
734.384-010......93926E
734.481-010......89199
734.584-010......91117
734.684-010......93998
734.684-014......93956
734.684-018......83005A
734.684-022......93998
734.684-026......93998
734.685-010......92998
734.685-014......92998
734.687-010......93956
734.687-014......93956
734.687-018......93956
734.687-022......98999A
734.687-026......83005A
734.687-030......83005A
734.687-034......93998
734.687-038......83005A
734.687-042......83005A
734.687-046......93998
734.687-050......93956
734.687-054......93953
734.687-058......93956
734.687-062......83005A
734.687-066......83005A
734.687-070......83005A
734.687-074......93956
734.687-078......93956
734.687-082......83005A
734.687-086......93926E
734.687-090......93956
734.687-094......83005A
735.381-010......89126E
735.381-014......89126E
735.381-018......89126C
735.587-010......83005A
735.681-010......89126E
735.684-010......93956
735.684-014......93953
735.684-018......93956
735.687-010......98999A
735.687-014......93956
735.687-018......93947E
735.687-022......93956
735.687-026......98999A
735.687-030......83005A
735.687-034......93956
735.687-038......93956
735.687-042......93956
736.131-010......81008
736.131-014......81008
736.131-018......81008
736.281-010......83002A
736.367-010......83005A
736.381-010......93197C
736.381-014......89999C
736.381-018......83002B
736.384-010......83005A
736.387-010......83005A
736.387-014......83005A

736.481-010 ..... 89999C
736.587-010 ..... 98999A
736.684-010 93956
736.684-014 93956
736.684-018 93953
736.684-022 93953
736.684-026 93997
736.684-030 93956
736.684-034 93956
736.684-038 ..... 93917A
736.684-042 ..... 83005A
736.687-010 ..... 98999A
736.687-014 ..... 83005A
736.687-018 ..... 83005A
737.131-010 81008
737.132-010 81008
737.134-010 81008
737.137-010 81008
737.137-014 81008
737.137-018 81008
737.137-022 81008
737.364-010 ..... 83005A
737.367-010 ..... 83005A
737.381-010 ..... 93197C
737.387-010 ..... 83005A
737.387-014 ..... 83005A
737.387-018 ..... 83005A
737.487-010 ..... 83005A
737.587-010 ..... 98999A
737.587-014 93956
737.587-018 ..... 98902A
737.684-010 93902
737.684-014 93956
737.684-018 93956
737.684-022 93956
737.684-026 ..... 83005A
737.684-030 93956
737.684-034 93956
737.684-038 93956
737.685-010 ..... 83005A
737.685-014 ..... 83005A
737.685-018 92998
737.687-010 93956
737.687-014 ..... 98902A
737.687-018 93956
737.687-022 93956
737.687-026 ..... 83005A
737.687-030 ..... 98902A
737.687-034 ..... 98999A
737.687-038 93956
737.687-042 93998
737.687-046 93956
737.687-050 ..... 98999A
737.687-054 ..... 83005A
737.687-058 ..... 83005A
737.687-062 ..... 83005A
737.687-066 ..... 83005A
737.687-070 93956
737.687-074 93956
737.687-078 93998
737.687-082 ..... 98999A
737.687-086 ..... 83005A
737.687-090 93998
737.687-094 ..... 98902A

737.687-098 93956
737.687-102 93956
737.687-106 ..... 83005A
737.687-110 93956
737.687-114 ..... 83005A
737.687-118 ..... 83005A
737.687-122 93956
737.687-126 ..... 83005A
737.687-130 ..... 93947E
737.687-134 93998
737.687-138 93998
739.130-010 81008
739.131-010 81008
739.131-014 81008
739.132-010 81008
739.134-010 81008
739.134-014 81008
739.137-010 81008
739.137-014 81008
739.137-018 81008
739.137-022 81008
739.261-010 ..... 89908D
739.281-010 ..... 89908B
739.281-014 ..... 83002A
739.361-010 ..... 89908D
739.381-010 ..... 89599C
739.381-014 ..... 89599C
739.381-018 89102
739.381-022 89102
739.381-026 ..... 83002A
739.381-030 ..... 93197C
739.381-034 85998
739.381-038 ..... 89908B
739.381-042 ..... 89999B
739.381-046 ..... 89905A
739.381-050 93956
739.381-054 85998
739.381-058 ..... 89999B
739.384-010 93997
739.384-014 ..... 93923B
739.384-018 93999
739.384-022 93956
739.387-010 ..... 83005A
739.387-014 ..... 83005A
739.484-010 ..... 83002A
739.484-014 85998
739.484-018 85998
739.587-010 ..... 83005A
739.664-010 92998
739.667-010 ..... 83005A
739.684-010 ..... 93944D
739.684-014 93956
739.684-018 93956
739.684-022 93997
739.684-026 93953
739.684-030 ..... 85999A
739.684-034 93956
739.684-038 93956
739.684-042 93956
739.684-046 93956
739.684-050 ..... 93905D
739.684-054 ..... 93917A
739.684-058 93956
739.684-062 93998

739.684-066......92314
739.684-070......93998
739.684-074......93953
739.684-078......93956
739.684-082......93956
739.684-086......93998
739.684-090......93956
739.684-094......93956
739.684-098......93998
739.684-102......93998
739.684-106......85998
739.684-110......85998
739.684-114......89511
739.684-118......93997
739.684-122......93998
739.684-126......93926E
739.684-130......93956
739.684-134......85119B
739.684-138......93956
739.684-142......93998
739.684-146......93956
739.684-150......93956
739.684-154......93956
739.684-158......93956
739.684-162......93923B
739.684-166......93956
739.684-170......93956
739.684-174......93956
739.684-178......93956
739.684-182......93998
739.684-186......85998
739.684-190......93956
739.685-010......92998
739.685-014......92998
739.685-018......92956
739.685-022......92944
739.685-026......92998
739.685-030......92705
739.685-034......92314
739.685-038......92998
739.685-042......92998
739.685-046......92198
739.685-050......92198
739.685-054......93998
739.685-058......92998
739.687-010......93956
739.687-014......93956
739.687-018......93956
739.687-022......93956
739.687-026......93956
739.687-030......93956
739.687-034......93956
739.687-038......83005A
739.687-042......83005A
739.687-046......93956
739.687-050......93926E
739.687-054......93944D
739.687-058......98999A
739.687-062......98905
739.687-066......93956
739.687-070......93998
739.687-074......93956
739.687-078......93998
739.687-082......83005A
739.687-086......93956
739.687-090......93998
739.687-094......98102
739.687-098......98999A
739.687-102......83005A
739.687-106......83005A
739.687-110......83005A
739.687-118......83005A
739.687-122......93956
739.687-126......93998
739.687-130......93956
739.687-134......93956
739.687-138......93998
739.687-142......83005A
739.687-146......83005A
739.687-150......92998
739.687-154......93998
739.687-158......93944D
739.687-162......93998
739.687-166......83005A
739.687-170......93947E
739.687-174......93947E
739.687-178......93947E
739.687-182......83005A
739.687-186......93956
739.687-190......93998
739.687-194......93956
739.687-198......85998
739.687-202......93956
739.687-206......93956
739.687-210......93998
740.221-010......31314
740.381-010......89911A
740.381-014......89911A
740.381-018......89911A
740.484-010......93947E
740.681-010......89911A
740.684-010......93947E
740.684-014......93947E
740.684-018......93947E
740.684-022......93947E
740.684-026......93947E
740.687-010......93947E
740.687-018......93947E
740.687-022......93947E
741.684-010......93947E
741.684-014......93947E
741.684-018......93947E
741.684-022......93947E
741.684-026......93947E
741.684-030......93947E
741.685-010......92953
741.687-010......83005A
741.687-014......98999A
741.687-018......93947E
741.687-022......93947E
742.134-010......81008
742.684-010......93947E
742.684-014......93947E
742.687-010......93947E
749.131-010......81008
749.131-014......81008
749.134-010......81008
749.137-010......81008
749.381-010 ..... 89911G
749.587-010 ..... 98999A
749.684-010 ..... 93947E
749.684-014 ..... 93947E
749.684-018 ..... 93947E
749.684-022 ..... 93947E
749.684-026 ..... 93947E
749.684-030 ..... 93947E
749.684-034 ..... 93947E
749.684-038 ..... 93947E
749.684-042 93999
749.684-046 ..... 93947E
749.684-050 92965
749.684-054 ..... 93947E
749.686-010 98502
749.687-010 ..... 93947E
749.687-014 ..... 93947E
749.687-018 93998
749.687-022 ..... 93947E
749.687-026 93999
749.687-030 93999
749.687-034 ..... 98999A
750.130-010 81008
750.132-010 81008
750.367-010 ..... 83005A
750.382-010 ..... 83002A
750.384-010 92911
750.384-014 93956
750.387-010 ..... 83005A
750.681-010 85953
750.684-010 92956
750.684-014 92911
750.684-018 ..... 83005A
750.684-022 93998
750.684-026 93998
750.684-030 ..... 83005A
750.684-034 ..... 93926E
750.684-038 93998
750.684-042 93956
750.684-046 93998
750.684-050 93998
750.685-010 92998
750.685-014 92998
750.687-010 93956
750.687-014 ..... 83005A
750.687-018 ..... 83005A
750.687-022 ..... 83005A
751.381-010 ..... 89114B
751.387-010 ..... 93926E
751.584-010 ..... 83005A
751.684-010 ..... 83005A
751.684-014 ..... 93926E
751.684-018 ..... 93926E
751.684-022 ..... 93926E
751.684-026 ..... 89908B
751.686-010 98502
751.687-010 ..... 93926E
752.684-010 93956
752.684-014 93956
752.684-018 93998
752.684-022 93953
752.684-026 ..... 93944D
752.684-030 93956
752.684-034 93998
752.684-038 93956
752.684-042 93998
752.684-046 93956
752.684-050 92998
752.685-010 92971
753.381-010 89511
753.467-010 ..... 83005A
753.584-010 ..... 93944D
753.587-010 ..... 83005A
753.684-010 92965
753.684-014 93956
753.684-018 93998
753.684-022 93998
753.684-026 89511
753.684-030 93998
753.687-010 ..... 93926E
753.687-014 93998
753.687-018 ..... 83005A
753.687-022 93956
753.687-026 93956
753.687-030 ..... 93944D
753.687-034 ..... 98999A
753.687-038 ..... 98902A
753.687-042 ..... 98999A
754.130-010 81008
754.137-010 81008
754.381-010 ..... 89911C
754.381-014 ..... 89114B
754.381-018 ..... 93197C
754.684-010 93956
754.684-014 93956
754.684-018 93953
754.684-022 ..... 93944D
754.684-026 93998
754.684-030 93953
754.684-034 93998
754.684-038 ..... 93944D
754.684-042 93956
754.684-046 85998
754.684-050 93956
754.685-010 92998
754.685-014 92198
754.687-010 93998
754.687-014 ..... 98999A
759.135-010 81008
759.137-010 81008
759.261-010 93114
759.364-010 ..... 83005A
759.381-010 ..... 83002A
759.384-010 85998
759.484-010 92956
759.664-010 92705
759.664-014 93956
759.664-018 92998
759.684-010 93956
759.684-014 93956
759.684-018 92998
759.684-022 92965
759.684-026 85799
759.684-030 93956
759.684-034 93998
759.684-038 93956
759.684-042 85998
759.684-046 93998
759.684-050 93956
759.684-054 85998
759.684-058 93998
759.684-062 93956
759.684-066 92956
759.684-070 93998
759.684-074 ..... 83005A
759.687-010 ..... 83005A
759.687-014 93956
760.684-010 93956
760.684-014 93956
761.130-010 81008
761.131-010 81008
761.281-010 ..... 89397B
761.281-014 89398
761.281-018 ..... 89397B
761.381-010 89398
761.381-014 ..... 89302C
761.381-018 89398
761.381-022 89305
761.381-026 89398
761.381-030 89398
761.381-034 ..... 89397B
761.381-038 ..... 89397B
761.682-010 92314
761.682-014 92314
761.682-018 92311
761.684-010 93953
761.684-014 93998
761.684-018 93956
761.684-022 93998
761.684-026 92965
761.684-030 92314
761.684-034 92314
761.684-038 93953
761.684-042 85998
761.684-046 93953
761.684-050 93998
761.684-054 92314
761.684-058 92998
761.687-010 93953
762.134-010 81008
762.384-010 ..... 83005A
762.484-010 93956
762.684-010 93956
762.684-014 93956
762.684-018 93956
762.684-022 ..... 93926E
762.684-026 93956
762.684-030 93956
762.684-034 93956
762.684-038 93956
762.684-042 93956
762.684-046 93956
762.684-050 93956
762.684-054 93956
762.684-058 93956
762.684-062 93956
762.684-066 93956
762.685-010 92956
762.686-010 98502
762.687-010 93998
762.687-014 ..... 83005A
762.687-018 ..... 83005A

762.687-022..... 93956
762.687-026..... 98999A
762.687-030..... 93956
762.687-034..... 93956
762.687-038..... 93956
762.687-042..... 93956
762.687-046..... 93956
762.687-050..... 93956
762.687-054..... 93956
762.687-058..... 93956
762.687-062..... 98999A
762.687-066..... 93998
762.687-070..... 93956
763.134-010..... 81008
763.134-014..... 81008
763.380-010..... 89314
763.381-010..... 89314
763.381-014..... 89314
763.681-010..... 89314
763.684-010..... 83005A
763.684-014..... 93956
763.684-018..... 93956
763.684-022..... 89314
763.684-026..... 93998
763.684-030..... 93998
763.684-034..... 89314
763.684-038..... 93956
763.684-042..... 93956
763.684-046..... 93956
763.684-050..... 93956
763.684-054..... 93997
763.684-058..... 93956
763.684-062..... 93956
763.684-066..... 93926E
763.684-070..... 83005A
763.684-074..... 93997
763.684-078..... 93956
763.687-010..... 98999A
763.687-014..... 83005A
763.687-018..... 93998
763.687-022..... 93947E
763.687-026..... 83005A
763.687-030..... 93926E
764.134-010..... 81008
764.387-010..... 83005A
764.387-014..... 83005A
764.684-010..... 92998
764.684-014..... 93997
764.684-018..... 93956
764.684-022..... 87102C
764.684-026..... 87102C
764.684-030..... 93956
764.687-010..... 98999A
764.687-014..... 93956
764.687-018..... 98999A
764.687-022..... 83005A
764.687-026..... 93947E
764.687-030..... 98999A
764.687-034..... 98999A
764.687-038..... 98999A
764.687-042..... 93998
764.687-046..... 98999A
764.687-050..... 98312
764.687-054..... 83005A
764.687-058......93956
764.687-062......93956
764.687-066......93998
764.687-070......93956
764.687-074......93956
764.687-078......93998
764.687-082......93956
764.687-086......83005A
764.687-090......93998
764.687-094......93998
764.687-098......93998
769.130-010......81008
769.134-010......81008
769.137-010......81008
769.137-014......81008
769.381-010......89905A
769.387-010......83005A
769.664-010......85119B
769.684-010......93956
769.684-014......85998
769.684-018......93998
769.684-022......83005A
769.684-026......93998
769.684-030......93998
769.684-034......93956
769.684-038......87102D
769.684-042......93926E
769.684-046......83005A
769.684-050......93956
769.684-054......93956
769.684-058......85998
769.685-010......92998
769.687-010......83005A
769.687-014......83005A
769.687-018......83005A
769.687-022......93998
769.687-026......83005A
769.687-030......83005A
769.687-034......83005A
769.687-038......98999A
769.687-042......83005A
769.687-046......83005A
769.687-050......83005A
769.687-054......98999A
769.687-058......83005A
770.131-010......81008
770.131-014......81008
770.261-010......89926A
770.261-014......89926A
770.267-010......83002A
770.281-010......89999C
770.281-014......89926A
770.381-010......89126E
770.381-014......89926A
770.381-018......89926A
770.381-022......89926A
770.381-026......89926A
770.381-030......89926A
770.381-034......89926A
770.381-038......89926A
770.381-042......89926A
770.382-010......89926A
770.382-014......89926A
770.582-010......92965
770.682-010......93953
770.682-014......92998
770.682-018......92965
770.682-022......93953
770.682-026......92998
770.684-010......93953
770.684-014......93953
770.684-018......93953
770.685-010......92965
770.685-014......92965
770.685-018......92965
770.685-022......93953
770.685-026......92965
770.685-030......92965
770.685-034......92965
770.687-010......93998
770.687-014......83002A
770.687-018......83002A
770.687-022......83005A
770.687-026......98999A
770.687-030......98999A
770.687-034......93998
771.137-010......81008
771.281-010......89908B
771.281-014......89905C
771.381-010......89905C
771.381-014......89905C
771.384-010......93926E
771.484-010......93953
771.684-010......93926B
772.281-010......89905D
772.381-010......89905D
772.381-014......89908B
772.381-018......89905D
772.381-022......89905D
772.482-010......92998
772.684-010......93998
772.684-014......93998
772.684-018......93998
772.684-022......93944D
772.687-010......93956
772.687-014......83005A
773.131-010......81008
773.381-010......89911B
773.487-010......93998
773.684-010......93947E
773.684-014......93947E
773.687-010......83005A
774.130-010......81008
774.381-010......89905F
774.382-010......92998
774.384-010......83005A
774.684-010......93997
774.684-014......93947E
774.684-018......93998
774.684-022......93956
774.684-026......93944D
774.684-030......93998
774.684-034......93998
774.684-038......93997
774.684-042......92965
774.684-046......93956
774.687-010......83005A
774.687-014......93998
774.687-018 ..... 83005A
774.687-022 93953
774.687-026 ..... 83005A
775.130-010 81008
775.131-010 81008
775.134-010 81008
775.281-010 92997
775.381-010 ..... 89911C
775.381-014 ..... 89911D
775.382-010 92965
775.584-010 ..... 93951B
775.664-010 93953
775.684-010 92965
775.684-014 93953
775.684-018 92965
775.684-022 ..... 93926D
775.684-026 ..... 93926D
775.684-030 92965
775.684-034 92965
775.684-038 93953
775.684-042 92965
775.684-046 ..... 93926E
775.684-050 93998
775.684-054 93953
775.684-058 92965
775.684-062 92965
775.685-010 92944
775.687-010 93998
775.687-014 93998
775.687-018 ..... 98999A
775.687-022 93953
776.487-010 ..... 83005A
776.667-010 ..... 83005A
776.684-010 93956
776.684-014 ..... 85119B
776.687-010 93998
777.081-010 ..... 89905A
777.131-010 81008
777.261-010 ..... 89908A
777.281-010 ..... 89908C
777.281-014 ..... 89908C
777.281-018 ..... 89908A
777.361-010 ..... 89908C
777.381-010 ..... 89908C
777.381-014 ..... 89908C
777.381-018 ..... 89908C
777.381-022 ..... 89126C
777.381-034 ..... 89905A
777.381-038 ..... 89905A
777.381-042 ..... 89908C
777.381-046 ..... 83002A
777.684-010 93998
777.684-014 ..... 93944A
777.684-018 ..... 93944A
779.131-010 81008
779.281-010 ..... 89908C
779.381-010 ..... 89999C
779.381-014 87308
779.381-018 ..... 31511D
779.381-022 ..... 89911E
779.387-010 ..... 83005A
779.387-014 ..... 83005A
779.584-010 ..... 93926D
779.681-010 ..... 93926E
779.684-010 ..... 93944D
779.684-014 ..... 93944D
779.684-018 93953
779.684-022 ..... 93926E
779.684-026 ..... 85119B
779.684-030 93953
779.684-034 93998
779.684-038 93998
779.684-042 93998
779.684-046 ..... 93944D
779.684-050 ..... 93944D
779.684-054 ..... 93926E
779.684-058 ..... 87899M
779.687-010 93998
779.687-014 93998
779.687-018 ..... 93947E
779.687-022 ..... 83005A
779.687-026 ..... 83005A
779.687-030 ..... 93926E
779.687-034 93998
779.687-038 ..... 98999A
780.131-010 81008
780.131-014 81008
780.134-010 81008
780.134-014 81008
780.137-010 81008
780.381-010 89508
780.381-014 89508
780.381-018 89508
780.381-022 89508
780.381-026 89508
780.381-030 89511
780.381-034 89508
780.381-038 89508
780.384-010 93956
780.384-014 89508
780.587-010 ..... 83005A
780.682-010 92721
780.682-014 92721
780.682-018 92721
780.684-010 93956
780.684-014 93956
780.684-018 93956
780.684-022 93956
780.684-026 93956
780.684-030 93956
780.684-034 93956
780.684-038 ..... 93926E
780.684-042 93998
780.684-046 93956
780.684-054 93956
780.684-058 93956
780.684-062 93956
780.684-066 93956
780.684-070 ..... 93923B
780.684-074 93956
780.684-078 93956
780.684-082 93956
780.684-086 93956
780.684-090 93956
780.684-094 93956
780.684-098 93956
780.684-102 93956
780.684-106 93956

780.684-110......93997
780.684-114......93956
780.684-118......93956
780.684-122......89508
780.684-126......93956
780.684-130......93956
780.684-134......93956
780.685-010......93956
780.685-014......92974
780.685-018......93956
780.687-010......93998
780.687-014......93956
780.687-018......93956
780.687-022......83005A
780.687-026......98999A
780.687-030......93956
780.687-034......93956
780.687-038......93956
780.687-042......93956
780.687-046......93956
780.687-050......93998
780.687-054......98999A
780.687-058......89514
780.687-062......93956
780.687-066......83005A
780.687-070......93956
781.131-010......81008
781.134-010......81008
781.287-010......93997
781.361-010......89502A
781.361-014......89502A
781.381-010......89502B
781.381-018......89511
781.381-022......89502A
781.381-030......89502A
781.381-034......89502A
781.384-014......93998
781.384-018......93926E
781.484-010......89502A
781.667-010......83005A
781.682-010......92705
781.684-010......93932
781.684-014......93928
781.684-018......93926E
781.684-022......83005A
781.684-026......83005A
781.684-030......93921
781.684-034......93926E
781.684-038......92705
781.684-042......93998
781.684-046......93926E
781.684-050......93956
781.684-054......93926E
781.684-058......93998
781.684-062......83005A
781.684-066......93997
781.684-070......93926E
781.684-074......93926E
781.684-078......93926E
781.685-010......92998
781.687-010......83005A
781.687-014......83005A
781.687-018......98999A
781.687-022......98999A
781.687-026......93926E
781.687-030......93926E
781.687-034......83005A
781.687-038......98999A
781.687-042......93998
781.687-046......93998
781.687-050......93926E
781.687-054......93947E
781.687-058......98999A
781.687-062......98999A
781.687-066......98999A
781.687-070......93926E
782.361-010......89505A
782.361-014......89502B
782.381-010......89599D
782.381-014......89599A
782.381-018......89599A
782.381-022......85956C
782.487-010......83005A
782.684-010......85956A
782.684-014......93956
782.684-018......93997
782.684-026......93998
782.684-030......93923B
782.684-034......93997
782.684-038......98999B
782.684-042......89599A
782.684-046......85956A
782.684-050......93923B
782.684-054......93947E
782.684-058......93923B
782.684-062......93998
782.687-010......98999A
782.687-014......98999A
782.687-018......93923B
782.687-022......93998
782.687-026......98999A
782.687-030......98999A
782.687-034......98999A
782.687-038......93926E
782.687-042......93998
782.687-046......92721
782.687-050......83005A
782.687-054......93998
782.687-058......93923B
783.131-010......81008
783.132-010......81008
783.261-010......89599B
783.361-010......89511
783.381-010......89599B
783.381-014......89599B
783.381-018......89511
783.381-022......89511
783.381-026......89511
783.384-010......83005A
783.387-010......83005A
783.681-010......93999
783.682-010......92721
783.682-014......92721
783.684-010......93956
783.684-014......93956
783.684-018......83005A
783.684-022......93926E
783.684-026......93956
783.684-030 93956
783.685-010 92998
783.685-014 92728
783.685-018 92998
783.685-022 92956
783.685-026 92998
783.687-010 93956
783.687-014 .....93926E
783.687-018 .....83005A
783.687-022 .....83005A
783.687-026 93956
783.687-030 .....98999A
784.130-010 81008
784.132-010 81008
784.261-010 .....89599D
784.361-010 .....89502D
784.387-010 .....83005A
784.387-014 .....83005A
784.587-010 .....83005A
784.682-010 92717
784.682-014 92717
784.684-010 .....93926E
784.684-014 93998
784.684-018 93956
784.684-022 .....93923B
784.684-026 93956
784.684-030 93956
784.684-034 93997
784.684-038 93956
784.684-042 .....93923B
784.684-046 .....85956A
784.684-050 .....93926E
784.684-054 93998
784.684-058 92998
784.684-062 93998
784.684-066 93998
784.684-070 93956
784.684-074 93956
784.684-078 93956
784.685-010 92705
784.685-014 92717
784.687-010 .....98999A
784.687-014 .....93947E
784.687-018 93998
784.687-022 93956
784.687-026 .....93926E
784.687-030 .....83005A
784.687-034 .....83005A
784.687-038 .....98999A
784.687-042 .....98902A
784.687-046 93998
784.687-050 .....83005A
784.687-054 .....93926E
784.687-058 .....93947E
784.687-062 93998
784.687-066 .....98999A
784.687-070 93998
784.687-074 93998
784.687-078 .....98999A
784.687-082 93956
784.687-086 .....98999A
784.687-090 93998
785.131-010 81008
785.261-010 .....89505A
785.261-014 .....89505B
785.261-018 .....89505A
785.261-022 .....89505B
785.361-010 .....89505B
785.361-014 .....89505A
785.361-018 .....89505A
785.361-022 .....89505A
785.361-026 .....89505A
786.132-010 81008
786.682-010 92717
786.682-014 92717
786.682-018 92717
786.682-022 92717
786.682-026 92717
786.682-030 92717
786.682-034 92717
786.682-038 92717
786.682-042 92717
786.682-046 92717
786.682-050 92717
786.682-054 92717
786.682-058 92717
786.682-062 92717
786.682-066 92717
786.682-070 92717
786.682-074 92717
786.682-078 92717
786.682-082 92717
786.682-086 92717
786.682-090 92717
786.682-094 92717
786.682-098 92717
786.682-102 92717
786.682-106 92717
786.682-110 92717
786.682-114 92717
786.682-118 92717
786.682-122 92717
786.682-126 92717
786.682-130 92717
786.682-134 92717
786.682-138 92717
786.682-142 92717
786.682-146 92717
786.682-150 92717
786.682-154 92717
786.682-158 92717
786.682-162 92717
786.682-166 92717
786.682-170 92717
786.682-174 92717
786.682-178 92717
786.682-182 92717
786.682-186 92717
786.682-190 92717
786.682-194 92717
786.682-198 92717
786.682-202 92717
786.682-206 92717
786.682-210 92717
786.682-214 92717
786.682-218 92717
786.682-222 92717
786.682-226 92717
786.682-230 92717
786.682-234 92717
786.682-238 92717
786.682-242 92717
786.682-246 92717
786.682-250 92717
786.682-254 92717
786.682-258 92717
786.682-262 92717
786.682-266 92717
786.682-270 92717
786.682-274 92717
786.682-278 92717
786.682-282 92717
786.682-286 92717
786.685-010 92717
786.685-014 92717
786.685-018 92717
786.685-022 92717
786.685-026 92717
786.685-030 92717
786.685-034 92717
786.685-038 92998
786.685-042 92717
787.132-010 81008
787.132-014 81008
787.132-018 81008
787.381-010 .....93923B
787.682-010 92721
787.682-014 92721
787.682-018 92721
787.682-022 92717
787.682-026 92721
787.682-030 .....85956A
787.682-034 92721
787.682-038 92721
787.682-046 92721
787.682-050 92721
787.682-054 92721
787.682-058 92721
787.682-066 92721
787.682-074 92717
787.682-078 92721
787.682-082 92721
787.682-086 92721
787.685-010 92721
787.685-014 92721
787.685-018 92721
787.685-022 92721
787.685-026 92721
787.685-030 92721
787.685-034 92721
787.685-038 92721
787.685-042 92721
787.685-046 92717
787.685-050 92721
787.685-054 92721
787.686-010 98502
788.131-010 81008
788.137-010 81008
788.222-010 31314
788.261-010 89511
788.281-010 .....89502A
788.381-010 89511

788.381-014..... 89511
788.384-010..... 83005A
788.387-010..... 83005A
788.584-010..... 83005A
788.584-014..... 93998
788.587-010..... 83005A
788.667-010..... 83005A
788.684-010..... 93956
788.684-014..... 93956
788.684-018..... 92998
788.684-022..... 93997
788.684-026..... 93956
788.684-030..... 93951C
788.684-034..... 93956
788.684-038..... 93926E
788.684-042..... 93926E
788.684-046..... 89511
788.684-050..... 93998
788.684-054..... 93923B
788.684-058..... 93956
788.684-062..... 93997
788.684-066..... 93947E
788.684-070..... 93998
788.684-074..... 93956
788.684-078..... 93956
788.684-082..... 93926E
788.684-086..... 93956
788.684-090..... 93956
788.684-094..... 93998
788.684-098..... 89511
788.684-102..... 93998
788.684-106..... 93998
788.684-110..... 93923B
788.684-114..... 92723
788.684-118..... 93998
788.684-122..... 93956
788.684-126..... 93998
788.684-130..... 93998
788.685-010..... 92998
788.685-014..... 92998
788.685-018..... 92998
788.685-022..... 92998
788.685-026..... 92998
788.685-030..... 92998
788.687-010..... 93998
788.687-014..... 93998
788.687-018..... 98999A
788.687-022..... 98999A
788.687-026..... 83005A
788.687-030..... 93956
788.687-034..... 83005A
788.687-038..... 93953
788.687-042..... 93926E
788.687-046..... 83005A
788.687-050..... 98999A
788.687-054..... 93956
788.687-058..... 98999A
788.687-062..... 98999A
788.687-066..... 98999A
788.687-070..... 98999A
788.687-074..... 93926E
788.687-078..... 93947E
788.687-082..... 98905
788.687-086..... 98999A
788.687-090......98999A
788.687-094......93956
788.687-098......93947E
788.687-102......93998
788.687-106......83005A
788.687-110......83005A
788.687-114......98999A
788.687-118......93956
788.687-122......98999A
788.687-126......98999A
788.687-130......98999A
788.687-134......98999A
788.687-138......93956
788.687-142......93998
788.687-146......98999A
788.687-150......93926E
788.687-154......93956
788.687-158......93998
788.687-162......93926E
788.687-166......93947E
789.132-010......81008
789.132-014......81008
789.132-018......81008
789.132-022......81008
789.132-026......81008
789.134-010......81008
789.134-014......81008
789.137-010......51002B
789.137-014......81008
789.222-010......31314
789.261-010......89599C
789.381-010......93923B
789.381-014......89502A
789.381-018......89599C
789.382-010......92944
789.387-010......83005A
789.387-014......93998
789.484-010......93932
789.484-014......93923B
789.487-010......83005A
789.587-010......83005A
789.587-014......83005A
789.587-018......98999A
789.587-022......83005A
789.587-026......58017
789.684-010......93998
789.684-014......93998
789.684-018......93997
789.684-022......93926E
789.684-026......93998
789.684-030......93998
789.684-034......93998
789.684-038......85956A
789.684-042......93998
789.684-046......93998
789.684-050......93926E
789.684-054......93998
789.685-010......92998
789.687-010......83005A
789.687-014......98999A
789.687-018......98999A
789.687-022......93998
789.687-026......83005A
789.687-030......93926E
789.687-034......83005A
789.687-038......83005A
789.687-042......83005A
789.687-046......98999A
789.687-050......83005A
789.687-054......93956
789.687-058......98999A
789.687-062......98999A
789.687-066......98999A
789.687-070......83005A
789.687-074......98999A
789.687-078......83005A
789.687-082......93956
789.687-086......83005A
789.687-090......98999A
789.687-094......98999A
789.687-098......93998
789.687-102......93956
789.687-106......98902A
789.687-110......98999A
789.687-114......83005A
789.687-118......98999A
789.687-122......98999A
789.687-126......93926E
789.687-130......93998
789.687-134......98999A
789.687-138......98999A
789.687-142......83005A
789.687-146......83005A
789.687-150......93926E
789.687-154......93956
789.687-158......98999A
789.687-166......98999A
789.687-170......93998
789.687-174......98999A
789.687-178......92728
789.687-182......98999A
790.134-010......81008
790.381-010......89899
790.684-010......93998
790.684-014......93997
790.684-018......93998
790.684-022......93997
790.687-010......93926E
790.687-014......83005A
790.687-018......83005A
790.687-022......93944D
790.687-026......83005A
790.687-030......93998
794.684-010......93998
794.684-014......93956
794.684-018......93956
794.684-022......93956
794.684-026......93997
794.684-030......93998
794.687-010......93956
794.687-014......93998
794.687-018......83005A
794.687-022......93998
794.687-026......93956
794.687-030......93956
794.687-034......98902A
794.687-038......98999A
794.687-042......93956
794.687-046 93956
794.687-050 ..... 98999A
794.687-054 93998
794.687-058 93998
794.687-062 ..... 93926E
795.684-014 93997
795.684-018 93998
795.684-022 93998
795.684-026 93956
795.687-010 92956
795.687-014 93956
795.687-018 93956
795.687-022 93956
795.687-026 93956
795.687-030 93956
800.662-010 92198
800.682-010 92198
800.684-010 ..... 87899D
800.684-014 ..... 87899D
800.687-010 ..... 98999A
801.131-010 ..... 81005A
801.131-014 81008
801.131-018 81008
801.134-010 ..... 81005A
801.137-010 81008
801.137-014 81008
801.261-010 93105
801.261-014 93108
801.261-018 93105
801.361-010 93105
801.361-014 87814
801.361-018 87814
801.361-022 87814
801.381-010 87814
801.381-014 93108
801.381-018 ..... 83002B
801.384-010 93956
801.663-010 ..... 98999B
801.664-010 ..... 85128A
801.664-014 ..... 85128A
801.664-018 93956
801.667-010 ..... 83005A
801.684-010 93956
801.684-014 93997
801.684-018 ..... 87899A
801.684-022 93902
801.684-026 87314
801.687-010 ..... 98999A
801.687-014 ..... 98999A
801.687-018 ..... 98999A
804.281-010 89132
804.281-014 89132
804.481-010 89132
804.684-010 ..... 93926E
804.684-014 93956
805.131-010 81002
805.137-010 81002
805.261-010 89135
805.261-014 89135
805.361-010 89135
805.361-014 89135
805.381-010 89135
805.664-010 ..... 98999B
805.667-010 ..... 83005A
805.687-010 ..... 98999A
806.130-010 81008
806.131-010 81008
806.131-014 81008
806.131-018 81008
806.131-022 81008
806.131-026 81008
806.131-030 81002
806.131-034 81008
806.131-038 81008
806.131-042 81008
806.134-010 81008
806.134-014 81008
806.137-010 81008
806.137-014 81008
806.137-018 81008
806.137-022 81008
806.261-010 ..... 83002B
806.261-014 85935
806.261-018 85935
806.261-022 ..... 83002B
806.261-026 ..... 85116C
806.261-030 ..... 83002B
806.261-034 ..... 83002A
806.261-038 ..... 83002B
806.261-042 ..... 83002A
806.261-046 ..... 83002A
806.261-050 ..... 83002A
806.264-010 ..... 83005A
806.264-014 ..... 83002A
806.281-010 ..... 83002B
806.281-014 89108
806.281-018 ..... 83002B
806.281-026 ..... 83002B
806.281-058 ..... 87102F
806.283-010 ..... 83005A
806.283-014 ..... 83002A
806.361-014 ..... 93102B
806.361-018 ..... 83002A
806.361-022 ..... 83002A
806.361-026 ..... 85302B
806.361-030 ..... 93102C
806.364-010 ..... 83005A
806.367-010 ..... 83005A
806.367-014 ..... 83005A
806.367-018 ..... 83005A
806.380-010 92197
806.381-014 ..... 93102C
806.381-018 ..... 93102C
806.381-022 93105
806.381-026 ..... 93102B
806.381-034 ..... 93102D
806.381-042 ..... 93102D
806.381-046 89121
806.381-050 89121
806.381-058 ..... 93197C
806.381-062 ..... 85116C
806.381-066 ..... 93102C
806.381-070 85938
806.381-074 ..... 83002A
806.381-078 ..... 93197C
806.381-082 ..... 93102C
806.383-010 ..... 83005A
806.384-014 ..... 83005A

806.384-022......98999B
806.384-030......93956
806.384-034......93956
806.384-038......85999G
806.387-014......83002B
806.464-010......93956
806.481-010......93197C
806.481-014......93105
806.667-010......98999A
806.684-010......93956
806.684-014......93956
806.684-018......93956
806.684-022......93956
806.684-026......93956
806.684-038......93956
806.684-046......93956
806.684-050......93956
806.684-054......93956
806.684-066......83005A
806.684-070......93956
806.684-074......93956
806.684-082......93956
806.684-086......93997
806.684-090......93956
806.684-094......93956
806.684-098......93956
806.684-102......93956
806.684-106......93956
806.684-114......93956
806.684-118......93956
806.684-122......98102
806.684-126......93956
806.684-130......93998
806.684-134......83005A
806.684-142......93997
806.684-146......93956
806.684-150......93926E
806.687-010......93956
806.687-018......83005A
806.687-022......98999A
806.687-026......83005A
806.687-030......83005A
806.687-034......93956
806.687-042......83005A
806.687-046......93956
806.687-050......98999A
807.137-010......81002
807.261-010......85323B
807.267-010......85305D
807.281-010......85305C
807.361-010......85305B
807.361-014......87102E
807.381-010......85305B
807.381-014......85323B
807.381-018......85308
807.381-022......85305C
807.381-026......85317
807.381-030......85305B
807.484-010......85308
807.664-010......85302B
807.667-010......98999A
807.684-010......91305
807.684-014......93956
807.684-018......85999G
807.684-022......85302B
807.684-026......93956
807.684-034......83005A
807.687-010......98102
807.687-014......98102
809.130-010......81008
809.130-014......81008
809.131-010......81008
809.131-014......81005A
809.131-018......81005A
809.134-010......81008
809.134-014......81008
809.261-010......93108
809.281-010......89117
809.381-010......93197C
809.381-014......89117
809.381-018......85321
809.381-022......87899K
809.381-026......87899K
809.381-030......89199
809.381-034......93197C
809.382-010......92997
809.484-010......93956
809.484-014......93998
809.664-010......87899A
809.667-010......93998
809.681-010......93197C
809.684-010......93956
809.684-014......93956
809.684-018......93998
809.684-022......93953
809.684-026......93953
809.684-030......93956
809.684-034......85998
809.684-038......93956
809.684-042......93956
809.687-010......93926E
809.687-014......98999A
809.687-018......83005A
809.687-022......98999A
809.687-026......98905
810.382-010......91702
810.384-010......93914B
810.384-014......93914B
810.664-010......93914A
810.684-010......93914A
811.482-010......91702
811.684-010......93914B
811.684-014......93914B
812.360-010......91702
812.682-010......91702
813.360-010......91708
813.360-014......91708
813.382-010......91708
813.382-014......91708
813.482-010......91711
813.682-010......93917B
813.684-010......93917B
813.684-014......93917A
813.684-018......93917A
813.684-022......93917A
813.684-026......93917A
813.684-030......93917A
813.685-010......91711
814.382-010......91705
814.682-010......91705
814.684-010......91705
815.380-010......91702
815.382-010......91702
815.382-014......91705
815.682-010......91705
815.682-014......91705
816.364-010......93914B
816.464-010......93914B
816.482-010......92197
816.682-010......92197
816.684-010......93914A
819.131-010......81008
819.131-014......81008
819.132-010......81008
819.281-010......93914C
819.281-014......93914C
819.281-018......83002A
819.281-022......93914C
819.361-010......93914C
819.361-014......93914C
819.381-010......93914C
819.384-010......93914B
819.384-014......93914B
819.664-010......93953
819.666-010......98999A
819.684-010......93914A
819.685-010......91705
819.686-010......98502
819.687-010......83005A
819.687-014......98999A
820.131-010......81002
820.137-010......81008
820.261-010......85721
820.261-014......85721
820.261-018......85721
820.361-010......87899A
820.361-014......93105
820.361-018......83002D
820.381-010......85714B
820.381-014......93114
820.662-010......95028
820.684-010......93905D
821.131-010......81002
821.131-014......81002
821.131-018......81002
821.131-022......81005A
821.131-026......81002
821.261-010......85599A
821.261-014......85723
821.261-018......85721
821.261-022......85723
821.261-026......85723
821.281-010......85702
821.361-010......85723
821.361-014......85911
821.361-018......85723
821.361-022......85723
821.361-026......85723
821.361-030......85723
821.361-034......85714C
821.361-038......85723
821.364-010......83005B
821.367-010......83005B
821.367-014......83005B
821.381-010......83002C
821.381-014......83002D
821.381-018......85714A
821.564-010......98102
821.667-010......98313
821.684-010......85911
821.684-014......98313
821.684-018......87899A
821.684-022......85723
821.687-010......87899J
822.131-010......81002
822.131-014......81002
822.131-018......81002
822.131-022......81002
822.131-026......81002
822.131-030......81002
822.261-010......85599A
822.261-014......22128
822.261-018......83002D
822.261-022......85726
822.261-026......83002D
822.267-010......83005B
822.281-010......85508
822.281-014......85502
822.281-018......85726
822.281-022......85502
822.281-026......85511
822.281-030......85599A
822.281-034......85599A
822.361-010......83002D
822.361-014......85502
822.361-018......87202A
822.361-022......87202A
822.361-026......83002D
822.361-030......83002D
822.381-010......85508
822.381-014......85702
822.381-018......85502
822.381-022......85502
822.664-010......98313
822.684-010......85505
822.684-014......98313
822.684-018......98102
823.131-010......81002
823.131-014......81002
823.131-018......81002
823.131-022......81002
823.131-026......81002
823.261-010......85599C
823.261-014......83099
823.261-018......85514
823.261-022......85599A
823.261-026......85717A
823.261-030......85599A
823.281-014......85514
823.281-018......85905
823.281-022......85599A
823.361-010......85708
823.684-010......87899A
824.137-010......81005A
824.137-014......81002
824.261-010......87202A
824.261-014......87202A
824.281-010......87202A
824.281-014......83002D
824.281-018......87202A
824.381-010......87202A
824.664-010......98102
824.681-010......87202A
824.683-010......83005A
824.684-010......93997
825.131-010......81005A
825.131-014......81002
825.137-010......81002
825.261-010......85511
825.261-014......85932
825.261-018......85728A
825.281-014......87202A
825.281-022......85728B
825.281-026......85728B
825.281-030......85932
825.281-034......85932
825.281-038......85326
825.361-010......85932
825.361-014......83002D
825.381-010......85728A
825.381-014......85302B
825.381-018......85728B
825.381-026......83002D
825.381-030......87202A
825.381-034......87202A
825.381-038......85723
825.664-010......98102
825.684-010......98313
825.684-014......98102
825.684-018......85714B
826.131-010......81002
826.131-014......81008
826.261-010......85914
826.361-010......93114
826.381-010......93114
826.384-010......85714B
826.684-010......93956
826.684-014......85714B
826.684-018......85714B
826.684-022......93956
827.131-010......81002
827.131-014......81008
827.131-018......81002
827.261-010......85711A
827.261-014......85711A
827.361-010......83002A
827.361-014......85902B
827.381-010......83002D
827.384-010......83005A
827.485-010......92998
827.584-010......93956
827.584-014......83005A
827.585-010......92974
827.661-010......85711B
827.684-010......93956
828.131-010......81002
828.161-010......81002
828.251-010......85717A
828.261-010......85708
828.261-014......85717A

828.261-018..... 22505B
828.261-022..... 85705
828.261-026..... 85705
828.281-018..... 85128A
828.281-022..... 85717A
828.281-026..... 85717A
828.381-010..... 85728B
828.381-018..... 93111B
829.131-010..... 81002
829.131-014..... 81005A
829.131-018..... 81002
829.131-022..... 81002
829.261-010..... 83002D
829.261-014..... 85908
829.261-018..... 87202A
829.281-010..... 85928C
829.281-018..... 85728A
829.281-022..... 85599C
829.361-010..... 85723
829.361-014..... 85723
829.361-018..... 83002D
829.381-010..... 85119B
829.667-010..... 98102
829.667-014..... 98102
829.684-010..... 85714B
829.684-014..... 85728B
829.684-018..... 93997
829.684-022..... 98313
829.684-026..... 98313
840.131-010..... 81005A
840.131-014..... 81005A
840.381-010..... 87402A
840.381-014..... 87402A
840.381-018..... 87402A
840.681-010..... 87402A
840.684-010..... 93947E
840.687-010..... 98314
841.137-010..... 81005A
841.381-010..... 87402B
841.684-010..... 87402B
842.131-010..... 81005A
842.131-014..... 81005A
842.131-018..... 81005A
842.134-010..... 81005A
842.361-010..... 87114
842.361-014..... 87114
842.361-018..... 87317
842.361-022..... 87317
842.361-026..... 87317
842.361-030..... 87108
842.381-014..... 87317
842.664-010..... 87111
842.665-010..... 87899D
842.684-010..... 93947E
842.684-014..... 87108
843.134-010..... 81005A
843.137-010..... 81005A
843.384-010..... 93998
843.482-010..... 91926
843.684-010..... 93997
843.684-014..... 93947E
844.364-010..... 87311
844.364-014..... 87311
844.461-010..... 87311
844.681-010......93944D
844.684-010......87311
844.687-010......98319
845.381-010......92947
845.381-014......92947
845.381-018......92947
845.681-010......92947
845.684-010......98905
845.684-014......98999B
849.137-010......81008
849.381-010......89599C
849.484-010......85126
849.665-010......87899D
849.684-010......93953
850.133-010......81005A
850.137-010......81005B
850.137-014......81005A
850.137-018......81005A
850.381-010......87905
850.387-010......83005B
850.467-010......87899D
850.662-010......87902A
850.662-014......87902A
850.663-010......97928
850.663-014......97938
850.663-018......97399A
850.663-022......97938
850.663-026......97923A
850.682-010......87949A
850.683-010......97938
850.683-014......97938
850.683-018......97926
850.683-022......97938
850.683-026......97923A
850.683-030......97923A
850.683-034......87902A
850.683-038......97938
850.683-042......97923A
850.683-046......97938
850.684-010......24599C
850.684-014......98319
850.684-018......85128B
851.137-010......81005A
851.137-014......81005A
851.262-010......87899H
851.362-010......39999H
851.383-010......87508
851.663-010......97923A
853.133-010......81005A
853.137-010......81005A
853.663-010......87708
853.663-014......87708
853.663-018......87708
853.663-022......87708
853.665-010......87899D
853.683-010......87708
853.683-014......87708
853.683-018......87708
853.685-010......87899D
859.133-010......81005A
859.137-010......81011
859.137-014......81005A
859.137-018......81005A
859.261-010......87905
859.267-010......83005B
859.281-010......83005A
859.362-010......87902B
859.682-010......87902A
859.682-014......87902A
859.682-018......87705
859.683-010......97956
859.683-014......97956
859.683-018......87714A
859.683-022......87708
859.683-026......87708
859.683-030......87708
859.684-010......87711
859.687-010......98323
860.131-010......81005A
860.131-014......81005A
860.131-018......81005A
860.131-022......81005A
860.131-026......81005A
860.137-010......81017
860.261-010......83002A
860.281-010......87102A
860.281-014......87102F
860.361-010......87102E
860.361-014......87102E
860.381-010......87105
860.381-022......87102A
860.381-026......87102A
860.381-030......87102B
860.381-034......87102A
860.381-038......87102A
860.381-042......87102B
860.381-046......87102B
860.381-050......87102F
860.381-054......87102F
860.381-058......87102E
860.381-062......87102E
860.381-066......87102C
860.381-070......87102C
860.664-010......87102D
860.664-014......98312
860.664-018......98312
860.681-010......87102D
860.684-010......87102D
860.684-014......87102D
860.684-018......98799B
860.684-022......93956
861.131-010......81005A
861.131-014......81005A
861.131-018......81005A
861.131-022......81005A
861.131-026......81005A
861.134-010......81002
861.361-010......87305B
861.361-014......87305B
861.381-010......87302
861.381-014......87302
861.381-018......87302
861.381-022......87302
861.381-026......87302
861.381-030......87305B
861.381-034......87605
861.381-038......87305B
861.381-042......87305B
861.381-046..... 87311
861.381-050..... 87311
861.381-054..... 87308
861.381-058..... 87308
861.381-062..... 87308
861.664-010..... 98311
861.664-014..... 98319
861.664-018..... 98311
861.684-010..... 87302
861.684-014..... 87302
861.684-018..... 87308
861.684-022..... 87302
861.687-010..... 98311
861.687-014..... 98311
862.131-010..... 81005A
862.131-014..... 81005A
862.131-018..... 81005A
862.131-022..... 81005A
862.132-010..... 81008
862.134-010..... 81008
862.134-014..... 81002
862.137-010..... 81005A
862.137-014..... 81002
862.137-018..... 81008
862.261-010..... 87502A
862.281-010..... 87502A
862.281-014..... 87502A
862.281-018..... 85902A
862.281-022..... 87502A
862.281-026..... 87502A
862.361-010..... 85902A
862.361-014..... 87502A
862.361-018..... 87502A
862.361-022..... 87502A
862.381-014..... 87502A
862.381-022..... 87502A
862.381-030..... 87502B
862.381-034..... 87502B
862.381-038..... 83002A
862.662-010..... 87899H
862.681-010..... 87502B
862.682-010..... 87899A
862.682-014..... 87899H
862.684-010..... 93997
862.684-014..... 98999B
862.684-018..... 98315
862.684-022..... 98315
862.684-026..... 87899A
862.684-030..... 85928A
862.684-034..... 87899A
862.687-010..... 83005A
862.687-014..... 83005A
862.687-018..... 83005A
862.687-022..... 98102
863.134-010..... 81005A
863.134-014..... 81005A
863.364-010..... 87802
863.364-014..... 87802
863.381-010..... 87802
863.381-014..... 87802
863.664-010..... 87802
863.684-010..... 87102D
863.684-014..... 87102D
863.685-010..... 87802
864.381-010..... 87602
864.481-010..... 87605
864.481-014..... 87605
864.684-010..... 87899D
864.687-010..... 98319
865.131-010..... 81005A
865.361-010..... 87811
865.381-010..... 87811
865.381-014..... 87811
865.684-010..... 85305A
865.684-014..... 93956
865.684-018..... 93956
865.684-022..... 93956
866.131-010..... 81005A
866.381-010..... 87808
866.381-014..... 87808
866.684-010..... 87808
869.131-010..... 81002
869.131-014..... 81005A
869.131-018..... 81005A
869.131-022..... 81005A
869.131-026..... 81008
869.131-030..... 81008
869.131-034..... 81005A
869.131-038..... 81005A
869.133-010..... 81005A
869.134-010..... 81005A
869.134-014..... 81005A
869.134-018..... 81005A
869.134-022..... 81005A
869.134-026..... 81005A
869.137-010..... 81008
869.137-014..... 81008
869.261-010..... 87899L
869.261-014..... 85123A
869.261-018..... 87899M
869.261-022..... 85938
869.261-026..... 22599C
869.281-010..... 85902A
869.281-014..... 87899M
869.281-018..... 83002A
869.287-010..... 83005B
869.361-010..... 87899F
869.361-014..... 87899G
869.361-018..... 87102B
869.367-010..... 81005A
869.367-014..... 49999B
869.367-018..... 83005B
869.381-010..... 87102A
869.381-014..... 87899A
869.381-018..... 87899A
869.381-022..... 85923
869.381-026..... 87899J
869.381-030..... 87899M
869.381-034..... 87102B
869.384-010..... 85938
869.387-010..... 83005A
869.463-010..... 87899C
869.481-010..... 87899A
869.484-010..... 87899A
869.484-014..... 87899B
869.484-018..... 87899B
869.487-010..... 87899D
869.564-010..... 83005A

869.567-010......98319
869.662-010......87899G
869.664-010......87899D
869.664-014......87505
869.664-018......87511
869.665-010......87899D
869.667-010......87899D
869.667-014......98999A
869.681-010......87899M
869.682-010......87899E
869.682-014......87899E
869.683-010......87708
869.683-014......97941
869.683-018......87708
869.684-010......93956
869.684-014......93956
869.684-018......87102D
869.684-022......87817
869.684-026......93956
869.684-030......87899A
869.684-034......87102D
869.684-038......87102D
869.684-042......87102D
869.684-046......87921
869.684-050......87108
869.684-054......87899J
869.684-058......87121
869.684-062......87102D
869.684-066......87102D
869.684-074......85938
869.684-078......93956
869.684-082......87899D
869.685-010......92923
869.687-010......98319
869.687-014......93956
869.687-018......98999A
869.687-022......93944D
869.687-026......87999
869.687-030......98102
869.687-034......98319
869.687-038......83005A
869.687-042......98312
891.131-010......81002
891.137-010......81002
891.137-014......81017
891.137-018......81017
891.564-010......85128A
891.684-010......98999B
891.684-014......99003
891.684-018......67005
891.684-022......87899D
891.685-010......87899D
891.687-010......67005
891.687-014......98905
891.687-018......67005
891.687-022......98905
891.687-030......98905
899.130-010......81002
899.131-010......81005A
899.131-014......81002
899.131-018......81005A
899.131-022......81017
899.133-010......81005A
899.134-010......81005A
899.137-010......81005A
899.137-014......81005A
899.137-018......81002
899.261-010......85999F
899.261-014......85132
899.281-010......85119A
899.364-010......87302
899.364-014......34038F
899.381-010......85132
899.384-010......31511D
899.484-010......85132
899.487-010......83005A
899.664-010......98319
899.664-014......87511
899.682-010......92998
899.684-010......85126
899.684-014......87711
899.684-018......93956
899.684-022......98102
899.684-026......87899H
899.684-030......93926E
899.684-034......87989A
899.684-038......93998
899.684-042......87102D
899.684-046......87899D
899.687-010......98999A
899.687-014......98999A
900.683-010......97102A
902.683-010......97102A
903.683-010......97102A
903.683-014......97102A
903.683-018......97102A
904.383-010......97102B
904.683-010......97102B
905.483-010......97102A
905.663-010......97102A
905.663-014......97102A
905.683-010......97102A
905.687-010......98799B
906.683-010......97105
906.683-014......97105
906.683-018......97105
906.683-022......97105
909.127-010......15023A
909.137-010......81011
909.137-014......81011
909.137-018......81011
909.663-010......97102A
909.687-014......98999A
910.137-010......51002A
910.137-014......81017
910.137-018......81017
910.137-022......81011
910.137-026......81017
910.137-034......81011
910.137-038......51002A
910.137-046......81011
910.167-010......97302
910.167-014......58005
910.263-010......83008A
910.362-010......97399B
910.363-010......97311
910.363-014......97305
910.363-018......97308
910.364-010.....97317A
910.367-010.....97317A
910.367-014.....55347
910.367-018.....58005
910.367-022.....97317B
910.367-026.....68028
910.367-030.....83008A
910.382-010.....97399B
910.384-010.....83008A
910.387-010.....83008D
910.387-014.....83008A
910.583-010.....97308
910.663-010.....87714A
910.664-010.....97317B
910.667-010.....83008A
910.667-014.....68028
910.667-018.....83008D
910.667-022.....83008D
910.667-026.....97317B
910.667-030.....98799B
910.677-010.....68028
910.683-010.....97308
910.683-014.....97314
910.683-018.....87714A
910.683-022.....97399A
910.684-010.....87714B
910.684-014.....87714B
910.687-010.....98999A
910.687-014.....98905
910.687-018.....98999A
910.687-022.....98905
910.687-026.....98999A
911.131-010.....81011
911.131-014.....97802
911.133-010.....97505
911.137-010.....97502A
911.137-014.....97502A
911.137-018.....81011
911.137-022.....81011
911.137-026.....81011
911.167-010.....58005
911.263-010.....97502A
911.362-010.....97802
911.363-010.....97502A
911.363-014.....97514
911.364-010.....97514
911.364-014.....97989A
911.584-010.....97517
911.663-010.....97511
911.663-014.....97902
911.664-010.....97899B
911.664-014.....97517
911.667-010.....98799B
911.667-014.....98999A
911.667-018.....98319
911.677-010.....98999A
911.687-010.....98999A
911.687-014.....98905
911.687-018.....97941
911.687-022.....97517
911.687-026.....98999A
911.687-030.....97517
912.167-010.....39002
912.364-010.....85132
912.367-010.....58008
912.367-014.....58011
912.662-010.....99003
912.663-010.....97899A
912.682-010.....99003
912.684-010.....93997
912.687-010.....98799B
913.133-010.....81011
913.133-014.....81011
913.167-010.....58005
913.167-014.....81011
913.167-018.....58008
913.363-010.....97108
913.367-010.....58005
913.463-010.....97108
913.463-014.....97314
913.463-018.....97114
913.663-010.....97114
913.663-014.....97108
913.663-018.....97105
913.683-010.....66023
914.131-010.....81011
914.132-010.....81011
914.132-014.....81011
914.132-018.....81011
914.132-022.....81011
914.134-010.....81011
914.137-010.....81011
914.137-014.....81011
914.137-018.....81011
914.167-010.....15023C
914.167-014.....58005
914.362-010.....95099
914.362-014.....83005A
914.362-018.....97914
914.382-010.....97908
914.382-014.....97905
914.382-018.....97905
914.382-022.....97911
914.384-010.....95017
914.485-010.....92974
914.585-010.....97953
914.665-010.....97953
914.665-014.....97953
914.667-010.....97905
914.682-010.....97953
914.685-010.....97989A
914.687-010.....98999A
914.687-014.....98799B
914.687-018.....98999A
915.133-010.....81011
915.134-010.....81002
915.137-010.....81017
915.467-010.....97805
915.473-010.....97808
915.477-010.....97805
915.583-010.....97808
915.587-010.....97805
915.667-010.....98905
915.667-014.....97808
915.684-010.....85953
915.687-010.....93956
915.687-014.....97805
915.687-018.....97805
915.687-022.....98905
915.687-026.....98905
915.687-030.....97805
915.687-034.....98905
919.162-010.....58005
919.223-010.....31314
919.363-010.....83008C
919.663-010.....97114
919.663-014.....97308
919.663-018.....97102A
919.663-022.....97105
919.663-026.....97102A
919.664-010.....79999P
919.682-010.....97802
919.683-010.....97511
919.683-014.....97114
919.683-018.....97399A
919.683-022.....97199
919.683-026.....97399A
919.683-030.....97199
919.687-010.....58017
919.687-014.....98905
919.687-018.....83008C
919.687-022.....98799B
920.130-010.....81008
920.132-010.....81008
920.132-014.....81008
920.137-010.....81008
920.137-014.....81008
920.137-018.....81008
920.137-022.....81008
920.137-026.....81008
920.380-010.....92997
920.387-010.....83005A
920.482-010.....92974
920.586-010.....98502
920.587-010.....98902A
920.587-014.....98999A
920.587-018.....98902A
920.587-022.....98902A
920.587-026.....92902B
920.665-010.....92974
920.665-014.....92974
920.667-010.....83005A
920.667-014.....83005A
920.680-010.....92997
920.684-010.....87102D
920.685-010.....92974
920.685-014.....92974
920.685-018.....92974
920.685-022.....93998
920.685-026.....92974
920.685-030.....92974
920.685-034.....92974
920.685-038.....92974
920.685-042.....92974
920.685-046.....92974
920.685-050.....92974
920.685-054.....92974
920.685-058.....92974
920.685-062.....92974
920.685-066.....92974
920.685-070.....92705
920.685-074.....92974

920.685-078 92974
920.685-082 92974
920.685-086 92974
920.685-090 92974
920.685-094 92974
920.685-098 92974
920.685-102 92998
920.685-106 92974
920.685-110 92974
920.685-114 92974
920.686-010 ..... 98999A
920.686-014 98502
920.686-018 98502
920.686-022 ..... 98999A
920.686-026 98502
920.686-030 98502
920.686-034 98502
920.686-038 98502
920.686-042 98502
920.686-046 98502
920.686-050 98502
920.687-010 ..... 98902A
920.687-014 ..... 98902A
920.687-018 ..... 98902A
920.687-022 ..... 93923B
920.687-026 ..... 98902A
920.687-030 ..... 98902A
920.687-034 ..... 98902A
920.687-038 ..... 98902A
920.687-042 ..... 98902A
920.687-046 ..... 98999A
920.687-050 ..... 83005A
920.687-054 ..... 83005A
920.687-058 ..... 83005A
920.687-062 ..... 98999A
920.687-066 ..... 98902A
920.687-070 ..... 83005A
920.687-074 ..... 98902A
920.687-078 ..... 98902A
920.687-082 93956
920.687-086 ..... 98902A
920.687-090 ..... 98902A
920.687-094 ..... 98902A
920.687-098 ..... 98999A
920.687-102 ..... 98999A
920.687-106 ..... 98999A
920.687-110 ..... 98902A
920.687-114 ..... 98902A
920.687-118 ..... 98902A
920.687-122 ..... 98902A
920.687-126 ..... 93951C
920.687-130 ..... 98902A
920.687-134 ..... 98902A
920.687-138 ..... 98999A
920.687-142 ..... 98902A
920.687-146 ..... 98902A
920.687-150 ..... 98902A
920.687-154 58017
920.687-158 ..... 98902A
920.687-166 ..... 98902A
920.687-170 ..... 98902A
920.687-174 ..... 98902A
920.687-178 ..... 93947E
920.687-182 98905

920.687-186 ...... 98999A
920.687-190 ...... 98999A
920.687-194 ...... 83005A
920.687-198 ...... 98902A
920.687-202 79858
921.130-010 ...... 81005A
921.131-010 ...... 72002F
921.132-010 81011
921.133-010 81011
921.133-014 81011
921.133-018 81011
921.137-010 81008
921.137-014 81011
921.260-010 85935
921.364-010 ...... 73099C
921.365-010 ...... 83005A
921.382-010 97951
921.563-010 97951
921.565-010 97951
921.583-010 97947
921.662-010 ...... 97989A
921.662-014 95099
921.662-018 97951
921.662-022 97941
921.662-026 97951
921.663-010 97944
921.663-014 97944
921.663-018 ...... 97989A
921.663-022 97944
921.663-026 97941
921.663-030 97941
921.663-034 ...... 97989B
921.663-038 97944
921.663-042 97944
921.663-046 97941
921.663-050 97941
921.663-054 97944
921.663-058 97944
921.663-062 97944
921.663-066 97941
921.663-070 97944
921.664-010 ...... 98999B
921.664-014 85935
921.665-010 ...... 97989A
921.667-010 ...... 98999A
921.667-014 ...... 73099C
921.667-018 ...... 97989A
921.667-022 ...... 98799B
921.667-026 ...... 98799B
921.682-010 ...... 97989A
921.682-014 97951
921.682-018 ...... 97989A
921.682-022 97941
921.683-010 97941
921.683-014 97951
921.683-018 97944
921.683-022 ...... 97923A
921.683-030 97941
921.683-034 97944
921.683-038 67011
921.683-042 97947
921.683-046 97941
921.683-050 97947
921.683-054 97941

921.683-058 97941
921.683-062 ...... 97989A
921.683-066 97944
921.683-070 97947
921.683-074 97944
921.683-078 97947
921.683-082 97941
921.683-086 97941
921.685-010 97941
921.685-014 97951
921.685-018 ...... 97989A
921.685-022 97951
921.685-026 97951
921.685-030 97951
921.685-034 97951
921.685-038 ...... 97989A
921.685-042 97941
921.685-046 97951
921.685-050 97951
921.685-054 ...... 83005A
921.685-058 ...... 97989A
921.685-062 97951
921.685-066 97951
921.685-070 97951
921.686-010 98502
921.686-014 98502
921.686-018 ...... 73099B
921.686-022 ...... 73099B
921.687-010 ...... 98799B
921.687-014 73005
921.687-018 ...... 98799B
921.687-022 ...... 73099B
921.687-026 98102
921.687-030 ...... 73099B
921.687-034 ...... 98999A
922.137-010 ...... 51002B
922.137-014 81008
922.137-018 81017
922.137-022 81008
922.137-026 81011
922.137-030 81008
922.587-010 ...... 98799B
922.665-010 ...... 97989A
922.665-014 ...... 97989A
922.667-010 ...... 98999A
922.684-010 ...... 98902A
922.686-010 98502
922.686-014 98502
922.687-010 ...... 98902A
922.687-014 ...... 98902A
922.687-018 ...... 83005A
922.687-022 ...... 98799B
922.687-026 ...... 98799B
922.687-030 ...... 98999A
922.687-034 ...... 98799B
922.687-038 ...... 83005A
922.687-042 58017
922.687-046 ...... 98902A
922.687-050 ...... 98799B
922.687-054 ...... 83005A
922.687-058 ...... 98999A
922.687-062 ...... 98999A
922.687-066 ...... 98999A
922.687-070 ...... 98799B

922.687-074 ..... 83005A
922.687-078 ..... 98799B
922.687-082 ..... 73099B
922.687-086 ..... 83005A
922.687-090 98702
922.687-094 ..... 98902A
922.687-098 ..... 98799B
922.687-102 ..... 98999A
929.131-010 81002
929.132-010 81011
929.133-010 81011
929.137-010 81008
929.137-014 81008
929.137-018 81008
929.137-022 81008
929.137-026 81008
929.137-030 81011
929.137-034 ..... 72002A
929.367-010 ..... 83005A
929.381-010 93932
929.382-010 ..... 83005A
929.583-010 97947
929.587-010 ..... 98999A
929.663-010 73011
929.683-014 97947
929.684-010 ..... 98902A
929.685-010 92971
929.685-014 92974
929.685-018 92974
929.686-014 ..... 98999A
929.686-018 98502
929.686-022 98502
929.687-010 ..... 93926E
929.687-014 ..... 98999A
929.687-018 ..... 98999A
929.687-022 ..... 98999A
929.687-026 ..... 98999A
929.687-030 ..... 98799B
929.687-034 ..... 98799B
929.687-038 ..... 98999A
929.687-042 ..... 98902A
929.687-046 ..... 83005A
929.687-050 ..... 83005A
929.687-054 ..... 98902A
929.687-058 ..... 98902A
929.687-062 ..... 83005A
930.130-010 ..... 81005B
930.131-010 ..... 81005B
930.134-010 ..... 81005B
930.167-010 ..... 24511B
930.261-010 87917
930.261-014 ..... 83002A
930.267-010 ..... 83002A
930.361-010 87917
930.363-010 97941
930.364-010 83099
930.382-010 87943
930.382-014 ..... 83005A
930.382-018 87911
930.382-022 87914
930.382-026 87911
930.382-030 97941
930.383-010 87943
930.482-010 87943

930.662-010 87943
930.663-010 87943
930.664-010 ..... 87989B
930.664-014 98323
930.665-010 ..... 87949A
930.666-010 98323
930.666-014 98323
930.667-010 98323
930.683-010 87941
930.683-014 87943
930.683-018 97941
930.683-022 ..... 97923A
930.683-026 87923
930.684-010 87943
930.684-014 ..... 87989A
930.684-018 87702
930.684-022 87908
930.684-026 98323
930.685-010 92965
930.687-010 98323
930.687-014 98319
930.687-018 ..... 98999A
931.261-010 87905
931.361-010 87905
931.361-014 87905
931.361-018 87905
931.382-010 87905
931.384-010 ..... 87989A
931.664-010 87905
931.667-010 87905
931.684-010 ..... 87989A
932.132-010 ..... 81005B
932.132-014 81011
932.167-010 58005
932.363-010 97941
932.664-010 ..... 97317B
932.664-014 ..... 98999B
932.667-010 ..... 98799B
932.667-014 ..... 85128B
932.683-010 ..... 97899B
932.683-014 97932
932.683-018 97932
932.683-022 97935
932.685-010 ..... 97923B
932.687-010 ..... 97989A
933.664-010 ..... 87989B
933.687-010 ..... 98999A
934.685-010 92962
934.685-014 92998
934.685-018 92962
934.685-022 92962
934.687-010 ..... 98999A
939.130-010 81008
939.131-010 ..... 81005B
939.131-014 81008
939.131-018 81011
939.132-010 ..... 81005B
939.132-014 ..... 81005B
939.137-010 ..... 51002A
939.137-014 ..... 81005B
939.137-018 ..... 81005B
939.137-022 ..... 81005B
939.167-010 81008
939.281-010 ..... 87989A

939.362-010......58005
939.362-014......95099
939.364-010......98323
939.382-010......87949A
939.462-010......87949B
939.485-010......87949A
939.585-010......83005A
939.663-010......98323
939.667-010......98799B
939.667-014......87989B
939.667-018......98799B
939.682-010......97953
939.682-014......87989A
939.684-010......87989A
939.684-014......87989A
939.684-018......98999B
939.685-010......92962
939.685-014......92962
939.686-010......97989A
939.687-010......83005A
939.687-014......98999A
939.687-018......98999A
939.687-022......98905
939.687-026......87989B
939.687-030......83005A
939.687-034......98999A
950.131-010......81008
950.131-014......81008
950.362-010......97953
950.362-014......95032
950.382-010......95032
950.382-014......97921
950.382-018......95032
950.382-022......87911
950.382-026......95032
950.382-030......95032
950.485-010......95032
950.562-010......95099
950.585-010......95099
950.585-014......92926
950.685-010......95032
950.685-014......92926
951.685-010......95023
951.685-014......92926
951.685-018......92926
951.686-010......98502
952.131-010......81008
952.132-010......81008
952.137-010......81008
952.137-014......81008
952.137-018......81002
952.137-022......81008
952.137-026......81008
952.167-010......58005
952.167-014......95028
952.261-010......83002D
952.362-010......95023
952.362-014......95028
952.362-018......95021
952.362-022......95026
952.362-026......95028
952.362-030......95028
952.362-034......95028
952.362-038......95028
952.362-042......95021
952.364-010......87202C
952.367-010......83005A
952.367-014......95028
952.381-010......87202C
952.382-010......95021
952.382-014......95021
952.382-018......95021
952.464-010......97953
952.567-010......83005A
952.665-010......98999A
952.667-010......98999A
952.687-010......79041
952.687-014......98999A
953.132-010......81008
953.137-010......81011
953.137-014......81008
953.137-018......81002
953.167-010......58005
953.281-010......85928A
953.362-010......95005B
953.362-014......95005A
953.362-018......95005B
953.364-010......85928D
953.367-010......83005A
953.367-014......83005A
953.367-018......83005A
953.382-010......97917
953.387-010......83005A
953.583-010......97102A
953.584-010......98999B
953.667-010......98999A
953.684-010......98999B
953.687-010......98102
954.130-010......81008
954.132-010......81008
954.362-010......79999B
954.367-010......58005
954.382-010......95002A
954.382-014......95002A
954.382-018......95099
954.385-010......92962
954.564-010......87899A
954.587-010......98905
955.130-010......81008
955.131-010......81008
955.133-010......81011
955.137-010......81011
955.167-010......58005
955.222-010......31314
955.362-010......95002A
955.362-014......95099
955.382-010......95002A
955.382-014......95002A
955.383-010......97989B
955.463-010......97938
955.585-010......95002B
955.667-010......98999A
955.685-010......92923
955.687-010......98905
955.687-014......98999A
955.687-018......98999A
955.687-022......98705
956.267-010......83005B
956.387-010 ..... 83005B
959.131-010 81008
959.137-010 ..... 51002B
959.137-014 ..... 51002A
959.137-018 ..... 51002B
959.137-022 ..... 51002A
959.167-010 58005
959.361-010 ..... 85928D
959.367-010 83099
959.367-014 ..... 85599B
959.367-018 ..... 85928D
959.574-010 ..... 85928D
959.684-010 93998
960.132-010 81008
960.362-010 92905
960.382-010 92905
961.364-010 ..... 34056B
961.367-010 ..... 49032B
961.667-010 ..... 49032B
961.667-014 ..... 34056B
962.132-010 34032
962.134-010 81008
962.137-010 81002
962.137-018 81008
962.137-022 81008
962.137-026 81008
962.162-010 ..... 34056K
962.167-010 ..... 22599A
962.167-014 ..... 34056F
962.167-018 55347
962.261-010 ..... 39999D
962.261-014 ..... 39999D
962.262-010 34032
962.267-010 ..... 39999D
962.281-010 ..... 87102A
962.281-014 ..... 39999D
962.281-018 ..... 39999D
962.361-010 34032
962.362-010 ..... 39999D
962.362-014 ..... 39999D
962.381-010 ..... 89502A
962.381-014 ..... 39999D
962.381-018 ..... 89908A
962.382-010 ..... 22599A
962.382-014 34032
962.384-010 ..... 98799A
962.664-010 85935
962.664-014 ..... 98799A
962.665-010 92998
962.684-010 85935
962.684-014 85935
962.684-018 ..... 98799A
962.684-022 ..... 98799A
962.687-010 ..... 98999A
962.687-014 ..... 98999A
962.687-018 ..... 98799A
962.687-022 ..... 98799A
969.137-010 81008
969.137-014 ..... 19999A
969.367-010 58023
969.381-010 ..... 89505A
969.664-010 ..... 39999H
969.685-010 92998
969.687-010 ..... 98999A
969.687-014 ..... 98999A
970.131-014 61005
970.137-010 81008
970.281-010 ..... 89914A
970.281-014 ..... 34035A
970.281-018 ..... 89914A
970.281-022 ..... 89911A
970.281-026 ..... 89911E
970.361-010 ..... 89911E
970.361-014 89712
970.361-018 ..... 34035B
970.381-010 ..... 89914A
970.381-014 ..... 89911A
970.381-018 89706
970.381-022 ..... 89911A
970.381-026 ..... 89911A
970.381-030 89712
970.381-034 ..... 89914A
970.381-038 ..... 89911E
970.381-042 ..... 89911E
970.581-010 ..... 89911E
970.661-010 ..... 89911E
970.661-014 ..... 89911E
970.664-010 ..... 98999B
970.681-010 ..... 89911B
970.681-014 ..... 93947E
970.681-018 ..... 89911E
970.681-022 ..... 89911E
970.681-026 ..... 89911A
970.681-030 ..... 89911A
971.131-010 81008
971.131-014 81008
971.261-010 89712
971.381-010 89712
971.381-014 89712
971.381-022 89712
971.381-026 89712
971.381-030 89712
971.381-034 89712
971.381-038 89712
971.381-040 89712
971.381-046 ..... 89799A
971.381-050 89717
971.381-054 89717
971.382-014 89712
971.382-018 89712
971.684-010 ..... 93947E
971.684-014 ..... 93947E
971.685-010 92545
971.687-010 ..... 98999A
972.137-010 81008
972.281-010 ..... 89719A
972.281-018 ..... 89719A
972.281-022 89717
972.282-010 89715
972.282-018 ..... 89719B
972.284-010 ..... 83005A
972.381-010 89718
972.381-014 89718
972.381-018 89128
972.381-022 89717
972.381-026 89718
972.381-030 89706
972.381-034 ..... 89799A
972.381-038 89706
972.382-010 89713
972.382-014 89713
972.382-018 89712
972.382-022 ..... 89719B
972.384-014 92545
972.681-010 89128
972.682-010 92545
972.682-014 92545
972.687-010 ..... 83005A
973.137-010 81008
973.381-010 89702
973.381-014 89702
973.381-018 89705
973.381-022 89705
973.381-026 89702
973.381-030 89702
973.681-010 89702
974.131-010 81008
974.381-010 ..... 89799B
974.381-014 ..... 89799B
974.382-010 ..... 89799B
974.382-014 ..... 89799B
974.682-010 91911
976.131-010 81008
976.131-014 81008
976.131-018 81008
976.131-022 81008
976.131-026 81008
976.132-010 81008
976.134-010 81008
976.137-014 81008
976.267-010 ..... 83005A
976.360-010 92997
976.361-010 ..... 89914B
976.362-010 ..... 83005A
976.380-010 92908
976.381-010 ..... 89914D
976.381-014 ..... 89799A
976.381-018 ..... 89914B
976.381-022 ..... 89914B
976.382-010 34026
976.382-014 92908
976.382-018 92908
976.382-022 ..... 89914B
976.382-030 92908
976.382-034 92908
976.382-038 92908
976.384-010 92908
976.384-014 92908
976.385-010 92908
976.487-010 93998
976.564-010 58008
976.567-010 55326
976.665-010 92908
976.667-010 93998
976.681-010 ..... 89914C
976.682-010 92908
976.682-014 92908
976.682-018 92908
976.682-022 56099
976.684-010 93997
976.684-014 92908
976.684-018 ..... 93926E

976.684-022 93998
976.684-026 93998
976.684-030 92908
976.684-034 ..... 93951C
976.684-038 92908
976.685-010 92944
976.685-014 92908
976.685-018 92908
976.685-022 92908
976.685-026 92908
976.685-030 92908
976.685-034 92908
976.685-038 92908
976.687-010 ..... 83005A
976.687-014 ..... 83005A
976.687-018 58028
976.687-022 ..... 83005A
977.381-010 89721
977.381-014 89721
977.684-010 85998
977.684-014 ...... 93947E
977.684-018 93956
977.684-022 ...... 93923B
977.684-026 93998
977.687-010 ...... 83005A
979.130-010 81008
979.130-014 81008
979.131-010 81008
979.131-014 81008
979.131-018 81008
979.132-010 81008
979.137-010 81008
979.137-014 81008
979.137-018 81008
979.137-022 81008
979.137-026 81008
979.281-010 89128
979.281-014 89128
979.281-018 89128
979.282-010 89707
979.360-010 92524
979.361-010 ...... 31511D
979.362-010 92543
979.380-010 ...... 92529D
979.381-010 89128
979.381-014 ...... 89799A
979.381-026 85112
979.381-030 89128
979.381-034 ...... 89911E
979.381-038 ...... 89908B
979.382-010 92549
979.382-014 ..... 92529D
979.382-018 ..... 89799A
979.382-022 92545
979.382-026 ..... 89799A
979.384-010 ..... 89799A
979.581-010 ..... 93951D
979.667-010 ..... 83005A
979.681-010 ..... 89911E
979.681-014 ..... 89799A
979.681-018 ..... 93951D
979.681-022 ..... 89908B
979.682-010 92549
979.682-014 92545
979.682-022 92545
979.682-026 92545
979.684-010 ..... 93951C
979.684-014 ..... 93951D
979.684-018 93998
979.684-022 92998
979.684-026 ..... 98999B
979.684-030 ..... 93951C
979.684-034 ..... 93951C
979.684-038 ..... 85119B
979.684-042 93956
979.685-010 92543
979.687-010 ..... 83005A
979.687-014 ..... 98999A
979.687-018 ..... 83005A
979.687-022 ..... 98999A
979.687-026 ..... 83005A
979.687-030 ..... 83005A
979.687-034 ..... 98999A

APPENDIX B
Guide For Occupational Exploration (GOE)
Interest Areas and Related Jobs

INTRODUCTION

You can use this appendix as a way to identify career interests. While it is not a career assessment test, it provides information that can help you clarify your career goals. To meet the needs of career counselors and others, the U.S. Department of Labor developed a system to organize jobs into major interest areas. This was considered a useful and intuitive way for people to explore career options. This system was used in a book published by the Department of Labor titled the ***Guide for Occupational Exploration*** (GOE).

Since then, a variety of occupational reference books, career assessment tests, and career information software has used the GOE system for organizing occupations. You may use some of these GOE-based materials and, even if you don't, the information in this appendix can help you clarify your career objectives.

The GOE uses a simple system to organize all jobs into just 12 major interest areas. These 12 interest areas are then divided into more specialized subgroups. Look over the 12 descriptions for the GOE Interest Areas that follow. As you do, decide which areas seem most interesting to you.

01. Artistic: An interest in the creative expression of feelings or ideas. You can satisfy this interest in several of the creative or performing arts. For example, if you enjoy literature, writing or editing might appeal to you. If you prefer work in the performing arts, you could direct or perform in drama, music, or dance. If you especially enjoy the visual arts, you could become a critic in painting, sculpture, or ceramics. You may prefer to use your hands to create or decorate products. Or you may like to model clothes or develop stage sets for plays.

02. Scientific: An interest in discovering, collecting, and analyzing information about the natural world, and in applying scientific research findings to problems in medicine, the life sciences, and the natural sciences. You can satisfy this interest by working with the knowledge and processes of the sciences. You may enjoy researching and developing new knowledge in mathematics, or perhaps solving problems in the physical or life sciences would appeal to you. You may wish to study medicine and help people or animals. If you want to work with scientific equipment and procedures, you could seek a job in a research or testing laboratory.

03. Plants and Animals: An interest in working with plants and animals, usually outdoors. You can satisfy this interest by working in farming, forestry, fishing, or related fields. You may like doing physical work outdoors, such as on a farm. You may enjoy animals; perhaps training or taking care of animals would appeal to you. If you have management ability, you could own, operate, or manage a farm or related business.

04. Protective: An interest in using authority to protect people and property. You can satisfy this interest by working in law enforcement, fire fighting, and related fields. For example, if you enjoy mental challenge and intrigue, you could investigate crimes or fires for a living. You may prefer to fight fires and respond to other emergencies. Or, if you want more routine work, perhaps a job in guarding or patrolling would appeal to you. If you have management ability, you could seek a leadership position in law enforcement and protective services.

05. Mechanical: An interest in applying mechanical principles to practical situations by use of machines or hand tools. You can satisfy your mechanical interest in a variety of careers, ranging from routine jobs to complex professional positions. If you enjoy working with ideas about things, you could seek a job in engineering or in a related technical field. You may instead prefer to deal directly with things: you could find a job in the crafts or trades, building, making, or repairing objects. You may like to drive or operate vehicles and special equipment. If you prefer routine or physical work in settings other than factories, perhaps work in mining or construction would appeal to you.

06. **Industrial: An interest in repetitive, concrete, organized activities done in a factory setting.** You can satisfy this interest by working in one of many industries that mass-produce goods. You may enjoy manual work, using your hands or hand tools. Perhaps you prefer to operate or take care of machines. You may like to inspect, sort, count, or weigh products. Using your training and experience to set up machines or supervise other workers may appeal to you.

07. **Business Detail: An interest in organized, clearly defined activities requiring accuracy and attention to details, primarily in an office setting.** You can satisfy this interest in a variety of jobs in which you attend to the details of a business operation. You may enjoy using your math skills; if so, perhaps a job in billing, computing, or financial record-keeping would satisfy you. If you prefer to deal with people, you may want a job in which you meet the public, talk on the telephone, or supervise other workers. You may like to operate computer terminals, typewriters, or bookkeeping machines. Perhaps a job in filing or recording would satisfy you. Or you may wish to use your training and experience to manage an office.

08. **Selling: An interest in bringing others to a particular point of view by personal persuasion, using sales and promotional techniques.** You can satisfy this interest in a variety of sales jobs. You may enjoy selling technical products or services, or perhaps a selling job requiring less technical knowledge. You may work in stores, sales offices, or customers' homes. You may wish to buy and resell products to make a profit. You can also satisfy this interest in legal work, business negotiations, advertising, and related fields.

09. **Accommodating: An interest in catering to the wishes and needs of others, usually on a one-to-one basis.** You can satisfy this interest by providing services for the convenience of others in hotels, restaurants, airplanes, and other locations. If you enjoy improving the appearance of others, perhaps working in the hair and beauty care field would satisfy you. Or you may wish to provide personal services such as taking tickets, carrying baggage, or ushering.

10. **Humanitarian: An interest in helping others with their mental, spiritual, social, physical, or vocational needs.** You can satisfy this interest by work in which caring for people's welfare is important. Perhaps the spiritual or mental well-being of others concerns you. If so, you would prepare for a job in religion or counseling. If you wish to help others with physical problems, you could work in the nursing, therapy, or rehabilitation fields. You may like to provide needed but less complicated care by working as an aide, orderly, or technician.

11. **Leading and Influencing: An interest in leading and influencing others by using high-level verbal or numerical abilities.** You can satisfy this interest through study and work in a variety of professional fields. You may enjoy the challenge and responsibility of leadership. You may like to help others learn, in which case working in education may appeal to you.

12. **Physical Performing: An interest in physical activities performed before an audience.** You can satisfy this interest through jobs in athletics, sports, and the performance of physical feats. Perhaps a job as a professional player or official would appeal to you. You may wish to develop and perform special acts such as acrobatics or wire walking.

GOE SUBGROUPS, PLUS RELATED OOH JOBS, DOT JOBS, SELF-EMPLOYMENT JOBS, AND EDUCATION AND TRAINING

The 12 major GOE Interest Areas are divided into 66 work groups and 348 even more specific subgroups of related jobs. All jobs are organized within these increasingly specific clusters of related jobs.

The GOE uses a system of number codes for the various groupings. Called "GOE Codes" these numbers can be used to cross-reference you to other occupational information systems that use the same organizational structure.

The information that follows gives you a variety of useful information. For each of the 12 major GOE Interest Areas it provides the following:

GOE Subgroups: Each of the 12 major GOE Interest Areas are further organized into subgroups of related jobs. Each subgroup has a four-digit GOE number that allows you to cross-reference it to information systems using the GOE structure.

Related OOH Occupations: For each GOE subgroup, we provide a listing of job titles found in the *Occupational Outlook Handbook* (OOH). This listing will give you a good idea of the major job titles related to each GOE Interest Area and subgroup. Note any OOH job titles that interest you and read the descriptions provided in the OOH for these jobs.

Related DOT Occupations: This list provides jobs found in the ***Dictionary of Occupational Titles*** (DOT) that are related to the GOE Interest Area. Many of these job titles are more specialized than the job titles used in the OOH, and we include them here to give you an idea of the wide range of job titles within the various GOE Interest Areas. You can identify job titles of particular interest and obtain more information on these jobs from the DOT.

Self-Employment Options: This list provides some jobs that offer self-employment opportunities related to each GOE Interest Area.

Related Education and Training: This list provides a partial listing of education and training programs, courses, majors, or topical areas that are related to the occupations in each GOE Interest Area.

We suggest that you pay particular attention to the GOE Interest Areas that are of most interest to you. We did not provide a cross-reference to the related O*NET occupations because you can identify the types of jobs that interest you most in the O*NET listing following the table of contents for this book. The O*NET descriptions will provide you with additional information that is helpful in focusing your career exploration efforts.

---

01 ARTISTIC: An interest in the creative expression of feelings or ideas.

GOE Subgroups

01.01 Literary Arts
01.02 Visual Arts
01.03 Performing Arts: Drama
01.04 Performing Arts: Music
01.05 Performing Arts: Dance
01.06 Craft Arts
01.07 Elemental Arts
01.08 Modeling

Related OOH Occupations

01.01 Literary Arts—Social Scientists and Urban Planners; Radio and Television Announcers and Newscasters; Writers and Editors; Actors, Directors, and Producers

01.02 Visual Arts—Marketing, Advertising, and Public Relations Managers; Adult Education Teachers; Designers; Photographers and Camera Operators; Visual Artists; Broadcast Technicians; Blue-Collar Worker Supervisors; Prepress Workers; Apparel Workers

01.03 Performing Arts: Drama—Adult Education Teachers; Radio and Television Announcers and Newscasters; Actors, Directors, and Producers; Secretaries

01.04 Performing Arts: Music—Adult Education Teachers; Actors, Directors, and Producers; Musicians

01.05 Performing Arts: Dance—Adult Education Teachers; Dancers and Choreographers

01.06 Craft Arts—Social Scientists and Urban Planners; Adult Education Teachers; Archivists and Curators; Designers; Photographers and Camera Operators; Visual Artists; Barbers and Cosmetologists; Industrial Machinery Repairers; Carpenters; Blue-Collar Worker Supervisors; Inspectors, Testers, and Graders; Jewelers; Prepress Workers; Bindery Workers; Apparel Workers; Shoe and Leather Workers and Repairers; Woodworking Occupations; Photographic Process Workers; Handlers, Equipment Cleaners, Helpers, and Laborers

01.07 Elemental Arts—Actors, Directors, and Producers

01.08 Modeling—Adult Education Teachers; Actors, Directors, and Producers

Related DOT Occupations

Actor/actress, announcer, art appraiser, art director, art teacher, artist, architect, biographer, cartoonist, choreographer, clothes designer, color expert, columnist, comedian, commentator, commercial artist, commercial designer, communications technician, composer, continuity writer, copyist, copy editor, copy writer, costuming supervisor, critic, crossword puzzle maker, dance instructor, dancer, delineator, director, disk jockey, display designer, drama teacher, editor, editorial assistant, editorial writer, English teacher, engraver, fashion artist, film editor, freelance writer, furniture designer, graphic arts technician, graphic designer, graphologist, greeting card editor, humorist, illustrator, interior designer, interpreter, jeweler, literature instructor, lyricist, magician, make-up artist, memorial designer, mime, model, model maker, music teacher, musician, novelist, offset-plate make, orchestrator, package designer, painter, playwright, producer, photoengraving etcher, photographer, photojournalist, poet, print maker, producer, puppeteer, quick sketch artist, radio director, reader, reporter, screen writer, sculptor, set decorator, set designer, singer, story editor, taxidermist, technical writer, translator, writer.

Self-Employment Options

Advertising person, aerial photography, airbrush artist/retoucher, art consultant/dealer, artist, art gallery, art instruction, artist's representative, arts and crafts instructor, book designer, eulogy writer, fashion designer, jewelry designer, mural maker, oil and water painting restorer, paste-up artist, short story author, sign painter, stained glass artist, tole painter.

Related Education and Training

Art, craft arts, drama, graphic arts, music, photography, modern dance, architecture, art history, theater arts, performing arts, commercial art, interior design, commercial photography, visual arts, illustration design, literature, journalism, humanities, English, creative writing, communications studies, language, philosophy, classics, broadcasting, and composition.

---

02 SCIENTIFIC: An interest in discovering, collecting, and analyzing information about the natural world, and in applying scientific research findings to problems in medicine, life sciences, and natural sciences.

GOE Subgroups

02.01 Physical Sciences

02.02 Life Sciences

02.03 Medical Sciences

02.04 Laboratory Technology

Related OOH Occupations

02.01 Physical Sciences—Engineering, Science, and Data Processing Managers; Metallurgical, Ceramic, and Materials Engineers; Surveyors; Mathematicians; Chemists; Geologists and Geophysicists; Meteorologists; Physicists and Astronomers; Social Scientists and Urban Planners; Science Technicians

02.02 Life Sciences—Inspectors and Compliance Officers, except Construction; Agricultural Scientists; Biological and Medical Scientists; Foresters and Conservation Scientists; Chemists; Physicists and Astronomers; Social Scientists and Urban Planners; Veterinarians; Dietitians and Nutritionists; Science Technicians; Farm Operators and Managers

02.03 Medical Sciences—Health Services Managers; Chiropractors; Dentists; Optometrists; Physicians; Podiatrists; Veterinarians; Speech-Language Pathologists and Audiologists

02.04 Laboratory Technology—Engineering, Science, and Data Processing Managers; Health Services Managers; Biological and Medical Scientists; Chemists; Pharmacists; Photographers and Camera Operators; Clinical Laboratory Technologists and Technicians; Radiologic Technologists; Engineering Technicians; Science Technicians; Medical Assistants; Inspectors, Testers, and Graders; Textile Machinery Operators; Photographic Process Workers

Related DOT Occupations

Aerial photograph interpreter, agronomist, anesthesiologist, animal scientist, archaeologist, astronomer, anthropologist, audiologist, biochemist, biologist, biological aide, biomedical engineer, botanist, chemist, chiropractor, coroner, crystallographer, cytologist, dairy scientist, dental hygienist, dentist, embalmer, environmental analyst, environmental research project manager, food chemist, food technologist, forest ecologist, geneticist, geodesist, geographer, geologist, geophysical prospector, geophysicists, hydrologist, laboratory assistant, laboratory technician, laboratory tester, mathematician, materials scientist, medical officer, medical laboratory assistant, medical technologist, metallurgist, meteorologist, microbiologist, mineralogist, nematologist, neurologist, nurse aide, optometrist, paleontologist, perfumer, petrologist, pharmacist, pharmacologist, physical metallurgist, physical science teacher, physical therapist, physician, physiologist, physicist, plant breeder, poultry scientist, radiologist, range manager, research dietitian, scientific helper, seismologist, soil conservationist, soil scientist, speech pathologist, stratigrapher, veterinarian, zoologist.

Self-Employment Options

Audiologist, biological laboratory operation, chiropractor, dentist, doctor, environmental services, geological consultant, herbalist, home health agency, home-visit nurse, medical lab technician, microscope rental/repair, personal home care, plant breeder, recycling services, solar consultant, solar systems designer, speech pathologist.

Related Education and Training

Biology, chemistry, anatomy, pharmacology, anesthesiology, radiology, biochemistry, toxicology, microbiology, nursing, chiropractic, human nutrition, dentistry, allied health professions, medical technology, physical therapy, physician assistant, astronomy, earth science, physics, geology, meteorology, archeology, mining/minerals engineering, geophysics, aerospace science, pure mathematics, planetary science, and paleontology.

---

03 PLANTS AND ANIMALS: An interest in working with plants and animals, usually outdoors.

GOE Subgroups

03.01 Managerial Work
03.02 General Supervision
03.03 Animal Training and Service
03.04 Elemental Work

Related OOH Occupations

03.01 Managerial Work—Plants and Animals; Construction Contractors and Managers; General Managers and Top Executives; Industrial Production Managers; Inspectors and Compliance Officers, except Construction; Foresters and Conservation Scientists; Science Technicians; Gardeners and Groundskeepers; Farm Operators and Managers; Fishers, Hunters, and Trappers

03.02 General Supervision—Plants and Animals; Science Technicians; Forestry and Logging Occupations; Blue-Collar Worker Supervisors

03.03 Animal Training and Service—Animal Caretakers, except Farm; Handlers, Equipment Cleaners, Helpers, and Laborers

03.04 Elemental Work—Plants and Animals; Science Technicians; Material Recording, Scheduling, Dispatching, and Distributing Occupations; Firefighting Occupations; Gardeners and Groundskeepers; Fishers, Hunters, and Trappers; Forestry and Logging Occupations; Blue-Collar Worker Supervisors; Butchers and Meat, Poultry, and Fish Cutters; Inspectors, Testers, and Graders; Woodworking Occupations; Material Moving Equipment Operators; Handlers, Equipment Cleaners, Helpers, and Laborers

Related DOT Occupations

Agriculture scientist, animal breeder/caretaker, animal keeper, animal trainer, animal trapper, artificial-breeding technician, barn boss, botanist, budder, cemetery worker, Christmas tree farm manager, comp tender, cowpuncher, cruiser, dairy farm manager, dog catcher, dog groomer, electric-fork operator, farm machine operator, farm worker, farming supervisor, field contractor, fish farmer, fish hatchery supervisor, forest nursery supervisor, forestry aide, forestry worker, game warden, greens superintendent, horse exerciser, fisher, forest ecologist, forester, game farm worker, gamekeeper, game preserve manager, greenskeeper, horse trainer, horseshoer, horticulture worker, landscape gardener, lawn service worker, livestock rancher, logger, logging supervisor, nursery manager, park ranger, plant propagator, park naturalist, parks and grounds groundskeeper, poultry breeder, poultry farm worker, range manager, seedling sorter, shellfish grower, soil conservationist, special effects gardener, stable attendant, tree cutter and trimmer, tree cutter, tree planter, tree surgeon, veterinarian assistant, wildlife biologist, wildlife control agent, woods boss, yard worker, zoo director, zoologist.

Self-Employment Options

Animal boarder, animal breeder, animal clipper, animal dipper, animal food depot owner, animal groomer, animal sitter, bee keeper, cattle farmer, dairy farmer, duck boarder and breeder, exterminator, greenhouse owner, farmer, florist, florist sales and service, flower arranger, flower bulb sales, gardener, gardening service owner, goat keeper, goldfish breeding, green plant maintenance, herb farming, horticulturist, landscape contractor, lawn maintenance service, mink farmer, pet groomer, pig farmer, poultry farmer, seed shop owner, sheep farmer, tack shop owner, taxidermist, trapper, tree maintenance service, vegetable farmer, veterinarian.

Related Education and Training

Wildlife technology, zoology, animal science, botany, landscaping, horticulture, agriculture, fisheries and wildlife services, wastewater technology, water resources, animal nutrition, environmental sciences, oceanography, farm management, animal grooming, biology, forestry, soil science, botany, agronomy, life sciences, agricultural economics, forest recreation, forestry and wildlife resources, environmental conservation, industrial forestry, and plan pathology.

---

04 PROTECTIVE: An interest in using authority to protect people and property.

GOE Subgroups

04.01 Safety and Law Enforcement

04.02 Security Services

Related OOH Occupations

04.01 Safety and Law Enforcement—General Managers and top executives; Inspectors and Compliance Officers, except Construction; Social Scientists and Urban Planners; Adult Education Teachers; Firefighting Occupations; Police Detectives, and Special Agents

04.02 Security Services—Inspectors and Compliance Officers, except Construction; Adjusters, Investigators, and Collectors; Dispatchers; Correction Officers; Firefighting Occupations; Guards; Police Detectives, and Special agents

Related DOT Occupations

Alarm investigator, airline security agent, armed services personnel, armored-car guard, bailiff, border guard, bodyguard, bouncer, chaperon, correctional officer, court deputy, customs inspector, customs patrol officer, deputy sheriff, detective, dispatcher, equal-opportunity representative, fire chief's aide, fire inspector, fire fighter, fire marshall, fire prevention bureau captain, fire ranger, fire warden, fish and gambling monitor, food and drug inspector, game warden, gate tender, house officer, immigration guard, internal security manager, jailer, lifeguard, merchant patroller, motorized squad commanding officer, narcotics investigator, parking enforcement office, park ranger, patroller, police academy instructor, police inspector, police officer, protective officer, repossessor, safety inspector, security guard, security guard dispatcher, school bus monitor, sheriff, ski patroller, smoke jumper, smoke jumper supervisor, special agent, state highway police officer, traffic sergeant, undercover operator, wildlife agent.

Self-Employment Options

Bodyguard, burglar alarm sales, collections agent, fire alarm system sales, fire extinguisher sales, fire investigator, firearms instructor, firearms repair/service, firearms safety instructor, firearms sales, fireworks manufacturing, investigative services, law-for-the-layperson instructor, loss adjustment services, martial arts training school, military equipment, private detective, security systems designer.

Related Education and Training

Criminology, law enforcement, fire science, political science, army ROTC, physical education, economics, correctional justice, state police academy, history, police science, correctional administration, and protective services.

---

05 MECHANICAL: An interest in applying mechanical principles to practical situations by use of machines or hand tools.

GOE Subgroups

05.01 Engineering
05.02 Managerial Work: Mechanical
05.03 Engineering Technology
05.04 Air and Water Vehicle Operation
05.05 Craft Technology
05.06 Systems Operation
05.07 Quality Control
05.08 Land and Water Vehicle Operation
05.09 Material Control
05.10 Crafts
05.11 Equipment Operation
05.12 Elemental Work: Mechanical

Related OOH Occupations

05.01 Engineering—Engineering, Science, and Data Processing Managers; Management Analysts and Consultants; Aerospace Engineers; Chemical Engineers; Civil Engineers; Electrical and Electronics Engineers; Industrial Engineers; Mechanical Engineers; Metallurgical, Ceramic, and Materials Engineers; Mining Engineers; Nuclear Engineers; Petroleum Engineers; Architects; Landscape Architects; Surveyors; Computer Scientists and Systems Analysts; Geologists and Geophysicists; Physicists and Astronomers; Designers; Engineering Technicians; Science Technicians; Manufacturers' and Wholesale Sales Representatives; Retail Sales Workers; Machinists and Tool Programmers

05.02 Managerial Work: Mechanical—Construction Contractors and Managers; Engineering, Science, and Data Processing Managers; General Managers and Top Executives; Industrial Production Managers; Inspectors and Compliance Officers, except Construction; Marketing, Advertising, and Public Relations Managers; Property and Real Estate Managers; Purchasers and Buyers; Industrial Engineers; Petroleum Engineers; Science Technicians; Services Sales Representatives; Dispatchers; Blue-Collar Worker Supervisors

05.03 Engineering Technology—Construction and Building Inspectors; Cost Estimators; Engineering, Science, and Data Processing Managers; Inspectors and Compliance Officers, except Construction; Purchasers and Buyers; Industrial Engineers; Mechanical Engineers; Surveyors; Aircraft Pilots; Air Traffic Controllers; Broadcast Technicians; Drafters; Engineering Technicians; Science Technicians; Material Recording, Scheduling, Dispatching, and Distributing Occupations; Blue-Collar Worker Supervisors; Inspectors, Testers, and Graders; Apparel Workers; Rail Transportation Workers

05.04 Air and Water Vehicle Operation—Inspectors and Compliance Officers, except Construction; Adult Education Teachers; Aircraft Pilots; Science Technicians; Fishers, Hunters, and Trappers; Water Transportation Occupations

05.05 Craft Technology—Health Services Managers; Industrial Production Managers; Management Analysts and Consultants; Adult Education Teachers; Dietitians and Nutritionists; Engineering Technicians; Chefs, Cooks, and Other Kitchen Workers; Aircraft Mechanics and Engine Specialists; Automotive Body Repairers; Automotive Mechanics; Diesel Mechanics; Commercial and Industrial Electronic Equipment Repairers; Communications Equipment Mechanics; Computer and Office Machine Repairers; Electronic Home Entertainment Equipment Repairers; Telephone Installers and Repairers; Elevator Installers and Repairers; Farm Equipment Mechanics; General Maintenance Mechanics; Heating, Air-Conditioning, and Refrigeration Technicians; Home Appliance and Power Tool Repairers; Industrial Machinery Repairers; Line Installers and Cable Splicers; Millwrights; Mobile Heavy Equipment Mechanics; Motorcycle, Boat, and Small Engine Mechanics; Musical Instrument Repairers and Tuners; Bricklayers and Stonemasons; Carpenters; Concrete Masons and Terrazo Workers; Drywall Workers and Lathers; Electricians; Painters and Paperhangers; Plasterers; Plumbers and Pipefitters; Sheetmetal Workers; Structural and Reinforcing Ironworkers; Tilesetters; Precision Assemblers; Blue-Collar Worker Supervisors; Inspectors, Testers, and Graders; Boilermakers; Jewelers; Machinists and Tool Programmers; Metalworking and Plastics-Working Machine Operators; Tool and Die Makers; Welders, Cutters, and Welding Machine Operators; Prepress workers; Printing Press Operators; Bindery Workers; Apparel Workers; Shoe and Leather Workers and Repairers; Upholsterers; Woodworking Occupations; Dental

Laboratory Technicians; Ophthalmic Laboratory Technicians; Handlers, Equipment Cleaners, Helpers, and Laborers

05.06 Systems Operation—Adult Education Teachers; Dispatchers; Blue-Collar Worker Supervisors; Inspectors, Testers, and Graders; Electric Power Generating Plant Operators and Power Distributors and Dispatchers; Stationary Engineers; Water and Wastewater Treatment Plant Operators; Material Moving Equipment Operators; Water Transportation Occupations; Handlers, Equipment Cleaners, Helpers, and Laborers

05.07 Quality Control—Construction and Building Inspectors; Inspectors and Compliance Officers, except Construction; Engineering Technicians; Clerical Supervisors and Managers; Material Recording, Scheduling, Dispatching, and Distributing Occupations; Firefighting Occupations; Forestry and Logging Occupations; Automotive Body Repairers; Communications Equipment Mechanics; Elevator Installers and Repairers; Line Installers and Cable Splicers; Inspectors, Testers, and Graders; Handlers, Equipment Cleaners, Helpers, and Laborers

05.08 Land and Water Vehicle Operation—Blue-Collar Worker Supervisors; Inspectors, Testers, and Graders; Rail Transportation Workers; Taxi Drivers and Chauffeurs; Truckdrivers; Water Transportation Occupations; Handlers, Equipment Cleaners, Helpers, and Laborers

05.09 Material Control—Cost Estimators; Inspectors and Compliance Officers, except Construction; Counter and Rental Clerks; Retail Sales Workers; Adjusters, Investigators, and Collectors; Clerical Supervisors and Managers; Material Recording, Scheduling, Dispatching, and Distributing Occupations; Dispatchers; Traffic, Shipping, and Receiving Clerks; Billing Clerks; Bookkeeping, Accounting, and Auditing Clerks; Library Assistants and Bookmobile Drivers; Industrial Machinery Repairers; Blue-Collar Worker Supervisors; Inspectors, Testers, and Graders; Handlers, Equipment Cleaners, Helpers, and Laborers

05.10 Crafts—Photographers and Camera Operators; Dispensing Opticians; Broadcast Technicians; Engineering Technicians; Clerical Supervisors and Managers; Material Recording, Scheduling, Dispatching, and Distributing Occupations; Order Clerks; Chefs, Cooks, and Other Kitchen Workers; Private Household Workers; Fishers, Hunters, and Trappers; Automotive Body Repairers; Automotive Mechanics; Commercial and Industrial Electronic Equipment Repairers; Communications Equipment Mechanics; Electronic Home Entertainment Equipment Repairers; Farm Equipment Mechanics; General Maintenance Mechanics; Heating, Air-Conditioning, and Refrigeration Technicians; Home Appliance and Power Tool Repairers; Industrial Machinery Repairers; Line Installers and Cable Splicers; Motorcycle, Boat, and Small Engine Mechanics; Vending Machine Servicers and Repairers; Bricklayers and Stonemasons; Carpenters; Carpet Installers; Concrete Masons and Terrazo Workers; Drywall Workers and Lathers; Electricians; Glaziers; Insulation Workers; Painters and Paperhangers; Plumbers and Pipefitters; Roofers; Roustabouts; Precision Assemblers; Blue-Collar Worker Supervisors; Butchers and Meat, Poultry, and Fish Cutters; Inspectors, Testers, and Graders; Metalworking and Plastics-Working Machine Operators; Welders, Cutters, and Welding Machine Operators; Prepress Workers; Printing Press Operators; Shoe and Leather Workers and Repairers; Woodworking Occupations; Painting and Coating Machine Operators; Photographic Process Workers; Handlers, Equipment Cleaners, Helpers, and Laborers

05.11 Equipment Operation—Janitors and Cleaners; Insulation Workers; Blue-Collar Worker Supervisors; Material Moving Equipment Operators; Rail Transportation Workers; Truckdrivers

05.12 Elemental Work: Mechanical—Clerical Supervisors and Managers; Stock Clerks; Chefs, Cooks, and Other Kitchen Workers; Janitors and Cleaners; Private Household Workers; Forestry and Logging Occupations; Aircraft Mechanics and Engine Specialists; Automotive Body Repairers; Automotive Mechanics; Farm Equipment Mechanics; Industrial Machinery Repairers; Line Installers and Cable Splicers; Carpenters; Insulation Workers; Roofers; Roustabouts; Tilesetters; Blue-Collar Worker Supervisors; Inspectors, Testers, and Graders; Boilermakers; Metalworking and Plastics-Working Machine Operators; Welders, Cutters, and Welding Machine Operators; Water and Wastewater Treatment Plant Operators; Prepress Workers; Printing Press Operators; Bindery Workers; Photographic Process Workers; Material Moving Equipment Operators; Rail Transportation Workers; Water Transportation Occupations; Handlers, Equipment Cleaners, Helpers, and Laborers

Related DOT Occupations

Aeronautical test engineer, air conditioning mechanic, aircraft mechanic, architect, automatic door mechanic, automobile body repairer, automobile mechanic, baggage handler, battery repairer, boilermaker, bookbinder, brake coupler, bricklayer, cabinetmaker, cable splicer, cable tester, carpenter, cleaner, clerical methods analyst, die designer, distribution field engineer, drafter, engraver, electrician, electronics assembler, engineer, estimator, excavator, facilities planner, film developer, floor layer, heavy equipment operator, janitor, land surveyor, laser technician, laundry worker, lodging facilities attendant, logistics engineer, machinist, maintenance mechanic, management analyst, mechanic, millwright, miner, offset press operator, optician, painter, pipe fitter, plasterer, plumber, production planner, quality control directory, refrigeration unit repairer, rug dyer, safety clothing and equipment developer, safety inspector, sales engineer, school plant consultant, scrap sorter, sewing machine operator, shore hand, silk screen repairer, stonemason, surveyor, tool and die maker, television/cable installer, tool designer, tool planner, welder, truck driver, vacuum cleaner repairer, warehouse worker, welder, welding technician.

Self-Employment Options

Appliance repairer, auto body rebuilder, auto mechanic, backhoe operator, cabinet maker, car wash owner, ceiling specialist, charter boat operator, chimney sweep, computer repair service, contractor, electronics repair shop, floor specialist, furniture maker, home remodeling service, investor, mason, mobile auto window service, mobile designer, motor bike repair and sales, plasterer, plumber, quick oil change shop, radio repairer, remodeler, restoration specialist, roofer, vacuum sales and service shop, vehicle tester.

Related Education and Training

Auto mechanics, engineering, mechanical drawing, electronics, industrial arts, shops/crafts, welding, architecture, heating and air conditioning, carpentry, masonry, pipe fitting, major appliance repair, heavy equipment maintenance, and building maintenance.

---

06 INDUSTRIAL: An interest in repetitive, concrete, organized activities done in a factory setting.

GOE Subgroups

06.01 Production Technology

06.02 Production Work

06.03 Quality Control

06.04 Elemental Work: Industrial

Related OOH Occupations

06.01 Production Technology—Material Recording, Scheduling, Dispatching, and Distributing Occupations; Dispatchers; Commercial and Industrial Electronic Equipment Repairers; Computer and Office Machine Repairers; Industrial Machinery Repairers; Motorcycle, Boat, and Small Engine Mechanics; Musical Instrument Repairers and Tuners; Precision Assemblers; Blue-Collar Worker Supervisors; Inspectors, Testers, and Graders; Jewelers; Metalworking and Plastics-Working Machine Operators; Tool and Die Makers; Welders, Cutters, and Welding Machine Operators; Printing Press Operators; Bindery Workers; Apparel Workers; Textile Machinery Operators; Woodworking Occupations; Ophthalmic Laboratory Technicians

06.02 Production Work—Adult Education Teachers; Clerical Supervisors and Managers; Aircraft Mechanics and Engine Specialists; Commercial and Industrial Electronic Equipment Repairers; Computer and Office Machine Repairers; Farm Equipment Mechanics; Industrial Machinery Repairers; Musical Instrument Repairers and Tuners; Carpenters; Painters and Paperhangers; Plumbers and Pipefitters; Precision Assemblers; Blue-Collar Worker Supervisors; Butchers and Meat, Poultry, and Fish Cutters; Inspectors, Testers, and Graders; Metalworking and Plastics-Working Machine Operators; Welders, Cutters, and Welding Machine Operators; Water and Wastewater Treatment Plant Operators; Prepress Workers; Printing Press Operators; Bindery Workers; Apparel Workers; Shoe and Leather Workers and Repairers; Textile Machinery Operators; Upholsterers; Woodworking Occupations; Dental Laboratory Technicians; Ophthalmic Laboratory Technicians; Painting and Coating Machine Operators; Photographic Process Workers; Material Moving Equipment Operators; Handlers, Equipment Cleaners, Helpers, and Laborers

06.03 Quality Control—Material Recording, Scheduling, Dispatching, and Distributing Occupations; Traffic, Shipping, and Receiving Clerks; Industrial Machinery Repairers; Blue-Collar Worker Supervisors; Butchers and Meat, Poultry, and Fish Cutters; Inspectors, Testers, and Graders; Metalworking and Plastics-Working Machine Operators; Prepress Workers; Apparel Workers; Handlers, Equipment Cleaners, Helpers, and Laborers

06.04 Elemental Work: Industrial—Adult Education Teachers; Material Recording, Scheduling, Dispatching, and Distributing Occupations; Janitors and Cleaners; Forestry and Logging Occupations; Aircraft Mechanics and Engine Specialists; Industrial Machinery Repairers; Musical Instrument Repairers and Tuners; Carpenters; Drywall Workers and Lathers; Painters and Paperhangers; Blue-Collar Worker Supervisors; Butchers and Meat, Poultry, and Fish Cutters; Inspectors, Testers, and Graders; Metalworking and Plastics-Working Machine Operators; Welders, Cutters, and Welding Machine Operators; Prepress Workers; Printing Press Operators; Bindery Workers; Apparel Workers; Textile Machinery Operators; Woodworking Occupations; Painting and Coating Machine Operators; Photographic Process Workers; Material Moving Equipment Operators; Handlers, Equipment Cleaners, Helpers, and Laborers

Related DOT Occupations

Alloy weigher, bakery worker, bench hand, bicycle assembler, binder, box tender, bowling ball grader and maker, butcher, carpet cutter, cloth grader supervisor, color matcher, electronics tester, furnace helper, gear-shover set-up operator, grinder operator, inspector and tester, kiln worker, knitting-machine operator, linen grader, locket maker, loom setter, machine setter, machinist, mannequin-mold maker, mixer, mill operator, picker, plumbing systems tester, punch-press operator, roller maker, rug inspector, sander, saw operator, sewing supervisor, solderer, spark tester, speedometer inspector, spring inspector, stocking inspector, stitcher, testing-machine operator, tire repairer, umbrella examiner, upholstery sewer, watch repairer, weaver, welder setter, zipper cutter.

Self-Employment Options

Accessories manufacturer, bookbinder, carpet cleaning service, carpet sales and installation store, customized draper, electronics consultant, film processor, gem engraver, house painting, industrial catalog preparation, industrial supplies rental, leather products sales, linen products manufacturer, luggage manufacturer, magazine binding, mobile locksmith, plastics designer, scrap dealer, sewing machine operator, silk screen printer, tool maker, toy designer, trucker, upholstery business, watch repair service.

Related Education and Training

Management training, supervision, mechanical shop, blueprint reading, math computing/shop math, machine shop, graphic processes (printing and bindery), sheetmetal shop, chemistry, forging/heat treating, sewing or upholstery, watch repair, foundry, glass blowing, wood shop or machining, electronics, auto body repair, electrical shop, diesel and auto mechanics, photographic laboratory production, printing press operations, leatherworking, meatcutting

---

07 BUSINESS DETAIL: An interest in organized, clearly defined activities requiring accuracy and attention to details, primarily in an office setting.

GOE Subgroups

07.01 Administrative Detail
07.02 Mathematical Detail
07.03 Financial Detail
07.04 Oral Communications
07.05 Records Processing
07.06 Clerical Machine Operation
07.07 Clerical Handling

Related OOH Occupations

07.01 Administrative Detail—Administrative Services Managers; Education Administrators; Inspectors and Compliance Officers, except Construction; Personnel, Training, and Labor Relations Specialists and Managers; Human Services Workers; Archivists and Curators; Counselors; Adjusters, Investigators, and Collectors; Clerical Supervisors and Managers; Credit Clerks and Authorizers; General Office Clerks; Material Recording, Scheduling, Dispatching, and Distributing Occupations; Postal Clerks and Mail Carriers; Billing Clerks; Bookkeeping, Accounting, and Auditing Clerks; Brokerage Clerks and Statement Clerks; Personnel Clerks; Secretaries; Teacher Aides; Police Detectives, and Special Agents

07.02 Mathematical Detail—Mathematicians; Cashiers; Counter and Rental Clerks; Adjusters, Investigators, and Collectors; Bank Tellers; Clerical Supervisors and Managers; General Office Clerks; Reservation and Transportation Ticket Agents and Travel Clerks; Material Recording, Scheduling, Dispatching, and Distributing Occupations; Stock Clerks; Traffic, Shipping, and Receiving Clerks; Billing Clerks; Bookkeeping, Accounting, and Auditing Clerks; Brokerage Clerks and Statement Clerks; Payroll and Timekeeping Clerks

07.03 Financial Detail—Cashiers; Counter and Rental Clerks; Retail Sales Workers; Adjusters, Investigators, and Collectors; Bank Tellers; Clerical Supervisors and Managers; Reservation and Transportation Ticket Agents and Travel Clerks; Mail Clerks and Messengers; Postal Clerks and Mail Carriers; Bookkeeping, Accounting, and Auditing Clerks

07.04 Oral Communications—Adult Education Teachers; Cashiers; Counter and Rental Clerks; Adjusters, Investigators, and Collectors; Clerical Supervisors and Managers; Credit Clerks and Authorizers; General Office Clerks; Hotel and Motel Clerks; Interviewing and New Accounts Clerk; Receptionists; Reservation and Transportation Ticket Agents and Travel Clerks; Mail Clerks and Messengers; Material Recording, Scheduling, Dispatching, and Distributing Occupations; Dispatchers; Library Assistants and Bookmobile Drivers; Order Clerks; Personnel Clerks; Telephone Operators; Firefighting Occupations; Police Detectives, and Special Agents; Blue-Collar Worker Supervisors

07.05 Records Processing—Writers and Editors; Medical Record Technicians; Adjusters, Investigators, and Collectors; Clerical Supervisors and Managers; Credit Clerks and Authorizers; General Office Clerks; Receptionists; Reservation and Transportation Ticket Agents and Travel Clerks; Mail Clerks and Messengers; Material Recording, Scheduling, Dispatching, and Distributing Occupations; Dispatchers; Stock Clerks; Traffic, Shipping, and Receiving Clerks; Postal Clerks and Mail Carriers; Bookkeeping, Accounting, and Auditing Clerks; File Clerks; Library Assistants and Bookmobile Drivers; Order Clerks; Personnel Clerks; Stenographers and Court Reporters; Typists, Word Processors, and Data Entry Keyers

07.06 Clerical Machine Operation—Clerical Supervisors and Managers; Computer and Peripheral Equipment Operators; Receptionists; Billing Clerks; Stenographers and Court Reporters; Typists, Word Processors, and Data Entry Keyers; Blue-Collar Worker Supervisors; Prepress Workers

07.07 Clerical Handling—Cashiers; Clerical Supervisors and Managers; General Office Clerks; Mail Clerks and Messengers; Material Recording, Scheduling, Dispatching, and Distributing Occupations; Traffic, Shipping, and Receiving Clerks; Billing Clerks; File Clerks; Library Assistants and Bookmobile Drivers; Inspectors, Testers, and Graders; Handlers, Equipment Cleaners, Helpers, and Laborers

Related DOT Occupations

Accountant, accounting analyst, accounting clerk, actuary, adding machine operator, administrative clerk, administrative secretary, admissions evaluator, admitting officer, advertising clerk, advice clerk, appraiser, archivist, audit clerk, auditor, bank teller, billing clerk, bond clerk, bookkeeper, brokerage clerk, budget clerk, bursar, buyer, cashier, checker, claims examiner, clerk typist, collator, collection clerk, collector, computer operator, controller, copyreader, credit analyst, credit counselor, court clerk, curator, data typist, dispatcher, examiner, field cashier, file clerk, financial aid counselor, financial analyst, information clerk, insurance adjuster, insurance clerk, keypunch operator, labor expediter, layaway clerk, legal assistant, legal secretary, librarian, loan counselor, loan officer, loan interviewer, mail censor, mail clerk, mail handler, market research analyst, medical records clerk, medical secretary, new accounts clerk, night auditor, officer helper, payroll clerk, personnel clerk, phototypesetter operator, postal clerk, procurement clerk, programmer, purchasing agent, radio officer, reader, real estate clerk, receptionist, reservation clerk, routing clerk, secretary, securities clerk, securities trader, shipping clerk, statistical clerk, statistician, stenographer, switchboard operator, systems analyst, tax clerk, telephone operator, test technician, ticket agent, title examiner, toll collector, tourist information assistant, travel clerk, typist, underwriter, vault cashier, word processor.

Self-Employment Options

Answering service, bookkeeping service, data processor, dictating/transcribing service, financial aid service, information broker, income tax preparer, indexer, mail order business, mail sorting service, medical claims processing, office equipment and supply sales, office permanent and temporary help agency, office record storage and shredding, secretarial service, utility/telephone bill auditing.

Related Education and Training

Secretarial science, legal assistance, data processing, typing, library science, computer science, stenography, legal secretary, court reporting, clerk-typist, general office practice, bookkeeping, accounting, banking, finance, insurance, real estate, business law, investments and securities, database management, and income tax.

08 SELLING: An interest in bringing others to a particular point of view by personal persuasion, using sales and promotional techniques.

GOE Subgroups

08.01 Sales Technology

08.02 General Sales

08.03 Vending

Related OOH Occupations

08.01 Sales Technology—Property and Real Estate Managers; Purchasers and Buyers; Insurance Agents and Brokers; Manufacturers' and Wholesale Sales Representatives; Retail Sales Workers; Securities and Financial Services Sales Representatives; Services Sales Representatives; Bank Tellers

08.02 General Sales—Manufacturers' and Wholesale Sales Representatives; Real Estate Agents, Brokers, and Appraisers; Retail Sales Workers; Securities and Financial Services Sales Representatives; Services Sales Representatives; Travel Agents; Blue-Collar Worker Supervisors; Truckdrivers

08.03 Vending—Photographers and Camera Operators; Retail Sales Workers

Related DOT Occupations

Advertising agent, auctioneer, auto sales worker, marketing consultant, business services sales agent, buyer, cigarette vendor, communications consultant, comparison shopper, computer and equipment systems sales representatives, demonstrator, estate planner, field contact technician, field representative, foreign banknote teller/trader, fund raiser, grain buyer, group-sales representative, hardware supplies salesperson, insurance agent, jewelry salesperson, leasing agent, lounge car attendant, membership solicitor, outside property agent, pawn broker, peddler, pharmaceutical dealer, placer, public relations specialist, real estate sales agent, sales agent, sales representative, shoe salesperson, song plugger, sporting goods salesperson, sales exhibitor, sales route driver, sandwich-board carrier, subscriptions crew leader, telephone solicitor, traffic agent, travel agent, vendor, wedding consultant, wholesale sales representative.

Self-Employment Options

Antiques dealer, bridal consultant, carpet sales, direct mail sales, direct sales from home, discount store owner, display specialties service, flea market, mutual fund sales, off-price retailing store, pawn shop, public relations service, real estate broker, sales instructor, sales representative, salesperson, telephone sales and service, travel agency, travel consultant, tour service manager, tourist guide/escort, video rental shop, vitamin sales, wedding service.

Related Education and Training

Public relations, advertising, marketing, retail management, public affairs, consumer behavior, sales force management, real estate, and industrial sales.

09 ACCOMMODATING: An interest in catering to the wishes and needs of others, usually on a one-to-one basis.

GOE Subgroups

09.01 Hospitality Services

09.02 Barber and Beauty Services

09.03 Passenger Services

09.04 Customer Services

09.05 Attendant Services

Related OOH Occupations

09.01 Hospitality Services—Recreation Workers; Social Workers; Adult Education Teachers; Archivists and Curators; Food and Beverage Service Occupations; Flight Attendants; Private Household Workers; Rail Transportation Workers

09.02 Barber and Beauty Services—Barbers and Cosmetologists

09.03 Passenger Services—Adult Education Teachers; Blue-Collar Worker Supervisors; Busdrivers; Rail Transportation Workers; Taxi Drivers and Chauffeurs

09.04 Customer Services—Retail Managers; Cashiers; Counter and Rental Clerks; Retail Sales Workers; Material Recording, Scheduling, Dispatching, and Distributing Occupations; Stock Clerks; Food and Beverage Service Occupations; Vending Machine Servicers and Repairers; Blue-Collar Worker Supervisors; Truckdrivers; Handlers, Equipment Cleaners, Helpers, and Laborers

09.05 Attendant Services—Clerical Supervisors and Managers; Reservation and Transportation Ticket Agents and Travel Clerks; Chefs, Cooks, and Other Kitchen Workers; Food and Beverage Service Occupations; Barbers and Cosmetologists; Private Household Workers; Handlers, Equipment Cleaners, Helpers, and Laborers

Related DOT Occupations

Alpine guide, automobile rental clerk, bagger, baker, bar attendant, barber, bartender, bellhop, bicycle rental clerk, bridge instructor, bus attendant, bus driver, butler, cab supervisor, caddie, cafeteria attendant, camp counselor, car wash attendant, cardroom attendant, caterer helper, chauffeur, clerk, cook, cosmetologist, counter attendant, curb attendant, delivery route drive, desk clerk, drive-in theater attendant, driving instructor, doorkeeper, elevator operator, escort, food service worker, flight attendant, funeral attendant, gate attendant, group worker, hair stylist, host/hostess, maid, manicurist, masseur/masseuse, newspaper carrier, page, parking-lot attendant, passenger service representative, pay station attendant, personal shopper, plant guide, platform attendant, porter, pullman conductor, real estate guide, recreation leader, sales attendant, scalp-treatment operator, skate shop attendant, social director, steward/stewardess, streetcar operator, taxi driver, ticket taker, usher, vault attendant, waiter/waitress.

Self-Employment Options

Beautician, beauty consultant, bed and breakfast inn, building/office cleaner, caterer, coffee and tea store, convenience food store, driver/chauffeur, gift basket store, hair care service, hair removal service, health food store owner, home economist, home shopper, hot meals provider, ice cream store, lunch cart operator, maid service, massage service, party planner, pool cleaning service, restaurant owner, sandwich delivery service, tour guide/escort.

Related Education and Training

Home economics, food service, cosmetology, dietetics, textiles/clothing, nutrition, consumer science, clothing and textile management, travel/tourism, catering, tailoring and alteration, food service, executive housekeeping.

---

10 HUMANITARIAN: An interest in helping others with their mental, spiritual, social, physical, or vocational needs.

GOE Subgroups

10.01 Social Services

10.02 Nursing, Therapy, and Specialized Teaching Services

10.03 Child and Adult Care

Related OOH Occupations

10.01 Social Services—Education Administrators; Personnel, Training, and Labor Relations Specialists and Managers; Psychologists; Human Services Workers; Social Workers; Protestant Ministers; Rabbis; Roman Catholic Priests; Counselors

10.02 Nursing, Therapy, and Specialized Teaching Services—Education Administrators; Health Services Managers; Personnel, Training, and Labor Relations Specialists and Managers; Recreation Workers; Adult Education Teachers; School Teachers—Kindergarten, Elementary, and Secondary; Occupational Therapists; Physical Therapists; Physician Assistants; Recreational Therapists; Registered Nurses; Respiratory Therapists; Cardiovascular Technologists and Technicians; Dental

Hygienists; Licensed Practical Nurses; Nuclear Medicine Technologists; Radiologic Technologists; Preschool Workers

10.03 Child and Adult Care—Cardiovascular Technologists and Technicians; EEG Technologists; Emergency Medical Technicians; Surgical Technologists; Dental Assistants; Medical Assistants; Nursing Aides and Psychiatric Aides; Preschool Workers; Homemaker-Home Health Aides; Private Household Workers

Related DOT Occupations

Ambulance attendant, anthropologist, astrologer, athletic trainer, blind aide, companion, case aide, caseworker, caseworker supervisor, child monitor, child welfare caseworker, child-care worker, children's tutor, clergy member, community health nursing director, counselor, Dean of Students, dental assistant, director of religious activities, Director of Placement, educational therapist technician, emergency medical technician, first-aid attendant, foreign student advisor, group work program aide, historian, home attendant, hypnotherapist, inservice coordinator, job analyst, manual-arts therapist, marriage counselor, music therapist, nurse, nurse's aide, occupational therapist, orderly, orientation therapist for the blind, parole officer, physical therapist, physician assistant, playroom attendant, preschool teacher, principal, program aide, radiologic technologist, recreational therapist, recreational worker, rehabilitation counselor, residence counselor, respiratory therapist, social worker, sociologist, teacher, teacher's aide, university professor, urban planner, veteran's contact representative.

Self-Employment Options

Baby-sitter, camp director, child therapist, child-care specialist, diet consultant, elderly care specialist, exceptional needs counselor, family counselor, foster parent, growth counselor, hypnotist, individual psychotherapist, instructor for the handicapped, marriage broker, nursery/daycare operator, nursing home operation, senior day care, stress management consultant, tutor, vocational advice.

Related Education and Training

Family studies, psychology, sociology, human development, social work, education, religious studies, teacher education, education administration, child care studies, special education, counseling, recreational therapy, geriatrics, human resources, and curriculum and instruction.

---

11 LEADING AND INFLUENCING: An interest in leading and influencing others by using high-level verbal or numerical abilities.

GOE Subgroups

11.01 Mathematics and Statistics

11.02 Educational and Library Services

11.03 Social Research

11.04 Law

11.05 Business Administration

11.06 Finance

11.07 Services Administration

11.08 Communications

11.09 Promotion

11.10 Regulations Enforcement

11.11 Business Management

11.12 Contracts and Claims

Related OOH Occupations

11.01 Mathematics and Statistics—Engineering, Science, and Data Processing Managers; General Managers and Top Executives; Management Analysts and Consultants; Actuaries; Computer Scientists and Systems Analysts; Operations Research Analysts; Statisticians; Computer Programmers; Science Technicians

11.02 Educational and Library Services—Education Administrators; Personnel, Training, and Labor Relations Specialists and Managers; Adult Education Teachers; Archivists and Curators ; College and University Faculty; Librarians ; School Teachers—Kindergarten, Elementary, and Secondary; Dietitians and Nutritionists; Library Technicians; Clerical Supervisors and Managers; General Office Clerks; Stock Clerks; Library Assistants and Bookmobile Drivers; Order Clerks; Teacher Aides; Homemaker-Home Health Aides

11.03 Social Research—Employment Interviewers; Personnel, Training, and Labor Relations Specialists and Managers; Social Scientists and Urban Planners; Economists and Marketing Research Analysts; Psychologists; Sociologists; Urban and Regional Planners; Archivists and Curators

11.04 Law—Personnel, Training, and Labor Relations Specialists and Managers; Lawyers and Judges; Paralegals

11.05 Business Administration—Administrative Services Managers; Engineering, Science, and Data Processing Managers; Financial Managers; General Managers and top executives; Health Services Managers; Industrial Production Managers; Inspectors and Compliance Officers, except Construction; Loan Officers and Counselors; Marketing, Advertising, and Public Relations Managers; Personnel, Training, and Labor Relations Specialists and Managers; Property and Real Estate Managers; Purchasers and Buyers; Restaurant and Food Service Managers; Retail Managers; Archivists and Curators; Public Relations Specialists; Writers and Editors; Actors, Directors, and Producers; Retail sales Workers; Blue-Collar Worker Supervisors

11.06 Finance—Accountants and Auditors; Budget Analysts; Financial Managers; Loan Officers and Counselors; Management Analysts and Consultants; Purchasers and Buyers; Underwriters; Economists and Marketing Research Analysts; Real Estate Agents, Brokers, and Appraisers; Securities and Financial Services Sales Representatives; Credit Clerks and Authorizers; Billing Clerks

11.07 Services Administration—Education Administrators; General Managers and Top Executives; Health Services Managers; Management Analysts and Consultants; Personnel, Training, and Labor Relations Specialists and Managers; Foresters and Conservation Scientists; Recreation Workers; Social Workers; Archivists and Curators; Counselors; Librarians; School Teachers—Kindergarten, Elementary, and Secondary; Public Relations Specialists

11.08 Communications—Mathematicians; Librarians; Radio and Television Announcers and Newscasters; Reporters and Correspondents; Writers and Editors; Actors, Directors, and Producers

11.09 Promotion—Education Administrators; General Managers and Top Executives; Marketing, Advertising, and Public Relations Managers; Personnel, Training, and Labor Relations Specialists and Managers; Public Relations Specialists; Actors, Directors, and Producers; Manufacturers' and Wholesale Sales Representatives; Services Sales Representatives; Police Detectives, and Special Agents

11.10 Regulations Enforcement—General Managers and top executives; Health Services Managers; Inspectors and Compliance Officers, except Construction; Personnel, Training, and Labor Relations Specialists and Managers; Science Technicians; Firefighting Occupations; Blue-Collar Worker Supervisors

11.11 Business Management—Financial Managers; Funeral Directors; Hotel Managers and Assistants; Marketing, Advertising, and Public Relations Managers; Personnel, Training, and Labor Relations Specialists and Managers; Property and Real Estate Managers; Restaurant and Food Service Managers; Retail Managers; Recreation Workers; Blue-Collar Worker Supervisors; Rail Transportation Workers

11.12 Contracts and Claims—Administrative Services Managers; Construction Contractors and Managers; Engineering, Science, and Data Processing Managers; Property and Real Estate Managers; Purchasers and Buyers; Lawyers and Judges; Services Sales Representatives; Adjusters, Investigators, and Collectors; Clerical Supervisors and Managers

Related DOT Occupations

Academic dean, account executive, actuary, administrative assistant, adult education teacher, advertising agent, airport manager, anthropologist, applied statistician, appraiser, arbitrator, audiovisual librarian, auditor, bibliographer, branch manager, business manager, career-guidance counselor, city planning aide, classifier, commissary manager, credit analyst, curator, department store manager, director of employment research and planning, director of vital statistics, district attorney, economist, education specialist, educational institution president, employment interviewer, education supervisor, ethnologist, executive director, fashion coordinator, federal aid coordinator, financial analyst, food service director, forms analyst, funeral director, genealogist, historian, historic sites supervisor, hospital administrator, hotel manager, information scientist, information system programmer, intelligence specialist, investigator, job analyst, judge, lawyer, library director, librarian, lobbyist, magistrate, maintenance supervisor, manager, mathematical statistician, mathematical technician, media specialist, membership director, newscaster, office manager, operations director, paralegal assistant, patent agent, pawnbroker, personnel manager, politician, postmaster, principal, production manager, program director, project director, psychologist, public relations specialist, records management director, reporter, reports analyst, retail store manager, risk and insurance manager, school administrator, securities trader, social welfare administrator, sociologist, special agent, sports director, supervisor, systems analyst, teacher, teacher's aide, ticket broker, traffic manager, training representative, translator, treasurer, underwriter, vocational training instructor, warden, wholesale sales representative.

Self-Employment Options

Auctioneer, audiovisual production, commodity broker, communications consultant, educational consultant, educational researcher, importer/exporter, information broker, information service, instruction-book preparation, insurance agent, insurance sales, investment consultant, language translator service, paralegal assistance service, researcher, seminar promotions, special projects coordinator.

Related Education and Training

Management science, business administration, economics, labor relations, international management, finance, law/ethics, public administration, small business management, hotel/motel management, urban planning, health care administration, computer science, banking, finance, business law, and investments and securities.

12 PHYSICAL PERFORMING: An interest in physical activities performed before an audience.

GOE Subgroups

12.01 Sports

12.02 Physical Feats

Related OOH Occupations

12.02 Actors, Directors, and Producers

Related DOT Occupations

Acrobat, aerialist, athletic trainer, automobile racer, charter, coach, dog track kennel manager, dude wrangler, flagger, golf course ranger, golf pro, head coach, health club worker, horse identifier, horse-race starter, horse-race timer, hunting guide, jockey, jockey-room custodian, juggler, lead pony rider, marshall, motorcycle racer, patrol judge, physical educational teacher, pit steward, professional athlete, professional athletes coach, professional sports scout, racetrack steward, recreation leader, rodeo performer, scorer, sports psychologist, sports instructor, stunt performer, sulky driver, tour guide, umpire, wire walker.

Self-Employment Options

Aerobics instructor, children's fitness center, coach, developing training/exercise equipment, gymnastics instructor, health spa director, horseback riding instructor, personal trainer, physical fitness center, sports equipment salesperson, sporting goods store, sports memorabilia shop, sports instructor, umpire/referee, yoga instructor.

Related Education and Training

Sports psychology, sports physiology, physical education, leisure studies, recreational administration, coaching, sports medicine, health and wellness, athletic training, outdoor recreation, driver education, and sports education.

APPENDIX C
Information on The O*NET Database's Structure And Development

This appendix is divided into two sections. The first, "The O*NET Content Model," provides a brief overview of the major types of information contained in the O*NET. This information would be helpful for anyone using this book. The second section, titled "The Development of the Occupational Information (O*NET) Analyst Database," provides detailed information on how the information in the O*NET was developed. This information will interest technical users of the O*NET.

When reviewing this appendix, keep in mind that the O*NET is a computerized database and that the *O*NET Dictionary of Occupational Titles* does not present the entire set of information available for each O*NET occupation.

We realize that some of you will want to know more about the technical elements of the O*NET database. This appendix provides information we consider helpful for understanding the logic for how the O*NET database has been constructed. Much of the information comes from support documentation provided by the U.S. Department of Labor's O*NET database made available to developers.

For that reason, some content in this appendix will refer to the "O*NET Analyst Database" or the "O*NET Database Viewer" rather than to the book you are holding.

The O*NET Content Model

The O*NET is a complex relational database, but there is an understandable logic to how it is constructed. The illustration that follows presents a visual image that can help you understand the major subcomponents to the O*NET database. Called the "O*NET Content Model," we've included it here as a reference for those who want a better understanding of the O*NET's structure. The Content Model includes the specific domains and elements in the O*NET database used to describe jobs. These components are based on psychological and job analysis research.

The illustration is followed by brief descriptions of the major elements in the model. Together, we hope this information provides you with a better understanding of the scope and complexity of the O*NET. At the same time, it should increase your appreciation of this printed version by JIST that strives to capture the essential information from this immense database.

The O*NET Content Model is subdivided into increasingly specific elements.

As indicated in the following illustration, the O*NET is organized into six major subgroups of information. Called "domains," they include the following:

- **Experience Requirements** composed of training, experience, any licensing requirements
- **Occupation Requirements** composed of generalized work activities, work context, and organizational context
- **Occupation-Specific Information** composed of tasks that are particular to a specific occupation, including knowledge, skills, work context, and machines, tools, and equipment
- **Occupation Characteristics** include details such as labor market information, occupational outlook, and wage information
- **Worker Characteristics** composed of abilities, interests, and work styles
- **Worker Requirements** composed of basic skills, cross-functional skills, general knowledge, and education

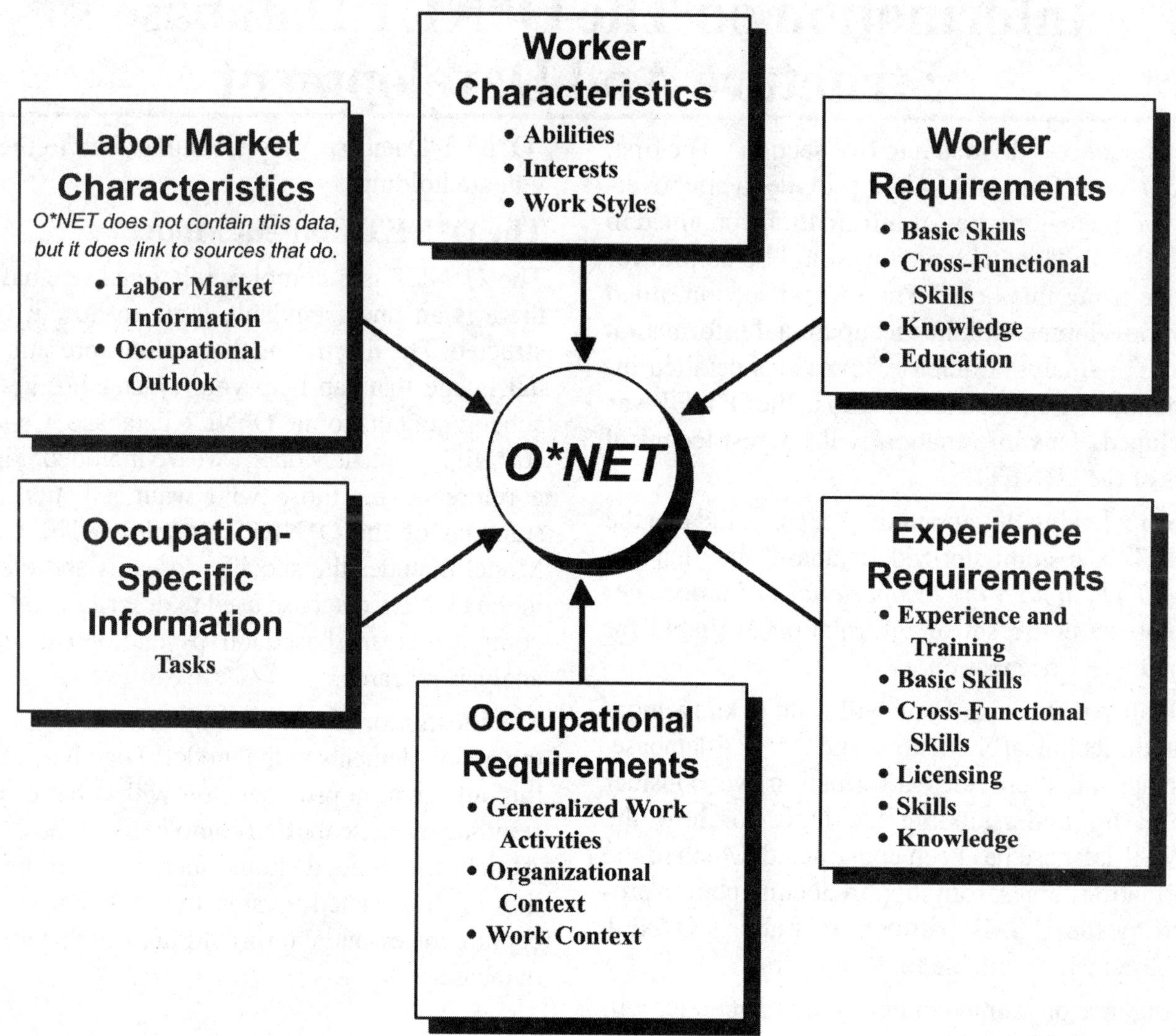

The O*NET Content Model

The O*NET Content Model has a hierarchical organization that provides for increasingly specific groupings of information. For example, abilities within Worker Characteristics consist of 52 elements grouped into four categories—cognitive, psychomotor, physical, and sensory.

For each element in the O*NET Content Model, such as Oral Comprehension, the O*NET database may include multiple variables, or scales. While a variety of these scales exist, the three scales used most often are as follows:

- **Level**, or the level of the ability needed to perform a job. Level scales differ for each element and have behavioral examples illustrating three or more points on the scale. The scale runs from 0, "Not Relevant at All for Performance on This Job," to a high of 7.
- **Importance**, or how important this ability is to perform on a job. Importance is measured on a scale of 1 to 5, from "Not Important" to "Extremely Important."

- **Frequency**, or how often the activity is performed on a job. Frequency is measured on a scale of 1 to 4, from "Almost Never" to "Always."

For each occupation, the scales associated with each variable provide a numerical value to show the relevance of that measure to the occupation. For example, for the job of Financial Managers, the O*NET element "Oral Comprehension" has a Level of 5.3 and an Importance of 4.8. Each O*NET occupation includes numerical measures for hundreds of elements.

While that works well for the information contained in a computerized database, imagine the difficulty of presenting all this information in a useful printed format. That is why we have carefully selected the information we provide for each of the O*NET occupations in this book—we wanted to give only the most relevant details needed to understand the job.

The Development of the Occupational Information (O*NET) Analyst Database

Developing the O*NET database was an immense task, and it will continue to be changed in the years to come. This section explains how the data in the O*NET database was obtained. The material that follows came directly from the U.S. Department of Labor's support materials for the O*NET database that was released to developers. We again remind you that internal references in the material that follows are to the computerized O*NET database and not to this book. We apologize for any confusion this may create but thought it best to present this information to you in its original form, straight from the (Department of Labor's) horse's mouth.

An important item to note is that the O*NET data was derived from information collected by field analysts for the previously published *Dictionary of Occupational Titles* (DOT). This demonstrates an important link between the DOT and O*NET—a link that JIST has tried to affirm in the development and publication of this book. By reading the remainder of this appendix, you will learn the details about how the transition from the *Dictionary of Occupational Titles* to O*NET was accomplished.

Overview

The database for O*NET 98 is based largely on data supplied by occupational analysts. Thus, it is known as the Analyst Database. To develop data for the O*NET Analyst Database, analysts evaluated and refined existing occupational data, then extrapolated these data to the O*NET content model. Development of the database involved four phases:

Transition from the *Dictionary of Occupational Titles* (DOT) to the O*NET System

Phase I: Developing Homogeneous Occupations for O*NET. First, the 11,761 *Dictionary of Occupational Titles* (DOT) occupations were grouped into categories based on Occupational Employment Statistics (OES) occupations. Because some of the 852 OES occupations were too broad, however, statistical clustering was used to divide some of them into two or more new categories that were more homogeneous in terms of required skills. Review and modification of the preliminary categories resulted in 1,122 defined O*NET Occupational Units (OUs).

Phase II: Developing Task Statements to Describe the OUs. To develop descriptive task statements for each OU, analysts began by examining the task statements for the DOT occupations that were grouped under the OU. The analysts combined and condensed the DOT statements, extracting a list of more general task statements to describe the OU.

Phase III: Rating OUs in Terms of O*NET Content Model Descriptors. In order to relate the OUs to the content model that forms the conceptual framework for O*NET, analysts rated each OU in terms of selected descriptors drawn from the content model. Ratings were based on examination of the OU task statements developed in Phase II. A particular descriptor was included only if non-incumbents would be able to determine a rating based solely on the task statements.

Phase IV: Evaluating the OU Task Statements. To evaluate the currency, relevance, and face validity of the OU task statements, analysts compared OU task statements to task data from existing occupational databases. The results suggested that the OU task statements are consistent with task content from widely used sources of occupational information. This appendix describes these phases in more detail.

Phase I: Developing Homogeneous Occupations for O*NET

The first phase of database development required analysts to group over 11,000 very specific DOT occupations into broader occupational categories that could be used for O*NET. The purpose of this regrouping of occupations was to make the O*NET more manageable and useful than the DOT by placing greater emphasis on the meaningful differences between occupations. Thus, it was essential to accurately group the DOT occupations and to ensure that the categories themselves were meaningful. In particular, each grouping of DOT occupations needed to display Belongingness—the work activities of each DOT occupation had to match the definition of the occupational category under which it was grouped; and Homogeneity—differences within a single category had to be less than differences between categories and all the DOT occupations within a single category had to show consistency of skill transferability.

Initial Crosswalking of DOT and OES Occupations

To ensure that the new O*NET System could be linked to current labor market information, a common taxonomy of occupations was needed as its developmental foundation. The OES provided the most feasible taxonomy for this purpose. Then, by linking, or "crosswalking" the OES taxonomy to other taxonomies, the O*NET System could have increased application.

To initiate the O*NET development process, job analysts evaluated the National Occupational Information Coordinating Committee (NOICC) Master Crosswalk. The NOICC crosswalk, which was created by the Bureau of Labor Statistics (BLS), identifies the relationships among individual DOT occupations and OES occupational categories and establishes direct links between the two classification systems. In some cases, the DOT occupations linked to an OES occupation were not sufficiently similar, with regard to skill requirements or work activities, to develop homogeneous occupations for O*NET. For many potential O*NET users, these broad OES occupations were too diverse to be meaningful or functional. Therefore, it was anticipated that some modification of the OES occupations would be needed. In general, however, the analysts agreed that the OES and the corresponding NOICC crosswalk could be used as a starting point to develop an occupation structure for O*NET.

To ensure that the linkages established between the DOT occupations and the OES occupations were sound, job analysts used a two-stage process: In the first stage, analysts evaluated OES occupations that were linked to four or fewer DOT occupations. In the second stage, they evaluated OES occupations that were linked to more than four DOT occupations.

Direct Analysis of Relatively Narrow OES Occupations

Analysts selected 220 OES occupations that they determined were accurately matched with DOT occupations and were linked to four or fewer DOT occupations. Of the 220, 140 of the OES occupations were crossed with only one DOT occupation. The remaining 80 OES occupations were crossed with two to four DOT occupations.

To confirm this crosswalk evaluation, the list of the OES and the associated DOT occupations was distributed to four additional job analysts. In this stage of the evaluation, analysts were provided with the OES and DOT codes, titles, and definitions, as well as supplemental information from the DOT for each occupation. This information included codes for General Educational Development (GED) and Specific Vocational Preparation (SVP), as well as the date when the occupational information was last updated. The analysts were asked to read the OES definition and DOT definitions and indicate the degree of match between the OES and DOT definition (where there was a 1:1 correspondence) or the degree of match between the OES title and group of DOT titles (where there were multiple DOT occupations matched to an OES occupation). Analysts rated these using the following rating scale: 1= "Very poor"; 2= "Poor"; 3= "Moderate"; 4= "Good"; 5= "Very-Good."

Out of the 220 linkages, 207 were found to be classified appropriately, yielding either "Good" or "Very Good" match ratings. The remaining 13 OES occupations were not represented in O*NET because the available DOT information was not sufficient to adequately represent the OES category.

Generation of Subclusters within Broad OES Occupations

Because of the complexity of the information involved, instances where more than four DOT occupations were linked with an OES occupation required a different method of evaluation. Thus, statistical clustering was performed to generate subclusters for each OES occupation that had more than four DOT occupations associated with it. Once the cluster analysis was conducted, three teams of three job analysts assessed the homogeneity and belongingness of the DOT occupations within each subcluster. The analysts then compared the subclusters and made final decisions on occupational structure. A detailed description of the methodology follows.

Selecting the variables. There were 28 variables used in the clustering procedure. These variables were based on job analysis components commonly used in the DOT to describe the dimensions of jobs. Specific variables were selected because of their relationships to specific parts of the O*NET content model as well as their usefulness in classifying occupations. These components are:

- Reasoning
- Mathematical
- Language
- Specific Vocational Preparation (SVP)
- Data
- People
- Things
- General Learning Ability
- Verbal Aptitude
- Numerical Aptitude
- Spatial Aptitude
- Form Perception
- Clerical Perception
- Motor Coordination
- Finger Dexterity
- Manual Dexterity
- Eye-Hand-Foot Coordination
- Color Discrimination
- Materials, Products, Subject Matter, and Services (3 Codes)
- Work Fields
- Directing
- People
- Influencing
- Expressing

Some variables (i.e., the GED dimensions, the SVP measure, the Worker Functions, and the Aptitudes) were selected because they were most closely related to skills. Others (i.e., the Materials, Products, Subject Matter, and Services [MPSMS] codes, the Work Field codes, and the Temperament variables) were selected because they provided necessary information about work context. Temperament variables most closely related to interpersonal skills, as defined in the content model, were actually included in the cluster analysis. These were Directing People, Influencing, and Expressing. Data for all the cluster variables came directly from the DOT.

Variable DOT Job Component

Selecting the proximity measure. To indicate the amount of similarity between individual occupations, a proximity or distance measure was used. Any one of several different types of similarity measures could have been used. The Euclidean distance measure was chosen because it tends to be less affected by potential anomalies often associated with categorical variables.

Selecting the method of analysis. Proximity measures for the 28 profile variables were cluster analyzed using Ward's Minimum Variance procedure. Twelve clustering trials, using a sample DOT data set, were conducted to select the most appropriate method. Observational analyses and comparisons of the results revealed that the Ward's procedures best represented the data. This algorithm also supported the primary objectives of the project. Ward's emphasizes clusters with small, roughly equal numbers of observations (SAS, 1989, pp. 56, 536) but minimizes the tendency to create single member clusters. A large number of single member clusters within an OES category would pose problems for this study, so a clustering procedure that minimized single member clusters was preferred. Further, Ward's has been widely used in the clustering literature, has been shown to be superior for recovering known spherical clusters (SAS, 1989, p. 56), and accepts a wide variety of similarity measures.

Determining whether to use raw or standardized profile variables. Additionally, analysts needed to determine whether raw (i.e., unstandardized) or standardized profile variables should be used in the computation of the Euclidean distance measure. To determine which method provided the most meaningful cluster structures, cluster analyses were conducted for a subset of 31 OES units using both methods. While the results for both methods were similar, some differences were apparent. A set of five analysts examined the solutions and determined that the use of raw unstandardized profiles yielded the most meaningful information.

Generating the subclusters. The clustering procedure described above (i.e., Ward's Minimum Variance, using Euclidean distance and unstandardized profile variables) was used to generate subclusters for each OES occupation with more than four associated DOT occupations. For each OES occupation, results were organized by DOT codes and titles under each resulting cluster number. These results were given to job analysts for subclustering review.

Review and Modification of the Subclusters

A group of three job analysts was presented with the OES code and definition, the DOT codes and titles, arranged by cluster results, and the DOT occupational definitions. Initially, the analysts reviewed the DOT definitions, familiarizing themselves with the definitions for all job titles within each subcluster. They focused on occupation-specific skills and knowledges (e.g., tasks performed, equipment used, subject-matter, etc.), noting the differences between the occupations. *The Occupational Outlook Handbook* (1990) was consulted, as needed, for information regarding training requirements.

Evaluating belongingness. After reviewing the DOT definitions, each analyst evaluated the belongingness of the DOT occupations, noting any DOT occupations that did not match the OES definition. These titles were discussed with the group and a consensus was reached as to whether or not to remove the DOT from the OES. If recommended for removal, a rationale for removal was included on a group worksheet along with a recommendation of the OES occupation to which the DOT title should be linked.

Evaluating homogeneity. After removing the mismatched DOT occupational titles from the list, the analysts then selected a seed DOT occupation (i.e., the most representative DOT occupation) for each subcluster. This occupational title was the one that most closely represented the OES definition. If more than one DOT title reflected the OES, then skill level was used as a second criterion. In these cases, the occupational title representing the highest appropriate skill level (based on GED and SVP rating) for all DOT occupations in the subcluster was selected. After recording their individual responses, the group discussed their selections until they reached a consensus on the seed DOT designation. This selection was then recorded on the group worksheet. Next, each analyst estimated the amount of retraining time required to make a career move from each DOT within the subcluster to the seed DOT. Retraining time was defined as the amount of time required by a worker to acquire—through either vocational or on-the-job training—the additional occupation-specific skills and knowledges needed to perform proficiently in the seed DOT. Retraining time estimates were used to assess the relative similarity of groups of DOTs within each subcluster. These estimates were not considered predictors of actual retraining time.

Analysts estimated retraining times using task statements and ratings from the DOT and training requirement information from the *Occupational Outlook Handbook*. Analysts were asked to: 1) identify the overlap of occupation-specific skills and knowledges; 2) identify the additional occupation-specific skills and knowledges required to perform proficiently in the seed DOT; and 3) estimate how much retraining time is required to gain these additional occupation-specific skills and knowledges. Retraining time was rated using the following scale: 1= "1 day up to 1 week"; 2= "1 week up to 1 month";

3= "1 month up to 3 months"; 4= "3 months up to 6 months"; 5= "6 months up to 1 year"; 6= "1 year up to 2 years"; 7= "more than 2 years." Individual estimates of retraining time were recorded on the individual worksheets. After group members made individual estimates, the group discussed the individual estimates until they reached a consensus on a retraining time estimate, which they recorded on the group worksheet. The group then compared retraining times of the DOT occupations within each subcluster to determine if the occupations had similar retraining time estimates. If a given DOT occupation differed significantly in terms of retraining time from the other occupations in the subcluster, the group estimated the time required to retrain to the seed occupation in each of the remaining subclusters of that OES occupation. The analysts then determined if the retraining time for the discrepant DOT occupation was closer to the retraining times of the occupational titles within any of the remaining subclusters. The DOT occupation was moved to the subcluster in which the retraining time to the seed occupation was the lowest. If an occupation did not fit any subcluster, the group re-evaluated belongingness to the OES occupational category. If the DOT occupation matched the OES occupational category (i.e., "belonged"), but did not fit any of the subclusters, it formed a cluster by itself. In contrast, if the DOT occupation did not match the OES category, the DOT occupation was moved to a more suitable OES category.

Finally, the group evaluated the subclusters once more. They compared the retraining times within subclusters of the OES units to retraining times across subclusters. The criteria for comparison was that there should be lower retraining time estimates within OES subclusters than between OES subclusters. The group determined if there was sufficient justification to maintain occupational subclusters or if the OES should form only one cluster. For cases in which there were no retraining time differences between and within OES subclusters, the subclusters were collapsed back into single clusters. On the group worksheet provided, the group stated the rationale for the formation of final subclusters, including estimates of retraining times within and across subclusters.

Defining the preliminary Occupational Units (OUs). The group was asked to name and provide a short definition for the subclusters. Each resulting subcluster was defined as an Occupational Unit (OU). These OUs, formed to maintain consistent levels of within group skills transferability between the DOT occupations, were homogeneous groupings of DOT occupations

Conducting a final review of the OU structure. As a result of the initial subcluster reviews described above, about one-third of the original OES categories were subclustered, yielding 1,350 OUs. One final review of the new OU structure was then conducted. Based on expected relevance and usage level, several single-member OUs were placed on a low priority list for inclusion in O*NET. These OUs were evaluated and 1) reassigned to a related OU, 2) reassigned to an "All Other" residual OU, or 3) targeted for further review. For example, the OU "Mule Team Driver" was expected to have relatively low employment and to be slightly dated. OUs such as this are now pending additional study before future inclusion in O*NET.

Assigning titles and definitions to the final OUs. The final version of the new OU structure included a total of 1,122 OUs, each with DOT occupations linked to it. Some of these OUs are identical to the OES occupation. If this process determined that an original OES occupation was homogeneous, the 5-digit code, title and definition were adopted as the OU code, title, and definition. If the clustering process resulted in a subclustered OES, then each subcluster became a separate OU. These OUs were assigned the original OES 5-digit code with an alphabetical suffix. This created a 6-character OU code for all subclustered OUs. The titles and definitions of these OUs were then developed in a manner consistent with the 1995 OES occupational titles and definitions. This naming convention made it easy to identify subclusters of the OES and show the relationship of OESs to OUs.

APPENDIX D
Definitions of the O*NET Database's Descriptive Elements

The introduction states that each O*NET occupation has 445 separate descriptors. Each Descriptive Element contains a numeric value, and we concluded that providing detailed information for 445 elements would be overwhelming in printed form. So we set out to find a logical process that would limit the data given, yet provide substantial, helpful information.

After careful analysis, we selected 218 elements to use in the descriptions in this book. These elements describe the ability level needed to perform effectively in an occupation. We did not include data elements that refer to how important the element is to the occupation. We feel that this distinction provided in the O*NET database is not important to most people. Our rationale is that a person must be able to perform at the required level regardless of how important the element is to job performance.

While cutting the number of Descriptive Elements to 218 helps, including detailed information on these 218 elements for the 1,172 O*NET occupations still would result in too much information for most users. So we went one step further by including only information for elements with above average ratings when compared to other occupations. For those who want a technical definition, "above average" refers to an element's value that is equal to or greater than one standard deviation above the mean.

Simply put, each element appearing in a description is one that requires a high level of performance as it relates to the occupation. We have classified these elements into categories in each job description titled as follows: knowledge; skills; general work activities; and job characteristics. These categories are similar to ones used in O*NET, but we simplified the names to make them more understandable to the average user of this book.

DEFINITIONS OF SELECTED DESCRIPTIVE ELEMENTS INCLUDED IN THE *O*NET DICTIONARY OF OCCUPATIONAL TITLES*™

Following is a list, in alphabetical order, of all 218 Descriptive Elements included in this book, along with brief definitions. Please refer to these definitions as needed to better understand the terms used. The definitions have been edited from those provided by the U.S. Department of Labor to increase clarity.

Active Learning—Working with new material or information to grasp its implications.

Active Listening—Listening to what other people are saying and asking questions as appropriate.

Administering—Administrative, staffing, monitoring, or controlling activities done while performing this job.

Administration and Management—Knowledge of principles and processes involved in business and organizational planning, coordination, and execution. This includes strategic planning, resource allocation, manpower modeling, leadership techniques, and production methods.

Analyzing Data or Information—Identifying underlying principles, reasons, or facts by breaking down information or data into separate parts.

Arm-Hand Steadiness—The ability to keep the hand and arm steady while making an arm movement or while holding the arm and hand in one position.

Arts and Humanities—Knowledge of facts and principles related to the branches of learning concerned with human thought, language, and the arts.

Assisting and Caring for Others—Providing assistance or personal care to others.

Auditory Attention—The ability to focus on a single source of auditory (hearing) information in the presence of other distracting sounds.

Bending or Twisting the Body—Bending or twisting the body.

Biology—Knowledge of plant and animal living tissue, cells, organisms, and entities, including their functions, interdependencies, and interactions with each other and the environment.

Building and Construction—Knowledge of materials, methods, and the appropriate tools to construct objects, structures, and buildings.

Category Flexibility—The ability to produce many rules so that each rule tells how to group (or combine) a set of things in a different way.

Chemistry—Knowledge of the composition, structure, and properties of substances and of the chemical processes and transformations that they undergo. This includes uses of chemicals and their interactions, danger signs, production techniques, and disposal methods.

Clerical—Knowledge of administrative and clerical procedures and systems such as word processing systems, filing and records management systems, stenography and transcription, forms design principles, and other office procedures and terminology.

Climbing Ladders, Scaffolds, Poles, etc.—Climbing ladders, scaffolds, poles, and so on.

Coaching and Developing Others—Identifying developmental needs of others and coaching or otherwise helping others to improve their knowledge or skills.

Common Protective or Safety Attire—Common protective or safety attire, such as safety shoes, glasses, gloves, hearing protection, hard-hat, or personal flotation device.

Communicating with Other Workers—Providing information to supervisors, fellow workers, and subordinates. This information can be exchanged face-to-face, in writing, or via telephone/electronic transfer.

Communicating with Persons Outside Organization—Communicating with persons outside the organization, representing the organization to customers, the public, government, and other external sources. This information can be exchanged face-to-face, in writing, or via telephone/electronic transfer.

Communicating/Interacting—Interacting with other people while performing this job.

Communications—Knowledge of the science and art of delivering information.

Communications and Media—Knowledge of media production, communication, and dissemination techniques and methods including alternative ways to inform and entertain via written, oral, and visual media.

Complex Problem Solving Skills—Developed capacities used to solve novel, ill-defined problems in complex, real-world settings.

Computers and Electronics—Knowledge of electric circuit boards, processors, chips, and computer hardware and software, including applications and programming.

Consequence of Error—Serious result if the worker made a mistake that was not readily correctable.

Contaminants—Contaminants (pollutants, gases, dust, odors, and so on).

Control Precision—The ability to quickly and repeatedly make precise adjustments in moving the controls of a machine or vehicle to exact positions.

Controlling Machines and Processes—Using either control mechanisms or direct physical activity to operate machines or processes (not including computers or vehicles).

Coordinate or Lead Others—Coordinate or lead others in accomplishing work activities (not supervision).

Coordinating Work & Activities of Others—Coordinating members of a work group to accomplish tasks.

Coordinating/Developing/Managing/Advising—Coordinating, managerial, or advisory activities done while performing this job.

Coordination—Adjusting actions in relation to others' actions.

Cramped Work Space, Awkward Positions—Cramped work space that requires getting into awkward positions.

Critical Thinking—Using logic and analysis to identify the strengths and weaknesses of different approaches.

Customer and Personal Service—Knowledge of principles and processes for providing customer and personal services including needs assessment techniques, quality service standards, alternative delivery systems, and customer satisfaction evaluation techniques.

Deal with External Customers—Deal with external customers (for example, retail sales) or the public in general (for example, police work).

Deal with Physical Aggressive People—Requires the worker to deal with physical aggression of violent individuals.

Deal with Unpleasant/Angry People—Requires the worker to deal with unpleasant, angry, or discourteous individuals as part of the job requirements.

Deductive Reasoning—The ability to apply general rules to specific problems to come up with logical answers. It involves deciding if an answer makes sense.

Degree of Automation—Indicate the level of automation of this job.

Depth Perception—The ability to judge which of several objects is closer or farther away from the observer, or to judge the distance between an object and the observer.

Design—Knowledge of design techniques, principles, tools and instruments involved in the production and use of precision technical plans, blueprints, drawings, and models.

Developing and Building Teams—Encouraging and building mutual trust, respect, and cooperation among team members.

Developing Objectives and Strategies—Establishing long-range objectives and specifying the strategies and actions to achieve these objectives.

Diseases/Infections—Diseases/infections (for example, patient care, some laboratory work, sanitation control, and so on).

Documenting/Recording Information—Entering, transcribing, recording, storing, or maintaining information in either written form or by electronic/magnetic recording.

Drafting & Specifying Technical Devices, etc.—Providing documentation, detailed instructions, drawings, or specifications to inform others about how devices, parts, equipment, or structures are to be fabricated, constructed, assembled, modified, maintained, or used.

Dynamic Flexibility—The ability to quickly and repeatedly bend, stretch, twist, or reach out with the body, arms, and/or legs.

Dynamic Strength—The ability to exert muscle force repeatedly or continuously over time. This involves muscular endurance and resistance to muscle fatigue.

Economics and Accounting—Knowledge of economic and accounting principles and practices, the financial markets, banking, and the analysis and reporting of financial data.

Education and Training—Knowledge of instructional methods and training techniques including curriculum design principles, learning theory, group and individual teaching techniques, design of individual development plans, and test design principles.

Engineering and Technology—Knowledge of equipment, tools, mechanical devices, and their uses to produce motion, light, power, technology, and other applications.

English Language—Knowledge of the structure and content of the English language including the meaning and spelling of words, rules of composition, and grammar.

Equipment Maintenance—Performing routine maintenance and determining when and what kind of maintenance is needed.

Equipment Selection—Determining the kind of tools and equipment needed to do a job.

Establishing & Maintaining Relationships—Developing constructive and cooperative working relationships with others.

Estimating Needed Characteristics—Estimating the characteristics of materials, products, events, or information: Estimating sizes, distances, and quantities, or determining time, costs, resources, or materials needed to perform a work activity.

Evaluating Information against Standards—Evaluating information against a set of standards and verifying that it is correct.

Explosive Strength—The ability to use short bursts of muscle force to propel oneself (as in jumping or sprinting), or to throw an object.

Extent Flexibility—The ability to bend, stretch, twist, or reach out with the body, arms, and/or legs.

Extremely Bright or Inadequate Lighting—Extremely bright or inadequate lighting conditions.

Far Vision—The ability to see details at a distance.

Fine Arts—Knowledge of theory and techniques required to produce, compose, and perform works of music, dance, visual arts, drama, and sculpture.

Finger Dexterity—The ability to make precisely coordinated movements of the fingers of one or both hands to grasp, manipulate, or assemble very small objects.

Flexibility of Closure—The ability to identify or detect a known pattern (a figure, object, word, or sound) that is hidden in other distracting material.

Fluency of Ideas—The ability to come up with a number of ideas about a given topic. It concerns the number of ideas produced and not the quality, correctness, or creativity of the ideas.

Food Production—Knowledge of techniques and equipment for planting, growing, and harvesting of food for consumption including crop rotation methods, animal husbandry, and food storage/handling techniques.

Foreign Language—Knowledge of the structure and content of a foreign (non-English) language including the meaning and spelling of words, rules of composition and grammar, and pronunciation.

Frequency in Conflict Situations—Frequency with which the job places the worker in conflict situations.

Frustrating Circumstances—The extent to which frustrating circumstances ("road blocks" to work that are beyond the worker's control) hinder the accomplishment of this job.

Geography—Knowledge of various methods for describing the location and distribution of land, sea, and air masses including their physical locations, relationships, and characteristics.

Getting Information Needed to do the Job—Observing, receiving, and otherwise obtaining information from all relevant sources.

Glare Sensitivity—The ability to see objects in the presence of glare or bright lighting.

Gross Body Coordination—The ability to coordinate the movement of the arms, legs, and torso together in activities where the whole body is in motion.

Gross Body Equilibrium—The ability to keep or regain one's body balance or stay upright when in an unstable position.

Guiding, Directing & Motivating Subordinates—Providing guidance and direction to subordinates, including setting performance standards and monitoring subordinates.

Handling and Moving Objects—Using one's own hands and arms in handling, installing, forming, positioning, and moving materials, or in manipulating things, including the use of keyboards.

Hazardous Conditions—Hazardous conditions (for example, high voltage electricity, combustibles, explosives, chemicals; does not include hazardous equipment or situations).

Hazardous Equipment—Hazardous equipment (for example, saws, machinery/mechanical parts include exposure to vehicular traffic, but not driving a vehicle).

Hazardous Situations—Hazardous situations involving likely cuts, bites, stings, or minor burns.

Health Services—Knowledge of principles and facts regarding diagnosing, curing, and preventing disease, and improving and preserving physical and mental health and well-being.

Hearing Sensitivity—The ability to detect or tell the difference between sounds that vary over broad ranges of pitch and loudness.

High Places—High places (for example, heights above 8 feet on ladders, poles, scaffolding, catwalks, and so on).

History and Archeology—Knowledge of past historical events and their causes, indicators, and impact on particular civilizations and cultures.

Idea Evaluation—Evaluating the likely success of an idea in relation to the demands of the situation.

Idea Generation—Generating a number of different approaches to problems.

Identification of Key Causes—Identifying the things that must be changed to achieve a goal.

Identify/Evaluating Job-Relevant Information—Interpreting information to perform this job.

Identifying Downstream Consequences—Determining the long-term outcomes of a change in operations.

Identifying Objects, Actions, and Events—Identifying information received by making estimates or categorizations, recognizing differences or similarities, or sensing changes in circumstances or events.

Implementation Planning—Developing approaches for implementing an idea.

Implementing Ideas, Programs, etc.—Conducting or carrying out work procedures and activities in accord with one's own ideas or information provided through directions/instructions for purposes of installing, modifying, preparing, delivering, constructing, integrating, finishing, or completing programs, systems, structures, or products.

Importance of Being Aware of New Events—Importance of being constantly aware of either frequently changing events (for example, security guard watching for shoplifters) or infrequent events (for example, radar operator watching for tornadoes).

Importance of Being Exact or Accurate—Importance of being very exact or highly accurate.

Importance of Being Sure All is Done—Importance of being sure that all the details of this job are performed and everything is done completely.

Importance of Repeating Same Tasks—Importance of repeating the same physical activities (for example, key entry) or mental activities (for example, checking entries in a ledger) over and over, without stopping.

Inductive Reasoning—The ability to combine separate pieces of information, or specific answers to problems, to form general rules or conclusions. It includes coming up with a logical explanation for why a series of seemingly unrelated events occur together.

Information Gathering—Knowing how to find information and identifying essential information.

Information Ordering—The ability to correctly follow a given rule or set of rules in order to arrange things or actions in a certain order. The things or actions can include numbers, letters, words, pictures, procedures, sentences, and mathematical or logical operations.

Information Organization—Finding ways to structure or classify multiple pieces of information

Information/Data Processing—Importance of processing information in the performance of this job.

Inspecting Equipment, Structures, Material—Inspecting or diagnosing equipment, structures, or materials to identify the causes of errors or other problems or defects.

Installation—Installing equipment, machines, wiring, or programs to meet specifications.

Instructing—Teaching others how to do something.

Interacting with Computers—Controlling computer functions by using programs, setting up functions, writing software, or otherwise communicating with computer systems.

Interacting with Others—Interactions with other persons or supervisory activities occur while performing this job.

Interpreting Meaning of Information to Others—Translating or explaining what information means and how it can be understood or used to support responses or feedback to others.

Job-Required Social Interaction—Requirement that the worker be in contact (face-to-face, by telephone, or otherwise) with others in order to perform it.

Judging Qualities of Things, Service, People—Making judgments about or assessing the value, importance, or quality of things or people.

Judgment and Decision Making—Weighing the relative costs and benefits of a potential action.

Keeping or Regaining Balance—Keeping or regaining balance.

Kneeling, Crouching or Crawling—Kneeling, stooping, crouching or crawling.

Law and Public Safety—Knowledge of regulations and methods for maintaining people and property free from danger, injury, or damage; the rules of public conduct established and enforced by legislation, and the political process establishing such rules.

Law, Government and Jurisprudence—Knowledge of laws, legal codes, court procedures, precedents, government regulations, executive orders, agency rules, and the democratic political process.

Learning Strategies—Using multiple approaches when learning or teaching new things.

Making Decisions and Solving Problems—Combining, evaluating, and reasoning with information and data to make decisions and solve problems. These processes involve making decisions about the relative importance of information and choosing the best solution.

Making Repetitive Motions—Making repetitive motions.

Management of Financial Resources—Determining how money will be spent to get the work done, and accounting for these expenditures.

Management of Material Resources—Obtaining and seeing to the appropriate use of equipment, facilities, and materials needed to do certain work.

Management of Personnel Resources—Motivating, developing, and directing people as they work, identifying the best people for the job.

Manual Dexterity—The ability to quickly make coordinated movements of one hand, a hand together with its arm, or two hands to grasp, manipulate, or assemble objects.

Manufacturing and Production—Knowledge of principles and facts related to the production, processing, storage, and distribution of manufactured and agricultural goods.

Mathematical Reasoning—The ability to understand and organize a problem and then to select a mathematical method or formula to solve the problem.

Mathematics—Knowledge of numbers, their operations, and interrelationships including arithmetic, algebra, geometry, calculus, statistics, and their applications

Mechanical—Knowledge of machines and tools, including their designs, uses, benefits, repair, and maintenance.

Medicine and Dentistry—Knowledge of the information and techniques needed to diagnose and treat injuries, diseases, and deformities. This includes symptoms, treatment alternatives, drug properties and interactions, and preventive health-care measures.

Memorization—The ability to remember information such as words, numbers, pictures, and procedures.

Monitor Processes, Material, Surroundings—Monitoring and reviewing information from materials, events, or the environment, often to detect problems or to find out when things are finished.

Monitoring—Assessing how well one is doing when learning or doing something.

Monitoring and Controlling Resources—Monitoring and controlling resources and overseeing the spending of money.

Multilimb Coordination—The ability to coordinate movements of two or more limbs together (for example, two arms, two legs, or one leg and one arm) while sitting, standing, or lying down. It does not involve performing the activities while the body is in motion.

Near Vision—The ability to see details of objects at a close range (within a few feet of the observer).

Negotiation—Bringing others together and trying to reconcile differences.

Night Vision—The ability to see under low light conditions.

Number Facility—The ability to add, subtract, multiply, or divide quickly and correctly.

Objective or Subjective Information—Objective or subjective information is communicated in this job.

Operating Vehicles or Equipment—Running, maneuvering, navigating, or driving vehicles or mechanized equipment, such as forklifts, passenger vehicles, aircraft, or water craft.

Operation and Control—Controlling operations of equipment or systems.

Operation Monitoring—Watching gauges, dials, or other indicators to make sure a machine is working properly.

Operations Analysis—Analyzing needs and product requirements to create a design.

Oral Comprehension—The ability to listen to and understand information and ideas presented through spoken words and sentences.

Oral Expression—The ability to communicate information and ideas in speaking so others will understand.

Organizing, Planning, and Prioritizing—Developing plans to accomplish work, and prioritizing and organizing one's own work.

Originality—The ability to come up with unusual or clever ideas about a given topic or situation, or to develop creative ways to solve a problem.

Pace Determined by Speed of Equipment—Pace is determined by the speed of equipment or machinery. (This does not refer to keeping busy at all times on this job.)

Perceptual Speed—The ability to quickly and accurately compare letters, numbers, objects, pictures, or patterns. The things to be compared may be presented at the same time or one after the other. This ability also includes comparing a presented object with a remembered one.

Performing Administrative Activities—Approving requests, handling paperwork, and performing day-to-day administrative tasks.

Performing Complex/Technical Activities—Skilled activities using coordinated movements are done to perform this job.

Performing for/Working with Public—Performing for people or dealing directly with the public, including serving persons in restaurants and stores, and receiving clients or guests.

Performing General Physical Activities—Performing physical activities that require moving one's whole body, such as in climbing, lifting, balancing, walking, stooping, where the activities often also require considerable use of the arms and legs, such as in the physical handling of materials.

Performing Physical & Manual Work Activities—Activities using the body and hands are done to perform this job.

Peripheral Vision—The ability to see objects or movement of objects to one's side when the eyes are focused forward.

Personnel and Human Resources—Knowledge of policies and practices involved in personnel/human resource functions. This includes recruitment, selection, training, and promotion regulations and procedures; compensation and benefits packages; labor relations and negotiation strategies; and personnel information systems

Persuade Someone to a Course of Action—Persuade someone to a course of action (informally) or influence others to buy something (to sell).

Persuasion—Persuading others to approach things differently.

Philosophy and Theology—Knowledge of different philosophical systems and religions, including their basic principles, values, ethics, ways of thinking, customs, and practices, and their impact on human culture.

Physics—Knowledge and prediction of physical principles, laws, and applications including air, water, material dynamics, light, atomic principles, heat, electric theory, earth formations, and meteorological and related natural phenomena.

Problem Identification—Identifying the nature of problems.

Problem Sensitivity—The ability to tell when something is wrong or is likely to go wrong. It does not involve solving the problem, only recognizing there is a problem.

Process—Procedures that contribute to the more rapid acquisition of knowledge and skill across a variety of domains.

Processing Information—Compiling, coding, categorizing, calculating, tabulating, auditing, verifying, or processing information or data.

Product Inspection—Inspecting and evaluating the quality of products.

Production and Processing—Knowledge of inputs, outputs, raw materials, waste, quality control, costs, and techniques for maximizing the manufacture and distribution of goods.

Programming—Writing computer programs for various purposes.

Provide a Service to Others—Provide a service to others (for example, customers).

Provide Consultation & Advice to Others—Providing consultation and expert advice to management or other groups on technical, systems-related, or process related topics.

Psychology—Knowledge of human behavior and performance, mental processes, psychological research methods, and the assessment and treatment of behavioral and affective disorders.

Public Safety and Security—Knowledge of weaponry, public safety, and security operations, rules, regulations, precautions, prevention, and the protection of people, data, and property.

Radiation—Radiation.

Rate Control—The ability to time the adjustments of a movement or equipment control in anticipation of changes in the speed and/or direction of a continuously moving object or scene.

Reaction Time—The ability to quickly respond (with the hand, finger, or foot) to one signal (sound, light, picture, and so on) when it appears.

Reading Comprehension—Understanding written sentences and paragraphs in work-related documents.

Reasoning/Decision Making—Decisions are made and problems solved in performing this job.

Repairing—Repairing machines or systems using the needed tools.

Repairing & Maintaining Electrical Equipment—Fixing, servicing, adjusting, regulating, calibrating, fine-tuning, or testing machines, devices, and equipment that operate primarily on the basis of electrical or electronic (not mechanical) principles.

Repairing & Maintaining Mechanical Equipment—Fixing, servicing, aligning, setting up, adjusting, and testing machines, devices, moving parts, and equipment that operate primarily on the basis of mechanical (not electronic) principles.

Resolving Conflict, Negotiating with Others—Handling complaints, arbitrating disputes, and resolving grievances, or otherwise negotiating with others.

Resource Management Skills—Developed capacities used to allocate resources efficiently.

Response Orientation—The ability to choose quickly and correctly between two or more movements in response to two or more signals (lights, sounds, pictures, and so on). It includes the speed with which the correct response is started with the hand, foot, or other body parts.

Responsibility for Outcomes and Results—Responsibility for work outcomes and results of other workers.

Responsible for Other's Health & Safety—Responsibility for others' health and safety on this job.

Sales and Marketing—Knowledge of principles and methods involved in showing, promoting, and selling products or services. This includes marketing strategies and tactics, product demonstration and sales techniques, and sales control systems.

Scheduling Work and Activities—Scheduling events, programs, and activities, as well as the work of others.

Science—Using scientific methods to solve problems

Selective Attention—The ability to concentrate and not be distracted while performing a task over a period of time.

Selling or Influencing Others—Convincing others to buy merchandise/goods, or otherwise changing their minds or actions.

Service Orientation—Actively looking for ways to help people.

Sitting—Sitting.

Social Perceptiveness—Being aware of others' reactions and understanding why they react the way they do.

Social Skills—Developed capacities used to work with people to achieve goals.

Sociology and Anthropology—Knowledge of group behavior and dynamics, societal trends and influences, cultures, their history, migrations, ethnicity, and origins.

Solution Appraisal—Observing and evaluating the outcomes of a problem's solution to identify lessons learned or redirect efforts.

Sound Localization—The ability to tell the direction from which a sound originated.

Sounds, Noise Levels Are Distracting, etc.—Sounds and noise levels that are distracting and uncomfortable.

Spatial Orientation—The ability to know one's location in relation to the environment, or to know where other objects are in relation to one's self.

Speaking—Talking to others to effectively convey information.

Special Uniform—A special uniform, such as that of a commercial pilot, nurse, police officer, or military personnel.

Specialized Protective or Safety Attire—Specialized protective or safety attire, such as breathing apparatus, safety harness, full protection suit, or radiation protection.

Speech Clarity—The ability to speak clearly so that it is understandable to a listener.

Speech Recognition—The ability to identify and understand the speech of another person.

Speed of Closure—The ability to quickly make sense of information that seems to be without meaning or organization. It involves quickly combining and organizing different pieces of information into a meaningful pattern.

Speed of Limb Movement—The ability to quickly move the arms or legs.

Staffing Organizational Units—Recruiting, interviewing, selecting, hiring, and promoting persons for the organization.

Stamina—The ability to exert one's self physically over long periods of time without getting winded or out of breath.

Standing—Standing.

Static Strength—The ability to exert maximum muscle force to lift, push, pull, or carry objects.

Supervise, Coach, Train Others—Supervise, coach, train, or develop other employees.

Synthesis/Reorganization—Reorganizing information to get a better approach to problems or tasks.

Systems Evaluation—Looking at many indicators of system performance, taking into account their accuracy.

Systems Perception—Determining when important changes have occurred in a system or are likely to occur.

Systems Skills—Developed capacities used to understand, monitor, and improve socio-technical systems.

Take a Position Opposed to Others—Take a position opposed to coworkers or others.

Teaching Others—Identifying educational needs, developing formal training programs or classes, and teaching or instructing others.

Technical Skills—Developed capacities used to design, set-up, operate, and correct malfunctions involving application of machines or technological systems.

Technology Design—Generating or adapting equipment and technology to serve user needs.

Telecommunications—Knowledge of transmission, broadcasting, switching, control, and operation of telecommunications systems.

Testing—Conducting tests to determine whether equipment, software, or procedures are operating as expected.

Therapy and Counseling—Knowledge of information and techniques needed to rehabilitate physical and mental ailments and to provide career guidance including alternative treatments, rehabilitation equipment and its proper use, and methods to evaluate treatment effects.

Thinking Creatively—Originating, inventing, designing, or creating new applications, ideas, relationships, systems, or products, including artistic contributions.

Time Management—Managing one's own time and the time of others.

Time Sharing—The ability to efficiently shift back and forth between two or more activities or sources of information (such as speech, sounds, touch, or other sources).

Transportation—Knowledge of principles and methods for moving people or goods by air, rail, sea, or road, including their relative costs, advantages, and limitations.

Troubleshooting—Determining what is causing an operating error and deciding what to do about it.

Trunk Strength—The ability to use one's abdominal and lower back muscles to support part of the body repeatedly or continuously over time without "giving out" or "fatiguing."

Updating & Using Job-Relevant Knowledge—Keeping up-to-date technically and knowing one's own jobs' and related jobs' functions.

Using Hands on Objects, Tools, Controls—Using hands to handle, control, or feel objects, tools or controls.

Very Hot—Very hot (above 90 degrees F) or very cold (under 32 degrees F) temperatures.

Visioning—Developing an image of how a system should work under ideal conditions.

Visual Color Discrimination—The ability to match or detect differences between colors, including shades of color and brightness.

Visualization—The ability to imagine how something will look after it is moved around or when its parts are moved or rearranged.

Walking or Running—Walking or running.

Whole Body Vibration—Whole body vibration (for example, operating a jackhammer or earthmoving equipment).

Work Output—Physical activities, equipment, vehicles, or complex/technical activities are used to accomplish job outputs.

Wrist-Finger Speed—The ability to make fast, simple, repeated movements of the fingers, hands, and wrists.

Writing—Communicating effectively with others in writing as indicated by the needs of the audience.

Written Comprehension—The ability to read and understand information and ideas presented in writing.

Written Expression—The ability to communicate information and ideas in writing so others will understand.

Annotated Bibliography of Useful Resources for Career Planning and Job Seeking

Compiled by Mike Farr

This is not a conventional bibliography. My comments are informal and admittedly biased, and I include only materials I like in some way. I developed this bibliography for a book I wrote titled *The Very Quick Job Search*. Because the bibliography was so well received there, I made a few changes and include it here for your information.

I've been looking at career materials for over 20 years, and it still amazes me how much junk is out there. A good example are resume books that still suggest that sending out many good-looking resumes is the way to get a job. While the advice on creating a resume may be good, the advice on *using* it is—too often—not. I tried to sort the wheat from the chaff, so materials that I do not consider good or useful are not listed.

I emphasize books you are most likely to find in a bookstore or good library. Materials published or distributed by JIST are among those listed, as are some that I have written. Of course, I tend to be enthusiastic about materials I have been involved in, although I try to be objective.

I organize the materials into categories and provide comments on many titles. Within categories, books are not presented in a particular order, although titles published by JIST are listed first. For brevity, I mention a publisher only if it is JIST. I don't provide publication dates, because materials are often updated regularly.

A good bookstore or library should be able to locate a book by its title and author. Most bookstores have a computer that allows them to find any book you want. Ask them to look up a desired title in "Books in Print." Some materials are rather obscure and not easy to obtain. Others are out of print (it's difficult to keep up with all this), although you may find them through an interlibrary loan program. Ask your librarian to help you locate something you *really* want.

So browse the descriptions that follow. Remember that this an informal list rather than a formal bibliography, but I hope you find it helpful.

General Advice on Finding Career and Job Search Information

As mentioned, many resource materials in this bibliography can be found in a good library. Libraries have more information than I can list, including journals, newspapers, books, CD-ROM databases, access to the Internet, and other resources. So here are some tips for using the library as your job search friend.

The librarian: Your friendly librarian can be one of your best sources of specific information during your job search. If you can ask the question, he or she can probably give you some ideas on where to find an answer.

Finding Facts Fast: Todd. Perhaps the best book on finding out about anything at the library or elsewhere. Great research aid.

Trade magazines and journals: Most libraries will have one or more professional journals related to a variety of major career areas. Staying current on the publications in your field will help you in the interviewing process. These publications sometimes have job listings.

You Can Get Anything You Want: Dawson.

Develop a Network of Contacts, Including Members of Professional and Trade Associations

You already know hundreds of people, and networking to meet more is covered in many job search books I recommend. Consider joining professional associations related to the job you want. Your membership gives you access to meetings, newsletters, and other information sources. But the biggest benefit is that other members are an excellent source of networking opportunities. They often hire or supervise people with similar skills—or know those who do. You can get access to membership lists and use the contact information to call members in your area or in any part of the country. Make lots of phone contacts, send JIST Cards, resumes, and thank-you notes—and get lots of interviews!

Directories

People who work in the careers that interest you can tell you which organizations to join. A good library will often have one or more helpful directories including the following:

Career Guide to Professional Associations: Garrett Park Press. Describes more than 2,500 professional associations. The information is more oriented to the job seeker than is the ***Encyclopedia of Associations,*** but some information may not be current.

Encyclopedia of Associations: Gale Research Company. A listing of more than 22,000 professional, trade, and other nonprofit organizations in the United States, representing more issues than you can imagine. It cross-references them in various helpful ways.

Encyclopedia of Associations—International Organizations: Gale Research. A listing of more than 11,000 organizations in 180 countries. Includes trade, business, and commercial associations, and associations of labor unions.

Professional & Trade Association Job Finder: By career category, details over 1,000 sources of information, referral, and more.

Newspapers and Professional Journals

While the want ads in newspapers represent relatively few of the available job openings—and allow almost everyone to apply for them—some people do get jobs from want ads. Newspapers also contain other useful employment information. Look for tips on new or expanding businesses and leads for unadvertised job openings. Articles about new or expanding companies can be valuable leads for new job possibilities.

If relocating is a possibility, look at newspapers from other areas. They can serve as a source of job leads as well as indicate some idea of the job market. The major out-of-town newspapers are sold in most large cities and are available in many public libraries.

Some newspapers such as *The New York Times, The Chicago Tribune,* and *The Financial Times* are national in scope. *The National Business Employment Weekly,* published by *The Wall Street Journal,* contains much information of interest to professional job seekers. But remember that competition for jobs advertised in these sources is fierce, so don't rely on them too heavily.

Review these sources for articles mentioning your target companies. Look for information on new products, expansions, consolidations, relocations, promotions, articles by executives in the companies, annual company earnings, and current problems.

Check back issues of newspapers for old want ads. They can provide important information on job duties, salary, and benefits. There may even be a want ad for a job in which you are interested. Perhaps the job was never filled or the person previously hired has already moved on.

Specialty newspapers such as *The National Business Employment Weekly* have a compilation of the previous week's want ads from the regional editions of *The Wall Street Journal,* plus its own want ads. *National Ad Search* is a weekly tabloid that has a compilation of want ads from 75 key newspapers across the U.S. Expect major competition for jobs listed this widely.

Back issues of major newspapers can be accessed on the Internet, allowing you to sort by key words or for specific geographic areas.

Here are some related resources.

Business Newsbank, Newsbank, Inc.: This service provides the narrative of articles from newspapers and business journals from 400 cities. It cross-references information by company name, individual's name, industry, or product category.

New York Times Index: A thorough index of all stories that appear in the *Times.*

Wall Street Journal Index: This is an important source of information on larger business and business trends.

Where the Jobs Are: 1200 Journals with Job/Career Openings: Feingold and Winkler. A unique resource providing tips on responding to journal ads and a cross-reference to specific journals by job type.

Where to Find Business Information: Brownstone and Curruth. Lists and describes the many newsletters, journals, computer databases, books, and other sources of business information.

I provide additional details on using the newspapers in the section titled "Getting Information on Specific Employers."

Job Search and Career Planning Books by Yours Truly

I've worked on many job search, career planning, and occupational information books, assessment tests, videos, and software over the years. Some are readily available in bookstores and libraries, while others are used by schools, institutions, and instructors. Most of my materials are published by JIST. Many are included in the various sections of this bibliography, along with brief descriptions.

I feel strongly that only two main issues in the career planning and job search field really matter. The first is that it is essential to select a career that will satisfy you. This involves knowing yourself well enough to select *the* job rather than *a* job. The second issue is, if you need to find a job, you might as well find a good one and do it in as little time as possible. My books incorporate these simple principles and tend to be practical and results-oriented. Here is a partial list, should this be of interest to you:

Books You Are Most Likely to Find in Bookstores and Libraries

- *The Very Quick Job Search—Get a Good Job in Less Time*
- *How to Get a Job Now!—Six Easy Steps to Getting a Better Job*
- *The Quick Resume and Cover Letter Book*
- *The Quick Interview and Salary Negotiations Book*
- *America's Top Resumes for America's Top Jobs*
- *America's Fastest Growing Jobs*
- *America's Top Jobs for College Graduates*
- *America's Top Jobs for People Without College Degrees*
- *America's Top Medical, Education, and Human Services Jobs*
- *America's Top Office, Management, Sales, & Professional Jobs*
- *Best Jobs for the 21st Century* (coauthored with LaVerne Ludden)

Occupational Reference Books

My name appears on several occupational reference books that can be found in libraries. These books are mostly based on information obtained from government sources. I was part of a team that made the information useful. Calling anyone an author of these books is a bit of a stretch, although I spent many hours working on them. These titles include the following:

- *The O*NET Dictionary of Occupational Titles*
- *The Enhanced Occupational Outlook Handbook*
- *The Complete Guide to Occupational Exploration*

Materials Used in Schools and Other Programs

One of my life's missions has been to improve the information and training that students and job seekers receive in career and job search programs. Here are some materials I have authored for this use—most are *not* available in bookstores but can be obtained from JIST.

The JIST Career Planning and Job Search Course: For instructors, a complete curriculum I wrote to support the use of *The Very Quick Job Search*. It includes lesson plans, over 50 overhead transparencies, and reproducible handout masters.

The JIST Course: The Young Person's Guide to Getting and Keeping a Good Job: Coauthored by Marie Pavlicko for use by high school students. It was field tested with thousands of students. Good graphics and easy-to-follow narrative. Accompanying instructor's guide and transparency set.

The Right Job for You: A thorough career planning book that includes lots of information and worksheets.

The Guide for Occupational Exploration Inventory: This is an interest "test" to help with career exploration.

The Work Book: Getting the Job You Want: This is my first job search book. Originally published in 1981, it has been revised several times and has sold over 300,000 copies. It remains popular in postsecondary schools and programs. An instructor's guide is available. Published by McGraw-Hill, Glencoe Division.

Job Finding Fast: A thorough book that includes sections on career decision making as well as job seeking. It was written to support a full course or program at the postsecondary or college level. An instructor's guide is available. Also published by McGraw-Hill, Glencoe Division.

Videos and software: I've written content scripts for numerous job search and career-related videos and have worked on a variety of career-related software.

Etcetera: I've worked on many workbooks and other projects over the years, including several series for youth coauthored with Susan Christophersen (The Living Skills Series and The Career and Life Skills Series). I have edited or helped to develop many others. It's been work and it's been fun.

Career Materials Published by JIST

I formerly listed career-related books published by JIST in a separate section, but the list became too long. Besides, I only included those JIST books that were likely to be found in a bookstore or library and excluded many videos, assessment tests, instructional materials, and books used in schools and institutions. The JIST books you are most likely to find in a bookstore or library are now included in the various subsections of this bibliography. If you want a more thorough list, contact JIST for a catalog. JIST's Internet site (www.JIST.com) provides free chapters of many books and links to other career-related sites.

Information on Occupations and Industries

Hundreds of books provide information on jobs, and most libraries have a basic selection. I suggest you begin with the general career references, and then look for more specific information on jobs that interest you most.

While most people focus their career-planning time on choosing an occupation, I suggest you also consider the industry where you want to work. For example, if you have experience in accounting (a career) and an interest in airplanes (an industry), perhaps accounting-oriented jobs in a flight-related industry such as airports, airplane manufacturing, or air-transportation regulation would be your best fit. I include industry references for this reason and recommend you browse some of them.

Best Sources of Information on Industries

Career Guide to America's Top Industries: Based on information from the U. S. Department of Labor, provides details on over 40 major industries. Easy-to-read and loaded with helpful information, it was written specifically to assist in career planning and job seeking. If you are going to use one book on industries, this is the one I recommend. JIST.

U.S. Industrial Outlook: Based on information from the U.S. Department of Commerce, it provides business forecasts for over 300 industries. Good source of information to review prior to interviews.

Standard Industrial Classification Manual (SIC): A standard reference developed by the U.S. Department of Commerce that lists all industries in an organized way. Accountants, banks, the IRS, and many others use it as a way to codify business. While I would not recommend this as light reading, it is useful for identifying more specialized industries for a job search or career exploration. Available from JIST.

North American Industrial Classification System (NAICS): A new system to replace the SIC Manual was introduced in 1998 and will be used in Mexico, the United States, and Canada. This book has similar uses to the older SIC manual. Available from JIST.

Best Sources of Information on Occupations

The Occupational Outlook Handbook: Highly recommended. Published by the U.S. Department of Labor and updated every other year, this book provides descriptions for 250 major jobs covering 87 percent of the workforce. The descriptions are well written and provide information on pay, working conditions, related jobs, projected growth, and more. A very helpful book for exploring career options or for job seeking. Available from JIST.

The Enhanced Occupational Outlook Handbook: Includes all the descriptions in the ***Occupational Outlook Handbook*** plus 3,000 descriptions of more specialized jobs and 5,000 additional titles. Easy to use. JIST.

America's Top Jobs Series. Each book in this series includes about 100 job descriptions plus a review of job market trends, career planning and job search advice, summary information on hundreds of additional jobs, and useful appendices. The job descriptions are based on those used in the ***Occupational Outlook Handbook*** and include details on pay, education required, working conditions, and more. All are published by JIST.

- *America's Fastest Growing Jobs:* J. Michael Farr.
- *America's Top Jobs for College Graduates:* J. Michael Farr.
- *America's Top Jobs for People Without College Degrees:* J. Michael Farr.
- *America's Top Medical, Education, and Human Services Jobs:* J. Michael Farr.
- *America's Top Office, Management, Sales, & Professional Jobs:* J. Michael Farr.
- *America's Federal Jobs*
- *America's Top Military Careers*

Best Jobs for the 21st Century: J. Michael Farr and LaVerne Ludden. Lists of jobs for best paying, highest earning at different education levels, and other criteria. Hundreds of job descriptions. JIST.

The Complete Guide for Occupational Exploration: The U.S. Department of Labor developed the GOE to help people explore careers based on interests. The CGOE narrows broad interests to the many specific jobs within each major category. It lists over 12,000 jobs by occupational cluster, interests, abilities, and traits required for successful performance. You can look up jobs by industry, types of skills or abilities required, values, related home/leisure activities, military experience, education required, or related jobs you have had. JIST.

The Enhanced Guide for Occupational Exploration: Similar to the CGOE, but also provides descriptions for 2,500 jobs. These jobs cover 95 percent of the workforce and few people will miss those that are not listed. JIST.

Dictionary of Occupational Titles: Published by the U.S. Department of Labor, the DOT provides brief descriptions for 12,741 jobs—more than any other reference. It is a large book, over 1,400 pages, and not particularly easy-to-use. But it is a standard reference that many other books cross-reference. Available from JIST.

More Career Information Books

Hundreds of books provide information on specific careers. I've selected representative titles, but you will find many others in a good library.

American Almanac of Jobs and Salaries: Wright. Useful data on pay and opportunities for hundreds of jobs.

Career Connection for College Education—A Guide to College Education and Related Career Opportunities, revised edition: Fred Rowe. Provides information on over 100 college majors and 1,000 occupations that are related to them. Includes information on salaries, course requirements, related high school courses, and other details useful in planning a college major. JIST.

Career Connection for Technical Education—A Guide to Technical Training and Related Career Opportunities: Fred Rowe. Similar to the above but provides information on 70 technical training majors and 450 related occupations. JIST

Career Finder—Pathways to Over 1,500 Entry-Level Jobs: Schwartz and Breckner.

Careers without College Series: A series of 11 books for those not planning on a four-year college degree. Topics on health care, fashion, cars, office, sports, and others.

Choosing an Airline Career: March.

Discover the Best Jobs for You!: Krannich and Krannich. Explores skills, interests, and explores specific jobs.

Encyclopedia of Careers: Ferguson Publishing. A series of books providing useful information on all major occupations.

Great Careers: The 4th of July Guide to Careers, Internships, and Volunteer Opportunities in the Non-Profit Sector: An enormous reference of books and programs covering jobs with a social cause.

High Paying Jobs in 6 Months or Less: For jobs requiring brief training.

High Tech Jobs for Non High Tech Grads: O'Brien. Good ideas for those without technical training.

Jobs Rated Almanac: Krantz. Ranks 250 jobs by pay, benefits, stress, and other criteria.

Occu-facts: Provides one-page descriptions for over 500 jobs in an easy-to-read format. Jobs are arranged into groups of similar occupations, which encourages its use as a career exploration tool.

Opportunities is . . . Series: A series books published by VGM Career Horizons. Each covers related jobs in that field, skills required, working conditions, pay, education required, jargon. Some of the careers covered are Secretarial; Health and Medical; Office Occupations; Data Processing; Computer Science; Travel; Hotel and Motel Management; Cable Television; Accounting.

Outdoor Careers: Shenk.

Peterson's Engineering, Science and Computer Jobs: An annual update of 900 employers, types of jobs, and more.

Professional Careers Series: Another series of books on a variety of professional jobs including finance, medicine, law, computers, accounting, business, and others.

Real Estate Careers: Jamic and Rejnis.

Revised Handbook for Analyzing Jobs: A technical book describing various coding systems used to quantify and categorize jobs. Available from JIST.

Worker Trait Data Book: Donald Mayall. A technical book that provides coded information on over 12,000 jobs in the ***Dictionary of Occupational Titles***. Much of this information is not available elsewhere. JIST.

Worker Trait Group Guide: A simpler version of the ***Guide for Occupational Exploration*** providing information on clusters of similar jobs. Available from JIST.

Career Planning and Job Search Books

There are innumerable job search and career planning books and more are published all the time. Most are written by corporate recruiters, headhunters, social workers, academics, and personnel experts who are well intentioned but have little practical experience in determining whether the job search methods they recommend actually work. Many books provide advice that would, if followed, actually slow down the job search process.

Generally, I discard books that suggest sending out resumes or answering want ads as good job search methods—or that do not include methods appropriate for approaching smaller businesses. The research clearly indicates the importance of these issues, and anyone who is not aware of this should not be considered an expert. So, in my humble opinion, here are some of the better books.

Highly Recommended Career Planning and Job Search Books

This is a short list that includes a few of my own books, a few books published by JIST, and a few books published by others that I like and are widely regarded as among the best books on their topics.

The Very Quick Job Search—Get a Good Job in Less Time: J. Michael Farr. This is my most thorough job search book, and it includes lots of information on career planning and, of course, job seeking. This is the book I would recommend to a friend who was out of work, if I had to recommend just one book. While written as a "bookstore" book, it is widely used in schools and colleges. There is an accompanying activities book, curriculum, and transparency set. This book has won a variety of awards including best career book of the year. JIST.

How to Get a Job Now!—Six Easy Steps for Getting a Better Job: J. Michael Farr. This is a short book that covers the basics in an interactive format. I included those things I believe most important to know if you want to get a better job in less time. JIST.

Using the Internet and the World Wide Web in Your Job Search: Fred Jandt and Mary Nemnich. For new or more experienced Internet users, it is full of information on getting career information, finding job listings, creating electronic resumes, networking with user groups, and other interesting techniques. Reviews all major career sites. JIST.

The PIE Method for Career Success—A New Job Search Strategy: Daniel Porot. The PIE method (Pleasure, Information, and Employment) uses a visual and creative format to present career planning and job search techniques. The author is one of Europe's major career consultants, and this book presents his powerful career planning and job seeking concepts in a memorable way. JIST.

Inside Secrets of Finding a Teaching Job: Jack and Diane Warner and Clyde Bryan. Practical advice for new and experienced teachers looking for a new job. JIST.

What Color Is Your Parachute?: Richard N. Bolles. This is the best-selling, career-changing book ever. Well written and entertaining, it is updated each year and includes a useful self-assessment section, "The Quick Job Hunting Map." Bolles is fun to read and the book is highly recommended.

The Complete Job Search Handbook: All the Skills You Need to Get Any Job, and Have a Good Time Doing It: Howard Figler. A solid book with lots of exercises to assess skills, values, and needs. Procedures for exploring careers and developing a job objective. An excellent book that is loaded with innovative ideas.

Other Career and Job Search Books for a General Audience

Getting the Job You Really Want: J. Michael Farr. Covers career planning and job seeking topics in a workbook format with lots of activities. Very popular in schools and job search programs and available in bookstores. An instructor's guide is also available. JIST.

Job Search 101—Getting Started on Your Career Path: Pat Morton and Marcia Fox. For college seniors and recent graduates seeking entry-level jobs. JIST.

Job Finding Fast: J. Michael Farr. A thorough career planning and job search workbook used in colleges. An instructor's guide is available. Available from JIST.

Job Strategies for Professionals: Based on advice provided by the U.S. Department of Labor, it provides job search advice for professionals and managers who have lost their jobs. JIST.

Job Rights and Survival Strategies—A Handbook for Terminated Employees: Paul Tobias and Susan Sauter. Covers legal rights and benefits as well as how to handle these traumatic situations with dignity. Distributed by JIST.

900,000 Plus Jobs Annually: Feingold and Winkler. Reviews 900+ periodicals that list openings and positions wanted in hundreds of fields.

Big Splash in a Small Pond—Finding a Great Job in a Small Company: Resnick and Pechter.

Change Your Job, Change Your Life: Krannich. Reviews jobs trends and job search methods.

Do What You Are—Discover the Perfect Career for You Through the Secrets of Personality Type: Tieger and Barron-Tieger.

Go Hire Yourself An Employer: Richard Irish. Lots of good stuff in this new revision. Covers skills identification, job search, resumes, interviews, the unemployment "blahs," succeeding on the next job, and other topics.

Guerrilla Tactics in the New Job Market: Tom Jackson.

Professional Careers Sourcebook, an Informational Guide for Career Planning: K. Savage and C. Dorgan.

Hardball Job Hunting Tactics: Dick Wright. From a trainer with lots of experience with the hard to employ. Excellent sections on completing applications (a topic not often covered well) and resumes. Brief but good section on job search. Tips for people with various "problems" and how to overcome them.

How to Get Interviews from Classified Job Ads: Elderkin.

Information Interviewing: What It Is and How to Use It in Your Career: Martha Stoodley.

Job & Career Building: Richard Germann and Peter Arnold. A good choice for laid-off professionals, managers, and others with more experience and training.

Job Hunters Sourcebook: Where to Find Employment Leads and Other Job Search Sources: Michelle LeCompte.

Marketing Yourself: The Ultimate Job Seeker's Guide: Dorothy Leeds.

New Network Your Way to Job and Career Success: Ron and Carol Krannich.

Re-Careering in Turbulent Times: Ronald Krannich. Lots of good material including employment trends, selecting a career, getting training and education, communication skills, sources of job leads, interviewing, resumes, relocation, public employment opportunities, and career advancement.

Robert Half On Hiring: Robert Half. Written to help employers select better employees. Most of the advice is based on a series of employer surveys providing unique insight into how employers make hiring decisions.

Selling On The Phone: Porterfield. Self-teaching guide for telemarketing and other sales approaches. Good ideas for reinforcing effective phone skills in the job search.

Starting Over: You in the New Workplace: Jo Danna.

The Complete Job Search Book: Richard Beatty.

The Job Bank Guide to Employment Services: Bob Adams.

The Only Job Hunting Guide You'll Ever Need: Kathryn Ross Petras.

Three Boxes of Life and How to Get Out of Them: Richard Bolles. Introduces the concepts of "life/work planning." Very thorough.

Where Do I Go From Here with the Rest of My Life?: John Crystal and Richard Bolles. John Crystal has died, but his techniques and insights into the career planning process helped to start an important movement that came to be called "Life/Work Planning."

Who's Hiring Who: Richard Lathrop. Solid, practical information for job seekers. Good self-assessment sections and excellent resume advice (he calls them "qualifications briefs"). I particularly like this book and respect Lathrop's work.

Specialized Career and Job Search Books

Many books have been written on specialized career and job search topics. For example, there are books to help various segments of our population gain a competitive edge; books on specialized job search methods (such as using the telephone); and books on getting certain types of jobs (such as those with small business or overseas jobs). Some of these materials are not easily categorized into one group, so look through the entire list for things related to your situation—there is probably something in here that fits.

Internet Job Search Books

The Internet is a growing source of information on all topics, but you can also waste a lot of time there unless you know where to look. Here are a few helpful guides to get you started.

***Using the Internet and the World Wide Web in Your Job Search*:** Fred Jandt and Mary Nemnich. A good book for both new and more experienced Internet users. Lists all major career sites and, more importantly, tells you how to use the Internet in effective ways. JIST.

The Quick Internet Guide to Career and College Information: Anne Wolfinger. A time-saving and brief guide for educators, counselors, and employment professionals to the best sites and how to use them. JIST.

Electronic Job Search Revolution: Kennedy and Morrow. Tips on using your computer and online services to get jobs.

Resources for Youth and Parents

An enormous amount of material is available for young people to help them explore career alternatives. I present only a few here. Most are not available in bookstores and are available only from the publishers. If you help youth I suggest you contact JIST and ask for its institutional catalog; it presents materials from a variety of publishers. I also include a few good books for parents to help their kids in their quest for a career (and, of course, to get them out of the house).

Helping Your Child Choose a Career: Luthor Otto. One of the most helpful books available on the topic for parents, teachers, and even kids. Comprehensive and sensible advice. JIST.

Young Person's OOH: For grades 6-10. Provides information on 250 jobs listed in the ***Occupational Outlook Handbook*** plus career exploration advice. JIST.

Young Person's Guide to Getting & Keeping a Good Job: J. Michael Farr and Marie Pavilicko. A practical workbook for high school students. A separate instructor's guide and overhead transparencies are also available. JIST.

Creating Your Life's Work Portfolio for High School Students: Good activities and content. JIST.

Career and Life Skills Series: J. Michael Farr and Susan Christophersen. Four books for grades 7-12 on career preparation. JIST.

HIRE Learning Series: Patricia Duffy and T. Walter Wannie. Three books for high school students on career planning, job seeking, and job success. JIST.

Dream Catchers: Norene Lindsay. A career exploration workbook for grades 5 to 8. JIST.

Pathfinder—Exploring Career and Educational Paths: Norene Lindsay. A workbook for high school students, with a separate instructor's guide. JIST.

***Secrets to Getting Better Grades*:** Brian Marshall and Wendy Ford. Teaches students to study smart, with lots of practical tips for notes, tests, papers, memory, and other techniques. JIST.

Exploring Careers—A Young Person's Guide to Over 300 Careers, revised edition: A revision of the original, published by the U.S. Department of Labor. An excellent resource for young people, providing details on over 300 jobs in an interesting format. JIST.

Career Coaching Your Kids: Montross et al. Tips on helping your children explore career options.

Career Discovery Encyclopedia: This is a six-volume set for grades 4 and up with reading level at about the 7th grade, appropriate through high school. Excellent, with over 1,000 pages and helpful ways to look up jobs. A school or other good library may have them. Excellent.

Children's Dictionary of Occupations: For elementary and middle school students; covers 300 occupations.

Directory of American Youth Organizations: Erickson. Lists more than 500 organizations.

Job Power: The Young People's Job Finding Guide: Haldane and Martin. One of our favorite books for group process ideas on skills identification and selecting a job objective. Simple, direct, useful for any age.

Joyce Lain Kennedy's Career Book: Kennedy and Laramore. A very thorough book, covering just about everything that a young person (or parent) would need to know about career and life decisions. Highly recommended.

***Parents With Careers Workbook*:** Good worksheets and advice on getting organized, child care, home management, single parents, dual careers, time use, and so on.

Summer Jobs for Students: Reviews sources for 20,000 summer jobs and explains how to use the Internet for additional information.

Working Parents and Couples

***Home But Not Alone—The Parents' Work-at-Home Handbook*:** Katherine Murray. A very good book that won an award for being one of the top three business books of the year. Lots of solid tips. JIST.

The Working Parents' Handbook—How to Succeed at Work, Raise Your Kids, Maintain a Home, and Still Have Time for You: Katherine Murray. An entertaining and helpful book providing advice on handling the multiple roles of working parents. Excellent. JIST.

Surviving Your Partner's Job Loss: Jukes and Rosenberg.

The Three Career Couple: Byalick and Saslow. On handling two jobs plus a family.

Books to Help Get Jobs in the Government, Education, and Nonprofit Sector

The Unauthorized Teacher's Survival Guide: Jack Warner, Clyde Bryan with Diane Warner. Great advice for new and experienced teachers telling you the things you did not learn in teacher's college. JIST.

Inside Secrets of Finding a Teaching Job: Jack Warner, Clyde Bryan with Diane Warner. Helpful techniques for finding a job in teaching, based on years of experience and interviews with many educators. JIST.

Alternative Careers for Teachers: Pollack and Beard. Good ideas on getting a job in another field using transferable skills.

Careers in Local and State Government: Zehring. Where they are, how to apply, take tests, and find internships and summer jobs. Job search tips.

Complete Guide to Public Employment: Krannich. Reviews opportunities with federal and local governments, associations, nonprofits, foundations, research, international, and many other institutions. Well done.

Doing Well by Doing Good—The First Complete Guide to Careers in the Non-Profit Sector: McAdam.

Moving Out Of Education: A Guide To Career Management & Change: Krannich and Banis. Good tips for this special situation from an ex-educator who moved out.

Take Charge of Your Own Career—A Guide to Federal Employment: Moore and Vanderwey.

Minorities and Immigrants

Best Companies for Minorities: Graham. Profiles of 85 companies.

Career Opportunities for Bilinguals and Multiculturals—A Directory of Resources in Education, Employment and Business: Wertsman. Over 3,500 listings.

Directory of Special Programs for Minority Group Members: Willis L. Johnson. Over 2,800 sources of training, jobs, scholarships, programs.

Finding a Job in the United States: Friedenberg and Bradley.

Minority Career Guide: Kastre, Kastre, and Edwards.

Minority Organizations—The Directory of Special Programs for Minority Group Members: Oakes. The largest source of information available covering over 5,800 professional organizations and resources.

Stepping Up: Placing Minority Women Into Managerial and Professional Jobs: Tips to replicate results of a program that increased the pay, advancement, and retention of minority women.

The Big Book of Minority Opportunities—Directory of Special Programs for Minority Group Members: Oakes. 4,000 sources of scholarships, financial aid, and special programs.

The Black Woman's Career Guide: Nivens. Good advice on over 50 good jobs, dress and grooming, skills identification, job search, and more.

The Colorblind Career: Stenson. Tips for African-American, Hispanic, and Asian-Americans to succeed.

Workers over 40, Displaced Workers, Retirement Issues

Arthur Young's Pre-Retirement Planning Book: Very well done book. Lots of worksheets.

Cracking the Over 50 Job Market: Conner. Good job search advice.

Getting a Job After 50: John S. Morgan. Age discrimination is real, and people over 50 need better than average job-seeking skills to overcome this.

Helping the Dislocated Worker: Ashley and Zahniser. Reviews suggested services and programs—helpful for program planners.

Job Hunting After 50: Strategies for Success: Samuel Ray.

Job Hunting for the 40+ Executive: Birsner. Good advice on the personal and job search needs of middle-aged executives.

Mid Career Job Hunting: Official Handbook of the 40+ Club: E. Patricia Birsner. Solid advice on getting back on track and getting a job.

Retirement Careers: Marsh.

Second Careers—New Ways to Work After 50: Bird. Analyzes career changes of over 6,000 people and how they worked out.

The Over 40 Job Guide: Petras.

People with Disabilities, Disadvantaged Groups, the Homeless

Know-How is the Key: Dixie Lee Wright. A job search program (student workbook and instructor's guide) for high school through young adult "special needs" students with learning and other disabilities. JIST.

Americans with Disabilities Act Handbook—and Technical Assistance Manual: Government publication providing comprehensive information on the Americans With Disabilities Act (ADA) and how it is interpreted. Available from JIST.

A Helping Hand—A Guide to Customized Support Services for Special Populations: Thorough guide for program operators who emphasize employment—JTPA, older workers, ex-offenders, and others.

Bouncing Back from Injury: How to Take Charge of Your Recuperation: Karen Klein and Carla Derrick Hope.

Career Success for People with Physical Disabilities: Kissane. Good advice for job seekers. Lots of exercises.

Complete Guide to Employing Persons with Disabilities: Henry McCarthy. From the National Rehabilitation Information Center; phone (800) 346-2742.

Job Hunting for the Disabled: Adele Lewis and Edith Marks. Interest surveys, programs, job descriptions, and job search tips.

Job Strategies for People with Disabilities: Witt. Good advice as well as lists of resource materials and programs.

Job-Hunting Tips for the So-Called Handicapped or People Who Have Disabilities: Richard N. Bolles.

No One is Unemployable: Angel and Harney. A good resource for welfare-to-work, ex-offender programs, and other "difficult" populations.

Recovery from Alcohol and Substance Abuse and Coping with Job Loss

Career Knockouts: How to Battle Back: Joyce Lain Kennedy. Avoiding, learning, and even benefiting from job failures.

Clean, Sober and Unemployed: Elliot. Good advice for recovering substance abusers.

Coping with Unemployment: Jud. Dealing with long-term unemployment.

Sacked! Why Good People Get Fired and How to Avoid It: Gould.

Termination Trap: Best Strategies for a Job Going Sour: Cohen. Excellent insights on avoiding or dealing with job loss.

The Career Seekers: Tannenbaum. For anyone recovering from codependency or in a recovery program.

People with Four-Year and Advanced Degrees and Technical Training

Finding a Job in Your Field: A Handbook for Ph.D.'s & M.A.'s

Jobs for English Majors and Other Smart People: Good tips for liberal arts grads.

The MBA's Guide to Career Planning: Ed Holton

The High-Tech Career Book: Collard.

Job Search for the Technical Professional: Moore. For programmers and engineers.

Military/Veterans

Many good materials are available to help vets transition to civilian employment. Following are some of the specific ones, but many of the career and job search books (such as *America's Top Resumes*) include veterans among their examples.

America's Top Military Careers: Based on Department of Defense information, this book provides details on 200 enlisted and officer occupations including civilian counterparts. JIST.

Complete Guide for Occupational Exploration: Among other things, this comprehensive career reference book cross-references military occupations to over 12,000 civilian job titles. JIST.

Jobs and the Military Spouse—Married, Mobile, and Motivated for the New Job Market: Farley.

Resume and Job Hunting Guide for Present and Future Veterans: DePrez. Helpful book with some good techniques.

Veteran's Survival Guide to Good Jobs in Bad Times: Grant's Guides.

You and the Armed Forces: Marrs. Better understand career options and what to expect from military life.

Young Person's Guide to Military Service: Bradley. Covers pros and cons of going into the services. Good sections for minorities and women.

Your Career in the Military: Gordan. Reviews advantages of education and money. Enlistment options and procedures.

Women

Women are in the workforce more than ever, and they tend to be better educated than average. But women without advanced educations and who are single heads of households are not doing as well. Special advice and resources are clearly needed; here are just a few.

Congratulations! You've Been Fired: Sound Advice for Women Who've Been Terminated, Pink Slipped, Downsized or Otherwise Unemployed: Emily Koltnow and Lynne S. Dumas.

Developing New Horizons for Women: Ruth Helm Osborn. Very good text to improve self-esteem, identify strengths, and develop long-range life and career plans.

Directory of Special Opportunities for Women: Over 1,000 resources for women entering and reentering the workforce. Recommended.

Good Enough for Mothers: Marshall. Balancing work and family.

Homemaker's Complete Guide to Entering the Job Market: Lussier. Useful techniques to transfer homemaking skills to the work world and find a job.

Resume Guide for Women of the '90s: Marino.

The Extra Edge: Mitchell. Success strategies for women, based on data from women grads of Harvard Business School.

The Woman's Job Search Handbook: Bloomburg and Holden. Well done career planning and job search techniques.

Time for a Change: A Woman's Guide to Non-Traditional Occupations: For women considering non-traditional jobs: exercises and narrative, plus a review of 10 growth-oriented jobs.

Winning the Salary Game: Salary Negotiations for Women: Sherry Chastain.

Yes to Career Success!: Hennekins.

International Jobs

If you want to work in another country, you had better do your homework in advance. For example, you should carefully consider personal and family issues that might impede a full adjustment to your host country. Here are some resources to help you consider this option.

Directory of European Industrial and Trade Associations: CBD Research, Kent, England. Lists the industrial and trade associations of Europe.

Directory of European Professional and Learned Societies: CBD Research, Kent, England. Similar in format but deals strictly with learned and professional societies.

Foreign Jobs: The Most Popular Countries: Casewit. Profiles desirable countries and how to get jobs there.

How to Get a Job in Europe—The Insider's Guide: Surrey Books. Gives country-by-country listings of newspapers, business directories, regulations, organizations, and other useful information.

How to Get a Job in the Pacific Rim: Surrey Books. Information similar to above, but for countries bordering the Pacific Ocean.

International agencies: These agencies maintain lists of people available to work as consultants, and you might want to register with one or more: World Bank; U.S. Aid for International Development (USAID); United Nations Development Program; United National Industrial Development Organization.

International Careers: Bob Adams, Inc. Information on finding government, corporate, and nonprofit jobs.

International Employment Hotline: Names and addresses of government and nongovernment hiring organizations.

International Jobs: Where They Are, How to Get Them: A Handbook for Over 500 Career Opportunities Around the World: Kocher.

Key British Enterprises: Dun and Bradstreet. Detailed information on the 50,000 British companies that together employ more than a third of the British workforce.

Passport to Overseas Employment—100,000 Job Opportunities Abroad: Information on overseas careers, study, and volunteer programs.

Principal International Businesses: Dun and Bradstreet. While not aimed at the job seeker, it provides details on more than 55,000 companies in 143 countries.

Teaching English Abroad: Griffith.

The Complete Guide to International Jobs and Careers: Your Passport to a World of Exciting and Exotic Employment: Ron and Carol Krannich

The Peace Corps: Wages are low and living conditions basic, but if you are interested in helping people, the Peace Corps is a possibility.

The U.S. government: Don't overlook government jobs; there are many foreign assignments. A larger library may have the publications ***Federal Career Opportunities*** or the ***Federal News Digest,*** which list openings. Federal jobs are listed on the Internet and available through most state employment service offices.

Interviewing and Salary Negotiations

The two most important parts of a job search are getting interviews and doing well in them. I suggest that *the* most important interview question to answer well is "Why should I hire you over someone else?" It takes considerable self-analysis to answer this well. Curling up with a good job search book will help you know that you *do* have good things to say about yourself. Then there is the interview issue of pay, which is where many people lose more money in 30 seconds than at any other time in their lives. Or, worse, they get a job they hate. So here are some good resources on interviewing and salary negotiations, in hopes that they are of help to you.

The Quick Interview and Salary Negotiation Book—Dramatically Improve Your Interviewing Skills and Pay in a Matter of Hours: Mike Farr. A substantial book, but I arranged it so that you can read the first section and do better in interviews later that day. Also covers career planning, job seeking, resumes, pay rates, and other topics of importance for a job seeker. JIST.

101 Dynamite Questions to Ask at Your Job Interview: Fein.

50 Winning Answers to Interview Questions: Albrecht.

American Almanac of Jobs and Salaries: Wright. Covers hundreds of careers in the public and private sector.

American Salaries and Wages Survey: Gale Research. Detailed information on salaries and wages for thousands of jobs, by region. Also gives cost-of-living data, which is helpful in determining what the salary differences really mean.

AMS Office, Professional and Data Processing Salaries Report: Administrative Management Society. Salary distributions for 40 occupations by company size, type of business, and geographic region.

Dynamite Answers to Interview Questions: Ron and Carol Krannich.

Getting To Yes: Negotiating Agreements Without Giving In: Fisher and Ury. Good negotiating tips for anything.

How To Have A Winning Job Interview: Bloch. Good advice in a readable format, with lots of activities.

How to Make $1000 a Minute—Negotiating Your Salaries and Raises: Jack Chapman. Tips on getting more money and benefits during the critical part of a job offer.

Interviewing for Success: Ron and Carol Krannich.

Interviews That Get Results: Vik. Good tips for job seekers.

Knock'em Dead: With Great Answers to Tough Interview Questions: Martin John Yate.

Make Your Job Interview A Success: Biegeleisen. Good checklists, interview answers, grooming tips, and other content.

Out Interviewing the Interviewer: Merman and McLaughlin. Good exercises, case studies, and tips for experienced and not-so-experienced job seekers.

Perks and Parachutes: Tarrant.

Power Interviewing: Job Winning Tactics from Fortune 500 Recruiters: Yeager and Hough.

Ready, Aim, You're Hired!: How to Job-Interview Successfully Anytime, Anywhere with Anyone: Hellman.

State and Metropolitan Area Data Book: Helpful details from the U.S. Department of Commerce providing unemployment rates, average income, employment and population growth, and other details for all major regions—important for those considering a move.

Sweaty Palms—The Neglected Art of Being Interviewed: Anthony Medley. Fun factual tips on illegal questions, problem interviews, appropriate dress and behaviors.

The Evaluation Interview: Richard Fear. Considered a classic for anyone who is, or wants to be, a professional interviewer.

The Five Minute Interview: Richard H. Beatty.

The Ultimate Interview: How to Get It, Get Ready, and Get the Job You Want: Caple.

When Do I Start?: Clearly written, good content.

White Collar Pay: Private Goods-Producing Industries: U.S. Department of Labor's Bureau of Labor Statistics. Good source of salary information for white collar jobs.

Winning The Salary Game: Salary Negotiations for Women: Chastain. Good strategies for men, too.

Resumes and Cover Letters

There are hundreds (thousands?) of resume books and most offer bad advice. They often suggest that a good/better/best/perfect resume, sent out to lots of people, will get interviews, but the research clearly indicates that this is not the case. In addition to bad job search advice, many resume books offer unnecessarily rigid advice about the resume itself (that their way is the one enlightened way to do a resume).

In contrast, I believe that resumes are an important tool in the job search but that active job search methods (such as contacting employers by phone) are more effective than passive ones (like sending unsolicited resumes). And I do not believe that one formula exists for a good resume. Like people, resumes can be different. Of course, JIST's resume books are included here; I think they are among the best available.

America's Top Resumes for America's Top Jobs: J. Michael Farr. This is a big book, with 381 sample resumes covering over 200 major jobs. Resumes were selected from submissions by professional resume writers from all over North America. I took this approach to provide a rich array of writing styles, designs, and approaches to solving resume problems. From entry-level to very experienced, there are good examples here for everyone. JIST.

The Quick Resume and Cover Letter Book—Write and Use an Effective Resume in Only One Day: J. Michael Farr. Starting with an "instant" resume worksheet and basic formats you can complete in an hour or so, this book then takes you on a tour of everything you need to know about resumes and, more importantly, how to use them in your job search. Lots of good examples plus advice on cover letters, the job search, and related matters. JIST.

The Resume Solution—How to Write (and Use) a Resume That Gets Results: David Swanson. Lots of good advice and examples for creating superior resumes. Very strong on resume design and layout and provides a step-by-step approach that is very easy to follow. JIST.

Gallery of Best Resumes: David Noble. Advice and over 200 examples from professional resume writers. Lots of variety in content and design; an excellent resource. I consider it to be the best resume library, because the resumes are organized into useful categories and are all different. JIST.

The Edge Resume & Job Search Strategy: Bill Corbin and Shelbi Wright. The only book I know of that includes sample resumes using special papers and die-cut shapes. Unique. Distributed by JIST.

Gallery of Best Resumes for Two-Year Degree Graduates: David Noble. An excellent selection of over 200 sample resumes submitted by professional resume writers. Good advice and lots of excellent samples. A very good resource book that organizes resumes by occupational category. JIST.

Professional Resumes for Executives, Managers, and Other Administrators: A New Gallery of Best Resumes by Professional Resume Writers: David Noble. Includes more than 200 resumes, organized by occupation. JIST.

The Federal Resume Guidebook: Kathryn Troutman. A thorough book covering the new procedures for applying for jobs with the federal government. JIST.

Using WordPerfect in Your Job Search: David Noble. A unique and thorough book that reviews how to use WordPerfect to create effective resumes, correspondence, and other job search documents including scannable and hypertext resumes. JIST.

100 Winning Resumes for $100,000+ Jobs: Enelow.

College Student's Resume Guide: Marino.

Complete Resume Guide: Faux. Some good ideas and examples.

Damn Good Resume Guide: Yana Parker. An irreverent title, but it has many good examples and an easy-to-follow process for creating resumes.

Developing a Professional Vita or Resume: McDaniels. Special resume advice for professionals with advanced education or experience.

Don't Use a Resume: Richard Lathrop. A booklet providing good examples and advice on a special resume that emphasizes skills.

Dynamic Cover Letters: Hanson. A very focused book, just on cover letters.

Dynamite Cover Letters: Ron and Carol Krannich. Good content.

Dynamite Resumes: Ron and Carol Krannich. Lots of good examples and advice.

Encyclopedia of Job Winning Resumes: Fournier and Spin. Lots of examples in a wide variety of jobs.

High Impact Resumes & Letters: Krannich and Banis. Good job search advice and lots of sample resumes and letters.

How to Write a Winning Resume: Bloch. Good examples for college grads, more experienced job seekers, and professionals.

Job Search Letters That Get Results: Ron and Carol Krannich. Good advice and over 200 sample letters.

Liberal Arts Power**:** Nadler. How to sell it on your resume.

Ready, Aim, Hired: Developing Your Brand Name Resume: Karson.

Resume Kit: Beatty. Better-than-average advice on putting together effective resumes and cover letters.

Resume Pro: The Professional Guide: Yana Parker. A how-to guide for those who help others write resumes.

Resumes for Computer Professionals: Shanahan. Many examples.

Resumes for Executives and Professionals: Shy and Kind.

Resumes for High School Graduates: VGM editors. An unusual but useful focus.

Resumes for Mid-Career Job Changes: VGM editors.

Resumes for Technicians: Shanahan. Examples, tips for use, and so on.

The No Pain Resume Workbook: Hiyaguha Cohen.

The Perfect Resume: Tom Jackson. Uses a workbook format, making it easy to identify job objective, skills, interests, and achievements. Good examples.

The Resume Catalog—200 Damn Good Resumes: Yana Parker. Organized by job objective. Good.

Writing a Job Winning Resume: John McLaughlin and Stephen Merman. A good book with examples showing how the resume covered a weakness.

Dress and Grooming Advice

One survey of employers I read found that about 40 percent of job seekers who made it through initial screening and got an interview then created a negative first impression based on dress and grooming. Another study found that candidates who made a negative impression within five minutes had virtually no chance of getting a job offer. So, put the two studies together, and you can see that a big problem exists with first impressions. How you dress and groom is only one issue, of course, but it is one that most people can easily change. So here are some books on that topic.

Always in Style with Color Me Beautiful: Pooser. By a noted color consultant, clothing styles, colors, and makeup for women. Many photos.

Big and Beautiful: Olds. Larger women can be gorgeous, too.

Color Me Beautiful: Jackson. Discover your "seasonal" colors and coordinate your look. Color photos. Well done.

Dress for Success: John Molloy. Some of the advice is dated, but this still gives good research-based advice on business attire.

Professional Image: Bixler. One of few on dress, grooming, body language, and details for both men and women.

Red Socks Don't Work: Karpinski. Dressing tips for men in formal corporate environments.

Women's Dress for Success: Molloy. Same thorough approach as for men.

Personal and Career Success and Advancement

There are thousands of personal and career success books and tapes. Some are very good, some are not. I include a selection of the better ones here.

Beat Stress with Strength—A Survival Guide for Work and Life: Stephanie Spera and Sandra Lanto. Includes a personal stress test and many tips for handling stress and achieving balance. JIST.

Career Satisfaction and Success—How to Know and Manage Your Strengths: Bernard Haldane. A complete revision of a classic by one of the founders of the modern career planning movement. It presents techniques for succeeding on the job and concepts that have changed many lives for the better, including defining your "motivated skills" and using them as a basis for career planning. JIST.

Dare to Change Your Job and Your Life: Carole Kanchier. Based on interviews with more than 5,000 adults, provides a proven self-help approach to developing a more meaningful career and more fulfilling life. JIST.

Job Savvy—How to Be a Success at Work: LaVerne Ludden. A workbook covering work-appropriate behaviors. JIST.

Jobscape—Career Survival in the New Global Economy: Colin Campbell. A well-written and fascinating book that presents the essential trends shaping the future workforce and how we can best prepare to benefit. JIST.

Networking for Everyone!: Michelle Tullier. More than for the job search, his book covers creating a network to help you through life—lots of motivational and practical tips. JIST.

Ready, Set, Organize!: Pipi Peterson. Time management strategies for your personal and work lives. Good advice and a fun read. JIST.

SuccessAbilities!—1,001 Practical Ways to Keep Up, Stand Out, and Move Ahead at Work: Paula Ancona. Short and motivational tips from Ancona's nationally syndicated column. JIST.

The Customer Is Usually Wrong!: Fred Jandt. Great tips for handling customers and doing the right thing. JIST.

The Perfect Memo!—Write Your Way to Career Success!: Patricia Westheimer. Good tips and activities for more effective business writing. JIST.

We've Got to Start Meeting Like This!: Roger Moskvick and Robert Nelson. An essential book for getting the most out of meeting time. JIST.

Brushing Up Your Clerical Skills: Steinberg. For new and returning office workers. Exercises on spelling, punctuation, typing, business letters, filing, and more.

Business Protocol: Yager. On-the-job manners.

Do What You Love, The Money Will Follow: Sinetar. For those who seek meaning as a first priority, there is hope that we can also make a living doing the things we really want to do.

Getting Things Done When You Are Not in Charge: Bellman.

How to Jump Start a Stalled Career: Prugh.

How to Make a Habit of Success: Bernard Haldane. Originally published many years ago, it was a best-seller and is still available. Many consider Haldane one of the founders of the career planning movement that began in the 1950s. This is an important book that has much good advice.

Improve Your Writing for Work: Chesla. Includes lots of samples and activities.

Love Your Work and Success Will Follow: Hirsch. For those who are not happy with their current career.

Moving Up—How To Get High Salaried Jobs: Djeddah. Techniques to get promoted or move out to a new job.

Not Just a Secretary: Morrow and Lebov. Techniques for doing well and getting ahead.

Secretary Today, Manager Tomorrow: How to Turn a Secretarial Job into a Managerial Position: Marrs.

Skills for Success: Scheele. Good advice on getting ahead in all sorts of careers.

Wish Craft: Barbara Sher. An upbeat book that provides activities and advice on setting goals and reaching your full potential.

Working Smart: Zehring. Advice on getting ahead, organizing time, dealing with people, developing leadership skills.

Would You Put That in Writing?: Booher. Good primer for improving your business communications.

Future Trends/Labor Market Information

Jobscape—Career Survival in the New Global Economy: Colin Campbell. A well-written and fascinating book that presents the essential trends shaping the future workforce and how we can best prepare to benefit. JIST.

Work in the New Economy: Robert Wegmann, Robert Chapman, and Miriam Johnson. A very well-researched book on where our economy is going and how we should adapt our career planning and job search methods to get better results. While this is now an older book, I consider Wegman's work to be among the best on the topic and much of the advice remains current. JIST.

Emerging Careers: New Occupations for the Year 2000 & Beyond: Based on years of research; details hundreds of new careers. Very good.

Megatrends: Nesbitt. A best-seller that provides a review of where the economy is heading.

The Work Revolution: Schwartz and Neikirk. Thorough and well done. Predicts retraining, education, and other needs of rapid change.

Work Force 2020—Work and Workers in the 21st Century: Richard Judy and Carol D'Amico of the Hudson Institute. A well-researched book predicting likely trends in the workforce.

Work in the 21st Century: Isaac Asimov and others. Anthology of well-done articles on work trends for the future. Stimulating.

Self-Employment, Starting Your Own Business, and Temporary, Part-Time, and Volunteer Jobs

More people are working for themselves, starting small businesses, or working in part-time, temporary, or volunteer jobs. There are hundreds of books on these topics, and a good library will have more resources than I can list. Here are a few suggestions.

Self-Employment: From Dream to Reality—An Interactive Workbook for Starting Your Small Business: Linda Gilkerson and Theresia Paauwe. A workbook to encourage "microenterprises," very small business started by those with little money or experience. Unique. JIST.

Mind Your Own Business—Getting Started as an Entrepreneur: LaVerne Ludden and Bonnie Maitlen. A good book for those considering their own business, with lots of good advice. JIST.

Be Your Own Business—The Definitive Guide to Entrepreneurial Success: Marsha Fox and LaVerne Ludden. JIST.

Franchise Opportunities Handbook: LaVerne Ludden. Lists over a thousand franchise companies and provides tips on selecting one that makes sense for a business.

America's New Breed of Entrepreneurs: Presents collective experiences of 48 successful entrepreneurs and how they achieved their goals.

Beginning Entrepreneur: Matthews.

Best Home Businesses for the '90s: Edwards and Edwards.

Directory of Microenterprise Programs: Lists loans and programs for low-income entrepreneurs.

Getting Business to Come to You: Edwards and Edwards. Low-cost marketing tips.

Home Sweet Office: Meade. Telecommunicating from home to a regular job.

How to Build a Successful One Person Business: Bautista.

How to Run Your Own Home Business: Kern and Wolfgram.

How to Start, Run, and Stay in Business: Kishel. Good primer for the school of hard knocks.

Inc. Yourself: How to Profit from Setting Up your Own Corporation: Shows financial and other advantages, plus how to set up.

Job Sharing Handbook: Smith. Provides guidelines for setting up a shared job, case histories, and so on. Good.

Making It on Your Own—What to Know Before Starting Your Own Business: Feingold.

Opportunities in Your Own Service Business: McKay.

Part-Time Professional: Good information on finding part time jobs, benefits, negotiating with employers, converting full-time to part-time jobs, and other tips.

Running a One Person Business: Whitmeyer, Rasberry, Phillips. Practical.

Side by Side: Cuozzo and Graham.

Starting on a Shoe String: Building a Business Without a Bankroll: Goldstein.

Ten Best Opportunities for Starting a Home Business Today: Reed Glenn.

The Mid-Career Entrepreneur: Mancuso.

The Small Business Administration: The U.S. Small Business Administration (SBA) offers loans, training, planning, and many useful publications. Its toll-free number is 1-800-U ASK SBA. In addition, its Service Corps of Retired Executives (SCORE) provides free help on how to set up and run a small business.

The Temp Track: Justice. Reviews the many opportunities for temporary jobs.

Volunteer America: Kipps. Lists over 1,400 organizations for training, service, and work experience.

Working from Home: Edwards and Edwards.

Places to Live or Move to

Some people will be unhappy wherever they live, but living in a place you like makes life more enjoyable. Here are a few books that provide details.

Best Towns In America: Bayless. 50 of the U.S.'s most desirable places plus ways to evaluate all communities.

Country Careers—Successful Ways to Live and Work in the Country: Rojak.

Finding Your Best Place To Live In America: Bowman and Guiliani. Another good book providing information on good places to live.

Greener Pastures Relocation Guide: Finding the Best State in the U.S. for You!

Places Rated Almanac: Richard Boyer and David Savagean. A thorough review of over 270 metropolitan areas with information on housing, education, climate, health services, recreation, arts, transportation, crime, and income.

Getting Information on Specific Employers

There are two basic reasons for you to be interested specific employers. The first has to do with identifying potential job search targets, and the second is to get more information on an employer prior to an interview.

Some books and businesses "sell" the idea of sending your resume to potential employers as a good thing. Some even sell lists in print or computer form, so you can mount a big mail campaign. And some sell the idea of having special lists of employers that you can buy from them. I do not think that sending unsolicited resumes to any list is a good idea. While any technique works for some people, you will be better off if your job search is more targeted and involves more direct contact.

You have to begin with knowing the type of job you want and the industries where you will find these jobs. Then and only then can you intelligently begin your search for specific employers.

Free Resources

The yellow pages: The best resource you can get is probably free: it's the yellow pages of the phone book. Think about it: it lists all the organizations by type and gives you what you need to contact them. All of my job search books tell you how to use the yellow pages as an effective tool. The yellow pages for regions throughout the country is also now available on the Internet, as are many other sources of information on organizations.

Networking: Another free resource of information is networking. If you want to know more about a particular job or place of employment, ask the people who do that kind of work or who work in that place. This is often the only source of information for small organizations not listed in the directories. A good book on networking is ***Networking for Everyone—Connecting with People for Career and Job Success*** by Michelle Tullier. It provides lots of practical advice for personal and business success and is published by JIST.

Chambers of commerce: Most are not staffed to provide specific information to job seekers, but many do provide information such as new businesses in the area, larger employers, and other details.

Contact the organization directly: For large organizations, contact the human resources or public relations departments. In smaller ones the receptionist or manager may be able to help. Get brochures, an annual report, description of relevant jobs, and anything else that describes the organization.

Annual reports: All publicly owned and many smaller organizations provide annual reports detailing earnings, trends, strategies, and other information. If one is available, it is an excellent source of information.

Other Resources

A good bookstore or library has many sources of information on specific businesses and other organizations. While many of these resources were not specifically developed for use by job seekers, they can work just fine.

You can use resource materials in several ways. The first is to get information on a specific organization as background for an interview. You can also get names of organizations as well as background information to use in making direct contact lists. With so many potential sources of information, ask a librarian to help you once you have a good idea of what you are looking for.

Following are just a few of the many books and other resources for obtaining information on employers. Some are organized by industry or region or in other ways that may be of help to you. If you use the Internet, more and more information is now available there. I suggest you read one of the Internet job search books published by JIST for the most useful sites.

100 Best Companies to Work for in America: Levering and Moscowitz.

America's Corporate Families, The Billion Dollar Directory: Describes 2,500 large corporate "families" and their 28,000 subsidiaries; provides information on each; and cross-references by location, business or product type, and other methods.

America's Fastest Growing Employers: Bob Adams. Lists more than 700 of the fastest-growing companies in the country.

American Business Information Inc. of Omaha, Nebraska: Publishes business directories for many different industries. Phone (402) 593-4600.

Bay Area 500: Hoover. An example of a regional listing, this one providing profiles of the largest companies in the San Francisco area.

Business Newsbank: Newsbank, Inc. This service provides the narrative of articles from newspapers and business journals from 400 cities. Cross-references by company name, individual's name, industry, or product category.

Business Organizations and Agencies Directory: Gale Research Company. Provides useful information to look up by business name and types of activity. Provides contact information.

Business Periodicals Index: Cross-references business articles from over 300 periodicals by subject and company name.

Career Guide—Dun's Employment Opportunities Directory: Aimed specifically at the professional job seeker, this book lists more than 5,000 major U.S. companies and their personnel directors, career opportunities, and benefits packages.

Chambers of commerce and local business associations: These often publish directories of local companies, available in libraries or by writing to the individual associations.

Contacts Influential: A series of directories providing information on smaller businesses. Allows look up by organization name or type to learn details of its operations and size.

Directory of Executive Recruiters: Joyce Lain Kennedy.

Directory of Executive Search Firms: Lists and cross-references 100s of these businesses, should they be appropriate for you.

Dun & Bradstreet Million Dollar Directory: Provides information on 180,000 of the largest companies in the country. Gives the type of business, number of employees, and sales volume for each. It also lists the company's top executives.

Hidden Job Market: A Guide to America's 2000 Little-Known Fastest Growing High-Tech Companies: Peterson's Guides. Concentrates on high-tech companies with good growth potential.

Hoover's Handbook of American Business: Profiles more than 750 larger companies.

Hoover's Handbook of Emerging Companies: Spain, Campbell, Talbot. Profiles of 250 entrepreneurial companies.

Job Bank Series: Bob Adams Inc. Series of books for job-seeking professionals, each covering a different large city or metropolitan area with details on economic outlook for the covered area, list of major companies, and positions within the company.

Job Hunter's Guide to 100 Great American Cities: Brattle Communications. Lists major employers for 100 of America's largest cities.

Little Known, Fastest Growing High-Tech Companies: Peterson's Guides.

Macrae's State Industrial Directories: Published for northeastern states, but similar volumes are produced for other parts of the country by other publishers. Each book lists thousands of companies, concentrating on those that produce products, rather than services. They include a large number of small firms, in addition to the larger ones listed in many other guides.

Million Dollar Directory: Dun's Marketing Services. Provides general information on over 115,000 businesses.

Moody's Industrial Manual: Provides detailed information on over 3,000 larger organizations.

Moody's Industrial News Reports: Provides articles related to each of the businesses listed in the related directory.

National Business Telephone Directory: Gale Research. An alphabetical listing of companies across the United States, with their addresses and phone numbers. It includes many smaller firms (20 employees minimum).

Peterson's Business and Management Jobs: An annual listing of 100s of employers plus essential background information on each.

Polk's Directories: R.L. Polk & Co. Each major city has its own Polk Directory created by door-to-door canvass of individuals and businesses in the area. Cross-references by name, address, type of business.

Reference Book of Corporate Management: Dun's Marketing Services. Provides information on the executives and officers of the 6,000 largest U.S. corporations.

Standard & Poor's Register of Corporations, Directors and Executives: Brief information on over 40,000 corporations and their key people cross-referenced by names, types of businesses, and other methods. Lists parent companies with subsidiaries and the interlocking affiliations of directors.

Thomas Register: Lists more than 100,000 companies across the country by name, type of product made, and brand name of product produced.

Many directories give information about firms in a particular industry. Here are just a few.

The Blue Book of Building and Construction
Directory of Advertising Agencies
Directory of Computer Dealers
McFadden American Bank Directory

School and Training Admissions, Financing, and Survival

Education pays. People with more education and training tend to earn substantially more. Most of the rapidly growing jobs require technical training beyond high school or a four-year college degree. While a four-year college degree makes sense for a lot of people, many occupations with high pay and rapid growth can be learned in two years or less.

More adults are going back to school to upgrade their career skills, and any young person should consider getting as much education and training as possible. Knowledge of computers is now important in most jobs and, if you have not kept up with the new developments in your field, it is important to do so as soon as possible. There are a wide variety of training options including technical schools, adult-education classes, workshops, formal college courses, and even classes you can take on the Internet.

You can finance postsecondary training or education in many ways, so don't let a lack of money be a barrier to getting what you need. If you want to do it, seek and ye shall find a way. Here are some resources.

Back to School: A College Guide for Adults: LaVerne Ludden. A comprehensive guide that includes self-assessment activities and good advice on setting goals, considering various degrees, selecting a college, juggling priorities, and much more. Includes a directory of 1,000 adult-friendly degree programs. JIST.

Ludden's Adult Guide to Colleges and Universities: LaVerne and Marsha Ludden. Good advice for adults going back to school, plus information on more than 1,500 degree programs. Includes many nontraditional programs that can be used to reduce the time required to get a degree. JIST.

Career Connection for College Education—A Guide to College Education and Related Career Opportunities: Fred Rowe. Information on over 100 college majors and 1,000 related occupations. Includes details on salaries, course requirements, related high school courses, and other details useful in planning a college major. JIST.

Career Connection for Technical Education—A Guide to Technical Training and Related Career Opportunities: Fred Rowe. Similar to the above, this book describes over 60 technical education majors and the careers they lead to. JIST.

Bear's Guide to Finding Money For College: John Bear. Well written, readable, helpful.

But What if I Don't Want to Go to College?: Unger. Reviews alternative education or training needed for hundreds of jobs.

College 101: Farrar. Primer for getting along in college.

College Admissions Data Handbook: Orchard House. The most thorough and up-to-date source of information on colleges available, four volumes cover different sections of the country.

College Degrees by Mail: John Bear. Brief descriptions for 100 nonresident schools.

College Degrees You Can Earn from Home: Frey.

College Guide for Students with Learning Disabilities: Sciafini and Lynch. Covers over 500 programs.

College Majors and Careers: A Resource Guide for Effective Life Planning: Phifer. Good information on college majors, skills, related leisure activities, personal attributes, and additional resource materials for major occupational interests.

College Survival Guide: Mayer. Well-done, new student orientation to basics of making it.

Earn College Credit for What You Know: Simosko. On nontraditional college credit programs: types, application procedures, and so on.

Electronic University: A Guide to Distance Learning Programs: Peterson's Guides.

Free Dollars From the Federal Government: Blum.

Free Money for College: A Guide to More Than 1,000 Grants and Scholarships: Blum.

Guide to Non-Traditional College Degrees: John Bear. Fun to read, well done, thorough.

Guide to Technical, Trade, and Business Schools: A four-volume set with thorough profiles of 2,200 accredited schools.

Historically Black Colleges and Universities: Details on all 91 such schools.

How to Apply to American Colleges and Universities: Brennan and Briggs.

Internships: 50,000 On-The-Job Training Opportunities for Students and Adults: Rushing.

Liberal Education and Careers Today: Howard Figler. "I dropped out of pre-med in my junior year of college (a long story) and got a degree in liberal arts—and I turned out OK." Figler makes a case for a liberal arts education with research and advice on how liberal arts is a good way to go.

Major Decisions—A Guide to College Majors: Orchard House. Provides brief descriptions for all college majors.

Minority Student Enrollments in Higher Education: Provides information on 500 schools with the highest minority enrollments.

New Horizons—Education and Career Guide for Adults: Haponski. Methods of seeking and using education to get ahead.

Paying Less for College: Peterson's College Money Handbook: Provides costs, types of aid, and other details from over 1,700 schools.

Person's College Money Handbook.

Peterson's Colleges and Programs for Students with Learning Disabilities: Mangrum and Strichart. Lists over 1,000 colleges with these programs.

Peterson's Internships: Lists 40,000 positions to get experience as interns.

Peterson's Scholarships, Grants, and Prizes.

Peterson's Competitive Colleges: Tips on getting into the top 300 schools.

Peterson's Guide to College Admissions: Student workbook on preparing and competing. Well done.

Peterson's Guide to Four-Year Colleges: 1,900 schools and 400 majors. Organized to select by many criteria, plus tips on applying.

Peterson's Guide to Two-Year Colleges: Details on over 1,400 schools with associate degrees.

Peterson's Independent Study Catalog: Guide to over 12,000 correspondence and Internet courses.

Peterson's National College Databank: Data in over 350 categories, a major source of data for colleges of all descriptions.

Tech Prep Guide: Technical, Trade, & Business School Data Handbook: Orchard House. The most thorough reference of its kind, providing complete information on over 1,600 schools plus summary information on another 3,000 schools. Four volumes cover different parts of the country.

Time for College—The Adult Student's Guide to Survival and Success: Siebert and Gilpin.

Who Offers Part-Time Degree Programs?: Peterson's Guides. Data on over 2,500 institutions.

Winning Money for College: High school student's guide to scholarship contests.

You Can Make It Without a College Degree: Roesch.

Instructor and Trainer Resources

While you should be able to find books on public speaking in most bookstores and libraries, more specific materials such as instructor's guides for a job search workshop are very hard to find. JIST publishes or distributes a variety of these more specialized materials, should you be interested.

Career Exploration Groups: A Facilitator's Guide: Garfield and Nelson. Includes group activities and exercises to aid in self-knowledge, career information, and decision making.

Career Information Service: Norris. One of the few texts for university level career counseling and development courses. Thorough book for career counselors.

Career Planning Workshop Manual: Instructor's guide for life/work planning workshops. Includes group exercises, worksheets.

Developing Vocational Instruction: Mager and Beach. Easy-to-understand, step-by-step guidelines to developing good curriculum.

How to Organize and Manage a Seminar: What to Do and How to Do It: Murray. Budgets, plans, staffing, promotion, and more. Very good.

Louder & Funnier: A Practical Guide for Overcoming Stage Fright: Nelson. Getting over fear of groups is a major obstacle to success as a trainer or presenter. Excellent.

Making Successful Presentations: Smith. Good for the new or moderately experienced trainer.

Making Vocational Choices: A Theory of Careers: John Holland. There are few career theory books, and this is one of the most influential. In plain and readable English, it presents the research, rationale, and practical uses of his theory of six personality types.

The Business of Public Speaking: Good tips on business aspects of doing presentations.

Where To Start: An Annotated Career Planning Bibliography: Thorough, helpful. Organized by topic.

Work in the New Economy: Robert Wegmann, Robert Chapman, and Miriam Johnson. Well-researched and written review of the research on labor market trends and how a job seeker is affected. Though written some time ago, I consider this the best book of its kind. JIST.

Career Interest Tests and Books on Test-Taking

Too many people think a magical solution exists to their career planning problems that does not require effort. Tests are only tools to provide you with information and can't tell you what to do. I prefer assessment instruments that are self-scored and encourage you to participate in the career decision-making process.

If you have access to a career counselor, ask about taking a career interest test. But remember that it can only provide you food for thought, not an answer to what you should do. Following are a few of the self-administered and self-scored interest inventories that I like. Most are available from JIST but in packages. Individuals must get them through a counselor, though several inventories are available as a package for individuals on JIST's Internet site at JIST.com. Test-related books are listed after the tests themselves.

Career Exploration Inventory (CEI): John Liptak. Uses a unique past/present and future orientation and results in scores that cross-reference to major occupational interest areas. Includes a large chart of occupational information, an action plan, and recommends sources of additional information. Spanish version available. JIST.

The Guide for Occupational Exploration Inventory (GOEI): J. Michael Farr. Uses an intuitive process to lead to one or more of the 12 career interest areas from the ***Guide for Occupational Exploration.*** A related information chart then provides substantial information on the jobs in each area, related courses, and leisure activities. Includes an action plan and suggests additional sources of information. JIST.

Leisure/Work Search Inventory (LSI): John Liptak. Ties leisure activities to related jobs, making this a good test for young people with limited work experience or adults looking for more interesting career options. Includes substantial chart of career information, an action plan, and other useful elements. JIST.

Occupational Clues—A Career Interest Survey. A thorough book that includes checklists for values, interests, activities, school subjects. and work experience—all cross-referenced to related job clusters. JIST.

Barriers to Employment Success Inventory (BESI): John Liptak. Self-scored inventory that helps identify barriers to employment—very helpful for programs. JIST.

The Job Search Attitude Inventory: John Liptak. A self-scored inventory that identifies potential problem areas for success in the job search. JIST.

***Career Decision-Making System* (CDM):** Thomas Harrington and Arthur J. O'Shea. A popular interest test that is easy to use, self-scoring and interpreted. Records occupational preferences, school subjects, job values, abilities, plans for future education, and training.

College Majors Finder: Cross-references Holland codes (which can be obtained from the ***SDS*** and ***CDM*** described in this section as well as from other devices) to over 900 college majors.

Self-Directed Search (SDS): John L. Holland. Widely used, responses result in recommended jobs in six major clusters. A separate booklet cross-references over 1,100 jobs in a logical manner.

American College Testing Program (ACT): Over 450 pages of skills, reviews, sample questions, study tips, and tips to raise ACT scores.

Book of U.S. Postal Exams: Bautista. Sample exams for 44 job categories.

Career Aptitude Tests: Klein and Outerman. Series of self-scored tests measuring aptitudes against over 250 jobs.

Career Finder: The Pathways to Over 1500 Entry-Level Jobs: Schwartz and Breckner. Checklists result in recommended jobs for more exploration. Lists salary, openings, and more.

Civil Service Test Tutor: Practice drills and samples for government tests for beginning office jobs such as accounting, file clerk, telephone operator.

Counselor's Guide to Vocational Guidance Instruments: Kappes and Mastie. Reviews of many tests.

Fairness in Employment Testing: National Academy of Sciences.

Guide to 75 Tests for Special Education: Up-to-date guide covering major tests and how to select, interpret, and use.

How to Get a Clerical Job in Government: Hundreds of sample questions and answers covering major topics on federal, state, and local exams.

How to Pass Employment Tests: How to do well in tests you may encounter in your job search plus tests given to evaluate advancement potential.

Making the Grade: Study habits and techniques for getting good grades by doing well on all sorts of tests.

Practice for Clerical, Typing, Steno Tests: Sample questions, drills, exercises to improve scores on most clerical tests.

Practice for the Armed Forces Tests: Drills, sample questions, test-taking tips, general review for all service tests.

Preparation for the GED: Thorough preparation to increase scores.

Preparation for the SAT: Thorough preparation to increase scores.

Career-Oriented Software

I formerly listed software that you could find for reasonable prices in a retail software store, but changes occur so rapidly that any list is quickly out-of-date. A number of good resume preparation programs are quite helpful in preparing basic resumes, though you won't need them if you have access to a good word processing program and a good resume book. Two good resume programs that have been consistently available are ***WinWay Resume on CD-ROM*** and ***PFS Resume Pro***—both are popular.

The major word processing programs include resume formats, but they force you to use formats that may not be the best for your situation. David Noble's book, ***Using WordPerfect in Your Job Search,*** shows you the many tricks you can do with a powerful word-processing program.

Another category of software that is very helpful in the job search is that of contact management programs such as ACT! or GoldMine. These are designed for individuals like sales people to follow up on their contacts and are well suited for any follow-up tasks including letters, schedules, and phone calls.

A growing number of career planning, occupational exploration, and related programs are becoming available. Some are poorly done while others seem helpful, so buyer beware.

JIST publishes a variety of software, but the software is priced for multiple users such as in schools or programs, and it is too expensive for individuals. JIST has a free job search program on its Internet site at www.JIST.com if you want to check it out.

To give you an idea of the types of information becoming available, here are some JIST-published programs followed by a few of the many available from other sources:

JIST's Career Explorer on CD-ROM: Answering a series of questions about your interests and other factors results in a list of the 20 jobs that best match your responses. The program then allows you to get information on each of these jobs. Takes about 15 minutes.

JIST's Multimedia Occupational Outlook Handbook: Very easy to use, this software includes descriptions for the 250 major jobs in the OOH, powerful search features, and color images and sounds.

Mike Farr's Get a Job Workshop on CD-ROM: Includes activities, text, video clips, and sound in an interactive format covering setting a job objective, details on all major jobs, identifying skills, job search methods, resumes, job survival, and related topics. JIST.

The Electronic Enhanced Dictionary of Occupational Titles: This is a sophisticated CD-ROM program that includes the complete content of the ***Dictionary of Occupational Titles***, the ***Occupational Outlook***

Handbook*, *The Complete Guide for Occupational Exploration, and additional details on over 12,000 jobs. While it is easy to use, it provides access to detailed technical information on over 12,000 jobs that has not been readily available in the past. JIST.

Young Person's Electronic Occupational Outlook Handbook: A lively and simple-to-use format provides basic information on 250 major jobs.

Free Phone CD-ROM: Toll-free numbers for over 1,000 business categories covering the entire country. Allows lookup by region and other criteria.

Information USA: Provides substantial information on federal jobs, government resources, agencies, grants, loans, scholarships, statistics.

Lovejoy's College Counselor CD-ROM: Provides details on thousands of colleges and technical schools, 2,500 scholarships, and video clips of many schools. Excellent.

Scholarships 101: Information on over 5,000 scholarship sources. Sorts by various criteria and helps write letters asking for additional information.

Select Phone CD-ROM: Includes all listings in the white and yellow pages directories for the entire U.S. Search by name, region, business heading, and so on.

Alphabetic Index Of O*NET Job Titles

If you have the correct O*NET job title, use this index for looking up its page number. For example, if you are looking for the O*NET description for "Accountant," you will find its page reference easily in the alphabetical listing that follows.

If you do not have the correct O*NET job title, looking up a given job may not be as simple. For example, suppose that you are looking for a job titled "Unemployment Benefits Counselor." That job is not listed under the first word "Unemployment," but a very similar O*NET job is listed under "Claims Takers, Unemployment Benefits."

Looking for this job under the first word "Claims" would probably not occur to you, although a similar O*NET job obviously exists. For this reason, we encourage you to use the list of O*NET occupations that immediately follows the table of contents in the front of this book. That list organizes jobs into clusters of similar jobs and, for most readers, will be a more helpful way to locate a job title that interests you.

Using that list has an additional benefit of introducing you to jobs that you might otherwise overlook. For example, for those interested in "Accountants," you will find there a variety of related jobs including "Treasurers, Controllers, and Chief Financial Officers," "Financial Managers, Branch or Department," "Auditors," and "Tax Preparers."

A

B

C

D

E

F

G

H

I

J

K

L

M

N

R

S

T

The Unauthorized Teacher's Survival Guide

By Jack Warner and Clyde Bryan, with Diane Warner

This is the most honest, helpful and practical book ever written for teachers. Two veteran educators share inside secrets, anecdotes, and practical advice destined to save colleagues years of frustrating trials and errors.

ISBN: 1-57112-068-8 · **$12.95** · Order Code: P0688

Inside Secrets of Finding a Teaching Job

By Jack Warner and Clyde Bryan, with Diane Warner

Tap the experts to get the inside track on your job search! Authors Warner and Bryan combine their 50 years of on-the-job teaching experience with advice from hundreds of teachers, administrators, and personnel professionals. The result: a powerful self-directed guide to landing your perfect teaching job.

ISBN: 1-57112-079-3 · **$12.95** · Order Code: P0793

Home but Not Alone

The Parents' Work-at-Home Handbook

By Katherine Murray

DREAM IT. DARE IT. DELIGHT IN IT. Maybe you've always wanted your own business. Or maybe you've been downsized, right-sized, or outsized from the corporate office. Either way, starting a home-based enterprise opens the door to a rewarding and challenging new lifestyle for you–and your family.

ISBN: 1-57112-080-7 · **$14.95** · Order Code: P0807

The Working Parents' Handbook

How to Succeed at Work, Raise Your Kids, Maintain a Home, and Still Have Time for You

By Katherine Murray

Kids are for keeps, and parenting is one of the most important jobs many of us will ever have. About 70 million men and women balance their roles as parents and workers. Balance. That's one of the topics Katherine Murray champions here. In a positive, friendly tone, she provides thoughtful advice on setting priorities and shows readers how to construct more balanced and satisfying lives.

ISBN: 1-57112-075-0 · **$14.95** · Order Code: P0750

We've Got to Start Meeting Like This!

A Guide to Successful Meeting Management

By Roger K. Mosvick & Robert B. Nelson

Upgrade your leadership skills! Have fewer meetings that get vastly better results! Details the six most common meeting mismanagement problems and offers practical solutions. Includes advice on appropriate settings, effective meeting formats, agendas, and much more.

ISBN: 1-57112-069-6 · **$14.95** · Order Code: P0696